THE QUOTABLE WOMAN
THE FIRST 5,000 YEARS

D0075454

Also by Elaine T. Partnow

Books

The Quotable Woman, 1800–1981
The Quotable Woman, Eve–1799
The New Quotable Woman
Breaking the Age Barrier
Photographic Artists and Innovators (with Turner Browne)
Everyday Speaking for All Occasions (with Susan Partnow)
The Female Dramatist (with Lesley Hyatt)

Plays

Hear Us Roar, A Woman's Connection
Hispanic Women Speak

THE QUOTABLE WOMAN
THE FIRST 5,000 YEARS

Compiled and Edited by
ELAINE T. PARTNOW

Checkmark Books®
An imprint of Facts On File, Inc.

The Quotable Woman: The First 5,000 Years

Copyright © 2001, 1992, 1986, 1985, 1983, 1977 by Elaine Partnow

This is a completely revised and updated edition of *The New Quotable Woman.*

All rights reserved. No part of this book may be reproduced or utilized in any form or by any means, electronic or mechanical, including photocopying, recording, or by any information storage or retrieval systems, without permission in writing from the publisher. For information contact:

Checkmark Books
An imprint of Facts On File, Inc.
11 Penn Plaza
New York NY 10001

Library of Congress Cataloging-in-Publication Data
The quotable woman : the first 5,000 years / compiled and edited by
    Elaine T. Partnow.
        p.   cm.
    Includes bibliographical references and index.
    ISBN 0-8160-4012-5 (hardcover : alk. paper) / ISBN 0-8160-4575-5 (pbk)
    1. Women—Quotations. 2. Quotations, English. I. Partnow, Elaine.
PN6081.5.Q65   2000
305.4—dc21   00-037660

Checkmark Books are available at special discounts when purchased in bulk quantities for businesses, associations, institutions, or sales promotions. Please call our Special Sales Department in New York at (212) 967-8800 or (800) 322-8755.

You can find Facts On File on the World Wide Web at http://www.factsonfile.com.

Text design by Joan M. Toro
Cover design by Cathy Rincon

Printed in the United States of America

VB FOF 10 9 8 7 6 5 4 3 2 1
  (pbk) 10 9 8 7 6 5 4 3 2 1

This book is printed on acid-free paper.

for Gina
my DB genie

Inscribed
to those women whose voices have been muted by
oppressive regimes, poverty and brutality

Addressed
to all women and all men
who long for a world in balance

Contents

Acknowledgments

To Gina Hicks: Gina, dear, what could I have done without you? It would have been like the dinosaur days, when I did everything on 5x8 index cards and it took me four years and there were all kinds of inconsistencies that I couldn't even see until after the book was in print, and even then there were some major mess-ups—until I got it all in the computer. Organized. Cross-referenced. Backed up. Integrated. Tabulated. Filterable. Reportable. Formidable. How do you do it, how do you do it, how do you do it? It's not just your wizardry with databases that dazzles me, though. It's your sense of equanimity, your reserve, your gentle humor, your infinite patience, your granite reliability. We've worked together, what? Five years now? Despite the loose hours and lousy pay, when I or Turner had a deadline, you never let us down. Thank you.

To Stephanie Fitz: Dear Stephanie. Thank you. It has brought great joy to my heart to have gotten to know you a little these past several months as you assisted me on *The Quotable Woman* as an intern for your understudies program in English and Women's Studies at the University of Washington. You impressed me from the start. High-spirited, organized, efficient, conscientious, loyal. I pushed you hard the last few weeks; you did not let me—nor yourself—down.

To Jessica Partnow: Jessica, I have harbored a secret delight ever since you started working for me and Uncle Turner in our business, because that brought us closer together, and few things in this world give me greater pleasure than being close to my goddess daughter. But to employ you in my life's work . . . Transposing the entire text of the fourth edition into my database was no small task. Your remarkable focus lent a speed and accuracy to the work for which I am very grateful. And scouting out the lyrics of contemporary songwriters like Ani DiFranco, Liz Phair, and Lauryn Hill was a great contribution that helps the book be more current. More, though, I'm grateful my work could be a conduit for exposing you to so many wonderful women of history—since you were a little girl, really.

Marissa Betz-Zall, another extremely focused young woman, you worked so diligently on finishing Jessica's task when she left for Europe, then going on to the tedious work of transposing the Subject Index. Kaila, still in high school, it renews my faith in the young to have encountered such a reliable, hard worker as yourself. The three of you, always pleasant, always conscientious, always full of life. Amy Nenneman and Rekha Kuver, you, too, contributed your share and won your work units for your undergraduate programs. You were my first exposure to working with interns, and a chamber of

ix

my heart unfolded at connecting with young people again. Thank you. Sarah Stuteville, my bubbling, passionate, warm-as-toast young friend, brief as your sojourn was with *The Quotable Woman*, your energy passed through its soul and became part of it.

Lesley Hyatt, adored niece, your help with the español made it possible to include several Latinas; what fun it's been for us to build this additional level with which to connect heart and mind. Dear sister Susan Partnow, you, too, with the languages—Spanish, French, German. And the quotes you e-mailed me. And your constant moral support and enthusiasm. Janice Price, we have you to thank for the Nelly Sachs poem; I think you enjoyed the process as much as I did.

Anne Savarese, my editor, who generously provided me with several of Facts On File's American Profiles and Global Profiles books, which proved invaluable to my research, and who showed constant patience and understanding with my several delays. Thank you so much.

Sheree Bykofsky, my agent, whose attention and energy during the inception of this project is not forgotten; Shelley Glendenning, who introduced me to the works of Meg Wheatley and Nel Nodding; compatriots from the International Partnership Center and The Partnership Way who sent me their favorite quotes and helped me make the selections for Riane Eisler — that was fun. All the wonderful literary critics who unwittingly did my work for me by culling out superb bon mots in their book reviews; Liz Bernstein at icbl.org helped with Nobel Prize–winner Jody Williams; Pat Cross, whose website Sunshine for Women (http://www.pinn.net/~sunshine/main.html) is a marvel of resources, which Pat shared generously with me, introducing me to Jenny P. d'Hericourt, piling me up with material on Mathilda Gage, and so much more; Kristina Lerman at USC Information Sciences Institute, who helped with Hildegarde von Bingen; poet Heather McHugh; Kim Caldwell for help with Anne Tyler; Denise Rohed-Trout and Keller W. Webster for a string of quotes; Lisa Lynch for help on Mary Oliver; and the Quick Information Desk at the main branch of the Seattle Public Library for their diligence, patience and generostiy of spirit. Carrie Rhodes, coming in at the 11th hour and volunteering to help me with proofreading galleys, made it possible to bring out this work without further delays; I thank you for your diligence and generosity of spirit.

As I sit at my desk, reading through the galleys, for what will be one of the last of the thousands of hours spent on this voluminous edition, tears suprise my cheeks and my body is suddenly racked with sobs. Mammoth project that it is, I've had to juggle doing it between working at the small business that my husband and I own and run for our daily bread. I am exhausted, I am relieved—I am grateful. Grateful to have been able to be a conduit in bringing forth the voices of women in history. May their spirits transform you, as they have me.

This book is for you, young women, middle-aged women, and old. And for you, Turner, my dear husband, my partner. Each of you is a poem, Emily Dickinson would say. I say you're a campfire. And the warmth and energy from each of you has carried me through these long, long months and days.

Thank you.

Elaine T. Partnow
Seattle, Washington

Introduction

It has become my custom to constantly collect materials for future editions of *The Quotable Woman*, even when I'm finishing a new revision. Whenever I find an article or review that warrants a closer look, I toss it in a cardboard box under my desk, which is plastered with old flyers advertising *The Quotable Woman*. I will never forget the day when, having just rolled out of bed and made a pot of tea, I entered the tiny, cluttered office next to my bedroom to find empty the precious box that had been tucked under my desk for years! The new housekeeper had mistaken my five-year collection of clippings for the recycling bin and dumped it in the trash! Still in my robe, I tore out of the house. In the rain, I raced into the alley way behind our rental, and, with trembling hands and cries of anguish, scrambled through the large green recycling bin till I had salvaged (I hoped) every precious clipping.

Years later, going through that box to find the jewels preserved there, I straighten out crumpled papers, taped-together reviews, smeared photographs of half-remembered faces, grateful for the retrieval of this almost lost—on so many levels—history.

Lots of things have happened since I sent off the fourth edition of *The Quotable Woman* in 1991: Toni Morrison was awarded the Nobel Prize in literature, the first woman of color to be so honored; feminist stalwart Bella Abzug died; Dr. Mae Jemison became the first African-American woman in space; and, for the first time ever, I've gone quote-hunting in cyberspace. What a difference a decade makes! Last edition, I tried to use the Internet for research and, at last, threw up my hands in despair. I couldn't make head nor tail of the Library of Congress card catalogue website; getting access to university archives meant a long labyrinthine journey that often led to dead ends. The Internet drove me mad! It was so garbled and bungled; I never used it, opting for the good old library instead. For this edition, however, I barely set foot in a library. The Internet's ease of use and plethora of resources make it a bonanza for researchers—and for readers. In several instances, I've cited websites instead of books or journals as the reference for the quote. I hope you look into those sites and enjoy them, as I did.

Among the tremendous number of changes that have taken place in the nine brief years since I concluded research on the fourth edition and undertook it for the fifth are subjects such as cyperspace, virtual books, gender identity, digital age, cross-dressing, genital mutilation, world paradigm, global thinking (though the concept isn't new; in 1921 Carrie Chapman Catt, in a commencement address, advised: "You must think internationally. You are members of the human race . . . Let us be a nation with sympathy enough to put war out of the world."), domestic violence, yuppies, ecofeminism. Protocol has demanded that we change from Afro-American to African American. Certain subjects are of much greater interest now, as per this chart:

SUBJECT	FOURTH EDITION	FIFTH EDITION
business	19	31
community	4	17
homosexual & lesbian	17	55
science & scientists	29	72

Happily, the proliferation of books by and about women has rendered my task virtually impossible; I am like a kid in a candy store with just a dollar to spend and five minutes to catch the school bus.

Yet, much as many things change, some, sadly, seem not to. More than 2,000 years ago, Sepulcia wrote:

> They are a little worried about me,
> afraid I might trip up,
> marry a nobody.

The old roles are still the expected roles, and this applies to women's professional life as well. In the professions, including literature, the canon is still dominated by men. The recipients of Pulitzer Prizes offer a simple example. Of the 35 awards granted for fiction since 1965, 11 have gone to women. All other categories in which the prizes are conferred were established in 1986. In 14 years, only one woman—Tina Rosenberg—has been awarded the prize in the category of nonfiction; in biography, two women; in history, three; in drama, three; and in poetry, four. In all, of 104 Pulitzer Prizes awarded, 24 have been bestowed upon women. Women still have a long way to go.

The first edition of *The Quotable Woman* was published December 1977 and included 1,334 women born from the year 1800. At 25, the American jockey Denise Boudrot was the youngest entrant; her youthful position in this fifth edition has been usurped by 20-year-old Zlata Filipovic, whose diary of the horrors she endured in Bosnia is quoted. The current edition is more inclusive than ever, with 3,667 women from all over the world—952 from non-English-speaking countries—sharing more than 18,000 of their thoughts, witticisms, ruminations, philosophies, perceptions, prejudices, feelings, anger, joy, love, care, hope, dreams and schemes. This, too, has been a remarkable increase over the last edition's 12,500 quotations. The women represent 128 nationalities and 14 ethnicities and come from all walks of life: from queens to courtesans, lawyers to welfare mothers, politicians to beauticians—and scientists. The latter were a major focus for me in this edition: 208 women in the sciences are represented in these pages (no small task, as many scientists, though often brilliant, are not necessarily eloquent).

CRITERIA

I posted a flyer on my office wall that I made to remind me of the requirements of quotations to be included:

> NOT ONLY INFORM BUT
> *INSPIRE!*
> NOT ONLY EMOTE BUT
> *MOVE!*
> NOT ONLY AMUSE BUT
> *DELIGHT!*
> NOT ONLY INTIMATE BUT
> *REVEAL!*

Selection of material is a demanding and humbling task. What seems appropriate one day, taken out of context, may be bewildering a week later. As always, my first gleanings are kept in check until, after a healthy separation from the feeder material, they are reread. A quotation that doesn't make sense without providing a lengthy context cannot be included. However, if merely a fillip of information is needed, a footnote fills the bill.

The book is heavily glossed. With several young interns and assistants working to help me in my research over these last 15 months, I have had to face the fact that as I am getting older, the readership is getting younger, and what is familiar territory to me exists in the Dark Ages for my young wards in this quickly spinning world. It is difficult for me to realize that there are young people today with whom I'm acquainted who have barely heard of the Vietnam War, and the Korean War (vague even to me when I was 19) is, as Emily Dickinson might say, rather oblique.

At the same time, it is easy for me, in our new cyberspace age, to imagine that people all over the world will have access to this English-language volume. For both these reasons and more, I have elected to gloss the quotations densely, for I see this work, not only as a research tool, but a learning tool. Also, as this work becomes more and more inclusive, and as the English language falls into more and more common use the world over, I have to realize (or should I say hope) that the readership will include many who, again, do not share my referential map. And so I glossed—and glossed. At what point does one decide to explicate Tiananmen Square but not the day John F. Kennedy or Martin Luther King Jr. or Medgar Evers was shot? Doesn't everybody know who Bill Clinton is? Isn't it possible that John Ford is as obscure to a Gen-Xer as Rutherford Hayes is to most of us? If I gloss one president, must I not gloss them all? With no pat answers, it was my choice to err on the side of more information. Some of you may know most of the information included in the footnotes—please, don't be insulted. For those who didn't know, they provide a context; for those who did not have prior knowledge, they will help them to learn, and what could be more important than that?

There are more than 2,000 footnotes scattered throughout the Quotations section. Many (about half) are simply cross-references to another of the book's contributors (it is wonderful how often women refer to the work of other women, but discouraging how reluctant men still are to cite women). The remaining half offers thumbnail sketches either of the person or the event cited in the quotation.

As always, there are scores of notable women who, for myriad reasons and despite their laudable achievements, were left out. Either I wasn't able to find English-language translations of their words or, as with Elizabeth Hazen, the brilliant American microbiologist, I could not find a passage that met the requirements I established. Others, although included, are not as well represented as I would have wished (Carolyn Heilbrun and Dale Spender come to mind). Then there are those women whom I've considered my personal intellectual and spiritual mentors (e.g., Riane Eisler, Emily Dickinson and Ursula K. LeGuin) who are, I fear, overrepresented—but I couldn't help myself. A work like this is ongoing; already my precious under-the-desk box is filling with materials for the sixth edition.

THE INDEXES

There are four indexes in this volume. The first, the Biographical Index, offers the briefest of looks at the contributors' accomplishments: their full name (whereas, in the Quotations section and other indexes, only their familiar name is used), notable family relations, major achievements and awards. The Career and Occupation Index follows. Under six broad-based professions, a directory of which appears at its head, the 829 occupations of the women in this book are gathered—from slave to freedwoman, from householder to head of state. It is not always apparent how to categorize an occupation. There were some struggles. Under what category, for example, does one place a madam or brothel keeper? The simple solution would be "Householders, Laborers, Slaves and Miscellaneous," although I was tempted to place them under "Adventurers, Frontier Settlers, Heroes and Pilots"; finally, I realized, acceptable or not, that these women were in the business of entertainment, and, in fact, were highly successful at it. So—"Arts and Entertainment" it was. Then there are the issues of gender-neutral language, vexing me in all the indexes. Do I use *draftsman, draftsperson, drafter; fisherman, fisherwoman, or fisher*? My most frequent choice was the most neutral—*drafter, fisher,* etc.

The Ethnicity and Nationality Index conveniently groups women for the ethnographic researcher. My protracted argument with myself as to whether or not to include an ethnicity index in this edition is antithetical to the argument I presented to my publishers in 1988, when I began work on the fourth edition. Why was it so important to me then? Is it still? If I name some ethnicities, why not all ethnicities; why stop at African Americans, Asian Americans, white South Africans; why not name Italian English, Polish Mexican, Irish American? While it isn't disparaging to name one's nationality, might it be to name one's ethnicity? Why do I still vacillate? The various aspects of this argument remain, for me, unresolved. I know only one thing: I long for the day when these identifications are no more a matter of interest than, in looking through a family album, one notes the color of one's grandparents' eyes or whether their hair was straight, curly, or *there*.

George Sand wrote, "Classification is Ariadne's clue through the labyrinth of nature" (*Nouvelles Lettres d'un Voyageur*, 1869). The Subject Index is the sluice for those pursuing a special interest. Unlike the more typical keyword or phrase index, it is an abstract subject index; each quotation has been examined and analyzed for meaning and indexed accordingly. Keywords can throw a hunter off track. Using *greetings* as the keyword for Juana Inez de la Cruz's "Greetings, greenest branch," for example, would not aid the peruser looking for material on the Virgin Mary, to whom this greeting is addressed. To further aid the researcher, the 4,000 or so subjects are subclassified (more than 12,000 of those!), so that one doesn't have to wade through hundreds of quotations about "love" to find those specifically about "familial love," or "work" to find those specifically about "woman/women, work and ~." Because I chose to retain the integrity of language used in the quotations, those about similar subjects may be found variously under, for instance, "avarice" or "greed." A generous sprinkling of cross-references are meant to aide those in pursuit of just the right gem.

SYNERGY

Aside from the obvious joy of perusing quotations of remarkable women, or the need to find a quotation by a certain woman—or women—in a certain field of endeavor, the layout of this book can be useful in other, unexpected ways. While each section is useful on its own, for advanced research, they are designed to work in concert.

When searching for remarks about the environment by Native American women, for example, first find the contributors in the Ethnicity and Nationality Index, then look for their contributor numbers under environment, ecology, ecofeminism, etc. in the Subject Index.

Looking for humorous quotations? Go to the Career and Occupation Index and find the humorists and comedians; look them up in the Quotations section.

Vaguely recall something some woman wrote about roses? Let the Subject Index be your guide.

Each section of the book is preceded by is own "Notes to . . . ", which explains the nuts and bolts of abbreviations, format, etc.

SEMANTICS

"A word is dead when it is said, some say—/ I say it just begins to live that day" (Emily Dickinson). New words pop up, receive wide currency, then promptly disappear: *empowerment* is less popular than it once was; *nurturing* lingers on; *conflict resolution* is very in; *ecofeminism* is practically newborn. And while *gender* has been around since the first edition, not until recently has it attained such lofty and abundant usage. It is certainly amusing and possibly instructive to look at the Subject Index in this way.

One of the challenges in categorizing quotations that range all over the map and whose contributors are rooted in so many different eras and ethnic and social backgrounds is using words that represent their thoughts with integrity, but without being offensive to today's sensibilities. *The Handbook of Non-Sexist Writing*[1] has been my Polaris through several editions now. I also consulted with professors of women's studies, African-American studies, and Hispanic studies at the University of Washington to try and gauge the best usage today. Only in rare instances, when it very obligingly represents one and all, have I used the female form of a word. Thus, *comedian* and *writer* refer to professionals of both genders, except where otherwise noted in subclassifications ("women~"); but *goddess* is in a class of its own, as is *heroine* (but in a telescoped mode: hero/ine: see Notes to Subject Index). This is a word I personally shun. I much prefer Maya Angelou's clever *shero*; perhaps in the next edition I'll brave it. Other choices: *brotherhood* and *sisterhood* where literally applicable, but *esprit de corps* for expressing the larger sense of "brotherhood" of all peoples. *Actor*, not *actress*, since the latter's use in the 17th century when it was first applied was pejorative; but *princess* since, historically, it has always been in use with no derogation intended; *humankind* rather than *man* (as a race).

The struggle is ongoing and help is always welcome. As Gloria Steinem said, "Finding language that will allow people to act together while cherishing each other's individuality is probably the most feminist and therefore truly revolutionary function of writers."

Aside from its obvious usage, the Subject Index offers an unexpected look at the fashion and usage of language. Since it is known that there are 3,671 contributors in the book, it doesn't take long to establish a rough time line for them:

From	To	Contr. #s
5,000 b.c.e.	1 c.e.	1–75
1 c.e.	1500	76–300
1500	1700	301–535
1700	1800	536–840
1800	1875	841–1380
1875	1920	1381–2150
1921	1940	2151–2835
1941	present	2836–3657

With this little chronology as a yardstick, one can examine the Subject Index and see when a certain word went out of fashion (from *avarice* to *greed*, for example) and others first came into use (this is not official, of course, but a strong indicator). *Sin*, for example, is practically abandoned from 1920 on. In 1952, Eleanor Roosevelt claimed, "Television has completely revised what should go on at a political convention." And Lois Gould was talking about

[1]Miller, Casey, and Kate Swift (New York: Lippincott & Crowell, 1980).

computers in her 1970 novel *Such Good Friends*. Even though she has since been proved wrong, around 1775 Eliza Haywood wrote an article for *The Female Spectator* entitled "Flying Machines, The Impossibility of Their Use" in which she stipulates:

> All that can be justly objected against any arguments made use of to prove the reasonableness of a belief in a plurality of worlds is, that is to us, that live in this, no matter of concern, since there is not a possibility of traveling to them, or of ever becoming acquainted with their inhabitants.

CONCLUSION

I have tried to be eclectic in my selection, with a goal to serve all who search here. I see this work as a conduit for inspiration and understanding. As such I have endeavored to include women of all races, religions, nations and eras so that among these pages everyone will find someone with whom to identify and use.

For the most part, I am in awe of the women I study. I read excerpts from the works of Hannah Arendt, Riane Eisler, Mathilda Gage, Elizabeth Cady Stanton, Marie Desborde-Valmore, Murasaki Shikibu and many others, and I want to fall down on my knees and sing their praises. Ahhh, I sigh to myself, how can I ever hope to inspire, illuminate, direct others with my own writings? But I am so grateful to them for sharing their thoughts, enabling me to enlarge my understanding of the world.

Lastly, I do see this book as a political tool. The world is out of joint: I deeply believe that gender balance, within each of us and within our immediate and global communities, is crucial for healing our planet. When I created the first edition of *The Quotable Woman*, published 23 years ago, it was the first collection of women's quotations; there have been a few others since. At that time the major collections of quotations hardly included women's voices: one-half of 1 percent of all the quotations in the 14th edition of Bartlett's *Familiar Quotations* were by women; a similar absence of women could be found in *The Home Book of Quotations, The Oxford Book of Quotations*, et al. Since that time, the mainstream collections have vastly improved. Yet still we are, as a sex, underrepresented in the upper echelons of government, business, science and the arts. My continued faith is that *The Quotable Woman* will assist in raising the voices of women, not in a monolithic way—there is no one voice speaking for all women—but in a diverse way, a way that helps to widen the path toward gender equity that began, as we can see in these pages, many hundreds of years ago, escalating with the centuries, so that now, each decade, we bear witness toward a rebalancing of the sexes.

Guidelines for Use

The women quoted are presented in chronological order according to the year of their birth, then by year of death, then alphabetically. Each contributor has been assigned a number; guides to these contributor numbers appear in the running heads throughout the Quotations Section and are used in lieu of page numbers in all four indexes.

Where actual years of birth and/or death are not known, but could be estimated with reasonably accuracy, dates are followed by a question mark; dates that are less certain are preceded by "c." (circa). Dates shown with a slash (1734/37) indicate birth or death having taken place within that range of years. When the year of birth is not known but the year of death is, the latter has been used for placement in the chronology. When neither year is known, a *floruit* is used and the woman is placed at the beginning of the decade or decades during which she was at her height (e.g., fl. c. 1760–1770). It is often most difficult to ascertain years of birth among emerging voices who have not yet been consigned to the dusty pages of history. Between the time the manuscript was submitted to the publisher and the proofreading of pages, new facts were found. Rather than omit this information in service to form, it has been included, putting some of the "fl. 1980s or 90s" contributors out of chronological order. This may cause annoyance at the end of the Quotations section, where some 50 or so contemporary women had to be listed as (fl. 1980s) or (fl. 1990s).

Quotations for each contributor are also laid out chronologically, in ascending order, based on year of *publication*. Parenthetical dates within a source indicate the time at which the quotation was originally spoken, written or published and, again, are laid out chronologically. When no date could be ascertained, the abbreviation *n.d.* (no date) appears; these quotations are placed at the end of entries with known dates.

Sic is used sparingly; for reasons of historical interest, whenever it would not muddle meaning, I have elected to maintain original spellings and references.

When possible, the location of a quotation within its source is given—chapter, stanza, act, etc. Abbreviations used in source citations are: Vol.—volume; Pt.—part; Bk.—Book; Ch.—Chapter; St.—Stanza; Sec.—Section; No.—Number; Sc.—Scene, l.—line; l.l.—last line(s); c.—circa; ed.—editor; tr.—translator.

When a quotation is taken from a book, an article or any work by a writer other than the contributor, it is indicated by the words "Quoted in," followed by the source and its author. In the anthologies, "Quoted in" is not used; instead, editors are identified.

Quotation marks around a quotation indicate it was dialogue in the original source. Every effort has been made to maintain the integrity of form in all poetry.

For further information on the Indexes, see the prefatory notes to each.

QUOTATIONS

1. Eve (pre-4000 B.C.E.)
1 The serpent beguiled me, and I did eat.
Genesis, 3:13 *c. ninth century* B.C.E.

2. Spider Woman (3500?–B.C.E.?)
1 That is the Sun. You are meeting your Father the Creator for the first time. You must always remember and observe these three phases of your Creation. This time of the three lights, the dark purple, the yellow, and the red reveal in turn the mystery, the breath of life, and warmth of love. These comprise the Creator's plan of life for you as sung over you in the Song of Creation.
"The Creation of Spider Woman," Quoted in *The Book of Hopi* by Frank Waters *1963*

3. Isis (3100?–B.C.E.?)
1 I am Nature, the universal Mother, mistress of all the elements, primordial child of time, sovereign of all things spiritual, queen of the dead, queen also of the immortals, the single manifestation of all gods and goddesses that are. My nod governs the shining heights of Heaven, the wholesome sea-breezes, the lamentable silences of the world below. Though I am worshiped in many aspects, known by countless names, and propitiated with all manner of different rites, yet the whole round earth venerates me.
"The Goddess Isis Intervenes," *The Golden Ass by Apuleius*, Robert Graves, tr. *1978*

4. Enheduanna (c. 2354–? B.C.E.)
1 O lady of all truths . . .
"Inanna* and An," adapted by Anne Draffkorn Kilmer, Quoted in *The Exaltation of Inanna* by William W. Hallo and J. J. A. van Dijk *1968*
*Sumerian goddess of love.

2 You are in all our great rites.
Who can understand you?
"Inanna and An," adapted by Aliki and Willis Barnstone, Ibid.

3 cries of labor I gave birth to this hymn . . .
"Inanna and An," adapted by Anne Draffkorn Kilmer, Ibid.

4 My honeyed tongue is tied with confusion
Untitled, adapted by Anne Draffkorn Kilmer, Ibid.

5. Hagar (2300?–c. 1850 B.C.E.)
1 Thou God seest me: ... Have I also here looked after him that seeth me?
Genesis, 16:13 *c. ninth century* B.C.E.

6. Inanna (fl. 2300 B.C.E.)
1 The shepherd! I will not marry the shepherd!
His clothes are coarse; his wool is rough.
I will marry the farmer.
The farmer grows flax for my clothes.
The farmer grows barley for my table.
Quoted in *Inanna* by Diane Wolkstein and Samuel Noah Kramer *1983*

2 He put his hand in her hand.
He put his hand to her heart.
Sweet is the sleep of hand-to-hand.
Sweeter still the sleep of heart-to-heart.
Ibid.

7. Kubatum (fl. c. 2030 B.C.E.)
1 my sweet and darling one with whom I would speak honey—
youth, I am in love with you!
"Love Song to King Shu-Suen," St. 6, Thorkild Jacobsen, tr., *Most Ancient Verse*, Thorkild Jacobsen and John A. Wilson, eds. *n.d.*

8. Sarah (1987?–1860 B.C.E.)
1 After I am waxed old shall I have pleasure, my lord being old also?
Genesis, 18:12 *c. ninth century* B.C.E.

2 God hath made me to laugh, so that all that hear will laugh with me.
21:6, Ibid.

9. Leah (fl. 18th century B.C.E.)

1   Is there yet an portion or inheritance for us [Leah and Rachel] in our father's house?

Are we not counted of him strangers? For he hath sold us, and hath quite devoured also our money.

For all the riches which God hath taken from our father, that is ours, and our children's . . .*

Genesis, 31:14–16* *c. ninth century* B.C.E.

*See 13.

10. Lot's daughter (the elder) (fl. 18th century B.C.E.)

1   Our father is old, and there is not a man in the earth to come in unto us after the manner of all the earth;

Come let us make our father drink wine, and we will lie with him, that we may preserve seed of our father.

Genesis, 19:31, 32 *c. ninth century* B.C.E.

11. Rebekah (fl. 18th century B.C.E.)

1   Drink my lord: . . .

I will draw water for thy camels also, until they have done drinking.

Genesis, 24:18,19
c. ninth century B.C.E.

2   Upon me be thy curse, my son: only obey my voice, and go fetch me them.

27:13,19, Ibid.

12. Eristi–Aya (1790?–1745 B.C.E.)

1   Even warriors seized as booty in war are treated humanely. At least, treat me like them!

"A Letter to Her Mother," Willis Barnstone, tr., *A Book of Women Poets*, Aliki and Willis Barnstone, eds. *1980*

13. Rachel (?–1732 B.C.E.?)

1   Give me children, or else I die.

Genesis, 30:1 *c. ninth century* B.C.E.

14. Hathshepsut (fl. c. 1500–d. 1482 B.C.E.)

1   My command stands firm like the mountains and the sun's disk shines and spreads rays over the titulary of my August person, and my falcon rises high above the kingly banner unto all eternity.

Quoted in *The Remarkable Women of Ancient Egypt* by Barbara Lesko *1978*

15. Ankhesenpaton (fl. c. 1390 B.C.E.)

1   My husband, Nib-khuruia,* has recently died, he and I have no son. But thy sons, they say, are many. If thou wilt send me a son of thine, he shall become my husband.

Letter to Shuppiluliuma, the Hittite king (62 B.C.E.),
Quoted in *When Egypt Ruled the East* by
George Steindorff and Keith C. Seele *1942*
*Official name of Tutankhamen, who ruled c. 1379-1362 B.C.E.

16. Miriam (fl. c. 1250–30 B.C.E.)

1   Sing ye to the Lord, for he hath triumphed gloriously; the horse and his rider hath he thrown into the sea.

Exodus, 15:21
c. ninth century B.C.E.

17. Pharaoh's daughter (fl. 1250s B.C.E.)

1   Because I drew him [Moses] out of the water.

Exodus, 2:10 *c. ninth century* B.C.E.

18. Five Daughters of Zelophehad: Mahlah, Noah, Hoglah, Milcah and Tirzah (fl. 1240s–1200 B.C.E.)

1   Our father died in the wilderness, and he was not in the company of them that hath gathered themselves together against the Lord in the company of Kôr-ah; but died in his own sin, and had no sons.

Why should the name of our father be done away from among his family, because he hath no son? Give unto us therefore a possession among the brethren of our father.

Numbers, 27:3, 4 *c. ninth century* B.C.E.

19. Zipporah (fl. c. 1230 B.C.E.)

1   Surely a bloody husband art thou to me . . .

A bloody husband thou art, because of the circumcision.

Exodus, 4:25, 26 *c. ninth century* B.C.E.

20. Penelope (1214?–? B.C.E.)

1   Careless to please, with insolence ye woo!

Quoted in *The Odyssey* by Homer *c. 800* B.C.E.

2   When have I not been dreading dangers more grievous than the reality? Love is a thing replete with anxious fears.

Quoted in *Epistulae Heroidum [Letters from Heroines]*
by Ovid *c. 20* B.C.E.

21. Daughter of Jephthah the Gileadite (fl. c. 1140 B.C.E.)

1   Let this thing be done for me: let me alone two months, that I may go up and down upon the mountains, and bewail my virginity.

Judges, 11:37 *c. 550* B.C.E.

22. Naomi (fl. c. 1100 B.C.E.)

1   Go, return each to her mother's house . . .*

Ruth, 1:8 *late fifth/fourth century* B.C.E.
*Spoken to her daughters-in-law, Ruth and Orpah. See 23.

23. Ruth (fl. c. 1100 B.C.E.)

1   Intreat me not to leave thee,* or to return from following after thee: for whither thou goest, I will go; and where thou lodgest, I will lodge: thy people shall be my people, and thy God my God:

Where thou diest, will I die, and there will I be buried: the Lord do so to me, and more also, if ought but death part thee and me.

Ruth, 1:16, 17 *late fifth/fourth century* B.C.E.
*Her mother-in-law, Naomi: see 22.

24. Delilah (fl. c. 1080 B.C.E.)

1   How canst thou say, I love thee, when thine heart is not with me? Thou hast mocked me these three times, and hast not told me wherein thy great strength lieth.

16:15, Judges *c. 550* B.C.E.

25. Wife of Manoah (fl. 1080 B.C.E.)

1   If the Lord were pleased to kill us, he would not have received a burnt offering and a meat offering at our hands, neither

would he have shewed us all these things, nor would as at this time have told us such things as these.

Judges, 13:23 *c. 550 b.c.e.*

26. First wife of Samson (fl. c. 1080 b.c.e.)

1 Thou dost but hate me, and lovest me not; thou hast put forth a riddle unto the children of my people, and hast not told it me.

Judges, 14:16 *c. 550 b.c.e.*

27. Deborah (fl. c. 1070 b.c.e.)

1 Speak, ye that ride on white asses, ye that sit in judgment, and walk by the way.

Judges, with Barak,* 5:10 *c. 550 b.c.e.*

*Leader who, with Deborah, delivered Israel from the Canaanites.

2 So let all think enemies perish, O Lord: but let them that love him be as the sun when he goeth forth in his might. And the land had rest forty years.

5:31, Ibid.

28. Jael (fl. c. 1070 b.c.e.)

1 Turn in, my Lord, turn in to me; fear not.

Judges, 4:18 *c. 550 b.c.e.*

29. Woman of Abel of Beth-maacah (fl. c. 1040–c. 970 b.c.e.)

1 . . . why wilt thou swallow up the inheritance of the Lord?

2 Samuel, 20:19 *c. 550 b.c.e.*

30. Hannah (1040 b.c.e.?–?)

1 My heart rejoiceth in the Lord, mine horn is exalted in the Lord: my mouth is enlarged over mine enemies; because I rejoice in thy salvation.

There is none holy as the Lord: for there is none beside thee: neither is there any rock like our God.

Talk no more so exceeding proudly; let not arrogancy come out of your mouth: for the Lord is a God of knowledge, and by him actions are weighed.

The bows of the mighty men are broken, and they that stumbled are girded with strength.

They that were full have hired out themselves for bread; and they that were hungry ceased: so that the barren hath born seven; and she that hath many children is waxed feeble.

The Lord killeth, and maketh alive: he bringeth down to the grave, and bringeth up.

The Lord maketh poor, and maketh rich: he bringeth low, and lifteth up.

He raiseth up the poor out of the dust, and lifteth up the beggar from the dunghill, to set them among princes, and to make them inherit the throne of glory: for the pillars of the earth are the Lord's, and he hath set the world upon them.

He will keep the feet of his saints, and the wicked shall be silent in darkness; for by strength shall no man prevail.

The adversaries of the Lord shall be broken to pieces; out of heaven shall he thunder upon them: the Lord shall judge the ends of the earth; and he shall give strength unto his king, and exalt the horn of his anointed.

1 Samuel, 2:1-10 *c. 550 b.c.e.*

31. Wife of Phinehas (1040?–970 b.c.e.)

1 The glory is departed from Israel: for the ark of God is taken.

Samuel, 4:22 *c. 550 b.c.e.*

32. Michal (fl. c. 1010–970 b.c.e.)

1 If thou save not thy life tonight, tomorrow thou shalt be slain.

Samuel, 19:11 *c. 550 b.c.e.*

33. Bathsheba (fl. c. 1000–970 b.c.e.)

1 And thou, my lord, O king, the eyes of all Israel are upon thee, that thou shouldest tell them who shall sit on the throne of my lord the king after him.

1 Kings, 1:20 *c. 550 b.c.e.*

34. Abigail (fl. 990s b.c.e.)

1 Behold, let thine handmaid be a servant to wash the feet of the servants of my lord.

1 Samuel, 25:41 *c. 550 b.c.e.*

35. Tamar (fl. c. 990 b.c.e.)

1 Nay, my brother, do not force me; for no such thing ought to be done in Israel: do not thou this folly.

2 Samuel, 13:12
c. 550 b.c.e.

36. Prostitute of Jerusalem (mother of the dead child) (fl. 950s b.c.e.)

1 Let it be neither mine nor thine, but divide it.

1 Kings, 3:26 *c. 550 b.c.e.*

37. Prostitute of Jerusalem (mother of the living child) (fl. c. 950 b.c.e.)

1 O my lord, give her the living child, and in no wise slay it: she is the mother thereof.

1 Kings, 3:26 *c. 550 b.c.e.*

38. Queen of Sheba (fl. 950s b.c.e.)

1 Howbeit I believed not the words, until I came, and mine eyes had seen it: and, behold, the half was not told me: thy wisdom and prosperity exceedeth the fame which I heard.

Kings, 10:7 *c. 550 b.c.e.*

39. Tekoa (fl. 940 c. b.c.e.)

1 For we must needs die, and are as water spilt on the ground, which cannot be gathered up again. . . .

2 Samuel, 14:14
c. 550 b.c.e.

40. Jezebel (fl. c. 870–853 b.c.e.)

1 . . . arise, and eat bread, and let thine heart be merry . . .

1 Kings, 21:7 *c. 550 b.c.e.*

41. Wife of Job (fl. eighth century b.c.e.)

1 Dost thou still retain thine integrity? Curse God, and die.

Job, 2:9 *c. early fifth century b.c.e.*

42. Semiramis (fl. eighth century b.c.e.)

1 Nature gave me the form of a woman; my actions have raised me to the level of the most valiant of men.

Quoted in *Women of Beauty and Heroism* by Frank B. Goodrich *1858*

43. Anna (fl. 720s B.C.E.)

1 Alas! I let you leave me, my child, you, the light of my eyes.

Tobit, 10:5 c. 175-164 B.C.E.

44. Sarah (fl. c. 720 B.C.E.)

1 I cannot cause my father a sorrow which would bring down his old age to the dwelling of the dead.

Tobit, 3:10 c. 175-164 B.C.E.

45. Edna (fl. c. 720 B.C.E.)

1 Courage, daughter! May the Lord of heaven turn your grief to joy! Courage, daughter!

Tobit, 7:16 c. 175–164 B.C.E.

46. Sappho (fl. c. 610–535 B.C.E.)

1 When anger spreads through the breast, guard thy tongue from barking idly.

Untitled fragment, Quoted in *Women in the Golden Ages*
by Amelia Gere Mason *1901*

2 . . . death is an evil; the gods have so judged; had it been good, they would die.

Ibid.

3 I do not expect to touch the heavens with my two arms

Untitled fragment, Quoted in *Distinguished Women Writers*
by Virginia Moore *1934*

4 Gentle ladies, you will remember till old age what we did together in our brilliant youth!

Ibid.

5 Now Eros has shaken my thoughts, like a wind among highland oaks.

Ibid.

6 Love, fatal creature. . . .

Ibid.

7 Now love the limb-loosener sweeps me away. . . .

Ibid.

8 Some say an army of horsemen
is the fairest sight
on this sluggish black earth,
others an army of foot-soldiers,
    and others a navy of ships,
but I say it is the one you love.

Ibid.

9 Like a mountain whirlwind
punishing the oak trees,
love shattered my heart.

Untitled fragment, *Greek Lyric Poetry*, Willis Barnstone, ed.
and tr. *1962*

10 all my flesh is wrinkled with age,
my black hair has faded to white,

my legs can no longer carry me,
once nimble like a fawn's,

but what can I do?
It cannot be undone,

no more than can pink-armed Dawn
not end in darkness on earth.

Untitled, Sts. 2-5, Ibid.

11 If I meet
you suddenly, I can't

speak—my tongue is broken;
a thick flame runs under
my skin; seeing nothing,
hearing only my own ears
drumming, I drip with sweat;
trembling shakes my body

and I turn paler than
dry grass. At such times
death isn't far from me.

Untitled, *The Penguin Book of Women Poets*, Carol Cosman, Joan Keefe and Kathleen Weaver, eds. *1978*

12 The angel of spring, the mellow-throated nightingale.

No. 39, Fragments n.d.

13 Art thou the topmost apple
The gatherers could not reach,
Reddening on the bough?
Shall I not take thee?

No. 53, Ibid.

47. Erinna (fl. c. 610–595 B.C.E.)

1 Little trails through my heart that are
Still warm—my remembrances of you.

"This Distaff," Marilyn Bentley Arthur, tr., *Women Poets of the World*, Joanna Bankier and Deirdre Lashgari, eds. *1983*

48. Mettika (fl. sixth century B.C.E.)

1 I sit here on this rock.
And over my spirit blows
The breath of liberty

"Though I am weak and tired now," *Therigatha,*
Uma Chakravarti and Kumkum Roy, trs. *80 B.C.E.*

49. Mutta (fl. sixth century B.C.E.)

1 So free am I, so gloriously free,
Free from three petty things—
From mortar, from pestle and from my twisted lord,

"So free am I, so gloriously free," *Therigatha,* Uma
Chakravarti and Kumkum Roy, trs. *80 B.C.E.*

50. Sumangalamata (fl. sixth century B.C.E.)

1 How wonderfully free, from kitchen drudgery.
Free from the harsh grip of hunger,
And from empty cooking pots

"A woman well set free! How free I am," *Therigatha,*
Uma Chakravarti & Kumkum Roy,
trs. *80 B.C.E.*

51. Judith (fl. sixth century–d. 495 B.C.E.)

1 If you cannot sound the depths of the heart of man or unravel the arguments of his mind, how can you fathom the God who made all things, or sound his mind or unravel his purposes?

Judith, 8:12-14 c. 150 B.C.E.

2   But you have no right to demand guarantees where the designs
of the Lord our God are concerned. For God is not to be coerced as man is, nor is he, like mere man, to be cajoled.

8:16, Ibid.

3   Her sandal ravished his eyes,
her beauty took his soul prisoner . . .
and the scimitar cut through his neck!

16:9, Ibid.

4   May your whole creation serve you!
For you spoke and things came into being,
you sent your breath and they were put together,
and no one can resist your voice.

16:14, Ibid.

5   A little thing indeed
is a sweetly smelling sacrifice. . . .

16:16, Ibid.

6   Woe to the nations
who rise against my race!

16:17, Ibid.

52. Huldah (fl. 580s B.C.E.)

1   Behold therefore, I will gather thee unto thy fathers, and thou
shalt be gathered into thy grave in peace; and thine eyes shall
not see all the evil which I will bring upon this place.

2 Kings, 22:20 c. 550 B.C.E.

53. Susanna (fl. c. 580–d. 538 B.C.E.)

1   But I prefer to fall innocent into your power than to sin in the
eyes of the Lord.

Daniel, 13:23 c. 167-164 B.C.E.

54. Ambapali (fl. c. 560–d. 480 B.C.E.)

1   Such was my body once. Now it is weary and tottering,
the home of many ills, an old house with flaking plaster.
Not otherwise is the world of the truthful.

Untitled, St. 9, The Wonder that was India,
A. L. Bashun, ed. and tr. 1959

2   The truth of the Truth-speaker's words
doesn't change.

"Therigatha XIII," St. 1 (refrain) n.d.

3   Swelling, round, firm, and high,
both my breasts were once splendid.
In the drought of old age, they dangle
like empty old water bags.

St. 14 n.d., Ibid.

55. Corinna (fl. c. 520–d. 420 B.C.E.)

1   When he sailed into the harbor
his ship became a snorting horse.

Untitled, St. 1, Greek Lyric Poetry, Willis Barnstone, ed.
and tr. 1962

2   asleep forever?
you were not like that, Corinna,
in the old days.

Untitled, John Dillon, tr., The Penguin Book of Women
Poets, Carol Cosman, Joan Keefe and Kathleen Weaver, eds.
1978

56. Esther (fl. c. 510–d. 465 B.C.E.)

1   . . . if I perish, I perish.

Esther, 4:16 c. 199-150 B.C.E.

2   . . . you, lord, chose
Israel out of all the nations
and our ancestors out of all the people of old times
to be your heritage for ever . . .

4:17, Ibid.

3   Never let men mock at our ruin.

Ibid.

57. Rebecca (fl. fifth century B.C.E.)

1   It is indeed better for us to live with wild beasts and perish of
hunger than to be compelled by Greeks and idolaters to fall
into the filth of marriage.

Acts of Xanthippe and Polyxena, XXXI, Ante-Nicene
Fathers edition, Alexander Roberts and James Donaldson,
eds. 1955 (repr).

58. Telesilla (fl. fifth century B.C.E.)

1   Run swiftly to escape
the rape of the hunter Alpheus.

Untitled, Greek Lyric Poetry, Willis Barnstone, ed. and tr.
1978

59. Xanthippe (fl. fifth century B.C.E.)

1   O beauty of the world! For that which we hitherto thought to
come of itself, we know now that all things are beautifully
fashioned by the beautiful One.

Acts of Xanthippe and Polyxena,* VI, Ante-Nicene Fathers
edition, Alexander Roberts and James Donaldson, eds.
1955 (repr.)

*See 84.

2   Why is his* walk quiet and equable, as of one who expects
to take in his arms one that is pursued? Why is his countenance kindly, as of one that tends the sick? Why does he
look so lovingly hither and thither, as one who desires to assist those who are seeking to flee from the mouths of
dragons?

VII, Ibid.

*St. Paul, the Apostle, biblical era.

60. Artemisia (fl. c. 480 B.C.E.)

1   Spare your ships, and do not risk a battle; for these people [the
Greeks] are as much superior to your people in seamanship, as
men to women.

Remark to King Xerxes,* Bk. VIII, Quoted in
The Persian Wars by Herodotus c. 450 B.C.E.
*519?–465 B.C.E., King of Persia (486–465 B.C.E.)

61. Praxilla (fl. c. 450 B.C.E.)

1   You gaze at me teasingly through the window:
a virgin—and below—a woman's thighs.

Untitled, Greek Lyric Poetry, Willis Barnstone, ed.
and tr. 1962

2   Loveliest of what I leave
is the sun himself
Next to that the bright stars
and the face of mother moon

Oh yes, and cucumbers in season,
    and apples, and pears.
      "Adonis Dying," John Dillon, tr., *The Penguin Book of*
      Women Poets, Carol Cosman, Joan Keefe and Kathleen
      Weaver, eds. *1978*

3 Watch out, my dear,
    there's a scorpion under every stone.
                    Untitled fragment, Ibid.

62. Aspasia (fl. c. 420 B.C.E.)

1 . . . if you don't endeavor that there be not a better husband
and wife in the world than yourselves, you will always be
wishing for that which you shall think best.
      Quoted by Socrates in *Dialogue of Aeschines* by Plato
                              c. 360–386 C.E.

2 Your great glory is not to be inferior to what God has made
you, and the greatest glory of a woman is to be least talked
about by men, whether they are praising you or criticizing you.
      Quoted in *History of the Pelopennesian War* by Thucydides
                              c. 413 B.C.E.

63. Theano (fl. 420s B.C.E.)

1 Put off your shame with your clothes when you go in to your
husband, and put it on again when you come out.
      Bk. VIII, Sec. 43, Quoted *in Lives, Teachings, and Sayings of*
      Famous Philosophers by Diogenes Laertius *c. 300 B.C.E.*

2 The gods could not be honored by lies.
      Quoted in *Biography of Distinguished Women* by Sarah
                          Josepha Hale* 1879
  *See 788.

64. Phyrne (fl. fourth century B.C.E.)

1 He* is not a man but a statue.
      Quoted in *Lives, Teachings, and Sayings of Famous Philoso-*
      phers by Diogenes Laertius *c. 300 B.C.E.*
  *The Greek philosopher Xenocrates.

65. Lais (?-340 B.C.E.)

1 I do not understand what is meant by the austerity of philosophers, for with this fine name, they are as much in my power
as the rest of the Athenians.
      Quoted in *Biography of Distinguished Women*
              by Sarah Josepha Hale* 1879
  *See 788.

66. Lady Ho (fl. 300 B.C.E.)

1 When a pair of magpies fly together
They do not envy the pair of phoenixes.
      "A Song of Magpies," *The Orchid Boat, Women Poets of*
      China, Kenneth Rexroth and Ling Chung, eds. and trs. *1972*

67. Anyte of Tegea (fl. c. 300 B.C.E.)

1 This place is sacred to the goddess.
Here her constant pleasure
is to watch the sea as it shimmers from the shore
      Quoted in *Classical Women Poets*, Josephine Balmer, tr. *1966*

68. Sibyl, the Jewish (fl. c. 190–d. 165 B.C.E.?)

1 . . . here is a city, Chaldean Ur,

Whence come a race of most upright men,
Who are ever right-minded and their works good.
They are neither concerned for the sun's course,
Nor the moon's, nor for monstrosities on earth,
Nor for satisfaction from ocean's depths,
Nor for signs of sneezing and the augury from birds;
Nor for soothsaying, nor sorcery, nor incantations;
Nor for deceitful follies of ventriloquists.
They do not, Chaldean fashion, astrologize,
Nor watch the stars. . . .
But they are concerned about rightness and virtue.
      The Fourth Book of Sibylline Oracles
                         c. 100 B.C.E.

69. Chuo Wên-chün (179?–117 B.C.E.)

1 Why should marriage bring only tears?
All I wanted was a man
With a single heart,
And we would stay together
As our hair turned white,
Not somebody always after wriggling fish
With his big bamboo rod.
      "A Song of White Hair," *The Orchid Boat*,
      Women Poets of China, Kenneth Rexroth and Ling
                         Chung, eds. and trs. *1972*

70. Mother of the Seven Brothers (164?–161 B.C.E.)

1 I do not know how you appeared in my womb; it was not I
who endowed you with breath and life, I had not the shaping
of your every part.
    It is the creator of the world, ordaining the process of
man's birth and presiding over the origin of all things.
      2 Maccabees, 7:22-23 *c. 41–44 C.E.*

2 I implore you, my child, observe heaven and earth, consider all
that is in them, and acknowledge that God made them out of
what did not exist, and that mankind comes into being the
same way.
                              Ibid., 7:28

71. Cornelia (fl. c. 160–140 B.C.E.)

1 These are all the jewels of which I can boast.*
      Quoted in *Biography of Distinguished Women* by Sarah
                          Josepha Hale** 1876
  *Referring to her sons, Tiberius and Gaius Gracchi. ** See 788.

72. Wife of Ch'in Chia (fl. first century B.C.E.)

1 I stood on tiptoe gazing into the distance
Interminably gazing at the road that had taken you.
      "Ch'in Chia's Wife's Reply," *Translations from the Chinese*,
                          Arthur Waley, tr. *1919*

73. Hsi-chün (fl. 100s B.C.E.)

1 Would I were a yellow stork
And could fly to my old home!
      "Lament of Hsi-chün," *Translations from the Chinese*,
                          Arthur Waley, tr. *1919*

74. Hortensia (85 B.C.E.–?)

1 . . . you assume the glorious title of reformers of the state, a
title which will turn to your eternal infamy, if, without the
least regard to the laws of equity, you persist in your wicked

resolution of plundering those [women] of their lives and fortunes, who have given you no just cause of offence.

        (c. 45 B.C.E.), Vol. IV, Quoted in *Civil Wars*
        by Appian of Alexandria *32–34 C.E.*

2   Why should we pay taxes when we have no part in the honors,
the commands, the state craft for which you contend?
        Speech before the Roman Triumvirate (42 B.C.E.), *Women in*
        World History Curriculum, http:womeninhistory.com,
        Lyn Reese, Director *1996–97*

75. Cleopatra VII (69 B.C.E.–30 C.E.)

1   Leave the fishing-rod, Great General, to us sovereigns of
Pharos and Canopus. Your game is cities and kings and continents.
        Remark to Marc Antony,* Quoted in Ch. 9,
        Cleopatra of Egypt by Philip W. Sergeant *1909*
*83?–30 B.C.E. Roman general

2   As surely as one day I shall administer justice on the Capitol . . . *
        Ch. 13, Ibid.
*Her favorite oath, referring to the capital of the Roman Empire.

3   Fool! Don't you see now that I could have poisoned you a hundred times had I been able to live without you!
        Remark to Marc Antony, Quoted in Ch. 5,
        Cleopatra's Daughter, the Queen of Mauretania
        by Beatrice Chanler *1934*

4   Nothing could part us while we lived, but death seems to
threaten to divide us. You, a Roman born, have found a grave
in Egypt. I, an Egyptian, am to seek that favour, and none but
that, in your country.
        Spoken over Marc Antony's tombstone, Ch. 20,
        Quoted in *The Life and Times of Cleopatra* by Arthur
        Weigall *1968*

76. Sulpicia (fl. c. 60 B.C.E.–14 C.E.)

1   Drat my hateful birthday
   to be spent in the boring old country.
        Untitled, John Dillon, tr., *The Penguin Book of Women*
        Poets, Carol Cosman, Joan Keefe and Kathleen Weaver, eds.
        1978

2   At last love has come. I would be more ashamed
   to hide it in cloth than leave it naked
        Untitled, *A Book of Women Poets*, Aliki and
        Willis Barnstone, eds. and trs. *1980*

3   Friends worry about me and are upset that somehow
   I might tumble into bed with a nobody.
        Ibid.

4   Trips are often poorly timed.
        Ibid.

5   At last. It's come. Love,
   the kind that veiling
   will give me reputation more
   than showing my soul naked to someone.
        Untitled (1), *Six Poems, from Corpus Tibullianum*, Lee T.
        Pearcy, tr. *1995*

6   indiscretion has its charms
        Ibid.

7   What is sweeter than the city?
        Untitled (2), Ibid.

77. Porcia (?–42 B.C.E.)

1   Brutus,* I am Cato's** daughter, and I was brought into thy
house, not, like a mere concubine, to share thy bed and board
merely, but to be a partner in thy troubles. Thou, indeed, art
faultless as a husband; but how can I show thee any grateful service if I am to share neither thy secret suffering nor the anxiety
which craves a loyal confidant? I know that a woman's nature is
thought too weak to endure a secret; but good rearing and excellent companionship go far towards strengthening the
character, and it is my happy lot to be both the daughter of Cato
and the wife of Brutus. Before this I put less confidence in these
advantages, but now I know that I am superior even to pain.***
        From *Parallel Lives* by Plutarch (c. 100 C.E.), Quoted in
        Plutarch's Lives, Vol. VI, B. Perrin, tr. *1914–1926*
*85?–42 B.C.E. Roman political and military leader. **95–46
B.C.E. Roman statesman. ***Spoken shortly before Caesar's murder, when she sensed Brutus' troubled mind; she wounded her
thigh with a small knife just before making the above speech.

78. Saint Elisabeth (fl. c. 20 B.C.E.–? C.E.)

1   Blessed art thou [Mary*] among women, and blessed is the
fruit of thy womb.
     And whence is this to me, that the mother of my Lord
should come to me?
     For, lo, as soon as the voice of thy salutation sounded in
mine ears, the babe [John the Baptist] leaped in my womb for
joy.
     And blessed is she that believed: for there shall be a perfor-
mance of those things which were told her from the Lord.
        Luke, 1:42-45 *c. 65-80 C.E.*
*See 79.

79. Mary (fl. 7 B.C.E.–25 C.E.)

1   My soul doth magnify the Lord, And my spirit hath rejoiced in
God my Savior.
     For he hath regarded the low estate of his handmaiden; for,
behold, from henceforth all generations shall call me blessed.
     For he that is mighty hath done to me great things; and
holy is his name.
     And his mercy is on them that fear him from generation to
generation.
     He hath shewed strength with his arm; he hath scattered
the proud in the imagination of their hearts.
     He hath put down the mighty from their seats, and exalted
them of low degree.
     He hath filled the hungry with good things; and the rich he
hath sent empty away.
     He hath helped his servant Israel, in remembrance of his
mercy;
     As he spake to our fathers, to Abraham, and to his seed for
ever.
        Luke, 1:46-55 *c. 65-80 C.E.*

80. Agrippina the Younger (14–59 C.E.)

1   No philosophy, my son [Nero*]; it is of no use to an emperor.
        Ch. 8, Quoted in *The Great Empress, A Portrait*
        by Maximilian Schele de Vere *1870*
*(37–68 C.E.), Emperor of Rome (54–68 C.E.).

2   Strike the womb that bore a monster!
        Ch. 11, Ibid.

81. Mary Magdalene (fl. c. 20 C.E.)

1 They have taken away the Lord out of the sepulchre, and we know not where they have laid him.

> John, 20:2 *100 C.E.*

82. Salome (fl. c. 20 C.E.)

1 I will that thou give me by and by in a charger the head of John the Baptist.

> Mark, 6:25 *68*

83. Samaritan Woman (fl. c. 20 C.E.)

1 How is it that thou [Christ], being a Jew, askest drink of me, which am a woman of Samaria? . . .

> John, 4:9 *100*

84. Polyxena (fl. c. 30 C.E.)

1 Would that I were as one of the wild beasts that I might not know what captivity is.

> *Acts of Xanthippe* and Polyxena*, XXVI, Ante-Nicene Fathers edition, Alexander Roberts and James Donaldson, eds. *1955 (repr.)*

*See 59.

2 No one sees or heeds or hears my groaning. Verily I shall beseech Him that sees the hidden things, for who is more pitiful and compassionate than He who always keeps watch over the oppressed?

> Ibid.

85. Boadicea (fl. c. 40–65 C.E.)

1 It will not be the first time, Britons, that you have been victorious under the conduct of your queen. For my part, I come not here as one descended of royal blood, not to fight for empire or riches, but as one of the common people, to avenge the loss of their liberty, the wrongs of myself and children.

> Speech, Quoted in *Biography of Distinguished Women* by Sarah Josepha Hale* *1876*

*See 788.

2 Roman lust has gone so far that not even our own persons remain unpolluted. If you weigh well the strengths of our armies, you will see that in this battle we must conquer or die. This is a woman's resolve. As for the men, they may live or be slaves.

> Quoted in *The Dinner Party, A Symbol of our Heritage* by Judy Chicago* *1979*

*See 2744.

86. Arria the Elder (?–42 C.E.)

1 It does not hurt, my Paetus.*

> Bk. III, epistle 16, Quoted in Epistles by Pliny the Younger *c. 100–109*

*Remark to her husband, who had been ordered to commit suicide, after she had stabbed herself.

87. Pan Chao (45?–115? C.E.)

1 The virtues of women are not brilliant talent, nor distinction and elegance. The virtues of women are reserve, quiet, chastity, orderliness, governing herself to maintain a sense of shame, and conducting herself according to the rules of Confucian etiquette.

> From *Nü Chieh* [Precepts for Women], Quoted in *Chinese Women: Yesterday and Today* by Florence Ayscough *1936*

2 Only needle-and-thread's delicate footsteps are truly broadranging yet without beginning!

> "Needle and Thread," St. 3, Richard Mather and Rob Swigart, trs., *Women Poets of the World*, Joanna Bankier and Deirdre Lashgari, eds. *1983*

3 How can those who count pennies calculate their worth? They may carve monuments yet lack all understanding.

> Ibid., St. 5

88. Lady Pan (45?–115?)

1 I took a piece of the rare cloth of Ch'i,
White silk glowing and pure as frost on
    snow,
and made you a fan of harmony and joy,
As flawlessly round as the full moon.

> "A Present from the Emperor's New Concubine," *Love and the Turning Year: One Hundred More Poems from the Chinese*, Kenneth Rexroth, ed. and tr. *1970*

89. Lydia (fl. 50s C.E.)

1 If ye have judged me to be faithful to the Lord, come into my house, and abide there.

> Acts, 16:15 *c. 85-95 C.E.*

90. Slave girl who was a soothsayer (fl. c. 50 C.E.)

1 These men are the servants of the most high God, which shew unto us the way of salvation.

> Acts, 16:17 *c. 85-95 C.E.*

91. Poppæa Sabina (fl. 50s–60 C.E.)

1 Rather die than see my beauty pass away!

> Ch. 9, Quoted in *The Great Empress, A Portrait* by Maximilian Schele de Vere *1870*

92. Sulpicia (80?–99 C.E.)

1 . . . Priscus Cato* held it of such deep import to determine whether the Roman stock would better be upheld by prosperity or adversity.—By adversity, doubtless; for when the love of country urges them to defend themselves by arms, and their wife held prisoner together with their household goods, they combine just like wasps, (a bristling band, with weapons all unsheathed along their yellow bodies,). . . .

> *Satire c. 90*

*Probably the same as Publius Valerius Cato, the first-century C.E. Roman poet and grammarian.

2 . . . when care-dispelling peace has returned, forgetful of labour, commons and fathers together lie buried in lethargic sleep.

> Ibid.

93. Pompeia Plotina (80?–122)

1 May the gods send me forth from this august palace, whenever I may be destined to leave it, even as I now enter it; and may the high destiny to which fortune now raises me leave me in possession of the same qualities with which I this day assume it.

> Speech (99), Quoted in *Biography of Distinguished Women* by Sarah Josepha Hale* *1876*

*See 788.

94. Myrta (fl. first century)

1 Paul the servant of the Lord will save many in Rome and will nourish many with the word. . . so that there will be great grace in Rome.

> Quoted in "Word, Spirit and Power: Women in Early Christian Communities" by Elisabeth Schüssler Fiorenza, *Women of Spirit*, Rosemary Ruether* and Eleanor McLaughlin, eds. *1979*

*See 2692.

95. Okkur Macatti (fl. first–third century)

1 In Jasmine country, it is evening
for the hovering bees,
but look, he hasn't come back.

He left me and went in search
of wealth.

> "What She Said," Speaking of Siva, A. K. Ramanujan, ed. and tr. *1973*

96. Venmanippūti (fl. first–third century)

1 my arms grow beautiful
in the coupling
and grow lean
as they come away
What shall I make of this?

> "What She Said to her Girlfriend," St. 2, *Interior: Landscape: Love Poems from a Classical Tamil Anthology*, A. K. Ramanujan, ed. and tr. *1967*

97. Ts'ai Yen (162?–239?)

1 Heaven was pitiless.
It sent down confusion and separation.
Earth was pitiless.
It brought me to birth in such a time.
War was everywhere.
Every road was dangerous.
Soldiers and civilians everywhere
Fleeing death and suffering.

> "Eighteen Verses Sung to a Tartar Reed Whistle," I:2, *The Orchid Boat, Women Poets of China*, Kenneth Rexroth and Ling Chung, eds. a nd trs. *1972*

2 Men here are as savage as giant vipers,
And strut about in armour, snapping their bows.

> II:1, Ibid.

98. Vivia Perpetua (180?–203)

1 "Father," said I, "do you see this vase here, for example, or water pot or whatever?"

"Yes, I do," said he.

And I told him: "Could it be called by any other name than what it is?"

And he said: "No."

"Well, so too I cannot be called anything other than what I am, a Christian."

> Ch. 3, Quoted in *Perpetua's Passion, The Death and Memory of a Young Roman Woman* by Joyce E. Salisbury* *1997*

*See 3023.

99. Zenobia of Palmyra (240–300)

1 By valor alone, by the force of arms only, can wars be brought to a close.

> Letter to Aurelian Augustus* (272), Quoted *in Women of Beauty and Heroism* by Frank B. Goodrich *1858*

*212?–75, Roman emperor (270–75).

100. Trieu Thi Trinh (fl. c. 270)

1 My wish is to ride the tempest, tame the waves, kill the sharks. I will not resign myself to the usual lot of women who bow their heads and become concubines.

> Remark (270), Quoted *in Women in World History Curriculum*, http://www.womeninhistory.com, Lyn Reese, Director *1996–97*

101. Auvaiyar (fl. third century?)

1 This is the womb that carried him,
like a stone cave,
lived in by a tiger and now abandoned.

> Untitled, George Hart, tr., *Women Poets of the World*, Joanna Bankier and Deirdre Lashgari, eds. *1983*

102. Kaccipēṭṭu Nānnakaiyār   (fl. third century?)

1 . . . a dream
that lied like truth.

> "What She Said," St. 1, *Interior Landscape: Love Poems from a Classical Tamil Anthology*, A. K. Ramanujan, ed. and tr. *1967*

2 I grow lean
in loneliness,
like a water lily
gnawed by a beetle.

> St. 3, Ibid.

103. Tzŭ Tzu Yeh (fl. third–fourth century)

1 I let down my silken hair
Over my shoulders
And open my thighs
Over my lover.
"Tell me, is there any part of me
That is not lovable?"

> "Song," II, *The Orchid Boat, Women Poets of China*, Kenneth Rexroth and Ling Chung, eds. and trs. *1972*

104. Monica (340–395)

1 Son, what I should here, and why I am here, I know not; the hope of this life is now quite spent.

> Quoted in *Biography of Distinguished Women* by Sarah Josepha Hale* *1876*

*See 788.

2 Nothing is far from God; and I do not fear that he will not know where to find me at the resurrection.

> Ibid.

105. Iwa no Hime (?–347)

1 In the autumn field,
Over the rice ears,
The morning mist trails,

Vanishing somewhere. . . .
Can my love fade too?
> "Longing for the Emperor," *The Penguin Book of Japanese Verse*, Goeffrey Bownas and Anthony Thwaite, eds. and trs. *1964*

106. Hypatia (370?–415)

1 Life is an unfoldment, and the further we travel the more truth we can comprehend. To understand the things that are at our door is the best preparation for understanding those that lie beyond.
> "Hypatia," Quoted in *Little Journeys to the Homes of Great Teachers* by Elbert Hubbard *1908*

2 Men will fight for a superstition quite as quickly as for a living truth—often more so, since a superstition is so intangible you cannot get at it to refute it, but truth is a point of view, and so is changeable.
> Ibid.

3 He who influences the thought of his times, influences all the times that follow. He has made his impress on eternity.
> Ibid.

4 It does not make much difference what a person studies—all knowledge is related, and the man who studies anything, if he keeps at it, will become learned.
> Ibid.

5 To rule by fettering the mind through fear of punishment in another world, is just as base as to use force.
> Ibid.

6 All formal dogmatic religions are fallacious and must never be accepted by self-respecting persons as final.
> Quoted in *4000 Years of Women in Science*, http://www.astr.ua.edu4000WS *1 August 1997*

7 Reserve your right to think, for even to think wrongly is better than not to think at all.
> Ibid.

8 To teach superstitions as truth is a most terrible thing.
> Ibid.

107. Egeria (fl. 380s–d. 384)

1 I saw many holy monks from those parts when they came to Jerusalem on pilgrimage to the holy places, and all they told me about Uz* made me eager to take the trouble to make a further journey to visit it—if one can really speak of trouble when one sees one's wishes fulfilled.
> From *Travels*, Quoted in *Egeria: Diary of a Pilgrimage*, George E. Gingras, ed. and tr. *1970*

*The Land of Uz was probably near Damascus, although there is little evidence of its actual location.

108. Aelia Pulcheria (399–454)

1 The more princes abstain from touching the wealth of their people, the greater will be their resources in the wants of the state.
> Quoted in *Biography of Distinguished Women* by Sarah Josepha Hale* *1876*

*See 788.

109. Brigid of Kildare (453–523)

1 I should like a great lake of ale
For the King of kings
> Prayer for the Heavenly Feast* *n.d.*, Attr.

*Her feast day was February 1, the first day of spring according to the pagan calendar; she was worshipped as a goddess. Her canonization was an effort by the church to convert her followers.

2 I would like to be a tenant to the Lord, so if I should suffer distress, he would confer on me a blessing. Amen.
> Ibid.

110. Basine (fl. c. 460)

Had I known a more valiant hero than yourself, I should have fled over the seas to his arms.
> Remark to Childeric [Merovingian king], Quoted in *Biography of Distinguished Women* by Sarah Josepha Hale* *1876*

*See 788.

111. Maximilla (fl. c. 460)

1 I am pursued like a wolf out of the sheep fold; I am no wolf: I am word and spirit and power.
> Quoted in "Word, Spirit and Power: Women in Early Christian Communities" by Elisabeth Schüssler Fiorenza, *Women of Spirit*, Rosemary Ruether* and Eleanor McLaughlin, eds. *1979*

*See 2692.

112. Theodora (508?–d. 547/8)

1 For a King, death is better than dethronement and exile.
> Remark (c. 532), Quoted in *Women in World History Curriculum*, http://womeninhistory.com/ Lyn Reese, Director *1996–97*

113. Saint Radegunda (518?–587)

1 If you do not understand what is read, it is because you do not ask solicitously for a mirror of the soul.
> Quoted in *Vita Radegundis* [Life of Radegunda] by Fortunatus *c. 580–600*

114. Bertegund (fl. 530)

1 Go home and govern our children. I will not return to you [her husband], for the married will not see the kingdom of heaven.
> Ch. 6, Quoted in *Histoire Française* by Gregory of Tours* *c. 538*

*French bishop and writer (538/39–594/95).

115. Al-Khansa (575–646)

1 He is dead, who was the buckler of our tribe.
> "For Her Brother," St. 3, E. Powys Mathers, tr., *The Penguin Book of Women Poets*, Carol Cosman, Joan Keefe and Kathleen Weaver, eds. *1978*

2 . . . every tribe is a journey to ruin
and every treaty is erased by time.
> "In Death's Field," Sts. 12, 13, Willis Barnstone, tr., *A Book of Women Poets*, Aliki and Willis Barnstone, eds. *1980*

116. Baudonivia (fl. sixth century)

1 I am but the least among the least, small is my understanding and timid my heart.
> Letter to her abbess, Dedimia, Quoted in *Women and Their Letters in the Early Middle Ages* by Eleanor Shipley Duckett *1965*

117. Saint Caesaria (fl. sixth century)

1 . . . you cannot fight lust if you do not flee from the presence of men.

> Ch. 6, Quoted in *Women in Frankish Society, Marriage and the Cloister, 500–900* by Suzanne Fonay Wemple *1981*

2 . . . read and hear assiduously the divine lessons. . . to gather from them precious daisies for your ears and make from them rings and bracelets.

> Ch. 8, Ibid.

118. Herchenfreda (fl. 600s)

1 What shall I, an unfortunate mother, do now that I have lost your brothers? If you were also to die, I would have no children left! But you, my most pious son, my sweetest, you must constantly guard yourself against murder, for now that I have lost your brothers, I cannot lose you too!

> Ch. 3, Quoted in *Women in Frankish Society, Marriage and the Cloister, 500–900* by Suzanne Fonay Wemple *1981*

119. Hind bint Utba (fl. c. 600–d. 635)

1 Rrrrrrrraaarghr
We have paid you back
Battle feeds battle
and war that follows war is always violent.

> "Fury Against the Moslems at Uhud," St. 1, Bridget Connelly and Deirdre Lashgari, trs., *Women Poets of the World*, Joanna Bankier and Deirdre Lashgari, eds. *1983*

120. Wu Tse-t'ien [Empress Wu] (624–705)

1 My thoughts are many and tumultuous,
As troubled as the tossing branches,
All for thinking of you.

> "A Love Song of the Empress Wu," *The Orchid Boat, Women Poets of China*, Kenneth Rexroth and Ling Chung, eds. and trs. *1972*

121. Laila Akhyaliyya (fl. c. 660–699/704)

1 They stay intoxicated at the springs as if
Drinkers dependent on Persian lords

> "They press to belly and breast the wings and hover a little at a favorite pool," *Diwan Antara ibn Shaddad ibn Qurad al Abs*, Arthur Wormhoudt, tr. *1974*

2 We left no joy for the stragglers,
neitther camps nor dripping blood.
We are Banu Khuwailid without compare;
the battle does not lie nor trifle.

> "We left no joy for the stragglers," Ibid.

3 He was honey—no, I see a beehive in his likeness

> "He reached the heights of things with ease," Ibid.

4 Our lungs are strong
when we wail with the first knives of dawn.

> "Laila Boasting," Willis Barnstone, tr., *A Book of Women Poets*, Aliki and Willis Barnstone, eds. *1980*

5 No life is favored
nor corpse reborn
Every youth passes through destruction to Allah.

> "Lamenting Tauba," Ibid., St. 3

122. Nukada (fl. c. 660–699)

1 When, loosened from the winter's bond, spring appears,
The birds that were silent

Come out and sing,
The flowers that were prisoned
Come out and bloom;
But the hills are so rank with trees
We cannot see the flowers,
And the flowers are so tangled with weeds
We cannot take them in our hands.

> Untitled, from *Manyō-Shū*, [Collection of Ten Thousand Leaves], Harold P. Wright, tr. *c. mid-eighth century*

123. Oku (661–701)

1 How will you cross
the autumn mountain
alone?
It was hard
for us,
even when we went
together.

> Untitled, Willis Barnstone, tr., *A Book of Women Poets*, Aliki and Willis Barnstone, eds. *1980*

124. Maysun (fl. 670s)

1 I love the Bedouin's tent, caressed by the murmuring breeze,
and standing amid boundless horizons
More than the gilded halls of marble in all their splendor
I prefer a desert cavalier, generous and poor,
to a fat lout in purple living behind closed doors.

> Untitled poem, *Islamic Literature: an Introductory History*, Najib Ullah, tr. *1963*

125. Safiya bint Musafir (fl. c. 670)

1 Emptied with weeping
my eyes are
two buckets of the waterman
as he walks among the orchard trees

> "At the Badr Trench,"* St.1, Bridget Connelly and Deirdre Lashgari, trs., *Women Poets of the World*, Joanna Bankier and Deirdre Lashgari, eds. *1983*

*Burial place for 14 Muslim martyrs killed at Battle of Badr at Medina (now in Saudi Arabia) in 674.

126. Yamatohime (fl. 670)

1 Others may forget you, but not I.
I am haunted by your beautiful ghost.

> Untitled, *One Hundred Poems from the Japanese*, Kenneth Rexroth and Ikuko Atsumi, eds. and trs. *1964*

127. Liadan (fl. seventh century)

1 Not vain,
it seemed, our choice,
to seek Paradise through pain.

> "Liadan Laments Cuirithir,"* St. 3, *The Penguin Book of Women Poets*, Carol Cosman, Joan Keefe and Kathleen Weaver, eds. *1978*

*Her lover who, after she became a nun, unknown to Liadan became a monk.

2 Gain without gladness
Is in the bargain I have struck

> Untitled, St. 1, Frank O'Connor, tr., *The Penguin Book of Irish Verse*, Brendan Kennelly, ed. *1981*

128. Mahodahi (fl. seventh–11th century)

1 The sun's charioteer is lost. . . .
> Untitled, Willis Barnstone, tr., *A Book of Women Poets*,
> Aliki and Willis Barnstone, eds. *1980*

129. Sila (fl. seventh–11th century)

1 We knew long evenings wet with the moon.
> Untitled, Willis Barnstone, tr., *A Book of Women Poets*,
> Aliki and Willis Barnstone, eds. *1980*

130. Silabhlaṭṭarika (fl. seventh–11th century)

1 I too am still the same;
> and yet with all my heart I yearn for the reedbeds by the
> stream
> which knew our happy, graceful
> unending bouts of love.
>> "The Wanton" (*Treasury of Well-Turned Verse*, comp. by
>> Vidya Kara, c. 1100), Quoted in *Sanskrit Poetry*,
>> Daniel H. H. Ingalls, ed. and tr. *1955*

131. Vidya (fl. seventh–11th century)

1 I praise the disc of the rising sun
> red as a parrot's beak, sharp-rayed,
> friend of the lotus grove,
> an earring for the goddess of the east.
>> "The Sun" (*Treasury of Well-Turned Verse*, comp.
>> by Vidya Kara, c.1100), Quoted in *Sanskrit Poetry*,
>> Daniel H. H. Ingalls, ed. and tr. *1955*

2 Friends,
> you are lucky you can talk
> about what you did as lovers:
> the tricks, the laughter, the words,
> the ecstasy.
> After my darling put his hand on the knot
> of my dress,
> I swear I remember nothing.
>> Untitled, *in toto*, Willis Barnstone, tr., *A Book of Women
>> Poets*, Aliki and Willis Barnstone,
>> eds. *1980*

132. Ōtomo no Sakano-e no Iratsume (700?–750)

1 Ah! I have handed over
> The jewel to its owner;
> So from henceforth, my dear pillow,
> Let us two sleep together.
>> "On the Marriage of a daughter," *in toto*, from *Manyō-Shū*,
>> Vol. IV, *An Anthology of Japanese Poems*,
>> Miyamori Asatarō, ed. and tr. *1938*

2 Do not smile to yourself
> Like a green mountain
> With a cloud drifting across it.
> People will know we are in love.
>> Untitled, *One Hundred Poems from the Japanese*, Kenneth
>> Rexroth and Ikuko Atsumi, eds. and trs. *1964*

3 My heart, thinking
> "How beautiful he is"
> Is like a swift river
> Which though one dams it and dams it
> Will still break through.
>> Untitled, from *Manyō-Shū*, Quoted in *Japanese Poetry:
>> The Uta*, Arthur Waley, ed. and tr. *1976*

133. Young Woman of Harima (fl. c. 710–20)

1 If you go away,
> why should I adorn myself?
>> Untitled, from the *Manyō-Shū*, Quoted in *Land of the
>> Reed Plains*, Kenneth Yashuda, ed. and tr. *1972*

134. Chigami Sanu (fl. c. 710–784)

1 These are the garments
> I, a helpless woman, sewed
> with troubled longings
> as a token of the day
> when we two shall meet again.
>> Untitled, from the *Manyō-Shū*, (c.800), Quoted in
>> *Land of the Reed Plains*, Kenneth Yashuda,
>> ed. and tr. *1972*

135. Rabi'a al-Adawiya (712/7–801)

1 My Lord
> if I worship Thee from fear of Hell
> burn me in Hell

> and if I worship Thee from hope of Paradise
> exclude me thence

> but if I worship Thee
> for Thine own sake alone
> do not withhold from me Thine Eternal Beauty
>> "A Prayer," Sts. 1-3, Quoted in *Rabi'a the Mystic
>> and Her Fellow Saints in Islam* by Margaret
>> Smith *1928*

2 O my Lord, the stars are shining and the eyes of men are
> closed, and kings have shut their doors
> and every lover is alone with his beloved,
> and here am I alone with Thee.
>> Prayer, Quoted in *Muslim Saints and Mystics*
>> by Farid al-Din Attar; A.J. Arberry, tr. *1966*

3 My peace, O my brothers, is in solitude
>> Untitled, Ibid.

4 I'd truly be ashamed to ask for worldly things from Him to
> whom the world belongs; so why would I ask for the same
> things from those to whom it does not belong?
>> Quoted in *Uppity Women of Medieval Times*
>> by Vicki León *1997*

136. Khosrovidoukht Koghtnatsi (?–737)

1 More astonishing to me
> than the lyrics made for you,
> more amazing than the music composed
> for your death,
> is the sound of the sobbing mourning.
>> "More Astonishing," St. 1 (737), *Anthology of Armenian
>> Poetry*, Diana Der Hovanessian and Marzbed Margossian,
>> eds. and trs. *1978*

137. Rabi'a bint Isma'il of Syria (?–755)

1 But if You consume me in fire, goal of my longing,
> where then lies my hope of You, and where my fear?
>> "Sufi Quatrain," St. 2, Deirdre Lashgari, tr., *Women Poets
>> of the World*, Joanna Bankier and Deirdre Lashgari,
>> eds. *1983*

138. Hsüeh T'ao (768–831)

1 Blossoms crowd the branches: too beautiful to endure.
Thinking of you, I break into bloom again.
"Spring-Gazing Song," Carolyn Kizer, tr., *A Book of
Women Poets*, Aliki and Willis Barnstone, eds. *1980*

2 He is gone, who knew the music of my soul.
Weaving Love Knots," St. 2, Ibid.

139. Xue Tao (768–831)

1 I'd heard of the hardships
in walled-off frontier towns.

But now at last
I've come to understand.

Ashamed, I take up
a song from your court

and sing it
for back-country boys
"On being banished to the Borderlands: Submitted to Commander Wei," *in toto*, *Brocade River Poems: Selected works
of the Tang Dynasty courtesan Xue Tao*
Jeanne Larsen, tr. and intro. *1987*

2 Then by chance she
took a nip
and bit a well-loved guest.

Now she no longer sleeps
upon his red silk rugs.
"Dog parted from her master," Sts. 3–4, Ibid.

3 Chirr after chirr,
as if in unison

But each perches
on its one branch
alone.
"But each pershes on its one branch, alone." [On cicadas],
Sts. 3–4, Ibid.

4 He's done with reading holy texts.
He want to play a bit.
"listening to a monk play the reed pipes," St. 3, Ibid.

140. Huneberc of Heidenheim (fl. 778–786)

1 I am but womanly, stained by the frailty and weakness of my
sex, and supported neither by pretense to wisdom nor by exalted aspiration to great power, but freely prompted by my
own willful impetuosity, like some ignorant child who at her
heart's discretion plucks a few small things from trees rich in
foliage and fruit. Nonetheless I would be pleased to pluck, collect, and display, with however small an art, a few tokens from
the lowest branches for you to keep in your memory.
Prologue (Thomas Head, tr.), *Hodoeporicon of St. Willibald*
pre-786

2 These men come from the West where the sun sets; we know
nothing of their country except that byond it lies nothing but
water.
Ibid., Text

3 Willibald, who was inquisitive and eager to see what this Hell
was like inside, wanted to climb to the top of the mountain

underneath which the crater lay; but he was unable to do so
because of the ashes . . .
Ibid.

141. Lady Ishikawa (fl. c. 780–800)

1 You were soaked, my lord,
with the drops of mountain dew:
how I wish that I were they!
Untitled, from the *Manyō-Shū*, (c.800), Quoted in *Land of
the Reed Plains*, Kenneth Yashuda, ed. and tr. *1972*

142. Chao Luan-luan (fl. eighth century)

1 Small cherries sip delicately
At the edge of the wine cup.
"Red Sandalwood Mouth," *The Orchid Boat, Women Poets
of China*, Kenneth Rexroth and Ling Chung,
eds. and trs. *1972*

2 Slender, delicate, soft jade,
Fresh peeled spring onions—
They are always hidden in emerald
Sleeves of perfumed silk.

"Slender Fingers," Ibid.

143. Egburg (fl. eighth century)

1 No sailor tossed by the tempest hopes so keenly for the harbour, not thus does the thirsty field wait for the rain, not so
eagerly does the anxious mother look from the curving shore
for the coming of her son, as, My Father, I long for the sight of
you.
Letter to St. Boniface (c. 716–726), Quoted in *Women and
Their Letters in the Early Middle Ages*
by Eleanor Shipley Duckett *1965*

144. Kasa no Iratsume (fl. eighth century)

1 To love someone
Who does not return that love
Is like offering prayers
Back behind a starving god
Within a Buddhist temple.
Untitled, from *Manyō-Shū*, (c.800; *Collection of Ten
Thousand Leaves*), Harold P. Wright,
tr. *c. mid-eighth century*

145. Lady Kii (fl. eighth century)

1 . . . the idle ways
of the beach.
Untitled, *The Burning Heart: Women Poets of Japan*,
Kenneth Rexroth and Ikuko Atsumi, eds. and trs. *1977*

146. Li Yeh (fl. eighth century)

1 It is good to get drunk once in a while.
What else is there to do?
"A Greeting to Lu Hung-Chien," *The Orchid Boat, Women
Poets of China*, Kenneth Rexroth and Ling Chung,
eds. and trs. *1972*

147. Sahakdoukht Siunetsi (fl. eighth century)

1 And spiritual orchard, bright flower,
you conceived from God, as from rains
flowing through the soul, the word,

and with the shield of your body
made it apparent to men.
> "Acrostic," St. 2, *Anthology of Armenian Poetry*, Diana Der
> Hovanessian and Marzbed Margossian, eds. and trs. *1978*

148. Kassiane (804?–867?)

1 You meet your friend, your face
brightens—you have struck gold.
> Untitled, Patrick Diehl, tr., *The Penguin Book of
> Women Poets*, Carol Cosman, Joan Keefe and
> Kathleen Weaver, eds. *1978*

2 Poverty? wealth? seek neither—
One causes swollen heads,
The other, swollen bellies.
> Ibid.

3 Better unborn than fool.
If born, spare earth your tread.
Don't wait. Go straight to hell.
> Ibid.

4 No remedy for fools,
No helping them, but death.
In office? puffed and strutting.
Acclaimed? beyond endurance.
Columns of stone will kneel
Before you change a fool.
> Ibid.

5 A nun—a door unopened.
> Ibid.

6 Wealth covers sin—the poor
are naked as a pin.
> "Epigrams" (ninth century), *Women Poets of the World*,
> Joanna Bankier and Deirdre Lashgari, eds. *1983*

7 "O what a night   what a night I've had!
Extravagant frenzy   in a moonless gloom,
craving the body.
> "Mary Magdalene," Aliki Barnstone, tr., *Wise Women:
> Over 2000 Years of Spiritual Writing by Women*,
> Susan Cahill, ed. *1996*

149. Ono no Komachi (834–880)

1 So lonely am I
My body is a floating weed
Severed at the roots.
Were there water to entice me,
I would follow it, I think.
> Untitled, *in toto*, from *Kokin Shū*, (905 C.E.), *Anthology of
> Japanese Literature*, Donald Keene, ed. and tr. *1955*

2 A thing which fades
With no outward sign—
Is the flower
Of the heart of man
In this world!
> Untitled, *Japanese Poetry: The Uta*, Arthur Waley,
> ed. and tr. *1976*

150. Empress Nijo (842–910)

1 Spring has already come round
While on the ground lies snow;

The frozen tears of uguisu*
Soon in the soft warm breeze will thaw.
> "The Tears of Uguisu," *in toto*, from *Kokin Shū*, Vol. I, *An An-
> thology of Japanese Poems*, Miyamori Asatarō, ed. and tr. *1938*
*A bird similar to a nightingale.

151. Yü Hsüan-chi (843?–868)

1 I lift my head and read their names
In powerless envy.
> "On a Visit to Ch'ung Chên Taoist Temple I See In the
> South Hall the List of Successful Candidates in the Imperial
> Examinations," *The Orchid Boat, Women Poets of China*,
> Kenneth Rexroth and Ling Chung, eds. and trs. *1972*

2 To find a rare jewel is easy.
To get a good man is harder.
> "For a Neighbor Girl," *A Book of Women Poets*,
> Aliki and Willis Barnstone, eds. *1980*

3 How do we get the life we want?
I am a loosed boat floating a thousand miles.
> "At the End of Spring," St. 2, Ibid.

4 Evening, page by page, I hum beneath my quilt.
> "Rhyming a Friend's Poem," St.3, Ibid.

5 Thinking hard, hunting rhymes, humming by my lamp,
Awake all night, I fear the cold quilt.
> "Sent to Wen T'ing on a Winter Night," St. 1, Ibid.

152. Han Ts'ui-p'in (fl. c. 850)

1 Red leaf, I order you—
Go find someone
In the world of men.
> "A Poem Written on a Floating Red Leaf," *The Orchid
> Boat, Women Poets of China*, Kenneth Rexroth
> and Ling Chung, eds. and trs. *1972*

153. Lady Ukon (fl. c. 860–899)

1 It does not matter
That I am forgotten,
But I pity
His foresworn life.
> "I am forgotten now," *Poems from the Japanese*,
> Kenneth Rexroth, tr. *1964*

2 You gave me your solemn word, and I was
sure you would be constant.
I am moved to call down on you the penalty
of death for abandoning me!
> Untitled, from *Waga* (Mine), Quoted in *Women Poets of
> Japan*, Kenneth Rexroth and Ikuko Atsumi, ed. *1977*

154. Lady Ise (875?–938?)

1 Not even in dreams
Can I meet him anymore. . . .
> Untitled, *Japanese Literature: An Introduction for
> Western Readers*, Donald Keene, ed. and tr. *1955*

2 . . . my reputation
reaches to the skies
like a dust storm.
> Untitled, *The Burning Heart: Women Poets of Japan*,
> Kenneth Rexroth and Ikuko Atsumi, eds. and trs. *1977*

3 And like the maple leaves
of autumn, when members
of the household
have scattered
in their own ways,
uncertainty
fills the air.
"Elegy: Ise Lamenting the Death of Empress Onshi," Etsuko
Terasaki with Irma Brandeis, tr., *A Book of Women Poets*,
Aliki and Willis Barnstone, eds. *1980*

155. Qernertoq (fl. ninth–14th century)

1 It seems as if
I'll never get beyond
the foot-prints that I made
"The Widow's Song," St. 2, *Eskimo Poets of Canada and
Greenland*, Tom Lowenstein, ed. and tr. *1973*

156. Vallana (fl. ninth–10th century)

1 who could save me from plunging into a sea
of shame
but the love god
who teaches us how to faint?
Untitled, Willis Barnstone, tr., *A Book of Women Poets*,
Aliki and Willis Barnstone, eds. *1980*

157. Hroswitha of Gandersheim (935?–1000)

1 I know that it is as wrong to deny a divine gift as to pretend
falsely that we have received it.
"Epistle of the Same to Certain Learned Patrons of this Book,"
The Plays of Roswitha, Christopher St. John, tr. *1923*

2 GALLICANUS. It is said that the face is the mirror of the soul.
Pt. I, Sc. 3, *Gallicanus*, Ibid.

3 IRENA. A God who can be bought cheap in the market-place,
what is he but a slave?
Sc. 1, *Dulcitius*, Ibid.

4 IRENA. Better far that my body should suffer outrage than my
soul.
Sc. 12, Ibid.

5 ANDRONICUS. . . .it is not in our power to attain a precise
knowledge of the causes of things.
Sc. 9, *Callimachus*, Ibid.

6 EPHREM. Out of the mouths of babes and sucklings!
Sc. 1, *Abraham*, Ibid.

7 ABRAHAM. It is human to sin, but it is devilish to remain in sin.
Sc. 7, Ibid.

8 DISCIPLES. It is better to know nothing than to be bewildered.
Sc. 1, *Paphnutius*, Ibid.

9 THAIS. Remorse has killed everything.
Sc. 3, Ibid.

10 THAIS. Rumour never delays.
Sc. 6, Ibid.

11 ANTONY. What pleasures God sends us, when we resign ourselves to have none!
Sc. 10, Ibid.

12 PAPHNUTIUS. Grace is the free gift of God and does not depend
on our merits. If it did, it could not be called grace.
Sc. 12, Ibid.

158. Daughter of Ki no Tsurayuki (fl. c. 940–967)

1 But if the uguisu* inquire
For their home, oh! what shall I say?
"The Uguisu's Home,"** from *Go Shūi Shū*, Vol. IX, *An An-
thology of Japanese Poems*, Miyamori Asatarō, ed. and tr. *1938*
*A bird similar to a nightingale. **Poem in response to Emperor
Murakami's order to transplant a plum tree from the poet's garden
to his own.

159. Mother of Michitsuna (fl. c. 950–974)

1 Every day he promises that it shall be tomorrow. And when
tomorrow comes, it is to be the day after. Of course I do not
believe him; yet each time that this happens I begin imagining
that he has repented,—that all has come right again. So day
after day goes by.
Diary Entry (970), *Kagero Nikki* [Gossamer Diary] *954–974*

2 Have you any idea
How long a night can last, spent
Lying alone and sobbing?
Untitled, *One Hundred Poems from the Japanese*, Kenneth
Rexroth and Ikuko Atsumi, eds. and trs. *1964*

160. 'Aisha bint Ahmad al-Qurtubiyya (fl. c. 960–999)

1 I am a lioness
and will never allow my body
to be anyone's resting place.
Untitled, Elene Margot Kolb, tr., *Women Poets of the
World*, Joanna Bankier and Deirdre Lashgari, eds. *1983*

162. Nieh Shen-ch'iung (fl. 960–1279)

1 I try to dream good dreams
But it is hard to do
"Farewell To Li," *The Orchid Boat, Women Poets of China*,
Kenneth Rexroth and Ling Chung, eds. and trs. *1972*

163. Sei Shonagon (966/67–1013?)

1 One writes a letter, taking particular trouble to get it up as prettily as possible; then waits for the answer, making sure every
moment that it cannot be much longer before something comes.
At last, frightfully late, is brought in—one's own note, still
folded or tied exactly as one sent it, but so fingermarked and
smudged that even the address is barely legible. "The family is
not in residence," the messenger says, giving one back the note.
Makura no Soshi [The Pillow-Book of Sei Shonagon], (c.
991–1100), Arthur Waley, tr. *1928*

2 Among the five thousand arrogants, you too will surely find a
place.
Ibid.

3 There is nothing in the whole world so painful as feeling that
one is not liked. It always seems to me that people who hate
me must be suffering from some strange form of lunacy.
Ibid.

4 Writing is an ordinary enough thing; yet how precious it is!
When someone is in a far corner of the world and one is terri-

bly anxious about him, suddenly there comes a letter, and one feels as though the person were actually in the room. It is really very amazing.

Ibid.

164. Lady Nakatsukasa (fl. c. 970)

1 Before they bloomed I longed for them;
After they bloomed I mourned that they must fade;
The mountain cherry-flowers
Sorrow alone for my poor heart have made.
"Pining for a Dead Child," *in toto*, from Go Shūi Shū, Vol. I,
An Anthology of Japanese Poems, Miyamori Asatarō,
ed. and tr. *1938*

165. Izumi Shikibu (974?–1030?)

1 I am a drop of dew
Hanging from a leaf
Yet I am not unrestful
For on this branch I seem to have existed
From before the birth of the world.
III, *The Diary of Izumi Shikibu*, Annie Shepley Omori and
Kochi Doi, trs. 1002-1003

2 Sleeves wet with tears are my bed-fellows.

Ibid.

3 Ah, when I count the years still left,
I find them quickly told;
In all the world is nought so sad
As growing old.
"At the Close of the Year," *in toto*, from Shin Kokin Shū,
Vol. VI, *An Anthology of Japanese Poems*,
Miyamori Asatarō, ed. and tr. *1938*

4 Perhaps
A heart in love
Becomes a deep ravine?
Untitled, Edwin A. Cranston, tr., *The Penguin Book of
Women Poets*, Carol Cosman, Joan Keefe and
Kathleen Weaver, eds. 1978

5 When you broke from me
I thought I let the thread
of my life break
Untitled, Willis Barnstone, tr., *A Book of Women Poets*,
Aliki and Willis Barnstone, eds. *1980*

6 I wore out the darkness
until lazy dawn.

Ibid.

166. Murasaki Shikibu (974–1031?)

1 . . . so quick was I at picking up the language [Chinese] that I was soon able to prompt my brother whenever he got stuck. At this my father used to sigh and say to me: "If only you were a boy how proud and happy I should be." But it was not long before I repented of having thus distinguished myself; for person after person assured me that even boys generally become very unpopular if it is discovered that they are fond of their books. For a girl, of course, it would be even worse. . . .
Murasaki Shikibu Nikki [The Diary of Murasaki Shikibu],
Hakubunkuwan text *c. 994–1010*

2 There [at Princess Senshi's Court] I should be allowed to live buried in my own thoughts like a tree-stump in the earth . . .

Ibid.

3 Who has told you that the fruit belies the flower? For the fruit you have not tasted, and the flower you know but by report.*

Ibid.

*Addressing Michinaga, the prime minister, and implying that he has neither read her book, *The Tale of Genji*, nor won her love.

4 The truth is I now find that I have not the slightest pleasure in the society of any but a few indispensable friends. They must be people who really interest me, with whom I can talk seriously on serious subjects, and with whom I am brought into contact without effort on my side in the natural course of everyday existence.

Ibid.

5 "We are told," answered Genji, "that everything which happens to us in this life is the result of our conduct in some previous existence. If this is to be taken literally I suppose I must now accept the fact that in a previous incarnation I must have misbehaved myself in some way."
"The Sacred Tree," Ch. 3, *Genji Monogatari* [The Tale of
Genji], (1001-1015), Vol.II, Arthur Waley, tr. *1925-1933*

6 "What is all this about criminals?" he growled. "Surely you know that some of the most distinguished men in history both here and in China have been forced at one time or another to retire from Court. There is nothing disgraceful about it."

Ibid.

7 "It is only as a background to music that the sound of the sea is tolerable."

Ch. 4, Ibid.

8 "A night of endless dreams, inconsequent and wild, is this my life; none more worth telling than the rest."

Ibid.

9 "You had best be quick, if you are ever going to forgive me at all; life does not last forever."

Ch. 5, Ibid.

10 Princes are the lamps that alight this world.

Ch. 9, Ibid.

11 "Though the snow-drifts of Yoshino were heaped across his path, doubt not that whither his heart is set, his footsteps shall tread out their way."

Vol. III, "A Wreath of Cloud," Ch. 1, Ibid.

12 Indeed, she had seen enough of the world to know that in few people is discretion stronger than the desire to tell a good story. . . .

Ch. 2, Ibid.

13 "Beauty without colour seems somehow to belong to another world."

Ibid.

14 "I have noticed that children of good families, assured of such titles and emoluments as they desire, and used to receive the homage of the world however little they do deserve it, see no advantage in fatiguing themselves by arduous and exacting studies."

Ch. 3, Ibid.

15 "You cannot simply disappear while people are talking to you."

Ch. 7, Ibid.

16 "But I have a theory of my own about what this art of the novel is, and how it came into being. . . . it happens because the storyteller's own experience of men and things, whether for good or ill . . . has moved him to an emotion so passionate that he can no longer keep it shut up in his heart."

Ibid.

17 "Some people have taken exception on moral grounds to an art [storytelling] in which the perfect and the imperfect are set side by side. But even in the discourses which Buddha in his bounty allowed to be recorded, certain passages contain what the learned call Upāya or 'Adapted Truth'. . . ."

Ibid.

18 "I have never thought there was much to be said in favour of dragging on long after all one's friends were dead."

Vol. IV, "Blue Trousers," Ch. 1, Ibid.

19 "It would be fatal, for example, if this situation were suddenly sprung upon the world in all its details. But allowed to leak out piecemeal, it will do very little harm. What matters is that people should have plenty of time to get used to one part of a scandal before the next is allowed to leak out."

Ibid.

20 "Now faithlessness, that once was held a crime, rules all the world, and he a half-wit is accounted whose heart is steadfast for an hour."

Ch. 4, Ibid.

21 But unfortunately, Genji reflected, people who do not get into scrapes are a great deal less interesting than those who do.

Ch. 6, Ibid.

22 "Though the body moves, the soul may stay behind."

Ch. 7, Ibid.

23 "Think not that I have come in quest of common flowers; but rather to bemoan the loss of one whose scent has vanished from the air."

Ch. 12, Ibid.

167. Andal (fl. 10th century)

1 Sing,
   but not too loudly, so he will come.
      Untitled, Willis Barnstone, tr., *A Book of Women Poets*,
         Aliki and Willis Barnstone, eds. *1980*

2 we will do good things,
   use good words,
   give away our possessions and live for him.

Ibid.

168. Akazome Emon (fl. 10th century)

1 When I was on my way to Ishiyama after the death of Masahira [her husband], I saw a new house that looked extremely dilapidated. I. . .was told that it had fallen into this state after the death of the occupant's father two years before. I wrote:
I had supposed
That I alone lamented
A neglected bed,
But here was another house
Bereft of its master.

Quoted in *Seeds in the Heart: Japanese Literature From Earliest Times to the Late Sixteenth Century* by Donald Keene *1993*

2 I wish I could live
Long enough to see him soar
High above the clouds
When his cloak of crane feathers
Has grown out with the years.
      "Composed after the birth of Masafusa,* on asking someone to sew baby clothes for him," Ibid.
*Oe no Masafusa (1041–1111), her great-grandson, who became a brilliant and noted scholar.

169. Gormley (fl. 10th century)

1 though I have loved twenty men
   this is not what women seek.
      "Gormley's Laments," St. 1, Joan Keefe, tr., *The Penguin Book of Women Poets*, Carol Cosman, Joan Keefe and Kathleen Weaver, eds. *1978*

2 I paid poets for their words
   before God took my riches.

St. 14, Ibid.

170. Rabi'a of Balkh (fl. 10th century)

1 My wish for you
   that God should make your love
   fall on a heart as cold and stony as
   your own
      Untitled, Deirdre Lashgari, tr., *Women Poets of the World*, Joanna Bankier and Deirdre Lashgari, eds. *1983*

171. Maryam bint Abi Ya'qub al-Ansari (fl. c. 1000–1035)

1 What can you expect
   from a woman with seventy-seven years,
   frail as the web of a spider?
      Untitled, Elene Margot Kolb, tr., *Women Poets of the World*, Joanna Bankier and Deirdre Lashgari, eds. *1983*

172. Wallada al-Mustakfi (fl. 1000s–d. 1035)

1 Expect my visit when the darkness comes.
   The night I think is best for hiding all.
   If the full moon felt like me she wouldn't rise;
   if the star, it wouldn't move;
   if the night, it wouldn't fall.
      Untitled, Quoted in *The Troubadours and Their World of the Twelfth and Thirteenth Centuries* by Jack Lindsay *1976*

2 Time passes, yet I see no end to your long absence,
   Nor does patience free me from the bondage of yearning!
      "A Correspondence to Ibn Zaidun:* #4," A. R. Nykul, tr., *The Penguin Book of Women Poets*, Carol Cosman, Joan Keefe and Kathleen Weaver, eds. *1978*
*Her lover, an Andalusian writer of classical Arabic poetry.

3 I will let my love touch my cheek, and I feel free to give my kisses to whomever asks for them.*
      Quoted in *Uppity Women of Medieval Times* by Vicki León *1997*
*This was said to have been calligraphed on the sleeves of her embroidered jacket.

173. Lady Sarashina (1008–1060?)

1 They will come back next spring—those cherry blooms

that scatter from the tree.
But how I yearn for her who left
And never will return!
As I Crossed a Bridge of Dreams: Recollections of Woman
in Eleventh Century Japan, Ivan Morris, tr. *1971*

2 There is no difference in their sounds—
This wind that blows across the Barrier now
And the one I heard so many years ago.
Ibid.

174. Lady Suo (fl. 1030–1065)
1 That spring night I spent
Pillowed on your arm
Never really happened
Except in a dream.
Unfortunately I am
Talked about anyway.
Untitled, *One Hundred Poems from the Japanese*, Kenneth
Rexroth and Ikuko Atsumi, eds. and trs. *1964*

175. Anna Comnena (1083–1153)
1 Indeed, so great a multitude of Gauls and Normans were cut
down by the Ishmaelite sword that when the dead bodies of the
killed, which were lying all about in the place, were brought together, they made a very great mound, or hill, or lookout place,
lofty as a mountain, and occupying a space very conspicuous for
its width and depth. So high did that mound of bones tower, that
some barbarians of the same race as the killed later used the
bones of the slain instead of stones in constructing a wall, thus
making that fortress a sort of sepulcher for them. It stands to this
day, an enclosure of walls built with mixed rocks and bones.
"On the Crusades," *Alexiad*, Vol. 10 *1138-48*

2 But since there were also Normans in his army, estimated at
about ten thousand men, these, separating themselves from the
rest of the body, devastated the region lying around the city of
Nicaea, rioting most cruelly in every way. For they tore some of
the children apart, limb from limb and, piercing others through
with wooden stakes, roasted them in fire; likewise, upon those
advanced in years they inflicted every kind of torture.
Ibid.

3 And as for the churches, woe is me—he called our sacred
churches the temples of devils, and our consecration of the
body and blood of our one and greatest High Priest and Victim he considered and condemned as worthless.
The Bogomils (c. 1110), *The Alexiad of the Princess Anna
Comnena*, Elizabeth A. S. Dawes, tr. *1918*

4 Her expression, which revealed her true character, demanded
the worship of the angels but struck terror among demons . . .
from *Alexiad, The Writings of Medieval Women*, Vol. 14,
M. Thiebaux, tr. and ed. *1987*

5 For my grandmother* really had the gift of conducting the affairs of state. She knew so well how to organize and administer that she was capable of governing not only the Roman Empire
but also every other kingdom under the sun. . . .
Ibid.

*Anna Dalassena, Byzantine Empress.

176. Li Qingzhao [Ch'ing-chao] (1081/84–1140/51)
1 My body is a prisoner
In this room above the misty

River, the jade green river,
That is the only companion
of my endless days.
Untitled, St. 2, *Love and the Turning Year: One Hundred
More Poems from the Chinese*, Kenneth Rexroth, ed. and tr.
1970

2 Who can
Take a letter beyond the clouds?
Untitled, Ibid.

3 Search. Search. Seek. Seek.
Cold. Cold. Clear. Clear.
Sorrow. Sorrow. Pain. Pain.
Hot flashes. Sudden chills.
Stabbing pains. Slow agonies.
"A Weary Song to a Slow Sad Tune," Ibid.

4 But I am startled by the breaking cup of Spring.
to the tune "A Hilly Garden," *The Orchid Boat, Women
Poets of China*, Kenneth Rexroth and Ling Chung, eds. and
trs. *1972*

5 Nothing is left of Spring but fragrant dust.
"Spring Ends," Ibid.

6 The jade
burner
is cold,
a companion
to
my
feelings,
which
are
water.
Untitled, St. 3, Willis Barnstone and Sun Chu-chin, trs., *A
Book of Women Poets*, Aliki and Willis Barnstone, eds.
1980

7 Dense
sleep
doesn't
fade
a wine
hangover.
Untitled, St. 2, Ibid.

8 There is no way to banish this feeling.
As it leaves the eyebrows,
it enters the heart.
to the tune "Yi chian mei," St. 3, Marsha Wagner, tr.,
Women Poets of the World, Joanna Bankier and
Deirdre Lashgari, eds. *1983*

177. Héloise (1098?–1164)
1 Can it be said, in fact, that one is truly penitent, whatever be
the bodily penances submitted to, when the soul still harbors
the thought of sin and burns with the same passions as of old?
Letter to Peter Abelard,* Quoted in *Women of
Medieval France* by Pierce Butler *1907*
*French theologian and philosopher (1079-1142)

2 The blessings promised to us by Christ were not promised to
those alone who were priests; woe unto the world, indeed, if
all that deserved the name of virtue were shut up in a cloister.
Ibid.

3   Riches and power are but gifts of blind fate, whereas goodness is the result of one's own merits.
> Letter to Peter Abelard, #2, *The Letters of Abelard and Héloise*, C. K. Scott Moncrieff, tr. *1925*

4   Prosperity seldom chooses the side of the virtuous . . .
> First Letter to Abelard (c.1122), *The World's Great Letters*, M. Lincoln Schuster, ed. *1940*

5   . . . I was more pleased with possessing your heart than with any other happiness . . . the man was the thing I least valued in you.
> Ibid.

6   We fluctuate long between love and hatred before we can arrive at tranquility.
> Ibid.

7   Banish me forever from your heart, it is the best advice I can give you.
> Letter to Peter Abelard, *The Letters of Abelard and Héloise*, C. K. Scott Moncrieff, tr. *1974*

8   I ought to deplore what we did—but I sigh only for what we have lost.
> Ibid.

9   To my lord/no/my father
my husband/no/my brother
his servant/no/his daughter
his wife/no/his sister
To my Abelard his Héloise.
> Untitled, Quoted in *Women in the Middle Ages* by Sibylle Harksen *1975*

10   When my self is not with you, it is nowhere.
> Letter to Peter Abelard, Ibid.

178. Hildegarde von Bingen (1098–1179)

1   Greetings, greenest branch
> Song 71, "About the Blessed Virgin Mary," St. 1, *Symphony of the Harmony of Heavenly Relations 1151–1158*

2   I am that supreme and fiery force that sends forth all living sparks. Death hath no part in me, yet I bestow death, wherefore I am girt about with wisdom as with wings. I am that living and fiery essence of the divine substance that glows in the beauty of the fields, and in the shining water, and in the burning sun and the moon and the stars, and in the force of the invisible wind, the breath of all living things, I breathe in the green grass and in the flowers, and in the living waters. . . . All these live and do not die because I am in them . . . I am the source of the thundered word by which all creatures were made, I permeate all things that they may not die. I am Life.
> *Book of Divine Works* c. 1167

3   When a woman is making love with a man, a sense of heat in her brain, which brings with it sensual delight, communicates the taste of that delight during the act and summons forth the emission of the man's seed. And when the seed has fallen into its place, that vehement heat descending from her brain draws the seed to itself and holds it, and soon the woman's sexual organs contract, and all the parts that are ready to open up during the time of menstruation now close, in the same way as a strong man can hold something enclosed in his fist.
> Ibid.

4   . . . man . . . rushes to woman like the stag to the spring, and the woman to him like the threshing floor of the barn, shaken and heated by the many blows of the flail when the grain is threshed.
> Quoted in *Women in the Middle Ages* by Sibylle Harksen *1975*

5   The prophetic spirit orders that God be praised with cymbals of jubilation and with the rest of the musical instruments which the wise and studious have created, since all of the arts (whose purpose is to fill uses and needs of man) are brought to life by that breath of life which God breathed into the body of man: and therefore it is just that God be praised in all things.
> Letter to Prelates of Mainz, Quoted in *Women in Music* by Carol Neuls-Bates *1982*

6   The earth which sustains humanity must not be injured. It must not be destroyed!
> Remark, Quoted in *Hildegarde of Bingen: a visionary life* by S. Flanagan *1989*

7   And it came to pass . . . when I was 42 years and 7 months old, that the heavens were opened and a blinding light of exceptional brilliance flowed through my entire brain. And so it kindled my whole heart and breast like a flame, not burning but warming . . . and suddenly I understood of the meaning of expositions of the books . . .
> *4000 Years of Women in Science*, http://www.astr.ua.edu/4000WS *11 July 1997*

8   But although I heard and saw these things, because of doubt and low opinion of myself and because of diverse sayings of men, I refused for a long time a call to write, not out of stubbornness but out of humility, until weighed down by a scourge of god, I fell onto a bed of sickness.
> Ibid.

179. Sugawara no Takasue no musume (fl. 11th century)

1   Even into the mind always clouded with grief,
There is cast the reflection of the bright moon.
> Quoted in "The Sarashina Diary," *Diaries of Court Ladies of Old Japan*, Annie Shepley Omori and Kochi Doi, trs. *1920*

180. Matilda (1100?–1135)

1   Do not, therefore, good and sainted father, give up your bodily strength by such inopportune fasting as this, for fear "The orator's gift is not only talent, but lung power." Once this is gone, your great spiritual eminence will soon be lost, and so would your great memory of the past and your ability to foresee the future. So much art, so much learning, so much invention, so much understanding of human affairs, as well as the clear wisdom of the divine, would soon be lost.
> Letter to Saint Anselm *c. 1100*

2   Just as spiritual drink and food are necessary to the soul, so are physical drink and food necessary for the soul.
> Ibid.

181. Sun Tao-hüsan (fl. 1100–1135)

1   The wind blows down from the emerald sky
A song like a string of pearls.

But the singer is invisible
Hidden behind her embroidered curtains.
"A Dream Song," *The Orchid Boat, Women Poets of China,*
Kenneth Rexroth and Ling Chung, eds. and trs. *1972*

182. Eleanor of Aquitaine (1122?–1204)

1 Trees are not known by their leaves, nor even by their blossoms, but by their fruits. In this wise we have known your cardinals.
Letter to Pope Celestine III (1192), Quoted in *Eleanor of Aquitaine* by Amy Kelly *1950*

2 I have lost the staff of my age, the light of my eyes.
Comment on the death of her son, Richard I* (1199), Ibid.
*Known as "Coeur de Lion" or "the Lion-Hearted" (1157–1199)

183. Sun Bu-er (1124–?)

1 When you've cooked the marrow of the sun and moon,
The pearl is so bright you don't worry about poverty.
"Projecting the Spirit," Thomas Cleary, tr., *Wise Women:
Over 2000 Years of Spiritual Writing by Women,* Susan
Cahill, ed. *1996*

184. Frau Ava (?–1127)

1 I am yours,
you are mine.
Of this we are certain.
You are lodged
in my heart,
the small key
is lost.
You must stay there
forever.
Attributed, attached to a letter to a cleric (c.1160),
A Book of Women Poets, Aliki and Willis Barnstone,
eds. *1980*

185. Lady Horikawa (fl. 1130–1165)

1 Will he always love me?
I cannot read his heart.
This morning my thoughts
Are as disordered
As my black hair.
Untitled, *One Hundred Poems from the Japanese,* Kenneth
Rexroth and Ikuko Atsumi, eds. and trs. *1964*

186. Tibors (1130?–1182)

1 nor did it ever come to pass, if you went off angry,
that I felt joy until you had come back
Untitled, from *Die Provenzalischen Dicterinnen* by Oscar
Schultz-Gora (1888), Quoted in *The Women Troubadours*
by Meg Bodin, tr. *1976*

187. Almucs de Castelnau (1140–?)

1 But if you want him dead let him receive the sacraments, to guarantee that he'll refrain from doing further injury.
Untitled, St. 1, with Iseut de Capio, Quoted in *The Women
Troubadours* by Meg Bodin, tr. *1976*

2 Still, if you can get him to repent his perfidy you'll have no trouble in converting me.
Untitled, St. 2, Ibid.

188. Azalais de Porcairages (1140?–?)

1 Now we are come to the cold time
Untitled, St. 1, Quoted in *The Women Troubadours* by Meg
Bodin, tr. *1976*

2 Handsome friend, I'll gladly stay
forever in your service—
such noble mien and such fine looks—
so long as you don't ask too much
Untitled, St. 5, Ibid.

189. Beatritz de Dia (1140?–post-1189?)

1 For times to come, I tell the plight
I've learned through loving in excess.
Untitled, Quoted in *The Troubadours and Their World of
the Twelfth and Thirteenth Centuries* by Jack Lindsay *1976*

2 If all the pangs are mine, I say
unequal parts in love we play.
Ibid.

3 Those bad-talking gossips
No one who counts
Pays any attention to them.
They are a fog that rises
Against the sunlight.
Untitled, St. 2, Doris Earnshaw, tr., *Women Poets of the
World,* Joanna Bankier and Deirdre Lashgari, eds. *1983*

190. Marula (fl. c. 1150)

1 She was troubled with indescribable love.
"Meeting after Separation," *Indian Love Poems,* Tambimuttu and R. Appalaswamy, eds. and trs. *n.d.*

191. Marie de France (1160?–1215?)

1 Whoever has received knowledge
and eloquence in speech from God
should not be silent or secretive
but demonstrate it willingly.
When a great good is widely heard of,
then, and only then, does it bloom,
and when that good is praised by man,
it has spread its blossoms.
Prologue, ll. 1-8, *The Lais of Marie de France,* Robert Hannings and Joan Ferrante, trs. *1978*

2 Whoever deals with good material
feels pain if it's treated improperly.
"Guigemar," ll. 1, 2, Ibid.

3 You have to endure what you can't change.
l. 410, Ibid.

4 But he who hides his sickness
can hardly be brought back to health;
love is a wound in the body,
and yet nothing appears on the outside.
ll. 481–484, Ibid.

5 But Fortune, who never forgets her duty, turns her wheel suddenly.
ll. 538–539, Ibid.

6 indeed, I condemned myself
when I slandered all womankind.
"Le Fresne [The Ash Tree]" ll. 79–80, Ibid.

7 whether it makes you weep or sing
 justice must be carried out.
> "Lanval," ll. 435–436, Ibid.

8 Whoever wants to tell a variety of stories
 ought to have a variety of beginnings.
> "Milun," ll. 1-2, Ibid.

9 With the two of them it was just
 as it is with the honeysuckle
 that attaches itself to the hazel tree:
 when it has wound and attached
 and worked itself around the trunk,
 the two can survive together;
 but if someone tries to separate them,
 the hazel dies quickly
 and the honeysuckle with it.
 "Sweet love, so it is with us:
 You cannot live without me, nor I without you."
> "Chevrefoil [The Honeysuckle]," ll. 68–78, Ibid.

10 "Whoever believes in a man is very foolish."
> "Eliduc," l. 1084, Ibid.

11 By men's words we know them.
> *Medieval Fables of Marie de France*, Jeanette Beer, tr. *1981*

12 Desire can blind us to the hazards of our enterprises.
> Ibid.

192. Marie de Ventadorn (1165?–?)

1 . . . the lady
 ought to do exactly for her lover
 as he does for her, without regard to rank;
 for between two friends neither one should rule.
> Untitled, St. 2, Quoted in *The Women Troubadours* by Meg
> Bodin, tr. *1976*

2 . . . to me it's nothing short of treason
 if a man says he's her equal *and* her servant.
> Untitled, St. 5, Ibid.

193. Alamanda (fl. 1165–1199)

1 I'm so angry that my body's
 all but bursting into flame.
> Untitled, St. 1, Quoted in *The Women Troubadours* by Meg
> Bodin, tr. *1976*

194. Aldrude (fl. c. 1170)

1 It is by those only who are truly great, that virtue is esteemed
 more than riches or honours, or that virtuous actions can be
 duly appreciated.
> (1172), Quoted in *Biography of Distinguished Women* by
> Sarah Josepha Hale* *1876*
 *See 788.

2 Courage is relaxed by delay.
> Ibid.

195. Garsenda de Forcalquier (1170?–?)

1 . . . it's you who stands to lose
 if you're not brave enough to state your case
> Untitled, St. 1, Quoted in *The Women Troubadours* by Meg
> Bodin, tr. *1976*

196. Isabella (1180?–?)

1 . . . if I sang your praises
 it wasn't out of love
 but for the profit I might get from it
> Untitled, St. 2, Quoted in *The Women Troubadours* by Meg
> Bodin, tr. *1976*

197. Chu Shu-chên (fl. c. 1180–1200)

1 I write poems, change and correct them,
 And finally throw them away.
> "Sorrow," *Love and the Turning Year: One Hundred More
> Poems from the Chinese*, Kenneth Rexroth, ed. and tr. *1970*

2 Like a flight of arrows the wind
 Pierces my curtain.
> "Stormy Night in Autumn," *One Hundred Poems from the
> Chinese*, Kenneth Rexroth, ed. and tr. *1971*

3 Alone in the dark, I am
 Going mad, counting my sorrow.
> Ibid.

4 It is easier to see Heaven
 Than to see you.
> "Spring Joy" (1182), *The Orchid Boat, Women
> Poets of China*, Kenneth Rexroth and Ling Chung, eds. and
> trs. *1972*

198. Lombarda (1190?–?)

1 but then when I remember what my name records,
 all my thoughts unite in one accord.
> Untitled, St. 3, Quoted in *The Women Troubadours* by Meg
> Bodin, tr. *1976*

199. Clare of Assisi (1193/94–1253)

1 . . . sisters beware of all pride, vain ambition, envy, greed, and
 of taking part in the cares and busy ways of the world.
> *Rule and Testament 1253*

200. Alais (fl. 12th century)

1 . . . shall I stay unwed? that would please me,
 for making babies doesn't seem so good,
 and it's too anguishing to be a wife.
> Untitled, St. 1, with Iselda and Carenza, Quoted in
> *The Women Troubadours* by Meg Bodin *1976*
 *See 203.

201. Domna H. (fl. 12th century)

1 for when a man is in love's grip
 it's wrong for him to knowingly
 ignore his lady's orders.
> Untitled, St. 2, Quoted in *The Women Troubadours* by Meg
> Bodin, tr. *1976*

202. Iselda (fl. 12th century)

Co-author with Alais. See 200.

203. Kasmuneh (fl. 12th–13th century)

1 A vine I see, and though 'tis time to glean,
 No hand is yet stretched forth to cull the fruit.
> "Overripe Fruit," *A Treasury of Jewish Poetry*, Nathan and
> Maryann Ausubel, eds. *1957*

204. Stewardess of the Empress Kōka Mon-in no Betto (fl. 12th century)

1   For the sake of a night
Short as the nodes
Of the reeds of Naniwa
Must I live on,
My flesh wasted with longing?
Untitled, *One Hundred Poems from the Japanese*, Kenneth
Rexroth and Ikuko Atsumi, eds. and trs. *1964*

205. Mahādēviyakka (fl. 12th century)

1   husband, inside,
lover outside.
I can't manage them both.
Untitled, *Speaking of Siva*, A. K. Ramanujan, ed. and tr. *1973*

2   When all the world is the eye of the lord,
onlooking everywhere, what can you
cover and conceal?
Ibid.

3   Till you know and lose this knowing
you've no way
of knowing
my lord white as jasmine.*
Ibid.

*Another name for the god Siva.

206. Mahsati (fl. 12th century)

1   Better to live as a rogue and a bum,
a lover all treat as a joke
to hang out with a crowd of comfortable drunks,
than crouch in a hypocrite's cloak.
Selected Quatrains, #1, Deirdre Lashgari, tr., *Women Poets
of the World*, Joanna Bankier and Deirdre Lashgari, eds.
1983

2   Gone are the games we played all night,
gone the pearls my lashes strung.
You were my comfort and my friend.
You've left, with all the songs I'd sung.
#4, Ibid.

207. T'ang Wan (fl. 12th century)

1   The world's love runs thin.
to the tune "The Phoenix Hairpin," *The Orchid Boat*,
Women Poets of China, Kenneth Rexroth and Ling Chung,
eds. and trs. *1972*

2   My troubled mind sways
Like the rope of a swing.
Ibid.

208. Shikishi (?–1201)

1   The blossoms have fallen.
I stare blankly at a world
Bereft of color.
Untitled, *Anthology of Japanese Literature*, Donald Keene,
ed. and tr. *1955*

209. Castelloza (1200?–?)

1   . . . at any moment I might
rediscover reason to rejoice.
Untitled, St. 4, Quoted in *The Women Troubadours* by Meg
Bodin, tr. *1976*

2   the more I sing
the worse I fare in love.
Untitled, St. 1, Ibid.

3   And if you left me now,
I wouldn't feel a thing,
for since no joy sustains me
a little pain won't drive me mad.
Untitled, St. 4, Ibid.

210. Beatrijs of Nazareth (c. 1200–1268)

1   Fear makes us work and suffer, act and be still out of dread of
the anger of our Lord, of the judgment of our righteous Judge,
of punishment in eternity or of chastizing in this life. But love,
in all that it does, strives for the purity and the exaltation and
the supreme excellence which is love's very nature and possession and delight: and it is this striving which love teaches to
those who serve love.
"Seven manieren van minne" (Seven Manners of
Loving), *Mediaeval Netherlands religious literature*, E.
Colledge, tr. and intro.. *1965*

2   . . . the soul is like a maiden who serves her master only for her
great love of him, not for any payment, sastisfied that she may
serve him and that he suffers her to serve. . .
Ibid.

3   It seems to the soul that the veins are bursting, the blood
spilling, the marrow withering, the bones softening, the
heart burning, the throat parching, so that the body in its
every part feels this inward heat, and this is the fever of
love. . .
Ibid.

4   And you may see that now the soul is like a housewife who
has put all her household in good order and prudently arranged it and well disposed it.
Ibid.

211. Bieiris de Romans (1200–1235)

1   Don't grant your love to a deceitful suitor.
Untitled, St. 3, Quoted in *The Women Troubadours* by Meg
Bodin, tr. *1976*

212. Clara d' Anduza (1200–1235)

for the love that has me in its spell wants me to lock you up
and guard you well; and I will . . .
Untitled, St. 3, Quoted in *The Women Troubadours* by Meg
Bodin, tr. *1976*

213. Elizabeth of Thuringia (1206/07–1231)

1   We must not sadden God with sullen looks.
Quoted in *Saint Elizabeth* by Elisabeth von Schmidt-Pauli;
Olga Marx, tr. *1932*

2   We are made loveless by our possessions.
Ibid.

3   We women were allowed to stand at the Cross. We saw His
wounds bleed and His eyes grow dim. As He was dying Jesus
put His faith in us, we were to carry His love through the
whole world and here we sit and have forgotten Him.
Ibid.

214. Mechtild von Magdeburg (1207–1283/97)

1 I come to my Beloved
Like dew upon the flowers.
Introduction, *Das fliessende Licht der Gottheit*
[The Flowering Light of God] *1344*

2 The fish cannot drown in the water, the bird cannot sink in the air, gold cannot perish in the fire, where it gains clear and shining worth. God has granted to each creature to cherish its own nature. How can I withstand my nature?
Ibid.

3 . . . a hungry man can do no deep study, and thus must God, through such default, lose the best prayers.
Ibid.

4 Those who would know much, and love little, will ever remain at but the beginning of a godly life.
Ibid.

5 I cannot dance, Oh, Lord, unless Thou lead me.
Ibid.

6 Of the heavenly things God has shown me, I can speak but a little word, not more than a honey bee can carry away on its feet from an overflowing jar.
Ibid.

215. Beruriah (fl. c. 1210–1280)

1 How do you make out [that such a prayer should be permitted]? Because it is written "Let *hattaim* [sins] cease"? Is it written *hottim* [sinners]? It is written *hattaim*! Further, look to the end of the verse "and let the wicked men be no more." Since the sins will cease, there will be no more wicked men! Rather pray for them that they should repent, and there will be no more wicked.
Quoted in *The Jewish Woman: New Perspectives*,
Elizabeth Koltun, ed. *1976*

216. Hadewijch of Brabant (fl. c. 1230–1260/65)

1 All things
Crowd me in!
I am so wide!
"All Things Confine," St. 1, Frans van Rosevelt, tr., *The Penguin Book of Women Poets*, Carol Cosman, Joan Keefe and Kathleen Weaver, eds. *1978*

2 Love appears every day
for one who offers love,
That wisdom is not enough.
"Poems on the Seven Names of Love," St. 2, Willis Barnstone and Elene Kolb, trs., *A Book of Women Poets*, Aliki and Willis Barnstone, eds. *1980*

3 Take care, you who wish
to deal with names
for love. Behind their sweetness
and wrath, nothing endures.
Nothing but wounds and kisses.
St. 10, Ibid.

4 Things of great wonder come to those who give their all to love.
Poem 12, *Strofische Gedichte* (Strophic Poems) *n.d.*

5 These things are beyond the mind of man: how the lover whom love has overwhelmed with love beholds the beloved so full of love.
Ibid.

6 For this is love's truth: she joins two in one being, makes sweet sour, strangers neighbors, and the lowly noble.
Poem 28, Ibid.

217. Guillelma de Rosers (fl. c. 1230–1265)

1 a man who keeps his word is worth much more
than one whose plans are constantly revised.
Untitled, St. 2, Quoted in *The Women Troubadours*
by Meg Bodin, tr. *1976*

2 . . . there's no such thing
as chivalry that doesn't spring from love.
Untitled, St. 3, Ibid.

218. Gertrude the Great (fl. c. 1250–d. 1302)

1 . . . growing in the knowledge of virtue like unto these trees, I flower in the greenness of good deeds . . .
from *Legacy of Divine Piety*, Quoted in *Women in the Middle Ages: Religion, Marriage and Letters* by Angela M. Lucas *1983*

2 . . . looking down on things earthly in free flight like these doves, I approach heaven, and with my bodily senses removed from external turmoil, apprehend thee with my whole mind . . .
Ibid.

219. Angela of Foligno (1250–1309)

1 In that time, by the will of God, my mother, who was a severe obstacle to me, died. Then my husband and all my children died within a brief period. Since I had taken the path of the religious life, and had begged God to be released from every worldly tie, their death was a great consolation for me.
The Book of Divine Consolation of the Blessed Angela of Foligno, Mary G. Steegmann, tr. *1908*

2 Sometimes I see the host as if I were seeing a neck or breast in nobility and beauty exceeding those of the sun, and seeming to come from within. In the face of this beauty I understand without a shadow of a doubt that I am seeing God.
Ibid.

3 . . . do not adore this idol any more, because in this idol lives the devil.
Ibid.

220. Lady Nijo (1258–1306?)

1 "Even consolation brings pain."
(1284), *The Confessions of Lady Nijo*, Karen Brazell, tr. *1973*

2 Its blossoms detaining travelers
The cherry tree guards the pass
On Osaka Mountain.
(1289), Ibid.

3 A roof of cedar branches,
Pine pillows, bamboo blinds,
If only these could screen me
From this world of sorrow.
Ibid.

221. Kuan Tao-shêng (1262–1319)

1   I am your clay.
    You are my clay.
    In life we share a single quilt.
    In death we will share one coffin.

> "Married Love," *The Orchid Boat, Women Poets of China*,
> Kenneth Rexroth and Ling Chung, eds. and trs. *1972*

222. Jeanne of Navarre (1271–1307/9?)

1   When you kill these Flemish boars, do not spare the sows;
    them I would have spitted.

> Attributed comment about revolt of Flanders (1302),
> Quoted in *Women of Medieval France* by Pierce Butler *1907*

223. Empress Eifuku (1271–1342)

1   we
    Were caught in bed by the dawn

> Untitled, *One Hundred More Poems from the
> Japanese*, Kenneth Rexroth and Ling Chung, eds.
> and trs. *1972*

224. Abutsu (?–1283?)

1   Between the pines of the shore hills on the eastern road/
    Even the waves rise in the image of flowers.

> "The Diary of the Waning Loon," *The Penguin Book of
> Women Poets*, Carol Cosman, Joan Keefe and Kathleen
> Weaver, eds. *1978*

225. Mahuat d' Artois (1285–1319)

1   . . . have pity upon me, a poor widow driven from her her-
    itage, and here without counsel! You see how your people
    besiege me, one barking on my right, another at my left, till I
    know not what to answer, in the great trouble of my mind.

> Plea before the Duke de Noirs, Quoted in *Women of
> Medieval France* by Pierce Butler *1907*

226. Marguerite Porète (1250?–1310)

1   . . . a soul annihilated in the love of the creator could and
    should grant to nature all that it desires.

> *Le Miroir des simples âmes* (The Mirror of the Simple Soul;
> repr. 1992) *c. 1296–1306*

2   Reason, you'll always be half-blind.

> Ibid.

3   Theologians and other clerks,
    You won't understand this book
    —however bright your wits—
    if you do not meet it humbly,
    and in this way Love and Faith
    make you surmount Reason:
    they are the mistresses of Reason's house.

> Introduction, Ibid.

4   Virtues, I take leave of you for evermore:
    I'll have a freer heart for that—more joyful too.
    Your service is too unremitting—indeed I know.
    . . . I have quit your tyrannies; now I am at peace

> Ch. 6, Ibid.

5   The divine school is held with the mouth closed, which the
    human mind cannot express in words.

> Ch. 66, Ibid.

6   But those are in good and profitable times who adore God not
    only in temples and monasteries, but adore Him in all places
    through union with the divine will.

> Ch. 69, Ibid.

7   All the Virtues are mothers.

> Ibid.

8   My heart is drawn so high and fallen so low at the same time
    that I cannot complete [this book]. For everything one can say
    or write about God or think about Him, God who is greater
    than what is ever said, [everything] is thus more like lying than
    speaking the truth.

> Ch. 119, Ibid.

9   Thought is no longer of worth to me,
    nor work, nor speech.
    Love draws me so high
    (thought is no longer of worth to me)
    with her divine gaze,
    that I have no intent.
    Thought is no longer of worth to me,
    nor work nor speech.

> Ch. 122, Ibid.

227. Mistress of Albrecht of Johannsdorf (fl. 13th century)

1   How can you combine two unlike things, to cross the sea and
    bide with me? You leave the tenderness of my heart, then how
    can you cherish it also?

> Quoted in *Saint Elizabeth* by Elisabeth von Schmidt-Pauli;
> Olga Marx, tr. *1932*

228. Mukta Bai (fl. 13th century)

1   What is beyond the mind,
    has no boundary,
    In it our senses end.

> Untitled, Willis Barnstone, tr., *A Book of Women Poets*,
> Aliki and Willis Barnstone, eds. *1980*

2   Mukta says: Words cannot contain him,
    yet in him all words are.

> Ibid.

229. La Compiuta Donzella (fl. 13th century)

1   To leave the world serve God
    make my escape from all pretension . . .
    That is my wish
    For what I see flourish and ascend
    the stalk is only
    insanity, low acts and lies of men.

> Untitled, Sts. 1-2, Laura Stortoni, tr., *Women Poets of the
> World*, Joanna Bankier and Deirdre Lashgari, eds. *1983*

2   . . . all men find evil
    a proper ornament.

> Untitled, St. 3, Ibid.

230. Duchess of Lorraine (fl. 13th century)

1   Churl death, who wars on all mankind,
    you have taken from me what I most loved.
    Now I am the Phoenix, alas! alone and bereft,
    the single bird of which they tell.

> "Elegy," St. 3, Quoted in *Medieval Lyrics of Europe*,
> Willard R. Trask, tr. *1969*

231. Wang Ch'ing-hui (fl. 13th century)

1   Suddenly, one day, war drums on horseback
    Came like thunder, tearing off the sky,
    And all glorious flowery days were gone forever.
        Untitled, *The Orchid Boat, Women Poets of China*, Kenneth
        Rexroth and Ling Chung, eds. and trs. *1972*

232. Bridget of Sweden (1303–1373)

1   Mary is the lily in God's garden.
        Revelations, Vol. III *1344–1349*

2   Pride alienates man from heaven; humility leads to heaven.
        "Book of Questions," Vol. V, Ibid.

3   The source of justice is not vengeance but charity.
        Ibid.

4   JUDGE: If the nobleman is superior to the commoner, the nobleman should fear that his ultimate Judgement will be the more severe, because God has given him more.
        Ibid.

5   To write well and speak well is mere vanity if one does not live well.
        Ibid.

6   Man, the author of evil, must bear it.
        Ibid.

7   I beheld a Virgin of extreme beauty wrapped in a white mantle and a delicate tunic . . . with her beautiful golden hair falling loosely down her shoulders. . . . She stood with uplifted hands, her eyes fixed on heaven, rapt, as it were, in an ecstasy of contemplation, in a rapture of divine sweetness. And while she stood in prayer, I beheld her Child move in her womb and . . . she brought forth her Son, from Whom such ineffable light and splendor radiated that the sun could not be compared to it. . . . And then I heard the wonderful singing of many angels. *
        Vol. VII, Ibid.
    *Her vision of the Nativity has become the standard, "influencing Western art, music, literature, and even the decisions at the Council of Trent." (Anthony Butkovich, *Revelations*, 1972).

8   Woe is me, I have become like a newborn whelp that cannot see, and cannot find the paps of its mother. Woe is me, for in my blindness I see that I shall never see God.
        "Written of the Devil," Vol. VIII, Ibid.

9   The world would have peace if the men of politics would only follow the Gospel.
        Prayer, "In Honor of our Lord Jesus Christ," Quoted in
        Revelations by Anthony Butkovich *1972*

233. Juliana of Norwich (1342?–1417/23)

1   He shewed me a little thing, the quantity of a hazel nut, lying in the palm of my hand. . . . I looked thereupon and thought: "What may this be?" And I was answered . . . thus: "It is all that is made. . . . It lasts and ever shall last because God loves it, and hath all-things its being through the love of God."
        Ch. 4, *Revelations of Divine Love 1373*

2   And then our good Lord opened my ghostly eye, and shewed me my soul in the midst of my heart. I saw the soul so large as it were an endless world, and also as it were a blessed kingdom. And by the conditions that I saw therein, I understood that it is a worshipful city.
        Ch. 68, Ibid.

3   He said not, "Thou shalt not be troubled, thou shalt not be travailed, thou shalt not be diseased;" but He said, "Thou shalt not be overcome"
        Ibid.

4   For it is God's will that we hold us in comfort with all our might: for bliss is lasting without end, and pain is passing and shall be brought to nought for them that shall be saved.
        The Seventh Revelation, Ch. XV, Ibid.

234. Catherine of Siena (1347–1380)

1   Every evil, harm, and suffering in this life or in the next comes from the love of riches.
        The Dialogue of the Seraphic Virgin Catherine of Siena,
        Algar Thorold, ed. and tr. *1896*

2   . . . the Devil invites men to the water of death . . . and blinding them with the pleasures and conditions of the world, he catches them with the hook of pleasure . . .
        Ch. 44, Ibid.

3   The Devil often places himself upon the tongues of creatures, causing them to chatter nonsensically . . .
        Ch. 66, Ibid.

4   Thy miseries are not hid from thee now, for the worm of conscience sleeps no longer . . .
        Ch. 132, Ibid.

5   . . . if thou wish to reach the perfection of love, it befits thee to set thy life in order.
        Letter to Monna Alessa dei Saracini, *Saint Catherine of Siena as Seen in her Letters*, Vida D. Scudder, ed. and tr. *1906*

6   Make two homes for thyself, my daughter. One actual home . . . and another spiritual home, which thou art to carry with thee always. . . .
        Ibid.

7   . . . perfection does not consist in macerating or killing the body, but in killing our perverse self-will.
        Letter to Daniella of Orvieto, Ibid.

8   . . . sometimes God works through rascally men, in order that they may execute justice on His enemy.
        Letter to Giovanna, Ibid.

9   *Vidi arcana Dei* [I have seen the hidden things of God].
        Quoted in *Catherine of Siena: Fire and Blood*
        by Igino Girodani, Thomas J. Tobin, tr. *1959*

10   My soul . . . can see no other remedy pleasing to God than peace. Peace, peace, therefore, for the love of Christ crucified!
        Letter to Pope Gregory XI, Ibid.

11   We are put here in this life like a battlefield and we must fight the good fight.
        Dialogue with Divine Providence n.d.

235. Jefimija (1348?–1405?)

1   The sorrow for him is burning steadily in my heart
    And I am overcome by my motherly ways.
        "The Lament Over the Dead Son Overcome by Her Motherly Ways," St. 3, *An Anthology of Medieval Serbian Literature in English*, Mateja Matejic and Dragan Milivojevic, eds. *1978*

236. A Northern Mother* (fl. c. 1350)

1 Laugh not to scorne nodir [neither] olde ne young,
   Be of good bering and have a good tongue
   "The Good Wife Taught Her Daughter," St. 2 *1350*

2 . . . good name is worth gold . . .
                                          St. 13, Ibid.

3 . . . their thrift wexis thin
   That spend more than they win
                                          St. 17, Ibid.

4 . . . better it is a childe to be unborne,
   Than for unteaching to be forlorne.
                                          St. 24, Ibid.

   *This is the only name by which the author is known. We assume
   she lived about the time of the date of her book, but the time may
   well have been earlier.

237. Leonor Lopez de Cordoba (1361–post-1414)

1 The rest of us were kept prisoner for nine years. . . . Our husbands had sixty pounds of iron each on their feet, and my
   brother Don Lope Lopez had a chain on top of the irons, in
   which there were seventy links. He was a child of thirteen
   years [when he died], the most beautiful creature there was in
   the world.

                                          Memorias 1412

238. Margaret of Nassau (fl. c. 1360)

1 Know, my love, that I should like to call you a thief, because
   you have stolen my heart. . . .
   Letter to Matilda of Cleves (1367), Quoted in *Women
   in the Middle Ages* by Sibylle Harsken
   1975

239. Lalleswari (fl. c. 1360–1399)

1 I set forth hopeful—cotton-blossom Lal.
   Untitled, George Grierson, tr., adapted by Dierdre Lashgari,
   Women Poets of the World, Joanna Bankier and
   Dierdre Lashgari, eds. *1983*

2 Good repute is water carried in a sieve.
                                          Untitled, George Grierson, tr., Ibid.

240. Margherita Datini (1360–1423)

1 You say, always sermonizing, that we will have a fine life, and
   every month and every week will be the one. You have told me
   this for ten years, and today it seems more timely than ever to
   reply: it is your fault. . . .
      If you delay so much, you will never seize this "fine life,"
   and if you say, "Look at the hardships that I undergo every
   day, never can one live in the world without them:" that is no
   excuse for not living a fine life for the soul and the body.
   Letter to [her husband] Francesco di Marco Datini (January
   1386), Quoted in *Women in the Middle Ages* by Frances
   and Joseph Gies *1978*

241. Chao Li-hua (fl. c. 1360–1644)

1 my boat goes west, yours east
   heaven's a wind for both journeys
   "Farewell," J.P. Seaton, tr., *A Book of Women Poets*, Aliki
   and Willis Barnstone, eds. *1980*

242. Christine de Pisan (1363/65–1430/31)

1 If justice were king,
   neither female nor male would lose,
   but mostly, I am certain
   custom reigns, rather than justice.
   La Livre de la Mutacion de Fortune, Vol. 1, (p. 21),
   Susan Groag Bell, tr. *1400*

2 If it were customary to send little girls to school and to teach
   them the same subjects as are taught to boys, they would learn
   just and fully and would understand the subtleties of all arts
   and sciences. Indeed, maybe they would understand them better . . . for just as women's bodies are softer than men's, so
   their understanding is sharper.
   Prologue, *La Cité des Dames* [The City
   of Women] *1404*

3 She [Lady Reason] replied, "Rest assured, dear friend, that
   many noteworthy and great sciences and arts have been discovered through the understanding and subtlety of women,
   both in cognitive speculation, demonstrated in writing, and in
   the arts, manifested in manual works of labor.
                                          Ibid.

4 [I wondered] . . . how it happened that so many different
   men—and learned men among them—have been and are so inclined to express both in speaking and in their treatises and
   writings so many wicked insults about women and their behavior.
                                          Sections I.1.1–I.1.2, Ibid.

5 . . . as says the Philosopher—he is not wise who knows not
   part of everything.
                                          Pt. II, Ch. 9, "La Livre des Trois Vertus" *1405*

6 She* seemeth fed by that same armour's touch,
   Nurtured on iron —
   Untitled poem, St. 1 (1429), Quoted in *Of Six Medieval
   Women* by Alice Kemp-Welch, tr. *1913*

7 Honour to Womankind! It needs must be
   That God loves Woman, since He fashioned Thee.*
                                          St. 2, Ibid.

   *References in quotes 7 and 8 to Joan of Arc; see 249.

8 I returned to the life which pleased me most naturally, that was
   to study in solitude and quiet.
   L'Avison-Christine, Sister Mary Louis Towner, ed.; Susan
   Groag Bell, tr. *1932*

9 Knowledge has sweet savory, honeyed things which precede in
   value all other treasures as sovereign . . .
                                          Ibid.

10 Ah childhood and youth, if you knew the bliss which resides in
   the taste of knowledge, and the evil and ugliness that lies in ignorance, how well you are advised to little complain of the
   pain and labor of learning.
                                          Ibid.

11 Where true love is, it showeth; it will not feign.
   "The Epistle of Othea to Hector," St. 27, *The Penguin Book
   of Women Poets*, Carol Cosman, Joan Keefe and Kathleen
   Weaver, eds. *1978*

12 He is too unwise that, for default of one,
   will therefore despise woman everyone.
   "The Epistle of Othea to Hector," St. 45, Ibid.

13 Trust not on fortune, called the great goddess;
....
Before men's eyes she casteth a great mist.
When they find her favourable, they think they be well;
And yet is it feeble to hold on a slipper eel.
> St. 74, Ibid.

14 I will not stay when you behave
harshly, insult me like a cur,
for things have changed. I won't concur
and won't reveal my sorrow, save
I'll always dress in black and rave.
> Untitled, St. 3, Willis Barnstone, tr., *A Book of Women Poets*, Aliki and Willis Barnstone, eds. *1980*

15 Alone am I, menaced by mourning,
Alone am I, dyed deeper than dark brown,
Alone am I, my love no longer living.
> Untitled, St. 4, Julie Allen, tr., Ibid.

16 This wise lady ought to persuade her husband if she can by kind words and sensible admonitions to agree to discuss their finances together and try to keep to such a standard of living as their income can provide and not so far above it that at the end of the year they find themselves in debt to their own people or other creditors. There is absolutely no shame in living within your income, however small it may be, but there is shame if creditors are always coming to your door to repossess their goods or if they are obliged to make nuisances of themselves to your men or your tenants or if they have to try by hook or by crook to get their payment.
> "How ladies and young women who live on their manors ought to manage their households and estates," *The Treasure of the City of Ladies: or The Book of the Three Virtues* (pp. 130–33; 1404), Sarah Lawson, tr. *1985*

17 All wives of artisans should be very painstaking and diligent if they wish to have the necessities of life. They should encourage their husbands or their workmen to get to work early in the morning and work until late, for mark our words, there is no trade so good that if you neglect your work you will not have difficulty putting bread on the table. And besides encouraging the others, the wife herself should be involved in the work to the extent that she knows all about it, so that she may know how to oversee his workers if her husband is absent, and to reprove them if they do not do well.
> "Of the wives of artisans and how they ought to conduct themselves," Ibid.

18 . . . help those who have need of it in humane compassion, remembering that you too will become powerless and weak if you live that long, and then you would surely wish to be comforted yourself. You should also do it for God as the greatest charity and almsgiving that there is, for there is no worse disease than old age.
> "How young women ought to conduct themselves towards their elders," Ibid.

19 . . . a woman with a mind is fit for any task . . .
> Quoted in *The Creation of Feminist Consciousness: From the Middle Ages to Eighteen-Seventy*, Gerda Lerner* *1993*
> *See 203.

243. Margery Kempe (1373–1438?)

1 She thought that she loved God more than He did her. She was smitten with the deadly wound of vainglory, and felt it not, for she many times desired that the crucifix should loosen His hands from the Cross, and embrace her in token of love.
> *The Book of Margery Kempe c. 1435*

2 "I have oftentimes told thee, daughter, that thinking, weeping, and high contemplation is the best life on earth, and thou shalt have more merit in Heaven for one year of thinking in thy mind than for a hundred years of praying with thy mouth. . . . "
> Ibid.

3 And sometimes those that men think were revelations, are deceits and illusions, and therefore it is not expedient to give readily credence to every stirring, but soberly abide . . .
> Ch. 89, Ibid.

244. Valentine Visconti (fl. c. 1390–1405)

1 There is nothing more for me, nothing matters more. *[Rien ne m'est plus, plus ne m'est rien.]*
> Motto, adopted after her husband's death (c. 1405), Quoted in *Women of Medieval France* by Pierce Butler *1907*

245. Padeshah Khatun (fl. 14th century)

1 Two yards of veil won't make any woman a lady
nor a hat make any head worthy of command
> "Sovereign Queen," Deirdre Lashgari, tr., *Women Poets of the World*, Joanna Bankier and Deirdre Lashgari, eds. *1983*

246. Mehri (1404?–1447)

1 Each subtlety hard for the pedant to solve
I found a drop of wine would dissolve.
> "Coming Across," Deirdre Lashgari, tr., *Women Poets of the World*, Joanna Bankier and Deirdre Lashgari, eds. *1983*

247. Alessandra de' Machingi Strozzi (1406–1471)

1 One has nothing to do now but to pay taxes. . . . It is miraculous how much money they extort from us, and yet we seem to gain no advantage.
> Letter to her son Lorenzo (1452), Quoted in *Famous Women of Florence* by Edgecumbe Staley, tr. *1909*

2 Those who have no money are bound to go down . . .
> Letter to her son Filippo (1464), Ibid.

3 A man, when he is a man indeed, makes a woman a woman.
> Letter (c. 1466), Ibid.

4 If I had no other interruptions in my work than my grandson, that would be more than enough, but I get so much pleasure from it. He follows me everywhere, like a chicken following a hen.
> Letter to her son, Quoted in *Uppity Women of Medieval Times* by Vicki León *1997*

5 I pray to God that he frees you from your fears—if all men were as afraid of marriage as you are, the world would have long since died out!
> Letter to her son Filippo, Ibid.

248. Catherine of Bologna (1413–1463)

1 Let every lover who loves the Lord
Come to the dance singing of love
Let her come dancing all afire

Desiring only him who created her
And separated her from the dangerous
worldly state.

> Preface, *The Seven Spiritual Weapons,* Hugh Feiss
> and Daniela Re, trs., *1998*

2   Whoever from deep within her noble and zealous heart wishes to take up the cross . . . , let her first take up the arms necessary for such battles.

> Text, Ibid.

3   My Lord, what should I do because I do not have my heart in the control of my free will and I cannot restrain the thoughts which come to me?

> Ibid.

249. Joan of Arc (1412?–1431)

1   Messire, I am but a poor village girl; I cannot ride on horseback nor lead men to battle.

> Attributed to vision of St. Michael (c.1425), Quoted in
> *Women of Beauty and Heroism* by Frank B. Goodrich *1858*

2   My brothers in Paradise tell me what to do.

> Remark, Ibid.

3   I know neither A nor B; but I come from God to deliver Orleans and consecrate the king.

> Ibid.

4   Children say that people are hung sometimes for speaking the truth.

> Defense at her tribunal (23 February 1431), Ibid.

5   If I am not [in a state of grace], God bring me there; if I am, God keep me there!

> Ibid.

250. Isotta Nogarola (1417–1461/68)

1   There are already so many women in the world! Why then . . . was I born a woman, to be scorned by men in words and deeds.

> Letter to Guarino Veronese, Quoted in "Book-Lined Cells,"
> Margaret King, tr., *Beyond Their Sex,* Patricia Labalme, ed.
> *1980*

2   Hence the woman, but only because she had been first deceived by the serpent's evil persuasion, did indulge in the delights of paradise; but she would have harmed only herself and in no way endangered human posterity if the consent of the first-born man had not been offered. Therefore Eve was no danger to posterity but [only] to herself; but the man Adam spread the infection of sin to himself and to all future generations. Thus Adam, being the author of all humans yet to be born, was also the first cause of perdition.

> Letter to Ludovico Foscarini (1451), Quoted in *Her Immaculate Hand* by Margaret L. King and Albert Rabil, Jr. *1991*

3   For where there is less intellect and less constancy, there is less sin . . .

> Ibid.

251. Lucrezia de' Medici (1425–1482)

1   Here is the mighty king
He has conquered the evil
Which has lasted many years,

And makes the earth tremble
removing sorrows from it
Thus filling the seats of paradise
To restore his court.

> "Here is the Mighty King," Claudia Alexander with Carlo
> Di Maio, trs., from *Laude,* Quoted in *Poesia italiana: Il quatrocento,* Giulio Ferroni, ed. *1978*

252. Costanza Varano Sforza (1426–1447)

1   Even the wisest and most famous men would fear to attempt to praise you adequately. What then can I, an ignorant, unlettered, and inexperienced girl hope to do?

> "Oration to Bianca Maria Visconti,"* Quoted in "Book-Lined Cells," Margaret King, tr., *Beyond Their Sex,* Patricia Labalme, ed. *1980*

*Last surviving member of the Visconti family of Milan, who dominated the history of northern Italy in the 14th and 15th centuries.

253. Sister Bertken (1427?–1514?)

1   I must sow lilies by the light of the dawn,
And start my work early as the new day is born.

> "A Ditty," St. 8, Jonathan Crewe, tr., *Women Poets of the World,* Joanna Bankier and Deirdre Lashgari, eds. *1983*

254. Margaret of Anjou (1430–1482)

1   The world is always disposed to consider what is done by a great and powerful monarch as of course right, and even when it would seem to them wrong they believe that its having that appearance is only because they are not in a position to form a just judgement on the question, not being full acquainted with the facts, or not seeing all the bearings of them.

> Ch. 9, Remark to Henry VI, her husband, Quoted in *The History of Marguerite d'Anjou* by Jacob Abbott *1861*

255. Macuilxochitl (1435–1499?)

1   Will my songs
be borne to his house
where he dwells in mystery?
Or do thy flowers bloom
here only?
Let the dance begin!

> "Battle Song," St. 2, Miguel León-Portilla and Catherine Rodriguez-Nieto, trs., *Trece poetas del mundo azteca* [Thirteen Poets of the Aztec World], Miguel León-Portilla, ed. *1967*

256. Elizabeth Woodville Grey (1437?–1492)

1   . . . desire of kingdom knoweth no kindred . . .

> Speech to Archbishop of Canterbury (1483), Quoted in *Chronicles* by Raphael Holinshed *1577*

2   . . . for as ye think I fear too much, be you well ware that you fear not as far too little.

> Ibid.

257. Margaret Mautby Paston (1441–1484)

1   I would that ye should not be too hasty to be married till ye were more sure of your livelode [livelihood], for ye must remember what charge ye shall have; and if ye have not [the means] to maintain it it will be a great rebuke. And therefore

labour that ye . . . be more in surety of your land ere than ye be married.

> Letter to her son, John Paston II (1469), *The Paston Letters and Papers of the Fifteenth Century*, Pt. II, Norman Davis, ed. *1976*

258. Catherine of Genoa (1447–1510)

1 I am so washed in the tide of His measureless love that I seem to be below the surface of a sea and cannot touch or see or feel anything around me except its water.

> *La Vita della B. Caterina Fiesca Adorna Dama Genouese* *1681*

2 My Me is God, nor do I recognize any other Me except my God himself.

> Quoted in *The Perennial Philosophy* by Aldous Huxley* *1945*

*British writer (1894-1963).

259. Elizabeth Clere (fl. c. 1450)

1 Cousin, think on this matter, for sorrow oftentime causeth women to beset them otherwise than they should do.

> Letter to John Paston I (c. 1450), *The Paston Letters and Papers of the Fifteenth Century*, Pt. II, Norman Davis, ed. *1976*

260. Isabella I (1451–1504)

1 Whoever hath a good presence and a good fashion, carries continual letters of recommendation.

> #99, Quoted in *Apophthagmes New and Old*, Francis Bacon, ed. *1625*

2 . . . kings who wish to reign have to labor . . .

> Quoted in *Isabella of Spain* by William Thomas Walsh *1930*

3 . . . in all human affairs there are things both certain and doubtful, and both are equally in the hands of God.

> Ibid.

4 Since . . . kings, like other men, are exposed to mortal accidents . . . they should be prepared for death . . .

> Letter* to Archbishop of Granada (1492/93), Ibid.
> *Occasioned by the attempted assassination of her husband, King Ferdinand V of Aragon.

5 Although I have never doubted it . . . the distance is great from the firm belief to the realization from concrete experience.

> Ibid.

261. Antonia Pulci (1452–1501)

1 SERVANT. All these husbands put their best forward: When their lady is engaged to them How humble, then, they wish to seem, and mild — At least until they've led her to their home.

> *The Plays of Saint Flavia Domitilla, Florentine Drama for Convent and Festival*, James Wyatt Cook, tr. and annot. *1997*

2 SERVANT. So is virginity the glory true. It wafts a sweet aroma up to God.

> Ibid.

3 SERVANT. Lo, some keep mistresses or concubines, and some their ladies batter painfully,

Torment them with harsh discipline so cruel; Many scornful outbursts, too, they bear; One needs to think through all things to their end—

> Ibid.

262. Juliana Berners (1460?–?)

1 A faythfulle frende wold I fayne finde, to fynde hym where he myghte be founde. But now is the worlde wext so unkynde, Yet frenship is fall to the grounde; (Now a Frende I have Founde) That I woll nother banne ne curse, But of all frendes in felde or towne Ever, gramercy, myn own purse.

> "Song," St.1, *Boke of Saint Albans 1486*

2 What are the means and the causes that lead a man into a merry spirit! Truly, in my best judgment, it seems that they are good sports and honest games in which a man takes pleasure without any repentance afterward. Thence it follows that good recreations and honorable pastimes are the cause of a man's fair old age and long life. And therefore, I will now choose among four good sports and honorable pastimes—to whit, among hunting, hawking, fishing and fowling. The best, in my simple judgment, is fishing, called angling, with a rod and a line and a hook.

> *The Treatise of Fishing With an Angle* (A Treatyse of Fysshynge Wyth an Angle) *1496*

3 Also you must not be too greedy in catching your said game, as in taking too much at one time . . . That could easily be the occasion of destroying your own sport and other men's also. When you have a sufficient mess, you should covet no more at that time. Also you should busy yourself to nourish the game in everything that you can, and to destroy all such things as are devourers of it.

> Ibid.

4 . . . you will avoid idleness, which is the principal cause inciting many to other vices, as is right well-known.

> Ibid.

263. Florencia del Pinar (fl. c. 1460–1499)

1 These birds were born singing for joy; such softness imprisoned gives me much sorrow — yet no one weeps for me.

> "To Some Partridges, Sent to Her Alive" (c.1511), Julie Allen, tr., *A Book of Women Poets*, Aliki and Willis Barnstone, eds. *1980*

264. Gwerfyl Mechain (1460?–1500)

1 Before the men who drink here, I offer a perfect world. I want nothing more. I walk among men, faultlessly, sing intimate songs and pour the mead.

> "Lady of the Ferry Inn," St. 2, Willis Barnstone, tr., *A Book of Women Poets*, Aliki and Willis Barnstone, eds. *1980*

2 Tiny snow of the stunningly cold black day is white flour,

is flesh of the earth,
cold lamb fleece on the mountain.
>> "In the Snowfall," St. 1, Ibid.

3   It's a sad state of affairs that a cock
completely deprives a woman of her senses.
>> "To Jealous Wives," St. 2, *Medieval Welsh Erotic Poetry*,
>> Dafydd Johnston, ed. and tr. *1991*

4   a girl's thick grove, circle of precious greeting,
lovely bush, God save it.
>> "The Female Genitals," Ibid.

5   I declare, the quim is fair
circle of broad-edged lips
it is a valley longer than a spoon or a hand
a ditch to hold a penis two hands long
>> Ibid.

265. Caterina Sforza (1462–1509)

1   Could I write all, the world would turn to stone.
>> Letter to her Dominican confessor (c.1501–1509),*
>> Quoted in *The Medici* by G.F. Young *1930*
>> *Written from her prison in the Castel Sant'Angelo, Rome.

2   War is not for ladies and children like mine.
>> Letter to her uncle, Ludovico Sforza il Moro (27 August
>> 1498), Quoted in *Caterina Sforza* by Ernst Breisach *1967*

266. Clemence Isaure (1464–1515/16)

1   . . . I, alas, plaintive and solitary,
I who have known only that I love, and that I suffer,
I must — a stranger to the world, to happiness —
Weep . . . and die.
>> Untitled, St. 2, Michael Fanning, tr., *Dictats de Dona*
>> *Clamenza Isaure 1505*

267. Elizabeth of York (1465/66–1503)

1   Delivered from sorrow, annexed to pleasance,
Of all comfort having abundance.
This joy and I, I trust, shall never twin—
My heart is set upon a lusty pin.
>> "My Heart Is Set Upon a Lusty Pin," St. 1, *The Women*
>> *Poets in English*, Ann Stanford, ed. *1972*

268. Cassandra Fedele (1465–1558)

1   Do that for which nature has suited you . . .
>> "Letter to Alessandra Scala," from *Clarissimae*
>> *feminae Cassandra Fidelis benetae epistolae et orationes*
>> *posthumae*, (1536), Quoted in "Book-Lined Cells,"
>> Margaret King, tr., *Beyond Their Sex*, Patricia Labalme, ed.
>> *1980*

2   . . . many of you no doubt will see it as audacious, that I, a
maiden . . . have come forth to speak in this radiance of
learned men . . .
>> "Oration delivered in Padua," Ibid.

269. Laura Cereta (1469–1499)

1   Burning with the fires of hatred, the more they gnaw others,
spewing forth words, the more are they wordless, gnawed
within.
>> from *Epistolae*, Ibid.

2   The free mind, not afraid to labor, presses on to attain the
good.
>> Ibid.

3   For knowledge is not given as a gift but by study. For a mind
free, keen, and unyielding in the face of hard work always rises
to the good, and the desire for learning grows in the depth and
breadth.
>> Letter to Bibolo Semproni, *Laura Cereta, Collected Letters*
>> *of a Renaissance Feminist*, Diana Robin, ed. & tr. *1997*

4   Nature has granted to all enough of her bounty; she opens to
all the gates of choice, and through these gates, reason sends
legates to the will, for it is through reason that these legates
transmit desires.
>> Ibid.

5   For some women worry about the styling of their hair, the
elegance of their clothes, and the pearls and other jewelry
they wear on their fingers. Others love to say cute little
things, to hide their feelings behind a mask of tranquillity, to
indulge in dancing, and to lead pet dogs around on a leash.
For all I care, other women can long for parties. . . . But
those women for whom the quest for the good represents a
higher value restrain their young spirits and ponder better
plans.
>> Letter to Bibolo Semproni (1488), Ibid.

6   Your mouth has grown foul because you keep it sealed so that
no arguments can come out of it that might enable you to
admit that nature imparts one freedom to all human beings
equally — to learn.
>> Ibid.

270. Elizabeth Brews (fl. c. 1470)

1   Cousin, it is but a simple oak that [is] cut down at the first
stroke.
>> Letter to John Paston III, her son-in-law (February 1477),
>> *Paston Letters, 1422-1509*, James Gairdner, ed. *1904*

271. Elisabetta Gonzaga (1471–1526)

1   Who is there among us whose conduct is so perfect as to close
the mouth of slanderers? . . . trouble yourself no more on the
subject, but . . . allow the wrong to recoil on the heads of those
who invent these slanders, and who, in my judgement, are sufficiently punished by seeing how hateful they become in the
eyes of all virtuous and honest persons.
>> Letter to Isabella d'Este* (1513), Quoted in *Isabella d'Este*,
>> Vol. II, by Julia Cartwright *1903*
>> *See 272.

272. Isabella d' Este (1474–1530)

1   This [Milan] is the school of the Master and of those who
know, the home of art and understanding.
>> (1492), Quoted in *Beatrice d'Este**
>> by Julia Cartwright *1899*
>> *See 273.

2   . . . the discontent of the people is more dangerous to a
monarch than all the might of his enemies on the battlefield.
>> Letter to her husband (Milan, February 1495), Ibid.

3   I am here in Mantua, but all my heart is in Rome.
>> Letter to Cardinal Bibbiena (1515), Quoted in
>> *Isabella d'Este*, Vol. II, by Julia Cartwright *1903*

4 Neither hope nor fear. (*Nec spe nec metu.*)
      Personal motto, Quoted in *Great Ages of Man:*
                 The Renaissance by John R. Hale *1964*

5 . . . resolve to think of nothing but . . . health in the first place
   and . . . honor and comfort in the second, because in this fickle
   world we can do nothing else, and those who do not know
   how to spend their time profitably allow their lives to slip
   away with much sorrow and little praise.
      Letter to Elisabetta of Urbino (1492), Quoted in
                 *Lucrezia Borgia** by Rachel Erlanger *1978*
   *See 277.

6 Your Excellency is indebted to me as never husband was to
   wife. Even if you loved and honored me more than anyone in
   the world, you could not repay my good faith.*
      Quoted in *Uppity Women of Medieval Times*
                 by Vicki León *1997*
   *Her reply to her husband's remark: "We're ashamed that it is
   our fate to have as wife a woman who is always ruled by her
   head."

273. Beatrice d' Este (1475–1497)

1 I cannot say much of the perils of the chase, since game is so
   plentiful here that hares are to be seen jumping out at every
   corner — so much so, that often we hardly know which way
   to turn to find the best sport.
      Letter to Isabella d'Este* (1491), Quoted in *Beatrice d'Este*
                 by Julia Cartwright *1899*
   *See 272.

2 Wherever I turn, in the house or out-of-doors, I seem to see
   your face before my eyes, and when I find myself deceived, and
   realize that you are really gone, you will understand how sore
   my distress has been — nay, how great it still is.
      Letter to Isabella d'Este, her sister (1495), Ibid.

274. Barbara Torelli (1475–1533)

1 Would that my fire might warm this frigid ice
   And turn with tears, this dust to living flesh
      Poem on the death of her husband* (1508), Quoted in
                 *Lucrezia Borgia** by Rachel Erlanger *1978*
   *Her second husband was murdered by the Bentivoglio, the family
   of her first husband. **See 277.

275. Giulia Farnese (1476–?)

1 We look as if we had despoiled Florence [Italy] of brocade.
      Letter to Pope Alexander VI, Quoted in *Lucrezia Borgia**
                 by Rachel Erlanger *1978*
   *See 277.

276. Agnes Paston (?–1479)

1 This world is but a thoroughfare, and full of woe; and when
   we depart therefrom, right nought bear with us but our good
   deeds and ill.
      Letter to her son John (c.1444), *The Paston Letters and
      Papers of the Fifteenth Century*, Pt. II, Norman Davis, ed.
                 1976

2 There knoweth no man how soon God will call him; and therefore it is good for every creature to be ready. Whom God
   visiteth, he loveth.
                 Ibid.

277. Lucrezia Borgia (1480–1519)

1 . . . my husbands have been very unlucky.
      Remark to her father after the murder of her second hus-
      band, Quoted in *Lucrezia Borgia* by Rachel Erlanger *1978*

2 The more I try to do God's will the more he visits me with misfortune.
      Remark upon hearing of the death of her brother, Ibid.

278. Margaret of Austria (1480–1530)

1 The time is troubled, but time will clear;
   After the rain one awaits fair weather.
      Untitled roundelay, St. 1, Quoted in *Margaret of Austria:
      Regent of the Netherlands* by Jane de Iongh,
                 M. D. Herternorton, tr. *1953*

2 All goes awry and lawless in the land,
   Where power takes the place of justice.
                 Ibid.

3 *Fortune. Infortune. Fort. Une.* (Fortune persecutes one
   harshly.)
                 Motto (1506), Ibid.

279. Catherine of Aragon (1485–1536)

1 . . . I am in debt in London. . . . So that, my lord, I am in the
   greatest trouble and anguish in the world. . . . I have now sold
   some bracelets to get a dress of black velvet, for I was all but
   naked; . . . certainly I shall not be able to live in this manner.
      Letter to King Ferdinand of Spain (1505), Quoted in
      Letters of Royal and Illustrious Ladies of Great Britain,
                 Vol. I, Mary Anne Everett Wood Green,* ed. *1846*
   *See 926.

2 Our time is ever passed in continual feasts.
      Letter to King Ferdinand of Spain (1509), Ibid.

3 They tell me nothing but lies here, and they think they can
   break my spirit. But I believe what I choose and say nothing. I
   am not so simple as I seem.
      Letter to King Ferdinand of Spain (1508), Quoted in
                 Catherine of Aragon by Garrett Mattingly *1941*

4 I came not into this realm as merchandise, nor yet to be married to any merchant.
      Letter replying to request she acquiesce to the marriage
                 of Henry VIII and Anne Boleyn* (1533), Ibid.
   *See 298.

280. Elisabeth of Brandenburg (1485–1545)

1 I believe in Him who made the sun and the moon and all the
   stars. . . . May he not tarry to fetch me. . . . I am so weary of
   life.
      Last words (1545), Quoted in *Women of the Reformation,
      Vol. I, Germany and Italy*, by Roland H. Bainton *1971*

281. Veronica Gambara (1485–1550)

1 until Nature falls in love with herself
   and delights to see the beauty she's made,
      "How dream-like, fleeting earthly things," St. 2, *Stanzas
                 1532–33*

2 It's Heaven's will we are without hope of
   renewal like everything else in nature,
   certain of nothing but that we must die,
                 St. 5, Ibid.

3   if without false emotion and sighs, we
    simply enjoyed what Heaven offers us,
    if we could live in modest, humble ways.

St. 14, Ibid.

4   but, afterwards the evil plague was born,
    born too envy, ambition's companion,
    and all at once the world was afflicted,
    a world at first so carefree, so joyful.

St. 19, Ibid.

5   I'll stand here, glad to be rid of all else,
    loving virtue and the soul as long as I live.

St. 27, last lines, Ibid.

6   . . . blissful in heaven you see dawn appear
    And under your feet you see the stars. . . .

Sonnet on the death of an unidentified poet, Claudia
Alexander with Carlo DiMaio, trs., from *Rime* (1759), *Poe-
sia italiana: il cinquecento*, Giulio Ferroni, ed. *1978*

282. Ursula Shipton (1488–1561)

1   Now shall the Mitered Peacock* first begin to plume, whose
Train shall make a great show in the World for a time, but
shall afterwards vanish away and his Honour come to nothing, which shall take its end at Kingston.

The Life, Prophecies and Death of the Famous
Mother Shipton 1687

*Reference to Cardinal Wolsey (?–1530), whose pride and retinue
of 800 followers inspired the metaphor, and whose death Shipton
foretold.

283. Argula von Grumbach (1492–post-1563)

1   Where do you read in the Bible that Christ, the apostles, and
the prophets imprisoned, banished, burned or murdered anyone?

Letter of protest to the faculty of the University of Ingolstadt
(1523), Quoted in *Women of the Reformation, Vol. I;
Germany and Italy*, by Roland H. Bainton *1971*

2   To obey my man indeed is fitting,
    But if he drives me from God's Word
    In Matthew ten it is declared
    Home and child we must forsake
    When God's honor is at stake.

Untitled, Ibid.

3   I am distressed that our princes take the Word of God no more
seriously than a cow does a game of chess.

Letter to her cousin, Adam von Torring, Ibid.

4   I have even heard some say, "If my father and mother were in
hell, I wouldn't want to be in heaven." Not me, not if all my
friends were down there.

Ibid.

284. Vittoria da Colonna (1492–1547/49)

1   Your virtue may raise you above the glory of being king. The
sort of honour that goes down to our children with real lustre
is derived from our deeds and qualities, not from power or titles.

Letter to Francesco, Marquis of Pescara, her husband,
Quoted in *Biography of Distinguished Women*
by Sarah Josepha Hale* *1876*

*See 788.

2   Thou knowest, Love, I never sought to flee
    From thy sweet prison, nor impatient threw
    Thy dear yoke from my neck, nor e'er withdrew
    what, that first day, my soul bestowed on thee. . . .

Untitled sonnet (c.1525–1529), in Letter to Francesco,
Marquis of Pescara (1529), Quoted in *A Princess of
the Italian Reformation: Giulia Gonzaga*
by Christopher Hare** *1912*

*See 304. **Pseudonym of Marian Andrews.

3   . . . the swaggering knights prepare to ride.
    The war begins. They gloat and cannot wait.
    They think they are masters of their fate.

Untitled sonnet (c.1529–1549), Quoted in *Women of
the Reformation, Vol. I; Germany and Italy*,
by Roland H. Bainton *1971*

4   By true humility we reach the light
    And know the sacred writings to be true.
    Read little, then, and believe the more.

Ibid.

5   One cannot have a lively faith, I trow,
    Of God's eternal promises if fear
    Has left the warm heart chilled and sear
    And placed a veil between the I and Thou.

Ibid.

6   A scissors cut the single noble thread
    which twisted our lives into one; he's gone
    and the life I lived through him is vanished.

"By losing myself in a deepening," St. 3, *Amaro Lagrimar,
The Sonnets of Vittoria Colonna*, Ellen Moody, tr. *1999*

7   I would like to be deaf to the world's noise,
    to hear with a clear fully absorbed mind,
    that lofty angelic music — sweet notes —
    tell us that real peace belongs to real love.

"I would like to be deaf to the world's noise," St. 1, Ibid.

8   What use are all these rhymes about
    his chivalry or my desperation?
    Helicon needs not my utterances.

"My voice was exhausted, and I could not," St. 3, Ibid.

9   See that lovely juniper, pressed so hard,
    angry winds swirl round her, but she'll not let
    her leaves fall or scatter; clenched, branches held
    high, she gathers strength; her refuge within.

"See that lovely juniper, pressed so hard," Ibid.

10 It's not that the heart must do this or how
    deeply she desires that; it's does she
    do what she can, in birth, life, and in death,

"Two times has the light of paradise shone," St. 2, Ibid.

11 Rather than beating on locked doors, open
    the one to oblivion, and shut off
    all possibility of another

"Why endlessly appeal to death's cold ear," St. 2, Ibid.

285. Marguerite of Navarre (1492–1549)

1   A father will have compassion on his son. A mother will
never forget her child. A brother will cover the sin of his sister. But what husband ever forgave the faithlessness of his
wife?

Mirror of the Sinful Soul 1531

2 spite will make a woman do more than love. . . .
        "Novel III, the First day," *The Heptameron, or Novels of the Queen of Navarre 1558*

3 I have heard much of these languishing lovers, but I never yet saw one of them die for love.
        Ibid.

4 To me it seems much better to love a woman as a woman, than to make her one's idol, as many do. For my part, I am convinced that it is better to use than to abuse.
        "Novel XIII, the Second Day," Ibid.

5 . . . all the lovers I have had have invariably begun by talking of my interests, and telling me that they loved my life, my welfare, and my honor, and the upshot of it has no less invariably been their own interest, their own pleasure, and their own vanity.
        "Novel XIV, the Second Day," Ibid.

6 . . . no one ever perfectly loved God who did not perfectly love some of His creatures in this world.
        "Novel XIX, the Second Day," Ibid.

7 . . . there is no greater ninny than a man who thinks himself cunning, nor any one wiser than he who knows that he is not so.
        "Novel XXIX, the Second Day," Ibid.

8 He who knows his own incapacity, knows something, after all. . . .
        Ibid.

9 . . . the first step man takes in self-confidence, removes him so far from the confidence he ought to have in God.
        "Novel XXX, the Third Day," Ibid.

10 Man is wise . . . when he recognizes no greater enemy than himself. . . .
        Ibid.

11 . . . God always helps madmen, lovers, and drunkards. . . .
        "Novel XXXVIII, the Fourth Day," Ibid.

12 . . . fools live longer than the wise, unless someone kills them. . . for . . . fools do not dissemble their passions. If they are angry they strike; if they are merry they laugh; but those who deem themselves wise hide their defects with so much care that their hearts are all poisoned with them.
        Ibid.

13 A prison is never narrow when the imagination can range in it at will.
        Ibid.

14 Blessed . . . is he who has it in his power to do evil, yet does it not.
        "Novel XLIII, the Fourth Day," Ibid.

15 Though jealousy be produced by love, as ashes are by fire, yet jealousy extinguishes love as ashes smother the flame.
        "Novel XLVIII, the Fifth Day," Ibid.

16 I never knew a mocker who was not mocked . . . a deceiver who was not deceived, or a proud man who was not humbled.
        "Novel LI, the Sixth Day," Ibid.

17 People pretend . . . not to like grapes when they are too high for them to reach.
        "Novel LIII, the Sixth Day," Ibid.

18 . . . some there are who are much more ashamed of confessing a sin than of committing it.
        "Novel LX, the Sixth Day," Ibid.

19 I did not know that love could grow through death. But now I know.
        Dialogue on the death of her brother, King Francis I (c.1547/48), Quoted in *Women of the Reformation, Vol. II: France and England*, by Roland H. Bainton *1973*

286. Mary of France (1496–1533)

1 God's will sufficeth me. (*La Volonté de Dieu me suffit.*)
        Personal motto (1514), Quoted in *Mary Tudor: The White Queen* by Walter C. Richardson *1970*

2 Sir, your Grace knoweth well that I did marry for your pleasure . . . and now I trust you will suffer me to marry as me liketh for to do.
        Letter to her brother, Henry VIII* (c.1514/15), Ibid.

        *King of England (1509–47) who broke from the Catholic Church in 1534 to form the Church of England.

287. Katherine Zell (1497/98–1562)

1 A disturber of the peace, am I? Yes indeed, of my own peace. Do you call this disturbing the peace? . . . Instead of spending my time in frivolous amusements, I have visited the plague-infested and carried out the dead . . .
        Letter to the city of Strasbourg *1557*

2 You remind me that the Apostle Paul told women to be silent in church. I would remind you of the word of this same apostle that in Christ there is no longer male nor female.
        "*Entschuldigung* [Apology of] *Katharina Schutzinn*" (1524), Quoted in *Women of the Reformation, Vol. I; Germany and Italy* by Roland H. Bainton *1971*

3 Faith is not faith which is not tried.
        "*Den Leyenden Christgläubigen*" [To Suffering Believers in Christ] (1524), Ibid.

4 Lead us not into the temptation of believing that we have truly forgiven, while rancor lingers . . .
        Ibid.

5 Besides food even the healthy wouldn't eat, the place [a local hospital] is so Godless that when an "Our Father" is said at the table, it's done so quietly that no one knows if it's a prayer or a fart . . .
        Quoted in *Uppity Women of Medieval Times* by Vicki León *1997*

288. Mirabai (1498–1547)

1 She drinks the honey of her vision.
        Untitled, St. 4, Willis Barnstone and Usha Nilsson, trs., *A Book of Women Poets*, Aliki and Willis Barnstone, eds. *1980*

2 Hari is an ocean,
    my eyes touch him.
    Mira is an ocean of joy.
    She takes him inside.

        Untitled, Ibid.

3   The energy that holds up mountains is the one Mirabai bows down to, He lives century after century, and the test I set for him he has passed.
> "The Clouds," *News of the Universe*, Robert Bly,* ed. and adapter *1980*

*American poet (1926–).

4   I have felt the swaying of the elephant's shoulders . . . and now you want me to climb on a jackass? Try to be serious!
> "Why Mira Can't Go Back to her Old House," *Ibid.*

5   Get up, dear child, the dawn has come, outside the door wait gods and men.
> Untitled, Usha Nilsson, tr., *Women Poets of the World*, Joanna Bankier and Deirdre Lashgari, eds. *1983*

289. Huang O (1498–1569)

1   Once more I will shyly
Let you undress me and gently
Unlock my sealed jewel.
> "A Farewell to a Southern Melody," *The Orchid Boat, Women Poets of China*, Kenneth Rexroth and Ling Chung, eds. and trs. *1972*

2   I will allow only
My lord to possess my sacred
Lotus pond, and every night
You can make blossom in me
Flowers of fire.
> to the tune "Soaring Clouds," *Ibid.*

3   Maybe you can fool some girls,
But you can't fool Heaven.
> to the tune "Red Embroidered Shoes," *Ibid.*

4   Go and make somebody else
Unsatisfied.
> *Ibid.*

290. Diane de Poitiers (1499–1566)

1   Farewell sweet kisses, pigeon-wise,
With lip and tongue, farewell again
The secret sports betwixt us twain
> "To Henry II Upon His Leaving for a Trip" (c.1552), Quoted in *The Life and Times of Catherine de Medici** by Francis Watson *1935*

*See 310.

2   The years that a woman subtracts from her age are not lost. They are added to the ages of other women.
> Attributed *n.d.*

291. Nahabed Kouchak (fl. 15th century)

1   My heart is turned into a wailing child,
In vain with sweets I seek to still its cries;
Sweet love, it calls for thee in sobbing wild
All day and night, with longing and with sighs.
What solace can I give it?
> "My Heart Is Turned into a Wailing Child," St. 1, *Armenian Legends and Poems*, Zabelle C. Boyajian, ed. *1916*

2   On the morning of thy birth
We were glad but thou wert wailing

See that when thou leav'st the earth
Thou art glad and we bewailing.
> "Birthday Song," St. 1, *Ibid.*

292. Agnes the Martyr (1500–1535)

O Eternall Governour, vouchsafe to open the gates of heaven once shut up against all the inhabitants of the earth . . .
> "The praier of Agnes the Martyr at hir death," *The Monument of Matrones conteining seven severall Lamps of Virginitie, or distinct treatises* . . . , Vol. I, Thomas Bentley, ed. *1582*

293. Honor Lisle (1500?–1550)

1   Good my lord, whereas in my former letters I have written to you that you should write to me with your own hand, whereof two lines should be more comfort to me than a hundred of another man's hand.
> Letter to Arthur Plantagenet (1539), Quoted *in Letters of Royal and Illustrious Ladies of Great Britain*, Vol. III, Mary Anne Everett Wood Green,* ed. *1846*

*See 926.

294. Caterina Cibo (1501–1557)

1   . . . all creatures are flames of love.
> Quoted in *Seven Dialogues* by Bernadino Orchino (n.d.), cited in *Women of the Reformation, Vol. I: Germany and Italy* by Roland H. Bainton *1971*

2   We have but a little knowledge of God. . . . We are like bats who cannot look upon the light of the sun. God is infinite, immense, uncircumscribed, but our intellect is finite, limited, imprisoned in this body of darkness, stained with primal sin.
> *Ibid.*

295. Maria of Hungary and Bohemia (1505–1558)

1   Full well I know
God is my sword,
And of my Lord
None is me relieving.
> Untitled, St. 1 (1529), Quoted in *Women of the Reformation, Vol. III: From Spain to Scandinavia* by Roland H. Bainton *1977*

296. Mihri Hatun (?–1506)

1   At one glance
I love you
With a thousand hearts
> Untitled, St. 1, Tâlat S. Halman, tr., *The Penguin Book of Women Poets*, Carol Cosman, Joan Keefe and Kathleen Weaver, eds. *1978*

2   Let the zealots think
Loving is sinful
Never mind
Let me burn in the hellfire
Of that sin
> St. 3, *Ibid.*

297. Hwang Chin-I (1506?–1544)

1   I cut in two
A long November night
> Untitled, Peter H. Lee, tr., *The Penguin Book of Women Poets*, Carol Cosman, Joan Keefe and Kathleen Weaver, eds. *1978*

2   Mountains are steadfast but the mountain streams
    Go by, go by
    And yesterdays are like the rushing streams,
    They fly, they fly,
    And the great heroes, famous for a day,
    They die, they die.

                                                    Ibid.

298. Anne Boleyn (1507–1536)

1   Commend me to the king, and tell him he is constant in his course of advancing me; from a private gentlewoman he made a marquise, and from a marquise a queen; and now, as he had left no higher degree of earthly honour, he hath made me a martyr.

         (19 May 1536), Quoted in *Apophthagmes New and Old*,
                     No. 9, Francis Bacon, ed. *1625*

2   I will rather lose my life than my virtue, which will be the greatest and best part of the dowry I shall bring my husband.

          Letter to Henry VIII,* Quoted in *Women of Beauty
              and Heroism* by Frank B. Goodrich *1858*

  *King of England (1509–47) who broke from the Catholic Church in 1534 to form the Church of England.

3   I have heard say the executioner is very good, and I have a little neck.

         Remark shortly before execution (19 May 1536), *Ibid.*

4   Alas! poor head, in a very brief space thou wilt roll in the dust upon the scaffold; and as in life thou didst not merit to wear the crown of a queen, so in death thou deservest not better doom than this.*

           Spoken at her execution (19 May 1536), *Ibid.*
  *The linen cap she placed over her head before submitting to the executioner.

5   What will be, will be, grumble who may. (*Ainsi sera, groigne qui groigne.*)

          Motto embroidered on servants' livery (c.1530/31),
            Quoted in *Anne Boleyn* by Marie Louise Bruce *1972*

6   I am her death, as she is mine.

         Said of Catherine of Aragon's* death (January 1536), *Ibid.*
  *See 279.

7   The people will have no difficulty in finding a nickname for me, I shall be Queen Anne Lack-Head.

         Spoken at her execution (19 May 1536), *Ibid.*

299. Tullia d'Aragona (1510–1556)

1   Yes, but I'll tell you something that's very true: when one is speaking of our mortal world, it's really not acceptable to introduce elements of the divine, because the latter is so perfect that we shall never be able to comprehend it, and each individual is entitled to pronounce his own opinion about it.

         (p. 63), *Dialogue on the Infinity of Love*, Rinaldina Russell
             and Bruce Merry, eds. and trs. (repr. 1997) *1547*

2   VARCHI. So you want me to bow to authority!
    TULLIA. No, Sir. I want you to bow to experience, which I trust by itself far more than all the reasons produced by the whole class of philosophers

                                          Ibid.

300. Elisabeth of Braunschweig (1510–1558)

1   Obey God, the emperor, and your mother.

         Treatise on government written for her son, Erich II, Quoted
          in *Women of the Reformation, Vol. I; Germany and Italy*
                  by Roland H. Bainton *1971*

2   Woe, woe, woe and again woe to you if you do not change.

                    Letter to her son, *Ibid.*

3   Better be hurt than to hurt.

                       Hymn, *Ibid.*

4   No one without the experience knows the anguish which children can cause and yet be loved.

         From *Book of Consolation for Widows*, *Ibid.*

301. Marina de Guevara (1510?–1559)

1   Better than the castigation of the flesh is the overcoming of pride and anger.

             Testimony before the Inquisition (1558/59),
          Quoted in *Women of the Reformation, Vol. III:
         From Spain to Scandinavia* by Roland H. Bainton *1977*

2   To bring the heart into tune with God is better than audible prayer.

                              Ibid.

302. Renée de France (1510–1575)

1   . . . Satan is the father of lies and God of the truth . . .

          Letter to John Calvin* (1564), Quoted in *Queen of
        *Navarre: Jeanne d'Albret** by Nancy Lyman Roelker *1968*
  *French religious reformer (1509–64). **See 324.

2   Had I had a beard I would have been the King of France. I have been defrauded by that confounded Salic law.*

           Quoted in *Women of the Reformation, Vol. I;
         Germany and Italy*, by Roland H. Bainton *1971*
  *European law (derived from a fifth-century Frankish code) preventing women from succeeding to a throne.

303. Catherine Parr (1512/13–1548)

1   A goodly example and lesson for us to follow at all times and seasons, as well in prosperity as in adversity, to have no will but God's will. . . . But we be yet so carnal and fleshly, that we run headlong like unbridled colts, without snaffle or bit.

    If we had the love of God printed in our hearts, it would keep us back from running astray. And until such time as it pleases God to send us this bit to hold us in, we shall never run the right way, although we speak and talk never so much of God and His word.

         "The Lamentation on or Complaint of a Sinner,"
                 The Lamentation of a Sinner 1545

2   We be so busy and glad to find and spy out other men's doings that we forget and can have no time to weigh and ponder our own.

                              Ibid.

3   . . . our cause now being just, and being inforced to entre into warre and bataile, we most humbly beseche the (O lorde god of hostes) so to turne the hertes of our ennemies to the desire of peace, that no christen blud be spilt, or els graunt (O lorde) that with small effusion of bloude, and to the litle hurt and domage of innocentis, we maye to thy glory optein victory: and that the warres being sone ended, we may al, with one herte

and mynde, knyt togyther in concorde and unitie, laude and prayse the, whiche livest and reignest, worlde without ende. Amen.

> "A Praier for men to say entring into battayle," *Prayers stirryng the mynd unto heavenlye medytacions 1545*

4   Set your affection on thynges that are above: and not on thinges, whiche are on the earthe.

> Epigraph, Ibid.

5   Let there be alwaye in me one wille, and one desire with the, & that I have no desire to will, or not to will, but as thou wilte.

> Untitled prayer, Ibid.

304. Giulia Gonzaga (1513–1566)

1   What mad credulity is ours! How infinite is the cupidity of mortals!

> Letter to Livia Negra, Quoted in *A Princess of the Italian Reformation: Giulia Gonzaga* by Christopher Hare* 1912
> *Pseudonym of Marian Andrews.

2   . . . what should we do if we had to remain in this world perpetually? We cannot inhabit a house for three days in this miserable world without being dissatisfied.

> Ibid.

3   The promises of the alchemist are like those of the astrologers, who boast that they can foretell future things, and do not even know the present or the past. . . . I do not know whether their fraud is more shameful, or our folly in believing, as we do . . .

> Ibid.

305. Chiara Cantarini Matraini (1514–post-1597)

1   Return soul of the sky, candid moon
To the first sphere, shining and beautiful,
And with your customary brilliance restore
The crown of silver to the darkened sky

> Untitled sonnet, Claudia Alexander with Carlo DiMaio, trs., from *Poemas* (1560), *Poesia Itlaiana: il cinquecento*, Giulio Ferroni, ed. *1978*

2   . . . that weak and tired vessel finding
Itself with broken mast and sail
Bereft of helmsman, tossed by monstrous waves,
Seems like my soul deprived of light, bereft of every hope.

> Ibid.

306. Teresa of Avila (1515–1582)

1   The hour I have long wished for is now come.

> Last words (1582), Quoted in *Distinguished Women Writers* by Virginia Moore *1934*

2   How is it that there are not many who are led by sermons to forsake open sin? Do you know what I think? That is because preachers have too much worldly wisdom. They are not like the Apostles, flinging it all aside and catching fire with love of God; and so their flame gives little heat.

> "Life" (1562), *The Complete Works of Saint Teresa of Jesus*, Vol. I, E. Allison Peers, ed. and tr. *1946*

3   I only wish I could write with both hands, so as not to forget one thing while I am saying another.

> "Way of Perfection," Ch. 20 (1579), Vol. II, Ibid.

4   . . . I believe that honour and money nearly always go together
. . . seldom or *never* is a poor man honoured by the world;

however worthy of honour he may be, he is apt rather to be despised by it.

> Ch. 22, Ibid.

5   How is it, Lord, that we are cowards in everything save in opposing Thee?

> "Exclamations of Soul to God" (1569), *Selected Writings of St. Theresa of Avila*, E. Allison Peers, tr.; William J. Doheny, ed. *1950*

6   It is true that we cannot be free from sin, but at least let our sins not be always the same. . . .

> "Conception of Love of God" (1571), Ibid.

7   If we plant a flower or a shrub and water it daily it will grow so tall that in time we shall need a spade and hoe to uproot it. It is just so, I think, when we commit a fault, however small, each day, and do not cure ourselves of it.

> Ibid.

8   Humility must always be doing its work like a bee making its honey in the hive: without humility all will be lost.

> "Interior Castle" (1577), Ibid.

9   Untilled soil, however fertile it may be, will bear thistles and thorns; and so it is with man's mind.

> "Maxim for Her Nuns," Ibid.

10   Accustom yourself continually to make many acts of love, for they enkindle and melt the soul.

> Ibid.

11   Be gentle to all and stern with yourself.

> Ibid.

12   Remember that you have only one soul; that you have only one death to die; that you have only one life, which is short and has to be lived by you alone; and there is only one glory, which is eternal. If you do this, there will be many things about which you care nothing.

> Ibid.

13   . . . about the injunction of the Apostle Paul that women should keep silent in church? Don't go by one text only.

> Letter, Quoted in *Women of the Reformation, Vol. III: From Spain to Scandinavia*, by Roland H. Bainton *1977*

14   Let nothing disturb thee,
Nothing affright thee;
All things are passing;
God never changeth.
Patient endurance
Attaineth to all things;
Who Good possesseth
In nothing is wanting;
Alone God sufficeth.

> "Nada te turbe" ("Nothing disturbs thee"; a.k.a. "Saint Theresa's Bookmark") *in toto*, Henry Wadsworth Longfe low,* tr., *An Anthology of Spanish Poetry*, John A. Crow, ed. *1979*
> *American poet (1807–1882).

15   God walks among the pots and pipkins.

> Attributed *n.d.*

307. Mary I of England (1516–1558)

1   When I am dead and opened, you shall find "Calais" lying on my heart.

> Quoted in *Chronicles*, Vol. III by Raphael Holinshed *1585*

2 . . . there are two things only, soul and body. My soul I offer to God, and my body to your Majesty's service.

> Letter to Edward VI (c. 1552), Quoted in *Catherine of Aragon** by Garrett Mattingly 1942
> *See 279.

3 May it please you to take away my life rather than the old religion.

> Ibid.

308. Laura Terracina (1519?–1577?)

1 . . . alas, who has taken you from me?
Who has torn you from my breast so brazenly
And locked such beauty in a little grave?

> Untitled sonnet, Claudia Alexander with Carlo DiMaio, trs., *Poesia italiana: il cinquecento*, Giulio Ferroni, ed. 1978

2 . . . I see virtue abandoned
and the muses enslaved by such baseness
that my brain is nearly overwhelmed.

> "Sonnet to Marcantonio Passero," Claudia Alexander, tr., Ibid.

309. Catherine Willoughby (1519/20–1580)

1 Undoubtedly the greatest wisdom is not to be too wise. . . .

> Letter to William Cecil (1559), Quoted in *Women of the Tudor Age* by Cecilie Gaff 1930

2 . . . though God wink. . . . He sleepeth not. . . .

> Ibid.

3 Christ's plain coat without a seam is fairer to the older eyes than all the jaggs* of Germany.

> Ibid.
> *A slash made in a garment to show a different color beneath.

4 God is a marvellous man.

> Quoted by Catherine Parr* in a letter to Thomas Seymour (c.1548), *Tudor Women* by Alison Plowdon 1979
> *See 303.

310. Catherine de' Medici (1519–1589)

1 Ah, sentiments of mercy are in unison with a woman's heart.

> Ch. 3, Quoted in *The Huguenots of France and America*, Vol. I by Hannah Farnham Lee* 1843
> *See 768.

2 . . . suppress this violence of emotion. I have always found it best *to appear to yield*. Assume a seeming conformity to your husband's will, even attend mass, and you will more easily get the reins into your own hands.

> Ch. 7, Remark to Queen of Navarre,* Ibid.
> *Jeanne d'Albret; see 324.

3 *Lachrymae hinc, hinc dolor.* (Tears henceforth, henceforth sadness.)

> Motto (1559), Quoted in *The Medici* by G.F. Young 1930

4 When I see these poor people burnt, beaten and tormented, not for thieving or marauding, but simply for upholding their religious opinions, when I see some of them suffer cheerfully, with a glad heart, I am forced to believe that there is something in this which transcendeth human understanding.

> Letter regarding persecution of Protestants (1559/60), Ibid.

5 If things were even worse than they are after all this war they might have laid the blame upon the rule of a woman; but if such persons are honest they should blame only the rule of men who desire to play the part of kings. In future, if I am not any more hampered, I hope to show that women have a more sincere determination to preserve the country than those who have plunged it into the miserable condition to which it has been brought.

> Letter to Ambassador of Spain (1570), Ibid.

6 . . . never did woman who loved her husband succeed in loving his whore. One must call a spade a spade, though the term is an ugly one on the lips.

> Letter (1583), Quoted in *Women of Power* by Mark Strange 1976

311. Pernette du Guillet (1520?–1545?)

1 True love, to whom my heart is prey,
How dost thou hold me in thy sway,
That in each day I find no fault
But daily wait for love's assault

> "Song," St. 1, William Stirling, tr. (1947), *Rhymes de Gentille et Vertueuse Dame de Pernette du Guillet* (Lyonaisse) 1545

2 As the body denies the means to look
Into the spirit or know its force,
Likewise Error for me drew
Around my eyes the blindfold of ignorance.

> "Epigram," Joan Keefe with Richard Terdiman, trs. (1978), Ibid.

3 I no longer need be concerned
whether daylight goes or night comes,
. . . because my Day,* with tender brilliance,
enlightens me through and through.

> "Epigram 8," Ann Rosalind Jones, tr. (1981), Ibid.
> *Allusion to the poet Maurice Scève, with whom she had a liaison.

312. Anne Askew (1520–1546)

1 . . . unadvised hasty judgement is a token apparent of a very slender wit.

> Testimony at inquisition (1545), Quoted in *Actes and monuments of these latter and perillous dayes* (a.k.a *The Book of Martyrs*) by John Foxe 1563

2 God has given me the bread of adversity and the water of trouble.

> Letter to King Henry VIII* (1546), Ibid.
> *King of England (1509–47) who broke from the Catholic Church in 1534 to form the Church of England.

3 . . . what God hath charged me with his mouth, that have I shut up in my heart.

> Ibid.

4 Like as the armed knight
Appointed to the field,
With this world will I fight,
And faith shall be my shield.

> "The Ballad Which Anne Askew Made and Sang When She Was in Newgate," St. 1 (1547), *The Women Poets in English*, Ann Stanford, ed. 1972

313. Isabella da Morra (1520–1546)

1 Once more, O arid valley
O wild river, O wretched, barbarous stones
You shall hear my eternal pain and weeping.

> Untitled sonnet, Claudia Alexander with Carlo DiMaio, trs., *Poesia italiana: il cinquecento*, Giulio Ferroni, ed. 1978

2 Turbid Siri,* now that my bitter end is here, proclaim my sor-
row. . . .
Tumultuously incite your waves
And say, "Not merely tears, but the copious weeping
Of Isabella increased me while she lived."

Untitled poem, Ibid.

*A river that runs between Calabria and Basilicata in southern
Italy.

314. Madeleine Fradonnet (1520?–1587)

1 Distaff, my pride and care, I vow to thee
That I shall love thee ever nor exchange
Thy homely virtue for a pleasure strange

"To My Distaff," with Catherine Fradonnet,* *Anthology of
European Poetry, 13th to 17th century*, William Stirling, tr.;
Mervyn Savill, ed. *1947*

*Her sister (1547–1587).

315. Ippolita Castiglione (?–1521)

1 My dear Lord, — I have got a little daughter, of which I think
you will not be sorry. I have been much worse than I was last
time, and have had three attacks of high fever, but to–day I
feel better, and hope to have no more trouble. I will not try to
write more, lest I overdo myself, but commend myself to you
with all my heart — Your wife who is a little tired out with
pain, your Ippolita.

Letter to Baldassare Castiglione, her husband
(24 August 1521; four days before her death),
Quoted in *Isabella d'Este** by Julia Cartwright
1903

*See 272.

316. Lucia dall'Orno Bertana (1521–1567)

. . . bless me Muse and I will go
Through thick woods and over pleasant hills
To bright fountains where I will find mercy.

Sonnet on her marriage, Claudia Alexander, tr., Quoted in *A
Women's Record* by Sarah Josepha Hale*
1855

*See 788.

317. Lucrezia Gonzaga (?–1552?)

1 . . . a poor man's life is like sailing near the coast, whereas that
of a rich man resembles the condition of those who are in the
main sea. The former can easily throw a cable on the shore,
and bring their ship safe into a harbour; whereas the latter cannot do it without much danger and difficulty.

Letter to Hortensio Lando, Quoted in *Woman's
Record* by Sarah Josepha Hale*
1855

*See 788.

2 . . . all things are good which are according to nature, and
what is there more natural to all men than death?

Letter to Ippolita Gonzaga (c.1552), Quoted in *A Princess
of the Italian Reformation: Giulia Gonzaga**
by Christopher Hare** *1912*

*See 304. **Pseudonym of Marian Andrews.

3 . . . he alone acts wisely who, being mortal, expects nothing
from this life of ours but mortal things.

Ibid.

318. Luisa Sigea (1522–1560)

1 You have written me a letter which . . . exudes the fragrance
of a life unspotted, which I would inhale were I not so
spoiled by the stench of the human as to be incapable of the
divine. . . .

Letter to a friend (n.d.), Quoted in *Women of the Reformation, Vol. III: From Spain to Scandinavia* by Roland H.
Bainton *1977*

2 Blaze with the fire that is never extinguished.

"Dialogue of Blesilla and Flaminia,"
Ibid.

319. Gaspara Stampa (1523–1554)

1 Love made me such that I live in fire
like a new salamander on earth
or like that other rare creature, the Phoenix,
who expires and rises at the same time.

Untitled sonnet, Lynne Lawner, tr., *The Penguin Book of
Women Poets*, Carol Cosman, Joan Keefe and Kathleen
Weaver, eds. *1978*

2 I hate who loves me, love who scorns me.

Ibid.

3 O love, what strange and wonderful fits:
one sole thing, one beauty alone,
can give me life and deprive me of wits.

Untitled sonnet, J. Vitiello, tr., *A Book of Women Poets*,
Aliki and Willis Barnstone, eds. *1980*

4 Deeply repentant of my sinful ways
And of my trivial, manifold desires,
Of squandering, alas, these few brief days
Of fugitive life in tending love's vain fires

Untitled sonnet, Lorna de'Lucchi, tr., *Women Poets of the
World*, Joanna Bankier and Deirdre Lashgari, eds. *1983*

320. Louise Labé (1524/25–1566)

1 O terrible fate! Suffering the scorpion to feast
on me, I seek protection from the pain
of poison by appealing to the beast
that stings me.

Sonnet I, *Oeuvres* (1555), *A Book of Women Poets*,
Aliki and Willis Barnstone, eds. *1980*

2 A woman's heart always has a burned mark.

Sonnet II, Ibid.

3 However much Love tries to batter us
our force congeals at every impetus,
becoming fresh with each attacking prong.

Sonnet IV, Ibid.

4 I live, I die, I burn myself and drown.

Sonnet VIII, Ibid.

5 Only outside my body can I live
or else in exile like a fugitive.

Sonnet XVII, Ibid.

6 Kiss me again, rekiss me, kiss me more,
give me your most consuming, tasty one,
give me your sensual kiss, a savory one,
I'll give you back four burning at the core.

Sonnet XVIII, Ibid.

7   What grandeur make a man seem venerable?
    What hair? What color of skin? What size?
    What kind of glance is best? What honeyed eyes?
> Sonnet XXI, Ibid.

8   Your brutal goal was to make *me* a slave
    beneath the ruse of being served by you.
    Pardon me, friend, and for once hear me through:
    I am outraged with anger and I rave.
> Sonnet XXIII, Ibid.

9   Don't blame me, ladies, if I've loved. No sneers
    if I have felt a thousand torches burn
> Sonnet XXIV, Ibid.

10 Since a time has come, Mademoiselle, when the severe laws of men no longer prevent women from applying themselves to the sciences and other disciplines, it seems to me that those of us who can, should use this long-craved freedom to study and to let men see how greatly they wronged us when depriving us of its honor and advantages. And if any woman becomes so proficient as to be able to write down her thoughts, let her do so and not despise the honor but rather flaunt it instead of fine clothes, necklaces, and rings. For these may be considered ours only by use, whereas the honor of being educated is ours entirely.
> Letter to a friend, Quoted in *Uppity Women of Medieval Times* by Vicki León 1997

321. Cicely Ormes (1525–1557)

1 . . . this my death is and shall be a witness of my faith unto you all here present. Good People! As many of you as believe as I believe, pray for me.
> Spoken at her execution (23 September 1557), Quoted in *Actes and monuments of these latter and perillous dayes* (a.k.a. *The Book of Martyrs*) by John Foxe 1563

322. Olimpia Morata (1526–1555)

1 Never does the same desire enlist us all.
  Tastes are not conferred by Zeus on all alike.
> Untitled (c.1542), Jules Bonnet and Roland H. Bainton, trs., Quoted in *Women of the Reformation, Vol. I: Germany and Italy* by Roland H. Bainton 1971

2 I, a woman, have dropped the symbols of my sex,
  Yarn, shuttle, basket, thread
> Ibid.

3 Remembering that the span of our life is but toil and trouble and we soon fly away, may I give myself to the contemplation of things eternal.
> Letter to her sister, Vittoria (c.1553), Ibid.

4 God is a light to our feet. Let us not be troubled by men, for what is man if not a fleeting shadow, a windblown leaf, a fading flower, and vanishing smoke!
> Last letter, to Lavinia della Rovere (1555), Ibid.

323. Elizabeth Hoby Russell (1528–post-1603)

1 No one need honor me with tears, or lament my burial! This is why! I go through the stars to God! (*Nemo me lachrymis decoret, neque funera fletio! Faxit cur! Vado perastra deo!*)
> Composed for and inscribed on her monument in Bisham Church near Great Marlow, England, John Williams, tr., Quoted in *Society Women of Shakespeare's Time* by Violet A. Wilson 1924

2 I beseech your Majesty, let me have Justice, and I will then trust the law.
> Spoken to King James I (1603), Quoted in *Diary of Lady Margaret Hoby,** Dorothy M. Meads, ed. 1930
> *See 368.

3 Though I be not so bad a bird as to defile mine own nest, yet I know my children. . . .
> Letter to [William Cecil, Lord] Burghley (n.d.), Ibid.

324. Jeanne d' Albret (1528–1572)

1 . . . arms once taken up should never be laid down, but upon one of three conditions — a safe peace, a complete victory, or an honourable death.
> Quoted in *Biography of Distinguished Women* by Sarah Josepha Hale* 1876
> *See 788.

2 . . . the task of women and men who do not bear arms . . . is to fight for peace . . . do your part, for God's sake. As for me I will spare nothing.
> Letter to Cardinal de Bourbon (1568), Quoted in *Queen of Navarre: Jeanne d'Albret* by Nancy Lyman Roelker 1968

3 . . . if religion separates us, does our common blood then separate? Do friendship and natural duty cease to exist? *Non, mon frère.*
> Ibid.

4 . . . in this world . . . I see nothing but vanity.
> Spoken during her last illness, Ibid.

5 Nothing is impossible to a valiant heart. (*À coeur valliant rien d'impossible*).
> Motto (adopted by her son, Henry IV*) n.d.
> *Known as "Henry of Navarre," King of France (1589–1610) who founded Bourbon royal line (1553–1610).

325. Anne Cooke Bacon (1528?–1610?)

1 Ignorance, especially of the heavenly things, is the greatest lack that can be seen in man.
> 15th sermon, *Sermons . . . concerning the predestination and election of God: very expedient to the setting forth of his glory among creatures* c. 1570

2 Simple ignorance hath not so much confused . . . wisdom, as Philosophie, which maketh men bold, unshamefaced, hot, lyers, proud, contentious, frenticke, foolysh, and wicked.
> 17th sermon, Ibid.

326. Margaret Bryan (fl. 1530s)

1 The minstrels played, and his grace [Edward VI] danced . . . so wantonly that he could not stand still, and was as full of pretty toys as ever I saw a child in my life.
> Letter to [Thomas] Cromwell* (1539), *Letters of Royal and Industrious Ladies of Great Britain*, Vol. III, Mary Anne Everett Wood Green,** ed. n.d.
> *Earl of Essex; English politician (1485?–1540). **See 926.

327. Maria Cazalla (fl. 1530s)

1 You do this to a woman? I dread more the affront than the pain.
> Testimony before the Inquisition (c.1531–1534), Quoted in *Women of the Reformation, Vol. III: From Spain to Scandinavia* by Roland H. Bainton 1977

328. Catherine Killigrew (1530?–1583)

1 In thee my soul shall own combined
   The sister and the friend.

   If from my eyes by thee detained
   The wanderer cross the seas,
   No more thy love shall soothe, as friend,
   No more as sister please.
   > Untitled, Sts. 2, 3, Quoted in *Women of the Reformation, Vol. III: From Spain to Scandinavia* by Roland H. Bainton *1977*

329. Anne Locke (1530?–1590?)

1 My many sinnes in nomber are encreast,
   With weight wherof in sea of depe despeire
   My sinking soule is now so sore opprest,
   That now in peril and in present fere,
   I crye: susteine me, Lord, and Lord I pray,
   With endlesse number of thy mercies take
   The endlesse number of my sinnes away.
   > *A Meditation of a Penitent Sinner: Written in Maner [sic] of A Paraphrase upon the 51. Psalme of David*, Vol. 13 *1560*

2 So foule is sinne and lothesome in thy sighte,
   So foule with sinne I see my selfe to be,
   That till from sinne I may be washed white,
   So foule I dare not, Lord, approche to thee.
   > Ibid.

3 . . . why (casting off all impediments that presseth down) do we not run on our course with cheerfulness and Hope, having Christ so mighty a King, for our captain and Guide?
   > Preface to her translation of *The Markes of the Children of God* by J. Taffin *1590*

330. Anne d' Este (1531–post–1563)

1 My sweet god, so much blood, surely some of it will fall upon our house.
   > Comment on the mass execution of conspirators (22 March 1560), Quoted in *Women of Power* by Mark Strange *1976*

331. Queen Elizabeth I of England (1533–1603)

1 Much suspected of me,
   Nothing proved can be,
   Quoth Elizabeth, prisoner.
   > Scratched with a Diamond on her Window at Woodstock Prison (c.1554–1555), Quoted in *Actes and monuments of these later and perillous dayes* (a.k.a. *The Book of Martyrs*) by John Foxe *1563*

2 I am your anointed Queen. I will never be by violence constrained to do anything. I thank God I am endued with such qualities that if I were turned out of the Realm in my petticoat I were able to live in any place in Christendom.
   > Speech, Deputation of Lords and Commons *October 1566*

3 The [use of the] sea and air is common to all; neither can a title to the ocean belong to any people or private persons, for as much as neither nature nor public use and custom permit any possession thereof.
   > Letter to the Spanish Ambassador *1580*

4 I know I have the body of a weak and feeble woman, but I have the heart and stomach of a king, and of a king of England too. . . .
   > Speech to the troops at Tilbury on the Approach of the Armada *8 August 1588*

5 Must! Is must a word to be addressed to princes? Little man, little man! Thy father, if he had been alive, durst not have used that word.
   > Remonstrance to Sir Robert Cecil, her secretary, Attributed *March 1603*

6 All my possessions for a moment of time.
   > Last words, Attributed *1603*

7 . . . I know they are most deceived that trusteth most in themselves. . . .
   > Letter to Edward Seymour, Lord Protector (21 February 1549), *The Sayings of Queen Elizabeth*, Frederick Chamberlain, ed. *1923*

8 For, what is a family without a steward, a ship without a pilot, a flock without a shepherd, a body without a head, the same, I think, is a kingdom without the health and safety of a good monarch.
   > Letter to King Edward VI (c.1551), Ibid.

9 I am more afraid of making a fault in my Latin, than of the Kings of Spain, France, Scotland, the whole House of Guise, and all of their confederates.
   > To the Archbishop of St. Andrews (n.d.), Ibid.

10 For the face, I grant, I might well blush to offer, but the mind I shall never be ashamed to present. For though from the grace of the picture the colours may fade by time, may give by weather, may be spotted by chance; yet the other nor time with her swift wings shall overtake, nor the misty clouds with their lowerings may darken, nor chance with her slippery foot may overthrow.
   > Letter to King Edward VI (15 May 1549–1553?), *The Letters of Queen Elizabeth the First*, G. B. Harrison, ed. *1935*

11 The king's word is more than any other man's oath.
   > Letter (1554), Ibid.

12 . . . I cannot but muse for my part, and blush for theirs, to see the rebellious hearts and devilish intents of Christians in name, but Jews in deed. . . .
   > Letter to Mary, Queen of Scots* (22 August 1556), Ibid.
   > *See 339.

13 And among earthly things I chiefly wish this one, that there were as good surgeons for making anatomies of hearts that might show my thought to your Majesty, as there are expert physicians of the bodies, able to express the inward griefs of their maladies to their patients.
   > Ibid.

14 You know a kingdom knows no kindred. . . .
   > Letter to Sir Henry Sidney (1565), Ibid.

15 A strength to harm is perilous in the hand of an ambitious head.
   > Ibid.

16 Where might is mixed with wit, there is too good an accord.
   > Ibid.

17 Brass shines as fair to the ignorant as gold to the goldsmith.
   > Letter to "the Monk" (c.1581), Ibid.

18 I hope you will remember that who seeketh two strings to one bow, he may shoot strong but never straight.
   > Letter to James VI [of Scotland] (1585), Ibid.

19 Eyes of youth have sharp sight, but commonly not so deep as those of elder age. . . .
> Letter to Robert Devereux, Earl of Essex (8 July 1597), Ibid.

20 My care is like a shadow in the sun —
Follows me flying, flies when I pursue it.
> "On the Departure of the Duke d'Alençon" (1582),
The Poems of Queen Elizabeth I, Leicester Bradner, ed.
1964

21 Never think you fortune can bear the sway
Where virtue's force can cause her to obey.
> "On Fortune," Ibid.

22 No crooked leg, no bleared eye,
 No part deformed out of kind,
Nor yet so ugly half can be
 As in the inward suspicious mind.
> Written in her French psalter,
Ibid.

23 'Twas God the word that spake it,
He took the bread and brake it;
And what the word did make it;
That I believe, and take it.
> Answer on being asked her opinion of Christ's presence in
the Sacrament, Ibid.

24 Though God has raised me high, yet this I count the glory of my crown that I have reigned with your loves. I do not so much rejoice that God has made me a Queen, as to be a Queen over so thankful a people.
> Quoted in *Uppity Women of Medieval Times*
by Vicki León *1997*

25 *Semper eadem.* [Ever the same].
> Motto *n.d.*

26 I am no lover of pompous title, but only desire that my name be recorded in a line or two, which shall briefly express my name, my virginity, the years of my reign, the reformation of religion under it, and my preservation of peace.
> To her ladies, discussing her
epitaph *n.d.*

332. Sofonisba Anguissola (1535/40?–1625)

1 It will be a great pleasure to me if I have gratified your Holiness's wish, but I must add that, if the brush could represent the beauties of the queen's [Isabel of Valois] soul to your eyes, they would be marvelous. However, I have used the utmost diligence to present what art can show, to tell your Holiness the truth.
> Letter to Pope Pius IV (16 September 1561),
Quoted in *The Lives of the Painters, Sculptors, and Architects*, Vol. III by Giorgio Vasari, A. B. Hinds,
tr. *1927*

333. Jane Grey (1537–1554)

1 Think not, O mortal, vainly gay,
That thou from human woes art free;
The bitter cup I drink today,
Tomorrow may be drunk by thee.
> Lines written on a prison wall at the Tower of London
(1554), Quoted in *Woman's Record*
by Sarah Josepha Hale* *1855*

*See 788.

2 One of the greatest benefits that ever God gave me is, that he sent me so sharp and severe parents and so gentle a schoolmaster.
> "The Scholemaster" (1569), *The English Works
of Roger Ascham*, William Aldis Wright, ed.
1904

334. Anna Maria of Braunschweig (fl. c. 1540)

1 I'd rather marry a wise old man than a young fool.
> Quoted in *Women of the Reformation,
Vol. I; Germany and Italy* by Roland H. Bainton
1971

335. Countess de Marcelle (fl. c. 1540)

1 By compelling us to return to the world, it is not liberty the Calvinists offer us, but bondage.*
> Ch. 26, Quoted in *The Huguenots of France and America*,
Vol. II by Hannah Farnham Lee** *1843*

*The Calvinists attempted to abolish monasteries and convents in France. **See 768.

336. Isabella Whitney (1540?–1573)

1 Some use the teares of Crocodiles,
contrary to their hart:
And yf they cannot alwayes weepe,
they wet their Cheekes by Art.
> "The admonition by the Auctor to all yong Gentilwomen:
And to al other Maids being in Love," Sts. 4–5,
Letter 1567?

2 And this (where so you shall become)
full boldly may you boast:
That once you had as true a Love,
as dwelt in any Coast.

Whose constantnesse had never quaild
if you had not begonne:
And yet it is not so far past,
but might agayne be wonne.
> "To her unconstant Lover," Sts. 3–4, Ibid.

3 Gold savours well, though it be got
with occupations vile:
If thou hast gold, thou welcome art,
though virtue thou exile.
> "The 103. Flower," *A Sweet Nosegay or Pleasant
Posye Containing a Hundred and Ten Phylosophicall
Flowers 1573*

4 Such poor folk as to law do go
are driven oft to curse:
But in mean while, the Lawyer thrives,
the money in his purse.
> "The 104. Flower," Ibid.

337. Lettice Knollys (1540–1634)

1 . . . country life is fittest for disgraced persons.
> Letter to her son, the Earl of Essex (c.1595–1598),
Quoted in *Queen Elizabeth's* Maids of Honor*
by Violet A. Wilson *n.d.*

*See 331.

338. Isabella de' Medici Orsini (1542–1576)

1   Make yourself happy where you are adored, and on no account seek another abode.
> Letter to her sister-in-law, Bianca Capello (24 September 1572), Quoted in *Famous Women of Florence* by Edgecumbe Staley, tr. *1909*

339. Mary of Scots (1542–1587)

1   I do not aspire to any public position, especially when I consider the pain and desperance which meet those who wish to do right, and act with justice and dignity in the midst of so perverse a generation, and when a whole world is full of crimes and troubles.
> Remark at her trial *October 1586*

2   I am no subject to Elizabeth, but an independent queen as well as she; and I will consent to nothing unbecoming the majesty of a crowned head.
> *Ibid.*

3   I would disdain to purchase all that is most valuable upon earth by the assassination of the meanest of the human race . . .
> *Ibid.*

4   If ever I have given consent by my words, or even by my thoughts, to any attempt against the life of the Queen of England, far from declining the judgment of men, I shall not even pray for the mercy of God.
> *Ibid.*

5   Time than fortune should be held more precious
For Fortune is as false as she is specious.
> "Book of Hours" *1579*

6   Give me, dear Lord, the true humility
And strengthen my too feeble halting faith;
Let but Thy Spirit shed his light on me —
Checking my fever with His purer breath.
> *Ibid.*

7   O Lord my God, I have trusted in thee;
O Jesus my dearest one, now set me free.
In prison's oppression, in sorrow's obsession,
I weary for thee.
With sighing and crying bowed down as dying,
I adore thee, I implore thee, set me free!
> Quoted in *Book of Devotion* by Algernon Swinburne* *February 1587*
> *British poet and critic (1837–1909).

8   I will that you do nothing by which any spot may be laid on my honor or conscience; but wait till God of His goodness shall put a remedy to it.
> Last words (8 February 1587), Quoted in *Women of Beauty and Heroism* by Frank B. Goodrich *1858*

9   Farewell, France! farewell beloved country, which I shall never more behold!
> (August 1559), *Ibid.*

10 Here the sun can never penetrate, neither does any pure air ever visit this habitation, on which descend drizzling damps and eternal fogs, to such excess that not an article of furniture can be placed beneath the roof, but in four days it becomes covered with green mould.
> Remark (1586/87) from her prison cell, *Ibid.*

11 No more tears now; I will think upon revenge.
> Remarking on the murder of her servant, David Riccio (1566), Quoted in *Memorials of Mary Stewart*, J. Stevenson, ed. *1883*

12 . . . the world is not that what we do make of it, nor yet are they most happy that continue longest in it.
> Remark to Lord Randolph (c. 1551), Quoted in *Calendar of State Papers Relating to Scottish Affairs*, J. Bain, ed. *1898*

13 Look to your consciences and remember that the theater of the world is wider than the realm of England.
> Remark at her trial (1586), Quoted in *The Tragedy of Fotheringhay* by Mrs. Maxwell–Scot *1905*

14 Ah! here are many counsellors, but not one for me.
> *Ibid.*

15 As a sinner I am truly conscious of having often offended my Creator and I beg him to forgive me, but as a Queen and Sovereign, I am aware of no fault or offence for which I have to render account to anyone here below.
> To Sir Amyas Paulet (October 1586), Quoted in *Mary, Queen of Scots* by Antonia Fraser* *1969*
> *See 2496.

16 In my end is my beginning. (*En ma fin est mon commencement.*)
> Motto, *Ibid.*

17 I do not desire vengeance. . . . I would rather pray with Esther* than take the sword with Judith.**
> Remark at her trial (October 1586), *Ibid.*
> *See 56. **See 51.

18 Whatever the hour of day
Be it dawn or the eventide
My heart still feels it yet
The eternal regret.
> "The Absent One" (poem on the death of Francis II, her first husband; 1561), *Ibid.*

19 Constancy does become all folks well, but none better than princes, and such as have rule over realms.
> Quoted in *Women of the Reformation, Vol. III: From Spain to Scandinavia*, by Roland H. Bainton *1977*

20 There is much ado in my realm about matters of religion.
> Recorded by John Knox *n.d.*

21 I will defend the Kirk of Rome, for it is, I think, the true Kirk of God.
> *Ibid.*

340. Mary Grey (1543/44–1578)

1   . . . the princes favor is not so soon gotten agayn, and . . . to be without it is such a greff to any true subjectes harte, as no turment can be greater. . . .
> Letter to William Cecil, Lord Burghley (written from prison, 1566), *Original Letters Illustrative of English History*, Vol. II, Henry Ellis, ed. *1824–1846*

341. Veronica Franco (1546–1591)

1   Now that my mind is bent on revenge,
my disrespectful, my rebellious lover,
step up and arm yourself with what you will.

What battlefield do you prefer? this place?
this secret hideaway where I have sampled —
unwarily—so many bitter sweets?
>> Untitled, Sts. 10, 11, Lynne Lawner, tr., *The Penguin Book of Women Poets*, Carol Cosman, Joan Keefe and Kathleen Weaver, eds. *1978*

2 Alas! I say now and always will say
That to live without you is cruel death to me
And pleasures to me are cruel torments.
>> "*Lontana dall'Amante e da Venezia*" ["Far from my Lover and from Venice"], Claudia Alexander with Carlo DiMaio, trs., *Poesia italiana: il cinquecento*, Giulio Ferroni, ed. *1978*

341.1 Catherine Fradonnet (1547–1589)
Coauther with Madeleine Fradonnet; see 314.

342. Idelette de Bure Calvin (?–1549)
1 O glorious resurrection! God of Abraham and of all our fathers! The faithful have in so many ages hoped in Thee, and not one has been disappointed! I will also hope!
>> Ch. 3, Dying words (1549), Quoted in *The Huguenots of France and America*, Vol. I by Hannah Farnham Lee* *1843*
>> *See 768.

343. Mother Benet (fl. c. 1550)
1 O man! be content, and let us be thankful; for God hath given us enough, if we can see it.
>> Quoted in *Actes and monuments of these latter and perillous dayes* (a.k.a. *The Book of Martyrs*) by John Foxe *1563*

2 I cannot firkin [store] up my butter, and keep my cheese in the chamber and wait a great price, and let the poor want, and so displease God.
>> Ibid.

344. Elizabeth Bowes (fl. c. 1550)
1 Alas, wretched woman that I am, for the self-same sins that reigned in Sodom and Gomorrah reign in me!
>> Letter to John Knox (c.1550), Quoted in *Women of the Reformation, Vol. III: From Spain to Scandinavia* by Roland H. Bainton *1977*

345. Zofia Olesnicka (fl. c. 1550)
1 Better to safeguard Thy treasure,
Which neither moth nor rust can corrupt
Than enmeshed in the ways of the world
To forfeit Thy favor forever.
>> Hymn, St. 5 (1556), Quoted in *Women of the Reformation, Vol. III: From Spain to Scandinavia* by Roland H. Bainton *1977*

346. Elizabeth Young (fl. c. 1550)
1 . . . I had rather all the world should accuse me, than mine own conscience.
>> Testimony at her first examination, Quoted in *Actes and monuments of these latter and perillous dayes* (a.k.a. *The Book of Martyrs*) by John Foxe *1563*

2 If ye take away my meat, I trust God will take away my hunger.
>> Testimony at her second examination, Ibid.

3 Here is my carcase: do with it what you will . . . ye can have no more but my blood.
>> Ibid.

4 No man can be the head of Christ's church; for Christ himself is the head, and his word is the governor of all.
>> Testimony at her seventh examination, Ibid.

347. Renée de Chateauneuf Rieux (1550–1587)
1 Marriage is a lottery in which men stake their liberty and women their happiness.
>> Attributed *n.d.*

348. Grace Sherrington (1552?–1620)
1 She [her governess] scoffed at all dalliance, idle talk, and wanton behaviour appertaining thereto. . . . She counseled us when we were alone so to behave ourselves as if all the worlde did looke upon us, and to doe nothing in secret whereof our conscience might accus us. . . .
>> Quoted in *Diary of Lady Margaret Hoby*,* Dorothy M. Meads, ed. *1930*
>> *See 368.

2 If all fathers and mothers were . . . provident and careful, and governors and governesses put in trust by them were diligent and faithful in performing their trust, so many parents should not be discomfited as they are in their age by the wickedness and misfortunes of their children.
>> Ibid.

349. Marguerite of Valois (1553–1615)
1 Joy takes far away from us the thoughts of our actions; sorrow it is that awakens the soul.
>> *Memoirs* (1594–1600) *1628*

2 . . . mistrust is the sure forerunner of hatred.
>> Letter IX, Ibid.

3 Adversity is solitary, while prosperity dwells in a crowd.
>> Letter XII, Ibid.

4 Science conducts us, step by step, through the whole range of creation, until we arrive, at length, at God.
>> Ibid.

5 In my sadness and solitude, I rediscovered the great gifts of study and devotion—gifts which, among the vanities and magnificence of my former good fortune, I had never truly tasted.
>> Ibid.

6 . . . the sight of you . . . is as necessary for me as is the sun for the spring flowers.
>> Letter to Jacques de Harlay, Marquess of Chanvallon (1582), Quoted in *A Daughter of the Medicis* by Jean H. Mariejol, John Peile, tr. *1929*

7 . . . let no one ever say that marriages are made in Heaven; the gods would not commit so great an injustice!
>> Letter to Jacques de Harlan (1582), Quoted in *Queen of Hearts* by Charlotte Haldane *1968*

350. Moderata Fonte (1555–1592)
1 And when it's said that women must be subject to men, the phrase should be understood in the same sense as when we say we are subject to natural disasters, diseases, and all the other accidents of this life: it's not a case of being subjected in the sense of obeying, but rather of suffering an imposition, not a case of serving them fearfully, but rather of tolerating them in

a spirit of Christian charity, since they have been given to us by God as a spiritual trial.

The Worth of Women (p. 59; repr. 1996) *1600**
*Fonte's daughter, Cecelia, published her mother's manuscript eight years after her death in childbirth at age 37.

2 Men were created before women. But that doesn't prove their superiority—rather, it proves ours, for they were born out of the lifeless earth in order that we could be born out of living flesh. And what's so important about this priority in creation, anyway? . . . Lowly seeds are nourished in the earth, and then later the ravishing blooms appear; lovely roses blossom forth and scented narcissi.

(p. 60) Ibid.

3 But we should not think that they behave like this only towards our sex, for even among themselves they deceive one another, rob one another, destroy one another, and try to do each other down. Just think of all the assassinations, usurpations, perjuries, the blasphemy, gaming, gluttony, and other such vicious deeds they commit all the time! Not to mention the murders, assaults, and thefts, and other dissolute acts, all proceeding from men! And if they have so few scruples about committing these kind of excesses, think of what they are like where minor vices are concerned: just give a thought to their ingratitude, faithlessness, falsity, cruelty, arrogance, lust, and dishonesty.

(p. 61) Ibid.

4 "Do you really believe," Cornelia replied, "that everything historians tell us about men—or about women—is actually true? You ought to consider the fact that these histories have been written by men, who never tell the truth except by accident."

(p. 77) Ibid.

5 The Romans in their day did not confer any important responsibilities on any man who did not have a wife; they did not allow him to take up a public office or to perform any serious duties relating to the Republic. Homer used to say that men without wives were scarcely alive.

(p. 91) Ibid.

6 For it was with a good end in mind—that of acquiring the knowledge of good and evil—that Eve allowed herself to be carried away and eat the forbidden fruit. But Adam was not moved by this desire for knowledge, but simply by greed: he ate it because he heard Eve say it tasted good, which was a worse motive and caused more displeasure. And that is the reason why God did not chase them from Paradise as soon as Eve sinned, but rather after Adam had disobeyed him—in other words, he didn't respond to Eve's action, but Adam's prompted him to give both the punishment they deserved, which was and is common to all humankind.

(p. 94) Ibid.

7 Couldn't we live without them? Couldn't we earn our living and manage our affairs without help from them? Come on, let's wake up, and claim back our freedom, and the honor and dignity that they have usurped from us for so long. Do you think that if we really put our minds to it, we would be lacking the courage to defend ourselves, the strength to fend for ourselves, or the talents to earn our own living?

(p. 237) Ibid.

8 And then, having achieved equality, we'll be in a sufficiently strong position to mock them as they now mock us; and we'll have a thing or two to say about how they spend a thousand years combing and setting the few paltry hairs they have on their heads and their chins . . .

Ibid.

351. Margaret Clitherow (1556?–1586)

1 They that think much and are not willing to do such base things [as housework], have little regard of well-doing or knowledge of themselves.

Quoted in *A True Report of the Life and Martyrdom of Mrs. Margaret Clitherow* by Fr. John Mush *1586*

2 God forbid that I should will any to do that in my house which I would not willingly do myself. . . .

Ibid.

3 . . . bear me company this night, not for any fear of death, for it is my comfort, but the flesh is frail.

Remark to a friend before her execution, Ibid.

352. Joyce Lewes (?–1557)

1 I thank my God that he will make me worthy to adventure my life in his quarrel.

At her execution (1557), Quoted in *Actes and monuments of these latter and perillous dayes* (a.k.a. *The Book of Martyrs*) by John Foxe *1563*

353. Anne Dacre Howard (1557–1630)

1 In sad and ashy weeds I sigh. . . .

Elegy on the Death of Her Husband, St. 1 (1595), *The Women Poets in English*, Ann Stanford, ed. *1972*

2 I envy aire because it dare
Still breathe, and he not so;
Hate earthe, that doth entomb his youth,
And who can blame my Owe?

St. 3, Ibid.

354. Wife of Prest (?–1558)

1 How save you souls, when you preach nothing but damnable lies. . . .

Testimony to examining bishop, Quoted in *Actes and monuments of these latter and perillous dayes* (a.k.a. *The Book of Martyrs*) by John Foxe *1563*

2 Farewell you with your salvation.

Ibid.

3 God forbid that I should lose the life eternal, for this carnal and short life.

At her execution (1558), Ibid.

355. Catherine de Bourbon (1559–1604)

1 . . . [King Henry of] Navarre can ill brook *words* when *deeds* are so much wanted.

Ch. 15, Remark to Count de Soissons, Quoted in *The Huguenots of France and America*, Vol. I by Hannah Farnham Lee* *1843*
*See 768.

2 Command me, my King, to make you a little page, for I fear that unless you command it yourself, he will not consent to lodge in my body.

Letter to her brother, Henry IV of France (18 August 1599), Quoted in *Queen of Navarre: Jeanne d'Albret,** Nancy Lyman Roelker, tr. *1968*
*See 324.

356. Blanche Parry (fl. c. 1560)

1 . . . madam . . . if you ever marry without the Queen's [Elizabeth I*] writing, you and your husband will be undone, and your fate worse than that of my Lady Jane.**
Letter to Lady Catherine Grey (c.1560), Quoted in *Queen Elizabeth's Maids of Honor* by Violet A. Wilson *n.d.*

*See 331. ****Sister of Lady Catherine, see 333; subsequently, Catherine was imprisoned after her secret marriage to the earl of Hertford.

357. Frances Walsingham (1560?–post-1603)

1 I will have more care of my self for your little one's sake.
Letter to her husband, the Earl of Essex (c.1599), Quoted in *Society Women of Shakespeare's Time* by Violet A. Wilson *1924*

2 Simple thankes is a slender recompens. . . .
Letter to Robert Cecil (December 1599), Ibid.

358. Mary Sidney Herbert (1561–1621)

1 My fellow, my companion, held most dear,
My soul, my other self, my inward friend
Psalm LV, "Exaudi, Deus," St. 4, *The Psalmes of David* (c.1593), C. Whittingham, ed. *1823*

2 There is a God that carves to each his own.
Psalm LVIII, "*Si Vere Utique*," St. 4, Ibid.

3 How thou hast been the target of my head
Psalm LXIII, St. 3, Ibid.

4 O sun, whom light nor flight can match,
Suppose thy lightful flightful wings
Thou lend to me,
And I could flee
As far as thee the ev'ning brings
Psalm CXXXIX, "Domine, Probasti," St. 5, Ibid.

5 If ever hapless woman had a cause
To breathe her plaints into the open air,
And never suffer inward grief to pause,
Or seek her sorrow-shaken soul's repair:
Then I, for I have lost my only brother,*
Whose like this age can scarcely yield another.
"If Ever a Hapless Woman Had a Cause," St. 1 (c.1599), Quoted in *The Woman Poets in English* by Ann Stanford *1972*

*The poet Sir Philip Sidney (1554–1586), who, in their joint translation of the psalms, translated the first 43.

359. Penelope Devereaux Rich (1562/63–post-1605)

1 . . . they will seem . . . such crafty workmen as will not only pull downe all the obstacles of theyr greatnes, but when they are in theyr full strengths (like gyants) make warr agaynst Heaven.
Letter to Queen Elizabeth I* (1599), Quoted *in Society Women of Shakespeare's Time* by Violet A. Wilson *1924*

*See 331.

2 Faction . . . careth not upon whose neck they buyld the walles of theyr owne fortunes . . .
Ibid.

360. Hŏ Nansŏrhŏn (1563–1589)

1 Yesterday I fancied I was young;
But already, alas, I am aging.
"A Woman's Sorrow," Peter H. Lee, tr., *The Penguin Book of Women Poets*, Carol Cosman, Joan Keefe and Kathleen Weaver, eds. *1978*

2 Numberless are the sorrowful.
Untitled, Ibid.

361. Elizabeth Grymeston (1563?–1603)

1 I resolved to break the barren soil of my fruitless brain.
Dedicatory letter to her son, Bernye Grymeston, *Miscelanea: Prayer, Meditations, Memoratives 1604*

2 I have prayed for thee, that thou mightest be fortunate in two hours of thy life time: in the hour of thy marriage, and at the hour of thy death.
Ibid.

3 Defer not thy marriage till thou comest to be saluted with a "God speed you, Sir," as a man going out of the world after forty; neither yet to the time of "God keep you, Sir," whilst thou are in thy best strength after thirty; but marry in the time of "You are welcome, Sir," when thou are coming into the world: for seldom shalt thou see a woman out of her own love to pull a rose that is full blown, deeming them always sweetest at the first opening of the bud.
Ibid.

4 Crush the serpent in the head,
Break ill eggs ere they be hatched.
Kill bad chickens in the tread,
Fledged they hardly can be catched.
In the rising stifle ill,
Lest it grow against thy will.
Ibid.

5 Our best life is to die well: for living her we enjoy nothing: things past are dead and gone: things present are always ending: things future always beginning: while we live we die; and we leave dying when we leave living.
Ch. 4, Ibid.

6 Epicurism is the fuel of lust; the more thou addest, the more she is enflamed.
Ch. 20, "Memoratives," Ibid.

7 If thou givest a benefit, keep it close; but if thou receivest one, publish it, for that invites another.
Ibid.

8 On the anvil of upbraiding is forged the office of unthankfulness.
Ibid.

9 Be not at any time idle. Alexander's* soldiers should scale molehills rather than rest unoccupied; it is the woman that sitteth still that imagineth mischief; it is the rolling stone that riseth clean, and the running water that remaineth clear.
Ibid.

*Alexander the Great or Alexander III (356–323 B.C.E.), king of Macedon; incontestably one of the greatest generals of all time.

10 There be four good mothers have four bad daughters: Truth hath Hatred; Prosperity hath Pride; Security hath Peril, and Familiarity hath Contempt.
Ibid.

11 A fair woman is a paradise to the eye, a purgatory to the purse, and a hell to the soul.

Ibid.

363. Marie le Jars de Gournay (1565–1645)

1 Suppose we believed that the Scriptures indeed order woman to submit to the authority of man because she cannot think as well as he can, see here the absurdity that would follow: women would be worthy of having been made in the likeness of the Creator, worthy of taking part in the holy Eurcharist, of sharing the mysteries of the Redemption, Paradise, worthy of the vision, even possession, of God, but not of the status and privileges of men. Wouldn't we be saying then that men are more precious and sacred than all these things, and wouldn't that be the most grievous blasphemy?

The Equality of Men and Women
1622

2 . . . I have known some [authors] who thoroughly despised all books written by women without even bothering to read them to see of what stuff they are made, and without wanting to find out first whether they themselves could produce books worthy to be read by all kinds of women.

The Ladies Grievance 1626

3 . . . even if a woman has only the name of being educated she will be evilly spoken of.

Proumenoir (1594), Quoted in *A Daughter of the Renaissance* by Marjorie Henry Ilsley
1963

4 I am on the side of those who believe that vice comes from stupidity and consequently that the nearer one draws to wisdom the farther one gets from vice.

Preface to *Essais* by Montaigne (1595), Ibid.

5 Pierre, your life is condemned
By the crime of a single moment:
While you believe that you are just for a whole year
Because you are good for a single day.

"Illusions Bigottes" (1626), Ibid.

6 Knowledge not based on ethics cannot . . . bring real honor nor profit to its master. . . .

"Advis" (1634), Ibid.

7 Since language and speech are the cement of human society whoever falsifies them should be punished for counterfeit or for poisoning the public water well.

Ibid.

8 What are our efforts but a flood-gate of reeds against the roaring torrent of fortune?

Ibid.

9 Society is a cage of idiots.

"A Lenten" (1634), Ibid.

364. Elizabeth Joceline (1566–1622)

1 . . . all the delight a Parent may take in a child is honey mingled with gall.

Introduction, *The Mothers Legacie to her Unborne Childe*
1624

2 Drunkennesse . . . is the highway to hell. . . .

Ch. 9, Ibid.

3 . . . there is nothing more contrary to our wicked nature than this loving our neighbour as our selves. Wee can with ease envie him if hee be rich, or scorne him if he be poore; but love him?

Ch. 10, Ibid.

365. Aemilia Lanyer (1569/70–1640/45?)

1 If Eve did err, it was for knowledge sake,
No subtle Serpent's falsehood did betray him,
If he would eat it, who had power to stay him?
Not Eve, whose fault was only too much love,
which made her give this present to her Dear,
That what she tasted, he likewise might prove,
Whereby his knowledge might become more clear

"Eve's Apology," *Salve Deus Rex Judeorum* (Hail, God,
King of the Jews) *1611*

2 Then let us [women] have our liberty again,
And challenge to your selves no sovereignty;
You came not in the world without our pain,
Make that a bar against your cruelty;
Your fault being greater, why should you disdain
Our being your equals, free from tyranny?

Ibid.

3 [There are] evil disposed men, who forgetting they were borne of women, nourished of women, and that if it were not by the means of women, they would be quite extinguished out of the world, and a final end of them all, do like Vipers deface the wombs wherein they were bred, only to give way and utterance to their want of discretion and goodness.

Introduction, Ibid.

4 As also in respect it pleased our Lord and Savior Jesus Christ, without the assistance of man, being free from original and all other sins, from the time of his conception, till the hour of his death, to be begotten of a woman, borne of a woman, nourished of a woman, obedient to a woman; and that he healed woman, pardoned women, comforted women: yea, even when he was in his greatest agony and bloody sweat, going to be crucified, and also in the last hour of his death, took care to dispose of a woman: after his resurrection, appeared first to a woman, sent a woman to declare his most glorious resurrection to the rest of his Disciples.

Ibid.

366. Mairi MacLeod (1569–1674?)

1 To Ullinish
with its white–hoofed herds,
Where once in childhood
I was nourished
On breast-milk
of smooth-skinned women

"A Complaint About Exile," ll. 11–16, Joan Keefe, tr.,
The Penguin Book of Women Poets, Carol Cosman,
Joan Keefe and Kathleen Weaver, eds. *1978*

367. Antoinette de Pons Guercheville (1570–1632)

1 If I am not noble enough to be your wife, I am too much so to be your mistress.

Remark to Henry IV,* Quoted in *Biography of Distinguished Women* by Sarah Josepha Hale** *1876*
*Known as "Henry of Navarre," King of France (1589–1610)
who founded the Bourbon royal line (1553–1610). **See 788.

2 A king, wherever he is, should always be master. As to myself,
I also choose to be free.

> Message to Henry IV, Ibid.

368. Margaret Hoby (1570–1633)

1 . . . it is not sufficient only to have faith . . . but I must likewise
pray especially for that virtue which is opposed to that vice
whereunto I am then tempted.

> Diary Entry (10 December 1599), *Diary of Lady Margaret
> Hoby*, Dorothy M. Meads, ed. *1930*

2 They are unworthy of God's benefits and special favors that
can find no time to make a thankful record of them.

> Diary Entry (1 April 1605), Ibid.

369. Katherine Stubbes (1571–1591/92)

1 I would rather be a door keeper in the house of my God, than
to dwell in the tents of the wicked.

> Spoken during her final illness (1591/92), Quoted in *Women
> of the Reformation, Vol. III: From Spain to Scandinavia*,
> by Roland H. Bainton *1977*

370. Elizabeth Clinton (1574–1630?)

1 Now who shall deny the own mother's suckling of their own
children to be their duty, since every godly matron hath
walked in these steps before them: Eve, the mother of all the
living; Sarah, the mother of all the faithful; Hannah, so graciously heard of God; Mary, blessed among women, and called
blessed of all ages.

> *The Countess of Lincoln's Nurserie* 1622

2 Whatsoever things are true, whatsoever things are honest . . .
whatsoever things are just, whatsoever things are pure, whatsoever things are of good report . . . think on these things;
these things do, and the God of peace shall be with you.

> Ibid.

3 Trust not other women whom wages hire . . . better than yourselves whom God and nature tie. . . .

> Ibid.

371. Beatrice Cenci (1577–1599)

1 I am no Turk and no dog that I should wish to shed my own
blood.

> Testimony at her trial (1599), Quoted in *Beatrice Cenci*
> by Corrado Ricci, Morris Bishop and Henry Longan Stuart,
> tr. *1925*

2 I no longer know what to do in order not to fall from one evil
into another, and even though I slew myself, I would fall under
the curse of the Holy Father.

> Letter to her defense lawyer, Prospero Farinaccio (1599), Ibid.

3 Alas! Alas! O Madonna *santissima*, aid me! . . . Let me down!
I will tell the truth.

> Remark during torture on the rack (1599), Ibid.

372. Jane Anger (fl. c. 1580)

1 Was there ever any so abused, so slandered, so railed upon, so
wickedly handled undeservedly, as are we women.

> Introduction, *For Protection for Women** 1589
> *Written in response to *Boke His Surfeit in Love, with a farwel to
> the folies of his own phantasie* (1588) by Thomas Orwin.

2 The Desire that every man has to show his true vain in writing
is unspeakable, and their minds are so carried away with the
manner, as no care at all is bad of the matter: they run so into
Rhetoric, as often times they overrun the bounds of their own
wits, and go they know not wither.

> "A Protection for Women Etc.,"
> Ibid.

3 Wild are men's lusts, false are their lips, besmeared with
flattery

> Ibid.

4 The man that is of Cuckolds lot afraid,
From Lechery he ought for to refrain,
Else shall he have the plague he does forlorn:
and ought (perforce constrained) to wear the horn.

> Ibid.

5 We are the grief of man, in that we take all the grief from
man: we languish when they laugh, we lie sighing when
they sit singing, and sit sobbing when they lie slugging and
sleeping.

> Ibid.

6 . . . our behaviors alter daily, because men's virtues decay
hourly.

> Ibid.

7 The lion rages when he is hungry, but man rails when he is
glutted.

> Ibid.

8 Deceit will give you fair words, & pick your pockets: nay he
will pluck out your hearts, if you be not wary.

> Ibid.

373. Anna of Saxony (fl. c. 1580)

1 . . . many pregnant women in confinement and small children of noble as well as of common rank are often miserably
neglected, injured, harmed and crippled at the time of the
birth or in the following six weeks, all through the clumsiness, arrogance, and rashness of the midwives and assisting
women; few sensible mid-wives are to be found in this country [Germany].

> (c. 1587), Quoted in *Women in the Middle Ages*
> by Sibylle Harksen *1975*

374. Mistress Bradford (fl. c. 1580)

1 As Hanna* did applie, dedicate, and give her first child and
sonne Samuel unto thee: even so doo I deere Father; beseeching thee, for Christ's sake, to accept this my gift.

> "The praier that maister Bradford's mother said and o ered
> unto God in his behalfe, a little before his martyrdom,"**
> *The Monument of Matrones conteining seven severall
> Lamps of Virginitie, or Distinct Treatises . . .* , Thomas
> Bentley, ed. *1582*
> *See 30. **Her son, John Bradford, executed c.1582 for heresy.

375. Anne Dowriche (fl. c. 1580)

1 O noble France (quod he) that bor'st sometime the bell,
And for thy pleasure and thy wealth all Nations didst ex-
cell!
How art thou now of late with mischiefe so possest,
That al the Realmes of Christendome thy falshoods do detest?

> *The French Historie* 1589

2   As winde disperse the wavring chaffe, and toss it quite away,
All worldly pompe shall so consume, and pass without delay.
"Dedicatory poem to her brother," Ibid.

3   Who thinke they swim in wealth (blinded by guile):
Yet wanting Truth; are wretched, poore and vile.
Epilogue: "Veritie purtraied by the French pilgrim," St. 1, Ibid.

4   . . . malicious Men devise
Torments for Truth. . . .
St. 2, Ibid.

376. Margaret Lambrun (fl. c. 1580)

1   I confess to you, that I suffered many struggles within my breast, and have made all possible efforts to divert my resolution from so pernicious a design, but all in vain; I found myself necessitated to prove by experience the certain truth of that maxim, that neither reason nor force can hinder a woman from vengeance, when she is impelled thereto by love.
Remark to Queen Elizabeth I* when caught attempting to assassinate her (1587), Quoted in *Biography of Distinguished Women* by Sarah Josepha Hale** *1876*
*See 331. **See 788.

2   Your majesty ought to grant me a pardon [without assurances from me]. . . . A favour given under . . . restraint is no more a favour; and, in so doing, your majesty would act against me as a judge.
Ibid.

377. Elizabeth Tyrwhit (fl. c. 1580)

1   . . . from Sathan deliver me, with the bread of Angels feede me, from fleshlie lusts purge me, from sudden death and deadlie sinne, O Lord take me.
"Another praier at our uprising," Morning and evening praiers, with divers, Psalmes, Hymnes, and Meditations, made and set forth by the Ladie Elizabeth Tyrwhit *1582*

2   Sweets dews from heven to earth God grant,
of peace and quiet mind,
That we may serve the living God, as his statutes doo bind.
"The Hymne or praier to he sonne of God," Ibid.

378. Elizabeth Vernon (158?–post-1647)

1   . . . ever you like best I should be, that place shall be most pleasing to me. . . .
Letter to her husband, Henry Wriothesley, 3rd Earl of Southampton (8 July 1599), Quoted in *Society Women of Shakespeare's Time* by Violet A. Wilson *1924*

379. Ann Wheathill (fl. c. 1580)

1   . . . humilitie . . . the beautiful flowre of vertue that groweth in the garden of man's soule. . . .
Prayer 9, *A Handfull of holesome (though homelie) Hearbs, gathered out of the Godlie Garden of Gods most Holie Word: for the common Benefit and comfortable Exercise of all such as are Devoutlie Disposed 1584*

2   The young chickens, when the kite striketh at them, have no other refuge but to run dickering under the wings of the hen:

no more hath mankind any other defense against his enemies, but onelie the covering of Thy grace, and the shaddowe of Thy most precious passion. . . .
Prayer 28, Ibid.

380. Alice Harvey (fl. c. 1580–1600)

1   All the speed is in the morning.
Quoted in *Commonplace Book* by Gabriel Harvey *c. 1580*

381. Lucy Harington (1581–1627)

1   Death be not proud, thy hand gave not this blow. . . .
"Elegy," l.1, Quoted in *The Woman Poets in English* by Ann Stanford *1972*

2   And teach this hymn of her with joy and sing,
The grave no conquest gets, Death hath no sting.
"Elegy," last line, Ibid.

382. Catalina de Erauso (1585–post-1624)

1   I went out of the convent; I found myself in the street, without knowing where to go; that was no matter; all I wanted was liberty.
Quoted in *Biography of Distinguished Women* by Sarah Josepha Hale* *1876*
*See 788.

2   In this attempt [to cross the deserts of the Andes] I *may* find death; by remaining here [in this sanctuary] I shall certainly find it.
Ibid.

383. Elizabeth Carew (1585?–1639)

1   CHORUS. Tis not enough for one that is a wife
To keep her spotless from an act of ill:
But from suspicion she should free her life,
And bare herself of power as well as will.
Act III, *The Tragedie of Mariam the Faire Queene of Jewry 1613*

2   For in a wife it is no worse to find
A common body, than a common mind.
Ibid.

3   CHORUS. The fairest action of our human life,
Is scorning to revenge an injury;
For who forgives without a further strife,
His adversary's heart to him doth tie:
And 't is a firmer conquest, truly said,
To win the heart, and overthrow the head.
Act IV, Sc. 1, Ibid.

4   When she hath spacious ground to walk upon
Why on the ridge should she desire to go?
Ibid.

5   . . . benefit upbraided, forfeits thanks.
Act V, Sc. 1, Ibid.

384. Feng Meng-lung (1574–1645)

1   When a crummy horse has no bridle, who enjoys the ride?
"My Old Man's Small," 1, Richard W. Bodman, tr. *World of Poetry,* Katharine Washburn and John S. Major, eds., Clifton Fadiman,* general ed. *1998*
*American writer and editor (1904–1999)

2   We share the same bedcurtains but not the same pillow.
                                                    2, Ibid.

3   But I rashly carried my lover into bed and out again
    The two of us sharing a single pair of shoes.
                                "Smart," Richard W. Bodman, tr., Ibid.

385. Mary Ward (1585–1645)
1   Fervour is not placed in feelings but in will to do well, which
    women may have as well as men. There is no such difference
    between men and women that women may not do great things
    as we have seen by example of many saints who have done
    great things.
                            Quoted in *The Life of Mary Ward* by
                            Mary Catherine Elizabeth Chambers *1884*

386. Mary Sidney Wroth (1586/87–1640/51)
1   . . . wounds still cureless, must my rulers be.
                    "Morea's Sonnet," St. 2, *The Countess of Montgomeries
                                                    Urania c. 1615*

2   Had I not happy been, I had not known
    So great a loss; a king deposed feels most
    The torment of a throne–like–want when lost . . .
                            "Pamphilia's Sonnet," St. 3, Ibid.

3   O Memory, could I but lose thee now . . .
                            "Lindamira's Complaint," last line, Ibid.

387. Francesca Caccini (1587–1640?)
1   I would rather lose my life before the desire to study and the
    affection I have always had for virtue, because this is worth
    more than all treasure and all grandeur.
                    Letter to Michelangelo Buonarroti the Younger (Genoa, 26
                    May 1617), Quoted in *Women in Music*
                                    by Carol Neuls–Bates *1982*

388. Elizabeth Compton (fl. c. 1590)
1   I would have two gentlewomen, lest one should be sick. . . . It
    is an indecent thing for a gentlewoman to stand mumping
    alone when God hath blessed their Lord and Lady with a great
    estate.
                    Letter to her husband William, earl of Northampton,
                    Quoted in *Court of King James* by Bishop Godfrey
                                            Goodman *1839*

389. Mary Harding (fl. c. 1590)
1   . . . how weary my lady of the courte, and what little gayne
    there is gotten in this tyme.
                    Letter to Countess of Rutland (1594), Quoted in
                    Queen Elizabeth's Maids of Honor by Violet A. Wilson
                                                    n.d.

    *See 331.

390. Maria de Zayas y Sotomayor (1590–1661/69)
1   In conclusion, I have held her penned up, in the condition that
    you have seen, for two years. She eats and drinks no more than
    that ration which was allotted to her today. A heap of straw is
    her only bed and the nook in which she stays is not any larger
    than the space occupied by her reclining body. Her sole com-
    panion is the skull of her treacherous, beloved cousin.
                    "Too Late for Disillusionment" *c. 1637–1647*

391. Anne Clifford (1590–1676)
1   I am like an owl in the desert.
                    Diary Entry (May 1616), *The Diary of the Lady
                    Anne Clifford*, Vita Sackville-West,* ed. *1923*
    *See 1637.

2   I . . . strived to sit as merry a face as I could upon a discon-
    tented heart . . . knowing that God often brings things to pass
    by contrary means.
                                Diary Entry (March 1617), Ibid.

392. Anne Hutchinson (1591–1643)
1   An oath, sir, is an end of all strife, and it is God's ordinance.
                    Spoken at her trial in Boston (1 November 1637), Quoted in
                    *Antinomianism in the Colony of Massachusetts Bay,
                    1636–1638*, Charles Francis Adams, ed. *1894*

2   I thinke the soule to be nothing but Light.
                                                    Ibid.

3   What from the Church at Boston? I know no such church, nei-
    ther will I own it. Call it the whore and strumpet of Boston, no
    Church of Christ!
                                    Remark (c. 1638), Ibid.

393. Margaret Winthrop (1591?–1647)
1   I have many reasons to make me love thee, whereof I will
    name two, first because thou lovest God, and secondly because
    that thou lovest me.
                    Letter to John Winthrop,* *The Winthrop Papers*, Samuel E.
                                    Morison et al., eds. *1929*
    *English colonial administrator (1588–1649); first governor of
    Massachusetts Bay Colony (1629–1649).

394. Sarah Copia Sullam (1592–1641)
1   The lying tongue's deceit with silence blight,
    Protect me from its venom, you, my Rock,
    And show the spiteful sland'rer by this sign
    That you will shield me with your endless might.
                    "My Inmost Hope," *A Treasury of Jewish Poetry*, Nathan
                                    and Maryann Ausubel, eds. *1957*

395. Artemisia Gentileschi (1593–1652/53)
1   I have the greatest sympathy for your lordship, because the name
    of a woman makes one doubtful until one has seen the work.
                    Letter to Don Antonio Ruffo, a patron (30 January 1649),
                    Quoted in *Women Artists: 1550–1950* by Ann Sutherland
                                    Harris and Linda Nochlin *1976*

2   As long as I live, I will have control over my being. . . .
                    Letter to Don Antonio Ruffo, a patron (March 1649), Ibid.

3   You will find the spirit of Caesar in the soul of this woman.
                    Letter to Don Antonio Ruffo, a patron (November 1649),
                                                    Ibid.

396. Gabrielle de Coignard (?–1594)
1   I'm dust and ashes, Lord; remember this.

    You are the wind and I am straw, or less,
    For you can sweep me into nothingness.
    Ah, do not let me fall in the abyss!
                    "Prayer," Sts. 3–4, Raymond Oliver, tr., *Women Poets of the
                    World*, Joanna Bankier and Deirdre Lashgari, eds. *1983*

397. Pocahontas (1595/97–1616/17)

1 You promised my father [Chief Powhatan] that whatever was yours should be his, and that you and he would be all one. Being a stranger in our country, you called Powhatan father; and I for the same reason will now call you so.

> Remark to Captain John Smith* (c. 1616), Quoted in
> *Women of Beauty and Heroism* by Frank B. Goodrich *1858*
> *English colonist, explorer and writer (1580–1631).

398. Rachel Speght (1597–post-1621)

1 Some dogs barke more upon custome then curstnesse; and some speake evill of others, not that the defamed deserve it, but because through custome and corruption of their hearts they cannot speak well of any.

> "Epistole Dedicatorie," *A Mouzell for Melastomus, the Cynicall Bayter of, and foule mouthed Barker against Evahs Sex. Or an apologeticall Answere to that Irreligius and Illiterate Pamphlet made by Jo[seph] Sw[etnam] and by him intituled, The Arraignment of Women 1617*

2 . . . man was created of the dust of the earth, but woman was made of a part of man, after that he was a living soule: yet was shee not produced from Adam's foote, to be his too low inferiour; nor from his head to be his superiour, but from his side, neare his heart, to be his equall. . . .

> "Essay," Ibid.

3 . . . then are those husbands to be blamed, which lay the whole burthen of domesticall affaires and maintenance on the shoulder of their wives. For, as yoake-fellowes they are to sustayne part of each others cares, griefs, and calamities. . . .

> Ibid.

4 For as Christ turned water into wine, a farre more excellent liquor . . . So the single man is by marriage changed from Batchelour to a Husband, a farre more excellent title: from a solitarie life unto a joyfull union. . . .

> Ibid.

5 Marriage is a merri–age, and this world's Paradise, where there is mutual love.

> Ibid.

6 Corne kept close in a garner feeds not the hungry; A candle put under a bushell doth not illuminate an house . . .

> Dedication, *Mortalitie's Memorandum, with a Dreame Prefixed, imaginarie in manner, reall in matter 1621*

7 Readers too common, and plentifull be;
For Readers they are that can read a, b, c.
And utter their verdict on what they doe view,
Though none of the Muses they yet euer knew.

> Prefatory Verse, *in toto*, Ibid.

8 And from the soul three faculties arise.
The mind, the will, the power; then wherefore shall
A woman have her intellect in vain
Or not endeavor Knowledge to attain.

> "A Dream," St. 14, Ibid.

9 All parts and faculties were made for us; The God of Knowledge nothing gave in vain.

> St. 15, Ibid.

10 If happinesse consist in length of dayes,
An Oke more happie then a man appeares;

> St. 118, Ibid.

399. Lucy Hay (1599–1660)

1 Spell well, if you can.

> *Thoughts n.d.*

400. Marie de L'Incarnation (1599–1672)

1 The air is excellent and in consequence this [Quebec] is an earthly paradise where crosses and thorns grow so lovingly that the more one is pricked by them, the more filled with tenderness is the heart.

> Letter to Mother Marie-Gillette Roland (1640), Quoted in
> *Word from New France* by Joyce Marshall *1967*

2 We see nothing, we walk gropingly, and . . . ordinary things do not come about as they have been foreseen and advised. One falls and, just when one thinks oneself at the bottom of an abyss, one finds oneself on one's feet.

> Letter to her son (1652), Ibid.

3 Everything is savage here [Quebec], the flowers as well as the men.

> Letter to her sister (1653), Ibid.

4 . . . if God strikes us with one hand, he consoles us with another.

> Letter to her son (1665), Ibid.

5 If practical affairs . . . cause some objects to pass through my imagination, these are but little clouds, like those that pass across the sun and remove it from our sight for a brief moment, leaving it bright as before.

> Letter to Father Poncet, S.J. (1670), Ibid.

6 Writing teaches us our mysteries. . . .

> Letter to her son (1670), Ibid.

401. Madeleine de Souvré de Sablé (1599–1678)

1 Study and research into truth often only serves to make us see by experience our natural ignorance.

> *The Maxims of Madame de Sablé*, Arthur Chandler, tr. *1665*

2 Instead of taking care to acquaint ourselves with others, we only think of making ourselves known to them. It would be better to listen to other people in order to become enlightened rather than to speak so as to shine in front of them.

> Ibid.

3 Often the desire to appear competent impedes our ability to become competent, because we are more anxious to display our knowledge than to learn what we do not know.

> Ibid.

4 We must accustom ourselves to the follies of others and not be astonished at the foolishness that takes place in our presence.

> Ibid.

5 Mean–spirited mediocrities, especially those with a smattering of learning, are the most likely to be opinionated. Only strong minds know how to correct their opinions and abandon a bad position.

> Ibid.

6 It is sometimes useful to pretend we are deceived, because when we show a deceiving man that we see through his artifices, we only encourage him to increase his deceptions.

> Ibid.

7 Honest and sincere acts mislead the wicked and cause them to lose their path to their own goals, because mean–spirited people usually believe that people never act without deceit.

Ibid.

8 It is such a great fault to talk too much that, in business and conversation, if what is good is also brief, it is doubly good, and one gains by brevity what one often loses by an excess of words.

Ibid.

9 The ties of virtue ought to be closer than the ties of blood, since the good man is closer to another good man by their similarity of morals than the son is to his father by their similarity of face.

Ibid.

10 Often our good deeds make enemies for us, and the ungrateful person despises us on two counts; for he is not only unwilling to acknowledge the gratitude he owes us: he does not want to have his benefactor as witness to his thankless behavior.

Ibid.

11 If we took as much trouble to be what we should be as we take to deceive others by disguising what we are, we could appear as we really are without having the trouble of disguising ourselves.

Ibid.

12 We think highly of men when we do not know the extent of their capabilities, for we always suppose that more exists when we only see half.

Ibid.

13 We nearly always make ourselves masters of those whom we know well, because he who is thoroughly understood is in some sense subject to those who understand him.

Ibid.

14 We judge matters so superficially that ordinary acts and words, done and spoken with some flair and some knowledge of worldly matters, often succeed better than the greatest cleverness.

Ibid.

15 Man's greatest wisdom consists in knowing his own follies.

Ibid.

16 To know how to unveil the inner workings of others, and how to hide one's own, is the great mark of the superior intellect.

Ibid.

17 Self-love is even deceived by self-love, because by looking out for our own interests and disregarding those of other people, we lose the advantage that comes with the exchange of favors.

Ibid.

18 Sometimes we praise the way things used to be in order to blame the present, and we esteem what is no longer in order to scorn what is.

Ibid.

19 Good fortune almost always makes some change in a man's behavior—in his manner of speaking and acting. It is a great weakness to want to bedeck oneself in qualities which are not his own. If he esteemed virtue above all other things, neither the favors of fortune nor the advantages of position would change a man's face or heart.

Ibid.

20 We would often rather seem dutiful to others than to succeed in our duties; and often we would rather tell our friends that we have done them good than to do good in actuality.

Ibid.

21 Wealth does not teach us to transcend the desire for wealth. The possession of many goods does not bring the repose of not desiring them.

Ibid.

402. Devorah Ascarelli (fl. c. 1600)

1 Although a beautiful shock of golden hair swings across her forehead
And love finds nourishment in her eyes
The chaste Susannah never strays from the right path
And harbors not one thought without the Lord.

Untitled poem, Quoted in *Written Out of History: Jewish Foremothers* by Sondra Henry & Emily Taitz *1990*

403. Lal Ded (fl. 16th century?)

1 Like water in goblets of unbaked clay
I drip out slowly,
and dry.

Untitled, Willis Barnstone, tr., *A Book of Women Poets*, Aliki and Willis Barnstone, eds. *1980*

2 I came by the way
but didn't go back by the way.

Ibid.

404. Lucrezia Marinella (fl. c. 1600)

1 It is an amazing thing to see in our city [Venice] the wife of a shoemaker, or a butcher, or a porter dressed in silk with chains of gold at the throat, with pearls and a ring of good value . . . and then in contrast to see her husband cutting the meat, all smeared with cow's blood, poorly dressed, or burdened like an ass, clothed with the stuff from which sacks are made . . . but whoever considers this carefully will find it reasonable, because it is necessary that the lady, even if low-born and humble, be draped with such clothes for her natural excellence and dignity, and that the man less adorned as if a slave, or a little ass, born to her service.

The Nobility and Excellence of Women together with the Defects and Deficiencies of Men 1600

405. Elizabeth Melvill (fl. c. 1600)

1 The brain of man most surely did invent
That purging place, he answer'd me again:
For greediness together they consent
To say that souls in torment may remain,
Till gold and goods relieve them of their pain.

Ane Godlie Dreame Complit in Scottish Meter be M.M., Gentilwoman in Cul Ross, at the Request of her Friendes, St. 1 *1606*

2 The fire was great, the heat did pierce me sore;
My faith was weak, my grip was wondrous small,
I trembled fast, my fear grew more and more. . . .

St. 8, Ibid.

406. Elizabeth Raleigh (fl. c. 1600)

1 I wish she would be as ambitious to do good as she is apt to the contrary.

Letter to Sir Robert Cecil (c.1601), Quoted in *Society Women of Shakespeare's Time* by Violet A. Wilson *1924*

407. Ann Sutcliffe (fl. c. 1600–1630)

1   . . . remember thy dayes of Darknes, for they are many.
*Meditations of Man's Moralitie, Or, a Way to
true Blessednesse*, 2nd ed. *1634*

2   . . . the Glory of this World, is but the singing of Syrens, sweet
but a deadly poison.
Ibid.

3   Pride, in it selfe doth beare a poyson'd breath. . . .
Ibid.

408. Brilliana Harley (1600–1643)

1   . . . that is the evil in [those who are] melancholy; it acts most,
inwardly; full of thoughts they are, but not active in expressions. Many times they are so long in studying what is fit for
them to do, that the opportunity is past.
Letter to her son, Edward (4 January 1638), *Letters of the
Lady Brilliana Harley*, Thomas Taylor Lewis, ed. *1854*

2   . . . man is so forgetful of his God, that all, and most of all
great men, live in prosperity as if they were lords of what they
had, forgetting that they are but tenants at will.
Letter to her son (29 November 1639), Ibid.

3   . . . keep your heart above the world, and then you will not be
troubled at the changes in it.
Letter to her son (15 July 1642), Ibid.

409. Anne of Austria (1601–1666)

1   God does not pay at the end of every week, but He pays.
Letter to Cardinal Mazarin, *Letters n.d.*

410. Priscilla Alden (1602?–pre-1687)

1   John, why do you not speak for yourself?*
Quoted in *Collections of American Epitaphs and Inscriptions
with Original Notes*, Vol. III, Rev. Timothy Alden, ed. *1814*
*Reply to John Alden, Pilgrim colonist (1559?–1687), who was
intervening on behalf of Miles Standish, English colonial settler in
America (1584?–1656).

411. María de Agreda (1602–1664/65)

1   Earth has 2,502 leagues, and up to the half of it, which is the
place or seat of Hell, there are 1,251 leagues of profundity. In
this center or middle of the Earth are the Purgatory and the
Limbo. Hell has many caverns and mansions of punishment,
and everything in there forms a big infernal cavern with a
mouth in it, and is a proven fact that there is a big stone, bigger than the mouth, to cover it, when Hell will be sealed with
all the sinners inside of it, where they have to suffer for all the
eternities to come.
Quoted in *Women in Myth and History* by Violeta Miqueli
1962

412. Violante do Céu (1602?–1693)

1   You fool yourself and live a crazy day or year, dizzy with ad-
ventures, and bent solely on pleasures! Know the argument or
rigid doom and find a wiser way.
"Voice of a Dissipated Woman Inside a Tomb, Talking to
Another Woman Who Presumed to Enter a Church with the
Purpose of Being Seen and Praised by Everyone, Who Sat
Down Near a Sepulchar Containing This Epitaph, Which
Curiously Reads," *Rimas Varias 1646*

2   . . . the end which ends with no way out.
Ibid.

413. Anna Maria Marchocka (1603–1652)

1   Humbly I beseech Thee, my Father. Cover me with Thy pinions, enlighten mine eyes that I wander not in a haze, knowing
not what to write nor where.
Prayer found in her *Autobiography*, Quoted in *Women of
the Reformation, Vol. III: From Spain to Scandinavia*
by Roland H. Bainton *1977*

414. Arcangela Tarabotti (1604–1652)

1   When women are seen with pen in hand, they are met immediately with shrieks commanding a return to that life of pain
which their writing had interrupted, a life devoted to the
women's work of needle and distaff.
Remark (1654), Quoted in *Women in World History Curriculum*, http://www.womeninworldhistory.com *1996–97*

415. Marcela de Carpio de San Feliz (1605–1688)

1   Love giving gifts
Is suspicious and cold;
I have all, my Belovèd,
When thee I hold.
"Amor Mysticus," St. 3, *The Catholic Anthology*, Thomas
Walsh, ed. *1927*

2   But in Thy chastising
Is joy and peace.
O Master and Love,
Let Thy blows not cease.
St. 8, Ibid.

416. A. M. Bigot de Cornuel (1605/14?–1694)

1   Turenne's small change. (*La monnaie de M. Turenne.*)*
Remark, Quoted in *Nouvelle Biographie Universelle
1853–1866*
*Reference to the eight generals appointed to take the place of the
great French marshal Henri de La Tour d'Auvergne, vicomte de
Turenne (1611–1675).

2   No man is a hero to his valet. (*Il n'y a point de héros pour son
valet de chambre.*)
Letter (13 August 1628), *Lettres de Mlle. Aissé*,* n.d.
*Charlotte Elizabeth Aissé; see 532.

417. Anna Maria van Schurman (1607–1678)

1   Whoever longs greatly for a solid and enduring occupation is
suited for the study of letters. And woman longs greatly for a
solid and enduring occupation.
"Arguments: IV," *Whether the Study of Letters Is Fitting for
a Christian Woman? 1645?*

2   Whatever fills the mind of man with distinguished and honest
delight is fitting for a Christian woman.
"Arguments: XIII," Ibid.

3   To whomever ignorance is not fitting, the study of letters is fitting.
"Arguments: XIV," Ibid.

4   Woman has the same erect countenance* as man, the same ideals, the same love of beauty, honor, truth, the same wish for

self-development, the same longing after righteousness, and yet she is to be imprisoned in an empty soul of which the very windows are shuttered.

Quoted in *The Dinner Party, A Symbol of our Heritage* by Judy Chicago** *1979*

*Probably a faulty translation; more likely, "stance" or "posture."
**See 2750.

418. Madeleine de Scudéry (1607–1701)

1 In order to represent the heroic spirit it is undoubtedly necessary to have the hero do something extraordinary, as in a moment of heroic rapture, but this should not continue too long or it will degenerate into something ridiculous and will not have any good effect on the reader.

Preface, *Ibrahim or the Illustrious Bassa, an Excellent New Romance 1652*

2 Since the body and the mind are so closely linked that one cannot suffer without the other, I fell ill.

Vol. I, Ibid.

3 It is certain that I am inconstant, but at the same time I am not troublesome. I never contradict anyone's opinions or stand in the way of his pleasures. I give to others the freedom that I would have them accord me. I do not find fault with constancy, although I myself am happier with change, and my soul is so passionate that I could never condemn anything connected with love.

Vol. II, Ibid.

4 Any road that can take us where we want to go is the right one. Don't trouble yourself in asking if what you do is just, but only if it is advantageous.

Ibid.

5 . . . among private citizens it is prudent not to rise above the average.

Vol. III, Ibid.

6 He who imposes unnecessary problems upon himself cannot complain because he is the sole cause of whatever ills befall him.

Vol. IV, Ibid.

7 When we know the truth in our own consciences it is unnecessary to be troubled about anything else.

Artamenes, or The Grand Cyrus, an Excellent New Romance, Vol. I *1653–1655*

8 I find nothing more extravagant than to see a husband still in love with his wife.

Vol. VI, Ibid.

9 I don't think that she has ever been indisposed on a day when there was a party to attend.

Vol. VII, Ibid.

10 . . . by staying in Babylon during the autumn and winter, in Susa during the spring, and in Ecbatana during the summer, he was able to live in an eternal springtime, feeling neither the great discomfort of the cold nor that of the heat.

Vol. X, Ibid.

11 I would, without a doubt, rather be a simple soldier than be a woman, because to be truthful, a soldier can become king, but a woman can never become free.

Celia, An Excellent New Romance, Vol. I *1656–1661*

12 It is better to find glory in one's own merit. In fact it is more important to have self-respect than to gain respect from others, and it is better to earn glory than to publicize it.

Vol. III, Ibid.

13 In losing a husband one loses a master who is often an obstacle to the enjoyment of many things.

Vol. IV, Ibid.

14 . . . the familiarity of married life does not encourage love to grow.

Vol. VI, Ibid.

15 . . . one always admires her at first but inevitably comes to the point of despising her.

Vol. IX, Ibid.

16 In fashioning a good portrait of an evil man one can sometimes instill a loathing for vice.

Ibid.

17 Victory follows me, and all things follow victory. (*La victoire me suit, et tout suit la victoire.*)

"Tyrannic Love" *n.d.*

419. Bathsua Makin (1608/12?–1674/75?)

1 . . . these men of Law and their confederates . . . the caterpillars of this Kingdom, who with their uncontrolled exactions and extortions, eat up the free-born people of this Nation. . . .

The Malady . . . and Remedy of Vexations and Unjust Arrests and Actions 1646

2 A Learned woman is thought to be a comet, that bodes mischief whenever it appears.

An Essay to Revive the Ancient Education of the Gentlewomen 1673

3 To ask too much is the way to be denied all.

Ibid.

4 One generation passeth away and another cometh, but the earth, the theatre on which we act, abideth forever.

Ibid.

5 Merely to teach gentlewomen to frisk and dance, to paint their faces, to curl their hair, to put on a whisk,* to wear gay clothes, is not truly to adorn, but to adulterate their bodies; yea (what is worse) to defile their souls.

Ibid.

*A woman's scarf, worn around the neck.

6 Had God intended women only as a finer sort of cattle, He would not have made them reasonable. Brutes, a few degrees higher than . . . monkeys . . . might have better fitted some men's lust, pride, and pleasure; especially those that desire to keep them ignorant to be tyrannized over.

Ibid.

7 . . . a little philosophy, carries a man from God, but a great deal brings him back again.

Ibid.

8 . . . a little knowledge, like windy bladders, puffs up, but a good measure of true knowledge, like ballast in a ship, settles down and makes a person move more even in his station; 'tis not knowing too much, but too little that causes irregularity.

Ibid.

9   Objection: Women do not desire learning.
    Answer: Neither do many boys . . . yet I suppose you do not
    intend to lay fallow all children that will not bring forth fruit
    of themselves.
                                                                    Ibid.

420. Queen Henrietta Maria (1609–1666)

1   Queens of England are never drowned.
            Written during a storm at sea (February 1642), *Letters of
            Queen Henrietta Maria*, Mary Anne Everett Wood Green,*
                                                            ed. 1857

    *See 926.

421. Constantina Munda (fl. c. 1610)

1   . . . things simply good
    Keep their essence, though they be withstood
    By all the compices of hell. . . .
            Prefatory poem, *The Worming of a Mad Dogge* 1617

2   . . . printing that was invented to be the storehouse of famous
    wits, the treasure of Divine literature . . . is become . . . the
    nursery and hospitall of every spurious and pernicious brat,
    which proceeds from base phreneticall brainesicke bablers.
                                                        (Text) Ibid.

3   . . . you lay open your imperfections . . . by heaping together
    the . . . fragments . . . of diverse english phrases . . . by scraping
    together the glaunder and . . . the refuse of idle-headed Au-
    thors and making a mingle-mangle gallimauphrie of them . . .
    let every bird take his owne feathers, and you would be as
    naked as Aesop's jay.
            Answer to Joseph Swetnam's "The Arraignment of Lewd,
                    Idle, Forward and Unconstant Women," Ibid.

422. Jane Owen (fl. c. 1610–1633?)

1   Among all the Passions of the mind, there is not any, which
    hath so great a sovereignty, and command over man, as the
    Passion of Feare.
            *An Antidote against Purgatory. Or Discourse, wherein is
            shewed that Good Workes, and Almes-Deeds, are a meanes
            for the preventing, or mitigating the Torments of Purgatory*
                                                            1634

423. Joane Sharp (fl. c. 1610)

1   Any answere may serve an impudent lyar,
    Any mangie scab'd horse doth fit a scab'd Squire
            "Epilogue: A Defence of Women, against the Author of the
            Arraignment of Women," Quoted in *Ester Hath Hang'd
            Haman: or an Answere to a lewd Pamphlet, entituled, The
            Arraignment of Women** by Ester Sowernam** 1617
    *Written by Joseph Swetnam in 1617. **See 424.

424. Ester Sowernam (fl. c. 1610)

1   The world is a large field, and it is full of brambles, bryers,
    and weedes.
            "To the Reader," *Ester* Hath Hang'd Haman: or An A
            swere to a lewd Pamphlet, entituled, The Arraignment of
            Women*** 1617
    *See 56. **Written by Joseph Swetnam in 1617.

2   In all dangers, troubles, and extremities, which fell to our
    Saviour, when all men fled from Him, living or dead, women
    never forsook Him.
                                                        Ch. 3, Ibid.

3   . . . forbeare to charge women with faults which come from
    the contagion of Masculine serpents.
                                                        Ch. 7, Ibid.

425. Anne Bradstreet (1612?–1672)

1   That there is a God my Reason would soon tell me by the won-
    drous workes that I see, the vast frame of the Heaven and the
    Earth, the order of all things, night and day, Summer and Win-
    ter, Spring and Autumn, the dayly providing for this great
    household upon the Earth, the preserving and directing of All
    to its proper end.
            Dedication, "To My Dear Children: Religious Experience
            and Occasional Pieces," *The Tenth Muse Lately Sprung Up
                                                    in America 1650*

2   I am obnoxious to each carping tongue
    Who says my hand a needle better fits,
    A Poet's pen all scorn I should thus wrong,
    For such despite they cast on Female wits:
    If what I do prove well, it won't advance,
    They'll say it's stoln, or else it was by chance.
            Prologue, St. 5, *Several Poems Compiled with Great Variety
                                            of Wit and Learning 1678*

3   Ye Cooks, your Kitchen implements I frame
    Your Spits, Pots, Jacks, what else I need not name
    Your dayly food I wholsome make, I warm
    Your shrinking Limbs, which winter's cold doth harm.
                                        "The Four Elements; Fire," Ibid.

4   But thou art bound to me, above the rest
    Who am thy drink, thy blood, thy sap and best. . . .
                                                        "Water," Ibid.

5   Man at his best estate is vanity.
                            "Of the Four Ages of Man: Middle Age," Ibid.

6   Let such as say our Sex is void of reason,
    Know 'tis Slander now, but once was Treason.
            "In Honour of that High and Mighty Princess, Queen Eliza-
                                                        beth",* Ibid.
    *See 331.

7   And he that knowes the most, doth still bemoan
    He knows not all that here is to be known.
                            "The Vanity of All Worldly Things," Ibid.

8   Thou ill-form'd offspring of my feeble brain. . . .
                                "From the Author to her Book," Ibid.

9   If ever two were one, than surely we.
    If ever man were lov'd by wife, than thee.
                            "To my Dear and Loving Husband," Ibid.

10 I had eight birds hatcht in one nest,
    Four Cocks there were, and Hens the rest,
    I nurst them up with pain and care,
    Nor cost nor labour did I spare.
                    "In reference to her Children" (23 June 1656?), Ibid.

11 More fool than I to look on that was lent
    As if mine own, when thus impermanent.
            "In Memory of my dear Child, Anne Bradstreet" (20 June
                                                        1669), Ibid.

12 There is no object that we see; no action that we do; no good
    that we enjoy; no evil that we feel, or fear, but we may make

some spiritual advantage of all: and he that makes such improvement is wise, as well as pious.

"Meditations Devine and Moral (1664)," *The Works of Anne Bradstreet in Prose and Verse*, John Harvard Ellis, ed. *1867*

13 A prosperous state makes a secure Christian, but adversity makes him Consider.

VIII, *Ibid.*

14 . . . those parents are wise that can fit their nurture according to their Nature.

X, *Ibid.*

15 Authority without wisdom is like a heavy axe without an edg[e], fitter to bruise than polish.

XII, *Ibid.*

16 Sweet words are like honey, a little may refresh, but too much gluts the stomach.

Ibid.

426. Henriette de Coligny (1613?–1673)

1 His cleverness in the art of love is unequaled.

He knows how to draw the soul out by the ear.

Untitled sonnet (c.1725), Quoted in *Precious Women* by Dorothy Backer *1974*

427. Margaret Askew Fell Fox (1614–1702)

1 We who are the People of God called Quakers, who are hated and despised, and every where spoken against, as people not fit to live, as they were that went before us, who were of the same spirit, power, & Life and were as we are, in that they were accounted as the off-scouring of all things, by that Spirit and Nature that is of the world, and so the Scripture is fulfilled, he that is born of the flesh persecuteth him that is born of the Spirit . . .

A Declaration and an Information 1660

2 We are a People that follow after those things that make for Peace, Love and Unity, it is our desire that others feet may walk in the same, and do deny and beare our Testimony against all Strife, and Wars, and Contentions that come from the Lusts that warr in the members, that warr against the Soul, which we wait for and watch for in all People, and love and desire the good of all; for no other cause but love to the Souls of all People, have our sufferings been . . .

Ibid.

3 Thus much may prove, that the Church of Christ is represented as a Woman; and those that speak against this Woman's speaking, speak against the Church of Christ, and the Seed of the Woman, which Seed is Christ; that is to say, Those that speak against the Power of the Lord, and the Spirit of the Lord speaking in a Woman, simply by reason of her Sex, or because she is a Woman, not regarding the Seed, and Spirit, and Power that speaks in her; such speak against Christ and his Church, and are of the Seed of the Serpent, wherein lodgeth Enmity.

Women's Speaking Justified 1667

4 For Christ in the Male and in the Female is one, and he is the Husband, and his Wife is the Church; and God hath said, that his Daughters should prophesie as well as his Sons: And where he hath poured forth his Spirit upon them, they must prophe-

sie, though blind Priests say to the contrary, and will not permit holy Women to speak.

Ibid.

5 And whereas it is said, I permit not a Woman to speak, as saith the Law: But where Women are led by the Spirit of God, they are not under the Law; for Christ in the Male and in the Female is one; and where he is made manifest in Male and Female, he may speak . . .

Ibid.

428. Dorothy Leigh (?–1616?)

1 . . . gather hony of each flowre,
   as doth the labrous Bee.
Shee looks not who did place the Plant,
   nor how the flowre did grow;
Whether so stately up aloft,
   or neere the ground below.
But where she finds it, there she workes,
   and gets the wholsome food,
And beares it home, and layes it up,
   to doe her Countrey good.

"Counsell to my Children," prefatory poem, *The Mother's Blessing 1616*

2 . . . Feare not to be poore with Lazarus, but feare a thousand times to be rich with Dives.*

"Counsell to my Children," Ch. 6, *Ibid.*

*Latin for rich; traditionally used as the name for the unnamed rich man in Luke 16:19 ff.

3 . . . have your Children brought up with much gentlenesse and patience . . . for forwardnes and curtnesse doth harden the heart of a child, and maketh him weary of vertue.

Ch. 11, *Ibid.*

4 . . . a woman fit to be a man's wife is too good to be his servant.

Ch. 13, *Ibid.*

429. Charlotte Bregy (1619?–1693)

1 I never oppose the opinions of any; but I must own that I never adopt them to the prejudice of my own.

Letters (1688), Quoted in *Biography of Distinguished Women* by Sarah Josepha Hale* *1876*

*See 788.

2 I am indolent; I never seek pleasure and diversions, but when my friends take more pains than I do to procure them for me, I feel myself obliged to appear very gay at them, though I am not so in fact.

Ibid.

430. Margareta Ruarowna (fl. c. 1620)

1 O King . . . The nations in Thy sight are as nothing and are esteemed as vain and empty. The world before Thee is as the quivering of the balance, as the drop of the morning dew when it lights upon the earth.

from *Prayer Book* (1621), Quoted in *Women of the Reformation, Vol. III: From Spain to Scandinavia*, by Roland H. Bainton *1977*

431. Eleanor Audeley (fl. c. 1620–1651)

1 POPE. Kings I Depose, and all their Race, to Raigne.
DIVELL. And Popes to Friers I can turne againe.

A Warning to the Dragon and all his Angels 1625

2 No man so well knowes his owne frailtie, as the Lord your God knowes how prone Devotion is to Superstition.

Ibid.

432. Lucy Hutchinson (1620–1671)

1 The greatest excellency she had was the power of apprehending and the virtue of loving him; so, as his shadow, she waited on him everywhere, till he was taken into that region of light which admits of none, and then she vanished into nothing.

Journal Entry, Quoted in *Leading Women of the Restoration* by Grace Johnstone *1891*

2 'Twas not her face he loved, her honour and her virtue were his mistresses. . . .

Ibid.

433. Ninon de Lenclos (1620–1705)

1 Old age is woman's hell. (*La vieillesse est l'enfer des femmes.*)

La Coquette vengée 1659

2 We should take care to lay in a stock of provisions, but not of pleasures: these should be gathered day by day.

Correspondance authentique de Ninon de Lenclos, Émile Colombey, ed. *1886*

3 The joy of the mind is the measure of its strength. (*La joie de l'espirit est marque de sa force.*)

Ibid.

4 What you priests tell us is sheer nonsense. I don't believe a single word of it.

Quoted in *The Immortal Ninon* by Cecil Austin *1927*

5 I put your consolations by,
And care not for the hopes you give:
Since I am old enough to die,
Why should I longer wish to live?

Untitled, Ibid.

6 Love never dies of starvation, but often of indigestion.

Ch. 3, *L'Espirit des autres n.d.*

434. Jane Cavendish (1621–1669)

1 LUCENAY. My distruction is that when I marry Courtly I shall bee condemn'd to looke upon my Nose, whenever I walke and when I sitt at meate confin'd by his grave winke to looke upon the Salt, and if it bee but the paireing of his Nales to admire him.

The Concealed Fansyes, with Elizabeth Brackley *c.1644–1646*

435. Hannah Woolley (1621/23?–1675/76?)

1 . . . blows are fitter for beasts than for rational creatures.

The Gentlewoman's Companion 1675

2 . . . a woman in this age is considered learned enough if she can distinguish her husband's bed from that of another.

Ibid.

436. Leonora Christina (1621–1685)

1 . . . in the twinkling of an eye much may change; the hand of God, in whom are the hearts of kings, can change everything.

Preface, *Memoirs of Leonora Christina*, F. E. Bunnet, tr. *1929*

2 The past is rarely remembered without sorrow, for it has been either better or worse than the present.

Ibid.

3 Many a one has acquired great learning in captivity, and has gained a knowledge of things which he could not master before. Yes, imprisonment leads to heaven. I have often said to myself: "Comfort thyself, thou captive one, thou art happy."

Ibid.

4 Who can have any care for a child when one does not love its father?

"A Record of the Sufferings of the Imprisoned Countess Leonora Christina" (1674–1685), Ibid.

5 The vanished hours can ne'er come back again,
Still may the old their youthful joys retain;
The past may yet within our memory live,
And courage vigor to the old may give.

"Contemplation on Memory and Courage, recorded to the honour of God by the suffering Christian woman in the sixty-third year of her life, and the almost completed 21st year of her captivity" (1684), Ibid.

6 I am but dust and ashes,
Yet one request I crave:
Let me not go unawares
Into the silent grave.

"A Mourning Hymn," St. 6, Ibid.

7 What is all our labour here,
The servitude and yoke we bear?
Are they aught but vanity?
Art and learning what are ye?
Like a vapour all we see

Spiritual song, St. 1 (1682), Ibid.

437. Anna Trapnel (1622?–?)

1 In another Vision she saw a great company of little children walking on the earth, and a light shining round about them, and a very glorious person in the midst of them, with a Crown on his head, speaking these words: These will I honour with my Reigning presence in the midst of them, and the Oppressor shall dye in the wilderness.

Strange and Wonderful Newes from White-Hall: or, The Mighty Visions Proceeding from Mistris Anna Trapnel . . . 1654

2 Thou art not only to receive pleasures at home, but to establish Righteousness abroad.

Ibid.

437.1. Elizabeth Brackley (1623?–1663)
Coauthor with jane Cavendish; see 376.

438. Margaret Cavendish (1623/24–1673/74)

1 Mirth laughing came, and running to me, flung
Her fat white arms about my neck. . . .

"Mirth and Melancholy," *Mirth, Poems & Fancies 1653*

2 My music is the buzzing of a fly.

Ibid.

3 Since all heroic actions, public employments, powerful governments, and eloquent pleadings are denied our sex in this age, or at least would be condemned for want of a custom . . . I write.

"An Epistle to My Readers," *Nature's Pictures, Drawn by Fancies Pencil to the Life 1656*

4 A man awalking did a lady spy;
   To her he went, and when he came hard by,
   Fair Lady, Said he, why walk you alone?
   Because, said she, my thoughts are then my own.
                          "The Effeminate Description," Ibid.

5 For had my brain fancies in 't
   To fill the world, I'd put them all *in print*:
   No matter whether they be well or ill exprest,
   My *will* is done, and that please woman best.
            The True Relation of My Birth, Breeding, and Life 1656

6 LADY HAPPY. Let me tell you, that Riches ought to be bestowed
   on such as are poor, and want means to maintain themselves;
   and Youth, on those that are old; Beauty, on those that are
   ill–favoured; and Virtue, on those that are vicious: So that if I
   should place my gifts rightly, I must Marry one that's poor,
   old, ill–favoured, and debauch'd.
                    Act I, Sc. 2, *The Convent of Pleasure c. 1662*

7 LADY HAPPY. I believe, the gods are better pleased with Praises
   then Fasting; but when the Senses are dull'd with abstinency, the
   Body weakned with fasting, the Spirits tir'd with watching, the
   Life made uneasie with pain, the Soul can have but little will to
   worship: only the Imagination doth frighten it into active zeal,
   which devotion is rather forced then voluntary; so that their
   prayers rather flow out of their mouth, then spring from their
   heart, like rain-water that runs thorow [through] Gutters . . .
                                                         Ibid.

8 DICK. The truth is, Sir, that Women are always unhappy in
   their thoughts, both before and after Marriage; for, before
   Marriage they think themselves unhappy for want of a Husband; and after they are Married, they think themselves
   unhappy for having a Husband.
                                            Act II, Sc. 1, Ibid.

9 COURT. They are not Civil Laws that punish Lovers.
   ADVISER. But those are Civil Laws that punish Adulterers.
   COURT. Those are Barbarous Laws that make Love Adultery.
   ADVISER. No, Those are Barbarous that make Adultery Love.
                                            Act II, Sc. 4, Ibid.

10 LADY VICTORIA. Now or never is the time to prove the courage
   of our sex, to get liberty and freedome from the Female Slavery,
   and to make our selves equal with men: for shall Men only sit in
   Honours chair, and Women stand as waiters by? Shall only Men
   in triumphant Chariots ride, and Women run as Captives by?
   Shall only men be Conquerors, and women Slaves? Shall only
   men live by Fame, and women dy in Oblivion?
                                       Bell in Campo, Playes 1662

11 LADY SANSPAREILLE. . . . some men are so inconsiderately wise,
   gravely foolish and lowly base, as they had rather be thought
   cuckolds, than their wives should be thought wits, for fear the
   world should think their wife the wiser of the two . . .
                      In Youth's Glory and Earth's Banquet, Ibid.

12 Many times married women desire children, as maids do husbands, more for honour than for comfort or happiness, thinking
   it a disgrace to live old maids, and so likewise to be barren.
                                         Sociable Letters 1664

13 Women's minds are like shops of small–wares, wherein some
   have pretty toys, but nothing of any great value.
                                                         Ibid.

14 But nature be thanked, she has been so bountiful to us as we
   oftener enslave men than men enslave us. They seem to govern

the world, but we really govern the world in that we govern
men. For what man is he that is not governed by a woman,
more or less?
                                            Letter XVI, Ibid.

15 . . . one may be my very good friend, and yet not of my opinion.
                                                         Ibid.

16 Everyone's conscience in religion is between God and themselves, and it belongs to none other.
                                                         Ibid.

17 . . . I think a bad husband is far worse than no husband, and
   to have unnatural children is more unhappy than to have no
   children.
                                            Letter XCIII, Ibid.

18 I had rather die in the adventure of noble achievements, than
   live in obscure and sluggish security.
         The Description of a New World Called the Blazing World
                                                         1666

19 Women make poems? burn them, burn them,
   Let them make bone-lace, let them make bone-lace
         (1662), Quoted in *Reconstructing Aphra** by Angeline
                                                  Goreau 1980
   *Aphra Behn; see 469.

20 Whereas in nature we have as clear an understanding as men,
   if we were bred in schools to mature our brains and to manure
   our understandings, that we might bring forth the fruits of
   knowledge.
                "The Preface to the Reader," *The World's Olio n.d.*

21 . . . for all the Brothers were Valiant, and all the Sisters virtuous.
                          Epitaph, Westminster Abbey *n.d.*

439. Mary of Warwick (1624–1678)

1 O Lord, from my soul I bless Thee for making me again remember the wormwood and the gall I had met with from all my
   worldly enjoyments, to which I had too much let out my heart,
   and from which I did foolishly expect too much comfort.
         Diary (December 2, 1672), Quoted in *Leading Women of
                       the Restoration* by Grace Johnstone 1891

2 I will begin my first rule of advice to your lordship, with desiring you not to turn the day into night . . . by sleeping so long
   in the morning. . . .
         Letter to George, Earl of Berkeley, "Rules for a Holy Life,"
                                                         Ibid.

3 This sweet river, which I looked upon with so much pleasure
   and delight, while it was smooth, serene, and calm, when a
   sudden tempest rose unexpectedly, and made it rough and
   troubled, proved rather frightful than delightful to me, and
   made me shut my window, and cease looking on it.
         "Upon looking out of my window at Chelsea, upon the
                                                   Thames" *n.d.*

440. Bessie Clarkstone (?–1625)

1 O for absolution! O for a drop to coole my tormented soule.
         Quoted in *The Conflict in Conscience of a deare Christian,
   named Bessie Clarkstone, in the Parish of Lanark, which she
   lay under three yeare & an half* by John Wreittoun 1631

2 Alas, I have long to live, and a wretched life . . . sighs helpe not, sobs helpe not, groanes helpe not, and prayer is faint.

Ibid.

441. Ann Fanshawe (1625–1680)

1 Endeavour to be innocent as a dove, but as wise as a serpent.

Memoirs of Ann, Lady Fanshawe
c. 1670

2 . . . it was never seen that a vicious youth terminated in a contented, cheerful old age. . . .

Ibid.

3 . . . reserve some hours daily to examine yourself and fortune; for if you embark yourself in perpetual conversation or recreation, you will certainly shipwreck your mind and fortune.

Ibid.

4 My glory and my guide, all my comfort in this life, is taken from me.* See me staggering in my path, because I expected a temporal blessing as a reward for the great innocence and integrity of his whole life.

Ibid.

*Referring to the death of her husband, Sir Richard Fanshawe (1608–1666), diplomat and author.

442. Christina of Sweden (1626–1689)

1 There is a star above us which unites souls of the first order, though worlds and ages separate them.

Maxims (1660–1680), Included in *Pensées de Christine, reine de Suède 1825*

2 Life becomes useless and insipid when we have no longer either friends or enemies.

Ibid.

3 Fools are more to be feared than the wicked.

Ibid.

4 We grow old more through indolence, than through age.

Ibid.

5 I love men, not because they are men, but because they are not women.

Ibid.

6 Confessors of princes are like men engaged in taming tigers and lions: they can induce the beasts to perform hundreds of movements and thousands of actions, so that on seeing them one might believe they were completely tamed; but when the confessor least expects it, he is knocked over by one blow of the animal's paw, which shows that such beasts can never be completely tamed.

Ibid.

7 Nuns and married women are equally unhappy, if in different ways.

Ibid.

8 As you know, no one over thirty years of age is afraid of tittle-tattle. I myself find it much less difficult to strangle a man than to fear him.

Letter (1657), Quoted in *Christina of Sweden* by Sven Stolpe *1960*

9 God has neither form nor shape under which we can know Him; when he speaks of Himself in metaphors and similes, He is adapting Himself to our foolishness, our limited capacity.

Marginal notes (c.1684), Ibid.

443. Marie de Sévigné (1626–1696)

1 I love you so passionately that I hide a great part of my love not to oppress you with it.

Letter to Françoise Marguerite, the Comtesse de Grignan,* her daughter, *Letters of Madame de Sévigné to Her Daughter and Friends 1811*

*See 472.

2 . . . the most astonishing, the most surprising, the most marvelous, the most miraculous, the most magnificent, the most confounding, the most unheard of, the most singular, the most extraordinary, the most incredible, the most unforeseen, the greatest, the least, the rarest, the most common, the most public, the most private till today . . . I cannot bring myself to tell you: guess what it is.

Letter to M. de Coulanges, Ibid.

3 If I inflict wounds, I heal them.

from letters to her daughter, Ibid.

4 There is no real evil in life, except great pain; all the rest is imaginary, and depends on the light in which we view things.

Ibid.

5 There is no person who is not dangerous for someone. (*Il n'y a personne qui ne soit dangereux pour quelqu'un.*)

Ibid.

6 . . . lonely as a violet, easy to be hid. . . .

Ibid.

7 When I step into this library, I cannot understand why I ever step out of it.

Ibid.

8 Ah, how easy it really is to live with me! A little gentleness, a little social impulse, a little confidence, even superficial, will lead me such a long way.

Ibid.

9 We like so much to hear people talk of us and our motives, that we are charmed even when they abuse us.

Ibid.

10 The desire to be singular and to astonish by ways out of the common seems to me to be the source of many virtues.

Ibid.

11 There is nothing so lovely as to be beautiful. Beauty is a gift of God and we should cherish it as such.

Ibid.

12 I have seen the Abbé de la Vergne; we talked about my soul; he says that unless he can lock me up, not stir a step from me, take me to and from church himself, and neither let me read, speak, nor hear a single thing, he will have nothing to do with me whatever.

Ibid.

13 It is sometimes best to slip over thoughts and not go to the bottom of them. (*Il faut glisser sur les pensées et ne pas les approfondir.*)

Ibid.

14 The mind should be at peace but the heart debauches it perpetually.

Ibid.

15 . . . long journeys are strange things: if we were always to continue in the same mind we are in at the end of a journey, we should never stir from the place we were then in; but Providence in kindness to us causes us to forget it. It is much the same with lying-in women. Heaven permits the forgetfulness that the world may be peopled, and that folks may take journeys to Provence.

(31 May 1671) Ibid.

16 True friendship is never serene.

(10 September 1671) Ibid.

17 Luck is always on the side of the big battalions. *(La fortune est toujours pour les gros battaillons.)*

(22 December 1673) Ibid.

18 . . . it seldom happens, I think, that a man has the civility to die when all the world wishes it.

(1 March 1680) Ibid.

19 . . . a lucky marriage pays for all.

(11 September 1680) Ibid.

20 . . . this life is a perpetual chequer-work of good and evil, pleasure and pain. When in possession of what we desire, we are only so much the nearer losing it; and when at a distance from it, we live in expectation of enjoying it again. It is our business, therefore, to take things as God is pleased to send them.

(22 September 1680) Ibid.

21 We are always on the side of those who speak last.

Letter to Marie de Rabutin-Chantal, Marquise de Sévigné (1671), Ibid.

444. Ann-Marie-Louise d'Orléans (1627–1693)

1 . . . self-love is scarcely conducive to piety.

"Self-Portrait," *Mademoiselle's Portrait Gallery*
1657

2 . . . fate has been more lacking in judgement than I, for had it had more sense it would doubtless have treated me better.

Ibid.

3 Children who are the object of great respect . . . usually become horribly puffed up.

From *Memoirs* (1652–1688), Quoted in *The Grand Mademoiselle*, Francis Steegmuller, tr. *1956*

4 Nothing so disfigures a person, to my taste, as the inability to *talk*. . . .

Ibid.

5 . . . there is no doubt that Cupid is French. . . .

Ibid.

6 The sight of a person of my quality exposing himself to danger always does wonders for a population.

Ibid.

7 There is nothing so tiresome as other people's business.

Ibid.

445. Dorothy Osborne (1627–1695)

1 . . . there are certain things that custom has made almost of absolute necessity, and reputation I take to be one of those . . .

Letter (c. 1653), *Letters*, E. A. Perry, ed. *1914*

2 All letters, methinks, should be as free and easy as one's discourse, not studied as an oration, nor made up of hard words like a charm.

Letter to Sir William Temple (October 1653), Ibid.

446. Alice Thornton (1627–1707)

1 Therefore it highly concerned me to enter into this greatest change of my life [marriage] with abundance of fear and caution, not lightly, nor unadvisedly, nor, as I may take my God to witness that knows the secrets of hearts, I did it not to fulfill the lusts of the flesh, but in chastity and singleness of heart, as marrying in the Lord.

The Autobiography of Mrs. Alice Thornton, of East Newton, Co. York 1875

447. Dorothy Berry (fl. c. 1630)

1 Whose Noble Praise
Deserves a Quill pluckt from an Angels wing,
And none to write it but a Crowned King.

Dedicatory Poem, Quoted in *A Chaine of Pearle. Or A Memoriall of the peerless Graces, and Heroick Vertues of Queene Elizabeth,* * *Glorious Memory* by Diana Primrose* *
1630

*Elizabeth I; see 331. **See 449.

2 Shee, Shee* it was, that gave us Golden Daies

Ibid.

*Elizabeth I. See 331.

448. Mary Dyer (fl. c. 1630s–1660)

1 In obedience to the will of the Lord I came and in His will I abide faithful to the death.

Last words on the gallows (Boston, 1 June 1660), Quoted in *Notable American Women*, Edward T. James, ed. *1971*

2 My life not availeth me in comparison of the liberty of the truth.

Carved on monument to Mary Dyer at the Boston Statehouse *n.d.*

449. Diana Primrose (fl. c. 1630)

1 . . . Great Eliza,* England's brightest Sun,

"The Induction," *A Chaine of Pearle. Or A Memoriall of the peerless Graces, and Heroick Vertues of Queene Elizabeth, of Glorious Memory 1630*

*Elizabeth I; see 331.

2 . . . that Vestall Fire
Still flaming, never would Shee condescend
To Hymen's* Rightes. . . .

"The Second Pearle. Chastity," Ibid.

*Eponymous god of fruitfulness; also, in Attic legend, representative of married life.

3 O Golden Age! O blest and happy years!
O music sweeter than that of the Spheres!
When Prince and People mutually agree
In sacred concord and sweet symphony!

"The Fourth Pearle. Temperance," Ibid.

450. Anne Wentworth (1630?–?)

1 I had spent out all my natural strength of body in obedience to satisfy the unreasonable will of my earthly Husband, and laid my body as the ground, and as the street for him to go over for 18 years together, and keep silent, for thou O Lord did'st it, and afflicted me less than I deserved, and now the Lord sees my Husband hath as much need of this as I had of his being so great a scourge and lash to me.
A true Account of Anne Wentworths Being cruelly, unjustly, and unchristianly dealt with by some of those people called Anabaptists . . . 1676

2 And there is no repentance in the Grave . . .
Revelation IX (9 April), *The Revelation of Jesus Christ,*
Vickie Taft, ed. 1676

3 Saints love God, and will love no other
Revelation XV (3 August), Ibid.

4 Some are guilty of so much, that they cannot enter, except God give them repentance.
Revelation I (6 September 1677), Ibid.

5 For my message is Truth, and in it there is no Lye,
But Mercy and Judgment, that is still the Cry.
You may take it or leave it, that is all one to me,
For Judgments will come, good and bad, you will see:
Revelation VI (8 March 1679), Ibid.

451. R. M. (?–1630?)

1 Women that are chaste when they are trusted, prove often wantons when they are Causelesse suspected.
"Live Within Compasse in Chastitie," *The Mothers Counsell or, Live within Compasse. Being the last Will and Testament to her dearest Daughter 1630*

2 There cannot be a greater clog to man than to be troubled with a wanton woman.
"Out of Compasse in Chastitie is Wantonesse," Ibid.

3 Heaven made Beauty like itselfe to view,
Not to be lockt up in a smokie mew:
A rosie vertuous cheeke is heavens gold,
Which all men joy to touch, all to behold.
"Live Within Compasse in Beautie," Ibid.

4 To frivolous questions silence is ever the best answer.
"Live Within Compasse in Humilitie," Ibid.

5 When Dogs fall on snarling, Serpents on hissing, and Women on weeping, the first meanes to bite, the second to sting, and the last to deceive.
"Out of Compasse in Humilitie is Pride," Ibid.

452. Katherine Fowler Philips (1631–1664)

1 Who to another does his heart submit,
Makes his own idol, and then worships it
"Against Love," St. 2, Poems, *By the Incomparable Mrs. K. P. 1664*

2 How soon we curse what erst we did adore.
"A Sea-Voyage From Tenby to Bristol, Begun September 5, 1652. Sent From Bristol to Lucasia, September 8, 1652,"
Ibid.

3 He who commands himself is more a prince,
Than he who nations keep in awe
Untitled, Ibid.

4 *Christ* will be King, but I ne'er understood
His Subjects built his Kingdom up with
Blood
"Upon the Double Murther of King Charles I in Answer to a Libellous Copy of Rimes by Vavasor Powell," *Poems. By the most deservedly Admired Mrs. Katherine Philips, the Matchless Orinda** . . . 1678
*Philips's pseudonym.

5 Slander must follow Treason. . . .
Ibid.

6 They are, and yet they are not, two.
"Friendship in Embleme, or the Seal. To my Dearest Lucasia," St. 6, Ibid.

7 Such horrid Ignorance benights the Times,
That Wit and Honour are become our Crimes.
"The Prince of Phancy",* Ibid.
*William Cartwright (1611–1643), poet, playwright, wit, scholar.

8 A Chosen Privacy, a cheap Content,
And all the Peace a Friendship ever lent,
A Rock which civil Nature made a Seat,
A Willow that repulses all the heat
"A Revery," Ibid.

9 He only dies untimely who dies late.
For if 'twere told to Children in the Womb,
To what a Stage of Mischiefs they must come
. . . .
what we call their Birth would count their Death.
"2 Cor. 5, 19. God was in Christ Reconciling the World to himself," Ibid.

10 I did but see him, and he dis-appear'd,
I did but pluck the Rose–bud and it fell
"Orinda upon little Hector Philips,"* St. 2, Ibid.
*Her son.

11 I'm so entangl'd and so lost a thing
By all the shocks my daily sorrow bring
"Orinda to Lucasia parting October, 1661, at London," Ibid.

12 But I can love, and love at such a pitch,
As I dare boast it will ev'n you enrich
"To my Lady M[argaret] Cavendish, chusing the Name of Polycrite," Ibid.
*See 438.

13 For kindness is a Mine, when great and true,
Of Nobler Ore than even *Indians* knew;
'Tis all that Mortals can on Heav'n bestow,
And all that Heav'n can value here below.
Ibid.

14 For my sake talk of Graves no more
"To my Atenor,* March 16, 1661/2," Ibid.
*Her friend, Philip James.

15 Death is as coy a thing as Love.
Ibid.

16 And when our Fortune's most severe,
The less we have, the less we fear.
Ibid.

17 Woes have their Ebb as well as Flood

               Ibid.

18 Friendship's an abstract of this noble flame,
   "Tis love refin'd, and purged from all its dross,
   "Tis next to angel's love, if not the same,
   As strong in passion is, though not so gross.

               "Friendship," *Ibid.*

19 Poets and friends are born to what they are.

               Ibid.

20 . . . we may generally conclude the Marriage of a Friend to be the Funeral of a Friendship. . . .

               Ibid.

21 Waste not in vain the crystal Day,
   But gather your Rose-buds while you may.

               Ibid.

453. Marie-Catherine Desjardins (1632–1683)

1 Beautiful lovers, hold your tongues, you err to the extreme;
   Taking turns a hundred times to say: I love you.
   In love, one must speak with elegance.

     "Madrigal," Elaine T. Partnow,* tr., Quoted in *Biography of Distinguished Women* by Sarah Josepha Hale** 1876
   *See 2870. **See 788.

2 A sweet languor takes me from my senses,
   I die away in the arms of my faithful lover,
   and in this death I rediscover life.
   (*Une douce langueur m'ôte le sentiment;*
   Je Meurs entre les bras de mon fidèle amant,
   Et c'est dans cette mort que je trouve la vie.)
     Untitled sonnet, Quoted in *Precious Women* by Dorothy Backer *1974*

454. Anne Wharton (1632?–1685)

1 May yours* excel the matchless Sappho's** name;
   May you have all her wit, without her shame.
            "The Temple of Death" *1695*
   *The English writer Aphra Behn; see 469. **See 46.

2 Sorrow may make a silent moan,
   But joy will be revealed.
     Untitled, St. 2, *Tooke's* Collection of Miscellaneous Poems* *n.d.*
   *Probably John Horne Tooke (1736–1812), English politician and philologist.

455. Kawai Chigetsu-Ni (1632–1736)

1 Grasshoppers
   Chirping in the sleeves
   Of a scarecrow.
     Untitled haiku, *The Burning Heart: Women Poets of Japan,* Kenneth Rexroth and Ikuko Atsumi, eds. and trs. *1977*

456. Catharina Regina von Greiffenberg (1633–1694)

1 You empress of the stars, the heaven's worthy crown,

   The world's great eye, and soul of all spreading earth
     "Spring–Joy Praising God. Praise of the Sun," St. 1, George C. Schoolfield, tr., *Anthology of German Poetry through the Nineteenth Century,* Alexander Gode and Frederick Ungar, eds. *1963*

2 You mirror-spectrum-glance, you many-colored gleam!
   You glitter to and fro, are incomprehensibly clear
     "On the Ineffable Inspiration of the Holy Spirit," St. 3, *Geistliche Sonnette* (1662), Michael Hamburger, tr., *The Penguin Book of Women Poets,* Carol Cosman, Joan Keefe and Kathleen Weaver, eds. *1978*

457. Marie Madeleine de La Fayette (1634–1692/93)

1 Most mothers think that to keep young people away from love-making it is enough never to speak of it in their presence.
        The Princess of Clèves, First Part *1678*

2 Ambition and love-making were the soul of this Court,* and obsessed the minds of men and women alike.

               Ibid.

   *The court of Henry II of France.

3 "If you judge by appearances in this place," replied Madame de Chartres, "you will often be deceived; what appears on the surface is almost never the truth."

               Ibid.

4 "I was wrong in believing there was a man capable of hiding what pleases his vanity."

            Third Part, *Ibid.*

5 " . . . all who marry Mistresses who love them tremble when they marry them, and have fears with regard to other men when they remember their wives' conduct with themselves. . . . "

            Fourth Part, *Ibid.*

6 The necessity of dying, which she saw close at hand, accustomed her to detaching herself from everything. . . .

               Ibid.

7 A new torment was added to those she had already: The Count of Tende became as enamored of her as if she hadn't been his wife; he never left her and wanted to retake all his rights, which he had previously spurned.
     La Comtesse de Tende, Christy Sheffield Sanford, tr. (on-line 1996) *1718*

8 The shame and the unhappiness of libertinism presented itself to her spirit; she saw the abyss, where she was hurling herself and she resolved to avoid it.

               Ibid.

9 One cedes easily to that which is pleasing; . . .

               Ibid.

458. Mary Evelyn (1634–1709)

1 Whoever has a mind to abundance of Trouble,
   Let him furnish himself with a Ship and a Woman,
   For no two things will find you more Employment,
   If once you begin to Rig them out with all their Streamers.
     A Voyage to Maryland; or, The Ladies Dressing-Room 1690

459. Mary Rowlandson (1635?–post-1678)

1 I had often before this said, that if the Indians should come, I should chuse rather to be killed by them than taken alive but when it came to the tryal my mind changed; their glittering weapons so daunted my spirit, that I chose rather to go along

with those (as I may say) ravenous Bears, then that moment to end my dayes.

The Sovereignty & Goodness of God, Together, with the Faithfulness of His Promises Displayed; Being a Narrative of the Captivity and Restauration of Mrs. Mary Rowlandson 1682

2 Now is the dreadful hour come, that I have often heard of (in time of war, as it was the case of others), but now mine eyes see it. Some in our house were fighting for their lives, others wallowing in their blood, the house on fire over our heads, and the bloody heathen ready to knock us on the head, if we stirred out.

Ibid.

3 It is a solemn sight to see so many Christians lying in their blood, some here, and some there, like a company of sheep torn by wolves, all of them stripped naked by a company of hell-hounds, roaring, singing, ranting, and insulting, as if they would have torn our very hearts out; yet the Lord by His almighty power preserved a number of us from death, for there were twenty-four of us taken alive and carried captive.

Ibid.

460. Françoise de Maintenon (1635–1719)

1 Nothing is more adroit than irreproachable conduct.

Motto, *Maximes de Mme de Maintenon 1686*

2 Delicacy is to love what grace is to beauty.

Ibid.

3 . . . teach them to be extremely moderate about reading, to always prefer work with the hands, the cares of the house, duties of their station. They need infinitely more to learn to conduct themselves in a Christian fashion in the world and to govern their families with wisdom than to play *savantes* and heroines.

Note to teachers at Saint-Cyr (p. 101), Quoted in *Madame de Maintenon et la Maison Royale de Saint-Cyr (1688–1793)* by Théophile Lavallée *1862*

4 Far from complaining and grumbling about the aid that war obliges [the state] to draw from its people, you should induce others to yield to it, because the general need of the State is that of each private person, who cannot be safe at home if not protected from enemies.

Note to Saint-Cyr graduate (pp. 334–35), Ibid.

5 Frankness does not consist in saying a great deal, but in saying everything, and this everything is soon said when one is sincere, because there is no need of a great flourish and because one does not need many words to open the heart.

Letter to Madame de Saint-Périer (21 October 1708), *Lettres sur l'education des filles 1854*

6 . . . thanks to the goodness of God, I have no passions, that is to say, I love no one to the point of being willing to do anything that God would not approve.

Remark to Madame Glapion (October 1708), *Lettres historiques et édifantes*, Vol. II *1856*

7 [I wish] to remain an enigma to posterity.

Correspondance générale de Mme de Maintenon, Vol. I, Théophile Lavallée, ed. *1865–1866*

8 The longer I live, the more I grow in the opinion that it is useless to pile up wealth.

Letter to Madame de Brinon (April 1683), Vol. II, Ibid.

9 There are few women who have sufficiently solid minds to carry great learning without a yet greater arrogance; furthermore, women never know but half-way, and the little they know generally renders them proud, disdainful, loquacious, and disgusted with essential matters.

Quoted in *Souvenirs d'une Bleue élève à Saint-Cyr . . .* (p. 104) *1897*

10 I spent my youth with what one calls *beaux esprits*, who, finding me to have a good memory, undertook to make me learned but, when I saw that the best usage a person of our sex can make of science is to hide it, I thought that it was very useless to tire oneself out in order to acquire a thing which one must never use.

Ibid.

11 You know that my mania is to make people hear reason.

Letter to Madame de Ventadour (February 1692), *Lettres*, Vol. I, Marcel Langlois, ed. *1935–1939*

12 I am determined to aid those who aid themselves, and to let the good-for-nothing suffer.

Ibid.

13 [Marriage is] a state that causes the misery of three quarters of the human race.

Letter to Gobelin (1 August 1674), Ibid.

14 I would not do it [domestic work] for anything in the world. Who, me? who has an enlightened wit? I would be stooping in these sorts of things. I can only enjoy myself with rhetoricians, philosophers, poets, in a word with *beaux esprits*.

from "Sur le bon esprit entre hit demoiselles," cited in "*Noblesse*, Domesticity, and Social Reform: The Education of Girls by Fénelon and Saint-Cyr" by Carolyn C. Lougee, *History of Education Quarterly Spring 1974*

461. Rachel Russell (1636–1723)

1 . . . so little we distinguish how, and why we love, to me it argues a prodigious fondness of one's self. . . .

Letter to Dr. Fitzwilliam, *Letters c. 1793*

2 I was too rich in possessions whilst I possessed him*. . . .

Ibid.

*Her husband, Lord William Russell, first Duke of Bedford.

3 . . . that biggest blessing of loving and being loved by those I loved and respected; on earth no enjoyment certainly to be put in the balance with it.

Letter to the Earl of Galway, Ibid.

4 . . . the conversation of friends . . . is the nearest approach we can make to heaven while we live in these tabernacles of clay; so it is in a temporal sense also, the most pleasant and the most profitable improvement we can make of the time we are to spend on earth.

Letter to Lady Sunderland, Ibid.

5 . . . who would live and not love?

Ibid.

462. Antoinette Deshoulières (1638–1694)

1 It isn't easy for one who thinks
To be honest, and yet play the game;
The desire for gain, a day and night occupation,

Is a dangerous spur
That goads one towards jeopardy.
> Untitled poem, Elaine T. Partnow,* tr., Quoted in *Biography of Distinguished Women* by Sarah Josepha Hale** *1876*
> *See 2870. **See 788.

2   Alas! little sheep, you are blessed!
You pass through our fields without care, without alarm.
> "Idylle," Elaine T. Partnow,* tr., from *Les Moutons* (1695), Ibid.
> *See 2870.

3   No one is satisfied with his fortune, nor dissatisfied with his intellect.
(*Nul n'est content de sa fortune; Ni mécontent de son esprit.*)
> "Epigram" *n.d.*

463. Makhfi (1639–1703)

1   I want to go to the desert
but modesty is chains on my feet.
> Untitled, Willis Barnstone, tr., *A Book of Women Poets*, Aliki and Willis Barnstone, eds. *1980*

2   My tears break forth, my will is overridden,
Reason retreats and resolutions wane;
The stormy bursts of weeping come unbidden,
Wayward and fitful as the April rain.
> Untitled, St. 2, Paul Whalley, tr., *Women Poets of the World*, Joanna Bankier and Deirdre Lashgari, eds. 1983

464. Johanna Cartwright (fl. c. 1640)

1   And that this Nation of England, with the Inhabitants of the Nether-lands, shall be the first and readiest to transport Izraells Sons & Daughters in their Ships to the Land promised to their fore-Fathers, Abraham, Isaac, and Jacob, for an everlasting Inheritance.
For the glorious manifestation whereof, and pyous meanes thereunto, your Petitioners humbly pray that the inhumane cruel Statute of banishment made against them, may be repealed, and they under the Christian banner of charity, and brotherly love, may again be received and permitted to trade and dwell amongst you in this Land, as now they do in the Nether-lands.
> *The Petition of the Jewes, For the Repealing of the Act of Parliament for their banishment out of England 1649*

465. Joane Hit-him-home (fl. c. 1640)

Coauthor with Mary Tattlewell; see 467.

466. Anna Hume (fl. c. 1640)

1   Reader, I have oft been told,
Verses that speak not Love are cold.
> "To the Reader," *The Triumphs of Love, Chastity, Death: translated out of Petrarch** 1644*
> *Italian poet (1304–74).

2   The fatal hour of her short life drew near,
That doubtful passage which the world doth fear
> "The Triumph of Death," Ch. 1, Ibid.

467. Mary Tattlewell (fl. c. 1640)

1   . . . what have we women done,
That any one who was a mother's sonne
Should thus affront our sex? Hath he forgot

From whence he came? or doth he seek to blot
His own conception?
> "Epistle to the Reader: Long Megge of Westminster, hearing the abuse, offeres to women to riseth out of her grave and thus speaketh," with Joane Hit–him–home* *1640*
> *See 465.

2   . . . the corrupt heart discovereth itself by the lewd tongue.
> Essay, Ibid.

3   Nature hath bestowed upon us two eares, and two eyes, yet but one tongue; which is an Embleme unto us that though we heare and see much, yet ought wee to speak but little. . . .
> Ibid.

4   . . . even fooles being silent have passed for wise men. . . .
> Ibid.

5   . . . hee never came to me empty mouth'd or handed; for he was never unprovided of stew'd Anagrams, bak'd Epigrams, sous'd Madrigalls, pickled Round delayes, broyld Sonnets, parboild Elegies, perfum'd poesies for Rings, and a thousand other such foolish flatteries, and knavish devices. . . .
> Ibid.

468. Ephelia (fl. c. 1640–1681?)

1   Beauty's but the smallest Grace,
Unless it be i'th' Mind as well as Face:
> "Acrostic," *Female Poems On Several Occasions 1679*

2   If you her Wit, or Plot, or Fancy blame,
When you Addresses make, She'll do the same;
But if you'll Clap the Play, and Praise the Rhyme,
She'll do as much for you another time.
> "Epilogue," Ibid.

3   Whole Months but hours seem, when you are here,
When absent, every Minute is a Year:
> "First Farewell to J.G.," Ibid.

4   Great Love, I yield; send no more Darts in vain,
I am already fond of my soft Chain;
Proud of my Fetters, so pleased with my state,
That I the very Thoughts of Freedom hate.
> "Love's First Approach," Ibid.

5   Be kind for once then to a Female Pen.
When you with women in discourse do sit,
Before their Faces you'll commend their wit,
Pray flatter now, the Poet heareth it:
> "Prologue to the Pair-Royal of Coxcombs," Ibid.

6   How strangely is my Life perplexed by fate!
I would not Love, and yet I cannot hate.
> "To a Gentleman that durst not pass the door while I stood there," last lines, Ibid.

7   Oh! if you Love not, plainly say you hate,
And give my Miseries a shorter date,
> "To J.G.," Ibid.

8   Why do I Love? go, ask the Glorious Sun
Why every day it round the world doth Run:
Ask *Thames* and *Tiber*, why they Ebb and Flow:
Ask Damask Roses, why in *June* they blow:
> "To one that asked me why I loved J.G." last lines, Ibid.

9 How Happy was the World before men found
  Those metals, Nature hid beneath the Ground!
  All Necessary things She placed in View,
  But this She wisely hid, because She knew
  That it destructive to her work would be,
  And jar the consort of her Harmony:

  "Wealth's Power," Ibid.

469. Aphra Behn (1640–1689)

1 Who is't that to women's beauty would submit,
  And yet refuse the fetters of their wit?

  Prologue, *The Forced Marriage* 1670

2 AMINITA. While to inconstancy I bid adieu, I find variety
  enough in you.

  Ibid.

3 This humour is not à la mode. . . .

  Prologue, *The Amorous Prince* 1671

4 . . . I have heard the most of that which bears the name of
  learning, and which has abused such quantities of ink and
  paper, and continually employs so many ignorant, unhappy
  souls, for ten, twelve, twenty years in a university (who yet
  poor wretches think they are doing something all the while) as
  logic, etc. and several other things (that shall be nameless lest I
  misspell them) are much more absolutely nothing than the er-
  rantist play that e'er was writ.

  " An Epistle to the Reader," *The Dutch Lover* 1673

5 ALONZO. . . . the natural itch of talking and lying. . . .

  Act. II, Sc. 6, Ibid.

6 OLINDA. . . . this marrying I do not like: 'tis like going on a
  long voyage to sea, where after a while even the calms are distasteful, and the storms dangerous: one seldom sees a new
  object, 'tis still a deal of sea, sea; husband, husband, every
  day,—till one's quite cloyed with it.

  Act. IV, Sc. 1, Ibid.

7 SIR TIMOTHY. The Devil's in her tongue, and so 'tis in most
  women's of her age; for when it has quitted the tail, it repairs
  to the upper tier.

  The Town Fop 1676

8 Come away! Poverty's catching.

  Act I, Sc. 1, *The Rover* 1677

9 WILMORE. There is no sinner like a young saint.

  Sc. 2., Ibid.

10 Variety is the soul of pleasure.

  Act II, Sc. 1, last line Ibid.

11 AGNILLICA BIANCA. Who made the laws by which you judge
   me? Men! Men who would rove and ramble require that
   women must be nice.

  Act, Sc. 2, Ibid.

12 Money speaks sense in a language all nations understand.

  Act III, Sc. 1, Ibid.

13 Conscience: a chief pretence to cozen fools withall. . . .

  Epilogue, Ibid.

14 Constancy, that current coin for fools.

  Ibid.

15 The play had no other Misfortune but that of coming out for a
   Womans: had it been owned by a Man, though the most dull
   Unthinking Rascally Scribler in Town, it had been a most ad-
   mirable Play.

  Epistle to the Reader, *Sir Patient Fancy* 1678

16 Sure he's too much a gentleman to be a scholar.

  Ibid.

17 She's a chick of the old cock.

  Act IV, Sc. 4, Ibid.

18 Quickest in finding all the subtlest ways
   To make your Joys, why not to make your Plays?

  Epilogue, Ibid.

19 The Devil take this curset plotting age,
   'T has ruin'd all our plots upon the stage;
   Suspicions, new elections, jealousies,
   Fresh informations, new discoveries,
   Do so employ the busy fearful town,
   Our honest calling here is useless grown:
   Each fool turns politician now, and wears
   A formal face, and talks of state-affairs.

  Prologue, *The Feigned Curtezans* 1679

20 Patience is a flatterer, sir—and an ass, sir.

  Act III, Sc. 1, Ibid.

21 'Tis not your saying that you love,
   Can ease me of my smart;
   Your actions must your words approve,
   Or else you break my heart.

  "Song," *Poems Upon Several Occasions* 1684

22 Take back your gold, and give me current love,
   The treasure of your heart, not of your purse.

  "On Desire," Ibid.

23 Love ceases to be a pleasure, when it ceases to be a secret.

  "Four O'Clock," *The Lover's Watch* 1686

24 All I ask, is the privilege for my masculine part, the poet in me
   . . . if I must not, because of my sex, have this freedom, I lay
   down my quill and you shall hear no more of me. . . .

  Preface, *The Lucky Chance* 1686

25 Too much curiosity lost Paradise.

  Act. III, Sc. 3, Ibid.

26 Faith, Sir, we are here to-day, and gone tomorrow.

  Act IV, Ibid.

27 Madam, 'twas a pious fraud, if it were one.

  Act V, Sc. 7, Ibid.

28 Advantages are lawful in love and war.

  Sc. 3, Ibid.

29 Of all that writ, he was the wisest bard,
   Who spoke this mighty truth—
   He that knew all that ever learning writ,
   Knew only this—that he knew nothing yet.

  Act I, Sc. 3, *The Emperor of the Moon* 1687

30 How many idiots has it [love] made wise! how many fools eloquent! how many homebred squires accomplished! how many
   cowards brave!

  The Fair Jilt 1688

31 . . . in that country . . . where the only crime and sin against a woman, is, to turn her off, to abandon her to want, shame, and misery; such ill morals are only practised in Christian countries, where they prefer the bare name of religion. . . .
Oroonko, The Royal Slave 1688

32 Love, like Reputation, once fled, never returns more.
History of the Nun 1689

33 . . . that perfect tranquility of life, which is nowhere to be found but in retreat, a faithful friend, a good library. . . .
The Lucky Mistake 1689

34 This money certainly is a most devilish thing!
The Court of the King Bantam 1696

470. Mary Coffyn Starbuck (1644/45–1717)

1 . . . such who believed once in Christ, were always in Him, without possibility of falling away; and whom He had once loved, He loved to the End . . .
Quoted in *An Account of the life of That Ancient Servant of Jesus Christ* by John Richardson *1757*

471. Nur Jahan (?–1646)

1 My eyes have one job: to cry.
Untitled, Willis Barnstone, tr., *A Book of Women Poets*, Aliki and Willis Barnstone, eds. *1980*

2 The key to my locked spirit is your laughing mouth.
Ibid.

472. Françoise de Grignan (1646/48?–1705)

1 We [women] have not enough reason to use all our strength.
(Nous n'avons pas assez de raison pour employer toute notre force.)
Letter to her mother [Mme. de Sévigné],* Quoted in *Letters of Madame de Sévigné to Her Daughter and Her Friends 1811*
*See 443.

473. Glückel of Hameln (1646–1724)

1 We sinful men are in the world as if swimming in the sea and in danger of being drowned. But our great, merciful and kind God, in his great mercy, has thrown ropes into the sea that we may take hold of them and be saved. These are our holy Torah where is written what are the rewards and punishments for good and evil deeds.
Memoirs (1692) 1896

2 The kernel of the Torah is: "Thou shalt love thy neighbour as thyself." But in our days we seldom find it so, and few are they who love their fellow men with all their heart. On the contrary, if a man can contrive to ruin his neighbour nothing pleases him more . . .
Ibid.

3 The best thing for you, my children, is to serve God from your heart without falsehood or deception, not giving out to people that you are one thing while, God forbid, in your heart you are another. Say your prayers with awe and devotion.
Ibid.

474. Maria Sibylla Merian (1647–1717)

1 From my youth I have been interested in insects. First I started with the silkworms in my native Frankfurt am Main. After

that . . . I started to collect all the caterpillars I could find in order to observe their changes . . . and I painted them very carefully on parchment.
Quoted in "A Surinam Portfolio," *Natural History December 1962*

475. Jeanne-Marie de la Motte Guyon (1648–1717)

1 But though my wing is closely bound,
My heart's at liberty;
My prison walls cannot control
The flight, the freedom of the soul.
"A Prisoner's Song," written while imprisoned at the Castle of Vincennes *c. 1695–1702*

2 There is nothing great, there is nothing holy, there is nothing wise, there is nothing fair, but to depend wholly on God, like a child who does and can do only what is bidden.
Lettres chrétiennes et spirituelles, Vol. III *1717–1718*

3 I know but one path, but one way, but one road, which is that of continual renouncement, of death, of nothingness. Everybody flies this way and seeks with passion all that makes us live; nobody is willing to be nothing, yet how shall we find what we are all seeking by a road which leads precisely wrong?
Ibid.

4 The soul is no longer either confined or possessed, nor does it possess or even enjoy; it perceives no difference between God and itself, sees nothing, possesses nothing, distinguishes nothing, even in God. God is the soul and the soul is God.
Vol. V, Ibid.

5 My condition in marriage was rather that of a slave than that of a free woman.
La Vie de Mme J.-M. B. de La Mothe Guion, écrite par elle-même [Autobiography], Vol. I *1720*

6 Let us love without reasoning about it, and we shall find ourselves filled with love before others have found out the reasons that lead to loving.
Ibid.

7 Love causes grief, but 'tis to move
And stimulate the slumbering mind;
And he has never tasted love
Who shuns a plan so graciously design'd.
"Divine Love Endures No Rival," St. 4, *The Works of William Cowper,* Comprising His Poems, Correspondence and Translations,* William Cowper, tr. *1835*
*Earl—(1664?–1773), English jurist.

8 Yet man, dim-sighted man, and rash as blind,
Deaf to the dictates of his better mind,
In frantic competition dares the skies,
And claims precedence of the Only wise.
"Glory to God Alone," St. 4, Ibid.

9 'Tis love unites what sin divides;
The centre, where all bliss resides;
"The Testimony of Divine Adoption," St. 6, Ibid.

476. Anna Tompson Hayden (1648?–1720?)

1 For none Can tell who shall be next,
Yet all may it expect;

Then surely it Concerneth all,
Their time not to neglect.
> "Upon the Death of the desireable young virgin, Elizabeth Tompson, Daughter of Joseph & Mary Tompson of Bilerika, who Deceased in Boston out of the house of Mr Legg, 24 August, 1712, aged 22 years," *Handkerchiefs from Paul: Being Pious and Consolatory Verses of Puritan Massachusetts,* Kenneth B. Murdock, ed. 1927

477. Maria Anna Mancini (1649–1714)

1 You weep, and you are the master! (*Vous pleurez, et vous êtes le maître!*)
> Remark to Louis XIV* (c.1658) in response to being sent away from Paris, *Memoires n.d.*
> *King of France (1638–1715; r. 1643–1715).

478. Anne Collins (fl. c. 1650)

1 As in a cabinet or chest
One jewel may exceed the rest.
> Untitled, St. 2, *Divine Songs and Meditacions* 1653

2 Cheerfulness
Doth express
A settled pious mind;
Which is not prone to grudging,
From murmuring refin'd.
> "Song," St. 5, Ibid.

479. Mary Morpeth (fl. c. 1650)

1 Perfection in a woman's work is rare;
From an untroubled mind should verses flow;
My discontent makes mine too muddy show;
And hoarse encumbrances of household care,
Where these remain, the Muses ne'er repair.
> "Til William Drummond, of Hawthornden," Quoted as Prefix to *Poems* by William Drummond 1656

480. Nell Gwyn (1650–1687)

1 Shall the dog lie where the deer once crouched?*
> Attributed 1685
> *Her alleged rejection of a suitor after Charles II's death; she was the king's mistress.

2 Here is a sad slaughter at Windsor, the young mens taking your Leaves and going to France, and, although they are none of my Lovers, yet I am loathe to part with the men.
> Letter to Madam Jennings (14 April 1684),
> Quoted in *The Story of Nell Gwynn* by Peter Cunningham 1892

481. Juana Inés de la Cruz (1651–1695)

1 Nothing could be funnier
Than the tale of him befouling
His own mirror, and then scowling
When the image was a blur.
> "Redondillas," St. 5, Garrett Strange, tr., *The Catholic Anthology,* Thomas Walsh, ed. 1927

2 The greater evil who is in—
When both in wayward paths are straying
The poor sinner for the pain,
Or he that pays for the sin?
> St. 9, Ibid.

3 Oh dreaded destiny and yet pursued!
> "Crimson lute that comest in the dawn . . . ," St. 4, *Anthology of Mexican Poetry,* Octavio Paz,* ed.; Samuel Beckett,** tr. 1958
> *Mexican writer (b. 1914) and Nobel laureate (1990).
> *(1906–89), Irish playwright, novelist.

4 I do not value wealth or riches,
Wherefore I shall be ever more content
To bring more richness to my mind
And not to keep my mind on riches.
> "*En perseguirme, mundo, ¿qué interesas?*" ["Oh World, Why do you thus pursue me?"], St. 2, Muriel Kittel, tr., *An Anthology of Spanish Poetry, from Garcilaso to García Lorca,* Angel Flores, ed. 1961

5 In my opinion, better far it be
To destroy vanity within my life
Than to destroy my life in vanity.
> St. 4, Ibid.

6 "*Diuturna enfermedad de la Esperanza . . .*" ("Perpetual Infirmity of Hope . . . ")
> Title of poem, Ibid.

7 Lure of the world, senescent lushness,
Imagination's decrepit verdure,
Today expected by the happy,
And by the hapless not before tomorrow.
> "Esperanza" ["Hope"], St. 2, Kate Flores, tr., Ibid.

8 What magical infusions, brewed
from herbals of the Indians
of my own country, spilled their old
enchantment over all my lines?
> "*En reconocimiento a las inimitables plumas de la Europa*" [In acknowledgment of the praises of European Writers"], St. 14, Constance Urdang, tr., Ibid.

9 Everything that you receive
is not measured according to
its actual size, but, rather, that
of the receiving vessel.
> St. 27, Ibid.

10 I believed, when I entered this convent, I was escaping from myself, but alas, poor me, I brought myself with me!
> Quoted in *Women in Myth and History* by Violeta Miqueli 1962

11 this in which flattery has undertaken
to extenuate the hideousness of years,
and, vanquishing the outrages of time,
to triumph o'er oblivion and old age,
is an empty artifice of care.
> Untitled, Samuel Beckett,* tr., *The Penguin Book of Women Poets,* Carol Cosman, Joan Keefe and Kathleen Weaver, eds. 1978

12 Critics: in your sight
no woman can win:
keep you out, and she's too tight;
she's too loose if you get in.
> Verses from "A Satirical Romance," St. 3, Ibid.

13 . . . sorting the reasons to leave you or hold you,
I find an intangible one to love you,
and many tangible ones to forego you.
> Untitled, Judith Thurman, tr., Ibid.

14 . . . as love is union, it knows no extremes of distance.
"*Repuesta a Sor Filotea*" ["Reply to Sister Philotea: 1691],
Quoted in *A Woman of Genius: The Intellectual Autobiog-
raphy of Sor Juana Inés de la Cruz* by Margaret Sayers
Peden *1982*

15 One will abide, and will confess that another is nobler than he,
that another is richer, more handsome, and even that he is
more learned, but that another is richer in reason scarcely any
will confess: *Rare is he who will concede genius.*
Ibid.

16 But, lady, as women, what wisdom may be ours if not the
philosophies of the kitchen? Lupercio Leonardo spoke well
when he said: how well one may philosophize when preparing
dinner. And I often say, when observing these trivial details:
had Aristotle* prepared victuals, he would have written more.
Ibid.

*Greek philosopher, logician and scientist (384 B.C.E.–322).

17 And I would add that a fool may reach perfection (if ignorance may tolerate perfection) by having studied his little of
philosophy and theology and by having some learning of
tongues, by which he may be a fool in many sciences and languages: a great fool cannot be contained solely by his mother
tongue.
Ibid.

18 For misuse is not the blame of art, but rather of the evil teacher
who perverts the arts, making of them the snare of the devil;
and this occurs in all the arts and sciences.
Ibid.

19 . . . in the formal and theoretical arts . . . each may illuminate
and open the way to others, by nature of their variations and
their hidden links, which were placed in this universal chain
by the wisdom of their Author in such a way that they conform and are joined together with admirable unity and
harmony.
Ibid.

20 On your most hallowed altars
no Sheban gums are burnt,
no human blood is spilt,
no throat of beast is slit,
for even warring desires
within the human breast
are a sacrifice unclean,
a tie to things material,
and only when the soul
is afire with holiness
does sacrifice glow pure,
is adoration mute.
"Phyllis," St. 2, Alan S. Trueblood, tr., *Lesbian Poetry*,
http://www.sappho.com/poetry/index.shtml
21 January 1996

21 That you're a woman far away
is no hindrance to my love:
for the soul, as you well know,
distance and sex don't count.
St. 3, Ibid.

22 When it comes to bravely posturing,
your witlessness must take the prize:
you're the child that makes a bogeyman,
and then recoils in fear and cries.
"You Men," St. 4, Ibid.

23 With you, no woman can hope to score;
whichever way, she's bound to lose;
spurning you, she's ungrateful—
succumbing, you call her lewd.
St. 7, Ibid.

24 In loss itself
I find assuagement:
having lost the treasure,
I've nothing to fear.
"Disillusionment," St. 5, Ibid.

25 No god is ever secure
against the lofty flight of human thought.
"My Divine Lysis," St. 1, Ibid.

26 Who has forbidden women to engage in private and individual
studies? Have they not a rational soul as men do? . . . I have
this inclination to study and if it is evil I am not the one who
formed me thus—I was born with it and with it I shall die.
Letter to Father Nunez (1681), *Women in World History
Curriculum*, http://home.earthlink.net/~womenwhist/
1996–97

27 . . . given the total antipathy I felt towards marriage, I deemed
convent life least unsuitable and the most honorable I could
elect if I were to ensure my salvation. . . . wishing to live alone,
and wishing to have no obligatory occupation to inhibit the
freedom of my studies, nor the sounds of a community to intrude upon the peaceful silence of my books.
4000 Years of Women in Science,
http://www.astr.ua.edu/4000WS *1 August 1997*

482. Anne Dacier (1651–1720)

1 Silence is the ornament of women.
Quoted in *Biography of Distinguished Women* by Sarah
Josepha Hale* *1876*
*See 788.

2 . . . let her [her granddaughter] conceal her learning with as
much care as she might crookedness or lameness.
Letter to her daughter, Quoted in *The Life of Lady Mary
Wortley Montagu* by Robert Halsband *1956*
*See 527.

483. Margaret Godolphin (1652–1678)

1 If you speake anything they like, say 'tis borrowed. . . .
Quoted in *The Life of Mrs. Godolphin* by John Evelyn;*
H. Sampson, ed. *1939*

2 . . . may the Clock, the Candle, may everything I see, teach and
instruct me some thing.
Ibid.

3 . . . children servants master father mouther, things that though
they are blessings yet often they prove otherwis, and the best
of them have days in which one thinkes one could live without
them. . . .
Ch. 8, Letter to John Evelyn* (July 1675), Quoted in
John Evelyn and Mrs. Godolphin by W. G. Hiscock *1951*

4 God knows a little pain makes one forget a long health, and
the unkindes of one frind maks one forget the frindship of
many for a time, for we by nateur are apter to grine than laugh,
the first sound we make is crying, our childhood is scarce anything els but frowardnes, and so but in a little more reasonable

maner we proceed till we dye, so that unles we had hops of a beter world we wear of all things most miserable. . . .

Ibid.

5 . . . our wholl life is, in my opinion, a search after remedys, which doe often, if not always, exchange rather than cuer a deseas. . . .

Ch. 11, Last letter to John Evelyn,* Ibid.
*English author and diarist (1620–1706).

484. Francisca Gregoria (1653–1710)

1 Fair plaything of the breeze tonight.
"Envying a Little Bird," *The Catholic Anthology*, Thomas Walsh, ed. *1927*

485. Elizabeth Bathurst (1655?–1685/91)

1 Oh! where was your patient Mind, that you could not hear what I had to say unto you, and have tried what Spirit I had been of, that so, if in Error, by sound Argument you might have convinced me.
"An Expostulatory Appeal to the Professors of Christianity" *1680*

486. Mary Chudleigh Lee (1656–1710)

1 MALE VOICE. Then blame us not if we our interest mind,
And would have knowledge to ourselves confined,
Since that alone pre-eminence does give,
And robbed of it we should unvalued live.
While you are ignorant, we are secure,
A little pain will your esteem procure.
The Ladies' Defence: Or, the Bride–Woman's Counsellor Answered: A Poem in a Dialogue between Sir John Brute, Sir William Loveall, Melissa, and a Parson 1701

2 The restless atoms play. . . .
Of them, composed with wondrous art,
   We are our selves a part,
And on us still they nutriment bestow;
   To us they kindly come, from us they swiftly go,
And through our veins in purple torrents flow.
   Vacuity is nowhere found,
Each place is full, with bodies we're encompassed round:
   In sounds they're to our ears conveyed,
In fragrant odors they our smell delight,
And in ten thousand curious forms displayed
   They entertain our sight.
"The Offering," Pt. One, Ibid.

3 Wife and servant are the same
But only differ in the name,
For when that fatal knot is tied,
Which nothing, nothing can divide,
When she the word *obey* has said,
And man by law supreme has made,
Then all that's kind is laid aside,
And nothing left but state and pride.
"To the Ladies," Ibid.

487. Frances Boothby (fl. c. 1660)

1 I'm hither come, but what d'ye think to say?
A Womans Pen present you with a Play:
Who smiling told me I'd be sure to see,
That once confirm'd, the House would empty be.
Not one yet gone!
Prologue, *Marcelia: or, The Treacherous Friend 1669*

2 You powerful Gods! if I must be
An injur'd offering to Love's deity,
Grant my revenge, this plague on men,
That woman ne'er may love again.
"Song," St. 1, Ibid.

488. Isobel Gowdie (fl. c. 1660)

1 When we would ride, we take windle-straws, or beanstalks, and put them betwixt our feet, and say thrice:
Horse and Hattock, horse and go,
Horse and pellattis, ho! Ho!
And immediately we fly away wherever we would.
Confession (1662), Quoted in "The Broomstick or Besom," *An ABC of Witchcraft, Past and Present* by Doreen Valiente* *1973*

*See 2219.

489. Anne Killigrew (1660?–1685)

1 More rich, more noble I will ever hold
The Muse's laurel, than a crown of gold.
"Upon the Saying That My Verses Were Made by Another," St. 2, *Poems 1686*

2 I willingly accept Cassandra's fate,
To speak the truth, although believed too late.
St. 6, Ibid.

3 But O, the laurel'd fool that doats on fame,
Who's hope's applause, whose
fear's to want a name:
Who can accept for pay
Of what he does, what others say
"The Discontent," St. 2, Ibid.

4 Too loud, O Fame! thy trumpet is too shrill
St. 3, Ibid.

5 Farewel to Unsubstantial Joyes,
Ye Gilded Nothings, Gaudy Toyes
"A Farewel to Worldly Joyes," Ibid.

6 When I am Dead, few Friends attend my Hearse,
And for a Monument, I leave my VERSE.
"An Epitaph on her Self," *in toto*, Ibid.

7 Ah! Who would them have deadly deem'd?
But Flowers do often Serpents hide.
"Complaint of a Lover," St. 6, Ibid.

8 We are *Diana's* Virgin-Train,
Descended of no Mortal Strain;
Our Bows and Arrows are our Goods,
Our Pallaces, the lofty Woods,
"On a Picture Painted by her self, representing two Nimphs of DIANA's, one in a posture to Hunt, the other Batheing," St. 1, Ibid.

9 Friendship, the Cement, that does faster twine
Two Souls, than that which Soul and Body joyn:
"The Miseries of Man," St. 4, Ibid.

10 The bloody Wolf, the Wolf does not pursue;
The Boar, though fierce, his Tusk will not embrue
In his own Kind, Bares, not on Bares do prey:
Then art thou, Man, more savage far than they.
St. 7, Ibid.

11 Now cursed Gold does lead the Man astray,
    False flatt'ring Honours do anon betray,
    Then Beauty does as dang'rously delude,
    Beauty, that vanishes, while 'tis pursu'd,
    That, while we do behold it, fades away,
    And even a Long Encomium will not stay.

                                    St. 11, Ibid.

12 How dares bold Vice unmasked walk,
    And like a Giant proudly stalk?

                         "To the Queen," St. 8, Ibid.

490. Honnamma (fl. c. 1660–1699)

1 Wasn't your mother a woman?
              Untitled, Willis Barnstone, tr., *A Book of Woman Poets*,
                           Aliki and Willis Barnstone, eds. *1980*

2 Here and in the other world
        happiness
   comes to a person, not a gender.

                                           Ibid.

491. Anne Finch (1661–1720/22?)

1 Alas! a woman that attempts the pen
   Such an intruder on the rights of men,
   Such a presumptuous Creature, is esteem'd
   The fault, can by no vertue be redeem'd.
       Introductory Verse, *Miscellany Poems on Several Occasions*
                                                      1713

2 . . . I have applied
   Sweet mirth, and music, and have tried
   A thousand other arts beside,
   To drive thee from my darkened breast,
   Thou, who has banished all my rest.
          "To Melancholy," *Miscellany Poems, Written by a Lady*
                                        1713 (repr. 1928)

3 Trail all your pikes, dispirit every drum,
   March in a slow procession from afar,
   Ye silent, ye dejected, men of war.
   Be still the hautboys, and the flute be dumb!
   Display no more, in vain, the lofty banner;
   For see where on the bier before ye lies
   The pale, the fall'n, the untimely sacrifice
   To your mistaken shrine, to your false idol
   Honour.
                       "Trail All Your Pikes," *in toto*, Ibid.

4 How gaily is at first begun
   Our life's uncertain race!
                           "Life's Progress," St. 1, Ibid.

5 To-morrow and to-morrow cheat our youth.
   In riper age, to-morrow still we cry,
   Not thinking that the present age we die,
   Unpracts'd all the good we have design'd:
   There's no to-morrow to a willing mind.
                                "No To-Morrow," Ibid.

6 Now the Jonquille o'ercomes the feeble brain;
   We faint beneath the aromatic pain.
                                    "The Spleen," Ibid.

7 He lamented for Behn,* o'er that
        place of her birth,

And said amongst women there was none
        on earth
Her superior in fancy, in language, or wit,
Yet owned that a little too loosely she writ.
                     "Aristomenes," The Introduction, Ibid.
   *Aphra Behn; see 469.

8 How are we fal'n, fal'n, by mistaken rules?
                                           Ibid.

9 Give me, O indulgent fate!
   Give me yet before I die
   A sweet, yet absolute retreat,
   'Mongst the paths so lost and trees so high
   That the world may ne'er invade
   Through such windings and such shade
   My unshaken liberty.
             "The Petition for an Absolute Retreat," Ibid.

492. Mary II of England (1662–1694)

1 There is but one command which I wish him* to obey; and
   that is, "*Husbands, love your wives.*" For myself, I shall follow the injunction, "*Wives, be obedient to your husbands in
   all things.*"
                     Quoted in *Biography of Distinguished Women*
                              by Sarah Josepha Hale** *1876*
   *Her husband, William III (1650–1702), king of England from
   1689 to 1702. **See 788.

493. Kata Szidónia Petröczi (1662–1708)

1 Hourly I howl the change in my fate.
          "Swift Floods," St. 1, Laura Schiff, tr, *Women Poets of the
                  World*, Joanna Bankier and Deirdre Lashgari, eds. *1983*

2 The winds of sadness lay siege
   To my forsaken mind, my wounded heart.
                                           St. 2, Ibid.

494. Delariviere Manley (1663/72–1724)

1 BELIRA. Poor cavillier, those who can jest with oaths can play
   with words.
            Act IV, Sc. ii, *The Lost Lover, or: The Jealous Husband*
                                                      1696

2 BELIRA. I would exchange thee for the last of men, and think
   the bargain cheap; would part with all that goodly form for
   honest ugliness, and think it fairer; thy youth for age, and doat
   upon his dotage, so in return I found but truth, mark well that
   word, that word has charms thou never knewest, and which
   out-weighs thine.

                                           Ibid.

3 WILMORE. What woman's fair after we find her faulty? What
   lady innocent when no longer chaste? Or who so vain to hope
   for honour, or for pity from that soul who wants it for herself?
                                           Ibid.

4 WILMORE. . . . vows that are made in love are writ in sand.
                                    Act V, Sc. iii, Ibid.

5 ACMAT (a eunuch, speaking to the prince of Homais of
       his lady's behavior toward the prince's portrait].
   How often have I seen this lovely Venus
   Naked, extended, in the gaudy Bed,
   Her snowy Breasts all panting with desire,

With gazing, melting Eyes, survey your Form,
And wish in vain, 't had Life to fill her Arms.
> *The Royal Mischief 1696*

495. Elizabeth Bradford (1663–1731)

For 'tis no humane knowledge gain'd by art,
But rather 'tis inspir'd into the heart
By divine means; for true divinity
Hath with this science great affinity
> Preface, "To the Reader, in Vindication of this Book,"
> Quoted in *War With the Devil* by Benjamin Keach *1707*

496. Elisabeth-Claude Jacquet de la Guerre (1664–1729)

1 He thinks he can escape the Lord by merely moving to a new place.
> Recitatif, St. 2, *Jonas Cantata n.d.*

2 Such adversity! It seems that the world is returning to its primal, chaotic state.
> Air, St. 1, Ibid.

497. Marie Jeanne L'Heritier (1664–1734)

1 You care for nothing but loving and joking.
> "Rondeau, to a Young Girl," Elaine T. Partnow,* tr.,
> Quoted in *Biography of Distinguished Women*
> by Sarah Josepha Hale** *1876*

*See 2870. **See 788.

498. Anne of England (1665–1714)

1 O, my dear brother, how I pity thee!
> Remark to her brother, the future King William III,*
> on her deathbed (20 July 1714), Quoted in *Biography of
> Distinguished Women* by Sarah Josepha Hale** *1876*

* (1650–1702; r. 1689–1702) **See 788.

499. Henrietta Johnston (1665?–1728/29)

1 . . . reason and conscience startle not.
> Letter to her husband (August 1713), Quoted in
> *Henrietta Johnston, America's First Pastellist*
> by Margaret Simons Middleton *1966*

500. Grisell Home (1665–1746)

1 When bonny young Johnnie cam' o'er the sea,
He said he saw naething sae lovely as me. . . .
> "Warena My Heart Licht I Wad Dee," *Scottish Song*,
> Mary Carlyle Aitken, ed. *1874*

501. Mary Griffith Pix (1666–1720?)

1 Deceiver Deceived, and Imposture cheated!. . . .
Our authoress, like true woman, showed her play
To some, who, like true wits, stole't half away.*
> Prologue, *The Deceiver Deceived 1698*

*Reference to the plagiarism charges she and playwright William Congreve brought against George Powell for his work, *The Imposture Defeated.*

2 The First Time she was grave, as well she might,
For Women will be damn'd sullen the first Night;
But faith, they'll quickly mend, so be n't uneasie:
To Night she's brisk, and trys New Tricks to please ye.
> Prologue, *The Spanish Wives 1696*

3 . . . instead of making his life easie with jolly *Bona-robas* [courtesans], [he] dotes on a Platonick Mistress, who never allows him greater favours than to read Plays to her, kiss her hand, and fetch Heart-breaking Sighs at her Feet.
> *The Innocent Mistress 1697*

4 MRS. RICH. . . . I quarrel daily with my destiny, that I was not at first a woman of quality . . . I had rather be the beggarliest countess in the town, than the widow of the richest banker in Europe.
> Act I, Sc. 1, *The Beau Defeated 1700*

5 LAURA. I find an Englishman true to one woman, nay even before he has had her is a miracle.
> Act II, Sc. ii, *The Adventures in Madrid 1706*

6 GAYLOVE. Oh the affairs of love are quite different from those of war. We yield to all conditions before the engagement, but end alike, for when we have taken the town, we seldom keep them.
> Act III, Sc. ii, Ibid.

502. Sophia Dorothea of Celle (1666–1726)

1 . . . my illness only comes from loving you, and I do not want to be cured of it.
> Letter to George I (c.1689–1694), Quoted in *Lives of the
> Hanoverian Queens of England* by Alice Drayton Greenwood *1909*

503. Sarah Kemble Knight (1666–1727)

1 May all that dread the cruel fiend of night
Keep on, and not at this curs't mansion light.
> Untitled (c.1704), *The Journal of Madame Knight*,
> Theodore Dwight, Jr., ed. *1825*

2 I ask thy Aid, O Potent Rum!
To charm these wrangling Topers Dum.
Thou hast their Giddy Brains possest—
The man confounded with the Beast—
And I, poor I, can get no rest.
Intoxicate them with thy fumes;
O still their Tongues till morning comes!
> "Resentments Composed because of the Clamor of Town
> Topers [drunkards] Outside My Apartment," *in toto*, Ibid.

504. Mary Astell (1666/8–1731)

1 Women are from their very infancy debarr'd those advantages [of education] with the want of which they are afterwards reproached, nursed up in those vices with which will hereafter be upbraided them. So partial are Men as to expect Bricks when they afford no straw.
> *A Serious Proposal to the Ladies for the Advancement of
> their True and Greatest Interest 1694*

2 They only who have felt it know the Misery of being forc'd to marry where they do not love; of being yok'd for life to a disagreeable Person and imperious Temper, where Ignorance and Folly (the ingredients of a Cockscomb, who is the most unsufferable Fool) tyrannizes over wit and Sense.
> *Some Reflections Upon Marriage* (repr. 1970) *1700*

3 . . . Beauty with all the Helps of Art, is of no long Date; the more it is help'd the sooner it decays. . . .
> Ibid.

4 . . . he who only or chiefly chose for Beauty, will in a little Time find the same Reason for another Choice.
> Ibid.

5 . . . Marriage in general is too sacred to be treated with Disrespect, too venerable to be the subject of Raillery and Buffonery. It is the Institution of Heaven, the only Honourable way of continuing Mankind, and far be it from us to think there could have been a better way than infinite Wisdom has found out for us.

Ibid.

6 But how can a Woman scruple entire Subjection, how can she forbear to affirm the Worth and Excellency of the Superior Sex, if she at all considers it! Have not all the great Actions that have been performed in the World been done by Men? Have they not founded Empires and over-turned them? Do they not make Laws and continually repeal and amend them? Their vast Minds lay Kingdoms waste, no Bounds or Measures can be prescribed to their Desires. . . . What is it they cannot do? They make Worlds and ruin them . . .

Ibid.

7 There is not anything so excellent, but some will carp at it. . . .

Quoted in Preface (18 December 1724), *Letters of the Right Honourable Lady Mary Wortley Montagu* 1767*

*See 527.

505. Susanna Centlivre (1667/9?–1723)

1 LUDOVICHO. I never strike Bargains in the Dark

Act I, Sc. 1, *The Perjur'd Husband 1700*

2 COUNT BASSINO. Why must his generous Passion thus be starv'd, And be confin'd to one alone? The Woman, whom Heaven sent as a Relief, To ease the Burden of a tedious Life, And be enjoy'd when summon'd by Desire, Is now become the Tyrant of our Fates.

Act I, Sc. 2, Ibid.

3 ARMANDO. . . . there's more Glory in subduing Our wild Desires, than an embattl'd Foe.

Act IV, Sc. 1, Ibid.

4 AMELIA. I have the best Proof in the World of it, ocular Demonstration.

Act III, Sc. 1, *The Beau's Duel 1702*

5 TOPER. Yesterday I carried to wait on a Relation of ours that has a Parrot, and whilst I was discoursing about some private Business, she converted the Bird, and now it talks of nothing but the Light of the Spirit, and the Inward man.

Ibid.

6 You see gallants 'it has been out Poets' care,
To shew what Beaus in their Perfection are,
By Nature *Cowards, foolish, useless Tools,*
Made *Men* by *Taylors* and by *Women, Fools.*

Epilogue, Ibid.

7 He surest strikes that smiling gives the blow.

Ibid.

8 Friendship's a noble name, 'tis love refined.

Act II, Sc. 2, *The Stolen Heiress 1702*

9 Writing is a kind of Lottery in this fickle Age. . . .

Preface, *Love's Contrivance 1703*

10 OCTAVIO. . . . for I find by the beating of my Pulse, the Motion of my Brain, and the Heavings of my Heart, I am very far gone

in that dangerous Distemper call'd Love, and you are the only Physician can save my life.

Act III, Sc. 1, Ibid.

11 LUCINDA. Once a week! I wou'd not for the World bed with you oftener; why 'tis not the Fashion, Sir Toby; and I assure you when I marry I hope to be my own Mistress, and follow my own Inclination, which will carry me to the utmost Pinnacle of the Fashion.

Act IV, Sc. 1, Ibid.

12 'Tis the defect of age to rail at the pleasures of youth.

Act I, *The Basset-Table 1705*

13 LADY REVELLER. Will you never be weary of these whimsies.
VALERIA. Whimsies! Natural philosophy a whimsy! Oh! The unlearned world.
LADY REVELLER. Ridiculous learning!
MRS. ALPIEW. Ridiculous indeed, for women. Philosophy suits our sex as jack-boots would do.
VALERIA. Custom would bring them as much in fashion as furbelows, and practice would make us as valiant as e'er a hero of them all, the resolution is in the mind—Nothing can enslave that.

Act II, Sc. 1, Ibid.

14 LADY LUCY. . . . nothing melts a Woman's Heart like gold.

Act IV, Ibid.

15 HECTOR. Love's Fever is always highest when the Cash is at an Ebb.

Act I, *The Gamester 1705*

16 VALERE. . . . there's nothing like ready Money to nick Fortune.

Act III, Ibid.

17 HECTOR. Lying is a thriving Vocation.

Ibid.

18 HECTOR. What Business had you to get Children, without you had Cabbage enough to maintain 'em?

Ibid.

19 All policy's allowed in war and love.

Act I, *Love at a Venture 1706*

20 And why this Wrath against the Women's Works? Perhaps you'll answer, because they meddle with things out of their Sphere: But I say, no; for since the Poet is born, why not a Woman as well as a Man?

Dedication, *The Platonic Lady 1707*

21 ISABINDA. The world cannot be more savage than our parents.

The Busie Body 1709

22 SIR GEORGE AIRY. . . . a Man that wants Money thinks none can be unhappy that has it. . . .

Act I, Ibid.

23 CHARLES. . . . Want, the Mistress of Invention, still tempts me on. . . .

Ibid.

24 MANAGE. . . . my present Profession is Physick—Now, when my Pockets are full, I cure a Patient in three Days; when they are empty, I keep him three months.

Act II, *The Man's Bewitched; or, The Devil to Do About Her 1709*

25   . . . my spouse who understands
     Nought to be good, but Bills and Bonds, The ready Cash, or
         fruitful Lands,
     Begins new Quarrels ev'ry Day,
     And frights my dear lov'd Muse away . . .
                                                          Ibid.

26   DON PERRIERA. . . . sure cuckoldom is so rank a Scent, that
     tho' I lived in *England*, where they scarce breathe any other
     Air, I cou'd distinguish it.
         Act I, Sc. 1, *Mar Plot, or, The Second Part of the Busy Body*
                                                          1711

27   MARPLOT. I had rather fathom the Depth of Man's Thoughts,
     than his Pocket. . . .
                                              Act III, Sc. 1, Ibid.

28   FLORELLA. . . . nobody can boast of Honesty till they are
     try'd. . . .
                                 Act III, Sc. 1, *The Perplex'd Lovers 1712*

29   DON LOPEZ. There is no Condition of Life without its Cares,
     and it is the Perfection of a Man to wear 'em as easy as he can.
     . . .
                         Act I, Sc. 1, *The Wonder: A Woman Keeps a Secret 1714*

30   'Tis my opinion every man cheats in his way, and he is only
     honest who is not discovered.
                                         Act V, *The Artifice 1724*

31   When the glowing of passion's over, and pinching winter
     comes, will amorous sighs supply the want of fire, or kind
     looks and kisses keep off hunger?
                                                          Ibid.

506. Susanna Wesley (1668?–1742)

1   Let every one enjoy the present hour.
                 Quoted in *The Women of Methodism: Its Three*
                         Foundresses . . . by Abel Stevens *1866*

2   [To subdue the will of the child] is the only strong and rational
     foundation of a religious education, without which both pre-
     cept and example will be ineffectual. But when this is
     thoroughly done, then a child is capable of being governed by
     the reason and piety of its parents till its own understanding
     comes to maturity, and the principles of religion have taken
     root in the mind.
                         Letter to her son, John Wesley,* Ibid.
     *English preacher; founder of Methodism (1703–1791).

3   God's prescience is no more the effective cause of the loss
     of the wicked than our foreknowledge of the rising of to-
     morrow's sun is the cause of its rising.
                                                          Ibid.

507. Joan Philips (fl. c. 1670–1682)

1   Thou dull companion of our active years,
     That chill'st our warm blood with thy frozen fears,
     How is it likely thou shouldst long endure,
     When thought itself thy ruin may procure?
                 "Maidenhead," *Female Poems on Several Occasions 1679*

2   Think me all man: my soul is masculine,
     And capable of as great things as thine.
                         "To Phylocles, Inviting Him to Friendship,"
                                                   St. 3, Ibid.

508. Sarah Fyge Field Egerton (1670–1723)

1   When Heav'n survey'd the Works that it had done,
     Saw Male and Female, but found Man
     alone, A barren Sex, and insignificant,
     then Heav'n made Woman to supply the want,
     And to make perfect what before was
     scant: Surely then she a Noble Creature is,
     Whom Heav'n thus made to consummate all Bliss.
         The Female Advocate, or An Answer to a Late Satyr Against
             *the Pride, Lust, and Inconstancy, &c. of Woman** 1683
     *Her response to Robert Gould's misogynist tract *A Late Satyr*
     Against the Pride, Lust, and Inconstancy, etc. of Woman.

2   For Adam most did of the guilt partake;
     While he from God's own mouth had the Command,
     But Woman had it at the second hand:
                                                          Ibid.

3   We find most Men have banish'd Truth for spight
                                                          Ibid.

509. Anne Baynard (1672–1697)

1   . . . it is a sin to be content with a little knowledge.
             Quoted in *Biography of Distinguished Women* by Sarah
                                         Josepha Hale* 1876
     *See 788.

2   I could wish that all young persons might be exhorted to . . .
     read the great book of nature, wherein they may see the wis-
     dom and power of the Creator, in the order of the universe,
     and in the production and preservation of all things.
                                         From her deathbed, Ibid.

510. Mary Davys (1674–1732)

1   As a Child born of a common Woman, has many Fathers, so
     my poor Offspring has been laid at a great many Doors. . . . I
     am proud they think it deserves a better Author.
             Preface, *The Northern Heiress; or, The Humours of York*
                                                          1716

2   LADY GREASY. Love is like a bug, the longer it sticks in the skin,
     the harder it is to pluck out.
                                                          Ibid.

3   The Pedant despises the most elaborate Undertaking, unless it
     appears in the World with *Greek* and *Latin* Motto's; a Man
     that would please him, must pore an Age over musty Authors,
     till his Brains are as worm-eaten as the Books he reads, and his
     Conversation fit for nobody else. . . .
             The Reformed Coquet; or, the Memoirs of Amoranda 1724

4   . . . the busy part of our Species, who are so very intent upon
     getting Money, that they lose the pleasure of spending it.
                                                          Ibid.

5   It is the way of the Damn'd, Madam, to desire all Mankind
     should be in their own miserable State. . . .
                                                          Ibid.

6   How many brave Men, courageous Women, and innocent
     Children did I see butcher'd, to do God good Service? . . . I
     went to the *Irish* Rebellion, where I saw more than three hun-
     dred thousand Souls murder'd in cold Blood . . . crying, *Nits
     will become Lice, destroy Root and Branch:* with a thousand

other Barbarities, too tedious as well as too dreadful to repeat, beside what has been transacted abroad.

"To Artander, November 10," *Familiar Letters, Betwixt a Gentleman and a Lady 1725*

7 . . . we Women as naturally love Scandal, as you Men do Debauchery; and we can no more keep up Conversation without one, than you can live an Age without t'other.

"To Artander, December 10," Ibid.

8 I cannot say I was ever so glutted with Pleasure in my Life, as to be weary of it, nor properly speaking, can any body say so; because, when once a Man is tir'd of a thing, it is no longer a Pleasure, but retiring from it is; so that a Person who has power to follow his own Inclinations, is always in Pleasure. . . .

"To Berina, December 26," Ibid.

9 . . . Love, like Edg'd-Tools, shou'd never be play'd with.

"To Artander, January 12," Ibid.

10 When Women write, the Criticks, now-a-days,
Are ready, e'er they see, to damn their Plays;
Wit, as the Men's Prerogative, they claim,
And with one Voice, the bold Invader blame.

Prologue, *The Self-Rival; A Comedy 1725*

11 MRS. FALLOW. So many Men and Women go together that, in all probability, could never have met.

Ibid.

12 I never was so vain, as to think they [her works] deserv'd a Place in the first Rank, or so humble, as to resign them to the last.

Works 1725

511. Elizabeth Rowe (1674–1736/37)

1 Thy numerous Works exalt Thee thus,
And shall I silent be?
No; rather let me cease to breathe,
Than cease from praising Thee!

"Hymn," St. 8, *Poems on Several Occasions by Philomela 1696*

2 . . . the studious follies of the great,
The tiresome farce of ceremonious state.

"Despair," Ibid.

3 By this thy glorious lineage thou dost prove
Thy high descent; for GOD himself is Love.

"Ode to Love," St. 11, *Miscellaneous Works in Prose and Verse 1739*

512. Elizabeth Thomas (1675/77?–1730/31)

1 Ah! strive no more to know what fate
Is pre-ordain'd foe thee:
'Tis vain in this my mortal state,
For Heaven's inscrutable decree
Will only be reveal'd in vast Eternity.

"Predestination; or the Resolution," *Miscellany Poems on Several Subjects 1722*

513. Rosalba Carriera (1675–1757)

1 . . . I think that pleasures should be enjoyed with great sobriety and moderation.

Ch. 6, Quoted in *Portraits and Backgrounds* by Evangeline Wilbour Blashfield *1917*

2 You may be sure that I know that there is a world, men, and bread beyond the lagoons [of Venice], but I submit to the will of heaven which has decreed that my journeys shall be only to my easel. I am contented with but little bread, while as to men, believe me there is nothing in the world that I think less of. . . .

Ibid.

3 . . . for three years I have been deprived of my sight. I wish you to learn from my own hand that thanks to the Divine Goodness I have recovered it. I see but as one sees after an operation, that is to say very dimly. Even this is a blessing for one who has had the misfortune to become blind. When I was sightless I cared for nothing, now I want to see everything. . . .

Ch. 7, Letter from Venice (23 August 1749), Ibid.

514. Penelope Aubin (1679–1731)

1 Love and Honour had a sharp contest, but at last Love got the Victory, and the rose.

Ch. 2, *The Life of the Lady Lucy 1726*

2 This is the vast difference betwixt doing well and ill; that in Vice the Pleasure is always momentary and of no duration, and the Remorse for having done it, sure and lasting; but in doing virtuous Deeds, tho' we may suffer Loss and Pain for some short time, yet we have always a secret Satisfaction within, that supports us under them, and the End brings us Honour and generally Reward, even in this world. . . .

Ch. 10, Ibid.

515. Catherine Trotter (1679–1749)

1 . . . when a Woman appears in the World under any distinguishing Character, she must expect to be the mark of ill nature.

Dedication to Princess Anne, *Fatal Friendship 1698*

2 . . . We tax our Judgement, when we cease to love.

Love at a Loss; or, Most Votes Carry It (a.k.a. *The Honourable Deceiver*) *1700*

3 LESBIA. Hands, and Seals, and Oaths cannot secure
A mind like Man's unfaithful and impure.

Epilogue, Ibid.

4 But who the useful art can teach,
When sliding down a steepy way,
To stop, before the end we reach?

"The Caution," St. 3, *The Female Wits*, Lucyle Hook, ed. *1704*

5 A heart whose safety but in flight does lie,
Is too far lost to have the power to fly.

"The Vain Advice," St. 2, *The Works of Mrs. Catharine Cockburn, Theological, Moral, Dramatic, and Poetical*, Thomas Birch, ed. *1751*

6 Being married in 1708, I bid adieu to the muses, and so wholly gave myself up to the cares of a family, and the education of my children, that I scarce knew, whether there was any such thing as books, plays, or poems stirring in Great Britain.

"Account of the Life of the Author," Ibid.

7 . . . when anything is written by a woman, that [men] cannot deny their approbation to, [they] are sure to rob us of the glory of it, by concluding 'tis not her own; or at least, that she had some assistance, which has been said in many instances to my knowledge unjustly.

Vol. II, Ibid.

8   Women are as capable of penetrating into the grounds of things and reasoning justly as men are who certainly have no advantage of us but in their opportunities of knowledge . . .
                                                                    Ibid.

9   You* were our Champion, and the Glory ours.
    Well you've maintain'd our equal right in Fame,
    To which vain Man had quite engrost the claim
              Commentary verses quoted in *The Royal Mischief* by Mary
                                    de la Rivière Manley* 1796

    *See 495.

516. Mrs. Taylor (fl. c. 1680)

1   . . . tears,
    Those springs that water Love.
              "Song," St. 2, *Miscellany, Being a Collection of Poems
                          by several Hands*, Aphra Behn,* ed. 1685
    *See 469.

2   Alas! it does my soul perplex,
         When I his charms recall,
    To think he should despise the sex,
         Or what's worse, love them all.
                                        "Song," St. 3, Ibid.

517. Eleonora von dem Knesebeck (fl. c. 1680–1713)

1   The [British] government must have done a deed of great in-
    justice since they stop my mouth, for if they can answer to all
    the world for what they have done . . . why am I not [allowed
    to] speak? If their judgements are righteous, how should I dare
    to speak wrongfully?
              (c. 1697), Quoted in *Lives of the Hanoverian Queens of
                          England* by Alice Drayton Greenwood 1891

518. Jane Barker (fl. c. 1680–1715)

1   Happy life . . .
    Fearless of twenty-five and all its train,
    Of slights and scorns, or being called old maid. . . .
    Ah lovely state how strange it is to see,
    What mad conceptions some have made of thee,
    As though thy being was all wretchedness,
    Or foul deformity in the ugliest dress.
                          "A Virgin Life," *Poetical Recreations* 1688

2   Poverty's the certain fate
    Which attends a poet's state.
                                "Poetical Recreations," Ibid.

3   . . . thus we see that Human Projects are mere Vapours, carried
    about with every Blast of cross Accidents. . . .
                                        Love Intrigues 1713

4   . . . Love is apt to interpret things in its own Favour. . . .
                                                    Ibid.

519. Elizabeth Haddon Estaugh (1680–1762)

1   I'll venture to say, few, if any, in a married State, ever lived in
    sweeter Harmony than we did.
              Quoted in Introduction to *A Call to the Unfaithful Profes-
                          sors of Truth* by John Estaugh 1744

2   I have received from the lord a charge to love thee, John Es-
    taugh.
              Attributed, Quoted in *Tales of a Wayside Inn* by Henry
                                    Wadsworth Longfellow* 1863

    *American poet (1807–1882).

520. Elizabeth Elstob (1683–1756)

1   . . . I shou'd think it as Glorious an Employment to instruct
    Poor Children as to teach the Children of the Greatest
    Monarch.
              Letter to George Ballard (c. 1740), Quoted in
                          A Galaxy of Governesses by Bea Howe
                                                    1954

2   . . . you can come into no company of Ladies and or Gentle-
    men, where you shall not hear an open and Vehement
    exclamation against Learned Women.
                          Letter to George Ballard (c. 1753), Ibid.

521. Jane Brereton (1685–1740)

1   Pope* is the emblem of true wit,
    The sunshine of the mind.
              "On Mr. Nash's** Picture at Full Length, Between the Busts
                          of Sir Isaac Newton*** and Mr. Pope," St. 4,
                                    Mrs. Jane Brereton's Poems 1744
    *British poet and satirist Alexander Pope (1688–1744). **British
    satirist and pamphleteer Thomas Nash (1567–1601). ***British
    physicist and mathematician (1643–1727).

2   I scorn this mean fallacious art
    By which you'd steal, not win, my heart
                                "To Damon," St. 1, Ibid.

3   . . . Cupid's empire won't admit
    Nor own, a Salic law.*
                                "To Philotinus," St. 2, Ibid.
    *European law of succession (derived from a 5th–century Frank-
    ish code), prohibiting daughters from inheriting land and women
    from succeeding to a throne.

522. Claudine Alexandrine de Tencin (1685–1749)

1   Unless God visibly interferes, it is physically impossible that
    the state [France] should not fall to pieces.
              Quoted in *Biography of Distinguished Women*
                          by Sarah Josepha Hale*
                                                    1876
    *See 788.

523. Mary Chandler (1687–1745)

1   Fatal effects of luxury and ease!
    We drink our poison and we eat disease.
              "Temperance," *The Female Poets of Great Britain*,
                                    Frederic Rowton, ed. 1853

524. Mary Collier (1689/90–post-1759)

1   In gleaning Corn, such is our frugal Care.
    When Night comes on, unto our Home we go,
    Our Corn we carry, and our Infant too;
    Weary indeed! but 'tis not worth our while
    Once to complain, or rest at ev'ry Stile;
    We must make haste, for when we home are come,
    We find again our Work has just begun;
    So many Things for our Attendance call,
    Had we ten hands, we could employ them all.
                                        The Woman's Labour 1739

2   Our Toil and Labour's daily so extreme,
    That we have hardly ever Time to Dream.
                                                    Ibid.

525. Mary Waite (?–1689)

1 All the
sinners in Sion shall be
afraid, fearfulnesse shall take hold on the
Hypocrite. Dread and
horror shall surprise them. O whither will
you unfaithful fly!
*A Warning to all Friends Who Professeth the Everlasting
Truth of God, which he hath Revealed and made manifest in
this his Blessed Day, (whether on this Side, or beyond the
Seas.) 1679*

2 For the Devil is the King of pride . . .
Ibid.

526. Eliza Haywood (1689/93–1756)

1 Criticks! be dumb to-night—no Skill display;
A dangerous Woman-Poet wrote the Play:
One, who not fears your Fury, tho' prevailing,
More than your match, in every thing, but Railing.
Give her fair Quarter, and whene'er she tries ye,
Safe in superior Spirit, she defies ye . . .
A Wife to Be Let 1723

2 Flattery is a Vice so much in Fashion, and, I am sorry to say, so
much encouraged, that there is nothing more difficult than to
find a Patron who not expects, nor would be pleased with it. . . .
Dedication, *The Rash Resolve 1724*

3 How little are the ill judging Multitude capable of chusing for
themselves! How far are Wealth and Beauty, the two great
Idols of the admiring world, from being real Blessings to the
Possessors of them!
The Mercenary Lover; or, the Unfortunate Heiresses 1726

4 The base are always Cowards, the same Meaness of Spirit
which makes them the one, inclines them to the other also;
they are ever in Fear, and while there remains even the smallest
Probability of Danger, peace is a Stranger to their Minds.
Ibid.

5 The natural Propensity which all People have to listen to any Arguments which may serve to excuse the Errors they commit. . . .
Ibid.

6 I am not without some share of that too common Foible of
Humanity, which makes us place less Value on the things we
are in possession of, than those above our reach. . . .
Pt. I, *The Secret History of the Present Intrigues of the
Court of Caramania 1727*

7 He represented to her, that the greatest Glory of a Monarch
was the Liberty of the People, his most valuable Treasures in
their crowded Coffers, and his securest Guard in their *sincere*
Affection.
Adventures of Eovaii, Princess of Ijaveo 1736

8 . . . nothing but Liberty was denied her.
"The History of Yximilla," Ibid.

9 To endure all the toils and hardships of the field with patience
and intrepidity, to be fearless of danger when the duties of his
post commanded, is highly laudable and emulative; but to run
into them without a call, and when bravery can be of no service, is altogether idle; and courage like all other virtues,
degenerates into a vice by being carried to an extreme.
"Effeminacy in the Army," *The Female Spectator
1744–1746*

10 Nature is in itself abhorrent of vice. . . .
"Masquerades, How Prejudicial," Ibid.

11 All that can justly be objected against any arguments made use
of to prove the reasonableness of a belief in a plurality of
worlds is, that to us, that live in this, it is no manner of concern, since there is not a possibility of travelling to them, or of
ever becoming acquainted with the inhabitants.
"Flying-Machines, The Impossibility of Their Use," Ibid.

12 Philosophy is the toil which can never tire the persons engaged
in it; all its ways are strewed with roses, and the farther you
go, the more enchanting objects appear before you and invite
you on.
"Study of Philosophy Recommended," Ibid.

13 I desire no other Revenge for my abused Sincerity, than that
you may, some time or other, find a Woman fair enough to create a real Passion in you; and as insensible of it, as you are of
mine.
"The History of Graciana," *Memoirs of a Certain Island
Adjacent to the Kingdom of Utopia 1775*

14 She was so exact an Economist, and made so good use of her
Time, that she had always an Opportunity of being happy with
the Man she lik'd, and never miss'd one with the Man whose
Purse was at her devotion.
"The History of Hortensia," Ibid.

15 That Generosity and open Candor, which is almost inseparable from good Sense, renders the Person possess'd of it, at once
incapable of a base Action himself, or of suspecting it in
others.
"The History of Count Orainos, and
Madame Del Millmonde," Ibid.

527. Mary Wortley Montagu (1689–1762)

1 But when the long hours of public are past,
And we meet with champagne and a chicken at last,
May every fond pleasure that moment endear;
Be banish'd afar both discretion and fear!
"The Lover: A Ballad (To Mr. Congreve),"* St. 4,
Six Town Ecologues 1747
*English playwright (1670–1729).

2 In crowded courts I find myself alone,
And pay my worship to a nobler throne.
"In Answer to a Lady who advised Retirement," St. 1, *The
London Magazine May 1750*

3 I enjoy vast delight in the folly of mankind; and, God be
praised, that is an inexhaustible source of entertainment.
Letter to Countess of Mar (n.d.), *Letters of the Right Honourable Lady Mary Wortley Montagu 1767*

4 Nature is seldom in the wrong, custom always.
Letter to Miss Anne Wortley (8 August 1709), Ibid.

5 . . . I hate the noise and hurry inseparable from great estates
and titles, and look upon both as blessings that ought only to
be given to fools, for 'tis only to them that they are blessings.
Letter to Wortley Montagu, her husband
(28 March 1710), Ibid.

6 General notions are generally wrong.
Ibid.,

7 A woman, till five-and-thirty, is only looked upon as a raw girl, and can possibly make no noise in the world till about forty.
>Letter to Lady R[ich], (Vienna, 20 September 1716), Ibid.

8 . . . if it were the fashion to go naked, the face would be hardly observed.
>(Sophia, Turkey, 1717), Ibid.

9 I am patriot enough to take pains to bring this useful invention [smallpox inoculation] into fashion in England; and I should not fail to write to some of our doctors very particularly about it, if I knew any one of them that I thought had virtue enough to destroy such a considerable branch of revenue for the good of mankind.
>Letter to Lady Mar [her sister], (Belgrade, 1 April 1717), Ibid.

10 . . . to be ever beloved, one must be ever agreeable.
>Letter to Mr. Wortley Montagu (c. 1720), Ibid.

11 The last pleasure that fell in my way was Madame de Sévigné's* letters; very pretty they are, but I assert without the least vanity, mine will be full as entertaining forty years hence. I advise you, therefore, to put none of them to the use of waste-paper.
>Letter to Lady Mar (1724), Ibid.
>*See 443.

12 I give myself sometimes admirable advice, but I am incapable of taking it.
>(1725), Ibid.

13 Nobody can deny but religion is a comfort to the distressed, a cordial to the sick, and sometimes a restraint on the wicked; therefore, whoever* would laugh or argue it out of the world, without giving some equivalent for it, ought to be treated as a common enemy.
>Letter to Countess of Bute [her daughter] (1752), Ibid.
>*Reference to Irish satirist Jonathan Swift (1667–1745).

14 . . . the knowledge of numbers is one of the chief distinctions between us and the brutes.
>(28 January 1753), Ibid.

15 True knowledge consists in knowing things, not words.
>Ibid.

16 People are never so near playing the fool as when they think themselves wise.
>(1 March 1755), Ibid.

17 Civility costs nothing and buys everything.
>(30 May 1756), Ibid.

18 . . . it is now eleven years since I have seen my figure in a glass, and the last reflection I saw there was so disagreeable, that I resolved to spare myself the mortification in the future.
>Letter (Venice, c. 1758–1761), Ibid.

19 It [her health] is so often impaired that I begin to be as weary of it as mending old lace; when it is patched in one place, it breaks out in another.
>Ibid.

20 Life is too short for any distant aim;
And cold the dull reward of future fame.
>"Epistle to the Earl of Burlington," *Poetical Works 1768*

21 Satire should, like a polished razor keen,
Wound with a touch that's scarcely felt or seen.
>"To the Imitator [Alexander Pope*] of the First Satire of Horace,"** Ibid.
>*English poet and satirist (1688–1744). **Roman poet (65–8 B.C.E.).

22 Be plain in dress, and sober in your diet;
In short, my dreary, kiss me! and be quiet.
>"In Summary of Lord Lyttleton's Advice to a Lady," Ibid.

23 But the fruit that will fall without shaking,
Indeed is too mellow for me.
>"To a Lady Making Love; or, Answered, for Lord Hamilton," Ibid.

24 Thou silver deity of secret night,
>"A Hymn to the Moon," St. 1, *The Letters and Works of Lady Mary Wortley Montagu*, Lord Wharncliffe, ed. 1861

25 Poets write morals—priests for martyrs preach—
Neither such fools to practice what they teach.
>"Epilogue to the Tragedy of Cato," St. 1, Ibid.

26 Since you, Mr. H**d, will marry black Kate,
Accept of good wishes for that blessed state:
May you fight all the day like a dog and a cat,
And yet ev'ry year produce a new brat.
Fal la!

May she never be honest—you never be sound;
May her tongue like a clapper be heard a mile round;
Till abandon'd by joy, and deserted by grace,
You hang yourselves both in the very same place.
Fal la!
>"Epithalamium," *in toto*, Ibid.

27 Let mules and asses in that circle tread,
And proud of trappings toss a feather'd head;
Leave you the stupid business of the state,
Strive to be happy, and despise the great:
>"Fragment To," Ibid.

28 "O youth! O spring of life, for ever lost!
>"Friday, The Toilette: Lydia," St. 2, Ibid.

29 Men that have not sense enough to show any superiority in their arguments, hope to be yielded to by a faith, that as they are men, all the reason that has been allotted to human-kind has fallen to their share. I am seriously of another opinion.
>"From the Nonsense of Common Sense," Ibid.

30 Fond virgin, thy power is lost,
On a race of rude Hottentot brutes;
What glory in being the toast
Of noisy dull 'squires in boots?
>"Melinda's Complaint," St. 4, Ibid.

31 Why should you think I live unpleas'd,
Because I am not pleas'd with you?
>"Song," St. 1, Ibid.

32 Show that true wit disdains all little art,
And can at once engage and mend the heart;
Knows even popular applause to gain,
Yet not malicious, wanton, or profane.
>"The Court of Dulness [sic]," St. 2, Ibid.

33 Let this great maxim be my virtue's guide;
In part she is to blame that has been try'd—
He comes too near, that comes to be deny'd.
                                    "The Lady's Resolve," Ibid.

34 Consider, friend, but coolly, and you'll find
Revenge the frailty of a feeble mind;
                                    "To the Same," St. 3, Ibid.

35 I show you all my heart without disguise;
But these are tender proofs that you despise—
I see too well what wishes you pursue;
You would not only conquer, but undo:
                    "Wednesday—The Tête-à-Tête: Dancinda," St. 1, Ibid.

36 A real marriage bears no resemblance to these marriages of interest or ambition. It is two lovers who live together. A priest
may well say certain words, a notary may well sign certain papers—I regard these preparations in the same way that a lover
regards the rope ladder that he ties to his mistress's window.
                                    Essay n.d.

528. Ariadne (fl. c. 1690)

1 [I] could not conquer the Inclination I had for Scribling from
my Childhood. And when our Island enjoyed the Blessing of
the incomparable Mrs. [Aphra] Behn,* even then I had much
ado to keep my muse from shewing her Impertinence; but,
since her death, has claim'd a kind of Privilege; and, in spite of
me, broke from her Confinement.
                            Preface, She Ventures and He Wins 1695
  *See 469.

2 Our Author hopes indeed,
You will not think, though charming
Aphra's* dead,
All Wit with her, and with Orinda's** fled.
                                    Prologue, Ibid.
  *The playwright Aphra Behn; see 469. **Pseudonym of the poet
  Katherine Philips; see 452.

3 (Enter CHARLOTTE and JULIANA in men's clothes.)
JULIANA. Faith, Charlotte, the breeches become you so well
'tis almost pity you should ever part with 'em.
CHARLOTTE. Nor will I, till I can find one can make better use
of them to bestow 'em on, and then I'll resign my title to 'em
for ever.
JULIANA. 'Tis well if you find it so easy for a woman once
vested in authority though 'tis by no other than her own making, does not willingly part with it.
                                    Act I, Sc. 1, Ibid.

529. Mary Barber (1690?–1757)

1 A richer present I design,
A finished form, of work divine,
Surpassing all the power of art;
A thinking head, a grateful heart.
            "On Sending my Son as a Present to Dr. [Jonathan] Swift,*
            Dean of St. Patrick's, on his Birthday," Poems on
                                    Several Occasions 1734
  *Irish satirist (1667–1745)

530. Francisca Josefa del Castillo y Guevara (1691?–1743)

1 The land grew bright in a single flower—
One great carnation rare. . . .
                    "Christmas Carol," St. 1, The Catholic Anthology,
                                    Thomas Walsh, ed. 1927

2 "My sin has led me far
As some wild thirsting bee
Beneath Thy meadow star,
Idly forgetting Thee;
But Thou dost call me home; I hear
Thy voice whose sweetness charms mine ear.
                            "The Holy Ecologue," St. 6, Ibid.

531. Martha Corey (?–1692)

1 Ye are all against me and I cannot help it.*
                    Remark (1692), Quoted in Notable American Women,
                                    Edward T. James, ed. 1971
  *Remark at her trial for witchcraft in Salem, Massachusetts.

532. Charlotte Elizabeth Aïssé (1694/95–1733)

1 We sup wretchedly, we have neither good fish nor good
friends.
                    Ch. 5, Letter, Quoted in Portraits and Backgrounds by
                                    Evangeline Wilbour Blashfield 1917

2 . . . I could never love where I could not respect.
                                    Ch. 5, Letter, Ibid.

3 It seems to be a natural human impulse to profit by the weakness of others. I do not know how to use such arts; I know
only one: to make life so sweet to him I love that he will find
nothing preferable to it.
                                    Ch. 6, Letter, Ibid.

533. Elizabeth Tollet (1694–1754)

1 The conscious moon and stars above
Shall guide me with my wandering love.
            "Winter Song," an Epistle to King Henry VIII, Poems on
                            Several Occasions, with Anne Boleyn* 1755
  *See 298.

2 'Tis vanished all! remains alone
The eyeless scalp of naked bone;
The vacant orbits sunk within;
The jaw that offers at a grin.
Is this the object, then, that claims
The tribute of our youthful flames?
                                    "On a Death's Head," Ibid.

534. Cornelia Bradford (1695?–1755)

1 The Punsters are of Opinion, that though we could not Cope
with the Rebellion at first, we shall make shift to Wade thro' it
at last.*
                    From article in American Weekly Mercury, Quoted in An-
                    drew Bradord, Colonial Journalist by A. J. DeArmond 1949
  *Neither Sir John Cope nor Field Marshal George Wade was suc-
  cessful in stemming the Jacobite invasion of 1745.

535. Frïederika Karoline Neuber (1697–1760)

1 Dear reader, here is something for you to read. To be sure, it is
not written by a great, scholarly man. Oh, no! It is by a mere
woman whose name you scarcely know and for whose station
in life you have to look among the most humble of people, for
she is nothing but a comedian. She cannot be responsible for
anything but her own art, though she does know enough to
understand another artist when he talks about his work. If you
should ask her why she writes at all, her answer will be the
customary feminine "Because." If any one asks you who

helped her, you had better answer, "I don't know"—for it may very well be that she did it all herself.

> Preface to the play *Vorspiel*, Quoted in *Enter the Actress* by Rosamond Gilder *1931*

536. Marie Anne du Deffand (1697–1780)

1 What more can you ask? He [Voltaire*] has invented history! (*Que voulez–vous de plus? Il a inventé l'histoire!*)

> Quoted in *L'Esprit dans histoire* by Fournier *1857*

*Pen name of François Marie Arouet (1694–1798), French philosopher and writer.

2 The distance is nothing: it is only the first step that is difficult.*

> Letter to Jean Le Rond d'Alembert (7 July 1763),
> *Correspondance inédite 1859*

*Refers to the legend that St. Denis, carrying his head in his hands, walked two leagues.

3 I do not know why Diogenes* went looking for a man: nothing could happen to him worse than finding one.

> Ibid.

*Greek philosopher (412?–323 B.C.E.)

4 . . . everything seems insupportable to me. This may very well be because I am insupportable myself.

> Ibid.

5 I hear nothings, I speak nothings, I take interest in nothing and from nothing to nothing I travel gently down the dull way which leads to becoming nothing.

> Ibid.

6 I remember thinking in my youth that no one was happy but madmen, drunkards and lovers.

> Ibid.

7 Faith is a devout belief in what one does not understand.

> Ibid.

8 I love nothing and that is the true case of my ennui.

> Ibid.

9 God is not more incomprehensible than you; but if he is not more just, it is hardly worth while believing in him.

> Ibid.

10 Vanity ruins more women than love.

> Quoted in *Lettres à Voltaire*, Joseph Trabucco, ed. *1922*

11 Women are never stronger than when they arm themselves with their weaknesses.

> Ibid.

537. Susanna Wright (1697–1784)

1 Flowers on thy breast, and round thy head,
With thee their sweets resign,
Nipp'd from their tender stalks, and dead,
Their fate resembles thine

> "On the Death of a Young Girl," St. 11 (1737), *Women Poets in Pre-Revolutionary America*, Patti Cowell, ed. *1981*

2 And what are they—a vision all the past,
A bubble on the water's shining face,
What yet remain, till the first transient blast,
Shall leave no more remembrance of their place.

> "My Own Birth-Day," St. 2 (1 August 1761), Ibid.

538. Kshetrayya (fl. 17th century)

1 He* set my heart floating on the honey stream of his words,
With his amorous kiss he burnt my lips,
And left me utterly alone, and unfulfilled.

> "Dancing-Girl's Song," St. 2, *Indian Love Poems*, Tambimuttu and R. Appalaswamy, eds. and trs. *n.d.*

*The god Krishna.

539. Marchioness de Tibergeau (fl. 17th century)

1 No, it isn't the point of poetry to write of the tenderness of love:
To pick away at it, finding just the right words,
Arranging all in perfect measure and rhyme,
Stripping the heart to feed the mind.

> Untitled, Elaine T. Partnow,* tr., Quoted in *Biography of Distinguished Women* by Sarah Josepha Hale** *1876*

*Author; see 2870. **See 788.

540. Wang Wei (fl. 17th century)

1 A traveler's thoughts in the night
Wander in a thousand miles of dreams.

> "Seeking a Mooring," *The Orchid Boat, Women Poets of China*, Kenneth Rexroth and Ling Chung, eds. and trs. *1972*

541. Jane Wiseman (fl. c. 1700)

1 The Reception it [her play] met with in the World, was not kind enough to make me Vain, nor yet so ill, to discourage my Proceeding.

> Dedication, *Antiochus the Great; or, The Fatal Relapse 1701*

542. Sarah Updike Goddard (1700?–1770)

1 . . . [the] mystick art of printing. . . .

> Untitled poem, from *Providence Gazette* (16 March 1765), Ch. 4, Quoted in *William Goddard, Newspaperman* by Ward L. Miner *1962*

2 Ye learned physicians, whose excellent skill,
Can save, or demolish, can cure, or can kill;
To a poor forlorn damsel contribute your aid,
Who is sick, very sick of remaining a maid.

> "The Distressed Maid" (30 August 1766), Ibid.

3 . . . every one who takes delight in publicly or privately taking away any person's *good name*, or striving to render him ridiculous, are in the gall of bitterness, and in the bonds of iniquity, whatever their pretences may be for it.

> Letter to her son, William Goddard, Ch. 5, Ibid.

543. Mary Delany (1700–1788)

1 Hail to the happy times when fancy led
My pensive mind the flow'ry path to tread,
And gave me emulation to presume,
With timid art, to race fair nature's bloom

> Preface, *Flora, or, Herbal n.d.*

544. Fukuzoyo Chiyo (1701/03?–1775)

1 The dew of the rouge-flower
When it is spilled
Is simply water.

> Untitled haiku, R.H. Blyth, tr., *The Penguin Book of Women Poets*, Carol Cosman, Joan Keefe and Kathleen Weaver, eds. *1978*

2 After a long winter
giving
each other nothing, we collide
with blossoms in our hands.
　　　Untitled, *in toto*, David Ray, tr., *A Book of Women Poets*,
　　　Aliki and Willis Barnstone, eds. *1980*

545. Sidqi (?–1703)
1 From the hand of Power Unbounded draineth he the Wine of
Life,
Aye inebriate with Knowledge, learning's light, desireth not.
　　　Untitled ghazel, *Wise Women: Over 2000 Years of
Spiritual Writing by Women*, Susan Cahill,
ed. *1996*

546. Judith Boulbie (?–1706)
1 O ye Bishops and Priests of this Nation, ye have for a long
time
covered your selves with the name of Christ's Ministers, but
now
your covering is too narrow, and your Profession will not hide
you,
for the Light of Christ is risen, and with it you are judged and
condemned, and seen to be Enemies to the cross of Christ and
Strangers to the Covenant of Promise . . .
　　　*A Testimony for Truth against all Hireling-Priests
and Deceivers: With a Cry to the Inhabitants of this Nation, to turn to the Lord, before his dread-ful Judgements
overtake them 1655*

2 And (you) . . . .scoffers (who say) those silly Quakers . . . setting up men and women's meeting their prescribing laws and
statutes . . . and decrees to what purpose is women's meetings
the men can do the business the women must be subject to
their husbands, but . . . there is a little remnant which is one
with our brethren and is entered into the work and service and
feels that heavenly reward in their bosoms which all that
world . . . can (not) . . . take it from us. Therefore my dear sisters let nothing discompose your minds . . .
　　　(p. 333), Quoted in *Visionary Women: Ecstatic Prophecy in
Seventeenth-Century England* by Phyllis Mack *1992*

547. Constantia Grierson (1706?–1733)
1 And if to wit, our courtship they pretend,
'Tis the same way that they a cause defend;
In which they give of lungs a vast expence,
But little passion, thought, or eloquence.
　　　"To Miss Laetitia Van Lewen (Afterwards Mrs. Pilking-
ton),* at a Country Assize," *Poems on Several Occasions*,
Mary Barber, ed.** *1734*
　*See 561. **See 529.

548. Mercy Wheeler (1706–1733?)
1 Poor, wretched and vile sinners all
Rank'd with the heathen nation,
Who unto God ne'er pray nor call,
For pardon and salvation.
　　　Untitled, St. 1 (1732), *Women Poets in Pre-Revolutionary
America*, Patti Cowell, ed. *1981*

549. Anna Williams (1706–1783)
1 When Delia strikes the trembling string,
She charms our list'ning ears;

But when she joins her voice to sing,
She emulates the spheres.
　　　"On a Lady Singing," St. 1, *Biography of Distinguished
Women* by Sarah Josepha Hale* *1876*
　*See 788.

550. Selina Hastings (1707–1791)
1 I am well; all is well—well for ever. I see, wherever I turn my
eyes, whether I live or die, nothing but victory.*
　　　Quoted in *The Women of Methodism: Its Three
Foundresses . . .* by Abel Stevens *1866*
　*Remark after a stroke that presaged her death.

2 My work is done; I have nothing left to do but to go to my Fa-
ther.*
　　　Ibid.
　*Some of her last words.

551. Jane Colman Turell (1708–1735)
1 My good fat Bacon, and our homely Bread,
With which my healthful Family is fed.
Milk from the Cow, and Butter newly churn'd,
And new fresh Cheese, with Curds and
Cream just turn'd.
　　　"An Invitation Into the Country, In Imitation of Horace,"
St. 4, *Reliquiae Turellae et Lachrymae Paternae*
[Relics of Turell and Paternal Tears] *1735*
　*Roman poet (65–8 B.C.E.).

2 Dauntless you undertake th' unequal strife,
And raise dead virtue by your verse to life.
A woman's pen strikes the curs'd serpent's head,
And lays the monster gaping, if not dead.
　　　"On Reading the Warning by Mrs. Singer",* *Women Poets
in Pre-Revolutionary America*, Patti Cowell, ed. *1981*
　*Elizabeth Singer Rowe; see 511.

3 . . . no pain is like a bleeding heart.
　　　"Part of the Fifth Chapter of Canticles Paraphras'd From
the 8th Verse," St. 1 (14 September 1725), Ibid.

4 Thrice in my womb I've found the
pleasing strife,
In the first struggles of my infant's life:
But O how soon by Heaven I'm call'd to mourn,
While from my womb a lifeless babe is torn?
Born to the grave ere it has seen the light,
Or with one smile had cheer'd my longing sight.
　　　"Lines on Childbirth," St. 2, Ibid.

552. Mary Washington (1708–1789)
1 I am not surprised at what George has done, for he was always
a very good boy.
　　　*Recollections and Private Memoirs of Washington by his
adopted son, George Washington Parke Curtis, with a
Memoir of the Author, by his daughter . . . 1860*

553. Lydia Fish Willis (1709–1767)
1 The gate is straight,—the way is narrow,—my heart is
hard,—my sins are great,—my strength is weak,—my faith is
so benighted with doubts, that I am ready to cast all offered
good away. . . .

Such languid, faint desires I feel,

Within this wicked, stupid heart,
I should, I would, but that, I will,
I hardly dare (with truth) assert.
> "Lines from an Undated Letter to her Niece," *Rachel's Sepulchre; Or, a Memorial of Mrs. Lydia Willis, taken Chiefly, from her Letters to Friends . . . 1767?*

554. Mary Hearne (fl. c. 1710–20)

1 Love . . . generally hurries us on without Consideration. . . .
> "The Third Day," *The Lover's Week 1718*

2 . . . Love and Reason, like a Fever and Ague, took their alternate Turns in my Breast. . . .
> "The Amours of Calista and Torismond," *The Female Deserters 1719*

3 . . . therefore You should not by the vulgar Notion of Marriage make yourself uneasy, since that Ceremony is nothing but a piece of Formality, introduced on purpose to bring Profit to the Church; and I think that Love is much more to be Esteem'd, which has no other Motive but mutual Affection.
> Ibid.

555. Sarah Pierpont Edwards (1710–1758)

1 My soul remained in a kind of heavenly elysium.
> Ch. XIV, Quoted in *The Works of President Edwards* (1738)*, Vol. I, Sereno E. Dwight, ed. *1830*
> *Jonathan Edwards, American theologian and philosopher (1703–1758).

2 I seemed to myself to perceive a glow of divine love come down from the heart of Christ in heaven, into my heart, in a constant stream, like a stream or pencil of sweet light. At the same time, my heart and soul all flowed out in love to Christ.
> Ibid.

556. Sarah Fielding (1710–1768)

1 " . . . the height of my distress lies in not knowing my own mind; if I could once find that out, I should be easy enough. I am so divided by the desire of riches on the one hand, and by my honour and the man I like on the other, that there is such a struggle in my mind I am almost distracted."
> *David Simple c. 1750*

2 "I hope to be excused by those gentlemen who are quite sure they have found one woman who is a perfect angel, and that all the rest are perfect devils. . . . "
> Ibid.

3 "I think there is nothing so pleasant as revenge; I would pursue a man who had injured me to the very brink of life. I know it would be impossible for me ever to forgive him; and I would have him live only that I might have the pleasure of seeing him miserable."
> Ibid.

557. Mary Singleton Copley Pelham (1710–1789)

1 Your fame, my dear son, is sounded by all who are lovers of the art you bid fair to excel in. May God prosper and cause you to succeed in all your undertakings, and enroll your name among the first in your profession.
> Letter to John Singleton Copley,* her son (Boston, 6 February 1788), Quoted in *The Domestic and Artistic Life of John Singleton Copley, R.A.* by Martha Babcock Amory *1882*
> *American loyalist painter (1738–1815) .

558. Catherine Clive (1711–1785)

1 WILLING. But don't your heart ache when you think of the first night, hey?
> *The Rehearsal: or, Boys in Petticoats 1753*

2 MRS. HAZARD. Oh fie, Miss! that will never do: you speak your words as plain as a parish girl: the audience will never endure you in this kind of singing; if they understand what you say. You must give your words the Italian accent.
> Ibid.

3 SIR ALBANY ODELOVE. If Men, who are properly graduated in Learning, who have swallow'd the Tincture of a polite Education, who, as I may say, are hand and glove with the Classics, if such Genius's as I'm describing, fail of Success in Dramatical Occurrences, or Performances, ('tis the same Sense in the Latin) what must a poor lady expect, who is ignorant as the dirt.
> Ibid.

4 Necessity or inclination brings every one to the stage.
> Quoted in *The Life of Mrs. Catherine Clive* by Percy Fitzgerald *1888*

5 I am at present in such health and such spirits, that when I recollect I am an old woman, I am astonished.
> Letter to Mr. [David] Garrick* (London, 14 April 1769), Ibid.
> *English actor and theater manager (1717–1779).

6 I have seen your lamb turned into a lion: by this your great labour was entertained; they thought they all acted very fine—they did not see you pull the wires.
> Letter to Mr. Garrick (Twickenham, 23 June 1776), Ibid.

559. Marie de Beauveau (1711–1786)

1 Say what you will in two
Words and get through.
> "Air: Sentir avec ardeur," St. 1, Ezra Pound,* tr., *Confucius to Cummings; An Anthology of Poetry*, Ezra Pound and Marcella Spann, eds. *1964*
> *American poet and critic (1885–1972).

2 An idiot
Will always
Talk a lot.
> St. 2, Ibid.

560. Ho Shuang-ch'ing (1712–?)

1 The hardest thing in the world
Is to reveal a hidden love.
> to the tune "A Watered Silk Dress," *The Orchid Boat, Women Poets of China*, Kenneth Rexroth and Ling Chung, eds. and trs. *1972*

561. Laetitia Pilkington (1712–1750/51)

1 Lying is an occupation
    Used by all who mean to rise;
Politicians owe their station
    But to well-concerted lies.

These to lovers give assistance
    To ensnare the fair one's heart;
And the virgin's best resistance
    Yields to this commanding art.

Study this superior science,
　　Would you rise in church or state;
Bid to truth a bold defiance,
　　'Tis the practice of the great.
　　　　"Song," *in toto*, *Memoirs of Mrs. Laetitia Pilkington,*
　　　　written by herself, Wherein are occasionally interspersed
　　　　all her Poems, with Anecdotes of several eminent
　　　　persons living and dead 1748

562. Alicia Cockburn (1713–1794)

1　I've seen the smiling of fortune beguiling,
　I've felt all its favours and found its decay;
　Sweet was its blessing and kind its caressing,
　But now it is fled—it is fled far away.
　　　　"The Flowers of the Forest,"* *Scottish Song,*
　　　　Mary Carlyle Aitken, ed. *1874*
　　*This is a reworking of a much older, anonymous song. (Cf. Jean El-
　liot, 586:1.) The reference is to the thousands of men led by James
　IV who were slain at the Battle of Flodden Field (9 September 1513).

2　The flowers of the forest are withered away.
　　　　　　　　　　　　　　　　Refrain, Ibid.

563. Mary Monk (?–1715)

1　O'er this marble drop a tear,
　Here lies fair Rosalind;
　All mankind were pleased with her,
　And she with all mankind.
　　　　"Lady of Pleasure," *Marinda: Poems and Translations on*
　　　　Several Occasions 1716

2　A just applause and an immortal name
　Is the true object of the Poet's aim
　　　　　　　　　"Epistle to Marinda," Ibid.

3　Say, shouldst thou grieve to see my sorrows end?
　Thou know'st a painful pilgrimage I've past;
　And shouldst thou grieve that rest is come at last?
　Rather rejoice to see me shake off life,
　And die as I have liv'd, thy faithful wife.
　　　　"Verses written on her deathbed at Bath, to her husband in
　　　　London," Ibid.

564. Abigail Colman Dennie (1715–1745)

1　Yet still my fate permits me this relief,
　To write to lovely Delia* all my grief.
　To you alone I venture to complain;
　From others hourly strive to hide my pain.
　　　　Lines from a letter to her sister, Jane Colman (23 March
　　　　1733), Quoted in *New England Historical and*
　　　　Genealogical Register, No. 14 *1860*
　　*Her sister, the poet Jane Colmam Turell; see 551.

565. Anne Steele (1717–1778/79)

1　Little monitor, by thee
　Let me learn what I should be;
　Learn the round of life to fill,
　Useful and progressive still.
　　　　"To My Watch," *Poems on Subjects Chiefly Devotional 1760*

566. Maria Theresa (1717–1780)

1　My son,* as you are the heir to all my worldly possessions, I
　cannot dispose of them; but my children are still, as they

have ever been, my *own*. I bequeath them to you; be to them a
father.
　　　　Last words (29 November 1780), Quoted in *Biography of*
　　　　Distinguished Women by Sarah Josepha Hale** *1876*
　*Joseph II (1741–1790), Holy Roman Emperor, 1765–1790.
　**See 788.

2　I want to meet my God awake.
　　　　Remark on her deathbed, refusing drugs; attributed by
　　　　Thomas Carlyle* November *1780*
　*Scottish–born author (1795–1881).

567. Elizabeth Carter (1717–1806)

1　For Wealth, the smiles of glad content,
　For Power, its amplest, best extent,
　An empire o'er the mind.
　　　　"Ode to Wisdom," St. 7, *Poems Upon Particular Occasions*
　　　　　　　　　　　　　　　　　　　1738

2　Beneath her clear discerning eye,
　The visionary shadows fly
　Of Folly's painted show:
　She sees, through every fair disguise,
　That all but Virtue's solid joys
　Is vanity and woe.

　　　　　　　　　　　　　　　　St. 16, Ibid.

3　I have nothing to assist me but industry; genius I have none,
　and I want mightily to know whether one can make any
　progress without it.
　　　　Quoted in *A Woman of Wit and Wisdom*
　　　　by Alice C. C. Gaussen *1906*

4　I am sick of people of sense because they can act like fools,
　and of fools because they cannot talk like people of sense, and
　of myself for being so absurd as to trouble my head about
　them.
　　　　　　　　Letter to a friend (1745), Ibid.

5　Do you want employment? Choose it well before you begin,
　and then pursue it. Do you want amusement? Take the first
　you meet with that is harmless, and never be attached to any.
　Are you in a moderate station? Be content, though not affect-
　edly so; be philosophical, but for the most part keep your
　thoughts to yourself. Are you sleepy? Go to bed.
　　　　　　　　　　　　　　　　　　　Ibid.

568. Maria Gaëtana Agnesi (1718–1799)

1　. . . proper clarity and simplicity . . . , that natural order which
　provides, perhaps, the best instruction and the greatest light.
　　　　Preface, *Instituzioni analitiche ad uso della gioventù*
　　　　italiana, Vol. 1 *1748*

2　With all the study, sustained by the strongest inclination to-
　wards mathematics, that I forced myself to devote to it on my
　own, I should have become altogether tangled in the great
　labyrinth of insuperable difficulty, had not [Rampinelli's*] se-
　cure guidance and wise direction led me forth from it . . . ; to
　him I owe deeply all advances (whatever they might be) that
　my small talent has sufficed to make.
　　　　　　　　　　　　　　　　　　　Ibid.

　*Ramiro Rampinelli, monk and mathematician.

569. Mary Draper (1718?–1810)

1　He [her son] is wanted and must go. You [her daughter] and I,
　Kate, have also service to do. Food must be prepared for the

hungry; for before to-morrow night, hundreds, I hope thousands, will be on their way to join the continental forces.

> Response to a call to arms (1776), Quoted in *The Women of the American Revolution* by Elizabeth F. Ellet *1848*

570. Peg Woffington (1720–1760)

1 I count time by your absence; I have not seen you all morning, and is it not an age since then?

> Ch. 6, Remark to David Garrick* (1776), Quoted in *Days of the Dandies* by J. Fitzgerald Molloy *n.d.*

*English actor and theater manager (1717–1779).

571. Frances Fulke Greville (1720–1789)

1 No peace nor ease the heart can know,
    Which, like the needle true,
Turns at the touch of joy or woe,
    But, turning, trembles too.

> "Prayers for Indifference,"* St. 6 (1753), *Maxims and Characters 1756*

*See Isabella Howard, 577:1, for reply poem.

2 And what of life remains for me
    I'll pass in sober ease;
Half pleased, contented I will be,
    Content but half to please.

> last stanza, Ibid.

572. Elizabeth Montagu (1720–1800)

1 Will an intelligent spectator not admire the prodigious structures of Stone–Henge because he does not know by what law of mechanics they were raised?

> *An Essay on the Writing and Genius of Shakespeare Compared with Greek and French Dramatic Poets . . . 1769*

2 To judge therefore of Shakespeare by Aristotle's* rule is like trying a man by the Laws of one Country who acted under those of another.

> Ibid.

*Greek philosopher (384–322 B.C.E.).

3 Shakespeare seemed to have had the art of the Dervish in the Arabian tales who could throw his soul into the body of another man and be at once possessed of his sentiments, adopt his passions and rise to all the functions and feelings of his situation.

> Ibid.

4 Gold is the chief ingredient in the composition of worldly happiness. Living in a cottage on love is certainly the worst diet and the worst habitation one can find out.

> *The Letters of Mrs. Elizabeth Montagu 1810–1813*

5 If she [Catherine the Great*] is not a good woman, she is a great Prince.

> Letter to Lord Lyttleton, Ibid.

*See 591.

6 . . . there is a much higher character from that of a wit or a poet or a savant, which is that of a rational sociable being, willing to carry on the commerce of life with all the sweetness and condescension, decency and virtue will permit.

> Letter to Mrs. William Robinson, her sister-in-law, Ibid.

7 Minds ripen at very different ages.

> Ibid.

8 I endeavor . . . to be wise when I cannot be merry, easy when I cannot be glad, content with what cannot be mended and patient when there is no redress.

> Letter (c. 1739), Ibid.

9 There are but two kinds of people I think myself at liberty to hate and despise, the first is of the class of *soi disant* philosophers who by sophistry would cheat the less acute out of their principles, the only firm basis of moral virtue; the seconds are witts who ridicule whatsoever things are lovely, whatsoever things are of good report.

> Letter (1768), Ibid.

10 It is surprizing what money I have spent out of a principle of economy; because they are cheap I have bought more shoes than a millipede could wear in VII years. By my caps you would think I had more heads than Hydra.

> Letter to her brother (1776), Ibid.

11 But where there has not subsisted a good form of government and a regular system of Laws and mode of manners the people in general never are of good character

> Letter to Mrs. Carter (1777), Ibid.

12 We are become a scoundrel nation worthy to be scorned and fit to cudgel'd.

> Letter (1779), Ibid.

13 Wit in women is apt to have bad consequences; like a sword without a scabbard, it wounds the wearer and provokes and assailants. I am sorry to say the generality of women who have excelled in wit have failed in chastity. . . .

> (1750), Quoted in *Reconstructing Aphra* by AngelineGoreau *1980*

573. Charlotte Lennox (1720–1804)

1 I am not cruel enough to wish his Death; say that I command him to live, if he can live without Hope.

> *Arabella; or, The Female Quixote*, Vol. I *1752*

2 "Oh! Sir," cried Sir George, "I have Stock enough by me, to set up an Author Tomorrow, if I please: I have no less than Five Tragedies, some quite, others almost finished; Three or Four Essays on Virtue, Happiness, etc., Three thousand Lines of an Epic Poem; half a Dozen Epitaphs; a few Acrostics; and a long String of Puns, that would serve to embellish a Daily Paper, if I was disposed to write one."

> Vol. II, Ibid.

3 The only excellence of Falsehood . . . is its Resemblance to Truth. . . .

> Ibid.

4 It is the Fault of the best Fictions, that they teach young Minds to expect strange Adventures and sudden Vicissitudes, and therefore encourage them often to Chance. A long Life may be passed without a single Occurrence that can cause much Surprize, or produce any unexpected Consequence of great Importance.

> Ibid.

5 Oh couldst thou teach the totur'd Soul to know,
With Patience, each Extream of human Woe

> "On reading [Francis] Hutcheson* on the Passions," *Poems on Several Occasions 4 November 1752*

*British philosopher and moralist (1694–1746) and author of "An Essay on the Nature and Conduct of the Passions and Affections . . . " (1728).

6 " . . . I believe there is an intelligent cause which governs the world by physical rules. As for moral attributes, there is no such thing; it is impious and absurd to suppose it."

Henrietta, Vol. II *1758*

7 "Whatever is, is best. The law of nature is sufficiently clear; and there is no need of supernatural revelation."

Ibid.

8 MISS AUTUMN. I protest I tremble at the idea, of being one day, what my stepmother is at present. Oh heavens! in the midst of wrinkles and grey hairs, to dream of gentle languishment, vows, ardors!—but there is some comfort yet, fifty and I are at an immense distance.

The Sister 1759

9 In a word, the savage is subject to none but natural evils. . . .

Euphemia, Vol. III *1790*

10 The life of a good man is a continual prayer.

Vol. IV, Ibid.

574. Jeanne-Antoinette Poisson de Pompadour (1721–1764)

1 The King and I have such implicit confidence in you* that we look upon you as a cat, or a dog, and go on talking as if you were not there.

Quoted in *The Memoirs of Louis XV and of Madame de Pompadour* by Mme du Hausset *1802*

*Mme du Hausset, her bed-chamber attendant and author; see 650.

2 It is a wolf who makes the sheep reflect.

Ibid.

3 After us the deluge! (*Après nous le déluge!*)

Her motto, Ibid.

4 Wait a moment, monsieur, and we will set forth together. (*Attendez–moi, monsieur le curé, nous partirons ensemble.*)

Last words, spoken to the priest, Ibid.

575. Anna Dorothea Lisiewska-Therbusch (1721–1782)

1 I would not have dared suggest it to you, but you have done well, and I thank you.*

(1767), Quoted by Denis Diderot in *Diderot Salons*, Vol. III, Jean Adhémar and Jean Seznec, eds. *1963*

*In response to Diderot's voluntary disrobing for his portrait bust by her; Diderot (1713–1784) was a French philosopher and writer.

576. Mary Leapor (1722–1746)

1 EMILIA. Our servile Tongues are taught to cry for Pardon
Ere the weak Senses know the Use of Words:
Our little Souls are tortur'd by Advice;
And moral Lectures stun our Infant Years:
Thro' check'd Desires, Threatnings, and Restraint
The Virgin runs; but ne'er outgrows her Shackles
They still will fit her, even to hoary Age.

The Unhappy Father 1751

2 And all the arts that ruin while they please.

"The Temple of Love—a Dream," St. 3, *Poems Upon Several Occasions*, Vol. II *1751*

577. Isabella Howard (1722?–1793/95?)

1 "I dare not change a first decree:
She's doomed to please, nor can be free:
Such is the lot of beauty!"

"Reply by the Countess of C—,"* St. 11 (c.1753), *The Female Poets of Great Britain*, Frederic Rowton, ed. *1853*

*Reply poem to Frances Greville's "Prayers for Indifference"; see 571:1–2.

578. Eliza Pinckney (1722?–1793)

1 Be particularly watchful against heat of temper; it makes constant work for repentance and chagrin.

Letter to Charles Pinckney* (1761), *Journal and Letters of Eliza Lucas Pinckney*, Harriet R. Holbrook, ed. *1850*

*Her husband, a politician and judge.

579. Janet Graham (1723/24–1805)

1 Alas! my son, you little know
The sorrows that from wedlock flow,
Farewell to every day of ease,
When you have got a wife to please.

"The Wayward Wife," *Scottish Song*, Mary Carlyle Aitken, ed. *1874*

2 Great Hercules* and Samson** too,
Were stronger men than I or you,
Yet they were baffled by their dears,
And felt the distaff and the shears.

Ibid.

*Greek hero. **Israelite judge of Old Testament.

580. Frances Sheridan (1724–1766)

1 I must take her down a peg or so.

Act IV, Sc. 4, *The Dupe 1760*

2 As quick as lightning.

Act I, Sc. 2, *The Discovery 1763*

3 What taught me silently to bear,
To curb the sigh, to check the tear,
When sorrow weigh'd me down?

'T was Patience!

"Ode to Patience," Sts. 3, 4, *The Female Poets of Great Britain*, Frederic Rowton, ed. *1853*

581. Sarah Ryan (1724?–1768)

1 My merciful God did not leave me to follow my own imaginations, but often checked me by that thought, "Must all men die? Must all have an end? And must I die?"

Quoted in *The Women of Methodism: Its Three Foundresses . . .* by Abel Stevens *1866*

582. Frances Brooke (1724–1789)

1 To be happy in this world, it is necessary not to raise one's ideas too high. . . .

Letter XV, *The History of Emily Montague*, Vol. I *1769*

2 I have said married women are, by my principles, forbidden fruit: I should have explained myself; I mean in England, for my ideas on this head change as soon as I land at Calais.

Letter XXXVI, Ibid.

3 We have been saying, Lucy, that 'tis the strangest thing in the world people should quarrel about religion, since we undoubtedly all mean the same thing; all good minds in every religion aim at pleasing the Supreme Being; the means we take differ according to where we are born, and the prejudices we imbibe from education; a consideration which ought to inspire us with kindness and indulgence to each other.

Letter L, Ibid.

4 Parents should chuse our company, but never even pretend to direct our choice. . . .

Letter LXV, Ibid.

5 A marriage where not only esteem, but passion is kept awake, is, I am convinced, the most perfect state of sublunary happiness: but it requires great care to keep this tender plant alive. . . .

Letter LXVIII, Ibid.

6 . . . this love is the finest cosmetik in the world.

Letter XCIII, Ibid.

7 . . . happiness is not to be found in a life of intrigue. . . .

Letter XCIX, Ibid.

8 In my opinion, the man who conveys, and causes to grow, in any country, a grain, a fruit, or even a flower, it never possessed before, deserves more praise than a thousand heroes: he is a benefactor, he is in some degree a creator.

Letter CXXI, Ibid.

9 It is a painful consideration, my dear, that the happiness or misery of our lives are generally determined before we are proper judges of either.

Letter CLII, Ibid.

10 Restrained by custom, and the ridiculous prejudices of the world, we go with the crowd, and it is late in life before we dare to think.

Ibid.

11 If the Supreme Creator had meant us to be gloomy, he would, it seems to me, have clothed the earth in black, not in that lively green, which is the livery of cheerfulness and joy.

Letter CXCIV, Vol. IV, Ibid.

12 ROSINA. Why should I repine? Heaven, which deprived me of my parents and my fortune, left me health, content, and innocence. Nor is it certain that riches lead to happiness. Do you think the nightingale sings the sweeter for being in a gilded cage?

Act I, Sc. 1, *Rosina: A Comic Opera 1783*

13 RUSTIC. . . . I hate money when it is not my own.

Act II, Sc. 1, Ibid.

14 ROSINA. Whoever offends the object of his love is not worthy of obtaining her.

Ibid.

583. Eva Maria Garrick (1725–1822)

1 Groans and complaints are very well for those who are to mourn but a little while; but a sorrow that is to last for life will not be violent or romantic.

Quoted by Hannah More* in *Biography of Distinguished Women* by Sarah Josepha Hale** 1876
*See 636. **See 788.

584. Bridget Fletcher (1726–1770)

1 God's only son by woman came,
   To take away our shame;
And so thereby, to dignify,
   Also to raise our fame.
   Hymn XXXVI: St. 1, "The Greatest Dignity of a Woman,
   Christ Being Born of One," *Hymns and Spiritual Songs 1773*

585. Hester Chapone (1727–1801)

1 "Love worketh no ill to his neighbour"; therefore, if you have true benevolence; you will never do any thing injurious to individuals, or to society. Now, all crimes whatever are (in their remoter consequences at least, if not immediately and apparently) injurious to the society in which we live.
   "The Two Commandments," *Letters on the Improvement of the Mind 1773*

2 Affectation is so universally acknowledged to be disgusting, that it is among the faults which the most intimate friends cannot venture gravely to reprove in each other; for to tell your friends that they are habitually affected, is to tell them that they are habitually disagreeable; which nobody can bear to hear.
   "Affectation," *Miscellanies in Prose and Verse 1775*

3 Thrice welcome, friendly Solitude,
O let no busy foot intrude,
Nor listening ear be nigh!
   "Ode to Solitude," St. 1, *A Volume of Miscellanies 1775*

4 I make no scruple to call romances the worst of all species of writing; unnatural representation of the passions, false sentiment, false precepts, false wit, false honour, and false modesty, with a strange heap of improbable, unnatural incidents mixed up with true history. . . .
   Letter to Elizabeth Carter (31 July 1750), *The Works of Mrs. Chapone*, Vol. I 1818

586. Jean Elliot (1727–1805)

1 I've heard them lilting, at the ewes milking.
Lasses a' lilting, before dawn of day;
But now they are moaning, on ilka green loaning;
The Flowers of the Forest* are a' wede away.
   "The Flowers of the Forest," *Scottish Song*,
   Mary Carlyle Aitken, ed. 1874
*The forces of James IV who were slain at Flodden Field (9 September 1513). See note on Alicia Cockburn, 562:1.

2 The prime of our land, lie cauld in the clay.

Ibid.

587. Hannah Griffitts (1727–1817)

1 Then for the sake of Freedom's name,
   (Since British wisdom scorns repealing)
Come sacrifice to Patriot fame,
   And give up tea by way of healing.
   "'Beware of the Ides of March,' Said the Roman Augur To
   Julius Caesar," St. 3 (1775), *Women Poets in Pre-
   Revolutionary America*, Patti Cowell, ed. 1981

2 Like a Newton,* sublimely he soar'd,
   To a summit before unattain'd,

New regions of science explor'd,
     And the palm of philosophy gain'd.
          "Inscription On A Curious Chamberstove In the
     Form of an Urn, Contriv'd in Such A Manner as to Make
     the Flame Descend Instead of Rising, Invented By The
          Celebrated B.F.,"** St. 1 (1776), Ibid.
*British physicist and mathematician (1642–1727). **Benjamin
Franklin, American printer and publisher, author, inventor and
scientist, and diplomat (1706–1790); poem also attributed to
Jonathan Odell.

588. Margaret Klopstock (1728–1758)

1   I could not speak, I could not play; I thought I saw nothing
    but Klopstock.*
         Letter to Samuel Richardson** (Hamburg, 14 March 1758),
                    Letters from the Dead to the Living post-1758
    *Her husband, the poet Friedrich Gottlieb Klopstock
    (1724–1803). **English novelist (1689–1761).

2   It is long since I made the remark that the children of geniuses
    are not geniuses.
             Letter to Samuel Richardson (26 August 1758), Ibid.

589. Mercy Otis Warren (1728–1758)

1   BRUTUS. . . . hoodwink'd justice
    Drops her scales, and totters from her basis.
                         Act I, Sc. 1, *The Adulateur 1773*

2   E------R. [sic.] Honors, places, pensions—
    'Tis all a cheat, a damn'd, a cruel cheat.
                                     Act V, Sc. 2, Ibid.

3   CRUSTY CROWBAR. I too am almost sick of the parade
    Of honours purchas'd at the price of peace.
                         Act I, Sc. 1, *The Group 1775*

4   MONSIEUR. So great the itch I feel for titl'd place
    Some honorary post, some small distinction,
    To save my name from dark oblivious jaws,
    I'll Hazard all, but ne'er give up my place.
                                     Act II, Sc. 1, Ibid.

5   HATEALL. Then the green Hick'ry, or the willow twig,
    Will prove a curse for each rebellious dame
    Who dare oppose her lord's superior will.
                                                 Ibid.

6   SECRETARY. What shifts, evasions, what delusive tales,
    What poor prevarication for rash oaths,
    What nightly watchings, and what daily cares
    To dress up falsehood in some fair disguise
                                                 Ibid.

7   VALENTINIAN. I fear no storms but from an injur'd wife.
                                 Act II, Sc. 1, *The Sack of
                                         Rome 1790*

8   GAUDENTIUS. Ambition, in a noble, virtuous mind,
    Is the first passion that the gods implant,
    And soars to glory till it meets the skies
                                     Sc. 2, Ibid.

9   GAUDENTIUS. Fate may do much before we meet again;
    She has a busy hand, and swiftly rides
    On revolution's wheel. . . .
                                     Act IV, Sc. 5, Ibid.

10 EDOXIA. Enough of life and all life's idle pomp—
    Nor by a tyrant's fiat will I live—
    I leave the busy, vain, ambitious world
    To cheat itself anew, and o'er and o'er
    Tread the same ground their ancestors have trod,
    In chace of thrones, of sceptres, or of crowns,
    'Till all these bubbles break in empty air,
    Nor leave a trace of happiness behind.
                                     Act V, Sc. 3, Ibid.

11 DON JUAN DE PADILLA. Let freedom be the mistress of thy heart.
                         Act I, Sc. 1, *The Ladies of Castile 1790*

12 DE HARO. But in the hero ne'er forget the man.
                                     Sc. 2, Ibid.

13 FRANCIS. Mistaken man!
                                     Sc. 5, Ibid.

14 MARIA. Today the cap of liberty's toss'd up—
    Tomorrow torn and given to the winds,
    And all their leaders, by the fickle throng
    Are sacrific'd by violence, or fraud.
                                     Act II, Sc. 4, Ibid.

15 DON JUAN. Most men are brave till courage has been try'd,
    And boast of virtue till their price is known. . . .
                                     Sc. 5, Ibid.

16 DON PEDRO. . . . the bubble freedom—empty name!—
    'Tis all a puff—a visionary dream—
    That kindles up this patriotic flame;
    'Tis rank self love, conceal'd beneath a mask
    Of public good. The hero's brain inflates—
    He cheats himself by the false medium,
    Held in virtue's guise, till he believes it just
                                                 Ibid.

17 DE HARO. Great souls—form's in the same etherial mould,
    Are ne'er at war—they, different paths
    Of glory may pursue, with equal zeal;
    Yet not a cruel, or malignant thought,
    Or rancorous design, deform the mind.
                                     Act III, Sc. 1, Ibid.

18 DON JUAN. To learn to die is an heroic work
                                     Act IV, Sc. 2, Ibid.

19 MARIA. Maternal softness weakens my resolve,
    And wakes new fears—thou dearest, best of men,
    Torn from my side, I'm levell'd with my sex.
    The wife—the mother—make me less than woman.
                                     Sc. 5, Ibid.

20 'Tis social converse, animates the soul.
         "To Fidelio,* Long Absent on the Great Public Cause, which
         Agitates All America," St. 1 (1776), *Miscellaneous Poems n.d.*
    *Pseudonym of James Warren, her husband, who fought in the
    Revolutionary War.

21 The balm of life, a kind and faithful friend.
                                                 Ibid.

22 Each humbler muse at distance may admire,
    But none to Shakespeare's fame e'er dare aspire.
         "To Mrs. Montague,* Author of 'Observation, On the Ge-
         nius and Writings of Shakespeare,'" St. 2 (Plymouth, 10 July
                                     1790), Ibid.
    *Elizabeth Robinson Montagu; see 572.

590. Sarah Prince Gill (1728–1771)

1   —Thou, thou art all!
    My soul flies up and down in thoughts of thee,
    And finds herself but at the center still!
    I AM, thy name! Existence, all thine own!
    Creation's nothing to Thee, the great Original!
        Untitled, St. 1, *Dying Exercises of Mrs. Deborah Prince and
            Devout Meditations of Mrs. Sarah Gill . . . 1784*

591. Catherine II of Russia (1729–1796)

1   For to tempt and to be tempted are things very nearly allied,
    and in spite of the finest maxims of morality impressed upon
    the mind, whenever feeling has anything to do in the matter,
    no sooner is it excited than we have already gone vastly far-
    ther than we are aware of.
        Memoirs, A. Herzen, ed. and tr. *1857*

2   I may be kindly, I am ordinarily gentle, but in my line of busi-
    ness I am obliged to will terribly what I will at all.
        Letter (30 August 1774), *Correspondance avec le Baron F.
            M. Grimm (1774–1796) 1878*

3   A great wind is blowing, and that gives you either imagination
    or a headache.
        Letter (29 April 1775), Ibid.

4   I am one of the people who love the why of things.
        Letter (20 January 1776), Ibid.

5   In my position you have to read when you want to write and
    to talk when you would like to read; you have to laugh when
    you feel like crying; twenty things interfere with twenty others,
    you have not time for a moment's thought, and nevertheless
    you have to be constantly ready to act with out allowing your-
    self to feel lassitude, either of body or spirit; ill or well, it
    makes no difference, everything at once demands that you
    should attend to it on the spot.
        Letter (23 August 1794), Ibid.

6   Your wit makes others witty. (*Votre esprit en donne aux
    autres.*)
        Letter to Voltaire,* *The Complete Works of Catherine II*,
            Evdokimov, ed. *1893*
        *François-Marie Arouet, French philosopher and writer
        (1694–1778).

7   I praise loudly, I blame softly.
        Letter, Ibid.

8   If Fate had given me in youth a husband whom I could have
    loved, I should have remained always true to him. The trouble is
    that my heart would not willingly remain one hour without love.
        Letter to Prince Potemkin (1774), Quoted in *Memoirs*,
            Katharine Anthony, ed. and tr. *1925*

9   At the age of fourteen she made the three-fold resolution, to
    please her Consort, [Empress] Elizabeth, and the Nation.
        Epitaph, written by herself (1789), Ibid.

10   To govern you have to have eyes and hands, and a woman has
    only ears.
        Quoted in *Daughters of Eve* by Gamaliel Bradford *1928*

11   The most sure, but at the same time the most difficult expedi-
    ent to mend the morals of the people, is a perfect system of
    education.
        Remark (1767), Quoted in *Women in World History Cur-
            riculum*, http://www.womeninworldhistory.com *1996–97*

592. Sarah Crosby (1729–1804)

1   The day after, at church, the Lord showed me that many things
    which I had thought were sins were only temptations, and also
    what a little thing it was for him to take the root of sin out of
    my heart.
        Quoted in *Women of Methodism: Its Three
            Foundresses . . .* , by Abel Stevens *1866*

593. Elizabeth Cooper (fl. 1730s)

1   BELLAIR. . . . Money is of no Value till 'tis used.
        The Rival Widows; or, Fair Libertine 1735

2   BELLAIR. We can talk of Murder, Theft, and Treason, without
    blushing: and surely there's nothing a–kin to Love that's half
    so wicked.
        Ibid.

594. Mrs. Weddell (fl. c. 1730–1740)

1   [I cannot] admit of making the People's Taste the Rule of Writ-
    ing, [for] it is known to all who consider the Intention of a
    Theater, That its peculiar Business is to correct a wrong Taste,
    instead of complying with it.
        Preface, *The City Farce 1737*

2   . . . [they are] a wise People, and fond of Liberty, who consider
    all Men as Denizens of the Earth's plenteous Blessings, nor
    think the casual Tincture of the Skin, differing from the Euro-
    pean Hue alienates any from the indubitable Right they are
    naturally entitled to, as Fellow Creatures.
        Preface, *Incle and Yarico 1742*

3   [Africa] . . .
    Where the Remembrance of the Multitudes
    Borne hence, to Slav'ry, by our Countrymen
    Must make each Man we meet an Enemy.
        Ibid.

595. Mary Masters (fl. 1730–1755)

1   What if the charms in him I see
    Only exist in thought
        "To Lucinda," St. 2, *Poems on Several Occasions 1733*

2   Love is a mighty god, you know,
        That rules with potent sway;
    And when he draws his awful bow,
        We mortals must obey.
        "To Lucinda," St. 6, Ibid.

596. Caterina Gabrielli (1730–1796)

1   In this case, your majesty has only to engage one of your field-
    marshals to sing.
        Reply to Catherine the Great's* response ("None of my
            field–marshals receive so enormous a sum!") to Gabrielli's
            fee of 5,000 ducats to sing, Quoted in *Biography of
            Distinguished Women* by Sarah Josepha Hale** *1876*
        *See 591. **See 788.

597. Sophie de la Briche Houdetot (1730–1813)

1   Youth, I loved you; those loveliest years,
    Brief as they were, when love was my only occupation.
        "Imitation de Marot," Elaine T. Partnow,* tr., Quoted in *Biog-
            raphy of Distinguished Women* by Sarah Josepha Hale** *1876*
        *See 2870. **See 788.

598. Marguerite Brunet (1730–1820)

1 Will I then really have no company here, and does the King absolutely insist that I sleep alone?

Remark upon entering her prison cell, Quoted in Enter the Actress *by Rosamond Gilder* 1931

2 . . . these special gala performances are always good for trade.

Remark, Ibid.

599. Lucy Terry (1731?–1822?)

1 Eunice Allen see the Indians comeing
And hoped to save herself by running
And had not her petticoats stopt her
The awful creatures had not cotched her
And tommyhawked her on the head
And left her on the ground for dead.

"Bars Fight,"* The Poetry of the Negro, 1746–1870, *Langston Hughes** and Arna Bontemps, eds.* 1949
*Refers to an Indian raid on Deerfield, Massachusetts (25 August 1746). **American poet, writer (1902–1967).

600. Martha Washington (1731–1802)

1 . . . the greater part of our happiness or misery depends on our dispositions, and not on our circumstances. We carry the seeds of the one or the other about with us in our minds wherever we go.

Letter to Mrs. Warren* (26 December 1789), Quoted in Lives of Celebrated Women *by Samuel Griswold Goodrich* 1844

*Probably Mercy Otis Warren; see 589.

2 It is all over now. I shall soon follow him. I have no more trials to pass through.*

Remark (1799), Ibid.

*Referring to the death of her husband, George Washington (1732–99), 1st president of the United States (1789–97).

3 I live a very dull life here . . . indeed I think I am more like a state prisoner than anything else. . . .

Letter to a relative, Quoted in Martha Washington *by Anne Hollingsworth Wharton* 1897

4 . . . steady as a clock, busy as a bee, and cheerful as a cricket. . . .

Letter to a friend, Ibid

601. Julie-Jeanne-Eléonore de Lespinasse (1732–1776)

1 There is a certain hour in the day when I wind up my moral machine as I wind my watch. And then, the movement once given, it goes more or less well. . . . What is curious is that no one suspects the effort required to appear what I am thought really to be.

Letter to Condorcet* (4 May 1771), Lettres inédites 1887
*Marquis de Condorcet, French philosopher and politician (1743–1794).

2 . . . people observe very little, and it is fortunate, for there is not much to be gained by seeing more than others do.

Ibid.

3 If you can attain repose and calm, believe that you have seized happiness. Alas! Is there any other! And can there be any when one has made one's existence dependent upon another? Were he a god, the sacrifice would be too great.

Letter (23 August 1772), Ibid.

4 I do nothing but love, I know nothing but love.

Letter to Guibert* (30 May 1773), Lettres 1906
*François-Apollini Guibert, French military reformer (1744–1790).

5 Ah! how the mind weakens when one loves.

Ibid.

6 The logic of the heart is absurd.

Letter (27 August 1774), Ibid.

7 You know that when I hate you, it is because I love you to a point of passion that unhinges my soul.

Letter (1774), Ibid.

602. Mary Knowles (1733–1807)

1 He [Dr. Johnson] gets at the substance of a book directly; he tears out the heart of it.

Letter (15 April 1778), Quoted in The Life of Samuel Johnson,* LL.D. *by James Boswell* 1791
*English author and lexicographer (1709–84).

603. Mrs. Pennington (1734–1759)

1 On glories greater glories rise.

"Ode to Morning," St. 1, The Female Poets of Great Britain, *Frederic Rowton, ed.* 1853

604. Louise Honorine de Choiseul (1734–1801)

1 You know you love me, but you do not feel it.

Letter to Marie du Deffand,* Correspondance complète de Mme du Deffand avec la duchesse de Choiseul, l'abbé Barthélemy et M. Craufurt 1866

*See 536.

2 It is well to love even a dog when you have the opportunity, for fear you should find nothing else worth loving.

Quoted in Portraits of Women *by Gamaliel Bradford* 1916

3 If I have learned anything, I owe it neither to precepts nor to books, but to a few opportune misfortunes. Perhaps the school of misfortunes is the very best.

Ibid.

4 He [Jean-Jacques Rousseau*] has always seemed to me to be a charlatan of virtue.

Ibid.

*French philosopher and writer (1712–1778).

5 He [Voltaire*] tells us he is faithful to his enthusiasms; he should have said, to his weaknesses. He has always been so cowardly where there was no danger, insolent where there was no motive, and mean where there was no object in being so. All which does not prevent his being the most brilliant mind of the century. We should admire his talent, study his works, profit by his philosophy, and be broadened by his teaching. We should adore him and despise him, as is indeed the case with a good many objects of worship.

Ibid.

*François Marie Arouet, French philosopher and writer (1694–1778).

6 My skepticism has grown so great that it falls over backward and from doubting everything I have become ready to believe anything.

Ibid.

7 We grow old as soon as we cease to love and trust.

Ibid.

8 Good-by, dear child, I wish you good sleep and a good digestion. I don't know anything better to desire for those I love.

Ibid.

605. Caroline Keppel (1735–?)

1 What's this dull town to me?
    Robin's not near—
He whom I wished to see,
    Wished for to hear;
Where's all the joy and mirth
    Made life a heaven on earth?
O! they're all fled with thee,
    Robin Adair

"Robin Adair" *n.d.*

606. Nancy Hart (1735?–1830)

1 Surrender your damned Tory carcasses to a Whig woman.

On her capture of five Loyalists, Quoted in *The Women of the American Revolution*, Vol. II by Elizabeth F. Ellet *1848*

607. Ann Lee (1736–1784)

1 By the Son, the *true* being and *true character* of the Father, was first revealed: and, the existence of the Son while it proved the existence of the Eternal *Father*, proved also the existence of the Eternal *Mother*.

Neither argument, nor illustration, would seem necessary to prove this. For, without both a *father* and a *mother*, there can be neither son nor daughter; either natural or spiritual, visible or invisible!

"The Order of Deity, Male and Female, in whose Image Man was Created," *Shaker Bible*, a.k.a. *Mother Ann's Bible c. 1774*

2 I converse with Christ; I feel him present with me, as sensibly as I feel my hands together.

Quoted in *The Testimony of Christ's Second Appearing* by Benjamin S. Youngs *1808*

3 It is not I that speak, it is Christ who dwells in me.

Ibid.

4 You can never enter into the Kingdom of God with hardness against anyone, for God is love, and if you love God you will love one another.

Remark, upon her release from prison (c. 1776), Quoted in *Wise Women: Over 2000 Years of Spiritual Writing by Women*, Susan Cahill, ed. *1996*

5 'Tis the gift to be simple,
'Tis the gift to be free,
'Tis the gift to come down where we ought to be,
And when we find ourselves in the place that's right
'Twill be in the valley of love and delight.

"Simple Gifts" (Shaker Hymn), Ibid.

608. Theodosia De Visme Burr (1736–1794)

1 Piety teaches resignation. . . . The better I am acquainted with it, the more claims I find.

Letter to her husband, Aaron Burr* (6 March 1781), *Memoirs of Aaron Burr*, Vol. I, Matthew L. Davis, ed. *1836–1837*
*American vice president (1801–1805) and politician (1756–1836); tried for treason.

2 I am impatient for the evening; for the receipt of your dear letter; for those delightful sensations which your expression of tenderness alone can excite. Dejected, distracted without them, elated, giddy even to folly with them, my mind, never at medium, claims everything from your partiality.

Letter to Aaron Burr (August 1786), Ibid.

609. Annis Stockton (1736–1801)

1 . . . future ages shall enroll thy name
In sacred annals of immortal fame.

"Addressed to General Washington* in the Year 1777 After the Battles of Trenton and Princeton," *Columbian Magazine January 1787*
*George Washington (1732–1799), first president of the United States (1789–1797).

2 For, oh! I find on earth no charms for me
But what's connected with the thought of thee!

"Epistle to Mr. S[tockton]," *Women Poets in Pre-Revolutionary America*, Patti Cowell, ed. *1981*

3 Thousands of heroes from this dust shall rise.

"On Hearing That General [Dr. Joseph] Warren Was Killed on Bunker Hill, the 17th of June, 1775," Ibid.

610. Mary Katherine Goddard (1736/38?–1816)

1 . . . [it is] their duty to inquire into everything that has a tendency to restrain the liberty of the Press. . . .

Letter to the Baltimore Committee of Safety (May/June 1776), Quoted in Ch. 8, *William Goddard, Newspaperman* by Ward L. Miner *1962*

2 The stoppage of the *Paper-Mill*, near this Town, for the Want of a Supply of Rags, and the enormous Prices demanded at the Stores here for PAPER, constrains us to print the *Maryland Journal* on this dark and poor Sort, which our Readers will, we are persuaded to excuse, for one Week at least, when they are assured, that rather than deprive them of *the important Intelligence of the Times*, by the Discontinuance of our *Journal*, we have given from *Forty* to *Fifty Pounds* a Week for the Article of Paper *alone*, an equal Quantity of which, might, formerly, have been purchased for *Eight Dollars*!

Notice in *Maryland Journal* (26 May 1778), Ibid.

611. Suzanne Chardon Necker (1737–1794)

1 . . . I cannot help thinking that the vows most women are made to take are very foolhardy. I doubt whether they would willingly go to the altar to swear that they will allow themselves to be broken on the wheel every nine months.

Quoted in *Mistress to an Age: A Life of Madame de Staël** by J. Christopher Herold *1958*
*See 717.

2 Governesses have always one great disadvantage; if they are qualified for their calling, they intercept the child's affection for its mother.

Ibid.

612. Elizabeth Graeme Ferguson (1737–1801)

1 A transient, rich, and balmy sweet
Is in thy fragrance found;
But soon the flow'r and scent retreat—
Thorns left alone to wound.

"On a Beautiful Damask Rose, Emblematical of Love and Wedlock," St. 3, *Columbian Magazine May 1789*

2 Thus over all, self-love presides supreme
"On the Mind's Being Engrossed By One Subject," Ibid.

3 Birth day odes to lords and kings,
Oft are strain'd and stupid things!
Poet laureate's golden lays,
Fulsome hireling's hackney'd praise!
"An Ode Written on the Birthday of Mr. Henry Ferguson By
His Wife When They Had Been Married Two Years, He
Aged 26 Years," St. 1 (12 March 1774), *Women Poets in
Pre-Revolutionary America*, Patti Cowell, ed. *1981*

4 . . . angel-like he spake, and God-like died.
"On the Death of Leopold, Hereditary Prince of Brunswick,
Who was Drowned in the Oder, April 17, 1785, in
Attempting to Save Some Children Whose Mother
had Left Them on the Banks of that River,"
(Montgomery County, 5 July 1785), Ibid.

613. Margaret Morris (1737?–1816)

1 A loud knocking at my door brought me to it. . . . I opened it,
and a half a dozen men, all armed, demanded the key of the
empty house. . . . I put on a very simple look and exclaimed—
"Bless me! I hope you are not Hessians!"*

"Do we look like Hessians?" asked one rudely.

"Indeed, I don't know."

"Did you ever see a Hessian?"

"No—never in my life; but they are *men*; and you are men;
and may be Hessians for aught I know!"
from her Journal (16 December 1776), Quoted in
The Women of the American Revolution, Vol. II
by Elizabeth F. Ellet *1848*
*German mercenaries hired by the British.

2 . . . there is a god of battle as well as a God of peace. . . .
(27 December 1776), Ibid.

614. Mary Fletcher (1739–1815)

1 I was deeply conscious it [religion] is one of the most delicate
subjects in the world, and requires both much wisdom and
much love, to extinguish false fire, and yet keep up the true.
Quoted in *The Women of Methodism: Its Three
Foundresses . . .* by Abel Stevens *1866*

2 I feel at this moment a more tender affection toward him* than
I did at that time [of her marriage], and by faith I now join my
hand afresh with his.
Journal entry (12 November 1809), Ibid.
*Her husband, Jean Guillaume de la Flechère; written during her
widowhood, on the anniversary of her marriage.

615. Madame de Charrière (1740–?)

1 I would prefer being my lover's laundress and living in a garret
to the arid freedom and the good manners of our great families.
Quoted in *Mistress to an Age: A Life of Madame de Staël**
by J. Christopher Herold *1958*
*See 717.

616. Mrs. Hoper (fl. 1740s)

1 The Stage shall flourish, Tragedy shall thrive,
And Shakespear's Scenes ne'er die whilst They* survive
Prologue, *Queen Tragedy Restores 1749*
Othello, Hamlet, Falstaff (Henry IV) and *Richard II.*

617. Sarah Parsons Moorhead (fl. c. 1740)

1 Despise the blest instructions of their tongue,
Conversion is become the drunkard's song;
God's glorious work, which sweetly did arise,
By this unguarded sad imprudence dies;
Contention spreads her harpy claws around,
In every church her hateful stings are found.
"To the Reverend Mr. James Davenport on His Departure
from Boston, By Way of a Dream," St. 1 *1742*

618. Martha Brewster (fl. 1740s–1757)

1 Oh!——he——is——gone.
"To the Memory of that worthy Man Liet. NATHANIEL
BURT of *Springfield* . . . [who died] in the Battle of Lake-
George in the Retreat, September 8th, 1753," *Poems on
Divers Subjects 1757*

2 There is a wheel within a wheel.
"A Farewell to Some of My Christian Friends at Goshen, in
Lebanon," St. 4 (5 April 1745), Ibid.

3 Dear friends, the life is more than meat,
The soul excels the clay;
O labor then for gospel food,
Which never shall decay.
St. 14, Ibid.

4 O absence! absence! sharper than a thorn
"A Letter to My Daughter Ruby Bliss," Ibid.

619. Clementina Rind (1740?–1774)

1 Open to ALL PARTIES, but Influenced by NONE
Motto, Quoted in *Virginia Gazette* (first issue) *16 May 1766*

620. Sophie Arnould (1740/4–1802)

1 We shall be rich as princes. A good fairy has given me a talisman to transform every thing into gold and diamonds at the
sound of my voice.
Quoted in *Queens of Song* by
Ellen Creathorne Clayton *1865*

2 Oh! that was the good time; I was very unhappy. (*Oh! c'était
le bon temps; j'étais bien malheureuse.*)
Remark to Claude-Carlomande Rulhière,* Quoted in
*Sophie Arnould; d'après sa correspondance et ses mémoirs
inédits*, Edmond and Jules de Goncourt, eds. *1884*
*French writer and historian (1734–1791).

3 They give themselves to God when the Devil will no longer
have them.
Ch. 4, Quoted in *Sophie Arnold: Actress and Wit* by Robert
B. Douglas *1898*

621. Martha Mica Moore (1740–1829)

1 Let the Daughters of Liberty nobly arise.
"The Female Patriots, Addressed to the Daughters of Liberty
in America," *William and Mary Quarterly April 1977*

622. Sarah Kirby Trimmer (1741–1810)

1 Happy would it be for the animal creation, if every human
being . . . consulted the welfare of inferior creatures, and neither spoiled them by indulgence, nor injured them by tyranny!
Happy would mankind be . . . by cultivating in their own

minds and those of their own children, the divine principle of general benevolence.

Fabulous Histories: or, The History of the Robins. Designed for the Instruction of Children, Respecting Their Treatment of Animals, 13th ed. *1821*

2 Every living creature that comes into the world has something allotted to him to perform, therefore he should not stand an idle spectator of what others are doing.

Ibid.

623. Hester Lynch Piozzi (1741–1821)

1 It is a maxim here [at Venice], handed down from generation to generation, that change breeds more mischief from its novelty than advantage from its utility.

"Observations on a Journey Through Italy," *Autobiography, Letters and Literary Remains*, Abraham Hayward, ed. *1861*

2 The tree of deepest root is found
Least willing still to quit the ground:
'Twas therefore said by ancient sages,
That love of life increased with years
So much, that in our later stages,
When pain grows sharp and sickness rages,
The greatest love of life appears.

"Three Warnings," Ibid.

3 Ah! he was a wise man who said Hope is a good breakfast but a bad dinner. It shall be my supper, however, when all's said and done.

Vol. II, Ibid.

4 A physician can sometimes parry the scythe of death, but has no power over the sand in the hourglass.

Letter to Fanny Burney* (12 November 1781), Ibid.
*See 661.

5 Johnson's conversation was by far much too strong for a person accustomed to obsequiousness and flattery; it was mustard in a young child's mouth.

(May 1781), Quoted in *Life of Samuel Johnson** by James Boswell *1791*

*British writer and lexicographer (1709–1794).

624. Dorcas Richardson (1741?–1834)

1 I do not doubt that men who can outrage the feelings of a woman by such threats, are capable of perpetrating any act of treachery and inhumanity towards a brave but unfortunate enemy. But conquer or capture my husband [Captain Richard Richardson], if you can do so, before you boast the cruelty you mean to mark your savage triumph! And let me tell you, meanwhile, that some of you, it is likely, will be in a condition to implore *his* mercy, before he will have need to supplicate, or deign to accept yours.

Remark to the British, Quoted by Dr. Joseph Johnson in *The Women of the American Revolution* by Elizabeth F. Ellet *1848*

625. Anna Seward (1742–1809)

1 O hours! more worth than gold
Untitled (December 1782), *Sonnets 1789*

2 This last and long enduring passion for Mrs. Thrale* was, however, composed of cupboard love, Platonic love, and vanity tickled and gratified.

Letter, *Letters*, Vol. II *n.d.*
*Allusion to Dr. Samuel Johnson's relationship with Hester Lynch Piozzi, a.k.a. Mrs. Thrale; see 623.

626. Darcy Maxwell (1742?–1810)

1 It is seldom that we go beyond our teachers.
Quoted in *The Women of Methodism: Its Three Foundresses . . .* by Abel Stevens *1866*

2 Suffice it to say, I was chosen in the furnace of affliction. The Lord gave me all I desired in this world, then took all from me;* but immediately afterward sweetly drew me to Himself.

Letter to a friend (c. 1776), Quoted in *Biography of Distinguished Women* by Sarah Josepha Hale** *1876*
*She was widowed at nineteen; six weeks later her only child died.
**See 788.

627. Isabella Graham (1742–1814)

1 Hail! thou state of widowhood,
State of those that mourn to God;
Who from earthly comforts torn,
Only live to pray and mourn.

"Widowhood" (1774), *Life and Writings n.d.*

628. Anne Home (1742–1821)

1 'Tis hard to smile when one would weep,
To speak when one would silent be;
To wake when one would wish to sleep,
And wake to agony.

"The Lot of Thousands," *Poems by Mrs. John Hunter 1802*

2 My mother bids me bind my hair
With bands of rosy hue,
Tie up my sleeve with ribbons rare,
And lace my bodice blue.
"For why," she cries, "sit still and weep,
While others dance and play?"
Alas! I scarce can go or creep
While Lubin is away.

"My Mother Bids Me Bind My Hair," Ibid.

629. Eibhlín Dhubh Ní Chonaill (1743–1790)

1 Till Art O'Leary returns
There will be no end to the grief
That presses down on my heart,
Closed up tight and firm
Like a trunk that is locked
And the key mislaid.

"The Lament for Arthur O'Leary," St. 35, Ellis Dillon, tr., *The Penguin Book of Women Poets*, Carol Cosman, Joan Keefe and Kathleen Weaver, eds. *1978*

630. Hannah Cowley (1743–1809)

1 DOILEY. No, no; you must mind your P's and Q's* with him, I can tell you.

Act I, Sc. 2, *Who's the Dupe? 1779*
*Originally abbreviation for "pints and quarts," used in taverns.

2 DOILEY. Well, good fortune never comes in a hurry. . . .
Ibid.

3 GRADUS. The charms of women were never more powerful—never inspired such achievements, as in those immortal periods, when they could neither read nor write.

Sc. 3, Ibid.

4 CHARLOTTE. You know very well, the use of language is to express one's likes and dislikes—and a pig will do this as

effectually by its squeak, or a hen with her cackle, as you with your Latin and Greek.

> *Ibid.*

5 GRADUS. Beauty is a talisman which works true miracles, and, without a fable, transforms mankind.

> *Act II, Sc. 1, Ibid.*

6 SAVILLE. Five minutes! Zounds! I have been five minutes too late all my life-time!

> *Act I, Sc. 1, The Belle's Strategem c. 1780s*

7 VILLERS. A lady at her toilette is as difficult to be moved as a quaker.

> *Sc. 3, Ibid.*

8 SIR GEORGE TOUCHWOOD. Heaven and earth! with whom can a man trust his wife in the present state of society? Formerly there were distinctions of character amongst ye; every class of females had its particular description! grandmothers were pious, aunts discreet, old maids censorious! but now, aunts, grandmothers, girls, and maiden gentlewomen, are all the same creature; a wrinkle more or less is the sole difference between ye.

> *Act II, Sc. 1, Ibid.*

9 COURTALL. But 'tis always so; your reserved ladies are like ice, 'egad!—no sooner begin to soften than they melt!

> *Sc. 2, Ibid.*

10 MRS. RACKET. Marry first and love will follow.

> *Act III, Sc. 1, Ibid.*

11 LADY FRANCIS TOUCHWOOD. Every body about me seem'd happy—but every body seem'd in a hurry to be happy somewhere else.

> *Sc. 4, Ibid.*

12 FLUTTER. O lord! your wise men are the greatest fools upon earth; they reason about their enjoyments, and analyse their pleasures, whilst the essence escapes.

> *Act IV, Sc. 1, Ibid.*

13 FLUTTER. "Live to love," was my father's motto: "Live to laugh," is mine.

> *Ibid.*

14 VILLERS. The charms that helped to catch the husband are generally laid by, one after another, till the lady grows a downright wife, and then runs crying to her mother, because she has transformed her lover into a downright husband.

> *Act V, Sc. 1, Ibid.*

15 MRS. RACKET. It requires genius to make a good pun—some men of bright parts can't reach it.

> *Sc. 5, Ibid.*

16 OLIVIA. But no gentle Katherine* will he find me, believe it. Katherine!—Why, she had not the spirit of a roasted chestnut. A few big words, an empty oath, and a scanty dinner, made her as submissive as a spaniel. My fire will not be so soon extinguished: it shall resist big words, oaths, and starving!

> *A Bold Stroke for a Husband 1784*

*Reference to Katharine in Shakespeare's *Taming of the Shrew*.

17 OLIVIA. He has a very pretty kind of conversation; 'tis like a parenthesis.
DON CAESAR. Like a parenthesis!
OLIVIA. Yes, it might be all left out, and never missed.

> *Ibid.*

18 OLIVIA. Dost think my husband shall contradict my will? Oh! I long to set a pattern to those milky wives, whose mean compliances degrade the sex!

> *Ibid.*

631. Ekaterina Vorontsova Dashkova (1743–1810)

1 As there were no other two women at the time, apart from the Grand Duchess* and myself, who did any serious reading, we were mutually drawn to each other; and the charm which she knew how to exert whenever she wanted to win over anyone, was too powerful for an artless little girl like myself, to refuse her the gift of my heart forevermore.

> *The Memoirs of Princess Dashkova*, Kyril Fitzlyon, tr. and ed. *1995*

*Reference to Catherine the Great; see 591.

2 My life had been spent in constant sacrifice of my own wishes and pleasures for the sake of my children.

> *Ibid.*

3 God himself, by creating me a woman, had exempted me from accepting the employment of a Director of an Academy of Sciences.*

> *Ibid.*

*She later founded and became director of the Russian Academy of Sciences.

632. Anna Letitia Barbauld (1743–1825)

1 While Genius was thus wasting his strength in eccentric flights, I saw a person of very different appearance, named Application.

> "The Hill of Science," *Miscellaneous Pieces in Prose 1773*

2 The most characteristic mark of a great mind is to choose some one important object, and pursue it for life.

> "Against Inconsistency in Our Expectations," *Ibid.*

3 The awakenings of remorse, virtuous shame and indignation, the glow of moral approbation—if they do not lead to action, grow less and less vivid every time they occur, till at length the mind grows absolutely callous.

> "An Inquiry Into Those Kinds of Distress Which Excite Agreeable Sensations," *Ibid.*

4 Education, in its largest sense, is a thing of great scope and extent. It includes the whole process by which a human being is formed to be what he is, in habits, principles, and cultivation of every kind. . . . You speak of *beginning* the education of our son. The moment he was able to form an idea his education was already begun. . . .

> "On Education," *Ibid.*

5 Let us confess a truth, humiliating perhaps to human pride;—a very small part only of the opinions of the coolest philosopher are the result of fair reasoning; the rest are formed by his education, his temperament, by the age in which he lives, by trains of thought directed to a particular track through some accidental association—in short, by *prejudice*.

> "On Prejudice," *Ibid.*

6 Forgotten rimes, and college themes,
Worm-eaten plans, and embryo schemes;—
A mass of heterogeneous matter.
A chaos dark, nor land nor water.

> "An Inventory of the Furniture in Dr. Priestley's* Study," *Poems 1773*

*The English chemist Joseph Priestley (1733–1804).

7   Who can resist those dumb beseeching eyes,
    Where genuine eloquence pervasive lies?
    Those eyes, where language fails, display thy heart
    Beyond the pomp of phrase and pride of art.
                                    "To A Dog," Ibid.

8   We neither laugh alone, nor weep alone,—
      why then should we pray alone?
        *Remarks on Mr. Gilbert Wakefield's Enquiry Into the Expe-
        diency and Propriety of Public or Social Worship 1792*

9   . . . still Afric bleeds,
    Unchecked, the human traffic still proceeds
        "Epistle to William Wilberforce, Esq."* (1791), *The Works
                        of Anna Letitia Barbauld*, Vol. I *1826*
    *English politician and abolitionist (1759–1833); the reference is
    to slavery.

10 Where seasoned tools of Avarice prevail,
    A Nation's eloquence, combined, must fail
                                              Ibid.

11 Yes, injured Woman! rise, assert thy right!
    Woman! too long degraded, scorned, opprest;
    O born to rule impartial Laws despite,
    Resume thy native empire o'er the breast!
                        "The Right of Woman," Ibid.

12 . . . separate rights are lost in mutual love.
                                              Ibid.

13 No line can reach
    To thy unfathomed depths. The reasoning sage
    Who can dissect a sunbeam, count the stars,
    And measure distant worlds, is here a child,
    And, humbled, drops his calculating pain.
                                    "Eternity," Ibid.

14 When trembling limbs refuse their weight,
    And films, slow gathering, dim the sight,
    And clouds obscure the mental light,—
    'Tis nature's precious boon to die.
        "A Thought on Death" (November 1814), Ibid.

15 To *repair* a ruin carries a better sound with it than to *build* a
    ruin, as we do in England.
            Letter to Dr. Aiken (Thoulouse [sic], 27 February 1786),
                                              Ibid.

16 Nobody ought to be too old to improve; I should be sorry if I
    was; and I flatter myself I have already improved considerably
    by my travels. First, I can swallow gruel soup, egg soup, and
    all manner of soups, without making faces much. Secondly, I
    can pretty well live without tea. . . .
            Letter to Miss Belshan (Geneva, 21 October 1785), Ibid.

17 Here dwell the true magicians. Nature is our servant. Man is
    our pupil. We change, we conquer, we create.
                "To Miss C.," *A Legacy for Young Ladies n.d.*

19 Finding out riddles is the same kind of exercise to the mind
    which running and leaping are to the body.
                                    "On Riddles," Ibid.

19 . . . Taste has one great enemy to contend with . . . Fashion—
    an arbitrary and capricious tyrant, who reigns with the most
    despotic sway over that department which Taste alone ought
    to regulate.
                "On Female Studies, Letter Two," Ibid.

20 . . . a forest was never planted.
                                    "On Plants," Ibid.

21 I often murmur, yet I never weep;
    I always lie in bed, yet never sleep;
    My mouth is large, and larger than my head,
    And much disgorges though it ne'er is fed;
    I have no legs or feet, yet swiftly run,
    And the more falls I get, move faster on.
                                    "On Riddles," Ibid.

22 How patiently does she support the various burdens laid upon
    her! We tear her plows and harrows, we crush her with castles
    and palaces; nay we penetrate her very bowels, and bring to
    light the veined marble, the pointed crystal, the ponderous ores
    and sparkling gems, deep hid in darkness the more to excite
    the industry of man. Yet, torn and harassed as she might seem
    to be, our mother Earth is still fresh and young, as if she but
    now came out of the hands of her Creator.
                                    "Earth," Ibid.

23 Between the greater part of those we call the different classes,
    there is only the difference of less and more. . . .
                "On Female Studies, Letter Two," Ibid.

24 Friends should consider themselves as the sacred guardians of
    each other's virtue; and the noblest testimony they can give of
    their affection is the correction of the faults of those they love.
                                "On Friendship," Ibid.

25 Happy is he to whom, in the maturer season of life, there re-
    mains one tried and constant friend. . . .
                                              Ibid.

633. Sarah Bache (1744–1808)

1   The subject now is Stamp Act, and nothing else is talked of.
    The Dutch talk of the "Stamp tack," the negroes of the
    "tamp"—in short, every body has something to say.
            Letter to Benjamin Franklin,* her father (c. November
            1764), Quoted in *The Women of the American Revolution*
                                by Elizabeth F. Ellet *1848*
    *American statesman, author, and scientist (1706–1790).

2   In this country there is no rank but rank mutton.
            Note to an Englishwoman who ran a school for girls
                        that Bache's daughters attended, Ibid.

634. Abigail Adams (1744–1818)

1   Do not put such unlimited power into the hands of the Hus-
    bands. Remember all Men would be tyrants if they could.
                        Letter to her husband, John Adams* *1776*

2   I am more and more convinced that man is a dangerous crea-
    ture . . . ; and that power, whether vested in many or a few, is
    ever grasping, and, like the grave, cries "Give, give."
            Letter to John Adams* (27 November 1775), *Letters of
                                        Mrs. Adams 1840*
    *(1735–1826) second president of the United States (1797–1801).

3   We are no ways dispirited here, we possess a Spirit that will
    not be conquered. If our Men are all drawn off and we should
    be attacked, you would find a Race of Amazons in America.
                                        (1776) Ibid.

4   If particular care and attention is not paid to the Ladies we
    are determined to foment a Rebellion, and will not hold our-

selves bound by any Laws in which we have no voice, or Representation.

(31 March 1776) Ibid.

5 Men of Sense in all Ages abhor those customs which treat us only as the vassals of your Sex.

Ibid.

6 [At] the court of St. James*. . . I seldom meet with characters so inoffensive as my Hens and chickings, or minds so well improved as my garden.

Letter to Thomas Jefferson (26 February 1788), Quoted in *The Papers of Thomas Jefferson*,** Julian P. Boyd, ed. *1955*
*Reference to James Madison (1751–1836), fourth president of the United States (1809–1817). **(1743–1826) third president of the United States (1801–1809).

7 . . . had nature formed me of the other Sex, I should certainly have been a rover.

Letter to Isaac Smith, Jr. (20 April 1771), *The Adams Papers*, L. H. Butterfield, ed. *1963*

8 The Natural tenderness and Delicacy of our Constitution, added to the many Dangers we are subject to from your Sex, renders it almost impossible for a Single Lady to travel without injury to her character.

Ibid.

635. Elizabeth Martin (1745?–post-1776)

1 Go, boys; fight for your country! fight till death, if you must, but never let your country be dishonored. Were I a man I would go with you.

Remark to her seven sons at the call to arms, Quoted in *The Women of the American Revolution* by Elizabeth F. Ellet *1848*

2 I wish I had fifty.

Reply to a British officer's query regarding her sons in arms, Ibid.

636. Hannah More (1745–1833)

1 I shall have nothing to do but go to Bath and drink like a fish.

Letter to David Garrick,* Quoted in *Garrick Correspondence*, Vol. II *1778*
*English actor and theater manager (1717–1779).

2 . . . dost thou know
The cruel tyranny of tenderness?

Percy 1778

3 Honor! O yes, I know him. 'Tis a phantom,
A shadowy figure, wanting bulk and life,
Who, having nothing solid in himself,
Wraps his thin form in Virtue's plundered robe,
And steals her title.

The Fatal Falsehood 1779

4 The keen spirit
Ceases* the prompt occasion,—makes the thought
Start into instant action, and at once
Plans and performs, resolves and executes!

Daniel 1782
*Seizes.

5 A crown! what is it?
. . . .
It is to sit upon a joyless height,

To ev'ry blast of changing fate expos'd!
Too high for hope! too great for happiness.

Pt. VI, Ibid.

6 No adulation; 'tis the death of virtue;
Who flatters, is of all mankind the lowest
Save he who courts the flattery.

Ibid.

7 O war!—what, what art thou?
At once the proof and scourge of man's fall'n state!
After the brightest conquest, what appears
Of all thy glories! for the vanquish'd chains!
For the proud victors, what? alas! to reign
O'er desolated nations!

Pt. V, Ibid.

8 Books, the Mind's food, not exercise!
"Conversation," St. 1, *The Bas Bleu* [The Blue Stocking] *1784*

9 But sparks electric only strike
On souls electrical alike

"Conversation," St. 2, Ibid.

10 He liked those literary cooks
Who skim the cream of others' books;
And ruin half the author's graces
By plucking *bon-mots* from their places.

Florio 1786

11 And Pleasure was so coy a prude,
She fled the more, the more pursued. . . .

Ibid.

12 He thought the world to him was known,
Whereas he only knew the *town*
In men this blunder still you find:
All think their little set—mankind.

Ibid.

13 The wretch who digs the mine for bread,
Or ploughs, that others may be fed,
Feels less fatigued than that decreed
To him who cannot think or read.

Pt. I, Ibid.

14 Fell luxury! more perilous to youth
Then storms or quicksands, poverty or chains.

"Belshazzar," *The Complete Works of Hannah More 1856*

15 That silence is one of the great arts of conversation is allowed by Cicero* himself, who says, there is not only an art, but even an eloquence in it.

"Thoughts on Conversation," *Essays on Various Subjects 1856*
*Roman statesman, orator and philosopher (106–43 B.C.E.)

16 Subduing and subdued, the petty strife,
Which clouds the colour of domestic life;
The sober comfort, all the peace which springs
From the large aggregate of little things;
On these small cares of daughter, wife or friend,
The almost sacred joys of home depend.

"Sensibility," *Poems 1856*

17 If faith produce no works, I see
That faith is not a living tree.

"Dan and Jane," Ibid.

18 Going to the opera, like getting drunk, is a sin that carries its own punishment with it.
> Letter to her sister (1775), *The Letters of Hannah More* 1925

19 My plan of instruction is extremely simple and limited. They learn, on week-days, such coarse works as may fit them for servants. I allow of no writing for the poor. My object is not to make fanatics, but to train up the lower classes in habits of industry and piety.
> Letter to the Bishop of Bath and Wells (1801), Ibid.

637. Esther De Berdt Reed (1746–1780)

1 . . . if these great affairs must be brought to a crisis and decided, it had better be in our time than our children's
> Letter to Dennis De Berdt, her brother (1775), Quoted in *The Life of Esther De Berdt, Afterwards Esther Reed* by William H. Reed 1853

638. Frederica de Riedesel (1746–1808)

1 Britons never retrograde.
> Quoted in *The Women of the American Revolution*, Vol. II by Elizabeth F. Ellet 1848

2 Seizing some maize, I begged our hostess to give me some of it to make a little bread. She replied that she needed it for her black people. "They work for us," she added, "and you come to kill us."
> Ibid.

3 It is astonishing how much the frail human creature can endure. . . . *
> Ibid.

*Referring to the breakout of a malignant fever in New York in 1780.

639. Stephanie Félicité Genlis (1746–1830)

1 For which reason, you may observe that the man whose probity consists in merely obeying the laws, cannot be truly virtuous or estimable; for he will find many opportunities of doing contemptible and even dishonest acts, which the laws cannot punish.
> "Laws," *Tales of the Castle c.* 1793

2 Hence it is that men act ill, and judge well. Feeble and corrupted, they give way to their passions; but when they are cool—that is to say, when they are uninterested—they instantly condemn what they have often been guilty of; they revolt against every thing that is contemptible; they admire every thing generous, and they are moved at every thing affecting.
> "Virtue," Ibid.

3 Can any one be a connoisseur in music, without knowledge of the science?
No; it is absolutely impossible.
> "Music," Ibid.

4 "A philosopher, desirous of praising a princess, who had been dead these fifty years, could not accomplish his purpose but at the expense of all the princesses, and all the women, who have ever existed or do exist; and that in a single phrase."
"He has been very laconic indeed."
"You shall hear—*Though a woman and a princess*, said he, *she loved learning!*"
"The orator ought to have been answered, that *though a philosopher*, and an academician, he did not, on this occasion, show either much politeness or equity."
> "The Two Reputations," Ibid.

640. Susanna Blamire (1747–1794)

1 And ye shall walk in silk attire,
And siller* ha'e to spare.
> "The Siller Crown," *The Poetical Works of Miss Susanna Blamire, the Muse of Cumberland* 1842

*Scottish for "silver."

2 Till soft remembrance threw a veil
Across these een o' mine,
I closed the door, and sobbed aloud,
To think on aul langsyne!
> "The Nabob," St. 4, Ibid.

3 I come, I come, my Jamie dear;
And O! wi' what good will
I follow wheresoe'er ye lead!
Ye canna lead to ill.
> "The Weafu' Heart," St. 5, Ibid.

4 Of aw things that is I think thout* is meast queer,
It brings that that's by-past and sets it down here.
> "Auld Robin Forbes," St. 1, Ibid.

*Thought.

641. Anna Gordon Brown (1747–1810)

1 O first he sang a merry song,
An then he sang a grave,
And then he peckd his feathers gray,
To her the letter gave.
> "The Gay Goshawk," St. 10, *The English and Scottish Popular Ballads*, Francis James Child, ed. 1898

642. Olympe de Gouges (1748–1793)

1 Observe the Creator in his wisdom; survey in all her grandeur that nature with whom you seem to want to be in harmony, and give me, if you dare, an example of this tyrannical empire. Go back to animals, consult the elements, study plants, finally glance at all the modifications of organic matter, and surrender to the evidence when I offer you the means; search, probe, and distinguish, if you can, the sexes in the administration of nature. Everywhere you will find them mingled; everywhere they cooperate in harmonious togetherness in this immortal masterpiece.
> *Declaration of the Rights of Woman and the Female Citizen** 1791

*Retort to Emmanuel Sieyès's *Declaration of the Rights of Man and the Citizen* (1789), preamble to the French Constitution (1791).

2 Bizarre, blind, bloated with science and degenerated—in a century of enlightenment and wisdom—into the crassest ignorance, he wants to command as a despot a sex which is in full possession of its intellectual faculties; he pretends to enjoy the Revolution and to claim his rights to equality in order to say nothing more about it.
> Ibid.

3 Postcript: Woman, wake up; the tocsin of reason is being heard throughout the whole universe; discover your rights.
> Ibid

4 Postcript: Marriage is the tomb of trust and love. The married woman can with impunity give bastards to her husband, and also give them the wealth which does not belong to them. The woman who is unmarried has only one feeble right; ancient and inhuman laws refuse to her for her children the right to

the name and the wealth of their father; no new laws have been made in this matter.

Ibid.

5 Article 6: The laws must be the expression of the general will; all female and male citizens must contribute either personally or through their representatives to its formation; it must be the same for all: male and female citizens, being equal in the eyes of the law, must be equally admitted to all honors, positions, and public employment according to their capacity and without other distinctions besides those of their virtues and talents.

Ibid.

6 Article 10: No one is to be disquieted for his very basic opinions; woman has the right to mount the scaffold; she must equally have the right to mount the rostrum, provided that her demonstrations do not disturb the legally established public order.

Ibid.

7 We,_____and_____, moved by our own will, unite ourselves for the duration of our lives, and for the duration of our mutual inclinations, under the following conditions: We intend and wish to make our wealth communal, meanwhile reserving to ourselves the right to divide it in favor of our children and of those toward whom we might have a particular inclination, mutually recognizing that our property belongs directly to our children, from whatever bed they come, and that all of them without distinction have the right to bear the name of the fathers and mothers who have acknowledged them . . .

Form for a Social Contract Between Man and Woman, Ibid.

643. Marie Letitia Bonaparte (1748–1836)

1 Napoleon has never given me a moment's pain, not even at the time which is almost universally woman's hour of suffering.*

Quoted in *Biography of Distinguished Women*
by Sarah Josepha Hale** 1876
*Reference to the birth of her son, Napoleon Bonaparte, French general and emperor (1769–1821). **See 788.

644. Charlotte Smith (1749–1806)

1 Queen of the silver bowl!

"To the Moon," *Elegiac Sonnets and Other Essays* 1782

2 Sweet poet of the woods.

"The Departure of the Nightingale," Ibid.

3 Another May new buds and flowers shall bring;
Ah! why has happiness—no second Spring?

"The Close of Spring," Ibid.

4 But Reason comes at—Thirty-eight.

"Thirty-Eight," St. 4, Ibid.

5 Stripp'd of their gaudy hues by Truth,
We view the glitt'ring toys of youth.

St. 7, Ibid.

6 Swift fleet the billowy clouds along the sky,
Earth seems to shudder at the storm aghast;
While only beings as forlorn as I,
Court the chill horrors of the howling blast.

"Montalbert," Ibid.

7 . . . the moon, mute arbitress of tides

"Sonnet Written in the Church-Yard at Middleton, in Sussex," Ibid.

8 He was stretched upon a sopha—with boots on—a terrier lay on one side of him, and he occasionally embraced a large hound, which licked his face and hands, while he thus addressed it.— Oh! thou dear bitchy—thou beautiful bitchy—damme, if I don't love thee better than my mother or my sisters."

Ch. 5, *Desmond*, Vol. I 1792

9 "'Tis an uneasy thing," said he, "a very uneasy thing, for a man of probity and principles to look in these days into a newspaper."

Ch. 6, Ibid.

10 "I reflect with concern on the power of national prejudice and national jealousy, to darken and pervert the understanding."

Ch. 9, Ibid.

11 "He [Henry IV of England] had not been taught, that to be born a king is to be born something more than man."

Ibid.

12 When the imagination soars into those regions, where the planets pursue each its destined course, in the immensity of space—every planet, probably, containing creatures adapted by the Almighty, to the residence he has placed them in; and when we reflect, that the smallest of these is of as much consequence in the universe, as this world of our's; how puerile and ridiculous do those pursuits appear in which we are so anxiously busied; and how insignificant the trifles we toil to obtain, or fear to lose.

Ch. 12, Ibid.

13 Were there, indeed, a sure appeal to the mercies of the rich, the calamities of the poor might be less intolerable; but it is too certain, that high affluence and prosperity have a direct tendency to harden the temper.

Ch. 10, Ibid.

14 Having never heard anything but her own praises, she really believed herself a miracle of knowledge and accomplishments. . . .

The Old Manor House 1793

15 The masters of a great school are apt to shew that pupils connected with title and fortune have a more than ordinary share of their regard; yet among boys of the same age there is always established a certain degree of equality. . . .

Ch. 3, *The Young Philosopher*, Vol. I 1798

16 . . . the wantonness of tyranny, that induces men to exercise power merely because they have it. . . .

Ibid.

17 "If my family are ashamed of me, they have only to leave me out of their genealogical table, as an unworthy branch of the tree, bent towards its native earth, and no longer contributing to their splendid insignificance."

Ch. 4, Ibid.

18 "And let me tell you, Mrs. Winslow," said the Doctor, "that you are too apt to fall into these fits of admiration."

Ch. 7, Ibid.

19 "These presentiments of evil are often the causes that evil really arrives. . . . "

Ch. 5, Vol. II, Ibid.

20 "Youth, even when deprived of all viable support—makes a long and often a successful stand against calamity."

Ch. 6, Ibid.

645. Gertrude Elizabeth Mara (1749–1833)

1 When I give a lesson in singing, I sing with my scholars; by so doing they learn in half the time they can if taught in the usual way—by the master merely playing the tune of the song on the piano. People cannot teach what they don't know—my scholars have my singing to imitate—those of other masters seldom any thing but the tinkling of a piano.

Quoted in *Queens of Song* by
Ellen Creathorne Clayton *1865*

646. Mary Jones (fl. 1750s)

1 How much of paper's spoil'd! what floods of ink!
And yet how few, how very few can think!

I. "Extract from an Epistle to Lady Bowyer," St. 1,
Miscellanies in Prose and Verse 1750

2 For what is beauty but a sign?
A face hung out, through which is seen
The nature of the goods within.

II. "To Stella, after the Small-Pox," St. 1, Ibid.

647. Judith Madan (fl. c. 1750)

1 Doubt not to reap, if thou canst bear to plough.

"Verses. Written in her brother's Coke upon
Littleton",* *The Female Poets of Great Britain*, Frederic
Rowton, ed. *1853*

*I. e., a copy of the commentary by the English jurist Sir Edward Coke on the *Tenures of Sir Thomas Littleton*.

648. Elizabeth Peabody (1750–?)

1 Lost to virtue, lost to humanity must that person be, who can view without emotion the complicated distress of this injured land. Evil tidings molest our habitations, and wound our peace. Oh, my brother! oppression is enough to make a wise people mad.

Letter to John Adams,* her brother-in-law, Quoted in
The Women of the American Revolution,
Vol. II, by Elizabeth F. Ellet *1848*

*(1735–1826), second U.S. president (1797–1801)

649. Sophia Burrell (1750?–1764)

1 Blindfold I should to Myra run,
And swear to love her ever;
Yet when the bandage was undone,
Should only think her clever.

With the full usage of my eyes,
I Chloe should decide for;
But when she talks, I *her* despise,
Whom, dumb, I could have died for!

"Chloe and Myra," Sts. 4–5,
Poems 1793

2 Cupid and you, it is said, are cousins,
(*Au faith** in stealing hearts by dozens,)

"To Emma," Ibid.

*Proficient.

3 And you should be arraign'd in court
For practising this cruel sport,
In spite of all the plaintiff's fury
Your smile would bribe both judge and jury.

Ibid.

650. Madame du Hausset (fl. c. 1750–1764)

1 Great people have had the bad habit of talking very indiscreetly before their servants.

(1802), Quoted in *The Memoirs of Louis XV, and of
Madame de Pompadour** 1910 ed.

*Jeanne-Antoinette Poisson de Pompadour; see 574.

2 See what the Court is; all is corruption there, from the highest to the lowest.

Remark to Mme de Pompadour, Ibid.

651. Sophia Lee (1750–1824)

1 Society, that first of blessings, brings with it evils death only can cure.

The Recess 1785

652. Anne Barnard (1750–1825)

1 The waes o' my heart fa' in showers frae my e'e,
While my gudeman lies sound by me.

"Auld Robin Gray" *1771*

2 My father couldna work, and my mother couldna spin;
I toiled day and night, but their bread I couldna win.

Ibid.

3 They gied him my hand, tho' my heart was at sea.

Ibid.

653. Caroline Herschel (1750–1848)

1 Many a half or whole holiday he* was allowed to spend with me was dedicated to making experiments in chemistry, where generally all boxes, tops of tea-canisters, pepper-boxes, teacups, etc, served for the necessary vessels and the sand-tub furnished the matter to be analyzed. I only had to take care to exclude water, which would have produced havoc on my carpet.

Memoir and Correspondence of Caroline Herschel, Mrs.
John Herschel, ed. *1876*

*Her nephew, the astronomer Sir John Frederick Herschel (1792–1871).

2 I am now so enured to receiving honours in my old age, that I take them all upon me without blushing.

Ibid.

654. Caroline Matilda (1751–1775)

1 O God, keep me innocent; make others great!

Scratched with a diamond on a window of the castle of
Frederiksborg, Denmark *n.d.*

655. Judith Sargent Murray (1751–1820)

1 To the absorbing grave I must resign,
All of my first born child that e'er was mine!

"Lines, Occasioned by the Death of an Infant," St. 4, *The
Massachusetts Magazine January 1790*

2 Will it be said that the judgement of a male two years old, is more sage than that of a female's of the same age? I believe the reverse is greatly observed to be true. But from that period what partiality! how is the one exalted and the other depressed, by the contrary modes of education which are adopted! the one is taught to aspire, and the other is early confined and limited.

"On the Equality of the Sexes," Ibid.

3 I know there are those who assert, that as the animal powers of the one sex are superiour, of course their mental faculties also must be stronger; thus attributing strength of mind to the transient organization of this earth born tenement. But if this reasoning is just, man must be content to yield the palm to many of the brute creation. . . .

Ibid.

4 I would be Cesar, or I would be nothing.
The Gleaner, Vol. I 1798

5 Religion is 'twixt God and my own soul,
Nor saint, nor sage, can boundless thought control.
"Lines Prefacing Essay No. XIX. A Sketch of the Gleaner's Religious Sentiment," Ibid.

6 I may be accused of enthusiasm, but such is my confidence in the sex, that I expect to see our young women forming a new era in female history.

Vol. III, Ibid.

656. Jeanne Isabelle Montolieu (1751–1832)

1 Here lies the child [Voltaire] spoiled by the world which he spoiled. *(Ci git l'enfant gâté du monde qu'il gâta.)*
"Epitaph on Voltaire"* *n.d.*
*François-Marie Arouet, French philosopher and writer (1694–1778).

657. Ann Eliza Bleecker (1752–1783)

1 New worlds to find, new systems to explore:
When these appear'd, again I'd urge my flight
Till all creation open'd to my sight.
"On the Immensity of Creation," St. 1 (Tomhanick, 1773), *The Posthumous Works of Ann Eliza Bleecker, in Prose and Verse*, Margaretta Faugeres, ed. 1793

2 My gods took care of me—not I of them!
"On Reading Dryden's *Virgil*" (1778), Ibid.

3 What art thou now, my love!—a few dry bones,
Unconscious of my availing moans
"Recollection," St. 2 (Tomhanick, 10 February 1778), Ibid.

4 But think not I dislike my situation here; on the contrary, I am charmed with the lovely scene the spring opens around me. Alas! the wilderness is within: I muse so long on the dead until I am unfit for the company of the living.

Letter (8 April 1780), Ibid.

5 . . . Oh leave the city's noxious air.
"To the Same," St. 1, Ibid.

6 You've broke th' agreement, Sir, I find;
(Excuse me, I must speak my mind)
It seems in your poetic fit
You mind not jingling, where there's wit
"To Mr. L***,*" Ibid.

658. Jemima Wilkinson (1752–1819)

1 Live peaceably with all men as much as possible; in an especial manner do not strive against one another for mastery, but all of you keep your ranks in righteousness, and let not one thrust another [aside].
The Universal Friend's Advice, to Those of the Same Religious Society 1784

2 It is a Sifting time; Try to be on the Lord's side. . . .
Letter to John and Orpha Rose (1789), Quoted in *Pioneer Prophetess* by Herbert A. Wisbey, Jr. 1964

3 . . . thou needest not Ask who Shall Ascend up into heaven for to Search the record of Eternity, thou mayest But Descend down into thine own heart and there read what thou art and what thou Shalt Be . . .
"Book of Conscience," Ibid.

4 . . . that way the tree inclineth while it groweth that way it pitcheth when it falleth and there it Lieth. . . . So we Lie down to Eternity whether it Be towards heaven or towards hell Being Once fallen there is no removing for as in war an Error is death So in death an Error is damnation therefore Live as you intend to die and die as you intend to Live
"As We Live So we Die," Ibid.

5 . . . I am weary of them that hate peace.
Letter to James Parker (1788), Ibid.

659. Jeanne Louise Campan (1752–1822)

1 I have put together all that concerned the domestic life of an unfortunate princess [Marie Antoinette*], whose reputation is not yet cleared of the stains it received from the attacks of calumny, and who justly merited a different lot in life, a different place in the opinion of mankind after her fall.
Memorandum, Quoted in *The Memoirs of Marie Antoinette*, editor reissue 1910
*See 668.

2 His [Louis XVI's*] heart, in truth, disposed him towards reforms; but his prejudices and fears, and the clamours of pious and privileged persons, intimidated him, and made him abandon plans which his love for the people had suggested.
Ch. 6, Ibid.
*King of France (1754–1793), r.. 1779–1792.

3 Tremble at the moment when your child has to choose between the rugged road of industry and integrity, leading straight to honour and happiness; and the smooth and flowery path which descends, through indolence and pleasure, to the gulf of vice and misery. It is then that the voice of a parent, or of some faithful friend, must direct the right course.
"To Her Only Son," *Familiar Letters to her Friends n.d.*

4 Learn to know the value of money. This is a most essential point. The want of economy leads to the decay of powerful empires, as well as private families. Louis XVI perished on the scaffold for a deficit of fifty millions. There would have been no debt, no assemblies of the people, no revolution, no loss of the sovereign authority, no tragical death, but for this fatal deficit.
Ibid.

660. Hannah Mather Crocker (1752–1829)

1 . . . the wise Author of nature has endowed the female mind with equal powers and faculties, and given them the same right of judging and acting for themselves, as he gave to the male sex.
Observations on the Real Rights of Women 1818

661. Fanny Burney (1752–1840)

1 "Do you come to the play without knowing what it is?" "O, yes, Sir, yes, very frequently. I have no time to read play-bills. One merely comes to meet one's friends, and show that one's alive."
Letter XX, *Evelina* 1778

2 "What a jabbering they make!" cried Mr. Braughton; "there's no knowing a word they say. Pray what's the reason they can't

as well sing [opera] in English?—but I suppose the fine folks would not like it, if they could understand it."

Letter XXI, Ibid.

3 Concealment, my dear Maris, is the foe of tranquility. . . .

Letter LX, Ibid.

4 . . . *Imagination* took the reins, and *Reason*, slow-paced, though sure-footed, was unequal to a race with so eccentric and flighty a companion.

Letter XVII, Ibid.

5 . . . but this is not an age in which we may trust to appearances, and imprudence is much sooner regretted than repaired.

Ibid.

6 "If Time thought no more of me, than I do of Time, I believe I should bid defiance, for one while, to old age and wrinkles,—for deuce take me if ever I think about it at all."

Letter LXXVII, Ibid.

7 I'd do it as soon as say "Jack Robinson."

Letter LXXXII, Ibid.

8 CECILIA. Oh, how unequally are we affected by the progress of time! Winged with the gay plumage of hope, how rapid seems its flight,—oppressed with the burden of misery, how tedious its motion!—yet it varies not,—insensible to smiles and callous to tears, its acceleration and its tardiness are mere phantasms of our disordered imaginations.

Act V, Sc. 1, The Witlings *1779?*

9 "But an old woman . . . is a person who has no sense of decency; if once she takes to living, the devil himself can't get rid of her."

Bk. I, Ch. 10, Cecilia *1782*

10 "How true is it, yet how consistent . . . that while we all desire to live long, we have all a horror of being old!"

Bk. II, Ch. 3, Ibid.

11 To a heart formed for friendship and affection the charms of solitude are very short-lived. . . .

Ch. 4, Ibid.

12 "Report is mightily given to magnify."

Ibid.

13 " . . . childhood is never troubled with foresight. . . . "

Bk. III, Ch. 2, Ibid.

14 Travelling is the ruin of all happiness! There's no looking at a building here after seeing Italy.

Bk. IV, Ch. 2, Ibid.

15 "But if the young are never tired of erring in conduct, neither are the older in erring of judgement. . . . "

Ch. 11, Ibid.

16 " . . . where concession is made without pain, it is often made without meaning. For it is not in human nature to project any amendment without a secret repugnance."

Ibid.

17 The shill I, shall I, of Congreve* becomes shilly shally.

Bk. V, Ibid.

*William Congreve, Restoration dramatist (1670–1729).

18 " . . . he looked around him for any pursuit, and seeing distinction was more easily attained in the road to ruin, he galloped along it, thoughtless of being thrown when he came to the bottom, and sufficiently gratified in showing his horsemanship by the way."

Ch. 7, Ibid.

19 "True, very true, ma'am," said he, yawning, "one really lives no where; one does but vegetate, and wish it all at an end."

Bk. VII, Ch. 5, Ibid.

20 The historian of human life finds less of difficulty and of intricacy to develop, in its accident and adventures, than the investigator of the human heart in its feelings and its changes.

Bk. I, Ch. 1, Camilla *1796*

21 " . . . there is nothing so pleasant as working the indolent; except, indeed, making the restless keep quiet. . . ."

Bk. II, Ch. 5, Ibid.

22 "Far from having taken any positive step, I have not yet even formed any resolution."

Ch. 13, Ibid.

23 "Happiness is in your power, though beauty is not; and on that to set too high a value would be pardonable only in a weak and frivolous mind; since, whatever is the involuntary admiration with which it meets, every estimable quality and accomplishment is attainable without it. . . . "

Bk. IV, Ch. 5, Ibid.

24 The artlessness of unadorned truth, however sure in theory of extorting admiration, rarely in practice fails inflicting pain and mortification.

Ch. 8, Ibid.

25 Whatever there is new and splendid, is sure of a run for at least a season.

Bk. X, Ch. 3, Ibid.

26 Indeed, the freedom with which Dr. [Samuel] Johnson* condemns whatever he disapproves is astonishing.

Diary Entry (23 August 1778), Diary and Letters of Madame D'Arblay, 1778–1840, *Vol. I, Charlotte Barrett, ed. 1904*

*English lexicographer and author (1709–1784).

27 'Tis best to build no castles in the air.

Diary entry, Vol. II, Ibid.

28 All the delusive seduction of martial music. . . .

Diary Entry (1802), Vol. VIII, Ibid.

662. Phillis Wheatley (1753?–1784)

1 Suppress the deadly serpent in its egg.
Ye blooming plants of human race divine,
An Ethiop tells you 'tis your greatest foe;
Its transient sweetness turns to endless pain,
And in immense perdition sinks the soul.

"To the University of Cambridge, in New-England," St. 3
(1767), *Poems on Various Subjects, Religious and Moral*
1773

2 Some view our sable race with scornful eye,
"Their colour is a diabolic dye."
Remember, *Christians*, *Negroes* black as Cain,
May be refin'd and join th' angelic train.

"On Being Brought From Africa to America" (c. 1768), *Ibid.*

3   I, young in life, by seeming cruel fate
    Was snatch'd from Afric's fancy'd happy seat:
    What pangs excruciating must molest,
    What sorrows labor in my parent's breast?
    Steel'd was that soul and by no misery mov'd
    That from a father seiz'd his babe belov'd:
    Such, such my case. And I can then but pray
    Others may never feel tyrannic sway?
    "To the Right Honourable William, Earl of Dartmouth, His
    Majesty's Principal Secretary of State for North America, &
    C.," St. 3, Ibid.

4   The land of freedom's heaven-defended race!
    "To His Excellency General Washington,"* St. 3, Ibid.
    *George Washington (1732–1799), first U.S. president (1789–1797).

5   . . . civil and religious liberty . . . are so inseparably united,
    that there is little or no enjoyment of one without the
    other: . . . in every human breast, God has implanted a princi-
    ple, which we call love of freedom; it is impatient of
    oppression and pants for deliverance. . . .
    Letter to Rev. Samson Occom (11 February 1774),
    Boston: Post-Boy 21 March 1774

663. Catharine Greene (1753–1815?)

1   If you expect to be an inhabitant of this country [Georgia],
    you must not think to sit down with your netting pins; but on
    the contrary, employ half your time at the toilet, one quarter
    to paying and receiving visits; the other quarter to scolding
    servants, with a hard thump every now and then over the head;
    or singing, dancing, reading, writing, or saying your prayers.
    The latter is here quite a phenomenon; but you need not tell
    how you employ your time.
    Letter to Miss Flagg (c. 1783), Quoted in *The Women of
    the American Revolution*, Vol. II by Elizabeth F. Ellet
    1848

664. Elizabeth Inchbald (1753–1821)

1   LADY MARY. Beauty in London is so cheap, and consequently
    so common to the men of fashion (who are prodigiously fond
    of novelty), that they absolutely begin to fall in love with the
    ugly women, by way of change.
    Act I, Sc. 1, *Appearance is Against Them 1785*

2   HUMPHRY. You can't be at a loss for words, while you are
    courting!—Women will always give you two for your one.
    Sc. 2, Ibid.

3   LADY EUSTON. There is as severe a punishment to men of gal-
    lantry (as they call themselves) as sword or pistol; laugh at
    them—that is a ball which cannot miss; and yet kills only their
    vanity.
    Act III, Sc. 1, *I'll Tell You What 1786*

4   LADY EUSTON. "You are the most beautiful woman I ever
    saw," said Lord *Bandy*; "and your Lordship is positively the
    most lovely of mankind"—"What eyes," cried he; "what
    hair," cried I; "what lips," continued he; "what teeth," added
    I; "What a hand and arm," said he; "and what a *leg* and *foot*,"
    said I—"Your Ladyship is jesting," was his Lordship's last
    reply; and he has never since paid me one compliment.
    Ibid.

5   MARQUIS. . . .love is a general leveller—it makes the king a
    slave; and inspires the slave with every joy a prince can taste.
    Act I, Sc. 1, *The Midnight Hour 1787*

6   GENERAL. . . .a man never looks so ridiculous as when he is
    caught in his own snare.
    Act III, Sc. 1, Ibid.

7   SIR LUKE TREMOR. . . .he is the slave of every great man, and
    the tyrant of every poor one.
    Act I, Sc. 1, *Such Things Are 1788*

8   MR. TWINEALL. Why, Madam, for instance, when a gentleman
    is asked a question which is either troublesome or improper to
    answer, you don't say you *won't* answer it, even though you
    speak to an inferior—but you say—"really it appears to me e-
    e-e-e-e-[mutters and shrugs]—that is—mo-mo-mo-mo-mo—
    [mutters]—if you see the thing—for my part—te-te-te-te—and
    that's all I can tell about it at *present*."
    Ibid.

9   DOCTOR. They have refused to grant me a *diploma*; forbid me
    to practice as a physician, and all because I do not know a par-
    cel of insignificant words; but exercise my profession
    according to the rules of *reason* and *nature*.—Is it not natural
    to die? Then, if a dozen or two of my patients *have* died under
    my hands, is not that natural?
    Act I, Sc. 1, *Animal Magnetism 1789*

10 MADAME TICASTIN. What misers are we all of our real pleasures!
    Act I, Sc. 1, *The Massacre 1792*

11 SIR ROBERT RAMBLE. We none of us endeavour to *be* happy, Sir,
    but merely to be *thought* so; and for my part, I had rather be in
    a state of misery, and envied for my supposed happiness, than in
    a state of happiness, and pitied for my supposed misery.
    Act I, Sc. 1, *Every One Has his Fault 1793*

12 LORD PRIORY. I know several women of fashion, who will visit
    six places of different amusement on the same night, have
    company at home besides, and yet, for want of something
    more, they'll be out of spirits. . . . .
    Act I, Sc. 1, *Wives as they Were, and Maids as they Are
    1797*

13 COTTAGER. Wife, Wife, never speak ill of the dead. Say what
    you please against the living, but not a word against the dead.
    COTTAGER'S WIFE. And yet, husband, I believe the dead care
    the last what is said about them—
    Act II, Sc. 1, *Lover's Vows 1798*

14 VERDUN THE BUTLER. Loss of innocence never sounds well ex-
    cept in verse.
    Act IV, Sc. 2, Ibid.

15 GIRONE. . . .women's power seldom lasts longer than their
    complexion.
    Act I, Sc. 1, *A Case of Conscience 1833*

16 GIRONE. My Lord, I *do* know, but I am sworn to secrecy; and
    'tis so unmanly to tell! But I will lead you to my wife, who
    knows also; and being a woman, she would unsex herself as
    much by keeping the secret, as I should by revealing it.
    Act II, Sc. 1, Ibid.

17 My present apartment is so small, that I am all over black and
    blue with thumping my body and limbs against my furniture
    on every side; but then I have not far to *walk* to reach any-
    thing I want, for I can kindle my fire as I lie in bed, and put on
    my cap as I dine. . . .
    from her Journal, Quoted in *English Women of Letters*,
    Vol. II by Julia Kavanagh* *1863*
    *See 965.

665. Frances Thynne (1699–1754)

1   To thee, all glorious, ever-blessed power,
I consecrate this silent midnight hour.
"A Midnight Hour," *Miscellanies*, Dr. Watt, ed. *n.d.*

666. Jeanne-Marie Roland (1754–1793)

1   O liberty! what crimes are committed in thy name!* *(O liberté! que de crimes on commêt dans ton nom!)*
Ch. LI, Last words before being guillotined (8 November 1793), Quoted in *Histoire des Girondins* by Alphonse Lamartine *1847*
*Words inscribed on front of Statue of Liberty in New York City; also recorded as: "O Liberty, how you have been trifled with!" (*O Liberté, comme on t'a jouée!*)

2   I shall soon be there [at the guillotine]; but those who send me there will follow themselves ere long. I go there innocent, but they will go as criminals; and you, who now applaud, will also applaud them.
Remark en route to execution (8 November 1793), Quoted in *Biography of Distinguished Women* by Sarah Josepha Hale* *1876*
*See 788.

3   The more I see of men, the more I admire dogs. *(Plus je vois les hommes, plus j'admire les chiens.)*
Attributed* *n.d.*
*Also attributed to Ouida (see 1053) and to Mme de Sévigné (see 443).

667. Eliza Wilkinson (1755?–?)

1   . . . they [soldiers] really merit every thing, who will fight from principle alone; for from what I could learn, these poor creatures had nothing to protect them, and seldom got their pay; yet with what alacrity will they encounter danger and hardships of every kind!
Quoted in *The Women of the American Revolution*, Vol. II by Elizabeth F. Ellet *1848*

668. Marie-Antoinette (1755–1793)

1   Let them eat cake.* *(Qu'ils mangent de la brioche.)*
Quoted in *Confessions* by Jean-Jacques Rousseau** *1740*
*Brioche, or "cake," was, in that day, equivalent to a round, hard-crusted bread. **French philosopher and writer (1712–1778).

2   Courage! I have shown it for years; think you I shall lose it at the moment when my sufferings are to end?
Remark (16 October 1793; on way to guillotine), Quoted in *Women of Beauty and Heroism* by Frank B. Goodrich *1858*

3   Adieu, once again, my children, I go to join your father.
Last words (16 October 1793), Ibid.

4   I have seen all, I have heard all, I have forgotten all.
Reply to inquisitors (October 1789), Quoted in *Biography of Distinguished Women* by Sarah Josepha Hale* *1876*
*See 788.

5   I was a queen, and you took away my crown; a wife, and you killed my husband; a mother, and you deprived me of my children. My blood alone remains: take it, but do not make me suffer long.
Remark at the revolutionary tribunal (14 October 1793), Quoted in *Biography of Distinguished* Women by Sarah Josepha Hale* *1876*
*See 788.

6   History is busy with us.
Ibid.

7   All have contributed to our downfall; the reformers have urged it like mad people, and others through ambition, for the wildest Jacobin seeks wealth and office, and the mob is eager for plunder. There is not one real patriot among all this infamous horde. The emigrant party have their intrigues and schemes; foreigners seek to profit by the dissensions of France; every one has a share in our misfortunes.
Ch. 22, *The Memoirs of Marie-Antoinette*, Jeanne Louise Campan,* ed. *1910*
*See 659.

8   There is nothing new except what has been forgotten.
Remark, Quoted in *Women in World History Curriculum*, http://www.womeninworldhistory.com *1996–97*

669. Anna Maria Lenngren (1755–1817)

1   'Tis plain to see what pride within her glance reposes,
And mark how nobly curved her nose is!
"The Portraits," St. 2, *Anthology of Swedish Lyrics from 1750–1915*, C.W. Stork, ed. and tr. *1917*

2   The fairer sex possessed a mind
Of sturdy fabric, like her cloak.
Now all is different in our lives—
Other fabrics, other mores!
Taffetas, indecent stories
"Other Fabrics, Other Mores!" Nadia Christensen and Mariann Tiblin, trs., *The Penguin Book of Women Poets*, Carol Cosman, Joan Keefe and Kathleen Weaver, eds. *1978*

670. Sarah Siddons (1755–1831)

1   I am, as you may observe, acting again: but how much difficulty to get my money! Sheridan* is certainly the greatest phenomenon that Nature has produced for centuries. Our theatre is going on, to the astonishment of everybody. Very few of the actors are paid, and all are vowing to withdraw themselves: yet still we go on. Sheridan is certainly omnipotent.
Letter to a friend (9 November 1796), Quoted in *Life of Mrs. Siddons*, Vol. II by Thomas Campbell *1834*
*Richard Brinsley Sheridan (1751–1816), playwright especially noted for *The School for Scandal*, and manager of the Drury Lane Theatre in London.

2   . . . I know, by sad experience, with what difficulty a mind, weakened by long and uninterrupted suffering, admits hope, much less assurance.
Letter to Mrs. FitzHugh (Preston, 14 July 1801), Ibid.

3   I pant for retirement and leisure, but am doomed to inexpressible and almost unsupportable hurry.
Letter to Rev. Sedgwick Whalley (Dublin, 21 June 1784), Quoted in *Journals and Correspondence of Thomas Sedgwick Whalley*, Vol. I, Rev. Hill Wickham, ed. *1863*

4   This woman* is one of those monsters (I think them) of perfection, who is an angel before her time, and is so entirely resigned to the will of heaven, that (to a very mortal like myself) she appears to be the most provoking piece of still life one had ever had the misfortune to meet.
(c. 1787) Ibid.
*The lead character in a new play by Bertie Greatheed.

5 . . . sorry am I to say I have often observed, that I have performed worst when I most ardently wished to do better than ever.
Letter to Rev. Whalley (Bristol, 16 July 1781), Quoted in
The Kembles, Vol. I, by Percy Fitzgerald *1871*

6 [I] . . . commenced my study of Lady Macbeth. As the character is very short, I thought I should soon accomplish it. Being then only twenty years of age, I believed, as many others do believe, that little more was necessary than to get the words into my head, for the necessity of discrimination, and the development of character, at that time of my life, had scarcely entered into my imagination.
Recollection (1785), Ibid.

7 I have paid severely for eminence.
Letter to the Rev. and Mrs. Whalley (15 March 1785), Ibid.

8 Alas! How wretched is the being who depends on the stability of public favour! *The Reminiscences of Sarah Kemble Siddons*,
(1824), William Van Lennep, ed. *1942* (repr.)

9 The awful consciousness that one is the sole object of attention to that immense space, lined as it were with human intellect from top to bottom, and on all sides round, may perhaps be imagined but can not be described, and never never to be forgotten. . . .
Ibid.

10 Alas, why had I enemies, but because to be prosperous is sufficient cause for enmity.
Ibid.

11 . . . . I believe one half of the world is born for the convenience of the other half. . . .
Ch. 5, Letter to Hester Lynch Piozzi* (27 August 1794),
Quoted in *Sarah Siddons, Portrait of an Actress*
by Roger Manvell *1970*
*See 623.

671. Renier Giustina Michiel (1755–1832)

1 For me ennui is among the worst evils—I can bear pain better.
Quoted in *Biography of Distinguished Women* by Sarah
Josepha Hale* *1876*
*See 788.

2 The world improves people according to the dispositions they bring into it.
Ibid.

3 Time is a better comforter than reflection.
Ibid.

672. Anne Grant (1755–1838)

1 Gem of the heath! whose modest bloom
Sheds beauty o'er the lonely moor
"On A Sprig of Heath," St. 3, *The Highlanders and Other
Poems 1808*

2 O where, tell me where, is your Highland laddie gone?
He's gone with streaming banners, where noble deeds are done,
And my sad heart will tremble till he comes safely home.
"O Where, Tell Me Where,"* *Scottish Song*,
Mary Carlyle Aitken, ed. *1874*
*Both this and "The Blue Bells of Scotland" by Dorothea Jordan (see 701:1) are variants on an older popular song.

673. Elisabeth Vigée-Lebrun (1755–1842)

1 I was so fortunate as to be on very pleasant terms with the Queen [Marie-Antoinette].* When she heard that I had something of a voice we rarely had a sitting without singing some duets . . . together, for she was exceedingly fond of music. . . .
(1835), *Memoirs of Madame Vigée-Lebrun*,
Lionel Strachey, tr. *1907*
*See 668.

2 The women reigned then; the Revolution dethroned them.
Ibid.

674. Henrietta Luxborough (?-1756)

1 Yon bullfinch, with unvaried tone,
Of cadence harsh, and accent shrill,
Has brighter plumage to atone
For want of harmony and skill.
"The Bullfinch in Town," St.2, *A Collection of Poems.
By Several Hands*, Robert Dodsley, ed. *1748*

675. Anna Young Smith (1756–1780?)

1 Blest be this humble strain if it imparts
The dawn of peace to but one pensive breast
"An Elegy to the Memory of the American Volunteers, who
Fell in the Engagement Between the Massachusetts-Bay
Militia, and the British Troops. April 19, 1775," St. 9
(2 May 1775), *Pennsylvania Magazine June 1775*

2 But should we know as much as they,
They fear their empire would decay;
For they know women heretofore
Gained victories, and envied laurel's war.
And now they fear we'll once again
Ambitious be to reign,
And so invade the territories of the brain.
Sylvia's Complaint of her Sex's Unhappiness 1788

3 But now, so oft filth chokes thy sprightly fire,
We loathe one instant, and the next admire—
Even while we laugh, we mourn thy wit's abuse,
And while we praise thy talents, scorn their use.
"On Reading Swift's* Works" (Philadelphia, 1774), *Universal Asylum & Columbian Magazine September 1790*
*Jonathan Swift, English satirist (1667–1745).

4 Teach my unskilled mind to sing
The feelings of my heart.
"An Ode to Gratitude," Pt. 1 (Philadelphia, 1770), *Women
Poets in Pre-Revolutionary America*, Patti Cowell, ed. *1981*

5 Oh Sensibility divine!
"Ode to Sensibility," Pt. 1 (Philadelphia, 1774), Ibid.

676. Hester Ann Rogers (1756–1794)

1 What I suffered is known only to God.
Quoted in *The Women of Methodism: Its Three
Foundresses . . .* by Abel Stevens *1866*

677. Georgiana Cavendish (1757–1806)

1 Their Liberty requir'd no rites uncouth,
No blood demanded, and no slaves enchain'd;
Her rule was gentle, and her voice was truth,
By social order form'd, by law restrain'd.
Passage of the Mountain of Saint Gothard, St. 26 *1802*

678. Augusta (1757–1831)

1 How can his [Napoleon's*] conscience be quite in abeyance, with so many thousands of lives sacrificed to his insane ambition? What would I not give to read his inner thoughts. If he will ever awake from his mad dream of power, God only knows, Who has permitted him to become the scourge of the nations of the earth.

> Diary Entry (26 January 1813), *In Napoleonic Days, Extracts from the private diary of Augusta, Duchess of Saxe-Coburg-Saalfeld, Queen Victoria's** maternal grandmother, 1806–1821*, H. R. H., the Princess Beatrice, ed. and tr. *1941*

*Emperor of the French (1769–1821; r. 1804–1814) *See 934.

2 When one gets old one is so thankful to be quiet.

> Diary entry (19 December 1817), Ibid.

679. Martha Wilson (1758–post-1848)

1 . . . let it never be forgotten by you that the reputation established by a boy at school and college, whether it be of merit or demerit, will follow him through life.

> Letter to C. S. Stewart, her nephew and adopted son (16 February 1811), Quoted in *The Women of the American Revolution*, Vol. II by Elizabeth F. Ellet *1848*

2 Press forward, my dear son, in the ways of wisdom—they are ways of pleasantness, and their end is peace.

> Letter to C. S. Stewart (31 May 1814), Ibid.

3 Industry is the handmaid of good fortune. . . .

> Ibid.

4 Man can do much for himself as respects his own improvement, unless self-love so blinds him that he cannot see his own imperfections and weaknesses.

> Ibid.

5 The exercise of a little self-denial for the time being will be followed by the pleasure of having achieved the greatest of triumphs—a triumph over one's self.

> Ibid.

680. Esther Hayden (?–1758)

1 I'm sore distress'd, and greatly 'press'd
With filthy Nature, Sin;
I cannot rise to view the Prize
Of happiness within.

> Untitled, *A Short Account of the Life, Death and Character of Esther Hayden, the Wife of Samuel Hayden of Braintree* (Mass.) *1759*

681. Henrietta O'Neill (1758–1793)

1 Hail, lovely blossom! thou canst ease
The wretched victims of Disease
Canst close those weary eyes in gentle sleep,
Which never open but to weep;
For oh! thy potent charm
Can agonizing Pain disarm;
Expel imperious Memory from her seat,
And bid the throbbing heart forget to beat.

> "Ode to Poppy," St. 5, Quoted in *Elegaic Sonnets and Other Essays*, Charlotte Smith, ed. *1782*

682. Mary Robinson (1758–1800)

1 Yet when love and hope are vanished,
Restless memory never dies.

> "Stanzas, written between Dover & Calais," St. 4, *Poems 1775*

2 I have wept to see thee weep.

> St. 13, Ibid.

3 The Snow-drop, Winter's timid child,
Awakes to life, bedew'd with tears.

> "The Snow-Drop," St. 1, Ibid.

4 For we were poor—and hearts of stone
Will never throb at misery's groan.

> "All Alone," St. 17, Ibid.

5 For what is all the world to me—
What are the dews and buds of morn?
Since she who left me sad, alone
In darkness sleeps, beneath yon stone!

> St. 23, Ibid.

6 The proudest of the purring band:—
So dignified in all her paces,
She seem'd a pupil of the Graces!
There never was a finer creature
In all the varying whims of Nature!

> "Mistress Gurton's Cat. A Domestic Tale," St. 1, Ibid.

7 For friends, whom trifling faults can sever,
Are valued most—when lost for ever!

> St. 12, Ibid.

8 When FATE in ruthless rage assail'd my breast,
And Heaven relentless seal'd the harsh decree;
HOPE, placid soother of the mind distress'd;
To calm my rending sorrows—gave me THEE

> "Sonnet. To My Beloved Daughter," Ibid.

9 The proud inheritor of Heaven's best gifts—
The mind unshackled, and the guiltless soul!

> "The Widow's Home," St. 5, last lines, Ibid.

10 Insatiate TIME shall steal those tints away,
Warp thy fine form, and bend thy beauties low:

But the rare wonders of thy polish'd MIND
Shall mock the empty menace of decay;

> "To Her Grace the Duchess of Devonshire," Sts. 2–3, Ibid.

683. Elizabeth Hamilton (1758?–1816)

1 "Those who wait till evening for sunrise," said Mrs. Mason, "will find that they have lost the day."

> Ch. 8, *The Cottagers of Glenburnie: A Tale for the Farmer's Ingle-nook 1808*

2 Of a' roads to happiness were ever tried,
There's nane half so sure as ane's ain fireside.
My ain fireside, my ain fireside,
O there's naught to compare wi' ane's ain fireside.

> "My Ain Fireside," *Scottish Song*, Mary Carlyle Aitken, ed. *1874*

3 With expectation beating high,
Myself I now desire to spy;
And straight I in a glass surveyed
An antique lady, much decayed

> Untitled, Quoted in *Biography of Distinguished Women* by Sarah Josepha Hale* *1876*

*See 788.

4 It is only by the love of reading that the evil resulting from the association with *little* minds can be counteracted.

> "The Benefits of Society," *Private Letters n.d.*

5 I perfectly agree with you in considering castles in the air as more useful edifices than they are generally allowed to be. It is only plodding matter-of-fact dullness that cannot comprehend their use.

"Imagination," Ibid.

684. Hannah Webster Foster (1758/59–1840)

1 An unusual sensation possesses my breast—a sensation which I once thought could never pervade it on any occasion whatever. It is *pleasure*, pleasure, my dear Lucy, on leaving my paternal roof.

Letter I, *The Coquette; or, The History of Eliza Wharton*
1797

2 In whatever situation we are placed, our greater or less degree of happiness must be derived from ourselves. Happiness is in a great measure the result of our own dispositions and actions.

Letter XXI, Ibid.

3 If the conviction of any misconduct on your part gives you pain, dissipate it by the reflection that unerring rectitude is not the lot of mortals; that few are to be found who have not deviated, in a greater or less degree, from the maxims of prudence. Our greatest mistakes may teach lessons which will be useful through life.

Letter XLIII, Ibid.

4 How can that be a diversion which racks the soul with grief, even though that grief be imaginary? The introduction of a funeral solemnity upon the stage is shocking indeed!

Letter LII, Ibid.

685. Jane West (1758–1852)

1 Great and sudden reverses of fortune are not frequent; yet little disappointments hourly occur, which fall with the greatest severity on those, whose amiable, though dangerous enthusiasm, induces them to expect too much, and to feel too severely.

Preface, *The Advantage of Education; or, The History of Maria Williams, a tale for Misses and their Mammas*, Vol. I
1793

2 " . . . your newly acquired taste for reading, prevents even the hazard of your ever perceiving time to be an intolerable burden."

Ch. 7, Ibid.

3 Oh! gather in life's early prime,
The produce which despises time;
Waste not in pleasure's soothing bowers
Youth's irrecoverable hours

Ch. 13, Untitled poem, St. 4, Ibid.

4 It is in the power of cunning to affect simplicity, but simplicity itself, when it would assume art, finds it too thin a disguise.

Ch. 1, Vol. II, Ibid.

5 When virtue loses its abhorrence of vice, she dismisses one of her most vigilant guards. Let but self-interest surmount principle, and her ruin is compleat.

Ch. 3, Ibid.

6 There are some secrets which scarcely admit of being disclosed even to ourselves.

Ch. 8, *A Gossip's Story*, Vol. I 1797

7 As wise people often defeat their aims by too great caution, cunning also frequently overshoots the mark by too much craft.

Ch. 11, Ibid.

8 Man. Lord of all, beneath the reign of time,
Awaits perfection in a nobler clime.

Ch. 24, "To a Rose Bush," Vol. II, Ibid.

9 "How disgraceful are these baby quarrels! how ridiculous these high theatrical passions, which subject them to the laugh of the neighbourhood! nay, worse, which point out to artful villany, means whereby it may *effectually* undermine domestick happiness."

Ch. 31, Ibid.

10 Early in life, before his character was formed, or his opinions methodized, Mr. Clermont entered into marriage; with vague, floating ideas of angelick goodness, and consummate bliss. In proportion as his romantick enthusiasm had raised the mortal nymph into a goddess, his cooler, but not more accurate judgement, as the infatuation of love subsided, magnified her errors into indelible offences.

Ch. 35, Ibid.

686. Anna Green Winslow (1759–1780)

1 Those golden arts* the vulgar never knew.

"To her Parents" (17 March 1772), *Diary of Anna Green Winslow: A Boston School Girl of 1771*,
Alice Morse Earle, ed. 1895

*Virtues.

687. Mary Wollstonecraft (1759–1797)

1 If the abstract rights of man will bear discussion and explanation, those of woman, by a parity of reasoning, will not shrink from the same test: though a different opinion prevails in the country.

Dedication, *A Vindication of the Rights of Women* 1792

2 Independence I have long considered as the grand blessing of life, the basis of every virtue; and independence I will ever secure by contracting my wants, though I were to live on a barren heath.

Ibid.

3 Perhaps the seeds of false-refinement, immorality, and vanity, have ever been shed by the great. Weak, artificial beings, raised above the common wants and defections of their race, in a premature and unnatural manner, undermine the very foundation of virtue, and spread corruption through the whole mass of society!

Introduction to 1st ed., Ibid.

4 . . . elegance is inferior to virtue. . . .

Ibid.

5 Virtue can only flourish among equals.

Ibid.

6 Children, I grant, should be innocent; but when the epithet is applied to men, or women, it is but a civil term for weakness.

Ch. 2, Ibid.

7 Standing armies can never consist of resolute robust men; they may be well-disciplined machines, but they will seldom contain men under the influence of strong passions, or with very vigorous faculties.

Ibid.

8 Women are told from their infancy, and taught by the example of their mothers, that a little knowledge of human weakness,

justly termed cunning, softness of temper, outward obedience and a scrupulous attention to a puerile kind of propriety, will obtain for them the protection of man.

Ibid.

9   Taught from infancy that beauty is woman's sceptre, the mind shapes itself to the body, and roaming round its gilt cage, only seeks to adorn its prison.

Ch. 3, Ibid.

10   What a weak barrier is truth when it stands in the way of an hypothesis!

Ibid.

11   It is a melancholy truth—yet such is the blessed affect of civilization!—the most respectable women are the most repressed. . . .

"Of the Pernicious Effects which Arise from the Unnatural Distinctions Established in Society," Ibid.

12   Would man but generously snap our chains, and be content with rational fellowship instead of slavish obedience, they would find us more observant daughters, more affectionate sisters, more faithful wives, more reasonable mothers—in a word, better citizens. We should then love them with true affection, because we should learn to respect ourselves. . . .

Ibid.

13   But a child, though a pledge of affection, will not enliven it, if both father and mother be content to transfer the charge to hirelings; for they who do their duty by proxy should not murmur if they miss the reward of duty—parental affection produces filial duty.

"Parental Affection," Ibid.

14   From the respect paid to property flow, as from a poisoned fountain, most of the evils and vices which render this world such a dreary scene to the contemplative mind.

Ibid.

15   The preposterous distinctions of rank, which renders civilization a curse by dividing the world between voluptuous tyrants and cunning envious dependents, corrupt, almost equally, every class of people. . . .

Ibid.

16   When poverty is more disgraceful than even vice, is not morality cut to the quick?

Ibid.

17   I . . . think schools, as they are now regulated, the hot-beds of vice and folly, and the knowledge of human nature supposedly attained there, merely cunning selfishness.

"On National Education," Ibid.

18   . . . only that education deserves emphatically to be termed cultivation of mind which teaches young people how to begin to think.

Ibid.

19   The imagination should not be allowed to debauch the understanding before it gains strength, or vanity will become the forerunner of vice: for every way of exhibiting the acquirements of a child is injurious to its moral character.

Ibid.

20   The mind will ever be unstable that has only prejudices to rest on, and the current will run with destructive fury when there are no barriers to break its force.

"The Prevailing Opinion of a Sexual Character Discussed," Ibid.

21   . . . as blind obedience is ever sought for by power, tyrants and sensualists are in the right when they endeavour to keep women in the dark, because the former only want slaves, and the latter a play-thing.

Ibid.

22   . . . females . . . have been stripped of the virtues that should clothe humanity . . . their sole ambition is to be fair, to raise emotion instead of inspiring respect; and this ignoble desire, like the servility in absolute monarchies, destroys all strength of character.

Ibid.

23   I begin to love this little creature, and to anticipate his birth as a fresh twist to a knot, which I do not wish to untie.

Letter to William Godwin, her husband (March 1797), Quoted in *Godwin and Mary* by Ralph M. Wardle *1966*

24   How I hate this crooked business! This intercourse with the world, which obliges one to see the worst side of human nature!

Letter XXX (29 December 1794), *Letters to Imlay* n.d.*
*Captain Gilbert Imlay, her lover.

25   Society fatigues me inexpressibly. So much so, that finding fault with everyone, I have only reason enough to discover that the fault is in myself.

Letter XXXVII (19 February 1795), Ibid.

26   I never wanted but your heart—That gone, you have nothing more to give.

Letter LXX (London, November 1795), Ibid.

688. Martha Laurens Ramsay (1759–1811)

1   . . . the bucks, the fops, the idlers of college. . . .

Letters to her son at college *n.d.*

2   . . . of all the mean objects in creation, a lazy, poor, proud gentleman, especially if he is a dressy fellow, is the meanest. . . .

Ibid.

689. Agnes Craig (1759–1841)

1   Talk not of love, it gives me pain,
     For love has been my foe;
     He bound me with an iron chain,
     And plunged me deep in woe.
     But friendship's pure and lasting joys,
     My heart was formed to prove.

"Talk Not of Love," *Scottish Song*, Mary Carlyle Aitken, ed. *1874*

690. Sarah Wentworth Morton (1759–1846)

1   When life hung quiv'ring on a single hair

"To Constantia," St. 1, *Massachusetts Magazine* May 1790

2   To the mere superficial observer, it would seem that man was sent into this breathing world for the purpose of enjoyment—woman for that of trial and suffering.

"The Sexes," *My Mind and Its Thoughts 1823*

3 More prized than wealth; than worlds more dear
      "Lines to the Breath of Kindness," St. 2, Ibid.

4 Expression in its finest utterance lives,
  And a new language to creation gives.
      "To Mr. [Gilbert] Stuart.* Upon Seeing Those Portraits
      Which were Painted by Him at Philadelphia, in the Begin-
            ning of the Present Century," St. 1, Ibid.
  *Famed American portrait painter (1755–1828).

5 Did all the Gods of Afric sleep,
  Forgetful of their guardian love,
  When the white tyrants of the deep
  Betrayed him in the palmy grove?
      "The African Chief," St. 2, Ibid.

691. Sally Sayward Wood (1759–1855)

1 Amelia was not a disciple of Mary Woolstonecraft* [sic], she
  was not a woman of fashion, nor a woman of spirit. She was
  an old-fashioned wife, and she meant to obey her husband:
  she meant to do her duty in the strictest sense of the word.
      Amelia; or, the Influence of Virtue 1802
  *See 687.

692. Dicey Langston (1760?–?)

1 Shoot me if you dare! I will not tell you.*
      Quoted by the Hon. B. F. Perry in *The Women of the Ameri-
      can Revolution*, Vol. II, by Elizabeth F. Ellet 1848
  *Response to Loyalist's demand for intelligence concerning the
  Whigs; Langston was 16 years old at the time.

693. Charlotte Charke (?–1760)

1 MRS. TRAGIC. 'Tis every Parent's Duty to breed their Children
  with every Advantage their Fortunes will admit of . . .
      The Art Management, or Tragedy Expelled 1735

2 Your two friends, PRUDENCE and REFLECTION, I am inform'd, have lately ventur'd to pay you a visit; for which I
  heartily congratulate you, as nothing can possibly be more joyous to the Heart than the Return of absent Friends, after a long
  and painful Peregrination.
      Dedication, *A Narrative of the Life of Mrs. Charlotte
      Charke* 1755

3 . . . forced again to . . . find fresh means of Subsistence . . . 'till
  even the last thread of Invention was worn out.
      Ibid.

4 Misfortunes are too apt to wear out Friendship. . . .
      Ibid.

5 An excellent Demonstration of the Humanity of those low-
  lived Wretches! Who have no farther Regard to the sons they
  employ, but while they are immediately serving 'em; and look
  upon Players like Pack-horses, though they live by 'em.
      Ibid.

694. Anne Douglas Howard (?–1760)

1 Nothing so like as male and female youth;
  Nothing so like as man and woman old
      "A defence to her sex in answer to [Alexander] Pope's*
      'Characters of Women'," *The British Female Poets*,
      George W. Bethune, ed. 1848
  *English poet and satirist (1688–1744).

2 In education all the difference lies; . . .
      Ibid.

3 Culture improves all fruits, all sorts we find,
  Wit, judgement, sense, fruits of the human mind.
      Ibid.

695. Ho Xuan Huong (fl. c. 1760–1799)

1 I am like a jackfruit on the tree.
  To taste you must pluck me quick, while fresh:
  the skin rough, the pulp thick, yes,
  but oh, I warn you against touching—
  the rich juice will gush and stain your hands.
      "The Jackfruit," *in toto*, *A Thousand Years of Vietnamese
      Poetry*, Nguyen Ngoc Bich, ed. and tr. 1975

2 Pray hard: you too can be a Superior
  And squat, proud, on a lotus.
      "A Buddhist Priest," Nguyen Ngoc Bich and Burton Raffel,
      trs., Ibid.

696. Margaret Shippen Arnold (1760–1804)

1 . . . my ambition has sunk with my fortune.
      Letter to E. Burd (15 August 1801), Quoted in "Life of
      Margaret Shippen" by Lewis Burd Walker, *Pennsylvania
      Magazine of History and Biography*, Vol. XXV 1901

2 At one period, when I viewed everything through a false
  medium, I fancied that nothing but the sacrifice of my life
  would benefit my children, for that my wretchedness embit-
  tered every moment of their lives; and dreadful to say, I was
  many times on the point of making the sacrifice.
      Letter to her father (1801), Ibid.

697. Anne Yearsley (1760–1806)

1 Earth by the grizzly tyrant desert made
  The feathered warblers quit the leafless shade;
  Quit those dear scenes where life and love began,
  And, cheerless seek the savage haunts of man.
      "Clifton Hill," St. 1 (January 1785), *The British
      Female Poets*, George W. Bethune, ed.
      1848

2 All Nature's sweets in joyous circles move
  And wake the frozen soul again to love.
      St. 2, Ibid.

3 The portals of the swelling soul ne'er ope'd
  By liberal converse, rude ideas strove
  Awhile for vent, but found it not, and died.
  Thus rust the mind's best powers.
      "A Poem on Mrs. Montague",* *The Female
      Poets of Great Britain*, Frederic Rowton, ed.
      1853
  *Mary Wortley Montagu; see 527.

698. Rebecca Franks (176-?–1823)

1 I have gloried in my rebel countrymen! Would to God I, too,
  had been a patriot!
      Remark to General Winfield Scott (c. 1816), Quoted in *Re-
      becca Franks: An American Jewish Belle of the Last Century*
      by Max J. Kohler 1894

699. Susannah Farnum Copley (fl. c. 1760–1836)

1 It was his* own inclination and persevering industry that brought him forward in the art of painting, for he had no instructor.

> Ch. 1, Letter, Quoted in *The Domestic and Artistic Life of John Singleton Copley, R.A.*, by Martha Babcock Amory** *1882*

*Her husband, the artist John Singleton Copley (1738–1815).
**Copley's granddaughter.

2 I tell [your father] I don't know what might be the effect if our comfort, as well as our delight, was not so interwoven with the arts, which it is mortifying to know do not find a place among the other refinements of our native country [the United States]. . . .

> Ch. 11, Letter to her daughter (1 June 1801), Ibid.

3 . . . but we find the law, as well as many other pursuits, requires much perseverance and patience to obtain the object; it is well for us that we do not always foresee the degree that it is necessary . . .

> (15 March 1805), Ibid.

4 A happy calm prevails after great apprehension of the reverse.
> Ch. 16, Letter to her daughter (22 March 1821), Ibid.

700. Mary Slocumb (1760–1836)

1 Allow me to observe and prophesy, the only land in these United States which will ever remain in possession of a British officer, will measure but six feet by two.

> Remark to a British colonel, Quoted in *The Women of the American Revolution*, Vol. II by Elizabeth F. Ellet *1848*

2 My husband is not a man who would allow a duke, or even a king, to have a quiet [titled] seat upon his ground.

> Ibid.

701. Dorothea Jordan (1762–1816)

1 'Oh, where, and Oh! where is your Highland laddie gone?'
'He's gone to fight the French, for King George upon the throne,
And it's Oh! in my heart, how I wish him safe at home!'
> "The Blue Bells of Scotland"* *n.d.*

*Both this and "Oh Where, Tell Me Where" by Anne Green are variants on an older popular song.

702. Susanna Haswell Rowson (1762–1824)

1 HENRY. This fellow will do some mischief, with his nonsensical prate.

> Act III, Sc. 1, *Slaves in Algiers, or a Struggle for Freedom 1794*

2 To raise the fall'n—to pity and forgive,
This is our noblest, best prerogative.
By these, pursuing nature's gentle plan,
We hold—in silken chains—the lordly tyrant man.
> Epilogue, Ibid.

3 Nay, start not, gentle stirs; indeed, 'tis true,
Poor woman has her rights as well as you;
And if she's wise, she will assert them too.
> "Rights of Women," *Miscellaneous Poems 1804*

703. Helen Maria Williams (1762–1827)

1 No riches from his scanty store
My lover could impart;

He gave a boon I valued more,
He gave me all his heart.
> "Song," St. 1, *An Ode to Peace and Other Poems 1782–1788*

2 The night is dark, the waters deep,
Yet soft the billows roll;
Alas! at every breeze I weep,
The storm is in my soul.

> St. 5, Ibid.

3 Come, gentle Hope! with one gay smile remove
The lasting sadness of an aching heart.
> "Sonnet to Hope," *Poems, moral, elegant and pathetic: viz. Essay on Man, by Pope* . . . And Original Sonnets* by Helen Maria Williams *1796*

*English poet and satirist (1688–1744).

4 Thy light can visionary thoughts impart,
And leaf the Muse to soothe a suffering heart.
> "Sonnet to the Moon," Ibid.

704. Mrs. Lyon (1762–1840)

1 Yet the doctors they do a' agree,
That whiskey's no the drink for me.
Saul! quoth Neil, 'twill spoil my glee,
Should they part me and whiskey, O
> "Neil Gow's Farewell to Whiskey," *Scottish Song*, Mary Carlyle Aitken, ed. *1874*

705. Joanna Baillie (1762–1851)

1 O! who shall lightly say that fame
Is nothing but an empty name?
> "The Legend of Christopher Columbus,"* St. 1, ix, *Fugitive Verses 1790*

*Italian explorer (1451–1506).

2 O lovely Sisters! is it true
That they are all inspired by you,
And write by inward magic charm'd,
And high enthusiasm warm'd?
> "Address to the Muses," St. xi, Ibid.

3 "Ah! happy is the man whose early lot
Hath made him master of a furnish'd cot;
Who trains the vine that round his window grows,
And after setting sun his garden hoes;
Whose wattled pails his own enclosure shield,
Who toils not daily in another's field."
> "A Reverie," St. iii, Ibid.

4 "What hollow sound is that?" approaching near,
The roar of many wheels breaks on his ear.
It is the flood of human life in motion!
> "London," St. iii, Ibid.

5 Sweet bud of promise, fresh and fair,
Just moving in the morning air.
The morn of life but just begun,
The sands of time just set to run!
Sweet babe with cheek of pinky hue,
With eyes of soft ethereal blue,
With raven hair like finest down
Of unfledged bird, and scant'ly shown
Beneath the cap of cumbrous lace,

That circles round thy placid face!
Ah, baby! little dost thou know
How many yearning blossoms glow,
How many lips in blessings move,
How many eyes beam looks of love
At sight of thee!

"To Sophia J. Baillie, an Infant," *in toto, Ibid.*

6   Busy work brings after ease;
Ease brings sport and sport brings rest;
For young and old, of all degrees,
The mingled lot is best.

"Rhymes," St. I, *Ibid.*

7   GEOFFRY. Some men are born to feast and not to fight:
Whose sluggish minds, e'en in fair honours field
Still on their dinner turn—
Let such pot-boiling varlets stay at home,
And wield a flesh-hook rather than a sword.

Act I, Sc. 1, *Basil* 1798

8   DUKE. But int'rest, int'rest, man's all-ruling pow'r. . . .

Act II, Sc. 3, *Ibid.*

9   COUNTESS OF ALBINI. For she who only finds her self-esteem
In other's admiration, begs in alms;
Depends on others for her daily food,
And is the very servant of her slaves. . . .

Sc. 4, *Ibid.*

10   COUNT ROSINBERG. The brave man is not he who feels no fear,
For that were stupid and irrational;
But he, whose noble soul its fear subdues,
And barely dares the danger nature shrinks from.

Act III, Sc. 1, *Ibid.*

11   SONG. Child, with many a childish wile,
Timid look, and blushing smile,
Downy wings to steal thy way,
Gilded bow, and quiver gay,
Who in thy simple mien would trace
The tyrant of the human race?

Sc. 3, *Ibid.*

12   Thinks't thou there are no serpents in the world
But those that slide along the grassy sod,
And sting the luckless foot that presses them?
There are who in the path of social life
Do bask their spotted skins in Fortune's sun,
And sting the soul.

Act I, Sc. 2, *De Monfort* 1798

13   A willing heart adds feather to the heel.

Act III, Sc. 2, *Ibid.*

14   COL. HARDY. Nay, heaven defend us from a violent woman;
for that is the devil himself!

Act IV, Sc. 1. *The Trial,* 1789

15   The bliss e'en of a moment still is bliss.

Act I, Sc. 2, *The Beacon* 1802

16   ETHWALD. He who will not give
Some portion of his ease, his blood, his wealth
For other's good is a poor frozen churl.

Act I, Sc. 2, *Ethwald,
Part Second* 1802

17   SIR CRAFTY SUPPLECOAT. Pride is a fault that great men
blush not to own: it is the ennobled offspring of self-love;
though, it must be confessed, grave and pompous vanity,
like a fat plebeian in a rove of office, does very often assume its name.

Act II, Sc. 4, *The Second Marriage* 1802

18   MAHOMET. In mortal man
I have no trust; they are all hollow slaves,
Who tremble and detest, and would betray.

Act III, Sc. 2, *Constantine Paleologus* 1804

19   WORSHIPTON. Curse your snug comfortable ways of living! my
soul abhors the idea of it. I'll pack up all I have in a knapsack
first, and join the wild Indians in America.

Act V, Sc. 2, *The Country Inn* 1804

20   The mind doth shape itself to its own wants
And can bear all things.

Rayner 1804

21   Still on it creeps,
Each little moment at another's heels,
Till hours, days, years and ages are made up
Of such small parts as these, and men look back
Worn and bewilder'd, wondering how it is.

Ibid.

22   EARL OF ARGYLL. That day will come,
When in the grave this hoary head of mine,
And many after heads, in death are laid;
And happier men, our sons, shall live to see it.
O may they prize it too with grateful hearts;
And, looking back on these our stormy days
Of other years, pity, admire, and pardon
The fierce, contentious, ill-directed valour
Of gallant fathers, born in darker time!

Act V, Sc. 4, *The Family Legend* 1810

23   BALTIMORE. O! hang them, but they won't laugh! I have seen
the day, when, if a man made himself ridiculous, the world
would laugh at him. But now, everything that is mean, disgusting and absurd, pleases them but so much the better!

Act I, Sc. 2, *The Election* 1811

24   Pampered vanity is a better thing perhaps than starved pride.

Act II, Sc. 2, *Ibid.*

25   ORRA. He was not all a father's heart could wish;
but oh, he was my son!—my only son.

Act III, Sc. 2, *Orra* 1812

26   CRAFTON. Fy, fy! let no man be on his knees but when he is at
his prayers.

Act V, Sc. 2, *The Alienated Manor* 1836

27   SANCHO. Me care for te laws when te laws care for me.

Ibid.

28   ROBINAIR. This will be triumph! this will be happiness! yea,
that very thing, happiness, which I have been pursuing all my
life, and have never yet overtaken.

Act IV, Sc. 1, *The Stripling* 1836

29   Words of affection, howso'er express'd,
The latest spoken still are deem'd the best.

"Address to Miss Agnes Baillie on Her Birthday,"
ll.125–126 *n.d.*

30 . . . Some still a thought,
And clip it round the edge, and challenge him
Whose 'twas to swear to it. To serve things thus
Is as foul witches to cut up old moons
Into new stars.

Festus n.d.

706. Empress Josephine (1763–1814)

1 Trust to me, ladies, and do not envy a splendor which does not
constitute happiness.

Quotes in *Lives of Celebrated Women* by Samuel Griswold
Goodrich *1844*

2 . . . patience and goodness will ever in the end conciliate the
goodwill of others.

Letter to her children (1794), Ibid.

707. Catherine Rilliet-Huber (1764–post-1810)

1 All I can say is that she [Germaine de Staël*] is as lively and
brilliant as ever—which proves the advantage of organizing
one's heart in a system of multiple hiding places.

Letter to Henri Meister (13 November 1810), Quoted in
Mistress to an Age: A Life of Madame de Staël
by J. Christopher Herold *1958*

*See 717.

708. Helene Marie Phillipine Elizabeth (1764–1794)

I am Elizabeth of France, the aunt of your king [Louis XVII].

In answer to request for her identity at her tribunal (May
10, 1794), Quoted in *Biography of Distinguished Women*
by Sarah Josepha Hale* *1876*

*See 788.

709. Anne Willing Bingham (1764–1801)

1 The women of France interfere in the politics of the Country,
and often give a decided Turn to the Fate of Empires.

Letter to Thomas Jefferson* (c.1783–1786), Quoted in *The
Papers of Thomas Jefferson*, Vol. XI, Julian P. Boyd, ed.
1955

*(1743–1826), third president of United States (1801–1809).

710. Sun Yün-fêng (1764–1814)

1 Under the waning moon
In the dawn—
A frosty bell.

"Starting at Dawn," *The Orchid Boat, Women Poets of
China*, Kenneth Rexroth and Ling Chung, eds. and trs. *1972*

2 Along the shore the willows
Wait for their Spring green.

"On the Road Through Chang-te," Ibid.

711. Ann Radcliffe (1764–1823)

1 At first a small line of inconceivable splendour emerged on the
horizon, which, quickly expanding, the sun appeared in all of
his glory, unveiling the whole face of nature, vivifying every
colour of the landscape, and sprinkling the dewy earth with
glittering light. The low and gentle responses of the birds,
awakened by the morning ray, now broke the silence of the
hour, their soft warbling rising by degrees till they swelled the
chorus of universal gladness.

The Romance of the Forest 1791

2 "We in Italy are not so apt to despair. . . . "

The Italian 1797

3 "From my mind the illusion which gave spirit to the colouring
of nature is fading fast. . . . "

Gaston de Blondeville 1826

4 Then let me stand amidst thy glooms profound
On some wild woody steep, and hear the breeze

"Night," St. 8, *Poems 1834*

712. Juliana Krudener (1764–1824)

1 Stay quiet; refuse nothing; flowers grow only because they
tranquilly allow the sun's rays to reach them. You must do the
same.

Remark to Germaine de Staël,* Quoted in
Mistress to an Age: A Life of Madame de Staël
by J. Christopher Herold *1958*

*See 717.

713. Mary Ann Lamb (1764–1847)

1 Who, that e'er could understand
The rare structure of a hand,
With its branching fingers fine,
Work itself of hands divine,
Strong, yet delicately knit,
For ten thousand uses fit

"Cleanliness," *Poetry for Children 1809*

2 His conscience slept a day or two,
As it is very apt to do

"The Boy and the Skylark," I, St. 5, Ibid.

3 An infant is a selfish sprite.

"The Broken Doll," St. 1, Ibid.

4 Reproof a parent's province is;
A sister's discipline is this;
By studied kindness to effect
A little brother's young respect.

St. 3, Ibid.

5 This place, methinks, resembleth well
The world itself in which we dwell.
Perils and snares on every ground,
Like these wild beasts, beset us round.

"The Beasts in the Tower,"* II, St. 2, Ibid.
*I.e., the cages in a zoo.

6 A child is fed with milk and praise.

"The First Tooth," Ibid.

7 Shut these odious books up, brother—
They have made you quite another
Thing from what you used to be;
Once you liked to play with me. . . .

"The Sister's Expostulation on the Brother's
Learning Latin," Ibid.

8 Know ye not, each thing we prize
Does from small beginnings rise?

"The Brother's Reply," I, Ibid.

9 O happy town-bred girl, in fine chaise going
For the first time to see the green grass growing!

"The First Sight of Green Fields," Ibid.

10 Honey and locusts were his* food,
And he was most severely good.
"Salome,"** St. 3 (1808/09), Ibid.
*John the Baptist. **See 82.

11 A child's a plaything for an hour.
"Parental Recollections," Ibid.

12 Thou straggler into loving arms,
Young climber up of knees,
When I forget thy thousand ways,
Then life and all shall cease.
"A Child," St. 3, Ibid.

13 . . . I do not expect or want you to be otherwise than you are,
I love you for the good that is in you, and look for no change.
Letter to Sarah Stoddart (21 September 1803), *The Letters
of Charles and Mary Lamb*, Vol. II, 1801–1809,
Edwin W. Marrs, Jr., ed. *1976*

14 . . . by secrecy I mean you both want the habit of telling each
other at the moment everything that happens,—where you
go—and what you do—that free communication of letters and
opinions, just as they arise, as Charles [her brother] and I do,
and which is after all the only groundwork of friendship. . . .
Ibid.

15 . . . I never have the power of altering or amending anything I
have once laid aside with satisfaction.
Letter to Dorothy Wordsworth* (7 May 1805), Ibid.
*See 745.

16 . . . I have lost all self confidence in my own actions & one
cause of my low spirits is that I never feel satisfied with anything I do—a perception of not being in a sane state
perpetually haunts me.
Letter to Sarah Stoddart (9-14 November 1805), Ibid.

17 It is but being once thourowly [sic] convinced one is wrong, to
make one resolve to do so no more. . . .
Letter to Sarah Stoddart (14 March 1806), Ibid.

18 Our love for each other* has been the torment of our lives
hitherto. I am most seriously intending to bend the whole force
of my mind to counteract this, and I think I see some prospect
of success.
Ibid.
*Referring to her brother, Charles Lamb, English essayist
(1775–1834).

19 I have known many single men I should have liked in my life
(if it had suited them) for a husband: but very few husbands
have I ever wished was mine which is rather against the state
[of marriage] in general [so] that one is never disposed to envy
wives their good husbands, So much for marrying—but however get married if you can.
(30 May–2 June 1806), Ibid.

20 If you fancy a very young man, and he likes an elderly gentlewoman, if he likes a learned & accomplished lady, and you
like a not very learned youth who may need a little polishing
which probably he will never acquire; it is all very well & God
bless you both together & may you both be very long in the
same mind.
(23 October 1806), Ibid.

21 . . . you must begin the world with ready money. . . .
(21? December 1807), Ibid.

714. Emma Hamilton (1765–1815)

1 When she [her daughter] comes and looks in my face and calls
me "mother," indead [sic] I then truly am a mother. . . .
Letter to Charles Greenville (June 1774),
Quoted in *Memoirs of Emma,
Lady Hamilton* 1815

715. Nancy Storace (1765–1815)

1 I have as good a right to show the power of my *bomba** as
anyone else.
Quoted in *Queens of Song* by
Ellen Creathorne Clayton *1865*
*Tremolo or vibrato.

716. Catherine Marie Fanshawe (1765–1834)

1 'Twas whisper'd in heaven, 'twas mutter'd in hell,
And echo caught faintly the sound as it fell;
On the confines of earth 'twas permitted to rest,
And the depths of the ocean its presence confess'd.
"Enigma: The Letter H," *Memorials*
1865

2 At their speed behold advancing
Modern men and women dancing;
Step and dress alike express
Above, below from heel to toe,
Male and female awkwardness.
"The Abrogation of the Birth-Night Ball," Ibid.

717. Germaine de Staël (1766–1817)

1 . . . inventiveness is childish, practice sublime.
Réflexions sur la paix intérieure (Reflections on internal
peace) *1795*

2 Love is the whole history of a woman's life, it is but an episode
in a man's.
Preface (1 July 1796), *De l'influence des passions sur le
bonheur des individus et des nations* (A Treatise on the
Influence of the Passions upon the Happiness of
Individuals and of Nations) *1796*

3 Intellect does not attain its full force unless it attacks
power.
*De la littérature considérée dans ses rapports avec les
institutions sociales* (The Influence of Literature
upon Society) *1800*

4 [Literature has] ceased to be a mere art; it [has] become a
means to an end, a weapon in the service of the spirit of
man.
Ibid.

5 Every time a new nation, America or Russia for instance, advances toward civilization, the human race perfects itself;
every time an inferior class emerges from enslavement and
degradation, the human race again perfects itself.
Ibid.

6 The decadence of empires is no more in the natural order of
things than is the decadence of literature and science.
Ibid.

7 Happy the land where writers are sad, the merchants satisfied,
the rich melancholic, and the populace content.
Ibid.

8 Scientific progress makes moral progress a necessity; for if man's power is increased, the checks that restrain him from abusing it must be strengthened.

Ibid.

9 Why should it not be possible some day to compile tables that would contain the answer to all questions of a political nature based on statistical knowledge, on positive facts gathered from every country?

Ibid.

10 Morality must guide calculation, and calculation must guide politics.

Ibid.

11 The entire social order . . . is arrayed against a woman who wants to rise to a man's reputation.

Ibid.

12 Between God and love, I recognize no mediator but my conscience.

Delphine 1802

13 "Follow me, let this instant decide our lives! There are decisions that must be made in the heat of passion, without giving bitter reflections the time to revive!"

Ibid.

14 A man must know how to defy opinion; a woman how to submit to it.

Ibid.

15 She liked to make others' lives as drab as possible, perhaps so as not to feel too much regret at the dissolution of her own.

Corinne, or Italy 1807

16 Love, supreme power of the heart, mysterious enthusiasm that encloses in itself all poetry, all heroism, all religion!

Ibid.

17 To understand all makes one very indulgent.

Ibid.

18 Wit lies in recognizing the resemblance among things which differ and the difference between things which are alike.

Pt. 3, Ch. 8, *Germany 1813*

19 Love is above the laws, above the opinion of men; it is the truth, the flame, the pure element, the primary idea of the moral world.

Zulma, and Other Tales 1813

20 Magnificence is the characteristic of everything one sees in Russia.

Dix années d'exil (Ten Years of Exile) *1813*

21 The phantom of *ennui* forever pursues me.

Quoted in *Lives of Celebrated Women* by Samuel Griswold Goodrich *1844*

22 Life resembles Gobelin tapestry; you do not see the canvas on the right side but when you turn it, the threads are visible.

Ibid.

23 The greatest happiness is to transform one's feelings into actions. . . .

Letter to de Pange (Coppet, c. May 1796), *Madame de Staël et François de Pange: lettres et documents inédits*, Jean de Pange, ed. *1925*

24 What I love about noise is that it camouflages life.

Letter to Eric Staël von Holstein, *Revue des Deux Mondes June/July 1932*

25 Money alone determines your entire life, political as well as private.

Letter to Benjamin Constant* (Coppet, April 1815), *Lettres à un ami*, Jean Mistler, ed. *1949*
*Baron d'Estourelles, French politician, diplomat and Nobel laureate (1832–1924)

26 The pursuit of politics is religion, morality, and poetry all in one.

Quoted in *Mistress to an Age: A Life of Madame de Staël* by J. Christopher Herold *1958*

27 Those gentlemen [Lafayette* and Sylvain Bailly, mayor of Paris] are like the rainbow; they always appear after the storm is over.

Ibid.
*French soldier and politician (1757–1834).

28 Genius has no sex!

Ibid.

29 Sir, I understand everything that deserves to be understood; what I don't understand is nothing.

Ibid.

30 There is a kind of physical pleasure in resisting as iniquitous power.

Ibid.

31 I never was able to believe in the existence of next year except as in a metaphysical notion.

Ibid.

32 In matters of the heart, nothing is true except the improbable.

Letter to her cousin Juliette, *Ibid.*

33 If one hour's work is enough to govern France, four minutes is all that is needed for Italy. There is no nation more easily frightened; even its poetic imagination predisposes it to fear, and they look upon power as on an image that fills them with terror.

(1804), *Ibid.*

34 I shall have to conquer myself once more, despite everything.

(near Blois, 27 September 1810), *Ibid.*

35 I must keep on rowing, not until I reach port but until I reach my grave.

Letter to Albertine Necker de Saussure, her daughter (Coppet, July 1814), *Ibid.*

36 How much past there is in a life, however brief it be.

Letter to Récamier (c. February 1816), *Ibid.*

37 You [America] are the vanguard of the human race. You are the world's future.

Spoken to George Ticknow* (c. Spring 1817), *Ibid.*
*American author and teacher of languages (1791–1871).

38   . . . I have always made it a point to adopt the opinions of the man whom I prefer.

> Letter to Adolph Ludvig Ribbing (c.1794), *Lettres à Ribbing*, Simone Balaye, ed. *1960*

39   The desire of the man is for the woman, but the desire of the woman is for the desire of the man.

> Attributed *n.d.*

718. Nancy Dennis Sproat (1766–1826)

1   How pleasant is Saturday night,
When I've tried all the week to be good,
Not spoken a word that is bad,
And obliged every one that I could.

> "How Pleasant is Saturday Night," *n.d.*

719. Betty Zane (1766?–1831?)

1   You have not one man to spare.*

> Quoted in *Chronicles of Border Warfare* by Alexander S. Withers *1831*

*Attributed remark as she volunteered to run a dangerous mission.

720. Carolina Nairne (1766–1845)

1   The Laird o' Cockpen, he's proud an' he's great,
His mind is ta'en up wi' things o' the State. . . .

> "The Laird o' Cockpen," St. 1, *Lays from Strathearn 1846*

2   A penniless lass wi' a lang pedigree.

> St. 2, Ibid.

3   Oh, ye may ca' them vulgar farin',
Wives and mithers maist despairin',
Ca' them lives o' men.

> "Caller* Herrin'," Ibid.

*Fresh.

4   Wi' a hundred pipers an' a', an' a',
Wi' a hundred pipers an' a', an' a',
We'll up an' gie them a blaw, a blaw,
Wi' a hundred pipers an' a', an' a'.

> "The Hundred Pipers," Ibid.

5   O, Charlie is my darling,
My darling, my darling;
Charlie is my darling,
The young Chevalier.

> "Charlie* Is My Darling," *Scottish Song*, Mary Carlyle Aitken, ed. *1874*

*The reference is to Charles Stuart, a.k.a. "Bonnie Prince Charlie," or The Young Pretender (1720–1788).

721. Barbara Frietschie (1766–1862)

1   "Shoot, if you must, this old gray head
But spare your country's flag"

> Attributed, Quoted by John Greenleaf Whittier* in "Barbara Fritchie," *Atlantic Monthly* (Boston) *October 1863*

*American poet (1807–1892).

722. Rachel Robards Jackson (1767–1828)

1   Believe me, this country [Florida] has been greatly overrated. One acre of our fine Tennessee land is worth a thousand here.

> Letter to friends, Quoted in *Dames and Daughters of the Young Republic* by Gamaliel Bradford *1901*

2   To tell you of this city [Washington, D.C.], I would not do justice to the subject. The extravagance is in dressing and running to parties; but I must say they regard the Sabbath and attend preaching, for there are churches of every denomination and able ministers of the gospel.

> Letter to a friend, Ibid.

723. Maria Edgeworth (1767–1849)

1   Man is to be held only by the *slightest* chains; with the idea that he can break them at pleasure, he submits to them in sport. . . .

> Letter I (1787), *Letters of Julia and Caroline 1795*

2   In strong minds, despair is an acute disease; the prelude to great exertion. In weak minds, it is a chronic distemper, followed by incurable indolence.

> Letter IV (1787), Ibid.

3   "Pleasing for a moment," said Helen, smiling, "is of some consequence; for, if we take care of the moments, the years will take care of themselves, you know."

> *Mademoiselle Panache 1795*

4   A man who marries a showy entertaining coquette, and expects she will make him a charming companion for life, commits as absurd a blunder as that of the famous nobleman who, delighted with the wit and humour of Punch at a puppet-show, bought Punch, and ordered him to be sent home for his private amusement.

> Ibid.

5   I've a great fancy to see my own funeral afore I die.

> Ch. 1, *Castle Rackrent 1800*

6   Nothing for nothing.

> Ibid.

7   "It is quite fitting that charity should *begin* at home," said Wright; "but then it should not *end* at home; for those that help nobody shall find none to help them in time of need."

> Ch. 2, *The Will 1800*

8   How success changes the opinion of men!

> Ch. 4, Ibid.

9   Business was his aversion; pleasure was his business.

> Ch. 2, *The Contrast 1801*

10   All work and no play makes Jack a dull boy,
All play and no work makes Jack a mere toy.

> *Harry and Lucy 1801*

11   When Paddy heard an English gentleman speaking of the fine echo at the lake of Killarney, which repeats the sound forty times, he very promptly observed, "Faith, that's nothing at all to the echo in my father's garden, in the county of Galway: if you say to it, 'how do you do, Paddy Blake?' it will answer, 'pretty well, I thank you, sir.'"

> Ch. 1, *Essay on Irish Bulls 1802*

12   Bishop Wilkins prophesied that the time would come when gentlemen, when they were to go on a journey, would call for their wings as regularly as they call for their boots.

> Ch. 2, Ibid.

13   Those who are animated by hope can perform what would seem impossibilities to those who are under the depressing influence of fear.

> *The Grateful Negro 1802*

14 "The law, in our case, seems to make the right; and the very reverse ought to be done—the right should make the law."

Ibid.

15 "Those who have lived in a house with spoiled children must have a lively recollection of the degree of torment they can inflict upon all who are within sight or hearing."

Ch. 1, *The Manufacturers 1803*

16 Children were pretty things at three years old; but began to be great plagues at six, and were quite intolerable at ten.

Ibid.

17 The facility at which I learned my lessons encouraged me to put off learning them till the last moment; and this habit of procrastinating, which was begun in presumption, ended in disgrace.

Ch. 1, *To-Morrow 1803*

18 I was ever searching for some *short cut* to the temple of Fame, instead of following the beaten road.

Ch. 3, Ibid.

19 I now attempted too much: I expected to repair by bustle the effects of procrastination.

Ch. 4, Ibid.

20 . . . when driven to the necessity of explaining, I found that I did not myself understand what I meant.

Ibid.

21 What a misfortune it is to be born a woman! . . . Why seek for knowledge, which can prove only that our wretchedness is irremediable? If a ray of light break in upon us, it is but to make darkness more visible; to show us the now limits, the Gothic structure, the impenetrable barriers of our prison.

Letter I, *Leonora 1805*

22 It is not so easy to do good as those who have never attempted it may imagine. . . .

Ch. 2, *Madame de Fleury 1805*

23 As a highwayman knows that he must come to the gallows at last, and acts accordingly, so a fashionably extravagant youth knows that, sooner or later, he must come to matrimony.

Ch. 2 (1804), *Ennui 1809*

24 "How virtuous we shall be when we have no name for vice!"

Ch. 10 (1804), Ibid.

25 " . . . sometimes the very faults of parents produce a tendency to opposite virtues in their children . . . "

Ch. 1, *Manoeuvring 1809*

26 Well! some people talk of morality, and some of religion, but give me a little snug property.

Ch. 2, *The Absentee 1812*

27 People usually revenge themselves for having admired too much, by afterward despising and depreciating without mercy—in all great assemblies the perception of ridicule is quickly caught, and quickly too revealed.

Ch. 3, Ibid.

28 "I believe in the rational, but not in the magical power of education."

Ch. 1, *Vivian 1812*

29 "My mother took too much, a great deal too much, care of me; she over-educated, over-instructed, over-dosed me with premature lessons of prudence: she was so afraid that I would ever do a foolish thing, or not say a wise one, that she prompted my every word, and guided my every action. So I grew up, seeing with her eyes, hearing with her ears, and judging with her understanding, till, at length, it was found out that I had no eyes, or understanding of my own."

Ibid.

30 "Fortune's wheel never stands still—the highest point is therefore the most perilous."

Ch. 2, *Patronage 1814*

31 "Whenever the honours of professions, civil, military, or ecclesiastical, are bestowed by favour, not earned by merit—whenever the places of trust and dignity in a state are to be gained by intrigue and solicitation—there is an end of generous emulation, and consequently of exertion. Talents and integrity, in losing their reward of glory, lose their vigour, and often their very existence."

Ch. 8, Ibid.

32 "Of all men, I think a dissipated clergyman is the most contemptible."

Ch. 19, Ibid.

33 Alarmed successively by every fashionable medical terror of the day, she dosed her children with every specific which was publicly advertised or privately recommended. No creatures of their age had taken such quantities of Ching's lozenges, Godbold's elixir, or Dixon's anti-bilious pills. The consequence was, that the dangers, which had at first been imaginary, became real: these little victims of domestic medicine never had a day's health: they looked, and were, more dead than alive.

Ch. 20, Ibid.

34 We must be content to begin at the beginning, if we would learn the history of our own mind; we must condescend to be even as little children, if we would discover or recollect those small causes which early influenced the imagination, and afterward become strong habits, prejudices, and passions.

Ch. 1, *Harrington 1817*

35 An orator is the worst person to tell a plain fact. . . .

Ch. 10, Ibid.

36 After a certain age, if one lives in the world, one can't be astonished—that's a lost pleasure.

Ch. 15, *Ormond 1817*

37 A bore is a biped, but not always *unplumed.*

Thoughts On Bores 1826

38 The everlasting quotation-lover dotes on the husks of learning. He is the infant-reciting bore in second childishness.

Ibid.

723.1. Madame Necker de Saussure (1768–1847)

1 . . . there are so many causes of excitement in early life, personal affections and the desire to win the love and esteem of others occupy the mind so fully, that the young rarely press steadily onward to the most elevated mark.

Quoted in *Biography of Distinguished Women*
by Sarah Josepha Hale* *n.d.*

*See 788.

724. Maria-Louisa Rose Petigny (1768–?)

1   How enviable, thy destiny
    Blessed, nimble butterfly!
    To live out a stable life,
    Then—so change yourself!
                "Le Papillon," St. 1, Elaine T. Partnow, tr.,* *Idylles n.d.*
    *See 2870.

725. Charlotte Corday (1768/69–1793)

1   I have done my task, let others do theirs.
                Reply during interrogation at Abbaye Prison,
                Paris (13 July 1793), Quoted in *Biography of
                Distinguished Women* by Sarah Josepha Hale*
                1876
    *See 788.

2   I considered that so many brave men need not come to Paris
    for the head of one man [Jean Paul Marat*]. He deserved not
    so much honour: the hand of a woman was enough. . . .
                Letter to Barbaroux (from Abbaye prison), Ibid.
    *Swiss-born French revolutionary (1743–93); assassinated by Cor-
    day.

3   . . . we do not execute well that which we have not ourselves
    conceived.
                Remark at her trial (17 July 1793), Ibid.

726. Caroline Amelia Elizabeth (1768–1821)

1   I find him* very fat and not half as handsome as his portrait.
                Ch. 1, Recorded by Lord Malmesbury, Quoted in *Caroline
                the Unhappy Queen* by Lord Russell of Liverpool *1967*
    *Her future husband, King George IV.

2   . . . my dear, Punch's wife is nobody when Punch is present.*
                Ch. 3, Recorded by Lady Charlotte Bury, Ibid.
    *Punch and Judy, traditional English puppets, derived from *com-
    media dell' arte* characters.

3   The wasp leaves his sting in the wound and so do I.
                Ch. 4, Recorded by a friend, Ibid.

727. Melesina Trench (1768–1827)

1   A fat, fair, and fifty card-playing resident of the Crescent.
                (18 February 1816), *Letters c. 1820*

728. Dolley Madison (1768–1849)

1   I would rather fight with my hands than my tongue.
                Memoirs and Letters of Dolley Madison 1886

2   You may imagine me the very shadow of my husband.*
                Letter to Mr. and Mrs. Barlow (1811), Ibid.
    *James Madison (1751–1836), fourth president of the United
    States (1809–1817).

3   How the crowd jostles!
                Quoted in *Dames and Daughters of the Young Republic* by
                Gamaliel Bradford *1901*

4   The profusion of my table is the result of the prosperity of my
    country, and I shall continue to prefer Virginia liberality to Eu-
    ropean elegance.
                Retort to the wife of a foreign minister, Ibid.

729. Anne Brunton Merry (1769–1808)

1   The business of the Theatre has been and is very, very bad indeed.
                Letter to Mrs. Thackerson, Quoted in *The Career of Mrs.
                Anne Brunton Merry in the American Theatre* by Gresdna
                Ann Doty *1971*

730. Amelia Opie (1769–1853)

1   Thy love, thy fate, dear youth, to share,
    Must ever be thy happy lot;
    But thou may'st grant this humble prayer,
    Forget me not! forget me not!
                "Go, Youth Beloved," St. 1 (1802), *The Warrior's Return &
                Other Poems 1808*

2   Yet still enchant and still deceive me,
    Do all things, fatal fair, but leave me.
                "Song," St. 1, Ibid.

3   . . . this *wilderness* of pleasure. . . .
                Quoted in *English Women of Letters*, Vol. II by Julia Ka-
                vanagh* *1863*
    *See 965.

4   It usually takes some time for the husband and wife to know
    each other's humours and habits, and to find what surrender
    of their own they can make with the least reluctance for their
    mutual good.
                "Two Years of Wedded Life," *A Wife's Duty n.d.*

5   Had I been an artful woman, and could I have condescended
    to make him doubtful of the extent of my love, by a few
    woman's subterfuges; could I have feigned a desire to return to
    the world, instead of owning, as I did, that all my enjoyment
    was comprised in home and him, I do think that I might have
    been, for a much longer period, the happiest of wives; but then
    I should have been, in my own eyes, despicable as a woman;
    and I was always tenacious of my own esteem.
                Ibid.

731. Anne Newport Royall (1769–1854)

1   Let them be bucktails or cowtails, the nether end of any ani-
    mal fits them well.
                *The Black Book; or, A Continuation of Travels in the United
                States*, Vol. I *1828*

2   . . . the evangelical-tractical-biblical-Sabbath School-prayer meet-
    ing—good, honest, pious, sound Presbyterians of Capitol Hill.
                Remarking on witness at her trial (28 November 1817),
                *Mrs. Royall's Pennsylvania; or, Travels Continued in the
                United States*, Vol. II *1829*

3   Cards subject you to bad company and bad hours. What is
    worse?
                Letter I, *Letters from Alabama 1830*

4   Hitherto I have only learned mankind in theory—but I am
    now studying him in practice. One learns more in a day, by
    mixing with mankind, than he can in an age shut up in a
    closet.
                Letter XIII (22 December 1817), Ibid.

5   . . . true to their nature, the people, or rabble, rather always think
    the greatest fool the wisest man. They have proved it in this in-
    stance, by their selecting him [a local politician] to make laws for
    them. Alas, for my country! all your citizens want is a rope.
                Letter XLIV (2 June 1821), Ibid.

6 The United States Bank [is] not a political machine! It is a despot. It is the rack. It is the inquisition. It is a monster of corruption.
> Quoted in "Anne Royall, Tireless Traveler and Common Nuisance," *Anne Royall's Letters from Alabama*, Lucille Griffith, ed. *1969*

732. Anna Elliott (fl. c. 1770)

1 [It is called] the rebel flower . . . because it always flourishes most when trampled upon.
> Remark to a British soldier, Quoted in *The Women of the American Revolution*, Vol. II by Elizabeth F. Ellet *1848*

2 Let not oppression shake your fortitude, nor the hope of a gentler treatment cause you for a moment to swerve from strict duty.
> Remark to her father, Thomas Ferguson, on his removal as a prisoner of war, Ibid.

733. Daniel Hall (fl. c. 1770–80)

1 What is it you wish to look for? [Treason, came the reply.] Then you may be saved the trouble of search, for you may find enough of it at my tongue's end.
> Upon handing over the key of her trunk to a British officer, Quoted in *The Women of the American Revolution*, Vol. II by Elizabeth F. Ellet *1848*

734. Margaret Holford (fl. c. 1770)

1 'T is man's pride,
His highest, worthiest, noblest boast,
The privilege he prizes most,
To stand by helpless woman's side.
> "Margaret of Anjou,"* *Fanny and Selina, Gresford Vale and Other Poems 1798*

*See 254.

735. Mary Lacy (fl. c. 1770)

1 Perceiving her forwardness I thought it was no wonder the young men took such liberties with the other sex when they gave them such encouragement . . . I must confess that if I had been a young man I could not have withstood the temptations which this young person laid in my way.
> *The History of the Female Shipwright 1773*

736. Mary Scott (fl. c. 1770)

1 Owl, that lov'st the cloudy sky,
Sure, thy notes are harmony!
> St. 1, "The Owl," *The Female Poets of Great Britain*, Frederic Rowton, ed. *1853*

737. Mrs. Richard Shubrick (fl. c. 1770–178-?)

1 To men of honor, the chamber of a lady should be sacred as a sanctuary!
> Remark to British soldiers hunting for an American hiding in her bedroom, Quoted in *The Women of the American Revolution*, Vol. II by Elizabeth F. Ellet *1848*

738. Ann Murry (fl. c. 1770–1799)

1 Mark but the hist'ry of a modern day,
Composed of nonsense, foppery, and play.
> "A Familiar Epistle," *Poems on Various Subjects 1779*

739. Martha Bratton (fl. c. 1770–1816)

1 It was I who did it.* Let the consequence be what it will, I glory in having prevented the mischief contemplated by the cruel enemies of my country.
> Quoted in *The Women of the American Revolution*, Vol. II by Elizabeth F. Ellet *1848*

*She set fire to a cache of ammunition to prevent its falling into the hands of the British.

740. Mary Wordsworth (1770–1859)

1 O My William! it is not in my power to tell thee how I have been affected by this dearest of all letters—it was so unexpected—so new a thing to see the breathing of thy inmost heart upon paper that I was quite overpowered. . . .
> Letter to William Wordsworth,* her husband (Grasmere, 1 August 1810), *The Love Letters of William and Mary Wordsworth*, Beth Darlington, ed. *1982*

*English poet (1770–1850).

2 Bad as this is, it is some satisfaction to think this act* could only be done by a Lunatic—We were fearful that it was some dreadful Plot which might now be raging, the first act only being gone through—Alas for this Country [England], Who have we now—I fear a shadow pated Creature** to take his Place. . . .
> (13–14 May 1812), Ibid.

*The assassination of British Prime Minister Spencer Perceval (1762–1812) in the House of Commons. **Robert Banks Jenkinson (1770–1828), second earl of Liverpool; Tory statesman and prime minister (1812–1827).

741. Maria Falconar (1771–?)

1 Once Superstition, in a fatal hour,
O'er Europe rais'd the sceptre of her power;
She reign'd triumphant minister of death,
And Peace and Pleasure faded in her breath;
Deep in monastic solitude entomb'd,
The bud of beauty wither'd ere it bloom'd
> Untitled, *Poems*, by Maria and Harriet Falconar* *1788*

*See 749.

742. Margaretta Van Wyck Faugères (1771–1801)

1 *There*, wrapt in musings deep, and steadfast gaze,
In solemn rapture hath she past the night.
> "Winter," *Essays in Prose and Verse 1795*

2 "When I am gone—ah! who will care for thee?"
> "Elegy to Miss Anna Dundass," Ibid.

743. Rachel Levin Varnhagen (1771–1833)

1 My whole day is a feast of doing good!
> *Letters n.d.*

744. Elizabeth Holland (1771–1845)

1 Your poetry is bad enough, so pray be sparing of your prose.
> Remark to Samuel Rogers,* Quoted in *Portraits of Women* by Gamaliel Bradford *1916*

*English poet (1763–1855) known for his wit.

2 I am sorry to hear you are going to publish a poem. Can't you suppress it?
> Remark to Lord Porchester, Ibid.

3 There is a sensation in a mother's breast at the loss of an infant that partakes of the feeling of instinct. It is a species of savage despair.

> Letter to her husband, Lord Holland, Ibid.

4 . . . as nobody can do more mischief to a woman than a woman, so perhaps might one reverse the maxim and say nobody can do more good.

> Ibid.

745. Dorothy Wordsworth (1771–1855)

1 The half dead sound of the near sheep-bell in the hollow of the sloping coombe, exquisitely soothing.

> *The Alfoxden Journal 1897*

2 I found a strawberry blossom in a rock. I uprooted it rashly and felt as if I had been committing an outrage, so I planted it again.

> Ibid.

3 One only leaf upon the top of a tree—the sole remaining leaf— danced round and round like a rag blown by the wind.

> (7 March 1798), Ibid.

746. Mary Tighe (1772–1810)

1 Oh! how impatience gains upon the soul,
When the long promised hour of joy draws near!
How slow the tardy moments seem to roll!
What specters rise of inconsistent fear!
To the fond doubting heart its hopes appear
Too brightly fair, too sweet to realize;
all seem but day-dreams of delight too dear!

> *Psyche, or the Legend of Love 1795–1805*

2 Change is the lot of all.

> Ibid.

3 Oh! have you never known the silent charm
That undisturb'd retirement yields the soul

> Ibid.

4 Yes, gentle Time, thy gradual, healing hand
Hath stolen from sorrow's grasp the en-venomed dart;
Submitting to thy skill, my passive heart

> "To Time," "Sonnet," *The British Female Poets*, George W. Bethune, ed. *1848*

5 Who can speak a mother's anguish

> "Hagar* in the Desert," St. 2, Ibid.

*See 5.

6 The careless eye can find no grace,
Nor beauty in the scaly folds,
Nor see within the dark embrace
What latent loveliness it hold.
Yet in that bulb, those sapless scales,
The lily wraps her silver vest.

> "The Lily," Sts. 2–3, *The Female Poets of Great Britain*, Frederic Rowton, ed. *1853*

747. Sophie Cottin (1773–1807)

1 We have resisted a little while, and we think we have done wonders; because we estimate the merit of our resistance, not by its duration, but by the difficulty it has cost us.

> Quoted in *Biography of Distinguished Women* by Sarah Josepha Hale* *1876*

*See 788.

2 It is in affliction that the imagination elevates itself to the great thoughts of eternity and supreme justice, and that it takes us of ourselves, to seek a remedy for our pains.

> Ibid.

3 But still, amidst the horror and gloom of an eternal winter, nature displays some of her grandest spectacles. . . .

> "The Exiles and their Home," *Elizabeth, or the Exile of Siberia n.d.*

748. Harriet Auber (1773–1862)

And His that gentle voice we hear,
Soft as the breath of even,
That checks each fault, that calms each
fear,
And speaks of heaven.

> "Our Blest Redeemer, ere He breathed," *Spirit of the Psalms 1829*

749. Harriet Falconar (1774–?)

1 Shall Britain view, unmov'd, sad Afric's shore
Delug'd so oft in streams of purple gore!

> Untitled, St. 2, *Poems*, by Maria and Harriet Falconar* *1788*

*See 741.

2 Britain, where science, peace, and plenty smile,
Virtue's bright seat, and freedom's favour'd isle!

> Ibid.

750. Cecile Renard (1774?–1794)

1 I wanted to see how a tyrant looks.

> Reply at inquiry on her attempted assassination of Robespierre* (1794), Quoted in *Biography of Distinguished Women* by Sarah Josepha Hale** *1876*

*French revolutionary leader (1758–1794); guillotined. **See 788.

2 We have five hundred tyrants, [but] I prefer one king.

> Ibid.

751. Elizabeth Seton (1774–1821)

1 Afflictions are the steps to heaven.

> *Notable American Women*, Edward T. James, ed. *1971*

752. Mary Moody Emerson (1774–1863)

1 Rose before light every morn; . . . commented on the Scriptures; . . . touched Shakespeare,—washed, carded, cleaned house, baked.

> Diary Entry (1805), *Notable American Women*, Edward T. James, ed. *1971*

2 Scorn trifles, lift your aims; do what you are afraid to do.

> Remark to Ralph Waldo Emerson,* Quoted in *Notable American Women*, Edward T. James, ed. *1971*

*American essayist and poet (1803–1882).

753. Jane Austen (1775–1817)

1 "Beware of the insipid Vanities and idle Dissipations of the Metropolis of England; Beware of the unmeaning Luxuries of Bath and of the stinking fish of South Hampton."

> Letter Fourth, *Love and Friendship 1790*

2   She was nothing more than a mere good-tempered, civil and obliging young woman; as such we could scarcely dislike her— she was only an Object of Contempt—.

Letter Thirteenth, Ibid.

3   She is probably by this time as tired of me, as I am of her; but as she is too polite and I am too civil to say so, our letters are still as frequent and affectionate as ever, and our Attachment as firm and sincere as when it first commenced.

Letter the Fourth, Lesley Castle 1792

4   An annuity is a very serious business.

Ch. 2, Sense and Sensibility 1811

5   "It is not time or opportunity that is to determine intimacy; it is disposition alone. Seven years would be insufficient to make some people acquainted with each other, and seven days are more than enough for others."

Ch. 12, Ibid.

6   I am afraid that the pleasantness of an employment does not always evince its propriety.

Ch. 13, Ibid.

7   Lady Middleton . . . exerted herself to ask Mr. Palmer if there was any news in the paper.
"No, none at all," he replied, and read on.

Ch. 19, Ibid.

8   "You mistake me, my dear. I have a high respect for your nerves. They are my old friends. I have heard you mention them with consideration these twenty years at least."

Ch. 1, Pride and Prejudice 1813

9   It is a truth universally acknowledged, that a single man in possession of a good fortune, must be in want of a wife.

Ibid.

10   A lady's imagination is very rapid; it jumps from admiration to love, from love to matrimony in a moment.

Ch. 6, Ibid.

11   "The power of doing anything with quickness is always much prized by the possessor, and often without any attention to the imperfection of the performance."

Ch. 10, Ibid.

12   "You have delighted us long enough."

Ch. 18, Ibid.

13   "It is particularly incumbent on those who never change their opinion, to be secure of judging properly at first."

Ibid.

14   "Is not general incivility the very essence of love?"

Ch. 25, Ibid.

15   . . . where other powers of entertainment are wanting, the true philosopher will derive benefit from such as are given.

Ch. 42, Ibid.

16   "You ought certainly to forgive them as a Christian, but never admit them in your sight, or allow their names to be mentioned in your hearing."

Ch. 57, Ibid.

17   I have been a selfish being all my life, in practice, though not in principle.

Ch. 58, Ibid.

18   An engaged woman is always more agreeable than a disengaged. She is satisfied with herself. Her cares are over, and she feels that she may exert all her powers of pleasing without suspicion. All is safe with a lady engaged; no harm can be done.

Ch. 5, Mansfield Park 1814

19   " . . . there is not one in a hundred of either sex who is not taken when they marry. Look where I will, I see that it *is* so; and I feel that it *must* be so, when I consider that it is, of all transactions, the one in which people expect most from others, and are the least honest themselves."

Ibid.

20   "What strange creatures brothers are!"

Ch. 6, Ibid.

21   "Those who see quickly, will resolve quickly, and act quickly. . . . "

Ibid.

22   "Selfishness must always be forgiven, you know, because there is no hope of a cure."

Ch. 7, Ibid.

23   To sit in the shade on a fine day, and look upon verdure is the most perfect refreshment.

Ch. 9, Ibid.

24   "Oh! do not attack me with your watch. A watch is always too fast or too slow. I cannot be dictated by a watch."

Ibid.

25   It is indolence. . . . Indolence and love of ease; a want of all laudable ambition, of taste for good company, or of inclination to take the trouble of being agreeable, which make men clergymen. A clergyman has nothing to do but be slovenly and selfish; read the newspaper, watch the weather, and quarrel with his wife. His curate does all the work and the business of his own life is to dine.

Ch. 11, Ibid.

26   But Shakespeare one gets acquainted with without knowing how. It is a part of an Englishman's constitution. His thoughts and beauties are so spread abroad that one touches them everywhere; one is intimate with him by instinct.

Ch. 34, Ibid.

27   An egg boiled very soft is not unwholesome.

Ch. 3, Emma 1815

28   'If I lay it down as a general rule, Harriet, that if a woman *doubts* as to whether she should accept a man or not, she certainly ought to refuse him. If she can hesitate as to 'Yes,' she ought to say 'No,' directly.'

Ch. 7, Ibid.

29   "Vanity working on a weak head produces every sort of mischief."

Ch. 8, Ibid.

30   The truth is, that in London it is always a sickly season. Nobody is healthy in London, nobody can be.

Ch. 12, Ibid.

31   It was a delightful visit—perfect, in being much too short.

Ch. 13, Ibid.

32   . . . but a sanguine temper, for ever expecting more good than occurs, does not always pay for its hopes by any proportion of

depression. It soon flies over the present failure, and begins to hope again.

Ch. 18, Ibid.

33 Nobody who has not been in the interior of a family can say what the difficulties of any individual of that family may be.

Ibid.

34 There is safety in reserve, but no attraction. One cannot love a reserved person.

Ch. 24, Ibid.

35 "But, my dear sir," cried Mr. Weston, "if Emma comes away early, it will be breaking up the party." "And no great harm if it does," said Mr. Woodhouse. "The sooner every party breaks up the better."

Ch. 25, Ibid.

36 It may be possible to do without dancing entirely. Instances have been known of young people passing many, many months successively without being at any ball of any description, and no material injury accrue either to body or mind; but when a beginning is made—when the felicities of rapid motion have once been, though slightly, felt—It must be a very heavy set that does not ask for more.

Ch. 29, Ibid.

37 Business, you know, may bring money, but friendship hardly ever does.

Ch. 34, Ibid.

38 The post-office had a great charm at one period of our lives. When you have lived to my age, you will begin to think letters are never worth going through the rain for.

Ibid.

39 "It is very difficult for the prosperous to be humble."

Ch. 50, Ibid.

40 "To look *almost* pretty is an acquisition of higher delight to a girl who has been looking plain the first fifteen years of her life than a beauty from the cradle can ever receive."

Ch. 1, *Northanger Abbey 1818*

41 "And what are you reading, Miss—?" "Oh! it is only a novel!" replies the young lady; while she lays down her book with affected indifference, or momentary shame. "It is only *Cecilia*, or *Camilla*, or *Belinda*"; or, in short, only some work in which the greatest powers of the mind are displayed, in which the most thorough knowledge of human nature, the happiest delineation of its varieties, the liveliest effusions of wit and humour, are conveyed to the world in the best chosen language.

Ch. 5, Ibid.

42 "... I am sure of *this*, that if everybody was to drink their bottle a day, there would be not half the disorders in the world there are now. It would be a famous good thing for us all."

Ch. 9, Ibid.

43 History, real solemn history, I cannot be interested in. . . . I read it a little as a duty; but it tells me nothing that does not either vex or weary me. The quarrels of popes and kings, with wars and pestilences in every page; the men all so good for nothing, and hardly any women at all.

Ch. 14, Ibid.

44 A woman, especially, if she have the misfortune of knowing anything, should conceal it as well as she can.

Ibid.

45 "But your mind is warped by an innate principle of general integrity, and, therefore, not accessible to the cruel reasonings of family partiality, or a desire for revenge."

Ch. 27, Ibid.

46 Personal size and mental sorrow have certainly no necessary proportions. A large bulky figure has as good a right to be in deep affliction as the most graceful set of limbs in the world. But, fair or not fair, there are unbecoming conjunctions, which . . . taste cannot tolerate —which ridicule will seize.

Persuasion 1818

47 How quick come the reasons for approving what we like!

Ch. 2, Ibid.

48 "In fact, as I have long been convinced, though every profession is necessary and honourable in its turn, it is only the lot of those who are not obliged to follow any, who can live in a regular way, in the country, choosing their own hours, following their own pursuits, and living on their own property, without the torment of trying for more; it is only *their* lot, I say, to hold the blessings of health and a good appearance to the utmost: I know no other set of men but what lose something of their personableness when they cease to be quite young."

Ch. 3, Ibid.

49 She had been forced into prudence in her youth, she learned romance as she grew older: the natural sequence of an unnatural beginning.

Ch. 4, Ibid.

50 "My idea of good company, Mr. Elliot, is a company of clever, well-informed people, who have a great deal of conversation; that is what I call good company."

"You are mistaken," said he, gently, "that is not good company; that is the best."

Ch. 16, Ibid.

51 One does not love a place the less for having suffered in it, unless it has been all suffering, nothing but suffering.

Ch. 20, Ibid.

52 "... I do not think I ever opened a book in my life which ad not something to say upon woman's inconstancy. Songs and proverbs all talk of woman's fickleness. But, perhaps, you will say, these were all written by men."

"Perhaps I shall . . . Yes, yes, if you please, no reference to examples in books . . . the pen has been in their hands. I will not allow books to prove anything."

Ch. 23, Ibid.

754. Mary Martha Sherwood (1775–1851)

1 "The book of Nature, my dear Henry, is full of holy lessons, ever new and ever varied; and to learn to discover these lessons should be the work of good education; for there are many persons who are exceedingly wise and clever in worldly matters, and yet with respect to spiritual things are wholly blind and dark, and are as unable to look on divine light as the bats and moles to contemplate the glory of the sun's rays at midday."

The History of Henry Milner, Pt. First, Ch. 16, from *The Works of Mrs. Sherwood*, Vol. I 1856

2 "... it is the very nature of sin to prevent man from meditating on spiritual things. . . . "

Pt. Second, Ch. 11, Ibid.

3   "We are getting too fine in this country, Lord H——; too fine in our habits. I doubt much whether our intellectual advancement bears a due proportion with the refinements of our habits. If that is the case, as I apprehend, there will be a reaction by-and-by—a reaction in which all that is mere tinsel in the state of society will be reduced to non-entity, and nothing will remain but that which is solid and real."

Pt. Third, Ch. 2, Ibid.

4   "Where the habits are simple, and the mind truly elevated, then is society in the best state. . . . "

Ibid.

5   O, how little do children know what parents sometimes endure for their sake!

"The Hedge of Thorns," Vol. III, Ibid.

6   "And why not?" returned the *fakeer*, "I can read books and men, too, and I tell you that the latter is a much more profitable branch of study than the former."

Arzoomund, Ch. 5, Ibid.

7   "To speak the plain truth, all religions seem alike to me, one mass of absurdities and lies— . . . I know that there is a God, but I know no more of him; and I believe that all those who are liars who pretend to know more than I do."

Ibid.

8   Humility becomes our fallen nature. . . .

Introductory, Vol. I, Ch. 2, *The Lady of the Conversations on the Subject of Confirmation intended for the use of the Middle and Higher Ranks of Young Female*, Vol. IX, Ibid.

9   " . . . whatever station the child may occupy, humility must be enforced, and enforced upon Christian principles. All education, however otherwise excellent, which fails in this point, has, in my opinion, a pernicious tendency; and, humanly speaking, can only produce, at the best, a species of worldly morality, or a mere profession of religion. . . . "

Ch. 7, Ibid.

10   . . . what is the zest of argument when the antagonist is not allowed to answer?

The Monk of Climiés, Ch. 5, Vol. XIV, Ibid.

11   " . . . my father has lived abroad till he has lost his judgement. . . . "

The History of John Marten, Ch. 1, Vol. XVI, Ibid.

12   . . . a dirty exterior is a great enemy to beauty of all descriptions.

Ch. 13, Ibid.

755. Louisa Catherine Adams (1775–1852)

1   Go flatter'd image tell the tale
Of years long past away;
Of faded youth, of sorrow wail,
Of times too sure decay. . . .

Ch. 3, "To my Sons with my Portrait by Stuart"* (18 December 1825), Quoted in *Portraits of John Quincy Adams** and His Wife* by Andrew Oliver 1970

*Gilbert Stuart, famed American portrait painter (1755–1828).
**Sixth president of the United States (1825–1829).

756. Hester Lucy Stanhope (1776–1839)

1   If you were to take every feature in my face, and lay them one by one on the table, there is not a single one that would bear examination. The only thing is that, put together and lighted up, they look well enough. It is homogeneous ugliness, and nothing more.

Quoted in *Little Memoirs of the Nineteenth Century*, Pt. I by George Paston 1902

2   . . . I shall go on making sublime and philosophical discoveries, and employing myself in deep, abstract studies.

Letter to Dr. Meryon (1827), Pt. II, Ibid.

3   Nobody is such a fool as to moider [waste] away his time in the slipslop conversation of a pack of women.

Remark, Ibid.

4   My roses are my jewels, the sun and moon my clocks, fruit and water my food and drink. I see in your face that you are a thorough epicure; how will you endure to spend a week with me?

Ibid.

757. Jane Porter (1776–1850)

1   Such, thought she, O Sun, art thou!—The resplendent image of the Giver of All Good. Thy cheering beams, like His All-cheering Spirit, pervades the very soul, and drives thence the despondency of cold and darkness.

Life of Sir William Wallace; or, The Scottish Chiefs* [a novel] 1810

*Scottish hero (c.1270–1305).

2   Bright was the summer of 1296. The war which had desolated Scotland was then at an end. Ambition seemed satiated; and the vanquished, after having passed under the yoke of their enemy, concluded they might wear their chains in peace. Such were the hopes of those Scottish noblemen who, early in the preceding spring, had signed the bond of submission to a ruthless conqueror, purchasing life at the price of all that makes life estimable,—liberty and honor.

Ch. 1, Ibid.

3   "The cruel are generally false."

Ch. 3, Ibid.

4   "Beloved of my soul! never shall this sword leave my hand till it has drunk the life-blood of thy murderer."

Ch. 4, Ibid.

5   "No country is wretched, sweet lady," returned the knight, "till by a dastardly acquiescence it consents to its own slavery."

Ch. 9, Ibid.

6   "You would teach confidence to Despair herself. . . . "

Ibid.

7   "For shame, Murray!" was the reply of Wallace; "they are dead, and our enemies no more. They are men like ourselves; and shall we deny them a place in that earth whence we all sprung?"

Ch. 13, Ibid.

8   "Earthly crowns are dross to him who looks for a heavenly one."

Ch. 33, Ibid.

9   "You are like a bad mirror that, from radical defect, always gives false reflections."

Ch. 17, *Thaddeus of Warsaw*, Vol. II 1835

10   "The man who dares to be virtuous and great, and appears so, arms the self-love of all common characters against him."

Ch. 22, Ibid.

11 That sickness which is the consequence of mental pain, usually vanishes with its cause.

> Ch. 33, Ibid.

758. Adelaide O'Keeffe (1776–1855?)

1 The butterfly, an idle thing,
Nor honey makes, nor yet can sing.

> "The Butterfly" *n.d.*

759. Sydney Owenson Morgan (c. 1776/83–1859)

1 There can be no individual happiness but that which harmonizes with the happiness of society—there may be virtue without felicity, but there can be no felicity without virtue. . . .

> *Ida of Athens 1808*

2 Literary fiction, whether directed to the purpose of transient amusement, or adopted as an indirect medium of instruction, has always in its most genuine form exhibited a mirror of the times in which it is composed; reflecting morals, customs, manners, peculiarity of character, and prevalence of opinion. Thus, perhaps, after all, it forms the best history of nations. . . .

> Preface, *O'Donnell: A National Tale*, Vol. I *1813*

3 He stood, indeed, at the head of that class of apathetic men of gallantry, *qui se laissent aimer* [who allow themselves to be loved]; . . . less anxious to be loved than to be adulated —to awaken a sentiment than to expose a triumph; . . .

> Ch. 1, Vol. III, Ibid.

4 "That you are an Irishman, *genuine* and thorough bred, there can be no doubt; with your porcupine spirit, rising before it is assailed, and throwing its quill before it receives a wound. . . . "

> Ch. 3, Ibid.

5 " . . . as is usual among the semi-barbarous, improvement is resisted as innovation; . . . the old muddling system must go on for ever in the same old muddling way."

> Ibid.

6 " . . . if foreigners won't understand one another, who do they expect will, I wonder."

> Ch. 1, *Florence Macarthy: An Irish Tale*, Vol. I *1819*

7 "Oh! *par exemple*, for fine men," said Lady Dunore, throwing herself into an arm chair, "I think they are really quite extinct with us altogether."

> Ch. 3, Vol. III, Ibid.

8 "South America," he observed, "is well known to us in the Spanish histories of its early discoverers, when Spain invaded it under the Simoniacal pretext of *religion*; letting loose, at the same time, *bloodhounds and apostles*, while they opened its mineral veins and exterminated its population . . . almost [depriving] these great regions of a place in the history of nations. . . . "

> Ibid.

9 "Temporary measures of expediency have nothing to do with general views," replied young Crawley to Mr. Daly's observation. "What is wisdom *to-day* in the conduct of a government may be madness *to-morrow*."

> Ibid.

10 "You are right, madam; the soul is of no sect, no party: it is, as you say, our passions and our prejudices, which give rise to our religious and political distinctions."

> Ch. 12, *The Novice of St. Dominick*, Vol. II *1823*

11 "All," said he mentally, "sweet child of nature, is pleasing to thee, because all is new: O youth, what a season of delight is thine."

> Ch. 19, Ibid.

12 "Dreadful to the soul is that moment when the lingering light of hope is finally extinguished, and all its sweet energies of fond expectations are buried in the gloom of despondency."

> Ch. 24, Vol. III, Ibid.

13 It is under the pressure of great and sudden exigencies that the faculties of a strong and comprehensive mind awaken to a full sense of their own power.

> Ch. 35, Vol. IV, Ibid.

14 "You see, madam, your wine is like the nepenthe of Helen, for it gives the cares as well as the senses of your guests to oblivion."

> Ch. 40, Ibid.

15 "For," says O'Brien, who worships his new found sister as a thing enskied, "with woman and music, Abbé, dear, you might proselytize all Ireland, far better than by all the peynals [sic] and all the persecutions that ever were invented:" and wonders that the government never hit upon it.

> Ch. 1, *The O'Briens and the O'Flahertys*, Vol. I *1827*

760. Anna Chamber (?–1777)

1 But modern quacks have lost the art,
And reach of life the sacred seat;
They know not how its pulses beat,
Yet take their fee and write their bill,
In barb'rous prose resolved to kill.

> "To the Duchess of Leeds, who, being ill, desired a copy of my verses to cure her," *Poems, printed at Strawberry Hill 1764*

761. Mary Brunton (1778–1818)

1 . . . —"Let them persecute me, and I will be a martyr." "You may be so now, to-day, every day," returned Mrs. Douglas. "It was not at the stake that these holy men began their self-denial. They had before taken up their cross daily; and whenever, from a regard to duty, you resign anything that is pleasing or valuable to you, you are for the time a little martyr."

> "Sketch of the Heroine," *Self-Control 1811*

2 . . . little acquainted with other minds, deeply studious of her own, she concluded that all mankind were like herself engaged in a constant endeavour after excellence. . . .

> Ibid.

3 The passion which we do not conquer will, in time, reconcile us to any means that can aid its gratification.

> "The Lover and his Declaration," Ibid.

762. Margaret Bayard Smith (1778–1844)

1 Ladies and gentlemen only had been expected at this Levee, not the people en masse. Of all tyrants, they are the most ferocious, cruel and despotic.

> Quoted in *First Ladies* by Betty Boyd Caroli *1987*

763. Margaret Hodson (1778–1852)

1 They are solemn and low, and none can hear
The whispers which come to Memory's ear!

> "On Memory; Written at Aix-la-Chapelle," St. 3, *Poems 1811*

2 "Bright success
May only for a while sustain Man's feeble spirit!"
4th canto, "Margaret of Anjou:* A Poem in Ten Cantos"
1816

*See 254.

3 "Let me Fate's awful page explore!
Leaf after leaf would I unfold,
E'en to the final word!—till *all* the tale be told!"
7th canto, Ibid.

4 And, hark! the signal!—Now begin,
Of those who lose and those who win,
The strife, the shout, the mortal din!
Behold!—they meet!—they clash!—they close!—
They mix!—Sworn friends and deadly foes,
In one dire mass, one struggling host,
All order and distinction lost,
Roll headlong, guideless, blind, like waves together toss'd!
Ibid.

5 "'Tis strange
How memory fails with fortune's change!"
10th canto, Ibid.

6 "Monsters! A mother's curse lie strong
And heavy on you! May the tongue,
The ceaseless tongue which well I ween
Live in the murderer's murky breast,
With goading whispers, fell and keen,
Make havoc of your rest!"
Ibid.

764. Angelica Catalani (1779–1848)

1 For when God has given to a mortal so extraordinary a talent as I possess, people ought to applaud and honour it as a miracle: it is profane to depreciate the gifts of Heaven!
Quoted in *Queens of Song* by Ellen Creathorne Clayton
1865

765. Elizabeth Fry (1780–1845)

1 Does Capital punishment tend to the security of the people?
By no means. It hardens the hearts of men, and makes the loss of life appear light to them; and it renders life insecure, inasmuch as the law holds out that property is of greater value than life.
From her Journal, Quoted in *Biography of Distinguished Women* by Sarah Josepha Hale* 1876

*See 788.

2 Punishment is not for revenge, but to lessen crime and reform the criminal.
Ibid.

766. Tabitha Moffatt Brown (1780–1858)

1 Worse than alone, in a savage wilderness, without food, without fire, cold and shivering, wolves fighting and howling all around me.
Letter (c. 1846), Quoted in *Women Pioneers* by Rebecca Stefoff 1995

2 Father Time is no respecter of persons, he is busily engaged in drawing furrows and disfiguring our faces to convince me that we are but mortal. Our next change will be from mortality to immortality. Oh, that we may all be prepared for this great and lasting change!
Letter (25 January 1858), Ibid.

767. Frances Milton Trollope (1780–1863)

1 "Is not amusement the very soul of life?"
Ch. 6, *The Life and Adventures of Michael Armstrong, the Factory Boy* 1839

2 "That's nonsense, Michael," said Fanny. "They can't keep us here for ever. When we die, we are sure to get away from them."
Ch. 17, Ibid.

3 "Times are altered with me now, nurse Tremlett," replied Mary; "I have left off living for myself, and I feel my temper improving already by it."
Ch. 22, Ibid.

768. Hannah Farnham Lee (1780–1865)

1 Astronomers tell us of countless worlds;—if we look within our own precincts we shall find an equal multiplication; every class of society talks of *the world*, and every class means something different.
Ch. 1, *Elinor Fulton* 1837

2 "I never could bear people that are always striving to rise."
Ibid.

3 No one can have any high degree of virtue, without self-respect; it is the twin-sister of virtue.
Ch. 8, Ibid.

4 Liberty has set her foot on our shore, and she is not to be restricted in her walks.
Ibid.

5 We have arrived at that period when there is no putting a padlock on the human mind; every one is contending for his rights, every one ready to strike for them.
Ibid.

6 "Our good and bad depend much on circumstances."
Ch. 9, Ibid.

7 "What is a new bonnet, or a new pelisse [fur piece], to the pleasure of feeling there is something in reserve that you may call your own! Blessings on the Savings Bank! It is truly, to those who resolutely deposit their earnings there, the purse of Fortunatus. . . . "
Ch. 11, Ibid.

8 . . . is there no exterminating the shoots of vanity where it has once taken root?
Ibid.

9 Fireside occupation is one of the rights of women that men may envy.
Ch. 13, Ibid.

10 A mere compilation of facts presents only the skeleton of History; we do but little for her if we cannot invest her with life, clothe her in the habiliments of her day, and enable her to call forth the sympathies of succeeding generations.
Preface, *The Huguenots in France and America*, Vol. I 1843

11 Unless history can be converted to moral uses, it is only "a little book got by heart."

Ibid.

12 He [John Calvin*], who had so loudly declaimed against the tyranny of Rome, was doomed to prove how dangerous an instrument is power in the hands of a human being.

Ch. 3, *Ibid.*

*French-born Swiss Protestant theologian and religious reformer (1509–1564).

13 It is amusing to observe in every age the ingenuity of dress in changing the human figure.

Ch. 13, *Ibid.*

14 It is those in whom the power of virtue is formed and matured, that are truly great. It matters not how many millions a man may command, the next day may strip him of all; but the *undying principle* of duty is his own, and can only be surrendered by his will.

Ch. 29, Vol. II, *Ibid.*

15 There are principles implanted in the breast that cannot be wholly eradicated. God does not leave himself without witnesses in the heart of every human being.

Ch. 31, *Ibid.*

16 Even under an absolute monarchy men will have an instinctive sense of justice.

Ch. 33, *Ibid.*

17 Trifling circumstances are exciting in still life.

Part First, *The Log-Cabin; or, the World Before You 1844*

18 " . . . keep your money if you can, but remember it hath wings . . . "

Ibid.

19 There is nothing old tolerated in this new world [America].

Part Second, *Ibid.*

20 . . . but has not my whole life been made up of trifles?

Ibid.

21 Causes are often disproportioned to effects.

Ibid.

22 "The school may do much; but alas for the child where the instructor is not assisted by the influences of home!"

Ibid.

23 Surely we ought to prize those friends on whose principles and opinions we may constantly rely—of whom we may say in all emergencies, "I know what they would think."

Ibid.

24 . . . a good nurse is of more importance than a physician.

Pt. Third, *Ibid.*

769. Mary Somerville (1780–1872)

1 And who shall declare the time allotted to the human race, when the generation of the most insignificant insect existed for unnumbered ages? Yet man is also to vanish in the ever-changing course of events. The earth is to be burnt up, and the elements to melt with fervent heat—to be again reduced to chaos—possibly to be renovated and adorned for other races of beings. These stupendous changes may be but cycles in

those great laws of the universe, where all is variable but the laws themselves and He who ordained them.

"God and His Works," *Physical Geography 1848*

2 . . . no circumstance in the natural world is more inexplicable than the diversity of form and colour in the human race.

"Varieties of the Human Race," *Ibid.*

3 . . . one of the greatest improvements in education is that teachers are now fitted for their duties by being taught the art of teaching.

"Benevolence," *Ibid.*

4 The moral disposition of the age appears in the refinement of conversation.

"Influence of Christianity," *Ibid.*

770. Janet Colquhoun (1781–1846)

1 This day I am thirty years old. Let me now bid a cheerful adieu to my youth. My young days are now surely over, and why should I regret them? Were I never to grow old I might be always here, and might never bid farewell to sin and sorrow.

Ch. 2, Diary entry (17 April 1811), Quoted in *A Memoir of Lady Colquhoun* by James Hamilton, D. D. *1851*

2 The world? it is nothing to me; its pomps, its pleasures, its vanities—all nothing, nothing.

(19 July 1816), *Ibid.*

3 I feel something within me that lives for God, that delights in God, that cannot exist without God, that must be derived from God.

Ch. 6, Diary entry (8 September 1844), *Ibid.*

771. Anna Jane Vardill (1781–1852)

1 Behold this ruin! 'Twas a skull
One of the ethereal spirit full!
This narrow cell was Life's retreat;
This place was Thought's mysterious seat!
What beauteous pictures fill'd that spot,
What dreams of pleasure, long forgot!
Nor Love, nor Joy, nor Hope, nor Fear,
Has left one trace, one record here.

"Lines to a Skull," *European Magazine* November *1816*

772. Lucy Aiken (1781–1864)

1 No! instead of aspiring to be inferior men, let us content ourselves with becoming noble women:. . . . but let not sex be carried into every thing. Let the impartial voice of History testify for us, that, when permitted, we have been the worthy associates of the best efforts of the best of men; let the daily observation of mankind bear witness, that no talent, no virtue, is masculine alone; no fault or folly exclusively feminine; . . . that there is not an endowment, or propensity, or mental quality of any kind, which may not be derived from her father to the daughter, to the son from his mother.

Introduction, *Epistles on Women, Exemplifying Their Character and Condition in Various Ages and Nations. With Miscellaneous Poems 1810*

2 I touch no sacred thing,
Or when was ever weakness in the right?
With passive reverence too I hail the law,
Formed to secure the strong, the weak to awe,

Impartial guardian of unerring sway,
Set up by man for woman to obey.

Epistle I, St. 3, Ibid.

3 Stretch wide and wider yet thy liberal mind,
And grasp the sisterhood of womankind:

Epistle II, St. 3, Ibid.

4 And smiling round, the daughter, mother, wife,
Fed the dear charities of social life.

Epistle III, St. 1, Ibid.

5 Their kindness cheer'd his drooping soul;
And slowly down his wrinkled cheek
The big round tears were seen to roll,
And told the thanks he could not speak.
The children, too, began to sigh,
And all their merry chat was o'er;
And yet they felt, they knew not why,
More glad than they had done before.

"The Beggar Man," Sts. 9–10, The Female Poets of Great
Britain, Frederic Rowton, ed. 1853

6 Shepherd people on the plain
Pitch their tents and wander free;
Wealthy cities they disdain,
Poor,—yet blest with liberty.

"Arabia," St. 3, Ibid.

7 That life may not be prolonged beyond the power of usefulness, is one of the most natural, and apparently of the most
reasonable wishes man can form for the future. . . .

"Memoirs" (of her father, Dr. Aiken), Quoted in Biography
of Distinguished Women by Sarah Josepha Hale* 1876
*See 788.

773. Susan Edmonstone Ferrier (1782–1854)

1 . . . petty ills; like a troup of locusts, making up by their number and their stings what they want in magnitude.

Ch. 6, Marriage 1818

2 . . . as . . . the surface was covered with flowers . . . who would
have thought of analysing the soil?

Ch. 28, Ibid.

3 There are some people who, furious themselves at opposition,
cannot understand the possibility of others being equally firm
and decided in a gentle manner.

Ch. 52, Ibid.

4 There are plenty of fools in the world; but if they had not been
sent for some wise purpose, they wouldn't have been here; and
since they are here they have as good a right to have elbow-
room in the world as the wisest.

Ch. 68, Ibid.

5 Oh, how easy it must be to be good when one has the power
of doing good!

Ch. 4, The Inheritance 1824

6 Ah! what will not the heart endure e'er it will voluntarily surrender the hoarded treasure of its love to the cold dictates of
reason or the stern voice of duty!

Ch. 33, Ibid.

7 . . . it is not the first stroke of grief, however heavy it may fall,
that can at once crush the native buoyance of youthful spirit; it

is the continuance of misery which renders its weight insupportable. . . .

Ch. 43, Ibid.

8 "The profane and licentious works of Lord B.* will live only
in the minds of the profane and impure, and will soon be
classed amongst worthless dross, while all that is fine in his
works will be culled by the lovers of virtue, as the bee gathers
honey from even the noxious plant, and leaves the poison to
perish with the stalk; so shall it be with Burns,** so shall it be
with More."***

Ch. 45, Ibid.

*Lord Byron (1788–1824), English poet. **Robert Burns
(1759–1796), Scottish poet. ***Henry More (1614–1687), English poet and philosopher.

9 ". . . the synagogin', the tabernaclin', the psalmin', that goes
on in this hoose, that's enough to break the spirits o' ony
young creature."

Ch. 46, Ibid.

10 ". . . passion without passion is an anomaly I cannot comprehend."

Ch. 72, Ibid.

11 . . . lovers, it is well known, carry the art of tautology to its utmost perfection, and even the most impatient of them can both
bear to hear and repeat the same things time without number,
till the sound becomes the echo to the sense or the nonsense
previously uttered.

Ibid.

12 "I am for everything starting into full-blown perfection at
once."

Ch. 79, Ibid.

13 ". . . there is no doctor like meat and drink. . . . "

Ch. 98, Ibid.

14 "Which of all the gifts a liberal Creator has endowed you with
would you exchange for those empty distinctions which one
creature bestows upon another? Would you exchange your
beauty for rank, your talents for wealth, your greatness of
mind for extended power; for all of them would you exchange
your immortal soul?'

Ch. 101, Ibid.

15 . . . the sickness of hope deferred crept like poison through her
veins.

Ch. 102, Ibid.

16 But who can count the beatings of the lonely heart?

Ibid.

17 "It was the saying, sir, of one of the wisest judges who ever sat
upon the Scottish bench, that a <i>poor</i> clergy made a <i>pure</i>
clergy—a maxim which deserves to be engraven in letters of
gold on every manse in Scotland."

"A Bustling Wife," Destiny, or the Chief's
Daughter 1831

18 The next day was Sunday—day of rest to the poor and the toil-
worn—of weariness to the rich and the idle.

"Sunday," Ibid.

19 "I am no friend to a premature knowledge of the world; it
comes soon enough to most of us."

Ch. 15, Ibid.

20 " . . . I do assure you, it is a very tiresome thing to be trained up to be a person of consequence. . . . "

Ch. 47, Ibid.

21 " . . . the stomach requires to be amused as well as the mind."

Ch. 55, Ibid.

22 No generous impulse ever led her beyond the strict line of duty. . . .

Ch. 71, Ibid.

23 " . . . there's no face like the face that loves us."

Ch. 78, Ibid.

24 There is no surer mark of a selfish character than that of shrinking from the truth."

Ch. 89, Ibid.

25 " . . . time and eternity are but different periods of the same states. . . . "

Ibid.

774. Ann Taylor (1782–1866)

1 'Tis a *credit* to any good girl to be neat,
But quite a disgrace to be *fine*.

"Neatness," *Original Poems for Infant Minds*, with Jane Taylor* 1804

2 Who ran to help me when I fell,
And would some pretty story tell,
Or kiss the place to make it well?
My Mother.

"My Mother," St. 6, Ibid.

3 Twinkle, twinkle, little star
How I wonder what you are,
Up above the world so high,
Like a diamond in the sky!

"The Star," St. 1, *Rhymes for the Nursery*, with Jane Taylor* 1806

4 Oh, that it were my chief delight
To do the things I ought!
Then let me try with all my might
To mind what I am taught.

"For a Very Little Child," *Hymns for Infant Minds*, with Jane Taylor* 1810

5 And willful waste, depend upon 't,
Brings, almost always, woeful want!

"The Pin," St. 6, Ibid.

6 So, while their bodies moulder here
Their souls with God himself shall dwell, —
But always recollect, my dear,
That wicked people go to hell.

"About Dying," with Jane Taylor* n.d.

*See 777.

775. Amelia (1783–1810)

1 Unthinking, idle, wild, and young,
I laugh'd and danc'd and talk'd and sung.

"Youth" n.d.

776. Theodosia Burr Alston (1783–1813)

1 What a charming thing a bustle is! Oh, dear, delightful confusion! It gives a circulation to the blood, an activity to the mind, and a spring to the spirits.

Letter to her father (December 1803), Quoted in *Memoirs of Aaron Burr,** Vol. II, Matthew L. Davis, ed. 1836–1837
*(1756–1836), third vice president of the United States (1801–1805), tried for treason.

2 You know, I love to convict you of an error, as some philosophers seek for spots in the sun.

Letter to her father (1 February 1809), Quoted in *The Private Journal of Aaron Burr*, Vol. I, Matthew L. Davis, ed. 1838

3 Alas! my dear father, I do live, but how does it happen? Of what am I formed that Live, and why? . . . You talk of consolation. Ah! you know not what you have lost. I think Omnipotence could give me no equivalent for my boy; no, none—none.

Letter to her father on the death of her son (12 August 1812), Vol. II, Ibid.

777. Jane Taylor (1783–1824)

1 Though man a thinking being is defined,
Few use the grand prerogative of mind.
How few think justly of the thinking few!
How many never think, who think they do!

"Prejudice, or, Essay on Morals and Manners," St. 45, *Original Poems for Infant Minds*, with Ann Taylor* 1804

2 How pleasant it is, at the end of the day,
No follies to have to repent;
But reflect on the past, and be able to say,
That my time has been properly spent.

"The Way to be Happy," *Rhymes for the Nursery*, with Ann Taylor* 1806

3 I like little Pussy, her coat is so warm;
And if I don't hurt her she'll do me no harm.

"I Like Little Pussy," St. 1, Ibid.

*See 774.

778. Mary Austin Holley (1784–1846)

1 How hard it is to be poor.

Texas: Observations Historical, Geographical and Descriptive 1833

2 Taste does not spring up in the wilderness, nor in prairies, nor in log cabins!

Quoted in *Letters of an Early American Traveller: Mary Austin Holley* by Mattie Austin Hatcher 1933

779. Caroline Lamb (1785–1828)

1 Then, for the first time, Camioli beheld, in one comprehensive view, the universal plan of nature—unnumbered systems performing their various but distinct courses, unclouded by mists, and unbounded by horizon—endless variety in infinite space!

Ch. 1, *Glenarvon*, Vol. I 1816

2 It is the common failing of an ambitious mind to over-rate itself. . . .

Ch. 2, Ibid.

3   . . . the sins of children rise up in judgement against their parents.

> Ch. 20, Ibid.

4   " . . . she is in love with ruin: it stalks about in every possible shape, she hails it:—woe is it; victim of prosperity, luxury and self indulgence."

> Ch. 28, Ibid.

5   Love's blighted flower, can never bloom again.

> Ch. 17, Vol. II, Ibid.

6   "I had rather be the cause of her laughter, than of her tears."

> Ch. 24, Ibid.

7   But, when the flame [of love] is unsupported by . . . pure feelings, it rages and consumes us, burns up and destroys every noble hope, perverts the mind, and fills with craft and falsehood every avenue to the heart.

> Ch. 72, Vol. III, Ibid.

8   Women, like toys, are sought after, and trifled with, and then thrown by with every varying caprice.

> Ch. 81, Ibid.

9   " . . . my mind is a world in itself, which I have peopled with my own creatures."

> Ch. 94, Ibid.

10 It is but the name of wife I hate.

> Ibid.

11 Mad, bad, and dangerous to know.*

> Journal n.d.

*Her description of her lover, Lord Byron, English poet (1788–1824).

780. Bettina von Arnim (1785–1859)

1   A purple sky my mind, a warm love-dew my words, the soul must come forth like a bride from her chamber, without evil, and avow herself.

> Various letters to Goethe,* Quoted in *Correspondence Between Goethe and a Young Girl 1835*

*Johann Wolfgang von Goethe, German poet, dramatist, novelist (1749–1832).

2   Without trust, the mind's lot is a hard one; it grows slowly and needily, like a hot plant betwixt rocks: thus am I—thus was I till today. . . .

> Ibid.

3   O yes! the ascending from out of unconscious life into revelation,—that is music!

> Ibid.

4   But this breaking forth of the mind to light, is it not art? This inner man asking for light, to have by the finger of God loosened his tongue; untied his hearing; awakened all sense to receive and to spend: and is love here not the only master, and we its disciples in every work which we form by its inspiration?

> Ibid.

5   They who fancy to understand it [art] will perform no more than what is ruled by understanding; but when senses are submitted to its spirit, he has revelation.

> Ibid.

6   Whoever is come to something in art, did forget his craftiness, his load of experience, became shipwreck, and despair led him to land on the right shore.

> Ibid.

7   To inhale the divine spirit is to engenerate, to produce; to exhale the divine breath is to breed and nourish the mind. . . .

> Ibid.

8   Body is art, art is the sensual nature engenerated into the life of the spirit.

> Ibid.

781. Caroline Anne Southey (1786–1854)

1   Sleep, little baby! sleep!
    Not in thy cradle bed,
    Not on thy mother's breast

> "To A Dying Infant," St. 1, *Solitary Hours, and Other Poems 1826*

2   She dwelt alone, a cloistered nun,
    In solitude and shade.

> "The Primrose," St. 5, Ibid.

3   O Grave! we come.

> "The Last Journey," St. 1, Ibid.

4   You must love—*not my faults*— but in *spite* of them, me,
        For the very caprices that vex ye;
    Nay, the more should you chance (as it's likely) to see
        'T is my special delight to perplex ye.

> "The Threat," St. 6, Ibid.

5   But I have drunk enough of life
        (The cup assign'd to me
    Dash'd with a little sweet at best,
        So scantily, so scantily)

> "To Death," St. 4, Ibid.

6   This weak, weak head! this foolish heart! they'll cheat me to
        the last:
    I've been a dreamer all my life, and now that life is past!

> "The Dying Mother to her Infant," St. 11, *Autumn Flowers, and Other Poems 1844*

7   How happily, how happily, the flowers die away!
    Oh, could we but return to earth as easily as they!

> "The Death of the Flowers," St. 1, Ibid.

782. María Augustín (1786–1857)

1   Death or victory!*

> Speech at siege of Zaragoza (2 June 1808), Quoted in *Women of Beauty and Heroism* by Frank B. Goodrich *1858*

*Cry that led the Spanish resistance to Napoleon's assault.

783. Marceline Desbordes-Valmore (1786–1859)

1   "Has any seen a little child astray among the crowd?
    The mother has been seeking it, and weeping long and loud."

> "The Lost Child," 1, St. 1 (refrain), *Elegies and Romances 1842*

2   "What?—find my vanished Eden?"

> "A Woman's Dream," St. 1, Ibid.

3   Shall I never play again in my mother's garden-close?

> "*Tristesse*," (Sadness), St. 1, Ibid.

4 Ah, when the soul is young,
  It is lightly filled with joy, and the taste is yet unknown
  Of the morsel steeped in tears, with honey overstrown,
  That leaves a bitter savor on the tongue.
  St. 10, Ibid.

5 Why are our joys remembered more bitter than our woes?
  St. 21, Ibid.

6 "I wonder who will take the oar
  When my poor bark is at last found"
  "To Alphonse de Lamartine,"* St. 6, Ibid.
  *French poet and statesman (1790–1869).

7 In the vain shows where wit doth win applause,
    Hushed lies the heart, and hidden:
  To please becomes the first of laws;
    To love is aye forbidden.
  Ch. 1, Untitled poem, St. 2, Quoted in *Memoirs of Madame Desbordes-Valmore* by C. A. Sainte-Beuve; Harriet W. Preston, tr. *1872*

8 "O strange caprice of the unstable crowd!"
  St. 3, Ibid.

9 "The scattered lights of fame!"
  St. 4, Ibid.

10 . . . money demoralizes even the giver.
  Remark, Ibid.

11 We must make our lives as we sew,—stitch by stitch.
  Ibid.

12 God will gather like bruised flowers
  The souls of babes and women who to him
  Are fled,—the air with outraged souls is dim,
  On earth men wade in blood,—Merciful Powers!
  Ch. 3, "Lyons," St. 2 (1834), Ibid.

13 Are we* not like the two volumes of one book?
  Ch. 4, Letter, Ibid.
  *Referring to her friend, Pauline Duchambge, composer, with whom Valmore frequently collaborated on songs.

14 I am climbing, as best I may, to the goal of an existence in which I speak very much oftener to God than to the world.
  Letter to M. Antoince de Latour (7 February 1837), Ibid.

15 All the miseries of Lyons are added to my own,—twenty or thirty thousand workmen begging daily for a little bread, a little fire, a garment, lest they die. Can you realize, monsieur, this universal and insurmountable despair which appeals to one in God's name, and makes one ashamed of daring to have food and fire and two garments, when these poor creatures have none? I see it all, and it paralyzes me.
  Ibid.

16 . . . the more I read, the farther I penetrate into the shadows which have hidden our great lights from me, the less I dare to write: I am smitten with terror,—I am like a glowworm in the sun.
  Letter to her son, Hippolyte (26 October 1840), Ibid.

17 It is certainly true that housekeeping cares bring with them a thousand endearing compensations. They are a woman's peculiar joy, and women are apt to be light-hearted.
  Letter to Hippolyte and Undine, her son and daughter (1 November 1840), Ibid.

18 . . . if I were not poor, you would not be so.
  Letter to her brother, Felix Desbordes (14 January 1843), Ibid.

19 In these days the rich will come and tell you their troubles with such utter candor, such bitter bewailings, that you are compelled to pity them more than you do yourself.
  Letter to Pauline Duchambge (10 February 1843), Ibid.

20 An attack of hope is the same for us as an attack of fever.
  Ibid.

21 Nothing is very clear in my memory, except that we were very happy, and very unhappy. . . .
  Letter to her brother (14 April 1843), Ibid.

22 But politics poison the mind.
  (28 September 1847), Ibid.

23 To gain in strength and elevation of mind, day by day; to shame, or at least to soften, those who have despised us, and render them glad to have been our allies and old friends,—there is something in all this which may yet sanctify life.
  Ibid.

24 . . . what are grace and wit and wisdom in times like these?
  (12 January 1848), Ibid.

25 To write what I think, is to betray myself.
  To write anything else is to deceive. . . .
  Letter to Mme. Derains (4 October 1852), Ibid.

26 This world of ours grows dizzy.
  Letter to her niece, Camille (26 March 1854), Ibid.

27 The last result of misfortune is to sow seeds of discord in families in which happiness would have united. When it becomes necessary for each member to work hard in order to escape absolute indigence, the wings of the soul are folded, and soaring is postponed to a future day.
  Letter to her niece (6 September 1854), Ibid.

28 . . . the sum and substance of volumes that I feel . . . will remain unwritten, like seeds put away in closets, which dry up and are never sown.
  Letter to Mme. Derains (c. September 1854), Ibid.

29 The rich are no worse than we, but they are utterly unable to understand how one can want for the humblest necessities of life.
  Letter to her sister, Cecile (9 November 1854), Ibid.

30 and what a hard stepmother is life. . . .
  Letter to Pauline Duchambge (27 December 1855), Ibid.

31 You say, my dear and true friend, that poetry is my consolation. On the contrary, it torments me, as with a bitter irony. I am like the Indian who sings at the stake.
  (15 January 1856), Ibid.

32 Are we not always young?
  (5 January 1857), Ibid.

33 Life may become wearisome, but it does not end.
  Ibid.

34 Ah, how many stabs are concealed by the smiles and sweet "goodmornings" of the world.
  (April 1857), Ibid.

35 The are times when one cannot lift a blade of grass without finding a serpent under it.

    (11 May 1857), Ibid.

36 "Flowers o' the home," says he,
    "Are daughters."

    "Mother and Maiden," St. 15, Idylles n.d.

37 And one hears best, methinks, when one hears blindly.

    St. 17, Ibid.

38 Their fragrance fills my gown this evening, still;
    All that remains of a scented
    souvenir.

    "The Roses of Sa'adi," St. 3, Elaine T. Partnow,* tr.,
    Les poètes maudits,** Paul Verlaine, ed. 1884
    *See 2870. **The dispossessed, exiled or cursed poets.

39 Do not write. Let us learn to die, as best we may.
    Did I love you? Ask God. Ask yourself. Do you know?
    To hear that you love me, when you are far away,
    Is like hearing from heaven and never to go.
        Do not write!

    "Apart," St. 2, Modern Poets of France: A Bilingual
    Anthology, Louis Simpson, ed. & tr. 1997

784. Mary Russell Mitford (1787–1855)

1 JULIAN. I have been
    Sick, brainsick, heartsick, mad I thought—I feared—
    It was a foretaste of the pains of hell
    To be so mad and yet retain the sense
    Of that which made me so.

    Act II, Sc. 1, Julian 1823

2 Of all living objects, children, out of doors, seem to me the most interesting to a lover of nature . . . Within doors . . . I am one of the many persons who like children in their places,—that is to say, anyplace where I am not. But out of doors there is no such limitation: from the gypsy urchins under a hedge, to the little lords and ladies in a ducal demesne, they are charming to look at, to watch, and to listen to. Dogs are less amusing, flowers are less beautiful, trees themselves are less picturesque.

    "The Carpenter's Daughter," Belford Regis; or, Sketches of a
    Country Town, Vol. I 1835

3 The grave equals all men. . . .

    No. III, Vol. II, Ibid.

4 COLONNA. The fool's grown wise—
    A grievous change.

    Act II, Sc. 1, Rienzi 1857

5 COLONNA. Joined! by what tie?
    RIENZI. By hatred—
    By danger—the two hands that tightest grasp
    Each other—the two cords that soonest knit
    A fast and stubborn tie: your true love knot
    Is nothing to it.

    Ibid.

6 I have discovered that out great favourite, Miss [Jane] Austen,* is my countrywoman . . . with whom mamma before her marriage was acquainted. Mamma says that she was then the prettiest, silliest, most affected, husband-hunting butterfly she ever remembers.

    Letter to Sir William Elford (3 April 1815), Quoted in Life of
    Mary Russell Mitford, Vol. I by Rev. A. G. L'Estrange, ed. 1870
    *See 753.

7 There is a thrilling awfulness, an intense feeling of simple power in that naked colorless beauty which falls on the earth, like the thoughts of death—death pure, and glorious, and smiling—but still death. Sculpture has always had the same affect on my imagination, and painting never. Colour is life.

    "Walks in the Country: Frost and Thaw," Our Village 1892

785. Eliza Leslie (1787–1858)

1 "The truth is," pursued Mr. Culpepper, "I am travelling for my health, and therefore I am taking cross-roads, and stopping at out of the way places. For there is no health to be got by staying in cities, and putting up at crowded hotels, and accepting invitations to dinner-parties and tea-parties, or in doing any thing else that is called fashionable."

    "The Red Box, or, Scenes at the General Wayne," Pencil
    Sketches; or Outlines of Character and Manners 1837

2 Servility and integrity rarely go together.

    Ibid.

3 "Certainly every body ought to feel on these occasions; but you know it is impossible to devote every moment between this and the funeral to tears and sobs. One cannot be crying all the time—nobody ever does."

    "Constance Allerton; or, the Mourning Suits," Ibid.

4 "Excuse me, but innovations on established customs ought only to be attempted by people of note—by persons so far up in society that they may feel at liberty to do any out-of-the-way thing with impunity."

    Ibid.

5 "There is no better cure for folly, and particularly for romantic folly, than a good burlesque. . . . "

    "The Serenades," Ibid.

6 "The pleasure of listening to delightful notes, with delightful words, uttered with taste and feeling by an accomplished and intellectual singer, is one of the most perfect that can fall to the lot of beings who are unable to hear the music of the spheres and the songs of Paradise."

    Ibid.

7 "Why, Pharaoh—my old fellow!" exclaimed Lindsay, "Is this really yourself?"
    "Can't say, masser," replied Pharaoh. "All people's much the same—Best not be too personal—But I b'lieve I'm he."

    "The Old Farm House," Ibid.

8 "And the Newman girls mix up their talk with all sorts of French words that sound very ugly to me. Instead of 'good night' they say bone swear,* and a 'trifle' they call a bag-tail,* and they are always talking about having a Gennessee Squaw,* though what they mean by that I cannot imagine; for I am sure I never saw any such thing in this part of the country."

    Ibid.

    *bon soir; bagatelle; je ne sais quoi.

9 " . . . you Americans always know more of every thing than you ought to. I don't wonder so few of you look plump and ruddy. You all wear yourselves out with headwork."

    "That Gentleman," Ibid.

10 " . . . there's a considerable difference between doing without a thing of your own accord, and being made to do without it."

    "Chase Loring. A Story of the Revolution," Ibid.

11 "Aunt Rhoda," observed Tudor, "a cause* that is sanctioned by the approval of so many wise and pious men cannot fail to prosper."

Ibid.

*Reference to the Boston Tea Party (16 December 1773).

12 Our anticipations cannot keep pace with the realities that are continually overtaking them. . . .

Godey's Lady's Book November 1845

13 Albert Colesbury, of Philadelphia, fell in love with Catherine Branchely, of New York, at a quarter past ten o'clock, while dancing opposite to her on the evening of his arrival at Ballston Springs. . . .

'Love at First Sight," *Kitty's Relations, and other pencil sketches 1847*

14 "Love at first sight is certainly a most amusing thing," remarked Mrs. Seabright, "at least to the by-standers."

Ibid.

15 "Some goes by coffee-grounds, which is low and vulgar; and some goes by the lines on the parms of your hands, which is nothing but plexity and puzzledom; and some goes by the stars and planipos [planets], which is too far off to be certain. But cards is the only true things, as all the best judges can scratify [certify]."

"The Fortune-Teller," *Leonilla Lynmore, and Mr. and Mrs. Woodbridge or A Lesson for young wives 1847*

786. Eliza Lee Follen (1787–1860)

1 The night comes on,
   And sleep upon this little world of ours,
   Spreads out her sheltering, healing wings; and man—
   The heaven-inspired soul of this fair earth,
   The bold interpreter of nature's voice,
   Giving a language even to the stars—
   Unconscious of the throbbings of his heart,—
   Is still

"Winter Scenes in the Country," St. 1, *Poems 1839*

787. Emma Hart Willard (1787–1870)

1 Rocked in the cradle of the deep
   I lay me down in peace to sleep;
   Secure I rest upon the wave,
   For Thou, O Lord! hast power to save.

"The Ocean Hymn," St. 1 (written at sea)   *14 July 1831*

2 'T is best to make the Law our friend.

Harry Guy 1848

3 In searching for the fundamental principles of the science of teaching, I find few axioms as indisputable as is the first principles of mathematics. One of these is this, HE IS THE BEST TEACHER WHO MAKES THE BEST USE OF HIS OWN TIME AND THAT OF HIS PUPILS. *For* TIME *is all that is given by God in which to do the work of Improvement.*

"How to Teach," Address to the Columbian Association *n.d.*

4 He is not necessarily the best teacher who performs the most labour; makes his pupils work the hardest, and bustle the most. A hundred cents of copper, though they make more clatter and fill more space, have only a tenth of the value of one eagle of gold.

Ibid.

5 Reason and religion teach us that we too are primary existences, that it is for us to move in the orbit of our duty around the holy center of perfection, the companions not the satellites of men.

Inscribed beneath her bust in the Hall of Fame of Great Americans, Bronx, New York *n.d.*

788. Sarah Josepha Hale (1788–1879)

1 O wondrous power! how little understood,
   —Entrusted to the mother's mind alone
   To fashion genius, form the soul for good,
   Inspire a West,* or train a Washington!**

The Genius of Oblivion and Other Poems 1823
*Benjamin West, American painter (1738–1820). **George W—
(1732–99) first president of the United States (1789–1797).

2 And bards and prophets tune their mystic lyres
   While listening to the music of the waves!

Ibid.

3 The great error of those who would sever the Union, rather than see a slave within its borders, is that they forget the master is their brother as well as the servant. . . .

Preface (5th edition, 1852), *Northwood, A Tale of New England 1828*

4 . . . . there is a period when nations as well as individuals quit their minority. . . .

Text, *Ibid.*

5 You may easily tell a rich Yankee farmer—he is always pleading poverty.

Ibid.

6 In this age of innovation perhaps no experiment will have an influence more important on the character and happiness of our society than the granting to females the advantages of a systematic and thorough education. The honour of this triumph, in favour of intellect over long established prejudice, belongs to the men of America.

Editorial, *The Ladies' Magazine and Literary Gazette January 1828**
*First issue of first woman's magazine in the United States.

7 There is no influence so powerful as that of the mother, but next in rank in efficacy is that of schoolmaster.

Ibid.

8 Victoria's reign will be one of the longest in English annals. . . .
   She may so stamp her influence on the period in which she flourishes that history shall speak of it as her own. . . .
   It will be the Victorian, as a former one now is the Elizabethan age . . . *

Ibid.

*Predicted two years before Victoria (see 934) ascended the throne.

9 She was a weak woman—too highly elated in prosperity, too easily depressed by adversity—not considering that *both* are situations of trial. . . .

"Walter Wilson," *Sketches of American Character 1829*

10 There is something in the decay of nature that awakens thought, even in the most trifling mind.

"A Winter in the Country,," *Ibid.*

11 Mary had a little lamb,
   Its fleece was white as snow,

And everywhere that Mary went
 The lamb was sure to go.

It followed her to school one day,
 Which was against the rule.
It made the children laugh and play
 To see a lamb at school.

"What makes the lamb love Mary so?"
 The eager children cry.
"Oh, Mary loves the lamb, you know,"
 The teacher did reply.
    "Mary's Little Lamb," *in toto, Poems for
             Our Children 1830*

12 O, beautiful rainbow, all woven of light!
 There's not in thy tissue one shadow of night;
 Heaven surely is open when thou dost appear,
 And bending above thee, the angels draw near,
 And sing—"the rainbow! the rainbow!
 The smile of God is here."
       "Beautiful Rainbow," *Ibid.*

13 We need not power or splendor;
 Wide hall or lordly dome;
 The good, the true, the tender,
 These form the wealth of home.
          "Home," *Ibid.*

14 Though Mind Aladdin's lamp might be,
 His Geni was the Hand.
      "The Hand and Its Work," *Ibid.*

15 I consider every attempt to induce women to think they have a just right to participate in the public duties of government as injurious to their best interests and derogatory to their character. Our empire is purer, more excellent and spiritual. . . .
   Editorial, *The Ladies' Magazine and Literary Gazette*
               February 1832

16 There is a deep moral influence in these periodical seasons of rejoicing, in which whole communities participate. They bring out, and together, as it were, the best sympathies in our natures.
        Traits of American Life 1835

17 Americans have two ardent passions; the love of liberty and the love of distinction.
              Ibid.

18 There is small danger of being starved in our land of plenty; but the danger of being stuffed is imminent.
              Ibid.

19 There can be no education without leisure, and without leisure education is useless.
      Godey's Lady's Book (passim) 1837–1877

20 The barbarous custom of wresting from women whatever she possesses, whether by inheritance, donation or her own industry, and conferring it all upon the man she marries, to be used at his discretion and will, perhaps waste it on his wicked indulgences, without allowing her any control or redress, is such a monstrous perversion of justice *by law*, that we might well marvel how it could obtain in a Christian community.
   "The Rights of Married Women," *Godey's Lady's Book
               May 1837*

21 . . . man in blessing others finds his highest fame!
         Ormond Grosvenor 1838

22 The temple of our purest thoughts is—silence!
              Ibid.

23 "You talk to me about educating my children; but what's the use of it. . . . The more they know the wuss it will be for 'em; for they won't keep company with their own color, and white folks won't associate with them, and thar they are shut up by themselves . . . and they won't be any thing but just what I am, a nigger that every body despises."
         Ch. 3, *Liberia 1853*

24 " . . . it's might hard for a man like me, that could be as good as any body, if his skin were a shade or two lighter, to be kept down so all the time, and not get drunk or wicked."
              Ibid.

25 " . . . what's de good of strong arms when de heart is a coward's?"
            Ch. 5, *Ibid.*

26 "Africa . . . is the home . . . of the mysterious Negro races yet lying dormant in the germ, destined, perhaps, to rule this earth when our proud Anglo-Saxon blood is as corrupt as that of the descendents of Homer* or Perricles** [sic]."
            Ch. 7, *Ibid.*
*Greek epic poet (fl. 850 B.C.E.). **Athenian leader (d. 429 B.C.E.)

27 The belief in witchcraft was and is universal, where the spirit of Christianity has not shed its blessed light.
            Ch. 9, *Ibid.*

28 If men cannot cope with women in the medical profession let them take an humble occupation in which they can.
   Editorial, *Godey's Lady's Book January 1853*

29 Lambs skip and bound, kittens and puppies seem wild with the joy of life; and little children naturally run, leap, dance and shout in the exuberance of that capacity for happiness which the young human heart feels as instinctively as the flower buds open to the sun. To repress their natural joyousness, not to direct and train it for good, seems to be the object of most parents.
              Ibid.

30 Growing old! growing old! Do they say it of me?
 Do they hint my fine fancies are faded and fled?
 That my garden of life, like the winterswept tree,
 Is frozen and dying, or fallen and dead?
   "Growing Old" [written on her 70th birthday], *Ibid.*

31 . . . the whole process of home-making, housekeeping and cooking, which ever has been woman's special province, should be looked on as an art and a profession. . . .
          Editorial, *Ibid.*

32 The most welcome guest in society will ever be the one to whose mind everything is a suggestion, and whose words suggest something to everybody.
          "Manners," *Ibid.*

33 The profession of teacher requires . . . as thorough and special training as that of any of the other intellectual professions. The great majority of our teachers are deficient in this training . . . the complaint on this head is indeed universal, and it is coupled with another complaint of the inadequate salaries almost every where paid to teachers, but more especially in rural districts.
          Editorial, *Ibid.*

34 What has made this nation great? Not its heroes but its households.

Ibid.

35 Every century has its particular tide of thought.

Woman's Record (earlier edition, *Biography of Distinguished Women*, 1876) *1877*

789. Ann Hasseltine Judson (1789–1826)

1 Either I have been made, through the mercy of God, a partaker of divine grace, or I have been fatally deceiving myself, and building upon a sandy foundation. Either I have, in sincerity and truth, renounced the vanities of this world, and entered the narrow path which leads to life, or I have been refraining from them for a time only, to turn again and relish them more than ever. God grant that the latter may never be my unhappy case!

Journal Entry (22 December 1806), Quoted in *Memoir of Mrs. Ann H. Judson, Late Missionary to Burma* by James D. Knowles *1829*

2 I find more real enjoyment in contrition for sin, excited by a view of the adorable moral perfections of God, than in all earthly joys.

Ibid.

790. Harriette Wilson (1789–1846)

1 I shall not say why and how I became, at the age of fifteen, the mistress of the Earl of Craven.

Memoirs (first sentence) *n.d.*

791. Marguerite Blessington (1789–1849)

1 "Och! Jim, and this is the way you keep the Bible oath you took over to Father Cahill last Easther Sunday, that you would not dhrink a dhrop in any sheban-house for a year and a day? . . ."

"I did not dhrink a dhrop in the sheban-house, for I put my head clean out the window while I was dhrinking, so my oath is safe. . . ."

Ch. 1, *The Repealers 1833*

2 "How is it, Jim dear, that I, who love you betther than ever I loved myself, and you, who say you love me—that we, who have but one heart, can have two minds?"

Ibid.

3 "Why liberty, cuishlamachree, manes to do every thing we like ourselves, and hinder everyone else from doing it."

Ch. 2, Ibid.

4 "Sure there's different roads from this to Dungarvan*—some thinks one road pleasanter, and some think another; wouldn't it be mighty foolish to quarrel for this?—and sure isn't it twice worse to thry to interfere with people for choosing the road they like best to heaven?"

Ibid.

*Seaport and seat of Waterford County, Ireland; dating back to seventh century.

5 "Imagination, which is the eldorado of the poet and of the novel-writer, often proves the most pernicious gift to the individuals who compose the talkers instead of the writers in society."

Ch. 40, Ibid.

6 Politeness, that cementer of friendship and soother of enmities, is nowhere so much required, and so frequently outraged, as in family circles. . . .

Ch. 57, Ibid.

7 " . . . chance, the very worst guardian a man can choose for his personal comfort."

Ch. 1, *The Two Friends 1835*

8 "My spaniel Dido is not more submissive," said Scamper; "for though I try Lady Janet by contradicting flatly to-day, what I maintained yesterday, it is all the same to her; she never has any opinion but mine: this is what I call the only solid foundation to build matrimonial happiness upon; and so I have made up my mind to marry."

Ch. 28, Ibid.

9 This is an autobiographical-loving age. . . .

The Confessions of an Elderly Gentleman 1836

10 . . . it is better to die young than to outlive *all* one loved, and *all* that rendered one lovable.

Ibid.

11 Love is, I think, like fever; one severe attack leaves the patient subject to relapses through youth; and each succeeding one renders him more weakened, and consequently, more exposed to future assaults.

"My Fourth Love," Ibid.

12 Happiness is a rare plant, that seldom takes root on earth: few ever enjoyed it, except for a brief period; the search after it is rarely rewarded by the discovery. But, there is an admirable substitute for it, which all may hope to attain, as its attainment depends wholly oneself—and that is, a contented spirit.

"Lady Mary Howard to Lady Augusta Vernon,"
The Victims of Society 1837

13 Injurious as are the examples of bad conduct, the impunity which too frequently attends the perpetration is still more fatally pernicious.

"Lord Delaward to Lady Delaward," Ibid.

14 . . . we [the French] believe that the people who support the ills of life with the most cheerfulness, and forget them with the greatest facility, are the happiest, and, consequently, the wisest. *You* [the English] are above this happiness, and *we* are superior to the *ennui* which sends half your nation wandering into every clime; as if locomotion could relieve a malady that arises in the discontented mind. . . .

"La Marquise Le Villeroi to Miss Montressor," Ibid.

15 You ask me whether English husbands are, in general, *bons et aimables? Pas du tout, ma chère; tout au contraire.* They are, as far as I can judge from the specimens I have seen, the most selfish beings imaginable.

"Miss Montressor to La Marquise Le Villeroi," Ibid.

16 It is the motive, and not the results, that constitutes the crime.

"La Marquise Le Villeroi to Miss Montressor," Ibid.

17 . . . with a good fortune, a brilliant position, and a weak, indulgent husband, what more could she desire?

Ibid.

18 How soothing is affection! and how do those who, like me, know little of this sweetener of life, turn, with awakened tenderness, to him who administers the cordial!

"The Countess of Anandale to La Marquise Le Villeroi," Ibid.

19 A mother's love! O holy, boundless thing!
Fountain whose waters never cease to spring!

"Affection," *Gems of Beauty 1837–1838*

20 People seem to lose all respect for the past; events succeed each other with such velocity that the most remarkable one of a few years gone by, is no more remembered than if centuries had closed over it.

The Confessions of an Elderly Lady 1838

21 . . . modern historians are all would-be philosophers; who, instead of relating facts as they occurred, give us their version, or rather perversions of them, always colored by their political prejudices, or distorted to establish some theory, and rendered obscure by cumbrous attempts to trace effect from cause.

Ibid.

22 . . . if those only wrote, who were sure of being read, we should have fewer authors; and the shelves of libraries would not groan beneath the weight of dusty tomes more voluminous than luminous.

Ibid.

23 There is no magician like Love. . . .

Ibid.

24 Time, that omnipotent effacer of *eternal* passions. . . .

Ibid.

25 Tears fell from my eyes—yes, weak and foolish as it now appears to me, I wept for my departed youth; and for that beauty of which the faithful mirror too plainly assured me, no remnant existed.

Ibid.

26 Novels and comedies end generally in a marriage, because, after that event, it is supposed that nothing remains to be told.

"The Honey-Moon," *The Works of Lady Blessington 1838*

27 They perceived that the love, unceasing and ecstatic, of which they had dreamt before their union, was a chimera existing only in imagination; and they awoke, with sobered feelings, to seek content in rational affection, instead of indulging in romantic expectations that never falls to the lot of human beings: each acknowledging, with a sigh, that even in a marriage of love, the brilliant anticipations of imagination are never realised; that disappointment awaits poor mortals even in that brightest portion of existence—The Honey-Moon.

Ibid.

28 Reason dissipates the illusions of life, but does not console us for their departure.

Desultory Thoughts and Reflections 1839

29 Love-matches are made by people who are content, for a month of honey, to condemn themselves to a life of vinegar.

Commonplace Book n.d.

30 When the sun shines on you, you see your friends. Friends are the thermometers by which one may judge the temperature of our fortunes.

Ibid.

31 Religion converts despair, which destroys, into resignation, which submits.

Ibid.

792. Eliza Townsend (1789-1854)

1 . . . let that come now,
Which soon or late must come. For light
    like this
Who would not dare to die?

"The Incomprehensibility of God," St. 1, *The Female Poets of America*, Rufus Griswold, ed. *1849*

793. Hannah Flagg Gould (1789–1865)

1 He went to the windows of those who slept,
And over each pane, like a fairy, crept;
Wherever he breathed, wherever he *stepped*
    By the light of the morn, were seen
Most beautiful things. . . .

"The Frost," *Poems 1832*

2 O Thou, who in thy hand dost hold
The winds and waves that wake or sleep,
Thy tender arms of mercy fold
Around the seamen on the deep.

"Changes on the Deep," Ibid.

794. Catherine Maria Sedgwick (1789–1867)

1 "There is some pure gold mixed with all this glitter; some here that seem to have as pure hearts and just minds as if they had never stood in the dazzling sunshine of fortune."

"The Opinions of a Yankee Spinster," *Redwood 1824*

2 " . . . contentment is a modest, prudent spirit; and . . . for the most part she avoids the high places of the earth, where the sun burns and the tempests beat, and leads her favourites along quiet vales to sequestered fountains."

Ibid.

3 He who should embody and manifest the virtues taught in Christ's sermon on the Mount, would, though he had never seen a drawing-room, nor even heard of the artificial usages of society, commend himself to all nations, the most refined as well as the most simple.

"True Politeness," Ibid.

4 The fountains are with the rich, but they are no better than a stagnant pool till they flow in streams to the labouring people.

"His Advice to his Children," *The Poor Rich Man and the Rich Poor Man 1836*

5 "If parents are civil and kind to one another, if children never hear from them profane or coarse language, they will as naturally grow up well-behaved, as that candle took the form of the mould it was run in.

"His Remarks on Manners," Ibid.

795. Charlotte Elliott (1789–1871)

1 Just as I am, without one plea
But that Thy blood was shed for me,
And that Thou bidd'st me to come to Thee,
    O Lamb of God, I come!

"Just As I Am," *Invalid's Hymn Book 1834*

2 "Christian! seek not yet repose,"
Hear thy guardian angel say;
Thou art in the midst of foes—
"Watch and pray."

"Christian! Seek Not Yet Repose," *Morning and Evening Hymns c. 1840*

796. Mary Cole (fl. c. 1790)

1 If all writers upon Cookery had acknowledged from whence they took their receipts, as I do, they would have acted with more candour by the public. Their vanity to pass for Authors, instead of Compilers, has not added to their reputation.

The Lady's Complete Guide 1791

797. Hannah Godwin (fl. c. 1790)

1 Good sense without vanity, a penetrating judgment without a disposition to satire, with about as much religion as my William likes, struck me with a wish that she [Miss Gay] was my William's wife.

> Letter to William Godwin,* her brother, Quoted in
> *William Godwin: His Friends and Contemporaries*
> by C. K. Paul *1876*

*English political philosopher (1756–1836); married to Mary Wollstonecraft; see 687.

798. Rahel Levin (fl. c. 1790–181-?)

1 Poor woman [Germaine de Staël*], she has seen nothing, heard nothing, understood nothing.

> Quoted in *Mistress to an Age: A Life of Madame de Staël*
> by J. Christopher Herold *1958*

*See 717.

799. Eleanor Anne Franklin (c.1790/97–1825)

1 "Thine icy heart I well can bear,
But not the love that others share."

> "Coeur de Lion,* an Epic Poem in Sixteen Cantos" *1822*

*Richard I (the Lion-Hearted; 1157–1199).

2 "The widow'd dove can never rest,
The felon kite has robb'd her nest;
With wing untir'd she seeks her mate,
To share or change his dreadful fate.

> Ibid.

800. Charlotte Elizabeth Tonna (1790–1846)

1 When we name the infliction of a wrong, we imply the existence of a right. Therefore, if we undertake to discuss the wrongs of women, we may be expected to set out by plainly defining what are the rights of women.

> Ch. 1, "Milliners and Dress-makers," *The Wrongs of
> Women*, Pt. I *1833–1834*

2 There is no presumption in taking God at his word: not to do so, is very impertinent. . . .

> Letter I, *Personal Recollections 1841*

3 There can be no doubt that the hand which first encloses the waist of a girl in these cruel contrivances [stays], supplying her with a fictitious support, where the hand of God has placed bones and muscles that ought to be brought into vigorous action, that hand lays the foundation of bitter suffering. . . .

> Letter II, Ibid.

4 How very much do they err who consider the absence of order and method as implying greater liberty or removing a sense of restraint!

> Letter IV, Ibid.

5 . . . the want of punctuality is a want of honest principle; for however people may think themselves authorised to rob God and themselves of their own time, they can plead no right to lay a violent hand on the time and duties of their neighbour.

> Ibid.

6 "And how do you feel when you have got absolution?" "I feel all right; and I go out and begin again." "And how do you know that God has really pardoned you?" "He doesn't pardon me directly; only the priest does. He [the priest] confesses my sins to the bishop, and the bishop confesses them to the pope, and the pope sees the Virgin Mary every Saturday night, and tells her to speak to God about it."

> Letter VII, Ibid.

7 Nothing rights a boy of ten or twelve years like putting him on his manhood. . . .

> Letter XIV, Ibid.

8 "He must be sworn. Boy, do you know the nature of an oath?"
The wretched child answered by repeating some of the most common and blasphemous modes of execration, which, to Richard's great horror, drew forth a peal of laughter, some on the bench more than smiling.
"Pho!" said the presiding magistrate, angrily, "Do you know, sir, what will become of those who take a false oath?"
"I have heard some say that it is bad to swear, sir."

> *Helen Fleetwood*, Ch. 14, from *The Works of
> Charlotte Elizabeth*, Vol. I *1844*

9 "The weight seemed to be not only on my head, but all over me; and then the sickening smell and the whirring noise—I'll tell you what, the first few days in a factory would make me ill, and when I got over that, I should become stupid."

> Ch. 19, Ibid.

10 Truth is a very aggressive principle; it does not stand still to be attacked, but marches on, under the conduct of faith, to assail the enemy, to make conquests, and to recover what falsehood has stolen, or violence wrested away.

> *Second Causes; or, Up and be Doing*, Ch. 7, Ibid.

11 Scorning the rude world's idle toys,
Its faithless vowes and treacherous joys. . . .

> "After a Tempest," St. 3, *Posthumous and
> Other Poems*, Ibid.

12 A self-sold, suicidal world.

> "The Watchman," St. 4, Ibid.

13 Man, the proud sleeper, will not wake.

> Ibid.

14 Look upon thy negro brother—
Be one moment *bound with him*,
Slave, in flesh and weary—
Ponder what thy need would be—
Ponder deep the touching query
That thy brother asks of thee!

> "Anti-Slavery Album," No. I, Ibid.

15 Haste to set thy people free;
Come; creation groans for thee!

> "The Millennium," St. 4, *The Female Poets of
> Great Britain*, Frederic Rowton, ed. *1853*

16 The fashion of poisoning people is getting too common.*

> Remark (1690), Quoted in *Life and Letters of Charlotte
> Elizabeth 1889*

*Reference to three deaths by poison at court.

801. Louisa Macartney Crawford (1790–1858)

1 Kathleen Mavourneen; what, slumbering still?
Oh, hast thou forgotten how soon we must sever?
O hast thou forgotten this day we must part?
It may be for years, and it may be for ever!
Oh, why art thou silent, thou voice of my heart?

> "Kathleen Mavourneen" (Attributed) *n.d.*

802. Rahel Morpurgo (1790–1871)

1   A woman's fancies lightly roam, and weave
    Themselves into a fairy web.
          Sonnet, *Ugab Rachel* (The Harp of Rachel), I. Castiglione,
          ed. *1890*

2   Wherever you go, you will hear all around:
    The wisdom of woman to the distaff is bound.
          Untitled, St. 4, Ibid.

3   Better to die—to rest in shadows folded,
    Than thus to grope amid the depths in vain!
          "And here also I have done nothing that they should put
          me into the dungeon" (a.k.a. "The Dark Valley"),
          St.1 (1867), Ibid.

4   I will tell thee an idea that has come into mind that "oil from
    the flinty rock"* is *petroleum*, and there is nothing new under
    the sun.
          Letter to Isaac Luzzatto (1869), Ibid.
    *From Deuteronomy 32:13.

5   Woe! my knowledge is weak,
    My wound is desperate.
          Last poem (1871), Ibid.

803. Ann Eliza Bray (1790–1883)

1   Never fear spoiling children by making them too happy. Happiness is the atmosphere in which all good affections grow . . . unhappiness—the chilling pressure which produces . . . "the mind's green and yellow sickness"—ill temper.
          Attributed *n.d.*

804. Sarah Martin (1791–1843)

1   I knew also that it sometimes seemed good in His sight to try the faith and patience of His servants, by bestowing upon them very limited means of support; as in the case of Naomi* and Ruth;** of the widow of Zarephath and Elijah; and my mind, in the contemplation of such trials, seemed exalted by more than human energy; for I had counted the cost; and my mind was made up.
          Article in *Edinburgh Review 1847*
    *See 22. **See 23.

805. Margaret Mercer (1791–1846)

1   *Conversation is to works what the flower is to the fruit.* A godly conversation shelters and cherishes the new-born spirit of virtue, as the flower does the fruit from the cold, chill atmosphere, of a heartless world; and the beauty of holiness expanding in conversation, gives rational anticipation of noble-minded principles ripening into the richest fruits of good works.
          Ethics n.d.

2   . . . I confess that the 'unidea-ed chatter of females' is past my endurance; they are very capable of better things, but what of that? Is it not yet more annoying that they will do nothing better?
          Quoted in *Memoirs* by Caspar Morris, M.D. *n.d.*

3   . . . steady laborious efforts to do good will doubtless be blessed, although we may in mercy be denied the luxury of seeing our work under the sun prosper.
          Ibid.

806. Eliza Vestris (1791\97–1856)

1   Before you hear a 'venturous woman bends—
    A warrior woman, who in strife embarks,

The first of all dramatic Joan-of-Arcs!
Cheer on the enterprize thus dared by me,
The first that ever led a company;
What though until this very hour and age,
A Lessee lady never owned a stage,
I'm that *Belle Sauvage*—only rather quieter—
Like Mrs. Nelson, turn'd a stage proprietor.
          Composed for her Olympic Theatre (London) debut (3 January 1831), Quoted in *Enter the Actress* by Rosamond Gilder *1931*

807. Lydia Howard Sigourney (1791–1865)

1   "I was a worm till I won my wings."
          "Butterfly on a Child's Grave," St. 2, *Poems 1834*

2   To evil habit's earliest wile
    Lend neither ear, nor glance, nor smile—
    Choke the dark fountain ere it flows,
    Nor e'en admit the camel's nose.
          "The Camel's Nose," St. 4, Ibid.

3   Not on the outer world
    For inward joy depend;
    Enjoy the luxury of thought,
    Make thine own self friend
          "Know Thyself," Ibid.

4   Flow on forever, in thy glorious robe
    Of terror and beauty.
          "Niagara," St. 1, *Zinzendorff, and Other Poems 1836*

5   *Death is the test of life.*—All else is vain.
          "The Test of Life," St. 1, Ibid.

6   Bid the long-prisoned mind attain
    A sphere of dazzling day,
    Bid her unpinion'd foot
       The cliffs of knowledge climb,
    And search for Wisdom's sacred root
       That mocks the blight of time.
          "Female Education," St. 3, Ibid.

7   They, perchance,
    Did look on woman as a worthless thing,
    A cloistered gem, a briefly-fading flower,
    Remembering not that she had kingly power
    O'er the young soul.
          "Establishment of a Female College in New-Grenada, South America," St. 1, Ibid.

8   Hope spreads her wing of plumage fair,
    Rebuilds the castle bas'd on air
          "The Soap Bubble," Ibid.

9   Death's shafts are ever busy.
          "Death of Mr. Oliver D. Cooke," St. 1, Ibid.

10   —See, life is but a dream. Awake! Awake!
    Break off the trance of vanity. . . .
          "Dreams," St. 4, Ibid.

11   Like wild flowers among the dells, or clefts of the rock, they [poems] sprang up wherever the path of life chanced to lead.
          Preface, *Select Poems 1841*

12   O Man! so prodigal of pride and praise,
    Thy works survive thee—dead machines perform

Their revolution, while thy scythe-shorn days
Yield thee a powerless prisoner to the worm—
"The Ancient Family Clock," St. 10, Ibid.

13 —I fear thee. Thou'rt a subtle husbandman,
Sowing thy little seed, of good or ill,
In the moist, unsunn'd surface of the heart.
"Thought," St. 2, Ibid.

14 Memory, with traitor-tread
Methinks, doth steal away
Treasures that the mind had laid
Up for a wintry day.
"Barzillai the Gileadite,"* St. 4, Ibid.
*Aged and wealthy citizen of the city of Gilead, who befriended David when he fled from Absalom (2 Samuel 17: 27–29; 19:32).

15 And yield the torn world to the angel of peace.
"The War Spirit," St. 5, Ibid.

16 This is the parting place; this narrow house
"The Tomb," St. 1, Ibid.

17 Thou who has toiled to earn
The fickle praise of far posterity,
Come, weigh it at the grave's brink, here with me,
If thou canst weigh a dream.
"The Dying Philosopher," St. 4, Ibid.

18 But their name is on your waters,
Ye may not wash it out.
"Indian Names," St. 1, Ibid.

19 For thou* dost teach us from the dead
A lesson that all pride should tame;
That genius high and morals base
Mar the great Giver's plan,
And, like a comet's flaming race,
Make visible that deep disgrace
Of His best gifts to man.
"The Western Home," St. 52, Poems 1854
*Aaron Burr (1756–1836), third vice president of the United States (1801–1805), who was tried for treason.

20 For fashion, for thirst of gold.
The venal hand may diamonds link,
In velvet pile the foot may sink
The lips from jewelled chalice drink,
Yet every nerve to joy be dead,
And all the life of feeling fled
In the heart's palsied atrophy.
St. 53, Ibid.

21 Man's warfare on the tree is terrible.
"Fallen Forests," St. 1, Ibid.

22 They say that the cell of the poet should be
Like the breast of the shell that remembers the sea
"The Muse," St. 1, Ibid.

23 Nature hath secret lore for those who lean
Upon her breast, with leisure in their soul
"Listen," St. 2, Ibid.

24 Language is slow.
"Unspoken Language," St. 1, Ibid.

25 We dream, but they awake
"The Holy Dead," St. 4, Ibid.

26 . . . the few who by examples teach,
Making a text-book of their own strong heart
And blameless life.
"The Ivy," St. 4, Ibid.

27 For every quarrel cuts a thread
That healthful love has spun.
"The Thriving Family," St. 3, Ibid.

28 The influence which is most truly valuable is that of mind over mind.
"Power of a Mother," Letters to Mothers n.d.

29 Admitting that it is the profession of our sex to teach, we perceive the mother to be first in point of precedence, in degree of power, in the faculty of teaching, and in the department allotted. For in point of precedence she is next to the Creator; in power over her pupil, limitless and without competitor; in faculty of teaching, endowed with the prerogative of a transforming love; while the glorious department allotted is a newly quickened soul and its immortal destiny.
Ibid.

30 This, then, is the patriotism of woman; not to thunder in senates, or to usurp dominion, or to seek the clarion-blast of fame, but faithfully to teach by precept and example that wisdom, integrity, and peace which are the glory of a nation.
"Woman's Patriotism," Ibid.

808. Eliza Ware Farrar (1791–1870)

1 The queen* and princesses were all such common-looking people that they upset my childish notions of royalty.
Ch. 2, Recollections of Seventy Years 1865
*Queen Charlotte (1744–1818), consort of George III of England.

2 . . . Sir William Ellis . . . was at the head of the great lunatic asylum for paupers at Handwell near London. . . . No strait-waistcoats, no strapping patients into beds or chairs, no punishments of any kind were used,—nothing but the personal influence of Sir William and Lady Ellis; and their power over all under their care was extraordinary. Even persons in the height of an attack of mania yielded to it. Part of their system was to keep the patients as fully and as happily employed as was possible, and the whole establishment was like a great school of industry.
Ch. 38, Ibid.

809. Anne Marsh (1791–1874)

1 To say nothing of that brief but despotic sway which every woman possesses over the man in love with her—a power immense, unaccountable, invaluable; but in general so evanescent as but to make a brilliant episode in the tale of life—how almost immeasurable is the influence exercised by wives, sisters, friends, and, most of all, by mothers!
"Woman's Influence," Angela 1848

2 He [without education] enters life an ill-trained steed; and the best that can be hoped for him is, that the severe lash of disappointment, contradiction, and suffering, will during the course of his career, supply the omissions of his youth, and train him at last, through much enduring, to that point from which a good education would have started him.
Ibid.

3 Oh, vice is a hideous thing.
A hideous, dark mystery—the mystery of iniquity! Its secret springs are hidden from our view. . . .
"Sin and its Consequences," Mordaunt Hall; or, A September Night 1849

4   He shall render a heavier account . . . [who] is great, and gifted, and wise, and powerful, and fitted to guide a state and rule the interests of a nation—he shall be the less forgiven, because in the plenitude of his powers he has chosen to step aside to crush a poor little insect in its humble path—he shall be the less forgiven, because the wider the knowledge, and the higher the intellect, and the larger the observation, so much the greater is the power of estimating the claims and appreciating the sufferings of whatever breathes; and that thoughtless cruelty which we lament and pardon in the untutored child, is odious, is execrable in the man!

"Seduction," Ibid.

5   Wherever or howsoever the sacredness of marriage is not reverenced, depend upon it, *there* the man will ever be found imperfectly developed.

"Illegitimacy," Ibid.

810. Caroline Symonds (1792–1803)

1   She planted, she lov'd it, she water'd its head,
And its bloom every rival defied;
But alas! what was beauty or virtue, soon fled,
In Spring they both blossom'd and died.

"The Faded Rose, which grew on the tomb of Zelida," St. 4,
The Female Poets of Great Britain, Frederic Rowton, ed.
1853

2   Scarce had thy velvet lips imbib'd the dew,
And nature hail'd thee, infant queen of May;
Scarce saw thy opening bloom the sun's broad ray,
And on the air its tender fragrance threw;
When the north wind enamour'd of thee grew,
And from his chilling kiss, thy charms decay.

"The Blighted Rosebud",* Ibid.
*Inscribed on the tomb of the writer, who died at the age of eleven.

811. Anne Isabella Milbanke (1792–1860)

1   Yes! Farewell—farewell forever!
Thou thyself has fixed our doom,
Bade hope's fairest blossoms wither,
Ne'er again for me to bloom.

"Fare Thee Well" (to Lord Byron*) *c. January 1816*
*English poet (1788–1824).

812. Sarah Moore Grimké (1792–1873)

1   . . . the false translation of some passages [of the New Testament] by the MEN who did that work, and against the perverted interpretation by the MEN who undertook to write commentaries thereon. I am inclined to think, when we [women] are admitted to the honor of studying Greek and Hebrew, we shall produce some various readings of the Bible a little different from those we now have.

Letter (Haverhill, 17 July 1837), *Letters on the Equality of the Sexes, and the Condition of Woman* 1838

2   Ah! how many of my sex feel . . . that what they have leaned upon has proved a broken reed at best, and oft a spear.

Ibid.

3   In most families, it is considered a matter of far more consequence to call a girl off from making a pie, or a pudding, than to interrupt her whilst engaged in her studies.

Letter (Brookline, 1837), Ibid.

4   There is another way in which the general opinion, that women are inferior to men, is manifested. . . . I allude to the disproportionate value set on the time and labor of men and women.

Ibid.

5   Woman, instead of being elevated by her union with man, which might be expected from an alliance with a superior being, is in reality lowered. She generally loses her individuality, her independent character, her moral being. She becomes absorbed into him, and henceforth is looked at, and acts through the medium of her husband.

Letter (Brookline, September 1837), Ibid.

6   Brute force, the law of violence, rules to a great extent in the poor man's domicile; and woman is little more than his drudge.

Ibid.

7   We cannot push Abolitionism forward . . . *until* we take up the stumbling block [women's rights] out of the road.

Letters of Theodore Dwight Weld, Angelina Grimké
Weld,** and Sarah Grimké, 1822–1844,* Vol. I, Gilbert
Hobbs Barnes and Dwight L. Dumonds, eds. *1934*
*American abolitionist (1803–1895). **See 871.

813. Virginie Ancelot (1792–1875)

1   "*There are no longer any women!* no, my dear, Count, there are no longer any women," mournfully exclaimed the Marchioness de Fontenay-Mareuil. . . .

Ch. 1, *Gabrielle 1840*

2   "Saloons* [sic] exist no longer; conversation has ceased; good taste has disappeared with it, and the mind has lost all its influences."

Ibid.

*Reference to the French term 'salons,' social gatherings of distinguished guests.

814. Harriet Grote (1792–1878)

1   Politics and theology are the only two really great subjects.

Bk. VIII, Ch. 1, Letter to Lord Rosebery* (16 September
1880), Quoted in *Life of Gladstone* by John Morley Morly
1903
*Archibald Philip Primrose, fifth earl of Rosebery, English statesman (1847–1929).

815. Felicia Dorothea Hemans (1793–1835)

1   We will give the names of our fearless race
To each bright river whose course we trace.

"Song of Emigration," *Works 1839*

2   The stately homes of England!
How beautiful they stand,
Amidst their tall ancestral trees,
O'er all the pleasant land!

"The Homes of England," St. 1, Ibid.

3   The boy stood on the burning deck,
Whence all but he had fled.

"Casabianca," St. 1, Ibid.

4   Life's best balm—forgetfulness.

"The Caravan in the Desert," Ibid.

5   Home of the Arts! where glory's faded smile
Sheds lingering light o'er many a mouldering pile.

"Restoration of the Works of Art to Italy," Ibid.

6 Oh! what a crowded world one moment may contain.
   "The Last Constantine," Ibid.

7 We endow
   Those whom we love, in our fond, passionate blindness,
   With power upon our souls too absolute
   To be a mortal's trust.
   "The Siege of Valencia," Ibid.

8 They grew in beauty side by side,
      They fill'd one home with glee;—
   Their graves are severed far and wide
      By mount, and stream, and sea.
   "The Graves of a Household," Ibid.

9 Oh, lightly, lightly tread!
   A holy thing is sleep.
   "The Sleeper," Ibid.

10 Talk not of grief till thou has seen the tears of warlike men!
    "Bernardo del Carpio," l. 26, Ibid.

11 Oh! call my brother back to me!
       I cannot play alone;
    The summer comes with flower and bee—
       Where is my brother gone?
    "The Child's First Grief," St. 1, Ibid.

12 Is *all* that we see or seem
    But a dream within a dream?
    "A Dream Within a Dream," ll., Ibid.

816. Catherine Spalding (1793–1858)

1 My heart still clings to the orphans.
   Notable American Women, Edward T. James, ed. *1971*

817. Sarah Taylor Austin (1793–1867)

1 It is the peculiar and invaluable privilege of a translator, as such, to have no opinions, and this is precisely what renders the somewhat toilsome business of translating attractive to one who has a profound sense of the difficulty of forming mature and coherent opinions, and of the presumption of putting forth crude and incongruous ones. . . .
   Translator's Preface, Quoted in *England in 1835: being a series of Letters written to friends in Germany . . . by* Frederick von Raumer *1836*

818. Sarah Alden Ripley (1793–1867)

1 What a vista! A whole new language!*
   Notable American Women, Edward T. James, ed. *1971*
   *Reaction to satirical novel *Don Quixote* by Miguel de Cervantes, Spanish writer (1547–1616).

2 The sun looks brighter . . . as the evening of life draws near.
   Letter to her sister-in-law, Ibid.

819. Rebecca Burton Burlend (1793–1872)

1 Whatever may have been our success in America, I can attribute little of it to myself; as I gave up the idea of ending my days in my own country with the utmost reluctance, and should never have become an emigrant, if obedience to my husband's wishes had left me any alternative.
   A True Picture of Emigration 1848

2 I observed several groups of slaves linked together in chains, and driven about the streets like oxen under the yoke.
   On arriving in New Orleans (1 November 1831), Ibid.

3 I was now going to be an alien among strangers.
   Ibid.

4 The nights in winter are at once inexpressibly cold, and poetically fine. The sky is almost invariably clear, and the stars shine with a brilliancy entirely unknown in the humid atmosphere of England.
   On Homesteading in Illinois, Ibid.

5 Every thing here bears the mark of ancient undisturbed repose. The golden age still appears, and when the woodsman with his axe enters these territories for the first time, he cannot resist the impression that he is about to commit a trespass on the virgin loveliness of nature, that he is going to bring into captivity what has been free for centuries.
   Ibid.

820. Lucretia Mott (1793–1880)

1 Then, in the marriage union, the independence of the husband and wife will be equal, their dependence mutual, and their obligations reciprocal.
   Discourse on Women 1850

2 Look at the heads of those [Quaker] women; they can mingle with men; they are not triflers; they have intelligent subjects of conversation.
   Women's Rights Convention, Proceedings 1853

3 Learning, while at school, that the charge for the education of girls was the same as that for boys, and that, when they became teachers, women received only half as much as men for their services, the injustice of this distinction was so apparent, that I resolved to claim for my sex all that an impartial Creator had bestowed, which, by custom and a perverted application of the Scriptures, had been wrested from woman.
   Letter, Quoted in *Biography of Distinguished Women* by Sarah Josepha Hale* *1876*
   *See 788.

4 The cause of Peace has had a share of my efforts, taking the ultra non-resistance ground—that a Christian cannot consistently uphold, and actively support, a government based on the sword, or whose ultimate resort is to the destroying weapon.
   Ibid.

5 . . . systems by which the rich are made richer, and the poor poorer, should find no favour among people professing to "fear God and hate covetousness."
   Ibid.

6 Truth for authority, not authority for truth.
   Motto, Quoted in *The Peerless Leader* by Paxton Hibben *n.d.*

821. Almira Lincoln Phelps (1793–1884)

1 What a pledge for virtuous conduct is the character of a mother!
   "The Mother's Hopes," *The Mother's Journal 1838*

2 So, in the physical world mankind are prone to seek an explanation of *uncommon* phenomena only, while the ordinary

changes of nature, which are in themselves equally wonderful, are disregarded.

"An Infant's First Ideas," Ibid.

3 The universe, how vast! exceeding far
The bounds of human thought; millions of suns,
With their attendant world moving around
Some common centre, gravitation strange!
Beyond the power of finite minds to scan!

"The Wonders of Nature," St. 1, *Poems n.d.*

4 Each opening bud, and care-perfected seed,
Is as a page, where we may read of God.

St. 3, Ibid.

822. Anna Brownwell Jameson (1794–1860)

1 To think of the situations of these women! . . . steeped in excitement from childhood, their nerves for ever in a state of terror between severe application and maddening flattery; cast on the world without chart or compass—with energies misdirected, passions uncontrolled, and all the inflammable and imaginative part of their being cultivated to excess as part of their profession—of their material!

"Women Artists—Singers—Actresses, & C.," *Visits and Sketches at Home and Abroad; With Tales and Miscellanies 1834*

2 It is this cold impervious pride which is the perdition of us English, and of England.

"English Pride," Ibid.

3 Conversation may be compared to a lyre with seven chords—philosophy, art, poetry, politics, love, scandal, and the weather.

"Conversation," Ibid.

4 Truth is the golden chain which links the terrestrial with the celestial, which sets the seal of heaven on the things of this earth, and stamps them with immortality.

The Loves of the Poets c. 1835

5 The true purpose of education is to cherish and unfold the seed of immortality already sown within us; to develop, to their fullest extent, the capacities of every kind with which the God who made us has endowed us.

"Education," *Winter Studies and Summer Rambles 1842*

6 He that seeks popularity in art closes the door on his own genius: as he must needs paint for other minds, and not for his own.

"Washington Allston,"* *Memoirs and Essays Illustrative of Art, Literature, and Social Mores 1846*
*American painter (1779–1843).

7 The only competition worthy a wise man is with himself.

Ibid.

8 A man may be as much a fool from the want of sensibility as the want of sense.

Detached Thoughts n.d.

9 As the rolling stone gathers no moss, so the roving heart gathers no affections.

"Sternberg's Novels," *Studies n.d.*

823. Caroline Gilman (1794–1888)

1 Changes! Sameness! What a perpetual chime those words ring on the ear of memory!

Ch. 1, *Recollections of a Southern Matron 1837*

2 One clear idea is too precious a treasure to lose.

Ch. 3, Ibid.

3 I know how the mind rushes back, in such moments, to infancy, when those stiffened hands were wrapped around us in twining love; when that bosom was the pillow of our first sorrows; when those ears, now insensible and soundless, heard our whispered confidence; when those eyes, now curtained by uplifted lids, watched our every motion. I know the pang that runs through the heart, and I can fancy the shrieking voice which says, "Thou mightst have done more for thy mother's happiness, for her who loved thee so!"

Ibid.

4 I must ask indulgence of general readers for mingling so much of the peculiarities of negroes with my details. Surrounded with them from infancy, they form a part of the landscape of a southern woman's life; take them away, and the picture would lose half its reality. They watch our cradles; they are the companions of our sports; it is they who aid our bridal decorations, and they wrap us in our shroud.

Ch. 14, Ibid.

5 . . . it is death—there is its stillness—its shroud—its fixed and pale repose; the voice tells not its wants—the eye knows not. We bend over the stiffened form, and turn away, and come not again, for it is death; perchance we lift the bloodless hand, or smooth the straying hair, but only once, for it is death, and we are chilled.

Ch. 23, Ibid.

6 . . . convert schools into places for *teaching* instead of *recitation.* . . . If the system continue as it its, the name of *teacher* should be changed to *lesson-hearer.*

Ch. 28, Ibid.

7 . . . sitting down to *one* plate, that loneliest of all positions. . . .

Ch. 35, Ibid.

8 To repress a harsh answer, to confess a fault, and to stop (right or wrong) in the midst of self-defence, in gentle submission, sometimes requires a struggle like life and death; but these *three* efforts are the golden threads with which domestic happiness is woven; once begin the fabric with this woof, and trials shall not break or sorrow tarnish it.

Ibid.

9 Space for the sunflower,
Bright with yellow glow
To court the sky.

"To The Ursulines," *Verses of a Life-Time 1849*

824. Maria Brooks (1795–1845)

1 My ills are my desert, my good thy gift.

'Hymn,' St. 3, *Judith,* * *Esther,* ** and Other Poems 1820*
*See 51. **See 56.

2 Day, in melting purple is dying.

"Song," St. 1, Ibid.

3 Looks are its food, its nectar sighs,
Its couch the lips, its throne the eyes,
The soul its breath: and so possest,
Heaven's raptures reign in mortal breast,
Fratello del mio cor. [Brother of my heart.]

"Friendship," St. 2, Ibid.

4 Who would not brave a fiend to share an angel's smile?
> Canto First, "Grove of Acadias," VIII, St. 1,
> *Zóphiël; or the Bride of Seven 1825*

5 Where passion is not found, no virtue ever dwelt.
> X, St. 1, Ibid.

6 "The bird that sweetest sings can least endure the storm."
> XIV, St. 1, Ibid.

7 But thou,* too bright and pure for mortal touch,
Art like those brilliant things we never taste
  Or see, unless with Fancy's lip and eye,
When maddened by her mystic spells, we waste
Life on a thought, and rob reality.
> XX, Sts. 1–2, Ibid.

*The passionflower.

8 . . . Reverie,
Sweet mother of the muses, heart and soul are thine!
> XXII, St. 1, Ibid.

9 Ye who beheld her hand forgot her face;
Yet in that face was all beside forgot
> Canto Second, "Death of Altheëtor," LI, St. 1, Ibid.

10 'Tis now the hour of mirth, the hour of love,
The hour of melancholy: Night, as vain
Of her full beauty, seems to pause above,
That all may look upon here ere it wane.
> Canto Third, "Palace of Gnomes," I, St. 1, Ibid.

11 Soul, I would rein thee in.
> XXXII, St. 1, Ibid.

12 Soul, what a mystery thou art! not one
Admires, or loves, or worships virtue more
Than I; but passion hurls me on, till torn
By keen remorse, I cool, to curse me and deplore.
> XXXIII, St. 1, Ibid.

13 How can I no longer bear my weary doom?
Alas! what have I gain'd for all I lost?
> CIX, St. 4, Ibid.

14 . . . cold ambition mimicks love so well,
That half the sons of heaven looked on deceived.
> Canto Fourth, "The Storm," XLVIII, St. 2, Ibid.

15 How thrills the kiss, when feeling's voice is mute!
> Canto Fifth, "Zameïa," III, St. 1, Ibid.

16 "Women may be
Enthrall'd by love, and often will forsake
  All other gods for love's idolatry."
> XXII, St. 3, Ibid.

17 "If evil things can give
Dreams such as mine, let me turn foe to good,
And make a God of *Evil* while I live!"
> XXIV, St. 1, Ibid.

18 And love and hope are twins. . . .
> XCVI, St. 1, Ibid.

19 '"The frailest hope is better than despair."
> CII, St. 1, Ibid.

20 But thousand evil things there are that hate
To look upon happiness
> Canto Sixth, "Bridal of Helon," IV, St. 1, Ibid.

825. Frances Wright (1795–1852)

1 The prejudices still to be found in Europe . . . which would confine . . . female conversation to the last new publication, new bonnet, and *pas seul* [nothing else] are entirely unknown here. The women are assuming their place as thinking beings. . . .
> *Views of Society & Manners in America 1821*

2 No man can see his own prejudices.
> *A Few Days in Athens 1822*

3 It is not as of yore. Eve puts not forth her hand to gather the fair fruit of knowledge. The wily serpent now hath better learned his lesson; and, to secure his reign in the garden, beguileth her *not* to eat.
> *Course of Popular Lectures 1829*

4 . . . whenever we establish our own pretensions upon the sacrificed rights of others, we do in fact impeach our own liberties, and lower ourselves in the scale of being!
> Ibid.

5 Equality! Where is it, if not in education? Equal rights! They cannot exist without equality of instruction.
> "Of Free Inquiry," Ibid.

6 Let us enquire—not if a mother be a wife, or a father a husband, but if parents can supply, to the creatures they have brought into being, all things requisite to make existence a blessing.
> (1828), Quoted in *Frances Wright, Free Enquirer* by A. J. G.
> Perkins and Theresa Wolfson *1939*

826. Frances Manwaring Caulkins (1795–1869)

1 The hand of God is seen in the history of towns as well as in that of nations. The purest and noblest love of the olden time is that which draws from its annals, motives of gratitude and thanksgiving for the past—counsels and warnings for the future.
> Preface, *History of New London, Connecticut 1852*

2 The tendency of man among savages, without the watch of his equals and the check of society, is to degenerate; to decline from the standard of morals, and gradually to relinquish all Christian observances.
> Ch. 6, Ibid.

827. Rebecca Cox Jackson (1795–1871)

1 I always believed that if the Lord had a work for His children to do, He was able to make it as plain as the light.
> From her *Autobiography* (1833–1836), *Gift of Powers,*
> *The Writings of Rebecca Jackson, Black Visionary,*
> *Shaker Eldresss*, Jean McMahon Humez, ed. *1981*

2 Jesus, the seed of the woman, is the manhood in which the seed of God dwells. Which seed is called the Godhead dwelling in manhood.
> Ibid.

3 The fear of God is the beginning of wisdom. . . .
> Ibid.

828. Sophia Smith (1796–1870)

1 It is my opinion that by the higher and more thoroughly Christian education of women, what are called their "wrongs" will be redressed, their wages will be adjusted, their weight of influence in reforming the evils of society will be greatly increased; as teachers, as writers, as mothers, as members of society, their power for good will be incalculably enlarged.

> Last Will and Testament of Sophia Smith,
> Late of Hatfield, Massachusetts *1871*

829. Kamamalu (1797?–1824)

1 O! heaven; O! earth; O! mountains; O! sea; O! my counsellors and my subjects, farewell! O! thou land for which my father suffered, the object of toil which my father sought. We now leave thy soil; I follow thy command; I will never disregard thy voice; I will walk by the command which thou hast given me.

> Farewell address to her people upon her departure to England* (27 November 1823), Quoted in *Biography of Distinguished Women* by Sarah Josepha Hale** *1876*

*She died in England, never returning to her native land. **See 788.

830. Katharine Augusta Ware (1797–1843)

1 I've looked on thee as thou wert calmly sleeping,
And wished—Oh, couldst thou ever be as blest
As now, when haply all thy cause of weeping
Is for a truant bird, or faded rose!

> "A New-Year Wish, to a child aged five years," St. 1,
> *The Power of the Passions, and Other Poems 1842*

831. Anette Elizabeth von Droste-Hülshoff (1797–1848)

1 At night, when heavenly peace is flying
Above the world that sorrow mars,
Ah, think not of my grave with sighing!
For then I greet you from the stars.

> "Last words," St. 3, *The Catholic Anthology*,
> Thomas Walsh, ed. *1927*

2 So still the pond in morning's gray,
A quiet conscience is not clearer.

> "Der Weiher" (The Pond), Herman Salinger, tr.,
> *An Anthology of German Poetry from Hölderlin to Rilke*, Angel Flores, ed. *1960*

3 O spirit free, entrancing youth,
Here at the very railing, I
Would wrestle, hip to hip, against
Your hold; become alive—or die.

> "Am Turme" (On the Tower), St. 1,
> James Edward Tobin, tr., Ibid.

4 If heaven listened to my plea,
Made me a man, even though small!
Instead, I sit here—delicate,
Polite, precise, well-mannered child.
Dreams shake my loosened hair—the wind
Lone listener to my spirit wild.

> Ibid.,

5 O slumber-waking strange, are you the certain
Curse of delicate nerves or yet their blessing?

> "Durchwachte Nacht" (Sleepless Night), St. 4,
> Herman Salinger, tr., Ibid.

6 . . . dreams release the soul's love urge

> St. 6, Ibid.

7 . . . all the ghosts within your breast
(Dead love, dead pleasure, and dead time)

> "Im Grase" (In the Grass), St. 2,
> James Edward Tobin, tr., Ibid.

8 The year is at its close,
A spindle ravels thinning thread;
One strand is left, a single hour.
And time, a glowing, pulsing rose,
Will crumble as a final flower,
Dusty and dead.

> "Am letzten Tage des Jahres" (The Last Day of the Year),
> St. 1, James Edward Tobin, tr., Ibid.

9 Minutes, like rivers, shake
The city walls, each house, each gate.

> Ibid.

832. Mary Lyon (1797-1849)

1 There is nothing in the universe that I fear but that I shall not know all my duty, or shall fail to do it.*

> Quoted in *Eminent Missionary Women*
> by Mrs. J. T. Gracey *1898*

*Inscribed on her monument at Mt. Holyoke College, which she founded (1837) in Hadley, Massachusetts.

2 When you choose your fields of labor go where nobody else is willing to go.

> Ibid.

3 Oh, how immensely important is this work of preparing the daughters of the land to be good mothers!

> Letter to her mother (Ipswich, 12 May 1834), Quoted in
> *Mary Lyon through Her Letters*, Marion Lansing, ed. *1937*

833. Mary Wollstonecraft Shelley (1797–1851)

1 . . . my dreams were all my own; I accounted for them to nobody; they were my refuge when annoyed—my dearest pleasure when free.

> Introduction (1831 edition), *Frankenstein (or, the Modern Prometheus) 1818*

2 Ah! It is well for the unfortunate to be resigned, but for the guilty there is no peace.

> Ibid.

3 Learn from me, if not by my precepts, at least by my example, how dangerous is the acquirement of knowledge, and how much happier that man is who believes his native town to be the world, than he who aspires to become greater than his nature will allow.

> Ch. 4, Ibid.

4 I felt that blank incapability of invention which is the greatest misery of authorship, when dull Nothing replies to our anxious invocations.

> Ibid.

5 I beheld the wretch—the miserable monster whom I had created.

> Ch. 5, Ibid.

6 "Of what a strange nature is knowledge! It clings to the mind, when it has once seized on it, like a lichen on the rock."

> Ch. 13, Ibid.

7 Life is obstinate and clings closest where it is most hated.
Ch. 23, Ibid.

8 His conversation was marked by its happy abundance.
Preface, *Collected Edition of Shelley 1839*

9 Mrs. Shelley was choosing a school for her son,* and asked the advice of this lady, who gave for advice—to use her own words to me—"Just the sort of banality, you know, one does come out with: 'Oh, send him somewhere where they will teach him to think for himself!'" . . . Mrs. Shelley answered: "Teach him to think for himself? Oh, my God, teach him rather to think like other people!"
Quoted in *Essays in Criticism, Second Series; Shelley* by Matthew Arnold *1888*
*Percy Bysshe Shelley, English poet and husband of Mary (1792–1822).

834. Therese Albertine Louise Robinson (1797–post-1852)

1 Not the untamed passion of the human heart, which, bursting out into a flame, spreading ruinously, destroys all barriers; not the unbridled force, which, in wild outbreaks of savage roughness, crushes under foot tender blossoms, lovely flowers,—not these constitute the greatest, the truest evil of the world; it is cold, creeping *egotism*, heartless *selfishness*; which with its attendants, treachery, deceit, and hypocrisy, easily bears away the palm, because it knows what it is doing, while passion, in blind fury, shatters its own weapons.
"Selfishness," *Life's Discipline; a Tale of the Annals of Hungary 1851*

2 Losing her faith in the moral worth of the man she loves, a woman loses all the *happiness* of love.
"Loving Unworthily," Ibid.

3 Love is dead. We are cured,—but are we happy?
Ibid.

835. Emily Eden (1797–1869)

1 People may go on talking for ever of the jealousies of pretty women; but for real genuine, hard-working envy, there is nothing like an ugly woman with a taste for admiration.
Pt. 1, Ch. 1, *The Semi-Attached Couple 1830*

2 "You will soon see how naturally one acquires a distaste for any ill-judging individual who presumes not to like one's husband."
Ch. 3, Ibid.

3 What could be more absurd than to assemble a crowd to witness a man and a woman promising to love each other for the rest of their lives, when we know what human creatures are,—men so thoroughly selfish and unprincipled, women so vain and frivolous?
Ch. 7, Ibid.

4 "I said to myself the other day, that one never hears anything new till it is old. . . . "
Ch. 17, Ibid.

5 There is nothing so catching as refinement. . . .
Ch. 48, Ibid.

6 "I often think, my dear, that it is a great pity you are so imaginative, and still a greater pity that you are so fastidious. You would be happier if you were as dull and as matter-of-fact as I am."
Ch. 1, *The Semi-Detached House c. 1860*

7 "Now is that so like the Post Office?" she said. "Letters that are of no consequence are always delivered directly, but when Arthur writes to me, they send his letters all over England."
Ch. 5, Ibid.

8 At last, there came the joyful whisper, "a fine boy," perhaps the only moment of a fine boy's existence in which his presence is more agreeable than his absence.
Ch. 18, Ibid.

836. Penina Moïse (1797–1880)

1 Lay no flowers on my grave. They are for those who live in the sun, and I have always lived in the shadow.
Last words, *Notable American Women*, Edward T. James, ed. *1971*

837. Sojourner Truth (1797?–1883)

1 Ef women want any rights more'n dey got, why don't dey jes' *take 'em*, and not be talkin' about it.
Comment *c. 1863*

2 I . . . can't read a book but I can read de people.
Address, Tremont Temple, Boston, Massachusetts *January 1871*

3 It is the mind that makes the body.
Interview, Battle Creek, Michigan *c. 1877*

4 Religion without humanity is a poor human stuff.
Ibid.

5 Wall, childern, whar dar is so much racket dar must be somethin' out o' kilter.
Speech, The Akron, Ohio, Convention (1851), *History of Woman Suffrage*, Vol. I, Elizabeth Cady Stanton,* Susan B. Anthony,** and Mathilda Gage*** *1881*
*See 907. **See 949. ***See 979.

6 Dat man ober dar say dat womin needs to be helped into carriages, and lifted ober ditches, and to hab de best place everywhar. Nobody eber helps me into carriages, or ober mud-puddles, or gibs me any best place! An a'n't I a woman? Look at me! Look at my arm! I have ploughed, and planted, and gathered into barns, and no man could head me! And a'n't I a woman? I could work as much and eat as much as a man—when I could get it—and bear de lash as well! And a'n't I a woman? I have borne thirteen chilern, and seen 'em mos' all sold off to slavery, and when I cried out with my mother's grief, none but Jesus heard me! And a'n't I a woman?
Ibid.

7 Den dat little man in black dar,* he say women can't have as much rights as men, 'cause Christ wasn't a woman! . . . Whar did your Christ come from? From God and a woman. Man had notin' to do wid Him.
Ibid.
*A clergyman in the audience.

8 If de fust woman God ever made was strong enough to turn the world upside down all alone, dese women togedder ought to be able to turn it back, and get it right side up again!
Ibid.

9 I know that it feels a kind o' hissin' and ticklin' like to see a colored woman get up and tell you about things, and Woman's Rights. We have all been thrown down so low that nobody thought we'd ever get up again; but we have been long enough trodden now; we will come up again, and now I am here.

Speech, The Mob Convention, Broadway Tabernacle (New York City, 8 September 1853), Ibid.

10 There is a great stir about colored men getting their rights, but not a word about the colored women; and if colored men get their rights, and not colored women theirs, you see the colored men will be masters over the women, and it will be just as bad as it was before. So I am for keeping the thing going while things are stirring; because if we wait till it is still, it will take a great while to get it going again.

Speech, Annual Meeting of Equal Rights Convention (New York City, 9 May 1867), Vol. II, Ibid.

11 I know that it is hard for one who has held the reins for so long to give up; it cuts like a knife. It will feel all the better when it closes up again.

Ibid.*

*Quotations have been printed as they appear in History of Woman Suffrage. One assumes that the difference inthe use of the vernacular and standard English has to do with the choice of the scribe at the event.

12 Truth burns up error.

Comment c. 1882

13 I will show my breast to the entire congregation. It is not my shame, but yours.*

Quoted in Women Suffragists by Diana Star Helmer 1998
*Her response when challenged by a heckler to show her breast to some of the ladies present to prove that, despite her deep voice, she was indeed a woman.

14 [In New York City] . . . the rich rob the poor and the poor rob one another.

Ibid.

15 I left everything behind. I wa'n't goin' to keep nothin' of Egypt on me. So I went to the Lord and asked him to give me a new name. And the Lord gave me Sojourner, because I was to travel up and down the land showin' the people their sins and bein' a sign unto them. Afterward, I told the Lord I wanted another name, 'cause everybody else had two names. And the Lord gave me Truth, because I was to declare the truth to the people.

Remark to Lucretia Mott,* Ibid.
*See 820.

16 I sell the shadow to support the substance.*

Ibid.

*Inscription of photographs of herself she sold to make money for food; she always spoke for free.

17 Now some people say, "Let the blacks take care of themselves." But you've taken everything away from them. They don't have anything left. I say, get the black people out of Washington! Get them off the government. Get the old people out and build them homes in the West, where they can feed themselves. Lift up those people and put them there. Teach them to read part of the time and teach them to work the other part of the time. Do that, and they will soon be a people among you.

Speech, American Equal Rights Association Convention (1867), Ibid.

18 I *am* a woman's rights. I am a woman's rights.

Ibid.

838. Louisa Caroline Tuthill (1798/99–1879)

1 Never ring for a servant unless it is absolutely necessary; consider whether you have a right to make even your own waiting-maid take forty steps to save yourself one.

"Behaviour to Servants," The Young Lady's Home n.d.

2 A cumbrous set of rules and maxims hung about one, like the charms which the gree-gree man* sells to the poor African, will not ward off the evils, nor furnish an antidote to the trials of life.

"Home Habits," Ibid.
*Voodoo witch.

839. Madame Pfeiffer (1799–post-1852)

1 A small affair would it have been for me to sail around the world, as many have done; it is my land journeys that render my tour a great undertaking, and invest it with interest.

Quoted in Biography of Distinguished Women by Sarah Josepha Hale* 1876
*See 788.

2 Never betray fear.

Motto, Ibid.

840. Catherine Gore (1799–1861)

1 Waterton, the naturalist . . . asserts that whenever he countered an alligator *tête-à-tête*, in the wilderness, he used to leap on his back, and ride the beast to death. This feat, so much discredited by the stay-at-home critics, was an act of neither bravery nor braggartry—but of necessity. Either the man or the alligator must have had the upper hand. *Il a fallu opter.**

Just so are we situated with regard to the world. Either we must leap upon its back, strike our spur into its panting sides, and, in spite of its scaly defenses, compel it to obey our glowing will, or the animal will mangle us with its ferocious jaws, leaving us expiring in the dust.

"How to Manage the World," Modern Chivalry n.d.
*He had to choose.

2 For the egoïst has so far the advantage over every other species of devotee, that his idol is ever present.

"Society," Ibid.

3 Thanks to the march of civilization, privacy has been exploded among us, and individuality effaced. People feel in thousands, and think in tens of thousands. No quiet nook of earth remaining for the modern Cincinnatus* to cultivate his own carrots and opinions, where humours may expand into excrescence, or originality let grow its beard!

Self n.d.
*Legendary Roman hero, political leader and farmer (fl. 460 B.C.E.).

841. Catharine Crowe (c.1799/1800–1876)

1 The great proportion of us live for this world alone, and think very little of the next . . . whilst . . . what is generally called the religious world, is so engrossed by its struggles for power or money, or by its sectarian disputes and enmities, and so narrowed and circumscribed by dogmatic orthodoxies, that is has neither inclination nor liberty to turn back or look around, and endeavour to gather up, from past records and present ob-

servation, such hints as are now and again dropt in our path, to give us an intimation of what the truth may be.

The Night-Side of Nature 1848

2 A great many things have been pronounced untrue and absurd, and even impossible, by the highest authorities in the age in which they lived, which have afterwards, and indeed, within a very short period, been found to be both possible and true.

Ibid.

842. Mary Howitt (1799–1888)

1 "Will you walk into my parlor?" said a Spider to a Fly;
"'Tis the prettiest little parlor that ever you did spy."

"The Spider and the Fly," *Poems c. 1822–1831*

2 Old England is our home and Englishmen are we,
Our tongue is known in every clime, our flag on every sea.

"Old England is Our Home," Ibid.

3 Yes! in the poor man's garden grow,
Far more than herbs and flowers,
Kind thoughts, contentment, peace of mind,
And joy for weary hours.

"The Poor Man's Garden," Ibid.

4 Make beauty a familiar guest.

Untitled, *Ballads and Other Poems 1847*

5 Hunger, and cold, and weariness, these are a frightful three,
But another curse there is beside, that darkens poverty;
It may not have one thing *to love*, how small soe'er it be!

"The Sale of the Pet Lamb," St. 6, Ibid.

6 Sixteen summers had she seen,
A rose-bud just unsealing

"Tibbie Inglis, or the Scholar's Wooing," St. 2, *The British Female Poets*, George W. Bethune, ed. *1848*

7 Snatches of delicious song,
Full of old love-sadness!

"Beatrice. A Lover's Lay," St. 9, Ibid.

8 Ye are neither deep nor wise;
Ye shall ne'er philosophize.

"Village Children," St. 1, Ibid.

9 Oh, hapless heirs of want and woe!

"Pauper Orphans," St. 5, *The Female Poets of Great Britain*, Frederic Rowton, ed. *1853*

10 I love the fields, the woods, the streams,
The wild flowers fresh and sweet,
And Yet I love, no less than these,
The crowded city street

"A City Street," St. 1, Ibid.

11 Our lives are all turmoil;
Our souls are in a weary strife and toil,
Grasping and straining—tasking nerve and brain,
—Both day and night for gain!
We have grown worldly: have made gold our god

"English Churches," St. 3, Ibid.

12 For visions come not to polluted eyes!

Ibid.

13 Oh! what had death to do with one like thee. . . . ?

"The Lost One," St. 3, Ibid.

14 Let us take our proper station;
We the rising generation,
Let us stamp the age as ours!

"The Children," St. 5, *Birds and Flowers; or, Lays and Lyrics of Rural Life 1873*

15 How pleasant the life of a bird must be,
Flitting about in a leafy tree;
And away through the air what a joy to go,
And to look on the green bright earth below.

"Birds in Summer," St. 3, Ibid.

16 Oh, tell me how my garden grows,
Where I no more may take delight,
And if some dream of me it knows,
Who dream of it by day and night.

"Oh, Tell Me How My Garden Grows," St. 5 *n.d.*

843. Frances Crowe (fl. c. 1800)

1 . . . keep on keeping on . . .

Quoted in "Karen Malpede," * *Interviews with Contemporary Women Playwrights*, Kathleen Betsko** and Rachel Koenig *1987*

*See 3057. **See 2739.

844. Ann Holbrook (fl. c. 1800)

1 An actress can never make her children comfortable . . . The mother returning with harassed frame and agitated mind, from the varying passions she has been portraying, instead of imparting healthful nourishment to her child, fills it with bile and fever, to say nothing of dragging them long journies, at all seasons of the year.

The Dramatist, or Memoires of the Stage 1809

845. Sarah Catherine Martin (fl. c. 1800)

1 Old Mother Hubbard
Went to the cupboard,
To get her poor dog a bone;
But when she came there
The cupboard was bare,
And so the poor dog had none.

"The Comic Adventures of Old Mother Hubbard" *1805*

846. Elizabeth Trefusis (fl. c. 1800)

1 Thus the vain man, with subtle feigning,
Pursues, o'ertakes poor woman's heart;
But soon his hapless prize disdaining,
She dies!—the victim of his art.

"The Boy and Butterfly," *Poems and Tales 1808*

847. Maria de Fleury (fl. c. 1800)

1 Thou soft-flowing Keedron,* by thy silver stream
Our Saviour at midnight, when Cynthia's pale beam
Shone bright on the waters, would often times stray,
And lose in thy murmurs the toils of the day.

"Thou Soft-Flowing Keedron" *1804*

*Stream on the east side of Jerusalem near Mount of Olives; a.s.a. Kidron, Kedron.

848. Maria Jane Jewsbury (1800–1833?)

1 But let not thy little heart think, Genie,
Childhood the prophet of life:

It may be life's minstrel, Genie,
And sing sweet songs and clear
'Birth-Day Ballad," St. 4, *Lays for Leisure Hours:
Phantasmagoria 1824*

2 When the tossed mind surveys its hidden world,
And feels in every faculty a foe,
United but in strife; waves urged and hurled
By passion and by conscience, winds of woe,
Till the whole being is a storm-swept sea—
There's none like thee, O Lord! there's none like thee!
"There Is None Like Unto Thee (Jeremiah X.6)," St. 3, Ibid.

3 Unfortunately, I was twenty-one before I became a reader, and I became a writer almost as soon; it is the ruin of all young talent of the day, that reading and writing are simultaneous. We do not educate ourselves for literary enterprise. I would gladly burn almost everything I ever wrote, if so be I might start now with a mind that has seen, read, thought, and suffered somewhat, at least, approaching to a preparation.
Letter to Felicia Hemans,* *Three Histories 1830*
*See 815.

849. Catharine Esther Beecher (1800–1878)

1 Woman's great mission is to train immature, weak, and ignorant creatures to obey the laws of God; the physical, the intellectual, the social, and the moral—first in the family, than in the school, then in the neighborhood, then in the nation, then in the world. . . .
"An Address to the Christian Women of America,"
Woman Suffrage and Women's Professions 1871

2 To open avenues to political place and power for all classes of women would cause [the] humble labors of the family and school to be still more undervalued and shunned.
Ibid.

3 . . . as if *reasoning* were *any kind* of writing or talking which tends to convince people that some doctrine or measure is true and right.
Ibid.

4 The delicate and infirm go for sympathy, not to the well and buoyant, but to those who have suffered like themselves.
"Statistics of Female Health," Ibid.

5 How many young hearts have revealed the fact that what they had been trained to imagine the highest earthly felicity was but the beginning of care, disappointment, and sorrow, and often led to the extremity of mental and physical suffering
Ibid.

850. Julia Crawford (1800–1885)

1 Kathleen Mavourneen! The grey dawn is breaking
The horn of the hunter is heard on the hill.
"Kathleen Mavourneen," St. 1 (Attributed) *1835*

2 Oh! Hast thou forgotten how soon we musts ever?
Oh! Hast thou forgotten this day we must part?
It may be for years, and it may be forever;
Then why art thou silent, thou voice of my heart?
Ibid.

851. Elizabeth Wallbridge (?–1801)

But when I consider what a high calling, what honor and dignity God has conferred upon me, to be called his child, to be

born of his Spirit, made an heir of glory, and joint heir with Christ; how humble and circumspect should I be in all my ways, as a dutiful and loving child to an affectionate and loving Father! When I seriously consider these things it fills me with love and gratitude to God, and I do not wish for any higher station, nor envy the rich. I rather pity them if they are not good as well as great.
Quoted in *The Women of Methodism: Its Three
Foundresses . . .* by Abel Stevens *1866*

852. Frederika Bremer (1801–1865)

1 Thou mayest own the world, with health
And unslumbering powers;
Industry alone is wealth,
What we do is ours.
"Home" *1885*

853. Jane Welsh Carlyle (1801–1866)

1 If peace and quiet be not in one's own power, one can always give oneself at least bodily fatigue—no such bad *succe daneum* [substitution] after all.
Journal entry (23 October 1855), *Letters and Memorials
1883*

2 All that senseless sighing of *Te Deum* before the battle has begun!
Letter, Ibid.

3 It's [society] like seasickness: one thinks at the time one will never risk it again, and then the impression wears off and one thinks perhaps one's constitution has changed and that this time it will be more bearable
Ibid.

4 He [Thomas Carlyle*] has his talents, his vast and cultivated mind, his vivid imagination, his independence of soul and his high-souled principles of honour. But then—ah, these Buts! Saint Preux never kicked the fireirons, nor made puddings in his tea cups.
Letter to a friend (July 1821), Ibid.

5 If they had said the sun and the moon was gone out of the heavens, it could not have struck me with the idea of a more awful and dreary blank in the creation than the words: Byron* is dead.
Letter to Thomas Carlyle** (1824), Ibid.
**English poet (1788–1824). *English essayist, historian (1795–1881).

6 . . . the only thing that makes one place more attractive to me than another is the quantity of *heart* I find in it. . . .
Letter (1829), Ibid.

7 Medical men all over the world having merely entered into a tacit agreement to call all sorts of maladies people are liable to, in cold weather, by one name; so that one sort of treatment may serve for all, and their practice thereby be greatly simplified.
Letter to John Welsh (4 March 1837), Ibid.

8 Some new neighbors, that came a month or two ago, brought with them an accumulation of all the things to be guarded against in a London neighborhood, viz., a pianofort, a lapdog, and a parrot.
Letter to Thomas Carlyle's mother (6 May 1839), Ibid.

9 It is sad and wrong to be so dependent for the life of my life on any human being as I am on you; that I cannot by any force of

logic cure myself at this date, when it has become second nature. If I have to lead another life in any of the planets, I shall take precious good care not to hang myself round any man's neck, either as a locket or a millstone.

Letter to Thomas Carlyle (1850), Ibid.

10 Never does one feel oneself so utterly helpless as in trying to speak comfort for great bereavement. I will not try it. Time is the only comforter for the loss of a mother.

(27 December 1853), Ibid.

11 When one has been threatened with a great injustice, one accepts a smaller as a favour.

(21 November 1855), Ibid.

12 Blessed be the inventor of photography! I set him above even the inventor of chloroform! It has given more positive pleasure to poor suffering humanity than anything else that has "cast up" in my time or is like to—this art by which even the "poor" can possess themselves of tolerable likenesses of their absent dear ones. And mustn't it be acting favourably on the morality of the country?

Letter (21 October 1859), *The Collected Letters of Thomas and Jane Welsh Carlyle 1970*

13 Men of England, look at your poor girls, many of them fading around you, dropping off in consumption or decline; or, what is worse, degenerating to sour old maids . . . Keep your girls' minds narrow and fettered, they will still be a plague and a care, sometimes a disgrace to you. Cultivate them—give them scope and work—they will be your gayest companions in health, your tenderest nurses in sickness, your most faithful prop in age.

Quoted in *I, Too, Am Here: Selected Letters of Jane Welsh Carlyle*, Alan & Mary Simpson, eds. *1977*

14 Of all god's creatures, Man alone is poor.

"To a Swallow Building Under Our Eaves," *n.d.*

854. Letitia Landon (1802–1838)

1 As beautiful as woman's blush—
As evanescent too.

"Apple Blossoms," *The Poetical Works of Miss Landon 1842*

2 Were it not better to forget
Than but remember and regret?

"Despondency," Ibid.

3 Ah tell me not that memory
Sheds gladness o'er the past;
What is recalled by faded flowers
Save that they did not last?

Ibid.

4 Childhood, whose very happiness is love.

"Erinna," Ibid.

5 I loved him too as woman loves—
Reckless of sorrow, sin or scorn.

"The Indian Bride," Ibid.

6 Few, save the poor, feel for the poor.

"The Poor," Ibid.

7 We might have been—These are but common words,
And yet they make the sum of life's bewailing.

"Three Extracts from the Diary of a Week," Ibid.

855. Harriet Martineau (1802–1876)

1 . . . there is no country in the world where there is so much boasting of the "chivalrous" treatment she enjoys. . . . In short, indulgence is given her as a substitute for justice.

"Women," *Society in America   1837*

2 Fidelity to conscience is inconsistent with retiring modesty. If it be so, let the modesty succumb. It can be only a false modesty which can be thus endangered.

Ibid.

3 If a test of civilisation be sought, none can be so sure as the condition of that half of society over which the other half has power—from the exercises of the right of the strongest.

Ibid.

4 Religion is a temper, not a pursuit.

Ibid.

5 . . . the sum and substance of female education in America, as in England, is training women to consider marriage as the sole object in life, and to pretend that they do not think so.

Ibid.

6 Persecution for opinion, punishment for all manifestations of intellectual and moral strength, are still as common as women who have opinions and who manifest strength. . . .

Ibid.

7 If there is any country on earth where the course of true love may be expected to run smooth, it is America.

"Marriage," Ibid.

8 Retribution is known to impend over violations of conjugal duty.

Ibid.

9 . . . nobody, I believe, defends the arrangement by which . . . divorce is obtainable only by the very rich. The barbarism of granting that as a privilege . . . !

Ibid.

10 In no country, I believe, are the marriage laws so iniquitous as in England, and the conjugal relation, in consequence, so impaired.

Ibid.

11 . . . the early marriages of silly children . . . where . . . every woman is married before she well knows how serious a matter human life is.

Ibid.

12 It is clear that the sole business which legislation has with marriage is with the arrangements of property; to guard the reciprocal rights of the children of the marriage and the community. There is no further pretence for the interference of the law, in any way.

Ibid.

13 Anyone must see at a glance that if men and women marry those whom they do not love, they must love those whom they do not marry.

Ibid.

14 Marriage . . . is still the imperfect institution it must remain while women continue to be ill-educated, passive, and subservient. . . .

Ibid.

15 I have no sympathy for those who, under any pressure of circumstances, sacrifice their heart's-love for legal prostitution.

Ibid.

16 For my own part, I had rather suffer any inconvenience from having to work occasionally in chambers and kitchen . . . than witness the subservience in which the menial class is held in Europe.

"Occupation," Ibid.

17 But is it not the fact that religion emanates from the nature, from the moral state of the individual? Is it not therefore true that unless the nature be completely exercised, the moral state harmonised, the religion cannot be healthy?

Ibid.

18 During the present interval between the feudal age and the coming time, when life and its occupations will be freely thrown open to women as to men, the condition of the female working classes is such that if its sufferings were but made known, emotions of horror and shame would tremble through the whole of society.

Ibid.

19 Readers are plentiful: thinkers are rare.

Ibid.

20 What office is there which involves more responsibility, which requires more qualifications, and which ought, therefore, to be more honourable, than that of teaching?

Ibid.

21 Everywhere they [Egyptian women] pitied us European women heartily. . . . They think us strangely neglected in being left so free, and boast of their spy system and imprisonment as tokens of the value in which they are held.

"The Harem," *Eastern Life: Present and Past 1848*

22 . . . in the history of human affections . . . the least satisfying is the fraternal. Brothers are to sisters what sisters can never be to brothers as objects of engrossing and devoted affection.

Ibid.

23 . . . I declare that if we are to look for a hell upon earth, it is where polygamy exists: and that, as polygamy runs riot in Egypt, Egypt is the lowest depth of this hell.

Ibid.

24 I am sure that no traveler seeing things through author spectacles can see them as they are. . . .

Harriet Martineau's Autobiography, Vol. I *1877*

25 I am in truth very thankful for not having married at all.

Ibid.

26 The older I have grown, the more serious and irremediable have seemed to me the evils and disadvantages of married life as it exists among us at this time.

Ibid.

856. Lydia Maria Child (1802–1880)

1 In most nations the path of antiquity is shrouded in darkness, rendered more visible by the wild, fantastic light of fable; but with us, the vista of time is luminous to its remotest point.

Ch. 1, *Hobomok 1824*

2 The old men gazed on them in their loveliness, and turned away with that deep and painful sigh, which the gladness of childhood, and the transient beauty of youth, are so apt to awaken in the bosom of the aged.

Ch. 8, Ibid.

3 "The fact is, passengers to heaven are in haste, and will walk one way or the other. If a man doubts of his way, Satan is always ready at hand to help him to a new set of opinions at every stage. . . ."

Ch. 13, Ibid.

4 England may well dam up the waters from the Nile with bulrushes as to fetter the step of Freedom, more proud and firm in this youthful land. . . .

Ch. 4, *The Rebels 1825*

5 I sometimes think the gods have united human beings by some mysterious principle, like the according notes of music,. Or is it as Plato* has supposed, that souls originally one have been divided, and each seeks the half it lost?

Ch. 1, *Philothea: A Romance 1836*
*Greek philosopher (427–399 B.C.E.).

6 Every human being has, like Socrates,* an attendant spirit; and wise are they who obey its signals. If it does not always tell us what to do, it always cautions us what not to do.

Ch. 6, Ibid.

*Greek philosopher (470–347 B.C.E.).

7 No music is so pleasant to my ears as that word—father. Zoroaster* tells us that children are a bridge joining this earth to a heavenly paradise, filled with fresh springs and blooming gardens. Blessed indeed is the man who hears many gentle voices call him father!

Ch. 19, Ibid.

*Persian philosopher (fl. sixth century).

8 Now twilight lets her curtain down
And pins it with a star.

Quoted in obituary for MacDonald Clark *1842*

9 It is right noble to fight with wickedness and wrong; the mistake is in supposing that spiritual evil can be overcome by physical means.

Letters from New York, Vol. I *1843*

10 There was a time when all these things would have passed me by, like the flitting figures of a theatre, sufficient for the amusement of an hour. But now, I have lost the power of looking merely on the surface. Everything seems to me to come from the Infinite, to be filled with the Infinite, to be tending toward the Infinite. Do I see crowds of men hastening to extinguish a fire? I see not merely uncouth garbs, and fantastic, flickering lights, of lurid hue, like a trampling troop of gnomes—but straightway my mind is filled with thoughts about mutual helpfulness, human sympathy, the common bond of brotherhood, and the mysteriously deep foundations on which society rests; or rather, on which it now reels and totters.

Letter 1 (19 August 1841), Ibid.

11 Reverence is the highest quality of man's nature; and that individual, or nation, which has it slightly developed, is so far unfortunate. It is a strong spiritual instinct, and seeks to form channels for itself where none exists; thus Americans, in the dearth of other objects to worship, fall to worshiping themselves.

Letter 18 (26 May 1842), Ibid.

12 Flowers have spoken to me more than I can tell in written words. They are the hieroglyphics of angels, loved by all men

for the beauty of the character, though few can decypher even fragments of their meaning.

> Letter 26 (1 September 1842), Ibid.

13 Not in vain is Ireland pouring itself all over the earth. . . . The Irish, with their glowing hearts and reverent credulity, are needed in this cold age of intellect and skepticism.

> No. 33 (8 December 1842), Ibid.

14 None speaks of the bravery, the might, or the intellect of Jesus; but the devil is always imagined as being of acute intellect, political cunning, and the fiercest courage.

> Ibid.

15 Whoso does not see that genuine life is a battle and a march has poorly read his origin and his destiny.

> Ibid., Vol. II 1852

16 Use is the highest law of our being, and it cannot be disobeyed with impunity.

> Ibid.

17 The nearer society approaches to divine order, the less separation will there be in the characters, duties, and pursuits of men and women. Women will not become less gentle and graceful, but men will become more so. Women will not neglect the care and education of their children, but men will find themselves ennobled and refined by sharing those duties with them; and will receive, in return, co-operation and sympathy in the discharge of various other duties, now deemed inappropriate to women. The more women become rational companions, partners in business and in thought, as well as in affection and amusement, the more highly will men appreciate home.

> Letter 34 (January 1843), Ibid.

18 Childhood itself is scarcely more lovely than a cheerful, kind, sunshiny old age.

> Letter 37 (March 1843), Ibid.

19 That man's best works should be such bungling imitations of Nature's infinite perfection, matters not much; but that he should make himself an imitation, this is the fact which Nature moans over, and deprecates beseechingly. Be spontaneous, be truthful, be free, and thus be individuals! is the song she sings through warbling birds, and whispering pines, and roaring waves, and screeching winds.

> Letter 38 (17 March 1843), Ibid.

20 Misfortune is never mournful to the soul that accepts it; for such do always see that every cloud is an angel's face. Every man deems that he has precisely the trials and temptations which are the hardest of all others for him to bear; but they are so, simply because they are the very ones he most needs.

> Letter 39 (27 April 1843), Ibid.

21 There are not many people who are conscientious about being kind in their relations with human beings; and therefore it is not surprising that still fewer should be considerate about humanity to animals. . . . The fact is, reasonable and kind treatment will generally produce a great and beneficial change in vicious animals as well as in vicious men.

> "Kindness to Animals," The Freedman's Book 1865

22 Ah, my friend, that is the only true church organization, when heads and hearts unite in working for the welfare of the human race!

> Letter to Theodore Weld 1880

23 Genius hath electric power
Which earth can never tame.

> "Marius Amid the Ruins of Carthage" n.d.

24 Over the river and through the wood,
To grandfather's house we'll go.

> "Thanksgiving Day," St. 1 n.d.

857. Dorothea Dix (1802-1887)

1 I have myself seen more than nine thousand idiots, epileptics and insane in the United States . . . bound with galling chains, bowed beneath fetters, lacerated with ropes, scourged with rods.

> First Petition to Congress c. 1848

2 In a world where there is so much to be done, I felt strongly impressed that there must be something for me to do.

> Letter (31 December 1944), Letters from New York, Vol. II,
> Lydia Maria Child,* ed. 1852

*See 856.

3 I think even lying in my bed, I can still do something.

> Quoted in Twelve American Women by E. Anticaglia 1975

858. Marjory Fleming (1803–1811)

1 the most Devilish thing is 8 times 8 and 7 times 7 it is what nature itselfe cant endure. . . .

> Diary of Marjory Fleming (repr. 1934) 1811

2 love is a very
papithatick thing as well as
troublesom and tiresome. . . .

> Ibid.

3 Sentiment is what I am not acquainted with.

> Ibid.

4 I confess that I have been
more like a little young
Devil than a creature. . . .

> Ibid.

859. Flora Tristan (1803–1844)

1 Ne me demandez pas d'où je viens. (Do not ask from where I come.)

> Pt. I, Méphis 1838

2 In the future, when woman is conscious of her power, she will free herself from the need for social approval, and those little tricks which today aid her to deceive men, will become useless; when that time comes, woman will say:—"I choose this man for my lover, because my love will be a powerful force on his intelligence, and our happiness will be reflected on others."

> Pt. II, Ibid.

3 To love one's fellow-man is rational self-love.

> Ibid.

4 What a revolting contrast exists in England between the slavery of women and the intellectual superiority of women writers.

> Ch. 17, Promenades Dans Londres (London Walks) 1840

860. Sarah B. Judson (1803–1845)

1 Then gird thine armour on, love,
Nor faint thou by the way—

Till the Boodh* shall fall, and Burmah's sons
Shall own Messiah's sway.
> Poem to her husband, departing on a long voyage, St. 3
> (c.1845), Quoted in *Biography of Distinguished Women*
> by Sarah Josepha Hale** *1876*

*Buddha: Judson was a missionary in Burma. **See 788.

861. Marie Lovell (1803–1877)

1   PARTHENIA. Clear be mine eyes, and thou, my soul, be steel!
> Act I, *Ingomar, the Barbarian* 1896

2   INGOMAR. Freedom is hunting, feeding, danger;
that, that is freedom—that it is which makes
the veins to swell, the breast to heave and glow.
Aye, that is freedom,—that is pleasure—life!
> Act II, Ibid.

3   INGOMAR.—This slavery
that gives thee freedom, brings along with it
so rich a treasure of consoling joy,
liberty shall be poor and worthless by its side.
> Act V, Ibid.

862. Maria McIntosh (1803–1878)

1   Beneficent Nature, how often does the heart of man, crushed beneath the weight of his sins or his sorrows, rise in reproach against thine unchanged serenity!
> Ch. 1, *Two Lives* 1846

2   ". . . there is selfishness in our hearts as long as we live; but while you watch over yourself, and pray earnestly to God against it, He will give you power always to act generously— to subdue your selfish feelings."
> "Florence Arnott," *Aunt Kitty's Tales* 1847

3   "Now, Jessie, there is some beauty and some goodness in every thing God has made, and he who has a pure conscience is like one looking into a clear stream; he sees it all; while him who has a bad conscience, all things look as you say they did in the muddy stream—black and ugly."
> "Jessie Graham," Ibid.

4   To the inhabitants of the Southern States, not only the New Englander, but everyone who dwelt north of the Potomac was a Yankee—a name which was with him a synonym of meanness, avarice and low cunning—while the native of the Northern States regarded his southern fellow-citizens as an indolent and prodigal race, in comparison with himself but half civilized, and far better acquainted with the sword and the pistol than with any more useful instrument.
> Ch. 1, *The Lofty and the Lowly* 1852

5   ". . . it is only death which is hopeless. . . "
> Ch. 19, Ibid.

863. Sarah Power Whitman (1803–1878)

1   And evening trails her robes of gold
Through the dim halls of the night.
> "Summer's Call" *n.d.*

2   Star of resplendent front! Thy glorious eye
Shines on me still from out yon clouded sky.
> "Arcturus (To Edgar Allan Poe*)" *n.d.*

*American poet, author (1809–1849).

3   Raven from the dim dominions
On the Night's Plutonian shore,
Oft I hear thy dusky pinions
Wave and flutter round my door.
> "The Raven" *n.d.*

864. Maria W. Stewart (1803–1879)

1   What if I am a woman? Is not the god of ancient times the god of these modern days? Did he not raise up Deborah,* to be a mother, and a judge in Israel? Did not queen Esther** save the lives of the Jews?
> Introduction, Essay (1835), *Spiritual Narratives*,
> Sue E. Houchins *1988*

*See 27. **See 56.

2   O, ye daughters of Africa, awake! awake! arise! no longer sleep nor slumber, but distinguish yourselves. Show forth to the world that ye are endowed with noble and exalted faculties . . . How long shall the fair daughters of Africa be compelled to bury their minds and talents beneath a load of iron pots and kettles?
> "Religion and the Pure Principles of Morality" (1831), Ibid.

865. Clara Brown (1803–1885)

1   All churches do the Lord's work.
> Quoted in *Women Pioneers* by Rebecca Stefoff *1995*

866. Susanna Moodie (1803–1885)

1   I had heard and read much of savages, and have since seen, during my long residence in the bush, somewhat of uncivilized life, but the Indian is one of Nature's gentlemen—he never says or does a rude or vulgar thing. The vicious, uneducated barbarians, who form the surplus of overpopulace European countries, are far behind the wild man in delicacy of feeling or natural courtesy.
> Ch. 1, *Roughing It in the Bush* 1852

2   A nose, kind sir! Sure, Mother Nature,
With all her freaks, ne'er formed this feature.
If such were mine, I'd try and trade it,
And swear the gods had never made it.
> Ch. 6, "Old Satan and Tom Wilson's Nose," Ibid.

3   But hunger's good sauce.
> Ch. 12, Ibid.

4   "I have no wish for a second husband. I had enough of the first. I like to have my own way—to lie down mistress, and get up master."
> Ibid.

5   I have a great dislike to removing, which involves a necessary loss, and is apt to give to the emigrant roving and unsettled habits.
> Ibid.

6   The pure beauty of the Canadian water, the somber but August grandeur of the vast forest that hemmed us in on every side and shut us out from the rest of the world, soon cast a magic spell upon our spirits, and we began to feel charmed with the freedom and solitude around us.
> Ch. 13, Ibid.

7   When hands are tightly clasped, 'mid struggling sighs
And streaming tears, those whisper'd accents rise,

Leaving to God the objects of our care
In that short, simple, comprehensive prayer-
ADIEU!

Ch. 25, Ibid.

8 I have given you a faithful picture of a life in the backwoods of Canada. . . . To the poor, industrious working man it presents many advantages; to the poor gentleman, *none*! The former works hard, puts up with coarse, scanty fare, and submits, with a good grace, to hardships that would kill a domesticated animal at home. Thus he becomes independent. . . . The gentleman can neither work so hard, live so coarsely, nor endure so many privations as his poorer but more fortunate neighbor.

Ibid.

9 Ah, Hope! what would life be, stripped of thy encouraging smiles, that teach us to look behind the dark clouds of to-day, for the golden beams that are to gild the morrow.

Ch. 1, *Life in the Clearing* 1853

10 To wean a fellow-creature from the indulgence of a gross sensual propensity, as I said before, we must first convince the mind: the reform must commence there. Merely withdrawing the means of gratification, and treating a rational being like a child, will never achieve a great moral conquest.

Ch. 2, Ibid.

11 The want of education and moral training is the only real barrier that exists between the different classes of men. Nature, reason, and Christianity recognize no other. Pride may say Nay; but Pride was always a liar, and a great hater of the truth.

Ch. 3, Ibid.

12 This is my tale of woe; and if thou wilt
Be warn'd by me, this sparkling cup resign;
A serpent lurks within the ruby wine,
Guileful and strong as him who erst betray'd
The world's first parents in their bowers of joy.

Ibid.

13 What a wonderful faculty is memory!—the most mysterious and inexplicable in the great riddle of life; that plastic tablet on which the Almighty registers with unerring fidelity the records of being, making it the depository of all our words, thoughts and deeds—this faithful witness against us for good or evil.

Ch. 15, Ibid.

14 Large parties given to very young children, which are so common in this country [Canada], are very pernicious in the way in which they generally operate upon youthful minds. They foster the passions of vanity and envy, and produce a love of dress and display which is very repulsive in the character of a child.

Ch. 19, Ibid.

15 The emigrant's hope of bettering his condition, and securing a sufficient competence to support his family, to free himself from the slighting remarks too often hurled at the poor gentleman by the practical people of the world, which is always galling to a proud man, but doubly so when he knows that the want of wealth constitutes the sole difference between him and the more favoured offspring of the same parent stock.

"Canada: A Contrast" 1871

16 We left one by one
the cities rotting with cholera,
one by one our civilized

distinctions
and entered a large darkness.
It was our own
ignorance we entered

Quoted in *The Journals of Susanna Moodie* by Margaret Atwood* 1970

*See 2736.

867. Sarah Childress Polk (1803–1891)

1 It is only the hope that you can live through the campaign that gives me a prospect of enjoyment.

Letter to her husband, James Polk* (1843), Quoted in *First Ladies* by Betty Boyd Caroli 1987

*J—Knox P—(1795–1849), 11th president of the United States (1845–1849).

868. Delphine de Girardin (1804–1855)

1 Business is other people's money.

Marguerite, Vol. II 1852

869. George Sand (1804–1876)

1 She is Choice at odds with Necessity; she is Love blindly butting its head against all the obstacles set in its path by civilization.

Preface, *Indiana*, (1900 ed.; George Burnham Ives, tr.) 1832

2 "I know that I am a slave, and you are my lord. The law of this country has made you my master. You can bind my body, tie my hands, govern my actions: you are the strongest, and society adds to your power; but with my will, sir, you can do nothing. God alone can restrain it and curb it. Seek then a law, a dungeon, an instrument of torture, by which you can hold it, it is as if you wished to grasp the air, and seize vacancy."

Ibid.

3 . . . self-love is a part of love just as self-interest is a part of friendship.

Pt. 1, Ch. IV, Ibid.

4 "But that's just like the stupid jealousy of the ordinary husband! They imagine everything and understand nothing."

Ch. VIII, Ibid.

5 "You women are all false and cunning just for the pleasure of being so."

Pt. II, Ch. IX, Ibid.

6 "What I say," rejoined Sir Ralph, "is not meant to be philanthropic at all; my point is that selfishness properly understood leads us to do good to others to prevent them injuring us. I am selfish myself, as everybody knows. I have accustomed myself not to blush for it, and, after analyzing all the virtues, I find personal interest at the foundation of them all. Love and devotion, which are two apparently generous passions, are perhaps the most selfish passions that exist; nor is patriotism less so, my word for it. I care little for men; but not for anything in the world would I undertake to prove it to them, my fear of them is inversely proportional to my esteem for them. We are both selfish therefore but I admit it, whereas you deny it."

Ibid.

7 . . . nothing resembles selfishness more closely than self-respect.

Ch. XV, Ibid.

8   The wit of small towns is, as you doubtless know, the most ill-natured in the world. Good people are always misunderstood there, superior minds are sworn foes of the public.

Pt. III, Ch. XIX, Ibid.

9   "When I feel that I am caught in a woman's net, I cannot break it quickly enough, in order to recover my repose and mental tranquillity."

Ch. XXII, Ibid.

10   "If I listened to the voice which God has placed in the depths of my heart, and to the noble instinct of a bold and strong nature, which perhaps is the genuine conscience, I should fly to the desert, I should learn to do without help, protection and love: I should go and live for myself in the heart of our beautiful mountains: I should forget the tyrants, the unjust and the ungrateful."

Ch. XXIII, Ibid.

11   Love is woman's virtue; it is for love that she glories in her sins, it is from love that she acquires the heroism to defy her remorse. The more dearly it costs her to commit the crime, the more she will have deserved at the hands of the man she loves. It is like the fanaticism that places the dagger in the hand of the religious enthusiast.

Ch. XXVII, Ibid.

12   She hoped to die; but grief rivets the chain of life instead of breaking it.

Ch. XXIX, Ibid

13   "Where love is absent there can be no woman."

Lelia, Vol. I *1833*

14   I had forgotten how to be young, and Nature had forgotten to awaken me. My dreams had moved too much in the world of sublimity, and I could no longer descend to the grosser level of fleshly appetites. A complete divorce had come about, though I did not realize it, between body and spirit.

Vol. II, Ibid.

15   What led to my loving him for so long . . . was a feverish irritation which took possession of my faculties as a result of never achieving personal satisfaction.

Ibid.

16   As things are, they [women] are ill-used. They are forced to live a life of imbecility, and are blamed for doing so. If they are ignorant, they are despised, and if learned, mocked. In love they are reduced to the status of courtesans. As wives they are treated more as servants than as companions. Men do not love them: they make use of them, they exploit them, and expect, in that way, to make them subject to the law of fidelity.

"La Fauvette du Docteur" (November 1844),
Almanach du Mois November 1844

17   "And yet," plied my friend, "nature has not changed. The night is still unsullied, the stars still twinkle, and the wild thyme smells as sweetly now as it did then. . . . We may be afflicted and unhappy, but no one can take from us the sweet delight which is nature's gift to those who love her and her poetry."

Preface, *La Petite Fadette* 1848

18   No one makes a revolution by himself; and there are some revolutions, especially in the arts, which humanity, accomplishes without quite knowing how, because it is everybody who takes them in hand.

Preface, *The Haunted Pool* 1851

19   Art is not a study of positive reality, it is the seeking for ideal truth. . . .

Ch. 1, Ibid.

20   It is sad, no doubt, to exhaust one's strength and one's days in cleaving the bosom of this jealous earth, which compels us to wring from it the treasures of its fertility, when a bit of the blackest and coarsest bread is, at the end of the day's work, the sole recompense and the sole profit attaching to so arduous a toil.

Ch. 2, Ibid.

21   He who draws noble delights from the sentiments of poetry is a true poet, though he has never written a line in all his life.

Ibid.

22   "One never knows how much a family may grow; and when a hive is too full, and it is necessary to form a new swarm, each one thinks of carrying away his own honey."

Ch. 4, Ibid.

23   "Parents . . . sacrifice all the time of youth, which is the best, to foreseeing what will happen to one at the age when one is no longer good for anything, and when it makes little difference whether one ends in one way or another."

Ch. 13, Ibid.

24   For everything, alas! is disappearing. During even my own lifetime there has been more progress in the ideas and customs of my village than had been seen during centuries before the Revolution.

Appendix, Ibid.

25   It is extraordinary how music sends one back into memories of the past—and it is the same with smells.

The Story of My Life, Vol. I *1856*

26   . . . since it always happens that one gives form and substance to the dangers upon which one broods to excess, the dread of the possibility became an accurate forecast of the future.

Ibid.

27   Once my heart was captured [by religion], reason was shown the door, deliberately and with a sort of frantic joy. I accepted everything, I believed everything, without struggle, without suffering, without regret, without false shame. How can one blush for what one adores?*

Pt. 3, Ch. 14, Vol. III, Ibid.
*Reference to her newfound religious faith.

28   Marriage is the ultimate goal of love. When love ceases, or is absent from the beginning, all that remains is sacrifice. . . . All very well for those who understand sacrifice . . . there is probably no middle way between the strength of the great-hearted, and that convenient negative attitude in which the poor-spirited find refuge—or, rather, there is a middle way, and its name is despair.

Vol. IV, Ibid.

29   I regard as a mortal sin not only the lying of the senses in matters of love, but also the illusion which the senses seek to create where love is only partial. I say, I believe, that one must love with all of one's being, or else live, come what may, a life of complete chastity.

Pt. 5, Ch. 7, Ibid.

30   "I hated the pride of men of rank, and thought that I should be sufficiently avenged for their disdain if my genius raised me

above them. Dreams and illusions all! My strength has not equalled my mad ambition. I have remained obscure; I have done worse—I have touched success, and allowed it to escape me. I thought myself great, and I was cast down to the dust; I imagined that I was almost sublime, and I was condemned to be ridiculous. Fate took me—me and my audacious dreams—and crushed me as if I had been a reed. I am a most wretched man!"

"The Marquise" 1869

31 The whole secret of the study of nature lies in learning how to use one's eyes. . . .

Nouvelles Lettres d'un Voyageur 1869

32 Classification is Ariadne's clue through the labyrinth of nature.

Ibid.

33 The beauty that addresses itself to the eyes is only the spell of the moment; the eye of the body is not always that of the soul.

Ch. 1, *Handsome Lawrence* 1872

34 Consciousness lies in the consciousness we have of it, and by no means in the way the future keeps its promises.

Ch. 3, Ibid.

35 Universal suffrage, that is to say the expression of the will of all, whether for good or ill, is a necessary safety-valve. Without it, you will get merely successive outbreaks of civil violence. This wonderful guarantee of security is there to our hands. It is the best social counterweight so far discovered.

Ibid.

36 I have had my belly full of great men (forgive the expression). I quite like to read about them in the pages of Plutarch,* where they don't outrage my humanity. Let us see them carved in marble or cast in bronze, and hear no more about them. In real life they are nasty creatures, persecuters, temperamental, despotic, bitter and suspicious.

Correspondence, Vol. II *1883*
*Greek biographer and philosopher (46–120).

37 There is only one happiness in life, to love and be loved. . . .

Letter to Lina Calamatta (31 March 1862), Vol. IV, Ibid.

38 Faith is an excitement and an enthusiasm: it is a condition of intellectual magnificence to which we must cling as to a treasure, and not squander on our way through life in the small coin of empty words, or in exact and priggish argument. . . .

Letter to Des Planches (25 May 1866), Vol. V, Ibid.

39 One is happy as a result of one's own efforts, once one knows the necessary ingredients of happiness—simple tastes, a certain degree of courage, self denial to a point, love of work, and, above all, a clear conscience. Happiness is no vague dream, of that I now feel certain.

Letter, Ibid.

40 One wastes so much time, one is so prodigal of life, at twenty! Our days of winter count for double. That is the compensation of the old.

Letter to Joseph Dessauer (5 July 1868), Ibid.

41 Liszt* said to me today that God alone deserves to be loved. It may be true, but when one has loved a man, it is very different to love God.

(1834), *The Intimate Journal of George Sand* 1926
*Franz L—, Hungarian composer (1811–1886).

42 But if these people of the future are better than we are, they will, perhaps, look back at us with feelings of pity and tenderness for struggling souls who once divined a little of what the future would bring.

Ibid.

43 I have the feeling now that one changes from day to day, and that after a few years have passed one has completely altered. Examine myself as I may, I can no longer find the slightest trace of the anxious, agitated individual of those years, so discontented with herself, so out of patience with others.

Ibid.

44 He is unaware that any man who is adored as a god is deceived, mocked and flattered.

(3 June 1837), Ibid.

45 Immodest creature, you do not want a woman who will accept your faults, you want one who pretends that you are faultless—one who will caress the hand that strikes her and kiss the lips that lie to her.

Ibid.

46 One approaches the journey's end. But the end is a goal, not a catastrophe.

"Final Comment by George Sand" (September 1868), Ibid.

47 Stupid men—you who believe in laws which punish murder by murder and who express vengeance in calumny and defamation!

Ibid.

48 The trade of authorship is a viokent, and indestructible obsession.

Letter to Jules Boucoiran (4 March 1831),
The Letters of George Sand 1930

49 No religion can be built on force.

Quoted in *Women: A Journal of Liberation* Fall 1970

50 She prided herself on being educated, erudite and eccentric. She had read a little of everything, even of politics and philosophy, and it was curious to hear her bringing out as her own, for the delectation of the ignorant, things that she had read that same morning in a book, or had heard the night before from the lips of some serious-minded man of her acquaintance.

"Horace" *n.d.*

51 Men do not wish to be shown for what they are, nor to be made to laugh at the masks they have assumed. If you are no longer capable of love, then you must lie, or draw a veil so close about you that no eye can penetrate it. You must treat your heart as aging libertines treat their bodies—hide it beneath the disguise of paint and subterfuge.

"Sketches and Hints" *n.d.*

52 Education will in time be the same for men and women, but it will be in the female heart par excellence, as it always has been, that love and devotion, patience and pity, will find their true home. On woman falls the duty, in a world of brute passions, of preserving the virtues of charity and the Christian spirit. . . . When women cease to play that role, life will be the loser.

Impressions Littéraires n.d.

53 The old woman I shall become will be quite different from the woman I am now. Another *I* is beginning, and so far I have not had to complain of her.

Isadora, Vol. II *n.d.*

870. Sarah Flower Adams (1805–1848)

1 And joys and tears alike are sent
To give the soul fit nourishment.
As comes to me or cloud or sun,
Father! thy will, not mine, be done.

"He Sendeth Sun, He Sendeth Shower" *n.d.*

2 Though like the wanderer,
the sun gone down,
Darkness be over me,
my rest a stone;
Yet in my dreams I'd be
Nearer, my God, to Thee,
Nearer to Thee.

"Nearer, My God, to Thee," St. 2 *n.d.*

3 Once have a priest for enemy, goodbye
To peace.

Act III, Sc. 2, *Vivia Perpetua** n.d.*

*See 98.

871. Angelina Grimké (1805–1879)

1 So precious a talent as intellect never was given to be wrapt in a napkin and buried in the earth.

"Appeal to the Christian Women of the South," *The Anti-Slavery Examiner* September 1836

2 . . . When the books and papers of the Anti-Slavery Society were thrown out of the windows of the office, one individual laid hold of the Bible and was about tossing it out to the ground, when another reminded him that it was the Bible he had in his hand. "O! 'Tis all one," he replied, and out went the sacred volume, along with the rest. We thank him for the acknowledgment.

Ibid.

3 It is through the tongue, the pen, and the press that truth is principally propagated.

Ibid.

4 . . . there is something in the heart of man which *will bend under moral suasion*. There is a swift witness for truth in his bosom, which *will respond to truth* when it is uttered with calmness and dignity.

Ibid.

5 What was the conduct of Shadrach, Meshach, and Abednago? . . . Did these men *do right in disobeying the law* of their sovereign? Let their miraculous deliverance from the burning fiery furnace answer. . . .

Ibid.

6 I have not placed reading before praying because I regard it more important, but because, in order to pray aright, we must understand what we are praying for. . . .

Ibid.

7 If a law commands me to *sin I will break it*; if it calls me to *suffer*, I will let it take its course *unresistingly*. The doctrine of blind obedience and unqualified submission to any human power, whether civil or ecclesiastical, is the doctrine of despotism, and ought to have no place 'mong Republicans and Christians.

Ibid.

8 Slavery always has, and always will, produce insurrections wherever it exists, because it is a violation of the natural order of things, and no human power can much longer perpetrate it. . . .

Ibid.

9 Our fathers waged a bloody conflict with England, because *they* were taxed without being represented. . . . *They* were not willing to be governed by laws which *they* had no voice in making; but this is the way in which women are governed in this Republic.

Letter No. 11, *Letters to Catherine Beecher,**
Isaac Knapp, ed. *1836*

*See 849.

10 I am not afraid to trust my sisters—not I.

Ibid.

11 Hitherto, instead of being a help meet to man, in the highest, noblest sense of the term, as a companion, a co-worker, an equal; she has been a mere appendage of his being, an instrument of his convenience and pleasure, the pretty toy with which he whiled away his leisure moments, or the pet animal whom he humored into playfulness and submission.

Letter No. 12, Ibid.

12 When human beings are regarded as *moral* beings, *sex*, instead of being enthroned upon the summit, administering upon rights and responsibilities, sinks into insignificance and nothingness. . . .

Ibid.

13 I recognize no rights but *human* rights—I know nothing of men's rights and women's rights; for in Christ Jesus there is neither male nor female. It is my solemn conviction that, until this principle of equality is recognized and embodied in practice, the church can do nothing effectual for the permanent reformation of the world.

Ibid.

14 Ought God to be *all in all* to us on *earth*? I thought so, and am frightened to find He is not, that is, I feel something else is necessary to my happiness. I laid awake thinking why it was that my heart longed and panted and reached after you as it does. Why my Savior and my God is not enough to *satisfy* me. Am I sinning, am I ungrateful, *am I an IDOLATOR*? I trust I am not, and yet—but I cannot tell how I feel. I am a mystery to myself.

Letter to Theodore Dwight Weld (February 1938), *Letters of Theodore Dwight Weld,** Angelina Grimké Weld, and Sarah Grimké,*** 1822–1844*, Vol. II, Gilbert Hobbs Barnes and Dwight L. Dumonds, eds. *1934*
*American abolitionist (1803–1895). **See 812.

15 . . . thou art blind to the danger of marrying a woman who feels and acts out the principle of equal rights. . . .

Ibid.

872. Jeanne-Françoise Deroine (1805–1894)

1 Because the revolutionary tempest, in overturning at the same time the throne and the scaffold, in breaking the chain of the black slave, forgot to break the chain of the most oppressed of all—of Woman, the pariah of humanity. . . .

Letter from Prison of St. Lazare (Paris, 15 June 1851), written with Pauline Roland, *History of Woman Suffrage*, Vol. I, Elizabeth Cady Stanton,** Susan B. Anthony,*** and Mathilda Gage**** *1881*
*See 1125. **See 907. ***See 949. ****See 979.

2 We have, moreover, the profound conviction that only by the power of association based on solidarity—by the union of the working classes of both sexes to organize labor—can be ac-

quired, completely and pacifically, the civil and political equality of women, and the social right for all.

Ibid.

873. Flora Hastings (1806–1839)

1 Grieve not that I die young. Is it not well
To pass away ere life hath lost its brightness?

"Swan Song" *n.d.*

874. Mary Ann Dwight (1806–1858)

1 Janus was invoked at the commencement of most actions; even in the worship of the other gods the voterie began by offering wine and incense to Janus. The first month in the year was named from him; and under the title of Matutinus he was regarded as the opener of the day.

"Janus," *Grecian and Roman Mythology 1864*

875. Elizabeth Barrett Browning (1806–1861)

1 Eve is a twofold mystery. . . .

"The Poet's Vow," Pt. I, St. 1, *The Seraphim and Other Poems 1838*

2 Is it thus,
Ambition, idol of the intellect?

"The Student," 1.56, *Ibid.*

3 But since he had
The genius to be loved, why, let him have
The justice to be honored in his grave.

"Crowned and Buried," St. 27 (1838),
Athenoeum 4 July 1840

4 And lips say "God be pitiful,"
Who ne'er said "God be praised."

"The Cry of the Human," St. 1, *Graham's American Magazine 1842*

5 There Shakespeare, on whose forehead climb
The crowns o' the world: O eyes sublime
With tears and laughters for all time!

"A Vision of Poets," 1.298, *Poems of 1844 1844*

6 Life treads on life, and heart on heart;
We press too close in church and mart
To keep a dream or grave apart. . . .

Conclusion, 1.820, *Ibid.*

7 Poets ever fail in reading their own verses to their worth.

"Lady Geraldine's Courtship," St. 42, *Ibid.*

8 Then we talked—oh, how we talked! her voice so cadenced in
the talking,
Made another singing—of the soul! a music without bars . . .

St. 45, *Ibid.*

9 Experience, like a pale musician, holds
A dulcimer of patience in his hand . . .

"Perplexed Music," *Ibid.*

10 Thou large-brained woman and large-hearted man. . . .

"To George Sand,* A Desire," *Ibid.*

*See 869.

11 Our Euripides,* the human,
With his dropping of warm tears,

And his touches of things common
Till they rose to touch the spheres!

"Wine of Cyprus," St. 12, *Ibid.*

*Greek dramatist (480–406 B.C.E.).

12 I tell you, hopeless grief is passionless. . . .

"Grief," *Ibid.*

13 "Yes," I answered you last night;
"No," this morning, sir, I say:
Colors seen by candle-light
Will not look the same by day.

"The Lady's 'Yes'," St. 1, *Ibid.*

14 What I do
And what I dream includes thee, as the wine
Must taste of its own grapes.

Sonnets from the Portuguese, I *1850*

15 Go from me. Yet I feel that I shall stand
Henceforward in thy shadow.

VI, *Ibid.*

16 Say thou dost love me, love me, love me—toll
The silver iterance!—only minding, Dear,
To love me also in silence, with thy soul.

XXI, *Ibid.*

17 Because God's gifts put man's best dreams to shame.

XXVI, *Ibid.*

18 How do I love thee? Let me count the ways.
I love thee to the depth and breadth and height
My soul can reach. . . .

XLIII, *Ibid.*

19 I love thee with a love I seemed to lose
With my lost saints,—I love thee with the breath,
Smiles, tears, of all my life!—and, if God choose,
I shall but love thee better after death.

Ibid.

20 Alas, this Italy has too long swept
Heroic ashes up for hour-glass sand. . . .

Pt. I, l. 187, *Casa Guidi Windows 1851*

21 If we tried
To sink the past beneath our feet, be sure
The future would not stand.

l. 416, *Ibid.*

22 But "Live the People," who remained and must,
The unrenounced and unrenounceable.
Long live the people! How they lived! and boiled
And bubbled in the cauldron of the street. . . .

Pt. II, l. 115, *Ibid.*

23 Life, struck sharp on death,
Makes awful lightning.

Bk. I, l. 210, *Ibid.*

24 The beautiful seems right
By force of Beauty, and the feeble wrong
Because of weakness.

l. 753, *Ibid.*

25 Whoever love true life, will love true love.

l. 1066, *Ibid.*

26 Men do not think
Of sons and daughters, when they fall in love. . . .

Bk. II, l. 608, Ibid.

27 God answers sharp and sudden some prayers,
And thrusts the thing we have prayed for in our face,
A gauntlet with the gift in 't.—Every wish
Is like a prayer, with God.

l. 952, Ibid.

28 How many desolate creatures on the earth
Have learnt the simple dues of fellowship
And social comfort, in a hospital. . . .

Bk. III, l. 1122, Ibid.

29 For poets (bear the word),
Half-poets even, are still whole democrats. . . .

Bk. IV, l. 413, Ibid.

30 A little sunburnt by the glare of life. . . .

l. 1140, Ibid.

31 Measure not the work
Until the day's out and the labor done. . . .

Bk. V, l. 76, Ibid.

32 Men get opinions as boys learn to spell,
By reiteration chiefly. . . .

Bk. VI, l. 6, Ibid.

33 Since when was genius found respectable?

l. 275, Ibid.

34 Earth's crammed with heaven,
And every common bush afire with God;
But only he who sees, takes off his shoes—
The rest sit round it and pluck blackberries. . . .

Bk. VII, l .820, Ibid.

35 Genuine government
Is but the expression of a nation, good
Or less good—even as all society,
Howe'er unequal, monstrous, crazed and cursed,
Is but the expression of men's single lives,
The loud sum of the silent units.

Bk. VIII, l. 867, Ibid.

36 The thinkers stood aside
To let the nation act.

"Napoleon III in Italy," St. 3, *Poems Before Congress* 1860

37 And each man stands with his face in the light
Of his own drawn sword,
Ready to do what a hero can.

St. 8, Ibid.

38 The world goes whispering to its own,
"This anguish pierces to the bone;"
And tender friends go sighing round,
"What love can ever cure this wound?"
My days go on, my days go on.

"De Profundis," St. 5, *Last Poems* 1862

39 We walked too straight for fortune's end,
We loved too true to keep a friend;
At last we're tired, my heart and I.

"My Heart and I," St. 9,
Ibid.

40 "What a monster have we here?
A great Deed at this hour of day?
A great just Deed—and not for pay?
Absurd,—or insincere."

"A Tale of Villafrance," St. 4, *Athenoeum*
24 September 1859

876. Julia Pardoe (1806–1862)

1 Raising his truncheon above his head, he broke it in the centre, and throwing the pieces among the crowd, exclaimed in a loud voice, "Le roi est moi!" Then seizing another staff, he flourished it in the air as he shouted, "Vive le Roi!"

Life of Louis XIV, Vol. III 1947

2 The heart is a free and fetterless thing—
A wave of the ocean, a bird on the wing.

"The Captive Greek Girl" *n.d.*

877. Nomura Motoni (1806–1867)

1 The whistle of the samurai's arrow is changing today to the thunder of the cannon.

Untitled Poem *1855*

2 This is a world that cages all warblers with a beautiful voice.

Ibid.

3 Many are the victims of the waves that rush in, then out of the beach.

Ibid.

4 The song of the warbler, joyful at his release has drawn forth the cry of many other birds.

Ibid.

878. Juliette Drouet (1806–1883)

1 I love you [Victor Hugo] *because* I love you, because it would be impossible for me not to love you. I love you without question, without calculation, without reason good or bad, faithfully, with all my heart and soul, and every faculty.

(1833), *Letters to Victor Hugo* 1915
*French poet, novelist (1802–1885).

2 It is wicked of me to torment you, yet I cannot help myself. My offence goes by the name of "jealousy."

(1834), Ibid.

3 If I were a clever woman, my gorgeous bird, I could describe to you how you unite in yourself the beauties of form, plumage, and song!

(1835), Ibid.

4 Love exalts as much as glory does.

(21 January 1838), Ibid.

5 There are no wrinkles in the heart, and you will see my face only in the reflection of your attachment, eh, Victor, my beloved?

(19 November 1841), Ibid.

6 In my opinion, infidelity does not consist in action only; I consider it already accomplished by the sole fact of desire.

(4 April 1847), Ibid.

7 I come to fetch my heart where I left it, that is to say in yours.

(14 December 1881), Ibid.

879. Maria Weston Chapman (1806–1885)

1 As *wives* and *mothers*, as *sisters* and *daughters*, we are deeply responsible for the influence we have on the human race. We are bound to exert it; we are bound to urge man to cease to do evil, and learn to do well. We are bound to urge them to regain, defend and preserve inviolate the rights of all, especially those whom they have most deeply wronged.

Address, Boston Female Anti-Slavery Society, Quoted in *Liberator* 13 August 1836

2 Grudge no expense—yield to no opposition—forget fatigue— till, by the strength of prayer and sacrifice, the spirit of love shall have overcome sectional jealousy, political rivalry, prejudice against color, cowardly concession of principle, wicked compromise with sin, devotion to gain, and spiritual despotism. . . .

Ibid.

3 Let us rise in the moral power of womanhood; and give utterance to the voice of outraged mercy, and insulted justice, and eternal truth, and mighty love and holy freedom.

Ibid.

4 Custom is never, by her nature, the handmaid of freedom.

Right and Wrong in Massachusetts 1839

5 Slavery can only be abolished by raising the character of the people who compose the nation; and that can be done only by showing them a higher one.

Address, "How Can I Help to Abolish Slavery," New York 1855

6 My disgust was unutterable . . . at the stupid schemes by which selfish men were then, as now, trying to make capital for themselves out of the sacred cause of human rights. . . . Hear them clamorously and meanly taking advantage of ignorance, for the promotion of self-interest.

Ibid.

7 In a republican land the power behind the throne is *the* power.

Ibid.

8 Don't drag the engine, like an ignoramus, but bring wood and water and flame, like an engineer.

Ibid.

9 We may draw good out of evil; we must not do evil, that good may come.

Ibid.

880. Elizabeth Oakes Smith (1806–1893)

1 Faith is the subtle chain
which binds us to the infinite.

"Faith" *n.d.*

2 Yes, this is life, and everywhere we meet,
Not victor crowns, but wailings of defeat.

"The Unattained" *n.d.*

3 My friends, do we realize for what purpose we are convened? Do we fully understand that we aim at nothing less than an entire subversion of the present order of society, a dissolution of the whole existing social compact?

Speech *n.d.*

881. Harriet Taylor Mill (1807/08–1858)

1 We deny the right of any portion of the species to decide for another portion what is and what is not their 'proper sphere.'

The proper sphere for all human beings is the largest and highest which they are able to attain to.

Remark (1850), Quoted in *Women in World History Curriculum*, http://womeninworldhistory.com *1996–97*

882. Helen Dufferin (1807–1867)

1 The poor make no new friends.

"Lament of the Irish Immigrant" *1894*

2 They say there's bread and work for all,
And the sun shines always there:
But I'll not forget old Ireland,
were it fifty times as fair.

Ibid.

883. Lucretia Maria Davidson (1808–1825)

1 Shakespeare, with all thy faults, (and few have more,)
I love thee still, and still will con thee o'er.
Heaven in compassion to a man's erring heart,
Gave thee a virtue, then a vice, apart,
Lest we, in wonder here, should bow before thee,
Break God's commandment, worship, and adore thee.

Untitled (1823), Quotes in *Lives of Celebrated Women* by Samuel Griswold Goodrich *1844*

2 O, say, amid this wilderness of life,
What bosom would have throbbed like thine for me?
Who would have smiled responsive? Who, in grief,
Would e'er have felt, and, feeling, grieved like thee?

"To My Mother" (November 1824), Ibid.

3 There is something which I dread;
It is a dark and fearful thing;
It steals along with withering tread,
Or sweeps on wild destruction's wing.

That thought comes o'er me in the hour
Of grief, of sickness, or of sadness;
'Tis not the dread of death; 'tis more,—
It is the dread of madness.

Untitled (1825), Ibid.

884. Caroline Sheridan Norton (1808–1877)

1 God made all pleasures innocent.

Pt. I, *The Lady of LaGaraye 1862*

2 Until I truly loved, I was alone.

Pt. II, Ibid.

3 They serve God well, who serve his creatures.

Conclusion, Ibid.

4 . . . (for ere the moon be risen
My body will be out of pain—my soul be out of prison). . . .

"Bingen on the Rhine," St. 1 *1883*

5 O Friend, I fear the lightest heart makes sometimes heaviest mourning.

Ibid.

6 A soldier of the legion lay dying in Algiers—
there was a lack of woman's nursing,
There was a dearth of woman's tears.

Ibid.

7 I do not love thee!—no! I do not love thee!
   And yet when thou art absent I am sad.
                          "I Do Not Love Thee" *n.d.*

8 Love not! Love not! Ye hapless sons of clay;
   Hope's gayest wreaths are made of earthly flowers—
   Things that are made to fade and fall away,
   Ere they have blossomed for a few short years.
                          "Love Not" *n.d.*

9 My beautiful, my beautiful! That standest meekly by,
   With thy proudly-arched and glossy neck, and dark and fiery
       eye!
                 "The Arab's Farewell to His Steed" *n.d.*

10 The stranger hath thy bridle-rein, thy master hath his gold;—
   Fleet limbed and beautiful, farewell; thou'rt sold, my steed,
       thou'rt sold.
                          Ibid.

885. Frances Dana Gage (1808–1884)

1 The home we first knew on this beautiful earth,
   The friends of our childhood, the place of our birth,
   In the heart's inner chamber sung always will be,
   As the shell ever sings of its home in the sea.
                          "Home" *n.d.*

886. Fanny Kemble (1809–1893)

1 . . . children are made of eyes and ears, and nothing, however
   minute, escapes their microscopic observation.
            *Journal of a Residence on a Georgian Plantation in
            1838–1839,* John Scott, ed. *1961*

2 Just in proportion as I have found the slaves on this plantation intellectual and advanced beyond the general brutish level of the
   majority, I have observed this pathetic expression of countenance
   in them, a mixture of sadness and fear, the involuntary exhibition
   of the two feelings, which I suppose must be the predominant experience of their whole loves, regret and apprehension. . . .
                          Ibid.

3 This is no place for me, since I was not born among slaves,
   and cannot bear to live among them.
                          Ibid.

4 For the last four years of my life that preceded my marriage I
   literally coined money, and never until this moment, I think,
   did I reflect on the great means of good, to myself and others,
   that I so gladly agreed to give up forever for a maintenance by
   the unpaid labor of slaves—people toiling . . . unpaid.
                          Ibid.

5 A sacred burden is this life ye bear;
   Look on it; lift it; bear it solemnly;
   Fail not for sorrow; falter not for sin;
   But onward, upward, till the goal ye win.
            "Lines to the Young Gentlemen Graduates at Lenox
                          Academy, Massachusetts" *n.d.*

6 Nature lay frozen dead,—and still and slow,
   A winding sheet fell o'er her body fair,
   Flakey and soft, from his wide wings of snow.
                          "Winter" *n.d.*

7 Maids must be wives and mother, to fulfill
   The entire and holiest end of woman's being.
                          "Woman's Heart" *n.d.*

8 Better trust all and be deceived,
   And weep that trust, and that deceiving,
   Than doubt one heart that, if believed,
   Had blessed one's life with true believing.
                          "Faith" *n.d.*

9 What shall I do with all the days and hours
   That must be counted ere I see thy face?
   How shall I charm the interval that lowers
   Between this time and that sweet time of grace?
                          "Absence" *n.d.*

887. Addison (fl. c. 1810)

1 Why is the Ass so stubborn grown!
   How many mount and then are thrown!
   Oh say ! that men forget, alas!
   Their Saviour rode upon an Ass.
            "Written for a School-piece," St. 1, *Poetry on
                          Different Subjects n.d.*

2 Yet one thing still I would advise,
       As much as in your power lies,
   Your father's love to gain;
       And as for trifles never mind,
   This consolation you will find,
       Reflection without pain.
            "Advice to a Youth," St. 2, Ibid.

888. Dorothea Primrose Campbell (fl. c. 1810)

1 The winds of heaven are hushed and mild
   As the breath of a slumbering child
                          "Moonlight," *Poems 1816*

2 I dreamed not that a fairer spot
   On earth's broad bosom lay;
   Nor ever wished my wand'ring feet
   Beyond its bounds to stray.
            "Address to Zetland [the Shetlands]," St. 4, Ibid.

889. La Pola (fl. c. 1810)

1 Although I am a woman and young, I have more than enough
   courage to suffer this death and a thousand more.
            Statement before execution in wars of independence (1817),
                          Women in World History Curriculum,
            http://www.womeninworldhistory.com *1996–97*

890. Mrs. Henry Rolls (fl. c. 1810–1825)

1 Whence is that sad, that transient smile
       That dawns upon the lip of owe;
   That checks the deep-drawn sigh awhile,
       And stays the tear that starts to flow?
   'Tis but a veil cast o'er the heart,
       When youth's gay dreams have pass'd away
   When joy's faint lingering rays depart,
       And the last gleams of hope decay!
            "Smiles," Sts. 7–8, *The Female Poets of Great Britain,* Fred-
                          eric Rowton, ed. *1853*

891. Margaret Fuller (1810–1850)

1 And knowing that there exists, in the world of men, a tone of
   feeling towards women as towards slaves, such as is expressed
   in the common phrase, "Tell that to women and children.". . .
            "The Great Lawsuit. Man Versus Men. Woman Versus
                          Women," *The Dial July 1843*

2 For human beings are not so constituted, that they can live without expansion; and if they do not get it one way, must another, or perish.

Ibid.

3 The well-instructed moon flies not from her orbit to seize on the glories of her partner.

Ibid.

4 Harmony exists in difference no less than in likeness, if only the same key-note govern both parts.

Ibid.

5 The especial genius of women I believe to be electrical in movement, intuitive in function, spiritual in tendency.

Ibid.

6 Male and female represent the two sides of the great radical dualism. But, in fact, they are perpetually passing into one another. Fluid hardens to solid, solid rushes to fluid. There is no wholly masculine man, no purely feminine woman.

Ibid.

7 If the negro be a soul, if the woman be a soul, apparelled in flesh, to one master only are they accountable.

Ibid.

8 . . . not a few believe, and men themselves have expressed the opinion, that the time is come when Euridice is to call for an Orpheus, rather than Orpheus for Euridice; that the idea of man, however imperfectly brought out, has been far more so than that of woman, and that an improvement in the daughters will best aid the reformation of the sons of this age.

Ibid.

9 In every-day life the feelings of the many are stained with vanity. Each wishes to be lord in a little world, to be superior at least over one; and he does not feel strong enough to retain a lifelong ascendant over a strong nature. Only a Brutus would rejoice in a Portia. . . .

Ibid.

10 Plants of great vigor will almost always struggle into blossom, despite impediments. But there should be encouragement, and a free genial atmosphere for those of more timid sort, fair play for each in its own kind.

Ibid.

11 George Sand* smokes, wears male attire, wishes to be addressed as Mon frère; perhaps, if she found those who were as brothers indeed, she would not care whether she were a brother or sister.

Ibid.

*See 869.

12 "You are not the head of your wife. God has given her a mind of her own."

"I am the head and she is the heart."

"God grant you play true to one another then."

Ibid.

13 It is a vulgar error that love, a love, to woman is her whole existence; she is also born for Truth and Love in their universal energy.

Ibid.

14 What I mean by the Muse is that unimpeded clearness of the intuitive powers, which a perfectly truthful adherence to every admonition of the higher instinct would bring to a finely organized human being.

Woman in the 19th Century 1845

15 It should be remarked that, as the principle of liberty is better understood, and more nobly interpreted, a broader protest is made in behalf of women. As men become aware that few [of them] have had a fair chance, they are inclined to say that no women have had a fair chance.

Ibid.

16 What woman needs is not as a woman to act or rule, but as a nature to grow, as an intellect to discern, as a soul to live freely and unimpeded, to unfold such powers as were given her when we left our common home.

Ibid.

17 It does not follow because many books are written by persons born in America that there exists an American literature. . . . Before such can exist, an original idea must animate this nation and fresh currents of life must call into life fresh thoughts along its shores.

Quoted in the *New York Tribune* 1846

18 Truth is the nursing mother of genius.

Ibid.

19 . . . the public must learn how to cherish the nobler and rarer plants, and to plant the aloe, able to wait a hundred years for its bloom, or its garden will contain, presently, nothing but potatoes and pot-herbs.

Ibid.

20 Essays, entitled critical, are epistles addressed to the public, through which the mind of the recluse relieves itself of its impressions.

"A Short Essay on Critics," *Art, Literature and the Drama* 1858

21 It is not because the touch of genius has roused genius to production, but because the admiration of genius has made talent ambitious, that the harvest is still so abundant.

Ibid.

22 POET. Yes, that is always the way. You [critics] understand me, who never have the arrogance to pretend that I understand myself.

"A Dialogue," Ibid.

23 . . . there are two modes of criticism. One which. . . crushes to earth without mercy all the humble buds of Phantasy, all the plants that, though green and fruitful, are also a prey to insects or have suffered by drouth. It weeds well the garden, and cannot believe the weed in its native soil may be a pretty, graceful plant. There is another mode which enters into the natural history of every thing that breathes and lives, which believes no impulse to be entirely in vain, which scrutinizes circumstances, motive and object before it condemns, and believes there is a beauty in natural form, if its law and purpose be understood.

"Poets of the People," Ibid.

24 The lives of the musicians are imperfectly written for this obvious reason. The soul of the great musician can only be expressed in music. . . . We must read them in their works; this, true of artists in every department, is especially so of the high priestesses of sound.

"Lives of the Great Composers," Ibid.

25 We cannot have expression till there is something to be expressed.
"American Literature," Ibid.

26 This was one of the rye-bread days, all dull and damp without.
Ch. 7, Diary Entry, Quoted in *Life of Margaret Fuller-Ossoli*
by Thomas Wentworth Higginson,* ed. *1884*
*American author and editor (1823–1922).

27 For precocity some great price is always demanded sooner or
later in life.
Ch. 18, Ibid.

28 Genius will live and thrive without training, but it does not the
less reward the watering-pot and pruning-knife.
Diary entry, Ibid.

29 It is so true that a woman may be in love with a woman, and a
man with a man. It is pleasant to be sure of it, because it is undoubtedly the same love that we shall feel when we are angels,
when we ascend to the only fit place for the Mignons, where *sie
fragen nicht nach Mann und Weib* [they ask not about men and
women].
Quoted in *Margaret Fuller, Whetstone of Genius*
by Mason Wade *1940*

30 They [the Irish] are looked upon with contempt for their want
of aptitude in learning new things; their ready and ingenious
lying; their eye-service. These are the faults of an oppressed
race, which must require the aid of better circumstances
through two or three generations to eradicate. . . .
Untitled Essay, Quoted in *The Feminist Papers* by Alice
Rossi* *1973*
*See 2213.

31 I myself am more divine than any I see.
Letter to Emerson (1 March 1838), Ibid.

32 Beware of over-great pleasure in being popular or even
beloved.
Letter to her brother, Arthur (20 December 1840), Ibid.

33 What a difference it makes to come home to a child!
Letter to friends (1849), Ibid.

892. Elizabeth Gaskell (1810–1865)

1 What's the use of watching? A watched pot never boils.
Ch. 31, *Mary Barton 1848*

2 A man. . . is *so* in the way in the house!
Ch. 1, *Cranford 1851–1853*

3 Bombazine would have shown a deeper sense of her loss.
Ibid.

4 There, economy was always "elegant," and money-spending
always "vulgar," and ostentatious—a sort of sour grapeism,
which made us very peaceful and satisfied.
Ibid.

5 Correspondence, which bears much the same relation to personal intercourse that the books of dried plants I sometimes
see ("Hortus Siccus," I think they called the thing) do to the
living and fresh flowers in the lanes and meadows. . . .
Ch. 3, Ibid.

6 One gives people in grief their own way.
Ch. 6, Ibid.

7 A little credulity helps one on through life very smoothly.
Ch. 11, Ibid.

8 I'll not listen to reason. . . . Reason always means what someone else has got to say.
Ch. 14, Ibid.

9 A wise parent humours the desire for independent action, so
as to become the friend and advisor when his absolute rule
shall cease.
Ch. 15, *North and South 1855*

10 My heart burnt within me with indignation and grief; we could
think of nothing else. . . . All night long we had only snatches
of sleep, waking up perpetually to the sense of a great shock
and grief. Every one is feeling the same. I never knew so universal a feeling.*
Letter to Harvard professor Charles E. Norton
28 April 1865
*Reference to the news of Lincoln's assassination reaching En-
gland.

11 He had not an ounce of superfluous flesh on his bones, and
leanness goes a great way towards gentility.
Ch. 4, *Wives and Daughters 1866*

12 To be sure a stepmother to a girl is a different thing to a second wife to a man!
Ch. 6, Ibid.

13 How easy it is to judge rightly after one sees what evil comes
from judging wrongly!
Ch. 43, Ibid.

14 People may flatter themselves just as much by thinking that
their faults are always present to other people's minds, as if
they believe that the world is always contemplating their individual charms and virtues.
Ch. 50, Ibid.

15 Sometimes one likes foolish people for their folly, better than
wise people for their wisdom.
Ch. 54, Ibid.

893. Ernestine Rose (1810–1892)

1 Oh, she [Frances Wright*] had her reward!—that reward of
which no enemies could deprive her, which no slanders could
make less precious—the eternal reward of knowing that she
had done her duty; the reward of springing from the consciousness of right, of endeavoring benefit unborn generations.
Convention Speech, "Petitions Were Circulated" (1860),
History of Woman Suffrage, Vol. I, Elizabeth Cady Stanton,** Susan B. Anthony,*** and Mathilda Gage**** *1881*
*See 825. **See 907. ***See 949. ****See 979.

894. Frances Sargent Osgood (1811–1850)

1 Work—for some good, be it ever so slowly;
Cherish some flower, be it ever so lowly;
Labor!—all labor is noble and holy!
Let thy great deeds be thy prayer to thy god!
"Laborare Est Orare," St. 6 *n.d.*

895. Fanny Fern (1811–1872)

1 The way to a man's heart is through his stomach.
"Willis Parton" *n.d.*

896. Harriet Beecher Stowe (1811–1896)

1 What makes saintliness in my view, as distinguished from ordinary goodness, is a certain quality of magnanimity and greatness of soul that brings life within the circle of the heroic.

"The Cathedral," *Atlantic Monthly* (Boston) 1846

2 "Well, I've got just as much conscience as any man in business can afford to keep—just a little, you know, to swear by as 't were. . . . "

Ch. 1, *Uncle Tom's Cabin* 1852

3 So long as the law considers all these human beings, with beating hearts and living affections, only as so many *things* belonging to the master—so long as the failure, or misfortune, or imprudence, or death of the kindest owner, may cause them any day to exchange a life of kind protection and indulgence for one of hopeless misery and toil—so long it is impossible to make anything beautiful or desirable in the best-regulated administration of slavery.

Ibid.

4 "I b'lieve in religion, and one of these days, when I've got matters tight and snug, I calculate to 'tend to my soul, and them are matters: . . ."

Ch. 8, Ibid.

5 "Treat 'em like dogs, and you'll have dogs' works and dogs' actions. Treat 'em like men, and you'll have men's works."

Ch. 11, Ibid.

6 If ever Africa shall show an elevated and cultivated race—and come it must, some time, her turn to figure in the great drama of human improvement—life will awake there with a gorgeousness and splendour of which our cold western tribes faintly have conceived.

Ch. 16, Ibid.

7 "Cause I's wicked—I is. I's mighty wicked, any how. I can't help it."

Ch. 20, Ibid.

8 "Who was your mother?"
"Never had none!" said the child, with another grin.
"Never had any mother? What do you mean? Where were you born?"
"Never was born!" persisted Topsy. . . .
"Do you know who made you?"
"Nobody, as I knows on," said the child with a short laugh . . . "I 'spect I grow'd. Don't think nobody never made me."

Ibid.

9 Whipping and abuse are like laudanum: You have to double the dose as the sensibilities decline.

Ibid.

10 "Knows all that, Mas'r St. Clare; Mas'r's been too good: but, Mas'r, I'd rather have poor clothes, poor house, poor everything, and have 'em *mine*, then have the best, and have 'em any man's else! I had so, Mas'r; I think it's natur, Mas'r!"

Ch. 28, Ibid.

11 For how imperiously, how coolly, in disregard of all one's feelings, does the hard, cold, uninteresting course of daily reality move on!

Ibid.

12 Who can speak the blessedness of that first day of freedom? Is not the sense of liberty a higher and finer one than any of the five? To move, speak, and breathe, go out and come in, unwatched and free from danger! Who can speak the blessings of that rest which comes down on the free man's pillow, under laws which ensure to him the rights that God has given to man?

Ch. 37, Ibid.

13 No one is so thoroughly superstitious as the godless man.

Ch. 39, Ibid.

14 "Ah, Miss Nina, we mustn't 'spect more of folks than dere is in them."
"Expect? I don't expect."
"Well, bless you, honey, bless you, honey, when you knows what folks *is*, don't let's worry. Ye can't fill a quart cup out of a thimble, honey, no way you can fix it. Dere's just where 'tis."

Ch. 6, *Dred* 1856

15 "They breed like rabbits! What God Almighty makes such people for, I don't know! I suppose He does. But there's these poor miserable trash have children like sixty; and there's folks living in splendid houses, dying for children, and can't have any. If they do manage one or two, the scarlet-fever or whooping cough makes off with 'em. Lord bless me, things go on in a terrible mixed-up way in this world."

Ch. 17, Ibid.

16 "Oh, I think," said Clayton, "the African race evidently are made to excel in that department which lies between the sensuousness and the intellectual—what we call the elegant arts. These require rich and abundant animal nature, such as they possess; and if ever they become highly civilised, they will excel in music, dancing and elocution."

Ch. 29, Ibid.

17 He declared that the gold made in it [slavery] was distilled from human blood, from mother's tears, from the agonies and dying groans of gasping, suffocating men and women, and that it would sear and blister the soul of him that touched it; in short, he talked as whole-souled, impractical fellows are apt to talk about what respectable people sometimes do. Nobody had ever instructed him that a slave-ship, with a procession of expectant sharks in its wake, is a missionary institution, by which closely-packed heathen are brought over to enjoy the light of the Gospel.

Ch. 1, *The Minister's Wooing* 1859

18 So we go, so little knowing what we touch and what touches us as we talk! We drop out a common piece of news, "Mr. So-and-so is dead, Miss Such-a-one is married, such a ship has sailed," and lo, on our right hand or on our left, some heart has sunk under the news silently—gone down in the great ocean of Fate, without even a bubble rising to tell its drowning pang. And this—God help us!—is what we call living!

Ch. 4, Ibid.

19 And ever and anon came on the still air the soft eternal pulsations of the distant sea—sound mournfulest, most mysterious, of all the harpings of Nature. It was the sea—the deep, eternal sea—the treacherous, soft, dreadful, inexplicable sea. . . .

Ch. 5, Ibid.

20 There are some people who receive from Nature as a gift a sort of graceful facility of sympathy, by which they incline to take on, for the time being, the sentiments and opinions of those with whom they converse, as the chameleon was fabled to change its hue with every surrounding. Such are often supposed to be willfully acting a part, as exerting themselves to flatter and deceive, when in fact they are only framed so sensitive to the sphere of

mental emanation which surrounds others that it would require an exertion not in some measure to harmonize with it. In approaching others in conversation, they are like a musician who joins a performer on an instrument—it is impossible for them to strike a discord; their very nature urges them to bring into play faculties according in vibration with those another is exerting.

Ch. 16, Ibid.

21 All systems [of thought] that deal with the infinite are, besides, exposed to danger from small, unsuspected admixtures of human error, which become deadly when carried to such vast results. The smallest speck of earth's dust, in the focus of an infinite lens, appears magnified among the heavenly orbs as a frightful monster.

Ch. 23, Ibid.

22 One would like to be grand and heroic, if one could; but if not, why try at all? One wants to be very something, very great, very heroic; or if not that, then at least very stylish and very fashionable. It is this everlasting mediocrity that bores me.

"Dress, or Who Makes the Fashions?," *Atlantic Monthly* (Boston) *1864*

23 . . . women are the real architects of society.

Ibid.

24 The pain of discipline is short, but the glory of the fruition is eternal.

"The Cathedral," Ibid.

25 In a good old age, Death, the friend, came and opened the door of this mortal state, and a great soul, that had served a long apprenticeship to little things, went forth into the joy of its Lord; a life of self-sacrifice and self-abnegation passed into a life of endless rest.

Ibid.

26 . . . she never saw her hero, and so never married.

Ibid.

27 Many a humble soul will be amazed to find that the seed it sowed in weakness, in the dust of daily life, has blossomed into immortal flowers under the eye of the Lord.

Ibid.

28 . . . these remarkable women of olden times are like the ancient painted glass—the art of making them is lost; my mother was less than her mother, and I am less than my mother.

"The Lady Who Does Her Own Work," Ibid.

29 Slavery, it is true was to some extent introduced into New England, but it never suited the genius of the people, never struck deep root, or spread so as to choke the good seed of self-helpfulness. . . . People, having once felt the thorough neatness and beauty of execution which came of free, educated, and thoughtful labor, could not tolerate the clumsiness of slavery.

Ibid.

30 Everyone confesses in the abstract that exertion which brings out all the powers of body and mind is the best thing for us all; but practically most people do all they can to get rid of it, and as a general rule nobody does much more than circumstances drive them to do.

Ibid.

31 "Take us the foxes, the little foxes, that spoil the vines: for our vines have tender grapes." . . . "Little Foxes," by which I mean those unsuspected, unwatched, insignificant *little* causes that

nibble away domestic happiness, and make home less than so noble an institution should be. . . . The reason for this in general is that home is a place not only of strong affections, but of entire unreserve; it is life's undress rehearsal, its backroom, its dressing room, from which we go forth to more careful and guarded intercourse, leaving behind us much *debris* of cast-off and everyday clothing.

Ch. 1, *Little Foxes 1865*

32 Irritability is, more than most unlovely states, a sin of the flesh. . . . It is a state of nervous torture; and the attacks which the wretched victim makes on others are as much a result of disease as the snapping and biting of a patient convulsed with hydrophobia.

Ch. 2, Ibid.

33 The bitterest tears shed over graves are for words left unsaid and deeds left undone.

Ibid.

34 I am speaking now of the highest duty we owe our friends, the noblest, the most sacred—that of keeping their own nobleness, goodness, pure and incorrupt. . . . If we *let* our friend become cold and selfish and exacting without a remonstrance, we are no true lover, no true friend.

Ibid.

35 A little reflection will enable any person to detect in himself that *setness in trifles* which is the result of the unwatched instinct of self-will and to establish over himself a jealous guardianship.

Ch. 4, Ibid.

36 Now, if the principle of toleration were once admitted into classical education—if it were admitted that the great object is to read and enjoy a language, and the stress of teaching were placed on the few things absolutely essential to this result, if the tortoise were allowed time to creep, and the bird permitted to fly, and the fish to swim, towards the enchanted and divine sources of Helicon—all might in their own way arrive there, and rejoice in its flowers, its beauty, and its coolness.

Ch. 5, Ibid.

37 Every human being has some handle by which he may be lifted, some groove in which he was meant to run; and the great work of life, as far as our relations with each other are concerned, is to lift each one by his own proper handle, and run each one in his own proper groove.

Ibid.

38 "For my part," said my wife, "I think one of the greatest destroyers of domestic peace is Discourtesy. People neglect, with their nearest friends, those refinements and civilities which they practice with strangers."

Ch. 6, Ibid.

39 One must be very much of a woman for whom a man can sacrifice the deepest purpose of his life without awakening to regret it.

Ch. 2, *Old Town Folks 1869*

40 The burning of rebellious thoughts in the little breast, of internal hatred and opposition, could not long go on without slight whiffs of external smoke, such as mark the course of subterranean fire.

Ch. 11, Ibid.

897. Sarah Boyle (1812–1869)

1 Here I come creeping, creeping everywhere. . . .

"The Voice of Grass" *n.d.*

898. Sarah Ellis (1812–1872)

1 To act the part of a true friend requires more conscientious feeling than to fill with credit and complacency any other station or capacity in social life.

Ch. 4, Pictures of Private Life 1834

899. Geraldine Jewsbury (1812–1880)

1 I wish that I had a good husband and a dozen children! Only the difficulty is that "women of genius" require very special husbands—men of noble character, not intellect, but of a character and nature large enough, and strong enough, and wise enough to take them and their genius too, without cutting them down to suit their own crochets, or reprobating half their qualities because they don't know what to do with them, or what they are intended for.

Selections from the Letters of Geraldine E. Jewsbury to Jane Welsh Carlyle, Ireland, ed. 1892

*See 853.

900. Ann Preston (1813–1872)

1 Wherever it is proper to introduce women as patients, there also it is in accordance with the instinct of truest womanhood for women to appear as physicians and students.

Quoted in The Liberated Woman's Appointment Calendar, Lynn Sherr and Jurate Kazickas, eds. 1975

901. Ellen Wood (1813–1887)

1 Petty ills try the temper worse than great ones.

Ch. 1, East Lynne (novel) 1861

2 Years ago, by dint of looking things steady in the face, and by economizing, he might have retrieved his position; but he had done what most people do in such cases—put off the evil day *sine die,* and gone on increasing his enormous list of debts. The hour of exposure and ruin was now advancing fast.

Ibid.

3 When folks act childishly, they must be treated as children.

Ch. 37, Ibid.

4 Nothing but stabs; nothing but stabs! Was her punishment ever to end?

Ch. 40, Ibid.

5 LEVISON. But there are moments when our hearts' dearest feelings break through the conventionalities of life, and betray themselves in spite of our sober judgement.

Act II, Sc. 1, East Lynne (play) 1862

6 ARCHIBALD. A woman may almost as well love herself as suffer herself to love unsought.

Ibid.

7 LEVISON. All stratagems are fair in love and war.

Act III, Sc. 2, Ibid.

8 "Afflictions are of two kinds—as I class them. The one we bring upon ourselves, through our own misconduct; the other is laid upon us by God for our real advantage. Yes, my boys, we receive many blessings in disguise. Trouble of this sort will only serve to draw out your manly energies, to make you engage vigorously in the business of life, to strengthen your self-dependence and your trust in God."

Ch. 3, The Channings, Vol. I 1862

9 Things often seem to go by the rule of contrary.

Ch. 8, Ibid.

10 One thing is certain: that natures are not all formed to *feel* in a like degree. While the shock of some great trouble, whether anticipated or falling unexpectedly, as the case may happen, is passed over lightly by one man—hardly seen when it comes; to another it is as a terrible agony, shattering the spirit for the time, leaving its marks until death.

Our Children 1876

11 Life has become to the most of us one swift, headlong race—a continuous fight in which there is so much to do that the half of it has to be left undone. . . . It is not so much what we have done amiss, as what we have left undone, that will trouble us, looking back.

Ibid.

12 We are truly indefatigable in providing for the needs of the body, but we starve the soul.

Ch. 1, About Ourselves 1883

902. Esther Hobart Morris (1813/4–1902)

1 Justice first, then after that the law.

Quoted in The 50 Most Influential Women in American Law by Dawn Bradley Berry 1996

*See 3435.

2 I have assisted in drawing a grand and petit jury, deposited a ballot, and helped canvass the voters after the electing, and in performing all those duties I do not know as I have neglected my family any more than in ordinary shopping.

Quoted in the Laramie Sentinel (1871), Ibid.

903. Elizabeth Phelps (1815–1852)

1 She found out there was no doctor for her like Dr. "Have-To."

"What Sent One Husband to California," The Tell-Tale 1853

2 "You gentleman," said she, "have such odd ideas of *housecleaning*! You imagine you can do it up just as you buy and sell—so much labor for so much money. Now, the fact is, the simple labor is the easiest part of it. It is the getting ready for labor—contriving, planning, arranging—that is so wearisome."

"The Old Leather Portfolio," Ibid.

3 Put in *your* oar, and share the sweat of the brow with which you must both start up the stream. You will richly enjoy the rest when you reach the harbor.

"First Trials of a Young Physician," Ibid.

904. Eliza Farnham (1815–1864)

1 Our own theological Church, as we know, has scorned and vilified the body till it has seemed almost a reproach and a shame to have one, yet at the same time has credited it with power to drag the soul to perdition.

Pt. I, Ch. 1, Woman and Her Era 1864

2 Again the human face is the organic seat of beauty. . . . It is the register of value in development, a record of Experience, whose legitimate office is to perfect the life, a legible language to those who will study it, of the majestic mistress, the soul. . . .

Ibid.

3   The ultimate aim of the human mind, in all its efforts, is to become acquainted with Truth.

> *Ibid.*

4   Each of the Arts whose office it is to refine, purify, adorn, embellish, and grace life is under the patronage of a Muse, no god being found worthy to preside over them.

> *Pt. II, Ch. 1, Ibid.*

905. Julia Margaret Cameron (1815–1879)

1   I longed to arrest all beauty that came before me, and at length the longing has been satisfied.

> *Annals of My Glass House 1874*

906. Anne Botta (1815–1891)

1   The honey-bee that wanders all day long . . .
Seeks not alone the rose's glowing breast,
The lily's dainty cup, the violet's lips,
But from all rank and noxious weed he sips
The single drop of sweetness closely pressed
Within the poison chalice.

> *"The Lesson of the Bee" n.d.*

907. Elizabeth Cady Stanton (1815–1902)

1   To make laws that men cannot, and will not obey, serves to bring all law into contempt.

> *Address 1861*

2   . . . we still wonder at the stolid incapacity of all men to understand that woman feels the invidious distinctions of sex exactly as the black man does those of color, or the white man the more transient distinctions of wealth, family, position, place, and power; that she feels as keenly as man the injustice of disfranchisement.

> *History of Woman Suffrage*, Vol. 1, with Susan B. Anthony*
> and Mathilda Gage** *1881*
> *See 949. **See 979.

3   Like all disfranchised classes, they began by asking to have certain wrongs redressed, and not by asserting their own right to make laws for themselves.

> *Ibid.*

4   But if a chivalrous desire to protect woman has always been the mainspring of man's dominion over her, it should have prompted him to place in her hands the same weapons of defense he has found to be most effective against wrong and oppression.

> *Ibid.*

5   In a republic where all are declared equal an ostracised class of half of the people, on the ground of a distinction founded in nature, is an anomalous position, as harassing to its victims as it is unjust, and as contradictory as it is unsafe to the fundamental principles of a free government.

> *Ibid.*

6   And here is the secret of the infinite sadness of women of genius; . . . [she] must ever be surprised and aggravated with his assumptions of leadership and superiority, a superiority she never concedes, an authority she utterly repudiates.

> *Ibid.*

7   The mind always in contact with children and servants, whose aspirations and ambitions rise no higher than the roof that shelters it, is necessarily dwarfed in its proportions.

> *Ibid.*

8   . . . the woman is uniformly sacrificed to the wife and mother.

> *Ibid.*

9   The more complete the despotism, the more smoothly all things move on the surface.

> *Ibid.*

10   *Declaration of Sentiments.* Now, in view of this entire disfranchisement of half the people of this country, through social and religious degradation—in view of the unjust laws above mentioned, and because women do feel themselves aggrieved, oppressed, and fraudulently deprived of their most sacred rights, we insist that they have immediate admission to all the rights and privileges which belong to them as citizens of the United States.

> *Ibid.*

11   *Declaration of Sentiments: Resolved,* That the same amount of virtue, delicacy, and refinement of behavior that is required of woman in the social station, should also be required of man, and the same transgressions should be visited with equal severity on both man and woman.

> *Ibid.*

12   It requires philosophy and heroism to rise above the opinion of the wise men of all nations and races. . . .

> *Ibid.*

13   Womanhood is the great fact in her life; wifehood and motherhood are but incidental relations.

> *Ibid.*

14   But the love of offspring . . . tender and beautiful as it is, can not as a sentiment rank with conjugal love.

> *Ibid.*

15   Two pure souls fused into one by an impassioned love—friends, counselors—a mutual support and inspiration to each other amid life's struggles, must know the highest human happiness;—this is marriage; and this is the only corner-stone of an enduring home.

> *Ibid.*

16   They who give the world a true philosophy, a grand poem, a beautiful painting or statue, or can tell the story of every wandering star . . . have lived to a holier purpose than they whose children are of the flesh alone, into whose minds they have breathed no clear perceptions of great principles, no moral aspiration, no spiritual life.

> *Ibid.*

17   Modern inventions have banished the spinning-wheel, and the same law of progress makes the woman of to-day a different woman from her grandmother.

> *Ibid.*

18   *Declaration of Sentiments*: . . . We hold these truths to be self-evident: that all men and women are created equal. . . .

> *Ibid.*

19   *Declaration of Sentiments: Resolved,* That all laws which prevent women from occupying such a station in society as her conscience shall dictate, or which place her in a position inferior to that of man, are contrary to the great precept of nature, and therefore of no force or authority.

> *Ibid.*

20   But standing alone we learned our power; we repudiated man's counsels forevermore; and solemnly vowed that there should

never be another season of silence until we had the same rights everywhere on this green earth, as man.

Ibid.

21 The prolonged slavery of women is the darkest page in human history.

Ibid.

22 . . . woman's discontent increases in exact proportion to her development.

Ibid.

23 Whenever the skilled hands and cultured brain of women have made the battle of life easier for man, he has readily pardoned her sound judgment and proper self-assertion.

Ibid.

24 The queens in history compare favorably with the kings.

Ibid.

25 . . . there is no force in the plea, that "if women vote they must fight." Moreover, war is not the normal state of the human family in its higher development, but merely a feature of barbarism lasting on through the transition of the race, from the savage to the scholar.

Ibid.

26 Reformers can be as bigoted and sectarian and as ready to malign each other, as the Church in its darkest periods has been to persecute its dissenters.

"The Kansas Campaign of 1867," *Ibid.*

27 The *ennui* and utter vacuity of a life of mere pleasure is fast urging fashionable young women to something better. . . .

"The Newport Convention," *Ibid.*

28 The tyrant, Custom, has been summoned before the bar of Common-Sense. His majesty no longer awes the multitude—his sceptre is broken—his crown is trampled in the dust—the sentence of death is pronounced upon him.

Speech, New York State Legislature (1854), *Ibid.*

29 Thus far women have been the mere echoes of men. Our laws and constitutions, our creeds and codes, and the customs of social life are all of masculine origin. The true woman is as yet a dream of the future.

Speech, International Council of Women *1888*

30 Religious superstitions of women perpetuate their bondage more than all other adverse influences . . .

Ibid.

31 The Bible teaches that woman brought sin and death into the world, that she precipitated the fall of the race, that she was arraigned before the judgement seat of Heaven, tried, condemned and sentenced. Marriage for her was to be a condition of bondage, maternity a period of suffering and anguish, and in silence and subjection, she was to play the role of a dependent on man's bounty for all her material wants. . . .

Pt. I, *Ibid.*

32 So long as tens of thousands of Bibles are printed every year, and circulated over the whole habitable globe, and the masses in all English-speaking nations revere it as the word of God, it is vain to belittle its influence.

Ibid.

33 If the Bible teaches the equality of women, why does the church refuse to ordain women to preach the gospel, to fill the offices of deacons and elders, and to administer the Sacraments...?

Ibid.

34 Why is it more ridiculous to arraign ecclesiastics for their false teaching and acts of injustice to women, than members of Congress and the House of Commons?

Ibid.

35 For so far-reaching and momentous a reform as her complete independence, an entire revolution in all existing institutions is inevitable.

Ibid.

36 Reformers who are always compromising, have not yet grasped the idea that truth is the only safe ground to stand upon.

Ibid.

37 The Bible and Church have been the greatest stumbling blocks in the way of woman's emancipation.

Quoted in *Free Thought Magazine* September *1896*

38 The memory of my own suffering has prevented me from ever shadowing one young soul with the superstitions of the Christian religion.

Eighty Years and More 1898

39 We found nothing grand in the history of the Jews nor in the morals inculcated in the Pentateuch. . . . I know of no other books that so fully teach the subjection and degradation of woman.

Ch. 24, *Ibid.*

40 They smiled at each other, and one said, "Well, after all, a mother's instinct is better than a man's reason." "Thank you, gentlemen, there was no instinct about it. I did some hard thinking. . . ."

Eighty Years and More, rev. ed. *1902*

41 Besides the obstinancy of the nurse, I had the ignorance of the physicians to contend with.

Ibid.

42 Though motherhood is the most important of all the professions—requiring more knowledge than any other department in human affairs—there was no attention given to preparation for this office.

Ibid.

43 So closely interwoven have been our lives, our purposes, and experiences that, separated, we have a feeling of incompleteness—united, such strength of self-assertion that no ordinary obstacles, differences, or dangers ever appear to us insurmountable.

Ibid.

44 I am at a boiling point! If I do not find someday the use of my tongue on this question I shall die of an intellectual repression, a woman's rights convulsion.

Elizabeth Cady Stanton, Vol. II, Theodore Stanton and Harriot Stanton Blatch, eds. *1922*

45 I never felt more keenly the degradation of my sex. To think that all in me of which my father would have felt a proper pride had I been a man, is deeply mortifying to him because I am a woman.

Ibid.

46 I think if women would indulge more freely in vituperation, they would enjoy ten times the health they do. It seems to me they are suffering from repression.

Ibid.

47 Last evening we spoke of the propriety of women being called by the names which are used to designate their sex, and not by those assigned to males. . . . I have very serious objections, dear Rebecca, to being called Henry. There is a great deal in a name. . . . The custom of calling women Mrs. John This and Mrs. Tom That, and colored men Sambo and Zip Coon, is founded on the principle that white men are lords of all. I cannot acknowledge this principle as just; therefore, I cannot bear the name of another.

Letter to Rebecca R. Eyster (1 May 1847), Ibid.

48 Women's degradation is in man's idea of his sexual rights.

Letter to Susan B. Anthony* (1860), Ibid.
*See 949.

49 I shall not grow conservative with age.

Ibid.

50 I have no sympathy with the old idea that children owe such immense gratitude to their parents that they can never fulfill their obligations to them. I think the obligation is all on the other side. Parents can never do too much for their children to repay them for the injustice of having brought them into the world, unless they have insured them high moral and intellectual gifts, fine physical health, and enough money and education to render life something more than one ceaseless struggle for necessities.

Diary entry (1880), Ibid.

51 I have come to the conclusion that the first great work to be accomplished for women is to revolutionize the dogma that sex is a crime, marriage a defilement and maternity a bane.

Diary entry (1881), Ibid.

52 I have been into many of the ancient cathedrals—grand, wonderful, mysterious. But I always leave them with a feeling of indignation because of the generations of human beings who have struggled in poverty to build these altars to the unknown god.

Diary entry (1882), Ibid.

53 I am weary seeing our laboring classes so wretchedly housed, fed, and clothed, while thousands of dollars are wasted every year over unsightly statues. If these great men must have outdoor memorials let them be in the form of handsome blocks of buildings for the poor.

Diary entry (1886), Ibid.

54 Our trouble is not our womanhood, but the artificial trammels of custom under false conditions. We are, as a sex, infinitely superior to men, and if we were free and developed, healthy in body and mind, as we should be under natural conditions, our motherhood would be our glory. That function gives women such wisdom and power as no male ever can possess. When women can support themselves, have their entry to all the trades and professions, with a house of their own over their heads and a bank account, they will own their bodies and be dictators in the social realm.

Diary entry (1890), Ibid.

55 I asked them why . . . one read in the synagogue service every week the 'I thank thee, O lord, that I was not born a woman.' " . . . It is not meant in an unfriendly spirit, and it is not in-tended to degrade or humiliate women." "But it does, nevertheless. Suppose the service read, 'I thank thee, O Lord, that I was not born into a jackass.' Could that be twisted in any way into a compliment to the jackass?"

Diary entry (1895), Ibid.

56 Men as a general rule have very little reverence for trees.

Diary entry (1900), Ibid.

57 I do not know whether the world is quite willing or ready to discuss the question of marriage. . . . I feel, as never before, that this whole question of women's rights turns on the pivot of the marriage relation, and, mark my word, sooner or later it will be the topic for discussion. I would not hurry it on, nor would I avoid it.

Letter to Susan B. Anthony* (1853), *Feminism: The Essential Historical Writings*, Miriam Schneir,** ed. 1972
*See 949. **See 2538.

58 We who like the children of Israel have been wandering in the wilderness of prejudice and ridicule for forty years feel a particular tenderness for the young women on whose shoulders we are about to leave our burdens.

Speech, International Council of Women (1888), Ibid.

59 No matter how much women prefer to lean, to be protected and supported, nor how much men desire to have them do so, they must make the voyage of life alone, and for safety in an emergency, they must know something of the laws of navigation.

Speech, "Solitude of Self," House Judiciary Committee (1892), Ibid.

60 Whatever is done to lift woman to her true position will help to usher in a new day of peace and perfection for the race.

Quoted in *Women Suffragists* by Diana Star Helmer 1998

61 In writing, we did better work together than either could alone. . . . She* supplied the facts and statistics, I the philosophy and rhetoric . . .

Ibid.

*Reference to Susan B. Anthony; see 949.

62 . . . one of the best gifts of the gods . . . a good, faithful housekeeper . . . But for this noble, self-sacrificing woman,* much of my public work would have been quite impossible.

Ibid.

*Amelia Willard, who worked for the Stantons for 31 years.

63 Surely a government of the most virtuous, educated men and women would better represent the whole, and protect the interests of all than could the representation of either sex alone.

Ibid.

64 I get more radical as I grow older, while [Susan*] seems to get more conservative.

Ibid.

*S—B. Anthony; see 949.

65 [Victoria Woodhull*] is a grand, brave woman [who] has done a work for women that none of us could have done. . . . She has risked and realized the sort of ignominy that would have paralyzed any of us . . . with a steadfast faith that glorious principle would triumph at last.

Ibid.

*See 1051.

66 . . . put it down in capital letters: SELF-DEVELOPMENT IS A HIGHER DUTY THAN SELF-SACRIFICE. The thing which

most retards and militates against women's self-development is self-sacrifice.

> Remark to reporter, Quoted in *In a Different Voice* by Carol Gilligan* 1982

*See 2628.

908. Harriet Tubman (1815/21?–1913)

1 I had crossed the line. I was *free*; but there was no one to welcome me to the land of freedom. I was a stranger in a strange land; and my home, after all, was down in Maryland; because my father, my mother, my brothers, and sisters, and friends were there. But I was free, and *they* should be free. I would make a home in the North and bring them there, God helping me.

> Quoted in *Scenes in the Life of Harriet Tubman* by Sarah H. Bradford 1869

2 When I found I had crossed dat *line*, I looked at my hands to see if I was de same pusson. There was such a glory ober ebery ting; de sun came like gold through the trees, and ober the fields, and I felt like I was in Heaben.

> Ibid.*

3 Don't you think we colored people are entitled to some credit for that exploit, under the lead of the brave Colonel Montgomery? We weakened the rebels somewhat on the Combahee River, by taking and bringing away *seven hundred and fifty-six* head of their most valuable live stock, known up in your region as "contrabands," and this, too, without the loss of a single life on our part, though we had good reason to believe that a number of rebels bit the dust. Of these seven hundred and fifty-six contrabands, nearly or quite all the able-bodied men have joined the colored regiments here. . . .

> Article in the *Boston Commonwealth* (30 June 1863), Ibid.

4 I tink dar's many a slaveholder'll git to Heaven. Dey don't know no better. Dey acts up to de light dey hab. You take dat sweet little child—'pears more like an angel dan anything else—take her down dere, let her nebber know nothing 'bout niggers but they was made to be whipped, an' she'll grow up to use the whip on 'em jus' like de rest. No, Missus, it's because dey don't know no better.

> Ibid.*

*Quotations have been printed as they appear in *Scenes from the Life of Harriet Tubman*. One assumes that the difference in the use of the vernacular and standard English has to do with the various scribes who recorded the events.

5 I had reasoned this out in my mind, there was two things I had a right to, liberty and death. If I could not have one, I would have the other, for no man should take me alive.

> Quoted in "Lost Women: Harriet Tubman—The Moses of her People" by Marcy Galen, *Ms.* (New York) August 1973

6 I never ran my train off the track, and I never lost a passenger.

> ThinkQuest, http://library.advanced.org/10320/ Tubman.html 1995

909. Ellen Sturgis Hooper (1816–1841)

1 I slept, and dreamed that life was Beauty;
I woke, and found that life was Duty.

> "Beauty and Duty" n.d.

2 The straightest path perhaps which may be sought,
Lies through the great highway men call "I ought."

> "The Straight Road" n.d.

910. Charlotte Brontë (1816–1855)

1 The human heart has hidden treasures,
In secret kept, in silence sealed;—
The thoughts, the hopes, the dreams, the pleasures,
Whose charms were broken if revealed.

> St. 1, "Evening Solace," *Poems by Currer, Ellis and Acton Bell** 1846

*Pseudonyms of Charlotte, Emily B— (see 917) and Anne B— (see 938).

2 Life, believe, is not a dream
So dark as sages say;
Oft a little morning rain
Foretells a pleasant day.

> "Life," St. 1 1846

4 Vain favour! coming, like most other favours long deferred and often wished for, too late!

> Ch. 3, *Jane Eyre* 1847

5 Consistency, madam, is the first of Christian duties.

> Ch. 4, Ibid.

6 It is in vain to say human beings ought to be satisfied with tranquility: they must have action; and they will make it if they cannot find it.

> Ch. 12, Ibid.

7 Little girl, a memory without blot or contamination must be an exquisite treasure—an inexhaustible source of pure refreshment: is it not?

> Ch. 14, Ibid.

8 "Dread remorse when you are tempted to err, Miss Eyre: remorse is the poison of life."

> Ibid.

9 "I grant an ugly *woman* is a blot on the fair face of creation; but as to the *gentlemen*, let them be solicitous to possess only strength and valour: let their motto be:—Hunt, shoot, and fight: the rest is not worth a fillip."

> Ch. 17, Ibid.

10 "Reason sits firm and holds the reins, and she will not let the feelings burst away and hurry her to wild chasms. The passions may rage furiously, like true heathens, as they are; and the desires may imagine all sorts of vain things, but judgment shall still have the last word in every argument, and the casting vote in every decision."

> Ch. 19, Ibid.

11 ". . . as much good-will may be conveyed in one hearty word as in many."

> Ch. 21, Ibid.

12 Feeling without judgment is a washy draught indeed; but judgment untempered by feeling is too bitter and husky a morsel for human deglutition [*sic*].

> Ibid.

13 "Laws and principles are not for the times when there is no temptation: they are for such moments as this, when body and soul rise in mutiny against their rigour; stringent are they; inviolate they shall be. If at my individual convenience I might break them, what would be their worth?"

> Ch. 28, Ibid.

14 The soul, fortunately, has an interpreter—often an unconscious, but still a truthful interpreter—in the eye.

> Ibid.

15 One does not jump, and spring, and shout hurrah! at hearing one has got a fortune, one begins to consider responsibilities, and to ponder business; on a base of steady satisfaction rise certain grave cares, and we contain ourselves, and brood over our bliss with a solemn brow.

Ch. 33, Ibid.

16 Reader, I married him.

Ch. 38, Ibid.

17 Prejudices, it is well known, are most difficult to eradicate from the heart whose soil has never been loosened or fertilized by education; they grow there, firm as weeds among stones.

Ibid.

18 An abundant shower of curates has fallen upon the north of England.

Ch. 1, Shirley 1849

19 Give him rope enough and he will hang himself.

Ch. 3, Ibid.

20 Look twice before you leap.

Ch. 9, Ibid.

21 But this I know; the writer who possesses the creative gift owns something of which he is not always master—something that at times strangely wills and works for itself. . . . If the result be attractive, the World will praise you, who little deserve praise; if it be repulsive, the same World will blame you, who almost as little deserve blame.

Preface, Quoted in *Wuthering Heights*
by Emily Brontë* 1850

*Her sister; see 917.

22 Alfred and I intended to be married in this way almost from the first; we never meant to be spliced in the hum-drum way of other people.

Ch. 42, Villete 1853

23 Yes—there is no Emily in Time or on Earth now—yesterday— we put her poor, wasted mortal frame quietly under the Church pavement. . . . —we feel she is at peace—no need now to tremble for the hard frost and keen wind—Emily does not feel them. She has died in a time of promise—we saw her taken from life in its prime—but it is God's will and the place where she is gone is better than that she has left.*

Letter to her friend, Ellen Nussey (23 December 1848),
Quoted in *The Brontës: A Life in Letters*
by Juliet Barker 1998

*See 917, Emily Brontë

911. Frances Brown (1816–1864/79)

1 It was the richest city in all the land; merchants from every quarter came there to buy and sell, and there was a saying that people had only to live seven years in it to make their fortunes. Rich as they were, however, Snowflower thought she had never seen so many discontented, covetous faces as looked out from the great shops, grand houses, and fine coaches . . .

Ch. 1, Granny's Wonderful Chair 1857

2 Oh! those blessed times of old! with their chivalry and state;
I love to read their chronicles, which such brave deeds relate. . . .

"Oh! The Pleasant Days of Old," St. 7 n.d.

912. Charlotte Saunders Cushman (1816–1876)

1 To me it seems as if when God conceived the world, that was Poetry; He formed it, and that was Sculpture; He colored it, and that was Painting, He peopled it with living beings, and that was the grand, divine, eternal Drama.

Quoted in *Charlotte Cushman* by Emma Stebbins 1879

2 Art is an absolute mistress; she will not be coquetted with or slighted; she requires the most entire self-devotion, and she repays with grand triumphs.

Ch. 10, Ibid.

3 There is a God! The sky his presence snares,
His hand upheaves the billows in their mirth,
Destroys the mighty, yet the humble spares
And with contentment crowns the thought of worth.

"There Is a God" n.d.

913. Priscilla Cooper Tyler (1816–1889)

1 I am considered "charmante" by the Frenchmen, "lovely" by the Americans and "really quite nice, you know" by the English.

Letter, Quoted in *First Ladies* by Betty Boyd Caroli 1987

914. Eliza "Mother" Stewart (1816–1908)

1 No power on earth or above the bottomless pit has such influence to terrorize and make cowards of men as the liquor power. Satan could not have fallen on a more potent instrument with which to thrall the world. Alcohol is king!

Ch. 1, Memories of the Crusade 1888

2 But you must know the class of sweet women—who are always so happy to declare "they have all the rights they want"; "they are perfectly willing to let their husbands vote for them"—are and always have been numerous, though it is an occasion for thankfulness that they are becoming less so.

Ch. 7, Ibid.

915. Jane Montgomery Campbell (1817–1879)

1 We plough the fields and scatter
The good seed on the land,
But it is fed and watered
By God's Almighty hand.

"We Plough the Fields," Garland of Songs n.d.

916. Mary Elizabeth Hewitt (1818–?)

1 A sumptuous dwelling the rich man hath.
And dainty is his repast;
But remember that luxury's prodigal hand
Keeps the furnace of toil in blast.

"A Plea for the Rich Man," St. 3, Poems 1853

2 Then hail! thou noble conqueror!
That, when tyranny oppressed,
Hewed for our fathers from the wild
A land wherein to rest.

"The Axe of the Settler," St. 5, Ibid.

3 . . . and what is life, alas!
But of the visions that we see?
Shadows of love, and hope, that pass
To mock us, like my dream of thee.

"Leonora Thinking of Tasso," Sts. 4–5, Ibid.

4 And I shall hear thy sound resound,
Till from his shackles man shall bound
And shout exultant, "LIBERTY!"
"The Songs of Our Land," St. 12, Ibid.

917. Emily Brontë (1818–1848)

1 No coward soul is mine,
No trembler in the world's storm-troubled sphere:
I see Heaven's glories shine,
And faith shines equally, arming me from fear.
"Last Lines," *Poems by Currer, Ellis, and Acton Bell** 1846
*Pseudonyms of Charlotte B— (see 910), Emily B— and Anne B—
(see 938).

2 Vain are the thousand creeds
That move men's hearts: unutterably vain. . . .
Ibid.

3 There is not room for Death.
Ibid.

4 Faithful, indeed, is the spirit that remembers
After such years of change and suffering!
"Remembrance" 1846

5 Once drinking deep of that divinest anguish,
How could I seek the empty world again?
Ibid.

6 Sleep not, dream not; this bright day
Will not, cannot, last for aye;
Bliss like thine is bought by years
Dark with torment and with tears.
"Sleep Not," St. 1 1846

7 Oh! dreadful is the check—intense the agony—
When the ear begins to hear, and the eye begins to see;
When the pulse begins to throb, the brain to think again;
The soul to feel the flesh, and the flesh to feel the chain.
"The Prisoner" 1846

8 I'll walk where my own nature would be leading—
It vexes me to choose another guide. . . .
"Often Rebuked" 1846

9 Love is like the wild-rose briar;
Friendship like the holly-tree.
The holly is dark when the rose-briar blooms,
But which will bloom most constantly?
"Love and Friendship" 1846

10 I've dreamt in my life dreams that have stayed with me ever after, and changed my ideas . . . and altered the color of my mind.
Wuthering Heights 1847

11 "Wretched inmates!" I ejaculated, mentally, "you deserve perpetual isolation from your species for your churlish inhospitality."
Ch. 2, Ibid.

12 "I am now quite cured of seeking pleasure in society, be it country or town. A sensible man ought to find sufficient company in himself."
Ch. 3, Ibid.

13 "A person who has not done one half his day's work by ten o'-clock, runs a chance of leaving the other half undone."
Ch. 7, Ibid.

14 A good heart will help you to a bonny face, my lad . . . and a bad one will turn the bonniest into something worse than ugly.
Ch. 7, Ibid.

15 Proud people breed sad sorrows for themselves.
Ibid.

16 "My love for Linton is like the foliage in the woods: time will change it, I'm well aware, as winter changes the trees. My love for Heathcliff resembles the eternal rocks beneath: a source of little visible delight, but necessary. Nelly, I *am* Heathcliff!"
Ch. 9, Ibid.

17 Having levelled my palace, don't erect a hovel and complacently admire your own charity in giving me that for a home.
Ch. 11, Ibid.

18 The tyrant grinds down his slaves and they don't turn against him, they crush those beneath them.
Ibid.

19 Any relic of the dead is precious, if they were valued living.
Ch. 13, Ibid.

20 Good things lost amid a wilderness of weeds, to be sure, whose rankness far over-topped their neglected growth; yet, notwithstanding, evidence of a wealthy soil, that might yield luxuriant crops under other and favourable circumstances.
Ch. 18, Ibid.

21 I lingered round them [tombstones], under that benign sky: watched the moths fluttering among the heath and harebells; listened to the soft wind breathing through the grass; and wondered how anyone could ever imagine unquiet slumbers for the sleepers in that quiet earth.
Conclusion, Ibid.

918. Elizabeth Prentiss (1818–1878)

1 Sleep, baby, sleep!
Thy father's watching the sheep,
Thy mother's shaking the dreamland tree,
And down drops a little dream for the.
Sleep, baby, sleep.
"Cradle Song" *n.d.*

919. Emily Collins (1818?–1879?)

1 It is ever thus; where Theology enchains the soul, the Tyrant enslaves the body.
Quoted in "Reminiscences of Emily Collins," *History of Woman Suffrage*, Vol. I, by Elizabeth Cady Stanton,
* Susan B. Anthony,** and Mathilda Gage*** 1881
*See 907. **See 949. ***See 979.

2 Every argument for the emancipation of the colored man was equally one for that of women; and I was surprised that all Abolitionists did not see the similarity in the condition of the two classes.
Ibid.

3 From press, and pulpit, and platform, she was taught that "to be unknown was her highest praise," that "dependence was her best protection," and "her weakness her sweetest charm."
Ibid.

4   . . . from the earliest dawn of reason I pined for that freedom of thought and action that was then denied to all womankind. I revolted in spirit against the customs of society and the laws of the State that crushed my aspirations and debarred me from the pursuit of almost every object worthy of an intelligent, rational mind.

Ibid.

5   Moral Reform and Temperance Societies may be multiplied *ad infinitum*, but they have about the same effect upon the evils they seek to cure as clipping the top of a hedge would have toward extirpating it.

Letter to Sarah C. Owen (23 October 1848), Ibid.

6   People are more willing to be convinced by the calm perusal of an argument than in a personal discussion.

Ibid.

920. Mary Todd Lincoln (1818–1882)

1   The change from this gloomy earth, to be forever reunited to my idolized husband & my darling Willie, would be happiness indeed!

Letter to Mrs. Slataper (29 September 1868), *The Mary Lincoln Letters*, Justin G. Turner, ed. *1956*

2   I am convinced, the longer I live, that life & its blessings are not so entirely unjustly distributed [as] when we are suffering greatly, we are inclined to suppose. My home for so many years was so rich in love and happiness; now I am so lonely and isolated—whilst others live on in a careless lukewarm state—not appearing to fill Longfellow's* measure: "Into each life, some rain must fall."

Ibid.

*Henry Wadsworth L—American poet (1807–1882).

3   Beautiful, glorious Scotland, has spoilt me for every other country!

Letter (21 August 1869), Ibid.

4   My evil genius Procrastination has whispered me to tarry 'til a more convenient season.

Letter (June 1841), *Mary Todd Lincoln: Her Life and Letters*, Justin G. Turner, ed. *1972*

5   My feelings & hopes are all so sanguine that in this dull world of reality 'tis best to dispell our delusive daydreams as soon as possible.

Letter to Mercy Levering (23 July 1840), Ibid.

6   Clouds and darkness surround us, yet Heaven is just & the day of triumph will *surely* come, when justice & truth will be vindicated. Our wrongs will be made right, & we will once more, taste the blessings of freedom, of which the degraded rebels, would deprive us.

Letter to James Gordon Bennet (October 25, 1861), Ibid.

921. Eliza Cook (1818–1889)

1   Better build schoolrooms for "the boy,"
     Than cells and gibbets for "the man."

"A Song for the Ragged Schools," St. 12 *n.d.*

2   I love it—I love it, and who shall dare
     To chide me for loving that old Arm-chair?

"The Old Arm-Chair" *n.d.*

3   Oh! much may be done by defying
     The ghosts of Despair and Dismay;

And much may be gained by relying
     On "Where there's a will there's a way."

"Where There's a Will There's a Way," St. 4 *n.d.*

4   Let Reason become your employer,
     And your body be ruled by your soul.

St. 3, Ibid., *n.d.*

5   Though language forms the preacher,
     'Tis "good works" make the man.

"Good Works" *n.d.*

6   'Tis well to give honour and glory to Age,
     With its lessons of wisdom and truth;
     Yet who would not go back to the fanciful page,
     And the fairytale read but in youth?

"Stanzas" *n.d.*

7   Whom do we dub as Gentleman? The
          Knave, the fool, the brute—
     If they but own full tithe of gold, and
          Wear a courtly suit.

"Nature's Gentleman," St. 1 *n.d.*

8   'Tis a glorious charter, deny it who can,
     That's birthed in the words, "I'm an Englishman."

"An Englishman" *n.d.*

9   Who would not rather trust and be deceived?

"Love On," St. 16 *n.d.*

10   Oh, how cruelly sweet are the echoes that start
     When Memory plays an old tune on the heart!

"Old Dobbin," St. 16, *The Journal*, Vol. IV *n.d.*

11   There's a star in the West* that shall never go down
     Till the Records of Valour decay,
     We must worship its light though it is not our own,
     For liberty burst in its ray.

"There's a Star in the West" *n.d.*

*Reference to George Washington (1732–1799), first president of United States (1789–1797).

12   On what strange stuff Ambition feeds!

"Thomas Hood"* *n.d.*

*British poet and editor (1799–1845).

13   Oh! Better, then, to die and give
     The grave its kindred dust,
     Than live to see Time's bitter change
     In those we love and trust.

"Time's Changes" *n.d.*

922. Maria Mitchell (1818–1889)

1   Why can not a man act himself, be himself, and think for himself? It seems to me that naturalness alone is power; that a borrowed word is weaker than our own weakness, however small we may be.

Diary entry (1867), *Maria Mitchell, Life, Letters, and Journals*, Phoebe Mitchell Kendall, ed. *1896*

2   We travel to learn; and I have never been in any country where they did not do something better than we do it, think some thoughts better than we think, catch some inspiration from heights above our own.

Diary entry (July 1873), Ibid.

3 For women there are, undoubtedly, great difficulties in the path, but so much the more to overcome. First, no woman would say, "I am but a woman!" But a woman! what more can you ask to be?

> Address to students (1874), Ibid.

4 This ignorance of the masses leads to a misconception in two ways; the little that a scientist can do, they do not understand—they suppose him to be god-like in his capacity, and they do not see results; they overrate him and they underrate him—they underrate his work.

> Diary entry (1874), Ibid.

5 The whole system is demoralizing and foolish. Girls study for prizes and not for learning, when "honors" are at the end. The unscholarly motive is wearying. If they studied for sound learning, the cheer which would come with every day's gain would be health-preserving.

> Address to students (13 March 1882), Ibid.

6 . . . to-day I am ready to say, "Give no scholarships at all." I find a helping-hand lifts the girl as crutches do; she learns to like the help which is not self-help. If a girl has the public school, and wants enough to learn, she will learn. It is hard, but she was born to hardness—she cannot dodge it. Labor is her inheritance.

> Diary entry (10 February 1887), Ibid.

7 Health of body is not only an accompaniment of health and mind, but is the cause; the converse may be true—that health of mind causes health of body; but we all know that intellectual cheer and vivacity act upon the mind. If the gymnastic exercise helps the mind, the concert or the theater improves the health of the body.

> Ibid.

8 . . . I do think, as a general rule, that teachers talk too much! A book is a very good institution! To read a book, to think it over, and to write our notes is a useful exercise; a book which will not repay some hard thought is not worth publishing.

> Diary entry (July 1887), Ibid.

9 Every formula which expresses a law of nature is a hymn of praise to God.

> Inscription on bust in the Hall of Fame, Bronx, N.Y. 1905

10 The eye that directs the needle in the delicate meshes of embroidery will equally well bisect a star with the spider web of the micrometer . . .

> Quoted in 4000 Years of Women in Science,
> http://www.astr.ua.edu/4000WS 27 September 1997

923. Lucy Stone (1818–1893)

1 The right to vote will yet be swallowed up in the real question, viz: has woman a right to herself? It is very little to me to have the right to vote, to own property, etc., if I may not keep my body, and its uses, in my absolute right.

> Letter to Antoinette Brown* 1855
> *Antoinette Brown Blackwell; see 975.

2 The widening of woman's sphere is to improve her lot. Let us do it, and if the world scoff, let it scoff—if it sneer, let it sneer. . . .

> Speech, "Disappointment Is the Lot of Women," (17–18
> October, 1855), History of Woman Suffrage, Vol. 1,
> Elizabeth Cady Stanton,* Susan B. Anthony**
> and Mathilda Gage*** 1881
> *See 907. **See 949. ***See 979.

3 I know not what you believe of God, but I believe He gave yearnings and longings to be filled, and that He did not mean all our time should be devoted to feeding and clothing the body.

> Ibid.

4 In education, in marriage, in religion, in everything, disappointment is the lot of women. It shall be the business of my life to deepen this disappointment in every woman's heart until she bows down to it no longer.

> Ibid.

5 We want rights. The flour-merchant, the house-builder, and the postman charge us no less on account of our sex; but when we endeavor to earn money to pay all of these, then, indeed, we find the difference.

> Ibid.

6 I expect some new phases of life this summer, and shall try to get the honey from each moment.

> Quoted in Antoinette Brown Blackwell:
> *Biographical Sketch by Sarah Gilson 1909
> *See 975.

7 Because I know that I shall suffer, shall I, for this, like Lot's wife, turn back? No, mother, if in this hour of the world's need I should refuse to lend my aid, however small it may be, I should have no right to think myself a Christian, and I should forever despise Lucy Stone. If, while I hear the wild shriek of the slave mother robbed of her little ones, or the muffled groan of the daughter spoiled of her virtue, I do not open my mouth for the dumb, am I not guilty?

> Letter to her mother (c.1847), Quoted in Ch. 6,
> Morning Star, Pt. II by Elinor Rice Hayes* 1961
> *See 1793.

8 I was a woman before I was an abolitionist. I must speak for the women.

> Letter to her mother (c. 1848), Ibid.

9 "We, the people of the United States." Which "We, the people?" The women were not included.

> Speech (New York Tribune, April 1853), Ibid.

10 My heart aches to love somebody that shall be all its own . . . [but] I shall not be married ever. I have not yet seen the person whom I have the slightest wish to marry, and if I had, it will take longer than my lifetime for the obstacles to be removed which are in the way of a married woman having any being of her own.

> Letter to Nettie Brown (1853), Ch. 9, Ibid.

11 I think God rarely gives to one man, or one set of men, more than *one* great moral victory to win.

> (c. 1867), Ch. 19, Pt. III, Ibid.

12 Our victory is sure to come, and I can endure anything but recreancy to principle.

> Ibid.

13 There was only one will in our home, and that was my father's.

> Quoted in Women Suffragists by Diana Star Helmer 1998

14 The great majority of women are more intelligent, better educated, and far more moral than multitudes of men whose right to vote no man questions.

> Ibid.

15 These men ought not to be allowed to vote before we do, because they will be just so much dead weight to lift.*
> Letter to Susan B. Anthony,** Ibid.
> *Reference to the 15th Amendment granting African-American men enfranchisement. **See 949.

16 Woman must marry for a home, and you men are the sufferers by this; for a woman who loathes you may marry you because you have the means to get money which she cannot have. But when woman can enter the lists with you and make money for herself, she will marry you only for deep and earnest affection. . . .
> Speech, National Women's Rights Convention (Cincinnati, 1855), Ibid.

17 For these years, I can only be a mother—no trivial thing, either. . . . This work will be worthy work to leave as my last.
> Letter to Antoinette Brown* (c. 1857), Ibid.
> *Antoinette Brown Blackwell; see 975.

18 Make the world better.
> Last words, spoken to her daughter Alice Stone Blackwell (18 October 1893), Ibid.

924. Amelia Jenks Bloomer (1818–1894)

1 Another cannot make fit to eat without wine or brandy. A third must have brandy on her apple dumplings, and a fourth comes out boldly and says she likes to drink once in a while too well. What flimsy excuses these! brandy and apple dumplings forsooth! That lady must be a wretched cook indeed who cannot make apple dumplings, mince pie, or cake palatable without the addition of poisonous substances.
> *Water Bucket* 1842

2 Like the beautiful flower from which it derives its name, we shall strive to make *The Lily* [a newspaper] the emblem of "sweetness and purity"; and may heaven smile on our attempt to advocate the great cause of Temperance reform!
> *The Lily* 1 January 1849

3 Man represents us, legislates for us, and now holds himself accountable for us! How kind in him, and what a weight is lifted from us! We shall no longer be answerable to the laws of God or man, no longer be subject to punishment for breaking them, no longer be responsible for any of our doings.
> Ibid.

4 Ah, how steadily do they who are guilty shrink from reproof!
> Ibid.

5 The costume of women should be suited to her wants and necessities. It should conduce at once to her health, comfort, and usefulness; and, while it should not fail also to conduce to her personal adornment, it should make that end of secondary importance.
> Letter to Charlotte A. Joy *3 June 1857*

6 Every woman who is tied to a confirmed drunkard should sunder the ties, and if she do it not otherwise, the law should compel it, especially if she has children.
> Speech, Woman's State Temperance Society Convention (Rochester, New York, Spring 1852), Quoted in *Women Suffragists* by Diana Star Helmer *1998*

7 It will not do to say that it is out of woman's sphere to assist in making laws, for if that were so, then it should be also out of her sphere to submit to them.
> Speech, Council Bluffs Methodist Church (Iowa, 7 December 1855), Ibid.

8 Why was the Negro made a voter?* Because, until he became such, there was no guarantee that his emancipation from slavery would not prove a cheat and a fraud.
> Letter to editors, Council Bluffs (Iowa, February 1867), Ibid.
> *Reference the 15th Amendment, giving African-American *males* the right to vote.

9 If women obeyed, ministers would have but few listeners.
> Speech, Ibid.

10 Adam first, then Eve, they say. To this we reply: Animals first—then Adam.
> Ibid.

11 Stitch! Stitch! Stitch!
in poverty, hunger and dirt—
sewing at once with a double thread
a shroud as well as a shirt.
> Song, sung during speech, Ibid.

12 Alas! Poor Adam! While it required all the persuasive powers and eloquence of the subtle tempter, all the promises of wisdom and knowledge and power to seduce the so-called "weaker" vessel from the right path, all that was necessary to secure *his* downfall was simply to offer him the apple.
> Speech, Ibid.

13 If then home be, indeed, the sphere of Woman, why has Man so wholly failed to make her supreme within its limits?
> Ibid.

925. Mrs. Cecil Frances Alexander (1818–1895)

1 Jesus calls us, o'er the tumult
Of our life's wild, restless sea.
> "Jesus Calls Us" *n.d.*

2 All things bright and beautiful,
All creatures great and small,
All things wise and wonderful,
The Lord God made them all.
> "All Things Bright" *n.d.*

3 The rich man at his castle,
The poor man at his gate,
God made them, high and lowly,
And ordered their estate.
> Ibid.

926. Mary A. E. Green (1818?–1895)

1 Of all the royal daughters of England who, by the weight of personal character, or the influence of advantageous circumstances, had exercised a permanent bearing on its destiny, few have occupied so prominent a place as Elizabeth, queen of Bohemia, the high-minded but ill-fated daughter of James I.
> Ch. I, *Elizabeth, Queen of Bohemia* 1855

927. Harriet Brent Jacobs (1818–1896)

1 It seems less degrading to give one's self, than to submit to compulsion. There is something akin to freedom in having a lover who has no control over you, except that which he gains by kindness and attachment.
> *Incidents in the Life of a Slave Girl*, Lydia Maria Child,* ed. 1861 (repr. 1973)
> *See 856.

2 You never knew what it is to be a slave; to be entirely unprotected by law or custom; to have the laws reduce you to the condition of a chattel, entirely subject to the will of another. You never exhausted your ingenuity in avoiding the snares, and eluding the power of a hated tyrant; you never shuddered at the sound of his footsteps, and trembled within hearing of his voice.

Ibid.

928. Amelia C. Welby (1819–1852)

1 As the dew to the blossom, the bud to the bee,
As the scent to the rose, are those memories to me.

"Pulpit Eloquence" *n.d.*

2 Ten thousand stars were in the sky,
Ten thousand on the sea.

"Twilight at Sea," St. 4 *n.d.*

929. Anna Cora Mowatt (1819–1870)

1 TRUEMAN. Fashion is an agreement between certain persons to live without using their souls! To substitute etiquette for virtue—decorum for purity—manners for morals!

Fashion 1845

930. George Eliot (1819–1880)

1 Hate is like fire—it makes even light rubbish deadly.

Scenes of Clerical Life 1857

2 Any coward can fight a battle when he's sure of winning; but give me the man who has pluck to fight when he's sure of losing. That's my way, sir; and there are many victories worse than a defeat.

"Janet's Repentance," Ch. 6, Ibid.

3 Opposition may become sweet to a man when he has christened it persecution.

Ch. 8, Ibid.

4 A toddling little girl is a centre of common feeling which makes the most dissimilar people understand each other.

Ibid.

5 Animals are such agreeable friends—they ask no questions, they pass no criticisms.

"Mr. Gilfi's Love Story," Ibid.

6 We hand folks over to God's mercy, and show none ourselves.

Adam Bede 1859

7 Our deeds determine us, as much as we determine our deeds.

Ibid.

8 I tell you there isn't a thing under the sun that needs to be done at all, but what a man can do better than a woman, unless it's bearing children, and they do that in a poor make-shift way; it had better ha' been left to the men.

Bk. 2, Ch. 21, Ibid.

9 It's them as take advantage that get advantage i' this world.

Bk. 4, Ch. 32, Ibid.

10 That's what a man wants in a wife, mostly; he wants to make sure o' one fool as 'ull tell him he's wise.

Bk. 6, Ch. 53, Ibid.

11 It's but a little good you'll do a-watering the last year's crop.

Ch. 18, Ibid.

12 It was a pity he couldna be hatched o'er again, an' hatched different.

Ibid.

13 A maggot must be born i' the rotten cheese to like it.

Ch. 29, Ibid.

14 I'm not denyin' the women are foolish: God almighty made 'em to match the men.

Ch. 43, Ibid.

15 I'm not one o' those as can see the cat i' the dairy an' wonder what she's come after.

Ch. 52, Ibid.

16 The law's made to take care o' raskills.

Bk. III, Ch. 4, *The Mill on the Floss 1860*

17 I've never any pity for conceited people, because I think they carry their comfort about them.

Bk. V, Ch. 4, Ibid.

18 If we use common words on a great occasion, they are the more striking, because they are felt at once to have a particular meaning, like old banners, or everyday clothes, hung up in a sacred place.

Bk. VI, Ch. 2, Ibid.

19 The happiest women, like the happiest nations, have no history.

Ch. 3, Ibid.

20 I should like to know what is the proper function of women, if it is not to make reasons for husbands to stay at home, and still stronger reasons for bachelors to go out.

Ch. 6, Ibid.

21 Jealousy is never satisfied with anything short of an omniscience that would detect the subtlest fold of the heart.

Ch. 10, Ibid.

22 Who has not felt the beauty of a woman's arm?—the unspeakable suggestions of tenderness that lie in the dimpled elbow, and all the varied gently-lessening curves, down to the delicate wrist, with its tiniest, almost imperceptible nicks in the firm softness.

Ibid.

23 More helpful than all wisdom is one draught of simple human pity that will not forsake us.

Bk. VII, Ch. 1, Ibid.

24 Nothing is so good as it seems beforehand.

Ch. 18, *Silas Marner 1861*

25 Justice is like the Kingdom of God—it is not without us as a fact, it is within us as a great yearning.

Romola 1862–63

26 There is a mercy which is weakness, and even treason against the common good.

Ibid.

27 In the vain laughter of folly wisdom hears half its applause.

Bk.1, Ch. 12, Ibid.

28 An ass may bray a good while before he shakes the stars down.

Ch. 50, Ibid.

29 When one wanted one's interests looking after whatever the cost, it was not so well for a lawyer to be over honest, else he might not be up to other people's tricks.
Introduction, *Felix Holt, The Radical 1866*

30 There are glances of hatred that stab, and raise no cry of murder.
Ibid.

31 The beginning of compunction is the beginning of a new life.
Ch. 13, Ibid.

32 Play not with paradoxes. That caustic which you handle in order to scorch others may happen to sear your own fingers and make them dead to the quality of things.
Ibid.

33 Speech is often barren; but silence also does not necessarily brood over a full nest. Your still fowl, blinking at you without remark, may all the while be sitting on one addled egg; and when it takes to cackling will have nothing to announce but that addled delusion.
Ch. 15, Ibid.

34 One way of getting an idea of our fellow-countrymen's miseries is to go and look at their pleasures.
Ch. 28, Ibid.

35 To act with doubleness towards a man whose own conduct was double, was so near an approach to virtue that it deserved to be called by no meaner name than diplomacy.
Ch. 29, Ibid.

36 The only failure a man ought to fear is failure in cleaving to the purpose he sees to be best.
Ch. 45, Ibid.

37 Life is measured by the rapidity of change, the succession of influences that modify the being.
Ch. 48, Ibid.

38 "Abroad," that large home of ruined reputations.
Epilogue, Ibid.

39 Particular lies may speak a general truth.
The Spanish Gypsy 1868

40 'Tis what I love determines how I love.
Bk. I, Ibid.

41 Best friend, my well-spring in the wilderness!
Bk. 3, Ibid.

42 Our words have wings, but fly not where we would.
Ibid.

43 Truth has rough flavors if we bite it through.
Sc. 2, *Armgart 1871*

44 Quarrel? Nonsense; we have not quarrelled. If one is not to get into a rage sometimes, what is the good of being friends?
Bk. 2, Ch. 12, *Middlemarch 1871–72*

45 Might, could, would—they are contemptible auxiliaries.
Bk. 2, Ch. 14, Ibid.

46 In the multitude of middle-aged men who go about their vocations in a daily course determined for them much in the same way as the tie of their cravats, there is always a good number who once meant to shape their own deeds and alter the world a little.
Ch. 15, Ibid.

47 One must be poor to know the luxury of giving!
Ch. 17, Ibid.

48 There is a sort of jealousy which needs very little fire; it is hardly a passion, but a blight bred in the cloudy, damp despondency of uneasy egoism.
Ch. 21, Ibid.

49 Failure after long perseverance is much grander than never to have a striving good enough to be called a failure.
Ch. 22, Ibid.

50 To be a poet is to have a soul so quick to discern, that no shade of quality escapes it, and so quick to feel, that discernment is but a hand playing with finely-ordered variety on the chords of emotion—a soul in which knowledge passes instantaneously into feeling, and feeling flashes back as a new organ of knowledge. One may have that condition by fits only.
Ibid.

51 With memory set smarting like a reopened wound, a man's past is not simply a dead history, an outworn preparation of the present: it is not a repented error shaken loose from the life: it is a still quivering part of himself, bringing shudders and bitter flavours and the tinglings of a merited shame.
Bk. 6, Ch. 61, Ibid.

52 Only those who know the supremacy of the intellectual life . . . can understand the grief of one who falls from that serene activity into the absorbing soul-wasting struggle with worldly annoyances.
Bk. 8, Ch. 73, Ibid.

53 She was no longer wrestling with the grief, but could sit down with it as a lasting companion and make it a sharer in her thoughts.
Ch. 80, Ibid.

54 Prophecy is the most gratuitous form of error.
Ch. 10, Ibid.

55 If we had keen vision of all that is ordinary in human life, it would be like hearing the grass grow or the squirrel's heart beat, and we should die of the roar which is the other side of silence.
Ch. 22, Ibid.

56 What loneliness is more lonely than distrust?
Ch. 44, Ibid.

57 Where women love each other, men learn to smother their mutual dislike.
"Finale," Ibid.

58 Gossip is a sort of smoke that comes from the dirty tobacco-pipes of those who diffuse it; it proves nothing but the bad taste of the smoker.
Daniel Deronda 1876

59 The Jews are among the aristocracy of every land; if a literature is called rich in the possession of a few classic tragedies, what shall we say to a national tragedy lasting for fifteen hundred years, in which the poets and actors were also the heroes.
Ibid.

60 Hostesses who entertain much must make up their parties as ministers make up their cabinets, on grounds other than personal liking.

Bk.1, Ch. 5, Ibid.

61 The desire to conquer is itself a sort of subjection.

Ch. 10, Ibid.

62 When we get to wishing a great deal for ourselves, whatever we get soon turns into mere limitation and exclusion.

Bk. 2, Ch. 14, Ibid.

63 A difference of taste in jokes is a great strain on the affections.

Ch. 15, Ibid.

64 ". . . I say that the strongest principle of growth lies in human choice."

Ibid.

65 There are some cases . . . in which the sense of injury breeds— not the will to inflict injuries and climb over them as a ladder, but—a hatred of all injury.

Ch. 16, Ibid.

66 Genius at first is little more than a great capacity for receiving discipline.

Bk. 3, Ch. 23, Ibid.

67 Excellence encourages one about life generally; it shows the spiritual wealth of the world.

Bk. 5, Ch. 36, Ibid.

68 A woman's heart must be of such a size and no larger, else it must be pressed small, like Chinese feet; her happiness is to be made as cakes are, by a fixed receipt.

Bk. 7, Ch. 51, Ibid.

69 You may try—but you can never imagine what it is to have a man's force of genius in you, and yet to suffer the slavery of being a girl.

Ibid.

70 And when a woman's will is as strong as the man's who wants to govern her, half her strength must be concealment.

Ibid.

71 The best augury of a man's success in his profession is that he thinks it the finest in the world.

Bk. 8, Ch. 58, Ibid.

72 Ignorant kindness may have the effect of cruelty; but to be angry with it as if it were direct cruelty would be an ignorant unkindness.

Ch. 59, Ibid.

73 Blessed is the man who, having nothing to say, abstains from giving wordy evidence of the fact.

Ch. 4, *The Impressions of Theophrastus Such 1879*

74 What a wretched lot of old shrivelled creatures we shall be by-and-by. Never mind—the uglier we get in the eyes of others, the lovelier we shall be to each other; that has always been my firm faith about friendship.

Letter (27 May 1852), *George Eliot's Life as Related in Her Letters and Journals 1885–86*

75 The years seem to rush by now, and I think of death as a fast approaching end of a journey—double and treble reason for loving as well as working while it is day.

Letter to Miss Sara Hennell (22 November 1861), Ibid.

76 I have the conviction that excessive literary production is a social offence.

Letter to Alexander Main (11 September 1871), Ibid.

77 Oh may I join the choir invisible
Of those immortal dead who live again
In minds made better by their presence.

"Oh May I Join the Choir Invisible," *Poems n.d.*

78 'Tis God gives skill,
But not without men's hands: He could not make
Antonio Stradivari's violins
Without Antonio.

"Stradivarius," l. 140, Ibid.

79 It is never too late to be what you might have been.

Quoted by Anna Quindlen* in her commencement speech, Mount Holyoke College (South Hadley, Mass.)
23 May 1999

* See 3366.

931. Susan Warner (1819–1885)

1 Many a bit we passed in our ignorance, in the days when we could see no metal but what glittered on the surface; and many a good time we went back again, long afterward, and broke our rejected lump with great exultation to find it fat with the riches of the mind.

Foreword, *The Law and the Testimony 1853*

2 One chapter a day was all we took. We searched that carefully, and noted down with miser eagerness everything which seemed to us to have an important bearing upon any point in our scheme. . . . But by dint of this practice we ourselves grew daily in the power of judging; and not only that, but the skill and the power of seeing, too; till by the time we were half through the Bible, we were just fit to begin again at the beginning. And so we did. . . .

Ibid.

3 "There is a world there, Winthrop—another sort of world— where people know something; where other things are to be done than running plow furrows; where men may distinguish themselves!—where men may read and write; and do something great; and grow to be something besides what nature made them!—I want to be in that world."

Ch. 1, *The Hills of the Shatemuc 1856*

4 "Did it ever happen to you to want anything you could not have, Miss Elizabeth?"
"No—never," said Elizabeth slowly.
"You have a lesson to learn yet."
"I hope I sha'n't learn it," said Elizabeth.
"It must be learned," said Mrs. Landholm gently. "Life would not be life without it. It is not a bad lesson either."

Ch. 10, Ibid.

5 "The back is fitted to the burden, they say; and I always *did* pray that if I had work to do, I might be able to do it; and I always was, somehow."

Ch. 3, *What She Could 1870*

6 "And I, Maria—am I not somebody?" her aunt asked.
"Well, we're all *somebody*, of course, in one sense. Of course we're not *nobody*."
"I am not sure what you think about it," said Mrs. Candy.
"I think that in your language, who isn't somebody, is nobody."

Ch. 7, Ibid.

7 "He who serves God with what costs him nothing, will do very
little service, you may depend on it."
Ch. 11, Ibid.

8 "Why should not a woman be as brave as a man, and as
strong—in one way?"
"I suppose, because she is not as strong in the other way."
Ch. 1, *The House in Town* 1871

932. Harriet Sewall (1819–1889)

1 Why thus longing, thus forever sighing
For the far-off, unattain'd and dim,
While the beautiful all round thee lying
Offers up its low, perpetual hymn?
"Why Thus Longing" *n.d.*

933. Louise Otto (1819–1895)

1 The history of all times, and of today especially, teaches
that . . . women will be forgotten if they forget to think about
themselves.
Women in World History Curriculum,
http://womeninworldhistory.com *1996–97*

934. Queen Victoria (1819–1901)

1 We are not interested in the possibilities of defeat.
Letter to A. J. Balfour *1899*

2 We are not amused.
Notebooks of a Spinster Lady 1900

3 I sat between the King and Queen. We left supper soon. My
health was drunk. I then danced one more quadrille with Lord
Paget. . . . I was *very* much amused.
Journal entry (16 June 1833), *The Girlhood of
Queen Victoria*, Vol. I, Viscount Esher, ed. *1912*

4 . . . I *too well* know its truth, from experience, that whenever
any poor Gipsies are encamped anywhere and crimes and rob-
beries &c. occur, it is invariably laid to their account, which is
shocking; and if they are always looked upon as vagabonds,
how *can* they become good people?
Journal entry (29 December 1836), Ibid.

5 *Russia* having *failed*, she *must see* that she *cannot* again *attempt* a similar coup d'etat. One of the first conditions should
therefore be to bring about a reconciliation. . . . Russia has
gravely compromised herself. . . . She will therefore be more
easily worked upon, for she cannot avow such monstrous conduct.
Letter to Marquis of Salisbury (25 August 1886), *The Letters of Queen Victoria*, Vol. I, George Earle Buckle, ed. *1930*

6 The Queen is most anxious to see the Government strengthened
and supported, and she *does* think that want of firmness in the
leader of the House of Commons is most detrimental to it.
(27 June 1890), Ibid.

7 . . . Now let me entreat you seriously not to do this, not to let
your feelings (very natural and usual ones) of momentary irritation and discomfort be seen by others; don't (as you so often
did and do) let every little feeling be read in your face and seen
in your manner, pray don't give way to irritability before your
ladies. All this I say with the love and affection I bear you—as
I know what you have to contend with and struggle against.
Letter to Princess Royal (27 September 1858),
Dearest Child, Roger Fulford, ed. *1964*

8 He (Mr. Gladstone)* speaks to Me as if I was a public
meeting.
Quoted in *Collection and Recollections* by G. W. E. Russell
n.d.
*William Ewart Gladstone (1809–1898), British prime minister
who served on four separate occasions between 1868 and 1894.

935. Louise Amelia Clappe (1819–1906)

1 . . . there is a certain fascination about the place (San Francisco), which our friends in the States find it difficult to
comprehend. For what with its many-costumed, many-
tongued, many-visaged populations; its flashy looking squares,
built one day and burnt the next; its wickedly beautiful gambling houses; its gay stores where the richest productions of
every nation can be found, and its wild, free, unconventional
style of living, it possesses for the young adventurer especially
a strange charm.
Letter to sister Molly (Rich Bar mining camp, 1849),
"Dame Shirley" letters, *The Pioneer* (1854–55),
The Shirley Letters 1933

2 I wish I could give you some faint idea of the majestic solitudes
through which we passed; where the pine trees rise so grandly
in their awful height, that they seem looking into Heaven itself. Hardly a living thing disturbed this solemnly beautiful
wilderness.*
(1851), Ibid.
*The forests of the Sierra Nevada.

3 I wet my feet, tore my dress, spoilt a new pair of gloves, nearly
froze my fingers, got an awful headache, took cold and lost a
valuable breastpin, in this my labor of love. I can assure you
that it is the last golden handiwork you will ever receive from
"Dame Shirley."*
Ibid.
*Reference to the $3.25 in gold dust she panned herself.

4 . . . no newspapers, no shopping, calling, nor gossiping, little
tea-drinkings; no parties, no balls, no picnics, no tableaux, no
charades, no latest fashions, no daily mail (we have an express
once a month), no promenades, no rides or drives; no vegetables but potatoes and onions, no milk, no eggs, no *nothing.*
Ibid.

5 My heart is heavy at the thought of departing forever from this
place. I like this wild and barbarous life; I leave it with regret.
The solemn fir trees . . . the watching hills, and the calmly
beautiful river, seem to gaze sorrowfully at me, as I stand in
the moon-lighted midnight, to bid them farewell . . .
(1852), Ibid.

6 I would gladly write something which the world would not
willingly let die.
(n.d), Ibid.

7 Though ye've not shaved your savage lips, nor cut your bar-
barous hair—
Ye are welcome, merry miners! All bearded as ye are.
Fourth of July Poem for Rich Bar miners (1852), Ibid.

936. Julia Ward Howe (1819–1910)

1 Mine eyes have seen the glory
Of the coming of the Lord
He is trampling out the vintage
Where the grapes of wrath are stored.
He hath loosed the fateful lightning

Of His terrible, swift sword;
His truth is marching on!
                    "The Battle Hymn of the Republic" 1862

2 In the beauty of the lilies
   Christ was born across the sea,
   With a glory of His bosom
   That transfigures you and me:
   As He died to make men holy.
   Let us die to make men free
   His truth is marching on!

                                        Ibid.

3 They are the mothers of the boys who are killed in war. They
   have the right to ask that the sons they love have a happy life.
   Cited in "Ahead of her time" by Rev. Dale Turner, *Seattle
   Times*, A8 *4 July 1992*

4 The peace crusade is going to take a long time. I will devote the
   rest of my life to world peace, but that will not be long enough. I
   will encourage others to carry on the work when I am done.
                                        Ibid.

5 All the sugar was in the bottom of the cup.
                              Last words, Ibid.

6 'Twas red with the blood of freemen and white with the fear of
   the foe;
   And the stars that fit in their courses 'gainst tyrants its symbols know.
                              "The Flag" *n.d.*

937. Mme. de Launey (fl. 1820s)
1 I forgive the *nonchalance* which you assume about receiving a
   pension. . . . It flatters both the vanity and the purse.
       Letter to Desbordes-Valmore* (1 November 1826), Quoted
       in Memoirs of Madame Desbordes-Valmore by C. A. Sainte-
                        Beuve; Harriet W. Preston, tr. *1872*
   *See 783.

938. Anne Brontë (1820–1849)
1 All true histories contain instruction; though, in some, the
   treasure may be hard to find, and when found, so trivial in
   quantity, that the dry, shrivelled kernel scarcely compensates
   for the trouble of cracking the nut.
                              Ch. II, *Agnes Gray 1847*

2 I would not send a poor girl into the world, . . . ignorant of the
   snares that beset her path; nor would I watch and guard her,
   till, deprived of self-respect and self-reliance, she lost the
   power or the will to watch and guard herself. . . .
                    Ch. III, *The Tenant of Wildfell Hall 1848*

3 "If you would have your son to walk honourable through the
   world, you must not attempt to clear the stones from his path,
   but teach him to walk firmly over them—not insist upon leading him by the hand, but let him learn to go alone."
                                        Ibid.

4 "Oh! I see," said he, with a bitter smile; "it's an act of Christian charity, whereby you hope to gain a higher seat in heaven
   for yourself, and scoop a deeper pit in hell for me."
                              Ch. XLVII, Ibid.

5 They say such tears as children weep
   Will soon be dried away;

That childhood's grief, however strong,
Is only for a day;
And parted friends, how dear so e'er,
Will soon forgotten be:
It may be so with other hearts;
It is not so with me.
       "An Orphan's Lament" (1 January 1841), *The Complete
            Poems of Anne Brontë*, Clement Shorter, ed. *1920*

6 Domestic peace! best joy of earth,
   When shall we all thy value learn?
              "Domestic Peace," St. 7 (11 May 1846), Ibid.

7 Nothing is lost that thou didst give,
   Nothing destroyed that thou hast done.
              "Severed and Gone," St. 15 (April 1847), Ibid.

8 But he that dares not grasp the thorn
   Should never crave the rose.
              "The Narrow Way," St. 4 (27 April 1848), Ibid.

939. Alice Cary (1820–1871)
1 Three little bugs in a basket,
   And hardly room for two.
                              "Three Bugs" *n.d.*

2 True worth is in *being*, not *seeming*—
   In doing, each day that goes by,
   Some little good—not in dreaming
   Of great things to do by and by.
                              "Nobility," St. 1 *n.d.*

3 We cannot bake bargains for blisses,
   Nor catch them like fishes in nets;
   And sometimes the thing our life misses,
   Helps more than the thing which it gets.
                                        St. 4, Ibid.

4 Work, and your house shall be duly fed:
   Work, and the rest shall be won;
   I hold that a man had better be dead
   Than alive when his work is done.
                              "Work" *n.d.*

5 Women and men in the crowd meet and mingle,
   Yet with itself every soul standeth single. . . .
                              "Life," St. 2 *n.d.*

6 How many lives we live in one,
   And how much less than one, in all!
                              "Life's Mysteries" *n.d.*

7 Kiss me, though you make believe;
   Kiss me, though I almost know
   You are kissing to deceive.
                              "Make Believe" *n.d.*

8 For the human heart is the mirror
   Of the things that are near and far;
   Like the wave that reflects in its bosom
   The flower and the distant star.
                              "The Time to Be" *n.d.*

940. Anna Sewell (1820–1878)
1 . . . if we see cruelty or wrong that have the power to stop, and
   do nothing, we make ourselves sharers in the guilt.
                              Black Beauty 1877

2   Though I am an old horse, and have seen and heard a great deal, I never yet could make out why men are so fond of this sport; they often hurt themselves, often spoil good horses, and tear up the fields, and all for a hare, or a fox, or a stag, that they could get more easily some other way; but we are only horses, and don't know.

Pt. I, Ch. 2, Ibid.

3   . . . he said that cruelty was the Devil's own trademark, and if we saw anyone who took pleasure in cruelty we might know who he belonged to, for the Devil was a murderer from the beginning, and a tormentor to the end.

Ch. 13, Ibid.

4   I am never afraid of what I know.

Pt. II, Ch. 29, Ibid.

5   I said, "I have heard people talk about war as if it was a very fine thing."
    "Ah!" said he, "I should think they never saw it. No doubt it is very fine when there is no enemy, when it is just exercise and parade, and sham fight. Yes, it is very fine then; but when thousands of good, brave men and horses are killed or crippled for life, it has a very different look."

Pt. III, Ch. 34, Ibid.

941. Urania Locke Bailey (1820–1882)

1   I want to be an angel,
    And with the angels stand
    A crown upon my forehead,
    A harp within my hand.

"I Want to Be an Angel," St. 1 n.d.

942. Jenny Lind (1820–1887)

1   I have a brightness in my soul, which strains toward Heaven. I am like a bird!

Quoted in *Jenny Lind: The Swedish Nightingale* by Gladys Denny Shultz 1962

2   I have appeared twice in *Norma*; and was called so many times before the curtain that I was quite exhausted. Bah! I don't like it. Everything should be done in moderation; otherwise it is not pleasing.

Letter (April 27, 1846), *The Lost Letters of Jenny Lind*, W. Porter Ware and Thaddeus C. Lockard, Jr., eds 1966

3   I have often wished for the blessing of motherhood, for it would have given me a much-needed focal point for my affections. With it, and through the varied experiences that accompany it, I could perhaps have achieved something better than that which I have attained up to now.

Letter (11 July 1849), Ibid.

4   My voice is still the same, and this makes me beside myself with joy! Oh, *mon Dieu*, when I think what I might be able to do with it!

Letter (10 January 1855), Ibid.

943. Jean Ingelow (1820–1897)

1   Oh Land where all the men are stones,
    Or all the stones are men.

"A Land that Living Warmth Disowns" n.d.

2   There's no dew left on the daisies and clover,
    There's no rain left in heaven:

I've said my "seven times" over and over,
Seven times one are seven.

"Seven Times One," St. 1, *Songs of Seven n.d.*

3   You Moon! Have you done something wrong in heaven,
    That God has hidden your face?

St. 4, Ibid.

4   A sweeter woman ne'er drew breath
    Than my sonne's wife Elizabeth.

"The High Tide on the Coast of Lincolnshire" n.d.

944. Margaret J. Preston (1820–1897)

1   Pain is no longer pain when it is past.

"Nature's Lesson" c. 1875

2   'Tis the motive exalts the action;
    'Tis the doing, not the deed.

"The First Proclamation of Miles Standish"* c.1875
*English colonial settler in America (1584?–1656).

3   Who so lives the holiest life
    Is fittest far to die.

"Ready" c. 1875

945. Lucretia Peabody Hale (1820–1900)

1   But behind the east wind is hidden the summer, and in these early spring days we feel a little of its breath, its warmth, and its languor. The invitation it gives to come out from winter activities and winter confinements, into its soft lassitude, and all its offers of freedom.

Ch. 4, *The Struggle for Life* 1867

2   All the years before, she had lived in a roving, aimless way, and the old love of change came up often to assert its power. Often came back the old longings to live where she would not be bound to anybody—where she might be free, even if she were only free to starve.

Ch. 18, Ibid.

3   It is so hard to melt away the influences of an early life, to counteract all the lessons of the first ten years, to tear up the weeds that are early planted. There are evil inheritances to be struggled with, childish prejudices, and fancies banished.

Ch. 33, Ibid.

946. Mary Ann Muller (1820–1900/02)

1   How long are women to remain a wholly unrepresented body of the people? This is a question that has of late been agitated in England, and women in this colony read, watch, and reflect . . . Why should not New Zealand also lead? . . . Why has a woman no power to vote, no right to vote, when she happens to possess all the requisites which legally qualify a man for that right?"

(1869), *Women in World History Curriculum*, http://www.womeninworldhistory.com 1996–97

947. Mathilde (1820–1904)

1   But I think him lost forever for any kind of locomotion. Nowadays it is only his mind that travels; his body stays behind on the bank.

Quoted in *Revue Bleu* 6 August 1863

2   He knew that his conversation had the power to fascinate, and he used it like a prodigal man who knew he had an everlasting fortune. . . .

Quoted in *Le Moniteur Universelle* 15 October 1869

3 I was born in exile—civically dead. . . .
    "Souvenirs de Années d'Exile," *La Revue des Deux Mondes*
    15 December 1927

948. Mary Livermore (1820?–1905)

1 For humanity has moved forward to an era when wrong and slavery are being displaced, and reason and justice are being recognized as the rule of life. . . . The age looks steadily to the redressing of wrong, to the righting of every form of error and injustice; and a tireless and prying philanthropy, which is almost omniscient, is one of the most hopeful characteristics of the time.
    Ch. 1, *What Shall We Do with Our Daughters?* *1883*

2 Other books have been written by men physicians. . . . One would suppose in reading them that women possess but one class of physical organs, and that these are always diseased. Such teaching is pestiferous, and tends to cause and perpetuate the very evils it professes to remedy.
    Ch. 2, Ibid.

3 Almost every one of the great religions of the world has made special provisions for them, and the woman who has preferred a celibate to a domestic life has been able to occupy a position of honor and usefulness.
    Ch. 7, Ibid.

4 Above the titles of wife and mother, which, although dear, are transitory and accidental, there is the title human being, which precedes and out–ranks every other.
    Ibid.

949. Susan B. Anthony (1820–1906)

1 Men their rights and nothing more; women their rights and nothing less.
    Motto, *The Revolution 1868*

2 . . . gentlemen. . . Do you not see that so long as society says a woman is incompetent to be a lawyer, minister, or doctor, but has ample ability to be a teacher, that every man of you who chooses this profession tacitly acknowledges that he has no more brains than a woman?
    Speech, State Convention of Schoolteachers, *History of
    Woman Suffrage*, Vol. 1, with Elizabeth Cady Stanton*
    and Mathilda Gage** *1881*
    * See 907. ** See 979.

3 Suffrage is the pivotal right.
    "The Status of Women, Past, Present and Future,"
    The Arena May 1897

4 Of all the old prejudices that cling to the hem of the woman's garments and persistently impede her progress, none holds faster than this. This idea that she owes service to a man instead of to herself, and that it is her highest duty to aid his development rather than her own, will be the last to die.
    Ibid.

5 . . . there never will be complete equality until women themselves help make laws and elect lawmakers.
    Ibid.

6 . . . The day will come when men will recognize woman as his peer, not only at the fireside, but in the councils of the nation. Then, and not until then, will there be the perfect comrade-ship, the ideal union between the sexes that shall result to the highest development of the race.
    Ibid.

7 . . . who can measure the advantages that would result if the magnificent abilities of [women] . . . could be devoted to the needs of government, society, home, instead of being consumed in the struggle to obtain their birthright of individual freedom?
    Ibid.

8 While in most states the divorce laws are the same for men and women, they never can bear equally upon both while all the property earned during the marriage belongs wholly to the husband.
    Ibid.

9 . . . and I shall earnestly and persistently continue to urge all women to the practical recognition of the old Revolutionary maxim, "Resistance to tyranny is obedience to God."
    Quoted in Courtroom Speech (18 June 1873), *Jailed for
    Freedom* by Doris Stevens *1920*

10 So, for the love of me and for the saving of the reputation of womanhood, I beg you, with one baby on your knee and another at your feet, and four boys whistling, buzzing, halooing, "Ma, Ma," set yourself about the work.
    *Elizabeth Cady Stanton,** Vol. II, Theodore Stanton
    and Harriot Stanton Blatch, eds. *1922*
    *See 907.

11 And yet, in the schoolroom more than any other place, does the difference of sex, if there is any, need to be forgotten.
    Ibid.

12 The fact is, women are in chains, and their servitude is all the more debasing because they do not realize it. O to compel them to see and feel and give them the courage and the conscience to speak and act for their own freedom, though they face the scorn and contempt of all the world for doing it!
    Quoted in *The Liberated Woman's Appointment Calendar*,
    Lynn Sherr and Jurate Kazickas, eds. *1975*

13 How I wish I had Mrs. Stanton* here, and I could galvanize her to make beautiful my crude glimmering of ideas.
    Quoted in *Women Suffragists* by Diana Star Helmer *1998*
    *Elizabeth Cady Stanton; see 907.

14 The preamble of the Federal Constitution says: We, the people of the United States . . . It was we, the people, not we, the white male citizens, nor we, the male citizens; but we, the whole people, who formed this Union.
    Ibid.

15 Whoever controls work and wages, controls morals.
    Ibid.

16 I would not consent that the man I loved . . . should unite his destinies in marriage with a political slave and pariah.
    Ibid.

17 Independence is happiness.
    Ibid.

18 Would you exalt your profession, exalt those who labor with you . . . increase the salaries of the women engaged in the noble work of educating our future presidents, senators and congressmen.
    Remark to men, Ibid.

19 I feel discouraged when I think of holding a Convention without Lucy* or Antoinette**—but they are bound to give themselves over to the ineffable joys of Maternity.
Diary entry (1857), Ibid.
*Reference to L— Stone (see 923). **A— Brown Blackwell (see 975).

20 Oh, the voice is stilled which I have loved to hear for fifty years. Always I have felt that I must have Mrs. Stanton's* opinion of things before I knew where I stood myself.
Letter to Ida Husted Harper (1902), Ibid.
*See 907; Stanton died 26 October 1902.

21 With such women as these consecrating their lives, failure is impossible.*
Remark to celebrants at her 86th birthday gala, Ibid.
*These words were the last Anthony spoke in public and became the watchwords of the suffrage movement.

950. Florence Nightingale (1820–1910)

1 No *man*, not even a doctor, ever gives any other definition of what a nurse should be than this—"devoted and obedient." This definition would do just as well for a porter. It might even do for a horse. It would not do for a policeman.
Notes on Nursing 1859

2 Merely looking at the sick is not observing.
Ibid.

3 But when you have done away with all that pain and suffering, which in patients are the symptoms, not of their disease, but of the absence of one or all of the essentials to the success of Nature's reparative processes, we shall then know what are the symptoms of, and the sufferings inseparable from, the disease.
Ibid.

4 It may seem a strange thing to begin a book with:—This Book is not for any one who has time to read it—but the meaning of it is: this reading is good only as a preparation for work. If it is not to inspire life and work, it is bad. Just as the end of food is to enable us to live and work, and not to live and eat, so the end of most reading perhaps, but certainly of mystical reading, is not to read but to work.
Preface, *Mysticism* 1873

5 For what is Mysticism? Is it not the attempt to draw near to God, not by rites or ceremonies, but by inward disposition? Is it not merely a hard word for "The Kingdom of Heaven is within?" Heaven is neither a place nor a time.
Ibid.

6 So I never lose an opportunity of urging a practical beginning, however small, for it is wonderful how often in such matters the mustard-seed germinates and roots itself.
"Health Missionaries for Rural India," *India* December 1896

7 Nothing ever laughs and plays [in Egypt]. Everything is grown up and grown old.
Quoted in *The Life of Florence Nightingale* by Sir Edward Cook 1913

8 I stand at the altar of murdered men, and, while I live, I fight their cause.
Private note (1856), Ibid.

9 Asceticism is the trifling of an enthusiast with his power, a puerile coquetting with his selfishness or his vanity, in the ab-

sence of any sufficiently great object to employ the first or overcome the last.
Letter to Dr. Sutherland (1857), Ibid.

10 I can stand out the war with any man.
Quoted in *The World Book Encyclopedia 1972*

11 What the horrors of war are, no one can imagine. They are not wounds and blood and fever, spotted and low, or dysentery, chronic and acute, cold and heat and famine. They are intoxication, drunken brutality, demoralisation and disorder on the part of the inferior . . . jealousies, meanness, indifference, selfish brutality on the part of the superior.
Letter to her family (5 May 1855), *Forever Yours, Florence Nightingale: Selected Letters 1989*

12 Instead of wishing to see more doctors made by women joining what there are, I wish to see as few doctors, either male or female, as possible. For, mark you, the women have made no improvement—they have only tried to be "men" and they have only succeeded in being third-rate men.
Letter to John Stuart Mill* (12 September 1860), Ibid.
*British philosopher and economist (1806–1873).

13 The martyr sacrifices *herself* (*him*self in a few instances) entirely in vain. Or rather not in vain; for she (or he) makes the selfish more selfish, the lazy more lazy, the narrow narrower.
Letter to the scholar Benjamin Jowett (c. 1867), Ch. 4, Ibid.

951. Anna Bartlett Warner (1820–1912)

1 Daffy-down-dilly came up in the cold. . . .
"Daffy-Down-Dilly *n.d.*

2 Jesus loves me, this I know
For the Bible tells me so.
"Jesus Loves Me" *n.d.*

952. Elizabeth Blackwell (1821–1910)

1 Social intercourse—a very limited thing in a half civilized country, becomes in our centers of civilization a great power. . . .
Medicine as a Profession for Women, with Emily Blackwell* 1860
*Her sister; see 975.

2 . . . Every advance in social progress removes us more and more from the guidance of instinct, obliging us to depend upon reason for the assurance that our habits are really agreeable to the laws of health, and compelling us to guard against the sacrifice of our physical or moral nature while pursuing the ends of civilization.
Ibid.

3 . . . health has its science as well as disease. . . .
Ibid.

4 Our school education ignores, in a thousand ways, the rules of healthy development . . .
Ibid.

5 For what is done or learned by one class of women becomes, by virtue of their common womanhood, the property of all women.
Ibid.

6 How often homes, which should be the source of moral and physical health and truth, are centers of selfishness and frivolity!
Ibid.

7 Medicine is so broad a field, so closely interwoven with general interests, dealing as it does with all ages, sexes, and classes, and yet of so personal a character in its individual applications, that it must be regarded as one of those great departments of work in which the cooperation of men and women is needed to fulfill all its requirements.

Ibid.

8 . . . the church, with its usual sagacity in availing itself of all talents, opens the attractive prospect of active occupation, personal standing and authority, social respect, and the companionship of intelligent co-workers, both men and women—the feeling of belonging to the world, in fact, instead of a crippled and isolated life. For though it is common to speak of the sisters as renouncing the world, the fact is that the members of these sisterhoods have a far more active participation in the interests of life than most of them had before.

Ibid.

9 As teachers, then, to diffuse among women the physiological and sanitary knowledge which they need, we found the first work for women physicians.

Ibid.

10 This failure to recognize the equivalent value of internal with external structure has led to such a crude fallacy as a comparison of the penis with such a vestige as the clitoris, whilst failing to recognize that the vast amount of erectile tissue, mostly internal, in the female, which is the direct seat of sexual spasm.

The Human Element in Sex 1894

11 . . . the total deprivation of it [sex] produces irritability.

Ibid.

12 . . . I, who so love a hermit life for a good part of the day, find myself living in public, and almost losing my identity.

Pioneer Work for Women 1914

13 I must have something to engross my thoughts, some object in life which will fill this vacuum and prevent this sad wearing away of the heart.

Ibid.

14 Do you think I care about medicine? Nay, verily, it's just to kill the devil, whom I hate so heartily—that's the fact, mother.

Letter to Mother, Quoted in *Those Extraordinary Blackwells** by Elinor R. Hays** 1967

*See 975 and 975.1. **See 1793.

953. Mary Baker Eddy (1821–1910)

1 Audible prayer can never do the works of spiritual understanding, which regenerates; but silent prayer, watchfulness, and devout obedience enable us to follow Jesus' example. Long prayers, superstition, and creeds clip the strong pinions of love, and clothe religion in human forms. Whatever materializes worship hinders man's spiritual growth and keeps him from demonstrating his power over error.

Ch. 1, *Science and Health, with Key to the Scriptures 1875*

2 Chastity is the cement of civilization and progress. Without it there is no stability in society, and without it one cannot attain the Science of Life.

Ch. 3, Ibid.

3 Give up the belief that mind is, even temporarily, compressed within the skull, and you will quickly become more manly or womanly. You will understand yourself and your Maker better than before.

Ch. 12, Ibid.

4 The basis of all health, sinlessness, and immortality is the great fact that God is the only Mind; and this Mind must be not merely believed, but it must be understood.

Ch. 14, Ibid.

5 Stand porter at the door of thought. Admitting only such conclusions as you wish realized in bodily results, you will control yourself harmoniously.

Ibid.

6 Divine love always has met and always will meet every human need.

Ibid.

7 God is Mind, and God is infinite; hence all is Mind.

Ibid.

8 We classify disease as error, which nothing but Truth or Mind can heal, and this Mind must be divine, not human.

Ibid.

9 The highest prayer is not one of faith merely; it is demonstration. Such prayer heals sickness, and must destroy sin and death.

Ibid.

10 Spirit is the real and eternal; matter is the unreal and temporal.

Ibid.

11 Disease is an image of thought externalized.

Ibid.

12 Christian Science explains all cause and effect as mental, not physical.

Ibid., *1910 ed.*

13 Then comes the question, how do drugs, hygiene, and animal magnetism heal? It may be affirmed that they do not heal, but only relieve suffering temporarily, exchanging one disease for another.

Ibid.

14 Disease is an experience of so-called mortal mind. It is fear made manifest in the body.

Ibid.

15 If materialistic knowledge is power, it is not wisdom. It is but a blind force.

Ibid.

16 Jesus of Nazareth was the most scientific man that ever trod the globe. He plunged beneath the material surface of things, and found the spiritual cause.

Ibid.

17 Sin brought death, and death will disappear with the disappearance of sin.

Ibid.

18 Health is not a condition of matter, but of Mind; nor can the material senses bear reliable testimony on the subject of health.

Ibid.

19 Truth is immortal; error is mortal.

Ibid.

20   I would no more quarrel with a man because of his religion
     than I would because of his art.
          Miscellaneous Writings (rev. as *The First Church of Christ,
          Scientist, and Miscellany* 1913) 1883–1896

21   How would you define Christian Science? As the law of God,
     the law of good, interpreting and demonstrating the divine
     Principle and rule of universal harmony.
          Rudimental Divine Science 1891

22   To live and let live, without clamor for distinction of recogni-
     tion; to wait on divine Love; to write truth first on the tablet
     of one's own heart—this is the sanity and perfection of living,
     and my human ideal.
          Message to the Mother Church 1902

23   To live so as to keep human consciousness in constant relation
     with the Divine, the spiritual and the eternal, is to individual-
     ize infinite power; and this is Christian Science.
          The First Church of Christ, Scientist and Miscellany 1913

24   My prayer, some daily good to do
     To Thine, for Thee—
     An offering of pure Love, whereto
     God leadeth me.
          "O'er Waiting Harp-Strings of the Mind," St. 7 *n.d.*

25   It matters not what be thy lot,
     So Love doth guide;
     For storm or shine, pure peace is Thine
     What'er betide.
          "Satisfied," St. 1 *n.d.*

954. Clara Barton (1821–1912)

1   It is wise statesmanship which suggests that in times of peace
    we must prepare for war, and it is no less wise benevolence
    that makes preparation in the hour of peace for assuaging the
    ills that are sure to accompany war.
          Ch. 1, *The Red Cross 1898*

2   An institution or reform movement that is not selfish, must
    originate in the recognition of some evil that is adding to the
    sum of human suffering, or diminishing the sum of happiness.
    I suppose it is a philanthropic movement to try to reverse the
    process.
          Ibid.

3   I have an almost complete disregard of precedent and a faith
    in the possibility of something better. It irritates me to be told
    how things always have been done . . . I defy the tyranny of
    precedent. I cannot afford the luxury of a closed mind. I go for
    anything new that might improve the past.
          Quoted in *A Chosen Faith* by Robin Lane Fox* *n.d.*
          *See 3101.

955. Lilly Martin Spencer (1822–1902)

1   . . . fame is as hollow and brilliant as a soap bubble, it is all
    colors outside and nothing worth kicking at inside.
          Letter to parents, *Women in the Arts*, Vol. X,
          No. 2 *Summer 1992*

956. Frances Cobbe (1822–1904)

1   The time comes to every dog when it ceases to care for people
    merely for biscuits or bones, of even for caresses, and walks out
    of doors. When a dog *really* loves, it prefers the person who gives

it nothing, and perhaps is too ill ever to take it out for exercise,
to all the liberal cooks and active dog-boys in the world.
          The Confessions of a Lost Dog 1867

2   I could discern clearly, even at that early age, the essential dif-
    ference between people who are *kind* to dogs and people who
    really *love* them.
          Ibid.

3   Is it to mock a world of woe
    The soft winds laugh, the clear streams flow?
    Is it a proof of wrath Divine
    That the earth is gilt by the bright sunshine?

    "*A Vale of Tears*"? Does not each sense
    Proclaim a good Omnipotence?
          "A Vale of Tears," Sts. 6–7, *Rest in the Lord 1887*

4   Then the Sorcerer Science entered, and where e'er he waved
       his wand
    Fresh wonders and fresh mysteries rose on every hand.
          "The Pageant of Time," St. 1 (December, 1859), Ibid.

5   . . . I must avow that the halo which has gathered round Jesus
    Christ obscures Him to my eyes.
          Ch. 15, *Life of Frances Power Cobbe*, Vol. II *1894*

957. Caroline Dall (1822–1912)

1   The solution of an old mystery must bring justification and
    proof to every assertion.
          Preface, *The Romance of the Association 1875*

2   I have seen no Hindu who seemed to me prepared intellectu-
    ally and morally for the freedom he would find in American
    society; nor are Americans prepared for the air of innocence
    and exaltation worn by very undeserving Orientals.
          The Life of Doctor Anandabai Joshee *1888*
          *See 1245.

3   It is not learning, intellect, subtlety, or imagination that is
    wanting in the average Hindu; it is purity, faith, and honesty.
          Ibid.

4   Why is it that human hearts are so dead to the heroic?
          Pt. 1, *Barbara Fritchie** 1892*
          *See 721.

5   It was the glorious function of [John Greenleaf] Whittier* to
    lift us nearer to the Infinite Spirit, to keep us intent upon our
    immortal destiny, and to fill us with that love of Beauty which
    is the love of God.
          "L'Envoi," Ibid.
          *(1807–1892) American poet and abolitionist.

958. Margaret Davidson (1823–1838)

1   When left alone, when thou art gone,
    Yet still I will not feel alone;
    Thy spirit still will hover near,
    And guard thy orphan daughter here.
          Untitled poem (ca. 1831), Quotes in *Lives of Celebrated
          Women* by Samuel Griswold Goodrich *1844*

2   My sister! With that thrilling word
    Let thoughts unnumbered wildly spring!
    What echoes in my heart are stirred,
    While thus I touch the trembling string.
          Untitled poem (1836), Ibid.

3 I cannot weep that thou are fled;
Forever blends my soul with thine

Ibid.

959. Mary Bokin Chesnut (1823–1886)

1 "You know how women sell themselves and are sold in marriage, from queens downwards, eh? You know what the Bible says about slaves, and marriage. Poor women, poor slaves."

(4 March 1861), *Diary from Dixie 1949*

2 I think this journal will be disadvantageous for me, for I spend my time now like a spider spinning my own entrails, instead of reading as my habit was in all spare moments.

(14 March 1861), Ibid.

3 You see, Mrs. Stowe* did not hit the sorest spot. She makes Legree a bachelor.

(27 August 1861), Ibid.

*See 896.

4 . . . those soul stirring Negro camp-meeting hymns. To me this is the saddest of all earthly music, weird and depressing beyond my power to describe.

(13 October 1861), Ibid.

5 I hate slavery. I even hate the harsh authority I see parents think it is their duty to exercise toward their children.

(28 November 1861), Ibid.

6 Conscription has waked the Rip Van Winkles. To fight and to be made to fight are different things.

(19 March 1862), Ibid.

7 Grief and constant anxiety kill nearly as many women as men die on the battlefield.

(9 June 1862), Ibid.

8 "Hysterical grief never moves me. It annoys me. You think yourself a miracle of sensibility; but self-control is what you need. That is all that separates you from those you look down upon as unfeeling."

(7 December 1863), Ibid.

9 Is the sea drying up? It is going up into mist and coming down on us in this water spout, the rain. It raineth every day, and the weather represents our tearful despair on a large scale.

(5 March 1865), Ibid.

10 We are scattered, stunned, the remnant of heart left alive in us filled with brotherly hate. We sit and wait until the drunken tailor [President Andrew Johnson] who rules the United States issues a proclamation and defines our anomalous position.

(16 May 1865), Ibid.

960. Caroline Mason (1823–1890)

1 Do they miss me at home—do they miss me?
'Twould be an assurance most dear,
To know that this moment some loved one
Were saying, "I wish he were here."

"Do They Miss Me at Home," St.1 *1850*

2 . . . like a story well-nigh told,
Will seem my life—when I am old.

"When I Am Old," St. 1 *n.d.*

3 Ere I am old, O! Let me give
My life to learning how to live,

St. 8, Ibid.

4 His grave a nation's heart shall be,
His monument a people free!

"President Lincoln's Grave" *n.d.*

961. Charlotte Yonge (1823–1901)

1 As the most striking lines of poetry are the most hackneyed, because they have grown to be the common inheritance of all the world, so many of the most noble deeds that earth can show have become the best known, and enjoyed their full meed of fame.

A Book of Golden Deeds 1864

962. Elizabeth Stoddard (1823–1902)

1 A woman despises a man for loving her, unless she returns his love.

Ch. 32, *Two Men 1888*

963. Julia Carney (1823–1908)

1 Little drops of water, Little grains of sand,
Make the mighty ocean, And the pleasant land.
So the little minutes, Humble tho' they be,
Make the mighty ages Of Eternity!

"Little Things," St. 1 *1845*

964. Phoebe Cary (1824–1871?)

1 Charley Church, was a preacher who praught,
Though his enemies called him a screecher who scraught.

"The Lovers" *n.d.*

2 I think true love is never blind
But rather brings an added light,
An inner vision quick to find
The beauties hid from common sight.

Ibid.

3 For all the hard things to bear and grin,
The hardest is being taken in.

"Kate Ketchem" *n.d.*

4 Sometimes, I think, the things we see
Are shadows of the things to be;
That what we plan we build. . . .

"Dreams and Realities," St. 7 *n.d.*

5 Give plenty of what is given to you,
And listen to pity's call;
Don't think the little you give is great
And the much you get is small.

"A Legend of the Northlands," I, St. 8 *n.d.*

6 Thou hast battled for the right
With many a brave and trenchant word
And shown us how the pen may fight
A mightier battle than the sword.

"John Greenleaf Whittier"* *n.d.*

*American poet and abolitionist (1807–1892).

7 There's many a battle fought daily
The world knows nothing about.

"Our Heroes," St. 2 *n.d.*

8 Be steadfast, my boy, when you're tempted,
   To do what you know to be right.
   Stand firm by the colors of manhood,
   And you will o'ercome in the fight.
                                    St. 3, Ibid.

9 And wouldn't it be nicer
   For you to smile than pout,
   And so make sunshine in the house
   When there is none without?
                                "Suppose," St. 2 n.d.

10 And isn't it, my boy or girl,
   The wisest, bravest plan,
   Whatever comes, or doesn't come,
   To do the best you can?
                                    St. 5, Ibid.

965. Julia Kavanagh (1824–1877)

1 Most children are aristocratic. . . .
                                Daisy Burns, Vol. I 1853

2 Alas! why has the plain truth the power of offending so many
   people. . . .
                                    Ch. 4, Ibid.

3 It is the culprit who must seek the glance of the judge, and not
   the judge that must look at the culprit.
                                    Ch. 1, Nathalie 1872

4 A beauty must regret the past; a noble-born and impoverished
   lady cannot look with favour on a new order of things.
                                    Ch. 2, Adele 1872

966. Sarah Anna Lewis (1824–1880)

1 The oblivious world of sleep—
   That rayless realm where Fancy never beams,
   That nothingness beyond the land of dreams.
                                "Child of the Sea" n.d.

967. Adeline Dutton Whitney (1824–1906)

1 I bow me to the thwarting gale:
   I know when that is overpast,
   Among the peaceful harvest days
   An Indian Summer comes at last.
                                "Equinoctal," St. 6 n.d.

968. Adelaide Proctor (1825–1864)

1 Dreams grow holy put in action.
     "Phillip and Mildred," The Poems of Adelaide Proctor 1869

2 One dark cloud can hide the sunlight;
   Loose one string, the pearls are scattered;
   Think one thought, a soul may perish;
   Say one word, a heart may break
                                    Ibid.

3 One by one the sands are flowing,
   One by one the moments fall;
   Some are coming, some are going;
   Do not strive to grasp them all.
                                "One by One," St. 1, Ibid.

4 See how time makes all grief decay.
                                "Life in Death," Ibid.

5 I know too well the poison and the sting
   Of things too sweet.
                                "Per Pacem ad Lucem," Ibid.

6 Now Time has fled—the world is strange,
   Something there is of pain and change;
   My books lie closed upon the shelf;
   I miss the old heart in myself.
                                    "A Student," Ibid.

7 Half my life is full of sorrow,
   Half of joy, still fresh and new;
   One of these lives is a fancy,
   But the other one is true.
                                "Dream-Life," Ibid.

8 Tell her that the lesson taught her
   Far outweighs the pain.
                                "Friend Sorrow," Ibid.

9 Rise! for the day is passing
   And you lie dreaming on. . . .
                                "Now," St. 1, Ibid.

10 The Past and the Future are nothing
   In the face of the stern To-day.
                                    Ibid.

11 O, there are Voices of the Past,
   Links of a broken chain,
   Wings that can bear me back to Times
   Which cannot come again. . . .
                                "Voices of the Past," Ibid.

12 Only heaven
   Means crowned, not conquered, when it says "Forgiven."
                                "A Legend of Provence," Ibid.

969. Laura Towne (1825–1901)

1 I want to agitate, even if I am agitated.
           Journal Entry (1877), Quoted in Woman's True Profession
                                    by Nancy Hoffman 1981

970. Mrs. Alexander (1825–1902)

1 ". . . it is impossible to rely on the prudence or common sense
   of any man. . . ."
                                Ch. 1, Ralph Wilton's Weird 1875

2 "There's nothing more mischievous than moping along and
   getting into the blue devils!—nothing more likely to drive a
   man to suicide or matrimony, or some infernal entanglement
   even worse!"
                                    Ch. 6, Ibid.

971. Frances Ellen Watkins Harper (1825–1911)

1 "Now, father, I do think it is a shame for this child to be a slave,
   when he is just as white as anybody; . . . He is so beautiful, I
   would like him for my brother; and he looks like us anyhow."
                                Minnie's Sacrifice 1869

972. Harriet Robinson (1825–1911)

1 What if she did hunger and thirst after knowledge? She could
   do nothing with it even if she could get it. So she made a fetish
   of some male relative, and gave him the mental food for which

she herself was starving; and devoted all her energies towards helping him to become what she felt, under better conditions, she herself might have been. It was enough in those early days to be the *mother* or *sister* of somebody.

"Early Factory Labor in New England," *Massachusetts in the Woman Suffrage Movement* 1883

2 Skilled labor teaches something not to be found in books or in colleges.

Ibid.

3 In those days there was no need of advocating the doctrine of the proper relation between employer and employed. *Help was too valuable to be ill-treated* . . .

Ibid.

973. Julia Dorr (1825–1913)

1 A new beatitude I write for thee,
"Blessed are they who are not sure of things."

"A New Beatitude," *Poems* 1897

2 Oh golden Silence, bid our souls be still,
And on the foolish fretting of our care
Lay thy soft touch of healing unaware!

"Silence" *n.d.*

3 What dost thou bring me, O fair To-day,
That comest o'er the mountains with swift feet?

"To-day" *n.d.*

4 The year grows rich as it groweth old,
And life's latest sands are its sands of gold!

"To the 'Bouquet Club'" *n.d.*

5 And the stately lilies stand
Fair in the silvery light,
Like saintly vestals, pale in prayer.

"A Red Rose" *n.d.*

6 Come, blessed Darkness, come and bring thy balm
For eyes grown weary of the garish day!
Come with thy soft, slow steps, thy garments grey,
Thy veiling shadows, bearing in thy palm
The poppy-seeds of slumber, deep and calm.

"Darkness" *n.d.*

7 Stars will blossom in the darkness,
Violets bloom beneath the snow.

"For a Silver Wedding" *n.d.*

8 O beautiful, royal Rose,
O Rose, so fair and sweet!
Queen of the garden art thou,
And I—the Clay at thy feet.

"The Clay to the Rose" *n.d.*

9 Grass grows at last above all graves.

"Grass-Grown" *n.d.*

974. Henrietta Heathorn (1825–1915)

1 Be not afraid, ye waiting hearts that weep,
For God still giveth His beloved sleep,
And if an endless sleep He wills—so best.*

"Browning's Funeral"** 1889

*Epitaph on T. H. Huxley's tombstone; English scientist and humanist (1825–1895). **Robert Browning, English poet (1812–1889).

2 To all the gossip that I hear
I'll give no faith; to what I see
But only half, for it is clear
All that led up is dark to me.
Learn we the larger life to live,
To comprehend is to forgive.

"Tout Comprendre, C'est Tout Pardonner" *n.d.*

975. Antoinette Brown Blackwell (1825–1921)

1 . . . the sexes in each species of beings . . . are always true equivalents—equals but not identicals. . . .

The Sexes Throughout Nature 1875

2 Any positive thinker is compelled to see everything in the light of his own convictions.

Ibid.

3 I do not underrate the charge of presumption which must attach to any woman who will attempt to controvert the great masters of science and scientific inference. But there is no alternative!

Ibid.

4 If woman's sole responsibility is of the domestic type, one class will be crushed by it, and the other throw it off as a badge of poverty. The poor man's motto, "Women's work is never done," leads inevitably to its antithesis—ladies work is never begun.

Ibid.

5 The brain is not, and cannot be, the sole or complete organ of thought and feeling.

Ibid.

6 The law of grab is the primal law of infancy.

Ibid.

7 That she is not his peer in all intellectual and moral capabilities, cannot at least be very well provided until she is allowed an equally untrammeled opportunity to test her own strength.

Ibid.

8 If Evolution, as applied to sex, teaches any one lesson plainer than another, it is the lesson that the monogamic marriage is the basis of all progress.

Ibid.

9 Mr. [Charles] Darwin . . . has failed to hold definitely before his mind the principle that the difference of sex, whatever it may consist in, must itself be subject to natural selection and to evolution.

Ibid.

10 Woman's share of duties must involve direct nutrition, man's indirect nutrition. She should be able to bear and nourish their young children, at a cost of energy equal to the amount expended by him as household provider. Beyond this, if human justice is to supplement Nature's provisions, all family duties must be shared equitably, in person or by proxy.

Ibid.

11 Women's thoughts are impelled by their feelings. Hence the sharp-sightedness, the direct instinct, the quick perceptions; hence also their warmer prejudices and more unbalanced judgements. . . . In this the child is more like the woman.

Ibid.

12 Every nursing mother, in the midst of her little dependent brood, has far more right to whine, sulk, or scold, as temperament dictates, because beefsteak and coffee are not prepared for her and exactly to her taste, than any man ever had or ever can have during the present stage of human evolution.

Ibid.

13 Nature is just enough; but men and women must comprehend and accept her suggestions.

Ibid.

14 Work, alternated with needful rest, is the salvation of man or woman.

Ibid.

15 All insect mothers act with the utmost wisdom and good faith, and with a beautiful instinctive love towards a posterity which they are directly never to caress or nurture. . . . These tiny creatures work with the skill of carpenters and masons, and often with a prudence and forethought which is even more than human; for they never suffer personal ease or advantage to prevent their making proper provision for their young.

Ibid.

16 It is difficult to perceive what self-adjusting forces, in the organic world, have developed men everywhere the superiors of women, males characteristically the superiors of females.

Ibid.

17 It has seemed to both Lucy Stone* and myself in our student days that marriage would be a hindrance to our public work.

Quoted in *Antoinette Brown Blackwell: Biographical Sketch* by Sarah Gibson *1909*

*See 923.

18 . . . you asked me one day if it [marriage] seemed like giving up much for your sake. Only leave me free, as free as you are and everyone ought to be, and it is giving up nothing.

Letter to future husband, Ibid.

975.1 Emily Blackwell (1826–1911)

Coauthor with Elizabeth Blackwell; see 952:1–9.

976. Dinah Mulock Craik (1826-1887)

1 For since it is a law of nature, admitting only rare exceptions, that the qualities of the ancestors should be transmitted to the race—the fact seems patent enough, that even allowing equal advantages, a gentleman's son has more chances of growing up a gentleman than the son of a working man.

Ch. I, *John Halifax, Gentleman 1856*

2 "Madam," said he, with a bow of perfect good-humor, and even some sly drollery, "you mistake; I never begged in my life—I am a person of independent property, which consists of my head and my two hands, out of which I hope to realize a large capital some day."

Ch. II, *Ibid.*

3 "I wonder," he said at last, "if, when I was born, my father was as young as I am; whether he felt as I do now. You cannot think what an awful joy it is to be looking forward to a child; a little soul of God's giving, to be made fit for His eternity. How shall we do it! we that are both so ignorant, so young— she will be only just nineteen when, please God, her baby is born. Sometimes, of an evening, we sit for hours on this bench, she and I, talking of what we ought to do, and how we ought to rear the little thing, until we fall into silence, awed at the blessing that is coming to us."

Ch. XXI, *Ibid.*

4 Yet, I think either parent would have looked amazed, had any one pitied them for having a blind child. The loss—a loss only to them, and not to her, the darling!—became familiar, and ceased to wound; the blessedness was ever new.

Ch. XXII, *Ibid.*

5 . . . a Brownie is a curious creature. . . .

The Adventures of a Brownie 1872

6 Altogether, his conscience pricked him a good deal; and when people's consciences prick them, sometimes they get angry with other people, which is very silly, and only makes matters worse.

Ibid.

7 Now, I have nothing to say against uncles in general. They are usually very excellent people, and very convenient to little boys and girls.

Ch. 2, *The Little Lame Prince 1875*

8 There is much that we do not know, and cannot understand— we big folks, no more than you little ones.

Ch. 6, *Ibid.*

9 "One cannot make oneself, but one can sometimes help a little in the making of somebody else."

Ch. 10, *Ibid.*

10 "You are a child. Accept the fact. Be humble—be teachable. Lean upon the wisdom of others till you have gained your own."

Ibid.

11 Friend, what years could us divide?

"A Christmas Blessing," *Thirty Years 1881*

12 Those rooks, dear, from morning till night,
They seem to do nothing but quarrel and fight,
And wrangle and jangle, and plunder.

"The Blackbird and the Rooks," *Ibid.*

13 And when I lie in the green kirkyard,
With mould upon my breast,
Say not that she did well—or ill,
Only "she did her best."

"Obituary" *1887*

14 Lo! All life this truth declares,
Laborare est orare;
And the whole earth rings with prayers.

"Labour is Prayer," St. 4 *n.d.*

15 Immortality
Alone could teach this mortal how to die.

"Looking Death in the Face" *n.d.*

16 Love that asketh love again
Finds the barter nought but pain;
Love that giveth in full store
Aye receives as much, and more.

"Love That Asketh Love Again" *n.d.*

17 A secret at home is like rocks under tide.

Sc. 2, *Magnus and Morna n.d.*

18 Silence is sweeter than speech.

Sc. 3, *Ibid.*

19 God rest ye, little children; let nothing you affright,
For Jesus Christ, your Saviour, was born this happy night;

Along the hills of Galilee the white blocks sleeping lay,
When Christ, the child of Nazareth, was born on Christmas
   day.
             "Christmas Carol," St. 2 *n.d.*

20 Hour after hour the passionless bright face
    Climbs up the desolate blue.
             "Moon-Struck" *n.d.*

21 Keep what is worth keeping—
    And with the breath of kindness
    Blow the rest away.
             "Friendship" *n.d.*

22 Oh my son's my son till he gets him a wife,
    But my daughter's my daughter all her life.
             "Young and Old" *n.d.*

23 O the green things growing, the green things growing,
    The faint sweet smell of the green things growing!
             "Green Things Growing" *n.d.*

24 Pierce with thy trill the dark,
    Like a glittering music spark.
             "A Rhyme About Birds" *n.d.*

25 Duty's a slave that keeps the keys,
    But Love the master goes in and out
    Of his goodly chambers with song and shout,
    Just as he pleases—just as he pleases.
             "Plighted" *n.d.*

26 Faith needs her daily bread.
             Ch. 10, *Fortune's Marriage n.d.*

977. Lucy Larcom (1826–1893)

1 He who plants a tree
    Plants a hope.
       "Plant a Tree," St. 1, *Poetical Works of Lucy Larcom 1885*

2 Canst thou prophesy, thou little tree,
    What the glory of thy boughs shall be?
             Ibid.

3 I do not own an inch of land,
    But all I see is mine.
             "A Strip of Blue," Ibid.

4 If the world seems cold to you,
    Kindle fires to warm it!
             "Three Old Saws," Ibid.

5 If the world's a wilderness,
    Go, build houses in it!
             Ibid.

6 There is light in shadow and shadow in light,
    And black in the blue of the sky.
             "Black in Blue Sky," St. 2, Ibid.

7 June falls asleep upon her bier of flowers.
             "Death of June," Ibid.

8 Oh, her heart's adrift, with one
    On an endless voyage gone!
    Night and morning
    Hannah's at the window binding shoes.
             "Hannah Binding Shoes," St. 2, Ibid.

9 Breathe thy balm upon the lonely,
    Gentle Sleep!
             "Sleep Song," Ibid.

10 Each red stripe has blazened forth
    Gospels writ in blood;
    Every star has sung the birth
    Of some deathless good.
             "The Flag," Ibid.

11 The land is dearer for the sea,
    The ocean for the shore.
             "On the Beach," St. 11, Ibid.

978. Jane Francesca Wilde (1826–1896)

1 We have now traced the history of women from Paradise to the nineteenth century and have heard nothing through the long roll of the ages but the clank of their fetters.
         "The Bondage of Women," *Social Studies 1893*

2 Weary men, what reap ye?—"Golden corn for the stranger."
    What sow ye?—"Human corpses that await for the Avenger."
    Fainting forms, all hunger-stricken, what see you in the offing?
    "Stately ships to bear our food away amid the stranger's scoff-
      ing."
    There's a proud array of soldiers—what do they round your
      door?
    "They guard our master's granaries from the thin hands of the
      poor."
            "Ballad of the Irish Famine" *n.d.*

979. Mathilda J. Gage (1826–1898)

1 This Book is *Inscribed* to the Memory of my Mother, who was at once mother, sister, friend: *Dedicated* to all Christian women and men, of whatever creed or name who, bound by Church or State, have not dared to Think for Themselves: *Addressed* to all Persons, who, breaking away from custom and the usage of ages, dare seek Truth for the sake of Truth. To all such it will be welcome; to all others, aggressive and educational.
    Dedication, *Woman, Church and State: A Historical Account of the Status of Woman Through the Christian Ages with Reminiscences of the Matriarchate* (repr. 1972) *1893*

2 . . . the most grievous wrong ever inflicted upon woman has been in the Christian teaching that she was not created equal with man, and the consequent denial of her rightful place in Church and State.
        Ch. I, "The Matriarchate" (p. 12), Ibid.

3 The whole ancient world recognized a female priesthood . . .
             Ibid.

4 While the inferior and secondary position of woman early became an integral portion of Christianity, its fullest efforts are seen in Church teaching regarding marriage. . . . . Had it not been for the fall, God would have found some way outside of this relation for populating the world, consequently marriage was regarded as a condition of peculiar temptation and trial; celibacy as one of especial holiness.
        Ch. II, "Celibacy" (pp. 49–50), Ibid.

5 One of the most revered ancient Scriptures, The Gospel according to the Hebrews, which was in use as late as the second century of the Christian era, taught the equality of the feminine in the Godhead; also that daughters should inherit with

sons. . . . The fact remains undeniable that at the advent of Christ, a recognition of the feminine element in the divinity had not entirely died out from general belief . .

(pp. 50–51), Ibid.

6   Without predetermined intention of wrong doing, man has been so molded by the Church doctrine of ages and the coordinate laws of State as to have become blind to the justice of woman's demand for freedom such as he possesses.

(p. 63), Ibid.

7   To the theory of "God the Father," shorn of the divine attribute of motherhood, is the world beholden for its most degrading beliefs, its most infamous practices.

(p. 69), Ibid.

8   No greater crime against humanity has ever been known than the division of morality into two codes, the strict for woman, the lax for man. Nor has woman been the sole sufferer from this creation of Two Moral Codes within the Christian Church. Through it man has lost fine discrimination between good and evil, and the Church itself as the originator of this distinction in sin upon the trend of sex, has become the creator and sustainer of injustice, falsehood, and the crimes into which its priests have most deeply sunk.

(p. 109), Ibid.

9   She was taught that sensual submission to man, and the bearing of children, were the two reasons for her having been created, and that the woman who failed in either had no excuse for longer encumbering the earth.

Ch. IV, "Marquette" (p. 155), Ibid.

10   The Parliament of Toulouse burned 400 witches at one time. Four hundred woman at one hour on the public square, dying the horrid death of fire for a crime which never existed save in the imagination of those persecutors and which grew in their imagination from a false belief in woman's extraordinary wickedness, based upon a false theory as to original sin.

Ch. V, "Witchcraft" (p. 228), Ibid.

11   In the fourteenth century the church decreed that any woman who healed others without having duly studied, was a witch and should suffer death; yet in that same century, 1527, at Basle, Paracelsus* threw all his medical works, including those of Hippocrates and Galen into the fire, saying that he knew nothing except what he had learned from witches.

(pp. 240–41), Ibid.
*German-Swiss alchemist and physician (1493–1541)

12   The superior learning of witches was recognized in the widely extended belief of their ability to work miracles. . . . As knowledge has ever been power, the church feared its use in woman's hands, and leveled its deadliest blows at her.

(p. 243–44), Ibid.

13   What was termed magic, among men, was called witchcraft in woman. The one was rarely, the other invariably, punished.

(p. 251), Ibid.

14   Woman is not regarded as a person but as a field, cultivable or not, as the possessor desires. As a field can neither have faith, nor intellect, nor a will of its own, it would be absurd for a man to occupy himself about what a woman believes, thinks, or wishes. She is absolutely nothing but her husband's domain. He cultivates it and reaps the harvest, for the harvest belongs to the proprietor.

(p. 321), Ibid.

15   When woman interprets the Bible for herself, it will be in the interest of a higher morality, a purer home. Monogamy is woman's doctrine, as polygamy is man's.

Ch. VII, "Polygamy" (p. 424), Ibid.

16   Man, ever unjust to woman, has been no less so in the entire field of work. He has not taken upon himself the entire work of the world, as commanded, but has ever imposed a large portion of it upon woman. Neither do all men labor; but thousands in idleness evade the "curse" of work pronounced upon all men alike.

Ch. VIII, "Women and Work" (pp. 432–35), Ibid.

17   Viewing her through the Christian Ages, we find woman has chiefly been regarded as an element of wealth; the labor of wife and daughters, the sale of the latter in the prostitution of a loveless marriage, having been an universally extended form of domestic slavery, one which the latest court decisions recognize as still extant.

Ibid.

18   Man in thrusting the enforcement of his "curse" upon woman in Christian lands has made her the greatest unpaid laborer of the world.

(p. 441), Ibid.

19   The individual and not the family is the social unit; the rights of individuals are foremost.

Ch. IX, "The Church of Today" (p. 498), Ibid.

20   It must be noted that the chief reason given by the church for assuming woman's greater guilt in committing adultery is not based upon the greater immorality of the act, per se, but the injury to property rights, succession, etc."

(p. 500), Ibid.

21   The most stupendous system of organized robbery known has been that of the church towards woman, a robbery that has not only taken her self-respect but all rights of person; the fruits of her own industry; her opportunities of education; the exercise of her own judgment, her own conscience, her own will.

Ch. X, "Past, Present, and Future" (p. 527), Ibid.

21   But woman is learning for herself that not self-sacrifice, but self-development, is her first duty in life; and this, not primarily for the sake of others but that she may become fully herself; a perfectly rounded being from every point of view; her duty to others being a secondary consideration arising from those relations in life where she finds herself placed at birth, or those which later she voluntarily assumes.

(pp. 530–31), Ibid.

22   The church and civilization are antipodal; one means authority, the other freedom; one means conservatism, the other progress; one means the rights of god as interpreted by the priesthood, the other the rights of humanity as interpreted by humanity. Civilization advances by free-thought, free speech, free men.

(p. 540), Ibid.

980. Dorothy Nevill (1826–1913)

1   It seems to be that, had the educational authorities attempted to keep alive these local industries by encouraging the children under their charge not to abandon them, they would have been doing much more good than by teaching smatterings of many totally useless subjects, which, imperfectly understood and

soon forgotted, have but served to convert the English rustic into a somewhat dissatisfied imitation of the Londoner, whilst thoroughly stamping out that local character and individuality which was such an admirable feature of old-time country life.

Ch. 3, *The Reminiscences of Lady Dorothy Nevill 1907*

2   The commercial class has always mistrusted verbal brilliancy and wit, deeming such qualities, perhaps with some justice, frivolous and unprofitable.

Ch. 8, Ibid.

3   Society to-day and Society as I formerly knew it are two entirely different things; indeed, it may be questioned whether Society, as the word used to be understood, now exists at all. . . . Now all is changed, and wealth has usurped the place formerly held by wit and learning. The question is not now asked, "Is So-and-so clever?" but, instead, "Is So-and-so rich?"

Ibid.

4   It is, I think, a good deal owing to the preponderance of the commercial element in Society that conversation has sunk to its present dull level of conventional chatter.

Ibid.

5   The French I think are improved, not so childish—how refined their manners and talk and how dirty their habits—morality and decency they know nothing of, but yet with benefit we might exchange a little of our morality for some of their cooking virtues. . . .

Letter to a Friend (1871), *The Life and Letters of Lady Dorothy Nevill*, Ralph Nevill, ed. *1919*

981. Ethel Lynn Beers (1827–1879)

1   All quiet along the Potomac to-night,
No sound save the rush of the river,
While soft falls the dew on the face of the dead,
The picket's off duty forever.

"The Picket Guard," St. 6 (1861), *All Quiet Along the Potomac and Other Poems 1879*

2   Art thou a pen, whose task shall be
To drown in ink
What writers think?
Oh, wisely write,
That pages white
Be not the worse for ink and thee.

"The Gold Nugget" *n.d.*

3   Oh, Mother! Laugh your merry note,
Be gay and glad, but don't forget
From baby's eyes look out a soul
That claims a home in Eden yet.

"Weighing the Baby" *n.d.*

4   Only a mother's heart can be
Patient enough for such as he.

"Which Shall It Be" *n.d.*

982. Rose Terry Cooke (1827–1892)

1   Yet courage, soul! nor hold thy strength in vain,
In hope o'er come the steeps God set for thee,
For past the Alpine summits of great pain
Lieth thine Italy.

"Beyond," St. 4 *n.d.*

2   Darlings of the forest!
Blossoming alone

When Earth's grief is sorest
For her jewels gone. . . .

"Trailing Arbutus" *n.d.*

983. Ellen Howarth (1827–1899)

1   Who hath not saved some trifling thing
More prized than jewels rare,
A faded flower, a broken ring,
A tress of golden hair.

"'Tis But a Little Faded Flower" *n.d.*

2   Where is the heart that doth not keep,
Within its inmost core,
Some fond remembrance hidden deep,
Of days that are no more?

Ibid.

984. Johanna Spyri (1827–1901)

1   "You mischievous child!" she cried, in great excitement. "What are you thinking of? Why have you taken everything off? What does it mean?"
     "I do not need them," replied the child, and did not look sorry for what she had done.

Ch. 1, *Heidi 1885*

2   "Oh, I wish that God had not given me what I prayed for! It was not so good as I thought."

Ch. 11, Ibid.

3   "One must wait," she said after a while, "and must always think that soon the good God will bring something to make one happier; that something will come out of the trouble, but I must keep perfectly quiet, and not run away."

Ch. 17, Ibid.

4   "If your ABC is not learned to-day,
Go to be punished to-morrow, I say."

Ch. 19, Ibid.

5   ". . . anger makes us all stupid."

Ch. 23, Ibid.

985. Martha Johnson Patterson (1828–1860s)

1   We are plain folks from Tennessee, called here by a national calamity. I hope not too much will be expected of us.

Comment after President Lincoln's* assassination, when her father, Andrew Johnson,** took office, Quoted in *First Ladies* by Betty Boyd Caroli *1987*
*(1809–1865), 16th president of the United States (1861–1865).
**(1808–1875), 17th president of the United States (1865–1869).

986. Elizabeth Charles (1828–1896)

1   To know how to say what others only know how to think is what makes men poets or sages; and to dare to say what others only dare to think makes men martyrs or reformers—or both.

Chronicle of the Schönberg-Cotta Family 1863

987. Margaret Oliphant (1828–1897)

1   The first thing which I can record concerning myself is, that I was born. . . . These are wonderful words. This life, to which neither time nor eternity can bring diminution—this everlasting living soul, *began*. My mind loses itself in these depths.

Bk. I, Ch. 1, *Memoirs and Resolutions of Adam Graeme, of Mossgray*, Vol. I *1852*

2 "I am perfectly safe—nobody can possibly be safer than such a woman as I am, in poverty and middle age," said this strange acquaintance. "It is an immunity that women don't often prize. Mr. Vincent, but it is very valuable in its way."
Ch. 9, "Salem Chapel" *1863*

3 ". . . the world does not care, though our hearts are breaking; it keeps its own time."
Ch. 18, Ibid.

4 "There ain't a worm but will turn when he's trod upon. . . ."
Ch. 20, *The Perpetual Curate*, Vol. II *1864*

5 The incomprehensibleness of women is an old theory, but what is that to the curious wondering observation with which wives, mothers, and sisters watch the other unreasoning animal in those moments when he has snatched the reins out of their hands, and is not to be spoken to! . . . It is best to let him come to, and feel his own helplessness.
"The Rector," Ch. 4, *Chronicles of Carlingford*, No. 1 *1866*

6 For everybody knows that it requires very little to satisfy the gentlemen, if a woman will only give her mind to it.
Ibid.

7 As for pictures and museums, that don't trouble me. The worst of going abroad is that you've always got to look at things of that sort. To have to do it at home would be beyond a joke.
"Phoebe, Junior," Ch. 26, No. 5, Ibid.

8 To have a man who can flirt is next thing to indispensable to a leader of society.
"Miss Marjoribanks," Ch. 13, No. 4, Ibid.

9 Oh, never mind the fashion. When one has a style of one's own, it is always twenty times better.
Ch. 31, No. 4, Ibid.

10 Temptations come, as a general rule, when they are sought.
Ch. 47, Ibid.

11 It, the thirteenth century, possessed few of the virtues of civilization, had little time for thought and none for speculation, and was marked by all the rudeness of manners and morals, indifference to human life and callousness to suffering which are almost inseparable from continuous and oft-repeated wars.
Introduction, *Francis of Assisi 1871*

12 She was not clever; you might have said she had no mind at all; but so wise and right and tender a heart, that it was as good as genius.
Ch. 1, *A Little Pilgrim 1882*

13 "And we who were the workers began to contend one against another to satisfy the gnawings of the rage that was in our hearts. For we had deceived ourselves, thinking once more that all would be well; while all the time nothing was changed."
Ch. 2, Ibid.

14 "One does not want to hear one's thoughts; most of them are not worth hearing."
Ch. 3, Ibid.

15 It *was* a bore to go out into these aimless assemblies where not to go was a social mistake, yet to go was weariness of the flesh and spirit.
Ch. 5, *A Country Gentleman and His Family*, Vol. III *1886*

16 "A girl who has been talked about is always at a disadvantage. She had much better keep quite quiet until the story has all died away."
Ch. 12, Ibid.

17 In the history of men and of commonwealth there is a slow progression, which, however faint, however deferred, yet gradually goes on, leaving one generation always a trifle better than that which preceded it, with some scrap of new possession, some right assured, some small inheritance gained.
Introduction, *The Literary History of England 1889*

18 There are many variations in degree of the greatest of human gifts, but they are few in kind.
Pt. IV, Ch. 3, *Royal Edinburgh 1890*

19 It has been my fate in a long life of production to be credited chiefly with the equivocal virtue of industry, a quality so excellent in morals, so little satisfactory in art.
Preface, *The Heir Presumptive and the Heir Apparent 1892*

20 The highest ideal [in the fifteenth century] was that of war, war no doubt sometimes for good ends, to redress wrongs, to avenge injury, to make crooked things straight—but yet always war, implying a state of affairs in which the last thing that men thought of was the Golden Rule, and the highest attainment to be looked for was the position of a protector, doer of justice, deliverer of the oppressed.
Ch. 1, *Jeanne d'Arc* 1896*
*See 249.

21 It is not necessary to be a good man in order to divine what in certain circumstances a good and pure spirit will do.
Ch. 17, Ibid.

22 I could not help but say that Mr. Carlyle* seemed the only virtuous philosopher we had. Upon which his wife** answered, "My dear, if Mr. Carlyle's digestion had been stronger, there is no saying what he might have been!"
Letter (May 1866), *Autobiography and Letters of Mrs. Margaret Oliphant 1899*
*Thomas Carlyle (1795–1881), English historian, writer. **Jane Welsh Carlyle ; see 853.

23 There is something very solemn in the thought of a great spirit like hers* entering the spiritual world which she did not believe in. If we are right in our faith, what a blessed surprise for her!
Letter (26 December 1880), Ibid.
*Reference to George Eliot (see 930), who had recently died.

24 Imagination is the first faculty wanting in those that do harm to their kind.
"Innocent" *n.d.*

988. Mary Jane Holmes (1828–1907)

1 ". . . but needn't tell me that prayers made up is as good as them as isn't. . . ."
Ch. 1, *The Cameron Pride 1867*

2 "Keep yourself unspotted from the world," Morris had said, and she repeated it to herself asking, "how shall I do that? how can one be good and fashionable too?"
Ch. 19, Ibid.

3 "If the body you bring back has my George's heart within it, I shall love you just the same as I do now. . . ."
Ch. 3, *Rose Mather 1868*

989. Elizabeth Doten (1829–?)

1 God of the granite and the rose,
    Soul of the sparrow and the bee,
    The mighty tide of being flows
    Through countless channels, Lord, from Thee.

                        "Reconciliation" *c.1870*

990. Edna Dean Proctor (1829–1923)

1 Now God avenges the life he gladly gave,
    Freedom reigns to-day!

                        "John Brown"* *n.d.*

    *American militant abolitionist (1800–1859).

2 O there are tears for him,*
    O there are cheers for him—
    Liberty's champion, Cid of the West.

                        "Cid of the West" *n.d.*

    *Referring to Theodore Roosevelt (1858–1919), 26th president of the United States (1901–1909).

3 The fasts are done; the Aves said;
    The moon has filled her horn,
    And in the solemn night I watch
    Before the Easter morn.

                        "Easter Morning" *n.d.*

991. Charlotte Barnard (1830–1869)

1 I cannot sing the old songs,
    Or dream those dreams again.

          "I Cannot Sing the Old Songs" *c. 1860*

2 Take back the freedom thou cravest,
    Leaving the fetters to me.

                  "Take Back the Heart" *c. 1860*

992. Helen Fiske Hunt Jackson (1830–1885)

1 There is nothing so skillful in its own defense as imperious pride.

                  Ch. 13, *Ramona* 1884

2 There cannot be found in the animal kingdom a bat, or any other creature, so blind in its own range of circumstance and connection, as the greater majority of human beings in the bosom of their families.

                             Ibid.

3 Wounded vanity knows when it is mortally hurt; and limps off the field, piteous, all disguises thrown away. But pride carries its banner to the last.

                             Ibid.

4 That indescribable expression peculiar to people who hope they have not been asleep, but know they have.

                      Ch. 14, Ibid.

5 Words are less needful to sorrow than to joy.

                      Ch. 17, Ibid.

6 My body, eh. Friend Death, how now?
    Why all this tedious pomp of writ?
    Thou hast reclaimed it sure and slow
    For half a century, bit by bit.

                  "Habeas Corpus," St. 1 *1885*

7 Father, I scarcely dare to pray,
    So clear I see, now it is done,

How I have wasted half my day,
And left my work but just begun.

                      "A Last Prayer" *n.d.*

8 But all lost things are in the angels' keeping. . . .

                  "At Last," St. 6 *n.d.*

9 Great loves, to the last, have pulses red;
    All great loves that have ever died dropped dead.

                      "Dropped Dead" *n.d.*

10 We sail, at sunrise, daily, "outward bound."

                    "Outward Bound." *n.d.*

11 She said: "The daisy by deceives;
    'He loves me not,' 'He loves me well,'
    One story no two daisies tell."
    Ah foolish heart, which waits and grieves
    Under the daisy's mocking spell.

                  "The Sign of the Daisy" *n.d.*

12 Who longest waits of all most surely wins.

                "The Victory of Patience" *n.d.*

13 Bee to the blossom, moth to the flame;
    Each to his passion; what's in a name?

                  "Vanity of Vanities" *n.d.*

14 O Sweet delusive Noon,
    Which morning climbs to find,
    O moment sped too soon,
    And morning left behind.

                  "Noon," *Verses n.d.*

15 Find me the men on earth who care
    Enough for faith or creed today
    To seek a barren wilderness
    For simple liberty to pray.

           "The Pilgrim Forefathers," St. 5 *n.d.*

16 Love has a tide!

                      "Tides" *n.d.*

17 Oh, write of me, not "Died in bitter pains,"
    But "Emigrated to another star!"

                    "Emigravit" *n.d.*

18 O suns and skies and clouds of June,
    And flowers of June together,
    Ye cannot rival for one hour
    October's bright blue weather.

          "October's Bright Blue Weather," St. 1 *n.d.*

19 The mighty are brought low by many a thing
    Too small to name. Beneath the daisy's disk
    Lies hid the pebble for the fatal sling.

                      "Danger" *n.d.*

993. Emily Dickinson (1830–1886)

1 Will you tell me my fault, frankly as to yourself, for I had rather wince, than die. Men do not call the surgeon to commend the bone, but to set it, Sir.

           Letter to Thomas Wentworth Higginson,* *The Letters of Emily Dickinson*, Vol. 2, Thomas H. Johnson, ed. *July 1862*
    *American clergyman, author and editor (1823–1911).

2 Success is counted sweetest
    By those who ne'er succeed.

                No. 67, St. 1 (c. 1859), Ibid.

3 Surgeons must be very careful
   When they take the knife!
   Underneath their fine incisions
   Stirs the Culprit—Life!

   No. 108, (c. 1859), Ibid.

4 To fight aloud is very brave,
   But gallanter, I know,
   Who charge within the bosom
   The Cavalry of Woe.

   No. 126, Ibid.

5 Just lost when I was saved!

   No. 160, St. 1 (c. 1860), Ibid.

6 "Faith" is a fine invention
   When Gentlemen can *see*—
   But *Microscopes* are prudent
   In an Emergency.

   No. 185 (c. 1860), Ibid.

7 "Hope" is the thing with feathers—
   That perches in the soul—
   And sings the tune without the words—
   And never stops—at all—

   No. 254, St. 1 (c. 1861), Ibid.

8 There's a certain Slant of light,
   Winter Afternoons—
   That oppresses like the Heft
   Of Cathedral Tunes—

   No. 258, St. 1 (c. 1861), Ibid.

9 A single Screw of Flesh
   Is all that pins the Soul

   No. 262 (c. 1861), Ibid.

10 I'm nobody, Who are you?
   Are you—Nobody—too?

   No. 288, St. 1 (1861), Ibid.

11 How dreary—to be—Somebody!
   How public—like a frog—

   St. 2, Ibid.

12 I tasted—careless—then—
   I did not know the Wine
   Came once a World—Did you?

   No. 296, St. 3 (c. 1861), Ibid.

13 I reason, Earth is short—
   And Anguish—absolute—
   And many hurt,
   But, what of that?

   No. 301, St. 1 (c. 1862), Ibid.

14 The Soul selects her own Society—
   Then—shuts the Door—

   No. 303, St. 1 (c. 1862), Ibid.

15 I'll tell you how the Sun rose—
   A Ribbon at a time—

   No. 318 (c. 1862), Ibid.

16 Some keep the Sabbath going to Church—
   I keep it, staying at Home—
   With a Bobolink for a chorister—
   And an Orchard, for a Dome—

   No. 324, St. 1 (c. 1860), Ibid.

17 After great pain, a formal feeling comes—

   No. 341, St. 1 (c. 1862), Ibid.

18 Much Madness is divinest Sense—
   To a discerning Eye—
   Much Sense—the starkest Madness—

   No. 435, St. 1 (c. 1862), Ibid.

19 This is my letter to the World
   That never wrote to Me—

   No. 441, St. 1 (c. 1862), Ibid.

20 I heard a Fly buzz—when I died—

   No. 465, St. 1 (c. 1862), Ibid.

21 I reckon—when I count at all—
   First—Poets—Then the Sun—
   Then Summer—Then the Heaven of God—
   And then—the List is done—

   No. 569, St. 1 (c. 1862), Ibid.

22 The Brain—is wider than the Sky—
   For—put them side by side—
   The one the other will contain
   With ease—and You—beside—

   No. 632, St. 1 (c. 1862), Ibid.

23 I dwell in Possibility—
   A fairer House than Prose—
   More numerous of Windows—
   Superior—for doors—

   No. 657, St. 1 (c. 1862), Ibid.

24 The Soul unto itself
   Is an imperial friend—
   Or the most agonizing Spy—
   An Enemy—could send—

   No. 683, St. 1 (c. 1862), Ibid.

25 Because I could not stop for Death—
   He kindly stopped for me—

   No. 712, St. 1 (c. 1863), Ibid.

26 My Life had stood—a Loaded Gun—
   In Corners. . .

   No. 754, St. 1 (c. 1863), Ibid.

27 Of Consciousness, her awful Mate
   The Soul cannot be rid—

   No. 894, Ibid.

28 If I can stop one Heart from breaking
   I shall not live in vain

   No. 919, St. 1 (c. 1864), Ibid.

29 I never saw a Moor—
   I never saw the Sea—
   Yet know I how the Heather looks
   And what a Billow be.

   No. 1052, St. 1 (c. 1865), Ibid.

30 The Sweeping up the Heart
   And putting Love away

   No. 1078, St. 2 (c. 1866), Ibid.

31 A great hope fell
   You heard no noise
   The Ruin was within

   No. 1123, St. 1 (c. 1868), Ibid.

32 Tell all the Truth but tell it slant—
   Success in Circuit lies
                    No. 1129, St. 1 (c. 1868), Ibid.

33 A word is dead
   When it is said,
   Some say.
   I say it just
   Begins to live
   That day.
                    No. 1212 in toto (1872?), Ibid.

34 A Deed knocks first at Thought
   And then—it knocks at Will—
   That is the manufacturing spot
                    No. 1216, St. 1 (c. 1872), Ibid.

35 There is no Frigate like a Book
   To take us Lands away
   Nor any Coursers like a Page
   Of prancing Poetry.
                    No. 1263, Ibid.

36 Not with a Club, the Heart is broken
   Nor with a Stone—
   A Whip so small you could not see it
   I've known
   To lash the Magic Creature
   Till it fell.
                    No. 1304, St. 1 (c. 1874), Ibid.

37 That short—potential stir
   That each can make but once—
                    No. 1307, St. 1 (1874), Ibid.

38 A little Madness in the Spring
   Is wholesome even for the King,
   But God be with the Clown—
                    No. 1333, St. 1 (c. 1875), Ibid.

39 Forbidden Fruit a flavor has
   That lawful Orchards mocks—
   How luscious lies within the Pod
   The Pea that Duty locks—
                    No. 1377 (c. 1876), Ibid.

40 To see the Summer Sky
   Is Poetry, though never in a Book it lie—
   True Poems flee—
                    No. 1472, Ibid.

41 The Pedigree of Honey
   Does not concern the Bee—
   A Clover, any time, to him,
   Is Aristocracy—
                    No. 1627, version II (c. 1884), Ibid.

42 Fame is a fickle food
   Upon a shifting plate.
                    No. 1659, Ibid.

43 The distance that the dead have gone
   Does not at first appear—
   Their coming back seems possible
   For many an ardent year.
                    No. 1742, Ibid.

994. Christina Rossetti (1830–1894)

1 Why strive for love when love is o'er. . . .
              "Hearts' Chill Between," St. 2, 22 September 1847

2 When I am dead, my dearest,
   Sing no sad songs for me;
   Plant thou no roses at my head,
   Nor shady cypress tree.
   Be the green grass above me
   With showers and dew drops wet:
   And if thou wilt, remember,
   And if thou wilt, forget
                    "Song," St. 1 12 December 1848

3 To-day is still the same as yesterday,
   To-morrow also even as one of them;
   And there is nothing new under the sun. . . .
                    "One Certainty" 2 June 1849

4 My friends have failed one by one,
   Middle-aged, young, and old,
   Till the ghosts were warmer to me
   Than my friends that had grown cold.
                    "A Chilly Night," St. 2 11 February 1856

5 Because the birth of my life
   Is come, my love is come to me.
                    "A Birthday," St. 2 1861

6 "Does the road wind up-hill all the way?"
   "Yes, to the very end."
   "Will the day's journey take the whole long day?"
   "From morn to night, my friend."
                    "Up-Hill," St. 1 1861

7 My heart is like a singing bird.
                    "A Birthday," St. 1 1861

8 We, one, must part in two:
   Verily death is this:
   I must die.
                    "Wife to Husband," St. 5 8 June 1861

9 Too late for love, too late for joy,
   Too late, too late!
   You loitered on the road too long,
   You trifled at the gate. . . .
              "The Prince's Progress," St. 1 11 November 1861

10 All earth's full rivers cannot fill
   The sea, that drinking thirsteth still.
                    "By the Sea," Goblin Market 1862

11 For there is no friend like a sister
   In calm or stormy weather;
   To cheer one on the tedious way,
   To fetch one if one goes astray,
   To lift one if one totters down,
   To strengthen whilst one stands.
                    "Goblin Market," Ibid.

12 One day in the country
   Is worth a month in town.
                    "Summer," Ibid.

13 Better by far that you should forget and smile
   Than that you should remember and be sad.
                    "Remember" (25 July 1849), Ibid.

14 "I ate his life as a banquet,
   I drank his life as new wine,
   I've fattened upon his leanness,
   Mine to flourish and his to pine."
                    "Cannot Sweeten," St. 7 8 March 1866

15 "For the nobility have blood, if you please, and the literary beggars are welcome to all the brains they've got" (the Doctor smiled, Allen winced visibly); "but you'll find it's us city men who've got backbone, and backbone's the best to wear. . . ."

Ch. 6, *Commonplace, a Tale of Today* 1870

16 So gradually it came to pass that, from looking back together, they took also to looking forward together.

Ch. 17, Ibid.

17 Glow-worms that gleam but yield no warmth in gleaming . . . .
"Till To-morrow," St. 2 *c.* 1882

18 If thou canst dive, bring up pearls. If thou canst not dive, collect amber.

Prefatory Note, *The Face of the Deep* 1892

19 Multitude no less than Unity characterizes various types of God the Holy Spirit.

Ch. 1, Ibid.

20 Rapture and rest, desire and satisfaction, perfection and progress, may seem to clash to-day: to-morrow the paradoxes of earth may reappear as the demonstrations of heaven.

Ch. 4, Ibid.

21 Well spake the soldier who being asked what he would do if he became too weak to cling to Christ, answered, "Then I will pray Him to cling to me."

Ch. 16, Ibid.

22 I might show facts as plain as day:
But, since your eyes are blind, you'd say,
"Where? What?" and turn away.

"A Sketch," St. 3 *n.d.*

23 No wonder that his soul was sad,
When not one penny piece he had.

"Johnny" *n.d.*

24 Hope is like a harebell trembling from its birth. . . .
"Hope is Like a Harebell" *n.d.*

25 Who has seen the wind!
Neither you nor I:
But when the trees bow down their heads,
The wind is passing by.

"Who Has Seen the Wind?", St. 2 *n.d.*

995. Louise Michel (1830–1905)

1 In rebellion alone, woman is at ease, stamping out both prejudices and sufferings; all intellectual women will sooner or later rise in rebellion.

Attributed *1890*

996. Harriet Hosmer (1830–1908)

1 Apropos of a Temple, I have long entertained the hope of seeing before I die a monument erected which shall record the great deeds of women wherever found and it is high time that such a memorial should assume form.

Quoted by Carole Simmons Oles, (p. 24)
The Women's Review of Books, XVI,
No. 2 *November 1998*

997. Sarah Agnes Pryor (1830–1912)

1 The public does not tolerate the intrusion of a man's personal joys and griefs into his official life.

Comment on Franklin Pierce's* inaugural speech (4 March 1853), Quoted in *First Ladies* by Betty Boyd Caroli 1987
* (1804–1869), 14th President of the United States (1853–1857).

998. Maria von Ebner Eschenbach (1830–1916)

1 HE. You apparently occupy yourself but little with reading?
I. Just enough to do penance for my sins, and to keep up my English.

The Two Countesses 1893

2 "Nothing is too strong to express the humiliation of knowing the being one looks up to—or rather one should look up to—to be a nonentity, or the hypocrisy of seeming to defer to him one knows to be one's inferior."

Ibid.

3 "Everyone plays at the game for a time, my dear Paula, because it is the correct thing to do. . . . But thinking persons cannot hide from themselves the consciousness of the hollowness of it all, and then they turn to the realities of life, often bitterly to repent of their wasted years."

Ibid.

4 "Good heavens!" said he, "if it be our clothes alone which fit us for society, how highly we should esteem those who make them."

Ibid.

5 He says a learned woman is the greatest of all calamities.

Ibid.

6 Accident is veiled necessity.

Aphorisms 1905

7 If there is faith that can move mountains, it is faith in your own power.

Ibid.

8 Many think they have a kind heart who only have weak nerves.

Ibid.

9 As far as your self-control goes, as far goes your freedom.

Ibid.

10 Even a stopped clock is right twice a day.

Ibid.

11 Conquer, but don't triumph.

Ibid.

12 No one is so eager to gain new experience as he who doesn't know how to make use of the old ones.

Ibid.

13 Privilege is the greatest enemy of right.

Ibid.

14 Those whom we support hold us up in life.

Ibid.

15 Only the thinking man lives his life, the thoughtless man's life passes him by.

Ibid.

16 You can stay young as long as you can learn, acquire new habits and suffer contradiction.

Ibid.

17 In youth we learn; in age we understand.

Ibid.

18 Fear not those who argue but those who dodge.

Ibid.

19 To be content with little is hard, to be content with much, impossible.

Ibid.

20 He who believes in freedom of the will has never loved and never hated.

Ibid.

21 Whenever two good people argue over principles, they are both right.

Ibid.

22 Imaginary evils are incurable.

Ibid.

23 We don't believe in rheumatism and true love until the first attack.

Ibid.

24 We are so vain that we even care for the opinion of those we don't care for.

Ibid.

25 Oh, say not foreign war! A war is never foreign.

Quoted in *War, Peace, and the Future* by Ellen Key* 1916
*See 1121.

999. Belva Lockwood (1830–1917)

1 I do not believe in sex discrimination in literature, law, politics, or trade—or that modesty and virtue are more becoming to women than to men, but wish we had more of it everywhere.

Quoted in Pt. II, Ch. 8, *Lady for the Defense* by Mary Virginia Fox 1975

2 I know we can't abolish prejudice through laws, but we can set up guidelines for our actions by legislation. If women are given equal pay for Civil Service jobs, maybe other employers will do the same.

Ch. 11, Ibid.

3 If nations could only depend on fair and impartial judgments in a world court of law, they would abandon the senseless, savage practice of war.

Ch. 15, Ibid.

4 No one can claim to be called Christian who gives money for the building of warships and arsenals.

Address at Westminster Hall, London (c.1886), Ibid.

5 I have been told that there is no precedent for admitting a woman to practice in the Supreme Court of the United States. The glory of each generation is to make its own precedents. As there was none for Eve in the Garden of Eden, so there need be none for her daughters on entering the colleges, the church, or the courts.*

Pt. III, Ch. 13, Ibid.

*Lockwood argued in favor of admitting women to practice in the U.S. Supreme Court, for which there was no precedent. In 1879 she became the first woman to do so.

6 Has God given one half of his creatures talents and gifts that are but a mockery—wings but not to fly?

Quoted in *The 50 Most Influential Women in American Law* by Dawn Bradley Berry* 1996
*See 3435.

1000. Helen Olcott Bell (1830–1918)

1 To a woman, the consciousness of being well-dressed gives a sense of tranquility which religion fails to bestow.

Letters and Social Aims: R. W. Emerson 1876
*Ralph Waldo E—, American poet and essayist (1803–1882).

1001. Mother Jones (1830–1930)

1 Sometimes I'm in Washington, then in Pennsylvania, Arizona, Texas, Alabama, Colorado, Minnesota. My address is like my shoes. It travels with me. I abide where there is a fight against wrong.

Congressional Hearing, Quoted in *The Rebel Girl*, Pt. II by Elizabeth Gurley Flynn* 1955
*See 1603.

2 Sit down and read. Educate yourself for the coming conflicts.

Quoted in *Ms.* (New York) *November 1981*

3 Pray for the dead and fight like hell for the living.

Motto *n.d.*

4 Get it right, I ain't a humanitarian. . . . I'm a hell-raiser!

Comment *n.d.*

1002. Amelia Edwards (1831–1889)

1 The Queen has lands and gold, Mother
The Queen has lands and gold,
While you are forced to your empty breast
A skeleton Babe to hold. . . .

"Give Me Three Grains of Corn, Mother," St. 4 *n.d.*

2 What has poor Ireland done, Mother,
What has poor Ireland done,
That the world looks on, and sees us starve,
Perishing one by one?

St. 5, Ibid.

1003. Lucy Webb Hayes (1831–1889)

1 Women's mind is as strong as man's—equal in all things and his superior in some.

Quoted in *First Ladies* by Betty Boyd Caroli 1987

1004. Elena Petrovna Blavatsky (1831–1891)

1 We live in an age of prejudice, dissimulation, and paradox, wherein, like dry leaves caught in a whirlpool, some of us are tossed helpless, hither and thither, ever struggling between our honest convictions and fear of that cruelest of tyrants—PUBLIC OPINION.

"A Paradoxical World," *Lucifer February 1889*

2 For fourteen years our Theosophical Society has been before the public. Born with the three-fold object of infusing a little more mutual brotherly feeling in mankind; of investigating the

mysteries of nature from the Spiritual and Psychic aspect. . . . If it did not do all the good that a richer Society might, it certainly did no harm.

"On Pseudo-Theosophy," Ibid.

3 We must prepare and study truth under every aspect, endeavoring to ignore nothing, if we do not wish to fall into the abyss of the unknown when the hour shall strike.

Quoted in *La Revue Theosophique* 21 March 1889

4 This idea of passing one's whole life in moral idleness, and having one's hardest work and duty done by another—whether God or man—is most revolting to us, as it is most degrading to human dignity.

Sec. 5, *The Key to Theosophy* 1893

5 And so the only reality in our conception is the hour of man's *post mortem* life, when, disembodied—during the period of that pilgrimage which we call "the cycle of re-births"—he stands face to face with truth and not the mirages of his transitory earthly existences.

Sec. 9, Ibid.

6 It is the worst of crimes and dire in its results. . . . Voluntary death would be an abandonment of our present post and of the duties incumbent on us, as well as an attempt to shirk karmic responsibilities, and thus involve the creation of new Karma.

Sec. 12, Ibid.

7 Just back from under the far-reaching shadow of the Eighth Wonder of the World—the gigantic iron carrot that goes by the name of the Eiffel Tower. Child of its country, wondrous in its size, useless in its object, as shaky and vacillating as the republican soil upon which it is built, it has not one single moral feature of its seven ancestors, not one trait of atavism to boast of.

"The Eighth Wonder," *Lucifer* October 1891

8 For in this age of crass and illogical materialism, the Esoteric Philosophy [theosophy] alone is calculated to withstand the repeated attacks on all and everything man holds most dear and sacred in his inner spiritual life.

Introduction, *The Secret Doctrine* (1893) 1918

9 If there were such a thing as a void, a vacuum in Nature, one ought to find it produced, according to a physical law, in the minds of helpless admirers of the "lights" of Science, who pass their time in mutually destroying their teachings.

Sec. 17, Ibid.

1005. Myra R. Bradwell (1831–1894/96)

1 [Mary Lincoln*] is no more insane than I am.

Comment, Quoted in *First Ladies*
by Betty Boyd Caroli 1987

*See 920.

1006. Henrietta Dobree (1831–1894)

1 Safely, safely, gather'd in,
Far from sorrow, far from sin.

"Child's Hymn Book" *n.d.*

1007. Isabel Burton (1831–1896)

1 Without any cant, does not Providence provide wonderfully for us?

Ch. 15, *Arabia Egypt India* 1879

2 Blessed be they who invented pens, ink, and paper!

Bk. I, Ch. II, *The Romance of Isabel, Lady Burton*, Vol. I,
W. H. Wilkins, ed. *1897*

3 Happy is she who meets at her first start the man who is to guide her for life, whom she is always to love. Some women grow fastidious in solitude, and find it harder to be mated than married. Those who fear and respect the men they love, those whose judgment and sense confirm their affection, are lucky.

Ch. IV, Ibid.

4 I have learnt since that often in a place one dislikes there will arise some circumstance that will prove the pivot on which part, or the whole, of one's life may turn, and that scene, that town, or that house will in after–years retain a sacred place in one's heart for that thing's sake, which a gayer or a grander scene could never win. And so it was with me.

Ibid.

5 It was not only his eyes* which showed the gypsy peculiarity; he had the restlessness which could stay nowhere long, nor own any spot on earth, the same horror of a corpse, deathbed scenes, and graveyards, or anything which was in the slightest degree ghoulish, though caring little for his own life, the same aptitude for reading the hand at a glance. With many he would drop their hands at once and turn away, nor would anything induce him to speak a word about them.

Ibid.

*Her husband, Sir Richard Burton, British explorer and Orientalist (1821–90).

6 They say it is time I married (perhaps it is); but it is never time to marry any man one does not love, because such a deed can never be undone.

Ch. V, Ibid.

7 I do not want to think it over [Burton's* proposal]. I have been thinking it over for six years, ever since I first saw you at Boulogne. I have prayed for you every morning and night, I have followed all your career minutely, I have read every word you ever wrote, and I would rather have a crust and a tent with you than be queen of all the world; and so I say now, 'Yes, yes, YES!'

Ch. VI, Ibid.

8 She freely unveiled before me. I was not impressed with her charms, and I thought what a fine thing the sheet and the veil would be to some of our European women.

Bk. II, Ch. X, Ibid.

9 I have no leisure to think of style or of polish, or to select the best language, the best English—no time to shine as an authoress. I must just think aloud, so as not to keep the public waiting.

Foreword, *The Life of Captain Sir Richard F. Burton* 1898

1008. Nora Perry (1831–1896)

1 But not alone with the silken snare
Did she catch her lovely floating hair,
For, tying a bonnet under her chin,
She tied a young man's heart within.

"The Love-Knot," St. 1 *n.d.*

2 Some day, some day of days, threading the street
With idle, heedless pace,
Unlooking for such grace,
I shall behold your face!

"Some Day of Days" *n.d.*

3   What silences we keep, year after year,
     With those who are most near to us,
     And dear!

                         "Too Late," St. 1 *n.d.*

4   Who knows the thoughts of a child?

                         "Who Knows," St. 1 *n.d.*

1009. Rebecca Harding Davis (1831–1910)

1   The idiosyncracy of this town is smoke. It rolls solemnly in
slow folds from the great chimneys of the iron foundries, and
settles down in black, slimy pools on the muddy streets. Smoke
on the wharves, smoke on the dinghy boats, on the yellow
river—clinging in a coating of greasy soot to the house-front,
the two faded poplars, the faces of the passers-by.

                         "Life in the Iron Mills," *Atlantic Monthly* (Boston) *April
                         1861*

2   Be just—not like man's law, which seizes on one isolated fact,
but like God's judging angel, whose clear, sad eye saw all the
countless cankering days of this man's life. . . .

                         Ibid.

3   "I tell you, there's something wrong that no talk of 'Liberté' or
'Egalité' will do away. If I had the making of men, these men
who do the lowest part of the world's work should be machines—nothing more—hands. It would be kindness. God help
them! What are taste, reason, to creatures who must live such
lives as that?"

                         Ibid.

4   Reform is born of need, not pity.

                         Ibid.

5   You, Egoist, or Pantheist, or Arminian, busy in making
straight paths for your feet on the hills, do not see it clearly—
this terrible question which men here have gone mad and died
trying to answer. I dare not put this secret into words. I told
you it was dumb. These men, going by with drunken faces and
brains full of unawakened power, do not ask it of Society or of
God. Their lives ask it; their deaths ask it.

                         Ibid.

6   There are moments when a passing cloud, the sun glinting on
the purple thistles, a kindly smile, a child's face, will rouse him
to a passion of pain—when his nature starts up with a mad cry
of rage against God, man, whoever it is that has forced this
vile, slimy life upon him.

                         Ibid.

7   He was . . . a man who sucked the essence out of a science or
philosophy in an indifferent gentlemanly way; who took Kant,
Novalis, Humboldt, for what they were worth in his own
scale; accepting all, despising nothing, in heaven, earth, or hell,
but one-idea'd men; with a temper yielding and brilliant as
summer water, until his Self was touched, when it was ice,
though brilliant still. Such men are not rare in the States.

                         Ibid.

8   Something is lost in the passage of every soul from one eternity
to the other—something pure and beautiful, which might have
been and was not: a hope, a talent, a love, over which the soul
mourns, like Esau deprived of his birthright.

                         Ibid.

9   Every child was taught from his cradle that money was Mam-
mon, the chief agent of the flesh and the devil. As he grew up

it was his duty as a Christian and a gentleman to appear to despise filthy lucre, whatever his secret opinion of it might be.

                         Ch. 1, *Bits of Gossip 1904*

10   Nowhere in this country, from sea to sea, does nature comfort
us with such assurance of plenty, such rich and tranquil beauty
as in those unsung, unpainted hills of Pennsylvania.

                         Ch. 4, Ibid.

11   North and South were equally confident that God was on their
side, and appealed incessantly to Him.

                         Ch. 5, Ibid.

12   We don't look into these unpleasant details of our great struggle [the Civil War]. We all prefer to think that every man who
wore the blue or gray was a Phillip Sidney at heart. These are
sordid facts that I have dragged up. But they are facts. And because we have hidden them our young people have come to
look upon war as a kind of beneficent deity, which not only
adds to the national honor but uplifts a nation and develops
patriotism and courage. That is all true. But it is only fair, too,
to let them know that the garments of the deity are filthy and
that some of her influences debase and befoul a people.

                         Ibid.

13   But while the light burning within may have been divine, the
outer case of the lamp was assuredly cheap enough. [Walt]
Whitman* was, from first to last, a boorish, awkward *poseur*.

                         Ch. 8, Ibid.

     *American poet (1819–1892)

1010. Amelia Barr (1831–1919)

1   "But what do we know of the heart nearest to out own? What
do we know of our own heart? Some ancestor who sailed with
Offa, or who fought with the Ironsides, or protested with the
Covenanters, or legislated with the Puritans, may, at this very
hour, be influencing us, in a way of which we never speak, and
in which no other soul intermeddles."

                         Ch. 1, *Jan Vedder's Wife 1885*

2   ". . . for still I see that forethought spares afterthought and
after-sorrow."

                         Ch. 5, Ibid.

3   "There is no corner too quiet, or too far away, for a woman to
make sorrow in it."

                         Ch. 9, Ibid.

4   "'Is she not handsome, virtuous, rich, amiable?' they asked,
'What hath she done to thee?' The Roman husband pointed to
his sandal. 'Is it not new, is it not handsome and well made?
But none of you can tell where it pinches me.' That old Roman
and I are brothers. Everyone praises 'my good wife, my rich
wife, my handsome wife,' but for all that, the matrimonial
shoe pinches me."

                         Ibid.

5   "Let me tell thee, time is a very precious gift of God; so precious that He only gives it to us moment by moment. He
would not have thee waste it."

                         Ch. 11, Ibid.

6   "It is a sin to be merciful to the wicked, it is that; and the kindness done to them is unblessed, and brings forth sin and
trouble."

                         Ibid.

7 "It is little men know of women; their smiles and their tears alike are seldom what they seem."

Ibid.

8 That is the greatest mistake about the affections. It is not the rise and fall of empires, the birth and death of kings or the marching of armies that move them most. When they answer from their depths, it is to the domestic joys and tragedies of life.

Ch. 14, Ibid.

9 It is only in sorrow bad weather masters us; in joy we face the storm and defy it.

Ibid.

10 But the lover's power is the poet's power. He can make love from all the common strings with which this world is strung.

Ch. 3, *The Belle of Bolling Green* 1904

11 The fate of love is that it always seems too little or too much.

Ch. 5, Ibid.

12 "When men make themselves into brutes it is just to treat them as brutes."

Ch. 8, Ibid.

13 I entered this incarnation on March-the-twenty-ninth, A.D. 1831, at the ancient town of Ulverston, Lancashire, England. My soul came with me. This is not always the case. Every observing mother of a large family knows that the period of spiritual possession varies. . . . I brought my soul with me—an eager soul, impatient for the loves and joys, the struggles and triumphs of the dear, unforgotten world.

Ch. 1, *All the Days of My Life* 1913

14 With renunciation life begins.

Ch. 9, Ibid.

15 The great difference between voyages rests not with the ships, but with the people you meet on them.

Ch. 11, Ibid.

16 What we call death was to him only emigration, and I care not where he now tarries. He is doing God's will, and more alive than ever he was on earth.

Ch. 23, Ibid.

17 Whatever the scientists may say, if we take the supernatural out of life, we leave only the unnatural.

Ch. 26, Ibid.

18 Old age is the verdict of life.

Ibid.

1011. Mary Woolsey (1832–1864)

1 I lay me down to sleep with little thought or care
   Whether my waking finds me here, or there.

"Rest" *n.d.*

1012. Louisa May Alcott (1832–1888)

1 A little kingdom I possess,
   Where thoughts and feelings dwell;
   And very hard the task I find
   Of governing it well.

"My Kingdom," St. 1 *c. 1845*

2 I do not ask for any crown
   But that which all may win;

Nor try to conquer any world
Except the one within.

St. 4, Ibid.

3 Above man's aims his nature rose.
   The wisdom of a just content
   Made one small spot a continent,
   And turned to poetry life's prose.

"Thoreau's Flute,"* St. 2, *Atlantic Monthly* (Boston)
September 1863
*Henry David Thoreau, American philosopher and writer (1817–1862).

4 "She would make a man of me. She puts strength and courage into me as no one else can. She is unlike any girl I ever saw; there's no sentimentality about her; she is wise, and kind, and sweet. She says what she means, looks you straight in the eye, and is as true as steel."

Ch. III, *Behind a Mask: or, A Woman's Power* 1866

5 ". . . rivalry adds so much to the charms of one's conquests."

Ch. VII, Ibid.

6 "I can't get over my disappointment in not being a boy."

Little Women 1868

7 "I shall have to toil and moil all my days, with only little bits of fun now and then, and get old and ugly and sour, because I'm poor, and can't enjoy my life as other girls do. It's a shame!"

Pt. I, Ibid.

8 "Christmas won't be Christmas without any presents."

Ibid.

9 ". . . It seems as if I could do anything when I'm in a passion. I get so savage I could hurt anyone and enjoy it. I'm afraid I *shall* do something dreadful some day, and spoil my life, and make everyone hate me. O Mother, help me . . . ."

Ibid.

10 . . . love is a great beautifier.

Ibid.

11 "You have a good many little gifts and virtues, but there is no need of parading them, for conceit spoils the finest genius. There is not much danger that real talent or goodness will be overlooked long, and the great charm of all power is modesty."

Ch. 7, Ibid.

12 "Housekeeping ain't no joke."

Ch. 11, Ibid.

13 . . . public opinion is a giant which has frightened stouter-hearted Jacks on bigger beanstalks than hers.

Pt. II, Ibid.

14 ". . . love is the only thing that we can carry with us when we go, and it makes the end so easy."

Ibid.

15 . . . she was one of those happily created beings who please without effort, make friends everywhere, and take life so gracefully and easily that less fortunate souls are tempted to believe that such are born under a lucky star.

Ibid.

16 . . . when a man has a great sorrow, he should be indulged in all sort of vagaries till he has lived it down.

Ibid.

17 It takes people a long time to learn the difference between talent and genius, especially ambitious young men and women.

Ibid.

18 . . . she had a womanly instinct that clothes possess an influence more powerful over many than the worth of character or the magic of manners

Ibid.

19 . . . when women are the advisers, the lords of creation don't take the advice until they have persuaded themselves that it is just what they intended to do; then they act upon it, and if it succeeds, they give the weaker vessel half the credit of it; if it fails, they generously give her the whole.

Ibid.

20 ". . . I'm not afraid of storms, for I'm learning how to sail my ship."

Ibid.

21 ". . . What *do* girls do who haven't any mothers to help them through their troubles?"

Ibid.

22 ". . . It's a great comfort to have an artistic sister."

Ibid.

23 ". . . elegance has a bad effect upon my constitution. . . ."

Ibid.

24 "It takes two flints to make a fire."

Ibid.

25 ". . . women have been called queens for a long time, but the kingdom given them isn't worth ruling."

An Old-Fashioned Girl 1869

26 I believe that it is as much a right and duty for women to do something with their lives as for men and we are not going to be satisfied with such frivolous parts as you give us.

Rose in Bloom 1876

27 "[Molly] remained a merry spinster all her days, one of the independent, brave and busy creatures of whom there is such need in the world to take care of other people's wives and children, and to do the many useful jobs that married folk have no time for."

Jack and Jill 1880

28 "[I'm] very glad and grateful that my profession will make me a useful happy and independent spinster."

Jo's Boys 1886

29 My definition [of a philosopher] is of a man up in a balloon, with his family and friends holding the ropes which confine him to the earth and trying to haul him down.

Louisa May Alcott: Her Life, Letters, and Journals, Edna D. Cheney, ed. *1889*

30 Resolved to take Fate by the throat and shake a living out of her.

Ch. 3, Ibid.

31 Father asked us what was God's noblest work. Anna said *men*, but I said *babies*. Men are often bad; babies never are.

Early diary kept at Fruitlands (1843), Ibid.

32 I have at last got the little room I have wanted so long, and am very happy about it. It does me good to be alone. . . .

(1846) Ibid.

33 Philosophers sit in their sylvan hall
And talk of the duties of man,
Of Chaos and Cosmos, Hegel and Kant,
With the Oversoul well in the van;
All on their hobbies they amble away
And a terrible dust they make;
Disciples devout both gaze and adore,
As daily they listen and bake.

"Philosophers" (1845), *Alcott and the Concord School of Philosophy*, Florence Whiting Brown, ed. *1926*

1013. Elizabeth Chase Akers (1832–1911)

1 Backward, turn backward, O Time, in your flight,
Make me a child again, just for to-night!

"Rock Me to Sleep, Mother" *1860*

2 I have grown weary of dust and decay—
Weary of flinging my soul-wealth away;—
Weary of sowing for others to reap;
Rock me to sleep, Mother—rock me to sleep!

St. 2, Ibid.

3 Unremembered and afar
I watched you as I watched a star,
Through darkness struggling into view,
I loved you better than you knew.

"Left Behind," St. 5 *n.d.*

4 Carve not upon a stone when I am dead
The praises which remorseful mourners give
To women's graves—a tardy recompense—
But speak them while I live.

"Till Death," St. 6 *n.d.*

5 Blush, happy maiden, when you feel
The lips that press love's glowing seal.
But as the slow years darker roll,
Grown wiser, the experienced soul
Will own as dearer far than they
The lips which kiss the tears away.

"Kisses" *n.d.*

6 Though we be sick and tired and faint and worn,—
Lo, all things can be borne!

"Endurance," St. 5 *n.d.*

1014. Lucretia Rudolph Garfield (1832–1918)

1 My heart almost broke with the cruel thought that our marriage was based upon the cold, stern word duty.

Letter to James Garfield* (1858), Quoted in *First Ladies* by Betty Boyd Caroli *1987*

*(1831–81), 20th president of the United States.

1015. Mary Walker (1832–1919)

1 If men were really what they profess to be they would not compell women to dress so that the facilities for vice would always be so easy.

Quoted in *Saturday Review* *1935*

1016. Gail Hamilton (1833–1896)

1   Every person is responsible for all the good within the scope of his abilities, and for no more, and none can tell whose sphere is the largest.

"Men and Women," *Country Living and Country Thinking* 1862

2   Whatever an author puts between two covers of his book is public property; whatever of himself he does not put there is his private property, as much as if he had never written a word.

Preface, Ibid.

3   What's virtue in man can't be virtue in a cat.

"Both Sides" *n.d.*

1017. Julia Woodruff (1833–1909)

1   Out of the strain of the Doing,
Into the race of the Done.

"Harvest Home," *Sunday at Home May 1910*

1018. Julia Harris May (1833–1912)

1   If we could know
Which of us, darling, would be the first to go,
Who would be first to breast the swelling tide
And step alone upon the other side—
If we could know!

"If We Could Know" *n.d.*

1019. Lillie Devereux Blake (1833–1913)

1   Among all these strong, pushing, busy men, there seemed no place, and no hope for a woman to expect justice and mercy. These resolute-browed, swift-going, strong-limbed animals, who represented the great brute force of nature, its resistless power, its relentless will could crush out so easily the gentler, more spiritual being, who represented the beauty, the grace, the harmony of creation!

Fettered for Life 1874; rev. 1997

2   Mr. Livingston regarded his daughter in astonishment, as much surprised as one would be, who should see a humming-bird, that was sporting in apparent contentment among the flowers, on a sudden ask to be transformed into an eagle, and aspire to reach the sun.

Ibid.

3   . . . my health is perfect . . . I am always unromantically well . . .

Ibid.

1020. Emily Miller (1833–1913)

1   They sing, young hearts that are full of cheer,
With never a thought of sorrow;
The old goes out, but the glad young year
Comes merrily in tomorrow.

"New Year Song," *The Little Corporal 1865*

2   I love to hear the story
Which angel voices tell.

"I Love to Hear," Ibid.

1021. Hedwig Dohm (1833–1919)

1   For me the beginning of all true progress in the woman question lies in women's right to vote . . . The stronger the emphasis on the difference between the sexes, the clearer the need for the specific representation of women.

Remark (*1873*), Quoted in *Women in World History Curriculum* http://www.womeninworldhistory.com *1996–97*

1022. Josephine Pollard (1834–1892)

1   Though he had Eden to live in,
Man cannot be happy alone.

"We Cannot Be Happy Alone," St. 5 *n.d.*

1023. Katherine Hankey (1834–1911)

1   Tell me the old, old story
Of unseen things above,
Of Jesus and His glory
Of Jesus and His love.

Hymn *n.d.*

1024. Annie Adams Fields (1834–1915)

1   Once men could walk these roads
And hear no sound
Save the sad ocean beating on the shore . . .

"Unchanged," *The Singing Shepherd 1895*

1025. Harriet Kimball (1834–1917)

1   A very rapturing of white;
A wedlock of silence and light:
White, white as the wonder undefiled
Of Eve just wakened in Paradise.

"White Azaleas" *n.d.*

1026. Virginia Backentoe Murphy (1834–1921)

1   O Mary I have not rote you half of the truble we have had but I have rote you anuf to let you now that you dont now what truble is but thank god we have all got throw. [sic]

Letter to her cousin (April 1847),* *Illinois Journal December 1847*

*First detailed account of the disastrous Donner Party trek westward.

2   It was a dreary, desolate, alkali waste; not a living thing was to be seen; it seemed as though the hand of death had been laid upon the country.

Article on the Donner Party (on reaching the shore of the Great Salt Lake, Utah), Quoted in *Century Magazine 1891*

1027. Ellen Palmer Allerton (1835–1893)

1   Beautiful faces are those that wear
Whole-souled honesty printed there

"Beautiful Things," *Walls of Corn, and Other Poems 1894*

1028. Harriet Emma Burton (fl. 1835)

1   The voice of death is on the breeze,
It is the deep-toned bell,
In measured tone so mournfully,
Proclaims the last farewell!

"The White-Rose Wreath," St. 1, *The White-Rose Wreath 1835*

2   Say; can no healing art restore
The pulse of health and life;
Or still, within this feeble frame,
The long, unequal strife?

St. 6, Ibid.

3 Long may endure the hallow'd vows of youth,
Each tender hope its soft fulfilment meet,
To love's first glow, succeed connubial truth,
And years far off, as these found hours, be sweet.
"The Bride," St. 4, Ibid.

4 She was thy comfort, and perhaps thy pride,
Whilst others moved progressive from thy side.
A sweet companion, duteous, grateful, kind,
Blameless in mortal sight, and pure in mind.
Link'd to her sisters and their youthful race,
By changeless love and each domestic grace.
"The Redeemed," St. 4, Ibid.

5 Love, indestructible as pure,
Till memory leaves her, will endure:
And each attempt to quench the flame,
But strenghens it within her frame:
With one calm, gradual, sacred light,
It burns ethereal, firm and bright.
"Woman's Love," St. 2, Ibid.

1029. Celia Thaxter (1835–1894)

1 Across the narrow beach we flit,
One little sandpiper and I.
"The Sandpiper," St. 1 *n.d.*

2 Sad soul, take comfort, nor forget
That sunrise never failed us yet!
"The Sunrise Never Failed Us Yet," St. 4 *n.d.*

3 Look to the East, where up the lucid sky
The morning climbs! The day shall yet be fair.
"Faith" *n.d.*

1030. Mary Bradley (1835–1898)

1 Of all the flowers that come and go
The whole twelve months together,
This little purple pansy brings
Thoughts of the sweetest, saddest things.
"Heartsease" *n.d.*

1031. Olympia Brown (1835–1900)

1 I comforted her [Mother Cobb] by telling her that while it was disagreeable and unreasonable to have our wearing apparel described in the papers, it was inevitable at this stage of woman's progress, editors and reporters being much more able to judge of our clothes than they were of our arguments.
Ch. 10, *Acquaintances, Old and New Among Reformers* 1912

2 When I read of the vain discussions of the present day about the Virgin Birth and other old dogmas which belong to the past, I feel how great the need is still of a real interest in the religion which builds up character, teaches brotherly love, and opens up to the seeker such a world of usefulness and the beauty of holiness . . . .
"Olympia Brown, An Autobiography," Gwendolen B. Willis,* ed. (1960), Quoted in Ch. 5, *The Annual Journal of the Universalist Historical Society*, Vol. 4 1963
*Daughter of Olympia Brown; see 1126.

3 Our women's colleges are filled with young women, many of whom, with proper encouragement, would make good ministers. We must present the needs of the church and the fitness of the profession for women to these students. The difficulties and discouragements in their way must be overcome by the indefatigable efforts of individual women, so that prejudices will be conquered and church rules, where necessary, amended.
Ibid.

4 I used to say that Susan B. Anthony* was my pole star until I learned to make no one my guide but to follow truth wherever it might lead and to do the duty of the hour at whatever cost.
Ibid.
*See 949.

5 The more we learn of science, the more we see that its wonderful mysteries are all explained by a few simple laws so connected together and so dependent upon each other, that we all see the same mind animating them all.
Sermon (Mukwonago, Wisconsin, 13 January 1895?), Ibid.

6 In communion with the highest, in *striving* for the best, in losing oneself in others, one is lifted above the common material furniture of life, above its gaudy trappings and encumbering paraphernalia, above its contentions and toils, its antagonisms and weariness into a realm of peace which passeth understanding.
Ibid.

7 Man does not live by bread alone, but by faith, by admiration, by sympathy. 'Tis very shallow to say that cotton or iron or silver or gold are kings of the world. There are rulers that will at any moment make these forgotten. Fear will, love will, character will!
Ibid.

8 How natural that the errors of the ancient should be handed down and, mixing with the principles and system which Christ taught, give to us an adulterated Christianity.
Ibid.

9 The Old Testament teems with prophecies of the Messiah, but nowhere is it intimated that that Messiah is to stand as a God to be worshiped. He is to bring peace on earth, to build up the waste places—to comfort the broken-hearted, but nowhere is he spoken of as a deity.
Ibid.

10 He who never sacrificed a present to a future good or a personal to a general one can speak of happiness only as the blind do of colors.
Ibid.

1032. Louise Moulton (1835–1908)

1 Bend low, O dusky night,
And give my spirit rest,
Hold me deep to your breast,
And put old cares to flight.
"Tonight" *n.d.*

2 Give me back the lost delight
That once my soul possessed,
When love was loveliest.
Ibid.

3 The month it was the month of May,
And all along the pleasant way,
The morning birds were mad with glee,
And all the flowers sprang up to see. . . .
"The Secret of Arcady" *n.d.*

4   This life is a fleeting breath . . . .
"When I Wander Away with Death" *n.d.*

1033. Augusta Evans (1835–1909)

1   Money is everything in this world to some people, and more than the next to other poor souls.
Ch. 2, *Beulah 1859*

2   Oh! Duty is an icy shadow. It will freeze you. It cannot fill the heart's sanctuary.
Ch. 13, *Ibid.*

3   Oh, has the foul atmosphere of foreign lands extinguished all your self-respect? Do you come back sordid and sycophantic, and the slave of opinions you would once have utterly detested?
Ch. 18, *Ibid.*

4   Human genius has accomplished a vast deal for man's temporal existence. . . . But . . . what has it affected for philosophy, that great burden which constantly recalls the fabled labors of Sisyphus and the Danaides? Since the rising of Bethlehem's star, in the cloudy sky of polytheism, what has human genius discovered of God, eternity, destiny?
Ch. 41, *Ibid.*

5   Fortuitous circumstances constitute the moulds that shape the majority of human lives, and the hasty impress of an accident is too often regarded as the relentless decree of all ordaining fate . . . .
Ch. 1, *Until Death Us Do Part 1869*

1034. Amanda Theodosia Jones (1835–1914)

1   Books were more necessary than daily bread to our parents.
A Psychic Autobiography 1910

2   I see how fruit can be canned without cooking it. The air must be exhausted from the cells and fluid made to take its place. The fluid must be airless also—a light syrup of sugar and water—that, or the juice of fruit.*
Ibid.

*Jones maintained that she awoke from a nap with these exact words in her mind.

1035. Ellen Gates (1835–1920)

1   Sleep sweet within this quiet room,
O thou! who'er thou art;
And let no mournful yesterday,
Disturb thy peaceful heart.
"Sleep Sweet" *n.d.*

1036. Harriet Spofford (1835–1921)

1   Beauty vanishes like a vapor,
Preach the men of musty morals.
"Evanescence" *n.d.*

2   Something to live for came to the place,
Something to die for maybe,
Something to give even sorrow a grace,
And yet it was only a baby!
"Only" *n.d.*

3   The awful phantom of the hungry poor.
"A Winter's Night" *n.d.*

1037. Frances Ridley Havergal (1836–1879)

1   Doubt indulged soon becomes doubt realized.
"The Imagination of the Thoughts of the Heart," *Royal Bounty n.d.*

2   Love understands love; it needs no talk.
"Loving Allegiance," *Royal Commandments n.d.*

3   Silence is not certain token
That no secret grief is there;
Sorrow which is never spoken
Is the heaviest load to bear.
"Misunderstood," St. 15 *n.d.*

1038. Mary Frances Butts (1836–1902)

1   Build a little fence of trust
Around today;
Fill the space with loving work,
And therein stay.
"Trust" *n.d.*

1039. Marietta Holley (1836?–1926)

1   We are blind creeters, the fur-seein'-est of us; weak creeters, when we think we are the strong-mindedest. Now, when we hear of a crime, it is easy to say that the one who committed that wrong stepped flat off from goodness into sin, and should be hung. It is so awful easy and sort of satisfactory to condemn other folks'es faults that we don't stop to think that it may be that evil was fell into through the weakness and blindness of a mistake.
"Kitty Smith and Caleb Cobb," *My Wayward Pardner; or My Trials with Josiah, America, the Widow Bump, and Etcetery 1880*

2   And then when we read of some noble, splendid act of generosity, our souls burn within us, and it is easy to say, the one who did that glorious deed should be throned and crowned with honor—not thinkin' how, mebby, unbeknown to us, that act was the costly and glitterin' varnish coverin' up a whited sepulchre. That deed was restin' on self-seekin', ambitious littleness.
Ibid.

3   Yes, this world is a curious place, very, and holler, holler as a drum. Lots of times the ground seems to lay smooth and serene under your rockin' chair, when all the time a earthquake may be on the very p'int of bustin' it open and swollerin' you up—chair and all.
"Josiah Allen Gits a Stray," *Ibid.*

4   But I am a-eppisodin' and a-eppisodin' to a length and depth almost onprecedented and onheard of—and to resoom and go on.
Ch. 4, *Samantha at the World's Fair 1893*

5   And I sez, "Children and trees have to be tackled young, Josiah, to bend their wills to the way you want 'em to go."
Ch. 18, *Around the World with Josiah Allen's Wife 1899*

1040. Isabella Mary Mayson Beeton (1837–1865)

1   We hear of those to whom a lawsuit is an agreeable relaxation, a gentle excitement. One of this class, when remonstrated with, retorted, that while one friend kept dogs, and another horses, he, as he had a right to do, kept a lawyer; and no one had a right to dispute his taste.
The Book of Household Management 1861

2 There should be a place for everything, and everything in its place.

Ibid.

1041. Rosalia de Castro (1837–1885)

1 Give back the flower its fragrant scent
When it is dry;
From the waves that kiss the seashore
And one by one caress it as they die,
Go gather all the murmurs that are spent
And on bronze plates their harmonies inscribe.

"El tiempo pasa" (Life Passes By), John A. Crow, tr. n.d.

1042. Jean Detourbey (1837–1908)

1 Is it necessary to have read Spinoza* in order to make out a laundry list?

Quoted in Forty Years of Partisan Society
by Arthur Meyer 1912
*Baruch or Benedict Spinoza, Dutch philosopher and theologian (1632–1677).

2 Of course, fortune has its part in human affairs, but conduct is really much more important.

Ibid.

3 So I cannot bear to be told that So-and-so is lucky. Too often the phrase is a covert attack upon the man; for what does it amount to in plain speech but that he is an idiot with nothing but his luck to recommend him?

Ibid.

1043. Mary Elizabeth Braddon (1837–1915)

1 ". . . it is easy to starve, but it is difficult to stoop."

Ch. 23, Lady Audley's Secret 1862

2 "Let any man make a calculation of his existence, subtracting the house in which he has been thoroughly happy—really and entirely at his ease, without one arrièr pensée to mar his enjoyment—without the most infinitesimal cloud to overshadow the brightness of his horizon. Let him do this, and surely he will laugh in utter bitterness of soul when he sets down the sum of his felicity, and discovers the pitiful smallness of the amount."

Ch. 25, Ibid.

3 There can be no reconciliation when there is no open warfare. There must be a battle, a brave boisterous battle, with pennants waving and cannon roaring, before there can be peace treaties and enthusiastic shaking of hands.

Ch. 32, Ibid.

4 ". . . exceptional talent does not always win its reward unless favoured by exceptional circumstances."

Ch. 4, Dead-Sea Fruit, Vol. II 1868

5 "Are there not, indeed, brief pauses of mental intoxication, in which the spirit releases itself from its dull mortal bondage, and floats starward on the wings of inspiration?"

Ch. 9, Ibid.

6 "I think that most wearisome institution, the honeymoon, must have been inaugurated by some sworn foe to matrimony, some vile misogynist, who took to himself a wife in order to discover, by experience, the best mode of rendering married life a martyrdom."

Ibid.

7 "A priest can achieve great victories with an army of women at his command."

Ch. 1, Hostages to Fortune, Vol. I 1875

8 "A London house without visitors is so triste."

Ch. 6, The White House 1906

9 He had compelled her to think of the sons of toil as she had never thought before, this world outside the world of Skepton, the lower-grade labour, the unskilled, uncertain, casual work; a life in which thrift would seem impossible, since there was nothing to save, cleanliness and decency impractical and drunken oblivion the only possible relief.

Ch. 15, Ibid.

10 It may be that Miranda had enjoyed too much of the roses and lilies of life, and that a girlhood of such absolute indulgence was hardly the best preparation for the battle which has to come in the lives of women—whatever their temporal advantage—the battle of the heart, or of the brain, the fight with fate, or the fight with man.

Bk. I, Ch. 2, Miranda 1913

11 "Love is life, love is the lamp that lights the universe: without that light this goodly frame the earth, is a barren promontory and man the quintessence of dust."

Bk. II, Ch. 9, Ibid.

12 When once estrangement has arisen between those who truly love each other, everything seems to widen the breach.

Ch. 8, Run to Earth 1915?

1044. Jane Ellice Hopkins (1837–1915)

1 Gift, like genius, I often think only means an infinite capacity for taking pains.

Work Amongst Working Men 1870

1045. Martha Gay Masterson (1837–1916)

1 He [the schoolteacher] marched around occasionally, and if he discovered any fun or idleness going on, down would come that switch causing the juveniles to draw themselves into small parcels to evade the rod.

One Woman's West (autobio., 2nd ed.), Lois Barton, ed. 1990

2 . . . everybody came to say goodbye to us. We took a last look at all, then closed our eyes on the scene and moved forward. Their wails reached us as we moved away.*

Ibid.

*On leaving Springfield, Missouri, for the Oregon Trail (1851).

3 . . . we had no news or word from home. So we originated our own news and mirth.

Ibid.

4 Usually an Indian woman told the whites when the men were preparing for war. I think they preferred peace to war.

Ibid.

5 The city [Spokane, Washington] was becoming very sickly, occasioned by the bad water. The outlet of the lake was not pure. The smelters were at the headwater of the lake and the minerals poisoned the water.

Ibid.

6 A man is soon ready for a journey. Packs his grip, gets his ticket and is off before a woman can decide on the color of her traveling dress.

Ibid.

1046. Kate Field (1838–1896)

1 They talk about a woman's sphere,
   As though it had a limit.
   There's not a place in earth or heaven,
   There's not a task to mankind given. . . .
   Without a woman in it.
                                  "Woman's Spirit" *n.d.*

1047. Mary Mapes Dodge (1838?–1905)

1 To her mind, the poor peasant-girl Gretel was not a human
   being, a God-created creature like herself—she was only something that meant poverty, rags, and dirt.
                    Preface, *Hans Brinker or the Silver Skates* 1865

2 . . . in Holland ice is generally an all-winter affair.
                                                    Ibid.

3 Should this simple narrative . . . cause even one heart to feel a
   deeper trust in God's goodness and love, or aid any in weaving
   a life, wherein, through knots and entanglements, the golden
   thread shall never be tarnished or broken, the prayer with
   which it was begun and ended will have been answered.
                                                    Ibid.

4 What a dreadful thing it must be to have a dull father. . . .
                                     "Boys and Girls," Ibid.

5 . . . the dame was filled with delightful anxieties caused by the
   unreasonable demands of ten thousand guilders' worth of new
   wants that had sprung up like mushrooms in a single night.
                                       "A Discovery," Ibid.

6 This kind of work is apt to summon Vertigo, of whom good
   Hans [Christian] Andersen writes—the same who hurls daring
   young hunters from the mountains, or spins them from the
   sharpest heights of the glaciers, or catches them as they tread
   the stepping-stones of the mountain torrent.
                            "Jacob Poot Changes the Plan," Ibid.

7 Ten year's dropped from a man's life are no small loss; ten
   years of manhood, of household happiness and care; ten years
   of honest labor, of conscious enjoyment of sunshine and outdoor beauty; ten years of grateful life—one day looking
   forward to all this; the next, waking to find them passed, and
   a blank.
                                    "The Father's Return," Ibid.

8 "It is an ugly business, boy, this surgery," said the doctor, still
   frowning at Hans, "it requires great patience, self-denial and
   perseverance."
                                     "Broad Sunshine," Ibid.

9 How faithfully those glancing eyes shall yet seek for the jewels
   that live hidden in rocky schoolbooks!
                                                    Ibid.

10 "Modern ways are quite alarming,"
    Grandma says, "but boys were charming"
    (Girls and boys she means, of course) "long ago."
                                     "The Minuet," St. 3 1879

11 She wants from me, my lady Earth,
    Smiles and waits and sighs.
                                     "How the Rain Comes" *n.d.*

12 All things ready with a will,
    April's coming up the Hill.
                             "Now the Noisy Winds Are Still" *n.d.*

13 Life is a mystery as deep as every death can be;
    Yet oh, how dear it is to us, this life we live and see!
                                "The Two Mysteries," St. 3 *n.d.*

14 But I believe that God is overhead;
    And as life is to the living, so death is to the dead.
                                                 St. 5, Ibid.

1048. Margaret E. Sangster (1838–1912)

1 And it isn't the thing you do, dear,
   It's the thing you leave undone
   Which gives you a bit of a headache
   At the setting of the sun.
                                "The Sin of Omission" *n.d.*

2 Never yet was a springtime
   When the buds forgot to blow.
                                        "Awakening" *n.d.*

3 Not always the fanciest cake that's there
   Is the best to eat!
                                "French Pastry," St. 3 *n.d.*

4 Out of the chill and the shadow,
   Into the thrill and the shine;
   Out of the dearth and the famine,
   Into the fullness divine.
                                      "Going Home" *n.d.*

5 Prophet and priest he stood
   In the storm of embattled years;
   The broken chain was his heart's refrain,
   And the peace that is balm for tears.
                           "John Greenleaf Whittier"* *n.d.*
   *American poet (1807–1892).

6 And hearts have broken from harsh words spoken
   That sorrow can ne'er set right.
                                     "Our Own," St. 1 *n.d.*

7 We have careful thought from the stranger,
   And smiles from the sometimes guest;
   But oft from "our own" the bitter tone,
   Though we love our own the best.
                                                 St. 3, Ibid.

1049. Mary E. Bryan (1838/46–1913)

1 Men, after much demur and hesitation, have given women liberty to write; but they cannot yet consent to allow them full
   freedom. They may flutter out of the cage, but it must be with
   clipped wings; they may hop about the smooth-shaven lawns,
   but must, on no account, fly.
                    "How Should Women Write?" (1860), *Hidden Hands:
                    An Anthology of American Women Writers, 1790–1870*,
                    Lucy M. Freibert and Barbara A. White, eds. 1985

2 Women are . . . . learning that genius has no sex. . . . How
   should a woman write? I answer, as men, as all should write to
   whom the power of expression has been given—honestly and
   without fear.
                                                    Ibid.

1050. Lydia Kamekeha Liliuokalani (1838–1917)

1 The Hawaiian people have been from time immemorial lovers
   of poetry and music, and have been apt in improvising historic

poems, songs of love, and chants of worship, so that praises of the living or wails over the dead were with them but the natural expression of their feelings.

Ch. 5, *Hawaii's Story* 1898

2 Oh, honest Americans, as Christians hear me for my downtrodden people! Their form of government is as dear to them as your is precious to you. Quite as warmly as you love your country, so they love theirs. . . . do not covet the little vineyards of Naboth's, so far from your shores, lest the punishment of Ahab fall upon you, if not in your day, in that of your children, for "be not deceived, God is not mocked."

Ch. 57, Ibid.

3 Farewell to thee, farewell to thee,
Thou charming one who dwells among the bowers,
One fond embrace before I now depart
Until we meet again.

"Aloha Oe" *n.d.*

1051. Victoria Claflin Woodhull (1838–1927)

1 While others of my sex devoted themselves to a crusade against the laws that shackle the women of the country, I asserted my individual independence; while others prayed for the good time coming, I worked for it; while others argued the equality of woman with man, I proved it by successfully engaging in business; while others sought to show that there was no valid reason why women should be treated, socially and politically, as being inferior to man, I boldly entered the arena of politics and business and exercised the rights I already possessed.

I now announce myself candidate for the Presidency.

Letter to the Editor, *New York Herald* 2 April 1870

2 I submit that I have established first, that by the mere fact of being citizens, women are possessed of the elective franchise; and second, that the elective franchise is one of the privileges of the 14th Amendment which the states shall not abridge.

Address to Judiciary Committee, House of Representatives *11 January 1871*

3 I have an inalienable constitutional and natural right to love whom I may, to love as long or as short a period as I can, to change that love every day if I please!

Article, *Woodhull and Claflin's Weekly* 20 November 1871

4 A Vanderbilt may sit in his office and manipulate stocks or declare dividends by which in a few years he amasses fifty million dollars from the industries of the country, and he is one of the remarkable men of the age. But if a poor, half-starved child should take a loaf of bread from his cupboard to appease his hunger, she would be sent to the tombs.

Campaign Speech *1872*

5 The wife who submits to sexual intercourse against her wishes or desires, virtually commits suicide; while the husband who compels it, commits murder. . . .

Speech, "The Elixir of Life," American Association of Spiritualists (Chicago, 1873), *Feminism: The Essential Historical Writings*, Miriam Schneir,* ed. 1972
*See 2538.

6 It is a fact terrible to contemplate, yet it is nevertheless true, and ought to be pressed upon the world for its recognition: that fully one-half of all women seldom or never experience any pleasure whatever in the sexual act. Now this is an impeachment of nature, a disgrace to our civilization.

Ibid.

7 Woman's ability to earn money is a better protection against the tyranny and brutality of man than her ability to vote.

Quoted in *Women Suffragists* by Diana Star Helmer 1998

8 All this talk of women's rights is moonshine. Women have every right. They have only to exercise them.

Ibid.

9 Yes, I am a free lover. . . . I am conducting a campaign against marriage, with the view of revolutionizing the present theory and practice.

Ibid.

10 Those who are called prostitutes . . . are free women, sexually, when compared to the slavery of the poor wife. They are at liberty, at least to refuse; but she knows no such escape . . . Yet marriage is held to be synonymous with morality! I say, eternal damnation sink such morality!

Ibid.

11 I never knew love was anything but free.

Ibid.

12 If the very next Congress refuses women all the legitimate results of citizenship, we mean treason! We mean secession. We are plotting revolution! We will overthrow this bogus Republic and plant a government of righteousness in its stead!

Speech, "Great Secession," Ibid.

13 Friends of the cause should act in concert. Their real power has never been felt.

Ibid.

14 So after all, I am a very promiscuous free lover. I want the love of you all, promiscuously. It makes no difference who or what you are, old or young, black or white, pagan, Jew, or Christian. I want to love you all and be loved by you all; and I mean to have your love.

Speech, "Tried as by Fire" (1874), Ibid.

15 Suffrage is only one phase of the larger question of woman's emancipation. More important is the question of her social and economic position.

Editorial, *The Humanitarian** (1896), Ibid.
*A weekly publication founded and operated by Woodhull.

16 If I want sexual intercourse with one hundred men, I shall have it.

Quoted in *Other Powers: The Age of Suffrage, Spiritualism, and the Scandalous Victoria Woodhull* by Barbara Goldsmith 1998

1052. Mary Clemmer (1839–1884)

1 I lie amid the Goldenrod,
I love to see it lean and nod.

"Goldenrod" *n.d.*

2 The Indian Summer, the dead Summer's soul.

"Presence" *n.d.*

3 Only a newspaper! Quick read, quick lost,
Who sums the treasure that it carries hence?
Torn, trampled under feet, who counts thy cost,
Star-eyed intelligence?

"The Journalist" *n.d.*

4 To serve thy generation, this thy fate:
"Written in water," swiftly fades thy name;

But he who loves his kind does, first or late,
A work too great for fame.

Ibid.

5   A shining isle in a stormy sea,
We seek it ever with smiles and sighs;
To-day is sad. In the bland To-be,
Serene and lovely To-morrow lies.

"To-morrow" *n.d.*

1053. Ouida (1839–1908)

1   . . . with peaches and women, it's only the side next the sun that's tempting.

Strathmore 1865

2   What is it that love does to a woman? Without it she only sleeps; with it alone, she lives.

Wisdom, Wit and Pathos 1884

3   A cruel story runs on wheels, and every hand oils the wheels as they run.

"Moths" (1880), Ibid.

4   She knew how to be "so naughty and so nice" in a way that society in London likes and never punishes.

Ibid.

5   To vice, innocence must only seem a superior kind of chicanery.

"Two Little Wooden Shoes" (1874), Ibid.

6   Fame has only the span of a day, they say. But to live in the hearts of the people—that is worth something.

"Signa" (1875), Ibid.

7   The song that we hear with our ears is only the song that is sung in our hearts.

"Ariadne" (1877), Ibid.

8   Petty laws breed great crimes.

"Pipistrello" (1880), Ibid.

9   Take hope from the heart of man, and you make him a beast of prey.

"A Village Commune" (1881), Ibid.

10   Christianity has ever been the enemy of human love.

"The Failure of Christianity" *n.d.*

11   Christianity has made of death a terror which was unknown to the gay calmness of the Pagan.

Ibid.

1054. Frances Willard (1839–1908)

1   Here's a recipe for the abolishment of the Blues which is worth a dozen medical nostrums:
Take one spoonful of Pleasant memories.
Take two spoonfuls of Endeavours for the Happiness of others.
Take two spoonfuls of Forgetfulness of Sorrow.
Mix well with half a pint of Cheerfulness.
Take a portion every hour of the day.

Journal entry (c.1860), Quoted in Ch. 2, *Frances Willard:
Her Life and Works* by Ray Strachey 1912

2   Geology teaches that death was in the world before sin, which is contrary to the Bible. But it is nowhere stated in the Bible that sin was the cause of the death of any save man: he only has sinned. Any other idea is a superstition and without foundation.

Ibid.

3   Germany is the purgatory of women and dogs.

Journal entry (November 30, 1868), Ch. 5, Ibid.

4   The world is wide, and I will not waste my life in friction when it could be turned into momentum.

Journal entry (c.1860), Ch. 6, Ibid.

5   Recognising that our cause is, and will be, combated by mighty, determined, and relentless forces, we will, trusting in Him who is the Prince of Peace, meet argument with argument, misjudgment with patience, denunciations with kindness, and all our difficulties and dangers with prayer.

Ch. 7, Ibid.

6   Everything is not in the temperance movement, but the temperance movement should be in everything.

Ch. 11, Ibid.

1055. Mary Louisa Molesworth (1839–1921)

1   Time indeed seemed to stand still in and all about the old house, as if it and the people who inhabited it had got so old that they could not get any older, and had outlived the possibility of change.

Ch. I, *The Cuckoo Clock* 1877

2   "What a *very* funny house it is, Aunt Grizzel," she said, as she followed her aunt down the steps. "Every room has so many doors, and you come back to where you were just when you think you are ever so far off. I shall never be able to find my way about."

Ibid.

3   "Why not?" said Griselda. "Lots of children have been there."
"I doubt it," said the cuckoo. "Some may have thought they had been there who hadn't really been there at all. And as to those who have been there, you may be sure of one thing—they were not taken, they found their own way. No one ever was taken to fairyland—to the real fairyland. They may have been taken to the neighbouring countries, but not to fairyland itself."

Ch. IV, Ibid.

1056. Ann Plato (fl. 1840s)

1   . . . a good education is another name for happiness.

Essays 1841

1057. Emilia Dilke (1840–1904)

1   [Artistic] work which is not done for its own sake, in which the chief place is claimed by the historical or the moral, in which attention is seized by the subject rather than the rendering of the subject . . . loses its aesthetic character, and cannot possess those poetic elements which fire the fancy and rouse the emotions.

Quoted in *The Saturday Review 23 August 1868*

2   It was put before me that if I wished to command respect I must make myself *the* authority on some one subject which interested me. I was told, and it was good counsel, not to take hack-work, and to reject even well-paid things that would lead me off the track.

Quoted in "Memoir" by Sir Charles Dilke,
The Book of Spiritual Life 1905

1058. Elizabeth York Case (1840?–1911)

1   There is no unbelief;
    Whoever plants a seed beneath the sod
    And waits to see it push away the clod,
    He trusts in God.

"There Is No Unbelief" n.d.

1059. Katharine Walker (1840–1916)

1   The elusiveness of soap, the knottiness of strings, the transitory nature of buttons, the inclination of suspenders to twist and of hooks to forsake their lawful eyes, and cleave only to the hairs of their hapless owner's head.

"The Total Depravity of Inanimate Things," *Atlantic Monthly* (Boston) *September 1864*

2   However divinity schools may refuse to "skip" in unison, and may butt and butter each other about the doctrine and origin of human depravity, all will join devoutly in the credo, I believe in the total depravity of inanimate things.

Ibid.

1060. Harriet King (1840–1920)

1   Measure thy life by loss instead of gain,
    Not by the wine drunk, but by the wine poured forth.

"The Disciples" n.d.

1061. Helena Modjeska (1840–1920)

1   Alas! it was not my fate to die for my country, as was my cherished dream, but instead of becoming the heroine I had to be satisfied with acting heroines, exchanging the armor for tinsel, and the weapon for words.

Pt. I, Ch. 1, *Memories and Impressions 1910*

2   It is never right to be more Catholic than the Pope.

Ch. 25, Ibid.

3   . . . the word "great" is not sufficient anymore, if you do not add to it, "Genius!" In Europe the word "genius" is only applied to the greatest of the world, but here [in America] it has become an everyday occurrence.

Pt. III, Ch. 51, Ibid.

4   We foreigners, born outside of the magic pale of the Anglo-Saxon race, place Shakespeare upon a much higher pedestal. We claim that, before being English, he was human, and that his creations are not bound either by local or ethnological limits, but belong to humanity in general.

Ibid.

5   It seems to me that there are only two schools, one of good acting, the other of bad acting.

Ibid.

1062. Marilla Ricker (1840–1920)

1   The only thing that ever came back from the grave that we know of was a lie.

The Philistine, Vol. XXV c. 1901

2   He [Thomas Paine]* was as democratic as nature, as impartial as sun and rain.

Ibid.

*British-born American writer and Revolutionary leader (1737–1809).

1063. Mary Branch (1840–1922)

1   So, I think, God hides some souls away,
    Sweetly to surprise us, the last day.

"The Petrified Fern" n.d.

1064. Elizabeth Wordsworth (1840–1932)

1   If all the good people were clever,
    And all the clever people were good,
    The world would be nicer than ever
    We thought that it possibly could.

    But somehow, 'tis seldom or never
    The two hit it off as they should;
    The good are so harsh to the clever,
    The clever so rude to the good.

"The Good and the Clever," *St. Christopher and Other Poems 1890*

1065. Sarah Sadie Williams (1841–1868)

1   Is it so, O Christ in heaven, that the highest suffer most,
    That the strongest wander farthest, and more hopelessly are lost,
    That the mark of rank in nature is capacity for pain,
    That the anguish of the singer makes the sweetness of the strain?

"Is It So, O Christ in Heaven?" n.d.

1066. Mathilde Blind (1841–1896)

1   Blossoms of humanity!

"The St.-Children's Dance" n.d.

2   The moon returns, and the spring; birds warble, trees burst into leaf,
    But love once gone, goes forever, and all that endures is the grief.

No. 3, *"Love Trilogy" n.d.*

3   The dead abide with us. Though stark and cold,
    Earth seems to grip them, they are with us still:
    They have forged our chains of being of good or ill,
    And their invisible hands these hands yet hold.

"The Dead" n.d.

1067. Mary Wood Allen (1841–1908)

1   Woman embroiders man's life—Embroidery is to beautify—
    The embroidery of cleanliness—Of a smile—Of gentle words.

Summary, *What a Young Girl Ought to Know 1897*

1068. Mary Lathbury (1841–1913)

1   Day is dying in the west;
    Heaven is touching earth with rest.

"Day Is Dying in the West," St. 1 *1877*

2   Children of yesterday,
    Heirs of tomorrow,
    What are you weaving?
    Labor and sorrow?

"Song of Hope," St. 1 *n.d.*

1069. Kate Brownlee Sherwood (1841–1914)

1   One heart, one hope, one destiny, one flag, from sea to sea.

"Albert Sidney Johnstone," *Dreams of the Ages 1893*

1070. Sarah Knowles Bolton (1841–1916)

1   He alone is great
Who by a life heroic conquers fate.

"The Inevitable" *n.d.*

1071. Eliza Burt Gamble (1841–1920)

1   . . . with the dawn of scientific investigation it might have been hoped that the prejudices resulting from lower conditions of human society would disappear, and that in their stead would be set forth not only facts, but deductions from facts, better suited to the dawn of an intellectual age . . . .

The ability, however, to collect facts, and the power to generalize and draw conclusions from them, avail little, when brought into direct opposition to deeply rooted prejudices.

The Evolution of Woman 1894

1072. Marie le Baron (1842–1894)

1   We point with proud, though bleeding hearts, to myriads of graves.
They tell the story of a war that ended Slavery's night;
And still women struggle for our Liberty, our Right.

"The Yellow Ribbon" *1876*

1073. Ellen Swallow (1842–1911)

1   The power of knowledge is appreciated by manufacturers. They take advantage of every new step in science. The woman must know something of chemistry in self-defense. . . . The housekeeper should know when to be frightened. . . . It is for women to institute reform.

Speech (1879), Quoted in *Ellen Swallow, The Woman Who Founded Ecology* by Robert Clarke *1973*

2   For this knowledge of right living, we have sought a new name. . . . As theology is the science of religious life, and biology the science of [physical] life . . . so let *Oekology* be henceforth the science of [our] normal lives . . . the worthiest of all the applied science which *teaches the principles on which to found . . . a healthy . . . and happy life.*

Speech (1892), Ibid.

3   Heretofore, civilized man has proclaimed, as his God-like privilege, and as a proof of his superiority to animals, the right to eat what he liked, whether it was suitable or not, and as a result, he has been compelled to employ a band of skilled magicians to exorcise the devils . . . invited to enter his body. But man is . . . only an upright animal, amenable to the same laws of growth and decay as others. . . . The science of human nutrition is to play a larger part in therapeutics than heretofore and it will be of great advantage to the physician [who] . . . at present has less confidence in the cook than in the druggist.

Ch. 13, *The New England Kitchen Magazine* (1893), Ibid.

4   The essential principles of health are not understood by the people . . . and, alas! not by all our physicians, who as a rule have been educated to cure disease, not to prevent it. Too many have been taught to fight Nature's Laws, not stand by . . . as her adjutant.

Ch. 15, Ibid.

5   Woman was originally the inventor, the manufacturer, the provider. She has allowed one office after another gradually to slip from her hand until she retains, with loose grasp, only the so called housekeeping. . . . she rightly feels that what is left is mere deadening drudgery, and that escape from this condition is essential to her well being as an individual.

The Outlook (magazine; 1897), Ibid.

6   It is hard to find anyplace in the world where the water does not show the effect of human agencies.

Ch. 17, Ibid.

1074. Mary Elizabeth Brown (1842–1917)

1   I'll go where you want me to go, dear Lord,
O'er mountain, or plain, or sea;
I'll say what you want me to say, dear Lord,
I'll be what you want me to be.

"I'll Go Where You Want Me to Go" *n.d.*

1075. May Riley Smith (1842–1927)

1   How these little hands remind us,
As in snowy grace they lie,
Not to scatter thorns—but roses—
For our reaping by and by.

"If We Knew," St. 3 *1867*

2   Let us gather up the sunbeams
Lying all around our path;
Let us keep the wheat and roses,
Casting out the thorns and chaff.

St. 6, Ibid.

3   Strange we never prize the music
Till the sweet-voiced bird is flown. . . .

St. 14, Ibid.

4   God's plan, like lilies pure and white, unfold.
We must not tear the close-shut leaves apart.
Time will reveal the calyxes of gold.

"Sometime," *Sometime and Other Poems* 1892

5   My life's a pool which can only hold
One star and glimpses of blue.

"My Life is a Bowl," St. 2 *n.d.*

1076. Ina Coolbrith (1842–1928)

1   He walks with God upon the hills!
And sees, each morn, the world arise
New-bathed in light of paradise.

"The Poet" *n.d.*

1077. Caroline Bigelow Le Row (1843–?)

1   But I will right of him who fights
And vanquishes his sins,
Who struggles on through weary years
Against himself and wins.

"True Heroism" *n.d.*

1078. Anna Hamilton (1843–1875)

1   This learned I from the shadow of a tree,
That to and fro did sway against a wall,
Our shadow selves, our influence, may fall
Where we ourselves can never be.

"Influence" *n.d.*

1079. Isabella S. Stephenson (1843–1890)

1   Holy Father, in Thy mercy,
Hear our anxious prayer,
Keep our loved ones, now far absent,
'Neath thy care.

"Holy Father, in Thy Mercy" *n.d.*

1080. Violet Fane (1843–1905)

1 Ah, "All things come to those who wait,"
  (I say these words to make me glad),
  But something answers soft and sad,
  "They come, but often come too late."

  "*Tout Vient à Qui Sait Attendre*" n.d.

2 Let me arise and open the gate,
  To breath the wild warm air of the heath,
  And to let in Love, and to let out Hate,
  And anger at living and scorn of Fate,
  To let in Life, and to let out Death.

  "Reverie" n.d.

3 Nothing is right and nothing is just;
  We sow in ashes and reap in dust.

  Ibid.

1081. Bertha von Suttner (1843–1914)

1 After the verb, "To Love," "To Help" is the most beautiful
  verb in the world!

  "Epigram," *Ground Arms* 1892

1082. Carmen Sylva (1843–1916)

1 Life was a radiant maiden, the daughter of the Sun, endowed
  with all the charm and grace, all the power and happiness,
  which only such a mother could give to her child.

  "The Child of the Sun," *Pilgrim Sorrow* 1884

2 But Truth was not in love, neither was it in renunciation, for I
  murmured and knew not why I should renounce.

  "A Life," Ibid.

3 "It seems to me," said a young man who, sitting by the fire in
  deep study over a roll of paper, had not yet spoken, "that in
  these tales of yours, only those came to harm who themselves
  sought after money, greedily, and merely for their own use. But
  methinks, after all, the best and safest way of getting wealth is
  to work for it. I, too, hope to find a pot of gold in the earth,
  but not by your manner of seeking it."

  "Seekers After Gold," *Legends from River
  and Mountain* 1896

4 "'Tis the ignorant who boast. . . ."

  "The Nixies' Cleft," Ibid.

5 Surely he could never have borne such a life, and must have
  died of misery, save for one only consolation. Every man must
  have some such, be it only a dog, a flower, or a spider. Ovid
  had a snake, a tiny, bewitching snake. . . .

  "The Serpent Isle," Ibid.

6 Complaints were heard no longer, for dull despair had reduced
  all men to silence; and when the starving people tore one another to pieces, no one even told of it.

  "*Rìul Doamnei,*" Ibid.

7 . . . he hesitated to pluck the fruit, for fear it should leave a bitter taste behind.

  "A Doubting Lover," Ibid.

8 "One cannot help those who will not help themselves, so we
  felt it would be quite useless for us to come again."

  "The Little People," *Real Queen's Fairy Tales* 1901

9 "Our work was only play, we never knew what it was to feel
  fatigue; and as for loving others, since it has been granted to
  us to see how all things are, and have been, and must ever be,
  how should any feeling but love and infinite compassion fill
  our hearts for all who live?"

  "The Swan Lake," Ibid.

10 There was another thing that did not exist in these islands; that
   was money. The swans would never have permitted anything
   so low and degrading to enter their domain. Gold they tolerated, but merely for ornamentation, where it could light up
   some dull surface. But to traffic with money, and to bargain,
   and barter—that was unheard of.

   Ibid.

11 "Ill could I resign myself to dwell forever shut in between four
   walls. I must be free, free to roam where I please, like the birds
   in the woodlands."

   "Carma, the Harp-Girl," Ibid.

12 The pangs
   Are hushed, for life is wild no more with strife,
   Nor breathless uphill work, nor heavy with
   The brewing tempests, which have torn away
   So much, that nothing more remains to fear.

   "A Friend," St. 3, *Sweet Hours* 1904

13 Our life is seldom open,
   For love and fear have shut it.

   "Out of the Deep," St. 2, Ibid.

14 Ye not dare tell
   Your heart what it has suffered, dare not look
   Into the past again, for fear of turning
   To stone, for white lipped fear of waking from
   Its sleep that heart to make it throb again,
   Like millstones.

   "Rest," Ibid.

15 Great Solitude
   Hath one thousand voices and a flood of light,
   Be not afraid, enter the Sanctuary,
   Thou wilt be taken by the hand and led
   To Life's own fountain, never-ending Thought!

   "Solitude," Ibid.

1083. Sarah Doudney (1843–1926)

1 Oh, the wasted hours of life
  That have drifted by!
  Oh, the good that might have been,
  Lost without a sigh.

  "The Lesson of the Water-Mill" 1864

2 "No," said Faith sternly, "we don't want this girl to be hanged;
  we wish her to spend a useful life, full of repentance and good
  deeds."

  Ch. 4, *Faith Harrowby; or, The Smuggler's Cave* 1871

3 "Ah, how good God is to me! He has not suffered me to be
  tried and tempted! Had I been in her place I might have done
  just the same."

  Ibid.

4 "There are no such thing as mermaids," exclaimed Frank, her
  schoolboy brother; "and if there are, their company wouldn't
  suit you, Ada. How do you suppose you would get on under
  the sea, with no circulating library, no dress-makers and
  milliners, and knick knacks and fallals?"

  Ch. 19, Ibid.

5 We love thee well, but Jesus loves thee best.
        "The Christians' Good-Night" *1892*

6 But the waiting time, my brothers,
  Is the hardest time of all.
        "The Hardest Time of All," *Psalms of Life n.d.*

1084. Bertha Buxton (1844–1881)

1 After all, the eleventh commandment (thou shalt not be found out) is the only one that is virtually impossible to keep in these days.
        Ch. 3, *Jenny of the Princes 1879*

1085. Sarah Winnemucca (1844–1891)

1 I would be the first Indian woman who ever spoke before white people, and they don't know what the Indians have got to stand sometimes.
        Newspaper interview (1879), Quoted in *Sarah Winnemucca of the Northern Paiutes* by Gae Whitney Canfield *1983*

2 I assure you that there is an Indian ring; that it is a corrupt ring, and that it has its head and shoulders in the treasury at Washington.
        Lecture, Ibid.

3 Everyone knows what a woman must suffer who undertakes to act against bad men. My reputation has been assailed, and it is done so cunningly that I cannot prove it to be unjust.
        Ibid.

4 If I possessed the wealth of several rich ladies whom you all know, I would place all the Indians of Nevada on ships in our harbor, take them to New York and land them there as immigrants, that they might be received with open arms, blessed with the blessings of universal suffrage, and thus placed beyond the necessity of reservation help and out of the reach of Indian agents.
        Lecture (1885), Ibid.

5 Most of teachers have but one object, *viz.* To draw their salary. I do not think that a teacher should have no salary. But I think they should earn it first and then think of it.
        Remark (1885), Ibid.

1086. Minna Canth (1844–1897)

1 HOMSANTUU. Your law and justice . . . These are what I ought to have shot.
        The Working Man's Wife 1885

1087. Elizabeth Stuart Phelps (1844–1911)

1 Who originated the most exquisite of inquisitions, the condolence system?
        Ch. 2, *The Gates Ajar 1869*

2 That a girl could possibly be pretty with straight hair, had never once entered her mind. All the little girls in story-books had curls. Whoever heard of the straight-haired maiden that made wreaths of the rosebud, or saw the fairies, or married the Prince?
        Ch. 1, *Gypsy Breynton 1876*

3 "There are several disadvantages in being a girl, my dear, as you will find out, occasionally," said Tom, with a lordly air.
        Ch. 4, Ibid.

4 I must say distinctly that, though after the act of dying I departed from the surface of the earth, and reached the confines of a different locality, I cannot yet instruct another *where* this place may be.
        Ch. 3, *Beyond the Gates 1883*

5 The meaning of liberty broke upon me like a sunburst. Freedom was in and of itself the highest law. Had I thought that death was to mean release from personal obedience? Lo, death itself was but the elevation of moral claims, from lower to higher.
        Ibid.

6 I mean that the *soul of a sense* is a more exquisite thing than what we may call the body of the sense, as developed to earthly consciousness.
        Ch. 11, Ibid.

7 The great law of denial belongs to the powerful forces of life, whether the case be one of coolish baked beans, or an unrequited affection.
        Ch. 1, *A Singular Life 1896*

8 She had accomplished nothing, that she could see, but keep her house in order. . . . Unsatisfied longings for something which she had not attained, often clouded what, otherwise, would have been a bright day to her; and yet the causes of these feelings seemed to lie in a dim and misty region, which her eye could not penetrate.
        The Angel Over the Right Shoulder n.d.

1088. Arabella Smith (1844–1916)

1 Oh, friends! I pray to-night,
  Keep not your roses for my dead, cold brow
  The way is lonely, let me feel them now.
        "If I Should Die To-Night" *n.d.*

1089. Sophie Tolstoy (1844–1919)

1 One can't live on love alone; and I am so stupid that I can do nothing but think of him.*
        (13 November 1862), *A Diary of Tolstoy's Wife, 1860–1891 1928*

  *Count Leo Tolstoy, Russian philospher and novelist (1820–1910).

2 Of course I am idle, but I am not idle by nature; I simply haven't yet discovered what I can do here. . . .
        Ibid.

3 As for me, I both *can* and *want* to do everything, but after a while I begin to realize there is nothing to want, and that I can't do anything beyond eating, drinking, sleeping, nursing the children, and caring for them and my husband. After all, this *is* happiness, yet why do I grow sad and weep, as I did yesterday?
        (25 February 1865), Ibid.

4 The thing to do is *not* to love, to be clever and sly, and to hide all one's bad points. . . .
        (12 September 1865), Ibid.

5 I want nothing but his love and sympathy, and he won't give it me; and all my pride is trampled in the mud; I am nothing but a miserable crushed worm, whom no one wants, whom no one loves, a useless creature with morning sickness, and a big belly, two rotten teeth, and a bad temper, a battered sense of dignity,

and a love which nobody wants and which nearly drives me insane.

(12 September 1867), Ibid.

6 It makes me laugh to read over this diary. It's so full of contradictions, and one would think I was such an unhappy woman. Yet is there a happier woman than I?

(31 July 1868), Ibid.

7 How deep is the unconscious hatred of even one's nearest people, and how great their selfishness.

(25 October 1886), Ibid.

8 He would like to destroy his old diaries and to appear before his children and the public only in his patriarchal robes. His vanity is immense!

(17 December 1890), Ibid.

9 It is sad that my emotional dependence on the man I love should have killed so much of my energy and ability; there was certainly once a great deal of energy in me.

(31 December 1890), Ibid.

10 I am a source of satisfaction to him, a nurse, a piece of furniture, a *woman*—nothing more.

(13 November 1893), Ibid.

1090. Madeline Bridges (1844–1920)

1 When Psyche's friend becomes her lover,
How sweetly these conditions blend!
But, oh, what anguish to discover
Her lover has become—her friend!

"Friend and Lover" *n.d.*

2 Then give to the world the best you have,
And the best will come back to you.

"Life's Mirror," St. 1 *n.d.*

3 And a smile that is sweet will surely find
A smile that is just as sweet.

St. 3, Ibid.

1091. Saint Bernadette (1844–1923)

1 I fear only bad Catholics.

Quoted in *Lourdes* by Edith Sanders *1940*

1092. Sarah Bernhardt (1844–1923)

1 Cloister existence is one of unbroken sameness for all . . . . The rumor of the outside world dies away at the heavy cloister gate.

Ch. 3, *Memories of My Life 1907*

2 For the theatre one needs long arms; it is better to have them too long than too short. An artiste with short arms can never, never make a fine gesture.

Ch. 6, Ibid.

3 Those who know the joys and miseries of celebrity . . . know . . . It is a sort of octopus with innumerable tentacles. It throws out its clammy arms on the right and on the left, in front and behind, and gathers into its thousand little inhaling organs all the gossip and slander and praise afloat to spit out again at the public when it is vomiting its black gall.

Ch. 22, Ibid.

4 I have, thanks to my travels, added to my stock all the superstitions of other countries. I know them all now, and in any

critical moment of my life, they all rise up in armed legions for or against me.

Ch. 8, *The Memoirs of Sarah Bernhardt 1977*

5 We must live for the few who know and appreciate us, who judge and absolve us, and for whom we have the same affection and indulgence. The rest I look upon as a mere crowd, lively or sad, loyal or corrupt, from whom there is nothing to be expected but fleeting emotions, either pleasant or unpleasant, which leave no trace behind them.

Ch. 9, Ibid.

1093. Margaret Sidney (1844–1924)

1 The little old kitchen had quieted down from the bustle and confusion of mid-day; and now, with its afternoon manners on, presented a holiday aspect, that as the principal room in the brown house, it was eminently proper it should have.

"A Home View," *Five Little Peppers and How They Grew 1881*

2 "It's better'n a Christmas," they told their mother, "to get ready for it!"

"Getting a Christmas for the Little Ones," Ibid.

3 ". . . we've got to do something 'cause we've begun. . . ."

Ibid.

4 "You're just the splendidest, *goodest* mamsie in all the world. And I'm a hateful cross old bear, so I am!"

"Polly's Dismal Morning," Ibid.

5 ". . . it can't be Christmas all the time."

"Christmas Bells," Ibid.

6 "And you're very impertinent, too," said Miss Jerusha; "a good child *never* is impertinent."

"New Friends," Ibid.

7 "Corners are for little folks; but when people who know better, do wrong, there aren't any corners they *can* creep into, or they'd get into them pretty quick!"

"Which Treats of a Good Many Matters," Ibid.

1094. Mary Cassatt (1844–1926)

1 I am independent! I can live alone and I love to work.

Quoted in *Sixteen to Sixty, Memoirs of a Collector* by Louise W. Havemeyer *1930*

2 A woman artist must be . . . capable of making the primary sacrifices.

Quoted in "Mary Cassatt" by Forbes Watson, *Arts Weekly 1932*

3 Yet in spite of the total disregard of the dictionary of manners, he [Paul Cézanne*] shows a politeness toward us which no other man here would have shown. . . . Cézanne is one of the most liberal artists I have ever seen. He prefaces every remark with *Pour moi* it is so and so, but he grants that everyone may be as honest, and as true to nature from their convictions; he doesn't believe that everyone should see alike.

Letter to Mrs. Stillman (1894), Quoted in *Mary Cassatt: A Biography of the Great American Painter* by Nancy Hale** *1975*

*French impressionist painter (1839–1906). **See 1919.

4 Why do people so love to wander? I think the civilized parts of the World will suffice for me in the future.

Letter to Louise Havemeyer (11 February 1911), Ibid.

1095. Susan Coolidge (1845–1905)

1 "A commonplace life," we say and we sigh;
But why would we sigh as we say?
The commonplace sun in the commonplace sky
Makes up the commonplace day.
"Commonplace" *n.d.*

2 Men die, but sorrow never dies;
The crowding years divide in vain,
And the wide world is knit with ties
Of common brotherhood in pain.
"The Cradle Tomb in Westminster Abbey" *n.d.*

3 Yesterday's errors let yesterday cover.
"Every New Morning" *n.d.*

4 New morn has come
And with the morn the punctual tide again.
"Floodtide" *n.d.*

5 Slow buds the pink dawn like a rose
From out night's gray and cloudy sheath;
Softly and still it grows and grows,
Petal by petal, leaf by leaf.
"The Morning Comes Before the Sun" *n.d.*

1096. Emily Hickey (1845–1913)

1 Beloved, it is morn!
A redder berry on the thorn,
A deeper yellow on the corn,
For this good day new-born!
"Beloved, It Is Morn" *n.d.*

2 Strive we, and do, lest by-and-by we sit
In that blind life to which all other fate
Is cause for envy. . . .
"Michael Villers, Idealist" *n.d.*

1097. Margaret Janvier (1845–1913)

1 You needn't try to comfort me—
I tell you my dolly is dead!
There's no use in saying she isn't, with
A crack like that in her head.
"The Dead Doll," St. 1 *n.d.*

1098. Tennessee Claflin (1845–1923)

1 At the ballot-box is not where the shoe pinches. . . . It is at home where the husband . . . is the supreme ruler, that the little difficulty arises; he will not surrender this absolute power unless he is compelled.
"Constitutional Equality, a Right of Women" *1871*

2 A *free* man is a noble being; a *free* woman is a contemptible being. . . . In other terms, the use of this one word, in its twofold application to men and to women, reveals the unconscious but ever present conviction in the public mind that men tend, of course, heavenward in their natures and development, and that women tend just as naturally hellward.
Article, *Woodhull and Claflin's Weekly 1871*

3 The revolt against any oppression usually goes to an opposite extreme for a time; and that is right and necessary.
Ibid.

4 When people had slaves, they expected that their pigs, chickens, corn, and everything lying loose about the plantation would be stolen. But the planters began by stealing the liberty of their slaves, by stealing their labor, by stealing, in fact, all they had; and the natural result was that the slaves stole back all they could.
"Which Is to Blame?", Ibid.

5 He or she who would be free must defy the enemy, and must be *ultra* enough to exhaust the possibilities of the enemy's assault; and it will not be until women can contemplate and accept unconcernedly whatsoever imputation an ignorant, bitter, lying and persecuting world may heap on them that they will be really free.
Article, Ibid.

6 The world enslaves our sex by the mere fear of an epithet; and as long as it can throw any vile term at us, before which we cower, it can maintain our enslavement.
Ibid.

1099. Marie Chona (1845?–1937?)

1 You see, we have power. Men have to dream to get power from the spirits and they think of everything they can—song and speeches and marching around, hoping that the spirits will notice them and give them some power. But we have power . . . Children. Can any warrior make a child, no matter how brave and wonderful he is?
Papago Woman, Ruth M. Underhill, ed. *1936 (rev. ed. 1979)*

2 It is not good to be old, not beautiful.
Ibid.

1100. Kazu-no-Michi (1846–1877)

1 Please understand the heart of one who leaves as the water in the streams; never to return again.
Untitled Poem *1861*

2 I wear the magnificent dress of brocade and damask in vain, now that you are not here to admire it.
Ibid.

3 I would cross the river with you, if there were no barrier to stop me.
Ibid.

1101. Carry Nation (1846–1911)

1 God is a politician; so is the devil.
The Use and Need of the Life of Carry A. Nation 1904

2 It's not possible to make a bad law. If it is bad, it is not a law.
Ibid.

3 The women and children of Barber County are calling to you men for bread, for clothes, and education. . . . [Instead] men in Medicine Lodge and other towns of Barber County are selling whiskey. . . . No wonder the women want the ballot.
Quoted in *Cyclone Carry* by Carleton Beals *1962*

4 Who hath sorrow? Who hath woe?
They who do not answer no;
They whose feet to sin incline,
While they tarry at the wine.
Ch. 12, Ibid.

5   A woman is stripped of everything by them [saloons]. Her husband is torn from her; she is robbed of her sons, her home, her
food, and her virtue; and then they strip her clothes off and
hang her up bare in these dens of robbery and murder. Truly
does the saloon make a woman bare of all things!

Ch. 14 (c. 1893), Ibid.

6   You have put me in here [jail] a cub, but I will come out roaring like a lion, and I will make all hell howl!

(c. 1901), Ibid.

1102. Katharine Bradley (1846–1914)

1   Come, mete out my loneliness, O wind,
For I would know
How far the living who must stay behind
Are from the dead who go.
"Mete Out My Loneliness," with Edith Cooper* n.d
* See 1225..

2   Sweet and of their nature vacant are the days I spend—
Quiet as the plough laid by at the furrow's end.
"Old Age," with E— C—* n.d.

3   The enchanting miracles of change.
"Renewal," with E— C—* n.d.

1103. Anna Dostoevsky (1846–1918)

1   From a shy, timid girl I had become a woman of resolute character, who could not longer be frightened by the struggle with
troubles.
(c. 1871), Dostoevsky* Portayed by His Wife 1926
*Feodor M. D—, Russian novelist (1821–1881).

2   It seems to me that he has never loved, that he has only imagined that he has loved, that there has been no real love on his
part. I even think that he is incapable of love; he is too much
occupied with other thoughts and ideas to become strongly attached to anyone earthly.
(1887), Ibid.

1104. Anna Green (1846–1935)

1   Hath the spirit of all beauty
Kissed you in the path of duty?
"On the Threshold" n.d.

1105. Leylâ Hanim (?–1847)

1   Leylâ, indulge in pleasure
With your lovely friend:
Enjoy yourself in this world,
Never mind what they say.
Untitled, St. 4, Tâlat S. Halman, tr., The Penguin Book of
Women Poets, Carol Cosman, Joan Keefe and Kathleen
Weaver, eds. 1978

1106. Mary Catherwood (1847–1901)

1   They [the Chippewa] were a people ruled only by persuasive
eloquence moving on the surface of their passion. . . .
Pt. I, The White Islander 1893

2   He reveled in the swimming of the wilderness. He had capacities
for woodcraft. It gave freedom to a repressed and manly part of
him, and in the darkness of the buried path he breathed largely.
Pt. II, Ibid.

3   "Oh God, since Thou hast shut me up in this world, I will do
the best I can, without fear or favor. When my task is done, let
me out!"
"The King of Beaver," Mackinac and Lake Stories 1899

4   She might struggle like a fly in a web. He wrapped her around
and around with beautiful sentences.
Ibid.

5   Two may talk together under the same roof for many years,
yet never really meet; and two others at first speech are old
friends.
"Marianson," Ibid.

6   Though in those days of the young century a man might become anything; for the West was before him, an empire, and
woodcraft was better than learning.
"The Black Feather," Ibid.

7   The world of city-maddened people who swarmed to this lake
for their annual immersion in nature. . . .
"The Cursed Patois," Ibid.

1107. Anna Howard Shaw (1847–1919)

1   Her work will not be finished, nor will her last word be spo-
ken, while there remains a wrong to be righted or a fettered
life to be free in all the earth.
Elegy at funeral of Susan B. Anthony* (13 March 1906),
Quoted in Women Suffragists by Diana Star Helmer 1998
* See 949.

1108. Julia A. Moore (1847–1920)

1   And now, kind friends, what I have wrote
I hope you will pass over,
And not criticize as some have done
Hitherto herebefore.
"To My Friends and Critics" n.d.

2   Leave off the agony, leave off style,
Unless you've got money by us all the while.
"Leave off the Agony in Style" n.d.

1109. Alice Christiana Meynell (1845/47–1922)

1   If there is a look of human eyes that tells of perpetual loneliness, so there is also the familiar look that is the sign of
perpetual crowds.
"Solitude," Essays 1914

2   Let a man turn to his own childhood—no further—if he will
renew his sense of remoteness, and of the mystery of change.
"The Illusion of Historic Time," Ibid.

3   A child is beset with long traditions. And his infancy is so old,
so old, that the mere adding of years in the life to follow will
not seem to throw it further back—it is already so far.
Ibid.

4   Spirit of place! It is for this we travel, to surprise its subtlety;
and where it is a strong and dominant angel, that place, seen
once, abides entire in the memory with all its own accidents,
its habits, its breath, its name.
"The Spirit of Place," Ibid.

5   The true colour of life is the colour of the body, the colour of
the covered red, the implicit and not explicit red of the living

heart and the pulses. It is the modest colour of the unpublished blood.

"The True Colour of Life," Ibid.

6   It is easy to replace man, and it will take no great time, when Nature has lapsed, to replace Nature.

Ibid.

7   It is principally for the sake of the leg that a change in the dress of man is so much to be desired. . . . The leg is the best part of the figure . . . and the best leg is the man's. . . . Man should no longer disguise the long lines, the strong forms, in those lengths of piping or tubing that are of all garments the most stupid.

"Unstable Equilibrium," Ibid.

8   A voice peals in this end of night
A phrase of notes resembling stars,
Single and spiritual notes of light.

"A Thrush Before Dawn" n.d.

9   Flocks of the memories of the day draw near
The dovecote doors of sleep.

"At Night" n.d.

10   With the first dream that comes with the first sleep
I run, I run, I am gathered to thy heart.

"Renouncement" n.d.

11   My heart shall be thy garden.

"The Garden" n.d.

12   I shall not hold my little peace; for me
There is no peace but one.

"The Poet to the Birds" n.d.

13   New every year,
New born and newly dear,
He comes with tidings and a song,
The ages long, the ages long.

"Unto Us a Son Is Given" n.d.

14   And when you go
There's loneliness in loneliness.

"Song" n.d.

15   Dear Laws, be wings to me!
The feather merely floats, O be it heard
Through weight of life—the skylark's gravity—
That I am not a feather, but a bird!

"The Laws of Verse" n.d.

16   I come from nothing: but from where
Come the undying thoughts I bear?

"The Modern Poet, or a Song of Derivations" n.d.

17   She walks—the lady of my delight—
A shepherdess of sheep
Her flocks are thoughts.

"The Shepherdess," St. 1 n.d.

18   The sense of humour has other things to do
than to make itself conspicuous in the act
of laughter.

"Laughter" n.d.

1110. Eliška Krásnohorská (1847–1926)

1   Remember the protests which broke out all over the country when the female teachers wanted to be paid the same as the male teachers. It was said, "It may seem unjust, but in spite of the fact that the same education and job responsibilities are required for female teachers as for male teachers, the male teacher needs more money to live on. But," she continued, "when the shopkeeper replaces a male shop assistant with a female shop assistant to do the same work but at a lower wage, will the displaced male worker then claim that the man has greater needs? Lower wages for women are just not just."

(pp. 16–17) Women Question 1871

2   Poor women worked all the time, despite the fact that the issues raised by the women's movement had not been addressed. Poor women had to work: they, quite literally, could not live any other way. On the other hand, rich women will never have to work for their daily bread even if there is much progress in the women's movement. It is in the middle-class, between the iron need of poverty and the comforts of wealth, where the women's movement finds its reason for existence and will be taken seriously. The problems which the women's movement seeks to cure are derived mainly from the needs of the lives of middle-class women, especially the need of middle-class women for job opportunities.

(pp. 18-19) Ibid.

3   It is impossible for a small artisan, a shopkeeper, or a clerk in normal times to feed not only his family, but all destitute kinswomen, and to secure an income sufficient for his wife and daughters to refrain from paid labor in the event of his death. . . . Not only does every father know this, but all men know it. Nonetheless, men are against the women's movement, calling it nonsense. They must have been born mad to be able to honor their prejudices by naming them "principles."

(p. 22) Ibid.

1111. Millicent Garrett Fawcett (1847–1929)

1   The Income-Tax presses more heavily on the possessors of small incomes than on the possessors of large incomes.

Political Economy for Beginners 1870

2   There are many excuses for the person who made the mistake of confounding money and wealth. Like many others they mistook the sign for the thing signified.

Ibid.

1112. Annie Wood Besant (1847–1933)

1   For I believe that the colour bar and all it implies are largely due to thoughtlessness, to silly pride, to the pride of race, which has grown mad in a country where there is no public opinion to check it.

Wake Up, India: A Plea for Social Reform 1913

2   There is no birthright in the white skin that it shall say that wherever it goes, to any nation, amongst any people, there the people of the country shall give way before it, and those to whom the land belongs shall bow down and become its servants. . . .

Ibid.

3   . . . when there shall be no differences save by merit of character, by merit of ability, by merit of service to the country. Those are the true tests of the value of any man or woman, white or coloured; those who can serve best, those who help most, those who sacrifice most, those are the people who will be loved in life and honoured in death, when all questions of colour are swept away and when in a free country free citizens shall meet on equal grounds.

Ibid.

4   No circumstances can ever make or mar the unfolding of the spiritual life. Spirituality does not depend upon the environment; it depends upon one's attitude towards life.
   Spiritual Life (rev. ed. *The Spiritual Life in the World*) *1991*

5   To call one day the Lord's Day is to deny that same lordship to every other day in the week and to make six parts of life outside the spiritual, while only one remains recognized as dedicated to the Spirit. And so common talk of sacred history and profane history, religious education and secular education, all these phrases that are so commonly used, hypnotize the public mind into a false view of the spirit and the world.
   Ibid.

6   The wheels of the world are turned by God, and we are only his hands, which touch the rim of the wheel.
   Ibid.

7   The clerk behind his counter and the doctor in the hospital are quite as much engaged in a divine activity as any preacher in his church. Until that is realized the world is vulgarized, and until we can see one life everywhere and all things rooted in that life, it is we who are hopelessly profane in attitude, we who are blind to the beatific vision which is the sight of the one life in everything, and all things as expressions of that life.
   Ibid.

8   If it is true that he is everywhere and in everything, then he is as much in the marketplace as in the desert, as much in the office as in the jungle, as easily found in the street of the crowded city as in the solitude of the mountain peak. . . .
   It is our weakness that the rush and the bustle of life in the city make us deaf to the Voice that is ever speaking. . . . That is the first thing to realize—that we do not find because our eyes are blinded.
   "Divinity Everywhere," Ibid.

9   The great mother-heart by which we are trained is ever dangling in front of us some attractive object, some prize for the child-spirit, turning outwards the powers that live within. In order to induce exertion, in order to make the effort by which alone those inward-turned powers will turn outwards into manifestation, we are bribed and coaxed and induced to make efforts by the endless toys of life scattered on every side.
   "Worldly Attractions," Ibid.

10   You grow, not by what you gain of outer fruit, by the inner unfolding necessary for your success in the struggle.
   Ibid.

1113. Catherine Liddell (1848–?)

1   "Isn't this Joseph's son?" —ah, it is He;
   Joseph the carpenter—same trade as me.
   "Jesus the Carpenter" *n.d.*

1114. Alice James (1848–1892)

1   Notwithstanding the poverty of my outside experience, I have always had a significance for myself, and every chance to stumble along my straight and narrow little path, and to worship at the feet of my Deity, and what more can a human soul ask for?
   (1892) *The Diary of Alice James*, Leon Edel, ed. *1964*

2   It is so comic to hear oneself called old, even at ninety I suppose!
   Letter to William James* (14 June 1889), Ibid.
   *American philosopher and psychologist (1842–1910), her brother.

3   . . . The immutable law that however great we may seem to our own consciousness no human being would exchange his for ours. . . .
   (7 July 1889), Ibid.

4   Ah! Those strange people who have the courage to be unhappy! *Are* they unhappy, by-the-way?
   Ibid.

5   How sick one gets of being "good," how much I should respect myself if I could burst out and make everyone wretched for twenty-four hours; embody selfishness.
   (11 December 1889), Ibid.

6   It is an immense loss to have all robust and sustaining expletives refined away from one! At . . . moments of trial refinement is a feeble reed to lean on.
   (12 December 1889), Ibid.

7   . . . who would ever give up the reality of dreams for relative knowledge?
   Ibid.

8   Every hour I live I become an intenser devotee to common-sense!
   (16 June 1890), Ibid.

9   I suppose one has a greater sense of intellectual degradation after an interview with a doctor than from any human experience.
   (27 September 1890), Ibid.

10   Having to look forward to something for a while seems to double the value of the event. . . .
   (1 June 1891), Ibid.

11   The grief is all for K. and H.,* who will *see* it all [her death], whilst I shall only feel it. . . .
   Ibid.
   *K. is Katherine Loring Peabody, her companion and nurse; H. is Henry James, novelist (1843–1916), her brother.

12   The difficulty about all this dying is that you can't tell a fellow anything about it, so where does the fun come in?
   Letter to William James* (11 December 1891), Ibid.
   *American philosopher and psychologist (1842–1910), her brother.

13   . . . physical pain however great ends in itself and falls away like dry husks from the mind, whilst moral discords and nervous horrors sear the soul.
   (4 March 1892), Ibid.

1115. Hubertine Auclert (1848–1914)

1   Ladies, we must remind ourselves that the weapon of the vote will be for us, just as it is for man, the only means of obtaining the reforms we desire. As long as we remain excluded from civic life, men will attend to their own interests rather than to ours.
   1879, *Women in World History Curriculum*, http://www.womeninworldhistory.com *1996–97*

1116. Annie Rankin Annan (1848–1925)

1   A dandelion in his verse,
   Like the first gold in childhood's purse.
   "Dandelions" *n.d.*

1117. Ellen Terry (1848–1928)

1 Imagination, industry, and intelligence—"the three I's"—are all indispensable to the actress, but of these three the greatest is, without any doubt, imagination.

Ch. 2, The Story of My Life 1908

2 Some people are "tone-deaf," and they find it physically impossible to observe the law of contrasts. But even a physical deficiency can be overcome by that faculty for taking infinite pains which may not be genius but is certainly a good substitute for it.

Ch. 4, Ibid.

3 What is a diary as a rule? A document useful to the person who keeps it, dull to the contemporary who reads it, invaluable to the student, centuries afterwards, who treasures it!

Ch. 14, Ibid.

4 Wonderful women! Have you ever thought how much we all, and women especially, owe to Shakespeare, for his vindication of women in these fearless, high-spirited, resolute and intelligent heroines?

"The Triumphant Women," Lecture (1911), Four Lectures on Shakespeare 1932

1118. Emma Lazarus (1849–1887)

1 Give me your tired, your poor,
Your huddled masses yearning to breathe free,
The wretched refuse of your teeming shore,
Send these, the homeless, tempest-tossed to me,
I lift my lamp beside the golden door!*

"The New Colossus" c. 1886
*Carved at the base of the Statue of Liberty in New York City.

2 Here at our sea-washed, sunset gates shall stand
A mighty woman with a torch, whose flame
Is the imprisoned lightning, and her name
Mother of exiles.

Ibid.

3 His cup is gall, his meat is tears,
His passion lasts a million years.

"Crowing of the Red Cock" n.d.

1119. Sarah Orne Jewett (1849–1909)

1 A harbor, even if it is a little harbor, is a good thing. . . . It takes something from the world and has something to give in return.

"River Driftwood," Country By-Ways 1886

2 This was one of those perfect New England days in late summer where the spirit of autumn takes a first stealthy flight, like a spy, through the ripening country-side, and, with feigned sympathy for those who droop with August heat, puts her cool cloak of bracing air about leaf and flower and human shoulders.

"The Courting of Sister Wisby," Atlantic Monthly (Boston) 1887

3 "Now I'm a believer, and I try to live a Christian life, but I'd as soon hear a surveyor's book read out, figgers an' all, as try to get any simple truth out o' most sermons."

Ibid.

4 The thing that teases the mind over and over for years, and at last gets itself put down rightly on paper—whether little or great, it belongs to Literature.

Preface, Letter to author Willa Cather, The Country of the Pointed Firs and Other Stories 1896
*See 1338.

5 Wrecked on the lee shore of age.

Ch. 7, Ibid.

6 Tact is after all a kind of mind reading.

Ch. 10, Ibid.

7 "Yes'm, old friends is always best, 'less you can catch a new one that's fit to make an old one out of."

Ch. 12, Ibid.

8 "T'ain't worthwhile to wear a day all out before it comes."

Ch. 16, Ibid.

9 The road was new to me, as roads always are, going back.

Ch. 19, Ibid.

10 So we die before our own eyes; so we see some chapters of our lives come to their natural end.

Ibid.

11 God bless them all who die at sea!
If they must sleep in restless waves,
God make them dream they are ashore,
With grass above their graves.

"The Gloucester Mother," St. 3 1908

12 A lean sorrow is hardest to bear.

Life of Nancy n.d.

1120. Frances Burnett (1849–1924)

1 "Are you a 'publican, Mary?" "Sorra a bit," sez I; "I'm the bist o' dimmycrats!" An' he looks up at me wid a look that ud go to yer heart, an' sez he: "Mary," sez he, "the country will go to ruin." An' nivver a day since thin has he let go by widout argyin' wid me to change me polytics.

Ch. 1, Little Lord Fauntleroy 1888

2 It is astonishing how short a time it takes for very wonderful things to happen.

Ch. 14, Ibid.

1121. Ellen Key (1849–1926)

1 Poverty hinders suitable marriages.

Ch. 1, The Century of the Child 1909

2 The emancipation of women is practically the greatest egoistic movement of the nineteenth century, and the most intense affirmation of the right of the self that history has yet seen.

Ch. 2, Ibid.

3 According to my method of thinking, and that of many others, not woman but the mother is the most precious possession of the nation, so precious that society advances its highest well-being when it protects the functions of the mother.

Ibid.

4 All philanthropy—no age has seen more of it than our own—is only a savoury fumigation burning at the mouth of a sewer. This incense offering makes the air more endurable to passersby, but it does not hinder the infection in the sewer from spreading.

Ibid.

5 For success in training children the first condition is to become as a child oneself, but this means no assumed childishness, no condescending baby-talk that the child immediately sees

through and deeply abhors. What it does mean is to be as entirely and simply taken up with the child as the child himself is absorbed by his life.

Ch. 3, Ibid.

6 At every step the child should be allowed to meet the real experiences of life; the thorns should never be plucked from his roses.

Ibid.

7 Nothing would more effectively further the development of education than for all flogging pedagogues to learn to educate with the head instead of with the hand.

Ibid.

8 Anyone who would the attempt the task of felling a virgin forest with a penknife would probably feel the same paralysis of despair that the reformer feels when confronted with existing school systems.

Ch. 5, Ibid.

10 I wrote in the sand [at age ten], "God is dead." In doing so I thought, If there is a God, He will kill me now with a thunderbolt. But since the sun continued to shine, the question was answered for the time being; but it soon turned up again.

Ch. 7, Ibid.

11 A destroyed home life, an idiotic school system, premature work in the factory, stupefying life in the streets, these are what the great city gives to the children of the under classes. It is more astonishing that the better instincts of human nature generally are victorious than the fact that this result is occasionally reversed.

Ch. 8, Ibid.

12 For outside the field of immutable laws, children ought not to be constrained nor coerced against their nature and their disposition, against their healthy egoism and against their especial taste.

"The Conventional Woman," The Morality of Woman and
Other Essays 1911

13 The discovery that each personality is a new world—which in Shakespeare found its Columbus, a Columbus after whom new mariners immediately undertook new conquests —this discovery of literature has yet only partially penetrated the universal consciousness, as a truth of experience.

"The Morality of Woman," Ibid.

14 Purity is the new-fallen snow which can be melted or sullied; chastity is steel tempered in the fire by white heat.

Ibid.

15 Not observation of a duty but liberty itself is the pledge that assures fidelity.

Ibid.

16 Love is moral without legal marriage, but marriage is immoral without love.

Ibid.

17 . . . everything which is exchanged between husband and wife in their life together can only be the free gift of love, can never be demanded by one or the other as a right. Man will understand that when one can no longer continue the life of love then this life must cease; that all the vows binding forever the life of feeling are a violence of one's personality, since one cannot be held accountable for the transformation of one's feeling.

Ibid.

18 When one paints an ideal, one does not need to limit one's imagination.

"The Woman of the Future," Ibid.

19 Conventionality is the tacit agreement to set appearance before reality, form before content, subordination before principle.

"The Conventional Woman," Ibid.

20 The educator must above all understand how to wait; to reckon all efforts in the light of the future, not the present.

Ibid.

21 Instead of defending "free love," which is a much-abused term capable of many interpretations, we ought to strive for the freedom of love; for while the former has come to imply freedom of any sort of love, the latter must only mean freedom for a feeling which is worthy the name of love. This feeling, it may be hoped, will gradually win for itself the same freedom in life as it already possesses in poetry.

Spreading Liberty and the Great Libertarians 1913

22 The home was a closed sphere touched only at its edge by the world's evolution.

Pt. I, Ch. 1, The Renaissance of Motherhood 1914

23 Woman, however, as the bearer and guardian of the new lives, has everywhere greater respect for life than man, who for centuries, as hunter and warrior, learned that the taking of lives may be not only allowed, but honourable.

Pt. I, Ch. 2, Ibid.

24 No emancipation must make women indifferent to sexual self-control and motherly devotion, from which some of the highest life values we possess on this earth have sprung.

Ch. 4, Ibid.

25 Art, that great undogmatized church.

Pt. 2, Ch. 1, Ibid.

26 . . . the child craves of the mother, the work craves of its creator: the vision, the waiting, the hope, the pure will, the faith, and the love; the power to suffer, the desire to sacrifice, the ecstacy of devotion. Thus, man also has his "motherliness," a compound of feelings corresponding to those with which the woman enriches the race, oftener than the work, but which in woman, as in man, constitutes the productive mental processes without which neither new works nor new generations turn out well.

Ibid.

27 Motherhood has . . . for many women ceased to be the sweet secret dream of the maiden, the glad hope of the wife, the deep regret of the ageing woman who has not had this yearning satisfied.

Ch. 3, Ibid.

28 The socially pernicious, racially wasteful, and soul-withering consequences of the working of mothers outside the home must cease. And this can only come to pass, either through the programme of institutional upbringing, or through the intimate renaissance of the home.

Pt. 3, Ch. 2, Ibid.

29 The belief that we shall some day be able to prevent war is to me one with the belief in the possibility of making humanity really human.

Preface, War, Peace, and the Future 1916

30 But the havoc wrought by war, which one compares with the havoc wrought by nature, is not an unavoidable fate before which man stands helpless. The natural forces which are the causes of war are human passions which it lies in our power to change.

Ch. 1, Ibid.

31 Formerly, a nation that broke the peace did not trouble to try and prove to the world that it was done solely from higher motives. . . . *Now war has a bad conscience.* Now every nation assures us that it is bleeding for a human cause, the fate of which hangs in the balance of its victory. All now declare themselves to be fighting for right, against might, the very thing that the pacifists urged. No nation will admit that it was solely to insure its own safety and to increase its power that it declared war. No nation dares to admit the guilt of blood before the world.

Ibid.

32 Everything, everything in war is barbaric. . . . But the worst barbarity of war is that is forces men collectively to commit acts against which individually they would revolt with their whole being.

Ch. 6, Ibid.

33 Every State that relies on its war-preparedness for its power, honour, and glory must look upon its mothers with the same eye as the first Napoleon, of whom someone had said that "he looked as if he wished to rive new war material out of the wombs of the mothers."

Ch. 9, Ibid.

34 Only calm thinking will lead one to the root of war. The peace movement that has only appealed to the emotions has never put the axe to the root of the problem. This movement, which was started in America and England, presupposed that Christianity is already realized.

Ch. 10, Ibid.

35 . . . feelings of sympathy and admiration are the indispensable mortar that holds the stones of international justice together.

Ch. 16, Ibid.

1122. Clara Shortridge Foltz (1849–1934)

1 A woman would be better off almost anywhere than home raising men like you.
Quoted by Sandra Day O'Connor* in Foreword, "First Women: Contribution of American Women to the Law," 28, *Valparaiso Law Review*, xiii *1994*
*See 2437.

2 They called me the lady lawyer—a dainty sobriquet—which enabled me to maintain a dainty manner as I browbeat my way through the marshes of ignorance and prejudice.
Quoted in *The 50 Most Influential Women in American Law* by Dawn Bradley Berry *1996*
*See 3435.

3 Narrow-gauge statesmen grew red as turkey gobblers mouthing their ignorance against the [women lawyers'] bill, and staid old grangers who had never seen the inside of a courthouse seemed to have been given the gift of tongues and delivered themselves of maiden speeches pregnant with eloquent nonsense.
Debate on California senate floor (c. 1876), Ibid.

1123. Marie de La Coste (1849–1936)

1 Into a ward of the whitewashed walls
Where the dead and dying lay—
Wounded by bayonets, shells, and balls—
Somebody's darling was borne one day.
"Somebody's Darling," St. 1 *n.d.*

2 Tenderly bury the fair young dead,
Pausing to drop on his grave a tear;
Carve on the wooden slab at his head,
"Somebody's darling lies buried here!"
St. 5, Ibid.

1124. Geneviève (1850–?)

1 The feminine chest was not made for hanging orders on.
Quoted in *Pomp and Circumstance* by E. de Gramont *1929*

1125. Pauline Roland (fl. 1850s)

Coauthor with Jeanne-Françoise Deroine.*
*See 872: 1–2.

1126. Abby Langdon Alger (1850–?)

1 In the beginning, God made Adam out of the earth, but he did not make Glūs-kābé (the Indian God). Glūs-kābé made himself out of the dirt that was kicked up in the creation of Adam. He rose and walked about, but he could not speak until the Lord opened his lips.

God made the earth and the sea, and then he took counsel with Glūs-kābé concerning them. He asked him if it would be better to have the rivers run up on one side of the earth and down on the other, but Glūs-kābé said, "No, they must all run down one way."

Then the Lord asked him about the ocean, whether it would do to have it always lie still. Glūs-kābé told him, "No!" It must always rise and fall, or else it would grow thick and stagnant.
In *Indian Tents: Stories Told by Penobscot, Passamaquoddy and Mimac Indians to Abby L. Alger 1897*

1127. Sofia Vasilyevna Kovalevskaya (1850–1891)

1 The meaning of these concepts I naturally could not yet grasp, but they acted on my imagination, instilling in me a reverence for mathematics as an exalted and mysterious science which opens up to its initiates a new world of wonders, inaccessible to ordinary mortals.

A Russian Childhood 1987

2 I began to feel an attraction for my mathematics so intense that I started to neglect my other studies.

Ibid.

3 Say what you know, do what you must, come what may.
Motto on her paper "On the Problem of the Rotation of a Solid Body about a Fixed Point," Cited in *4000 Years of Women in Science*, http://www.astr.ua.edu/4000WS *1 August 1997*

1128. Margaret Collier Graham (1850–1910)

1 "Harvest's a poor time fer wishin'; it's more prof'table 'long about seedin'-time. . . ."
"Idy," *Stories of the Foot-hills 1875*

2 . . . it's no more 'n fair to be civil to a man when you're getting' the best of 'im; but I hain't.
"The Withrow Water Right," Ibid.

3 The mind of the most logical thinker goes so easily from one point to another that it is not hard to mistake motion for progress.

Gifts and Givers 1906

4 People need joy quite as much as clothing. Some of them need it far more.

Ibid.

5 We are all held in place by the pressure of the crowd around us. We must all lean upon others. Let us see that we lean gracefully and freely and acknowledge their support.

Ibid.

6 Conscience, as I understand it, is the impulse to do right because it is right, regardless of personal ends, and has nothing whatever to do with the ability to distinguish between right and wrong.

"A Matter of Conscience," *Do They Really Respect Us?
And Other Essays 1911*

7 If any good results to a man from believing a lie, it certainly comes from the honesty of his belief.

"Some Immortal Fallacy," Ibid.

1129. Frances Xavier Cabrini (1850–1917)

1 But I don't think that my Institute can be confined to one city or one diocese. The whole world is not wide enough for me.

Quoted by Bishop Gelmini in Pt. I, Ch. 3, *Too Small a
World* by Theodore Maynard *1945*

2 To become perfect, all you have to do is to obey perfectly. When you renounce your personal inclinations you accept a mortification countersigned with the cross of Christ.

Ibid.

3 I want all of you to take on wings and fly swiftly to repose in that blessed peace possessed by a soul that is all for God.

Diary (1889) Pt. II, Ch. 7, Ibid.

4 God commands, the sea obeys. If also in religion every Sister would obey her superior—with perfect submission, that is, without relying on her own judgement—what peace, what paradisal sweetness would be hers.

Ibid.

5 Love is not loved, my daughters! Love is not loved! And how can we remain cold, indifferent and almost without heart at this thought? . . . If we do not burn with love, we do not deserve the title which ennobles us, elevates us, makes us great, and even a portent to the angels in heaven.

Diary (1891), Ibid.

1130. Emma Carleton (1850–1927)

1 Reputation is a bubble which a man bursts when he tries to blow it for himself.

The Philistine, Vol. IX, No. 82 *n.d.*

1131. Florence Earle Coates (1850–1927)

1 Age, out of heart, impatient, sighed;—
"I ask what will the *Future* be?"
Youth laughed contentedly, and cried:—
"The future leave to me!"

"Youth and Age" *n.d.*

2 Fear is the fire that melts Icarian wings.

"The Unconquered Air" *n.d.*

3 He turned with such a smile to face disaster
That he sublimed defeat.

"The Hero" *n.d.*

4 I love, and the world is mine!

"The World Is Mine" *n.d.*

5 The soul hath need of prophet and redeemer:
Her outstretched wings against her prisoning bars,
She waits for truth; and truth is with the dreamer,—
Persistent as the myriad light of stars!

"Dream the Great Dream" *n.d.*

6 Though his beginnings be but poor and low,
Thank God a man can grow!

"Per Aspera" *n.d.*

7 Death—Life's servitor and friend—the guide
That safely ferries us from shore to shore!

"Sleep" *n.d.*

8 Ah me! the Prison House of Pain!—what lessons there are bought!—
Lessons of a sublimer strain than any elsewhere taught.

"The House of Pain" *n.d.*

1132. Jane Harrison (1850–1928)

1 Youth and Crabbed Age stand broadly for the two opposite poles of human living, poles equally essential to any real vitality, but always contrasted. . . . The whole art of living is a delicate balance between the two tendencies.

"Crabbed Age and Youth," *Alpha and Omega 1915*

2 Your thoughts are—for what they are worth—self-begotten by some process of parthenogenesis. But there comes often to me, almost always, a moment when alone I cannot bring them to birth, when, if companionship is denied, they die unborn.

"Scientlae Sacra Fames," Ibid.

3 A child's mind is, indeed, throughout the best clue to understanding of savage magic . . . Like the artist, he goes forth to the work of creation, gloriously alone.

"Darwinism and Religion," Ibid.

4 To be womanly is one thing, and one only; it is to be sensitive to man, to be highly endowed with the sex instinct; to be manly is to be sensitive to woman.

"Homo Sum," Ibid.

5 Whenever at an accusation blind rage burns up within us, the reason is that some arrow has pierced the joints of our harness. Behind our shining armour of righteous indignation lurks a convicted and only half-repentant sinner . . . [and] we may be almost sure some sharp and bitter grain of truth lurks within it, and the wound is best probed.

"Epilogue on the War," Ibid.

6 Old age, believe me, is a good and pleasant thing. It is true you are gently shouldered off the stage, but then you are given such a comfortable front stall as spectator. . . .

"Conclusion," *Reminiscences of a Student's Life 1925*

7 If I think of Death at all it is merely as a negation of life, a close, a last and necessary chord. What I dread is disease, that is, bad disordered life, not Death, and disease, so far, I have escaped. I have no hope whatever of personal immortality, no desire even for a future life. My consciousness began in a very

humble fashion with my body; with my body, very quietly, I hope it will end.

     Ibid.

8 Here was a big constructive imagination; here was a mere doctor laying bare the origins of Greek drama as no classical scholar had ever done, . . . for generations almost every branch of human knowledge will be enriched and illumined by the imagination of Freud.

     Ibid.

9 I have elsewhere tried to show that Art is not the handmaid of Religion, but that Art in some sense springs out of Religion, and that between them is a connecting link, a bridge, and that bridge is Ritual.

     Ibid.

10 Marriage, for a woman at least, hampers the two things that made life to me glorious—friendship and learning.

     Ibid.

1133. Rose Hartwick Thorpe (1850–1939)

1 And her face so sweet and pleading, yet with sorrow pale and worn,
  Touched his heart with sudden pity—lit his eye with misty light;
  "Go, your lover lives!" said Cromwell; "Curfew shall not ring tonight!"

     "Curfew Shall Not Ring Tonight" *1866*

1134. Laura Howe Richards (1850–1943)

1 "And the storm went on. It roared, it bellowed, and it screeched: it thumped and it kerwhalloped. The great seas would come bunt agin the rocks, as if they were bound to go right though to Jersey City, which they used to say was the end of the world."

     Ch. 2, *Captain January 1890*

2 "There's times when a man has strength given to him, seemin'ly, over and above human strength. 'Twas like as if the Lord ketched holt and helped me: maybe he did, seein' what 'twas I was doing. Maybe he did!"

     Ibid.

3 "A cap'n on a quarterdeck's a good thing; but a cap'n on a pint o' rock, out to sea in a northeast gale, might just as well be a fo'c'sle hand and done with it."

     Ibid.

4 Be you clown or be you King,
  Still your singing is the thing.

     "Dedication," *Tirra Lirra 1890*

5 Every little wave has its nightcap on.

     "Song for Hal," Refrain, Ibid.

6 Once there was an elephant
  Who tried to use the telephant—
  No! No! I mean an elephone
  Who tried to use the telephone.

     "Eletelephony," St. 1, Ibid.

7 Ponsonby Perks,
  He fought with Turks,
  Performing many wonderful works.

     "Nonsense Verses," St. 2, Ibid.

8 Great is truth and shall prevail,
  Therefore must we weep and wail.

     "The Mameluke and the Hospodar," St. 4, Ibid.

9 "Mighty poor country up that way. Some say the Rome folks don't see any garden-truck from year's-end to year's-end, and that if you ask a Rome girl to cook you up a mess of string beans, she takes the store beans and runs 'em on a string, and boils 'em that way. . . ."

     Pt. II, *Narcissa 1892*

1135. Nellie Cashman (1851–1904)

1 When I saw something that needed doing, I did it.

     Interview, *Daily British Colonist 1898*

1136. Kate Chopin (1851–1904)

1 The mother-women seemed to prevail that summer at Grand Isle. It was easy to know them, fluttering about with extended, protecting wings when any harm, real or imaginary, threatened their precious brood. They were women who idolized their children, worshipped their husbands, and esteemed it a holy privilege to efface themselves as individuals and grow wings as ministering angels.

     Ch. 4, *The Awakening 1889*

2 The voice of the sea speaks to the soul. The touch of the sea is sensuous, enfolding the body in its soft, close embrace.

     Ch. 6, Ibid.

3 A certain light was beginning to dawn dimly within her—the light which, showing the way, forbids. . . . But the beginning of things, of a world especially, is necessarily vague, tangled, chaotic, and exceedingly disturbing. How few of us ever emerge from such beginning! How many souls perish in its tumult!

     Ibid.

4 "Pirate gold isn't a thing to be hoarded or utilized. It is something to squander and throw to the four winds, for the fun of seeing the golden specks fly."

     Ch. 12, Ibid.

5 The past was nothing to her; offered no lesson which she was willing to heed. The future was a mystery which she never attempted to penetrate. The present alone was significant. . . .

     Ch. 15, Ibid.

6 "The way to become rich is to make money, my dear Edna, not to save it. . . ."

     Ch. 18, Ibid.

7 It sometimes entered Mr. Pontellier's mind to wonder if his wife were not growing a little unbalanced mentally. He could see plainly that she was not herself. That is, he could not see that she was becoming herself and daily casting aside that fictitious self which we appear before the world.

     Ch. 19, Ibid.

8 . . . "a wedding is one of the most lamentable spectacles on earth."

     Ch. 22, Ibid.

9 Alcée Arobin's manner was so genuine that it often deceived even himself.

     Ch. 25, Ibid.

10 ". . . when I left her today, she put her arms around me and felt my shoulder blades, to see if my wings were strong, she

said. 'The bird that would soar above the level plain of tradition and prejudice must have strong wings. It is a sad spectacle to see the weaklings bruised, exhausted, fluttering back to earth.'"

Ch. 27, Ibid.

11 "There are some people who leave impressions not so lasting as the imprint of an oar upon the water."

Ch. 34, Ibid.

12 "The years that are gone seem like dreams—if one might go on sleeping and dreaming—but to wake up and find—oh! well! perhaps it is better to wake up after all, even to suffer, rather than to remain a dupe to illusions all one's life."

Ch. 38, Ibid.

13 The children appeared before her like antagonists who had overcome her; who had overpowered and sought to drag her into the soul's slavery for the rest of her days.

Ch. 39, Ibid.

14 In entering upon their new life they decided to be governed by no precedential methods. Marriage was to be a form, that while fixing legally their relation to each other, was in no wise to touch the individuality of either; that was to be preserved intact. Each was to remain a free integral of humanity, responsible to no dominating exactness of so-called marriage laws. And the element that was to make possible such a union was trust in each other's love, honor, courtesy, tempered by the reserving clause of readiness to meet the consequences of reciprocal liberty.

"A Point at Issue!" *1889*

15 Only the birds had seen, and she could count on their discretion.

"A Shameful Affair" *1891*

16 What could love, the unsolved mystery, count for in face of this possession of self-assertion which she suddenly recognized as the strongest impulse of her being!

"The Story of an Hour" *1894*

17 There would be no one to live for her during these coming years; she would live for herself. There would be no powerful will bending hers in that blind persistence with which men and women believe they have a right to impose a private will upon a fellow-creature.

Ibid.

18 "I don't hate him," Athenaise answered. . . . "It's jus' being married that I detes' an' despise."

"Athenaise" *1895*

19 I trust it will not be giving away professional secrets to say that many readers would be surprised, perhaps shocked, at the questions which some newspaper editors will put to a defenseless woman under the guise of flattery.

"On Certain Brisk Days," *St. Louis Post-Dispatch* (26 November 1899), *The Complete Works of Kate Chopin*, Vol. 2, *1970*

1137. Mary Augusta Ward (1851–1920)

1 "Propinquity does it"—as Mrs. Thornburg is always reminding us.

Bk. I, Ch. 2, *Robert Elsmer 1888*

2 "Every man is bound to leave a story better than he found it."

Ch. 3, Ibid.

3 One may as well preach a respectable mythology as anything else.

Ch. 5, Ibid.

4 This Laodicean* cant of tolerance . . .

Bk. II, Ch. 12, Ibid.

*Lukewarm.

5 In my youth people talked about Ruskin; now they talk about drains.

Ibid.

6 "Put down enthusiasm." . . . The Church of England in a nutshell.

Ch. 16, Ibid.

7 Conviction is the Conscience of the Mind.

Bk. IV, Ch. 26, Ibid.

8 All things change, creeds and philosophies and outward system—but God remains!

Ch. 27, Ibid.

9 Truth has never been, can never be, contained in any one creed.

Bk. VI, Ch. 38, Ibid.

10 A great movement, in which this household is engaged, is now beginning to put women on the land, and so replace the agricultural labourers who have gone either into the armies or the munition factories. And meanwhile all the elderly men and women of the countryside are sitting on War Committees, or working for the Red Cross. Our lives are penetrated by the war; our thoughts are never free from it.

Ch. I, *England's Effort*, Vol. II *1918*

11 For there we come to the root of everything—*the unpreparedness of England*—and what it meant. It meant simply that as a nation we never wished for war with Germany, and, as a nation, we never expected it.

Ch. II, Ibid.

12 For that final clash -- that Armageddon that all think must come, our sailors wait, not despising their enemy, knowing very well that they -- the Fleet—are the pivot of the situation, that without the British Navy, not all the valour of the Allies in France or Russia could win the war, and that with it, Germany's hope of victory is vain. While the Navy lives, England lives, and Germany's vision of a world governed by the ruthless will of the scientific soldier is doomed.

Ch. IV, Ibid.

1138. Anna Garlin Spencer (1851–1931)

1 And when her biographer says of an Italian woman poet, "during some years her Muse was intermitted," we do not wonder at the fact when he casually mentions her ten children.

Woman's Share in Social Culture 1912

2 It is not alone the fact that women have generally had to spend most of their strength in caring for others that has handicapped them in individual effort; but also that they have almost universally had to care wholly for themselves.

Ibid.

3 A successful woman preacher was once asked "what special obstacles have you met as a woman in the ministry?" "Not one," she answered, "except the lack of a minister's wife."

Ibid.

4   The failure of woman to produce genius of the first rank in most of the supreme forms of human effort has been used to block the way of all women of talent and ambition for intellectual achievement in a manner that would be amusingly absurd were it not so monstrously unjust and socially harmful.

Ibid.

5   The whole course of evolution in industry, and in the achievements of higher education and exceptional talent, has shown man's invariable tendency to shut women out when their activities have reached a highly specialized period of growth.

Ibid.

1139. Mariana Griswold Van Rensselaer (1851–1934)

1   Let us shun self-analyzation, self-consciousness, morbidness, affectation, attitudinizing. Let us look ahead as little as possible, keeping our eyes on our brushes and on the world of beauty around us.

"Some Aspects of Contemporary Art," *Lippincott's* [Philadelphia] *December 1878*

2   . . . we also, and not our artists only, have a duty to perform if we wish the stream of progress to grow wider, deeper, swifter. We must give ourselves more earnestly and intelligently and generously than we have to the happy duty of appreciation.

The Book of American Figure Painters 1886

1140. Mary A. Barr (1852–?)

1   I sing the Poppy! The frail snowy weed!
The flower of Mercy! That within its heart
Doth keep "a drop serene" of human need,
A drowsy balm of every bitter smart.
For happy hours the rose will idly blow
The Poppy hath a charm of pain and woe.

"White Poppies" *n.d.*

1141. Qurrat al-'Ayn (?–1852)

1   The tangled curls of thy darling's hair, and thy saddle and steed are thine only care;
In thy heart the Infinite hath no share, nor the thought of the poor man's poverty.

Untitled ghazal, *Wise Women: Over 2000 Years of Spiritual Writing by Women*, Susan Cahill, ed. *1996*

2   The country of "I" and "We" forsake; thy home in Annihilation make,
Since fearing not this step to take, thou shalt gain the highest felicity.*

Ibid.

*This is the core philosophy of Babism, a "systemized Sufism," of which Qurrat was a leader and martyred saint.

1142. Martha Jane Burke (1852–1903)

1   During the month of June I acted as a pony express rider carrying the U.S. mail between Deadwood and Custer, a distance of fifty miles. . . . It was considered the most dangerous route in the hills, but as my reputation as a rider and quick shot was well known, I was molested very little, for the toll gatherers looked on me as being a good fellow, and they knew that I never missed my mark.

Life and Adventures of Calamity Jane 1896

2   I Jane Hickok Burke better known as Calamity Jane of my own free will and being of sound mind do this day June 3,

1903 make this confession. I have lied about my past life. . . . People got snoopy so I told them lies to hear their tongues wag. The women are all snakes and none of them I can call friends.

Document to James O'Neill (2 June 1903), Quoted in *Calamity Was the Name for Jane* by Glenn Clairmonte *1959*

1143. Emilia Pardo Bazan (1852–1921)

1   Nature, they call you a mother; they ought to call you a cruel stepmother.

La madre naturaleza (Mother Nature) *1887*

2   I don't know how men are different from hogs. . . . They chase after the same things: food, drink, women. In short, we're all made of the same stuff.

Ibid.

3   Men can hardly form an idea of how difficult it is for a woman to acquire culture and to fill in her education by teaching herself. Boys, from the age they can walk and talk, attend elementary schools, then secondary institutes, the academies, the university. . . . For them, all advantages; for women, all obstacles.

"*Apuntes autobiograficos,*" Quoted in *Emilia Pardo Bazan* by R. E. Osborne *1964*

4   . . . those of us who came into the world a third of a century after Concepcion Arenal found public opinion just as hostile (perhaps more so) to women who were called poetesses or bluestockings, and we read every day furious articles intended to demonstrate that the object of woman's life is to darn socks.

"*La Lectura*" (1907), Ibid.

1144. Mary Wilkins Freeman (1852–1930)

1   . . . it took her a long time to prepare her tea; but when ready it was set forth with as much grace as if she had been a veritable guest to her own self.

A New England Nun 1891

2   Louisa's feet had turned into a path . . . so straight and unswerving that it could only meet a check at her grave, and so narrow that there was no room for anyone at her side.

Ibid.

3   She gazed ahead through a long reach of future days strung together like pearls in a rosary, every one like the others, and all smooth and flawless and innocent, and her heart went up in thankfulness.

Ibid.

1145. Augusta Gregory (1852–1932)

1   CHRISTIE. It's a grand thing to be able to take your money in your hand and to think no more of it when it slips away from you than you would of a trout that would slip back into the stream.

Twenty Five 1903

2   MRS. TARPEY. Business, is it? What business would the people here have but to be minding one another's business?

Spreading the News 1905

3   MRS. DELANE. I'm not one that blames the police. Sure, they have their own bread to earn like every other one. And indeed it is often they will let a thing pass.

Hyacinth Halvey 1906

4 MRS. DONOHOE. There is many a thing in the sea is not decent, but cockles is fit to put before the Lord!

The Workhouse Ward 1908

5 HAZEL. To have no power of revenge after death! My strength to go nourish weeds and grass!

Coats 1910

6 MRS. BRODERICK. A splendid shot he was; the thing he did not see he'd hit it the same as the thing he'd see.

The Full Moon 1910

7 DARBY. I am maybe getting your meaning wrong, your tongue being a little hard and sharp because you are Englified, but I am without new learnments and so I speak flat.

The Bogiemen 1912

8 O'MALLEY. Well, there's no one at all, they do be saying, but is deserving of some punishment from the very minute of his birth. . . . Sure it is allotted to every Christian to meet with his share of trouble.

Act II, Shanwalla 1915

9 1ST POLICEMAN. There's nothing in the world more ignorant than to give any belief to ghosts. I am walking the world these twenty years, and never met anything worse than myself!

Act III, Ibid.

10 GIANT. Fru, Fa, Fashog! I smell the smell of a melodious lying Irishman!

Act I, Sc. 4, The Golden Apple 1916

11 GIANT. One person to know it, and you to know him to know it, is the same as if it was known to all the world.

Act II, Sc. 2, Ibid.

12 MOTHER. Them that have too much of it [learning] are seven times crosser than them that never saw a book.

Act I, Aristotle Bellows 1921

13 CELIA. It is better to be tied to any thorny bush than to be with a cross man.

Ibid.

14 JESTER. There's more learning than is taught in books.

Act I, The Jester 1923

15 OGRE. I'll take no charity! What I get I'll earn by taking it. I would feel no pleasure it being given to me, any more than a huntsman would take pleasure in being made a present of a dead fox, in place of getting a run across country after it.

Act II, Sc. 1, Ibid.

16 JOEL. That's the way of it! All the generations looking for him, and praying for him. We wanted him, and we got him, and what we did with him was to kill him. And that is the way it will be ever and always, so long as leaves grow upon the trees!

Act III, The Story Brought by Brigit 1924

17 A theater with a base of reality and an apex of beauty.

Quoted in "Karen Malpede,"* *Interviews with Contemporary Women Playwrights*, Kathleen Betsko**
and Rachel Koenig *1987*

* See 3057. ** See 2739.

1146. Gertrude Kasebier (1852–1934)

1 . . . from the first days of dawning individuality, I have longed unceasingly to make pictures of people . . . to make likenesses that are biographies, to bring out in each photograph the es-

sential personality that is variously called temperament, soul, humanity.

Quoted in *The Woman's Eye* by Anne Tucker* *1973*
*See 3073.

1147. Vera Figner (1852–1942)

1 Generally speaking, there was in her* nature both feminine gentleness and masculine severity. Tender, tender as a mother with the working people, she was exacting and severe toward her comrades and fellow-workers, while toward her political enemies, the government, she could be merciless. . . .

Memoirs of a Revolutionist 1927
*Reference to Sofia Perovskaya; see 1148.

1148. Sofia Perovskaya (1853–1881)

1 . . . my lot is not at all such a dark one. I have lived as my convictions have prompted me; I could not do otherwise; therefore I await what is in store for me with a clear conscience.

Letter to her Mother, *Woman as Revolutionary*,
Fred C. Giffin, ed. *1973*

1149. Octavia Victoria Rogers Albert (1853–1889/90)

1 None but those who resided in the South during the time of slavery can realize the terrible punishments that were visited upon the slaves. Virtue and self-respect were denied them.

. . . Much has been written concerning the negro, and we must confess that the moral standing of the race is far from what it should be; but who is responsible for the sadly immoral condition of this illiterate race in the South? I answer unhesitatingly, Their masters. Consider that here in this Bible land, where we have the light, where the Gospel was preached Sunday after Sunday in all portions of the South, and where ministers read from the pulpit that God had made of one blood all nations of men, etc., that nevertheless, with the knowledge and teachings of the word of God, the slaves were reduced to a level with the brute.

Ch. I, The house of bondage, or, Charlotte Brooks and other slaves 1890

2 "The white people thought in slave-time we poor darkies had no soul, and they separated us like dogs. So many poor colored people are dead from grieving at the separation of their children that was sold away from them."

Ch. IV, Ibid.

3 "I tell you, I have seen black people, in slave-time, drove along—may be one hundred in a drove—just like hogs to be sold. Sometimes men were sold from their wives and mothers from their children. I saw a white man in Virginia sell his own child he had by a colored woman there. They say a 'Merican man never would take care of his children he would have in slave-time by the black women, as a Frenchman would here in Louisiana."

Ch. VIII, Ibid.

1150. Lillie Langtry (1853–1929)

1 The sentimentalist ages far more quickly than the person who loves his work and enjoys new challenges.

Quoted in the *New York Sun 1906*

2 Anyone who limits his vision to his memories of yesterday is already dead.

Quoted in *Because I Love Him* by Noel B. Gerson *1971*

1151. Mary Lease (1853–1933)

1 What you Kansas farmers ought to do is to raise less corn and raise more hell.

Political Speech 1890

1152. Emilie Poulsson (1853–1939)

1 Books are keys to wisdom's treasure;
Books are gates to lands of pleasure;
Books are paths that upward lead;
Books are friends. Come, let us read.

Inscription in Children's Reading Room,
Hopkington, Massachusetts n.d.

1153. Jennie Jerome Churchill (1854–1921)

1 Of all nationalities, Americans are the best in adapting themselves. With them, to see is to know—and to know is to conquer.

Quoted in the New York World-Telegram 13 October 1908

2 The best society does not necessarily mean the "smart set."

Ibid.

3 You may be a princess or the richest woman in the world, but you cannot be more than a lady.

Ibid.

4 ALMA. I rather suspect her of being in love with him.
MARTIN. Her own husband? Monstrous! What a selfish woman!

His Borrowed Plumes 1909

5 All natures are in nature.

Ibid.

6 Italians love—sun, sin, and spaghetti.

Ibid.

7 What is love without passion?—A garden without flowers, a hat without feathers, tobogganing without snow.

Ibid.

8 BASIL. But remember, a man ends by hating the woman who he thinks has found him out.

Ibid.

9 It is so tempting to try the most difficult thing possible.

Quoted in the Daily Chronicle (London) 8 July 1909

10 We don't elope nowadays, and we don't divorce, except out of kindness.

The Bill 1913

11 Your castle in Spain has no foundations, that is why it is so easily built. . . .

"Mars and Cupid,"
Pearson's September 1915

12 . . . we owe something to extravagance, for thrift and adventure seldom go hand in hand. . . .

"Extravagance" October 1915

13 Treat your friends as you do your pictures, and place them in their best light.

"Friendship," Small Talk on Big Subjects 1916

14 There is no such thing as a moral dress. . . . It's people who are moral or immoral.

Quoted in Daily Chronicle (London) 16 February 1921

15 It's a wise virgin who looks after her own lamp.

Quoted in Bystander 6 July 1921

16 But I suppose experience of life will in time teach you that tact is a very essential ingredient in all things.

Letter to Winston Churchill* (4 October 1895), Quoted in
Jennie, Vol. II by Ralph G. Martin 1971

17 Life is not always what one wants it to be, but to make the best of it as it is, is the only way of being happy. . . .

Letter to Lord Kitchener (27 November 1896), Ibid.

18 You seem to have no real purpose in life and won't realize at the age of twenty-two that for a man life means work, and hard work if you mean to succeed.

Letter to Winston Churchill* (26 February 1897), Ibid.
*(1874–1965) British statesman, prime minister (1940–1945 and
1951–1955), her son.

19 . . . be modest. . . . One must be tempted to talk of oneself . . . but resist. Let them drag things out.

(November 4, 1897), Ibid.

20 If we can eliminate sufferings and at the same time comfort the many aching and anxious hearts at home, shall we not be fulfilling our greatest mission in life? These are "Women's Rights" in the best sense of the word. We need no others.

Speech, First Meeting of General Committee for Hospital
Ship (18 November 1899), Ibid.

21 One is forever throwing away substance for shadows.

Letter to her sister, Leonie Leslie
(24 July 1914), Ibid.

1154. Edith Thomas (1854–1925)

1 How on the moment all changes!

"Optimi Consiliarii Mortui, XXXIV," Sts. 1–2, The Inverted Torch 1890

2 When the wind through the trees makes a path for the moon!
Praise June!

"Praise June," In Sunshine Land 1894

3 And Heaven gave me strivings blind
By Justice to be schooled,
And purpose branded in the mind,
To rule not, nor be ruled. . . .

"Of the Middle World," St. 2, The Guest at the Gate 1909

4 They troop to their work in the gray of the morning,
Each with a shovel swung over his shoulder . . .
You have cut down their wages without any warning—
Angry? Well, let their wrath smolder!

"The Argument," St. 2, Ibid.

5 The God of Music dwelleth out of doors.

"The God of Music" n.d.

1155. Eva March Tappan (1854–1930)

1 We drove the Indians out of the land,
But a dire revenge those Redmen planned,
For they fastened a name to every nook,
And every boy with a spelling book
Will have to toil till his hair turns gray
Before he can spell them the proper way.

"On the Cape," St. 1 n.d.

1156. Margaret Wolfe Hungerford (1855?–1897)

1   Beauty is in the eye of the beholder.

Molly Bawn 1878

1157. Alice Freeman Palmer (1855–1902)

1   Exquisite child of the air.

"The Butterfly" *n.d.*

1158. Ella Wheeler Wilcox (1855–1919)

1   Laugh and the world laughs with you;
    Weep, and you weep alone;
    For the sad old earth must borrow its mirth,
    But has trouble enough of its own.

"Solitude" St. 1, *New York Sun*
25 February 1883

2   'Tis easy enough to be pleasant,
    When life flows along like a song;
    But the man worth while is the one who will smile
    When everything goes dead wrong.

"Worth While" *n.d.*

3   But with every deed you are sowing a seed,
    Though the harvest you may never see.

"You Never Can Tell," St. 2 *n.d.*

4   Give us that grand word "woman" once again,
    And let's have done with "lady"; one's a term
    Full of fine force, strong, beautiful, and firm,
    Fit for the noblest use of tongue or pen;
    And one's a word for lackeys.

"Woman" *n.d.*

5   I love your lips when they're wet with wine
    And red with wicked desire.

"I Love You," St. 1, *n.d.*

6   It ever has been since time began,
    And ever will be, till time lose breath,
    That love is a mood—no more—to man,
    And love to a woman is life or death.

"Blind," St. 1 *n.d.*

7   Let there be many windows to your soul,
    That all the glory of the world
    May beautify it.

"Progress," St. 1 *n.d.*

8   Tear away
    The blind of superstition; let the light
    Pour through fair windows broad as Truth itself
    And high as God.

Ibid.

9   Sweep up the debris from decaying faiths;
    Sweep down the cobwebs of worn-out beliefs,
    And throw your soul open to the light
    Of Reason and Knowledge.

St. 2, Ibid.

10 Love lights more fires than hate extinguishes,
    And men grow better as the world grows old.

"Optimism" *n.d.*

11 Come, cuddle your head on my shoulder, dear,
    Your head like the golden-rod,
    And we will go sailing away from here
    To the beautiful land of Nod.

"The Beautiful Land of Nod" *n.d.*

12 With care, and skill, and cunning art,
    She parried Time's malicious dart,
    And kept the years at bay,
    Till passion entered in her heart
    And aged her in a day!

"The Destroyer" *n.d.*

13 All love that has not friendship for its base,
    Is like a mansion built upon the sand.

"Upon the Sand" *n.d.*

14 Keep on with your weary battle against triumphant might;
    No question is ever settled until it is settled right.

"Settle the Question Right" *n.d.*

15 The splendid discontent of God
    With chaos, made the world.
    And from the discontent of man
    The world's best progress springs.

"Discontent" *n.d.*

16 We flatter those we scarcely know,
    We please the fleeting guest,
    And deal full many a thoughtless blow
    To those who love us best.

"Life's Scars," St. 3 *n.d.*

17 Whatever is—is best.

"Whatever Is—Is Best" *n.d.*

1159. Olive Schreiner (1855–1920)

1   The troubles of the young are soon over; they leave no external mark. If you wound the tree in its youth the bark will quickly cover the gash; but when the tree is very old, peeling the bark off, and looking carefully, you will see the scar there still. All that is buried is not dead.

Pt. 1, Ch. 13, *The Story of an African Farm* 1883

2   To us, from the beginning, Nature has been but a poor plastic thing, to be toyed with this way or that, as man happens to please his deity or not; to go to church or not; to say his prayers right or not; to travel on a Sunday or not. Was it possible for us in an instant to see Nature as she is—the flowing vestment of an unchanging reality?

Pt. 2, Ch. 1, Ibid.

3   How hard it is to make your thoughts look anything but imbecile fools when you paint them with ink on paper.

Ch. 4, "Lyndall," Ibid

4   Everything has two sides—the outside that is ridiculous, and the inside that is solemn.

Ibid.

5   A little weeping, a little wheedling, a little self-degradation, a little careful use of our advantages, and then some man will say—"Come, be my wife!" With good looks and youth marriage is easy to attain. There are men enough; but a woman who has sold herself, even for a ring and a new name, need hold her skirt aside for no creature in the street. They both earn their bread in one way. Marriage for love is the beautifullest external symbol of the union of souls; marriage without it is the uncleanliest traffic that defiles the world.

Ibid.

6   Power! You may dam up the fountain of water, and make it a stagnant marsh, or you may let it run free and do its work; but you cannot say whether it shall be there; it is there. And it will act, if not openly for good, then covertly for evil; but it will act.

Ibid.

7   They are called finishing-schools and the name tells accurately what they are. They finish everything. . . .

Ibid.

8   "The surest sign of fitness is success."

Ibid.

9   "*We* bear the world, and we make it. . . . There was never a great man who had not a great mother—it is hardly an exaggeration."

Ibid.

10   "Men are like the earth and we are the moon; we turn always one side to them, and they think there is no other, because they don't see it—but there is."

Ibid.

11   I have seen some souls so compressed that they would have fitted into a small thimble, and found room to move there—wide room.

Ibid.

12   "It is delightful to be a woman; but every man thanks the Lord devoutly that he isn't one."

Ibid.

13   "Wisdom never kicks at the iron walls it can't bring down."

Ibid.

14   "Look at this little chin of mine, Waldo, with the dimple in it. It is but a small part of my person; but though I had a knowledge of all things under the sun, and the wisdom to use it, and the deep loving heart of an angel, it would not stead me through life like this little chin. I can win money with it, I can win love; I can win power with it, I can win fame."

Ibid.

15   "We fit our sphere as a Chinese woman's fits her shoe, exactly as though god had made both; and yet He knows nothing of either."

Ibid.

16   "We were equals once when we lay newborn babes on our nurse's knees. We shall be equals again when they tie up our jaws for the last sleep."

Ibid.

17   "If the bird *does* like its cage, and *does* like its sugar, and will not leave it, why keep the door so very carefully shut?"

Ibid.

18   Perhaps the old monks were right when they tried to root love out; perhaps the poets are right when they try to water it. It is a blood-red flower, with the colour of sin; but there is always the scent of a god about it.

Ch. 8, Ibid.

19   I said to God, "What are they doing?"
   God said, "Making pitfalls into which their fellows may sink."
   I said to God, "Why do they do it?"

God said, "Because each thinks that when his brother falls he will rise."

"Across My Bed," *Dreams 1890*

20   I saw a woman sleeping. In her sleep she dreamt life stood before her, and held in each hand a gift—in the one hand love, in the other freedom. And she said to the woman, "Choose." And the woman waited long: and she said, "Freedom." And life said, "Thou hast well chosen. If thou hadst said "love" I would have given thee that thou didst ask for; and I would have gone from thee, and returned to thee no more. Now, the day will come when I shall return. In that day I shall bear both gifts in one hand." I heard the woman laugh in her sleep.

"Three Dreams in a Desert" (1887), Ibid.

21   And he said, "I take it, ages ago the Ages-of-Dominion-of-Muscular-Force found her, and when she stooped low to give suck to her young, and her back was broad, he put his burden of subjection on to it, and tied it on with the broad band of Inevitable Necessity.

Ibid.

22   All day, where the sunlight played on the seashore, Life sat.

"The Lost Joy," Ibid.

23   "No woman has the right to marry a man if she has to bend herself out of shape for him. She might wish to, but she could never be to him with all her passionate endeavor what the other woman could be to him without trying. Character will dominate over all and will come out at last."

"The Buddhist Priest's Wife," *Stories, Dreams, and Allegories 1892*

24   "There are only two things that are absolute realities, love and knowledge, and you can't escape them."

Ibid.

25   "I suppose the most absolutely delicious thing in life is to feel a thing needs you, and to give at the moment it needs. Things that don't need you, you must love from a distance."

Ibid.

26   "There is nothing ridiculous in love."

Ibid.

27   If Nature here wishes to make a mountain, she runs a range for five hundred miles; if a plain, she levels eighty; if a rock, she tilts five thousand feet of strata on end; our skies are higher and more intensely blue; our waves larger than others; our rivers fiercer. There is nothing measured, small nor petty in South Africa.

Ch. 1, *Thoughts on South Africa 1892*

28   There are artists who, loving their work, when they have finished it, put it aside for years, that, after the lapse of time, returning to it and reviewing it from the standpoint of distance, they may judge of it in a manner which was not possible while the passion of creation and link of unbroken emotion bound them to it. What the artist does intentionally, life often does for us fortuitously in other relationships.

Ibid.

29   St. Francis of Assisi preached to the little fishes: we eat them. But the man who eats fish can hardly be blamed, seeing that the eating of fishes is all but universal among the human race!—if only he does not pretend that while he eats them he preaches to them!

Ch. 4, Ibid.

30 "Yes, the life of the individual is short, but the life of the nation is long; and it is longer, and stronger, more vigorous and more knit, if it grows slowly and spontaneously than if formed by violence or fraud. The individual cannot afford to wait but the nation can and must wait for true unity, which can only come as the result of internal growth and union of its atoms, and in no other way whatsoever."

Ch. 8, Ibid.

31 I know there will be spring; as surely as the birds know it when they see above the snow two tiny, quivering green leaves. Spring cannot fail us.

"The Woman's Rose" 1893

32 I suppose there is no man who to-day loves his country who has not perceived that in the life of the nation, as in the life of the individual, the hour of external success may be the hour of irrevocable failure, and that the hour of death, whether to nations or individuals, is often the hour of immortality.

The English South African's View of the Situation c. 1899

33 The greatest nations, like the greatest individuals, have often been the poorest; and with wealth comes often what is more terrible than poverty—corruption.

Ibid.

34 We have in us the blood of a womanhood that was never bought and never sold; that wore no veil and had no foot bound; whose realized ideal of marriage was sexual companionship and an equality in duty and labor.

Woman and Labor 1911

35 We have always borne part of the weight of war, and the major part. . . . Men have made boomerangs, bows, swords, or guns with which to destroy one another; we have made the men who destroyed and were destroyed! . . . *We pay the first cost on all human life.*

Ch. 4, Ibid.

1160. Mary Dow Brine (1855?–1925?)

1 She's somebody's mother, boys, you know,
For all she's aged, and poor, and slow.
"Somebody's Mother," St. 15, Harper's Weekly 2 March 1878

1161. Alexandra Gripenberg (1856/57–1911/13)

1 The miracle has happened! On May the 29th the Finnish Diet agreed to an Imperial proposal from the Czar concerning changes in the constitution of Finland, which changes also include political suffrage and eligibility to the Diet for Women, married and unmarried, on the same conditions as for men.
Statement (1906), Women in World History Curriculum, http://www.womeninworldhistory.com 1996–97

1162. Kate Douglas Wiggin (1856–1923)

1 Women never hit what they aim at: but if they just shut their eyes and shoot in the air they generally find themselves in the bull's eye.
New Chronicles of Rebecca 1907

2 My heart is open wide tonight
For stranger, kith or kin.
I would not bar a single door
When love might enter in.
"The Romance of a Christmas Card" n.d.

1163. Elisabeth Marbury (1856–1933)

1 I began to realize that the world was divided into three groups: wasters, mollusks, and builders.
Ch. 1, My Crystal Ball 1923

2 "Ah, daughter," said Mother, "where there is room in the heart, there is always room on the hearth."
Ibid.

3 I began to realize the woefulness of ignorance. Things of unimportance fell into their proper places. I was inoculated with beauty and my feet became shod with a sense of its value. . . .
Ch. 3, Ibid.

4 Throughout my life, I have always found that events which seemed at the time disastrous ultimately developed into positive blessings. In fact, I have never known one instance when this has not proved to be the case.
Ch. 5, Ibid.

5 The praise of injudicious friends frequently fosters bad mannerisms.
Ch. 6, Ibid.

6 The richer your friends, the more they will cost you.
"Careers for Women" n.d.

7 A caress is better than a career.
Ibid.

8 No influence so quickly converts a radical into a reactionary as does his election to power.
Ibid.

1164. Lizette Reese (1856–1935)

1 A book may be a flower that blows;
A road to a far town;
A roof, a well, a tower;
A book
May be a staff, a crook.
"Books" n.d.

2 Creeds grow so thick along the way,
Their boughs hide God.
"Doubt" n.d.

3 The old faiths light their candles all about,
But burly Truth comes by and puts them out.
"Truth" n.d.

4 When I consider life and its few years—
A wisp of fog betwixt us and the sun;
A call to battle, and the battle done
Ere the last echo dies within our ears,
I wonder at the idleness of tears.
"Tears" n.d.

5 We that are twain by day, at night are one.
A dream can bring me to your arms once more.
"Compensation" n.d.

6 Fame is a bugle call
Blown past a crumbling wall.
"Taps" n.d.

1165. Mrs. N. F. Mossell (1856–1946)

1 . . . keeping a clean house will not keep a man at home.
The Work of the Afro-American Women 1894

2 . . . women must not be blamed because they are not equal to the self-sacrifice of always meeting husbands with a smile.
Ibid.

1166. Mary Lee Demarest (1857–1888)

1 Like a bairn to his mither, a wee birdie to its nest,
I wud fain be ganging nod unto my Saviour's breast;
For he gathers in his bosom witless, worthless lambs like me
An' he carries them himsel' to his ain countree
"My Ain Countree" *n.d.*

1167. Edna Lyall (1857–1903)

1 Two is company, three is trumpery, as the proverb says.
Ch. 24, *Wayfaring Men 1897*

1168. Fannie Farmer (1857–1915)

1 Progress in civilization has been accompanied by progress in cookery.
Ch. 2, *The Boston Cooking-School Cookbook 1896*

2 I certainly feel that the time is not far distant when a knowledge of the principles of diet will be an essential part of one's education. Then mankind will eat to live, be able to do better mental and physical work, and disease will be less frequent.
Preface to the First Edition, *Ibid.*

3 . . . France, that land to which we ever look for gastronomic delights. . . .
Ch. 1, *Chafing Dish Possibilities 1898*

1169. Klara Zetkin (1857–1933)

1 . . . women must remain in industry despite all narrow-minded caterwauling; in fact the circle of their industrial activity must become broader and more secure daily. . . .
The Question of Women Workers and Women in the Present Time 1889

2 The organization and enlightenment of working women, the struggle to attain their economic and political equal rights is not only desirable for the socialist movement. It is and will become more and more a life-and-death question for it. . . .
Ibid.

3 In agreement with the class-conscious, political and trade union organizations of the proletariat of their respective countries, the Socialist women of all countries will hold each year a Women's Day, whose foremost purpose it must be to aid the attainment of women's suffrage. This demand must be handled in conjunction with the entire women's question according to Socialist precepts. The Women's Day must have an international character and is to be prepared carefully.
Proposal to the Second International Women's Conference (Copenhagen, 27 August 1910), *Die Gleicheit* (Stuttgart), with Käthe Duncker and Comrades *29 August 1910*

4 The beginnings of the class-conscious organized proletarian woman's movement in Germany are indissolubly bound up with the coming into being and maturing of the socialist conception of society in the proletariat. . . .
Zur Geschichte der proletarischen Frauenbewegung Deutschlands 1928

5 . . . as the liberation of the proletariat is possible only through the abolition of the capitalist productive relation, so too the emancipation of woman is possible only through doing away with private property.
Ibid.

6 All roads led to Rome. Every truly Marxist analysis of an important part of the ideological superstructure of society, of an outstanding social phenomenon, had to lead to an analysis of bourgeois society and its foundation, private property. It should lead to the conclusion that "Carthage must be destroyed."
"My Recollections of Lenin"* (1925), Quoted in *The Emancipation of Women 1966*
*Vladimir L—, Russian revolutionary leader and statesman (1870–1924).

7 The reasons for the constantly growing use of female laborers have been repeatedly pointed out: their cheapness and the improvement of the mechanical means and methods of production. The automatic machine . . . works with the powers of a giant, possesses unbelievable skill, speed and exactness and renders muscle power and acquired skills superfluous. The capitalist entrepreneur can employ only female labor at those places where he previously had to use male employees. And he just loves to hire women because female labor is cheap, much cheaper than male labor.
"Women's Work and the Trade Unions" (*Die Gleicheit*), (Stuttgart, 1 November 1893), *The Organization of Trade Unions n.d.*

8 . . . women are house as well as factory slaves and are forced to bear a double workload.
Ibid.

9 The larger the number of organized female workers who fight shoulder to shoulder with their comrades from the factory or workshop for better working conditions, the sooner and the greater will women's wages rise so that soon there may be the realization of the principle: Equal pay for equal work regardless of the difference in sex.
Ibid.

10 As far as the proletariat is concerned, capitalism has changed blessing into curse and wealth into bitter poverty.
Ibid.

11 How extensive is just the number of women who slave away as domestic servants!
Ibid.

12 If during the Age of the Family, a man had the right . . . to tame his wife occasionally with a whip, capitalism is now taming her with scorpions. In former times, the rule of a man over his wife was ameliorated by their personal relationship. Between an employer and his worker, however, exists only a cash nexus.
Speech, "Only in Conjunction with the Proletarian Woman Will Socialism Be Victorious," presented to Party Congress of the Social Democratic Party of Germany (Gotha, 16 October 1896), *Ibid.*

13 The women's question . . . is only present within those classes of society who are themselves the products of the capitalist mode of production. Thus it is that we find no women's question in peasant circles . . . [but among] the women of the proletariat, the bourgeoisie, the intelligentsia and the Upper Ten Thousand.
Ibid.

14 . . . the social suppression of women coincided with the creation of private property.

Ibid.

15 As far as the proletarian woman is concerned, it is capitalism's need to exploit and to search incessantly for a cheap labor force that's created the women's question.

Ibid.

16 Once the family as an economic unit will vanish and its place will be taken by the family as a moral unit, the woman will become an equally entitled, equally creative, equally goal-oriented, forward-stepping companion of her husband; her individuality will flourish while at the same time, she will fulfill her task as wife and mother to the highest degree possible.

Ibid.

17 The competition of the women in the professional world is the driving force for the resistance of men against the demands of bourgeois women's rights advocates. It is, pure and simple, the fear of competition. All other reasons which are listed against the mental work of women, such as the smaller brain of women or their allegedly natural avocation to be a mother are only pretexts. This battle of competition pushes the women of these social strata towards demanding their political rights so that they may, by fighting politically, tear down all barriers which have been created against their economic activity.

Ibid.

1170. Martha Thomas (1857–1935)

1 Women are one-half of the world but until a century ago . . . it was a man's world. The laws were man's laws, the government a man's government, the country a man's country. . . . The man's world must become a man's and a woman's world. Why are we afraid? It is the next step forward on the path to the sunrise, and the sun is rising over a new heaven and a new earth.

Address, North American Woman Suffrage Association,
(Buffalo, New York) *October 1908*

1171. Ada Alden (1857–1936)

1 Can this be Italy, or but a dream
Emerging from the broken waves of sleep? . . .
This world of beauty, color, and perfume,
Hoary with age, yet of unaging bloom.

"Above Salerno" *n.d.*

2 The years shall right the balance tilted wrong,
The years shall set upon his* brows a star.

"Ave" *n.d.*

*Reference to Woodrow Wilson, (1856–1924), 28th president of the United States (1913–1921).

1172. Minna Irving (1857–1940)

1 He's cheerful in weather so bitterly cold
It freezes your bones to the marrow;
I'll admit he's a beggar, a gangster, a bum,
But I take off my hat to the sparrow.

"The Sparrow" *n.d.*

2 The flowery frocks and the ancient trunk,
And Grandmother Granger, too, are dust,
But something precious and sweet and rare
Survives the havoc of moth and rust.

"The Wedding Gift," St. 6 *n.d.*

3 A nation thrills, a nation bleeds,
A nation follows where it leads,
And every man is proud to yield
His life upon a crimson field
For Betsy's battle flag.

"Betsy's Battle Flag" *n.d.*

1173. A. Mary F. Robinson (1857–1944)

1 You hail from dream-land, Dragon-fly?
A stranger hither? So am I.

"To a Dragonfly" *n.d.*

2 When I was young the twilight seemed too long.

"Twilight" *n.d.*

1174. Ida Tarbell (1857–1944)

1 The first and most imperative necessity in war is money, for money means everything else—men, guns, ammunition.

Ch. 1, *The Tariff in Our Times 1906*

2 There is no man more dangerous, in a position of power, than he who refuses to accept as a working truth the idea that all a man does should make for rightness and soundness, that even the fixing of a tariff rate must be moral.

Ch. 12, Ibid.

3 Sacredness of human life! The world has never believed it! It has been with life that we settled our quarrels, won wives, gold and land, defended ideas, imposed religions. We have held that a death toll was a necessary part of every human achievement, whether sport, war, or industry. A moment's rage over the horror of it, and we have sunk into indifference.

Ch. 3, *New Ideals in Business 1914*

4 Those who talk of the mine, the mill, the factory as if they were inherently inhuman and horrible are those who never have known the miner, the weaver, or the steel or iron worker.

Ch. 7, Ibid.

5 There is no more effective medicine to apply to feverish public sentiment than figures. To be sure, they must be properly prepared, must cover the case, not confine themselves to a quarter of it, and they must be gathered for their own sake, not for the sake of a theory. Such preparation we get in a national census.

Ch. 1, *The Ways of Woman 1914*

6 A mind which really lays hold of a subject is not easily detached from it.

Ch. 5, Ibid.

7 A mind truly cultivated never feels that the intellectual process is complete until it can reproduce in some media the thing which it has absorbed.

Ibid.

8 They did not understand it [culture] to be ripeness and sureness of mind, it was not taste, discrimination, judgement; it was an acquisition—something which came with diplomas and degrees and only with them.

Ibid.

9 "Yes, sir; he was what I call a *godly* man. Fact is, I never knew anybody I felt so sure would walk straight into Heaven, everybody welcomin' him, nobody fussin' or fumin' about his bein' let in, as Abraham Lincoln."

In Lincoln's Chair 1920

10   "There are more men who see clear now how hard it is for
people to rule themselves, more people to determine government by the people shan't perish from the earth, more people
willin' to admit that you can't have peace when you've got a
thing like slavery goin' on. That something, that's goin' to help
when the next struggle comes."

Ibid.

1175. Myrta Lockett Avary (1857–1946)

1   Memoirs and journals written not because of their historical
or political significance, but because they are to the writer the
natural expression of what life has meant to him in the moment of living, have a value entirely apart from literary quality.
They bring us close to the human soul —the human soul in
undress.

Introduction, *A Virginia Girl in the Civil War, 1861-1865*,
ed. *1903*

1176. Gertrude Atherton (1857–1948)

1   We love the lie that saves their pride, but never the unflatter-
ing truth.

Bk. III, Ch. 6, *The Conqueror 1902*

2   To put a tempting face aside when duty demands every faculty
. . . is a lesson which takes most men longest to learn.

Ibid.

3   The perfect friendship of two men is the deepest and highest
sentiment of which the finite mind is capable; women miss the
best in life.

Ch. 12, Ibid.

4   No matter how hard a man may labor, some woman is always
in the background of his mind. She is the one reward of virtue.

Bk. IV, Ch. 3, Ibid.

5   Better extirpate the whole breed, root and branch. And this,
unless the German people come to their senses, is what we propose to do.

The New York Times 18 August 1918

1177. Alice Brown (1857–1948)

1   Praise not the critic, lest he think
You crave the shelter of his ink.

"The Critic" *n.d.*

2   Yet thou, O banqueter on worms,
Who wilt not let corruption pass!—
Dost search out mildew, mound and stain,
Beneath a magnifying-glass.

"The Slanderer" *n.d.*

3   And led by silence more majestical
Than clash of conquering arms, He comes! He comes!
And strikes out flame from the adoring hills.

"Sunrise on Mansfield Mountain" *n.d.*

1178. Marie Konsantinovna Bashkirtseff
   (1858/60–1884)

1   Ah, when one thinks what a miserable creature man is! Every
other animal can, at his will, wear on his face the expression
he pleases. He is not obligated to smile if he has a mind to
weep. When he does not wish to see his fellows he does not see
them. While man is the slave of everything and everybody!

(6 May 1873) *The Journal of a Young Artist 1884*

2   To say that my grief will be eternal would be ridiculous—nothing is eternal.

(17 October 1873) Ibid.

3   Let us love dogs; let us love only dogs! Men and cats are unworthy creatures. . . .

(16 July 1874) Ibid.

4   In the studio all distinctions disappear. One has neither name
nor family; one is no longer the daughter of one's mother, one
is one's self—an individual—and one has before one art, and
nothing else. One feels so happy, so free, so proud.

(5 October 1877) Ibid.

5   . . . I write down everything, everything, everything. Otherwise
why should I write?

(1 May 1884) Ibid.

6   If I had been born a man, I would have conquered Europe. As
I was born a woman, I exhausted my energy in tirades against
fate, and in eccentricities.

(25 June 1884) Ibid.

7   For my own part I think love—impossible—to one who looks at
human nature through a microscope, as I do. They who see only
what they wish to see in those around them are very fortunate.

(1 August 1884) Ibid.

8   Mama was doing housework, which makes me furious. I
would like to see her elegant and beautiful instead of looking
like a cleaning-woman in an old dress and with Dina's dirty
monkey on her shoulder, hanging on to a cucumber.

*I Am the Most Interesting Book of All: The Diary of Marie
Bashkirtseff*, Vol. 1, Phyllis Howard Kernberger with
Katherine Kernberger, tr. *1997*

9   I was born to be a remarkable woman; it matters little in what
way or how . . . I shall be famous or I will die.

Ibid.

1179. Edith Nesbit (1858–1924)

1   Little brown brother, oh! little brown brother,
Are you awake in the dark?

"Baby Seed Song" *n.d.*

2   The chestnut's proud, and the lilac's pretty,
The poplar's gentle and tall,
But the plane tree's kind to the poor dull city—
I love him best of all!

"Child's Song in Spring" *n.d.*

1180. Eva Rose York (1858–1925?)

1   I shall not pass this way again;
Then let me now relieve some pain,
Remove some barrier from the road,
Or brighten some one's heavy load.

"I Shall Not Pass This Way Again," St. 2, *n.d.*

2   . . . I have drunk the cup of bliss
Remembering not that those there be
Who drink the dregs of misery.

St. 3, Ibid.

1181. Emmeline Pankhurst (1858–1928)

1   We are here, not because we are law-breakers; we are here in
our efforts to become law-makers.

Speech, at her trial in London *21 October 1908*

2 Those men and women are fortunate who are born at a time when a great struggle for human freedom is in progress.
My Own Story 1914

3 It was rapidly becoming clear to my mind that men regarded women as a servant class in the community, and that women were going to remain in the servant class until they lifted themselves out of it.
Ibid.

4 Women had always fought for men, and for their children. Now they were ready to fight for their own human rights. Our militant movement was established.
Ibid.

5 "I have never felt a prouder woman than I did one night when a police constable said to me, after one of these demonstrations, 'Had this been a man's demonstration, there would have been bloodshed long ago.' Well, my lord, there has not been any bloodshed except on the part of the women themselves—these so-called militant women. Violence has been done to us, and I who stand before you in this dock have lost a dear sister in the course of this agitation."
Ibid.

6 Why is it that men's blood-shedding militancy is applauded and women's symbolic militancy punished with a prison-cell and the forcible feeding horror?
Ibid.

7 There is something that governments care far more for than human life, and that is the security of property, and so it is through property that we shall strike the enemy.
Speech, "I Incite This Meeting to Rebellion" (17 October 1912), Ibid.

8 One thing is essential to an army, and that thing is made up of a two-fold requirement. In an army you need unity of purpose. In an army you also need unity of policy.
Ibid.

9 How different the reasoning is that men adopt when they are discussing the cases of men and those of women.
Speech, "When Civil War Is Waged by Women" (London, 13 November 1913), Ibid.

10 You have to make more noise than anybody else, you have to make yourself more obtrusive than anybody else, you have to fill all the papers more than anybody else, in fact you have to be there all the time and see that they do not snow you under, if you are really going to get your reform realized.
Ibid.

11 I am what you call a hooligan!
Speech (1909), Quoted in *The Fighting Pankhursts**
by David Mitchell *1967*
*See Christabel P—, 1454; Adela P—, 1505; Sylvia P—, 1485.

12 I have no sense of guilt. I look upon myself as a prisoner of war. I am under no moral obligation to conform to, or in any way accept, the sentence imposed upon me.
Speech to the Court (April 1913), Ibid.

13 Over one thousand women have gone to prison in the course of this agitation, have suffered their imprisonment, have come out of prison injured in health, weakened in body, but not in spirit. . . . I ask you . . . if you are prepared to go on doing that kind of thing indefinitely, because that is what is going to hap-

pen. There is absolutely no doubt about it. . . . We are women, rightly or wrongly convinced that this is the only way in which we can win power to alter what for us are intolerable conditions, absolutely intolerable conditions. From the moment I leave this court I shall deliberately refuse to eat food—I shall join the women who are already in Holloway [Women's Prison] on the hunger strike. I shall come out of prison, dead or alive, at the earliest possible moment; and once again, as soon as I am physically fit I shall enter into this fight again. Life is very dear to all of us. I am not seeking, as was said by the Home Secretary, to commit suicide. I do not want to commit suicide. I want to see the women of this country enfranchised, and I want to live until that is done.
Speech to the Court (2 April 1913), *Shoulder to Shoulder*, Midge Mackenzie, ed. *1975*

14 In time of war the rules of peace must be set aside and we must put ourselves without delay upon a war basis, let the women stand shoulder to shoulder with the men to win the common victory which we all desire.
Speech, London Pavilion (5 October 1915), Ibid.

15 Better that we should die fighting than be outraged and dishonoured. . . . Better to die than to live in slavery.
Speech, Army and Navy Hall, Petrograd (August 1917), Ibid.

1182. Dorothy Gurney (1858–1932)

1 The kiss of sun for pardon,
The song of the birds for mirth—
One is nearer God's Heart in a garden
Than anywhere else on earth.
"The Lord God Planted a Garden," St. 3 *n.d.*

1183. Selma Lagerlöf (1858–1940)

1 There were no accusers; there could be no judge.
The Story of Gösta Berling 1891

2 Burdensome are the ways men have to follow here on earth. They lead through deserts, and through marshes, and over mountains. Why is so much sorrow allowed to go on without interruption, until it loses itself in the desert or sinks in the bog, or is killed in the mountains? Where are the little flower-pickers, where are the little princesses of the fairy tale about whose feet roses grow; where are they who should strew flowers on the weary path?
Pt. II, Ch. 2, Ibid.

3 She began to weep because she would never reach her journey's end. Her whole life long she would travel, travel, travel, and never reach the end of her journey.
Bk. I, Ch. 7, *The Miracles of Anti-Christ 1899*

4 Women can do nothing that has permanence.
Bk. II, Ch. 2, Ibid.

5 Just fancy what an effect his violin could have! It made people quite forget themselves. It was a great power to have at his disposal. Any moment he liked he could take possession of his kingdom.
"The Story of a Country House," Ch. 1, *From a Swedish Homestead 1901*

6 The fair sun is like a mother whose son is about to set out for a far-off land, and who, in the hour of the leave-taking, cannot take her eyes from the beloved.
"Astrid," Ch. 3, Ibid.

7   In that reign of terror, in that great desert, there had at any rate grown one flower that had comforted him with fragrance and beauty, and now he felt that love would dwell with him forever. The wildflower of the desert had been transplanted into the garden of life, and had taken root and grown and thriven, and when he felt this he knew he was saved; he knew that the darkness had found its master.
Ch. 6, Ibid.

8   Anyone who has ever sat in a train as it rushes through a dark night will know that sometimes there are long minutes when the coaches slide smoothly along without so much as a shudder. All rustle and bustle cease and the sound of the wheels becomes a soothing, peaceful melody. The coaches no longer seem to run on rails and sleepers but glide into space.
Acceptance Speech, Nobel Prize (Stockholm) 1909

9   "I have come to ask you for advice, Father," I will say, "for I am very heavily in debt. . . . but it is not money that I owe, Father. . . . [and] It is not too much to ask that you should help, Father, for it was all your fault right from the beginning. Do you remember how you used to play the piano and sing Bellman's songs to us children and how, at least twice every winter, you would let us read Tegnér and Runeberg and Andersen? It was then that I first fell into debt. Father, how shall I ever repay them for teaching me to love fairy tales and sagas of heroes, the land we live in and all of our human life, in all its wretchedness and glory?"
Ibid.

10   There is nothing so terrible as perjury. There is something uncanny and awful about that sin. There is no mercy or condonation for it.
"The Girl from the Marsh Croft," The Girl from the Marsh Croft 1911

11   "When I see a stream like this in the wilderness," he thought, "I am reminded of my own life. As persistent as this stream have I been in forcing my way past all that has obstructed my path. Father has been my rock ahead, and Mother tried to hold me back and bury me between moss-tufts, but I stole past both of them and got out in the World. Hey—ho, hi, hi!"
"The Musician," Ibid.

12   Thinking is never so easy as when one follows a plow up a furrow and down a furrow.
Bk. I, Ch. 1, Jerusalem 1915

13   "It has been said, as you know," Hellgum went on, "that if somebody strikes us on one cheek we must turn the other cheek also, and that we should not resist evil, and other things of the same sort; all of which none of us can live up to. Why, people would rob you of your house and home, they'd steal your potatoes and carry off your grain, if you fail to protect what was yours."
Bk. II, Ibid.

14   "The ways of Providence cannot be reasoned out by the finite mind," he mused. "I cannot fathom them, yet seeking to know them is the most satisfying thing in all the world."
Ibid.

15   There isn't much that tastes better than praise from those who are wise and capable . . .
Ch. 5, The Wonderful Adventures of Nils, Velma Swanston Howard, tr. 1922

16   It is thus with children: they never think any further ahead than the length of their tiny noses. That which lies nearest them they want promptly, with never a thought as to what it may cost them.
Ch. 6, Ibid.

17   Could I ever be happy again now that I knew there was so much evil in the world?
(24 March 1872) The Diary of Selma Lagerlöf 1936

18   To be sure, I believe in the power of the dead, but I also know that Selma Otilla Lovisa Lagerlöf is inclined to imagine things that are utterly impossible.
(26 March 1872), Ibid.

1184. Beatrice Potter Webb (1858–1943)

1   The underlying principle of the industrial revolution—the creed of universal competition—the firm faith that every man free to follow his own self-interest would contribute most effectively to the common weal, with the converse proposition that each man should suffer the full consequences of his own actions—this simple and powerful idea was enabling a rising middle class to break up and destroy those restraints on personal freedom, those monopolies for private gain, with which a Parliament of landowners had shackled the enterprise and weighted the energies of the nation.
Ch. 1, The Cooperative Movement in Great Britain 1891

2   For the committee-man or the officer who accepts a bribe or neglects his duty must be fully aware that he is not simply an indifferently honest man, like many of his fellows in private trade, but the deliberate betrayer of the means of salvation to thousands of his fellow-countrymen of this and all future generations.
Ch. 7, Ibid.

3   The hand-to-mouth existence of the casual labourer . . . the restlessness or mortal weariness arising from lack of nourishment, tempered by idleness, or intensified by physical exhaustion, do not permit the development, in the individual or the class, of the qualities of democratic association and democratic self-government.
Ch. 8, Ibid.

4   The caprices of fashion, the vagaries of personal vanity and over-indulged appetites can find no satisfaction in an organization of industry based on the supply of rational and persistent wants.
Ibid.

5   But evidence drawn empirically from facts, though it may justify the action of the practical man, is not scientifically conclusive.
"The Economics of Factory Legislation," Socialism and the National Minimum 1909

6   All along the line, physically, mentally, morally, alcohol is a weakening and deadening force, and it is worth a great deal to save women and girls from its influence.
Ch. 10, Health of Working Girls 1917

7   The inevitability of gradualness . . .
Presidential Address, British Labour Party Congress 1923

8   Beneath the surface of our daily life, in the personal history of many of us, there runs a continuous controversy between an Ego that affirms and an Ego that denies. On the course of this

controversy depends the attainment of inner harmony and consistent conduct in private and public affairs.

Introduction, *My Apprenticeship 1926*

9 Religion is love; in no case is it logic.

Ch. 2, Ibid.

10 For any detailed description of the complexity of human nature, of the variety and mixture in human motive, of the insurgence of instinct in the garb of reason, of the multifarious play of the social environment of the individual ego and of the individual ego on the social environment, I had to turn to novelists and poets. . . .

Ch. 3, Ibid.

11 . . . if I had been a man, self-respect, family pressure and the public opinion of my class would have pushed me into a money-making profession; as a mere woman I could carve out a career of disinterested research.

Ch. 8, Ibid.

12 . . . what we had to do was . . . to make medical treatment not a favour granted to those in desperate need but to compel all sick persons to submit to it . . . to treat illness, in fact, as a public nuisance to be suppressed in the interests of the community.

Quoted by Anne Fremantle in *Woman as Revolutionary*, Fred C. Giffin, ed. *1973*

1185. Ethel Mary Smyth (1858-1944)

1 The habit some writers indulge in of perpetual quotation is one it behooves lovers of good literature to protest against, for it is an insidious habit which in the end must cloud the stream of thought, or at least check spontaneity. If it be true that *le style c'est l'homme*, what is likely to happen if *l'homme* is for ever eking out his own personality with that of some other individual?

"The Quotation-Fiend," *Streaks of Life 1924*

2 Because I have conducted my own operas and love sheep-dogs; because I generally dress in tweeds, and sometimes, at winter afternoon concerts, have even conducted in them; because I was a militant suffragette and seized a chance of beating time to "The March of the Women" from the window of my cell in Holloway Prison with a tooth-brush; because I have written books, spoken speeches, broadcast, and don't always make sure that my hat is on straight; for these and other equally pertinent reasons, in a certain sense I am well known.

Epilogue, *As Time Went On 1936*

1186. Agnes Repplier (1858–1950)

1 . . . the children of to-day are favored beyond their knowledge and certainly beyond their deserts.

"Children, Past and Present," *Books and Men 1888*

2 But self-satisfaction, if as buoyant as gas, has an ugly trick of collapsing when full blown, and facts are stony things that refuse to melt away in the sunshine of a smile.

"Some Aspects of Pessimism," Ibid.

3 It is a humiliating fact that, notwithstanding our avaricious greed for novelties, we are forced, when sincere, to confess that "*les anciens ont tout dit*," and that it is probable that the contending schools of thought have always held the same relative positions they do now: Optimism glittering in the front ranks as a deservedly popular favorite; pessimism speaking

with a still, persistent voice to those who, unluckily for themselves, have the leisure and the intelligence to attend.

Ibid.

4 The pessimist, however—be it recorded to his credit—is seldom an agitating individual. His creed breeds indifference to others, and he does not trouble himself to thrust his views upon the unconvinced.

Ibid.

5 Memory cheats us no less than hope by hazing over those things that we would fain forget; but who that has plodded on to middle age would take back upon his shoulders ten of the vanished years, with their mingled pleasures and pains? Who would return to the youth he is forever pretending to regret?

Ibid.

6 In the stress of modern life, how little room is left for that most comfortable vanity that whispers in our ears that failures are not faults! Now we are taught from infancy that we must rise or fall upon our own merits; that vigilance wins success, and incapacity means ruin.

"On the Benefits of Superstition," Ibid.

7 There is nothing in the world so enjoyable as a thorough-going monomania . . .

"The Decay of Sentiment," Ibid.

8 Amusement is merely one side of pleasure, but a very excellent side, against which, in truth, I have no evil word to urge. The gods forbid such base and savorless ingratitude!

"Pleasure: A Heresy," *Points of View 1891*

9 Sensuality, too, which used to show itself coarse, smiling, unmasked and unmistakable, is now serious, analytic, and so burdened with a sense of its responsibility that it passes muster half the time as a new type of asceticism.

"Fiction in the Pulpit," Ibid.

10 We have but the memories of past good cheer, we have but the echoes of departed laughter. In vain we look and listen for the mirth that has died away. In vain we seek to question the gray ghosts of old-time revelers.

"Humors of Gastronomy," *Essays in Miniature 1892*

11 A villain must be a thing of power, handled with delicacy and grace. He must be wicked enough to excite our aversion, strong enough to arouse our fear, human enough to awaken some transient gleam of sympathy. We must triumph in his downfall, yet not barbarously nor with contempt, and the close of his career must be in harmony with all of its previous development.

"A Short Defense of Villains," Ibid.

12 Philadelphians are every whit as mediocre as their neighbours, but they seldom encourage each other in mediocrity by giving it a more agreeable name.

Introduction, *Philadelphia: The Place and the People 1898*

13 It is hard for us who live in an age of careless and cheerful tolerance to understand the precise inconveniences attending religious persecution.

Ch. 1, Ibid.

14 Necessity knows no Sunday. . . .

Ch. 18, Ibid.

15 It is not what we learn in conversation that enriches us. It is the elation that comes of swift contact with tingling currents of thought.

"The Luxury of Conversation," *Compromises 1904*

16 Anyone, however, who has had dealings with dates knows that they are worse than elusive, they are perverse. Events do not happen at the right time, nor in their proper sequence. That sense of harmony with place and season which is so strong in the historian—is lamentably lacking in history, which takes no pains to verify his most convincing statements.

Ch. 1, To Think of Tea! 1932

17 It has been well said that tea is suggestive of a thousand wants, from which spring the decencies and luxuries of civilization.

Ch. 2, Ibid.

18 The English do not strain their tea in the fervid fashion we [Americans] do. They like to see a few leaves dawdling about the cup. They like to know what they are drinking.

Ch. 13, Ibid.

19 People who cannot recognize a palpable absurdity are very much in the way of civilization.

Ch. 9, In Pursuit of Laughter 1936

20 It is not depravity that afflicts the human race so much as a general lack of intelligence.

Ibid.

21 Humour brings insight and tolerance. Irony brings a deeper and less friendly understanding.

Ibid.

22 Science may carry us to Mars, but it will leave the earth peopled as ever by the inept.

Ibid.

1187. Anna Julia Cooper (1858/68–1964)

1 Let our girls feel that we expect something more of them than that they merely look pretty and appear well in society. Teach them that there is a race with special needs which they and only they can help; that the world needs and is already asking for their trained, efficient forces.

Preface, A Voice from the South; By a Black Woman of the South 1892

2 If these broken utterances can in any way help to a clearer vision and a truer pulse-beat in studying our Nation's Problem, this Voice by a Black Woman of the South will not have been raised in vain.

Ibid.

3 I would beg to add my plea for the Colored *Girls* of the South:—that large, bright, promising fatally beautiful class . . . so full of promise and possibilities, yet so sure of destruction; often without a father to whom they dare apply the loving term, often without a stronger brother to espouse their cause and defend their honor with his life's blood; in the midst of pitfalls and snares, waylaid by the lower classes of white men, with no shelter, no protection.

Ibid.

4 We take our stand on the solidarity of humanity, the oneness of life, and the unnaturalness and injustice of all special favoritisms, whether of sex, race, country, or condition. . . . The colored woman feels that woman's cause is one and universal; and that . . . not till race, color, sex, and condition are seen as accidents and the pursuit of happiness is conceded to be inalienable to all; not till then is woman's . . . cause won—not the white woman's nor the black woman's, not the red

woman's but the cause of every man and of every woman who has writhed silently under a mighty wrong.

Speech (1893), Quoted in The Woman That I Am, The Literature and Culture of Contemporary Women of Color, D. Soyini Madison, ed. 1976

1188. Lettie Burlingame (1859–1890)

1 I have determined to make a specialty of equity. It is very interesting to me, and a very nice subject for a lady to pursue.

Diary Entry, Quoted in The 50 Most Influential Women in American Law by Dawn Bradley Berry 1996*

*See 3435.

1189. Eleanora Duse (1859–1924)

1 Before passing my lips each word seemed to have coursed through the ardor of my blood. There wasn't a fiber in me that did not add its notes to the harmony. Ah, grace—the state of grace!

Quoted in Il Fuoco by Gabriele D'Annunzio 1900*

*Italian writer, poet and Fascist activist (1863–1938).

2 To save the theatre, the theatre must be destroyed, the actors and actresses must all die of the plague. They poison the air, they make art impossible. It is not drama that they play, but pieces for the theatre. We should return to the Greeks, play in the open air; the drama dies of stalls and boxes and evening dress, and people who come to digest their dinner.

"Eleanora Duse," Quoted in Studies in Seven Arts by Arthur Symons 1906

3 I know nothing, nothing! I have everything to learn. Twelve years ago, when I left the theatre, I did so with no regrets. I was tired of living for others; I wanted to live for myself and learn and learn!

Quoted in Errinerungen, Betrachtungen, und Brief by Edouard Schneider 1921

4 I did not use paint, I made myself up morally.

Quoted in Le Gaulois by Louis Schneider 27 July 1922

5 I'm only a little Italian actress. Nobody would understand me abroad. Let me first perfect myself in my art which I dearly love, and don't try to lead me astray.

Quoted in Le Matin 12 April 1924

6 Do you think one can speak about art? It would be like trying to explain love. There are many ways of loving and there are as many kinds of art. There is the love that elevates and leads to good—there is the love that absorbs all one's will, all one's strength and intelligence. In my opinion this is the truest love—but it is certainly fatal. . . . So it is with art. . . .

Quoted in Eleanora Duse by C. Antonia-Traversi 1926

7 Oh, art, that consumes my life! But what resource! I could not bear to live if I did not have it.

Quoted by Olga Resnevic (1884) in Signorelli 1938

8 The strongest is the loneliest and the loneliest is the strongest.

Quoted in Vita de Arrigo Boito by Piero Nardi 1942

9 Work means so many things! So many! Among other things Work also means Freedom. . . . Without it even the miracle of love is only a cruel deception.

Ibid.

10 When moral sensibility alone is in question, I am won; but as soon as doctrinal intransigence and a purely ecclesiastical point of view enter in, I rebel.

Quoted in *The Mystic in the Theatre: Eleanora Duse* by Eva Le Gallienne* 1965

* See 1752.

1190. Katherine Lee Bates (1859–1929)

1 O beautiful for spacious skies,
For amber waves of grain,
For purple mountains majesties
Above the fruited plain!
America! America!
God shed his grace on thee
And crown thy good with brotherhood
From sea to shining sea!

"America the Beautiful." St. 1 *1893*

2 O beautiful for patriot dream
That sees beyond the years.
Thine alabaster cities gleam
Undimmed by human tears!

St. 4, Ibid.

3 Nay, brother of the sod,
What part hast thou in God?
What spirit art thou of?
It answers, "Love."

"Laddie" *n.d.*

4 Spirit long shaping for sublime endeavor,
A sword of God, the gleaming metal came
From stern Scotch ancestry, where whatsoever
Was true, was pure, was noble, won acclaim.

"Woodrow Wilson"* *n.d.*

*American politician (1856–1924), 28th president of the United States (1913–1921).

5 Dawn love is silver,
Wait for the west:
Old love is gold love—
Old love is best.

"For a Golden Wedding" *n.d.*

1191. Florence Kelley (1859–1932)

1 . . . the utter unimportance of children compared with products in the minds if the people. . . .

"My Philadelphia," *The Survey Graphic 1 October 1926*

1192. Helen Gray Cone (1859–1934)

1 A song of hate is a song of Hell;
Some there be who sing it well.

"Chant of Love for England" *1945*

2 Bind higher, grind higher, burn higher with fire,
Cast her ashes into the sea,—
She shall escape, she shall aspire,
She shall arise to make men free.

Ibid.

3 Peerless, fearless, an army's flower!
Sterner soldiers the world never saw,
Marching lightly, that summer hour,
To death and failure and fame forever.

"Greencastle Jenny," St. 4 *n.d.*

4 Upon a showery night and still,
Without a second of warning,
A trooper band surprised the hill,
And held it in the morning.
We were not waked by bugle notes,
No cheer our dreams invaded,
And yet at dawn their yellow coats
On the green slopes paraded.

"The Dandelions" *n.d.*

1193. Nora Archibald Smith (1859–1934)

1 They'd knock on a tree and would timidly say
To the spirit that might be within there that day:
"Fairy fair, Fairy fair, wish thou me well;
'Gainst evil witcheries weave me a spell!"

"Knocking on Wood," St. 3 *n.d.*

1194. Louise de Koven Bowen (1859–1947)

1 By the time I made my entry into society I was ignorant of everything and accomplished in nothing.

Ch. 1, *Growing Up with a City 1926*

2 I hated myself because I smelt of onions and meat, and I seriously considered suicide in the cistern which supplied the house.

Ibid.

3 It is always a real satisfaction to know that politics has not yet dominated the Juvenile Court of Cook County; that we still have these judges who are incorruptible and devoted to their work.

Ch. 4, Ibid.

1195. Carrie Chapman Catt (1859–1947)

1 There are two kinds of restrictions upon human liberty—the restraint of law and that of custom. No written law has ever been more binding than unwritten custom supported by popular opinion.

Speech, "For the Sake of Liberty" (8–14 February 1900),
Quoted in *History of Woman Suffrage*, Vol. IV,
by Susan B. Anthony* and Ida Husted *1902*

*See 949.

2 The sacrifice of suffering, of doubt, of obloquy, which has been endured by the pioneers in the woman movement will never be fully known or understood. . . .

Ibid.

3 The Government evidently nurses a forlorn hope that by delay it may tire out the workers and destroy the force of the campaign.

Speech, "Is Woman Suffrage Progressing?" Stockholm *1911*

4 There they swell that horrid, unspeakably unclean peril of civilisation, prostitution—augmented by the White Slave Traffic and by the machinations of the male parasites who live upon the earnings of women of vice. . . . We must be merciful, for they are the natural and inevitably consequence of centuries of false reasoning concerning woman's place in the world. . . . Upon these women we have no right to turn our backs. Their existence is part of our problem. They have been created by the very injustice against which we protest.

Ibid.

5 Once, this movement represented the scattered and disconnected protests of individual women. . . . Happily those days

are past; and out of that incoherent and seemingly futile agitation, which extended over many centuries, there has emerged a present-day movement possessing a clear understanding and a definite, positive purpose.

Ibid.

6   When a just cause reaches its flood-tide, as ours has done in that country, whatever stands in the way must fall before its overwhelming power.

Ibid.

7   Parliaments have stopped laughing at woman suffrage, and politicians have begun to dodge! It is the inevitable premonition of coming victory.

Speech, International Woman Suffrage Association (1913), *Women in World History Curriculum*, http://www. womeninworldhistory.com *1996–97*

8   Women are not in rebellion against men. They are in rebellion against worn-out traditions.

Quoted in *Women Suffragists* by Diana Star Helmer *1998*

9   When I was nearly twelve years old . . . on Election Day, my father drove past the house . . . taking the men to vote. When he returned home, I asked him, "Why didn't Mother go to vote?"

Ibid.

10   My husband used to say that he was as much a reformer as I, but that he couldn't work at reforming and earn a living at the same time . . . what he could do was to earn a living enough for two and free me from all economic burden, and thus I could reform for two. That was our bargain, and we happily understood each other.

Ibid.

11   You must think internationally. You are members of the human race . . . Let us be a nation with sympathy enough to put war out of the world.

Speech, Iowa State College graduation (1921), Ibid.

12   It was not an antagonistic public sentiment, nor yet an uneducated or indifferent public sentiment—it was the control of public sentiment, the deflecting and the thwarting of public sentiment, through the trading and the trickery, the buying and the selling of American politics . . . combines of interests that systematically fought suffrage with politics and effectively delayed suffrage for years.

(1923), Ibid.

13   We [Caucasians] stole land, whole continents.

(c. 1940s), Ibid.

1196.   Alice Eastwood (1859–1953)

1   My own destroyed work I do not lament, for it was a joy to me while I did it, and I can still have the same joy in starting it again . . . *

(p 96), Quoted in *Alice Eastwood's Wonderland: The Adventures of a Botanist* by Carol Wilson *1955*

*Reference to the destruction, by the San Francisco earthquake of 1906, of her meticulously gathered botanical collections at the California Academy of Sciences where she was curator of botany.

2   . . . there is a part of me that will not die . . .

(p. 222), Ibid.

3   Never in all my experience have I had the slightest discourtesy and I have never had any fear. I believe that fear brings danger.*

Quoted in "Alice Eastwood" by Marcia Bonta (pp. 10–15), *American Horitculturist* October *1983*

*Reference to her travels to the Western frontier in the 1880s.

1197.   Mary Gardiner Brainard (fl. 1860s)

1   I would rather walk with God in the dark than go alone in the light.

"Not Knowing," St. 1 *n.d.*

2   And what looks dark in the distance may brighten as I draw near.

St. 2, Ibid.

1198.   Jenny P. d'Hericourt (fl. 1860s)

1   To emancipate woman is not to acknowledge her right to use and abuse love; such an emancipation is only the slavery of the passions; the use of the beauty and youth of woman by man; the use of man by woman for his fortune or credit.

To emancipate woman is to acknowledge and declare her free, the equal of man in the social and the moral law, and in labor.

Preface, *A Woman's Philosophy of Woman; or Woman Affranchised 1864*

2   In marriage, woman is a serf.
In public instructions, she is sacrificed.
In labor, she is made inferior.
Civilly, she is a minor.
Politically, she has no existence.
She is the equal of man only when punishment and the payment of taxes are in question.
I claim the rights of woman, because it is time to make the nineteenth century ashamed of its culpable denial of justice to half the human species . . .

Ibid.

3   I have no heart, you say. I am lacking in it, perhaps, towards tyrants, but the conflict that I undertake proves that I am not lacking in it toward their victims; I have therefore a sufficient quantity of it, the more, inasmuch as I neither desire to please you, nor care to be loved by any among you.

"To My Adversaries," Ibid.

4   You tell the child that lies, "it is wrong to deceive; you would not wish others to deceive you."

You tell the child that pilfers, "it is wrong to steal; you would not wish others to steal from you."

You tell the child that take advantage of his strength and knowledge to torment his younger companion, "you would not wish others to do these things to you; you are wicked and cowardly."

These are good lessons. Why then, when the child has become a young man, do you say: *Young men must sow their wild oats?*

To sow their wild oats is to deceive young girls, to destroy their future, to practice adultery, to keep mistresses, to visit brothels.

Yet mothers, women thus consent to the profanation of their sex!

Ch. 6, "Love; Its Functions in Humanity," I, Ibid.

5   Love, my child, undergoes transformations which we should expect and to which we should submit; in the beginning it is a fever of the soul; but fever is a condition which cannot last without destroying life.

II, Ibid.

6   MOTHER. You know, my children, that humanity advances only by forming itself an ideal and endeavoring to realize it. Every passion has its ideal, which, is modified by that of the whole.

III, Ibid.

1199. Henrietta Zolde (1860–1915)

1 In the life of the spirit there is no ending that is not a beginning.

Comment *n.d.*

1200. Florence Kling Harding (1860–1924)

1 If the career is the husband's, the wife can merge her own with it, if it is to be the wife's as it undoubtedly will be in an increasing proportion of cases, then the husband may, with no sacrifice of self respect or of recognition by the community, permit himself to be the less prominent and distinguished member of the combination.

Remark (1922), Quoted in *First Ladies*
by Betty Boyd Caroli *1987*

2 They can't hurt you now.

Posthumous remark to her husband, Warren Harding,* Ibid.
*(1865–1923), 29th president of the United States (1921–1923).

1201. Annie Oakley (1860–1926)

1 I can shoot as well as you [her husband].

Quoted in Ch. 4, *Annie Oakley: Woman at Arms* by Courtney Ryley Cooper *1927*

2 The contents of his [Sitting Bull's*] pockets were often emptied into the hands of small, ragged little boys, nor could he understand how so much wealth should go brushing by, unmindful of the poor.

Quoted in Ch. 7, Ibid.
*Dakota Indian leader (1834?–1890).

1202. Juliette Low (1860–1927)

1 To put yourself in another's place requires real imagination, but by doing so each Girl Scout will be able to live among others happily.

Letter to Girl Scouts of America (31 October 1923*),
Juliette Low and the Girl Scouts, Anne Hyde Choate
and Helen Ferris, eds. *1928*
*Low's 63rd birthday.

2 I hope that during the coming year we shall all remember the rules of this Girl Scouting game of ours. To play for your side and not for yourself. And as for the score, the best thing in a game is the fun and not the result. . . .

(31 October 1924*), Ibid.
*Low's 64th birthday.

3 I am like the old woman who lived in the shoe! And now the shoe has become too small for the many children and we must have a building that will be large enough for us all.

Ibid.

1203. Ellen Thorneycroft Fowler (1860–1929)

1 Though outwardly a gloomy shroud,
The inner half of every cloud
Is bright and shining:
I therefore turn my clouds about
And always wear them inside out
To show the lining.

"Wisdom of Folly" *n.d.*

1204. Jane Addams (1860–1935)

1 We are thus brought to a conception of Democracy not merely as a sentiment which desires the well-being of all men, nor yet as a creed which believes in the essential dignity and equality of all men, but as that which affords a rule of living as well as a test of faith.

Introduction, *Democracy and Social Ethics 1902*

2 The new growth in the plant swelling against the sheath, which at the same time imprisons and protects it, must still be the truest type of progress.

"Filial Relations," Ibid.

3 In our pity for Lear, we fail to analyze his character. . . . His paternal expression was one of domination and indulgence, without the perception of the needs of his children, without any anticipation of their entrance into a wider life, or any belief that they could have a worthy life apart from him.

Ibid.

4 Doubtless the clashes and jar which we feel most keenly are those which occur when two standards of morals, both honestly held and believed in, are brought sharply together.

Ibid.

5 The word "non-resistance" is misleading, because it is much too feeble and inadequate. It suggests passivity, the goody-goody attitude of ineffectiveness. The words "overcoming," "substituting," "re-creating," "readjusting moral values," "forming new centres of spiritual energy" carry much more of the meaning implied. For it is not merely the desire for a conscience at rest, for a sense of justice no longer outraged, that would pull us into new paths where there would be no more war nor preparations for war. There are still more strenuous forces at work reaching down to impulses and experiences as primitive and profound as are those of struggle itself.

Ch. I, *Newer Ideals of Peace 1907*

6 A little examination will easily show that in spite of the fine phrases of the founders, the Government became an entity by itself away from the daily life of the people. There was no intention to ignore them nor to oppress them. But simply because its machinery was so largely copied from the traditional European Governments which did distrust the people, the founders failed to provide the vehicle for a vital and genuinely organized expression of the popular will.

Ch. II, Ibid.

7 It has been discovered that the city which is too careless to provide playgrounds, gymnasiums, and athletic fields where the boys legitimately belong and which the policeman is bound to respect, simply puts a premium on lawlessness.

Ibid.

8 A city is in many respects a great business corporation, but in other respects it is enlarged housekeeping. . . . May we not say that city housekeeping has failed partly because women, the traditional housekeepers, have not been consulted as to its multiform activities?

Ch. VII, Ibid.

9 Old-fashioned ways which no longer apply to changed conditions are a snare in which the feet of women have always become readily entangled.

Ibid

10 To point to the achievement of the past as a guarantee for continuing what has since become shocking to us is stupid business; it is to forget that progress itself depends upon adaptation, upon a nice balance between continuity and change . . . We have come to realize that the great task of pushing forward

social justice could be enormously accelerated if primitive methods as well as primitive weapons were once for all abolished.

Ch. VIII, Ibid.

11 Unless our conception of patriotism is progressive, it cannot hope to embody the real affection and the real interest of the nation.

"Utilization of Women in City Government," *Ibid.*

12 We were often distressed by the children of immigrant parents who were ashamed of the pit whence they were digged, who repudiated the language and customs of their elders, and counted themselves successful [when] they were able to ignore the past.

Twenty Years at Hull House 1910

13 You do not know what life means when all the difficulties are removed! I am simply smothered and sickened with advantages. It is like eating a sweet dessert the first thing in the morning.

Ibid.

14 Private beneficence is totally inadequate to deal with the vast numbers of the city's disinherited.

Ibid.

15 Perhaps I may record here my protest against the efforts, so often made, to shield children and young people from all that has to do with death and sorrow, to give them a good time at all hazards on the assumption that the ills of life will come soon enough. Young people themselves often resent this attitude on the part of their elders; they feel set aside and belittled as if they were denied the common human experiences.

Ibid.

16 Only in time of fear is government thrown back to its primitive and sole function of self-defense and the many interests of which it is the guardian become subordinated to that.

"Women, War and Suffrage," *Survey 6 November 1915*

17 Each exponent in this long effort to place law above force was called a dreamer and a coward, but each did his utmost to express clearly the truth that was in him, and beyond that human effort cannot go.

Ibid.

18 Civilization is a method of living, an attitude of equal respect for all men.

Speech, Honolulu 1933

1205. Charlotte Perkins Gilman (1860–1935)

1 I do not want to be a fly,
I want to be a worm!

"A Conservative," *In This Our World 1893*

2 The female of the genus homo is economically dependent on the male. He is her food supply.

Ch. 1, Women and Economics 1898

3 The labor of women in the house, certainly, enables men to produce more wealth than they otherwise could; and in this way women are economic factors in society. But so are horses.

Ibid.

4 The women who do the most work get the least money, and the women who have the most money do the least work.

Ibid.

5 To be surrounded by beautiful things has much influence upon the human creature: to make beautiful things has more.

Ch. 4, Ibid.

6 Specialization and organization are the basis of human progress.

Ibid.

7 We have built into the constitution of the human race the habit and desire of taking, as divorced from its natural precursor and concomitant of making.

Ch. 6, Ibid.

8 When we see great men and women, we give credit to their mothers. When we see inferior men and women—and that is a common circumstance—no one presumes to the question of the motherhood which has produced them.

Ch. 9, Ibid.

9 Maternal instinct, merely as an instinct, is unworthy of our superstitious reverence.

Ibid.

10 A family unity which is only bound together with a table-cloth is of questionable value.

Ch. 11, Ibid.

11 The child learns more of the virtues needed in modern life—of fairness, of justice, of comradeship, of collective interest and action—in a common school that can be taught in the most perfect family circle.

Ch. 13, Ibid.

12 Work the object of which is merely to serve one's self is the lowest. Work the object of which is merely to serve one's family is the next lowest. Work the object of which is to serve more and more people, in widening range . . . is social service in the fullest sense, and the highest form of service we can reach.

Ibid.

13 A baby who spent certain hours of every day among other babies, being cared for because he was a baby and not because he was "my baby," would grow to have a very different opinion of himself from that which is forced upon each new soul that comes among us by the ceaseless adoration of his own immediate family.

Ibid.

14 You cannot teach every mother to be a good school educator or a good college educator. Why should you expect every mother to be a good nursery educator?

Ibid.

15 Eternity is not something that begins after you are dead. It is going on all the time. We are in it now.

Quoted in *The Forerunner Magazine 1909–1916*

16 I am the squaw—the slave—the harem beauty—
I serve and serve, the handmaid of the world.

Introduction, Pt. I, "Two Callings," *The Home 1910*

17 So when the great word "Mother!" rang once more,
I saw at last its meaning and its place;
Not the blind passion of the brooding past,
But Mother—the World's Mother—come at last,
To love as she had never loved before—
To feed and guard and teach the human race.

Pt. II, Ibid.

18 The original necessity for the ceaseless presence of the woman to maintain the altar fire—and it was an altar fire in very truth at one period—has passed with the means of prompt ignition; the matchbox has freed the housewife from that incessant service, but the *feeling* that women should stay at home is with us yet.

Ch. 3, Ibid.

19 It will be a great thing for the human soul when it finally stops worshipping backwards.

Ibid.

20 You may observe mother instinct at its height in a fond hen sitting on china eggs—instinct, but no brains.

Ibid.

21 Human life consists in mutual service. No grief, pain, misfortune, or "broken heart," is excuse for cutting off one's life while any power of service remains. But when all usefulness is over, when one is assured of an unavoidable and imminent death, it is the simplest of human rights to choose a quick and easy death in place of a slow and horrible one.

Suicide Note *17 August 1935*

22 One may have a brain specialized in its grasp of ethics, as well as of mechanics, mathematics or music.

The Living of Charlotte Perkins Gilman 1935

23 Death? Why all this fuss about death. Use your imagination, try to visualize a world *without* death! . . . Death is the essential condition of life, not an evil.

Ibid.

24 . . . love grows by service.

Ibid.

25 We are told to hitch our wagons to a star, but why pick on Betelgeuse?*

Ibid.

*Largest star in the galaxy.

26 . . . New York . . . that unnatural city where everyone is an exile, none more so than the American.

Ibid.

27 There is no female mind. The brain is not an organ of sex. As well speak of a female liver.

Quoted in *The Liberated Woman's Appointment Calendar*, Lynn Sherr and Jurate Kazickas, eds. *1975*

28 Until we see what we are, we cannot take steps to become what we should be.

Quoted in *Feminist Theorists*, Dale Spender,* ed. *1983*
*See 2971.

29 A concept is stronger than a fact.

"Human Work" *n.d.*

30 The people people have for friends
Your common sense appall,
But the people people marry
Are the queerest folks of all.

"Queer People" *n.d.*

1206. Harriet Monroe (1860–1936)

1 Great ages of art come only when a widespread creative impulse meets an equally widespread impulse of sympathy. . . .

The people must grant a hearing to the best poets they have else they will never have better.

Quoted in "Harriet Monroe," *Famous American Women* by Hope Stoddard *1970*

2 . . . poetry, "The Cinderella of the Arts."

Ibid.

3 . . . poetry might become the fashion—a real danger, because the poets need an audience not fitful and superficial, but loyal and sincere.

Ibid.

4 Poetry has been left to herself and blamed for inefficiency, a process as unreasonable as blaming the desert for barrenness.

Ibid.

1207. Amy Leslie (1860–1939)

1 No animal is so inexhaustible as an excited infant.

Amy Leslie at the Fair 1893

2 When these marvels of art and architecture begin to crumble the hearts of nations will stand still. Now the city blooms apace like a great white rose perfuming the clouds and smiling out upon the waters, but it is to fade! It is to die and that it one of its most exquisite enchantments.

Ibid.

3 Those who make the most memorable racket are of two classes—wary diplomats looking for the best of a business proposition and irresponsible parrots who croak and yell and chatter simply because exclamation points and interrogatories swim through the misty Chicago air.

Ibid.

4 As a singer you're a great dancer.

Quoted by George Primrose in *They All Sang* by E. W. Marks *1934*

1208. Grandma Moses (1860–1961)

1 I don't advise any one to take it [painting] up as a business proposition, unless they really have talent, and are crippled so as to deprive them of physical labor. Then with help they might make a living, But with taxes and income tax there is little money in that kind of art for the ordinary artis [sic]. But I will say that I have did remarkable for one of my years, and experience. As for publicity, that Im [sic] too old to care for now. . .

"How Do I Paint?" *The New York Times 11 May 1947*

2 What a strange thing is memory, and hope; one looks backward, the other looks forward. The one is of today, the other is the Tomorrow. Memory is history recorded in our brain, memory is a painter, it paints pictures of the past and of the day.

Ch. 1, *Grandma Moses, My Life's History*, Aotto Kallir, ed. *1947*

3 If I didn't start painting, I would have raised chickens.

Ch. 3, Ibid.

1209. Minna Antrim (1861–?)

1 A homely face and no figure have aided many women heavenward.

Naked Truth and Veiled Allusions 1902

2 Man forgives woman anything save the wit to outwit him.

Ibid.

3 Experience has no text books nor proxies. She demands that her pupils answer her roll-call personally.

Ibid.

4 To know one's self is wisdom, but to know one's neighbor is genius.

Ibid.

5 Smiles are the soul's kisses. . . .

Ibid.

6 To control a man a woman must first control herself.

Ibid.

7 Golden fetters hurt as cruelly as iron ones.

Ibid.

8 A fool bolts pleasure, then complains of moral indigestion.

Ibid.

9 An epigram is a flashlight of a truth; a witticism, truth laughing at itself.

Ibid.

10 The difference between a saint and a hypocrite is that one lies for his religion, the other by it.

Ibid.

11 To be loved is to be fortunate, but to be hated is to achieve distinction.

Ibid.

12 Enthusiasms, like stimulants, are often affected by people with small mental ballast.

Ibid.

13 The drama of life begins with a wail and ends with a sigh.

Ibid.

14 The "Green-Eyed Monster" causes much woe, but the absence of this ugly serpent argues the presence of a corpse whose name is Eros.

Ibid.

15 Experience is a good teacher, but she sends in terrific bills.

Ibid.

16 Between flattery and admiration there often flows a river of contempt.

Ibid.

17 Satiety is a mongrel that barks at the heels of plenty.

Ibid.

1210. Mary Byron (1861–?)

1 On gossamer nights when the moon is low,
   And stars in the mist are hiding,
   Over the hill where the foxgloves grow
   You may see the fairies riding.

"The Fairy Thrall" *n.d.*

1211. Jessie Brown Pounds (1861–?)

1 Somewhere, Somewhere, Beautiful Isle of Somewhere,
   Land of the true, where we live anew,
   Beautiful Isle of Somewhere.

"Beautiful Isle of Somewhere" *1901*

1212. Mary Coleridge (1861–1907)

1 The fruits of the tree of knowledge are various; he must be strong indeed who can digest all of them.

Gathered Leaves from the Prose of Mary E. Coleridge 1910

2 Solitude effects some people like wine; they must not take too much of it, for it flies to the head.

Ibid.

3 And in her lurid eyes there shone
   The dying flame of life's desire,
   Made mad because its hope was gone,
   And kindled at the leaping fire
   Of jealousy, and fierce revenge,
   And strength that could not change nor tire.

"The Other Side of the Mirror," St. 4 *n.d.*

4 Mother of God! No lady thou:
   Common woman of common earth!

"Our Lady" *n.d.*

5 We were young, we were merry, we were very, very wise,
   And the door stood open at our feast,
   When there passed us a woman with the West in her eyes,
   And a man with his back to the East.

"Unwelcome" *n.d.*

6 Into the land of dreams I long to go.
   Bid me forget!

"Mandragora" *n.d.*

7 Where is delight? and what are pleasures now?—
   Moths that a garment fret.

Ibid.

1213. Nettie Maria Stevens (1861–1912)

1 How could you think your questions would bother me? They never will, so long as I keep my enthusiasm for biology; and that, I hope, will be as long as I live.

Letter to a student, Quoted in "Nettie Maria Stevens" by Marilyn Bailey Oglivie and Clifford J. Choquette (p. 373), *Proceedings of the American Philosophical Society*, Vol. 125, No. 4 *August 1981*

1214. Alice Hubbard (1861–1915)

1 [Thomas] Paine* was a Quaker by birth and friend by nature. The world was his home, mankind were his friends, to do good was his religion.

Introduction, *An American Bible 1911*

*English-born American revolutionary leader (1737–1809).

1215. Louise Imogen Guiney (1861–1920)

1 To be Anonymous is better than to be Alexander. Cowley said it engagingly, in his little essay on *Obscurity*: "*Bene qui latuit, bene vixit*; he lives well that has lain well hidden." The pleasantest condition of life is in Incognito.

"The Delights of an Incognito," *Patrins 1897*

2   Quotations (such as have point and lack triteness) from the great old authors are an act of filial reverence on the part of the quote, and a blessing to a public grown superficial and external.
>   *Quoted in Scribner's Magazine January 1911*

3   A certain sesquipedalianism* is natural to Americans: witness our press editorials, our Fourth of July orations, and the public messages of all our Presidents since Lincoln.
>   *Ibid.*

*Use of long words.

4   The fears of what may come to pass,
I cast them all away,
Among the clover scented grass,
Among the new-mown hay.
>   "A Song from Sylvan," St. 2 *n.d.*

5   He has done with roofs and men,
Open, Time, and let him pass.
>   "Ballad of Kenelm" *n.d.*

6   To fear not sensible failure,
Nor covet the game at all,
But fighting, fighting, fighting,
Die, driven against the wall.
>   "The Kings" *n.d.*

7   A short life in the saddle, Lord!
Not long life by the fire.
>   "The Knight Errant," St. 2 *n.d.*

8   High above hate I dwell,
O storms! Farewell.
>   "The Sanctuary" *n.d.*

9   The fool who redeemed us once of our folly,
And the smiter who healed us, our right John Brown!*
>   "John Brown: A Paradox" *n.d.*

*American abolitionist (1800–1859).

1216. Katharine Tynan Hinkson (1861–1931)

1   O you poor folk in cities,
A thousand, thousand pities!
>   "June Song" *n.d.*

2   To me the wonderful charge was given,
I, even a little ass, did go
Bearing the very weight of heaven;
So I crept cat-foot, sure and slow.
>   "The Ass Speaks" *n.d.*

1217. Corinne Roosevelt Robinson (1861–1933)

1   Though Love be deeper, Friendship is more wide. . . .
>   "Friendship," *The Call of Brotherhood and Other Poems 1912*

2   Stretch out your hand and take the world's wide gift
Of Joy and Beauty.
>   "Stretch Out Your Hand," Ibid.

3   Serene amid the clamor and the strife
She bore the lily of a blameless life!
>   "To F.W.," Ibid.

4   Is life worth living?
Aye, with the best of us,

Heights of us, depths of us,—
Life is the test of us!
>   "Life, A Question," *One Woman to Another 1914*

5   Nothing is as difficult as to achieve results in this world if one is filled full of great tolerance and the milk of human kindness. The person who achieves must generally be a one-ideaed individual, concentrated entirely on that one idea, and ruthless in his aspect toward other men and other ideas.
>   Ch. 1, *My Brother Theodore Roosevelt* 1921

*(1858–1919) 26th president of the United States (1901–1909).

6   Thy love was like a royal accolade. . . .
>   "Afterward," *Out of Nymph 1930*

7   Spirit of the air,
And of the seas, and of the fragrant earth,
I thank thee that thou didst attend my birth
To dower me with wonder. . . .
>   "The Gift of Wonder," Ibid.

1218. Gracy Hebard (1861–1936)

1   These Indians [Shoshones] believe also that God pulled out the upper teeth of the elk because the elk were meant to be eaten by the Indians, and not the Indians by the elk.
>   *Washakie 1930*

2   The buffaloes were the original engineers, as they followed the lay of the land and the run of the water. These buffalo paths became indian trails, which always pointed out the easiest way across the mountain barriers. The white man followed in these footpaths. The iron trail finished the road.
>   Ch. 9, *The Pathbreakers from River to Ocean 1932*

3   While we are enjoying the luxuries of this new era of the great west let us not forget to honor those who endured hardships and privations, encountered dangers and peril; yes, even gave up their lives to make these things possible. . . . It is all a story that has never had its equal in the world's history. The great American desert is no more.
>   Ibid.

1219. Ernestine Schumann-Heink (1861–1936)

1   One can never either hear or see himself, and there is a need—if one would make real progress in art—for constant criticism.
>   Quoted in *Schumann-Heink, The Last of the Titans* by Mary Lawton 1935

2   This shall be my parting word—know what you want to do—then do it. Make straight for your goal and go undefeated in spirit to the end.
>   Ibid.

1220. Frances Greville (1861–1938)

1   Love and Misery proverbially go together. There is a popular notion . . . that a lover could not get along without a little misery. . . .
>   Quoted in *Anglo-Saxon Review June 1900*

1221. Helen Herron Taft (1861–1943)

1   I have thought that a woman should be independent and not regard matrimony as the only thing to be desired in life.
>   Diary entry (at 22), Quoted in *First Ladies* by Betty Boyd Caroli 1987

2   I do not dislike teaching when the boys behave themselves.

Ibid.

1222. Edith Carow Roosevelt (1861–1948)

1   Women who marry pass their best and happiest years in giving life and fostering it.

American Backlogs, Quoted in *First Ladies* by Betty Boyd Caroli *1987*

1223. Dorothy Dix (1861–1951)

1   It is only the women whose eyes have been washed clear with tears who get the broad vision that makes them little sisters to all the world.

Introduction, *Dorothy Dix, Her Book 1926*

2   I have learned in the great University of Hard Knocks a philosophy that no woman who has had an easy life ever acquires. I have learned to live each day as it comes, and not to borrow trouble by dreading tomorrow. It is the dark menace of the future that makes cowards of us.

Ibid.

3   Now one of the great reasons why so many husbands and wives make shipwreck of their lives together is because a man is always seeking for happiness, while a woman is on a perpetual still hunt for trouble.

Ch. 1, Ibid.

4   So many persons think divorce a panacea for every ill, who find out, when they try it, that the remedy is worse than the disease.

Ch. 13, Ibid.

5   Confession is always weakness. The grave soul keeps its own secrets, and takes its own punishment in silence.

Ch. 20, Ibid.

6   In reality, the mother who rears her children up to be monsters of selfishness has no right to expect appreciation and gratitude from them because she has done them as ill a turn as one human being can do another. She has warped their characters.

Ch. 44, Ibid.

7   Extravagance. The price of indulging yourself in your youth in the things you cannot afford is poverty and dependence in your old age.

Ch. 53, Ibid.

8   Women have changed in their relationship to men, but men stand pat just where Adam did when it comes to dealing with women.

Ch. 59, Ibid.

9   For in all the world there are no people so piteous and forlorn as those who are forced to eat the bitter bread of dependency in their old age, and find how steep are the stairs of another man's house.

Ch. 69, Ibid.

10   Nobody wants to kiss when they are hungry.

News Item *n.d.*

11   The reason that husbands and wives do not understand each other is because they belong to different sexes.

Ibid.

1224. Susan Cocroft (1862–?)

1   Don't be ashamed of your desire for beauty.

(p. 14), *A New Method of Physical Culture for the Face 1912*

2   The women of today, yesterday, and tomorrow are the same, but our horizons are broadening. And this will not make us mannish. We can be as sweet and dear and lovable in the street as in the home.

"Miss Cocroft Tells How to Build a Neck," *The New York Times 21 April 1915*

1225. Edith Cooper (1862–1913)

Co-author with Katharine Bradley. See 1102:1–2.

1226. Loie Fuller (1862–1928)

1   "Light" and "Color" thrown on great masses of silk, was my real representation and not dancing at all...called dance for want of a more appropriate title.

Fifteen Years of My Life 1913

2   Education is wonderful but nobody wants it rubbed in...when you don't even know what they are talking about & you don't want to know.

Ibid.

1227. Ida B. Wells (1862–1931)

1   Let the Afro-American depend on no party, but on himself for his salvation. Let him continue to develop his education, character, and above all, put money in his purse.

"Iola's Southern Field," *The New York Age 11 November 1892*

2   The first excuse given to the civilized world for the murder of unoffending Negroes was the necessity of the white man to repress and stamp out "race riots." . . . It was always a remarkable feature in these insurrections and riots that only Negroes were killed during the rioting, and that all the white men escaped unharmed.

The Red Record 1895

3   True chivalry respects all womanhood. . . . Virtue knows no color lines, and the chivalry which depends upon complexion of skin and texture of hair can command no honest respect.

Ibid.

4   I felt that one had better die fighting against injustice than to die like a dog or a rat in a trap. I had already determined to sell my life as dearly as possible if attacked. I felt if I could take one lyncher with me, this would even up the score a little bit.

Crusade for Justice: The Autobiography of Ida B. Wells, Alfreda M. Duster, ed. *1970*

5   Not all or nearly all of the murders done by white men, during the past thirty years in the South, have come to light, but the statistics as gathered and preserved by white men, and which have not been questioned, show that during these years more than ten thousand Negroes have been killed in cold blood without the formality of judicial trial and legal execution.

Black Women in White America, Gerda Lerner,* ed. *1972*
* See 2160.

1228. Ada Leverson (1862–1933)

1   Absurdly improbable things happen in real life as well as in weak literature.

The Twelfth Hour 1907

2 Before he left, Aunt William pressed a sovereign into his hand guiltily, as if it were conscience money. He, on his side, took it as though it were a doctor's fee, and both ignored the transaction.

"Aunt William" 1907

1229. Edith Wharton (1862–1937)

1 A New York divorce is in itself a diploma of virtue. . . .

Ch. 1, "The Other Two," *The Descent of Man 1904*

2 "It feels uncommonly queer to have enough cash to pay one's bills. I'd have sold my soul for it a few years ago!"

Ch. 3, Ibid.

3 "I don't know as I think a man is entitled to rights he hasn't known how to hold on to. . . ."

Ch. 4, Ibid.

4 Her pliancy was beginning to sicken him. Had she really no will of her own . . . ? She was "as easy as an old shoe"—a shoe that too many feet had worn.

Ibid.

5 If he paid for each day's comfort with the small change of his illusions, he grew daily to value the comfort more and set less store upon the coin.

Ibid.

6 She keeps on being queenly in her own room with the door shut.

The House of Mirth 1905

7 When she spoke it was only to complain, and to complain of things not in his power to remedy; and to check a tendency of impatient retort he had first formed the habit of not answering her, and finally of thinking of other things while she talked.

Ch. 4, *Ethan Frome 1911*

8 Almost everybody in the neighborhood had "troubles," frankly localized and specified; but only the chosen had "complications." To have them was in itself a distinction, though it was also, in most cases, a death-warrant. People struggled on for years with "troubles," but they almost always succumbed to "complications."

Ch. 7, Ibid.

9 "Oh, what good'll writing do? I want to put my hand out and touch you. I want to do for you and care for you. I want to be there when you're sick and when you're lonesome."

Ch. 9, Ibid.

10 . . . they seemed to come suddenly upon happiness as if they had surprised a butterfly in the winter woods. . . .

Ibid.

11 Mrs. Ballinger is one of the ladies who pursue Culture in bands, as though it were dangerous to meet it alone.

"Xingu," *Xingu and Other Stories 1916*

12 There's no such thing as old age, there is only sorrow.

"A First Word," *A Backward Glance 1934*

13 "I can imagine being in love at 60."

Buccaneers 1938

14 "A sweet lass she were, even though she were a harlot."

Ibid.

15 I think sometimes that it is almost a pity to enjoy Italy as much as I do, because the acuteness of my sensations makes them rather exhausting; but when I see the stupid Italians I have met here, completely insensitive to their surroundings, and ignorant of the treasures of art and history among which they have grown up, I begin to think it is better to be an American, and bring to it all a mind and eye unblunted by custom.

Letter (8 March 1903), *The Letters of Edith Wharton 1988*

16 My first few weeks in America are always miserable, because the tastes I am cursed with are all of a kind that cannot be gratified here, & I am not enough in sympathy with our "gros public" to make up for the lack on the aesthetic side. One's friends are delightful; but we are none of us Americans, we don't think or feel as the Americans do, we are the wretched exotics produced in a European glass-house, the most *déplacé* & useless class on earth!

Letter to Sara Norton (5 June 1903), Ibid.

17 I despair of the Republic!* Such dreariness, such whining sallow women, such utter absence of the amenities, such crass food, crass manners, crass landscape!!

. . . What a horror it is for a whole nation to be developing without the sense of beauty, & eating bananas for breakfast.

(19 August 1904), Ibid.

*The republic of the United States.

18 After all, one knows one's weak points so well, that it's rather bewildering to have the critics overlook them & invent others.*

Letter (19 November 1907), Ibid.

*Reference to reviews of her recently published work, *The Fruit of the Tree*.

19 I wonder, among all the tangles of this mortal coil, which one contains tighter knots to undo, & consequently suggests more tugging, & pain, & diversified elements of misery, than the marriage tie.

Letter (12 February 1909), Ibid.

20 We who knew him* well know how great he would have been if he had never written a line.

Letter of condolence (1 March 1916), Ibid.

*Henry James, American novelist (1843–1916).

21 How much longer are we going to think it necessary to be "American" before (or in contradistinction to) being cultivated, being enlightened, being humane, & having the same intellectual discipline as other civilized countries? It is really too easy a disguise for our shortcomings to dress them up as a form of patriotism!

Letter (19 July 1919), Ibid.

22 It's a turgid welter of pornography (the rudest schoolboy kind) & unformed & unimportant drivel; & until the raw ingredients of a pudding make a pudding, I shall never believe that the raw material of sensation & thought can make a work of art without the cook's intervening.*

Letter to Bernard Berenson** (6 January 1923), Ibid.

*Reference to James Joyce's (1882–1941) novel *Ulysses* (1922).
**Lithuanian art critic and historian (1865–1959).

23 I have never known a novel that was good enough to be good in spite of its being adapted to the author's political views.

Letter to Upton Sinclair* (19 August 1927), Ibid.

*American novelist and socialist reformer (1878–1968).

24 My little dog:
A heartbeat at my feet.

"A Lyrical Epigram" *n.d.*

25 There are two ways of spreading light: to be
The candle or the mirror that receives it.
"Vesalius in Zante" *n.d.*

1230. Ella Higginson (1862–1940)

1 Forgive you?—Oh, of course, dear,
A dozen times a week!
"Wearing Out Love," St. 1 *n.d.*

2 It's what you do, unthinking,
That makes the quick tear start;
The tear may be forgotten—
But the hurt stays in the heart.
St. 2 *n.d., Ibid.*

3 One leaf is for hope, and one is for faith,
And one is for love, you know,
And God put another in for luck.
"Four-Leaf Clover," St. 2 *n.d.*

1231. Chang Ts'ai-t'ien (1862–1945)

1 . . . I wanted to study and not to marry. My brother and Mao
Tse-tung also hated marriage and declared they would never
marry. . . .
Quoted in *Women in Modern China*
by Helen Foster Snow* 1967

*See 1903.

1232. Helen Bannerman (1862-1946)

1 But the Tiger said, "What would your shoes be to me? I've got
four feet, and you've got only two; you haven't got enough
shoes for me."
But Little Black Sambo said, "You could wear them on
your ears."
"So I could," said the Tiger: "that's a very good idea. Give
them to me, and I won't eat you this time."
The Story of Little Black Sambo 1899

2 And there he saw all the Tigers fighting, and disputing which
of them was the grandest. And at last they got so angry that
they jumped up and took off all the fine clothes, and began to
tear each other with their claws, and bite each other with their
great big white teeth.
Ibid.

1233. Carrie Jacobs Bond (1862–1946)

1 When God made up this world of ours,
He made it long and wide,
And meant that it should shelter all,
And none should be denied.
"Friends," St. 1, *Little Stories in Verse 1905*

2 Kind words smooth all the "Paths o' Life"
And smiles make burdens light,
And uncomplainin' friends can make
A daytime out o' night.
"The Path o' Life," St. 11, *Ibid.*

3 And we find at the end of a perfect day,
The soul of a friend we've made.
"A Perfect Day," St. 2 *1926*

1234. Kishida Toshiko (1863–1901)

1 If it is true that men are better than women because they are
stronger, why aren't our sumo wrestlers in the government?
Remark *n.d.*

1235. Annie Fellows Johnston (1863–1931)

1 Her ideas of grandfathers, gained from stories and observation, led her to class them with fairy godmothers. She had
always wished for one.
Ch. III, *The Little Colonel 1895*

1236. Belle Kearney (1863–1939)

1 The popular delusion is that the ante-bellum Southern woman,
like Christ's lilies, "toiled not." Though surrounded by the
conditions for idleness she was not indolent after she became
the head of her own household. Every woman sewed, often
making her own dresses; the clothing of all the slaves on a
plantation was cut and made by negro seamstresses under her
direct supervision, even the heavy coats of the men; she minis-
tered personally to them in cases of sickness, frequently
maintaining a well managed hospital under her sole care. She
was a most skillful housekeeper, though she did none of the
work with her own hands, and her children grew up around
her knees; however, the black "mammy" relieved her of the
actual drudgery of child-worry.
Ch. 1, *The Slaveholders' Daughter 1900*

2 There was born in me a sense of the injustice that had always
been heaped upon my sex, and this consciousness created and
sustained in me a constant and ever increasing rebellion. The
definite idea of the political emancipation of woman, as a
happy and logical solution of the vexed question, did not present itself to me in a positive guise until some time after my
entrance upon the list of wage-earners.
Ch. 11, *Ibid.*

3 There are moments when one cannot weep, nor speak, nor
pray,—only be quiet before God.
Ch. 22, *Ibid.*

1237. Annie Jump Cannon (1863–1941)

1 . . . a life spent in the routine of science need not destroy the
attractive human element of a woman's nature.
Quoted in *Science 30 June 1911*

2 They [streaks of light in spectrograms] aren't just streaks to me.
Each new spectrum is the gateway to a wonderful new world.
(p. 17), Quoted in *Science: Contributions of Women* by
Diane Emberlin *1977*

3 In these days of great trouble and unrest, it is good to have
something outside our own planet, something fine and distant
and comforting to troubled minds. Let people look to the stars
for comfort.
Interview (c. 1941; p. 27), *Ibid.*

4 Classifying the stars has helped materially in all studies of the
structure of the universe. No greater problem is presented to
the human mind. Teaching man his relatively small sphere in
the creation, it also encourages him by its lessons of the unity
of Nature and shows him that his power of comprehension allies him with the great intelligence overreaching all.
4000 Years of Women in Science,
http://www.astr.ua.edu/4000WS *11 July 1997*

1238. Elaine Goodale (1863–1953)

1 We feel our savage kind,—
And thus alone with conscious meaning wear
The Indian's moccasin.
"Moccasin Flower," *In Berkshire with the Wild Flowers 1879*

2 Nature lies, disheveled, pale,
With her feverish lips apart,—
Day by day the pulses fail,
Nearer to her bounding heart.

"Goldenrod" *n.d.*

3 Bronzed and molded by wind and sun,
Maddening, gladdening everyone
With a gypsy beauty full and fine,—
A health to the crimson columbine!

"Columbine" *n.d.*

1239. Mary Church Terrell (1863–1954)

1 Lynching is the aftermath of slavery.
"Lynching from a Negro's Point of View," *North American Review June 1904*

2 The whole country seems tired of hearing about the black man's woes. The wrongs of the Irish, of the Armenians, of the Roumanian and Russian Jews, of the exiles of Russia and of every other oppressed people upon the face of the globe, can arouse sympathy and fire the indignation of the American public, while they seem to be all but indifferent to the murderous assaults upon the negroes in the South.

Ibid.

3 I cannot help wondering sometimes what I might have become and might have done if I had lived in a country which had not circumscribed and handicapped me on account of my race, but had allowed me to reach any height I was able to attain.
A Colored Woman in a White World 1940

4 No matter what I say, I shall be accused either of "whining" too much or boasting too much.

Ibid.

5 Holding human beings in slavery seems to have been part of the divine plan to bring out the best there is in them.

Ibid.

6 As a colored woman I might enter Washington any night, a stranger in a strange land, and walk miles without finding a place to lay my head, . . . The colored man alone is thrust out of the hotels of the national capital like a leper.
"What It Means to Be Colored in the Capital of the United States" (1907), Ibid.

7 It is impossible for any white person in the United States, no matter how sympathetic and broad, to realize what life would mean to him if his incentive to effort were suddenly snatched away. To the lack of incentive for effort, which is the awful shadow under which we live, may be traced the wreck and ruin of scores of colored youth.

Ibid.

8 Please stop using the word "Negro" . . . We are the only human beings in the world with fifty-seven variety of complexions who are classed together as a single racial unit. Therefore, we are really truly colored people, and that is the only name in the English language which accurately describes us.
Letter to the Editor, *The Washington Post* (14 May 1949), Ibid.

9 Hanging, shooting, and burning black men, women and children in the United States have become so common that such occurrences create but little sensation and evoke but slight comment now.
Black Women in White America, Gerda Lerner,* ed. *1972*
*See 2160.

10 Colored women are the only group in this country who have two heavy handicaps to overcome, that of race as well as of sex.
Quoted in *Women Suffragists* by Diana Star Helmer *1998*

11 The injustice involved in denying woman the suffrage is not confined to the disenfranchised sex alone, but extends to the nation as well, in that it is deprived of the excellent service which woman might render.

Ibid.

12 If we do not use the franchise, we shall give our enemies a stick with which to break our heads, and we shall not be able to live down the reproach of our indifference for 100 years. Hold meetings! Every time you meet a woman, talk to her about going to the polls to vote.
Speech to Women's Republican League, Ibid.

1240. Elinor Glyn (1864–1943)

1 Marriage is the aim and end of all sensible girls, because it is the meaning of life.
"Letters to Caroline," *Harper's Bazaar September 1913*

1241. Margot Asquith (1864–1945)

1 Riches are overestimated in the Old Testament: the good and successful man received too many animals, wives, apes, she-goats, and peacocks.
Ch. 7, *The Autobiography of Margot Asquith*, Vols. I and II *1920–1922*

2 Rich men's houses are seldom beautiful, rarely comfortable, and never original. It is a constant source of surprise to people of moderate means to observe how little a big fortune contributes to Beauty.

Ch. 17, Ibid.

3 To marry a man out of pity is folly; and, if you think you are going to influence the kind of fellow who has "never had a chance, poor devil," you are profoundly mistaken. One can only influence the strong characters in life, not the weak; and it is the height of vanity to suppose that you can make an honest man of anyone.

Ch. 7, Vol. 1, Ibid.

4 The first element of greatness is fundamental humbleness (this should not be confused with servility); the second is freedom from self; the third is intrepid courage, which, taken in its widest interpretation, generally goes with truth; and the fourth—the power to love—although I have put it last, is the rarest.

Ch. 8, Ibid.

5 From the happy expression on their faces you might have supposed that they welcomed the war. I have met with men who loved stamps, and stones, and snakes, but I could not imagine any man loving war.*

Ch. 7, Vol. 2, Ibid.

*Reference to the crowds outside Downing Street, on the eve of the declaration of World War I (3 August 1914).

6 Journalism over here [in America] is not only an obsession but a drawback that cannot be overrated. Politicians are frightened of the press, and in the same way as bull-fighting has a brutalising effect upon Spain (of which she is unconscious), headlines of murder, rape, and rubbish, excite and demoralise the American public.

Ch. 10, *My Impressions of America 1922*

7 It is always dangerous to generalise, but the American people, while infinitely generous, are a hard and strong race and, but for the few cemeteries I have seen, I am inclined to think they never die.

Ch. 14, Ibid.

8 The ingrained idea that, because there is no king and they despise titles, the Americans are a free people is pathetically untrue. . . . There is a perpetual interference with personal liberty over there that would not be tolerated in England for a week.

Ch. 17, Ibid.

9 . . . her one idea was to exercise a moderating influence; and without knowing it she would in a subtle and disparaging manner check the enthusiasm, dim the glow, and cramp the extravagance of everyone around her.

Ch. 1, *Octavia* 1928

10 "Women are like horses and should never be ridden on the curb."

Ch. 9, Ibid.

11 She wanted to *give* life; to warm the blood and kindle the hope of drab and cautious people. You could not make others live unless you had life yourself.

Ch. 12, Ibid.

12 She was not an individual when she was with him, she was an audience—

Ibid.

13 Life was cruel, demanding wisdom from the young before they had the chance of acquiring it! Innocence was admired, ignorance despised: yet, in their effects, they had a dangerous resemblance.

Ch. 22, Ibid.

14 He could not see a belt without hitting below it.*

Introduction, Quoted in *Margot Asquith, Autobiography*
by Mark Bonham Carter 1962
*Reference to British prime minister (1916–22) David
Lloyd George.

1242. Mary Berenson (1864–1945)

1 Love in whatever form it comes is a god, and even if it destroys all one's so-called "moral nature," it remolds the world nearer to the heart's desire. Why should we put faithfulness above it?

Diary Entry (1895), *Mary Berenson: A Self-Portrait
from Her Letters and Diaries*, Barbara Strachey
and Jayne Samuels, eds. 1984

1243. Margaret P. Sherwood (1864–1955)

1 Whisper some kindly word, to bless
A wistful soul who understands
That life is but one long caress
Of gentle words and gentle hands.

"In Memoriam—Leo: A Yellow Cat" *n.d.*

1244. Louisa Thomas (1865–?)

1 Charm is the measure of attraction's power
To chain the fleeting fancy of the hour.

"What Is Charm?" St. 1 *n.d.*

1245. Anandabai Joshee (1865–1887)

1 Holes are bored through the lower part of the left nostril for the nose-ring, and all around the edge of the ear for jewels.

This may appear barbarous to the foreign eye; to us it is a beauty! Everything changes with the clime.

Letter to Mrs. Carpenter (1880), Quoted in *The Life of
Anandabai Joshee* by Caroline H. Dall 1888

2 When I think over the sufferings of women in India in all ages, I am impatient to see the Western light dawn as the harbinger of emancipation.

Ibid.

3 Your American widows may have difficulties and inconveniences to struggle with, but weighed in the scale against ours, all of them put together are but as a particle against a mountain.*

Ibid.

*Reference to the now illegal act or practice of suttee (or sati),
wherein a Hindu widow cremates herself on her husband's funeral
pyre in order to fulfill a marital duty.

4 Had there been no difficulties and thorns in the way, then man would have been in his primitive state and no progress made in civilization and mental culture.

Letter to her aunt (27 August 1881), Ibid.

5 . . . I regard irreligious people as pioneers. If there had been no priesthood the world would have advanced ten thousand times better than it has now.

Ibid.

1246. Laurence Hope (1865–1904)

1 For this is wisdom: to love, to live,
To take what Fate, or the Gods, may give.

"The Teak Forest," *India's Love Lyrics* 1922

2 Speed passion's ebb as you greet its flow—
To have, to hold, and in time let go!

Ibid.

3 Less than the dust beneath thy chariot wheel,
Less than the weed that grows beside thy door,
Less than the rust that never stained thy sword,
Less than the need thou hast in life of me,
Even less am I.

"Less Than the Dust," St. 1, Ibid.

4 Pale hands I loved beside the Shalimar,
Where are you now? Who lies beneath your spell?

"Kashmiri Song," St. 1, Ibid.

5 Your work was waste? Maybe your share
Lay in the hour you laughed and kissed;
Who knows but that your son shall wear
The laurels that his father missed?

"The Masters" *n.d.*

6 Often devotion to virtue arises from sated desire.

"I Arise and Go Down to the River," St. 6 *n.d.*

7 Men should be judged, not by their tint of skin,
The Gods they serve, the Vintage that they drink,
Nor by the way they fight, or love, or sin,
But by the quality of thought they think.

"Men Should Be Judged" *n.d.*

8 Yet I, this little while ere I go hence,
Love very lightly now, in self-defense.

"Verse by Taj Mahomed" *n.d.*

1247. Edith Louisa Cavell (1865–1915)

1 I realize that patriotism is not enough. I must have no hatred or bitterness towards anyone.

Last Words, Quoted in The Times *(London) 23 October 1915*

1248. Kathe Schirmacher (1865–1930)

1 In the greater part of the world woman is a slave and a beast of burden. . . . In most cases she is overworked, exploited, and (even when living in luxury) the oppressed sex. . . . These conditions are opposed by the woman's right movement. . . . Most men do not understand this ideal; they oppose it with unconscious egotism.

The Modern Rights Movement 1905

1249. Nellie Melba (1865?–1931)

1 The first rule in opera is the first rule in life: see to everything yourself.

Melodies and Memories 1925

2 One of the drawbacks of Fame is that one can never escape from it.

Ibid.

3 Music is not written in red, white and blue. It is written in the heart's blood of the composer.

Ibid.

1250. Minnie Fiske (1865–1932)

1 "Bosh! Do not talk to me about the repertory idea. It is an outworn, needless, impossible, *harmful* scheme. . . . This, my friend, is an age of specialization, and in such an age the repertory theatre is an anachronism, a ludicrous anachronism."

Quoted in Ch. 1, *Mrs. Fiske* by Alexander Woollcott* *1917*

2 The essence of acting is the conveyance of truth through the medium of the actor's mind and person. The science of acting deals with the perfecting of that medium. The great actors are the luminous ones. They are the great conductors of the stage.

Ch. 5, Ibid.

3 But there are times when the actor is an artist far greater and more creative than his material. . . .

Ibid.

4 You must make your own blunders, must cheerfully accept your own mistakes as part of the scheme of things. You must not allow yourself to be advised, cautioned, influenced, persuaded, this way and that.

Letter to Alexander Woollcott* (1908), Ibid.
*American columnist, critic (1887–1943).

5 Among the most disheartening and dangerous of . . . advisors, you will often find those closest to you, your dearest friends, members of your own family, perhaps, loving, anxious, and knowing nothing whatever. . . .

Ibid.

1251. Mrs. Patrick Campbell (1865–1940)

1 I believe I was impatient with unintelligent people from the moment I was born: a tragedy—for I am myself three-parts a fool.

Ch. 2, *My Life and Some Letters 1922*

2 I remember a certain dinner party given for me by a well-known Jewish financier, and being asked by him at table in an earnest, curious voice, what I kept in a small locket I wore on a chain round my neck. Everyone stopped talking and listened for my answer. I replied gravely, "One hair of a Jew's moustache."

Ch. 6, Ibid.

3 To be made to hold his [George Bernard Shaw's*] tongue is the greatest insult you can offer him—though he might be ready with a poker to make you hold yours.

Ch. 16, Ibid.
*Irish-born English author (1856–1950).

4 There can be a fundamental gulf of gracelessness in a human heart which neither our love nor our courage can bridge.

Ch. 19, Ibid.

5 Wedlock—the deep, deep peace of the double bed after the hurly-burly of the chaise-longue.

(1914), Quoted in *Jennie*, Vol. II by Ralph G. Martin *1971*

6 It doesn't matter what you do in the bedroom as long as you don't do it in the street and frighten the horses.

Attributed *n.d.*

1252. Yvette Guilbert (1865–1944)

1 Try to make a woman who does badly on the stage understand that she might do better in trade, or in any other occupation. She will never believe you. It seems impossible to her to make linen garments or millinery, but very simple to enact the dandy on the stage.

La Vedette 1902

2 One cannot remain the same. Art is a mirror which should show many reflections, and the artist should not always show the same face, or the face becomes a mask.

Ibid.

3 Caper without cease, and caper again. . . . You are gaiety, which passes away.

Ibid.

4 All women are alike. All demand stimulation for their senses . . . . These ladies of society also feel the need of language strong enough to stimulate them. . . . Licentiousness takes them all in the same manner.

Ibid.

1253. Emily James Putnam (1865–1944)

1 But the typical lady everywhere tends to the feudal habit of mind. In contemporary society she is an archaism, and can hardly understand herself unless she knows her own history.

Introduction, *The Lady 1910*

2 Until changing economic conditions made the thing actually happen, struggling early society would hardly have guessed that woman's road to gentility would lie through doing nothing at all.

Ibid.

3 Sentimentally the lady has established herself as the criterion of a community's civilisation. . . . When it is flatly put to her that she cannot become a human being and yet retain her privileges as a non-combatant, she often enough decided for etiquette.

Ibid.

4 Maternity is on the face of it an unsocial experience. The selfishness that a woman has learned to stifle or to dissemble where she alone is concerned, blooms freely and unashamed on behalf of her offspring.

Ibid.

1254. Baroness Orczy (1865–1947)

1 A surging, seething, murmuring crowd of beings that are human only in name, for to the eye and ear they seem naught but savage creatures, animated by vile passions and by the lust of vengeance and of hate.

Ch. 1, *The Scarlet Pimpernel* 1905

2 Marguerite St. Just was from principle and by conviction a republican—equality of birth was her motto—inequality of fortune was in her eyes a mere untoward accident, but only inequality she admitted was of talent. "Money and titles may be hereditary," she would say, "but brains are not. . . ."

Ch. 6, Ibid.

3 "I sometimes wish you had not so many lofty virtues. . . . I assure you little sins are far less dangerous and uncomfortable."

Ch. 7, Ibid.

4 "We seek him here, we seek him there,
Those Frenchies seek him everywhere.
Is he in heaven?—Is he in hell?
That damned elusive Pimpernel?"

Ch. 12, Ibid.

5 It is only when we are very happy that we can bear to gaze merrily upon the vast and limitless expanse of water, rolling on and on with such persistent, irritating monotony, to the accompaniment of our thoughts, whether grave or gay. When they are gay, the waves echo their gaiety; but when they are sad, then every breaker, as it rolls, seems to bring additional sadness, and to speak to us of hopelessness and of the pettiness of all our joys.

Ch. 21, Ibid.

6 The weariest nights, the longest days, sooner or later must perforce come to an end.

Ch. 22, Ibid.

7 An apology? Bah! Disgusting! cowardly! beneath the dignity of any gentleman, however wrong he might be.

Prologue, *I Will Repay* 1906

8 To love, for us men, is to clasp one woman with our arms, feeling that she lives and breathes just as we do, suffers as we do, thinks with us, loves with us, and, above all, sins with us.

Ch. 7, Ibid.

9 Your mock saint who stands in a niche is not a woman if she have not suffered, still less a woman if she have not sinned. Fall at the feet of your idol as you wish, but drag her down to your level after that—the only level she should ever reach, that of your heart.

Ibid.

10 "We are not masters of our heart, Messire."

Bk. I, Ch. 3, *Leatherface* 1918

11 "But a wife! . . . What matters what she thinks and feels? if she be cold or loving, gentle or shrewish, sensitive to a kind word or callous to cruelty? A wife! . . . Well! so long as no other man hath ever kissed her lips—for that would hurt masculine vanity and wound the pride of possession!"

Ibid.

12 This, mayhap, was not logic, but it was something more potent, more real than logic—the soft insinuating voice of Sentiment . . .

Bk. II, Ch. 5, Ibid.

13 A blind, unreasoning rage, an irresistible thirst for revenge: a black hatred of all those placed in authority; of all those who were rich, who were independent or influential, filled André Vallon's young soul to the exclusion of every other thought and every other aspiration.

Bk. II, Ch. 5, *A Child of the Revolution* 1932

14 "My dear, since the beginning of all times, men have perpetrated horrors against one another. It is the devil in them, but the devil would have no power over men if God did not allow it. Could He not, if He so willed, quell this revolution with His Word? Must we not rather bow to His will and try to realize that something great, something good, something, at any rate, that is in accordance with the great scheme of the universe must in the end come out of all this sorrow?"

Bk. III, Ch. 31, Ibid.

1255. Wenonah Stevens Abbott (1865–1950)

1 To-day the journey is ended,
I have worked out the mandates of fate;
Naked, alone, undefended,
I knock at the Uttermost Gate.

"A Soul's Soliloquy" *n.d.*

1256. Evangeline Booth (1865–1950)

1 Drink has drained more blood,
Hung more crepe,
Sold more houses,
Plunged more people into bankruptcy,
Armed more villains,
Slain more children,
Snapped more wedding rings,
Defiled more innocence,
Blinded more eyes,
Twisted more limbs,
Dethroned more reason,
Wrecked more manhood,
Dishonored more womanhood,
Broken more hearts,
Blasted more lives,
Driven more to suicide, and
Dug more graves than any other poisoned
Scourge that ever swept its death—
Dealing waves across the world.

"Good Housekeeping" *n.d.*

1257. Elsie De Wolfe (1865–1950)

1 It is the personality of the mistress that the home expresses. Men are forever guests in our home, no matter how much happiness they may find there.

Ch. 1, *The House in Good Taste* 1920

2 What a joyous thing is color! How influenced we all are by it, even if we are unconscious of how our sense of restfulness has been brought about.

Ch. 6, Ibid.

3 It does not matter whether one paints a picture, writes a poem, or carves a statue, simplicity is the mark of a master-hand.

Don't run away with the idea that it is easy to cook simply. It requires a long apprenticeship.

"Why I Wrote This Book," *Recipes for Successful Dining*
1934

1258. Voltairine de Cleyre (1866–1912)

1 [Anarchism is] . . . not only the denial of authority, not only a new economy, but a revision of the principles of morality. It means . . . self-responsibility, not leader-worship.

"The Burial of My Past Self" (1885), *The Selected Works of Voltairine de Cleyre* 1914

2 Consider the soul reflected on the advertising page. . . . Commercial man has set his image therein; let him regard himself when he gets time.

Ibid.

3 [Language] . . . this great instrument which men have jointly built . . . Every word the mystic embodiment of a thousand years of vanished passion, hope, desire, thought.

Ibid.

4 And Now Humanity, I turn to you;
I consecrate my service to the world!

Ibid.

5 Do I repent? Yes, I do; but wait till I tell you of what I repent and why. I repent that I ever believed a man could be anything but a living lie!

"Betrayed," Ibid.

6 I had never seen a book or heard a word to help me in my loneliness.

"The Making of an Anarchist," Ibid.

7 I die, as I have lived, a free spirit, an Anarchist, owing no allegiance to rulers, heavenly or earthly. . . . If my comrades wish to do aught for my memory, let them print my poems.

Journal (1912), Ibid.

1259. Dora Read Goodale (1866–1915)

1 The earth and sky, the day and night
Are melted in her depth of blue.

"Blue Violets" *n.d.*

2 The modest, lowly violet
In leaves of tender green inset,
So rich she cannot hide from view,
But covers all the bank with blue.

"Spring Scatters Far and Wide" *n.d.*

1260. Annie Johnson Flint (1866–1932)

1 Have you come to the Red Sea place in your life
Where, in spite of all you can do,
There is no way out, there is no way back,
There is no other way but through?

"At the Place of the Sea," St. 1 *n.d.*

2 The thrones are rocking to their fall—
It is the twilight of the Kings!

"The Twilight of the Kings" *n.d.*

1261. Eleanor Prescott Hammond (1866–1933)

1 Prone on my back I greet arriving day,
A day no different than the one just o'er;

When I will be, to practically say,
Considerably like I have been before.
Why then get up? Why wash, why eat, why pray?
—Oh, leave me lay!

"Oh, Leave Me Lay," *Atlantic Monthly* (Boston) *August
1922*

1262. Annie Sullivan (1866–1936)

1 I have thought about it a great deal, and the more I think the more certain I am that obedience is the gateway through which knowledge, yes, and love, too, enter the mind of the child.

Letter (11 March 1887), Quoted in *The Story of My Life*
by Helen Keller* 1903

*See 1458.

3 I am beginning to suspect all elaborate and special systems of education. They seem to me to be built on the supposition that every child is a kind of idiot who must be taught to think.

Letter (8 May 1887), Ibid.

4 It is a rare privilege to watch the birth, growth, and first feeble struggles of a living mind. . . .

Letter (22 May 1887), Ibid.

5 It's queer how ready people always are with advice in any real or imaginary emergency, and no matter how many times experience has shown them to be wrong, they continue to set forth their opinions, as if they had received them from the Almighty!

Letter (12 June 1887), Ibid.

6 It's a great mistake, I think, to put children off with falsehoods and nonsense, when their growing powers of observation and discrimination excite in them a desire to know about things.

Letter (28 August 1887), Ibid.

7 . . . people seldom see the halting and painful steps by which the most insignificant success is achieved.

Letter (30 October 1887), Ibid.

8 She likes stories that make her cry—I think we all do, it's so nice to feel sad when you've nothing in particular to be sad about.

Letter (12 December 1887), Ibid.

9 I see no sense in "faking" conversation for the sake of teaching language. It's stupid and deadening to pupil and teacher. Talk should be natural and have for its object an exchange of ideas.

Letter (1 January 1888), Ibid.

10 The truth is not wonderful enough to suit the newspapers; so they enlarge upon it and invent ridiculous embellishments.

Letter (4 March 1888), Ibid.

11 Why, it is as easy to teach the name of an idea, if it is clearly formulated in the child's mind, as to teach the name of any object.

Letter (15 May 1888), Ibid.

12 Language grows out of life, out of its needs and experiences . . . . *Language* and *knowledge* are indissolubly connected; they are interdependent. Good work in language presupposes and depends on a real knowledge of things.

Speech, American Association to Promote the Teaching of
Speech to the Deaf (July 1894), Ibid.

13 I have never taught language for the PURPOSE of teaching it; but invariably used language as a medium for the communica-

tion of *thought*; thus the learning of language was *coincident* with the acquisition of knowledge.

Ibid.

1263. Mary Elizabeth Arnim (1866–1941)

1 I suppose the fact is that no friendship can stand the breakfast test. . . .Civilisation has done away with curl-papers, yet at that hour the soul of the Hausfrau is as tightly screwed up in them as was ever her grandmother's hair, and though my body comes down mechanically, having been trained that way by punctual parents, my soul never thinks of beginning to wake up for other people till lunch-time, and never does so completely till it has been taken out of doors and aired in the sunshine. Who can begin conventional amiability the first thing in the morning? It is the hour of savage instincts and natural tendencies; it is the triumph of the Disagreeable and the Cross. I am convinced that the Muses and the Graces never thought of having breakfast anywhere but in bed.

"September 15th," *Elizabeth and Her German Garden* 1898

2 A marriage, she found, with someone of a different breed is fruitful of small rubs. . . .

Ch. 1, *Mr. Skeffington* 1940

3 Life was certainly a queer business—so brief, yet such a lot of it; so substantial, yet in a few years, which behaved like minutes, all scattered and anyhow.

Ibid.

4 She had been dragged in the most humiliating of all dusts, the dust reserved for older women who let themselves be approached, on amorous lines, by boys. . . . It had all been pure vanity, all just a wish, in these waning days of hers, still to feel power, still to have the assurance of her beauty and its effects.

Ch. 3, Ibid.

5 . . . without it [love], without, anyhow, the capacity for it, people didn't seem to be much good. Dry as bones, cold as stones, they seemed to become, when love was done; inhuman, indifferent, self-absorbed, numb.

Ch. 5, Ibid.

6 Strange that the vanity which accompanies beauty—excusable, perhaps, when there is such great beauty, or at any rate understandable—should persist after the beauty is gone.

Ch. 6, Ibid.

7 How could one live, while such things were going on? How could one endure consciousness, except by giving oneself up wholly and forever to helping, and comforting, and at last, at last, perhaps healing?

Ch. 11, Ibid.

1264. Martha Dickinson Bianchi (1866–1943)

1 Deeper than chords that search the soul and die,
Mocking to ashes color's hot array,—
Closer than touch,—within out hearts they lie—
The words we do not say.

"The Words We Do Not Say" *n.d.*

1265. Beatrix Potter (1866–1943)

1 Once upon a time there were four little Rabbits, and their names were—Flopsy, Mopsy, Cottontail, and Peter.

The Tale of Peter Rabbit 1904

2 The water was all slippy-sloppy in the larder and the back passage. But Mr. Jeremy liked getting his feet wet; nobody ever scolded him, and he never caught a cold.

The Tale of Mr. Jeremy Fisher 1906

1266. Emmeline Pethick-Lawrence (1867–?)

1 Under the flagstones of the pavements in London lie the dormant seeds of life—ready to spring into blossom if the opportunity should ever occur. And under our cruel and repressive financial and economic system lie dormant human energy and joy that are ready to burst into flower. So far as a drop may be compared to the ocean, we witnessed in many individual cases that releasing of the spirit that is possible when the conditions of life afford some modicum of dignity and of leisure.

Ch. 7, *My Part in a Changing World* 1938

2 I find in many writers of the present day a persistent inclination to refer to the suffrage movement as inspired by enmity towards men. So far as my own experience goes, during the six years with which I was connected with the campaign no effort was spared to instruct the public that we had no enemy except a Government that was false to its professions. We refused to have any quarrel even with the police who, acting under their orders, did us violence, or the prison officials and doctors who became the agents of torture in prison because their livelihood depended upon their obedience.

Ch. 19, Ibid.

3 A change of heart is the essence of all other change and it is brought about by a re-education of the mind.

Ch. 23, Ibid.

1267. Pearl Craigie (1867–1906)

1 To love is to know the sacrifices which eternity exacts from life.

Ch. 25, *Schools of Saints* 1897

2 Women may be whole oceans deeper than we are, but they are also a whole paradise better. She may have got us out of Eden, but as a compensation she makes the earth very pleasant.

Act III, *The Ambassador* 1898

3 A false success made by the good humor of outside influences is always peaceful; a real success made by the qualities of the thing itself is always a declaration of war.

The Dream and the Business 1906

1268. C.J. Walker (1867–1919)

1 We must not let our love of our country, our patriotic loyalty, cause us to abate one whit in our protest against wrong and injustice.

Speech, "Women's Duty to Women,"
Walker Convention* 1917
*More than 200 agents of Walker's beauty business attended.

2 I am not ashamed of my past; I am not ashamed of my humble beginning. Don't think because you have to go down in the wash-tub that you are any less a lady!

Quoted in Ch. 3, *Hope in a Jar, The Making of America's Beauty Culture* by Kathy Peiss* 1998
*See 3275.

3 I am a woman who came from the cotton fields of the South. I was promoted from there to the washtub. Then I was pro-

moted to the cook kitchen, and from there I promoted *myself* into the business of manufacturing hair goods and preparations. I have built my own factory on my own ground.

Quoted in *Women Inventors* by Linda Jacobs Altman *1997*

1269. Marie Curie (1867–1934)

1 All my life through, the new sights of Nature made me rejoice like a child.

*Pierre Curie** 1923

*French chemist, her partner and husband (1859–1906).

2 . . . I was taught that the way of progress is neither swift nor easy. . . .

Ibid.

3 You cannot hope to build a better world without improving the individuals. To that end each of us must work for his own improvement, and at the same time share a general responsibility for all humanity, our particular duty being to aid those to whom we think we can be most useful.

Ibid.

4 One never notices what has been done; one can only see what remains to be done. . . .

Letter to her brother (18 March 1894), Ibid.

5 Men of moral and intellectual distinction could scarcely agree to teach in schools where an alien attitude was forced upon them.

Ibid.

6 After all, science is essentially international, and it is only through lack of the historical sense that national qualities have been attributed to it.

"Intellectual Co-operation," *Memorandum* (magazine) *16 June 1926*

7 Indeed, if the mentality of the scholars of the various countries, as revealed by the recent war, often appears to be on a lower level than that of the less cultured masses, it is because there is a danger inherent in all power that is not disciplined and directed toward the higher aims which alone are worthy of it.

Ibid.

8 I have no dress except the one I wear every day. If you are going to be kind enough to give me one, please let it be practical and dark so that I can put it on afterwards to go to the laboratory.

Letter to a Friend (1849?), Quoted in "She Did Not Know How to Be Famous," *Party of One* by Clifton Fadiman* *1955*

*American writer, editor and radio host (1904–1999).

9 It was like a new world opened to me, the world of science, which I was at last permitted to know in all liberty.

Quoted in Lecture by Nanny Fröman, Royal Academy of Sciences (Stockholm) *28 February 1996*

10 The shattering of our voluntary isolation was a cause of real suffering for us and had all the effects of disaster.*

27 September 1997, Ibid.

*In response to the enormous interest from the public and the media after she and her husband won the Nobel Prize in 1903.

11 I am 38 and able to support myself.*

Remark (1906), Ibid.

* Reference to her refusal of a pension after Pierre was killed by a horse-drawn wagon; at the time her daughters Irène and Ève (see 1844) were nine and two years old.

12 Nothing in life is to be feared. It is only to be understood.

Ibid.

13 Life is not easy for any of us. But what of that? We must have perseverance and above all confidence in ourselves. We must believe that we are gifted for something, and that this thing, at whatever cost, must be attained.

Ibid.

1270. Ellen O'Grady (1867–1938)

1 Crime takes but a moment but justice an eternity.

Quoted in "Woman Police Deputy Is Writer of Poetry" by Djuna Barnes,* *New York Sun Magazine 1918*

* See 1638.

1271. Käthe Kollwitz (1867–1945)

1 No longer diverted by other emotions, I work the way a cow grazes.

(April 1910), *Diaries and Letters*, Hans Kollwitz, ed. *1955*

2 Sensuality is burgeoning. . . . I feel at once grave, ill at ease and happy as I watch our children—our *children*—growing to meet the greatest of instincts. May it have mercy on them!

(5 May 1910), Ibid.

3 For the last third of life there remains only work. It alone is always stimulating, rejuvenating, exciting and satisfying.

(1 January 1912), Ibid.

4 Where do all the women who have watched so carefully over the lives of their beloved ones get the heroism to send them to face the cannon?

(27 August 1914), Ibid.

5 I do not want to die . . . until I have faithfully made the most of my talent and cultivated the seed that was placed in me until the last small twig has grown.

Ibid.

6 When we married, we took a leap in the dark. . . . There were grave contradictions in my own feelings. In the end I acted on this impulse: jump in—you'll manage to swim.

(1916), Ibid.

7 Men without joy seem like corpses.

(19 September 1918), Ibid.

8 Age remains age, that is, it pains, torments and subdues. When others see my scant achievements, they speak of a happy old age. I doubt that there is such a thing as a happy old age.

(1 January 1932), Ibid.

9 I am afraid of dying—but being dead, oh yes, that to me is often an appealing prospect.

(December 1941), Ibid.

10 Although my leaning toward the male sex was dominant, I also felt frequently drawn toward my own sex—an inclination which I could not correctly interpret until much later on. As a matter of fact I believe that bisexuality is almost a necessary factor in artistic production; at any rate, the tinge of masculinity within me helped me in my work.

(1942), Ibid.

1272. Laura Ingalls Wilder (1867–1957)

1 It was so hard to be good all the time, every day, for a whole year.

Ch. 4, *Little House in the Big Woods 1932*

2   "Did little girls have to be as good as that?" Laura asked, and Ma said: "It was harder for little girls. Because they had to behave like little ladies all the time, not only on Sundays. Little girls could never slide downhill, like boys. Little girls had to sit in the house and stitch on samplers."

Ch. 5, Ibid.

3   "That machine's a great invention!" he said. "Other folks can stick to old-fashioned ways if they want to, but I'm all for progress. It's a great age we're living in."

Ch. 12, Ibid.

1273. Edith Hamilton (1867–1963)

1   The fundamental fact about the Greek was that he had to use his mind. The ancient priests had said, "Thus far and no farther. We set the limits of thought." The Greeks said, "All things are to be examined and called into question. There are no limits set on thought."

The Greek Way 1930

2   The Greeks were the first intellectualists. In a world where the irrational had played the chief role, they came forward as the protagonists of the mind.

Ch. 1, Ibid.

3   The anthropologists are busy, indeed, and ready to transport us back into the savage forest where all human things . . . have their beginnings; but the seed never explains the flower.

Ibid.

4   Mind and spirit together make up that which separates us from the rest of the animal world, that which enables a man to know the truth and that which enables him to die for the truth.

Ibid.

5   The spirit has not essentially anything to do with what is outside of itself. It is mind that keeps hold of reality.

Ch. 3, Ibid.

6   The English method [of poetry] is to fill the mind with beauty; the Greek method was to set the mind to work.

Ch. 4, Ibid.

7   None but a poet can write a tragedy. For tragedy is nothing less that pain transmuted into exaltation by the alchemy of poetry, and if poetry is true knowledge and the great poet's guides safe to follow, this transmutation has arresting implications.

Ch. 11, Ibid.

8   A people's literature is the great textbook for real knowledge of them. The writings of the day show the quality of the people as no historical reconstruction can.

Preface, The Roman Way 1932

9   Theories that go counter to the facts of human nature are foredoomed.

Ch. 1, Ibid.

10 A good-humored crowd, those people who filled the Roman theatre in its first days of popularity, easily appealed to by any sentimental interest, eager to have the wicked punished—but not too severely—and the good live happily after. No occasions wanted for intellectual exertion, no wit for deft malice; fun such as could be passably enjoyed, broad with a flavor of obscenity. Most marked characteristic of all, a love of mediocrity, a complete satisfaction with the average. The people who applauded these plays wanted nothing bigger than their own small selves. They were democratic.

Ch. 2, Ibid.

11 There are few efforts more conducive to humility than that of the translator trying to communicate an incommunicable beauty. Yet, unless we do try, something unique and never surpassed will cease to exist except in the libraries of a few inquisitive book lovers.

Introduction, Three Greek Plays 1937

12 No facts however indubitably detected, no effort or reason however magnificently maintained, can prove that Bach's music is beautiful.

Witness to the Truth 1948

13 Christ must be rediscovered perpetually.

Ch. 1, Ibid.

14 So Socrates loved the truth and so he made it live. He brought it down into the homes and hearts of men because he showed it to them in himself, the spirit of truth manifest in the only way that can be, in the flesh.

Ibid.

15 "Bless me," he [Socrates*] said, looking around the market where all an Athenian wanted lay piled in glowing profusion, "what a lot of things there are a man can do without."

Ibid.

*Greek philosopher (470?–399 B.C.E.).

16 A life can be more lasting than systems of thought.

Ch. 2, Ibid.

17 Ages of faith and of unbelief are always said to mark the course of history.

Ch. 9, Ibid.

18 But it is not hard work which is dreary; it is superficial work. That is always boring in the long run, and it has always seemed strange to me that in our endless discussions about education so little stress is ever laid on the pleasure of becoming an educated person, the enormous interest it adds to life. To be able to be caught up in the world of thought—that is to be educated.

Quoted in the Bryn Mawr School Bulletin 1959

1274. Queen Mary (1867–1963)

1   God grant we may not have a European war thrust upon us, and for such a stupid reason too, no I don't mean stupid, but to have to go to war on account of tiresome Servia beggars belief.

Letter to her aunt, Princess Augusta, Grand-Duchess of Mecklenburg-Strelitz (Germany) 28 July 1914

1275. Guida Diehl (1868–?)

1   Never did Hitler* promise to the masses in his rousing speeches any material advantage whatever. On the contrary he pleaded with them to turn aside from every form of advantage-seeking and serve the great thought: Honor, Freedom, Fatherland!

The German Woman and National Socialism 1933

*Adolf H—, Austrian-born Nazi dictator (1889–1945).

2   We long to see Men and Heroes who scorn fate. . . . Call us to every service, even to weapons!

Ibid.

1276. Eleanor H. Porter (1868–1920)

1 "Oh, yes, the game was to just find something about everything to be glad about—not matter what 'twas," rejoined Pollyanna earnestly. "And we began right then—on the crutches."

"Well, goodness me! I can't see anythin' ter be glad about—getting' a pair of crutches when you wanted a doll!"

"Goosey! Why, just be glad because you *don't—need—'em*!"

Ch. 5, *Pollyanna* 1912

2 "Oh, but Aunt Polly, Aunt Polly, you haven't left me any time at all just to—to live."

"To live, child! What do you mean? As if you weren't living all the time!"

"Oh, of course I'd be *breathing* all the time I was doing those things, Aunt Polly, but I wouldn't be living. You breath all the time you're sleep, but you aren't living. I mean *living*—doing the things you want to do. . . . That's what I call living, Aunt Polly. Just breathing isn't living!"

Ch. 7, Ibid.

3 "What men and women need is encouragement. . . . Instead of always harping on a man's faults, tell him of his virtues. Try to pull him out of his rut of bad habits. Hold up to him his better self, his *real* self that can dare and do and win out . . . People radiate what is in their minds and in their hearts."

Ch. 5, Ibid.

4 ". . . he said, too, that he wouldn't *stay* a minister a minute if 'twasn't for the rejoicing texts. . . . Of course the Bible didn't name 'em that. But it's all those that begin 'Be glad in the Lord,' or 'Rejoice greatly,' or 'Shout for joy,' and all that, you know—such a lot of 'em. Once, when father felt specially bad, he counted 'em. There were eight hundred of 'em."

Ch. 22, Ibid.

1277. Mary Parker Follett (1868–1933)

1 Majority rule rests on numbers; democracy rests on the well-grounded assumption that society is neither a collection of units nor an organism but a network of human relations.

The New State—Group Organisation, the Solution for Popular Government (p. 7) 1918

2 Conflict is resolved not through compromise, but through invention.

Ibid.

3 The essential feature of common thought is not that it is held in common but that it has been produced in common...The core of the social process is not likeness, but the harmonizing of differences through interpenetration.

Ibid.

4 We cannot put the individual on one side and society on the other, we must understand the complete interrelation of the two. Each has no value, no existence without the other. The individual is created by that process. There is no such thing as a self-made Man.

Ibid.

5 It is only in a complex state of society that any large degree of freedom is possible, because nothing else can supply the many opportunities necessary to work out freedom.

Ibid.

6 I am free when I am functioning here in time and space as the creative will...freedom by our definition is obedience to the law of one's nature.

Ibid.

7 ...we are learning to think of society as a psychic process. This conception must replace the old and wholly erroneous idea of society as a collection of units, and the later and only less misleading theory of society as an organism.*

Ibid.

*In a footnote, she clarifies her use of "later" because the biological analogy was different from the organism of medieval doctrine.

8 We want the single voice but not the single note; that is the secret of the group. The enthusiasm and unanimity of a mass-meeting may warm an inexperienced heart, but the experienced know that this unanimity is largely superficial and is based on the spread of similar ideas, not the unifying of differences.

Ibid.

9 Our rate of progress, then, and the degree in which we actualize the perfect democracy, depend upon our understanding that man has the power of creating, and that he gets this power through his capacity to join with others to form a real whole, a living group.

Ibid.

10 The unifying of opposites is the eternal process.

Ch. II, Ibid.

11 The object of a conference is not to get at a lot of different ideas, as is often thought, but just the opposite—to get at one idea. There is nothing rigid or fixed about thoughts, they are entirely plastic, and ready to yield themselves completely to their master—the group spirit.

Ibid.

12 But compromise is still on the same plane as fighting. War will continue—between capital and labor, between nation and nation—until we relinquish the ideas of compromise and concession.

Ibid.

13 The essence of society is difference, related difference. "Give me your difference" is the cry of society to-day to every man.

Ch. III, Ibid.

14 Imitation is for the shirkers, like-mindedness for the comfort lovers, unifying for the creators.

Ibid.

15 Man's biological inheritance is not his only life. And the progress of man means that this inheritance shall occupy a less and less important place relatively.

Ibid.

16 Unity, not uniformity, must be our aim. We attain unity only through variety. Differences must be integrated, not annihilated, nor absorbed.

Ibid.

17 The higher the degree of social organization the more it is based on a very wide diversity among its members.

Ibid.

18 I think it better when practicable to keep to verbs; the value of nouns is chiefly for post mortems.

(p. 88), *Creative Experience* 1924

19 The paradox of American democracy has been that its slogan of equal opportunity has meant, often, equal opportunity to get power over your fellows.

(p. 180) Ibid.

20 All majority control is getting power over. Genuine control is activity between, not influence over.

(p. 186) *Ibid.*

21 We can confer authority; but power or capacity, no man can give or take.

Lecture, "Power," Bureau of Personnel Administration conference (New York, January 1925), *Dynamic Administration: The Collected Papers of Mary Parker Follett*, Henry C. Metcalf and L. Urwick, eds. *1941*

1278. Mary Hunter Austin (1868–1934)

1 When a woman ceases to alter the fashion of her hair, you guess that she has passed the crisis of her experience.

The Land of Little Rain 1903

2 It is a still field, this of my neighbor's, though so busy, and admirably compounded for variety and pleasantness,—a little sand, a little loam, a grassy plot, a stony rise or two, a full brown stream, a little touch of humanness, a footpath trodden out by moccasins. Naboth expects to make town lots of it and his fortune in one and the same day; but when I take the trail to talk with old Seyavi at the campoodie, it occurs to me that though the field may serve a good turn in those days it will hardly be happier. No, certainly not happier.

"My Neighbor's Field," *Ibid.*

3 Choose a hill country for storms. There all the business of the weather is carried on above your horizon and loses its terror in familiarity. When you come to think about it, the disastrous storms are on the levels, sea or sand or plains. There you get only a hint of what is about to happen, the fume of the gods rising from their meeting place under the rim of the world; and when it breaks upon you there is no stay nor shelter. The terrible mewings and mouthings of a Kansas wind have the added terror of viewlessness. You are lapped in them like uprooted grass; suspect them of a personal grudge. But the storms of hill countries have other business.

"Nurslings of the Sky," *Ibid.*

4 The increase of wild creatures is in proportion to the things they feed upon: the more carrion the more buzzards. The end of the third successive dry year bred them beyond belief. The first year quail mated sparingly; the second year the wild oats matured no seed; the third, cattle died in their tracks with their heads towards the stopped watercourses. And that year the scavengers were as black as the plague all across the mesa and up the treeless, tumbled hills.

"The Scavengers," *Ibid.*

5 Life set itself to new processions of seed-time and harvest, the skin newly turned to seasonal variations, the very blood humming to new altitudes. The rhythm of walking, always a recognizable background for our thoughts, altered from the militaristic stride to the jog of the wide unrutted earth.

The American Rhythm 1923

6 What need has he of clocks who knows
When highest peaks are gilt and rose
Day has begun?

"Clocks and Calendars," St. 1 *n.d.*

7 Oh, the Shepards in Judea!
Do you think the shepards know
How the whole round world is brightened
In the ruddy Christmas glow?

"The Shepards in Judea" *n.d.*

8 Never was it printed on a page,
Never was it spoken, never heard.

"Whisper of the Wind" *n.d.*

1279. Agnes Lee (1868–1939)

1 Bed is the boon for me!
It's well to bake and sweep,
But hear the word of old Lizette:
It's better than all to sleep.

"Old Lizette on Sleep," St. 1 *n.d.*

2 But I'll not venture in the drift
Out of this bright security,
Till enough footsteps come and go
To make a path for me.

"Convention" *n.d.*

3 Oh, mine was rosy as a bough
Blooming with roses, sent, somehow,
To bloom for me!
His balmy fingers left a thrill
Deep in my breast that warms me still.

"Motherhood," St. 5 *n.d.*

1280. Florence Prag Kahn (1868–1948)

1 Preparedness never caused a war and unpreparedness never prevented one.

Quoted in *American Political Women* by Esther Stineman *1980*

1281. Maude Glasgow (1868–1955)

1 When new-born humanity was learning to stand upright, it depended much on its mother and stood close to her protecting side. Then women were goddesses, they conducted divine worship, woman's voice was heard in council, she was loved and revered and genealogies were reckoned through her. . . .
As the race grew older, rationality flourished at the expense of moral sense.

The Subjection of Women and the Traditions of Men 1940

1282. Caroline Otero (1868–1965)

1 . . . Paco took care of me; protected me; taught me to dance and sing, and was my lover. It was the first time in over two years that I knew where I was going to sleep every night, and the first time in my life that I knew there would be something for me to eat when I woke up. Then Paco fell in love with me; wanted me to marry him, and spoiled everything.

Quoted in *The Pittsburgh Leader 11 April 1904*

2 There are two things in Spain which are not found elsewhere— flowers, lovely flowers in such abundance, and bull fights. I love both.

Quoted in *New York World 10 May 1908*

1283. Alexandra David-Néel (1868–1969)

1 I wish to live philosophy on the spot and undergo physical and spiritual training, not just read about them.

Quoted in "Walker in the Sky" by Jane Dedman, *Quest May/June 1978*

2 Whatever those unacquainted with it may think, solitude and utter loneliness are far from being devoid of charm. Words cannot convey the almost voluptuous sweetness of the feelings

experience . . . Mind and senses develop their sensibility in this contemplative life made up of continual observations and reflections. Does one become a visionary or, rather, is it not that one has been blind until them?

Ibid.

3 To the one who knows how to look and feel, every moment of this free wandering life is an enchantment.

Ibid.

1284. Anna Bunston De Bary (1869–?)

1 Close to the sod there can be seen
A thought of God in white and green.

"The Snowdrop" *n.d.*

1285. Margaret Fairless Barber (1869–1901)

1 . . . Earth, my Mother, whom I love.

Dedication, *The Roadmender*, Vol. I *1900*

2 The people who make no roads are ruled out from intellectual participation in the world's brotherhood.

Ch. 5, Ibid.

3 Necessity can set me helpless on my back, but she cannot keep me there; nor can four walls limit my vision.

Ch. 6, Vol. II, Ibid.

4 Revelation is always measured by capacity.

Ch. 3, Vol. III, Ibid.

5 To look backward for a while is to refresh the eye, to restore it, and to render it the more fit for its prime function of looking forward.

Ibid.

6 This place is peace and would be silent peace were it not for an Eisteddfod of small birds outvying each other with an eagerness which cannot wait until the last candidate has finished.

Letter (19 May 1900), *The Complete Works of Michael Fairless 1932*

7 "In my Father's house are many mansions," and I suppose we are stripped of something in each till at last we can do without the Tree of Life and the candle and the sun and the protecting gates, in the innermost mansion which is the Beatific Vision.

Ibid.

1286. Charlotte Mew (1869–1928)

1 When us was wed she turned afraid
Of love and me and all things human;
Like the shut of a winter's day.

"The Farmer's Bride," *Collected Poems 1916*

2 . . . Oh! my God! the down,
The soft young down of her, the brown,
The brown of her. . . .

St. 5, Ibid.

1287. Corra May Harris (1869–1935)

1 The deadly monotony of Christian country life . . .

Ch. 3, *A Circuit Rider's Wife 1910*

2 This is the wonderful thing about the pure in heart—they do see God.

Ch. 6, Ibid.

3 No one has yet had the courage to memorialize his wealth on his tombstone. A dollar mark would not look well there.

Ch. 11, Ibid.

4 So long as a man attends to his business the public does not count his drinks. When he fails they notice if he takes even a glass of root beer.

Ch. 6, *Eve's Second Husband 1910*

5 Adam was a man who could believe any statement he could evolve out of his ambitious imagination easier than he could believe the literal facts of his life.

Ch. 7, Ibid.

6 "The world smacks most of us out of shape so soon."

Ch. 14, Ibid.

7 A woman would rather visit her own grave than the place where she has been young and beautiful after she is aged and ugly.

Ibid.

1288. Nadezhda Konstanitovna Krupskaia (1869–1939)

1 Solidarity among the male and female workers, a general cause, general goals, a general path to that goal—that is the solution to the "woman" question in the working-class environment.

Editorial, *Rabotnitsa* (Woman Worker) *1913*

1289. Emma Goldman (1869–1940)

1 In taking out an insurance policy one pays for it in dollars and cents, always at liberty to discontinue payments. If, however, woman's premium is a husband, she pays for it with her name, her privacy, her self-respect, her very life, "until death doth part."

"Marriage and Love," *Anarchism and Other Essays 1910*

2 Only when human sorrows are turned into a toy with glaring colors will baby people become interested—for a while at least. The people are a very fickle baby that must have new toys every day.

"The Traffic in Women," Ibid.

3 Anarchism is the only philosophy which brings to man the consciousness of himself; which maintains that God, the State, and society are non-existent, that their promises are null and void, since they can be fulfilled only through man's subordination. Anarchism is therefore the teacher of the unity of life; not merely in nature, but in man.

"Anarchism: What It Really Stands For," Ibid.

4 The State is the altar of political freedom and, like the religious altar, it is maintained for the purpose of human sacrifice.

Ibid.

5 The political arena leaves one no alternative, one must either be a dunce or a rogue.

Ibid.

6 Poor human nature, what horrible crimes have been committed in thy name!

Ibid.

7 Crime is naught but misdirected energy.

Ibid.

8 Rather would I have the love songs of romantic ages, rather Don Juan and Madame Venus, rather an elopement by ladder and rope on a moonlight night, followed by the father's curse, mother's moans, and the moral comments of neighbors, than correctness and propriety measured by yardsticks.
"The Tragedy of Women's Emancipation," Ibid.

9 The higher mental development of woman, the less possible it is for her to meet a congenial male who will see in her, not only sex, but also the human being, the friend, the comrade and strong individuality, who cannot and ought not lose a single trait of her character.
Ibid.

10 There is no hope even that woman, with her right to vote, will ever purify politics.
Ibid.

11 True, the movement for women's rights has broken many old fetters, but it has also forged new ones.
Ibid.

12 Merely external emancipation has made of the modern woman an artificial being. . . . Now, woman is confronted with the necessity of emancipating herself from emancipation, if she really desires to be free.
Ibid.

13 Politics is the reflex of the business and industrial world. . . .
Ibid.

14 These internal tyrants [conscience] . . . these busybodies, moral detectives, jailers of the human spirit, what will they say?
Ibid.

15 If love does not know how to give and take without restrictions, it is not love, but a transaction that never fails to lay stress on a plus and a minus
Ibid.

16 . . . true emancipation begins neither at the polls nor in courts. It begins in woman's soul.
Ibid.

17 . . . the most vital right is the right to love and be loved.
Ibid.

18 Man has bought brains, but all the millions in the world have failed to buy love. Man has subdued bodies, but all the power on earth has been unable to subdue love. Man has conquered whole nations but all his armies could not conquer love. Man has chained and fettered the spirit, but he has been utterly helpless before love. High on a throne, with all the splendor and pomp his gold can command, man is yet poor and desolate, if love passes him by. And if it stays, the poorest hovel is radiant with warmth, with light and color. Thus love has the magic power to make of a beggar a king. Yes, love is free; it can dwell in no other atmosphere. In freedom it gives itself unreservedly, abundantly, completely.
"Marriage and Love," Ibid.

19 The important and only God of practical American life: Can the man make a living? Can he support a wife? That is the only thing that justifies marriage.
Ibid.

20 Capitalism . . . has . . . grown into a huge insatiable monster.
"The Social Aspect of Birth Control,"
Mother Earth April 1916

21 . . . the soldier's business is to take life. For that he is paid by the State, eulogized by political charlatans and upheld by public hysteria. But woman's function is to give life, yet neither the State nor politicians nor public opinion have ever made the slightest provision in return for the life woman has given.
Ibid.

22 No, it is not because woman is lacking in responsibility, but because she has too much of the latter that she demands to know how to prevent conception.
Ibid.

23 After all, that is what laws are for, to be made and unmade.
Ibid.

24 But even judges sometimes progress.
Ibid.

25 Anarchy stands for the liberation of the human mind from the dominion of religion; the liberation of the human body from the dominion of property; liberation from the shackles and restraints of government.
Anarchism 1917

26 . . . no great idea in its beginning can ever be within the law. How can it be within the law? The law is stationary. The law is fixed. The law is a chariot wheel which binds us all regardless of conditions or place or time.
"Address to the Jury," Mother Earth July 1917

27 . . . democracy must first be safe for America before it can be safe for the world.
Ibid.

28 . . . the experience of Russia, more than any theories, has demonstrated that all government, whatever its forms or pretenses, is a dead weight that paralyzes the free spirit and activities of the masses.
My Disillusionment in Russia 1923

29 The ultimate end of all revolutionary social change is to establish the sanctity of human life, the dignity of man, the right of every human being to liberty and well-being.
My Further Disillusionment in Russia 1924

30 Since every effort in our educational life seems to be directed toward making of the child a being foreign to itself, it must of necessity produce individuals foreign to one another, and in everlasting antagonism with each other.
"The Child and Its Enemies," Mother Earth
(New York, April 1906), Pt. 2, Ibid.

31 The history of progress is written in the blood of men and women who have dared to espouse an unpopular cause, as, for instance, the black man's right to his body, or woman's right to her soul.
"What I Believe" (New York World, 1908), Pt. 1, Ibid.

32 Every daring attempt to make a great change in existing conditions, every lofty vision of new possibilities for the human race, has been labeled Utopian.
Lecture, "Socialism: Caught in the Political Trap"
(c. 1912), Ibid.

33 Jealousy is indeed a poor medium to secure love, but it is a secure medium to destroy one's self-respect. For jealous people, like dope-fiends, stoop to the lowest level and in the end inspire only disgust and loathing.
Lecture, "Jealousy: Causes and a Possible Cure" (c. 1912),
Pt. 2, Ibid.

34 It is essential that we realize once and for all that man is much more of a sex creature than a moral creature. The former is inherent, the other is grafted on.

> Lecture, "The Social Importance of the Modern School" (c. 1912), Ibid.

35 Heaven must be an awfully dull place if the poor in spirit* live there.

> "The Failure of Christianity," *Mother Earth* (New York, April 1913), Ibid.
> * Reference to first beatitude, "Blessed are the poor in spirit for theirs is the kingdom of heaven" (New Testament, Matthew 5:3).

36 Revolution is but thought carried into action.

> Quoted in *The Feminist Papers* by Alice Rossi* 1973
> *See 2213.

37 There's never been a good government.

> Quoted by Katherine Anne Porter* in *The Los Angeles Times* 7 July 1974
> *See 1608.

1290. Carolyn Wells (1869–1942)

1 Total is a book. We find it
Just a little past its prime;
And departing leaves behind it
Footprints on the sands of time.

> "Four," St. 3, *At the Sign of the Sphinx* 1896

2 "Women are all right, in their place—which, by the way, is not necessarily in the home—but a family feud, of all things, calls for masculine management and skill!"

> Ch. 1, *In the Onyx Lobby* 1920

3 "I'll bet Sherlock Holmes could find a lot of data just by going over the floor with a lens."

"He could in a story book—and do you know why? Because the clews and things, in a story, are all put there for him by the property man. Like a salted mine. But in real life, there's nothing doing of that sort."

> Ch. 5, Ibid.

4 There was a young man of St. Kitts
Who was very much troubled with fits;
The eclipse of the moon
Threw him into a swoon,
When he tumbled and broke into bits.

> "Limericks," No. 3, *The Book of Humorous Verse* 1920

5 A Tutor who tooted the flute
Tried to teach two young tutors to toot;
Said the two to the Tutor,
"Is it harder to toot, or
To tutor two tutors to toot?"

> "Limericks," No. 6, Ibid.

6 The earth has rolled around again and harvest time is here,
The glory of the seasons and the crown of all the years.

> "The Meaning of Thanksgiving Day" 1922

7 I love the Christmas–tide, and yet;
I notice this, each year I live;
I always like the gifts I get,
But how I love the gifts I give!

> "A Thought" *n.d.*

8 When Venus said "Spell no for me,"
"N-O" Dan Cupid wrote with glee,

And smiled at his success:
"Ah, child," said Venus, laughing low,
"We women do not spell it so,
We spell it Y-E-S."

> "The Spelling Lesson" *n.d.*

9 But Woman is rare beyond compare,
The poets tell us so;
How little they know of Woman
Who only Women know!

> "Woman" *n.d.*

10 A canner can can
Anything that he can,
But a canner can't can a can, can he?

> "The Canner" *n.d.*

11 The books we think we ought to read are poky, dull, and dry;
The books that we would like to read we are ashamed to buy;
The books that people talk about we never can recall;
And the books that people give us, oh, they're the worst of all.

> "On Books" *n.d.*

1291. Else Lasker-Schüler (1869–1945)

1 We shall rest from love like two rare beasts
In the high reeds behind this world.

> "A Love Song" (c. 1902), *The Other Voices*, Carol Cosman, ed. 1975

2 MEPHISTO. Let me ask you, Doctor Faust, with all due respect, why He created me, the Devil, from slime and scorn to live forever?

> Ibid.

4 Theater is theater! Theater isn't a lecture hall for medicine or any other scientific discipline....We do not want to go home from a performance saddened or refined but rather shaken by the joy of sorrow or even pleasure.

> "Das Konzert" (1920–32) in *Gesammelte Werke*, Vol. 2, Nos. 635–38 (1962), cited in, *The Divided Home/Land: Contemporary German Women's Plays*, Sue-Ellen Case,* ed. 1988
> *See 3625.

1292. Jessie Rittenhouse (1869–1948)

1 I worked for a menial's hire,
Only to learn, dismayed,
That any wage I had asked of life,
Life would have paid.

> "My Wage" *n.d.*

2 My debt to you, Beloved,
Is one I cannot pay
In any coin of any realm
On any reckoning day.

> "Debt" *n.d.*

1293. Elsa Barker (1869–1954)

1 They never fail who light
Their lamp of faith at the unwavering flame
Burnt for the altar service of the Race
Since the beginning.

> "The Frozen Grail" *1910*

1294. Nancy Ford Cones (1869–1962)

1 Lonely? Dull? At Road's End [her home]? Not as long as I can see the catkins from my door and our maple trees in early spring, or tramp through the misty April wood in search of wildflowers to photograph and color, or watch the birds nesting about our house. Not as long as I can have our friends gather around our fireplace or about our stone tables for a picnic under the maples in the summer.

Quoted in "Rediscovering the Lady from Loveland" by Owen Findsen, *The Cincinnati Enquirer* 9 November 1980

1295. Olive Dargan (1869–1968)

1 Be a God, your spirit cried;
Tread with feet that burn the dew;
Dress with clouds your locks of pride;
Be a child, God said to you.

"To William Blake"* *n.d.*

*English artist and poet (1757–1827).

2 The mountains lie in curves so tender
I want to lay my arm about them
As God does.

"Twilight" *n.d.*

1296. Alice Hamilton (1869–1970)

1 In those days [her childhood] children invented their own games; grownups looked after health, studies, manners, and morals, but amusement was not their responsibility.

(p. 25), *Exploring the Dangerous Trades* (autobiography) 1943

2 I had to accept the thinly veiled contempt of many of my teachers and fellow students because I was at once a woman and an American, therefore uneducated and incapable of real study.*

(p. 47), Ibid.

*Reference to the time when she and her sister, Edith, studied in Germany in 1894.

1297. Elizabeth Botume (fl. 1870s)

1 It was not an unusual thing to meet a woman coming from the fields, where she had been hoeing cotton, with a small bucket or cup on her head, and a hoe over her shoulder, contentedly smoking a pipe and briskly knitting as she strode along. I have seen, added to all these, a baby strapped to her back.

First Days Amongst the Contrabands 1893

1298. Clara Dolliver (fl. 1870s)

1 No merry frolics after tea,
No baby in the house.

"No Baby in the House," *No Baby in the House and Other Stories for Children* 1868

1299. Mary Pyper (fl. c. 1870)

1 I sat me down; 'twas autumn eve,
And I with sadness wept;
I laid me down at night, and then
'Twas winter, and I slept.

"Epitaph: A Life" *n.d.*

1300. Sarah Ann Sewell (fl. c. 1870)

1 It is a man's place to rule, and a woman's to yield. He must be held up as the head of the house, and it is her duty to bend so unmurmuringly to his wishes, that the rest of the household will follow her example, and treat him with the due respect his sex demands.

Woman and the Times We Live In 1869

1301. Lucia Clark Markham (1870–?)

1 To-night from deeps of loneliness I wake in wistful wonder
To a sudden sense of brightness, an immanence of blue.

"Bluebells" *n.d.*

1302. Laura Lee Davidson (1870–1949)

1 If I have learned nothing else in all these months in the woods, I have thoroughly learned to keep hands off the processes of nature.

A Winter of Content 1922

1303. Grace Hibbard (1870?–1911)

1 "An Honest Lawyer"—book just out—
What can the author have to say?
Reprint perhaps of ancient tome—
A work of fiction anyway.

"Books Received" *n.d.*

1304. Rosa Luxemburg (1870–1919)

1 . . . profits are springing, like weeds, from the fields of the dead.

The Crisis in the German Social Democracy 1919

2 Shamed, dishonored, wading in blood and dripping with filth, thus capitalist society stands.

Ibid.

3 Self-criticism, cruel, unsparing criticism that goes to the very root of the evil, is life and breath for the proletarian movement.

Ibid.

4 Reduced to its objective historic significance, the present world war as a whole is a competitive struggle of a fully developed capitalism for world supremacy, for the exploitation of the last remnant of noncapitalist world zones.

Ibid.

5 The high state of world-industrial development in capitalistic production finds expression in the extraordinary technical development and destructiveness of the instruments of war. . . .

Ibid.

6 It is a foolish delusion to believe that we need only live through the war, as a rabbit hides under the bush to await the end of a thunderstorm, to trot merrily off in his old accustomed gait when all is over.

Ibid.

7 Victory or defeat? It is the slogan of all-powerful militarism in every belligerent nation. . . . And yet, what can victory bring to the proletariat?

Ibid.

8 This madness will not stop, and this bloody nightmare of hell will not cease until the workers . . . will drown the bestial chorus of war agitators and the hoarse cry of capitalist hyenas with the mighty cry of labor, "Proletarians of all countries, unite!"

Ibid.

9   Passive fatalism can never be the role of a revolutionary
    party. . . .

                                                          Ibid.

10 . . . we will be victorious if we have not forgotten how to
    learn.

                                                          Ibid.

11 If the proletariat learns *from* this war and *in* this war to exert
    itself, to cast off its serfdom to the ruling classes, to become
    the lord of its own destiny, the shame and misery will not have
    been in vain.

                                                          Ibid.

12 Freedom for supporters of the government only, for the mem-
    bers of one party only—no matter how big its membership
    may be—is not freedom at all. Freedom is always freedom for
    the man who thinks differently.

        Quoted in *Die Russische Revolution* by Paul Froelich *1940*

13 Without general elections, without freedom of the press, free-
    dom of speech, freedom of assembly, without the free battle of
    opinions, life in every public institution withers away, becomes
    a caricature of itself, and bureaucracy rises as the only decid-
    ing factor.

                                                          Ibid.

14 That is Lenin.* Look at the self-willed, stubborn head. A real
    Russian peasant's head with a few faintly Asiatic lines. That
    man will try to overturn mountains. Perhaps he will be crushed
    by them. But he will never yield.

             Remark to Klara Zetkin,* *Reminiscences of Lenin* (1929),
             Quoted in Ch. 4, *Not By Politics Alone*, Tamara Deutsch,
                                                     ed. *1973*
    *Vladimir Ilich Lenin (1870–1924), Russian founder of the Bol-
    sheviks and leader of the Russian Revolution, and first head of the
    U.S.S.R. (1917–24). **See 1169.

15 I hope to die at my post; on the street, or in prison.
                              Letter to Sonia Liebnicht* *n.d.*
    *Wife of Karl L—(1871–1919), German journalist and politician.

1305. Marie Lloyd (1870–1922)

1   A little of what you fancy does you good.

                                                      Song *n.d.*

2   I'm one of the ruins that Cromwell* knocked about a bit.
                                                          Ibid.
    *English military, political and religious leader (1599–1658).

1306. Mary Johnston (1870–1936)

1   "I am weary of swords and courts and kings. Let us go into
    the garden and watch the minister's bees."
                              Ch. 9, *To Have and To Hold* *1899*

1307. Maud Younger (1870–1936)

1   "See here. How am I ever going to get experience if everyone
    tells me that I must have it before I begin?"
               "New York, May 6, 1907," *McClure's Magazine* *1907*

2   It is not pleasant to have a stranger doubt your respectability.
                                                          Ibid.

3   We have so many ideas about things we have never tried.
                                                          Ibid.

4   I did not know the working classes were so united. There is
    more affection and loyalty toward one another than among
    other people. Perhaps this is because the working people feel
    that there is a class struggle, and the leisure class does not
    know it yet.
                                       "New York, May 15, 1907," Ibid.

5   "Then why don't all girls belong to unions?" I asked, feeling
    very much an outsider; but she of the gents' neckwear replied:
    "Well, there's some that thinks it ain't fashionable; there's
    some that thinks it ain't no use; and there's some that never
    thinks at all."
                                        "New York, June 8," Ibid.

6   A trade unionist—of course I am. First, last, and all the time.
    How else to strike at the roots of the evils undermining the
    moral and physical health of women? How else grapple with
    the complex problems of employment, overemployment, and
    underemployment alike, resulting in discouraged, undernour-
    ished bodies, too tired to resist the onslaughts of disease and
    crime?
               Speech, Quoted in *Ms.* (New York) *January 1973*

1308. Jessie Tarbox Beals (1870–1942)

1   Too many photographers try too hard. They try to lift photog-
    raphy into the realm of Art, because they have an inferiority
    complex about their Craft. You and I would see more interest-
    ing photography if they would stop worrying, and instead,
    apply horse-sense to the problem of recording the look and
    feel of their own era.
                                       Quoted in *PM Magazine*
                                                   April 1941

2   I have learned that to get a job done and have fun in it is all
    you can get out of life.
             Quoted in *Jessie Tarbox Beals: First Woman News
                         Photographer* by Alexander Alland *1978*

3   I had too many keys that opened too many doors in too many
    places.
                                                          Ibid.

4   Mere feminine, delicate, Dresden china type of women get
    nowhere in business or professional life. They marry million-
    aires, if they are lucky. But if a woman is to make headway
    with men, she must be truly masculine.
                                                          Ibid.

5   I miss New York with its fairy-like towers
    With Liberty's torch high in the air
    I'd give all of California's damn flowers
    For the sight of Washington Square.
                                       Poem in diary (1936), Ibid.

1309. Alice Caldwell Rice (1870–1942)

1   Life is made up of desires that seem big and vital one minute,
    and little and absurd the next. I guess we get what's best for us
    in the end.
                             Ch. 2, *A Romance of Billy-Goat Hill* *1912*

2   To him work appeared a wholly artificial and abnormal ac-
    tion, self-imposed and unnecessary. The stage of life presented
    so many opportunities for him to exercise his histrionic ability,
    that the idea of settling down to a routine of labor seemed a
    waste of talent.
                                                   Ch. 6, Ibid.

3 The arbitrary division of one's life into days and weeks and hours seemed, on the whole, useless. There was but one day for the men, and that was pay day, and one for the women, and that was rent day. As for the children, every day was theirs, just as it should be in every corner of the world.

Ch. 15, Ibid.

4 "Fer my part I can't see it's to any woman's credit to look nice when she's got the right kind of a switch and a good set of false teeth. It's the woman that keeps her good looks without none of them luxuries that orter be praised."

Ch. 2, *Calvary Alley 1918*

5 When one has a famishing thirst for happiness, one is apt to gulp down diversions wherever they are offered. The necessity of draining the dregs of life before the wine is savored does not cultivate a discriminating taste.

Ch. 14, Ibid.

1310. Sharlot Mabridth Hall (1870–1943)

1 I stayed not, I could not linger; patient, resistless, alone,
I hewed the trail of my destiny deep in the hindering stone.
"Song of the Colorado," *Cactus Pine 1910*

1311. Maria Montessori (1870–1952)

1 The teacher must derive not only the capacity, but the desire, to observe natural phenomena. In our system, she must become a passive, much more than an active, influence, and her passivity shall be composed of anxious scientific curiosity and of absolute *respect* for the phenomenon which she wishes to observe. The teacher must understand and *feel* her position of observer: the activity *must lie in the phenomenon*.

The Montessori Method, Anne Everett George, tr. *1912*

2 The first idea that the child must acquire, in order to be actively disciplined, is that of the difference between *good* and *evil*; and the task of the educator lies in seeing that the child does not confound *good* with *immobility*, and *evil* with activity.

Ibid.

3 The observation of the way in which the children pass from the first disordered movements to those which are *spontaneous and ordered*—this is the book of the teacher; this is the book which must inspire her actions; it is the only one in which she must read and study if she is to become a real educator.

Ibid.

4 The prize and the punishment are incentives toward unnatural or forced effort, and, therefore we certainly cannot speak of the natural development of the child in connection with them. The jockey offers a piece of sugar to his horse before jumping into the saddle, the coachman beats his horse that he may respond to the signs given by the reins; and, yet, neither of these runs so superbly as the free horse of the plains.

Ch. I, Ibid.

5 It is my belief that the thing which we should cultivate in our teachers is more the *spirit* than the mechanical skill of the scientist; that is, the *direction* of the *preparation* should be toward the spirit rather than toward the mechanism.

Ibid.

6 Our servants are not our dependents, rather it is we who are dependent upon them.

Ch. V, Ibid.

7 Discipline must come through liberty. . . . If discipline is founded upon liberty, the discipline itself must necessarily be active. We do not consider an individual disciplined only when he has been rendered as artificially silent as a mute and as immovable as a paralytic. He is an individual annihilated, not disciplined.

Ibid.

8 But if for the physical life it is necessary to have the child exposed to the vivifying forces of nature, it is also necessary for his psychical life to place the soul of the child in contact with creation, in order that he may lay up for himself treasure from the directly educating forces of living nature. The method for arriving at this end is to set the child at agricultural labour, guiding him to the cultivation of plants and animals, and so to the intelligent contemplation of nature.

Ch. X, Ibid.

9 If one considers the charm of human speech one is bound to acknowledge the inferiority of one who does not possess a correct spoken language; and an aesthetic conception in education cannot be imagined unless special care be devoted to perfecting articulate language.

Ch. XVIII, Ibid.

10 We have belittled the son of man by giving him foolish and degrading toys, a world of idleness where he is suffocated by a badly conceived discipline.

Ch. XXII, Ibid.

11 If physical care leads the child to take pleasure in bodily health, intellectual and moral care make possible for him the highest spiritual joy, and send him forward into a world where continual surprises and discoveries await him; not only in the external environment, but in the intimate recesses of his own soul.

Ibid.

12 All adults stand accused...the society responsible for the welfare of children has been put on trial. There is something apocalyptic about this startling accusation; it is mysterious and terrible like the voice of the Last Judgment: "What have you done to the children I entrusted to you?"

The Secret of Childhood 1936

13 The child endures all things.

The Absorbent Mind 1949

14 The only language men ever speak perfectly is the one they learn in babyhood, when no one can teach them anything!

Ch. 1, Ibid.

15 If help and salvation are to come, they can only come from the children, for the children are the makers of men.

Ibid.

16 We teachers can only help the work going on, as servants wait upon a master.

Ibid.

17 The babies . . . sought to render themselves independent of adults in all the actions which they could manage on their own, manifesting clearly the desire not to be helped, except in cases of absolute necessity. And they were seen to be tranquil, absorbed and concentrating on their work, acquiring a surprising calm and serenity.

The Child in the Family 1956

18 Love and the hope of it are not things one can learn; they are a part of life's heritage.

The Absorbent Mind 1967 ed.

19 The Absorbent Mind welcomes everything, puts its hope in everything, accepts poverty equally with wealth, adopts any religion and the prejudices and habits of its countrymen, incarnating all in itself.

Ibid.

20 Strange, is it not, that among all the wonders man has worked, and the discoveries he has made, there is only one field to which he has paid no attention; it is that of the miracle that God has worked from the first: the miracle of children.

Ibid.

21 The greatness of the human personality begins at the hour of birth. From this almost mystic affirmation there comes what may seem a strange conclusion: that education must start from birth.

Ibid.

22 And so we discovered that education is not something which the teacher does, but that it is a natural process which develops spontaneously in the human being.

Ibid.

23 . . . humanity is still far from that stage of maturity needed for the realizations of its aspiration, for the construction, that is, of a harmonious and peaceful society and the elimination of wars. Men are not yet ready to shape their own destinies, to control and direct world events, of which—instead—they become the victims.

Ibid.

24 And if education is always to be conceived along the same antiquated lines of a mere transmission of knowledge, there is little to be hoped from it in the bettering of man's future. For what is the use of transmitting knowledge if the individual's total development lags behind?

Ibid.

1312. Helena Rubinstein (1870–1965)

1 The cosmetic business is interesting among modern industries in its opportunities for women. Here they have found a field that is their own province—working for women with women, and giving that which only women can give—an intimate understanding of feminine needs and feminine desires.

"Manufacturing—Cosmetics," *An Outline of Careers for Women*, Doris Fleischman Bernays, ed. *1928*

2 I have always felt that a woman had the right to treat the subject of her age with ambiguity until, perhaps, she passed into the realm of over ninety. Then it is better she be candid with herself and with the world.

Pt. I, Ch. 1, *My Life for Beauty 1965*

3 There are no ugly women, just lazy ones.

Pt. II, Ch. 1, Ibid.

4 But what parent can tell when some such fragmentary gift of knowledge or wisdom will enrich her children's lives? Or how a small seed of information passed from one generation to another may generate a new science, a new industry—a seed which neither the giver nor the receiver can truly evaluate at the time.

Ch. 10, Ibid.

5 Production on a small scale is now practically prohibitive.

(c. 1920), Quoted in *Hope in a Jar, The Making of America's Beauty Culture* by Kathy Peiss* *1998*

*See 3275.

1313. Florence Hurst Harriman (1870–1967)

1 Next to entertaining or impressive talk, a thoroughgoing silence manages to intrigue most people.

Ch. 4, *From Pinafore to Politics 1924*

1314. Ella Stewart (1871–?)

1 The real goddesses of Liberty in this country do not spend a large amount of time standing on pedestals in public places; they use their torches to startle the bats in political cellars.

Quoted in *New Directions for Women*
November/December 1980

1315. Pamela Glenconnor (1871–1928)

1 Giving presents is a talent; to know what a person wants, to know when and how to get it, to give it lovingly and well. Unless a character possesses this talent there is no moment more annihilating to ease than that in which a present is received and given.

Ch. 5, *Edward Wyndhan Tennant: A Memoir 1919*

2 Bitter are the tears of a child:
Sweeten them.
Deep are the thoughts of a child:
Quiet them.
Sharp is the grief of a child:
Take it from him.
Soft is the heart of a child:
Do not harden it.

"A Child" *n.d.*

1316. Agnes C. Laut (1871–1936)

1 They had reached the fine point where it is better for the weak to die trying to overthrow strength, than to live under the iron heel of brute oppression.

Ch. 4, *Vikings of the Pacific 1905*

2 Countless hopes and fears must have animated at the breasts of the Frenchmen.* It is so with every venture that is based on the unknown. The very fact that possibilities *are* unknown gives scope to unbridled fancy and the wildest hopes; gives scope, too, when the pendulum swings the other way to deepest distrust.

Ch. 7, *The Conquest of the Great Northwest 1908*
*Radisson and Groseiller's voyage in 1668 to Hudson Bay.

3 The ultimate umpire of all things in life is—Fact.

Ch. 20, Ibid.

4 Canada's prosperity is literally overflowing from a cornucopia of superabundant plenty. Will her Constitution, wrested from political and civil strife; will her moral stamina, bred from the heroism of an heroic past, stand the strain, the tremendous strain of the new conditions? . . . Above all, will she stand the strain, the tremendous strain, of prosperity, and the corruption that is attendant on prosperity? *Quien sabe?*

Ch. 16, *Canada, the Empire of the North 1909*

5 Yet when you come to trace when and where national consciousness awakened, it is like following a river from the ocean to its mountain springs. . . . You can guess the eternal striving, the forward rush and the throwback that have carved a way through the solid rock; but until you have followed the river to its source and tried to stem its current you can not know.

Ch. 1, *The Canadian Commonwealth 1915*

1317. Georgiana Goddard King (1871–1939)

1 English spelling is an affair of memory, not of reason.
The Bryn Mawr Spelling Book 1909

2 Like other things that came out of the East, it [architecture] is always a little intoxicating.
"Castles in Spain," *The Journal of the American Institute of Architects*, Vol. 9 *1921*

1318. Margaret Floy Washburn (1871–1939)

1 One of the difficulties in writing these recollections has been that the present is so much more interesting than the past. It is hard to keep one's attention on reminiscence.
4000 Years of Women in Science,
http://www.astr.ua.edu/4000WS *27 September 1997*

1319. B. M. Bower (1871/4–1940)

1 Do you like children? In other words, are you human?
Ch. I, *The Ranch at the Wolverine 1914*

2 Marthy was clumsy with words, and she was always coming to the barrier between her powers of expression and the thoughts that were prisoned and dumb.
Ibid.

3 "I didn't know there was a woman in the world like you," Ward said irrelevantly and looked into the fire. "I thought women were just soft things a man had to take care of and carry along through life, a dead weight when they weren't worse. I never knew a woman could be a friend—the kind of friend a man can be."
Ch. IV, Ibid.

4 "Maybe I started wrong, but for a kid with nobody to point the trail for him, I don't think I did so worse—till old Dame Fortune spotted me in the crowd and proceeded to use me for a football."
Ibid.

5 "You know you belong to me, don't you? And I belong to you—body and soul. You know that, don't you? I've known it ever since the world was made. I knew it when God said, 'Let there be light,' and there was light. You were it."
Ch. IX, Ibid.

6 It is not always cowardice which makes a man extremely careful not to fall into the hands of his enemy. There is a small matter of pride involved.
Ch. XI, Ibid.

1320. Maxine Elliott (1871–1940)

1 Beauty, what is that? There are phalanxes of beauty in every comic show. Beauty neither buys food nor keeps up a home.
News Item *1908*

1321. Emily Carr (1871–1945)

1 I wonder why we are always sort of ashamed of our best parts and try to hide them. We don't mind ridicule of our "sillinesses" but of our "sobers," oh! Indians are the same and even dogs.
(November 23, 1930), *Hundreds and Thousands 1966*

2 Life's an awfully lonesome affair. . . . You come into the world alone and you go out of the world alone yet it seems to me you are more alone while living than even going and coming.
"The Elephant" (16 July 1933), Ibid.

3 Oh, the glory of growth, silent, mighty, persistent, inevitable! To awaken, to open up like a flower to the light of a fuller consciousness!
(17 October 1933), Ibid.

4 It is not all bad, this getting old, ripening. After the fruit has got its growth it should juice up and mellow. God forbid I should live long enough to ferment and rot and fall to the ground in a squash.
(12 December 1933*), Ibid.

*The eve of her 62nd birthday.

5 B-a-a-a-, old sheep, bleating for fellows. Don't you know better by now?
(6 April 1934), Ibid.

6 Twenty can't be expected to tolerate sixty in all things, and sixty gets bored stiff with twenty's eternal love affairs.
(12 August 1934), Ibid.

7 It is wonderful to feel the grandness of Canada in the raw, not because she is Canada but because she is something sublime that you were born into, some great rugged power that you are a part of.
(16 April 1937), Ibid.

8 I am not half as patient with old women now that I am one.
(6 March 1940), Ibid.

9 Everything holds its breath except spring. She bursts through as strong as ever.
(7 March 1941), Ibid.

1322. Florence Sabin (1871–1953)

1 The prohibition law, written for weaklings and derelicts, has divided the nation, like Gaul, into three parts—wets, drys and hypocrites.
Speech *9 February 1931*

1323. Margaret Witter Fuller (1871–1954)

1 I am immortal! I know it! I feel it!
Hope floods my heart with delight!
Running on air, mad with life, dizzy, reeling,
Upward I mount—faith is sight, life is feeling,
Hope is the day-star of might!
"Dryad Song" *n.d.*

2 It was thy kiss, Love, that made me immortal.
Ibid.

1324. Eleanor Rathbone (1872–1946)

1 Pluck from under the family all the props which religion and morality have given it, strip it of the glamour, true or false, cast round it by romance, it will still remain a prosaic, indisputable fact, that the whole business of begetting, bearing and rearing children, is the most essential of all the nation's business.
The Disinherited Family 1924

1325. Mary Reynolds Aldis (1872–1949)

1 They flush joyously like a cheek under a lover's kiss;
They bleed cruelly like a dagger—wound in the breast;
They flame up madly of their little hour,
Knowing they must die.
"Barberries" *n.d.*

1326. Eva Gore-Booth (1872–1949)

1   The little waves of Breffney go stumbling through my soul.
"The Little Waves of Breffney," *Poems n.d.*

1327. Aleksandra Kollontai (1872–1952)

1   In place of the indissoluble marriage based on the servitude of women, we shall see rise the free union, fortified by the love and the mutual respect of the two members of the workers' state, equal in their rights and in their obligations.
Communism and the Family 1918

2   The practice of [political] appointments rejects completely the principle of collective work; it breeds irresponsibility.
The Workers' Opposition in Russia c. 1921

3   . . . beginning with the appointment of a sovereign for the state and ending with a sovereign director for the factory. This is the supreme wisdom of bourgeois thought.
Ibid.

4   . . . the middle class with their hostility toward communism, and with their predilections toward the immutable customs of the past, with resentments and fears toward revolutionary acts—these are the elements that bring decay into our Soviet institutions, breeding there an atmosphere altogether repugnant to the working class.
Ibid.

5   The "upper" elements may divert the masses from the straight road of history which leads toward communism only when the masses are mute, obedient, and when they passively and credulously follow their leaders.
Ibid.

6   Bureaucracy, as it is, is a direct negation of mass self-activity. . . .
Ibid.

7   Fear of criticism and freedom of thought by combining together with bureaucracy quite often produce ridiculous forms.
Ibid.

1328. Maude Adams (1872–1953)

1   If I smashed the traditions it was because I knew no traditions.
Quoted in *Maude Adams: A Biography* by Ada Patterson *1907*

2   Genius is the talent for seeing things straight. It is seeing things in a straight line without any bend or break or aberration of sight, seeing them as they are, without any warping of vision. Flawless mental sight! That is genius.
Ibid.

1329. Leonora Speyer (1872–1956)

1   You gave me wings to fly;
Then took away the sky.
Introduction, Pt. V, *Fiddler's Farewell 1926*

2   Let me declare
That music never dies;
That music never dies.
"Fiddler's Farewell," St. 13, *Ibid.*

3   Love has a hundred gentle ends.
"Two Passionate Ones Part," St. 5, *Ibid.*

4   I'll sing, "Here lies, here lies, here lies—"
Ah, rust in peace below!
Passers will wonder at my words,
But your dark dust will know.
"I'll Be Your Epitaph," *Ibid.*

5   Poor patch-work of the heart,
This healing love with love;
Binding the wound to wound,
The smart to smart!
"Therapy," St. 3, *Ibid.*

6   Houses are like the hearts of men,
I think;
They must have life within,
(This is their meat and drink),
They must have fires and friends and kin,
Love for the day and night,
Children in strong young laps:
Then they live—then!
"Abrigada," St. 10, *Ibid.*

7   I do not think that too severe comment is good teaching.
"On the Teaching of Poetry," *The Saturday Review of Literature 1946*

8   I believe in anthologies, although I know they offer only a glimpse.
Ibid.

9   . . . I quote a great deal in my talks. . . . I do like to call upon my radiant cloud of witnesses to back me up, saying the thing I would say, and saying it so much more eloquently.
Ibid.

10   . . . no amount of study will contrive a talent, that being God's affair; but having the gift, "through Grace," as John Masefield says, it must be developed, the art must be learned.
Ibid.

11   There is not much stitching and unstitching in some of the hasty and cocksure writing of today.
Ibid.

12   . . . to be exact has naught to do with pedantry or dogma. . . .
Ibid.

13   Sky, be my depth;
Wind, be my width and my height;
World, my heart's span:
Loneliness, wings for my flight!
"Measure Me, Sky" *n.d.*

14   Thunder crumples the sky,
Lightning tears at it.
"The Squall" *n.d.*

1330. Julia Morgan (1872–1957)

1   I don't think you understand just what my work has been here. The decorative part was all done by a New York firm. My work was structural [on the rebuilding of the Fairmont Hotel following the 1906 earthquake].
Quoted in *San Francisco Call 1907*

2   The building should speak for itself.
Quoted in "Some Examples of the Work of Julia Morgan" by Walter T. Steilberg, *Architect and Engineer November 1918*

259

3   Never turn down a job because you think it's too small, you don't know where it can lead.

                                                                    Ibid.

1331. Winifred Kirkland (1872–1943)

1   We are each launched in life with an elfin shipmate—set jogging upon earth beside a fairy comrade. When our ears are clear, he pipes magic music; when our feet are free he pleads with us to follow him on witching paths. We cannot often hear, we cannot often follow, but when we do, we know him for what he is; when we sail or run or fly with him, we know him for the gladdest fellow with whom life ever paired us, a companion rarely glimpsed, but glorious, for he is our own true Self.

       Foreword, "The Ego in the Essay," *The Joys of Being a
       Woman and Other Papers 1918 (repr. 1968)*

2   Of all literary forms the personal essay appears the most artless, a little boat that sails us into pleasant havens, without any sound of machinery and without any chart or compass.

1332. Grace Seton-Thompson (1872–1959)

1   . . . the outfit I got together for my first [hunting] trip appalled that good man, my husband, while the number of things I had to learn appalled me.

                                           Ch. 1, *A Woman Tenderfoot 1900*

2   I know what it means to be a miner and a cowboy, and have risked my life when need be, *but*, best of all, I have felt the charm of the glorious freedom, the quick rushing blood, the bounding motion, of the wild life, the joy of the living and of the doing, of the mountain and the plain; I have learned to know and feel some, at least, of the secrets of the Wild Ones.

                                                       Ch. 19, Ibid.

3   If I must suffer more re-birth
    Upon the weary plain of earth,
    Grant that my rest be deep,
    And happy be my sleep
    Until the turning Wheel of Life
    Wakes me to Illusion's strife.
           "Goddess of Mercy," St. 1, *The Singing Traveler 1947*

4   Beckon, dreams of passion, luring snare!
    Your guileful bed of satin-white
    Calls to lustful ease.
                                   "Opium Poppy," St. 2, Ibid.

5   What is an eye?
    A strange device,
    A bit of film and nerve, the first camera obscura,
    A wonder steeped in mystery . . .
    Recording scenes and filing prints in cabinets of the brain?
                                 "Windows of the Soul," St. 1, Ibid.

6   Many times I have looked into the eyes of wild animals
    And we have parted friends.
    What did they see, and recognize,
    Shining through the windows of a human soul?
                                                    St. 9, Ibid.

7   Butterflies and birds fly over me unconcerned . . .
    The forest accepts me.
                                          "Forest," St. 4, Ibid.

8   My Mother is everywhere . . .
    In the perfume of a rose,

The eyes of a tiger,
The pages of a book,
The food that we partake,
The whistling wind of the desert,
The blazing gems of sunset,
The crystal light of the moon,
The opal veils of sunrise.
                                    "Hindu Chant," St. 4, Ibid.

9   Courage! Speed the day of world perfection.
    Straining from the Wheel of Things,
    Let us break the bonds of lost direction!
    Godward! Borne on Freedom's wings!
                                    "The Wheel of Life," St. 6, Ibid.

1333. Mildred Howells (1872–1966)

1   And so it criticized each flower,
    This supercilious seed;
    Until it woke one summer hour,
    And found itself a weed.
                                  "A Different Seed." St. 5 *n.d.*

1334. Mary Elizabeth Crouse (1873–?)

1   How often do the clinging hands, though weak,
    Clasp round strong hearts that otherwise would break.
                                     "Strength of Weakness" *n.d.*

1335. Daisy, Princess of Pless (1873–?)

1   Either of my parents would have done anything in the world for me—except tell me the truth.
                             Ch. 1, *Daisy, Princess of Pless 1923*

2   How seldom people find their happiness on a darkened stage; they must turn up all the limelights to find it.
              Entry (16 August 1903), *From My Private Diary 1926*

3   No theater is prosperous, or a play complete, unless there is a bedroom scene in the second act. . . .
                                     Entry (28 April 1904), Ibid.

4   It is no use having illusions about life. Life, as we live it, *is* commonplace unless one chooses to renounce the world, and live out of it, and therefore be different from others.
                                                              Ibid.

5   The souls we have loved here, we may love and meet again because we have once loved them; but our intercourse with them will not be tainted with the remembrance of this heart-breaking little world; we shall not recognize them in their personal limitations.
                                       (13 February 1907), Ibid.

6   I was always frank by nature and cannot understand the absurd reticences which many people seem to consider so necessary.
                                    Ch. 1, *Better Left Unsaid 1931*

7   For each of us, after middle-age, the world is always emptying.
                                                       Ch. 3, Ibid.

8   The Irish sit by a peat fire; the English by a coal one. That is the unbridgeable difference between the two peoples: We prefer the glamorous, the quick, the pungent; they the lasting and substantial.
                                     Ch. 1, *What I Left Unsaid 1936*

1336. Marie Dressler (1873–1934)

1 Fate cast me to play the role of an ugly duckling with no promise of swanning. Therefore, I sat down as a mere child—fully realizing how *utterly* "mere" I was—and figured out my life early. Most people do it, but they do it too late. At any rate, from the beginning I have played my life as a comedy rather than the tragedy many would have made of it.

Ch. 1, *The Life Story of an Ugly Duckling* 1924

2 . . . poor had no terror for me! It was pie for me! My whole life had been a fight!

Ch. 5, Ibid.

3 I was born serious and I have earned my bread making other people laugh.

Ch. 1, *My Own Story* 1934

4 In order to represent life on the stage, we must rub elbows with life, live ourselves.

Ch. 3, Ibid.

5 Love is not getting, but giving. It is sacrifice. And sacrifice is glorious! I have no patience with women who measure and weigh their love like a country doctor dispensing capsules. If a man is worth loving at all, he is worth loving generously, even recklessly.

Ch. 7, Ibid.

6 By the time we hit fifty, we have learned our hardest lessons. We have found out that only a few things are really important. We have learned to take life seriously, but never ourselves.

Ch. 17, Ibid.

7 There is a vast difference between success at twenty-five and success at sixty. At sixty, nobody envies you. Instead, everybody rejoices generously, sincerely, in your good fortune.

Ibid.

1337. Janet Scudder (1873–1940)

1 I don't believe artists should be subjected to experiences that harden the sensibilities; without sensibility no fine work can ever be done.

Ch. 2, *Modeling My Life* 1925

2 Someone has said that even criticism is better than silence. I don't agree to this. Criticism can be very harmful unless it comes from a master; and in spite of the fact that we have hundreds of critics these days, it is one of the most difficult of professions.

Ibid.

1338. Willa Cather (1873–1947)

1 No one can build his security upon the nobleness of another person.

Ch. 8, *Alexander's Bridge* 1912

2 There are only two or three human stories, and they go on repeating themselves as fiercely as if they had never happened before.

Pt. II, Ch. 4, *O Pioneers!* 1913

3 The history of every country begins in the heart of a man or woman.

Ibid.

4 I like trees because they seem more resigned to the way they have to live than other things do.

Pt. II, Ch. 8, Ibid.

5 "I don't see why anybody wants to marry an artist, anyhow."

The Song of the Lark 1915

6 "I tell you there is such a thing as creative hate!"

Pt. I, Ibid.

7 Artistic growth is, more than it is anything else, a refining of the sense of truthfulness. The stupid believe that to be truthful is easy; only the artist, the great artist, knows how difficult it is.

Pt. IV, Ch. 11, Ibid.

8 "Oh, better I like to work out of doors than in the house. . . . I not care that your grandmother says it makes me like a man. I like to be like a man.

My Ántonia 1918

9 There seemed to be nothing to see; no fences, no creeks or trees, no hills or fields. If there was a road, I could not make it out in the faint starlight. There was nothing but land: not a country at all, but the material out of which countries are made.

Ibid.

10 That is happiness; to be dissolved into something completely great.

Bk. I, Ch. 2, Epitaph, Ibid.

11 Winter lies too long in country towns; hangs on until it is stale and shabby, old and sullen.

Bk. II, Ch. 7, Ibid.

12 It was not that symphonies, as such, meant anything in particular to Paul, but the first sigh of the instruments seemed to free some hilarious spirit within him; something that struggled there like the Genius [sic] in the bottle found by the Arab fisherman.

"Paul's Case," *Youth and the Bright Medusa* 1920

13 It was a highly respectable street, where all the houses were exactly alike, and where business men of moderate means begot and reared large families of children, all of whom went to sabbath-school and learned the shorter catechism, and were interested in arithmetic; all of whom were as exactly alike as their homes, and of a piece with the monotony in which they lived.

Ibid.

14 Perhaps it was because, in Paul's world, the natural nearly always wore the guise of ugliness, that a certain element of artificiality seemed to him necessary to beauty.

Ibid.

15 He . . . knew now, more than ever, that money was everything, the wall that stood between all he loathed and all he wanted.

Ibid.

16 This was a lie, but Paul was quite accustomed to lying; found it, indeed, indispensable for overcoming friction.

Ibid.

17 Art, it seems to me, should simplify. That, indeed, is very nearly the whole of the higher artistic process; finding what conventions of form and what details one can do without and yet preserve the spirit of the whole. . . .

On the Art of Fiction 1920

18 There was this to be said for Nat Wheeler, that he liked every sort of human creature; he liked good people and honest people, and he liked rascals and hypocrites almost to the point of loving them.

Bk. I, Ch. 1, *One of Ours* 1922

19 The sun was like a great visiting presence that stimulated and took its due from all animal energy. When it flung wide its cloak and stepped down over the edge of the fields at evening, it left behind it a spent and exhausted world.

> Bk. II, Ch. 6, Ibid.

20 The dead might as well try to speak to the living as the old to the young.

> Ibid.

21 Yes, inside of people who walked and worked in the broad sun, there were captives dwelling in darkness,—never seen from birth to death.

> Bk. III, Ch. 6, Ibid.

22 "When I'm in normal health, I'm a Presbyterian, but just now I feel that even the wicked get worse than they deserve."

> Bk. IV, Ch. 9, Ibid.

23 They were mortal, they were unconquerable.

> Bk. V, Ch. 18, Ibid.

24 Theoretically he knew that life is possible, maybe even pleasant, without joy, without passionate griefs. But it had never occurred to him that he might have to live like that.

> The Professor's House 1925

25 When kindness has left people, even for a few moments, we become afraid of them as if their reason had left them. When it has left a place where we have always found it, it is like shipwreck; we drop from security into something malevolent and bottomless.

> My Mortal Enemy 1926

26 That irregular and intimate quality of things made entirely by the human hand.

> Bk.1, Ch. 3, Death Comes for the Archbishop 1927

27 The miracles of the church seem to me to rest not so much upon faces or voices or healing power coming suddenly near to us from afar off, but upon our perceptions being made finer, so that for a moment our eyes can see and our ears can hear what is there about us always.

> Ch. 4, Ibid.

28 The universal human yearning for something permanent, enduring, without shadow of change.

> Bk. III, Ch. 3, Ibid.

29 CECILE. Do you think it wrong for a girl to know Latin?
PIERRE. Not if she can cook a hare or partridge as well as Mademoiselle Auclaire! She may read all the Latin she pleases.

> Shadows on the Rock 1931

30 Only solitary men know the full joys of friendship. Others have their family; but to a solitary and an exile his friends are everything.

> Bk. III, Ch. 5, Ibid.

31 One made a climate within a climate; one made the days—the complexion, the special flavor, the special happiness of each day as it passed; one made life.

> Ch. 3, Ibid.

32 Sometimes a neighbor who we have disliked a lifetime for his arrogance and conceit lets fall a single commonplace remark that shows us another side, another man, really; a man uncertain, and puzzled, and in the dark like ourselves.

> Epilogue, Ibid.

33 "Nothing really matters but living—accomplishments are the ornaments of life; they come second."

> Lucy Gayheart 1935

34 To note an artist's limitations is but to define his talent. A reporter can write equally well about everything that is presented to his view, but a creative writer can do his best only with what lies within the range and character of his deepest sympathies.

> "Miss Jewett," Not Under Forty 1936

35 Religion and art spring from the same route and are close kin. Economics and art are strangers.

> On Writing 1949

36 The revolt against individuals naturally calls artists severely to account, because the artist is of all men the most individual; those who were not have long been forgotten.

> Ibid.

37 The condition every art requires is, not so much freedom from restriction, as freedom from adulteration and from the intrusion of foreign matter.

> "Four Letters: Escapism" (1936), Ibid.

38 Give the people a new word and they think they have a new fact.

> Ibid.

39 Writing ought either to be the manufacture of stories for which there is a market demand—a business as safe and commendable as making soap or breakfast foods—or it should be an art, which is always a search for something for which there is no market demand, something new and untried, where the values are intrinsic and have nothing to do with standardized values.

> "On the Art of Fiction" (1920), Ibid.

40 The fact that I was a girl never damaged my ambitions to be a pope or an emperor.

> Quoted by Joan Acocella in "Cather and the Academy," The New Yorker 27 November 1995

41 So blind is life, so long at last is sleep,
And none but love to bid us laugh or weep.

> "Evening Song" n.d.

42 Where are the loves that we have loved before
When once we are alone, and shut the door?

> "L'Envoi" n.d.

43 Oh, this is the joy of the rose:
That it blows,
And goes.

> "In Rose-Time" n.d.

44 Whatever is felt upon the page without being specifically named there—that, one might say, is created. It is the inexplicable presence of the thing not named, of the overtone divined by the ear but not heard by it, the verbal mood, the emotional aura of the fact or the thing or the deed, that gives high quality to the novel or the drama, as well as to poetry itself.

> Essay, "The Novel Démeublé" n.d.

1339. Margaret Baillie Saunders (1873–1949?)

1 I've often known people more shocked because you are not bankrupt than because you are.

> A Shepherd of Kensington 1907

2 One's old acquaintances sometimes come upon one like ghosts—and most people hate ghosts.

Ibid.

3 Very few men care to have the obvious pointed out to them by a woman.

Ibid.

1340. Nellie McClung (1873–1951)

1 When they felt tired, they called it laziness and felt disgraced and thus they had spent their days, working, working from the grey dawn, until the darkness came again, and all for what? When in after years these girls, broken in health and in spirits, slipped away to premature graves, or, worse still, settled into chronic invalidism, of what avail was the memory of the cows they milked, the mats they hooked, the number of pounds of butter they made.

Sowing Seeds in Danny 1908

2 "While we are side by side" the violins sang, glad, triumphant, that old story that runs like a thread of gold through all life's patterns; that old song, old yet ever new, deathless, unchangeable, which maketh the poor man rich and without which the richest becomes poor!

Ibid.

1341. Colette (1873–1954)

1 All those beautiful sentiments I've uttered have made me feel genuinely upset.

"The Journey" 1905

2 Privation prevents all thought, substitutes for any other mental image that of a hot, sweet-smelling dish, and reduces hope to the shape of a rounded loaf set in rays of glory.

Music Hall Sidelights 1913

3 A bed, a nice fresh bed, with smoothly drawn sheets and a hot-water bottle at the end of it, soft to the feet like a live animal's tummy.

Ibid.

4 I look like a discouraged beetle battered by the rains of a spring night. I look like a moulting bird. I look like a governess in distress. I look—Good Lord, I look like an actress on tour, and that speaks for itself.

"On Tour," Ibid.

5 How can one help shivering with delight when one's hot fingers close around the stem of a live flower, cool from the shade and stiff with newborn vigor!

Ibid.

6 Nothing ages a woman like living in the country.

Ibid.

7 Life is nothing but a series of crosses for us mothers.

Cheri 1920

8 The divorce will be gayer than the wedding.

Ibid.

9 . . . her smile was like a rainbow after a sudden storm.

Ibid.

10 Give me a dozen such heart-breaks, if that would help me to lose a couple of pounds.

Ibid.

11 You aren't frightened when a door slams, though it may make you jump. It's a snake creeping under it that's frightening.

Ibid.

12 . . . The sudden desire to look beautiful made her straighten her back. "Beautiful? For whom? Why for myself, of course."

Ibid.

13 Let's go out and buy playing-cards, good wine, bridge-scorers, knitting needles—all the paraphernalia to fill a gaping void, all that's required to disguise that monster, an old woman.

Ibid.

14 I hate guests who complain of the cooking and leave bits and pieces all over the place and cream-cheese sticking to the mirrors.

Ibid.

15 Years of close familiarity rendered silence congenial. . . .

Ibid.

16 Those love children always suffer because their mothers have crushed them under their stays trying to hide them, more's the pity. Yet after all, a lovely unrepentant creature, big with child, is not such an outrageous sight.

"My Mother and Illness," My Mother's House 1922

17 But at my age there's only one virtue: not to make people unhappy.

Ibid.

18 It's pretty hard to retain the characteristics of one's sex after a certain age.

Ibid.

19 You'll understand later that one keeps on forgetting old age up to the very brink of the grave.

Ibid.

20 Oh, for those young embroiderers of bygone days, sitting on a hard little stool in the shelter of their mother's ample skirts! Maternal authority kept them there for years and years, never rising except to change the skein of silk or to elope with a stranger.

"The Seamstress," Ibid.

21 . . . great joys must be controlled.

Ibid.

22 If there be a place of waiting after this life, then surely she who so often waited for us has not ceased to tremble for those two who are yet alive.

"Where Are the Children," Ibid.

23 "What a nuisance! Why should one have to eat? And what shall we eat this evening?"

"Jealousy," Ibid.

24 Blushing beneath the strands of her graying hair, her chin trembling with resentment, this little elderly lady is charming when she defends herself without so much as a smile against the accusations of a jealous sexagenarian. Nor does he smile either as he goes on to accuse her of "gallivanting." But I can still smile at their quarrels because I am only fifteen and have not yet divined the ferocity of love beneath his old man's eyebrows, or the blushes of adolescence upon her fading cheeks.

Ibid.

25 "What are you thinking about, Bel-Gazou?"
"Nothing, Mother."
An excellent answer. The same that I invariably gave when I was her age.

"The Priest on the Wall," Ibid.

26 It is not a bad thing that children should occasionally, and politely, put parents in their place.

Ibid.

27 . . . the telephone shone as brightly as a weapon kept polished by daily use. . .

Ibid.

28 If one wished to be perfectly sincere, one would have to admit there are two kinds of love—well-fed and ill-fed. The rest is pure fiction.

Ibid.

29 I instinctively like to acquire and store up what promises to outlast me.

Break of Day 1928

30 "Love is not a sentiment worthy of respect."

Ibid.

31 As for an authentic villain, the real thing, the absolute, the artist, one rarely meets him even once in a lifetime. The ordinary bad hat is always in part a decent fellow.

Ibid.

32 Shall we never have done with that cliché, so stupid that it could only be human, about the sympathy of animals for man when he is unhappy? Animals love happiness almost as much as we do. A fit of crying disturbs them, they'll sometimes imitate sobbing, and for a moment they'll reflect our sadness. But they flee unhappiness as they flee fever, and I believe that in the long run they are capable of boycotting it.

Ibid.

33 Whenever I feel myself inferior to everything about me, threatened by my own mediocrity, frightened by the discovery that a muscle is losing its strength, a desire its power, or a pin the keen edge of its bite, I can still hold up my head and say to myself: . . . "Let me not forget that I am the daughter of a woman who bent her head, trembling, over a cactus, her wrinkled face full of ecstasy over the promise of a flower, a woman who herself never ceased to flower, untiringly, during three quarters of a century."
Ibid.

34 A second place [setting] . . . If I say that it is to be taken away for good, no pernicious blast will blow suddenly from the horizon to make my hair stand on end and alter the direction of my life as once it did. If that plate is removed from my table, I shall still eat with appetite.

Ibid.

35 My true friends have always given me that supreme proof of devotion, a spontaneous aversion for the man I loved.

Ibid.

36 I have suffered, oh yes, certainly I learned how to suffer. But is suffering so very serious? I have come to doubt it. It may be quite childish, a sort of undignified pastime—I'm referring to the kind of suffering a man inflicts on a woman or a woman on a man. It's extremely painful. I agree that it's hardly bearable. But I very much fear that this sort of pain deserves no consideration at all.

Ibid.

37 The lovesick, the betrayed, and the jealous all smell alike.

"The South of France," Ibid.

38 I am seized with the itch to possess the secrets of a being who has vanished forever. . . .

"The Savages," Sido 1929

39 He was such an inoffensive little boy, she could find no fault with him, except his tendency to disappear.

Ibid.

40 When ordinary parents produce exceptional children they are often so dazzled by them that they push them into careers that they consider superior, even if it takes some lusty kicks on their behinds to achieve this result.

Ibid.

41 . . . that wild, unknown being, the child, who is both bottomless pit and impregnable fortress. . . .

"Look!" 1929

42 Smokers, male and female, inject and excuse idleness in their lives every time they light a cigarette.

The Pure and the Impure 1933

43 Perhaps the only misplaced curiosity is that which persists in trying to find out here, on this side of death, what lies beyond the grave.

Ibid.

44 It is wise to apply the oil of refined politeness to the mechanism of friendship.

Ch. 9, Ibid.

45 This life's idiotic: we're seeing far too much of each other and yet we never see each other properly.

The Cat 1933

46 He shut his eyes while Sasha [the cat] kept vigil, watching all the invisible signs that hover over sleeping human beings when the light is put out.

Ibid.

47 . . . that provisional tomb where the living exile sighs, weeps, fights, and succumbs, and from which he rises, remembering nothing, with the day.

Ibid.

48 She [the cat] hasn't had her full ration of kisses-on-the-lips today. She had the quarter-to-twelve one in the Bois, she had the two o'clock one after coffee, she had the half-past-six one in the garden, but she's missed tonight's.

Ibid.

49 He loved his dreams and cultivated them.

Ibid.

50 "She never misses an opportunity to shrink away from anything that can be tasted or touched or smelled."

"Armande" 1944

51 He wondered why sexual shyness, which excites the desire of dissolute women, aroused the contempt of decent ones.

Ibid.

52 . . . one word escaped, crisp and lively, and made a beeline for Jean, the word "crisis." Sometimes it entered ceremoniously,

like a lady dressed up to give away prizes, with an *h* behind its ear and a *y* tucked into its bodice: Chrysis, Chrysis Salutari.
                              "The Sick Child" *1944*

53 A boiled egg raised its little lid and revealed its buttercup yolk.
                                                    Ibid.

54 A mouth is not always a mouth, but a bit is always a bit, and it matters little what it bridles.
                              "The Sick Child" *1944*

55 Sorrow, fear, physical pain, excessive heat and excessive cold, I can still guarantee to stand up to all these with decent courage. But I abdicate in the face of boredom, which turns me into a wretched and, if necessary, ferocious creature.
                        "The Photographer's Missus" *1944*

56 . . . He was always ready to part with twenty francs or even a "banknote," so much so that he died poor, in the arms of his unsuspected honesty.
                                                    Ibid.

57 "Don't be too nice to me. When anyone's too nice to me, I don't know what I'm doing—I boil over like soup."
                                                    Ibid.

58 The unexpected sound of sobbing is demoralizing.
                                                    Ibid.

59 It is easy to relate what is of no importance.
                                                    Ibid.

60 "But once I had set out, I was already far on my way."
                                                    Ibid.

61 "Madame, people very seldom die because they lost someone. I believe they die more often because they haven't had someone."
                                                    Ibid.

62 A pretty little collection of weaknesses and a terror of spiders are our indispensable stock-in-trade with the men.
                                              Gigi 1944

63 "Explain yourself without gestures. The moment you gesticulate you look common."
                                                    Ibid.

64 "Boredom helps one to make decisions."
                                                    Ibid.

65 . . . pessimists have good appetites.
                                                    Ibid.

66 "They [men] forgive us—oh! for many things, but not for the absence in us of their own feelings."
                                                    Ibid.

67 "Don't ever wear artistic jewelry; it wrecks a woman's reputation."
                                                    Ibid.

68 "If only her brain worked as well as her jaws!"
                                                    Ibid.

69 "Call your mother, Gigi! Liane d'Exelmans has committed suicide."
         The child replied with a long drawn-out "Oooh!" and asked, "Is she dead?"
         "Of course not. She knows how to do these things."
                                                    Ibid.

70 "The telephone is of real use only to important businessmen or to women who have something to hide."
                                                    Ibid.

71 "Instead of marrying 'at once,' it sometimes happens that we marry 'at last'."
                                                    Ibid.

72 "All that's in the past. All that's over and done with."
    "Of course, Tonton, until it begins again."
                                                    Ibid.

73 . . . writing leads only to writing.
                              "The Blue Lantern" *1949*

74 A line of verse need not necessarily be beautiful for it to remain in the depths of our memory and occupy maliciously the place overrun by certain condemnable but unerasable melodies.
                                                    Ibid.

75 You must not pity me because my sixtieth year finds me still astonished. To be astonished is one of the surest ways of not growing old too quickly.
              Speech, Belgian Academy,* Pt. 4, "Lady of Letters,"
                     Earthly Paradise, Robert Phelps, ed. *1966*
    *On the occasion of her election to the Academy.

76 Girls usually have a papier mâché face on their wedding day.
                              "Wedding Day," Pt. 2, Ibid.

77 There is no need to waste pity on young girls who are having their moments of disillusionment, for in another moment they will recover their illusion.
                                                    Ibid.

78 The writer who loses his self-doubt, who gives way as he grows old to a sudden euphoria, to prolixity, should stop writing immediately: the time has come for him to lay aside his pen.
                              "Lady of Letters," Pt. 4, Ibid.

79 No temptation can ever be measured by the value of its object.
                                    "Temptations," Ibid.

80 Researchers, with science as their authority, will be able to cut [animals] up, alive, into small pieces, drop them from a great height to see if they are shattered by the fall, or deprive them of sleep for sixteen days and nights continuously for the purposes of an iniquitous monograph. . . . "Animal trust, undeserved faith, when at last will you turn away from us? Shall we never tire of deceiving, betraying, tormenting animals before they cease to trust us?"
         "Animals," *Quatre Saisons* (c. 1928), *Journey for Myself*
                                                         1971

81 January, month of empty pockets! . . . Let us endure this evil month, anxious as a theatrical producer's forehead.
                                  "Empty Pockets," Ibid.

82 It's nothing to be born ugly. Sensibly, the ugly woman comes to terms with her ugliness and exploits it as a grace of nature. To become ugly means the beginning of a calamity, self-willed most of the time.
                                       "Beauties," Ibid.

1342. Elizabeth Cutter Morrow (1873–1955)

1   My friend and I have built a wall
    Between us thick and wide:

The stones of it are laid in scorn
And plastered high with pride.

"Wall," St. 1 *n.d.*

2   There is no lover like an island shore
For lingering embrace;
No tryst so faithful as the turning tide
At its accustomed place.

"Islands," St. 1 *n.d.*

1343. Virginia Taylor McCormick (1873–1957)

1   Not any leaf from any book
Can give what Pan, in going took.

"Regret from Pan" *n.d.*

2   Now she is dead she greets Christ with a nod,—
(He was a carpenter)—*but she knows God.*

"The Snob" *n.d.*

1344. Dorothy Miller Richardson (1873–1957)

1   "There; how d'ye like that, eh? A liberal education in twelve volumes, with an index."

Ch. 24, *Pilgrimage*, Vol. II *1938*

2   If there was a trick, there must be a trickster.

Ibid.

3   It will all go on as long as women are stupid enough to go on bringing men into the world. . . .

Ibid.

4   No future life could heal the degradation of having been a woman. Religion in the world had nothing but insults for women.

Ibid.

5   They invent a legend to put the blame for the existence of humanity on women and, if she wants to stop it, they talk about the wonders of civilizations and the sacred responsibilities of motherhood. They can't have it both ways.

Ibid.

6   . . . women stopped being people and went off into hideous processes.

Ibid.

7   *Coercion.* The unpardonable crime.

Ch. 9, Vol. IV, Ibid.

8   "Women carry all the domesticity they need about with them. That is why they can get along alone so much better than men."

Ibid.

9   With the familiar clothes, something of his essential self seemed to have departed.

Ibid.

10   "Religious people in general are in some way unsatisfactory. Not fully alive. Exclusive. Irreligious people are unsatisfactory in another way. Defiant."

Ibid.

11   . . . she saw how very slight, how restricted and perpetually baffled must always be the communication between him and anything that bore the name of woman. Saw the price each

one had paid with whom he had been intimate either in love or friendship, in being obliged to shut off . . . three-fourths of their being.

Ibid.

12   In and out of every year of his ascent her life had been woven. She had been a witness, and was now a kind of compendium for him of it all, one of his supports, one of those who through having known the beginnings, through representing them every time she appeared, brought to him a realization of his achievements.

Ibid.

13   . . . men want recognition of their work, to help them to believe in themselves.

Ibid.

1345. Edith Franklin Wyatt (1873–1958)

1   Every true poem is a lone fount, of whose refreshment the traveler himself must drink, if he is to quench his thirst for poetry.

"Modern Poetry," *Art and the Worth-While*, Baker Brownell, ed. *1929*

2   Our criticism is always devoting itself to . . . watching the sticks and straws on the surface of the current, without interest, apparently, in the natural force of the stream, the style and turn of the whole composition, its communicative social imagination.

Ibid.

1346. Emily Post (1873–1960)

1   Considering manners even in their superficial aspect, no one—unless he be a recluse who comes in contact with no other human being—can fail to reap the advantage of a proper, courteous and likeable approach, or fail to be handicapped by an improper, offensive and resented one.

Ch. 1, *Etiquette 1922*

2   Ideal conversation must be an exchange of thought, and not, as many of those who worry most about their shortcomings believe, an eloquent exhibition of wit or oratory.

Ch. 6, Ibid.

3   To do exactly as your neighbors do is the only sensible rule.

Ch. 33, Ibid.

4   To the old saying that man built the house but woman made it a "home" might be added the modern supplement that woman accepted cooking as a chore but man has made of it a recreation.

Ch. 34, Ibid.

5   The honor of a gentleman demands the inviolability of his word, and the incorruptibility of his principles. He is the descendant of the knight, the crusader; he is the defender of the defenseless and the champion of justice—or he is not a gentleman.

Ch. 48, Ibid.

6   To tell a lie in cowardice, to tell a lie for gain, or to avoid deserved punishment—are all the blackest of black lies. On the other hand, to teach him to try his best to avoid the truth—even to press it when necessary toward the outer edge of the rainbow—for a reason of kindness, or of mercy, is far closer to the heart of truth than to repeat something accurately and mercilessly that will cruelly hurt the feelings of someone.

Ch. 11, *Children Are People 1940*

7   The natural impulses of every thoroughbred include his sense of honor; his love of fair play and courage; his dislike of pretense and of cheapness.

> Ch. 30, Ibid.

1347. Lily Montagu (1873–1963)

1   Organized religion has a part in the evolution of personal religion. It is the material upon which personal religion is grafted, but the process of grafting must be individual. Every human soul must, through thought, prayer, and study, cultivate his [sic] own religion to suit himself.

> Sermon to the Reform Synagogue, Berlin (1928), *Four Centuries of Jewish Women's Spirituality: A Sourcebook,* Ellen M. Umansky and Dianne Ashton, eds. *1992*

1348. Isabel La Howe Conant (1874–?)

He who loves an old house
Never loves in vain.

> "Old House," St. 1 *n.d.*

1349. Mrs. Edmund Craster (?–1874)

1   The Centipede was happy quite,
Until the Toad in fun
Said, "Pray which leg goes after which?"
And worked her mind to such a pitch,
She lay distracted in a ditch
Considering how to run.

> "Pinafore Poems," *Cassell's Weekly 1871*

1350. Ch'iu Chin (1874–1907)

1   We'll follow Joan of Arc—*
With our own hands our land we shall regain!

> "Ch'iu Chin—A Woman Revolutionary" (1905), Quoted in *Women of China* by Fan Wen-Lan *1956*
>
> *See 249.

2   We want to unite our two hundred million sisters into a solid whole, so that they can call to each other. Our journal will act as the mouthpiece for our women. It is meant to help our sisters by giving their life a deeper meaning and hope and to advance rapidly toward a bright, new society. We Chinese women should become the vanguard in rousing the people to welcome enlightenment.

> Ibid.

1351. Yamamuro Kieko (1874–1915)

1   . . . I realize that were I a man, I would be at the battlefront fighting amidst bullets and explosives, instead of sitting serenely at my desk.

> Untitled Essay *1895*

1352. Josephine Preston Peabody (1874–1922)

1   That you should follow our poor humanhood,
Only because you would!

> "To a Dog," *Collected Poems of Josephine Preston Peabody 1927*

2   . . . The elements rehearse
Man's urgent utterance, and his words traverse
The spacious heav'ns like homing birds.

> "Wireless," Ibid.

3   The little Road says, Go;
The little House says, Stay;
And oh, it's bonny here at home,
But I must go away.

> "The House and the Road," Ibid.

1353. Amy Lowell (1874–1925)

1   Brave idolatry
Which can conceive a hero! No deceit,
No knowledge taught by unrelenting years,
Can quench this fierce, untamable desire.

> "Hero-Worship," *A Dome of Many-Coloured Glass 1912*

2   For books are more than books, they are the life
The very heart and core of ages past,
The reason why men lived and worked and died,
The essence and quintessence of their lives.

> "The Boston Athenoeum," Ibid.

3   Marshalled like soldiers in gay company,
The tulips stand arrayed. Here infantry
Wheels out into the sunlight.

> "A Tulip Garden," *Sword Blades and Poppy Seeds 1914*

4   My words are little jars
For you to take and put upon a shelf.

> Ibid.

5   Happiness, to some, elation;
Is, to others, mere stagnation.

> "Happiness," Ibid.

6   Every castle of the air
Sleeps in the fine black grains, and there
Are seeds for every romance, or light
Whiff of a dream for a summer night.

> "Sword Blades and Poppy Seeds," Ibid.

7   All books are either dreams or swords,
You can cut, or you can drug, with words.

> St. 3, Ibid.

8   My God, but you keep me starved! You write "No Entrance Here," over all the doors. . . .
Hating bonds as you do, why should I be denied the rights of love if I leave you free?

> "The Basket" III, Ibid.

9   You are beautiful and faded,
Like an old opera tune
Played upon a harpsichord.

> "A Lady," St. 1, Ibid.

10   The cost runs into millions, but a woman must have something to console herself for a broken heart.

> "Malmaison," V, *Men, Women, and Ghosts 1916*

11   I too am a rare
Pattern. As I wander down
The garden paths.

> "Patterns," Ibid.

12   A pattern called a war.
Christ! What are patterns for?

> St. 7, Ibid.

13 Art is the desire of a man to express himself, to record the reactions of his personality to the world he lives in.
Tendencies in Modern American Poetry 1917

14 Youth condemns; maturity condones.
Ibid.

15 All Naples prates of this and that, and runs about its little business, shouting, bawling, incessantly calling its wares.
"Sea-Blue and Blood-Red," II, *Can Grande's Castle 1918*

16 Let the key-guns be mounted, make a brave
show of waging war, and pry off the lid of
Pandora's box once more.
"Gun's as Keys: And the Great Gate Swings," Pt. I, Ibid.

17 A wise man,
Watching the stars pass across the sky,
Remarked:
In the upper air the fireflies move more slowly.
"Meditation," *Picture of the Floating World 1919*

18 If failure, then another long beginning.
Why hope,
Why think that Spring must bring relenting.
"A Legend of Porcelain," St. 25, *Legends 1921*

19 "The sun weaves the seasons," thought Many Swans, "I have
been under and over the warp of the world. . . ."
"Many Swans," Ibid.

20 There are few things so futile, and few so amusing,
As a peaceful and purposeless sort of perusing
Of old random jottings set down in a blank-book
You've unearthed from a drawer as you looked for your bank-
book. . . .
"A Critical Fable," St. 1, *A Critical Fable 1922*

21 Heart-leaves of lilac all over New England,
Roots of lilac under all the soil of New England,
Lilac in me because I am New England.
"Lilacs," St. 4, *What's O'Clock 1925*

22 And the sight of a white church above thin trees in a city
square
Amazes my eyes as though it were the Parthenon.
"Meeting-House Hills," Ibid.

23 I went a-riding, a-riding,
Over a great long plain.
And the plain went a-sliding, a-sliding
Away from my bridle-rein.
"Texas," St. 1, Ibid.

24 And what are we?
We, the people without a race,
Without a language;
Of all races, and of none;
Of all tongues, and one imposed;
Of all traditions and all pasts,
With no tradition and no past.
A patchwork and an altar-piece. . . .
"The Congressional Liberty," St. 1, Ibid.

25 Love is a game—yes?
I think it is a drowning. . . .
"Twenty-four Hokku on a Modern Theme," XIX, Ibid.

26 Sappho* would speak, I think, quite openly,
And Mrs. Browning** guard a careful silence,
But Emily*** would set doors ajar and slam them
And love you for your speed of observation.
"The Sisters," St. 2, Ibid.
*See 46; **Elizabeth Barrett B—, see 875; ***E— Dickinson, see
993.

27 Finally, most of us [imagist poets] believe that concentration is
the very essence of poetry.
"Imagist Poetry" *n.d.*

28 Time! Joyless emblem of the greed
Of millions, robber of the best
Which earth can give . . .
"New York at Night" *n.d.*

29 Moon!
Moon!
I am prone before you.
Pity me,
And drench me in loneliness.
"On a Certain Critic" *n.d.*

1354. Roselle Mercier Montgomery (1874–1933)

1 I would always be with the thick of life,
Threading its mazes, sharing its strife;
Yet—somehow, singing!
"Somehow, Singing," *Ulysses Returns 1925*

2 Never a ship sail out of the bay
But carries my heart as a stowaway.
"The Stowaway," Ibid.

3 Put by, O waiting ones, put by your weaving,
Unlike Ulysses, love is unreturning.
"Counsel," Ibid.

4 The fates are not quite obdurate.
They have a grim sardonic way
Of granting men who supplicate
The things they wanted—yesterday!
"The Fates," *Many Devices 1929*

5 Companioned years have made them comprehend
The comradeship that lies beyond a kiss.
"For a Wedding Anniversary" *n.d.*

1355. Zona Gale (1874–1938)

1 They were all dimly aware that something was escaping them,
some inheritance of joy which they had meant to share. How
was it they were not sharing it?
Ch. 1, *Birth 1918*

2 Loving, like prayer, is a power as well as a process. It's cura-
tive. It is creative.
Ch. 3, Ibid.

3 DWIGHT. Energy—it's the driving power of the nation.
Act I, Sc. 1, *Miss Lulu Bett 1920*

4 NINIAN. Education: I ain't never had it and I ain't never missed it.
Sc. 2, Ibid.

5 DWIGHT. I tell you of all history the most beautiful product is
the family tie. Of it are born family consideration. . . .
Act II, Sc. 2, Ibid.

6   He faced the blind wall of human loneliness. He was as one who, expecting to be born, is still-born, and becomes aware not of the cradle, but of eternity.
    "The Biography of Blade," *Century Magazine 1924*

7   Always he had wanted to tell somebody about his life, but when he had tried, his confidante had looked at him.
    "Evening," *The Book Man 1925*

8   The unexpressed, then, is always of greater value than the expressed.
    "Modern Prose," *Art and the Worth-While*,
    Baker Brownell, ed. *1929*

9   He was integrated into life,
    He was a member of life,
    He was harmonized, orchestrated, identified with the program
        of being.
    "Walt Whitman"* *n.d.*

    * American poet (1819–1892).

1356. Alice Duer Miller (1874–1942)

1   And now too late, we see these things are one:
    The art is sacrifice and self-control,
    And who loves beauty must be stern of soul.
    "An American to France," *Welcome Home 1928*

2   Frenchmen, when
    The ultimate menace comes, will die for France
    Logically as they lived.
    "Forsaking All Others," XXI, *Forsaking All Others 1931*

3   When a woman like that who I've seen so much
    All of a sudden drops out of touch,
    Is always busy and never can
    Spare you a moment, it means a Man.
    Ibid.

4   They make other nations seem pale and flighty,
    But they do think England is God almighty,
    And you must remind them now and then
    That other countries breed other men.
    "The White Cliffs," *The White Cliffs 1940*

5   The white cliffs of Dover, I saw rising steeply
    Out of the sea that once made her [England] secure.
    St. 1, Ibid.

6   Good manners are the techniques of expressing consideration for the feelings of others.
    "I Like American Manners," *Saturday Evening Post
    13 August 1932*

1357. Lucy Maud Montgomery (1874–1942)

1   "Isn't it splendid to think of all the things there are to find out about? It just makes me feel glad to be alive—it's such an interesting world. It wouldn't be half so interesting if we knew all about everything, would it? There'd be no scope for imagination then, would there?"
    Ch. 2, *Anne of Green Gables 1908*

2   "There's such a lot of different Annes in me. I sometimes think that is why I'm such a troublesome person. If I was just one Anne it would be ever so much more comfortable, but then it wouldn't be half so interesting."
    Ch. 20, Ibid.

3   "As for Horace Baxter, he was in financial difficulties a year ago last summer, and he prayed to the Lord for help; and when his wife died and he got her life insurance he said he believed it was the answer to his prayer. Wasn't that like a man?"
    Ch. 15, *Anne's House of Dreams 1917*

4   "When a man is alone he's mighty apt to be with the devil—if he ain't with God. He has to choose which company he'll keep, I reckon."
    Ibid.

5   The point of good writing is knowing when to stop.
    Ch. 24, Ibid.

6   "They say that the only thing she was ever known to give away was a crock of butter made out of cream a rat had fell into. She contributed it to a church social. Nobody found out about the rat until afterwards."
    Ch. II, *Rainbow Valley 1919*

7   What had seemed easy in imagination was rather hard in reality.
    Ch. XII, Ibid.

8   "Mrs. Leander Crawford is always crying in church," said Susan contemptuously. "She cries over every affecting thing the minister says. But you do not often see her name on a subscription list, Mrs. Dr. dear. Tears come cheaper."
    Ibid.

9   All cats are mysterious but Dr. Jekyll-and-Mr. Hyde—"Doc" for short—were trebly so. He was a cat of double personality—or else, as Susan vowed, he was possessed by the devil.
    Ch. I, *Rilla of Ingleside 1921*

10 "The only thing I envy a cat is its purr," remarked Dr. Blythe once, listening to Doc's resonant melody. "It is the most contented sound in the world."
    Ibid.

11 Certainly, Monday's looks were not his strong point. Black spots were scattered at random over his yellow carcass, one of them blotting out an eye. His ears were in tatters, for Monday was never successful in affairs of honour. But he possessed one talisman. He knew that not all dogs could be handsome or eloquent or victorious, but that every dog could love. Inside his homely hide beat the most affectionate, loyal, faithful heart of any dog since dogs were; and something looked out of his brown eyes that was nearer akin to a soul than any theologian would allow.
    Ch. II, Ibid.

12 "We know the real charm of night here as town-dwellers never do. Every night is beautiful in the country—even the stormy ones. I love a wild night storm on this old gulf shore. As for a night like this, it is almost too beautiful—it belongs to youth and dreamland and I'm half afraid of it."
    Ch. III, Ibid.

1358. Olive Custance (1874–1944)

1   Spirit of Twilight, through your folded wings
    I catch a glimpse of your averted face,
    And rapturous on a sudden, my soul sings
    "Is not this common earth a holy place?"
    "Twilight" *n.d.*

1359. Theodosia Garrison (1874–1944)

1 I never crossed your threshold with a grief
   But that I went without it.
   > "The Closed Door," St. 1 *n.d.*

2 The hardest habit of all to break
   Is the terrible habit of happiness.
   > "The Lake" *n.d.*

3 When the red wrath perisheth, when the dulled swords fail,
   These three who have walked with death—these shall prevail.
   Hell bade all its millions rise; Paradise sends three:
   Pity, and self-sacrifice, and charity.
   > "Three Shall Prevail" *n.d.*

4 I have known laughter—therefore I
   May sorrow with you far more tenderly
   Than those who never guess how sad a thing
   Seems merriment to one's heart's suffering.
   > "Knowledge" *n.d.*

5 At first cock-crow the ghost must go
   Back to their quiet graves below.
   > "The Neighbors" *n.d.*

6 The kindliest thing God ever made,
   His hand of very healing laid
   Upon a fevered world, is shade.
   > "The Shade," St. 1 *n.d.*

1360. Lou Henry Hoover (1874–1944)

1 My chief hobbies are my husband and my children.
   > Comment, Quoted in *First Ladies*
   > by Betty Boyd Caroli *1987*

2 Boys, remember you are just as great factors in the home making of the family as are the girls.
   > Radio speech to 4-H Club (June 1929), Ibid.

1361. Rose O'Neill (1874–1944)

1 Remember, men of guns and rhymes,
   And kings who kill so fast,
   That men you kill too many times
   May be too dead at last.
   > "When the Dead Men Die," *The Master's Mistress 1922*

2 "My face is a caricature of her, and her soul is a caricature of mine. In fact, she has no soul. She is my substance. She robbed me of substance in the womb. That's why I named her Narcissa. . . . She grew her beauty on me like a flower on a dunghill. She is my material. I am her soul. We are that perilous pair."
   > Ch. 1, *Garda 1929*

3 "When we are in bed, or floating in water, is the only time when we are really out of pain. In every other situation there is always some stress."
   > Ch. 5, Ibid.

4 They lose least who have least to lose.
   > Ch. 11, Ibid.

5 Her mind was as spry as a hummingbird, but its beak was not so long for the inward flower of things. Still, she had always been looked upon as a wit; and when a creature is witty enough, he will occasionally say something that smacks of the profound.
   > Ibid.

6 It was not her way to invent obstacles, that blood-thinning process of the sickly imaginative.
   > Ch. 15, Ibid.

1362. Ellen Glasgow (1874–1945)

1 And the spring passed into Nicholas also. The wonderful renewal of surrounding life thrilled through the repression of his nature. With the flowing of the sap the blood flowed more freely in his veins. New possibilities were revealed to him; new emotions urged him into fresh endeavours. All his powerful, unspent youth spurred on to manhood.
   > Bk. II, Ch. 3, *The Voice of the People 1900*

2 It was not the matter of the work, but the mind that went into it, that counted—and the man who was not content to do small things well would leave great things undone.
   > Ch. 4, Ibid.

3 "A farmer's got to be born, same as a fool. You can't make a corn pone out of flour dough by the twistin' of it."
   > Ibid.

4 "What a man marries for's hard to tell," she returned; "an' what a woman marries for's past findin' out."
   > Bk. III, Ch 1, Ibid.

5 "I ain't never seen a head so level that it could bear the lettin' in of politics. It makes a fool of a man and a worse fool of a fool. The government's like a mule, it's slow and it's sure; it's slow to turn, and it's sure to turn the way you don't want it."
   > Ch. 2, Ibid.

6 "I d'clare if it don't beat all—one minute we're thar an' the next we're here. It's a movin' world we live in, ain't that so, Mum?"
   > Bk. I, Ch. 1, *The Deliverance 1904*

7 "Maria has been so long at her high-and-mighty boarding-school," he said, "that I reckon her head's full of fancies as a cheese is of maggots."
   > Ch. 3, Ibid.

8 I haven't much opinion of words. . . . They're apt to set fire to a dry tongue, that's what I say.
   > Bk. II, Ch. 4, Ibid.

9 "I hate lies, I have had so many of them, and I shall speak the truth hereafter, no matter what comes of it. Anything is better than a long, wearing falsehood, or than those hideous little shams that we were always afraid to touch for fear they would melt and show us our own nakedness."
   > Bk. IV, Ch. 2, Ibid.

10 I wondered why anyone so rich and so beautiful should ever be unhappy—for I had been schooled by poverty to believe that money is the first essential of happiness—and yet her unhappiness was as evident as her beauty, or the luxury that enveloped her.
   > "The Past," *Good Housekeeping 1920*

11 "But the war wasn't the worst thing," he concluded grimly. "The worst thing is this sense of having lost our way in the universe. The worst thing is that the war has made peace seem so futile. It is just as if the bottom had dropped out of idealism. . . ."
   > Pt. I, Ch. 1, *They Stooped to Folly 1929*

12 "Oh, but it feels so nice to be hard! If I had known how nice it felt, I should have been hard all my life."

Ch. 12, Ibid.

13 After all, you can't expect men not to judge by appearances.

The Sheltered Life 1932

14 Shadows are not enough.

Ibid.

15 Women like to sit down with trouble as if it were knitting.

Pt. 3, Sct. 3, Ibid.

16 No idea is so antiquated that it was not once modern. No idea is so modern that it will not someday be antiquated.

Address, Modern Language Association *1936*

17 To seize the flying thought before it escapes us is our only touch with reality.

Ibid.

18 "Grandpa says we've got everything to make us happy but happiness."

Pt. I, Ch. 1, *In This Our Life 1941*

19 "Heaven knows, I'm not a snob, and I realize it's the fashion nowadays to climb down and not up; but all the radicals you see in the newspaper look so untidy, and I'm afraid when he gets middle-aged he will never want to brush his hair or wash his face."

Ch. 9, Ibid.

20 "I don't like human nature, but I do like human beings."

Pt. II, Ch. 1, Ibid.

21 "We didn't talk so much about happiness in my day. When it came, we were grateful for it, and, I suppose, a little went farther than it does nowadays. We may have been all wrong in our ideas, but we were brought up to think other things more important than happiness."

Ch. 10, Ibid.

22 No matter how vital experience might be while you lived it, no sooner was it ended and dead than it became as lifeless as the piles of dry dust in a school history book.

Pt. III, Ch. 9, Ibid.

23 Tilling the fertile soil of man's vanity.

A Certain Measure 1943

1363. Gertrude Stein (1874–1946)

1 "I never wanted to be a hero, but on the other hand I am not anxious to cultivate cowardice."

"Adele," *Q. E. D.,* Bk. I *1903*

2 Honesty is a selfish virtue. Yes, I am honest enough.

Ibid.

3 "You are so afraid of losing your moral sense that you are not willing to take it through anything more dangerous than a mud puddle."

Ibid.

4 "I could undertake to be an efficient pupil if it were possible to find an efficient teacher."

Ibid.

5 I simply contend that the middle-class ideal which demands that people be affectionate, respectable, honest and content, that they avoid excitements and cultivate serenity is the ideal that appeals to me, it is in short the ideal of affectionate family life, of honorable business methods.

Ibid.

6 One must either accept some theory or else believe one's instinct or follow the world's opinion.

"Helen," Bk. III, Ibid.

7 I am writing for myself and strangers. This is the only way that I can do it.

The Making of Americans 1906–1908

8 "Rose is a rose is a rose is a rose."

"Sacred Emily" *1913*

9 I suppose I pose I expose, I repose, I close the door when the sun shines so, I close the door when the wind is so strong and the dust is not there. . . .

"Mildred's Thoughts" *1922*

10 Pigeons on the grass alas.

Four Saints in Three Acts (opera) *1927*

11 Saint Therese something like that.
Saint Therese something like that.
Saint Therese something like that.
Saint Therese would and would and would.
Saint Therese something like that.
Saint Therese.
Saint Therese half in doors and half out doors.
Saint Therese not knowing of other saints.

Ibid.

12 "Before the flowers of friendship faded friendship faded."

Story title *1931*

13 Remarks are not literature.

The Autobiography of Alice B. Toklas 1933

14 She always says she dislikes the abnormal, it is so obvious. She says the normal is so much more simply complicated and interesting.

Ibid.

15 America is my country and Paris is my hometown. And it is as it has come to be. After all anybody is as their air and land is. Anybody is as the sky is low or high, the air heavy or clear and anybody is as there is wind or no wind there. It is that which makes them and the arts they make and the work they do and the way they eat and the way they drink and the way they learn and everything. And so I am an American and I have lived half my life in Paris, not the half that made me but the half in which I made what I made.

"An American and France" *1936*

16 In the United States there is more space where nobody is than where anybody is. That is what makes America what it is.

The Geographical History of America 1936

17 Everybody knows if you are too careful you are so occupied in being careful that you are sure to stumble over something.

Ch. 1, *Everybody's Autobiography 1937*

18 . . . native always means people who belong somewhere else, because they had once belonged somewhere. That shows that

the white race does not really think they belong anywhere because they think of everybody else as a native.

Ibid.

19 . . . one never discusses anything with anybody who can understand, one discusses things with people who cannot understand. . . .

Ibid.

20 . . . if anything is a surprise then there is not much difference between older or younger because the only thing that does make anybody older is that they cannot be surprised.

Ch. 2, Ibid.

21 . . . money . . . is really the difference between men and animals, most of the things men feel animals feel and vice versa, but animals do not know about money, money is a purely human conception and that is very important to know very very important.

Ibid.

22 . . . considering how dangerous everything is nothing is really very frightening.

Ibid.

23 . . . what is the use of thinking if after all there is to be organization.

Ibid.

24 It takes a lot of time to be a genius, you have to sit around so much doing nothing, really doing nothing.

Ibid.

25 A distraction is to avoid the consciousness of the passage of time.

Ibid.

26 More great Americans were failures than they were successes. They mostly spent their lives in not having a buyer for what they had for sale.

Ibid.

27 It is funny the two things most men are proudest of is the thing that any man can do and doing does in the same way, that is being drunk and being the father of their son.

Ibid.

28 . . . understanding is a very dull occupation.

Ibid.

29 I am always ready to sign anything a bank tells me to sign but anything else fills me with suspicion.

Ch. 3, Ibid.

30 America is not old enough yet to get young again.

Ibid.

31 The minute you or anybody else knows what you are you are not it, you are what you or anybody else knows you are and as everything in living is made up of finding out what you are it is extraordinarily difficult really not to know what you are and yet to be that thing.

Ibid.

32 I am also fond of saying that a war or fighting is like a dance because it is all going forward and back, and that is what everybody likes; they like that forward and the back movement, that is the reason that revolutions and Utopias

are discouraging they are up and down and not forward and back.

Ibid.

33 Too few is as many as too many.

Ibid.

34 That is natural enough when nobody has had fathers they begin to long for them and then when everybody has had fathers they begin to long to do without them.

Ibid.

35 Counting is the religion of this generation it is its hope and its salvation.

Ibid.

36 I understand you undertake to overthrow my undertaking.

Ibid.

37 . . . I do want to get rich but I never want to do what there is to do to get rich.

Ibid.

38 . . . what is the use of being a little boy if you are going to grow up to be a man.

Ch. 4, Ibid.

39 If things happen all the time you are never nervous it is when they are not happening that you are nervous.

Ibid.

40 In America if they do not do it right away they do not do it at all in France they very often seem not to be going to do it at all but if it has ever really been proposed at all sometimes it really is done.

Ibid.

41 The only thing that anybody can understand is mechanics and that is what makes everybody feel that they are something when they talk about it. About every other thing nobody is of the same opinion nobody means the same thing by what they say as the other one means and only the one who is talking thinks he means what he is saying even though he knows very well that that is not what he is saying.

Ibid.

42 . . . it is a peaceful thing to be one succeeding.

Ibid.

43 She was thinking about it she was thinking about life. She knew it was just like that through and through.

She never did not want to leave it.

She did not want to stop thinking about it thinking about life, so that is what she was thinking about.

"Ida" *1941*

44 One does not get better but different and older and that is always a pleasure.

Letter to F. Scott Fitzgerald* (22 May 1925), *The Crack-Up*, Edmund Wilson,** ed. *1945*

*American writer (1896–1940). **American literary critic (1895–1972).

45 A saint a real saint never does anything, a martyr does something but a really good saint does nothing and so I wanted to have Four Saints that did nothing and I wrote the *Four Saints in Three Acts* and they did nothing and that was everything.

Realistically speaking anybody is more interesting doing nothing than doing anything.
> Quoted in Introduction, *Last Operas and Plays*
> by Carl Van Vechten* *1949*
> *American music critic and novelist (1880–1964).

46 Nothing has happened today except kindness. . . .
> "A Diary," *Alphabets and Birthdays 1957*

47 A diary means yes indeed. . . .
> Ibid.

48 Oh, I wish I were a miser; being a miser must be so occupying.
> Quoted by Thornton Wilder* in *Writers at Work*
> (First Series), Malcom Cowley, ed. *1958*
> *American novelist and playwright (1897–1975).

49 Communists are people who fancied that they had an unhappy childhood.
> Ibid.

50 What is the answer? (I was silent.) In that case, what is the question?
> Quoted in *What Is Remembered* by Alice B. Toklas* *1963*
> *See 1414.

51 All of you young people who served in the war. You are a lost generation. . . . You have no respect for anything. You drink yourselves to death.
> Remark to Ernest Hemingway,* Quoted in
> Ch. 3, *A Moveable Feast 1964*
> *American writer (1899–1961).

52 Nature is commonplace. Imitation is more interesting.
> Ch. 20, Quoted in *My Autobiography*
> by Charlie Chaplin* *1964*
> *British-born comic film actor and director (1889–1977).

53 You know very well that it is not necessary to explain to an intelligent person—one only explains to a stupid one.
> Quoted in *Playing on Alone: Letters of Alice B. Toklas*,
> Ed Burns, ed. *1973*

54 And how do you look backward. By looking forward. And what do they see. As they look forward. They see what they had to do before they could look backward. And there we have it all.
> "Thoughts on an American Contemporary Feeling" (1932),
> *Reflection on the Atomic Bomb*, Vol. I *1973*

55 Everybody gets so much information all day long that they lose their common sense.
> Untitled essay (1946), Ibid.

56 The United States is just now the oldest country in the world, there always is an oldest country and she is it, it is she who is the mother of the twentieth century civilization. She began to feel herself as it just after the Civil War. And so it is a country the right age to have been born in and the wrong age to live in.
> "Why I Do Not Live In America" (*Transition*, Fall 1928),
> *How Writing Is Written*, Robert Bartlett Haas, ed. *1974*

57 Americans are very friendly and very suspicious, that is what Americans are and that is what always upsets the foreigner, who deals with them, they are so friendly how can they be so suspicious they are so suspicious how can they be so friendly but they just are.
> "The Capital and Capitals of the United States of America,"
> *New York Herald Tribune* (9 March 1935), *How Writing
> Is Written*, Robert Bartlett Haas, ed. *1974*

58 The unreal is natural, so natural that it makes of unreality the most natural of anything natural. That is what America does, and that is what America is.
> "I Came and Here I Am" (*Cosmopolitan*, New York,
> February 1936), Ibid.

59 A writer must always try to have a philosophy and he should also have a psychology and a philology and many other things. Without a philosophy and a psychology and all these various other things he is not really worthy of being called a writer. I agree with Kant and Schopenhauer and Plato and Spinoza and that is quite enough to be called a philosophy. But then of course a philosophy is not the same thing as a style.
> "Style," Quoted in *Voices: A Memoir* by Frederic Prokosch
> *1983*

1364. Etsu Inagaki Sugimoto (1874?–1950)

1 A careless or perturbed state of mind always betrays itself in the intricate shadings of ideographs, for each one requires absolute steadiness and accuracy of touch. Thus, in careful guidance of the hand were we children taught to hold the mind in leash.
> Ch. 2, *A Daughter of the Samurai 1925*

2 "Look in the mirror every day," she said, "for if scars of selfishness or pride are in the heart, they will grow into the lines of the face. Watch closely."
> Ch. 6, Ibid.

1365. Beatrice Hinkle (1874–1953)

1 Fundamentally the male artist approximates more to the psychology of woman, who, biologically speaking, is a purely creative being and whose personality has been as mysterious and unfathomable to the man as the artist has been to the average person.
> "The Psychology of the Artist," *Recreating the Individual*
> *1923*

2 . . . woman is a being dominated by the creative urge and . . . no understanding of her as an individual can be gained unless the significance and effects of that great fact can be grasped.
> Ibid.

3 When one looks back over human existence, however, it is very evident that all culture has developed through an *initial resistance against adaptation to the reality in which man finds himself.*
> Ibid.

4 The creator does not create only for the pleasure of creating but . . . he also desires to subdue other minds.
> Ibid.

5 The attitude and reactions of artists toward their children reveal an attitude similar to that which mothers in general possess toward their children. There is the same sensitivity to any criticism, the same possessive pride, the same devotion and love, with the accompanying anxiety and distress concerning them.
> Ibid.

6 The amount which cannot be harnessed and domesticated, but insists on its own form of activity rather than one which is offered ready made, is the energy used for the creation of art.
> Ibid.

7 . . . the artist has always been and still is a being somewhat apart from the rest of humanity.
> Ibid.

8 The mystics are the only ones who have gained a glimpse into what is possible. . . .

> Ibid.

1366. Anne Crawford Flexner (1874–1955)

1 MRS. WIGGS. The worse Mr. Wiggs would act, the harder I would pat him on the back. And as for the children, I always did use compliments on 'em instead of switches.

> Act I, *Mrs. Wiggs of the Cabbage Patch* 1903

2 MRS. FROST. If there were no women in the world, what would become of you men?
FROST. We would be scarce, Emily, but we might be happier.

> Act I, *The Marriage Game* 1913

3 KEATS. One must have health! You may banish money—banish sofas—banish wine! but right Jack Health, true Jack Health, honest Jack Health—banish health, and you banish all the world!

> Act II, Sc. 3, *Aged Twenty-six* 1937

1367. Bettina von Hutten (1874–1957)

1 A good many women are good tempered simply because it saves the wrinkles coming too soon.

> *The Halo* 1907

2 Everybody in the world ought to be sorry for everybody else. We all have our little private hell.

> Ibid.

1368. Angela Morgan (1874?–1957)

1 O thrilling age,
O willing age!

> "Today," St. 1 *n.d.*

2 The signals of the century
Proclaims the things that are to be—
The rise of woman to her place,
The coming of a nobler race.

> St. 3, Ibid.

3 To be alive in such an age—
To live in it,
To give to it!

> St. 4, Ibid.

4 I will hew new windows for my soul.

> "Room" *n.d.*

5 Praised be the gods that made my spirit mad;
Kept me aflame and raw to beauty's touch.

> "June Rapture" *n.d.*

6 Work!
Thank God for the swing of it,
For the clamoring, hammering ring of it,
Passion of labor daily hurled
On the mighty anvils of the world.

> "Work: A Song of Triumph" *n.d.*

7 God, when you thought of a pine tree,
How did you think of a star?

> "God, the Artist," St. 1 *n.d.*

8 A courage mightier than the sun—
You rose and fought and, fighting, won!

> "Know Thyself" *n.d.*

9 Lad, you took the world's soul,
Thrilled it by your daring,
Lifted the uncaring
And made them joyous men.

> "Lindbergh"* *n.d.*

* Charles August Lindbergh, American aviator who made first solo nonstop transatlantic flight (1902–1974).

1369. Dorothy Reed Mendenhall (1874–1964)

1 My early life had been fed with dreams and a deep feeling that if I waited, did my part and was patient, love would come to me and with it such a family life as fiction depicted and romance built up. It seems to me that I have always been waiting for something better—sometimes to see the best I had snatched from me.

> Quoted in "Dorothy Mendenhall: 'Childbirth is Not a Disease'" by Gena Corea, *Ms.* (New York) *April 1974*

2 When hurry in the attendant meets fear in the mother, the combination . . . militates against safe and sane obstetrics.

> Ibid.

1370. María Martínez Sierra (1874–1974)

1 SISTER JOANNA OF THE CROSS. They say canaries are born in cages and, see, how he doesn't care to fly away.
SISTER MARÍA. Then you're a great fool, birdie. God made the air for wings and He made wings to fly with. While he might be soaring away above the clouds, he is satisfied to stay here all day shut up in his cage, hopping between two sticks and a leaf of lettuce! What sense is there in a bird?

> Act I, *The Cradle Song*, with Gregorio Martínez Sierra* 1911

2 ANTONIO. . . .there is no longer in the world either far or near.

> Act II, Ibid.

3 DON GUILLERMO. When we have once peeped into the Garden of Knowledge, even at the tiniest gate, it is astounding what marvelous voyages we are able to make, and what sights we can see, without taking the trouble of leaving our chairs.

> Act II, *Madame Pepita*, with Gregorio Martínez Sierra* 1912

4 DOÑA PAQUITA. Oh . . . I love flowers. And the earth will always give something in return for one's care of it, will it not? It is easier to strive with than the hearts of men.

> Act II, *The Two Shepherds*, with Gregorio Martínez Sierra* 1913

5 RAMÓN. Just as sure as you name a street after a man, he goes and disgraces himself afterwards . . .

> Act I, *Wife to a Famous Man*, with Gregorio Martínez Sierra* 1914

6 MARIANA. I want you to stop talking humbug. As you always lie like a newspaper it doesn't matter much what sort of tale you tell, for no one's going to believe you.

> Act II, Ibid.

7 LORENZO. María Isabel . . . children are not an idle gift.
MARÍA ISABEL. What do you mean?
LORENZO. I mean that they are not our own just to do as we like with.
MARÍA ISABEL. So like a man! Easy to see that you don't suffer to bring them into the world.

LORENZO. We sweat blood though, sometimes, to keep them alive in it. But we owe them more than that. Did we so deliberately plan to bring them into the world? They are ours through our frailty.

MARÍA ISABEL. Frailty!

LORENZO. What else? And if they are the fruit of our happiness what right have we to deny them their own . . . unless they seek it in evil ways?

Act I, The Kingdom of God, with Gregorio Martínez Sierra* 1915

8 SISTER GRACIA. It is by no will of his that some are poor and neglected while some are set up in pride. For God is Love and he loves us all and to each one he gives a share in heaven and in this earth.

FELIPE. Don't listen to her . . . she's just preaching lies to you. Nuns have all sold themselves to the rich. Do they ever go hungry? And as long as they can get us to keep up the sham they're left to stuff themselves with food in peace.

Act III, Ibid.

9 SISTER DIONISIA. But where are you going . . . what are you going to do?

FELIPE. What men do . . . take by force what we can't get by asking nicely.

Ibid.

10 IRENE. He's the untidiest man in the world, and the one thing he won't stand is untidiness. That's where his secretary comes in. He'll go out leaving his writing strewn all over the place, pages unnumbered, books on the floor, torn up paper in the drawers and his notes in the waste paper basket. But when he comes back, he likes to find everything just so.

Act II, Romantic Young Lady, with Gregorio Martínez Sierra* 1918

* Her husband, famed Spanish novelist, poet, essayist, theatrician (1881–1947); shortly before his death it was revealed that María had been his constant collaborator and had, in many instances, been the principal author of their dramatic works.

1371. Anne Goodwin Winslow (1875–?)

1 And how can curses make him yours
When kisses could not make him so?

"The Beaten Path" *n.d.*

1372. Abbie Farwell Brown (1875–1927)

1 No matter what my birth may be,
No matter where my lot is cast,
I am the heir in equity
Of all the precious past.

"The Heritage," St. 1 *n.d.*

2 They named their rocky farmlands,
Their hamlets by the sea,
For the mother-towns that bred them
In racial loyalty.

"Names," St. 7 *n.d.*

1373. Alice Ruth Dunbar-Nelson (1875–1935)

1 In its dark bosom many secrets lie buried. It is like some beautiful serpent, languorous, sinister. It ripples in the sunshine, sparkles in the moonlight, glooms in the dusk and broods in the dark. But it thinks unceasingly, and below its brightest sparkle you feel its unknown soul.

Sketch about a Louisiana bayou, *The Schomburg Library of Nineteenth-Century Black Women Writers*, Henry Louis Gates, Jr., ed. *1988*

1374. Anna Hempstead Branch (1875–1937)

1 His screaming stallions maned with whistling wind.

"Nimrod Wars with the Angels" *1910*

2 Oh, grieve not, ladies, if at night
Ye wake to feel your beauty going.
It was a web of frail delight,
Inconstant as an April snowing.

"Grieve Not, Ladies," St. 1 *n.d.*

3 Order is a lovely thing;
On disarray it lays its wing,
Teaching simplicity to sing.

"The Monk in the Kitchen" *n.d.*

4 God wove a web of loveliness,
Of clouds and stars and birds,
But made not anything at all
So beautiful as words.

"Songs for My Mother: Her Words," St. 5 *n.d.*

5 If there is no God for thee
Then there is no God for me.

"To a Dog" *n.d.*

1375. Elie Faure (1875–1937)

1 The stamping out of the artist is one of the blind goals of every civilization. When a civilization becomes so standardized that the individual can no longer make an imprint on it, then that civilization is dying. The "mass mind" has taken over and another set of national glories is heading for history's scrap heap.

Quoted in *Forbes* magazine *n.d.*

1376. Margaret Eliza Ashmun (1875–1940)

1 We are the whirlwinds that winnow the West—
We scatter the wicked like straw!
We are the Nemeses, never at rest—
We are Justice, and Right, and the Law!

"The Vigilantes," *Pacific Monthly* 1907

1377. Marie Lenéru (1875–1940)

1 To be deaf is perhaps not to hear, but certainly it is this: to hold your tongue. Whatever spontaneous feelings may move you, to resist the impulse to communicate them, to remember that *your* world, your moment, are not other people's: to hold your tongue . . . a *haute école* of self-control, of nonspontaneousness, of solitude and indifference.

Journal 1945

2 One *sees* intelligence far more than one hears it. People do not always say transcendental things, but if they are *capable* of saying them, it is always visible.

Ibid.

3 I will never abdicate. I shall always want everything. To accept my life I must prefer it.

(1898), Ibid.

4 If I were honest, I would admit that money is one half of happiness; it makes it so much more attractive!

Ibid.

5 Books, books, these are the only things that have come to my aid! In the end, it makes one terribly arrogant, always to do without one's equals!

Ibid.

6 Isolation has led me to reflection, reflection to doubt, doubt to a more sincere and intelligent love of God.

Ibid.

7 I have discovered that in an intellectual society individual intelligence is no more frequent than anywhere else, and its absence is more tedious, for not to speak in a superior manner of superior subjects is both boring and ridiculous.

Ibid.

8 To succeed is nothing, it's an accident. But to feel no doubts about oneself is something very different: it is character.

Ibid.

1378. Helen Huntington (1875?–1950)

1 With the bitter past I will deck to-morrow.

"The Wayfarer" n.d.

1379. Vilda Sauvage Owens (1875–1950)

1 If ever I have time for things that matter,
If ever I have the smallest chance,
I'm going to live in
Little Broom Gardens,
Moat-by-the-Castle,
Nettlecomb, Hants.

"If Ever I Have Time for Things That Matter," St. 1 n.d.

1380. Mary McLeod Bethune (1875–1955)

1 If our people are to fight their way up out of bondage we must arm them with the sword and the shield and the buckler of pride. . . .

"Clarifying Our Vision with the Facts," *Journal of Negro History January 1938*

2 Mr. Lincoln* had told our race we were free, but mentally we were still enslaved.

"Faith That Moved a Dump Heap," *Who, The Magazine About People June 1941*
*Abraham Lincoln (1809–1865), 16th president of the United States (1861–65); assassinated.

3 I never stop to plan. I take things step by step.

Ibid.

4 For I am my mother's daughter, and the drums of Africa still beat in my heart. They will not let me rest while there is a single Negro boy or girl without a chance to prove his worth.

Ibid.

5 "For God so loved the world, that He gave His only begotten Son, that whosoever believeth in Him should not perish, but have everlasting life." With these words the scales fell from my eyes and the light came flooding in. My sense of inferiority, my fear of handicaps, dropped away. "Whosoever," it said. No Jew nor Gentile, no Catholic nor Protestant, no black nor white; just "whosoever." It meant that I, a humble Negro girl, had just as much chance as anybody in the sight and love of God. These words stored up a battery of faith and confidence and determination in my heart, which has not failed me to this day. . . .

Ibid.

6 The true worth of a race must be measured by the character of its womanhood. . . .

Address, "A Century of Progress of Negro Women" (Chicago Women's Federation, 3 June 1933), *Black Women in White America*, Gerda Lerner,* ed. *1972*
*See 2160.

7 [The African American woman] has been quick to seize every opportunity which presented itself to come more and more into the open and strive directly for the uplift of the race and nation. In that direction, her achievements have been amazing . . .

Ibid.

8 I do feel, in my dreamings and yearnings, so undiscovered by those who are able to help me. . . . The burden is so heavy just now, the task is so great, that speedy reinforcement is needed. My mind is overtaxed. Brave and courageous as I am I feel that creeping on of that inevitable thing, a breakdown, if I cannot get some immediate relief. I need somebody to come and get me.

Letter to George R. Arthur (1 November 1930), Ibid.

9 I leave you love...hope...the challenge of developing confidence in one another...a thirst for education...a respect for the uses of power...faith...racial dignity...a desire to live harmoniously with your fellow men...a responsibility to our young people.

Last will and testament, Quoted in "Chronicles of Black Courage" by L. Bennett, *Ebony December 1982*

1381. Louise Driscoll (1875–1957)

1 Power and gold and fame denied,
Love laughs glad in the paths aside.

"The Highway" n.d.

2 There you will find what
Every man needs,
Wild religion
Without any creeds.

"Spring Market," St. 5 n.d.

3 When youth is spent, a penny at a fair,
The old men tell of the bargains there.
There was this and that for a price and a wage,
But when they came away they had all bought age.

"Bargain" n.d.

4 Some men die early and are spared much care,
Some suddenly, escaping worse than death;
But he is fortunate who happens where
He can exult and die in the same breath.

"The Good Hour" n.d.

1382. Minnie Haskins (1875–1957)

1 And I said to the man who stood at the gate of the year:
"Give me a light that I may tread safely into the Unknown."
And he replied: "Go out into the darkness and put your hand
Into the hand of God. That shall be to you better than light
And safer than a known way."

"The Desert" 1908

1383. Belle Livingstone (1875–1957)

1 That winter two things happened which made me see that the world, the flesh, and the devil were going to be more powerful influences in my life after all than the chapel bell. First, I tasted champagne; second, the theater.

Belle Out of Order 1959

2 Like Moses, I wasn't born. I was found.

Pt. I, Ch. 1, Ibid.

3 Odd how the erotic appeal has swung away from legs; today a smart girl takes her legs for granted and gets herself a good sweater.

Ch. 2, Ibid.

4 The courtesan, alas, is gone, extinct as the American buffalo . . . . Anyone can become a mistress; one has to be born a courtesan.

Ibid.

5 Much has been written about the beauty, the stillness, the terror of the desert but little about its flies.

Ch. 5, Ibid.

6 Oddly enough, a gambler never entertains the thought of loss. He can't afford to. No one who has never gambled can possibly understand the projects, plans, dreams a gambler can create on the turn of a card or the chance of a horse going to the post.

Ch. 9, Ibid.

7 . . . I had swallowed the sugar-coated pill of Rabelaisian philosophy—that life is its own justification and we need not live depriving ourselves of anything.

Pt. II, Ch. 1, Ibid.

8 It is a truism that most people take their adventures vicariously.

Epilogue, Ibid.

1384. Christopher St. John (1875?–1960)

1 WINIFRED. The majority of men in this country shouldn't for years have kept alive the foolish superstition that all women are supported by men. For years we have told them it was a delusion, but they could not take our arguments seriously.

How the Vote Was Won 1909

1385. Sally Kinsolving (1876–?)

1 Ships, young ships,
I do not wonder men see you as women—
You in the white length of your loveliness
Reclining on the sea!

"Ships," *Many Waters* 1942

1386. Mata Hari (1876–1917)

1 The dance is a poem of which each movement is a word.

Scrapbook 1905

2 The [military] officer is a being apart, a kind of artist breathing the grand air in the brilliant profession of arms, in a uniform that is always seductive. . . . To me the officer is a separate race.

Life 1906

3 I firmly believe that the only means of living in beauty consists in avoiding the thousand and one daily annoyances which interfere with an existence in the full ideal. That is why I cannot tolerate European things, not even the religion.

Quoted in *Mata Hari* by Major Thomas Coulson, O.B.E. (1917) 1930 (reissue)

4 I am a woman who enjoys herself very much; sometimes I lose, sometimes I win.

Quoted in *Mata Hari, The True Story* by Russell Howe 1986

1387. Norah M. Holland (1876–1925)

1 Life has given me of its best—
Laughter and weeping, labour and rest,
Little of gold, but lots of fun;
Shall I then sigh that all is done?

"Life" *n.d.*

1388. Grace Fallow Norton (1876–1926)

1 I have loved many, the more and the few—
I have loved many that I might love you.

"Song of the Sum of All" *n.d.*

2 Take me upon thy breast,
O River of Rest.
Draw me down to thy side,
Slow-moving tide.

"O Sleep" *n.d.*

1389. Elinore Pruitt Stewart (1876–1933)

1 I am very enthusiastic about women homesteading....Any woman who can stand her own company, can see the beauty of the sunset, loves growing things, and is willing to put in as much time at careful labor as she does over the washtub, will certainly succeed; will have independence, plenty to eat all the time, and a home of her own in the end.

Article, *Atlantic Monthly* (Boston) 1913

2 I had not thought I should ever marry again. Jerrine was always such a dear little pal, and I wanted to just knock about footloose and free to see life as a gypsy sees it. I had planned to see the Cliff-Dwellers' home; to live right there until I caught the spirit of the surrounding enough to live over their lives in imagination anyway. I had planned to see the old missions and to go to Alaska; to hunt in Canada. I even dreamed of Honolulu. Life stretched out before me one long, happy jaunt. I aimed to see all the world I could, but to travel unknown bypaths to do it.

Letters of a Woman Homesteader 1914

3 I have had more than half a century of such happiness. A great deal of worry and sorrow, too, but never a worry or sorrow that was not offset by a purple iris, a lark, a bluebird, or a dewy morning glory.

Letter to a friend, Quoted in *Women Pioneers* by Rebecca Stefoff 1995

1390. Helen L. Sumner (1876–1933)

1 . . . the history of women's work in this country shows that legislation has been the only force which has improved the working conditions of any large number of women wage-earners.

Senate Report, *History of Women in Industry in the United States*, Vol. IX 1911

2 The story of women's work in gainful employment is a story of constant changes or shifting of work and workshop, accompanied by long hours, low wages, insanitary conditions, overwork, and the want on the part of the woman of training, skill, and vital interest in her work.

Ibid.

1391. Susan Glaspell (1876/82–1948)

1 STEPHEN. If you're going to separate from psychoanalysis, there's no reason why I should separate from you!
MABEL. What am I supposed to do with my suppressed desires?
STEPHEN. Mabel, you just keep right on suppressing them!

Suppressed Desires 1914

2 HENRIETTA. It is through suppression that hells are formed in us.

Sc. 1, Ibid.

3 MABEL. Why, if it wasn't for psychoanalysis you'd never find out how wonderful your own mind is!

Sc. 2, Ibid.

4 We live close together and we live far apart.
Trifles 1916

5 "We all go through the same things—it's all just a different kind of the same thing!"
"A Jury of Her Peers," *Every Week 1917*

6 FATHER. But in a world that won't have visions—why not study Sanscrit while such a world is being made over—into another such world.
Act I, *Bernice 1919*

7 Those who were neither mourning nor rejoicing were being kept awake by mourners or rejoicers. All the while, diluted whiskey that could be bought on the quiet was in use for the deadening or the heightening of emotion.
"Government Goat," *The Pictorial Review 1919*

8 GRANDMOTHER. That's the worst of a war—you have to go on hearing about it so long.
Act I, *Inheritors 1921*

9 GRANDMOTHER. Seems nothing draws men together like killing other men.
Ibid.

10 HOLDEN. And I think a society which permits things to go on which I can prove go on in our federal prisons had better stop and take a fresh look at itself. To stand for that and then talk of democracy and idealism—oh, it shows no mentality, for one thing.
Act. II, Sc. 2, Ibid.

11 A new town was only the same town in a different place. . . .
"His Smile," *The Pictorial Review 1921*

1392. Helen Rowland (1876–1950)

1 Woman: the peg on which the wit hangs his jest, the preacher his text, the cynic his grouch, and the sinner his justification.
Reflections of a Bachelor Girl 1903

2 When you see what some girls marry, you realize they must hate to work for a living
Ibid.

3 Love, the quest; marriage, the conquest; divorce, the inquest.
Ibid.

4 Marriage: a souvenir of love.
Ibid.

5 The follies which a man regrets most in his life are those which he didn't commit when he had the opportunity.
Ibid.

6 It takes a woman twenty years to make a man of her son, and another woman twenty minutes to make a fool of him.
Ibid.

7 One man's folly is another man's wife.
Ibid.

8 Variety is the spice of love.
Ibid.

9 "Home" is any four walls that enclose the right person.
Ibid.

10 The tenderest spot in a man's make-up is sometimes the bald spot on top of his head.
Ibid.

11 Nowadays love is a matter of chance, matrimony a matter of money and divorce a matter of course.
Ibid.

12 Between lovers a little confession is a dangerous thing.
Ibid.

13 When a girl marries, she exchanges the attentions of all the other men of her acquaintance for the inattention of just one.
Ibid.

14 Never trust a husband too far, or a bachelor too near.
The Rubáiyat of a Bachelor 1915

15 Every man wants a woman to appeal to his better side, his nobler instincts and his higher nature—and another woman to help him forget them.
"Second Interlude," *A Guide to Men 1922*

16 A Bachelor of Arts is one who makes love to a lot of women, and yet has the art to remain a bachelor.
"Bachelors," Ibid.

17 No girl who is going to marry need bother to win a college degree; she just naturally becomes a "Master of Arts" and a "Doctor of Philosophy" after catering to an ordinary man for a few years.
"Cymbals and Kettle-drums," Ibid.

18 A husband is what is left of a lover, after the nerve has been extracted.
"Prelude," Ibid.

19 After marriage, a woman's sight becomes so keen that she can see right through her husband without looking at him, and a man's so dull that he can look right through his wife without seeing her.
"First Interlude," Ibid.

20 A fool and her money are soon courted.
Ibid.

21 Before marriage, a man will go home and lie awake all night thinking about something you said; after marriage, he'll go to sleep before you finish saying it.
Ibid.

22 It is easier to keep half a dozen lovers guessing than to keep one lover after he has stopped guessing.
"Third Interlude," Ibid.

23 To be happy with a man you must understand him a lot and love him a little. To be happy with a woman you must love her a lot and not try to understand her at all.
"Fourth Interlude," Ibid.

24 When two people decide to get a divorce, it isn't a sign that they "don't understand" one another, but a sign that they have, at last, begun to.
"Divorces," Ibid.

25 Call the bald man, "Boy"; make the sage thy toy;
Greet the youth with solemn face; praise the fat man for his grace.
"Maxims of Cleopatra," No. 10, Ibid.

26 Telling lies is a fault in a boy, an art in a lover, an accomplishment in a bachelor, and second-nature in a married man.
"Syncopations," Ibid.

27 Wedding: the point at which a man stops toasting a woman and begins roasting her.
Ibid.

28 Falling in love consists merely in uncorking the imagination and bottling the common-sense.
"Variations," Ibid.

29 France may claim the happiest marriages in the world, but the happiest divorces in the world are "made in America."
"What Every Woman Wonders," Ibid.

30 A widow is a fascinating being with the flavor of maturity, the spice of experience, the piquancy of novelty, the tang of practised coquetry, and the halo of one man's approval.
"Widows," Ibid.

31 Courtship is a republic; marriage, a monarchy; divorce, a soviet.
"Personally Speaking," *The Book of Diversion*, F. P. Adams, D. Taylor, J. Bechdolt, eds. *1925*

32 At twenty, a man feels awfully aged and blasé; at thirty, almost senile; at forty, "not so old"; and at fifty, positively skittish.
Ibid.

33 Alas, why will a man spend months trying to hand over his liberty to a woman—and the rest of his life trying to get it back again?
Ibid.

34 Marriage is the only thing that affords a woman the pleasure of company and the perfect sensation of solitude at the same time.
Ibid.

35 The woman who appeals to a man's vanity may stimulate him; the woman who appeals to his heart may attract him; but it's the woman who appeals to his imagination who *gets* him.
Ibid.

1393. Mary Sinton Leitch (1876–1954)

1 And deaf, he sings of nightingales
Or, blind, he sings of stars.
"The Poet" *n.d.*

2 He who loves the ocean
And the ways of ships
May taste beside a mountain pool
Brine on his lips.
"He Who Loves the Ocean" *n.d.*

3 They would not be the great, were not the cause
They love so great that it must needs be lost.
"Pity the Great" *n.d.*

4 While far below men crawl in clay and cold,
Sublimely I shall stand alone with God.
"The Summit, Mt. Everest" *n.d.*

1394. Mary Ritter Beard (1876–1958)

1 The prosecution of modern wars rests completely upon the operation of labor in mines, mills and factories, so that labor fights there just as truly as the soldiers do in the trenches.
Ch. 1, *A Short History of the American Labor Movement* *1920*

2 The trade agreement has become a rather distinct feature of the American labor movement. It does not represent any revolutionary tendency in industry. It is based on the idea that labor shall accept the capitalist system of production and makes terms of peace with it.
Ch. 9, Ibid.

3 Viewed narrowly, all life is universal hunger and an expression of energy associated with it.
Ch. 1, *Understanding Women* *1931*

4 In their quest for rights they [women] have naturally placed emphasis on their wrongs, rather than their achievements and possessions, and have retold history as a story of their long Martyrdom.
Ibid.

5 Unless one's philosophy is all-inclusive, nothing can be understood.
Ch. 4, Ibid.

6 In matters pertaining to the care of life there has been no marked gain over Greek and Roman antiquity.
Ch. 5, Ibid.

7 The emphasis in Communism, if its ideal is realized, will be on woman as a worker, and the opportunities for a life of leisure, patronage, noblesse oblige, religious service, and idle curiosity will vanish.
Ch. 6, Ibid.

8 If this analysis of history is approximately sound and if the future like the past is to be crowded with changes and exigencies, then it is difficult to believe that the feminism of the passing generation, already hardened into dogma and tradition, represents the completed form of woman's relations to work, interests and society.
Ibid.

9 In other words, those who sit at the feast will continue to enjoy themselves even though the veil that separates them from the world of toiling reality below has been lifted by mass revolts and critics.
Ibid.

10 The dogma of women's complete historical subjection to men must be rated as one of the most fantastic myths ever created by the human mind.
Woman as a Force in History 1946

11 . . . history has been conceived—and with high justification in the records—as the human struggle for civilization against barbarism in different ages and places, from the beginning of human societies.
Ch. 12, Ibid.

12 Beneath the surface of civilian interests and capitalistic enterprises smoldered embers of the world's war spirit—humanity's traditional flare—now to be inflamed by new instruments for fighting and the associated aspiration for world trade and world power.
Ch. 9, *The Force of Women in Japanese History 1963*

1395. Mary Roberts Rinehart (1876–1958)

1 Conscription may form a great and admirable machine, but it differs from the trained army of volunteers as a body differs

from a soul. But it costs a country heavy in griefs, does a volunteer army; for the flower of the country goes.

    Introduction, *Kings, Queens, and Pawns* 1915

2 It is easier to die than to send a son to death.

    Ch. 37, Ibid.

3 What do I want to do? You may say what you like, a lot of married women get into things they never meant to simply because they are kind-hearted and hate to be called quitters.

    "Affinities," *Affinities and Other Stories* 1920

4 "You're a perfect child, a stubborn child! Your mind's in pigtails, like your hair."

    "The Family Friend," Ibid.

5 LIZZIE. I've stood by you through thick and thin—I stood by you when you were a Vegetarian—I stood by you when you were a Theosophist—and I seen you through Socialism, Fletcherism and Rheumatism—but when it comes to carrying on with ghosts—

    Sc. 1, *The Bat* (play based on her novel, *The Circular Staircase*, 1908), with James Avery Hopwood 1920

6 The great God endows His children variously. To some He gives intellect—and they move the earth. To some he allots heart—and the beating pulse of humanity is theirs. But to some He gives only a soul, without intelligence—and these, who never grow up, but remain always His children, are God's fools, kindly, elemental, simple, as if from His palette the Artist of all had taken one colour instead of many.

    "God's Fool," *Love Stories* 1920

7 "Nurses in hospitals are there to carry out the doctor's orders. Not to think or to say what they think unless they are asked."

    "Twenty-Two," Ibid.

8 Men deceive themselves; they look back on the children who were once themselves, and attempt to reconstruct them. But they can no longer think like the child, and against the unpleasant and the horrid the mind has set up the defensive machinery of forgetfulness.

    Ch. 1, *My Story* 1931

9 But it is interesting to see how the Socialist becomes the conservative when given power; Mussolini, Briand, Masaryk, all considered radicals at one time. Or is it that our own ideas change, and that we are after all moving slowly toward a greater justice?

    Ch. 40, Ibid.

10 Will we never learn? Is our cupidity greater than our patriotism? And is our generosity greater than our common sense?

    Ch. 19, *My Story*, Rev. Ed. 1948

1396. Sarah Norcliffe Cleghorn (1876–1959)

1 The golf links lie so near the mill
That almost every day
The laboring children can look out
And watch the men at play.

    "The Conning Tower," *New York Herald Tribune*
    1 January 1915

2 Since more than half my hopes came true
And more than half my fears
Are but the pleasant laughing–stock
Of these my middle years . . .

Shall I not bless the middle years?
Not I for youth repine
While warmly round me cluster lives
More dear to me than mine.

    "Contented at Forty" *1916*

3 Come, Captain Age,
With your great sea-chest full of treasure!
Under the yellow and wrinkled tarpaulin
Disclose the carved ivory
And the sandalwood inlaid with pearl:
Riches of wisdom and years.

    "Come, Captain Age," *Three Score* 1936

4 "The unfit die—the fit both live and thrive."
Alas, who say so? They who do survive.

    "Survival of the Fittest" *n.d.*

1397. Josephine Dodge Bacon (1876–1961)

1 "Girls, it isn't likely that we'll win, *but we can give 'em something to beat!*"

    "The Emotions of a Sub-Guard," *Smith College Stories*
    1900

2 Life in all its phases possessed for him unsounded depths of entertainment, and in the intervals of uncontrolled laughter at the acts and words of his astonished elders he gave way to frequent subtle smiles resulting from subjectively humorous experiences unguessed by the world at large.

    Ch. 2, *The Memoirs of a Baby* 1904

3 You musn't say anything that won't be perfectly true when he's grown up, you see. It's learning two sets of things that makes a child distrust you.

    Ch. 6, Ibid.

4 You mark my words, Toots, if you ever hear a darn-fool thing to-day, you can make up your mind some woman said it that writes books. . . . It ought to be a crime for any woman to have children that writes books.

    Ch. 2, *The Biography of a Boy* 1910

5 Starved once and forever,
By a cruel love.
I lost my life—
The public gained it.

    Ch. 15, *Truth o' Women* 1923

6 I do not see how there can be any real respect,
Or any real privacy such as women love,
When you marry a man.
A man makes trouble.

    Ch. 20, Ibid.

7 To you in reality dead,
Dragging your bodies after you,
Persistently vital,
I say this:
Death will come. Be patient.

    Ch. 42, Ibid.

1398. Anne Bronaugh (1876-1961)

1 Life is a patchwork—here and there,
Scraps of pleasure and despair
Join together, hit or miss.

    "Patchwork" *n.d.*

1399. Elizabeth Baker (1876–1962)

1 MAGGIE. Office work is awf'lly monotonous.
MRS. MASSEY. Of course it is. So is all work. Do you expect work to be pleasant? Does anybody ever like work? The idea is absurd. Anyone would think work was to be pleasant. You don't come into the world to have pleasure. We've got to do our duty, and the more cheerfully we can do it, the better for ourselves and everybody else.

Act III, Chains 1909

1399.1. Gwendolen Willis (1876–1969)

1 When we write the history of our feminists we must begin not with them but with their mothers.

Quoted by Nancy S. Prichard in a letter to Elaine T. Partnow* from Unitarian Universalist Women's Federation *17 December 1981*

*See 2870.

1400. Natalie Clifford Barney (1876–1972)

1 Renouncement: the heroism of mediocrity.

"Gods," *Adam*, No. 299 *1962*

2 Would that well-thinking people should be replaced by thinking ones.

Ibid.

3 We know all their gods; they ignore ours. What they call our sins are our gods, and what they call their gods, we name otherwise.

Ibid.

4 Eternity—waste of time.

Ibid.

5 There are . . . intangible realities which float near us, formless and without words; realities which no one has thought out, and which are excluded for lack of interpreters.

"On Writing and Writers," Ezra Pound,* tr. from French, Ibid.

*American poet, critic (1885–1972).

6 Novels are longer than life.

Ibid.

7 It is time for dead languages to be quiet.

Ibid.

8 Most virtue is a demand for greater seduction.

"My Country 'tis of Thee," Ibid.

9 Why grab possessions like thieves, or divide them like socialists when you can ignore them like wise men?

Ibid.

10 To be one's own master is to be the slave of self.

"Samples from Almost Illegible Notebooks," Ibid.

11 The advantage of love at first sight is that it delays a second sight.

Ibid.

12 Youth is not a question of years: one is young or old from birth.

Ibid.

13 If we keep an open mind, too much is likely to fall into it.

Ibid.

14 Fatalism is the lazy man's way of accepting the evitable.

Ch. 10, Quoted in *The Amazon of Letters* by George Wickes *1976*

15 Time engraves our faces with all the tears we have not shed.

Ibid.

16 How many inner resources one needs to tolerate a life of leisure without fatigue.

Ibid.

17 Lovers should also have their days off.

Ibid.

1401. Mathilda von Kemnitz (1877–?)

1 Since the fundamental principle of eroticism imperiously governs every human life, since the manner of the first erotic happiness determines in a far-reaching manner the laws of the individual's eroticism throughout his entire life, the majority of men have become entirely incapable of concentrating their erotic will consistently on one human being; therefore, they have become incapable of monogamy.

The Triumph of the Immortal Will 1932

2 The man experiences the highest unfolding of his creative powers not through asceticism but through sexual happiness.

Ibid.

1402. Isabelle Eberhardt (1877–1904)

1 For those who know the value and the exquisite taste of solitary freedom (for one is only free when alone), the act of leaving is the bravest and most beautiful of all.

Journal entry, Quoted in *The Destiny of Isabelle Eberhardt* by Cecily Mackworth *1975*

2 I love to dive into the bath of street life, the waves of the crowds flowing over me, to impregnate myself with the fluids of the people.

Ibid.

3 In the staid costume of a European girl I would never have seen anything. The world would have been closed to me, for . . . external life seems to have been made for man, not for woman.

Ibid.

4 Death does not frighten me, but dying obscurely and above all uselessly does.

Ibid.

1403. Anne Shannon Monroe (1877–1942)

1 I have never been much cheered by the "stenciled smile," the false front, the pretending that there was no trouble when trouble stalked, that there was no death when Death laid his cold hand upon one dearer to us than life: but I have been tremendously cheered by the *brave* front; the imagination that could travel past the trouble and see that there were still joys in the world. . . .

Ch. 1, *Singing in the Rain*, with Adolph Green *1926*

2 For loneliness is but cutting adrift from our moorings and floating out to the open sea; an opportunity for finding ourselves, our *real* selves, what we are about, where we are heading during our little time on this beautiful earth.

Ch. 6, Ibid.

3 "Don't get hung up on a snag in the stream, my dear. Snags alone are not so dangerous—it's the debris that clings to them that makes the trouble. Pull yourself loose and go on."

Ch. 13, Ibid.

1404. Rosika Schwimmer (1877–1948)

1 I am no uncompromising pacifist. . . . I have no sense of nationalism, only a cosmic consciousness of belonging to the human family.

Court testimony, Citizenship Hearing *1928*

2 Women's rights, men's rights—human rights—all are threatened by the ever-present spectre of war so destructive now of human material and moral values as to render victory indistinguishable from defeat.

Speech, Centennial Celebration of Seneca Falls Convention of Women's Rights *July 1948*

3 Women's function of homemaker, we once dreamed, would extend into politics and economics our highest creative and conserving instincts. Let us go back to the task of building that safe, decent and wholesome home for the entire human family to which we once pledged ourselves.

Ibid.

4 We who successfully freed half of the human race without violence must now undertake with equal devotion, perseverance and intelligence the supreme act of human statesmanship involved in the creation of institutions of government on a world scale.

Ibid.

1405. Laura Simmons (1877–1949)

1 The face within that passport book
Will rise to haunt you yet.

"Your Passport Picture" *n.d.*

1406. Marian Le Sueur (1877–1954)

1 The American destiny is what our fathers dreamed, a land of the free, and the home of the brave; but only the brave can be free. Science has made the dream of today's reality for all the earth if we have the courage and vision to build it. American Democracy must furnish the engineers of world plenty—the builders of world peace and freedom.

Quoted in *Crusaders* by Meridel Le Sueur* *1955*

* Her daughter; see 1778.

1407. Maude Royden (1877–1956)

1 The belief that the personality of men and women are of equal dignity in the sight of God is necessary to a right moral standard.

The Church and Woman c. 1920

1408. Rose Fyleman (1877–1957)

1 There are fairies at the bottom of our garden.

"The Fairies," St. 1 *n.d.*

2 The Fairies have never a penny to spend,
They haven't a thing put by,
But theirs is the dower of bird and of flower,
And theirs are the earth and the sky.

"The Fairies Have Never a Penny to Spend," St. 1 *n.d.*

1409. Teresa Billington-Greig (1877–1964)

1 The early suffragists believed men when they said that success for women would lie in reason and justice, in presenting their case in an appropriate manner, but this has proved to be a hoax which has taken up women's time and energy and has led nowhere.

The Militant Suffrage Movement 1911

2 The only time that power changes hands, there is a struggle.

Ibid.

3 It will be the fact that women are in revolt, rather than the revolt itself, which will win the day.

Ibid.

1410. Katharine Anthony (1877–1965)

1 Personal ambitions and disappointments, personal desire and weaknesses, personal shrewdness or slackness play their part in these narrow homes as they do in more spacious ones.

Ch. 8, *Mothers Who Must Earn 1914*

2 For mothers who must earn, there is indeed no leisure time problem. The long hours of earning are increased by the hours of domestic labor, until no slightest margin for relaxation or change of thought remains.

Ch. 6, Ibid.

3 Beyond all superficial differences and incidental forms, the vision of the emancipated woman wears the same features, whether she be hailed as *frau*, *fru*, or *woman*.

Ch. 1, *Feminism in Germany and Scandinavia 1915*

4 The cult of "arms and the man" must reckon with a newer cult, that of "schools and the woman." Schools, which exalt brains above brawn, and women, who exalt life-giving above life-taking, are the natural allies of the present era.

Ch. 2, Ibid.

5 The struggle for self-consciousness is the essence of the feminist movement. Slowly but inevitably, the soul of a sex is emerging from the dim chamber of instinct and feeling into the strong sunshine of reason and will.

Ch. 9, Ibid.

6 There can be no doubt as to who began the literary war between the sexes. Also there is no comparison between the severity and harshness of the tone of criticism in the opposing camps. If we search the polemic writings of the most militant feminists, we can nowhere find expressions which compare in venom and ruthlessness with the woman-hating sentiments of certain medieval "saints" and modern "philosophers."

Ibid.

7 The generosity of childless people toward the children of near relatives and favorite friends strikes one as mere justice and propriety, after all, and such voluntary acts of evening-up between one generation and the next are not at all uncommon among the families and classes who can afford to be kind.

Preface, *The Endowment of Motherhood 1920*

8 Principles are a dangerous form of social dynamite. . . .

Introduction, Ibid.

9 Foremost among the barriers to equality is the system which ignores the mother's service to Society in making a home and rearing children. The mother is still the unchartered servant of

the future, who receives from her husband, at *his* discretion, a share in *his* wages.

                                                              Ibid.

10 Persons who are born too soon or born too late seldom achieve the eminence of those who are born at the right time.
                              "Writing Biography," *The Writer's Book*,
                                            Helen Hull, ed. *1950*

11 The lovers of romance can go elsewhere for satisfaction but where can the lovers of truth turn if not to history?

                                                              Ibid.

12 To the biographer all lives bar none are dramatic constructions.

                                                              Ibid.

13 . . . people . . . seem to think that life began with the achievement of personal independence.

                                                              Ibid.

1411. Grace Noll Crowell (1877–1965?)

1 I am one ever journeying toward the "light that never was on land or sea," and yet ever beckons one onward and upward to the glory ahead.
                      Foreword, "Focus," St. 7, *Grace Noll Crowell 1938*

2 The woman who can move about a house,
   Whether it be a mansion or a camp,
   And deftly lay a fire, and spread a cloth,
   And light a lamp,
   And by the magic of a quick touch give
   The look of home wherever she may be—
   Such a woman always will seem great
   And beautiful to me.
                              "The Home Makers," St. 1 *n.d.*

3 Home may be near,
   Home may be far—
   But it is anywhere love
   And a few plain household treasures are.

                                                              Ibid.

4 God wrote His loveliest poem on the day
   He made the first tall silver poplar tree.
                              "Silver Poplars," St. 1 *n.d.*

1412. Virginia Gildersleeve (1877–1965)

1 Medicine is a profession which naturally appeals deeply to women, as they are instinctively concerned with conserving life.
                  "The Advancement of Women," *Many a Good Crusade*
                                                              1954

2 Now our witch-hunters are trying to drive students and teachers into conformity with a rigid concept of Americanism defined by ignorant and irresponsible politicians. If we do not check this movement, we shall become a totalitarian state like the Fascist and Communist models and our colleges and universities will produce frightened rabbits instead of scholars with free minds.
                              "The Inescapable Desert," Ibid.

3 The delicate first moment of dawn, before its mystery is invaded by the clatter of daily living, the bright hour of sunset before it is quenched in darkness, the last days of health unbroken, the last year of man's assurance that his civilization

moves "ever upward and onward"—these are the moments, hours, days, years that have for us a poignant significance.
                              "The Turning of the Tide," Ibid.

1413. Mary Garden (1877?–1967)

1 It was my first real flutter. I am sure Mr. Smith never knew, for he never paid the slightest attention to me except as a pupil. But *I* knew—I was in such a state of excitement every time I came for a lesson; but my Mr. Smith never noticed it and to the end was as correct as a metronome, and as cold.
                  Ch. 1, *Mary Garden's Story*, with Louis Biancolli *1951*

2 I have never been nervous in all my life and I have no patience with people who are. If you know what you're going to do, you have no reason to be nervous. And I knew what I was going to do.

                                                  Ch. 3, Ibid.

3 If I ever had complete charge of an opera house, the chances are I wouldn't get anybody to sing for me. I would be very emphatic about some things. I would never have a curtain call. I would never allow an encore. I would never permit a claque. There would be only art in my theatre.

                                                  Ch. 11, Ibid.

4 I used my voice to color my roles. Salomé was blood red. Melissande was ice, melting ice. . . .

                                                  Ch. 21, Ibid.

1414. Alice B. Toklas (1877–1967)

1 What is sauce for the goose may be sauce for the gander, but it is not necessarily sauce for the chicken, the duck, the turkey, or the guinea hen.
                              The Alice B. Toklas Cook Book 1954

2 She quoted a friend who used to say any advice is good as long as it is strong enough.
                      Letter to Carl Van Vechten* (3 September 1946),
                                  Staying On Alone, Ed Burns, ed. *1973*
   *American music critic and satirical writer (1880–1964).

3 I am staying on here alone now.*
                      Letter to Julian Beck (8 September 1946), Ibid.
   *Her partner Gertrude Stein (see 1363) had recently died.

4 Now I ask you what is the impulse that comes from the possession of even the kindest heart compared to real faith in God and a hereafter. Without it one just plods on. . . .
                      Letter to Fania Marinoff Van Vechten
                                      (21 February 1948), Ibid.

5 Austerity has gone so far that the population has become submissive through lack of physical resistance.
                      Letter to Donald Gallup (12 October 1948), Ibid.

6 . . . he [Baskets, a dog] has filled the corners of the room and the minutes and me so sweetly these last years.
                      Letter to Thornton Wilder* (5 April 1949), Ibid.
   *American playwright and novelist (1897–1975).

7 Well, I've gotten to the end of the subject—of the page—of your patience and my time.
                      Letter to Elizabeth Hansen (19 July 1949), Ibid.

8 I love Spain and things Spanish and Picasso!*
                      Letter to Louise Taylor (16 August 1951), Ibid.
   *Pablo Picasso, renowned Spanish painter (1881–1973).

9   The young men of today seem mostly to be interested in the manner rather than the matter.
> Letter to Mark Lutz (16 August 1951), Ibid.

10   Haven't you learned yet that it isn't age but lack of experience that makes us fall off ladders or have radiators fall on us.
> Letter to Princess Dilkusha de Rohan (5 March 1955), Ibid.

11   . . . the past is not gone—nor is Gertrude.*
> Letter to Samuel Steward (7 August 1958), Ibid.
> *Gertrude Stein; see 1363.

12   Dawn comes slowly but dusk is rapid.
> Letter to Virginia Knapik (9 August 1958), Ibid.

1415. Adelaide Crapsey (1878–1914)

1   If I'd as much money as I can tell,
I never would cry my songs to sell.
> "Vendor's Song" *n.d.*

2   These be
Three silent things:
The falling snow . . . the hour
Before the dawn . . . the mouth of one
Just dead.
> "Cinquain: Triad" *n.d.*

3   Wouldst thou find my ashes? Look
In the pages of my book;
And, as this thy hands doth turn,
Know here is my funeral urn.
> "The Immortal Residue" *n.d.*

4   Is it as plainly in our living shown,
By slant and twist, which way the wind hath blown?
> "On Seeing Weather-Beaten Trees" *n.d.*

1416. Isadora Duncan (1878–1927)

1   You were once wild here. Don't let them tame you!
> Curtain speech, Symphony Hall (Boston) *1922*

2   America has all that Russia has not. Russia has things America has not. Why will America not reach out a hand to Russia, as I have given my hand?
> Ibid.

3   All Puritan vulgarity centers in Boston. The Back Bay conservatives are impoverished by customs and taboo. They are the lifeless and sterile of this country.
> Interview (Boston) *1922*

4   . . . [I] would rather live in Russia on black bread and vodka than in the United States at the best hotels. America knows nothing of food, love, or art.
> Interview aboard ship *1922*

5   So ends my first experience with matrimony, which I always thought a highly overrated performance.
> Interview, *The New York Times 1923*

6   . . . when I listened to music the rays and vibrations of the music streamed to this one fount of light within me—there they reflected themselves in Spiritual Vision, not the brain's mirror, but the soul's, and from the vision I could express them in Dance. . . .
> *My Life 1927*

7   With what a price we pay for the glory of motherhood. . . .
> Ibid.

8   . . . the artist is the only lover, he alone has the pure vision of beauty, and love is the vision of the soul when it is permitted to gaze upon immortal beauty. . . .
> Ibid.

9   I have discovered the dance. I have discovered the art which has been lost for two thousand years.
> Ibid.

10   . . . I believe, as a wage-earning woman, that if I make the great sacrifice of strength and health and even risk my life to have a child, I should certainly not do so if, on some future occasion, the man can say that the child belongs to him by law and he will take it from me and I shall see it only three times a year!
> Ibid.

11   Any intelligent woman who reads the marriage contract, and then goes into it, deserves all the consequences.
> Ibid.

12   No composer has yet caught this rhythm of America—it is too mighty for the ears of most.
> Ibid.

13   And this dance will have nothing in it of the inane coquetry of the ballet, or the sensual convulsion of the Negro. It will be clean.
> Ibid.

14   . . . now that I had discovered that Love might be a pastime as well as a tragedy, I gave myself to it with pagan innocence. Men seemed to hungry for Beauty, hungry for that love which refreshes and inspires without fear or responsibility.
> Ibid.

15   . . . if you have a body in which you are born to a certain amount of pain . . . why should you not, when the occasion presents, draw from this same body the maximum of pleasure?
> Ibid.

16   Virtuous people are simply those who have . . . not been tempted sufficiently, because they live in a vegetative state, or because their purposes are so concentrated in one direction that they have not had the leisure to glance around them.
> Introduction, Ibid.

17   I had learned to have a perfect nausea for the theatre: the continual repetition of the same words and the same gestures, night after night, and the caprices, the way of looking at life, and the entire rigmarole disgusted me.
> Ch. 5, Ibid.

18   It is unheard-of, uncivilized barbarism that any woman should still be forced to bear such monstrous torture. It should be remedied. It should be stopped. It is simply absurd that, with our modern science, painless childbirth does not exist as a matter of course. . . . I tremble with indignation when I think of . . . the unspeakable egotism and blindness of men of science who permit such atrocities when they can be remedied.
> Ch. 19, Ibid.

19   It seems to me monstrous that anyone should believe that the jazz rhythm expresses America. Jazz rhythm expresses the primitive savage.
> Ch. 30, Ibid.

20 The real American type can never be a ballet dancer. The legs are too long, the body too supple and the spirit too free for this school of affected grace and toe walking.

Ibid.

21 People do not live nowadays—they get about ten percent out of life.

"Memoirs" (1924), *This Quarter* (Paris) *Autumn 1929*

22 The whole world is absolutely brought up on lies. We are fed nothing but lies. It begins with lies and half our lives we live with lies.

Ibid.

23 So long as little children are allowed to suffer, there is no true love in this world.

Ibid.

24 Others loved themselves, money, theories, power: Lenin* loved his fellow men. . . . Lenin was God, as Christ was God, because God is Love and Christ and Lenin were all Love!

Ibid.

*Vladimir Ilich Ulanov (1870–1920), leader of the Bolsheviks.

25 Art is not necessary at all. All that is necessary to make this world a better place to live in is to love—to love as Christ loved, as Buddha loved.

Ibid.

1417. Amelia Burr (1878–1940?)

1 Because I have loved life, I shall have no sorrow to die.

"A Song of Living," St. 3, *Life and Living 1916*

2 Spring comes laughing down the valley
All in white, from the snow
Where the winter's armies rally
Loath to go.

"New Life," Ibid.

3 But I have certainty enough,
For I am sure of you.

"Certainty Enough" *n.d.*

4 Swift and sure go the lonely feet,
And the single eye seems cold and true,
And the road that has room and to spare for one
May be sorely narrow for two.

"The Lovers" *n.d.*

1418. Ethel Watts Mumford (1878–1940)

1 God gives us our relatives—thank God we can choose our friends.

Pt. 1, *The Cynic's Calendar*, with Addison Mizner and
Oliver Herford *1903*

2 There was a young lady from Skye,
With a shape like a capital I;
She said, "It's too bad!
But then I can pad,"
Which shows you that figures can lie.

"Appearances Deceitful," *The Limerick Up to Date Book*
1903

3 There was a young lady named Julie,
Who was terribly fond of patchouli;
She used bottles seven,

'Til smelt up to heaven,
Which made all the angels unruly.

"Lavishness," Ibid.

4 There was a young damsel named Nell,
Who considered herself quite a belle.
She sat on the sand,
And held her own hand,
And never got on to the swell.

"Self-Sufficiency," Ibid.

5 There was a young person of Tottenhem,
Whose manners, good Lord! she'd forgotten 'em.

"Good Manners," Ibid.

6 Said a Rooster, "I'd have you all know
I am nearly the whole of the show;
Why, the Sun every morn
Gets up with the dawn
For the purpose of hearing me crow!"

"Know Your Own Worth," Ibid.

7 In the midst of life we are in debt.*

The Altogether New Cynic's Calendar, with Addison Mizner
and Oliver Herford *1907*

*A parody of *The Book of Common Prayer* anthem: "In the midst
of life we are in death" (1662).

1419. Florence Ayscough (1878–1942)

1 Ideals determine government, and government determines social life, and social life, with all that the term connotes, is the essence of every literature.

Introduction, *Fir-Flower Tablets 1921*

1420. Mary Grant Bruce (1878–1958)

1 "An' town ladies can't never compre'end country children, any'ow. Our little maid's jus' grown up like a bush flower, an' all the better she is for it."

Ch. I, *Mates at Billabong*
1911

2 "It's the most extraordinary place I was ever at," he told himself later, dressing for dinner, in the seclusion of his own room....."Absolutely no class limits whatever, and no restrictions—why, she kept me waiting for my second cup while she looked after that fat old black in the dirty white turban!"

Ch. XI, Ibid.

3 "Five weeks on my back, Murty!—and goodness knows how much ahead. It doesn't suit me."
"I will admit there's some on the station 'twould suit better," Murty answered. "Dave here, now—sure, he shines best whin he's on his back! an' I can do a bit av that same meself. ("You can that!" from the outraged Mr. Boone.) But y' had the drawback to be born widout a lazy bone in y'r body, so 'tis a hardship on y'."

Ch. XX, Ibid.

1421. Grace H. Conkling (1878–1958)

1 I have an understanding with the hills.

"After Sunset" *n.d.*

2 Mountains are good to look upon
But do not look too long.
They are made of granite. They will break your heart.

"Mountains" *n.d.*

3   The forest looks the way
Nightingales sound.
"Frost on a Window" *n.d.*

4   I wonder if it *is* a bird
That sings within the hidden tree,
Or some shy angel calling me
To follow far away?
"Nightingale" *n.d.*

5   Over the stones to lull and leap
Herding the bubbles like white sheep;
The claims of worry to deny,
And whisper sorrow into sleep.
"The Whole Duty of Berkshire
Brooks" *n.d.*

6   To build the trout a crystal stair.
Ibid.

7   Invisible beauty has a world so brief
A flower can say it or a shaken leaf,
But few may ever snare it in a song.
"After Sunset" *n.d.*

1422. Rachel Crothers (1878–1958)

1   WELLS (reading a book review). Her first work attracted wide attention when we thought Frank Ware was a man, but now that we know she is a woman we are more than ever impressed by the strength and scope of her work.
Act I, *A Man's World* 1910

1423. Bertha Runkle (1878–1958)

1   We own the right of roaming, and the world is wide.
"Songs of the Sons of Essau" *n.d.*

1424. Edith Ronald Mirrielees (1878–1962)

1   In the thinking out of most stories, the thing the story is about, as apart from merely what happens in it, is of the utmost importance. For a story is not the sum of its happenings.
"The Substance of the Story,"
Story Writing 1947

2   Incident piled on incident no more makes life than brick piled on brick makes a house.
Ibid.

3   Experience shows that exceptions are as true as rules.
Ibid.

4   . . . belief that persistence is all and is bound to be rewarded has no . . . foundation.
Ibid.

1425. Elizabeth Arden (1878–1966)

1   The great days of the salons are over.
"I Am a Famous Woman in This Industry,"
Fortune October 1938

2   Nothing that costs only a dollar is worth having.
Quoted in "In Cosmetics the Old Mystique is No Longer
Enough" by Eleanore Carruth, Ibid.

1426. Lise Meitner (1878–1968)

1   Women have a great responsibility...to try...to prevent another war. I hope...that we will be able to use this great [atomic] energy...for peaceful work.
Frontispiece, Quoted in *Twentieth-Century
Women Scientists* by Lisa Yount 1996

2   It is an unfortunate accident that this discovery [fission] came about in time of war....You must not blame us scientists for the use to which war technicians have put our discoveries.*
Interview, Ibid.

*Her oft-said response about the atomic bomb.

3   It's tempting to speculate...about uranium-charged trains and flivvers [cars], and—why not?—about a trip to the moon...in rockets propelled by atomic energy. But...neither our generation nor the next one will sample the possibilities of atomic energy.
Interview (1946), Ibid.

4   I got so frightened, my heart almost stopped beating. I knew that the Nazis had just declared open season on Jews, that the hunt was on. For ten minutes I sat there and waited, minutes that seemed like so many hours.*
Ibid.

*Reference to the occasion when a military patrol took her passport as she was fleeing Germany.

1427. Beth Slater Whitson (1879–1930)

1   Meet me in Dreamland, sweet dreamy Dreamland,
There let my dreams come true.
"Meet Me To-Night in Dreamland" 1909

1428. Katherine Gerould (1879–1944)

1   There are only three things worth while—fighting, drinking, and making love.
"The Tortoise," *Vain Oblations* 1914

2   The commonest field may be chosen by opposing generals to be decisive; and in a day history is born where before only the quiet wheat has sprung.
"The Case of Paramore," Ibid.

3   You don't care about this State: you want to put it into white petticoats and see it across a muddy street.
"The Knight's Move," *Atlantic Monthly* (Boston) 1917

4   . . . it is one thing to sow your wild oats in talk, and quite another to live by your own kaleidoscopic paradoxes. The people who frowned on the manifestations of "temperament" were merely those logical creatures who believed that if you expressed your opinions regardless of other people's feelings, you probably meant what you said. They did not know the pathology of epigram, the basic truth of which is that word-intoxicated people express an opinion long before they dream of holding it.
"Tabu and Temperament," *Modes and Morals* 1920

5   . . . I have always, privately and humbly, thought it a pity that so good a word [as culture] should go out of the best vocabularies; for when you lose an abstract term, you are very apt to lose the thing it stands for.
"The Extirpation of Culture," Ibid.

6   We were a plutocracy; which means that so long as a man had the house and the drinks, you asked no questions. The same

rule holds—allowing for their dizzier sense of figures—in New York and Chicago.

"French Eva," *Scribner's 1920*

7 Politics, which, the planet over, are the fly in the amber, the worm in the bud, the rift in the loot, had, with great suddenness, deprived Wharton Cameron of a job.

Ch. 1, *Conquistador 1923*

8 Codes cohabit easily until it comes to women. Then jungle and steppe, delta and forest, proceed to argue their differences.

Ch. 5, Ibid.

1429. Catherine Carswell (1879–1946)

1 . . . it wasn't a woman who betrayed Jesus with a kiss.

The Savage Pilgrimage 1932

1430. Huda Shaarawi (1879/82–1947)

1 Men have singled out women of outstanding merit and put them on a pedestal to avoid recognizing the capabilities of all women.

Remark (1924), Quoted in *Women in World History Curriculum*, http://www.womeninworldhistory.com
1996–97

1431. Sarojini Naidu (1879–1949)

1 *To-day it is spring!*

"Ecstasy," *The Golden Threshold 1890*

2 The voice of the wind is the voice of our fate.

"Wandering Singers," St. 3, Ibid.

3 And spirits of Truth were the birds that sang,
And spirits of Love were the stars that glowed,
And spirits of Peace were the streams that flowed
In that magical wood in the land of sleep.

"Song of a Dream," St. 1, Ibid.

4 O Bird of Time on your fruitful bough
What are the songs you sing?

"The Bird of Time," St. 1, *The Bird of Time 1912*

5 Shall hope prevail where clamorous hate is rife,
Shall sweet love prosper or high dreams find place
Amid the tumult of reverberant strife.

"At Twilight," St. 2, Ibid.

6 What do you know in your blithe, brief season
Of dreams deferred and a heart grown old?

"A Song in Spring," St. 2, Ibid.

7 The Indian woman of to-day is once more awake and profoundly alive to her splendid destiny as the guardian and interpreter of the Triune Vision of national life—the Vision of Love, the Vision of Faith, the Vision of Patriotism.

Foreword, *The Broken Wing 1916*

8 Thy changing kings and kingdoms pass away
The gorgeous legends of a bygone day,
But thou dost still immutably remain
Unbroken symbol of proud history, unageing priestess of old
mysteries
Before whose shrine the spells of Death are vain.

"Imperial Delhi," St. 2, Ibid.

9 Can ye measure the grief of the tears I weep
Or compass the woe of the watch I keep?

"The Gift of India," St. 3, Ibid.

10 Two gifts for our portion
We ask thee, O Fate,
A maiden to cherish,
A kinsman to hate.

"A Song of the Khyber Pass," St. 2, *The Feather of the Dawn 1927*

11 What, O my heart, though tomorrow be tragic,
Today is inwoven of rapture and magic.

"Spring in Kashmir," St. 9, Ibid.

1432. Lillian Leveridge (1879–1953)

1 Over the hills of home, laddie, over the hills of home.

"A Cry from the Canadian Hills," St. 9, *Over the Hills of Home 1918*

2 Laddie! Laddie! Laddie! "Somewhere in France" you sleep,
Somewhere 'neath alien flowers and alien winds that weep,
Bravely you marched to battle, nobly your life laid down,
You unto death were faithful, laddie; yours is the victor's crown.

Ibid.

1433. Frieda Lawrence (1879–1956)

1 Everything he* met had the newness of a creation, just that moment come into being.

Not I, But the Wind 1934

*D. H. Lawrence, English author (1885–1930).

2 In spite of his age and strong passions he [D.H. Lawrence] had never let himself go. Sex was suppressed in him with ferocity. He had suppressed it so much, put it away so entirely, that now, married, it overwhelmed him.

Frieda Lawrence: The Memoirs and Correspondence,
E. W. Tedlock, ed. *1961*

3 . . . he hated me for being miserable, not a moment of misery did he put up with; he denied all the suffering and suffered all the more. . . .

Letter to Edward Garnett (c. 1914), Ibid.

4 He loved me absolutely, that's why he hates me absolutely. . . .

Ibid.

5 But it was nice to feel him at the back of her days, solid and firm her rock of ages. He bored her a bit occasionally.

Letter (1938/39), Ibid.

6 Of course in war all madnesses come out in a man, that is the fault of war not of a man or a nation.

Letter (c. 13 September 1914), *The Letters of D. H. Lawrence*, Vol. 2, George J. Zytaruk and James T. Boulton, eds. *1979*

1434. Grace Goodhue Coolidge (1879–1957)

1 This was I and yet not I—this was the wife of the President of the United States and she took precedence over me; my personal likes and dislikes must be subordinated to the consideration of those things which were required of her.

Quoted in *First Ladies*
by Betty Boyd Caroli *1987*

1435. Dorothy Canfield Fisher (1879–1958)

1 "He divides us all into two kinds: the ones that get what they want by taking it away from other people—those are the dolichocephalic blonds—though I believe it doesn't refer to the color of their hair. The other kind are the white folks, the unpredatory ones who have scruples, and get pushed to the wall for their pains."

Bk. I, Ch. 5, *The Bent Twig* 1915

2 No European could have conceived how literally it was true that the birth or wealth of social position of a child made no difference in the estimation of his mates. There were no exceptions to the custom of considering the individual on his own merits.

Ch. 7, Ibid.

3 "I am thinking that I am being present at a spectacle which cynics say is impossible, the spectacle of a woman delighting—and with most obvious sincerity—in the beauty of another."

Bk. III, Ch. 23, Ibid.

4 A mother is not a person to lean on but a person to make leaning unnecessary.

Her Son's Wife 1926

5 This was a nightmare memory, one of those that never comes to you at all in daylight, but when you get about so far asleep, start to unroll themselves in the dark.

Pt. I, Ch. 2, *The Deepening Stream* 1930

6 "Father sticks to it that anything that promises to pay too much can't help being risky."

Pt. II, Ch. 1, Ibid.

7 "I've seen children before who'd had too great a fright. They are always imbeciles. . . ." There had been long periods in her youth when she too had crept into a corner and turned her face away from what life seemed to be.

Pt. III, Ch. 11, Ibid.

8 The skull of life suddenly showed through its smile.

Bonfire 1933

9 Freedom is not worth fighting for if it means no more than license for everyone to get as much as he can for himself. And freedom *is* worth fighting for. Because it does mean more than unrestricted grabbing. He saw in imagination those young faces looking up at him attentively, and told them, "Laugh in the faces of the Fascist priests who chant the new Black Mass, when they tell you boys and girls that democratic government means nothing but license for the money-getters."

Seasoned Timber 1939

1436. Ethel Barrymore (1879–1959)

1 That's all there is, there isn't any more.

Curtain speech after a performance of *Sunday* 1904

2 For an actress to be a success she must have the face of Venus, the brains of Minerva, the grace of Terpsichore, the memory of Macaulay, the figure of Juno, and the hide of a rhinoceros.

Quoted in *The Theatre in the Fifties*
by George Jean Nathan* 1953
*American art critic (1882–1958).

3 I never let them cough. They wouldn't dare.

New York Post 7 June 1956

4 You grow up the day you have your first real laugh at yourself.

Comment *n.d.*

1437. Wanda Landowska (1879–1959)

1 Music of the past has become a distant and vague country where everything is totally different from our surroundings, our life, our art, our impressions, and our concepts.

"Music of the Past" (1905), *Landowska on Music*, Denise Resout, ed. 1964

2 Obviously the good lady [melody] has a tough constitution. The more attempts made against her, the more she blooms with health and rotundity. It is interesting to note that all those accused of being her murderers are becoming, in turn, her benefactors and saviors.

"Why Does Modern Music Lack Melody?" (9 February 1913), Ibid.

3 In this obstinate race after the original—while avoiding thoroughly that which has already been said and taking refuge on an island that we thought was uninhabited—do we not risk running into a good old acquaintance who has just been dropped? . . . Is it really indispensable to believe with such seriousness that every little change will, at last, bring the definitive salvation? If it gives us a thrill, it is already delightful enough; and if this thrill reminds us of the dear caresses of old, it is all for the best!

Book review (1923), Ibid.

4 To embrace an epoch in all its splendor and truth, to understand the fluctuations of taste, one needs perspective.

Letter (8 September 1948), Ibid.

5 But I cannot help it if, having never stopped working, I have learned a great deal, especially about this divine freedom that is to music the air without which it would die. What would you say of a scientist or of a painter who, like stagnant water, would stop his experimentation and remain still?

Letter to a former pupil (1950), Ibid.

6 The most beautiful thing in the world is, precisely the conjunction of learning and inspiration. Oh, the passion for research and the joy of discovery!

Ibid.

1438. Mabel Dodge (1879–1962)

1 . . . I knew instinctively that the strongest, surest way to the soul is through the flesh.

Lorenzo in Taos 1932

2 . . . she [Frieda Lawrence*] had to see life from the sex center, she endorsed or repudiated experience from that angle. She was the mother of orgasm and of the vast, lively mystery of the flesh. But no more.

Ibid.

*See 1433.

3 The groping, suffering, tragic soul of man was so much filthiness to that healthy creature.

Ibid.

4 The womb behind the womb—the significant, extended and transformed power that succeeds in primary sex, that he [D. H. Lawrence]* was ready, long since, to receive from woman.

Ibid.

*British novelist (1885–1930).

5   A mania of love held me enthralled. . . . Nothing counted for me but Reed* . . . to lie close to him and to empty myself over and over, flesh against flesh. And I was proud I had saved so much to spill lavishly, without reckoning, passion unending.

Movers and Shakers 1936
*John "Jack" Reed, American poet, adventurer, revolutionary writer (1887–1920).

6   Something in us wants men to be strong, mature, and superior to us so that we may admire them, thus consoled in a measure for our enslavement to them. But something else in us wants them to be inferior, and less powerful than ourselves, so that obtaining the ascendancy over them we gain possession, not only of them, but of our own souls, once more.

Quoted in "The Passions of Mabel Dodge" by Rusty Brown, *Ms.* (New York) March *1984*

7   Nature is so strong here [Taos, New Mexico] that one has to be on one's guard not to be absorbed by it.

Ibid.

1439. Nancy Astor (1879–1964)

1   I can conceive of nothing worse than a man-governed world—except a woman-governed world.

"America," Ch. 1, *My Two Countries 1923*

2   It is no use blaming the men—we made them what they are—and now it is up to try and make ourselves—the makers of men—a little more responsible.

Ibid.

3   In passing, also, I would like to say that the first time Adam had a chance he laid the blame on woman. . . .

Ibid.

4   I believe that the safest and surest way to get out of war is to join some sort of league of nations. That misrepresented and much despised League has already prevented three small wars, it has registered over one hundred treaties, has repatriated nearly four hundred thousand prisoners—not a bad record for only half a league.

"America," Ch. 2, Ibid.

5   Real education should educate us out of self into something far finer—into a selflessness which links us with all humanity. Political education should do the same.

Ch. 7, Ibid.

6   The most practical thing in the world is common sense and common humanity.

Ibid.

7   A fool without fear is sometimes wiser than an angel with fear.

Ch. 8, Ibid.

8   My vigor, vitality and cheek repel me. I am the kind of woman I would run from.

News Item *1955*

1440. Alma Mahler–Werfel (1879–1964)

1   Mahler, ascetic though he was, had a lurid reputation. In fact, he was a child and women were his dread. It was only because I was a stupid, inexperienced girl that I took him off his guard.

"First Meeting," *Gustav Mahler* *1946*
*Her first husband, Austrian composer (1860–1911).

2   He soured my enjoyment of life and made it an abomination. That is, he tried to. Money—rubbish! Clothes—rubbish! Beauty—rubbish! Traveling—rubbish! Only the spirit was to count. I know today that he was afraid of my youth and beauty. He wanted to make them safe for himself by simply taking from me any atom of life in which he himself played no part. I was a young thing he had desired and whose education he now took in hand.

"Marriage and Life Together," Ibid.

3   I can never forget his dying hours and the greatness of his face as death drew nearer. His battle for the eternal values, his elevation about trivial things and his unflinching devotion to truth are an example of the saintly life.

"The End," Ibid.

4   . . . we exchanged a voluptuous glance—for a long, wonderful moment—regardless of on-lookers. Such a glance can be stunningly sensual—and he's the very picture of a man....There's good stock for you. Mahler* can't compete with that.

Diaries 1898-1902, Selected and tr., Antony Beaumont *1999*

5   Why are boys *taught* to use their brains, but not girls?...My mind has not been schooled, which is why I have such frightful difficulty with everything.

Ibid.

6   I sucked on his mouth. Suddenly I felt him salivate—again and again—& I drank eagerly from his mouth—blessed impregnation!*

Ibid.

*A rendezvous with artist Zemlinsky; more probably an illusion to fellatio.

7   The text* is excellent, the melody a little impoverished, but the structure firm and effective. I can imagine some passages sounding quite passable.

Ibid.

*Gustav Mahler's *Klagende Lied.*

8   No one will ever succeed in completely describing me; not even I myself succeeded. I am full of enigmas that can't be solved. In distant days, they'll say of me: She was a sphinx.

Quoted by Berndt Wessling, her chief biographer, Ibid.

1441. Margarete Bieber (1879–1978)

1   Hope for the best, and expect the worst.

Quoted in "Margarete Bieber: An Archaeologist in Two Worlds" by Larissa Bonfante, *Women as Interpreters of the Visual Arts*, Claire Richter Sherman, ed. *1981*

2   Sweets are good for the nerves.

Ibid.

1442. Mary F. Armstrong (fl. 1880s)

1   Paint and powder, however skillfully their true names may be concealed under the mask of "Liquid Bloom," or "Lily Enamel," can never change their real character, but remain always unclean, false, unwholesome.

(p. 31), *On Habits and Manners 1888*

1443. Ophelia Guyon Brown (fl. 1880s)

1   She knows Omnipotence has heard her prayer
And cries, "It shall be done—sometime, somewhere."

"Pray Without Ceasing," *Singing with Grace 1882*

1444. E. T. Corbett (fl. 1880s)

1   Ef you want to be sick of your life,
    Jest come and change places with me a spell—for I'm an inventor's wife.

The Inventor's Wife 1883

1445. Meta Orred (fl. 1880s)

1   In the gloaming, O, my darling!
    When the lights are dim and low,
    And the quiet shadows falling
    Softly come and softly go.

"In the Gloaming" *1890*

1446. Alice Williams Brotherton (fl. 1880s–1930)

1   Books we must have though we lack bread.
    "Ballade of Poor Bookworms" *n.d.*

2   Heap high the board with plenteous cheer, and gather to the feast,
    And toast the sturdy Pilgrim band whose courage never ceased.
    "The First Thanksgiving Day" *n.d.*

1447. Ellen M. Hutchinson (fl. 1880s–1933)

1   They are all in the lily-bed, cuddled close together—
    Purple, yellow-cap, and baby-blue;
    How they ever got there you must ask the April weather,
    The morning and the evening winds, the sunshine and the dew.
    "Vagrant Pansies" *n.d.*

1448. Radclyffe Hall (1880–1943)

1   Acknowledge us, o God, before the whole world. Give us also the right to our existence.

The Well of Loneliness 1928

2   "You're neither unnatural, nor abominable, nor mad; you're as much a part of what people call nature as anyone else; only you're unexplained as yet—you've not got your niche in creation."

Ibid.

3   But the intuition of those who stand midway between the two sexes is so ruthless, so poignant, so accurate, so deadly as to be in the nature of an added scourge.

Ibid.

4   They had sought among the ruins of a dead civilization for the beauty they missed subconsciously in their own.

Ch. 1, *A Saturday Life 1930*

5   But when told that to appear naked in a drawing-room might be considered somewhat odd, since it was no longer the custom, she had argued that our bodies were very unimportant, only there so that people might perceive us. "We couldn't see each other without them, you know," she had said, smiling up at her mother.

Ibid.

6   At a time of great strain and unhappiness a comparatively insignificant event may discover the chink in our armour; an event connected, as likely as not, with an equally insignificant person. . . .

Ch. 25, *The Master of the House 1932*

7   Cry out until the world shook with her cries: "You shall not take him, I care nothing for honour. I care only for the child

that my womb has held, that my pain has brought forth, that my breasts have nourished. I care nothing for your wars. He was born of love; shall the blossom of love be destroyed by your hatreds? I care nothing. . . ."

Ch. 41, Ibid.

1449. Maria Jotuni (1880–1943)

1   Life is laughable indeed, if one takes it seriously.
    Tohvelisankarin rouva (The Wife of the Henpecked Man) *1924*

1450. Elizabeth Kenny (1880/86-1952)

1   . . . panic plays no part in the training of a nurse.
    And They Shall Walk, with Martha Ostenso* 1943
    *See 1775.

2   . . . it is easier to recount grievances and slights than it is to set down a broad redress of such grievances and slights. The reason is that one fears to be thought of as an arrant braggart.

Ibid.

3   The record of one's life must needs prove more interesting to him who writes it than to him who reads what has been written.

Foreword, Ibid.

4   O sleep, O gentle sleep, I thought gratefully, Nature's gentle nurse!

Ch. 2, Ibid.

5   Fortunately, perhaps, I was completely ignorant of the orthodox theory of the disease [polio-myelitis].

Ibid.

6   He looked at the book, took my name, and consulted his records. Then he informed me that I had been lost at sea and was dead. Under the circumstances, he could not possibly give me any money. . . . Even the fact that he was dealing with someone who had been dead for several days failed to awaken the slightest interest in his official heart.

Ch. 3, Ibid.

7   I was wholly unprepared for the extraordinary attitude of the medical world in its readiness to condemn anything that smacked of reform or that ran contrary to approved methods of practice.

Ch. 6, Ibid.

8   Some minds remain open long enough for the truth not only to enter but to pass on through by way of a ready exit without pausing anywhere along the route.

Ibid.

9   My mother used to say, "He who angers you, conquers you!" But my mother was a saint.

Ch. 7, Ibid.

10   His response was remarkable for its irrelevance, if for nothing else.

Ibid.

11   A measure of victory has been won, and honors have been bestowed in token thereof. But honors fade or are forgotten, and monuments crumble into dust. It is the battle itself that matters—and the battle must go on.

Ch. 14, Ibid.

1451. Edith Lewis (1880?–1955?)

1 . . . it is not in any form of biographical writing, but in art alone, that the deepest truth about human beings is to be found.

Willa Cather* Living 1953

*See 1338.

1452. Miles Franklin (1880–1956)

1 Bravely you jog along with the rope of class distinction drawing closer, close, tighter, tighter, around you. . . . I see it and know it, but I cannot help you. . . . I am only an unnecessary, little, bush commoner, I am only a—woman.

My Brilliant Career 1901

1453. Christabel Pankhurst (1880–1958)

1 We are not ashamed of what we have done, because, when you have a great cause to fight for, the moment of greatest humiliation is the moment when the spirit is proudest. The women we do pity, the women we think unwomanly, the women for whom we have almost contempt, if our hearts could let us have that feeling, are the women who can stand aside, who take no part in the battle—and perhaps even more, the women who know what the right path is and will not tread it, who are selling the liberty of other women in order to win the smiles and favour of the dominant sex.

Speech, Albert Hall (London) *19 March 1908*

2 We are here to claim our rights as women, not only to be free, but to fight for freedom. It is our privilege, as well as our pride and our joy, to take some part in this militant movement, which, as we believe, means the regeneration of all humanity. Nothing but contempt is due to those people who ask us to submit to unmerited oppression. We shall not do it.

Speech *23 March 1911*

3 Some people are tempted to say that all war is wrong, and that both sides in every war must be in the wrong. I challenge that statement and deny it utterly, absolutely, and with all the power I have at my disposal. All wars are not wrong. Was your war against a British Government wrong? As an Englishwoman, I say that when you fought us for the principle of freedom, for the right of self-government, you did right. I am glad you fought us and I am glad you beat us.

Speech, "America and the War," Carnegie Hall (New York) *25 October 1915*

4 What we suffragettes aspire to be when we are enfranchised is ambassadors of freedom to women in other parts of the world, who are not so free as we are.

Ibid.

5 I have known passion that strengthens one for endurance, shakes one with its mighty force, makes human's god-like, fills them with creative force. The passion of my life has been for the freeing of women, not only for reasons political and economic.

"Confessions of Christabel: Why I Never Married," *Weekly Dispatch* (London) *April 1921*

6 Never lose your temper with the Press or the public is a major rule of political life.

Unshackled 1959

7 The spirit of the movement was wonderful. It was joyous and grave at the same time. Self seemed to be laid down as the women joined us. Loyalty, the greatest of the virtues, was the keynote of the movement—first to the cause, then to those who were leading, and member to member. Courage came next, not simply physical courage, though so much of that was present, but still more the moral courage to endure ridicule and misunderstandings and harsh criticism and ostracism. There was a touch of the "impersonal" in the movement that made for its strength and dignity. Humour characterized it, too, in that our militant women were like the British soldier who knows how to joke and smile amid his fighting and trials.

Ibid.

8 I go about with the Bible in one hand and a newspaper in the other. The two go well together, for the concentrated study of the newspaper is a Christian's duty as this Age draws to its close.

Speech, Albert Hall, London (September 1926), Quoted in *The Fighting Pankhursts** by David Mitchell *1967*

*See Adela P—, 1505; Emmeline P—, 1181; Syvia P—, 1485.

9 We are suffering today from a greed for knowledge of evil. Moral disease and sin is rampant. Groups here and there are striving to keep us from slipping back into barbarism. But nothing can save us but divine intervention. . . .

California Speech, (1930), Ibid.

10 Remember the dignity of your womanhood. Do not appeal, do not beg, do not grovel. Take courage, join hands, stand beside us, fight with us.

Remark, Quoted in *Women in World History Curriculum*, www.womeninworldhistory.com/1996–97

1454. Marie Carmichael Stopes (1880–1958)

1 The surface freedom of our women has not materially altered the pristine purity of a girl of our northern race.

Married Love 1918

2 Each heart knows instinctively that it is only a mate who can give full comprehension of all the potential greatness in the soul, and have tender laughter for all the childlike wonder that lingers so enchantingly even in the white-haired.

Ch. 1, Ibid.

3 An impersonal and scientific knowledge of the structure of our bodies is the surest safeguard against prurient curiosity and lascivious gloating.

Ch. 5, Ibid.

4 . . . each coming together of man and wife, even if they have been mated for many years, should be a fresh adventure; each winning should necessitate a fresh wooing.

Ch. 10, Ibid.

5 London, scarred mistress of proud Freedom's heart,
The love we bear you has no counterpart.

"London," *Joy and Verity 1952*

6 So deeply are we woven I can lend
You outwardly to other hands who clutch
Small corners of your heart, greedy that such
Resplendence should its rays to darkness send.

"You," St. 2, Ibid.

7 We are not much in sympathy with the typical hustling American business man, and we have often felt compunction for him, seeing him nervous and harassed, sleeplessly, anxiously hunting dollars, and all but overshadowed by his over-dressed,

extravagant and idle wife, who sometimes insists that her spiritual development necessitates that she shall have no children. Such husbands and wives are also found in this country; they are a growing produce of the upper reaches of the capitalist system. Yet such wives imagine that they are upholding women's emancipation.

Article in *Dreadnought* (c.1919), Quoted in *The Fighting Pankhursts** by David Mitchell *1967*
*See Adela P—, 1505; Christabel P—, 1454; Emmeline P—, 1181; Syvia P—, 1485.

1455. Sophie Kerr (1880–1965)

1 Freud and his three slaves, Inhibition, Complex and Libido.
"The Age of Innocence," *Saturday Evening Post 9 April 1932*

2 The longing to produce great inspirations didn't produce anything but more longing.
Ch. 1, *The Man Who Knew the Date 1951*

3 If peace, he thought (as he had often thought before), only had the music and pageantry of war, there'd be no more wars.
Ch. 8, Ibid.

1456. Kathleen Thompson Norris (1880–1966)

1 "If you have children, you never have anything else!"
Ch. 2, *Mother 1911*

2 We cooked, cleaned, labored, worried, planned, we wept and laughed, we groaned and sang—but we never despaired. All this was but a passing phase; "we will certainly laugh at this someday," we all said buoyantly, laughing even then.
Ch. 1, *Noon 1924*

3 And so came middle-age, for I have discovered that middle-age is not a question of years. It is that moment in life when one realizes that one has exchanged, by a series of subtle shifts and substitutes, the vague and vaporous dreams of youth for the definite and tangible realization.
Ch. 3, Ibid.

4 Never in the history of the big round world has anything like us occurred. A country without caste, without serfs, peons or slaves, without banishment or exile or whipping post, without starvation and oppression!
Home 1928

5 Home ought to be our clearinghouse, the place from which we go forth lessoned and disciplined, and ready for life.
Ibid.

6 When they were going to be flagrantly, brutally selfish, how men did love to talk of being fair!
Ch. 2, *Bread into Roses 1936*

7 But somehow one never had time to stop and savor the taste of life as the stream of it flowed by. It would be good to find some quiet inlet where the waters were still enough for reflection, where one might sense the joy of the moment, rather than plan breathlessly for a dozen mingled treats in the future.
Ch. 11, Ibid.

8 The bright panorama was only a panorama, that was the trouble. Under its undeniable joy and excitements . . . there was a strange emptiness, a feeling that somehow reality was escaping

her, that the business of being amused was altogether too successful. Life wasn't, after all, only amusement—or was it?
Ibid.

9 "There seems to be so much more winter than we need this year."
Ch. 14, Ibid.

1457. Helen Keller (1880–1968)

1 . . . we could never learn to be brave and patient, if there were only joy in the world.
Atlantic Monthly (Boston) *May 1890*

2 There is no king who has not had a slave among his ancestors, and no slave who has not had a king among his.
Pt. 1, Ch. 1, *The Story of My Life 1903*

3 There is nothing more beautiful, I think, than the evanescent fleeting images and sentiments presented by a language one is just becoming familiar with—ideas that flit across the mental sky, shaped and tinted by capricious fancy.
Ch. 16, Ibid.

4 I hung about the dangerous frontier of "Guess," avoiding with infinite trouble to myself and others the broad valley of reason.
Ch. 17, Ibid.

5 Knowledge is happiness, because to have knowledge—broad, deep knowledge—is to know true ends from false, and lofty things from low. To know the thoughts and deeds that have marked man's progress is to feel the great heart-throbs of humanity through the centuries; and if one does not feel in these pulsations a heavenward striving, one must indeed be deaf to the harmonies of life.
Ch. 20, Ibid.

6 There is much in the Bible against which every instinct of my being rebels, so much that I regret the necessity which has compelled me to read it through from beginning to end. I do not think that the knowledge which I have gained of its history and sources compensates me for the unpleasant details it has forced upon my attention.
Ch. 21, Ibid.

7 Literature is my Utopia. Here I am not disenfranchised. No barrier of the senses shuts me out from the sweet, gracious discourse of my book friends. They talk to me without embarrassment or awkwardness.
Ibid.

8 I sometimes wonder if the hand is not more sensitive to the beauties of sculpture than the eye. I should think the wonderful rhythmical flow of lines and curves could be more subtly felt than seen. Be this as it may, I know that I can feel the heart-throbs of the ancient Greeks in their marble gods and goddesses.
Ch. 22, Ibid.

9 Everything has its wonders, even darkness and silence, and I learn, whatever state I may be in, therein to be content.
Ibid.

10 . . . a people's peace—a peace without victory, a peace without conquests or indemnities.
Ibid.

11 . . . militarism . . . is one of the chief bulwarks of capitalism, and the day that militarism is undermined, capitalism will fail.
Ibid.

12 The hands of those I meet are dumbly eloquent to me. The touch of some hands is an impertinence. I have met people so empty of joy, that when I clasped their frosty fingertips, it seemed as if I were shaking hands with a northeast storm. Others there are whose hands have sunbeams in them, so that their grasp warms my heart.

Ch. 23, Ibid.

13 Now I feel as if I should succeed in doing something in mathematics, although I cannot see why it is so very important. . . . The knowledge doesn't make life any sweeter or happier, does it?

Pt. 2, Letter to Laurence Hutton, Ibid.

14 Toleration is the greatest gift of the mind; it requires the same effort of the brain that it takes to balance oneself on a bicycle.

Pt. 3, "Personality," Ibid.

15 "I never fight," she replied, "except against difficulties."

Ibid.

16 I know that daisies and pansies come from seeds which have been put in the ground; but children do not grow out of the ground. I am sure. I have never seen a plant child. . . .

Quoted in Annie Sullivan's* Report of 1891, Ibid.

*See 1262.

17 One can never consent to creep when one feels an impulse to soar.

Speech (Mt. Airy), Ibid.

18 The highest result of education is tolerance.

Optimism 1903

19 Study the hand, and you shall find in it the true picture of man, the story of human growth, the measure of the world's greatness and weakness.

"The Hand of the World," *American Magazine December 1912*

20 . . . as the eagle was killed by the arrow winged with his own feather, so the hand of the world is wounded by its own skill.

Ibid.

21 How to reconcile this world of fact with the bright world of my imagining? My darkness has been filled with the light of intelligence, and behold, the outer day-light world was stumbling and groping in social blindness.

Quoted in *The Cry for Justice*, Upton Sinclair,* ed. *1915*

*American writer and reformer (1878–1968).

22 Let us start a world-encircling revolt, a revolt which shall make a junk heap out of the civilization of Kaisers and Kings and all the things that make of man a brute and of God a monster.

Speech (New York City) *19 December 1915*

23 The few who profit from the labor of the masses want to organize the workers into an army which will protect the interests of the capitalists.

Ibid.

24 I look upon the whole world as my fatherland, and every war has to me a horror of a family-feud. I look upon true patriotism as the brotherhood of man and the service of all to all.

"Menace of the Militarist Program," *New York Call 20 December 1915*

25 The only moral virtue of war is that it compels the capitalist system to look itself in the face and admit it is a fraud. It com-

pels the present society to admit that it has no morals it will not sacrifice for gain.

Ibid.

26 The burden of war always fall heaviest on the toilers.

Ibid.

27 We may have found a cure for most evils; but it has found no remedy for the worst of them all—the apathy of human beings.

Pt. I, Ch. 6, *My Religion 1927*

28 Security is mostly a superstition. It does not exist in nature, nor do the children of men as a whole experience it. Avoiding danger is no safer in the long run than outright exposure. Life is either a daring adventure, or nothing.

The Open Door 1957

1458. Ruth St. Denis (1880–1968)

1 I used to say that if a person wanted to keep alive, in distinction to merely existing, he should change his occupation every ten years.

Ch. 3, *Ruth St. Denis: An Unfinished Life 1939*

2 I want to dance always, to be good and not evil, and when it is all over not to have the feeling that I might have done better.

Ch. 6, Ibid.

3 I am a child of nature. Too much civilization and a touch of luxury have only depressed me. I must find a way to live more simply.

Ibid.

4 We were a Poet* and a Dancer; and we became lovers. And let it be said of us that Beauty was our god whom we worshipped in rites of such pure loveliness that he became my Emperor and I became Moon to his Imperial Sun. Poems, like shy white birds, rose from our union: records of the strange drama of our love.

Ch. 15, Ibid.

*Reference to her husband, Ted Shawn.

5 The human tragedy of artists must, at some time, bring itself to the attention of all earnest thinkers and seekers after truth. That something is terribly wrong with the whole round of artists' lives must be apparent to anyone who takes the trouble to observe it.

Ibid.

1459. Ruth Sawyer (1880—1970)

1 Perhaps you have discovered this for yourself; you may have in mind this minute some of the stories that you wished had begun long before they did—and others that ended before you thought they had any business doing so. These have a very unpleasant way of leaving your expectations and your interest all agog; and I have not a doubt that you have always blamed the author. This is not fair. In a matter of this kind an author is just as helpless as a reader, and there is no use in trying to coax or scold a story into telling itself her way. As sure as she tries the story gets sulky or hurt, picks up its beginning and ending, and trails away, never to come back; and that story is lost for all time.

Ch. I, *This Way to Christmas 1916*

1460. Nancy Byrd Turner (1880–1971)

1 Burn, wood, burn—
Wood that once was a tree, and knew

Blossom and sheaf, and the Spring's return,
Nest, and singing, and rain, and dew—
Burn, wood, burn!

"Flame Song" n.d.

2   Death is only an old door
Set in a garden wall.

"Death Is a Door" n.d.

3   Men climb tall hills to suffer and die.

"Hills" n.d.

1461. Jeannette Rankin (1880–1973)

1   If the hogs of the nation are ten times more important than the children, it is high time that women should make their influence felt.

Campaign Speech* 1916
*Reference to the government's appropriation of $300,000 to study fodder for hogs and only $30,000 to study children's needs.

2   We're half the people, we should be half the congress.

Remark (1966), Quoted in Jeannette Rankin: First Lady in Congress by Hannah Josephson 1974

3   The individual woman is required . . . a thousand times a day to choose either to accept her appointed role and thereby rescue her good disposition out of the wreckage of her self-respect, or else follow an independent line of behavior and rescue her self-respect out of the wreckage of her good disposition.

Ch. 3, Ibid.

4   As a woman I can't go to war, and I refuse to send anyone else.

Congressional remark (December 1941), Ibid.

5   You take people as far as they will go, not as far as you would like them to go.

Prologue (c.1941), Ibid.

6   Establish democracy at home, based on human rights as superior to property rights. . . .

Ch. 6, Ibid.

7   You can no more win a war than you can win an earthquake.

Ch. 8, Ibid.

8   Men and women are like right and left hands: it doesn't make sense not to use both.

Quoted in American Political Women by Esther Stineman 1980

9   At the beginning of this country's history, men gave their lives for a principle. It was: Taxation without representation is tyranny! Women struggle now for the same principle: "No taxation without representation."

Speech, Montana state legislature (11 February 1911), Quoted in Women Suffragists by Diana Star Helmer 1998

10   If they are going to have a war, they ought to take the old men and leave the young men to carry on the race.

Campaign speech (1916), Ibid.

11   Today as never before, the nation needs it women, needs the work of their hands and their hearts and their minds. Are we now going to refuse these women the opportunity to serve, in the face of their plea, in the face of the nation's great need?…The boys at the front know something of the democracy for which they are fighting. These courageous lads who are paying with their lives testified to their sincerity when they sent home their ballots in the New York election and voted two to one in favor of woman suffrage and democracy at home. Can we afford to permit a doubt as to the sincerity of our protestations of democracy?

Speech to Congress presenting the Anthony Amendment* (10 January 1918), Ibid.
*After Susan B. A— (see 949), the 19th Amendment was commonly referred to as such.

12   . . . [women have] been worms. They let their sons go off to war because they're afraid their husbands will lose their jobs in industry if they protest.

Newspaper interview (c. 1967), Ibid.

13   We could have peace in one year if women were organized.

Acceptance speech, NOW* Hall of Fame (12 February 1972), Ibid.
*She was the first member of the National Organization for Women's Susan B. Anthony Hall of Fame.

14   Money shouldn't be a factor in our lives…I give all my money to the peace movement.

Interview, The New York Times (1972), Ibid.

15   It was women's work which was destroyed by war. Their work was raising human beings, and war destroyed human beings to protect profits and property.

Ibid.

16   You can't settle disputes by shooting nice young men.

Ibid.

17   You give us the responsibility of raising children, but we have nothing to say about the laws that affect our children.

Ibid.

18   [I believed that World War I was] a commercial war, that none of the idealistic hopes would be carried out, and I was aware of the falseness of much of the propaganda.

Ibid.

19   Might it not be that the men who have spent their lives thinking in terms of commercial profit find it hard to adjust themselves to thinking in terms of human needs? Might it not be that a great force that has always been thinking in terms of human needs and that always will think in terms of human needs has not been mobilized? Is it not possible that the women of the country have something of value to give the nation at this time?

Ibid.

20   What one decides to do in a crisis depends on one's philosophy in life, and that philosophy cannot be changed by an accident. If one hasn't any philosophy, in crises others make the decision. The most disappointing feature of working for a cause is that so few people have a clear philosophy of life. We used to say, in the suffrage movement, that we could trust the woman who believed in suffrage, but we could never trust the woman who just wanted to vote.

Letter to friend, Ibid.

1462. Margaret Widdemer (1880–1978)

1   I have shut my little sister in from light and life
(For a rose, for a ribbon, for a wreath across my hair),
I have made her restless feet still until the night,
Locked from sweets of summer and from wild spring air.

"The Factories," St. 1 c.1916

2 The old road to Paradise
   Easy it is missed!
   "The Old Road to Paradise," St. 2 *1919*

3 To grown people a girl of fifteen and a half is a child still; to
   herself she is very old and very real; more real, perhaps, than
   ever before or ever after. . . .
   "The Changeling," *The Boardwalk 1920*

4 But the young are improvident—not having yet learned how
   hard to come by money is and of how little account are other
   things.
   "The Congregation," *Ibid.*

5 No one had told them that Age was a place
   Where you sat with a curious mask on your face.
   "Old Ladies," St. 6, *Hill Garden 1936*

6 "It only was gifts that I let them take.
   I never gave dreams away."
   "Spendthrift Nancy," St. 3, *Ibid.*

7 Love and grief and motherhood,
   Fame and mirth and scorn—
   These are all shall befall
   Any woman born.
   "A Cyprian Woman" *n.d.*

8 And all that you are sorry for is what you haven't done.
   "De Senectute" n.d.

9 I am the Dark Cavalier; I am the Last Lover:
   My arms shall welcome you when other arms are tired.
   "The Dark Cavalier" *n.d.*

1463. Grace Stone Coatés (1881–?)

1 Now, no doubt, my friend and I
   Will proceed to lie and lie
   To ourselves, till we begin
   To act the truth and call it sin.
   "As It Is" *n.d.*

1464. Mary Webb (1881–1927)

1 To many women marriage is only this. It is merely a physical
   change impinging on their ordinary nature, leaving their mentality untouched, their self-possession intact. They are not
   burnt by even the red fire of physical passion—far less by the
   white fire of love.
   Ch. 18, *The Golden Arrow
   1916*

2 The past is only the present become invisible and mute; and
   because it is invisible and mute, its memoried glances and its
   murmurs are infinitely precious. We are tomorrow's past.
   Foreword, *Precious Bane 1924*

3 It made me gladsome to be getting some education, it being
   like a big window opening.
   Bk. I, Ch. 5, *Ibid.*

4 Saddle your dreams afore you ride 'em.
   Ch. 6, *Ibid.*

5 If you stop to be kind, you must swerve often from your
   path.
   Bk. II, Ch. 3, *Ibid.*

6 It's the folks that depend on us for this and for the other that
   we most do miss.
   Bk. IV, Ch. 4, *Ibid.*

1465. Crystal Eastman (1881–1928)

1 A good deal of tyranny goes by the name of protection.
   Equal Rights 1924

2 . . . with the feminist ideal of education accepted in every home
   and school, and with all special barriers removed in every field
   of human activity, there is no reason why women should not
   become almost a human thing.
   Quoted in *The 50 Most Influential Women in
   American Law* by Dawn Bradley Berry* *1996*
   *See 3435.

3 . . . establish new values, to create an overpowering sense of the
   sacredness of life, so that war would be unthinkable.
   Remark (c. 1914–17), *Ibid.*

1466. Anna Pavlova (1881–1931)

1 . . . although one may fail to find happiness in theatrical life, one
   never wishes to give it up after having once tasted its fruits. To
   enter the School of the Imperial Ballet is to enter a convent
   whence frivolity is banned, and where merciless discipline reigns.
   "Pages of My Life," *Pavlova: A Biography*,
   A. H. Franks, ed. *1956*

2 To tend, unfailingly, unflinchingly, toward a goal, is the secret
   of success. But success? What exactly is success? For me it is to
   be found not in applause, but in the satisfaction of feeling that
   one is realising one's ideal. When a small child . . . I thought
   that success spelled happiness. I was wrong. Happiness is like
   a butterfly which appears and delights us for one brief moment, but soon flits away.
   Ibid.

3 As is the case in all branches of art, success depends in a very
   large measure upon individual initiative and exertion, and cannot be achieved except by dint of hard work. Even after having
   reached perfection, a ballerina may never indulge in idleness.
   Ibid.

1467. Eleanor Patterson (1881–1948)

1 Perhaps a woman editor is resented because an editor is supposed to possess wisdom, and something in the masculine
   mind objects to the suggestion that a woman can know anything except what she has already been told by a man.
   Quoted in *Cissy* by Ralph G. Martin *1979*

1468. Mary Antin (1881–1949)

1 "So at last I was going to America! Really, really going, at last!
   The boundaries burst. The arch of heaven soared. A million
   suns shone out of every star. The winds rushed out into outer
   space, roaring in my ears, 'America! America!'"
   The Promised Land 1912

1469. Alice Corbin (1881–1949)

1 I know we grow more lovely
   Growing wise.
   "Two Voices" *n.d.*

2 Then welcome Age, and fear not sorrow;
   Today's no better than tomorrow.
   Ibid.

1470. Esther Lape (1881–1949)

1 We have no illusions about the flexibility of the Nobel Committee. Its statements reflect a rigidity *extraordinaire*.

> Letter to A. David Gurewitsch (30 December 1964), Quoted in *Eleanor:* * *The Years Alone* by Joseph P. Lash *1972*
> *E— Roosevelt; see 1513.

1471. Rose Macaulay (1881–1958)

1 "You, you see, have seemed equally happy for a time, equally unhappy after a time, in all the creeds of no-creeds. And equally good, my dear. I suppose I may say that I believe in none of them, or believe in all. In any case, it matters very little."

> Pt. I, Ch. 14, *Told by an Idiot 1923*

2 Decades have a delusive edge to them. They are not, of course, really periods at all, except as any other ten years would be. But we, looking at them, are caught by the different name each bears, and give them different attributes, and tie labels on them, as if they were flowers, in a border.

> Pt. II, Ch. 1, Ibid.

3 Cranks live by theory, not by pure desire. They want votes, peace, nuts, liberty, and spinning-looms not because they love these things, as a child loves jam, but because they think they ought to have them. That is one element which makes the crank.

> "Cranks," *A Casual Commentary 1925*

4 Sleeping in a bed—it is, apparently, of immense importance. Against those who sleep, from choice or necessity, elsewhere society feels righteously hostile. It is not done. It is disorderly, anarchical.

> "Beds and 'Omes," Ibid.

5 Does conduct rank with food, wine, and weather as a department of life in which goodness is almost universally admired?

> "A Platonic Affection," Ibid.

6 Yet, because prolonged anarchy is impossible to man's law-bound nature, as to that of the universe which bore him, each attempt at it defeats itself. . . .

> *Catchwords and Claptrap 1926*

7 In our attacks on conduct we mislike, we wave the corpses of women and children about us like banners as we charge.

> Ibid.

8 . . . he desired to exaggerate. And here we have what may be called a primary human need, which should be placed by psychologists with the desire for nourishment, for safety, for sense—gratifications, and for appreciation, as one of the elemental lusts of man.

> Ibid.

9 "The century of the common man": ominous phrase, that he and his friends like to turn on their tongues with relishing distaste; lacking this bogy, this sense of there being massed against them a Philistine, vocal army terrible with slogans, illiterate cries, and destructive leveling aims, the young gentlemen would have been less happy, less themselves.

> Ch. 2, *The World My Wilderness 1950*

10 . . . the desire not to work; indeed, I share it to the full. As to one's country, why should one feel any more interest in its welfare than in that of any other countries? And as to the family, I have never understood how that fits in with any of the other ideals at all. A group of closely related persons living under one roof; it is a convenience, often a necessity, sometimes a pleasure, sometimes the reverse; but who first exalted it as admirable, an almost religious ideal?

> Ch. 20, Ibid.

11 "Take my camel, dear," said my aunt Dot, as she climbed down from this animal on her return from High Mass.

> Ch. 1, *The Town of Trebizond 1956*

1472. Mountain Wolf Woman (1881–1960)

1 I cried as loud as I could and cried as much as I wanted to. That is the way I cried. Then when I got enough crying, I stopped crying. When I stopped crying my anxiety seemed to be relieved. Then, after I cried it out, this pain in my heart, I felt better.

> *Mountain Wolf Woman, Sister of Thunder*, Nancy Oestreich Lurie, ed. *1961*

2 I do not know why, but whatever the white people say, that is the way it has to be. I guess it must be that way.

> Ibid.

1473. Marie L. Bonaparte (1881–1962)

1 On the one hand, then, in the reproduction functions proper—menstruation, defloration, pregnancy, and parturition—woman is biologically doomed to suffer. Nature seems to have no hesitation in administering her strong doses of pain, and she can do nothing to submit passively to the regimen prescribed. On the other hand, as regards sexual attraction, which is necessary for the act of impregnation, and as regards the erotic pleasure experienced during the act itself, the woman may be on equal footing with the man.

> "Passivity, Masochism, and Femininity" (1934), *International Journal of Psycho-Analysis*, Vol. 16 *1935*

2 The residue of virility in the woman's [sexual] organism is utilized by nature in order to eroticize her: otherwise the functioning of the maternal apparatus would wholly submerge her in the painful tasks of reproduction and motherhood.

> Ibid.

3 Now every living organism dreads invasion from without, and this is a dread bound up with life itself and governed by the biological law of self-preservation. Moreover . . . little girls . . . bear imprinted on their minds from earliest childhood the terrifying vision of a sexual attack by a man upon a woman, which they believe to be the cause of the [menstrual] bleeding. It follows therefore that, in spite of the instinct, which urges them forward, they draw back from the feminine erotic function itself, although of all the reproductive functions of woman this is the only one which should really be free from suffering and purely pleasurable.

> Ibid.

1474. Margaret Sackville (1881–1963)

1 When all is said and done, monotony may after all be the best condition for creation.

> Introduction, *The Works of Susan Ferrier,** Vol. I *1929*
> *See 773.

2 Great imaginations are apt to work from hints and suggestions and a single moment of emotion is sometimes sufficient to create a masterpiece.

> Ibid.

3 . . . extreme modernity is apt very quickly to become old-fashioned.

> Ibid.

4 Noble natures can adapt themselves to any change without loss of dignity; but those who are naturally insignificant make themselves ridiculous by taking refuge in their own sense of self-importance.

Ibid.

5 Laughter is ever young, whereas tragedy, except the very highest of all, quickly becomes haggard.

Ibid.

1475. Mary Breckinridge (1881–1965)

1 To meet the needs of the frontiersman's child, you must begin before he is born and carry him through the hazards of childbirth. His care not only means the care of the mother before, during and after his birth, but the care of his whole family as well. . . . Health teaching must also be on a family basis—in the homes.

Quoted in "Birth Control Gains in the Mountains of Kentucky" by Kenneth Reich, *Los Angeles Times 9 May 1975*

1476. Mary Heaton Vorse (1881–1966)

1 "Some folks is born in the world feeling it and knowing it in their hearts that creation don't stop where the sight of the eyes stop, and the thinner the veil is the better, and something in them sickens when the veil gets too thick."

"The Other Room," *McCall's 1919*

2 He had seized the one loophole that life had given her and had infused her relentless courage into another's veins.

"The Wallow of the Sea," *Harper's* (New York) *1921*

1477. Anzia Yezierska (1881/6–1970)

1 "If you have no luck in this world, then it's better not to live."

"The Fat of the Land," *Hungry Hearts and Other Stories 1920*

2 "The world is a wheel always turning," philosophized Mrs. Pelz. "Those who were high go down low, and those who've been low go up higher."

Ibid.

3 The trouble with us is that the ghetto of the Middle Ages and the children of the twentieth century have to live under one roof.

Ibid.

4 A man is free to go up as high as he can reach up to; but I, with all my style and pep, can't get a man my equal because a girl is always judged by her mother.

Ibid.

5 Without comprehension, the immigrant would forever remain shut—a stranger in America. Until America can release the heart as well as train the hand of the immigrant, he would forever remain driven back upon himself, corroded by the very richness of the unused gifts within his soul.

"How I Found America," *Ibid.*

6 Give a beggar a dime and he'll bless you. Give him a dollar and he'll curse you for withholding the rest of your fortune. Poverty is a bag with a hole at the bottom.

Ch. 9, *Red Ribbon on a White Horse 1950*

1478. Winifred Letts (1882–?)

1 Age after age the children give
Their lives that Herod still may live.

"The Children's Ghosts," *Hallow-e'en, and Poems of War 1916*

2 God rest you, happy gentlemen,
Who laid your good lives down,
Who took the khaki and the gun
Instead of cap and gown.

"The Spires of Oxford," St. 4, *The Spires of Oxford and Other Poems 1917*

3 I do be thinking God must laugh
The time he makes a boy,
All element the creatures are,
And divilment and joy.

"Boys," *Ibid.*

4 That God once loved a garden
We learn in Holy writ.
And seeing gardens in the spring
I well can credit it.

"Stephen's Green," St. 1 *n.d.*

1479. Mabel Ulrich (1882?–?)

1 It can't be so easy being the husband of a "modern" woman. She is everything his mother wasn't—and nothing she was.

"A Doctor's Diary, 1904–1932," *Scribner's June 1933*

2 But, oh, what a woman I should be if an able young man would consecrate his life to me as secretaries and technicians do to their men employers.

Ibid.

3 Verily what bishops are to the English, bankers are to Americans.

Ibid.

4 A man, it seems, may be intellectually in complete sympathy with a woman's aims. But only about ten percent of him is his intellect—the other ninety his emotions.

Ibid.

1480. Virginia Verona (1882–?)

1 I blame the unions, first, last and all the time. The nation has gotten to the place where unskilled labor is getting paid more than skilled. The unions have gone too far. They rule this country, and they have no compassion, no mercy for people, not even other union members.

Quoted in "Fighting for Her—and Our—Rights" by Ursula Vils, *Los Angeles Times 5 January 1975*

2 People are too easygoing. The American people will not stand up for their rights. They'll be violent, of course, but they will not stand up for their rights.

Ibid.

1481. Virginia Woolf (1882–1941)

1 One of the signs of passing youth is the birth of a sense of fellowship with other human beings as we take our place among them.

"Hours in a Library," *Times Literary Supplement* (London) *30 November 1916*

2 But when the self speaks to the self, who is speaking?—the entombed soul, the spirit driven in, in, in to the central catacomb; the self that took the veil and left the world—a coward perhaps, yet somehow beautiful, as it flits with its lantern restlessly up and down the dark corridors.

"An Unwritten Novel," *Monday or Tuesday 1921*

3 Life's bare as a bone.

Ibid.

4 The eyes of others our prisons; their thoughts our cages.

Ibid.

5 The older one grows the more one likes indecency.

"The String Quartet," Ibid.

6 Each had his past shut in him like the leaves of a book known to him by heart; and his friends could only read the title, James Spalding, or Charles Budgeon, and the passengers going the opposite way could read nothing at all—save "a man with a red moustache," "a young man in grey smoking a pipe."

Ch. 5, *Jacob's Room* 1922

7 In people's eyes, in the swing, tramp, and trudge; in the bellow and uproar; the carriages, motor cars, omnibuses, vans, sandwich men shuffling and swinging; brass bands; barrel organs; in the triumph and the jingle and the strange high singing of some aeroplane overhead was what she loved; life; London; this moment in June.

Mrs. Dalloway 1925

8 Rigid, the skeleton of habit alone upholds the human frame.

Ibid.

9 The man who is aware of himself is henceforward independent; and he is never bored, and life is only too short, and he is steeped through and through with a profound yet temperate happiness. He alone lives, while other people, slaves of ceremony, let life slip past them in a kind of dream.

"Montaigne," *The Common Reader* (First Series) 1925

10 We all indulge in the strange, pleasant process called thinking, but when it comes to saying, even to someone opposite, what we think, then how little we are able to convey! The phantom is through the mind and out of the window before we can lay salt on its tail, or slowly sinking and returning to the profound darkness which it has lit up momentarily with a wandering light.

Ibid.

11 Once conform, once do what other people do because they do it, and a lethargy steals over all the finer nerves and faculties of the soul.

Ibid.

12 Humour is the first of the gifts to perish in a foreign tongue.

"On Not Knowing Greek," Ibid.

13 The good diarist writes either for himself alone or for a posterity so distant that it can safely hear every secret and justly weigh every motive. For such an audience there is need neither of affectation nor of restraint. Sincerity is what they ask, detail, and volume; skill with the pen comes in conveniently, but brilliance is not necessary; genius is a hindrance even; and should you know your business and do it manfully, posterity will let you off mixing with great men, reporting famous affairs, or having lain with the first ladies in the land.

"Rambling Round Evelyn," Ibid.

14 We are nauseated by the sight of trivial personalities decomposing in the eternity of print.

"The Modern Essay," Ibid.

15 A good essay must have this permanent quality about it; it must draw its curtain round us, but it must be a curtain that shuts us in not out.

Ibid.

16 The word-coining genius, as if thought plunged into a sea of words and came up dripping.

"An Elizabethan Play," Ibid.

17 Those comfortably padded lunatic asylums which are known, euphemistically, as the stately homes of England.

"Lady Dorothy Nevill," Ibid.

18 For love . . . has two faces; one white, the other black; two bodies; one smooth, the other hairy. It has two hands, two feet, two tails, two, indeed, of every member and each one is the exact opposite of the other. Yet, so strictly are they joined together that you cannot separate them.

Ch. 2, *Orlando* 1928

19 Every secret of a writer's soul, every experience of his life, every quality of his mind is written large in his works.

Ch. 4, Ibid.

20 Where the Mind is biggest, the Heart, the Senses, Magnanimity, Charity, Tolerance, Kindliness, and the rest of them scarcely have room to breathe.

Ibid.

21 Men felt a chill in their hearts; a damp in their minds. In a desperate effort to snuggle their feelings into some sort of warmth, one subterfuge was tried after another . . . sentences swelled, adjectives multiplied, lyrics became epics.

Ch. 5, Ibid.

22 When the shrivelled skin of the ordinary is stuffed out with meaning, it satisfies the senses amazingly.

Ch. 6, Ibid.

23 Different though the sexes are, they inter-mix. In every human being a vacillation from one sex to the other takes place, and often it is only the clothes that keep the male or female likeness, while underneath the sex is very opposite of what it is above.

Ibid.

24 Suppose...that men were only represented in literature as the lovers of women, and were never the friends of men, soldiers, thinkers, dreamers; how few parts in the plays of Shakespeare could be allotted to them; how literature would suffer! We might perhaps have most of Othello; and a good deal of Antony; but no Caesar, no Brutus, no Hamlet, no Lear, no Jacques—literature would be incredibly impoverished, as indeed literature is impoverished beyond our counting by the doors that have been shut upon women.

A Room of One's Own 1929

25 What a vision of loneliness and riot the thought of Margaret Cavendish brings to mind! As if some giant cucumber had spread itself over all the roses and carnations in the garden and choked them to death...the Duchess* became a bogey to frighten clever girls with.

Ibid.

*See 438.

26 The first duty of a lecturer—to hand you after an hour's discourse a nugget of pure truth to wrap up between the pages of your notebooks and keep on the mantelpiece for ever.

Ch. 1, Ibid.

27 One cannot think well, love well, sleep well, if one has not dined well.

Ibid.

28 A woman must have money and a room of her own if she is to write fiction.

Ibid.

29 Yet it is in our idleness, in our dreams, that the submerged truth sometimes comes to the top.

Ch. 2, Ibid.

30 Women have served all these centuries as looking-glasses possessing the magic and delicious power of reflecting the figure of a man at twice its natural size.

Ibid.

31 Indeed, I thought, slipping the silver into my purse, it is remarkable, remembering the bitterness of those days, what a change of temper a fixed income will bring about.

Ibid.

32 If truth is not to be found on the shelves of the British Museum, where, I asked myself, picking up a notebook and a pencil, is truth?

Ibid.

33 Why are women . . . so much more interesting to men than men are to women?

Ibid.

34 Who shall measure the heat and violence of the poet's heart when caught and tangled in a woman's body?

Ch. 3, Ibid.

35 It is the nature of the artist to mind excessively what is said about him. Literature is strewn with the wreckage of men who have minded beyond reason the opinions of others.

Ibid.

36 . . . for fiction, imaginative work that it is, is not dropped like a pebble upon the ground, as science may be; fiction is liked a spider's web, attached ever so lightly perhaps, but still attached to life at all four corners. . . . But when the web is pulled askew, hooked up at the edge, torn in the middle, one remembers that these webs are not spun in midair by incorporeal creatures, but are the work of human beings and are attached to grossly material things, like health and money and the houses we live in.

Ibid.

37 When, however, one reads of a witch being ducked, of a woman possessed by devils, of a wise woman selling herbs, or even a very remarkable man who had a mother, then I think we are on the track of a lost novelist, a suppressed poet . . . indeed, I would venture to guess that Anon, who wrote so many poems without signing them, was often a woman.

Ibid.

38 The history of men's opposition to women's emancipation is more interesting perhaps than the story of that emancipation itself.

Ibid.

39 It would be a thousand pities if women wrote like men, or lived like men, or looked like men, for if two sexes are quite inadequate, considering the vastness and variety of the world, how should we manage with one only? Ought not education to bring out and fortify the differences rather than the similarities? For we have too much likeness as it is, and if an explorer should come back and bring word of other sexes looking through the branches of other trees at other skies, nothing

would be of greater service to humanity; and we should have the immense pleasure into the bargain of watching Professor X rush for his measuring-rods to prove himself "superior."

Ch. 5, Ibid.

40 Novels so often provide an anodyne and not an antidote, glide one into torpid slumbers instead of rousing one with a burning brand.

Ibid.

41 It is fatal to be a man or woman pure and simple; one must be woman-manly or man-womanly.

Ch. 6, Ibid.

42 Let a man get up and say, "Behold, this is the truth," and instantly I perceive a sandy cat filching a piece of fish in the background. Look, you have forgotten the cat, I say.

The Waves 1931

43 Things have dropped from me. I have outlived certain desires; I have lost friends, some by death . . . others through sheer inability to cross the street.

(p. 132), Ibid.

44 Some people go to priests; others to poetry; I to my friends.

(p. 189), Ibid.

45 There is the old brute, too, the savage, the hairy man who dabbles his fingers in ropes of entrails; and gobbles and belches; whose speech is guttural, visceral—well, he is here. He squats in me.

(p. 205), Ibid.

46 On the outskirts of every agony sits some observant fellow who points.

Ibid.

47 Against you I will fling myself, unvanquished and unyielding, O Death!

Final words,* Ibid.
*Her husband, Leonard Woolf, chose these words as her epitaph at her burial-place and former home, Monk's House, Rodmell, Sussex, England. Woolf committed suicide by drowning on 28 March 1941.

48 I have sometimes dreamt, at least, that when the Day of Judgement dawns and the great conquerors and lawyers and statesmen come to receive their rewards—their crowns, their laurels, their names carved indelibly upon imperishable marble—the Almighty will turn to Peter and will say, not without a certain envy when he sees us coming with our books under our arms, "Look, these need no reward. We have nothing to give them here. They have loved reading."

"How Should One Read a Book?" The Second Common Reader 1932

49 But what have I done with my life? thought Mrs. Ramsay, taking her place at the head of the table, and looking at all the plates making white circles on it.

To the Lighthouse 1937

50 If people are highly successful in their professions they lose their senses. Sight goes. They have no time to look at pictures. Sound goes. They have no time to listen to music. Speech goes. They have no time for conversation. They lose their sense of proportion—the relations between one thing and another. Humanity goes. . . .

Three Guineas 1938

51 To depend upon a profession is a less odious form of slavery than to depend upon a father.

(p. 20), Ibid.

52 Inevitably we look upon society, so kind to you, so harsh to us, as an ill-fitting form that distorts the truth; deforms the mind; fetters the will.

(p. 121), Ibid.

53 For such will be our ruin if you, in the immensity of your public abstractions, forget the private figure, or if we in the intensity of our private emotions forget the public world. Both houses will be ruined, the public and the private, the material and the spiritual, for they are inseparably connected.

(p. 163), Ibid.

54 We can best help you to prevent war not by repeating your words and following your methods but by finding new words and creating new methods.

(p. 164), Ibid.

55 "I will not cease from mental fight," Blake* wrote. Mental fight means thinking against the current, not with it. The current flows fast and furious. It issues a spate of words from the loudspeakers and the politicians. Everyday they tell us that we are a free people fighting to defend freedom. That is the current that has whirled the young airman up into the sky and keeps him circulating there among the clouds. Down here, with a roof to cover us and a gas mask handy, it is our business to puncture gas bags and discover the seeds of truth.

Article in *The New Republic* 21 October 1940
*William Blake, English poet and engraver (1757–1827).

56 There can be no two opinions as to what a highbrow is. He is the man or woman of thoroughbred intelligence who rides his mind at a gallop across country in pursuit of an idea.

"Middlebrow," *The Death of the Moth* 1942

57 Almost any biographer, if he respects facts, can give us much more than another fact to add to our collection. He can give us the creative fact; the fertile fact; the fact that suggests and engenders.

"The Art of Biography," Ibid.

58 If you do not tell the truth about yourself you cannot tell it about other people.

The Moment and Other Essays 1952

59 It is worth mentioning, for future reference, that the creative power which bubbles so pleasantly in beginning a new book quiets down after a time, and one goes on more steadily. Doubts creep in. Then one becomes resigned. Determination not to give in, and the sense of an impending shape keep one at it more than anything.

(11 May 1919), *A Writer's Diary*, Leonard Woolf, ed. 1954

60 I mark Henry James's* sentence: observe perpetually. Observe the oncome of age. Observe greed. Observe my own despondency. By that means it becomes serviceable.

(8 March 1941), Ibid.
*American novelist (1843–1916).

61 That great Cathedral space which was childhood.

"A Sketch of the Past," *Moments of Being* (1939–40), Jeanne Schulkind, ed. 1976

62 A masterpiece is . . . something said once and for all, stated, finished, so that it's there complete in the mind, if only at the back.

Letter (1 January 1933), *The Sickle Side of the Moon: Letters of Virginia Woolf*, Vol. V, Nigel Nicolson, ed. 1979

63 He's like an express train running through a tunnel—one shriek, sparks, smoke and gone.

Letter to poet Stephen Spender (25 June 1935), Ibid.

64 My own brain is to me the most unaccountable of machinery—always buzzing, humming, soaring, roaring, diving, and then buried in mud.

(8 March 1941), Ibid.

65 One has to secrete a jelly in which to slip quotations down people's throats—and one always secretes too much jelly.

Letter (4 July 1938), *Leave the Letters Till We're Dead: Letters of Virginia Woolf*, Vol. 6, Nigel Nicolson, ed. 1980

66 Boredom is the legitimate kingdom of the philanthropic.

Letter (10 September 1918), *The Diary of Virginia Woolf*, Vol. 1, Anne O. Bell, ed. 1982

67 The thing about Proust* is his combination of the utmost sensibility with the utmost tenacity. He searches out these butterfly shades to the last grain. He is as tough as catgut and as evanescent as a butterfly's bloom.

(8 April 1925), Vol. 3, Ibid.
*Marcel P—, French novelist (1871–1922).

68 What I like, or one of the things I like, about motoring is the sense it gives one of lighting accidentally, like a voyager who touches another planet with the tip of his toe, upon scenes which would have gone on, have always gone on, will go on, unrecorded, save for this chance glimpse. Then it seems to me I am allowed to see the heart of the world uncovered for a moment.

(21 August 1927), Ibid.

69 At 46 one must be a miser; only have time for essentials.

(22 March 1928), Ibid.

70 This is not "writing" at all. Indeed, I could say that Shakespeare surpasses literature altogether, if I knew what I meant.

(13 April 1930), Ibid.

71 These are the soul's changes. I don't believe in ageing. I believe in forever altering one's aspect to the sun. Hence my optimism.

(2 October 1932), Vol. 4, Ibid.

72 Now, aged 50, I'm just poised to shoot forth quite free straight & undeflected my bolts whatever they are.

Ibid.

1482. Sigrid Undset (1882–1949)

1 After all, the people of our peninsula form a distinct part of the world. Our forests and our mountains run into each other and our rivers carry their waters from one country to the other. Our houses in Norway resemble those in Sweden. God be praised! We have always lived in a great number of small, private dwellings spread all over our countries. Modern technology has not yet completely intruded on the humanity of the North.

Acceptance speech, Nobel Prize Ceremonies (Sweden) 1928

2 My mother had no choice but to send me to a commercial school in Christiania. I did not like it there but it had one great

advantage over my old school; no one there expected me to like anything!

Autobiographical Essay, Nobel Lectures *1928*

1483. Anne O'Hare McCormick (1882?–1954)

1 Whoever goes to Russia discovers Russia.

Ch. 1, *The Hammer and the Scythe 1927*

2 The peasant wanders; he is still a nomad, a creature of pilgrimages and excursions, harnessed to rather than rooted in the soil.

Ch. 6, Ibid.

3 There is no place where you can see more human nature in a few hours than in a season of the Parliament of Italy.

"A Papal Consistory and a Political Debut" (24 July 1921), *Vatican Journal, 1921–1954*, Marion Turner Sheehan, ed. *1957*

4 A new Italy demands a new Rome.

"A New Rome Arises to Rival the Old" (16 January 1927), Ibid.

5 One little angry, brooding man [Hitler] has put the whole world on wartime. A man who could never keep step with anybody has forced millions of free and intelligent human beings to keep the time he sets.

"Reflections in Time of War" (4 April 1942), Ibid.

6 For what is the naked issue of the most universal war in history but the right of man to be himself?

"Where the Christmas Lights Are Out" (25 December 1943), Ibid.

1484. Emma Jung (1882–1955)

1 Neither arrogance nor presumption drives us to the audacity of wanting to be like God—that is, like man; we are not like Eve of old, lured by the beauty of the fruit of the tree of knowledge, nor does the snake encourage us to enjoy it. No, there has come to us something like a command; we are confronted with the necessity of biting into the apple, whether we think it good to eat or not, confronted with the fact that the paradise of naturalness and unconsciousness, in which many of us would only too gladly tarry, is gone forever.

"On the Nature of Animus" (1931), *Animus and Anima 1957*

2 And now we come to the magic of words. A word, also, just like an idea, a thought, has the effect of reality upon undifferentiated minds. Our Biblical myth of creation, for instance, where the world grows out of the spoken word of the Creator, is an expression of this.

Ibid.

3 Learning to cherish and emphasize feminine values is the primary condition of our holding our own against the masculine principle. . . .

Ibid.

4 The real thinking of woman . . . is pre-eminently practical and applied. It is something we describe as sound common sense, and is usually directed to what is close at hand and personal . . . . In general, it can be said that feminine mentality manifests an undeveloped, childlike, or primitive character; instead of the thirst for knowledge, curiosity; instead of judgment, prejudice; instead of thinking, imagination or dreaming; in-

stead of will, wishing. Where a man takes up objective problems, a woman contents herself with solving riddles; where he battles for knowledge and understanding, she contents herself with faith or superstition, or else she makes assumptions.

Ibid.

5 For by her unconsciousness, woman exerts a magical influence on man, a charm that lends her power over him. Because she feels this power instinctively and does not wish to lose it, she often resists to the utmost the process of becoming conscious. . . . Many men take pleasure in woman's unconsciousness. They are bent on opposing her development of greater consciousness in every possible way, because it seems to them uncomfortable and unnecessary.

Ibid.

6 Very frequently, feminine activity also expresses itself in what is largely a retrospectively oriented pondering over what we ought to have done differently in life, and how we ought to have done it; or, as if under compulsion, we make up strings of causal connections. We like to call this thinking; though, on the contrary, it is a form of mental activity that is strangely pointless and unproductive, a form that really leads only to self-torture.

Ibid.

1485. Sylvia Pankhurst (1882–1960)

1 English is the most modern of the great languages, the most widely spoken, and the most international. . . . Its swiftness and transparent accuracy of expression, and especially the fact that it has shed most of the old grammatical forms which time has rendered useless and scarcely intelligible, have made English a model, pointing the way which must be followed in building the Interlanguage. . . .

Ch. 5, *Delphos 1926*

2 The Interlanguage will provide a means by which the thoughts and emotions of mankind, as expressed in language, may achieve a world-comprehension, which is to-day possible only in music. There is work here for our teachers and students, our pacifists, and our sociologists. Let them rally to the standard of Interlanguage—to perfect it, and to advance it.

Ch. 7, Ibid.

3 We do not make beams from the hollow, decaying trunk of the fallen oak. We use the upsoaring tree in the full vigour of its sap.

Quoted in *The Evening Standard* (London) *5 March 1930*

4 Hourly the War drew nearer; threat followed threat; ultimatum, ultimatum. My mind shrank from the menace sweeping down on us, as children's do from belief in death and misfortune, vainly clinging to the fancy that great disasters only happen to other people.

Ch. 1, *The Home Front 1932*

5 The machinery of succor might be preparing; but the people were hungry.

Ch. 2, Ibid.

6 I could not give my name to aid the slaughter in this war, fought on both sides for grossly material ends, which did not justify the sacrifice of a single mother's son.

Ch. 25, Ibid.

7 Racked with pain, prostrate with headache, at times I might be, yet within me was a rage at this merciless War, this squalor

of poverty! Oh! that all the wealth and effort the nation was squandering might be to rebuild these slums, to restore these faded women, these starved and stunted children.

Ch. 58, Ibid.

8 The cause of Ethiopia cannot be divorced from the cause of international justice, which is permanent and is not to be determined by ephemeral military victories. . . . *New Times* is opposed to the conception of dictatorship. It understands that Fascism destroys all personal liberty and is in fundamental opposition to all forms of intellectual and moral progress.

Quoted in the *New Times & Ethiopia News* 5 May 1936

9 My belief in the growth and permanence of democracy is undimmed. I know that the people will cast off the new dictatorship as they did the old. I believe as firmly as in my youth that humanity will surmount the era of poverty and war. Life will be happier and more beautiful for all. I believe in the GOLDEN AGE.

Essay in *Myself When Young*, Margot Asquith,* ed. *1938*
*See 1241.

10 The discerning traveler who records what appears to the citizens of a country [to be] commonplace performs a service to posterity.

Preface, *Ethiopia 1955*

11 I am proud to call myself a Bolshevist.

Article in *Dreadnought* (1918), Quoted in
*The Fighting Pankhursts** by David Mitchell *1967*
*See Adela P—, 1505; Christabel P—, 1454; Emmeline P—, 1181.

12 We have only one life in this world. Can't we see the revolution in our time? Can't we live in it and enjoy it? I want to see the beginning. I want to see something done. When are you going to begin? If the police came here tonight and killed some of us, I think it would do a great deal of good!

Speech, "Hands Off Russia" Rally, (London; January 1919), Ibid.

13 . . . but all my experience showed that it was useless trying to palliate an impossible system. It is a *wrong* system and has got to be smashed. I would give my life to smash it. You cannot frighten me with any sentence you may impose. . . . You will not stop this agitation. The [*Dreadnought*] will be as common as daily bread.

Courtroom speech (28 October 1919), Ibid.

14 I have gone to war too. . . . I am going to fight capitalism even if it kills me. It is wrong that people like you should be comfortable and well fed while all around you people are starving.

Courtroom Speech (January 1921), Ibid.

15 Love and freedom are vital to the creation and upbringing of a child. I do not advise anyone to rush into either legal or free marriage without love, sympathy, understanding, friendship and frankness. These are essential, and having these, no legal forms are necessary.

Article in *News of the World* (April 1928), Ibid.

16 Socialism is the greatest thing in life for me. You will never crush it out of me or kill it. I am only one of thousands or millions. Socialists make it possible to practice what you say in church, that we should love our neighbors as ourselves. If you work against socialism, you are standing with reaction against life, standing with the dead past against the coming civilization.

Pt. II, Ch. 4, Ibid.

17 The emancipation of today displays itself mainly in cigarettes and shorts. There is even a reaction from the ideal of an intellectual and emancipated womanhood, for which the pioneers toiled and suffered, to be seen in painted lips and nails, and the return of trailing skirts and other absurdities of dress which betoken the slave-woman's intelligent companionship.

Pt. V, Ch. 3, Ibid.

1486. Charlotte Brown (1882–1961)

1 As a part of my argument for education for Negroes I used the incident as illustration that most white people looked upon every Negro, regardless of his appearance, modulated tones that reflected some culture and training, as a servant. . . .

Autobiographical Sketch, *Black Women in White America*,
Gerda Lerner,* ed. *1972*
*See 2160.

2 Now that things are turning and many are opening their eyes to what I've tried to do and desiring to have a share in the same, the question in my heart and mind, and God only knows how it hurts, is just what are they going to ask me to submit to as a negro woman to get their interest for there are some men who occupy high places who feel that no negro woman whether she be cook, criminal, or principal of a school should ever be addressed as *Mrs.*

Letter Fragment, Ibid.

3 . . . I propose the raising of dollars to $500,000 as an endowment. . . . This seems tremendous, I know, for me to undertake but folks don't seem to pay much attention nowadays to anything that's small and a fund like this places a sort of permanence to the thing.

Letter to Mr. and Mrs. Galen Stone (19 June 1920), Ibid.

4 A few of us must be sacrificed perhaps in order to get a step further.

Letter to F. P. Hobgood, Jr. (19 October 1921), Ibid.

1487. Frances Perkins (1882–1965)

1 In America, public opinion is the leader.

Sec. I, *People at Work 1934*

2 But with the slow menace of a glacier, depression came on. No one had any measure of its progress; no one had any plan for stopping it. Everyone tried to get out of the way.

Sec. IV, Ibid.

3 The quality of his [F.D. Roosevelt*] being one with his people, of having no artificial or naural barriers between him and them, made it possible for him to be a leader without ever being or thinking of being a dictator.

Ch. 7, *The Roosevelt I Knew 1946*

4 To one who believes that really good industrial conditions are the hope for a machine civilization, nothing is more heartening that to watch conference methods and education replacing police methods.

Sec. VIII, Ibid.

5 He [F. D. Roosevelt*] didn't like concentrated responsibility. Agreement with other people who he thought were good, right-minded, and trying to do the right thing by the world was almost as necessary to him as air to breathe.

Ch. 12, Ibid.
*(1882–1945), 32nd president of the United States (1933–1945).

1488. Mina Loy (1882–1966)

1 Pig Cupid his rosy snout
Rooting erotic garbage
"Once upon a time"
"Songs to Johannes," *The Lost Lunar Baedeker: The Poems
of Mina Loy*, Roger L. Conover, ed. *1996*

2 Proto-plasm was raving made
Evolving us
Ibid.

3 Curie*
of the laboratory
of vocabulary
she crushed
the tonnage
of consciousness
congealed to phrases
to extract
a radium of the word
"Homage to Gertrude Stein,"** Ibid.
*Reference to Marie C—; see 1269; **see 1363.

4 Silver, circular corpse
your decease
infects us with unendurable ease
"Moreover, the Moon——," St. 3, Ibid.

5 I am the centre
Of a circle of pain
Exceeding its boundaries in every direction
"Parturition" (1914), Ibid.

6 the eye-white sky-light
white-light district
of lunar lusts
"Lunar Baedeker," St. 6, Ibid.

1489. Gisela Richter (1882–1972)

1 . . . a series of failures may culminate in the best possible result.
My Memoirs: Recollection of an Archaeologist's Life 1972

1490. Clementine Hunter (1883?–?)

1 My papa taught me how to pick cotton when I was 8 years old. I didn't mind it. I'd rather pick cotton than to paint.
Quoted in "Clementine Hunter" by Mimi Read,
Dixie Magazine 14 April 1985

2 Work don't kill nobody. It make you tired though.
Ibid.

1491. Frances Newman (1883?–1928)

1 . . . she did not understand how her father could have reached such age and such eminence without learning that all mothers are as infallible as any pope and more righteous than any saint.
The Hard-Boiled Virgin 1926

2 For the first time, she realised that conversation might have been entirely satisfactory if women had been allowed to admit they understood the limited number of subjects men were interested in, and she was so excited by her idea that she almost committed the social crime of allowing a conversation to pause.
Ibid.

3 But she was disturbed when her mind astonished something which she did not think was her mind, and which she called herself.
Dead Lovers Are Faithful Lovers 1928

4 And while she wondered at all the things civilization can teach a woman to endure, she was able to take Mrs. Abbott's departing hand, and to watch Mrs. Abbott walk out of a door into the temporary silence civilization would require of her until she found another acquaintance on whom her conversation could pour as if she were emerging from a year and a day of solitary confinement.
Ibid.

1492. Marguerite Wilkinson (1883–1928)

1 God bless pawnbrokers!
They are quiet men.
"Pawnbrokers" *n.d.*

2 My father got me strong and straight and slim
And I give thanks to him.
My mother bore me glad and sound and sweet,
I kiss her feet!
"The End" *n.d.*

1493. Bella da Costa Greene (1883–1950)

1 . . . every woman who comes within a mile of J.P.* immediately loses her head. . . . They flock to him all day long in rapid and sickening succession. Each one pluming her feathers and thinking she is the hen pheasant, when in reality she is forgotten before her successor appears.
Quoted in *Morgan, American Financier*
by Jean Strouse** *1999*
*John Pierpont Morgan (1837–1913), American financier and philanthropist. **See 3071.

1494. Nannie Helen Burroughs (1883–1961)

1 What every woman who bleaches and straightens out needs, is not her appearance changed, but her mind. She has a false notion as to the value of color and hair in solving the problem of her life. Why does she wish to improve her appearance? Why not improve her real self?
"Not Color but Character," *Voice of the Negro July 1904*

2 Many Negroes have colorphobia as badly as the white folk have Negrophobia.
Ibid.

3 In fact, America will destroy herself and revert to barbarism if she continues to cultivate the things of the flesh and neglect the higher virtues.
"With All They Getting," *The Southern Workman July 1927*

4 When the Negro learns what manner of man he is spiritually, he will wake up all over. He will stop playing white even on the stage. He will rise in the majesty of his own soul. He will glorify the beauty of his own brown skin. He will stop thinking white and go to thinking straight and living right. He will realize that wrong-reaching, wrong-bleaching and wrong-mixing have "most nigh ruin't him" and he will redeem his body and rescue his soul from the bondage of that death. . . .
Ibid.

5 Don't wait for deliverers. . . . I like that quotation, "Moses, my servant, is dead. Therefore arise and go over Jordan."

There are no deliverers. They're all dead. We must arise and go over Jordan. We can take the promised land.
Article, Louisiana Weekly 23 December 1933

6 Chloroform your "Uncle Toms." The Negro must unload the leeches and parasitic leaders who are absolutely eating the life out of the struggling, desiring mass of people. Negroes like that went out of style seventy years ago. They are relics and good for museums.
Ibid.

7 This nation openly endorses, tolerates and legalizes the very abuses against which she originally waged a bloody revolution. A colored boy, a nickel penknife and a screaming woman were no more the cause of the Harlem uprising in 1935 than was a shipload of tea in the Boston harbor, in 1773, the cause of the Revolutionary War.
"Declaration of 1776 Is Cause of Harlem Riot," The Afro-American 13 April 1935

8 The framers of the Declaration of Independence prophesied that uprisings would occur "in the course of human events," if people are denied those inalienable rights to which the "laws of nature and of nature's God entitle them." Reread their prophecy. . . . If that's Red, then the writers of the Declaration of Independence were very Red. They told Americans not to stand injustice after "patient sufferance."
Ibid.

9 We specialize in the wholly impossible
Motto, National Training School for Girls (Washington D.C., c.1909), Black Women in White America, Gerda Lerner,* ed. 1972

*See 2160.

1495. Mabel Louise Robinson (1883?–1962)

1 "Can't you have sense?"
Thankful, [the girl] hurried him on. "Not if I can have anything else."
Pt. I, Bright Island 1937

2 What if the truth does make them sad, what if it haunts them? Better be saddened than dead.
"Writing for the Younger Generation," The Writer's Book, Helen Hull, ed. 1950

3 We have thought that because children are young they are silly. We have forgotten the blind stirrings, the reaching outward of our own youth.
Ibid.

4 If this generation, like those before it, repeats the blunders of the past, we might possibly be to some degree at fault.
Ibid.

5 From the dog's point of view his master is an elongated and abnormally cunning dog.
Quoted in The New York Times Magazine 14 May 1967

1496. Elsa Maxwell (1883–1963)

1 Fade little searchlight, fade forever.
Please go without a fuss,
For you don't interfere
With the Zeppelins, dear,
But you do interfere with us.
"Shine Little Searchlights" 1912

2 First I want a woman guest to be beautiful. Second, I want her to be beautifully dressed. Third, I demand animation and vivacity. Fourth, not too many brains. Brains are always awkward at a gay and festive party.
Interview, New York Mirror 1938

3 I married the world—the world is my husband. That is why I'm so young. No sex. Sex is the most tiring thing in the world.
"I Married the World," This Fabulous Century: 1930–1940 1940

4 Most rich people are the poorest people I know.
Ch. 1, R.S.V.P. 1954

5 I have lived by my wits all my life and I thank the Lord they are still in one, whole piece. I don't need glasses, Benzedrine or a psychiatrist.
Ch. 16, Ibid.

6 Giving parties is a trivial avocation, but it pays the dues for my union card in humanity.
Ibid.

7 Intolerance of mediocrity has been the main prop of my independence. . . .
Ibid.

8 Yet "old friend" always seemed a contradiction to me. Age cannot wither nor custom stale the infinite variety of friends who, as long as you know them, remain as vibrant and stimulating as the day you first met them.
Ibid.

9 Anatomize the character of a successful hostess and the knife will lay bare the fact that she owes her position to one of the three things: either she is liked, or she is feared, or she is important.
Ch. 3, How to Do It 1957

1497. Margaret Sanger (1883–1966)

1 Women of the working class, especially wage workers, should not have more than two children at most. The average working man can support no more and the average working woman can take care of not more in decent fashion.
Family Limitations 1914

2 A mutual and satisfied sexual act is of great benefit to the average woman, the magnetism of it is health giving. When it is not desired on the part of the woman and she gives no response, it should not take place. The submission of her body without love or desire is degrading to the woman's finer sensibility, all the marriage certificates on earth to the contrary notwithstanding.
"Coitus Interruptus," Ibid.

3 The basic freedom of the world is woman's freedom.
Women and the New Race 1920

4 A free race cannot be born of slave mothers.
Ibid.

5 Woman must not accept; she must challenge. She must not be awed by that which has been built up around her; she must reverence that woman in her which struggles for expression.
Ibid.

6 She goes through the vale of death alone, each time a babe is born.
Ibid.

7 When we voice, then, the necessity of setting the feminine spirit utterly and absolutely free, thought turns naturally not to rights of the woman, nor indeed of the mother, but to the rights of the child—of all children in the world.
Ibid.

8 . . . behind all the slogans and shibboleths coined out of the ideals of the peoples for the uses of imperialism, women must and will see the iron hand of that same imperialism, condemning women to breed and men to die for the will of the rulers.
Ibid.

9 Behind all war has been the pressure of population . . . let countries become overpopulated and war is inevitable. It follows as daylight follows the sunrise. . . .
Ibid.

10 The problem of birth control has arisen directly from the effort of the feminine spirit to free itself from bondage.
Ibid.

11 Women are too much inclined to follow in the footsteps of men, to try to think as men think, to try to solve the general problems of life as men solve them. . . . The woman is not needed to do man's work. She is not needed to think man's thoughts. . . . Her mission is not to enhance the masculine spirit, but to express the feminine; hers is not to preserve a man-made world, but to create a human world by the infusion of the feminine element into all of its activities.
Ibid.

12 Diplomats make it their business to conceal the facts. . . .
Ibid.

13 Upon women the burden and the horrors of war are heaviest. . . . When she sees what lies behind the glory and the horror, the boasting and the burden, and gets the vision, the human perspective, she will end war. She will kill war by the simple process of starving it to death. For she will refuse longer to produce the human food upon which the monster feeds.
Ibid.

14 When motherhood becomes the fruit of a deep yearning, not the result of ignorance or accident, its children will become the foundation of a new race.
Ibid.

15 Like begets like. We gather perfect fruit from perfect trees. . . . Abused soil brings forth stunted growths.
Ibid.

16 Custom controls the sexual impulse as it controls no other.
Interview, American Mercury 1924

17 . . . we were dispossessed by the law as a "public nuisance." In Holland the clinics were called "public utilities."
"A Public Nuisance," My Fight for Birth Control 1931

18 . . . There was not a darkened tenement, hovel, or flat but was brightened by the knowledge that motherhood could be voluntary; that children need not be born into the world unless they are wanted and have a place provided for them.
Ibid.

19 I seemed chained hand and foot, and longed for an earthquake or a volcano to shake the world out of its lethargy into facing these monstrous atrocities.
"Awakening and Revolt," Ibid.

20 "Yes, yes—I know, Doctor," said the patient with trembling voice, "but," and she hesitated as if it took all of her courage to say it, "what can I do to prevent getting that way again?"
"Oh, ho!" laughed the doctor good naturedly. "You want your cake while you eat it too, do you? Well, it can't be done. . . . I'll tell you the only sure thing to do. Tell Jake to sleep on the roof!"
Ibid.

21 The menace of another pregnancy hung like a sword over the head of every poor woman. . . .
Ibid.

22 Awaken the womanhood of America to free the motherhood of the world!
Ibid.

23 I am resolved to seek out the root of the evil, to do something to change the destiny of mothers whose miseries were as vast as the sky.
An Autobiography 1938

24 No woman can call herself free who does not own and control her body. No woman can call herself free until she can choose consciously whether she will or will not be a mother.
Quoted in Parade (New York) 1 December 1963

25 Woman was and is condemned to a system under which the lawful rapes exceed the unlawful ones a million to one.
Lawyer's Wit and Wisdom, Bruce Nash, Allan Zullo, eds.; Kathryn Zullo, compiler 1995

26 Many people are horrified at the idea of birth control. Why, to me, it is simply the keynote of a new moral program.
"100 Years of Great Women," ABC News Special with Barbara Walters* 30 April 1999

*See 2480.

1498. Coco Chanel (1883–1971)

1 Fashion is made to become unfashionable.
Life (New York) 19 August 1957

2 A fashion for the young? That is a pleonasm: there is no fashion for the old.
Quoted in Coco Chanel, Her Life, Her Secrets by Marcel Haedrich 1971

3 My friends, there are no friends.
Ibid.

4 Since everything is in our heads, we had better not lose them.
Ibid.

5 "Where should one use perfume?" a young woman asked. "Wherever one wants to be kissed," I said.
Ibid.

6 Fashion is architecture; it is a matter of proportions.
Ibid.

7 Elegance does not consist in putting on a new dress.
Ch. 21, Ibid.

8 I am no longer what I was. I will remain what I have become.
Ibid.

9 Silence is the cruelty of the provincial.
Ibid.

10 Legend is the consecration of fame.

Ibid.

11 Great loves must be endured.

Ibid.

12 Youth is something very new: twenty years ago no one mentioned it.

Ibid.

13 There goes a woman who knows all the things that can be taught and none of the things that cannot be taught.

Ibid.

14 In order to be irreplaceable one must always be different.

Ibid.

15 Nothing is ugly as long as it is alive.

Ibid.

16 I am doing an optimistic collection because things are going badly.

Ibid.

17 You see, that's what fame is: solitude.

Ibid.

1499. Sara Murphy (1883–1975)

1 It was like a great fair, and everybody was so young.*
    Quoted in *Everybody Was So Young: Gerald and Sara Murphy—A Lost Generation Love Story* by Amanda Vaill 1998
    *Paris in the 1920s.

2 I don't think the world is a very nice place. And all there seems to be left to do is to make the best of it while we are here, & be VERY grateful for one's friends because they are the best there is, & make up for many another thing that is lacking.

Ibid.

1500. Imogen Cunningham (1883–1976)

1 People who are living aren't famous—they're just infamous.
    Quoted in *Never Give Up* (film) by Ann Hershey 1975

2 One thing about being born without beauty—you don't look for it.

Ibid

1501. Dorothy Brett (1883–1977)

1 She [Mabel Dodge*] had an insatiable appetite for tasting life in all its aspects. She tasted and spat it out.
    "My Long and Beautiful Journey," *South Dakota Review* Summer 1967

    * See 1438.

1502. Florida Scott-Maxwell (1883–1979)

1 Age puzzles me. I thought it was a quiet time. My seventies were interesting and fairly serene, but my eighties are passionate. I grow more intense as I age.
    The Measure of My Days 1972

2 No matter how old a mother is she watches her middle-aged children for signs of improvement.

Ibid.

3 I wonder why love is so often equated with joy when it is everything else as well. Devastation, balm, obsession, granting and receiving excessive value, and losing it again. It is recognition, often of what you are not but might be. It sears and it heals. It is beyond pity and above law. It can seem like truth.

Ibid.

4 Is life a pregnancy? That would make death a birth.

Ibid.

5 We who are old know that age is more than a disability. It is an intense and varied experience, almost beyond our capacity at times, but something to be carried high. If it is a long defeat it is also a victory . . .

Ibid.

6 When a new disability arrives I look about me to see if death has come, and I call quietly, "Death, is that you? Are you there?" So far the disability has answered, "Don't be silly, it's me."

Ibid.

7 If a grandmother wants to put her foot down, the only safe place to do it these days is in a note book.
    The Measure of My Days 1972

8 I have made others suffer, and if there are more lives to be lived, I believe I ought to do penance for the suffering I have caused. I should experience what I have made others experience. It belongs to me, and I should learn it.

Ibid.

9 Age is a desert of time—hours, days, weeks, years perhaps—with little to do. So one has ample time to face everything one has had, been, done; gather them all in: the things that came from outside, and those from inside. We have time at last to make them truly ours.

Ibid.

10 Is there any stab as deep as wondering where and how much you failed those you loved?

Ibid.

11 Order, cleanliness, seemliness make a structure that is half support, half ritual, and—if it does not create it—maintains decency.

Ibid.

12 You need only claim the events of your life to make yourself yours. When you truly possess all you have been and done, which may take some time, you are fierce with reality.

Ibid.

1503. Caroline Giltinan (1884–?)

1 Betrayer of the Master,
    He sways against the sky,
    A black and broken body,
    Iscariot—or I?

"Identity" n.d.

2 Let me keep my eyes on yours;
    I dare not look away
    Fearing again to see your feet
    Cloven and of clay.

"Disillusioned" n.d.

1504. Rose Henniker Heaton (1884–?)

1 She left no little things behind
Except loving thoughts and kind.

"The Perfect Guest" *n.d.*

1505. Adela Pankhurst (1885–1961)

1 We have no religious doctrine to preach, only a morality that is big enough to include all religions and that should give offence to none.

Quoted in *The Fighting Pankhursts** by David Mitchell *1967*

2 Profits and prostitution—upon these empires are built and kingdoms stand. . . .

"Communism and Social Purity," *Dreadnought* (London; February 1921), Ibid.

3 Their [politicians'] most outstanding characteristic, I should say, would be their inability to manage anything properly. What industry have they ever promoted but the gambling industry? What have they ever produced but strife and deficits? What resolve have they shown but a determination to grab for themselves, their friends and supporters whatever is available to grab?

Speech (c.1929), Ibid.

4 Capital and labour in alliance will require neither government control nor political interference, and the vast network of government which is impoverishing us today will become useless and will shrivel up and die away.

Ibid.

*See Christabel P—, 1454; Emmeline P—, 1181; Syvia P—, 1485.

1506. Sophie Tunnell (1884–?)

1 Fear is a slinking cat I find
Beneath the lilacs of my mind.

"Fear" *n.d.*

1507. Ruth Mason Rice (1884–1927)

1 An oval, placid woman who assuaged men's lives;
Her comely hands wrought forth a century
Of oval, placid women who engaged, as wives,
In broideries and tea.

"Queen Victoria," *Afterward 1927*

2 Where are you going, multitude of feet?

"New York," Ibid.

3 But now—a loaf's an easy thing;
Made quickly by a blind machine;
And still—I find me hungering
For fare—unseen.

"Daily Bread," Ibid.

1508. Texas Guinan (1884–1933)

1 Fifty million Frenchmen can be wrong.

Quoted in the *New York World-Telegram* 21 March 1931

2 I've been married once on the level, and twice in America.

Nightclub Act *n.d.*

3 Success has killed more men than bullets.

Ibid.

1509. Sara Teasdale (1884–1933)

1 Let it be forgotten for ever and ever,
Time is a kind friend, he will make us old.

"Let It Be Forgotten," St. 1 *1921*

2 Stephen's kiss was lost in jest,
Robin's lost in play,
But the kiss in Colin's eyes
Haunts me night and day.

"Look," St. 2. *n.d.*

3 When I am dead and over me bright April
Shakes out her rain-drenched hair,
Though you should lean above me broken-hearted,
I shall not care.

"I Shall Not Care," St. 1 *n.d.*

4 One by one, like leaves from a tree,
All my faiths have forsaken me.

"Leaves" *n.d.*

5 Of my own spirit let me be
In sole though feeble mastery.

"Mastery" *n.d.*

6 I shall not let a sorrow die
Until I find the heart of it,
Nor let a wordless joy go by
Until it talks to me a bit.

"Servitors" *n.d.*

7 O beauty, are you not enough?
Why am I crying after love?

"Spring Night" *n.d.*

8 Joy was a flame in me
Too steady to destroy.

"The Answer" *n.d.*

9 I found more joy in sorrow
Than you could find in joy.

Ibid.

10 My soul is a broken field
Ploughed by pain.

"The Broken Field" *n.d.*

11 No one worth possessing
Can be quite possessed.

"Advice to a Girl" *n.d.*

12 Spend all you have for loveliness.

"Barter" *n.d.*

13 Then, like an old-time orator
Impressively he rose;
"I make the most of all that comes
And the least of all that goes."

"The Philosopher," St. 4 *n.d.*

14 When I can look Life in the eyes,
Grown calm and very coldly wise,
Life will have given me the Truth,
And taken in exchange—my youth.

"Wisdom" *n.d.*

1510. Anna Wickham (1884–1947)

1 It is well within the order of things
That man should listen when his mate sings;

But the true male never yet walked
Who liked to listen when his mate talked.
"The Affinity," *The Contemplative Quarry 1915*

2 When I am sick, then I believe in law.
"Self-Analysis," Ibid.

3 I desire Virtue, though I love her not—
I have no faith in her when she is got:
I fear that she will bind and make me slave
And send me songless to the sullen grave.
St. 3, Ibid.

4 I smother in the house in the valley below,
Let me out to the night, let me go!
"Divorce," *The World Split Open*,
Louise Bernikow,* ed. *1974*
*See 2780.

5 Because of the body's hunger we are born,
And by contriving hunger we are fed;
Because of hunger is our work well done,
And so our songs well sung, and things well said.
"Sehnsucht" *n.d.*

6 Desire and longing are the whips of God.
Ibid.

7 I have been so misused by chaste men with one wife
That I would live with satyrs all my life.
"Ship Near Shoals" *n.d.*

8 If I had peace to sit and sing,
Then I could make a lovely thing. . . .
"The Singer" *n.d.*

9 Oh, give me a woman of my race
As well controlled as I,
And let us sit by the fire,
Patient till we die!
"The Tired Man" *n.d.*

10 Think how poor Mother Eve was brought
To being as God's afterthought.
"To Men" *n.d.*

11 Alas! For all the pretty women who marry dull men,
Go into the suburbs and never come out again.
"Meditation at Kew" *n.d.*

1511. Fanny Heaslip Lea (1884–1955)

1 It's odd to think we might have been
Sun, moon and stars unto each other—
Only, I turned down one little street
As you went up another.
"Fate," St. 5 *n.d.*

1512. Edith Summers Kelley (1884–1956)

1 . . . the barnyard was an expression of something that was real, vital, and fluid, that . . . was of natural and spontaneous growth, that . . . turned with its surroundings, that . . . was a part of the life that offered itself to her.
Weeds 1923

2 The only break in what would seem to an outsider an intolerable stretch of tedium was the dinner. This usually consisted of salt hog meat, fried or boiled potatoes and some other vegetable, followed by a heavy-crusted apple pie or a soggy boiled pudding.
Ibid.

1513. Eleanor Roosevelt (1884–1962)

1 No one can make you feel inferior without your consent.
This Is My Story 1937

2 A democratic form of government, a democratic way of life, presupposes free public education over a long period; it presupposes also an education for personal responsibility that too often is neglected.
"Let Us Have Faith in Democracy," *Land Policy Review*,
Department of Agriculture *January 1942*

3 I think if the people of this country can be reached with the truth, their judgement will be in favor of the many, as against the privileged few.
Quoted in *Ladies' Home Journal May 1942*

4 Perhaps in His wisdom the Almighty is trying to show us that a leader may chart the way, may point out the road to lasting peace, but that many leaders and many peoples must do the building.
"My Day," Syndicated newspaper column *16 April 1945*

5 Perhaps nature is our best assurance of immortality.
Ibid.

6 It is very difficult to have a free, fair and honest press anywhere in the world. In the first place, as a rule, papers are largely supported by advertising, and that immediately gives the advertisers a certain hold over the medium which they use.
If You Ask Me 1946

7 We must be willing to learn the lesson that cooperation may imply compromise, but if it brings a world advance it is a gain for each individual nation.
"My Day," Syndicated newspaper column *21 January 1946*

8 I am sorry that Governments in all parts of the world have not seen fit to send more women as delegates, alternates or advisors to the Assembly [U.N.]. I think it is in these positions that the women of every nation should work to see that equality exists.
Ibid. *28 January 1946*

9 None of us has lived up to the teachings of Christ.
Ibid. *14 February 1946*

10 It is not fair to ask of others what you are not willing to do yourself.
Ibid.

11 If I do not run for office, I am not beholden to my Party. What I give, I give freely and I am too old to want to be curtailed in any way in the expression of my own thinking.
"Why I Do Not Choose to Run," *Look* (New York)
9 July 1946

12 . . . a trait no other nation seems to possess in quite the same degree that we do—namely, a feeling of almost childish injury and resentment unless the world as a whole recognizes how innocent we are of anything but the most generous and harmless intentions.
"My Day," Syndicated newspaper column *11 November 1946*

13 It is not that you set the individual apart from society but that you recognize in any society that the individual must have rights that are guarded.
Quoted in *The New York Times* 4 February 1947

14 I used to tell my husband that, if he could make *me* understand something, it would be clear to all the other people in the country.
"My Day," syndicated newspaper column *12 February 1947*

15 The economy of Communism is an economy which grows in an atmosphere of misery and want.
Ibid.

16 . . . I deplore . . . the attitude of self-righteous governments. . . . Our own Government's position has never gone beyond pious hopes and unctuous words.
"My Day," Syndicated newspaper column *26 April 1947*

17 Justice cannot be for one side only, but must be for both. . . .
Ibid. *15 October 1947*

18 . . . certain rights can never be granted to the government, but must be kept in the hands of the people.
Quoted in *The New York Times* 3 May 1948

19 A society in which everyone works is not necessarily a free society and may indeed be a slave society; on the other hand, a society in which there is widespread economic insecurity can turn freedom into a barren and vapid right for millions of people.
Speech, "The Struggle for Human Rights," (Paris) *27 September 1948*

20 My own feeling is that the Near East, India and many of the Asiatic people have a profound distrust of white people. This is understandable since the white people they have known intimately in the past have been the colonial nations and in the case of the United States, our businessmen. . . .
*Report to President Truman** 1950*
*Harry S. T— (1884–1972), 33rd president of the United States (1945–53).

21 We must preserve our right to think and differ. . . . The day I'm afraid to sit down with people I do not know because five years from now someone will say five of those people were Communists and therefore you are a Communist—that will be a bad day.
Speech, Americans for Democratic Action *2 April 1950*

22 For it isn't enough to talk about peace. One must believe in it. And it isn't enough to believe in it. One must work at it.
Broadcast, *Voice of America 11 November 1951*

23 There is a small articulate minority in this country which advocates changing our national symbol which is the eagle to that of the ostrich and withdrawing from the United Nations.
Speech, Democratic National Convention *23 July 1952*

24 Too often the great decisions are originated and given form in bodies made up wholly of men, or so completely dominated by them that whatever of special value women have to offer is shunted aside without expression.
Speech, United Nations *December 1952*

25 You have to accept whatever comes and the only important thing is that you meet it with courage and with the best that you have to give.
Essay in, *This I Believe*, Edward P. Morgan, ed. *1953*

26 The only hope for a really free press is for the public to recognize that the press *should* not express the point of view of the owners and the writers but be factual; whereas the editorials *must* express the opinions of owners and writers.
It Seems to Me 1954

27 A mature person is one who does not think only in absolutes, who is able to be objective even when deeply stirred emotionally, who has learned that there is both good and bad in all people and in all things, and who walks humbly and deals charitably with the circumstances of life, knowing that in this world no one is all-knowing and therefore all of us need both love and charity.
Ibid.

28 Life has got to be lived—that's all there is to it. At 70, I would say the advantage is that you take life more calmly. You know that "this, too, shall pass!"
Quoted in *The New York Times* 8 October 1954

29 Could we have the vision of doing away in this great country with poverty? . . . what can make us not only the nation that has some of the richest people in the world, but the nation where there are no people that have to live at a substandard level. That would be one of the very best arguments against Communism that we could possibly have.
Speech, Democratic National Convention *13 August 1956*

30 You always admire what you really don't understand.
"Meet the Press," NBC TV *16 September 1956*

31 I have always felt that anyone who wanted an election so much that they would use those* methods did not have the character that I really admired in public life.
Ibid.
*Reference to Richard Nixon's smear campaign against Helen Gahagan Douglas; see 1781.

32 Where, after all, do universal human rights begin? In small places, close to home—so close and so small that they cannot be seen on any maps of the world. Yet they *are* the world of the individual persons; the neighborhood he lives in; the school or college he attends; the factory, farm or office where he works. Such are the places where every man, woman and child seeks equal justice, equal employment, equal dignity without discrimination. Unless these rights have meaning there, they have little meaning anywhere. Without concerned citizen action to uphold them close to home, we shall look in vain for progress in the larger world.
Speech, "The Great Question," United Nations *1958*

33 You can't move so fast that you try to change the mores faster than people can accept it. That doesn't mean you do nothing, but it means that you do the things that need to be done according to priority.
On My Own 1958

34 We cannot exist as a little island of well-being in a world where two-thirds of the people go to bed hungry every night.
Speech, Democratic Fund-Raising Dinner *8 December 1959*

35 Everybody wants something.
Interview with Maureen Corr *1960*

36 You gain strength, courage, and confidence by every experience in which you really stop to look fear in the face.
"You Learn by Living" *1960*

37 You must do the thing you think you cannot do.
Ibid.

38 We have to face the fact that either all of us are going to die together or we are going to learn to live together and if we are to live together we have to talk.
> Quoted by A. David Gurewitsch in *The New York Times*
> *15 October 1960*

39 . . . I could not, at any age, be content to take my place by the fireside and simply look on. Life was meant to be lived. Curiosity must be kept alive. The fatal thing is the rejection. One must never, for whatever reason, turn his back on life.
> Quoted by Emma Bugbee in the *New York Herald Tribune*
> *11 October 1961*

40 Both the President and his wife can never give way to apprehension even though they are probably more aware than most citizens of the dangers which may surround us. If the country is to be confident, they must be confident.
> "My Day," Syndicated newspaper column *29 May 1962*

41 They [Israelis] are still dreamers, but they make their dreams come true. . . .
> Quoted by Ruth G. Michaels in *Hadassah December 1962*

42 This I know. This I believe with all my heart. If we want a free and peaceful world, if we want to make the deserts bloom and man grow to greater dignity as a human being—*we can do it*!
> *Tomorrow Is Now 1963*

43 I think, at a child's birth, if a mother could ask a fairy godmother to endow it with the most useful gift, that gift would be curiosity.
> *Today's Health* (Chicago) *2 October 1966*

44 I'm glad I never *feel* important, it does complicate life.
> Ch. 2, Quoted in *Eleanor: The Years Alone* by Joseph P.
> Lash *1972*

45 . . . when you know to laugh and when to look upon things as too absurd to take seriously, the other person is ashamed to carry through even if he was serious about it.
> Letter to Harry S. Truman* (14 May 1945), Ibid.

46 So—against odds, the women inch forward, but I'm rather old to be carrying on this fight!
> Letter to Joseph P. Lash (13 February 1946), Ibid.

47 Not all Jewish people want a nation and a national home. . . .
> Letter to Miss Siegel (5 September 1946), Ibid.

48 . . . we do not always like what is good for us in this world.
> Letter to Miss Binn (24 October 1947), Ibid.

49 . . . perhaps man's spirit, his striving, is indestructible. It is set back but it does not die and so there is a reason why each one of us should do our best in our own small corner. Do you think I'm too optimistic?
> Letter to A. David Gurewitsch (18 December 1947), Ibid.

50 I cannot believe that war is the best solution. No one won the last war, and no one will win the next war.
> Letter to Harry S. Truman* (22 March 1948), Ibid.

51 Our real battlefield today is Asia and our real battle is the one between democracy and communism. . . . We have to prove to the world and particularly to downtrodden areas of the world which are the natural prey to the principles of communist eco-

nomics that democracy really brings about happier and better conditions for the people as a whole.
> Memo to Harry S. Truman* (28 December 1948), Ibid.
> *(1884–1972), 33rd president of the United States (1945–53).

52 Spiritual leadership should remain spiritual leadership and the temporal power should not become too important in any Church.
> Letter to Cardinal Francis Spellman (23 July 1949), Ibid.

53 We need our heroes*. . . .
> Letter to Joseph Lash (21 January 1952), Ibid.
> *Reference to General Dwight D. Eisenhower (1890–1969), 34th president of the United States (1954–61).

54 The Jews in their own country are doing marvels and should, once the refugee problem is settled, help all the Arab countries.
> Letter to Maude Gray (5 March 1952), Ibid.

55 Television has completely revolutionized what should go on at a convention.
> Letter to Frank E. McKinney (13 July 1952), Ibid.

56 . . . I have spent many years of my life in opposition and I rather like the role.
> Letter to Bernard Baruch* (18 November 1952), Ibid.
> *B— Mannes B— (1870–1965), American financier and political advisor.

57 I believe that it is essential to our leadership in the world and to the development of true democracy in our country to have no discrimination in our country whatsoever. This is most important in the schools of our country.
> Letter to Richard Bolling (20 January 1956), Ibid.

58 I doubt if Eisenhower can stand a second term and I doubt if the country can stand Nixon as President.
> Letter to Lord Elibank (20 January 1956), Ibid.

59 Mr. Dulles* has just frightened most of our allies to death with a statement that there is an art in actually threatening war and coming to the brink but retreating from the brink.
> Letter to Gus Ranis (23 January 1956), Ibid.
> *John Foster Dulles (1888–1959), American diplomat and politician; secretary of state (1953–1959).

60 It seems to me . . . we have reached a place where it is not a question of "can we live in the same world and cooperate" but "we must live in the same world and learn to cooperate."
> Letter to Queen Juliana* of the Netherlands
> (14 February 1958), Ibid.
> *See 1943.

61 When you cease to make a contribution you begin to die.
> Letter to Mr. Horne (19 February 1960), Ibid.

62 I cannot, of course, ever feel safe . . . because with Mr. Nixon* I always have the feeling that he will pull some trick at the last minute.
> Letter to John F. Kennedy** (27 August 1960), Ibid.
> *Richard M. Nixon (1913–1994), 37th president of the United States (1969–74), resigned. **(1917–1963) 35th president of the United States (1961–63), assassinated.

63 To say he [John F. Kennedy]* would not make mistakes would be silly. Anyone would make mistakes with the problems that lie ahead of us.
> Letter to Peter Kamitchis (21 October 1960), Ibid.

64 . . . on the whole, life is rather difficult for both the children and their parents in the "fish bowl" that lies before you.
> Letter to Jacqueline Kennedy* (1 December 1960), Ibid.
> *Later, Jacqueline Kennedy Onassis; see 2403.

65 You seem to think that everyone can save money if they have the character to do it. As a matter of fact, there are innumerable people who have a wide choice between saving and giving their children the best possible opportunities. The decision is usually in favor of the children.
> Letter to Franklin Roosevelt III (15 January 1962), Ibid.

66 This is a strange little complacent country, in many ways a U.S.A in miniature but of course nearer the center of disturbance!
> Letter to her daughter Anna (Geneva, 2 May 1951),
> *Mother and Daughter: The Letters of Eleanor and Anna Roosevelt 1982*

67 It has always been so somber a business for me (living I mean) and I guess this quality of abandon is a grand thing to have.
> Letter to Lorena Hickok* (1936), *Empty Without You:
> The Intimate Letters of Eleanor Roosevelt and
> Lorena Hickok*, Roger Streitmatter, ed. *1998*
> *Her longtime secretary and companion; see 1654.

1514. Phyllis Bottome (1884–1963)

1 In my early life, and probably even today, it is not sufficiently understood that a child's education should include at least a rudimentary grasp of religion, sex, and money. Without a basic knowledge of these three primary facts in a normal human being's life—subjects which stir the emotions, create events and opportunities, and if they do not wholly decide must greatly influence an individual's personality—no human being's education can have a safe foundation.
> Ch. 9, *Search for a Soul 1947*

1515. Florence Ellinwood Allen (1884–1966)

1 Liberty cannot be caged into a charter and handed on ready made to the next generation. Each generation must re-create liberty for its own times. Whether or not we establish freedom rests with ourselves.
> *This Constitution of Ours 1940*

2 The attainment of justice is the highest human endeavor.
> Quoted in *The 50 Most Influential Women in American
> Law* by Dawn Bradley Berry* *1996*
> *See 3435.

1516. Sophie Tucker (1884–1966)

1 Success in show business depends on your ability to make and keep friends.
> Ch. 4, *Some of These Days*, with Dorothy Giles *1945*

2 From birth to age eighteen, a girl needs good parents. From eighteen to thirty-five, she needs good looks. From thirty-five to fifty-five, she needs a good personality. From fifty-five on, she needs good cash.
> Attributed *1953*

3 Keep breathing.
> Anniversary Speech *13 January 1964*

1517. Laura Benét (1884–1979)

1 Lost in the spiral of his conscience, he
Detachedly takes rest.
> "The Snail" *n.d.*

2 No voice awoke. Dwelling sedate, apart
Only the thrush, the thrush that never spoke,
Sang from her bursting heart.
> "The Thrush" *n.d.*

1518. Alice Roosevelt Longworth (1884–1980)

1 He [Coolidge*] looks as if he had been weaned on a pickle.
> *Crowded Hours 1934*
> *Calvin C— (1872–1933), 30th president of the United States (1923–29).

2 Were it not for Czolgosz [the assassin of President McKinley*], we'd all be back in our brownstone-front houses. That's where we'd be. And I would have married for money and been divorced for good cause.
> Quoted by Jean Vanden Heuvel in the *Saturday
> Evening Post 4 December 1965*
> *William M— (1843–1901), 25th president of the United States (1897–1901).

3 I have a simple philosophy. Fill what's empty. Empty what's full. And scratch where it itches.
> Quoted in *The Best* by Peter Russell and Leonard Ross *1974*

1519. Helene Deutsch (1884–1982)

1 They have an extraordinary need of support when engaged in any *activity directed outward*, but are absolutely independent in such feeling and thinking as related to their inner life, that is to say, in their *activity directed inward*. Their capacity for identification is not an expression of inner poverty but of inner wealth.
> *The Psychology of Women*, Vol. I *1944–1945*

2 After all, the ultimate goal of all research is not objectivity, but truth.
> Ibid.

3 It is interesting to note that in every phase of life feminine masochism finds some form of expression.
> Ch. 1, Ibid.

4 . . . adolescence is the period of the decisive last battle fought before maturity. The ego must achieve independence, the old emotional ties must be cast off, and new ones created.
> Ch. 2, Ibid.

5 The very fact that the youthful soul feels insecure strengthens its active aspiration to master its insecurity.
> Ibid.

6 It is no exaggeration to say that among all living creatures, only man, because of his prehensile appendages, is capable of rape in the full meaning of this term—that is, sexual possession of the female against her will.
> Ch. 6, Ibid.

7 The vagina—a completely passive, receptive organ—awaits an active agent to become a functioning excitable organ.
> Ibid.

8 She [Rosa Luxembourg] was too great to be considered "only a woman," even by her enemies.
> Ch. 7, Ibid.

9 All observations point to the fact that the intellectual woman is masculinized; in her, warm, intuitive knowledge has yielded to cold unproductive thinking.
> Ch. 8, Ibid.

10 Psychoanalysis was my last and most deeply experienced revolution; and Freud, who was rightly considered a conservative on social and political issues, became for me the greatest revolutionary of the century.

Ch. 10, Ibid.

11 The embattled gates to equal rights indeed opened up for modern women, but I sometimes think to myself: "That is not what I meant by freedom-it is only 'social progress.'"

Ch. 1, Confrontations with Myself 1973

1520. Aline Triplett Michaelis (1885–?)

1 Alone, yet never lonely,
Serene, beyond mischance,
The world was his, his only,
When Lindbergh flew to France.

"Lindbergh"* *n.d.*

*Charles A. L—, American aviator (1902-1974) who made the first nonstop solo trans-Atlantic flight.

1521. Clare Sheridan (1885–?)

1 At the end of her days, she became superbly squaw-like, and would sit impassively for hours, staring into the fire, her head shrouded in a shawl. A figure of great moral fortitude and self-oblation was gradually fading out.

To the Four Winds 1955

1522. Gladys Cromwell (1885–1919)

1 Sorrow can wait,
For there is magic in the calm estate
Of grief; lo, where the dust complies
Wisdom lies.

"Folded Power" *n.d.*

1523. Elinor Wylie (1885–1928)

1 I was, being human, born alone;
I am, being woman, hard beset;
I live by squeezing from a stone
The little nourishment I get.

In masks outrageous and austere
The years go by in single file;
And none has merited my fear,
And none has quite escaped my smile.

"Let No Charitable Hope," Sts. 2–3 (1923),
Collected Poems 1932

2 Honeyed words like bees,
Gilded and sticky, with a little sting.

"Pretty Words," Ibid.

3 I love smooth words, like gold-enameled fish
Which circle slowly with a silken swish. . . .

Ibid.

4 The worst and best are both inclined
To snap like vixens at the truth;
But, O, beware the middle mind
That purrs and never shows a tooth!

"Nonsense Rhyme," St. 2, Ibid.

5 I've played the traitor over and over;
I'm a good hater but a bad lover.

"Peregrine," Ibid.

6 Avoid the reeking herd,
Shun the polluted flock,
Live like that stoic bird
The eagle of the rock.

"The Eagle and the Mole," St. 1 (1921), Ibid.

7 If you would keep your soul
From spotted sight and sound,
Live like the velvet mole,
Go burrow underground.

St. 5, Ibid.

8 If any has a stone to throw
It is not I, ever or now.

"The Pebble," Ibid.

1524. Elizabeth Madox Roberts (1885–1941)

1 The wind found out my coat was thin.
It tried to tear my clothes away.
And the cold came in.

"Cold Fear," St. 3, *Under the Tree 1922*

1525. Constance Rourke (1885–1941)

1 Ardent and tired and overwrought, in that sensitive state where the imagination grows fluid, where the inner and outer motives coalesce. . . .

The Trumpets of Jubilee 1927

2 An emotional man may possess no humor, but a humorous man usually has deep pockets of emotion, sometimes tucked away or forgotten.

Ch. 1, American Humor 1931

3 Comic resilience swept through them in waves, transcending the past, transcending terror, with a sense of comedy, itself a wild emotion.

Ch. 2, Ibid.

4 It is a mistake to look for the social critic—even Manqué—in Mark Twain. In a sense the whole American comic tradition had been of social criticism: but this had been instinctive and incomplete, and so it proved to be in Mark Twain. . . . He was primarily a *raconteur*. . . . He was never the conscious artist, always the improviser.

Ch. 7, Ibid.

5 In comedy, reconcilement with life comes at the point when to the tragic sense only an inalienable difference or dissension with life appears.

Ch. 8, Ibid.

6 Humor has been a fashioning instrument in America, cleaving its way through the national life, holding tenaciously to the spread elements of that life. Its mode has often been swift and coarse and ruthless, beyond art and beyond established civilization. It has engaged in warfare against the established heritage, against the bonds of pioneer existence. Its objective—the unconscious objective of a disunited people—has seemed to be that of creating fresh bonds, a new unity, the semblance of a society and the rounded completion of an American type.

Ch. 9, Ibid.

1526. Karen Horney (1885–1952)

1 Psychoanalysis is the creation of a male genius, and almost all those who have developed his ideas have been men. It is only

right and reasonable that they should evolve more easily a masculine psychology and understand more of the development of men than of women.

"The Flight from Womanhood," *Feminine Psychology 1926*

2 Is not the tremendous strength in men of the impulse to creative work in every field precisely due to their feeling of playing a relatively small part in the creation of living beings, which constantly impels them to an overcompensation in achievement?

Ibid.

3 Like all sciences and all valuations, the psychology of women has hitherto been considered only from the point of view of men.

Ibid.

4 It seems to me impossible to judge to how great a degree the unconscious motives for the flight from womanhood are reinforced by the actual social subordination of women.

Ibid.

5 . . . it is necessary not to be too easily satisfied with ready-at-hand explanations for a disturbance.

Self-Analysis 1942

6 . . . a person who feels helplessly caught in his neurotic entanglements tends to hope against hope for a miracle.

Ibid.

7 . . . concern should drive us into action and not into a depression.

Ibid.

8 But miracles occur in psychoanalysis as seldom as anywhere else.

Ibid.

9 Fortunately [psycho]analysis is not the only way to resolve inner conflicts. Life itself still remains a very effective therapist.

Our Inner Conflicts 1945

1527. Marie Laurencin (1885–1956)

1 Why should I paint dead fish, onions and beer glasses? Girls are so much prettier.

Quoted in *Time* (New York) *18 June 1956*

1528. Isak Dinesen (1885–1962)

1 "What is man, when you come to think upon him, but a minutely set, ingenious machine for turning, with infinite artfulness, the red wine of Shiraz* into urine?"

Seven Gothic Tales 1934

*City in Iran famous for its wine.

2 Woman. I understand the word itself, in that sense, has gone out of the language. Where we talk of woman . . . you talk of women, and all the difference lies therein. . . .

"The Old Chevalier," Ibid.

3 I do not know if you remember the tale of the girl who saves the ship under mutiny by sitting on the power barrel with her lighted torch . . . and all the time knowing that it is empty? This has seemed to me a charming image of the women of my time. There they were, keeping the world in order . . . by sitting on the mystery of life, and knowing themselves that there was no mystery.

Ibid.

4 "If only I could so live and so serve the world that after me there should never again be birds in cages. . . ."

"The Deluge at Norderney,"
Ibid.

5 I thought that it would be a pleasant thing to be laid out to the sun and the stars, and to be so promptly, neatly and openly picked and cleansed; to be made one with Nature and become a common component of a landscape.*

Out of Africa 1938

*Commenting on a native custom of leaving deceased bodies to decompose in the bush.

6 I have seen a herd of elephants travelling through dense native forest . . . pacing along as if they had an appointment at the end of the world.

Pt. I, Ch. 1, Ibid.

7 The giraffe, in their queer, inimitable, vegetating gracefulness, as if it were not a herd of animals but a family of rare, long-stemmed, speckled gigantic flowers slowly advancing.

Ibid.

8 If I knew a song of Africa—I thought of the giraffe, and the African new moon lying on her back, of the plows in the fields, and the sweaty faces of the coffee-pickers—does Africa know a song for me?

Ch. 4, Ibid.

9 "The true aristocracy and the true proletariat of the world are both in understanding with tragedy. To them it is the fundamental principle of God, and the key, the minor key, to existence. They differ in this way from the bourgeoisie of all classes, who deny tragedy, who will not tolerate it, and to whom the word tragedy means in itself unpleasantness."

Pt. V, Ch. 1, Ibid.

10 "All Natives are masters in the art of the pause, and thereby give perspective to a discussion."

Ibid.

11 When Africans speak of the personality of God, they speak like the Arabian Nights or the last chapters of the Book of Job; it is . . . the infinite power of imagination with which they are impressed.

Ibid.

12 I have before seen other countries, in the same manner, give themselves to you when you are about to leave them.

Ibid.

13 "But the trouble is not as you think now, that we have put up obstacles too high for you to jump, and how could we possibly do that, you great leaper? It is that we have put up no obstacles at all. The great strength is in you, Lulu, and the obstacles are within you as well, and the thing is, that the fullness of time has not yet come."

Ibid.

14 She was like a man who has been given an elephant gun and asked to shoot little birds.

Winter's Tales 1942

15 But she was badly hurt and disappointed because the world was not a much greater place . . . and because nothing more colossal, more like the dramas of the stage, took place in it.

Ibid.

16 I don't believe in evil, I believe only in horror. In nature there is no evil, only an abundance of horror: the plagues and the blights and the ants and the maggots.
> "Phantoms," *Prokosch, Voices: A Memoir* 1983

1529. Malvina Hoffman (1885–1966)

1 My true center of work was not commissions. It was an enormous capacity for falling in love with everything around me. . . .
> Quoted in "Malvina Hoffman," *Famous American Women* by Hope Stoddard 1970

2 . . . at heart we are really working for the angels. . . . What counts is the lasting integrity of the artist and the enduring quality of his work.
> Ibid.

1530. Helen M. Cam (1885–1968)

1 We must not read either law or history backwards.
> Introduction, *Selected Essays of F. W. Maitland*, H. D. Hazeltine, G. Gapsley. P. H. Winfield, eds. 1936

2 The authority of a statute made in Parliament is universally recognized as superior to that of any other legislative act.
> Ch. 12, *England Before Elizabeth* 1950

3 Feudalism, for all its insistence on priority and place, had proved inadequate for the needs of government, however much its traditions of deference and responsibility might linger in the English social system.
> Ibid.

4 Law offers a guiding thread to us . . . one of purpose—and a purpose infinitely worthwhile, for in the long view it is more important that human beings should learn to get on with each other than that they should be more comfortable materially and safer physically.
> Lecture, "Law as It Looks to a Historian," Girton College *18 February 1956*

5 If civilisation is the art of living together with people not entirely like oneself, the first step in civilisation is not so much the invention of material tools as the regularisation of social habits. As soon as you begin to say "We always do things this way" the foundations are laid. "Custom is before all law." As soon as you begin to say "We have always done things this way—perhaps *that* might be a better way," conscious law-making is beginning. As soon as you begin to say "*We* do things this way—*they* do things that way—what is to be done about it?" men are beginning to feel towards justice, that resides between the endless jar of right and wrong.
> Ibid.

6 Historical fiction is not only a respectable literary form: it is a standing reminder of the fact that history is about human beings.
> *Historical Novel* 1961

7 . . . every historian knows that belief itself is a historical fact, and that legend and myth cannot be left out of account in tracing the sequence of cause and effect.
> Lecture, "Magna Carta—Event or Document?" Old Hall of Lincoln's Inn *7 July 1967*

1531. Marjorie Allen Seiffert (1885–1968)

1 And when I search my soul until
I see too deeply and divine

That you can never love me—Still
I hold you fast for you are mine!
> "Possession," St. 3, *A Woman of Thirty* 1919

2 For to your heart
Beauty is a burned-out torch,
And Faith, a blind pigeon,
Friendship, a curious Persian myth,
And love, blank emptiness,
Bearing no significance
Nor any reality.

Only Weariness is yours. . . .
> "Singalese Love Song, II" Sts. 2-3, Ibid.

3 Sorrow stands in a wide place,
Blind—blind—
Beauty and joy are petals blown
Across her granite face,
They cannot find sight or sentience in stone.

Yesterday's beauty and joy lie deep
In sorrow's heart, asleep.
> "Sorrow," Ibid.

4 Spring raged outside, but ghostly in my bed
A dead self lay and knew itself for dead.
> "A Full Storm," *The King with Three Faces and Other Poems* 1929

5 We are damned with the knowledge of good and evil: they,
Whose new estate is freedom, suffer worse
And find life empty, trivial and boring,
A sort of game that every one must play,
And no one knows the rules, and no one's scoring,
And nothing's at stake, for youth has lost its purse.
> "Youth Visits Our Inferno," Ibid.

6 And love is worth what it cost you, nothing more.
> "The Horse-Leech's Daughter," Ibid.

7 Lust is the oldest lion of them all.
> "An Italian Chest" *n.d.*

1532. Billie Burke (1885–1970)

1 To survive there, you need the ambition of a Latin-American revolutionary, the ego of a grand opera tenor, and the physical stamina of a cow pony.
> Quoted in *Filmgoer's Companion* by Leslie Halliwell 1984

1533. Frances Parkinson Keyes (1885–1970)

1 Women were cats, all of them, unless they were fools, and there was no way of getting even with them, even, except by walking off with the men they wanted. . . .
> Pt. I, Ch. 3, *The Great Tradition* 1939

2 "Well, it's a good thing to trust in Providence. But I believe the Almighty likes a little cooperation now and again."
> Pt. III, Ch. 10, Ibid.

3 "I can't see that the Nazis are any different from the Communists, except that they're cleaner and better looking and better drilled. They're both stirring up trouble, they're both bent on destruction and despotism, they're both ready to go to any lengths to gain their ends!"
> Pt. V, Ch. 15, Ibid.

4 Folks with their wits about them knew that advertisements were just a pack of lies—you had only to look at the claims of patent medicines!

Pt. I, Ch. 3, *Blue Camellia 1957*

5 ". . . young folks, them, don' never think 'bout nothin' only spend, spend, spend money, instead of save, save, save money, like us used to do, us. It's education, or either it's clothes, or either it's something else, as long as somebody got to spend, spend, spend. Boys is plenny bad, I got to admit, yes, but girls is even worser."

Pt. V, Ch. 22, Ibid.

1534. Anna Louise Strong (1885–1970)

1 Some day I shall go by the world's highest mountains and most secret waters, traveling with the nomads in the heart of Asia!

The Road to the Gray Pamir 1931

1535. Sophie Treadwell (1885/90–1970)

1 PRISON BARBER (to Woman). You'll submit my lady, right to the end, you'll submit.

Episode 9, *Machinal 1928*

1536. Alice Gerstenberg (1885–1972)

1 HARRIET. I am what you wish the world to believe you are.
HETTY. You are the part of me that has been trained.
HARRIET. I am your educated self.
HETTY. I am the rushing river; you are the ice over the current.

Overtones 1915*

*Harriet/Hetty are the conscious/unconscious of the same character; this was the first depiction of the subconscious on stage and made a tremendous impact on expressionism and psychological realism in theater.

1537. Ettie Lee (1885–1974)

1 Every child has a right to a good home.

Quoted in *The Los Angeles Times* 27 April 1974

1538. Alice Paul (1885–1977)

1 Equality of rights under the law shall not be denied or abridged by the United States or by any State on account of sex.

Equal Rights Amendment 1923*

*The wording of the proposed amendment was likely contributed to by several members of the National Woman's Party, of which Paul was founder and president.

2 It is better, as far as getting the vote is concerned I believe, to have a small, united group than an immense debating society.

Letter to Eunice R. Oberly (6 March 1914), Quoted in *Alice Paul and the National Woman's Party, 1912–1920* by Loretta Ellen Zimmerman *1964*

3 I have never doubted that equal rights was the right direction. Most reforms, most problems are complicated. But to me there is nothing complicated about ordinary equality. Which is a nice thing about our campaign. It really is true, at least to my mind, that only good will come to everybody with equality. . . . It seems to me it is not our problem how women use their equality or how men use their equality.

Quoted in *Women Suffragists* by Diana Star Helmer *1998*

4 You can't have peace in a world in which some women or some men or some nations are at different stages of development.

Ibid.

5 I think every reform movement needs people who are full of enthusiasm. It's the first thing you need. I was full of enthusiasm, and I didn't want any lukewarm person around.

Ibid.

6 There had never been a procession of women for any cause under the sun.*

Ibid.

*Reference to 3 March 1913, the day before Woodrow Wilson's inauguration as 28th United States president; 8,000 marchers, 10 bands, five squadrons of cavalry with chariots, 26 floats, and more, gathered together to demand women's suffrage.

7 Until women vote, every piece of legislation undertaken by the administration is an act of injustice to them. All laws affect the interests of women.

Motto, The *Suffragist,** Ibid.
*Official publication of the Congressional Committee of NAWSA, debut edition (November 1913)

8 It is not a war of women against men, for the men are helping loyally, but a war of women and men together against the politicians.

Ibid.

9 If we had universal suffrage throughout the world, we might not even have wars.

Ibid.

1539. Bess Truman (1885–1982)

1 A woman's place in public is to sit beside her husband, be silent, and be sure her hat is on straight.

Quoted in *Bess W. Truman* by Margaret Truman* *1986*
*Her daughter; see 2259.

2 I'm not used to this awful public life.

Comment to Frances Perkins,* Quoted in *First Ladies* by Betty Boyd Caroli *1987*
*See 1487.

1540. Frances Darwin Cornford (1886–?)

1 O fat white woman whom nobody loves,
Why do you walk through the fields in gloves?

"To a Fat Lady Seen from the Train" *n.d.*

2 Magnificently unprepared
For the long littleness of life.

"Rupert Brooke"* *n.d.*

*English poet (1837–1915).

1541. Florence Kiper Frank (1886?–?)

1 The canny among the publishers know that an enormous popular appetite for the insulting of the famous must be gratified, and the modern biographer emerges from the editorial conference a sadist and a wiser man.

Morrow's Almanac 1929

2 Pooh-men!
We are done with them now,
Who had need of them then,-
I and you!

"Baby" *n.d.*

1542. Hazel Hall (1886–1924)

1 *I am the dream of youth, and life is fair!*
Footfall, footfall;

I am a dream, divinely unaware!
Footfall, footfall;
I am the burden of an old despair!
Footfall.

"Footsteps" *n.d.*

1543. Zoë Akins (1886–1958)

1 LADY HELEN. To accuse is so easy that it is infamous to do so where proof is impossible!

Act I, *Déclassé* 1919

2 LADY HELEN. My life is like water that has gone over the dam and turned no mill wheels. Here I am, not happy, but not unhappy, as my days run on to the sea, idly—but not too swiftly—for I love living.

Ibid.

3 LADY HELEN. Englishmen are like that. They love life more and value it less than any other people in the world.

Act II, Ibid.

4 SOLOMON. Like a fool I thought I was the arbiter of her destiny; and all the time Fate had happier plans for her.

Act III, Ibid.

5 EDITH. . . . there's a great strangeness about love. . . . Yes, I'm very sure that love is the strangest thing in the world—much stranger than death—or—or just life.

Act I, *Daddy's Gone A-Hunting* 1921

6 OSCAR. But you've got a wife. It's all right to tell a wife the brutal truth, but you've got to go sort of easy with your lady-love.

Act II, Ibid.

7 MRS. DAHLGREN. Shutting one's eyes is an art, my dear. I suppose there's no use trying to make you see that—but that's the only way one *can* stay married.

Ibid.

8 EDITH. This world is a very unsafe place. It's all shifting sands, Ned. Shifting sands and changing winds.

Act III, Ibid.

9 TILLERTON. "To him that hath it shall be given—" She hath . . . that's all. That's greatness.
PRESCOTT. One sort of greatness, maybe.
TILLERTON. Even the great can have only their own sort of greatness.
PRESCOTT. And it's often only that they're great sponges. . . .
TILLERTON. Often, yes, or great roses for whose blooming the trees have been pruned and stripped. But they make the beauty of the world and that's enough.

Act I, *Greatness* 1922

10 CANAVA. The success-haters. . . . That's what I call them—the people who have never got what they want and turned sour on everybody who has. The world's full of them. . . . As soon as you've made good they begin to watch for you to fail. . . .

Ibid.

11 TILLERTON. And I wonder if peace is enough for any man. . . .

Act II, Ibid.

12 RAYMOND. No one can ever help loving anyone.

Act III, Ibid.

13 SENTONI. My cousin Cleofante does not believe in inspiration. She shuns the false energy of all stimulants, even those of criticism and sympathy, when she sets herself to a task. What she does, she does alone—unencouraged, unadvised, unmoved.

The Portrait of Tiero 1924

14 CLEOFANTE. Work alone qualifies us for life, Sentoni.

Ibid.

15 CHARLOTTE. Tina, Tina, why must you always think that people are interested in you?
TINA. Why shouldn't I? Aren't they?
DELIA. My dear! What will people think of you if you talk like that?
CHARLOTTE. Just what she deserves, probably.

4th episode, *The Old Maid** 1935

*This play, which won Akins the Pulitzer Prize, was an adaptation of a story by Edith Wharton (see 1229).

16 Mine was a love so exquisite that I
Rather than watch it wither chose to die:
So dress my grave, O friend, with no poor flower
Which in your quiet garden blooms an hour!

"Epitaph," *The Hills Grow Smaller* 1937

17 And have we lost the right
To look on a blooming bough
Without remembering how
Once with high promising
We were a part of spring—
We who are now the dead
Leaves of other years strewn where flowers spread?

"Jazz Nocturne," St. 3, Ibid.

18 I know not where I go; I scarcely feel
The menacing fatigue about my feet,
The skies that scourge, the distances that cheat,
The constant wounds that neither hurt nor heal.

"Lethargy," St. 2, Ibid.

19 And they shall know that in the ordering
Of every world to come the law shall read
That he who dares be lawless wears the wing

Of bird and prophet and his light shall lead
On through the darkness to eventual light,
To undiscovered wealth, to newer need. . . .

"The Anarchist, III," Sts. 15–16, Ibid.

20 Indifference to all the fun of chance
I watched black spiders of inertia spin
The far-flung web which I was strangling in.

"Indifference," St. 1, Ibid.

21 In all my locked-up songs
No one but you belongs.

"To H. R.," St. 1, Ibid.

1544. Hilda Doolittle (1886–1961)

1 "Why couldn't I have a dog? Cats are girls' animals."

"Old Tommy," *The Comrade* 30 April 1911

2 "Well, young man, if I'm not much mistaken, you'll have to begin at the beginning, if ever you want to get to the end. That's a platitude, if you know what that means. That means that it's seven times seven times true, if you know how true that is. And I'll tell you this, you'd better hurry and begin at

the beginning, or you can be quite sure you'll be pretty well forgotten at the end."

Ibid.

3   "If he can't be happy in his own house, he won't be any more so on the far seas."

Ibid.

4   "There never is anything a boy can do when he's not allowed to go out because it rains. There never is anything a boy can do!"

Ibid.

5   "Oh, go away; this is the garden of make-believe and you can't enter here unless you have the key."

Ibid.

6   "I wonder how girls get such fun out of nothing!"

Ibid.

7   Why not let the pears cling
to the empty branch?
All your coaxing will only make
a bitter fruit—
let them cling, ripen of themselves,
test their own worth,
nipped, shrivelled by the frost,
to fall at last but fair
with a russet coat.

"Sheltered Garden," St. 6, Sea Garden 1916

8   beauty without strength,
chokes out life

St. 8, Ibid.

9   Ah kingly kiss—
no more regret
nor old deep memories
to mar the bliss.

"Leda" 1919

10   I who still kept of wisdom's meagre store
a few rare songs and some philosophising,
offered you these for I had nothing more

"Let Zeus Record," IV, St. 2, Red Roses for Bronze 1931

11   My thoughts tear me,
I dread their fever.
I am scattered in its whirl.
I am scattered like
the hot shrivelled seeds

"Mid-Day" n.d.

12   Egypt had maimed us,
offered dream for life,
an opiate for a kiss,
and death for both.

"Egypt" n.d.

13   O wind, rend open the heat,
cut apart the heat,
rend it to tatters.

"Heat" n.d.

1545. Margaret Ayer Barnes (1886–1967)

1   There they were. Opinions. Jane bumped into them, tangible obstacles in her path, things to be recognized, and accepted or evaded, as the exigencies of the situation demanded.

Pt. 1, Ch. 1, Years of Grace 1930

2   "Curious, isn't it," he went on airily, "that 'talking with the right people' means something so very different from 'talking with the right person'?"

Pt. 3, Ch. 1, Ibid.

3   Childless women, Olivia reflected, slipped gracefully into middle age. There was no one particular awkward moment when they climbed up on the shelf.

Ch. 1, Westward Passage 1931

4   "There's nothing half so real in life as the things you've done," she whispered. "Inexorably, unalterably done."

Ch. 4, Ibid.

5   Sentiment, crystallized, grows into sentimentality. It lost all spontaneity, which was the essence of feeling. It was dated—old-fashioned.

"Prelude," Within This Present 1933

6   "Character comes before scholarship. . . ."

Pt. I, Ch. 1, Ibid.

1546. Frances Marion (1886–1973)

1   The thought had taken root in his imagination and grown as a tree grows from a tiny seed until it crowded out all other thoughts in his mind.

Pt. I, Ch. 1, Westward the Dream 1948

2   The land around San Juan Capistrano is the pocket where the Creator keeps all his treasures. Anything will grow there, from wheat and beans to citrus fruit.

Ch. 3, Ibid.

3   "Do we really know anybody? Who does not wear one face to hide another?"

Ch. 10, Ibid.

4   What a strange pattern the shuttle of life can weave. . . .

Pt. II, Ch. 14, Ibid.

5   This is not dead land, it is only thirsty land.

Pt. II, Ch. 22, Ibid.

6   "A coin, Mr. Fox, can only fall heads or tails, and I'll gamble on heads, they last longer."

Off with Their Heads 1972

7   I shall refrain from mentioning to our southern neighbors that San Franciscans look upon the City of the Queen of the Angels as California's floating kidney transplanted from the Middle West.

"1914 Through 1924," Ibid.

8   Promises that you make to yourself are often like the Japanese plum tree—they bear no fruit.

Ibid.

9   We have a little catch phrase in our family which somehow fits almost everyone in the movie colony: "Spare no expense to make everything as economical as possible."

Ibid.

10   One thing you learned when you wrote for the movies: all nationalities were sensitive except Americans. The Arabs were always to be pictured as sweet, friendly people. So were the

Greeks, the Dutch, Turks, Laps, Eskimos, and so on down the line. Everyone was honest and virtuous, except Americans. You could make them the most sinister villains and never hear a word of protest from Washington, Chicago, Kalamazoo, or all points south. But should you describe a villain belonging to any country but America, you found yourself spread-eagled between the Board of Censors and the diplomatic service of some foreign power.

"1925 Through 1928," Ibid.

1547. Ida Rosenthal (1886–1973)

1 Nature made woman a bosom, so nature thought it was important. Why argue with nature?...A sister shouldn't look like a brother.*

Quoted in *Women Inventors* by Linda Jacobs Altman *1997*
*Discoursing her reasons for rejecting the flattening bandeau of the 1920s and devising the modern-day bra.

1548. Mary Wigman (1886–1973)

1 Art is communication spoken by man for humanity in a language raised above the everyday happening.

"The New German Dance," *Modern Dance*,
Virginia Stewart, ed. *1935*

2 During the process of artistic creation, man descends into the primordial elements of life. He reverts to himself to become lost in something greater than himself, in the immediate, indivisible essence of life.

Ibid.

3 Strong and convincing art has never arisen from theories.

Ibid.

1549. Helen Hoyt (1887–?)

1 My heart led me past and took me away;
And yet it was my heart that wanted to stay.

"In the Park" *n.d.*

1550. Florence Luscomb (1887–?)

1 . . . there is no end to what you can accomplish if you don't care who gets the credit.

Quoted in *Moving the Mountain* by Ellen Cantarow *1980*

2 The tragedy in the lives of most of us is that we go through life walking down a high–walled land with people of our own kind, the same economic situation, the same national background and education and religious outlook. And beyond those walls, all humanity lies, unknown and unseen, and untouched by our restricted and impoverished lives.

Oral History Project, University of Rhode Island (1972/73), Ibid.

3 And when women are working side by side with them on all the great public issues, and carrying on the life of humanity, I think that men are going to get comradeship that only the really advanced men have now. And when we have amended the Declaration of Independence so that it reads, "All men and women are created equal," this new force of men and women will be able to go forward and create a society of peace and of social justice and of beauty we haven't ever known in this world.

Ibid.

4 I have come face-to-face with the question, "Is America still a democracy? Is it ruled by the people, by their votes?" and I have been forced to answer, "No." Behind the screen of the ballot, the real holders of power who decide national policies and laws, and control public opinion by their ownership of all the mass media of information are the great industrial and monetary monopolies who own our national economic life. They, together with the armed forces—the military industrial complex—are the real rulers of our country today.

Ibid.

5 Capitalism, by definition, sets money as the sole model of power which keeps us running. Every man for himself. From my lifetime experiences, I have reached the firm conviction that the only possible basis for a successful, just, and peaceful world society is a cooperative economy of production for human needs, not for individual profits. That is the basic principle of communism.

Ibid.

6 It is subversive to set up inquisitions like this, state or national, into the thoughts and consciences of Americans. . . . It is subversive for commissions like this to spread hysteria and intimidation throughout the land that Americans are afraid to sign petitions, afraid to read progressive magazines, afraid to make out checks for liberal causes, afraid to join organizations, afraid to speak their mind on public issues. Americans dare not be free citizens! This is the destruction of democracy.

Statement to Commission to Investigate Communism in Massachusetts (7 January 1955), Ibid.

1551. Agnes Meyer (1887–1970?)

1 When you travel through the wheat fields of Kansas for a day and a night and see endless herds grazing on the pastureland, when you have spent weeks visiting factory after factory in city after city producing at top speed, when you have seen the tireless effort, the intelligent application of management and labor and their ever-increasing co-operation, you realize that there are enough resources, actual and potential, enough brains and good will in this country to turn the whole world into a paradise.

"Juvenile Delinquency and Child Labor," *Washington Post*
14 March 1943

2 What the Nation must realize is that the home, when both parents work, is non-existent. Once we have honestly faced the fact, we must act accordingly.

"Living Conditions of the Woolworker," *Washington Post*
10 April 1943

3 We have forgotten that democracy must live as it thinks and think as it lives.

Introduction, *Journey Through Chaos 1943*

4 An orderly existence creates primarily an unconscious relation to the silent progression of the days, seasons, and the music of the spheres.

Out of These Roots 1953

5 Fortunate are the people whose roots are deep.

Ch. 1, Ibid.

6 In the pursuit of an educational program to suit the bright and the not-so-bright we have watered down a rigid training for the elite until we now have an educational diet in many of our public high schools that nourishes neither the classes nor the masses.

Ch. 2, Ibid.

7 Let us hope that in the process of integration in our society, which fortunately is now well underway, the Negro will not

allow the American steam roller of conformity to destroy his creative gifts.

Ch. 8, Ibid.

8 The children are always the chief victim of social chaos.

Ch. 13, Ibid.

9 Science was the method used in the struggle by which mankind has passed from habit, routine, and caprice, from efforts to use nature magically, to intellectual self-control.

Lecture, "Democracy and Clericalism" 21 May *1954*

10 Christianity must now rise above the limits of orthodoxy just as the free world must rise above the limitations of nationalism if we are not to pull the civilized world down around our ears.

Ibid.

11 We Americans must now throw off our childishness and parochialism and create a new idea of man acceptable to thinking people the world over.

Ch. 1, *Education for a New Morality 1957*

12 There is a need for heroism in American life today.

Ibid.

13 We can never achieve absolute truth but we can live hopefully by a system of calculated probabilities. The law of probability gives to natural and human sciences—to human experience as a whole—the unity of life we seek.

Ch. 3, Ibid.

14 From the nineteenth-century view of science as a god, the twentieth century has begun to see it as a devil. It behooves us now to understand that science is neither one nor the other.

Ibid.

15 We are immoral in America today precisely because our existing institutions do not perform their function of abolishing our inherited dualism between thought and action, between our American ideals and what we do about them. Let us bear in mind that idealism when separated from empirical methods and experimental utilization in concrete social situations is vague, semantic mouthing. . . .

Ch. 16, Ibid.

16 It certainly must have been a relief for the women of the country to realize that one could be a woman and a lady and yet be thoroughly political.

Letter to Eleanor Roosevelt* (25 July 1952}, Quoted in *Eleanor: The Years Alone* by Joseph P. Lash *1972*

*See 1513.

1552. Rebecca Shelley (1887–?)

1 Humanity above all nations!

"Bicentennial Prayer for Peace" *1976*

1553. Ruth Benedict (1887–1948)

1 No man ever looks at the world with pristine eyes. He sees it edited by a definite set of customs and institutions and ways of thinking.

Ch. 1, *Patterns of Culture 1934*

2 If we justify war, it is because all peoples always justify the traits of which they find themselves possessed, not because war will bear an objective examination of its merits.

Ibid.

3 War is, we have been forced to admit, even in the face of its huge place in our own civilization, an asocial trait.

Ibid.

4 "Hybrid vigor" has been shown in studies of American Indian-White mixture, stature in the half-breeds being greater than that of either race contributing to the cross. Mixed bloods also show over and over again evidence of increased fertility. . . . Nature apparently does not condemn the half-caste to physiological inferiority. The rule for the breeding of good human stock is that both parents be of good physique and good mental ability.

Ch. 4, Ibid.

5 Racism is the new Calvinism which asserts that one group has the stigmata of superiority and the other has those of inferiority. . . . For racism is an *ism* to which everyone in the world today is exposed; for or against, we must take sides. And the history of the future will differ according to the decision which we make.

Ch. 1, *Race: Science and Politics 1940*

6 Racism in its nationalistic phase, therefore, has been a politician's plaything. . . . It is a dangerous plaything, a sword which can be turned in any direction to condemn the enemy of the moment.

Ch. 7, Ibid.

7 But the Thai have an indestructible conviction that existence is good, and they have characteristically placed the promised rewards of Buddhism in this life rather [than] in the life to come.

Pt. II, Ch. 5, *Thai Culture and Behavior 1943*

8 Everybody repeats the proverbial maxim: "In this world everything changes except good deeds and bad deeds; these follow you as the shadow follows the body."

Ibid.

9 The Japanese are, to the highest degree, both aggressive and unaggressive, both militaristic and aesthetic, both insolent and polite, rigid and adaptable, submissive and resentful of being pushed around, loyal and treacherous, brave and timid, conservative and hospitable to new ways.

Ch. 1, *The Chrysanthemum and the Sword 1946*

10 Love, kindness, generosity, which we value just in proportion as they are given without strings attached, necessarily must have their strings in Japan. And every such act received makes one a debtor.

Ch. 5, Ibid.

11 A man's indebtedness . . . is not virtue; his repayment is. Virtue begins when he dedicates himself actively to the job of gratitude.

Ch. 6, Ibid.

12 We turn in our sleep and groan because we are parasites—we women—because we produce nothing, say nothing, find our whole worth in the love of a man.—For shame! We are become the veriest Philistines—in this matter of woman's sphere. I suppose it is too soon to expect us to achieve perspective on the problem of women's rights. . . .

Quoted in *An Anthropologist at Work* by Margaret Mead* *1951*

*See 1802.

13 . . . the passionate belief in the superior worth-whileness of our children. It is stored up in us as a great battery charged by the accumulated instincts of uncounted generations.

Ibid.

14 I have always used the world of make-believe with a cezrtain desperation.

Ibid.

15 If we are not to have the chance to fulfill our one potentiality—the power of loving—why were we not born men? At least we could have had an occupation then.

(October 1912), Ibid.

16 Life was a labyrinth of petty turns and there was no Ariadne who held the clue.

Ibid.

17 The trouble is not that we are never happy—it is that happiness is so episodical.

Ibid.

18 We hurt each other badly, for words are clumsy things, and he is inexorable. But, at any rate, he does not baby me, and honesty helps even when it is cruel.

(Christmas 1916), Ibid.

19 I long to speak out the intense inspiration that comes to me from the lives of strong women.

(January 1917), Ibid.

20 . . . work even when I'm satisfied with it is never my child I love nor my servant I've brought to heel. It's always busy work I do with my left hand, and part of me watches grudging the wastes of a lifetime.

(9 June 1934), Ibid.

21 If any society wishes to pay that cost for its chosen and congenial traits, certain values will develop within this pattern, however "bad" it may be. But the risk is great, and the social order may not be able to pay the price. It may break down beneath them with all the consequent wanton waste of revolution and economic and emotional disaster.

Quoted in *4000 Years of Women in Science*, http://www.astr.ua.edu *27 September 1997*

1554. Edith Sitwell (1887–1964)

1 Every one hundred years or so it becomes necessary for a change to take place in the body of poetry. . . . A fresh movement appears and produces a few great men, and once more the force and vigour die from the results of age; the movement is carried on by weak and worthless imitators, and a change becomes necessary again.

Poetry and Criticism 1926

2 Still falls the Rain—
Dark as the world of man, black as our loss—
Blind as the nineteen hundred and forty nails
Upon the Cross.

"Still Falls the Rain," *Night and Dawn 1940*

3 Daisy and Lily
Lazy and silly. . . .

"Façade" (1922), *Façade and Other Poems 1920–1935 1950*

4 But a word stung him like a mosquito. . . .

"I do like to be beside the Seaside" (1922), Ibid.

5 I have often wished I had time to cultivate modesty . . . . But I am too busy thinking about myself.

Quoted in *Observer* (London) *30 April 1950*

6 My poems are hymns of praise to the glory of life.

"Some Notes on My Poetry," *Collected Poems 1954*

7 I'm not the man to baulk at a low smell,
I'm not the man to insist on asphodel.
This sounds like a He-fellow, don't you think?
It sounds like that. I belch, I brawl, I drink.

"One-Way Song," Ibid.

8 Jane, Jane
Tall as a crane,
The morning light creaks down again.

"Aubade," Ibid.

9 The air still seems to reverberate with the wooden sound of numskulls being soundly hit.

"Dylan Thomas,"* *Atlantic Monthly* (Boston) February *1954*
*Welsh poet (1914–1953).

10 He had full eyes . . . giving at first the impression of being unseeing, but seeing all, looking over immeasurable distances.

Ibid.

11 Alas, that he who caught and sang the sun in flight, yet was the sun's brother, and never grieved it on its way, should have left us with no good-bye, good night.

Ibid.

12 A lady asked me why, on most occasions, I wore black. "Are you in mourning?"
"Yes."
"For whom are you in mourning?"
"For the world."

Ch. 1, *Taken Care Of 1965*

13 . . . I have never, in all my life, been so odious as to regard myself as "superior" to any living being, human or animal. I just walked alone—as I have always walked alone.

Ch. 2, Ibid.

14 By the time I was eleven years old, I had been taught that nature, far from abhorring a Vacuum, positively adores it.

Ch. 3, Ibid.

15 I have lived through the shattering of two civilizations, have seen two Pandora's boxes opened. One contained horror, the other emptiness. . . . In both the new worlds hatched in those Pandora's boxes, mud and flies had taken over the spirit.

Ch. 7, Ibid.

16 At last the day drifted into a long lacquered afternoon.

Ch. 13, Ibid.

17 MR. MUGGLEBY LION. I hate to disturb you, but I have just finished a *Little Sonnet*, that I *must* read to you.
HIERATIC WOMAN (coldly). It can't be a *Little* Sonnet, Mr. Muggleby Lion. Sonnets are all of the same size.

Ibid.

18 Rhythm is one of the principal translators between dreams and reality. Rhythm might be described, as to the world of sound, what light is to the world of sight. It shares and gives new meaning. Rhythm was described by Schopenhauer as melody deprived of its pitch.

Ch. 14, Ibid.

19 A pompous woman of his acquaintance, complaining that the head-waiter of a restaurant had not shown her and her hus-

band immediately to a table, said, "We had to tell him who we were." Gerald [Lord Berners], interested, enquired, "And who were you?"

Ch. 15, Ibid.

20 Eccentricity is not, as dull people would have us believe, a form of madness. It is often a kind of innocent pride, and the man of genius and the aristocrat are frequently regarded as eccentrics because genius and aristocrat are entirely unafraid of and uninfluenced by the opinions and vagaries of the crowd.

Ibid.

21 Vulgarity is, in reality, nothing but a modern, chic, pert descendant of the goddess Dullness.

Ch. 19, Ibid.

22 Then all will be over, bar the shouting and the worms.

Ch. 22, Ibid.

23 Winter is the time for comfort, for good food and warmth, for the touch of a friendly hand and for a talk beside the fire: it is the time for home.

Ibid.

24 I do not know how to address you. I cannot call you a goose, as geese saved the capitol of Rome, and no amount of cackling on your part would awaken anybody! Nor can I call you an ass, since Balaam's constant companion saw an angel, and recognized it.

Ibid.

25 . . . the heartless stupidity of those who have never known a great and terrifying poverty.

Ibid.

26 When we think of cruelty, we must try to remember the stupidity, the envy, the frustration from which it has arisen.

Ibid.

27 Remember only this of our hopeless love
That never till time is done
Will the fire of the heart and the fire of the mind be one.

"Heart and Mind" n.d.

1555. Jessie Chambers (1887–1965)

1 So instead of a release and deliverance from bondage, the bondage was glorified and made absolute. His [D. H. Lawrence's] mother conquered indeed, but the vanquished one was her son.

D. H. Lawrence: A Personal Record* 1935
*D. H. Lawrence, English author (1885–1930).

1556. Elizabeth Drew (1887–1965)

1 In spite of equal education and equal opportunity, the *scope* of woman remains still smaller than the scope of man. . . . Just as it is still in her close personal relationships that woman most naturally uses her human genius and her artistry in life, so it is still in the portrayal of those relationships that she perfects her most characteristic genius in writing.

"Is There a 'Feminine' Fiction?," *The Modern Novel* 1926

2 The test of literature is, I suppose, whether we ourselves live more intensely for the reading of it. . . .

Ibid.

3 The world is not run by thought, nor by imagination, but by opinion. . . .

"Sex Simplexes and Complexes," Ibid.

4 Sown in space like one among a handful of seeds in a suburban garden, the earth exists; a revolving, tepid sphere, whose every rotation brings it relentlessly nearer to the moon's dim, white, rotten desolation. Dwelling in this spinning island of terror, under immutable sentence of death, is Man, who, whether we regard him with the Psalmist as a little lower than the angels, or as "an ape, reft of his tail and grown rusty at climbing"; whether we see him shouting exultantly that he is the captain of his soul, or meeting his fate with all the lumbering discomfort of a cow being hustled into a railway truck, remains yet the ultimate mystery.

"The New Psychology," Ibid.

5 But though personality is a skin that no writer can slip, whatever he may write about: though it is a shadow which walks inexorably by his side, so also is the age he lives in.

"The Novel and the Age," Ibid.

6 How poetry comes to the poet is a mystery.

Quoted in "On the Teaching of Poetry" by Leonora Speyer,*
The Saturday Review of Literature 1946
*See 1329.

7 We read poetry because the poets, like ourselves, have been haunted by the inescapable tyranny of time and death; have suffered the pain of loss, and the more wearing, continuous pain of frustration and failure; and have had moods of unlooked-for release and peace. . . . . Sympathy and empathy, feeling with and feeling into, are the bases for his search for the true embodiment in words of his perception, great and small.

Pt. II, Ch. 7, *Poetry: A Modern Guide to Its Understanding and Enjoyment* 1959

8 The pain of loss, moreover, however agonizing, however haunting in memory, quiets imperceptibly into acceptance as the currents of active living and of fresh emotions flow over it.

Ch. 9, Ibid.

9 Propaganda has a bad name, but its root meaning is simply to disseminate through a medium, and all writing therefore is propaganda for *something*. It's a seeding of the self in the consciousness of others.

Ch. 10, Ibid.

10 The torment of human frustration, whatever its immediate cause, is the knowledge that the self is in prison, its vital force and "mangled mind" leaking away in lonely, wasteful self-conflict.

Ch. 13, Ibid.

11 The inspired scribbler always has the gift for gossip in our common usage . . . he or she can always inspire the commonplace with an uncommon flavor, and transform trivialities by some original grace or sympathy or humor or affection.

"The Literature of Gossip," *The Literature of Gossip* 1964

12 How frail and ephemeral . . . is the material substance of letters, which makes their very survival so hazardous. Print has a permanence of its own, though it may not be much worth preserving, but a letter! Conveyed by uncertain transportation, over which the sender has no control; committed to a single individual who may be careless or inappreciative; left to the mercy of future generations, of families maybe anxious to suppress the past, of the accidents of removals and house-cleanings, or of mere ignorance. How often it has been by the veriest chance that they have survived at all.

Ibid.

1557. Edna Ferber (1887–1968)

1 Roast Beef, Medium, is not only a food. It is a philosophy. Seated at Life's Dining Table, with a menu of Morals before you, your eye wandering a bit over the entrées, the hors d'oeuvres, and the things *à la carte* though you know that the Roast Beef, Medium, is safe and sane, and sure.

Foreword, Roast Beef, Medium 1911

2 From supper to bedtime is twice as long as from breakfast to supper.

Ch. 1, Ibid.

3 Even in her childhood she extracted from life double enjoyment that comes usually only to the creative mind. "Now I am doing this. Now I am doing that," she told herself while she was doing it. Looking on while she participated.

Ch. 1, So Big 1924

4 "There are only two kinds of people in the world that really count. One kind's wheat and the other kind's emeralds."

Ibid.

5 But young love thrives on colour, warmth, beauty. It becomes prosaic and inarticulate when forced to begin its day at four in the morning . . . and to end that day at nine, numb and sodden with weariness, after seventeen hours of physical labour.

Ch. 8, Ibid.

6 "Woman's work! Housework's the hardest work in the world. That's why men won't do it."

Ibid.

7 "But 'most any place is Baghdad if you don't know what will happen in it."

Ch. 10, Ibid.

8 "Any piece of furniture, I don't care how beautiful it is, has got to be lived with, kicked about, and rubbed down, and mistreated by servants, and repolished, and knocked around and dusted and sat on or slept in or eaten off of before it develops its real character," Salina said. "A good deal like human beings."

Ch. 15, Ibid.

9 But his gifts were many, and not the least of them was the trick of appearing sartorially and tonsorially flawless when dishevelment and a stubble were inevitable in any other male.

Ch. 1, Show Boat 1926

10 They . . . never exchanged civilities. This state of affairs lent spice to an existence that might otherwise have proved too placid for comfort. The bickering acted as a safety valve.

Ch. 5, Ibid.

11 Faro was not a game with Ravenal—it was for him at once his profession, his science, his drug, his drink, his mistress. He had, unhappily, as was so often the case with your confirmed gambler, no other vice.

Ch. 13, Ibid.

12 "Don't you believe 'em when they say that what you don't know won't hurt you. Biggest lie ever was. See it all and go your own way and nothing'll hurt you. If what you see ain't pretty, what's the odds! See it anyway. Then next time you don't have to look."

Ibid.

13 Wasn't marriage, like life, unstimulating and unprofitable and somewhat empty when too well ordered and protected and

guarded. Wasn't it finer, more splendid, more nourishing, when it was, like life itself, a mixture of the sordid and the magnificent; of mud and stars; of earth and flowers; of love and hate and laughter and tears and ugliness and beauty and hurt?

Ch. 19, Ibid.

14 It had no definite expression. It was not in their bearing; it could not be said to look out from the dead, black, Indian eye, nor was it anywhere about the immobile, parchment face. Yet somewhere black implacable resentment smoldered in the heart of this dying race

Ch. 3, Cimarron 1929

15 "The difference in America is that the women have always gone along. When you read the history of France you're peeking through a bedroom keyhole. The history of England is a joust. The womenfolks were always Elaineish and anemic, it seems. . . . But here in this land, Sabra, my girl, the women, they've been the real hewers of wood and drawers of water. You'll want to remember that."

Ibid.

16 "The gaudiest star-spangled cosmic joke that ever was played on a double-dealing government burst into fireworks today when, with a roar that could be heard for miles around, thousands of barrels of oil shot into the air on the miserable desert land known as the Osage Indian reservation and occupied by those duped and wretched—!"

Ch. 20, Ibid.

17 "If American politics are too dirty for women to take part in, there's something wrong with American politics."

Ch. 23, Ibid.

18 "I am not belittling the brave pioneer men, but the sunbonnet as well as the sombrero has helped to settle this glorious land of ours."

Ibid.

19 KITTY (a social climber). I was reading a book the other day...It's all about civilization or something. A nutty kind of a book. Do you know that the guy said that machinery is going to take the place of every profession?
CARLOTTA (a former stage star). Oh my dear. That's something you need never worry about.

Dinner at Eight, with George S. Kaufman 1932

20 The calla lilies are in bloom again.

Stage Door, with George S. Kaufman 1936

21 America—rather, the United States—seems to me to be the Jew among the nations. It is resourceful, adaptable, maligned, envied, feared, imposed upon. It is warm-hearted, overfriendly; quick-witted, lavish, colorful; given to extravagant speech and gestures; its people are travelers and wanderers by nature, moving, shifting, restless; swarming in Fords, in ocean liners; craving entertainment; volatile. The schnuckle among the nations of the world.

Ch. 1, A Peculiar Treasure 1939

22 Only amateurs say that they write for their own amusement. Writing is not an amusing occupation. It is a combination of ditch-digging, mountain-climbing, treadmill and childbirth. Writing may be interesting, absorbing, exhilarating, racking, relieving. But amusing? Never!

Ibid.

23 The goat's business is none of the sheep's concern.

Ch. 2, Saratoga Trunk 1941

24 Adventurers, both. . . . They were like two people who, searching for buried treasure, are caught in a quicksand. Every struggle to extricate themselves only made them sink deeper.

Ch. 6, Ibid.

25 "Men often marry their mothers. . . ."

Ibid.

26 "You lose in the end unless you know how the wheel is fixed or can fix it yourself."

Ch. 14, Ibid.

27 It was part of the Texas ritual. We're rich as son-of-a-bitch stew but look how homely we are, just as plain-folksy as Grandpappy back in 1836. We know about champagne and caviar but we talk hog and hominy.

Ch. 2, *Giant* 1952

28 "Texas air is so rich you can nourish off it like it was food."

Ch. 9, Ibid.

29 A woman can look both moral and exciting—if she also looks as if it was quite a struggle.

Quoted in *The Reader's Digest* December 1954

1558. Violet Bonham-Carter (1887–1969)

1 [He] has a brilliant mind until it is made up.*

Quoted in Ch. 12, *The Fine Art of Political Wit*
by Leon Harris 1964

*Reference to British Labour politician Sir Stafford Cripps.

1559. Violet Jessop (1887–1971)

1 One awful moment of empty, misty blackness enveloped us in its loneliness, then an unforgettable, agonizing cry went up from 1500 despairing throats, a long wail and then silence and our tiny craft tossing about at the mercy of the ice field.

Titanic Survivor, John Maxtone-Graham, ed.
& annot. 1997

1560. Marianne Moore (1887–1972)

1 The monkeys
winked too much and were afraid of snakes. The zebras, supreme in
their abnormality; the elephants, with their fog-colored skin and strictly practical appendages were there.

"The Monkeys" 1921

2 There is a great amount of poetry in unconscious fastidiousness.

"Critics and Connoisseurs," *Collected Poems* 1935

3 The deepest feeling always shows itself in silence;
not in silence, but restraint. . . .

"Silence," Ibid.

4 I, too, dislike it; there are things that are important beyond all this fiddle.

"Poetry," St. 1, Ibid.

5 I wonder what Adam and Eve
think of it by this time.

"Marriage," Ibid.

6 My father used to say,
"Superior people never make long visits,

Have to be shown Longfellow's* grave
or the glass flowers at Harvard."

"Silence," Ibid.

*Henry Wadsworth Longfellow, American poet (1807–82).

7 Denunciations do not affect
the culprit; nor blows, but it
is torture to him not to be spoken to.

"Spenser's* Ireland,"
St. 1, Ibid.

*Edmund Spenser, English poet (1552?–99).

8 I'm troubled, I'm dissatisfied, I'm Irish.

Ibid.

9 . . . you're not free
until you've been made captive by
supreme belief...

St. 4, Ibid.

10 What is our innocence
what is our guilt? All are
naked, none is safe.

"What are Years?" St. 1, Ibid.

11 . . . satisfaction is a lowly
thing, how pure a thing is joy.

St. 3, Ibid.

12 Among animals, one has a sense of humor.
Humor saves a few steps, it saves years.

"The Pangolin," St. 1, Ibid.

13 there never was a war that was
not inward

"In Distrust of Merits," Ibid.

14 As contagion
of sickness make sickness,
contagion of trust can make trust.

St. 2, Ibid.

15 . . . "When a man is prey to anger,
he is moved by outside things; when he holds
his ground in patience patience
patience, that is action or
beauty."

St. 6, Ibid.

16 . . . The world's an orphan's home. . . .

St. 7, Ibid.

17 Beauty is everlasting
And dust is for a time.

Ibid.

18 Three foremost aids to persuasion which occur to me are humility, concentration, and gusto.

Speech, "Humility, Concentration, and Gusto,"
Grolier Club 21 December 1948

19 [The] whirlwind fife-and-drum of the storm
bends the salt
marsh grass, disturbs stars in the sky and
the star on the steeple; it is a privilege to
see so much confusion.

"The Steeple-Jack," *Collected Poems* 1951

20 Verbal felicity is the fruit of art and diligence and refusing to be false.

Quoted in "Reading Contemporary Poetry" by
Louise Bogan,* *College English February 1953*
*See 1716.

21 One must be as clear as one's natural reticence allows one to be.

Ibid.

22 Since writing is not only an art but a trade embodying principles attested by experience, we would do well not to forget that it is an expedient for making oneself understood and that what is said should at least have the air of having meant something to the person who wrote it—as is the case with Gertrude Stein and James Joyce.

Lecture, "Idiosyncrasy and Technique,"
Oxford University *June 1956*

23 Camels are snobbish
and sheep, unintelligent;
water buffaloes, neurasthenic-
even murderous.
Reindeer seem over-serious.

"The Arctic Fox (or Goat)," *O to Be a Dragon 1959*

24 To wear the arctic fox
you have to kill it.

Ibid.

25 O to be a dragon
a symbol of the power of Heaven—of silkworm
size or immense; at times invisible.
Felicitous phenomenon!

"O to Be a Dragon," Ibid.

26 Fanaticism? No. Writing is exciting
and baseball is like writing.
You can never tell with either
how it will go
or what you will do;

"Baseball and Writing," St. 1, *The Complete Poems
of Marianne Moore 1961*

27 Assign Yogi Berra* to Cape Canaveral;
he could handle any missile.

"Baseball and Writing," St. 4, Ibid.
*Lawrence Peter Berra, known as "Yogi," baseball player and
manager (1925–).

28 The power of the visible   is the invisible

"He 'Digesteth Harde Yron'," St. 8, Ibid.

29 the greenest place I've never seen.
Every name is a tune.

"Spenser's* Ireland," St. 1, Ibid.
*Edmund Spener, English poet (1552–1599)

30 Writers entrapped by
teatime fame and by
commuters' comforts...

"The Paper Nautilus," St. 1, Ibid.

31 He fights and he writes.

Is there something I have missed?
He is a smiling pugilist.

Liner notes, "On Muhammed Ali",* *I Am the Greatest*
(album), Cassius Clay *1963*
*American boxer (né Cassius Clay; 1942–).

32 A writer is unfair to himself when he is unable to be hard on himself.

Interview in *Writers at Work* (Second Series),
George Plimpton,* ed. *1963*
*American writer and editor (1917–).

33 Poetry, that is to say the poetic, is a primal necessity.

"Comment," *Dial*, No. 81 (New York, August 1926),
Complete Prose 1987

34 Egotism is usually subversive of sagacity.

No. 82 (New York, March 1927), Ibid.

35 When one cannot appraise out of one's own experience, the temptation to blunder is minimized, but even when one can, appraisal seems chiefly useful as appraisal of the appraiser.

No. 85 (New York, October 1928), Ibid.

36 War is pillage versus resistance and if illusions of magnitude could be transmuted into ideals of magnanimity, peace might be realized.

No. 86 (New York, April 1929), Ibid.

37 Mole* says while anyone wants anything of us we "dare" not be too tired to give it.

Letter to John Warner Moore** (12 December 1915),
The Selected Letters of Marianne Moore,
Bonnie Costello, ed. *1997*
*Her mother, Mary Warner (1862–1947). **Her brother
(1908–).

38 I accept mongrel art but a flavor of the exceptional must be there along with the negligible.

Letter to Ezra Pound* (10 May 1921), Ibid.
*American poet (1885–1972).

39 Those who are deaf to the sublime, have to be without it; that is their honorarium.

Letter to e.e. cummings* (5 March 1938), Ibid.
*American poet (1894–1962).

40 With its baby rivers and little towns, each with its
abbey or its cathedral,
with voices-one voice perhaps, echoing through
the transept—The
criterion of suitability and convenience.

"England" *n.d.*

1561. Georgia O'Keeffe (1887–1986)

1 Those hills! They go on and on—it was like looking at two miles of gray elephants.

Quoted in *Time* (New York) *12 October 1970*

2 . . . nobody sees a flower—really—it is so small—we haven't time—and to see takes time like to have a friend takes time. If I could paint the flower exactly as I see it no one would see what I see because I would paint it small like the flower is small. So I said to myself—I'll paint what I see—what the flower is to me but I'll paint it big and they will be surprised into taking time to look at it—I will make even busy New Yorkers take time to see what I see of flowers. . . . Well, I made you take time to look at what I saw and when you took time to really notice my flower you hung all your own associations with flowers on my flower and you write about my flower as if I think and see what you think and see of the flower—and I don't.

(c.1939), Quoted in *Georgia O'Keeffe* by Lloyd Goodrich
and Doris Bry *1970*

3 I grew up pretty much as everybody else grows up, and one day . . . [in 1916] found myself saying to myself—I can't live where I want to—I can't go where I want to—I can't do what I want to—I can't even say what I want to—School and things that painters have taught me even keep me from painting as I want to. I decided I was a very stupid fool not to at least paint as I wanted to and say what I wanted to when I painted as that seemed to be the only thing I could do that didn't concern anybody but myself—that was nobody's business but my own. . . .

Ibid.

4 . . . that Blue [of the sky] . . . will always be there as it is now after all man's destruction is finished.

Quoted in "Flowers, Bones, and the Blue" by Alfred
Frankenstein (c.1919), San Francisco Chronicle
14 March 1971

5 This is the only place that I really belonged [the Texas panhandle], that I really felt at home. This is my country—terrible winds and wonderful emptiness.

Ibid.

6 I don't very much enjoy looking at paintings in general. I know too much about them. I take them apart.

Quoted in "An Artist of Her Own School" by Alexander
Fried, San Francisco Chronicle 16 March 1971

7 The desert is the last place you can see all around you. The light out here makes everything close, and it is never, never the same. Sometimes the light hits the mountains from behind and front at the same time, and it gives them the look of Japanese prints, you know, distances in layers.

Quoted in "A Visit with Georgia O'Keeffe" by Beth Coffelt,
San Francisco Examiner & Chronicle 11 April 1971

8 Where I was born, and where and how l lived is unimportant. It is what I have done and where I have been that should be of interest.

Georgia O'Keeffe 1985

9 My first memory is of the brightness of light, light all around.

Ibid.

10 Marks on paper are free—free speech-press-pictures all go together I suppose.

Letter to Anita Pollitzer (14 January 1916), Quoted in
Portrait of an Artist by Laurie Lisle 1986

11 One can not be an American by going about saying that one is an American. It is necessary to feel America, like America, love America and then work.

Chicago Evening Post (2 March 1926), Ibid.

12 Singing has always seemed to me the most perfect means of expression. It is so spontaneous. And after singing, I think the violin. Since I cannot sing, I paint.

New York Sun (5 December 1922), Ibid.

13 Before I put a brush to canvas, I question, "Is this mine? . . . Is it influenced by some idea which I have acquired from some man?" . . . I am trying with all my skill to do a painting that is all of women, as well as all of me.

Debate reported in New York World (16 March 1930), Ibid.

14 I hate flowers—I paint them because they're cheaper than models and they don't move.

New York Herald Tribune (18 April 1954), Ibid.

1562. Olga Knopf (1888–?)

1 The art of being a woman can never consist of being a bad imitation of a man.

The Art of Being a Woman 1932

2 . . . the sexes are living, we might say, in a vast communal neurosis; a highly contagious neurosis which parents pass on to their children and men and women pass on to each other.

Ibid.

3 The outer limitations to woman's progress are caused by the fact we are living in a man's culture.

Women on Their Own 1935

1563. Agnes Sligh Turnbull (1888–1982)

1 "Now ain't that funny! I thought it was you, an' you thought is was me; an' begob, it's nayther of us!"

Bk. I, Ch. 6, The Rolling Years 1936

2 "The older I get, Jeannie, the more I wonder whether a life shouldn't perhaps be like a river—flowing along in the channel God gave it. Not too many radical deflections."

Bk. II, Ch. 1, Ibid.

3 "It's the trail of the old Puritan over us. We assume that the only natural course of events is the wrath of God and the miseries of this life. We're afraid to believe that the Creator might sometimes actually wish us well!"

Ch. 4, Ibid.

4 That's it! The long look ahead. Doesn't it change things, though? Staking neck or nothing on a life to come! Keeps us from being too fussy over affairs here, I guess."

Ibid.

5 "There is still vitality under the winter snow, even though to the casual eye it seems to be dead."

Ibid.

6 "The trouble with the average human being is that he never goes on mountain journeys. He stops at the first way station and refuses to believe there is country beyond."

Ch. 5, Ibid.

7 "You must learn to drink the cup of life as it comes, Connie, without stirring it up from the bottom. That's where the bitter dregs are!"

Ibid.

8 "Wasn't it [religion] invented by man for a kind of solace? It's as though he said, 'I'll make me a nice comfortable garment to shut out the heat and the cold; and then it ends by becoming a straitjacket."

Ch. 6, Ibid.

9 "I don't know that I care so much about going far," he said at last; "but I should like to go deep where I go."

Epilogue, Ibid.

10 "You can put city polish on a man, but by golly, it seems you can't ever rub it off him."

Ch. 2, The Golden Journey 1955

11 "The ideas of perfection always gives one a chance to talk without knowing facts."

Ch. 4, Ibid.

12 "The older you get the more you realize that gray isn't such a bad color. And in politics you work with it or you don't work at all."

Ch. 7, Ibid.

13 There would seem to be a law operating in human experience by which the mind once suddenly aware of a verity for the first time immediately invents it again.

Ch. 10, Ibid.

14 Oh, the utter unpredictability of a quarrel! How inflammable words were to ignite each other until the blaze of them scorched and seared.

Ibid.

15 "Do you know that the tendrils of graft and corruption have become mighty interlacing roots so that even men who would like to be honest are tripped and trapped by them?"

Ch. 11, Ibid.

16 Defeat in itself was part and parcel of the great gambling game of politics. A man who could not accept it and try again was not of the stuff of which leaders are made.

Ch. 12, Ibid.

17 . . . she *was* a widow, that strange feminine entity who had once been endowed with a dual personality and was now only half of what she had been.

Ch. 1, *The Flowering* 1972

18 "Dogs' lives are too short. Their only fault, really."

Ch. 2, Ibid.

19 "If you keep things long enough, some fool or other will come along an' buy 'em."

Ch. 3, Ibid.

20 Girls! Girls! Girls!
With platted hair an' mebbe curls
Singin' in a *chorus*!
Lord have mercy o'er us.

Ch. 4, Ibid.

1564. Katherine Mansfield (1888–1923)

1 Make it a rule of life never to regret and never to look back.

"Bliss," *Bliss and Other Stories* 1920

2 How idiotic civilization is! Why be given a body if you have to keep it shut up in a case like a rare, rare fiddle?

Ibid.

3 ". . . Why! Why! Why is the middle-class so stodgy—so utterly without a sense of humour!"

Ibid.

4 . . . roses are the only flowers that impress people at garden-parties; the only flowers that everybody is certain of knowing.

"The Garden Party" 1922

5 "If you're going to stop a band playing every time someone has an accident, you'll lead a very strenuous life."

Ibid.

6 There lay a young man, fast asleep—sleeping so soundly, so deeply, that he was far, far away from them both. Oh, so remote, so peaceful. He was dreaming. Never wake him up again.

Ibid.

7 Fancy cream puffs so soon after breakfast. The very idea made one shudder. All the same, two minutes late Jose and Laura were licking their fingers with that absorbed inward look that only comes from whipped cream.

Ibid.

8 Hundreds, yes, literally hundreds, had come out in a single night; the green bushes bowed down as if they had been visited by archangels.

Ibid.

9 Although over six years had passed away, the boss never thought of the boy except as lying unchanged, unblemished in his uniform, asleep forever.

"The Fly," *The Dove's Nest 1923*

10 How on earth could he have slaved, denied himself, kept going all those years without the promise for ever before him of the boys stepping into his shoes carrying on where he left off?

Ibid.

11 It is as though God opened his hand and let you dance on it a little, and then shut it . . . so tight that you could not even cry.

(February 1914), *The Journal of Katherine Mansfield 1927*

12 Oh, the times when she had walked upside down on the ceiling . . . Floated on a lake of light . . . !

(31 December 1918), Ibid.

13 Everything in life that we really accept undergoes a change. So suffering must become Love. That is the mystery.

(19 December 1920), Ibid.

14 As in the physical world, so in the spiritual world, pain does not last forever.

Ibid.

15 There is no limit to human suffering. When one thinks "Now I have touched the bottom of the sea—now I can go no deeper," one goes deeper. . . . Suffering is boundless, is eternity. One pang is eternal torment. Physical suffering is—child's play.

Ibid.

16 I want, by understanding myself, to understand others. I want to be all that I am capable of becoming. . . . This all sounds very strenuous and serious. But now that I have wrestled with it, it's no longer so. I feel happy—deep down. *All is well.*

(1922), Ibid.

17 Whenever I prepare for a journey I prepare as though for death. Should I never return, all is in order. This is what life has taught me.

Ibid.

18 "Do you know what individuality is?"
"No."
"Consciousness of will. To be conscious that you have a will and can act."
Yes, it is. It's a glorious saying.

(30 September 1922), Ibid.

19 *Important.* When we can begin to take our failures nonseriously, it means we are ceasing to be afraid of them. It is of immense importance to learn to laugh at ourselves.

(October 1922), Ibid.

20 By health I mean the power to live a full, adult, living, breathing life in close contact with . . . the earth and the wonders thereof—the sea—the sun.

(14 October 1922), Ibid.

21 Nearly all improved health is pretence—acting. What does it amount to? . . . I am an absolutely helpless invalid. What is my life? It is the existence of a parasite.

Ibid.

22 Risk! Risk anything! Care no more for the opinions of others, for those voices. Do the hardest thing on earth for you. Act for yourself. Face the truth.

Ibid.

23 Now perhaps you understand what "indifference" means. It is to learn not to mind, and not to show your mind.

(17 October 1922), Ibid.

24 To be wildly enthusiastic or deadly serious—both are wrong. Both pass. One must keep ever present a sense of humor.

Ibid.

25 I feel like a fly who has been dropped into the milk-jug and fished out again, but is still too milky and drowned to start cleaning up yet.

Katherine Mansfield's Letters to John Middleton Murry,* 1913–1922 1951
*British critic, editor, pacifist (1889–1957), her husband.

26 Would you not like to try *all* sorts of lives—one is so very small-but that is the satisfaction of writing—one can impersonate so many people.

Letter (24 April 1907), *Collected Letters*, Vol. 1, Vincent O'Sullivan and Margaret Scott, eds. *1984*

27 To work—to work! It is such infinite delight to know that we still have the best things to do.

Letter to Bertrand Russell* (December 1916), Ibid.
*English mathematician and philosopher (1872–1970).

28 I'm a writer first and a woman after.

Letter to her husband John Middleton Murry (3 December 1920), Ibid.

29 Were we positive, eager, real—alive? No, we were not. We were a nothingness shot with gleams of what might be.

Letter to her husband, John Middleton Murry (11 October 1922), Ibid.

1565. Aline Murray Kilmer (1888–1941/44)

1 I'm sorry you are wiser,
I'm sorry you are taller;
I liked you better foolish,
And I liked you better smaller.

"For the Birth of a Middle-Aged Child," St. 1 *n.d.*

2 I cannot see myself as I once was;
I would not see myself as I am now.

"To Aphrodite: With a Mirror" *n.d.*

3 I sing of little loves that glow
Like tapers shining in the rain,
Of little loves that break themselves
Like moths against the window-pane.

"Prelude" *n.d.*

4 When people inquire I always just state,
"I have four nice children and hope to have eight."

"Ambition" *n.d.*

5 For there is only sorrow in my heart;
There is no room for fear.

But how I wish I were afraid again,
My dear, my dear.

"I Shall Not Be Afraid" *n.d.*

6 Things have a terrible permanence
When people die.

"Things," St. 6 *n.d.*

1566. Clare Kummer (1888–1948)

1 ETHEL. Did you sell your verses to Binder?
JENNINGS. No—he seemed to think they were indecent and when I explained to him that they weren't he lost interest in them—so that's all.

Act I, *Good Gracious, Annabelle 1916*

2 STEIN. It's the public. You can't count on it. Give 'em something good and they'll go to see something bad. Give 'em something bad and they don't like that either.

Act I, Sc. 1, *Rollo's Wild Oat 1922*

3 STEIN. Pictures are a great business. You take a picture and you got something.
MRS. PARK-GALES. Yes, but what?
STEIN. You get all through with the actors and there they are playing for you every night. If they are sick or dead, it don't make any difference. They are working just the same.
LUCAS. Anything to make us work for nothing!

Sc. 2, Ibid.

4 AUNT MIN. He should have started worrying before he had things to worry about.

Act I, *Her Master's Voice 1933*

5 QUEENA. Don't you know when people are in love they don't think? Merciful heavens!
AUNT MIN. Well, they ought to. I don't know of any time when it's more important for them to think. In love! In foolishness!

Act II, Ibid.

6 Oh, there was a woman-hater hated women all he could,
And he built himself a bungle in a dingle in the wood;
Here he lived and said of ladies things I do not think he should,
"If they're good they're not good-looking; if good-looking, they're not good."

"In the Dingle-Dongle Bell" *n.d.*

1567. Marjorie Bowen (1888–1952)

1 "But will it last?"
"What a ridiculous question," returned the colonel blandly. "Will you, or I, or anything last? Flesh is grass, my dear Count."

Ch. 1, *General Crack 1928*

2 "If you live in the world you must live on the world's terms."

Ch. 10, Ibid.

3 "If you can't command your own soul, how can I give you enlightenment how to do so?"

Ibid.

4 Useless for one who did not believe in Heaven to renounce the World: that would be to fall into a void.

Ibid.

5 "What is the most dangerous possession in the world, Mr. Falkland?"

"No use at riddles," replied the young man cautiously.
Dobree picked up the speaking tube.
"Someone else's secret," he remarked. . . .

Ch. 2, *The Shadow on Mockways* 1932

6 "If I continue to drink I shall soon be like these—how long
would it take? It has not really got hold of me yet. I could stop
it if I wanted. Sometimes I take nothing for days together—
yes, if it were worth while and something else offered, I could
stop. But it is not worth while and nothing else offers."

Moss Rose 1935

7 . . . she was cured of love as she was cured of drunkenness. Indulgence had soon brought her to a point of nausea; she had
never given anyone tenderness or affection, and the recollection of dead passions that had ended in disgust or rage was
like the recollection of the stench of decay.

Ibid.

8 "It is more difficult, my lord, to rule the King's favourites that
for the favourites to rule the King."

Ch. 1, *My Tattered Loving* 1937

9 Meanwhile, he continued to search for a brisk and subtle poison, for it seemed to him that one who could make the
discovery of such a weapon as this would be more powerful
than the greatest of kings.

Ch. 2, Ibid.

10 But it had not needed much of a turn of fortune's wheel for the
Frenchman to have been the quack counting up his illicit gains
and the Englishman to have been the courtly physician to
whom all the great ones ran for help in their distresses.

Ibid.

11 Flattery is so necessary to all of us that we flatter one another
just to be flattered in return. . . .

"The Art of Flattery,"
World's Wonder 1937

12 As civilisation advanced, people began to discover that more
was to be gained by flattery than by force—and that flattery
had a larger purchasing power than coin of the realm.

Ibid.

13 "Rich and free," Barbara repeated to herself. It was hard to
accept the meaning of the words. There was no one to thwart
her, to scold her, to warn her, to advise her; there was only Mr.
Bompast who had no authority over her and whose dry prudence would be ignored. She could not even be checked if she
did anything eccentric.

Ch. 1, *Mignonette* 1948

14 "Leave well alone, my dear Miss Lawne."
"But perhaps we are leaving evil alone," replied the lady,
smiling.
"In that case, also, have nothing to do with it."

Ibid.

15 Custom reclaimed her. . . . So, insidiously, her middle-class respectability hemmed in Barbara Lawne. . . . Only in her
dreams did she explore wild and darkling landscapes. . . .

Ch. 2, Ibid.

16 Even a fool can deceive a man—if he be a bigger fool than himself.

"The Glen o' Weeping" *n.d.*

1568. Sophie Hutchinson Drinker (1888–1968)

1 Music gives access to regions in the subconscious that can be
reached in no other way.

Music and Women 1948

2 Great music has always been rooted in religion—when religion is understood as an *attitude* toward superhuman power
and the mysteries of the universe.

Ibid.

1569. Vicki Baum (1888–1960)

1 GRUSINSKAYA. I want to be alone.

Grand Hotel (play) 1930

2 Fame always brings loneliness. Success is as ice cold and lonely
as the north pole.

Grand Hotel (novel) 1931

3 A woman who is loved always has success.

Ibid.

4 Pity is the deadliest feeling that can be offered to a woman.

And Life Goes On 1932

5 Marriage always demands the greatest understanding of the
art of insincerity possible between two human beings.

Ibid.

6 To be a Jew is a destiny.

Ibid.

1570. Clemence Dane (1888–1965)

1 SYDNEY. It's extraordinary to me—whenever you middle-aged
people want to excuse yourselves for anything you've done
that you know you oughtn't have done, you say it was the war.

Act I, *A Bill of Divorcement* 1921

2 HILARY. I was a dead man. You know what the dead do in
heaven? They sit on their golden chairs and sicken for home.

Ibid.

3 It's the things I might have said that fester.

Act II, Ibid.

4 DR. ALLIOT. That young, young generation found out, out of
their own unhappiness, the war taught them, what peace
couldn't teach us—that when conditions are evil it is not your
duty to submit—that when conditions are evil, your duty, in
spite of protests, in spite of sentiment, your duty, though you
trample on the bodies of your nearest and dearest to do it,
though you bleed your own heart white, your duty is to see
that those conditions are changed. If your laws forbid you, you
must change your laws. If your church forbids you, you must
change your church. And if your God forbids you, why then,
you must change your God.

Ibid.

5 ZEDEKIAH. How else should I treat an idol but tread on it?

Act I, Sc. 1, *Naboth's Vineyard* 1925

6 JEZEBEL. How often must I stoop to hold you up?

Sc. 2, Ibid.

7 JEZEBEL. Toss back the ball! Shall I flinch because a heavy hand
flings it? At least it is a friend's hand.

Ibid.

8 JEZEBEL. What is it to sit on a throne? Weariness! But to shift the dolls that sit there, that's a game. Jehu, for a man or a woman! Let me teach you my game!

Act II, Sc. 1, Ibid.

9 I think of our century as a sixty-year-old housewife in love with modern ideas.

Speech, "Approach to Drama," London 1961

10 I suppose there is not one of us here who has not, at some time or other, evoked the good in which we believe to take our part, to speak for us, to put our case to the invisible evil (if it is evil) that thwarts and destroys our efforts toward happiness. . . .

Ibid.

1571. Mary Day Winn (1888–1965)

1 Sex is the tabasco sauce which an adolescent national palate sprinkles on every course in the menu.

Adam's Rib 1931

2 In the argot of the sub-deb, "U.S.A." has long ago lost its patriotic meaning. It now stands for "Universal Sex Appeal."

Ibid.

1572. Carlotta Monterey O'Neill (1888–1970)

1 To understand his [Eugene O'Neill's*] work you must understand the man, for the work and the man are one.

Quoted in O'Neill by Arthur and Barbara Gelb 1960
*American playwright (1888–1953), her husband.

2 I had to work like a dog. I was Gene's secretary, I was his nurse. His health was always bad. I did everything. He wrote the plays, but I did everything else. I loved it. It was a privilege to work with him, because he was mentally stimulating. My God, how many women have husbands who are very stimulating?

Ch. 4, Ibid.

3 He got a racing car, a Bugatti, and when he was very nervous and tired he would go out in it and drive ninety-five miles an hour and come back looking nineteen years old and perfectly relaxed.

Ibid.

4 O'Neill was a tough mick and never loved a woman who walked. He loved only his work. But he had respect for me. I had an independent income, and I told him I'd marry him if he would let me pay half of all the household expenses. . . . He said he needed a home. "I want a home properly run," he told me. And that is what I did for him, I saw to it that he was able to work.

Ibid.

1573. M. Esther Harding (1888–1971)

1 The chief characteristic of the goddess in her crescent phase is that she is a virgin. Her instinct is not used to capture or possess the man whom she attracts. . . . Her divine power does not depend on her relation to a husband-god, and thus her actions are not dependent on the need to conciliate such a one or to accord with his qualities and attitudes. For she bears her divinity in her own right.
In the same way, the woman who is virgin, one-in-herself, does what she does—not because of any desire to please, not to be liked, or to be approved, even by herself; not because of any desire to gain power over another, to catch his interest or love, but because what she does is true.

Woman's Mysteries 1935

1574. Edith Evans (1888–1976)

1 When a woman behaves like a man, why doesn't she behave like a nice man?

Quoted in "Sayings of the Week," Observer (London 30 September 1956

1575. Lotte Lehman (1888–1976)

1 But to me the actual sound of the words is all important; I feel always that the words complete the music and must never be swallowed up in it. The music is the shining path over which the poet travels to bring his song to the world.

"The Singing Actor," Players at Work, Morton Eustis, ed. 1937

2 I have never understood the star who enjoys playing with a mediocre cast in order to shine out the more brilliantly himself, for the essence of any fine dramatic or operatic production is harmonious integration of all performances.

Ibid.

3 Do not become paralyzed and enchained by the set patterns which have been woven of old. No, build from your own youthful feeling, your own groping thought and your own flowering perception—and help to further that beauty which has grown from the roots of tradition.

Introduction, More Than Singing 1945

4 For what mission can be greater than that of giving the world hours of exaltation in which it may forget the misery of the present, the cares of everyday life and lose itself in the eternally pure world of harmony. . . .

Ibid.

5 That fine God-given instrument—the voice—must be capable of responding with the greatest subtlety to every shade of each emotion. But it must be subordinate, it must only be the foundation, the soil from which flowers true art.

Ibid.

6 Imitation is, and can only be, the enemy of artistry. Everything which breathes the breath of life is changeable. . . . Only from life itself may life be born.

Ibid.

1576. Anita Loos (1888–1981)

1 "She always believed in the old adage: "Leave them while you're looking good."

Ch. 1, Gentlemen Prefer Blondes 1925

2 "I really think that American gentlemen are the best after all, because . . . kissing your hand may make you feel very, very good, but a diamond and sapphire bracelet lasts forever."

Ch. 4, Ibid.

3 So this gentlemen said, "A girl with brains ought to do something else with them besides think."

Ibid.

4 . . . I always say that a girl never really looks as well as she does on board a steamship, or even a yacht.

Ibid.

5 ADDIE. I've always been my own best company, Mr. Bishop.

Act I, Happy Birthday 1947

6 JUDGE. Always go to a solitary drinker for the truth!

Ibid.

7 ADDIE. I was making love to a man, a man I hardly even know. He was kissing the face off me and I was kissing the face off him. And I found it highly satisfactory.

Act II, Ibid.

8 ADDIE. Why, Benjamin Franklin says a man without a woman is like a half a pair of scissors.

Act III, Ibid.

9 Of course, everybody knows that the greatest thing about Motherhood is the "Sacrifices," but it is quite a shock to find out that they begin so far ahead of time.

Ch. 1, A Mouse is Born 1951

10 So after a Star has received five or six million of those Fan letters, you begin to realize you must be wonderful without having to read all those monitinous [sic] letters.

Ibid.

11 For the most outstanding shock that Tourists ever get is to find out that "Hollywood" is meerly [sic] one of unnumerable other spots, which we Citizens term "Hollywood" as a "cover-up" for the whole accumilation [sic].

Ch. 6, Ibid.

12 So I am beginning to wonder if maybe girls wouldn't be happier if we stopped demanding so much respeckt for ourselves and developed [sic] a little more respeckt for husbands.

Ch. 19, Ibid.

13 "Why, with a mental equipment which allows me to tell the difference between hot and cold, I stand out in this community like a modern-day Cicero. Dropped into any other city of the world, I'd rate as a possibly adequate night watchman. And let's be fair, old pal, you yourself, a leader of public thought in Hollywood, wouldn't have sufficient mental acumen anywhere else to hold down a place in a bread line!"

Ch. 3, No Mother to Guide Her 1961

14 "Childish is the word with which the intelligentsia once branded Hollywood. And yet, those movies which depicted Life as life can never be, were fairy tales for us to believe in, and this is possibly a reason for the universal prevalence of mental crack-up. Yes, if we were childish in the past, I wish we could be children once again.

Ch. 10, Ibid.

15 . . . the Welsh are a very peculiar breed, poetic, unpredictable, remote, and fiercely independent. For such a man [D. W. Griffith]* to be in love must be terribly frustrating, because his deepest instinct is to be a loner.

A Girl Like I 1966

*American film director (1875–1948).

16 The people I'm furious with are the Women's Liberationists. They keep getting up on soapboxes and proclaiming women are brighter than men. That's true, but it should be kept quiet or it ruins the whole racket.

Observer (London) 30 December 1973

17 . . . memory is more indelible than ink.

Ch. 1, Kiss Hollywood Goodbye 1974

18 Pleasure that isn't paid for is as insipid as everything else that's free.

Ch. 2, Ibid.

19 Show business is the best possible therapy for remorse.

Ch. 13, Ibid.

20 That our popular art forms become so obsessed with sex has turned the U.S.A. into a nation of hobbledehoys; as if grown people don't have more vital concerns, such as taxes, inflation, dirty politics, earning a living, getting an education, or keeping out of jail. It's true that the French have a certain obsession with sex, but it's a particularly adult obsession. France is the thriftiest of all nations; to a Frenchman sex provides the most economical way to have fun. The French are a logical race.

Ch. 21, Ibid.

21 There's nothing colder than chemistry.

Ibid.

22 If we have to tell Hollywood good-by, it may be with one of those tender, old-fashioned, seven-second kisses exchanged between two people of the opposite sex, with all their clothes on.

Ibid.

1577. Mildred Cram (1889–?)

1 Publicity tripped upon the heels of publicity.

"Billy," Harper's Bazaar 1924

2 He was capitalized, consolidated, incorporated, copyrighted, limited, protected, insured, and all rights reserved, including the Scandinavian.

Ibid.

3 "I am vulgar, my friend! I mix tears with idiocy. I put the grotesque into love. I tickle sluggish minds. My recipe is a mixture of legend and pep, pantomime and beauty, artifice and art."

Ibid.

1578. Sarah "Sadie" Delany (1889–1999)

1 We were good citizens, good Americans! We loved our country, even though it didn't love us back.

Having Our Say, The Delany Sisters' First 100 Years, with Elizabeth Delany and Amy Hill Hearth 1993*
*Her sister; see 1610.

2 I never let prejudice stop me from what I wanted to do in this life.

Ibid.

3 Well, we didn't order any credit cards! We don't spend what we don't have . . . Imagine a bank sending credit cards to two ladies over a hundred years old! What are those folks thinking!

Ibid.

4 Your job is to help somebody.

Family motto, Ibid.

1579. Dorothy McCall (1889–?)

1 One cannot have wisdom without living life.

Quoted in The Los Angeles Times 14 March 1974

2 Technology dominates us all, diminishing our freedom.

Ibid.

3 Lawmakers and employers should not be allowed to continue their shameful practice of punishing still-producing and competent people merely because of age.

Ibid.

1580. Julia Seton (1889–?)

1 Dancing is a universal instinct—zoölogic, a biologic impulse, found in animals as well as in man.

"Why Dance?" *The Rhythm of the Redman 1930*

2 In its natural, primitive form, dancing is vigorous muscular action to vent emotion. Originally, it was the natural expression of the basic impulses of a simple form of life. Triumph, defeat, war, love, hate, desire, propitiation of the gods—all were danced by the hero or the tribe to the rhythm of beaten drums.

"Dance in the Animal World," Ibid.

3 I have listened by a thousand fires as the Buffalo Wind blew through our lives. . . . And so would come a flood of revelation, an unceasing flow of inspiration such as could not be courted. Many a time have I sat by the embers, in motionless silence for hours, while the words came in unhesitating rhythm of passionate life—for we did not measure our life together with a shallow cup. Each time we dipped, we brought up the chalice brimming full and running over.

Prologue, *By a Thousand Fires 1967*

4 But life has taught me that it knows better plans than we can imagine, so that I try to submerge my own desires, apt to be too insistent, into a calm willingness to accept what comes, and to make the most of it, then wait again. I have discovered that there is a Pattern, larger and more beautiful than our short vision can weave. . . .

Epilogue, Ibid.

1581. Agnes E. Benedict (1889–1950)

1 The only thing better than education is more education.

Progress to Freedom 1942

2 A democratic home is the foundation of a democratic state.

The Happy Home 1948

1582. Elsie Janis (1889–1956)

1 When I think of the hundreds of things I might be,
I get down on my knees and thank God that I'm me.

"Compensation," *Poems Now and Then* c. 1927

2 Why do we do it?
Oh, Hell! What's the use?
Why battle with the universe?
Why not declare a truce?

"Why," Ibid.

3 Up and down the burning sidewalks
Praying ever for a job,
In my heart a curse for mankind,
In my pocket not a bob.

"The Actor's Lament," Ibid.

4 It was Mother who fought. Fought! To keep me up to par! To make me study and improve. Fought! To keep my name in the large type she believed I merited. Fought for heat in trains to protect my health. Fought to make ends meet, when each week she had finished sending money to the many dependents that automatically arrived on the high heels of success. Invincible! best describes her.

Pt. I, *So Far, So Good! 1931*

5 I realize, at least, that I have never been really virtuous, I have only been egotistical.

Pt. IV, Ibid.

6 Life is marvelous! There is no death! It's a pity, everything that goes up must come down.

Ibid.

1583. Gabriela Mistral (1889–1957)

1 Let me be more maternal than a mother; able to love and defend with all of a mother's fervor the child that is not flesh of my flesh. Grant that I may be successful in molding one of my pupils into a perfect poem, and let me leave within her deepest-felt melody that she may sing for you when my lips shall sing no more.

"La Oracion de la Maestra" (The Teacher's Prayer), *Desolacion 1922*

2 Let me make my brick schoolhouse into a spiritual temple. Let the radiance of my enthusiasms envelop the poor courtyard and the bare classroom. Let my heart be a stronger column and my goodwill purer gold than the columns and gold of rich schools.

Ibid.

3 A son, a son, a son! I wanted a son of yours and mine, in those distant days of burning bliss when my bones would tremble at your least murmur and my brow would glow with a radiant mist.

"Poem of the Son," St. 1, Ibid.

4 he kissed me and now I am someone else

"He Kissed Me," St. 1, Ibid.

5 My grief and my smile begin in your face, my son.

"Eternal Grief," St. 2, Ibid.

6 Blushing, full of confusion, I talked with her about my
worries and the fear in my body. I fell on her breast,
and all over again I became a little girl sobbing in her
arms at the terror of life.

"Mother," St. 2, Ibid.

7 The crimson rose
plucked yesterday,
the fire and cinnamon
of the carnation,

the bread I baked
with anise seed and honey,
and the goldfish
flaming in its bowl.

All these are yours, baby born of woman,
if you'll only go to sleep.

"If You'll Only Go to Sleep," Sts. 1-3, *Tenura* (Tenderness) *1924*

8 I have a true happiness
and a happiness betrayed,
the one like a rose,
the other like a thorn.

"Richness," *Tala* (Felling) *1938*

9 And I wished I were born with them.
Could it not be so another time?
To leap from a clump of banana plants
one morning of wonders—
a dog, a coyote, a deer;
to gaze with wild pupils, to run, to stop, to run, to fall,
to whimper and whine and jump with joy,

riddled with sun and with barking,
a hallowed child of God, his secret, divine servant.
    "*Ocho Perritos*" (Eight Puppies), Ibid.

10 Of the enemies of the soul—
the world, the devil, the flesh—
the *world* is the most serious and most dangerous.
    "*Todas Ibamos a Ser Reinas*" (We Were All to Be Queens),
    Ibid.

11 I have all that I lost
and I go carrying my childhood
like a favorite flower
that perfumes my hand
    Ibid.

12 I love the things I never had
along with those I have no more.
    "Things," St. 1, Ibid.

13 As a daughter of Chilean democracy, I am moved to have before me a representative of the Swedish democratic tradition, a
tradition whose originality consists in perpetually renewing itself within the framework of the most valuable creations of
society. The admirable work of freeing a tradition from deadwood while conserving intact the core of the old virtues, the
acceptance of the present and the anticipation of the future,
these are what we call Sweden, and these achievements are an
honour to Europe and an inspiring example for the American
continent.
    Acceptance speech, Nobel Prize Awards (Stockholm) *1945*

14 At this moment, by an undeserved stroke of fortune, I am the
direct voice of the poets of my race and the indirect voice for
the noble Spanish and Portuguese tongues. Both rejoice to
have been invited to this festival of Nordic life with its tradition of centuries of folklore and poetry.
    Ibid.

15 I will leave behind me the dark ravine, and climb up gentler
slopes toward that spiritual mesa where at last a wide light
will fall upon my days. From there I will sing words of hope,
without looking into my heart. As one who was full of compassion wished: I will sing to console men.
    Quoted in Introduction to *Tala, Selected Poems of Gabriela*
    Mistral, Doris Dana, tr. and ed. rev. ed. *1971*

1584. Mabel Walker Willebrandt (1889–1963)

1 When we sum up the columns that make "success" for the boy
on the one hand and the girl on the other, you find the girl has
the much longer column to add.
    "Give Women a Fighting Chance," *The Smart Set 1930*

2 Why the devil they have to put on that "girly-girly" tea party
description every time they tell anything about a professional
woman is more than I can see.
    Quoted in *The 50 Most Influential Women in American*
    Law by Dawn Bradley Berry* *1996*

    *See 3435.

1585. Fannie Hurst (1889–1968)

1 It's hard for a young girl to have patience for old age sitting
and chewing all day over the past.
    "Get Ready the Wreaths," *Cosmopolitan* (New York) *1917*

2 "I always say he wore himself out with conscientiousness."
    "She Walks in Beauty," *Cosmopolitan* (New York) *1921*

3 It is doubtful if in all its hothouse garden of women the Hotel
Bon Ton boasted a broken finger-nail or that little brash place
along the forefinger that tattles so of potato peeling or aspara-
gus scraping.
    Ibid.

4 To housekeep, one had to plan ahead and carry items of motley nature around in the mind and at the same time preside, as
mother had, at table, just as everything, from the liver and
bacon, to the succotash, to the French toast and strawberry
jam, had not been matters of forethought and speculation.
    Ch. 2, *Imitation of Life 1932*

5 He had always said of himself that people first tasted the command in his voice and then came nibbling at his products.
    Ch. 14, Ibid.

6 "I know it, and when I know a thing wid my knowin', I knows
it."
    Ch. 33, Ibid.

7 "Honey-chile, it will shore seem a funny world up dar widout
washin'. If de Lawd's robes only needed launderin', I'd do his
tucks de way He's never seen 'em done."
    Ch. 36, Ibid.

8 The history of [women's] role in this desperate struggle [World
War II] will not be written in lipstick.
    Article, *New York Times Magazine 29 March 1942*

9 Papa lived so separately within himself that I retreated to Mama,
who wore herself on the outside. Everything about her hung in
view like peasant adobe houses with green peppers and little
shrines, drying diapers and cooking utensils on the façade.
    Bk. I, *Anatomy of Me 1958*

10 This anatomy of me is serving the double purpose of revealing
me to myself.
    Bk. III, Ibid.

1586. Enid Bagnold (1889–1981)

1 A loneliness beyond anything she had ever known settled upon
Fanny. She found comfort in a look, a cry, a whistle. The smiles
of strange men upon the road whom she would never see again
became her social intercourse. The lost smiles of kind Americans, the lost, mocking whistles of Frenchmen, the scream of a
nigger, the twittering surprise of a Chinese scavenger.
    Pt. I, Ch. 1, *The Happy Foreigner 1920*

2 On and on and on rolled the days, and though one might add
them together and make them seven, they never made Sunday.
For there is no Sunday in the French Army, there is no bell at
which tools are laid aside, and not even the night is sacred.
    Ibid.

3 "Yes, they're good boys," said the old woman, "but one
doesn't want other people's children always in one's life."
    Ibid.

4 EARTH has her usual delights--which can be met with six
days out of the seven. But here and there upon grey earth there
exist, like the flying of sunlight, celestial pleasures also--and
one of these is the heaven of success.
    Pt. II, Ch. III, Ibid.

5 "She keeps 'er brains in 'er 'eart. An' that's where they ought
ter be. An' a man or woman who does that's one in a million
an' 'as got my backing."
    National Velvet 1935

6 "Things come suitable to the time. Childbirth. An' bein' in love. An' death. You can't know 'em till you come to them. No use guessing an' dreading."

Ibid.

7 "There's men . . . as can see things in people. There's men . . . as can choose a horse, an' that horse'll win. It's not the look of the horse, no, nor of the child, nor of the woman, it's the thing *we* can see. . . .

Ibid.

8 "Love don't seem dainty on a fat woman."

Ibid.

9 MADRIGAL. Truth doesn't ring true in a court of law.
The Chalk Garden 1953

10 JUDGE. A judge does not always get to the bottom of a case.
MADRIGAL. No. It takes the pity of God to get to the bottom of things.

Ibid.

11 MADRIGAL. One can lie, but truth is more interesting.

Ibid.

12 MAITLAND. Madame loves the unusual! It's a middle-class failing—she says—to run away from the unusual.

Act I, Ibid.

13 MRS. ST. MAUGHAM. You can't fit false teeth to a woman of character. As one gets older and older, the appearance becomes such a bore.

Ibid.

14 MRS. ST. MAUGHAM. Privilege and power make selfish people—but gay ones.

Ibid.

15 MAITLAND. Praise is the only thing that brings to life again a man that's been destroyed.

Ibid.

16 OLIVIA. The thoughts of a *daughter* are a kind of memorial.

Act III, Ibid.

17 SHE. Women are so dutiful and the best men make them work so hard for them. I have yet to find out what a day is like when I'm not planning the next one!

The Chinese Prime Minister 1964

18 ALICE. What is this ghastly difference between men and women? What is this closeness that works—and doesn't work! That boils, that burns and blisters, and is so near love!

Ibid.

19 BENT. You were meant to be a single woman. Women of individuality are damned uncomfortable for men.

Ibid.

20 ALICE. Oh—a girl's looks are *agony*!

Act I, Sc. 1, Ibid.

21 SIR GREGORY. Marriage. The beginning and the end are wonderful. But the middle part is hell.

Act II, Ibid.

22 BENT. So few people achieve the final end. *Most* are caught napping.

Act III, Ibid.

23 SHE. We were so different that when two rooms separated us for half an hour—we met again as strangers.

Ibid.

24 SHE. And if I die in ten years—or ten minutes—you can't measure Time! In ten minutes everything can be felt! In four minutes you can be born! Or live. In two minutes, God may be understood! And what one woman grasps—all men may get nearer to.

Ibid.

25 To note, to pin down, to build up, to create, to be astonished at nothing, to cherish the oddities, to let nothing go down the drain, to make something, to make a great flower out of life, even if it's a cactus.

Ch. 3, *Autobiography 1969*

26 The theatre is a gross art, built in sweeps and over-emphasis. Compromise is its second name.

Ibid.

27 A father is always making his baby into a little woman. And when she is a woman he turns her back again.

Ch. 4, Ibid.

28 The pleasure of one's effect on other people still exists in age—what's called making a hit. But the hit is much rarer and made of different stuff.

Ch. 5, Ibid.

29 Sex—the great inequality, the great miscalculator, the great Irritator.

Ch. 6, Ibid.

30 In marriage there are no manners to keep up, and beneath the wildest accusations no real criticism. Each is familiar with that ancient child in the other who may erupt again. . . . We are not ridiculous to ourselves. We are ageless. That is the luxury of the wedding ring.

Ibid.

31 If a dog doesn't put you first where are you both? In what relation? A dog needs God. It lives by your glances, your wishes. It even shares your humour. This happens about the fifth year. If it doesn't happen you are only keeping an animal.

Ch. 10, Ibid.

32 MRS. BASIL. There is no end of an end of an end—to her discontent.

A Matter of Gravity 1978

33 MRS. BASIL. I think it's snobbery and a sort of outrage to despise people for the way they were born.

Ibid.

34 MRS. BASIL. Intelligence is such an easy thing—one knows at once. But the stuff that shoulders a life and a wife is harder to discern.

Ibid.

35 . . . [cheese-making is] a sort of science and a sort of legend, evolved from man's necessities and from the empirical advices and observations of women long dead and gone—a mixture today of higher mathematics and decimals of acidity, mixed with witchcraft and a sort of rough luck. Now and then you throw up a good cheese like a good poem.

Journal entry, Quoted in *Enid Bagnold: The Authorized Biography* by Anne Sebba 1986

36 I am sick, sick of the war, sick of the unending misery in these hospitals here...I am unable to turn pain and loss to an account . . . I am not inspired to any turn of thought. I find nothing provocative, nothing suggestive.

Ibid.

1587. Susan Hamilton Ardagh (fl. 1890s)

1 What are necessaries? What are luxuries? For I need hardly point out to any one who has felt the grip of an English winter, that what constitutes riches in Capri would mean poverty and privation in a climate like ours. So much depends on the class we happen to associate with, and the sky under which we live.

The Modern Marriage Market 1897

2 Beauty and evanescence are two of the chief characteristics of existence—beauty which the human eye may never see, and evanescence which oft-times enhances that very beauty we desire or regret.

Ibid.

3 The exhilarating and stimulating effect of certain minds upon our own is within the experience of most of us, while another perhaps superior intellect may leave us cold and dull.

Ibid.

1588. Mary E. Buell (fl. 1890s)

1 Something made of nothing, tasting very sweet,
A most delicious compound, with ingredients complete;
But if, as on occasion, the heart and mind are sour,
It has no great significance and loses half its power.

"The Kiss" *n.d.*

1589. Harriet L. Childe-Pemberton (fl. 1890s)

1 As I allays say to my brother,
If it isn't one thing it's the tother.
"Geese: A Dialogue," *Dead Letters and Other Narrative and Dramatic Pieces 1896*

2 Whenever any one tells me that he or she has a headache, has business letters to write,—doesn't want to be disturbed,—I take it for granted that he or she is engaged in something nothing less than wicked—and naturally I don't want to know anything about it!

"Smoke: A Monologue," *Ibid.*

3 MRS. CATERMOLE MACFADIE. No one will deny that things that are wrong frequently have their roots in things that are right; therefore, things that are right are things that are wrong. We are nothing if not logical; and when you have once become a member of the Sour Grape Club, of the Ishmaelites Club, and of the Clean-Sweepers League, you will understand these matters with a more enlightened apprehension.

"The Deuce of Clubs," *Ibid.*

4 MURIEL. In fact you expect me to submit to your unreasonableness because you haven't the courage to be honest. How like a man!

Ibid.

5 O sensitive Air who are one with Thought,
To my seeking soul you have brought
(On wings of silence or breeze or gale,)
Your manifold messages. . . .
"Songs of Air," X, St. 1, *Nenuphar 1911*

6 O beautiful Earth! alive, aglow,
With your million things that grow,
I would lay my head on your ample knee. . . .
"Songs of Earth," St. 1, Ibid.

7 Earth rules all her children by the solar clock;—
Should they dare to mock,
Running loose before she gives them leave,
They assuredly will grieve.
II, St. 2, Ibid.

8 "There is no fear for those who truly see
What is, or will be, springs from all that was,—
How all that happens fitly has to be,
And what ye name 'effect' and 'cause'
Make up but one degree."
"Songs of Fire," IX, St. 7, Ibid.

9 For passion has come to the verge and leaps
Headlong to the blind abyss,
Yet gathers thereby the strength of deeps,
And eddies a moment and swirls and sweeps
Till peril is one with bliss!
"Songs of Water," IV, St. 4, Ibid.

1590. Anne Hocking (189?–?)

1 Other sins only speak,
Murder cries out.
Death Leaves a Shining Mark 1943

1591. Beatrice Llewellyn-Thomas (1890–?)

1 O We have a desperate need of laughter!
Give us laughter, Puck!*
"To Puck" *n.d.*
*Character from Shakespeare's *A Midsummer's Night Dream*.

1592. Anita Owen (fl. 1890s)

1 And in these eyes the love-light lies
And lies—and lies and lies!
"Dreamy Eyes" *c. 1894*

2 . . . Daisies won't tell.
"Sweet Bunch of Daisies" *1894*

1593. Mary A. Owen (fl. 1890s)

1 "To be strong in de haid"—that is, of great strength of will—is the most important characteristic of a "conjurer" or "voodoo". Never mind what you mix—blood, bones, feathers, grave-dust, herbs, saliva, or hair—it will be powerful or feeble in proportion to the dauntless spirit infused by you, the priest or priestess, at the time you represent the god or "Old Master".
Among the Voodoos 1891

1594. Fradel Schtok (1890–193–?)

1 She sensed the truth of what was said when the wedding trumpet sounds, "This too will be your fate, this too will be your fate..." and the fiddle laments, "Oh, how you will be blighted!" while the bass angrily booms, "Just like this, just like this."
"The Veil," *Found Treasures: Stories by Yiddish Women Writers*, Frieda Forman, Ethel Raicus, Sarah Silberstein Swartz and Margie Wolf, eds. *1994*

1595. Hattie Starr (fl. 1890s)

1   Nobody loves me, well do I know,
Don't all the cold world tell me so?
"Nobody Loves Me" 1893

2   Somebody loves me; How do I know?
Somebody's eyes have told me so!
"Somebody Loves Me" 1893

1596. Ellen West (1890?–1923?)

1   I am twenty-one years old and am supposed to be silent and
grin like a puppet.
Diary entry (c. 1911), Quoted in Women and Madness by
Phyllis Chesler* 1972
*See 2787.

1597. Lina Eckenstein (fl. 1890s–1931)

1   The contributions of nuns to literature, as well as incidental
remarks, show that the curriculum of study in the nunnery
was as liberal as that accepted by the monks, and embraced
all available writing whether by Christian or profane authors.
Women Under Monasticism 1896

1598. Rachel (1890–1931)

1   Like a bird in the butcher's palm you flutter in my hand, insolent pride.
"Revolt," Poems from the Hebrew, Robert Mezey, ed. 1973

2   This is a bond nothing can ever loosen.
What I have lost: what I possess forever.
"My Dead," Ibid.

1599. Frances Noyes Hart (1890–1943)

1   "I cried at first . . . and then, it was such a beautiful day, that I
forgot to be unhappy."
"Green Garden," Scribner's 1921

2   Death cannot alter facts, only feelings.
The Crooked Lane 1933

1600. Aimee Semple McPherson (1890–1944)

1   O Hope! dazzling, radiant Hope!—What a change thou
bringest to the hopeless; brightening the darkened paths, and
cheering the lonely way.
Pt. I, Ch. 1, This Is That 1923

2   We are all making a crown for Jesus out of these daily lives of
ours, either a crown of golden, divine love, studded with gems
of sacrifice and adoration, or a thorny crown, filled with the
cruel briars of unbelief, or selfishness, and sin, and placing it
upon His brow.
Pt. II, "What Shall I Do with Jesus," Ibid.

3   "Pit-a-pat! Pit-a-pat!"—say the hundreds and thousands of
feet, surging by the church doors of our land. "Pat! Pat! Pit-a-
pat!"—hurrying multitudes, on business and pleasure bent.
"Is Jesus Christ the Great 'I Am' or Is He the Great
'I Was'?" Ibid.

4   Right here let us make it plain, that each individual is either a
sinner or a saint. It is impossible to be both; it is impossible to
be neutral; there is no half-way business with God. Either you

are the child of the Lord or you are serving the devil—there is
no middle territory.
"The Two Houses," Ibid.

1601. Madeline Talmage Astor (fl. 1890s–1945)

1   [Being helped over the rail of the Titanic*] I rang for ice, but
this is ridiculous!
Attributed 15 April 1912
*British luxury passenger liner that sank during its maiden voyage
after it struck an iceberg near Newfoundland; 1,513 lives were
lost.

1602. Maria, Grand Duchess of Russia (1890–1958)

1   . . . death, the mysterious disillusion and disappearance, of a
human being.
Ch. 1, Education of a Princess 1930

2   Girls' games never had any interest for me; I hated dolls; the
congealed expression on their porcelain faces provoked me. It
was with lead soldiers that we played, without ever growing
tired.
Ch. 3, Ibid.

3   The mouthpieces of the so-called public opinion; those men,
who by high-sounding formulas had so impressed the densely
ignorant masses. . . . They had neither sufficient moral force
nor experience necessary to build up a new system. Their mental store was limited to theories, often excellent but
inapplicable to reality.
Ch. 8, Ibid.

4   Russia still writhed and stumbled. The wave of revolts and uprisings, the constant agitations, the incessant inflammatory
orations of men possessed of little political competence. . . .
Ibid.

1603. Elizabeth Gurley Flynn (1890–1964)

1   He was an agitator, born of the first national awakening of
American labor. The shame of servitude and the glory of strug-
gle were emblazoned in the mind of every worker who heard
[Eugene V.] Debs.*
"Eugene V. Debs," Debs, Haywood, Ruthenberg 1939
*American socialist leader and pacifist (1855–1926).

2   We study their lives to understand better the past, as lessons
for the present and inspiration for the future. The past is the
background, the struggle part. . . .
Conclusion, Ibid.

3   Time was, when the ACLU was young, they were Anarchists,
Socialists, Christian pacifists, trade unionists, I.W.W., Quaker,
Irish, Republican and Communist! Today, they are no longer
heretics, non-conformists, radicals,—they are respectable.
"I Am Expelled from Civil Liberties!,"
Sunday Worker 17 March 1940

4   History has a long-range perspective. It ultimately passes stern
judgement on tyrants and vindicates those who fought, suffered, were imprisoned, and died for human freedom, against
political oppression and economic slavery. Pioneers who were
reviled, persecuted, ridiculed, and abused when they fought
for free public schools, woman's suffrage against chattel slavery, for labor unions, are honored and revered today.
Labor's Own: William Z. Foster* 1949
*American labor leader and Communist Party leader
(1881–1961).

5 We know that the solid foundation of a Communist Party are the workers and that our Party must be rooted in their struggle. . . . A study of the inner workings of capitalism with all its failures and contradictions, its excesses and abuses, will convince them that capitalism's days are numbered; it has been tried and found wanting; it hampers progress. . . . Negro and white workers, young workers, women workers—will come to understand the need of being a member of the Communist Party. . . .

Ibid.

6 We hated the rich, the trusts they owned, the violence they caused, the oppression they represented.

Pt. I, *The Rebel Girl* 1955

7 I said then and am still convinced that the full opportunity for women to become free and equal citizens with access to all spheres of human endeavor cannot come under capitalism, although many demands have been won by organized struggle.

Ibid.

8 "What freedom?" we asked again. To be wage-slaves, hired and fired at the will of a soulless corporation, paid low wages for long hours, driven by the speed of a machine? What freedom? To be clubbed, jailed, shot down—and while we spoke, the hoofs of the troopers' horses clattered by on the street.

Pt. III, Ibid.

9 So confident was he [Nicola Sacco*] of his innocence that sunny afternoon that he had no fear. He was sure when he told his story in court he would go free. He did not know that he was approaching the valley of the shadow of death. He feared no evil because the truth was with him. But greed, corruption, prejudice, fear and hatred of radical foreign-born workingmen were weaving a net around him.

Pt. VII, Ibid.

*Italian-born American anarchist (1891-1927); executed.

10 I was a convict, a prisoner without rights, writing a censored letter. But my head was unbowed. Come what may, *I was a political prisoner* and proud of it, at one with some of the noblest of humanity who had suffered for conscience's sake. I felt no shame, no humiliation, no consciousness of guilt. To me my number 11710 was a badge of honor.

Ch. 3, *The Alderson Story* 1963

*The Federal Reformatory for Women at Alderson, West Virginia.

11 One of my correspondents asked me: "What do you think are the main differences between a women's prison and a men's prison?" I replied: "You would never see diapers hung on a line at a men's prison or hear babies crying in the hospital on a quiet Sunday afternoon." The physiological differences—menstruation, menopause, and pregnancy—create intense emotional problems among many women in prison.

Ch. 13, Ibid.

12 A popular saying at Alderson went as follows: "They work us like a horse, feed us like a bird, treat us like a child, dress us like a man—and then expect us to act like a lady."

Ch. 25, Ibid.

13 We who are members of the Communist Party repudiate the exclusive identification of democracy with capitalism. We declare that democracy can be widened, take on new aspects, become truly a rule of the people, only when it is extended to the economic life of the people, as in the Soviet Union. As far

as women are concerned, the U.S.S.R. is a trailblazer for equal rights and equal opportunities.

Defense Speech (7 May 1940), *The Trial of Elizabeth Gurley Flynn by the American Civil Liberties Union*, Corliss Lamont, ed. 1968

1604. Hedda Hopper (1890–1966)

1 His footprints* were never asked for, yet no one has ever filled his shoes.

From Under My Hat 1952

*Reference to D. W. Griffith, American filmmaker (1875–1948), and Grauman's Theatre in Hollywood.

2 In Hollywood gratitude is Public Enemy Number One.

Ibid.

3 At one time I thought he wanted to be an actor. He had certain qualifications, including no money and a total lack of responsibility.

Ibid.

4 I decided that [Arthur] Brisbane* was a member of the 7–H club—Holy howling hell, how he hates himself.

Ibid.

*American newspaper editor infamous for yellow journalism (1864–1936).

1605. Hallie Flanagan (1890–1969)

1 We were a violent lot,* a thorn in the body bureaucratic. Possibly that is one function of art in society. In the midst of learning the necessary lingo of procedures, allotments, authorizations, we found time for exchange of ideas, ideas for salvaging the quickly receding past of our country, capturing it in plays, pictures, books; ideas for penetrating and illuminating our own age, finding quicksilver ways in which to express the mercurial present.

"Danger: Men Not Working," *Arena, The Story of the Federal Theatre* 1940

*The Federal Theatre of the New Deal's WPA (Work Projects Administration).

2 We live in a changing world: man is whispering through space, soaring to the stars in ships, flinging miles of steel and glass into the air. Shall the theatre continue to huddle in the confines of a painted box set? The movies, in their kaleidoscopic speed and juxtaposition of external objects and internal emotions are seeking to find visible and audible expression for the tempo and psychology of our time. The stage too must experiment—with ideas, with psychological relationships of men and women, with speech and rhythm forms, with dance and movement, with color and light—or it must and should become a museum product.

Comment at meeting (8/9 October 1935), Ibid.

3 It was ended because Congress, in spite of protests from many of its own members, treated the Federal Theatre not as a human issue or a cultural issue, but as a political issue.

"Blasting: Work Suspended," Ibid.

4 The greatest achievement of these public theatres was in their creation of an audience of many millions, a waiting audience. . . . Neither should the theatre in our country be regarded as a luxury. It is a necessity because in order to make democracy work the people must increasingly participate; they can't participate unless they understand; and the theatre is one of the greatest mediums of understanding.

Ibid.

1606. Blanche Stuart Scott (1892–1970)

1   Something must have happened to the throttle block.*
      Quoted in Introduction, *Women Aviators* by Lisa Yount
                                                      1995
      *Excuse she made to her instructor, who had blocked the throttle,
      upon safely landing an unauthorized solo flight.

1607. Daisy Ashford (1890?–1972)

1   I am parshial [sic] to ladies if they are nice. I suppose it is my
      nature. I am not quite a gentleman but you would hardly no-
      tice it.
                                  Ch. 1, *The Young Visitors** 1919
      *Written when the author was nine years old.

2   My life will be sour grapes and ashes without you.
                                                  Ch. 8, Ibid.

1608. Katherine Anne Porter (1890–1980)

1   She had set down and read the letter over again; but there were
      phrases that insisted on being read many times, they had a life
      of their own separate from the others. . . .
                  "Theft," *Flowering Judas and Other Stories 1930*

2   In this moment she felt that she had been robbed of an enor-
      mous number of valuable things, whether material or
      intangible: things lost or broken by her own fault, things she
      had forgotten and left in houses when she moved: books bor-
      rowed from her and not returned, journeys she had planned
      and had not made, words she had waited to hear spoken to
      her and had not heard, and the words she meant to answer
      with. . . .
                                                         Ibid.

3   . . . all that she had had, and all that she had missed, were lost
      together, and were twice lost in this landslide of remembered
      losses.
                                                         Ibid.

4   She laid the purse on the table and sat down with the cup of
      chilled coffee, and thought: I was right not to be afraid of any
      thief but myself, who will end by leaving me nothing.
                                                         Ibid.

5   "*What* could you buy with a hundred dollars?" she asked fret-
      fully.
         "Nothing, nothing at all," said their father, "a hundred
      dollars is just something you put in the bank."
                                  Pt. II, "Old Morality" *1936*

6   "It don't *look* right," was his final reason for not doing any-
      thing he did not wish to do.
                                                  Noon Wine 1937

7   "I don't see no reason to hold it against a man because he went
      loony once or twice in his lifetime and so I don't expect to take
      no steps about it. Not a step. I've got nothin' against the man,
      he's always treated me fair. They's things and people," he went
      on, "'nough to drive any man loony. The wonder to me is,
      more men don't wind up in straitjackets, the way things are
      going these days and times."
                                                         Ibid.

8   "Adam," she said, "the worst of war is the fear and suspi-
      cion and the awful expression in all the eyes you meet . . . as
      if they had pulled down the shutters over their minds and
      their hearts and were peering out at you, ready to leap if you

make one gesture or say one word they do not understand
instantly."
                                  Pale Horse, Pale Rider 1939

9   Nothing is mine, I have only nothing but it is enough, it is
      beautiful and it is all mine. Do I even walk about in my own
      skin or is it something I have borrowed to spare my modesty?
                                                         Ibid.

10 After working for three years on a morning newspaper she had
      an illusion of maturity and experience; but it was fatigue
      merely. . . .
                                                         Ibid.

11 "The mind and the heart sometimes get another chance, but if
      anything happens to the poor old human frame, why, it's just
      out of luck, that's all."
                                                         Ibid.

12 No more war, no more plague, only the dazed silence that fol-
      lows the ceasing of the heavy guns; noiseless houses with the
      shades drawn, empty streets, the dead cold light of tomorrow.
      Now there would be time for everything.
                                                         Ibid.

13 All believed they were bound for a place for some reason more
      desirable than the place they were leaving, but it was necessary
      to make the change with the least possible delay and expense.
      Delay and expense had been their common portion at the
      hands of an army of professional tip-seekers, fee-collectors,
      half-asleep consular clerks and bored migration officials who
      were not in the least concerned whether the travelers gained
      their ship or dropped dead in their tracks.
                                  Pt. I, *Ship of Fools 1962*

14 "People on a boat, Mary, can't seem to find any middle ground
      between stiffness, distrust, total rejection, or a kind of evasive,
      gnawing curiosity. Sometimes it's a friendly enough curiosity,
      sometimes sly and malicious, but you feel as if you were being
      eaten alive by fishes."
                                                  Pt. II, Ibid.

15 They exchanged one or two universal if minor truths—plea-
      sure was so often more exhausting than the hardest work; they
      had both noticed that a life of dissipation sometimes gave to a
      face the look of gaunt suffering spirituality that a life of asceti-
      cism was supposed to give and quite often did not.
                                                  Pt. III, Ibid.

16 Miracles are instantaneous, they cannot be summoned, but
      come of themselves, usually at unlikely moments and to those
      who least expect them.
                                                         Ibid.

17 "The real sin against life is to abuse and destroy beauty, even
      one's own—even more, one's own, for that had been put in
      our care and we are responsible for its well-being. . . ."
                                                         Ibid.

18 You can't write about people out of textbooks, and you can't
      use jargon. You have to speak clearly and simply and purely in
      a language that a six-year-old child can understand; and yet
      have the meanings and the overtones of language, and the im-
      plications, that appeal to the highest intelligence.
      Writers at Work, Second Series, George Plimpton,* ed. *1963*
      *American writer and editor (1927–).

19 A cultivated style would be like a mask. Everybody knows it's
      a mask, and sooner or later you must show yourself—or at

least, you show yourself as someone who could not afford to show himself, and so created something to hide behind. . . . You do not create a style. You work, and develop yourself; your style is an emanation from your own being.

Ibid.

20 There seems to be a kind of order in the universe, in the move-ment of the stars and the turning of the earth and the changing of the seasons, and even in the cycle of human life. But human life itself is almost pure chaos. Everyone takes his stance, as-serts his own rights and feelings, mistaking the motives of others, and his own.

Ibid.

21 Human life itself may be almost pure chaos, but the work of the artist—the only thing he's good for—is to take these hand-fuls of confusion and disparate things, things that seem to be irreconcilable, and put them together in a frame to give them some kind of shape and meaning. Even if it's only his view of a meaning. That's what he's for—to give his view of life.

Ibid.

22 Our being is subject to all the chances of life. There are so many things we are capable of, that we could be or do. The potentialities are so great that we never, any of us, are more than one-fourth fulfilled.

Ibid.

23 It is disaster to have a man fall in love with me. They aren't content to take what I can give; they want everything from me.
Quoted in "A Lioness of Literature Looks Back" by Henry Allen, *Los Angeles Times* 7 July 1974

24 No man can be explained by his personal history, least of all a poet.

Ibid.

25 Such ignorance. All the boys were in military schools and all the girls were in the convent, and that's all you need to say about it.

Ibid.

26 I do not understand the world, but I watch its progress.

Ibid.

27 My grandmother, when she heard that Mr. Lincoln had abol-ished slavery and the Negroes were free, was heard to say "I hope it works both ways," and lived to realize that it did not.
"Notes on the Texas I Remember," *The Atlantic March 1975*

1609. Rose Fitzgerald Kennedy (1890–1995)

1 The secret of the Kennedy successes in politics was not money but meticulous planning and organization, tremendous effort and the enthusiasm and devotion of family and friends.
Times to Remember 1974

2 Sedentary people are apt to have sluggish minds. A sluggish mind is apt to be reflected in flabbiness of body and in a dull-ness of expression that invites no interest and gets none.

Ibid.

3 Birds sing after a storm; why shouldn't people feel as free to delight in whatever remains to them?

Ibid.

4 We cannot always understand the ways of Almighty God—the crosses which He sends us, the sacrifices which He demands of

us. . . . But we accept with faith and resignation His holy will with no looking back to what might have been, and we are at peace.
"After Robert Kennedy's Death" (Television Broadcast; 1968), Ibid.

1610. A. Elizabeth "Bessie" Delany (1891–1995)

1 We've outlived those old rebby boys!* They're turning in their graves while Sadie** and me are getting the last word, in this book.
Having Our Say, The Delany Sisters' First 100 Years, with Sarah Delaney** and Amy Hill Hearth *1993*
*Term they used to call racist white men [probably stemming from Civil War]. **Sarah Delany, her sister; see 1578.

2 When Negroes are average, they fail, unless they are very, very lucky. Now, if you're average and *white*, honey, you can go far. Just look at Dan Quayle.* If that boy was colored he'd be washing dishes somewhere.

Ibid.
*James Danforth Quayle, 41st vice president of United States (1947–).

3 Oppressed people have a good sense of humor. Think of the Jews. They know how to laugh, and to laugh at themselves! Well, we colored folks are the same way. We colored folks are survivors.

Ibid.

4 The first thing I would do if I was President would be to say that people over 100 years of age no longer have to pay taxes! Ha ha! Lord knows I've paid my share.

Ibid.

5 As a child, every time I encountered prejudice—which was rubbed in your face, once segregation started under Jim Crow*—I would feel it down to my core. I would go home and sit on my bed and weep and weep and weep, the tears streaming down my face.

Ibid.
*The practice of discriminating against and segregating black peo-ple.

1611. Vivian Yeiser Laramore (1891–?)

1 Talk to me tenderly, tell me lies;
I am a woman and time flies.
"Talk to Me Tenderly" *n.d.*

2 I've shut the door on yesterday
And thrown the key away-
To-morrow holds no fears for me,
Since I have found to-day.
"To-day" *n.d.*

1612. Fanny Brice (1891–1951)

1 Your audience gives you everything you need. They tell you. There is no director who can direct you like an audience.
Quoted in Ch. 6, *The Fabulous Fanny* by Norman Katkov *1952*

2 Being a funny person does an awful lot of things to you. You feel that you mustn't get serious with people. They don't ex-pect it from you, and they don't want to see it. You're not entitled to be serious, you're a clown, and they only want you to make them laugh.

Ch. 9, Ibid.

3 When love is out of your life, you're through in a way. Because while it's there it's like a motor that's going, you have such vitality to do things, big things, because love is goosing you all the time.

Ch. 19, Ibid.

4 Let the world know you as you are, not as you think you should be, because sooner or later, if you are posing, you will forget the pose, and then where are you?

Ch. 24, Ibid.

5 Men always fall for frigid women because they put on the best show.

Bk. 5, "Don Juan in Hollywood," Quoted in *A Child of the Century* by Ben Hecht* 1954
*American playwright, screenwriter, writer (1894–1964).

1613. Zora Neale Hurston (1891–1960)

1 JOHN. So this is the woman I've been wearing over my heart like a rose for twenty years! She so despises her own skin that she can't believe anyone else could love it!

Color Struck 1926

2 Now, women forget all those things they don't want to remember and remember everything they don't want to forget. The dream is the truth. Then they act and do things accordingly.

Their Eyes Were Watching God 1937

3 Ships at a distance have every man's wish on board. For some they come in with the tide. For others they sail forever on the horizon, never out of sight, never landing, until the Watcher turns his eyes away in resignation, his dreams mocked to death by Time. That is the life of men.

Ch. 1, Ibid.

4 There is no agony like bearing an untold story inside you.

Dust Tracks on a Dirt Road (autobiography) 1942

5 I do not belong to that sobbing school of Negro-hood who hold that nature somehow has given them a lowdown dirty deal.

Ibid.

6 I used to climb to the top of one of the huge chinaberry trees which guarded our front gate and look out over the world. The most interesting thing that I saw was the horizon...It grew upon me that I ought to walk out to the horizon and see what the end of the world was like.

Ibid.

7 "You love like a coward. Don't take no steps at all. Just stand around and hope for things to happen outright. Unthankful and unknowing like a hog under an acorn tree. Eating and grunting with your ears hanging over your eyes, and never even looking up to see where the acorns are coming from."

Seraph on the Suwanee 1948

8 "I'll bet when you get down on them rusty knees and get to worrying God, He goes in His privy-house and slams the door. That's what he thinks about *you* and *your* prayers."

Ch. 15, Ibid.

9 She had the misfortune to be too good-looking and too available for women to take to her, but not pretty enough for any man to excuse her generosity and want to protect her. Nor had she the avarice nor the hardness to turn her position to profit.

Ibid.

10 "Don't you realize that the sea is the home of water? All water is off on a journey unlessen it's in the sea, and it's homesick, and bound to make its way home someday."

Ch. 27, Ibid.

1614. Irene Rutherford McLeod (1891–1964?)

1 I'm a lean dog, a keen dog, a wild dog, and alone.

"Lone Dog," *Songs to Save a Soul* 1919

1615. Anne Nichols (1891–1966)

1 MRS. COHEN. How early it is of late!

Act I, *Abie's Irish Rose* 1922

2 FATHER WHALEN. Shure, we're all trying to get to the same place when we pass on. We're just going by different routes. We can't all go on the same train.
RABBI. And just because you are not riding on my train, why should I say your train won't get there?

Act II, Ibid.

1616. Ruth Law Oliver (1891–1970)

1 I had a great desire to take off and go somewhere in flight, never having done it.

Ch. 4, *The American Heritage History of Flight* 1962

1617. Nelly Sachs (1891–1970)

1 Butterflies fluttering
soon feel at home in the sea—
This stone
inscribed with the 'fly
has placed itself in my hand—

In place of a homeland
I hold out for the world to transform—

Acceptance speech poem, Nobel Prize Awards (Stockholm),
Janice Price with Elaine T. Partnow, trs. 1966

2 In the spring of 1940, after tortuous months, we [she and her mother] arrived in Stockholm. The occupation of Denmark and Norway had already taken place. The great novelist was no more. We breathed the air of freedom without knowing the language or any person.

Acceptance speech, Nobel Prize Awards (Stockholm; 1966),
Ruth and Matthew Mead tr. Quoted in *O the Chimneys*
1967

3 Peoples of the earth,
leave the words at their source,
for it is they that can nudge
the horizons into the true heaven. . . .

"Peoples of the Earth," St. 4, Ibid.

4 O you chimneys,
O you fingers
And Israel's body as smoke through the air!

"O the Chimneys," St. 4, Ibid.

5 When sleep leaves the body like smoke
and man, sated with secrets,
drives the overworked nag of quarrel
out of its stall,
then the fire-breathing union begins anew. . . .

"When Sleep Enters the Body Like Smoke,"
St. 3, Ibid.

6 But how shall time be drawn
from the golden threads of the sun?
Wound
for the cocoon of the silken butterfly
night?
"Hunter," *The Seeker and Other Poems* 1970

7 You, the inexperienced, who learn nothing in the nights.
Many angels are given you
But you do not see them.
"Chorus of Clouds," Ibid.

8 Are graves breath-space for longing?
"Are Graves Breath-Space for Longing?," Ibid.

1618. Agatha Christie (1891–1975)

1 Every murderer is probably somebody's old friend.
The Mysterious Affair at Styles 1920

2 The evidence of a woman devoted to him would not have been enough—you hinted as much yourself. But I know something of the psychology of crowds. Let my evidence be wrung from me, as an admission, damning me in the eyes of the law, and a reaction in favor of the prisoner would immediately set in.
Witness for the Prosecution 1924

3 Curious things, habits. People themselves never knew they had them.
Ibid.

4 It is completely unimportant. That is why it is so interesting.
The Murder of Roger Ackroyd 1926

5 To say that crime brings its own punishment is by way of being a platitude, and yet in my opinion nothing can be truer.
The Tuesday Club Murders 1933

6 Crime is terribly revealing. Try and vary your methods as you will, your tastes, your habits, your attitude of mind, and your soul is revealed by your actions.
Ch. 17, *The ABC Murders* 1936

7 There is nothing so dangerous for anyone who has something to hide as conversation! . . . A human being, Hastings, cannot resist the opportunity to reveal himself and express his personality which conversation gives him. Every time he will give himself away.
Ch. 31, Ibid.

8 Achievement brings with it its own anticlimax.
They Came to Baghdad 1951

9 She lied with fluency, ease and artistic fervor.
Ibid.

10 LADY ANGKATELL. People are quite right when they say nature in the mild is seldom raw.
Act I, *The Hollow* 1952

11 LADY ANGKATELL. Tradespeople are just like gardeners. They take advantage of your not knowing.
Ibid.

12 GUDGEON. The trouble is there are no proper *employers* anymore.
Ibid.

13 HENRIETTA. I say the word, you know, over and over again to myself. Dead-dead-dead-dead—and soon it hasn't any meaning, it hasn't any meaning at all. Just a funny little word like the breaking of a rotten branch. Dead-dead-dead-dead-dead.
Act II, Sc. 2, Ibid.

14 An archaeologist is the best husband any woman can have: the older she gets, the more interested he is in her.
Attributed by Sir Max Mallowan, her husband, news item 9 March *1954*

15 CLARISSA. Oh dear, I never realized what a terrible lot of explaining one has to do in a murder!
Spider's Web 1956

16 SIR ROWLAND. You must know better than I do, Inspector, how very rarely two people's account of the same thing agrees. In fact, if three people were to agree exactly, I should regard it as suspicious. Very suspicious, indeed.
Act II, Sc. 2, Ibid.

17 TREVES. In my experience, pride is a word often on women's lips—but they display little sign of it where love affairs are concerned.
Act I, *Towards Zero* 1957

18 TREVES. If one sticks too rigidly to one's principles one would hardly see anybody.
Ibid.

19 Evil is not something superhuman, it's something less than human.
The Pale Horse 1961

20 One doesn't recognize in one's life the really important moments —not until it's too late.
Endless Night 1967

21 Is there ever any particular spot where one can put one's finger and say, "It all began that day, at such a time and such a place, with such an incident."
Ch. 1, Ibid.

22 One of the oddest things in life, I think, is the things one remembers.
Bk I, Ch. 3, Ibid.

23 . . . money isn't so hot, after all. What with incipient heart attacks, lots of bottles of little pills you have to take all the time, and losing your temper over the food or the service in hotels. Most of the rich people I've known have been fairly miserable.
Ibid.

24 I didn't want to work. It was as simple as that. I distrusted work, disliked it. I thought it was a very bad thing that the human race had unfortunately invented for itself.
Ibid.

25 "Look here," I said, "people like to collect disasters."
Ch. 5, Ibid.

26 To put it quite crudely . . . The poor don't really know how the rich live, and the rich don't know how the poor live, and to find out is really enchanting to both of them.
Bk. II, Ch. 9, Ibid.

27 "Doctors can do almost anything nowadays, can't they, unless they kill you first while they're trying to cure you."
Ch. 11, Ibid.

28 Every Night and every Morn
    Some to Misery are born.
    Every Morn and every Night
    Some are born to Sweet Delight,
    Some are born to Endless Night.

    Ch. 14, Ibid.

29 Where large sums of money are concerned, it is advisable to
    trust nobody.

    Ch. 15, Ibid.

30 It's astonishing in this world how things don't turn out at all
    the way you expect them to!

    Ibid.

1619. Katherine Stinson (1891–1977)
1   When I began to talk about flying, she already had confidence
    in me. My mother never warned me not to do this or that for
    fear of being hurt. Of course I got hurt, but I was never afraid.

    Quoted in *Women Aviators* by Lisa Yount *1995*

2   It's all right if your automobile goes wrong while you are driv-
    ing it. You can get out in the road and tinker with it. But if
    your airplane breaks down, you can't sit on a convenient cloud
    and tinker with *that*!

    Article, *American Magazine* (1917), Ibid.

1620. Laura Gilpin (1891–1979)
1   A river seems a magic thing. A magic, moving, living part of
    the very earth itself—for it is from the soil, both from its depth
    and from its surface, that a river has its beginning

    Introduction, *The Rio Grande 1949*

2   . . . much earnest philosophical thought is born of the life
    which springs from close association with nature.

    "The Source," Ibid.

3   Since the earliest-known existence of human life in the West-
    ern World, all manner of men have trod the river's banks. With
    his progressing knowledge and experience, man has turned
    these life-giving waters upon the soil, magically evoking an in-
    creasing bounty from the arid land. But through misuse of its
    vast drainage areas—the denuding of forest lands and the de-
    struction of soil-binding grasses—the volume of the river has
    been diminished, as once generous tributaries have become
    parched *arroyos*. Will present and future generations have the
    vision and wisdom to correct these abuses, protect this her-
    itage, and permit a mighty river to fulfill its highest destiny?

    "The Delta," Ibid.

1621. Victoria Ocampo (1891–1979)
1   He [T. E. Lawrence] was of the same stuff as the saints, and
    like them he had to find perfection in himself, and not like a
    great artist in the work he had conceived and executed.

    "Childhood," *33817TE (Lawrence of Arabia)* 1947*
    *T. E. Lawrence, British soldier and writer (1888–1935).

2   Morality, like physical cleanliness, is not acquired once and
    for all: it can only be kept and renewed by a habit of constant
    watchfulness and discipline.

    "Scruples and Ambitions," Ibid.

3   . . . there is a touch of optimism in every worry about one's
    own moral character.

    Ibid.

4   Some regions of the earth, which are not rich or picturesque,
    attract us because of a mysterious relationship we have with
    them.

    "A Man of the Desert," Ibid.

5   In literature homosexuality is always the occasion for detailed
    grandiloquent justifications and scientific reflections, or of ob-
    scure unclean explanation mixed up with a sense of guilt, or a
    weakness which turns out to be bragging. You apologize and
    then preen yourself upon it.

    "Homosexuality," Ibid.

6   Sadism, masochism, neuroses, suppressed desires, complexes,
    all those things which psychoanalysis invents in order to de-
    bunk the scruples and ardent aspirations of mankind and their
    rebirth in secular disguises, are not sufficient to explain them.

    "The Flesh," Ibid.

7   The eagerness to seek hidden but necessary connections, con-
    nections that revealed a close relationship between the world
    where I was born in the flesh and the other worlds where I was
    reborn, has been the enterprise of my whole life.

    Speech, American Academy of Arts and Letters, New York
    1973

1622. Margaret Culkin Banning (1891–1982)
1   I get a little angry about this highhanded scrapping of the
    looks of things. What else have we to go by? How else can the
    average person form an opinion of a girl's sense of values or
    even of her chastity except by the looks of her conduct?

    Letters to Susan 1936

2   It isn't easy to be the person who sometimes has to try to pre-
    serve your happiness at the expense of your fun.

    Ibid.

3   You wouldn't be caught wearing cheap perfume, would you?
    Then why do you want to wear cheap perfume on your con-
    duct?

    Ibid.

4   Did it ever occur to you that there's something almost crooked
    in the way decent girls nowadays use the shelter of their estab-
    lished respectability to make things awkward for men?

    Ibid.

5   The women's magazines are advertising mediums as well as
    publishers of fiction and articles on current subjects. They are
    fashion and marketing experts, instructors in home economics.

    Ibid.

1623. Marie Rambert (1891–1982)
1   We want to create an atmosphere in which creation is possible.

    Quoted in "Ballet Rambert: The Company That Changed Its
    Mind" by John Percival, *Dancemagazine* February *1973*

2   I don't do cartwheels any more, but I still do a *barre* to keep
    supple.

    Quoted in "Old School Tights" by Beryl Hilary Ostlere,
    Ibid.

1624. Storm Jameson (1891–1986)
1   Think of all the really successful men and women you know.
    Do you know a single one who didn't learn very young the
    trick of calling attention to himself in the right quarters?

    Ch. 7, *A Cup of Tea for Mr. Thorgill 1957*

2 Mere human beings can't afford to be fanatical about anything. . . . Not even about justice or loyalty. The fanatic for
justice ends by murdering a million helpless people to clear a
space for his law-courts. If we are to survive on this planet,
there must be compromises.

Ch. 28, Ibid.

1625. Mary Ambrose (1892–?)

1 The true vocation [of a nun is] settled on the day a girl looks
around her and sees a young woman her own age in pretty
clothes wheeling a baby carriage by the convent. Then her
heart takes an awful flop and she knows what it is God really
is asking of her.

Quoted in *Life* (New York) *15 March 1963*

1626. Mary Baker (1892–197-?)

1 Women must organize and think strategically about creating
ongoing pressure for change. Access is easy. Getting in law
schools and getting a job is easy. To actually change the structure at law schools and law firms is really difficult.

"Back to the Future," *Perspectives Fall 1997*

1627. Lady Willie Forbus (1892–)

1 But now that I'll be 100 years old, I think it's about time that I
get out of the profession. I don't know any lawyers who are
practicing at 100.

Quoted in "Lawyer observes 100 years" by Robert L.
Jamieson, Jr., *Seattle Post-Intelligencer*, B1 *24 August 1992*

2 I thought I'd go out West because it was more up-to-date.
More open and receptive to women.*

Ibid.

*Reference to the difficulty for a woman lawyer to find a position
c. 1916.

3 When you become 100, life changes completely.

Ibid.

1628. Bessie Coleman (1892-1926)

1 I decided blacks should not have to experience the difficulties I
had faced, so I decided to open a flying school and teach other
black women to fly.

Memoir, Quoted in *Ladybirds* by Henry M. Holden *1991*

2 I wasn't going to let them humiliate *my* people, who were coming to see me. I told them I would not fly until they let the
blacks through the same gate as the whites.

Remark to Waxahachie, Texas stadium managers (1925),
Quoted in *Women Aviators* by Lisa Yount *1995*

3 Tell them all that as soon as I can walk I'm going to fly!

Ibid.

1629. Stella Benson (1892–1933)

1 Call no man foe, but never love a stranger.
Build up no plan, nor any star pursue.
Go forth in crowds, in loneliness is danger.
Thus nothing fate can send,
And nothing fate can do
Shall pierce your peace, my friend.

"To the Unborn," St. 3, *This Is the End 1917*

2 Family jokes, though rightly cursed by strangers, are the bond
that keeps most families alive.

Ch. 9, *Pipers and a Dancer 1924*

1630. Alfonsina Storni (1892–1938)

1 Miles overhead there is a light in space:
He sees a star; aroused, inspired, he reaches up to hold it,
And then another hand cuts off the hand he raises.

"Man," John A. Crow, tr., *El duce dano* (The sweet injury)
1918

2 I gutted your belly as I would a doll's
Examining its artifice of cogs
And buried deep within its golden pulleys
I found a trap bearing this label: sex.

"To Eros," *Mask and Trefoil* c. *1930*

3 . . . Ah, one favor:
If he telephones again,
Tell him it's no use, that I've gone out. . . .

"I Shall Sleep",* *La Nacion* (Buenos Aires) *1938*
*Sent to *La Nacion* the day before she drowned herself.

4 You want me to be white
(God forgive you)
You want me to be chaste
(God forgive you)
You want me to be immaculate!

"You Want Me White" *n.d.*

5 I was in your cage, little man
Little man, what a cage you have given me,
I say little because you do not understand me;
You will never understand me.

"Dear Little Man" *n.d.*

6 To tell you, my love, that I desired you
With no instinctive hypocritic blush,
I was incapable, as tightly bound as Prometheus,
Until one day I burst my bonds.

"Twenty Centuries" *n.d.*

1631. Marina Tsvetaeva (1892–1941)

1 HENRIETTE.* God created his marvelous world in a week.
A woman is a hundred worlds. With one breath,
How can I become a woman in just one day?
Yesterday a hussar—in spurs and sword.
Today, a lace and satin angel.
And tomorrow, perhaps, who knows?

Priklyuchenie (An Adventure) *1923*
*The playwright's spin on Casanova's mysterious French lover;
Giovanni Jacopo C— de Seingalt was an Italian adventurer and
jack-of-all-trades who established a legendary reputation as a
lover (1725–1798).

2 HENRIETTE. I am a moonbeam, free to go wherever I choose.

Ibid.

1632. Edna St. Vincent Millay (1892–1950)

1 Strange how few,
After all's said and done, the things that are
Of moment.

"Interim," St. 8, *Renascence and Other Poems 1917*

2 I think our heart-strings were, like warp and woof
In some firm fabric, woven in and out. . . .

St. 12, Ibid.

3 Not Truth, but Faith, it is
That keeps the world alive.

St. 15, Ibid.

4 For my omniscience paid I toll
In infinite remorse of soul.

"Renascence," St. 2, Ibid.

5 A grave is such a quiet place.

St. 4, Ibid.

6 God, I can push the grass apart
And lay my finger on Thy heart.

St. 7, Ibid.

7 The soul can split the sky in two,
And let the face of God shine through.

St. 8, Ibid.

8 Who told me time would ease me of my pain!

"Time does not bring relief," Ibid.

9 Life goes on forever like the gnawing of a mouse.

"Ashes of Life," St. 3, Ibid.

10 COLUMBINE. I cannot *live*
Without a macaroon!

Aria Da Capo *1919*

11 PIERROT. I am become a socialist. I love Humanity; but I hate
people.

Ibid.

12 PIERROT. Your mind is made of crumbs. . . .

Ibid.

13 COLUMBINE. Why, Pierrot, I can't act.

PIERROT. Can't act? Can't act? La, listen to the woman!
What's that to do with the price of furs?—
You're blonde,
Are you not?—you have no education, have you?—
Can't act! You under-rate yourself my dear!

COLUMBINE. Yes, I suppose I do.

Ibid.

14 PIERROT. You see, I am always wanting
A little more than what I have,—or else
A little less.

Ibid.

15 CORYDON. *Your* sheep! You are mad, to call them
Yours—mine—they are all one flock!

Ibid.

16 CORYDON. We seem to be forgetting
It's only a game. . . .
But one of us has to take a risk, or else,
Why, don't you see?—the game goes on forever!

Ibid.

17 Was it for this I uttered prayers,
And sobbed and cursed and kicked the stairs,
That now, domestic as a plate,
I should retire at half-past eight?

"Grown-Up," *A Few Figs from
Thistles* 1920

18 Whether or not we find what we are seeking
Is idle, biologically speaking.

"I shall forget you presently," Ibid.

19 Cut if you will, with Sleep's dull knife,
Each day to half its length, my friend,—
The years that time takes off my life,
He'll take from off the other end!

"Midnight Oil," Ibid.

20 After the feet of beauty fly my own.

"Oh, think not I am faithful," Ibid.

21 With him for a sire and her for a dam,
What should I be but just what I am?

"The Singing-Woman from the Wood's Edge," St. 9, Ibid.

22 The fabric of my faithful love
No power shall dim or ravel
Whilst I stay here,—but oh, my dear,
If I should ever travel!

"To the Not Impossible Him,"
St. 3, Ibid.

23 My candle burns at both its ends;
It will not last the night;
But oh, my foes, and oh, my friends—
It gives a lovely light.

"First Fig," Ibid.

24 I had a little Sorrow,
Born of a little Sin.

"The Penitent," St. 1, Ibid.

25 I am waylaid by Beauty.

"Assault," St. 2, *Second April 1921*

26 Spring will not ail nor summer falter;
Nothing will know that you are gone. . . .

"Elegy Before Death," St. 3, Ibid.

27 Longing alone is singer to the lute. . . .

"Into the golden vessel of great song," Ibid.

28 Life in itself
Is nothing,
An empty cup, a flight of uncarpeted stairs.

"Spring," Ibid.

29 *Down you mongrel, Death!*
Back into your kennel!

"The Poet and His Book," St. 1, Ibid.

30 Read me, do not let me die!
Search the fading letters, finding
Steadfast in the broken binding
All that once was I!

St. 6, Ibid.

31 Many a bard's untimely death
Lends unto his verses breath. . . .

"To a Poet That Died Young," St. 3, Ibid.

32 I turn away reluctant from your light,
And stand irresolute, a mind undone,
A silly, dazzled thing deprived of sight
From having looked too long upon the sun.

"When I too long have looked upon your face," Ibid.

33 And what did I see I had not seen before?
Only a question less or a question more. . . .

"Wild Swans," Ibid.

34 All my life,
  Following Care along the dusty road,
  Have I looked back at loveliness and sighed. . . .
                              "Journey," St.1, Ibid.

35 I make bean-stalks, I'm
  A builder, like yourself.
                      "The Bean-Stalk," St. 4, Ibid.

36 Life is a quest and love a quarrel. . . .
                              "Weeds," St. 1, Ibid.

37 Life must go on;
  I forgot just why.
                              "Lament," Ibid.

38 Always I climbed the wave at morning,
  Shook the sand from my shoes at night,
  That now am caught beneath great buildings,
  Stricken with noise, confused with light.
                              "Exiled," St. 4, Ibid.

39 Your body was a temple to Delight. . . .
              "As to some lovely temple tenantless," Ibid.

40 Oh, oh, you will be sorry for that word!
  Give back my book and take my kiss instead.
  Was it my enemy or my friend I heard,
  "What a big book for such a little head!"
              "Oh, oh, you will be sorry for that word!," The Harp-
                        Weaver and Other Poems 1923

41 She said at length, feeling the doctor's eyes,
  "I don't know what you do exactly when a person dies."
              "Sonnets from an Ungrafted Tree" XVI, Ibid.

42 He laughed at all I dared to praise,
  And broke my heart, in little ways.
                      "The Spring and the Fall," St. 2, Ibid.

43 I would blossom if I were a rose.
      "Three Songs from the Lamp and the Bell," I, St. 1, Ibid.

44 I only know that summer sang in me
  A little while, that in me sings no more.
      "What lips my lips have kissed, and where, and why," Ibid.

45 Pity me that the heart is slow to learn
  What the swift mind beholds at very turn.
                  "Pity me not because the light of day," Ibid.

46 If I ever said, in grief or pride,
  I tired of honest things, I lied. . . .
                          "The Goose-Girl," Ibid.

47 I know I am but summer to your heart,
  And not the full four seasons of the year. . . .
              "I know I am but summer to your heart," Ibid.

48 I drank at every vine.
  The last was like the first.
  I came upon no wine
  So wonderful as thirst.
                              "Feast," St. 1, Ibid.

49 Music my rampart, and my only one.
      "On Hearing a Symphony of Beethoven,"* St. 1, The Buck
                            in the Snow 1928
  *Ludwig van B—, German composer (1770–1827).

50 The anguish of the world is on my tongue.
  My bowl is filled to the brim with it; there is more than I can
      eat.
  Happy are the toothless old and the toothless young,
  That cannot rend this meat.
                              "The Anguish," St. 2, Ibid.

51 Not for you was the pen bitten,
  And the mind wrung, and the song written.
                      "To Those Without Pity," Ibid.

52 Unnatural night, the shortest of the year,
  Farewell! 'Tis dawn. The longest day is here.
              "Fatal Interview," XIII, Fatal Interview 1931

53 Youth, have no pity; leave no farthing here
  For age to invest in compromise and fear.
                              XXIX, Ibid.

54 Desolate dreams pursue me out of sleep;
  Weeping I wake; waking, I weep, I weep.
                              XXXIII, Ibid.

55 My kisses now are sand against your mouth,
  Teeth in your palm and pennies on your eyes.
                              XXXIX, Ibid.

56 Breed, crowd, encroach, expand, expunge yourself, die out,
  Homo called sapiens.
              "Apostrophe to Man," Wine from These Grapes 1934

57 Childhood is the Kingdom Where Nobody Dies.
      "Childhood Is the Kingdom Where Nobody Dies," III, Ibid.

58 To be grown up is to sit at the table with people who have
  died, who neither listen nor speak. . . .
                              St. 6, Ibid.

59 Soar, eat ether, see what has never been seen; depart, be lost,
  But climb.
                      "On Thought in Harness," St. 3, Ibid.

60 All skins are shed at length, remorse, even shame.
              "Time, that renews the tissues of this frame," Ibid.

61 I shall die, but that is all that I shall do for Death; I am not on
  his pay-roll.
                          "Conscientious Objector,"
                              St. 3, Ibid.

62 Am I a spy in the land of the living, that I should deliver men
  to Death?
                              St. 4, Ibid.

63 . . . what frosty fate's in store
  For the warm blood of man,—man, out of ooze
  But lately crawled, and climbing up the shore?
                  "Epitaph for the Race of Man," III, Ibid.

64 Man, with his singular laughter, his droll tears,
  His engines and his conscience and his art,
  Made but a simple sound upon your ears. . . .
              "Oh Earth, unhappy planet born to die," IV, Ibid.

65 O Life, my little day, at what cost
  Have you been purchased!
      "Be sure my coming was a sharp offense," Huntsman, What
                              Quarry? 1939

66 Even the bored, insulated heart,
  That signed so long and tight a lease,
  Can break its contract, slump in peace.
              "Theme and Variations," IV, St. 6, Ibid.

67 Infinite Space lies curved within the scope
  Of the hand's cradle.
              "Truce for a Moment," St. 2, Ibid.

68 Wisdom enough to leech us of our ill
  Is daily spun; but there exists no loom
  To weave it into fabric. . . .
              "Upon this age, that never speaks its mind," Ibid.

69 Ease has demoralized us, nearly so; we know
  Nothing of the rigours of winter. . . .
              "Underground System," St. 2, Ibid.

70 Heart, do not stain my skin
  With bruises; go about
  Your simple function. Mind,
  Sleep now; do not intrude;
  And do not spy; be kind.

  Sweet blindness, now begin.
              "Theme and Variations," II, Sts. 5–6, Ibid.

71 . . . my heart is set
  On living—I have heroes to beget
  Before I die. . . .
              "Thou famished grave, I will not fill thee yet," Ibid.

72 No, no, not love, not love. Call it by name,
  Now that it's over, now that it is gone and cannot hear us.
  It was an honest thing. Not noble. Yet no shame.
              "What Savage Blossom," Sts. 3-4, Ibid.

73 Parrots, tortoises and redwoods
  Live a longer life than men do,
  Men a longer life than dogs do,
  Dogs a longer life than love does.
              "Pretty Love I Must Outlive You," Ibid.

74 See how these masses mill and swarm
  And troop and muster and assail:
  God! we could keep this planet warm
  By friction, if the sun should fail.
              "Three Sonnets in Tetrameter," I, Ibid.

75 Love does not help to understand
  The logic of the bursting shell.
                              III, Ibid.

76 You think we build a world; I think we leave
  Only these tools, wherewith to strain and grieve.
              "Count them unclean, these tears that turn no mill," Ibid.

77 Any person who publishes a book willfully appears before the
  populace with his pants down. . . .
              Letters of Edna St. Vincent Millay, Allen R. Macdougall, ed.
                              1952

78 It's not true that life is one damn thing after another—it's one
  damn thing over and over.
                              Ibid.

79 After all, my erstwhile dear,
  My no longer cherished,

Need we say it was not love,
Now that love is perished?

              "Passer Mortuus Est" n.d.

1633. Ruth Suckow (1892–1960)

1 To have someone tell his boys to do this and that! To take away
  his help on the farm just when he needed it most! To have somebody just step in and tell him where they had to go! Was that
  what happened in this country? Why had his people left the old
  country, then if things were going to be just the same?
              Pt. II, Ch. 4, *Country People 1924*

2 All women were that way—except his mother and sister and
  aunt, whom he unconsciously excluded (since they need not
  count in the way of desire) and did not place under the head of
  "Woman." He scorned, so he thought, all that had to do with
  them, and declared only "men's books" worth reading—adventure, travel; scorned "Woman" for not having brains, and
  despised the ones who had,
              Pt. IV, Ch. 2, *The Odyssey of a Nice Girl 1925*

3 To most of the people it [World War I] had seemed far away,
  something that could never come close. Some resented it, others seized upon it now to help break up the long monotony of
  everyday living—more terribly thrilling than a fire in the business district, a drowning in the river, or the discovery that the
  cashier of the Farmers' Bank had been embezzling. Something
  had come, it seemed, to shake up that placid, solid, comfortable life of home, changing things around, shifting values that
  had seemed to be fixed.
                              Ch. 3, Ibid.

4 That would be the most terrible thing of all, if she began to
  forget. Then her heart would have to close. Yes, but if she kept
  it open, to feel the happiness, then she would have to feel the
  rest, too. . . . She would have to feel again, like blows on her
  open heart, every cruel detail of Harold's suffering, and the
  awful blank fact of his death.
              "Experience," *Children and Other People 1931*

5 Exercises, songs and recitations—pieces by children whose
  mothers would be offended if they were left off the program:
  good or bad, the audience clapped.
              "Eminence," Ibid.

1634. Vita Sackville-West (1892–1962)

1 So prodigal was I of youth,
  Forgetting I was young;
  I worshipped dead men for their strength,
  Forgetting I was strong.
              "MCMXIII," St. 1, *Poems of West and East 1917*

2 We have tasted space and freedom, frontiers falling as we
  went,
  Now with narrow bonds and limits, never could we be content,
  For we have abolished boundaries, straitened borders we rent,
  And a house no more confines us than the roving nomads' tent.
              "Nomads," St. 6, Ibid.

3 For observe, that to hope for Paradise is to live in Paradise, a
  very different thing from actually getting there.
              Ch. 1, *Passenger to Teheran 1926*

4 Travel is the most private of pleasure. There is no greater bore
  than the traveller to bore. We do not in the least want to hear
  what he has seen in Hong-Kong.
                              Ibid.

5 This question of horizon, however; how important it is; how it alters the shape of the mind; how it expresses, essentially, one's ultimate sense of country! That is what can never be told in words: the exact size, proportion, contour; the new standard to which the mind must adjust itself.

Ch. 4, Ibid.

6 If you are wise you will not look upon the long period of time thus occupied in actual movement as the mere gulf dividing you from the end of your journey, but rather as one of those rare and plastic seasons of your life from which, perhaps, in after times, you may love to date the moulding of your character—that is, your very identity. Once feel this, and you will soon grow happy and contented in you saddle home.

Ch. 6, Ibid.

7 . . . besides, the fingers which had once grown accustomed to a pen soon itched to hold one again: it is necessary to write, if the days are not to slip emptily by. How else, indeed, to clap the net over the butterfly of the moment? for the moment passes, it is forgotten; the mood is gone; life itself is gone. That is where the writer scores over his fellows: he catches the changes of his mind on the hop. Growth is exciting; growth is dynamic and alarming. Growth of the soul, growth of the mind. . . .

Ch. 1, *Twelve Days* 1928

8 Those who have never dwelt in tents have no idea either of the charm or of the discomfort of a nomadic existence. The charm is purely romantic, and consequently very soon proves to be fallacious.

Ch. 6, Ibid.

9 Perhaps it would be better to go the whole hog and cut oneself off entirely from the outside world. A merely negative form of protest, I feel, against conditions one does not like; for resentment is vain unless one has an alternative to offer. Flight is no alternative; it is only a personal solution. But as a personal experiment it certainly offers material for reflection to the curious.

Ch. 15, Ibid.

10 If this is Society, thought Anguetil, God help us, for surely no fraud has ever equalled it.

Ch. 1, *The Edwardians* 1930

11 Among the many problems which beset the novelist, not the least weighty is the choice of the moment at which to begin his novel.

Ibid.

12 All the world of feminine voluptuousness seemed to be gathered up and released in that one divine curving of the loosened lips. There was no humour in it, but there was an indescribable caress.

Ch. 3, Ibid.

13 For a young man to start his career with a love affair with an older woman was quite *de rigueur*. . . . Of course, it must not go on too long.

Ibid.

14 The inner knowledge that he was behaving not only badly but histrionically increased his obstinacy. He was acutely ashamed of himself, since, for the first time in his life, he saw himself through other eyes; and saw his selfishness, his self-indulgence, his arrogance, his futile philandering, for what they were worth. Still, he would not give way.

Ch. 4, Ibid.

15 Click, clack, click, clack, went their conversation, like so many knitting-needles, purl, plain, purl, plain, achieving a complex pattern of references, cross-references, Christian names, nicknames, and fleeting allusions. . . .

Ch. 6, Ibid.

16 And as her legal authority shrivelled, so did her personal authority turn suddenly into a thing which had never enjoyed any real existence.

Ch. 7, Ibid.

17 Men do kill women. Most women enjoy being killed; so I'm told.

All Passion Spent 1931

18 Now to my little death the pestering clock
Beckons—but who would sleep when he might wake?

"Solitude" 1938

19 It is very necessary to have makers of beauty left in a world seemingly bent on making the most evil ugliness.

Country Notes 1940

20 Nothing shows up the difference between the things said or read, so much as the daily experience of it.

Ibid.

21 I have grown wise, after many years of gardening, and no longer order recklessly from wildly alluring descriptions which make every annual sound easy to grow and as brilliant as a film star. I now know that gardening is not like that.

"January," *In Your Garden Again* 1953

22 I have come to the conclusion, after many years of sometimes sad experience, that you cannot come to any conclusion at all.

"May," Ibid.

23 Ambition, old as mankind, the immemorial weakness of the strong.

No Signposts in the Sea 1961

24 "It is lucky for some people," I say to Laura, "that they can live behind their own faces."

Ibid.

25 When, and how, and at what stage of our development did spirituality and our strange notions of religion arise? the need for worship which is nothing more than our frightened refuge into propitiation of a Creator we do not understand? A detective story, the supreme Who-done-it, written in indecipherable hieroglyphics, no Rosetta stone supplied, by the consummate mystifier to tease us poor fumbling unravellers of his plot.

Ibid.

26 My whole curse has been a duality with which I was too weak and too self-indulgent to struggle.

Quoted in *Portrait of a Marriage* by Nigel Nicolson* 1973
*Her son.

27 Women, like men, ought to have their youth so glutted with freedom they hate the very idea of freedom.

Letter to her husband, diplomat and author Harold Nicolson (1 June 1919), Ibid.

28 You have met and understood me on every point. It is this which binds me to you through every storm, and makes you so unalterably the one person whom I trust and love.

(1 November 1919), Ibid.

29 . . . I hold the conviction that as centuries go on, and the sexes become more nearly merged on account of their increasing resemblances, I hold the conviction that such connections will to a very large extent cease to be regarded as merely unnatural, and will be understood far better, at least in their *intellectual* if not in their physical aspects.
"Autobiography" (27 September 1920), Ibid.

30 Since "unnatural" means "removed from nature," only the most civilized, because the least natural, class of society can be expected to tolerate such a product of civilization.
Ibid.

31 I advance, therefore, the perfectly accepted theory that cases of dual personality do exist, in which the feminine and masculine elements alternately preponderate. I advance this in an impersonal and scientific spirit, and claim that I am qualified to speak with the intimacy a professional scientist could acquire only after years of study and indirect information, because I have the object of study always at hand, in my own heart.
Ibid.

32 Things were not tragic for us then, because although we cared passionately we didn't care deeply.
(29 September 1920), Ibid.

33 Of course I wish now that I had never made these discoveries. One doesn't miss what one doesn't know, and now life is made wretched by privations. I often long for ignorance and innocence.
Ibid.

1635. Ivy Compton-Burnett (1892–1969)

1 "But a gentlewoman is not able to spin gold out of straw; it required a full princess to do that."
Ch. 1, *A House and Its Head 1935*

2 "We do not discuss the members of our family to their faces. . . ."
Ch. 11, Ibid.

3 "It is no good to think that other people are out to serve our interests."
Ch. 1, *Elders and Betters 1944*

4 "It is a lonely business, waiting to be translated to another sphere."
Ch. 7, Ibid.

5 "The relationship is only a shadow, but a shadow is not always easy to elude."
Ch. 3, *Two Worlds and Their Ways 1949*

6 "I do like approving of things. It is disapproving of them that is disturbing."
Ch. 4, Ibid.

7 "We will let the dead past bury its dead, and go back to the old days and the old ways and the old happiness."
Ch. 5, Ibid.

8 "Parents have too little respect for their children, just as the children have too much for the parents. . . ."
Ibid.

9 "We can build upon foundations anywhere, if they are well and truly laid."
Ch. 7, Ibid.

10 "If I were not a child with my parents, they would be more unloving towards me," said Gwendolen.
Ibid.

11 "My youth is escaping without giving me anything it owes me."
Ch. 1, *A Heritage and Its History 1959*

12 "There is no change. That is your trouble. You want me to be altered by my father's death. And I have not been, and shall not be. I am what I am."
Ch. 3, Ibid.

13 "Civilised life exacts its toll."
Ch. 9, Ibid.

14 "A thing is not nothing, when it is all there is."
Ch. 10, Ibid.

15 "There is no need to act on a truth that might never have emerged. It would not have in most cases, should not have, to my mind. Many must lie unsaid. We can put it from us and go forward."
Ibid.

16 "She should be thinking of higher things."
"Nothing could be higher than food," said Leah.
Ch. 1, *The Mighty and Their Fall 1961*

17 "Destiny is over all of us, high or low."
Ch. 2, Ibid.

18 "They must release each other in time for their lives to grow."
Ch. 3, Ibid.

19 "You and Ninian will have each other," said Hugo. "That foolish thing that is said, when that is all people have. As if they did not know it! It is the whole trouble."
"It is not only trouble," said Ninian, smiling at Teresa. "Or it is trouble shared and therefore less."
Ch. 13, Ibid.

20 I have had such an uneventful life that there is little to say.
A Family and a Fortune 1962

21 Life makes great demands on people's characters, and gives them great opportunities to serve their own ends by the sacrifice of other people. Such ill doing may meet with little retribution, may indeed be hardly recognized, and I cannot feel so surprised if people yield to it.
Quoted in *The Life of Ivy Compton-Burnett* by Elizabeth Sprigge *1973*

22 When an age is ended you see it as it is.
Ibid.

1636. Pearl S. Buck (1892–1973)

1 It is better to be first with an ugly woman than the hundredth with a beauty.
Ch. 1, *The Good Earth 1931*

2 "We will eat meat that we can buy or beg, but not that which we steal. Beggars we may be but thieves we are not."
Ch. 12, Ibid.

3 "Hunger makes a thief of any man."
Ch. 15, Ibid.

4 "I do not need to tell you that there are no honorable rulers, and the people cry out under the cruelties and oppression of those who ought to treat them as fathers treat their sons."

Sons 1932

5 "Now we revolutionists are against every sort of god; our own or foreign, we are against them all and someday we will tear down temples, we will tear down gods. But if men in their ignorance must believe for a while in some god, let it be their own and not a foreign superstition such as these preach."

Ch. 6, *The Young Revolutionist 1932*

6 "Men do not take good iron to make nails nor good men to make soldiers."

Ch. 8, Ibid.

7 "There was an old abbot in one temple and he said something of which I think often and it was this, that when men destroy their old gods they will find new ones to take their place."

Ch. 15, Ibid.

8 Man was lost if he went to a usurer, for the interest ran faster than a tiger upon him...

"The Frill," *First Wife and Other Stories 1933*

9 "A woman must learn to obey. We must not ask why. We cannot help our birth. We must accept it and do the duty that is ours in this lifetime."

"The First Wife," Ibid.

10 "But that land—it is one thing that will still be there when I come back—land is always there.

Ch. 1, *A House Divided 1935*

11 They were all trying so hard to live as they felt it beautiful to live, and their houses were so small—too small and too close, so that they had constantly to hush the crying of their children and their own laughter or anger or weeping as well. They had only silence to keep them private from each other. And they needed privacy, since they were not ignorant people and since decency was a necessity to them. They could make a joke of poverty and did.

Ch. 1, *The Proud Heart 1938*

12 Travel, the casual come and go of strange faces, people for whom she cared nothing and who did not care for her, these were not her life. She had to live not in that passing world but in her own deeps.

Ch. 2, Ibid.

13 You who have already so recognized your own Selma Lagerlöf,* and have long recognized women in other fields, cannot perhaps wholly understand what it means in many countries that it is a woman who stands here at this moment. But I speak not only for writers and for women, but for all Americans, for we all share in this.

Acceptance speech, Nobel Prize Awards (Stockholm) *1938*
*See 1183.

14 The minds of my own country and of China, my foster country, are alike in many ways, but above all, alike in our common love of freedom. And today more than ever, this is true, now when China's whole being is engaged in the greatest of all struggles, the struggle for freedom.

Ibid.

15 Freedom—it is today more than ever the most precious human possession.

Ibid.

16 I feel no need for any other faith than my faith in human beings.

I Believe 1939

17 There were many ways of breaking a heart. Stories were full of hearts broken by love, but what really broke a heart was taking away its dream—whatever that dream might be.

Pt. II, *The Patriot 1939*

18 "We shall fight until all anti-Japanese feeling is stamped out and the Chinese are ready to cooperate with us."

I-wan stared at him, not believing what he heard.

"You mean," he repeated, "you will kill us and bomb our cities—and—and—rape our women—until we learn to love you?"

Ibid.

19 . . . the basic discovery about any people is the discovery of the relationship between its men and women.

Ch. 1, *Of Men and Women 1941*

20 When hope is taken away from the people moral degeneration follows swiftly after.

Letter to the Editor, *The New York Times 14 November 1941*

21 None who have always been free can understand the terrible fascinating power of the hope of freedom to those who are not free.

What America Means to Me 1942

22 Every era of renaissance has come out of new freedoms for peoples. The coming renaissance will be greater than any in human history, for this time all the peoples of the earth will share in it.

Introduction, Ibid.

23 Race prejudice is not only a shadow over the colored—it is a shadow over all of us, and the shadow is darkest over those who feel it least and allow its evil effects to go on.

Ch. 1, Ibid.

24 Every great mistake has a halfway moment, a split second when it can be recalled and perhaps remedied.

Ch. 10, Ibid.

25 But when you remember the suffering, which you have not deserved, do not think of vengeance, as the small man does. Remember, rather, as the great remember, that which they have unjustly suffered, and determine only that such suffering shall not be possible again for any human being anywhere.

"A Letter to Colored Americans," *American Unity and Asia 1942*

26 One faces the future with one's past. . . .

Lecture, "China Faces the Future," New York *14 March 1942*

27 For our democracy has been marred by imperialism, and it has been enlightened only by individual and sporadic efforts at freedom.

Speech, "Freedom for All" (New York) *14 March 1942*

28 I remember as a child hearing my impatient missionary father . . . [as] he explained to an elderly Chinese gentlemen, "Does it mean nothing to you that if you reject Christ you will burn in hell?"

The Chinese gentleman smiled as he replied, "If, as you say, my ancestors are all in hell at this moment, it would be unfilial of me not to be willing to suffer with them."

Speech, "The Chinese Mind and India" (Boston) *28 April 1942*

29 There is no one way of dividing us. We are different races, and that is a division. We are of different nations, and that is a division. Religion is a division, and wealth is a division, and education is a division. Climate and geography and food have their dividing effects, and so has history. But war is the great simplifier.

"The Spirit Behind the Weapon," *Survey Graphics*
November 1942

30 Fate proceeds inexorably . . . only upon the passive individual, the passive people. . . . Fate may be foreseen unacknowledged.
Address to Nobel Prize Winners (New York) *10 December 1942*

31 "Who knows what you'll tell?" Wang Ma said severely.
"I never tell anything I know," Peony said demurely.
Wang Ma put down the bowl. "What do you know?" she inquired.
"Now you want me to tell," Peony said, smiling.
Ch. 1, *The Bondsmaid 1949*

32 "Believing in gods always causes confusion."
Ibid.

33 She had been too wise to tell him all she thought and felt, knowing by some intuition of her own womanhood, that no man wants to know everything of any woman.
Ch. 4, Ibid.

34 Endurance can be a harsh and bitter root in one's life, bearing poisonous and gloomy fruit, destroying other lives. Endurance is only the beginning. There must be acceptance and the knowledge that sorrow fully accepted brings its own gifts. For there is an alchemy in sorrow. It can be transmuted into wisdom. . . .
Ch. 1, *The Child Who Never Grew 1950*

35 Americans are all too soft. I am not soft. It is better to be hard, so that you can know what to do.
Ibid.

36 Ours is an individualistic society, indeed, and the state must do for the individual what the family does for the older civilizations.
Ch. 2, Ibid.

37 Euthanasia is a long, smooth-sounding word, and it conceals its danger as long, smooth words do, but the danger is there, nevertheless.
Ibid.

38 Children who never grow are human beings, and suffer as human beings, inarticulately but deeply nevertheless. The human creature is always more than an animal.
Ch. 3, Ibid.

39 Introversion, at least if extreme, is a sign of mental and spiritual immaturity.
"In Search of Readers," *The Writer's Book*, Helen Hull, ed.
1950

40 There are people who honestly do not see the use of books in the home, either for information—have they not radio and even television?—or for decoration—is there not wallpaper?
Ibid.

41 The average person, fool that he often is, interests and amuses me more than the rare and extraordinary individual. The ways of common people are enchanting and funny and profound.
Ibid.

42 We had no police and needed none, because the family was responsible for all its members. . . . The child in Asia is loved not only for its own sake but as a symbol of hope for the future of both family and nation.
Ch. 1, *Children for Adoption 1964*

43 The American woman, when she is an unmarried mother, simply disappears for a while from her community and then comes back, childless, her secret hidden for life.
Ibid.

44 What is a neglected child? He is a child not planned for, not wanted. Neglect begins, therefore, before he is born.
Ch. 3, Ibid.

45 The community must assume responsibility for each child within its confines. Not one must be neglected whatever his condition. The community must see that every child gets the advantages and opportunities which are due him as a citizen and as a human being.
Ch. 4, Ibid.

46 The problem of the mixed-race child, born displaced in the world community, must be faced in its entirety. It can be no credit to the United States to have half-American children running about as beggars and potential criminals in the streets of Asian cities and on the islands of the Pacific.
Ch. 7, Ibid.

47 If our American way of life fails the child, it fails us all.
Ch. 9, Ibid.

48 Praise out of season, or tactlessly bestowed, can freeze the heart as much as blame.
"First Meeting," *To My Daughters, With Love 1967*

49 The bitterest creature under heaven is the wife who discovers that her husband's bravery is only bravado, that his strength is only a uniform, that his power is but a gun in the hands of a fool.
"Love and Marriage," Ibid.

50 It is indeed exasperating to have a memory that begins too young and continues too long. I know, because this is my memory. It goes back too far, it holds everything too fast, it does not forget anything—a relentless, merciless, disobedient memory, for there are some things I would like to forget. But I never forget.
Ch. 1, *China, Past and Present 1972*

51 Nothing and no one can destroy the Chinese people. They are relentless survivors. They are the oldest civilized people on earth. Their civilization passes through phases but its basic characteristics remain the same. They yield, they bend to the wind, but they never break.
Ibid.

52 Ah well, perhaps one has to be very old before one learns how to be amused rather than shocked.
Ch. 6, Ibid.

53 No one really understood music unless he was a scientist, her father had declared, and not just a scientist, either, oh, no, only the real ones, the theoreticians, whose language was mathematics. She had not understood mathematics until he had explained to her that it was the symbolic language of relationships. "And relationships," he had told her, "contained the essential meaning of life."
Pt. I, *The Goddess Abides 1972*

54 I contemplate death as though I were continuing after its arrival. I, therefore, survive since I can contemplate myself afterward as well as before.

Ibid.

55 "A hand is not only an implement, it's a sense organ. It's the eye of a blind man, it's the tone of those who cannot speak."

Pt. II, Ibid.

56 Be born anywhere, little embryo novelist, but do not be born under the shadow of a great creed, not under the burden of original sin, nor under the doom of salvation.

"Advice to Unborn Novelists" *n.d.*

57 Go out and be born among gypsies or thieves or among happy workaday people who live with the sun and do not think about their souls.

Ibid.

1637. Janet Flanner (1892–1978)

1 Paris is now the capital of limbo.
"Paris, Germany," *The New Yorker* 7 December 1940

2 The German passion for bureaucracy—for written and signal forms, for files, statistics, and lists, and for printed permissions to do this or that, to go here or there, to move about, to work, to exist—is like a steel pin pinning each French individual to a sheet of paper, the way an entomologist pins each specimen insect past struggling to his laboratory board.

Ibid.

3 Never have nights been more beautiful than these nights of anxiety. In the sky have been shining in trinity the moon, Venus and Mars. Nature has been more splendid than man.
"Letter from Paris," Ibid.

4 In place of certainty there is only a vast, tangled ball of rumor. In place of sensible, humane procedure, now destroyed by wars, revenge, suspicion and power politics, petty official strictures have been built up against which the individual is as helpless as a caged animal.
"The Escape of Mrs. Jeffries," Ibid.

5 By jove, no wonder women don't love war nor understand it, nor can operate in it as a rule; it takes a man to suffer what other men have invented . . . Women have invented nothing in all that, except the men who were born as male babies and grew up to be men big enough to be killed fighting.
Letter to Natalia Danesi Murray (1944), *Darlinghissima: Letters to a Friend* 1985

1638. Djuna Barnes (1892–1982)

1 She knew what was troubling him, thwarted instincts, common beautiful instincts that he was being robbed of.
"A Night Among the Horses," *The Little Review* 1918

2 She wanted to be the reason for everything and so was the cause of nothing.

Nightwood 1936

3 She defied the very meaning of personality in her passion to be a person.

Ibid.

4 No man needs curing of his individual sickness; his universal malady is what he should look to.

Ibid.

5 No, I am not a neurasthenic; I haven't that much respect for people—the basis, by the way, of all neurasthenia.

Ibid.

6 Dreams have only the pigmentation of fact.

Ch. 5, Ibid.

7 The heart of the jealous knows the best and most satisfying love, that of the other's bed, where the rival perfects the lover's imperfections.

Ibid.

8 The night is a skin pulled over the head of day that the day may be in torment.

Ibid.

9 Sleep demands of us a guilty immunity. There is not one of us who, given an eternal incognito, a thumbprint nowhere set against our souls, would not commit rape, murder and all abominations.

Ibid.

10 I'm a fart in a gale of wind, a humble violet, under a cow pat.

Ibid.

11 We are beginning to wonder whether a servant girl hasn't the best of it after all. She knows how the salad tastes without the dressing, and she knows how life's lived before it gets to the parlor door.
"The Home Club: For Servants Only," (*Brooklyn Daily Eagle*, 12 October 1913), *Djuna Barnes's New York* 1989

12 New York is the meeting place of the peoples, the only city where you can hardly find a typical American.
"Greenwich Village As It Is" (*Pearson's Magazine*, October 1916), Ibid.

1639. Rebecca West (1892–1983)

1 I myself have never been able to find out precisely what feminism is: I only know that people call me a feminist whenever I express sentiments that differentiate me from a doormat.
(1913), Quoted in Introduction, *Backlash: The Undeclared War Against American Women* by Susan Faludi* 1991
*See 3455.

2 Literature must be an analysis of experience and a synthesis of the findings into a unity.

Ending in Earnest 1931

3 When a book of great literary merit is denounced the first line of defense always is to point out that that kind of book, which conscientiously analyzes a human experience and gives its findings honestly, cannot do those who read it any harm, since it adds to the knowledge of reality by which man lives.
"Concerning the Censorship," Ibid.

4 Yes, if an age would deal fairly well with its children and let them do what they can!
"*Manibus Date Lilia Plenis*," Ibid.

5 Infantilism is not a happy state. The childhood of the individual and the race is full of fears, and panic-stricken attempts to avert what is feared by placating the gods with painful sacrifices.
"Journey's End," Ibid.

6 Most works of art, like most wines, ought to be consumed in the district of their fabrication.

"Journey's End Again," Ibid.

7 "That's what's wrong with us!" he exclaimed, getting up and walking about the room. "We can't talk. Nobody but writers know how to put things into words, and everybody goes around stuffed up with things they want to say and can't." It seemed to him that he had put his finger on the secret of all human sorrow.

Life Sentence 1935

8 It was true that her avarice operated continuously, collecting from him jewels and furs over and above her regular allowance at regular periods, but as at the beginning it was always as nicely calculated in relation to his means as if she had a highly-paid statistician working for her.

The Abiding Vision 1935

9 "We're on a permanent plateau of prosperity. There's never been anything like it before. It's America."

Ibid.

10 "The point is that nobody likes having salt rubbed into their wounds, even if it is the salt of the earth."

Ch. 2, *The Salt of the Earth 1935*

11 "But then what did you want me to forgive you for?"

"I want you to forgive me for being mean," he said, "and having to be what I am, and do what I have done." A smile passed over his lips. "Just as you might ask me to forgive you for being you."

Ibid.

12 "Why must you always try to be omnipotent, and shove things about? Tragic things happen sometimes that we just have to submit to."

Ibid.

13 It is queer how it is always one's virtues and not one's vices that precipitate one into disaster.

Ch. 1, *There Is No Conversation 1935*

14 There is no such thing as conversation. It is an illusion. There are intersecting monologues, that is all.

"The Harsh Voice," Sct. 1, *Ibid.*

15 It appears that even the different parts of the same person do not converse among themselves, do not succeed in learning from each other what are their desires and their intentions.

Ch. 2, *Ibid.*

16 . . . exchanging platitudes, as Frenchmen do, for the pleasure of feeling their mouths full of the good meat of common sense.

Ch. 3, *The Thinking Reed 1936*

17 In England and America a beard usually means that its owner would rather be considered venerable than virile; on the continent of Europe it often means that its owner makes a special claim to virility.

Ch. 10, *Ibid.*

18 All good biography, as all good fiction, comes down to the study of original sin, of our inherent disposition to choose death when we ought to choose life.

Time and Tide 1941

19 There is . . . the mystic who went into the desert because his head was so full of ideas about the spiritual world that everyday talk was in his ears as a barrel-organ playing outside a concert-hall is to a musician, the mystic who does not want to eat or drink or sleep with women because that is to take time

off from the ecstatic pleasure of pursuing the ramifications of good and evil through his bosom and through the universe . . . If a naked woman appeared before him, she would not be a temptation but an offence, offending as a person in a library who begins chatting to a student who has found a long-sought reference a few minutes before closing time. Life is not long enough for these men to enjoy the richness of their own perceptions, to transmute them into wisdom.

"Old Serbia," *Black Lamb and Grey Falcon 1941*

20 But there are other things than dissipation that thicken the features. Tears, for example.

"Serbia," *Ibid.*

21 We all drew on the comfort which is given out by the major works of Mozart, which is as real and material as the warmth given up by a glass of brandy.

Ibid.

22 There is no wider gulf in the universe than yawns between those on the hither and thither side of vital experience.

Ibid.

23 But the Slav knows . . . that life . . . is an essence unpredictable, that she often produces events for which there are no apt prescription, and that she can be as slippery as an eel when wise men attempt to control her; and they know that it is life, not power or authority, that gives us joy, and this often when she is least predictable.

"Dalmatia," *Ibid.*

24 Now different races and nationalities cherish different ideals of society that stink in each other's nostrils with an offensiveness beyond the power of any by the most monstrous private deed.

Epilogue, *Ibid.*

25 The intellectual world is largely of English creation, yet our authors write of ideas as if they were things to pick and choose, even though the choice might be pushed to the extremity of martyrdom, as if they could be left alone, as if they came into play only as they were picked and chosen. But that ideas are the symbols of relationships among real forces that make people late for breakfast, that take away their breakfast, that makes them beat each other across the breakfast-table, is something which the English do not like to realize. Lazy, bone-lazy, they wish to believe that life is lived simply by living.

Ibid.

26 All the world over, the most good-natured find enjoyment in those who miss trains or sit down on frozen pavements.

"A Day in the Town," *The New Yorker 25 January 1941*

27 Just how difficult it is to write biography can be reckoned by anybody who sits down and considers just how many people know the real truth about his or her love affairs.

"The Art of Skepticism," *Vogue (New York 1 November 1952*

28 . . . any authentic work of art must start an argument between the artist and his audience.

Pt. I, Ch. 1, *The Court and the Castle 1957*

29 But humanity is never more sphinx-like than when it is expressing itself.

Pt. II, Ch. 1, *Ibid.*

30 It is so difficult to become a specialist that the mediocre man has been very eager to cry wolf to the specialist, often before it was actually necessary.

Speech, "McLuhan and the Future of Literature" *1969*

31 I cannot think that espionage can be recommended as a technique for building an impressive civilisation. It's a lout's game.
Introduction, *The Meaning of Treason* 1949 rev. *1982*

32 Men must be capable of imagining and executing and insisting on social change if they are to reform or even maintain civilization, and capable too of furnishing the rebellion which is sometimes necessary if society is not to perish of immobility.
Pt. 4, "Conclusion," Ibid.

33 All men should have a drop of treason in their veins, if nations are not to go soft like so many sleepy pears.
Ibid.

34 He is every other inch a gentleman.*
Pt. 3, Ch. 5, Quoted in *Rebecca West: A Life*
by Victoria Glendinning *1987*
*Reference to Bulgarian-born English novelist Michael Arlen (1895–1956).

35 Motherhood is the strangest thing, it can be like being one's own Trojan horse.
Pt. 5, Ch. 8, Letter (20 August 1959), Ibid.

36 Everyone realizes that one can believe little of what people say about each other. But it is not so widely realized that even less can one trust what people say about themselves.
Quoted in *Sunday Telegraph* (London, 1975), Epigraph, Ibid.

1640. Brenda Ueland (1892–1985)

1 Everybody is talented, original and has something important to say.
Ch. 1, *If You Want To Write 1938*

2 You know how all children have this creative power. You have all seen things like this: the little girls in our family used to give play after play. . . . these small ten-year-olds were working with feverish energy and endurance. . . . If they had worked that hard for school it probably would have killed them. They were working for nothing but fun, for that glorious inner excitement. It was the creative power working in them. It was hard, hard work but there was no pleasure or excitement like it and it was something never forgotten
Ibid.

3 For when you come to think of it, the only way to love a person is not, as the stereotyped Christian notion is, to coddle them and bring them soup when they are sick, but by listening to them and seeing and believing in the god, in the poet, in them. For by doing this, you keep the god and the poet alive and make it flourish.
Ibid.

4 . . . orthodox criticism . . . is a murderer of talent. And because the most modest and sensitive people are the most talented, having the most imagination and sympathy, these are the first ones to get killed off. It is the brutal egotists that survive.
Ibid.

5 Self-trust is so important. When you launch on a story, make your neck loose, feel free, good-natured. And be lazy. Feel that you are going to throw it away. Try writing utterly unplanned stories and see what comes out.
Ch. 16, Ibid.

6 When we are listened to, it creates us, makes us unfold and expand. Ideas actually begin to grow within us and come to life.
Strength to Your Sword Arm 1993

1641. Diana Cooper (1892–1986)

1 Naturally good until now, I had never lied, for nothing tempted me to lie except fear of wounding and I had nothing to fear. But now with the advent of the young men—benign serpents—came the apple . . . Childhood was over.
Ch. 5, *The Rainbow Comes and Goes 1958*

2 In astrology there is room for precaution and obstruction; the disaster is not inevitable. One can dodge the stars in their courses.
Trumpets from the Steep 1960

3 Childhood is stamped on the fair face of one's uncluttered memory as clearly as morning, and a heart beating with love, enterprise and procreancy seemed recordable, but when I come to armies clashing in the dark, to destruction, to the rulers and their strength, shortcomings or ambivalence . . . I am lost in a rabble of stampeding thought that can never be rounded up.
Ch. 2, Ibid.

4 It helped me in the air to keep my small mind contained in earthly human limits, not lost in vertiginous space and elements unknown.
Ch. 5, Ibid.

5 I'll write no more memories. They would get too sad, tender as they are. Age wins and one must learn to grow old. As I learnt with the loss of a nurse to put childish things behind me, as I learnt when the joys of dependence were over to embrace with fear the isolation of independence, so now I must learn to walk this long unlovely wintry way, looking for spectacles, shunning the cruel looking-glass, laughing at my clumsiness before others mistakenly condole, not expecting gallantry yet disappointed to receive none, apprehending every ache or shaft of pain, alive to blinding flashes of mortality, unarmed, totally vulnerable.
Ch. 8, Ibid.

1642. Lillian Day (1893–?)

1 A lady is one who never shows her underwear unintentionally.
Kiss and Tell 1931

1643. Marie Gilchrist (1893–?)

1 But the life of poetry lies in fresh relationships between words, in the spontaneous fusion of hitherto unrelated words.
Ch. 1, *Writing Poetry 1932*

2 All American Indian poems are songs, and an Indian was once asked which came first, the words or the music. "They come together," he replied.
Ch. 3, Ibid.

3 Nouns and verbs are almost pure metal; adjectives are cheaper ore.
Quoted in "On the Teaching of Poetry" by Leonora Speyer,*
The Saturday Review of Literature 1946
*See 1329.

1644. Margery Eldredge Howell (1893–1946)

1 There's dignity in suffering—
Nobility in pain—
But failure is a salted wound
That burns and burns again.
"Wormwood" *n.d.*

1645. Emily Beatrix Jones (1893–?)

1 The pools of art and memory keep
Reflections of our fallen towers,
And every princess there asleep,
Whom once we kissed, is always ours.

"Middle-Age" n.d.

1646. Hesper Le Gallienne (1893–?)

1 The loose foot of the wanderer
Is curst as well as blest!
It urges ever, ever on
And never gives him rest.

"The Wanderer" n.d.

1647. Laura Frost Smith (1893–?)

1 No one at home has the faintest idea how they are getting
killed [here]. . . . I'm sure no one realizes the suffering of the
boys. It's their spirit that affects me. I can watch them ampu-
tate a leg and dress a wound that is open from the hip down,
but when a boy tells you he is sorry he lost [his leg] because it
puts him out and he can't go back, well I have to walk away.

Letter, cited in "Witness to War" by Carol Smith, *Seattle
Post-Intelligencer*, E1-5 *24 September 1998*

2 At the end of my ward there were several wounded German
prisoners, young towheaded, blue-eyed boys. A guard stood
over them with a .45. Having American and German patients
together brought home the fact of how stupid any war is.

Ibid.

3 Finally, one day, the 11th of November,* everything became
quiet about 11 a.m. And you wondered what was different.
There wasn't a sound, for there were no birds to sing, or no
cows to moo. We still couldn't believe it possible, as we had so
many patients. A group of French trumpeters came in the afternoon and played for us, so that was the only celebration we
had.

Ibid.

*Armistice Day, 1918; the end of World War I.

4 [On hearing her home town was displaying a flag for the
nurses:] I'm glad someone appreciates the nurses. The patients
are the only ones here that do. . . . We just have to fight for our
very existence here.

Ibid.

5 It really was a wonderful parade. . . . They didn't say much
about the nurses in it. We thought we were the whole show.
They just said 400 [women] marched and there were at least
1,400. It is funny, because a paper usually exaggerates so much.

Letter (6 July 1918), cited in "Witness to War"
by Carol Smith,* *Ibid.*

*Carol Smith is the granddaughter of Laura Frost Smith.

1648. Dora Carrington (1893–1932)

1 Yesterday evening I spent mending my patchwork counter-
pane, with more patches. I think it's a strangely romantic
occupation—these faded pieces of cotton, twenty, or fifty years
ago the print dress of some lovely welsh servant, the frock of a
young girl of fifteen, the pinafore of a little girl of six, the
apron of a plain fat girl in a Baker's shop, the petticoat of Mrs.
Slater's mother...the purple flowered drawers of Mrs. Slater's
niece who died when she was twelve...

Letter to Gerald Grenan, Quoted in *The Art of
Dora Carrington* by Jane Hill *1994*

1649. Helen Hathaway (1893–1932)

1 More tears have been shed over men's lack of manners than
their lack of morals.

Manners for Men n.d.

1650. Dorothy L. Sayers (1893–1957)

1 "A man goes and fights for his country, gets his insides gassed
out, and loses his job, and all they give him is the privilege of
marching past the Cenotaph once a year and paying four
shillings in the pound income-tax."

Ch. 1, *The Unpleasantness at the Bellona Club 1928*

2 The planet's tyrant, dotard Death, had held his gray mirror before them for a moment and shown them the image of things
to come.

Ch. 2, *Ibid.*

3 "I'm determined never to be a parent. Modern manners and
the break-up of the fine old traditions have simply ruined the
business. I shall devote my life and fortune to the endowment
of research on the best method of producing human beings
decorously and unobtrusively from eggs. All parental responsibility to devolve upon the incubator."

Ch. 3, *Ibid.*

4 "Very dangerous things, theories."

Ch. 4, *Ibid.*

5 "But I don't believe women ever get sensible, not even through
prolonged association with their husbands."

Ch. 8, *Ibid.*

6 "And a continued atmosphere of hectic passion is very trying
if you haven't got any of your own."

Ch. 10, *Ibid.*

7 "I quite thought he was honest when he said he didn't believe
in marriage—and then it turned out that it was a test, to see
whether my devotion was abject enough.

Strong Poison 1930

8 Death seems to provide the minds of the Anglo-Saxon race with
a greater fund of amusement than any other single subject.

Introduction, *The Third Omnibus of Crime 1935*

9 "'If you want to set up your everlasting rest, you are far more
likely to find it in the life of the mind than any other subject. . . .'"

Gaudy Night 1936

10 "Once lay down the rule that the job comes first, and you
throw that job open to every individual . . . who is able to do
that job better than the rest of the world."

Ibid.

11 "A desire to have all the fun," he says, "is nine-tenths of the
law of chivalry."

Ibid.

12 "People who make some other person their job are dangerous."

Ibid.

13 "There is perhaps one human being in a thousand who is passionately interested in his job for the job's sake. The difference
is that if that one person in a thousand is a man, we say, simply, that he is passionately keen on his job; if she is a woman,
we say she is a freak."

Ibid.

14 ". . . of all devils let loose in the world there [is] no devil like devoted love. . . ."

Ibid.

15 ". . . love's a nervous, awkward, overmastering brute; if you can't rein him in it's best to have no truck with him."

Ibid.

16 ". . . a human being must have occupation if he or she is not to become a nuisance to the world."

Busman's Honeymoon 1947

17 The "passionate intellect" is really passionate. It is the only point at which ecstasy can enter.

Ibid.

18 "The only sin passion can commit is to be joyless."

Ibid.

19 "Except ye become as little children," except you can wake on your fiftieth birthday with the same forward-looking excitement and interest in life that you enjoyed when you were five, "ye cannot enter the kingdom of God." One must not only die daily, but every day we must be born again.

"Strong Meat," *Creed or Chaos? and Other Essays in Popular Mythology 1947*

20 "Many words have no legal meaning. Others have a legal meaning very unlike their ordinary meaning. For example, the word 'daffy-down-dilly.' It is a criminal libel to call a lawyer a 'daffy-down-dilly.' Ha! Yes, I advise you never to do such a thing. No, I certainly advise you *never* to do it."

Ch. 14, *Unnatural Death 1955*

21 "Contrast," philosophized Lord Peter sleepily, "is life. . . ."

Ch. 1, *Clouds of Witness 1956*

22 ". . . What? Sunday morning in an English family and no sausages? God bless my soul, what's the world coming to, eh . . . ?"

Ch. 2, Ibid.

23 "Lawyers enjoy a little mystery, you know. Why, if everybody came forward and told the truth, the whole truth, and nothing but the truth straight out, we should all retire to the workhouse."

Ch. 3, Ibid.

24 "She always says, my lord, that facts are like cows. If you look them in the face hard enough they generally run away."

Ch. 4, Ibid.

25 "But after all, what's money?"

"Nothing, of course," said Peter. "But if you've been brought up to havin' it, it's a bit awkward to drop it suddenly. Like baths, you know."

Ch. 7, Ibid.

26 ". . . And the w'y they speak—that took some getting's used to. Call that English, I useter say, give me the Frenchies in the Chantycleer Restaurong, I ses."

Ch. 11, Ibid.

27 "Well-bred English people never have imagination. . . ."

Ibid.

28 "Time and trouble will tame an advanced young woman, but an advanced old woman is uncontrollable by any earthly force."

Ch. 16, Ibid.

29 There is no waste with God. He cancels nothing but redeems all.

Quoted in *Dorothy L. Sayers: Her Life and Soul* by Barbara Reynolds *1993*

30 I am not to be called a fisher of men.

Ibid.

31 How do we say that God creates, and how does this compare with the act of creation by an artist?

Ibid.

32 . . . the lovely satisfying unity of things—the wedding of the thing learnt and the thing done—the great intellectual fulfillment.

Ibid.

33 . . . passionate flesh and passionate intellect fused together in. . .a furnace of the passionate spirit. . . . Dante is sublime, intellectual, and on occasion, grim; but we must also be prepared to find him simple, homely, humorous, tender and bubbling over with ecstasy.

Ibid.

34 This is what he [Dante]* thought reality was like, when got to the *eterna fontana* at the center of it: this laughter, this inebriation, this riot of charity and hilarity.

Ibid.

*Alighieri D—, Italian poet (1265–1321).

35 What we make is more important than what we are, particularly if making is our profession.

Letter to John Anthony, her son (c. 1930s), Ibid.

36 People are always imagining that if they get hold of the writer himself and, so to speak, shake him long enough and hard enough, something exciting and illuminating will drop out of him. But it doesn't. What's due to come out has come out, in the only form in which it ever can come out.

Ibid.

37 I have a foolish complex against allying myself publicly with anything labeled feminist. . . . The more clamor we make about "the women's point of view," the more we ram into people that the women's point of view is different, and frankly I do not think it is.

Letter to her agent (1936), Ibid.

38 If it were not for the war,
This war
Would suit me down to the ground.

"London Calling: Lord I Thank Thee" *n.d.*

39 . . . [detective fiction] softly persuades that love and hatred, poverty and unemployment, finance and international politics are problems capable of being dealt with and solved in the same manner as the death in the library.

"Problem Picture" (essay) *n.d.*

40 [In the mystery novel]. . .the murderer's motive has been detected, but nothing at all has been said about the healing of his murderous soul. . . . There is no solution to death. . . . Life intends to kill us.

Ibid.

41 The keeping of an idle woman is a badge of superior social status.

Essay *n.d.*

1651. Clara Thompson (1893–1958)

1 The women of past generations had no choice but to bear children. Since their lives were organized around this concept of duty, they seldom became aware of dislike of the situation, but there must have been many unwanted children then. Nowadays, when women have a choice, the illusion is to the effect that unwanted children are less common, but women still from neurotic compulsion bear children they cannot love.

> "The Role of Women in This Culture," *Psychology*, Vol. IV
> *1941*

2 The question that is raised in any study of change, whether by evolution or revolution, takes the form: Can one say that people are more benefitted or harmed?

> Ibid.

3 The question of her inferiority scarcely troubles her when her life is happily fulfilled, even though she lives in relative slavery.

> Ibid.

4 Sexual freedom [for women] can be an excellent instrument for the expression of neurotic drives arising outside the strictly sexual sphere, especially drives expressive of hostility to men, or of the desire to be a man. Thus promiscuity may mean the collecting of scalps with the hope of hurting men, frustrating them, or taking away their importance, or in another case it may mean to the woman that she is herself a man.

> Ibid.

5 Although this is a special group within the culture [the upper classes], it is an important group because, on the whole, it is a thinking group, nonconformist, and seeking to bring about changes in the cultural situation.

> Ibid.

6 Industry has been taken out of the home.

> Ibid.

7 People who have low self-esteem . . . have a tendency to cling to their own sex because it is less frightening.

> "Changing Concepts of Homosexuality in Psychoanalysis,"
> *A Study of Interpersonal Relations, New Contributions to Psychiatry*, Patrick Mullahy, ed. *1949*

8 The fact that one is married by no means proves that one is a mature person.

> Ibid.

1652. Evelyn Scott (1893–1963)

1 If I could only *feel* the child! I imagine the moment of its quickening as a sudden awakening of my own being which has never before had life. I want to *live* with the child, and I am as heavy as a stone.

> *Escapade 1913*

2 I realized a long time ago that a belief which does not spring from a conviction of the emotions is no belief at all.

> Ibid.

3 It is impossible to control creation.

> Ibid.

4 Inwardly shrinking and cold with an obscure fear, I make it a point to look very directly at all the men who speak to me. I want to shame them by the straightforwardness of my gaze.

> Ibid.

5 Yes, I want to be an outcast in order to realize fully what human beings are capable of. Now I know that fear and cruelty underlie all of society's protestations in favor of honesty and moral worth.

> Ibid.

6 To have one's individuality completely ignored is like being pushed quite out of life. Like being blown out as one blows out a light.

> Ibid.

7 He was too young to want milk but I held his face against my breast. In all my desire for him I was conscious of a heavy sensuality, a massiveness of appreciation.

> Ibid.

8 . . . pain is timeless, absolute. It has removed itself from space. It always has been and always will be for it exists independent of relations.

> Ibid.

9 People think that in order to give up financial security one must be intoxicated.

> Ibid.

10 If nobody recognizes me, then it is a sign that I have ceased to exist.

> Ibid.

1653. Dorothy Parker (1893–1967)

1 (All your life you wait around for some damn man!)

> "Chant for Dark Hours," *Enough Rope 1927*

2 By the time you swear you're his,
Shivering and sighing,
And he vows his passion is
Infinite, undying—
Lady, make a note of this:
One of you is lying.

> "Unfortunate Coincidence," Ibid.

3 Four be the things I am wiser to know:
Idleness, sorrow, a friend, and a foe.

Four be the things I'd be better without:
Love, curiosity, freckles, and doubt.

> "Inventory," Sts. 1–2, Ibid.

4 Men seldom make passes
At girls who wear glasses.

> "News Item," Ibid.

5 Oh, life is a glorious cycle of song,
A medley of extemporanea;
And love is a thing that can never go wrong;
And I am Marie of Roumania.

> "Comment," Ibid.

6 Razors pain you
Rivers are damp;
Acids stain you;
And drugs cause cramp.
Guns aren't lawful;
Nooses give;
Gas smells awful;
You might as well live.

> "Resumé," Ibid.

7   Scratch a lover, and find a foe.
                "Ballade of a Great Weariness," St. 1, Ibid.

8   Where's the man could ease a heart
    Like a satin gown?
                "The Satin Dress," St. 1, Ibid.

9   Authors and actors and artists and such
    Never know nothing, and never know much.
                "Bohemia," *Sunset Gun 1928*

10 Byron and Shelley and Keats
    Were a trio of lyrical treats.
                "A Pigs-Eye View of Literature," Ibid.

11 Her mind lives tidily, apart
    From cold and noise and pain,
    And bolts the door against her heart,
    Out wailing in the rain.
                "Interior," St. 3, Ibid.

12 They sicken of the calm, who knew the storm.
                "Fair Weather," St. 1, Ibid.

13 This living, this living, this living,
    Was never a project of mine.
                "Coda," Ibid.

14 There was nothing separate about her days.
    Like drops upon a window-pane, they ran together and trick-
        led away.
                "Big Blonde," Pt. 1, *Laments for the Living 1929*

15 She was always pleased to have him come and never sorry to
    see him go.
                "Big Blonde," Pt. II, Ibid.

16 She had spent the golden time in grudging its going.
                "The Lovely Leave," Ibid.

17 He [Ernest Hemingway]* has a capacity for enjoyment so vast
    that he gives away great chunks to those about him, and never
    even misses them. . . . He can take you to a bicycle race and
    make it raise your hair.
                Quoted in *The New Yorker 30 November 1929*
    *American novelist (1899–1961).

18 Scratch a king and find a fool!
                "Salome's Dancing-Lesson," St. 3, *Death and Taxes 1931*

19 There was nothing more fun than a man!
                "The Little Old Lady in Lavender Silk," St. 3, Ibid.

20 That woman speaks eighteen languages and can't say No in
    any of them.
                "Our Mrs. Parker," Quoted in *While Rome Burns*
                by Alexander Woollcott* 1934
    *American drama critic and journalist (1887–1943).

21 Brevity is the soul of lingerie.
                Ibid.

22 Those who have mastered etiquette, who are entirely, impecca-
    bly right, would seem to arrive at a point of exquisite dullness.
                "Mrs. Post Enlarges on Etiquette," *The New Yorker*
                (31 December 1927), *The Portable Dorothy Parker 1944*

23 Sorrow is tranquility remembered in emotion.
                "Sentiment," Ibid.

24 Hollywood money isn't money. It's congealed snow, melts in
    your hand, and there you are.
                Interview in *Writers at Work* (First Series),
                Malcolm Cowley, ed. *1958*

25 There's a helluva distance between wisecracking and wit.
    Wit has truth in it; wisecracking is simply calisthenics with
    words.
                Ibid.

26 As artists they're rot, but as providers they're oil wells; they
    gush. Norris* said she never wrote a story unless it was fun to
    do. I understand Ferber** whistles at her typewriter. And there
    was that poor sucker Flaubert*** rolling around on his floor
    for three days looking for the right word.
                Ibid.
    *Kathleen Thompson Norris; see 1457. **Edna Ferber; see
    1557. ***Gustave Flaubert (1821–80), French novelist.

27 It's not the tragedies that kill us, it's the messes.
                Ibid.

28 Gratitude—the meanest and most sniveling attribute in the
    world.
                Ibid.

29 I misremember who first was cruel enough to nurture the cock-
    tail party into life. But perhaps it would be not too much to
    say, in fact it would be not enough to say, that it was not worth
    the trouble.
                Quoted in *Esquire* (New York) *November 1964*

30 She [Katherine Hepburn*] runs the gamut of emotions from A
    to B.
                Quoted in *Publisher's Weekly 19 June 1967*
    *See 1942.

31 This is not a novel to be tossed aside lightly. It should be
    thrown with great force.
                Quoted in *Algonquin Wits*, Robert E. Drennan, ed. *1968*

32 I heard someone say, and so I said it too, that ridicule is the
    most effective weapon. Well, now I know. I know that there
    are things that never have been funny, and never will be. And I
    know that ridicule may be a shield, but it is not a weapon.
                Quoted in *You Might As Well Live* by John Keats *1970*

33 I love to drink Martinis,
    Two at the very most
    Three, I'm under the table;
    Four, I'm under the host.
                The New Yorker, Quoted in *Shaken Not Stirred*,
                Anistatia R. Miller and Jared M. Brown *1997*

34 Drink, and dance and laugh and lie,
    Love the reeling midnight through,
    For tomorrow we shall die!
    (But, alas, we never do.)
                "The Flaw in Paganism" *n.d.*

35 Why is it no one ever sent me yet
    One perfect limousine, do you suppose?
    Ah no, it's always just my luck to get
    One perfect rose.
                "One Perfect Rose" *n.d.*

36 Excuse my dust.
                "Epitaph" *n.d.*

1654. Lorena A. Hickok (1893–1968)

1 [The giant redwoods* made me feel] almost prayerful, and, above all, I wanted to be quiet. However, we were surrounded, not only by tourists, but guides, who kept hurling statistics at us. . . . The final indignity, so far as I was concerned, was to name one of those trees—which was probably a sapling when Christ walked this earth—after General Sherman. Or anyone else. To me, it seemed positively sacrilegious. And I said so, right out loud.
(p. 170), *Empty Without You: The Intimate Letters of Eleanor Roosevelt** and Lorena Hickok*, Roger Streitmatter, ed. *1998*
*In California. **See 1513.

2 What is it you offer to send me, a Bible or a Girdle?...Since you mention it right after something about your riding and spell it with a small "b"—it might be a bridle. On the other hand, I have no horse, so a Bible would make better sense. I'm very curious!
Letter (20 May 1937), Ibid.

1655. Vera Brittain (1893–1970)

1 I thought that spring must last forevermore,
For I was young and loved, and it was May.
"May Morning," St. 4 (May 1916), *Poems of the War and After 1934*

2 I found in you a holy place apart,
Sublime endurance, God in man revealed,
Where mending broken bodies slowly healed
My broken heart.
"Epitaph on My Days in Hospital" (1919), Ibid.

3 Hope has forsaken me, by death removed,
And love that seemed so strong and gay has proved
A poor crushed thing, the toy of cruel chance.
"May Morning," St. 7 (May 1916), Ibid.

4 He was of those whose vanity untold
Builds up complacency to shut out loss
Who, snatching after dross, believe in gold,
And throw away unvalued gold as dross.
"The Fool," St. 1 (1920), Ibid.

5 Meek wifehood is no part of my profession;
I am your friend, but never your possession.
"Married Love" (1926), Ibid.

6 For the courage of greatness is adventurous and know not withdrawing,
But grasps the nettle, danger, with resolute hands,
And ever again.
Gathers security from the sting of pain.
"Evening in Yorkshire," St. 4 (December 1932), Ibid.

7 Have I so changed, since sorrow set her seal
On my lost youth, and left me solitary. . . .
"After Three Years," St. 2, Ibid.

8 For though I must die, youth itself is immortal; its star begins to ascend the heaven of the future as mine sinks below the brief zenith of my generation.
Ch. 24, *England's Hour 1941*

9 The idea that it is necessary to go to a university in order to become a successful writer, or even a man or woman of letters (which is by no means the same thing), is one of those phantasies that surround authorship.
Ch. 2, *On Being an Author 1948*

10 His secret realisation of his physical cowardice led him to underrate his exceptional moral courage. . . .
Pt. I, Ch. 1, *Born 1949*

11 He had never been afraid of death, which was still unreal to him, but he dreaded the end of the world.
Pt. I, Ch. 6, Ibid.

12 "There is a spiritual fellowship in suffering which unites men and women as nothing else can. Perhaps it will be by the world-wide members of this fellowship, in which those whom we call our enemies share, that the temple of civilisation will be rebuilt when peace returns."
Pt. II, Ch. 8, Ibid.

13 The history of men and women in the past fifty years suggests that the old conflict between male and female will ultimately reach reconciliation in a new synthesis which is already in sight. The organic type of human being which will emerge from that synthesis may well be the constructive achievement of the next half-century.
Ch. 1, *Lady into Woman 1953*

14 It is probably true to say that the largest scope for change still lies in men's attitudes to women, and in women's attitudes to themselves.
Ch. 15, Ibid.

15 Politics are usually the executive expression of human immaturity.
Ch. 1, *The Rebel Passion 1964*

16 The pacifists' task today is to find a method of helping and healing which provides a revolutionary constructive substitute for war.
Ch. 12, Ibid.

17 Nuclear weapons immediately vitiated campaigning methods of the secular pacifist society, since the individual renunciation of war, while retaining its moral authority, had lost its political validity. Wars would not now cease if the common man refused to fight when government possessed weapons which were capable of annihilating both the enemy and his opponent.
Ibid.

18 At no previous period has mankind been faced by a half-century which so paradoxically united violence and progress. Its greater and lesser wars and long series of major assassinations have been strangely combined with the liberation of more societies and individuals than ever before in history, and by the transformation of millions of second-class citizens—women, workers and the members of subject races—to a stage at which first-rate achievement is no longer inhibited even if opportunities are not yet complete.
Ibid.

19 I know one husband and wife who, whatever the official reasons given to the court for the break up of their marriage, were really divorced because the husband believed that nobody ought to read while he was talking and the wife that nobody ought to talk while she was reading.
"The Battle Done," *Violets and Vinegar*, Jilly Cooper and Tom Hartman, eds. *1980*

20 All that a pacifist can undertake—but it is a very great deal—is to refuse to kill, injure or otherwise cause suffering to another human creature, and untiringly to order his life by the rule of love though others may be captured by hate.
"What Can We Do In Wartime?," Foreword (Scotland, 9 September 1939), *Wartime Chronicle: Vera Brittain's Diary 1939–1945 1989*

1656. Margaret Anderson (1893–1973)

1 My unreality is chiefly this: I have never felt much like a human being. It's a splendid feeling.

My Thirty Years' War 1930

2 I didn't know what to do about life—so I did a nervous breakdown that lasted many months.

Ibid.

3 I have never been able to accept the two great laws of humanity—that you're always being suppressed if you're inspired and always being pushed into a corner if you're exceptional. I won't be concerned and I won't stay suppressed.

Ibid.

4 I have always had something to live besides a private life.

Ibid.

5 In real love you want the other person's good. In romantic love you want the other person.

The Fiery Fountains 1969

1657. Tehilla Lichtenstein (1893–1973)

1 God has given us the physical eye, a miraculous instrument, with which to behold reality, the world about us, but he has given us the still more miraculous instrument of the imagination, he has given us the power of visualization, with which to create new and greater realities...

"Believing is Seeing" (p. 181), *Four Centuries of Jewish Women's Spirituality: A Sourcebook*, Ellen M. Umansky and Dianne Ashton, eds. *1992*

1658. Margaret Leech (1893–1974)

1 England was the friend whose policy stood like a bulwark against Continental animosity to the ambitions of the American republic.

Ch. 11, *In the Days of McKinley* 1959
*William McKinley, 25th president of the United States (1897–1901); assassinated (1901).

2 Charity stood ready to atone for the heartlessness of the War Department.

Ch. 13, Ibid.

3 The colonial fever was mildly infectious in Washington. Some of the President's closest friends and counselors came down with it.

Ch. 17, Ibid.

4 Never in history had the Union of the States been joined in such universal sorrow. North and South, East and West, the people mourned [William McKinley] a father and a friend, and the fervent strains of "Nearer, My God, to Thee"* floated, like a prayer and a leave-taking, above the half-masted flags in every city and town.

Ch. 26, Ibid.

*McKinley's favorite hymn and last words.

5 Yet, for a space, Americans turned from the challenge and the strangeness of the future. Entranced and regretful, they remembered McKinley's firm, unquestioning faith; his kindly, frock-coated dignity; his accessibility and dedication to the people: the federal simplicity that would not be seen in Washington.

Ibid.

6 The nation felt another leader, less nervous, aggressive, and strong. Under command of a bold young captain [Theodore Roosevelt*], America set sail on the stormy voyage of the twentieth century.

Epilogue, Ibid.

1659. Bessie Breuer (1893–1975)

1 The habit of worry had settled so firmly into her mother's being that her worries were her aspects of love. . . .

Ch. 1, *The Actress 1955*

2 Hollywood . . . scripts . . . a medium where both syntax and the language itself were subjected to horrid mutilation by young men who thought of themselves as writers and who proved it by the enormous salaries they received from those higher up who were even less knowledgeable of the mother tongue.

Ch. 15, Ibid.

3 When they first brought the baby in to her . . . she stared, inert, and thought, This is the author of my pain.

Ch. 21, Ibid.

4 Did I stay with him the very next night because I, way deep down, thought I would learn the secret of acting by sleeping with him; was that it—the way women are always snatching at poets and composers and writers to bedizen themselves with a rag, a knuckle, a toe, the sacred toe of art?

Ch. 32, Ibid.

5 Lust, this muscular dilation and contraction, this in itself, was that it—the *ding an sich*, memory of a college course?

Ch. 36, Ibid.

1660. Faith Baldwin (1893–1978)

1 The kiss was so much a part of the routine that it embarrassed him to withhold it.

Ch. 2, *Alimony 1928*

2 "Compromises aren't enough."
"But," he protested, stupidly, "they're life, aren't they?"
"If they are, then life isn't enough either!"

Ch. 8, Ibid.

3 He made more money than he could spend. His tastes were sound, not extravagant. There was no one dependent on him. He had a few close friends among his colleagues and a thousand pleasant acquaintances. Women had been kind to him and he had so arranged his life that he had been able to enjoy their generosity with discretion. He had recreations. . . . He liked to travel. . . . He liked his work. In short, the world with a fence around it was his.

Pt. I, Ch. 3, *Medical Center 1938*

4 Sometimes entering the ward he felt himself a god, with the gifts of life, of hope, of alleviation, of promise in his hands.

Pt. V, Ch. 28, Ibid.

5 The shadow of fear and uncertainty lies over most of us; for us the future seems far from being as clear and open as we believed it would be.

"Writing for the Women's Magazines," *The Writer's Book*, Helen Hull, ed. *1950*

6 . . . it is hard to convince editors . . . that people of—or past—forty are not senile, and might even have problems, emotions and—*mirabile dictu*—romances, licit and illicit.

Ibid.

7   Oh well, one must adopt a New England attitude, saying not yea, nor nay, but perhaps, maybe, and sometimes.

Ibid.

8   One thing I know about March—whether it storms or shines, it is the key to spring. It can be a sun-warmed key, or a wet one, or a cold; but a key just the same.

"March," *Harvest of Hope 1962*

9   Men's private self-worlds are rather like our geographical world's seasons, storm, and sun, deserts, oases, mountains and abysses, the endless-seeming plateaus, darkness and light, and always the sowing and the reaping.

"April," *Ibid.*

10 Character builds slowly, but it can be torn down with incredible swiftness.

"July," *Ibid.*

11 . . . my temperament's temperature does not rise and fall with thermometers or barometers.

"September," *Ibid.*

12 Gratitude is a humble emotion. It expresses itself in a thousand ways, from a sincere thank you to friend or stranger, to the mute, upreaching acknowledgment to God—not for the gifts of this day only, but for the day itself; not for what we believe will be ours in the future, but for the bounty of the past.

"December," *Ibid.*

13 I think that life has spared these mortals much—
And cheated them of more—who have not kept
A breathless vigil by the little bed
Of some beloved child.

"Virgil" *n.d.*

1661. Sylvia Townsend Warner (1893–1978)

1   Blest fertile Dullness! mothering surmise, rumor, report, as stagnant water, flies, whose happy votaries, stung by every hatch, divinely itch, and more divinely scratch!

Opus Seven 1931

2   "PANSY. *Phoenix pheonixissima formosissima arabiana.* This rare and fabulous bird is UNIQUE. The World's Old Bachelor. Has no mate and doesn't want one. When old, sets fire to itself and emerges miraculously reborn. Specially imported from the east."

"The Phoenix," *The Cat's Cradle-Book 1940*

3   . . . Audrey carried in *The Daily Telegraph.* Mother turned with avidity to the Deaths. When other helpers fail and comforts flee, when the senses decay and the mind moves in a narrower and narrower circle, when the grasshopper is a burden and the postman brings no letters, and even the Royal Family is no longer quite what it was, an obituary column stands fast.

"Their Quiet Lives," *Swans on an Autumn River 1966*

4   There are some women . . . in whom conscience is so strongly developed that it leaves little room for anything else. Love is scarcely felt before duty rushes to encase it, anger impossible because one must always be calm and see both sides, pity evaporates in expedients, even grief is felt as a sort of bruised sense of injury, a resentment that one should have grief forced upon one when one has always acted for the best.

"Total Loss," *Ibid.*

5   It was the ambiguous interval of winter nightfall when one seems to be wading through darkness as through knee-high water while there is still light overhead.

"A Stranger with a Bag," *Ibid.*

6   But no one would possibly listen to her. No one ever listened to one unless one said the wrong thing.

"Fenella," *Ibid.*

7   . . . somewhere out to sea . . . was a bell buoy, rocking and ringing. It seemed as though a heart was beating—a serene, impersonal heart that rocked on a tide of salt water.

"Healthy Landscape with Dormouse," *Ibid.*

8   Efficient people are always sending needless telegrams.

"The View of Rome," *Ibid.*

9   You are only young once. At the time it seems endless, and is gone in a flash; and then for a very long time you are old.

"Swans on an Autumn River," *Ibid.*

1662. Mary Pickford (1893–1979)

1   I was forced to live far beyond my years when just a child, now I have reversed the order and I intend to remain young indefinitely.

Quoted in "How Mary Pickford Stays Young" by Athene Farnsworth, *Everybody's Magazine May 1926*

2   I left the screen because I didn't want what happened to Chaplin* to happen to me. When he discarded the little tramp, the little tramp turned around and killed him.

Quoted in "America's Sweetheart Lives" by Aljean Harmetz, *The New York Times 28 March 1971*
*Charlie (Sir Charles Spencer) Chaplin, English actor and director (1889–1977)

1663. Mae West (1893–1980)

1   Come up 'n' see me some time.

Diamond Lil 1928

2   "You're a fine woman, Lou, one of the finest women that ever walked the streets."

She Done Him Wrong 1932

3   TIRA. She's the kind of girl who climbed the ladder of success, wrong by wrong.

I'm No Angel 1933

4   It is better to be looked over than overlooked.

Belle of the Nineties (screenplay) *1934*

5   FRISCO DOLL. Between two evils, I always pick the one I never tried before.

Klondike Annie 1936

6   It ain't no sin if you crack a few laws now and then just so long as you don't break any.

Every Day's a Holiday (screenplay) *1937*

7   FLOWER BELLE LEE. I generally avoid temptation unless I can't resist it.

My Little Chickadee 1940

8   The various men in my life can claim a great many things, but never that they had a dull time. I have never posed as the definitive expert on the sexes, but I have done my own field work.

Goodness Had Nothing to Do with It 1959

9   It wasn't what I did, but how I did it. It wasn't what I said, but how I said it and how I looked when I did it and said it. I had evolved into a symbol and didn't even know it.

Ibid.

10 I've always had a weakness for foreign affairs.
Quoted in *Time* (New York) *1959*

11 I believe in the single standard for men and women.
The Wit and Wisdom of Mae West, Joseph Weintraub, ed.
1967

12 He who hesitates is last.
Ibid.

13 It's hard to be funny when you have to be clean.
Ibid.

14 A man in the house is worth two in the street.
Ibid.

15 Women are as old as they feel, and men are old when they lose their feelings.
Ibid.

16 When women go wrong, men go right after them.
Ibid.

17 It's not the men in my life that counts—it's the life in my men.
Ibid.

18 Too much of a good thing can be wonderful.
Ibid.

19 I used to be Snow White . . . but I drifted.
Ibid.

20 The best way to hold a man is in your arms.
Ibid.

21 Right now I think censorship is necessary; the things they're doing and saying in films right now just shouldn't be allowed. There's no dignity anymore and I think that's very important.
Interview, *Take One* (Quebec) *22 January 1974*

22 My advice to those who think they have to take off their clothes to be a star is, once you're boned, what's left to create the illusion? Let 'em wonder. I never believed in givin' them too much of me.
Ch. 4, *Mae West on Sex, Health and ESP 1975*

23 When it comes to finances, remember that there are no withholding taxes on the wages of sin.
"Last Word," Ibid.

24 There are no good girls gone wrong, just bad girls found out.
Ibid.

25 A man in love is like a clipped coupon—it's time to cash in.
"That Four-Letter Word!," Ibid.

26 Personality is the glitter that sends your little gleam across the footlights and the orchestra pit into that big black space where the audience is.
Ch. 2, Ibid.

27 Is that a gun in your pocket, or are you just glad to see me?
Sextette 1978

28 I've made it my business to make business my business.
Quoted in "My Side" by M. George Haddad, *Working Woman February 1979*

29 Men have structured society to make a woman feel guilty if she looks after herself. Well, I beat men at their own game. I don't look down on men but I certainly don't look up to them either. I never found a man I could love—or trust—the way I loved myself.
Ibid.

1664. Madame Sun Yat-sen (1893–1981)

1 Liberty and equality, those two inalienable rights of the individual . . . but there is still Fraternity to be acquired. . . . And it may be for China, the oldest of nations, to point the way to this Fraternity.
Quoted in *The Wesleyan April 1912*

2 In the last analysis, all revolutions must be social revolutions, based upon fundamental changes in society; otherwise it is not revolution, but merely a change of government. . . .
Article in *The People's Tribune 14 July 1927*

3 Let us exert every ounce of man's energy and everything produced by him to ensure that everywhere the common people of the world get their due from life. This is to say that our task does not end until every hovel has been rebuilt into a decent house, until the products of the earth are within easy reach of all, until the profits from the factories are returned in equal amount to the effort exerted, until the family can have complete medical care from the cradle to the grave.
Address, "The Chinese Women's Fight for Freedom"
(21 September 1949), *Asia July–August 1956*

4 . . . I want especially to say to our young people . . . learn from Sun Yat-sen!* Imbibe his continuous zeal, study his demand for constant progress, emulate his lack of subjectiveness, his humbleness and his closeness to the people. Make these characteristics part of your own makeup. With these you can surely go forward to build a great socialist China.
Ibid.

*Her husband, Chinese politician and revolutionary leader (1866–1925), who served as provisional president of the Republic after the fall of the Manchu dynasty (1911–1912).

5 Civil war cannot bring unity, liberation or livelihood. . . . The peasants will support the Communists, who give them land and lower taxes. . . . Why then do the reactionaries inflame a war which *they cannot win*?
Public Statement (1947), Quoted in *Women in Modern China* by Helen Foster Snow* *1967*

*See 1903.

1665. Suzanne LaFollette (1893–1983)

1 There is nothing more innately human than the tendency to transmute what has become customary into what has been divinely ordained.
"The Beginnings of Emancipation," *Concerning Women 1926*

2 The revolutionists did not succeed in establishing human freedom; they poured the new wine of beliefs in equal rights for all men into the old bottle of privilege for some; and it soured.
Ibid.

3 . . . where divorce is allowed all . . . society demands a specific grievance of one party against the other. . . . The fact that marriage may be a failure spiritually is seldom taken into account.
Ibid.

4 If responsibility for the upbringing of children is to continue to be vested in the family, then the rights of children will be secured only when parents are able to make a living for their families with so little difficulty that they may give their best thought and energy to the child's development. . . .

Ibid.

5 All political and religious systems have their root and their strength in the innate conservatism of the human mind, and its intense fear of autonomy.

Ibid.

6 . . . to institutionalize means to a great degree to mechanize.

Ibid.

7 For the wage-earner gets his living on sufferance: while he continues to please his employer he may earn a living. . . .

Ibid.

8 . . . the economic conditions brought about by the State operate to make marriage the State's strongest bulwark. . . .

Ibid.

9 . . . most people, no doubt, when they espouse human rights, make their own mental reservations about the proper application of the word "human."

Ibid.

10 . . . laws are felt only when the individual comes into conflict with them.

Ibid.

11 . . . where is the society which does not struggle along under a dead weight of tradition and law inherited from its grandfathers?

Ibid.

12 For man, marriage is regarded as a station; for women, as a vocation.

"Women and Marriage," Ibid.

13 . . . nothing could be more grotesquely unjust than a code of morals, reinforced by laws, which relieves men from responsibility for irregular sexual acts, and for the same acts drives women to abortion, infanticide, prostitution, and self-destruction.

Ibid.

14 . . . when one hears the argument that marriage should be indissoluble for the sake of children, one cannot help wondering whether the protagonist is really such a firm friend of childhood. . . .

Ibid.

15 The claim for alimony...implies the assumption that a woman is economically helpless...

Ibid.

16 No system of government can hope to survive the cynical disregard of both law and principle which government in America regularly exhibits.

"What Is to Be Done," Ibid.

17 It is impossible for a sex or a class to have economic freedom until everybody has it, and until economic freedom is attained for everybody, there can be no real freedom for anybody.

Ibid.

18 Rights that depend on the sufferance of the State are of uncertain tenure. . . .

Ibid.

19 People never move towards revolution; they are pushed towards it by intolerable injustices in the economic and social order under which they live.

"Institutional Marriage and its Economic Aspects," Ibid.

20 It is necessary to grow accustomed to freedom before one may walk in it sure-footedly.

Ibid.

21 No one . . . who has not know that inestimable privilege can possibly realize what good fortune it is to grow up in a home where there are grandparents.

Letter to Alice Rossi* (July 1971), The Feminist Papers, Alice Rossi,* ed. 1973

*See 2213.

22 I . . . watch with growing concern the disintegration of the Western World—above all our own country—and the steady growth of totalitarian influence and power. . . .

Ibid.

1666. Elizabeth Coatsworth (1893–1986)

1 Only of one thing I am sure:
when I dream
I am always ageless

Personal Geography 1976

2 To a life that seizes
Upon content,
Locality seems
But accident.

"To Daughters, Growing Up," St. 1 n.d.

1667. Elizabeth Cotton (1893–1987)

1 But I didn't know people could take songs from you.

Quoted by Stephen March in Southern Voices
August/September 1974

2 Freight train, freight train, goin' so fast. . . .

"Freight Train" n.d.

3 This life I been livin' is very hard.
Work all the week, honey
and I give it all to you.
Honey, baby, what more can I do?

"Babe, It Ain't No Lie" n.d.

1668. Freya Madeline Stark (1893–1993)

1 Perhaps the best function of parenthood is to teach the young creature to love with safety, so that it may be able to venture unafraid when later emotion comes; the thwarting of the instinct to love is the root of all sorrow and not sex only but divinity itself is insulted when it is repressed. To disapprove, to condemn-the human soul shrivels under barren righteousness.

Ch. 10, Traveller's Prelude 1934

2 The great and almost only comfort about being a woman is that one can always pretend to be more stupid than one is and no one is surprised.

Ch. 2, The Valleys of the Assassins 1934

3 The slightest living thing answers a deeper need than all the works of man because it is transitory. It has an evanescence of life, or growth, or change: it passes, as we do, from one stage to the other, from darkness to darkness, into a distance where

we, too, vanish out of sight. A work of art is static; and its value and its weakness lie in being so: but the tuft of grass and the clouds above it belong to our own travelling brotherhood.

Ch. 14, *Perseus in the Wind* 1948

4 Pain and fear and hunger are effects of causes which can be foreseen and known: but sorrow is a debt which someone else makes for us.

Ch. 16, Ibid.

5 The true gardener then brushes over the ground with slow and gentle hand, to liberate a space for breath round some favourite; but he is not thinking about destruction except incidentally. It is only the amateur like myself who becomes obsessed and rejoices with a sadistic pleasure in weeds that are big and bad enough to pull, and at last, almost forgetting the flowers altogether, turns into a Reformer.

Ch. 17, Ibid.

6 I have met charming people, lots who would be charming if they hadn't got a complex about the British and everyone has pleasant and cheerful manners and I like most of the American voices. On the other hand I don't believe they have any God and their hats are frightful. On balance I prefer the Arabs.

Letter to Field-Marshal Lord Wavell (19 February 1944), *Over the Rim of the World: Selected Letters*, Caroline Moorehead, ed. 1988

1669. Agnes Kendrick Gray (1894–?)

1 Sure, 'tis God's ways is very quare,
   An' far beyont my ken,
   How o' the selfsame clay he makes
   Poets an' useful men.

"The Shepherd to the Poet," St. 4 *n.d.*

1670. Pascalina (1894–?)

1 The Pope* should stop all overt political activity by the clergy.

Ch. 5, Quoted in *La Popessa* by Paul I. Murphy with R. Rene Arlington 1983

*Pius XII (1876–1958), pope of Roman Catholic Church (1939–1958).

2 Pius spurned ecumenism and feared the increasing democratization of ecclesiastical decision-making. The vernacular Mass, the growing role of the laity in Church policies, and the rising debate over the Holy See's sexual ethics [are] signs of decadence and profanation of Catholic heritage.

Epilogue, Ibid.

1671. Katherine Bowditch (1894–1933)

1 And what am I but love of you made flesh,
   Quickened by every longing love may bring,
   A pilgrim fire, homeless and wandering.

"Reincarnation" *n.d.*

1672. Rachel Lyman Field (1894–1942)

1 You won't know why, and you can't say how
   Such a change upon you came,
   But—once you have slept on an island
   You'll never be quite the same!

"If Once You Have Slept on an Island," *Taxis and Toadstools* 1926

2 Doorbells are like a magic game,
   Or the grab-bag at a fair—

You never know when you hear one ring
Who may be waiting there.

"Doorbells" *n.d.*

1673. Genevieve Taggard (1894–1948)

1 Try tropic for your balm,
   Try storm,
   And after storm, calm.
   Try snow of heaven, heavy, soft and slow,
   Brilliant and warm.
   Nothing will help, and nothing do much harm.

"Of the Properties of Nature for Healing an Illness," St. 1 *n.d.*

1674. Agnes Smedley (1894?–1950)

1 The gossips specialized most of all in the gruesome . . .

Bk. I, "The Pattern," *Battle Hymn of China* 1943

2 I have always detested the belief that sex is the chief bond between man and woman. Friendship is far more human.

Ibid.

3 The belief in immortality has always seemed cowardly to me. When very young I learned that all things die, and all that we wish of good must be won on this earth or not at all.

Ibid.

4 There's something dreadfully decisive about a beheading.

Bk. IX, "Farewell!," Ibid.

5 . . . Commercialism seemed to have eaten into the very heart of American life and culture.

Bk. X, "Hong Kong," Ibid.

6 There was waste and softness on every hand.

Ibid.

1675. Osa Johnson (1894–1953)

1 When I was most tired, particularly after a hot safari in the dry, dusty plains, I always found relaxation and refreshment in my garden. It was my shop window of loveliness, and Nature changed it regularly that I might feast my hungry eyes upon it. Lone female that I was, this was my special world of beauty: these were my changing styles and my fashion parade.

Ch. 9, *I Married Adventure* 1940

2 "A woman that's too soft and sweet is like tapioca pudding—fine for them as likes it."

Ch. 10, Ibid.

3 Theirs, it might be said, was a Utopian existence, for they [pygmies] showed neither hate, greed, vanity, not any other of the dominatingly unpleasant emotions of our so-called civilized world. Each dusky hop-o'-my-thumb plays his pleasant game of life with no desire to interfere with, and caring little about, the conduct of his fellows.

Ch. 27, Ibid.

4 "We must string him up in the presence of the chief and the villagers. . . . We have to break this murder madness on the island; we must make a show of force that they will remember every time they want to go on a rampage and give them a picture of retribution they can't doubt and will not forget."

Ch. 1, *Bride in the Solomons* 1944

5 "Animals and primitive people are alike in one thing," he said. "They know when you are friendly, they can sense it. . . . They can even smell fear."

Ch. 18, Ibid.

1676. Dorothy Thompson (1894–1961)

1 But I do not think that Communism as a belief, apart from overt and illegal actions, can be successfully combatted by police methods, persecution, war, or a mere anti-spirit. The only force that can overcome an idea and a faith is another and better idea and faith, positively and fearlessly upheld.

Quoted in *The Ladies' Home Journal* October *1954*

2 The United States is the only great and populous nation-state and world power whose people are not cemented by ties of blood, race or original language. It is the only world power which recognizes but one nationality of its citizens—American. . . . How can such a union be maintained except through some idea which involves loyalty.

Quoted in *The Ladies' Home Journal October 1954*

3 They have not wanted *Peace* at all; they have wanted to be spared war—as though the absence of war was the same as peace.

On the Record May 1958

4 It is not the fact of liberty but the way in which liberty is exercised that ultimately determines whether liberty itself survives.

Ibid.

5 Of all forms of government and society, those of free men and women are in many respects the most brittle. They give the fullest freedom for activities of private persons and groups who often identify their own interests, essentially selfish, with the general welfare.

Ibid.

6 Great states, able to defend *themselves*, do not entrust matters of life and death to a head count of states that can do neither. The "sovereign equality of all states" is an illusion. A universal "rule of Law" can neither be formulated in a manner acceptable to people with different concepts of law nor enforced under present conditions except by war.

"The Discrepancy Between Democratic Ideals and Realities," *The Ladies' Home Journal October 1960*

1677. Esther Forbes (1894–1967)

1 Women have almost a genius for anticlimaxes.

O Genteel Lady! 1926

2 Most American heroes of the Revolutionary period are by now two men, the actual man and the romantic image. Some are even three men—the actual man, the image, and the debunked remains.

Paul Revere* 1942

*American silversmith, engraver and Revolutionary War hero (1735–1818).

1678. Jean Rhys (1890–1979)

1 . . . Miss Bruce, passing by a shop, with the perpetual hunger to be beautiful and that thirst to be loved which is the real curse of Eve. . . . Then must have begun the search for *the* dress, the perfect Dress, beautiful, beautifying, possible to be worn. And lastly, the search for illusion—a craving, almost a vice, the stolen waters and the bread eaten in secret of Miss Bruce's life.

"Illusion," *The Left Bank 1927*

2 She respected Americans: they were not like the English, who, under a surface of annoying moroseness of manner, were notoriously timid and easy to turn round your finger.

"Mannequin," Ibid.

3 For the first time she had dimly realized that only the hopeless are starkly sincere and that only the unhappy can either give or take sympathy—even some of the bitter and dangerous voluptuousness of misery.

"In the Rue de l'Arrivée," Ibid.

4 "But I do not wish to sell my pictures. And, as I do not wish to sell them, exhibiting is useless. My pictures are precious to me. They are precious, most probably, to no one else."

"Tea with an Artist," Ibid.

5 "I don't get any *kick* out of Anglo-Saxons," she said out loud. "They don't . . . they *don't* stimulate my imagination!"

"Tout Montparnasse and Lady," Ibid.

6 The feeling of Sunday is the same everywhere, heavy, melancholy, standing still. Like when they say, "As it was in the beginning, is now, and ever shall be, world without end."

Act IV, *Voyage in the Dark 1934*

7 We can't all be happy, we can't all be rich, we can't all be lucky—and it would be so much less fun if we were. Isn't it so, Mr. Blank? There must be the dark background to show off the bright colours. Some must cry so that others may be able to laugh the more heartily. Sacrifices are necessary. . . .

Pt. I, *Good Morning, Midnight 1939*

8 Saved, rescued, fished-up, half-drowned, out of the deep, dark river, dry clothes, hair shampooed and set. Nobody would know I had ever been in it. Except, of course, that there always remains something. Yes, there always remains something. . . . Never mind, here I am, sane and dry, with my place to hide in. What more do I want?

Ibid.

9 Next week, or next month, or next year I'll kill myself. But I might as well last out my month's rent, which has been paid up, and my credit for breakfast in the morning.

Pt. II, Ibid.

10 "I often want to cry. That is the only advantage women have over men—at least they can cry."

Ibid.

11 She could give herself up to the written word as naturally as a good dancer to music or a fine swimmer to water. The only difficulty was that after finishing the last sentence she was left with a feeling at once hollow and uncomfortably full. Exactly like indigestion.

"The Insect World," *Sleep It Off, Lady 1976*

1679. Dora Russell (1894–1986)

1 Marriage, laws, the police, armies and navies are the mark of human incompetence.

The Right to Be Happy 1927

2 We have never yet had a Labour Government that knew what taking power really means; they always act like second-class citizens.

Quoted in *Observer* (London) *30 January 1983*

3   We do not want our world to perish. But in our quest for knowledge, century by century, we have placed all our trust in a cold, impartial intellect which only brings us nearer to destruction. We have heeded no wisdom offering guidance. Only by learning to love one another can our world be saved. Only love can conquer all.*
> Ch. 14, *Challenge to the Cold War*, Vol. 3 *1985*
> *Final words of final volume of her autobiography.

1680. Adela Rogers St. Johns (1894–1988)

1   Before he left, Aunt William pressed a sovereign into his hand guiltily, as if it were conscience money. He, on his side, took it as though it were a doctor's fee, and both ignored the transaction.
> "Aunt William," *The Twelfth Hour 1970*

2   People don't think the only American saint is a woman [Mother Cabrini].* I knew her and didn't know she was a saint. She didn't know, either. She built the first school and first hospital in every town.
> *Some Are Born Great 1974*
> *Saint Frances Xavier Cabrini (1850–1917); see 1129.

3   Mrs. [Margaret] Sanger* said the best birth control is to make your husband sleep on the roof.
> Ibid.
>
> *See 1497; Sanger *reported* this advice—she did not give it.

4   Roosevelt* had great class. He not only handled them [the press], he used them. F.D.R. would send for reporters and pick their brains. . . . He adored Eleanor.** He had mistresses, but let's face facts. If more people would face facts, there'd be fewer broken marriages.
> Quoted in "She's Had the Last Word for Sixty Years" by Joyce Haber, *Los Angeles Times 13 October 1974*
> *Franklin Delano R— (1882–1945), 32nd president of the United States (1933–1945). **See 1513.

5   Why keep the [Watergate]* tapes around? It's like you left the corpse in the bullring.
> Ibid.
>
> *Reference to the series of scandals in July 1972 emanating from President Richard Nixon's administration (1969–1974).

6   I've often thought with Nixon* that if he'd made the football team, his life would have been different.
> Ibid.
>
> *Richard Milhous N— (1913–1994), 37th president of the United States (1969–1974); resigned.

7   The modern woman is the curse of the universe. A disaster, that's what. She thinks that before her arrival on the scene no woman ever did anything worthwhile before, no woman was ever liberated until her time, no woman really ever amounted to anything. . . .
> Quoted in "Some Are Born Great" by Mert Guswiler, *Los Angeles Herald-Examiner 13 October 1974*

8   About twenty-five years ago . . . I made three resolutions of what I would never do again. They were: to put on a girdle, to wear high heels, and to go out to dinner.
> Ibid.

9   I think every woman's entitled to a middle husband she can forget.
> Ibid.

10   I wish women would stand together and shackle the men who want to move us backwards.
> Quoted in *Time* (New York) *22 August 1988*

1681. Martha Graham (1894–1991)

1   Nothing is more revealing than movement.
> "The American Dance," *Modern Dance*, Virginia Stewart, ed. *1935*

2   America does not concern itself with Impressionism. We own no involved philosophy. The psyche of the land is to be found in its movement. It is to be felt as a dramatic force of energy and vitality. We move; we do not stand still. We have not yet arrived at the stock-taking stage.
> Ibid.

3   We look at the dance to impart the sensation of living in an affirmation of life, to energize the spectator into keener awareness of the vigor, the mystery, the humor, the variety, and the wonder of life. This is the function of the American dance.
> Ibid.

1682. Dorothea Lange (1895–1965)

1   These [country women] are women of the American soil. They are a hardy stock. They are the roots of our country. . . . They are not our well-advertised women of beauty and fashion. . . . These women represent a different mode of life. They are of *themselves* a very great American style. They live with courage and purpose, a part of our tradition.
> Quoted in *The Women's Eye* by Anne Tucker* *1973*
> *See 3073.

2   The camera is an instrument that teaches people how to see without a camera.
> Quoted in "The Photographer Who Showed Americans How to See Themselves" by Robert Kirsch, *Los Angeles Times 13 August 1978*

3   . . . being disabled gave me an immense advantage. People are kinder to you. It puts you on a different level than if you go into a situation whole and secure.
> Ibid.

4   The megalopolis is not just an American phenomenon, it's international and we are creating this environment, teeming with unfamiliar ways of living, almost without scrutiny.
> Ibid.

1683. Babette Deutsch (1895–1974)

1   But the poet's job is, after all, to translate God's poem (or is it the Fiend's?) into words.
> "Poetry at the Mid-Century," *The Writer's Book*, Helen Hull, ed. *1950*

2   . . . the poet . . . like the lover . . . is a person unable to reconcile what he knows with what he feels. His peculiarity is that he is under a certain compulsion to do so.
> Ibid.

3   The poets were among the first to realize the hollowness of a world in which love is made to seem as standardized as plumbing, and death is actually a mechanized industry. . . .
> Ibid.

4   Their memories: a heap of tumbling stones,
Once builded stronger than a city wall.
> "Old Women" *n.d.*

5   You, also laughing one,
Tosser of balls in the sun,

Will pillow your bright head
By the incurious dead.

"A Girl" *n.d.*

1684. Bessie Rowland James (1895–1974)

1   No matter how lofty you are in your department, the responsibility for what your lowliest assistant is doing is yours.

Quoted in *Adlai's Almanac*, Adlai Ewing Stevenson* *1952*
*American politican, governor of Illinois (1900–1965).

1685. Anna Freud (1895–1982)

1   The war acquires comparatively little significance for children so long as it only threatens their lives, disturbs their material comfort or cuts their food ration. It becomes enormously significant the moment it breaks up family life and uproots the first emotional attachments of the child within the family group.

War and Children, with Dorothy Burlingham *1943*

2   . . . it is normal for an adolescent to behave for a considerable length of time in an inconsistent and unpredictable manner; to fight his impulses and to accept them; to ward them off successfully and to be overrun by them; to love his parents and to hate them; to revolt against them and to be dependent on them; to be deeply ashamed to acknowledge his mother before others and, unexpectedly, to desire heart-to-heart talks with her; to thrive on imitation of and identification with others while searching unceasingly for his own identity; to be more idealistic, artistic, generous, and unselfish than he will ever be again, but also the opposite: self-centered, egoistic, calculating. Such fluctuation between extreme opposites would be deemed highly abnormal at any other time of life. At this time they may signify no more than that an adult structure of personality takes a long time to emerge . . .

"Adolescence," *The Psychoanalytic Study of the Child*,
Vol. 13 *1958*

1686. Alberta Hunter (1895–1984)

1   I didn't care what time my time was up [at work]. If my patient was restless, I'd stay there and try to soothe my patient to sleep, no matter how long it took. Then when they'd go to sleep, I'd go on home.

Quoted in *Alberta Hunter: A Celebration in Blues* by Frank C. Taylor with Gerald Cook *1987*

2   It upset me so to think that they have rules that make you leave something that you love.*

Ibid.

*Reference to her forced retirement as a nurse when, according to hospital records, she'd reached the age of seventy (actually she was eighty-two].

3   I gotta man, he's kinda old and thin.
But there are plenty of good tunes left
in an old violin'

"Workin' Man" (song) *n.d.*

1687. Susanne K. Langer (1895–1985)

1   Feeling, in the broad sense of whatever is felt in any way, as sensory stimulus or inward tension, pain, emotion or intent, is the mark of mentality.

Pt. I, Ch. 1, *Mind, An Essay on Human Feeling*, Vol. I *1967*

2   Art is the objectification of feeling.

Pt. II, Ch. 4, Ibid.

3   The secret of the "fusion" is the fact that the artist's eye sees in nature . . . an inexhaustible wealth of tension, rhythms, continuities and contrasts which can be rendered in line and color; and those are the "internal forms" which the "external forms"—painting, musical or poetic compositions or any other works of art—expresses for us.

Ibid.

4   Every artistic form reflects the dynamism that is constantly building up the life of feeling. It is this same dynamism that records itself in organic forms; growth is its most characteristic process, and is the source of almost all familiar living shape. Hence the kinship between organic and artistic forms, though the latter need not be modeled on any natural object at all. If a work of art is a projection of feelings, that kinship with organic nature will emerge, no matter through how many transformations, logically and inevitably.

Ch. 7, Ibid.

5   "Consciousness" is not an entity at all, let alone a special cybernetic mechanism. It is a condition built up out of mental acts of a particular life episode. . . .

Ch. 11, Ibid.

1688. Rose Franken (1895–1988)

1   CLAUDIA. Nothing, and no one really belongs to anyone.
DAVID. If you've learned that, you've learned a lot, my dearest.

Act III, *Claudia 1941*

1689. Juana de Ibarbourou (1895–1989)

1   I give you my naked soul
Like a statue unveiled.

"The Hour," *Diamond Tongues 1919*

2   For if I am so rich, if I have so much,
If they see me surrounded by every luxury,
It is because of my noble lineage
That builds castles on my pillow.

"Small Woman," Ibid.

1690. Dolores Ibarruri (1895–1989)

1   It is better to die on your feet than to live on your knees!

Radio Speech *18 July 1936*

2   It is better to be the widow of a hero than the wife of a coward.

Speech (Valencia, Spain) *1936*

3   . . . the working people of the whole world know that if fascism were to triumph in Spain, every democratic country in the world would be confronted with the fascist danger.

Speeches and Articles, 1936–1938 1938

4   Women have always played a prominent part, supporting the men in the struggle for liberty and showing them by their example that it is better to die than to bow to the butchers and oppressors of the people.

Ibid.

5   Never shall we see you again, yet we feel your closeness.

Ibid.

6   Wherever they pass they [the fascists] sow death and desolation.

Ibid.

7   We dip our colors in honor of you, dear women comrades, who march into battle together with the men.

Ibid.

8   *!No pasaran!*
    Quoted in Ch. 4, *Passionate War, the Narrative History of the Spanish Civil War (1936–39)* by Peter Wyden *1983*

9   I am a simple woman; granddaughter, daughter and sister of miners. A woman who has fought much and hard to bring socialism to Spain.
    Quoted in "Entrevista" by Antonio del Corral, *Carta de España*, Hélène Lopez, tr. *15 December 1985*

1691. Monica Baldwin (1896–?)

1   . . . all the magic of the countryside which is ordained from the healing of the soul.
    I Leap Over the Wall 1950

2   You might have been standing in the heart of an iceberg, so strange it was, so silent, so austere.
    Ibid.

1692. Dixie Willson (1896–?)

1   He may look just the same to you,
    And he may be just as fine,
    But the next-door dog is the next-door dog,
    And mine—is—mine!
    "Next-Door Dog" *n.d.*

1693. Tina Modotti (1896–1942)

1   . . . I never realized before that a letter—a mere sheet of paper—could be such a spiritual thing—could emanate so much feeling—you gave a soul to it!
    Letter to Edward Weston* (25 April 1921), Quoted in Ch. 1, *Tina Modotti, A Fragile Life* by Mildred Constantine *1975*
    *American photographer (1850–1936) with whom she collaborated and who was her companion.

2   The love of revolutionaries is not separate from their other activities; it is related to their political ideals.
    Courtroom Interrogation* (16 January 1929), Ibid.
    *After the shooting death of Julio Antonio Mella, Cuban revolutionary, in Mexico, who was her companion.

3   I consider myself a photographer, nothing more . . . Photography, precisely because it can only be produced in the present and because it is based on what exists objectively before the camera, takes its place as the most satisfactory medium of registering life in all its aspects, and from this comes its documental value. If to this is added sensibility and understanding and, above all, a clear orientation as to the place it should have in the field of historical development, I believe that the result is something worthy of a place in social production, to which we should all contribute.
    Comment at exhibition, Mexico City (December 1929), Ibid.

1694. Gordon Daviot (1896–1952)

1   JOHN OF GAUNT. He holds England in his two hands and laughs like a wicked child and men pause and hold their breath.
    Richard Bordeaux (play) *1932*

1695. Marjorie Kinnan Rawlings (1896–1953)

1   You can't change a man, no-ways. By the time his mammy turns him loose and he takes up with some innocent woman and marries her, he is what he is.
    "Benny and the Bird-Dogs,"
    When the Whippoorwill 1931

2   When she settled down for a life-time's quarreling at him, it was for the same reason syrup sours—the heat had just been put to her too long.
    Ibid.

3   There was something about the most fertile field that was beyond control. A man could work himself to skin and bones, so that there was no flesh left on him to make sweat in the sun, and a crop would get away from him. There was something about all living that was uncertain.
    Ch. 3, *South Moon Under 1933*

4   Sorrow was like the wind. It came in gusts, shaking the woman. She braced herself.
    Ch. 9, Ibid.

5   It seemed a strange thing to him, when earth was earth and rain was rain, that scrawny pines should grow in the scrub, while by every branch and lake and river there grew magnolias. Dogs were the same everywhere, and oxen and mules and horses. But trees were different in different places.
    Ch. 1, *The Yearling 1938*

6   The game seemed to him to be two different animals. On the chase, it was the quarry. He wanted only to see it fall. . . . When it lay dead and bleeding, he was sickened and sorry. . . . Then when it was cut into portions . . . his mouth watered at its goodness. He wondered by what alchemy it was changed, so that what sickened him one hour, maddened him with hunger the next. It seemed as though there were either two different animals or two different boys.
    Ch. 8, Ibid.

7   "A woman has got to love a bad man once or twice in her life, to be thankful for a good one."
    Ch. 12, Ibid.

8   "You figgered I went back on you. Now there's a thing ever' man has got to know. Mebbe you know it a'ready. 'Twa'n't only me. 'Twa'n't only your yearlin' deer havin' to be destroyed. Boy, life goes back on you."
    Ch. 33, Ibid.

9   Living was no longer the grief behind him, but the anxiety ahead.
    Ibid.

10 "Ever' man wants life to be a fine thing, and a easy. 'Tis fine, boy, powerful fine, but 'tain't easy. Life knocks a man down and he gits up and it knocks him down again. I've been uneasy all my life."
    Ibid.

11 He was the delight of fine cooks, who mistook his absent-minded capacity for appreciation.
    Ch. 1, *The Sojourner 1953*

12 He found himself denying this so-called force of gravity. It could not be what tied men to earth. It was a heavy weight, an unendurable pressure from the outer-land, and if a man could once break through it, soar high like a bird, he would be free,

would meet, would join, something greater than he, and be completed at last.

Ch. 15, Ibid.

13 They were all too tightly bound together, men and women, creatures wild and tame, flowers, fruits and leaves, to ask that anyone be spared. As long as the whole continued, the earth could go about its business.

Ch. 20, Ibid.

1696. Gerty Cori (1896–1957)

1 For a research worker the unforgotten moments of life are those rare ones, which come after years of plodding work, when the veil over nature's secret seems suddenly to lift and when what was dark and chaotic appears in a clear and beautiful light pattern.

Radio interview,* Quoted in "Gerty Cori"
by John Parascandola, *Notable American Women 1980*

*This interview was played at her memorial service.

2 I believe that in art and science are the glories of the human mind. I see no conflict between them.

Ibid.

1697. Martha Martin (1896–1959)

1 I killed a sea otter today. I actually did kill a sea otter. I killed him with the ax, dragged him home, and skinned him.

O Rugged Land of Gold 1952

2 I told her the deer are our helpers and our friends, our subjects and our comfort, and they will give us food and clothing according to our needs. I told her of the birds. . . . Told her of the fishes. . . . Told her of the mink and the otter, and the great brown bear with his funny, furry cub. Told her of the forest and of the things it will give us . . . of the majestic mountain uprising behind us with a vein of goldbearing ore coming straight from its heart. Told her that all these things were ours to have and to rule over and to care for.

Ibid.

3 The Indians have come, good, good Indians. Shy, fat, smelly, friendly, kindhearted Indians.

Ibid.

4 This awful deep snow and hard cold is going to kill off much of our wild life. Poor creatures, what a pity they can't all be like bears and sleep the winter through.

Ibid.

5 I have never seen a child born. I always felt inadequate to help and was too modest to want to be a spectator. I have never seen anything born—not even a cat. . . . I am no longer afraid, yet I do wish someone were with me to help me take care of the child. . . .

Ibid.

6 My darling little girl-child, after such a long and troublesome waiting I now have you in my arms. I am alone no more, I have my baby.

Ibid.

1698. Beata Rank (1896–1967)

1 Because she is so barren of spontaneous manifestations of maternal feelings, she studies vigilantly all the new methods of upbringing and reads treatises about physical and mental hygiene.

"Adaptation of the Psychoanalytic Technique . . .,"
American Journal of Orthopsychiatry January 1949

2 . . . examine the personality of the mother, who is the medium through which the primitive infant transforms himself into a socialized human being.

Ibid.

1699. Betty Smith (1896–1972)

1 There's a tree that grows in Brooklyn. Some people call it the Tree of Heaven. No matter where its seed falls, it makes a tree which struggles to reach the sky. It grows in boarded-up plots and out of neglected rubbish heaps. It grows up out of cellar gratings. It is the only tree that grows out of cement. It grows lushly . . . survives without sun, water, and seemingly without earth. It would be considered beautiful except that there are too many of it.

A Tree Grows in Brooklyn 1943

2 "If it makes her feel better to throw it away rather than to drink it, all right. *I* think it's good that people like us can waste something once in a while and get the feeling of how it would be to have lots of money and not have to worry about scrounging."

Ch. 1, Ibid.

3 "My Francie wears no hair bow but her hair is long and shiny. Can money buy things like that? That means there must be something bigger than money."

Ch. 27, Ibid.

4 Miss Gardner had nothing in all the world excepting a sureness about how right she was.

Ch. 42, Ibid.

5 "The difference between rich and poor," said Francie, "is that the poor do everything with their own hands and the rich hire hands to do things."

Ch. 45, Ibid.

6 "Is it not so that a son that is bad to his mother," he said, "is bad to his wife?"

Ch. 1, *Maggie—Now 1958*

7 She felt, vaguely, that she had given away her childhood that night. She had given it to him or he had taken it from her, and made it into something wonderful. In a way, her life was his now.

Ch. 23, Ibid.

8 ". . . I can never give a 'yes' or a 'no.' I don't believe everything in life can be settled by a monosyllable."

Ch. 39, Ibid.

1700. Elsa Schiaparelli (1896–1973)

1 So fashion is born by small facts, trends, or even politics, never by trying to make little pleats and furbelows, by trinkets, by clothes easy to copy, or by the shortening or lengthening of a skirt.

Ch. 9, *Shocking Life 1954*

2 A good cook is like a sorceress who dispenses happiness.

Ch. 21, Ibid.

3 Eating is not merely a material pleasure. Eating well gives a spectacular joy to life and contributes immensely to goodwill

and happy companionship. It is of great importance to the morale.

Ibid.

4 The moment that people stop copying you, it means that you are no longer any good, and that you have ceased to be news.

Ibid.

5 Courtesans used to know more about the soul of men than any philosopher. The art is lost in the fog of snobbism and false respectability.

Ibid.

1701. Vivien Kellems (1896–1975)

1 Our tax law is a 1,598-page hydra-headed monster and I'm going to attack and attack and attack until I have ironed out every fault in it.

Quoted in Los Angeles Times 26 January 1975

2 . . . the IRS has stolen from me over the past 20 years because I am single. It is unconstitutional to impose a penalty tax of 40 percent on me because I have no husband.

Quoted in "Unforgettable Vivien Kellems" by Gloria Swanson, Reader's Digest October 1975

3 Of course I'm a publicity hound. Aren't all crusaders? How can you accomplish anything unless people know what you're trying to do?

Ibid.

4 Men always try to keep women out of business so they won't find out how much fun it really is.

Ibid.

1702. Charlotte Whitton (1896–1975)

1 Whatever women do they must do twice as well as men to be thought half as good. Luckily, this is not difficult.

Quoted in Canada Month June 1963

1703. Mamie Doud Eisenhower (1896–1979)

1 I stayed busy all the time and loved being in the White House, but I was never expected to do all the things you have to do.

Comment to Rosalyn Carter* (1977), Quoted in First Ladies by Betty Boyd Caroli 1987

*See 2330.

1704. Ida P. Rolf (1896–1979)

1 Word's going around Esalen that Ida Rolf thinks the body is all there is. Well, I want it known that I think there's more than the body, but the body is all you can get your hands on.

Quoted in The Protean Body by Don Johnson 1977

2 Form and function are a unity, two sides of one coin. In order to enhance function, appropriate form must exist or be created.

Preface, Rolfing: The Integration of Human Structures 1977

3 Twentieth-century medicine, which has worked so many miracles, has been chemically not structurally oriented. Hence, the lay mind thinks of chemistry as the only outstanding healing medium—a drug for this, a shot for that. But any mirror photograph would reveal that a great many problems are matters of structure, of physics . . .

Ibid.

4 An effective human being is a whole that is greater than the sum of its parts.

Ibid.

1705. Ruth Gordon (1896–1985)

1 MAX. I *always* get seventy-eight. No more, no less. It's nerve-wracking. I'd almost rather flunk once in a while.

Act I, Over Twenty-One 1943

2 POLLY. People like us and people born to be soldiers are kind of getting to be one and the same.
GOW. They are not—they're just all dressing alike. A uniform doesn't make a soldier. It takes aptitude, just like anything else.

Act II, Ibid.

3 JOE. You hit it! The truth's no good to me, Polly! History just isn't practical. . . . We can't stick to history. History's unbelievable! And it's up to us to make it seem real.
POLLY. Honest to God, Joe, you must have a brain of solid popcorn.

Ibid.

4 MAX. Say, is it too early for a drink?
POLLY. What's early about it? It's tomorrow in Europe and yesterday in China.

Act III, Ibid.

5 POLLY. Do you realize you've come damn close to breaking a man's spirit?
GOW. Well, it was his spirit or my bank account.

Ibid.

6 RUTH. I got anything I want to have; but I'll never have anything at all if trouble makes me go and give up!

Years Ago 1946

7 FATHER. . . . there's always plenty of room at the bottom.

Ibid.

8 CLYDE. Nothing dates one so dreadfully as to think someplace is uptown. . . . At our age one must be watchful of these conversational gray hairs.

Act I, The Leading Lady 1948

9 CLYDE. I'm sure the way to be happy is to live well beyond your means!

Ibid.

10 CLYDE. The best impromptu speeches are the ones written well in advance.

Ibid.

11 GAY. So easy to fall into a rut, isn't it? Why should ruts be so comfortable and so unpopular?

Act II, Ibid.

12 BENJY. The kiss. There are all sorts of kisses, lad, from the sticky confection to the kiss of death. Of them all, the kiss of an actress is the most unnerving. How can we tell if she means it or if she's just practicing?

Ibid.

13 MRS. GILSON. Up and the world is your oyster! This time you can't miss! Whack comes down the old shillaly and you're down again bitin' the dust! Can't face it! Screeching into your pillow nights! Put back your smile in the morning, trampin' to managers' offices! Home again in the evenin' ready to give up

the ghost. Somebody come by, to tell you: "Go see Frohman nine-thirty sharp!" Luck's turned, you're on the trolley again! Curl up your ostrich feathers! Sponge off the train of your skirt! Because it's all aboard tomorrow. . . .

Act III, Ibid.

14 MRS. GILSON. The circle comes around for everyone. It dips, but it comes round. Seven lean years and seven fat ones. And seven lean and seven fat. It doesn't always have to be seven, but some number! Never knew anyone didn't have the balloon go up and down.

Ibid.

15 At seventy-four I look better than seventy-three. If you make it through seventy-four years, can it be that things shape up?

"Myself Among Others," *Myself Among Others 1970*

16 To get it right, be born with luck or else make it. *Never* give up. Get the knack of getting people to help you and also pitch in yourself. A little money helps, but what *really* gets it right is to *never*—I repeat—*never* under any condition face the facts.

Ibid.

17 The good that men do lives after them. That's a quote from myself. I know the correct one, but I don't think so. I think the *good* lives after. The evil gets accepted or forgotten. Or becomes hearsay. The *good* lives on and does us all some good.

"The Good That Men Do," Ibid.

1706. Wallis Simpson Windsor (1896–1986)

1 I don't remember any love affairs. One must keep love affairs quiet.

Quoted in *Los Angeles Times 11 April 1974*

2 One can never be too thin or too rich.

Comment *n.d.*

1707. Dodie Smith (1896–1990)

1 ROGER. You know, you women with this skinny complex are laying up a wretched old age for yourselves. String, that's what you'll be. Stringy and desiccated.
DOROTHY. Well, that's better than having two double chins and three double stomachs.
ROGER. I have no stomach whatsoever.
DOROTHY. How inconvenient.

Call It a Day 1935

2 I have found that sitting in a place where you have never sat before can be inspiring.

I Capture the Castle 1948

3 Noble deeds and hot baths are the best cure for depression.

Ch. 3, Ibid.

4 Oh, it was the most glorious morning! I suppose the best kind of spring morning is the best weather God has to offer. It certainly helps one to believe in Him.

Ch. 6, Ibid.

5 . . . miserable people cannot afford to dislike each other. Cruel blows of fate call for extreme kindness in the family circle.

Ibid.

6 ". . . she happens to belong to a type [of American woman] I frequently met—it goes to lectures. And entertains afterwards. . . . Amazing, their energy," he went on. "They're perfectly ca-

pable of having three or four children, running a house, keeping abreast of art, literature and music—superficially of course, but good lord, that's something—and holding down a job into the bargain. Some of them get through two or three husbands as well, just to avoid stagnation."

Ch. 7, Ibid.

7 What a difference there is between wearing even the skimpiest bathing-suit and wearing nothing! After a few minutes I seemed to live in every inch of my body as fully as I usually do in my head and my hands and my heart. I had the fascinating feeling that I could think as easily with my limbs as with my brain. . . .

Ch. 12, Ibid.

8 Perhaps the effect wears off in time, or perhaps you don't notice it if you are born to it, but it does seem to me that the climate of richness must always be a little dulling to the senses. Perhaps it takes the edge off joy as well as off sorrow.

Ch. 14, Ibid.

9 ". . . I don't like the sound of all those lists he's making—it's like taking too many notes at school; you feel you've achieved something when you haven't."

Ch. 15, Ibid.

1708. Ruth Pitter (1897–?)

1 I go about, but cannot find
The blood-relations of the mind.

"The Lost Tribe," St. 1 *n.d.*

2 Though our world burn, the small dim words
Stand here in steadfast grace,
And sing, like the indifferent birds
About a ruined place.

"On an Old Poem," St. 2 *n.d.*

1709. Margaret Chase Smith (1897–1995)

1 I believe that in our constant search for security we can never gain any peace of mind until we secure our own soul.

Essay, *This I Believe*, Raymond Swing, ed. *1952*

2 My creed is that public service must be more than doing a job efficiently and honestly. It must be a complete dedication to the people and to the nation with full recognition that every human being is entitled to courtesy and consideration, that constructive criticism is not only to be expected but sought, that smears are not only to be expected but fought, that honor is to be earned but not bought.

"My Creed," *Quick 11 November 1953*

3 In these perilous hours, I fear that the American people are ahead of their leaders in realism and courage—but behind them in knowledge of the facts because the facts have not been given to them.

Address, U.S. Senate *21 September 1961*

4 Strength, the American way, is not manifested by threats of criminal prosecution or police state methods. Leadership is not manifested by coercion, even against the resented. Greatness is not manifested by unlimited pragmatism, which places such a high premium on the end justifying *any* methods.

Address, National Republican Women's Conference Banquet *16 April 1962*

5 In today's growing, but tragic, emphasis on materialism, we find a perversion of the values of things in life as we once knew

them. For example, the creed once taught children as they grew up was that the most important thing was not in whether you won or lost the game but rather in "how you played the game." That high level attitude that stresses the moral side no longer predominates in this age of pragmatic materialism that increasingly worships the opposite creed that "the end justifies the means" or the attitude of get what you can in any way, manner, or means that you can.

> RCA Victor Recording *1964*

6 There are enough mistakes of the Democrats for the Republicans to criticize constructively without resorting to political smears. . . . Freedom of speech is not what it used to be in America.

> "Nuclear Test Ban Treaty," *Declaration of Conscience 1972*

7 Before you can become a statesman you first have to get elected, and to get elected you have to be a politician pledging support for what the voters want.

> Ibid.

8 We are rapidly approaching a day when the United States will be subject to all sorts of diplomatic blackmail and a strategy of terror waged by the Soviet Union.

> "It's Time to Speak Up for National Defense," *Reader's Digest March 1972*

9 We are sick to death of war, defense spending and all things military. We are disgusted with and weary of the vilification that has been heaped upon us, at home as well as abroad, for our attempts to block communist enslavement in Southeast Asia. We yearn to turn away from foreign entanglements and to begin making our own house a better place to live in

> Ibid.

10 The key to security is public information.

> Ibid.

1710. Amelia Earhart (1897–1937)

1 There are two kinds of stones, as everyone know, one of which rolls.

> Ch. 1, *20 Hours: 40 Minutes—Our Flight in the Friendship 1928*

2 There is so much that must be done in a civilized barbarism like war.

> Ibid.

3 In soloing—as in other activities—it is far easier to start something than it is to finish it.

> Ch. 2, Ibid.

4 Of course I realized there was a measure of danger. Obviously I faced the possibility of not returning when first I considered going. Once faced and settled there really wasn't any good reason to refer to it again.

> Ch. 5, Ibid.

5 Courage is the price that Life exacts for granting
  peace,
The soul that knows it not, knows no release
From little things.

> "Courage" (1927), Quoted in Ch. 1, *The Sound of Wings* by Mary S. Lovell *1989*

6 The effect of having other interests beyond those domestic works well. The more one does and sees and feels, the more

one is able to do, and the more genuine may be one's appreciation of fundamental things like home, and love, and understanding companionship.

> Ch. 11, Ibid.

7 The woman who can create her own job is the woman who will win fame and fortune.

> *The New York Times* (29 July 1928), Ch.12, Ibid.

8 Women must try to do things as men have tried. When they fail their failure must be but a challenge to others.

> Ch. 21, Ibid.

9 Ours is a reasonable and contented partnership, my husband with his solo jobs and I with mine; but the system of dual control works satisfactorily, and our work and our play is a great deal together.

> Quoted in *Women Aviators* by Lisa Yount *1995*

10 [I'm] getting housemaid's knee kneeling here gulping beauty.

> Comment in logbook (1928), Ibid.

11 You must know again my reluctance to marry, my feeling that I shatter thereby chances in work which means most to me. . . Please let us not interfere with the other's work or play. . . . I may have to keep some place where I can go to be by myself now and then, for I cannot guarantee to endure at all times the confinement of even an attractive cage.

> Letter to her future husband, George Putnam, Ibid.

12 I cruised inland until I found a suitable pasture. I landed there after frightening all the cows in the neighborhood and rolled up to the farmer's front door.*

> Quoted on "100 Years of Great Women," *ABC News Special with Barbara Walters** 30 April 1999*
> *Comment on landing after piloting the first trans-Atlantic flight by a woman. **See 2480.

1711. Elizabeth Asquith Bibesco (1897–1945)

1 Being in a hurry is one of the tributes he pays to life.

> "Balloons" *1922*

2 I have made a great discovery.
What I love belongs to me. Not the chairs and
tables in my house, but the masterpieces of the world.
It is only a question of loving them enough.

> Ibid.

3 You are such a wonderful Baedeker to life. All the stars are in the right places.

> Ch. 13, *The Fir and the Palm 1924*

4 It is sometimes the man who opens the door who is the last to enter the room.

> Ibid.

5 It is never any good dwelling on good-byes. It is not the being together that it prolongs, it is the parting.

> Ch. 15, Ibid.

1712. Catherine Cate Coblentz (1897–1951)

1 Life is an archer, fashioning an arrow
With anxious care, for in it life must trust;
A single flash across the earthly spaces
Straight to the throat of death—one conquering thrust!

> "Life" *n.d.*

1713. Irène Joliot-Curie (1897–1956)

1   That one must do some work seriously and must be independent and not merely amuse oneself in life—this our mother [Marie Curie]* has told us always, but never that science was the only career worth following.
> Quoted in Ch. 10, *A Long Way from Missouri*
> by Mary Margaret McBride** *1959*
*See 1269. **See 1746.

1714. Dawn Powell (1897–1965)

1   . . . the tragedy of the Attick poets, Keats, Shelley, Burns,* was not that they died young but that they were obliged by poverty to do all their own writing.
> *A Time to Be Born 1942*
*English poets John Keats (1895–1921), Percy Bysse Shelley (1892–1922), and Scottish poet Robert Burns (1759–96).

2   She knew exactly what she wanted from life, which was, in a word, everything.
> Ibid.

3   She had a genuine distaste for sexual intimacy . . . but there were so many things to be gained by trading on sex and she thought so little of the process that she itched to use it as currency once again.
> Ibid.

4   I reflected that he* [her husband] was the only person in the world I found it always a kick to run into on the street.
> Diary entry, Quoted in *Dawn Powell* by Tim Page *1998*
*Reference to her husband, Joseph Gousha.

1715. Lillian Smith (1897–1966)

1   Man is a broken creature, yes; it is his nature as a human being to be so; but it is also his nature to create relationships that can span the brokenness. This is his first responsibility; when he fails, he is inevitably destroyed.
> Foreword, *Killers of the Dream* (rev. ed., 1961) *1949*

2   *Segregation* . . . A word full of meaning for every person on earth. A word that is both symbol and symptom of our modern, fragmented world. We, the earth people, have shattered our dreams, yes; we have shattered our own lives, too, and our world.
> Ibid.

3   . . . I am caught again in those revolving doors of childhood.
> Ibid.

4   The warped, distorted frame we have put around every Negro child from birth is around every white child also. Each is on a different side of the frame but each is pinioned there . . . what cruelly shapes and cripples the personality of one is as cruelly shaping and crippling the personality of the other.
> Pt. 1, Ch. 1, Ibid.

5   The human heart dares not stay away too long from that which hurt it most. There is a return journey to anguish which few of us are released from making.
> Ch. 1, Ibid.

6   When . . . [people] unite in common worship and common fear of one idea we know it has come to hold deep and secret meanings for each of them, as different as are the people themselves. We know it has woven itself around fantasies at a level difficult for the mind to touch, until it is a part of each man's internal defense system, embedded like steel in his psychic fortifications. And, like the little dirty rag or doll that an unhappy child sleeps with, it has acquired inflated values. . . .
> Ch. 4, Ibid.

7   Man, born of woman, has found it a hard thing to forgive her for giving him birth. The patriarchal protest against the ancient matriarch has borne strange fruit through the years. . . .
> Pt. II, Ch. 4, Ibid.

8   It is a man's dreams that make him human or inhuman and a man who knows few words to dream with, who has never heard, in words said aloud, other men's dreams of human dignity and freedom and tender love, and brotherhood, who has never heard of man the creator of truth and beauty, who has never even seen man-made beauty, but has heard only of man the killer, and words about sex and "race" which fill him with anger and fear and lust, and words about himself that make him feel degraded, or blow him up crazily into paranoid "superiority"—how can he know the meaning of *human*! How can he know that?
> Pt. III, Ch. 1, Ibid.

9   Faith and doubt both are needed—not as antagonists but working side by side—to take us around the unknown curve.
> *The Journey 1954*

10   To believe in something not yet proved and to underwrite it with our lives: it is the only way we can leave the future open. Man, surrounded by facts, permitting himself no surprise, no intuitive flash, no great hypothesis, no risk, is in a locked cell. Ignorance cannot seal the mind and imagination more securely.
> Ibid.

11   For men tied fast to the absolute, bled of their differences, drained of their dreams by authoritarian leeches until nothing but pulp is left, become a massive, sick Thing whose sheer weight is used ruthlessly by ambitious men. Here is the real enemy of the people: our own selves dehumanized into "the masses." And where is the David who can slay this giant?
> Prologue, Ibid.

12   To find the point where hypothesis and fact meet; the delicate equilibrium between dream and reality; the place where fantasy and earthly things are metamorphosed into a work of art; the hour when faith in the future becomes knowledge of the past; to lay down one's power for others in need; to shake off the old ordeal and get ready for the new; to question, knowing that never can the full answer be found; to accept uncertainties quietly, even our incomplete knowledge of God; this is what man's journey is about, I think.
> Ch. 15, Ibid.

13   When you stop learning, stop listening, stop looking and asking questions, always new questions, then it is time to die. . . .
> "Bridges to Other People," *Redbook* (New York)
> *September 1969*

14   Education is a private matter between the person and the world of knowledge and experience, and has little to do with school or college. . . .
> Ibid.

1716. Louise Bogan (1897–1970)

1   The water will always fall, and will not fall,
And the tipped bell make no sound.
> "Medusa," St. 4, *Bookman 1922*

2   Eat it, and you will taste more than the fruit:
    The blossom, too,
    The sun, the air, the darkness at the root,
    The rain, the dew,
        "The Crossed Apple," St. 7, *Dark Summer 1929*

3   . . . the opened mouth of love.
        "Baroque Comment," St. 2, *Sleeping Fury 1937*

4   The spectacle of a poet's work invigorated by his lifelong
    struggle against the artistic inertia of his nation is one that
    would shed strong light into any era.
        "William Butler Yeats,"* *Atlantic Monthly* (Boston)
        May 1938
    *Irish writer, world renowned poet, and cofounder of Irish Na-
    tional Theatre (1865–1939).

5   Yeats's faith in the development of his own powers has never
    failed.
        Ibid.

6   Where so much of the spirit of art had to be revivified, so
    many of its forms repaired, and so tight a mould of fanaticism
    broken, a man was needed who had in himself some of the
    qualities of the fanatic—a man who was, above all else, an
    artist, capable of making an occasional compromise with a
    human being, but incapable of making one with the informing
    essence of his art.
        Ibid.

7   At midnight tears

    Run into your ears.
        "Solitary Observation Brought Back From a Sojourn in
        Hell," *in toto, Poems and New Poems, 1941 1941*

8   Women have no wilderness in them,
    They are provident instead,
    Content in the tight hot cell of their hearts
    To eat dusty bread.
        "Women," St. 1, *Body of this Death 1943*

9   The art of one period cannot be approached through the atti-
    tudes (emotional or intellectual) of another.
        "Reading Contemporary Poetry," *College English*
        February 1953

10 True revolutions in art restore more than they destroy.
        Ibid.

11 It is a dangerous lot, that of the charming, romantic public
    poet, especially if it falls to a woman. . . . it is almost impos-
    sible for the poetess, once laurelled, to take off the crown
    for good or to reject the values and taste of those who ten-
    der it.*
        "Unofficial Feminine Laureate" (1939), *Selected Criticism:*
        Poetry and Prose 1955
    *Reference to Edna St. Vincent Millay; see 1632.

12 But childhood prolonged, cannot remain a fairyland. It be-
    comes a hell.*
        "Childhood's False Eden" (1940), Ibid.
    *Reference to Katherine Mansfield; see 1564.

13 This mouth will yet know song
    And words move on this tongue.
        "Homunculus," Sts. 3–4, *The Blue Estuaries:*
        Poems 1923–1968 1968

14 It lacks but life...
        Ibid.

15 I would not wake at your word, I had tears to say.
    I clung to the bars of the dream and they were said,
        "Tears in Sleep," Ibid.

16 I burned my life, that I might find
    A passion wholly of the mind
        "The Alchemist," St. 1, Ibid.

17 Once form has been smashed, it has been smashed for good,
    and once a forbidden subject has been released it has been re-
    leased for good.
        "Experimentalists of a New Generation" (1957), *A Poet's*
        Alphabet 1970

18 How fortunate the rich and/or married, who have servants and
    wives to expedite matters.
        What the Woman Lived: Selected Letters 1920–1970,
        Ruth Limmer, ed. *1974*

19 I don't like quintessential certitude.
        Letter to Rolfe Humphries, Ibid.

20 A second blooming and the bough can scarcely bear it.
        Ibid.

21 I cannot believe that the inscrutable universe turns on an axis
    of suffering; surely the strange beauty of the world must some-
    where rest on pure joy!
        Letter to John Hall Wheelock, Ibid.

22 To be quiet in the fern
    Like a thing gone dead and still,
    Listening to the prisoned cricket
    Shake its terrible dissembling
    Music in the granite hill
        "Men Loved Wholly Beyond Wisdom" *n.d.*

1717. Catherine Drinker Bowen (1897–1973)

1   I know what these people want; I have seen them pick up my
    violin and turn it over in their hands. They may not know it
    themselves, but they want music, not by the ticketful, the
    purseful, but music as it should be had, music at home, a part
    of daily life, a thing as necessary, as satisfying, as the midday
    meal. They want to *play*. And they are kept back by the ab-
    surd, the mistaken, the wicked notion that in order to play
    an instrument one must be possessed by that bogey called
    Talent. . . .
        Ch. 2, *Friends and Fiddlers 1934*

2   "We don't want her to take music too seriously." Real concern
    came into her voice. "We don't want her to become intense
    over something, and warped and queer. Such women are un-
    happy in later life. They don't" she rang the bell for more tea,
    "they don't make good wives."
        Ch. 4, Ibid.

3   Many a man who has known himself at ten forgets himself ut-
    terly between ten and thirty.
        Ch. 9, Ibid.

4   Holmes divided lawyers into kitchen knives, razors, and stings.
    Brandeis, he said, was a sting.
        Yankee from Olympus 1944

5 The professors laugh at themselves, they laugh at life; they long ago abjured the bitch-goddess Success, and the best of them will fight for his scholastic ideals with a courage and persistence that would shame a soldier. The professor is not afraid of words like *truth*; in fact he is not afraid of words at all.

Ch. 5, *Adventures of a Biographer 1946*

6 There is a marvelous turn and trick to British arrogance; its apparent unconsciousness makes it twice as effectual.

Ch. 14, Ibid.

7 In writing biography, fact and fiction shouldn't be mixed. And if they are, the fictional points should be printed in red ink, the facts printed in black ink.

Quoted in *Publishers Weekly 24 March 1958*

8 People who carry a musical soul about them are, I think, more receptive than others. They smile more readily. One feels in them a pleasant propensity toward the lesser sins, a pleasing readiness also to admit the possibility that on occasion they may be in the wrong—they may be mistaken.

Speech, "The Nature of the Artist" Scripps College *27 April 1961*

9 Your great artist looks on his talent as a responsibility laid on him by God, or perhaps a curse set on him by the devil. Whichever way he looks at it, while he is writing that book or composing that symphony, DOOM hangs over him. He is afraid something will interfere to stop him. . . . Artists often think they are going to die before their time. They seem to possess a heightened sense of the passing of the hours. . . . I think . . . artists dread death because they love life. Artists, even at their gloomiest, seem to maintain a constant love affair with life, marked by all the ups and downs, the depressions and ecstasies of infatuation. Artists have so much to do, and so little time to do it!

Ibid.

10 Great artists treasure their time with a bitter and snarling miserliness.

Ibid.

11 The things we believe in and want done will not be done until women are in elective office.

Quoted in *National Business Week September 1974*

1718. Caroline Lejeune (1897–1973)

1 Nothing is said that can be regretted. Nothing is said that can even be remembered.

"Dietrich* as an Angel," *The Observer* (London) *1936*
*See 1809.

2 In a world as ravaged as ours there is still room for joy over the maturing of a great talent.

"The Little Man Grows Up," *The Observer* (London) *1940*

3 For a good book has this quality, that it is not merely a petrification of its author, but that once it has been tossed behind, like Deucalion's little stone, it acquires a separate and vivid life of its own.

Introduction, *Chestnuts in Her Lap, 1936–1946 1947*

4 It's odd how large a part food plays in memories of childhood. There are grown men and women who still shudder at the sight of spinach, or turn away with loathing from stewed prunes and tapioca. . . . Luckily, however, it's the good tastes one remembers best.

Ch. 1, *Thank You for Having Me 1964*

5 Sometimes it seems to me as if the only quality admired in modern writing, or play-making, or film-making, is truth-and-ugliness. This, for some reason, is described as realism; as if nothing could be real that is not sordid, disagreeable or violent.

Ch. 21, Ibid.

6 When you finish with a job it is wiser to make the break completely. Cut off the old life, clean and sharp. If your mind is tired, that is the only way. If your mind is lively you will soon find other interests.

Ch. 22, Ibid.

1719. Dorothy Day (1897–1980)

1 We do not really know how much pride and self-love we have until someone whom we respect or love suddenly turns against us. Then some sudden affront, some sudden offense we take, reveals to us in all its glaring distinctness our self-love, and we are ashamed.

Introduction, *From Union Square to Rome 1938*

2 Tradition! We scarcely know the word anymore. We are afraid to be either proud of our ancestors or ashamed of them. We scorn nobility in name and in fact. We cling to a bourgeois mediocrity which would make it appear we are all Americans, made in the image and likeness of George Washington.

Pt. 1, *The Long Loneliness 1952*

3 . . . who were the mad and who were the sane? . . . People sold themselves for jobs, for the pay check, and if they only received a high enough price, they were honored. If their cheating, their theft, their lies, were of colossal proportions, it were successful, they met with praise, not blame.

Pt. I, Ibid.

4 One of the greatest evils of the day among those outside of prison is their sense of futility. Young people say, What is the sense of our small effort? They cannot see that we must lay one brick at a time, take one step at a time; we can be responsible only for the one action of the present moment. But we can beg for an increase of love in our hearts that will vitalize and transform all our individual actions, and know that God will take them and multiply them, as Jesus multiplied the loaves and fishes.

Ch. 16, *Loaves and Fishes 1963*

5 In our disobedience we were trying to obey God rather than men, trying to follow a higher obedience. We did not wish to act in a spirit of defiance and rebellion.

Ibid.

6 The greatest challenge of the day is: how to bring about a revolution of the heart, a revolution which has to start with each one of us? When we begin to take the lowest place, to wash the feet of others, to love our brothers with that burning love, that passion, which led to the Cross, then we can truly say, "Now I have begun."

Ch. 19, Ibid.

7 The best thing to do with the best things in life is to give them up.

Quoted in "Saints Among Us," *Time* (New York) *29 December 1975*

8 If you feed the poor, you're a saint. If you ask why they're poor, you're a Communist.

Entertaining Angels (bio pic] *1996*

9 I . . . was not going to have her [her daughter] floundering through many years as I had done, doubting . . . undisciplined, and amoral.

Ibid.

1720. Margaret Mahler (1897–1985)

1 . . . the emotional growth of the mother in her parenthood, her emotional willingness to let go of the toddler—to give him, as the mother bird does, a gentle push, as encouragement toward independence—is enormously helpful. It may even be a *sine qua non* of normal (healthy) individuation.

The Psychological Birth of the Human Infant 1975

1721. Hermione Gingold (1897–1987)

1 My father dealt in stocks and shares and my mother also had a lot of time on her hands.

Pt. I, *The World is Square 1945*

2 To call him a dog hardly seems to do him justice, though inasmuch as he had four legs, a tail, and barked, I admit he was, to all outward appearances. But to those of us who knew him well, he was a perfect gentleman.

Pt. II, *Ibid.*

3 This isn't a recipe for soup, although it can land you right in the *potage* if you aren't careful.

"I Make Summer Stock," *Sirens Should Be Seen and Not Heard 1963*

4 "Have you anything to back up your theory?"
  "I cannot truthfully say I have," Mr. Smith replied. "I just believe implicitly."
  "Well," I said, "I suppose it's like believing in the creation. There is much less to back up that theory these scientific days, and yet in spite of everything people still believe."

"The Bomb That Had Mr. Smith's Name on It," *Ibid.*

1722. Madame Chiang Kai-shek (1898–?)

1 Of all the inventions that have helped to unify China perhaps the airplane is the most outstanding. Its ability to annihilate distance has been in direct proportion to its achievements in assisting to annihilate suspicion and misunderstanding among provincial officials far removed from one another or from the officials at the seat of government.

"Wings Over China," *Shanghai Evening Post 12 March 1937*

2 The faults of a government can be removed by the citizens, but the citizens must first remove their own faults, and learn in full what self-sacrifice really means. They must be self-reliant, and have self-respect.

Article in the *Birmingham Post*, England (1938), Quoted in *War Messages and Other Selections 1938*

3 My friends, the world situation is so grave that we can no longer afford to congratulate each other upon the splendid success that we have achieved internationally. It is imperative that we be frank, honest, and effective. As a first step, I propose that we recognize our failure mercilessly, even at the expense of our personal pride. We are guilty, every one of us. Let us say "mea culpa" and not blame the rest of the world for what is happening around us.

Speech, International Women's Conference (Sydney, Australia, February 1938), *Ibid.*

4 This changing world is rolling towards the abyss of self-destruction with a breath-taking rapidity.

Ibid.

5 There is no shadow of protection to be had by sheltering behind the slender stockades of visionary speculation, or by hiding behind the wagon-wheels of pacific theories.

Quoted in *New York Herald Tribune 1 March 1938*

6 No nation that descends to murder, rape and rapine can expect to prosper or be respected.

Article in the *Birmingham* [England] *Post*, (May 1938), *Ibid.*

7 Machinery should be used to make necessities which hands cannot make, but there it should stop.

Letter to a Friend (14 May 1938), *Ibid.*

8 Out of the ashes which the Japanese are spreading over our country will arise a phoenix of great national worth.

"People's Spiritual Mobilization" (18 March 1939), *Ibid.*

9 Hammered out on the anvil of experience are four cardinal principles of life, as we Chinese understand life: 1. The way in which human beings behave one toward another. 2. Justice for all classes within our social framework. 3. Honesty in public administration and in business. 4. Self-respect, and a profound sense of the value of personality.

Sec. I, Ch. 1, *This Is Our China 1940*

10 I am convinced that we must train not only the head, but the heart and hand as well.

Sec. II, *Ibid.*

11 If one task is more outstandingly important than any other in connection with the reform and rehabilitation of our country it must be the eradication of the criminal stagnation that has for so many generations stifled the natural development of our economic life and stood upon our horizon like a grim spectre of predestined rule.

Pt. I, Ch. 6, *China Shall Rise Again 1941*

12 Cliques seem to hold sway in many places. They are like dry rot in the administration. They stifle enterprise and initiative. They operate to oust honesty and efficiency by preventing a patriotic "outsider," or a stranger to the clique, from gaining a position, no matter how capable he may be. And they eject, or try to, anyone of any independence of character or mind who may happen to be near them but not of them. Every clique is a refuge for incompetence. It fosters corruption and disloyalty, it begets cowardice, and consequently is a burden upon and a drawback to the progress of the country. Its instincts and actions are those of the pack.

Ch. 8, *Ibid.*

13 They [the Chinese people] will remember never to believe in international promises or professions—no matter how well-intentioned they may appear to be; no matter how many imposing-looking seals may adorn the documents. To be sure this new wisdom has been dearly paid for; it will have to be paid for over and over again in more loss of blood and life. But, then I suppose they will have to learn the lesson of life that where there are no pains, there can be no real gains.

Pt. III, Ch. 23, *Ibid.*

14 America is not only the cauldron of democracy, but the incubator of democratic principles.

Speech, United States House of Representatives *18 February 1943*

15 The universal tendency of the world as represented by the United Nations is as patent and inexorable as the enormous

sheets of ice which float down the Hudson in winter. The swift and mighty tide is universal justice and freedom.

Speech, Madison Square Garden (New York) *3 March 1943*

16 For is it not true that human progress is but a mighty growing pattern woven together by the tenuous single threads united in a common effort?

Speech, Wellesley College *7 March 1943*

17 . . . is it not true that faith is the substance of things hoped for, the evidence of things not seen?

Speech, (Chicago) *22 March 1943*

18 Truth requires that each people live according to its own traditions in a climate of human liberty and dignity. That has been the soul of Chinese civilization.

Radio Address (New York), *9 January 1950*

19 China's struggle now is the initial phase of a gigantic conflict between good and evil, between liberty and communism.

Ibid.

1723. Helen Sekaquaptewa (1898–?)

1 We were as stubborn about going back to the old ways as they were about changing their way.

Me and Mine 1969

2 I was stuck here, so I might as well learn everything.

Interview (3 June 1981), Quoted in *American Indian Women, Telling Their Lives*, Gretchen M. Bataille and Kathleen Mullen Sands, eds. *1984*

1724. Bessie Smith (1898–1937)

1 No time to marry, no time to settle down;
I'm a young woman, and I ain't done runnin' aroun'.

"Young Woman's Blues" *1927*

2 I woke up this mornin', can't even get out of my do',
There's enough trouble to make a poor girl wonder where she wanna go.

"Back Water Blues" *1927*

3 While you're living in your mansion, you don't know what hard times mean.
Poor working man's wife is starving; your wife is living like a queen.

"Poor Man's Blues" *1930*

4 It's a long old road, but I know I'm gonna find the end.

"Long Old Road" *1931*

1725. Cecily R. Hallack (1898–1938)

1 Make me a saint by getting meals; and washing up the plates!

"The Divine Office of the Kitchen," St. 1 c. *1928*

1726. Dorothy Speare (1898–1951)

1 The intoxication of rouge is an insidious vintage known to more girls than mere man can ever believe.

Dancers in the Dark 1922

1727. Anna Moore Shaw (1898–1975)

1 We were not allowed to speak the Pima tongue at school. Some students would report on those who spoke in Indian and as a

punishment our mouths would be taped. We did not mind, for the matron, teachers, and other employees were good to us, despite our naughty ways.

A Pima Past 1974

2 The educations they had strived so hard to give us had prepared us to bring in money from the white man's work; it would be wrong to waste all those years of schooling on a life of primitive farming.

Ibid.

1728. Golda Meir (1898–1978)

1 Can we today measure devotion to husband and children by our indifference to everything else? Is it not often true that the woman who has given up all the external world for her husband and her children has done it not out of a sense of duty, out of devotion and love, but out of incapacity, because the soul is not able to take into itself the many-sidedness of life, with its sufferings but also with its joys?

The Plough Woman c. 1930

2 I want to say to you, friends, that the Jewish community in Palestine is going to fight to the very end. If we have arms to fight with, we will fight with those, and if not, we will fight with stones in our hands.

"In the Midst of Battle: 1948," Speech, Council of Jewish Federations (Chicago) *21 January 1948*

3 We desire nothing more than peace, but we cannot equate peace merely with an apathetic readiness to be destroyed. If hostile forces gather for our proposed destruction, they must not demand that we provide them with ideal conditions for the realization of their plans. . . . The concept of annihilating Israel is a legacy of Hitler's war against the Jewish people, and it is no mere coincidence that the soldiers of Nasser had an Arabic translation of *Mein Kampf* in their knapsacks.

"The Israeli Action in Sinai: 1956," Statement, General Assembly of United Nations *5 December 1956*

4 We have not the slightest doubt that eventually there will be peace and cooperation between us. This is a historic necessity for both peoples. We are prepared; we are anxious to bring it about now.

"A Solemn Appeal to the Arabs," Statement, General Assembly of United Nations *7 October 1957*

5 . . . The deserts of the Middle East are in need of water, not bombers.

Ibid.

6 I can honestly say that I was never affected by the question of the success of an undertaking. If I felt it was the right thing to do, I was for it regardless of the possible outcome.

Quoted in *Golda Meir: Woman with a Cause* by Marie Syrkin *1964*

7 There are not enough prisons and concentration camps in Palestine to hold all the Jews who are ready to defend their lives and property.

Speech (2 May 1940), Ibid.

8 Hebrew is our language, just as English is your language, just as French is the language of the French and Chinese the language of China. None of these probably would be questioned as to why they spoke their language.

Address, Anglo-American Committee of Inquiry (25 March 1946), Ibid.

9 The spirit is there. This spirit alone cannot face rifles and machine guns. Rifles and machine guns without spirit are not worth very much. But spirit without these in time can be broken with the body.
Address, Council of Jewish Federation (21 January 1949), Ibid.

10 We are not a better breed; we are not the best Jews of the Jewish people. It so happened that we are there and you are here. I am certain that if you were there and we were here, you would be doing what we are doing there, and you would ask us who are here to do what you will have to do.
Ibid.

11 Religious families have sons as well as daughters. If army life is degrading why are they not concerned for the morals of their sons?
Address (1953), Ibid.

12 Those that perished in Hitler's gas chambers were the last Jews to die without standing up to defend themselves.
"In the Hour of Deliverance: 1967," Speech, United Jewish Appeal rally at Madison Square Garden (New York) 11 June 1967

13 But the individual was not a tool for something. He was the maker of tools. He was the one who must build. Even for the best purpose it is criminal to turn an individual into simply a means for some ultimate end. A society in which the dignity of the individual is destroyed cannot hope to be a decent society.
"The Zionist Purpose," Speech at Dropise College 26 November 1967

14 When peace comes we will perhaps in time be able to forgive the Arabs for killing our sons, but it will be harder for us to forgive them for having forced us to kill their sons.
Press conference (London) 1969

15 I want to be able to live without a crowded calendar. I want to be able to read a book without feeling guilty, or go to a concert when I like. . . . But I do not intend to retire to a political nunnery.
Statement of Resignation, As Good as Golda, Israel and Mary Shenker, eds. 1970

16 A leader who doesn't hesitate before he sends his nation into battle is not fit to be a leader.
(1967), Ibid.

17 Being seventy is not a sin.
Quoted in "The Indestructible Golda Meir" by David Reed, Reader's Digest July 1971

18 We intend to remain alive. Our neighbors want to see us dead. This is not a question that leaves much room for compromise.
Ibid.

19 Women's Liberation is just a lot of foolishness. It's the men who are discriminated against. They can't bear children. And no one's likely to do anything about that.
Quoted in Newsweek (New York] 23 October 1972

20 I hate fashion. I've always hated it. Fashion is an imposition, a rein on freedom.
Quoted by Oriana Fallaci* in L'Europeo 1973
*See 2416.

21 Show me a sensible person who likes himself or herself! I know myself too well to like what I see. I know but too well that I'm not what I'd like to be.
Ibid.

22 If you knew how often I say to myself: to hell with everything, to hell with everybody, I've done my share, let the others do theirs now, enough, enough, enough!
Ibid.

23 I believe there are a couple of gross injustices in the world: against African blacks and against Jews. Moreover, I think these two instances of injustice can only be remedied by Socialist principles.
Ibid.

24 At work, you think of the children you've left at home. At home, you think of the work you've left unfinished. Such a struggle is unleashed within yourself: your heart is rent.
Ibid.

25 Those who do not know how to weep with their whole heart don't know how to laugh either.
Ibid.

26 I must govern the clock, not be governed by it.
Ibid.

27 . . . old age is like a plane flying through a storm. Once you're aboard, there's nothing you can do. You can't stop the plane, you can't stop the storm, you can't stop time. So one might as well accept it calmly, wisely.
Ibid.

28 . . . there's no difference between one's killing and making decisions that will send others to kill. It's exactly the same thing, or even worse.
Ibid.

29 For me party discipline is a sacred matter, not just lust for power as some people claim: I was brought up that way all my life.
Statement upon resignation as prime minister of Israel 11 April 1974

30 I have had enough.
Ibid.

31 We only want that which is given naturally to all peoples of the world, to be masters of our own fate, only of our fate, not of others, and in cooperation and friendship with others.
Address, Anglo-American Committee of Inquiry (25 March 1946), Quoted in Golda Meir: Woman with a Cause by Marie Syrkin 1984

32 From my early youth I believed in two things: one, the need for Jewish sovereignty, so that Jews...can be master of their own fate; and two, a society based on justice and equality without exploitation. But I was never so naïve or foolish as to think that if you merely believe in something it happens. You must struggle for it.
Quoted in Twentieth-Century Women Political Leaders by Claire Price-Groff 1998

33 The only alternative to war is peace and the only road to peace is negotiations.
Ibid.

34 I think women often get not so much an unfair deal as an illogical one. Once in the Cabinet we had to deal with the fact

that there had been an outbreak of assaults on women at night. One minister (a member of an extreme religious party) suggested a curfew. Women should stay home after dark. I said: "But it's the men who are attacking the women. If there's to be a curfew, let the men stay at home, not the women."

Speech n.d.

1729. Katharine "Katie" Burr Blodgett (1898–1979)

1   A woman who wants to do something in science must have three things besides formal training—patience, persistence and a knack at solving problems, or at least the desire to try to solve them. A girl who is not interested in the little problems of everyday life will not find it easy to learn to solve the problems of work in a laboratory.

Quoted in Women Inventors
by Linda Jacobs Altman 1997

2   That formaldehyde polyvinyl—
    If you eat it, you're certain to dine ill.
        One night at a party,
        When the guests all ate hearty,
    By actual count it made nine ill.

Ibid.

1730. Gracie Fields (1898–1979)

1   You can get good fish and chips at the Savoy; and you can put up with fancy people once you understand that you don't have to be like them.

Ch. 4, Sing as We Go 1960

2   Now sometimes it can be a very dangerous thing to go in search of a dream for the reality does not always match it. . . .

Ibid.

1731. Rachel Brown (1898–1980)

1   Recently I had a severe shock. A high school girl who wanted to [study] biology was advised by her counselor not to do so because "the opportunities are few for women." It is hard to understand why the many life sciences should not offer just the right chances for women to express themselves. Consider Rachel Carson's* Silent Spring . . .

Comment (15 April 1977), Quoted in
Women Inventors by Linda Jacobs Altman
1997

*See 1904.

1732. Isabel Briggs Myers (1898–1980)

1   We cannot safely assume that other people's minds work on the same principles as our own. All too often, others with whom we come in contact do not reason as we reason, or do not value the things we value, or are not interested in what interests us.

Pt. I, Ch. 1, Gifts Differing,
with Peter B. Myers 1980

2   Whatever the circumstances of your life, whatever your personal ties, work, and responsibilities, the understanding of type can make your perceptions clearer, your judgements sounder, and your life closer to your heart's desire.

Pt. IV, Ch. 19, Ibid.

1733. Ariel Durant (1898–1981)

1   You* love me because you know I love you to distraction.

Quoted in "The Philosopher and the Schoolgirl"
by Jim Bishop, Reader's Digest October 1969

*Since the lion's share of Ms. Durant's monumental work was in collaboration with her husband, historian Will Durant, (1885?–1981), little can be found that is purely her own work.

1734. Lotte Lenya (1898–1981)

1   [I have] a heavenly vase full of autumn leaves today. They looks so beautiful. How much closer to God can one get? And a beautiful blue heron flew over the brook. Nature can make me cry faster than anything.

Letter to Mary Daniel (April 1957), Quoted in Lenya,
a Life by Donald Spoto 1989

2   I don't like holidays, not here [the United States]—it's a giant supermarket, and I'm thinking with nostalgia of my childhood with a tiny Christmas tree . . .

Christmas card to Hilde Halpern (1980), Ibid.

1735. Lily Pincus (1898–1981)

1   Why not acknowledge and satisfy without shame the baby needs stirred up by bereavement?

Death and the Family 1974

2   Regression in grief must be seen and supported as a means toward adaptation and health.

Ibid.

1736. Beatrice Lillie (1898–1989)

1   I'll simply say here that I was born Beatrice Gladys Lillie at an extremely tender age because my mother needed a fourth at meals.

Ch. 1, Every Other Inch a Lady 1927

2   I took up knitting from time to time as a relaxation, but I always put it down again before going out to buy a rocking chair.

Ch. 15, Ibid.

3   The vows one makes privately are more binding than any ceremony or even a Shubert contract.

Ibid.

4   In my experience, anyone can paint if he doesn't have to. . . . During my apprentice days, I felt encouraged by the advice of Winston Churchill, who used to say, "Don't be afraid of the canvas." I have now reached the point where the canvas is afraid of me.

Ibid.

1737. Berenice Abbott (1898–1991)

1   Photography can never grow up if it imitates some other medium. It has to walk alone; it has to be itself.

"It Has to Walk Alone," Infinity (magazine) 1951

2   If a medium is represented by nature of the realistic image formed by a lens, I see no reason why we should stand on our heads to distort that function. On the contrary, we should take hold of that very quality, make use of it, and explore it to the fullest.

Ibid.

3   I took to photography like a duck to water. I never wanted to do anything else. Excitement about the subject is the voltage

which pushes me over the mountain of drudgery necessary to produce the final photograph.

Preface, *The Berenice Abbott Portfolio 1976*

4   Photography helps people to see.

Quoted in "Berenice Abbott: An American Master,"
ASMP Bulletin October 1989

5   I am so fascinated with this century it will help keep me alive. I'll be there until the last minute, fighting.

Ibid.

1738. Judith Anderson (1898–1992)

1   There is nothing enduring in the life of a woman except what she builds in a man's heart.

News item *8 March 1931*

1739. Indra Devi (1899–?)

1   Like an ugly bird of prey, tension hovers over the heads of millions of people, ready to swoop down on all its victims at any time and in any place. More and more men, women, and even children are caught up in its cold grip and held for years, sometimes for the whole of their lives. Tension, in fact, is probably one of the greatest menaces the civilized world must face these days.

Ch. 1, *Renewing Your Life Through Yoga 1963*

2   Tranquilizers . . . dull the keen edge of the angers, fears, or anxiety with which we might otherwise react to the problems of living. Once the response has been dulled, the irritating surface noise of living muted or eliminated, the spark and brilliance are also gone.

Ibid.

3   Like water which can clearly mirror the sky and the trees only so long as its surface is undisturbed, the mind can only reflect the true image of the Self when it is tranquil and wholly relaxed.

Ibid.

4   Our body is a magnificently devised, living, breathing mechanism, yet we do almost nothing to insure its optimal development and use. . . . The human organism needs an ample supply of good building material to repair the effects of daily wear and tear.

Ch. 2, Ibid.

5   Yoga is not a religion, nor is it a magic formula or some form of calisthenics. In the country of its origin it is called a science—the science of living a healthy, meaningful, and purposeful life—a method of realizing the true self when the body, mind, and spirit blend into one harmonious whole. . . . Yoga is a philosophy, a way of life, and organized religion forms no part of it.

Ch. 10, Ibid.

1740. Hildegarde Flanner (1899–?)

1   I saw a hawk devour a screaming bird,
Devour the little ounce sugared with song.

"Hawk Is a Woman,"
If There is Time 1942

2   May she, the very she, may that hawk hear
The ugly female laughter of a hawk.

Ibid.

1741. Emily Kimbrough (1899–?)

Co-author of *Our Hearts Were Young and Gay* with Cornelia Otis Skinner; see 1803.

1742. Helen Hill Miller (1899–?)

1   France prides itself on being very old, on being not only the first-born among the modern nations but the heir of the ancient world, the transmitter to the West of Mediterranean civilization.

Pamphlet, "The Spirit of Modern France" *1934*

2   Logical clarity is the genius of the French language.

Ibid.

3   Then, the word tyrant did not carry the pejorative meaning it conveys today. Tyrants seized and held their power by force, exercised it subject to no restraint, and perpetuated notorious cruelties. But many of them were great generals who fought wide-sweeping wars, lavish patrons of the arts, public figures who brought their cities riches and renown. The times combined civilization and savagery.

Sicily and Western Colonies of Greece 1965

4   It isn't very often that a person who has been at the very center of one period in the life of a political party has the forward-lookingness and the resilience to note the transition to a new time, much less to bring it forcefully to the attention to the current members of the party.

Letter to Eleanor Roosevelt* (1956), Quoted in
Eleanor: The Years Alone by Joseph P. Lash *1972*
*See 1513.

1743. Anna Akhmatova (1899–1966)

1   There is a sacred, secret line in loving which attraction and even passion cannot cross,—

Untitled, St. 4 (1915), *White Flock*, Jane Kenyon, tr. *1917*

2   I remember how the gods turned people into things, not killing their consciousness.
And now, to keep those glorious sorrows alive,
you have turned into my memory of you.

Untitled, St. 3 (1916), Ibid.

3   How quiet is it after the volley!
Death sends patrols into every courtyard.

Untitled (1917), Ibid.

4   O great language we love:
It is you, Russian tongue, we must save, and we swear
We will give you unstained to the sons of our sons.

"Courage" *1942*

5   What hangs in the balance is nowise in doubt;
We know the event and we brave what we know;
Our clocks are all striking the hour of courage.

Ibid.

6   Only my voice, like a flute, will mourn
at your dumb funeral feast.

"In Memory of M. B.," St. 2, *Poems of Akhmatova*,
Stanley Kunitz and Max Hayward, intro. and trs. *1967*

7   It is not with the lyre of someone in love
that I go seducing people.
The rattle of the leper
is what sings into my hands.

Untitled, *in toto*, *Twenty Poems of Anna Akhmatova*,
Jane Kenyon, tr. *1985*

8 And the sun goes down in waves of ether in such a way that I
     can't tell
   if the day is ending, or the world,
   or if the secret of secrets is within me again.
                                    "On the Road," St. 3 (1964), Ibid.

1744. Gertrude Berg (1899–1966)

1 MOLLY GOLDBERG. So who's to know?
                                                    Me and Molly 1948

2 It is impossible to improve on reality. The good radio story
   should never escape reality and the problems of real people.
              Quoted in *Who's Who in Comedy* by Ronald L. Smith 1992

1745. Elizabeth Bowen (1899–1973)

1 "The best type of man is no companion."
                                                    The Hotel 1928

2 "I have a horror, I think, of not being, and of my friends not
   being, quite perfectly balanced."
                                                             Ibid.

3 Intimacies between women go backwards, beginning with revelations and ending up in small talk without loss of esteem.
                           Pt. 2, Ch. 1, *The Death of the Heart* 1938

4 Only in a house where one has learnt to be lonely does one have
   this solicitude for things. One's relation to them, the daily seeing
   or touching, begins to become love, and to lay one open to pain.
                                                       Ch. 2, Ibid.

5 The heart may think it knows better: the senses know that absence blots people out. We really have no absent friends. The
   friend becomes a traitor by breaking, however unwillingly or
   sadly, out of our own zone: a hard judgment is passed on him,
   for all the pleas of the heart.
                                                             Ibid.

6 Pity the selfishness of lovers: it is brief, a forlorn hope; it is impossible.
                                                       Ch. 4, Ibid.

7 Nobody can be kinder than the narcissist while you react to
   life in his own terms.
                                                 Pt. 3, Ch. 3, Ibid.

8 The charm, one might say the genius of memory, is that it is
   choosy, chancy, and temperamental: it rejects the edifying
   cathedral and indelibly photographs the small boy outside,
   chewing a hunk of melon in the dust.
                         Article, *Vogue* (New York) 15 September 1955

9 "There being nothing was what you were frightened of all the
   time, eh? Yes."
                                                 The Little Girls 1963

10 "Did you exchange embraces of any kind?"
    "No. She was always in a hurry."
                                                    Eva Trout 1968

1746. Mary Margaret McBride (1899–1976)

1 Yes, we have a good many poor tired people here already, but
   we have plenty of mountains, rivers, woods, lots of sunshine
   and air, for tired people to rest in. We have Kansas wheat and
   Iowa corn and Wisconsin cheese for them to eat, Texas cotton

for them to wear. So give us as many as come—we can take it,
and take care of them.
                                       Ch. 1, *America for Me* 1941

2 This country began with people moving, and we've been moving ever since. . . . As long as we keep at that I guess we'll be
   all right.
                                                    Ch. 2, Ibid.

3 "Terrible things happen to young girls in New York City. . . ."
                              Ch. 1, *A Long Way from Missouri* 1959

1747. Marguerite Harris (1899–1978)

1 In tidy terminal homes,
   agape at the stalking Rorschach
   shapes that menace our cosmos,
   pawns, now, we itch and surmise.
              "The Chosen," St. 1, *The East Side Scene*, Allen de Loach,
                                                           ed. 1968

1748. Gloria Swanson (1899–1983)

1 When I die, my epitaph should read: *She Paid the Bills.* That's
   the story of my private life.
                   Quoted in "Gloria Swanson Comes Back" by S. Frank,
                                 Saturday Evening Post 22 July 1950

1749. Louise Nevelson (1899–1988)

1 The freer that women become, the freer will men be. Because
   when you enslave someone—you *are* enslaved.
                            Quoted in *AFTRA Magazine* Summer 1974

1750. Diana Vreeland (1899/1904?–1989)

1 Elegance is innate . . . it has nothing to do with being well
   dressed.
                        Quoted in *Time* (New York) 4 September 1989

1751. Bella Spewack (1899–1990)

1 BENSON. You were saying that this is one of the greatest pic-
   ture scripts ever written.
   C.F. Now, just a minute—
   LAW. And do you know why? Because it's the same story Larry
   Toms has been doing for years.
   BENSON. We *know* it's good.
   LAW. Griffith used it. Lubitsch used it. And Eisenstein's coming
   around to it.
   BENSON. Boy meets girl. Boy loses girl. Boy gets girl.
   LAW. The great American fairy-tale. Sends the audience back to
   the relief rolls in a happy frame of mind.
   BENSON. And why not?
   LAW. The greatest escape formula ever worked out in the his-
   tory of civilization . . .
   C.F. Of course, if you put it that way...but, boys, it's hack-
   neyed.
   LAW. You mean classic.
   C.F. *Hamlet* is a classic—but it isn't hackneyed!
   LAW. *Hamlet* isn't hackneyed? Why, I'd be ashamed to use that
   poison gag. He lifted that right out of the Italians.
                                          Sc. 4, *Boy Meets Girl* 1935

1752. Eva Le Gallienne (1899–1991)

1 . . . no mechanical device can ever, it seems to me, quite take
   the place of that mysterious communication between players

and public, that sense of an experience directly shared, which gives to the living theater its unique appeal.

> Ch. 1, *The Mystic in the Theater: Eleanora Duse* 1965*
> *See 1189.

2   Innovators are inevitably controversial.

> Ibid.

3   People who are born even-tempered, placid and untroubled—secure from violent passions or temptations to evil—those who have never needed to struggle all night with the Angel to emerge lame but victorious at dawn, never become great saints.

> Ch. 2, Ibid.

4   But the breathtaking part of it all was not so much the planning as the fantastic skill with which the planning was concealed.

> Ch. 5, Ibid.

5   There can be no generalizations as far as the art of acting is concerned. There can be no over-all "method"—above all no short cuts. Each actor must find his own way for himself.

> Ch. 6, Ibid.

1753. Grace Adams (1900–?)
1   Whenever serious intellectuals, psychologists, sociologists, practicing physicians, Nobel prize novelists take time off from their normal pursuits to scrutinize and appraise the Modern American Woman, they turn in unanimously dreary reports.

> "American Women Are Coming Along," *Harper's*
> (New York) *1939*

1754. Ellen Eglui (fl. late 19th century)
1   You know I am black and if it was known that a Negro woman patented the invention white ladies would not buy the wringer,* I was afraid to be known because of my color, in having it introduced into the market, that is the only reason.

> "The Innovative Woman" (p. 10), *New Scientist*
> *24 May 1984*
> *Hand-cranked roller device used to squeeze water out of fabric.

1755. Elizabeth, Queen Mother (1900–)
1   The children will not leave unless I do. I shall not leave unless their father does, and the King will not leave the country in any circumstances whatever.

> Attributed *1940*

2   I'm glad we've been bombed [Buckingham Palace]. It makes me feel I can look the East End in the face.

> Pt. 3, Ch. 6, Remark (September 1940),* Quoted in
> *King George VI* by John Wheeler-Bennett *1958*
> *Reference to the bombing of Buckingham Palace. The East End (London) bore the brunt of the bombing during the blitz in World War II.

1756. Joanna Field (1900–1998)
1   . . . the growth of understanding follows an ascending spiral rather than a straight line.

> *A Life of One's Own 1934*

2   I used to trouble about what life was for—now being alive seems sufficient reason.

> (8 June), Ibid.

3   I feel we have picked each other from the crowd as fellow-travellers, for neither of us is to the other's personality the end-all and the be-all.

> (20 September), Ibid.

4   . . . as soon as you are happy enjoying yourself, something hunts you on—the hounds of heaven—you think you'll be lost—damned, if you are caught. . . .

> (10 October), Ibid.

5   I came to the conclusion then that "continual mindfulness" . . . must mean, not a sergeant-major-like drilling of thoughts, but a continual readiness to accept whatever came.

> Ibid.

6   I began to suggest that thought, which I had always before looked on as a cart-horse to be driven, whipped and plodding between shafts, might be really a Pegasus, so suddenly did it alight beside me from places I had no knowledge of.

> Ibid.

1757. Lillian Gideon (1900?–)
1   Stay in school, no matter how hard it is for you. Get an education. And try to get along with each other, help each other.

> "Her dream: Give hope a chance" by Judi Hunt,
> *Seattle Post-Intelligencer*, C1–2 *18 January 1993*

2   Racial discrimination hasn't ended, it's just become more difficult to prove. It's subtle, unspoken, covert.

> Ibid.

3   You know, we're all going in the same direction, or at least trying to. So we need to live together, get along together and give each other enough space to be comfortable on that road.
>
> No one should crowd anyone else on that road.

> Ibid.

4   Whatever our race, we can't let our young be immobilized with anger and hopelessness. Then we're handing the other guy the stick with which to crack us across the head, and, believe me, they'll use it.

> Ibid.

5   It must be very tempting to join the drug culture when you're second or third generation on welfare, you have nothing, not even enough to eat.
>
> It has to be difficult, if not impossible, to say "no" when he's suddenly offered $200 a week to deliver or deal drugs. I don't know if I were in the same situation if I could say "no."

> Ibid.

1758. Guion Griffis Johnson (1900–)
1   Government existed for the best people—the intelligent, educated, and wealthy. In a society where all are equally free and share alike in political privileges, there are some more fit for the exercise of good government than others.

> "Southern Paternalism Toward Negroes After Emancipation," *The Journal of Southern History November 1957*

2   The argument against mixing in the schools stresses again the concept of superior and inferior races and the obligation of the superior to give the inferior equal but separate facilities so that the Negro may have the opportunity to rise within his own social system.

> Ibid.

3 It was always the responsibility of the strong, so ran the benevolent paternalist's argument, to bear the burden of the weak. The strong race by virtue of its superior intelligence, culture, and wealth was the national protector of the Negro.

Ibid.

1759. Wilhelmina Kemp Johnstone (1900–)

1 But how glad I am, how very glad and grateful for that window looking out upon the sea!

"My Window," *Bahamian Jottings 1973*

2 The dawn artist was already out, tipping the clouds with glory, and transforming the sky into a glow of wonder.

"Our Trip to Green Cay," Ibid.

3 Pride, we are told, my children, "goeth before a fall," and oh, the pride was there and so the fall was not far away!

"The Old Ship's Story," Ibid.

1760. Eva Lathbury (fl. early 1900s)

1 The fall, like the serpent, was mythical: the apple was sound and Eve hysterical.

My Meyer's Pupil 1907

2 I can't help it . . . that's what we all say when we don't want to exert ourselves.

Ibid.

1761. Estée Lauder (1900?–)

1 I would give the woman a sample of whatever she did not buy as a gift. It might be a few teaspoonfuls of powder in a wax envelope. I just knew, even though I had not yet named the technique, that a gift with a purchase was very appealing.

Estée: A Success Story 1985

1762. Barbara Morgan (1900–1992)

1 The Navajo and Pueblo Indian tribes who danced the rituals . . . as partners in the cosmic process, attuned me to the universally primal—rather than to either the "primitive" or the "civilized."

Quoted in *The Woman's Eye* by Anne Tucker* 1973
*See 3073.

2 . . . as the life style of the Space Age grows more inter-disciplinary, it will be harder for the "one-track" mind to survive. . . . I see simultaneous intake, multiple awareness, and synthesized comprehension as inevitable, long before the year 2000 A.D.

Ibid.

1763. Moira O'Neill (fl. early 1900s)

1 Youth's for an hour,
Beauty's a flower,
But love is the jewel that wins the world.

"Beauty's a Flower," *Songs of the Glens of Antrim 1901*

2 The memory's fairly spoilt on me
Wild mindin' to forget.

"Forgettin'," St. 5, Ibid.

1764. Frances Partridge (1900–)

1 It is a purely relative matter where one draws the plimsoll-line of condemnation, and . . . if you find the whole of humanity

falls below it you have simply made a mistake and drawn it too high. And are probably below it yourself.

Ch. 17, Entry (3 September 1959), *Julia 1983*

1765. Qui Jin (fl. 1900s)

1 Today the two hundred million men in our country are entering into a civilized new world . . . but we, the two hundred million women, are still kept down in the dungeon.

Remark (1907), Quoted in *Women in World History Curriculum*, www.womeninworldhistory.com/ 1996–97

1766. Violet Alleyn Storey (1900–?)

1 I have a small-town soul.
It makes me want to know
Wee, unimportant things
About the folks that go
Past on swift journeys.

"Ironical" *n.d.*

1767. Opal Whiteley (1900?–)

1 The mamma where I love
says I am a new sance.
I think it is something grown-ups
don't like to have around.

The Story of Opal 1920
*Written between the ages of five and twelve.

2 Potatoes are very interesting folks
I think they must see a lot
of what is going on in the earth
They have so many eyes.

Ibid.

3 And this I have learned
grown-ups do not know the language of shadows.

Ibid.

4 It is such a comfort to have a friend near.
when lonesome feels do come.

Ibid.

5 Some days are long.
Some days are short.
The days that I have to stay in the house
are the most long days of all.

Ibid.

6 I led her toward a shadow
that was coming our way.
It did touch her cheeks
with its velvety fingers.
And now she too
does have likings for shadows.
And her fear that was is gone.

Ch. 15, Quoted in *Women Who Run With the Wolves* by Clarissa Pinkola Estés* 1992
*See 2938.

1768. Frances Winwar (1900–)

1 In her [Eleanora Duse]* intellectual acquisitiveness she selected people as a bee chooses its flowers, for what they had to offer. Her lack of formal education made her the eternal disciple.

Ch. 14, *Wingless Victory 1956*
*See 1189.

1769. Lena Guilbert Ford (fl. early 1900s– d. 1916?)

1 Keep the home fires burning,
  While your hearts are yearning,
  Though your lands are far away
  They dream of home.
  There's silver lining
  Through the dark cloud shining:
  Turn the dark cloud inside out,
  Till the boys come home.

  "Keep the Home Fires Burning" 1915

1770. Lady Troubridge (fl. early 1900s– d. 1946)

1 A bad woman always has something she regards as a curse—a real bit of goodness hidden away somewhere.

  The Millionaire 1907

2 If I had had a pistol I would have shot him—either that or fallen at his feet. There is no middle way when one loves.

  Ibid.

3 It is far easier to love a woman in picturesque rags than in the common place garments of respectability.

  Ibid.

4 A girl can't analyze marriage, and a woman—daren't.

  Ibid.

1771. Zelda Fitzgerald (1900–1948)

1 Women, despite the fact that nine out of ten of them go through life with a death-bed air either of snatching-the-last-moment or with martyr-resignation, do not die tomorrow—or the next day. They have to live on to any one of many bitter ends.

  "Eulogy on the Flapper," *Metropolitan Magazine*
  (New York) *June 1922*

2 Most people hew the battlements of life from compromise, erecting their impregnable keeps from judicious submissions, fabricating their philosophical drawbridges from emotional retractions and scalding marauders in the boiling oil of sour grapes.

  Ch. 1, *Save Me the Waltz 1932*

3 Possessing a rapacious, engulfing ego, their particular genius swallowed their world in its swift undertow and washed its cadavers out to sea. New York is a good place to be on the up-grade.

  Ch. 2, Ibid.

4 Women sometimes seem to share a quiet, unalterable dogma of persecution that endows even the most sophisticated of them with the inarticulate poignancy of the peasant.

  Ibid.

5 Wasn't any art the expression of the inexpressible? And isn't the inexpressible always the same, though variable—like the *Time* in physics?

  Ch. 3, Ibid.

6 "Lives aren't as hard as professions," she gasped.

  Ibid.

7 "By the time a person has achieved years adequate for choosing a direction, the die is cast and the moment has long since passed which determined the future."

  Ch. 4, Ibid.

8 ". . . We grew up founding our dreams on the infinite promise of American advertising. I *still* believe that one can learn to play the piano by mail and that mud will give you a perfect complexion."

  Ibid.

9 "Oh, the secret life of man and woman—dreaming how much better we would be than we are if we were somebody else or even ourselves, and feeling that our estate has been unexploited to its fullest. I have reached the point where I can only express the inarticulate, taste food without taste, smell whiffs from the past, read statistical books, and sleep in uncomfortable positions."

  Ibid.

10 Why do we spend years using up our bodies to nurture our minds with experience and find our minds turning then to our exhausted bodies for solace?

  Ibid.

11 It's very expressive of myself. I just lump everything in a great heap which I have labeled "the past," and, having thus emptied this deep reservoir that was once myself, I am ready to continue.

  Ibid.

12 Home is the place to do the things you want to do. Here we eat just when we want to. Breakfast and luncheon are extremely moveable feasts. It's terrible to allow conventional habits to gain a hold on a whole household; to eat, sleep and live by clock ticks.

  Interview in the *Baltimore Sun*, Quoted in *Zelda*
  by Nancy Milford* 1970
  *See 1854.

13 Your entire life will soon be accounted for but the toils we have so assiduously woven—your leisure is eaten up by habits of leisure, your money by habitual extravagance, your hope by cynicism and mine by frustration, your ambition by too much compromise.

  Letter to her husband, F. Scott Fitzgerald* (undated), Ibid.
  *American writer (1896– 1940).

14 I don't want to live—I want to love first, and live incidentally.
  Letter to F. Scott Fitzgerald (March 1919), Pt. 1, Ch. 4, Ibid.

15 Mr. Fitzgerald—I believe that is how he spells his name—seems to believe that plagiarism begins at home. …On one page, I recognized a portion of an old diary of mine which mysteriously disappeared shortly after my marriage.
  Tribune review of F. Scott Fitzgerald's *The Beautiful and
  Damned* (New York, 2 April 1922), Pt. 2, Ch. 7, Ibid.

16 I wish I could write a beautiful book to break those hearts that are soon to cease to exist: a book of faith and small neat worlds and of people who live by the philosophies of popular songs.

  Pt. 3, Ch. 17, Ibid.

17 Don't you think I was made for you? I feel like you had me ordered—and I was delivered to you—to be worn—I want you to wear me, like a watch-charm or a button-hole boquet [sic]—to the world.

  Letter to F. Scott Fitzgerald (1919), Ibid.

18 I don't seem to know anything appropriate for a person of thirty. . . .

  Letter to F. Scott Fitzgerald (1930), Ibid.

19 . . . I have often told you that I am that little fish who swims about under a shark and, I believe, lives indelicately on its offal. Anyway, that is the way I am. Life moves over me in a vast black shadow and I swallow whatever it drops with relish . . .

Letter to F. Scott Fitzgerald (1932), Ibid.

20 I take a sun bath and listen to the hours, formulating, and disintegrating under the pines, and smell the resiny hardi-hood of the high noon hours. The world is lost in a blue haze of distances and the immediate sleeps in a thin and finite sun.

Journal (1938), Ibid.

1772. Margaret Mitchell (1900–1949)

1 Land is the only thing in the world that amounts to anything, for 'tis the only thing in this world that lasts, ... 'Tis the only thing worth working for, worth fighting for—worth dying for.

Pt. I, Ch. 2, *Gone With the Wind* 1936

2 "I'm tired of everlastingly being unnatural and never doing anything I want to do. I'm tired of acting like I don't eat more than a bird, and walking when I want to run and saying I feel faint after a waltz, when I could dance for two days and never get tired. I'm tired of saying 'How wonderful you are!' to fool men who haven't got one-half the sense I've got and I'm tired of pretending I don't know anything, so men can tell me things and feel important while they're doing it. . . ."

Ch. 5, Ibid.

3 "Until you've lost your reputation, you never realize what a burden it was or what freedom really is."

Pt. II, Ch. 9, Ibid.

4 "What most people don't seem to realize is that there is just as much money to be made out of the wreckage of a civilization as from the upbuilding of one."

Ibid.

5 Fighting is like champagne. It goes to the heads of cowards as quickly as of heroes. Any fool can be brave on a battlefield when it's be brave or else be killed.

Pt. IV, Ch. 31, Ibid.

6 The Irish . . . are the damnedest race. They put so much emphasis on so many wrong things.

Ch. 34, Ibid.

7 Southerners can never resist a losing cause.

Ch. 35, Ibid.

8 Now he disliked talking business with her as much as he had enjoyed it before they were married. Now he saw that she understood entirely too well and he felt the usual masculine indignation at the duplicity of women. Added to it was the usual masculine disillusionment in discovering that a woman has a brain.

Ch. 36, Ibid.

9 If! If! If! There were so many ifs in life, never any certainty of anything, never any sense of security, always the dread of losing everything and being cold and hungry again.

Ch. 38, Ibid.

10 "Death and taxes and childbirth! There's never any convenient time for any of them!"

Ibid.

11 "Everybody's mainspring is different. And I want to say this— folks whose mainsprings are busted are better off dead."

Ch. 40, Ibid.

12 "You kin polish a mule's feets an' shine his hide an' put brass all over his harness an' hitch him ter a fine cah'ige. But he a mule jes' de same. He doan fool nobody."

Ch. 48, Ibid.

13 "My pet, the world can forgive practically anything except people who mind their own business."

Ibid.

14 "Life's under no obligation to give us what we expect. We take what we get and are thankful it's no worse than it is."

Pt. V, Ch. 53, Ibid.

15 "I won't think of it now. I can't stand it if I do. I'll think of it tomorrow at Tara. Tomorrow's another day."

Ch. 57, Ibid.

16 "What's broken is broken—and I'd rather remember it as it was at its best than mend it and see the broken places as long as I lived."

Ch. 63, Ibid.

17 "You're so brutal to those who love you, Scarlett. You take their love and hold it over their heads like a whip."

Ibid.

18 I wish I could care what you do or where you go, but I can't. My dear, I don't give a damn.

Ibid.

1773. Lisa Gardiner (1900–1956)

1 And remember, expect nothing and life will be velvet.

Quoted in *Don't Fall Off the Mountain* by
Shirley MacLaine* 1970

*See 2569.

1774. Polly Adler (1900–1962)

1 Too many cooks spoil the brothel.

A House is Not a Home 1953

2 . . . I am one of those people who can't help getting a kick out of life—even when it's a kick in the teeth.

Ch. 1, Ibid.

3 The degree to which a pimp, if he's clever, can confuse and delude a prostitute is very nearly unlimited.

Ch. 4, Ibid.

4 What it comes down to is this: the grocer, the butcher, the baker, the merchant, the landlord, the druggist, the liquor dealer, the policeman, the doctor, the city father and the politician—these are the people who make money out of prostitution, these are the real reapers of the wages of sin.

Ch. 9, Ibid.

5 My home is in whatever town I'm booked.

Ibid.

6 The women who take husbands not out of love but out of greed, to get their bills paid, to get a fine house and clothes and jewels; the women who marry to get out of a tiresome job, or to get away from disagreeable relatives, or to avoid being

called an old maid—these are whores in everything but name. The only difference between them and my girls is that my girls gave a man his money's worth.

Ch. 10, Ibid.

1775. Martha Ostenso (1900–1963)

1 Far overhead sounded a voluminous prolonged cry, like a great trumpet call. Wild geese flying still farther north, to a region beyond human warmth . . . beyond even human isolation.

Ch. 1, *Wild Geese 1925*

2 The garden cost Amelia no end of work and worry; she tended the delicate tomato vines as though they were new born infants, and suffered momentary sinking of the heart whenever she detected signs of weakness in any of the hardier vegetables. She was grateful for the toil in which she could dwell as a sort of refuge from deeper thought.

Ch. 7, Ibid.

3 Wherever the wind was bound, Elsa thought, there the whole world seemed to be going.

Ch. 4, *The Mad Carews 1927*

4 Some clear intuition bade her fight the emotions which his coming stirred within her. It was a fight against that irresistible force which sought ever to turn back to the earth that which was the earth's; a struggle to evade the trap which would close her forever within Elder's Hollow.

Ch. 6, Ibid.

5 She was especially happy in the violence, the stride of the great, obstreperous city [Chicago], the fierce roar of the wind that was its voice, the white-green tumult of the waves breaking on the shore of Lake Michigan, its soul.

Ch. 21, Ibid.

6 "You have stirred the soil with our plow, my friend. It will never be the same again."

Ch. 4, *O River, Remember 1943*

7 It came to him sharply then that his mother had gradually discarded every vestige of her immigrant past, while his father was still—well, what *was* his father? Surely an American now, but with the best, the most vigorous and honest and spiritually simple qualities of the old land giving something to the new.

Ch. 8, Ibid.

8 Pity the Unicorn,
Pity the Hippogriff,
Souls that were never born
Out of the land of If!

"The Unicorn and the Hippogriff," St. 1 *n.d.*

1776. Loran Hurnscot (1900?–1970)

1 There are times when I feel I can no longer bear that grey room where I go once a week or fortnight in order to discover (presumably) how to turn from one person into another sort of person.

A Prison, a Paradise, Vol. II *1959*

2 It came over me, blindingly, for the first time in my life, that suicide was a wrong act, was indeed "mortal sin." In that moment, God stopped me. I did not want my life, but I knew I was suddenly forbidden by something outside myself to let it go.

(9 July 1939), Ibid.

3 It had always been pride that had held me off from Him. Now it was broken the obstacle was gone. One is never simple enough, while things go well.

Ibid.

4 And suddenly I was swept out of myself—knowing, knowing, knowing. Feeling the love of God burning through creation, and an ecstasy of bliss pouring through my spirit and down into every nerve.

(4 October 1939), Ibid.

1777. Paula Ludwig (1900–1974)

1 Because I betrayed myself there in the dim
no leaf moved
no drop fell
But in the stillness could be heard
my hands growing toward you.

"To the Dark God," St. 3, Candice L. McRee, tr. *n.d.*

1778. Malvina Reynolds (1900–1978)

1 Where are you going, my little one, little one,
Where are you going, my baby, my own?
Turn around and you're two,
Turn around and you're four,
Turn around and you're a young girl going out of my door.

"Turn Around" *1958*

2 Everybody thinks my head's full of nothing,
Wants to put his special stuff in,
Fill the space with candy wrappers,
Keep out sex and revolution,
But there's no hole in my head,
Too bad.

"No Hole in My Head" *1965*

3 While that baby is a child it will suffer from neglect,
Be picked up and pecked, run over and wrecked,
And its head will be crowned with the thorn,
But while it's inside her it must remain intact,
And it cannot be murdered till it's born.

"Rosie Jane" *1973*

4 There's inflation and pollution.
Everything's been bought on credit
In this rotten institution.
And they waste the gentle people
'Cause the system has no soul.
They've got the world in their pocket,
But the pocket's got a hole.

"World in Their Pocket," Verse 1 *1975*

5 Celebrate my death for the good times I've had,
For the work that I've done and the friends that I've made.
Celebrate my death, of whom it could be said,
"She was a working class woman, and a red."

Last song, untitled *1978*

1779. Cecilia Helena Payne-Gaposchkin (1900–1979)

1 The reward of the young scientist is the emotional thrill of being the first person in the history of the world to see something or to understand something. Nothing can compare with that experience; it engenders what Thomas Huxley* called the Divine Dipsomania. The reward of the old scientist is the sense of having seen a vague sketch grow into a masterly landscape.

Not a finished picture, of course; a picture that is still growing in scope and detail with the application of new techniques and new skills. The old scientist cannot claim that the masterpiece is his own work. He may have roughed out part of the design, laid on a few strokes, but he has learned to accept the discoveries of others with the same delight that he experienced his own when he was young.

Acceptance speech, Henry Norris Russell Prize,
American Astronomical Society *1977*

*English biologist (1825–95).

1780. Dorothy Arzner (1900–1980)

1   It is my theory that if you have authority, know your business and know you have authority, you have the authority.

Quoted in *The New York Times* 15 June *1972*

2   I was led by the grace of God to the movies. I would like the industry to be more aware of what they're doing to influence people. . . .

Quoted in *Popcorn Venus* by Marjorie Rosen* *1973*

*See 2920.

1781. Helen Gahagan Douglas (1900–1980)

1   If I go to Congress, it won't be to spar with anybody, man or woman. I'm not a wit. I'm not a fencer. I don't enjoy that kind of thing. It's all nonsense and an insult to the intelligence of the American people.

News item *1944*

2   Such pip-squeaks as Nixon and McCarthy are trying to get us so frightened of Communism that we'll be afraid to turn out the lights at night.

Speech *1950*

3   The Eleanor Roosevelt I shall always remember was a woman of tenderness and deep sympathy, a woman with the most exquisite manners of anyone I have known—one who did what she was called upon to do with complete devotion and rare charm.

The Eleanor Roosevelt We Remember 1963

4   I know the force women can exert in directing the course of events.

Ibid.

5   Would Eleanor Roosevelt* have had to struggle to overcome this tortuous shyness if she had grown up secure in the knowledge that she was a beautiful girl? If she hadn't struggled so earnestly, would she have been so sensitive to the struggles of others? Would a beautiful Eleanor Roosevelt have escaped from the confinements of the mid-Victorian drawing room society in which she was reared? Would a beautiful Eleanor Roosevelt have wanted to escape? Would a beautiful Eleanor Roosevelt have had the same need to be, to do?

Ibid.

*See 1513.

6   . . . the first step toward liberation of *any* group is to use the power in hand. . . . And the power in hand is the vote.

Quoted in "Helen Gahagan Douglas" by Lee Israel, *Ms.* (New York) *October 1973*

7   If the national security is involved, anything goes. There are no rules. There are people so lacking in roots about what is proper and what is improper that they don't know there's anything wrong in breaking into the headquarters of the opposition party.

Ibid.

1782. Kathryn Hulme (1900–1981)

1   I saw more of them [concentration-camp brands] on that first day. I saw so many that I was sure my memory was branded forever and that never again would I be able to think of mankind with that certain friendly ease which characterizes Americans like a birthright.

Ch. 2, *The Wild Place 1953*

2   Interior silence, she repeated silently. That would be her Waterloo. How without brain surgery could you quell the rabble of memories? Even as she asked herself the question, she heard her psychology professor saying quite clearly across a space of years, "No one, not even a saint, can say an *Ave* straight through without some association creeping in; this is a known thing."

Ch. 1, *The Nun's Story 1956*

3   "You must never lose the awareness that in yourself you are nothing, you are only an instrument. An instrument is nothing until it is lifted."

Ch. 8, Ibid.

4   Her defeat had so many facets, she could not define it all at once, but only her scorching shame for being a hypocrite in the religious life, for wearing the garb of obedience while flaunting the Holy Rule, and the Cross of Christ above a heart filled with hate.

Ch. 18, Ibid.

5   "I believe, Father," she said, "that even the smallest gesture of charity made in the world, with joy, would be ten times more pleasing to God than all the work I do here under the Holy Rule I only pretend to obey."

Ibid.

6   Then there had been the inspection of their child from head to toe as he watched Annie undress the baby before bedtime. The tiny perfect fingernails and toenails astonished him the most. They were like the small pink shells you scuffed up in the sands of tropical beaches, he whispered, counting them.

Ch. 9, *Annie's Captain 1961*

7   Their fright seemed to turn them into children.

Ch. 18, Ibid.

8   Annie clung to life like a shipwrecked soul on a slender spar adrift in an ocean of pain. She denied the pains but the doctor guessed them when she began refusing all medicines for fear he would slip in the morphine he had promised not to give until she herself asked. Her fortitude surpassed anything he had ever encountered and it turned him into a cursing madman every time he came downstairs. "She'd go through hell to keep her wits clear until *he* comes," he groaned. "God damn that bloody old scow."

Ibid.

1783. Elizabeth Goudge (1900–1984)

1   Her birthdays were always important to her; for being a born lover of life, she would always keep the day of her entrance into it as a very great festival indeed. . . .

Bk. I, Pt. II, Ch. 1,
Green Dolphin Street 1944

2   His hatred of his wife horrified him. It was the first hatred of his life, it was growing in bitterness and intensity day by day, and he had no idea what to do about it.

Pt. III, Ch. 1, Ibid.

3 The elements were "seeking" each other in rage and confusion, and in the fury of the conflict boastful man was utterly humiliated, sucked down, drowned.

Bk. II, Pt. III, Ch. 2, Ibid.

4 She had a deep sense of justice and sometimes this made her feel as uncomfortable in her spirit if she deserved a whipping and did not get it as she felt it on her body if she did get it, and of the two she preferred to suffer in body.

Bk. I, Ch. 1, *The Child
from the Sea* 1970

5 Butterflies . . . not quite birds, as they were not quite flowers, mysterious and fascinating as are all indeterminate creatures.

Ch. 2, Ibid.

6 Peace, she supposed, was contingent upon a certain disposition of the soul, a disposition to receive the gift that only detachment from self made possible.

Ch. 7, Ibid.

7 "All true glory, while it remains true, holds it. It is the maintaining of truth that is so hard."

Pt. III, Ch. 2, Ibid.

8 ". . . The travail of creation of course exaggerates the importance of our work while we engage in it; we know better when the opus is finished and the lion is perceived to be only a broken-backed mouse. . . ."

Ibid.

9 "All we are asked to bear we can bear. That is a law of the spiritual life. The only hindrance to the working of this law, as of all benign laws, is fear."

Ch. 17, Ibid.

1784. Taylor Caldwell (1900–1985)

1 ". . . I knew you would not betray us. Not because of—honor. But profit. And profits are not bedfellows of honor."

Bk. I, Ch. 12, *Dynasty of Death* 1938

2 "Honest men live on charity in their age; the almshouses are full of men who never stole a copper penny. Honest men are the fools and the saints, and you and I are neither."

Ibid.

3 "Protestantism forgets that men are men, and that there are appetites that it is better to wink at, provided that certain duties are observed. We don't strain at a gnat and swallow a camel, nor swim in an ocean and drown in a puddle."

Bk. II, Ch. 70, Ibid.

4 Men who retain irony are not to be trusted, thought Ernest. They can't always resist an impulse to tickle themselves.

Ch. 78, Ibid.

5 "He that hath no rule over his own spirit is like a city that is broken down and without walls."

Pt. I, Ch. 5, *This Side of Innocence* 1946

6 A civilization based purely on agriculture was a civilization which never went hungry. But a raucous and ruthless civilization, dependent on the churning of the "devil machines" within brick walls, was vulnerable to every sensitive wind that blew from Wall Street.

Pt. III, Ch. 43, Ibid.

7 Despair, Philip thought, is sometimes the great energizer of the mind, though sometimes its flowering may be sterile.

Ch. 45, Ibid.

8 "Shakespeare speaks of 'lean and hungry men,' but he never seemed to notice that a lot of women are lean and hungry, too, and much more vulturous than many men."

Ch. 16, *The Late Clara Beame* 1957

9 "It never pays to complicate a woman's mind too much."

Ibid.

10 Why, hadn't Pa often told him that no one could understand a person who had a gift? They lived in a world of their own, beyond criticism, beyond the knowing of other men. . . . "In Germany we understand these things, these geniuses," Mr. Enger had often told Edward dolefully. "But not in America. America has no soul."

Pt. I, Ch. 1, *The Sound of Thunder* 1957

11 "Learning," he would say, "should be a joy and full of excitement. It is life's greatest adventure; it is an illustrated excursion into the mind's noble and learned men, not a conducted tour through a jail. So its surroundings should be as gracious as possible, to complement it."

Ch. 9, Ibid.

12 But what was a body? Dust, dung, urine, itches. It was the light within which was important, and it was not significant if that light endured after death, or if the soul was blinded eternally in the endless night of the suspired flesh.

Pt. I, Ch. 1, *Great Lion of God* 1970

13 One, if one is sensible, blames government, not the servers of the government, not those entangled in their governments.

Ch. 10, Ibid.

14 Every object . . . burned with a blinding radiance as if each were being consumed by the sun. A very holocaust of flaming scintillation hovered over all things, appeared to emanate even from the pebbles of the paths. And the heat mounted.

Pt. II, Ch. 24, Ibid.

15 ". . . it is not always wise to appear singular."

Pt. III, Ch. 35, Ibid.

16 Is it not deplorable that a few heedless zealots can bring calamity to their law-abiding fellows?

Ch. 43, Ibid.

17 The old [Roman] gods understood that life was reasonable and favors were exchanged for favors, and that is how it should be.

Ch. 53, Ibid.

18 At the end—and as usual—God had betrayed the innocent and had left them comfortless.

Pt. I, Ch. 1, *Captains and the Kings* 1972

19 It was business, and none of them had allegiances or attachments or involvements with any nation, not even their own . . . Joseph immediately called them "the gray and deadly men," and did not know why he detested them, or why he found them the most dangerous of all among the human species.

Ch. 21, Ibid.

20 "Once power is concentrated in Washington—admittedly not an immediate prospect—America will take her place as an em-

pire and calculate and instigate wars, for the advantage of all concerned. We all know, from long experience, that progress depends on war."

Ibid.

21 "Mankind is the most selfish species this world has ever spewed up from hell, and it demands, constantly, that neighbors and politicians be 'unselfish,' and allow themselves to be plundered—for its benefit."

Pt. II, Ch. 13, Ibid.

1785. Laura Z. Hobson (1900–1986)

1 It was the rhythm of all living, apparently, and for most people. Happiness, and then pain. Perhaps then happiness again, but now, with it, the awareness of its own mortality.

Ch. 1, *Gentlemen's Agreement* 1946

2 Did it never occur to one of them to write about a fine guy who was Jewish? Did each one feel some savage necessity to pick a Jew who was a swine in the wholesale business, a Jew who was a swine in the movies, a Jew who was a swine in bed?

Ch. 3, Ibid.

3 Where did ideas come from, anyway? This one leaped at him when he'd been exhausted, AWOL* from his search.

Ch. 4, Ibid.

*Absent without leave.

4 We are born in innocence. . . . Corruption comes later. The first fear is a corruption, the first reaching for something that defies us. The first nuance of difference, the first need to feel better than the different one, more loved, stronger, richer, more blessed—these are corruptions.

Ch. 6, Ibid.

5 The anti-Semite offered the effrontery—and then the world was ready with harsh yardsticks to measure the self-control and dignity with which you met it. You were insensitive or too sensitive; you were too timid or too bellicose; they gave you at once the wound and the burden of proper behavior toward it.

Ch. 8, Ibid.

6 What trouble it was to be young! At sixty you grieved for the world; in youth you grieved for one unique creature.

Ch. 13, Ibid.

7 What was it, this being "a good father"? To love one's sons and daughters was not enough; to carry in one's bone and blood a pride in them, a longing for their growth and development—this was not enough. One had to be a ready companion to games and jokes and outings, to earn from the world this accolade. The devil with it.

Pt. I, Ch. 2, *The First Papers* 1964

8 She forced herself to stop thinking. . . . She was disciplined enough to do this nonthinking for short stretches, during the daytime at least. She had done it in other crises of her life; at times it was the only way to manage.

Consenting Adults 1975

9 It was all happening in a great, swooping free fall, irreversible, free of decision, in the full pull of gravity toward whatever was to be.

Ibid.

10 "Dear Mama. . . . I have something to tell you that I guess I better not put off any longer . . . you see, I am a homosexual. I

have fought it off for months and maybe years, but it just grows truer. . . ."

Ibid.

11 Why didn't children ever see that they could damage and harm their parents as much as parents could damage and harm children?

Ibid.

1786. Vijaya Lakshmi Pandit (1900–1990)

1 I feel torn in two between my duty to the children and the other duties of serving the country which, in our case, has come to mean long months of imprisonment.

(17 March 1943), *Prison Days 1946*

2 It [political imprisonment] is a slow daily sacrifice which can be so much more deadly than some big heroic gesture made in a moment of emotional upheaval. . . .

(3 May 1943), Ibid.

3 When my public activities are reported it is very annoying to read how I looked, if I smiled, if a particular reporter liked my hair style.

Quoted in *The Statesman* (Glasgow) *29 August 1955*

4 You know, what happens to anybody who has been in these two places [Moscow and Washington D.C.] and looked at them objectively, is the horrifying thought—if I may use that word in quotes—that they are so similar. . . . Take that passion for science—they're both absolutely dedicated to the machine, they are both extroverts, they both function in much the same way. . . .

Ibid.

5 It has simply been taken for granted that men and women are equal [in India] and even though woman functioned as a free citizen in her own right and her re-emergence after India's independence, the theoretical acceptance of equality has always remained.

"The Second Sex," *Punch 16 May 1962*

6 Difficulties, opposition, criticism—these things are meant to be overcome, and there is a special joy in facing them and in coming out on top. It is only when there is nothing but praise that life loses its charm and I begin to wonder what I should do about it.

Quoted in *The Envoy Extraordinary* by Vera Brittain* 1965

*See 1655.

7 The Indian temperament exceeds in emotionally worded epistles, which keep one in suspense as to what the aim of the writer is, until one has waded through a sea of beautiful metaphors to the final paragraphs.

(c. 1963), Ibid.

8 Freedom is not for the timid.

(c. 1964), Ibid.

1787. Helen Hayes (1900–1992)

1 An actress's life is so transitory—suddenly you're a building.*

News item *November 1955*

*Reference to a New York theater named for her.

2 We rely upon the poets, the philosophers, and the playwrights to articulate what most of us can only feel, in joy or sorrow. They illuminate the thoughts for which we only grope; they

give us the strength and balm we cannot find in ourselves. Whenever I feel my courage wavering I rush to them. They give me the wisdom of acceptance, the will and resilience to push on.

Introduction, *A Gift of Joy*, with Lewis Funke *1965*

3 One has to grow up with good talk in order to form the habit of it.

Ibid.

4 I was once the typical daughter, then the easily recognizable wife, and then the quintessential mother. I seem always to have reminded people of someone in their family. Perhaps I am just the triumph of Plain Jane.

On Reflection, with Sandford Dody *1968*

5 Actors cannot choose the manner in which they are born. Consequently, it is the one gesture in their lives completely devoid of self-consciousness.

Ch. 1, Ibid.

6 When I was very young, I half believed one could find within the pages of these [biographical] memoirs the key to greatness. It's rather like trying to find the soul in the map of the human body. But it is enlightening—and it does solve some of the mysteries.

Ch. 6, Ibid.

7 Yes, I have doubted. I have wandered off the path. I have been lost. But I always returned. It is beyond the logic I seek. It is intuitive—an intrinsic, built-in sense of direction. I seem always to find my way home. My faith has wavered but has saved me.

Ch. 15, Ibid.

8 When I get panicky at rehearsals, I reassure myself, "They wouldn't dare fire me. It would be like spitting on the American flag."

Remark (1966), Cited in "'First Lady of Theater'..." by Rayer Pike, *Seattle Post-Intelligencer 18 March 1993*

1788. Meridel Le Sueur (1900–1996)

1 In the mid-center of America a man can go blank for a long, long time. There is no community to give him life; so he can go lost as if he were in a jungle. No one will pay any attention. He can simply be as lost as if he had gone into the heart of an empty continent.

"Corn Village" (1930), *Salute to Spring 1940*

2 "I put my hand where you lie so silently. I hope you will come glistening with life power, with it shining upon you as upon the feathers of birds. I hope you will be a warrior and fierce for change, so all can live."

"Annunciation," Ibid.

3 Every generation must go further than the last or what's the use of it?

"The Dead in Steel," Ibid.

4 Hard times ain't quit and we ain't quit.

"Salute to Spring," Ibid.

5 "They can kill the bodies of Sacco and Vanzetti* but they can't kill what they stand for—the working class. It is bound to live. As certainly as this system of things, this exploitation of man by man, will remain, there will always be this fight, today and always..."

"Farewell," Ibid.

*Niccola S— (1891–1927) and Bartolomeo V— (1988–1927), Italian-born American anarchists, executed for a double murder. During the six years between sentencing and execution, worldwide protests were made in their behalf.

6 ... there is only one force that creates value and that is labor, and one manner of expropriation of wealth, the exploitation of labor and the natural resources.

Crusaders 1955

7 ... for there is no cruelty like that of the oppressor who feels his loss of the bit on those it has been his gain to oppress.

Ch. 3, Ibid.

8 ... the history of an oppressed people is hidden in the lies and the agreed-upon myth of its conquerors.

Ibid.

9 Security seemed to be something you had more of by being true to your beliefs. A house was only a house—it was nothing you gave your life to have, or sacrificed an idea to protect; the same with a job.

Ch. 5, Ibid.

10 The funeral has long been an instrument also of conveying history that has become hidden, of subtly informing the young, and of mining and blowing the mineral of collective poetry and courage.

Ch. 6, Ibid.

11 For none shall die who have the future in them.

Ibid.

12 Memory in America suffers amnesia.

Ibid.

13 Money is only money, beans tonight and steak tomorrow. So long as you can look yourself in the eye.

Ch. 7, Ibid.

14 Now that I am older it is even more wonderful to look at the gathering of this anthology, like some excavation of lost testaments, the transformation of silence into language.

Afterword, *Ripening: Selected Work* (2nd ed.) *1990*

15 Perhaps women like me of another generation are a bridge. Pass over, use the energy of the root in our witness and our singing. So we will never be gone. You have more tools now. The fog is lifting over the illusions. You have begun to tell it. You will bear sharper witness. Be bold. Tell it all. Don't spare the horses. The earth is waiting to hear you. All the children and the ancients are waiting. We shall come home together.

Ibid.

16 Pears cannot ripen alone. So we ripened together.

Ibid.

17 [I am] obsessed with a feeling of making some kind of repository, a mine like a gold mine far underground but accessible of women's merging consciousness so different than patriarchal consciousness, and it is collective...the only consciousness that can save the world literally, physically.

Quoted in "Remembering Meridel" by Florence Howe, *The Women's Review of Books*, Vol. XIV, No. 7 *April 1997*

1789. Nathalie Sarraute (1900–1999)

1 Those who live in a world of human beings can only retrace their steps.

"From Dostoevski to Kafka" (October 1947), *The Age of Suspicion*, Maria Jolas, tr. (1963) *1956*

2   Neither reproaches nor encouragements are able to revive a faith that is waning.

> "The Age of Suspicion" (February 1950), Ibid.

3   Suspicion . . . is one of the morbid reactions by which an organism defends itself and seeks another equilibrium.

> Ibid.

4   . . . what is hidden beneath the exterior monologue: an immense profusion of sensations, images, sentiments, memories, impulses, little larval actions that no inner language can convey, that jostle one another on the threshold of consciousness, gather together in compact groups, and loom up all of a sudden, then immediately fall apart, combine otherwise and reappear in new forms; while unwinding inside us, like the ribbon that come clattering from a telescriptor slot, in an uninterrupted flow of words.

> "Conversation and Sub-conversation" (January–February 1956), Ibid.

5   "We're swallowed up only when we are willing for it to happen."

> The Planetarium, Maria Jolas, tr. 1959

6   "But there are no more holy of holies, no more sacred places, no more magic, no more mirages for the thirsty, no more unsatisfied desires . . ."

> Ibid.

7   "There are people we should not allow to come near us, not for anything. Parasites who devour our very substance . . . Microbes that settle on us . . ."

> The Golden Fruits, Maria Jolas, tr. 1963

1790. Yocheved Bat-Miriam (1901–1980)

1   Singing like a hope, shining like a tear,
    Silent the echo of what will befall.

> "Parting," St. 1, Poems from the Hebrew, Robert Mezey, ed. 1973

2   I shall put on my dead face with a silence free
    Of joy and of pain forevermore,
    And dawn will trail like a child after me
    To play with shells on the shore.

> St. 5, Ibid.

3   Not to be, to be gone—I pray for this.
    At the gates of infinity, like a fey child.

> "Distance Spills Itself," St. 5, Ibid.

1791. Miriam Beard (1901–)

1   "Haven't you some small item I could send her, very attractive—typically American?"
    The sales expert looked depressed. . . .
    "American, you say? . . . Why, my dee-ur, we don't carry those Colonial goods. All our things are imported."

> Ch. 1, Realism in Romantic Japan 1930

2   A country honeycombed with agitation and a life made vivid by unending clash and controversy—that is what the traveler finds in Japan to-day.

> Ch. 5, Ibid.

1792. Barbara Cartland (1901–)

1   What did we in our teens realize of war? Only that we were unsatisfied after our meals, bored, in the selfishness of youth, with mourning and weeping, sick of being told plaintively that the world would "never be the same again."

> Ch. 1, The Isthmus Years 1942

2   I have always found women difficult. I don't really understand them. To begin with, few women tell the truth.

> Ibid.

3   I always say what I think and feel—it's got me into a lot of trouble but only with women. I've never had a cross word with a man for speaking frankly but women don't like it—. I can't think why, unless it's natural love of subterfuge and intrigue.

> Ch. 8, Ibid.

4   Only through freedom will man find salvation, only through freedom can civilization survive and progress. We shall win, I am as sure of that as I am that England with all her faults, her mistakes, her snobbery and her social injustices is worth any individual sacrifice—this England which means far more in the sum total of human existence than a small green island surrounded by blue seas.

> Epilogue, Ibid.

5   Every man has been brought up with the idea that decent women don't pop in and out of bed; he has always been told by his mother that "nice girls don't." He finds, of course, when he gets older that this may be untrue—but only in a certain section of society.

> Interview, Quoted in Speaking Frankly by Wendy Leigh 1978

6   A man will teach his wife what is needed to arouse his desires. And there is no reason for a woman to know any more than what her husband is prepared to teach her. If she gets married knowing far too much about what she wants and doesn't want then she will be ready to find fault with her husband.

> Ibid.

7   The great majority of people in England and America are modest, decent and pure-minded and the amount of virgins in the world today is stupendous.

> Ibid.

8   To sleep around is absolutely wrong for a woman; it's degrading and it completely ruins her personality. Sooner or later it will destroy all that is feminine and beautiful and idealistic in her.

> Ibid.

9   France is the only place where you can make love in the afternoon without people hammering on your door.

> The Guardian (London) 24 December 1984

10 Only the English and the Americans are improper. East of Suez everyone wants a virgin.

> Attributed n.d.

1793. Elinor Hayes (1901?–)

1   It was not childbearing that wore away women's lives. There were slower erosions.

> Pt. I, Ch. 1, Morning Star 1961

2   Those most dedicated to the future are not always the best prophets.

> Pt. IV, Ch. 29, Ibid.

1794. Grace Moore (1901–1947)

1   There, in repressed defiance, lies the natural instinct to tell the world where to get off: an instinct, alas, that too often takes itself out in the tardy report framed *sotto voce* , or the year-in, year-out threat mumbled to oneself, "Just wait till I write that book!"

Ch. 1, You're Only Human Once 1944

2   I think that to get under the surface and really appreciate the beauty of any country, one has to go there poor.

Ch. 4, Ibid.

1795. Gertrude Lawrence (1901–1952)

1   In London I had been by turns poor and rich, hopeful and despondent, successful and down-and-out, utterly miserable and ecstatically dizzily happy. I belonged to London as each of us can belong to only one place on this earth. And, in the same way, London belonged to me.

Ch. 1, A Star Danced 1945

2   "So this is America!" I exclaimed. "Look at that bath, will you? Feel that delicious warmth. Central heating, my girl. No wonder they call this the most luxurious country on earth."

Ch. 11, Ibid.

3   Perhaps you have to be born an Englishwoman to realize how much attention American men shower on women and how tremendously considerate all the nice ones among them are of a woman's wishes.

Ch. 12, Ibid.

1796. Jan Struther (1901–1953)

1   It took me forty years on earth
To reach this sure conclusion:
There is no Heaven but clarity,
No Hell except confusion.

"All Clear," The Glass Blower and Other Poems 1940

2   She saw every personal religion as a pair of intersecting circles. . . . Probably perfection is reached when the area of the two outer crescents, added together, is exactly equal to that of the leaf-shaped piece in the middle. On paper there must be some neat mathematical formula for arriving at this; in life, none.

Mrs. Miniver 1940

1797. Ruth Rowland Nichols (1901–1961)

1   Many newspaper articles . . . discussed the supposed rivalry between Amelia Earheart* and me. I have no hesitation in stating that they were exaggerated or slanted or untrue. . . . We were united by common bond of interest. We spoke each other's language—and that was the language of pioneer women of the air.

Wings for Life 1957

*See 1710.

2   It was a great source of concern, to put it mildly, when I finally had reached my altitude peak and discovered that I was down to my last five gallons of gasoline.

Quoted in Ch. 7, The American Heritage History of Flight 1960

1798. Nina Berberova (1901–1993)

1   I had learnt to seek intensity rather than happiness, not joys and prosperity but *more of life*, a concentrated sense of life, a strengthened feeling of existence, fullness and concentration of *pulse*, energy, growth, flowering, beyond the image of happiness or unhappiness.

The Italics Are Mine 1969

2   If the payment has sometimes been excessive, it was after all the payment *for life,* and there cannot be and is no excessive payment for life.

Ibid.

3   Not losing time has been my permanent concern since I was three years old, when it dawned on me that time is the warp of life, its very fabric, something that you cannot buy, trade, steal, falsify, or obtain by begging.

Ibid.

1799. Doris Fleeson (1901–1970)

1   It is occasionally possible to charge Hell with a bucket of water but against stupidity the gods themselves struggle in vain.

Newspaper column 17 February 1964

1800. Marie-Luise Fleisser (1901–1974)

1   OLGA. Oh, that we fall every day into a world of viciousness, just as we fell into our bodies, and now we're stuck with them.

Sc. 5, Purgatory in Ingolstadt, Annie Castledine, tr. (1991) 1924

1801. Edith Mendel Stern (1901–1975)

1   The role of the housewife is, therefore, analogous to that of the president of a corporation who would not only determine policies and make over-all plans but also spend the majority of his time and energy in such activities as sweeping the plant and oiling the machines.

For a woman to get a rewarding sense of total creation by way of the multiple monotonous chores that are her daily lot would be as irrational as for an assembly line worker to rejoice that he had created an automobile because he tightened a bolt.

"Women Are Household Slaves," American Mercury January 1949

1802. Margaret Mead (1901–1977)

1   The negative cautions of science are never popular.

Ch. 1, Coming of Age in Samoa 1928

2   The Samoan background which makes growing up so easy, so simple a matter, is the general casualness of the whole society. For Samoa is a place where no one plays for very high stakes, no one pays very heavy prices, no one suffers for his convictions or fights to the death for special ends. . . . No one is hurried along in life or punished harshly for slowness of development. Instead the gifted, the precocious, are held back, until the slowest among them have caught the pace. And in personal relations, caring is as slight.

Ch. 13, Ibid.

3   Chief among our gains must be reckoned this possibility of choice, the recognition of many possible ways of life, where other civilizations have recognized only one. Where other civilizations give a satisfactory outlet to only one temperamental type, be he mystic or soldier, business man or artist, a civilization in which there are many standards offers a possibility of satisfactory adjustment to individuals of many different temperamental types, of diverse gifts and varying interests.

Ch. 14, Ibid.

4 A society which is clamouring for choice, which is filled with many articulate groups, each urging its own brand of salvation, its own variety of economic philosophy, will give each new generation no peace until all have chosen or gone under, unable to bear the conditions of choice. The stress is in our civilization. . . .

Ibid.

5 To insist that there are no sex-differences in a society that has always believed in them and depended upon them may be as subtle a form of standardizing personality as to insist that there are many sex-differences.

Sex and Temperament in Three Primitive Societies 1935

6 Just as a festive occasion is the gayer and more charming if the two sexes are dressed differently, so it is in less material matters.

Ibid.

7 An occupation that has no basis in sex-determined gifts can now recruit its ranks from twice as many potential artists.

Ibid.

8 . . . we may say that many, if not all, of the personality traits which we have called masculine or feminine are as lightly linked to sex as are the clothing, the manners, and the form of headdress that a society at a given period assigns to either sex.

Ibid.

9 The knowledge that the personalities of the two sexes are so-cially produced is congenial to every programme that looks forward toward a planned order of society. It is a two-edged sword. . . .

Ibid.

10 The removal of all legal and economic barriers against women's participating in the world on an equal footing with men may be in itself a standardizing move towards the whole-sale stamping-out of the diversity of attitudes that is such a dearly bought product of civilization.

Ibid.

11 If we are to achieve a richer culture, rich in contrasting values, we must recognize the whole gamut of human potentialities, and so weave a less arbitrary social fabric, one in which each diverse human gift will find a fitting place.

Ibid.

12 We must recognize that beneath the superficial classifications of sex and race the same potentialities exist, recurring genera-tion after generation, only to perish because society has no place for them.

From the South Seas 1939

13 If little boys have to meet and assimilate the early shock of knowing that they can never create a baby with the sureness and incontrovertibility that is a woman's birthright, how does that make them more creatively ambitious, as well as more de-pendent upon achievement?

Male and Female 1948

14 It is of very doubtful value to enlist the gifts of women if bring-ing women into fields that have been defined as male frightens the men, unsexes the women, muffles and distorts the contri-bution women could make. . . .

Ibid.

15 Furthermore, the little girl learns that she will have a baby not because she is strong or energetic or initiating, not because she

works and struggles and tries, and in the end succeeds, but simply because she is a girl and not a boy, and girls turn into women, and in the end—if they protect their femininity—have babies.

Ibid.

16 We know of no culture that has said, articulately, that there is no difference between men and women except in the way they contribute to the creation of the next generation. . . .

Ibid.

17 Living in the modern world, clothed and muffled, forced to convey our sense of our bodies in terms of remote symbols like walking sticks and umbrellas and handbags, it is easy to lose sight of the immediacy of the human body plan.

Ibid.

18 Man's role is uncertain, undefined, and perhaps unnecessary. By a great effort, man has hit upon a method of compensating himself for his basic inferiority.

Ibid.

19 Women, it is true, make human beings, but only men can make men.

Ibid.

20 So women are scolded both for being mothers and for not being mothers, for wanting to eat their cake and have it too, and for not wanting to eat their cake and have it too.

Ch. 8, Ibid.

21 Coming to terms with the rhythms of women's lives means coming to terms with life itself, accepting the imperatives of the body rather than the imperatives of an artificial, man-made, perhaps transcendentally beautiful civilization. Emphasis on the male work-rhythm is an emphasis on infinite possibilities; emphasis on the female rhythms is an emphasis on a defined pattern, on limitation.

Ibid.

22 When human beings have been fascinated by the contempla-tion of their own hearts, the more intricate biological pattern of the female has become a model for the artist, the mystic, and the saint. When mankind turns instead to what can be done, altered, built, invented, in the outer world, all natural properties of men, animals, or metals become handicaps to be altered rather than clues to be followed.

Ibid.

23 The liberals have not softened their view of actuality to make themselves live closer to the dream, but instead sharpen their perceptions and fight to make the dream actuality or give up the battle in despair.

Ch. 12, Ibid.

24 The suffering of either sex—of the male who is unable, because of the way in which he was reared, to take the strong initiating or patriarchal role that is still demanded of him, or of the fe-male who has been given too much freedom of movement as a child to stay placidly within the house as an adult—this suffer-ing, this discrepancy, this sense of failure in an enjoined role, is the point of leverage for social change.

Ch. 15, Ibid.

25 Each home has been reduced to the bare essentials—to barer essentials than most primitive people would consider possible. Only one woman's hands to feed the baby, answer the tele-phone, turn off the gas under the pot that is boiling over,

soothe the older child who has broken a toy, and open both doors at once. She is a nutritionist, a child psychologist, an engineer, a production manager, an expert buyer, all in one. Her husband sees her as free to plan her own time, and envies her; she sees him as having regular hours and envies him.

Ch. 16, Ibid.

26 When we stopped short of treating women as people after providing them with all the paraphernalia of education and rights, we set up a condition whereby men also become less than full human beings and more narrowly domestic.

"American Man in a Woman's World," The New York Times Magazine 10 February 1957

27 Women want mediocre men, and men are working to be as mediocre as possible.

Quoted in Quote Magazine 15 May 1958

28 Early domesticity has always been characteristic of most savages, of most peasants and of the urban poor.

Quoted in "New Look at Early Marriages," U.S. News & World Report 6 June 1960

29 The first step in the direction of a world rule of law is the recognition that peace no longer is an unobtainable ideal but a necessary condition of continued human existence.

The New York Times Magazine 26 November 1961

30 I was brought up to believe that the only thing worth doing was to add to the sum of accurate information in the world.

Quoted in The New York Times 9 August 1964

31 A tribal people will be jealous of their women, or will offer them to male visitors in ways that are hard to resist, but tribal women do not fear that a woman anthropologist will take their men.

Field Work in the Pacific Islands, 1925–1967 1967

32 The prophet who fails to present a bearable alternative and yet preaches doom is part of the trap that he postulates. Not only does he picture us caught in a tremendous man-made or God-made trap from which there is no escape, but he must also listen to him day in, day out, describe how the trap is inexorably closing. To such prophecies the human race, as presently bred and educated and situated, is incapable of listening. So some dance and some immolate themselves as human torches; some take drugs and some artists spill their creativity in sets of randomly placed dots on a white ground.

Introduction, Culture and Commitment 1970

33 It is an open question whether any behavior based on fear of eternal punishment can be regarded as ethical or should be regarded as merely cowardly.

Quoted in Redbook (New York) February 1971

34 . . . most people prefer to carry out the kinds of experiments that allow the scientist to feel that he is in full control of the situation rather than surrendering himself to the situation, as one must in studying human beings as they actually live.

Blackberry Winter 1972

35 . . . I had no reason to doubt that brains were suitable for a woman. And as I had my father's kind of mind—which was also his mother's—I learned that the mind is not sex-typed.

Ibid.

36 There were options and turning points throughout cosmic and biological evolution. If you look seriously at the process of evolution, it did not have to take the present course. It could have taken many others.

"Our Open Ended Future," The Next Billion Years, Lecture Series, University of California at Los Angeles 1973

37 We are living beyond our means. As a people we have developed a life-style that is draining the earth of its priceless and irreplaceable resources without regard for the future of our children and people all around the world.

"The Energy Crises—Why Our World Will Never Again Be the Same," Redbook (New York) April 1974

38 The contempt for law and the contempt for the human consequences of lawbreaking go from the bottom to the top of American society.

Quoted in "Impeachment?" by Claire Safran, Ibid.

39 A city is a place where there is no need to wait for next week to get the answer to a question, to taste the food of any country, to find new voices to listen to and familiar ones to listen to again.

Ch. 2, World Enough 1975

40 If you associate enough with older people who do enjoy their lives, who are not stored away in any golden ghettos, you will gain a sense of continuity and of the possibility for a full life.

Quoted in "Growing Old in America" by Grace Hechinger, Family Circle 26 July 1977

41 Our treatment of both older people and children reflects the value we place on independence and autonomy. We do our best to make our children independent from birth. We leave them all alone in rooms with the lights out and tell them, "Go to sleep by yourselves." And the old people we respect most are the ones who will fight for their independence, who would sooner starve to death than ask for help.

Ibid.

42 In this country, some people start being miserable about growing old while they are still young.

Ibid.

43 There are far too many children in America who are badly afraid of older people because they never see any. Old people are not a regular part of their everyday lives.

Ibid.

44 The city as a center where, any day in any year, there may be a fresh encounter with a new talent, a keen mind or a gifted specialist—this is essential to the life of a country. To play this role in our lives a city must have a soul—a university, a great art or music school, a cathedral or a great mosque or temple, a great laboratory or scientific center, as well as the libraries and museums and galleries that bring past and present together. A city must be a place where groups of women and men are seeking and developing the highest things they know.

Quoted in Redbook (New York) August 1978

45 If I were to be taken hostage, I would not plead for release nor would I want my government to be blackmailed. I think certain government officials, industrialists and celebrated persons should make it clear they are prepared to be sacrificed if taken hostage. If that were done, what gain would there be for terrorists in taking hostages?

Quoted in "Comment," Parade Magazine 20 May 1979

46 It seems to me as if culture were rather like a cake the ingredients of which we are ignorant, and the main thing is to get a

big slice home, not give it chemicals to test whether it is made of butter or oleomargarine.

(c. 1938, p. 191), Quoted in *Margaret Mead: A Life* by Jane Howard* *1984*

*See 2596.

47 The first thing we have to get rid of is this horrible independent little misery called the suburban home. It is using up an unprecedented amount of hardware, creating an unprecedented amount of pollution, and producing unhappy people.

Quoted by Joni Seager* in "Blueprints for inequality," *The Women's Review of Books*, Vol. X, No. 4 *January 1993*

*See 3610.

48 . . . [to] nest in the gale [means] being able to be at home anywhere in the world, in any house, in any time band, eating any different kind of food, learning new languages as needed, never afraid of the new, sad to leave anywhere where one has been at home for a few days, but glad to go forward.

Letter, Library of Congress *n.d.*

1803. Cornelia Otis Skinner (1901–1979)

1 I can enjoy flowers quite happily without translating them into Latin. I can even pick them with success and pleasure. What, frankly, I can't do is arrange them.

"Floral Piece," *Dithers and Jitters 1937*

2 There are compensations for growing older. One is the realization that to be sporting isn't at all necessary. It is a great relief to reach this stage of wisdom.

"Bonnie Boating Weather," Ibid.

3 It's not that I don't want to be a beauty, that I don't yearn to be dripping with glamour. It's just that I can't see how any woman can find time to do to herself all the things that must apparently be done to make herself beautiful and, having once done them, how anyone without the strength of mind of a foreign missionary can keep up such a regime.

"The Skin-Game," Ibid.

4 We were young enough still to harbor the glad illusion that organized forms of get-together were commendable.

Our Hearts Were Young and Gay, with Emily Kimbrough* *1942*

*See 1741.

5 One of the most incongruous facets of the nature of *homo* not so *sapien* is the delight with which he wallows in temporary orgies of utter misery.

"Crying in the Dark," *Bottoms Up! 1950*

6 That food has always been, and will continue to be, the basis for one of our greater snobbisms does not explain the fact that the attitude toward the food choice of others is becoming more and more heatedly exclusive until it may well turn into one of those forms of bigotry against which gallant little committees are constantly planning campaigns in the cause of justice and decency.

"Your Very Good Health," Ibid.

7 It is disturbing to discover in oneself these curious revelations of the validity of the Darwinian theory. If it is true that we have sprung from the ape, there are occasions when my own spring appears not to have been very far.

"The Ape in Me," *The Ape in Me 1959*

8 Courtesy is fine and heaven knows we need more and more of it in a rude and frenetic world, but mechanized courtesy is as pallid as Pablum . . . in fact, it isn't even courtesy. One can put up with "Service with a Smile" if the smile is genuine and not mere compulsory tooth baring. And while I am hardly advocating "Service with a Snarl," I find myself occasionally wishing for "Service with a Deadpan," or just plain Service, executed with efficiency and minus all the Charm School garnish.

"Production-Line Courtesy," Ibid.

9 . . . that amenity which the French have developed into a great art . . . conversation.

Ch. 4, *Elegant Wits and Great Horizontals 1962*

10 These were clever and beautiful women, often of good background, who through some breach of the moral code or the scandal of divorce had been socially ostracized but had managed to turn the ostracism into profitable account. Cultivated, endowed with civilized graces, they were frankly—kept women, but kept by one man only, or, at any rate, by one man at a time.

Ch. 8, Ibid.

11 Woman's virtue is man's greatest invention.

Quoted in *Paris '90 n.d.*

1804. Margaret Craven (1901–1980)

1 The tide-book open by the compass because you came with the tide, you went with the tide, you waited for the tide, and sometimes you prayed for the tide.

Pt. I, Ch. 1, *I Heard the Owl Call My Name 1973*

2 "Where there is no written language, anything which must be remembered must be said."

Ch. 2, Ibid.

3 "Here in the village my people are at home as the fish in the sea, as the eagle in the sky. When the young leave, the world takes them, and damages them. They no longer listen when the elders speak. They go, and soon the village will go also."

Pt. II, Ch. 8, Ibid.

4 "The church belongs in the gutter. It is where it does some of its best work."

Pt. III, Ch. 12, Ibid.

5 Here every bird and fish knew its course. Every tree had its own place upon this earth. Only man had lost his way.

Ch. 16, Ibid.

6 Past the village flowed the river, like time, like life itself, waiting for the swimmer [salmon] to come again on his way to the climax of his adventurous life, and to the end for which he had been made.

"*Wa Laum* (That is all)," Pt. IV, Ch. 23, Ibid.

1805. Edith Summerskill (1901–1980)

1 Nagging is the repetition of unpalatable truths.

Speech, Married Women's Association, House of Commons, London *14 July 1960*

2 The breach of promise . . . I can think of no action more basically insincere than one conducted with the maximum publicity, for damages for a broken heart by a young woman who must already loathe the man who has rejected her.

Ch. 4, *A Woman's World 1967*

3 I learned that economics was not an exact science and that the most erudite men would analyze the economic ills of the world

and derive a totally different conclusion. . . . [Yet] governments still pin their faith to some new economic nostrum which is produced periodically by some bright young man. Only time proves that his alleged magic touch is illusory.

Ch. 5, Ibid.

4   Prize-fighting is still accepted as a display worthy of a civilized people despite the fact that all those connected with it are fully aware it caters to the latent sadistic instincts.

Ch. 12, Ibid.

5   The practice of abortion is as old as pregnancy itself. . . . Today, literate people of the space age, in well-populated countries, are not prepared to accept taboos without question; and in the matter of abortion the human rights of the mother with her family must take precedence over the survival of a few weeks' old foetus without sense or sensibility.

Ch. 19, Ibid.

6   There are those who believe that a divorce is better than subjecting a child to frequent scenes and quarrels but I am not among them. According to the report of some Judges sitting in custody, it is at the moment of the break-up of the home that the child shows signs of serious deterioration in bad behaviour and speech defects.

Ch. 20, Ibid.

1806. Irene Handle (1901/02–1987)

1   "The Dauphin has a truly terrifying sense of gratitude. You'll be annihilated by it, my poor Vince. Nothing can stand up against this terrible, slow gratitude of the Dauphin."

The Sioux 1965

1807. Nicola Abbagnano (1901–1990)

1   Reason itself is fallible, and this fallibility must find a place in our logic.

The Daily Telegraph (London) 14 September 1990

1808. Laura Riding (1901–1991)

1   We must distinguish better
Between ourselves and strangers.

"The Why of the Wind," *Collected Poems* 1938

2   I met God.
"What." he said, "you already?"
"What," I said, "you still?"

"Then Follows," Ibid.

3   You have pretended to be seeing.
I have pretended that you saw.

"Benedictory," Ibid.

4   Conversation succeeds conversation,
Until there's nothing left to talk about
Except truth, the perennial monologue,
And no talker to dispute it but itself.

"The Talking World," Ibid.

5   I do not doubt you.
I know you love me.
It is a fact of your indoor face. . . .

"In Due Form," Ibid.

6   The mercy of truth—it is to be truth.

"The Last Covenant," Ibid.

7   There can be no literary equivalent to truth.

"Extracts from Communication," *The Telling* 1967

8   In our unwilling ignorance we hurry to listen to stories of old human life, new human life, fancied human life, avid of something to while away the time of unanswered curiosity.

"The Telling," Ibid.

9   May our Mayness become All-embracing. May we see in one another the All that was once All-one rebecome One.

Ibid.

10   Until the missing story of ourselves is told, nothing besides told can suffice us: we shall go on quietly craving it.

Ibid.

11   Indeed, between Act and Matter-of-Fact
Was such consanguineous sympathy
That the displeasure of the matronymic
In the third generation of pure logic
Did not detract from the authority
Of this and later versions
Of the original progenitive argument.

"That Ancient Line," *Laura Riding: Selected Poems in Five Sets* 1970

12   To a poet the mere making of a poem can seem to solve the problem of truth. . . . but only a problem of art is solved in poetry.

Preface, *Selected Poems: In Five Sets* 1975

13   Art, whose honesty must work through artifice, cannot avoid cheating truth.

Ibid.

14   Father, I have begun to think.
Come and listen at my head.
It is frightful, like being dead
and having to hide.

"Addresses," *First Awakenings, The Early Poems...*, Elizabeth Friedmann, Alan J. Clark and Robert Nye, eds. 1993

15   Measure me by myself
And now by time or love or space
Or beauty. Give me this last grace:
That I may be on my low stone
A gage unto myself alone.
I would not have these old faiths fall
To prove that I was nothing at all.

"Dimensions," Ibid.

16   It would not be enough to say of "The White Goddess" that it is a...profession of poetic faith enacted with pseudo-naïve mind-immersing in glittering expanses of shallow poetic theorizing, into which is poured a foamy grandiose effusion of nothingish spiritualistics affecting learnedness in the meaning of *woman* in the cosmic totality; and to say that, as such, it is *deserved* by the modern intellectual populace that has emptied consciousness of a reality "soul" and invited "in," for replacement, poetically inflated psychological theory and literally and anthropologically recycled "myth." ..."The White Goddess" is worse than this. It is a personal infliction, an act of revenge.

"The White Goddess" (1933–35), *The Word "Woman" and Other Related Writings*, Elizabeth Friedmann and Alan J. Clark, eds. 1993

17   Man is an outside, an outdoor creature—indoors is not a serious idea to him.

"The Word 'Woman'" (1933–35), Ibid.

18 To woman the whole universe is, ultimately, an indoor place; it is her work to bring it all indoors. When woman becomes an outdoor creature, either physically or intellectually, she is "smart"…or clever or "interesting," but she ceases to be effective; she is no longer a comprehensive being.

> Ibid.

1809. Marlene Dietrich (1901–1992)

1 The average man is more interested in a woman who is interested in him than he is in a woman—any woman—with beautiful legs.

> News item *13 December 1954*

2 Latins are tenderly enthusiastic. In Brazil they throw flowers at you. In Argentina they throw themselves.

> Quoted in *Newsweek* (New York) *24 August 1959*

3 Sex. In America an obsession. In other parts of the world a fact.

> "Sex," *Marlene Dietrich's ABC 1962*

4 A new kind of award has been added—the deathbed award. It is not an award of any kind. Either the recipient has not acted at all, or was not nominated, or did not win the award the last few times around. It is intended to relieve the guilty conscience of the Academy members and save face in front of the public. The Academy has the horrible taste to have a star, choking with emotion, present this deathbed award so that there can be no doubt in anybody's mind why the award is so hurriedly given. Lucky is the actor who is too sick to watch the proceedings on television.

> "Academy Award," Ibid.

5 A country without bordels* is like a house without bathrooms.
> "Bordel," Ibid.

*Same as bordello, or house of prostitution.

6 There is a gigantic difference between earning a great deal of money and being rich.

> "Earning," Ibid.

7 Once a woman has forgiven her man, she must not reheat his sins for breakfast.

> "Forgiveness," Ibid.

8 There comes a time when suddenly you realize that laughter is something you remember and that you were the one laughing.

> "Laughter," Ibid.

9 To be completely woman you need a master, and in him a compass for your life. You need a man you can look up to and respect. If you dethrone him it's no wonder that you are discontented, and discontented women are not loved for long.

> "Married Love," Ibid.

10 Victory is gay only back home. Up front it is joyless.
> "Victory," Ibid.

11 The weak are more likely to make the strong weak than the strong are likely to make the weak strong.

> "Weakness," Ibid.

12 He is gentle, as all real men are gentle; without tenderness, a man is uninteresting.

> Ch. 1, *Papa Hemingway*,* A. E. Hotchner *1966*

*Ernest H—, American writer and journalist (1899–1961).

1810. Stella Gibbons (1902–1995)

1 Graceless, Pointless, Feckless and Aimless waited their turn to be milked.

> Ch. 3, *Conference at Cold Comfort Farm 1932*

2 Something nasty in the woodshed.

> Ch. 8, Ibid.

1811. Madeline Gray (1902–)

1 Sex, as I said, can be summed up in three P's: procreation, pleasure, and pride. From the long-range point of view, which we must always consider, procreation is by far the most important, since without procreation there could be no continuation of the race. . . . So female orgasm is simply a nervous climax to sex relations . . . and as such it is a comparative luxury from nature's point of view. It may be thought of as a sort of pleasure-prize like a prize that comes with a box of cereal. It is all to the good if the prize is there, but the cereal is valuable and nourishing if it is not.

> *The Normal Woman 1967*

1812. Leni Riefenstahl (1902–)

1 I state precisely: it is *film-verité*. It reflects the truth that was then, in 1934, history. It is therefore a documentary. Not a propaganda film. Oh! I know very well what propaganda is. That consists of recreating certain events in order to illustrate a thesis or, in the face of certain events, to let one thing go in order to accentuate another.

> Quoted by Michael Delahaye in *Cahiers du Cinema*, No. 5 *1966*

2 My life became a tissue of rumors and accusations through which I had to beat a path. . . .

> Ibid.

3 I only know how happy it makes me when I meet good men, simple men. But it repulses me so much to find myself faced with false men that it is a thing to which I have never been able to give artistic form.

> Ibid.

4 Whatever is purely realistic, slice-of-life, what is average, quotidian, doesn't interest me. Only the unusual, the specific, excites me.

> Ibid.

1813. Christina Stead (1902–1983)

1 The City is a machine miraculously organized for extracting gold from the seas, airs, clouds, from barren lands, holds of ships, mines, plantations, cottage hearth-stones, trees and rocks; and he, wretchedly waiting in the exterior halls, could not even get his finger on one tiny, tiny lever.

> "The Sensitive Goldfish," *The Salzburg Tales 1934*

2 . . . the waste, the insane freaks of these money men, the cynicism and egotism of their life . . . I'll show that they are not brilliant, not romantic, not delightful, not intelligent.

> *The House of All Nations 1938*

3 "I know your breed; all your fine officials debauch the young girls who are afraid to lose their jobs: that's as old as Washington."

> Ch. 4, *The Man Who Loved Children 1940*

4 "There are so many ways to kill yourself, they're just old-fashioned with their permanganate: do you think I'd take per-

manganate? I wouldn't want to burn my insides out and live to tell the tale as well: idiots! It's simple, I'd drown myself. . . . Why be in misery at the last?"

Ch. 5, Ibid.

5 "Anyone would think a thin stick like me, weak and miserable, would go down with everything: do you think I get more than my old cough every winter? I bet I live till ninety, with all my aches and pains. To think that's fifty more years of the Great I-Am."

Ibid.

6 "I do not want to go to heaven; I want my children, forever children, and other children, stalwart adults, and a good, happy wife, that is all I ask, but not paradise; earth is enough for me: it is because I believe earth is heaven, Naden, that I can overcome all my troubles and face down my enemies.'

Ch. 7, Ibid.

7 "A mother! What are we worth really? They all grow up whether you look after them or not. That poor miserable brat of his is growing up, and I certainly licked the hide off her; and she's seen marriage at its worst, and now she's dreaming about 'supermen' and 'great men.' What is the good of doing anything for them?"

Ch. 10, Ibid.

8 She was able to feel active creation going on around her in the rocks and hills, where the mystery of lust took place; and in herself, where all was yet only the night of the senses and wild dreams, the work of passion was going on.

For Love Alone 1944

9 "We are primitive men; we taboo what we desire and need. How did the denying of love come to be associated with the idea of morality?"

Ibid.

10 "When Europe's ruined after the war and the kids are starving and the old people dropping dead like flies, everybody sick, and without any hats or shoes, you'll see, we'll make a fortune."

A Little Tea, A Little Chat 1948

11 A cat and dog life it was; we didn't think we'd be able to stick it out. Eh, what a bloody egotist, love. . . .

Dark Places of the Heart 1966

12 "It's all bourgeois waste and caprice anyway. Someone taking the ideas of some Frenchman, great blocks of flats with angles and courtyards, a brick prison, it won't suit England; no fireplaces, no chimney and everything laid on from a center. . . . With this Corbusier there'll be no relaxing and no dreaming; only a soulless measured-off engineer's world with no place for us."

Ibid.

13 "Ye want to tell the plain truth all your life, woman, and speak straight and see straight; otherwise ye get to seein' double."

Ibid.

14 "Loneliness is a terrible blindness."

Ibid.

1814. Marya Zaturenska (1902–?)

1 The cold dream melts, the frost
Dissolves—the dream has sown
A harvest never lost.

"Song," St. 5 1960

2 Once they were flowers, and flame, and living bread;
Now they are old and brown and all but dead.

"Spinners at Willowsleigh" n.d.

1815. Stevie Smith (1902–1971)

1 I'm sorry to say my dear wife is a dreamer,
And as she dreams she gets paler and leaner.
Then be off to your Dream, with his fly-away hat,
I'll stay with the girls who are happy and fat.

"Be Off!" n.d.

2 Fourteen-year-old, why must you giggle and dote,
Fourteen-year-old, why are you such a goat?
I'm fourteen years old, that is the reason,
I giggle and dote in season.

"The Conventionalist" n.d.

3 This Englishwoman is so refined
She has no bosom and no behind.

"This Englishwoman" n.d.

4 O lovers true
And others too.
Whose best is only better
Take my advice
Shun compromise
Forget him and forget her.

To the tune of "The Coventry Carol," St. 4 n.d.

1816. Jessamyn West (1902–1984)

1 "After a good heart," she said, " the least a woman can do is pick a face she fancies. Men's so much alike and many so sorry, that's the very least. If a man's face pleasures thee, that doesn't change. That is something to bank on."

"Lead Her Like a Pigeon," The Friendly Persuasion 1945

2 She intended to forgive. Not to do so would be un-Christian; but she did not intend to do so soon, nor forget how much she had to forgive.

"The Buried Leaf," Ibid.

3 "Men ain't got any heart for courting a girl they can't pass—let alone catch up with."

"A Likely Exchange," Ibid.

4 "It's better to learn to say good-by early than late. . . ."

"Learn to Say Good-by," Love, Death, and the Ladies' Drill Team 1955

5 Being consistent meant not departing from convictions already formulated; being a leader meant making other persons accept these convictions. It was a narrow track, and a one-way, but a person might travel a considerable distance on it. A number of dictators have.

Ch. 7, To See the Dream 1956

6 We want the facts to fit the preconceptions. When they don't, it is easier to ignore the facts than to change the preconceptions.

Introduction, The Quaker Reader 1962

7 Friends [Quakers] refused to take legal oaths, since by doing so they acquiesced in the assumption that, unless under oath, one was not obliged to tell the truth.

Ibid.

8 A religious awakening which does not awaken the sleeper to love has roused him in vain.

Ibid.

9 Fiction reveals truths that reality obscures.
Quoted in *Reader's Digest* April 1973

10 "He should have put his wife to work. That's the way doctors and lawyers pay for their education nowadays."
Ch. 1, *Hide and Seek* 1973

11 Visitors to Los Angeles, then and now, were put out because the residents of Los Angeles had the inhospitable idea of building a city comfortable to live in, rather than a monument to astonish the eye of jaded travelers.
Ch. 22, Ibid.

1817. Elsa Lanchester (1902–1986)

1 If I can't be a good artist without too much pain, then I'm damned if I'll be an artist at all.
Charles Laughton and I 1938

2 Comedians on the stage are invariably suicidal when they get home.
Ibid.

3 Every artist should be allowed a few failures.
Ibid.

4 Perhaps the beginning of our interest in each other was first shown by the fact that although we are both the kind of people who can usually express ourselves and our ideas with great ease in conversation, we were practically dumb when we were alone together . . .
Ch. 3, Ibid.

5 One has to let slimmers act of their own free will. If you wag a finger and say: "Now, now, you must not eat cake," it is quite enough to make anyone immediately eat a cake.
Ch. 11, Ibid.

6 To complain too bitterly of the load of mischief that notoriety brings with it would mean that you are unsuited to the position you have made for yourself.
Ch. 20, Ibid.

7 As the film actor is seen by thousands of people simultaneously all over the world he is, compared to the stage actor, relatively independent of the critics. His fame depends upon something much less secure than the opinion of one man or the approval of one town; it depends on his capacity to keep up with public taste.
Ch. 21, Ibid.

8 She* looked as though butter wouldn't melt in her mouth—or anywhere else.
Attributed *n.d.*
*Reference to American actor Maureen O'Hara (1920–).

1818. Alva Reimer Myrdal (1902–1986)

1 An established tendency to drive values underground, to make the analysis appear scientific by omitting certain basic assumptions from the discussion, has too often emasculated the social sciences as agencies for rationality in social and political life. To be truly rational, it is necessary to accept the obvious principles that a social program, like a practical judgement, is a conclusion based upon premises of values as well as upon facts
Pt. I, Ch. 1, *Nation and Family* 1941

2 In the new era the scope of social policy will be widened to include general social solicitude for all human beings, not only for the indigent.
Pt. II, Ch. 10, Ibid.

3 The family of old could rightly be called the mutually supported family. All family members, without calculation as to exact shares, took part in both production and consumption. The nature and the degree of dependency were relatively similar for all. Only in the transition stage, when the male heads of households had surrendered to industrialism but that process had not yet markedly changed the functions of women, did the special dilemma of wives [as wage earner] appear.
Ch. 22, Ibid.

4 The plight of the hitherto less privileged nations is beginning to weigh heavily on our conscience. Today, when all the modern means of communication keep us supplied with an incessant, vivid flow of information, we can no longer ignore that plight, as our forefathers did. Such is the dilemma of our time . . .
"A Scientific Approach to International Welfare," *America's Role in International Welfare* 1955

5 The overpopulation scourge is the very symptom of an unbalanced development. It is as if it were Nature's own revenge when humans interfere in an unskillful way. The connection is a simple one: some of the most easily instituted measures of welfare lead to decreased mortality. This overthrows the balance which at a very low existence level is upheld by high mortality and high fertility checking each other.
Ibid.

6 It's not worthy of human beings to give up.
Quoted in "Sissela Bok,"* *A World of Ideas* by Bill Moyers 1989
*See 2552.

1819. Iris Origo (1902–1988)

1 But one resource is still left to man: a brotherly love and solidarity, a fearless recognition of the truth, untainted by praise or blame, which alone will render him capable of facing the insensibility of nature.
Ch. 13, *Leopardi* 1935

2 It is only comparatively seldom that the so-called "turning points" in a country's history—so convenient to the historian—are actually observable by those present at the time.
(2 February 1943), *War in Val d'Orcia* 1947

3 We are being governed by the dregs of the nation—and their brutality is so capricious that no one can feel certain that he will be safe tomorrow.
(28 November 1943), Ibid.

4 It is odd how used one can become to uncertainty for the future, to a complete planlessness, even in one's most private mind. What we shall do and be, and whether we shall, in a few month's time, have any home or possessions, or indeed our lives, is so clearly dependent on events outside our own control as to be almost restful.
(9 February 1944), Ibid.

5 What fraction of even that small part of us of which we are fully aware have we ever succeeded in communicating to any other human being?
Introduction, *A Measure of Love* 1957

6 A life-sentence can be pronounced in many ways; and there are as many ways of meeting it. What is common to all who have received it—the consumptive, the paralyzed, the deaf, the blind—is the absence of a fixed point on the mind's horizon.

Ibid.

7 It is the extreme concreteness of a child's imagination which enables him, not only to take from each book exactly what he requires—people, or genii, or tables and chairs—but literally to furnish his world with them.

Pt. II, Ch. 6, Ibid.

8 I write because, exacting as it may be to do so, it is still more difficult to refrain, and because—however conscious of one's limitations one may be—there is always at the back of one's mind, an irrational hope that this next book will be different: it will be the rounded achievement, the complete fulfillment. It never has been: yet I am still writing.

Ch. 8, Ibid.

9 All of my life that has not faded into mist has passed through the filter, not of my mind, but of my affections.

Images and Shadows 1970

1820. Barbara McClintock (1902–1992)

1 They* thought I was crazy, absolutely mad.

Quoted in "Honoring a Modern Mendel" by
Claudia Wallis, *Time* (New York) *24 October 1983*
*The National Academy of Sciences (1944), in response to her theory that genes could "jump" around in a chromosome; she later won the Nobel Prize for medicine (1983).

2 When you know you're right, you don't care what others think. You know sooner or later it will come out in the wash.

Ibid.

3 I know [my corn plants] intimately, and I find it a great pleasure to know them.

Quoted in *A Feeling for the Organism: The Life and Work of Barbara McClintock* by Evelyn Fox Keller* *1983*
*See 2635.

4 I would solve some of the problems [in science class at high school] in ways that weren't the answers the instructor expected. I would ask the instructor, "Please, let me…see if I can't find the standard answer" and I'd find it. It was a tremendous joy, the whole process of dinging that answer, just pure joy.

(p. 26), Ibid.

5 Well, you know, when I look at a cell I get down in that cell and look around.

(p. 69), Ibid.

6 You let the material tell you where to go.

Quoted in *Twentieth-Century Women Scientists*
by Lisa Yount *1996*

7 It seems a little unfair to reward a person for having so much pleasure over the years.*

Ibid.

*Her response to having received the Nobel Prize.

8 I start with the [corn] seedling, and I don't want to leave it. I don't feel I really know the story if I don't watch the plant all the way along. So I know every plant in the field. I know them intimately, and I find it a great pleasure to know them.

Ibid.

9 The initial association of the three of us,* followed subsequently by inclusion of any interested graduate student, formed a close-knit group eager to discuss all phases of genetics, including those being revealed or suggested by our own efforts. The group was self-sustaining in all ways. For each of us this was an extraordinary period. Credit for its success rests with Professor Emerson** who quietly ignored some of our seemingly strange behaviors.

Over the years, members of this group have retained the warm personal relationship that our early association generated. The communal experience profoundly affected each one of us.

Autobiographical Essay, *The Electronic Nobel Museum*,
http://www.nobel.se/enm-index.html *1999*
*George W. Beadle, American biologist (a Nobel laureate; 1903–89) and Marcus M. Rhoades. **Rollins A. E—, geneticist.

10 Only twenty-one years had passed since the rediscovery of Mendel's* principles of heredity. Genetic experiments, guided by these principles, expanded rapidly in the years between 1900 and 1921. The results of these studies provided a solid conceptual framework into which subsequent results could be fitted. Nevertheless, there was reluctance on the part of some professional biologists to accept the revolutionary concepts that were surfacing. This reluctance was soon dispelled as the logic underlying genetic investigations became increasingly evident.

Ibid.

*Gregor Johann M—, German botanist and founder of the science of genetics (1822–1884).

1821. Marian Anderson (1902–1993)

1 Where there is money, there is fighting.

Quoted in *Marian Anderson, a Portrait*
by Kosti Vehanen *1941*

2 Now I understood, if the good Lord doesn't like to behold the misery of the earth, He takes the clouds and covers it from His sight; but where human beings dwell there is always a dark shadow.

Ibid.

3 I had gone to Europe . . . to reach for a place as a serious artist, but I never doubted that I must return. I was—and am—an American.

Quoted in "Marian Anderson," *Famous American Women*
by Hope Stoddard *1970*

4 I could see that my significance as an individual was small. . . . I had become, whether I liked it or not, a symbol, representing my people. I had to appear. . . . I could not run away from this situation.

Ibid.

5 As long as you keep a person down, some part of you has to be down there to hold him down, so it means you cannot soar as you otherwise might.

Interview on CBS-TV *30 December 1957*

6 Sometimes it's [prejudice] like a hair across your cheek. You can't see it. You can't find it with your fingers, but you keep brushing at it because the feel of it is irritating.

Interview (1960), Cited in "Death stills voice…" (AP),
Seattle Post-Intelligencer, A9 *9 April 1993*

1822. Edna Gardner Whyte (1902–1993)

1 I must have been competitive from the day I was born.

Rising Above It 1991

2 Teaching was the best way to learn.

Ibid.

3 A shrinking violet would not last a day in a career in aviation. If the men didn't browbeat her to death the other women would.

Ibid.

4 I want to fly until I'm 100.

Ibid.

5 I hope that I have helped hold open the door to [the] sky so that every woman can "rise above it."

Ibid.

6 Just watch, all of you men. I'll show you what a woman can do. . . . I'll go across the country, I'll race to the moon. . . . I'll never look back.

Reflections after her first solo flight, New Year's Day, 1931,
Ibid.

1823. Brooke Astor (1903–)

1 I am beginning to think 1929 is going to be a great year for us. There is nothing that makes me feel more alive than making money.

The Last Blossom on the Plum Tree 1986

1824. Ella J. Baker (1903–?)

1 I don't think it ever occurred to our immediate family to in-doctrinate children against sharing. Because they had had the privilege of growing up where they'd raised a lot of food. They were never hungry. They could share their food with people. And so, you share your *lives* with people.

Quoted in *Moving the Mountain* by Ellen Cantarow *1980*

2 The best country in the world, you hear them say. I guess it may be. I haven't lived anywhere else. But it's not good enough as far as I'm concerned.

Ibid.

1825. Jessie Shirley Bernard (1903–1996)

1 Women may think like men, act like men, live the rules of the male world, and think they live in the male world until some-thing happens that shows how wide the chasm really is.

The Female World 1981

2 Many women find female solidarity hard to reconcile with al-most any other of the many competing pulls on them; ethnic, racial, religious—and male. Perhaps especially male. Men seem better able to "gang up" against women than vice versa.

Ibid.

3 There are two marriages, then, in every marital union, his and hers.

The Future of Marriage 1982

1826. Dorothy Dow (1903–1979)

1 Shall I tremble at a gray hair. . . .

"Unbeliever," *Time and Love* 1942

2 Things that are lovely
Can tear my heart in two—
Moonlight on still pools,
You.

"Things," Ibid.

1827. Elizabeth Hawkes (1903–)

1 Everyone is basically two-sexed. . . . Most people are taught that homosexuality is absolutely dreadful without ever being told that everyone has some of it in him, or her. . . . Some peo-ple are even alarmed when they find themselves having feelings or behaving in some way culturally considered as belonging to the opposite sex.

Fashion Is Spinach 1938?

2 Dress to please yourself. . . . Forget you are what you wear. . . . Wear what you are.

Ibid.

3 Dressing can be great fun, but what's the good if it's only a one-sex street?

It's Still Spinach 1954

4 As for the bright hues in clothes, men always snort..."Only pansies wear colored clothes!" So I say to myself, heaven help the American male with his complex of having to be mascu-line.

Article in *Reader's Digest* (1938), Cited in "Early Feminist Fashion" by Bettina Berch, *Ms.* (New York) March *1987*

1828. Virginia Moore (1903–1993)

1 Fortunately there is excess in greatness: it can lose more than mediocrity possesses, and still be great.

"Sappho,"* *Distinguished Women Writers* 1934
*See 46.

2 A poet is a state of mind.

"Saint Teresa,"* Ibid.
*See 306.

3 Suspicion is the badge of base-born minds,
And calculation never understands.

"Tragic Conclusions" *n.d.*

1829. Nagako (1903–2000)

1 We have always been trained in the past to a life of service and I am afraid that as these new changes come about there may be a loss of real values.

*Meeting with Eleanor Roosevelt** (1953), Quoted in
Eleanor: The Years Alone by Joseph P. Lash *1972*
*See 1513.

1830. Teng Ying-ch'ao (1903–)

1 . . . in order to fight the Japanese we must study Japanese!

Quoted in *Women in Modern China* by Helen Foster Snow*
1967
*See 1903.

1831. Nelly Ptaschkina (1903–1920)

1 Youth does not know how to concentrate, and, on the other hand, does not want to confide in others. Hence the diary. The old work out everything in themselves.

(23 January 1918), *The Diary of Nelly Ptaschkina* 1923

2 I am mentally short-sighted because, after all, I am but a child. . . .

(25 January 1918), Ibid.

3 Whatever I neglect now I shall have to pay for later.

(26 January 1918), Ibid.

4   It seems to me that man at birth does not represent a lump of clay, which can be shaped at will: for instance, either he is born intelligent or he is born stupid. Goodness can, on the other hand, be acquired.

> Ibid.

5   I shall drive away my thoughts as soon as they touch upon dangerous ground. I . . . I shall *deceive myself.*

> (5 March 1918), Ibid.

6   Give women scope and opportunity, and they will be no worse than men.

> (1 October 1918), Ibid.

7   Marriage is slavery. . . . Human personality must develop quite freely. Marriage impedes this development; even more than that, it often drives one to "moral crimes," not only because forbidden fruit is sweet, but because the new love, which could be perfectly legitimate, becomes a crime.

> (25 October 1918), Ibid.

8   . . . love must and can only be an appendix to life, it certainly must not form its substance.

> (21 April 1919), Ibid.

9   Yes, one must renounce that which is too emotional. There is no need for these moods, this longing, these *attendrissements*. . . . Work is waiting for us.

> (27 May 1919), Ibid.

1832. Bettina Ballard (1903–1961)

1   Steichen* had a talent for making people drop their affectations and pretensions so that what came through on his film were true portraits, whether that was what the sitter wanted or not. Steichen himself was incapable of pretense.

> Ch. 1, *In My Fashion* 1960

*Edward S— , American photographer and pioneer in fine art photography (1879–1973).

2   Fashions are born and they die too quickly for anyone to learn to love them.

> Ibid.

3   None of the people I wrote about were as exciting in reality as I imagined them to be.

> Ch. 3, Ibid.

4   The feeling about time and what to do with it has changed. What has become of those long hours when we brushed our hair, fooled with our nails, tried for the most effective place of a beauty spot? Fashion is just one of the great sacrifices of the jet age—there just isn't time to play at it.

> Ch. 21, Ibid.

5   Fashion is sold by loud-voiced barkers who claim magic claims for their wards; the superlatives mount to a higher pitch with each season. There is no privacy to fashion—no exclusivity.

> Ibid.

1833. Thyra Samter Winslow (1903–1961)

1   Platonic love is love from the neck up.

> Quoted by James Simpson in *Interview 19 August 1952*

1834. Tallulah Bankhead (1903–1968)

1   I have three phobias which, could I mute them, would make my life as slick as a sonnet, but as dull as ditch water: I hate to go to bed, I hate to get up, and I hate to be alone.

> Ch. 1, *Tallulah* 1952

2   It's one of the tragic ironies of the theatre that only one man in it can count on steady work—the night watchman.

> Ibid.

3   Cocaine habit-forming? Of course not. I ought to know. I've been using it for years.

> Ch. 4, Ibid.

4   Let's not quibble! I'm the foe of moderation, the champion of excess. If I may lift a line from a die-hard whose identity is lost in the shuffle, "I'd rather be strongly wrong than weakly right."

> Ibid.

5   Here's a rule I recommend. Never practice two vices at once.

> Ibid.

6   No man worth his salt, no man of spirit and spine, no man for whom I could have any respect, could rejoice in the identification of Tallulah's husband. It's tough enough to be bogged down in a legend. It would be even tougher to marry one.

> Ch. 14, Ibid.

7   I've been called many things, but never an intellectual.

> Ch. 15, Ibid.

8   I've tried several varieties of sex. The conventional position makes me claustrophobic and the others give me a stiff neck or lockjaw.

> Quoted in *Miss Tallulah Bankhead* by Lee Israel 1972

9   If you really want to help the American theater, don't be an actress, dahling, be an audience!

> Quoted by Liz Smith, newsday.com 29 April 1999

10   I am as pure as the driven slush.

> Comment *n.d.*

1835. Kathleen Yardley Lonsdale (1903–1971)

1   Any country that wants to make full use of all its potential scientists and technologists could do so, but it must not expect to get the women quite so simply as it gets the men. It seems to me that marriage and motherhood are at least as socially important as military service. Government regulations are framed to ensure (in the United Kingdom) that a man returning to work from military service is not penalized by his absence. Is it Utopian, then, to suggest that any country that really wants married women to return to a scientific career when her children no longer need her physical presence should make special arrangements to encourage her to do so?

> Quoted in "Women in Science: Reminiscences and Reflections" by Kathleen Lonsdale, *Impact of Science on Society*, Vol. 20 1970

1836. Barbara Hepworth (1903–1975)

1   . . . I rarely draw what I see. I draw what I feel in my body.

> Quoted by A. M. Hammersmith in *The World of Art Series* 1968

1837. Anaïs Nin (1903–1977)

1 Mystical geometry. The arithmetic of the unconscious which impelled this balancing of events.

Winter of Artifice 1945

2 He wove a veritable spider web about himself. No man was ever more completely installed in the realm of possessions. . . . He had prepared a fortress against need, war and change.

Ibid.

3 She could not believe in that which she wanted others to believe in—in a world made as one wanted it, an ideal world.

Ibid.

4 . . . all elegant women have acquired a technique of weeping which has no . . . fatal effect on the make-up.

Ibid.

5 This enthusiasm which must be held in check was a great burden for a child's soul. . . . to restrain meant to kill, to bury.

Ibid.

6 The imagination is far better at inventing tortures than life because the imagination is a demon within us and it knows where to strike, where it hurts. It knows the vulnerable spot, and life does not, our friends and loves do not, because seldom do they have the imagination equal to the task.

Ibid.

7 He had a mania for washing and disinfecting himself. . . . For him the only danger came from the microbes that attacked the body. He had not studied the microbe of conscience which eats into the soul.

Ibid.

8 Certain gestures made in childhood seem to have eternal repercussions.

"Birth," *Under a Glass Bell 1948*

9 No need to hate. No need to punish. . . . The little girl in her was dead. . . . The woman was saved. And with the little girl died the need of a father.

Ibid.

10 When one is pretending the entire body revolts.

Ibid.

11 He wants to interfere with his instruments, while I struggle with nature, with myself, with my child and with the meaning I put into it all, with my desire to give and to hold, to keep and to lose, to live and to die.

Ibid.

12 There is blood in my eyes. A tunnel. I push into this tunnel, I bite my lips and push. There is a fire and flesh ripping and no air. Out of the tunnel! All my blood is spilling out. Push! Push! Push! It is coming! It is coming! I feel the slipperiness, the sudden deliverance, the weight is gone.

Ibid.

13 She hated him because she could not remain detached. . . .

Ibid.

14 I stopped loving my father a long time ago. What remained was the slavery to a pattern.

Ibid.

15 I was so filled with love for her I did not notice my effect on her.

(30 December 1931), *The Diary of Anaïs Nin*, Vol. I *1966*

16 I want the firsthand knowledge of everything, not fiction, intimate experience only. . . . I don't care for films, newspapers, "reportages," the radio. I only want to be involved while it is being lived.

Ibid.

17 Too much awareness, without accompanying experience, is a skeleton without the flesh of life.

(February 1937), *The Diary of Anaïs Nin*, Vol. II *1967*

18 Analysis does not take into account the creative products of neurotic desires.

Ibid.

19 The face is masklike. It does not smile. It does not want to charm the mirror, or deceive the mirror, or flirt with it and gain a false answer. . . . You can never catch the face alive, laughing or loving.

(March 1937), Ibid.

20 I can remember what I did but not the reflection of what I did.

Ibid.

21 I am not interested in fiction. I want faithfulness.

(August 1937), Ibid.

22 For the womb has dreams. It is not as simple as the good earth.

Ibid.

23 Woman does not forget she needs the fecundator, she does not forget that everything that is born of her is planted in her.

Ibid.

24 Electric flesh-arrows . . . traversing the body. A rainbow of color strikes the eyelids. A foam of music falls over the ears. It is the gong of the orgasm.

(October 1937), Ibid.

25 The crowd is a malleable thing, it can be dominated, dazzled, it's a public, it is faceless. This is the opposite of relationship.

Ibid.

26 Inner chaos, like those secret volcanoes which suddenly lift the neat furrows of a peacefully plowed field, awaited behind all disorders of face, hair, and costume, for a fissure through which to explode.

A Spy in the House of Love 1968

27 Those who live for the world . . . always lose their personal, intimate life.

(January 1943), *The Diary of Anaïs Nin*, Vol. III *1969*

28 What I consider my weaknesses are feminine traits: incapacity to destroy, ineffectualness in battle.

Ibid.

29 One handles truths like dynamite. Literature is one vast hypocrisy, a giant deception, treachery. All writers have concealed more than they revealed.

The Diary of Anaïs Nin, Vol. V *1974*

30 How wrong it is for women to expect the man to build the world she wants, rather than set out to create it herself.

Ibid.

31 The role of the writer is not to say what we can all say but what we are unable to say.

Ibid.

32 Memory is a great betrayer.

Letter to Geismar, Ibid.

33 This year I finally achieved objectivity, very difficult for a romantic.

Ibid.

34 What I cannot love, I overlook. It that real friendship?

"San Francisco," Ibid.

35 . . . we cannot cure the evils of politics with politics. . . . Fifty years ago if we had gone the way of Freud (to study and tackle hostility within ourselves) instead of Marx, we might be closer to peace than we are.

Ibid.

36 If we are unable to make passion a relationship of duration, surviving the destruction and erosions of daily life, it still does not divest passion of its power to transform, transfigure, transmute a human being from a rather limited, petty, fearful creature to a magnificent figure reaching at moments the status of a myth.

Ibid.

37 Anxiety is love's greatest killer, because it is like the strangle hold of the drowning.

Ibid.

38 The alchemy of fiction is, for me, an act of embalming.

"Sierra Madre," Ibid.

39 The drugs, instead of bringing fertile images which in turn can be shared with the world . . . have instead become a solitary vice, a passive dreaming which alienates the dreamer from the whole world, isolates him, ultimately destroys him.

Ibid.

1838. Fanny Ellen Holtzman (1903–1980)

1 I don't follow precedent, I establish it.

Quoted in *The 50 Most Influential Women in American Law* by Dawn Bradley Berry *1996*

1839. Margaret Fishback (1903/4–1985)

1 At six weeks Baby grinned a grin
That spread from mouth to eyes to chin,
And Doc, the smartie, had the brass
To tell me it was only gas!

"Infant Prodigy," *Look Who's a Mother 1945*

2 The same old charitable lie
Repeated as the years scoot by
Perpetually makes a hit—
"You really haven't changed a bit!"

"The Lie of the Land" *n.d.*

1840. Clare Boothe Luce (1903–1987)

1 Lying increases the creative faculties, expands the ego, lessens the friction of social contacts. . . . It is only in lies, wholeheartedly and bravely told, that human nature attains through words and speech the forbearance, the nobility, the romance, the idealism, that—being what it is—it falls so short of in fact and in deed.

Vanity Fair (New York) *October 1930*

2 SECRETARY. I wish I could get a man to foot my bills. I'm sick and tired, cooking my own breakfast, sloshing through the rain at 8 A.M., working like a dog. For what? Independence? A lot of independence you have on a woman's wages. I'd chuck it like that for a decent, or an indecent home.

The Women 1936

3 CHRYSTAL. There's a name for you ladies, but it isn't used in high society...outside of a kennel.

Ibid.

4 A man has only one escape from his old self: to see a different self—in the mirror of some woman's eyes.

Act I, Ibid.

5 MAGGIE. Marriage is a business of taking care of a man and rearing his children. . . . It ain't meant to be no perpetual honeymoon.

Act II, Ibid.

6 MARY. Reno's full of women who all have their pride.

Ibid.

7 LITTLE MARY. You know, that's the only good thing about divorce; you get to sleep with your mother.

Act III, Ibid.

8 EDITH. Always remember, Peggy, it's matrimonial suicide to be jealous when you have a really good reason.

Ibid.

9 Indeed the swastika never burns more brightly or savagely in the Schwarzwald than the Fiery Cross of the Klan once burned in the bayous and cypress swamps of Dixie.

Introduction, *Kiss the Boys Good-Bye* (play) *1938*

10 You see few people here in America who really care very much about living a Christian life in a democratic world.

Ch. 12, *Europe in the Spring 1940*

11 Much of what Mr. [Vice-President Henry] Wallace calls his global thinking is, no matter how you slice it, still Globaloney.

Speech, U.S. House of Representatives *9 February 1943*

12 To put a woman on the ticket would challenge the loyalty of women everywhere to their sex, because it would be made to seem that the defeat of the ticket meant the defeat for a hundred years of women's chance to be truly equal with men in politics.

Quoted in *Vanity Fair 28 June 1948*

13 Communism is the opiate of the intellectuals [with] no cure except as a guillotine might be called a cure for dandruff.

Newsweek (New York) *24 January 1955*

14 I am for lifting everyone off the social bottom. In fact, I am for doing away with the social bottom altogether.

Quoted in *Time* (New York) *14 February 1964*

15 NORA. Know what Freud wrote in his diary when he was 77? "What do women want? My God, what do they want?" Fifty years this giant brain spends analyzing women. And he still can't find out want they want. So this makes him the world's greatest expert on female psychology?

Slam the Door Softly 1970

16 BLACK WOMAN'S VOICE. There's no human being a man can buy anymore—except a woman.

Ibid.

17 NORA. But if God had wanted us to think with our wombs, why did He give us a brain?

> Ibid.

18 NORA. When a man can't explain a woman's actions, the first thing he thinks about is the condition of her uterus.

> Ibid.

19 The American Republic is now almost 200 years old, and in the eyes of the law women are still not equal with men. The special legislation which will remedy that situation is the Equal Rights Amendment. Its language is short and simple: *Equality of rights under the law shall not be abridged in the United States or by any state on account of sex.**

> Quoted in the *Bulletin of the Baldwin School* (Pennsylvania)
> *September 1974*

*See Alice Paul, 1538.

20 A man's home may seem to be his castle on the outside; inside, it is more often his nursery.

> Ibid.

21 In politics women . . . type the letters, lick the stamps, distribute the pamphlets and get out the vote. Men get elected.

> Quoted in *Saturday Review/World 15 September 1974*

22 Male supremacy has kept women down. It has not knocked her out.

> Ibid.

23 My early disadvantages spurred me on to accept the challenges of life, to look for avenues of expression, to be the best I could be in whatever I tried. Coming as far as I have, I see each day's dawning as a triumph, with the curtain rising on a tremendously exciting show. I love every minute of it.

> Quoted in "Clare Boothe Luce in Hawaii" by
> Marshall Berges (p. 12), *National Retired Teachers
> Association Journal July–August 1979*

24 I hope I shall have ambition to the day I die.

> Quoted in *Rage for Fame: The Ascent of Clare Boothe Luce*
> by Sylvia Jukes Morris *1997*

25 I'll marry for money. Lots of it...Damned if I'll ever love any mere man. Money! I need it and the power it brings, and someday you shall hear my name spoken of as famous.

> *Diary entry, Ibid.*

26 I do not like to go to bed without you. But somehow, lately, even when I'm with you, I seem to go to bed without you.

> Letter to her husband, Henry Luce,* Ibid.

*American editor and publisher; founder of *Time, Life, Fortune* and *Sports Illustrated* (1898–1967).

27 There are times when a man or woman does better to act with sense than to react with sensibility.

> Ibid.

28 Most everyone that knew me casually preferred to think of me as a cold, remote, shrewd and ambitious woman: I have always contrived to behave so in their company.

> Note to her husband, Henry Luce, Ibid.

29 A badly burnt child I am so afraid of happiness, that let a perfect moment begin to unfold like a rose in my hands, and I instantly try to crush it.

> Ibid.

30 If he touched you it was like he was tearing you apart. I suppose today I would have given him a handbook of sex, but in those days women were expected to keep quiet.

> Recollection of her husband, Henry Luce, Ibid.

31 What rage for fame attends both great and small.

> School yearbook entry, Ibid.

32 The women who inspired this play [*The Women*] deserved to be smacked across the head with a meat axe. And that, I flatter myself, is exactly what I smacked them with.

> Quoted in *The Female Dramatist* by Elaine T. Partnow,*
> with Lesley Hyatt *1998*

*See 2870.

1841. Marguerite Yourcenar (1903–1987)

1 One reaches all great events of life a virgin.

> *Fires 1935*

2 One doesn't know what to do with delirium while experimenting with the mingling and mixing of bodies.

> Ibid.

3 And you are going? You are going? . . . No, you are not going: I am keeping you . . . You leave your soul, like a coat, in my hands.

> Ibid.

4 We say: mad with joy. We should say: wise with grief.

> Ibid.

5 To possess is the same thing as to know: the Bible is always right.

> Ibid.

6 Thieves are only after our rings, lovers our bodies, preachers our souls, murderers our lives.

> Ibid.

7 The worst examples of savage ferocity only harden the auditor that much more, and since the human heart has about as much softness as a stone anyhow I see no need for going further in that direction. Our men were certainly not lacking in invention either, but so far as I was concerned I preferred to deal out death without embellishment, as a rule. Cruelty is the luxury of those who have nothing to do, like drugs or racing stables. In the matter of love, too, I hold for perfection unadorned.

> *Coup de Grâce 1939*

8 The successive phases of love follow a monotonous course; what they still seem to me to resemble the most are the endless but sublime repetitions and returns in Beethoven's Quartets.

> Ibid.

9 There is so little basic difference between total innocence and complete degradation. . . .

> Ibid.

10 "Life is atrocious, we know. But precisely because I expect little of the human condition, man's periods of felicity, his partial progress, his efforts to begin over again and continue, all seem to me like so many prodigies which nearly compensate for the monstrous mass of ills and defeats, of indifference and error. Catastrophe and ruin will come; disorder will triumph, but order will too, from time to time."

> *Memoirs of Hadrian 1954*

11 This morning it occurred to me for the first time that my body, my faithful companion and friend, truly better known to me than my own soul, may be after all only a sly beast who will end by devouring his master.

"Animula Vagula Blandula," Ibid.

12 I have done much rebuilding. To reconstruct is to collaborate with time gone by, penetrating or modifying its spirit, and carrying it toward a longer future. Thus beneath the stones we find the secret of the springs.

"Tellus Stabilita," Ibid.

13 Nothing seemed simpler: a man has the right to decide how long he may usefully live. . . . [But] sickness disgusts us with death, and we wish to get well, which is a way of wishing to live. But weakness and suffering, with manifold bodily woes, soon discourage the invalid from trying to regain ground: he tires of those respites which are but snares, of that faltering strength, those ardors cut short, and that perpetual lying in wait for the next attack.

"Patientia," Ibid.

14 The memory of most men is an abandoned cemetery where lie, unsung and unhonored, the dead whom they have ceased to cherish. Any lasting grief is reproof of their forgetfulness.

"Saeculum Aureum," Ibid.

15 I have often thought that men who care passionately for women attach themselves at least as much to the temple and to the accessories of the cult as to their goddess herself. . . . I should have desired more: to see the human creature unadorned, alone with herself as she indeed must have been at least sometimes, in illness or after the death of a first-born child, or when a wrinkle began to show in her mirror. A man who reads, reflects, or plans belongs to his species rather than to his sex; in his best moments he rises above the human.

"Varius Multiplex Multi Formis," Ibid.

16 We are so used to seeing in wisdom a residue of dead passions that it's difficult to recognize in it the hardest and most condensed form of ardor, the gold nugget pulled out of the fire, not the ashes.

Essay on Constantine Cavafy, Quoted in *Marguerite Yourcenar; Inventing a Life* by Josyane Savigneau, tr. by Joan E. Howard 1993

17 It takes time to get to know this great country [America], at once so spread out and so secret.

Letter to Jean Lambert (1956), Ibid.

18 Until such time as one has managed to create on this continent, as Grace* and I have done, a domain, however small it may be, governed by fantasy or one's personal wishes, what the transplanted European finds here...is quite simply a poorer, harsher Europe, devoid of all the refinements that make Europe what it is for us...

Ibid.

*Grace Frick (d. 1979), translator, Yourcenar's companion of 40 years.

19 My life's choice is not that of America against France. It translates a taste for a world stripped of all borders.

Remark to visitors, Ibid.

1842. Leonor Kretzer Sullivan (1903–1988)

1 Millions of American women would like to see the nation which can dress men in the garments necessary to withstand the hostile environment of the moon help women to get through a day without a bag, sag, wrinkle or tear in an expensive and frequently essential article of wearing apparel here on earth.

The Congressional Record 1970

2 A woman with a woman's viewpoint is of more value than when she forgets she's a woman and begins to act like a man.

Ibid.

1843. Elaine Frances Burton (1904–)

1 A woman in authority is often unpopular, only because she is efficient.

What of the Women? 1941

2 If you get a good woman, you get the finest thing on earth.

Ibid.

1844. Eve Curie (1904–)

1 We discovered that peace at any price is no peace at all. . . . We discovered that life at any price has no value whatever; that life is nothing without the privileges, the prides, the rights, the joys which make it worth living, and also worth giving. And we also discovered that there is something more hideous, more atrocious than war or than death; and that is to live in fear.

Address, American Booksellers Association, New York 9 April 1940

2 Let's face it: however old-fashioned and out of date and devaluated the word is, we like the way of living provided by democracy.

Ibid.

3 Public opinion waged the war. Statesmen, diplomats, government officials waged the war. To beat the Axis, it was not enough to win battles in the field, to kill millions of men. We also had to kill ideas that knew no frontiers and spread like diseases.

Pt. V, Ch. 26, *Journey Among Warriors* 1943

1845. Lilly Daché (1904–1989)

1 When I was six I made my mother a little hat—out of her new blouse.

Newspaper interview 3 December 1954

2 Glamour is what makes a man ask for your telephone number. But it also is what makes a woman ask for the name of your dressmaker.

Quoted in *Woman's Home Companion* July 1955

1846. Molly Keane (1904–1996)

1 The list of sons of the right sort, still available in this country, was miserably short in comparison with that of the golden lads who had come to dust in Flanders and other places.

Queen Lear 1989

1847. Marya Mannes (1904–1990)

1 "I think funerals are barbaric and miserable. Everything connected with them—the black, the casket, the shiny hearse, the sepulchral tones of the preacher—is destructive to true memory."

"The First Days," *Message from a Stranger* 1948

2 Promiscuous. . . . That was a word I had never applied to myself. Possibly no one ever does, for it is a sordid word, reducing many valuable moments to nothing more than dog-like copulation.

"The Second Month," Ibid.

3 They had no serenity, for true serenity comes after knowledge of pain. They had only the stillness of spiritual inertia. They were half alive.

"The Seventh Month," Ibid.

4 The real demon is success—the anxieties engendered by this quest are relentless, degrading, corroding. What is worse, there is no end to this escalation of desire. . . .

"The Roots of Anxiety in Modern Women," *Journal of Neuropsychiatry* May 1964

5 What I call the destructive anxieties are not the growth of women's minds and powers, but quite the contrary: the pressures of society and the mass media to make woman conform to the classic and traditional images in men's eyes.

Ibid.

6 Who's kidding whom? What's the difference between Giant and Jumbo? Quart and *full* quart? Two-ounce and *big* two-ounce? What does Extra Long mean? What's a *tall* 24-inches? And what busy shopper can tell?

"New Bites by a Girl Gadfly," *Life* (New York) *12 June 1964*

7 The art of flirtation is dying. A man and woman are either in love these days or just friends. In the realm of love, reticence and sophistication should go hand in hand, for one of the joys of life is discovery.

Ibid.

8 Affluent as it was for the majority, the society we had produced was not admirable. It might be better than others, but it was nowhere near what it should have been. It was, in fact, going rotten. The private gain had for so long triumphed over the public need that the cities had become unlivable, the country desecrated, the arteries choked, and pollution—of air, of water, yes, of spirit too—a daily, oppressive fact. And who else but our generation (if not ourselves) had made it so?

Them 1968

9 "Well, my theory has always been," said Lev, "that if each of our senses—sight, hearing, touch, smell, taste—was developed to its utmost capacity we would then have attained not only total physical awareness, as in animals, but total spiritual development, as in man. Ideal man. Everything," pursued Lev, "atrophies without use."

Ibid.

10 Timing and arrogance are decisive factors in the successful use of talent. The first is a matter of instinct, the second part carapace and part self-hypnosis; the shell that protects, the ego that assumes, without question, that the talent possessed is not only unique but important, the particular vision demanding to be shared.

Preface, *Out of My Time* 1971

11 The barbarian weapon is fission: the splitting asunder. It has been perfected for death. Our only weapon is fusion: an imperfect process still, though designed for life.

Ch. 9, Ibid.

12 While the young fight the official barbarism of unsentient power—the insanities of war and the ruinous priorities imposed by leaders and organizations in the *name* of reason, perhaps our last duty is to fight for the civilization *of* reason.

Ibid.

1848. Anne Roe (1904–1991)

1 Nothing in science has any value to society if it is not communicated. . . .

Ch. 1, *The Making of a Scientist* 1952

2 Freedom breeds freedom. Nothing else does.

Ch. 16, Ibid.

1849. Charlotte Wolff (1904–1986)

1 I have no doubt that lesbianism makes a woman virile and open to *any* sexual stimulation, and that she is more often than not a more adequate and lively partner in bed than a "normal" woman.

Love Between Women 1971

2 A niggling feeling of discomfort and unease follows masturbation, even in those who do not feel guilty about it.

Ibid.

1850. Hayashi Fumiko (1904–1951)

1 Kin refused to forget her femininity.
Death itself was preferable to the
blowsiness of the average old woman.
There was a poem—composed, they said, by
some famous woman of the past—
Never could human form
Aspire, I know,
To beauty ripe as that now bends
This rose. Yet, somewhere here,
I see myself.

"Late Chrysanthemum," John Bester, tr. 1948

2 Love in itself, she felt should be like the creation of a succession of works of art.

Ibid.

1851. Margery Allingham (1904–1966)

1 Lying, they say, is a new modern art of the enemy's, but telling the truth is not easy.

Preface, *The Oaken Heart* 1941

2 We—he and thee and the parson and all the other lads of the village—constitute the public, and the politicians are our servants. They apply for the job (often rather obsequiously, we notice with instant suspicion), we give it to them, we pay them in honours or cash, and we judge them solely by results.

Ch. 1, Ibid.

3 "Do you know it occurred to me when I was listening to him that both in a past and in a future age this tremendous insistence of ours upon the nice importance of manners and breeding may well have seemed and still seem again to be absurd."
. . . "Fashion!" he repeated, as if the word had annoyed him. "I'll wager it goes far deeper than fashion."
"Few things go deeper than fashion," objected Castor.

Ch. 8, Ibid.

4 It is always difficult to escape from youth; its hopefulness, its optimistic belief in the privileges of desire, its despair, and its

sense of outrage and injustice at disappointment, all these spring on a man inflicting indelicate agony when he is no longer prepared.

Ch. 21, Ibid.

5 Normally he was the happiest of men. He asked so little of life that its frugal bounty amazed and delighted him. . . . He believed in miracles and frequently observed them, and nothing astonished him. His imagination was as wild as a small boy's and his faith ultimate. In ordinary life he was, quite frankly, hardly safe out.

Ch. 2, *The Tiger in the Smoke* 1952

6 Chemists employed by the police can do remarkable things with blood. They can find it in shreds of cloth, in the interstices of floor boards, on the iron of a heel, and can measure it and swear to it and weave it into a rope to hang a man.

Ch. 9, Ibid.

7 . . . nobody wants a prosaic explanation of fraud and greed.

The Villa Marie Celeste 1960

1852. Virgilia Peterson (1904–1966)

1 In Reno, there is always a bull market, never a bear market for the stocks and bonds of happiness.

A Matter of Life and Death 1961

2 A lady, that is an enlightened, cultivated, liberal lady—the only kind to be in a time of increasing classlessness—could espouse any cause: wayward girls, social diseases, unmarried mothers, and/or birth control with impunity. But never by so much as the shadow of a look should she acknowledge her own experience with the Facts of Life.

Ibid.

3 European society . . . automatically assumes its superiority to Americans whether they have money or not, but money tends to blur the sharpness of the distinction.

Ibid.

1853. Dorothy Eugenia Miner (1904–1973)

1 The book with pages was the stimulus to everything that we think of when we discuss book design.

The History of Bookbinding, 525–1950 A.D. 1957

2 . . . labels—a favorite device by which insignificant things can *reflect* significance.

Letter to Eleanor P. Spencer (3 November 1970), Quoted in "The Varied Career of a Medievalist" by Claire Richter Sherman, *Women As Interpreters of the Visual Arts*, Claire Richter Sherman, ed. 1981

1854. Nancy Mitford (1904–1973)

1 "I simply don't see the point of getting up at six all the time you are young and working eighteen hours a day in order to be a millionaire, and then when you are a millionaire still getting up at six and working eighteen hours a day. . . . What does it all mean?"

Ch. 1, *Pigeon Pie* 1940

2 All the heat there was seemed to concentrate in the Hons' cupboard, which was always stifling. Here we would sit, huddled up on the slatted shelves, and talk for hours about life and death.

Ch. 2, *The Pursuit of Love* 1945

3 Uncle Matthew's four years in France and Italy between 1914 and 1918 had given him no great opinion of foreigners. "Frogs," he would say, "are slightly better than Huns or Wops, but abroad is unutterably bloody and foreigners are fiends."

Ch. 15, Ibid.

4 "Always remember, children, that marriage is a very intimate relationship. It's not just sitting and chatting to a person; there are other things, you know."

Pt. I, Ch. 14, *Love in a Cold Climate* 1949

5 An aristocracy in a republic is like a chicken whose head has been cut off: it may run about in a lively way, but in fact it is dead.

Noblesse Oblige 1956

6 Americans relate all effort, all work, and all of life itself to the dollar. Their talk is of nothing but dollars. The English seldom sit happily chatting for hours on end about pounds. In England, public business is its own reward, nobody would go into Parliament in order to become rich, neither do riches bring public appointment.

Ibid.

7 The fact is with me, my love of shrieking* is greater than my *amour-propre* . My skin is thick. And, great protection, I never take myself seriously as a *femme de lettres*.

Letter to Evelyn Waugh*,* *Love From Nancy, The Letters of Nancy Mitford*, Charlotte Mosely, ed. 1993

*Her word for hysterical laughter. **British writer (1903–1966).

8 The reason for my resignation is that I'm no use to you. When things go badly you don't need me, when they go well you turn to other, prettier, ladies. So I seem to have no function—*le portefeuille est vide.**

Letter to Gaston Palewski** (1858), Ibid.

*An empty pocketbook. **A French diplomat of Polish descent; both married to others, he was the love of her life.

1855. Adelle Davis (1904–1974)

1 Nutrition is a young subject; it has been kicked around like a puppy that cannot take care of itself. Food faddists and crackpots have kicked it cruelly. . . . They seem to believe that unless food tastes like Socratic hemlock, it cannot build health. Frankly, I often wonder what such persons plan to do with good health in case they acquire it.

Ch. 1, *Let's Eat Right to Keep Fit* 1954

2 When the blood sugar is extremely low, the resulting irritability, nervous tension, and mental depression are such that a person can easily go berserk. . . . Add a few guns, gas jets, or razor blades, and you have the stuff murders and suicides are made of. The American diet has become dangerous in many more ways than one.

Ch. 2, Ibid.

3 Thousands upon thousands of persons have studied disease. Almost no one has studied health.

Ch. 29, Ibid.

4 If this country is to survive, the best-fed-nation myth had better be recognized for what it is: propaganda designed to produce wealth but not health.

Ch. 30, Ibid.

5 You can't eat well and keep fit if you don't shop well.

Quoted in "The Great Adelle Davis Controversy" by Daniel Yergin, *The New York Times Magazine* 20 May 1973

6   People in nutrition get the idea that they are going to live to be a hundred and fifty. And they never do.

Ibid.

7   Nutrition research, like a modern star of Bethlehem, brings hope that sickness need not be a part of life.

Ibid.

1856. Malka Lee (1904/05–1976)

1   Each person was given a number. When the nurse noticed that I was embarrassed to undress, she jumped on me like a vixen and spoke very rudely, puling my underwear from me... [A] man in a white smock sprayed me with a liquid chemical which went into my eyes, my hair and on all parts of my naked body . . .

After a while, we were asked for our number and in exchange were each handed our own bag of disinfected clothing.

I pulled my dress out of the bag. My mother's embroidered sailor collar had shrunk into a wrinkled rag. I began to cry like a child.

"Through the Eyes of Childhood," Found Treasures: Stories by Yiddish Women Writers, Frieda Forman, Ethel Raicus, Sarah Silberstein Swartz & Margie Wolf, eds. 1994

1857. Helen Lawrenson (1904–1982)

1   They are a curious mixture of Spanish tradition, American imitation, and insular limitation. This explains why they never catch on to themselves.

"Latins Are Lousy Lovers," Esquire (New York) October 1939

2   A skirt is no obstacle to extemporaneous sex, but it is physically impossible to make love to a girl while she is wearing trousers.

"Androgyne, You're a Funny Valentine," Latins Are Still Lousy Lovers 1968

3   Any definition of sophistication must include the word "worldliness"; and how can people be worldly who seem to have no inkling of what's going on in the world?

"Latins Are Lousy Lovers," Ibid.

4   Most of today's film actresses are typical of a mass-production age: living dolls who look as if they came off an assembly line and whose uniformity of appearance is frequently a triumph of modern science, thanks to which they can be equipped with identical noses, breasts, teeth, and hair.

"Where Did It Go?," Ibid.

1858. Sally Stanford (1904–1982)

1   No, no one sets out to be a madam; but madams answer the call of a well-recognized and very basic human need. Their responsibilities are thrust upon them by the fundamental nitwittedness and economic shortsightedness of most hustling broads. And they become tempered and sharpened and polished to the highest degree of professional awareness by constant intercourse with men devoutly dedicated to the policy of getting something for nothing.

Prologue, The Lady of the House 1966

2   Well, there's a Book that says we're all sinners and I at least chose a sin that's made quite a few people happier than they were before they met me, a sin that's left me with very little time to consider other extremely popular moral misdemeanors, like usury, intolerance, bearing false tales, extortion,

racial bigotry, and the casting of the first stone. And, I might add, a hell of a lot worse.

Ch. 4, Ibid.

3   No man can be held throughout the day by what happens throughout the night.

Ch. 13, Ibid.

4   Romance without finance is a nuisance. Few men value free merchandise. Let the chippies fall where they may.

Ibid.

1859. Sheilah Graham (1904–1988)

1   . . . you have to really drink a lot to enjoy parties.

Quoted in "Sheilah Graham: Still Upwardly, Verbally Mobile" by Kathleen Hendrix, The Los Angeles Times 13 October 1974

2   You just never know when you're going into eternity.

Ibid.

3   I think people still want to marry rich. Girls especially. . . . [It's] simple. Don't date poor boys. Go where the rich are. . . . You don't have to be rich to go where they go.

Ibid.

4   I won't be remembered for my writing. I'll be remembered as Scott's* mistress.

Comment, Quoted in Milestones Section, Time (New York) 28 November 1988

*F. Scott Fitzgerald, American writer (1896–1940).

1860. Mary Steichen Calderone (1904–1998)

1   Sex had to be brought out of the Victorian closet—freed from the guilt and fear, bigotry and misconceptions which shrouded it, if America was to recover from its deep-rooted sexual trouble.

SIECUS* Fund-raising Letter 1979

*Sex Information and Education Council of the United States.

2   Interference with self-pleasure is a very bad thing for children.

60 Minutes, CBS-TV 25 October 1981

3   I don't want to control anybody's mind or anybody's heart—I just want to help free people from the concept of sex as evil instead of a gift from God.

Ibid.

4   The significance of revolutions never lies in what they are against, but in what the are for.

Friends and Womankind (pamphlet, Friends General Conference) 1984

5   Being a Quaker lays on one the responsibility for engaging in a continuing internal process of finding out what one really believes in, and relentlessly tracking down one's own bigotries, prejudices, inconsistencies, blindnesses, and refusals to recognize truth and accept it as such.

Ibid.

1861. Shulamit Aloni (1905–)

1   Thus the Israeli woman, like her American counterpart, pushes aside all youthful enthusiasm and ambition to develop an active personality and instead copies the model with which she is presented—an agreeable beautiful doll and cheap servant. One

day, when the children have grown up, she comes face to face with the emptiness and looks for fulfillment in language courses, ceramics and art circles, volunteer work and charity, wrapped around a cup of coffee watching a fashion show.

Article, Quoted in Israel Magazine *April 1971*

2 According to civil law, women are equal to men. But I have to go to a religious court as far as personal affairs are concerned. Only men are allowed to be judges there—men who pray every morning to thank God He did not make them women. You need prejudice before you open your mouth. And because they believe women belong in the home, you are doubly discriminated against if you work.

Quoted in "Women in Israel" (November 1973), Crazy Salad *by Nora Ephron* 1975*

*See 2849.

1862. Viña Delmar (1905–1990)

1 "We have strict orders on how to teach. There are certain methods that must be employed. Your way is easier to learn, but it hasn't been approved by the school board for use in the classroom."

The Becker Scandal 1968

2 . . . her plumpness was so neat and firm that she was rather like one of the better apples that are purchased for fruit-bowl display.

Ibid.

3 It must be true that whenever a sensational murder is committed there are people who—though they are, quite properly, of no interest to law enforcers, attorneys, or newspaper reporters—weep, lie sleepless, and realize at last that their lives have been changed by a crime in which they played no part.

Ibid.

1863. Enchi Fumiko (1905–?)

1 Chigako had no interest in pornographic pictures and books; even in the first days of their marriage, when Keisaku had shown her his private store of pictures she had, far from enjoying them, ended by shutting the book unread, thus affording her husband simultaneously both disappointment and a sense of relief at his wife's lack of the lecherous instinct.

"Enchantress," John Bestor, tr. n.d.

2 . . . their daughter was gone, Kiriko had been invaluable—a solid, flesh-and-blood barrier between them. Now she had vanished, and the gap she had left must, whatever happened, be filled with something else.

Ibid.

3 Spectacles, false teeth eventually, false locks made of other people's hair—all kinds of things foreign to her own flesh which she donned like armor in her hungry craving to appear young, to be beautiful. What kind of creature was she?

Ibid.

1864. Ethel Jacobson (1905?–)

1 Behind every man who achieves success
Stands a mother, a wife, and the IRS.

Quoted in Reader's Digest *April 1973*

1865. Maggie Kuhn (1905–1995)

1 Our [old people's] citizenship is not served when we take ourselves out of the mainstream of society and consign ourselves

to a life of play. . . . Arbitrary retirement at a fixed age ought to be negotiated and decided according to the wishes of the people involved. Mandatory retirement ought to be illegal.

Quoted in "Profile of a Gray Panther" by Carol Offen, Retirement Living *December 1972*

2 Ageism is any discrimination against people on the basis of chronological age—whether old or young. It's responsible for an enormous neglect of social resources.

Ibid.

3 We want to give old folks a new sense of power and worth. We've been brainwashed by the youth cult to keep up youthful appearances, and to be ashamed of our age.

Ibid.

4 Men and women approaching retirement age should be recycled for public service work, and their companies should foot the bill. We can no longer afford to scrap-pile people.

"Gray Panthers Versus Ageism," Ms. *(New York) July 1973*

5 One reason our society has become such a mess is that we're isolated from each other. The old are isolated by government policy. So we have all sorts of stereotypes floating around about blacks, old people, and women.

Quoted in "How to Forget Age Bias," Ibid.

6 Power should not be concentrated in the hands of so few, and powerlessness in the hands of so many.

Ibid.

7 I think of age as a great universalizing force. It's the only thing we all have in common. It doesn't begin when you collect your social security benefits. Aging begins with the moment of birth, and it ends only when life itself has ended. Life is a continuum; only, we—in our stupidity and blindness—have chopped it up into little pieces and kept all those little pieces separate.

Quoted in "Liberating Aging" by Ken Dychtwald, New Age *February 1979*

8 There are lots of people and programs that have purported to serve us but instead treat us like wrinkled babies, powerless and dependent. Our goal should be responsible adulthood. We're the elders of the tribe, and the elders are charged with the tribe's survival and well being!

Ibid.

9 Our technological society scrap-piles old people as it does automobiles. . . .

Ibid.

10 Old age is not a disease—it is strength and survivorship, triumph over all kinds of vicissitudes and disappointments, trials and illnesses.

Ibid.

11 I'm having a glorious old age. One of my greatest delights is that I have outlived most of my opposition.

Speech, Vermont state legislature 1991

12 Learning and sex until *rigor mortis.*

Motto n.d.

1866. Eileen O'Casey (1900–1995)

1 I was liberated but not too liberated. I was Catholic, you see, and my conscience always bothered me.

Quoted in "Eileen O'Casey Remembers" by Lee Grant, The Los Angeles Times *13 November 1974*

2 Unless it's right next door, people don't notice killing and bloodshed. We take it in like the sun shines and the rain falls.
Ibid.

1867. Mary Renault (1905–)

1 Miss Searle had always considered boredom an intellectual defeat.
Ch. 1, *North Face 1948*

2 Exchanging ideas with women was always an illusion; they tagged everything on to some emotion, they were all incapable of the thing in itself.
Ch. 5, Ibid.

3 Which of youth's pleasures can compare with the making ready for one's first big war?
Bk. II, Ch. 3, *The King Must Die 1958*

4 Man born of woman cannot outrun his fate. Better then not to question the Immortals, nor when they have spoken to grieve one's heart in vain. A bound is set to our knowing, and wisdom is not to search beyond it. Men are only men.
Bk. V, Ch. 2, Ibid.

5 "Go with your fate, but not beyond. Beyond leads to dark places."
"Marathon," *The Bull from the Sea 1962*

6 I thought of my life, the good and evil days; of the gods, and fate; how much of a man's life and of his soul they make for him, how much he makes for himself. . . . Fate and will, will and fate, like earth and sky bringing forth the grain together; and which the bread tastes of, no man knows.
"Skyros," Ibid.

7 Sometimes I look round a lot of housewives shopping, or businessmen's wives stuck at some awful party when the men go off talking shop and leave them to go on about knitting or servants or something…and I have a terribly sad feeling like looking at a lot of animals that have moulted and got silly from being kept in a cage.
Letter (p. 176), Quoted in *Mary Renault: A Biography* by David Sweetman *1993*

8 Men have more fun.
Ibid.

9 . . . Shakespeare and Beethoven & Co do seem to have, as men, some extra reserve of neural strength, some capacity for sustained intensity and inner drive, which women do not possess. I will believe otherwise when given evidence.
Ibid.

1868. Anna F. Trevisan (1905–)

1 ELZA. Some things are very important and some are very unimportant. To know the difference is what we are given life to find out. . . .
Easter Eve 1946

2 ELZA. The mother! She is what keeps the family intact. . . . It is proved. A fact. Time and time again. The father, no matter how good . . . a father cannot keep the family intact.
Ibid.

3 MRS. BRENTA. When they're grown up, you might just as well not have them. They come home and they go out. This is like a railroad station and a restaurant.
Ibid.

4 ANNIE. Give me first the courage and the strength to bear my lot. And all the mothers the world over, who have sons acrost the seas.
In the Valley of the Shadow 1946

5 BARRY. He'll be ruined tied to yer apron and yer teachin's. Pamperin' and pettin', pettin' and pamperin'.
Ibid.

6 ANNIE. How was they to know the ould war would take them so soon and last so long?
Ibid.

7 MRS. GRISWOLD. The world is exhausted.
Ibid.

1869. Gretta Brooker Palmer (1905–1935)

1 Happiness is a by-product of an effort to make someone else happy.
Permanent Marriage n.d.

1870. Frances Frost (1905–1959)

1 I am the keeper of wall and sill,
I kneel on the hearth to a tempered fire:
(Flesh that was wild can learn to be still,
But what of a heart that was born to briar?)
"Capture," St. 4, *Hemlock Wall 1929*

2 But the trees that lost their apples
In the early windy year-
Hard-checked little apples,
Round and green and clear,-
They have nothing more to lose
And nothing more to fear.
"Loss," St. 2, Ibid.

3 Grow, white boy! Drink deep of living,
Deeper yet of mirth,
For there is nothing better than laughter
Anywhere on earth!
"White Boy," St. 3, Ibid.

1871. Adelaide Johnson (1905–1960)

1 The neurotic needs of the parent . . . are vicariously gratified by the behavior of the child.
"The Genesis of Antisocial Acting Out in Children and Adults," *Psychoanalytic Quarterly*, Vol. 21 *1952*

2 Firmness bespeaks a parent who has learned . . . how all of his major goals may be reached in some creative course of action. . . .
Ibid.

1872. Erika Mann (1905–1969)

1 "I want the child to become a human being, a good and decent man who knows the difference between lies and truth, aware of liberty and dignity and true reason, not the opportunistic reason 'dictated by policy' which turns black white if it's useful at the moment. I want the boy to become a decent human being—a man and not a Nazi!"
Prologue, *School for Barbarians 1938*

2 But the Hitler Youth organization, that third circle around the child, is the most expansive, most important, and by far the most comprehensive of his influences.
"The State Youth," Ibid.

3 "There's absolutely no discipline in the democracies. The other day our propaganda minister said that the democracies strike him as being a collection of comical old fogies. But I've got to say it myself; they're rotten and corrupt to the marrow."
"The City," *The Lights Go Down* 1940

4 The nightmare dreamer is delivered up to the horror he him-self has created, and derives not the slightest relief from the neutral world, such as would be granted by feeling that it is hot or windy, that other people are present, or that the day or the night is coming to an end. The dreamer knows and per-ceives nothing but the horror of his dream.
Quoted in *The Last Year of Thomas Mann,** a Revealing Memoir by His Daughter* 1958

5 Music, theater, the beauty of men and things, a fine day, a child, an attractive animal—from all these he [Thomas Mann]* drew much pleasure, provided he was getting on with his work. Without work—that is, without active hope—he would not have known how to live.
Ibid.

*German writer (1875–1955) who won the Nobel Prize (1929).

1873. Margaret Webster (1905–1972)

1 When an actor says a line, he makes his point and his thought moves on to the next; but a singer has to repeat the same words over a dozen times, the emotional shading varying with the music, the thought progressing only in terms of sound.
Don't Put Your Daughter On the Stage 1972

2 Revivals at the Met are unmitigated torture for the stage direc-tor and an almost total waste from his point of view.
Ibid.

1874. Vera Fedorovna Panova (1905–1973)

1 SHEMETOVA. Sometimes, when the accustomed pattern of things is suddenly broken…like today's emergency landing…as if you were going along and suddenly: Stop! and you look up…and it's terrifying—why has this happened to us? But it's only for a moment; no more. You, too, know how it is: you fall asleep, see something terrible, and you make yourself wake up.
Act III, *It's Been Ages! (Skolko let, skolko zhit!)* 1966

1875. Jane Ace (1905–1974)

1 Home wasn't built in a day.
Comment, "Easy Aces" radio show (c.1928–1945), Quoted in *The Fine Art of Hypochondria* by Goodman Ace* 1966
*American humorist and radio personality; her husband.

2 Familiarity breeds attempt
Ibid.

3 He's a ragged individualist.
Ibid.

4 Time wounds all heels.
Ibid.

1876. Dorothy Fields (1905–1974)

1 Gee, I'd like to give you something swell, baby,
Diamond bracelets Woolworth's doesn't sell, baby.
Till that lucky day, you know darn well, baby,
That I can't give you anything but love.
"I Can't Give You Anything But Love,"
with Jimmy McHugh *c.* 1920

2 Now I know why mother
Taught me to be true
She knew I'd meet someone
Exactly like you.
"Exactly Like You," *The International Revue,*
with Jimmy McHugh 1930

3 Grab your hat and grab your coat,
Leave your worries on the doorstep.
Just direct your feet
To the sunny side of the street.
"The Sunny Side of the Street," Ibid.

4 SISSY (singing). Obviously, love is an old established track.
Ten million suckers walk the plank.
If you land on your tail
Every time you fall
There must be a reason for it all.
Love is the reason for it all.
"Love Is the Reason," *A Tree Grows in Brooklyn**
(musical), with Arthur Schwartz 1951
*Based on novel by Betty Smith; see 1695: 1–5.

5 To think the highest-brow,
Which I must say is he,
Should pick the lowest-brow,
Which there's no doubt is me . . .
"If My Friends Could See Me Now," Act I, Sc. 6,
Sweet Charity 1966

6 No matter where I run,
I meet myself there.
"Where Am I Going?" Act II, Sc. 6, Ibid.

1877. Ivy Baker Priest (1905–1975)

1 We women ought to put first things first. Why should we mind if men have their faces on the money, as long as we get our hands on it?
Ch. 1, *Green Grows Ivy* 1958

2 We seldom stop to think how many peoples' lives are entwined with our own. It is a form of selfishness to imagine that every individual can operate on his own or can pull out of the gen-eral stream and not be missed.
Ch. 18, Ibid.

3 My father had always said that there are four things a child needs—plenty of love, nourishing food, regular sleep, and lots of soap and water—and after those, what he needs most is some intelligent neglect.
Ch. 11, Ibid.

1878. Ilka Chase (1905–1978)

1 She thought of all foreign lands as lands of promise, and with the same yearning that so many Europeans had for America.
Ch. 1, *I Love Miss Tilli Bean* 1946

2 She knew that no human being is immune to sorrow and she wanted me to be tough, the way a green branch is tough, and to be independent, so that if anything happened to her I would be able to take hold of my own life and make a go of it.
Ch. 6, Ibid.

3 People are subject to moods, to temptations and fears, lethargy and aberration and ignorance, and the staunchest qualities

shift under the stresses and strains of daily life. Like liberty, they are not secured for all time. They are not inevitable.

Ch. 1, *Free Admission 1948*

4 There are various theories as to what characteristics, what combination of traits, what qualities in our men won the war. The democratic heritage is highly thought of; the instinctive mechanical know-how of thousands of our young men is frequently cited; the church and Coca-Cola, baseball, and the movies all come in for their share of credit; but, speaking from my own observation of our armed forces, I should say the war was won on coffee.

Ch. 10, Ibid.

5 The very fact that we make such a to-do over golden weddings indicates our amazement at human endurance. The celebration is more in the nature of a reward stamina. . . .

Ch. 15, Ibid.

6 When he said we were trying to make a fool of him, I could only murmur that the Creator had beat us to it.

"Mrs. Crankhurst," *Violets and Vinegar*, Jilly Cooper and Tom Hartman, eds. *1980*

1879. Phyllis McGinley (1905–1978)

1 Oh, shun, lad, the life of an author.
It's nothing but worry and waste.
Avoid that utensil,
The laboring pencil,
And pick up the scissors and paste.

"A Ballad of Anthologies," *A Ballad of Anthologies 1941*

2 Forever that Ode on the Urn, sir,
Has headed the publisher's list.
But the name isn't Keats
On the royalty sheets
That go out to the anthropologist,
My lad,
The sedulous anthologist.

Ibid.

3 Mere wealth, I am above it.
It is the reputation wide,
The playwrights pomp, the poet's pride
That eagerly I covet.

Ibid.

4 Gossip isn't scandal and it's not merely malicious. It's chatter about the human race by lovers of the same. Gossip is the tool of the poet, the shop-talk of the scientist, and the consolation of the housewife, wit, tycoon and intellectual. It begins in the nursery and ends when speech is past.

"A New Year and No Resolutions," *Woman's Home Companion January 1957*

5 Kindness is a virtue neither modern nor urban. One almost unlearns it in a city. Towns have their own beatitude; they are not unfriendly; they offer a vast and solacing anonymity or an equally vast and solacing gregariousness. But one needs a neighbor on whom to practice compassion.

"A Garland of Kindness," *The Province of the Heart 1959*

6 Nothing fails like success; nothing is so defeated as yesterday's triumphant Cause.

"How to Get Along with Men," Ibid.

7 Women are the fulfilled sex. Through our children we are able to produce our own immortality, so we lack that divine restlessness which sends men charging off in pursuit of fortune or fame or an imagined Utopia. That is why we number so few geniuses among us. The wholesome oyster wears no pearl, the healthy whale no ambergris, and as long as we can keep on adding to the race, we harbor a sort of health within ourselves.

"Some of My Best Friends . . .," Ibid.

8 Sometimes I have a notion that what might improve the situation is to have women take over the occupations of government and trade and to give men their freedom. Let them do what they are best at. While we scrawl interoffice memos and direct national or extranational affairs, men could spend all their time inventing wheels, peering at stars, composing poems, carving statues, exploring continents—discovering, reforming, or crying out in a sacramental wilderness. Efficiency would probably increase, and no one would have to worry so much about the Gaza Strip or an election.

Ibid.

9 Of course we women gossip on occasion. But our appetite for it is not as avid as a man's. It is in the boys' gyms, the college fraternity houses, the club locker rooms, the paneled offices of business that gossip reaches its luxuriant flower.

Ibid.

10 It's this no-nonsense side of women that is pleasant to deal with. They are the real sportsmen. They don't have to be constantly building up frail egos by large public performances like over-tipping the hat-check girl, speaking fluent French to the Hungarian waiter, and sending back the wine to be recooled.

Ibid.

11 I do not know who first invented the myth of sexual equality. But it is a myth willfully fostered and nourished by certain semi-scientists and other fiction writers. And it has done more, I suspect, to unsettle mar happiness than any other false doctrine of this myth-ridden age.

"The Honor of Being a Woman," Ibid.

12 We have not owned our freedom long enough to know exactly how it should be used.

Ibid.

13 Frigidity is largely nonsense. It is this generation's catchword, one only vaguely understood and constantly misused. Frigid women are few. There is a host of diffident and slow-ripening ones.

Ibid.

14 Our bodies are shaped to bear children, and our lives are a working out of the processes of creation. All our ambitions and intelligence are beside that great elemental point.

Ibid.

15 Compromise? Of course we compromise. But compromise, if not the spice of life, is its solidity. It is what makes nations great and marriages happy and Spruce Manor the pleasant place it is.

"Suburbia, of Thee I Sing," Ibid.

16 Sin . . . has been made not only ugly but passé. People are no longer sinful, they are only immature or under privileged or frightened or, more particularly, sick.

"In Defense of Sin," Ibid.

17 Who could deny that privacy is a jewel? It has always been the mark of privilege, the distinguishing feature of a truly urbane culture. Out of the cave, the tribal tepee, the pueblo, the community fortress, man emerged to build himself a house of his own with a shelter in it for himself and his diversions. . . . But in each civilization, as it advanced, those who could afford it chose the luxury of a withdrawing-place.

> "A Lost Privilege," Ibid.

18 The Enemy, who wears
Her mother's usual face
And confidential tone,
Has access; doubtless stares
Into her writing case
And listens on the phone.

> "Fourteenth Birthday," *Times Three: 1932–1960* 1960

19 The thing to remember about fathers is, they're men.
A girl has to keep it in mind.

> "Girl's-Eye View of Relatives: First Lesson," Ibid.

20 Sisters are always drying their hair.
Locked into rooms, alone,
They pose at the mirror, shoulders bare,
Trying this way and that their hair,
Or fly importunate down the stair
To answer the telephone.

> "Girl's-Eye View of Relatives: Triolet against Sisters," Ibid.

21 Oh, high is the price of parenthood,
And daughters may cost you double.
You dare not forget, as you thought you could,
That youth is a plague and a trouble.

> "Homework for Anabelle," Ibid.

22 The knowingness of little girls
Is hidden underneath their curls.

> "What Every Woman Knows," Ibid.

23 For little boys are rancorous
When robbed of any myth,
And spiteful and cantankerous
To all their kin and kith.
But little girls can draw conclusions
And profit from their lost illusions.

> Ibid.

24 These are my daughters, I suppose.
But where in the world did the children vanish?

> "Ballade of Lost Objects," Ibid.

25 Time is the thief you cannot banish.

> St. 4, Ibid.

26 Oh! *do* you remember Paper Books
When paper books were thrilling,
When something to read
Was seldom Gide
Or Proust or Peacock
Or Margaret Mead
And seldom Lionel Trilling?

> "Dirge for an Era," St. 4, Ibid.

27 When blithe to argument I come,
Though armed with facts, and merry,
May Providence protect me from
the fool as adversary,
Whose mind to him a kingdom is.

Where reason lacks dominion,
Who calls conviction prejudice
And prejudice opinion.

> "Moody Reflections," Ibid.

28 Buffet, ball, banquet, quilting bee,
Wherever conversation's flowing,
Why must I feel it falls on me
To keep things going?

> "Reflections at Dawn," St. 3, Ibid.

29 Senor Dali,
Born delirious,
Considers it folly
To be serious. . . .

> "Spectator's Guide to Contemporary Art," St. 3, Ibid.

30 I'm a middle-bracket person with a middle-bracket spouse
And we live together gaily in a middle-bracket house.
We've a fair-to-middlin' family; we take the middle view;
So we're manna sent from heaven to internal revenue.

> "The Chosen People," St. 1, Ibid.

31 . . . "I am he
Who champions total liberty—
Intolerance being, ma'am, a state
No tolerant man can tolerate."

> "The Angry Man," St. 2, Ibid.

32 Pressed for rules and verities
All I recollect are these:
Feed a cold to starve a fever.
Argue with no true believer.
Think too-long is never-act.
Scratch a myth and find a fact.

> "A Garland of Precepts," St. 2, Ibid.

33 We might as well give up the fiction
That we can argue any view.
For what in me is pure Conviction
Is simple Prejudice to you.

> "Note to My Neighbor," Ibid.

34 Wit is not the prerogative of the unjust, and there is truly laughter in holy places.

> "Aspects of Sanctity," *Saint-Watching* 1969

35 History must always be taken with a grain of salt. It is, after all, not a science but an art. . . .

> Ibid.

36 We live in the century of the Appeal. . . . One applauds the industry of professional philanthropy. But it has its dangers. After a while the private heart begins to harden. We fling letters into the wastebasket, are abrupt to telephone solicitations. Charity withers in the incessant gale.

> Ibid.

37 For the wonderful thing about saints is that they were *human*. They lost their tempers, got hungry, scolded God, were egotistical or testy or impatient in their turns, made mistakes and regretted them. Still they went on doggedly blundering toward heaven.

> "Running to Paradise," Ibid.

38 A lady is smarter than a gentleman, maybe,
She can sew a fine seam, she can have a baby,
She can use her intuition instead of her brain,
But she can't fold a paper in a crowded train.

> "Trial and Error" *n.d.*

39 Meek-eyed parents hasten down the ramps
To greet their offspring, terrible from camps.
"Ode to the End of Summer" *n.d.*

40 Benevolent, stormy, patient, or out of sorts.
God knows which God is the God God recognizes.
"The Day After Sunday" *n.d.*

1880. Ayn Rand (1905–1982)

1 "Civilization is the progress toward a society of privacy. The savage's whole existence is public, ruled by the laws of his tribe. Civilization is the process of setting man free from men."
The Fountainhead 1943

2 "Creation comes before distribution—or there will be nothing to distribute."
Ibid.

3 "Has any act of selfishness ever equaled the carnage perpetrated by disciples of altruism?"
Ibid.

4 Great men can't be ruled.
Ibid.

5 If you learn how to rule one single man's soul, you can get the rest of mankind.
Ibid.

6 Kill reverence and you've killed the hero in man.
Ibid.

7 "Throughout the centuries there were men who took first steps down new roads armed with nothing but their own vision.. Their goals differed, but they all had this in common: that the step was first, the road new, the vision unborrowed, and the response they received—hatred. The great creators—the thinkers, the artists, the scientists, the inventors—stood alone against the men of their time."
Ibid.

8 "We are one in all and all in one.
There are no men but only the great WE.
One, indivisible and forever."
Ch. 1, *Anthem 1946*

9 My happiness is not the means to any end. It is the end. It is its own goal. It is its own purpose. Neither am I the means to any end others may wish to accomplish. I am not a tool for their use. I am not a servant of their needs. I am not a bandage for their wounds. I am not a sacrifice on their altars.
Ch. 9, Ibid.

10 The word which can never die on this earth, for it is the heart of it and the meaning and the glory. The sacred word: EGO.
Ch. 12, Ibid.

11 The only real moral crime that one man can commit against another is the attempt to create, by his words or actions, an impression of the contradictory, the impossible, the irrational, and thus shake the concept of rationality in his victim.
Atlas Shrugged 1957

12 If I were to speak your kind of language, I would say that man's only moral commandment is: Thou shalt think. But a 'moral commandment' is a contradiction in terms. The moral is the cho-sen, not the forced; the understood, not the obeyed. The moral is the rational, and reason accepts no commandments.
Ibid.

13 They did not know...that the same force that had made him tolerant, was now the force that made him ruthless—that the justice which would forgive miles of innocent errors of knowledge, would not forgive a single step taken in conscious evil.
Ibid.

14 A rational process is a moral process.
Ibid.

15 "Disunity, that's the trouble. It's my absolute opinion that in our complex industrial society, no business enterprise can succeed without sharing the burden of the problems of other enterprises."
Pt. I, Ch. 3, Ibid.

16 "The entire history of science is a progression of exploded fallacies, not of achievements."
Pt. II, Ch. 1, Ibid.

17 "To demand 'sense' is the hallmark of nonsense. Nature does not make sense. Nothing makes sense."
Ibid.

18 "People don't look for *kinds* of work anymore, ma'am," he answered impassively. "They just look for work."
Ch. 10, Ibid.

19 The modern mystics of muscle who offer you the fraudulent alternative of "human rights" versus "property rights," as if one could exist without the other, are making a last, grotesque attempt to revive the doctrine of soul versus body. Only a ghost can exist without material property; only a slave can work with no right to the product of his effort.
Pt. III, Ch. 7, Ibid.

20 Man's unique reward, however, is that while animals survive by adjusting themselves to their background, man survives by adjusting his background to himself.
For the New Intellectual 1961

21 Professional intellectuals are the voice of a culture and are, therefore, its leaders, its integrators and its bodyguards.
Ibid.

22 Ever since Kant divorced reason from reality, his intellectual descendants have been diligently widening the breach.
"The Cashing-In: The Student Rebellion,"
The New Left 1968

23 The hippies were taught by their parents, their neighbors, their tabloids, and their college professors that faith, instinct and emotion are superior to reason—and they obeyed. They were taught that material concerns are evil, that the State or the Lord will provide, that the Lilies of the Field do not toil—and they obeyed. They were taught that love, indiscriminate love, for one's fellow-men is the highest virtue—and they obeyed. They were taught that the merging of one's self with a herd, a tribe or a community is the noblest way for men to live—and they obeyed. There isn't a single basic principle of the Establishment which they do not share—there isn't a belief which they have not accepted.
"Apollo and Dionysus," Ibid.

1881. Lillian Hellman (1905–1984)

1 MRS. MORTAR. But the cinema is a shallow art. It has no—no—no fourth dimension.

Act I, *The Children's Hour 1934*

2 HANNAH. Lucy, there were people made to think and people made to listen. I ain't sure either you or Lundee were made to do either.

Act I, *Days to Come 1936*

3 EASTER. When you got nothin' to do, we can't do it for you.

Act. II, Sc. 1, Ibid.

4 WILKIE. You're a noble lady and I am frightened of noble ladies. They usually land the men they know in cemeteries.

Sc. 3, Ibid.

5 ANDREW. Polite and blind, we lived.

Act III, Ibid.

6 Cynicism is an unpleasant way of saying the truth.

Act I, *The Little Foxes 1939*

7 God forgives those who invent what they need.

Ibid.

8 ADDIE. Well, there are people who eat the earth and eat all the people on it like in the Bible with the locusts. And other people who stand around and watch them eat it. Sometimes I think it ain't right to stand an' watch them do it.

Act III, Ibid.

9 Fashions in sin change.

Watch on the Rhine 1941

10 SARA MÜLLER. It's an indulgence to sit in a room and discuss your beliefs as if they were a juicy piece of gossip.

Act II, Ibid.

11 KOYLA. You are what you are. It is my opinion the trouble in the world comes from people who do not know what they are, and pretend to be something they're not.

The North Star 1942

12 MARCUS. Carry in your own valise, son. It is not seemly for a man to load his goods on other men, black or white.

Act I, *Another Part of the Forest 1946*

13 BIRDIE. You lose your manners when you're poor.

Act II, Ibid.

14 LAVINIA. But maybe half a lie is worse than a real lie.

Act III, Ibid.

15 LAVINIA. I'm not going to have any Bibles in my school. That surprise you all. It's the only book in the world but it's just for grown people, after you know it don't mean what it says.

Ibid.

16 I am not willing, now or in the future, to bring bad trouble to people who, in my past association with them, were completely innocent of any talk or any action that was disloyal or subversive. . . . I cannot and will not cut my conscience to fit this year's fashions, even though I long ago came to the conclusion that I was not a political person and could have no comfortable place in any political group.

Letter to the House Committee on Un-American Activities, *The Nation* (New York) *31 May 1952*

17 JULIAN. Success isn't everything but it makes a man stand straight.

Act I, *Toys in the Attic 1959*

18 CARRIE. Not like the country. My. I never heard anybody say a thing like that before. It takes courage to just up and say you don't like the country. Everybody likes the country.

Ibid.

19 ALBERTINE. You do too much. Go and do nothing for a while. Nothing.

Act II, Ibid.

20 CARRIE. I read in a French book that there was nothing so abandoned as a respectable young girl.

Ibid.

21 CARRIE. There are lives that are shut and should stay shut. . . .

Act III, Ibid.

22 ANNA. Well, people change and forget to tell each other. Too bad—causes so many mistakes.

Ibid.

23 They're fancy talkers about themselves, writers. If I had to give young writers advice, I would say don't listen to writers talking about writing or themselves.

The New York Times 21 February 1960

24 I didn't know what she was saying when she moved her lips in a Baptist church or a Catholic cathedral or, less often, in a synagogue, but it was obvious that God could be found anywhere. . . .

An Unfinished Woman 1969

25 Mamma seemed to do only what my father wanted, and yet we lived the way my mother wanted us to live.

Ibid.

26 . . . the first sexual stirrings of little girls, so masked, so complex, so foolish as compared with the sex of little boys.

Ibid.

27 Intellectuals can tell themselves anything, sell themselves any bill of goods, which is why they were so often patsies for the ruling classes in nineteenth-century France and England, or twentieth-century Russia and America.

Ch. 13 (30 April 1967), Ibid.

28 It is a mark of many famous people that they cannot part with their brightest hour.

"Theatre," *Pentimento 1973*

1882. Greta Garbo (1905–1990)

1 There are many things in your heart you can never tell to another person. They are you, your private joys and sorrows, and you can never tell them. You cheapen yourself, the inside of yourself, when you tell them.

Quoted in *The Story of Greta Garbo* by Bruce Biery *1928*

2 I never said, "I want to be alone." I only said, "I want to be *left* alone." There is all the difference

Quoted in *Garbo* by John Bainbridge *1955*

3 Why can't we avoid being followed and examined? It is cruel to bother people who want to be left in peace. This kills beauty for me.

Newspaper Interview (Naples, 1938), Ibid.

1883. Agnes de Mille (1905–1993)

1 I learned three important things in college—to use a library, to memorize quickly and visually, to drop asleep at any time given a horizontal surface and fifteen minutes. What I could not learn was to think creatively on schedule.

Dance to the Piper 1952

2 No trumpets sound when the important decisions of our life are made. Destiny is made known silently.

Ibid.

3 Without the smell of iris and budding acacia coming through the windows, the sound of scholasticism filling my dreams with a reassuring hum, I sank deeper and deeper into a kind of cerebral miasma as I postponed all vital decisions.

Ibid.

4 Dancing is not taught as an art in any university. There it is still in the gymnasium.

Ibid.

5 A good education is usually harmful to a dancer. A good calf is better than a good head.

News item *1 February 1954*

6 Theater people are always pining and agonizing because they're afraid that they'll be forgotten. And in America they're quite right. They will be.

Quoted in *Life* (New York) *15 November 1963*

7 The truest expression of a people is in its dances and its music. Bodies never lie.

"Do I Hear a Waltz?," *The New York Times Magazine 11 May 1975*

1884. Dorothy Gillam Baker (1906–)

1 We are living today at the climax of history, when the main line of human history has converged to a balance of terror between the two superpowers. The United States and the Soviet Union find themselves in an accelerating arms race beyond their power to control, and appear trapped by the binding power of tradition, habit, and the very nature of power. In the past no dominant political, economic, religious or military power has voluntarily relinquished its position.

Transformation or Catastrophe? 1978

2 I am convinced that the promise of harmonious resolution as a united people of the world, capable of living on a higher level of consciousness . . . is not a utopian vision, but the new revolutionary form that lies within our grasp.

Ibid.

1885. Catherine Cookson (1906–1998)

1 "Catholic, be damned! They tell 'em to have bairns, but do they bloody well keep them?"

Ch. 1, *The Fifteen Streets 1952*

2 God knew there was no happiness came out of a mixed marriage. With a Church of England one it would be bad enough, but with a Spiritualist! . . . And yet . . . what was the obstacle of religion compared with the obstacle of class?

Ch. 7, Ibid.

3 "It's no good saying one thing and thinking another."

Ch. 8, Ibid.

1886. Gertrude Ederle (1906–)

1 To me, the sea is like a person—like a child that I've known a long time. It sounds crazy, I know, but when I swim in the sea I talk to it. I never feel alone when I'm out there.

New York Post 5 September 1956

1887. Mrs. Robert Henrey (1906–)

1 One must leave one's parents early, especially one's mother. Mothers are never any good for their daughters. They forget they were just as ugly and silly and scraggy when they were little girls.

Ch. 3, *Paloma 1951*

1888. Hsieh Ping-ying (1906–2000)

1 Ah! Mother really loved me, but why did she beat me so hard? Is not a child a person too? Can she never have her own way? Must she obey every word a grown-up says? These questions went round and round in my head.

Girl Rebel, Adet & Anor Lin, trs. *1940*

2 The spring came, warm and intoxicating, and planted the seeds of love in the hearts of many young boys and girls. But it also sprayed the dew of blood on the young bodies of boy and girl soldiers. The call to "fight on" had waked young people from their dreams. They came out of the pink palace of romance, going to the social front which was covered in corpses and reeked with the smell of blood. They gave up their ideas of love, and substituted for it the love of the masses suffering under suppression, the love of the poor, the love of their comrades.

Ibid.

1889. Mirra Komarovsky (1906–1999)

1 It is possible, of course, that the only effect of . . . sheltering is to create in women a generalized dependency which will then be transferred to the husband and which will enable her all the more readily to accept the role of wife in a family which still has many patriarchal features.

"Functional Analysis of Sex Roles," *American Sociological Review August 1950*

2 What is important to a relationship is a harmony of emotional roles and not too great a disparity in the general level of intelligence.

Women in the Modern World 1953

3 A social order can function only because the vast majority have somehow adjusted themselves to their place in society and perform the functions expected of them.

Ibid.

4 What are we educating women for? To raise this question is to face the whole problem of women's role in society. We are uncertain about the end of women's education precisely because the status of women in our country is fraught with contradictions and confusion.

Ibid.

5 Today the survival of some . . . stereotypes is a psychological straitjacket for both sexes.

Ibid.

6 For an interest to be rewarding, one must pay in discipline and dedication, especially through the difficult or boring stages which are inevitably encountered.

Ch. 4, Ibid.

7 Were our knowledge of human relationships a hundredfold more reliable than it is now, it would still be foolish to seek ready-made solutions for problems of living in the index of a book.

Ch. 6, *Ibid.*

8 The most elusive knowledge of all is self-knowledge and it is usually acquired laboriously through experience outside the classroom.

Ibid.

9 The greatest danger of traditional education is that learning may remain purely verbal.

Ch. 7, *Ibid.*

10 The price of concentrating on home-making involves the sacrifices of other instruction.

Ibid.

11 Controversy both within and between disciplines is an inevitable feature of scientific development. . . . But not all intellectual controversy is equally beneficial. Pseudo-issues produced by verbal and logical ambiguities are much too frequent and waste our resources. They are usually occasioned by the failure to discern the tacit assumption of the contending positions.

Introduction, *Common Frontiers of the Social Sciences* 1957

1890. Anne Morrow Lindbergh (1906–)

1 Travelers are always discoverers, especially those who travel by air. There are no signposts in the sky to show a man has passed that way before. There are no channels marked. The flier breaks each second into new uncharted seas.

Ch. 1, *North to the Orient* 1935

2 One can never pay in gratitude; one can only pay "in kind" somewhere else in life.

Ch. 19, *Ibid.*

3 . . . the fundamental magic of flying, a miracle that has nothing to do with any of its practical purposes—purposes of speed, accessibility, and convenience—and will not change as they change.

Ch. 23, *Ibid.*

4 Lost time was like a run in a stocking. It always got worse.

Ch. 3, *The Steep Ascent* 1944

5 Perhaps middle-age is, or should be, a period of shedding shells; the shell of ambition, the shell of material accumulations and possessions, the shell of the ego.

Gift from the Sea 1955

6 One cannot collect all the beautiful shells on the beach.

Ibid.

7 It isn't for the moment you are struck that you need courage, but for the long uphill climb back to sanity and faith and security.

Hours of Gold, Hours of Lead 1973

8 Is there *anything* as horrible as *starting* on a trip? Once you're off, that's all right, but the last moments are earthquake and convulsion, and the feeling that you are a snail being pulled off your rock.

Letter to mother, Mrs. Charles Long Cutty (2 January 1930), *Ibid.*

9 For miles out in the China Sea you see mud from the Yangtse River, then suddenly you are on China, and you gasp at the flat fields stretching as far as you can see, the great flat river. . . There is something magnificent about it. A feeling of its grandeur and age. . . .

(26 September 1931), *Ibid.*

10 . . . suffering . . . no matter how multiplied . . . is always individual.

Quoted by Dorothea Lange in *The Woman's Eye*, by Anne Tucker* 1973

*See 3073.

11 Love is a force. . . . It is not a result; it is a cause. It is not a product; it produces. It is a power, like money, or steam or electricity. It is valueless unless you can give something else by means of it.

Locked Rooms and Open Doors 1974

12 People talk about love as though it were something you could give, like an armful of flowers.

Ibid.

1891. Rita Boumy Pappas (1906–)

1 I did not let them nail my soul as they do butterflies.

"Roxane M." 1975

2 My fine days? Oh, a few fleeting birds,
I had no other treasure than my tears.
That is why none of those who tortured me
have seen me weep.

Ibid.

1892. Ting Ling (1906–1985)

1 In the Chinese family system, there is superficial quiet and calmness and quarreling is frowned upon, but in reality all is in conflict.

Quoted in *Women in Modern China* by Helen Foster Snow* 1967

*See 1903.

2 I wanted to escape from love but didn't know how.

Ibid.

3 The Red Army soldiers are a totally new type that cannot be found anywhere else in China. They have never known anything but revolution. Because they originally lived in the Sovietized areas, they have no ideology of private property and no domestic ideas. No unhappiness ever comes to mind. They think only of how to overcome the difficulties of their work and never of their troubles.

Ibid.

1893. Dilys Laing (1906–1960)

1 Vague, submarine, my giant twin
swims under me, a girl of shade
who mimics me.

"Ego," *Collected Poems* 1967

2 Time is illumined with inverted light:
the past all whole, the present weird with fault.

"Lot's Daughter," St. 3, *Ibid.*

3 The end will be, perhaps, the end of me,
which will, I humbly guess, be his beginning.

"Private Entry in the Diary of a Female Parent," *Ibid.*

4 The women took a train
   away away from herself.

   "The Double Goer," St. 1, Ibid.

5 and I
   grow younger as I leave
   my me behind.

   St. 2, Ibid.

6 She faced the crowd and cried:
   I love you all but one:
   the one who wears my face.
   She is the one I fled from.

   St. 6, Ibid.

7 Proud inclination of the flesh,
   most upright tendency, salute
   in honor of the secret wish.

   "Villanelle," St. 1, Ibid.

8 . . . memory is a storm I can't repel.

   "Venus Petrified," St. 3, Ibid.

9 I was a child who clutched the amulet
   of childhood in a terror of time. I saw
   archangels, worshipped trees, expected God

   "The Little Girls," St. 2, Ibid.

10 Women receive
   the insults of men
   with tolerance,
   having been bitten
   in the nipple
   by their toothless gums.

   "Veterans," Ibid.

11 To be a woman and a writer
   is double mischief, for
   the world will slight her
   who slights "the servile house," and who would rather
   make odes than beds.

   "Sonnet to a Sister in Error,"
   St. 2, Ibid.

1894. Margaret Bourke-White (1906–1971)

1 Usually I object when someone makes overmuch of men's work and women's work, for I think it is the excellence of the results which counts.

   Portrait of Myself 1963

2 . . . war correspondents . . . see a great deal of the world. Our obligation is to pass it on to the others.

   Quoted in *The Woman's Eye* by Anne Tucker* 1973
   *See 3073.

3 . . . to understand another human being you must gain some insight into the conditions which made him what he is.

   Ibid.

4 What makes Soviet Russia the new land of the machine are the new social relationships of the men and women around the machine. The new man . . . and with him, on equal footing, the new woman—operating drill presses, studying medicine and engineering—are integral parts of a people working collectively toward a common goal.

   Ibid.

1895. Maria Goeppert Mayer (1906–1972)

1 No one has ever seen, nor probably ever will see, an atom, but that does not deter the physicist from trying to draw a plan of it, with the aid of such clues to its structure as he has.

   "The Structure of the Nucleus," *Scientific American*
   March 1951

2 Of course my father always said I should have been a boy. He said, Don't grow up to be a woman, and what he meant by that was, a housewife . . . without any interests.

   Quoted in "Maria Goeppert-Mayer," *A Life of One's Own*
   by Joan Dash 1973

3 Mathematics began to seem too much like puzzle solving. Physics is puzzle solving, too, but of puzzles created by nature, not by the mind of man.

   Ibid.

1896. Hannah Arendt (1906–1975)

1 In an ever-changing, incomprehensible world the masses had reached the point where they would . . . think that everything was possible and that nothing was true.

   The Origins of Totalitarianism 1951

2 Only the mob and the elite can be attracted by the momentum of totalitarianism itself. The masses have to be won by propaganda.

   Ch. 3, Sct. 11, Ibid.

3 Totalitarianism is never content to rule by external means, namely, through the state and a machinery of violence; thanks to its peculiar ideology and the role assigned to it in this apparatus of coercion, totalitarianism has discovered a means of dominating and terrorizing human beings from within.

   Ch. 10, Sct. 1, Ibid.

4 Total loyalty is possible only when fidelity is emptied of all concrete content, from which changes of mind might naturally arise.

   Ibid.

5 The concentration camps, by making death itself anonymous (making it impossible to find out whether a prisoner is dead or alive), robbed death of its meaning as the end of a fulfilled life. In a sense they took away the individual's own death, proving that henceforth nothing belonged to him and he belonged to no one. His death merely set a seal on the fact that he had never existed.

   Pt. 3, Ch. 12, Sct. 3, Ibid.

6 Thought . . . is still possible, and no doubt actual, wherever men live under the conditions of political freedom. Unfortunately . . . no other human capacity is so vulnerable, and it is in fact far easier to act under conditions of tyranny than it is to think.

   The Human Condition 1958

7 Freedom from labor itself is not new; it once belonged among the most firmly established privileges of the few. In this instance, it seems as though scientific progress and technical developments had been only taken advantage of to achieve something about which all former ages dreamed but which none had been able to realize.

   Prologue, Ibid.

9 Wherever the relevance of speech is at stake, matters become political by definition, for speech is what makes man a political being.

   Ibid.

10 Man cannot be free if he does not know that he is subject to necessity, because his freedom is always won in his never wholly successful attempts to liberate himself from necessity.

Pt. 3, Ch. 16, Ibid.

11 The human condition is such that pain and effort are not just symptoms which can be removed without changing life itself; they are the modes in which life itself, together with the necessity to which it is bound, makes itself felt. For mortals, the "easy life of the gods" would be a lifeless life.

Ch. 16, "Labor," Ibid.

12 We have almost succeeded in leveling all human activities to the common denominator of securing the necessities of life and providing for their abundance.

Pt. 3, Ch. 17, Ibid.

13 Action without a name, a "who" attached to it, is meaningless.

Ch. 24, "Action," Ibid.

14 The new always happens against the overwhelming odds of statistical laws and their probability, which for all practical, everyday purposes amounts to certainty; the new therefore always appears in the guise of a miracle.

Pt. 5, Ch. 24, Ibid.

15 In contrast to revenge, which is the natural, automatic reaction to transgression and which, because of the irreversibility of the action process can be expected and even calculated, the act of forgiving can never be predicted; it is the only reaction that acts in an unexpected way and thus retains, though being a reaction, something of the original character of action.

Ch. 33, "Action," Ibid.

16 Poets . . . are the only people to whom love is not only a crucial, but an indispensable experience, which entitles them to mistake it for a universal one.

(footnote), Ibid.

17 Love, by reason of its passion, destroys the in-between which relates us to and separates us from others. As long as its spell lasts, the only in-between which can insert itself between two lovers is the child, love's own product. The child, this in-between to which the lovers now are related and which they hold in common, is representative of the world in that it also separates them; it is an indication that they will insert a new world into the existing world. Through the child, it is as though the lovers return to the world from which their love had expelled them. But this new worldliness, the possible result and the only possibly happy ending of a love affair, is, in a sense, the end of love, which must either overcome the partners anew or be transformed into another mode of belonging together.

Pt. 5, Ch. 33, Ibid.

18 Love, by its very nature, is unworldly, and it is for this reason rather than its rarity that it is not only apolitical but antipolitical, perhaps the most powerful of all antipolitical human forces.

Ibid.

19 With the loss of tradition we have lost the thread which safely guided us through the vast realms of the past, but this thread was also the chain fettering each successive generation to a predetermined aspect of the past. It could be that only now

will the past open up to us with unexpected freshness and tell us things that no one as yet has ears to hear.

Nomos I: Authority, Carl J. Frederich, ed. *1958*

20 Have we now come to the point where it is the children who are being asked to change or improve the world?

"Reflections on Little Rock" *1959*

21 Our tradition of political thought had its definite beginning in the teachings of Plato* and Aristotle.** I believe it came to a no less definite end in the theories of Karl Marx.***

Ch. 1, *Between Past and Future 1961*

*Greek philosopher (427–347 B.C.E.). **Greek philosopher (384–322 B.C.E.) ***Karl M—, German political philosopher and economist (1818–83).

22 Immortality is what nature possesses without effort and without anybody's assistance, and immortality is what the mortals must therefore try to achieve if they want to live up to the world into which they were born, to live up to the things which surround them and to whose company they are admitted for a short while.

Ch. 2, Ibid.

23 The ceaseless, senseless demand for original scholarship in a number of fields, where only erudition is now possible, has led either to sheer irrelevancy, the famous knowing of more and more about less and less, or to the development of a pseudo-scholarship which actually destroys its object.

"On Violence," *Crises of the Republic 1963*

24 The banality of evil.

Eichmann in Jerusalem 1963

25 . . . under conditions of terror most people will comply but *some people will not* . . . . Humanly speaking, no more is required, and no more can reasonably be asked, for this planet to remain a place fit for human habitation.

Ch. 14, Ibid.

26 It is quite gratifying to feel guilty if you haven't done anything wrong: how noble! Whereas it is rather hard and certainly depressing to admit guilt and to repent.

Ch. 15, Ibid.

27 No punishment has ever possessed enough power of deterrence to prevent the commission of crimes. On the contrary, whatever the punishment, once a specific crime has appeared for the first time, its reappearance is more likely than its initial emergence could ever have been.

Epilogue, Ibid.

28 The trouble with Eichmann* was precisely that so many were like him, and that the many were neither perverted nor sadistic, that they were, and still are, terribly and terrifyingly normal. . . . This new type of criminal, who is in actual fact *homo generis humani*, commits his crimes under circumstances that make it well-nigh impossible for him to know or to feel that he is doing wrong.

Ibid.

*Adolf E—, German Nazi official who as head of the Gestapo's Jewish section from 1939 to 1945 was responsible for the slaughter of millions of Jews during World War II, (1906–1962).

29 Wars and revolutions . . . have outlived all their ideological justifications. . . . No cause is left but the most ancient of all, the one, in fact, that from the beginning of our history has de-

termined the very existence of politics, the cause of freedom versus tyranny.

Introduction, *On Revolution* 1963

30 . . . What makes it so plausible to assume that hypocrisy is the vice of vices is that integrity can indeed exist under the cover of all other vices except this one. Only crime and the criminal, it is true, confront us with the perplexity of radical evil; but only the hypocrite is really rotten to the core.

Ch. 2, Ibid.

31 Opinions are formed in a process of open discussion and public debate, and where no opportunity for the forming of opinions exists, there may be moods—moods of the masses and moods of individuals, the latter no less fickle and unreliable than the former—but no opinion.

Ch. 6, Ibid.

32 Economic growth may one day turn out to be a curse rather than a good, and under no conditions can it either lead into freedom or constitute a proof for its existence.

Ch. 6, Ibid.

33 . . . be loyal to life, don't create fiction but accept what life is giving you, show yourself worthy of whatever it may be by recollecting and pondering over it, thus repeating it in imagination: "this is the way to remain alive."

Men in Dark Times 1968

34 The more dubious and uncertain an instrument violence has become in international relations, the more it has gained in reputation and appeal in domestic affairs, specifically in the matter of revolution.

"On Violence," *Crises of the Republic* (rev. ed.) 1972

35 The Third World is not a reality but an ideology.

Ibid.

36 The chief reason warfare is still with us is neither a secret death-wish of the human species, nor an irrepressible instinct of aggression, nor, finally and more plausibly, the serious economic and social dangers inherent in disarmament, but the simple fact that no substitute for this final arbiter in international affairs has yet appeared on the political scene.

Ibid.

37 The heritage of the American Revolution is forgotten, and the American government, for better and for worse, has entered into the heritage of Europe as though it were its patrimony— unaware, alas, of the fact that Europe's declining power was preceded and accompanied by political bankruptcy, the bankruptcy of the nation-state and its concept of sovereignty.

Ibid.

38 Predictions of the future are never anything but projections of present automatic processes and procedures, that is, of occurrences that are likely to come to pass if men do not act and if nothing unexpected happens; every action, for better or worse, and every accident necessarily destroys the whole pattern in whose frame the prediction moves and where it finds its evidence.

Ibid.

39 Power and violence are opposites; where the one rules absolutely, the other is absent. Violence appears where power is in jeopardy, but left to its own course it ends in power's disappearance.

Ibid.

40 The point, as Marx* saw it, is that dreams never come true.**

Ibid.

*Karl M—, *German political philosopher and economist (1818–1883). **Reference to the student rebellions in the 1960s.

41 The most radical revolutionary will become a conservative the day after the revolution.

"Civil Disobedience," Ibid.

42 Promises are the uniquely human way of ordering the future, making it predictable and reliable to the extent that this is humanly possible.

Ibid.

43 There is all the difference in the world between the criminal's avoiding the public eye and the civil disobedient's taking the law into his own hands in open defiance. This distinction between an open violation of the law, performed in public, and a clandestine one is so glaringly obvious that it can be neglected only by prejudice or ill will.

Ibid.

44 No civilization . . . would ever have been possible without a framework of stability, to provide the wherein for the flux of change. Foremost among the stabilizing factors, more enduring than customs, manners and traditions, are the legal systems that regulate our life in the world and our daily affairs with each other.

Ibid.

45 The defiance of established authority, religious and secular, social and political, as a world-wide phenomenon may well one day be accounted the outstanding event of the last decade.

Ibid.

46 What really distinguishes this generation in all countries from earlier generations . . . is its determination to act, its joy in action, the assurance of being able to change things by one's own efforts.

"Thoughts on Politics and Revolution," Ibid.

47 For the trouble with lying and deceiving is that their efficiency depends entirely upon a clear notion of the truth that the liar and deceiver wishes to hide. In this sense, truth, even if it does not prevail in public, possesses an eradicable primacy over all falsehoods.

"Lying in Politics," Ibid.

48 There are no dangerous thoughts; thinking itself is dangerous.

The Life of the Mind, Vol. 1 1978

49 Death not merely ends life, it also bestows upon it a silent completeness, snatched from the hazardous flux to which all things human are subject.

Pt. 3, Ch. 16, "Thinking," Ibid.

50 When we were young enough to have children, we had no money. And when we had money, we were too old.

Quoted in *Hannah Arendt: For Love of the World* by Elisabeth Young-Burial 1981

51 The universal demand for happiness and the widespread unhappiness in our society (and these are but two sides of the same coin) are among the most persuasive signs that we have begun to live in a labor society which lacks enough laboring to keep it contented. For only the *animal laborans*, and neither the craftsman nor the man of action, has ever demanded to be "happy" or thought that mortal man could be happy.

Quoted in "Balance gives both labor and leisure their meaning" by Paul Greenberg, *Seattle Post-Intelligencer*, A7 *3 September 1990*

1897. Josephine Baker (1906–1975)

1 I like Frenchmen very much, because even when they insult you they do it so nicely.

Remark *n.d.*

1898. Anna Roosevelt Halsted (1906–1975)

1 There are so many indignities to being sick and helpless. . . .

Letter to David Gray (1 November 1962), Quoted in
Eleanor:* *The Years Alone* by Joseph P. Lash *1972*
*Eleanor Roosevelt; see 1513.

1899. Jacqueline Cochran (1906/10–1980/81)

1 I have found adventure in flying, in world travel, in business, and even close at hand... Adventure is a state of mind—and spirit. It comes with faith, for with complete faith there is no fear of what faces you in life or death.

Article, *Guideposts* magazine *1954*

2 I can cure your men of walking off the [flight] program. Let's put on the girls.

Quoted in Ch. 8, *The American Heritage History of Flight*
1962

3 [My deprived childhood gave me] a kind of cocky confidence. . . . *I could never have so little that I hadn't had less.* It took away my fear.

Quoted in *Women Aviators* by Lisa Yount *1995*

4 The objective in every one of my flights was to go faster or farther through the atmosphere or higher into it than anyone else and to bring back some new information about plane, engine, fuel, instruments, air, or pilot that would be helpful in the conquest of the atmosphere.

Ibid.

5 I'd have given my right eye to be an astronaut.

Ibid.

6 To live without risk for me would be tantamount to death.

Ibid.

1900. Grace Murray Hopper (1906–1992)

1 We're just getting started. We're just beginning to meet what will be the future—we've got the model T.

60 Minutes, CBS-TV *24 August 1986*

2 It's just as well to be told you're too old at 40. Then you're over it.*

Quoted by Sara C. Medina in *Time* (New York)
25 August 1986
*Reference to regular Navy's rejection of her in 1946.

3 Go ahead and do it. It's much easier to apologize after something's been done than to get permission ahead of time.*

Business Watch (p. 87), *Working Woman* magazine
May 1987
*Speaking at her retirement from the U.S. Navy.

1901. Kathryn Murray (1906–1999)

1 Don't try to teach a whole course in one lesson.

Training Manual, The Arthur Murray Dance Studios
1950–60

2 Put a little fun into your life. Try dancing.

Motto, *The Arthur Murray Party* (radio and TV
syndicated show) *1950–60*

1902. Helen Dick Megaw (1907–)

1 Much has been said about the difficulties of women in science, but I would like to say explicitly that I at least was never or rarely aware of discrimination. Perhaps I was particularly lucky, in that everyone who advised me on my education and guided my career assumed that women should be given the same opportunities as men. First and foremost I am thankful to my parents for this, and then to those far-sighted women of earlier generations who founded Girton College as a college for women, within Cambridge University and an integral part of it

Acceptance Speech, Roebling Medal of the Mineralogical
Society of America (1989), *American Mineralogist*, Vol. 75
1990

1903. Helen Foster Snow (1907–1997)

1 The war between the artist and writer and government or orthodoxy is one of the tragedies of humankind. One chief enemy is stupidity and failure to understand anything about the creative mind. For a bureaucratic politician to presume to tell any artist or writer how to get his mind functioning is the ultimate in asininity. The artist is no more able to control his mind than is any outsider. Freedom to think requires not only freedom of expression but also freedom from the threat of orthodoxy and being outcast and ostracized.

"Women and Kuomintang," *Women in
Modern China 1967*

2 To be a Marxist does not mean that one becomes a Communist party member. There are as many varieties of Marxists as there are of Protestants.

Ibid.

3 . . . one can judge a civilization by the way it treats its women.

"Bound Feet and Straw Sandals," Ibid.

1904. Rachel Carson (1907–1964)

1 To stand at the edge of the sea, to sense the ebb and the flow of the tides, to feel the breath of a mist moving over a great salt marsh, to watch the flight of shore birds that have swept up and down the surf lines of the continents for untold thousands of years,...is to have knowledge of things that are as nearly eternal as any earthly life can be.

Under the Sea Wind 1941

2 Beginnings are apt to be shadowy and so it is the beginnings of that great mother of life, the sea.

Pt. I, Ch. 1, *The Sea Around Us 1951*

3 For the sea lies all about us. . . . In its mysterious past it encompasses all the dim origins of life and receives in the end, after its many, many transmutations, the dead husks of that same life. For all at last return to the sea—to Oceanus, the ocean river, like the everflowing stream of time, the beginning and the end.

Pt. III, Ch. 14, Ibid.

4 Always the edge of the sea remains an elusive and indefinable boundary. The shore has a dual nature, changing with the swing of the tides, belonging now to the land, now to the sea.

"The Marginal World," *The Edge of the Sea 1955*

5 The discipline of the writer is to learn to be still and listen to what his subject has to tell him.

Speech, American Association of University Women
22 June 1956

6   In every outthrust headland, in every curving beach, in every
grain of sand there is a story of the earth.
"Our Ever-Changing Shore," *Holiday July 1958*

7   As cruel a weapon as the cave man's club, the chemical barrage has been hurled against the fabric of life.
Silent Spring 1962

8   For the first time in the history of the world, every human
being is now subjected to contact with dangerous chemicals,
from the moment of conception until death.
Ch. 3, Ibid.

9   If we are going to live so intimately with these chemicals—eating and drinking them, taking them into the very marrow of
our bones—we had better know something about their nature
and their power.
Ibid.

10   Under the philosophy that now seems to guide our destinies,
nothing must get in the way of the man with the spray gun.
Ch. 7, Ibid.

11   Over increasingly large areas of the United States, spring now
comes unheralded by the return of the birds, and the early
mornings are strangely silent where once they were filled with
the beauty of bird song.
Ch. 8, Ibid.

12   The "control of nature" is a phrase conceived in arrogance, born
of the Neanderthal age of biology and convenience of man.
Ch. 17, Ibid.

13   This is an era of specialists, each of whom sees his own problems
and is unaware or intolerant of the larger frame into which it
fits. It is also an era dominated by industry, in which the right to
make a dollar at whatever cost is seldom challenged.
(p. 228), Quoted in *The House of Life: Rachel Carson
at Work* by Paul Brooks *1972*

1905. Eugenia Ginzburg (1907?–1967)

1   Maternal feelings are a splendid rationale for misbehavior.
Pt. I, Ch. 1, *Eugenia Ginzburg: Within the
Whirlwind* (1979), Ian Boland, tr. *1981*

2   When you have lived for years on end without any sense of the
future or any real feeling for the reality of the morrow, the whole
idea of putting something aside, of saving, goes clean out of your
head. There had been periods when we had been earning quite a
lot of money. We could have saved up for a rainy day. But when
every day is rainy, you somehow don't think about it. And now
we were ourselves astonished at where all the money had gone;
all at once we were without means.
Pt. II, Ch. 14, Ibid.

3   One way or another the book had entered upon a new phase
in its existence . . . The total alienation of the product from its
author had been accomplished. The book had become a
grown-up daughter off on her continental tour, without so
much as a look over her shoulder or a thought to spare for her
old mother left to fend for herself at home.
Epilogue, Ibid.

1906. Dorothy Baker (1907–1968)

1   In the first place maybe he shouldn't have got himself mixed
up with Negroes. It gave him a funny slant on things and he
never got over it. It gave him a feeling for undisciplined expression, a hot, direct approach, a full-throated ease that never
did him any good in his later dealings with those of his race,
those whom civilization has whipped into shape, those who
can contain themselves and play what's written.
Bk. I, Ch. 1, *Young Man with a Horn 1938*

2   It left him a little fluttery in the stomach, things like that are so
close. You're thrown out for insubordination or else you
aren't, and where the actual line of demarcation stands out
clear, God Himself only can know. . . . All he knew was that
recognition, that sweet thing, had been given to him because
he had been doing some good playing. It's a simple formula:
do your best and somebody might like it.
Bk. III, Ch. 2, Ibid.

3   Fortune, in its workings, has something in common with the
slot-machine. There are those who can bait it forever and
never get more than an odd assortment of lemons for their
pains; but once in a while there will come a man for whom all
the grooves will line up, and when that happens there's no end
to the showering down.
Bk. IV, Ch. 2, Ibid.

4   "Now, the easy thing to say is that they wrote great poetry because they had these weaknesses. . . . It's much too easy. We
could make a grand tour of all the jails right now, and find a
thousand drug addicts and homosexuals who never wrote a
line of poetry in their lives and never will. It isn't because of
these things that her poems were great, it's in spite of them."
Trio 1945

5   "She wastes herself, she drifts, all she wants to do with her life
is lose it somewhere."
Cassandra at the Wedding 1962

6   "Same thing everywhere I'd looked. Large amounts of safety,
very few risks. Let nothing endanger the proper marriage, the
fashionable career, the nonirritating thesis that says nothing
new and nothing true."
Ibid.

1907. Violette Leduc (1907–1972)

1   "She is killing me and there's nothing I can accuse her of."
La Bâtarde 1965

2   I was and I always shall be hampered by what I think other
people will say.
Ibid.

3   To give oneself, one must annihilate oneself.
Therese and Isabelle 1968

4   The pearl wanted what I wanted. I was discovering the little
male organ we all of us have. A eunuch taking heart again.
Ibid.

5   "I desire, am only able to desire, myself."
Mad in Pursuit 1971

6   "I walk without flinching through the burning cathedral of the
summer. My bank of wild grass is majestic and full of music. It
is a fire that solitude presses against my lips."
Ibid.

7   "Will you sell your sex for the sake of your pen? . . . I would
sell everything for greater exactness."
Ibid.

8 To write is to inform against others.

Ibid.

1908. Lee Miller (1907–1977)

1 I'm not Cinderella. I can't force my foot into the glass slipper.
Quoted in *The Lives of Lee Miller* by Anthony Penrose* 1985
*Her son.

2 In all the great sieges, the defenders eat rats, and if I have to eat rats, they are going to be well spiced!*

Ibid.

*Remark to store manager on purchasing a basketful of spices at start of the Blitz in London, 1940.

1909. Mary Chase (1907–1981)

1 VETA. It's our dreams that keep us going. That separate us from the beasts. I wouldn't even want to live if I thought it was all just eating and sleeping and taking off my clothes.

Harvey 1943

2 It's quite possible to leave your home for a walk in the early morning air and return a different person—beguiled, enchanted.

Introduction, *Bernardine* 1952

1910. Edith Head (1907–1981)

1 The subjective actress thinks of clothes only as they apply to her; the objective actress thinks of them only as they affect others, as a tool for the job.

The Dress Doctor, with Jane Kesner Ardmore 1959

1911. Daphne du Maurier (1907–1989)

1 . . . like most sleepers I knew that I dreamed.

Ch. 1, *Rebecca* 1938

2 We can never go back again, that much is certain. The past is still too close to us. The things we have tried to forget and put behind us would stir again, and that sense of fear, of furtive unrest . . . might in some manner unforeseen become a living companion, as it had been before.

Ch. 2, Ibid.

3 We were like two performers in a play, but we were divided, we were not acting with one another. We had to endure it alone, we had to put up this show, this miserable, sham performance for the sake of all these people I did not know and did not want to see again.

Ch. 17, Ibid.

4 MRS. DANVERS. Why don't you go? Why don't you leave Manderley? He doesn't need you. He's got his memories. He doesn't love you. He wants to be alone again, with her. You've nothing to stay for. You've nothing to live for, really, have you? (*Pointing to the sea, several stories below.*) Look down there. It's easy, isn't it? Why don't you, why don't you..Go on, go on, don't be afraid...

Rebecca (screenplay) 1940

5 "Corruption continues with us beyond the grave," she said, "and then plays merry hell with all ideals..."

Mary Anne 1954

6 Forgotten the lies, the deceit, the sudden bursts of temper. Forgotten the wild extravagance, the absurd generosity, the vitriolic tongue. Only the warmth remained, and the love of living.

Pt. I, Ch. 1, Ibid.

7 She could not separate success from peace of mind. The two must go together; her observation pointed to this truth. Failure meant poverty, poverty meant squalor, squalor led, in the final stages, to the smells and stagnation of Bowling Inn Alley.

Ch. 10, Ibid.

8 One second's hesitation. Tears, or laughter? Tears would be an admission of guilt, so laughter was best.

Pt. II, Ch. 7, Ibid.

9 All courtiers gossip madly, it's part of their business.

Pt. III, Ch. 5, Ibid.

10 The pair were playing a game that defied intervention, they were matched like reel and rod and there was no unwinding. They juggled in jargon, dabbled in *double-entendres*, wallowed in each other's witticisms, and all at the expense of the Defendant.

Pt. IV, Ch. 2, Ibid.

11 How replace the life of a loved lost child with a dream?

Don't Look Now 1970

12 . . . The little festive atmosphere of strangeness, of excitement, that only a holiday bedroom brings. This is ours for the moment, but no more. While we are in it we bring it life. When we have gone it no longer exists, it fades into anonymity.

Ibid.

13 "The trouble is," said Laura, "walking in Venice becomes compulsive once you start. Just over the next bridge, you say, and then the next one beckons."

Ibid.

14 God knows I have no desire to be rich, but my husband possesses nothing in this world but his army pay.
Letter to Victor Gollancz (her publisher), Quoted in *Daphne du Maurier; The Secret Life of the Renowned Storyteller* by Margaret Forster 1993

1912. Barbara Stanwyck (1907–1990)

1 Sponsors obviously care more about a ninety-second commercial and *want* to pay you more than any guest star gets for a ninety-minute *acting* performance.

Quoted in *McCall's* March 1965

2 There is a point in portraying surface vulgarity where tragedy and comedy are very close.
Quoted in *Starring Miss Barbara Stanwyck* by Ella Smith 1974

3 My only problem is finding a way to play my fortieth fallen female in a different way from my thirty-ninth.
Interview with Hedda Hopper,* Ibid.
*See 1604.

4 They don't seem to write . . . comedy anymore—just a series of gags.

Ibid.

1913. Fay Wray (1907–1995)

1 Only in your imagination can you revise.
Quoted in *International Herald Tribune* (Paris)
22 February 1989

1914. Anna Anastasi (1908–1997)

1 . . . it is apparent that we cannot speak of inferiority and supe-riority, but only of specific differences in aptitudes and personality between the sexes. These differences are largely the result of cultural and other experiential factors. . . .

Differential Psychology 1937

1915. Harriette Arnow (1908–)

1 "If a religion is unpatriotic, it ain't right."

Ch. 4, *The Dollmaker 1954*

2 "I've been readen th Bible an a hunten God fer a long while—off an on—but it ain't so easy as picken up a nickel off th floor."

Ch. 15, *Ibid.*

3 "Who inu hell," I said to myself, "wants to try to make pies like Mother makes when it's so much simpler to let Mother make um inu first place?"

Ch. 28, *Ibid.*

4 "You never did see them ads an signs an letters beggen all th people back home to come up here an save democracy far you all. They done it ina last war, too. Now you can git along with-out us, so's you cain't git shet a us quick enough. Want us to go back an raise another crop a youngens at no cost to you an Detroit, so's they'll be all ready to save you when you start an-other war—huh?"

Ch. 33, *Ibid.*

5 There was something frantic in their blooming, as if they knew that frost was near and then the bitter cold. They'd live through all the heat and noise and stench of summertime, and now each widely opened flower was like a triumphant cry, "We will, we will make seed before we die."

Ch. 34, *Ibid.*

6 Christ had had no money, just his life. Life and money: could a body separate the two? What had Judas done for his money? Whispered a little, kept still as she did now.

Ch. 37, *Ibid.*

7 "Supposen the rebels lose. They'll try again. Supposen they win? How can they ever stick together in one nation? They'll be jarren and fighten around over slavery, trade and a lot of other things. Right now the East don't want the West, and the North is a different world from the South. And they've got Spain on their doorstep. But supposen they do clean out Spain, kill every Indian, plow up every acre a ground from the At-lantic to the Pacific? They'll still have their wars."

The Kentucky Trace 1974

1916. Eve Langley (1908–1974)

1 It is a thought as sweet as heaven to know that in the minds of each of us the may by the fence still blooms in an eternal springtime; that the snowdrop has in our hearts a triple birth, and blooms in three separate minds, faultlessly. . . . So that if all the flowers and grasses and hollows and hills of the old house were razed and mutilated—as they are now, I suppose—we keep them intact in three minds, each depending on the other to supply it with the delicate minutiae of remembrance.

First Part, I, *Not Yet the Moon 1946*

2 The sun was a warrior whom I gladly contested and whom I overthrew. Dazzling and magnificent was the sun's army on my back and joyous were the blades of sweat that came from my pores and vanquished him.

Second Part, X, *Ibid.*

1917. Constance Carrier (1908–1991)

1 They recognize their own elect discriminate, appraise, con-demn, and, with no hint of disrespect, almost unconsciously they come to change *One should be* to *I am.*

"Seminary," St. 5, *The Middle Voice 1955*

1918. Martha Gellhorn (1908–1998)

1 I see mysteries and complications wherever I look, and I have never met a steadily logical person.

Introduction, *The Face of War 1959*

2 It took nine years, and a great depression, and two wars end-ing in defeat, and one surrender without war, to break my faith in the benign power of the press. Gradually I came to realize that people will more readily swallow lies than truth, as if the taste of lies was homey, appetizing: a habit.

Ibid.

3 Unless they are immediate victims, the majority of mankind behaves as if war was an act of God which could not be pre-vented; or they behave as if war elsewhere was none of their business. It would be a bitter cosmic joke if we destroy our-selves due to atrophy of the imagination.

Ibid.

4 People may correctly remember the events of twenty years ago (a remarkable feat), but who remembers his fears, his disgusts, his tone of voice? It is like trying to bring back the weather of that time.

"The War in Finland,"
Introduction, *Ibid.*

5 After all this time I still cannot think calmly about that war. It was the only war I reported on the wrong side.

"The War in Vietnam—Vietnam Again, 1986," *Ibid.*

6 America has made no reparation to the Vietnamese, nothing. We are the richest people in the world and they are among the poorest. We savaged them, though they had never hurt us, and we cannot find it in our hearts, our honor, to give them help—because the government of Vietnam is Communist. And perhaps because they won.

Ibid.

1919. Nancy Hale (1908–1988)

1 After my mother's* death I began to see her as she had really been. . . . It was less like losing someone than discovering someone.

"A Good Light," *The Life in the Studio 1957*
*Reference to Lillian Westcolt H—, American artist (1881–1963).

2 Like all real artists', her objective had been to create riches with modest means; squandering seemed to her a kind of stupidity. Since she never had but one standard, perfection—which in the nature of things fits art better than life—she often gave a mis-leading impression of Yankee parsimony.

Ibid.

3 "Your father used to say, 'Never give away your work. People don't value what they don't have to pay for.'"

"Eyes or No Eyes, or The Art of Seeing," *Ibid.*

4 She could never get used to the idea that most people don't use their eyes except to keep from running into things.

Ibid.

5 . . . the cynicism of the young about society is as nothing to the cynicism of young artists for the art establishment.
> Pt. I, Ch. 4, *Mary Cassatt:* A Biography of the
> *Great American Painter 1975*
> *See 1094.

6 . . . This mysterious thing, artistic talent; the key to so much freedom, the escape from so much suffering.
> Ibid.

7 An artist's originality is balanced by a corresponding conservatism, a superstitiousness, about it; which might be boiled down to "What worked before will work again."
> Pt. II, Ch. 6, Ibid.

8 The best work of artists in any age is the work of innocence liberated by technical knowledge. The laboratory experiments that led to the theory of pure color equipped the impressionists to paint nature as if it had only just been created.
> Ch. 7, Ibid.

9 I had wanted to say then to the young man, "Painting one picture—even a mediocre picture—is more important than collecting a hundred." I'd wanted to say, "You couldn't have any collections at all unless you first had pictures."
> Epilogue, Ibid.

1920. Josephine Jacobsen (1908–)

1 Kneel at the window.
Wait under the thorn tree
for the sun. Go away
carrying your difference, you cannot leave it.
Say, Not God
himself would dare to lay it on you without
relief.
Tell your secret bones: Wait.
> "Short Views of Africa" *n.d.*

2 Galaxies are simpler. There is an awful grace
in such mystery.
> "Presence I" *n.d.*

3 Life is absolutely brimming with terror.
> Quoted in interview by Betty Parry, *Belles Lettres May/June*
> *1986*

4 For me, it's like Jacob wrestling with the angel. In every encounter with a poem there is a possibility of an abysmal failure. It's like the difficulty of trying to climb a mountain: the chances that you are going to fall are very steep, and the sense of triumph if you get there is very strong.
> Ibid.

5 The essence of poetry is the unique view—the unguessed relationship, suddenly manifest. Poetry's eye is always aslant, oblique.
> Lecture, "One Poet's Poetry," Ibid.

1921. Jean Sutherland MacLeod (1908–)

1 Oh! why does the wind blow upon me so wild?
Is it because I'm nobody's child?
> "Nobody's Child" *1954*

1922. Madeline Mason-Manheim (1908–1958)

1 Know you Silence, my friend?
It is the dumbness of the tongue when the heart would be heard;

It is the muteness of the lips when the spirit speaks loudest.
It is the uttering of the unutterable.
> "Silence," St. 1, *Hill Fragments 1925*

2 You destiny, O River,
It is even as the destiny of man.
O, ye are brethren,
Souls unharboured,
Seeking to regain the Sea.
> "The River," Ibid.

3 Sleep, companion of Silence, walks in her garden;
Walks 'midst her deathless poppies and gathers them to her breast.
> "Sleep," Ibid.

4 They call you barren
Who, unseeing, gaze upon you.
Yet! Time's most secret thoughts,
The jewels of the ages
Are buried in your breast
As in your loneliness you lie
Beneath the everlasting heights.
> "The Desert," St. 1, Ibid.

5 I share the heart-ache of the traveler
Who would retrace his steps
And find the way he came.
> "Aspiration," Ibid.

6 My heart sings while I weep.
My heart knows
That Sorrow is a trail of dreams
To farther worlds.
> "Compensation," St. 3, Ibid.

7 How shall you speak of parting?
How shall the bands be loosened
That Friendship fastened round you?
> "Parting," St. 3, Ibid.

8 Yours the voice
Sounding ever in my ears.
> "To My Mother," St. 1, Ibid.

1923. Kathleen Jessie Raine (1908–)

1 I couldn't claim that I have never felt the urge to explore evil, but when you descend into hell you have to be very careful.
> *Times* (London) 18 April *1992*

1924. Ann Ronell (1908–1993)

1 Who's afraid of the big bad wolf?
> "Who's afraid of the big bad wolf?," *Walt Disney's*
> *Three Little Pigs 1933*

1925. Yang Ping (1908–)

1 That I should think, even now, of wanting to continue to exist only as the vessel of a chemical experimentation heartlessly, inexorably formulating itself within me! And against my will . . . And yet I love this little life! With all the pain of it, I long for the wonderful thing to happen, for a tiny human creature to spring from between my limbs bravely out into the world. I need it, just as a true poet *needs* to create a great undying work.
> "Fragment from a Lost Diary," *Fragment from a Lost Diary*
> *and Other Stories*, Naomi Katz and Nancy Milton,
> eds. *1973*

2 Women and revolution! What tragic, unsung epics of courage lie silent in the world's history!

Ibid.

3 Only when the beat of life is lifted to this pitch, this fury, and this danger, only when destiny (here in my case it is but a wayward sperm carrying its implacable microscopic chromosomes, but nevertheless it is a form of destiny!) poses the choice between irreconcilable desires at a given moment, only when a human being feels the necessity of ignoring personal feeling in the decision taken—only then can one talk of a revolutionary awakening!

Ibid.

1926. Amy Johnson (1908?–1941)

1 Had I been a man I might have explored the Poles or climbed Mount Everest, but as it was my spirit found outlet in the air.

Essay in *Myself When Young*, Margot Asquith,* ed. *1938*
*See 1241.

1927. Betty MacDonald (1908–1958)

1 Men are quite humorless about their own businesses.

"I Learn to Hate Even Baby Chickens," *The Egg and I 1945*

2 Gammy used to say, "Too much scrubbing takes the life right out of things" . . .

Ibid.

3 Nobody know how old Mrs. Piggle-Wiggle is. She says she doesn't know herself. She says, "What difference does it make how old I am when I shall never grow any bigger?"

Ch. 1, *Mrs. Piggle-Wiggle 1947*

1928. Rita Angus (1908–1970)

1 You have been trying to make me into a legend. I am a painter and paintings are paintings—line, tone, form and colour, mass, light. You cannot make a legend out of a painting.

Remark, Quoted at exhibition, Security Pacific Art Gallery,
Seattle *1992*

1929. Amy Vanderbilt (1908–1974)

1 We must learn which ceremonies may be breached occasionally at our convenience and which ones may never be if we are to live pleasantly with our fellow man.

Introduction, Pt. I, *New Complete Book of Etiquette 1963*

2 Ceremony is really a protection, too, in times of emotional involvement, particularly at death. If we have a social formula to guide us and do not have to extemporize, we feel better able to handle life.

Ibid.

3 Good manners have much to do with the emotions. To make them ring true, one must feel them, not merely exhibit them.

Introduction, Pt. II, Ibid.

4 One face to the world, another at home makes for misery.

Introduction, Pt. VI, Ibid.

5 The civilian once under the mantle of officialdom, wherever it may be, is subject to the rules governing civilian behavior under official circumstances.

Introduction, Pt. VIII, Ibid.

1930. Joan Fleming (1908–1980)

1 "It's the money," Molly said clumsily, "if you've once had no money, and I mean no money at all, it means something always ever afterwards."

Ch. 7, *The Chill and the Kill 1964*

2 "Folks love being told things about themselves they already know."

Ibid.

3 His despondent mood led to unusual frankness when he told Molly that, when he grew up, a murder at the end of a party was the regular thing but you didn't expect it of gentry; it made you lose heart, really it did.

Ibid.

1931. Hildegarde Dolson (1908–1981)

1 Perhaps the surest way to tell when a female goes over the boundary from childhood into meaningful adolescence is to watch how long it takes her to get to bed at night.

"How Beautiful with Mud," *We Shook the Family Tree*
1946

2 I too would be beautiful. I would also be Flower-Fresh, Fastidious and Dainty—a triple-threat virtue obviously prized above pears by the entire male sex, as depicted in the *Ladies' Home Journal*.

Ibid.

1932. Peace Pilgrim (1908–1981)

1 I wish that every child could have growing space because I think children are a little like plants. If they grow too close together they become thin and sickly and never obtain maximum growth. We need room to grow.

Ch. 1, *Peace Pilgrim: Her Life and Work in Her Own Words 1982*

2 I don't eat junk food and I don't think junk thoughts.

Ch. 2, Ibid.

3 This is the way of peace—overcome evil with good, and falsehood with truth, and hatred with love.

Motto, Ch. 3, Ibid.

4 Truth is the pearl without price. . . . Those who have the truth would not be packaging it and selling it, so anyone who is selling it, really does not possess it.

Ch. 3, Ibid.

5 Life is like a mirror. Smile at it and it smiles back at you.

Ibid.

6 If you feed a man a meal, you only feed him for a day—but if you teach a man to grow food, you feed him for a lifetime.

Ibid.

7 Prayer is a concentration of positive thought.

Ibid.

8 I would say to the military: yes, we need to be defended; yes, we need you. The Air Force can clean up the air, the Marines can take care of the despoiled forests, the Navy can clean the oceans, the Coast Guard can take care of the rivers, and the Army can be used to build adequate drainage projects to prevent disastrous floods, and other such benefits for mankind.

Ch. 8, Ibid.

9 We seem always ready to pay the price for war. Almost gladly we give our time and our treasures—our limbs and even our lives—for war. But we expect to get peace for nothing.

Ibid.

10 The price of peace is to abandon fear and replace it with faith—faith that if we obey God's laws we will receive God's blessing. The price of peace is to abandon hate and allow love to reign supreme in our hearts—love for all our fellow human beings over the world. The price of peace is to abandon arrogance and replace it with repentance and humility, remembering that the way of peace is the way of love. The price of peace is to abandon greed and replace it with giving, so that none will be spiritually injured by having more than they need while others in the world still have less than they need.

Ibid.

11 You have much more power when you are working for the right thing than when you are working against the wrong thing.

Ch. 11, *Ibid.*

1933. Sylvia Ashton-Warner (1908–1984)
1 Love interferes with fidelities.

Teacher 1963

2 When love turns away, now, I don't follow it. I sit and suffer, unprotesting, until I feel the tread of another step.

Ibid.

3 Ah, the simple rapture of fulfillment at my work being understood that cold morning. What unutterable reward for my labor.

Ibid.

4 I'll follow them into their own minds and fraternize there. . . .

(February 1941), *Myself 1967*

5 I've got to relearn what I was supposed to have learned.

Ibid.

6 I flung my tongue round like a cat-o'-nine-tails so that my pleasant peaceful infant room became little less than a German concentration camp as I took out on the children what life should have got.

(August 1941), *Ibid.*

7 I am my own Universe. I my own Professor.

Ibid.

8 The *need* to study, to do, to make, to think, *arises* from being married. I need to be married to work.

(22 March 1942), *Ibid.*

9 Your work means more to me than my own does to me because your work involves your contentment and that comes before my work with me.

Ibid.

10 The intellect is the tool to find the truth. It's a matter of sharpening it.

Ibid.

11 Love has the quality of informing almost everything—even one's work.

(12 November 1942), *Ibid.*

12 I'm happy, not because I'm coming home to welcome and warmth but because I'm not. I have no home and am better off without one.

Three 1970

13 "Quite nice women suddenly have to wear this title with the stigma on it and a crown of thorns. We're so frightened of it that we change our nature to avoid it and in so doing we end up the classical mother-in-law we feared in the first place; so gravely have we twisted ourselves."

Ibid.

14 What can be heavier in wealth than freedom?

Ibid.

15 "Women are so illogical. They find their baking going wrong and blame the baking powder but they haven't read the directions. They can't see a thing objectively. They react subjectively. They don't act, they react."

Ibid.

16 In mind I lay a hand on his arm but only in mind. That would be revealing a feeling, an offense against London.

Ibid.

17 As the blackness of the night recedes so does the nadir of yesterday. The child I am forgets so quickly.

Ibid.

18 "God, the illogic! The impossibility of communicating in this house. The sheer operation alone of getting something through to somebody."

Ibid.

1934. Ethel Merman (1908–1984)
1 Broadway has been very good to me—but then, I've been very good to Broadway.

Quoted in "She Had Rhythm and Was the Top" by William A. Henry III, *Time* (New York) 27 February *1984*

2 I take a breath when I have to.

Ibid.

1935. Alice Neel (1908–1984)
1 But we are all creatures in a way, aren't we? And both men and women are wretched.

Quoted in "Alice Neel: Portraits of Four Decades" |by Cindy Nemser, *Ms.* (New York) October *1973*

2 You can't leave humanity out. If you didn't have humanity, you wouldn't have anything.

Ibid.

3 You may use your penis but I use a paint brush.*

Cited by Ann Sutherland Harris in "Portrait of a lady," *New Directions for Women*, Vol. XIV, No. 4 *January 1997*

*Her retort to the men who taunted her as a young woman artist by telling her she needed a penis to paint.

1936. Simone de Beauvoir (1908–1986)
1 To attain his truth, man must not attempt to dispel the ambiguity of his being but, on the contrary, accept the task of realizing it. He rejoins himself only to the extent that he agrees to remain at a distance from himself.

Ch. 1, *The Ethics of Ambiguity 1948*

2 . . . the time that one gains cannot be accumulated in a storehouse; it is contradictory to want to save up existence, which, the fact is, exists only by being spent, and there is a good case for showing that airplanes, machines, the telephone, and the

radio do not make men of today happier than those of former times.

> Ch. 3, Ibid.

4 A man would never get the notion of writing a book on the peculiar situation of the human male.

> *The Second Sex 1953*

5 For him she is sex—absolute sex, no less. She is defined and differentiated with reference to man and not he in reference to her; she is the incidental, the inessential as opposed to the essential. He is the Subject, he is the Absolute—she is the Other.

> Ibid.

6 . . . the only public good is that which assures the private good of the citizens. . . .

> Ibid.

7 There is no justification for present existence other than its expansion into an indefinitely open future.

> Ibid.

8 Refusal to make herself the object is not always what turns women to homosexuality; most lesbians, on the contrary, seek to cultivate the treasures of their femininity. . . .

> Ibid.

9 Between women love is contemplative. . . . There is no struggle, no victory, no defeat; in exact reciprocity each is at once subject and object, sovereign and slave; duality becomes mutuality.

> Ibid.

10 Society, being codified by man, decrees that woman is inferior; she can do away with this inferiority only by destroying the male's superiority.

> Ibid.

11 All oppression creates a state of war.

> Ibid.

12 . . . justice can never be done in the midst of injustice.

> Ibid.

13 . . . the effort to inhibit all sex curiosity and pleasure in the child is quite useless; one succeeds only in creating repressions, obsessions, neuroses.

> Ibid.

14 . . . when we abolish the slavery of half of humanity, together with the whole system of hypocrisy that it implies, then the "division" of humanity will reveal its genuine significance and the human couple will find its true form.

> Ibid.

15 To make oneself an object, to make oneself passive, is a very different thing from being a passive object.

> Bk. 2, Pt. 4, Ch. 3, Ibid.

16 "Ah! if only there were two of me," she thought, "one who spoke and one who listened, one who lived and the other who watched, how I would love myself! I'd envy no one."

> Prologue, Ch. 1, *All Men Are Mortal 1955*

17 This stale taste of my life will never change. Always the same past, the same feelings, the same rational thoughts, the same boredom. For thousands of years! Never will I escape from myself!

> Bk. III, Ibid.

18 She was trying to get rid of a religious hangover.

> Pt. IV, *Memoirs of a Dutiful Daughter 1959*

19 "There won't be a war. The gap between the capitalist and the socialist countries will soon be done away with. Because now we're in the great twentieth-century revolution: producing is more important than possessing."

> Ch. 1, *Les Belles Images 1966*

20 Whatever the country, capitalist or socialist, man was everywhere crushed by technology, made a stranger to his own work, imprisoned, forced into stupidity. The evil all arose from the fact that he had increased his needs rather than limited them; . . . As long as fresh needs continued to be created, so new frustrations would come into being. When had the decline begun? The day knowledge was preferred to wisdom and mere usefulness to beauty. . . . Only a moral revolution—not a social or political revolution—only a moral revolution would lead man back to his lost truth.

> Ch. 3, Ibid.

21 It's frightening to think that you mark your children merely by being yourself. . . . It seems unfair. You can't assume the responsibility for everything you do—or don't do.

> Ibid.

22 I had grown very fond of this dying woman [her mother]. As we talked in the half-darkness I assuaged an old unhappiness; I was renewing the dialogue that had been broken off during my adolescence and that our differences and our likenesses had never allowed us to take up again. And the early tenderness that I had thought dead forever came to life again. . . .

> *A Very Easy Death 1966*

23 I find it absurd to assume that all coitus is rape. By saying that, one agrees to the masculine myth that a man's sex is a sword, a weapon.

> Quoted in "The Radicalization of Simone de Beauvoir" by Alice Schwarzer, *The First Ms. Reader*, Francine Klagsbrun, ed. 1972

24 Both today and throughout history, the class struggle governs the manner in which old age takes hold of a man: there is a great gulf between the aged slave and the aged patrician, . . . and these two classes are brought into being by the conflict between the exploiters and the exploited. Any statement that claims to deal with old age as a whole must be challenged, for it tends to hide this chasm.

> *The Coming of Age 1972*

25 . . . it is old age, rather than death, that is to be contrasted with life. Old age is life's parody, whereas death transforms life into a destiny: in a way it preserves it by giving it the absolute dimension—"And into himself eternity changes him at last." Death does away with time.

> Conclusion, Ibid.

26 One is not born a genius, one becomes a genius.

> Quoted in *The Woman's Eye* by Anne Tucker* 1973
> *See 3073.

27 I tore myself away from the safe comfort of certainties through my love for truth; and truth rewarded me.

> *All Said and Done 1974*

28 Patience [is one of those] "feminine" qualities which have their origin in our oppression but should be preserved after our liberation.

> Interview by Alice Schwarzer, *Marie-Claire* October 1976

1937. Bette Davis (1908–1989)

1 I have always been driven by some distant music—a battle hymn no doubt—for I have been at war from the beginning. I've never looked back before. I've never had the time and it has always seemed so dangerous. To look back is to relax one's vigil.

Ch. 1, *The Lonely Life 1962*

2 The sweetness of first love. It still clings like ivy to the stone walls of this institution called Bette Davis. Stonewall Davis! Alma Mater! You can't mortar bricks with treacle but I tried.

Ch. 9, Ibid.

3 The male ego with few exceptions is elephantine to start with.

Ibid.

4 Love is not enough. It must be the foundation, the cornerstone-but not the complete structure. It is much too pliable, too yielding.

Ibid.

5 Discipline is a symbol of caring to a child. He needs guidance. If there is love, there is no such thing as being too tough with a child. A parent must also not be afraid to hang himself. If you have never been hated by your child, you have never been a parent.

Ibid.

6 The act of sex, gratifying as it may be, is God's joke on humanity. It is man's last desperate stand at superintendency.

Ch. 20, Ibid.

7 I was always eager to salt a good stew. The trouble was that I was expected to supply the meat and potatoes as well.

Ibid.

8 The weak are the most treacherous of us all. They come to the strong and drain them. They are bottomless. They are insatiable. They are always parched and always bitter. They are everyone's concern and like vampires they suck our life's blood.

Ibid.

9 But my biggest problem all my life was men. I never met one yet who could compete with the image the public made out of Bette Davis.

Quoted in "Bette Davis," *Conversations in the Raw* by Rex Reed *1969*

10 This became a credo of mine . . . attempt the impossible in order to improve your work.

Ch. 10, *Mother Goddamn 1974*

11 They say this is a dope town, but then, we live in a dope nation now. There's no discipline, no love of work, no standards, little kindness. I'm lucky I'm not starting out now. The whole movie industry is out in space somewhere. There's no romance, no love.

Quoted in "The Story of a Winner" by Dotson Rader, *Parade Magazine 6 March 1983*

12 If you don't work, what the hell do you do? Sit around and rot! The retirement age of 65 has milled *millions*. Luckily, I'm in an industry with no retirement. They only retire you if you don't make money for them.

Ibid.

13 Writers don't know how to write scripts today. They don't know what to write about. . . . There are no scripts. That's why they all do these damn docu-dramas, because our lives are more interesting than anything they can make up.

Ibid.

14 Don't you hate people who drink white wine? I mean, my dear, every alcoholic in town is getting falling-down drunk on white wine. They think they aren't drunks because they only drink wine. Never, never trust anyone who asks for white wine. It means they're phonies.

Ibid.

15 I am a woman meant for a man, but I never found a man who could compete.

Newspaper interview *n.d.*

1938. Beatrice M. Murphy (1908–1992)

1 Not until you live more years and
Acquire deeper wisdom will you know
They paved and pointed the way
You are now impatient to go.

"To Any Negro Youth," St. 2. *The Rocks Cry Out*

2 All I know of the South
Is what I've been told
And the telling has filled
My veins with brackish hate
And made my blood run cold.

"Disclaimer," St. 2, Ibid.

3 Please send me a miracle
By noon tomorrow.

"Deadline for Miracles," St. 1, Ibid.

4 The almost universal cry today is that youth has something to say and no one will listen.

Preface, *Today's Negro Voices*, ed. *1970*

1939. M. F. K. Fisher (1908–1992)

1 Sharing food with another human being is an intimate act that should not be indulged in lightly.

"A Is for Dining Alone," *An Alphabet for Gourmets 1949*

2 A true karmic force is supposed to build up its strength through centuries of both evil and good, in order to prevent its transmigration into another and lesser form, and this may well explain why Marseilles has always risen anew from the ashes of history.

Ch. 1, *A Considerable Town 1964*

3 "In France we have lived with the law for so long that we know how and when to make use of it. We are not afraid of it. In your country you are still so inexperienced, that you are in awe of it. The law is your stern parent, like God, and you fear its punishment. Here we respect it, but only if we respect ourselves more. We use it when we need it."

Ch. 5, Ibid.

4 There are many people like me who believe firmly if somewhat incoherently that pockets on this planet are filled with what humans have left behind them, both good and evil, and that any such spiritual accumulation can stay there forever, past definition of such a stern word. . . . There are kindlier and even restorative places, which like the bad or merely disturbing ones influence people whether or not they are aware of their vulnerability before such old forces.

Ch. 8, Ibid.

5 . . . our dispassionate acceptance of attribution [by age needs to] be matched by a full use of everything that has ever happened in all the long wonderful-ghastly years to free a person's mind from his body . . . to use the experience, both great and evil, so that physical annoyances are surmountable in an alert and even mirthful appreciation of life itself.

Sister Age 1983

6 "There is a communion of more than our bodies when bread is broken and wine is drunk. And that is my answer when people ask me: Why do you write about hunger, and not wars or love?"

Quoted in "With Bold Pen and Fork" by Mimi Sheraton, *Time* (New York) *26 January 1987*

1940. Anne Fremantle (1909–)

1 Among the most truly responsible of all people are artists and revolutionaries, for they most of all are prepared to pay with their lives.

Introduction, *Woman as Revolutionary*, Fred C. Giffin, ed. *1973*

2 The revolutionary attempts a secular denial of mortality, the artist a spiritual one.

Ibid.

1941. Eleanor Hamilton (1909–)

1 Good lovers have known for centuries that the hand is probably the primary sex organ.

Quoted in "Hue & Cry," *San Francisco Chronicle* *29 October 1978*

1942. Katharine Hepburn (1909–)

1 The average Hollywood film star's ambition is to be admired by an American, courted by an Italian, married to an Englishman and have a French boyfriend.

New York Journal-American 22 February 1954

2 Only the really plain people know about love—the very fascinating ones try so hard to create an impression that they very soon exhaust their talents.

Look (New York) *18 February 1958*

3 I can remember walking as a child. It was not customary to say you were fatigued. It was customary to complete the goal of the expedition.

Quoted in "Hepburn: She Is the Best," *The Los Angeles Times 24 November 1974*

4 It's such a cuckoo business. And it's a business you go into because you're egocentric. It's a very embarrassing profession.

Ibid.

5 Television, which sank the picture industry, has turned the Academy Awards into a big television show. I think it should be an intimate honor.

Ibid.

6 To keep your character intact you cannot stoop to filthy acts. It makes it easier to stoop the next time.

Ibid.

7 To be loved is very demoralizing.

Dick Cavett Show, ABC-TV *4 April 1975*

8 Without discipline, there's no life at all.

Ibid.

9 You never feel that you have fame. It's always in back of you.

Ibid.

10 Trying to be fascinating is an asinine position to be in.

Ibid.

11 I always wear slacks because of the brambles and maybe the snakes. And see this basket? I keep everything in it. So I look ghastly, do I? I don't care—so long as I'm comfortable.

Quoted in *Kate* by Charles Higham *1975*

12 . . . plain women know more about men than beautiful ones do.

Ibid.

13 As for me, prizes mean nothing. My prize is my work.

Ibid.

14 Our Constitution was not intended to be used by . . . any group to foist its personal religious beliefs on the rest of us.

Planned Parenthood Federation fund-raising letter *November 1981*

1943. Queen Juliana (1909–)

1 You people of the United States of America have the wonderfully farseeing conception of being Democracy's material and spiritual arsenal, to save the world's highest values from annihilation.

Radio address, NBC *13 April 1941*

2 I want to emphasize that for a queen the task of being a mother is just as important as it is for every other Netherlands woman.

Inauguration address, Amsterdam *6 September 1948*

3 Though previous generations were also inspired by the fervent will to improve the world, they failed because they did not call a final halt to the forces of destruction. To do this is precisely the task of the present generation. . . .

Address, University of Paris *25 May 1950*

1944. Rita Levi-Montalcini (1909–1989)

1 . . . I [had] decided to become a writer and describe Italian saga "à la Lagerlöf".* But things were to take a different turn.

Autobiographical essay, *Les Prix Nobel 1986*
*See 1183.

2 The four of us enjoyed a most wonderful family atmosphere, filled with love and reciprocal devotion. Both parents were highly cultured and instilled in us their high appreciation of intellectual pursuit. It was, however, a typical Victorian style of life, all decisions being taken by the head of the family, the husband and father. He loved us dearly and had a great respect for women, but he believed that a professional career would interfere with the duties of a wife and mother. He therefore decided that the three of us—Anna, Paola and I—would not engage in studies which open the way to a professional career and that we would not enroll in the University.

Ibid.

3 At twenty, I realized that I could not possibly adjust to a feminine role as conceived by my father, and asked him permission to engage in a professional career. In eight months I filled my gaps in Latin, Greek and mathematics, graduated from high school, and entered medical school in Turin.

Ibid.

4 Wrapped in a black mantle, he bowed before the king and, for a moment, lowered the veil covering his face. We recognized each other in a matter of seconds when I saw him looking for me among the applauding crowd. He then replaced his veil and disappeared as suddenly as he had appeared.*

In Praise of Imperfection (autobiography) *1988*
*Her description of receiving the Nobel Prize from the King of Sweden; the "he" in the passage refers to NGF (nerve growth factor), the discovery for which she received the prize.

5 The answer* lies in the desperate...desire of human beings to ignore what is happening in situations where full awareness might lead one to self-destruction.

Quoted in *Twentieth-Century Women Scientists* by Lisa Yount *1996*
*Explaining how she, a Jew in hiding, could concentrate on research when Mussolini and the Germans took over Italy.

6 For a long time [in the late 1960s and early 1970s] people didn't mention how NGF* was discovered. . . . People repeated my experiment and didn't mention my name! I am not a person to be bitter, but it was astonishing to find it completely canceled.

Ibid.
*Nerve growth factor, which she discovered in 1950.

1945. Gabrielle Roy (1909–1983)

1 The city was made for couples, not for four or five silly girls with their arms interlaced, strolling up St. Catherine Street, stopping at every shop-window to admire things they would never own.

Ch. 1, *The Tin Flute 1947*

2 When there was enough money for their needs, the ties between them had been strong, but once the money was lacking, what a strain was put on their love!

Ch. 32, Ibid.

3 The Christian Scientists held that it was not God who wanted sicknesses, but man who puts himself in the way of suffering. If this were the case, though, wouldn't we all die in perfect health?

Ch. 3, *The Cashier 1955*

4 How clearly he realized that men did not like what they called love. That most embarassing of subjects between men they approached with half-utterances, with false carelessness, or else with a vulgar leer, never easily and comfortably.

Ch. 8, Ibid.

5 Oh! The matchless release of the man asleep! Who has not realized through experience that sleep tells the truth about us? In sleep a human being is finally brought back to himself, having sloughed off everything else. Bound hand and foot fettered with fatigue, he at last drifts toward the cavern of the unknown. Some men have returned therefrom with poems fully written, or with equations solved.

Ch. 12, Ibid.

1946. Eudora Welty (1909–)

1 These people cherished something here that he could not see, they withheld some ancient promise of food and warmth and light. Between them they had a conspiracy.

"Death of a Travelling Salesman," *A Curtain of Green and Other Stories 1936*

2 I have been sick and I found out, only then, how lonely I am. Is it too late?

Ibid.

3 He did not like illness, he distrusted it, as he distrusted the road without signposts.

Ibid.

4 This time, when his heart leapt, something—his soul—seemed to leap too, like a little colt invited out of a pen.

Ibid.

5 How intensified, magnified, really vain all attempt at expression becomes in the afflicted!

"The Key," Ibid.

6 Radio, sewing machine, bookends, ironing board and that great big piano lamp—peace, that's what I like. Butterbean vines planted all along the front where the strings are.

"Why I Live at the P.O.," Ibid.

7 "No, babe, it ain't the truth. . . . Truth is something worse, I ain't said what, yet. It's something that hasn't come to me, but I ain't saying it won't."

"Powerhouse," Ibid.

8 There was a need in all dreams for something to stay far, far away, never to torment with the rest, and the bright moon now was that.

"At the Landing," *The Wide Net and Other Stories 1943*

9 She was calm the way a child is calm, with never the calmness of a spirit. But like distant lightning that silently bathes a whole shimmering sky, one awareness was always trembling about her: one day she would be free to come and go. . . .

Ibid.

10 "We're walking along in the changing-time," said Doc. "Any day now the change will come. It's going to turn from hot to cold. . . . Old Jack Frost will be pinching things up. Old Mr. Winter will be standing in the door. Hickory tree there will be yellow. Sweet-gum red, hickory yellow, dogwood red, sycamore yellow. . . . Persimmons will all git fit to eat, and the nut will be dropping like rain all through the woods here. And run, little quail, run, for we'll be after you too."

"The Wide Net," Ibid.

11 In a shadowy place something white flew up. It was a heron, and it went away over the dark treetops. William Wallace followed it with his eyes and Brucie clapped his hands, but Virgil gave a sigh, as if he knew that when you go looking for what is lost, everything is a sign.

Ibid.

12 His memory could work like the slinging of a noose to catch a wild pony.

"First Love," Ibid.

13 "I rather a man be anything, than a woman be mean."

"Livvie," Ibid.

14 Haven't you noticed it prevail, in the world in general? Beware of a man with manners.

Ch. 1, *The Golden Apples 1949*

15 She yearned for her heart to twist. But it didn't, not in time.

Ch. 4, Ibid.

16 Attrition was their wisdom.

Ch. 7, Ibid.

17 She was dead as a doornail. And she'd died laughing. I could have shaken her for it. She'd never laughed for Uncle Daniel before in her life. And even if she had, that's not the same thing as smiling; you may think it is, but I don't.

The Ponder Heart 1954

18 He loved being happy! He loved happiness like I love tea.

Ibid.

19 Ah, I'm a woman that's been clear around the world in my rocking chair.

"Circe," *The Bride of Innisfallen and Other Stories 1955*

20 "Never think you've seen the last of anything. . . ."

Pt. I, Ch. 1, *The Optimist's Daughter 1969*

21 "I'm afraid my [minister] husband's running a little late. You know people like *this* don't die every day in the week. He's sitting home in his bathrobe now, tearing his hair, trying to do him justice."

Pt. II, Ch. 2, Ibid.

22 All they could see was sky, water, birds, light and confluence. It was the whole morning world. And they themselves were a part of the confluence. Their own joint act of faith had brought them here at the very moment and matched its occurrence, and proceeded as it proceeded. Direction itself was made beautiful, momentous. They were riding as one with it, right up front.

Pt. IV, Ibid.

23 What I do in the writing of any character is to try to enter into the mind, heart and skin of a human being who is not myself. Whether this happens to be a man or a woman, old or young, with skin black or white, the primary challenge lies in making the jump itself. It is the act of a writer's imagination that I set most high.

Preface, *The Collected Stories of Eudora Welty 1980*

24 Whoever the murderer is, I know him: not his identity, but his coming about, in this time and place. That is, I ought to have learned by now, from here, what such a man, intent on such a deed, had going on in his mind.

Preface to "Where is the Voice Coming From?",* Ibid.
*Written on the night of Medgar Evers's murder. Evers was an African-American civil rights activist (1925–1963).

25 He knew that the best he could make would be, after it was apart from his hand, a dead thing and not a live thing, never the essence, only the sum of parts; and that it would always meet with a stranger's sight, and never be one with the beauty in any other man's head in the world. As he had seen the bird most purely at its moment of death, in some fatal way, in his care for looking outward, he saw his long labor most revealingly at the point where it met its limit.

"A Still Moment," Ibid.

26 . . . listening to the magical percussion, the world beating in their ears. They heard through falling rain the running of the horse and bear, the stroke of the leopard, the dragon's crusty slither, and the glimmer and the trumpet of the swan.

"June Recital," Ibid.

27 So then Uncle Rondo says, "I'll thank you from now on to stop reading all the orders I get on postcards and telling everybody in China Grove what you think is the matter with them," but I says, "I draw my own conclusions and will continue in the future to draw them." I says, "If people want to write their inmost secrets on penny postcards, there's nothing in the wide world you can do about it, Uncle Rondo."

"Why I Live at the P.O.," Ibid.

28 She has spent her life trying to escape from the parlor-like jaws of self-consciousness.

"Old Mr. Marblehall," Ibid.

29 They were not really old—they were only 50; still, their lives were filled with tiredness, with a great lack of necessity to speak, with poverty which may have bound them like a disaster too great for any discussion but left them still separate and undesirous of sympathy. Perhaps, years ago, the long habit of silence may have been started in anger and passion. Who could tell now?

"The Whistle," Ibid.

30 "Fannie, I'd rather Eudora didn't hear that." "That" would be just what I was longing to hear, whatever it was. "I don't want her exposed to gossip"—as if gossip were measles and I could catch it. I did catch some of it but not enough.

One Writer's Beginning 1983

31 I had to grow up and learned to listen for the unspoken as well as the spoken—and to know a truth. I also had to recognize a lie.

Ibid.

1947. Gale Wilhelm (1909–)

1 "I'm going to turn on the light and we'll be two people in a room looking at each other and wondering why on earth they were afraid of the dark."

We Too Are Drifting 1953

1948. Simone Weil (1909–1943)

1 Just as a person who is always asserting that he is too good-natured is the very one from whom to expect, on some occasion, the coldest and most unconcerned cruelty, so when any group sees itself as the bearer of civilization this very belief will betray it into behaving barbarously at the first opportunity.

"Hitler and Roman Foreign Policy," *Nouveaux Cahiers*
1 January 1940

2 I would suggest that barbarism be considered as a permanent and universal human characteristic which becomes more or less pronounced according to the play of circumstances.

Ibid.

3 There is something else which has the power to awaken us to the truth. It is the works of writers of genius. . . . They give us, in the guise of fiction, something equivalent to the actual density of the real, that density which life offers us every day but which we are unable to grasp because we are amusing ourselves with lies.

"Morality and Literature," *Cahiers du Sud January 1944*

4 A right which goes unrecognized by anybody is not worth very much.

L'Enracinment (The Need for Roots, 1952) *1949*

5 Punishment must be an honour. It must not only wipe out the stigma of the crime, but must be regarded as a supplementary form of education, compelling a higher devotion to the public good. The severity of the punishment must also be in keeping with the kind of obligation which has been violated, and not with the interest of public security.

Ibid.

6 Culture is an instrument wielded by teachers to manufacture teachers, who, in their turn, will manufacture still more teachers.

Pt. 2, "Uprootedness in the Towns," Ibid.

7 Those who are unhappy have no need for anything in this world but people capable of giving them their attention.

"Reflections on the Right Use of School Studies,"
Waiting on God 1950

8 The capacity to give one's attention to a sufferer is a very rare and difficult thing; it is almost a miracle; it is a miracle. Nearly all those who think they have this capacity do not possess it. Warmth of heart, impulsiveness, pity are not enough.

Ibid.

9 With no matter what human being, taken individually, I always find reasons for concluding that sorrow and misfortune do not suit him; either because he seems too mediocre for anything so great, or, on the contrary, too precious to be destroyed.

Letter 4, Ibid.

10 Obvious and inexorable oppression that cannot be overcome does not give rise to revolt but to submission.

Factory journal, "The Mystery of the Factory" (1934–35),
La Condition Ouvrière 1951

11 Nothing is less instructive than a machine.

Ibid.

12 Bourgeois society is infected by monomania: the monomania of accounting. For it, the only thing that has value is what can be counted in francs and centimes. It never hesitates to sacrifice human life to figures which look well on paper, such as national budgets or industrial balance sheets.

"La Rationalisation" (1937), Ibid.

13 Purity is the power to contemplate defilement.

"Attention and Will" (1947), Gravity and Grace 1952

14 In solitude we are in the presence of mere matter (even the sky, the stars, the moon, trees in blossom), things of less value (perhaps) than a human spirit. Its value lies in the greater possibility of attention. If we could be attentive to the same degree in the presence of a human being . . .

Ibid.

15 A test of what is real is that it is hard and rough. Joys are found in it, not pleasure. What is pleasant belongs to dreams.

"Illusions" (1947), Ibid.

16 We must prefer real hell to an imaginary paradise.

Ibid.

17 The role of the intelligence—that part of us which affirms and denies and formulates opinions—is merely to submit.

"Intelligence and Grace" (1947), Ibid.

18 The mysteries of faith are degraded if they are made into an object of affirmation and negation, when in reality they should be an object of contemplation.

Ibid.

19 Two prisoners whose cells adjoin communicate with each other by knocking on the wall. The wall is the thing which separates them but is also their means of communication. It is the same with us and God. Every separation is a link.

"Metaxu" (1947), Ibid.

20 Money destroys human roots wherever it is able to penetrate, by turning desire for gain into the sole motive. It easily manages to outweigh all other motives, because the effort it demands of the mind is so very much less. Nothing is so clear and so simple as a row of figures.

"L'Enracinement," Pt. II (1949), The Need for Roots 1952

21 Propaganda is not directed towards creating an inspiration; it closes, seals up all the openings through which an inspiration might pass; it fills the whole spirit with fanaticism.

Pt. III, Ibid.

22 Evil becomes an operative motive far more easily than good; but once pure good has become an operative motive in the mind, it forms there a fount of a uniform and inexhaustible impulsion, which is never so in the case of evil.

Ibid.

23 Misfortunes leave wounds which bleed drop by drop even in sleep; thus little by little they train man by force and dispose him to wisdom in spite of himself. Man must learn to think of himself as a limited and dependent being; and only suffering teaches him this.

Pt. 1, Ch. 2, La Source Grecque 1953

24 One must always be ready to change sides with justice, that fugitive from the winning camp.

Quoted in The Unadjusted Man by Peter Viereck 1956

25 The idea of a snare set for man by God is also the meaning of the myth of the labyrinth . . . that path where man, from the moment he enters upon it, loses his way and finds himself equally powerless, at the end of a certain time, to return upon his steps or to direct himself anywhere. He errs without knowing where, and finally arrives at the place where God waits to devour him.

Intimations of Christianity, Elizabeth Chase Geissbuhler, ed.
1957

26 The only hope of socialism resides in those who have already brought about in themselves, as far as is possible in the society of today, that union between manual and intellectual labor which characterizes the society we are aiming at.

Ch. 1, Oppression and Liberty 1958

27 War, which perpetuates itself under the form of preparation for war, has once and for all given the State an important role in production.

"Revolution Proletarienne" (25 August 1933), Ibid.

28 . . . man alone can enslave man.

"Reflections Concerning the Causes of Liberty and
Social Oppression" (1934), Ibid.

29 He [Marx*] labeled this dream "dialectical materialism." This was sufficient to shroud it in mystery. These two words are of an almost impenetrable emptiness. A very amusing game—though rather a cruel one—is to ask a Marxist what they mean.

"Is There a Marxist Doctrine?" (1943), Ibid.
*Karl M—, German political philosopher and economist (1818–83).

30 The payment of debts is necessary for social order. The non-payment is quite equally necessary for social order. For centuries humanity has oscillated, serenely unaware, between these two contradictory necessities.

"On Bankruptcy" (1937), Selected Essays (1934–1953),
Richard Rees, ed. 1962

31 What a country calls its vital economic interests are not the things which enable its citizens to live, but the things which enable it to make war. Petrol is more likely than wheat to be a cause of international conflict.
"The Power of Words" (Nouveaux Cahiers,
1 & 15 April 1937), Ibid.

32 When once a certain class of people has been placed by the temporal and spiritual authorities outside the ranks of those whose life has value, then nothing comes more naturally to men than murder.
Letter to author Georges Bernanos (c. 1938), Ibid.

33 Who were the fools who spread the story that brute force cannot kill ideas? Nothing is easier. And once they are dead they are no more than corpses.
"Three Letters on History: Théophile de Viau"
(c. 1938/39), Ibid.

34 The appetite for power, even for universal power, is only insane when there is no possibility of indulging it; a man who sees the possibility opening before him and does not try to grasp it, even at the risk of destroying himself and his country, is either a saint or a mediocrity.
"Cold War Policy in 1939" (1939), Ibid.

35 It is not the cause for which men took up arms that makes a victory more just or less, it is the order that is established when arms have been laid down.
"The Great Beast: Conclusion" (1939–40), Ibid.

36 Every new development for the last three centuries has brought men closer to a state of affairs in which absolutely nothing would be recognized in the whole world as possessing a claim to obedience except the authority of the State. The majority of people in Europe obey nothing else.
Ibid.

37 Humanism was not wrong in thinking that truth, beauty, liberty, and equality are of infinite value, but in thinking that man can get them for himself without grace.
"The Romanesque Renaissance," (Marseilles,
Cahiers du Sud, ca. 1941/42), Ibid.

38 At the bottom of the heart of every human being from earliest infancy to the tomb, there is something that goes on indomitably expecting, in the teeth of all experience of crimes committed, suffered, and witnessed, that good and not evil will be done to him. It is this above all that is sacred in every human being.
"Human Personality" (1943; La Table Ronde,
December 1950), Ibid.

39 One cannot imagine St. Francis of Assisi* talking about rights.
Ibid.

*Italian friar; founder of the Franciscan Order (1182?–1226).

40 The only way into truth is through one's own annihilation; through dwelling a long time in a state of extreme and total humiliation.
Ibid.

41 Beauty always promises, but never gives anything.
Ibid.

42 A man whose mind feels that it is captive would prefer to blind himself to the fact. But if he hates falsehood, he will not do so; and in that case he will have to suffer a lot. He will beat his head against the wall until he faints. He will come to again and look with terror at the wall, until one day he begins afresh to beat his head against it; and once again he will faint. And so on endlessly and without hope. One day he will wake up on the other side of the wall.
Ibid.

43 Real genius is nothing else but the supernatural virtue of humility in the domain of thought.
Ibid.

44 The afflicted are not listened to. They are like someone whose tongue has been cut out and who occasionally forgets the fact. When they move their lips no ear perceives any sound. And they themselves soon sink into impotence in the use of language, because of the certainty of not being heard.
Ibid.

45 To set up as a standard of public morality a notion which can neither be defined nor conceived is to open the door to every kind of tyranny.
Ibid.

46 There is one, and only one, thing in modern society more hideous than crime—namely, repressive justice.
Ibid.

47 A mind enclosed in language is in prison.
Ibid.

48 When science, art, literature, and philosophy are simply the manifestation of personality they are on a level where glorious and dazzling achievements are possible, which can make a man's name live for thousands of years. But above this level, far above, separated by an abyss, is the level where the highest things are achieved. These things are essentially anonymous.
Ibid.

49 It is only the impossible that is possible for God. He has given over the possible to the mechanics of matter and the autonomy of his creatures.
"A War of Religions" (1943), Ibid.

50 Whenever a human being, through the commission of a crime, has become exiled from good, he needs to be reintegrated with it through suffering. The suffering should be inflicted with the aim of bringing the soul to recognize freely some day that its infliction was just.
"Draft for a Statement of Human Obligation" (1943), Ibid.

51 The needs of a human being are sacred. Their satisfaction cannot be subordinated either to reasons of state, or to any consideration of money, nationality, race, or color, or to the moral or other value attributed to the human being in question, or to any consideration whatsoever.
Ibid.

52 Equality is the public recognition, effectively expressed in institutions and manners, of the principle that an equal degree of attention is due to the needs of all human beings.
Ibid.

53 . . . when a man's life is destroyed or damaged by some wound or privation of soul or body, which is due to other men's actions or negligence, it is not only his sensibility that suffers but also his aspirations toward the good. Therefore there has been a sacrilege towards that which is sacred in him.
Ibid.

54   The poison of skepticism becomes, like alcoholism, tuberculosis, and some other diseases, much more virulent in a hitherto virgin soil.
"East and West" (1943), Ibid.

55   There can be a true grandeur in any degree of submissiveness, because it springs from loyalty to the laws and to an oath, and not from baseness of soul.
"The Great Beast," Pt. 3, Ibid.

56   Whatever debases the intelligence degrades the entire human being.
Letter (30 March 1936), *Seventy Letters 1965*

57   In struggling against anguish one never produces serenity; the struggle against anguish only produces new forms of anguish.
Draft of letter to André Weil (1940), Pt. 2, No. 39, Ibid.

58   Evil is neither suffering nor sin; it is both at the same time, it is something common to them both. For they are linked together; sin makes us suffer and suffering makes us evil, and this indissoluble complex of suffering and sin is the evil in which we are submerged against our will, and to our horror.
"Some Thoughts on the Love of God" (October 1940– May 1942), *On Science, Necessity, and the Love of God*, Richard Rees, ed. *1968*

59   The future is made of the same stuff as the present.
Ibid.

60   . . . if we are suffering from illness, poverty, or misfortune, we think we shall be satisfied on the day it ceases. But there too, we know it is false; so soon as one has got used to not suffering one wants something else.
Ibid.

61   Learn to reject friendship, or rather the dream of friendship. To want friendship is a great fault. Friendship ought to be a gratuitous joy, like the joys afforded by art, or life (like aesthetic joys). I must refuse it in order to be worthy to receive it.
The Pre-War Notebook (1933-39), *First and Last Notebooks*, Richard Rees, ed. *1970*

62   Art is the symbol of the two noblest human efforts: to construct . . . and to refrain from destruction.
Ibid.

63   Nothing can have as its destination anything other than its origin. The contrary idea, the idea of progress, is poison.
"The New York Notebook" (1942), Ibid.

64   Every perfect life is a parable invented by God.
Ibid.

65   Evil being the root of mystery, pain is the root of knowledge.
Ibid.

66   To get power over is to defile. To possess is to defile.
Ibid.

67   Charity. To love human beings in so far as they are nothing. That is to love them as God does.
Ibid.

68   Truth is not discovered by proofs but by exploration. It is always experimental. But necessity also is an object of exploration.
Ibid.

69   Joy fixes us to eternity and pain fixes us to time. But desire and fear hold us in bondage to time, and detachment breaks the bond.
Ibid.

70   The most important part of teaching = to teach what it is to *know*.
" London Notebook" (1943, pub. 1950), Ibid.

71   The proper method of philosophy consists in clearly conceiving the insoluble problems in all their insolubility and then in simply contemplating them, fixedly and tirelessly, year after year, without any hope, patiently waiting.
Ibid.

72   In relation to God, we are like a thief who has burgled the house of a kindly householder and been allowed to keep some of the gold. From the point of view of the lawful owner this gold is a gift; From the point of view of the burglar it is a theft. He must go and give it back. It is the same with our existence. We have stolen a little of God's being to make it ours. God has made us a gift of it. But we have stolen it. We must return it.
" New York Notebook" (1950), Ibid.

73   Human beings are so made that the ones who do the crushing feel nothing; it is the person crushed who feels what is happening. Unless one has placed oneself on the side of the oppressed, to feel with them, one cannot understand.
Pt. 3, Ch. 2, *Lectures on Philosophy 1978*

74   Force is as pitiless to the man who possesses it, or thinks he does, as it is to its victims; the second it crushes, the first it intoxicates. The truth is, nobody really possesses it.
"The Iliad or the Poem of Force" (*Cahiers du Sud*, Marseilles, December 1940/January 1941), *Simone Weil: An Anthology*, Sian Miles, ed.; Mary McCarthy, tr. *1986*

75   To write the lives of the great in separating them from their works necessarily ends by above all stressing their pettiness, because it is in their work that they have put the best of themselves.
Pt. 5, Ch. 4, "Otto Rühle: Karl Marx," *La Critique Sociale*, No. 11 (March 1934), *Oeuvres Complètes*, Vol. 2, No. 1 *1988*

76   In the Church, considered as a social organism, the mysteries inevitably degenerate into beliefs.
Ch. 9, Quoted in *Simone Weil: Utopian Pessimist* by David McLellan *1989*

1949. Dora Alonso (1910–)

1   The shadow, the color of the man, and the kind of living, all are the same; black in one hundred tones, either so light as to be cinnamon flesh or as dark as black coffee, it carries the sign of subjection.
"Times Gone By," *Fragment from a Lost Diary and Other Stories*, Naomi Katz and Nancy Milton, eds. *1973*

2   Life goes on, buried in pain for those who wait; swollen with haughtiness and arrogance for those who fear.
Ibid.

3   Her body broke down like the collapse of forked poles which could no longer bear the weight of an entire life dedicated to obedience, without a single pillar of rebellion to hold up the structure.
Ibid.

4 There's no higher right than might, and I am mighty.
"Time Gone By," Ibid.

1950. Bertha Adams Backus (fl. 1910s)

1 Build for yourself a strong-box,
Fashion each part with care;
When it's strong as your hand can make it,
Put all your troubles there.
"Then Laugh," St. 1 *1911*

1951. Myrtie Lillian Barker (1910–)

1 The idea of strictly minding my own business is moldy rubbish. Who could be so selfish?
I Am Only One 1963

1952. Janet Begbie (fl. 1910s)

1 Carry on, carry on, for the men and boys are gone,
But the furrow shan't lie fallow while the women carry on.
"Carry On" *n.d.*

1953. Mary Ingraham Bunting (1910–1998)

1 When her last child is off to school, we don't want the talented woman wasting her time in work far below her capacity. We want her to come out running.
Quoted in *Life* (New York) *13 January 1961*

1954. Katherine Dunlap Cather (fl. 1910s–20s)

1 When the time of rising came, I climbed joyfully into my mother's warm bed, and never did I listen to more beautiful fairy tales than at those hours. They became instinct with life to me and have always remained so. . . . It is a singular thing that actual events which happened in those early days have largely vanished from my memory, but the fairy tales I heard and secretly experienced became firmly impressed on my mind.
(p. 22), *Educating by Story-telling 1918*

2 Wherever there is no written language, wherever the people are too unlettered to read what is written, they still believe the legends. They love to hear them told and retold. . . . As it is with unlettered peasants today, as it was with tribesmen in primitive times and the great in medieval castle halls, it still is with the child.
(pp. 5–6), Ibid.

1955. Hilda Conkling (1910–1986)

1 The hills are going somewhere;
They have been going on the way a long time.
They are like camels in a line
But they move more slowly.
"Hills" *n.d.*

2 The world turns softly
Not to spill its lakes and rivers.
"Water" *n.d.*

3 Poems come like boats
With sails for wings;
Crossing the sky swiftly
They slip under tall bridges
Of cloud.
"Poems" *n.d.*

1956. Esther Lillian Duff (fl. 1910s)

1 Some of the roofs are plum-color
Some of the roofs are gray,
Some of the roofs are silverstone,
And some are made of clay;
But under every gabled close
There's a secret hid away.
"Not Three, But One," *Bohemian Glass 1916*

1957. Edith Starrett Green (1910–1987)

1 I have never believed that race, sex, religion, or national origin are valid criteria for either "favorable" or "unfavorable" treatment. This is one reason why I have been opposed to programs which give an advantage in job consideration and promotion to members of those groups who have suffered historic discrimination.
Speech, Brigham Young University *1977*

2 I've always argued that it is just as desirable, just as possible, to have philosopher plumbers as philosopher kings.
Quoted in *American Political Women*
by Esther Stineman *1980*

1958. Margaret Halsey (1910–1997)

1 . . . she blushed like a well-trained sunrise.
With Malice Toward Some 1938

2 These people . . . talk simply because they think sound is more manageable than silence.
Ibid.

3 . . . it takes a great deal to produce ennui in an Englishman and if you do, he only takes it as convincing proof that you are well-bred.
Ibid.

4 The attitude of the English . . . toward English history reminds one a good deal of the attitude of a Hollywood director toward love.
Ibid.

5 Such leaping to foot, such opening of doors, such lightning flourishes with matches and cigarettes—it is all so heroic, I never quite get over the feeling that someone has just said, "To the lifeboats!"
Ibid.

6 . . . the English think of an opinion as something which a decent person, if he has the misfortune to have one, does all he can to hide.
Ibid.

7 Humility is not my forte, and whenever I dwell for any length of time on my own shortcomings, they gradually begin to seem mild, harmless, rather engaging little things, not at all like the staring defects in other people's characters.
Ibid.

8 All of Stratford, in fact, suggests powdered history—add hot water and stir and you have a delicious, nourishing Shakespeare.
Ibid.

9 . . . in England, having had money . . . is just as acceptable as having it, since the upper-class mannerisms persist, even after the bankroll has disappeared. But never having had money is

unforgivable, and can only be atoned for by never trying to get any.

Ibid.

10 The boneless quality of English conversation, which, so far as I have heard it, is all form and no content. Listening to Britons dining out is like watching people play first-class tennis with imaginary balls.

Pt. 1, "12 June," Ibid.

11 I doused the fatal instrument [a cigarette] with lightning promptitude, but it was a good seven minutes before the last indignant handkerchief had folded its wings and gone back to its reticule and the last manufactured cough died protestingly away.

Pt. 2, "20 June," Ibid.

12 He has the common feeling of his profession. He enjoys a statement twice as much if it appears in fine print, and anything that turns up in a footnote . . . takes on the character of divine revelation.

"26 June," Ibid.

13 . . . there is not enough loving-kindness afloat in the continental United States to see a crippled old lady across an Indian trail.

The Folks at Home 1952

14 The role of a do-gooder is not what actors call a fat part.

Ibid.

15 The whole flavor and quality of the American representative government turns to ashes on the tongue, if one regards the government as simply an inferior and rather second-rate sort of corporation.

Ibid.

16 What I know about money, I learned the hard way—by having had it.

Ibid.

1959. Annie Kenney (fl. 1910s)

1 . . . Paradise would be there once the vote* was won! I honestly believed every word I said. I had yet to learn that Nature's works are very slow but very sure. Experience is indeed the best though the sternest teacher.

Memoirs of a Militant 1924
*Woman's suffrage was granted in 1918 in Great Britain, subject to limitations; full enfranchisement came in 1928.

2 Prison. It was not a prison for me. Hunger-strikes. They had no fears for me. Cat and Mouse Act. I could have laughed. A prison cell was quiet—no telephone, no paper, no speeches, no sea sickness, no sleepless nights. I could lie on my plank bed all day and all night and return once more to my day dreams.

Ibid.

3 I was once told that the lesson I had to learn in life was patience. If that is true, I can only say I began life very badly indeed!

Ibid.

1960. Mary Keyserling (1910–1997)

1 Occupationally women are relatively more disadvantaged today than they were twenty-five years ago. . . . This deterioration has occurred despite the increase in women's share of total employment over the same period and the rising number of women who enroll in and graduate from institutions of higher education.

Windows on Day Care 1972

2 There shouldn't be a single little child in America left alone to fend for himself.

Ch. 2, Ibid.

3 Our ultimate goal as a nation should be to make available comprehensive, developmental childcare services to all families that wish to use them.

Ch. 9, Ibid.

1961. Elizabeth Layton (1910–1993)

1 I never did dislike the world. I just dislike myself.

Quoted in "A Hidden Talent" by Michael Ryan,
Parade Magazine 28 May 1989

2 There's a wonderful story. There was a little sparrow, lying out on the ground with his feet up in the air. Somebody asked him what he was doing, and he said, "The sky is going to fall." And this person said, "What do you think you can do about it?" And the little sparrow said, "One must do what one can."

Ibid.

1962. Alicia Markova (1910–)

1 . . . glorious bouquets and storms of applause. . . . These are the trimmings which every artist naturally enjoys. But to *move* an audience in such a role, to hear in the applause that unmistakable note which breaks through good theatre manners and comes from the heart, is to feel that you have won through to life itself. Such pleasure does not vanish with the fall of the curtain, but becomes part of one's own life.

Ch. 18, *Giselle and I 1960*

1963. Adeline Wanatee (1910–?)

1 Men have visions, women have children.

Oral interview (28 February 1980), Quoted in Ch. 2, *American Indian Women, Telling Their Lives* by Gretchen M. Bataille & Kathleen Mullen Sands 1984

1964. Margaret R. Wilcox (1910?–)

1 Children ask the world from us.

Women's Action of Nuclear Disarmament (WAND), Boston
n.d.

1965. Hsiang Chin-yu (fl. 1910s–1927)

1 . . . the emancipation of women can only come with a change in the social structure which frees men and women alike.

Quoted in *Women in Modern China* by
Helen Foster Snow* 1967
*See 1903.

1966. Frida Kahlo (1910–1954)

1 I never painted dreams. I painted my own reality.

Quoted in *Frida: A Biography of Frida Kahlo*
by Hayden Herrera 1983

2 I'd rather sit on the floor in the market of Toluca and sell tortillas, than to have anything to do with these "artistic" bitches of Paris. They sit for hours on the "cafes" warming their pre-

cious behinds, and talk without stopping about "culture" "art" "revolution" and so forth thinking themselves the gods of the world. . . . Gee whiz! It was worthwhile to come here only to see why Europe is rottening.

> Letter to Nikolas Muray (1939), Ibid.

3 If a masterpiece can be made only by a master and a master is defined as "a man having control or authority,": you can see what we're up against. Considering the history of slavery, we suggest changing the word to "massa" and "massa's piece."

> Quoted in *Confessions of the Guerilla Girls* by Guerilla Girls *1995*

1967. Elizabeth Gould Davis (1910–1974)

1 The deeper the archaeologists dig, the further back go the origins of man and society—and the less sure we are that civilization has followed the steady upward course so thoroughly believed in by the Victorians. It is more likely that the greatest civilizations of the past have yet to be discovered.

> Prologue, *The First Sex 1971*

2 Maleness remains a recessive genetic trait like color-blindness and hemophilia, with which it is linked. The suspicion that maleness is abnormal and that the Y chromosome is an accidental mutation boding no good for the race is strongly supported by the recent discoveries by the geneticists that congenital killers and criminals are possessed of not one but *two* Y chromosomes, bearing a double dose, as it were, of genetically undesired maleness.

> Pt. I, Ch. 1, Ibid.

3 When man substituted God for the Great Goddess he at the same time substituted authoritarian for humanistic values.

> Ch. 7, Ibid.

4 It is men, not women, who have promoted the cult of brute masculinity; and because men admire muscle and physical force, they assume that women do too.

> Pt. IV, Ch. 21, Ibid.

5 If the human race is unhappy today, as all modern philosophers agree that it is, it is only because it is uncomfortable in the mirror image society man has made—the topsy-turvy world in which nature's supporting pillar is forced to serve as the cornice of the architrave, while the cornice struggles to support the building.

> Ch. 22, Ibid.

1968. Joyce Phipps Grenfell (1910–1979)

1 They look quite promising in the shop; and not entirely without hope when I get them back into my wardrobe. But then, when I put them on they tend to deteriorate with a very strange rapidity and one feels so sorry for them.

> "Stately as a Galleon," *English Lit. 1978*

2 Progress everywhere today does seem to come so very heavily disguised as Chaos.

> Ibid.

1969. Pauli Murray (1910–1985)

1 The lesson of history that all human rights are indivisible and that the failure to adhere to this principle jeopardizes the rights of all is particularly applicable here. A built-in hazard of an aggressive ethnocentric movement which disregards the interests of other disadvantaged groups is that it will become

parochial and ultimately self-defeating in the face of hostile reactions, dwindling allies, and mounting frustrations.

> "The Liberation of Black Women" (p. 102), *Voices of the New Feminism*, Mary Lou Thompson, ed. *1970*

1970. Millicent Fenwick (1910–1992)

1 The curious fascination in this job* is the illusion that either you are being useful or you could be—and that's so tempting.

> *60 Minutes,* CBS-TV *1 February 1981*

*U.S. Representative.

2 When you're old, everything you do is sort of a miracle.

> Ibid.

3 Party organization matters. When the door of a smoke-filled room is closed, there's hardly ever a woman inside.

> Ibid.

4 It has been said that one man's loophole is another man's livelihood. Even if this is true, it certainly is not fair, because the loophole-livelihood of those who are reaping undeserved benefits can be the economic noose of those who are paying more than they should.

> *Speaking Up 1982*

5 Being old isn't for sissies.

> Quoted in obituary, *Seattle Post-Intelligencer 20 September 1992*

6 We cannot continue to deny American women the full rights and responsibilities of citizenship.

> Quoted by the National Women's Political Caucus *n.d.*

1971. Dorothy Crowfoot Hodgkin (1910–1994)

1 There are certain letters which I dread to open, and when I saw one from Buckingham Palace I left it sealed, fearing that they wanted to make me Dame Dorothy.

> Remark to Max Perutz, Quoted in his obituary of her, *The Independent* (London) *1994*

1972. Jessie Hawkes (1910–1996)

1 The young are now kinder than they were and are more tender towards old age, more aware perhaps with the growth of self-consciousness that it will come also to them.

> *A Land 1952*

2 We live in a world made seemingly secure by the four walls of our houses, the artificiality of our cities, and by the four walls of habit. Volcanoes speak of insecurity, of our participation in progress. They are openings not any longer into a properly appointed hell, but into an equally alarming abysm of thought.

> Ibid.

3 . . . we do in fact maintain our fragile lives on a wafer balanced between a hellish morass and unlimited space.

> Ibid.

4 . . . the universe is substantially homogeneous, and shooting stars are chips from globes very much like our own. They are, as the label in the Geological Museum soberly states, "fragments of former worlds."

> Ibid.

5 The only inequalities that matter begin in the mind. It is not income levels but differences in mental equipment that keep people apart, breed feelings of inferiority.

> Quoted in *New Statesman* (London) *January 1957*

6 This dedication to a Goddess involved also a glorification of the meaning of sex. Fertility and abundance were the purpose and the desire, sex was the instrument, and for this reason its symbols were everywhere.

Dawn of the Gods 1968

1973. Mother Teresa (1910–1997)

1 Loneliness and the feeling of being unwanted is the most terrible poverty.

Quoted in "Saints Among Us," *Time* (New York)
29 December 1975

2 Our intellect and other gifts have been given to be used for God's greater glory, but sometimes they become the very god for us. That is the saddest part: we are losing our balance when this happens. We must free ourselves to be filled by God. Even God cannot fill what is full.

Ibid.

3 To keep a lamp burning we have to keep putting oil in it.

Ibid.

4 Our work brings people face to face with love.

Ibid.

5 The poor are somehow or other—we ourselves.

"Who Are the Poor?," *Life in the Spirit*, Kathryn Spink, ed.
1986

6 The spiritual poverty of the western world is much greater than the physical poverty of our people.

Ibid.

7 Jesus loved every one, but he loved children most of all. Today we know that unborn children are the targets of destruction. We must thank our parents for wanting us, for loving us and for taking such good care of us.

Speech, Awakening Conference,
Colorado *15 June 1986*

8 I don't claim anything of the work. It is his work. I am like a little pencil in his hand. That is all. He does the thinking. He does the writing. The pencil has nothing to do with it. The pencil has only to be allowed to be used.

Ibid.

9 We have very little, so we have nothing to be preoccupied with. The more you have, the more you are occupied, the less you give. But the less you have, the more free you are. Poverty for us is a freedom.

Ibid.

10 The hunger for love is much more difficult to remove than the hunger for bread.

Ibid.

1974. Annie Dodge Wauneka (1910–1997)

1 I ask them [Navajo youth], "What is your biggest problem?" They tell me alcohol, drugs.

I ask them, "What is the most beautiful machine?" They tell me they don't know how to answer.

I tell them it's their heads, and they must not let alcohol and drugs ruin that machine.

Quoted in "'Our Mother' Shepherds a Nation of Navajos"
by Rusty Brown, *The Albuquerque Tribune 1 May 1984*

1975. Virginia Mae Axline (1911–1988)

1 Out again into the night where the dulled light obscures the decisive lines of reality and casts over the immediate world a kindly vagueness. . . . The darkened sky gives growing room for softened judgments, for suspended indictments, for emotional hospitality. What *is*, seen in such light, seems to have so many possibilities that definitiveness becomes ambiguous.

Ch. 2, *Dibs: In Search of Self 1965*

2 "So much to say. And so much not to say! Some things are better left unsaid. But so many unsaid things can become a burden."

Ch. 8, *Ibid.*

3 Asking questions in therapy would be so helpful if anyone ever answered them accurately. But no one ever does.

Ch. 12, *Ibid.*

1976. Sybille von Schoenbeck Bedford (1911–)

1 A part, a large part, of travelling is an engagement of the ego v. the world. . . . The world is hydra headed, as old as the rocks and as changing as the sea, enmeshed inextricably in its ways. The ego wants to arrive at places safely and on time.

"The Quality of Travel," *Esquire* (repr. in *As It Was*, 1990)
November 1961

1977. Hortense Calisher (1911–)

1 A happy childhood can't be cured. Mine'll hang around my neck like a rainbow, that's all, instead of a noose.

Pt. I, *Queenie 1971*

2 Every sixteen-year-old is a pornographer, Miss Piranesi. We had to know what was open to us.

Ibid.

3 But now, even to be anything anti-anti, you still have to do it with the body; anything purely mental is insincere. And I agree, oh, I agree—but why can I only do it mentally?

Ibid.

4 An *oeuvre* is a body of work which, like a true body, interacts with itself, and with its own growth. We here in America are not allowed the sweet sense of growing them in life; even after death, the obituary quickly picks over the works for "what will last." Yet if a writer's work has a shape to it—and most have a repetition like a heartbeat—the *oeuvre* will begin to construct him.

Pt. I, *Herself 1972*

5 . . . the circulation of money is different from the circulation of the blood. Some eras obscure that; not that it was nakedly appearing. I began to understand why the banker had jumped. A circulatory failure.

Ibid.

6 She [Colette*] is no more essentially feminine as a writer than any man is essentially masculine as a writer—certain notable attempts at the latter notwithstanding. She uses the psychological and concrete dossier in her possession as a woman, not only without embarrassment but with the most natural sense of its value, and without any confusion as to whether the sexual balance of her sensitivity need affect the virility of her expression when she wants virility there. Reading her, one is reminded that art—whether managed as a small report on a wide canvas or vice versa—is a narrow thing in more senses than one, and that the woman writer, like any other,

does her best to accept her part in the human condition, and go on from there.

Pt. II, Ibid.

*See 1341.

7 Every art is a church without communicants, presided over by a parish of the respectable. An artist is born kneeling; he fights to stand. A critic, by nature of the judgement seat, is born sitting.

Pt. IV, Ibid.

8 When anything gets freed, a zest goes round the world.

Ibid.

9 When you come to the end of the past—no more peroration. Tolerate life—a poem which annoys when it falls into grandeur. The past will come round again.

Pt. V, Ibid.

1978. Raya Dunayevskaya (1911?–1987)

1 Ever since the myth of Eve giving Adam the apple was created, women have been presented as devils or as angels, but definitely not as human beings.

"We Speak in Many Voices," *Notes on Women's Liberation 1970*

2 It is not labor or "socialism" which acted as catalyst for . . . The anti-war movement and, indeed, gave birth to a whole new generation of revolutionaries, but the black revolution which was both catalyst and reason, *and continue to be that ceaseless movement today.*

Ibid.

3 The first act of liberation is to demand back our own heads.

Ibid.

1979. Josephine Miles (1911–1985)

1 All our footsteps, set to make
Metric advance,
Lapse into arcs in deference
To circumstance.

"On Inhabiting an Orange," St. 2, *Poems (1930–1960) 1960*

2 This weight of knowledge dark on the brain is never
To be burnt out like fever.

"*Physiologus*," St. 2, Ibid.

3 Where is the world? not about.
The world is in the heart
And the heart is closed in the sea lanes out of port.

"Merchant Marine," St. 1, Ibid.

4 How conduct in its pride
Maintains a place and sits
At the head of the table at the head of the hall
At the head of the hosts and guests.

"Conduct," St. 1, Ibid.

5 I chewed on a straw hoping it would get sweeter.
It got drier and drier
And gradually caught on fire.

"Loser," St. 2, Ibid.

6 My pride should affect your escape.
It carries every key.

Its own trusty, and a good chiseling trusty,
It can at its own price set everybody free.

"Pride," St. 1, Ibid.

7 Little things make Germany a lovely place. . . .

"Germany," *House and Home 1961*

8 Accustomed as we are to change, or unaccustomed, we think of a change of heart, of clothes, of life, with some uncertainty. We put off the old, put on the new, yet say that the more it changes the more it remains the same. Every age is an age of transition.

Introduction, *Poetry and Change 1974*

9 True, translation may use the value terms of its own tongue in its own time; but it cannot force these on a truly alien text.

Ch. 12, Ibid.

1980. Matilda White Riley (1911–)

1 People are aging better than they used to. Already about one-third of the average American's adult life is spent in retirement. A structural revolution is needed.

"Matilda Riley's revolution," *AARP Bulletin*, Vol. 33, No. 11 *December 1992*

2 There shouldn't be a certain age for learning, a certain age for working and a certain age for retiring.

Ibid.

3 I see a society where the structural revolution has provided more choices and more varied roles for older people. A society where lifelong learning replaces the lockstep of traditional education, a society where the burdens of the middle generation are spread over the life course.

Ibid.

1981. Anna Russell (1911–)

1 The reason that there are so few women comics is that so few women can bear being laughed at.

Quoted in *The Sunday Times* (London) *25 August 1957*

1982. Barbara Castle (1911–)

In politics, guts is all.

The Castle Diaries 1974–1976 1980

1983. Viola Spolin (1911?–)

1 Through spontaneity we are re-formed into ourselves. It creates an explosion that for the moment frees us from handed-down frames of reference, memory choked with old facts and information and undigested theories and techniques of other people's findings. Spontaneity is the moment of personal freedom when we are faced with reality, and see it, explore it and act accordingly. In this reality the bits and pieces of ourselves function as an organic whole. It is the time of discovery, of experiencing, of creative expression.

Ch. 1, *Improvisation for the Theater 1963*

2 We learn through experience and experiencing, and no one teaches anyone anything. This is as true for the infant moving from kicking to crawling to walking as it is for the scientist with his equations. If the environment permits it, anyone can learn whatever he chooses to learn; and if the individual permits it, the environment will teach him everything it has to teach.

Ibid.

3 In a culture where approval/disapproval has become the predominant regulator of effort and position, and often the substitute for love, our personal freedoms are dissipated.

Ibid.

4 It stands to reason that if we direct all our efforts towards reaching a goal, we stand in grave danger of losing everything on which we have based our daily activities. For when a goal is superimposed on an activity instead of evolving out of it, we often feel cheated when we reach it.

Ibid.

5 The audience is the most revered member of the theater. Without an audience there is no theater. . . . They are our guests, our evaluators, and the last spoke in the wheel which can then begin to roll. They make the performance meaningful.

Ibid.

6 It is the avant-garde teachers who . . . have come to realize that body release, not body control, is what is needed for natural grace to emerge, as opposed to artificial movement.

Ch. 5, Ibid.

7 There are few places outside his own play where a child can contribute to the world in which he finds himself. His world: dominated by adults who tell him what to do and when to do it—benevolent tyrants who dispense gifts to their "good" subjects and punishment to their "bad" ones, who are amused at the "cleverness" of children and annoyed by their "stupidities."

Ch. 13, Ibid.

8 The physical is the known; through it we may find our way to the unknown, the intuitive, and perhaps beyond that to man's spirit itself.

Quoted in "Spolin Game Plan for Improvisational Theater" by Barry Hyams, *The Los Angeles Times* 26 May *1974*

9 One must be chary of words because they turn into cages.

Ibid.

10 First teach a person to develop to the point of his limitations and then—pfft!—break the limitation.

Ibid.

1984. Kay Thompson (1911–1999)

1 The Plaza is the only hotel in New York that will allow you to have a turtle.

Eloise; a book for precocious grown-ups 1955

2 There is absolutely nothing but rooms in the Plaza.

Ibid.

3 Getting bored is not allowed.

Ibid.

1985. Yang Chiang (1911–)

1 SHEN. In the spring the flower blooms in the sun, the spring breeze blows it away where it will—ideals, love: they're nothing more than spring sunlight and spring breeze. Tomorrow that blossom will fall to earth, sprout, grow roots, nothing more than seed—if the environment lets it live. . . . There are botanical types that don't know their place. Here they fly, there they fly, thinking they have so much strength, that they're in charge! The law-abiding ones, like rice and wheat, have already quietly let themselves rot in the soil and turn into fertilizer for the next generation.

Act I, Fen hsü (Windswept Blossoms) 1946

1986. Hsiao Hung (1911–1941)

1 "I've never abused her all the time she's been in my home. Where else will you find another family that has not abused its child-bride by giving her beatings and tongue lashings all day long? Now I may have beaten her a little, just to get her started off on the right foot, and I only did that for a little over a month. Maybe I beat her pretty severely sometimes, but how was I expected to make a well-mannered girl out of her without being severe once in a while? Believe me, I didn't enjoy beating her so hard, what with all her screaming and carrying on. But I was doing it for her own good, because if I didn't beat her hard, she'd never be good for anything."

"The Child Bride," *Tales of the Hulan River*, Howard Goldblatt, tr. *1940*

2 "Each of the 360 trades in this world of ours has its share of miseries."

Ibid.

1987. Leah Goldberg (1911–1970)

1 There is a law of life in her hands milking,
For quiet seamen hold a rope like her.

"Of Bloom," Pt. II, St. 2, *Poems from the Hebrew*, Robert Mezey, ed. *1973*

2 Land of low clouds, I belong to you.
I carry in my heart your every drop of rain.

"Song of the Strange Woman," Pt. III, St. 1, *Ibid.*

1988. Mahalia Jackson (1911–1972)

1 It's easy to be independent when you've got money. But to be independent when you haven't got a thing—that's the Lord's test.

Ch. 1, Movin' On Up, with Evan McLoud Wylie 1966

2 Gospel music in those days of the early 1930s was really taking wing. It was the kind of music colored people had left behind them down south and they liked it because it was just like a letter from home.

Ch. 5, Ibid.

3 Blues are the songs of despair, but gospel songs are the songs of hope.

Ch. 6, Ibid.

4 Someday the sun is going to shine down on me in some faraway place.

Quoted in "Unforgettable Mahalia Jackson" by Mildred Falls, *Reader's Digest March 1973*

5 The grass is still green. The lawns are as neat as ever. The same birds are still in the trees. I guess it didn't occur to them to leave just because we moved in.

Ibid.

1989. Ruth McKenney (1911–1972)

1 If modern civilization had any meaning it was displayed in the fight against Fascism.

Letter to George Seldes, *The Great Quotations*, George Seldes, ed. *1960*

2   Man has no nobler function than to defend the truth.

Ibid.

1990. Rosalind Russell (1911–1976)

1   . . . taste. You cannot buy such a rare and wonderful thing. You can't send away for it in a catalogue. And I'm afraid it's becoming obsolete.

Quoted in "Rosalind Russell: Screen's Career Career Girl,"
The Los Angeles Times 31 March 1974

2   Sex for sex's sake on the screen seems childish to me, but it's violence that really bothers me. I think it's degrading. It breeds something cancerous in our young people. We have a great responsibility to the future in what we're communicating.

Ibid.

3   The sex symbol always remains, but the sophisticated woman has become old hat.

Ibid.

1991. Elizabeth Bishop (1911–1979)

1   It is like what we imagine knowledge to be:
dark, salt, clear, moving, utterly free,
drawn from the cold hard mouth
of the world, derived from the rocky breast
forever, flowing and drawn, and since
our knowledge is historical, flowing, and flow.

"At the Fishhouses," *A Cold Spring* 1955

2   The Seven Wonders of the World are tired
and a touch familiar, but the other scenes,
innumerable, though equally sad and still, are foreign.

"Over 2000 Illustrations and a Complete Concordance,"
Ibid.

3   Icebergs behoove the soul
(Both being self-made from elements least visible)
to see themselves: fleshed, fair, erected indivisible.

"The Imaginary Iceberg," *North and South* 1955

4   We stand as still as stones to watch the leaves and ripples
while light and nervous water hold their interview.

"*Quai d'Orleans*," Ibid.

5   Time is an *Etoile*; the hours diverge
so much that days are journeys round the suburbs,
circles surrounding stars, overlapping circles.

"Paris, 7 A.M.," Ibid.

6   Democracy in the contemporary world demands, among other things, an educated and informed people. Up until now, Brazil has not had one. Illiteracy, slow communication, and a consequent lack of awareness among the people have made it possible for determined groups of men to control the affairs of the country without the general consent—even the knowledge—of the Brazilian people as a whole.

Ch. 9, *Brazil* 1962

7   Brazilians are very quick, both emotionally and physically. Like the heroes of Homer, men can show their emotions without disgrace.

Ch. 1, Ibid.

8   The masses of poor people in the big cities, and the poor and not-so-poor of the "backlands," love their children and kill them with kindness by the thousands. The wrong foods, spoiled foods, warm medicines, sleeping syrups—all exact a terrible toll. . . .

Ibid.

9   Apparently they have reached their destination.
It would be hard to say what brought them here,
commerce or contemplation.

"Large Bad Picture," St. 9,
Questions of Travel 1965

10   You left North Haven, anchored in its rock,
afloat in mystic blue . . . And now, you've left
for good. You can't derange, or rearrange,
your poems again. (But the sparrows can their song.)
The words won't change again. Sad friend, you cannot change.

"North Haven (in memoriam—Robert Lowell)," St. 6, Ibid.

11   For Time is nothing if not amenable.

"Shampoo," St. 2, Ibid.

12   There is a magic made by melody:
A spell of rest, and quiet breath, and cool
Heart, that sinks through fading colors deep
To the subaqueous stillness of the sea,

Sonnet, Ibid.

13   Should we have stayed at home and thought of here?
Where should we be today?
Is it right to be watching strangers in a play
in this strangest of theatres?

"Questions of Travel," Ibid.

14   What childishness is it that while there's breath of life
in our bodies, we are determined to rush
to see the sun the other way around?

Ibid.

15   these regions now have little to say for themselves
except in thousands of light song-sparrow songs floating upward
freely, dispassionately, through the mist, and meshing
in brown-wet, fine torn fish-nets.

"Cape Breton," St. 3, *The Complete Poems 1927–1979*
1983

16   Why should I be my aunt,
or me, or anyone?
What similarities—
boots, hands, the family voice
I felt in my throat, or even
the National Geographic
and those awful hanging breasts—
held us all together
or made us all just one?

"In the Waiting Room," St. 4, Ibid.

17   The waves are running in verses this fine morning.

"Invitation to Miss Marianne Moore,"* St. 2, Ibid.
*See 1560.

18   Come with the pointed toe of each black shoe
trailing a sapphire highlight,
with a black capeful of butterfly wings and bon-mots,
with heaven knows how many angels all riding
on the broad black brim of your hat,
please come flying.

St. 3, Ibid.

19 The art of losing isn't hard to master
    so many things seem filled with the intent
    to be lost that their loss is no disaster.
    > "One Art," St. 1, Ibid.

20 The whole shadow of Man is only as big as his hat,
    > "The Man Moth," St. 1, Ibid.

21 the sweet peas cling
    to their wet white string
    on the whitewashed fences;
    bumblebees creep
    inside the foxgloves,
    and evening commences.
    > "The Moose," St. 9, Ibid.

22 I think that when something like that happens I'm so over-come with remorse, before I even get drunk, that that's why I get to feeling so damned sick—and it's much more the mental aftermath than the physical.
    > Letter, *One Art*, Robert Giroux, ed. 1994

23 I sometimes wish that I had nothing, or little more, to do but write letters to the people who are not here.
    > Letter (c. 1930), Ibid.

1992. Lucille Ball (1911–1989)

1 Luck? I don't know anything about luck. I've never banked on it, and I'm afraid of people who do. Luck to me is something else: Hard work—and realizing what is an opportunity and what isn't.
    > Quoted in Ch. 1, *The Real Story of Lucille Ball*
    > by Eleanor Harris 1954

2 I think knowing what you can *not* do is more important than knowing what you can do. In fact, that's good taste.
    > Ch. 7, Ibid.

3 I expected to only do the show for a year and then have some, like, home movies to show the baby that I had just had.*
    > "100 Years of Great Women," *ABC News Special*
    > *with Barbara Walters* 30 April 1999
    *Reference to *I Love Lucy*, a television comedy that ran from 1951 to 1956.

1993. Julia Child (1912–)

1 Sometimes . . . It takes me an entire day to write a recipe, to communicate it correctly. It's really like writing a little short story.
    > Quoted in "The Making of a Masterpiece" by Patricia
    > Simon, *McCall's* October 1970

2 Learn how to cook! That's the way to save money. You don't save it buying hamburger helpers, and prepared food; you save it buying fresh foods in season or in large supply, when they are cheapest and usually best, and you prepare them from scratch at home. Why pay for someone else's work, when if you know how to do it, you can save all that money for yourself?
    > Introduction, *Julia Child's Kitchen* 1975

1994. Lucille Fletcher (1912–1973)

1 Such amazing things happen to the female sex on an ocean cruise. The sea air acted like an aphrodisiac. Or maybe it was the motion. Or the carnival atmosphere. Whatever it was, and he had never seen it otherwise, the ladies, married or single,

young or old, simply went to pieces aboard the S.S. *Columbia*. They toppled like tenpins—into bed.
    > Ch. 2, *The Girl in Cabin B54* 1968

2 "The brain, of course, is still an unknown country in many re-spects—like outer space. And as a psychologist, I myself can believe that certain people, extraordinarily sensitive people, may possess special mental equipment which can tune in, as it were, certain waves, vibrations, even imagery, which other people cannot sense at all."
    > Ch. 8, Ibid.

1995. Martha Wright Griffiths (1912–)

1 This amendment [the Equal Rights Amendment*], if passed, would be like a beacon which should awaken nine sleeping Rip Van Winkles to the fact that the twentieth century is pass-ing into history. It is a different world and they [the Supreme Court] should speak for justice, not prejudice. . . . I seek jus-tice, not in some distant tomorrow, not in some study commission, but now while I live.
    > Quoted in *American Political Women*
    > by Esther Stineman 1980
    *See Alice Paul, 1538.

2 My grandmother wanted to live long enough to vote for a woman president. I'll be satisfied if I live to see a woman go before the Supreme Court and hear the justices acknowledge, "Gentlemen, she's human. She deserves the protection of our laws."
    > Ibid.

1996. Lady Bird Johnson (1912–)

1 It all began so beautifully. After a drizzle in the morning, the sun came out bright and clear. We were driving into Dallas. In the lead car were President and Mrs. Kennedy. . . .
    > (22 November 1963),* *A White House Diary* 1970
    *The day John F. Kennedy, 35th president of the United States, was assassinated.

2 It's odd that you can get so anesthetized by your own pain or your own problem that you don't quite fully share the hell of someone close to you.
    > (8 February 1964), Ibid.

3 As I record this several days later, I must say that being with President Truman* those days has been one of the biggest pluses of this period of my life. It has been an insight into his-tory for me, a joy to see a man who has lived through so much public rancor and condemnation and has emerged philo-sophic, salty, completely unembittered, a happy man—and vindicated by history on most of his major decisions.
    > (12 March 1964), Ibid.
    *Harry S. T—, politician (1884–1972); 33rd president of the United States (1945–1953).

4 The first lady is, and always has been, an unpaid public ser-vant elected by one person, her husband.
    > (14 March 1968), Ibid.

5 This was one of those terrific, pummeling White House days that can stretch and grind and use you—even I, who only live on the periphery. So what must it be like for Lyndon!*
    > Ibid.
    *Lyndon Baines Johnson (1908–1973), 36th president of the United States (1963–69).

6 Lyndon [Johnson] acts like there was never going to be tomorrow.

(29 November 1964), Quoted in
The New York Times Magazine 1970

7 I've had a long love affair with the environment. It is my sustenance, my pleasure, my joy. Flowers in a city are like lipstick on a woman—it just makes you look better to have a little color.

Quoted in *Time* (New York) *5 September 1989*

1997. Dena Justin (1912–)

1 Mythologically speaking, the ancients scooped our modern-day biologists by unknown thousands of years in their recognition of the female principle as the primal creative force. And they too buried the truth, restructuring the myths to accommodate male ideology.

"From Mother Goddess to Dishwasher,"
Natural History February 1973

2 Although the witch, incarnate or in surrogate mother disguise, remains a universal bogey, pejorative aspects of the wizard, her masculine counterpart, have vanished over the patriarchal centuries. The term *wizard* has acquired reverential status—wizard of finance, wizard of diplomacy, wizard of science.

Ibid.

3 It is remarkable how many legends survive among preliterate cultures of an earlier matriarchal period and a violent uprising by men in which they usurped female authority.

Ibid.

4 The earth Mother, the womb from which all living things are born and to which all return at death, was perhaps the earliest representation of the divine in protohistoric religions.

Ibid.

1998. Mary Lavin (1912–1996)

1 "Take my own father! You know what he said in his last moments? On his deathbed, he defied me to name a man who had enjoyed a better life. In spite of the dreadful pain, his face *radiated* happiness!" said Mother, nodding her head comfortably. "Happiness drives out pain, as fire burns out fire."

"Happiness," *The New Yorker 14 December 1968*

2 Our father, while he lived, had cast a magic over everything, for us as well as for her. He held his love up over us like an umbrella and kept off the troubles that afterward came down on us, pouring cats and dogs!

Ibid.

3 "Life is a vale of tears," they said. "You are privileged to find it out so young!" Ugh! After I staggered onto my feet and began to take hold of life once more, they fell back defeated. And the first day I gave a laugh—pouf, they were blown out like candles. They weren't living in a real world at all; they belonged to a ghostly world where life was easy: all one had to do was sit and weep. It takes effort to push back the stone from the mouth of the tomb.

Ibid.

4 Her theme was happiness: what it was, what it was not; where we might find it, where not; and how, if found, it must be guarded. Never must we confound it with pleasure. Nor think sorrow its exact opposite.

Ibid.

5 . . . a new noise started in her head; the noise of a nameless panic that did not always roar, but never altogether died down.

"Via Violetta," *A Memory and Other Stories 1972*

1999. Pat Nixon (1912–1993)

1 I have sacrificed everything in my life that I consider precious in order to advance the political career of my husband.

Quoted in *Women at Work* by Betty Medsger *1975*

2000. Ann Petry (1908–)

1 It took me quite a while to realize that there were fashions in literary criticism and that they shifted and changed much like the fashions in women's hats.

"The Novel as Social Criticism," *The Writer's Book*,
Helen Hull, ed. *1950*

2 It seems to me that all truly great art is propaganda. . . .

Ibid.

3 Time that enemy of labels...

Ibid.

4 I told myself that if I were a maker of perfumes I would make one and call it "Spring," and it would smell like this cool, sweet, early-morning air and I would let only beautiful young brown girls use it, and if I could sing I would sing like the song sparrow and I would let only beautiful young brown boys hear me.

"The New Mirror," *Miss Muriel and Other Stories 1971*

2001. Anne Barbara Ridler (1912–)

1 CRANMER. A scholar, you know, is a wingless creature
More tortoise than bird.
MARGARET. But with a bird's domain...

Sc. 1, *The Trial of Thomas Cranmer 1956*

2 And when our baby stirs and struggles to be born
It compels humility: what we began
Is now its own.

"For a Child Expected" *n.d.*

2002. May Sarton (1912–1995)

1 Learning is such a very painful business. It requires humility from people at an age where the natural habit is arrogance.

The Small Room 1961

2 Excellence costs a great deal.

Ibid.

3 It's hard to be growing up in this climate where sex at its most crude and cold is O.K. but feeling is somehow indecent.

Mrs. Stevens Hears the Mermaids Singing 1965

4 The Lord is not my shepherd. I shall want.

Ibid.

5 We are all monsters, if it comes to that, we women who have chosen to be something more and something less than women.

Ibid.

6 "There was such a thing as women's work and it consisted chiefly, Hilary sometimes thought, in being able to stand constant interruption and keep your temper. . . ."

Ibid.

7 Women's work is always toward wholeness.

Ibid.

8 Women have moved and shaken me, but I have been nourished by men.

Ibid.

9 True feeling justifies, whatever it may cost.

Ibid.

10 The poet must be free to love or hate as the spirit moves him, free to change, free to be a chameleon, free to be an enfant terrible. He must above all never worry about his effect on other people. Power requires that one do just that all the time. Power requires that the inner person never be unmasked. No, we poets have to go naked. And since this is so, it is better that we stay private people; a naked public person would be rather ridiculous, what?

Pt. 2, *Ibid.*

11 The creative person, the person who moves from an irrational source of power, has to face the fact that this power antagonizes. Under all the superficial praise of the "creative" is the desire to kill. It is the old war between the mystic and the non-mystic, a war to the death.

Ibid.

12 May we agree that private life is irrelevant? Multiple, mixed, ambiguous at best—out of it we try to fashion the crystal clear, the singular, the absolute, and that is what is relevant; that is what matters.

Ibid.

13 The woman who needs to create works of art is born with a kind of psychic tension in her which drives her unmercifully to find a way to balance, to make herself whole. Every human being has this need: in the artist it is mandatory. Unable to fulfill it, he goes mad. But when the artist is a woman she fulfills it at the expense of herself as a woman.

Ibid.

14 It is the privilege of those who fear love to murder those who do not fear it!

Ibid.

15 A man with a talent does what is expected of him, makes his way, constructs, is an engineer, a composer, a builder of bridges. It's the natural order of things that he construct objects outside himself and his family. The woman who does so is aberrant. . . . We have to *expiate* for this cursed talent someone handed out to us, by mistake, in the black mystery of genetics.

Ibid.

16 Self-respect is nothing to hide behind. When you need it most it isn't there.

"Epilogue: Mar", *Ibid.*

17 The strange effect of all these "lovers" is to make me feel not richer, but impoverished and mean.

Journal of a Solitude 1973

18 I would predicate that in all great works of genius masculine and feminine elements in the personality find expression, whether this androgynous nature is played out sexually or not.

Ibid.

19 My faults too have been those of excess; I too have made emotional demands, without being aware of what I was asking; I too have imagined that I was giving when I was battering at someone for attention.

Ibid.

20 I think men do not want women poets to talk about their feelings. It's the *feminine* poet men don't like.

Quoted in *May Sarton: A Biography* by Margot Peters 1997

21 One of the things I have got to find out is why love for me has always been a *wound*.

Ibid.

22 I don't think I shall ever be destroyed by emotion; it is my business to build into it.

Ibid.

23 I know my biographer will be my enemy.

Cited in "Licking her wounds" by Brenda Wineapple, *The Women's Review of Books*, Vol. XIV, No. 8 *May 1997*

2003. Kate Simon (1912–1990)

1 Girls' prayers counted for nothing; like animals, they had no souls and no voices to God's ear.

Bronx Primitive: Portraits in A Childhood 1982

2 One assumes that foreign ladies, English and Americans particularly, because they are tremulous, neurotic bags of bones reduced by sexual malnutrition, find all Italians irresistible.

Italy: The Places In Between n.d.

3 Here I stand, hobbled in a sack of doom, determined to tear out of it, knowing that I will.

A Wider World: Portraits in Adolescence 1986

4 I had no time for step-by-step projects; the urgent need was for swift voyages, with short stops at many ports of call.

Ibid.

5 The susurrus of silks dragging through pools of blood, chivalric elegance living with bestiality in high places, the silver rose boxed with the dagger, fidelity bedded with perfidy, remain a collage whose fascination has never quite faded.

A Renaissance Tapestry: The Gonzaga of Mantua 1988

6 Her impressive knowledge of Virgil, every line, didn't matter, nor did her command of Greek, and so what if she could explain the propositions of Euclid? Her vocation was marriage.

Ibid.

7 His new rules [Cardinal Ercole] called for severe restrictions in the consumption of peacocks, pheasants, and other game birds; only two kinds of roast and poultry were to be served at one time; no fish or oysters were to be offered with meats; dishes were not to be ornamented with figurines, fine inlays, bits of gold, as was the court custom.

Ibid.

2004. Claire Trevor (1912–2000)

1 What a holler would ensue if people had to pay the minister as much to marry them as they have to pay a lawyer to get them a divorce.

Quoted in *New York Journal-American 12 October 1960*

2005. Charleszetta Waddles (1912–)

1 You can't give people pride, but you can provide the kind of understanding that makes people look to their inner strengths and find their own sense of pride.

> Quoted in "Mother Waddles: Black Angel of the Poor" by Lee Edson, *Reader's Digest October 1972*

2 God knows no distance.

> Ibid.

2006. Pamela Hansford Johnson (1912–1981)

1 There are few things more disturbing than to find, in somebody we detest, a moral quality which seems to us demonstrably superior to anything we ourselves possess. It augurs not merely an unfairness on the part of creation, but a lack of artistic judgement. . . . Sainthood is acceptable only in saints.

> Ch. 23, *Night and Silence, Who is Here?— An American Comedy 1963*

2 You slam a politician, you make out he's the devil, with horns and hoofs. But his wife loves him, and so did all his mistresses.

> Ibid.

3 We demand that people should be true to the pictures we have of them, no matter how repulsive those pictures may be: we prefer the true portrait (as we have conceived it), in all its homogeneity, to one with a detail added which refuses to fit in.

> Ibid.

2007. Amalia Fleming (1912–1986)

1 So much sorrow should certainly not come to a man who has given so much of value to humanity.

> Letter to Ben May (5 November 1949), Quoted in *The Life of Sir Alexander Fleming** by André Maurois *1959*
> *English bacteriologist (1881–1955).

2 I am working on a problem which fascinates me but I keep failing to do what I try. Still there is an end even to failures.

> (December 1954), Ibid.

3 He, too, I thought, possesses, like Pasteur, and in the highest degree, the art of choosing the crucial experiment and of grasping the capital importance of a chance observation. . . . But . . . for Fleming there was a wide world lying beyond the confines of his lab. The appearance of a new flower in his garden was as interesting to him as the work he might be engaged on. . . . [He] felt himself to be an infinitesimal part of nature, and from that feeling was born his refusal to indulge in self-importance and his dislike of big words. It was almost possible to say that he was a genius in spite of himself, and reluctantly.

> Ch. 16, Ibid.

4 I respect every idealogy, including communism, provided they are not trying to impose their will through force. I am against any totalitarian regime.

> Quoted in *Newsweek* (New York) 11 October *1971*

5 The innocent people who have nothing to say are tortured the most because when a prisoner admits something, the torture stops.

> Quoted in "Greece: Survival of the Shrewdest" by Susan Margolis, *Ms.* (New York) *October 1973*

2008. Madeline Bingham (1912–1988)

1 In every country the organization of society is like a section of a rock face, with new layers and old layers built one upon the other. The decay of old ways of behaving and old laws does not take place within a few years; it is a gradual process of erosion.

> Ch. 2, *Scotland Under Mary Stuart** 1971
> *See 339.

2 Once the fervour has gone out of it, a revolution can turn out to be dull work for the ordinary people.

> Ch. 7, Ibid.

3 A country which is engaged in constant war, both internal and external, does not provide good ground in which the arts may flourish.

> Ch. 12, Ibid.

4 Too many cooks may spoil the broth, but it only takes one to burn it.

> *The Bad Cook's Guide n.d.*

5 There may be as many good fish in the sea as ever came out of it, but cooking them is even more difficult than catching them.

> Ibid.

2009. Mary McCarthy (1912–1989)

1 I felt caught in a dilemma that was new to me then but which since has become horribly familiar: the trap of adult life, in which you are held, wriggling, powerless to act because you can see both sides. On that occasion, as generally in the future, I compromised.

> *Memories of a Catholic Girlhood 1946*

2 The American, if he has a spark of national feeling, will be humiliated by the very prospect of a foreigner's visit to Congress—these, for the most part, illiterate hacks whose fancy vests are spotted with gravy, and whose speeches, hypocritical, unctuous, and slovenly, are spotted also with the gravy of political patronage, these persons are a reflection on the democratic process rather than of it; they expose it in its underwear.

> "America the Beautiful," *Commentary* (New York) *September 1947*

3 The immense popularity of American movies abroad demonstrates that Europe is the unfinished negative of which America is the proof.

> Ibid.

4 The strongest argument for the un-materialistic character of American life is the fact that we tolerate conditions that are, from a negative point of view, intolerable. What the foreigner finds most objectionable in American life is its lack of basic comfort. No nation with any sense of material well-being would endure the food we eat, the cramped apartments we live in, the noise, the traffic, the crowded subways and buses. American life, in large cities, is a perpetual assault on the senses and the nerves; it is out of asceticism, out of unworldliness, precisely, that we bear it.

> Ibid.

5 The happy ending is our national belief.

> Ibid.

6 In verity . . . we are the poor. This humanity we would claim for ourselves is the legacy, not only of the Enlightenment, but

of the thousands and thousands of European peasants and poor townspeople who came here bringing their humanity and their sufferings with them. It is the absence of a stable upper class that is responsible for much of the vulgarity of the American scene. Should we blush before the visitor for this deficiency?

Ibid.

7 . . . freedom to criticize is held to compensate for the freedom to err—this is the American system...One is assured, gently, that one has the freedom to criticize, as though this freedom, *in itself*, as it attaches to a single individual, counterbalanced the unjust law on the books. This sacred right of criticism is always invoked whenever abuses are mentioned, just as the free circulation of ideas and works of art is offered as evidence of a basic cultural freedom.

"No News, or What Killed the Dog,"
The Reporter July 1952

8 . . . Elinor was always firmly convinced of other people's hypocrisy since she could not believe that they noticed less than she did.

Ch. 1, *The Group 1954*

9 "You mustn't force sex to do the work of love or love to do the work of sex."

Ch. 2, Ibid.

10 Despite the fact that she had had no sexual experience, she had a very clear idea of the male member, and she could not help forming a picture of Put's as pale and lifeless, in the coffin of his trousers, a veritable *nature morte*.

Ch. 6, Ibid.

11 "Medicine seems to be all cycles," continued Mrs. Hartshorn. "That's the bone I pick with Sloan. Like what's his name's new theory of history. First we nursed our babies; then science told us not to. Now it tells us we were right in the first place. Or were we wrong then but would be right now? Reminds me of relativity, if I understand Mr. Einstein."

Ch. 10, Ibid.

12 She had tried to bind him with possessions, but he slipped away like Houdini.

Ch. 13, Ibid.

13 Sometimes she felt that he was postponing being a success till he could wear out her patience; as soon as she gave up and left him, his name would mock her in lights.

Ibid.

14 The things of this world reveal their essential absurdity when they are put in the Venetian context. In the unreal realm of the canals, as in a Swiftian Lilliput, the real world, with its contrivances, appears as a vast folly.

Ch. 1, *Venice Observed 1956*

15 A wholly materialistic city is nothing but a dream incarnate. Venice is the world's unconscious, a miser's glittering hoard, guarded by a Beast whose eyes are made of white agate, and by a saint who is really a prince who has just slain a dragon.

Ch. 2, Ibid.

16 Labor is work that leaves no trace behind it when it is finished, or if it does, as in the case of the tilled field, this product of human activity requires still more labor, incessant, tireless labor, to maintain its identity as a "work" of man.

"The *Vita Activa*," *The New Yorker 18 October 1958*

17 Bureaucracy, the rule of no one, has become the modern form of despotism.

Ibid.

18 There are no new truths, but only truths that have not been recognized by those who have perceived them without noticing. A truth is something that everybody can be shown to know and to have known, as people say, all along.

Ibid.

19 The labor of keeping house is labor in its most naked state, for labor is toil that never finishes, toil that has to be begun again the moment it is completed, toil that is destroyed and consumed by the life process.

Ibid.

20 When an American heiress wants to buy a man, she at once crosses the Atlantic.

On The Contrary 1961

21 In violence we forget who we are.

Pt. 3, "Characters in Fiction" (1961), Ibid.

22 Anti-Semitism is a horrible disease from which nobody is immune, and it has a kind of evil fascination that makes an enlightened person draw near the source of infection, supposedly in a scientific spirit, but really to sniff the vapors and dally with the possibility.

Pt. 3, "Settling the Colonel's Hash," Ibid.

23 An unrectified case of injustice has a terrible way of lingering restlessly, in the social atmosphere like an unfinished question.

"My Confession," Ibid.

24 Every age has a keyhole to which its eye is pasted.

Ibid.

25 The horror of Gandhi's* murder lies not in the political motives behind it or in its consequences for Indian policy or for the future of non-violence; the horror lies simply in the fact that any man could look into the face of this extraordinary person and deliberately pull a trigger.

Pt. 1, "Gandhi" (1949), Ibid.

*Mohandas G—, Indian nationalist leader and father of nonviolent resistance; assassinated (1869–1948).

26 The Crucifixion and other historical precedents notwithstanding, many of us still believe that outstanding goodness is a kind of armor, that virtue, seen plain and bare, gives pause to criminality. But perhaps it is the other way around.

Ibid.

27 A society person who is enthusiastic about modern painting or Truman Capote is already half a traitor to his class. It is middle-class people who, quite mistakenly, imagine that a lively pursuit of the latest in reading and painting will advance their status in the world.

Pt. 2, "Up the Ladder from *Charm* to *Vogue*" (1950), Ibid.

28 Liberty, as it is conceived by current opinion, has nothing inherent about it; it is a sort of gift or trust bestowed on the individual by the state pending good behavior.

Speech, "The Contagion of Ideas" (1952), Ibid.

29 Maybe any action becomes cowardly once you stop to reason about it. Conscience doth make cowards of us all, eh, *mamma mia*? If you start an argument with yourself, that makes two

people at least, and when you have two people, one of them starts appeasing the other.

"Epistle from Mother Carey's Chicken,"
Birds of America 1965

30 Being abroad makes you conscious of the whole imitative side of human behavior. The ape in man.

Ibid.

31 He had never outgrown the feeling that a quest for information was a series of maneuvers in a game of espionage.

"Winter Visitors," Ibid.

32 In politics, it seems, retreat is honorable if dictated by military considerations and shameful if even <i>suggested</i> for ethical reasons.

"Solutions," Vietnam 1967

33 . . . Americans do not dissemble what they are up to. They do not seem to feel the need, except through verbiage, <i>e.g.</i>, napalm has become "Inciderjell," which makes it sound like Jello-O. And defoliants are referred to as weed-killers—something you use in your driveway. The resort to euphemism denotes, no doubt, a guilty conscience or—the same thing nowadays—a twinge in the public relations nerve.

"The Home Program," Ibid.

34 In the Stalinist* days, we used to detest a vocabulary that had to be read in terms of antonyms—"volunteers," denoting conscripts, "democracy," tyranny, and so on. Insensibly, in Vietnam, starting with the little word "advisors," we have adopted this slippery Aesopian language ourselves…

"Language," Hanoi 1968

*Josef Stalin, Soviet leader (1879–1953), premier of U.S.S.R. (1941–1953).

35 It has to be acknowledged that in capitalist society, with its herds of hippies, originality has become a sort of fringe benefit, a mere convention, accepted obsolescence, the Beatnik model being turned in for the Hippie model, as though strangely obedient to capitalist laws of marketing.

Ibid.

36 I was born as a mind during 1925, my bodily birth having taken place in 1912.

How I Grew 1987

37 My grandmother had statutory ages for everything, sixteen for boys, fourteen for real, non-ribbed silk stockings, fifteen perhaps for lipstick.

Ibid.

2010. Barbara Tuchman (1912–1989)

1 Publicly his [the Kaiser's] performance was perfect; privately he could not resist the opportunity for fresh scheming.

Ch. 1, The Guns of August 1962

*Wilhelm II (1859–1941) emperor of Germany and King of Prussia (1888–1918)

2 Dead battles, like dead generals, hold the military mind in their dead grip.

Ch. 2, Ibid.

3 Although the defects of the Russian Army were notorious, although the Russian winter, not the Russian Army, had turned

Napoleon back from Moscow,…a myth of its invincibility prevailed.

Ch. 5, Ibid.

4 Alone in Europe Britain had no conscription. In war she would be dependent on voluntary enlistment…[Therefore] it was a prime necessity for Britain to enter war with a united government.

Ch. 7, Ibid.

5 Honor wears different coats to different eyes. . . .

Ibid.

6 No more distressing moment can ever face a British government than that which requires it to come to a hard, fast and specific decision.

Ch. 9, Ibid.

7 The will to defend the country outran the means…

Ch. 11, Ibid.

8 . . . out of the excited fancy produced by the fears and exhaustion and panic and violence of a great battle a legend grew. . . .

Ibid.

9 For one August in its history Paris was French—and silent.

Ch. 20, Ibid.

10 When every autumn people said it could not last through the winter, and when every spring there was still no end in sight, only the hope that out of it all some good would accrue to mankind kept men and nations fighting. When at last it was over, the war had many diverse results and one dominant one transcending all others: disillusion.

Ibid.

11 In April 1917 the illusion of isolation was destroyed, America came to the end of innocence, and of the exuberant freedom of bachelor independence. That the responsibilities of world power have not made us happier is no surprise. To help ourselves manage them, we have replaced the illusion of isolation with a new illusion of omnipotence.

"How We Entered World War I," The New York Times
Magazine</i> 5 May 1967</div>

12 We're being made to look like Lolitas and lion tamers.

Quoted in The Beautiful People by Marilyn Bender* 1968

*See 2270.

13 Reasonable orders are easy enough to obey; it is capricious, bureaucratic or plain idiotic demands that form the habit of discipline.

Pt. I, Ch. 1, Stilwell* and the American Experience in
China: 1911–1945</i> 1970</div>

*Joseph W. S—, American army general (1883–1946).

14 Through all changing circumstances and conditions in the coming period this remained the purpose of American aid and it retained the original flaw: the American purpose was not the Chinese purpose.

Pt. II, Ch.9, Ibid.

15 China was a problem from which there was no American solution. The American effort to sustain the status quo could not supply an outworn government with strength and stability or popular support. It could not hold up a husk nor long delay the cyclical passage of the mandate of heaven. In the end China went her own way as if the Americans had never come.

Pt. II, Ch.20, Ibid.

16 In a country where misery and want were the foundation of the social structure, famine was periodic, death from starvation common, disease pervasive, thievery normal, and graft and corruption taken for granted, the elimination of these conditions in Communist China is so striking that negative aspects of the new rule fade in relative importance.

Ch. 1, *Notes from China 1972*

17 The farmer is the eternal China.

Ch. 3, Ibid.

18 Diplomacy means all the wicked devices of the Old World, spheres of influence, balances of power, secret treaties, triple alliances, and, during the interwar period, appeasement of Fascism.

"If Mao Had Come to Washington in 1945," *Foreign Affairs October 1972*

19 Friendship of a kind that cannot easily be reversed tomorrow must have its roots in common interests and shared beliefs, and even between nations, in some personal feeling.

"Friendship with Foreign Devils," *Harper's* (New York) *December 1972*

20 The open frontier, the hardships of homesteading from scratch, the wealth of natural resources, the whole vast challenge of a continent waiting to be exploited, combined to produce a prevailing materialism and an American drive bent as much, if not more, on money, property, and power than was true of the Old World from which we had fled.

"On Our Birthday—America As Idea," *Newsweek* (New York) *12 July 1976*

21 In the United States we have a society pervaded from top to bottom by contempt for the law.

Ibid.

22 Our government . . . learns no lessons, employs no wisdom and corrupts all who succumb to the Potomac fever.

Ibid.

23 Our sins in the twentieth century—greed, violence, inhumanity—have been profound, with the result that the pride and self-confidence of the nineteenth century have turned to dismay and self-disgust.

Ibid.

24 Every French town has an Avenue Victor Hugo.* We never have a Mark Twain** Street.

Quoted in "Nothing Wicked About Being Elite . . ." by Nan Robertson, *The New York Times 28 February 1979*
*French novelist (1801–1885). **Pen name of American author and humorist Samuel Langhorne Clemens (1835–1910).

25 To a historian libraries are food, shelter, and even muse. They are of two kinds: the library of published material, books, pamphlets, periodicals, and the archive of unpublished papers and documents.

"The Houses of Research," *Practising History 1981*

26 Halfway "between truth and endless error," the mold of the species is permanent.

The First Salute 1988

27 I ask myself, have nations ever declined from a loss of moral sense rather than from physical reasons or the pressure of barbarians? I think that they have.

"Barbara Tuchman," Quoted in *A World of Ideas* by Bill Moyers *1989*

28 You can't govern without having the training in it. Even Plato said that a long time ago. You need to be trained in government, to exercise it, to practice it. But the American public is now satisfying itself with entertainers.

Ibid.

29 We're a public that is brought up on deception, through advertising. . . . We're accustomed to being deceived. We allow ourselves to be deceived. Advertising is really responsible for a lot in the deterioration of American public perceptions.

Ibid.

30 We have gained a lot in social freedom and individual rights, which is the thing that I personally believe in more intensely than anything else—the right of the individual to guide his own life, to think for himself, to live where he wants. We have created a society in which the individual is self-managing and insofar as he can economically manage, he can determine his own fate.

Ibid.

31 Nineteen-fourteen was the birthday of us all, the moment when the clock struck, and the war that followed is the chasm between our world and a world that died forever.

Interview (1962), Quoted in "Noted historian Tuchman dies," Knight-Ridder Newspapers *7 February 1989*

2011. Chien Shiung Wu (1912–1997)

1 . . . even the most sophisticated and seemingly remote basic nuclear physics research has implications beneficial to human welfare.

4000 Years of Women in Science, http://www.astr.ua.edu/4000WS *16 October 1998*

2 There is only one thing worse than coming home from the lab to a sink full of dirty dishes, and that is not going to the lab at all.

Contributions of 20th Century Women to Physics, UCLA, http://www.physics.ucla.edu/~cwp *16 March 1999*

2012. Virginia Graham (1912–1998)

1 It will be the firm intention of your hosts to take you, as soon as possible, away from their homes. Remember, they do not know what on earth to do with you and have been arguing about it for weeks, so do not be difficult and announce that all you want to do is sit still and look at the view. They are irrevocably determined you should be entertained, and it is a matter of little importance whether you wish to be or whether you don't.

Ch. 1, *Say Please 1949*

2 As hunting takes place in the open air and is ever so English and ever so traditional, the word bitch can be frequently employed without offence, and indeed is a rare pleasure for a lady to be able to look fearlessly into the eyes of another lady, even though she be on four legs, and say loudly and clearly, "Bitch!"

Ch. 3, Ibid.

3 Good shot, bad luck, and hell are the five basic words to be used in a game of tennis, though these, of course, can be slightly amplified.

Ch. 8, Ibid.

4 Words, like fashions, disappear and recur throughout English history, and one generation's phraseology, while it may seem abominably second-rate to the next, becomes first-rate to the third...

Ch. 14, Ibid.

5 In society it is etiquette for ladies to have the best chairs and get handed things. In the home the reverse is the case. That is why ladies are more sociable than gentlemen.

Ibid.

6 Be blind. Be stupid. Be British. Be careful.

Ch. 25, Ibid.

2013. Eleanor Clark (1913–1996)

1 "He was the kind of man, if a mule kicked somebody down the street, he'd work till he gut it on his conscience."

Pt. III, Ch. 2, *Baldur's Gate 1955*

2 "We Occidentals have a congenital, it may even be fatal, need for good manners, or you might say ceremony, in our approach to meaning, I suppose to make up for our crudeness in living."

Ch. 3, Ibid.

3 In the darkness, who would answer for the
color of a rose,
Or the vestments of the May moth and the pilgrimage it goes?

"The Blind Girl," St. 1 *n.d.*

4 The little *and*, the tiny *if*,
The ardent *ahs* and *ohs*,
They haunt the lane of poesy,
The boulevards of prose.

"Alliances" *n.d.*

5 Great is the rose
That challenges the crypt,
And quotes millenniums
Against the grave.

"Song from Tadmor" *n.d.*

6 He wooed the daunted odalisques,
He kissed each downcast nude;
He whispered that an angel's robe
Is mostly attitude.

"The First Reformer" *n.d.*

2014. Nathalia Crane (1913–)

1 But my heart is all aflutter like the washing on the line.

"The Flathouse Roof," St. 1 *n.d.*

2 Crumpling a pyramid, humbling a rose,
The dust has its reasons wherever it goes.

"The Dust" *n.d.*

3 There is a glory
In a great mistake.

"Imperfection" *n.d.*

4 You cannot choose your battlefield,
The gods do that for you,
But you can plant a standard
Where a standard never flew.

"The Colors" *n.d.*

2015. Ruth Beebe Hill (1913–)

1 I live in a world of reason and choice as opposed to faith and force.

Quoted in "'Hanta Yo': The Book of the Indian" by Kathleen Hendrix, *The Los Angeles Times 4 February 1979*

2 Bear with me. I'll get back on the track. Actually I'm not off the track. I'm off the train, but not off the track.

Ibid.

3 I own my life. And only mine. And so I shall appreciate my person. And so I shall make proper use of myself.

Hanta Yo 1979

4 I am Ahbleza. I own the earth.

Ibid.

2016. Elizabeth Janeway (1913–)

1 Such simplicity cannot be taught. But it can be denied and lost.

Ch. 1, *The Writer's Book*, Helen Hull, ed. *1950*

2 For there is always this to be said for the literary profession—like life itself, it provides its own revenges and antidotes.

Ch. 24, Ibid.

3 . . . it is through the ghost [writer] that the great gift of knowledge which the inarticulate have for the world can be made available.

Ch. 29, Ibid.

4 Poets are the leaven in the lump of civilization.

Ch. 30, Ibid.

5 As long as mixed grills and combination salads are popular, anthologies will undoubtedly continue in favor.

Ch. 32, Ibid.

6 After all, every circle has a point for a center. The size of the circle is determined by the energy with which it is expanded, not by the magnificence of what it may or may not take off from.

Ch. 40, Ibid.

7 Unable to dedicate herself to her husband—why, we shall never be sure—she ended by dedicating herself to his work...On the basis of an unusual if not unsatisfactory marriage was built an edifice of cooperation, of mutual aid and respect which was of immeasurable influence.

"This I Remember," *Accident on Route 37 1964*

8 . . . it is almost shockingly delightful to read a book which could have been written by absolutely no one else in the world than the great and important figure whose name is signed to it...

Ibid.

9 The Goddamn human race deserves itself, and as far as I'm concerned it can have it.

"Charles Benedict," Ibid.

10 I admire people who are suited to the contemplative life. . . . They can sit inside themselves like honey in a jar and just be. It's wonderful to have someone like that around, you always feel you can count on them. You can go away and come back, you can change your mind and your hairdo and your politics, and when you get through doing all these upsetting things, you look around and there they are, just the way they were, just being.

"Elizabeth Jowett," Ibid.

11 After the city, where we had always lived, those country years were startling. . . . The surprise of animals . . . in and out, cats and dogs and a milk goat and chickens and guinea hens,

all taken for granted, as if man was intended to live on terms of friendly intercourse with the rest of creation instead of huddling in isolation on the fourteenth floor of an apartment house in a city where animals occurred behind bars in the zoo.

"Steven Benedict," Ibid.

12 If every nation gets the government it deserves, every generation writes the history which corresponds with its view of the world.

"Reflections on the History of Women,"
Women: Their Changing Roles 1973

13 American women are not the only people in the world who manage to lose track of themselves, but we do seem to mislay the past in a singularly absent-minded fashion.

Ibid.

14 Like their personal lives, women's history is fragmented, interrupted; a shadow history of human beings whose existence has been shaped by the efforts and the demands of others.

Ibid.

15 Perhaps it is just a hangover from the past, but even those writers who declare that the importance of sex is its sheer pleasure do so with an evangelical zeal that is directive rather than permissive.

Between Myth and Morning 1974

16 . . . reaction isn't action—that is, it isn't truly creative.

Ibid.

17 Sex cannot be contained within a definition of physical pleasure, it cannot be understood as merely itself for it has stood for too long as a symbol of profound connection between human beings.

Ibid.

18 Confronted with the possibility of public catastrophe, every tyrant will opt to let permissiveness rule in private. Besides, will not such permissiveness turn the attention of the people away from public problems to private pleasures? One can image a modern Machiavelli suggesting to his prince that sex would make a very good opiate for the people.

Ibid.

19 Young or old, skepticism about conventional wisdom can give way all too early to a relapse into credulity before the allurements of new certainties.

Ibid.

20 Love between women is seen as a paradigm of love between equals, and that is perhaps its greatest attraction.

Ibid.

21 We have to see, I think, that questioning the values of old rules is different from simply breaking them.

Ibid.

22 When dealing with adultery becomes a matter of private choices instead of public rules, middle-class morality, that bastion of social stability, has ceased to function.

Ibid.

23 With the old rules for masculine superiority fading in the public sphere, how can men face the feminine superiority they have posited in the private world?

Ibid.

24 Philosophically, incest asks a fundamental question of our shifting mores: not simply what is normal and what is deviant, but whether such a thing as deviance exists at all in human relationships if they seem satisfactory to those who share them.

"Incest: A Rational Look at the Oldest Taboo," *Ms.*
(New York) *November 1981*

25 Growing up human is uniquely a matter of social relations rather than biology. What we learn from connections within the family takes the place of instincts that program the behavior of animals; which raises the question, how good are these connections?

Ibid.

26 Loyalty, friendship, family ties, the duty owed to an ideal—in our time, these obligations seem to have lost their force as motivators and connectors.

Ibid.

27 I am not sure how many "sins" I would recognize in the world. Some would surely be defused by changed circumstances. But I can imagine none that is more irredeemably sinful than the betrayal, the exploitation, of the young by those who should care for them.

Ibid.

28 Whatever class and race divergences exist, top cats are tom cats.

Improper Behavior 1987

29 To prepare for the future we need to interpret the past. I wish people would read more history. So many people believe that if something happened more than five years ago, it doesn't matter anymore.

"Trendspotters" (p. 59), *Working Woman Magazine*
July 1987

30 Women must do their part to invent the future. We must start thinking of ourselves as the people responsible for making public policy.

Ibid.

2017. Attia Hosain (1913–)

1 "Listen to me child. You will be a woman soon and must behave well and modestly. The Kazi will ask you three times whether you will marry Kalloo Mian. Now don't you be shameless, like these modern educated girls, and shout gleefully "Yes." Be modest and cry softly and say 'Hoon.'"

Phoenix Fled, introduction by Anita Desai *1953*
(repr. 1988)

2 My life changed. It had been restricted by invisible barriers almost as effectively as the physically restrictive lives of my aunts in the *zenana*. A window had opened here, a door there, a curtain had been drawn aside; but outside lay a world narrowed by one's field of vision.

Sunlight on a Broken Column, introduction by
Anita Desai *1961 (repr. 1988)*

2018. Mary Morris (1913–1986)

1 "It's like dependency on foreign oil. . . . We should be able to live alone, even if we don't want to."

"Summer Share," *The Bus of Dreams 1985*

2 . . . how easy it is for a heart to turn to stone.

"The Hall of Meteorites," Ibid.

2019. Tillie Olsen (1913–)

1 And when is there time to remember, to sift, to weigh, to estimate, to total?
> "I Stand Here Ironing," (1954) *Tell Me a Riddle 1960*

2 My wisdom came too late.
> Ibid.

3 Now suddenly she was Somebody, and as imprisoned in her difference as she had been in her anonymity.
> Ibid.

4 It is destroying, dissolving him utterly, this helpless warmth against him, this feel of a child. . . .
> "Hey Sailor, What Ship?" (1955), Ibid.

5 . . . the Law and the Wall: only so far shall you go and no further, uptown forbidden, not your language, not your people, not your country.
> Ibid.

6 In the beginning there had been youth and the joy of raising hell...And later there were memories to forget, dreams to be stifled, hopes to be murdered.
> Ibid.

7 There are worse words than cuss words, there are words that hurt.
> Ibid.

8 That's what I want to be when I grow up, just a peaceful wreck holding hands with other peaceful wrecks. . . .
> Ibid.

9 "Not everybody feel religion the same way. Some it's in their mouth, but some it's like a hope in their blood, their bones."
> "O Yes" (1956), Ibid.

10 It is a long baptism into the seas of humankind, my daughter. Better immersion than to live untouched. . . .
> Ibid.

11 For forty-seven years they had been married. How deep back the stubborn, gnarled roots of the quarrel reached, no one could say—but only now, when tending to the needs of others no longer shackled them together, the roots swelled up visible, split the earth between them, and the tearing shook even the children, long since grown.
> Ch. 1, "Tell Me a Riddle" (1960), Ibid.

12 He could not, could not turn away from this desire: to have the troubling of responsibility, the fretting with money, over and done with; to be free, to be *care*free where success was not measured by accumulation. . . .
> Ibid.

13 The television is shadows, Mrs. Enlightened! Mrs. Cultured! A world comes into your house—and it is shadows. People you would never meet in a million lifetimes. Wonders.
> Ibid.

14 Like the hide of a drum shall you be, beaten in life, beaten in death.
> Ibid.

15 "Vinegar he poured on me all his life; I am well marinated; how can I be honey now?"
> Ibid.

16 Heritage. How have we come from the savages, now no longer to be savages—this to teach. To look back and learn what humanizes man—this to teach. To smash all ghettos that divide us—not to go back, not to go back—this to teach.
> Ch. 2, Ibid.

17 "Remember your advice, easy to keep your head above water, empty things float. Float."
> Ch.3, Ibid.

18 ". . . life may be hated or wearied of, but never despised."
> Ch.4, Ibid.

19 Always roused by the writing, always denied.
. . . My work died.
> *Silences: When Writer's Don't Write 1965*

20 It is distraction, not meditation, that becomes habitual; interruption, not continuity; spasmodic, not constant toil.
> Ibid.

21 . . . the circumstances for sustained creation are almost impossible.
> Ibid.

22 More than in any other human relationship, overwhelmingly more, motherhood means being instantly interruptible, responsive, responsible. . . .
> Ibid.

23 Time granted does not necessarily coincide with time that can be most fully used.
> Ibid.

24 The mute inglorious Millions: those whose waking hours are all struggle for existence; the barely educated; the illiterate; women—their silence the silence of centuries as to how life was, is, for most of humanity.
> Ibid.

25 "The joy, the reason to believe," my mother said, "the hope for the world, the baby, holy with possibility, that is all of us at birth." And she began to cry, out of the dream and its telling now.
"Still I feel the baby in my arms, the human baby," crying now so I could scarcely make out the word, "the human baby, before we are misshapen; crucified into a sex, a color, a walk of life, a nationality . . . and the world yet warring and winter."
> "Dream-Vision," *Mother to Daughter,*
> *Daughter to Mother 1984*

2020. Rosa Parks (1913–)

1 My only concern was to get home after a hard day's work.*
> Quoted in *Time* (New York) *15 December 1975*
> *Reference to her refusal to give up her seat on a bus in Montgomery, Alabama, in 1955 to a white who was standing. From her act of defiance grew the Montgomery bus boycott and the leadership of Martin Luther King, Jr.

2 In these times, none of us seem safe from this type of treatment and violation by a sick-minded person.*
> "Nation," A3, *Seattle Post-Intelligencer 1 September 1994*
> *Remark after having been robbed and beaten in Detroit.

3 I had been pushed as far as I could stand.
> Quoted in "Women Who Could Be President" by
> Jane Ciabattari, *Parade Magazine 7 February 1999*

2021. Sylvia Porter (1913–1991)

1 The average family exists only on paper and its average budget is a fiction, invented by statisticians for the convenience of statisticians.

Ch. 1, Sylvia Porter's Money Book 1975

2 Money never remains just coins and pieces of paper. It is constantly changing into the comforts of daily life. Money can be translated into the beauty of living, a support in misfortune, an education, or future security. It also can be translated into a source of bitterness.

Ibid.

3 We are into an "era of aspirations" in our economy. In this era, most of us will spend a shrinking share of our income on the traditional necessities of food, clothing, shelter, and transportation while we spend a steadily increasing share of our income for goods and services which reflect our hopes and wants.

Ibid.

4 For millions, the retirement dream is in reality an economic nightmare. For millions, growing old today means growing poor, being sick, living in substandard housing, and having to scrimp merely to subsist. And this is the prospect not for the one out of every ten Americans now over sixty-five . . . but also for the sixty-five million who will reach retirement age within the next thirty-three years.

Ch. 19, Ibid.

2022. Nancy Reeves (1913–)

1 Today the hemisphere of the public has been assigned to the male and the hemisphere of the private to the female. Each sex has become a symbol for its territory. The conflict between them can then be seen as a reflection of the longing of each to be part of the other's sphere, to link the public with the private in our schizoid world, to embrace the whole of life.

Womankind Beyond the Stereotypes 1971

2023. Ruby Rohrlich-Leavitt (1913–)

1 With no voice in the laws that were passed primarily to protect the wealth and power of the elite groups, [women in ancient Sumer] were deprived of education and ousted from lucrative and prestigious professions. Segregated from the kinship group, they were made totally dependent on the male heads of the patrilineal family.

"Women in Transition," *Becoming Visible*,
Renate Bridenthal and Claudia Koonz, eds. *1977*

2024. Honor Tracy (1913–1989)

1 He was a member of the eccentric race of fiscophobes, Englishmen who would do anything and live anywhere, no matter how bored and miserable they might be, rather than stay at home and pay English taxes.

Ch. 1, The Butterflies of the Province 1970

2 "Early upbringing," David moaned. "One struggles against it in vain."

Ch. 5, Ibid.

2025. Margo Jones (1913–1955)

1 Neither the building, nor the organization, not the finest plays and actors in the whole world will help you create a fine theatre if you have no consistent approach of your own, a true philosophy of the theater.

Theatre in the Round 1951

2 Everything in life is theatre.

Quoted in The New York Times 26 July 1955

3 The theatre has given me a chance not only to live my own life but a million others. In every play there is a chance for one great moment, experience or understanding.

Ibid.

4 With imagination and a tremendous willingness for hard work, it is possible to create a great theatre, a vigorous and vital theatre, in the second half of the twentieth century.

"Theatre '50: A Dream Come True," *Ten Talents in the American Theatre*, David H. Stevens, ed. *1957*

5 There are two kinds of theatre, good and bad. Much as I should like to see theatre in America, I would rather have no theatre than bad theatre. What we must strive for is perfection and come as close to it as is humanly possible.

Ibid.

6 We have seen too much defeatism, too much pessimism, too much of a negative approach. The answer is simple: if you want something very badly, you can achieve it. It may take patience, very hard work, a real struggle, and a long time; but it can be done. That much faith is a prerequisite of any undertaking, artistic or otherwise.

Ibid.

2026. Dorothy Kilgallen (1913–1965)

1 The chief product of Baghdad is dates . . . and sheiks.

Girl Around the World 1936

2 The world is grand, awfully big and astonishingly beautiful, frequently thrilling. But I love New York.

Ibid.

3 Doorman—a genius who can open the door of your car with one hand, help you in with the other, and still have one left for the tip.

"Come Away, Poverty's Catching," *Violets and Vinegar*,
Jilly Cooper and Tom Hartman, eds. *1980*

2027. Vivien Leigh (1913–1967)

1 In Britain, an attractive woman is somehow suspect. If there is talent as well it is overshadowed. Beauty and brains just can't be entertained; someone has been too extravagant.

Quoted by Robert Ottaway in *Light of a Star* by Gwen Robyns *1968*

2028. Barbara Pym (1913–1980)

1 My thoughts went round and round and it occurred to me that if I ever wrote a novel it would be of the 'stream of consciousness' type and deal with an hour in the life of a woman at the sink.

Excellent Women 1952

2 I began piling cups and saucers on to a tray. I suppose it was cowardly of me, but I felt that I wanted to be alone, and what better place to choose than the sink, where neither of the men would follow me?

Ibid.

3 The burden of keeping three people in toilet paper seemed to me rather a heavy one.

Ibid.

4 I suppose an unmarried woman just over 30, who lives alone and has no apparent ties, must expect to find herself involved or interested in other people's business, and if she is also a clergyman's daughter then one might really say that there is no hope for her.

Ibid.

5 Miss Doggett again looked puzzled; it was as if she had heard that men only wanted one thing, but had forgotten for the moment what it was.

Jane and Prudence 1953

6 I should have liked the kind of life where one ate food flavoured with garlic, but it was not to be.

Ibid.

7 I'm not one of those excellent women, who can just go home and eat a boiled egg and make a cup of tea and be very splendid, she thought, but how useful it would be if I were!

Less Than Angels 1955

8 "Research with a good-looking man. That's an enviable lot."

No Fond Return of Love 1961

9 "You were lucky to find [a poet] so obscure that not even the Americans had done him. It's quite serious, this shortage of obscure poets."

Ibid.

10 "I imagine few tasks more distasteful than making an index for someone for whom one no longer cares."

Ibid.

11 It was at this point that somebody came to the unoccupied table, but as she was a woman of about forty, ordinary-looking and unaccompanied, nobody took much notice of her. As it happened, she was a novelist; indeed, some of the occupants of the tables had read and enjoyed her books, but it would never have occurred to them to connect her name, even had they ascertained it from the hotel register, with that of the author they admired. They ate their stewed plums and custard and drank their thimble-sized cups of coffee, quite unconscious that they were being observed.

Ibid.

2029. Muriel Rukeyser (1913–1980)

1 Women and poets see the truth arrive,
Then it is acted out,
then lives are lost, and all the newsboys shout.

"Letter to the Front," *Beast in
View 1944*

2 Women in drudgery knew
They must be one of four:
Whores, artists, saints, and wives.

"Wreath of Women," *Ibid.*

3 A poem does invite, it does require. What does it invite? A poem invites you to feel. More than that: it invites you to respond. And better than that: a poem invites a total response.

The Life of Poetry 1949

4 The continent in its voices is full of song; it is not to be heard easily, it must be listened for; among its shapes and weathers, the country is singing, among the lives of its people, its industries, its wild flamboyant ventures, its waste, its buried search. The passion is sung, beneath the flatness and the wild sexual

fevers, contorted gothic of the Middle West; the passion is sung, under the regret and violence and fiery flowers of the south; the passion is sung, under the size and range and golden bareness of the Western Coast, and the split acute seasons of the cities standing east.

Ibid.

5 The universe of poetry is the universe of emotional truth. Our material is in the way we feel and the way we remember.

Ibid.

6 Anyone dealing with poetry and the love of poetry must deal...with the hatred of poetry, and perhaps even more with the indifference.

Ibid.

7 However confused the scene of our life appears,
however torn we may be who now do face that scene,
it can be faced, and we can go on to be whole.

Ibid.

8 . . . second cry I woke
fully and gave to feed and fed on feeding.

"Night Feeding," *Selected Poems
1951*

9 You will enter the world which eats itself
Naming faith, reason, naming love, truth, fact.

"Nine Poems for the Unborn Child," VII, St. I,
Waterlily Fire (1935–1962) 1962

10 . . . the seeking marvelous look
Of those who lose and use and know their lives.

II, *Ibid.*

11 The strength, the grossness, spirit and gall of choice.

VI, *Ibid.*

12 Those women who stitch their lives to their machines
and daughters at the symmetry of looms.

"Ann Burlak," St. 4, *Ibid.*

13 The spies who wait for the spy at the deserted crossing,
a little dead since they are going to kill.

Ibid.

14 Years when the enemy is in our state,
and liberty, safe in the people's hands,
is never safe and peace is never safe.

Ibid.

15 Escape the birthplace; walk into the world
Refusing to be either slave or slaveholder.

"Secrets of American Civilization," St. 3,
The Speed of Darkness 1968

16 No more masks! No more mythologies!

"The Poem as Mask," St.3, *Ibid.*

17 Overtaken by silence

But this same silence Is become speech
With the speed of darkness.

"The Speed of Darkness," II, *Ibid.*

18 The universe is made of stories,
not of atoms.

IX, St. 2, *Ibid.*

19 I have forgotten what it was
that I have been trying to remember.
> "Women as Market," Ibid.

20 the revolutionary look
that says   I am in the world
to change the world.
> St. 2, Ibid.

21 A theme may seem to have been put aside,
but it keeps returning—
the same thing modulated,
somewhat changed in form.
> II, St.2, Ibid.

22 I believe
that bisexuality
is almost   a necessary factor
in artistic production...
> St. 6, Ibid.

23 my lifetime
listens to yours.
> "Käthe Kollwitz,"* I, St. 1, Ibid.

*See 1271.

24 What would happen if one woman told the truth about her
life?
The world would split open.
> III, St. 4, Ibid.

25 Whatever we stand against
We will stand feeding and seeding.
> "Wherever," St. 3, *Breaking Open* 1973

26 The collective unconscious is the living history brought to the
present in consciousness.
> Quoted in "Rare Battered She-Poet" by Louise Bernikow,
> *Ms.* (New York) April 1974

2030. Elizabeth Smart (1913–1986)

1 I am over-run, jungled in my bed, I am infested with a
menagerie of desires: my heart is eaten by a dove, a cat scram-
bles in the cave of my sex, hounds in my bed obey a
whipmaster who cries nothing but havoc as the hours test my
endurance with an accumulation of tortures. Who, if I cried,
would hear me among the angelic orders?
> Pt. 1, *By Grand Central Station I Sat Down and Wept* 1945

2 Vanity is a vital aid to nature: completely and absolutely necessary to life. It is one of nature's ways to bind you to the
earth.
> Journal entry (25 June 1933), Pt. 1, Ch. 2, *Necessary
> Secrets*, Alice Van Wart, ed. 1991

3 O I know they make war because they want peace; they hate
so that they may live; and they destroy the present to make the
world safe for the future. When have they not done and said
they did it for that?
> (18 February 1941), Ibid.

2031. May Swenson (1913/19–1989)

1 The summer that I was ten—
Can it be there was only one summer that I was ten? It must
have been a long one then—
> "The Centaur," Sts. 1 & 2, *To Mix with Time* 1963

2 I was the horse and the rider . . .
> St. 13, Ibid.

3 We play in the den of the Gods and snort at death
> "To Confirm a Thing," St. 2, *New and Selected Things
> Taking Place* 1978

4 Look closer. By April, at the hub of each wheel
of petals a green knob swells, erects a hairlike
stem with infant leaf attached.
> "Look Closer," *Nature: Poems Old
> and New* 1994

5 . . . Lake is our bathtub, dish-sink,
drinking jug, and (since the boat's head doesn't work,
—the ice box, either—the bilge pump barely)
lake is water closet, too. Little I knew
a gale this night would wash, and then
wind-wipe my rump hung over the rail.
> "The Beauty of the Head,"
> Ibid.

6 Stop bleeding   said the knife.
I would if I   could said the cut.
> "Bleeding", Ibid.

7 "Feel that I do right in not trying,
as you insist, to stay on your side. There is the wide
gateway and the splendid tower, and you implore me
to wait here, with the worms!"
> "Feel Me," Ibid.

8 . . . Elemental form simplified as an egg,
you held perfectly still on your artificial perch. You, too,
might be a crafty fake, stuffed or carved. Except your eyes.
Alive,
enormous, yellow circles containing black circles, clear, slick,
heartstopping double barrels of concentrated rage pointed
at me.
> "The Snowy," Ibid.

9 Intermittent moon
that we say climbs
or sets, circles only.
> "Sleeping Overnight on the Shore," Ibid.

2032. Agnes "Sis" Cunningham (1914–1968)

1 We . . . were young radicals who felt that by singing ideas
straightforwardly we could get more said in five minutes than
in hours, or days, of talking.
> "Songs of Hard Years" with Madeline B. Rose, *Ms.*
> (New York) *March 1974*

2 Oh, it's good to be living and working
when we know the land's our own
To know that we have got a right to
all the crops we've grown.
> "When We Know the Land's Our Own" *n.d.*

2033. Joan Littlewood (1914–)

1 I do not believe in the supremacy of the director, designer,
actor, or even of the writer. It is through collaboration that this
knockabout art of theatre survives and kicks.
> "A Goodbye Note from Joan," *Encore* (Natl. Assoc. of
> Dramatic and Speech Arts) *October 1961*

2034. Abigail McCarthy (1914?–)

1   For those of us whose lives have been defined by others—by wifehood and motherhood—there is no individual achievement to measure, only the experience of life itself.
Private Faces/Public Places 1972

2035. Molly Yard (1914–)

1   Don't buy the garbage that you're over the hill at 50. This country makes such a big thing about age, particularly if you're a woman. What I think is relevant is your experience, what you have to offer. I hope people will recognize that and keep going.
(p. 71), *Time* (New York) *3 August 1987*

2   I thought it would be different in this country [than it is in China], but I learned quickly that females weren't valued in this society, either. It is indeed a worldwide problem.
Quoted in "NOW Head Assails President's Policies" by Alex Tizon, *Seattle Times February 1989*

2036. Etty Hillesum (1914–1943)

1   And the thought that I will have to leave S., not even grief about the longing I shall feel for him but grief about the longing he will feel for me.
Entry (1942), *An Interrupted Life: The Diaries of Etty Hillesum 1941–1943*, Arno Pomerans, tr. *1983*

2   It is good to have such moments of despair and of temporary extinction; continuous calm would be superhuman.
Ibid.

3   When I pray, I never pray for myself, always for others, or else I hold a silly, naive or deadly serious dialogue with what is deepest inside me, which for the sake of convenience I call God. Praying to God for something for yourself strikes me as being too childish for words. . . . To pray for another's well-being is something I find childish as well; one should only pray that another should have enough strength to shoulder his burden. If you do that, you lend him some of your own strength.
Ibid.

4   The soul has a different age from that recorded in the register of births and deaths. At your birth, the soul already has an age that never changes. One can be born with a 12-year-old soul. One can also be born with a thousand-year-old soul. . . . I believe the soul is that part of man that he is least aware of. . .
Entry (12.10.42), Ibid.

5   Sometimes I try my hand at turning out small profundities and uncertain short stories, but I always end up with just one single word: God.
Entry , Westerbork,* 18 August [1943], Ibid.
*A transit camp in the eastern Netherlands, the last stop before Auschwitz.

2037. Julia de Burgos (1914/16–1953)

1   You are the bloodless doll of social lies
And I the virile spark of human truth...
"To Julia de Burgos," *The Nation* (New York) *1972*

2   You curl your hair and paint your face.
Not I:
I am curled by the wind, painted by the sun.
Ibid.

2038. "Babe" Didrikson Zaharias (1914–1956)

1   Boy, don't you men wish you could hit a ball like that!
Quoted in "'Babe' Didrikson Zaharias," *Famous American Women* by Hope Stoddard *1970*

2   All my life I've been competing—and competing to win. I came to realize that in this way, this cancer was the toughest competition I'd faced yet. I made up my mind that I was going to lick it all the way. I not only wasn't going to let it kill me, I wasn't even going to let it put me on the shelf.
Ibid.

3   It's not enough to just swing at the ball. You've got to loosen your girdle and really let fly.
"100 Years of Great Women," *ABC News Special with Barbara Walters 30 April 1999*

2039. Gypsy Rose Lee (1914–1970)

1   Mother, in a feminine way, was ruthless. She was, in her own words, a jungle mother, and she knew too well that in a jungle it doesn't pay to be nice. "God will protect us," she often said to June and me. "but to make sure," she would add, "carry a heavy club."
Ch. 1, *Gypsy 1957*

2   [He] often said I was the greatest no-talent star in the business.
Ibid.

2040. Barbara Ward (1914–1981)

1   All archaic societies feel themselves bound to a "melancholy wheel" of endless recurrence. . . . No vision of reality as progressing forward to new possibilities, no sense of the future as better and fuller than the present, tempered by the underlying fatalism of ancient civilization. It is only in the Jewish and Christian faith that a Messianic hope first breaks upon mankind.
Ch. 1, *The Rich Nations and the Poor Nations 1962*

2   It is very much easier for a rich man to invest and grow richer than for the poor man to begin investing at all. And this is also true of nations.
Ibid.

3   There is no human failure greater than to launch a profoundly important endeavor and then leave it half done. This is what the West has done with its colonial system. It shook all the societies in the world loose from their old moorings. But it seems indifferent whether or not they reach safe harbour in the end.
Ch. 2, Ibid.

4   To me, one of the most vivid proofs that there is a moral governance in the universe is the fact that when men or governments work intelligently and far-sightedly for the good of others, they achieve their own prosperity too.
Ch. 6, Ibid.

5   . . . mankind must go beyond the limits of purely national government and begin to find out what the "post-national community" is like...[But] it cannot, must not, mean a suppression of all variety and a civilization so standardized that we all end up hideously the same.
"Only One Earth," *Who Speaks for Earth?*, Maurice F. Strong, ed. *1973*

6   We . . . live in an epoch in which the solid ground of our preconceived ideas shakes daily under our uncertain feet.
Ibid.

7 We can all cheat on morals. . . . But today the morals of respect and care and modesty come to us in a form that we cannot evade. We cannot cheat on DNA. We cannot get round photosynthesis. We cannot say I am not going to give a damn about phytoplankton. All these tiny mechanisms provide the preconditions of our planetary life. To say we do not care is to say in the most literal sense that "we choose death."

Ibid.

2041. Catherine Marshall (1914–1983)

1 Often God has to shut a door in our face, so that He can subsequently open the door through which He wants us to go.

Ch. 2, *A Man Called Peter* 1951

2 . . . truth could never be wholly contained in words. All of us know it: At the same moment the mouth is speaking one thing, the heart is saying another . . .

Prologue, *Christy* 1967

3 So once I shut down my privilege of disliking anyone I chose and holding myself aloof if I could manage it, greater understanding, growing compassion came to me. . . .

Ch. 12, *Ibid.*

4 . . . in rejecting secrecy I had also rejected the road to cynicism.

Ch. 33, *Ibid.*

5 . . . I learned that true forgiveness includes total acceptance. And out of acceptance wounds are healed and happiness is possible again.

Ibid.

6 Usually passion wants to grab and to yank.

Ibid.

2042. Billy Tipton (1914–1989)

1 Some people might think I'm a freak or a hermaphrodite. I'm not. I'm a normal person. This has been my choice.*

Quoted in *Suits Me: The Double Life of Billy Tipton*
by Diane Wood Middlebrook *1998*
*Tipton lived most of her life as a man.

2043. Jiang Ching (1914–1991)

1 There cannot be peaceful coexistence in the ideological realm. Peaceful coexistence corrupts.

Remark (April 1967), Quoted in Ch. 15, *Mao and China:
From Revolution to Revolution* by Stanley Karnow *1972*

2044. Dixy Lee Ray (1914–1994)

1 My answer to why did I choose the Democratic Party is that I spent three years in Washington under a Republican administration.

Quoted in *The Wall Street Journal 15 March 1976*

2 Everybody's in favor of resolving the energy crisis and everybody is in favor of preserving the environment. But the people in the Northwest, where the big coal deposits are, don't want their terrain upset; and the people in the Northeast, who need heating fuel the most, don't want an oil port and refineries on their coast, and some of the Nader people don't want any nuclear plants at all generating electric power because of some theoretical dangers. I understand these conflicts, but this isn't

a perfect world. Somebody—and I mean every one of us—has to make some sacrifices.

Interview (1974), Quoted in *American Political Women*
by Esther Stineman *1980*

3 The reality is that zero defects in products plus zero pollution plus zero risk on the job is equivalent to maximum growth of government plus zero economic growth plus runaway inflation.

Speech, Scientist and Engineers for Secure Energy
(1980), *Ibid.*

2045. Hazel Brannon Smith (1914–1994)

1 I ain't no lady. I'm a newspaperwoman.

Quoted in "The 11-Year Siege of Mississippi's Lady Editor"
by T. George Harris, *Look* (New York) *16 November 1965*

2 I can't think of but one thing that's worse than being called a nigger-lover. And that's a nigger-hater!

Ibid.

3 A crusading editor is one who goes out and looks for the wrongs of the world. I just try to take care of things as they come up. I try to make them a little better.

Ibid.

4 I've always been too interested in what is happening in the present and what is going to happen to be much concerned about the past.

Ibid.

2046. Marguerite Duras (1914–1996)

1 "Do you think it is ever possible to be successful in love, if one doesn't make an effort to help things along?"

The Vice-Consul, Eileen Ellenbogen, tr. *1966*

2 One must talk. That's how it is. One must.

Ibid.

3 Thousands on the causeways, carrying their loads, laying them down, returning empty-handed. People surrounding the bare, watery spaces of the rice-field, fields of upright stalks. People everywhere, ten thousand, a hundred thousand, crowded like grains of millet, walking along the causeways, an endless procession, continually on the move, each one with his tools of naked flesh hanging down on either side.

Ibid.

4 CLAIRE. I am not intelligent enough for the intelligence within me.

The Lovers of Viorne 1971

5 Clarity is a disease of the French. They believe in it, it is everywhere!

Quoted in *Current Biography Yearbook*, Charles Moritz, ed.
1980–85

6 Journalism without a moral position is impossible. Every journalist is a moralist. It's absolutely unavoidable. A journalist is someone who looks at the world and the way it works, someone who takes a close look at things every day and reports what she sees, someone who represents the world, the event, for others. She cannot do her work without judging what she sees.

Foreword, *Outside: Selected Writings 1984*

7 From time to time, I wrote for the outside world, when the outside world overwhelmed me, when things outside in the street, drove me crazy.

Introduction, *Ibid.*

8 She represents the unavowed aspiration of the male human being, his potential infidelity—and infidelity of a very special kind, which would lead him to the opposite of his wife, to the "woman of wax" whom he could model at will, make and unmake in any way he wished, even unto death.
"Queen Bardot,"* *France-Observateur* (Paris, 1958), Ibid.
*Reference to Brigitte Bardot; see 2551.

9 Paradoxically, the freedom of Paris is associated with a persistent belief that nothing ever changes. Paris, they say, is the city that changes least. After an absence of twenty or thirty years, one still recognizes it.
"Tourists in Paris," *France-Observateur* (Paris, 1957), Ibid.

10 Nowhere is one more alone than in Paris . . . and yet surrounded by crowds. Nowhere is one more likely to incur greater ridicule. And no visit is more essential.
Ibid.

11 I'm still there watching . . . as far away from the mystery now as I was then. I've never written, though I thought I wrote, never loved, though I thought I loved, never done anything but wait outside the closed door.
The Lover 1984

12 No other human being, no woman, no poem or music, book or painting can replace alcohol in its power to give man the illusion of real creation.
"Alcohol," *Practicalities 1987*

13 Alcohol doesn't console, it doesn't fill up anyone's psychological gaps, all it replaces is the lack of God. It doesn't comfort man. On the contrary, it encourages him in his folly, it transports him to the supreme regions where he is master of his own destiny.
Ibid.

14 The woman is the home. That's where she used to be, and that's where she still is. You might ask me, What if a man tries to be part of the home—will the woman let him? I answer yes. Because then he becomes one of the children.
"House and Home," Ibid.

15 I believe that always, or almost always, in all childhoods and in all the lives that follow them, the mother represents madness. Our mothers always remain the strangest, craziest people we've ever met.
Ibid.

16 In heterosexual love there's no solution. Man and woman are irreconcilable, and it's the doomed attempt to do the impossible, repeated in each new affair, that lends heterosexual love its grandeur.
"Men," Ibid.

17 Before they're plumbers or writers or taxi drivers or unemployed or journalists, before everything else, men are men. Whether heterosexual or homosexual. The only difference is that some of them remind you of it as soon as you meet them, and others wait for a little while.
Ibid.

18 Heterosexuality is dangerous. It tempts you to aim at a perfect duality of desire.
Ibid.

19 You have to be very fond of men. Very, very fond. You have to be very fond of them to love them. Otherwise they're simply unbearable.
Ibid.

20 In homosexual love the passion is homosexuality itself. What a homosexual loves, as if it were his lover, his country, his art, his land, is homosexuality.
Ibid.

21 Frigidity is desire imagined by a woman who doesn't desire the man offering himself to her. It's the desire of a woman for a man who hasn't yet come to her, whom she doesn't yet know. She's faithful to this stranger even before she belongs to him. Frigidity is the non-desire for whatever is not him.
Ibid.

22 It was the men I deceived the most that I loved the most.
"The Chimneys of India Song," Ibid.

23 A writer is a foreign country.
"The M.D. Uniform," Ibid.

24 The best way to fill time is to waste it.
"Wasting Time," Ibid.

25 I see journalists as the manual workers, the laborers of the word. Journalism can only be literature when it is passionate.
"Walesa's* Wife," Ibid.
*Reference to wife of Lech Walesa, Polish labor leader and president of Poland (1990–1995) who won the Nobel Peace Prize (1983).

26 Acting doesn't bring anything to a text. On the contrary, it detracts from it.
International Herald Tribune (Paris) 28 March *1990*

2047. Hortensia Bussi de Allende (1915–)

1 We want a Chile where the rights of man will be fully respected. Our message is not fear but hope, not hate but joy. It is not the past, but the future, that we will build together.
Speech, Santiago, Chile 24 September *1988*

2048. Phyllis Shand Allfrey (1915–)

1 She went out on the portico and looked down on the land, sighing as if her heart had broken and the wind was whistling through it. "Beauty grows like a weed here," she said, "and so does disease."
The Orchid House 1953

2049. Caroline Bird (1915–1986)

1 The contraceptive pill may reduce the importance of sex not only as a basis for the division of labor, but as a guideline in developing talents and interests.
Foreword, *Born Female 1968*

2 A career woman who has survived the hurdle of marriage and maternity encounters a new obstacle: the hostility of men.
Ch. 3, Ibid.

3 Secretaries may be specially prized, and the top secretaries exceptionally well paid, because they give men who can afford to pay well the subservient, watchful and admiring attention that Victorian wives used to give their husbands.
Ch. 4, Ibid.

4 Equity speaks softly and wins in the end. But it is expedience, with its loud voice, that sets the time of victory.
Ch. 10, Ibid.

5 Femininity appears to be one of those pivotal qualities that is so important no one can define it.

Ch. 11, Ibid.

6 Feminism has never been deader than it was during the 1950s, when the marriage rate hit a new high, the age of marriage a new low, and the ideal of universal, compulsory marriage boomed marriage counseling, psychiatric therapy and romantic portrayals of married life.

"The Case Against Marriage," New Woman
September 1971

7 To keep the mammoth plants financially solvent, many [educational] institutions have begun to use hard-sell, Madison Avenue techniques to attract students. They sell college like soap . . .

The Case Against College 1975

8 . . . just as society had systematically damaged women by insisting that their poper place was in the home, so we may be systematically damaging 18-year-olds by insisting that their proper place is in college.

Ibid.

9 The big advantage of getting your college money in cash now is that you can invest it in something that has a higher return than a diploma.

Ibid.

10 A liberal-arts education is supposed to provide you with a value system, a standard, a set of ideas, not a job. The fact is, of course, that the liberal arts are a religion in every sense of that term. [And if] the liberal arts are a religious faith, the professors are its priests.

Ibid.

11 Equalizing opportunity through universal higher education subjects the whole population to the intellectual mode natural only to a few. It violates the fundamental egalitarian principle of respect for the differences between people.

Ibid.

12 In fact there is no real evidence that the higher income of college graduates is due to college. College may simply attract people who are slated to earn more money anyway: those with higer IQs, better family backgrounds, a more enterprising temperment.

Ibid.

13 College, then, may be a good place for those few young people who are really drawn to academic work, who would rather read than eat, but it has become too expensive, in money, time and intellectual effort, to serve as a holding pen for large numbers of our young. We ought to make it possilbe for those reluctant, unhappy students to find alternative ways of growing up, and more realistic preparation for the years ahead.

Ibid.

2050. Marie-Louise von Franz (1915–)

1 Unfortunately the conscious representation we make of the Godhead undergoes the same fate as all other contents of our consciousness: it suffers from the tendency to wear out, and becomes mere words which lose their emotional and feeling substructure.

Ch. 4, Individuation in Fairytales 1977

2 The inner experience consolidates, and instead of being a kind of emotional spiritual experience, it becomes a realization in the most literal sense of the word. We use the word "realization" rather too lightly; but if we "realize" something in its basic meaning, it becomes a real thing forever.

Ch. 5, Ibid.

3 The only way the Self can manifest is through conflict. To meet one's insoluble and eternal conflict is to meet God, which would be the end of the ego with all its blather.

Alchemy: An Introduction to the Symbolism and
the Psychology 1980

4 You think God has published general rules which He keeps Himself, and we think He is a living spirit appearing in man's psyche who can always create something new. . . . To a theologian God is bound to His own books and is incapable of further publications. That is where we lock horns.

Ibid.

5 Every content of the unconscious with which one is not properly related tends to obsess one for it gets at us from behind. If you can talk to it you get into a relationship with it. You can either be possessed by a content constellated in the unconscious, or you can have a relationship to it. The more one represses it, the more one is affected by it.

Redemption Motifs in Fairytales n.d.

2051. Janet Harris (1915–)

1 I'm the ultimate in the throwaway society, the disposable woman.

The Prime of Ms. America 1975

2 . . . one searches the magazines in vain for women past their first youth. The middle-aged face apparently sells neither perfume nor floor wax. The role of the mature woman in the media is almost entirely negative.

Ibid.

3 We were born in an era in which it was a disgrace for women to be sexually irresponsible. We matured in an era in which it was an obligation

Ibid.

4 Quite a few women told me, one way or another, that they thought it was sex, not youth, that's wasted on the young. . . .

Ibid.

5 At its most basic root, the death or disintegration of one's parents is a harsh reminder of one's own mortality.

Ibid.

6 We are anonymous—graphed but not acknowledged, a shadowy presence—hinted at, but never defined.

Ibid.

7 Reared as we were in a youth—and beauty-oriented society, we measured ourselves by our ornamental value.

Ibid.

8 We were brought up with the value that as we sow, so shall we reap. We discarded the idea that anything we did was its own reward.

Ibid.

9 . . . with the beginnings of the middle years, we face an identity crisis for which nothing in our past has prepared us.

Ibid.

2052. Lena May Jeger (1915–)

1 . . . no legislation can compel anybody to give an unmarried mother what she usually most needs—friendship, understanding and companionship in what is almost inevitably a lonely and deeply traumatic experience.

> Foreword, *Illegitimate Children and Their Parents* 1951

2 The child is different, not because he is illegitimate, but because he is fatherless and he is going to miss a father in the same way that any child who loses his father early, through death or separation, misses him.

> Ibid.

3 . . . we feel that there is often too little concern with the unmarried father. In our social records he is an elusive figure, often anonymous, alternately reviled, beloved or blackmailed. . . . Often he needs as much help as the mother to regain a mental and emotional equilibrium and so to make subsequently a good husband to somebody, if not to the mother of his first child.

> Ibid.

2053. Margaret Ellis Millar (1915–1994)

1 As soon as she opened her eyes Priscilla could feel in her bones that it was Saturday. The air smelled different, and it seemed to quiver with anticipation.

> "A Problem in Economics," *It's All in the Family* 1948

2 "And when I was eleven and wanted ten cents I went out and got me a ten-cent task to do."
"I can't think of any ten-cent tasks except just being good."
"In this world, you don't get paid for being good."

> Ibid.

2054. Nien Cheng (1915–)

1 I would rather die than tell a lie.

> *Life and Death in Shanghai* 1987

2 The [Chinese] leaders who ordered this killing of innocent people* will never ever recover the good reputation they'd worked so hard for and gained in the eyes of the world and the Chinese people.

> Quoted in "China Hears a Voice of Experience" by Judi
> Hunt, *Seattle Post-Intelligencer* 10 June 1989

*Reference to the gunning down by the military of Chinese students and workers demonstrating for democracy in Tiananmen Square, Beijing, 4 June 1989.

3 I think the democratic movement will be repressed for now, only to erupt again somewhere down the line.
And more blood will be shed, just like it was when Americans fought and died to bring independence, democracy, and freedom to the United States. It's not something you can sit back and wait for someone to give to you voluntarily.

> Ibid.

2055. Janet Mary Riley (1915–)

1 We [women law students] bore the burden of representing womankind, whether we liked it or not.
If you goofed, if you failed, if you cried in public or received bad grades, they'd say, "What do you expect: She's only a woman."
So we didn't cry in public. We didn't get bad grades. The result was that the woman students did remarkably well. For years, the women were the tops in their class.

There was a lot of self-inflicted pressure not to cry. But I did my share of crying in the women's lounge.

> Quoted in "Women Win Their Case as Legal Eagles"
> by Jean Blake, *The Times/Picayune* (New Orleans)
> *2 November 1986*

2 The role of mother is probably the most important career a woman can have.

> Ibid.

2056. Natalie Shainess (1915–)

1 At a recent meeting devoted to the theme of dissent, a Negro analyst pointed to the analyst's blind spot, in studying only the dissenters, but not the people or ideas dissented against. How valid a perception!

> "A Psychiatrist's View: Images of Woman—Past and
> Present, Overt and Obscured," *American Journal
> of Psychotherapy January 1969*

2 As we have become a thing-oriented, impulse-ridden, narcissistically self-preoccupied people, we are increasingly dedicated to the acquisition of things, and cultivate little else.

> Ibid.

3 It seems that the rewards of an affluent society turn bitter as gall in the mouth.

> Ibid.

4 In the generally progressive alienation of our times, we are back to the laws of the jungle, but without the gratification of biologic fulfillment.

> Ibid.

2057. Margaret Walker (1915–1998)

1 For my people thronging 47th Street in Chicago and Lenox
Avenue in New York and Rampart Street in New
Orleans, lost disinherited dispossessed and happy
people filling the cabarets and taverns and other
people's pocket. . . .

> "For My People," St. 6, *For My People* 1942

2 Let a new earth rise. Let another world be
born. Let a bloody
peace be written in the sky. Let a second
generation
full of courage issue forth;
let a people loving free—
dom come to growth.

> St. 10, Ibid.

3 Now this here gal warn't always tough
Nobody dreamed she'd turn out rough.

> "Kissie Lee," St. 2, Ibid.

4 Old women working by an age-old plan to make
their bread in ways as best they can.

> "Whores," St. 1, Ibid.

5 There were bizarre beginnings in old lands for
the making
of me.

> "Dark Blood" St. 1, Ibid.

6 I like it fine in Jail
And I don't want no Bail.

> "Girl Held Without Bail," St.2, *Prophets for a
> New Day 1970*

7   . . . the filthy
    privies marked "For Colored Only"
    and the drinking-soda-fountains
    tasting dismal and disgusting
    with a dry and dusty flavor
    of the deep humiliation. . . .

                                      "Now," Ibid.

8   Time to wipe away the slime.
    Time to end this bloody crime.

                                      St.2, Ibid.

9   Hurry up, Lucille, Hurry up
    We're Going to Miss Our Chance to go to Jail.
                                      "Street Demonstration," Ibid.

10 Everything I have ever written or hoped to write is dedicated
    . . . to our hope of peace and dignity and freedom in the world,
    not just as black people, or as Negroes, but as free human be-
    ings in a world community.
           Quoted in *By a Woman Writt*, Joan Goulianos, ed. *1974*

2058. Helen Yglesias (1915–)

1   They never ask the patient. The patient is anesthetized on the
    operating table, cut open. They call in the husband. "We think
    it best to remove this precancerous breast. Since this is your
    hunk of meat, do we have your permission, husband?"
                                      Ch. 1, *How She Died 1972*

2   "Life is too short to understand God altogether, especially
    nowadays."
                                      Ibid.

3   I wanted to pull him toward me and comfort him with my
    body as I had when he was a child, but that time was over. We
    could only be to each other what any two human beings might
    be, close or far, quick or dull, yielding or hard.
                                      Ch. 11, Ibid.

4   "I like to beat people at chess, and get better marks, and be
    elected to everything. It's disgusting to want those things. A
    person like that could do anything."
                                      Ibid.

5   Listening was a three times a day ritual with her, the news
    made even more nightmarish in the repetition: the war, the
    official statements, the enemy's denial, the traffic deaths,
    conspiracy charges, abortion reform rights, kidnappings, ter-
    rorism, peace talks, negotiations of all kinds, hijackings,
    charges and countercharges of anti-Semitism, Panther trials,
    civilian massacre trials, murder trials, riots, demonstrations,
    flaring wars between nations in corners of the world that
    didn't seem to really exist, the nonsense item they always
    found to end each broadcast with—and then the weather, re-
    ported as if every dip of the wind was a judgement day
    warning.
                                      Ch. 16, Ibid.

2059. Ethel Rosenberg (1915–1953)

1   Together we hunted down the answers to all the seemingly
    insoluble riddles which a complex and callous society pre-
    sented. . . . And yet for the sake of these answers, for the
    sake of American democracy, justice and brotherhood, for
    the sake of peace and bread and roses, and children's laugh-
    ter, we shall continue to sit here [in prison] in dignity and in
    pride—in the deep abiding knowledge of our innocence be-

fore God and man, until the truth becomes a clarion call to
all decent humanity.
                Letter to Julius Rosenberg, Sing Sing (27 May 1951),
          Death House Letters of Ethel and Julius Rosenberg 1953

2   Work and build, my sons, and build
    a monument to love and joy,
    to human worth, to faith we kept
    for you, my sons, for you.
                                      "If We Die" (24 January 1953), Ibid.

2060. Billie Holiday (1915–1959)

1   Southern trees bear a strange fruit,
    Blood on the leaves and blood at the root,
    Black bodies swinging in the Southern breeze,
    Strange fruit hanging from the poplar trees.
                                      "Strange Fruit" *1939*

2   Mama may have
    Papa may have
    But God bless the child that's got his own
    That's got his own.
                                      "God Bless the Child" *1941*

3   And when you're poor, you grow up fast.
                Ch. 1, *Lady Sings the Blues*, with William Dufty
                                      1956

4   I can't stand to sing the same song the same way two nights in
    succession, let alone two years or ten years. If you can, then it
    ain't music, it's close-order drill or exercise or yodeling or
    something, not music.
                                      Ch. 4, Ibid.

5   You can be up to your boobies in white satin, with gardenias
    in your hair and no sugar cane for miles, but you can still be
    working on a plantation.
                                      Ch. 11, Ibid.

6   Sometimes it's worse to win a fight than to lose.
                                      Ch. 13, Ibid.

7   People don't understand the kind of fight it takes to record
    what you want to record the way you want to record it.
                                      Ibid.

8   If you think dope is for kicks and for thrills, you're out of your
    mind. There are more kicks to be had in a good case of para-
    lytic polio or by living in an iron lung. If you think you need
    stuff to play music or sing, you're crazy. It can fix you so you
    can't play nothing or sing nothing.
                                      Ch. 23, Ibid.

9   In this country, don't forget, a habit is no damn private hell.
    There's no solitary confinement outside of jail. A habit is hell
    for those you love. And in this country it's the worst kind of
    hell for those who love you.
                                      Ch. 24, Ibid.

2061. Isobel Lennart (1915–1971)

1   FANNY. Look, suppose all you ever had for breakfast was
    onion rolls. All of a sudden one morning, in walks a bagel.
    You'd say, "Ugh! What's that?" Until you tried it. *That's* my
    trouble. I'm a bagel on a plate full of onion rolls!
                                      Act I, Sc. 3, *Funny Girl 1964*

2 NICK. Success is something to enjoy—to flaunt! Otherwise, why work so hard to get it?

> Sc. 10, Ibid.

3 NICK. Fanny, would you say you were a woman of—wide experience?...
FANNY...I've been too busy. What about you? *Hundreds* of girls, huh?
NICK. The count is in mere dozens. Of very minor entanglements. I like to feel free.
FANNY. You can get lonesome—being that free.
NICK. You can get lonesome—being that busy.

> Sc. 11, Ibid.

4 FANNY. It's wonderful to hear an audience applaud, but you can't take an audience home with you!

> Sc. 14, Ibid.

2062. Jean Stafford (1915–1979)

1 There were two objects of conversation; one was the food they were eating and the other was the food they had eaten at other times . . .

> "Maggie Meriwether's Rich Experience,"
> *The Innocents Abroad*, from *The Collected Stories
> of Jean Stafford 1969*

2 Abby's preconception of gambling derived from scenes in movies, and as she moved from table to table, endeavoring to understand the games, she realized that either her memory was at fault or Hollywood had carelessly added an apocryphal glitter and subtracted an essential gloom.

> "The Children's Game," Ibid.

3 . . . "From time to time, I need a rest from the exercitation of my intellect."

> "The Echo and the Nemesis," Ibid.

4 . . . (they revered education and, even when married, even when pregnant, took graduate courses in political science and Eastern philosophy), . . .

> "Polite Conversation," *The Bostonians*, Ibid.

2063. Fawn M. Brodie (1915–1981)

1 There is, of course, a gold mine or a buried treasure on every mortgaged homestead. Whether the farmer ever digs for it or not, it is there, haunting his daydreams when the burden of debt is most unbearable.

> Ch. 2, *No Man Knows My History 1945*

2 The paradise of the prophet [Joseph Smith]* had much of the earth in it.

> Ch. 13, Ibid.

*American prophet and founder of Mormons (1805–1844).

3 Mormon theology was never burdened with otherworldliness. There was a fine robustness about it that smelled of the frontier and that rejected an asceticism that was never endemic to America.

> Ibid.

4 A man's memory is bound to be a distortion of his past in accordance with his present interests, and the most faithful autobiography is likely to mirror less what a man was than what he had become.

> Ch. 19, Ibid.

5 A passion for politics stems usually from an insatiable need, either for power, or for friendship and adulation, or a combination of both.

> Ch. 1, *Thomas Jefferson** 1974

*American political philosopher, educator and architect (1743–1826), third president of the United States (1801–1809).

6 Show me a character whose life arouses my curiosity, and my flesh begins crawling with suspense.

> Quoted in "Home Q&A" by Marshall Berger in *The Los
> Angeles Times Home Magazine 20 February 1977*

7 Housework is a breeze. Cooking is a pleasant diversion. Putting up a retaining wall is a lark. But teaching is like climbing a mountain.

> Ibid.

2064. Ketti Frings (1915–1981)

1 EUGENE. If he hates it so much here, why does he stay?
BEN. You stupid little fool, it's like being caught in a photograph. Your face is there, and no matter how hard you try, how are you going to step out of a photograph?

> Act I, Sc. 1, *Look Homeward, Angel** 1957

*Stage adaptation of Thomas Wolfe's 1929 novel. In 1978, Frings collaborated on a musical version of her adaptation by the same name.

2065. Eleanor Perry (1915–1981)

1 "We've all known each other so long there's not even anyone to flirt with."

> *The Swimmer* (screenplay) *1967*

2 "That's your hang-up, Neddy-boy. You're afraid the sky will fall down if everybody doesn't love you. You'll lose the popularity contest, you won't be elected Head Boy—as if the whole world's a prep school!"

> Ibid.

3 Rape has become a kind of favor done to the female—a fairly commonplace male fantasy.

> Quoted in "Rebirth" by Kay Loveland and Estelle
> Changas, *The Hollywood Screenwriters*, Richard Corliss,
> ed. *1972*

4 . . . so long as a woman is dependent on a man for her self-image or her self-esteem she will remain without any sense of her own worth—can never be a fully realized human being.

> Ibid.

5 I believe that "the unexamined life is not worth living"— and what a glorious medium film is on which to conduct our examinations!

> Ibid.

6 Given a skillful cinematographer and technical staff almost any creative person can direct a film.

> Ibid.

2066. Ingrid Bergman (1915–1982)

1 . . . I saw my wrinkles in their wrinkles. You know, one looks at herself in the mirror every morning, and she doesn't see the difference, she doesn't realize that she is aging. But then she finds a friend who was young with her, and the friend isn't

461

young anymore, and all of a sudden, like a slap on her eyes, she remembers that she, too, isn't young anymore.

Quoted in "Ingrid Bergman," *The Egotists*
by Oriana Fallaci* 1963

*See 2416.

2 I've never sought success in order to get fame and money; it's the talent and the passion that count in success.

Ibid.

3 Things came to me asking to be done, and I did them—spontaneously, without asking whether it was wise or not. And the day after, I could say, "Maybe I shouldn't have done it." But years later, I always realized I was right in doing them.

Ibid.

2067. Dorothy Salisbury Davis (1916–)

1 There are seasons in Washington when it is even more difficult than usual to find out what is going on in the government. Possibly it is because nothing is going on, although a great many people seem to be working at it.

Ch. 1, *Old Sinners Never Die* 1959

2 We are all at the mercy of God as well as one another. And for that we can be grateful, He has so much more of it than we have.

Ch. 7, *Black Sheep Among White Lambs* 1963

3 She dressed more severely than was her fashion, needing herringbone for backbone . . .

"The Purple Is Everything," *Ellery Queen's
Mystery Magazine* 1964

4 The law is above the law you know.

Ch. 8, *The Little Brothers* 1973

5 You know what truth is, gentlemen? Truth is self-justification. That is everybody's truth. . . .

Ibid.

2068. Penelope Fitzgerald (1916–2000)

1 The dangerous and the ridiculous were necessary to his life, otherwise tenderness would overwhelm him.

Offshore 1978

2 [She] cared nothing for the future, and had, as a result, a great capacity for happiness.

Ibid.

3 The crucial moment when children realise that their parents are younger than they are had long since been passed by Martha.

Ibid.

4 Tenderly responsive to the self-deceptions of others, he was unfortunately too well able to understand his own.

Ibid.

5 The resulting uncertainty as to whether she was coming or going had made her, to some extent, mentally unstable.

Ibid.

6 His moral standards were much the same as Richard's; only he did not feel he was well enough off to apply them as often, and in such a wide range of conditions...

Ibid.

7 She was known to be one of the little ones who had filled in their colouring books irreverently, making our Lord's beard purple, or even green, largely, to be sure, because she never bothered to get hold of the best crayons first.

Ibid.

8 "She wants an Arts Centre. How can the arts have a centre? But she thinks they have, and she wishes to dislodge you."

The Bookshop 1979

9 She had once seen a heron flying across the estuary and trying, while it was on the wing, to swallow an eel which it had caught. The eel, in turn, was struggling to escape from the gullet of the heron and appeared a quarter, a half, or occasionally three-quarters of the way out. The indecision expressed by both creatures was pitiable.

Ibid.

10 Broadcasting House was in fact dedicated to the strangest project of the war, or of any war, that is, telling the truth.

Human Voices 1980

11 . . . hers must have been the last generation to fall in love without hope in such an unproductive way. After the war the species no longer found it biologically useful, and indeed it was not useful to Annie. Love without hope grows in its own atmosphere, and should encourage the imagination, but Annie's grew narrower.

Ibid.

12 The nation defended itself by counting large numbers of small things into separate containers.

Ibid.

13 Without prompting, the BBC had decided that truth was more important than consolation, and, in the long run, would be more effective.

Ibid.

14 Truth ensures trust, but not victory, or even happiness.

Ibid.

15 [The BBC operated like] a cross between a civil service, a powerful moral force, and an amateur theatrical company that wasn't too sure where next week's money was coming from . . .

Ibid.

16 "When the Germans arrive, and at best it will be in a few weeks, don't think of resistance, don't think of history. Nothing is so ungrateful as history. Think of yourselves, your homes and gardens . . . "

Ibid.

17 Lise replied that she was a psychic, with the result that she had a certain sensation in the points of her breasts whenever Fred was near at hand.

Ibid.

18 . . . England's wheezing before the autumn fogs began.

Ibid.

19 All her life she had been at a great disadvantage in finding it so much more easy to give than to take. Hating to see anyone in want, she would part without a thought with money or possessions, but she could accept only with the caution of a half-tamed animal.

The Gate of the Angels 1990

20   "... women like to live on their imagination. It's all they can afford, most of them."

Ibid.

21   They looked at each other in despair, and now there seemed to be another law or regulation by which they were obliged to say to each other what they did not mean and to attack what they wished to defend.

Ibid.

22   Over-prescriptions brought drama to the patients' tedious day. Too much antimony made them faint, too much quinine caused buzzing in the ears, too much salicylic acid brought on delirium...

Ibid.

23   Twigs snapped and dropped from above, sticky threads drifted across from nowhere, there seemed to be something like an assassination, on a small scale, taking place in the tranquil heart of summer.

Ibid.

24   ... how dangerous generosity is to the giver...

Ibid.

25   If they don't depend on true evidence, scientists are no better than gossips.

Ch. 3, Ibid.

26   However, no two people see the external world in exactly the same way. To every separate person a thing is what he thinks it is—in other words, not a thing, but a think.

Ch. 6, Ibid.

27   It's very good for an idea to be commonplace. The important thing is that a new idea should develop out of what is already there so that it soon becomes an old acquaintance. Old acquaintances aren't by any means always welcome, but at least one can't be mistaken as to who or what they are.

Ch. 20, Ibid.

28   They [the children] ought either to be quieter or more noisy than before, and it was disconcerting that they seemed to be exactly the same.

The Beginning of Spring 1997

29   A great many shots had hit people for whom they were not intended.

Ibid.

30   "The universe, after all, is within us. The way leads inwards, always inwards."

Ibid.

31   The benign indifference of the universe...

Ibid.

32   Now that he saw everything was going well, his mind was turning to his next charitable enterprise. With the terrible aimlessness of the benevolent, he was casting round for a new misfortune.

Ibid.

2069. Françoise Giroud (1916–)

1   Are there still virgins? One is tempted to answer no. There are only girls who have not yet crossed the line, because they want to preserve their market value. . . . Call them virgins if you wish, these travelers in transit.

Quoted in *Coronet*
November 1960

2   Nothing is more difficult than competing with a myth.

I Give You My Word 1974

3   ... the present evolution of women ... is to my mind the most profound revolution that highly developed societies will have to contend with. . . .

Ibid.

4   As though femininity is something you can lose the way you lose your pocketbook: hmm, where in the world did I put my femininity?

Ibid.

5   ... I don't for one moment believe that over the centuries some universal plot has been hatched by men to keep women in a state of servitude.

Ibid.

6   When mores are no longer founded on the law of civilization but on habit, then comes the revolt.

Ibid.

2070. Ruth Handler (1916–)

1   Domestic chores bored me silly. I missed the fast-paced business world and the adrenaline rush that came with closing a tough sale and delivering a gigantic order on time.

Quoted in *Women Inventors* by Linda Jacobs
Altman *1997*

2   I was—I *am*—a fiercely independent woman, one who has always felt the need to prove myself, even when I was just a child.

Ibid.

3   ... the most gratifying memories...from my sixteen years with Nearly Me* are the many times...I stood toe to toe in fitting rooms with women I was really helping. ...some came in depressed, confused, self-pitying. I'd fit them, and sometimes they would cry when they saw how Nearly Me had restored their looks.

Ibid.

*A company she founded that produced prosthetic breasts she designed for mastectomy patients.

2071. Elizabeth Hardwick (1916–)

1   Letters are above all useful as a means of expressing the ideal self; and no other method of communication is quite so good for this purpose. . . . In letters we can reform without practice, beg without humiliation, snip and shape embarrassing experiences to the measure of our own desires. . . .

"Anderson, Millay, and Crane* in Their Letters" (1953),
A View of My Own 1962

*Margaret A—, see 1656; Edna St. Vincent—, see 1632; Nathalia C—, see 2014.

2   Mothers born on relief have their babies on relief. Nothingness, truly, seems to be the condition of these New York people. . . . They are nomads going from one rooming house to another, looking for a toilet that functions.

"The Insulted and Injured: Books About Poverty," Ibid.

3 The fifties—they seem to have taken place on a sunny afternoon that asked nothing of you except a drifting belief in the moment and its power to satisfy.

"Domestic Manners," *Bartleby in Manhattan and Other Essays 1968*

4 The language of the younger generation . . . has the brutality of the city and an assertion of threatening power at hand, not to come. It is military, theatrical, and at its most coherent probably a lasting repudiation of empty courtesy and bureaucratic euphemism.

"The Apotheosis of Martin Luther King," Ibid.

5 *Hedda [Gabler]*,* rather than Nora [of *A Doll's House*],** was the real prophecy.

Seduction and Betrayal: Women in Literature 1974
*Play by Norwegian playwright Henrik Ibsen (1828–1906).
**Play by Swedish playwright August Strindberg (1849–1912)

6 Women, wronged in one way or another, are given the overwhelming beauty of endurance, the capacity for high or low suffering, for violent feeling absorbed, finally tranquilized, for the radiance of humility, for silence, secrecy, impressive acceptance. Heroines are, then, heroic.

Ibid.

7 The raging productivity of the Victorians, shattered nerves and punctured stomachs, but it was a thing noble, glorious, awesome in itself.

Ibid.

8 They [the F. Scott Fitzgeralds]* had created themselves together, and they always saw themselves, their youth, their love, their lost youth and lost love, their failures and memories, as a sort of living fiction.

Ibid.
*American author (1896–1940) and his wife Zelda; see 1771.

9 Sex can no longer be the germ, the seed of fiction. Sex is an episode, most properly conveyed in an episodic manner, quickly, often ironically. It is a bursting forth of only one of the cells in the body of the omnipotent "I," the one who hopes by concentration of tone and voice to utter the sound of reality.

Address, "Seduction and Betrayal" (1972), Ibid.

10 Stoicism...cannot be without its remaining uses in life and love; but if we read contemporary fiction we learn that improvisation is better.

Ibid.

11 You cannot seduce anyone when innocence is not a value. Technology annihilates consequence. Heroism hurts and no one easily consents to be under its rule.

Ibid.

12 The curious modernity of the plot [*Hedda Gabler*] is that the workings of destiny have shrunk to yawning boredom.

Ibid.

13 The "book"—a plaguing growth that does not itself grow, but attaches, hangs on, a tumorous companion made up of the deranged cells of learning, experience, thinking.

Sleepless Nights 1979

2072. Jane Jacobs (1916–)

1 But look what we have built . . . Low-income projects that become worse centers of delinquency, vandalism, and general social hopelessness than the slums they were supposed to replace. . . . Cultural centers that are unable to support a good bookstore. Civic centers that are avoided by everyone but bums. . . . Promenades that go from no place to nowhere and have no promenades. Expressways that eviscerated great cities. This is not the rebuilding of cities. This is the sacking of cities.

Introduction, *The Death and Life of Great American Cities 1961*

2 There is a quality even meaner than outright ugliness or disorder, and this meaner quality is the dishonest mask of pretended order, achieved by ignoring or suppressing the real order that is struggling to exist and to be served.

Ibid.

3 Streets and their sidewalks, the main public places of a city, are its most vital organs...If a city's streets are safe from barbarism and fear, the city is thereby tolerably safe from barbarism and fear...To keep the city safe is a fundamental task of a city's streets and its sidewalks.

Pt. I, Ch. 2, Ibid.

4 Conventionally, neighborhood parks or park-like open spaces are considered boons conferred on the deprived populations of cities. Let us turn this thought around, and consider city parks deprived places that need the boon of life and appreciation conferred on them.

Ch. 5, Ibid.

5 The main responsibility of city planning and design should be to develop—insofar as public policy and action can do so—cities that are congenial places for...[a] great range of unofficial plans, ideas and opportunities to flourish, along with the flourishing of...public enterprises.

Pt. III, Ch.13, Ibid.

6 Innovating economies expand and develop. Economies that do not add new kinds of goods and services, but continue only to repeat old work, do not expand much nor do they, by definition, develop.

Ch. 2, *The Economy of Cities 1969*

7 A city that is large for its time is always an impractical settlement because size greatly intensifies whatever serious practical problems exist in an economy at a given time.

Ch. 3, Ibid.

8 But because development subverts the status quo, the status quo soon subverts governments.

Ch. 8, Ibid.

9 The bureaucratized, simplified cities, so dear to present-day city planners and urban designers, and familiar also to readers of science fiction and utopian proposals, run counter to the processes of city growth and economic development. Conformity and monotony, even when they are embellished with a froth of novelty, are not attributes of developing and economically vigorous cities. They are attributes of stagnant settlements.

Ibid.

2073. Natasha Josefowitz (1916–)

1 Even though awareness must precede action, they are very different processes, and what we are experiencing today is the time lag between the two. For modern women, the time lag between heightened awareness and the need for action presents a new problem. Many are experiencing a real gap between how

they are supposed to feel and act and how they actually feel and act. All these discrepancies reinforce the inability of many women to identify the cause of their powerlessness.

Ch. 1, *Paths to Power 1980*

2   Speaking is the most visible of the four uncommon skills. You may not be well read, you may not know how to count, you may write poorly, but as soon as you open your mouth people get an impression of you based on both the content of your message and one the way you deliver it.

Ch. 4, Ibid.

2074. Florynce R. Kennedy (1916–2000)

1   . . . There can be no real pervasive system of oppression, such as that in the United States, without the consent of the oppressed.

"Institutionalized Oppression vs. the Female," *Sisterhood Is Powerful*, Robin Morgan,* ed. *1970*
*See 2864.

2   Women are dirt searchers; their greatest worth is eradicating rings on collars and tables. Never mind real-estate boards' corruption and racism, here's your soapsuds. Everything she is doing is peripheral, expendable, crucial, and nonnegotiable. Cleanliness is next to godliness.

Ibid.

3   Every form of bigotry can be found in ample supply in the legal system of our country. It would seem that Justice (usually depicted as a woman) is indeed blind to racism, sexism, war and poverty.

Ibid.

4   Oppressed people are frequently very oppressive when liberated.

Ibid.

5   Being a mother is a noble status, right? Right. So why does it change when you put "unwed" and "welfare" in front of it?

Quoted in "The Verbal Karate of Florence R. Kennedy, Esq." by Gloria Steinem,* *Ms.* (New York) *March 1973*
*See 2581.

6   The biggest sin is sitting on your ass.

Ibid.

7   Don't agonize. Organize.

Ibid.

8   If men could get pregnant, abortion would be a sacrament.

Ibid.

9   Niggerization is the result of oppression—and it doesn't just apply to black people. Old people, poor people, and students can also get niggerized.

Ibid.

10   There are very few jobs that actually require a penis or vagina. All other jobs should be open to everybody.

Quoted in "Freelancer with No Time to Write" by John Brady, *Writer's Digest February 1974*

11   If you have a child, you know that when he gets quiet, that's when you start to worry. That's why the Establishment should be worried about the antiestablishmentarians—the women, the Blacks, the youth, the aged, all the people who have no full part in the system, those I call the "niggers" of this country.

They are planning campaigns in each legislative district. They are moving out of the streets and into the executive suites.

Quoted in "Impeachment?" by Claire Safran, *Redbook* (New York) *April 1974*

2075. Bella Lewitzky (1916–)

1   Making social comment is an artificial place for an artist to start from. If an artist is touched by some social condition, what the artist creates will reflect that, but you can't force it.

Quoted in "Modern Dance Group Plants Western Roots" by Didi Moore, *San Francisco Chronicle 4 March 1979*

2   When you dance, it's only for now. When you choreograph, it's with you day and night. But when you get through, the creation leaves you like a child.

Ibid.

2076. Patricia McLaughlin (1916–)

1   Discoveries have reverberations. A new idea about oneself or some aspect of one's relations to others unsettles all one's other ideas, even the superficially related ones. No matter how slightly, if shifts one's entire orientation. And somewhere along the line of consequences, it changes one's behavior.

Quoted in *American Scholar Autumn 1972*

2077. Elizabeth Catlett Mora (1916?–)

1   I like to interpret women: women's ideas, women's feelings. The female aestheticism is more sensitive, and I'm happy to be a part of it.

Quoted in "Breaking the Mold" by Sharon Fitzgerald, *Ms.* (New York) *September/October 1996*

2078. Cicely Saunders (1916–)

1   Deception is not as creative as truth. We do best in life if we look at it with clear eyes, and I think that applies to coming up to death as well.

Quoted in "Dying with Dignity" by David Brand, *Time* (New York) *5 September 1988*

2079. Anya Seton (1916–)

1   People in England seemed to think nothing of false teeth, even when they got them from the National Health.

Pt. I, Ch. 1, *Green Darkness 1972*

2   "As I grew up I got cynical. I'd see Mother enthusiastic and involved with charlatans. Numerologists and astrologers who charged five hundred dollars for a 'reading' which was so vague you could twist the meaning any way you wanted. And faith healers who couldn't seem to heal themselves, and a Yogi in California who preached purity, sublimity, and continence, and then tried to seduce me one day while Mother was out."

Ch. 2, Ibid.

3   "Truth is naturally universal," said Akananda, "and shines into many different windows, though some of them are clouded."

Pt. III, Ch. 19, Ibid.

2080. Frances Silverberg (1916–)

1   It was better not to speak, not let your face or eyes show what you were feeling, because if people didn't know how you felt

about them, or things, or maybe thought you had no feelings at all, they couldn't hurt you as much, only a little.
"Rebecca by Any Other Name," American Scene: New Voices, Don Wolfe, ed. 1963

2081. Annie Skau (1916?–)

1 The old Christian who has lived and walked with the Lord for many years is living in a treasure chamber.
Quoted in "Saints Among Us," Time (New York) 29 December 1975

2082. Mary Stewart (1916–)

1 It is harder to kill a whisper than even a shouted calumny.
Bk.1, Ch. 1, The Last Enchantment 1979

2 There are few men more superstitious than soldiers. They are, after all, the men who live closest to death.
Bk. 2, Ch. 3, Ibid.

2083. Patricia Swerda (1916–)

1 Go to nature. Once you learn how plants grow, you will know how to arrange them.
Quoted in "Ikebana, a Zen way with flowers" by Karen Mathieson, Pacific Magazine 28 May 1989

2 The only difference between a rut and a grave are the dimensions.
Ibid.

2084. Hiltgunt Zassenhaus (1916–)

1 If they bomb my home in Hamburg, all I have left is what I can carry with me. . . . [But] there was something no suitcase could hold. It was intangible and the prisoners hungered for it. Only our minds and hearts could give truth and hope.
Walls: Resisting the Third Reich—One Woman's Story 1974

2085. Natalia Ginzburg (1916–1991)

1 I haven't managed to become learned about anything, even the things I've loved most in life: in me they remain scattered images, which admittedly feed my life of memories and feelings, but fail to fill my empty cultural wasteland.
"He and I" (1963), Italian Writing Today, Raleigh Trevelyan, ed. 1967

2 . . . it hurts me not to love music, because I feel my spirit is hurt by not loving it. But there's nothing to be done about it; I shall never understand music, and never love it. If I occasionally hear music I like, I can't remember it; so how could I love a thing I can't remember.
Ibid.

3 My tidiness, and my untidiness, are full of regret and remorse and complex feelings.
Ibid.

4 As far as the education of children is concerned I think they should be taught not the little virtues but the great ones. Not thrift but generosity and an indifference to money; not caution but courage and a contempt for danger; not shrewdness but frankness and a love of truth; not tact but love for one's neighbour and self-denial; not a desire for success but a desire to be and to know.
"The Little Virtues" (1962), The Little Virtues, Dick Davis, tr. 1985

5 A vocation is man's one true wealth and salvation.
Ibid.

6 The great can also contain the little, but by the laws of nature there is no way that the little can contain the great.
Ibid.

7 In these days, when a dialogue between parents and their children has become possible...it is necessary that in this dialogue we show ourselves for what we are, imperfect, in the hope that our children will not resemble us but be stronger and better than us.
Ibid.

8 Not too soon and not too late; the secret of education lies in choosing the right time to do things.
Ibid.

9 The true defense against wealth is not a fear of wealth—of its fragility and of the vicious consequences that it can bring—the true defense against wealth is an indifference to money. There is no better way to teach a child this indifference than to give him money to spend when there is money—because then he will learn to part with it without worrying about it or regretting it.
Ibid.

10 The money we give our children should be given for no reason; it should be given indifferently so that they will learn to receive it indifferently; but it should be given not so that they learn to love it, but so that they learn not to love it, so that they realize its true nature and its inability to satisfy our truest desires, which are those of the spirit. When we elevate money into a prize, a goal, an object to be striven for, we give it a position, an importance, a nobility, which it should not have in our children's eyes. We implicitly affirm the principle—a false one—that money is the crowning reward for work, its ultimate objective.
Ibid.

11 School should be from the beginning the first battle which a child fights for himself, without us; from the beginning it should be clear that this is his battlefield and that we can give him only very slight and occasional help there. And if he suffers from injustice there or is misunderstood it is necessary to let him see that there is nothing strange about this, because in life we have to expect to be constantly misunderstood and misinterpreted, and to be victims of injustice; and the only thing that matters is that we do not commit injustices ourselves.
Ibid.

12 He says they're all play-acting; and maybe he's right. Because, in the midst of my tears and his rages, I am completely calm. Over my real sorrows I never weep.
Ibid.

13 The birth and development of a vocation needs space, space and silence, the free silence of space.
Ibid.

14 What we must remember above all in the education of our children is that their love of life should never weaken.
Ibid.

15 . . . sometimes I wonder if we were those two people nearly twenty years ago along via Nazionale; two people who talked so politely, so urbanely, in the sunset; who chatted about everything, and nothing; two pleasant talkers, two young

intellectuals out for a walk; so young, so polite, so distracted, so ready to judge each other with absent kindliness, so ready to say goodbye for ever, in that sunset, on that street corner.

Ibid.

2086. Eve Merriam (1916–1992)

1 MARY JONES. I asked a man in prison once how he happened to be there and he said that he had stolen a pair of shoes. I told him if he had stolen a railroad he would be a United States Senator.

Out of Our Fathers' House, with Paula Wagner and Jack Hofsiss *1975*

2 It's up to women to shed our old habits, our old self-pity. We cannot afford to waste our energies in "What will men think? How will they respond? We have to do what is necessary to be done. We have to stop apologizing and stop being cute. We have to become *acute*.

Quoted in *Interviews with Contemporary Women Playwrights* by Kathleen Betsko* and Rachel Koenig *1987*
*See 2739.

3 Poetry is the liveliest use of language, and nobody knows more instinctively how to take delight in that playfulness than children.

"Serious Play: Reading Poetry with Children,"
The Academy of American Poets Web Site,
http://www.poets.org *April 1999*

2087. Betty Furness (1916–1994)

1 You fellows have got to get this [phosphate-pollution problem] straightened out, because the laundry's piling up.

Quoted in *Bella!** Mel Ziegler, ed. *1972*
*Reference to B— Abzug, see 2180.

2088. Maeve Brennan (1917–)

1 She had found that the more the child demanded of her, the more she had to give. Strength came up in waves that had their source in a sea of calm and unconquered devotion. The child's holy trust made her open her eyes, and she took stock of herself and found that everything was all right, and that she could meet what challenges arose and meet them well, and that she had nothing to apologize for—on the contrary, she had every reason to rejoice.

"The Eldest Child," *The New Yorker 23 June 1968*

2 She . . . enjoyed the illusion that life had nothing to teach her.

Ibid.

3 He wished they could go back to the beginning and start all over again, but the place where they had stood together, where they had been happy, was all trampled over and so spoiled that it seemed impossible ever to make it smooth again.

Ibid.

2089. Gwendolyn Brooks (1917–2000)

1 What she wanted was to donate to the world a good Maude Martha. That was the offering, the bit of art, that could not come from any other. She would polish and hone that.

Ch. 6, *Maude Martha 1943*

2 She had a tremendous impatience with other people's ideas—unless those happened to be exactly like hers; even then, often as not, she gave hurried, almost angry, affirmative, and flew onto emphatic illumination of her own.

Ch. 23, *Ibid.*

3 Abortions will not let you forget.
You remember the children you got that you did not get. . . .

"The Mother," St. 1, *A Street in Bronzeville 1945*

4 That the trouble with grown-ups was that under the magnificent shell of
adulthood, just under,
Waited the baby full of tantrums.

"A Bronzeville Mother Loiters in Mississippi. Meanwhile, a Mississippi Mother Burns Bacon," St. 2, *Ibid.*

5 He whispered something to her, did the Fine Prince, something about love and night and intention.
She heard no hoof-beat of the horse and saw no flash of the shining steel.

St. 10, *Ibid.*

6 I hold my honey and I store my bread
In little jars and cabinets of my will.
I label clearly, and each latch and lid
I bid, Be firm till I return from hell.
I am very hungry. I am incomplete.
And none can tell when I may dine again.

"My dreams, my works, must wait till after hell," *Ibid.*

7 People like definite decisions,
Tidy answers, all the little ravellings
Snipped off, the lint removed, they
Hop happily among their roughs
Calling what they can't clutch insanity
Or saintliness.

"Memorial to Ed Blanc," St. 3, *Annie Allen 1949*

8 Two who are Mostly Good.
Two who have lived their day,
But keep on putting on their clothes
And putting things away.

"The Bean Eaters," St. 2, *The Bean Eaters 1960*

9 We real cool. We
Left school. We

Lurk late. We
Strike straight. We

Sing sin. We
Thin gin. We

Jazz June. We
Die soon.

"We Real Cool," *Ibid.*

10 I wonder if the elephant
Is lonely in his stall
When all the boys and girls are gone
And there's no shout at all,
And there's no one to stamp before,
No one to note his might.
Does he hunch up, as I do,
Against the dark of night?

"Pete at the Zoo," *Ibid.*

11 He opened us—
who was a key,

who was a man.

"Malcolm X,"* Sts. 4-5, *In the Mecca 1968*
*Assumed name of Malcolm Little, American Black activist and founder of the Organization of Afro-American Unity (1964); assassinated (1925–1965).

12 Does man love Art? Man visits Art, but squirms
Art hurts. Art urges voyages—
and it is easier to stay at home,
the nice beer ready.
"The Chicago Picasso," St. 1, Ibid.

13 The worthy poor. The very very worthy
And beautiful poor. Perhaps just not too swarthy?

Perhaps just not too dirty nor too dim
Nor—passionate.
"The Lovers of the Poor" (1944), *The Woman That I Am,
The Literature and Culture of Contemporary Women
of Color*, D. Soyini Madison, ed. *1994*

14 Their League is allotting largess to the Lost.
But to put their clean, their pretty money, to put
Their money collected from delicate rose-fingers
Tipped with their hundred flawless rose-nails seems . . .
Ibid.

15 Already I am no longer looked at with lechery or love.
My daughters and sons have put me away with marbles and
dolls,
Are gone from the house.
My husband and lovers are pleasant or somewhat polite
And night is night.
"A Sunset of the City," Sts. 1–2 *n.d.*

16 Live not for battles won.
Live not for the-end-of-the-song.
Live in the along.
"Speech to the Young : Speech to the Progress-Toward,"
St. 2 *n.d.*

17 Love.
Complete
your pledges, reinforce your aides, renew
stance, testament.
"The Good Man," St. 1 *n.d.*

18 You did not know the Black continent
that had to be reached
was you.
"To the Diaspora," St. 2 *n.d.*

2090. Leonora Carrington (1917–)
1 Sentimentality is a form of fatigue.
"The Happy Corpse Story" (*Le Nouveau
Commerce*, No. 31, 1975), *The Seventh Horse
and Other Tales 1988*

2091. Anne Cumming (1917–)
1 Sex is a short cut to everything.
Ch. 1, *The Love Quest* (autobio.) *1991*

2092. Barbara Deming (1917–1984)
1 It is particularly hard on us as pacifists, of course, to face our
own anger. It is particularly painful for us—hard on our pride,
too—to have to discover in ourselves murderers.
"On Anger," *We Cannot Live Without Our Lives 1974*

2 If men put from them in fear all that is "womanish" in them,
then long, of course, for that missing part of their natures, so
seek to possess it by possessing us; and because they have

feared it in their own souls seek, too, to dominate it in us—
seek even to slay it—well, we're where we are now, aren't we?
"Two Perspectives on Women's Struggles," Ibid.

2093. Phyllis Diller (1917–)
1 Cleaning your house while your kids are still growing
Is like shoveling the walk before it stops snowing.
Phyllis Diller's Housekeeping Hints 1966

2 Never go to bed mad. Stay up and fight.
Ibid.

3 You know you're getting old, when your back starts going out
more than you do.
Quoted in Earl Wilson's syndicated "Broadway" column
8 September 1978

2094. Katherine Graham (1917–)
1 If one is rich and one's a woman, one can be quite misunder-
stood.
Quoted in "The Power That Didn't Corrupt" by
Jane Howard,* *Ms.* (New York) *October 1974*
*See 2596.

2 So few grown women like their lives.
Ibid.

3 To love what you do and feel that it matters—how could anything be more fun?
Ibid.

4 Bromidic though it may sound, some questions *don't* have answers, which is a terribly difficult lesson to learn.
Ibid.

2095. Han Suyin (1917–)
1 What we loved best about England was the grass—the short,
clean, incredibly green grass with its underlying tough, springy
turf, three hundred years growing.
Ch. 2, *Destination Chungking 1942*

2 The city hums with noise and work and hope. This is Chungking, not dead Pompeii—five hundred thousand Chinese with a
will to withstand, to endure and build again. Next year, next
spring, the planes will lay it waste again. Next autumn we shall
be building. . . .
Ch. 12, Ibid.

3 "Your laws are ineffective," Wen declared. "Why? Because no
system of control will work as long as most of those administering the law against an evil have more than a finger dipped
into it themselves."
Ch. 13, Ibid.

4 "I'd sell my love for food any day. The rice bowl is to me the
most valid reason in the world for doing anything. A piece of
one's soul to the multitudes in return for rice and wine does
not seem to me a sacrilege."
Preface, *A Many-Splendored Thing 1950*

5 "For sages and wise men have been mute for many centuries,
and their names are forgotten. But drunkards leave a resound-
ing echo after them."
Ch. 7, Ibid.

6 Our feelings are very much governed by commonplace associations, and often influenced by that sort of short-term logic which renders steady thinking superfluous.

Pt. II, Ch. 1, Ibid.

7 Foolish, mad, invulnerable in lunacy, having forgotten what I knew the winter before; that no one is invulnerable to repeated suggestion; that I was no different, no stronger, no more able to withstand reiteration than others...

Pt. III, Ch. 8, Ibid.

8 Afterwards, as happens when a man is safely dead, they sang his praise.

Pt. IV, Ibid.

9 This is Malaya. Everything takes a long, a very long time, in Malaya. Things get done, occasionally, but more often they don't, and the more in a hurry you are, the quicker you break down.

Ch. 2, *And the Rain My Drink* 1956

10 Barbed wire fences the clearings where man survives, and outside it is the grey-green toppling surge, all-engulfing, of the jungle.

Ch. 8, Ibid.

11 "I'm nicely dead," she told Leo, and it was his turn to find nothing to say.

Pt. I, Ch. 1, *The Mountain Is Young* 1958

12 ... all humans are frightened of their own solitude. Yet only in solitude can man learn to know himself, learn to handle his own eternity of aloneness. And love from one being to another can only be that two solitudes come nearer, recognize and protect and comfort each other.

Pt. V, Ch. 1, Ibid.

13 She was plunged in this new consciousness where vision and hearing was all, in which there was total forgetting of self, the body moving without knowing itself in movement, wholly transported in this same ecstasy, the trance concentration which here made her one with all the thousands gathered.

Pt. II, Ch. 13, Ibid.

14 How few of us really try to find out what we're like, really, inside?

Winter Love 1962

15 The world needs the artist who records, with dispassionate compassion, more than the missionary who proclaims with virulence unreal crusades against reality, especially those who want to put the clock back to an ideal past that never was.

Pt. I, Ch. 1, *The Crippled Tree* 1965

16 For exploitation and oppression is not a matter of *race*. It is the system, the apparatus of world-wide brigandage called imperialism, which made the Powers behave the way they did. I have no illusions on that score, nor do I believe that any Asian nation or African nation, in the same state of dominance, and with the same system of colonial profit-amassing and plunder, would have behaved otherwise.

Ch. 9, Ibid.

17 These ways to make people buy were strange and new to us, and many bought for the sheer pleasure at first of holding in the hand and talking of something new. And once this was done, it was like opium, we could no longer do without this new bauble, and thus, though we hated the foreigners and though we knew they were ruining us, we bought their goods. Thus I learned the art of the foreigners, the art of creating in the human heart restlessness, disquiet, hunger for new things, and these new desires became their best helpers.

Ch. 15, Ibid.

18 A country is not truly betrayed to the enemy outside its gates unless there are also traitors within. For money, for power, these can be found.

Ch. 17, Ibid.

19 Looking back now, with the hindsight of history, I can understand it so much better,. But understanding is also effacement, a vagueness, which explains, but explains away the minute agonies, the grief that warps a life, which accepts, as a tree, crippled at its root by some voracious stabbing insect and for ever after bearing the mark of the beast upon its unfolding, is accepted in the landscape.

Pt. II, Ch. 18, Ibid.

20 "Goldfish are flowers," said Papa, "flowers that move."

Ch. 26, Ibid.

21 Pain occupies its verbal niche in a construction of words, building a life after it has been lived, for what is lived is encountered in a retrospect of sentences made to fit what happened shaped by what was.

Ch. 30, Ibid.

22 On the railway...beneficent dragons champing docile impatience on the iron tracks, insides of fire so still, hooting melody of the night proclaiming life, life roaring, life waiting to pounce.

Ibid.

2096. Lena Horne (1917–)

1 It's ill-becoming for an old broad to sing about how bad she wants it. But occasionally we do.

Quoted in *Time* (New York) 17 October 1988

2 Always be smarter than the people who hire you.

Remark *n.d.*

2097. Estelle R. Ramey (1917–)

1 ... What is human and the same about the males and females classified as *Homo sapiens* is much greater than the differences.

"Men's Monthly Cycles (They Have Them Too, You Know)," *The First Ms. Reader*, Francine Klagsbrun, ed. *1972*

2 In man, the shedding of blood is always associated with injury, disease, or death. Only the female half of humanity is seen to have the magical ability to bleed profusely and still rise phoenix-like each month from the gore.

Ibid.

3 Women's chains have been forged by men, not by anatomy.

Ibid.

4 I don't mind ... The fun and games of being treated like a fragile flower. But as a physiologist working with the unromantic scientific facts of life, I find it harder to delude myself about feminine frailty.

Quoted in *The Prime of Ms. America* by Janet Harris* *1975*
*See 2051.

5 It is said, for instance, that men are innately more aggressive than women. But conditioning, not sex hormones, makes them that way. Anyone seeing women at a bargain-basement sale —where aggression is viewed as appropriate, even endearing— sees aggression that would make Attila the Hun turn pale.
> Quoted in "Are Men and Women Different?" by Judith Viorst,* *Redbook* (New York) *November 1978*
> *See 2479.

2098. Christiane Rochefort (1917–)

1 CELINE. It's not only that you are killing grass and trees. . . . You are killing LIFE.
> *Les Stances à Sophie 1970*

2 JULIA. Never argue with them. You're always forgetting you're a woman. They never listen to what you're saying, they just want to listen to the music of your voice.
> Ibid.

3 CELINE. Don't you read the paper? Don't you know that men don't hit their wives any more?
> Ibid.

4 . . . when someone tells you that you're paranoic in a situation that is not socialized yet, you feel you are.
> Quoted in "Les Stances à Sophie" by Annette Levy, *Women and Film* (Vol. I, Nos. 3 and 4) *1973*

5 You can go to the hospital. If you don't go to the hospital, you can go to marriage. And if you don't go to marriage you can go to the women's movement.
> Ibid.

2099. Helen Suzman (1917–)

1 Liberalism has a future in South Africa, but fundamental changes will take a lot longer than most people think.
> Quoted in World Notes, *Time* (New York) *29 May 1989*

2100. Raisa Davydovna Orlova (1917–1964)

1 Beliefs and convictions reach out from the past, and they cannot be altered by fervent desire alone. They possess their own logic and illogic, their own organic existence, their own rhythm of development.
> Introduction, *Memoirs*, Samuel Cioran, tr. *1983*

2 The fate of a song that had become part of folklore is inscrutable.
> Ch. 10, Ibid.

3 The working morning. Now I love the morning more than the evening, the spring more than the fall. The promise more than the fulfillment.
> Ch. 24, Ibid.

2101. Carson McCullers (1917–1967)

1 "There are those who know and those who don't know. And for every ten thousand who don't know there's only one who knows. That's the miracle of all time—that these millions know so much but don't know this."
> Pt. I, Ch. 1, *The Heart is a Lonely Hunter 1940*

2 The inside room was a very private place. She could be in the middle of a house full of people and still feel like she was locked up by herself.
> Pt. II, Ch. 5, Ibid.

3 "Today we are not put up on the platforms and sold at the courthouse square. But we are forced to sell our strength, our time, our souls during almost every hour that we live. We have been freed from one kind of slavery only to be delivered into another."
> Ch. 6, Ibid.

4 "Say a man died and left his mule to his four sons. The sons would not wish to cut up the mule into four parts and each take his share. They would own and work the mule together. That is the way Marx says all of the natural resources should be owned—not by one group of rich people but by all the workers of the world as a whole."
> Ibid.

5 An army post in peacetime is a dull place. Things happen, but then they happen over and over again. . . . But perhaps the dullness of a post is caused most of all by insularity and by a surfeit of leisure and safety, for once a man enters the army he is expected only to follow the heels ahead of him.
> Ch. 1, *Reflections in a Golden Eye 1941*

6 Three words were in the captain's heart. He shaped them soundlessly with his trembling lips, as he had not breath to spare for a whisper: "I am lost." And having given up life, the Captain suddenly began to live.
> Ch. 3, Ibid.

7 His preoccupation with the soldier grew in him like a disease. As in cancer, when the cells unaccountably rebel and begin the insidious self-multiplication that will ultimately destroy the body, so in his mind did the thoughts of the soldier grow out of all proportion to their normal sphere.
> Ch. 4, Ibid.

8 This August she was twelve and five-sixths years old. She was five feet and three-quarter inches tall, and she wore a Number 7 shoe. . . . If she reached her height on her eighteenth birthday, she had five and one-sixth growing years ahead of her. Therefore, according to mathematics and unless she could somehow stop herself, she would grow to be over nine feet tall. And what would be a lady who was over nine feet high? She would be a Freak.
> Pt. I, *The Member of the Wedding 1946*

9 This was the summer when for a long time she had not been a member. She belonged to no club and was a member of nothing in the world. Frankie had become an unjoined person who hung around in the doorways, and she was afraid.
> Ibid.

10 "We all of us somehow caught. We born this way or that way and we don't know why. But we caught anyhow. . . . And maybe we wants to widen and bust free. But no matter what we do we still caught. Me is me and you is you and he is he. We each one of us somehow caught all by ourself."
> Pt. II, Ch. 2, Ibid.

11 "I see a green tree. And to me it is green. And you would call the tree green also. And we would agree on this. But is the colour you see as green the same colour I see as green? Or say we both call a colour black. But how do we know that what you see as black is the same colour I see as black?"
> Ibid.

12 F. Jasmine did not want to go upstairs, but she did not know how to refuse. It was like going into a fair booth, or fair ride, that once having entered you cannot leave until the exhibition

or the ride is finished. Now it was the same with this soldier, this date. She could not leave until it ended.

Ch. 3, Ibid.

13 FRANKIE. The trouble with me is that for a long time I have been just an "I" person. . . . All people belong to a "we" except me...Not to belong to a "we" makes you too lonesome.

The Member of the Wedding (play) 1950

14 . . . the anodyne of time...

"The Sojourner," *The Ballad of the Sad Café* 1951

15 His own life seemed so solitary, a fragile column supporting nothing amidst the wreckage of the years.

Ibid.

16 Was it indeed true that at one time he had called this stranger, Elizabeth, Little Butterduck during nights of love, that they had lived together, shared perhaps a thousand days and nights and —finally—endured in the misery of sudden solitude the fiber by fiber (jealousy, alcohol and money quarrels) destruction of the fabric of married love.

Ibid.

17 "*L'improvisation de la vie humaine,*" he said. "There's nothing that makes you so aware of the improvisation of human existence as a song unfinished. Or an old address book."

Ibid.

18 Sweet, casual intimacy, the soft-fleshed loveliness indisputably possessed.

Ibid.

19 Ferris glimpsed disorder of his life: the succession of cities, of transitory loves; and time, the sinister glissando of the years, time always.

Ibid.

20 It is a curious emotion, this certain homesickness I have in mind. With Americans, it is a national trait, as native to us as the rollercoaster or the jukebox. It is no simple longing for the home town or country of our birth. The emotion is Janus-faced: we are torn between a nostalgia for the familiar and an urge for the foreign and strange. As often as not, we are homesick most for the places we have never known.

"Look Homeward, Americans" (*Vogue*, New York, 1 December 1940), *The Mortgaged Heart*, Margarita G. Smith, ed. 1972

21 All men are lonely. But sometimes it seems to me that we Americans are the loneliest of all. Our hunger for foreign places and new ways has been with us almost like a national disease. Our literature is stamped with a quality of longing and unrest, and our writers have been great wanderers.

Ibid.

2102. Violeta Parra (1917–1967)

1 I do not play the guitar for applause. I sing the difference that there is between what is true and is false; otherwise I do not sing.

Remark *n.d.*

2103. Fannie Lou Hamer (1917–1977)

1 Ain' no such thing as I can hate anybody and hope to see God's face.

Quoted in Introduction (p. xi), *Civil Wars* by June Jordan* 1981

*See 2634.

2 Let's face it. What's hurtin' the Black folks that's without, is hurtin' the white folks that's without. If the white folk fight for theyself, and the Black folk for theyself, we gonna crumble apart. These are things that we gonna have to fight together. We got to fight in America for ALL the people . . . and I'm perfectly willing to make this country what it have to be.

Slogan, Women for Racial & Economic Equality *n.d.*

2104. Marie Vassiltchikov (1917–1978)

1 After dinner we had a long discussion with a famous zoologist about the best way to get rid of Adolf.* He said that in India natives use tigers' whiskers chopped very fine and mixed with food. The victim dies a few days later and nobody can detect the cause. But where do we find a tiger's whiskers?

Diary entry, *Berlin Diaries, 1940–45* 1987

*Reference to Adolf Hitler, Austrian-born German Nazi dictator (1889–1945).

2 If they [the royals] don't stand up for their beliefs, where will all this end?

Diary entry (c. 1944), Ibid.

2105. Sybil Leek (1917–1982)

1 You can't be sure who the Devil is these days. He might be a TV or movie producer in disguise.

Ch. 1, *Diary of a Witch* 1968

2 Perhaps telepathy will remain a mystery for many more years but it has always been within the power of a few people in every generation to transmit and receive thoughts. People in love often claim this power. Maybe we are being forced to realize that love is in itself a magical power and that awareness may be instrumental in preventing our own destruction.

Ch. 6, Ibid.

3 We are about to move into the Aquarian age of clearer thinking. Astrology and witchcraft both have a contribution to make to the new age, and it behooves the practitioners of both to realize their responsibilities and obligations to the science and the religion.

Ch. 11, Ibid.

5 Reincarnation is nothing more than the law of evolution applied to the consciousness of the individual. . . . The spirit is our only link with the Godhead, the divine force of life, and it is the indestructible part of ourselves.

Ch. 12, Ibid.

6 We seem to be trapped by a civilization that has accelerated many physical aspects of evolution but has forgotten that other vital part of man—his mind and his psyche.

Ch. 13, Ibid.

2106. Indira Gandhi (1917–1984)

1 Peace we want because there is another war to fight against poverty, disease and ignorance. We have promises to keep to our people of work, food, clothing, and shelter, health and education.

Radio Broadcast (26 January 1966), Quoted in *Indira Gandhi* by Mithrapuram K. Alexander 1968

2 The young people of India must recognize that they will get from their country tomorrow what they give her today.

Ibid.

3 You cannot shake hands with a clenched fist.
   Press Conference, New Delhi (19 October 1971), Quoted in
   Indira Speaks by Dhiren Mullick *1972*

4 Martyrdom does not end something; it is only the beginning.
   Address to Parliament, New Delhi (12 August 1972), Ibid.

5 One cannot but be perturbed when fire breaks out in a neighbor's house.
   Address to Kremlin, Moscow (28 September 1971), Ibid.

6 To natural calamities of drought, flood, and cyclone has been added the man-made tragedy of vast proportions. I am haunted by tormented faces in our overcrowded refugee camps reflecting grim events, which have compelled exodus of these millions from East Bengal.
   Meeting with Richard Nixon* (Washington, D.C., 4
   November 1971), Ibid.
   *American politician (1913–1994); 37th president of the United States (1969–74); resigned.

7 No Government, no Head of Government can last if the people feel that this Government is not going to defend the security of the country.
   Address, Columbia University (7 November 1971), Ibid.

8 We know the true value of democracy, peace and freedom, since it was denied us for so long . . . We have been slaves and will not allow others to make slaves of us again.
   Address, New Delhi (12 December 1971), Ibid.

9 There are many kinds of wars. One war has just ended but I do not know if peace has come.
   Address, Ambala (24 December 1971), Ibid.

10 The times have passed when any nation sitting three or four thousand miles away could give orders to Indians on the basis of their colour superiority to do as they wished. India has changed and she is no more a country of natives.
   Address, Workers' Congress, New Delhi (2 December 1971),
   Ibid.

11 There are moments in history when brooding tragedy and its dark shadows can be lightened by recalling great moments of the past.
   Letter to Richard Nixon (16 December 1971), Ibid.

12 Is it possible, was it ever possible, to keep alive in India the beautiful dream of parliamentarian democracy the British imported along with five o'clock tea?
   Quoted in "Indira's Coup" by Oriana Fallaci,* *New York
   Review of Books 18 September 1975*
   *Italian journalist (b. 1930); see 2416

13 To bear many children is considered not only a religious blessing but also an investment. The greater their number, some Indians reason, the more alms they can beg.
   Ibid.

14 In a traditional society like India's, scandals are unavoidable. There is, in fact, the first consequence of the most ancient of social diseases: corruption.
   Ibid.

15 There exists no politician in India daring enough to attempt to explain to the masses that cows can be eaten.
   Ibid.

16 My father* was a statesman, I'm a political woman. My father was a saint. I'm not.*
   Ibid.
   *Pandit Jawaharlal Nehru (1889–1964), Indian prime minister (1947–64).

17 As for Western women, it seems to me that they have often had to struggle to obtain their own rights. That did not leave them much time to prove their abilities. The time will come.
   Quoted in "Conversation with Indira Gandhi," by José-Luis
   de Villalonga, *Oui 1975*

18 I think that the highly industrialized Western world has neglected to the utmost degree to leave room for man. The infernal production-consumption cycle has completely dehumanized life. The individual has become a tool. He hardly has any contact with nature anymore. That is, with himself. He has lost his soul and is not even trying to find it again.
   Ibid.

19 Never forget that when we are silent, we are one. And when we speak, we are two.
   Ibid.

20 I have no admiration for military feats. Defeats are always pitiful. Victories are always last resources.
   Ibid.

21 Every democratic system evolves its own conventions. It is not only the water but the banks which make the river.
   Remark (1967), Quoted in *Speeches and Writings 1975*

22 You must learn to be still in the midst of activity and to be vibrantly alive in repose.
   Quoted in "The Embattled Woman" by James Shepherd,
   People 30 June 1975

23 Even if I died in the service of the nation, I would be proud of it. Every drop of my blood . . . will contribute to the growth of this nation and to make it strong and dynamic.
   Speech, Delhi *30 October 1984**
   *The eve of her assassination by Sikh militants.

24 People tend to forget their duties but remember their rights.
   Last words *1984*

25 If I die a violent death as some fear and a few are plotting, I know the violence will be in the thought and the action of the assassin, not in my dying...*
   Diary entry (30 October 1984), Quoted in *Twentieth-
   Century Women Political Leaders* by
   Claire Price-Groff *1998*
   *Gandhi was assassinated by two of her own security guards the following day, as she strolled through her garden.

26 In India democracy has given too much license to the people. Sometimes bitter medicine has to be administered to a patient to cure him.
   Ibid.

2107. Lindy Boggs (1916–)

1 In the past we in the United States had thought we could escape direct participation in world events, but there was no way we could do so again.
   Ch. 6, *Washington Through a Purple Veil, Memoirs of a
   Southern Woman*, with Katherine Hatch *1994*

2 Our presidents often depict themselves as trying to save the people from Congress or the Supreme Court or both.

Ch. 14, Ibid.

2108. Jessica Mitford (1917–1996)

1 Things on the whole are much faster in America; people don't *stand for election*, they *run for office*.

Ch. 11, *Sons and Rebels* 1960

2 O death where is thy sting? O grave where is thy victory? Where, indeed? Many a badly stung survivor, faced with the aftermath of some relative's funeral, has ruefully considered that the victory has been won hands down by a funeral establishment—in disastrously unequal battle.

The American Way of Death 1963

3 [Undertakers have] successfully turned the tables in recent years to perpetrate a huge, macabre and expensive practical joke on the American public.

Ibid.

4 No doubt prison administrators sense that to permit the media and the public access to their domain would result in stripping away a major justification for their existence: that they are confining depraved, brutal creatures.

Ch. 1, *Kind and Unusual Punishment* 1971

5 What of homosexuality, recognized by everyone in Corrections as an inevitable consequence of long-term segregation of the sexes? Having driven them to it, why punish for it?

Ch. 2, Ibid.

6 When is conduct a crime, and when is a crime not a crime? When Somebody Up There—a monarch, a dictator, a Pope, a legislator—so decrees.

Ch. 5, Ibid.

7 One of the nicest American scientists I know was heard to say, "Criminals in our penitentiary are fine experimental material—much cheaper than chimpanzees." I hope the chimpanzees don't come to hear of this.

Ch. 9, Ibid.

8 No doubt like schools, old-age homes, mental hospitals, and other closed institutions that house the powerless, prisons afford a very special opportunity to employees at all levels for various kinds of graft and thievery.

Ch. 10, Ibid.

9 Radical and revolutionary ideologies are seeping into the prisons. Whereas formerly convicts tended to regard themselves as unfortunates whose accident of birth at the bottom of the heap was largely responsible for their plight, today many are questioning the validity of the heap.

Ch. 13, Ibid.

10 Those of us on the outside [of prisons] do not like to think of wardens and guards as our servants. Yet they are, and they are intimately locked in a deadly embrace with their human captives behind the prison walls. By extension so are we. A terrible double meaning is thus imparted to the original question of human ethics: Am I my brother's keeper?

Ch. 15, Ibid.

2109. Peg Bracken (1918–)

1 . . . unnecessary dieting is because everything from television to fashion ads have made it seem wicked to cast a shadow.

This wild, emaciated look appeals to some women, though not to many men, who are seldom seen pinning up a *Vogue* illustration in a machine shop.

The I Hate to Cook Book 1960

2110. Gertrude Louise Cheney (1918–)

1 All people are made alike.
They are made of bones, flesh and dinners.
Only the dinners are different.

"People" 1927

2111. Jeane L. Dixon (1918–1998)

1 The rare and beautiful experiences of divine revelation are moments of special gifts. Each of us, however, lives each day with special gifts which are a part of our very being, and life is a process of discovering and developing these God-given gifts within each of us.

Ch. 4, *My Life and Prophecies*, with Rene Noorbergen 1969

2112. Betty Ford (1918–)

1 . . . I wouldn't be surprised [if her daughter had an affair]. I think she's a perfectly normal human being like all young girls. If she wanted to continue, I would certainly counsel and advise her on the subject. And I'd want to know pretty much about the young man...whether it was a worthwhile encounter...She's pretty young to start affairs, [but] she's a big girl.

Interview on *60 Minutes*, CBS-TV *10 August 1975*

2 In our society, we get to know each other over drinks, we associate feast and celebrations with liquor. We think we have to drink, that it's a social necessity . . . It's romantic as long as you can handle it—for years I could and did—but it's misery when you become addicted.

The Times of My Life, with Chris Chase 1978

3 My makeup wasn't smeared, I wasn't disheveled, I behaved politely, and I never finished off a bottle, so how could a be an alcoholic? And I wasn't on heroin or cocaine, the medicines I took—the sleeping pills, the pain pills, the relaxer pills, the pills to counteract the side effects of other pills—had been prescribed by doctors, so how could I be a drug addict?

Ch. 2, *Glad Awakening*, with Chris Chase 1987

4 . . . a woman . . . told us she was forever getting herself into trouble. "But I just keep coming back," she said. "I just keep showing up for my life."

Showing up for life. Being blessed with the rebirth that recovery brings.

One day at a time.

Ch. 17, Ibid.

2113. Cecelia Helen Goetz (1918?–)

1 Once you put on a robe, the male-female distinction disappears, at least as far as the people who appear before you are concerned. They don't see you as either male or female.

Quoted in *The 50 Most Influential Women in American Law* by Dawn Bradley Berry* 1996

*See 3435.

2114. Doris Isaac Grumbach (1918–)

1 I am ready to begin the end.

Last lines, *Coming Into the End Zone* 1991

2 . . . keeping a journal thins my skin. I fall open to everything...
Extra Innings 1993

3 Is it unpopular, unsociable perhaps, to confess that one hates being old?
Ibid.

4 The end of life is too often like this, mean, without the grace in which a woman like this must have lived.*
Ibid.

*Reference to a former Harvard art professor who was moved to a nursing home.

5 [Perhaps it's] time to let go of one's passions and assign them to the realm of memory. I have grown too demanding of these ruins, too impatient with the behavior of everyone but myself and my traveling companions.
Ibid.

6 [I have] abandoned the barricades for the veranda, the foxhole for the hammock.
Ibid.

7 . . . children are most apt to discover their inner selves in moments of misery.
The Book of Knowledge 1995

8 They lay still, filled with the anguish of threatened, requited love.
Ibid.

2115. Fay Kanin (1918–)

1 JUDGE. Now, where were we? Oh, yes, plaintiff and defendant were in bed—talking.
His and Hers, with Michael Kanin *1948*

2 While other [film] crafts have to sit around chewing their fingernails waiting for a movie to be put together, writers have one great strength. They can sit down and generate their own employment and determine their own fate to a great extent by the degree of their disciplines, their guts, and their talents.
Quoted in "Fay Kanin," Quoted in *The Screenwriter Looks at the Screenwriter* by William Froug *1972*

3 Only an insatiable ego or an intolerable sense of inferiority could lead a director to ignore the basic creativity of the man or woman who thought it up, sweated it out, and delivered those precious pages into his hands.
Ibid.

4 She* was an early activist for freedom of expression. She stood up for what she believed in and fought all the negative elements. What recommended her to me was that she made sex fun. She put humor into sex, and I found that absolutely delicious.
Quoted in "Mae West still figures prominently . . . "
Associated Press *17 August 1993*
*Reference to Mae West; see 1663.

5 For myself, I think the word auteur has been used, misused, paraded, fought over, intellectualized, and interpreted to the point of boredom. As I understand from my French, auteur means author. And I cannot see how someone is an author who, having a concept for a film, does not at some point sit down and write it . . .
Quoted in "The Playwright" by Fields, *American Women Playwrights, 1900–1950* by Yvonne Shafer *1995*

6 It's my feeling that the highest aspiration of the [screen] writer is to be a writer-executive in the sense that he goes on to control his material in one further aspect by producing or directing it. I believe every writer who can should try to accomplish that. Because it's the best way he can get his work done well.
Ibid.

7 . . . every adult in the world has to tell the truth to the young, if we are to have a world at all.
Ibid.

2116. Corita Kent (1918–1986)

1 There are so many hungry people that God cannot appear to them except in the form of bread.
"Enriched Bread" (silkscreen) *1965*

2 One of the things Jesus did was to step aside from the organized religion of his time because it had become corrupt and bogged down with rules. Rules became more important than feeding the hungry.
Quoted in "A Time of Transition for Corita Kent"
by Lucie Kay Scheuer, *The Los Angeles Times*
11 July 1974

3 Women's liberation is the liberation of the feminine in the man and the masculine in the woman.
Ibid.

4 The real circus with acrobats, jugglers, and bareback riders = also an empty field transformed, and in the tent artists and freaks, children and pilgrims and animals are gathered in communion = us
Poster, New York Urban Coalition, Inc. *n.d.*

2117. Madeleine L'Engle (1918–)

1 It was not simple as darkness, or absence of light. Darkness has a tangible quality; it can be moved through and felt; in darkness you can bark your shins; the world of things still exists around you. She was lost in a horrifying void.
Ch. 4, *A Wrinkle in Time 1962*

2 "It's my worst trouble, getting fond. If I didn't get fond I could be happy all the time."
Ch. 6, Ibid.

3 "On Camazotz we are all happy because we are all alike. Differences create problems. You know that, don't you, dear sister?"
"No," Meg said.
"Oh, yes, you do. You've seen at home how true it its. You know that's the reason you're not happy at school."
"*I'm* different, and I'm happy," Calvin said.
"But you pretend that you *aren't* different."
"I'm different and I like being different." Calvin's voice was naturally loud.
"Maybe I don't like being different," Meg said, but I don't want to be like everybody else, either."
Ch. 8, Ibid.

4 A self is not something static, tied up in a pretty parcel and handed to the child, finished and complete. A self is always becoming. *Being* does mean becoming, but we run so fast that it is only when we seem to stop—as sitting on the rock at the brook—that we are aware of our own *isness*, of being. But eventually this is not static, for this awareness of being is

always a way of moving from the selfish self—the self-image—towards the real.

Who am I, then? Who are you?

A Circle of Quiet 1972

5   I found myself earnestly explaining to the young minister that I did not believe in God, "but I've discovered that I can't live as though I didn't believe in him."

Ibid.

6   I was in that area of despair where one is incapable of being ontological. In my definition, this is sin.

Ibid.

7   Her father said, "You know, my dears, the world has been abnormal for so long that we've forgotten what it's like to live in a peaceful and reasonable climate. If there is to be any peace or reason, we have to create it in our own hearts and homes."

Ch. 1, *A Swiftly Tilting Planet 1978*

8   "You know Where we are, then? I mean—When we are? Is it time gone, or time to be?"

"It is, I think, what you would call Once Upon a Time and Long Ago."

"So we're not in the present."

"Of course we are. Whenever we are is present."

"We're not in *my* present. We're not When we were when you came to me."

"When I was called to you," Guadior corrected. "And When is not what matters. It's what happens in the When that matters. Are you ready to go?"

Ch. 3, Ibid.

9   "Everything that happens within the created Order, no matter how small, has its effect. If you are angry, that anger is added to all the hate with which the Echthroi would distort the melody and destroy the ancient harmonies. When you are loving, that lovingness joins the music of the spheres."

Ibid.

10   "Hate hurts the hater more'n the hated."

Ch. 9, Ibid.

2118. Ann Landers (1918–)

1   Women complain about sex more often than men, Their gripes fall into two major categories: (1) Not enough. (2) Too much.

Ch. 2, *Ann Landers Says Truth Is Stranger . . . 1968*

2   What the vast majority of American children need is to stop being pampered, stop being indulged, stop being chauffeured, stop being catered to. In the final analysis it is not what you do for your children but what you have taught them to do for themselves that will make them successful human beings.

Ch. 3, Ibid.

3   All married couples should learn the art of battle as they should learn the art of making love. Good battle is objective and honest—never vicious or cruel. Good battle is healthy and constructive, and brings to a marriage the principle of equal partnership.

Ch. 11, Ibid.

4   The mail grew me up in a hurry.

Quoted in "Living By the Letter" by Elizabeth Taylor, *Time* (New York) *21 August 1989*

5   I don't want anybody calling me Ms.

Ibid.

6   At every party there are two kinds of people—those who want to go home and those who don't. The trouble is, they are usually married to each other.

International Herald Tribune (Paris) *19 June 1991*

7   The Lord does not take vacations. He is always on the job.

Advice column, *Seattle Post-Intelligencer*, C2 *17 March 1994*

8   Trouble is a great equalizer. No matter what our differences, in time of trouble the differences fade, and we become brothers and sisters. We want to reach out and help one another. The Internet has given us a unique opportunity to do just that.

Ann Landers Advice, *Seattle Post-Intelligencer* *17 November 1998*

9   Tact is the art of making people feel at home when that's where you wish they were.

Ann Landers Advice, *Seattle Post-Intelligencer* *22 December 1998*

10   The real test of class is how you treat people who cannot possibly do you any good.

Ann Landers Advice, *Seattle Post-Intelligencer* *22 January 1999*

11   Divorce makes its mark on children both in the short term and the long term. . . . Long after the divorce is final, children of divorce often have trouble entering into committed relationships of their own, fearing their relationships will end as they parents' did.

Ann Landers Advice, *Seattle Post-Intelligencer* *3 February 1999*

2119. Ida Lupino (1918–1995)

1   Movies, today, are made up of festivals, cannibalism, the idiocy they call lack of communication, intellectuals who always make out that they're teaching something and undervalue the public, forgetting that the public is composed—all right—of insecure individuals, but, put together, these insecure individuals become a miracle of intelligence. And intelligence won't put up with being led by the nose by imbeciles who preach from the pulpit.

Quoted in "Anna Magnani,"* *The Egotists* by Oriana Fallaci** *1963*

*See 2125; **see 2416.

2   And believe me, *Bring it in on time* is such a major factor in television that I'd sometimes get absolutely sick to my stomach days beforehand. . . . So any ladies who want to take over men's jobs—if that's what they really want—had better have strong stomachs.

Quoted in *Popcorn Venus* by Marjorie Rosen* *1973*

*See 2920.

2120. Mary McGrory (1918–)

1   But he [Richard M. Nixon]* was like a kamikaze pilot who keeps apologizing for the attack.

Syndicated newspaper column *8 November 1962*

2   Somehow it sounded as though his [Richard M. Nixon's]* zeal in providing a generation of peace rather than his efforts to cover up a generation of corruption had gotten him into trouble.

Syndicated newspaper column *9 August 1974*

*American politician (1913–1994); 37th president of the United States (1969–74); resigned.

3   He [John F. Kennedy]* came on, composed as a prince of the blood, chestnut thatch carefully brushed, facts straight, voice steady. "Look at him," breathed the proud Irishman next to me in the audience. "He's a thoroughbred."

Ibid.

*American politican (1917–1963); 35th president of the United States (1961–63); assassinated.

4   Hitlerism was a cult, too. Germany was a country of Branch Davidians,* dying to die for a psychopath.
"Holocaust Museum holds appalling relevance today,"
Seattle Post-Intelligencer, Op-Ed 27 April 1993
*A survivalist/religious cult based near Waco, Texas, burned alive in a pitched battle with federal law enforcement (1993).

5   The Holocaust* happened because a whole nation lined up behind a madman. Germany had a rich culture and vaunted family values. Germans prided themselves on their immaculate houses and their obedient children. Yet they tolerated the most horrendous mass murder of the 20th century.

Ibid.

*The genocide of European Jews and others by the Nazis during World War II.

6   And the propensity of weak and empty people to follow a leader into the darkness from which there is no return is still flourishing, as ever.

Ibid.

7   The Iran-Contra* hearings did not deserve, and did not get, any knights. The leaders had resolved there would be no impeachment no matter what they found out about Ronald Reagan.**   The committee danced to the tune of Oliver North,*** who blinked and croaked his way to celebrity while his senatorial inquisitors were clearing their throats.
"Congress drowns in soup of impeachment,"
Washington Post 10 January 1999
*Controversial secret government arrangement to provide funds to the Nicaraguan contra rebels with profits gained by selling arms to Iran that shook the Reagan administration and the nation in 1986. **American politician, actor (1911–), 40th president of the United States (1981–89). ***U.S. Marine officer (1943–) at the heart of Iran–contra affair.

2121. Penelope Mortimer (1918–1999)

1   In all the years of her marriage, a long war in which attack, if not happening, was always imminent, she had learned an expert cunning. The way to avoid being hurt, to dodge unhappiness, was to run away.

Ch. 1, *Daddy's Gone A-Hunting* 1958

2   "There is an obsessive tenderness and passion, an eating out of one's heart, a sense of longing, an affliction, which remains buried and unchanged from childhood, this is what is called falling in love. The longing is for reciprocation, the affliction is in knowing that reciprocation is forbidden."

Ch. 5, Ibid.

3   "I thought I was supposed to lie on a couch and you wouldn't say a word. It's like the Inquisition or something. Are you trying to make me feel I'm wrong? Because I do that for myself."

Ch. 1, *The Pumpkin Eater* 1962

4   It was intensely boring, but they all made a great fuss over me and I began to think that perhaps it was better to be bored and admired than interested and miserable.

Ch. 10, Ibid.

5   "What do your patients do while you're away? Commit suicide, murder their wives, or do they just sit and cry and take pills and think about what they told you last time? . . . If I'm sane enough to be left alone with my *thoughts* for two weeks then I'm too sane to need these futile, boring conversations—because my God, they bore me—at six guineas a time."

Ch. 11, Ibid.

6   "I have arguments with myself."
"About what?"
"Between the part of me that believes in things and the part of me that doesn't"
"And which wins?"
"Sometimes one. Sometimes the other."
"Then stop arguing."

Ch. 23, Ibid.

7   I was, and still am, running away from the person to whom . . . I had addressed my life.

Long Distance 1974

8   Grief is a very antisocial state...

Ibid.

2122. June Singer (1918–)

1   And so Multi-Media Man, the contemporary successor to Renaissance Man . . .
Ch. 1, *Boundaries of the Soul, The Practice of June's Psychology* 1972

2   As a man's image of the world changes, so a man changes himself.

Ibid.

3   In learning to sail you do not change the current of the water nor do you have any effect on the wind, but you learn to hoist your sail and turn it this way and that to utilize the greater forces which surround you. By understanding them, you become one with them, and in doing so are able to find your own direction—so long as it is in harmony with, and does not try to oppose, the greater forces in being.

Ibid.

4   The modern man needs to rescue himself from his cultural provincialism.

Ch. 4, Ibid.

5   Despite the continuing expansion or even explosion of information, there will forever be limits beyond which the devices of science cannot lead a man.

Ch. 13, Ibid.

6   To begin with, I was first attracted by psychology in general around the age of twelve when I discovered that the psychology books in the public library were kept under lock and key in a glass case and you could only see the titles. That rather intrigued me.
Interview (27 October 1982), *Contemporary Authors* 1983

2123. Muriel Spark (1918–)

1   Being over seventy is like being engaged in a war. All our friends are going or gone and survive amongst the dead and the dying as on a battlefield.

Ch. 4, *Memento Mori* 1959

2 "If I had my life over again I should form the habit of nightly composing myself to thoughts of death. I would practise, as it were, the remembrance of death. There is no other practise which so intensifies life. Death, when it approaches, ought not to take one by surprise. It should be part of the full expectancy of life."

Ch. 11, Ibid.

3 There was altogether too much candour in married life; it was an indelicate modern idea, and frequently led to upsets in a household, if not divorce.

Ch. 12, Ibid.

4 Daylight was appearing over London, the great city of bachelors. Half-pint bottles of milk began to be stood at the doorsteps of houses containing single apartments from Hampstead Heath to Greenwich Park, from Wanstead Flats to Putney Heath; but especially in Hampstead, especially in Kensington.

Bachelor 1960

5 "Give me a girl at an impressionable age, and she is mine for life."

Ch. 1, *The Prime of Miss Jean Brodie 1961*

6 "One's prime is elusive. You little girls, when you grow up, must be on the alert to recognize your prime at whatever time of your life it may occur. You must then live it to the full."

Ibid.

7 "Art and religion first; then philosophy; lastly science. That is the order of the great subjects of life, that's their order of importance."

Ch. 2, Ibid.

8 "To me education is a leading out of what is already there in the pupil's soul. To Miss Mackay it is a putting in of something that is not there, and that is not what I call education, I call it intrusion…"

Ibid.

9 Miss Brodie said: "Pavlova* contemplates her swans in order to perfect her swan dance, she studies them. That is true dedication. You must all grow up to be dedicated women as I have dedicated myself to you."

Ch. 3, Ibid.

*Anna P—, see 1466.

10 It is not to be supposed that Miss Brodie was unique…There were legions of her kind during the nineteen-thirties, women from the age of thirty and upward who crowded their war-bereaved spinsterhood with voyages of discovery into new ideas and energetic practices in art or social welfare, education or religion.

Ibid.

11 "Nothing infuriates people more than their own lack of spiritual insight, Sandy, that is why the Moslems are so placid, they are full of spiritual insight."

Ch. 4, Ibid.

12 "It is impossible to persuade a man who does not disagree, but smiles."

Ibid.

13 Long ago in 1945 all of the nice people in England were poor…

The Girls of Slender Means 1963

14 Oh, the trifles, the people, that get on your nerves when you have a neurosis!

"Come Along, Marjorie," *Collected Stories: I 1968*

15 Now I realised the distinction between neurosis and madness, and in my agitation I half-envied the woman beyond my bedroom wall, the sheer cool sanity of her behaviour within the limits of her impracticable mania.

Ibid.

16 She did not know then that the price of allowing false opinions was the gradual loss of one's capacity for forming true ones.

"Bang-Bang You're Dead," Ibid.

17 For some years she had been thinking she was not much inclined towards sex…It is not merely a lack of pleasure in sex, it is dislike of the excitement. And it is not merely dislike, it is worse, it is boredom.

Ibid.

18 A house in which there are no people—but with all the signs of tenancy—can be a most tranquil good place.

"The Portobello Road," Ibid.

19 Kathleen, speaking from the Catholic point of view which takes some getting used to, said, "She was at Confession only the day before she died—wasn't she lucky?"

Ibid.

20 New York, home to the vivisectors of the mind, and of the mentally vivisected still to be reassembled, of those who live intact, habitually wondering about their states of sanity, and home of those whose minds have been dead, bearing the scars of resurrection. . . .

Ch. 1, *The Hothouse by the East River 1973*

21 "Sex," she says, "is a subject like any other subject. Every bit as interesting as agriculture."

Ch. 4, Ibid.

22 So far as I knew to date, forever was slip-stitch, split-stitch, cross-stitch, back-stitch; and also buttonhole and running stitches . . . all along the dipping and rising hemline, as if for always and always.

"The Dragon," *The Stories of Muriel Spark 1985*

23 I wouldn't take the Pope too seriously. He's a Pole first, a pope second, and maybe a Christian third.

International Herald Tribune (Paris) *29 May 1989*

24 Her parents had searched through the past, consulted psychiatrists, took every moment to bits. In no way should she [their daughter] be explained.

Reality and Dreams 1997

25 "Everything I do is basically connected with my work. Everything."

Ibid.

2124. Abigail Van Buren (1918–)

1 People who fight fire with fire usually end up with ashes.

"Dear Abby" newspaper column *7 March 1974*

2 Some people are more turned on by money than they are by love. . . . In one respect they're alike. They're both wonderful as long as they last.

"Dear Abby" newspaper column *26 April 1974*

3 Religion, like water, may be free, but when they pipe it to you, you've got to help pay for the piping. And the piper!

"Dear Abby" newspaper column *28 April 1974*

4 The best index to a person's character is (a) how he treats people who can't do him any good, and (b) how he treats people who can't fight back.

"Dear Abby" newspaper column *16 May 1974*

5 Psychotherapy, unlike castor oil, which will work no matter how you get it down, is useless when forced on an uncooperative patient.

"Dear Abby" newspaper column *11 July 1974*

2125. Anna Magnani (1918–1973)

1 Great passions, my dear, don't exist: they're liars' fantasies. What do exist are little loves that may last for a short or a longer while.

Quoted in "Anna Magnani," *The Egotists*
by Oriana Fallaci* *1963*
*See 2416.

2 . . . I might use foul language, but I do hate bad breeding.

Ibid.

3 Children are like puppies: you have to keep them near you and look after them if you want to have their affection.

Ibid.

2126. Tove Ditlevsen (1918–1976)

1 When you have
once had
a great joy
it lasts always
quivers gently
on the edge of all the
insecure adult days
subdues inherited dread
makes sleep deeper.

"Self-Portrait," St. 1, Ann Freeman, tr., *In the Midst of Winter: Selections from the Literature of Mourning*,
Mary Jane Moffat,* ed. *1982*
*See 2719.

2127. Martha Mitchell (1918–1976)

1 I'm not certain that we should have Democrats in the Cabinet.

Interview, *Tonight Show* NBC-TV *11 February 1971*

2 I've never said I was against integration. It should have started right after the Civil War. But why single out the South? The South has been imposed on long enough. It's the orphan of the nation.

Quoted in *Martha: The Mouth That Roared* by
Charles Ashman and Sheldon Engelmayer *1973*

2128. Selma Fraiberg (1918–1981)

1 But the neurotic conscience behaves like a gestapo headquarters within the personality, mercilessly tracking down dangerous or potentially dangerous ideas and every remote relative of these ideas, accusing, threatening, tormenting in an interminable inquisition to establish guilt for trivial offenses or crimes committed in dreams. Such guilt feelings have the effect of putting the entire personality under arrest. . . .

The Magic Years 1959

2129. Pearl Bailey (1918–1986)

1 There are two kinds of talent, man-made talent and God-given talent. With man-made talent you have to work very hard. With God-given talent, you just touch it up once in a while.

Newsweek (New York) *4 December 1967*

2 There's a period of life when we swallow a knowledge of ourselves and it becomes either good or sour inside.

Ch. 13, *The Raw Pearl 1968*

3 The fact is that it takes more than ingredients and technique to cook a good meal. A good cook puts something of *himself* into the preparations—he cooks with enjoyment, anticipation, spontaneity, and he is willing to experiment.

Preface, *Pearl's Kitchen 1973*

4 My kitchen is a mystical place, a kind of temple for me. It is a place where the surfaces seem to have significance, where the sounds and odors carry meaning that transfers from the past and bridges to the future.

"Sanctuary," Ibid.

5 Hungry people cannot be good at learning or producing anything, except perhaps violence.

Epilogue, Ibid.

2130. Faith Bandler (1918–)

1 My father was taken from his island, which is the island of Ambrym, that makes up the eighty odd islands of the nation of Vanuatu, at a very young age. He was about twelve or thirteen in the year eighteen eighty-three and he was forcibly taken with other men and women and brought to McKay.

Wacvie 1977

2 [The constitutional amendment] will be of tremendous advantage to the indigenous Australian. It will mean that opportunities will be made available for better housing, for permanent employment and perhaps the most important of all is that of education.

Comment (1967), quoted in profile by Victor Chang,
Australians http://www.abc.net.au/btn/australians/
f.bandler.htm *2000*

2131. Gertrude B. Elion (1918–1999)

1 I was a child with an insatiable thirst for knowledge and remember enjoying all of my courses almost equally. When it came time at the end of my high school career to choose a major in which to specialize I was in a quandary. One of the deciding factors may have been that my grandfather, whom I loved dearly, died of cancer when I was 15. I was highly motivated to do something that might eventually lead to a cure for this terrible disease.

Autobiographical Essay, *Les Prix Nobel 1988*

2 . . . [I] entered graduate school at New York University in the fall of 1939. I was the only female in my graduate chemistry class but no one seemed to mind, and I did not consider it at all strange.

Ibid.

3 When we began to see the results of our efforts in the form of new drugs which filled real medical needs and benefited patients in very visible ways, our feeling of reward was immeasurable.

Ibid.

2132. Isidora Aguirre (1919–)

1 CAROLINA. Besides when I say "nothing," what I mean is: everything.

    Carolina (a.k.a. *Express for Santiago*) *1955*

2 CARLOS. Remember: don't start conversations with strangers on a trip. No way of getting rid of them later!

    Ibid.

3 CAROLINA. It's awful to be the wife of a lawyer.

    Ibid.

2133. E. Margaret Burbidge (1919–)

1 Suddenly I saw my fascination with the stars...linked to my other delight, large numbers. I decided then and there that the occupation I most wanted to engage in 'when I was grown up' was to determine the distances of the stars.

    "Watcher of the Skies," *Annual Review of Astronomy and Astrophysics 1994*

*Upon receiving astronomy books from her grandfather when she was 12.

2 I often think about the joys of work in an open [observatory] dome, under the stars, next to the telescope, joys denied to most younger astronomers.*

    Ibid.

*Today, like so many other sciences, much of the study of astronomy is via computers.

3 A guiding operational principle in my life [is that]...if frustrated in one's endeavor by a stone wall or any kind of blockage, one must find a way around—another route toward one's goal.

    Quoted in *Twentieth-Century Women Scientists* by Lisa Yount *1996*

2134. Betty Comden (1919–)

1 I'm singing in the rain,/
Just singing in the rain./
What a glorious feeling,/
I'm happy again.

    "Singin' in the Rain," *Singin' in the Rain* with Adolph Green *1952*

2 Moses supposes his toeses are roses
But Moses supposes erroneously.

    "Elocution," Ibid.

3 ELLA (singing). The party's over—
It's time to call it a day—
No matter how you pretend
You knew it would end this way.
It's time to wind up the masquerade—
Just make your mind up—
The piper must be paid.

    Act II, Sc. 4, "The Party's Over," *Bells Are Ringing*, with Adolph Green *1960*

2135. Jessie Lopez De La Cruz (1919–)

1 I'd hear them scolding their kids and fighting their husbands and I'd say, "Gosh! Why don't you go after the people that have you living like this? Why don't you go after the growers that have you tired from working out in the fields at low wages and keep us poor all the time? Let's go after them! *They're* the cause of our misery!"

    Quoted in *Moving the Mountain* by Ellen Cantarow *1980*

2 They tell us there's no money for food stamps for poor people. But if there is money enough to fight a war in Vietnam, and if there is money enough for Governor Reagan's wife* to buy a $3.000 dress for the Inaugural Ball, there should be money enough to feed these people. The nutrition experts say surplus food is full of vitamins. . . . But you know, we don't call them vitamins, we call them weevils!

    Ibid.

*Nancy Reagan (see 2188), wife of Ronald Reagan, American politician, actor (1911–), governor of California (1967–75), 40th president of the United States (1980–88).

3 America was built with small farms. They keep saying that the farmer is the country's backbone. I never heard anything about agribusiness being the backbone of the country, or corporations being the backbone.

    Ibid.

2136. Zsa Zsa Gabor (1919–)

1 I never hated a man enough to give him his diamonds back.

    Quoted in *Observer* (London) *28 August 1957*

2 Husbands are like fires. They go out when unattended.

    Quoted in *Newsweek* (New York) *28 March 1960*

3 A man in love is incomplete until he has married—then he's finished.

    Ibid.

4 I'm a vunderful housekeeper. Effry time I get a divorce I keep the house.

    Remark *n.d.*

2137. Uta Hagen (1919–)

1 More than in the other performing arts the lack of respect for acting seems to spring from the fact that every layman considers himself a valid critic.

    Introduction, Pt. I, *Respect for Acting 1973*

2 The American theatre poses endless problems for any actor who wants to call himself an artist, who wants to be part of an art form.

    Ibid.

3 Talent is an amalgam of high sensitivity; easy vulnerability; high sensory equipment (seeing, hearing, touching, smelling tasting—*intensely*); a vivid imagination as well as a grip on reality; the desire to communicate one's own experience and sensations, to make one's self heard and seen.

    Ch. 1, Ibid.

4 To maintain one's ideals in ignorance is easy. . . .

    Ibid.

5 Rebellion or revolt does not necessarily find its expression in violence. A gentle, lyric stroke may be just as powerful a means of expression.

    Pt. 1, Ch. 1, Ibid.

6 We must overcome the notion that we must be *regular*...It robs you of the chance to be extraordinary and leads you to the mediocre.

    Ch. 2, Ibid.

7 A great danger is to take the five senses for granted. Most people do. Once you become aware that the sources which move

in on you when you truly touch, taste, smell, see and hear are endless, you must also realize that self involvement deadens the senses, and vanity slaughters them until you end up playing alone—and meaninglessly.

Ch. 6, Ibid.

8 The teaching of others forced me into clarifications of my personal work. It raised my standards. In upholding honesty in the work of others, denying their right to be superficial or to take shortcuts, one can't allow oneself to cheat. I'm far more nervous when students are in the audience than when the critics are there, because the students know more about the craft than the critics do. . . . I would like to disagree with George Bernard Shaw's statement that "He who *can*, does. He who *cannot*, teaches" to express my personal belief that "Only he who *can* should teach!"

Prologue, *A Challenge for the Actor* 1991

9 Since the time of the ancient Greeks a democracy has depended on its philosophers and creative artists. It can only flourish by continuous probing, prodding, and questioning of the social conditions under which man exists and tries to better himself. One of the first moves of a dictatorship is to stifle the artists and thinkers who have the ability to stir up dissent from any prescribed dogma which might enslave them. Because the artist can arouse the curiosity and conscience of his community, he becomes a threat to those who have taken power.

Ch. 1, "The Actor's World," Ibid.

10 Let's face the fact that since the disappearance of the golden age of the actor-manager in the 1800s, the acting profession as a whole has relinquished its responsibility to the theatre. It has willingly accepted the role of subservient child to a kind of parental control exercised by managers, producers, directors, even its own agents.

Ibid.

11 The desire to perform in order to attain fame or fortune *or* romantic dreams of starring in the classics are not real goals but notions that rattle in the void.

Ch. 2, "The Actor's Goals," Ibid.

12 I truly believe there is *nothing* larger than life.

Ch. 3, "The Actor's Techniques," Ibid.

13 Read out loud. Learn to relish the explosive ideas and phenomenal imagery contained in a body of contemporary and classic literature. Let language take shape on your tongue until it begins to spring from your soul.

Ibid.

14 *I am only impressed when the actor's technique is so perfect that it has become *invisible* and has persuaded the audience that they are in the presence of a living human being who makes it possible for them to empathize with all his foibles and struggles as they unfold in the play.

Ibid.

2138. Pauline Kael (1919–)

1 The first prerogative of an artist in any medium is to make a fool of himself.

"Is There a Cure for Film Criticism?" *I Lost It at the Movies* 1965

2 One of the surest signs of the Philistine is his reverence for the superior tastes of those who put him down.

"Zeitgeist and Poltergeist," Ibid.

3 Good movies make you care, make you believe in possibilities again.

Pt. I, Ch. 1, *Going Steady* 1968

4 Technique is hardly worth talking about unless it's used for something worth doing...

Ch. 2, Ibid.

5 Trash has given us an appetite for art.

Ch. 5, Ibid.

6 Unsupervised enjoyment is probably not the only kind there is but it may feel like the only kind. Irresponsibility is part of the pleasure of all art, it is the part the schools cannot recognize.

Ibid.

7 Movies have been doing so much of the same thing—in slightly different ways—for so long that few of the possibilities of this great hybrid art have yet been explored.

Ibid.

8 If big film directors are to get credit for doing badly what others have been doing brilliantly for years with no money, just because they've put it on a big screen, then businessmen are greater than poets and theft is art.

Ch. 8, Ibid.

9 Art is still what teachers and ladies and foundations believe in, it's civilized and refined, cultivated and serious, cultural, beautiful, European, Oriental; it's what America isn't, and it's especially what American movies are not.

Pt. II, Ch. 4, Ibid.

10 The lowest action trash is preferable to wholesome family entertainment. When you clean them up, when you make movies respectable, you kill them. The wellspring of their *art*, their greatness, is in not being respectable.

Pt. II, Ch. 6, Ibid.

11 The words "Kiss Kiss Bang Bang," which I saw on an Italian movie poster, are perhaps the briefest statement imaginable of the basic appeal of movies.

Title note, *Kiss Kiss Bang Bang* 1968

12 Watching old movies is like spending an evening with those people next door. They bore us, and we wouldn't go out of our way to see them; we drop in on them because they're so close. If it took some effort to see old movies, we might try to find out which were the good ones, and if people saw only the good ones maybe they would still respect old movies. As it is, people sit and watch movies that audiences walked out on thirty years ago. Like Lot's wife, we are tempted to take another look, attracted not by evil but by something that seems much more shameful—our own innocence.

"Movies on Television," Ibid.

13 It seems likely that many of the young who don't wait for others to call them artists, but simply announce that they are, don't have the patience to make art.

Pt. 1, Ibid.

14 What they think is creativity is simply the excitement of success, the exhilaration of power.

Ibid.

15 . . . banality and luxuriant wastefulness . . . are so often called the superior "craftsmanship" of Hollywood.

Pt. I, Ibid.

16 . . . advertising determines what is accepted as art.

Pt. III, Ibid.

17 What makes movies a great popular art form is that certain artists can, at moments in their lives, reach out and unify the audience—educated and uneducated—in a shared response. The tragedy in the history of movies is that those who have this capacity are usually prevented from doing so.

Ibid.

18 We may be reaching the end of the era in which individual movies meant something to people. In the new era, movies may just mean a barrage of images.

Pt. V, Ibid.

19 In the arts, the critic is the only independent source of information. The rest is advertising.

Newsweek (New York) *December 1973*

20 Los Angeles, a mock paradise, is so perversely beautiful and so fundamentally unsatisfying that maybe just about everybody there secretly longs to see it come rattling down.

"The Current Cinema," *The New Yorker 2 December 1974*

21 Robert Redford . . . has turned almost alarmingly blond—he's gone past platinum, he must be into plutonium; his hair is co-ordinated with his teeth.

Pt. 2, "The Sting," *Reeling 1976*

2139. Libby Koontz (1919–)

1 . . . like steel that has been passed through fire, the century will be stronger for having been tested.

Quoted in "Impeachment?" by Claire Safran, *Redbook* (New York) *April 1974*

2140. Doris Lessing (1919–)

1 It is terrible to destroy a person's picture of himself in the interests of truth or some other abstraction.

Ch. 2, *The Grass is Singing 1950*

2 "If people dug up the remains of this civilization a thousand years hence, and found Epstein's* statues and that man Ellis,** they would think we were just savages."

Pt. I, Ch. 1, *Martha Quest 1952*
*Jacob E—, American-born British sculptor (1880–1959).
**(Henry) Havelock E—. British psychologist and writer (1859–1939).

3 "Died of gas from the war, she says. Pity those War Office blokes never understood that people could be ill because of the war, and it only showed afterwards. He got no compensation, she says. Damned unfair."

Pt. II, Ch. 2, Ibid.

4 "In university they don't tell you that the greater part of the law is learning to tolerate fools."

Pt. III, Ch. 2, Ibid.

5 . . . she envied her lost capacity for making the most of time— that was how she put it, as if time were a kind of glass measure which one could fill or not.

Pt. IV, Ch. 1, Ibid.

6 What of October, that ambiguous month, the month of tension, the unendurable month?

Ibid.

7 . . . he went on to remark gently that some women seemed to imagine birth control was a sort of magic; if they bought what was necessary and left it lying in a corner of a drawer, nothing more was needed. To this attitude of mind, he said, was due a number of births every year which would astound the public.

Pt. I, Ch. 1, *A Proper Marriage 1952*

8 Love had brought her here, to lie beside this young man; love was the key to every good; love lay like a mirage through the golden gates of sex.

Ibid.

9 There is something in the word "meeting" which arouses an instinctive and profound distrust in the bosoms of British people at this late hour of their history.

Pt. IV, Ch. 2, Ibid.

10 Africa belongs to the Africans; the sooner they take it back the better. But a country also belongs to those who feel at home in it. Perhaps it may be that love of Africa the country will be strong enough to link people who hate each other now. Perhaps . . .

Going Home 1957

11 "Sometimes I look at a young man in the States who has a certain resemblance, and I ask myself: Perhaps he is my son? Yes, yes, my friend, this is a question that every man must ask himself, sometimes, is it not?"

Ch. 3, *The Habit of Loving 1957*

12 The smell of manure, of sun on foliage, of evaporating water, rose to my head; two steps farther, and I could look down into the vegetable garden enclosed within its tall pale of reeds— rich chocolate earth studded emerald green, frothed with the white of cauliflowers, jeweled with the purple globes of eggplant and the scarlet wealth of tomatoes.

Ch. 9, Ibid.

13 Effort, after days of laziness, seemed impossible.

Ch. 15, Ibid.

14 Pleasure resorts are like film stars and royalty who—or so one hopes—must be embarrassed by the figures they cut in the fantasies of people who have never met them.

Ch. 17, Ibid.

15 Bed is the best place for reading, thinking, or doing nothing.

"A Room," *A Man and Two Women 1958*

16 . . . she was thirty-nine. . . . No, she did not envy her eighteen-year-old self at all. But she did envy, envied every day more bitterly, that young girl's genuine independence, largeness, scope, and courage.

"Between Men," Ibid.

17 They separated gently, but the movements both used...were more like a fitting together.

"Each Other," Ibid.

18 "There's nothing in sight, not one object or building anywhere, that is beautiful. Everything is so ugly and mean and graceless that it should be bulldozed into the earth and out of the memory of man."

"England Versus England," Ibid.

19 . . . the satisfied fervour of one who has at last pinned a label on a rare specimen: "She is, of course, one of your typical En-

glish spinsters."..."I suppose she has given up?" "Given up what?" I asked...

> "Our Friend Judith," Ibid.

20 Above all, intelligence forbids tears.

> "To Room 19," Ibid.

21 A high price has to be paid for the happy marriage with the four healthy children in the large white gardened house.

> Ibid.

22 Some people had to live with crippled arms, or stammers, or being deaf. She would have to live knowing she was subject to a state of mind she could not own.

> Ibid.

23 "Small things amuse small minds. . . ."

> "A Woman on a Roof," Ibid.

24 "Don't you think there's something awful in two grown people stuck together all the time like Siamese twins?"

> "A Man and Two Women," Ibid.

25 . . . he hated her for his ineptitude.

> "One Off the Short List," Ibid.

26 . . . the rifle, justified by utility. . . .

> Ibid.

27 MARY. If a man marries, he marries a woman, but if a woman marries, she marries a way of life.

> Play With a Tiger 1962

28 It seems to me like this. It's not a terrible thing—I mean it may be terrible, but it's not damaging, it's not poisoning to do without something one really wants...What's terrible is to pretend that the second-rate is first-rate. To pretend that you don't need love when you do; or you like your work when you know quite well you're capable of better.

> The Golden Notebook 1962

29 After a certain age—and for some of us that can be very young—there are no new people, beasts, dreams, faces, events: it has all happened before . . . and everything is an echo and a repetition; and there is no grief even that it is not a recurrence of something long out of memory.

> Ch. 2, Particularly Cats 1967

30 If a fish is the movement of water embodied, given shape, then cat is a diagram and pattern of subtle air.

> Ibid.

31 Oh cat; I'd say, or pray: be-ooootiful cat! Delicious cat! Exquisite cat! Satiny cat! Cat like a soft owl, cat with paws like moths, jeweled cat, miraculous cat! Cat, cat, cat, cat.

> Ibid.

32 What is charm then? The free giving of a grace, the spending of something given by nature in her role of spendthrift...Charm is something extra, superfluous, unnecessary, essentially a power thrown away—given.

> Ch. 9, Ibid.

33 Literature is analysis after the event.

> "Afterword," Children of Albion:
> Poetry of the Underground in Britain, Sct. 2,
> Michael Horovitz, ed. 1969

34 ". . . that is what learning is. You suddenly understand something you've understood all your life, but in a new way."

> The Four-Gated City 1969

35 . . . it isn't either or at all, it's and, and, and, and, and, and.

> Briefing for a Descent into Hell 1971

36 Thinking? She would not have said so. She was trying to catch hold of something, or to lay it bare so she could look and define; for some time now she had been "trying on" ideas like so many dresses off a rack.

> The Summer Before the Dark 1973

37 "The way to learn a language is to breathe it in. Soak it up! Live it!"

> Ibid.

38 . . . older woman, younger man! Popular wisdom claims that this particular class of love affair is the most poignant, tender, poetic, exquisite one there is, altogether the choicest on the menu.

> Ibid.

39 . . . should one judge people by the attitudes expected of them by virtue of the years they had lived, their phase or stage as mammals, or as items in society? Well, that is how most people have to be judged; only a few people are more than that.

> Ibid.

40 Nonsense, it was all nonsense: this whole damned outfit, with its committees, its conferences, its eternal talk, talk, talk, was a great con trick; it was a mechanism to earn a few hundred men and women incredible sums of money.

> Ibid.

41 Laughter is by definition healthy.

> Ibid.

42 And what authority even the creases in a suit can convey...

> Ibid.

43 This was a happy and satisfactory marriage because both she and Michael had understood, and very early on, that the core of discontent, or of hunger, if you like, which is unfailingly part of every modern marriage . . . was fed and heightened by what people were educated to expect of marriage, which was a very great deal because the texture of ordinary life . . . was thin and unsatisfactory. Marriage had had a load heaped on it which it could not sustain.

> Ibid.

44 You are young, and then you are middle-aged, but it is hard to tell the moment of passage from one state to the next. Then you are old, but you hardly know when it happened.

> Ibid.

45 There was nothing to prevent one or all of us becoming victims at any moment.

> The Memoirs of a Survivor 1975

46 [I wanted] a simultaneous knowledge of vastness and of smallness.

> Ibid.

47 It's almost impossible for anyone in the West not to see the West as the God-given gift to the world.

> Quoted in "Doris Lessing on Feminism, Communism and
> 'Space Fiction'" by Lesley Hazleton, The New York Times
> Magazine 25 July 1982

48 There are certain types of people who are political out of a certain kind of religious reason. I think it's fairly common among socialists: they are, in fact, God-seekers, looking for the kingdom of God on earth. A lot of religious reformers have been like that, too. It's the same psychological set, trying to abolish the present in favor of some better future—always taking it for granted that there is a better future. If you don't believe in heaven, then you believe in socialism.

Ibid.

49 The human community is evolving. . . . We can survive anything you care to mention. We are supremely equipped to survive, to adapt and even in the long run to start thinking.

Ibid.

50 This world is run by people who know how to do things. They know how things work. They are equipped. Up there, there's a layer of people who run everything. But we—we're just peasants. We don't understand what's going on, and we can't do anything.

(p. 330), *The Good Terrorist* 1985

51 Space or science fiction has become a dialect for our time.

The Guardian (London) 7 November 1988

52 When the time comes…to make the first trip home, it means stripping off new skin and offering exposed and smarting flesh to—the past.

African Laughter: Four Visits to Zimbabwe 1992

53 Surely it is better to be poor here, in this sunlight, this beauty, than, let's say, Bradford or Leeds.

Ibid.

54 I expected a period of incompetence. I expected every kind of mess and muddle. I knew nothing would work for a time. How could it when they didn't have trained people? But what I didn't expect was that these bastards would get into power and then not care about anything but feathering their own nests. There are dozens of them, noses in the trough, getting rich quick.

Ibid.

55 When the War ended, every black person who had supported Mugabe* because of his promises, and many who had not, waited for land, and for Paradise to begin…

Ibid.

*Robert Gabriel M—, Zimbabwean political leader (1924–).

56 The great secret that all old people share is that you really haven't changed in seventy or eighty years. Your body changes, but you don't change at all. And that, of course, causes great confusion.

Sunday Times: Books (London) 10 May 1992

57 Political correctness is the natural continuum from the party line. What we are seeing once again is a self-appointed group of vigilantes imposing their views on others. It is a heritage of communism, but they don't seem to see this.

Ibid.

58 . . . the slums of Nairobi stretch as far as the eye can see and nobody gives a damn.

Quoted in "Zimbabwe's poor are rich in hope"
by David Morgan (Reuters), *Seattle Post-Intelligencer*,
C1 & 4 10 November 1992

59 Children are very physical in what they see and feel. It's only afterward that you get intellectual about it.

Ibid.

60 I was born with skins too few. Or they were scrubbed off me by . . . robust and efficient hands.

Under My Skin: My Autobiography to 1949, Vol. 1 1994

61 . . . we have not yet developed a system of education that is not a system of indoctrination.

Ibid.

62 If you try and claim your own life by writing an autobiography, at once you have to ask, But is this the truth?

Ibid.

63 "I understand what it means to be ill with love. '*My heart hurts, it hurts…*'"

Love, Again 1996

64 The ichors that flooded her body created behind the face of Sarah, the face she and everyone knew, a younger face, that shone out, smiling. Her body was alive and vibrant, but also painful. Her breasts burned, and the lower part of her abdomen ached. Her mouth threatened to seek kisses—like a baby's mouth turning and turning to find the nipple.

Ibid.

65 People carry round with them this weight of longing, usually, thank heavens, well out of sight and "latent"—like an internal bruise?—and then, for no obvious reason, just like that, there he was (who?), and onto him is projected this longing, with love.

Ibid.

66 He* experienced me as a sanctimonious wincing idiot.

*Walking in the Shade: Vol. Two of My Autobiography,
1949–1962* 1997

*Reference to Henry Kissinger, German-born American scholar and government official (1923–); U.S. Secretary of State (1973-77).

67 [The British suffer from] a reluctance to understand extreme experience.

Ibid.

68 . . . memory's little tricks…how it simplifies, tidies up, makes sharp contrasts of light and shade.

Ibid.

69 Briefly and in passing: it is a sad thing that what is written has permanence, whereas what is said is often unnoticed. Something written is reprinted, becomes part of theses. Decades later it is quoted back at you. It is a millstone around your neck, and there is nothing you can do. "But you said, on page 123…"

Ibid.

70 Philistinism is endemic in Britain, and most particularly in London. As I write, the favourite pastime at the dinner tables is to recite—with pride—the list of great books you haven't read and have no intention of reading.

Ibid.

71 For years—decades—perhaps centuries—women have been complaining about men's lack of sensitivity, their unkindness, but no sooner have women acquired power than they permit, even sanctify, some of the nastiest manifestations of human nature.

Ibid.

72 Projectiles that could carry diseases designed to kill all the people in a country or city? What were these ancient peoples, that they could do such things?

Mara and Dann: An Adventure 1998

73 There was a recklessness about the ways they used their soil and their water.

Ibid.

2141. Françoise Parturier (1919–)

1 In general all curvaceousness strikes men as incompatible with the life of the mind.

Open Letter to Men
1968

2 And the more deodorants there are in the drugstores, the worse [woman] smells in literature.

Ibid.

3 That the most intelligent, discerning and learned men, men of talent and feeling, should finally put all their pride in their crotch, as awed as they are uneasy at the few inches sticking out in front of them, proves how normal it is for the world to be crazy. . . .

Ibid.

4 . . . we've never been in a democracy; we've always been in a phallocracy!

Ibid.

5 To tell a woman using her mind that she is thinking with a man's brain means telling her that she can't think with her own brain; it demonstrates your ineradicable belief in her intellectual inadequacy.

Ibid.

6 A real woman is a young, pretty, sexy, tender woman who is no taller than five feet six who adores you.

Ibid.

7 You say being a housewife is the noblest call in the world . . . You remind me of those company executives who . . . praise the "little guys" of their organization in their speeches . . .

Ibid.

8 You men can't stand the truth, sir, as soon as it embarrasses your interests or your pleasure . . .

Ibid.

2142. June Wayne (1919?–)

1 My art deals with information systems and astrophysical space because it is the new wilderness, the next frontier, a wilderness of an immensity we have yet to comprehend.

Quoted in "June Wayne," Exposures, Women & Their Art
by Ann Brown & Arlene Raven* 1989
*See 3020.

2143. Louise Young (1919–)

1 Life altered the atmosphere and gentled the sunlight. It turned the naked rocks of the continents into friable soil and clothed them with a richly variegated mantle of green which captured the energy of our own star for the use of living things on earth, and it softened the force of the winds. In the seas life built great reefs that broke the impact of storm-driven waves. It sifted and piled up shining beaches along the shores. Working with amazing strength and endurance life transformed an ugly and barren landscape into a benign and beautiful place.

(p.76), The Unfinished Universe *1986*

2144. Eva Duarte Perón (1919–1952)

1 Our president [General Juan Perón]* has declared that the only privileged person in our country are the children.

Speech, "My Labour in the Field of Social Aid," American
Congress of Industrial Medicine 5 December 1949
*Her husband, Argentinean soldier and politican (1895–1974),
president (1945–1955 and 1973–74).

2 Almsgiving tends to perpetuate poverty; aid does away with it once and for all. Almsgiving leaves a man just where he was before. Aid restores him to society as an individual worthy of all respect and not as a man with a grievance. Almsgiving is the generosity of the rich; social aid levels up social inequalities. Charity separates the rich from the poor; aid raises the needy and sets him on the same level with the rich.

Ibid.

3 When a woman goes into politics, the man eats cold *puchero* [stew].

Speech, Quoted in Twentieth-Century Women Political
Leaders *by Claire Price-Groff 1998*

4 Without fanaticism one cannot accomplish anything.

Ibid.

2145. Joy Adamson (1919–1980)

1 How could she [Elsa, the lion] know that it needed all the strength of my love for her to leave her now and give her back to nature—to let her learn to live alone until she might find her pride—her real pride?

"The Second Release," Born Free *1960*

2146. Ella Grasso (1919–1981)

1 I'm opposed to abortion because I happen to believe life deserves the protection of society.

Quoted in "Ella Grasso of Connecticut" by
Joseph B. Treaster, Ms. *(New York) October 1974*

2 I would not be President because I do not aspire to be President. But I'm sure that a woman will be President. When? I don't know. It depends. I don't think the woods are full of candidates today.

Quoted in Newsweek *(New York) 4 November 1974*

3 I keep my campaign promises, but I never promised to wear stockings.

Quoted in Time *(New York) 18 November 1974*

4 In Connecticut I'm just an old shoe.

Ibid.

2147. Margot Fonteyn (1919–1991)

1 I have never wanted to live to be old, so old I'd run out of friends or money.

Attributed n.d.

2148. Casey Geddes Miller (1919–1997)

1 Language screens reality as a filter on a camera screens light waves.

Words and Women 1976

2149. Iris Murdoch (1919–1999)

1 "What are you famous *for?*"
"For nothing. I am just famous."

The Flight from the Enchanter 1955

2 "We can only learn to love by loving. . . ."
The Bell 1958

3 "Only lies and evil come from letting people off..."
A Severed Head 1961

4 "You cannot have both civilization and truth. . . ."
Ibid.

5 In almost every marriage there is a selfish and an unselfish partner. A pattern is set up and soon becomes inflexible, of one person always making the demands and one person always giving way.
Ch. 2, Ibid.

6 Falling out of love is chiefly a matter of forgetting *how* charming someone is.
Ch. 24, Ibid.

7 There is no substitute for the comfort supplied by the utterly taken-for-granted relationship.
Ch. 28, Ibid.

8 "To be a complete victim may be another source of power."
The Unicorn 1963

9 I think being a woman is like being Irish. . . . Everyone says you're important and nice, but you take second place all the same.
Ch. 2, *The Red and the Green 1965*

10 Munching the substance of one's life as if it were a fruit with a thin soft furry exterior and a firm sweet fleshy inside.
The Nice and the Good 1968

11 Love can't always do work. Sometimes it just has to look into the darkness.
Ibid.

12 Being good is just a matter of temperament in the end.
Ch. 14, Ibid.

13 Happiness is a matter of one's most ordinary everyday mode of consciousness being busy and lively and unconcerned with self. To be damned is for one's ordinary everyday mode of consciousness to be unremitting agonising preoccupation with self.
Ch. 22, Ibid.

14 No love is entirely without worth, even when the frivolous calls to the frivolous and the base to the base.
Ch. 39, Ibid.

15 Bereavement is a darkness impenetrable to the imagination of the unbereaved.
The Sacred and Profane Love Machine 1974

16 He led a double life. Did that make him a liar? He did not feel a liar. He was a man of two truths.
Ibid.

17 Human affairs are not serious, but they have to be taken seriously.
Pt. 2, "The Great Teacher," *Henry and Cato 1976*

18 The priesthood is a marriage. People often start by falling in love, and they go on for years without realizing that that love must change into some other love which is so unlike it that it can hardly be recognised as love at all.
Ibid.

19 He . . . was a sociologist; he had got into an intellectual muddle early on in life and never managed to get out.
"The Events in Our Town," *The Philosopher's Pupil 1983*

20 Possibly, more people kill themselves and others out of hurt vanity than out of envy, jealousy, malice or desire for revenge.
Ibid.

21 The sin of pride may be a small or a great thing in someone's life, and hurt vanity a passing pinprick, or a self-destroying or ever murderous obsession.
Ibid.

22 Moralistic is not moral. And as for truth—well, it's like brown—it's not in the spectrum. . . .Truth is *sui generis*.
Ibid.

23 All art is a struggle to be, in a particular sort of way, virtuous.
Quoted in *Novelists in Interview*, John Haffenden, ed. *1985*

24 PLATO. Art is the final cunning of the human soul which would rather do anything than face the gods.
"Art and Eros: A Dialogue about Art" (first performed on stage, February 1980), *The Nice and the Good* (play) *1986*

25 SOCRATES. In philosophy if you aren't moving at a snail's pace you aren't moving at all.
"Above the Gods: A Dialogue about Religion," Ibid.

26 Philosophy! Empty thinking by ignorant conceited men who think they can digest without eating!
Pt. 1, "Midsummer," *The Book and the Brotherhood 1987*

27 They [bars and pubs] are universal places, like churches, hallowed meeting places of all mankind.
Pt. 2, "Midwinter," Ibid.

28 We shall be better prepared for the future if we see how terrible, how *doomed* the present is.
Ibid.

29 But fantasy kills imagination, pornography is death to art.
Pt. 1, *The Message to the Planet 1989*

30 Every man needs two women, a quiet home-maker, and a thrilling nymph.
Ibid.

31 I daresay anything can be made holy by being sincerely worshipped.
Pt. 5, Ibid.

32 The notion that one will not survive a particular catastrophe is, in general terms, a comfort since it is equivalent to abolishing the catastrophe.
Pt. 6, Ibid.

33 Perhaps when distant people on other planets pick up some wave-length of ours all they hear is a continuous scream.
Ibid.

34 A bad review is even less important than whether it is raining in Patagonia.
News Item *6 July 1989*

2150. Rosemary Brown (1920–)

1 I'm not committed to welfare measures. I don't think they get at the root of the problem. I'm committed to the eradication of all poverty, to its being wiped out. I'm not hung up on guaranteed incomes and that sort of thing, because I don't think that's the solution. We've got to change the system and make it impossible to be poor.

Quoted in "The Radical Tradition of Rosemary Brown" by Sharon Batt, *Branching Out July/August 1975*

2 We cannot swing our vote. We have to swing our party.

Ibid.

2151. Liz Carpenter (1920–)

1 I thought that we would wake up this morning and have the same rights as our husbands, grandsons and garbagement—but we are still begging to be let into our country's Constitution.*

Speech, Thursday Caucus (New York City) *22 March 1979*
*After the defeat of the Equal Rights Amendment; see Alice Paul, 1538:2.

2 And what was a shy, retiring homebody like me doing, bounding around between fifteen unratified states? I do it because I can't not do it. I do it because of indignation that women were left out in the first place and have always fought other people's battles in lieu of their own. I do it because I figure life has been good to me and I have the chance to say thanks. The Lord won't like me very well if I don't. And I won't like myself very well, either.

Speech, National Women's Political Caucus Conference (Albuquerque, New Mexico) *July 1981*

2152. Mary Carolyn Davies (fl. 1920s–30s)

1 Men are the devil—they all bring woe.
In winter it's easy to say just "No."
Men are the devil, that's one sure thing,
But what are you going to do in spring?

"Men Are the Devil" *n.d.*

2 If I had known what trouble you were bearing;
What griefs were in the silence of your face;
I would have been more gentle, and more caring,
And tried to give you gladness for a space.

"If I Had Known" *n.d.*

3 The talking oak
to the ancient spoke.
But any tree
Will talk to me.

"Be Different to Trees" *n.d.*

4 Women are doormats and have been,
The years these mats applaud—
They keep the men from going in
With muddy feet to God.

"Door-Mats" *n.d.*

5 Let me be joy, be hope! Let my life sing!

"A Prayer for Every Day" *n.d.*

6 May I forget
What ought to be forgotten; and recall
Unfailing, all
That ought to be recalled, each kindly thing,
Forgetting what might sting.

Ibid.

7 As oft as on the earth I've lain
I've died and come to life again.

"Out of the Earth" *n.d.*

8 Three can laugh and doom a king,
Three can make the planets sing.

"Three" *n.d.*

9 A trap's a very useful thing:
Nature in our path sets Spring.

"Traps" *n.d.*

10 Iron, left in the rain
And fog and dew,
With rust its covered.—Pain
Rusts into beauty too.

Ibid.

2153. Jean Edelstein (192?–)

1 I think that art is an internal investigation of who you are, what motivates you. It can't be something out there, it has to be something totally inside.

Quoted in "Jean Edelstein," *Exposures, Women & Their Art* by Ann Brown & Arlene Raven* 1989
*See 3020.

2 My Marxist background certainly didn't prepare me for the Goddess! Then everything I had been doing finally came to fruition—my work became a temple for the Goddess.

Ibid.

3 Whenever they talk about a male artist and his female model, they always talk about her as if she were something less, an object, something there for his satisfaction, not an individual who is really working with the person. I feel my working relationship with Camille* as a model is a totally different experience—two women working together.

Ibid.

*C— Ertoleto, acupressurist, model. **See 3020.

2154. Mary J. Elmendorf (fl. 1920s)

1 Beauty's the thing that counts
In women; red lips
And black eyes are better than brains.

"Beauty's the Thing" *n.d.*

2155. Barbara Guest (1920–)

1 I wonder if this new reality is going to destroy me.

"The Hero Leaves His Ship," St. 1, *The Location of Things 1962*

2 I am talking to you
With what is left of me written off,
On the cuff, ancestral and vague,
As a monkey walks through the many fires
Of the jungle while the village breathes in its sleep.

"Sunday Evening," St. 3, Ibid.

3 Then you took my hand. You told me that love was a sudden disturbance of the nerve ends that startled the fibers and made them new again.

"Sadness," St. 3, Ibid.

4 Where goes this wandering blue,
This horizon that covers us without a murmur?

Let old lands speak their speech,
Let tarnished canopies protect us.

In the Alps" St. 1, Ibid.

2156. Mary Anne Guitar (1920?–)

1 We have to stop being so teacher-centered, and become student-centered. It's not what you think they need but what they think they need. That's the functional approach.

"College Marriage Courses—Fun or Fraud?"
Mademoiselle February 1961

2157. Leona Helmsley (1920/21–)

1 We don't pay taxes. Only the little people pay taxes.*

Remark, Quoted in *The New York Times 12 July 1989*
*She was jailed for tax evasion.

2158. Helen Hudson (1920–)

1 A white casket with silver handles, she thought. Not a soft bed with a pink quilt but four sides and a lid that closes. To be shipped like a shoe in a box from this world to the next.

"Sunday Morning," *American Scene: New Voices,*
Don Wolfe, ed. *1963*

2 As he worked, putting the mask of sleep over the faces of death, he felt a vague excitement, as though he were, indeed, reviving her, as though the eyes he had closed so carefully might open again and see him, without reproach: a kindly man who knew his trade and did it well.

Ibid.

2159. P. D. James (1920–)

1 A politician is required to listen to humbug, talk humbug, condone humbug. The most we can hope is that we don't actually believe it.

A Taste for Death 1986

2160. Gerda Lerner (1920–)

1 Black people cannot and will not become integrated into American society on any terms but those of self-determination and autonomy.

Preface, *Black Women in White America 1972*

2 . . . black women . . . are trained from childhood to become workers, and expect to be financially self-supporting for most of their lives. They know they will have to work, whether they are married or single; work to them, unlike to white women, is not a liberating goal, but rather an imposed lifelong necessity.

Ibid.

3 The appeal of the New Right is simply that it seems to promise that nothing will change in the domestic realm. People are terrified of change there, because it's the last humanizing force left in society, and they think, correctly, that it must be retained.

Quoted in "On the Future of Our Past" by Catharine R.
Stimpson,* *Ms. (New York) September 1981*
*See 2653.

4 Long-term commitment to an intimate relationship with one person of whatever sex is an essential need that people have in order to breed the qualities out of which nurturant thought can rise.

Ibid.

5 . . . American social movements: they rise fast, they wane fast, and they seem to disappear. History tells us that this is not really true.

Ibid.

6 . . . women's history is the primary tool for women's emancipation.

Ibid.

7 Today, we can be defeated in regards to laws, to appropriations, to representation, but if we are truly transforming consciousness, we cannot be defeated.

Ibid.

8 Everything that explains the world has in fact explained a world that does not exist, a world in which men are at the center of the human enterprise and women are at the margin "helping" them. Such a world does not exist—never has.

Ibid.

9 [By the late 1700s] Authorization [for women] to speak, inspired speech, and the right to learn and to teach.

*The Creation of Feminist Consciousness: From the
Middle Ages to Eighteen-Seventy 1993*

10 [There is a] depth and urgency of the search of Jewish and Christian women for connection to the Divine, which found expression in more than 1000 years of feminist Bible criticism and religious re-visioning.

Ibid.

11 . . . religion was the primary arena on which women fought for hundreds of years for feminist consciousness.

Ibid.

12 Elitism, the polar opposite of "open access," has respectable and ancient antecedents.

Why History Matters: Life and Thought 1997

13 All of us, ultimately, will join one of the most despised, neglected and abused groups in [American] society—the old and the sick.

Ibid.

14 I learned first hand what it means to be defined as 'the Other,' the deviant. I was a respectable, bourgeois person, with class privileges...[a]nd then within weeks I was defined as a Jew, nothing else.

Address, Awards ceremony (Vienna), Ibid.

2161. Frances Maule (fl. 1920s)

1 It is just as impossible to pick out a single feminine type and call it "woman," as it is to pick out a single masculine type and call it "man."

"The 'Woman' Appeal'," *J. Walter Thompson
News Bulletin,* No. 105 January *1924*

2162. Elaine Morgan (1920–)

1 The trouble with specialists is that they tend to think in grooves.

Ch. 1, *The Descent of Woman 1972*

2 We had taken the first step along the tortuous road that led to the sex war, sado-masochism, and ultimately to the whole contemporary snarl-up, to prostitution, prudery, Casanova, John Knox, Marie Stopes, white slavery, women's liberation, *Play-*

boy magazine, *crimes passionels*, censorship, strip clubs, alimony, pornography, and a dozen different brands of mania. This was the Fall. It had nothing to do with apples.

> Ch. 4, Ibid.

3   . . . everyone knows that you can't relieve an itch by stroking it gently.

> Ch. 5, Ibid.

4   Housewives and mothers seldom find it practical to come out on strike. They have no union, anyway.

> Ch. 11, Ibid.

2163. Marjorie Newlin (1920–)

1   I see some people so terrified about getting older, but it's going to happen if you're still alive.

> Quoted in "Sure, You'll Get Older. So What" by Jean-Noel Bassior, *Parade Magazine* 22 November 1998

2   I just can't go and find somebody to ask for help every time I want to lift a finger.

> Ibid.

3   People say, "When you get to this age, you can't do this and you can't do that," but that's not the way it is. I never considered my age when I went to the gym.

> Ibid.

2164. Gabriela Roepke (1920–)

1   AMANDA. I just can't seem to go on—without a good morning in a big baritone voice.

> *A White Butterfly* 1960

2   SMITH. . . . the reflection in my shaving mirror tells me things nobody else would.

> Ibid.

3   OLD LADY. The best thing others can do for us is to tell us lies.

> Ibid.

4   SMITH. You lose an umbrella. You can also lose time.

> Ibid.

2165. Katsuko Saruhashi (1920–)

1   He* didn't care if it was a man or a woman. If a researcher had drive, he would do as much as he could for them.

> Quoted in *Twentieth-Century Women Scientists* by Lisa Yount 1996

*Yasuo Miyake, meteorologist and professor.

2   There are many women who have the ability to become great scientists. I would like to see the day when women can contribute to science and technology on an equal footing with men.

> Ibid.

3   Each winner* has been not only a successful researcher but...a wonderful human being as well. They have become role models for those who will follow in their footsteps.

> Ibid.

*Reference to the Saruhashi Prize, which she established in 1980 to be awarded to a Japanese woman 50 years old or younger who has made important contributions to the natural sciences.

2166. Elizabeth Shane (fl. 1920s)

1   But every road is tough to me
That has no friend to cheer it.

> "Sheskinbeg" *n.d.*

2167. Dinah Shore (1920–1995)

1   I earn and pay my own way as a great many women do today. Why should unmarried women be discriminated against—unmarried men are not.

> Quoted in "Dinah," *The Los Angeles Times* 16 April 1974

2   I have never thought of participating in sports just for the sake of doing it for exercise or as a means to lose weight. And I've never taken up a sport just because it was a social fad. I really enjoy playing. It is a vital part of my life.

> Ibid.

2168. Eileen Jackson Southern (1920–)

1   Who are our true rulers? The Negro poets, to be sure. Do they not set the fashion, and give laws to the public taste? Let one of them, in the swamps of Carolina, compose a new song, and it no sooner reaches the ear of a white amateur, than it is written down, amended (that is, almost spoilt), printed, and then put upon a course of rapid dissemination, to cease only with the utmost bounds of Anglo-Saxondom, perhaps with the world. Meanwhile, the poor author digs away with his hoe, utterly ignorant of his greatness.

> *Knickerbocker Magazine* (1845), *The Music of Black Americans* 1971

2169. Mabel Elsworth Todd (fl. 1920s–30s)

1   In the expiratory phase lies renewal of vigor through some hidden form of muscular release. . . .

> *The Balancing of Forces in the Human Body* 1929

2   Emotion constantly finds expression in bodily position. . . .

> Ibid.

2170. Harriet Van Horne (1920–)

1   Cooking is like love. It should be entered into with abandon or not at all.

> Quoted in *Vogue* October 1956

2171. Dottie Walters (192-?–)

1   Speaking—speaking *well*—is like a great dance involving your audiences, your customers and the great minds of all the ages.

> Ch. 1, *Speak and Grow Rich*, and Lilly Walters* 1997

2   Goals are dreams with deadlines.

> Ch. 12, Ibid.

*See 3469.

2172. Jane Screven Heyward (fl. 1920s–1939)

1   More brightly must my spirit shine
Since grace of Beauty is not mine.

> "The Spirit's Grace" *n.d.*

2   The dear old ladies whose cheeks are pink
In spite of the years of winter's chill,
Are like the Autumn leaves, I think,
A little crumpled, but lovely still.

> "Autumn Leaves" *n.d.*

2173. Margaret Turnbull (fl. 1920s–1942)

1 No man is responsible for his father. That is entirely his mother's affair.

Alabaster Lamps 1925

2 When a man confronts catastrophe on the road, he looks in his purse—but a woman looks in her mirror.

The Left Lady 1926

2174. Rosalind Elsie Franklin (1920–1958)

1 This was my first continental holiday by car . . . and I confirmed my impression that cars are undesirable. . . . Travelling around in a little tin box isolates one from the people and the atmosphere of the place in a way that I have never experienced before. I found myself eyeing with envy all rucksacks and tents.

Quoted in Saint Elizabeth by Anne Sayre 1975

2175. Shirley Jackson (1919–1965)

1 School was recently over for the summer, and the feeling of liberty sat uneasily on most of them...

The Lottery, or, The Adventures of James Harris 1949

2 "Listening to the young folks, nothing's good enough for *them*. Next thing you know, they'll be wanting to go back to living in caves, nobody work anymore, live *that* way for a while."

Ibid.

3 I believe that all women, but especially housewives, tend to think in lists. . . . The idea of a series of items, following one another docilely, forms the only possible reasonable approach to life if you have to live it with a home and a husband and children, none of whom would dream of following one another docilely.

Pt. II, Life Among the Savages 1953

4 "Cocoa," she said. "Cocoa. Damn miserable puny stuff, fit for kittens and unwashed boys. Did *Shakespeare* drink cocoa?"

Pt. I, The Bird's Nest 1954

5 . . . I saw that Beth now, looking about her and drawing herself together, was endeavoring to *form* herself, as it were; let my reader who is puzzled by my awkward explanations close his eyes for no more than two minutes, and see if he does not find himself suddenly not a compact human being at all, but only a consciousness on a sea of sound and touch; it is only with the eyes open that a corporeal form returns, and assembles itself firmly around the hard core of sight.

Pt. IV, Ibid.

7 Her manner of dress, of speech, of doing her hair, of spending her time, had not changed since it first became apparent to a far younger Morgen that in all her life to come no one was, in all probability, going to care in the slightest how she looked, or what she did, and the minor wrench of leaving humanity behind was more than compensated for by her complacent freedom from a thousand small irritations.

Pt. V, Ibid.

8 . . . February, when the days of winter seem endless and no amount of wistful recollecting can bring back any air of summer . . .

Pt. II, Raising Demons 1956

9 It has long been my belief that in times of great stress, such as a four-day vacation, the thin veneer of family unity wears off almost at once, and we are revealed in our true personalities. . . .

Pt. IV, Ibid.

10 She looked out the window . . . savoring the extreme pleasure of being on a moving train with nothing to do for six hours but read and nap and go to the dining-car, going farther and farther every minute from the children, from the kitchen floor, with even the hills being incredibly left behind, changing into fields and trees too far away from home to be daily.

"Pillar of Salt," *The Magic of Shirley Jackson*, Stanley Edgar Hyman, ed. *1966*

11 She walked quickly around her one-room apartment. . . . After more than four years in this one home she knew all its possibilities, how it could put on a sham appearance of warmth and welcome when she needed a place to hide in, how it stood over her in the night when she woke suddenly, how it could relax itself into a disagreeable unmade, badly-put-together state, mornings like this, anxious to drive her out and go back to sleep.

"Elizabeth," Ibid.

2176. Ruth Morgan (1920–1978)

1 Pregnant women! They had that weird frisson, an aura of magic that combined awkwardly with an earthy sense of duty. Mundane, because they were nothing unique on the suburban streets; ethereal because their attention was ever somewhere else. Whatever you said was trivial. And they had that preciousness which they imposed wherever they went, compelling attention, constantly reminding you that they carried the future inside, its contours already drawn, but veiled, private, an inner secret.

Ch. 13, *Andrew's Revenge 1975*

2177. Hazel Scott (1920–1981)

1 There's only one free person in this society, and he is white and male.

Quoted in "Great (Hazel) Scott!" by Margo Jefferson, *Ms.* (New York) *November 1974*

2 Who ever walked behind anyone to freedom? If we can't go hand in hand, I don't want to go.

Ibid.

3 There's a time when you have to explain to your children why they're born, and it's a marvelous thing if you know the reason by then.

Ibid.

4 If you reach for something and find out it's the wrong thing, you change your program and move on.

Ibid.

2178. Alice Childress (1920–1994)

1 OLDTIMER. Child, when hard luck fall it just keep fallin'.

Wine in the Wilderness 1969

2 TOMMY. I'm independent as a hog on ice and a hog on ice is dead, cold, well-preserved and don't need a mother'grabbin' thing.

Ibid.

3 TOMMY. I'm just sick-a hair, hair, hair. Do it this way, don't do it, leave it natural, straighten it, process, no process. I get sick-a hair and talkin' 'bout it and foolin' with it. That's why I wear the wig.

Ibid.

4 TOMMY. Accessories. Something you add on or take off. The real thing is takin' place on the inside...that's where the action is.

Ibid.

5   We think of poverty as a condition simply meaning a lack of funds, no money, but when one sees fifth, sixth, and seventh generation poor, it is clear that poverty is as complicated as high finance.
        A Hero Ain't Nothin' But a Sandwich 1973

6   I write about those who come in second, or not at all—the four hundred and ninety-nine and the intricate and magnificent patterns of a loser's life. No matter how many celebrities we may accrue, they cannot substitute for the masses of human beings.
        "A Gale in a Gale Wind" (p. 112), *Black Women Writers (1950-1980): A Critical Evaluation*, Mari Evans,* ed. *1984*
        *See 2225.

7   Today our youngsters can freely discuss sex. Soon they will even be able to openly discuss one of the results of sex-life.
        "Alice Childress," *Interviews with Contemporary Women Playwrights*, Kathleen Betsko* and Rachel Koenig *1987*
        *See 2739.

8   . . . "the good old days." The only good days are ahead.
        Ibid.

9   I think women need kindness more than love. When one human being is kind to another, it's a very deep matter.
        Ibid.

10 [I create] characters who feel rejected and have to painfully learn how to deal with other people, because I believe all human beings can be magnificent once they realize their full importance.
        Speaking for Ourselves: Autobiographical Sketches by Notable Authors of Books for Young Adults, Donald R. Gallo, ed. *1990*

2179. Amy Clampitt (1920–1994)

1   Think of it
    undermining
    the computer's
    cheep, the time
    clock's hiccup,
    the tectonic
    inchings of it
    toward some
    general crackup!
    Think of it, think of
    water running, running,
    running till it
        falls!
        "Times Square Water Music," St. 7 *1987*

2   . . . the worn reed of
    individual survival.
        "Urn-Burial and the Bitterly Migration," St. 2 *1987*

3   My dead brother, when we were
    kids, fed milkweed caterpillars
    in Mason jars, kept bees, ogled
    the cosmos through a backyard
    telescope. But then the rigor
    of becoming throttled our pure
    ignorance to mere haste
    toward something else.
        St. 5, Ibid.

4   O drifting apotheosis of dust
    exhumed, who will unseal
    the crypt locked up within

    the shimmer of the chromosomes
        St. 11, Ibid.

5   names have been
    given   (revelation
    kif   nirvana
    syncope)   for
    whatever gift
    unasked
    gives birth to

    torrents
    fixities/reincarnations of
    the angels
        "A Silence," Sts. 6–7, *A Silence Opens 1994*

2180. Bella Abzug (1920–1998)

1   Woman's place is in the house—the House of Representatives.
        Motto *1970*

2   I am not elevating women to sainthood, nor am I suggesting that all women share the same views, or that all women are good and all men bad. Women have screamed for war. Women, like men, have stoned black children going to integrated schools. Women have been and are prejudiced, narrow-minded, reactionary, even violent. *Some* women. They, of course, have a right to vote and a right to run for office. I will defend that right, but I will not support them or vote for them.
        Speech, National Women's Political Caucus (Washington, D.C.) *10 July 1971*

3   I've been described as a tough and noisy woman, a prize fighter, a man-hater, you name it. They call me Battling Bella, Mother Courage, and a Jewish mother with more complaints than Portnoy. There are those who say I'm impatient, impetuous, uppity, rude, profane, brash, and overbearing. Whether I'm any of those things, or all of them, you can decide for yourself. But whatever I am—and this ought to be made very clear at the outset—I am a very serious woman.
        Introduction, *Bella!*, Mel Ziegler, ed. *1972*

4   One thing that crystallized for me like nothing else this year is that Congress is a very *unrepresentative* institution. . . . Those men in Congress . . . represent their *own* point of view—by reason of their sex, background, and class.
        Epilogue, Ibid.

5   You can't have a Congress that responds to the needs of the workingman when there are practically no people here who represent him. And you're not going to have a society that understands its humanity if you don't have more women in government.
        Quoted in "Impeachment?" by Claire Safran, *Redbook* (New York) *April 1974*

6   We don't so much want to see a female Einstein become an assistant professor. We want a woman schlemiel to get promoted as quickly as a male schlemiel.
        "Lois Gordon and Alan Gordon," *American Chronicle 1987*

7   I was running [for Congress] not because I happened to be a woman but because I was a woman.
        Induction Speech, National Women's Hall of Fame (Seneca Falls, New York) *24 September 1943*

2181. Lynn D. Compton (1921–)

1 I think the law became an ass the day it let the psychiatrists get their hands on the law.*

Quoted in *The Los Angeles Times* 14 April 1969

*Summation at trial of Sirhan B. Sirhan, assassin of Senator Robert F. Kennedy (1968).

2182. Carol Emshwiller (1921–)

1 As a mother I have served longer than I expected.

"Autobiography," *Joy in Our Cause* 1974

2 Mother wants me to write something nice she can show to her friends.

Ibid.

2183. Betty Friedan (1921–)

1 The problem lay buried, unspoken for many years in the minds of American women. It was a strange stirring, a sense of dissatisfaction, a yearning that women suffered in the middle of the twentieth century in the United States. Each suburban housewife struggled with it alone. As she made the beds, shopped for groceries, matched slipcover material, ate peanut butter sandwiches with her children, chauffeured Cub Scouts and Brownies, lay beside her husband at night, she was afraid to ask even of herself the silent question: "Is this all?"

Ch. 1, *The Feminine Mystique* 1963

2 Over and over women heard in voices of tradition and Freudian sophistication that they could desire no greater destiny that to glory in their own femininity [and] to pity the neurotic, unfeminine, unhappy women who wanted to be poets or physicians or presidents.

Ibid.

3 The suburban housewife—she was the dream image of the young American women and the envy, it was said, of women all over the world. The American housewife—freed by science and labor-saving appliances from the drudgery, the dangers of childbirth, and the illnesses of her grandmother . . . had found true feminine fulfillment.

Ibid.

4 And strange new problems are being reported in the growing generations of children whose mothers were always there, driving them around, helping them with their homework—an inability to endure pain or discipline or pursue any self-sustained goal of any sort, a devastating boredom with life.

Ibid.

5 It can be less painful for a woman not to hear the strange, dissatisfied voice stirring within her.

Ibid.

6 American women no longer know who they are.

Ch. 3, Ibid.

7 How did Chinese women, after having their feet bound for many generations, finally discover they could run?

Ch. 4, Ibid.

8 The most powerful influence on modern women, in terms of both functionalism and the feminine protest, was Margaret Mead.* . . . She was, and still is, the symbol of the woman thinker in America.

Ch. 6, Ibid.

9 Female biology, women's "biological career-line," may be changeless . . . but the nature of the human relationship to biology *has* changed.

Ibid.

10 For, of course, the natural childbirth-breastfeeding movement Margaret Mead* helped to inspire was not at all a return to primitive earth-mother maternity. It appealed to the independent, educated, spirited . . . woman . . . because it enabled her to experience childbirth not as a mindless female animal, an object manipulated by the obstetrician, but as a whole person, able to control her own body with her aware mind.

Ibid.

*See 1802.

11 Anthropologists today are less inclined to see in primitive civilization a laboratory for the observation of our own civilization, a scale model with all the irrelevancies blotted out; civilization is just not that irrelevant.

Ibid.

12 There is little or no intellectual challenge or discipline involved in merely learning to adjust.

Ch. 7, Ibid.

13 A mystique does not compel its own acceptance.

Ch. 8, Ibid.

14 How to put the libido back, restore the lost spontaneity, drive, love of life, the individuality, that sex in America seems to lack?

Ch. 9, Ibid.

15 The glorification of the "woman's role," then, seems to be in proportion to society's reluctance to treat women as complete human beings; for the less real function that role has, the more it is decorated with meaningless details to conceal its emptiness.

Ch. 10, Ibid.

16 That we have not made any respectable attempt to meet the special educational needs of women in the past is the clearest possible evidence of the fact that our educational objectives have been geared exclusively to the vocational patterns of men.

Ch. 11, Ibid.

17 Women, because they are not generally the principal breadwinners, can be perhaps most useful as the trail blazers, working along the bypaths, doing the unusual job that men cannot afford to gamble on.

Ibid.

18 Instead of fulfilling the promise of infinite orgastic bliss, sex in the America of the feminine mystique is becoming a strangely joyless national compulsion, if not a contemptuous mockery.

Ibid.

19 The feminine mystique has succeeded in burying millions of American women alive.

Ch. 13, Ibid.

20 A woman is handicapped by her sex, and handicaps society, either by slavishly copying the pattern of man's advance in the professions, or by refusing to compete with man at all.

Ch. 14, Ibid.

21 It is easier to live through someone else than to become complete yourself.

Ibid.

22 The problem that has no name—which is simply the fact that American women are kept from growing to their full human capacities—is taking a far greater toll on the physical and mental health of our countries than any known disease.

Ibid.

23 It is better for a woman to compete impersonally in society, as men do, than to compete for dominance in her own home with her husband, compete with her neighbors for empty status, and so smother her son that he cannot compete at all

Ch. 18, Ibid.

24 If divorce has increased one thousand percent, don't blame the women's movement. Blame our obsolete sex roles on which our marriages were based.

Speech *20 January 1974*

25 Sexual war against men is an irrelevant, self-defeating acting out of rage.

The Second Stage 1981

26 The most important effect of transcending those old sex roles may be an evolution of morality and religious thought. . . .

Ibid.

27 The uneasy sense of battles won, only to be fought over again, of battles than should have been won, according to all the rules, and yet are not, of battles that suddenly one does not really want to win, and the weariness of battle altogether—how many women feel it?

Ibid.

28 Today the problem that has no name,* is how to juggle work, love, home and children.

Ibid.

*See quotation 22.

29 In 1993 we've broken through the feminine mystique. Twenty-five years ago we doorbelled for politicians. Today, women are making policy. There are more women in Congress than ever before. Women have discovered the power to change their own lives.

Speech, Overlake Hospital (Bellevue, Washington, 28 January), Cited in "Age of Growth" by Susan Phinney, *Seattle Post-Intelligencer*, C1–2 *30 January 1993*

30 There's such a denial of people over 60 in this country. . . . We weren't dying.

Ibid.

31 Say "no" to the fountain of youth and turn on the fountain of age.

Ibid.

2184. Janet Jagan (1921–)

1 There was much hatred and malice against me because I was a white person [married to a non-white], but also, they claimed that I was the brains behind Jagan* that wrote all his speeches. They were trying to say only white people had brains.

Quoted in "Cheddi Jagan's widow…" by Bert Wilkinson, Associated Press *1 April 1997*

*Reference to her husband, Cheddi Jagan (d. 1972), Guyanese prime minister (1971–1972).

2 I haven't even been an American citizen since 1947. I live here [Guyana] and I will die here.

Ibid.

2185. Juanita Kreps (1921–)

1 I'd like to get to the point where I can be just as mediocre as a man.

Quoted in *American Political Women* by Esther Stineman *1980*

2186. Eeva-Liisa Manner (1921–)

1 MAIJA. Artfulness is a kind of capital.

Act I, Sc. 1, *Snow in May 1966*

2 PAAVO. Modesty makes women insincere.

Ibid.

3 LASSI. Women are awful—they know everything. Though they don't understand anything.

Sc. 2, Ibid.

4 LASSI. I love uncertain things…things that are certain bore me, make me depressed, like everlasting rain. And reliable and safe people are as boring as textbooks. Incalculable people are lovable, although they cause suffering too.

Ibid.

5 LASSI. Love makes *intelligent* beings depressed and flat. Only women, ostriches and monkeys are made happy by love. Oh yes, and parrots.

Act II, Sc. 1, Ibid.

6 LASSI. The female is designed on the same principle as the starfish. Those creatures that the woman doesn't swallow she melts outside her body until the soft parts dissolve and only the shell remains.

Ibid.

7 PAAVO. Illusions! Illusions. Illusion of innocent love. Illusion of the heart's goodness, illusion of the sacredness of the pure life. But your virtuousness is only love of comfort, bourgeois self-satisfaction. Give up what you hold so dear: your illusions, and you can return to reality and become your real self.

Sc. 2, Ibid.

8 HELENA. If hope shows the depth of sorrow, then hopelessness must cure sorrow.

Ibid.

9 PAAVO. Great men are born in stable straw and they are put in a basket of reeds for the river to carry away. They are allowed to form their own souls—God looks after their bodies. They're not fed with warm milk, they must drink from the streams of the world, they do dirty work; the polisher of the mirror has dirty hands.

Sc. 3, Ibid.

10 LASSI. Women! There isn't anything so bad that they don't soon start to enjoy it. Even if they lived in a barrel of shit they'd start making a home out of it, with everything nice and cozy.

Act III, Sc. 1, Ibid.

11 LASSI. Nothing is ever voluntary. Even when a person thinks he's doing something of his own free will, he's being compelled to do it. Only the dead are free, the chain is broken…but perhaps they miss their chains?

Ibid.

12 sleep builds stepping stones.

"Untitled Poem," *The Other Voices*, Carol Cosman, ed. *1975*

13 The whole intelligence of a poem is in futility…

> Ibid.

2187. Del Martin (1921–)

1   To understand the lesbian as a sexual being, one must understand woman as a sexual being.

> *Lesbian/Woman*, with Phyllis Lyon* 1972

*See 2250.

2   It is only when she can denounce the idiocy of religious scriptures and legal strictures that bind her and can affirm her Lesbian nature as but a single facet of her whole personality that she can become fully human.

> Ibid.

3   There is nothing mysterious or magical about lesbian lovemaking . . . The mystery and the magic come from the person with whom you are making love.

> Ibid.

4   Most human sexual behavior is *learned*. It is only in the lower animals that it is totally instinctive. The higher on the evolutionary scale you are, the less instinctive are your sexual relations. So our life experiences "teach" us our sexuality, which may turn out to be hetero, homo, or bi.

> Ibid.

5   At a time when women, the forgotten sex, are voicing their rage and demanding their personhood, it is fitting that we [lesbians] emerge from the shadows.

> Ibid.

6   Much polarity between men and women has centered around [sic] procreation. But the sex act itself is neither male nor female: it is a human being reaching out for the ultimate in communication with another human being.

> Ibid.

7   As leaders…we could not display fear. In the process we overcame our own fears.

> Ibid.

2188. Nancy Reagan (1921–)

1   I must say acting was good training for the political life which lay ahead for us.

> *Nancy* 1980

2   The Sixties, of course, was the worst time in the world to try and bring up a child. They were exposed to all these crazy things going on.

> Quoted in "Reflections of a Woman in Love" by Dotson Rader, *Parade Magazine* 8 November 1981

3   Where would we be without the movies?

> Filmex Tribute to Elizabeth Taylor,* Quoted in "The Great Life" by George Cristy, *The Hollywood Reporter* November 1981

*See 2513.

2189. Mona Van Duyn (1921–)

1   Have made my peace
because am just plain done for and have no doubt
that the Lord will come any day with my release.

> "Letters from a Father," I, *Letters From a Father and Other Poems* 1982

2   So the world woos its children back for an evening kiss.

> VI, Ibid.

3   For what is story if not relief from the pain
of the inconclusive, from dread of the meaningless?

> "Endings," *Firefall* 1992

4   and not even the daffodils know if it's safe to come
up for air in this crazy, hot-and-cold weather.

> "Notes from a Suburban Heart," St. 3`, *If It Be Not I: Collected Poems 1959–1982* 1994

5   I pray that the great world's flowering
stay as it is.

> "The Gardener to His God," St. 1, *A Time of Bees n.d.*

6   There is no disorder but the heart's.

> St. 2, Ibid.

2190. Rosalyn Yalow (1921–)

1   Through the years my mother has told me that it was fortunate that I chose to do acceptable things, for if I had chosen otherwise no one could have deflected me from my path.

> Autobiographical entry, *Les Prix Nobel Yearbook*, Tore Frängsmyr, ed. 1977

2   It is of interest from this brief history that neither Sol* nor I had the advantage of specialized post-doctoral training in investigation. We learned from and disciplined each other and were probably each other's severest critic. I had the good fortune to learn medicine not in a formal medical school but directly from a master of physiology, anatomy and clinical medicine. This training was essential if I were to use my scientific background in areas in which I had no formal education.

> Ibid.

*Dr. Solomon A. Berson (d. 1972)

3   I have never aspired to have, nor do I now want, a laboratory or a cadre of investigators-in-training which is more extensive than I can personally interact with and supervise.

> Ibid.

4   Whether we like it or not, women, even now, must exert greater total effort than men for the same degree of success.

> Quoted in *The Lady Laureates* (p. 229) by Olga S. Opfell 1978

5   I've always had time for my children. I went home every day for lunch. When the children were small, if I worked on weekends, they came to the laboratory with me. When they were older, I took them to museums, on trips…

> Quoted in "Winner Woman!" by Letitia Kent (p. 174), *Vogue* (New York) *January* 1978

6   We must believe in ourselves or no one else will believe in us.*

> Acceptance speech, Nobel Prize, Quoted in *Mothers of Invention* (p. 131) by Ethlie Ann Vare and Greg Ptacek 1988

*Her challenge to young women in the sciences.

7   We still live in a world in which a significant fraction of people, including women, believe that a woman belongs—and wants to belong—exclusively in the home. . . . The world cannot afford the loss of the talents of half its people if we are to solve the many problems which beset us.

> Ibid.

2191. Hannah Senesh (1921–1944)

1 One needs something to believe in, something for which one can have whole-hearted enthusiasm. One needs to feel that one's life has meaning, that one is needed in this world.

    Diary entry (1938), *Hannah Senesh: Her Life and Diary* 1966

2 I dream and plan as if there was nothing happening in the world, as if there was no war, no destruction, as if thousands upon thousands were not being killed daily. . . .

    Diary entry (2 November 1940), Ibid.

3 There are events without which one's life becomes unimportant, a worthless toy; and there are times when one is commanded to do something, even at the price of one's life.

    Diary entry (25 December 1943), Ibid.

2192. Simone Signoret (1921–1985)

1 Chains do not hold a marriage together. It is threads, hundreds of tiny threads which sew people together through the years. That is what makes a marriage last—more than passion or even sex!

    Daily Mail (London) *4 July 1978*

2193. Donna Reed (1921–1986)

1 If nuclear power plants are safe, let the commercial insurance industry insure them. Until these most expert judges of risk are willing to gamble with their money, I'm not willing to gamble with the health and safety of my family.

    Quoted in *The Los Angeles Times 12 March 1974*

2194. Mirija Gimbutas (1921–1994)

1 . . . the world of myth was not polarized into female and male as it was among the Indo-Europeans and many other nomadic and pastoral people of the steppes [in Neolithic Times]. Both principals were manifest side by side. The male divinity in the shape of a young man or male animal appears to affirm and strengthen the forces of the creative and active female. Neither is subordinate to the other: by complementing one another, their power is doubled.

    (p. 237), *Gods and Goddesses of Old Europe* 1981

2 The difficulty with the term *matriarchy* in twentieth-century anthropological scholarship is that it is assumed to represent a complete mirror image of patriarchy or androcracy—that is to say, a hierarchical structure with women ruling by force in place of men. This is far from the reality of Old Europe. Indeed, we do not find in Old Europe, nor in all of the Old World, a system of autocratic rule by women with an equivalent suppression of men. Rather, we find a structure in which the sexes are more or less on equal footing, a society that could be termed a gylany.*

    (p. 324), *The Civilization of the Goddess* 1991
    *Term coined by Riame Eisler; see 2459.

2195. Alison Wyrley Birch (1922–)

1 There are sounds to seasons. There are sounds to places, and there are sounds to every time in one's life.

    Quoted in *The Christian Science Monitor 23 January 1974*

2196. Ruth Brinker (1922–)

1 You have to go out and beg.*

    Quoted in "Open Heart, Open Hand," *Time* (New York) *9 January 1989*
    *Reference to fund-raising for her Project Open Hand, which feeds people with AIDS.

2197. Helen Gurley Brown (1922–)

1 You may marry or you may not. In today's world that is no longer the big question for women. Those who glom onto men so that they can collapse with relief, spend the rest of their days shining up their status symbol and figure they never have to reach, stretch, learn, grow, face dragons, or make a living again are the ones to be pitied. They, in my opinion, are the unfulfilled ones.

    Sex and the Single Girl 1963

2198. Vinnette Carroll (1922–)

1 They told me that I had one-third less chance because I was a woman and a third less chance again because I was black, but I tell you, I'm going to do one hell of a lot with that remaining one third.

    Newspaper article by S. Patterson, Billy Rose Collection, New York Public Library at Lincoln Center *n.d.*

2199. Eugenie Clark (1922–)

1 Not many appreciate the ultimate power and potential usefulness of basic knowledge accumulated by obscure, unseen investigators who, in a lifetime of intensive study, may never see any practical use for their findings but who go on seeking answers to their unknown without thought of financial or practical gain.

    Ch. 1, *The Lady and the Sharks* 1969

2 In the beginning, I wanted to enter what was essentially a man's field. I wanted to prove I could do it. Then I found that when I did as well as the men in the field I got more credit for my work because I am a woman, which seems unfair.

    Quoted in "Shark Tamer" by Madeleine Lundberg, *Ms.* (New York) *August 1979*

3 It seems as though women keep growing. Eventually they can have little or nothing in common with the men they chose long ago.

    Ibid.

2200. Judith Crist (1922–)

1 The critics who love are the severe ones . . . we know our relationship must be based on honesty.

    Introduction, *The Private Eye, the Cowboy, and the Very Naked Girl* 1968

2 In this lovely land of corrugated cartons and plastic bags, we want our entertainment packaged as neatly as the rest of our consumer goods: an attractive label on the outside, a complete and accurate detailing of contents there or on the inside, no loose ends, no odd parts, nothing left out.

    "*Hud*: Unpackaged Reality" (2 June 1963), Ibid.

3 In this era of affluence and of permissiveness, we have, in all but cultural areas, bred a nation of overprivileged youngsters, saturated with vitamins, television, and plastic toys. But they are nurtured from infancy on a Dick-and-Jane literary and artistic level; and the cultural drought, as far as entertainment is concerned, sets in when they are between six and eight.

    "Forgotten Audience: American Children" (2 May 1965), Ibid.

4 . . . the outcry against the current spate of sadism and violence in films is . . . more than justified by the indecencies that we are being subjected to on the big screen (and more and more on the little one at home), by the puddles of blood and piles of

guts pouring forth from the quivering flesh that is being lashed and smashed, by the bouncing of breast and the grinding of groin, by the brutalizing of men and the desecration of women being fed to us by the hour for no possible social, moral or intellectual purpose beyond our erotic edification and sensual delight and, above all, the almighty box-office return.

"Against the Groin" (December 1967), Ibid.

2201. Mavis Gallant (1922–)

1   Flor looked at his closed fist. "Why do people keep things?" she said.

"I don't know," said George. "I guess it proves you were somewhere."

Ch. 1, *Green Water, Green Sky* 1959

2   Success can only be measured in terms of distance traveled. . . .

Ibid.

3   No people are ever as divided as those of the same blood. . . .

Its Image on the Mirror 1964

4   Until the time of my own marriage I had sworn I would settle for nothing less that a certain kind of love. However, I had become convinced, after listening to my mother and to others as well, that a union of that sort was too fantastic to exist; nor was it desirable. The reason for its undesirability was never plain. It was one of the definite statements of rejection young persons must learn to make; "Perfect love cannot last" is as good a beginning as any.

Ibid.

5   I was always putting myself in my sister's place, adopting her credulousness, and even her memories, I saw, could be made mine. It was Isobel I imagined as the eternal heroine—never myself. I substituted her feelings for my own, and her face for any face described. Whatever the author's intentions, the heroine was my sister.

Ibid.

6   We admitted we loved her—we who dread the word. We would rather say we adore: it is so exaggerated it can't be true. Adore equals like, but love is compromising, eternal.

Ibid.

7   The Knights had been married nearly sixteen years. They considered themselves solidly united. Like many people no longer in love, they cemented their relationship with opinions, pet prejudices, secret meanings, a private vocabulary that enabled them to exchange amused glances over a dinner table and made them feel a shade superior to the world outside the house.

"Bernadette," *My Heart Is Broken* 1964

8   The world drew into itself, became smaller and smaller, was limited to her room, her table in the dining room, her own eyes in the mirror, her own hand curved around a glass. Dreams as thick as walls rose about her bed and sheltered her sleep...

"The Moabitess," Ibid.

9   "What is the appeal about cats? he said kindly. "I've always wanted to know." . . .

"They don't care if you like them. They haven't the slightest notion of gratitude, and they never pretend. They take what you have to offer, and away they go...It would be interesting to see what role the cat fancier *is* trying on," said Walter..."He says he likes cats because they don't like anyone. I suppose he is proving he is so tough he can exist without affection."

"An Unmarried Man's Summer," Ibid.

10   They were young and ambitious and frightened; and they were French, so that their learned behavior was all smoothness. There was no crevice where an emotion could hold.

"The Cost of Living," Ibid.

11   "Don't cry whilst writing letters. The person receiving the letter is apt to take it as a reproach. Undefined misery is no use to anyone. Be clear, or, better still, be silent. If you must tell the world about your personal affairs, give examples. Don't just sob in the pillow hoping someone will overhear."

Ch. 1, *A Fairly Good Time* 1970

12   Swedish films had given her the impression that conversation in an unknown tongue consisted of nothing except "Where is God?" and "Should one have children?" although, in reality, everyone in those foreign countries was probably saying "How much does it cost?" and "Pass the salt."

Ch. 5, Ibid.

13   She had the loaded handbag of someone who camps out and seldom goes home, or who imagines life must be full of emergencies.

Ibid.

14   [They] had been in a war they had not believed in and that was not officially a war at all. They were not veterans and not entitled to pensions. Privilege, a token income...were allowed for veterans of both world wars, the survivors of Indo-China, the old soldiers of the resistance. But the combatants of Algeria seemed like bad weather. They were not a useful memory.

Ch. 8, Ibid.

15   Good profession, good family, no money, foul temper—oh, the best of husbands.

Ch. 9, Ibid.

16   Nobody in movies ever runs out of cigarettes or has to look for parking space.

Ch. 12, Ibid.

17   The worst punishment I can imagine must be solitary confinement with nothing for entertainment except news of the world.

Ibid.

18   Everyone is lying; he will invent his own truth. Is it important if one-tenth of a lie is true? Is there a horror in a memory if it was only a dream?

"Ernst in Civilian Clothes," *The Pegnitz Junction* 1973

19   She had gone into captivity believing in virtue and learned she could steal. Went in loving the poor, came out afraid of them; went in generous, came out grudging; went in with God, came out alone.

"The Pegnitz Junction," Ibid.

20   Now that he was rich he was not thought ignorant any more, but simply eccentric.

Ibid.

2202. Blanche H. Gelfant (1922–)

1   Friendships, like geraniums, bloom in kitchens. Love runs up and down a flight of stairs and enters one flat and another in the housing projects.

Quoted in *Women Writing in America: Voices in Collage* 1985

2 [I have a] preference for criticism that is open-ended, capable of surprise, and subversive of traditional standards and forms . . . Juxtaposition of disparate pieces allows for new ways of seeing, for re-vision [sic], the activity central to feminine criticism.

> Ibid.

2203. Grace Hartigan (1922–)

1 . . . the face the world puts on that sells itself to the world.
> Quoted by Cindy Nemser in *Art Talk* (magazine) *1975*

2 I'd like to think that there are some things that . . . can't be analyzed to the point where they're finished off, either.
> Ibid.

3 There's a time when what you're creating and the environment you're creating it in come together.
> Ibid.

4 . . . I don't mind being miserable as long as I'm painting well.
> Ibid.

2204. Gladys Heldman (1922–)

1 Players are always in the foreground, and they should be . . . anything else would be like Sol Hurok* thinking that *he* was the star when it is really the ballet.
> Quoted in "Queen of the Long-Way Babies" by Dan Rose,
> *Signature August 1974*
> *Russian-born American impresario (1888–1974).

2 It's a mental attitude you have about winning, about dying before you're willing to lose.
> Ibid.

2205. Gertrude Himmelfarb (1922–)

1 The old feminism spoke the language of liberation. . . . The new feminism speaks the language of power.
> Quoted in "Are Women Leaders Wielding Power Differently
> Than Men?" by Georgia Anne Geyer,* *Seattle Times
> 14 May 1989*
> *See 2592.

2206. Eda J. Le Shan (1922–)

1 . . . most of us carry into marriage not only our childlike illusions, but we bring to it as well the demand that it *has* to be wonderful, because it's *supposed* to be. Of course the biggest illusion of all is that we are going to do the job of parenthood so well: it will all be fun and always deeply satisfying.
> Ch. 2, *How to Survive Parenthood 1965*

2 We are learning that there are no longer any simple patterns or easy definitions. Each of us has to discover who and what we are, and our own special qualities; what makes us feel womanly. Passivity and weakness do not describe the feminine woman; devotion to kitchen or nursery serves us no better as a definition—where and what is the indefinable something our feminist grandmothers were so eager to give up and we are so anxious to recapture?
> Ch. 8, Ibid.

3 Psychotherapy can be one of the greatest and most rewarding adventures, it can bring with it the deepest feelings of personal worth, of purpose and richness in living. It doesn't mean that one's life situation will change dramatically or suddenly. . . . It

does mean that one can develop new capacities and strengths with which to meet the natural vicissitudes of living; that one may gain a sense of inner peace through greater self-acceptance, through a more realistic perspective on one's relationships and experiences.
> Ch. 11, Ibid.

4 . . . in all our efforts to provide "advantages" we have actually produced the busiest, most competitive, highly pressured and over-organized generation of youngsters in our history—and possibly the unhappiest. We seem hell-bent on eliminating much of childhood.
> Ch. 1, *The Conspiracy Against Childhood 1967*

5 Babies are necessary to grown-ups. A new baby is like the beginning of all things—wonder, hope, a dream of possibilities. In a world that is cutting down its trees to build highways, losing its earth to concrete . . . babies are almost the only remaining link with nature, with the natural world of living things from which we spring.
> Ch. 2, Ibid.

6 The reason the young child learns [to talk] so well and so fast is that *his* way of learning is his own best way. When he is allowed this freedom to explore the world of language, he pursues his own interest and curiosity...He comes at things from many directions and is therefore more likely to see the way they fit together and relate to one another...He learns not to please others, but to please himself.
> Ibid.

7 Because Maria Montessori* was herself a creative thinker, I cannot believe that she would be at all happy about what is being done in her name. The passionate fervor of today's Montessori proponents, their single-minded dependence on a narrow formulation and program despite all that has been learned about children and education since Dr. Montessori was alive, does not represent an objective or thoughtful pooling of all the resources at our disposal...
> Ch. 3, Ibid.
> *See 1311.

8 Instead of focusing our attention on developing readiness for academic achievement promulgating middle-class standards and behavior, we ought to be spending our time and our money on ways in which to help every child to feel that he is a person, that he is lovable and that he can contribute something of value to others.
> Ch. 4, Ibid.

9 We are not asking our children to do their own best but to be *the* best. Education is in danger of becoming a religion based on fear; its doctrine is to compete. The majority of our children are being led to believe that they are doomed to failure in a world which has room only for those at the top.
> Ch. 5, Ibid.

10 Excellence in life seems to me to be the way in which each human being makes the most of the adventure of living and becomes most truly and deeply himself, fulfilling his own nature in the context of a good life with other people...What he knows and what he feels have equal importance in his life...
> Ch. 9, Ibid.

11 We have kept our children so busy with "useful" and "improving" activities that we are in danger of raising a generation of young people who are terrified of silence, of being alone with their own thoughts...
> Ch. 11, Ibid.

2207. Nancy Lord (1922–)

1 People in traditional cultures consider time differently from those of us raised on Western standards, who learned to be "on time," not to waste time, and sometimes to "kill" time. These concepts have no meaning in Native cultures, where time just *is*.

(p. 14), *Fishcamp: Life on an Alaskan Shore 1997*

2 In our separate times and places, there isn't much we've witnessed together—only our single sun, the scatter of stars, that round or sliced or darkened orb moving through its phases, and the overarching vault of heaven.

(p. 86), Ibid.

3 Tonight the moon, tugging quiet water down the inlet, has me in its hold. Millions of years after the ancestors of land dwellers first crawled ashore, my blood remains as salty as the sea. I am eighty percent water, and my cells bulge toward the moon.

(p. 87), Ibid.

4 I want people to know that salmon exist, as food and more than food. I fear less the future of individual fishermen, myself included, than I do a future in which people don't know or care what a wild salmon requires, a future in which we don't do what we must to ensure that rives run clean and unimpeded, that oceans be nurseries instead of strip mines and dumps. Only when we provide for salmon will they provide for us—will we live in a world where it's possible to continue.

(p. 258), Ibid.

5 *. . . there's no picking out any one thing without finding it hitched to absolutely everything else.*

Ibid.

2208. Carmen McRae (1922–)

1 Blues is to jazz what yeast is to bread—without it, it's flat.

Speech, "Blues is a Woman," Newport Jazz Festival, Avery Fisher Hall, New York City *2 July 1980*

2209. Liz Moore (1922–)

1 [My parents] both taught me, very early on, two things: one was that you respected anyone who was good at whatever he or she did, no matter what it was; and the second was that, if you were lucky, you gave something back.

Quoted in "Liz Moore: Giving HMOs a Checkup" by Vickie L. Bane, *Ms.* (New York) *November/December 1997*

2 You have these moments, I guess you call it epiphany...I thought, "This is the answer." I had been documenting how bad and how high the costs are of traditional energy, particularly coal, and here is the benign source [solar energy]. All we have to do is learn to harvest it in an economic way.

Ibid.

2210. Grace Paley (1922–)

1 He had had a habit throughout the twenty-seven years of making a narrow remark which, like a plumber's snake, could work its way though the ear down the throat, halfway to my heart. He would then disappear, leaving me choking with equipment.

Enormous Changes at the Last Minute 1960

2 . . . a very large family. Four brothers and three sisters, they wouldn't touch birth control with a basement beam. Orthodox. Constructive fucking. Builders, baby.

Ibid.

3 I don't believe civilization can do a lot more than educate a person's senses. If it's truth and honor you want to refine, I think the Jews have some insight. Make no images, imitate no God. After all, in His field, the graphic arts, He is pre-eminent. Then let that One who made the tan deserts and blue Van Allen belt and the green mountains of New England be in charge of Beauty, which He obviously understands, and let man, who was full of forgiveness at Jerusalem, and full of survival at Troy, let man be in charge of good.

Ibid.

4 Rosiness is not a worse windowpane than gloomy gray when viewing the world.

Ibid.

5 They were busy as bees in a ladies' murmur about life and lives. They worked. They took vital facts from one another and looked as dedicated as a kibbutz.

Ibid.

6 The man has the burden of the money. It's needed day after day. More and more of it. For ordinary things and for life. That's why holidays are a hard time for him. Another hard time is the weekend, when he's not making money or furthering himself.

Ibid.

7 I was a fantastic student until ten, and then my mind began to wander.

Quoted in "Grace Paley: 'Art Is on the Side of the Underdog'" by Harriet Shapiro, *Ms.* (New York) March *1974*

8 There isn't a story written that isn't about blood or money. People and their relationship to each other is the blood, the family. And how they live, the money of it.

Ibid.

9 . . . I think art, literature, fiction, poetry, whatever it is, makes justice in the world. That's why it almost always has to be on the side of the underdog.

Ibid.

10 If you live an autonomous life you never really are repressed.

Ibid.

11 Nobody lives without a personal life.

"Grace Paley: Fragments for a Portrait in Collage," Quoted in *Women Writing in America: Voices in Collage* by Blanche H. Gelfant* *1984*

*See 2202.

12 I believe in a kind of fidelity to your own early ideas; it's a kind of antagonism in me to prevailing trends.

Ibid.

13 "But the fun of talking, Ruthy. What about that? It's as good as fucking lots of times. Isn't it?"
"Oh boy," Ruth said, "if it's that good, then it's got to be that bad."

"The Expensive Moment," *Later the Same Day 1985*

14 The table was the enameled table common to our class, easy to clean, with wooden undercorners for indigent and old cockroaches that couldn't make it to the kitchen sink.

"The Long Distance Runner," *The Collected Stories 1994*

15 First they make something, then they murder it. Then they write a book about how interesting it is.

Ibid.

16 I wanted to have been married forever to one person, my ex-husband or my present one. Either has enough character for a whole life, which as it turns out is really not such a long time. You couldn't exhaust either man's qualities or get under the rock of his reasons in one short life.

                                       "Wants," Ibid.

17 I often see through the appearance of things right to the apparition itself.

                                       Just As I Thought 1998

18 What is man that woman lies down to adore him?

                                       Ibid.

19 If you're a feminist, it means that you've noticed that male ownership of the direction of female lives has been the order of the day for a few thousand years, and it isn't natural.

                                       Ibid.

20 I'm not very good at Friends meetings. My mind refuses to prevent my eyes from looking at the folks around me, and I'm often annoyed because I can't get the drift of the murmur of private witness. I did hear one young man near me say, "May your intercession here today be the fruit of our action." I think this means "God helps those that help themselves," a proverb that sounds meaner than it really is.

                                       Ibid.

21 I had this idea that Jews *were* supposed to be better. I'm not saying they were, but they were *supposed* to be, and it seemed to me on my block that they often were. I don't see any reason in being in this world actually if you can't in some way be better, repair it somehow. . . . So to be like all the other nations seems to me a waste of nationhood, a waste of statehood, a waste of energy, and a waste of life.

                                       Ibid.

22 If there are prisons, they ought to be in the neighborhood, near a subway—not way out in distant suburbs, where families have to take cars, buses, ferries, trains, and the population that considers itself innocent forgets, denies, chooses to never know that there is a whole huge country of the bad and the unlucky and the self-hurters, a country with a population greater than that of many nations in our world.

                                       Ibid.

23 It's a terrible thing to die young. Still, it saves a lot of time.

                                       Ibid.

24 Let us go forth with fear and courage and rage to save the world.

                                       Ibid.

25 Though the world cannot be changed by talking to one child at a time, it may at least be known.

                                       Ibid.

26 Don't put yourself on a platter. What are you—a roast duck, everything removable with a lousy piece of flatware? Be secret. Turn over on your side. Let them guess if you're stuffed. That's how I got where I am.

                                       Ibid.

27 Wherever you turn someone is shouting give me liberty or I give you death.

                                       Ibid.

28 Hindsight, usually looked down upon, is probably as valuable as foresight, since it does include a few facts.

                                       Ibid.

29 [By the late seventies] some feminists were sometimes racist, some African Americans were sometimes misogynist, some Jews did sometimes act as though they were in charge of suffering, and almost everybody arrived too slowly at the reality of the destruction of species, water, and air.

                                Introduction, Ibid.

2211. Marie Birmingham Ponsot (1922–)

1 Each stroke starts a far drumming
   clumping the kelp, helping
shells and rubbish decay into sand.

             "Separate in the Swim," *The Bird Catcher* 1998

2 In this stretch of the Atlantic
   the whole Atlantic operates

                                       Ibid.

2212. Vera Randal (1922–)

1 Time, dough in a bowl, rose, doubling, trebling in bulk, and I was in the middle of the swelling, yeasty mass—lost.

                   "Alice Blaine," *The Inner Room* 1964

2 " . . . If this is July, what, precisely, happened to June, and a sizable slice of May?"

                                       Ibid.

3 "John is dead."
   "Yes."
   "I am also dead," I said numbly.
   "You're not dead. You're very far from dead."
   "I feel dead."
   "That's different."
   "Is it?" I said. "Is it really?"
   "It is. Really."

                                       Ibid.

4 "I believe in people, which I suppose is a way of believing in God."

                                       Ibid.

5 . . . I opened my eyes to the nightmare from which I knew, with a knowledge deeper and surer than words, I would not wake.

                                       Ibid.

6 Fury gathered until I was swollen with it.

                                       Ibid.

2213. Alice Rossi (1922–)

1 The emancipation or liberation of women involves more than political participation and the change of any number of laws. Liberation is equally important in areas other than politics; economics, reproduction, household, sexual and cultural emancipation are relevant.

                             Preface, *The Feminist Papers* 1973

2 Scholars all too often move in a world as restricted as that in which their subjects lived or from which they escaped.

          Pt. I, "The Making of a Cosmopolitan Humanist," Ibid.

3 A really radical break from the confinement of sex roles might lie in women's search for mates from very different social and intellectual circles, men who are not vain, self-centered and ambitious but tenderly devoted to home and children and the living of life.

                                       Ibid.

4 It is curious that it may be the help of a housekeeper and a friend that facilitates a woman's life's work, while the closest analogy . . . one would find from the pen of a man is typically a tribute to his wife.

"A Feminist Friendship," Ibid.

5 Equal pay for equal work continues to be seen as applying to equal pay for men and women in the same occupation, while the larger point of continuing relevance in our day is that some occupations have depressed wages because women are the chief employees. The former is a pattern of sex discrimination, the latter of institutionalized sexism.

Ibid.

6 The single most impressive fact about the attempt by American women to obtain the right to vote is how long it took.

"Along the Suffrage Trail," Ibid.

7 Without the means to prevent, and to control the timing of conception, economic and political rights have limited meaning for women. If women cannot plan their pregnancies, they can plan little else in their lives. . . .

"The Right to One's Body," Ibid.

8 Abridgement of any published book or essay is an assault, a cutting or pruning by one mind of the work of another.

"Guiness and Locks," Ibid.

9 While social class rests on economic factors of income and power, social status rests on less tangible cultural factors of life styles.

Pt. II, Introduction, Ibid.

10 Alcohol was a threat to women, for it released men from the moral control they had learned from a diet of preaching and scolding from ministers and mothers alike.

Ibid.

11 As economic affluence increased with the growth of the new industrialism and expansion of trade, women's worth declined as producers and increased as consumers.

Ibid.

12 It has become more "reasonable" to argue that Adam was made from Eve than vice versa.

"The 'Militant Madonna," Ibid.

13 The focus on heaven can be a lifetime pursuit, and there is no way to test whether the goal was worth the effort . . .

"The Blackwell Clan,"* Ibid.

*See Antoinette Brown Blackwell, 975; Elizabeth Blackwell, 952; Emily Blackwell, 975.1

14 Students of women's lives have sometimes claimed that spinsterhood and childlessness are the price such women paid for the unusual career paths they pursued.

Ibid.

15 For every war widow there may be several dozen wives who cope with the physical and emotional damage inflicted by war on their husbands and sons.

Pt. IV, Introduction, Ibid.

16 . . . sons forget what grandsons wish to remember . . .

Ibid.

17 The drum-beating martial mood of wartime is often followed by a pot-stirring and baby-rocking domestic ethos in its aftermath.

Ibid.

18 "Understanding" . . . is not a foundation for action if the terms in which a problem is "understood" tend toward acceptance of the status quo . . .

Ibid.

19 Understanding through mastery and control versus understanding through empathetic projection and the absorption of the views of others . . . may be a comparison that frequently differentiates the sexes . . .

"Cultural Stretch," Ibid.

2214. Joyce Treiman (1922?–)

1 You ask why I paint? Why do I breathe?

Quoted in "Joyce Treiman," *Exposures, Women & Their Art* by Ann Brown & Arlene Raven* 1989

*See 3020.

2 There has to be something elusive, something metaphorical, something unexpected. First you have to be hit on the head, really struck by it. Then you say, "Gee, what is this really about?" You have to be able to walk away with the image, carry it with you. That's something I call the "after-image." You have to be able to conjure it up later from your memory, like the Great Masters' images, such as Rembrandt's "Nightwatch."

Ibid.

3 The major challenge is to be able to articulate and perform all of it—subject and concept and media. That's really tough. And that's the difference between painting and the performing arts. For instance, in theater, the authors, producers, directors and performers are separate. But in painting, you have to come up with the idea, and be the performer and producer—they're tied up together. It's wonderful to be able to do them all.

Ibid.

2215. Renee Winegarten (1922–)

1 The book of the faults and complexities of the present cannot be closed like that containing the difficulties and errors of the past. . . .

"The Idea of Decadence," *Commentary* (New York) *September 1974*

2 The mighty are fallen and we shall not look upon their like again.

Ibid.

3 We still tend to share the idea that civilization must be either growing and pressing ever upwards, or else disintegrating into nothingness, instead of going on, variously developing and changing in a multitude of different areas, in ways not always perceptible to the human eye.

Ibid.

4 . . . the quest for origin and end, zenith and nadir, growth and decline, rise and fall, florescence and decadence. Where would writers be without these essential props for their narratives?

Ibid.

5 Old age cannot be cured. An epoch or a civilization cannot be prevented from breathing its last. A natural process that happens to all flesh and all human manifestations cannot be arrested. You can only wring your hands and utter a beautiful swan song.

Ibid.

6 Extremist movements...have played skillfully and successfully upon panic terrors and cultural decay and decadence.

Ibid.

7   What lies behind the concept of decadence to render it so ap-
    pealing to the imagination?

                                                        Ibid.

8   If epochs can grow old and die, what is to prevent them from
    becoming subject to disease?

                                                        Ibid.

9   The sad, dim shades of twilight seemed so much more moving
    than the clarity of day.

                                                        Ibid.

2216. Shelley Winters (1922–)

1   Every now and then, when you're on stage, you hear the best
    sound a player can hear. It's a sound you can't get in movies or
    in television. It is the sound of a wonderful, deep silence that
    means you've hit them where they live.

                                        Theatre Arts June 1956

2   It was so cold I almost got married.

                            Quoted in *The New York Times 29 April 1956*

2217. Judy Garland (1922–1969)

1   I was born at the age of twelve on a Metro-Goldwyn-Mayer
    lot.

                        Quoted in *Observer* (London) *18 February 1951*

2   . . . they [MGM] had us working days and nights on end.
    They'd give us pep-up pills to keep us on our feet long after we
    were exhausted. Then they'd take us to the studio hospital and
    knock us cold with sleeping pills—Mickey [Rooney] sprawled
    out on one bed and me on another. Then after four hours
    they'd wake us up and give us the pep-up pills again so we
    could work another seventy-two hours in a row. Half of the
    time we were hanging from the ceiling, but it became a way of
    life for us.

                        Quoted in Ch. 11, *Judy Garland,* Anne Edwards* 1975
    *See 2334.

3   Before every free conscience in America is subpoenaed, please
    speak up!

                                            Ch. 19 (c. 1947), Ibid.

4   How strange when an illusion dies
    It's as though you've lost a child. . . .

                                            "An Illusion," Ibid.

5   For 'twas not into my ear you whispered but into my heart.
    'Twas not my lips you kissed, but my soul.

                                            "My Love Is Lost," Ibid.

2218. Ava Gardner (1922–1990)

1   Deep down, I'm pretty superficial.

                        Ch. 8, Quoted in *Ava* by Roland Flamini *1983*

2219. Doreen Valiente (1922–1999)

1   The Christian Mass is a ritual involving bread and wine, which
    the Christians believe to be changed mystically into the body
    and blood of Christ; but the pagan does not believe this. In-
    deed, to celebrate the Black Mass, one has not only to be a
    Christian, but a Roman Catholic, who believes in the real
    Mass. Otherwise, as Gerald Gardner* has pointed out, one is
    going to a great deal of trouble to insult a piece of bread.

                        "The Black Mass," *An ABC of Witchcraft 1973*
    *G- Brosseau G-, English witch, author, historian (1884–1964).

2   Dancing is one of the activities, like poetry and music, which
    are essentially magical. All primitive people have ritual dances,
    not only for enjoyment, but with some purpose behind them.
    . . .Witches have the idea that the gods enjoy seeing people
    happy, and this is therefore an acceptable form of worship.

                        "Dancing, Its Uses in Witchcraft," Ibid.

3   . . . human nature and the human mind are basically the same
    beneath the sky-scrapers of New York in modern times, as they
    were centuries ago, in narrow medieval streets or remote villages.

                                            "Evil Eye," Ibid.

4   In our present-day "permissive society," sex is blazoned forth
    everywhere, usually in some more or less commercialised
    form. . . .And yet, how . . . many, beneath their surface gaiety,
    are loveless, insecure, neurotic and miserable? Perhaps the old
    idea of the sacredness of sex was not so foolish after all? To
    degrade sex is to degrade life itself.

                                            "Fertility, Worship of," Ibid.

5   The heart of paganism is a philosophy based upon Nature, and
    veiled in symbol and myth.

                                            "The Horned God," Ibid.

6   The gods of paganism are not remote. Their living symbols
    can be found close at hand in the world of Nature. But this
    does not preclude the god who is immanent being also tran-
    scendent, beyond the veil of manifested Nature.

                                                        Ibid.

7   Many people, and perhaps especially educated people, have an
    entirely wrong conception of what magic is. They think of it as
    something which miraculously violates the laws of Nature.
    Therefore, they say, it is absurd and impossible. But magic
    does not work like this at all. . . . By developing their powers,
    the magician or witch develop themselves. They aid their own
    evolution, their growth as a human being; and in so far as they
    truly do this, they aid the evolution of the human race.

                                            "Magic," Ibid.

8   As the most conspicuous luminary of the night, and the near-
    est heavenly body to our earth, the moon has hung like a
    shining magic mirror, reflecting man's dreams. From the Stone
    Age to the age of space travel, she has bewitched and allured
    mankind.

                                            "Moon Worship," Ibid.

9   The diamond of Truth is a jewel with many facets, flashing
    now one colour and now another; but the jewel does not
    change.

                                            "Reincarnation," Ibid.

10 The origin of torture and execution in the name of religion is
    the certainty that your religion is true, and therefore any other
    religion must be false. This being so, you must regard people
    who profess a different religion than your own as heretics, and
    as inevitably damned (as Saint Augustine did). It is your reli-
    gious duty to persecute them; and because their crime is
    against God, no cruelty is too great to use towards them. In-
    deed, anyone who urges mercy towards heretics is suspect
    himself. The evidence of history shows overwhelmingly that
    witches were persecuted, not because they had done harm, but
    because their crime was *heresy.* Hence the heavy involvement,
    from the beginning, of the Church in witchcraft trials.

                                            "Torture used on witches," Ibid.

11 An important point about witchcraft is that it *is* a craft, in the
    old sense of the word, the Anglo-Saxon *craeft*, implying art,

skill, knowledge. The word 'witch' means 'wise one'; and a person cannot be *made* wise, they have to *become* wise.

> "Witchcraft," Ibid.

12 The gods and goddesses are personifications of the powers of nature; or perhaps one should say, of super-nature, the powers which govern and bring forth the life of our world, both manifest and hidden. In other words, we live upon a plane of forms, superior to which is a plane of forces, upon which the gods move, because by personifying those forces to ourselves as gods we can establish a relationship with them.

> "The Old Gods," *Witchcraft for Tomorrow* 1978

13 Spaceship Earth is in deep trouble; when that happens, we need to get in touch with our base.

> Our base is the Divine Life of the universe. Our means of keeping in touch with it cannot be through any man-made dogma, but through nature, which man did not make. Men's hands wrote all the holy books and sacred scriptures; only the book of nature was written by divinity.

> "Witch Ethics," Ibid.

14 I remember in a radio interview once being asked, wasn't there a lot of *sex* in witchcraft? I pointed out that there was a lot of sex in human life. Witches are not responsible for this fact, so those who object to it must direct their complaint to a higher power.

> "Witch Signs and Symbols," Ibid.

15 Witchcraft does not need to apologize for involving sex magic. It is other religions which need to apologize for the miseries of puritanical repression they have inflicted on humanity.

> "Witch and Sex Magic," Ibid.

16 The birth and rebirth of all nature,
The passing of winter and spring,
We share with the life universal,
Rejoice in the magical ring.

> "The Witches' Creed," St. 3, in "Liber Umbrarum— A Book of Shadows," Ibid.

17 The dark and the light in succession,
The opposites each unto each,
Shown forth as a God and a Goddess:
Of this did our ancestors teach.

> St. 10, Ibid.

2220. Ylena Georgievna Bonner (1923–)

1 Since I never at any time anywhere under any circumstances deliberately spread slanderous fabrications defaming the Soviet state or social system or other countries, or private persons, I will not participate in the investigation and will not answer the question.

> *Alone Together* 1986

2 Living under the surveillance of the KGB* is very strange and unpleasant. Wherever you go, you feel the KGB watching, sometimes making films, sometimes harassing.

> Ibid.

*Komitet Gosudarstvennoy Bezopasnosti (Committee of State Security), Soviet intelligence agency.

2221. Ursula Reilly Curtiss (1923–)

1 It was the old principle of getting back on the horse that had thrown you (although why, Kate had always wondered? Why not just take up some other sport?) but sometimes, like a number of laudable things, it was wearing.

> Ch. 1, *The Wasp* 1963

2 After a second's astonishment, Kate let the lie stand. Like most lies it was much easier than the truth, and to contradict it might turn out to be a very wearying affair.

> Ch. 3, Ibid.

3 This was not love; it was exactly what Georgia had said: ownership. If you owned a race horse, you got the winner's stakes. If you owned a play, you got the royalties. If you owned a son. . . .

> Ch. 17, Ibid.

2222. Carolina Maria de Jesus (1923?–)

1 Actually we are slaves to the cost of living.

> Diary entry (15 July 1955), *Child of the Dark: The Diary of Carolina Maria de Jesus* 1962

2 I classify Sao Paulo this way: The Governor's Palace is the living room. The mayor's office is the dining room and the city is the garden. And the *favela** is the back yard where they throw the garbage.

> Diary entry (15 May 1958), Ibid.

*Barrio or ghetto.

3 "You had faith, and now you don't have it any more?"
"No, my son, democracy is losing its followers. In our country everything is weakening. The money is weak. Democracy is weak and politicians are very weak. Everything that is weak dies one day."

> Diary entry (20 May 1958), Ibid.

4 She neglects children and collects men.

> Diary entry (1 June 1958), Ibid.

5 A child is the root of the heart.

> Ibid.

2223. Antoinette DeWit (1923–)

1 Grab the Hope when it flies by, we* say.

> Letter to Elaine T. Partnow** *16 June 1989*

*Enabled Artists Guild, Portland, Oregon. **See 2870.

2 I really cannot, and never will, presume to "educate" the public . . . that being disabled never means "disabled en toto," but to recognize that "disabled" also means "enabled," and that I would like to see the public become more aware of.

> Quoted in "She's Got Art and Soul" by Kathy Brock, *Lake Oswego Review* (Oregon) *April 1989*

2224. Dorothy Dinnerstein (1923–)

1 . . . a sense of deep strain between women and men has been permeating our species' life as far back into time as the study of myth and ritual permits us to trace human feeling.

> *The Mermaid and the Minotaur* 1977

2 So long as the first parent is a woman, then, woman will inevitably be pressed into the dual role of indispensable quasi-human supporter and deadly quasi-human enemy of the human self. She will be seen as naturally fit to nurture other people's individuality; as the born audience in whose awareness other people's subjective existence can be mirrored; as the being so peculiarly needed to confirm other people's worth, power, significance that if she fails to render them this service she is a monster, anomalous and useless. And at the same time she will also be seen as the one who will not let other people be, the one who beckons her loved ones back from selfhood,

who wants to engulf, dissolve, drown, suffocate them as autonomous persons.

Ibid.

3 . . . renunciation of what has been inexorably outlived is by definition affirmative.

Ibid.

2225. Mari Evans (1923-)

1 It don't do
to wake up
quick . . .

"The Alarm Clock," I Am a Black Woman 1970

2226. Clara Fraser (1923–)

1 People hear that word [socialism] and they think "rhetoric. Karl Marx."* People's eyes get that kind of glazed look. [Socialism] is when the whole family is sitting around the dinner table, sharing and everyone gets alike.

Quoted in "Still active" by Florangela Davila,
Seattle Times, B2 17 March 1996

*German political philosopher and economist (1818–83).

2 Capitalism is constant change, but when you advocate change, people cry out, "That's revolutionary! Subversive!" And my favorite: "Un-American!" Of all the people who should be shocked—Americans. How the hell do they think they got here?

Ibid.

3 Capitalism is approaching a crisis. Everyone senses it. That's why they say "Throw out the immigrants. Put up tariff walls. Send women home. Get rid of affirmative action. Build more prisons."

Ibid.

4 As long as you are out there battling the establishment, the politicians, the cops, the right wing, the bosses...we're not going to get encrusted by empty theory. That's why we're still alive.

Ibid.

2227. Nadine Gordimer (1923–)

1 That was one of the things she held against the missionaries: how they stressed Christ's submission to humiliation, and so had conditioned the people of Africa to humiliation by the white man.

"Not for Publication," Not for Publication and
Other Stories 1965

2 It had proved impossible to anthropomorphize him into a handsome, dignified, well-behaved bully-boy; and somewhere along the unsuccessful process, he had lost the instincts of a dog, into the bargain.

"The Pet," Ibid.

3 He was a Nyasa with a face so black that the blackness was an inverted dazzle—you couldn't see what he was thinking.

Ibid.

4 I'm forty-nine but I could be twenty-five except for my face and my legs.

"Good Climate, Friendly Inhabitants," Ibid.

5 These [teenage] girls had dropped childhood, with its bond of physical dependency on parents, behind them. They had for-gotten what they had been, and they did not know that they would become what their parents were. For the brief hiatus they occupied themselves with preparations for a state of being very different—a world that would never exist.

"Vital Statistics," Ibid.

6 The two women gazed out of the slumped and sagging bodies that had accumulated around them.

Ibid.

7 Time is change; we measure its passage by how much things alter.

The Late Bourgeois World 1966

8 Why am I idiotically timid before such people, while at the same time so critical of their limitations?

Ibid.

9 Oh we bathed and perfumed and depilated white ladies, in whose wombs the sanctity of the white race is entombed! What concoction of musk and boiled petals can disguise the dirt done in the name of that sanctity?

Ibid.

10 "There's nothing moral about beauty."

Ibid.

11 Come to think of it all the earth is a graveyard, you never know when you're walking over heads—particularly this continent [Africa], cradle of man, prehistoric bones and the bits of shaped stone...that were weapons and utensils.

The Conservationist 1975

12 To keep anything the way you like it for yourself, you have to have the stomach to ignore—dead and hidden—whatever intrudes...

Ibid.

13 It is in opposition (the disputed territory of the argument, the battle for self-definition that goes on beneath the words) . . . that intimacy takes place.

Ibid.

14 She filled her house with blacks, and white parsons who went around preaching Jesus was a revolutionary, and then when the police walked in she was surprised.

Ibid.

15 She examines his body minutely and without shame, and he wakes to see her at it, and smiles without telling her why: she is the first not to pretend the different colours and textures of their being is not an awesome fascination. How can it be otherwise? The laws that have determined the course of life for them are made of skin and hair, the relative thickness and thinness of lips...skin and hair. It has mattered more than anything else in the world.

A Sport of Nature 1987

16 In the beginning was the Word. The Word was with God, signified God's Word, the word that was Creation. But over the centuries of human culture the word has taken on other meanings, secular as well as religious. To have the word has come to be synonymous with ultimate authority, with prestige, with awesome, sometimes dangerous persuasion, to have Prime Time, a TV talk show, to have the gift of the gab as well as that of speaking in tongues. The word flies through space, it is bounced from satellites, now nearer than it has ever been to the heaven from which it was believed to have come. But its

most significant transformation occurred for me and my kind long ago, when it was first scratched on a stone tablet or traced on papyrus, when it materialized from sound to spectacle, from being heard to being read as a series of signs, and then a script; and traveled through time from parchment to Gutenberg. For this is the genesis story of the writer. It is the story that wrote her or him into being.

Nobel lecture, "Writing and Being" (Johannesburg, 7 December 1991), *The Electronic Nobel Museum*, http://www.nobel.se/enm-index.html *1996*

17 The writer is of service to humankind only insofar as the writer uses the word even against his or her own loyalties, trusts the state of being, as it is revealed, to hold somewhere in its complexity filaments of the cord of truth, able to be bound together, here and there, in art: trusts the state of being to yield somewhere fragmentary phrases of truth, which is the final word of words, never changed by our stumbling efforts to spell it out and write it down, never changed by lies, by semantic sophistry, by the dirtying of the word for the purposes of racism, sexism, prejudice, domination, the glorification of destruction, the curses and the praise-songs.

Ibid.

18 Writing is always and at once an exploration of self and of the world; of individual and collective being.

Ibid.

19 Humans, the only self-regarding animals, blessed or cursed with this torturing higher faculty, have always wanted to know why.

Ibid.

20 [Myth] has made a whirling comeback out of Space, an Icarus in the avatar of Batman and his kind, who never fall into the ocean of failure to deal with the gravity forces of life. These new myths, however, do not seek so much to enlighten and provide some sort of answers as to distract, to provide a fantasy escape route for people who no longer want to face even the hazard of answers to the terrors of their existence. (Perhaps it is the positive knowledge that humans now possess the means to destroy their whole planet, the fear that they have in this way themselves become the gods, dreadfully charged with their own continued existence, that has made comic-book and movie myth escapist.)

Ibid.

21 Writers themselves don't analyze what they do; to analyze would be to look down while crossing a canyon on a tightrope. To say this is not to mystify the process of writing but to make an image out of the intense inner concentration the writer must have to cross the chasms of the aleatory and make them the word's own, as an explorer plants a flag.

Ibid.

22 Any writer of any worth at all hopes to play only a pocket-torch of light—and rarely, through genius, a sudden flambeau—into the bloody yet beautiful labyrinth of human experience, of being.

Ibid.

23 The question of for whom do we write nevertheless plagues the writer, a tin can attached to the tail of every work published. Principally it jangles the inference of tendentiousness as praise or denigration.

Ibid.

24 The edict of a world religion has sentenced a writer to death.
      For more than three years, now, wherever he is hidden, wherever he might go, Salman Rushdie* has existed under the
Ibid.

25 There is no privacy more inviolable than that of the prisoner. To visualize that cell in which he is thinking, to reach what he alone knows; that is a blank in the dark.

The House Gun 1997

26 Justice is a performance.

Ibid.

27 . . . nothing from the past could be more remote than this present.

Ibid.

28 As the couple emerge into the foyer of the courts, vast and lofty cathedral echoing with the susurration of its different kind of supplicants gathered there, Claudia suddenly breaks away, disappearing towards the sign indicating toilets. Harold waits for her among these people patient in trouble, no choice to be otherwise, for them, he is one of them, the wives, husbands, fathers, lovers, children of forgers, thieves and murderers.

Ibid.

2228. Jean Harris (1923–)

1 The problems of administering a prison or living in one as an inmate appear to me to be quite similar . . . mental illness, physical illness, ignorance, drugs and alcohol, racism, overcrowding, inadequate vocational training, incompetent staff and homosexuality.
      Were I to be asked to choose, I would put mental illness at the top of the list. There are days on my floor when the shrieks and screams and banging on the metal doors and throwing of furniture against a wall make my blood run cold, leave me touching a blanket or a book or something that represents sanity and a degree of permanence in a world gone mad.

"They Always Call Us Ladies": Stories from Prison 1988

2 My own observation is that many of the women here [in Bedford Hills Correctional Facility, New York] fall loosely into two groups. The first made up of those so damaged in childhood they have never learned to trust or love or even feel small pangs of compassion for others; the second made up of those in whom the need to love and be loved is the overriding drive in their lives.

Ibid.

3 Don't ever be sanguine about justice, Shane. Who the hell can say what it is?

Marking Time* 1992
*A book of letters to journalist Shana Alexander (see 2265).

2229. Marcella Hazan (1923–)

1 You don't cook? What do you do? Starve?

Quoted in "Battling Spaghetti O Taste Buds" by Cathy Booth, *Time* (New York) *29 May 1989*

2 Cooking is an art, but you can eat it too.

Ibid.

2230. Shirley Kaufman (1923–)

1 Through every night we hate,
preparing the next day's
war. . . .

"Mothers, Daughters," *The Floor Keeps Turning 1970*

2 We gnaw at each other's
skulls. Give me what's mine.
I'd haul her back, choking
myself in her, herself
in me.

Ibid.

3   What lets us be who we most are?
Suppose we only had to know
the climate, what grows where,
how rich or shallow the soil is.
A kind of field guide
for dislocated souls:
> "Lemon Sponge" (p. 139), *Roots in the Air:*
> *New and Selected Poems 1996*

4   Even now
in this sweet flesh
isn't there something starting to withdraw?
> "Milk" (1993) (p. 157), *Ibid.*

5   before
I could be her daughter,
she turned me into her mother.
Taught me the names of love
in her language: grief
and sorrow, sorrow and grief.
> "Leftovers" (p. 160), *Ibid.*

6   You have to get used to fear,
not fear exactly, but a long unease
> "Bread and Water," *Ibid.*

2231. Jean Kerr (1923–)

1   I'm tired of all this nonsense about beauty being only skin-deep. That's deep enough. What do you want—an adorable pancreas?
> "Mirror, Mirror, on the Wall," *The Snake Has*
> *All the Lines 1958*

2   I feel about airplanes the way I feel about diets. It seems to me that they are wonderful things for other people to go on.
> *Ibid.*

3   Marrying a man is like buying something you've been admiring for a long time in a shop window. You may love it when you get it home, but it doesn't always go with everything else in the house.
> "The Ten Worst Things About a Man," *Ibid.*

4   MARY. Being divorced is like being hit by a Mack truck. If you live through it, you start looking very carefully to the right and to the left.
> Act I, *Mary, Mary 1960*

5   BOB. I think success has no rules, but you can learn a great deal from failure.
> *Ibid.*

6   TIFFANY. Practically everybody Daddy knows is divorced. It's not that they're worse than other people, they're just richer.
> *Ibid.*

7   MARY…if you were absolutely convinced that you had no feeling in your hand, you'd be relieved to burn your fingers.
> Act II, *Ibid.*

8   MARY. It was hard to communicate with you. You were always communicating with yourself. The line was busy.
> *Ibid.*

9   A lawyer is never entirely comfortable with a friendly divorce, any more than a good mortician wants to finish the job and then have the patient sit up on the table.
> Quoted in *Time* (New York) 14 April *1961*

10   SYDNEY. You don't seem to realize that a poor person who is unhappy is in a better position than a rich person who is unhappy. Because the poor person has hope. He thinks money would help.
> Act I, *Poor Richard 1963*

11   SYDNEY. Even though a number of people have tried, no one has yet found a way to drink for a living.
> *Ibid.*

12   RICHARD. See, I believe in words. I think when they're put together they should mean something. They have an exact meaning, a precise meaning. There is more precision in one good sonnet than there is in an Atlas missile.
> Act III, *Ibid.*

13   SYDNEY. Our generation isn't looking for love. We're looking for desperation. We think it isn't real unless we have a fever of 103.
> *Ibid.*

14   JEFF. Man is the only animal that learns by being hypocritical. He pretends to be polite and then, eventually, he *becomes* polite.
> Act I, *Finishing Touches 1973*

15   KATY. If there is a fifty-fifty chance of immortality, why not play it with the believers?…I think you should impose standards and disciplines on yourself so that you might just possibly slip into eternity with Thomas More instead of going to hell with Hitler.
> Act II, *Ibid.*

16   FELICIA. Hope is the feeling you have that the feeling you have isn't permanent.
> Act III, *Ibid.*

2232. Liz Smith (1923–)

1   Gossip is news running ahead of itself in a red satin dress.
> "American Way" (syndicated column) *3 September 1985*

2   Most good gossip columnists have a touch of Savonarola* in them.
> "American Way" (syndicated column) *c. 1991*
*Girolamo S— (1452–98), Italian reformer and Dominican friar who gained a vast following and drove the Medici family out of Florence in 1494. He was later excommunicated and executed for criticizing Pope Alexander VI.

2233. Amy Swerdlow (1923–)

1   In the eighth grade my stomach churned and I thought I would faint as I had to stand up on the auditorium stage and refuse a bronze medal for coming in third in a potato race with the statement "I cannot accept a medal from William Randolph Hearst."*
> (p. 250), *Red Diapers: Growing Up in the Communist Left,*
> Judy Kaplan and Linn Shapiro, eds. *1998*
*American newspaper and magazine publisher (1863–1951).

2234. Wislawa Szymborska (1923–)

1   One monkey stares and listens with mocking disdain
the other seems to be dreaming away —
but when it's clear I don't know what to say
he prompts me with a gentle
clinking of his chain.
> "Brueghel's Two Monkeys," St. 3,
> *Calling Out to Yeti 1957*

2 Why does this written doe bound through these written woods?
For a drink of written water from a spring
whose surface will xerox her soft muzzle?
"The Joy of Writing," St. 1, *No End of Fun*,
Stanislaw Baranczak and Clare Cavanagh, trs. *1967*

3 The joy of writing.
The power of preserving.
Revenge of a mortal hand.
St. 6, Ibid.

4 For all its charms, the island is uninhabited,
and the faint footprints scattered on its beaches
turn without exception to the sea.

As if all you can do here is leave
and plunge, never to return, into the depths.

Into unfathomable life.
"Utopia," last lines, *A large number*, Stanislaw Baranczak
and Clare Cavanagh, trs. *1976*

5 With smiles and kisses, we prefer
to seek accord beneath our star,
although we're different (we concur)
just as two drops of water are.
"Nothing Twice," last stanza *1980*

6 I think that dividing literature or poetry into women's and
men's poetry is starting to sound absurd. Perhaps there was a
time when a woman's world did exist, separated from certain
issues and problems, but at present there are no things that
would not concern women and men at the same time. We do
not live in the boudoir anymore.
Interview with Beata Chmiel, *Ex Libris* (Poland) *1984*

7 All those bulbs, pods,
tentacles, fins, tracheae,
nuptial plumage, and winter fur
show that it has fallen behind
with its halfhearted work.
"On Death, Without Exaggeration," St. 7, *The People
on the Bridge*, Stanislaw Baranczak and
Clare Cavanagh, trs. *1986*

8 In vain it tugs at the knob
of the invisible door.
As far as you've come
can't be undone.
St. 10, Ibid.

9 When I pronounce the word Future,
the first syllable already belongs to the past.

When I pronounce the word Silence,
I destroy it.

When I pronounce the word Nothing,
I make something no non-being can hold.
"The Three Oddest Words," *in toto*, *Nära ögat*, Stanislaw
Baranczak and Clare Cavanagh, trs. *1996*

10 The poet as a person is in a way self-conceited: she has to believe in herself and hope she has something to say.
News conference *October 1996*

11 All imperfection is easier to tolerate if served up in small
doses.
Nobel lecture, "The Poet and the World," Stanislaw Baranczak
and Clare Cavanagh, trs., *The Electronic Nobel Museum*,
http://www.nobel.se/enm_index.html *7 December 1996*

12 Bureaucrats and bus passengers respond with a touch of in-
credulity and alarm when they find out that they're dealing
with a poet.
Ibid.

13 Films about painters can be spectacular, as they go about recreating every stage of a famous painting's evolution . . . Music
swells in films about composers . . . Of course this is all quite
naive and doesn't explain the strange mental state popularly
known as inspiration, but at least there's something to look at
and listen to.

But poets are the worst. Their work is hopelessly unphoto-
genic. Someone sits at a table or lies on a sofa while staring
motionless at a wall or ceiling. Once in a while this person
writes down seven lines only to cross out one of them fifteen
minutes later, and then another hour passes, during which
nothing happens . . . Who could stand to watch this kind of
thing?
Ibid.

14 . . . inspiration is not the exclusive privilege of poets or
artists generally. There is, has been, and will always be a certain group of people whom inspiration visits. It's made up of
all those who've consciously chosen their calling and do
their job with love and imagination. It may include doctors,
teachers, gardeners —and I could list a hundred more professions. Their work becomes one continuous adventure as
long as they manage to keep discovering new challenges in
it. Difficulties and setbacks never quell their curiosity. A
swarm of new questions emerges from every problem they
solve. Whatever inspiration is, it's born from a continuous
"I don't know."
Ibid.

15 And any knowledge that doesn't lead to new questions quickly
dies out: it fails to maintain the temperature required for sustaining life.
Ibid.

16 But in the language of poetry, where every word is weighed,
nothing is usual or normal. Not a single stone and not a single
cloud above it. Not a single day and not a single night after it.
And above all, not a single existence, not anyone's existence in
this world
Ibid.

17 Out of every hundred people, ...

Getting nothing out of life except things:
thirty
(though I would like to be wrong).

Balled up in pain
and without a flashlight in the dark:
eighty-three, sooner or later.
"A Word on Statistics," Sts. 1 & 14-15, Joanna Trzeciak, tr.
1997

18 I prefer myself liking people
to myself loving mankind
"Possibilities," ll. 5, 6, *Nothing Twice*, Stanislaw Baranczak
and Clare Cavanagh, trs. *1997*

19 I prefer the absurdity of writing poems
to the absurdity of not writing poems.
I prefer, where love's concerned, nonspecific anniversaries
that can be celebrated every day.
ll. 17–20, Ibid.

20 I prefer the earth in civvies.

l. 24, Ibid.

21 trash does not pretend to be anything better than it is

"Kitschy" *n.d.*

2235. Katherine Tait (1923–)

1 Reason, progress, unselfishness, a wide historical perspective, expansiveness, generosity, enlightened self-interest. I had heard it all my life, and it filled me with despair.

Afterword, Quoted in *Bertrand Russell** by Caroline Moorehead *1992*

*English mathematician and philosopher (1872–1970).

2236. Inge Trachtenberg (1923?–)

1 . . . my tenth year is marked as the year in which Adolf Hitler came to power in Germany. . . . Yet, when that event took place, Father wasn't sure that it was such a bad thing for Germany. Adolf Hitler had promised bread and order; Father was in favor of bread and order…I, for one, had no premonition of bad things to come

Ch. 4, *So Slow the Dawning 1973*

2 Decent was more than moral, decent was also being a good sport, a good friend, having a sense of humor, being tough.

Ch. 14, Ibid.

3 I did a lot of writing that winter. . . . Putting things down lent them a sense of permanence, it seemed to stem the feeling of rushing time which was suddenly so compelling that I fancied hearing its sound.

Ch. 16, Ibid.

2237. May Yamada (1923–)

1 Not only the young, but those who feel powerless over their own lives know what it is like not to make a difference on anyone or anything. The poor know it only too well, and we women have known it since we were little girls.

"Invisibility Is an Unnatural Disaster" (1981), *This Bridge Called My Back: Writings by Radical Women of Color*, Cherríe Moraga* and Gloria Anzaldúa,** eds. *1983*
*See 3336. **See 2891.

2 The Japanese have an all-purpose expression in their language for this attitude of resigned acceptance: "Shikataganai." "It can't be helped." "There's nothing I can do about it." It is said with the shrug of the shoulders and tone of finality, perhaps not unlike the "those-were-my-orders" tone that was used at the Nuremberg trials.

Ibid.

3 Asian American women still remain in the background and we are heard but not really listened to. Like Musak, they think we are piped into the airwaves by someone else.

Ibid.

4 Thank you people
of the village, if it had not been for your
kindness
in refusing me a bed
for the night
these humble eyes would never
have seen this
memorable sight.

Camp Notes and Other Poems 1992

2238. Diane Arbus (1923–1971)

1 I really believe there are things nobody would see if I didn't photograph them.

Diane Arbus 1972

2 Most people go through life dreading they'll have a traumatic experience. Freaks are born with their trauma. They've already passed it. They're aristocrats.

Ibid.

3 My favorite thing is to go where I've never been.

Ibid.

4 Something is ironic in the world and it has to do with the fact that what you intend never comes out like you intend it.

Ibid.

5 . . . the camera is a kind of license.

Ibid.

6 It gets to seem as if way back in the Garden of Eden after the Fall, Adam and Eve had begged the Lord to forgive them and He, in his boundless exasperation, had said, "All right, then. Stay. Stay in the Garden. Get civilized. Procreate. Muck it up." And they did.

Ibid.

7 A photograph is a secret about a secret. The more it tells you the less you know.

Preface, Quoted in *Diane Arbus: A Biography* by Patricia Bosworth *1985*

2239. Virginia Cassidy Kelley (1923–1994)

1 [I wanted to] show [Hillary]* how to bring out all that natural beauty she was covering up by going natural.

Leading with My Heart: My Life, with James Morgan *1994*
*Reference to Hillary Rodham Clinton (see 3139), wife of William Jefferson Clinton, 42nd president of the United States, her then future daughter-in-law.

2 He's a mighty good man, and it's not only due to my being perfect.*

Ibid.

*Reference to her son, William Jefferson Clinton (1946-), 42nd president of United States (1993–2001).

3 When I die, if I open my eyes and I'm standing in the middle of Marshall Field's makeup department, I'll know I made it to heaven.

Ibid.

2240. Denise Levertov (1923–1997)

1 Images
split the truth
in fractions.

"A Sequence," III, St. 2, *The Jacob's Ladder 1961*

2 To reach those shining pebbles,
that soil where uncommon men
have labored in their virtue
and left a store
of seeds for planting!

"A Common Ground," Sts. 3–4, Ibid.

3 Man gets his daily bread
in sweat, but no one said

in daily death. Don't eat
those nice green dollars your wife
gives you for breakfast.
>   "The Parts," Sts. 7–8, Ibid.

4   two by two in the ark of
the ache of it.
>   "The Ache of Marriage," *O Taste and See 1963*

5   living in the orchard and being

hungry, and plucking
the fruit
>   "O Taste and See," Sts. 5–6, Ibid.

6   Long after you have swung back
away from me
I think you are still with me
>   "Losing Track," St. 1, *Poems 1960–1967 1964*

7   Two girls discover
the secret of life
in a sudden line of
poetry.

I who don't know the
secret wrote
the line.
>   "The Secret," Sts. 1–2, Ibid.

8   "Life after life after life goes by
without poetry,
without seemliness,
without love."
>   "The Mutes," *The Sorrow Dance 1966*

9   No one had missed him, no one was in pursuit.
He himself must be
the key, now, to the next door,
the next terrors of freedom and joy.
>   "St. Peter and the Angel," St. 4, *Oblique Prayers 1984*

10   No, God's in the wilderness next door
—that huge tundra room, no walls and a sky roof—
busy at the loom.
>   "The Task," Ibid.

11   When shall we
dare to fly?
>   "Standoff," St. 8, *Breathing the Water 1987*

12   We must breathe time as fishes breathe water.
>   "Variation and Reflection on a Theme by Rilke,"* Ibid.
>   *Rainer Maria Rilke, German poet (1875–1926).

13   The bees
care for the allium, if you don't-
hear them now, doing their research,
humming the arias
of a honey opera . . .
>   "In Praise of Allium," Pt. VI, Ibid.

14   The day's blow
rang out, metallic—or it was I, a bell awakened,
and what I heard was my whole self
saying and singing what it knew: I *can*.
>   "Variation on a Theme by Rilke," Pt. I, Ibid.

15   I hear the books in all the rooms
breathing calmly
>   "August Daybreak," St. 1, Ibid.

16   Much happens when we're not there.
>   "Window-Blind," Pt. II, Ibid.

17   Every day, every day I hear
enough to fill
a year of nights with wondering.
>   "Every Day," Pt. III, St. 6, Ibid.

18   Not for one second
will my self hold still, but wanders
anywhere,
everywhere it can turn. Not you,
it is I am absent.
>   "Flickering Mind," *A Door in the Hive 1989*

19   He must return,
first, in Divine patience, and know
hunger again, and give
to humble friends the joy
of giving Him food—fish and a honeycomb.
>   "Ikon: The Harrowing of Hell ," Ibid.

20   Skies ever-blue,
daily sunshine, disgusted us like smile-buttons.
>   "In California During the Gulf War," St. 4, *Evening Train 1992*

21   . . . I have just enough faith to believe it exists.
>   "Work That Enfaiths," *New and Selected Essays 1992*

22   Every work of art is an "act of faith" in the vernacular sense of
being a venture into the unknown. The artist must dive into waters whose depths are unplumbed, and trust that he or she will
neither be swallowed up nor come crashing against a cement surface four foot down, but will rise and be buoyed upon them.
>   Ibid.

23   Invisible wings are given to us too, by which, if we would dare
to acknowledge and use them, we might transcend the duali-
ties of time and matter—might be upheld to walk on water.
Instead, we humans persistently say no, and persistently experience our wings only as a dragging weight on our backs.
>   Ibid.

24   Thus for me the subject is really reversed: not "faith that
works" but "work that enfaiths."
>   Ibid.

25   . . . I have engaged in building my own belief structure step by
step. They are poems written on the road to an imagined destination of faith. That imagination of faith acts as yeast in my
life as a writer: in that sense I do experience "faith that *works*"
as well as "work that enfaiths."
>   Ibid.

26   We call it "Nature"; only reluctantly
admitting ourselves to be "Nature" too.
>   "Sojourns in the Parallel World," *Sands of the Well 1996*

27   She's gathered up all the time in the world
—nothing else—and waits for scanty trophies,
complete in herself as a heron
>   "The Great Black Heron," Ibid.

28   Fully occupied with growing—that's
the amaryllis.
>   "The Métier of Blossoming," St. 1, *This Great Unknowing:
>   Last Poems 1998*

29 If humans could be
    that intensely whole, undistracted, unhurried,
    swift from sheer
    unswerving impetus! If we could blossom
    out of ourselves, giving
    nothing imperfect, withholding nothing!

                                             Ibid.

30 I'll dig in
    into my days, having come here to live, not to visit.
    Grey is the price
    of neighboring with eagles, of knowing
    a mountain's vast presence, seen or unseen.

                                      "Settling" n.d.

2241. Lauren Bacall (1924–)

1 The purity of Jewish upbringing—the restrictions that one carries through life being a "nice Jewish girl"—what a burden.

                            Lauren Bacall By Myself 1978

2 A man's illness is his private territory and, no matter how
   much he loves you and how close you are, you stay an outsider. You are healthy.

                                             Ibid.

3 I think your whole life shows in your face and you should be
   proud of that.

                        The Daily Telegraph (London) 2 March 1988

4 Looking at yourself in a mirror isn't exactly a study of life.

                        Daily Mail (London) 1 November 1990

2242. Sarah Caldwell (1924–)

1 If you approach an opera as though it were something that always went a certain way, that's what you get. I approach an
   opera as though l didn't know it.

              Quoted in "Sarah Caldwell: The Flamboyant of the Opera"
                    by Jane Scovell Appleton, Ms. (New York) May 1975

2 We must continually discipline ourselves to remember how it
   felt the first moment.

                                             Ibid.

3 It [Tanglewood, summer home of the Boston Symphony Or-
   chestra] was a place where gods strode the earth.

              Quoted in "Music's Wonder Woman," Time (New York)
                                            10 November 1975

2243. Nina Cassian (1924–)

1 With a triumphant smile,
   I confront time
   as its edged diamond
   sculpts my features.

                      "Poets," Cheerleader for a Funeral 1992

2 What's that tiny star on your left temple?
   Maybe a bird scratched it with tender claws
   to prod you into flying.

                      "Youthing," Take My Word For It 1998

2244. Shirley Chisholm (1924–)

1 It is not heroin or cocaine that makes one an addict, it is the
   need to escape from a harsh reality. There are more television
   addicts, more baseball and football addicts, more movie addicts, and certainly more alcohol addicts in this country than
   there are narcotics addicts.

                    Testimony, House Select Committee on Crime
                                         17 September 1969

2 As there were no black Founding Fathers, there were no
   founding mothers—a great pity on both counts.

                    Joint Resolution 264, Congressional Record
                                           10 August 1970

3 Of my two "handicaps," being female put many more obstacles in my path than being black.

                              Unbought and Unbossed 1970

4 Some members of Congress are the best actors in the world.

                                             Ibid.

5 When morality comes up against profit, it is seldom that profit
   loses.

                                             Ibid.

6 Tremendous amounts of talent are being lost to our society
   just because that talent wears a skirt.

                                             Ibid.

7 [In] working toward our own freedom, we can help others
   work free from the traps of their stereotypes. In the end, antiblack, antifemale and all forms of discrimination are equivalent to the same thing—anti-humanism. . . . We must reject
   not only the stereotypes that others have of us but also those
   we have of ourselves and others.

                                             Ibid.

8 I was well on the way to forming my present attitude toward
   politics as it is practiced in the United States; it is a beautiful
   fraud that has been imposed on the people for years, whose
   practitioners exchange gilded promises for the most valuable
   thing their victims own, their votes. And who benefits most?
   The lawyers.

                                      Pt. I, Ch. 4, Ibid.

9 The seniority system keeps a handful of old men, many of
   them southern whites hostile to every progressive trend, in
   control of the Congress. These old men stand implacably
   across the paths that could lead us toward a better future. But
   worse than they, I think, are the majority of members of both
   Houses who continue to submit to the senility system. Apparently, they hope they, too, will grow to be old.

                                      Pt. II, Ch. 8, Ibid.

10 The difference between de jure and de facto segregation is the
    difference between open, forthright bigotry and the shame-
    faced kind that works through unwritten agreements between
    real estate dealers, school officials, and local politicians.

                                      Pt. IV, Ch.14, Ibid.

11 I am particularly struck by the number of aged men who repre-
    sent America. It seems we are not taking into consideration what
    is happening in this country today. We are not giving bright
    young people—who are often so much in touch with the time—
    a sufficient chance to break into politics and be heard.

                      Quoted in Shirley Chisholm: A Biography
                                by Susan Brownmiller* 1971

    *See 2586.

12 I am a candidate for the Presidency of the United States. I
    make that statement proudly, in the full knowledge that, as a
    black person and as a female person, I do not have a chance of
    actually gaining that office in this election year.

                                      Speech 4 June 1972

13 I ran because someone had to do it first. In this country everyone is supposed to be able to run for President, but that's never been really true. I ran *because* most people think the country isn't ready for a black candidate, not ready for a woman candidate. Some day...

Ch. 1, *The Good Fight* 1973

14 Richard M. Nixon*...has a deeper concern for his place in history than for the people he governs. And history will not fail to note that fact.

Ch. 11, Ibid.

*Richard M. Nixon, American politician (1913–1994), 37th president of the United States (1969–74); resigned.

15 We Americans have a chance to become someday a nation in which all racial stocks and classes can exist in their own selfhoods, but meet on a basis of respect and equality and live together, socially, economically, and politically. We can become a dynamic equilibrium, a harmony of many different elements, in which the whole will be greater than all its parts and greater than any society the world has seen before. It can still happen.

Ch. 14, Ibid.

16 We must get the message out that on these issues, child care, abortion and women in the labor force, white women must get in line behind us. The issue is survival.

Speech, Eastern Regional Conference on Black Feminism
30 November 1973

17 When I decided to run for Congress, I knew I would encounter both antiblack and antifeminist sentiments. What surprised me was the much greater virulence of the sex discrimination. . . . I was constantly bombarded by both men and women exclaiming that I should return to teaching, a woman's vocation, and leave politics to men.

(p. 248), Quoted in *The Black 100: A Ranking of the Most Influential African–Americans, Past and Present* by Columbus Salley 1993

2245. Janet Frame (1924–)

1 Every morning I woke in dread, waiting for the day nurse to go on her rounds and announce from the list of names in her hand whether or not I was for shock treatment, the new and fashionable means of quieting people and of making them realize that orders are to be obeyed and floors are to be polished without anyone protesting and faces are made to be fixed into smiles and weeping is a crime.

Ch. 1, *Faces in the Water* 1961

2 Electricity, the peril the wind sings to in the wires on a gray day.

Ch. 2, Ibid.

3 For in spite of the snapdragons and the dusty millers and the cherry blossoms, it was always winter.

Ibid.

4 . . . very often the law of extremity demands an attention to irrelevance...

Ch. 3, Ibid.

5 "For your own good" is a persuasive argument that will eventually make man agree to his own destruction.

Ch. 4, Ibid.

6 It would be nice to travel if you knew where you were going and where you would live at the end or do we ever know, do we ever live where we live, we're always in other places, lost, like sheep.

"The Day of the Sheep," *You Are Now Entering the Human Heart* 1983

7 Writing a novel is not merely going on a shopping expedition across the border to an unreal land: it is hours and years spent in the factories, the streets, the cathedrals of the imagination.

Ch. 20, *The Envoy from Mirror City*, Vol. 1 1985

2246. Patricia Roberts Harris (1924–)

1 I am one of the [society's disadvantaged citizens]. I am a black woman, the daughter of a dining car waiter. You do not seem to understand who I am.

Congressional Confirmation Hearings (addressing Senator William Proxmire*) 25–26 July 1979

*American politician (1915–   ).

2247. Ruth Hubbard (1924–)

1 Every theory is a self-fulfilling prophecy that orders experience into the framework it provides.

"Have Only Men Evolved?," *Women Look at Biology Looking at Women*, Ruth Hubbard, Mary Sue Henifin and Barbara Fried, eds. 1979

2 The mythology of science asserts that with many different scientists all asking their own questions and evaluating the answers independently, whatever personal bias creeps into their individual answers is cancelled out when the large picture is put together. This might conceivably be so if scientists were women and men from all sorts of different cultural and social backgrounds who came to science with very different ideologies and interests. But since, in fact, they have been predo- minantly university-trained white males from privileged social backgrounds, the bias has been narrow and the product often reveals more about the investigator than about the subject being researched.

Ibid.

3 To overturn orthodoxy is no easier in science than in philosophy, religion, economics, or any of the other disciplines through which we try to comprehend the world and the society in which we live.

Ibid.

4 Without words to objectify and categorize our sensations and place them in relation to one another, we cannot evolve a tradition of what is real in the world.

Ibid.

2248. Alice Koller (1924–)

1 I stare into the mirror. I don't have a life: I'm just using up a number of days somehow. There is no *reason* for me to be here.

An Unknown Woman 1981

2 If I could learn how to see with my own eyes, I'd be able to make a comparable leap, leaving behind everybody else's rules. . . . I don't know what I want, or want to do. I don't know how to use my own evidence . . . I don't know what to look for inside me. I don't know how to identify that I'm feeling something, let alone give it a name. I think I've been anesthetized, deadened.

Ibid.

2249. Cloris Leachman (1924–)

1 Why can't we build orphanages next to homes for the elderly? If someone's sitting in a rocker, it won't be long before a kid will be in his lap.

Quoted in "I Love My Career and I Love My Children . . ." by Jane Wilkie, *Good Housekeeping* October 1973

2250. Phyllis Lyon (1924–)
Co-author with Del Martin; see 2187.

2251. Lisel Mueller (1924–)

1 This poem is endless
  the odds against us are endless,
  our chances of being alive together
  statistically nonexistent.
  > "Alive Together," *Alive Together: New and
  > Selected Poems 1996*

2 I started out as a girl
  without a shadow, in iron shoes;
  now, at the end of the world
  I am a woman full of rain.
  The journey back should be easy; if this reaches you, wait for
  me.
  > "Letter from the End of the World," *Ibid.*

3 I know enough to refuse to say
  that life is good,
  but I act as though it were,
  and skeptical about love, I survive
  by the witness of my own.
  > "On Reading an Anthology of Postwar
  > German Poetry," *Ibid.*

4 Memory is the only
  afterlife I can understand.
  > "Pillar of Salt," *Ibid.*

5 There are two of us here.
  Touch me.
  > "There are two of us here," *Ibid.*

6 In any age, life has to be lived
  Before we know what it is.
  > "Triumph of Life," *Ibid.*

7 Your story does not end with the wedding dance, it goes on.
  > "Voices from the Forest," *Ibid.*

8 I...
  placed my grief
  in the mouth of language,
  the only thing that would grieve with me.
  > "When I Am Asked," *Ibid.*

9 Because the story of our life
  becomes our life

  Because each of us tells
  the same story
  but tells it differently

  and none of us tells it
  the same way twice...
  > "Why We Tell Stores," *Ibid.*

10 Speaking of marvels, I am alive
  together with you, when I might have been / alive with anyone
  under the sun . . .
  > "Alive Together," *Ibid.*

11 How swiftly the strained honey
  of afternoon light
  flows into darkness
  > "In Passing," *in toto, Ibid.*

2252. Bess Myerson (1924–)

1 . . . the accomplice to the crime of corruption is frequently our
  own indifference.
  > Quoted in "Impeachment?" by Claire Safran, *Redbook*
  > (New York) *April 1974*

2 It's always time for a change for the better, and for a good fight
  for the full human rights of every individual.
  > Quoted in *AFTRA Magazine Summer 1974*

2253. Harriet Rochlin (1924–)

1 "Laughter can be more satisfying than honor; more precious
  than money; more heart cleansing than prayer."
  > Ch. 1, *So Far Away 1981*

2 "Family life is a training ground," intoned Miss O'Hara, "for
  life in the world. Learn to get along at home, and you can get
  along everywhere."
  > Ch. 8, *Ibid.*

3 "A Jew is supposed to chase God, not gold."
  > Ch. 18, *Ibid.*

2254. Alma Routsong (1924–)

1 Time enough later to teach her that it's better to be a real
  woman than an imitation man, and that when someone chooses a woman to go away with it's because a woman is what's
  preferred.
  > *A Place for Us 1969*

2 [I] wonder if what makes men walk lordlike and speak so mas-
  terfully is having the love of women.
  > *Ibid.*

2255. Miriam Schapiro (1924–)

1 A woman can make the choice to be an artist and decide to go
  all the way, but there is still tremendous guilt. You feel as
  though you're stealing power.
  > Quoted in "Miriam Schapiro," *Exposures, Women &
  > Their Art* by Ann Brown and Arlene Raven* *1989*
  > *See 3020.

2 Throughout history, many women who became artists trained
  in their fathers' studios . . . [Mine] had a passion for art that
  was very deep.
  > *Ibid.*

3 If you were to survey celebrated women, with every step toward real success there came a baby.
  > *Ibid.*

4 Revisionist art history that would incorporate the contributions
  of women has just barely begun. We female artists, critics, journalists, art historians, must stick together. If we don't voice what
  we're feeling, thinking and experiencing, we'll never educate the
  public and there will continue to be a one-sided view of what
  mainstream art is. My philosophy is always to keep mainstream
  thinking open to the thinking of "the others."
  > *Ibid.*

5 During the 1970s when the women's movement was taking
  hold, everyone was divorcing. Women were afraid that if they
  upset the barrel . . . they would be standing in front of a house
  with a little suitcase, not knowing what to do. [Paul]* sustained me through it all.
  > Quoted in "Miriam in Wonderland" by Kate Mulligan,
  > *Parade Magazine 1998*
  > *Her husband, Paul Brach, artist, arts administrator.

6 I felt that by making a large canvas magnificent in color, design and proportion, filling it with fabrics and quilt blocks, I could raise a housewife's lowered consciousness.*

Ibid.

*At the center of this artwork is a small, white rectangle with the embroidered words: "Welcome to our home."

7 The great thing about that quilt [the AIDS Names quilt] is that everybody and their brother and sister made those pieces without any thought of whether they had talent. You have art giving you a healing process. You have art giving you redemption.

Ibid.

2256. Phyllis Schlafly (1924–)

1 The advance planning and sense stimuli employed to capture a $10 million cigarette or soap market are nothing compared to the brainwashing and propaganda blitzes used to ensure control of the largest cash market in the world: the Executive Branch of the United States Government.

Ch. 1, *A Choice Not an Echo* 1964

2 The moral sickness of the Federal Government becomes more apparent every day. Public officials are caught in a giant web of payoffs, bribes, perversion, and conflicts of interest, so that few dare to speak out against the establishment.

Ch. 1, *Safe—Not Sorry* 1967

3 America is waiting for an Attorney General who will enforce the law—and a President with the courage to demand that he do so.

Ch. 8, Ibid.

4 The urgent need today is to develop and support leaders on every level of government who are independent of the bossism of every political machine—the big-city machine, the liberal Democrat machine, and the Republican king maker machine.

Ch. 9, Ibid.

5 The left wing forces—both obvious and hidden—which have been running our country for the last seven years understand and appreciate the importance of *political action*. Their long tentacles reach out in many fields: to "orchestrate" propaganda through the communications media, to indoctrinate youth in our schools and universities, to create a Socialist intellectual climate through tax-exempt foundations, and to bend business into line with Government contracts.

Ch. 12, Ibid.

6 One of the favorite slogans of the liberals is "U for Unity must precede V for Victory." Those who play this game forget that U and V are both preceded by P for Principle.

Ch. 13, Ibid.

7 The claim that American women are downtrodden and unfairly treated is the fraud of the century.

Quoted by Lisa Cronin Wahl in *Ms.* (New York) March 1974

2257. Efua Theodora Sutherland (1924–)

1 AMPONA. I declare to earth and sky and water, and all things with which we shall soon be one, that I am slave to your flesh and happy so to be.*

Edufa 1962

*Ampona is volunteering to die in her husband's place.

2 LABARAN. I was impatient at the beginning; in haste. Seeing the raggedness of my people's homes, I was ashamed, even

angry. I heard it, screamed: Progress! Development! I wanted it far and everywhere.

But now I have learned that I can roam all I please, and nothing will change. I can talk all I please—who cares? Friends, when you talk to people and see blankness in their faces, you have to give up. In these you can read the sum of their souls and whether or not they understand. From that derives the patience of which I speak.

Act I, *Foriwa* 1962

2258. Betty Shingler Talmadge (1924–)

1 If you love the law and you love good sausage, don't watch either of them being made.

Quoted in *The Reader* 25 November 1977

2259. Margaret Truman (1924–)

1 I know from experience that the barbs of the critics are more painful for a President's family to endure than they are for the President.

Women of Courage 1977?

2260. Sally Weinraub (1924–)

1 Architects believe less and less in doors these days, so that houses were becoming like beehives, arches leading into chambers and more arches. It was lucky that Americans were still puritan in their habits. You could be alone in the bathroom.

"Knifed with a Black Shadow," *American Scene: New Voices*, Don Wolfe, ed. 1963

2261. Wakako Yamauchi (1924–)

1 YO. What is there to fear? Life? Death? Just roll with the punches.

12–1-A 1982

2 YO. In a war, Obasan, one country wins; the other loses. . . . We all look the same to them. We lost both ways.

Act I, Sc. 1, Ibid.

3 [The internment camp] was a terrible place. You couldn't run away from it because you'd die in the desert*—*if* you escaped the bullets from the sentries. . . . I felt very bitter there, and very closed in.

Between Worlds: Contemporary Asian-American Plays, Misha Berson, ed. 1990

*Yamauchi and her family were interred at a camp in 1941 in Poston, Arizona.

2262. Bette Clair Graham (1924–1980)

1 As a young woman with a son to raise alone, I suffered greatly with extreme lack [of funds]. I was a Christian Scientist and had tried to work this problem out by turning to God, but I never seemed to get anywhere until I was willing to humbly let go of my fear of, and dependency on, matter.

Quoted in *Women Inventors* by Linda Jacobs Altman 1997

2 In ten years we have come from production in a kitchen . . . to a corporation employing many people . . .

Excerpt from company speech (1968), Ibid.

3 Each employee's contribution was regarded as equal in importance and value.

Interview, *Christian Science Journal*, Ibid.

2263. Pamelia Dillin Fergus (1924–1987)

1 I know we like to count dollars and cents but what are they to a little enjoyment the short time we stay here on earth.

Letter (April 1961), Quoted in Women Pioneers
by Rebecca Stefoff 1995

2264. Etel Adnan (1925–)

1 The human race is going to the cemetery
in great upheavals

"The Beirut-Hell Express" (1991), The Woman That I Am,
The Literature and Culture of Contemporary Women
of Color, D. Soyini Madison, ed. 1994

2 In the evening when darkness moves
as slow as mud
I watch the prostitutes
it is forbidden that women
think

Ibid.

3 City more unreal than the wind
although pregnant with the sins of
the world
it is in your belly that foreigners
exercise the alchemy of treason

Ibid.

4 we have mornings with no memories

Ibid.

2265. Shana Alexander (1925–)

1 Faithful horoscope-watching, practiced daily, provides just the sort of small but warm and infinitely reassuring fillip that gets matters off to a spirited start.

"A Delicious Appeal to Unreason" (May 1966), in
The Feminine Eye 1970

2 The sad truth is that excellence makes people nervous.

"Neglected Kids—the Bright Ones" (June 1966), Ibid.

3 A plane, if you're traveling alone, is also a good place to be melancholy . . . A plane is a bad place for an all-out sleep, but a good place to begin rest and recovery from the trip to the far-away places you've been, a decompression chamber between Here and There. Though a plane is not the ideal place really to think, to reassess or reevaluate things, it is a great place to have the illusion of doing so, and often the illusion will suffice.

"Overcuddle and Megalull" (February 1967), Ibid.

4 Mankind still has monsters, of course. The trouble is that they are no longer mythological. Rather, they are the terrifying things man creates with his technology, and then cannot control—things like Peenemünde; things like smog, that foul thousand-mile blob visible from any jet; things like the cataclysmic, coiling, deadly dragon that is Vietnam.

"More Monsters, Please!" (December 1967), Ibid.

5 Roughly speaking, the President of the United States knows what his job is. Constitution and custom spell it out, for him as well as for us. His wife has no such luck. The First Lady has no rules; rather each new woman must make her own.

"The Best First Lady" (December 1968), Ibid.

6 . . . when two people marry they become in the eyes of the law one person, and that one person is the husband!

Introduction, State-by-State Guide to Women's Legal Rights
1975

7 The law changes and flows like water, and . . . the stream of women's rights law has become a sudden rushing torrent.

Ibid.

2266. Dede Allen (1925–)

1 Editing [film] is really a creative art. Any editor needs to know certain techniques, but the real decisions are made in her or his head.

Quoted in "The Power Behind the Screen" by
Geraldine Febrikant, Ms. (New York) February 1974

2267. Svetlana Alliluyeva (1925–)

1 Moscow, breathing fire like a human volcano with its smoldering lava of passion, ambition and politics, its hurly-burly of meetings and entertainment. . . . Moscow seethes and bubbles and gasps for air. It's always thirsting for something new, the newest events, the latest sensation. Everyone wants to be the first to know. It's the rhythm of life today.

Introduction (16 July 1963), Twenty Letters to a Friend 1967

2 He is gone, but his shadow still stands over all of us. It still dictates to us and we, very often, obey.*

Ch. 2, Ibid.

*Reference to her father, Josef Stalin, Soviet Communist revolutionary and political leader (1879–1953).

3 . . . as a result of half a century of Soviet rule people have been weaned from a belief in human kindness.

"The Journey's End," Only One Year 1969

2268. Helen Barolini (1925–)

1 When you don't read, you don't write.

The Dream Book: An Anthology of Writings by Italian
American Women, ed. 1985

2 . . . the Italian American experience...is the American paradigm. It is the story of the lonely figure outside mainstream society; it is the story of having to make difficult choices, of losses and gains and paying the price. It is alienation, a staple of literature.

"Afterthoughts on Italian American Women Writers,"
Chiaroscuro: Essays of Identity 1997

3 What they can't express verbally, they show. Show and Tell: that is the level of a people in a linguistic backwater, in a backwater of old outdated attitudes; of a people uneducated in values beyond the blatant materialistic one that seduces so many newcomers to America: get rich and make good, defend your property values.

"Buried Alive by Language" (p. 52), Ibid.

4 It was not just the Convent School that taught me to efface myself before the male partner who was surely more important, worthier, better. It was also my Italian American education which upheld the eternal sacrificial position of the woman. We were the uprights of the home; we were there to give ourselves for our men and for our children. We were not there for ourselves.

"Shutting the Door on Someone" (p. 62), Ibid.

2269. Nina Bawden (1925–)

1 . . . memory had its own logic; a code which was hard to break sometimes.

Family Money 1991

2   Wars give ordinary people a chance to be more than just ordinary. . . . You can save your friend's life or betray him.
The Real Plato Jones 1993

3   . . . harder than belonging to a tribe . . . [is to be] A Citizen of the World.
Ibid.

4   All writers are liars. . . . They make use of their own tragedies to make a better story. They batten on their relations
In My Own Time: Almost An Autobiography 1995

5   . . . family stories . . . tell us who we are and help to shape our lives.
Ibid.

6   A writer's work may be a coded autobiography, but only a very close friend could decipher it.
Last chapter, Ibid.

2270. Marilyn Bender (1925–)

1   Female clothing has been disappearing literally and philosophically.
Ch. 1, *The Beautiful People 1967*

2   To whip up desire for something that people don't really need, at least not in endless quantity, glamorous idols are essential. If desire begets need, then envy begets desire. The stimulation of envy or a longing to imitate is the function of the idol. The fashion industry, through its press agents and an eagerly cooperative, self-serving press, had to manufacture new goddesses.
Ch. 3, Ibid.

3   What caused this...renaissance of the dandy in an era of technology? Pessimists attributed it to male decline. As women became more aggressive, invaded masculine professions and usurped male prerogatives, men fell back on being peacocks, they reasoned. With clothes, men were reconstructing their diminished manhood.
Ch. 10, Ibid.

4   Just as the court flunky tasted the king's food to screen it for poison, so today the corporate sovereign has his literary fare digested and presented in capsule form or laced into his speeches by his ghost writer.
"The Business of Reading About Business," *Saturday Review of the Society April 1973*

5   Any survey of what businessmen are reading runs smack into the open secret that most businessmen aren't. Reading books, that is.
Ibid.

2271. Barbara Bush (1925–)

1   I got away with murder [as Second Lady]. I'm now slightly more careful about what I say. Slightly.
Quoted in "The Silver Fox" by Michael Duffy, *Time* (New York) *23 January 1989*

2   Why would he tell me any secrets when he says I begin every sentence with "Don't tell George* I told you this, but . . ."
Ibid.

3   What happens in your house is more important than what happens in the White House.
Attributed by George Bush,* Cited in "A troubled Bush..." by Marianne Means, *Seattle Post-Intelligencer*, A7 *3 August 1992*
*Her husband, G— Bush (1924–), 41st president of the United States (1989–1992).

4   I'm feisty as the dickens.
Quoted in "The Best Days of their Wives" by Michael Duffy, *Time* (New York) *24 August 1992*

5   The fact that this comes up [accusations of adultery] every four years is not an enormous surprise to me, but it's a disappointing one...I know it's a lie, so it doesn't bother me. But it bothers me that we've come to this.
Ibid.

6   The personal things should be left out of, in my opinion, out of platforms at conventions...You can argue yourself blue in the face, and you're not going to change each other's minds. It's a waste of your time and my time.
Ibid.

2272. Kathryn Clarenbach (1925?–)

1   The overemphasis on protecting girls from strain or injury and underemphasis on developing skills and experiencing teamwork fits neatly into the pattern of the second sex. . . . Girls are the spectators and the cheerleaders. . . . Perfect preparation for the adult role of woman—to stand decoratively on the sidelines of history and cheer on the men who make the decisions.
Sex Role Stereotyping in the Schools 1973

2   Women who have had the regular experience of performing before others, of learning to win and lose, of cooperating in team efforts, will be far less fearful of running for office, better able to take public positions on issues in the face of public opposition.
Quoted in "Old School System Curbed Sportswomen," *The Los Angeles Times 24 April 1974*

2273. Pam Gems (1925–)

1   FISH (suicide note). My loves, what are we to do? We won't do as they want anymore, and they hate it. What are we to do?
Dusa, Fish, Stas and Vi (a.k.a. *Dead Fish*) *1976*

2   SUSANNAH. You've never been off the tit. Eleven-plus, scholarships, research fellowship project grant. You're free—white and male. And you've caved in.
Loving Women 1984

3   All the stories have been told long ago. Your job is retelling. Relighting.
Quoted in "Pam Gems," *Interviews with Contemporary Women Playwrights* by Kathleen Betsko* and Rachel Koenig *1987*
*See 2739.

4   The nature of the dramatic mode is the withholding of information, in the creation of a puzzle for the audience to solve. Clues.
Ibid.

5   What you have to control, in the writing, is silence. You have to orchestrate that important member of the cast, the audience. Orchestrate, and conduct. One joke too many and they become flatulent, blowzy. One thought too many and they begin to move, restless, oppressed. The audience *must* be

working, as hard as the actors. The audience must be alive, must create the play.

Ibid.

6 Art is of necessity. Which is why we need women playwrights just now very badly. We have our own history to create, and to write.
Introduction to *Queen Christina, Plays by Women*, Vol. 8, Mary Remnant, ed. *1990*

2274. Julie Harris (1925–)

1 I've been very fortunate and had many wonderful things to do, but nothing can compare with real beauty.
"Veteran actress personifies her characters . . . ,"
Seattle Times, L3 *16 August 1992*

2 I learned faith from Ethel [Waters*]. . . . She was a great wheel to hold on to, an anchor. I always liken her to a phenomenon of nature, a Niagara Falls.

Ibid.

*African-American singer and actor (1896–1977).

3 Courage. What is that? It's like faith. But you can't teach it to anybody. Only life teaches you courage.

Ibid.

2275. Eleanor Hoover (1925?–)

Coauthor with Marie Edwards; see 2296.

2276. Huang Zongying (1925–)

1 The woman growing wild herbs* aroused my interest for some unknown reason. Perhaps for her frankness, her composure, or perhaps because she looked as ordinary as any country mid-wife, who interrupts her pig-feeding and washes her hands before picking up her sterilized instruments.
"The Flight of the Wild Geese," Yu Fanqin & Wang Mingjie, trs., *Seven Contemporary Chinese Women Writers*, Gladys Yang,** ed. *1982*
*Quin Guanshu, Chinese botanist (1929–); see 2392. **See 2452.

2 God! In the world of plants, no two leaves have the same pattern of veins. But in the world of human beings, people have to be classified and tagged all over the country. But how can these tags express the complications of Chinese society? After all, class origin is not terribly important.

Ibid.

2277. Barbara Kanner (1925–)

1 The institutional techniques of starvation, cold, flogging and fisticuffs were among the chief mechanisms for turning boys into brave, self-reliant, self-governing gentlemen committed to masculine ideals.
Introduction, *Women in English Social History 1800–1914*
1990

2277.1. Carol Kaye (1925–)

Co-author with Elizabeth Douvan; see 2294: 1-2.

2278. Carolyn Kizer (1925–)

1 We don't lack people here on the Northern coast,
But they are people one meets, not people one cares for.
"Amusing Our Daughters," St. 1, *Knock Upon Silence 1963*

2 We waken and count our daughters.
Otherwise, nothing happens.
St. 3, Ibid.

3 Our masks, always in peril of smearing or
cracking,
In need of continuous check in the mirror or
silverware,
Keep us in thrall to ourselves, concerned with our surfaces.
"Pro Femina," Ibid.

4 Unfortunately we live in a society which cheers at naked self-exposure, and cares little if the stripper burns or freezes. But I care, as all people who love poetry for itself…care.
Proses on Poems and Poets 1994

2279. Maxine Kumin (1925–)

1 I find it good to line my gut
With tidy octagons of grit.
No loophole and no chink
Make vents in it.
"Grace," St. 3, *The Atlantic Monthly*, Vol. 208, No. 4
October 1961

2 Now under the ice, under twelve knee-deep layers
of mud in last summer's pond
the packed hearts of peepers are beating
barely, barely repeating
themselves enough to hang on.
"January 25th," St. 3, *The Atlantic Monthly*, Vol. 215,
No. 1 *January 1965*

3 I plucked the memory splinter from your spine
as we played at being normal, who
had eased each other in the cold zoo
of childhood.
"The Man of Many L's," *Our Ground Time Here
Will Be Brief 1982*

4 They've
been here
for thousands of years.
You're
the visitor
"You Are in Bear Country," *The Long Approach 1985*

5 Cherish
your wilderness.

Ibid.

6 Everything pays for growing tame
"Sunday in March," Ibid.

7 caring is small
susceptible fits in a pocket
not is it one thing to save animals
and people another
but seamless

"Caring: A Dream," Ibid.

8 Already we have had snow lucid,
snow surprising, snow bees
and lambswool snow.
"Getting Through," Ibid.

9 Let me put my faith in the bean.
"Shelling Jacob's Cattle Beans," Ibid.

10 I'm going home the old way with a light hand on the reins
making the long approach.
"The Long Approach," Ibid.

11 three smacks for failing in long division,
one more to instill the meaning of humble.
As the twig is bent, said your harridan nuns.
                    "The Nuns of Childhood: Two Views," 1., St. 2, *The At-
                    lantic Monthly*, Vol. 269, No. 2 *February 1992*

12 In the most direct, overt, and uncomplicated way, my writing
depends on the well-being that develops from...chores undertaken and completed.
                    "Menial Labor and the Muse," *Women, Animals,
                    and Vegetables 1994*

13 ... the vixen in the bottom meadow
I ride across allows me under cover
of horse scent to observe the education
of her kits, how they dive for the burrow
on command, how they re-emerge at another
word she uses, a word I am searching for.
                    "The Word," St. 5, *The Atlantic Monthly*, Vol. 273,
                    No. 3 *March 1994*

14 My children came, the rigorous bond of blood.
                    "Letters," *Connecting the Dots: Poems 1996*

15 A benevolent rain swells tomorrow's cucumbers
and reddening tomatoes (what else must I save?)
as the axis turns, spilling us into fall
until, in tears now with his have it?
the tired baby will have it all.
                    "In once a time," Ibid.

16 The animals talk in reasonable tones that children
can understand
                    Ibid.

17 when even the hostile soldiers throw back
bewildered babies that have dropped
from the arms of exhausted women, how tender
the earth is and we on it face up.
                    "After the Cleansing of Bosnia," Ibid.

18 We're assayed kindly
to see if we're
still competent
to keep house, mind
the calendar
connect the dots.
                    "Connecting the Dots," Ibid.

2280. Geraldine Fredritz Mock (1925-)

1 If I don't get out of this house, I'll go nuts.
                    "Shades of Amelia," *Newsweek* (New York) *30 March 1964*
                    *The remark that purportedly launched her career as an aviator.

2 The tiny plane* raced down the runway and...leaped into the
air, eager to explore the world.
                    Three-Eight Charlie 1970
                    *Her Cessna 180, officially dubbed the Spirit of Columbus.

3 [I] felt like a queen.... My subjects, the foamy clouds and
glowing rainbows, put on a command performance just for
me. It was worth all the hard work, worry, and sleepless
nights.... After Christopher Columbus* discovered America,
he became the Admiral of the Ocean Seas. In my red-and-white
Spirit of Columbus,.... I became Queen of the Ocean Skies.
                    Ibid.

                    *Christopher Columbus (1451–1506), Italian navigator and explorer
                    who, in 1492, opened the path from the Old World to the New.

4 I don't know if I'll ever settle down. I don't know where I'll be
a year from now...and I don't want to know.
                    Interview (1989), Quoted in *Women Aviators*
                    by Lisa Yount 1995

2281. Tharon Musser (1925-)

1 It's the lighting of moving sculpture....
Dance is heaven to light ...
                    Quoted in "The Facts of Light" by Arnold Aronson,
                    American Theatre (New York) *January 1986*

2 All design in theatre is a supportive art. It's there to help, to
underline, to emphasize.
                    Ibid.

2282. Beah Richards (1925/28?-)

1 Having grown up in a racist culture where two and two are
not five, I have found life to be incredibly theatrical and theatre to be profoundly lifeless.
                    Preface, *A Black Woman Speaks and Other Poems 1974*

2 ... nature is neither reasonable nor just. Nature is exact.
                    Ibid.

3 Heaven and earth!
How is it that bodies join
but never meet?
                    "It's Time for Love," St. 2, Ibid.

4 Lord,
there is no death,
no numb, no glacial sorrow
like the love of loveless love,
a tender grunting, sweating horror of obscenity.
                    "Love Is Cause It Has to Be," St. 6, Ibid.

5 If I cannot with my blind eyes see
that to betray or deny my brother
is but to diminish me
then you may pity me...
                    "The Liberal," St. 11, Ibid.

2283. Ru Zhijuan (1925-)

1 The desolate grassland stretched out as if to the end of the
world. On a piece of uncultivated land as vast as this, one
could have made straight for anywhere ...
                    "The Path Through the Grassland," Yu Fanqin, tr., *Seven Con-
                    temporary Chinese Women Writers*,Gladys Yang,* ed. 1982
                    *See 2452.

2 The hardest thing for a person to bear is not a dressing-down
or a beating, but loneliness, ostracism.
                    Ibid.

3 Love needed a full stomach, but the two were quite different
things.
                    Ibid.

2284. Naomi Streshinsky (1925-)

1 The danger of a gift is an intriguing concept. Primitive man
may have believed that the gift contained the spirit of the
donor and therein lay its potential harm. The belief in the
donor's spirit dissolved for modern man but the danger is still
very much present.
                    Ch. 2, *Welfare Rights Organizations 1970*

2 Political acceptability of social welfare can be translated to mean what the general public will permit to be granted, out of its tax money to poor people, just because they are in need and with no strings attached. Attitudes of hostility toward and derogation of the assisted poor puts serious obstacles in the way of future programs and are precisely the ones which contribute to the present bind.

Ch. 6, Ibid.

2285. Margaret Thatcher (1925–)

1 No woman in my time will be Prime Minister or Chancellor or Foreign Secretary—not the top jobs. Anyway I wouldn't want to be Prime Minister. You have to give yourself 100%.*

Interview in *Sunday Telegraph* (London) *26 October 1969*
*Ten years later she became England's first female prime minister; prior to that, she served in a cabinet post.

2 One of the things being in politics has taught me is that men are not a reasoned or reasonable sex.

BBC interview *14 January 1972*

3 I owe nothing to Women's Lib.

Remark (1982), Quoted in *Observer* (London) *1 December 1974*

4 In politics, if you want anything said, ask a man. If you want anything done, ask a woman.

Quoted in *People 15 September 1975*

5 We want a society where people are free to make choices, to make mistakes, to be generous and compassionate. This is what we mean by a moral society; not a society where the state is responsible for everything, and no one is responsible for the state.

Speech *1977*

6 *Détente* sounds a fine word. And, to the extent that there has really been a relaxation in international tension, it is a fine thing. But the fact remains that throughout this decade of *détente*, the armed forces of the Soviet Union have increased, are increasing, and show no signs of diminishing.

Speech, Chelsea Conservative Association (July 1975), Quoted in *Margaret Thatcher, A Tory and her Party* by Patrick Cosgrave *1978*

7 I have reason to believe that the tide is beginning to turn against collectivism, socialism, statism, dirigism, whatever you call it. And this turn is rooted in a revulsion against the sour fruit of socialist experience.

Speech, Zurich Economic Society (March 1977), Ibid.

8 I am extraordinarily patient provided I get my own way in the end.

Quoted in *Observer* (London) *2 January 1983*

9 I'll stay until I'm tired of it. So long as Britain needs me, I shall never be tired of it.*

Remark (1982), Ibid.
*She was England's prime minister from 1979 to 1990.

10 It was then that the iron entered my soul.*

Remark (1982), Quoted in *Observer* (London) *27 March 1983*
*Reference to her nickname, "The Iron Lady," of her time in Edward Heath's cabinet (1970–74); Thatcher and Heath became political antagonists.

11 I always cheer up immensely if an attack is particularly wounding because I think, well, if they attack one personally, it means they have not a single political argument left.

Quoted in *The Daily Telegraph* (London) *1986*

12 No one would remember the Good Samaritan if he'd only had good intentions. He had money as well.

Television interview (6 January 1986), *The Times* (London) *12 January 1986*

13 There is no such thing as society: there are individual men and women, and there are families.

Woman's Own (London) *31 October 1987*

14 People think that at the top there isn't much room. They tend to think of it as an Everest. My message is that there is tons of room at the top.

Interview in *The Daily Telegraph* (London) *30 September 1988*

15 You will only achieve higher growth, only release enterprise, only spur people to greater effort, only obtain their full-hearted commitment to reform, when people have the dignity and enjoyment of personal and political liberty, when they have the freedom of expression, freedom of association and the right to form free and independent trade unions.

Remark to Gen. Wojciech Jaruzelski,* state banquet (Warsaw) *3 November 1988*
*Polish military and political leader (1923–); premier (1982–1985), president (1985–1990).

16 To me, consensus seems to be the process of abandoning all beliefs, principles, values and policies. So it is something in which no one believes and to which no one objects.

Pt. 4, Ch. 23, Quoted in *The Time of My Life* by Denis Healey *1989*

17 The cocks may crow, but it's the hen that lays the egg.

Interview in *Sunday Times* (London) *9 April 1989*

18 Most women defend themselves. It is the female of the species—it is the tigress and lioness in you—which tends to defend when attacked.

Daily Mail (London) *4 May 1989*

19 The best compliment they [men] can give a woman is that she thinks like a man. I say she does not; she thinks like a woman.

Quoted in interview, *The Los Angeles Times 9 May 1989*

20 The great battle now is to prevent the smaller minority ruining the lives of the majority by violence, by dirtiness, by graffiti, by everyday surliness . . . .Graciousness has been replaced by surliness in much of everyday life.

Quoted in interview *The Washington Post 25 May 1989*

21 Battles in life are never won. I mean, you don't have your household budget permanently balanced; you have to balance it every year. Life's a continuous business, and so is success, and requires continuous effort.

Quoted in interview (London), *The New York Times 28 September 1989*

22 I am in politics because of the conflict between good and evil, and I believe that in the end good will triumph.

The Guardian (London) *23 October 1990*

23 I seem to smell the stench of appeasement in the air.

Independent (London) *31 October 1990*

24 No great goal was ever easily achieved.

Quoted in *Twentieth-Century Women Political Leaders* by Claire Price-Groff *1998*

25 Unless we change our ways and our direction, our greatness as a nation will soon be a footnote in the history books, a distant

memory of an offshore island, lost in the mists of time like Camelot, remembered kindly for its noble past.

Campaign Speech, Ibid.

26 If you have a sense of purpose and a sense of direction, I believe people will follow you. Democracy isn't just about deducing what the people want. Democracy is leading the people as well.

Ibid.

2286. Mai Zetterling (1925–)

1 Women are on the whole more sensual than sexual, men are more sexual than sensual.

Times (London) *17 May 1989*

2287. Flannery O'Connor (1925–1964)

1 In such a place you have to expect them all to sleep around. This is not a sin but Experience, and if you do not sleep with the opposite sex, it is assumed that you sleep with your own. . . . You survive in this atmosphere by minding your own business and by having plenty of your business to mind.

Letter (of the Yaddo Artist Colony) *c. 1948*

2 . . . the help was morally superior to all the guests.

Ibid.

3 The old man would point to his grandson, Haze. He had a particular disrespect for him because his own face was repeated almost exactly in the child's and seemed to mock him.

Ch. 1, *Wise Blood 1949*

4 "I'm going to preach there was no Fall because there was nothing to fall from and no Redemption because there was no Fall and no Judgement because there wasn't the first two. Nothing matters but that Jesus was a liar."

Ch. 6, Ibid.

5 I preach there are all kinds of truth, your truth and somebody else's. But behind all of them there is only one truth and that is that there's no truth.

Ch. 10, Ibid.

6 She felt justified in getting anything at all back that she could, money or anything else, as if she had once owned the earth and been dispossessed of it. She couldn't look at anything steadily without wanting it, and what provoked her most was the thought that there might be something valuable hidden near her, something she couldn't see.

Ch. 14, Ibid.

7 Living had got to be such a habit with him that he couldn't conceive of any other condition.

"A Late Encounter with the Enemy," *A Good Man Is Hard to Find 1955*

8 Mr. Head stood very still and felt the action of mercy touch him again but this time he knew that there were no words in the world that could name it. He understood that it grew out of agony, which is not denied to any man and which is given in strange ways to children. He understood it was all a man could carry into death to give his Maker and he suddenly burned with shame that he had so little of it to take with him. He stood appalled, judging himself with the thoroughness of God, while the action of mercy covered his pride like a flame and consumed it.

"The Artificial Nigger," Ibid.

9 "I call myself The Misfit," he said, "because I can't make what all I done wrong fit what all I gone through in punishment."

"A Good Man is Hard to Find," Ibid.

10 "Lady, a man is divided into two parts, body and spirit. . . . A body and a spirit," he repeated. "The body, lady, is like a house it don't go anywhere; but the spirit, lady, is like a automobile: always on the move, always. . . ."

"The Life You Save May Be Your Own," Ibid.

11 He had schooled him in the evils that befall prophets; in those that come from the world, which are trifling, and those that come from the Lord and burn the prophet clean; for he himself had been burned clean and burned clean again. He had learned by fire.

Pt. I, Ch. 1, *The Violent Bear It Away 1955*

12 Then the revelation came, silent, implacable, direct as a bullet. He did not look into the eyes of any fiery beast or see a burning bush.

Ch. 3, Ibid.

13 Manners are of such great consequence to the novelist that any kind will do. Bad manners are better than no manners at all, and because we are losing our customary manners, we are probably overly conscious of them; this seems to be a condition that produces writers.

"The Fiction Writer and His Country," *The Living Novel: A Symposium*, Granville Hicks, ed. *1957*

14 "Knowing who you are is good for one generation only."

"Everything That Rises Must Converge," *Everything That Rises Must Converge 1965*

15 She was a good Christian woman with a large respect for religion, through she did not, of course, believe any of it was true.

"Greenleaf," Ibid.

16 He had stuffed his own emptiness with good work like a glutton.

"The Lame Shall Enter First," Ibid.

17 Once or twice I have been asked what the peacock is "good for"—a question which gets no answer from me because it deserves none.

"Peacocks Are a Puzzle," *Mystery and Manners 1969*

18 It seems that the fiction writer has a revolting attachment to the poor, for even when he writes about the rich, he is more concerned with what they lack than with what they have.

"The Teaching of Literature," Ibid.

19 I have found that anything that comes out of the South is going to be called grotesque by the Northern reader, unless it is grotesque, in which case it is going to be called realistic.

Address, "Some Aspects of the Grotesque in Southern Fiction," Wesleyan College for Women (Macon, Ga., Fall 1960), Ibid.

20 There was a time when the average reader read a novel simply for the moral he could get out of it, and however naïve that may have been, it was a good deal less naïve than some of the limited objectives he has now. Today novels are considered to be entirely concerned with the social or economic or psychological forces that they will by necessity exhibit, or with those details of daily life that are for the good novelist only means to some deeper end.

Ibid.

21 While the South is hardly Christ-centered, it is most certainly Christ-haunted.

Ibid.

22 Being a Georgia author is a rather specious dignity, on the same order as, for the pig, being a Talmadge ham.
"The Regional Writer" (*Esprit*, Winter 1963), Ibid.

23 Faith is what you have in the absence of knowledge.
Letter to Alfred Corn (30 May 1962),
The Habit of Being 1978

24 If you want your faith, you have to work for it. It is a gift, but for very few is it a gift given without any demand for equal time devoted to its cultivation.
Ibid.

25 One of the effects of modern liberal Protestantism has been gradually to turn religion into poetry and therapy, to make truth vaguer and vaguer and more and more relative, to banish intellectual distinctions, to depend on feeling instead of thought, and gradually to come to believe that God has no power, that he cannot communicate with us, cannot reveal himself to us, indeed has not done so, and that religion is our own sweet invention.
Letter to Alfred Corn (16 June 1962), Ibid.

26 I find it reasonable to believe, even though these beliefs are beyond reason.
Ibid.

27 I believe that there are many rough beasts now slouching toward Bethlehem to be born and that I have reported the progress of a few of them.
Flannery O'Connor: Collected Works,
Sally Fitzgerald, ed. *1988*

28 The Catholic sacramental view of life is one that maintains and supports at every turn the vision that the storyteller must have if he is going to write fiction of any depth.
Wise Women: Over 2000 Years of Spiritual Writing by Women, Susan Cahill,* ed. *1996*
*See 2782.

2288. Linda Goodman (1925?–1970)

1 It seems to be quite a leap from the . . . lost continent of Atlantis to the jet-propelled twentieth century. But how far is it really? Perhaps only a dream or two.
Afterword, *Linda Goodman's Sun Signs 1968*

2 Alone among the sciences, astrology has spanned the centuries and made the journey intact. We shouldn't be surprised that it remains with us, unchanged by time—because astrology is truth—and truth is eternal.
Ibid.

3 Astrological language is a golden cord that binds us to a dim past while it prepares us for an exciting future of planetary explorations.
Ibid.

2289. Rosario Castellanos (1925–1974)

1 Indians are human beings no different from whites. They simply live in very different—and unfavorable—circumstances.
Introduction, Quoted in *Selected Works of Rosario Castellanos* by Myralyn F. Allgood *1990*

2 Since [Indians] are weaker, they have more potential for evil—violence, treachery, and hypocrisy—than whites.
Ibid.

3 . . . dáme la muerte que me falta . . . (. . . give me the death I need)
Quoted in Ch. 5, *Women Who Run With the Wolves* by Clarissa Pinkola Estés* *1992*
*See 2938.

2290. Clarice Lispector (1925–1977)

1 Her curiosity instructed her more than the answers she was given.
"Preciousness" (1960), *Family Ties*, Giovanni Pontiero, tr. *1972*

2 In the empty house, alone with the maid, she no longer walked like a soldier, she no longer needed to exercise caution. But she missed the battle of the streets: the melancholy of freedom, with the horizon still so very remote.
Ibid.

3 Since she had thought about nothing, she did not realize how the time had slipped by.
Ibid.

2291. Melina Mercouri (1925–1994)

1 When you are born and they tell you "what a pity that you are so clever, so intelligent, so beautiful but you are not a man," you are ashamed of your condition as a woman. I wanted to act like a man because the man was the master.
Quoted in "Greece: Survival of the Shrewdest" by Susan Margolis, *Ms.* (New York) *October 1973*

2292. Helen Bamber (1926–)

1 Above all else, there was the need to tell you everything, over and over and over again. And this was the most significant thing for me, realizing that you had to take it all.*
Quoted in *The Good Listener: Helen Bamber, a Life Against Cruelty* by Neil Belton *1999*
*Reference to survivors of the Holocaust, the genocide of European Jews and others by the Nazis during World War II.

2 When you walk with a limp, when you can't sit comfortably, when you can't eat properly because your mouth has been damaged, or you can't hear because your ears are damaged, you are reminded daily of what happened to you, and you need a way to put that in some form to rest.
Returning to some kind of strength means that you are going to want your needs to be recognized, and that there has to be a journey from being a victim to being a survivor. I know that there's a lot of sentimentality about—and a lot of talk about—not using the word victim and only using the word survivor, and so on, but for me, there is often a journey to be made from being a victim to being a survivor.
Interview with history editor Sunny Delaney, Amazon.com *1999*

3 There may be ways in which we can work for change. We don't have to do dramatic things or devote our entire lives to it. We can lead normal lives but at the same time try hard not to be bystanders.
Ibid.

4 I don't know how I would have behaved in Germany under the Nazis if I had been a German. I don't know—I can't make guarantees there. I don't think any of us can, as to our courage and so on. I don't pretend to know. But there are situations in our own society where the dangers are not so great and yet people are still bystanders. And these are the people who worry me.
Ibid.

5 Torture is not only about broken bodies and broken teeth and damaged limbs. It's about loss; it's about being helpless in the

face of other people's torture. It's hearing the screams of others. It's the helplessness of torture that is so difficult to bear. To begin to live a normal life again is a monumental task!

Ibid.

6   The bystander, I think, is somebody who will find good reason not to take part, not to intervene, not to take an individual decision of their own to stand up and be counted.

Ibid.

2293. Gina Berriault (1926–)

1   "I try to imagine them when they were girls, but I can't," she told the head nurse, Nancy and the nurse, already verging into that same anonymity of aging, turned her head for Angela to see her deliberately uncomprehending face. "Why would you ever think to do that anyway?"

"Women in Their Beds" (p. 7), *Women in Their Beds 1996*

2   Just remember the beds where you wished you weren't and the bed where you wished you were, and then name any spot on this earth that's a bed for some woman at this very hour. A bed of stones and a bed of earth trampled by soldiers and a bed of ashes, and where you're lying now, where you never wanted to imagine yourselves. If I'd wished for a bed of roses and feathers, and *I did, I did*, now I don't want it so much anymore.

(p. 15), *Ibid.*

3   The young man was now no one, as he'd feared he already was when alive. The absolute unwanted, that's who the dead become.

"Who Is It Can Tell Me Who I Am?" *Ibid.*

4   "Don't get scared, but in this box is all that remains of Clara Ruchenski. . . . she's in the palm of my hand," he said. "That's why I kept this. She's harmless. She's nothing. If I took the ashes between my fingers, it would powder off into air. But I'm alive, God damn it, and that means something."

"Around the Dear Ruin" (p. 221), *Ibid.*

2294. Elizabeth Douvan (1926–)

1   The dream of college apparently serves as a substitute for more direct preoccupation with marriage: girls who do not plan to go to college are more explicit in their desire to marry, and have a more developed sense of their own sex role.

"Motivational Factors in College Entrance," *The American College*, with Carol Kaye* 1987

*See 2430.

2295. Rosalyn Drexler (1926–)

1   [My characters] have all been invented only in order to rush madly around, armed to the teeth with language and also with the capacity to be quick-change artists, con men and false prophets, wolves in sheep's clothing and the reverse, so that they might do nothing else than establish an atmosphere of freedom...they make up new worlds of farce whose highly serious intention, as in all true examples of the genre, is to liberate us from the way things are said to be.

Quoted in *The Line of Least Existence and Other Plays*, Richard Gilman, ed. *1967*

2   WOMAN. You want it because it's mine. . . . And you think that I belong to you too, and that's why you want me. You want me and my art reproduction. you want my art reproduction and my entire reproduction system. You hate both my systems. The HOW TO LIE FOREVER System and the HOW TO LIVE HARMONIOUSLY AS A WOMAN system.

Skywriting 1968

3   Working with women is a new adventure; it is exciting. We are pioneering, beginning again. There is a feeling of conspiracy, that we are going to forge ahead.

Quoted in *AFTRA Magazine Summer 1974*

4   We reject the notion that the work that brings in more money is not more valuable. The ability to earn money, or the fact that one already has it, should carry more weight in a relationship.

The Cosmopolitan Girl 1975

5   "I'm just a dog. Look, no opposable thumb."

Ibid.

6   He visited the Museum of Modern Art, and was standing near the pool looking at his dark reflection when a curator of the museum noticed him. "My, my, what a fine work of art that is!" the curator said to himself. "I must have it installed immediately."

Ibid.

7   Acknowledging the body is acknowledging what is real. . . . It's such a strain, a struggle, to appear to be without physical blemish . . . to remain young as the relentless years add up. It's time consuming and emotionally depleting.

Quoted in "Rosalyn Drexler," *Interviews with Contemporary Women Playwrights* by Kathleen Betsko* and Rachel Koenig *1987*

*See 2739.

8   As Hemingway* once said, or was thought to have said, [to write well] one must have a built-in shit detector. But to have that, one must have smelled shit at least a few times.

Ibid.

*Ernest H——, American writer (1899–1961).

9   Pornography is not a safety valve, it is a writ of permission. . . .

Ibid.

2296. Marie Edwards (1926?–)

1   Books, magazines, counselors, therapists sell one message to unmarrieds: "Shape up, go where other singles are, entertain more, raise your sex quotient, get involved, get closer, be more open, more honest, more intimate, above all, find Mr. Right or Miss Wonderful and *get married.*

The Challenge of Being Single, with Eleanor Hoover* 1975

*See 2275.

2   "...an intense, one-to-one involvement is as socially conditioned as a hamburger and malt..."

Ibid.

2297. Queen Elizabeth II of England (1926–)

1   My whole life, whether it be long or short, shall be devoted to your [the public's] service and the service of our great imperial family to which we all belong. But I shall not have the strength to carry out this resolution alone unless you join in it with me.

Radio Broadcast *21 April 1947*

2   These wretched babies don't come until they are ready.*

Quoted in *Today* (London) *4 August 1988*

*Reference to the expected birth of her fifth grandchild, Beatrice, born five days later, the first child of the Duke and Duchess of York.

3   Like all the best families, we have our share of eccentricities, of impetuous and wayward youngsters and of family disagreements.

Quoted in *Daily Mail* (London) *19 October 1989*

4 It's all to do with the training: you can do a lot if you're properly trained.
Television documentary, BBC 1 *6 February 1992*

2298. Sissy Farenthold (1926–)

1 I am working for the time when unqualified blacks, browns and women join the unqualified men in running our government.
Quoted in the *The Los Angeles Times 18 September 1974*

2 There is no question that under the Equal Rights Amendment there will be debates at times, indecision at times, litigation at times. Has anyone proposed that we rescind the First Amendment on free speech because there is too much litigation over it? Has anyone suggested the same for the Fourteenth Amendment (I don't suppose there has ever been a constitutional amendment with so much litigation)?
Speech for International Women's Year, "Legal Rights," Vermont College *26 February 1977*

3 You change laws by changing lawmakers.
Quoted in "Interview with Sissy Farenthold" by Dave Anast, *The Bakersfield Californian 22 April 1978*

2299. Wilma Scott Heide (1926–)

1 The only jobs for which no man is qualified are human incubator and wet nurse. Likewise, the only job for which no woman is or can be qualified is sperm donor.
Quoted in NOW* Official Biography *1971*

2 . . . we whose hands have rocked the cradle, are now using our heads to rock the boat. . . .
Ibid.

3 . . . we will no longer be led only by that half of the population whose socialization, through toys, games, values and expectations, sanctions violence as the final assertion of manhood, synonymous with nationhood.
Ibid.

4 To date, we have taught men to be brave and women to care. Now we must enlarge our concepts of bravery and caring. Men must be *brave enough to care* sensitively, compassionately and contrary to the masculine mystique about the quality and equality of our society. Women must *care enough* about their families and all families to *bravely assert* their voices and intellects to every aspect of every institution, whatever the feminine mystique. Every social trait labeled masculine or feminine is in truth a human trait. It is our human right to develop and contribute our talents whatever our race, sex, religion, ancestry, age. Human rights are indivisible!
Ibid.

5 The path to freedom for women *or* men does *not* lie *down* the bunny trail!
Ibid.

6 The pedestal is immobilizing and subtly insulting whether or not some women yet realize it. We must move up from the pedestal.
Ibid.

7 As your president [of NOW]* . . . I am one of thousands of us privileged to experience the joy, the risks, the gratifications, bone weariness, tragedies and triumphs of activist feminism. There are women and men and children in our lives and whose lives we touch who may never know how profoundly we care about ourselves and them and the quality of the world we must share and make livable for all. We are self–helpers with the courage of our commitment.
Quoted in NOW* Accomplishments *1973*

8 Now that we've organized [NOW]* . . . all over the United States and initiated an international movement and actions, it must be apparent that feminism is no passing fad but indeed a profound, universal behavior revolution.
Quoted in "About Women," *The Los Angeles Times 12 May 1974*

*National Organization for Women.

2300. Carolyn G. Heilbrun (1926–)

1 In former days, everyone found the assumption of innocence so easy; today we find fatally easy the assumption of guilt.
Quoted in *Poetic Justice* by Amanda Cross* *1970*
*Her pseudonym.

2 Ideas move fast when their time comes.
Toward a Recognition of Androgyny 1973

3 What is important now is that we free ourselves from the prison of gender and, before it is too late, deliver the world from the almost exclusive control of the masculine impulse.
Introduction, Ibid.

4 Most of us nowadays regard the Victorian age as part of the very remote past…yet in the matter of sexual polarization and the rejection of androgyny we still accept the convictions of Victorianism; we view everything, from our study of animal habits to our reading of literature, through the paternalistic eyes of the Victorian era.
Ibid.

5 Androgyny suggests a spirit of reconciliation between the sexes; it suggests, further, a full range of experience open to individuals who may as women be aggressive, as men, tender; it suggests a spectrum upon which human beings choose their places without regard to propriety to custom.
Ibid.

6 Great periods of civilization, however much they may have owed their beginning to the aggressive dominance of the male principle, have always been marked by some sort of rise in the status of women. This in its turn is a manifestation of something more profound: the recognition of the importance of the "feminine" principle, not as other, but as necessary to wholeness.
Pt. I, Ibid.

7 Today's shocks are tomorrow's conventions.
Pt. II, Ibid.

8 Routine, disposable novels, able to provide relief or distraction but not in themselves valuable—like the smoked cigarette, the used whore, the quick drink—are exactly suited to the conventions of their consumers.
Ibid.

9 . . . ardent, intelligent, sweet, sensitive, cultivated, erudite. These are the adjectives of praise in an androgynous world. Those who consider them epithets of shame or folly ought not to be trusted with leadership, for they will be men hot for power and revenge, certain of right and wrong.
Pt. III, Ibid.

10 Queens may rule either as monarchs or as nationalized angels in the house.
Ibid.

11 From the critics of the past I have learned the futility of concerning oneself with the present.
Afterword, Ibid.

12 Only a marriage with partners strong enough to risk divorce is strong enough to avoid it. . . .
"Marriage Is the Message," *Ms.* (New York) *August 1974*

13 The genuine solitaries of life fear intimacy more than loneliness. The married are those who have taken the terrible risk of intimacy and, having taken it, know life without intimacy to be impossible.
Ibid.

14 Marriage today must...be concerned not with the inviolable commitment of constancy and unending passion, but with the changing patterns of liberty and discovery.
Ibid.

15 Women must continue to invade the domains of power in order to change institutions as we know them, in order to offer places to other women...and to do justice to themselves.
Reinventing Womanhood 1979

16 . . . artists of pen and brush, must essentially scorn those who are not themselves creative, the more so if they are threateningly kind.
"Generous to a fault," *The Women's Review of Books,*
Vol. XI, No. 1 *October 1993*

17 . . . catch courage...
The Last Gift of Time: Life Beyond Sixty 1997

18 We read...as women read about women who have braved the terrors and hopes we share, at least to some degree. Courage in women always catches me up, moves me to compassion, and the desire [to offer women] succor, sustenance, if possible.
"An Unmet Friend" (essay–portrait of Maxine Kumin*),
Ibid.
*See 2279.

19 To be alone if one has not been doomed to aloneness is a temptation so beguiling that it carries with it the guilt of adultery, and the promise of consummation.
"The Small House," Ibid.

20 . . . if we could discover a word that meant "adventure" and did not mean "romance," we in our last decades [would not connect] yearning and sex.
"Sex and Romance," Ibid.

2301. Aileen Clarke Hernandez (1926–)

1 My comments to the thousands of persons at the peace march [the 1971 Another Mother for Peace march in Los Angeles] were directed not just against the Vietnam War, but against *all* war, against the masculine mystique which glorifies violence as a solution to problems, and against the vast diverting of American energies and resources from socially needed programs into social destructive wars.
Letter to Eve Norman, Quoted in the NOW* Newsletter
29 April 1971

2 There are no such things as women's issues! All issues are women's issues. The difference that we bring to existing issues of our society, the issues of war and peace; the issues of poverty; the issues of child care; the issues of political power— the difference that we bring is that we are going to bring the full, loud, clear determined voice of women into deciding how those issues are going to be addressed.
Address, National Conference of NOW* (Los Angeles)
3–6 September 1971

3 We need to get about the business of becoming persons. We need to get about the business of addressing the major issues of society as full-fledged human beings in a society that puts

humanity at the head of its list, rather than masculinity at the head of its list.
Ibid.

4 This movement . . . is the last stage of the drive for equality for women. We are determined that our daughters and granddaughters will live as free human beings, secure in their personhood, and dedicated to making this nation and the world a humane place in which to live.
Ibid.
*National Organization for Women.

2302. Elizabeth Jennings (1926–)

1 At last now you can be
What the old cannot recall
And the young long for in dreams,
Yet still include them all.
"Accepted," *Growing Pains 1975*

2 Do they know they're old,
These two who are my father and my mother
Whose fire from which I came, has now grown cold?
"One Flesh" *n.d.*

2303. Sue Kaufman (1926–)

1 Now Accounts is really a very good word. Accounts in its reportorial not calculative sense. Account, accounting—an account of what is going on. Better than journal or diary by far. *Diary* makes me think of those girls at camp. . . . *Journal* makes me think of all those college Lit courses . . . Anyway, *Accounts* is good. Accounts is best. Yes, Accounts does very well indeed.
"Friday, September 12," *Diary of a Mad Housewife 1967*

2 I was afraid that if I opened my mouth, like Gerald McBoing-Boing, terrible inhuman sounds would come out—brakes screeching, metal clashing, tires skidding, trains roaring past in the night.
"Saturday, October 7," Ibid.

3 People. Along with doormen, elevator men and headwaiters, the opinions of People matter greatly to Jonathan these days. And who are People? His great secret public—strangers, anybody he doesn't know.
"Monday, October 30," Ibid.

4 "Make yourself a nice hot toddy, and while you sip it, read Proust.* Proust is the only thing when you're sick." . . . I skipped the hot toddy, but by God it worked. Saved me. Was the antibiotic which wouldn't "touch" the Thing I had. Marvelous crazy poet. Marvelous Proust.
"Friday, November 17," Ibid.
*Marcel Proust, French writer (1871–1922)

5 "You must give him your views of what both working roles in a successful marriage should be—he'll be thrilled by the brilliant simplicity of it all. You know—the Forceful Dominant Male, the Submissive Woman? The Breadwinner who has every right to expect the Obedient Wife to carry out all his orders? He'll lap it up."
"Thursday, December 7," Ibid.

6 Burt told her that he loved her, she told him that she loved him. She thought she didn't mean it. She thought she was being very advanced, very pre-liberated, shattering the damned double standard and lying while she did it, if that's what was required.
Falling Bodies 1974

7 "I loved my mother. And she died a horrible death. In unspeakable agony."

"She was *not* in agony when she died . . . And you didn't love her. You wanted to love her and tried to love her, though God only knows why—but you *hated* her. With damned good reason. She was a castrating bitch, who cut your poor father's nuts off and finally drove him to drink himself to death . . . It makes my blood run cold just imagining what that poor guy must've gone through, and what you must've gone through as a child. I've always felt it was proof of your terrific strength that you'd managed to come out of that relatively unscathed. But now she's finally gotten at you anyway. Finally did it by dying, the bitch—and screw that business about not speaking ill of the dead: she was a *bitch*."

Ibid.

8 Ever since she had gotten out of the hospital, her eyes kept seeking out and fastening on the cruel, the ugly, the sordid—trying to turn every nasty little incident or detail into some sort of concrete proof of just how rotten the world had become.

Ibid.

9 "In violent and chaotic times such as these, our only chance for survival lies in creating our own little islands of sanity and order, in making little havens of our homes."

Ibid.

2304. Gertrude Lemp Kerbis (1926–)

1 It was hell for women architects then. They didn't want us in school or in the profession. . . . One thing I've never understood about this prejudice is that it's so strange in view of the fact that the drive to build has always been in women.

Quoted in *Women at Work* by Betty Medsger *1975*

2305. Jeane Kirkpatrick (1926–)

1 Vietnam presumably taught us that the United States could not serve as the world's policeman; it should also have taught us the dangers of trying to be the world's midwife to democracy when the birth is scheduled to take place under conditions of guerrilla war.

"Dictatorship and Double Standards," *Commentary* (New York) *November 1979*

2 Tyranny and anarchy are alike incompatible with freedom, security, and the enjoyment of opportunity.

Speech, Third Committee of United Nations General Assembly *24 November 1981*

3 Personal virtue is a good in itself, but it is not a sufficient means to the end of good government.

Speech (Washington D.C.) *29 September 1982*

4 [Democrats] can't get elected unless things get worse—and things won't get worse unless they get elected.

Quoted in *Time* (New York) *17 June 1985*

5 It is a fact that successive presidents find so many different reasons not to appoint specific women to specific positions in specific Cabinets. And it is a fact that men always get irritable if they get pressed about this.

Cited by Solveig Torvik in "Clinton can't please everyone," *Seattle Post-Intelligencer*, Op-Ed, A7 *30 December 1992*

6 We have war when at least one of the parties to a conflict wants something more than it wants peace.

Quoted in *Reader's Digest 1994*

2306. Elizabeth Kübler–Ross (1926–)

1 The more we are making advancements in science, the more we seem to fear and deny the reality of death.

Ch. 1, *On Death and Dying 1969*

2 . . . we have to ask ourselves whether medicine is to remain a humanitarian and respected profession or a new but depersonalized science in the service of prolonging life rather than diminishing human suffering. . . .

Ch. 2, *Ibid.*

3 There is not much sense in suffering, since drugs can be given for pain, itching, and other discomforts. The belief has long died that suffering here on earth will be rewarded in heaven. Suffering has lost its meaning.

Ibid.

4 Acceptance should not be mistaken for a happy stage. It is almost void of feelings. It is as if the pain had gone, the struggle is over. . . .

Ch. 7, *Ibid.*

5 Guilt is perhaps the most painful companion of death.

Ch. 9, *Ibid.*

6 It is difficult to accept death in this society because it is unfamiliar. In spite of the fact that it happens all the time, we never see it.

Ch. 2, *Death: The Final Stage of Growth 1975*

7 Dying is hard under any circumstances, but dying in the familiar surroundings of one's home, with those you love and who love you, can take away much of the fear.

Ch. 3, *Ibid.*

8 Those who have been immersed in the tragedy of massive death during wartime, and who have faced it squarely, never allowing their senses and feelings to become numbed and indifferent, have emerged from their experiences with growth and humanness greater than that achieved through almost any other means.

Ch. 5, *Ibid.*

9 Dying is something we human beings do continuously, not just at the end of our physical lives on this earth.

Ch. 6, *Ibid.*

10 It is not the end of the physical body that should worry us. Rather, our concern must be to *live* while we're alive—to release our inner selves from the spiritual death that comes with living behind a façade designed to conform to external definitions of who and what we are.

"Omega," *Ibid.*

11 The world is in desperate need of human beings whose own level of growth is sufficient to enable them to learn to live and work with others cooperatively and lovingly, to care for others—not for what those others can do for you or for what they think of you, but rather in terms of what you can do for them.

Ibid.

12 Death is the final stage of growth in this life. There is no total death. Only the body dies. The self or spirit, or whatever you may wish to label it, is eternal.

Ibid.

13 Learn to get in touch with silence within yourself and know that everything in this life has a purpose. There are no mistakes, no coincidences; all events are blessings given to us to learn from. There is no need to go to India or anywhere else to find peace. You will find that deep place of silence right in your room, your garden or even your bathtub.

Speech (1976), Quoted in "Elizabeth Kübler-Ross" by Lennie Kronisch, Yoga Journal November/December 1976

2307. Margaret Laurence (1926–)

1 The bird had no name. She did not believe in bestowing names upon non-humans, for a name to her meant a christening, possible only for Christians.

"The Sound of Singing," Winter's Tales, A. D. Maclean, ed. 1963

2 Privacy is a privilege not granted to the aged or the young.

Ch. 1, The Stone Angel 1964

3 Even if heaven were real, and measured as Revelation says, so many cubits this way and that, how gimcrack a place it would be, crammed with its pavements of gold, its gates of pearl and topaz, like a gigantic chunk of costume jewelry.

Ch. 4, Ibid.

4 Each day dies with sleep.

Ch. 3, A Jest of God (a.k.a. Rachel, Rachel) 1966

5 Holidays are enticing only for the first week or so. After that, it is no longer such a novelty to rise late and have little to do.

Ch. 4, Ibid.

6 "The prime purpose of a funeral director is not all this beautician deal which some members of the profession go in for so much. No. It's this—to take over. Reassure people."

Ch. 7, Ibid.

7 "Presentation is all—that's what I believe. Everybody knows a product has to be attractively packaged—it's the first rule of sales—isn't that so?"

Ibid.

8 "Death's unmentionable?"
"Not exactly unmentionable, but let's face it, most of us could get along without it."
"I don't see how."

Ibid.

9 How strange to have to keep on retreating to the only existing privacy, the only place one is permitted to be unquestionably alone, the lavatory.

Ch. 9, Ibid.

10 I was always afraid that I might become a fool. Yet I could almost smile with some grotesque light-headedness at that fool of a fear, that poor fear of fools, now that I really am one.

Ch. 10, Ibid.

11 "You are out of danger," he said. I laughed, I guess, and said, "How can I be—I don't feel dead yet."

Ch. 11, Ibid.

12 God's mercy on reluctant jesters. God's grace on fools. God's pity on God.

Ch. 12, Ibid.

2308. Harper Lee (1926–)

1 The day was twenty-four hours long but seemed longer. There was no hurry, for there was nowhere to go, nothing to buy and no money to buy it with, nothing to see outside the boundaries of Maycomb County. But it was a time of vague optimism for some of the people: Maycomb County had recently been told that it had nothing to fear but fear itself.

Ch. 1, To Kill a Mockingbird 1960

3 "People in their right minds never take pride in talents," said Miss Maudie.

Ch. 10, Ibid.

4 "The one thing that doesn't abide by majority rule is a person's conscience."

Ch. 11, Ibid.

5 "Folks don't like to have somebody around knowin' more than they do. It aggravates 'em. You're not gonna change any of them by talkin' right, they've got to want to learn themselves, and when they don't want to learn there's nothing you can do but keep your mouth shut or talk their language."

Ch. 12, Ibid.

6 Never, never, never, on cross-examination ask a witness a question you don't already know the answer to, was a tenet I absorbed with my baby-food. Do it, and you'll often get an answer you don't want, an answer that might wreck your case.

Ch. 17, Ibid.

7 "Our courts have their faults, as does any human institution, but in this country our courts are the great levelers, and in our courts all men are created equal. I'm no idealist to believe firmly in the integrity of our courts and in the jury system— that is no ideal to me, it is a living, working reality. Gentlemen, a court is no better than each man of you sitting before me on this jury. A court is only as sound as its jury, and a jury is only as sound as the men who make it up."

Ch. 20, Ibid.

8 In the absence of eye-witnesses, there's always a shadow of a doubt. The law says "reasonable doubt," but I think a defendant's entitled to the shadow of a doubt. There's always the possibility, no matter how improbable, that he's innocent.

Ibid.

9 "As you grow older, you'll see white men cheat black men every day of your life, but let me tell you something and don't you forget it—whenever a white man does that to a black man, no matter who he is, how rich he is, or how fine a family he comes from, that white man is trash."

Ch. 23, Ibid.

2309. Pat Loud (1926–)

1 College for women was a refinement whose main purpose was to better prepare you for your ultimate destiny . . . to make you a more desirable product.

Pat Loud: A Woman's Story, with Nora Johnson 1974

2 Life was diapers and little jars of pureed apricots and bottles and playpens and rectal thermometers, and all those small dirty faces and all those questions.

Ibid.

3 A miserable marriage can wobble along for years until something comes along and pushes one of the people over the brink.

It's usually another man or woman. For me, it was a whole production staff and camera crew.

Ibid.

4 Housework isn't bad in itself—the trouble with it is that it's inhumanely lonely.

Ibid.

2310. Alison Lurie (1926–)

1 "You see, actually, Roger, the very second a plant is cut from its roots, or pulled out of the ground, it starts to die and lose its nutritive values. That's why I've got started growing my own, as much as I've got room for, and so's Elsie."

Ch. 16, *Imaginary Friends* 1967

2 But intellectual and personal force—even genius—are not guarantees of sanity.

Ch. 17, Ibid.

3 Then last year, when Jeffrey turned fourteen and Matilda twelve, they had begun to change; to grow rude, coarse, selfish, insolent, nasty, brutish, and tall. It was as if she were keeping a boarding house in a bad dream, and the children she had loved were turning into awful lodgers—lodgers who paid no rent, whose leases could not be terminated.

Ch. 1, *The War Between the Tates* 1974

4 Since she is an authority on children's literature, people assume that Vinnie must love children, and that her own lack of them must be a tragedy. For the sake of public relations, she seldom denies these assumptions outright. But the truth is otherwise. In her private opinion most contemporary children—especially American ones—are competitive, noisy, and shallow, at once jaded and ignorant as a result of overexposure to television, baby-sitters, advertising, and video games. Vinnie wants to be a child, not to have one; she isn't interested in the parental role, but in an extension or recovery of what for her is the best part of life.

Ch. 5, *Foreign Affairs* 1984

5 As an American friend of hers once put it at a high point of their brief relationship . . . "Sometimes I think we're the same person." "Oh, I know," Vinnie had replied, equally deluded. . . .

Even more often, outsiders conflate the couple, and credit them with each other's characteristics. If a radical takes up with a conservative, both will be perceived as more moderate politically, regardless of whether their views have in fact altered. The man or woman who becomes involved with a much younger person seems younger, the latter more mature.

Ch. 9, Ibid.

6 Without sex and death humans may become as angels.

Don't Tell the Grown-Ups 1990

7 [The world is] going to hell in a nonbiodegradable plastic handbasket.

The Last Resort 1998

8 "Nature can seem cruel, but she balances her books."

Ibid.

9 . . . to refuse to look at a writer's work is always a deadly insult.

Ibid.

10 "You don't have to be intellectually brilliant to be a famous American poet. It's a handicap, sometimes. Innocent egotism, good looks, romantic sensibility, a thrilling speaking voice, and a nice little lyric gift, that's what makes it with the reviewers and the public."

Ibid.

2311. Joyce McDougall (1926–)

1 Psychic reality will always be structured around the poles of absence and difference; and . . . human being will always have to come to terms with that which is forbidden and that which is impossible.

Quoted in *Necessary Losses* by Judith Viorst* 1986
*See 2479.

2312. Jan Morris (1926–)

1 I was loved and I was loving, brought up kindly and sensibly, spoiled to a comfortable degree, weaned at an early age on *Huck Finn* and *Alice in Wonderland,* taught to cherish my animals, say grace, think well of myself, and wash my hands before tea.

Ch. 1, *Conundrum* 1974

2 To me gender is not physical at all, but is altogether insubstantial. It is soul, perhaps, it is talent, it is taste, it is environment, it is how one feels, it is light and shade, it is inner music. . . .

Ch. 3, Ibid.

3 I had reached the conclusion myself that sex was not a division but a continuum, that almost nobody was altogether of one sex or another, and that the infinite subtlety of the shading from one extreme to the other was one of the most beautiful of nature's phenomena. Sex was like a biological pointer, but the gauge upon which it flickered was that very different device, gender.

Ch. 5, Ibid.

4 Intercourse seemed to me a tool, a reproductive device, and at the same time, in its symbolical fusion of bodies, a kind of pledge or surrender, not to be lightly given, still less thrown away in masquerade.

Ch. 6, Ibid.

5 But I have come to see within the mystery of the African genius, veiled as it is by superstition, fear, and resentment, something of the magic of the earth itself.

Ch. 11, Ibid.

6 Englishmen . . . found the [sexual] ambiguity in itself beguiling . . . Frenchmen were curious, and tended to engage me in inquisitive conversation. . . . Italians, frankly unable to conceive the meaning of such a phenomenon, simply stared boorishly, or nudged each other in piazzas. Greeks were vastly entertained. Arabs asked me to go for walks with them. Scots looked shocked. Germans looked worried. Japanese did not notice.

Ch. 12, Ibid.

7 We are told that the social gap between the sexes is narrowing, but I can only report that having, in the second half of the twentieth century, experienced life in both roles, there seems to me no aspect of existence, no moment of the day, no contact, no arrangement, no response, which is not different for men and for women.

Ch. 17, Ibid.

8 Why, the garbage thrown away in this city every day—every *day*—would feed the whole of Europe for a week.

Manhattan '45 1987

9 " . . . a bum who ain't drunk by midnight ain't trying."

Ibid.

10 Where else, in 1945, could you have your photograph taken by an unmanned machine (the Photomaton), or go to a theatre on the fiftieth floor of a skyscraper (the Chanin Building), or for that matter get an electric shock just from touching a door handle, in a city so charged with energy that the very air tingled with it?

Ibid.

11 Nothing is more flexibly resilient than Chineseness.
Hong Kong 1988

12 It seems to me that down the centuries only religion has given the continent any lasting common identity. Judaism has sometimes been powerful in Europe, the threat and presence of Islam has crucially affected its history; but paganism and Christianity have been the continent's universal defining factors, and the one long ago mastered the other.
Fifty Years of Europe: An Album 1997

13 It takes guts to be a martyr, to have arrows stuck all over you or be pulled apart on racks: but it perhaps takes true holiness to be laughed at by louts for your convictions.
Ibid.

2313. Patricia Neal (1926–)

1 It [Hollywood] always sounds glamorous when you're young.
Quoted in *Time* (New York) *20 March 1964*

2 It's very important not to pamper or indulge them [brain-injured or handicapped children] or to treat them differently from the other children in the family. But this is very difficult . . .
Quoted in "Triumph Over Tragedy" by Patricia Baum,
Parents' Magazine November 1975

3 Tennessee hillbillies don't conk out that easily.
Ibid.

4 In mid-life the man wants to see how irresistible he still is to younger women. How they turn their hearts to stone and more or less commit a murder of their marriage I just don't know, but they do.
Quoted in *The Daily Telegraph* (London) *22 June 1988*

2314. Charlotte Painter (1926–)

1 We are looking for some way to live in a world gone mad. We have left America the beautiful. But not because we know a better place.
Confession from the Malaga Madhouse 1971

2 If a thing is absolutely true, how can it not also be a lie? An absolute must contain its opposite.
Ibid.

3 I don't know where in this shrunken world to take you, son, to let you grow to manhood.
Ibid.

4 Not persuaded enough against violence to go to jail for it. Not persuaded he can kill either. Not interested in that Army, that War, sure enough of himself only to know that he doesn't yet know the Way . . .
Ibid.

5 The passion for destruction, glorious destruction. Must we seek grace in violence, more than any other way?
Ibid.

6 . . . as awareness increases, the need for personal secrecy almost proportionately decreases.
Afterword, *Revelations: Diaries of Women*,
with Mary Jane Moffat* *1974*

*See 2719.

7 Psychic bisexuality is a de-conditioning process, which can eventually eliminate sexist limitations for both men and women.
Ibid.

8 To a lover of literature, life tends to will o'wisp on either side of the poem, the story, the play.
Ibid.

9 If we can distinguish between specialized art, as designed for an intellectual, educated group, and primitive art, as created through a group's unconscious symbols, then perhaps we can talk about some diaries as primitive.
Ibid.

10 Habits do not like to be abandoned, and besides they have the virtue of being tools.
Ibid.

2315. R. Rajalakshmi (1926–)

1 . . . many of the ideas I advanced during my research career . . . which were received somewhat skeptically by some scientists in the field are now accepted as commonplace.
Quoted in *Twentieth-Century Women Scientists*
by Lisa Yount *1996*

2 . . . my capacity for insight and intuition . . . made [me] think of common-sense solutions to seemingly complex problems.
Ibid.

3 It is time we realized that ultimately the future of this planet earth and the beings it houses depends on the promotion of the welfare of all.
Speech (1982), Ibid.

2316. Gerlind Reinshagen (1926–)

1 BUBLITZ. What is it
That's taking hold of me now
Hanging around my neck like a stone
Like a millstone, pulling, pulling
Like I don't know what.
Pt. One, 3, *Ironheart (Eisenherz)*, Sue-Ellen Case*
and Arlene A. Teraoka, trs. *1981*

2 When photography was invented, painters reacted very subjectively with impressionism and expressionism. In contrast, in this country [Germany], [theater] people try to excel the suspense on television, often even the special effects. The discrepancy between imagination and reality, the persistent pursuit of the inner image, and the failure of the original concept—for all this I would like to find a form.
Interview by Anke Roeder, *The Divided Home/Land:*
Contemporary German Women's Plays,
Sue-Ellen Case,* ed. *1992*

*See 3625.

3 Drama is only a revolt if it moves away from this [true to life] reality, if it forces people to think differently. I don't want to repeat the pragmatic way of life on stage.
Ibid.

2317. Cynthia Propper Seton (1926–)

1 To Angela her grandmother was old but had not grown older and was never younger. This is a usual way with grandmothers.
Ch. 1, *The Sea Change of Angela Lewes 1971*

2   Well, banality is a terribly likely consequence of the underuse of a good mind. That is why in particular it is a female affliction.

Ch. 9, Ibid.

3   "It sometimes looks to me," said Angela, "that a middle-class marriage is a careful mismatching of two innocents—and the game is called Making the Best of It, while in actual fact each one does a terrible thing to the spirit of the other. . . . And you wonder why they endure each other, why they stand for it? And the explanation is that they really answer each other's needs, unconscious needs, and are in fact often admirably suited to each other, and that, unbelievable as it might seem from the outside, they do really *love* each other."

Ch. 12, Ibid.

4   Angela was spinning off, and Charlie was letting her. The shift in their marital relationship was remarkable for the absence of tension, of conflict—a peaceful *de*-consummation devoutly to be wished in the generality of aging marriages. Angela was becoming her own person, her own woman, and was alternately exhilarated and complacent . . .

Ch. 18, Ibid.

5   "Holding hands is a very intimate thing to do," she found herself whispering. "Even to hold a child's hand. It's very touching."

Ch. 25, Ibid.

6   To pursue yourself is an interesting and absorbing thing to do. Once you have caught the scent of a hidden being, your own hidden being, you won't readily be deflected from the tracking down of it.

Ibid.

7   She had trouble defining herself independently of her husband, tried to talk to him about it, but he said nonsense, he had no trouble defining her at all.

The Half-Sisters 1974

2318. Dorothy E. Smith (1926–)

1   In the social sciences the pursuit of objectivity makes it possible for people to be paid to pursue a knowledge to which they are otherwise indifferent.

"Women's perspective as a radical critique of sociology,"
Sociological Inquiry 44 1974

2   The exclusion of women from the making of our culture is not the product of a biological deficiency or a biological configuration of some kind. As we learn more of our women's history we discover that a powerful intellectual and artistic current moves like an underground stream through the history of the last few centuries. It appears sometimes merely as a missing potentiality . . . We learn of the subordination of genius to the discipline of service in the home and in relation to children, and of the fragmentary realization of extraordinary powers of mind and dedication. . . .

Ch. 1, The Everyday Woman as Problematic 1987

2319. Nancy Spero (1926–)

1   The male standard has been universal. Images in art are images that men have made. The correction is simple—equally a female standard with images in art that women make.

Quoted in "Nancy Spero," *Exposures, Women & Their Art*
by Ann Brown & Arlene Raven* 1989

*See 3020.

2   There are many more male political prisoners than female. . . . Both men and women are sexually abused, but with women sexual assault is always central to attacks upon the body. Woman has had the status of victim "par excellence" from time immemorial.

Ibid.

3   Only recently has women's history been uncovered. I'm recovering the past through all kinds of images by women, from goddesses to victims. An artist has power, if she has a voice that can enter the public discourse.

Ibid.

2320. Joan Sutherland (1926–)

1   If I weren't reasonably placid, I don't think I could cope with this sort of life. To be a diva, you've got to be absolutely like a horse.

Quoted in "Joan Sutherland," *Divas: Impressions of Six*
Opera Superstars by Winthrop Sargeant 1959

2   I know I'm not exactly a bombshell, but one has to make the best of what one's got.

Ibid.

3   But I think Australians have a sort of independence, and I think that, rightly or wrongly, they tend to make their own decisions as to how a thing has gone. Pioneers are apt to be like that. I think that it's not a bad idea. You can listen to what everybody says, but the fact remains that you've got to get out there and do the thing yourself.

Ibid.

2321. Johnnie Tillmon (1926–)

1   I'm a woman. I'm a black woman. I'm a poor woman. I'm a fat woman. I'm a middle-aged woman. And I'm on welfare. In this country, if you're any one of those things, you count less as a person. If you're *all* those things, you just don't count, except as a statistic.

"Welfare is a Woman's Issue," *The First Ms. Reader*,
Francine Klagsbrun, ed. 1972

2   Women aren't supposed to work. They're supposed to be married.

Ibid.

3   Wages are the measure of dignity that society puts on a job.

Ibid.

4   Welfare is like a traffic accident. It can happen to anybody, but especially it happens to women.

Ibid.

2322. Itka Frajiman Zygmuntowicz (1926–)

1   My childhood world was gone, but not from my heart and mind. Nothing dies as long as it is remembered and transmitted from person to person, from generation to generation. Or, as my beloved grandmother used to say, "My child, you only have what you choose to give away!"

"Survival and Memory" (p. 290), *Four Centuries of Jewish*
Women's Spirituality: A Sourcebook, Ellen M. Umansky
and Dianne Ashton, eds. 1992

2323. Marilyn Monroe (1926–1962)

1   I've been on a calender, but never on time.

Quoted in *Look* (New York) 16 January 1962

2 Unfortunately, I am involved in a freedom ride protesting the loss of the minority rights belonging to the few remaining earthbound stars. All we demanded was our right to twinkle.*

> Telegram to Mr. and Mrs. Robert Kennedy** *13 June 1962*
> *Response to a party invitation. **American politician; assassinated (1925–1968).

3 Fame will go by and, so long, I've had you, fame. If it goes by, I've always known it was fickle. So at least it's something I experienced, but that's not where I live.

> *Life* (New York) *3 August 1962*

4 I hope at some future time to make a glowing report on the wonders that psychiatrists can do for you.

> Quoted in "Marilyn: The Woman Who Died Too Soon" by Gloria Steinem,* *The First Ms. Reader*, Francine Klagsbrun, ed. *1972*
> *See 2581.

5 A career is born in public—talent in privacy.

> Ibid.

6 I have too many fantasies to be a housewife. . . . I guess I *am* a fantasy.

> Ibid.

7 I don't want to make money. I just want to be wonderful.

> Ibid.

8 I am always running into peoples' unconscious.

> Quoted in *Marilyn* by Norman Mailer* *1973*
> *American writer (1923–).

9 My work is the only ground I've ever had to stand on. I seem to have a whole superstructure with no foundation—but I'm working on the foundation.

> "Acting," *Marilyn Monroe In Her Own Words 1990*

10 Hollywood's a place where they'll pay you a thousand dollars for a kiss, and fifty cents for your soul. I know, because I turned down the first offer often enough and held out for the fifty cents.

> Ibid.

11 Husbands are chiefly good as lovers when they are betraying their wives.

> "Weddings & Divorces," Ibid.

2324. Ingeborg Bachmann (1926–1973)

1 For the facts that make up the world need the non-factual as a vantage point from which to be percieved.

> *Der Fall Franza* (The Franza Case), Jan van Heurck, tr. *n.d.*

2 He has taken my possessions from me. My laughter, my tenderness, my ability to feel joy, my compassion, my ability to help, my animality, my radiance; he has stamped out every sprout of all these things, until they stopped sprouting. But why does someone do that, I don't understand.

> Ibid.

3 The whites are coming. The whites are landing. And if they are repulsed again, they will return again once more. No revolution and no resolution and no foreign currency statute will help; they will come in spirit if they can no longer come in any other way. And they will be resurrected in a brown and a black brain; it will still always be the whites, even then. They will continue to own the world in this roundabout way.

> Ibid.

4 your heart has business elsewhere
your mouth is annexing new languages.

> "Explain to Me, Love," St. 1, Jan van Heurck, tr. *n.d.*

5 Explain nothing to me. I see the salamander
go through every fire.
No shudder pursues him, and nothing gives him pain.

> St. 6, Ibid.

2325. Carolyn Leigh (1926–1983)

1 When you arouse the need in me
My heart says yes, indeed, to me
Proceed with what you're leading me to

> "Witchcraft" *n.d.*

2 Out of the tree of life
I done picked me a plum

> "The Best is Yet to Come" *n.d.*

3 It's hard, you will find
To be narrow of mind
If you're young at heart

> "Young at Heart" *n.d.*

2326. Toni Carabillo (1926–1997)

1 But powerlessness is still each woman's most critical problem, whether or not she is a social activist. It is at the root of most of her psychological disorders.

> Address, "Power Is the Name of the Game," California NOW* State Conference (San Diego) *28 October 1973*

2 The sudden acquisition of power by those who have never had it before can be intoxicating, and we run the risk of becoming absorbed in petty power games with our organization [NOW]* that in the last analysis can only be self-defeating.

> Ibid.

3 But powerlessness is still each woman's most critical problem, whether or not she is a social activist. It is at the root of most of her psychological disorders.

> Ibid.

4 . . . women are not a special interest group in the usual sense of the term. We are half the population. When the image of women presented in the media is offensive, it is offensive to women of all social classes, races, religions and ethnic origins.

> Address, "Womanpower and the Media," National Association of Broadcasters *1974*

5 . . . we have learned from the experience of the first feminist movement that to stop short of the basic reordering of society, as it is reflected in sex role stereotypes, is too small a victory.

> Ibid.

6 Rock music consistently degrades women and makes it clear her place in this man's world is limited to the kitchen and the bedroom. Rock music has been rightly characterized, in our view, as a "frenzied celebration of masculine supremacy."

> Ibid.

7 We know that poverty in this country is primarily the problem of *all* women—that most women are only a husband away from welfare.

> Address, "Sharing the Power, the Glory—And the Pain," NOW* Western Regional Conference (Long Beach, California) *24 November 1974*

8   . . . we must learn that we can disagree with each other on issues, without becoming deadly enemies, and without totally
devastating our opposition. We can in fact continue to acknowledge and admire the skills and dedication, the genuine
accomplishments and contributions of those with whom we
are otherwise in dissent.

Ibid.

9   For the one equality women all over the world have already
achieved is the *Equality of Consequences.* No inventory of
the major challenges and crises of our times discloses any
from whose effects women will be exempt by virtue of our
sex.

Ibid.

10 Not only the CIA, but the FBI,** as well as many state and
community police departments, have devoted vast resources to
monitoring the activities of concerned citizens working in concert to make social changes within our system. The "flatfoot
mentality" insists that any individual or organization that
wants to change *anything* in our present system is somehow
subversive of "the American way," and should be under continuous surveillance—a task that appears to absorb most of
our resources for fighting genuine crime.

"The Flatfoot Mentality," Hollywood NOW* News
August 1975
*National Organization for Women. **Central Intelligence
Agency and the Federal Bureau of Investigation.

2327. Mary Mamie O'Brien (1926–1998)

1   . . . we have a substantial intellectual movement, bearing the
name if not always the perception of Marx, based on the necessity of subsistence. We have another body of thought,
exemplified by the followers of Freud, resting upon the imperatives of human sexuality. We have a further body of thought,
existentialism, resolutely anticipating the absurd necessity of
death. We have no philosophy of birth.

The Politics of Reproduction 1981

2   Man Alone is a subject which has long preoccupied Western
thought; woman alone is a welfare problem.

Cited in obituary, *New Directions for Women,* Vol. XVI,
No. 4, p. 4 *January 1999*

2328. Erma Bombeck (1927–1996)

1   Guilt: the gift that keeps on giving.

Quoted in *Time* (New York) *2 July 1984*

2   Humorists can never start to take themselves seriously. It's literary suicide.

Article, *Detroit Free Press 10 August 1978*

3   You hear a lot of dialogue on the death of the American family. Families aren't dying. They're merging into big conglome-
rates.

"Empty Fridge, Empty Nest," *San Francisco Examiner*
1 October 1978

4   I worry about scientist discovering that lettuce has been fattening all along. . . .

If Life is a Bowl of Cherries—What am I Doing
in the Pits? 1978

5   The Rose Bowl is the only bowl I've ever seen that I didn't have
to clean.

Remark *n.d.*

2329. Joyce Brothers (1927/28–)

1   Marriage is not just spiritual communion and passionate embraces; marriage is also three-meals-a-day and remembering to
carry out the trash.

"When Your Husband's Affection Cools,"
Good Housekeeping May 1972

2   Anger repressed can poison a relationship as surely as the cruelest words.

Ibid.

2330. Rosalyn Carter (1927–)

1   My greatest disappointment in all the projects I worked on
during the White House years was the failure of the Equal
Rights Amendment to be ratified . . . Why all the controversy
and why such difficulty in giving women the protection of the
Constitution that should have been theirs long ago?

First Lady From Plains 1984

2   Jimmy* and I were always partners.

Remark, Quoted in *First Ladies* by Betty Boyd Caroli *1987*
*James Carter, her husband (1924–), 39th president of the United
States (1977–81).

3   If we have not achieved our early dreams, we must either
find new ones or see what we can salvage from the old. If we
have accomplished what we set out to do in our youth, then
we need not weep like Alexander the Great* that we have
no more worlds to conquer. There is clearly much left to be
done, and whatever else we are going to do, we had better
get on with it.

Something to Gain 1987
*Greek military and political leader (356–323 B.C.E.); King of
Macedon (336–323 B.C.E.).

4   I had already learned from more than a decade of political life
that I was going to be criticized no matter what I did, so I
might as well be criticized for something I wanted to do. (If I
had spent all day "pouring tea," I would have been criticized
for that too).*

Ibid.
*Response to criticism of her attendance at Cabinet meetings,

2331. Theo E. Colborn (1927–)

1   In my business [science research], you measure your respect by
the enemies you make.

Interview with Bob Taylor, Quoted in, *Seattle Post-*
Intelligencer, C1 *2 April 1996*

2332. Nora Dauenhauer (1927–)

1   Trying to write
about you is like dragging
a fishing line through bushes.
I go a short distance
and my line hooks
on underbrush.

"Jessy," *in toto, That's What She Said,* Rayna Green, ed.
1984
*See 2800.

2333. Midge Decter (1927–)

1   Shifts in prejudice can work both ways.

Pt. I, Ch. 3, *The Liberated W*
oman and Other Americans 1971

2   Ideas are powerful things, requiring not a studious contemplation but an action, even if it is only an inner action. Their acquisition obligates each man in some way to change his life, even if it is only his inner life. They demand to be stood for. They dictate where a man must concentrate his vision. They determine his moral and intellectual priorities. They provide him with allies and make him enemies. In short, ideas impose an interest in their ultimate fate which goes far beyond the realm of the merely reasonable.

Pt. II, Ch. 2, Ibid.

3   . . . because I am a New Yorker, my experience is the more truly, the more typically, American one. It is my America that is moving in on them [Middle America]. God is about to bless them with an opportunity, and may He also save them from it, but there is no turning back now.

Pt. III, Ch. 6, Ibid.

4   The hatred of the youth culture for adult society is not a disinterested judgment but a terror-ridden refusal to be hooked into the, if you will, ecological chain of breathing, growing, and dying. It is the demand, in other words, to remain children.

Ch. 1, The New Chastity and Other Arguments Against Women's Liberation 1972

5   The fundamental impulse of the movement is neither masturbatory nor concretely lesbian—although it of course offers warm houseroom to both these possibilities; it is an impulse to maidenhood—to that condition in which a woman might pretend to a false fear or loathing of the penis in order to escape from any responsibility for the pleasure and well-being of the man who possesses it.

Ch. 2, Ibid.

6   Women's Liberation calls it enslavement but the real truth about the sexual revolution is that it has made of sex an almost chaotically limitless and therefore unmanageable realm in the life of women.

Ibid.

7   Consciousness-raising groups are of a piece with a whole cultural pattern that has been growing up. This pattern begins with the term growing up. This pattern begins with the term "rapping"—which is a process in which people in groups pretend that they are not simply self-absorbed because they are talking to each other.

Speech, Women's National Book Association, Quoted in "On Consciousness-Raising," *Crazy Salad* by Nora Ephron* *1973*

*See 2849.

8   It might sound a paradoxical thing to say—for surely never has a generation of children occupied more sheer hours of parental time—but the truth is that we neglected you. We allowed you a charade of trivial freedoms in order to avoid making those impositions on you that are in the end both the training ground and proving ground for true independence. We pronounced you strong when you were still weak in order to avoid the struggles with you that would have fed your true strength. We proclaimed you sound when you were foolish in order to avoid taking part in the long, slow, slogging effort that is the only route to genuine maturity of mind and feeling. Thus, it was no small anomaly of your growing up that while you were the most indulged generation, you were also in many ways the most abandoned to your own meager devices by those into whose safe-keeping you had been given.

Ch. 1, Liberal Parents/Radical Children 1975

9   All they wished for her was that she should turn herself into a little replica of them.

Ch. 3, Ibid.

2334. Anne Edwards (1927–)

1   What a difficult swallowing of ego and pride she [Judy Garland*] must have suffered with each pill—what a frightening loss of self.

Judy Garland 1975

*See 2217.

2   That was, of course, the problem—she *begged*, not demanded. She wanted a happy world and everyone in it happy, but she was at a loss as to how to accomplish this.

Ibid.

2335. Althea Gibson (1927–)

1   I always wanted to be somebody. I guess that's why I kept running away from home when I was a kid even though I took some terrible whippings for it.

Ch. 1, I Always Wanted to Be Somebody 1958

2   I was excited. I was confident, too. I don't mean that I wasn't nervous, because I was. But I was nervous and confident at the same time, nervous about going out there in front of all those people, with so much at stake, and confident that I was going to go out there and win.

Ch. 8, Ibid.

3   I don't want to be put on a pedestal. I just want to be reasonably successful and live a normal life with all the conveniences to make it so. I think I've already got the main thing I've always wanted, which is to be somebody, to have identity. I'm Althea Gibson, the tennis champion. I hope it makes me happy.

Ch. 9, Ibid.

2336. Ann Jellicoe (1927–)

1   TOLEN. Intuition is, to some degree, inborn, Colin. One is born with an intuition as to how to get women. But this feeling can be developed with experience and confidence, in certain people, Colin, to some degree. A man can develop the knack. First you must realize that women are not just individuals but types. No, not even types, just women. They want to surrender but they don't want the responsibility of surrendering.

The Knack 1961

2   The impulse to create is linked with the aggressive instinct.

Article by Carol Dix, Quoted in *The Guardian* (London) *1972*

2337. Ruth Prawer Jhabvala (1927–)

1   ". . . what she wants is a live guru—someone to inspire her . . . snatch her up and out of herself—simultaneously destroy and create her."

Travelers 1973

2   "It is only," he says, "when you have given up all enjoyment that it is no longer enjoyment, it is only then that you can have these things back again."

Ibid.

3   "India . . . is not a place that one can pick up and put down again as if nothing had happened. In a way it's not so much a

country as an experience, and whether it turns out to be a good or a bad one depends, I suppose, on oneself."

Ibid.

4   These diseases that people get in India, they're not physical, they're purely psychic. We only get them because we try to resist India—because we shut ourselves up in our little Western egos and don't want to give ourselves. But once we learn to yield, then they must fall away.

Ibid.

5   "Take me, make what you will of me, I have joy in my submission."

Ibid.

6   [India] was like being not in a different part of this world but in another world altogether, in another reality.

Heat and Dust 1983

7   I had come to India to be in India. I wanted to be changed. Henry didn't—he wanted a change, that's all, but not to be changed.

"An Experience of India," Out of India 1986

2338. Beverly Jones (1927–)

1   Now, as always, the most automated appliance in a household is the mother.

"The Dynamics of Marriage and Motherhood," The Florida Paper on Women's Liberation 1970

2   If enforced wakefulness is the handmaiden and necessary precursor to serious brainwashing, a mother—after her first child—is ready for her final demise.

Ibid.

3   Romance, like the rabbit at the dog track, is the illusive, fake, and never-attained reward which for the benefit and amusement of our masters keeps us running and thinking in safe circles.

Ibid.

4   We who have been raised on pap must develop a passion for honest appraisal.

Ibid.

5   Automation and unions have led to a continuously shortened day for men but the work day of housewives with children has remained constant.

Ibid.

2339. Coretta Scott King (1927–)

1   There is a spirit and a need and a man at the beginning of every great human advance. Each of these must be right for that particular moment of history, or nothing happens.

Ch. 6, My Life with Martin Luther King, Jr.* 1969

2   My husband* often told the children that if a man had nothing that was worth dying for, then he was not fit to live.

Press Conference (April 1968), Ibid.

*American clergyman and civil rights leader (1929–68); assassinated.

3   We are concerned not only about the Negro poor, but the poor all over America and all over the world. Every man deserves a right to a job or an income so that he can pursue liberty, life, and happiness. Our great nation, as he often said, has the resources, but his question was: Do we have the will?

Speech, Memphis City Hall, Ibid.

4   The more visible signs of protest are gone, but I think there is a realization that the tactics of the late sixties are not sufficient to meet the challenges of the seventies.

Speech, Quoted in the The Los Angeles Times 14 May 1974

2340. Mathilde Krim (1927–)

1   Now we [American Foundation for AIDS Research] can have theater benefits, cocktail parties, dinners, and people will come.* They're not as afraid anymore. It's as if, all of a sudden, it's chic to behave decently.

Quoted in "When No One Dared" by Michael Ryan, Parade Magazine 5 June 1988

*Since actor Elizabeth Taylor (see 2513) became honorary chair.

2   I've never known a virus that discriminates.

Ibid.

3   There were some friends who didn't want to associate with me after I became identified with AIDS. But then, they weren't friends, were they?

Ibid.

2341. Lolita Lebron (1927–)

1   I did not come here to kill, I came here to die.*

Quoted in A Message from God in the Atomic Age by Irene Vilar; * Gregory Rabassa, tr. 1996

*Reference to 24 February 1954, when Lebron and three male companions opened fire on the U.S. House of Representatives in protest against U.S. colonial rule; she spent 27 years in prison. **See 3492.

2   There is no victory without pain.

Ibid.

2342. Jean Baker Miller (1927–)

1   . . . it is extremely important to recognize that the pull toward affiliation that women feel in themselves is not wrong or backward. . . . What has not been recognized is that this psychic starting point contains the possibilities for an entirely different (and more advanced) approach to living and functioning—very different, that is, from the approach fostered by the dominant culture. . . . It allows for the emergence of the truth: that for everyone—men as well as women—individual development proceeds *only* by means of affiliation.

Toward a New Psychology of Women 1976

2   The power of another person, or group of people was generally seen as dangerous. You had to control them or they would control you. But in the realm of human development, this is not a valid formulation. Quite the reverse.

(p. 115), Ibid.

3   Women are quite validly seeking something more complete than autonomy as it is defined by men, a fuller not lesser ability to encompass relationships to others, simultaneously with the fullest development of oneself.

Ibid.

4   Most so-called women's work is not recognized as real activity. One reason for this attitude may be that such work is usually associated with helping others' development, rather than with self-enhancement or self-employment. This is seen as *not doing anything.*

Ch. 5, Ibid.

5   The very essence of all life is growth, which means change. . . . Some societies, particularly ours, attempt to divert the need for change by entertainment, and a rapid succession of fads. All of these "circuses" may convey the illusion of change, but in fact they accomplish the opposite. They do not meet the need for growth and enlargement of the mind. Instead, they often confuse us so much that we overlook the terrible frustration of this true need. They thwart rather than fulfill it.

Ibid.

6   Practically everyone now bemoans the Western man's sense of alienation, lack of community, and inability to find ways of organizing society for human ends. We have reached the end of the road that built on the set of traits held out for male identity—advance at any cost, pay any price, drive out all competitors, and kill them if necessary.

Ch. 8, *Ibid.*

7   Authenticity and subordination are totally incompatible.

Ch. 9, *Ibid.*

8   A backlash may be an indication that women really have had an effect, but backlashes occur when advances have been small, before changes are sufficient to help many people. . . . It is almost as if the leaders of backlashes use the fear of change as a threat before major change has occurred.

Quoted in Introduction, *Backlash: The Undeclared War Against American Women* by Susan Faludi* *1991*

*See 3455.

2343. Patsy Takemoto Mink (1927–)

1   We self-righteously expect all others to admire us for our democracy and our traditions. We are so smug about our superiority, we fail to see our own glaring faults, such as prejudice and poverty amidst affluence.

Speech, National Association of Student Affairs Conference (Atlanta) *May 1972*

2   National security is not only building war machines to kill. National security is as much a policy of the living who prefer life over death, wellness over sickness, work over idleness, education over illiteracy, and food over hunger.

"Gazette News," *Ms.* (New York) *October 1981*

2344. Leontyne Price (1927–)

1   I think that recording is in a way much more personal than stage performance. In a theater the audience sees and hears you. So the costumes and the general *mise en scène* help you do the job, because they can see. In recording, you have to see and hear for them with the voice—which makes it much more personal.

Quoted in "Leontyne Price," *Divas: Impressions of Six Opera Superstars* by Winthrop Sargeant *1959*

2   All token blacks have the same experience. I have been pointed at as a solution to things that have not *begun* to be solved, because pointing at us token blacks eases the conscience of millions, and I think this is dreadfully wrong.

Ibid.

3   I feel that you have to rest the voice and avoid pressure for considerable periods. You have to reflect, too . . . If I do have some success, I'd like to try to enjoy it, for heaven's sake! What is the point of having it otherwise? Everybody else gets excited, but *you're* the one who's always tired. That's not life. That's not living.

Ibid.

4   [Marian Anderson's*] vocal and other professional triumphs were only a small part of what this great diva contributed to human understanding.

Interview (1960), Cited in "Death stills voice . . . " (AP), *Seattle Post-Intelligencer*, A9 *9 April 1993*

*See 1821.

2345. Lillian Ross (1927–)

1   Good will was stamped on the faces of all, but there was no indication as to whom or what it was directed toward. As they entered, the guests exchanged quick glances, as though they were assuring each other and themselves that they were there.

Ch. 1, *Picture 1952*

2   His name was not engraved on a brass plate on his door; it was typed on a white card placed in a slot, from which it could easily be removed.

Ch. 3, *Ibid.*

2346. Vera C. Rubin (1927?–)

1   I returned to the subject of my Master's thesis, which had been believed by very few astronomers. But now I obtained my own data to look for large scale motions in the universe. This paper was also believed by very few, but the subject became a major branch of extragalactic astronomy a few years later.

"Motion of the Galaxy and the Local Group Determined from the Velocity Anisotropy of Distant Sc I Galaxies," *Astrophysical Journal* 289: 81 : 687 and 719 *1976*

2   I discovered from observations . . . that in the single disk of this galaxy, half the stars orbit clockwise, and half the stars orbit counterclockwise, both systems intermingled.

"Cospatial Counterrotating Stellar Disks in the Virgo . . . ,"with J. A. Graham and J. P. D. Kennedy, *Astrophysical Journal* 394: L9-L12 *1992*

2347. Una Stannard (1927–)

1   Woman's mask of beauty is the face of the child, a revelation of the tragic sexual immaturity of both sexes in our culture.

"The Mask of Beauty," *Woman in Sexist Society*, Vivian Gornick* and Barbara Moran, eds. *1971*

*See 2594.

2   Woman officially lost her head in Judeo-Christian cultures in Genesis 3, interestingly enough, for trying to acquire knowledge, for which sin God decided that a woman's head was good for nothing since it only got men into trouble.

Mrs. Man 1977

3   . . . wives are a dying breed.

Ibid.

4   Freud, living at a time when women were proving their heads were no different from men's, substituted the penis for the head as the organ of male superiority, an organ women could never prove they had.

Ibid.

2348. Arie P. Taylor (1927/28–)

1   When men restrict who can fight and die for America, they restrict who can run America.*

Letter to Sara Hammel, *Women Cross Generations to Talk About Family, Work, Sex, Love and the Future of Feminism*, Anna Bondoc and Meg Daly, eds. *1999*

*In response to being asked why women would choose to be in combat.

2349. Lillian Vernon (1927–)

1 Mail order is truly an American business.

Ch. 1, *An Eye for Winners* 1996

2 I maintain that the occasional honest outburst isn't a bad way to manage. . . . Risk brings entrepreneurs close to their emotional edge, and they find themselves beset with anxieties. An eruption, caused by even the smallest thing going wrong, is a natural release.

Ch. 6, Ibid.

3 Here is where some entrepreneurs fail. They are filled with creative juices and total commitment to their business, but too often they don't understand that they must also be managers, administrators, even gofers—at least for a while.

Afterword, Ibid.

2350. Jane Wagner (1927–)

1 LILY.* One thing I have no worry about is whether
God exists.
But it has occurred to me that God has Alzheimer's and has forgotten
we exist.

Pt. 1, *The Search for Signs of Intelligent Life in the Universe* 1986

*Lily Tomlin; see 2654.

2 KATE. I am sick of being the victim of trends I reflect
but don't even understand.

Ibid.

3 TRUDY. See, it's not so much what we know,
but how we know, and what
it is about us that needs to know.
The intriguing part: Of all the things we've learned, we still haven't learned
where did this desire to want to know come from?

Pt. II, Ibid.

2351. Doreen Gandy Wiley (1927–)

1 The feet of the enemy march like thunder. Swift as lightning, they deliver overwhelming change. The familiar is transformed into something strange, threatening. . . . This is not real. This is not real. As in a bad dream, the dreamer asks, "When will it end?" When will it end? A litany in the mass mind of a conquered people.

Fires of Survival 1994

2352. Lynn Caine (1927–1987)

1 Our society is set up so that most women lose their identities when their husbands die.

Widow 1974

2 After my husband died, I felt like one of those spiraled shells washed up on the beach . . . Poke a straw through the twisting tunnel, around and around, and there is nothing there. No flesh. No life. Whatever lived there is dried up and gone.

Ibid.

3 "Widow" is a harsh and hurtful word. It comes from the Sanskrit and it means "empty." I have been empty too long.

Ibid.

2353. Maya Angelou (1928–)

1 Of all the needs (there are none imaginary) a lonely child has, the one that must be satisfied, if there is going to be hope and a hope of wholeness, is the unshaking need for an unshakable God.

Ch. 4, *I Know Why the Caged Bird Sings* 1969

2 She said that I must always be intolerant of ignorance but understanding of illiteracy. That some people, unable to go to school, were more educated and even more intelligent than college professors. She encouraged me to listen carefully to what country people called mother wit. That in those homely sayings was couched the collective wisdom of generations.

Ch. 15, Ibid.

3 Children's talent to endure stems from their ignorance of alternatives.

Ch. 17, Ibid.

4 I find it interesting that the meanest life, the poorest existence, is attributed to God's will, but as human beings become more affluent, as their living standard and style begin to ascend the material scale, God descends the scale of responsibility at a commensurate speed.

Ch. 18, Ibid.

5 The needs of a society determine its ethics, and in the Black American ghettos the hero is that man who is offered only the crumbs from his country's table but by ingenuity and courage is able to take for himself a Lucullan feast.

Ch. 29, Ibid.

6 The fact that the adult American Negro female emerges a formidable character is often met with amazement, distaste and even belligerence. It is seldom accepted as an inevitable outcome of the struggle won by survivors, and deserves respect if not enthusiastic acceptance.

Ch. 34, Ibid.

7 Then the question began to live under my blankets: How did lesbianism begin? What were the symptoms? The public library gave information on the finished lesbian—and that woefully sketchy—but on the growth of a lesbian, there was nothing. I did discover that the difference between hermaphrodites and lesbians was that hermaphrodites were "born that way." It was impossible to determine whether lesbians budded gradually, or burst into being with a suddenness that dismayed them as much as it repelled society.

Ch. 35, Ibid.

8 My life has been one great big joke,
A dance that's walked
A song that's spoke,
I laugh so hard I almost choke
When I think about myself.

"When I Think About Myself," *Just Give Me a Cool Drink of Water 'fore I Diiie* 1971

9 For Africa to me . . . is more than a glamorous fact. It is a historical truth. No man can know where he is going unless he knows exactly where he has been and exactly how he arrived at his present place.

Quoted in *The New York Times* 16 April 1972

10 A textured guilt was my familiar, my bed mate to whom I had turned my back. My daily companion whose hand I would not hold. The Christian teaching dinned into my ears. . . .

Preface, *Gather Together in My Name* 1974

11 We had won. Pimps got out of their polished cars and walked the streets of San Francisco only a little uneasy at the unusual

exercise. Gamblers, ignoring their sensitive fingers, shook hands with shoeshine boys. . . . Beauticians spoke to the shipyard workers, who in turn spoke to the easy ladies. . . . I thought if war did not include killing, I'd like to see one every year. Something like a festival.

Prologue, Ibid.

12 "I probably couldn't learn to cook creole food, anyway. It's too complicated."

"Sheeit. Ain't nothing but onions, green peppers and garlic. Put that in everything and you got creole food."

Ch. 3, Ibid.

13 Self-pity in its early stage is as snug as a feather mattress. Only when it hardens does it become uncomfortable.

Ch. 6, Ibid.

14 "You a cherry, ain't you?"

"Yes." Lying would get me nothing.

"Well, that's a thirty-second business. When you turn the first trick, you'll be a 'ho. A stone 'ho. I mean for life. . . . I'm a damn good one. I'm a mud kicker. In the street I make more money by accident than most bitches make on purpose."

Ch. 27, Ibid.

15 Separate from my boundaries, I had not known before that he had and would have a life beyond being my son, my pretty baby, my cute doll, my charge. In the plowed farmyard near Bakersfield, I began to understand the uniqueness of the person. He was three and I was nineteen, and never again would I think of him as a beautiful appendage of myself.

Ch. 29, Ibid.

16 As far as I knew white women were never lonely, except in books. White men adored them, Black men desired them and Black women worked for them.

Ch. 1, *Singin' and Swingin' and Gettin' Merry Like Christmas* 1976

17 A bizarre sensation pervades a relationship of pretense. No truth seems true. A simple morning's greeting and response appear loaded with innuendo and fraught with implications. . . . Each nicety becomes more sterile and each withdrawal more permanent.

Ch. 5, Ibid.

18 Oh, the holiness of always being the injured party. The historically oppressed can find not only sanctity but safety in the state of victimization. When access to a better life has been denied often enough, and successfully enough, one can use the rejection as an excuse to cease all efforts.

Ch. 9, Ibid.

19 There is a very fine line between loving life and being greedy for it.

Interview, *Black Scholar January–February 1977*

20 While the rest of the world has been improving technology, Ghana has been improving the quality of man's humanity to man.

Interview, "Involvement in Black and White," *Oregonian* (Portland, 17 February 1971), *Conversations with Maya Angelou 1989*

21 The white American man makes the white American woman maybe not superfluous but just a little kind of decoration. Not really important to turning around the wheels of the state. Well the black American woman has never been able to

feel that way. No black American man at any time in our history in the United States has been able to feel that he didn't need that black woman right against him, shoulder to shoulder—in that cotton field, on the auction block, in the ghetto, wherever.

Interview, "A Conversation with Maya Angelou" (21 November 1973), Ibid.

22 The sadness of the women's movement is that they don't allow the necessity of love. See, I don't personally trust any revolution where love is not allowed.

"Listening to Maya Angelou" (*California Living,* 14 May 1975), Ibid.

23 Life loves the liver of it.

"The Black Scholar Interviews Maya Angelou" (January–February 1977), Ibid.

24 I love to see a young girl go out and grab the world by the lapels. Life's a bitch. You've got to go out and kick ass.

Interview, "Kicking Ass," *Girl About Town* (13 October 1986), Ibid.

25 There's a world of difference between truth and facts. Facts can obscure the truth.

Quoted in *I Dream a World* by Brian Lanker 1989

26 We allow our ignorance to prevail upon us and make us think we can survive alone, alone in patches, alone in groups, alone in races, even alone in genders.

Address to Centenary College of Louisiana, Reported in *The New York Times 11 March 1990*

27 You, created only a little lower than
the angels, have crouched too long in
The bruising darkness.
Have lain too long
Face down in ignorance.
Your mouths spilling words

Armed for slaughter.
The Rock cries out today, you may stand on me,
But do not hide your face.

"A Rock, A River, A Tree"* Sts. 3–4, *On The Pulse of Morning* 1993

*Commissioned for the inaugural of President William J. Clinton (20 January 1993).

28 History, despite its wrenching pain,
Cannot be unlived, and if faced
With courage, need not be lived again.

Sts. 9–10, Ibid.

29 Lift up your eyes upon
The day breaking for you.
Give birth again
To the dream.

Ibid.

30 When you learn, teach.
When you get, give.
As for me,

I shall not be moved.

"Our Grandmothers" (1990), *The Woman That I Am, The Literature and Culture of Contemporary Women of Color*, D. Soyini Madison, ed. 1994

31 No one, no, nor no one million
   ones dare deny me God. I go forth
   alone, and stand as ten thousand.

   The Divine upon my right
   impels me to pull forever
   at the latch on Freedom's gate.

                                          Ibid.

32 The night has been long,
   The wound has been deep,
   The pit has been dark,
   And the walls have been steep.
   "A poem from the Million Man March,"

                                    * Refrain *n.d.*

   *Held 16 October 1995 in Washington, D.C.

33 Dressing in purples and pinks and greens
   Exotic as rum and Cokes
   Living our lives with flash and style
   Ain't we colorful folks?

                              "Ain't That Bad?" *n.d.*

34 Televised news turns
   a half-used day into
   a waste of desolation.

                              "Televised," St. 1 *n.d.*

35 You dwell in whitened castles
   with deep and poisoned moats
   and cannot hear the curses
   which fill your children's throats.

                  "These Yet to be United States," St. 2 *n.d.*

36 You may write me down in history
   With your bitter, twisted lies,
   You may trod me in the very dirt
   But still, like dust, I'll rise.

                              "Still I Rise," St. 1 *n.d.*

37 Does my sexiness upset you?
   Does it come as a surprise
   That I dance like I've got diamonds
   At the meeting of my thighs?

                                          St. 7, Ibid.

38 When we come to it
   We must confess that we are the possible
   We are the miraculous, the true wonders of this world
   That is when, and only when
   We come to it.

                              "A Brave and Startling Truth," l.l. *n.d.*

2354. Shirley Temple Back (1928–)

1 Our whole way of life today is dedicated to the *removal of risk*. Cradle to grave we are supported, insulated, and isolated from the risks of life—and if we fall, our government stands ready with Band-Aids of every size.

   Speech, Kiwanis International Convention, Texas (June 1967), Quoted in *The Sinking of the Lollipop* by Rodney G. Minott *1968*

2 Won't the new "Suggested for Mature Audience" protect our youngsters from such films? I don't believe so. I know many forty-five-year-old men with the mentalities of six-year-olds, and my feeling is that they should not see such pictures, either.

   Quoted in *McCall's* (New York) *January 1967*

3 No country has washed more dirty laundry in public than we have.

   Quoted in *American Political Women* by Esther Stineman *1980*

4 I stopped believing in Santa Claus when I was six. Mother took me to see him in a department store and he asked for my autograph.

   Quoted in *Halliwell's Filmgoer's Companion* by Leslie Halliwell *1984*

5 I was very sophisticated when I was 17. When I was 14, I was the oldest I ever was.

   Quoted in "What Do You Do After You've Been Shirley Temple?" by Dotson Rader, *Parade Magazine* *7 December 1986*

6 One has to handle these negative experiences alone.* You can't get help from your friends and family. You're finally alone with it, and you have to come to grips with the misfortune and go on.

                                          Ibid.

   *Reference to her mastectomy.

2355. Antonia Brenner (1928–)

1 The Lord was a prisoner, just as you are a prisoner. You have something in common.

   Comment to a prisoner, Quoted in "She Brings Hope to Prisoners" by Arnie Weissman, *Parade Magazine* *19 January 1986*

2 I lived what most people call the good life. I was happy, but deep inside I always felt that, with the short amount of time we are given to live and love in this world, we spend too much time loving things instead of people.

                                          Ibid.

3 I love America, but charity knows no border.

                                          Ibid.

2356. Anita Brookner (1928–)

1 I shall settle down now. I shall have to, for I doubt if I have anything more to look forward to.

   Hotel du Lac 1984

2 [She went to a] quiet hotel . . . in which she could be counted upon to retrieve her serious and hard-working personality and to forget the unfortunate lapse which had led to this brief exile.

                                          Ibid.

3 She was a handsome woman of forty-five and would remain so for many years.

                                          Ch. 4, Ibid.

4 Good women always think it is their fault when someone else is being offensive. Bad women never take the blame for anything.

                                          Ch. 7, Ibid.

5 You have no idea how promising the world begins to look once you have decided to have it all for yourself. And how much healthier your decisions are once they become entirely selfish.

                                          Ibid.

6 The lessons taught in great books are misleading. The commerce in life is rarely so simple and never so just.

   Novelists in Interview, John Haffenden, ed. *1985*

7 There are moments when you feel free, moments when you have energy, moments when you have hope, but you can't rely on any of these things to see you through. Circumstances do that.
                                                                    Ibid.

8 Writing novels preserves you in a state of innocence—a lot passes you by—simply because your attention is otherwise diverted.
                                                                    Ibid.

9 Great writers are the saints for the godless.
                                                                    Ibid.

10 Like many rich men, he thought in anecdotes; like many simple women, she thought in terms of biography.
                                              Ch. 1, *The Misalliance 1986*

11 Time misspent in youth is sometimes all the freedom one ever has.
                                                        Ch. 10, Ibid.

12 Women don't sit at home any more, you know, dreaming of Prince Charming. They don't do it because they've found out that he doesn't exist. As you should have found out. I live in the real world, the world of deceptions. You live in the world of illusions.
                                              A Friend from England 1987

13 One thought of her not exactly as a woman but as some sort of animal known for its unassuming qualities, a heifer, perhaps.
                                                                    Ibid.

14 I had resolved at a very early stage never to be reduced to any form of emotional beggary, never to plead, never to impose guilt, and never to consider the world well lost for love. I think of myself as a plain dealer and I am rather proud of the honesty of my transactions.
                                                                    Ibid.

15 A man of such obvious and exemplary charm must be a liar.
                                                        Ch. 3, Ibid.

16 The essence of romantic love is that wonderful beginning, after which sadness and impossibility may become the rule.
                                                        Ch. 10, Ibid.

17 It will be a pity if women in the more conventional mould are to be phased out, for there will never be anyone to go home to.
                                                                    Ibid.

18 No blame should attach to telling the truth. But it does, it does.
                                                                    Ibid.

19 What is interesting about self-analysis is that it leads nowhere—it is an art form in itself.
                              Interview, *Writers at Work* (Eighth Series),
                                      George Plimpton,* ed. *1988*
*American writer and editor (1927–).

20 Existentialism is about being a saint without God; being your own hero, without all the sanction and support of religion or society.
                                                                    Ibid.

21 All good fortune is a gift of the gods, and . . . you don't win the favor of the ancient gods by being good, but by being *bold*.
                                                                    Ibid.

22 Accountability in friendship is the equivalent of love without strategy.
                                Women Writers Talk, Olga Kenyon, ed. *1989*

23 Romanticism is not just a mode; it literally eats into every life. Women will never get rid of just waiting for the right man.
                                                                    Ibid.

24 Real love is a pilgrimage. It happens when there is no strategy, but it is very rare because most people are strategists.
                                                                    Ibid.

25 Always let them think of you as singing and dancing.
                                                            Dolly 1993

26 . . . slender pillars of English virtue.
                                                                    Ibid.

27 . . . explanations for absence that were infinitely more mystifying than the truth would have been. . . .
                                                        Altered States 1996

28 . . . there are no rewards, and few consolations.
                                                                    Ibid.

29 For a moment I wondered what [my aunts] were doing at Angela's wedding, until I remembered that it was my wedding as well.
                                                                    Ibid.

30 All that was left was for them to find some middle way, between acceptance and defeat.
                                                            Visitors 1997

31 There must be some consolation for being an onlooker. The role is not always an enviable one.
                                                        Falling Slowly 1998

2357. Barbara B. Brown (1928–)

1 The critical and quite new element that biofeedback brings to medical and psychologic therapeutics is the capacity to manipulate one's own body (and mind) by one's own mind. The implications of this newly discovered capacity are enormous. The uses are obvious, but the misuses are not obvious at all.
                          *New Mind, New Body, Bio-Feedback: New Directions
                                                    for the Mind 1974*

2 Inner misery does not officially qualify for the curing magic of the healing arts. Yet we are not well at all.
                                  Prologue, *Between Health and Illness 1974*

3 Stress is a phenomenon generated almost exclusively by society's mad pace of the twentieth century. Diminished well being is the social Pac-Man that devours coping and psychic energy and inner strength. Before it wins the game of our lives, it needs some serious, sober attention.
                                                                    Ibid.

2358. Mary Daly (1928–)

1 It is the creative potential itself in human beings that is the image of God.
                                      Ch. 1, *Beyond God the Father 1973*

2 . . . "God's plan" is often a front for men's plans and a cover for inadequacy, ignorance and evil.
                                                                    Ibid.

3 If God is male, then male is God. The divine patriarch castrates women as long as he is allowed to live on in the human imagination.

Ibid.

4 The becoming of androgynous human persons implies a radical change in the fabric of human consciousness and in styles of human behavior.

Ibid.

5 People attempt to overcome the threat of nonbeing by denying the self. The outcome of this is ironic: that which is dreaded triumphs, for we are caught in the self-contradictory bind of shrinking our being to avoid nonbeing.

Ibid.

6 Courage to be is the key to the revelatory power of the feminist revolution.

Ibid.

7 . . . tokenism does not change stereotypes of social systems but works to preserve them, since it dulls the revolutionary impulse.

Ibid.

8 Why indeed must "God" be a noun? Why not a verb—the most active and dynamic of all.

Ch. 2, Ibid.

9 It is not good enough to talk about evil abstractly while lending implicit support to traditional images that legitimate specific social evils.

Ibid.

10 The image of Mary as Virgin, moreover, has an (unintended) aspect of pointing to independence for women. This aspect of the symbol is of course generally unnoticed by theologians.

Ch. 3, Ibid.

11 Sexist society maintains its grasp over the psyche by keeping it divided against itself.

Ch. 4, Ibid.

12 . . . we will look upon the earth and her sister planets as being *with* us, not for us. One does not rape a sister.

Ch. 6, Ibid.

13 I had explained that a woman's asking for equality in the church would be comparable to a black person's demanding equality in the Ku Klux Klan.

"New Autobiographical Preface" (1968), *The Church and the Second Sex 1975*

14 The liberation of language is rooted in the liberation of ourselves.

Ibid.

15 Phallic lust is seen as a fusion of obsession and aggression. As obsession it specializes in genital fixation and fetishism, causing broken consciousness, broken heartedness, broken connections among women and between women and the elements. As aggression it rapes, dismembers, and kills women and all living things within its reach. Phallic lust begets phallocratic society, that is sadosociety, which is, in fact, pseudo-society.

Introduction, *Pure Lust 1984*

16 Elemental female Lust is intense longing/craving for the cosmic concrescence that is creation. It is charged, tense, in tension with the tenses of fabricated "father time." Incensed, it burns through the shallow impressions of insipid senses, sensing the Sources, Astral Forces, Angels and Graces that call from the Deep. This Lusting is divining: foreseeing, foretelling, forecasting. Unlike the dim divines and divinities, the deadheads of deadlands whose ill-illuminations blind us, Lusty women portend with luster, our radiance from within that radiates from and toward Original Powers of creation.

Ibid.

17 The tidiness inflicted upon women, together with orders to impose this torture upon each other, combine to produce a climate of tidy torture.

Ch. 8, Ibid.

18 Even if there were only one or two men with 20 women [in a classroom], the young women would be constantly on an overt or a subliminal level giving their attention to the men because they've been socialized to nurse men.

Quoted in "Let men into class or quit, ultra-feminist professor told" by Robin Estrin (AP), *Seattle Post-Intelligencer 26 February 1999*

2359. Takako Doi (1928–)

1 The people are aware of how politics affects their daily life. It's the politicians who are behind the times.

Quoted in "A Mountain Moves" by Jill Smolowe, *Time* (New York) *7 August 1989*

2360. Muriel Fox (1928–)

1 Women and men have to fight together to change society—and both will benefit. We [her husband and herself] are strongly pro-marriage. I think it is a grave mistake for young girls to think that it has to be a career versus marriage, equality versus love. Partnership, not dependence, is the real romance in marriage.

Quoted in "Wait Late to Marry" by Barbara Jordan Moore, *New Woman October 1971*

2 Total commitment to family and total commitment to career is possible, but fatiguing.

Ibid.

3 I realize that what happened to my mother was very wrong. She got pigeonholed in the wrong job. That job was housewife. She hated it and was a tragically inefficient housekeeper. There was no valid reason why she should have got stuck in that job when she could have filled many others with distinction.

Ibid.

4 While you don't need a formal written contract before you get married, I think it's important for both partners to spell out what they expect from each other . . . . There are always plenty of surprises—and lots of give and take—once you're married.

Ibid.

2361. Griselda Gambaro (1928–)

1 FUNCTIONARY. Art is all that deserves to last—lofty sentiments, things and beings coming to life. You haven't smashed the doll so as to assure that there will be beauty in the world, order. In a word: so the trees can keep growing and putting forth new leaves, so the earth does not become a desolate wasteland.

The Walls (Las Paredes), Marguerite Feitlowitz, tr. *1964*

2 LORENZO (a Siamese twin). What happens in operations like these, is that they can't save them both. One of them is ruined. In order to leave one of them in perfect condition, they have to ruin the other. They have to.

The Siamese Twins (Los siameses) 1965

3 LORENZO. But who is capable of distinguishing between us? I can't. We're the same. That's our tragedy. We're so similar that our actions become confused.

Ibid.

4 ANTÍGONA. Let the laws, these vile laws! drag me to a grave that will be my tomb. No one will hear my weeping; no one will be aware of my suffering. They will live in the light as though nothing were happening. . . . I will be . . . uncounted among the living and among the dead. I will disappear from the world, alive.

Antígona Furiosa 1986

5 Through balkanization, regimes are able to employ horror and fear. The fact that everybody is isolated helps the purpose of any dictatorship. Every dictatorship is based on that principle. One starts being afraid of one's shadow.

"Griselda Gambaro," Albert Minero, tr.,
Interviews with Contemporary Women Playwrights,
Kathleen Betsko *and Rachel Koenig
1987

*See 2739.

6 . . . What feminism means is to change our optic, our vision, which means we must also change our ethics.

Ibid.

7 Theater is very much connected with the society, with the social situation. . . . A theater piece, of itself, demands a confrontation with an audience. It demands that you connect with other people; it demands a collective and social effort with the company and later with the audience.

Ibid.

8 This is a schizophrenic country, a country that lives two lives. The courteous and generous have their counterpart in the violent and the armed who move among the shadows . . . One never really knows what country one is living in, because the two co-exist . . .

Quoted in "Two Argentine Writers" by
Marguerite Feitlowitz, *Bomb*, No. 32 *Summer 1990*

2362. Shoshana Kalisch (1928?–)

1 These songs became a witnessing message, a means to express sorrow and to give courage and hope. It's a personal matter to me. Somehow I could not free myself until I sang songs of the Holocaust.*

Quoted in "Raising her Voice" by Janet Wallfisch
(p. G–3), *Times-Picayune* (New Orleans)
1 May 1988

*The genocide of European Jews and others by the Nazis during World War II.

2 I realized that refusing to look [at those being marched to the gas chamber] would have been tantamount to abandoning these human beings during their last hours. And so, every evening at roll call in Auschwitz, we [her sister, Nany] shared with our eyes and hearts the fate of those about to die.

Ibid.

2363. Joan Kelly-Gadol (1928–)

1 . . . there was no renaissance for women—at least not during the Renaissance.

"Did Women Have a Renaissance?" *Becoming Visible:
Women in European History*, Renate Bridenthal and
Claudia Koonz, eds. *1976*

2 What emerges [in historic perspective] is a fairly regular pattern of relative loss of status for women precisely in those periods of so-called progressive change.

"The Social Relation of the Sexes: Methodological Implications of Women's History," *Signs: A Journal of Women in
Culture and Society*, Vol. 1 *1976*

2364. Eva Clara Keuls (1928–)

1 Like a slave, a woman [in classical Athenian society] had virtually no protection under the law except in so far as she was the property of a man. She was, in fact, not a person under the law. The dominance of male over female was as complete during the period in question as that of master over slave.

*The Reign of the Phallus: Sexual Politics in
Ancient Athens 1993*

2 The governing principle in a phallocracy is that the human race is essentially male, the female being a mere adjunct, unfortunately required for the purpose of reproduction. The natural consequence of this notion is the elimination of the female from all social processes.

Ibid.

3 Rape is the ultimate translation of phallicism into action. Rape is committed not for pleasure or procreation, but in order to enact the principle of domination by means of sex.

Ibid.

2365. Rita Liljestrom (1928–)

1 What good does it do to treat women and men alike if the whole system is permeated by a male culture? If all of society's prioritized values rest on a collective male consciousness, then what is equality but assimilation in the dominant culture?

Quoted in *Sisterhood is Global*, Robin Morgan,* ed. *1984*
*See 2864.

2366. Cynthia Macdonald (1928–)

1 You genuflect?
Have you forgotten I was Jewish?
That made my heavenly Father Jewish,
Mary and Joseph, too.

"Jesus Returns," *I Can't Remember 1997*

2 You think the way I speak is not poetic,
no sweeping phrases? Remember I must use the language of today.

Ibid.

3 What is in back of the back?
Pleasure hidden behind flesh.

"Mary Cassatt's* Twelve Hours in the Pleasure Quarter:
Woman Bathing," Ibid.
*See 1094.

4 My working methods are to sit on my tail till inspiration,
that horsefly, bites. Then if I can, to throw the buzz away
and keep the path of flight.

"Poet-Chicken Answers," Ibid.

5   Jingle words like coins, the change,
        or covering
    for dead eyes. Fingers fiddle. Don't
        pick.
    How many times have I told you not to?
    Don't pick. But can choose.
                    "The Weekend He Died," Ibid.

6   She hangs in Dresden.
    Perhaps she is a sibyl reading of the
        firebombing
    three hundred years hence, of the light
    that caused flashcars, flashparks,
        flashpeople
    to run, burning . . .
              "Vermeer's* Lady Reading at an Open Window," Ibid.
    *Jan V— (a.s.a. van der Meer), Dutch painter (1632–1675).

7   . . . stone yields
    the language everyone
    understands but no one speaks.

    There are statues celebrating
    family life: stone mothers holding
    babies stirring pots, stone fathers
    tossing balls to sons, stone lovers
    reading Il Paradiso, releasing

    their tears only in the rain . . .
                "What No One Should Want to Have," Ibid.

2367. Jeanne Moreau (1928–)

1   Success is like a liberation or the first phase of a love story. . . .
            Quoted in "Jeanne Moreau," The Egotists by
                    Oriana Fallaci* 1963
    *See 2416.

2   I don't think success is harmful, as so many people say. Rather,
    I believe it indispensable to talent, if for nothing else than to
    increase the talent.
                            Ibid.

3   I have always liked things that are difficult, I have always had
    the urge to open forbidden doors, with a curiosity and an ob-
    stinancy that verge on masochism.
                            Ibid.

4   For me it's not possible to forget, and I don't understand peo-
    ple who, when the love is ended, can bury the other person in
    hatred or oblivion. For me, a man I have loved becomes a kind
    of brother.
                            Ibid.

5   Acting deals with very delicate emotions. It is not putting up a
    mask. Each time an actor acts he does not hide; he exposes
    himself.
                        The New York Times 30 June 1976

6   When people are alive, they have many deaths: not only cow-
    ards die a million deaths. What is incredible about existence is
    its toughness in extremity.
                    Quoted in "Profiles: A Sense of Dream" by
                    Penelope Gilliatt,* The New Yorker 13 March 1978
    *See 2493.

7   Mystery is a taste that we have lost, but it will come back. Maybe
    the longing to see the naked body is a longing to know every-

thing about someone. But you find then that the body itself is a
cover. That's the reason the way one is dressed has meaning.
                            Ibid.

8   Some people are addicts. If they don't act, they don't exist.
            International Herald Tribune (Paris) 15 November 1989

2368. Thea Musgrave (1928–)

1   Music is a human art, not a sexual one. Sex is no more impor-
    tant than eye color.
            Quoted in "A Matter of Art, Not Sex," Time (New York)
                        10 November 1975

2369. Anna Maria Ortese (1928?–)

1   It was the easiest and at the same time the most sinister thing
    possible that was happening to me: when one thing recalls an-
    other, and so on, till your present vanishes, and everything
    before you is purely past, the echo of a life that was more real
    than this one.
                    "The Lights of Genoa," Italian Writing Today,
                        Raleigh Trevelyna, ed. 1967

2   I was searching for a piece of luggage that seemed to have been
    mislaid, as my own life had for some time seem slightly mis-
    laid. . . .
                            Ibid.

3   . . . in order to feel anything you need strength. . . .
                            Ibid.

4   I felt desolate at the thought of the inevitable rudeness or rau-
    cousness that, in Rome or to some extent anywhere else, greets
    anyone who is lost and stops someone to ask the way.
                            Ibid.

5   People were alone, and at the same time never alone, at least
    not in the terrible way you are in Milan and in Rome, where,
    if you aren't socially eminent or rich or important, others sim-
    ply don't notice you, and if you're ill you could be thrown out
    with the rubbish . . .
                            Ibid.

2370. Cynthia Ozick (1928/31–)

1   He had once demonstrated that, since God had made the world,
    and since there was no God, the world in all logic could not exist.
                        Pt. I, Ch. 1, Trust 1966

2   It is true that money attracts; but much money repels.
                        Ch. 7, Ibid.

3   "He knows nothing about literature—most great writers
    don't; all they know is life."
                        Pt. III, Ch. 1, Ibid.

4   Superfluity, excess of custom, and superstition would climb
    like a choking vine on the Fence of the Law if skepticism did
    not continually hack them away to make freedom for purity.
                    "The Pagan Rabbi" (1966), The Pagan Rabbi
                        and Other Stories 1971

5   " . . . Paradise is only for those who have already been there."
                    "Envy; or, Yiddish in America" (1969), Ibid.

6   It was the old recurrent groan of life. It was the sound of na-
    ture turning on its hinge. Everyone had a story to tell him.

What resentments, what hatreds, what bitterness, how little good will!

"The Doctor's Wife" (1971), Ibid.

7 The usefulness of madmen is famous: they demonstrate society's logic flagrantly carried out down to its last scrimshaw scrap.

"The Hole/Birth Catalog," *The First Ms. Reader*,
Francine Klagsbrun, ed. *1972*

8 If the fish had stuck to its gills there would have been no movement up to the land.

Ibid.

9 The engineering is secondary to the vision.

Ibid.

10 Wondrous hole! Magical hole! Dazzlingly influential hole! Noble and effulgent hole! From this hole everything follows logically: first the baby, then the placenta, then, for years and years and years until death, a way of life. It is all logic, and she who lives by the hole will live also by its logic. It is, appropriately, logic with a hole in it.

Ibid.

11 Judaism has no dying god, no embalming of dead bodies, above all no slightest version of death-instinct—"Choose life."

Ibid.

12 Language makes culture, and we make a rotten culture when we abuse words.

"We Are the Crazy Lady and Other Feisty Feminist Fables,"
Ibid.

13 Moral: In saying what is obvious, never choose cunning. Yelling works better.

Ibid.

14 I'm not afraid of facts, I welcome facts *but a congeries of facts is not equivalent to an idea*. This is the essential fallacy of the so-called "scientific" mind. People who mistake facts for ideas are incomplete thinkers; they are gossips.

Ibid.

15 [The writer is like a] a beast howling inside a coal-furnace, heaping the coals on itself to increase the fire.

Writers at Work (Eighth Series), George Plimpton,* ed. *1988*
*American writer and editor (1927–).

16 After a certain number of years our faces become our biographies. We get to be responsible for our faces.

Ibid.

17 Summer without end, a mistake!

The Shawl 1989

18 Because she fears the past she distrusts the future—it, too, will turn into the past. As a result she has nothing.

Ibid.

19 . . . coiled in the bottommost pit of every driven writer is an impersonator—protean, volatile, restless, and relentless.

Fame and Folley: Essays 1996

20 A novel is like the physicist's premise of an expanding universe . . . a play is just the reverse.

"Old Hand as Novice," Ibid.

21 . . . real apprenticeship is ultimately always to the self.

Ibid.

22 Her heart beat for law, even for tax law.

The Puttermesser Papers 1997

23 . . . it was possible for brains to break the heart.

Ibid.

24 [T]he brain is the seat of the emotions . . .

Ibid.

25 It happens that in the several seconds before we die, the well of the ribs opens, and a crystal pebble is thrown in; then there is a distant tiny splash, no more than the chirp of a droplet. This seeming pebble is the earthly equal of what astrophysicists call a black hole—a dead sun that has collapsed into itself, shrinking from density to deeper density, until it is smaller than the period at the end of this sentence. Until it is less than infinitesimal.

"Puttermesser in Paradise," Ibid.

26 Joyce's Molly rejoicing. Bellow fanning fire, Updike fingering apertures, Oates wildly sowing, Roth wroth. And so on.*

Ibid.

*James Joyce, Irish writer (1882–1941); Saul Bellow, Canadian-born American writer (1915–); Joyce Carol Oates (see 2722); Philip Roth, American novelist (1933).

27 . . . dying, even agonized dying, generates its own amnesia.

Ibid.

28 Paradise is a dream bearing the inscription on Solomon's seal: *This, too, will pass.*

Ibid.

29 His intelligence was a version of cynicism. He rolled irony like an extra liquid in his mouth.

Quoted by John Leonard in "Amazing Grace," *The Nation*
(New York) *11 May 1998*

2371. Franca Rame (1928/9–)

1 MOTHER. I went to see the corpse of one of those young policemen murdered by my son's comrades. Yes, I went to the funeral parlor. Because it's too easy to complain about things if you don't see them at first-hand.

La Madre 1983

2 WIFE (to audience). "Listen Luigi," I said, "You get mad about how nobody pays you for your traveling time but what about me? Do I get paid for all the working and slaving I do at home? No I do not. And believe you me everything I do here is for the multinational, oh yes! . . . We recondition you, regenerate you . . . reproduce you! And all for free!"

"Waking Up," *Orgasmo Adulto Escapes from the Zoo*
(a.k.a. *Female Parts*, Olwen Wymark, tr., 1981),
Estelle Parsons, tr. *1983*
*American stage and screen actor (1927–).

3 PROLOGUE. Beautiful, no? Man elevated his member to his image and likeness. It is him, his thing, his power . . . the power assoluto! If we think a little, the world does not revolve around the United States . . . or Russia: The world revolves around the Grand Phallsa! The real tiger, not the paper one, is what is it! Notwithstanding its modest proportions . . .

Prologue, Ibid.

2372. Agnes Varda (1928–)

1 You ask me, is it difficult to be a woman director? I'd say that it's difficult to be a director, period! It's difficult to be free; it's

difficult not to be drowned in the system. It's difficult for women, and it's difficult for men, the same way.

> Quoted in an "Interview with Agnes Varda" by
> Barbara Confino, *Saturday Review* 12 August 1972

2 The image of woman is crucial, and in the . . . movies that image is always switching between the nun and the whore, the mama and the bitch. We have put up with that for years, and it has to be changed. It is the image that is important, not so much who is making the film.

> Ibid.

2372.1 Ruth Westheimer (1928–)

1 If you love to eat steak, you still wouldn't want to eat it every night for dinner, even if you didn't like the other foods as much. Why? Because if you ate steak every day, you'd become bored with it and there would come a time you'd never want to eat it again. The same effect can happen with sex, which is why it is good to throw in some variety, even if only once in a while.

> Dr. Ruth www.drruth.com/ 1997

2 Today we do know that from a scientific point of view that for many women masturbation is the best way for them to learn how to give themselves permission to have an orgasm.

> Ibid.

3 I don't believe that science has proved the existence of male menopause, but if it did exist, my philosophy would be the same as for femal menopause: You should do everything possible not to let your body dictate your actions.

You can either give in to negative feelings or fight them, and I'm of the belief that you should fight them. To risk wrecking a marriage because you allow some supposed chemical change to rule your life is just not worth it!

> Ibid.

4 Considering that I was to become famous as an advocate of contraception, it's somewhat ironic that my parents didn't use it at precisely the point when they should have.

> Ibid.

2373. Marion Woodman (1928–)

1 As human creatures, not gods, we must go for the grey, the steady solid line that makes its serpentine way only slightly to left and right down the middle course between the opposites
And that's the differential ego, whether male or female, cutting a course between wind and water.

> Ch. 1, *Addiction to Perfection, The Still Unravished Bride* 1982

2 It takes great courage to break with one's past history and stand alone

> Ch. 2, Ibid.

3 The aim in analysis is to bring the magnificent energy of the wild horse under the control of the rider, without using a whip that will kill its spirit.

> Ch. 5, Ibid.

4 The experience of the feminine is the psychological key to both the sickness of our time and its healing.

> Ch. 7, Ibid.

5 Moreover, perfectionist standards do not allow for failure. They do not even allow for life, and certainly not for death.

> Ibid.

6 Leap—leap—remembering my journal that looks like a Beethoven manuscript—blots, blue ink, red, yellow and green, pages torn by an angry pen, smudged with tears, leaping with joy from exclamation marks to dashes that speak more than the words between, my journal that dances with the heartbeat of a process in motion. How does one fashion a pipe that can contain that honesty, and be at the same time professionally credible?

> Introduction, *The Pregnant Virgin, A Process of Psychological Transformation* 1985

7 Without an understanding of myth or religion, without an understanding of the relationship between destruction and creation, death and rebirth, the individual suffers the mysteries of life as meaningless mayhem—alone.

> Ch. 1, Ibid.

8 Many people can listen to their cat more intelligently than they can listen to their own despised body. Because they attend to their pet in a cherishing way, it returns their love. Their body, however, may have to let out an earth-shattering scream in order to be heard at all.

> Ibid.

9 Rage and bitterness do not foster femininity. They harden the heart and make the body sick.

> Ch. 5, Ibid.

10 Healing depends on listening with the inner ear—stopping the incessant blather, and *listening*. Fear keeps us chattering—fear that wells up from the past, fear of blurting out what we really fear, fear of future repercussions. It is our very fear of the future that distorts the *now* that could lead to a different future if we dared to be whole in the present.

> Ch. 6, Ibid.

11 Detachment liberates the heart from the past and from the future. It gives us the freedom to be who we are, loving others for who they are. It is the leap into *now*, the stream of Being in which everything is possible. It is the domain of the pregnant virgin.

> Ibid.

12 New Year's Eve is not one of my favorite celebrations, never has been. The old year with all its surprises and disappointments, triumphs and mistakes, has become a friend—congenial, undemanding. A new year stretches ahead, fresh as white snow, pristine, perfectly void.

> "Crossing the Threshold: Fear or Feelings,"
> *The Fabric of the Future: Women Visionaries of Today Illuminate the Path to Tomorrow*,
> M.J. Ryan, ed. 1998

2374. Zong Pu (1928–)

1 "But I can't play the cello all day long. I must read some books too. Since I can't find any good ones, I'm reading these, even though they're bad. It's like food. When there's nothing delicious, I eat anything. So there!"

> Ch. 3, "Melody in Dreams," Song Shouquan, tr.,
> *Seven Contemporary Chinese Women Writers*,
> Gladys Yang,* ed. 1982

*See 245.

2 Yuejun was outraged thinking how many families had been ruined by the gang*; how many young people had been deprived of their lives. They wouldn't even leave the premier** alone. Our great hero had left nothing of himself after his

death. Even his ashes had been scattered over the mountains and rivers. Now they intended to blacken his reputation.

Ch. 4, Ibid.

*Reference to the "Gang of Four," the term of aspersion used by the Chinese authorities after the Cultural Revolution (1966–1969) to identify those held responsible for its excesses. **Mao Tse Tung (a.s.a. Mao Zedong), Chinese communist leader (1893–1976).

2375. Anne Sexton (1928–1974)

1 . . . I gather
guilt like a young intern
his symptoms, his certain evidence.

"The Double Image," *To Bedlam and Partway Back* 1960

2 love your self's self where it lives.

Ibid.

3 You, Dr. Martin,* walk from breakfast to madness.

"You, Dr. Martin," St. 1, Ibid.

*Martin Luther King, Jr., American civil rights leader, (1929–68); assassinated.

4 I am queen of all my sins forgotten. Am I still lost?

Last St., Ibid.

5 I say *Live, Live* because of the sun,
the dream, the excitable gift.

"Live," *Live or Die* 1966

6 lovers sprouting in the yard
like celery stalks . . .

Ibid.

7 Today life opened inside me like an egg. . . .

Ibid.

8 The trouble with being a woman,
Skeezis,
is being a little girl
in the first place.

"Hurry Up Please It's Time," *The Death Notebooks* 1974

9 Even without wars, life is dangerous.

Ibid.

10 What is death, I ask: What is life, you ask.

Ibid.

11 I would have taken care of daisies, giving them an aspirin every hour and cutting their stems properly, but with roses I'm reckless. When they arrive in their long white box, they're already in the death house.

"A Small Journal" (November 6, 1971), *The Poet's Story*, Howard Moss, ed. 1974

12 Generally speaking, mental hospitals are lonely places, they are full of televisions and medications.

(November 8, 1971), Ibid.

13 I took the radio, my vigil keeper, and played it for my waking, sleeping ever since. In memoriam. It goes everywhere with me like a dog on a leash.

Ibid.

14 The sea is mother-death and she is a mighty female, the one who wins, the one who sucks us all up.

(Entry for 19 November 1971), Ibid.

15 It doesn't matter who my father was; it matters who I remember he was.

(1 January 1972, 12:30 A.M.), Ibid.

16 God owns heaven
but He craves the earth.

"The Earth," St. 2, *The Awful Rowing Toward God* 1975

17 The eyes, opening and shutting like cameras and never forgetting, recording by thousands . . .

St. 3, Ibid.

18 The tongue, the Chinese say,
is like a sharp knife:
it kills
without drawing blood.

"The Dead Heart," St. 3, Ibid.

19 I am tired of being brave.

"The Truth the Dead Know," St. 1, *The Complete Poems* 1981

20 I have gone out, a possessed witch,
haunting the black air, braver at night;
dreaming evil . . .

"Her Kind," St. 1, Ibid.

21 Watching my mother slowly die I knew my first release

"My Friend, My Friend," Ibid.

22 Beauty is a simple passion,
but, oh my friends, in the end
you will dance the fire dance in iron shoes.

"Snow White and the Seven Dwarfs," St. 2, Ibid.

23 Pride pumped in her like poison.

Ibid.

24 But suicides have a special language.
Like carpenters they want to know which tools.
They never ask why build.

"Wanting to Die," St. 3, Ibid.

25 Each night I am nailed into place and forget who I am.

"Sleeping Beauty" *n.d.*

2376. Betty Boothroyd (1929–)

1 Everyone thinks it [touring in a dance company] was all men drinking champagne from your shoes. But, like politics, it was damned hard and taught me about teamwork.

Article by Judith Newman and Ellin Stein, quoted in *People* 28 February 1994

2 You've got to ensure that the holders of an opinion, however unpopular, are allowed to put across their points of view.

Ibid.

2377. Violeta Barrios de Chamorro (1929–)

1 Isn't it strange that during Somoza* we were called a yellow, communist paper. Now we are called a Reagan paper.

Quoted in "Once-lively paper is dead under Sandinistas" by Rick Raber, *The Times/Picayune* (New Orleans) 22 February 1987

*Anastasio Somoza, soldier/politician (1896–1956); was dictator of Nicaragua (1936–1956); succeeded by son, Luis Anastasio Somoza (1922–1967), president (1957–1963).

2   We [the newspaper staff] will die here.

Ibid.

3   When you run a paper under a dictatorship, it's very difficult and dangerous.

Quoted in "I Had To Be Strong From the Beginning" by Larry Smith, *Parade Magazine* 17 February 1991

4   Before, it was one person who decided everything, who managed everybody, and a fly could not fly and a cat could not walk without asking permission from the dictator. Now that we are making democracy, it's completely different. . . . There's an explosion, we could say, a certain excess of liberty. After 50 years, *la gente*—the people—now want everything to be done quickly.

Ibid.

5   Pero, mi señor! But sir—we are a beginning democracy. If there were not strikes, this would not be a democracy.

Ibid.

6   I think problems can be solved through dialogue, looking for solutions, but I want no intervention and no interference— from nobody!

Ibid.

7   There cannot be sovereignty without peace; no sovereignty without liberty. But to have liberty you must respect the rule of the law, other people's morals and opinions, and private property as well.

Quoted in *Twentieth-Century Women Political Leaders* by Claire Price-Groff 1998

8   Reconciliation is more beautiful than victory.

Ibid.

2378. Marilyn French (1929–)

1   One thing that makes art different from life is that in art things have a shape . . . it allows us to fix our emotions on events at the moment they occur, it permits a union of heart and mind and tongue and tear.

Ch. 3, *The Women's Room* 1977

2   There are thousands of snails, and mussels too, among the heaped boulders, clustering together like inhabitants of an ancient city . . . they don't have to create their order, they don't have to create their lives, those things are just programmed into them. All they have to do is live.

Ch. 4, Ibid.

3   And something happened sexually in marriage—the swearing to forsake all others, despite its slight observance, had a profound effect. Some people felt trapped by it, impelled to assert what they called freedom. Some accepted it like a rein, and in the effort to avoid pain in the form of hopeless desire, cut off occasions of desire, avoided having long talks at parties with attractive members of the opposite sex. In time, all feeling for the opposite sex was cut off, and intercourse limited to the barest politenesses. . . . But something happened to you when you did that, a kind of death seeped up from the genitals to the rest of the body, till it showed in the eyes, the gestures, in a certain lifelessness.

Ch. 5, Ibid.

4   Whatever they may be in public life, whatever their relations with men, in their relations with women, all men are rapists and that's all they are. They rape us with their eyes, their laws, their codes.

Ibid.

5   "Well, love is insanity. The ancient Greeks knew that. It is the taking over of a rational and lucid mind by delusion and self-destruction. You lose yourself, you have no power over yourself, you can't even think straight."

Ch. 10, Ibid.

6   "And this goddamned school is antifemale, they look down on women, especially women my age. It's a goddamned monas-tery that's been invaded by people in skirts and the men who run it only hope that the people in skirts are pseu-domen, so they won't disturb things, won't insist that feeling is as important as thinking and body is as important as mind. . . ."

Ch. 12, Ibid.

7   "When they kept you out it was because you were black; when they let you in, it is because you are black. That's progress?"

Ch. 19, Ibid.

8   "I hate discussions of feminism that end up with who does the dishes," she said. So do I. But at the end, there are always the damned dishes.

Ch. 21, Ibid.

9   In a patriarchal world, power is not just the highest but the only value.

Beyond Power; On Men, Women, and Morals 1985

10   And I thought: so that is what a peasant is. Or anyway, what *peasant* meant to my grandmother. Subhuman. The man may have been intelligent enough—he certainly knew crops and weather, and animal husbandry—things I didn't know. But intelligence didn't appear on his gaping face; I could not imagine him speaking. He was a creature immured in blue sky, the wind, wheat fields, shaky wood—fenced yards full of dung. Circumscribed within nature and benighted, benighted. I was shocked by him. I was shocked that the word *subhuman* crossed his mind. So this is what they meant, the old ones, when they talked of peasants.

Pt. I, Ch. 2, Sec. 3, *Her Mother's Daughter* 1987

11   . . . When the juices are running strong, it seems sinful not to let them run their course. It seems a waste of youth and vigor, and damming up what should run free.

Ch. 3, Sec. 2, Ibid.

12   The truth is it's not the sins of the fathers that descend unto the third generation, but the sorrows of the mother.

Pt. II, Ch. 6, Sec. 4, Ibid.

13   Losing the future was the best thing that ever happened to me.

A Season in Hell 1998

14   I cannot say I am happy I was sick, but I am happy that sickness, if it had to happen, brought me to where I am now.

Ibid.

2379. Lee Grant (1929–)

1   This is a period of great *angst*. The impermanence and flimsiness of houses built on faults, subject to landslides, add to a former apartment dweller's sense of insecurity. The stage-set quality of the streets, the green and blue spotlights illuminating every sallow palm in front of Hollywood court apartments, the 40-foot neon cross overlooking the freeway.

"Selling Out to Hollywood, or Home," *The New York Times* 12 August 1973

2 The more stringent the conditions are, the more the actor uses them—like hurdlers, or emotional stuntmen.

Ibid.

3 One's art adjusts to economic necessity if your metabolism does.

Ibid.

4 As more of us [actresses] are moving into producing and directing, the level of creativity among women has become very high, and therefore our relationships have changed—have themselves become more creative.

"Art Catches Up to Life," *Ms.* (New York) *November 1975*

5 . . . art always seems to be catching up to life.

Ibid.

2380. Shirley Ann Grau (1929–)

1 She thought of all the distance between the two parts of her, the white and the black. And it seemed to her that those two halves would pull away and separate and leave her there in the open, popped out like a kernel from its husk.

"Margaret," *The Keepers of the House 1964*

2 There's only one night like that—ever—where you're filled with wonder and excitement for no other reason but the earth is beautiful and mysterious and your body is young and strong . . . We hadn't really been friends before. It just sort of happened that we found ourselves together. It wasn't anything personal. It would have been the same with any man. . . . It happens like that and it's not the less precious. It's the thing you value and not the man. It happened that way with me.

Ibid.

3 And isn't it funny, she thought, that it takes two generations to kill off a man? . . . First him, and then his memory. . . .

Ibid.

4 Why does it take so much trouble to keep your stomach full and quiet?

Ibid.

5 I know that I shall hurt as much as I have been hurt. I shall destroy as much as I have lost. It's a way to live, you know. It's a way to keep your heart ticking under the sheltering arches of your ribs. And that's enough for now.

"Abigail," *Ibid.*

6 To hell with love, Margaret thought. It's an ache in my stomach, it's a terrible feeling in my head, it's a skin-crawling fear that I've done something wrong. I've forgotten the password. And the frog isn't going to change into Prince Charming, the secret door isn't going to open. And the world is going to end any minute.

"Margaret," *The Condor Passes 1971*

7 Her Father was waiting. When she saw him, she felt the usual shift in her feelings. A lift, a jump, a tug. Pleasure, but not totally. Love, but not completely. Dependence. Fear, familiarity, identification. That's part of me there, walking along. Tree from which I sprang. His spasm produced me. Shake of his body and here I am. . . .

Ibid.

8 Why, she thought, do I always get angry at my mother? For not leaving me a memory, for being so vague and gentle and so busy with her job of procreating that she hardly noticed her children once they left her womb . . .

"Anna," *Ibid.*

9 Before, I used to like it [the highway], especially the sounds: the tires whistling and singing on the wet, and hissing on the dry. The soft growling sound—kind of like a sigh—when some trucker tested his air brakes. The way horns echo way off in the distance. The thin little screech of car brakes, too, almost like a laugh. And something else—a steady even whisper. Day and night, no difference. It ran like electric wires singing. Or maybe kind of like breathing . . . But I didn't like the highway anymore . . . Like Joe would say, the highway brought everything to us, and took it away too.

"The Last Gas Station," *Ibid.*

10 It hurts to worry this much, she thought. It really hurts like a cut, or a broken bone. It hurts more than my broken arm when I fell off the climbing bars in the third grade. A lot more than that. It hurts so much that it can't hurt any more.

"Sea Change," *Ibid.*

11 Later on things did stop and time ended, and she perched on a single spot, weightless and empty in herself. Quite detached from her body, her mind stole out, prowling like a cat in the shadows, searching. And it found that there was nothing on any side of her, that she hung like a point, like a star in the empty sky.

Ibid.

12 Took as much skill to get rid of a girl as to get one. He was learning how to do both.

"Robert," *Ibid.*

13 "Haven't you ever noticed how highways always get beautiful near the state capital?"

"The Way Back," *Ibid.*

14 Trees come out of acorns, no matter how unlikely that seems. An acorn is just a tree's way back into the ground. For another try. Another trip through. One life or another. And what came out of sex now. Love maybe. But that wasn't as sure as a tree. Or maybe a tree was as unsure as Love. One capsule life or another.

Ibid.

15 He had to humor his body occasionally so that the rest of the time it obeyed his will.

"The Old Man," *Ibid.*

16 Me? What am I? Nothing. The legs on which dinner comes to the table, the arms by which cocktails enter the living room, the hands that drive cars. I am the eyes that see nothing, the ears that don't hear. I'm invisible too. They look and don't see me. When they move, I have to guess their direction and get myself out of the way. If they were to walk into me—all six feet of black skin and white bone—they'd never again be able to pretend that I wasn't there. And I'd be looking for another job.

"Stanley," *Ibid.*

17 "You forget places you've been and you forget women you've had, but you don't forget fighting."

"Homecoming," *The Wind Shifting West 1973*

18 Nothing in life has bells ringing or choruses singing. I've long ago stopped looking for glamour and drama. Life isn't like that. As a matter of fact, it's the search for instant gratification that is so harmful to young writers . . . The realization that something is good material for a story is no big bang. No need to dignify it with an explosion. Instant bangs never happen. No writer I know talks about it in those terms. Nonwriters

tend to think of it that way, but writing is day to day grubby hard work. It's isolated and time consuming.

Quoted in "Profile . . . Shirley Ann Grau" by Louis Gallo,
New Orleans February 1974

19 A lot more people can write than do. I think writers are only *born* a small sense. You're born with a feeling for words and writers deliberately set out to develop this innate feeling. If you are born with or acquire this feeling for words, then you can become a writer.

Ibid.

20 Women's lib is one of those great amorphous things. I don't think that you can characterize it as a single movement. It's really rather strange . . . [But] you can't legislate equality. Until the basic feelings of people are changed, the facts won't change.

Ibid.

21 One of my current pet theories is that the writer is a kind of evangelist, more subtle than Billy Graham,* of course, but of the same stuff.

Ibid.

*American evangelist (1918–)

22 Women use children as excuses not to do anything.

Ibid.

2381. Elizabeth Dodson Gray (1929–)

1 It is not accidental that in the Genesis 2 account of creation Adam "named" all the animals. Naming is power, the power to shape reality into a form that serves the interest and goals of the one doing the naming.

Sunday School Manifesto 1988

2382. Barbara Marx Hubbard (1929–)

1 As the human potential movement studied human wellness, the social potential movement studies and fosters peaks of social creativity, solutions, breakthroughs, and projects that are already working to heal and evolve our world.

"At the Crossroad: Living in Between,"
*The Fabric of the Future: Women Visionaries
of Today Illuminate the Path to Tomorrow,*
M.J. Ryan, ed. *1998*

2 We have not really changed very much in thousands of years. However, the social and technological environment into which we have been born has transformed, even in the last fifty years, since the understanding of the atom, the gene, the brain. We now have the actual power to co-create or to co-destroy our world, and we are entering the first age of *conscious* evolution, from passive to active participation in evolution itself.

Ibid.

3 It's the third great human drive: from self-preservation to self-reproduction to self-evolution.

Ibid.

4 It has taken fifteen billion years of evolution, from the Big Bang to the present to develop a planetary species on Earth that is aware of itself as a whole and must become responsible for the future of the whole system. The entire story of creation has led to the birth of a species which must learn to cooperate and co-create on a planetary scale.

Ibid.

2383. Elaine Jackson (1929–)

1 WOMAN. You see, the color *black* has within itself many colors. It is a very complex color and at the same time simple and delicate. It can be made to appear formidable and mysterious in a dark, unlit cave, or can appear as bright and inviting as the twinkling eyes of a child.

Paper Dolls n.d.

2384. Jill Johnston (1929–)

1 It's necessary in order to attract attention, to dazzle at all costs, to be disapproved of by serious people and quoted by the foolish.

Lesbian Nation: The Feminist Solution 1973

2 Bisexuality is not so much a copout as a fearful compromise.

Ibid.

3 I had the correct instinct to fuck things up but no political philosophy to clarify a course of action.

Ibid.

4 I have a case of the most exquisite paranoia. It's a wonderful feeling. For a female lesbian bastard writer mental case I'm doing awfully well.

Ibid.

5 I never said I was a dyke even to a dyke because there wasn't a dyke in the land who thought she should be a dyke or even thought she was a dyke so how could we talk about it.

Ibid.

6 . . . we womenfolk can't as I see it be all that smug and satisfied about where we're at anyhow until the ascending female principle is better established at large.

Gullible's Travels 1974

7 . . . i want these women in office who're in touch with their feelings and who know perfectly well when they're bullshitting and who don't have to displace their concealed feelings by dropping bombs on people who live thousands of miles away. . . .

Ibid.

2385. Ursula K. Le Guin (1929–)

1 When action grows unprofitable, gather information; when information grows unprofitable, sleep.

Ch. 3, *The Left Hand of Darkness 1969*

2 Legends of prediction are common throughout the whole Household of Man. Gods speak, spirits speak, computers speak. Oracular ambiguity or statistical probability provides loopholes, and discrepancies are expunged by Faith.

Ch. 4, Ibid.

3 A man wants his virility regarded, a woman wants her femininity appreciated, however indirect and subtle the indications of regard and appreciation. On [the planet] Winter they will not exist. One is respected and judged only as a human being. It is an appalling experience.

Ch. 7, Ibid.

4 . . . Primitiveness and civilization are degrees of the same thing. If civilization has an opposite, it is war. Of these two things, you have either one, or the other. Not both.

Ch. 8, Ibid.

5 To oppose something is to maintain it.

Ch. 11, Ibid.

6 It is a terrible thing, this kindness that human beings do not lose. Terrible because when we are finally naked in the dark and cold, it is all we have. We who are so rich, so full of strength, wind up with that small change. We have nothing else to give.

Ch. 13, Ibid.

7 What is more arrogant than honesty?

Ch. 15, Ibid.

8 It is good to have an end to journey towards; but it is the journey that matters, not the end.

Ibid.

9 I certainly wasn't happy. Happiness has to do with reason, and only reason earns it. What I was given was the thing you can't earn, and can't keep, and often don't even recognize at the time; I mean joy.

Ch. 18, Ibid.

10 He could also, now he was listening, hear doors, typewriters, voices, toilets flushing, in offices all up and down the hall and above him and underneath him. The real trick was to learn how not to hear them. The only solid partitions left were inside the head.

Ch. 2, *The Lathe of Heaven 1971*

11 "What the brain does by itself is infinitely more fascinating and complex than any response it can make to chemical stimulation . . ."

Ch. 3, Ibid.

12 A person is defined solely by the extent of his influence over other people, by the sphere of his interrelationships; and morality is an utterly meaningless term unless defined as the good one does to others, the fulfilling of one's function in the sociopolitical whole.

Ch. 5, Ibid.

13 He was not interested in detached knowledge, science for science's sake: there was no use learning anything if it was of no use. Relevance was his touchstone.

Ibid.

14 He had grown up in a country run by politicians who sent the pilots to man the bombers to kill the babies to make the world safe for children to grow up in.

Ch. 6, Ibid.

15 A person who believes, as she did, that things fit: that there is a whole of which one is a part, and that in being a part one is whole: such a person has no desire whatever, at any time, to play God. Only those who have denied their being yearn to play at it.

Ch. 7, Ibid.

16 He knew that in so far as one denies what is, one is possessed by what is not, the compulsions, the fantasies, the terrors that flock to fill the void.

Ch. 9, Ibid.

17 The quality of the will to power is, precisely, growth. Achievement is its cancellation. To be, the will to power must increase with each fulfillment, making the fulfillment only a step to a further one. The vaster the power gained the vaster the appetite for more.

Ibid.

18 Love doesn't just sit there, like a stone, it has to be made, like bread; re-made all the time, made new.

Ch. 10, Ibid.

19 Outside the locked room is the landscape of time, in which the spirit may, with luck and courage, construct the fragile, makeshift, improbable roads and cities of fidelity: a landscape inhabitable by human beings.

The Dispossessed 1975

20 "What would we do with freedom if we had it, Kosta? What has the West done with it? Eaten it, put it in it's belly. A great wondrous belly, that's the West."

"A Week in the Country," *The Little Magazine Spring 1976*

21 "Night. Country's the only place where they have night left."

Ibid.

22 It seems a pity to have a built-in rite of passage* and to dodge it, evade it, and pretend nothing has changed. That is to dodge and evade one's womanhood, to pretend one's like a man. Men, once initiated, never get the second chance. They never change again. That's their loss, not ours. Why borrow poverty?

"The Space Crone," *The Co-Evolution Quarterly Summer 1976*

*Menopause.

23 Virginity is now a mere preamble or waiting room to be got out of as soon as possible; it is without significance. Old age is similarly a waiting room, where you go after life's over and wait for cancer or a stroke. The years before and after the menstrual years are vestigial: the only meaningful condition left to women is that of fruitfulness.

Ibid.

24 Men are afraid of virgins, but they have a cure for their own fear and the virgin's virginity: fucking. Men are afraid of crones, so afraid that their cure for virginity fails them; they know it won't work. Faced with the fulfilled crone, all but the bravest men wilt and retreat, crestfallen and cock–a–droop.

Ibid.

25 The men thought everything, did everything, ran everything, made everything, made the laws, broke the laws, punished the lawbreakers; and there was no room left for the women. Nowhere, nowhere, but in their own rooms, alone.

Ch. 1, *The Eye of the Heron 1978*

26 "His soul is about the size of a toenail."

Ch. 7, Ibid.

27 Theory is not enough. There must be stones.

Introduction, *The Language of the Night, Essays on Fantasy and Science Fiction*, Susan Wood, ed. and intro. *1979*

28 Art, like sex, cannot be carried on indefinitely solo; after all they have the same mutual enemy, sterility.

Pt. I, "A Citizen of Mondath," Ibid.

29 For the story—from *Rumplestilskin* to *War and Peace*—is one of the basic tools invented by the mind of man, for the purpose of gaining understanding. There have been great societies that did not use the wheel, but there have been no societies that did not tell stories.

Pt. II, "On Fantasy and Science Fiction," Ibid.

30 Almost anything carried to its logical extreme becomes depressing, if not carcinogenic.

Pt. III, Introduction to *The Left Hand of Darkness*, Ibid.

31 Pop art, so called, was the pure essence of art as commodity: soup cans. Genuine newness, genuine originality, is suspect.

Unless it's something familiar rewarmed, or something experimental in form but clearly trivial or cynical in content, it is unsafe. And it must be safe. It mustn't hurt the consumer. It mustn't change the consumer. . . . The publishers, the gallery owners, the entrepreneurs, the producers, the marketers, . . . are happier if art is not taken seriously. Soup cans are much easier. They want products to sell, quick turnover, built-in obsolescence. They do not want large, durable, real, frightening things.

Pt. V, "The Stalin in the Soul," Ibid.

32 Now, I doubt that the imagination can be suppressed. If you truly eradicated it in a child, he would grow up to be an eggplant. Like all our evil propensities, the imagination will out. But if it is rejected and despised, it will grow into wild and weedy shapes; it will be deformed.

"Why are Americans Afraid of Dragons?" Ibid.

33 Fake realism is the escapist realism of our time. And probably the ultimate escapist reading is that masterpiece of total unreality, the daily stock market report.

Ibid.

34 Sure it's simple, writing for kids. Just as simple as bringing them up.

"Dreams Must Explain Themselves," Ibid.

35 Fantasy is nearer to poetry, to mysticism, and to insanity than naturalistic fiction is. It is a real wilderness, and those who go there should not feel too safe.

"From Elfland to Poughkeepsie," Ibid.

36 In art, "good enough" is not good enough.

Ibid.

37 The worst walls are never the ones you find in your way. The worst walls are the ones you put there—you build yourself. Those are the high ones, the thick ones, the ones with no doors in.

"The Stone Ax and the Muskoxen," Ibid.

38 We like to think we live in daylight, but half the world is always dark; and fantasy, like poetry, speaks the language of the night.

"Fantasy, Like Poetry, Speaks the Language of the Night,"
World Magazine 21 November 1979

39 Hating gets going, it goes round, it gets older and tighter and older and tighter until it holds a person inside it like a fist holds a stick.

Four Histories, "Old Woman Hating," *Always Coming Home 1985*

40 O brave new world that has no people in it!

"Time in the Valley," Ibid.

41 Almost everything is double like that for adolescents; their lies are true and their truths are lies, and their hearts are broken by the world. They gyre and fall; they see through everything, and are blind.

"Stone Telling," Pt. II, Ibid.

42 To me the "female principle" is, or at least historically has been, basically anarchic. It values order without constraint, rule by custom not by force.

"Is Gender Necessary?" *Aurora* (Susan Anderson and Vonda McIntyre, eds., 1976), *Dancing at the Edge of the World 1989*

43 If we can get that realistic feminine morality working for us, if we can trust ourselves and so let women think and feel that an unwanted child or an oversize family is wrong—not ethically wrong, not against the rules, but morally wrong, all wrong, wrong like a thalidomide birth, wrong like taking a wrong step that will break your neck—if we can get feminine and human morality out from under the yoke of a dead ethic, then maybe we'll begin to get somewhere on the road that leads to survival.

Speech, "Moral and Ethical Implications of Family Planning," Planned Parenthood Symposium (March 1978, Portland, Maine), Ibid.

44 There's a good deal in common between the mind's eye and the TV screen, and though the TV set has all too often been the boob tube, it could be, it can be, the box of dreams.

"Working on '*The Lathe*'" (*Horizon*, New York, 1980), Ibid.

45 The pornography of violence of course far exceeds, in volume and general acceptance, sexual pornography, in this Puritan land of ours. Exploiting the apocalypse, selling the holocaust, is a pornography. . . .

Address, "Facing It," Portland Fellowship of Reconciliation, Maine (December 1982), Ibid.

46 The preservation of life seems to be rather a slogan than a genuine goal of the anti-abortion forces; what they want is control. Control over behavior: power over women. Women in the anti-choice movement want to share in male power over women, and do so by denying their own womanhood, their own rights and responsibilities.

Address, "The Princess," National Abortion Rights Action League (Portland, Maine, *January* 1982), Ibid.

47 Translation is entirely mysterious. Increasingly I have felt that the art of writing is itself translating, or more like translating than it is like anything else. What is the other text, the original? I have no answer. I suppose it is the source, the deep sea where ideas swim, and one catches them in nets of words and swings them shining into the boat . . . where in this metaphor they die and get canned and eaten in sandwiches.

Address, "Reciprocity of Prose and Poetry," Poetry Series, Folger Shakespeare Library, (Washington, D.C., 1983), Ibid.

48 Our roots are in the dark; the earth is our country. Why did we look up for blessing—instead of around, and down? What hope we have lies there. Not in the sky full of orbiting spy-eyes and weaponry, but in the earth we have looked down upon. Not from above, but from below. Not in the light that blinds, but in the dark that nourishes, where human beings grow human souls.

"A Left-Handed Commencement Address," Mills College (1983), Ibid.

49 If you want your writing to be taken seriously, don't marry and have kids, and above all, don't die. But if you have to die, commit suicide. They approve of that.

Address, "Prospects for Women in Writing," Conference on Women in the Year 2000 (Portland, Maine, September 1986), Ibid.

50 The misogyny that shapes every aspect of our civilization is the institutionalized form of male fear and hatred of what they have denied and therefore cannot know, cannot share: that wild country, the being of women.

Address, "Woman/Wilderness," University of California at Davis (June 1986), Ibid.

51 Literature takes shape and life in the body, in the wombs of the mother tongue: always: and the Fathers of Culture get anxious about paternity. They start talking about legitimacy. They steal the baby. They ensure by every means that the artist, the writer, is male. This involves intellectual abortion by centuries of women artists, infanticide of works by women writers, and a whole medical corps of sterilizing critics working to purify the Canon, to reduce the subject matter and style of literature to something Ernest Hemingway could have understood.

Address, Bryn Mawr Commencement (1986), Ibid.

52 We are volcanoes. When we women offer our experience as our truth, as human truth, all the maps change. There are new mountains.

Ibid.

53 If science fiction is the mythology of modern technology, then its myth is tragic.

"The Carrier Bag Theory of Fiction" (Women of Vision, Denise M. Du Pont, ed., 1988), Ibid.

54 The unread story is not a story; it is little black marks on wood pulp. The reader, reading it, makes it live: a live thing, a story.

"Where Do You Get Your Ideas From?" Ibid.

55 My imagination makes me human and makes me a fool; it gives me all the world and exiles me from it.

"Winged: the Creatures on my Mind," Harper's (New York) August 1990

2386. Joanna Macy (1929–)

1 The Third Turning, I think, will be what Robinson Jeffers* called "falling in love outward." Our mission is not to escape from our world, or fix things by remote control, looking at charts and pushing buttons, and pulling levers, but to fall in love with our world. We are made for that, because we co-arise with her—in a dance where we discover ourselves and lose ourselves over and over.

World As Lover, World As Self 1990
*American poet (1887–1962).

2 Greed and fear are very isolating. They make us crazy. We have to see through them and refuse to be pitted against each other. Only through all beings and with all beings can we awaken to our peace and joy. Our daily adventure is to realize that.

Ibid.

3 In my mind I still hear the local Sarvodaya* workers, in their village meetings and district training centers. Development is not imitating the West. Development is not high-cost industrial complexes, chemical fertilizers and mammoth hydroelectric dams. It is not selling your soul for unnecessary consumer items or schemes to get rich quick. Development is waking up—waking up our true potential as persons and as a society.

(p. 132), Ibid.
*A Buddhist practice that means "everybody wakes up."

4 No magic bullet, not even the Internet, can save us from population explosion, deforestation, climate disruption, poison by pollution, and wholesale extinctions of plant and animal species. We are going to have to want different things, seek different pleasures, pursue different goals, than those that have been driving us and our global economy.

New values must arise now, while we still have room to maneuver—and that is precisely what is happening. They are emerging at this very moment, like green shoots through the rubble.

"The Great Turning," The Fabric of the Future: Women Visionaries of Today Illuminate the Path to Tomorrow, M. J. Ryan, ed. 1998

5 We are opening our senses to the web of relationships, the deep ecology, in which we have our being. Like our primordial ancestors, we begin again to see the world as our body and (whether we say the word or not) as sacred.

Ibid.

2387. Imelda Marcos (1929–)

1 I was no Marie Antoinette,* I was not born to nobility, but I had a human right to nobility.

Quoted on 60 Minutes with Diane Sawyer,** CBS-TV 21 September 1986
*See 668. **See 3066.

2 If you know how much you've got, you probably haven't got much.

Ibid.

3 Life is not a matter of place, things or comfort; rather, it concerns the basic human rights of family, country, justice and human dignity.

Quoted in Newsweek (New York) 12 June 1989

4 I get so tired listening to one million dollars here, one million dollars there, it's so petty.*

Quoted in The Times (London) 22 June 1990
*Response to witnesses' testimony against her during her trial in New York on charges of embezzlement.

2388. Jane S. Mayer (1929–)

1 The full story of his* confirmation thus raises questions not only about who lied and why, but, more important, about what happens when politics becomes total war and the truth—and those who tell it—are merely unfortunate sacrifices on the way to winning.

Strange Justice; The Selling of Clarence Thomas 1994
*Clarence Thomas, American jurist (1928–); appointed Associate Supreme Court Justice of the United States, 1991.

2 Historically, many black men felt that black women had succeeded at their expense and so owed them special deference.

Ibid.

2389. Ellen James Morphonios (1929–)

1 I have a saying—there's no justice in the law.

Lawyer's Wit and Wisdom, Bruce Nash, Allan Zullo, eds.; Kathryn Zullo, compiler 1995

2390. Nel Noddings (1929–)

1 Many of the practices embedded in the masculine curriculum masquerade as essential to the maintenance of standards, . . . [but in fact] they accomplish quite a different purpose: the systematic dehumanization of both female and male children through the loss of the feminine.

Caring 1984

2 It is time for the voice of the mother to be heard in education.

Ibid.

3   We are afraid that, if students prepare for something particular, they may change their minds and all that preparation will be wasted. Thus we busily prepare them uniformly for nothing.
"A Morally Defensible Mission for Schools in the 21st Century," Phi Delta Kappan January 1995

4   In direct opposition to the current emphasis on academic standards, a national curriculum, and national assessment, I have argued that our main educational aim should be to encourage the growth of competent, caring, loving, and lovable people.
Ibid.

5   We need to give up the notion of *a single* ideal of the educated person and replace it with a multiplicity of models designed to accommodate the multiple capacities and interests of students. We need to recognize multiple identities.
Ibid.

6   Programs for the noncollege-bound should be just as rich, desirable, and rigorous as those for the college-bound.
Ibid.

7   Artificially separating the emotional, academic, and moral care of children into tasks for specially designated experts contributes to the fragmentation of life in schools.
"Teaching Themes of Care," Phi Delta Kappan May 1995

8   Teachers can be very special people in the lives of children, and it should be legitimate for them to spend time developing relations of trust, talking with students about problems that are central to their lives, and guiding them toward greater sensitivity and competence across all the domains of care.
Ibid.

9   In an age when violence among school-children is at an unprecedented level, when children are bearing children with little knowledge of how to care for them, when the society and even the schools often concentrate on materialistic messages, it may be unnecessary to argue that we should care more genuinely for our children and teach them to care. However, many otherwise reasonable people seem to believe that our educational problems consist largely of low scores on achievement tests.
Ibid.

2391. Vivian Gussin Paley (1929–)

1   Children do not pretend to be storytellers; they are storytellers. It is their intuitive approach to all occasions. It is the way they think.
The Girl With the Brown Crayon: How Children use Stories to Shape Their Lives 1997

2   Clearly, we do not understand most of what motivates children.
The Kindness of Children 1999

3   No longer am I tested each day as I was in the classroom. *There* it was quite impossible to cover my mistakes; here, upon this podium, the illusion of virtue comes easily.
Ibid.

2392. Quin Guanshu (1929–)

1   Wasting time is an unbearable punishment.
Quoted by Huang Zongying* in "The Flight of the Wild Geese," Yu Fanqin & Wang Mingjie, trs., *Seven Contemporary Chinese Women Writers*, Gladys Yang,** ed. *1982*
*See 2276. **See 2452.

2393. Adrienne Rich (1929–)

1   Facts could be kept separate
by a convention; that was what
made childhood possible. Now knowledge finds me out;
in all its risible untidiness . . .
"From Morning-Glory to Petersburg" (1954), Snapshots of a Daughter-in-Law 1963

2   We who were loved will never
unlive that crippling fever.
"After a Sentence in 'Malte Laurids Brigge,'" (1958), Ibid.

3   Bemused by gallantry, we hear our mediocrity over-praised,
indolence read as abnegation,
slattern thought styled intuition,
every lapse forgiven, our crime
only to cast too bold a shadow
or smash the mould straight off.
Pt. III, St. 1, Ibid.

4   A thinking woman sleeps with monsters.
"Snapshots of a Daughter-in-Law," Pt. III, St. 1 (1958–1960), Ibid.

5   Only to have a grief
equal to all these tears!
"Peeling Onions," St. 1 (1961), Ibid.

6   Nothing changes. The bones of the mammoths are still in the earth.
"End of an Era," St. 1 (1961), Ibid.

7   The future reconnoiters in dirty boots
along the cranberry-dark horizon.
"Autumn Sequence," Pt. III, St. 4 (1964), Necessities of Life 1966

8   I'd call it love if love
didn't take so many years
but lust too is a jewel
a sweet flower. . . .
"Two Songs," Pt. I (1964), Ibid.

9   The mind's passion is all for singling out.
Obscurity has another tale to tell.
"Focus," St. 7 (1965), Ibid.

10   Only where there is language is there world.
"The Demon Lover," Leaflets 1969

11   Desire. Desire. The nebula
opens in space, unseen
your heart utters its great beats
in solitude . . .
Ibid.

12   Posterity trembles like a leaf
and we go on making heirs and heirlooms.
Ibid.

13   I am an instrument in the shape of a woman
trying to translate pulsations into images
for the relief of the body and the reconstruction of the mind.
"Planetarium," St. 14 (1968), The Will to Change 1971

14   . . . A language is a map of our failures.
"The Burning of Paper Instead of Children" (1968), Ibid.

15 Humans lived here once; it became sacred only when they
went away.
"Shooting Script Part I," Pt. IV, St. 9
(November 1969–February 1971), Ibid.

16 The victory carried like a corpse
from town to town
begins to crawl in the casket.
"Letters: March 1969: I," Ibid.

17 the moment of change is the only poem. . . .
"Images for Godard,"* Pt. V, St. 7 (1970), Ibid.
*Jean Luc G—, French filmmaker (1930–).

18 Rape is a part of war; but it may be more accurate to say that
the capacity for dehumanizing another which so corrodes male
sexuality is carried over from sex into war.
"Caryatid," *American Poetry Review* (repr. in *On Lies,
Secrets, and Silence*, 1980) *May–June 1973*

19 The woman I needed to call my mother was silenced before I
was born.
"Reforming the Crystal," *Poems: Selected
and New (1950–1974) 1974*

20 A friend I can trust is the one who will let me have my death.
The rest are actors who want me to stay and further the plot.
Untitled (1960s), Ibid.

21 Finality broods upon the things that pass . . .
"Walk by the Charles" (1950s), Ibid.

22 . . . Love, our subject:
we've trained it like ivy to our walls
baked it like bread in our ovens
worn it like lead on our ankles
Untitled (1970s), Ibid.

23 Every journey into the past is complicated by delusions, false
memories, false namings of real events.
Foreword, *Of Woman Born: Motherhood As Experience
and Institution 1976*

24 In order to live a fully human life we require not only control
of our bodies (though control is a prerequisite); we must touch
the unity and resonance of our physicality, our bond with the
natural order, the corporeal grounds of our intelligence.
Ch. 1, Ibid.

25 My children cause me the most exquisite suffering of which
I have any experience. It is the suffering of ambivalence: the
murderous alternation between bitter resentment and raw-
edged nerves, and blissful gratification and tenderness.
Some- times I seem to myself, in my feelings toward these
tiny guiltless beings, a monster of selfishness and intolerance.
Ibid.

26 Narrowed down by her early editors and anthologists, reduced
to quaintness or spinsterish oddity by many of her commenta-
tors, sentimentalized, fallen-in-love with like some gnomic
Garbo,* still unread in the breadth and depth of her full range
of work, she was, and is, a wonder to me when I try to imagine myself into that mind.*
"Vesuvius at Home: The Power of Emily Dickinson,"*
Parnassus: Poetry in Review (repr. in *On Lies, Secrets,
and Silence*, 1980) *Fall-Winter 1976*
*See 1882. **See 993.

27 As her sons have seen her: the mother in patriarchy:
controlling, erotic, castrating, heart-suffering, guilt-ridden,
and guilt-provoking; a marble brow, a huge breast, an avid
cave; between her legs snakes, swampgrass, or teeth; on her
lap a helpless infant or a martyred son. She exists for one purpose: to bear and nourish the son.
Ch. 8, *Of Woman Born: Motherhood As Experience
and Institution 1976*

28 The ocean, whose tides respond, like women's menses, to the
pull of the moon, the ocean which corresponds to the amniotic
fluid in which human life begins, the ocean on whose surface
vessels (personified as female) can ride but in whose depths
sailors meet their death and monsters conceal themselves . . . it
is unstable and threatening as the earth is not; it spawns new
life daily, yet swallows up lives; it is changeable like the moon,
unregulated, yet indestructible and eternal.
Ch. 4, Ibid.

29 The word "revolution" itself has become not only a dead relic of
Leftism, but a key to the deadendedness of male politics: the "rev-
olution" of a wheel which returns in the end to the same place;
the "revolving door" of a politics which has "liberated" women
only to use them, and only within the limits of male tolerance.
Introduction, "Power and Danger: Works of a Common
Woman," *The Work of a Common Woman: The Collected
Poetry of Judy Grahn,* 1964–1977 1977*
*See 2799.

30 How we dwelt in two worlds
the daughters and the mothers
in the kingdom of the sons.
"Sibling Mysteries"(1963), *The Dream of a Common
Language, Poems (1974–1977) 1978*

31 how sister gazed at sister
reaching through mirrored pupils
back to the mother
Pt. IV, St. 6, Ibid.

32 Whatever happens with us, your body
will haunt mine—
"(The Floating Poem, Unnumbered)," from *Twenty-One
Love Poems*, Ibid.

33 For months for years each one of us
had felt her own yes growing in her
slowly forming as she stood at windows waited
For trains mended her rucksack combed her hair
"Phantasia for Elvira Shatayev*"
Ibid.
*Leader of a women's climbing team, all of whom died in a storm
on Lenin Peak (August 1974).

34 No one lives in this room
without confronting the whiteness of the wall
behind the poems, planks of books,
photographs of dead heroines,
Without contemplating last and late
the true nature of poetry. The drive
to connect. The dream of a common language.
"Origins and History of Consciousness" (1972–1974), Ibid.

35 They can rule the world while they can persuade
us
our pain belongs in some order.
Is death by famine worse than death by suicide,
than a life of famine and suicide . . . ?
"Power. Hunger," Pt. 1, Ibid.

36 She* died a famous woman denying
  her sounds
  denying
  her wounds came from the same
  source as her power
                    "Power," Pt. I (1974), Ibid.
    *Marie Curie; see 1269.

37 Marriage is lonelier than solitude.
    Pt. III, "Paula Becker to Clare Westhoff" (1975–1976), Ibid.

38 But gentleness is active
  gentleness swabs the crusted stump
  invents more merciful instruments
  to touch the wound beyond the wound
          "Natural Resources," Pt. VIII, Sts. 3–4 (1979), Ibid.

39 But to be a female human being trying to fulfill traditional female functions in a traditional way *is* in direct conflict with the subversive function of the imagination.
                    On Lies, Secrets and Silence 1979

40 I am a feminist because I feel endangered, psychically and physically, by this society and because I believe that the women's movement is saying that we have come to an edge of history when men—insofar as they are embodiments of the patriarchal idea—have become dangerous to children and other living things, themselves included.
                                        Ibid.

41 It seems to me that the form of many communications in academia, both written and verbal, is such as to not only obscure the influence of the personal or subjective but also to give the impression of divine origin—a mystification composed of syballine statements—from beings supposedly emptied of the "dross" of the self.
                                        Ibid.

42 It is . . . crucial that we understand lesbian/feminism in the deepest, most radical sense: as that love for ourselves and other women, that commitment to the freedom of all of us, which transcends the category of "sexual preference" and the issue of civil rights, to become a politics of asking women's questions, demanding a world in which the integrity of all women—not a chosen few—shall be honored and validated in every respect of culture.
                                        Foreword, Ibid.

43 The connections between and among women are the most feared, the most problematic, and the most potentially transforming force on the planet.
            "Disloyal to Civilization: Feminism, Racism, Gynophobia,"
                                        Chrysalis, No. 7, Ibid.

44 In the middle-class United States, a veneer of "alternative lifestyles" disguises the reality that, here as everywhere, women's apparent "choices" whether or not to have children are still dependent on the far from neutral will of male legislators, jurists, a male medical and pharmaceutical profession, well-financed lobbies, including the prelates of the Catholic Church, and the political reality that women do not as yet have self-determination over our bodies and still live mostly in ignorance of our authentic physicality, our possible choices, our eroticism itself.
              "Motherhood: The Contemporary Emergency and the
              Quantum Leap," Future of Mothering Conference,
                    (Columbus, Ohio, 2 June 1978), Ibid.

45 No woman is really an insider in the institutions fathered by masculine consciousness. When we allow ourselves to believe we are, we lose touch with parts of ourselves defined as unacceptable by that consciousness; with the vital toughness and visionary strength of the angry grandmothers, the shamanesses, the fierce marketwomen of the Ibo's Women's War, the marriage-resisting women silkworkers of prerevolutionary China, the millions of widows, midwives, and the women healers tortured and burned as witches for three centuries in Europe.
        "What Does a Woman Need to Know?" *Blood, Bread, and
                    Poetry: Selected Prose 1979-1985* 1986

46 There is the falsely mystical view of art that assumes a kind of supernatural inspiration, a possession by universal forces unrelated to questions of power and privilege or the artist's relation to bread and blood. In this view, the channel of art can only become clogged and misdirected by the artist's concern with merely temporary and local disturbances. The song is higher than the struggle.
                    "Blood, Bread and Poetry," Ibid.

47 Lesbian existence comprises both the breaking of a taboo and the rejection of a compulsory way of life. It is also a direct or indirect attack on the male right of access to women.
            "Compulsory Heterosexuality and Lesbian Existence," Ibid.

48 White men need a history that does not simply "include" peoples of color and white women, that shows the process by which the arrogance of hierarchy and the celebration of violence have reached a point of destructiveness almost out of control.
              Lecture, Scripps College (Claremont, Calif.,
                                February 1983), Ibid.

49 Memory is a nutriment, and seeds stored for centuries can still germinate.
                                        Ibid.

50 To say yes, over and over, to our integrity, we need to know where we have been: we need our history.
                                        Ibid.

51 we move
  but our words stand
  become responsible

  and this is verbal privilege
                    "North American Time," *Your Native Land,
                              Your Life : Poems* 1986

52 This is the oppressor's language, yet I need it to talk to you.
                    Quoted in *Yearning* by bell hooks* 1990
    *See 3399.

53 Catch if you can your country's moment, begin
  where any calendar's ripped-off: Appomattox
  Wounded Knee, Los Alamos
  Selma, the last airlift from Saigon
          An Atlas of the Difficult World : Poems 1988–1991 1991

54 [The] impulse to enter, with other humans, through language, into the order and disorder of the world, is poetic at its root as surely as it is political at its root . . .
              *What Is Found There: Notebooks on Poetry
                              and Politics* 1993

55 I see the life of North American poetry at the end of the century as a pulsing, racing convergence of tributaries—regional,

ethnic, racial, social, sexual—that, rising from lost or long-blocked springs, intersect and infuse each other while reaching back to the strengths of their origins.

Ibid.

56 We have rarely, if ever, known what it is to tremble with fear, to lament, to rage, to praise, to solemnize, to say We have done this, to our sorrow; to say Enough, to say We will, to say We will not. To lay claim to poetry.

Ibid.

57 We must use what we have to invent what we desire.

Ibid.

58 . . . poetry can break open locked chambers of possibility, restore numbed zones to feeling, recharge desire . . .

Ibid.

59 [Maya Lin's* Vietnam Memorial is] the only great public monument that allows the anesthetized holes in the heart to fill with a truly national grief.

Ibid.

　　*See 3458.

60 To say that a poet is responsive, responsible—what can that mean? To me it means that she or he is free to become artistically most complex, serious and integrated when most aware of the great questions of her, of his, own time.

Ibid.

61 I am suspicious—first of all, in myself—of adopted mysticisms of glib spirituality, above all of white people's tendency to . . . vampirize American Indian, or African, or Asian, or other "exotic" ways of understanding.

Ibid.

62 When does a life bend toward freedom? grasp its direction?
Dark Fields of the Republic 1995

63 MIRACLE's truck comes down the little avenue,
　Scott Joplin ragtime strewn behind it like pearls,
　and, yes, you can feel happy
　with one piece of your heart.
"Miracle Ice Cream," Ibid.

64 Motherhood is the key role, the keystone in the patriarchal arch, for it is also the site of wresting of power from women.
Quoted in *Fruitful: a Real Mothern in the Modern World*
by Anne Roiphe* 1996

　　*See 2605.

65 Art . . . means nothing if it simply decorates the dinner-table of power which holds it hostage. The radical disparities of wealth and power in America are widening at a devastating rate. A president cannot meaningfully honor certain token artists while the people at large are so dishonored.
Letter to Jane Alexander,* Quoted in "No thanks, NEA,**
Ms. (New York) *November/December 1997*

　　*Chair, NEA; see 2734. **National Endowment for the Arts. Rich's explanation for her refusal to accept the prestigious National Medal of Arts, awarded annually by the president of the United States.

66 [I am trying] to face the terrible with hope, in language as complex as necessary, as communicative as possible—a poetics which can work as antidote to complacency, self-involvement, and despair. I have wanted to assume a theater of voices rather than the restricted I. To write both for readers I know exist

and those I can only imagine, finding their own salvaged beauty as I have found mine.
Preface, *Midnight Salvage: Poems 1995–1998* 1999

67 I wanted to go somewhere
　the brain had not yet gone
"Letters to a Young Poet," Ibid.

2394. Nafis Sadik (1929–)

1 More than one-half the world cannot be denied.
Cited in "Population blueprint criticized" (AP), *Seattle Post-
Intelligencer*, A14 *5 April 1994*

2 We should invest in people, especially in women, and let them make choices about family size.
Ibid.

2395. Johanna Levelt Sengers (1929–)

1 As an immigrant to the United States I have found at the "national Bureau of Standards [now NIST] a work environment where I felt welcome and accepted, where even in the 1960's women scientists had successful careers, where special arrangements were made for me while I was raising my family, and where I was given all support to succeed."
American Men and Women of Science 1990–1993

2396. Louise Shivers (1929–)

1 He was holding me, and for the first time I had the feeling. The feeling of wanting to push, to push myself into another person. *So this is what it is*, I thought. *This is why people do the things they do.* The feeling made me sick, scared me, and I pulled away . . .
　　But he knew how to wait, and just how to work me, and unbutton me.
　　By harvest time in the fall I'd be there waiting for him. He'd walk up and put his hand behind my neck and slowly pull me to him.
　　I remember thinking, *I am a rider on an ancient horse.*
A Whistling Woman 1993

2 I remember that old saying, "A whistling woman and a crowing hen never come to any good end." Well, I don't believe that just means that men want women to be quiet, or that if a woman whistles she's acting like a man. I've thought and thought on it. I believe that some women, most women, *know* so much that they never tell, know so many secret things that sometimes they're just making a little slow, low whistling sound of warning. Don't mess with a whistling woman.
Ibid.

2397. Beverly Sills (1929–)

1 In a way, retarded children are satisfying. Everything is a triumph. Even getting Bucky to manage to get a spoon to his mouth was a triumph. God compensates.
Quoted in "Beverly Sills," *Divas: Impressions of Six Opera
Superstars* by Winthrop Sargeant 1959

2 I would willingly give up my whole career if I could have just one normal child. . . .
Ibid.

3 I don't want to be an exhibitionistic coloratura who merely sings notes. I'm interested in the *character*.
Ibid.

551

4 There is something in me—I just can't stand to admit defeat.
Interview, *60 Minutes*, CBS-TV *1975*

5 My singing is very therapeutic. For three hours I have no troubles—I know how it's all going to come out.
Ibid.

6 A happy woman is one who has no cares at all; a cheerful woman is one who has cares but doesn't let them get her down.
Ibid.

2398. Patricia Meyer Spacks (1929–)

1 Theories by women about women have only recently begun to appear in print. Theories by men about women are abundant.
Ch. 1, *The Female Imagination 1975*

2 Dependency invites encroachment.
Ch. 2, *Ibid.*

3 Like the adolescent, the artist is a dreamer and a revolutionary; like the adolescent, he often finds his accomplishment inadequate to his imaginings. But his dream, setting him apart, helps him to escape the burden of the real.
Ch. 5, *Ibid.*

4 The cliché that women, more consistently that men, turn inward for sustenance seems to mean, in practice, that women have richly defined the ways in which imagination creates possibility; possibility that society denies.
"Afterword," *Ibid.*

5 One discourses from a height, gossips around the kitchen table.
"In Praise of Gossip," *Hudson Review*, 35 *1982*

6 Gossip, like poetry and fiction, penetrates to the truth of things.
Ibid.

7 . . . in religious and secular contexts, by standards of morality and of decorum, loose talk about people is deplorable. Few activities so nearly universal have been the object of such sustained and passionate attack.
Ibid.

2399. Alisa Wells (1929–)

1 Now the real beginnings of the "freedom" which we have discussed for many years—and a heady freedom it is, coming after so many years of reaching outward for it—to finally discover all I had to do was reach inward, and it was there waiting all the time for me!
Quoted in *The Woman's Eye* by Anne Tucker* *1973*
*See 3073.

2 I understood not a word he spoke that first night, and little in the endless ones following; but his words, gestures, challenges were speaking to something, someone deep within me.
Ibid.

2400. Christa Wolf (1929–)

1 Ten years of war. That was long enough to forget completely the question of how the wars started. In the middle of a war you think of nothing but how it will end. And put off living. When large numbers of people do that, it creates a vacuum within us, which the war flows in to fill.
Cassandra, Jan van Heurck, tr. *1983*

2 I could not have dreamed what my limbs replied to the question of his lips, or what unknown inclinations his scent would confer on me. And what a voice my throat had at its command.
Ibid.

3 "Try to understand, Mother," he said. "We want to spare you. The things we have to talk about in our council, now in wartime, are no longer the concern of women."
"Quite right," said Anchises. "Now they are the concern of children."
Ibid.

4 . . . We foreigners . . . incapable of deciphering even the signs outside the shops, must rely on pictures, smells.
But isn't the word the very thing that has taken over control of our inner life? The fact that I lack words here: doesn't this mean that I am losing myself? How quickly does lack of speech turn into lack of identity?
Ibid.

5 The atomic threat, if it has brought us to the brink of annihilation, must then have brought us to the brink of silence too, to the brink of endurance, to the brink of reserve about our fear and anxiety, and our true opinions.
"3: A Work Diary, about the Stuff Life and Dreams Are Made Of,"
Ibid.

6 About reality. The insane fact that in all the "civilized" industrialized nations, literature, if it is realistic, speaks a completely different language from any and all public disclosures. As if every country existed twice over. As if every resident existed twice over: once as himself and as the potential perceiver of an artistic presentation; second, as an object of statistics, publicity, agitation, advertisement, political propaganda.
Ibid.

7 To what extent is there really such a thing as "women's writing?" To the extent that women, for historical and biological reasons, experience a different reality than men. Experience a different reality than men and express it. To the extent that women belong not to the ruler but to the ruled, and have done so for centuries. To the extent that they are the objects of objects, second-degree objects, frequently the objects of men who are themselves objects, and so, in terms of their social position, unqualified members of the subculture. To the extent that they stop wearing themselves out trying to integrate themselves into the prevailing delusional systems. To the extent that, writing and living, they aim at autonomy. In this case they encounter the men who aim at autonomy. Autonomous people, nations, and systems can promote each other's welfare; they do not have to fight each other like those whose inner insecurity and immaturity continually demand the demarcation of limits and postures of intimidation.
Ibid.

8 Magic, though, was once exclusively the art of women (who, when driven to lovelessness, revert, not without reason, to magic spells). It was the art of the female tribal elders in the early agricultural societies; then, for a long time, of the priestesses, from whom the first priest could entice away the ritual only by pushing their way into the magical clothing of women. It would seem comical to me to point out these things in a tone of indignation, for humanity could not stay at the level of magic and sorcery. But what I ask myself is: Was it nec-

essary that man should come to stand "alone" before Nature—opposite Nature, not in it?*

"4: A Letter about Unequivocal and Ambiguous Meaning, Definiteness and Indefiniteness; about Ancient Conditions and New View-Scopes; about Objectivity," Ibid.

*Reference to Goethe's *Faust*, Act 5, Pt. II: "If, Nature, I stood before you a man alone."

9 Awe is composed of reverence and dread. I often think that people today have nothing left but the dread.

Ibid.

10 We lied and kowtowed and railed and slandered and we lusted for slavery and pleasure.

What Remains 1990

11 Whoever causes the people to lay hands on what they hold sacred makes himself their enemy.

Medea: A Modern Retelling 1998

12 It had seemed to me unbearable to be given the choice between two evils. I was a fool. Now I could only choose between two crimes.

Ibid.

13 Conscience no longer has any significance when the same words, the same deeds, can mean either rescue or betrayal.

Ibid.

2401. Anne Frank (1929–1945)

1 I soothe my conscience now with the thought that it is better for hard words to be on paper than that Mummy should carry them in her heart.

Entry (2 January 1944), *The Diary of a Young Girl 1947* (tr. 1952)

2 I think what is happening to me is so wonderful, and not only what can be seen on my body, but all that is taking place inside. I never discuss myself or any of these things with anybody; that is why I have to talk to myself about them.

Ibid.

3 Laziness may *appear* attractive, but work *gives* satisfaction.

Entry (6 January 1944), Ibid.

4 Mummy herself has told us that she looked upon us more as her friends than her daughters. Now that is all very fine, but still, a friend can't take a mother's place. I need my mother as an example which I can follow, I want to be able to respect her.

Entry (15 January 1944), Ibid.

5 The best remedy for those who are afraid, lonely or unhappy is to go outside, somewhere where they can be quiet, alone with the heavens, nature and God. Because only then does one feel that all is as it should be and that God wishes to see people happy, amidst the simple beauty of nature. As long as this exists, and it certainly always will, I know that then there will always be comfort for every sorrow, whatever the circumstances may be. And I firmly believe that nature brings solace in all troubles.

Entry (23 February 1944), Ibid.

6 The radio . . . goes on early in the morning and is listened to at all hours of the day, until nine, ten and often eleven o'clock in the evening. This is certainly a sign that the grown-ups have infinite patience, but it also means that the power of absorp-

tion of their brains is pretty limited, with exceptions, of course—I don't want to hurt anyone's feelings. One or two news bulletins would be ample per day! But the old geese, well—I've said my piece!

Entry (27 March 1944), Ibid.

7 I don't believe that the big men, the politicians and the capitalists alone are guilty of the war. Oh, no, the little man is just as keen, otherwise the people of the world would have risen in revolt long ago! There is an urge and rage in people to destroy, to kill, to murder, and until all mankind, without exception, undergoes a great change, wars will be waged, everything that has been built up, cultivated and grown, will be destroyed and disfigured, after which mankind will have to begin all over again.

Entry (3 May 1944), Ibid.

8 Is discord going to show itself while we are still fighting, is the Jew once again worth less than another? Oh, it is sad, very sad, that once more, for the umpteenth time, the old truth is confirmed: "What one Christian does is his own responsibility, what one Jew does is thrown back at all Jews."

Entry (22 May 1944), Ibid.

9 We all live with the objective of being happy; our lives are all different and yet the same.

Entry (6 July 1944), Ibid.

10 Parents can only give good advice or put them on the right paths, but the final forming of a person's character lies in their own hands. . . .

Entry (15 July 1944), Ibid.

11 It's really a wonder that I haven't dropped all my ideals because they seem so absurd and impossible to carry out. Yet, I keep them, because in spite of everything I still believe that people are really good at heart. I simply can't build up my hopes on a foundation consisting of confusion, misery, and death. I see the world gradually being turned into a wilderness, I hear the ever-approaching thunder, which will destroy us too, I can feel the sufferings of millions and yet, if I look up into the heavens, I think that it will all come right, that this cruelty too will end, and that peace and tranquility will return again.

Ibid.

12 And finally I twist my heart round again, so that the bad is on the outside and the good is on the inside, and keep on trying to find a way of becoming what I would so like to be, and could be, if . . . there weren't any other people living in the world.

Entry (1 August 1944), Ibid.

13 I'm awfully scared that everyone who knows me as I always am will discover that I have another side, a finer and better side. I'm afraid they'll laugh at me, think I'm ridiculous and sentimental, not take me seriously . . . *

Ibid.

*Last words of last entry. Three days after writing this entry, Anne Frank was arrested and sent to a concentration camp in Germany

2402. Audrey Hepburn (1929–1993)

1 Keep trying. Take care of the small circle around you. When you have succeeded with them, then move outwards, one small step at a time.

Quoted by her son, Sean Hepburn Ferrer* in *Seattle Post-Intelligencer 1994?*

*At the founding of the Audrey Hepburn Hollywood for Children Fund, Los Angeles.

2 For attractive lips, speak words of kindness.
For lovely eyes, seek out the good in people.
For a slim figure, share your food with the hungry.
For beautiful hair, let a child run his or her fingers through it
once a day.
For poise, walk with the knowledge you'll never walk alone.
"Beauty Tips" *n.d.*

3 Remember, if you ever need a helping hand, you'll find one at
the end of your arm. As you grow older, you will discover that
you have two hands, one for helping yourself, the other for
helping others.
Ibid.

2403. Jacqueline Kennedy Onassis (1929–1994)

1 If you bungle raising your children, I don't think whatever else
you do well matters very much.
Pt. 4, Ch. 15, Quoted in *Kennedy* by
Theodore C. Sorenson *1965*

2 Minimum information given with maximum politeness.*
Quoted in *A Hero for Our Time* by Ralph G. Martin *1983*
*Her guidelines for dealing with the media.

3 The one thing I do not want to be called is First Lady. It sounds
like a saddle horse.
Pt. 3, Ch. 2, Quoted in *The Kennedys* by Peter Collier
and David Horowitz *1984*

4 How can I explain these people [the Kennedys]? They were
like carbonated water, and other families might be flat.
Letter to friend, reported in "A Woman Named Jackie,"
Pt. 1, by C. David Heymann, *Seattle Post-Intelligencer*
23 May 1994

5 The main thing for me was to do whatever my husband
wanted. He couldn't—and wouldn't—be married to a woman
who tried to share the spotlight with him.
Pt. 2, Ibid. *24 May 1994*

6 We're nothing but sitting ducks in a shooting gallery.
Remark on attempted assassination (1960), Reported in
"The threat of danger . . ." by C. David Heymann, Ibid.
25 May 1994

7 It is a rare thing to be able to vote for one's husband as president of the United States, and I didn't want to dilute it by
voting for anyone else.
Remark to Arthur Schlesinger* (1960),
Reported in "The threat of danger . . . ,"
by C. David Heymann, Ibid.
*American historian and presidential adviser (1888–1965).

8 I'm almost glad it happened* because it's given me a second
life. I laugh and enjoy things so much more.
Quoted in "America's First Lady" by Peggy Noonan,**
Time (New York) *30 May 1994*
*Reference to her discovery that she had non-Hodgkin's lym-
phoma (cancer). **See 3273.

9 Do you think seeing the coffin can upset me, doctor? I've seen
my husband die, shot in my arms. His blood is all over me.
How can I see anything worse than I've seen?
Quoted by physician at Parkland
Memorial Hospital,* Ibid.
*The hospital in Dallas, Texas where John F. Kennedy's body was
taken after having been shot.

10 For a while I thought history was something that bitter old
men wrote. But then I realized history made Jack* what he
was. You must think of him as this little boy, sick so much of
the time, reading in bed, reading history, reading the Knights
of the Round Table, reading Marlborough. For Jack, history
was full of heroes. And if it made him this way—if it made him
see the heroes—maybe other little boys will see. Men are such
a combination of good and bad. Jack had this hero idea of history, this idealistic view.
Interview with Theodore White** (1963), Ibid.
*Her husband, John F. Kennedy (1917–63), 35th U.S. presi-
dent (1961–63); assassinated. **American political journalist
(1915–1986).

11 I feel strongly that publicity in this era has gotten completely
out of hand—and you must really protect the privacy of me
and my children.
Memo to press secretary (1961), quoted in "The Stylishness
of Her Privacy" by Lance Morrow, Ibid.

12 I think my biggest achievement is that after going through a
rather difficult time, I consider myself comparatively sane. I'm
proud of that.
Remark (1979), "Portrait of a Friendship" by John Russell,
Ibid.

2404. Ida Applebroog (193?–)

1 Artmaking is like riding naked through the streets—it's the
most risk-taking.
Quoted in "Ida Applebroog," *Exposures, Women &
Their Art* by Ann Brown & Arlene Raven* *1989*
*See 3020.

2 I know that everyone brings to the work his or her own experiences and background and may interpret the piece like a
rorschach, in their own way.
Ibid.

2405. Nguyen Thi Binh (1930–)

1 I was tortured [in the 1950s] by the Vietnamese, with the
French directing, just as now it is with the Americans direct-
ing.
Quoted in "Madame Binh" by Beca Wilson, *New York
Review of Books 25 June 1975*

2 We tell our children that the bombs cannot kill everyone, that
they must not be afraid. . . . We know our sacrifice is necessary. If the bombs do not fall on you, they fall on friends. We
accept fate. We are calm. It is useless to be a pessimist. Some
day we will win a beautiful life, if not for ourselves, then for
our children.
Ibid.

3 We were moving from one place to another, always moving . . . we lived underground often, never coming into the air
except at night. 1957 through 1959: those were the black
years. By 1960 the people could not bear it any longer. They
demanded the right to fight and protect themselves.
Ibid.

2406. Denise Bonal (193–?–)

1 VINCENT. Yeah, being forty isn't so easy . . .
MOTHER. True, it was pretty hard for me, too, at forty.
. . . Forty years old when Charles died! No man ever slept be-
side me since. Winter nights are the worst. Summer nights are

violent. You keep cats. And you learn never to look at a couple kissing again.

A Picture Perfect Sky (Passions et Prairie), Timothy Johns, tr. *1987*

2407. Box Car Bertha (fl. 1930s)
1 Our family never had any hard luck, because nothing ever seemed hard luck to it.

Sister of the Road 1937

2408. Marion Zimmer Bradley (1930–)
1 And as men believe, so their world goes. And so the worlds which once were one are drifting apart.

Bk. I, Ch. 1, *The Mists of Avalon 1982*

2 . . . one of the old priestesses had once said that the House of Maidens was for little girls whose whole duty in life was to spill things, break things, and forget things, the rules of their daily life among them, until they had spilled, broken, and forgotten everything they could, and thus made room in their lives for a little wisdom.

Ch. 12, Ibid.

3 Some knowledge and some song and some beauty must be kept for those days before the world again plunges into darkness.

Bk. IV, Ch. 7, Ibid.

4 "The truth is not so good a story."

Prologue, *The Firebrand 1987*

5 Men had no divine power; they neither bred nor bore; yet somehow they felt they had some natural right in the fruit of their women's bodies, as if coupling with a woman gave them some power of ownership, as if children did not naturally belong to the woman whose body had sheltered and nourished them.

Ibid.

2409. E. M. Broner (1930–)
1 "Here's your last chance. Mary, the Virgin, is visited by the Angel. He has an announcement to make. Mary will give birth to a baby, a son, who will be the son of God."
"Gee," says Mary, "I wanted a girl."
"That's good, Mother," says my eldest, patting me.

"Joking Around," *Ghost Stories 1995*

2410. Eva Burrows (1930–)
1 If we're not growing,* we must feel guilty, because we are not fulfilling Christ's demand.

Quoted in "A New General Takes Charge" by Richard N. Ostling, *Time* (New York) *11 August 1986*
*Reference to the Salvation Army.

2411. Maria Castellani (fl. 1930s)
1 Fascism recognizes women as part of the life force of the country, laying down a division of duties between two sexes, without putting obstacles in the way of those women who by their intellectual gifts reach the highest positions.

Italian Women, Past and Present 1937

2412. Blythe M. Clinchy (1930–)
See Mary Belenky, 2522: 1–4.

2413. Shirley Trusty Corey (193-?–)
1 The arts must be considered an essential element of education, not an optional or lesser element in the consideration of time, materials, or appropriate teaching staff. They are the content and process by which we bring unity to isolated knowledge and feelings. They are tools for living life reflectively, joyfully, and with the ability to shape the future.

Letter to Elaine T. Partnow* *19 December 1989*
*See 2870.

2 The arts personalize knowledge and visions, demanding an ever growing development of the mind and spirit. We do our children and our country ill service by not supporting them adequately in our schools.

Ibid.

2414. Elisabeth Craigin (fl. 1930s)
1 A so-called Lesbian alliance can be of the most rarefied purity, and those who do not believe it are merely judging in ignorance of the facts.

Either is Love 1937

2415. Mildred Spiewak Dresselhaus (1930–)
1 All the hardships I encountered provided me with the determination, capacity for hard work, efficiency, and a positive outlook on life that have been so helpful to me in realizing my professional career.

Quoted in *Contemporary Women Scientists of America* by Iris Noble *1979*

2 [I] became more and more of an expert in an increasingly narrow field.

"Perspectives on the Presidency of the American Physical Society" (p. 38), *Physics Today July 1985*

3 Follow your interests, get the best available education and training, set your sights high, be persistent, be flexible, keep your options open, accept help when offered, and be prepared to help others.

Letter to author, Quoted in *Women Scientists* by Nancy J. Veglahn *1991*

2416. Oriana Fallaci (1930–)
1 Listening to someone talk isn't at all like listening to their words played over on a machine. What you hear when you have a face before you is never what you hear when you have before you a winding tape.

Foreword, *The Egotists 1963*

2 If I were to give human semblance to the America of today, this hated and often misunderstood country, I would choose Norman Mailer to be the model. . . . One tries to catch America—Mailer's stare—and one doesn't know which eye to choose, which eye to respond to. As a result one cannot reach a moral decision about him. But the practical dilemma remains: Should one be his friend or his enemy? Most people consider him an enemy; to be his friend is anything but easy.

"Norman Mailer,"* Ibid.
*American author (1923–).

3 Glory is a heavy burden, a murdering poison, and to bear it is an art. And to have that art is rare.

"Federico Fellini,"* Ibid.
*Italian film director (1920–1993).

4 We are all going to become Swedish, and we do not understand these Americans who, like adolescents, always speak of sex, and who, like adolescents, all of a sudden have discovered that sex is good not only for procreating children.

"Hugh Hefner,"* Ibid.

*American magazine publisher (1926–)

5 He [Nguyen Cao Ky*] is the most famous man in South Vietnam and also the most hated. Reactionaries hate him because he is the most hostile enemy of the reactionaries; liberals hate him because he is the most hostile enemy of the liberals; Americans hate him because the most hostile enemy of the Americans.

"Nguyen Cao Ky," Ibid.

*Vietnamese political leader (1930–)

6 Every time she passed a mirror she was unable to resist the temptation of looking at the one thing that interested her most in the world—herself. And every time she was a bit disappointed—almost as if the girl facing her was some other person.

Ch. 1, *Penelope at War 1966*

7 But, with the optimism of those beings who will not give up even in the face of obvious defeat and who blindly raise their heads again after defeat thinking that it might have been worse and all is not lost, Giovanna did not want to understand—far less withdraw in good order.

Ch. 5, Ibid.

8 I'm going to show you the real New York—witty, smart, and international—like any metropolis. Tell me this—where in Europe can you find old Hungary, old Russia, old France, old Italy? In Europe you're trying to copy America, you're almost American. But here you'll find Europeans who immigrated a hundred years ago—and we haven't spoiled them. Oh, Gio! You must see why I love New York. Because the whole world's in New York. . . .

Ch. 8, Ibid.

9 "You know that everyone else is at home—with his beer, his wife, his children, those children dressed like elves, in yellow, red, that well dressed wife looking at the TV, that cool beer, that family, that is safe because they listen to the transistor radio, because they believe in business and civil religion, because they conform in a country where conformity means salvation . . . Lastly, you understand why the rule of God and of America is the rule of selection, why it's a man-made law, why spiritual values are earthly values, why America is God equals America equals Business equals America equals God. And there's no alternative: you have to be on the side of God equals America equals Business equals America equals God, or else you're alone. Alone and damned like me, understand?"

Ch. 10, Ibid.

10 "America's a hard school, I know, but hard schools make excellent graduates."

Ch. 16, Ibid.

11 "I think when men die they do what the trees do in winter when they go dry, but then spring comes and they're reborn. So life must be something else."

Ch. 1, *Nothing, and So Be It 1972*

12 But here's what I learned in this war, in this country, in this city: to love the miracle of having been born.

Ch. 3, Ibid.

13 Have you ever thought that war is a madhouse and that everyone in the war is a patient? Tell me, how can a normal man get up in the morning knowing that in an hour or a minute he may no longer be there? How can he walk through heaps of decomposing corpses and then sit down at the table and calmly eat a roll? How can he defy nightmare-like risks and then be ashamed of panicking for a moment?

Ch. 6, Ibid.

14 It was a big magnolia, with big branches and big leaves and big flowers which opened like clean handkerchiefs. . . .

Letter to a Child Never Born 1975

15 Equality, Child, like freedom, exists only where you are now. Only as an egg in the womb are we all equal.

Ibid.

16 But what is this life by which you, who exist still incomplete, count for more than I, who exist completely already? What is this respect for you that removes respect for me? What is this right of yours to exist that takes no account of my right to exist?

Ibid.

17 To have realized your dream makes you feel lost

Ibid.

2417. Maureen Fiedler (193-?–)

1 Why organize? First, because it ends isolation. Many women feel treated as second-class citizens—in church, in society. In organizing we lose the sense of being alone. Second, in organizing the whole is greater than the sum of its parts, and our energy is increased when we come together. And third, we are building base communities which struggle for change and give us a place to talk.

Speech, Annual Conference, National Assembly of Religious Women *1985*

2418. Målfrid Grude Flekkøy (193-?–)

1 It's not a law that says parents will be punished for striking their child.* It's an attitude–creating piece of legislation. It says that society does not approve of physically punishing children.

Quoted in "Who Speaks for Children?" by Michael Ryan, *Parade Magazine 8 July 1990*

*Reference to a law passed by Parliament at her urging.

2 . . . children are seen as people, with their own needs and their own rights—rights equal, but not identical, to those of adults.

Ibid.

3 Children are people of equal value—human beings with equal rights, including the right to state their own opinions and views on things. The important thing is to give them a channel through which they can be heard.

Ibid.

2419. Maria Irene Fornés (1930–)

1 "Let Me Be Wrong, but also Not Know It"

Song title, *The Successful Life of 3 1965*

2 DR. KHEAL. Opposites, contradictions compress so that you don't know where one stops and the other begins.

Dr. Kheal 1968

3 DR. KHEAL. We can only do what is possible for us to do. But still it is good to know what the impossible is.

Ibid.

4 FEFU. Women have to find their natural strength and when they do find it, it comes forth with bitterness and it's erratic. . . . Women are restless with each other. They are like live wires . . . either chattering to keep themselves from making contact or else, if they don't chatter, they avert their eyes like Orpheus . . . as if a god once said "and if they shall recognize each other, the world will be blown apart . . ."
Fefu and Her Friends 1977

5 FEFU. Women are always eager for the men to arrive. When they do, they can put themselves at rest, tranquilized. . . . That's the closest they can be to feeling wholesome. The danger is gone, but the price is the mind and the spirit.
Ibid.

6 . . . the playwright is the "woman" of the theater . . . The playwright is the woman and the director is the husband.
Quoted in "Maria Irene Fornes," *Interviews with Contemporary Women Playwrights* by Kathleen Betsko* and Rachel Koenig *1987*
*See 2739.

7 I feel that the older I get, the more shameless I feel. And in a sense, more pure.
Ibid.

8 Writing is an intellectual process, so it is good to *root* the process into your stomach, your heart, your bowels.
Ibid.

9 When I'm not doing something that comes deeply from me, I get bored. When I get bored I get distracted, and when I get distracted, I become depressed. It's a natural resistance, and it insures your integrity. You die when you are faking it, and you are alive when you are truthful.
Ibid.

2420. Lydia Gottschewski (fl. 1930s)

1 It is a curious fact that pacifism . . . is a mark of an age weak in faith, whereas the people of religious times have honored war as God's rod of chastisement . . . Only the age of enlightenment has wished to decide the great questions of world history at the table of diplomats.
Women in the New State 1934

2421. Francine Du Plessix Gray (1930–)

1 Woman—as tender of the hearth, custodian of most ethnic rituals and religious customs, safe-guarded of tribal memory—stands in contrast to man the explorer, innovator, technocrat, who in his nomadic obsession for power and control tends to neglects many time-honored traditions.
"Women's Rites," *Vogue* (New York) *September 1980*

2 If I were to describe the decline in quality of life enjoyed by women in the West, I'd say it decreased in proportion to the decrease of meaningful rituals in their lives.
Ibid.

3 This is indeed the nadir of women's history, the idle and lonely housewife, surrounded by kitchen appliances, who increasingly resorts, as medical figures show, to Valium and alcohol and the equally drugging effects of daytime television to relieve her sense of powerlessness and isolation.
Ibid.

4 The act of nutrition is not a purely physiological event. It remains, in its more civilized form, a way of communion. The family meal is a formality that cultivates in us from earliest age a curb of natural greed, a capacity for sharing, thoughtfulness, a talent for civilized conversation. It is a custom that can enrich our knowledge of our historic roots by carefully prepared food from our own ethnic tradition, that can enlarge our love of literature by readings of poetry easily adaptable to the beginning or the end of a meal.
Ibid.

5 In the terrifying orgies of his fictions he gave free rein to those darker inclinations, to the impulses that can compel us to regress if only in our fantasies to an archaic, animal-like stage, liberated from even the most fundamental taboos—incest, cannibalism—imposed by civilization.
At Home with the Marquis de Sade 1998
*Donatien Alphone Françoise de S—, French writer (1740–1814). The word "sadism" derives from the marquis.

2422. Barbara C. Harris (1930–)

1 A fresh wind is blowing across this church* of ours.
Sermon, Church of the Advocate (Philadelphia), Quoted in "First Anglican Woman Bishop . . ." by Bruce Rule, Associated Press *26 September 1988*
*Anglican Communion.

2423. Lorraine Hine (1930–)

1 Women don't have halos built in.
Quoted in "Cleaning house in government . . ." by Carol M. Ostrom, *Seattle Times*, A1–9 *2 August 1992*

2424. Jean Houston (193-?–)

1 Thus the hero/heroine always lives in a time of dyings, the dyings of the self, of the social sanctions, of society's forms, the dying of standard-brand religions, standard-brand governments, economics, psychologies, relationships. She or he, however, discovers the courage to undergo new birth and then serves as midwife for the continuum of births necessary to redeem both time and society to a higher level.
"Living in One's and Future Myths" (1995), *The Fabric of the Future: Women Visionaries of Today Illuminate the Path to Tomorrow*, M.J. Ryan, ed. *1998*

2 When mythological symbols no longer work, there's the sense of alienation from the society often followed by a desperate question to replace the lost meaning of the once-power myth. So currently we are seeing quickie replacement programs—yoga, Eastern philosophies, macrobiotic diets, shamanic rituals, drumming—being tried on and often discarded like so many cross-cultural garments that frankly don't fit our needs very well, as they too were growing in a different mythic soil.
Ibid.

3 We look to our myths to discover what to do to recreate our world and, most importantly, what *not* to do to raise up monsters and apparitions. To call genetics and geologies into being is to play God. And so we return to the divine plays of myth to discover the scenarios that await us.
Ibid.

4 A myth is something that never was but is always happening . . . and that happening is upon us and within us, declaring its continued presence in whatever medium we choose to receive the news of the world.
Ibid.

2425. Maureen Howard (1930–)

1 When I go home my mother and I play a cannibal game; we eat each other over the years, tender morsel by morsel, until there is nothing left but dry bone and wig.

Bridgeport Bus 1966

2 . . . my mother is soothed at last by her television, watching lives much more professional than ours.

Ibid.

3 I started that book but something happened, my brother's children, my mother's gall bladder, something happened so I never finished.

Ibid.

4 . . . they spoke to me. That happens now and again, even when you become a sophisticated reader with all kinds of critical impedimenta: you read something that is so direct, so pertinent to exactly where you are—the way you feel and your precise frame of mind.

Ibid.

5 I have a world now, about the size of a circle of light thrown by a desk lamp, that is mine and safe from my mother and the zipper company and my brother's children.

Ibid.

6 . . . the ivy remembered another season, though I suppose it was the future that I really admired in them, because I had none.

Ibid.

7 She was a survivor, frail, helpless, but a survivor: the past was one prop, the bottle another.

"Three Cheers for Mr. Spears," *Before My Time* 1974

8 "The process of losing my faith was so gradual," said Mr. Spears, "I didn't seem to notice it. I've thought since that it was a counterpart of attaining my physical growth, which I never noticed either. One day it was complete—my height and my loss of faith—and it was easy, painless. I wish that I had suffered."

Ibid.

2426. Dolores Huerta (1930–)

1 . . . if you haven't forgiven yourself something, how can you forgive others?

Quoted in "Stopping Traffic: One Woman's Cause" by Barbara L. Baer, *The Progressive September 1975*

2 Don't be a marshmallow. Walk the street with us into history. Get off the sidewalk. Stop being vegetables. Work for justice. *Viva* the boycott!

Ibid.

3 How do I stop eleven million people from buying the grape?

Ibid.

4 But we want to change people's lives. Farmworkers kill themselves working, living nowhere, traveling all the time, putting up with the pesticides because the growers want it that way. It's a feudal system which higher wages won't change. *We* know the work can be organized so people settle down in one place with their families, and control their lives through political power and their own union—which they run themselves.

Quoted in "Dolores Huerta: *La Pasionaria** of the Farmworkers" by Judith Coburn, *Ms.* (New York) *November 1976*

*Dolores Ibarruri (see 1690) was known as *La Pasionaria* during the Spanish Civil War.

5 I consider myself a feminist, and the Women's Movement has done a lot toward helping me not feel guilty about my [two] divorces. But among poor people, there's not any question about women being strong—even stronger than men—they work in the fields right along with the men. When your survival is at stake, you don't have these questions about yourself like middle-class women do.

Ibid.

6 Women are getting afraid to have kids. I still believe you are supposed to conceive children. Don't you want to leave something of yourself, belong to something, do that for your man?

Ibid.

7 That's why Cesar* always reminds us of that *dicho: Hay mas tiempo que vida* (the saying: there is more time than life).

Ibid.

*Cesar Chavez, American migrant worker, labor leader, union organizer (1927–1993).

2427. Sandra Weinstein Jacobson (1930–)

1 Wasting limited assets by encouraging protracted litigation is a cause of, not a cure for, the feminization of poverty.

"Restricting Divorce Hurts Children and Women," *The New York Times 21 February 1996*

2428. Selma James (1930–)

1 It is not women's fault if we are so tender. It is in the nature of the lives we live. And further, it would be a terrible catastrophe if men had to live men's lives and women's also. Which is precisely what has happened today—to women.

Ch. 1, *The Ladies and the Mammies: Jane Austen* & Jean Rhys*** 1983

*See 753. **See 1678.

2 Revolutions are notorious for allowing even non-participants—even women!—new scope for telling the truth since they are themselves such massive moments of truth, moments of such massive participation.

Ibid.

3 We have needed to define ourselves by reclaiming the words that define us. They have used language as weapons. When we open ourselves to what they say and how they say it, our narrow prejudices evaporate and we are nourished and armed.

Ibid.

2429. Jennifer Johnston (1930–)

1 [She] . . . didn't succumb to his enormous charm. [Or] . . . perhaps she had indeed succumbed, and thereafter had to protect herself from it.

The Invisible Worm 1992

2430. Priscilla Galloway (1930–)

1 I left you in a snowstorm in December
Nearly six years ago.
I write this for you, Bev, because
Somehow our marriage
Endures, and
Sometimes we go out together.
Sometimes we dance.

"Sometimes We Dance," St. 3, 25 October 1984

2 The bicycle of my mood
Wavers,

Wobbles, as I
Uncertain rider, uneasy,
Seek surety in slowness
"The Bicycle of My Mood," St. 1 (1975), *Cross-Canada
Writers' Quarterly* 7 (#1): 31 *February 1985*

3 What are the special properties of sand? It shifts, moves out from under you. With sand there is no stability, no permanence. Things are not what they appear to be. Sand insinuates itself everywhere. It slips in, grain by gritty grain. In calm weather, you live with it under your fingernails, in your pubic hair. When the dry wind rises, sand beats on your every door, into nostrils, under eyelids. The woman's dress of old Islam was created as a desperate defence against the invasion of sand, not the lascivious eyes of men.

In sandy places, the habit of silence develops early. Its alternative is a mouth forever full of grit. Those who cannot, will not learn to be silent, pay for their chatter with early loss of their worn-down teeth.
"A Bed of Peas," *Truly Grim Tales 1996*

4 Jack takes the harp and runs. I am feeling very light. In a little while I will float. Part of my mother's mystery has been explained. I've been grappling with the knowledge for more than a month. Unnatural images haunt me. My husband is sunken far in his own problems, or he would have noticed. A dozen times, I've started to tell him and my mouth has closed on the words.

I've had my own bones tested, and I'm only half human, though I am fully human size. I am half pygmy myself: a freak.
Ibid., "Blood and Bone"

5 "You did this carving?" Daedalus asked. It was obvious he did not believe her.

"Certainly." Hebe flushed. "Why do you doubt it?"

"A woman! Who taught you?"

"My mother, who else? My father also. My family have been carvers and workers in wood and metal for generations. Jewellers, sculptors, potters, sometimes a needlewoman or a weaver. My mother was a great artist, and artists are honured at this court. Why are you surprised? Are there no women in Athens who do this work?"

"Needlecrafts or weaving, yes. Those are women's work. The others, no."

Hebe snorted. "And people call Athens a civilized land!"
Daedalus and the Minotaur 1997

6 It seemed to me that paradise ought to be more attractive than hell. The experience of paradise, if one may speak thus about a concept, must surely be preferable to the experience of hell. It is one of the paradoxes of literature, however, that hell is the best seller. There is a fascination about the anatomy of sin. Dante's *Inferno* satisfied my adolescent appetitie for gothic images on a far more profound level than Frankenstein or Dracula.
Confessions of a Book Junkie n.d.

2431. Abbey Lincoln (1930–)
1 The fact that white people readily and proudly call themselves "white," glorify all that is white, and whitewash all that is glorified, becomes unnatural and bigoted in its intent only when these same whites deny persons of African heritage who are Black the natural and inalienable right to readily—proudly—call themselves "black," glorify all that is black, and blackwash all that is glorified.
"Who Will Revere the Black Woman?," *Negro Digest
September 1966*

2432. Gay Gaer Luce (1930–)
1 Swept along in the concepts of their business-oriented culture, many people berate themselves if they are not as consistent and productive as machines.
Preface, *Body Time 1971*

2 . . . people are beginning to resist the rhythm of the machine and suspect that the path of inner harmony and health demands an inward attention.
"Trust Your Body Rhythms," *Psychology Today*
(New York) *April 1975*

3 Even as small children we are trained not to listen to our bodies or trust our sensations.
Ibid.

4 Our harmony is maintained by nature, since we are not closed systems, but are part of the turning earth, the sun, moon and cosmos beyond. In contradiction with our inner clockwork, our urban culture bids us to forget our sources of health and harmony and live by artificial clocks.
Ibid.

2433. Ann McGovern (1930–)
1 Dumb. Dumb. Tiny drum beats. Dumb. Dumb. Her sister's favorite word. She called her dumb more than she called her Jane.
"Wonder is Not Precisely Knowing," *American Scene:
New Voices*, Don Wolfe, ed. *1963*

2 She shared much with her sister—the absence of a father, the presence of a shadowy unhappy mother. They had one bike and one sled between them and had learned long ago that these possessions were not worth the fights.
Ibid.

3 In those days, people did not think it was important for girls to read. Some people thought too much reading gave girls brain fever.
The Secret Soldier 1975

2434. Norma Meacock (193-?–)
1 . . . in all my life I have never found reasoning satisfactory as a means of progress.
Thinking Girl 1968

2 If the texture of our daily life gets any thinner, it'll disappear up its own arsehole.
Ibid.

3 Being human, we should bear all we can.
Ibid.

2435. Alice Miller (193-?–)
1 Society chooses to disregard the mistreatment of children, judging it to be altogether normal because it is so commonplace.
"Childhood and Creativity," *Pictures of a Childhood*,
Hildegarde Hannum, tr. *1986*

2 Technical mastery and skill may be helpful to many, but they are not necessarily so. They can even become a prison for those who are afraid to express themselves, for such artists may cling to their technical proficiency and hide behind it. I have seen drawings that are true to nature down to the last detail, with

scarcely a single flaw, yet they seem lifeless because the person who drew them is not sensed there at all.

Ibid.

3 We are often imprisoned in a cage of our own abilities and routines, which provides us with a sense of security. We are afraid to break free; yet we must gasp for air and keep seeking our way, probably over and over again, if we do not want to be smothered in the womb of what is familiar and well known to us, but rather to be born along with our new work.

Ibid.

2436. Frances Newton (fl. 1930s)

1 There, in that manufactured park with its ghoulish artificiality, with its interminable monuments to bad taste, wealth and social position, we were planning to place the body of a beautiful and dignified old man who had lived generously and loved beauty.

Light, Like the Sun 1937

2 I can stand what I know. It's what I don't know that frightens me.

Ibid.

2437. Sandra Day O'Connor (1930–)

1 There is no question that the [Supreme] Court has now made clear that it will no longer view as benign archaic and stereotypic notions concerning the roles and abilities of males and females. Despite the encouraging and wonderful gains and the changes for women which have occurred in my lifetime, there is still room to advance and to promote correction of the remaining deficiencies and imbalances.

Conference Speech (Atlanta), Quoted in *The New York Times* 12 February 1989

2 The more education a woman has, the wider the gap between men's and women's earnings for the same work.

Phoenix Magazine 1971

2438. Minako Ohba (1930–)

1 I was still in my twenties, but I felt like the old cedar tree that had been standing at the foot of the Three Sisters for thousands of years. . . . I was born and raised in Japan, an ancient country with a long history, but when I lived there I had never felt like an old cedar. Yet when I separated from my country a strange part of me, which seemed to have been covered by moss before, revealed itself. I became aware of a power inside me, informing me of things I had no way of knowing.

"Candle Fish," *Unmapped Territories, New Women's Fiction from Japan*, ed. & tr. 1991

2 We are the creatures who dream about things we cannot attain. Our dreams do not exist in reality.

Ibid.

3 And even if I could really disappear like vapor, leaving my husband and child to sleep soundly like the earth itself, I would fall again somewhere, sometime. It is not possible even for smoke to become nothing.

Ibid.

4 "If you try to kill someone, you can't complain about being killed yourself, can you? By putting his hand around my neck, he slowly strangled himself."

Ibid.

5 It seems we discover the meaning of our unconscious behavior only when we are confronted with the unconscious behavior of others.

Ibid.

6 "But we don't learn from other people, I guess. If I were ten years younger, I'm sure I would do the same thing all over again. That's why I don't want to be younger. Why do people want to bring their youth back? For my part, I'm glad it's gone for good."

Ibid.

2439. Dory Previn (1930–)

1 men wander
women weep
women worry
while men are asleep

"Men Wander" 1971

2 I said
your words
till my throat
closed up
and I had
no choice
but to do your song
I was you baby
I was you too long

"I Was You" 1971

3 Would you care to stay till sunrise
it's completely your decision
it's just the night cuts through me like a knife
would you care to stay awhile and save my life?

"The Lady With the Braid" 1971

4 What most of us want is to be heard, to communicate—which are in the ballads of the wandering minstrel.

Quoted in "Sexism Seen But Not Heard" by Tracy Hotchner, *The Los Angeles Times* 26 May 1974

5 The infiltration of women writers into film will bring new life to it because "the male idea" is in a state of terminal perfection . . . Films by and about women will now answer the questions raised by male films and then there will be a cycle when men will answer back.

Ibid.

2440. Carmen M. Pursufull (1930–)

1 I traded in my almost disappearing wings
withdrawing to the borough of restraint.
It was a barren place.

"First Stop/City of Senses," St. 12 (1986), *The Woman That I Am, The Literature and Culture of Contemporary Women of Color*, D. Soyini Madison, ed. 1994

2441. Ruth Rendell (1930–)

1 The worst has happened . . . it's rather liberating.

The Crocodile Bird 1993

2442. Muriel Resnik (193–?–)

1 JOHN. . . . that's nothing but a tax dodge! . . . This is what the Internal Revenue Service expects. It's all part of the game. They play their part, we have to play ours. It's our duty as American citizens!

Act I, Sc. 1, *Any Wednesday 1963*

2 HELEN . . . it's so horrible to be—oh God—*thirty* . . . Today is a turning point in my life, the beginning of the end. It's pushing forty—and menopause out there waiting to spring—and before you can even turn around you're a senior citizen.

Ibid.

3 JOHN. But she doesn't *know* I'm hurting her, so I'm not. Is that a happy woman? Is she? You see? We're not hurting her, we're not taking anything away from her. In point of fact, having you in my life makes me happy, a happy husband for Dorothy! Far from hurting her, pet, we're *helping* her.
ELLEN. We are?
JOHN. Of course! If I didn't have you, Dorothy would be *miserable*!

Act II, Sc. 1, Ibid.

4 JOHN. I'll tell you about babies. Whenever I see one, I want to give it a cigar and discuss the Common Market.

Sc. 2, Ibid.

5 JOHN. I happen to feel that suburbia is as much of a blight as billboards on country roads.

Ibid.

2443. Rachel Rosenthal (1930?–)

1 I look at performing as transcendental lovemaking. I put everything in it—I put who I am in it, all my passion, all my vulnerability, all my intelligence. When I come on stage and I feel the energy of the audience, all my fears disappear and the performance becomes a ritual of communion. In that way, it is extremely nourishing.

Quoted in "Rachel Rosenthal," *Exposures, Women & Their Art* by Ann Brown & Arlene Raven* 1989
*See 3020.

2 I need to know that the earth is given a chance to survive and that she will continue long after we are gone.

Ibid.

2444. Dorothy Semenow (1930–)

1 I share with the client how I arrive at my responses. In doing so, I demonstrate that analytical methods are knowable and imply that the client too can master them. This demystifies my utterances and punctures the myth often held over from childhood by the client (and by many of the rest of us too) that *big people*, originally *her parents* and now *the analyst*, can read her mind and heart with their powerful X-ray vision and thus know her sins *and* her destiny.

Address, "Principles of Feminist Psychoanalysis," Cedars-Sinai Hospital, Los Angeles *May 1975*

2 As early as possible in our analytic journey we try to sketch what kind of treasures the client wants to build into her life. True, she often comes to analysis caught up and spilling over with what is wrong. But buried in the suffering of those wrongs is some notion of stunted rights. We uncover those rights lost in the client's yesterdays and add to them her hopes for her tomorrow.

Ibid.

2445. Alice M. Shepard (fl. 1930s)

1 They shall not pass, tho' battleline
May bend, and foe with foe combine,
Tho' death rain on them from the sky
Till every fighting man shall die,
France shall not yield to German Rhine.

"They Shall Not Pass" *n.d.*

2446. June L. Tapp (1930–)

1 Now about the totalitarian liberal. . . . What I found . . . were groups who in principle or on paper were committed to religious values that looked liberal, but who held those views with a ferocity that would not, could not, allow for a truly democratic interpretation of the rights of others. Their liberality was more apparent than real.

Quoted in "The Notion of Conspiracy Is Not Tasty to Americans" by Gordon Bermant, *Psychology Today* (New York) *May 1975*

2 The liberal view, it seems to me, encourages a diversity of views and open confrontation among them. . . . The due process of law as we use it, I believe, rests squarely on the liberal idea of conflict resolution.

Ibid.

3 Public participation—as in the jury trial—is the cornerstone in the administration of justice and vital to our system of law.

Ibid.

4 . . . I cannot accept the idea of law as merely repressive or punitive. It can be expressive and conducive to the development of social values.

Ibid.

5 If I had to describe something as divine it would be what happens between people when they really get it together. There is a kind of spark that makes it all worthwhile. When you feel that spark, you get a good deep feeling in your gut.

Quoted in "By Law Possessed" by Carol Tavris, Ibid.

2447. Maria Elena Walsh (1930–)

1 4. Because your mother is a saint, but all other women are witches. (4. Porque su mamá es una santa, por lo tanto las demás mujeres son unas brujas.)

"Know Why You Are a Male Chauvinist," *1980*

2 9. Because the whole matter of gestation and birth scares and disgusts you, like sex ed at the Ministry of Education. (9. Porque todo ese asunto de la gestación y el parto le da miedo y asquete, como la educación sexual al Ministro de Educación.)

Ibid.

2448. C. DeLores Tucker (1930–)

1 Dr. King's* dream has become a nightmare not only for our children but for their parents and our whole society. People are frightened and fearful because of the culture of the gangstas**. . . . they're not afraid because of the enemy he had to fight, but because of their own brothers and sisters who are paid to glorify drugs and guns, to call black women obscene names.

Cited in "Black Activist crusades . . . ," *Seattle Times*, A12 *6 February 1994*
*Martin Luther King Jr., American civil rights leader (1929–68); assassinated. **A genre of music noted for driving beat and "talksing" modality, it is also a conduit for raunchy language and portrayals of violence.

2 Maybe it is wrong, but it is a way of life.*

Ibid.

*Reference to her acceptance of $65,000 in fees for speeches while holding state office.

3 We spent $500 billion on that war on Iraq, and Hussein* still lives. We could have spent $6,000 and sent the boys in the 'hood over there, and they would have taken care of Hussein and taken care of him permanently.

TV interview, Cited in "Black activist crusades . . . ," Ibid.
*Iraqi military and political leader (1937–), president of Iraq (1979–).

2449. Barbara G. Walker (1930–)

1 Through making God in his own image, man has almost forgotten that woman once made the Goddess in hers. This is the deep secret of all mythologies . . .

Introduction, The Woman's Encyclopedia of Myths and Secrets 1983

2 Our culture has been deeply penetrated by the notion that "man"—*not* woman—is created in the image of God. This notion persists, despite the likelihood that the creation goes in the other direction: that God is a human projection of the image of man.

Ibid.

3 From a biological viewpoint, patriarchal religion denied women the natural rights of every other mammalian female: the right to choose her stud, to control the circumstances of her mating, to occupy and govern her own nest, or to refuse all males when preoccupied with the important business of raising her young.

Ibid.

4 The rack and stake were replaced in the 18th and 19th centuries by more subtle abuses, aimed at suppressing women legally, politically, economically, and psychologically.

Ibid.

5 The church declared from the first that the Great Goddess "whom Asia and all the world worshippeth" must be despised "and her magnificence destroyed" (Acts 19:27). This is virtually the only Gospel tenet that churches followed through all their centuries with no deviation or contradiction. It seemed necessary to hide the fact that Christianity itself was an offshoot of Middle-Eastern Goddess worship . . .

Ibid.

6 Naturally, the secret most deeply concealed by Christianized history was the many-named Goddess, the original Holy Trinity who created and governed the world, gave birth to its Saviors, sent her tablets of divine law to the prophets, and watched over every life from womb to tomb, according to pre-Christian belief. Today she is viewed as "mythical," having been replaced by a God (equally mythical, but more acceptable to a male-dominated culture), who took over most of her attributes.

Ibid.

2450. Shirley Williams (1930–)

1 No test tube can breed love and affection. No frozen packet of semen ever read a story to a sleepy child.

Daily Mirror (London) *2 March 1978*

2 The Catholic Church has never really come to terms with women. What I object to is being treated either as Madonnas or Mary Magdalenes.*

Observer (London) *22 March 1981*

*See 79 and 81.

2451. Hilma Wolitzer (1930–)

1 I was drawn into the back seat of his father's green Pontiac and the pattern of those seat covers stays in my head forever.

"Waiting for Daddy," *Esquire* (New York) *July 1971*

2 It seemed strange that I could do all those things with him, discover all those sensations and odors and that new voice that came from the dark pit of my throat *Don't—oh yes, oh God* and that my mother and grandmother didn't know.

Ibid.

3 There is something terrific about not knowing your father because it opens up possibilities . . .

Ibid.

4 Their kitchen was full of piecework and vague hope.

Ibid.

2452. Gladys Yang (1930?–fl. 1950s–1980s)

1 In China, literature is not viewed as a form of entertainment or simply as a source of aesthetic enjoyment, but as an effective means of education, of inspiring readers with high ideals and the belief that these can be attained.

Preface, *Seven Contemporary Chinese Women Writers 1982*

2453. Elyce Zenoff (1930–)

1 The insanity defense is a key in part of our criminal justice system which is founded on the belief that [people] normally choose whether or not to obey the law.

U.S. News & World Report 5 July 1982

2454. Bertye Young Williams (fl. 1930s–d. 1951)

1 He who follows Beauty
Breaks his foolish heart.

"Song Against Beauty" *n.d.*

2455. Lorraine Hansberry (1930–1965)

1 WALTER. Baby, don't *nothing* happen for you in this world 'less you pay *somebody* off!

Act I, Sc. 1, *A Raisin in the Sun 1958*

2 BENEATHA. Why do you give money at church for the missionary work?
MAMA. Well, that's to help save people.
BENEATHA. You mean save them from *Heathenism* . . . I'm afraid they need more salvation from the British and the French.

Sc. 2, Ibid.

3 LINDER. And at the moment the overwhelming majority of our people out there feel that people get along better, take more of a common interest in the life of the community, when they share a common background. I want you to believe me when I tell you that race prejudice simply doesn't enter into it.

Act II, Sc. 3, Ibid.

4 ASAGAI. Ah, I like the look of packing crates! A household in preparation for a journey! . . . Something full of the flow of life. . . . Movement, progress. . . .

Act. III, Ibid.

5 BENEATHA. While I was sleeping in my bed in there, things were happening in this world that directly concerned me—and nobody asked me, consulted me—they just went out and did things—and changed my life.

Ibid.

6 BENEATHA. Don't you see there isn't any real progress, Asagai, there is only one large circle that we march in, around and around, each of us with our own little picture—in front of us—our own little mirage that we think is the future.

Ibid.

7 LENA. Child, when do you think is the time to love somebody the most; when they done good and made things easy for everybody?

Well then you ain't through learning—because that ain't the time at all. It's when he's at his lowest and can't believe in hisself 'cause the world done whipped him so. When you starts measuring somebody, measure him right, child, measure him right. Make sure you done taken into account what hills and valleys he come through before he got to wherever he is.

Ibid.

8 TOUSSAINT. The Europeans will always underestimate us. They will believe again and again that they have come to fight slaves. They will be fighting free men thinking they are fighting slaves, and again and again—that will be their undoing.

Toussaint (uncompleted work) 1961

9 It really doesn't matter whether you are talking about the oppressed or the oppressor. An oppressive society will dehumanize and degenerate everyone involved . . . and in certain very poetic and very true ways at the same time it will tend to make if anything the oppressed have more stature . . . because at least they are arbitrarily placed in the situation of overwhelming that which is degenerate . . . in this instance the slave society.

Television interview with Frank Perry, *Playwright at Work*
21 May 1961

10 GLORIA. Things as they are as they are and have been and will be that way because they got that way because things were as they were in the first place.

The Sign in Sidney Brustein's Window 1964

11 There is both joy and beauty and illumination and communion between people to be achieved through dissection of personality. That's what I want to do. I want to reach a little closer to the world, which is to say people, and see if we can share some illuminations together about each other.

Quoted in *To Be Young, Gifted and Black*
by Robert Nemiroff* 1969

*Hansberry's husband.

12 TSHEMBE. Abioseh, I know the tale of Jesus. But I think now if there was such a man he must have been what all men are: the son of man who died the death of men. And if the legend is true at all, that he was a good man, then he must have despised the priests of the temples of complicity!

Act I, Sc. 2, *Les Blancs* 1972

13 MARTA. I've lived without a confidante for years: it really isn't the strain it's painted to be.

Act II, Sc. 1, Ibid.

14 TSHEMBE. Ntali, there are men in this world—I don't know how to say this so you will understand—who *see* too much to take sides.

Sc. 2, Ibid.

15 TSHEMBE. I said racism is a device that, of itself, explains nothing. It is simply a means. An invention to justify the rule of some men over others.

Ibid.

16 TSHEMBE. I am simply saying that a device *is* a device, but that it also has consequences: once invented it takes on a life, a reality of its own. So, in one century, men invoke the device of religion to cloak their conquests. In another, race. Now in both cases you and I may recognize the fraudulence of the device, but the fact remains that a man who has a sword run through him because he refuses to become a Moslem or a Christian—or who is shot in Zatembe or Mississippi because he is black—is suffering the utter *reality* of that device. And it is pointless to pretend that it doesn't *exist*—merely because it is a *lie*!

Ibid.

17 ABIOSEH. That is what you think, but God is raging in you, fighting for you!
TSHEMBE. Why does He always tell you and not me what He is doing!

Sc. 4, Ibid.

18 DEKOVEN. We do not look down on the black because we really think he is lazy, we look down on him because he is wise enough to resent working for us. The problem, therefore, has been how *not* to educate him at all and—at the same time—teach him just enough to turn a dial and know which mining lever to raise. It has been as precise as that—and that much a failure. Because, of course, it is *impossible*! When a man knows that the abstraction *ten* exists—nothing on earth can stop him from looking for the fact of *eleven*.

Sc. 5, Ibid.

2456. Marjorie Tuite (193-?–1986)

1 I think to work on one issue is a luxury in a global analogy. Because there is a basic problem: militarism out of a patriarchal structure, a world view of militarism that nurtures cultural violence.

Speech, Annual Convention, National Assembly of Religious Women 1985

2457. Julie Anne Bovasso (1930–1991)

1 BEBE. I want to know you. And I want you to know me and understand me. What good is love without understanding? How can we love each other if we don't know each other and understand each other? And how can we know each other if we don't love each other?

Schubert's Last Serenade
1972

2 BEBE. I didn't take it all back: I simply adjusted my initial reaction.

Ibid.

2458. Geraldyn Cobb (1931–)

1 Even before [we] . . . had reached 300 feet, I recognized that the sky would be my home. I tumbled out of the airplane with stars in my eyes.*

Woman into Space 1963
*Her first flight, piloted by her father, taken when she was twelve years old.

2 . . . to marry . . . would be to cage an eagle.

Ibid.

3 I saw the bluest sky I'd ever known*. . . . There was no horizon, no boundary. . . . I felt that I could reach up to the sun, or touch the stars that were hidden in its glow.

Ibid.

* Her record-setting flight in 1957 when she reached an altitude of 30,560 feet.

4 I believe that . . . space exploration will reveal God's creations and purposes more clearly to us.

Ibid.

2459. Riane Eisler (1931–)

1 The root of [society's] problem lies in a social system in which the power of the Blade is idealized—in which both men and women are taught to equate true masculinity with violence and

dominance and to see men who do not conform to this ideal as "too soft" or "effeminate."
Introduction, *The Chalice and the Blade* 1987

2 . . . all the modern, post-Enlightenment movement for social justice, be they religious or secular, as well as the more recent feminist, peace, and ecology movements, are part of an underlying thrust for the transformation of a dominator to a partnership system. Beyond this, in our time of unprecedentedly powerful technologies, these movements may be seen as part of our species' evolutionary thrust for survival.
Ibid.

3 . . . the amazing world of our hidden past . . . reveal[s] a long period of peace and prosperity when our social, technological, and cultural evolution moved upward: many thousands of years when all the basic technologies on which civilization is built were developed in societies that were not male dominant, violent, and hierarchic.
Ibid.

4 . . . as evidenced by both sociological and psychological studies, human hierarchies based on a force or the threat of force not only inhibit personal creativity but also result in social systems in which the lowest (basest) human qualities are reinforced and humanity's higher aspiration (traits such as compassion and empathy as well as the striving for truth and justice) are systematically suppressed.
fn. 5, *Ibid.*

5 And if the central religious image [in Neolithic times] was a woman giving birth and not, as in our time, a man dying on a cross, it would not be unreasonable to infer that life and the love of life—rather than death and the fear of death—were dominant in society as well as art.
Ch. 2, "Messages from the Past: The World of the Goddess," *Ibid.*

6 Particularly in our age, when we are trying to create a peaceful society, it is instructive to know that the pen can be as mighty as the sword. For in the end it was this seemingly puny tool that was to literally stand reality on its head.
Ch. 5, "Memories of a Lost Age: The Legacy of the Goddess," *Ibid.*

7 In essence, the search of so many people today for the mystical wisdom of an earlier time is the search for the kind of spirituality characteristic of a partnership rather than a dominator society.
Ibid.

8 Still more arresting, when compared to our modern world, is that in these prehistoric partnership societies technological advances were used primarily to make life more pleasurable rather than to dominate and destroy.
Ibid.

9 . . . one of the best-kept historical secrets is that practically all the material and social technologies fundamental to civilization were developed before the imposition of a dominator society.
Ibid.

10 Like travelers through a time warp, we have, through archaeological discoveries, journeyed into a different reality. O the other side we found not the brutal stereotypes of an eternally depraved "human nature" but amazing vistas of possibilities for a better life. . . .

The old love for life and nature and the old ways of sharing rather than taking away, of caring for rather than oppressing, and the view of power as responsibility rather than domination did not die out. But, like women and qualities associated with femininity, they were relegated to a second place.
Ch. 8, "The Other Half of History: Pt. I," *Ibid.*

11 Rather than being any longer a threat to the established androcratic order, Christianity became what practically all this earth's religions, launched in the name of spiritual enlightenment and freedom, have also become: a powerful way of perpetuating that order.
Ch. 9, "The Other Half of History: Pt. II," *Ibid.*

12 . . . something went terribly wrong with Christianity's original gospel of love. How otherwise could such a gospel be used to justify all the torture, conquest, and bloodletting carried out by devout Christians against others, and against one another, that makes up so much of our Western history?
Ibid.

13 History as taught in most schools is largely a matter of the struggle for power among men and nations. It is the dates of battles and the names of kings and generals noted for alternately constructing and destroying fortresses, palaces, and religious monuments.
Ch. 10, "The Patterns of the Past: Gylany and History," *Ibid.*

14 It is hardly surprising that our conventional histories systematically omit anything relating to women or "femininity" when only a very short time ago not one American university even had a women's studies program. . . . It is thus also not surprising that most "educated" people still find it hard to believe there were any women who mattered in history or that anything as peripheral as women and "feminine" values could be a central force, not only to our past, but also to our prospects for a better future.
Ibid.

15 In making it possible for more women than ever before to gain at least a partial foothold in the world outside their homes, this [19th century feminist] movement vastly humanized society as a whole.
Ibid.

16 The evidence mounting from every quarter is that the prevailing [dominator] system is rapidly nearing its logical evolutionary end, the end of the line for a five-thousand-year androcratic detour. What may lie ahead is the final bloodbath of this dying system's violent efforts to maintain its hold. But the death throes of androcracy could also be the birth pains to gylany and the opening of a door into a new future.
Ch. 11, "Breaking Free: The Unfinished Transformation," *Ibid.*

17 In its radical departure from the older view in which men's social position and wealth were basically a function of birth, of being born a nobleman, a craftsman, or a serf, capitalism was in fact a move toward a freer society. It fundamentally challenged the rigid hierarchies of the earliest or protoandrocratic social organization in which the strongest most brutal and violent men, the warrior-conquerors, and their descendants, the nobles and kings, exerted despotic powers justified by religious ideologies as divinely ordained.
Ibid.

18 . . . the clear message from population experts worldwide [is] that if population planning is to succeed, creating satisfying

and socially rewarded roles for women other than those of wives and mothers is even more important than the availability of birth control education.

Ch. 12, "The Breakdown of Evolution:
A Dominator Future," Ibid.

19 Although a rigidly hierarchical social structure like androcracy, which imprisons both halves of humanity in inflexible and circumscribed roles, is quite appropriate for species of very limited capacity like social insects, it is truly inappropriate for humans. And at this juncture in our technological evolution, it may also be fatal.

Ibid.

20 For millennia of recorded history, the human spirit has been imprisoned by the fetters of androcracy. Our minds have been stunted, and our hearts have been numbed. And yet our striving for truth, beauty, and justice has never been extinguished. As we break out of these fetters, as our minds, hearts, and hands are freed, so also will be our creative imagination.

Ch. 13, "Breakthrough in Evolution: Toward a
Partnership Future," Ibid.

21 But ours is a time when "man's conquest of nature" threatens all life on our planet, when a dominator mind-set and advanced technology are a potentially lethal mix, when all around us institutions designed to maintain domination and exploitation are proving incapable of coping with the massive social, economic, and ecological problems they have created.

Introduction, *Sacred Pleasure: Sex, Myth, and the Politics
of the Body* 1995

22 . . . sex is to a very large degree socially constructed.

Ch. 1, "From Ritual to Romance: Sexuality, Spirituality, and
Society," Ibid.

23 But it is one thing to recognize the destructive side of nature, and ourselves, and the fact that sometimes people are violent and abusive. It is quite another to organize society so that—in order to maintain rigid rankings of domination—violence and abuse become institutionalized . . .

Ibid.

24 Is it just accidental that *passion* is the word we use for both sexual and mystical experiences? Or is there some long-forgotten but still powerful connection?

Ibid.

25 Indeed, if we view evolution as a giant creative experiment—of which we humans are one of the latest, and most amazing, results—we see an extraordinary pageant in which the evolution of both sex and consciousness plays an important part. For between the appearance of simple one-celled organisms three and a half billion years ago and the emergence sixty-five million years ago of the order of primates to which we humans belong, we see the unfolding of life from stationary blobs of matter to ever more complex crawling, flying, walking, and more recently tool-making, talking, and acutely self-aware creatures—life forms capable not only of joining nature in altering our physical environment but also, through our phenomenal human capacity for learning, of fundamentally altering ourselves and our social structures.

Ch. 2, "Animal Rites and Human Choices: The Roots of
Dominator and Partnership Sex," Ibid.

26 For with consciousness and choice comes the possibility of change.

Ibid.

27 It is hard for us to imagine an art where scenes of men killing are virtually absent, where the act of giving birth is depicted as sacral in sculptures and paintings of the Goddess herself, and where . . . the act of coitus is a religious rite. It is also not easy for us to imagine menstrual blood as a divine gift, as we are not used to thinking of the human body, much less sex, as spiritual. And it is particularly hard for us to see woman's sexuality, her vagina, her pregnancy, her birth giving—as associated with a deity rather than as something shameful, unfit for polite discussion, much less religious art.

Ch. 3, "Sex as Sacrament: The Divine Gifts of Life,
Love, and Pleasure," Ibid.

28 For to people who saw sex as a sacramental act of communion with nature and one another, our sexual images of men humiliating, degrading, mutilating, enslaving, and even killing women in the name of sexual pleasure would have been totally incomprehensible—and patently insane.

Ibid.

29 Laws are extremely useful indicators of the behaviors that are at a particular time and place considered acceptable or unacceptable. Of course, they do not tell us how people actually behave. but far more clearly than literary and historical accounts, laws do tell us what kinds of attitudes and behaviors the people who make the laws (and who have the power to enforce them) want to encourage or discourage.

Ch. 6, "The Reign of the Phallus: War, Economics,
Morality, and Sex," Ibid.

30 But to change our realities, we also have to change our myths. As history amply demonstrates, myths and realities go hand in hand.

Ch. 7, "The Sacred Marriage in a Dominator World:
The Metamorphosis of Sex, Death, and Birth," Ibid.

31 Certainly the earlier, more partnership-oriented societies of our pre-history were not ideal. But they were societies where our most intimate connections—the physical connection of women and children through birth and of women and men through sex—were still understood as sacred rather than profane. And they were societies where even at the dawn of human civilization, women and men already seem to have sensed the wisdom that lies at the core of our most exalted mystical and religious traditions: that is only through connection, through love (be it of a divinity or another human) that we can attain our highest potentials.

Ch. 8, "The Last Traces of the Sacred Marriage: Mysticism,
Masochism, and the Human Need for Love," Ibid.

32 Indeed, what better way of justifying male dominance than the biblical dogma that man derives his control over woman from a heavenly Father, God, or Lord in whose image he was made? And what better rationale for excluding women from the priesthood (and thus from positions of moral and, what was often the same, legal authority) than the Judeo-Christian and Muslim equation of divine power exclusively with maleness?

Ibid.

33 But I am also convinced that if we are to construct a society where sex will be linked not with violence and domination but with the truly erotic—with the life-and-pleasure-giving powers within us and around us in the world—we need to fully extricate ourselves from all that has for so long unconsciously bound us to painful and unhealthy myths and realities. We need an understanding of what I have here called the politics of the body, and of how this relates to what has conventionally been defined as political.

Ch. 10, "Waking from the Dominator Trance: The Revolution in consciousness and the Sexual Revolution," Ibid.

34 It is easy under the guise of sexual (or any other) freedom for those who hold power to more effectively dominate that who have been socially disempowered.

Ibid.

35 Still another manifestation of the strong resistance to the mounting partnership thrust has been an intensive campaign for a return to "traditional family values"—the new code name for an authoritarian, male-dominated, patriarchal family designed to teach both boys and girls to obey orders from above, no matter how unjust or unloving they may be. This campaign has mainly come from fundamentalist and other religious groups who are still told by their leaders that the ranking of man over woman is divinely ordained.

Ibid.

36 . . . the deforming binding of girls' feet practiced for many centuries in prerevolutionary China functioned to teach women to accept, as the very essence of their sense of self, the most painful bending of not only their minds but their bodies to the will of others.

Ibid.

37 Although there have always been those who rebel, who consciously reject cruelty and injustice in all its forms, most people conditioned from childhood on to accept chronic human rights violations as normal are not likely to create a society where human rights are not also chronically violated.

Ibid.

38 So at the time that the Church continued to mouth Jesus' message of peace and love, it could command the institution of the brutal Inquisition and the Crusades. It could continue to preach that we are all "brothers" through Jesus Christ, and at the same time condone the virtual enslavement of women to their husbands, along with the enslavement of men by men and nation by nation. And at the same time that the princes of the Church spoke of men's liberation from the "tyranny" of the flesh through abstention from any sexual pleasure, they could also enact the most complex, cruel and manifestly absurd rules to tyrannically control the most intimate sexual behaviors and even sexual thoughts of the women and men in their "earthly flock." And it is this control over people's bodies that is the ultimate mainstay of dominator social organi- zation.

Ch. 11, "Bondage or Bonding: Sex, Spirituality, and Repression," Ibid.

39 But Rousseau* did not see how his view of sex as an acting out of domination and submission affected not only his behaviors but his thinking—so much so that he could write of repression as natural for half our species, at the same time that he argued that freedom is an inalienable human right.

Ibid.

*French philosopher and writer (1712–1788).

40 But while public torture (and even the torture behind closed doors of political prisoners) is today properly condemned by almost everyone in the "civilized" world, some people still indignantly defend private (and now even public, as in the so-called torture circuses) sadomasochism as long as it has a sexual component. In other words, as long as it is contextualized in the relationship of men and women, or of homosexuals taking the traditional dominator-dominated roles of men and women, it is not condemned as torture—but defended as freedom.

Ibid.

41 For how can we speak of a free and democratic society with equality and justice for all at the same time that the domina- tion of one half of humanity over the other half is accepted as only proper and right?

Ibid.

42 Changes in consciousness are a very strange thing. Suddenly we see what was there all the time. And we wonder how it could for so long have been invisible to us.

Ibid.

43 This double standard has for millennia been justified by the teachings that in the eyes of God men are of a higher spiritual order than women. It manifests itself in the fact that although men are in Christian dogma deemed to be more spiritual than women, women are in actual practice expected to be far more spiritual than men—more noble, giving, and self-sacrificing. Under this double standard, no matter how kind and caring a woman is, unless she completely sacrifices her own welfare (even her life) for that of others (particularly her husband and children), she can never hope to be considered the spiritual equal of man. And even then, she will only be looked on as the exception to the rule that woman is less spiritually and morally evolved than man.

Ibid.

44 In short, be they secular or religious, Christian or Muslim, ancient or modern, Eastern or Western, the times and places where we find the greatest sexual repression of women are generally also the times and places where political repression is most severe. Yet even today the system's connection between freedom or repression for women and political freedom or repression is still generally ignored.

Ibid.

45 . . . how essential it is for us to ensure that the voices of the women who century after century managed to trust *not* what they were told but their own observations, experiences, and feelings are not lost again.

Ch. 14, "Getting Out of Prince Charming's Slipper: Sex, Femininity, and Power," Ibid.

46 . . . while reproductive sex is something we share with other species that reproduce through sexual intercourse, there are aspects of human sexuality—including the human female's capacity for year-round sexual activity and both the female's and male's capacity for prolonged sexual passion, sexual love, and erotic spirituality—that are uniquely human.

Ibid.

47 Indeed, even though many women have internalized the view that women should not dominate others, they have often also internalized a value system in which the power to dominate others is most highly valued

Ibid.

48 This notion that man can, and should, have absolute dominion over the "chaotic" powers of nature and woman . . . is what ultimately lies behind man's famous "conquest of nature"—a conquest that is today puncturing holes in the earth's ozone layer, destroying our forests, polluting our air and water, and increasingly threatening the welfare, and even survival, of thousands of living species, including our own.

Ch. 15, "Sex, Lies, and Stereotypes: Changing Views of Nature, the Body, and Truth," Ibid.

49 . . . the view of the world as a pyramid ruled from above by a remote, other-worldly deity robs both women's and men's day-to-day experiences of wonder and meaning, investing only that which distances us from life with holiness.

Ibid.

50 But, once again, the men who head the world's powerful religious hierarchies remain conspicuously silent about uncaring and violent sex—even when it is as extreme as genital mutilation and rape. Instead of pressuring world leaders to hold men fully accountable for rape, they expend their considerable resources on trying to stop women and men from the "sins" of contraception and abortion.

Ch. 16, "Morality, Ethics, and Pleasure: Sex and Love in the Age of AIDS," Ibid.

51 . . . despite the fact that even though there are important official Catholic statements on the need for a more just redistribution of wealth, the Vatican has yet to redistribute its enormous wealth or, as attested by former priests who did join such grass-roots struggles, to actively support those who in many Catholic countries are fighting for just that.

Ibid.

52 But here too there is enormous opposition from the religious right, once again on the grounds that to educate young people about sex is immoral.

Actually, if we stop to think about it, what is immoral is *not* to educate young people about sex. Because for no other matter of importance in our lives—and sex is obviously of tremendous importance—would anyone think of advocating ignorance.

Ibid.

53 Today, at least in principle, the ownership of one person's body by another, the appropriation of a person's services, and the negation of a person's right to make fundamental life choices is almost universally condemned. But there is one area where, even in principle, all this has been particularly resistant to change. When it comes to women's bodies, women's services, and women's choices, the traditional notion that men should hold power, men should make choices, and men should control women's bodies is still ideologically, legally, and economically in place throughout much of our world today.

Ch. 17, "Sex, Power, and Choice: Redefining Politics and Economics," Ibid.

54 And this exclusion of "women's work" continues, despite United Nations data gathered since 1975 (the beginning of the UN* Decade for Women) indicating that women globally contribute two-thirds of the world's work hours, for which—given the imbalanced, unjust, and truly peculiar nature of the accounting characteristic of dominator economics—they globally earn only one-tenth of what men do and own a mere one-hundredth of the world's property.

Ibid.

*United Nations.

55 For as long as human beings are forced to live in a system that at every turn impedes the fulfillment of their basic human needs—not only for love but for creative and spiritual expression—they will try to compensate for this in other ways, including the compulsive acquisition of ever more material goods.

Ibid.

56 . . . one of the most important developments in modern politics has been the unprecedented phenomenon of masses of people organizing, not just against those who violently oppress them, but against the oppression of others—and even against the use of violence itself.

Ch. 18, " Toward a Politics of Partnership: Our Choices for the Future," Ibid.

57 I now think of this courage to challenge unjust authority from a position of love rather than hate as spiritual courage. I think of it as the courage to question our most hallowed and sanctified norms—as the young Jew named Jesus did almost two thousand years ago when he defied the religion and secular authorities of his day. And I think of it as the kind of courage today being displayed by countless women and men in all walks of life who are through their lives and actions defying still firmly entrenched millennia-old dominator traditions.

Ch. 19, "The New Eves and the New Adams: The Courage to Question, the Will to Choose, and the Power to Love," Ibid.

58 . . . to heal ourselves we also have to heal society.

Ibid.

59 This reclamation of divinity for Mary is particularly important, since we obviously need to leave behind the idealization of a family in which only the father and the son, and not the mother, are divine. In fact, we also need to add to the pantheon of a holy family a divine daughter. For only then will we have a model for families in which all members are equally valued and respected.

Ibid.

60 We all hunger for stories. Stories give form to our desires, feelings, and goals, molding how we view just about everything—from our own bodies to what is sacred or profane, good or bad, possible or impossible. Stories give us figures to emulate, imitate, admire, or abhor. And it is from the stories we are told that we in turn unconsciously fashion our own life scripts.

Ibid.

61 We must have the courage to open our eyes to the needs, suffering, and hopes of children worldwide, to question prescribed conventions, and to become the architects of a partnership future for generations to come through an enlightened, empathic global public education.

Tomorrow's Children: a Blueprint For Partnership Education in The 21st Century 1999

62 Partnership education helps students look beyond conventional social categories, such as capitalism versus communism, right versus left, religious versus secular, and even industrial versus preindustrial or postindustrial. They can instead begin to focus on relationships, and on the underlying question of what kinds of beliefs and social structures support or inhibit relations of violence or nonviolence, democracy or authoritarianism, justice or injustice, caring or cruelty, environmental sustainability or collapse.

Ibid.

63 I have chosen the phrase meaningful evolution to describe a view of evolution in which we can find a larger sense of purpose. . . . It is an approach that draws from an emerging body of scientific findings pointing to the evolutionary roots of caring for others and caring for what happens to future generations. It highlights that what we do in this lifetime is meaningful because it advances the evolution of our species and fulfills our responsibilities to this planet.

Ibid.

2460. Sally Gearhart (1931–)

1 I look forward with great anticipation to the death of the church. The sooner it dies, the sooner we can be about the business of living the gospel.

"The Lesbian and God-the-Father or All the Church Needs Is a Good Lay—on Its Side" 1972

2 Falling asleep, she thought. Sheer contentment, always, even with another Spooned body. But, she mused, there's a special

balm to doing it in a wide bed all alone, with the margins of
your body quite unbounded. . . .
"Flossie's Flashes," *Lesbian Love Stories*, Irene Zahava, ed.
1989

2461. Patricia Goedicke (1931–)

1 even the spiral notebooks I fill
with inky scratches to keep count.

From minute to minute disappear,

erase themselves from the mind's liquid,
dissolving pages.
"Uncharted," *Invisible Horses 1996*

2 . . . she lives in me like a crowd
of love songs and loud static . . .
"Because My Mother Was Deaf She Played the Piano," Ibid.

3 the flesh you live in is an anchor
of damp stones, you cannot move with or without it
"Recipe," Ibid.

4 The mind holds hands with itself in music
Untitled, Ibid.

2462. Ossie Guffy (1931–)

1 I'm a woman, I'm black, I'm a little under forty, and I'm more
of black America than Ralph Bunche* or Rap Brown** or
Harry Belafonte,*** because I'm one of the millions who ain't
bright, militant, or talented.
Ossie: The Autobiography of a Black Woman 1971
*American founder and key diplomat of the United Nations and
recipient of the 1950 Nobel Peace Prize (1904–1971). **H. Rap
Brown, American Black militant (194?–). ***West Indian-born
American actor, singer, director (1927–).

2 I got more children than I can rightly take care of, but I ain't
got more than I can love.
Ibid.

2463. Shirley Hazzard (1931–)

1 How long women take to leave a room, Tancredi thought.
They can't simply get up and walk out—all this shambling and
turning back on their tracks, chattering and embracing . . .
Ch. 1, *The Evening of the Holiday 1965*

2 When we are young, she thought, we worship romantic love
for the wrong reasons . . . and, because of that, subsequently
repudiate it. Only later, and for quite other reasons, we discover its true importance. And by then it has become tiring
even to observe.
Ch. 2, Ibid.

3 One would always want to think of oneself as being on the side
of love, ready to recognize it and wish it well—but, when confronted with it in others, one so often resented it, questioned its
true nature, secretly dismissed the particular instance as folly or
promiscuity. Was it merely jealousy, or a reluctance to admit so
noble and enviable a sentiment in anyone but oneself?
Ch. 9, Ibid.

4 "Sometimes, surely, truth is closer to imagination—or to intelligence, to love—than to fact? To be accurate is not to be
right."
Ch. 11, Ibid.

5 "Perhaps if we lived with less physical beauty we would develop our true natures more."
Ch. 13, Ibid.

6 "Do you ever notice," asked Luisa, "how easy it is to forgive
a person any number of faults for one endearing characteristic, for a certain style, or some commitment to life—while
someone with many good qualities is insupportable for a single defect if it happens to be a boring one?"
Ibid.

7 Algie was collecting contradictions in terms: to a nucleus of
"military intelligence" and "competent authorities" he had
added such discoveries as the soul of efficiency, easy virtue,
enlightened self-interest, Bankers Trust, and Christian Scientist.
"Nothing in Excess," *People in Glass Houses 1967*

8 Mr. Bekkus frequently misused the word "hopefully." He
also made a point of saying locate instead of find, utilize instead of use, and never lost an opportunity to indicate or
communicate; and would slip in a "basically" when he felt
unsure of his ground.
Ibid.

9 Pylos' first official act was to name his new department. The
interim titles that had been used—"Economic Relief of
Under Privileged Territories" and "Mission for Under-De-
veloped Lands"—were well enough in their way, but they
combined a note of condescension with initials which, when
contracted, proved somewhat unfortunate.
"The Story of Miss Sadie Graine," Ibid.

10 Children . . . seldom have a proper sense of their own
tragedy, discounting and keeping hidden the true horrors of
their short lives, humbly imagining real calamity to be some
prestigious drama of the grown-up world.
Ch. 1, *The Bay of Noon 1970*

11 When I was a child . . . I would think it must be marvelous
to issue those proclamations of experience—"It was at least
ten years ago" or "I hadn't seen him for twenty years." But
chronological prestige is tenacious: once attained, it can't be
shed; it increased moment by moment, day by day, pressing
its honours on you until you are lavishly, overly endowed
with them. Until you literally sink under them.
Ibid.

12 Had I been accompanied, I might have laughed out
loud . . . but solitude, which is held to be a cause of eccentricity, in fact imposes excessive normality, at least in
public . . .
Ibid.

13 Words would have been as presumptuous as an embrace: yet
the inadequacy of silence was painful.
Ch. 6, Ibid.

14 Like many men who are compulsively cruel to their womenfolk, he also shed tears at the cinema, and showed a
dispropor- tionate concern for insects.
Ch. 7, Ibid.

15 "People resort to violence," she said. . . . "not to relieve their
feelings but their thoughts. The demand for comprehension
becomes too great, one would rather strike somebody than
have to go on wondering about them."
Ch. 8, Ibid.

16 The ultimate impression they made was of innocence—the novelty of passions not yet turned to slogans, of gifts not deployed for gain, of goodwill not turned to self-importance.

Ch. 9, Ibid.

17 He himself had strengthened this impression by the defences . . . he had constructed; had become their victim, like those heavily fortified towns that invite their own downfall by suggesting that there is something within to be assaulted.

Ch. 13, Ibid.

18 Although I wished I hadn't come, it did not occur to me to go back. In matters of importance there is no such thing as "best avoided"—avoidance is only a vacuum that something else must fill. Everything is the inevitable.

Ch. 15, Ibid.

2464. Margaret O'Shaughnessy Heckler (1931–)

1 When you undermine faith in a system, your child may not necessarily see the difference between the politician who is no longer respected and the policeman, the teacher, the parent.

Quoted in "Impeachment?" by Claire Safran, *Redbook* (New York) *April 1974*

2 Once you start to separate public service from the enormous influence of the fat cats of society, you rob the vested interests of their most powerful weapons.

Ibid.

3 Women are the one minority group it is still considered fashionable to discriminate against.

Quoted on p. 134 *Women of Congress: A Twentieth-Century Odyssey* by Marcy Kaptur 1996

2465. Kristin Hunter (1931–)

1 "A landlord is supposed to be brutal, stingy, insulting, and arrogant. Like the police, like the magistrates, like all the authority-figures of white society. That's what we're used to. That's what we understand. We're accustomed to our enemies, we know how to deal with them. A landlord who tries to be a friend only confuses us."

The Landlord 1966

2 "Love can't last around poverty. Neither can a woman's looks."

Ibid.

3 "But generally speaking I've always been too confused about who I was to decide who I was better than."

Ibid.

4 The most amazing thing about little children, Elgar decided . . . was their fantastic adaptability.

Ibid.

5 "First it is necessary to stand on your own two feet. But the minute a man finds himself in that position, the next thing he should do is reach out his arms."

Ibid.

6 Borden [the psychiatrist], his one stable reference point in reality. The way sailors needed the North Star to guide them through black seas, Elgar needed Borden to help him find his way out of the gathering chaos.

Ibid.

7 Phosdicker was as honest as the day was long. He was an old-fashioned, dedicated civil servant; a fine, upright, honorable old man, Elgar thought. God help us all. A monster.

Ibid.

8 "How does a person become an outlaw, DuBois?" Elgar inquired mildly . . .

"One is born to the calling," DuBois answered. "Many are called, but few choose. You see, society decides which of its segments are going to be outside its borders. Society says, 'These are the legitimate channels to my rewards. They are closed to you forever.' So then the outlawed segments must seek rewards through illegitimate channels. In other words, once my Great White Father declared me illegitimate, I had to be a bastard."

"Is Uncle Sam your Great White Father?"

"Exactly. The white society is my father and, in a figurative sense, every Negro's father. Our mother being Africa."

Ibid.

2466. Adrienne Kennedy (1931–)

1 SARAH. As for myself I long to become even a more pallid Negro than I am now; pallid like Negroes on the cover of American Negro magazines; soulless, educated and irrelevant. I want to possess no moral value, particularly value as to my being. I want not to be. I ask nothing except anonymity.

Funnyhouse of a Negro 1962

2 SARAH. I find there are no places only my *funnyhouse.*

Ibid.

3 SARAH. I wanted to live in Genesis in the midst of golden savannas, nim and white frankopenny trees and white stallions roaming under a blue sky. I wanted to walk with a white dove. I wanted to be a Christian.

Ibid.

4 SARAH. For, like all educated Negroes—out of life and death essential—I find it necessary to maintain a stark fortress versus recognition of myself. My white friends like myself will be shrewd, intellectual and anxious for death. Anyone's death.

Ibid.

5 SARAH. . . . for relationships was one of my last religions.

Ibid.

6 I bleed.

A Lesson in Dead Language 1964

7 To me, menstrual periods, no matter how long you've been having them, are traumatic—simply the fact that you bleed once a month. I wanted to write about the fear* . . . the fear that you will get blood on your clothes.

"Adrienne Kennedy," *Interviews with Contemporary Women Playwrights*, Kathleen Betsko** and Rachel Koenig 1987

*In her play *Lesson in a Dead Language*. **See 2739.

2467. Ella Leffland (1931–)

1 How could [the diplomats] keep from flinging themselves across the table and smashing each other's faces? Why had [innocent families] been killed if these leaders didn't even let go with a clenched fist? In such restraint, in such cordiality, there was something more horrifying than death itself.

Rumors of Peace 1979

2 Each century was the same; history was the same record played over and over. War was war, and peace was preparation for war; it was as if man were crazy, had always been, would always be. And the people on the street were man in his daily and abiding craziness.

Ibid.

2468. Jo Ann McNamara (1931–)

1 They [nuns] served their god and their church and in doing so they fulfilled themselves and laid a foundation for all women. Without the daring and sacrifice of these nuns, it is impossible to imagine the feminist movements of modern times finding any purchase in the public world. They created the image and reality of the autonomous woman. They formed the professions through which that autonomy was activated.

Sisters in Arms: Catholic Nuns Through Two Millennia 1996

2469. Toni Morrison (1931–)

1   "Which you want? A whipping and no turnips or turnips and no whipping?"

The Bluest Eye 1961

2 The difference between white and black females seemed to me an eminently satisfactory one. White females were *ladies*, said the sign maker, worthy of respect. And the quality that made ladyhood worthy? Softness, helplessness and modesty—which I interpreted as a willingness to let others do their labor and their thinking. Colored females, on the other hand, were *women*—unworthy of respect, independent and immodest.

"What the Black Woman Thinks About Women's Lib,"
The New York Times Magazine 22 August 1971

3 . . . she lived out her days exploring her own thoughts and emotions, giving them full reign, feeling no obligation to please anybody unless their pleasure pleased her . . .

Sula 1974

4   "I sure did live in this world."
    "Really? What have you got to show for it?"
    "Show? To who? Girl, I got my mind. And what goes on in it. Which is to say, I got me."
    "Lonely, ain't it?"
    "Yes. But my lonely is *mine*. Now your lonely is somebody else's. Made by somebody else and handed to you. Ain't that something? A secondhand lonely."

Ibid.

5 And like any artist with no art form, she became dangerous.

Ibid.

6   "I don't know everything, I just do everything."

Ibid.

7   "I know what every colored woman in this country is doing."
    "What's that?"
    "Dying."

Ibid.

8 He meant that if you take a life, then you own it. You responsible for it. You can't get rid of nobody by killing them. They still there, and they yours now.

Song of Solomon 1977

9   "How come it [peacock] can't fly no better than a chicken?" Milkman asked.

"Too much tail. All that jewelry weighs it down. Like vanity. Can't nobody fly with all that shit. Wanna fly, you got to give up the shit that weighs you down."

Ch. 8, *Ibid.*

10 Bryn Mawr had done what a four–year dose of liberal education was designed to do: unfit her for eighty per cent of the useful work of the world.

Ch. 9, *Ibid.*

11   "Grab this land! Take it, hold it, my brothers, make it, my brothers, shake it, squeeze it, turn it, twist it, beat it, kick it, kiss it, whip it, stomp it, dig it, plow it, seed it, reap it, rent it, buy it, sell it, own it, build it, multiply it, and pass it on—can you hear me? Pass it on!"

Ch. 10, *Ibid.*

12 . . . "I wish I'd a knowed more people. I would of loved 'em all. If I'd a knowed more, I would a loved more."

Ch. 15, *Ibid.*

13 Fog came to that place in wisps sometimes, like the hair of maiden aunts. . . .

Tar Baby 1981

14 What they took for inattentiveness was a miracle of concentration.

Ibid.

15 Of course I'm a black writer. . . . I'm not just a black writer, but categories like black writer, woman writer and Latin American writer aren't marginal anymore. We have to acknowledge that the thing we call "literature" is more pluralistic now, just as society ought to be. The melting pot never worked. We ought to be able to accept on equal terms everybody from the Hasidim* to Walter Lippmann**, from the Rastafarians*** to Ralph Bunche.****

Quoted in *Newsweek* (New York) 30 March 1981
*(1) A movement of strictly adherent Jews; **(2) American journalist who won Pulitzer Prizes in 1958 and 1962 (1889–1974); ***(3) religious-cultural movement that began in the 1930s in Jamaica; ****(4) American founder and key diplomat of the United Nations and recipient of the 1950 Nobel Peace Prize (1904–1971).

16 But I think women dwell quite a bit on the duress under which they work, on how hard it is just to do it at all. We are traditionally rather proud of ourselves for having slipped creative work in there between the domestic chores and obligations. I'm not sure we deserve such big A-pluses for all that.

Quoted in "Toni Morrison's Black Magic" by Jean Strouse,*
Newsweek (New York) 30 March 1981
*See 3071.

17 To make the story appear oral, meandering, effortless, spoken—to have the reader *feel* the narrator without *identifying* the narrator, or hearing him or her knock about, and to have the reader work with the author in the construction of the book—is what's important. What is left out is as important as what is there.

"Rootedness: The Ancestor as Foundation," *Black Women Writers (1950-1980)*, Mari Evans,* ed. 1983
*See 2225.

18 That's a pejorative term in critical circles now: if a work of art has any political influence in it, somehow it's tainted. My feeling is just the opposite: if it has none, it is tainted.

The problem comes when you find harangue passing off as art. It seems to me that the best art is political and you ought to be able to make it unquestionably political and irrevocably beautiful at the same time.

Ibid.

19 "How come everybody run off from Sweet Home can't stop talking about it? Look like if it was so sweet you would have stayed."

"Girl, who you talking to?"

Paul D laughed. "True, true. She's right, Sethe. It wasn't sweet and it sure wasn't home." He shook his head.

"But it's where we were," said Sethe. "All together. Comes back whether we want it to or not."

Pt. I, Beloved 1987

20 Once upon a time she had known more and wanted to.

Ibid.

21 She couldn't read clock time very well, but she knew when the hands were closed in prayer at the top of the face she was through for the day.

Pt. II, Ibid.

22 "Tell me this one thing. How much is a nigger supposed to take? Tell me. How much?"

"All he can," said Stamp Pad. "All he can."

"Why? Why? Why? Why? Why?"

Ibid.

23 Two parents can't raise a child any more than one. You need a whole community—everybody—to raise a child. And the little nuclear family is a paradigm that just doesn't work. It doesn't work for white people or for black people. Why we are hanging onto it, I don't know. It isolates people into little units—people need a larger unit.

Quoted in "The Pain of Being Black" by Bonnie Angelo,
Time (New York) 22 May 1989

24 How soon country people forget. When they fall in love with a city it is forever, and it is like forever. As though there never was a time when they didn't love it. The minute they arrive at the train station or get off the ferry and glimpse the wide streets and the wasteful lamps lighting them, they know they are born for it. There, in a city, they are not so much new as themselves: their stronger, riskier selves.

Ch. 2, Jazz 1991

25 In this country American means white. Everybody else has to hyphenate.

The Guardian (London) 29 January 1992

26 . . . huge silences in literature, things that had never been articulated, printed or imagined [inspired me] and they were the silences about black girls, black women.

It was into that area that I stepped and found it to be enormous.

Quoted in "Morrison wins a Nobel" by Michael Brown
(AP), Seattle Post–Intelligencer, A1, 7 8 October 1993

27 Winning as an American is very special—but winning as a black American is a knockout.

Ibid.

28 Oppressive language does more than represent violence; it is violence; does more than represent the limits of knowledge; it limits knowledge.

Nobel Prize acceptance speech (7 December 1993),
Cited by John Darnton, The New York Times
8 December 1993

29 In my country children have bitten their tongues and use bullets instead to iterate the voice of speechlessness.

Ibid.

30 We die. That may be the meaning of life. But we do language. That may be the measure of our lives.

Ibid.

31 For her a dead language is not only one no longer spoken or written, it is unyielding language content to admire its own paralysis. Like statist language, censored and censoring. Ruthless in its policing duties, it has no desire or purpose other than maintaining the free range of its own narcotic narcissism, its own exclusivity and dominance. However moribund, it is not without effect for it actively thwarts the intellect, stalls conscience, suppresses human potential. . . . . Official language smitheryed to sanction ignorance and preserve privilege is a suit of armor polished to shocking glitter, a husk from which the knight departed long ago. Yet there it is: dumb, predatory, sentimental. Exciting reverence in schoolchildren, providing shelter for despots, summoning false memories of stability, harmony among the public.

Nobel lecture (Princeton, New Jersey, 7 December 1993),
The Electronic Nobel Museum,
http://www.nobel.se/enm–index.html 7 December 1996

32 The vitality of language lies in its ability to limn the actual, imagined and possible lives of its speakers, readers, writers. Although its poise is sometimes in displacing experience it is not a substitute for it. It arcs toward the place where meaning may lie.

Ibid.

33 "Our inheritance is an affront. You want us to have your old, blank eyes and see only cruelty and mediocrity. Do you think we are stupid enough to perjure ourselves again and again with the fiction of nationhood? How dare you talk to us of duty when we stand waist deep in the toxin of your past?"

Ibid.

34 Passion is never enough; neither is skill.

Ibid.

35 "Don't tell us what to believe, what to fear. Show us belief's wide skirt and the stitch that unravels fear's caul."

Ibid.

36 They shoot the white girl first. With the rest they can take their time. No need to hurry out here. They are seventeen miles from a town which has ninety miles between it and any other. Hiding places will be plentiful in the Convent, but there is time and the day has just begun.

Paradise 1998

2470. Alice Munro (1931–)

1 Lovers. Not a soft word, as people thought, but cruel and tearing.

"Something I've Been Meaning to Tell You," Something I've
Been Meaning to Tell You 1974

2 If they had been married, people would have said they were very happy.

Ibid.

3 But I never cleaned thoroughly enough, my reorganization proved to be haphazard, the disgraces came unfailingly to light, and it was clear how we failed, how disastrously we fell

short of that ideal of order and cleanliness, household decency which I as much as anybody else believed in.
“Winter World,” Ibid.

4 Now that she was sure of getting away, a layer of loyalty and protectiveness was hardening around every memory she ever had.
The Beggar Maid 1981

5 They were intimate. They had found out so much about each other that everything had got cancelled out by something else. That was why the sex between them could seem so shamefaced, merely and drearily lustful, like sex between siblings.
The Progress of Love 1986

6 Moments of kindness and reconciliation are worth having, even if the parting has to come sooner or later.
Ibid.

7 So you see against what odds, and with what unpromising-looking persons, love takes root and flourishes.
Selected Stories 1996

8 [It is] a landscape that has an enchantment on it, making it kindly, ordinary and familiar while you are looking at it, but changing it, once your back is turned, into something you will never know, with all kinds of weathers, and distances you cannot imagine.
“Walker Brothers Cowboy,” Ibid.

9 What if people really did that—sent their love through the mail to get rid of it? What would it be that they sent? A box of chocolates with centers like the yolks of turkey’s eggs. A mud doll with hollow eye sockets. A heap of roses slightly more fragrant than rotten. A package wrapped in bloody newspaper that nobody would want to open.
“Before the Change,” *The Love of a Good Woman 1998*

10 But once in a while came a moment when everything seemed to have something to say to you. The rocking bushes, the bleaching light. All in a flash, in a rush, when you couldn’t concentrate. Just when you wanted summing up, you got a speedy, goofy view, as from a fun-ride.
“Jakarta,” Ibid.

11 My father and my father’s family had no real interest in music. They didn’t quite know this. They thought that the intolerance or even hostility they felt towards a certain type of music (this showed even in the way they pronounced the word “classical”) was based on a simple strength of character, an integrity and a determination not to be fooled. As if music that departed from a simple tune was trying to put something over on you, and everybody knew this, deep down, but some people—out of pretentiousness, from want of simplicity and honesty—would never admit that it was so. And out of this artificiality and spineless tolerance came the whole world of symphony orchestras, opera, and ballet, concerts that put people to sleep.
“My Mother’s Dream,” Ibid.

2471. Nisa (1931–)

1 There isn’t a child whose birth is painless. It hurts like a terrible sickness.
Quoted in *The Life and Words of a !Kung Woman* by Marjorie Shostak *1981*

2 When your child dies, you think . . . “This God . . . his ways are foul! Why did he give me a little one and then take her away?”

It is the same if it is your mother. You cry for her as you do for your child. You pull off your beads and ornaments so your neck and body are bare. You mourn for her, you miss her, and your heart is miserable.
Ibid.

3 Babies, yes . . . the day your baby is about to be born, that day your heart is miserable. But once it is lying on the sand, a baby is a wonderful thing. Your heart is very happy because you love children. You and your child talk together, even if it is just tiny.
Ibid.

2472. Elaine Roulet (1931–)

1 When a man goes to prison the woman keeps the home together. But when the woman goes to prison, many times the home falls apart.
Quoted in “Sister Elaine” by Sherrye Henry, *Parade Magazine 29 March 1987*

2 People in prison have been so put down, they just don’t realize how holy they are.
Ibid.

3 Our lives may be the only Gospel some people ever read.
Ibid.

2473. Amanda Row (1931–)

1 Jocelyn’s childhood stood on the bookcase: *Pollyanna, The Bobbsey Twins, Now We Are Six, Black Beauty*, and *The Little Minister* beside *Heidi*.
Where No Sea Runs 1963

2474. Jane Rule (1931–)

1 “. . . I think everything has value, absolute value, a child, a house, a day’s work, the sky. But nothing will save us. We were never meant to be saved.”
“What were we meant for then?”
“To love the whole damned world . . .”
Desert of the Heart 1964

2 Ann did not want to accept the view of the world she sometimes revealed to herself.
Ibid.

3 I believe only in art and failure.
This is Not for You 1970

4 Cleaving is an activity which should be left to snails for cleaning ponds and aquariums.
Introduction, *Lesbian Images 1975*

5 I didn’t want to be a boy, ever, but I was outraged that his height and intelligence were graces for him and gaucheries for me.
Ibid.

6 I had never been as resigned to ready-made ideas as I was to ready-made clothes, perhaps because, although I couldn’t sew, I could think.
Ibid.

7 Morality, like language, is an inverted structure for conserving and communicating order. And morality is learned, like language, by mimicking and remembering.
“Myth and Morality, Sources of Law and Prejudice,” Ibid.

8 What is is my domain. What ought to be is the business of politicians and preachers.

> "Lesbian and Writer," *A Hot-Eyed Moderate 1985*

2475. Maxine Singer (1931–)

1 . . . Science is one of the grand human activities. It uses the same kind of talent and creativity as painting pictures and making sculptures. It's not really very different, except that you do it from a base of technical knowledge.

Science is not an inhuman or superhuman activity. It's something that humans invented, and it speaks to one of our great needs—to understand the world around us.

> Quoted in *A World of Ideas* by Bill Moyers *1989*

2 A society that turns its back on science has to face decay and deterioration.

> Ibid.

3 The reasons we know that we will discover things that we can't describe now is that this has been the history of science. We do things to learn something we can define, and we wind up knowing things we never imagined even asking about.

> Ibid.

4 If the knowledge that is gained is misused, it is not because of science or the scientists, it is because of the same old human problems that have caused evil for eons. . . . And whether evil uses technology that's new or technology that's old, what motivates it are human problems that have nothing to do with the developments in technology.

> Ibid.

2476. Kabita Sinha (1931–)

1 I was the first
rebel—
banished from paradise,
exiled.
I learned
that human life
was greater
than paradise.
I was first
to know.

> "*Ishwarke Eve*" (Eve Speaks to God), *Poetry Is the Supreme Being*, Pritish Nandy, tr. *1976*

2477. Merlin Stone (1931–)

1 It is difficult to grasp the immensity and significance of the extreme reverence paid to the Goddess over a period of (at least) seven thousand years and over miles of land cutting across national boundaries and vast expanses of sea. Yet it is vital to do just that to fully comprehend the longevity as well as the widespread power and influence this religion once held.

> *When God Was A Woman 1976*

2 We may find ourselves wondering to what degree the suppression of women's rites has actually been the suppression of women's rights.

> Ibid.

3 They had so hoped that when the beings of Earth began to think about a very long past, it would help them to concieve of a very long future ahead.

> "The Plasting Project," *Hear the Silence*, Irene Zahava, ed. *1986*

2478. Jolene Unsoeld (1931–)

1 I think fewer of the women [in politics] have deliberately set out to be on a leadership track the way many of our male colleagues have. We want to work on the issues that drove us to office.

> Quoted in "Cleaning house in government . . . " by Carol M. Ostrom, *Seattle Times*, A1–9 *2 August 1992*

2 For some darn reason, society seems to think that men—I don't know why, because they wear the pants?—are effective, but women have to prove it.

Even after you've done a whale of a good job in a term of office, you have to prove it all over again . . . as though somehow your past work were a fluke.

> Ibid.

3 Reproductive health is at the very core of a woman's existence in its importance. If you want to be brutally frank what it compares [with] is if you had health care plans that did not cover any illness related to male testicles.

> "Unsoeld 'brutally frank' on issue," *Seattle Post-Intelligencer 13 May 1994*

2479. Judith Viorst (1931–)

1 The honeymoon is over
And we find that dining by candlelight makes us squint,
And that all the time
I was letting him borrow my comb and hang up his wet raincoat in my closet,
I was really waiting
To stop letting him.

> "The Honeymoon Is Over," *It's Hard to Be Hip Over Thirty and Other Tragedies of Married Life 1968*

2 With four walk-in closets to walk in,
Three bushes, two shrubs, and one tree,
The suburbs are good for the children,
But no place for grown-ups to be.

> "The Suburbs Are Good for the Children," Ibid.

3 But it's hard to be hip over thirty
When everyone else is nineteen . . .

> "It's Hard to Be Hip Over Thirty," Ibid.

4 And I'm working all day and I'm working all night
To be good-looking, healthy, and wise.
And adored.
And contented.
And brave.
And well-read.
And a marvelous hostess,
Fantastic in bed,
And bilingual,
Athletic,
Artistic . . .
Won't someone please stop me?

> "Self-Improvement Program," St. 4, *How Did I Get to Be Forty and Other Atrocities 1973*

5 Love is much nicer to be in than an automobile accident, a tight girdle, a higher tax bracket or a holding pattern over Philadelphia.

> "What IS This Thing Called Love?" *Redbook* (New York) *February 1975*

6 Brevity may be the soul of wit, but not when someone's saying, "I love you."

> Ibid.

7 Guilt: Although it is sometimes better to sin and feel guilty than never to sin at all, it is pretty ratty to sin and not feel guilty.

Love and Guilt and the Meaning of Life 1979

8 The world could maybe come to an end on next Tuesday.
The ceiling could maybe come crashing on my head.
I maybe could run out of things for me to worry about.
And then I'd have to do my homework instead.

"Fifteen, Maybe Sixteen Things to Worry About ," St. 2, *If I Were in Charge of the World and Other Worries . . . 1981*

9 My mom says I'm her sugarplum.
My mom says I'm her lamb.
My mom says I'm completely perfect
Just the way I am.
My mom says I'm a super-special wonderful terrific little guy.
My mom just had another baby.
Why?

"Some Things Don't Make Any Sense at All," *in toto, Ibid.*

10 When we think of loss we think of the loss, through death, of people we love. But loss is a far more encompassing theme in our life. For we lose not only through death, but also by leaving and being left, by changing and letting go and moving on. And our losses include not only our separations and departures from those we love, but our conscious and unconscious losses of romantic dreams, impossible expectations, illusions of freedom and power, illusions of safety—and the loss of our own younger self, the self that thought it would always be unwrinkled and invulnerable and immortal.

Introduction, *Necessary Losses 1986*

11 We begin life with loss. We are cast from the womb without an apartment, a charge plate, a job or a car. We are sucking, sobbing, clinging, helpless babies. Our mother interposes herself between us and the world, protecting us from overwhelming anxiety. We shall have no greater need than this need for our mother.

Ch. 1, *Ibid.*

12 Growing up means letting go of the dearest megalomaniacal dreams of our childhood. Growing up means knowing they can't be fulfilled. Growing up means gaining the wisdom and the skills to get what we want within the limitations imposed by reality—a reality which consists of diminished powers, restricted freedoms and, with the people we love, imperfect connections.

Ch. 11, *Ibid.*

13 It's true love because
If he said quit drinking martinis but I kept on drinking them
and the next morning I couldn't get out of bed,
He wouldn't tell me he told me.

True Love n.d.

2480. Barbara Walters (1931–)

1 . . . I happen to disagree with the well-entrenched theory that the art of conversation is merely the art of being a good listener. Such advice invites people to be cynical with one another and full of fake; when a conversation becomes a monologue, poked along with tiny cattle-prod questions, it isn't a conversation anymore.

How to Talk with Practically Anybody About Practically Anything 1970

2 Celebrities used to be found in clusters, like oysters—and with much the same defensive mechanisms.

Ch. 1, *Ibid.*

3 Don't confuse being stimulating with being blunt . . .

Ch. 2, *Ibid.*

4 If we could harness the destructive energy of disagreements over politics, we wouldn't need the bomb.

Ch. 3, *Ibid.*

5 Most old people . . . are disheartened to be living in the ailing house of their bodies, to be limited physically and economically, to feel an encumbrance to others—guests who didn't have the good manners to leave when the party was over.

Ch. 4, *Ibid.*

6 Parents of young children should realize that few people, and maybe no one, will find their children as enchanting as they do.

Ibid.

7 It's a fact that it is much more comfortable to be in the position of the person who has been offended than to be the unfortunate cause of it.

Ch. 6, *Ibid.*

8 A great many people think that polysyllables are a sign of intelligence . . .

Ch. 8, *Ibid.*

9 The origin of a modern party is anthropological: humans meet and share food to lower hostility between them and indicate friendship.

Ch. 9, *Ibid.*

10 Success can make you go one of two ways. It can make you a prima donna, or it can smooth the edges, take away the insecurities, let the nice things come out.

Quoted in "Barbara Walters—Star of the Morning," *Newsweek* (New York) *6 May 1974*

2481. Kathleen Collins (1931–1988)

1 MARIETTA. Dear Pop, always so full of fire, the need to be different . . . First colored to get a job with the Post Office, first colored to own property in Riverview . . . Kept us all in an uproar . . . He had such dreams, saw each of us living in angry defiance of all Negro rules, always standing tall and sturdy as the first of the first of the first of the coloreds . . . Dear Pop, he was so full of fire, none of us could breathe . . .

Act III, Sc. 2, *The Brothers 1982*

2482. Anouk Aimée (1932–)

1 You can only perceive real beauty in a person as they get older.

The Guardian (London) *24 August 1988*

2483. Liliane Atlan (1932–)

1 We have all become little sharks.

The Carriage of Flames and Voices 1971

2 My goal is to arrive at a nonegoistic type of writing: objective writing which would reawaken a love of life. I would like to be able to write for an *empty heart*, that is, emptied of myself—but filled with others.

Theater Winter 1981

3 At first, men wrote on the walls of their caves, then on papyrus, then paper; why, in an age such as ours, should we not write with waves of sound and light?

"Liliane Atlan," Antoine Bootz and Catherine Ruello, trs., *Interviews with Contemporary Women Playwrights*, Kathleen Betsko* and Rachel Koenig *1987*

*See 2739.

4 Video is a great instrument—the cassette and television are small and intimate. I am convinced that the new mode of communication is not the theater play, the novel, or cinema, but videotexts.

Ibid.

5 When we return to pure language we are given great visions.

Ibid.

2484. Bai Fengxi (1932?–)

1 Women are not the moon. Emit your own light.

Return of an Old Friend on a Stormy Night 1983

2 If a woman is strong, there will be no peace in the house.

Ibid.

3 My love of the stage is like my love for my mother: a love that grows with age . . .

"Bai Fengxi" by Corinne Jacker,* *Interviews with Contemporary Women Playwrights*, Kathleen Betsko** and Rachel Koenig *1987*

*See 2532. **See 2739.

4 I don't think a writer can give an answer, or make a judgement as to which solution is right or wrong. All a writer can do is raise the question.

Ibid.

2485. Beverly Butcher Byron (1932–)

1 Legislation is not going to change discrimination. That is like trying to legislate morality. The quality of representation is neither hindered nor helped by gender; the quality is with the individual.

Speech, 96th Congress *January 1979*

2486. Olga Connolly (1932–)

1 Society feels that sport must be justified, and we have gotten away from the Greek concept of mind and body. That is the failure of the physical education process.

Quoted in "Women in Sports: The Movement Is Real," *The Los Angeles Times 23 April 1974*

2 Women must be accepted as human beings, and it can't be done until women are physically strong enough to stand on their own feet.

Ibid.

2487. Shirley Conran (1932–)

1 I make no secret of the fact that I would rather lie on a sofa than sweep beneath it. But you have to be efficient if you're going to be lazy.

"The Reason Why," *Superwoman 1975*

2 Life is too short to stuff a mushroom.

Epigraph, Ibid.

2488. Patricia Cumming (1932–)

1 We thought we could banish
the faceless
dark, the sticky
cobwebs in the hall:
we thought the
hollowness would go away.

"Further Notes for the Alumni Bulletin," Sts. 3–4, *Quartet*, Vol. VI, Nos. 15–16 *Winter/Spring 1974*

2489. Alice Thomas Ellis (1932–)

1 Death is the last enemy: once we've got past that I think everything will be alright.

"In the Psychiatrist's Chair," BBC Radio 4 *19 August 1992*

2 Humans were useful for breeding, when you could catch one, and every now and then . . . he ate one, but otherwise he avoided them on the whole . . . .

Fairy Tale 1998

2490. Eva Figes (1932–)

1 The "cured" [psychiatric] patient is actually brainwashed, a walking automaton, as good as dead.

Patriarchal Attitudes 1970

2 Sadly, man recognizes that the ideal, submissive woman he has created for himself is somehow not quite what he wanted.

Ibid.

3 Either one goes on gradually liberating the divorce laws, until marriage stands exposed as a hollow sham in which no one would wish to engage, or one takes a short cut and abolishes marriage altogether . . .

Ibid.

4 When modern woman discovered the orgasm it was (combined with modern birth control) perhaps the biggest single nail in the coffin of male dominance.

Quoted in *The Descent of Woman* by Elaine Morgan* *1972*

*See 2162.

5 The law of individualism and private enterprise is that God helps those who help themselves; what is more, He is actually on their side, since it is a sin not to make use of the talents God gave you. So poverty definitely implies not only laziness but a fall from grace: God disapproves of paupers.

Ibid.

6 Providing for one's family as a good husband and father is a water-tight excuse for making money hand over fist. Greed may be a sin, exploitation of other people might, on the face of it, look rather nasty, but who can blame a man for "doing the best" for his children?

"A View of My Own," *Nova January 1973*

7 . . . unless society recognises that its responsibility extends far beyond the provision of free schooling, the money spent on state education is largely wasted. School becomes just another way of institutionalising the poor.

Ibid.

8 Helping her to run the [women's] clinic had taught me to view our lives as a sort of battleground, and every day as a skirmish in an unending war.

The Seven Ages 1987

9 The much vaunted male logic isn't logical, because they display prejudices—against half the human race—that are considered prejudices according to any dictionary definition.
Women Writers Talk, Olga Kenyon, ed. *1989*

2491. Antonia Fraser (1932–)

1 . . . As with all forms of liberation, of which the liberation of women is only one example, it is easy to suppose in a time of freedom that the darker days of repression can never come again.
"Epilogue: How Strong?" *The Weaker Vessel 1984*

2 It is however an almost universal fact of history that women have done well in wartime when they have been able or compelled to act as substitutes for men, showing themselves resourceful, courageous and strong in every sense of the words; in short displaying without much difficulty all those qualities generally described as masculine. It is another fact that the postwar period has generally seen a masculine retreat from this view of the female sex when the vacuum no longer needs to be filled.
Ibid.

2492. Shirley Gee (1932–)

1 MOTHER. There's too much hate in the world. I'll not be part of it. Sometimes that's hard, but how I try to think of it is this. The boys on the streets, the soldiers. With them it's not so much the boredom, it's the tension of that boredom. And nobody wants them, and they feel it. That makes explosions in them, trapped inside them, not allowed to burst. So when they get the chance, there's a bit of trouble, then they let it out, they're full of spite, smash things, smash people.
Act I, *Never in My Lifetime 1983*

2493. Penelope Gilliatt (1932–)

1 The reason why her face was unlined was perhaps that no expression ever passed through it, the owner having developed a reputation for herself as a sort of Delphic presence simply by a habit of nonparticipation that had begun as a defence against the efforts of a boisterous English nanny to boot her into vivacity.
Pt. I, Ch. 3, *A State of Change 1967*

2 "Why is it that beautiful women never seem to have any curiosity?"
"Is it because they know they're classical? With classical things the Lord finished the job. Ordinary ugly people know they're deficient and they go on looking for the pieces."
Pt. II, Ch. 8, Ibid.

3 MRS. GREVILLE. Darling, you keep throwing in your hand because you haven't got the whole thing. There *is* no whole thing. One has to make it work.
"Monday," *Sunday Bloody Sunday 1971*

4 ALEX. I can't see why having an affair with someone on and off is any worse that being married for a course or two at mealtimes.
Ibid.

5 ALEX. I've had this business that anything is better than nothing. There are times when nothing has to be better than anything.
"Saturday," Ibid.

6 Gossip columnists at it again. What a lousy job, thriving on invented rows.
Quoted in "Rebirth?" by James Childs, *The Hollywood Screenwriters*, Richard Corliss, ed. *1972*

7 Critics are probably more prone to clichés than fiction writers who pluck things out of the air.
Ibid.

8 I do wish people wouldn't call English people eccentric!
Ibid.

9 The odd thing is, whatever you've been stingy about is something you never use anyway. It's like life itself . . . spend it—spend it because you have it.
Ibid.

10 It would be difficult for a woman to be, I should think, the production head of a studio or a manager without being called a bull-dyke.
Ibid.

2494. Hannah Green (1932–)

1 "On my surface . . . there must be no sign showing, no seam—a perfect surface."
Ch. 1, *I Never Promised You a Rose Garden 1964*

2 A child's independence is too big a risk for the shaky balance of some parents.
Ch. 5, Ibid.

3 She had opened her mind to the words the way an eye used to darkness, veiled with its lashes, opens cautiously to the light, and, finding it even a little blinding, closes itself too late. The light had come, and come invincibly, even after the eye had renounced it. It was too late to unsee.
Ch. 8, Ibid.

4 "Look here," Furii said. "I never promised you a rose garden. I never promised you perfect justice. . . ."
Ch. 13, Ibid.

5 When she was this great soaring creature it seemed as if it was the earth ones who were damned and wrong, not she, who was so complete in beauty and anger. It seemed to her that they slept and were blind.
Ch. 16, Ibid.

6 "I had known all those years and years how sick I was, and nobody else would admit it."
"You were asked to mistrust even the reality to which you were closest and which you could discern as clearly as daylight. Small wonder that mental patients have so low a tolerance for lies."
Ch. 17, Ibid.

7 Later, they began to explore the secret idea that Deborah shared with all the ill—that she had infinitely more power than the ordinary person and was at the same time also his inferior.
Ibid.

8 "If I can teach you something, it may mean that I can count at least somewhere."
Ibid.

9 Outside the doors of study . . . an angel waits.
Ch. 20, Ibid.

10 "Besides, I like an anger that is not fearful and guilty . . ."
Ch. 21, Ibid.

11 "And if I fight, then for *what*?"

"For nothing easy or sweet, and I told you that last year and the year before that. For your own challenge, for your own mistakes and the punishment for them, for your own definition of love and sanity—a good strong self with which to begin to live."

Ibid.

12 Now that she held this tremulous but growing conviction that she was alive, she began to be in love with the new world.

Ch. 23, Ibid.

13 The girl . . . was a gentle, generous veteran of mechanical psychiatry in a dozen other hospitals. Her memory had been ragged, but her sickness was still intact.

Ch. 27, Ibid.

14 "The senses are not discreet!"

Ch. 28, Ibid.

2495. Barbara Howar (1932/35–)

1 . . . the cocktail party remains a vital Washington institution, the official intelligence system.

Ch. 5, *Laughing All the Way* 1973

2 In our long history of shooting politicians . . . I have come to feel that Washington politicians look upon these events as little more than temporary setbacks in the continuing process of government.

Ch. 12, Ibid.

3 Eventually most television stations around the country achieved their minority quota by hiring "twofers," which is a trade expression meaning a "black, female, on-air personality," two television unthinkables, at one salary—a salary, I might add, that generally falls short of the "equal pay for equal work" cliché.

Ch. 15, Ibid.

4 Kissinger* likes intrigue rather than confrontation . . . [He] believes all power begins in the White House. It is his firm belief that he and the President know what is best; the rest of us are to be patient and they will announce our destiny.

Ch. 16, Ibid.

*Henry K—, German-born American diplomat (1923–) who shared the 1973 Nobel Peace Prize.

5 Those complicated people that make Washington the mysterious jungle it is, those famous men and women who to the rest of the world are glamorous and powerful, even ruthless, public figures, have in them a specialness that is inconsistent with the city's official image—a combination of worldly involvement and personal commitment that makes Washington genuine despite its reach for power.

Ch. 21, Ibid.

2496. Jacquelyne Jackson (1932–)

1 Those black males who try to hold women down are expressing in sexist terms the same kinds of expression in racist terms which they would deny. . . .

Speech, First National Conference of Black Women *March 1974*

2497. Rona Jaffe (1932–)

1 A blonde in a red dress can do without introductions—but not without a bodyguard.

"Bottled in Blonde," *Roundabout 1962*

2498. Jenny Joseph (1932–)

1 When I am an old woman I shall wear purple
With a red hat which doesn't go, and doesn't suit me,
And I shall spend my pension on brandy and summer globes
And satin sandals, and say we've no money for butter.
I shall sit down on the pavement when I'm tired
And gobble up samples in shops and press alarm bells
And run my stick along the public railings
And make up for the sobriety of my youth.

"Warning," St. 1, *The Oxford Book of Twentieth Century English Verse*, Phillip Larkin, ed. 1973

2499. Lucille Chernos Kallen (1932–)

1 A lawyer's relationship to justice and wisdom . . . is on a par with a piano tuner's relationship to a concert. He neither composes the music, nor interprets it—he merely keeps the machinery running.

Lawyer's Wit and Wisdom, Bruce Nash, Allan Zullo, eds.; Kathryn Zullo, compiler 1995

2500. Nancy Kassebaum (1932–)

1 The professional politician, with his eye on the next election, quite naturally seeks to temporize or completely avoid potentially controversial issues. . . . The result is often the subjugation of the nation's common welfare.

Quoted in *American Political Women* by Esther Stineman 1980

2501. Judith Krantz (1932–)

1 "It's that or get fat again," she told herself, as she walked up Rodeo or down Camden, feeling a sexual buzz as she searched the windows for new merchandise. The thrill was in the trying on, in the buying. The moment after she had acquired something new it became meaningless to her. . . .

Ch. 6, *Scruples 1978*

2 Billy thought privately that the rich are different only because people treat them as if they were. Sometimes she wondered why people bothered. It was not as if knowing someone rich rubbed off on them, put more money in their own bank accounts. Yet, it was there, that slight self-consciousness, the faint over-consideration, that eagerness to charm, the instinctive putting-the-best-foot-forward that she heard all day.

Ch. 8, Ibid.

2502. Loretta Lynn (1932–)

1 A woman's two cents worth is worth two cents in the music business.

Quoted in "Sexism Seen But Not Heard" by Tracy Hotchner, *The Los Angeles Times 26 May 1974*

2503. Miriam Makeba (1932–)

1 I look at an ant and I see myself: a native South African, endowed by nature with a strength much greater than my size so I might cope with the weight of a racism that crushes my spirit. I look at a bird and I see myself: a native South African, soaring above the injustices of apartheid on wings of pride, the pride of a beautiful people. I look at a stream and I see myself: a native South African, flowing irresistibly over hard obstacles until they become smooth and, one day, disappear—flowing from an origin that has been forgotten toward an end that will never be.

Prologue, *Makeba, My Story*, with James Hall 1987

2 Ours was a marriage, a love affair—the land would nurture us, and we would honor the land.

But the land was too rich and too good. The powerful and greedy invaders saw this at once. . . . We Africans were not consulted or even paid attention to. We were pushed aside, robbed of our land. When we protested we were massacred. A handful of whites took power, and with their boots they pressed the faces of an entire people to the dirt.

Ibid.

3 "*Age ain't nothin' but a number.*" But age is other things, too. It is wisdom, if one has lived one's life properly. It is experience and knowledge. And it is getting to know all the ways the world turns, so that if you cannot turn the world the way you want, you can at least get out of the way so you won't get run over.

Ch. 16, Ibid.

4 Africa has her mysteries, and even a wise man cannot understand them. But a wise man respects them.

Ch. 20, Ibid.

5 People in the United States still have a "Tarzan" movie view of Africa. That's because in the movies all you see are jungles and animals or occasionally the pictures from South Africa of people being beaten by the police. You don't realize that we live "normal" lives there, just as Americans and Europeans do. We watch television and listen to the radio and go to dances and fall in love.

Quoted in "Miriam Makeba is set to take the U.S. by Storm Once Again" by J. Poet, *The New York Times* Syndicate
18 August 1988

2504. Vivienne Malone-Mayes (1932–1995)

1 . . . every day: definitions, theorem, proof, then example; it was almost like a little song . . . once you began to understand it, the beauty of it began to shine through.

Quoted in *Women in Mathematics: The Addition of Difference* by Claudia Henrion* 1997

*See 3446.

2505. Joan Manley (1932–)

1 The best direction is the least possible direction.

Quoted in "Hooked on Books" by Jurate Kazickas, *Working Woman February 1979*

2 Selling is the final step of the creative process—since I didn't have the ability to be in on the beginning of a book, the writing of it, then I wanted to be in on the end.

Quoted in "Wistful View From the Corporate Heights" by Lynn Darling, *The Washington Post 8 April 1979*

3 I would have made a terrible mother. For one thing, I hate to repeat myself.

Ibid.

4 Sometimes you wonder how you got on this mountain. But sometimes you wonder, "How will I get off?"

Ibid.

2506. Nobuko Mori (1932–)

1 Let the voice from the kitchen be heard in government.

Quoted in "A Mountain Moves" by Jill Smolowe, *Time* (New York) *7 August 1989*

2507. Edna O'Brien (1932–)

1 "Any news?" she said suddenly. When she said this I always felt obliged to entertain her, even if I had to tell lies.

Ch. 3, *The Country Girls 1960*

2 "Are you fast?" Baba asked bluntly.

"What's fast?" I interrupted. The word puzzled me.

"It's a woman who has a baby quicker than another woman," Baba said quickly, impatiently.

Ch. 9, Ibid.

3 He had what I call a very religious smile. An inner smile that came on and off, governed as it were by his private joy in what he heard or saw . . .

The Love Object 1963

4 I would mend and with vengeance.

Ibid.

5 That was the first time it occurred to me that all my life I had feared imprisonment, the nun's cell, the hospital bed, the places where one faced the self without distraction, without the crutches of other people . . .

Ibid.

6 . . . it is a shocking fact that although absence does not make love less it cools down our physical need for the ones we love.

Ibid.

7 "I am committing suicide through lack of intelligence, and through not knowing, not learning to know, how to live."

Ibid.

8 It is impossible to insist that bad news delivered in a certain manner and at a certain time will have a less awful effect.

Ibid.

9 Bad moments, like good ones, tend to be grouped together . . .

Ibid.

10 I did not sleep. I never do when I am over-happy, over-unhappy, or in bed with a strange man.

Ibid.

11 When something has been perfect . . . there is a tendency to try hard to repeat it.

Ibid.

12 There is something about holding on to things that I find therapeutic.

Ibid.

13 I suppose you wonder why I torment myself like this, but I need it, I cannot let go of him now, because if I did, all our happiness and my subsequent pain . . . will have been for nothing, and nothing is a dreadful thing to hold on to.

Ibid.

14 . . . she longed for him as she stood in the street and thought the wickedest thing he had done was to come like that and give her false hope, and renew her life for an evening when she had resigned herself to being almost dead.

Ch. 3, *August is a Wicked Month 1965*

15 Later she came in the house and sat in front of the telephone, staring at it, waiting for it to come to life, hoping, beseeching, lifting it from time to time to make sure it was not out of order, then, relieved at its regular purr, she would drop it suddenly in case he should be dialing at that very moment, which he wasn't.

Ibid.

16 "After the rich, the most obnoxious people in the world are those who serve the rich."

Ch. 8, Ibid.

17 Kindness. The most unkindest thing of all.

Ch. 11, Ibid.

18 She thought of the bigness and wonder of destiny, meeting him in a packed train had been a fluke, and this now was a fluke, and things would either convene to shut that door, or open it a little, or open and close it alternately, and they would be together, or not be together as life the gaffer thought fit.

"A Journey," *A Scandalous Woman 1974*

19 . . . at heart she was quite willful and rebellious . . . She had developed these traits of niceness and agreeableness simply to get away from people—to keep them from pestering her.

"Honeymoon," Ibid.

20 Do you know what I hate about myself, I have never done a brave thing, I have never risked death.

"Over," Ibid.

21 There are times when the things we are seeing changes before our very eyes, and if it is a landscape we praise nature, and if it is spectre, we shudder or cross ourselves, but if it is a loved one that defects, we excuse ourselves and say we have to be somewhere, and are already late for our next appointment.

"A Scandalous Woman," Ibid.

22 But it is not good to repudiate the dead because they do not leave you alone, they are like dogs that bark intermittently at night.

"Love-Child," Ibid.

23 In the evenings when I had a drink or two I would allow myself to think of her, as I might a painting or a beautiful garden. I would dwell on her body the way I never allowed myself to dwell on my own, exploring it with invisible hands, invisible eyes, touching her tentatively and without shame.

The High Road 1988

24 It hurt, with a raw hurt, to recall our gadfly days, and yet I did, our days, nights, beaded jackets, shawls, sometimes had our hands read . . . those days when every new love affair brought us, as we thought, to the brink of a sustained happiness. I thought of the day I too had gone a bit mad, slipped from behind this girl with all these hopes to the woman who would count in morsels from that moment onward the pleasures and excitements of her life.

Ibid.

25 I would grow to forget him, the him that I believed had broken my heart, but in my saner moments I recognized as being probably the last to partake with me at that fount of sensuality, and vertigo and earthly love.

Ibid.

26 In every question and every remark tossed back and forth between lovers who have not played out the last fugue, there is one question and it is this: "Is there someone new?"

"Long Distance," *Lantern Slides 1990*

2508. Linda Pastan (1932–)

1 Grief is a circular staircase

"The Five Stages of Grief," *The Five Stages of Grief 1978*

2 You have grown wings of pain
and flap around the bed like a wounded gull
calling for water, calling for tea, for grapes
whose skins you cannot penetrate.
Remember when you taught me
how to swim? Let go, you said,
the lake will hold you up.
I long to say, Father let go
and death will hold you up . . .

"Go Gentle," *PM/AM 1982*

3 what we want
is never simple

"Meditation by the Stove," *Carnival Evening : New and Selected Poems : 1968–1998 1998*

4 I have banked the fires of my body

Ibid.

2509. Sylvia Brinton Perera (1932–)

1 . . . so much of the power and passion of the feminine has been dormant in the underworld—in exile for five thousand years.

Introduction, *Descent of the Goddess, A Way of Initiation for Women 1981*

2 For what has been valued in the West in women has too often been defined only in relation to the masculine: the good, nurturant mother and wife; the sweet, docile, agreeable daughter; the gently supportive or bright, achieving partner. As many feminist writers have stated through the ages, this collective model (and the behavior it leads to) is inadequate for life; we mutilate, depotentiate, silence, and enrage ourselves trying to compress our souls into it, just as surely as our grandmothers deformed their fully breathing bodies with corsets for the sake of an ideal.

Ch. 1, Ibid.

3 Our planet is passing through a phase—the rebirth of the goddess . . .

Ibid.

2510. Harriet Rosenstein (1932?–)

1 . . . violent outrage and equally violent despair seem inevitable responses to our era. All the horrors committed in the name of national honor or the sanctity of the family or individual integrity have caught up with us.

"Reconsidering Sylvia Plath,"* *The First Ms. Reader,* Francine Klagsbrun, ed. *1972*
*See 2517.

2 . . . the novel . . . traditionally, at least, had depended on the pretense of objectivity to lend it the status of truth: a little world seen full and clear.

Ibid.

3 Destiny is something men select; women achieve it only by default or stupendous suffering.

Quoted in *Ms.* (New York) *July 1974*

4 Fiction, it seems, even living fiction, excuses just about anything.

Ibid.

2511. Alix Kates Shulman (1932–)

1 It was always the girl who was kept in the house after school if a boy molested her, never the boy. Ostensibly she was kept in

for protection, but how was it different from punishment if she couldn't even play on the street?

Memoirs of an Ex-Prom Queen 1972

2 They say it's worse to be ugly. I think it must only be different. If you're pretty, you are subject to one set of assaults; if you're plain, you are subject to another.

Ibid.

3 "Come on, Sasha, you're torturing me," he would say. But it was really he who was torturing me, squeezing me between two guilts.

Ibid.

4 Why was everything nice he did for me a bribe or a favor, while my kindnesses to him were my duty?

Ch. 1, Ibid.

5 If, as the girls always said, it's never too early to think about whom to marry, then it could certainly not be too early to think about who to be. Being somebody had to come first, because, of course, somebody could get a much better husband than nobody.

Ch. 2, Ibid.

6 In Columbia [University] waters I had to swim carefully to avoid being caught in the net laid for nonconforming traffickers in capitalism.

Ch. 6, Ibid.

7 The minute I heard feminism articulated, I recognized it as an explanation of all my puzzles. Until then, I only felt the anguish of it, and felt that it was demeaning to complain. This was my fate: I was a woman, I was a mother, and to complain about it would be beneath me. So I couldn't complain about it. But I had my secret thoughts.

Quoted in "The Liberation of An Ex-Prom Queen" by Leora Tanenbaum, *Ms.* (New York) *November/December 1997*

8 The protagonists of all my novels are in some sense me. And yet these are very different people. I feel quite ruthlessly free to raid my life for anything that might be useful for my fiction.

Ibid.

2512. Muriel Siebert (1932–)

1 I know a twenty-eight-year-old woman, a recent graduate of Harvard Business School. She asked me the other day if I wasn't afraid of what people will say if I associate with the women's movement. What she doesn't understand is that it's because of the movement and people like me that it's now not as difficult for her to make it.

Quoted in *Women at Work* by Betty Medsger *1975*

2513. Elizabeth Taylor (1932–)

1 When people say: she's got everything, I've only one answer: I haven't had tomorrow.

Elizabeth Taylor 1965

2 My God, I was on a merry-go-round for so long. Now I've stopped spinning. I'm not afraid of myself. I'm no longer afraid of what I will do. I have absolute faith in our future. Richard [Burton]* has given me all this.

Ibid.

*Welsh actor (1925–1984) to whom she was twice married.

3 I want to be known as an actress. I'm not royalty.

Interview in *The New York Times* (1964), Quoted in *Elizabeth* by Dick Sheppard *1974*

2514. Megan Terry (1932–)

1 CHESTER. My God, the human baby! A few weeks after birth, any other animal can fend for itself. But *you*! A basket case till you're twenty-one.

The Magic Realist 1968

2 CHESTER. Fourteen mewling brats and not a business brain in a bucketful.

Ibid.

3 CHESTER. Tighten the belt. Tough it out, fellow Americans, tough it out!

Ibid.

4 Theater is profoundly physically rewarding

Quoted in *The American Woman Playwright, A View of Criticism and Characterization* by Judith Olauson *1981*

5 Broadway is just a showcase for television now. Broadway is no longer the place I was taught about when I went to college, i.e., the place where The Theater was kept alive, the Theater of Ideas. A place where one could be in touch with human feelings, where you could see yourself, where society could see itself. Broadway is now a place for the tourists to go and be beguiled by stagecraft.

Quoted in "Megan Terry," *Interviews with Contemporary Women Playwrights* by Kathleen Betsko* and Rachel Koenig *1987*

*See 2739.

6 I think you have to *submit* to art. One must submit the ego to the work, or the work never gets done. That's the positive side of submission. The only utopias that ever lasted very long were those where people submitted to an idea greater than the individual.

Ibid.

7 I think that people are too rarified in New York. They've been too long away from animals and plants and trees.

Ibid.

8 Isn't it strange that this American culture has valued everything but the people who create something out of thin air? What is left when a civilization dies? Only its art and a few tool fragments.

Ibid.

2515. Maruxa Vilalta (1932–)

1 SEVEN. You're not eating?
NINE. I'm not hungry.
SEVEN. I'm dying of hunger!
NINE. Dying is going a bit far.
SEVEN. Well, I *am*.
NINE. Don't be so vain. Dying is going too far.

El 9 (Number Nine) *1965*

2516. Robin Worthington (1932–)

1 Mental health, like dandruff, crops up when you least expect it.

Thinking About Marriage 1971

2 The battle to keep up appearances unnecessarily, the mask—whatever name you give creeping perfectionism—robs us of our energies.

Ibid.

2517. Sylvia Plath (1932–1963)

1 Apparently, the most difficult feat for a Cambridge male is to accept a woman not merely as feeling, not merely as thinking, but as managing a complex, vital interweaving of both.

"Isis" 6 May 1956

2 I shut my eyes and all the world drops dead;
I lift my eyes and all is born again.

"Mad Girl's Love Song"
6 May 1956

3 His ardor snares me, lights the trees,
And I run flaring in my skin;

"Pursuit" (1956), The Colossus 1960

4 'There sits no higher court
Than man's red heart.'

"Dialogue between ghost and priest," St. 10 (1956), Ibid.

5 She judged petals in disarray,
The whole season, sloven.

"Spinster," St. 2 (1956), Ibid.

6 each day demands we create our whole world over,
disguising the constant horror in a coat
of many-colored fictions . . .

"Tale of a Tub," St. 5 (1956), Ibid.

7 King Egg-Head saw his domain crack,
His crown usurped by the low brow
Of the base, barbarous Prince Ow.

"Natural History," St. 3 (1957), Ibid.

8 Two virtues ride, by stallion, by nag,
To grind our knives and scissors:
Lantern-jawed Reason, squat Common Sense,
One courting doctors of all sorts,
One, housewives and shopkeepers.

"The death of myth-making," St. 1 (1957), Ibid.

9 . . . hearing the cut flowers
Sipping their liquids from assorted pots,
Pitchers and Coronation goblets
Like Monday drunkards.

"Leaving early," Ibid.

10 These poems do not live: it's a sad diagnosis.
They grew their toes and fingers well enough,
Their little foreheads bulged with concentration.
If they missed out on walking about like people
It wasn't for any lack of mother-love.

"Stillborn," St. 1 1960

11 Skin doesn't have roots, it peels away easy as paper.
When I grin, the stitches tauten. I grow backward. I'm twenty . . .

"Face Lift," St. 3 1961

12 Now she's done for, the dewlapped lady
I watched settle, line by line, in my mirror . . .

St. 4 Ibid.

13 The woman is perfected
Her dead
Body wears the smile of accomplishment.

"Edge"* 1963

*Her last poem, written a week before her suicide.

14 . . . they all wanted to adopt me in some way, and, for the price of their care and influence, have me resemble them.

The Bell Jar 1963

15 "What does a woman see in a woman that she can't see in a man?" Doctor Nolan paused. Then she said, "Tenderness."

Ibid.

16 I pushed myself into a flight I knew I couldn't stop by skill or any belated access of will.

Ibid.

17 . . . I guess I feel about a hot bath the way those religious people feel about holy water. . . . The longer I lay there in the clear hot water the purer I felt, and when I stepped out at last and wrapped myself in one of the big, soft, white, hotel bath-towels I felt pure and sweet as a new baby.

Ch. 2, Ibid.

18 "Do you know what a poem is, Esther?"
"No, what?" I would say.
"A piece of dust."
Then just as he was smiling and starting to look proud, I would say, "So are the cadavers you cut up. So are the people you think you're curing. They're dust as dust as dust. I reckon a good poem lasts a whole lot longer than a hundred of those people put together."

Ch. 5, Ibid.

19 I never wanted to get married. The last thing I wanted was infinite security, and to be the place an arrow shoots off from. I wanted change and excitement and to shoot off in all directions myself, like the colored arrows from a Fourth of July rocket.

Ch. 7, Ibid.

20 If neurotic is wanting two mutually exclusive things at one and the same time, then I'm neurotic as hell. I'll be flying back and forth between one mutually exclusive thing and another for the rest of my days.

Ch. 8, Ibid.

21 . . . I had followed the green, luminous course of the second hand and the minute hand and the hour hand of the bedside clock through their circles, their circles and semi-circles, every night for seven nights, without missing a second, or a minute, or an hour.

Ch. 10, Ibid.

22 They understood things of the spirit in Japan. They disemboweled themselves when anything went wrong . . . It must take a lot of courage to die like that.

Ch. 11, Ibid.

23 I stored the fact . . . in the corner of my mind the way a squirrel stores a nut.

Ch. 15, Ibid.

24 Sunday—the doctor's paradise! Doctors at country clubs, doctors at the seaside, doctors with mistresses, doctors with wives, doctors in church, doctors in yachts, doctors everywhere resolutely being people, not doctors.

Ch. 19, Ibid.

25 I took a deep breath and listened to the old brag of my heart. I am, I am, I am.

Ch. 20, Ibid.

26 If the moon smiled, she would resemble you.
 You leave the same impression
 Of something beautiful, but annihilating.
                              "The Rival," St. 1 (1961),
                                          Ariel 1965

27 Love set you going like a fat gold watch.
                              "Morning Song," Ibid.

28 A living doll, everywhere you look.
 It can sew, it can cook,
 It can talk, talk, talk.

 It works, there is nothing wrong with it.
 You have a hole, it's a poultice
 You have an eye, it's an image.
 My boy, it's your last resort.
 Will you marry it, marry it, marry it.
                              "The Applicant," Ibid.

29 Out of the ash
 I rise with my red hair
 and I eat men like air.
                              "Lady Lazarus," Ibid.

30 Dying
 Is an art, like everything else.
 I do it exceptionally well.
 I do it so it feels like hell.
 I do it so it feels real.
 I guess you could say I've a call.
                                          Ibid.

31 Viciousness in the kitchen!
                              "Lesbos," Ibid.

32 How long can I be a wall around my green property?
 How long can my hands
 Be a bandage to his hurts, and my words
 Bright birds in the sky, consoling? consoling?
 It is a terrible thing
 To be so open: it is as if my heart
 Put on a face and walked into the world. . . .
                      "A Poem for Three Voices" 1968

33 Spiderlike, I spin mirrors,
 Loyal to my own image,
 Uttering nothing but blood.
                      "Childless Woman" 1968

34 What would the dark
 Do without fever to eat?
 What would the light
 Do without eyes to knife . . .
                      "The Jailor," *Encounter* 1969

35 Widow. The word consumes itself. . . .
                      "Widow," *Crossing the Water* 1971

36 Every woman adores a Fascist,
 The boot in the face, the brute
 Brute heart of a brute like you.
                      "Daddy," St. 10 (12 October 1962),
                      Collected Poems/ Sylvia Plath,
                      Ted Hughes,* ed. *1981*
 *Plath's British-born husband (1930–2000), Poet Laureate of En-
 gland (1984).

37 I am no drudge
 Though for years I have eaten dust
 and dried plates with my dense hair.
                      "The Babysitters," Ibid.

38 Is there no way out of the mind?
                      "Apprehensions" *n.d.*

2518. Dian Fossey (1932–1985)

1 The more you learn about the dignity of the gorilla, the more
 you want to avoid people.
        Quoted in "Case of the Gorilla Lady Murder" by William E.
        Smith, *Time* (New York) 1 September 1986

2519. Raisa Maxima Gorbachev (1932–1999)

1 Soviet people are putting into practice plans of revolutionary
 restructuring. We want our public life . . . to be worthy of a
 human being.
                      Quoted in *Time* (New York) 20 March 1989

2 The calamity of war, wherever, whenever and upon whomever
 it descends, is a tragedy for the whole of humanity.
                                          I Hope 1991

3 No war, not even to punish an aggressor, is a good thing.
 Today people must learn to take into account each others' interests, if only for the sake of survival.
                                          Ibid.

4 Every woman dreams of her own political career and her own
 place in life.
        Remark (1990), Quoted in "Raisa Gorbachev Dies of
        Leukemia at 67" by Adam Tanner, *Yahoo! News*,
        http://dailynews.yahoo.com 20 September 1999

2520. Corazon Aquino (1933–)

1 The politicians think that I have not included enough of
 them; the nonpoliticians think that I have gone back to the
 old ways; and the mass public groups think I have forgotten
 them.
        Interview with Sandra Burton,* Quoted in *Time* (New York)
                                          10 March 1986
        *See 2553.

2 No one can say Cory did not give it her all.
                                          Ibid.

3 It wasn't until we [she and her incarcerated husband]* got
 over the self-pity that we were able to accept suffering as part
 of our life with Christ. A man or woman reaches this plane
 only when he or she ceases to be the "hero" playing to the
 gallery and becomes the humble Christian praying to God to
 fix the direction of his or her actions.
        Speech (1984), Quoted in "The Passage of Corazon
        Aquino" by Gail Sheehy,** *Parade Magazine* 8 June 1986
        *Benigno ("Ninoy") Aquino Jr., Philippine senator and hero
        (1933–1983). **See 2650.

4 Marcos* underestimated me—and look where it got him!
        Interview with Diane Sawyer,** *60 Minutes*, CBS-TV
                                          14 September 1986
        *Ferdinand Marcos, Philippine politician (1917–1989); president
        of the Philippines (1966–1986); husband of Imelda (see 2387).
        **See 3066.

5 I think Ninoy's joy is the knowledge that he pulled a fast one on me. Once more he has gone on his merry way and left me to pick up the mess.

Speech, St. Ignatius Roman Catholic Church (Newton, Massachusetts) *21 September 1986*

6 So long as I believe I have to do certain things, I will just go right ahead. That's how I run my life.

Quoted in *Twentieth-Century Women Political Leaders* by Claire Price-Groff *1998*

7 Faith is not simply a patience which passively suffers until the storm is past. Rather, it is a spirit which bears things—with resignation, yes, but above all with blazing serene hope.

Ibid.

2521. Beryl Bainbridge (1933–)

1 The carnage was horrid. Men died posed like the statues in Mr. Blundell's glass-house.

Master Georgie 1998

2 I didn't know what cause I was promoting, or why it was imperative to kill.

Ibid.

3 Some pictures would only cause alarm to ordinary folk.

Ibid.

4 The authoritarian voice, the ring of confidence, is not for me. I'm not bothered with causes or hard facts; my preoccupation is not with the immediate how and why of the lives we lead, but rather with a raking over of the life we once knew.

Something Happened Yesterday 1998

2522. Mary Field Belenky (1933–)

1 Language—even literacy—alone does not lead automatically to reflective, abstract thought. In order for reflection to occur, the oral and written forms of language must pass back and forth between persons who both speak and listen or read and write—sharing, expanding, and reflecting on each other's experiences. Such interchanges lead to ways of knowing that enable individuals to enter into the social and intellectual life of their community. Without them, individuals remain isolated from others; and without tools for representing their experiences, people also remain isolated from the self.

Pt. I, Ch. 1, *Women's Ways of Knowing, The Development of Self, Voice, and Mind*, with Blythe McVicker Clinchy, * Nancy Rule Goldberger,** and Jill Mattuck Tarule*** *1986*
*See 2412; **see 2561; ***see 2972.

2 That they can strengthen themselves through the empowerment of others is essential wisdom often gathered by women.

Ch. 2, Ibid.

3 Connected knowers do not measure other people's words by some impersonal standard. Their purpose is not to judge but to understand.

Ch. 6, Ibid.

4 Parents who enter into a dialogue with their children, who draw out and respect their opinions, are more likely to have children whose intellectual and ethical development proceeds rapidly and surely.

Pt. II, Ch. 8, Ibid.

5 Really listening and suspending one's own judgment is necessary in order to understand other people on their own terms. As we have noted, this is a process that requires trust and builds trust.

Ibid.

6 When a tradition has no name people will not have a rich shared language for articulating and reflecting on their experiences with the tradition. Poorly articulated traditions are likely to be fragile.

A Tradition That Has No Name: Nurturing the Development of People, Families and Communities, with Lynne A. Bond and Jacqueline S. Weinstock *1997*

2523. Maureen Duffy (1933–)

1 We all have to rise in the end, not just one or two who were smart enough, had will enough for their own salvation, but all the halt, the maimed and the blind of us which is most of us.

The Microcosm 1966

2 All reduction of people to objects, all imposition of labels and patterns to which they must conform, all segregation can lead only to destruction.

Rites 1969

3 ADA. Bastard men! Get a man she says. I'll get him right where I want him.

Ibid.

4 The pain of love is the pain of being alive. It's a perpetual wound.

Wounds 1969

5 Love is the only effective counter to death.

Ibid.

6 I think basically I just think I want everyone and don't really want anybody.

Love Child 1971

7 You will be wondering, putative reader, why I have reported all this. The answer is quite simple: it interests me, and you, forgive me, don't you. I am not trying to tell you anything; I am at my childlike, priestlike task of creation.

Ibid.

2524. Joycelyn Elders (1933–)

1 The most pervasive form of violence in America is interpersonal—domestic violence, partner abuse, abuse of children and adolescents, the elderly. If we ever expect to put an end to violence and victimization in America, we have to start where the violence starts—in our homes, in our families.

"Violence begins in the home . . . ," *Seattle Post-Intelligencer*, B1 *12 February 1993*

2 The only person that could have designed this [Medicaid] system was a white male slave owner.*

Ibid.

*Reference specifically to the plan's policy of paying for low-birth-weight babies but not for birth control methods.

3 When you are dancing with a bear, you do not sit down when you are tired; you sit down when the bear is tired.

Ibid.

4 We taught them what to do in the front seat of a car. Now it's time to teach them what to do in the back seat.

> Quoted in "Blunt Style of Teen Sex And Health" by Philip J. Hilts, *The New York Times* 14 September 1993

5 I am not of the opinion that just because you have a condom, you are going to go out and have sex. There is not a person in this room that doesn't have car insurance, but you're not going to go out and have a wreck because of it.

> Ibid.

6 I feel that denying young people health education, denying them the availability of contraceptives, and saying to them that you have to take this kind of risk, is almost child abuse.

> Ibid.

7 Society wants to keep all sexuality in the closet.

> Interview, *The Advocate* March 1994

8 I feel that God meant sex for more than procreation.

> Ibid.

2525. Cynthia Fuchs Epstein (1933–)

1 During World War II, for instance, when the young men were off at war, dating did not consume the time of the college co-ed and she redirected her energies to study. . . . Work became an alternative even for those who did marry. Once engaged in an occupation, many had so firm a foothold they were loath to give it up.

> *Woman's Place* 1970

2526. Pozzi Escot (1933–)

1 In our [Peruvian] schools we teach Bach, Beethoven and Brahms but nothing that has been composed in the past 70 years.

> Quoted in "A Matter of Art, Not Sex," *Time* (New York) 10 November 1975

2527. Elizabeth Evatt (1933–)

1 I believe every woman should have the right to live in a home *free* of deadly weapons.

> Interview with Robin Morgan,* *Ms.* (New York) March/April 1993

*See 2864.

2 . . . one brave person has to stand up, to be exposed to the limelight, go through the trauma of a sex harassment or rape case. But the force of an actual individual case can be very strong indeed, a bargaining tool, a powerful influence for change.

> Ibid.

3 You have to see human rights as an all-embracing concept. It could be something that would unite the world, if it could only be seen in that light.

> Ibid.

2528. Dianne Feinstein (1933–)

1 This city [San Francisco] typifies the American dream of a sense of tolerance and openness, with different people living closely together, carefully, with respect for the law, not impinging their will on others but living with a growing mutual respect.

> Quoted in "Dianne Feinstein: Learning the Lessons of the Phoenix" by Mildred Hamilton, *San Francisco Examiner* 4 March 1979

2 Toughness doesn't have to come in a pinstripe suit.

> *Time* (New York) 4 June 1984

3 I've been the first [woman] four times now: once as president of the Board of Supervisors [in San Francisco], as mayor, as the first gubernatorial candidate in my state, the first woman Senator from my state. What I've learned is there is a testing period that goes on—particularly in an executive capacity.

> I think it [takes someone] with the ability to run a campaign well, put together a platform that resounds with the American people and someone with the stamina, the staying power, the determination and enthusiasm to carry it off.

> Quoted in "Women Who Could Be President" by Jane Ciabattari, *Parade Magazine* 7 February 1999

4 It really comes down to a question of blood or guts—the blood of innocent people or the Senate of the United States having the guts to do what we should do when we take that oath to protect the welfare of our citizens.*

> (p. 85), Quoted in *Politics in America* 1998 by Philip D. Duncan 1999

*Reference to the legislative ban of assault weapons which she championed that was signed into law in 1994.

2529. Barbara C. Gelpi (1933–)

1 . . . the masculine and feminine principles are not simply arbitrary manila folders for filing certain qualities; they are transcendent functions, spiritual realities which must be taken into account in the psychological makeup of every human being.

> "The Androgyne," *Women and Analysis*, Jean Strouse,* ed. 1974

*See 3071.

2 If women could help society to throw off the heavy yoke of the Fathers they might eventually move humankind forward. . . .

> Ibid.

3 With myths, dreams, visions, poems, stories, conversations we must imagine a race in which both mind and soul are of equal importance and may be equally fulfilled for both sexes.

> Ibid.

4 Consciousness, as we tend to conceive of it, brings humanity into being—and that is good—but has certain negative consequences as well. Though it is man's triumph, it is divisive, separating him from the natural rhythms of life by virtue of the fact that he can observe those rhythms, looking forward and backward. He becomes then subject to the peculiarly human fear of death and the human affliction of boredom. He becomes also aware of his separateness, his individuality—and that is an achievement—but at the same time becomes competitive, suffering all the endless human misery which competition involves.

> Ibid.

2530. Ruth Bader Ginsberg (1933–)

1 In commercial law, the person duped was too often a woman. In a section on land tenure, one 1968 textbook explains that "land, like women, was meant to be possessed."

> Quoted in "Portia Faces Life—The Trials of Law School" by Susan Edmiston, *Ms.* (New York) April 1974

2 The emphasis must not be on the right to abortion but on the right to privacy and reproductive control.

> Ibid.

3 Civil rights groups hold no monopoly position among those discontent with legislative or executive action who seek the aid of the courts.

15 Georgia Law Review 539 1981

4 The judiciary has been the forum of ultimate resort for individuals and organizations representing almost every position on the political spectrum.

Ibid.

5 There can be no doubt that our Nation has had a long and unfortunate history of sex discrimination. Traditionally, such discrimination was rationalized by an attitude of "romantic paternalism" which, in practical effect, put women, not on a pedestal, but in a cage . . . our statute books gradually became laden with gross stereotyped distinctions between the sexes . . .

Supreme Court decision (1973), Quoted in
The Encyclopedia of Women's History in America
by K. Cullen-DuPont *1987*

6 A judge steps out of the proper judicial role most conspicuously and dangerously when he or she flinches from a decision that is legally right because the decision is not the one the home crowd wants.

Quoted in *The 50 Most Influential Women in American Law* by Dawn Bradley Berry* *1996*
*See 3435.

7 I do think that being the second* woman is wonderful, because it is a sign that being a woman in a place of importance is no longer extraordinary.

Remark to *ABA Journal*, Ibid.
*She was the second woman appointed to the U.S. Supreme Court; Sandra Day O'Connor (see 2437) was the first.

2531. Faye Joan Girsh (1933–)

1 [Dying] using to happen at home, children and pets would be on the dying person's bed, and it would be a natural, family-centered event. Now it occurs for most people alone, in a sterile hospital environment. Dying people should be able to have their loved ones present, say their good-bye's and I-love-you's, and die peacefully and gently with the help of a doctor.

"Kevorkian* serves public need," *USA Today*
24 November 1998
*Jack K—, American pathologist and activist who spearheaded a movement for physician-assisted suicide.

2532. Corinne Jacker (1933–)

1 LOIS. I write down significant things about beginnings. See— I'm trying to get it all straight. All my life it turns out that I've come in at the middle. Korea, Viet Nam, the energy crisis. And when I try to talk about it, they say, "You don't understand. That wasn't when it really began." But when I ask when the start was, nobody knows.

Act I, Sc. 1, *Harry Outside 1975*

2 STEVE. I came back here to be safe, and it's not safe here either.

Domestic Issues 1980

3 It's true that women tend to think of domestic, encapsulated incidents as crucial. We look at the microcosm rather than the macrocosm. . . . Perhaps women find their metaphors in domestic experience because we are still new to the world of action.

"Corinne Jacker," *Interviews with Contemporary Women Playwrights*, Kathleen Betsko* and Rachel Koenig *1987*
*See 2739.

2533. Devaki Jain (1933–)

1 I suggest that, without rethinking and specifying the philosophy, the vision, and the specific vocabularies, including the basic syllabus of education, it is not useful to draw women into education.

Essay, Quoted in *The Politics of Women's Education:*
Perspectives from Asia, Africa, and Latin America
by Jill Ker Conway and Susan C. Bourque *1993*

2 We were naïve and realized too late that this great goodness, development, into which our mandate had been to integrate women, and that this great public world, which men occupy and into which we were to bring women through employment and health strategies, was dangerous, even devastating.

Ibid.

2534. Penelope Lively (1933–)

1 Chronology irritates me. There is no chronology inside my head. I am composed of a myriad of Claudias who spin and mix and part like sparks of sunlight on water.

Moon Tiger 1987

2 . . . the rainbow experience we all have lost but of which we occasionally retrieve a brilliant glimpse.

Oleander, Jacaranda: A Childhood Perceived:
A Memoir 1994

3 There are realities which for most of us are beyond imagination.

The Five Thousand and One Nights 1996

4 I want to be somewhere else.

One, Two, Three, Jump! 1998

5 In her trade [anthropology], you travelled most fruitfully if you travelled alone. And it helped if you were footloose and singularly unfettered by personal possessions.

Spiderweb 1999

6 A small ancient-looking chapel of perfect simplicity perched above a hedgebank that sparkled with flowers. Sometimes it was difficult to take this landscape seriously—to remember that it had evolved from centuries of agricultural endeavour and blithe environmental disregard.

Ibid.

7 I am no longer in business. I am a part of the landscape like everyone else. And some of us are more tenuously placed within that landscape than others.

Ibid.

2535. Yoko Ono (1933–)

1 Everybody's an artist. Everybody's God. It's just that they're inhibited. I believe in people so much that if the whole of civilization is burned so we don't have any memory of it, even then people will start to build their own art. It is a necessity—a function. We don't need history.

Interview with Abram Deswaan, Dutch TV *October 1968*

2 I wonder why men can get serious at all. They have this delicate long thing hanging outside their bodies, which goes up and down by its own will. . . . If I were a man I would always be laughing at myself.

"On Film No. 4" (1967), *Grapefruit 1970*

3 Keep your intentions in a clear bottle
and leave it on the shelf when you rap.

"Peter the Dealer" *n.d.*

4   What a bastard the world is.
                    "What a Bastard the World Is" *n.d.*

5   I'm a sphinx
    Stamped on the Hilton poster
    Hoping to see the desert . . .
                    "A Thousand Times Yes" *n.d.*

6   The no that was hanging over the buildings
    Faded like the moon at dawn.
                                        Ibid.

7   I have a woman inside my soul.
                    "I Have a Woman Inside My Soul" *n.d.*

8   On a windy day let's go flying
    There may be no trees to rest on
    There may be no clouds to ride
    But we'll have our wings and the wind will be with us
    That's enough for me, that's enough for me.
                    "Song for John"* *n.d.*
    *Her husband, John Lennon, British singer-songwriter, member of
    the Beatles; murdered (1940–1980).

9   The bed is shining like an old scripture
    That's never been opened before.
                    "Winter Song" *n.d.*

10 Don't be too clever or we'll scratch your goodies out . . . or
    we'll blow your sillies off.
                    "Catman" *n.d.*

2536. Suzy Parker (1933–)

1   I thank God for high cheekbones every time I look in the mir-
    ror in the morning.
                    Quoted in *This Fabulous Century*
                    (1950–1960) 1970

2537. Ann Richards (1933–)

1   Poor George,* he can't help it. He was born with a silver foot
    in his mouth.
                    Quoted in *Independent* (London)
                    20 July 1988
    *George H. W. Bush, American politician (1924–); 41st U.S. pres-
    ident (1989–93).

2   Bill Clinton* isn't the first man I've had to forgive, and he isn't
    apt to be the last.
                    Cited by Susan Paynter in *Seattle Post-Intelligencer*, B1
                    28 October 1996
    *William Jefferson Clinton, American politician and lawyer
    (1946–), 42nd president of the U.S. (1993–2001).

3   They* go up there and forget who brung 'em to the dance.
                                        Ibid.
    *Reference to congressional representatives in Washington, D.C.

4   When you think you've come so far and achieved so much,
    your impatience begins to take over. To give you a context,
    my grandmother, for a period of her life, couldn't vote. The
    law said [that] "imbeciles, idiots, the insane and women"
    could not vote in Texas. And, within that same single life-
    time, I became the governor of Texas. What an incredible
    change that is.
                                        Ibid.

5   Many of us are held back by the constraints of what we think
    society will think and how we will be judged. That was not a
    problem for Alice Paul,* thank God.
                    "100 Years of Great Women," *ABC News Special*
                    *with Barbara Walters*** 30 April 1999
    *See 1538. **See 2480.

2538. Miriam Schneir (1933–)

1   The decline of feminism after the First World War is at-
    tributable at least in part to the eventual concentration of the
    women's movements on the single narrow issue of suffrage—
    which was won.
                    Introduction, *Feminism: The Essential Historical*
                    Writings 1972

2   . . . centuries of slavery do not provide a fertile soil for intellec-
    tual development or expression.
                                        Ibid.

2539. Mary Jane Sherfey (1933–)

1   The nature of female sexuality as here presented makes it clear
    that . . . woman's inordinate orgasmic capacity did not evolve
    for monogamous, sedentary cultures.
                    "A Theory on Female Sexuality," *Journal of the American*
                    Psychoanalytical Association 1966

2   The strength of the drive determines the force required to sup-
    press it.
                                        Ibid.

3   There is a great difference between satisfaction and satiation.
                                        Ibid.

4   There is no such thing as a vaginal orgasm distinct from a cli-
    toral orgasm. The nature of the orgasm is the same regardless
    of the erotogenic zone stimulated to produce it.
                                        Ibid.

2540. Susan Sontag (1933–)

1   The truth is always something that is told, not something that
    is known. If there were no speaking or writing, there would be
    no truth about anything. There would only be what is.
                    Ch. 1, *The Benefactor 1963*

2   Ambition if it feeds at all, does so on the ambition of others.
                                        Ibid.

3   I was not looking for my dreams to interpret my life, but
    rather for my life to interpret my dreams.
                    Ch. 4, Ibid.

4   The love of the famous, like all strong passions, is quite ab-
    stract. Its intensity can be measured mathematically, and it is
    independent of persons.
                    Ch. 9, Ibid.

5   *Transparence* is the highest, most liberating value in art—
    and in criticism—today. Transparence means experiencing
    the luminousness of the thing in itself, of things being what
    they are.
                    "Against Interpretation" (*Evergreen Review*, December
                    1964), *Against Interpretation 1966*

6   Interpretation is the revenge of the intellect upon art.
                                        Ibid.

7 In good films, there is always a directness that entirely frees us from the itch to interpret.
Ibid.

8 The aim of all commentary on art now should be to make works of art—and, by analogy, our own experience—more, rather than less, real to us. The function of criticism should be to show *how it is what it is*, even *that it is what it is*, rather than to *show what it means*.
Ibid.

9 Ours is a culture based on excess, on overproduction; the result is a steady loss of sharpness in our sensory experience. All the conditions of modern life—its material plenitude, its sheer crowdedness—conjoin to dull our sensory faculties.
Ibid.

10 Real art has the capacity to make us nervous. By reducing the work of art to its content and then interpreting that, one tames the work of art. Interpretation makes art manageable, conformable.
Ibid.

11 The whole point of Camp is to dethrone the serious. Camp is playful, anti-serious. More precisely, Camp involves a new, more complex relation to "the serious." One can be serious about the frivolous, frivolous about the serious.
"Notes on 'Camp'," Note 41 (1964), Ibid.

12 Intelligence . . . is really a kind of taste: taste in ideas.
Note 54, Ibid.

13 The discovery of the good taste of bad taste can be very liberating. The man who insists on high and serious pleasures is depriving himself of pleasure; he continually restricts what he can enjoy; in the constant exercise of his good taste he will eventually price himself out of the market, so to speak. Here Camp taste supervenes upon good taste as a daring and witty hedonism. It makes the man of good taste cheerful, where before he ran the risk of being chronically frustrated. It is good for the digestion.
Ibid.

14 The relation between boredom and Camp taste cannot be overestimated. Camp taste is by its nature possible only in affluent societies, in societies or circles capable of experiencing the psychopathology of affluence.
Ibid.

15 Camp is a vision of the world in terms of style. . . . It incarnates a victory of 'style' over 'substance,' 'aesthetics' over 'morality,' or irony over tragedy.
Ibid.

16 The truth is balance, but the opposite of truth, which is unbalance, may not be a lie.
"Simone Weil,"* Ibid.
*See 1948.

17 Science fiction films are not about science. They are about disaster, which is one of the oldest subjects of art.
"The Imagination of Disaster," Ibid.

18 Unfortunately, moral beauty in art—like physical beauty in a person—is extremely perishable. It is nowhere so durable as artistic or intellectual beauty. Moral beauty has a tendency to decay very rapidly into sententiousness or untimeliness.
"Camus' Notebooks"* (1963), Ibid.
*Albert C—, French writer and philosopher (1913–1960); recipient of Nobel Prize (1957).

19 How does an inexpressive face age? More slowly, one would suppose.
Death Kit 1967

20 Wiser and wiser. The scrim was raised. The gauzy light became, suddenly, knife-sharp. Almost gouged out his heart. Wiser. And suffering, for the first time. But not truly wise, wise enough to transcend suffering; and never likely to be.
Ibid.

21 Persons who merely have-a-life customarily move in a dense fluid. That's how they're able to conduct their lives at all. Their living depends on not seeing.
Ibid.

22 The becoming of man is the history of the exhaustion of his possibilities.
"'Thinking Against Oneself': Reflections on Cioran," *Styles of Radical Will* 1969

23 The truth is that Mozart, Pascal, Boolean algebra, Shakespeare, parliamentary government, baroque churches, Newton, the emancipation of women, Kant, Marx, and Balanchine ballets don't redeem what this particular civilization has wrought upon the world. The white race *is* the cancer of human history.
"What's Happening in America (1966)," (*Partisan Review*, Winter 1967), Ibid.

24 American "energy". . . is the energy of violence, of free-floating resentment and anxiety unleashed by chronic cultural dislocations which must be, for the most part, ferociously sublimated. This energy has mainly been sublimated into crude materialism and acquisitiveness. Into hectic philanthropy. Into benighted moral crusades, the most spectacular of which was Prohibition. Into an awesome talent for uglifying countryside and cities. Into the loquacity and torment of a minority of gadflies: artists, prophets, muckrakers, cranks, and nuts. And into self-punishing neuroses. But the naked violence keeps breaking through, throwing everything into question.
Ibid.

25 I do not think white America is committed to granting equality to the American Negro . . . this is a passionately racist country; it will continue to be so in the foreseeable future.
Ibid.

26 Foreigners extol the American "energy," attributing to it both our unparalleled economic prosperity and the splendid vivacity of our arts and entertainments. But surely this is energy bad at its source and for which we pay too high a price, a hypernatural and humanly disproportionate dynamism that flays everyone's nerves raw.
Ibid.

27 What pornographic literature does is precisely to drive a wedge between one's existence as a full human being and one's existence as a sexual being—
"The Pornographic Imagination," Sct. 3, Ibid.

28 Tamed as it may be, sexuality remains one of the demonic forces in human consciousness—pushing us at intervals close to taboo and dangerous desires, which range from the impulse to commit sudden arbitrary violence upon another person to the voluptuous yearning for the extinction of one's consciousness, for death itself.
Ibid.

29 Experiences aren't pornographic; only images and representations—structures of the imagination—are.
Ibid.

30 Bending the mind and shaking loose the body makes someone a less willing functionary of the bureaucratic machine. Rock, grass, better orgasms, freaky clothes, grooving on nature—really grooving on anything—unfits, maladapts a person for the American way of life.

Quoted in Recreation *by Mark Estrin 1971*

31 Most men experience getting older with regret, apprehension. But most women experience it even more painfully: with shame. Aging is a man's destiny, something that must happen because he is a human being. For a woman, aging is not only her destiny . . . it is also her vulnerability.

"The Double Standard of Aging," *Saturday Review October 1972*

32 Much of modern art is devoted to lowering the threshold of what is terrible. By getting us used to what, formerly, we could not bear to see or hear, because it was too shocking, painful, or embarrassing, art changes morals.

"America, Seen Through Photographs, Darkly," *On Photography 1977*

33 The freakish is no longer a private zone, difficult of access. People who are bizarre, in sexual disgrace, emotionally violent are seen daily on the newsstands, on TV, in the subways. Hobbesian man roams the streets, quite visible, with glitter in his hair.

Ibid.

34 Boredom is just the reverse side of fascination: both depend on being outside rather than inside a situation, and one leads to the other.

Ibid.

35 Industrial societies turn their citizens into image-junkies; it is the most irresistible form of mental pollution. Poignant longings for beauty, for an end to probing below the surface, for a redemption and celebration of the body of the world. Ultimately, having an experience becomes identical with taking a photograph of it.

"In Plato's Cave," *Ibid.*

36 Guns have metamorphosed into cameras in this earnest comedy, the ecology safari, because nature has ceased to be what it always had been—what people needed protection from. Now nature tamed, endangered, mortal—needs to be protected from people.

Ibid.

37 Using a camera appeases the anxiety which the work-driven feel about not working when they are on vacation and supposed to be having fun. They have something to do that is like a friendly imitation of work: they can take pictures.

Ibid.

38 Nature in America has always been suspect, on the defensive, cannibalized by progress. In America, every specimen becomes a relic.

"Melancholy Objects," *Ibid.*

39 The past itself, as historical change continues to accelerate, has become the most surreal of subjects—making it possible . . . to see a new beauty in what is vanishing.

Ibid.

40 Though collecting quotations could be considered as merely an ironic mimetism—victimless collecting, as it were . . . in a world that is well on its way to becoming one vast quarry, the collector becomes someone engaged in a pious work of salvage. The course of modern history having already sapped the traditions and shattered the living wholes in which precious objects once found their place, the collector may now in good conscience go about excavating the choicer, more emblematic fragments.

Ibid.

41 Fewer and fewer Americans possess objects that have a patina, old furniture, grandparents' pots and pans—the used things, warm with generations of human touch, . . . essential to a human landscape. Instead, we have our paper phantoms, transistorized landscapes. A featherweight portable museum.

Ibid.

42 Illness is the night-side of life, a more onerous citizenship. Everyone who is born holds dual citizenship, in the kingdom of the well and in the kingdom of the sick. Although we all prefer to use only the good passport, sooner or later each of us is obliged, at least for a spell, to identify ourselves as citizens of that other place.

Opening words, Illness As Metaphor *1978*

43 . . . cancer patients are lied to, not just because the disease is (or is thought to be) a death sentence, but because it is felt to be obscene—in the original meaning of the word: ill-omened, abominable, repugnant to the senses.

Ch. 1, Ibid.

44 A large part of the popularity and persuasiveness of psychology comes from its being a sublimated spiritualism: a secular, ostensibly scientific way of affirming the primacy of "spirit" over matter.

Ch. 7, Ibid.

45 For those who live neither with religious consolations about death nor with a sense of death (or of anything else) as natural, death is the obscene mystery, the ultimate affront, the thing that cannot be controlled. It can only be denied.

Ibid.

46 Any important disease whose causality is murky, and for which treatment is ineffectual, tends to be awash in significance.

Ch. 8, Ibid.

47 "At the beginning of the world, everything was America." How far from the beginning are we? When did we first start to feel the wound?

I, Etcetera *1978*

48 Sisyphus, I. I cling to my rock, you don't have to chain me. Stand back! I roll it up—up, up. And . . . down we go. I knew that would happen. See, I'm on my feet again. See, I'm starting to roll it up again. Don't try to talk me out of it. Nothing, nothing could tear me away from this rock.

"Debriefing," I (American Review, *September 1973), Ibid.*

49 This city [New York] is neither a jungle nor the moon. . . . In long shot: a cosmic smudge, a conglomerate of bleeding energies. Close up, it is a fairly legible printed circuit, a transistorized labyrinth of beastly tracks, a data bank for asthmatic voice-prints.

Ibid.

50 Although none of the rules for becoming more alive is valid, it is healthy to keep on formulating them.

Ibid.

51 The best emotions to write out of are anger and fear or dread. . . . The least energizing emotion to write out of is admiration. It is very difficult to write out of because the basic feeling that goes with admiration is a passive contemplative mood.
"On Writing" (1980), Quoted in *With William Burroughs:* *A Report from the Bunker* by Victor Bockris *1981*
*American writer (1914–1977).

52 Communism is fascism with a human face.
Speech, Forum for Poland's Solidarity (New York City) *1982*

53 The writer is either a practising recluse or a delinquent, guilt-ridden one; or both. Usually both.
"When Writers Talk among Themselves," *The New York Times 5 January 1986*

54 Like the effects of industrial pollution and the new system of global financial markets, the AIDS crisis is evidence of a world in which nothing important is regional, local, limited; in which everything that can circulate does and every problem is, or is destined to become, worldwide.
AIDS and its Metaphors 1989

55 War-making is one of the few activities that people are not supposed to view "realistically"; that is, with an eye to expense and practical outcome. In all-out war, expenditure is all-out, unprudent-war being defined as an emergency in which no sacrifice is excessive.
Ch. 1, Ibid.

56 It is not suffering as such that is most deeply feared but suffering that degrades.
Ch. 4, Ibid.

57 The fact that illness is associated with the poor—who are, from the perspective of the privileged, aliens in one's midst—reinforces the association of illness with the foreign: with an exotic, often primitive place.
Ch. 5, Ibid.

58 Authoritarian political ideologies have a vested interest in promoting fear, a sense of the imminence of takeover by aliens—and real diseases are useful material.
Ch. 6, Ibid.

59 AIDS obliges people to think of sex as having, possibly, the direst consequences: suicide. Or murder.
Ch. 7, Ibid.

60 One set of messages of the society we live in is: Consume. Grow. Do what you want. Amuse yourselves. The very working of this economic system, which has bestowed these unprecedented liberties, most cherished in the form of physical mobility and material prosperity, depends on encouraging people to defy limits.
Ibid.

61 I envy paranoids; they actually feel people are paying attention to them.
Quoted in *Time Out* (London) *19 August 1992*

62 Nations are communities that are always being imagined, reconceived, reasserted, against the pressure of a defining Other. The specter of a nation without borders, an infinitely porous nation, is bound to create anxiety. Europe needs its overbearing America.
"Why Are We In Kosovo," *The New York Times Magazine 2 May 1999*

63 Not all violence is equally reprehensible; not all wars are equally unjust.
Ibid.

64 The principal instances of mass violence in the world today are those committed by governments within their own legally recognized borders.
Ibid.

65 War is a culture, bellicosity is addictive, defeat for a community that imagines itself to be history's eternal victim can be as intoxicating as victory.
Ibid.

2541. Rosalie Sorrels (1933–)

1 Let her discover all the things that she can do.
Sooner or later, she's gonna discover
She can do without you.
"She Can Do Without You" *1974*

2 What can I say, but that it's not easy?
I cannot lift the stones out of your way,
And I can't cry your bitter tears for you.
I would if I could, what can I say?
"Apple of My Eye" *1974*

3 There's no more rooms to retire to,
I've got to move, there's no place to stay.
I've nothing that's mine but my shadow,
If you need one, I'll give that away.
"Travelin' Lady" *1974*

4 I like to sing for my friends; I don't want to sing in fucking stadiums. I like to be able to see who I'm singing too, look them right in the eye and talk to them. . . . I can't get into that thing where you keep swelling up bigger and bigger, publicity, super-hype, higher prices, more equipment. . . . If you come around with a seven-piece band, three roadies, a manager, and groupies . . . you lose your mobility and miss all the *good* times.
Quoted in "Rosalie Sorrels" by Amie Hill, *Rolling Stone* (New York) *28 January 1975*

5 It's not that I don't love the darlings
I'd do anything for my kids, but
If I had to go through all that one more time
I'd jump off the Golden Gate Bridge tra la la.
"Mother's Day Song" *1980*

2542. Joanna T. Steichen (1933–)

1 Sometimes the widows of consuming overachievers . . . learn skillfully to manipulate the would-be users and fabricate a life spun out on others' . . . but it is a precarious existence. Some pour their energies into building his work into an active career for themselves. Some look for the most convincing facsimile they can find and marry him. A few make the selfish choice that I did and, before he dies, plunge back into challenging work of their own.
  To make the choice for independent survival, the great man's wife has to become convinced of her own intrinsic worth.
"Jacqueline Picasso* and Me" (p. 76), *Ms.* (New York) *March 1987*
*Wife of Spanish artist Pablo Picasso (1881–1973).

2543. Minnie Thomas (1933?–)

1 Crack has taken away these women's pride.
    By the time they find their way here,* they'll beg, steal and trade their bodies to the dope man for more.
        Quoted in "A Hand and a Home for Pregnant Addicts"
        by Dennis Wyss, *Time* (New York) 27 February 1989
*Mandela House, a halfway house for pregnant crack addicts in Oakland, California.

2 I tell the women constantly that I'm part of them. I tell them, "I was you."
                                                                    Ibid.

2544. Dorothy Uhnak (1933–)

1 The only people left when the blacks and Puerto Ricans came spilling in were the old people who still paid nearly the same rents as they had for more than twenty-five years. Who had been fixed in income, fixed in a particular neighborhood, in a particular building, in a particular apartment. They stayed as though serving a life sentence; their next and only move would be in a box.
                                        Pt. I, Ch. 7, *The Investigation* 1977

2 I like to deliver more than I promise instead of the other way around. Which is just one of my many trade secrets.
                                                            Ch. 13, Ibid.

3 He maintained that the case was lost or won by the time the final juror had been sworn in; his summation was set in his mind before the first witness was called. It was all in the orchestration, he claimed: in knowing how and when to pitch each and every particular argument; who to intimidate; who to trust, who to flatter and court; who to challenge; when to underplay and exactly when to let out all the stops.
                                                            Ch. 14, Ibid.

4 There weren't many unusual events to clutter up her memory, so she hung on to the ones she had.
                                                    Pt. II, Ch. 10, Ibid.

2545. Helen Vendler (1933–)

1 It is a crushing burden . . . to reinterpret in a personal, and personally acceptable, way every conventional liturgical and religious act; to make devotion always singular, never simply communal . . . to particularize, not to merge; to individuate, not to accede.
                            Introduction, *The Poetry of George Herbert** 1975
*English metaphysical poet (1593–1633).

2 The micro-levels of stylistic change . . . need to be attended to quite as much as the macro-levels . . . such micro-levels of change from poem to poem reflect changes of feeling, changes of aesthetic perception, or changes of moral stance in the poet.
                            The Breaking of Style : Hopkins, Heaney,**
                            Graham**** 1996
*Gerald Manley Hopkins, English poet (1844–1889); **Seamus Justin Heaney, Irish poet (1939–); ***Jorie Graham, American poet (1951–).

3 When the mind becomes one gigantic cacophony of groans, in eight-beat sprung rhythm lines prolonging themselves into one undifferentiated monosyllabic vocal disharmony, we have come to the last agony of the stylistic body of poetry.
                                                            (p. 40), Ibid.

4 Perhaps total immersion in the Sonnets—that is to say, in Shakespeare's mind—is a mildly deranging experience to anyone.
                                    *The Art of Shakespeare's Sonnets** 1997
*William Shakespeare, English playwright and poet (1564–1616).

2546. Nina Voronel (1933–)

1 In Russia today, anything new is dangerous.
                    Quoted in "Russia: No Exit for These Four Women"
                    by Ruth Gruber, *Ms.* (New York) April 1974

2 The echoes of pogroms sob in my verses
  Making contacts with history.
                                                "I Am a Jew," Ibid.

3 . . . I believe devoutly in the word. The Word can save all, destroy all, stop the inevitable, and express the inexpressible.
                                                                    Ibid.

2547. Fay Weldon (1933–)

1 The New Women! I could barely recognise them as being of the same sex as myself, their buttocks arrogant in tight jeans, openly inviting, breasts falling free and shameless and feeling no apparent obligation to smile, look pleasant or keep their voices low. And how they live! Just look at them to know how! If a man doesn't bring them to orgasm, they look for another who does. If by mistake they fall pregnant, they abort by vacuum aspiration. If they don't like the food, they push the plate away. If the job doesn't suit them, they hand in their notice. They are satiated by everything, hungry for nothing. They are what I wanted to be; they are what I worked for them to be: and now I see them, I hate them.
                                                        Ch. 2, *Praxis* 1978

2 We shelter children for a time; we live side by side with men; and that is all. We owe them nothing, and are owed nothing. I think we owe our friends more, especially our female friends.
                                                            Ch. 19, Ibid.

3 You end up as you deserve. In old age, you must put up with the face, the friends, the health and the children you have earned.
                                                            Ch. 21, Ibid.

4 WASP. I never thought happiness was a goal worth achieving—cows are happy.
  EDWIN. You make jokes when people's hearts are breaking
                                                    After the Prize 1981

5 Women who live by the good will of men have no control over their lives, and that's the truth of it.
                                            The Heart of the Country 1989

6 The heart of the country is rotten.
                                                                    Ibid.

7 I am an ordinary person, but carried to extremes.
                                                Leader of the Band 1989

8 I make myself deaf to the pleas of the unborn. As many as my father brought into existence, I will keep out of it.
                                                                    Ibid.

9 The ability to respond to words [is] rather like having red hair or blue eyes—[it] tends to run in the family.
                                        Current Biography Yearbook 1990 1991

10 I always worked on the basic assumption that the world was peopled by females.

Ibid.

11 Apart from the fact that it is mostly lies, [advertising] teaches you form.

Ibid.

12 Life Force . . . leaping . . . like electricity, from this one to that one, burning us up, wearing us out, making us old, passing on, its only purpose its own survival . . . the best thing that ever happened to us.

Life Force 1991

13 How can he possibly choose her while I was on offer?
"Ind Aff,'" *Moon Over Minneapolis: Or Why She Couldn't Say* 1991

14 Young women especially have something invested in being nice people, and it's only when you have children that you realise you're not a nice person at all, but generally a selfish bully.

Quoted in *Independent on Sunday* (London) *5 May 1991*

15 "We're all Serbs and Croats and Bosnians at heart."
Trouble 1993

16 " You're wearing scent, so I know that in your calculating way you have sex with me planned for tonight."

Ibid.

17 . . . there was no such thing as a defeat. If you didn't accept it.
Worst Fears 1996

18 "How you've grown lately, Rex, and I haven't even noticed. I've been so busy with other things."
Nobody Likes Me! 1997

19 The past may be another country, but there are frequent international flights from there to here.
Wicked Women 1997

20 "You don't need to hear my excuses. They are the same that everyone makes to themselves when faced with the misery of others, and though they would like to do the right thing . . . look after themselves instead."

Ibid.

21 Platform soles are the opposite of stiletto heels. Girls want to be looked at, marveled at, but have lost interest in enticement.
Big Girls Don't Cry 1998

22 "I'll be frank with you. I have no time for women's-libbers. They make someone like me feel I've wasted my life, following rules they now laugh at."

Ibid.

2548. Nancy Makepeace Tanner (1933–1989)

1 Offspring [during early paleolithic times] with mothers intelligent enough to find, gather, premasticate, and share sufficient food with them had the selective advantage. Among those surviving children, those best able to learn and improve on their mother's techniques, and those who, like their mothers, were willing to share, in turn had the children who were most likely to live long enough to reproduce.

On Becoming Human 1981

2549. Freda Adler (1934–)

1 Woman throughout the ages has been mistress to the law, as man has been its master. . . . the controversy between rule of law and rule of men was never relevant to women—because, along with juveniles, imbeciles, and other classes of legal non-persons, they had no access to law except through men.

Sisters in Crime 1975

2 The phenomenon of female criminality is but one wave in this rising tide of female assertiveness—a wave which has not yet crested and may even be seeking its level uncomfortably close to the high–water mark set by male violence.

Prologue, Ibid.

3 The type of fig leaf which each culture employs to cover its social taboos offers a twofold description of its morality. It reveals that certain unacknowledged behavior exists and it suggests the form that such behavior takes.

Ch. 3, Ibid.

4 There is another side to chivalry. If it dispenses leniency, it may with equal justification invoke control.

Ch. 4, Ibid.

5 Of all the tyrannies which have usurped power over humanity, few have been able to enslave the mind and body as imperiously as drug addiction.

Ch. 5, Ibid.

6 Stripped of ethical rationalizations and philosophical pretensions, a crime is anything that a group in power chooses to prohibit.

Ch. 7, Ibid.

7 That man is a creature who needs order yet yearns for change is the creative contradiction at the heart of the laws which structure his conformity and define his deviancy.

Ch. 8, Ibid.

8 It is little wonder that rape is one of the least reported crimes. Perhaps it is the only crime in which the victim becomes the accused and, in reality, it is she who must prove her good reputation, her mental–soundness, and her impeccable propriety.

Ch. 9, Ibid.

2550. Eileen Atkins (1934–)

1 It's a damn shame we have this immediate ticking off in the mind about how people sound. On the other hand, how many people really want to be operated upon by a surgeon who talks broad cockney?

The Daily Telegraph (London) *5 February 1992*

2551. Brigitte Bardot (1934–)

1 I leave before being left. I decide.
Quoted in *Newsweek* (New York) *5 March 1973*

2 I am leaving the town* to the invaders: increasingly numerous, mediocre, dirty, badly behaved, shameless tourists.
International Herald Tribune (Paris) *10 August 1989*
*On leaving her home at Saint Tropez.

3 I gave my youth and beauty to men. Now I give the best of my wisdom and experience to animals.
Quoted in "Bardot Flies Again," *Parade Magazine 3 May 1992*

2552. Sissela Ann Bok (1934–)

1 If you combine lying and secrecy, and if you also bring in violence so that secrecy covers up for schemes of lying and violence, then I think a republic can die. I don't think it's possible for citizens to have much of an effect if they literally don't know what's going on.

> Quoted in *A World of Ideas* by Bill Moyers *1989*

2 The predicament we're in now and that we have been in for some time is the threat of extinction from nuclear weapons, and the threat of extinction from environmental sources. It has simply never been the case before in human history that all of life—not just human life but really all of life—could be wiped out. That has made an enormous change for us. At the same time, this is also an extraordinary opportunity.

> Ibid.

3 Our century has been unbelievably violent and brutal and filled with tyranny, but it has also brought forth countervailing powers. We've had popular movements seeking to change nonviolently and, in fact, succeeding more and more often. . . . We have better history. We know much more how wars start and how they can get out of hand.

> Ibid.

2553. Sandra Burton (1934?–)

1 [Marcos*] was the kind of lawyer you would hire to get you off if you were really in trouble—particularly if you were guilty.

> *Impossible Dream: the Marcoses, the Aquinos,** and the Unfinished Revolution 1989*
> *Ferdinand Marcos (1917–1989), Philippine president (1966–1986).
> **See Corazon Aquino, 2520.

2554. Diana Chang (1934–)

1 The old are girlish now
Going to their grooms
They marry mysteries

> "On Seeing My Great-Aunt in a Funeral Parlor," St. 5, *The American Scholar*, Vol. 28, No. 1 *Winter 1958/59*

2 I am the thin edge I sit on.
I begin to gray—white and black and in between.
My hair is America.

> "Second Nature," St. 7, *The Woman That I Am, The Literature and Culture of Contemporary Women of Color*, D. Soyini Madison, ed. *1994*

2555. Inga Clendinnen (1934–)

1 I was especially terrified of Germans, because they clearly gloried in their wickedness: they wore black uniforms, flaunted an insignia of a human skull couched on human bones, and unabashedly proclaimed themselves "Nasties." At a time when Australia stood in real and present danger from the Japanese, my dreams were full of the stolid minions of the men in black . . . invading across the back paddock, through the back gate and into the kitchen to kill us all.

> *Reading the Holocaust 1999*
> *The genocide of European Jews and others by the Nazis during World War II.

2 . . . the theological struggle to comprehend the Holocaust as an episode in an enigmatic deity's intentions regarding his chosen people continues to shadow putatively secular debate.

> Ibid.

3 In my view understanding does not require anything so heroic as "identification," which is at best a slapdash procedure and too often a misleading one.

> Ibid.

4 Villains are rarely simple men.

> Ibid.

5 Fractured identity is not confined to the innocent.

> Ibid.

6 We will not understand an Eichmann* unless we grasp not only the individual character, but the exhilaration infused into that drab character by his context of revolutionary excitement and urgent high purpose, so that bullying brutal action was transformed into heroism.

> Ibid.
> *Adolf Eichmann, German Nazi official (1906–62).

7 What most disquiets about a too-shrill insistence on the uniqueness of the Holocaust is the danger that, if the Holocaust were indeed to be accepted as unique, it would risk falling out of history.

> Ibid.

2556. Sherry Suib Cohen (1934–)

1 What have been the costs of blind, cutthroat, unaffiliating competition? Lagging productivity, as the import figures reveal, a huge turnover of the best people, distrust and suspicion within the ranks, political infighing and sabotage, workers who expect to be ignored and who expect to fail (and who do exactly these two things). These are the costs the American corporation is paying.

> Ch. 3, *Tender Power 1989*

2 Power is not a sorority for working women alone. A certain inner confidence is to be gained when, knowing one is following one's strongest instincts, one chooses, in defiance of current dogma, to stay home. For some, heeding that call is power. Moreover, those who decide they can afford to stay home, at least for a few years, are not alone in the wisdom of their decision.

> Ch. 10, Ibid.

2557. Arlene Croce (1934?–)

1 At least some of the men who write sex books admit they really don't understand female sexuality. Freud* was one. Masters** is another—that was why he got Johnson.***

> Quoted in *Commentary n.d.*
> *Sigmund Freud, Austrian physician and founder of psychoanalysis (1856–1939). **William H. Masters, gynecologist (1915–) and Virginia E. Johnson,*** psychologist (1925–), pioneering American research team in human sexuality.

2558. Margaretta D'Arcy (1934–)

1 SINGER (to the air "Long Lankin").
The cold rain of Ireland blows over the water
To furrow the face of fair England's proud daughter.

How long will it fall, O as sharp as a knife?
Till the dogteeth of England let go of our life.

Let go of our heart and the voice in our throat:
Till the day of that good-morning, no end to the fight . . .

> Prologue, *Vandaleur's Folly*, with John Arden* *1978*
> *British dramatist (1930–), her husband and collaborator.

2 I am not sure whether there is a connection between the loss of the concept of "play" and our present-day mechanistic bums-on-seats "task-profit" syndrome where the finished commodity of the cultural production-line is all that matters and to hell with the personal growth and vision of the workers.
Quoted by Elaine Turner in *Contemporary Dramatists*,
5th ed., K.A. Berney, ed. *1993*

2559. Diane Di Prima (1934–)

1 We buy the arms and the armed men, we have placed them
on all the thrones of South America
we are burning the jungles, the beasts will rise up against us
"Goodbye Nkrumah," St. 1, *Intrepid #VI 1966*

2 When the radio told me there was dancing in
the streets, I knew we had engineered
another coup; Bought off another army.
Ibid.

3 Had you lived longer than your twenty-six years
You, too, would have come up against it like a wall—
That the Beauty you saw was bought
At too great a price
Even in those days. . . .
"Ode to Keats," St. 1, *The East Side Scene*,
Allen de Loach, ed. *1968*

4 Don't forget, however great your visioning and your inspiration, you need the techniques of the craft and there's nowhere, really, to get them . . . they are passed on person to person and back then the male naturally passed them on to the male. I think maybe I was one of the first women to break through that in having deep conversations with Charles Olson* and Frank O'Hara.**
Quoted in *Women of the Beat Generation* by
Brenda Knight *1996*
*American avant garde poet and literary theorist (1910–1970).
**American poet (1926–1966).

2560. Sheila Fugard (1932?–)

1 In a way it is much simpler to take upon oneself a discipline without the consolation of a visionary guide.
I believe now that there is no need to find him, the Buddhist, that all I must do is progress in the knowledge of the void, the perennial nothingness of the moment.
Pt. III, l.l., *The Castaways 1972*

2 I talk of the lives of others. I am fertilized, but not fulfilled, and my life insists on its own voice.
Pt. I, *A Revolutionary Woman 1985*

3 Racism is enshrined here.*
Ibid.
*Reference to the Union of South Africa.

4 The Karoo* is all space. The trees fail to fill the emptiness, and the fences are useless too. The Karoo swallows up everything; Brahmins and Untouchables, the flocks of sheep and goats, as well as the houses and possessions. There is much to contend with here.
Ibid.
*The harsh landscape of South Africa.

5 The butcher is mistaken. Justice is not weighed on a scale like a pound of steak. I'm aware of the cost of justice, and it's not measured in pounds. It's got to do with men's hearts.
Pt. III, Ibid.

2561. Nancy Rule Goldberger (1934–)
See Mary Field Belenky, 2522: 1–4.

2562. Barbara Grizzuti Harrison (1934/41–)

1 Profoundly ignorant, we are obliged to invent.
"Talking Dirty," *Ms.* (New York) *October 1973*

2 Fantasies are more than substitutes for unpleasant reality; they are also dress rehearsals, plans. All acts performed in the world begin in the imagination.
Ibid.

3 To offer the complexities of life as an excuse for not addressing oneself to the simpler, more manageable (trivial) aspects of daily existence is a perversity often indulged in by artist, husbands, intellectuals—and critics of the Women's Movement.
Introduction, *Unlearning the Lie: Sexism in School 1973*

4 True revolutionaries are like God—they create the world in their own image. Our awesome responsibility to ourselves, to our children, and to the future is to create ourselves in the image of goodness, because the future depends on the nobility of our imaginings.
Ch. 9, Ibid.

5 I refuse to believe that trading recipes is silly. Tuna-fish casserole is at least as real as corporate stock.
"Secrets Women Tell Each Other," *McCall's August 1975*

6 Women's propensity to share confidences is universal. We confirm our reality by sharing.
Ibid.

7 . . . to have a crisis, and act upon it, is one thing. To dwell in perpetual crisis is another.
Ibid.

8 Kindness and intelligence don't always deliver us from the pitfalls and traps: there are always failures of love, of will, of imagination. There is no way to take the danger out of human relationships.
Ibid.

9 Memories gather around puzzles, passions and possession.
Introduction, *An Accidental Autobiography 1996*

10 A linear autobiography would falsify because it would cast things in a mold and present me with the temptation to find formal patterns where none exist.
Ibid.

11 . . . all that one [really] wants [is] to be seen; what one does not want is to be invented.
Ibid.

12 I love my body when I'm having sex, nice body, so obedient, so capable. . . . I rise, like yeast . . . so beautifully able to give and to take . . .
Ibid.

13 We hunt for things and experiences for states of grace, satiety, security, self-definition, immortality . . . out of love and lovingly, and for motives of snobbery . . . with graceful intuition, perception and integrity and with an urge to cherish and preserve . . . out of avarice, greed, lust, hunger, fear, boredom, restlessness, . . . out of a simple sense of entitlement . . .
Ibid.

14 At Swaine & Adeney, Her Majesty's whip and leather makers, the Queen Mother's umbrella makers (185 Piccadilly), "Listen, madam, hear it rustle, listen, hear it rustle," Mr. Johnson says. Sibilant and reverent, Mr. Johnson of Swaine & Adeney opens and closes a black silk taffeta umbrella, hand stitched, with a rosewood handle (£500); he caresses umbrellas with ostrich handles and umbrellas with pigskin handles, umbrellas with crocodile handles and snakeskin handles, umbrellas of Malacca, birch, and ash . . .

> Ibid.

15 (Did you ever doubt there was a censoring wily writerly presence behind the words you read?)

> Ibid.

2563. Nancy M. Henley (1934–)

1 The humiliation of being a subordinate is often felt most sharply and painfully when one is ignored or interrupted while speaking, towered over or forced to move by another's bodily presence or cowed unknowingly into dropping the eyes, the head, the shoulders. Conversely, the power to manipulate others' lives, to take graft, price gouge, or plan the bombing of far-off peasants is conferred in part by others' snapping to attention in one's presence, their smiling, fearing to touch or approach, their following one around for information or favors. These are the trivia that make up the batter for that great stratified waffle that we call our society.

> Ch. 1, *Body Politics: Power, Sex, and Non-Verbal Communication 1977*

2 Feminine atmosphere projects the image of immobility; these accoutrements are ones that one can only look beautiful in, not move, feel strong, or be active in. . . . It is no accident that coffins puff out with satin pads, lace, and frills . . .. and the funeral parlor is filled with flowers. These signs of femininity, common also to the beauty parlor, are symbolic of the powerlessness of the dead, as they are of the powerlessness of women.

> Ch. 4, Ibid.

3 "Polite" company, that is, the social elite and those who would imitate them, are so removed from their bodies undoubtedly a sign of spirituality and near-divinity that they are expected not to feel the need to itch, belch, or fart.

> Ch. 6, Ibid.

4 The history of power in fact shows us that victims of unfathomable oppression have arisen to claim their rights, that power is persistently being broken down and overturned. Every new insight into its workings may provide a new road to its overthrow.

> Ch. 11, Ibid.

2564. Marilyn Horne (1934–)

1 Ninety percent of what's wrong with singers today is that they don't breathe right.

> Quoted in "Marilyn Horne," *Divas: Impressions of Six Opera Superstars* by Winthrop Sargeant *1959*

2 The thing to do [for insomnia] is to get an opera score and read *that*. That will bore you to death.

> Ibid.

3 You have to know exactly what you want out of your career. If you want to be a star, you don't bother with other things.

> Ibid.

4 I've been a general for so long in many male roles, it's time I became emperor!

> Highlights, *Modern Maturity December 1991/January 1992*

5 Give me good health and I'll take care of the rest.

> Ibid.

2565. Jeanne Wakatsuki Houston (1934–)

1 As the months at Manzanar* turned to years, it became a world unto itself, with its own logic and familiar ways. In time, staying there seemed far simpler than moving once again to another, unknown place. It was as if the war were forgotten, our reason for being there forgotten. The present, the little bit of busywork you had right in front of you, became the most urgent thing. In such a narrowed, world, in order to survive, you learn to contain your rage and your despair, and you try to re-create, as well you can, your normality, some sense of things, continuing. The fact that America had accused us, or excluded us, or imprisoned us, or whatever it might be called, did not change the kind of world we wanted. Most of us were born in this country; we had no other models.

> *Farewell to Manzanar, and James D. Houston 1973*
> *Owens Valley, California: the first permanent internment camp for Japanese, set up after the bombing of Pearl Harbor in 1941.

2566. Louise Kapp Howe (1934–)

1 Despite the focus in the media on the affluent and the poor, the average man is neither. Despite the concentration in TV commercials on the blond, blue-eyed WASP, the real American prototype is of Italian or Irish or Polish or Greek or Lithuanian or German or Hungarian or Russian or any of the still amazing number of national origins represented in this country—a "white ethnic," sociologists somberly call him.

> Introduction, *The White Majority 1970*

2 . . . if the error of the sixties was that the people of the white majority were never given a concrete personal reason for social advance, the clear and present danger of the seventies is that they won't be warned in time against the threat of social repression being waged in their name.

> Afterword, Ibid.

3 We all know what the American family is supposed to look like. We can't help it. The picture has been imprinted on our brains since we were tiny, . . . Now, the striking point about our model family is not simply the compete-compete, consume-consume style of life it urges us to follow. . . . The striking point, in the face of all the propaganda, is how few Americans actually live this way.

> Introduction, *The Future of the Family 1972*

4 . . . the assumption of a male-breadwinner society . . . ends up determining the lives of everyone within a family, whether a male breadwinner is present or not, whether one is living by the rules in suburbia or trying to break them on a commune.

> Ibid.

5 While politicians carry on about the sanctity of the American family, we learn . . . that in the scale of national priorities our children and families really come last. After freeways. After pork subsidies. After the billions spent on munitions in the name of national defense. It is now time . . . to reverse the usual procedure. It is time to *change the economy* to meet the needs of American families.

> Ibid.

2567. Diane Johnson (1934–)

1 A lesser life does not seem lesser to the person who leads one. His life is very real to him; he is not a minor figure in it. He looks out of his eyes at our poet, our chronicled statesman. . . . And he is our real brother.

"Lesser Lives," The True History of the First Mrs. Meredity and Other Lesser Lives 1972

2 We are surrounded by the enraged.

The Shadow Knows 1974

3 Waiting to be murdered has given me you might say something to live for.

Ibid.

4 Men are generally more law-abiding than women . . . Women have a feeling that since they didn't make the rules, the rules have nothing to do with them.

Lying Low 1978

5 Great dramas, your perspective on life, your life altered for all time and at the end you have to get into a car and drive home.

Persian Nights 1987

6 Of course she had not really believed Iran would be a foreign land. She saw the deficiency in her imagination, that she had not been able to imagine with sufficient intensity the alien condition. A well-traveled American with no anxieties about hotels, headwaiters, planes—her imagination had provided her with no more than a benign region of camels, and mosques, and well-run hospitals of the American kind . . . She had assumed she could put things right . . . Now she saw that this presumption was naïve.

Ibid.

7 . . . life underneath is everywhere similar . . .

Ibid.

2568. Sophia Loren (1934–)

1 Getting ahead in a difficult profession requires avid faith in yourself. You must be able to sustain yourself against staggering blows and unfair reversals. There is no code of conduct to help beginners. That is why some people with mediocre talent, but with great inner drive, go much further than people with vastly superior talent. I'm convinced that this inner drive is something you are born with, and no one can teach you how to acquire it.

Quoted in Sophia: Living and Loving by A. E. Hotchner 1979

2 Sex appeal is fifty percent what you've got and fifty percent what people think you've got.

Quoted in Halliwell's Filmgoer's Companion by Leslie Halliwell 1984

2569. Shirley MacLaine (1934–)

1 The pain of leaving those you grow to love is only the prelude to understanding yourself and others.

Don't Fall Off the Mountain 1970

2 I asked, "Why, because a tree's arm got sick, did they have to cut down the whole body?" And they told me the tree doctor had said it was the right thing to do.

Ch. 1, Ibid.

3 For if the talent or individuality is there, it should be expressed. If it doesn't find its way out into the air, it can turn inward and gnaw like the fox at the Spartan boy's belly.

Ch. 4, Ibid.

4 In Japan, courtesy had an esthetic value far greater than good manners in the West. A negative truth is frequently subordinate to the virtue of courtesy. Courtesy, therefore, is more of a virtue than honesty.

Ch. 5, Ibid.

5 The more I traveled the more I realized that fear makes strangers of people who should be friends.

Ch. 13, Ibid.

6 Africa seems the harmonious voice of creation. Everything alive was inextricably intertwined until death. And even death was part of the life harmony.

Ibid.

7 India is a paradox, passionate, pulsating, even humorous in her poverty. And in her villages the subhuman drama plays itself out against a backdrop of such beauty that it seems grotesque mockery.

Ch. 14, Ibid.

8 Freedom, with her front windows open and unlocked, with breezes and challenges blowing in. I wished that she [MacLaine's daughter, Sasha] would know herself through freedom. I wished that underneath she would understand that there is no such thing as being safe—that there are no safe havens for anyone who wants to know the TRUTH, *whatever* it is, about himself or others.

Ch. 19, Ibid.

9 If you attach yourself to one person, you ultimately end up having an unhealthy relationship.

"The Odyssey of Shirley MacLaine," Quoted by Arthur Bell in Viva 1974

10 The notion of good and evil being fought outside the confines of our responsibility is anathema to me. Good and evil is in us. Good and evil is what we decide it should be. I have more faith in human beings than that. We can figure out what we're doing. We don't have to shove it off on God and the fucking devil.

Ibid.

11 Hollywood always had a streak of the totalitarian in just about everything it did.

Ch. 2, You Can Get There from Here 1975

12 . . . the more I became involved in "big time" politics the more I realized how vicious the in-fighting could get in the desire to "make things better."

Ch. 11, Ibid.

13 China was proud now—of herself and of her potential. She had pulled herself to dignity and unity and that spirit literally pervaded the communes, the backbone of China. The Chinese countryside was where the revolution was won and the countryside was the secret of China's future.

Ch. 20, Ibid.

14 I realized that if what we call human nature can be changed, then absolutely *anything* is possible. And from that moment, my life changed.

Epilogue, Ibid.

15 Perhaps Western values, for the past five hundred years, had been a human distortion, perhaps competition was simply not compatible with harmony, not conducive to human happiness, perhaps the competitive urge came only from the exaggerated

emphasis on the individual. Maybe the individual was simply not as important as the group.

Ibid.

16 In some ways, America has grown up to be a masterpiece of self-concern.

Ibid.

17 I was not a soldier or a philosopher or a politician; I could cure no disease, solve no economic problems or lead any revolution. But, I could dance. I could sing. I could make people laugh. I could make people cry.

Ibid.

18 Within the family environment was every human conflict that could ultimately lead to a willingness, or a nonwillingness, to wage war. Most attitudes of, and toward, violence and hostility are spawned in the family. Just as attitudes of love and compassion are.

Ch. 2, *Dancing in the Light* 1985

19 Experimentation in front of the big black giant* is enough to reduce an accomplished and seasoned performer to the rank of blithering idiot. . . . The audience never responds to artifice. They can detect sham immediately and just as swiftly respond positively to something you do that comes out of your gut. They want you to be real. That's what they're there for.

Ch. 6, Ibid.

*Reference to song "The Big Black Giant" from Rodgers and Hammerstein's musical *Me and Juliet*.

20 Nothing should be permanent except struggle with the dark side within ourselves.

Ch. 11, Ibid.

21 If I could know me, I could know the universe.

Epilogue, Ibid.

2570. Janet Malcolm (1934–)

1 Every journalist who is not too stupid or too full of himself to notice what is going on knows that what he does is morally indefensible. He is a kind of confidence man, preying on people's vanity, ignorance, or loneliness, gaining their trust and betraying them without remorse.

The Journalist and the Murderer 1990

2 When we talk with somebody, we are not aware of the language we are speaking. Our ear takes it in as English, and only if we see it transcribed verbatim do we realize that it is a kind of foreign tongue.

"Afterword," Ibid.

3 Fidelity to the subject's thought and to his characteristic way of expressing himself is the sine qua non of journalistic quotation.

Ibid.

4 The dominant and most deep-dyed trait of the journalist is his timorousness. Where the novelist fearlessly plunges into the water of self-exposure, the journalist stands trembling on the shore in his beach robe. . . . The journalist confines himself to the clean, gentlemanly work of exposing the griefs and shames of others.

Ibid.

2571. Winnie Madikizela-Mandela (1934–)

1 I am a living symbol of whatever is happening in the country. I am a living symbol of the white man's fear.

"My Little Siberia," *Part of My Soul Went With Him*,
Anne Benjamin, ed. *1984*

2 The Afrikaner in the Free State—for him a black is something that sits on their tractor or plods behind their plough. What is more important to that farmer is his tractor and not that laborer. . . .

Ibid.

3 We never had him* physically to share that love he exudes so much of. I knew when I married him that I married the struggle, the liberation of my people.

"Life With Him Was Always a Life Without Him," Ibid.

*Nelson Mandela, South African political and civil rights leader (1918–); incarcerated (1962–1990); president (1994–1999).

4 There is an anger that wakes up in you when you are a child and it builds up and determines the political consciousness of the black man.

Ibid.

5 Together, hand in hand, with that stick of matches, with our necklace*, we shall liberate this country.

Speech in black townships, Quoted in *The Guardian*
(London) *15 April 1986*

*Slang for the practice of lighting a gasoline filled tire thrown around a victim's neck.

6 It dawned on me that you either had to survive apartheid or you had to perish with it. I decided to survive.

Quoted in *Twentieth-Century Women Political Leaders*
by Claire Price-Groff *1998*

2572. Peggy McIntosh (1934–)

1 [White privilege is] . . . an invisible package of unearned assets . . . an invisible weightless knapsack of special provisions, assurance, tools, maps, guides, codebooks, passports, visas, clothes, compass, emergency gear, and blank checks.

Quoted in "Making Systems of Privilege Visible," *Privilege*
Revealed: How Invisible Preference Undermines America
by Stephanie M. Wildman* *1996*

*See 3240.

2573. Marianne Means (1934–)

1 Conservatives are used to strong women; they just aren't used to strong women who don't give men all the credit.

"Conservatives make much of Clinton . . . ," *Seattle Post-*
Intelligencer, A15 *12 February 1993*

2 In politics, the more things change, the more they remain the same.

Syndicated column *8 September 1997*

3 It is not surprising that young people feel their views will not be heard in distant, isolated Washington. Older adults feel that way, too. Such alienation is inevitable in an enormous nation of vast geographic contrasts, ethnic diversity and technical specialization.

"What's impeachment effect on younger set?," *Seattle Post-*
Intelligencer, E2 *24 January 1999*

2574. Kate Millet (1934–)

1 . . . the threadbare tactic of justifying social and temperamental differences by biological ones.

Sexual Politics 1969

2 The care of children, even from the period when their cognitive powers first emerge, is infinitely better left to the best-trained

practitioners of both sexes who have chosen it as a vocation, rather than to harried and all too frequently unhappy persons with little time or taste for the work of educating minds however young or beloved . . . The family, as that term is presently understood, must go.

Ibid.

3 . . . I see the function of true Erotica (writing which is pro—, not antisexual) as one not only permissible but worthy of encouragement and social approval, as its laudable and legitimate function is to increase sexual appetite just as culinary prose encourages other appetites.

Ibid.

4 . . . the female is rendered innocuous by her socialization. Before assault she is almost universally defenseless both by her physical and emotional training.

Ibid.

5 Perhaps nothing is so depressing an index of the inhumanity of the male supremacist mentality as the fact that the more genial human traits are assigned to the underclass: affection, response to sympathy, kindness, cheerfulness.

Ibid.

6 For our highly repressive and Puritan tradition has almost hopelessly confused sexuality with sadism, cruelty, and that which is in general inhumane and antisocial. This is a deplorable state of affairs.

Ibid.

7 Many women do not recognize themselves as discriminated against; no better proof could be found of the totality of their conditioning.

Ibid.

8 Sexual congress in a Mailer* novel is always a matter of strenuous endeavor, rather like mountain climbing—a matter of straining after achievement.

Ibid.

*Norman Mailer, American writer (1923–).

9 Prostitution, when unmotivated by economic need, might well be defined as a species of psychological addiction, built on self-hatred through repetitions of the act of sale by which a whore is defined.

Ch. 3, Ibid.

10 However muted its present appearance may be, sexual dominion obtains nevertheless as perhaps the most pervasive ideology of our culture and provides its most fundamental concept of power.

Ibid.

11 It is a further irony that our legal ethic prosecutes those who are forced (economically or psychologically) to offer themselves for sale as objects, but condones the act of buying persons as objects.

The Prostitution Papers 1971

12 Whores are the political prisoners of the feminist movement . . . They are considered criminals for no other reason than the fact that they are women . . . men aren't jailed for solicitation . . . women are jailed. And they're jailed because they have cunts.

Quoted in *Radical Lifestyles* by Claudia Dreifus* 1971
*See 2997.

13 Aren't women prudes if they don't and prostitutes if they do?

Speech, Women's Writer's Conference (Los Angeles)
22 March 1975

14 Isn't privacy about keeping taboos in their place?

Ibid.

2575. Marlo Morgan (1934–)

1 Little is gained in a lifetime if what you believe at age seven is still how you feel at age thirty-seven . . . New things cannot come where there is no room.

Mutant Mess Down Under 1994

2576. Sister Nirmala (1934–)

1 I remember [when I was in college] the church bells ringing, it was the bells of Angelus, and my roommate suddenly knelt down right there and prayed. At that moment, something happened in my heart. Jesus came alive in me.

Quoted in "Life in the shadow of Mother Teresa"*
by John Stackhouse, *Seattle Post-Intelligencer*, A12
5 September 1998

2 We have decided collectively to keep that title for Mother* only. For me it is definite. I like to be a sister. I like being sister to my sisters. When you are a sister, you can play with the sisters.

Ibid.

*See 1973.

2577. Carol Lee Sanchez (1934–)

1 For fifty years, children in this country have been raised to kill Indians mentally, subconsciously through the visual media, until it is an automatic reflex. That shocks you? Then I have made my point . . . The cheap western is still rolling out of Hollywood, the old shoot-'em-up westerns playing on afternoon kid shows, late night T.V. Would you allow your children to play Nazis and Jews? Blacks and KKKs?*

"Sex, Class and Race Intersections Visions of Women of
Color," *A Gathering of Spirit*, Beth Brant,** ed. *1984*

*Ku Klux Klan, a secret, militant, white supremacist society, founded in 1915 in the U.S. state of Georgia. **See 2842.

2 We have been displaced, relocated, removed, terminated, educated, acculturated, and in our hearts and minds we will always "go back to the blanket" as long as we are still connected to our families, our Tribes and our land.

Ibid.

3 yo soy india
pero no soy
yo soy anglo
pero no soy
yo soy arabe
pero no soy
yo soy chicana
pero no soy
(I am indian/but I am not/I am anglo/but I am not/I am arabic/but I am not/I am chicana/but I am not)

"Tribal Chant," St. 5, *That's What She Said*, Rayna Green,*
ed. *1984*

*See 2800.

4 how come you kees me by
the reever, & on the strit
jou don told me hallo?

"The Way I Was. . . ." St. 2, Ibid.

5 love longs to touch the ordinary places—
momentary what-nots scattered through the years
from dresser drawer
to china closet
and way up high on the linen
closet shelf.

Untitled, St. 2, Ibid.

2578. Sonia Sanchez (1934–)

1 Slow is not always dumb, and fast is not always smart.
The Adventures of Fathead, Smallhead, and Squarehead
1973

2 I've always known that if you write from a black experience,
you're writing from a universal experience as well . . . I know
you don't have to whitewash yourself to be universal.
Black Women Writers at Work, Claudia Tate, ed. *1983*

3 I sang unbending
songs and gathered gods.
"Past," St. 1, *The Woman That I Am, The Literature
and Culture of Contemporary Women of Color,*
D. Soyini Madison, ed. *1994*

4 tell me how I have become, became
this woman with razor blades between
her teeth.
"Past," 1. Woman, St. 1, Ibid.

5 I want my body to carry my words like aqueducts.
I want to make the world my diary
and speak rivers.
Ibid.

6 Catch the fire . . . and live
live
livelivelivelive
"Catch the Fire," *Wounded in the House of a Friend 1995*

7 let my journey sign a path they sang
o I will purchase my brother's whisper.
o I will reward my brother's tongue.
Does Your House Have Lions? 1997

8 you held me so close
we were like the singing coming off drums.
you made me squeeze muscles
lean back on the sound
of corpuscles sliding in blood. I heard my thighs singing
Untitled, *Like the Singing Coming Off the Drums 1997*

9 . . . I ammmmmmmm
the universe knows that
I ammmmmmm
hiv positive but I ammm
still. woman. lover. mother.
sistah. artist. organizer. activist.
woman . . .
Ibid.

2579. Carolyn See (1934–)

1 Explosions wait in all of us, and we're just as surprised as everyone else when they go off.
Dreaming: Hard Luck and Good Times in America 1995

2 Scorn was my career.
Ibid.

3 If I were a Republican on a golf course, I'd want a working
class that was efficient but subdued, hardworking but depressed. I'd want them to have a low energy level.
Ibid.

4 Her boyfriend Tony bored her to tears. He was good and kind,
but his idea was: go to work. Go to the movies. Take a class,
hear a lecture, buy a few beers, smoke some dope, zone out in
front of the TV, sleep, surf, be peaceful.
Ibid.

5 Don't do as we did. Do what it was we wanted to do when we
started our lives. Adhere to *those* high ideals. . . . Learn from
our mistakes.
Ibid.

2580. Patricia Simon (1934–)

1 An old French farm built on levels up and down a hillside near
Grasse—overlooking, in the middle distance, the quiet cluster
of the town and, in the further distance, hills, and beyond them
other hills, and other hills, in a gentle, fertile, dreamlike landscape that continued forever—the Alpes-Maritimes.
"The Making of a Masterpiece," *McCall's October 1970*

2 Flowers and sunlight, air and silence—"*luxe, calme et
volupté.*"
Ibid.

2581. Gloria Steinem (1934–)

1 We [women] are not more moral, we are only less corrupted
by power.
"A New Egalitarian Life Style," *The New York Times
Book Review 26 August 1971*

2 . . . no man can call himself liberal, or radical, or even a conservative advocate of fair play, if his work depends in any way
on the unpaid or underpaid labor of women at home, or in the
office.
Ibid.

3 The first problem for all of us, men and women, is not to learn,
but to unlearn.
Ibid.

4 It's clear that most American children suffer too much mother
and too little father.
Ibid.

5 The status quo protects itself by punishing all challengers.
"Sisterhood," *The First Ms. Reader*, Francine Klagsbrun, ed.
1972

6 As for logic, it's in the eye of the logician.
Ibid.

7 We are human beings first, with minor differences from men
that apply largely to the act of reproduction. We share the
dreams, capabilities, and weaknesses of all human beings, but
our occasional pregnancies and other visible differences have
been used—even more pervasively, if less brutally, than radical
differences have been used—to mark us for an elaborate division of labor that may once have been practical but has since
become cruel and false. The division is continued for clear reason, consciously or not: the economic and social profit of men
as a group.
Ibid.

8 God knows (*she* knows) that women try.

Ibid.

9 I have met brave women who are exploring the outer edge of human possibility, with no history to guide them, and with a courage to make themselves vulnerable that I find moving beyond words.

Ibid.

10 The long history of antiobscenity laws makes it very clear that such laws are most often invoked against political and lifestyle dissidents.

"Gazette News: Obscene?" *Ms.* (New York) *October 1973*

11 The definition of women's work is shitwork.

Quoted in "Freelancer with No Time to Write" by John Brady, *Writer's Digest February 1974*

12 . . . intelligence at the service of poor instinct is really dangerous . . .

Ibid.

13 . . . the new women in politics seem to be saying that we already know how to lose, thank you very much. Now we want to learn how to win.

"Victory with Honor," *Ms.* (New York) *April 1974*

14 A government's responsibility to its young citizens does not magically begin at the age of six. It makes more sense to extend the free universal school system downward—with the necessary reforms and community control that child care should have from the start.

Ibid.

15 Ten years from now, as I see it, either the movements for change will be totally annihilated, dispirited or ground down—or they will really have entered the mainstream and created major changes. It has come to the point of maximum push.

Quoted in "Impeachment?" by Claire Safran, *Redbook* (New York) *April 1974*

16 Erotic is about sexuality, but pornography is about power and sex-as-weapon—in the same way we have come to understand that rape is about violence, and not really about sex at all.

"Erotic and Pornography, A Clear and Present Difference," *Ms.* (New York) *November 1978*

17 . . . the family is the basic cell of government: it is where we are trained to believe that we are human beings or that we are chattel, it is where we are trained to see the sex and race divisions and become callous to injustice even if it is done to ourselves, to accept as biological a full system of authoritarian government.

Speech, National Women's Political Caucus Conference (Albuquerque, New Mexico) *July 1981*

18 We must understand the difference between what we mean by family and what the Right Wing means by family. . . . Women are the means of production, owned by the husband. Children are the labor, owned by the husband. And that's what they mean by family. Consequently, they oppose any direct guarantee of right between wife and the law or children and the law, because that is antithetical to their definition of the family.

Ibid.

19 Some of us are becoming the men we wanted to marry.

Speech, Yale University *23 September 1981*

20 If the men in the room would only think how they would feel graduating with a "spinster of arts" degree they would see how important this [language reform] is.

Ibid.

21 . . . the authority of any governing institution must stop at its citizen's skin.

"Night Thoughts of a Media-Watcher," *Ms.* (New York) *November 1981*

22 Dying seems less sad than having lived too little.

Outrageous Acts and Everyday Rebellion 1983

23 Evil is obvious only in retrospect.

Ibid.

24 Finding language that will allow people to act together while cherishing each other's individuality is probably the most feminist and therefore truly revolutionary function of writers.

Introduction, Ibid.

25 Living in India made me understand that a white minority of the world has spent centuries conning us into thinking a white skin makes people superior, even though the only thing it really does is make them more subject to ultraviolet rays and wrinkles.

"If Men Could Menstruate" (1978), Ibid.

26 Logic has nothing to do with oppression.

Ibid.

27 What has the women's movement learned from [Geraldine Ferraro's]* candidacy for vice president? Never get married.**

Quoted in *Boston Globe 14 May 1987*

*See 2591. **Reference to the damage done to Ferraro's candidacy due to her husband's financial misdeeds.

28 If men started taking care of children, the job will become more valuable.

Quoted in "Onward, Women!" by Claudia Wallis, *Time* (New York) *4 December 1989*

29 However sugar-coated and ambiguous, every form of authoritarianism must start with a belief in some group's greater right to power, whether that right is justified by sex, race, class, religion, or all four. However far it may expand, the progression inevitably rests on unequal power and airtight roles within the family.

Revolution From Within 1992

30 It's an incredible con job when you think about it, to believe something now in exchange for something after death. Even corporations with their reward systems don't try to make it posthumous.

Ibid.

31 At age 11, girls are sure of what they know. But at 12 or 13, when they take on the feminine role, they become uncertain. They begin to say, "I don't know." Their true selves go underground. . . . We women become ourselves again after 50. When the feminine role is over, we re-emerge.

Quoted in "A Day To Take Our Daughters to Work," *Parade Magazine 17 May 1992*

32 I thought seriously about whether the world still needs *Ms.* magazine. And I went out and picked up armloads of women's magazines and I looked at them and I thought: "Yes. The world does still need *Ms.* Magazine."

Quoted in "*Ms.* to balance today's 'women's' magazines" by Kimberly Mills, *Seattle Post-Intelligencer 13 December 1998*

33 A woman without a man is like a fish without a bicycle.

Attributed n.d.

2582. Shirley Hill Witt (1934–)

1 I want to weep for La Vieja*
Two booths away,
But I can't: she is me.
"Punto Final," St. 6, *That's What She Said,* Rayna Green,**
ed. *1984*

*The old woman. **See 2800.

2 The campesinos* tend to smooth out the wrinkled places of
legend for the better telling and also for their own better understanding. In this way, they discharge those questions left
unanswered in their time as so much uselessness: the tale
weaves better the more simply told, anyway.
"La Mujer de Valor" (The Brave Woman), Ibid.

*farmers or farmworkers.

2583. Nellie Wong (1934–)

1 when I was growing up, I hungered
for American food, American styles,
coded: white and even to me, a child
born of Chinese parents, being Chinese
was feeling foreign, was limiting,
was unAmerican.
"When I Was Growing Up," St. 7 (1981), *The Woman
That I Am, The Literature and Culture of Contemporary
Women of Color,* D. Soyini Madison, ed. *1994*

2 and now in my hours of awakening
as my hair turns white
my anger moves, a storm into the sunlight
where women and men fight alongside each other
"For an Asian Woman Who Says My Poetry Gives Her a
Stomach-ache," St. 8 (1989), Ibid.

2584. Audre Lorde (1934–1992)

1 Since Naturally black is Naturally Beautiful
I must be proud
And, naturally,
Black and
Beautiful

Who always was a trifle
Yellow
And plain though proud
Before.
"Naturally," St. 1, *Cables to Rage 1970*

2 call me
roach and presumptuous
nightmare on your white pillow
your itch to destroy
the indestructible
part of yourself.
"The Brown Menace or Poem to the Survival of Roaches,"
The New York Head Shop and Museum 1974

3 There are so many roots to the
tree of anger
that sometimes the branches
shatter
before they bear.
"From a Land Where Other People Live," *From a Land
Where Other People Live 1975*

4 . . . Which me will survive all these liberations.
Ibid.

5 . . . it is axiomatic that if we do not define ourselves for ourselves, we will be defined by others—for their use and to our
detriment.
Zami: A New Spelling of My Name 1983

6 *It was in high school that I came to believe that I was different
from my white classmates, not because I was Black, but because I was me.*
Ibid.

7 I remember how being young and Black and gay and lonely
felt. A lot of it was fine, feeling I had the truth and the light
and the key, but a lot of it was purely hell.
Ibid.

8 "And don't I have the scars to prove it," she sighed. "Makes
you tough though, babe, if you don't go under. And that's
what I like about you; you're like me. We're both going to
make it because we're both too tough and crazy not to!" And
we held each other and laughed and cried about what we had
paid for that toughness, and how hard it was to explain to
anyone who didn't already know it that soft and tough had to
be one and the same for either to work at all, like our joy and
the tears mingling on the one pillow beneath our heads.
Ibid.

9 "Oh," says a voice from the Black community, "but being
Black is NORMAL!" Well, I and many Black people of my age
can remember grimly the days when it didn't used to be!
"There is No Hierarchy of Oppressions," *The Council on
Interracial Books for Children Bulletin,* Vol. 14,
nos. 3 and 4, Leonore Gordon, ed. *1983*

10 The sharing of joy, whether physical, emotional, psychic, or
intellectual, forms a bridge between the sharers that can be the
basis for understanding much of what is not shared between
them, and lessens the threat of their difference.
"Uses of the Erotic: The Erotic as Power," *Sister/Outsider:
Essays and Speeches 1984*

11 We have been raised to fear the yes within ourselves, our deepest cravings. . . . The fear of our desires keeps them suspect
and indiscriminately powerful, for to suppress any truth is to
give it strength beyond endurance. The fear that we cannot
grow beyond whatever distortions we may find within ourselves keeps us docile and loyal and obedient, externally
defined . . .
Ibid.

12 There is, for me, no difference between writing a good poem
and moving into sunlight against the body of a woman I love.
Ibid.

13 There are no new ideas, just new ways of giving those ideas we
cherish breath and power in our own living.
Speech, "Learning from the 60s," Harvard University
(*February* 1982), Ibid.

14 Militancy no longer means guns at high noon, if it ever did. It
means actively working for change, sometimes in the absence
of any surety that change is coming. It means doing the unromantic and tedious work necessary to forge meaningful
coalitions, and it means recognizing which coalitions are possible and which coalitions are not. It means knowing that
coalition, like unity, means the coming together of whole, self-

actualized human beings, focused and believing, not fragmented automatons marching to a prescribed step. It means fighting despair.

Ibid.

15 . . . nothing neutralizes creativity quicker than tokenism, that false sense of security fed by a myth of individual solutions.

Ibid.

16 You do not have to be me in order for us to fight alongside each other. I do not have to be you to recognize that our wars are the same. What we must do is commit ourselves to some future that can include each other . . .

Ibid.

17 One of the most basic Black survival skills is the ability to change, to metabolize experience, good or ill, into something that is useful, lasting, effective. Four hundred years of survival as an endangered species has taught most of us that if we intend to live, we had better become fast learners.

Ibid.

18 The answer to cold is heat, the answer to hunger is food. But there is no simple monolithic solution to racism, to sexism, to homophobia. There is only the conscious focusing within each of my days to move against them, wherever I come up against these particular manifestations of the same disease.

Ibid.

19 In the 60s, White America—racist and liberal alike—was more than pleased to sit back as spectator while Black militant fought Black Muslim, Black Nationalist badmouthed the nonviolent, and Black women were told that our only useful position in the Black Power movement was prone.

Ibid.

20 Decisions to cut aid for the terminally ill, for the elderly, for dependent children, for food stamps, even school lunches, are being made by men with full stomachs who live in comfortable houses with two cars and umpteen tax shelters.

Ibid.

21 Revolution is not a one-time event.

Ibid.

22 Black feminism is not white feminism in blackface.
"Sexism: An American Disease in Blackface," Ibid.

23 What woman here is so enamoured of her own oppression that she cannot see her heelprint upon another woman's face?
"Uses of Anger," Ibid.

24 For women, then, poetry is not a luxury. It is a vital necessity of our existence. It forms the quality of the light within which we predicate our hopes and dreams toward survival and change, first made into language, then into idea, then into more tangible action. Poetry is the way we help give name to the nameless so it can be thought.
"Poetry Is Not a Luxury," Ibid.

25 What do we want from each other
after we have told our stories
"There Are No Honest Poems About Dead Women," *Our Dead Behind Us* 1986

26 *I am not afraid to say
unembellished
I am dying*

*but I do not want to do it
looking the other way.*

Today is not the day.
It could be
but it is not.
Today is today
"Today Could Be the Day," Sts. 2–3, *The Marvelous Arithmetics of Distance: Poems 1987–1992* 1993

27 Afrekete Afrekete my beloved
feel the sun of my Days surround you
binding our pathways

we have water to carry
honey to harvest
bright seed to plant for the next fair . . .
"Today is Not the Day," Ibid.

28 As my tongue unravels

in what pitch
will the scream hang unsung
or shiver like lace on the borders
"Echoes," Sts. 7–8, Ibid.

29 The master's tools will never bring down the master's house.
Quoted in "Harryette Mullen's* *écriture féminine*" by Mike Jackman, Twentieth Century Literature Conference (Louisville, Kentucky) *26–28 February 1998*
*See 3363.

2585. Trisha Brown (1935?–)
1 Yes, I am still dancing and still enraptured by it. In spite of the stereotype, I believe my dancing in some ways is better than ever. It got more amazing and deeper. Like everything.
Quoted in "Choreographer returns to NW . . . " by R.M. Campbell, D1, *Seattle Post-Intelligencer*, What's Happening *9 April 1993*

2 Dancing on the edge is the only place to be. Living there is wearing.

Ibid.

2586. Susan Brownmiller (1935–)
1 Man's discovery that his genitalia could serve as a weapon to generate fear must rank as one of the most important discoveries of prehistoric times, along with the use of fire and the first crude stone axe. From prehistoric times to the present, I believe, rape has played a critical function. It is nothing more or less than a conscious process of intimidation by which all men keep all women in a state of fear.
Against Our Will: Men, Women, and Rape 1975

2 It has been argued that, when killing is viewed as not only permissible but heroic behavior sanctioned by one's government or cause, the fine distinction between taking a human life and other forms of impermissible violence gets lost, and rape becomes an unfortunate but inevitable by-product of the necessary game called war.

Ibid.

3 My purpose in this book has been to give rape its history. Now we must deny it a future.

Ibid.

2587. Gretchen Cryer (1935–)

1 Music is my one salvation
Singin' is my celebration
And playin' with a rock 'n roll band
Is a natural high
　　"Natural High," *I'm Getting My Act Together And Taking It On The Road* 1977

2 MOTHER. I prayed and prayed that my father would die before mother so that she could have a little time to herself, a little time to be happy. But he didn't, he held on, the old coot. Finally she died first and he died the next day. He just couldn't let her have anything.
　　Ibid.

3 HEATHER. You see, men would rather have a shitty thing than a good thing. It's less binding. As long as a relationship is shitty, they have a sense of freedom because they can say to themselves, "This is shitty and I really should get out of it." But if a relationship is good, that's very frightening, because then they don't have an excuse to get out. So the trick becomes to stay in a relationship and keep it shitty so the door is always open.
　　Ibid.

4 TRIO. If you smile in just the right way
You'll make a pretty wife
And someone will take care of you
For all your pretty life
If you smile, smile, smile.
If you smile
　　Ibid.

5 Until men learn that nurturing is all part of the human condition, and that they have an equal responsibility to share in it, they are going to be stuck with their wars.
　　"Gretchen Cryer," *Interviews with Contemporary Women Playwrights*, Kathleen Betsko* and Rachel Koenig *1987*
　　*See 2739.

6 It's lucky happenstance that women's liberation came along just when it did so that women can participate in the world arena and rescue the planet. Just in the nick of time.
　　Ibid.

2588. Joan Didion (1935–)

1 New York is full of people on this kind of leave of absence, of people with a feeling for the tangential adventure, the risk adventure, the interlude that's not likely to end in any double-ring ceremony.
　　"New York: The Great Reprieve," *Mademoiselle February 1961*

2 Was there ever in anyone's life span a point free in time, devoid of memory, a night when choice was any more than the sum of all the choices gone before?
　　Ch. 4, *Run River 1963*

3 "I think nobody owns land until their dead are in it. . . ."
　　Ch. 8, Ibid.

4 She *knew* clocks weren't supposed to stop, don't be silly. She knew they needed a clock. But she could not work with it going every second. When it was going every second that way she could not seem to take her eyes off it, and because it made no noise she found herself making the noise for it in her mind.
　　Ch. 18, Ibid.

5 In a nation which increasingly appears to prize social virtues, Howard Hughes* remains not merely antisocial but grandly, brilliantly, surpassingly, asocial. He is the last private man, the dream we no longer admit.
　　"7000 Romaine, Los Angeles," *Slouching Towards Bethlehem 1968*
　　*American business tycoon (1905–1976).

6 The secret point of money and power in America is neither the things that money can buy nor power for power's sake . . . but absolute personal freedom, mobility, privacy. It is the instinct which drove America to the Pacific, all through the nineteenth century, the desire to be able to find a restaurant open in case you want a sandwich, to be a free agent, live by one's own rules.
　　Ibid.

7 Americans are uneasy with their possessions, guilty about power, all of which is difficult for Europeans to perceive because they are themselves so truly materialistic, so versed in the uses of power.
　　Ibid.

8 There has always been that divergence between our official and our unofficial heroes. It is impossible to think of Howard Hughes without seeing the apparently bottomless gulf between what we say we want and what we do want, between what we officially admire and secretly desire, between, in the largest sense, the people we marry and the people we love.
　　Ibid.

9 We are well advised to keep on nodding terms with the people we used to be, whether we find them attractive company or not. Otherwise they turn up unannounced and surprise us, come hammering on the mind's door at 4am of a bad night and demand to know who deserted them, who betrayed them, who is going to make amends. We forget all too soon the things we thought we could never forget.
　　"On Keeping a Notebook," Ibid.

10 Because when we start deceiving ourselves into thinking not that we want something or need something, not that it is a pragmatic necessity for us to have it, but that it is a *moral imperative* that we have it, then is when we join the fashionable madmen, and then is when the thin whine of hysteria is heard in the land, and then is when we are in bad trouble. And I suspect we are already there.
　　"On Morality" (1965), Ibid.

11 To have that sense of one's intrinsic worth which constitutes self-respect is potentially to have everything: the ability to discriminate, to love and to remain indifferent. To lack it is to be locked within oneself, paradoxically incapable of either love or indifference.
　　"On Self-Respect" (1961), Ibid.

12 Most of our platitudes notwithstanding, self-deception remains the most difficult deception. The tricks that work on others count for nothing in that very well-lit back alley where one keeps assignations with oneself: no winning smiles will do here, no prettily drawn lists of good intentions.
　　Ibid.

13 . . . the day I did not make Phi Beta Kappa nonetheless marked the end of something, and innocence may well be the word for it. I lost the conviction that lights would always turn green for me . . . lost a certain touching faith in the totem pole of good manners, clean hair, and proven competence on the Stanford-

Binet scale. To such doubtful amulets had my self-respect been pinned, and I faced myself that day with the nonplussed apprehension of someone who has come across a vampire and has no crucifix at hand.

Ibid.

14 As an adjective, the very word "Hollywood" has long been pejorative and suggestive of something referred to as "the System." . . . the System not only strangles talent but poisons the soul, a fact supported by rich webs of lore.

"I Can't Get That Monster Out of My Mind" (1964), *Ibid.*

15 . . . California is a place in which a boom mentality and a sense of Chekovian loss meet in uneasy suspension; in which the mind is troubled by some buried but ineradicable suspicion that things had better work here, because here, beneath that immense bleached sky, is where we run out of continent.

"Notes from a Native Daughter" (1965), *Ibid.*

16 In the absence of a natural disaster we are left again to our own uneasy devices.

"A Problem of Making Connections," *Life* (New York) 5 December 1969

17 "I am what I am. To look for 'reasons' is beside the point."

Play It As It Lays 1970

18 Each believed the other a murderer of time, a destroyer of life itself.

Ch. 4, *Ibid.*

19 Whether or not Carter could afford the rent, whether it was a month like this one when he was making a lot of money or a month when the lawyers were talking about bankruptcy, the boy came twice a week to vacuum the pool and the man came four days a week to work on the roses and the water in the pool was 85 degrees.

Ibid.

20 The way he looked was the problem. He looked exactly the same. He looked untouched, and she did not.

Ch. 10, *Ibid.*

21 . . . they would exchange the addresses of new astrologers and the tag lines of old jokes.

Ibid.

22 "Hear that scraping, Maria?" the doctor said. "That should be the sound of music to you. . . ."

Ch. 25, *Ibid.*

23 She had to have a telephone. There was no one to whom she wanted to talk but she had to have a telephone.

Ch. 35, *Ibid.*

24 "I'm sorry."
"I know you're sorry. I'm sorry."
"We could try," one or the other would say after a while.
"We've already tried," the other would say.

Ch. 37, *Ibid.*

25 Maria could never keep up her end of the dialogue with hairdressers.

Ch. 45, *Ibid.*

26 She had watched them in supermarkets and she knew the signs. At 7:00 on a Saturday evening they would be standing in the checkout line reading the horoscope in *Harper's Bazaar* and in their carts would be a single lamb chop and maybe two cans of cat food and the Sunday morning paper, the early edition with the comics wrapped outside.

Ch. 46, *Ibid.*

27 . . . she had deliberately not counted the months but she must have been counting them unawares, must have been keeping a relentless count somewhere, because this was the day, the day the baby would have been born.

Ch. 54, *Ibid.*

28 She did not much like him but she liked his not knowing her.

Ch. 60, *Ibid.*

29 To hear someone's voice she looked in the telephone book and dialed a few prayers . . .

Ibid.

30 By the end of a week she was thinking constantly about where her body stopped and the air began, about the exact point in space and time that was the difference between *Maria* and *other*.

Ch. 65, *Ibid.*

31 I am not much engaged by the problems of what you might call our day but I am burdened by the particular . . .

Ch. 68, *Ibid.*

32 Some nights he said that he was tired, and some nights she said that she wanted to read, and other nights no one said anything.

Ch. 69, *Ibid.*

33 My father advised me that life itself was a crap game: it was one of the two lessons I learned as a child. The other was that overturning a rock was apt to reveal a rattlesnake. As lessons go those two seem to hold up, but not to apply.

Ch. 74, *Ibid.*

34 I know something about dread myself, and appreciate the elaborate systems with which some people manage to fill the void, appreciate all the opiates of the people.

Quoted in *Ms.* (New York) *January 1973*

35 I know Las Vegas to be a theater dedicated to the immediate gratification of every impulse, but I also know it to be a theater designed to numb those very impulses it promised to gratify. Nobody in this theater rushes the stage.

"Getting the Vegas Willies," *Esquire* (New York) *May 1977*

36 The apparent ease of California life is an illusion, and those who believe the illusion will live here in only the most temporary way.

"Holy Water," *The White Album* 1979

37 A pool is, for many of us in the West, a symbol not of affluence but of order, of control over the uncontrollable. A pool is water, made available and useful, and is, as such, infinitely soothing to the western eye.

Ibid.

38 The fancy that extraterrestrial life is by definition of a higher order than our own is one that soothes all children, and many writers.

"Doris Lessing,"* *Ibid.*

*See 2140.

39 There is in Hollywood, as in all cultures in which gambling is the central activity, a lowered sexual energy, an inability to de-

vote more than token attention to the preoccupations of the society outside. The action is everything, more consuming than sex, more immediate than politics; more important always than the acquisition of money, which is never, for the gambler, the true point of the exercise.

"In Hollywood," Ibid.

40 Of course great hotels have always been social ideas, flawless mirrors to the particular societies they service.

"In the Islands," Ibid.

41 A place belongs forever to whoever claims it hardest, remembers it most obsessively, wrenches it from itself, shapes it, renders it, loves it so radically that he remakes it in his own image.

Ibid.

42 Ask anyone committed to Marxist analysis how many angels on the head of a pin, and you will be asked in return to never mind the angels, tell me who controls the production of pins.

"The Women's Movement," Ibid.

43 . . . the freeway experience . . . is the only secular communion Los Angeles has. . . . Actual participation requires a total surrender, a concentration so intense as to seem a kind of narcosis, a rapture-of-the-freeway. The mind goes clean. The rhythm takes over. A distortion of time occurs. . . .

"Bureaucrats" (1976), Ibid.

44 We were the generation called "silent," but we were silent neither, as some thought, because we shared the period's official optimism nor, as others thought, because we feared its official repression. We were silent because the exhilaration of social action seemed to us just one more way of escaping the personal, of masking a while that dread of the meaningless which was man's fate.

"On the Morning After the Sixties" (1970), Ibid.

45 We all have the same dreams.

Pt. II, Ch. 1, *The Book of Common Prayer 1979*

46 Many people I know in Los Angeles believe that the Sixties ended abruptly on August 9, 1969,* ended at the exact moment when word of the murders on Cielo Drive traveled like brushfire through the community, and in a sense this is true. The tension broke that day. The paranoia was fulfilled.

"The White Album: A Chronicle of Survival in the Sixties," *New West 4 June 1979*

*Day of the Tate–LaBianca murders, committed by Charles Manson (1937–) and his followers.

2589. Sylvia A. Earle (1935–)

1 We have become frighteningly effective at altering nature.

Quoted in "Call of the Sea" by Roger Rosenblatt, *Time* (New York) *5 October 1998*

2 Far and away the greatest threat to the ocean, and thus to ourselves, is ignorance. But we can do something about that.

Ibid.

3 [The sea is] the place where the history of life actually can be found, not in fossils but in living creatures that represent life as it has been, perhaps, from the beginning of time.

Ibid.

4 Look at the bark of a redwood, and you see moss. If you peer beneath the bits and pieces of the moss, you'll see toads, small

insects, a whole host of life that prospers in that miniature environment. A lumberman will look at a forest and see so many board feet of lumber. I see a living city.

Ibid.

5 [Marine exploration is] like having a chance to dive into your own circulatory system and swim around and see how it all fits together.

Ibid.

2590. Ann Faraday (1935–)

1 I believe we have entered a new age of self-reliance and personal responsibility in which former reticence about the inner life is being abandoned and the demand for external conformity is being relaxed. The need in this new age is for more deliberate inquiry into the hidden forces of the personality which shapes our waking behavior and for communication of our insights for public discussion.

Introduction, *Dream Power 1972*

2 In forming a bridge between body and mind, dreams may be used as a springboard from which man can leap to new realms of experience lying outside his normal state of consciousness and enlarge his vision not only of himself, but also of the universe in which he lives.

Pt. I, Ch. 1, Ibid.

3 Thus, learning to understand our dreams is a matter of learning to understand our heart's language.

The Dream Game 1974

2591. Geraldine A. Ferraro (1935–)

1 I don't think unnecessary suffering builds character at all. It doesn't make you a better person, it makes you a bitter person . . .

Ferraro: My Story, with Linda Bird Francke *1985*

2 I'm a competitive person, but I have never understood people's competitiveness at the expense of their colleagues.

Ibid.

3 Politics can be an ugly game . . .

Ibid.

4 If you play by the rules, you deserve a fair day's pay for a fair day's work.

Ibid.

5 Any society that cannot respect its past by granting those who built it financial security faces moral bankruptcy in the future.

Ibid.

2592. Georgia Anne Geyer (1935–)

1 . . . Not only does the world scarcely know who the Latin American man is, the world has barely *cared*.

Introduction, *The New Latins 1970*

2 . . . the more revolutions occur, the less things change.

Ibid.

3 Orderly northern man looked south and he saw a cluster of basically untroubled countries with simple, passionate people; a fiesta of the senses; people unencumbered by the moral chains of the Puritan North; men living out their lives in sensual celebration.

Ibid.

4 Because it was when "reporters" became "journalists" and when "objectivity" gave way to "searching for truth," that an aura of distrust and fear arose around the New Journalist.

"Whatever Happened to Lois Lane?," *The Los Angeles Times 4 February 1979*

5 Would women leaders wield power differently? Would they be more humane? Would they perhaps even usher in some gleaming, renascent era? And would men accept them?

Now that we have this veritable club of women leaders across the globe—ruling, scheming, changing the rules and the world—we can begin to answer those questions. But the answers are no simpler than the questions themselves.

"Are Women Leaders Wielding Power Differently Than Men?," *Seattle Times 14 May 1989*

2593. Ellen Gilchrist (1935–)

1 "Well, for God's sake, find somebody with money," Sudie said. "Being married is bad enough without having to be poor at the same time. Whenever I get tired of Johnny's allergies I just go look at his Merrill Lynch portfolio. It turns me on. I swear it does."

Ch. 5, *The Annunciation 1983*

2 "I just know life isn't supposed to be a holding action."

Ch. 6, Ibid.

3 "I don't know what is wrong with me or right with me. I didn't make my nature. I didn't create my needs and ambitions. Neither will I deny or regret them. I am what I am."

Ch. 8, Ibid.

4 Maybe that's all we really are, she thought, cold determined organisms moving through our days, chewing and swallowing, feeding, shivering, subterranean, secret, alone.

Ch. 10, Ibid.

5 "Work is the thing that stays. Work is the thing that sees us through."

Ch. 14, Ibid.

6 "Watch out for fame, Sissy. It ruined my life. I've spent my whole life watching men be jealous of me. It's dangerous to do something everyone else wishes they could do, to be the thing they wish they could be."

Ch. 25, Ibid.

7 "There are rules, Amanda, whether you like it or not. There are perimeters and prices to pay."

Ibid.

8 Don't ruin the present with the ruined past.

Ch. 27, Ibid.

2594. Vivian Gornick (1935/8–)

1 Behind the "passive" exterior of many women there lies a growing anger over lost energies and confused lives, an anger so sharp in its fury but so diffuse in its focus that one can only describe it as the price society must pay for creating a patriarchal system in the first place, and for now refusing to let it go. And make no mistake, it is not letting go.

"Why Women Fear Success," *The First Ms. Reader*, Francine Klagsbrun, ed. 1972

2 If the word for London is decency and the word for New York is violence, then, beyond doubt, the word for Cairo is tenderness. Tenderness is what pervades the air here.

Pt. I, *In Search of Ali-Mahmoud 1973*

3 I lived once in the American desert. The solitude opens up. It becomes an enormous surrounding comfort. But the solitude in the city is a confusing and painful thing.

Pt. II, Ibid.

4 There is a desperate lack of variety to the poverty here [Egypt], a kind of stupor of simplicity, an aimlessness that covers the people in a thick expressionless haze . . .

Ibid.

5 Suddenly, I see that the diffused love, which is the deepest lesson of the East, has within it the seeds of nonpossessive love. And with a surprised weariness I remember my own country. For God knows, those clutched, nonseparating marriages of the West don't indicate *love*.

Pt. IV, Ibid.

6 The subjection of women, in my view, lies most deeply in the ingrained conviction—shared by both men and women—that for women marriage is the pivotal experience. It is this conviction, primarily, that reduces and ultimately destroys in women that flow of psychic energy that is fed in men from birth by the anxious knowledge given them that one is alone in this world; that one is never taken care of; that life is a naked battle between fear and desire, and that fear is kept in abeyance only through the recurrent urge of desire. . . .

"Toward a Definition of the Female Sensibility," *The Village Voice 31 May 1973*

7 She takes daily walks on the land that was once the bottom of the sea, marking and classifying, sifting through her thoughts the meaning of the jagged edge of discontent that has begun to make inroads anew insider her.

"Stillness at the Center," *Ms.* (New York) *October 1973*

8 "Young man, I am a Jew and a socialist. I think that's more than enough for one lifetime, don't you?"

Fierce Attachments 1987

9 The streets attest to the power of the narrative drive: its infinite capacity for adaptation in the most inhospitable of times.

"On the Street," *Approaching Eye Level 1996*

10 This is a population in a permanent state of intermittent attachment. Inevitably, the silent apartment waits.

"On Living Alone," Ibid.

11 . . . hot with shame, a loneliness that tells you you're a fool and a loser. Everyone else is feasting, you alone cannot gain a seat at the table.

Ibid.

12 Loneliness, when it came, came . . . like a surge of physical illness.

Ibid.

13 Loneliness was the evaporation of inner life. Loneliness was me cut off from myself. Loneliness was the thing nothing out there could cure.

Ibid.

14 [She] would rather go senile than give up [her] rage."

"Tribute," Ibid.

15 It was the Catskills,* not early socialist teaching at my father's knee, that made me a Marxist.

"The Catskills Remembered," Ibid.

*A once popular, mountainous resort area frequented in large part by Jews, sometimes referred to as the borscht-belt.

16 . . . the Syndrome of the Approximate Response . . . acclimating daily to the repeated sound of the phrase, the nuance, the sentence spoken by a colleague or a neighbor that makes one shrivel rather than expand. It is a kind of death in life to which university people become inured.

"At the University," Ibid.

17 These sentences are born of a concentration in the writer that runs so deep, is turned so far inward, it achieves the lucidity of the poet. . . . The material is at one with the voice speaking.

On Grace Paley,* *The End of the Novel of Love* 1997
*See 2210.

2595. Sandra G. Harding (1935–)

1 Scientific and technological change are inherently political, since they redistribute costs and benefits of access to nature's resources in new ways. They tend to widen any pre-existing gaps between the haves and the have-nots unless issues of just distribution are directly addressed.

Is Science Multicultural? Postcolonialisms, Feminisms, and Epistemologies 1998

2 . . . identifying eurocentric and androcentric elements in the conceptual frameworks used to think about scientific and technological change . . . expands our knowledge of nature, sciences, and social relations.

Ibid.

2596. Jane Howard (1935–)

1 An encounter group is a gathering, for a few hours or a few days, of twelve to eighteen personable, responsible, certifiably normal and temporarily smelly people. Their destination is intimacy, trust and awareness of why they behave as they do in groups; their vehicle is candor.

"Whatever Possessed Me," *Please Touch* 1970

2 Group philosophy—wise group philosophy, anyway—does not prescribe that you run to inform your old landlord that everyone secretly thinks he's effeminate, or your boss that you have always thought he was a stupid tyrant. The aim is first to know, in your head and below it, what you think and feel, and then to reflect on newly unearthed alternatives to your accustomed ways of being. Once it is unlocked, the door between your feelings and the cosmos need not be kept yawning open. It can be left ajar.

"Back Home," Ibid.

3 The re-entry from encounter groups to reality, and the business of keeping alive the elusive benefits of sensitivity training, are problems that preoccupy every student of the human potential movement.

Ibid.

4 The genealogy of the human potential movement is as hard to trace as a foundling baby's. Foundlings have no known ancestors, but the movement is alleged to have preposterously many.

"Notes Toward History," Ibid.

5 Parents, however old they and we may grow to be, serve among other things to shield us from our sense of doom. As long as they are around, we can avoid the fact of our mortality; we can still be innocent children.

A Different Woman 1973

6 New links must be forged as old ones rust.

Ch. 1, Ibid.

7 I wish women in the gay liberation movement God-speed, although I take issue with their premise that all men, without exception, are intruding vandals bent only on the oppression of womankind. I submit that some of them can be welcome guests.

Ch. 9, Ibid.

8 Wholesomeness is exotic to me. I pretended to like the era of strobe lights and deafening acid rock in discotheques but a lot of that sixties frenzy really just made me nervous. More and more I am drawn toward stillness.

Ch. 34, Ibid.

2597. Beverly Hungry Wolf (1935–)

1 In the years since I began following the ways of my grandmothers I have come to value the teachings, stories, and daily examples of living which they shared with me. I pity the younger girls of the future who will miss out on meeting some of these fine old women.

The Ways of My Grandmothers 1980

2598. Sarah Kirsch (1935–)

1 This autumn the atomic mushrooms became such a common sight in the newspapers that aesthetic categories began to form.

"Year's End," St. 1, Jan van Heurck, tr. *n.d.*

2599. Myrna Lamb (1935–)

1 [I want to see] an ultimate revolution . . . the liberation of the female of the species so that the male of the species may be freed forever from supermasculine compulsion and may join his sister in full and glorious humanity.

Introduction, *The Mod Donna, A Space-Age Musical Soap Opera with Breaks for Commercials* 1970

2 Let us not be compliant earth to willful seed
Let us cast another god from our true vision
Our true need
LIBERATION LIBERATION LIBERATION

Ibid.

2600. Myra MacPherson (1935?–)

1 Above all, Vietnam was a war that asked everything of a few and nothing of most in America.

Epilogue, *Long Time Passing: Vietnam and the Haunted Generation* 1984

2601. Dacia Maraini (1936–)

1 He talked and talked because he didn't know what to say.

Ch. 1, *The Holiday* 1962

2 "Our strength is like the sea," Pompei announced, lifting his chin up proudly. "Nothing can divert it."

Ch. 8, Ibid.

3 The nausea of being the thing I was leapt from my throat like sobbing. . . .

"His Foot on the Sand," *Crudelta all Aria' Aperia (Open Cruelty)* 1966

4 the disgust with myself, weak and weary
throughout my intestines
I couldn't stop it nor vomit it . . .

Ibid.

5 A woman who writes poetry and knows
  she is woman, has no choice but to hang on
    tight
to contents because the sophistication
of forms is something that belongs to power
and the power that woman has is always an
un-power, a scorching inheritance never entirely
    hers.

Her voice may be hard and earthen
but it is the voice of a lioness that has been
reared too long a sensible sheep . . .
    "Woman's Poetry," *Donne Mie* (My Dear Woman) *1974*

2602. E. Annie Proulx (1935–)

1 "Life cripples us in different ways but it gets to everybody
. . . Gets you again and again and one day it wins."
    Postcards 1991

2 She imagined a diaphanous sparkling angel rising from Mrs.
Nipple's black underground corpse, but couldn't hold the image,
and thought instead of the body dissolving into the earth,
thought of the earth crawling with invisible hungry mites that
devoured rotting bits, that cleaned the bones of dead enaimals,
sucked the fire from consumed logs and the dew from the grass,
all the effluvium of plants and animals, rock and rain. Where
does it go, she thought, all those rivers of menstrual blood and
the blood of wounds and injuries from the beginning of the
world, imagining a deep, stiff lake of coagulated blood.
    Ch. 11, Ibid.

3 "I'm not going to end up on your goddamn farm pouring slops
to the pigs and looking a hundred years old before I'm forty
with a big belly every year and kids all over the place. I'll go
just so far with you, and then, if you want what I got, you
come the rest of the way with me."
    Ch. 12, Ibid.

4 His blood, urine, feces and semen, the tears, strands of hair,
vomit, flakes of skin, his infant and childhood teeth, the clippings of finger and toenails, all the effluvia of his body were in
that soil, part of that place. The work of his hands had
changed the shape of the land, the weirs in the steep ditch beside the lane, the ditch itself, the smooth field were echoes of
himself in the landscape, for the laborer's vision and strength
persists after the labor is done.
    Ibid.

5 The alchemist sea changed fishermen to wet bones, sent boats
to drift among the cod, cast them on the landwash.
    Ch. 4, "Cast Away," *The Shipping News 1993*

6 Challenged children, Got up a petition, called meetings, ah,
she said, they wrote letters asking for the special education
class. And got it. A three-year-old girl in No Name Cove had
never learned to walk. But could learn, did learn. Rescuing lost
children, showing them ways to grasp life. She squeezed her
hands together, showing him that anyone alive could clench
possibilities.
    Ch. 18, "Lobster Pie," Ibid.

7 What he knew was that women were shaped like leaves and
men fell.
    Ibid.

8 No, they didn't have any money, the sea was dangerous and men
were lost, but it was a satisfying life in a way people today do
not understand. There was a joinery of lives all worked together,
smooth in places, or lumpy, but joined. The work and the living
you did was the same things, not separated out like today.
    Ch. 20, "Gaze Island," Ibid.

9 "They used to say 'A man's set up in life if he's got a pig, a
punt and a potato patch.' What do they say now? Every man
for himself."
    Ch. 25, "Oil," Ibid.

10 "Nobody, nobody in their right mind would go back to them
hard, hard times. People was only kind because life was so
dirty you couldn't afford to have any enemies. It was all swim
or all sink. A situation that make people very sweet.
    Ibid.

11 "Herold," said Waves, "was a womanizer. He treated me body
like a trough. Come and swill and slobber in me after them. I felt
like he was casting vomit in me when he come to his climax."
    Ch. 37, "Slingstones," Ibid.

12 He'd call him up that night. Tell him. What? That he was wondering if love came in other colors than the basic black of none
and the red heat of obsession?
    Ibid.

13 Archie was an expert at dividing the affairs of life into men's
business and women's business. An empty cupboard and a full
plate were the man's business, a full cupboard and an empty
plate the concern of the woman.
    Ch. 38, "The Sled Dog Driver's Dream," Ibid.

14 "But, m'dear, if they don't know what death is how can they
understand the deep part of life? The seasons and nature and
creation "
    Ch. 39, "Shining Hubcaps," Ibid.

2603. Deborah Remington (1935–)

1 . . . I saw that representation was not my direction. My imagination was too grand. I didn't want to be stuck with shapes
that already existed, I wanted my own shapes and space.
    Quoted in "Deborah Remington," *Exposures, Women &*
    Their Art by Ann Brown & Arlene Raven* 1989
    *See 3020.

2604. Joan Rivers (1935–)

1 The psychic scars caused by believing you are ugly have a permanent mark on your personality.
    Quoted in "An Ugly Duckling Complex" by Lydia Lane,
    The Los Angeles Times 10 May 1974

2 There is not one female comic who was beautiful as a little
girl.
    Ibid.

3 Diets, like clothes, should be tailored to you.
    Ibid.

4 I hate housework! You make the beds, you do the dishes—and
six months later you have to start all over again.
    "Work," *Woman Talk*, Michèle Brown and
    Ann O'Connor, eds. *1984*

5 Your anger can be 49 percent and your comedy 51 percent, and
you are okay. If the anger is 51 percent, the comedy is gone.
    1986

6   Thank God we're living in a country where the sky's the limit, the stores are open late and you can shop in bed thanks to television.

International Herald Tribune (Paris) *31 May 1989*

7   My routines come out of total unhappiness. My audiences are my group therapy.

Television broadcast, BBC 2 *23 February 1990*

8   Can we talk?

Catchphrase *n.d.*

2605. Anne Roiphe (1935–)

1   . . . despite my concern for civil liberties, for equality, for justice in Mississippi—I am blond, and blond is still beautiful, and if I have one life to lead it will be as a white, and I am a mass of internal contradictions, all of which cause me to attempt some rite which will bring salvation, save me from a system I despise but still carry within me like any other of my vital organs.

"Out of Week One," *Up the Sandbox!* 1970

2   "What the world needs," he said, "is not a Joan of Arc,* the kind of woman who allows herself to be burned on the cross. That's just a bourgeois invention meant to frighten little girls into staying home. What we require is a real female military social leader."

"But that"—I smiled at him—"is just impossible. Women are tied to husband and children. Women are constructed to be penetrated; a sword or a gun in their hands is a joke or a mistake. They are open holes in which things are poured. Occasionally, it's true, a woman can become a volcano, but that's about it."

"Out of Week Two," Ibid.
    *See 249.

3   What I'm doing in this car flying down these screaming highways is getting my tail to Juarez so I can legally rid myself of the crummy son-of-a-bitch who promised me a tomorrow like a yummy fruitcake and delivered instead wilted lettuce, rotted cucumber, a garbage of a life.

Long Division 1972

4   She tried to be respectable because respectability kept away the chaos that sometimes overwhelmed her, causing her to call out in her sleep, screaming wild sounds, a warning to the future, a mourning for the past.

Ibid.

5   Reader, you forget that economics precedes religion; worship grew out of eating, not the other way around.

The Pursuit of Happiness 1991

6   . . . family stories are not morality plays, although they are about morality. . . . Perhaps we are all here to make good stories.

Ibid.

7   `Be careful. . . . There's a reason he's still available."

If You Knew Me 1993

8   We were squeezed between that proverbial rock and hard place. Motherhood by definition requires tending of the other, a sacrifice of self-wishes for the needs of a helpless, hapless human being, and feminism by definition insists on attention being paid to the self, to the full humanity, wishes, desires, capacities of the self. This basic contradiction is not simply the nasty work of a sexist society. It is the lay of the land, the mother of all paradoxes, the irony we cannot bend with mere wishing or might of will. Here are the ingredients of our private and public human tragedy.

Nevertheless I still wanted more children.

Fruitful: A Real Mother in the Modern World 1996

9   The only thing I know for sure is that I would rather have a child than a book . . .

Ibid.

10   Gender might not require a woman to stay home and raise the kids but it was clear that biology could not be erased just like that. . . . The pull to reproduce was not a political decision but deeply primordial, a response to rhythms and tides not always accessible to reason.

Ibid.

11   . . . isn't it also probable that the Devil has her feminine wiles?

Ibid.

12   The God who would do this to him deserved only silence.

1185 Park Avenue: A Memoir 1999

13   He told me he would never do to his son what had been done to him . . .

Ibid.

14   I am a writer, and burning bridges behind me is part of the cost of the work.

Ibid.

2606. Judith Rossner (1935–)

1   "Being a witch is like royalty," I said calmly. "You have to inherit it from someone."

Pt. I, *Nine Months in the Life of an Old Maid* 1969

2   As Lily had lost me years before from not caring, you lost me that day from caring but not nearly enough.

Ibid.

3   A nightmare is terrifying because it can never be undone . . . While in the beautiful well-ordered lie of our everyday lives there was almost nothing we could not do.

Ibid.

4   Identity is a bag and a gag. Yet it exists for me with all the force of a fatal disease. Obviously I am here, a mind and a body. To say there's no proof my body exists would be arty and specious and if my mind is more ephemeral, less provable, the solution of being a writer with solid (touchable, tearable, burnable) books is as close as anyone has come to a perfect answer.

Pt. II, Ibid.

5   "I've been accused of selling out so often that it's made me realize what extraordinary resources people saw in me in the first place. It's why I can afford to sell out my ideas; I know something new'll spring up to replace the ones I'm unloading."

Ibid.

6   It is easier to betray than to remain loyal. It takes far less courage to kill yourself than it takes to make yourself wake up one more time. It's harder to stay where you are than to get out. (For everyone but you, that is.)

Ibid.

7 Love is the direct opposite of hate. By *definition* it's something you can't feel for more than a few minutes at a time, so what's all this bullshit about loving somebody for the rest of your life?

Ibid.

8 So often I heard people paying blind obeisance to change—as though it had some virtue of its own. Change or we will die. Change or we will stagnate. Evergreens don't stagnate.

Ibid.

9 What was she to say now to her father, who thought change was the only serious mistake that could be made in a life?

Any Minute I Can Split 1972

10 "That's the New York thing, isn't it. People who seem absolutely crazy going around telling you how crazy they used to be before they had therapy."

Ibid.

11 "Self-government is a form of self-control, self-limitation. It goes against our whole grain. We're [Americans] supposed to go after what we want, not question whether we really need it."

Ibid.

12 He always said she was smart, but their conversations were a mined field in which at any moment she might make the wrong verbal move and find her ignorance exploding in her face.

Looking for Mr. Goodbar 1975

13 A lie was something that didn't happen but might just as well have.

Ibid.

14 "But I've been miserable ever since I came back. From Puerto Rico, that's where I had it [the abortion], it was like a vacation. It's almost like—it's not supposed to be that easy. It's too big a sin to get off that lightly."

Ibid.

15 "The point is," Evelyn said, "we're taught that we have to be perfect. Like objects in a museum, not people. People don't have to be perfect, only objects do."

Ibid.

16 Sometimes she thought that the TV wasn't so much an escape as a filter through which he saw and heard everything but was kept from being affected by it too much.

Ibid.

2607. Sara Ruddick (1935–)

1 I seemed to learn new ways of attending to the natural world and to people, especially children. This kind of attending was intimately concerned with caring; because I cared I reread slowly, then I found myself watching more carefully, listening with patience, absorbed by gestures, mood, and thoughts. The more I attended, the more deeply I cared. The domination of feeling by thought, which I had worked so hard to achieve, was breaking down. Instead of developing arguments that could bring my feelings to heel, I allowed feeling to inform my most abstract thinking.

"New Combinations: Learning from Virginia Woolf,"*
Between Women, with C. Asher and L. DeSalvor *1984*
*See 1481.

2 When their children flourish, almost all mothers have a sense of well-being.

Maternal Thinking: Towards a politics of peace 1989

3 What mother wouldn't want the power to keep her children healthy . . . to create hospitals, schools, jobs, day care, and work schedules that serve her maternal work?

Ibid.

2608. Françoise Sagan (1935–)

1 It is healthier to see the good points of others than to analyze our own bad ones.

Pt. I, Ch. 5, *A Certain Smile 1956*

2 Jazz music is an intensified feeling of nonchalance.

Pt. 1, Ch. 7, *Ibid.*

3 "Look here, why don't you love me? I should feel so much more peaceful. Why not put up that pane of glass called passion between us? It may distort things at times, but it's wonderfully convenient." But no, we were two of a kind, allies and accomplices. In terms of grammar, I could not become the object, or he the subject. He had neither the capacity nor the desire to define our roles in any such way.

Pt. II, Ch. 2, *Ibid.*

4 We had the same gait, the same habits and lived in the same rhythm; our bodies suited each other and all was well. I had no right to regret his failure to make the tremendous effort required of love, the effort to know and shatter the solitude of another.

Ibid.

5 It seems to me that there are two kinds of trickery: the "fronts" people assume before one another's eyes, and the "front" a writer puts on the face of reality.

Interview, *Writers at Work* (First Series), Malcolm Cowley,*
ed. *1958*

*American writer, editor and literary critic (1898–1989).

6 Writing is a question of finding a certain rhythm. I compare it to the rhythms of jazz. Much of the time life is a sort of rhythmic progression of three characters. If one tells oneself that life is like that, one feels it less arbitrary.

Ibid.

7 After Proust,* there are certain things that simply cannot be done again. He marks off for you the boundaries of your talent.

Ibid.

*Marcel P—, French writer (1871–1922).

8 Of course the illusion of art is to make one believe that great literature is very close to life, but exactly the opposite is true. Life is amorphous, literature is formal.

Ch. 9, *La Chamade 1965*

9 To jealousy, nothing is more frightful than laughter.

Ibid.

2609. Shen Rong (1935–)

1 Never having imagined love could be so intoxicating, she almost regretted not finding it earlier.

"At Middle Age," Ch. 3 (1980) Yu Fanqin and Wang Mingjie, trs., *Seven Contemporary Chinese Women Writers*, Gladys Yang,* ed. *1982*
*See 2452.

2 "Who are you?" Liu was really half tipsy. "You live in cramped quarters and slave away regardless of criticism, not seeking fame or money. A hard-working doctor like you is an

ox serving the children, as Lu Xun said, eating grass and providing milk."

Ch. 9, Ibid.

3 "I don't want a medal or a citation. I just wish your hospital understood how hard it is to be a doctor's husband. As soon as the order comes to go off on medical tours or relief work, she's up and off, leaving the family. She comes back so exhausted from the operating theater, she can't raise a finger to cook a meal. That being the case, if I don't go into the kitchen, who will? I should really be grateful to the 'cultural revolution' for giving me all that time to learn to cook."

Ibid.

4 "There's no pleasing you!" laughed Jiang. "When you're not used, you complain that your talents are wasted, you live at the wrong time. When you're fully used, you gripe that you're overworked and underpaid!"

Ibid.

5 She had performed such operations umpteen times, but every time she picked up her instruments, she felt like a raw recruit on the battlefield.

Ch. 13, Ibid.

6 So this was dying, no fear, no pain, just life withering away, the senses blurring, slowly sinking, like a leaf drifting on a river.

Ch. 17, Ibid.

2610. Carol Shields (1935–)

1 The things Mrs. Turner doesn't know would fill the Saschers' new compost pit, would sink a ship, would set off a tidal wave, would make her want to kill herself.

"Mrs. Turner Cutting the Grass," *Various Miracles* 1988

2 This business of being a guy, it never lets up.

The Republic of Love 1991

3 The smell of food fattened the air.

Ibid.

4 Belief, Fay knows, is sometimes perverse.

Ibid.

5 [She has] a restless anger and a sense of undelivered messages.

Happenstance 1993

6 . . . men spend whole lifetimes preparing answers to certain questions that will never be asked of them.

Ibid.

7 . . . the clean preserving gel of history.

Ibid.

8 Life is an endless recruiting of witnesses.

The Stone Diaries 1993

9 When we say a thing or an event is real, never mind how suspect it sounds, we honor it. But when a thing is made up—regardless of how true and just it seems—we turn up our noses. That's the age we live in. The documentary age. As if we can never get enough facts. We put on the television set and what we hear is the life cycles of birds.

Ibid.

10 "Life is a book each of us must write alone."

Larry's Party 1997

11 And he's tired—tired of his name, tired of being a man, tired of the ghostly self he's chained to and compelled to drag around.

Ibid.

12 He would fall asleep, finally, to the rhythm of those strange voices: Stu and Dot Weller, his silent poetic parents, coming awake in the soundwaves of their own muffled words, made gracefully by what they chose to say in the long darkness.

Ibid.

13 . . . a snail, a scribble, a doodle on the earth's skin with no other directed purpose but to wind its sinuous way around itself.

Ibid.

2611. Joan Micklin Silver (1935–)

1 Standing erect, like overgrown bookends on either side of Mr. MacAfee's desk, were two Air Force officers.

Ch. 1, *Limbo*, with Linda Gottlieb* 1972

*See 2854.

2 Just as war bound together the men under fire, Mary Kaye thought, it united the women left behind back home.

Ch. 5, Ibid.

3 The mother of an eighteen-year-old boy who had had to secure his mother's consent for enlisting in the Army, she now cried at the slightest provocation. "How could I tell him not to go?" she once asked Fay Clausen, the tears brimming in her eyes. "He always loved guns—from the time he was a little boy he would play with toy guns, BB guns—you know, pretended he was in the marines and things. I once got him that big illustrated history of the Second World War—it cost seventeen dollars—from American Heritage, and he read it over and over again."

Ch. 8, Ibid.

4 Red Fortner felt an unaccustomed clutch in his throat. Those savages over there! We ought to bomb the hell out of them, blast them from the face of the earth! He wished some of his dove colleagues at the office could hear this girl, so young, so pretty, so brave, without even a father for her child! They'd change their tune all right.

Ch. 21, Ibid.

2612. Audrey Thomas (1935–)

1 How could I tell her that she was wrong about things when essentially she was right? Life was cruel, people hurt and betrayed one another, grew old and died alone.

Songs My Mother Taught Me 1973

2 . . . cats everywhere asleep on the shelves like motorized bookends.

Ibid.

2613. Taeko Tomioka (1935–)

1 My favorite question was, "What would you do if we had a baby?" I always asked this question after I'd had sex with a young man, and I always looked forward to hearing their responses.

"Straw Dogs," *Unmapped Territories, New Women's Fiction from Japan*, ed. and tr. 1991

2 I've always wondered whether a relationship can be established simply by the entry of part of a stranger's body into mine.

Ibid.

3 I wanted to pull out the guts of his dark mood and devour them with my teeth.

Ibid.

4 There is really nothing two strangers, a male and a female, can do but have sex.

Ibid.

5 Through sex I try to discover something metaphysical about my and my partner's body. This is why I allow my body to be completely exposed, like a bag being turned inside out, with my sex organ as the opening. I'm curious to know if there are such things as spirituality and maliciousness hidden in the corners of this bag, waiting to be revealed when the bag is turned inside out by a stranger's sex organ.

Ibid.

6 Izumi hadn't seemed to be aware of the possibility that his penis was there to excite the woman and give her pleasure, that he could pierce the woman and her pleasure together like a skewer for barbecuing chicken and onions.

Ibid.

2614. Marina von Neumann Whitman (1935–)

1 I never took a lifetime view at 20 and decided where I wanted to be at 50. Since I was trailblazing, there weren't many rules about what you were and were not supposed to be. Young women today feel such a burden to prove themselves.

Quoted in "The Corporate Guru of Global Economics" by Beth McGoldrick, *Working Woman November 1988*

2 I've learned only that you never say never.

Ibid.

2615. Monique Wittig (1935/36–)

1 There was a time when you were not a slave, remember that . . . You say there are no words to describe this time. You say it does not exist. But remember. Make an effort to remember. Or, failing that, invent.

Les Guérillières* 1969

*Female guerrilla warriors.

2 The women say that they perceive their bodies in their entirety. They say that they do not favor any of its parts on the grounds that it was formerly a forbidden object. They say that they do not want to become prisoners of their own ideology.

Ibid.

3 The language you speak poisons your glottis tongue palate lips. They say, the language you speak is made up of words that are killing you. They say, the language you speak is made up of signs that rightly speaking designate what men have appropriated.

Ibid.

2616. Madeleine Albright (1936–)

1 Force, and the credible possibility of its use, are essential to defend our vital interests and to keep America safe. But force alone can be a blunt instrument, and there are many problems it cannot solve.

Speech (7 *February* 1997), *Vital Speeches of the Day 15 April 1997*

2 When it comes to lectures, it is more blessed to give than to receive.

Quoted in "Albright sees a struggle ahead" by Ed Offley, *Seattle Post-Intelligencer, A2 30 October 1998*

3 Only in America could a refugee girl from Europe become Secretary of State.

"Albright retakes citizenship oath" (p. 19A), *USA Today 11 November 1998*

4 The United States will never apologize for speaking or publishing the truth.

"Albright chides China . . . ," *Seattle Post-Intelligencer 2 March 1999*

5 Societies are more, not less, likely to be stable when citizens have an outlet to express their political views.

Ibid.

6 We determined some time ago that it was not a good idea to link human rights and trade, and that we actually make better progress in both when they are not linked.

Ibid.

2617. Jean M. Auel (1936–)

1 "You cannot see the spirit of your totem because he is part of you, inside you. Yet, he will tell you. Only you must learn to understand. If you have a decision to make, he will help you. He will give you a sign if you make the right choice. . . . It may be a stone you have never seen before or a root with a special shape that has meaning to you. You must learn to understand with your heart and mind, not your eyes and ears, then you will know.

Ch. 9, *The Clan of the Cave Bear 1980*

2 Six men, pitifully weak by comparison, using skill and intelligence and cooperation and daring, had killed the gigantic creature no other predator could. No matter how fast or how strong or how cunning, no four-legged hunter could match their feat.

Ch. 14, Ibid.

3 Zoug's pride was the pride of a true teacher for a pupil who had exceeded; a student who paid attention, learned well, and then did the master one better.

Ch. 15, Ibid.

2618. Rose Bird (1936–1999)

1 The courts hold a unique position among our democratic institutions. In a sense, they represent one of our last bastions of participatory democracy, in which disputants go directly before a judge or jury to resolve an issue. In no other governmental context does an individual have the opportunity to take a problem to a decision-maker who represents the full force and power of that particular branch of government. This direct interchange between the individual and the state is at the heart of the democratic process. . . . We must protect this unique heritage and strive to preserve the values it represents.

The Los Angeles Times 16 November 1977

2 If our courts lose their authority and their rulings are no longer respected, there will be no one left to resolve the divisive issues that can rip the social fabric apart. . . . The courts are a safety valve without which no democratic society can survive.

The Los Angeles Times 11 September 1978

3 The role of the press and the protections which we afford it are today more important than ever before, because we dwell in a society where belief in our governments and in the strength of our institutions is declining.

Quoted in "Hue & Cry," *San Francisco Chronicle 13 May 1979*

4   We must use our courage to ensure a judiciary not governed by the daily polls but by the rules of law, serving not the special interest of the few but the best interest of all, devoted not to self-preservation, but to the preservation of those great constitutional principles which history has bequeathed to us.

The Los Angeles Times 20 July 1982

5   The courts are an easy scapegoat because at a time when everything has to be boiled down to easy slogans, we speak in subtleties.

Newsweek (New York) *9 August 1982*

6   My role isn't to be politically smart. My role is to do what is right under the Constitution.

Quoted in "Rose Bird Runs for Her Life" by Edwin Chen, *The Nation* (New York) *18 January 1986*

7   When you have majority rule, often you are protecting the rights of people who are unpopular. It is always the minorities who aren't part of the mainstream, who define what the limits of the majority are going to be.

Ibid.

8   In an age of television, of personalities and black-and-white issues, we [judges] are a collegial body that speaks through the written work and in complexities.

Quoted in "Calm at the center of the storm," by Anthony Lewis, The New York Times News Service 23 October 1986

9   Courts are an aristocratic institution in a democracy. That's the dilemma for an institution that has the function of reviewing the will of the people. We're bound to be "anti-majoritarian."

Ibid.

2619. Martha Gross Boesing (1936–)

1   ABIGAIL. I have this malady: I try to make sense out of everything that happens to me. I cling to the neurotic belief that if I could understand what events mean, then I could stop obsessing about them.

Act I, *The Web 1981*

2620. Jean Shinoda Bolen (1936–)

1   There is a potential heroine in every woman.

Ch. 14, *Goddesses in Every Woman: A New Psychology of Women 1984*

2   . . . the necessity of choosing a "path with heart." I feel that one must deliberate and then act, must scan every life choice with rational thinking but then base the decision on whether one's heart will be in it. No other person can tell you if your heart is involved, and logic cannot provide an answer.

Ibid.

3   An estimated forty million baby-boomer generation women turn fifty in the few years preceding and following the year 2000, joining those women's movement-women who led the way a decade earlier. This could very well constitute a critical mass of women of wisdom, authority, and action who may determine the direction that humanity will take. What we do or fail to do at this liminal time will not only shape the course of our personal lives, but collectively will affect the third millennium and with that, the future of the planet.

"Wisewomen at the Crossroad," *The Fabric of the Future: Women Visionaries of Today Illuminate the Path to Tomorrow*, M. J. Ryan, ed. 1998

4   There is a stirring in the psyches of a generation of women's movement-influenced older women, one that calls on us to be an influence, to say what we know, to enter the phase of the wisewoman, whose concern is for other generations and the greater good.

Ibid.

2621. Sandy Boucher (1936–)

1   My father's voice says, Watch out for little men. They are more aggressive, meaner, nastier, trickier, more combative. A big man is secure in his strength, so he doesn't push it. A little man is always proving something. The same goes for little dogs versus big dogs.

"Mountain Radio," *Assaults and Rituals 1975*

2   Thus we were equally, though differently, sophisticated, and our game was the same: not to *care*—to arrive at each other without being there.

Ibid.

2622. Carol Burnett (1933–)

1   When someone who is known for being comedic does something straight, it's always "a big breakthrough" or "a radical departure." Why is it no one ever says that if a straight actor does comedy? Are they presuming comedy is easier?

Quoted in "Death by 'Friendly Fire' and a Mother's Search" by Ellen Farley, *San Francisco Chronicle 5 October 1978*

2   I don't consider [the Equal Rights Amendment] a political issue. It is a moral issue as far as I am concerned. Where are women mentioned in the Constitution except in the Nineteenth Amendment, giving us the right to vote? When they said all *men* were created equal, they really meant it—otherwise, why did we have to fight for the Nineteenth Amendment?

Quoted in "Hue & Cry," *San Francisco Chronicle 29 April 1979*

2623. A. S. Byatt (1936–)

1   Pain hardens, and great pain hardens greatly, whatever the comforters say, and suffering does not ennoble, though it may occasionally lend a certain rigid dignity of manner to the suffering frame.

Quoted in *The Daily Telegraph* (London) *21 July 1986*

2624. Lucille Clifton (1936–)

1   . . . the bond of live things everywhere.

"Cutting Greens," *An Ordinary Woman 1974*

2   . . . things don't fall apart. Things hold. Lines connect in ways that last and last and lives become generations made out of pictures and words just kept.

Generations 1976

3   how otherwise
could i, a sleek old
traveler
curl one day safe and still
beside You
at Your feet, perhaps
but, amen, Yours

The Book of Light 1993

4   the question for you is
what have you ever traveled toward
more than your own safety?

"further note to clark" from notes to clark kent, Ibid.

5 . . . come celebrate
with me that everyday
something has tried to kill me
and has failed.
                                    "Song at Midnight," Ibid.

6 sweet attic of a woman,
repository of old songs.
                                    "Thel," Ibid.

7 "what is the splendor of one breast
on one woman?" she asks,
 "if there are no cherry blossoms
can there be a cherry tree?"
                        The Terrible Stories: Poems 1996

8 children
when they ask you
why is your mama so funny
say
she is a poet
she don't have no sense
                                    "admonitions " n.d.

9 maybe i should have wanted less.
maybe i should have ignored the bowl in me
burning to be filled.
                                    "climbing" n.d.

10 i am accused of tending to the past
as if i made it,
as if i sculpted it
with my own hands. i did not.
                "i am accused of tending to the past" n.d.

11 i will keep the door unlocked
until something human comes.
                        "leaving fox," A Dream of Foxes n.d.

12 if the little girl lies
still enough
shut enough
hard enough
shapeshifter may not
walk tonight
                            "shapeshifter poems," 3 n.d.

13 her hair
is white with wonderful.
                                "song at midnight" n.d.

14 . . . it was not
the animal blood i was hiding from,
it was the poet in her, the poet and
the terrible stories she could tell.
                        "telling our stories," St. 4 n.d.

15 the time i dropped your almost body down
down to meet the waters under the city
and run one with the sewage to the sea
what did i know about waters rushing back
what did i know about drowning
or being drowned
                                "the lost baby poem" n.d.

16 it is the great circulation
of the earth's body, like the blood
of the gods, this river in which the past

is always flowing. every water
is the same water coming round.
                "the mississippi river empties into the gulf" n.d.

2625. Elizabeth Hanford Dole (1936–)

1 The time is ripe for a woman President. Definitely in our lifetime. There are many women who are prepared.
            Quoted in "Women Who Could Be President" by
        Jane Ciabattari, Parade Magazine 7 February 1999

2626. Nell Dunn (1936–)

1 JOSIE. He made me wild last night, we was having it and I was
really getting into it and enjoying, when he's come. "Hold up!"
I says. "What about me?" Well, after that I made him plate me
for an hour till I come, every time he lifts his head I push it
back down—I wouldn't even let him up to breathe . . . I can
feel it from the bottom of my toes to the top of my skull. It's as
if something pealed right through my body . . . I hadn't come
like that for months. It did me the world of good.
                                    Sc. 1, Steaming 1981

2627. Sandra Gilbert (1936–)

1 Examining the psychosocial implications of a "haunted" ancestral mansion, such a tale* explores the tension between
parlor and attic, the psychic split between the lady who submits to male dicta and the lunatic who rebels. But in examining
these matters the paradigmatic female story inevitably considers also the equally uncomfortable spatial options of expulsion
into the cold outside or suffocation in the hot indoors, and in
addition it often embodies an obsessive anxiety both about
starvation to the point of disappearance and about monstrous
inhabitation.
            (p. 86), The Madwoman in the Attic: The Woman Writer
                and The Nineteenth-Century Literary Imagination,
                            with Susan Gubar** 1979
*Jane Eyre by Charlotte Brontë; see 910:3–23. **See 3004.

2 I wanted to fall, I was falling, I had fallen
into the hissing crevices, the lanes of ice

where I knew you wandered, shivering
even in your Irish sweater.
        "October 6, 1991: Seattle, Looking for Mount Rainier,"
                                    Ghost Volcano 1995

3 If you've lost a gorgeous orange, no number of delicious apples can replace its glow and sweetness.
                Wrongful Death: A Medical Tragedy 1995

2628. Carol Gilligan (1936–)

1 Implicitly adopting the male life as the norm, they have tried
to fashion women out of a masculine cloth. It all goes back, of
course, to Adam and Eve—a story which shows, among other
things, that if you make a woman out of man, you are bound
to get into trouble. In the life cycle, as in the Garden of Eden,
the woman has been the deviant.
                            Ch. 1, In a Different Voice 1982

2 The blind willingness to sacrifice people to truth, however, has
always been the danger of an ethics abstracted from life. This
willingness links Gandhi to the biblical Abraham, who prepared to sacrifice the life of his son in order to demonstrate the
integrity and supremacy of his faith. Both men, in the limitations of their fatherhood, stand in implicit contrast to the

woman* who comes before Solomon and verifies her motherhood by relinquishing truth in order to save the life of her child. . . . The ethics of . . . adulthood . . . has become principled at the expense of care. . . .

Ch. 3, Ibid.

*Prostitute of Jerusalem, mother of the living child; see 37.

3   Thus changes in women's rights change women's moral judgements, seasoning mercy with justice by enabling women to consider it moral to care not only for others but for themselves.

Ch. 5, Ibid.

4   . . . while men represent powerful activity as assertion and aggression, women in contrast portray acts of nurturance as acts of strength.

Ch. 6, Ibid.

5   While an ethic of justice proceeds from the premise of equality—that everyone should be treated the same—an ethic of care rests on the premise of nonviolence—that no one should be hurt.

Ibid.

2629. Natalya Gorbanevskaya (1936–)

1   Opening the window, I open myself.

Untitled poem, *Poems, the Trial, Prison* 1972

2   I am awaiting the birth of my child quite calmly, and neither my pregnancy nor the birth will prevent me from doing what I wish—which includes participating in every protest against any act of tyranny.

Red Square at Noon 1972

2630. Judith Guest (1936–)

1   The small seed of despair cracks open and sends experimental tendrils upward to the fragile skin of calm holding him together.

Ch. 1, *Ordinary People* 1976

2   Riding the train gives him too much time to think, he has decided. Too much thinking can ruin you.

Ch. 4, Ibid.

3   He had left off being a perfectionist then, when he discovered that not promptly kept appointments, not a house circumspectly clean, not membership in Onwentsia, or the Lake Forest Golf and Country Club, or the Lawyer's Club, not power, or knowledge, or goodness—not *anything*—cleared you through the terrifying office of chance; that it is chance and not perfection that rules the world.

Ch. 11, Ibid.

4   How would you describe your marriage, in terms of knowing each other? In terms of being friends? Of understanding that hopelessly intricate network of clash and resolution that has been woven over the last twenty years? Two separate, distinct personalities, not separate at all, but inextricably bound, soul and body and mind, to each other, how did we get so far apart so fast?

Ch. 19, Ibid.

5   "Geez, if I could get through to you, kiddo, that depression is not sobbing and crying and *giving vent*, it is plain and simple *reduction of feeling*. Reduction, see? Of all feeling. People who keep stiff upper lips find that it's damn hard to smile.

Ch. 27, Ibid.

2631. Sandra Hochman (1936–)

1   What I wanted
Was to be myself again.

"The Inheritance," *Love Letters from Asia* 1967

2632. Xaviera Hollander (1936?–)

1   *Mundus vult decipi decipiatur ergo.* The world wants to be cheated, so cheat.

Ch. 1, *The Happy Hooker*, with Robin Moore and Yvonne Dunleavy 1972

2   For me the madam life has become a big ego trip. I enjoy the independence and what's more, for me prostitution is not just a way to make a living, but a real calling, which I enjoy.

Ch. 10, Ibid.

3   There is only one other profession that outranks bankers as dedicated clients, and that is the stockbroker. . . . When the stocks go up, the cocks go up!

Ch. 11, Ibid.

4   Actually, if my business was legitimate, I would deduct a substantial percentage for depreciation of my body.

Ch. 14, Ibid.

5   . . . if my business could be made legal . . . I and women like me could make a big contribution to what Mayor Lindsay* calls "Fun City," and the city and state could derive the money in taxes and licensing fees that I pay off to crooked cops and political figures.

Ibid.

*John V. Lindsay, American politican (1921–2000), mayor of New York City (1966–1974).

2633. Sonia Johnson (1936?–)

1   I liked the *name* of the amendment. I couldn't help feeling uneasy that the church was opposing something with a name as beautiful as the *Equal Rights* Amendment.

From Housewife to Heretic 1981

2   In our patriarchal world, we are all taught—whether we like to think we are or not—that God, being male, values maleness much more than he values femaleness . . . that in order to propitiate God, women must propitiate men. After all, God won't like us if we don't please those nearest to his heart, if we don't treat his cronies well.

Ibid.

3   I am a warrior in the time of women warriors; the longing for justice is the sword I carry, the love of womankind is my shield.

Ibid.

4   Women cannot serve two masters at once who are urgently beaming antithetical orders. . . . Either we believe in patriarchy—the rule of men over women—or we believe in equality.

Ibid.

2634. June Jordan (1936–)

1   There was no loneliness in the living room. So it was a good part, and maybe the best part of the house.

New Life, New Room 1975

2   "But what's more important. Building a bridge or taking care of a baby?"

Ibid.

3   I been scheming about my people
    I been scheming about sex
    I been dreaming about Africa
    Nightmaring Oedipus the Rex
                    "Alla That's All Right, But" *1980*

4   . . . the intimate face of the universal struggle. You begin with
    your family and the kids on the block, and next you open your
    eyes to what you call your people and that leads you into land
    reform, into Black English, into Angola, leads you back to
    your own bed where you lie by yourself, wondering if you de-
    serve to be peaceful.
                    Civil Wars 1981

5   The purpose of polite behavior is never virtuous. Deceit, sur-
    render, and concealment: these are not virtues. The goal of the
    mannerly is comfort, per se.
                    "Civil Wars" (1972), Ibid.

6   Self-determination has to mean that the leader is your individ-
    ual gut, and heart, and mind or we're talking about power,
    again, and its rather well-known impurities.
                    Ibid.

7   We do not deride the fears of prospering white America. A na-
    tion of violence and private property has every reason to dread
    the violated and the deprived.
                    "Black Studies: Bringing Back the Person" *(Evergreen
                    Review,* October 1969), *Moving Towards Home:
                    Political Essays 1989*

8   As a poet and writer, I deeply love and I deeply hate words. I
    love the infinite evidence and change and requirements and
    possibilities of language; every human use of words that is joy-
    ful, or honest or new, because experience is new. . . . But as a
    Black poet and writer, I hate words that cancel my name and
    my history and the freedom of my future: I hate the words that
    condemn and refuse the language of my people in America.
                    "White English/Black English: The Politics of Translation"
                    (1972), Ibid.

9   Language is political. That's why you and me, my Brother and
    Sister, that's why we sposed to choke our natural self into the
    weird, lying, barbarous, unreal, white speech and writing
    habits that the schools lay down like holy law. Because, in
    other words, the powerful don't play; they mean to keep that
    power, and those who are the powerless (you and me) better
    shape up—mimic/ape/suck-in the very image of the powerful,
    or the powerful will destroy you—you and our children.
                    Ibid.

10 When we heard about the hippies, the barely more than boys
    and girls who decided to try something different . . . we
    laughed at them. Smug in our certain awareness that . . . com-
    munal life must be more difficult even than nuclear family life,
    which we know, to our very nerve endings, is disastrous, we
    condemned them, our children, for seeking a different future.
    We hated them for their flowers, for their love, and for their
    unmistakable rejection of every hideous, mistaken compro-
    mise that we had made throughout our hollow, money-bitten,
    frightened, adult lives.
                    Address, "Old Stories: New Lives," Child Welfare League
                    of America (1978), Ibid.

11 In the name of motherhood and fatherhood and education and
    good manners, we threaten and suffocate and bind and en-
    snare and bribe and trick children into wholesale emulation of
    our ways.
                    Ibid.

12 I am a feminist, and what that means to me is much the same
    as the meaning of the fact that I am Black: it means that I must
    undertake to love myself and to respect myself as though my
    very life depends upon self-love and self-respect.
                    Address, "Where Is the Love?," Black Writers' Conference,
                    Howard University (1978), Ibid.

13 South Africa used to seem so far away. Then it came home to
    me. It began to signify the meaning of white hatred here. That
    was what the sheets and the suits and the ties covered up, not
    very well. That was what the cowardly guys calling me names
    from their speeding truck wanted to happen to me, to all of
    me: to my people. That was what would happen to me if I
    walked around the corner into the wrong neighborhood. That
    was Birmingham. That was Brooklyn. That was Reagan. That
    was the end of reason. South Africa was how I came to under-
    stand that I am not against war; I am against losing the war.
                    "South Africa: Bringing It All Back Home" (1981), Ibid.

14 In America, you can segregate the people, but the problems
    will travel.
                    "Problems of Language in a Democratic State" (1982), Ibid.

15 If any of us hopes to survive, s/he must meet the extremity of
    the American female condition with immediate and political
    response. The thoroughly destructive and indefensible subju-
    gation of the majority of Americans cannot continue except at
    the peril of the entire body politic.
                    "The Case for the Real Majority" (1982), Ibid.

16 When that devil's bullet lodged itself inside the body of Martin
    Luther King, he had already begun an astonishing mobiliza-
    tion of poor, Black, white, Latino Americans who had nothing
    to lose. They would challenge our government to eliminate ex-
    ploitative, merciless, and war-mongering policies, nationwide,
    or else "tie up the country" through "means of civil disobedi-
    ence." Dr. King intended to organize those legions into
    "coercive direct actions" that would make of Babylon a dys-
    functional behemoth begging for relief. Is it any wonder he
    was killed?
                    Lecture, "The Mountain and the Man Who Was Not God,"
                    Stanford University (California, 20 *January* 1987), Ibid.

17 "Mos anytime you see whitemen spose to fight each other an'
    you not white, well you know you got trouble, because they
    blah-blah loud about Democrat or Republican an' they huffin'
    an' puff about democracy someplace else but relentless, see,
    the deal come down evil on somebody don' have no shirt an'
    tie, somebody don' live in no whiteman house no whiteman
    country."
                    "White Tuesday" (1989), Ibid.

18 what I wanted was
    to braid my hair/bathe and bedeck my
    self so fully be—
    cause what I wanted was
    your love
    not pity
                    "The Talking Back of Miss Valentine Jones: Poem # one,"
                    St. 4, *Naming Our Destiny: New and Selected Poems 1989*

19 It sure did seem she wanted him to lose
    his job because she could not find
    the keys
    he could not find
                    "War and Memory," I, St. 1 (1989), *The Woman That
                    I Am, The Literature and Culture of Contemporary
                    Women of Color,* D. Soyini Madison, ed. *1994*

20 Crowd counts at the rallies.
Body counts on the news.
Ketchup on the steps of universities.
Blood on the bandages around the head of the Vietnamese
woman shot between the eyes.
Big guys.
             "War and Memory," V, St. 2 (1989), Ibid.

21 Who invented these Americans with pony
tails and Afros and tee shirts and statistical
arguments against the mining of the harbors
of a country far away?
             St. 3, Ibid.

22 I sometimes called the Operator
asking for Police
to beat my father up for beating me
so bad
but no one listened to
a tattletale
like me:
             VII, St. 2, Ibid.

23 and I
lust for justice
and I
make that quest arthritic/pigeon-toed/however
and I
invent the mother of the courage I require not to quit
             VII, St. 6, l.l., Ibid.

24 New World means non-European; it means new; it means big;
it means heterogeneous; it means unknown; it means free; it
means an end to feudalism, caste, privilege, and the violence of
power.
        Quoted in "New World Writing," *A World That Will Hold
All the People* by Suzanee Gardinier* 1996
    *See 3496.

25 I saw him as some kinda clown
a first class
colored fool
an Uncle Tom
a Peeping Tom
a creepy eager pornographic Tom
a hypocrite
a liar and a fake
a make-
believe Black man
a mediocre mediocrity of apple polish
brown nose cut-throat
      "Letter to Mrs. Virginia Thomas, Wife of Whatzhisname*
Lamentably Appointed to the Supreme Courte, U.S.A.," St.
1, *Kissing God Goodbye: New Poems 1991–1996* 1997
    *Reference to Clarence Thomas (1948–), appointed in 1991.

26 Most people search all
of their lives
for someplace to belong to
as you said
but I look instead
into the eyes of anyone
who talks to me
             "Untitled," St. 1 (27 May 1997), Ibid.

27 Because romance carried the rose inside a fist
Because she hungered for the fragrance of the rose
          "What Grief Has Made the Empress Mute," St. 5, Ibid.

28 Quit?
Save?
Sign Off?
Cancel?
ARE YOU SURE?

ARE YOU SURE?
      "Poem Against the Temptations of Ambivalence," *in toto*
3 October 1997

29 I'm saying that calculated racialization of poverty, inequality,
immigration, and education colors these realities so that too
many of us perceive these issues as strictly equivalent to this or
that race/this or that language/this or that ethnic heritage
when, actually, the issue is how we . . . devise a democratic,
and peaceable, means to go on, or not!
      "Affirmative Acts," *Affirmative Acts* 1999

30 momma/momma/mammy/nanny/granny
woman/mistress/sista luv
            "Trying to Get Over" *n.d.*

2635. Evelyn Fox Keller (1936–)

1 [Barbara McClintock]* didn't adopt a masculine ideal, nor did
she adopt a purely feminine ideal. She made use of the full
range of human capacity . . . and all her intuitive strengths, in
the service of science. . . . It doesn't matter that she was a
woman. One could find men in that tradition as well.
      Quoted in *A Feeling for the Organism: The Life and Work
of Barbara McClintock* 1983
    *See 1820.

2 The need to dominate nature is, in this view, a project of the
need to dominate other human beings.
         Reflections on Gender and Science 1985

3 In my vision of science, it is not the taming of nature that is
sought, but the taming of hegemony.
             Ibid.

2636. Florence King (1936–)

1 We want a president who is as much like an American tourist
as possible. Someone with the same goofy grin, the same innocent intentions, the same naive trust; a president with no
conception of foreign policy and no discernible connection to
the U.S. government, whose Nice Guyism will narrow the gap
between the U.S. and us until nobody can tell the difference.
      "Nice Guyism," *Reflections in a Jaundiced Eye* 1989

2 Chinks in America's egalitarian armor are not hard to find.
Democracy is the fig leaf of elitism.
           "Democracy," Ibid.

3 Owning your own home is America's unique recipe for avoiding revolution and promoting pseudo-equality at the same
time. To keep citizens puttering in their yards instead of sput-
tering on the barricades, the government has gladly deprived
itself of billions in tax revenues by letting home "owners"
deduct mortgage interest payments.
             Ibid.

4 Self-help books are making life downright unsafe. Women desperate to catch a man practice all the ploys recommended by
these authors. Bump into him, trip over him, knock him down,
spill something on him, scald him, but *meet him.*
          "Does Your Child Taste Salty?," Ibid.

5   American couples have gone to such lengths to avoid the interference of in-laws that they have to pay marriage counselors to
interfere between them.

Ibid.

6   The proliferation of support groups suggests to me that too
many Americans are growing up in homes that do not contain
a grandmother. A home without a grandmother is like an egg
without salt and Helpists know it. They have jumped into the
void left by the disappearance of morbid old ladies from the
bosom of the American family.

Ibid.

7   The American woman's concept of marriage is a clearly etched
picture of something uninflated on the floor. A sleeping-bag
without air, a beanbag without beans, a padded bra without
pads. To work on it, you start pumping—what the magazines
call "breathing life into your marriage." Do enough of this and
the marriage becomes a kind of Banquo's ghost, a quasi-living
entity.

"From Captain Marvel to Captain Valium," Ibid.

8   Once the vitamin became a pill, it became "real" according to
the precepts of American Cartesianism: "I swallow it, therefore it is."

Ibid.

9   America is not a democracy, it's an absolute monarchy ruled
by King Kid. In a nation of immigrants, the child is automatically more of an American than his parents. . . . Americans
regard children as what Mr. Hudson in "Upstairs, Downstairs" called "betters." Aping their betters, American adults
do their best to turn themselves into children. Puerility exercises *droit de seigneur* everywhere.

"Good King Herod," Ibid.

10   Any hope that America would finally grow up vanished with
the rise of fundamentalist Christianity.

Ibid.

11   He travels fastest who travels alone, and that goes double for
she. Real feminism is spinsterhood.

"Spinsterhood Is Powerful," Ibid.

12   Humor inspires sympathetic good-natured laughter and is favored by the "healing-power" gang. Wit goes for the jugular,
not the jocular, and it's the opposite of football; instead of
building character, it tears it down.

"The State of the Funny Bone," Ibid.

2637. Deena Metzger (1936–)

1   Stories are like a body. We can touch them and they touch the
very heart of us.

"Writing for Your Life," *Ms.* (New York) *March/April 1993*

2   Maintaining a spiritual practice is an ordeal like climbing a
mountain, and it demands the same of us: commitment, discipline, endurance, focus, and awareness. There at the top is the
sky and, perhaps, the large vision, but ultimately the meaning
is in the climbing, in the "angels" who accompany us, and in
the specific rituals and activities that take us to the summit
and sustain us along the way, both going up and coming down.

Ibid.

3   Following the creative is a path, but it is not a known path. It
has to be carved out by each individual practitioner. . . . Each
practitioner must discover her own prayers, sacrifices, offer-

ings, rituals—everything has to be invented from the beginning.
And so, as in the mystery religions, one travels with one's eyes
closed, utterly alone, into the unknown.

Ibid.

4   Understanding and vision cannot be fully cultivated until the
ego, the will, or the worldly self defers to other ways of being
and knowing.

Ibid.

2638. Barbara Ann Mikulski (1936–)

1   America is not a melting pot. It is a sizzling cauldron.

Speech, First National Conference of the National Center
for Urban and Ethnic Affairs, Quoted in *American
Political Women* by Esther Stineman *1980*

2   As we move from an economy of affluence to an economy of
scarcity, we must be careful that the people who make $5,000
a year are not pitted against those who make $25,000 a year
by those who make $900,000. The two-martinis-for-lunch
bunch would love for us to fight each other over the resources
they have made scarce.

Campaign Speech (1974), Ibid.

2639. Jane O'Reilly (1936–)

1   . . . the click! of recognition, that parenthesis of truth around a
little thing that completes the puzzle of reality in women's
minds—the moment that brings a gleam to our eyes and means
the revolution has begun.

"The Housewife's Moment of Truth," *The First Ms. Reader*,
Francine Klagsbrun, ed. *1972*

2   . . . housewives, the natural people to turn to when there is
something unpleasant, inconvenient or inconclusive to be
done.

Ibid.

3   Men will always opt for things that get finished and stay that
way—putting up screens, but not planning menus.

Ibid.

4   Parables are unnecessary for recognizing the blatant absurdity
of everyday life. Reality is lesson enough.

Ibid.

2640. Rochelle Owens (1936–)

1   CY. I wasn't near people. They came to me and looked under
my trousers all the way up to their dirty hearts! They minded
my *own* life.

Futz 1958

2   CY. I don't want no sow with two feet but with four! Them repeats true things with their grunts not like you
human-daughter.

Sc. 1, Ibid.

3   CY. And I have no hate for anybody, but wanting to love the
animals the way I do. *They*, mean folks, hate my face.

Ibid.

4   MRS. LOOP. A son and his mother are godly.

Sc. 2, Ibid.

5   KATKA. Depression is often a sign of worthy pleasure.

Sc. 5, Ibid.

6   ALICE. Hypocrites, what hypocrites! Jerusalem is always a pre-text for getting to Constantinople!
> Sc. 2, *Istanbul 1965*

7   BECLCH. Your lesson to your son is a hangnail to us—we don't need it.
> Act I, Sc. 1, *Beclch 1966*

8   BECLCH. No, sweet Jose . . . a cock fight is not cruel . . . for me . . . us to see . . . it's simply an evil reality . . . that's all . . .
> Sc. 2, Ibid.

9   BECLCH. Persecution is a fact of the condition of being a monarch!
> Act II, Sc. 2, Ibid.

10   MARX. Labor! Sucking Capital! Capital! The exploiting class! The milking class—the ruling class!
> *The Karl Marx* Play 1971*
> *German political philosopher and economist (1818–83).

11   MARX. Little rolls with butter is good! Viennese torte is Good! And a revolution is good!
> Ibid.

12   MARX . . . the bourgeoisie, the fat enemy will get their reactionary asses *schutupped* up with horseshit and whipped cream! A new era will dawn.
> Ibid.

13   MARX. Beware the eternal, unredeemed Jew, the everlasting bargainers! They are hot for buying and selling, they would kill my beautiful revolution!
> Ibid.

14   MARX. Economics is not only a cause. But the *only* cause for all human rancor. All human exploitation.
> Ibid.

15   Any woman . . . who dares to write in areas of human experience which are considered raw or terrifying or investigative . . . is chastised, disciplined, ridiculed.
> Quoted in "Five Important Playwrights Talk About Theatre Without Compromise and Sexism," *Mademoiselle 75 August 1972*

16   CHUCKY. My own failings are enmeshed in the times . . .
> *Chucky's Hunch 1981*

17   It's as if I was a chemist, an alchemist, mixing and playing around with fluids, living tissue, vapors, always testing the viability of the matter—language.
> "Rochelle Owens," *Interviews with Contemporary Women Playwrights*, Kathleen Betsko* and Rachel Koenig *1987*
> *See 2739.

2641. Marge Piercy (1936–)

1   Reflecting the values of the larger capitalistic society, there is no prestige whatsoever attached to actual working. Workers are invisible.
> "The Grand Coolie Damn," *Sisterhood Is Powerful*, Robin Morgan,* ed. *1970*
> *See 2864.

2   The ruling class isn't dissatisfied: they are healthy, well-fed, live in beauty, enjoy their own importance: fun-loving cannibals
> Ibid.

3   One trouble: to be a professional anything in the United States is to think of oneself as an expert and one's ideas as semi-sacred, and to treat others in a certain way—professionally.
> Ibid.

4   In an elitist world, it's always "women and children last."
> Ibid.

5   The manipulator liberates only
the mad bulldozers of the ego to level the ground.
> "Song of the Fucked Duck" (1969), Ibid.

6   The will to be totally rational
is the will to be made out of glass and steel:
and to use others as if they were glass and steel.
> Ibid.

7   There are lies that glow so brightly we consent to give a finger and then an arm to let them burn.
> Ibid.

8   "You and I both have livers, large and small intestines, kidneys, spines, blood vessels, nerves, spleens, stomachs, hearts and, I had thought, brains in common. What conclusions do you draw from anatomy? That I am about to take you to the cleaners?"
> *Small Changes 1973*

9   "You're not pretty, Miriam-mine, so you better be smart. But not too smart."
> Ibid.

10   "All women hustle. Women watch faces, voices, gestures, moods. The person who has to survive through cunning."
> Ibid.

11   She must learn again to speak
starting with I
starting with We
starting as the infant does
with her own true hunger
and pleasure
and rage.
> "Unlearning to Not Speak," *To Be of Use 1973*

12   She never felt much in common with gay men; it was like telling her she ought to feel empathy with child molesters because they were both defined by the law as sexual deviants.
> Ch. 3, *The High Cost of Living 1978*

13   As I kneel to put the seeds in
careful as stitching, I am in love.
You are the bed we all sleep on.
You are the food we eat, the food
we ate, the food we will become.
We are walking trees rooted in you.
> "The Common Living Dirt," St. 3, *Stone, Paper, Knife 1983*

14   We lack the knowledge we showed ten
thousand years past, that you live
a goddess but mortal, that what we take
must be returned; that the poison we drop
in you will stunt our children's growth.
> St. 6, Ibid.

15   we must come again to worship you
on our knees, the common living dirt.
> St. 11, Ibid.

16 "We did make a new world. Just not exactly the one we intended. It's a bigger job than we realized, to make things good and fair. It won't be us who finish it. But we gave it a pretty good start before we lost our way."
City of Darkness, City of Light 1996

17 She was sensual without being jaded, accomplished without a hint of whorishness. . . . but she did not admire him as he liked to be admired. . . . She had a critical eye he disliked in a woman. . . . She was good at sex, but he did not think she would be good at loving.
Ibid.

18 "I remember and I make sure my daughters know, it was old biddies like we are now and young women who brought the King down. We are the Revolution, ladies, and we carry it in our blood to the future."
Ibid.

19 She left early in the morning, not lingering for breakfast or expecting a present.
Ibid.

20 Americans live in an increasingly violent society that is . . . inured to violence (as eighteenth-century France was) and one in which the top is growing ever richer and further in every way from the vast bulk of the population. I thought looking at a society in crisis so very strange in some ways and so familiar in others might illuminate our own situation.
Author's note, Ibid.

21 Heaven and earth observe how we cherish or spoil our world.
"(Interpretation of the) She'ma,"* *The Art of Blessing the Day 1999*

*A holy Jewish prayer.

22 Bless what brought us through
the sea and the fire; we are caught
in history like whales in polar ice.
Yet you have taught us to push against the walls,

to reach out and pull each other along . . .
1, Ibid.

23 Bless the teaching of how to open
in love so all the doors and windows of the
body swing wide on their rusty hinges
and we give ourselves with both hands.
2, Ibid.

24 Bless the gift of memory
that breaks unbidden, released
from a flower or a cup of tea
so the dead move like rain through the room.
Ibid.

25 We will try to be holy,
We will try to repair the world given to us to hand on.
Precious is this treasure of words and knowledge and deeds
that moves inside us.
Holy is the hand that works for peace and for justice,
holy is the mouth that speaks for goodness
holy is the foot that walks toward mercy.
3, Ibid.

2642. Sharon Pollock (1936–)

1 SITTING BULL. In the beginning . . . was given . . . to everyone a cup . . . a cup of clay. And from this cup we drink our life. We all dip in the water, but the cups are different . . . My cup is broken. It has passed away.
Act III, *Walsh 1973*

2 [A play] is a theatrical impression of an historical event seen through the optique of the stage and the mind of the playwright.
Introduction, *The Komagata Maru Incident 1978*

2643. Estela Portillo (1936–)

1 The village of Lago de San Lorenzo is a stepchild; it is a stepchild to the Esquinas hacienda, for the hacienda has been a frugal mother and a demanding father. Its name comes from the yearly ritual of the saint-day of San Lorenzo when all the young women gather around the lake to wash their hair and bathe in promise of a future husband. The tempo of life, unbroken, conditioned, flavors its heartbeat with dramas and myths. The hacienda is the fiber upon which existence hangs. The church, the fluid rose, assures the future promise of Elysian fields. No one dares ask for life.
"The Day of the Swallows," Introduction (1973), *The Woman That I Am, The Literature and Culture of Contemporary Women of Color*, D. Soyini Madison, ed. 1994

2 In earnest belief, they wash their hair in spring water to insure future marriages made in heaven. It is true, no one has seen a marriage made in heaven, but each girl hugs the private truth that hers will be the one.
Ibid.

2644. Mary Quant (1936–)

1 Having money is rather like being a blond. It is more fun but not vital.
Quoted in *Observer* (London) *2 November 1986*

2645. Aishah Rahman (1936/7–)

1 GIRL. It's only in the head of a musician that I begin to understand. Only a musician can make sense for me. Only a musician knows how to connect shoes with cardboard to cover holes to P.S. 184 on 116th Street and Lenox Avenue to the red taste of watermelon and mocking white smiles to Anthony's smiles and smell of Florida Water to late night loneliness and . . . this . . . [her unborn baby].
Unfinished Woman Cry in No Man's Land While a Bird Die in a Gilded Cage 1984

2 BIRD. My pain is not unbearable. In none of my secret places inside of me have I condemned myself.
Ibid.

3 PREGNANT GIRL. One day we will not have to be afraid of our dreams.
Ibid.

4 Such categories [as gender, culture, or sexual orientation] are only literary apartheid that marginalizes specific groups of writers. They are false commercial distinctions that have nothing to do with the quality of writing. There are only two kinds of writing. Good and bad.
Quoted in *Moon Marked and Touched by Sun* by Sydné Mahone 1994

2646. Margaret Randall (1936–)

1 In order to effectively reverse the centuries-old paradigm of male = ownership = control, versus female = dependence =

powerlessness, we must begin to deal with the ways women have been made to *feel* about money.

The Price You Pay 1996

2   . . . the management of memory—how it may be preserved, mishandled, abused, or offered as a touchstone to the understanding of history.

"Eyes on the prizewinner," *The Women's Review of Books*,
Vol. XV, No. 12 *September 1998*

2647. Jill Robinson (1936–)

1   The fame fraud is so complete that all the Hollywood kids think everyone else has money. It is the suburban delusion. But then, suburbia was invented by Hollywood.

Pt. I, *Bed/Time/Story 1974*

2   I could hear the lovely, tiny swallowing gulps—you cover all ages in the sex-play cycle, from nursing infant to death in one terrifying swoop of the sexual plot.

Ibid.

3   Somewhere there was a gentle man with a cock that wore a jaunty grin and stayed long enough for you to get to know him.

Ibid.

4   And grownups have to act as if they know. That's how they show they love you, by knowing more stuff; it makes you feel secure.

Pt. II, Ibid.

5   The transcontinental jet flight is a condensed metaphor of the escapist's Geographical Change. One starts out with the gorgeous hope that the self one abhors can be left behind. Three thousand miles is a powerful distance; such speed, such height should get you away before that self can catch up.

Ibid.

6   We have to get where we are going. In New York the getting is the thing.

Ibid.

7   "Ambition is destruction, only competence matters . . . "

Ibid.

8   "Everyone's parent is only a fantasy finally, neither as magical as, forgive me, you are, nor as prosaic. It is the image one has created in the head that one is fighting. Not the real parent at all."

Ibid.

9   "It's a big risk—to stop drinking, going straight. Who knows? What you've got in mind could be very boring."

Ibid.

2648. Betty Rollin (1936–)

1   . . . biological *possibility* and desire are not the same as biological *need*. For them to choose not to use the equipment is no more blocking what is instinctive than it is for a man who, muscles or no, chooses not to be a weightlifter.

"Motherhood: Who Needs It," *Look* (New York)
16 May 1971

2   How can birth-control programs really be effective as long as the concept of glorious motherhood remains unchanged? (Even poor old Planned Parenthood has to euphemize—why not Planned Unparenthood?)

Ibid.

3   Motherhood affords an instant identity. First, through wifehood, you are somebody's wife; then you are somebody's mother. Both give not only identity and activity, but status and stardom of a kind.

Ibid.

2649. Sandra Marie Schneiders (1936–)

1   The gender of god, god's presumed masculinity, has functioned as the ultimate religious legitimization of the unjust social structures which victimize women.

Women and the Word 1986

2650. Gail Sheehy (1936/37–)

1   For there is no more defiant denial of one man's ability to possess one woman exclusively than the prostitute who refuses to be redeemed.

Ch. 1, *Hustling 1971*

2   Into this anonymous pit they climb—a fumbling, frightened, pathetic man and a cold, contemptuous, violated woman—prepared to exchange for twenty dollars no more than ten minutes of animal sex, untouched by a stroke of their common humanity.

Ch. 3, Ibid.

3   It is a silly question to ask a prostitute why she does it. . . . These are the highest-paid "professional" women in America.

Ch. 4, Ibid.

4   The prostitutes continue to take all the arrests, the police to suffer frustration, the lawyers to mine gold, the operators to laugh, the landowners to insist they have no responsibility, the mayor to issue press releases. The nature of the beast is, in a word, greed.

Ch. 5, Ibid.

5   . . . the upper East Side of Manhattan. This is the province of Let's Pretend located in the state of Anomie.

Ibid.

6   The difference between the call girl and the courtesan . . . comes down to one word. Discipline.

Ch. 9, Ibid.

7   The best way to attract money, she had discovered, was to give the appearance of having it.

Ibid.

8   It is fitting that speed should be our chemical superstar. With the only certainty of our daily existence being change, and a rate of change growing always faster in a kind of technological leapfrog game, speed helps people to think they are keeping up.

Speed Is of the Essence 1971

9   We hear the haunting presentiment of a dutiful middle age in the current reluctance of young people to select any option except the one they feel will impinge upon them the least.

Pt. II, Ch. 5, *Passages 1976*

10   It is a paradox that as we reach our prime, we also see there is a place where it finishes.

Pt. IV, Ch. 17, Ibid.

11   Safe but stifled, these are the most familiar men.

Pt. V, Ch. 15, Ibid.

12 The secret of a leader lies in the tests he has faced over the whole course of his life and the *habit of action* he develops in meeting those tests.

"Looking for Mikhail Gorbachev,"
Gorbachev 1991

13 Democratization is not democracy; it is a slogan for the temporary liberalization handed down from an autocrat. Glasnost is not free speech; only free speech, consitutionally guaranteed, is free speech.

Ibid.

14 The source of continuing aliveness was to find your passion and pursue it, with whole heart and single mind.

"Coalescence," *The Silent Passage: Menopause 1991*

15 Once she is no longer confined to the culture's definition of woman as a primarily sexual object and breeder, a full unity of her feminine and masculine sides is possible. As she moves beyond gender definition, she gains new license to speak her mind and initiate action.

Ibid.

16 Transformation also means looking for ways to stop pushing yourself so hard professionally or inviting so much stress. . . . This momentous passage invites meditation and spiritual exploration. A wisewoman will make time to contemplate things eternal and appreciate the life she has.

"The Menopause Getaway," Ibid.

17 When both ovaries are removed the abrupt and total, rather than gradual, shutting down of ovarian function can be devastating, placing the woman at risk of serious depression. It also extinguishes sexual desire.

"The Need to Know and the Fear of Knowing," Ibid.

18 Menopause may be the last taboo.

Ibid.

19 It used to be that a reliable guide to when you might expect menopause is when your mother experienced it. But the mothers of today's groundbreaking women knew nothing like the level of workplace stress and environmental toxins we live with today. Acute or prolonged and severe stress can reduce ovarian function and precipitate a temporary menopause at any time from the late thirties on.

"The Perimenopause Panic," Ibid.

2651. Becky Simpson (1936–)

1 What I wanted was justice for poor people. Then I realized that can also mean putting a good pair of shoes on somebody's feet, a meal on their table, clothes on their back—that's justice to me. I know it's ground level, but that's where I want to be.

Quoted in "You Just Have to Try" by Michael Ryan,
Parade Magazine
28 May 1989

2652. Carol Springer (1936–)

1 We're going to do exactly the same thing we would do if there were no gender issue. You do your job.*

"Arizona's 'girl thing' . . . " (p. 6A), *USA Today*
11 November 1998
*Referring to 1998 election of five women to top state government offices.

2653. Catharine R. Stimpson (1936–)

1 Women's Studies ought to invest in hope, not dread. For the social changes that helped to create it are irresistible.

"Annual Report on Women and Feminism," *The Women's Review of Books 1989*

2 Identity politics is contemporary shorthand for a group's assertion that it is a meaningful group; that it differs significantly from other groups; that its members share a history of injustice and grievance; and that its psychological and political mission is to explore, act out, act on and act up its group identity. What makes a group a group may be race, ethnicity, religion, class, gender, sexual preference or any one of a number of conditions. . . . Identity politics offers stability in a shifting, swiftly changing world.

"Acting Up and Opting Out," *The Nation* (New York)
18 December 1995

2654. Lily Tomlin (1936–)

1 If you have a psychotic fixation and you go to the doctor and you want these two fingers amputated, he will not cut them off. But he *will* remove your genitals. I have more trouble getting a prescription for Valium than I do having my uterus lowered and made into a penis.

Quoted by David Felton in *Rolling Stone* (New York)
24 October 1974

2 If you can't be direct, why be?

"Mary Jean,"* Ibid.

3 Once poor, always wantin'. Rich is just a way of wantin' bigger.

"Wanda V.,"* Ibid.

4 Lady . . . Lady, I do not make up things. That is lies. Lies is not true. But the truth could be made up if you know how. And that's the truth.

"Edith Ann,"* Ibid.
*Characters created by Lily Tomlin.

5 Thanks to medical technology, major breakthroughs in psychiatric care, I'm no longer a woman obsessed with an unnatural craving. Just another normal . . . very socially acceptable . . . alcoholic.

"Rubber Freak," Ibid.

6 If you win the rat race, you're still a rat.

Quoted by Anna Quindlen* in her Commencement Speech,
Mount Holyoke College *23 May 1999*
* See 3366.

2655. Jill Tweedie (1936–)

1 It is easy and dismally enervating to think of opposition as merely perverse or actually evil—far more invigorating to see it as essential for honing the mind, and as a positive good in itself. For the day that moral issues cease to be fought over is the day the word "human" disappears from the race.

Independent (London) *May 1989*

2656. Meredith "Marty" Walton (1936–)

1 It has only been recently that feminist consciousness has affected the Society of Friends just as it has affected the world at large. The old boys' network has been as much a factor in the Society of Friends as it has in the general society.

Cited by Barbara Findlen, *Ms.* (New York) *March 1987*

2 There have been women models in Quaker history that have perhaps made it easier for women to assume leadership positions now.

Ibid.

2657. Joan Myers Weimer (1936–)

1 She knows the Underworld like the palm of her hand.

Back Talk: Teaching Lost Selves to Speak 1994

2 I think the biggest secret I've kept from myself is my hunger for a spiritual life.

Ibid.

2658. Nancy Willard (1936–)

1 For me there is a very strong connection between listening to literature and telling stories and writing them. Finding your own voice grows out of hearing the spoken word.

"Far from just kid stuff" by Berthe Amoss, *Times-Picayune* (New Orleans), E7 *27 March 1988*

2 I like to work with my hands. Especially in connection with fantasy where you have to imagine so much; place, the geography, everything. It helps me to make a model of the thing about which I am writing.

Ibid.

3 . . . I found out it is not what happens, it is how you tell it and who does the telling.

Ibid.

4 . . . fairy tales, which were originally told, at least the Grimm's fairy tales, by grown-ups to other grown-ups; they were told by women to other women as they sat in the spinning rooms of their houses passing time.

Ibid.

5 You know the work will not go well
If you should mispronounce a spell.
A single lapse in common sense
can have a fatal consequence.

The Sorcerer's Apprentice 1993

6 [she] teaches them to say
the spell she worked out yesterday
for turning pencils into pails
and failures into fairy tales.

Ibid.

2659. Elizabeth Wilson (1936–)

1 Postmodernism refuses to privilege any one perspective, and recognizes only difference, never inequality, only fragments, never conflict.

Ch. 23, *Hallucinations 1988*

2660. Barbara Jordan (1936–1996)

1 I never intended to become a run-of-the-mill person.

Quoted in *Newsweek* (New York) *4 November 1974*

2 Politicians don't talk about "wielding power." That's so crass. The only thing I can hope is that I will continue to be able to influence the Congress by . . . persuasion . . . Nothing heavy-handed. Just openness and good relations.

Quoted in "Barbara Jordan" by Charles L. Sanders, *Ebony February 1975*

3 . . . if I have anything special that makes me "influential" I simply don't know how to define it. If I knew the ingredients I would bottle them, package them and sell them, because I want everyone to be able to work together in a spirit of cooperation and compromise and accommodation without, you know, any caving in or anyone being woefully violated personally or in terms of his principles.

Ibid.

4 If you're going to play the game properly you'd better know every rule.

Ibid.

5 The code of morality is to do unto others as you would have them do unto you. If you make that the central theme of your morality code, it will serve you well as a moral individual.

Quoted in "Where is Barbara Jordan Today?" by Malcolm Boyd, *Parade Magazine 16 February 1986*

6 I live a day at a time. Each day I look for a kernel of excitement. In the morning, I say: "What is my exciting thing for today?" Then, I do my day. Don't ask me about tomorrow.

Ibid.

7 Today, I am an inquisitor. I shall not sit here and be an idle spectator to the diminution, the subversion, the destruction of the Constitution.

Speech, House Judiciary Committee hearings (25 July 1974),* Quoted in *Barbara Jordan, American Hero* by Mary Beth Rogers *1998*

8 We must exchange the philosophy of excuses—what I am is beyond my control—for the philosophy of responsibility.

Quoted in *Twentieth-Century Women Political Leaders* by Claire Price–Groff *1998*

9 I am neither a black politician nor a female politician, just a politician.

Ibid.

10 When the Constitution was completed on the Seventeenth of September in 1787, I was not included in that "We, the people . . . "

Speech, House Judiciary Committee hearings (1974),* Ibid.
*Jordan was an African-American woman.

11 [Impeachment] is to be used for high crimes and misdemeanors. For great misdemeanors. The President* is sworn to uphold the Constitution and all the laws the Constitution protects.

Ibid.

*Reference to Richard M. Nixon (1913–94), 37th U.S. president (1969–74); resigned.

12 One hundred and forty-four years ago, members of the Democratic Party met for the first time in a convention to select their Presidential candidate. Since that time, Democrats have continued to convene once every four years to draft a party platform and nominate a Presidential candidate. Our meeting this week continues that tradition. There is something different and special about this opening night. I am a keynote speaker.*

Opening words, Keynote Address, Democratic National Convention (12 July 1976), Ibid.

*Reference to to her race and gender, both firsts at any major national party convention.

13 Are we to be one people bound together by common spirit . . . or will we become a divided nation?

Ibid.

14 We are a people in a quandary about the present and in search of the future . . . We are a people in search of a national community.

Closing words, Ibid.

2661. Sidney Abbot (1937–)

1 Lesbianism is far more than a sexual preference: it is a political stance.

Sappho * *Was a Right-on Woman*, with Barbara J. Love** *1972*

*See 46. **See 2681.

2 . . . a woman who wants a woman usually wants a woman.

Ibid.

3 Multiple relationships made it possible to comprehend people, not acquire them or own them.

Ibid.

2662. JoAnne Akalaitis (1937–)

1 JESSICA. One evening, I asked my evening school teacher to tell me the real difference between "I was writing" and "I have written" . . . "Well," he said grandly, "The imperfect tense refers to what WAS, while the present perfect tense refers to what HAS BEEN."

Act I, "English," *Green Card 1986*

2663. Bella Akhmadulina (1937–)

1 But your eyes have changed
since those terrible old days
a hundred years ago,
when you died, alone in the house here,
poor, without work or friends."

"A Dream," Sts. 6–7, adapted by Jean Valentine, quoted in *Poets on Street Corners* by Olga Carlisle *1968*

2664. Ann Arensberg (1937–)

1 Accepting a sexless marriage is a gradual process, subject to lapses. Every night brings a fresh opportunity for regression, reviving the hope that two bodies lying side by side will catch fire spontaneously. When proximity fails to work its remembered magic, every night is a new occasion for disappointment.

Incubus 1998

2 Ancient peoples bared themselves to the moon in adoration, but they knew, while we have forgotten, that the moon rules over death as well as fruitfulness.

Ibid.

2665. Margaret Lowe Benston (1937–)

1 In sheer quantity, household labor, including child care, constitutes a huge amount of socially necessary production. Nevertheless, in a society based on commodity production, it is not usually considered as "real work" since it is outside of trade and the marketplace. . . . In a society in which money determines value, women are a group who work outside the money economy.

"The Political Economy of Women's Lib," *Monthly Review September 1969*

2 Once women are freed from private production in the home, it will probably be very difficult to maintain for any long period of time a rigid definition of jobs by sex.

Ibid.

3 Industrialization is, in itself, a great force for human good; exploitation and dehumanization go with capitalism and not necessarily with industrialization.

Ibid.

2666. Sallie Bingham (1937–)

1 . . . he wondered again, how much of her desire was passion and how much grasping: girls used sex to get a hold on you, he knew—it was so easy for them to pretend to be excited.

"Winter Term," *Mademoiselle July 1958*

2 The clock would never let him forget the amount of time he was wasting . . .

Ibid.

2667. Nora Brooks Blakely (1937?–)

1 Night sits inside and defeats the sun.

"To Grandmother's House We Go," St. 3 (1984), *The Woman That I Am, The Literature and Culture of Contemporary Women of Color*, D. Soyini Madison, ed. *1994*

2668. Elena Castedo-Ellerman (1937–)

1 "The best way to get where you want to be is to please those who own the road."

Paradise 1990

2669. Hélène Cixous (1937–)

1 Write your self. Your body must be heard.

"The Laugh of the Medusa," Keith Cohen and Paula Cohen, trs., *Signs: A Journal of Women in Culture and Society 1976*

2 I, too, overflow: my desires have invented new desires, my body knows unheard-of songs.

(p.487), Ibid.

3 Nearly the entire history of writing is confounded with the history of reason."

(p. 484), Ibid.

4 To Write [would be] an act which will not only "realize" the decensored relation of woman to her sexuality, . . . it will give her back her goods, her pleasures, her organs, her immense bodily territories which have been kept under seal . . .

Ibid.

5 [Women] take pleasure in jumbling the order of space, in disorienting it, in changing around the furniture, dislocating things and values, breaking them all up, emptying structures, and turning propriety upside down.

Ibid.

6 You only have to look at the Medusa
straight on to see her,
And she's not deadly. She's beautiful
and she's laughing.

Ibid.

2670. Maryse Condé (1937–)

1 I can't understand why I placed all my hopes in this man whom I didn't know from Adam. Probably because he came from Elsewhere. From over there. From the other side of the

water. He wasn't born on our island of malice that has been left to the hurricanes and the ravages caused by the spitefulness in the hearts of black folks.

Traversé de la Mangrove (*Crossing the Mangrove*, tr. 1995),
Richard Philcox, tr. *1989*

2   . . . the wounds of childhood do not heal.

Ibid.

3   "Maman, all that about slavery and shackles, that's ancient history. You've got to live with your times."

Ibid.

2671. Jane Fonda (1937–)

1   I don't care about the Oscar. I make movies to support the causes I believe in, not for any honors. I couldn't care less whether I win an Oscar or not.

Quoted in Prologue, *Jane: An Intimate Biography of Jane Fonda* by Thomas Kiernan *1973*

2   I didn't like what I saw the acting profession do to people who went into the theater. All the young actresses I've met are obsessed with the theater. They think and talk only about one thing. Nothing else matters to them. It's terribly unhealthy to sacrifice everything—family, children—for a goal. I hope I never get that way. I don't believe in concentrating your life in terms of one profession, no matter what it is.

Pt. II, Ch. 8 (c. 1958), Ibid.

3   Before I went into analysis, I told everyone lies—but when you spend all that money, you tell the truth. . . . Analysis has also taught me that you should know who to love and who to hate and who to just plain like, and it's important to know the difference.

Ch. 13, Ibid.

4   You can do one of two things: just shut up, which is something I don't find easy, or learn an awful lot very fast, which is what I tried to do.

Pt. IV, Ch. 22, Ibid.

5   Prostitutes are the inevitable product of a society that places ultimate importance on money, possessions and competition.

Ch. 24 (c.1970), Ibid.

6   All I can say is that through the people I've met, the experiences I've had, the reading I've done, I realize the American system must be changed. I see an alternative to the usual way of living and relating to people. And this alternative is a total change of our structures and institutions—through Socialism. Of course I am a Socialist. But without a theory, without an ideology.

Ch. 26 (c.1971), Ibid.

7   But the whole point of liberation is that you get out. Restructure your life. Act by yourself.

Quoted in "At Home with Tom* and Jane" by Danae Brook, *Los Angeles Weekly 28 November– 4 December 1980*

*Reference to Tom Hayden, American politician and activist (1941–) who was one of the Chicago Seven in 1968 and later became a state legislator of California; once married to Fonda.

8   When a child enters the world through you, it alters everything on a psychic, psychological and purely practical level. You're just not free anymore to do what you want to do. And it's not the same again. Ever.

Ibid.

9   I am not a do-gooder. I am a revolutionary. A revolutionary woman.

Comment (1971), Ibid.

10   [Coco Chanel]* freed us from the corset. You know, the foot in the back, Scarlett O'Hara,** whalebone corset. If you get a strong emotion, be it fear, sadness, anger, what happens? You pass out. Women don't pass out today. You know why? We can breathe. She stripped us of the corset. She put the A-frame dress on us, showed our legs, removed the focus from the waist, bobbed our hair, and we were off and running.

"100 Years of Great Women," *ABC News Special with Barbara Walters*** 30 April 1999*

*See 1498. **Reference to central character in Margaret Mitchell's *Gone with the Wind*; see 1772:1–18. ***See 2480.

2672. Kathleen Fraser (1937–)

1   He is all of him urge.

Untitled poem, *What I Want 1974*

2   I think you have many shelves
but never put love there.

Ibid.

3   "Personal things is all I care about."

Ibid.

2673. Nancy Friday (1937–)

1   Anger broke the pane of glass between us.

Ch. 1, *My Mother, My Self 1977*

2   Spontaneous and honest love admits errors, hesitations, and human failings; it can be tested and repaired. Idealized love ties us because we already intuit that it is unreal and are afraid to face this truth.

Ibid.

3   The older I get, the more of my mother I see in myself.

Ibid.

4   We are the loving sex; people count on us for comfort, nurturing warmth. We hold the world together with the constant availability of our love when men would tear it apart with their needs for power.

Ibid.

5   It was the promise of men, that around each corner there was yet another man, more wonderful than the last, that sustained me. You see, I had men confused with life. . . . You can't get what I wanted from a man, not in this life.

Ch. 8, Ibid.

2674. Gail Godwin (1937–)

1   "The only reason people forget is because they want to. If we were all clear, with no aberrations, we could remember everything, before we were born, even."

Ch. 1, *The Perfectionists 1970*

2   Anchored by the heavy bright heat, she closed her eyes and ears and let it press her down. *Let* the sun bake her senseless in the hottest part of the day. Let it broil her brain free of all complexities. Let it burn her back into the same earth which held the bones of ancient peasants and the decayed petals of bygone flowers. She did not wish to compete, or to understand or to participate anymore . . . She felt tight in the head,

like something was growing—a flower someone planted in a pot too small.

Ch. 2, Ibid.

3 "You sort of glitter rather than glow. Small talk comes easy to you. You dress well. You are all crisp, sharp edges. You look like one of those young career women on the go."

Ch. 8, Ibid.

4 "With a husband you have to keep up appearances. I don't care who says not. They have their aura, we have ours. They are eternally different auras."

Ch. 12, Ibid.

5 . . . though all came to horrible ends, they kept track of themselves so beautifully along the way.

The Odd Woman 1974

6 . . . trying to organize the loneliness and the weather and the long night into something of abiding shape and beauty.

Ibid.

7 . . . life is a disease. . . .

Ibid.

8 "Good teaching is one-fourth preparation and three-fourths theatre. . . ."

Ibid.

9 I turn into an anachronism every time I come home, she thought angrily. I start measuring myself by standards thirty, fifty, a hundred years old.

Ibid.

10 I believe that dreams transport us through the undersides of our days, and that if we wish to become acquainted with the dark side of what we are, the signposts are there, waiting for us to translate them. Dreams say what they mean, but they don't say it in daytime language.

Ch. 1, The Finishing School 1984

11 Actors between plays are like ghosts looking for bodies to inhabit.

Ch. 7, Ibid.

12 Did I have to drive one hundred miles, and another hundred back, to discover that memory does not reside in places? Places have their own continuing lives. Memory lives in the brain of the rememberer.

Ibid.

13 Death is not the enemy; age is not the enemy. These things are inevitable, they happen to everybody. But what we ought to fear is the kind of death that happens in life. It can happen at any time. You're going along, and then, at some point, you congeal. You solidify at a certain point and from then on your life is doomed to be a repetition of what you have done before. That's the enemy.

Ibid.

14 "The best antidote I have found is to yearn for something. As long as you yearn, you can't congeal: there is a forward motion to yearning."

Ibid.

15 "I was thinking how nice it would be to be a character in one of your novels . . . you take care of [your characters] so nicely. You let them suffer a little, just enough to improve their char-

acters, but you always rescue them from the abyss at the last minute and reward them with love or money or the perfect job—or sometimes all three."

A Southern Family 1987

16 " . . . the Great Uncouth has taken up permanent residence inside me."

The Good Husband 1994

17 Mates are not always matches and matches are not always mates.

Ibid.

2675. Lois Gould (1937–)

1 Danny Mack got past the nurses at two-fifteen by impersonating a doctor. All he did was clip four ballpoint pens on his vest pocket and march in looking preoccupied.

Such Good Friends 1970

2 "Hogamous, Higamous, men are polygamous, Higamous, Hogamous, women monogamous."

Ibid.

3 Life is the only sentence which doesn't end with a period.

Ibid.

4 *Things* have squatter's rights; why else do we call them *belongings*?

Ibid.

5 . . . you can't . . . sneak around trying to correct the conjugal imbalance sheet: doing unto others what I did last night. The sheer symmetry of it scares people; how can they tell the victims from the perpetrators? In the dark they are all to blame.

Ibid.

6 " . . . the city *requires* a funeral . . . All the ordinances are designed with your friendly funeral directors in mind—not to mention the cemeteries and coffin makers and gravestone cutters."

Ibid.

7 What it is, I guess, is that I don't really miss *him*; I miss something that must have been *us*. Because we *were* something, in spite of each other, weren't we?

Ibid.

8 One of the new computers in the billing department had gone berserk, possibly from the strain of replacing five elderly bookkeepers, and a hundred thousand dollars' worth of credit had been erroneously issued to delinquent charge account customers before anyone caught it.

Necessary Objects 1972

9 Making love as if it were something one could make, as if it were making do or making believe. Hating her own hands, hating the thin desperate clinging body that responded by heart to echoes of old movements, like a mechanical toy . . . Its working was an unbearable affront; it accused her. It made her admit the truth. I don't care if it still works, I hate it—*I don't want it any more*.

Ibid.

10 "We are selling elegance. The idea of elegance. Throwaway chic, we are the last *word* in throwaway chic . . . We have an image. I have. Either we can afford to be subtle, either we live *up* to the image, or we're just another tacky dress shop. I mean, if we've got it, I say we don't *have* to flaunt it."

Ibid.

11 Amos Lowen taught his daughters carefully that poor was a curse word, and that if money couldn't buy happiness—a point he never conceded—there were still plenty of other selections.

Ibid.

12 She hated the powdered oil smell they put on the baby. Rubbing away all his natural sourness and anointing him with foreign substances that were all ironically labeled *Baby*. So that he would never recognize his own body in the dark, the way she could recognize hers now. Small victory, discovering your acrid identity after eighteen years. Buried alive under thousands of layers of powdered oil.

Ibid.

13 "Why the hell don't women ever make a scene? Men are *always* making scenes, yelling in the halls. Why can't *you* yell in the halls?"

"Because," she sighed, "women don't get away with yelling in the halls. They call you a hysterical bitch if you yell in the halls."

"Also," Sophy noted wryly, "they fire you. It's *their* halls."

Final Analysis 1974

14 "Women always run away," she said. "That's why women never get to run anything else. They can't stand the heat, so they get *back* in the kitchen."

Ibid.

15 She burst into tears. Just like a woman. Tears of rage: the ultimate toy weapon.

Ibid.

16 Make up. Meaning invent. Make up something more acceptable, because that face you have on right there will not do.

Ibid.

17 The only reason I hated him was that I had needed him so much. That's when I found out about need. It goes much better with hate than with love.

Ibid.

2676. Brooke Hayward (1937–)

1 I thought for a whole minute while my heart stopped and my eyes blinked and my face flushed with fury. It was a trick question, two-sided, flipping back and forth, now-you-see-it-now-you-don't, the trick of a supreme magician who could—with cunning legerdemain under a silk handkerchief —transform a few seconds of tranquility into an eternity of chaos. The truth: no, I did not, under any circumstances whatsoever, wish to share the doll's house with Bridget. . . . Or the truth: yes, of course I wanted to share the doll's house with Bridget, because not only would that please mother and demonstrate how generous and grown up I really was but because I knew that I loved Bridget very deeply and identified with her yearning as she tentatively touched the miniature grandfather's clock in the miniature hallway. (Get your nasty little fingers out of there, I wanted to scream, until I give you permission.)

Haywire 1978

2677. Bessie Head (1937–)

1 But in a society like this, which man cared to be owned and possessed when there were so many women freely available? And even all the excessive love-making was purposeless, aimless, just like tipping everything into an awful cesspit where no one really cared to take a second look.

Ch. 8, *When Rain Clouds Gather* 1968

2 And if the white man thought that Asians were a low filthy nation, Asians could still smile with relief—at least, they were not Africans. And if the white man thought that Africans were a low, filthy nation, Africans in southern Africa could still smile—at least, they were not bushmen. They all have their monsters.

Pt. I, *Maru* 1971

3 He wanted a flower garden of yellow daisies because they were the only flower which resembled the face of his wife and the sun of his love.

Ibid.

4 Love is mutually feeding each other, not one living on another like a ghoul.

A Question of Power 1973

2678. Tina Howe (1937–)

1 SANDY. When I looked in the mirror this morning, I saw an old lady. Not old old, just used up.

Birth and After Birth, with Honor Moore* 1974
*See 3061.

2 Young mothers inhabit rather wild territory.

"Tina Howe," *Interviews with Contemporary Women Playwrights*, Kathleen Betsko* and Rachel Koenig 1987
*See 2739.

3 The reason to pick up the pen or the paint brush is to fight back.

Ibid.

4 I've always thought women were much more dangerous than men.

Ibid.

2679. Ann Jones (1937–)

1 As we drove on toward Lovedu* land, we tried to imagine what it might mean to be a queen in Africa. All around us, all along the way, we saw women doing nothing but work. Debo,** who had been filming *Women at Work*, had footage of women hoeing, planting crops, weeding, harvesting, gathering wild edibles, shucking maize, pounding maize, grinding maize at the mill, carrying maize meal home, chopping wood, gathering firewood, carrying firewood home on their heads or on their backs, building fires, cooking, serving food, washing dishes, scouring pots, making clothes, buying clothes, washing clothes (after first carrying the laundry to the river, or carrying the river water home), selling clothes and just about anything else in the marketplace or beside the road, building houses, painting houses, gathering thatch, preparing mud plaster, polishing floors with cattle dung (to keep out insects), scrubbing floors, weaving palm fibers, making mats, making baskets, making hats, dyeing fabrics, sewing, knitting, embroidering, making pots, minding children, doctoring children, teaching children, feeding children, washing children, dressing children, plaiting hair, milking cows, feeding chickens, butchering chickens, shopping, making brooms, sweeping houses, sweeping yards, cleaning churches, cleaning wells, planting trees and keeping accounts. So far she had no footage at all of women being queen. What would a queen *do*?

"Finding the Lovedu," *The Women's Review of Books*, Vol. XV, No. 5 February 1998
*A Southern African people. **Debo Kinsland, Australian–born British-based filmmaker.

2 . . . the Lovedu believe that only a fool fails to find peaceable compromise, and only the truly stupid come to blows. Com-

promise, appeasement, reconciliation, tolerance, peace. The great ideals of Lovedu culture.

Ibid.

3 And I remember how she'd laughed and what she'd said in response to Debo's last question: "Your majesty, is there something of importance that you and your people could teach the people of the West?"

"Yes," the Queen said. "We could teach you to dance."

Ibid.

2680. Jan Karon (1937–)

1 God wastes nothing.

Quoted in "Down-home Jan Karon..," Nanci Helmlmich,
USA Today 14 April 1999

2 You used to have to be a rock star to be a celebrity; but there's such a craving for celebrity now that just any old body can be one.

Ibid.

3 There were times when he didn't like being a priest, always on the front line for justice and mercy and forgiveness and redemption; trying to figure out the mind of God; giving the Lord his personal agenda, then standing around waiting for it to be fulfilled. He didn't have an agenda for Morris Love, anymore; he was giving up the entire self-seeking, willful notion.

A New Song 1999

2681. Barbara J. Love (1937–)

Coauthor with Sidney Abbot; see 2661: 1–4.

2682. Lois Lowry (1937–)

1 . . . it was the sort of thing one didn't ask a friend about because it might have fallen into that uncomfortable category of "being different." Asher took a pill each morning; Jonas did not. Always better, less rude, to talk about things that were the same.

The Giver 1993

2 "Why can't everyone see them? Why did colors disappear?"
The Giver shrugged. "Our people made that choice, the choice to go to Sameness . . . .We gained control of many things. But we had to let go of others."

Ibid.

2683. Lydia Phindile Makhubu (1937–)

1 In my opinion, the major reason for the survival of the traditional system [of African medicine] in spite of the modern ways of life, is its approach. It is a holistic system utilizing treatment which focuses not only on symptoms but also on psychological and sociological factors.

The Traditional Healer 1978

2 I'm very concerned about the appreciation of science, not only among those who had a formal education in science but the nation as a whole . . . because I think there is a very strong relationship between our everyday life and science.

Ibid.

3 Some of Africa's greatest concerns today include finding ways to increase food production, to manage natural resources and the environment, nutrition, improved health and education. These areas are in many ways related to those in which women have traditionally found their functions.

Ibid.

2684. Marabel Morgan (1937–)

1 Be prepared mentally and physically for intercourse every night this week.

The Total Woman 1973

2685. Liane Norman (1937–)

1 If conscience is regarded as imperative, then compliance with its dictates commends a society not to forgive, but to celebrate, its conscientious citizens.

"Selective Conscientious Objection," *The Center Magazine May/June 1972*

2 While the State may respectfully require obedience on many matters, it cannot violate the moral nature of a man, convert him into a serviceable criminal, and expect his loyalty and devotion.

Ibid.

3 Whenever government's interests become by definition more substantial than the humanity of its citizens, the drift toward government by divine right gathers momentum.

Ibid.

4 To kill implies that the claims of some men to life are better than others . . .

Ibid.

2686. Eleanor Holmes Norton (1937–)

1 Racial oppression of black people in America has done what neither class oppression nor sexual oppression, with all their perniciousness, has ever done: destroyed an entire people and their culture.

"For Sadie and Maude," *Sisterhood Is Powerful*, Robin Morgan,* ed. *1970*

*See 2864.

2 There is no reason to repeat bad history.

Ibid.

3 With children no longer the universally accepted reason for marriage, marriages are going to have to exist on their own merits.

Ibid.

4 On the road to equality there is no better place for blacks to detour around American values than in forgoing its example in the treatment of its women and the organization of its family life.

Ibid.

5 The only way to make sure people you agree with can speak is to support the rights of people you don't agree with.

Quoted in *New York Post 28 March 1970*

6 There are not many males, black or white, who wish to get involved with a woman who's committed to her own development.

Quoted in "The Black Family and Feminism" by C. Ware, *The First Ms. Reader*, Francine Klagsbrun, ed. *1972*

7 The essence of a free life is being able to choose the style of living you prefer free from exclusion and without the compulsion of conformity or law.

Commencement address, Barnard College *6 June 1972*

8 But feminist change is both irresistible and irreversible. American women are part of an international movement that affects virtually every country in the world.

Speech, National Women's Political Caucus Conference (Albuquerque, New Mexico) *July 1981*

2687. Mary Oliver (1935–)

1 You do not have to be good.
You do not have to walk on your knees
for a hundred miles through the desert, repenting.
You only have to let the soft animal of your body
love what it loves
> "Wild Geese," *Dream Work* 1986

2 Whoever you are, no matter how lonely,
the world offers itself to your imagination,
calls to you like the wild geese, harsh and exciting—
over and over announcing your place
in the family of things.
> Ibid.

3 One day you finally knew
what you had to do, and began,
though the voices around you
kept shouting
their bad advice—
> "The Journey," Ibid.

4 Is the soul solid, like iron?
or is it tender and breakable, like
the wings of a moth in the beak of an owl?
> "Some Questions You Might Ask," *New and
Selected Poems* 1992

5 This morning the green fists of the peonies are getting ready to
break my heart

as the sun rises,

as the sun strokes them with his old, buttery fingers
> "Peonies," Ibid.

6 Do you love this world?

Do you cherish your humble and silky life?

Do you adore the green grass, with its terror beneath?
> Ibid.

7 [The writing of poetry is] a kind of possible love affair between something like the heart (that courageous but also shy factory of emotion) and the learned skills of the conscious mind.
> *A Poetry Handbook* 1995

8 . . . creative work needs the whole sky to fly in, and no eye watching until it comes to that certainty which it aspires to . . .
> *Blue Pastures: New and Selected Poems* 1995

9 I put my face close to the lily, where it stands just above the grass, and give it a good greeting from the stem of my heart.
> Ibid.

10 How can I hope to be friends
with the hard white stars
whose flaring and hissing are not speech
but a pure radiance?
How can I hope to be friends
with the yawning spaces between them
where nothing, ever, is spoken?"
> "Stars," *West Wind* 1998

11 the sunlight and shadows are chasing each other
> "The Dog Has Run Off Again," Ibid.

12 little curls little shafts
of letters words
little flames leaping
> "Forty Years," Ibid.

13 The world is made up of cats, and cattle, and fenceposts!
> *Winter Hours* 1999

14 Only oddly, and not naturally . . . are we found, while awake, in the posture of deliberate or hapless inaction. But such is the posture of the poet, poor laborer.
> Ibid.

15 . . . the nudge, the prick of the instant, the flame of appreciation that shoots from my heels to my head when compass grass bends its frilled branches and draws a perfect circle on the cold sand.
> Ibid.

16 Everything is all right, say the meter and the rhyme; everything is not all right, say the words.
> Essay on Robert Frost,* Ibid.

*American poet (1874–1963).

17 But I am devoted to Nature too, and to consider Nature without this appetite—this other–creature-consuming appetite—is to look with shut eyes upon the miraculous interchange that makes things work . . . .
> "Sister Turtle," Ibid.

2688. Alicia Suskin Ostriker (1937–)

1 Anyway, what is the soul
But a dream of itself?
> "Message from the Sleeper at Hell's Mouth," *A Woman
Under the Surface* 1982

2 Fearful, I see my hand is on the latch
I am the woman, and about to enter.
> "A Meditation in Seven Days," *Green Age* 1989

3 Was I succulent? Was I juicy?
> "Mastectomy," *The Crack in Everything* 1996

4 Like one of those trees with a major limb lopped,
I'm a shade more sublime today than yesterday
> "Normal," *The Little Space : Poems Selected and New,
1968–1998* 1998

5 What woman doesn't die in childbirth
What child doesn't murder the mother.
> "Surviving," Ibid.

6 How can the broken mothers teach us?
> Ibid.

7 As if there could be a world
Of absolute innocence
In which we forget ourselves
> "The Dogs at Live Oak Beach, Santa Cruz ," Ibid.

8 this wounded
World that we cannot heal, that is our bride.
> "The Eighth and Thirteenth," Ibid.

9 Whatever I can grasp of human experience within my art—the good and beautiful, the evil and chaotic. I tell my students that they must write what they are afraid to write; and I attempt to do so myself.
> Ibid.

10 Art destroys silence

Ibid.

11 My proposals, or should I say requirements,
    Include at least one image of a god,
    Virile, beard optional, one of a goddess
    Nubile, breast size approximating mine,
    One divine baby, one lion, one lamb,
    All nude as figs, all dancing wildly . . .

"Everywoman Her Own Theology," Ibid.

12 we would need an archaeology
    Of pain to trace the course of this frozen river.

"The War of Men and Women," Ibid.

13 Express your anger like a swan.

"About Time," Ibid.

14 The painting is never what is *there*,
    It throbs with the mystery
    Of your own sick-to-death soul
    Which demands, like everything alive,
    Love.

"From the Prado Rotunda: The Family of Charles IV, and
Others," Ibid.

2689. Tey Diana Rebolledo (1937–)

1 Privileging the theoretical discourse de-privileges ourselves.

"The Politics of Poetics . . . ," *The Americas Review*, 16
1988

2 We have internalized the dominant ideology so that only by
    talking theory (construed as a superior form of logic) can our
    literature and our cultural practices be intellectually viable,
    that is, acceptable within the traditional academic canon as
    "legitimate."

Ibid.

3 We have entered into the "Age of Criticism" which could be
    defined as a preoccupation with theoretical structures often
    not internalized: we feel that theory is power.

Ibid.

4 While contemporary writers may feel that they are seeing the
    world anew, those of us who are searching out our literary
    roots are finding women writers who were raising many of the
    same concerns women voice today—written in a different tone
    and style and conforming to a different mode; nevertheless,
    contemporary writers have not arisen from a complete void. If
    the written word did not survive in enough texts to be known
    today, nonetheless the oral forms of women's concerns, of
    women's images have lived in the tradition from one genera-
    tion, from one century to another. Thus the critic as literary
    historian is able to fill in the lacunae and to connect the past
    and the present.

Ibid.

5 In the search for our own aesthetic, for our own analytical direc-
    tion, we need to look to each other, to recognize that our
    literature and our cultural production does not need legitimiza-
    tion from the academy, that it already is legitimate in itself.

Ibid.

2690. Caryl Rivers (1937–)

1 . . . a more apt animal metaphor [for the media] . . . might be
    Garfield—fat, cynical, slovenly, hanging on the screen door by

his toenails for lack of anything better to do, thinking *Bored.
Bored. Bored. I'm so bored I could* scream!

*Slick Spins and Fractured Facts: How Cultural Myths
Distort the News* 1996

2 The laziness of pack journalism allows cultural stereotypes to
    multiply like bacteria on the locker-room floor. Your best bet,
    if you'd really like a glimpse of the press at work, is just to put
    the Friskies out on the porch.

Ibid.

3 In newsrooms all across the country interest in the powerless
    and the wretched is waning.

Ibid.

4 The picture of the poor—welfare mothers in particular—that
    has emerged from the media as I write has been one that is so
    savage, so lacking in compassion, that it takes my breath
    away . . . .So what if white-collar crooks make off with mil-
    lions, and the welfare queen bilks us out of a couple of thou?
    She's the one we'd like to throttle. . . . [we] hate welfare
    mothers.

Ibid.

2691. Jill Ruckelshaus (1937–)

1 It occurred to me when I was thirteen and wearing white
    gloves and Mary Janes and going to dancing school, that no
    one should have to dance backward all their lives.

Speech 1973

2 The family is the building block for whatever solidarity there
    is in society.

Quoted in "Jill Ruckelshaus: Lady of Liberty" by Frederic
A. Birmingham, *Saturday Evening Post* 3 March 1973

3 The best way to win an argument is to begin by being right . . .

Ibid.

4 What the emergence of woman as a political force means is
    that we are quite ready now to take on responsibilities as
    equals, not protected partners.

Ibid.

5 I have no hostility towards men. Some of my best friends are
    men. I married a man, and my father was a man.

Ibid.

6 Women's rights in essence is really a movement for freedom, a
    movement for equality, for the dignity of all women, for those
    who work outside the home and those who dedicate them-
    selves with more altruism than any profession I know to being
    wives and mothers, cooks and chauffeurs, decorators and child
    psychologists and loving human beings.

Ibid.

7 The Equal Rights Amendment * is designed to establish in our
    Constitution the clear moral value judgment that all Ameri-
    cans, women and men, stand equal under the law . . . It will
    give woman's role in the home new status, recognizing that the
    homemaker's role in a marriage has economic value . . . Critics
    say ERA will open the draft to women. At the moment, the
    United States has an oversubscribed volunteer army, many of
    whom are women. ERA means that women who serve will get
    equal benefits.

Quoted in "Forum," *Ladies' Home Journal* August 1975
*See Alice Paul, 1538.

2692. Rosemary Radford Ruether (1937–)

1 Feminist theology cannot be done from the existing base of the Christian Bible.

Womanguides: Reading Toward a Feminist Theology 1985

2 It is through generating stories of our own crisis and hope and telling them to one another that we light the path.

Ibid.

3 Vulgar Catholicism meant dogmatic, narrow-minded pastors who made you feel like you were on the road to hell if you ate hamburger on Friday and nuns who were shocked because, as an art student, I was drawing nudes at the age of 13. Authentic Catholicism was intellectually sophisticated and united with deep sacramental and contemplative spirituality and corporal works of mercy.

"A Wise Woman," The Christian Century 17 February 1993

4 The center of [my mother's] being was cultured leisure, in the sense of the cultivation of the mind, heart and soul through prayer, intellectual thought and service. This was more a state of being than of particular activities.

Ibid.

5 I went to college to cultivate my mind, and it was the purest accident that this turned out also to be preparation for employment.

Ibid.

2693. Dinae B. Schulder (1937–)

1 Law is a reflection and a source of prejudice. It both enforces and suggests forms of bias.

"Does the Law Oppress Women?," Sisterhood Is Powerful, Robin Morgan,* ed. 1970

*See 2864.

2 Legislation and case law still exist in some parts of the United States permitting the "passion shooting" by a husband of a wife; the reverse, of course, is known as homicide.

Ibid.

3 . . . prejudice (the mythology of class oppression) is enshrined in laws. Laws lead to enforcement of practices. Practices reinforce and lead to prejudice. The cycle continues . . .

Ibid.

2694. Evelyn Elizabeth Smith (1937?–)

1 Enemies whispered that he had bewitched the voting machines, but that wasn't true; he'd won fair and square through mass hypnosis.

The Martian and the Magician 1952

2 That's always the way when you discover something new; everybody thinks you're crazy.

Ibid.

3 It turned out that all the scientists had been doing the same thing, making a lot of hoopla about inventing stuff—atom bombs, jet planes, television—when actually they did it all with witchcraft. Seems all the magicians had gone underground since the Age of Enlightenment and had been passing off their feats as science—except for a few unreconstructed gypsies.

Ibid.

2695. Margo St. James (1937–)

1 A conservative estimate would be that 90 percent of politicians patronize public women. Imagine the wealth of information available for bringing "undercover" pressure to bear regarding passage of certain legislation concerning minors, women, minorities, religious and political freedoms.

Quoted in The Realist, No. 94 October 1972

2 I did not find the business [prostitution] all that disgusting. You pick your customers, you meet interesting people and youth is not a prerequisite.

Quoted in "St. James Still Hustling In Grand Old Party Style" by Allison Engel, San Jose Mercury 23 October 1978

3 Punishing the prostitute promotes the rape of all women. When prostitution is a crime, the message conveyed is that women who are sexual are "bad," and therefore legitimate weapons of sexual assault.

Quoted in "Margo" by Mildred Hamilton, San Francisco Examiner 29 April 1979

2696. Rita Süssmuth (1937–)

1 . . . we can expect from women different approaches and solutions to a number of problems connected with people living together . . . [because] women tend to approach problems in a more pragmatic and action-oriented way which is more closely related to real life.

Quoted in the Kölner Staadt-Arzeiger, weekend edition, 4 2–3 October 1993

2697. Jennifer Tipton (1937–)

1 I often do feel that theatre might truly save the world. It is that expression on a stage in front of an audience—not the global communication that film and television can give—that tells us how we see ourselves, how we can better ourselves. It doesn't mean that all plays should be beautiful—we can better ourselves by picturing the worst, too. I'm deeply committed to theatre in all its forms.

Quoted in "The Facts of Light" by Arnold Aronson, American Theatre (New York) January 1986

2 You have to see the dancer to know what is going on, whereas in theatre that's not necessarily true; information can come from language.

Ibid.

2698. Diane Wakoski (1937–)

1 thinking how cage life drove an animal into mazes of himself, his cage mates chosen for him his life circumscribed and focused
on eating, his play watched by it-doesn't-matter-whom, just watched, always watched.

"The Birds of Paradise Being Very Plain Birds," St. 5, The East Side Scene, Allen de Loach, ed. 1968

2 It happens all the time, I told her,
some of us have bad vision, are crippled, have defects, and our reality is a different one, not the correct and ascertainable one, and sometimes it makes us dotty and lonely but also it makes us poets.

St. 9, Ibid.

3 My face
that my friends tell me is so full of character;
my face
I have hated for so many years;
my face

I have made an angry contract to live with
though no one could love it.
"I Have Had to Learn to Live with My Face," St. 2, *The
Motorcycle Betrayal Poems 1971*

4   I wonder how we learn to live
without faces?
They must hide so much pain,
so many deep trenches of blood,
so much that would terrorize and drive others
    away, if they
could see it. The struggle to control it
articulates the face
St. 12, Ibid.

5   When I touch the man
I love,
I want to thank my mother for giving me
piano lessons
all those years,
keeping the memory of Beethoven,
a deaf tortured man,
in mind;
of the beauty that can come
from even an ugly
past.
"Thanking My Mother For Piano Lessons," St. 12, Ibid.

6   Mother-love: that is the only kind of love women are supposed
to have; more importantly, there is no metaphor for women to
be writers, singers, Orphic voices echoing the beauty of their
longing and lost desire for the perfect mate or lost love.
"Lost and found," *The Women's Review
of Books*, Vol. XII, Nos. 10–11
July 1995

2699. Jill Paton Walsh (1937–)
1   . . . no money has ever been minted which could pay for such
conduct.
Grace 1994

2   Morning knowledge is different from evening knowledge.
[Morning knowledge deals with] the nature of a straight line;
evening knowledge is knowing that no line in the world is really straight.
A Knowledge of Angels 1995

3   Things just are.
Ibid.

4   "The world is more fun by far now it has you in it!"
When I Was Little Like You 1997

2700. Eleanor Wilner (1937–)
1   The woman, says the holy man, can never
escape from *maya*; it grows in her like maggots
in tainted meat, and drives her from his holy ground.
"maya" (p. 290), *maya 1979*

2   birds came down
to feed and sing the summer into grass.
"See–Saw" (p. 239), Ibid.

3   You can be chosen
or you can choose. Not both.
"Sarah's Choice" (p. 166), *Sarah's Choice 1989*

4   as the bombs drop, as the world
splits open, as the mothers
reach for their own
in the night of the falling
sky, madness in
method, nature gone
into reverse.
"Bat Cave" (p. 96), *Otherwise 1993*

5   young men . . . filing into the black
belly of a huge cargo plane, each with a woman
in his wallet, her words on lilac paper,
her distant image as his aphrodisiac
in hell.
"Ume: Plum," (p. 100), Ibid.

6   for there is no enlightenment
without immersion.
"Blessing," *Reversing the Spell 1997*

7   Shall we paste up the placards
of a revolution in which we no
longer believe?
"Up Against It" (p. 66), Ibid.

2701. Zhang Jie (1937–)
1   What do a few lies on TV matter? They can be swallowed, digested and excreted, or follow people when they doze off to
sink into oblivion.
"What's Wrong with Him?," *As Long as Nothing Happens,
Nothing Will 1981*

2   I am thirty, the same age as our People's Republic. For a re-
public thirty is still young. But a girl of thirty is virtually on
the shelf.
"Love Must Not Be Forgotten" (1979) Gladys Yang,* tr.,
Seven Contemporary Chinese Women Writers, Gladys
Yang,* ed. 1982
*See 2452.

3   Though not bound together by earthly laws or morality,
though they never once clasped hands, each possessed the
other completely. Nothing could part them. Centuries to come,
if one white cloud trails another, two grasses grow side by side,
one wave splashes another . . . believe me, that will be them.
Ibid.

4   I long to shout: "Mind your own business! Let us wait patiently for our counterparts. Even waiting in vain is better than
willy-nilly marriage. To live single is not such a fearful disaster.
I believe it may be a sign of a step forward in culture, education and the quality of life."
Ibid.

5   No human emotion can transcend the social conditions
around it.
Quoted in "The Art of the Chinese Writer" by
Bruce Shenitz, *Newsweek* (New York) *26 May 1986*

6   In China since the founding of the People's Republic, women
have won equal rights in the social and economical spheres.
But in social consciousness there is still a skepticism of women's
abilities and there is still a degree of disrespect for women's dignity. But I don't think this problem can be solved by feminism
alone. It depends on the progress of mankind as a whole, and
that includes both material and spiritual progress.
Ibid.

7 . . . there's no absolute freedom anywhere in the world. Freedom is always relative.

> Ibid.

2702. Jane Chambers (1937–1983)

1 ELLIE. When I was your age, "lesbian" was a dictionary word used only to frighten teenage girls and parents. Mothers fainted, fathers became violent, landlords evicted you, and nobody would hire you. A Lesbian was like a vampire: she looked in the mirror and there was no reflection.

> *A Late Snow 1974*

2703. Renata Adler (1938–)

1 The writer has a grudge against society, which he documents with accounts of unsatisfying sex, unrealized ambition, unmitigated loneliness, and a sense of local and global distress. The square, overpopulation, the bourgeois, the bomb and the cocktail party are variously identified as sources of the grudge. There follows a little obscenity here, a dash of philosophy there, considerable whining overall, and a modern satirical novel is born.

> "Salt into Old Scars" (22 June 1963), *Toward a Radical Middle 1969*

2 If anything has characterized the [peace] movement, from its beginning and in all its parts, it has been a spirit of decentralization, local autonomy, personal choice, and freedom from dogma.

> "Early Radicalism: The Price Of Peace Is Confusion" (11 December 1965), Ibid.

3 . . . nothing defines the quality of life in a community more clearly than people who regard themselves, or whom the consensus chooses to regard, as mentally unwell.

> "The Thursday Group" (15 April 1967), Ibid.

4 I . . . doubt that film can ever argue effectively against its own material: that a genuine antiwar film, say, can be made on the basis of even the ugliest battle scenes. . . . the medium is somehow unsuited to moral lessons, cautionary tales or polemics of any kind. If you want to make a pacifist film, you must make an exemplary film about peaceful men.

> "The Movies Make Heroes of Them All" (7 January 1968), *A Year in the Dark: Journal of a Film Critic, 1968–69 1970*

5 At six one morning, Will went out in jeans and frayed sweater to buy a quart of milk. A tourist bus went by. The megaphone was directed at him. "There's one," it said. That was in the 1960s. Ever since, he's wondered. There's one what?

> *Speedboat 1976*

6 In the strange heat all litigation brings to bear on things, the very process of litigation fosters the most profound misunderstandings in the world.

> *Lawyer's Wit and Wisdom*, Bruce Nash, Allan Zullo, eds.; Kathryn Zullo, compiler *1995*

2704. Ti-Grace Atkinson (1938?–)

1 The continuance of the inheritance idea—the idea of living on through things, property, children—subverts any possibility of the communal society succeeding. For people to live communally instead of competitively, the bonds of inheritance must be completely broken.

> Quoted in "The Second Feminist Wave" by Martha Weinman Lear, *The New York Times Magazine 10 March 1968*

2 Love is the victim's response to the rapist.

> Quoted in "Rebellion," *Sunday Times Magazine* (London) *14 September 1969*

3 Feminism is the theory; Lesbianism is the practice.

> Attributed *n.d.*

2705. Rona Barrett (1938–)

1 It's ironic, but until you can free those final monsters within the jungle of yourself, your life, your soul is up for grabs.

> Prologue, *Miss Rona: An Autobiography 1974*

2 . . . the *healthy*, the *strong* individual, is the one who asks for help when he needs it. Whether he's got an abscess on his knee or in his soul.

> Ch. 15, Ibid.

2706. Simone Benmussa (1938?–)

1 ALBERT NOBBS. I thought that regrets had passed away with the petticoats. But you've awakened the woman in me. You've brought it all up again.

> "Albert Nobbs' Tale," *The Singular Life of Albert Nobbs 1977*

2 That a woman must cease to be a woman in order to assert her right to work is a fact too often forgotten in the class struggle, a fact which appears in a different form today [than in the nineteenth century], but which is still as tenacious.

> Quoted in *Feminism and Theatre* by Sue-Ellen Case* *1988*
> *See 3625.

2707. Mary Frances Berry (1938–)

1 When it comes to justice, I take no prisoners and I don't believe in compromising.

> *Lawyer's Wit and Wisdom*, Bruce Nash, Allan Zullo, eds.; Kathryn Zullo, compiler *1995*

2708. Judy Blume (1938–)

1 "Are you there God? It's me, Margaret.
I just told my mother I want a bra.
Please help me grow God. You know where.
I want to be like everyone else."

> *Are You There God? It's Me, Margaret 1970*

2709. Helen Caldicott (1938–)

1 We are the curators of life on earth. We hold it in the palm of our hand.

> Remark *n.d.*

2710. Caryl Churchill (1938–)

1 CLEGG (speaking of his successful wife). It's very like having a talking dog, and it's on the front page at breakfast, the radio at dinner, the television at night—that's mine, look, that's my clever dog. But a time comes when you say, Heel. Home. Lie down.

> *Owners 1972*

2 MARION. I can't be a failure just to help.

> Ibid.

3 WIFE. But women can't preach. We bear children in pain, that's why. And they die. For our sin. Eve's sin. That's why we have

pain. We're not clean. We have to obey. The man, whatever he's like. If he beats us that's why. We have blood, we're shameful, our bodies are worse than a man's. All bodies are evil but ours is worst. That's why we can't speak [in church].
Light Shining in Buckinghamshire 1976

4   I rapidly left the interesting theory that witchcraft had existed as a survival of suppressed pre-Christian religions and went instead for the theory that witchcraft existed in the minds of its persecutors, that "witches" were a scapegoat in times of stress like Jews and blacks. I discovered for the first time the extent of Christian teaching against women and saw the connections between medieval attitudes to witches and continuing attitudes to women in general.
Quoted in Introduction to *Vinegar Tom 1976*

5   JOAN. Women, children, and lunatics can't be Pope.
Act I, Sc. 1, *Top Girls 1982*

6   NELL. Because that's what an employer is going to have doubts about with a lady as I needn't tell you, whether she's got the guts to push through to a closing situation. They think we're too nice. They think we listen to the buyer's doubts. They think we consider his needs and his feelings.
Act II, Sc. 1, Ibid.

7   Mrs. Thatcher* . . . has succeeded because she has taken on male values and has not, by her success, done anything for the oppressed women of Britain. Women achieving things isn't success if it entails the exploitation of men and women.
Program notes, A Contemporary Theatre (A.C.T.), Seattle, Washington *June 1984*
*See 2285.

8   Most theaters are still controlled by men and people do tend to be able to see promise in people who are like themselves.
"Caryl Churchill," *Interviews with Contemporary Women Playwrights*, Kathleen Betsko* and Rachel Koenig *1987*
*See 2739.

9   [Margaret] Thatcher* had just become prime minister; there was talk about whether it was an advance to have a woman prime minister if it was someone with policies like hers: She may be a woman but she isn't a sister, she may be a sister but she isn't a comrade.
Ibid.
*See 2285.

2711. Colette Dowling (1938–)
1   I tell you, the great divide is still with us, the awful split, the Us and Them. Like a rubber band tautened to the snapping point, the polarization of the sexes continues, because we lack the courage to face our likenesses and admit to our real need.
"A Woman Sounds Off on Those Sexy Magazines," *Redbook* (New York) *April 1974*

2   Here it was—the Cinderella Complex. It used to hit girls of sixteen or seventeen, preventing them, often, from going to college, hastening them into early marriages. Now it tends to hit women after college—after they've been out in the world a while. When the first thrill of freedom subsides and anxiety rises to take its place, they begin to be tugged by that old yearning for safety: the wish to be saved.
The Cinderella Complex 1982

3   Without being conscious of it, she looks for a situation in which she can give up her façade of self-sufficiency and ease

back into that warm, cradled state reminiscent of childhood that's so seductive to a woman—a home.
Ch. 3, Ibid.

4   Like the youngest child obsessing on the negative treatment received from the family, women use the unfairness with which they've historically been treated to wall themselves off from further negative treatment. Isolated by their feelings of victimization, they remain trapped.
Ch. 4, Ibid.

5   Once a man is on hand, a woman tends to stop believing in her own beliefs.
Ch. 6, Ibid.

2712. Mary Ann Glendon (1938–)
1   Laws are ways that society makes sense of things.
Quoted in *A World of Ideas* by Bill Moyers *1989*

2   Certainly, the American woman is very well off as an individual and a possessor of rights. But many European women are better off as mothers and members of interdependent family units. This difference of opinion on what better off means makes it very difficult to say what is a feminist in the United States at the present time.
Ibid.

3   Apparently we just don't feel that all American children of all colors and social classes are our children, the way I think a Swede quite easily feels that a child up in Lapland is very precious to a worker in Stockholm.
Ibid.

4   Pro-choice has some silent support among men who don't want to take responsibility for fatherhood, among persons involved in a profit-making abortion industry, and, maybe saddest of all, among taxpayers who see abortion as a way of keeping down the size of an underclass. So there's a lot of unspoken support for the status-quo. On the other hand, pro-life has this dark side of puntitiveness toward women that I find absolutely incomprehensible, but it seems to be there, as well as a certain unwillingness to recognize that if you're going to be pro-life, it shouldn't be with a view that life begins at conception and ends at birth. You have to be pro-life all the way, and that means supporting maternity, childbirth, and child raising, which has become very difficult in our society, where both parents are usually in the labor force.
Ibid.

5   There is always the danger that if you speak a language that recognizes only individual rights, you will become a people that can think only about individuals.
Ibid.

2713. Shusha Guppy (1938–)
1   It is very important not to become hard. The artist must always have one skin too few in comparison to other people, so you feel the slightest wind.
Interview, *The Guardian* (London) *6 April 1988*

2714. Judith Partnow Hyman (1938–)
1   The birth of a mother and a father is initiated by the Promethean event of the birth of the first child.
"Shifting Patterns of Fathering in the First Year of Life," *Becoming A Father*, Jerrold Lee Shapiro, Michael J. Diamond, and Martin Greenberg, eds. *1995*

2 The modern mother's dual interests in both briefcases and babies also has a significant influence on the way in which men make the transition to fatherhood; among other things, there is generally an increased vacuum in the care of the child, and decreased pressure for him to be the sole provider. In this intermediate area a potential space is emerging that provides an opportunity for men to be engaged in the procreation and early care of children.

Ibid.

3 . . . dramatic shifts in the delivery room from the total absence of the expectant father, traditionally pacing back and forth in the alienated bareness of the maternity waiting room, to his ubiquitous presence and emotional involvement in the birthing experience.

Ibid.

4 . . . the reawakened nurturance of the actively involved father whose infant is being breastfed is faced with a quandary: How does he cope with the fact that his partner is able to achieve a degree of intimacy with the infant of which he is totally denied? He has to deal with the paradox of being more involved, as he is expected to be, while simultaneously being excluded from the most intimate contact with his new baby.

Ibid.

2715. Cheris Kramarae (1938–)

1 For many feminists, pornography is the theory and rape is the practice.

A Feminist Dictionary, with Paula A. Treichler* 1987
*See 2974.

2716. Jane Kramer (1938–)

1 Prophecy today is hardly the romantic business that it used to be. The old tools of the trade, like the sword, the hair shirt, and the long fast in the wilderness, have given way to more contemporary, mundane instruments of doom—the book, the picket and the petition, the sit–in . . . at City Hall.

"The Ranks and Rungs of Mrs. Jacobs' Ladder," *Off Washington Square* 1963

2 Dawia maintained that Europeans were . . . favored by Allah because Allah liked automobiles and was hoping that the Europeans would bring their cars to heaven with them. Omar, however, said no, Allah loved the Europeans because the Europeans always got to their appointments on time.

Pt. I, *Honor to the Bride* 1973

3 "It is a burden to have daughters," Dawia said, sighing. "My husband looks at Jmaa now and he says, 'What can I expect from her? More of the same problems I have suffered with the first two.'"

"He has a point," Musa remarked. "Having daughters is not profitable."

Pt. II, Ibid.

2717. Betty Bao Lord (1938–)

1 "If your heart did not break now and then, Spring Moon, how would you know it is there? Hearts break, then mend and break and mend again in a cycle without beginning, without end. As surely as dawn sows the evening, twilight sows the morn."

Prologue, *Spring Moon* 1981

2 "I fear, Lustrous Jade, that in broadening your mind, you have narrowed your heart."

Ch. 27, "Jade Phoenix," Ibid.

3 "If mortals wait until the gods remake the world to their liking to be happy, they are already in hell."

Ch. 38, "Sowing Dawn," Ibid.

4 "There is a season for sun, another for shadow. A season to sing, another to be silent. And, in all seasons, parting and reunion.

"In yielding we are like the water, by nature placid, conforming to the hollow of the smallest hand; in time, shaping even the mountains to its will.

"Thus we keep duty and honor. We cherish clan and civilization.

"We are Chinese."

Ibid.

2718. Glenna C. Matthews (1938–)

1 Would-be public women need more than just the removal of barriers to their access. They need imaginative new social arrangements so that they do not have to choose between the welfare of their loved ones and their public responsibilities. . . . Finally, we all need to recognize that women who stand up in public are still subject to scrutiny of their personal lives to an extent that often goes beyond what men experience. . . . Public woman will take her place alongside of public men only after the last residue of such unequal treatment has been obliterated.

The Rise of Public Woman: Woman's Power and Woman's Place in the United States 1630–1970 1993

2719. Mary Jane Moffat (1938?–)

1 Why do women keep diaries? . . . The form has been an important outlet for women partly because it is an analogue to their lives: emotional, fragmentary, interrupted, modest, not to be taken seriously, private, restricted, daily, trivial, formless, concerned with self, as endless as their tasks.

Foreword, *Revelations: Diaries of Women*, with Charlotte Painter* 1974

*See 2314.

2720. A. G. Mojtabai (1937–)

1 Everything sags near the end: the earlobes flatten, lie close along the skull, the jaw goes slack, the head lolls, too heavy to lift; secretions pool and thicken in the throat, the fingers, before this so restlessly seeking, fold in and are still.

Soon: Tales from Hospice 1998

2 It's the place—he's relieved—*his* place, the spot they'd promised him, it's waiting. Looming above him: Our Lady of the Fields, standing waist deep in wheat. Barberry hedge, cottonwoods and cedars, and the stones of his friends extending in widening circles around him.

"Tour," Ibid.

2721. Karen O'Connor (1938–)

1 [The] abortion issue may not be all that different from other policy issues, including civil rights and the environment. All such policy issues have gone off on tangents, incurred violence, and, ultimately, moved toward neutral ground. It appears that the abortion issue is now reaching that stage of equilibrium.

No Neutral Ground? Abortion Politics in an Age of Absolutes 1996

2722. Joyce Carol Oates (1938–)

1 "Personal relationships start off so cleanly but then become too involved."

"Norman and the Killer," *Upon the Sweeping Flood and Other Stories* 1965

2 "Nothing can be right and balanced again until justice is won—the injured party has to have justice. Do you understand that? Nothing can be right, for years, for lifetimes, until that first crime is punished. Or else we'd all be animals."

Ibid.

3 Those sobs filled the air in a way that the singing had not—the air was crowded and breathless with these sobs of guilty people, and the melody they made was one Clara understood better than she had understood the words of that song.

She understood something then: that these people had done something bad, something wrong, and that they would never get over it.

A Garden of Earthly Delights 1967

4 Anger always excited and pleased them; it was sacred.

Pt. I, Ch. 1, Ibid.

5 The only trouble was that here an odor of harsh antiseptic was everywhere, floating everywhere . . . it seemed to be eating its way into your lungs to get you clean even if it killed you.

Ch. 8, Ibid.

6 She felt like a plant of some kind, like a flower on a stalk that only looked slender but was really tough, tough as steel, like the flowers in fields that could be blown down flat by the wind but yet rose again slowly coming back to life.

Pt. II, Ch. 6, Ibid.

7 Whoever was stupid was beneath worry or thought; you did not have to figure them out. This eliminated hundreds of people. In this life you had time only for a certain amount of thinking, and there was no need to waste any of it on people who were not threatening.

Pt. III, Ch. 7, Ibid.

8 I was a child murderer.

I don't mean child-murderer, though that's an idea. I mean child murderer, that is, a murderer who happens to be a child, or a child who happens to be a murderer. You can take your choice. When Aristotle notes that man is a rational animal one strains forward, cupping his ear, to hear which of those words is emphasized—rational animal, rational animal? Which am I? Child murderer, child murderer?

Expensive People 1968

9 This is a work of history in fictional form—that is, in personal perspective, which is the only kind of history that exists.

Author's note, *Them* 1969

10 Shakily he thought of the future: that night, and the next day, and the real future. The future was important, not the present. These minutes spent around the supper table, these ten or fifteen minutes he had to get through, were not important except as they were part of a process leading to the future, a future that would be a good surprise, he felt sure.

Pt. I, Ch. 9, Ibid.

11 She ransacked her mind, but there was nothing in it.

Ch. 15, Ibid.

12 "I admit that I have no fixed income like your friend, and I have no desire for it," he said to Faye. "I like adventure. I don't dare prophesy where my liking for adventure will lead."

Pt. II, Ch. 2, Ibid.

13 ". . . women don't understand these things. They only understand money when they can see it. They're very crude essentially. They don't understand where money comes from or what it means or how a man can be worth money though he hasn't any at the moment. But a man understands all that."

Ibid.

14 She would have a baby with her husband, to make up for the absence of love, to locate love, to fix herself in a certain place, but she would not really love him.

Pt. III, Ch. 1, Ibid.

15 You're such a virgin, a sweet perpetual virgin. You're so perfect that you turn other people hard as ice . . .

Ch. 15, *Do With Me What You Will* 1970

16 Premeditated crime: the longer the meditating, the dreaming, the more triumphant the execution!

Pt. I, Ch. 1, Ibid.

17 "I don't think that California is a healthy place. . . . Things disintegrate there."

Ch. 8, Ibid.

18 The plaque at the front of the courtroom, high on the wall, was permanent and yet its words were new each time Jack read them, read them half against his will, his eyes moving restlessly forward and up to them while testimony droned on:*Conscience Speaks the Truth.*

Pt. II, Ch. 6, Ibid.

19 The worst cynicism: a belief in luck.

Ch. 15, Ibid.

20 . . . he believed in the justice of his using any legal methods he could improvise to force the other side into compromise or into dismissals of charges, or to lead a jury into the verdict he wanted. Why not? He was a defense lawyer, not a judge or a juror or a policeman or a legislator or a theoretician or an anarchist or a murderer.

Ibid.

21 . . . like all virtuous people he imagines he must speak the truth. . . .

Ibid.

22 Nothing is accidental in the universe—this is one of my Laws of Physics—except the entire universe itself, which is Pure Accident, pure divinity.

"The Summing Up: Meredith Dawe," Ibid.

23 What relationship had a dagger to the human hand, that it must be invented, imagined out of the shape of the hand? -where did the sharpness come from, was it from the soul and its unstoppable imaginings? -because the hand in itself was so defenseless, so vulnerable in its flesh.

"Elena," Ibid.

24 He hated her for the selfishness of her death and for her having eclipsed him forever, obliterated him as if she had smashed an insect under her shoe.

"The Wheel of Love" (1967), *The Wheel of Love and Other Stories* 1970

25 "Loneliness is dangerous, it's bad for you to be alone, to be lonely, because if aloneness does not lead to God, it leads to the devil. It leads to the self."

"Shame" (1968), Ibid.

26 Night comes to the desert all at once, as if someone turned off a light.

> "Interior Monologue" (1969), *Ibid.*

27 Minutes pass in silence, mysteriously. It is those few minutes that pass after we make love that are most mysterious to me, uncanny.

> "Unmailed, Unwritten Letters" (1969), *Ibid.*

28 When a marriage ends, who is left to understand it?

> *Ibid.*

29 . . . the necessity for patience had aged her magically; she was content in her age.

> "Bodies" (1970), *Ibid.*

30 Before falling in love, I was defined. Now I am undefined, weeds are growing between my ribs.

> "I Was in Love" (1970), *Ibid.*

31 The ringing of a telephone is always louder in an empty house.

> *Ibid.*

32 "We're off! Another week come and gone! Month in, month out! Even, odd—black, white—life, death—father, son. The cycles continue!"

> "Wild Saturday" (1970), *Ibid.*

33 Old women snore violently. They are like bodies into which bizarre animals have crept at night; the animals are vicious, bawdy, noisy. How they snore! There is no shame in their snoring. Old women turn into old men.

> "What Is the Connection Between Men and Women?"
> *Mademoiselle February 1970*

34 In love there are two things: bodies and words.

> *Ibid.*

35 Her mind churns so that she can't hear, she can't think.

> *Ibid.*

36 . . . it is a fever, this racing, this constant thought.

> *Ibid.*

37 "Things move from invisibility to visibility," he said slowly. "There are tremendous forces, like hurricanes or floods, that people have inside them. Sometimes there is a break and the force rushes out. It can't be stopped. . . . But then there's calm again. It's as if there were terrible ghosts inside us that were always prodding and testing our skins, looking for weaknesses. Then one day they rush out into the world, outside us. And so a 'crime' is committed."

> *Do With Me What You Will 1973*

38 . . . she had been turning over and over in her mind a conversation she and Andrew had had, walking along the beach after breakfast—his passionate admission that, for him, ideas were the only reality—the only permanent reality—the rational side of mankind the only really explored except by a few individuals, isolated, uncertain of their connection with one another: the future of mankind was only through reason, logic, awakened capacities in the brain that were now dormant in nearly everyone.

> *The Assassins 1975*

39 . . . there is nothing but time in the desolation of my soul.

> *Son of the Morning 1977*

40 I think of the improbable precision of the eye: the perfection of the iris, the pupil, the mirroring brain.

> *Ibid.*

41 She has always been absurdly superstitious: she believes that anything she might come upon, in such a situation, could have great bearing upon her life—could alter the course of her life. (Always, when she has been most unhappy, she has wandered into libraries, often into the libraries of unfamiliar cities; she has spent hours like this, rather like a blind woman, drawing at random to open. . . .)

> *Unholy Loves 1979*

42 It is not her body that he wants but it is only through her body that he can take possession of another human being, so he must labor upon her body, he must enter her body, to make his claim.

> "In the Founders' Room," *Ibid.*

43 Leah doubted that any man was capable of a love so profound it could lie silent, like a forest pond; Gideon doubted that any woman was capable of comprehending the nature of a man's passion, which might tear through him, rendering him broken and exhausted, as vulnerable as a small child . . .

> *Bellefleur 1980*

44 No one seems to have said that it was an appropriate death though we know that all deaths are appropriate.

> *Cybele 1980*

45 There are tears of grief that are tears of fury as well. But they are not cleansing. Nor does the earth greedily soak them up.

> *Ibid.*

46 "The joyous fulfillment of your sex : the sacred duties of beloved wife, and helpmeet, and mother. In opposition to the vulgar and mercantile hurly-burly of the great world, the idyllic pleasures of the domestic hearth—the which, I firmly believe, make of one small room an everywhere, indeed; and provide us with that small measure of bliss, which is, if we are greatly fortunate, and deserving, Our Lord's promise to us, of the Heaven to come."

> *A Bloodsmoor Romance 1982*

47 Xavier said: "But then, is not your life criminal too? Is it not predicated upon lies, hypocrisy, and subterfuge of every sort? For, by your own acknowledgment, you prefer guilty clients; you are most comfortable with crime; and derive your energies from it. How would you defend your life, erected upon such a foundation?"

> *Mysteries of Winterthurn 1984*

48 "Look: in my family suicide isn't that significant. . . . it's simply a way of asserting control at the proper time. When you've lived through all there is for you to live through, when you're burnt out, thoroughly, and the mere notion of returning to life, and doing it all again, the seasons, the years, the decades, O dear Christ. . . . When you're balked, nullified, stalled, it isn't a significant gesture, it isn't at all emotional, it's just something, you know, you do. And then it's over."

> *Solstice 1984*

49 Our enemy is by tradition our savior, in preventing us from superficiality.

> "Master Race," *Partisan Review 50th Anniversary Edition*, William Phillips, ed. *1985*

50 The television screen, so unlike the movie screen, sharply reduced human beings, revealed them as small, trivial, flat, in two banal

dimensions, drained of color. Wasn't there something reassuring about it!—that human beings were in fact merely images of a kind registered in one another's eyes and brains, phenomena composed of microscopic flickering dots like atoms. They were atoms—nothing more. A quick switch of the dial and they disappeared and who could lament the loss?

Pt. 1, Ch. 13, *You Must Remember This* 1987

51   The shopping excursions began when Nola was a small child but did not acquire their special significance until she was twelve or thirteen years old and capable of serious, sustained shopping with her mother.

"Shopping" (short story), *Ms.* (New York) *March 1987*

52   She knows no more of how love ends than she knew as a child, she knows only of how love begins—in the belly, in the womb, where it is always present tense.

Ibid.

53   When Mrs. Dietrich was pregnant with Nola she'd been twenty-nine years old and she and Mr. Dietrich had tried to have a baby for nearly five years. She'd lost hope, begun to despise herself, then suddenly it happened: like grace. Like happiness swelling so powerfully it can barely be contained.

Ibid.

54   Our house is made of glass . . . and our lives are made of glass; and there is nothing we can do to protect ourselves.

American Appetites 1988

55   Mr. Kreuzer had revealed to C.A. and a very small number of other privileged boys the secret of the X-factor, which democracy and Christianity and "archaic ethical remnants" sought to deny, but which manifested itself in the very genes and chromosomes of the biological organism—that approximately one tenth of one percent of the species Homo sapiens was destined to rule the rest, by way of superiority of intellect, personality, spiritual and physical strength, and that intangible element in the human psyche known as will. "Will is the conduit of fate," Mr. Kreuzer said. C.A. had not at first—for he was very young, a mere boy, a mere angel boy in whom his devil twin still slumbered!—comprehended. Will is the conduit of fate.

Soul/Mate 1989

56   I used to think getting old was about vanity—but actually it's about losing people you love. Getting wrinkles is trivial.

"Master Race," Interview in *The Guardian* (London)
18 August 1989

57   As, dreaming, we are the dreams we dream, and cannot escape from them except by the metaphysical impossibility of becoming someone other than ourselves . . .

Snake Eyes 1991

58   Staring at the hawks actually weeping to see the hawks, those predators visible only from this place of shame her heart lifting in joy seeing their strength, their beauty, riding the air, cunning in their use of the wind, always watchful though seemingly unhurried, even languid in their graceful curving motions now rising to the top of an invisible spiral so high in the air . . .

Foxfire 1993

59   She who boasted she was capable of reading her husband's and children's faces with the patience, shrewdness and devotion of a Sanskrit scholar pondering ancient texts

We Were the Mulvaneys 1996

60   *Fear is good, fear is normal. Fear will save your life.*

First Love 1996

61   From your mother you will inherit the belief that you can journey to your fate, there's a place to be located on a map that's destiny. If only you can get there. If only it isn't too late. If no one stops you.

Ibid.

62   It's the men who treat you like shit you're crazy for. For only they can tell you your punishment is just. This is not the testimony I would give to the police, and at the trial. This is the secret testimony only you may know.

Man Crazy 1997

63   Covet where you wish, but never in vain.
     Would this earthly globe were but the size of an apple, that it might be plucked, devoured!
     (By one who has the courage to pluck, and to bite hard.)

My Heart Laid Bare 1998

64   Past?—but the graveyard of Future.
     Future?—but the womb of Past.

Ibid.

65   Seeing the little man made me realize that the physical world that gives birth to us, nurtures and contains and defines us, is not really *our* world. It is not the world we would have invented.

"The Omen," *The Collector of Hearts* 1999

2723. Lyudmila Petrushevskaya (1938–)

1   YURA. . . . the family no longer exists. There is just the female tribe with their young ones, and lone males.

The Stairwell 1983

2   All men are brothers.
     Not all—some are sisters!

Three Girls in Blue (Tri devshki v golubom) 1983

2724. Diane Ravitch (1938–)

1   The ladder was there, "from the gutter to the university," and for those stalwart enough to ascend it, the schools were a boon and a path out of poverty.

The Great School Wars 1974

2725. Janet Reno (1938–)

1   Just as there should be a federal remedy for racial discrimination and for gender discrimination, I think in this instance somehow or another there has got to be a federal response to interference through physical conduct which restrains access to a woman's right to choose.

Interview at swearing in ceremony (12 March),
in "Reno takes an oath . . . ," *Seattle Post-Intelligencer*, A3
13 March 1993

2   I made the decision. I'm accountable.*

Speech, Press Conference
24 April 1993

*Reference to to the Waco, Texas debacle with the Branch Davidians, a survivalist/religious cult, who were burned alive in a pitched battle with federal law enforcement (1993).

3   If the [video] industry doesn't clean itself up, we'll have to look at doing it.

Cited in "Black activist crusades . . . ," *Seattle Times*, A12
6 February 1994

2726. Nancy Simpson (1938–)

1 In hearing distance of a wave's yes, earth is a woman with plans.

"Skin Underwater," *Night Student 1985*

2727. Zulu Sofola (1938–)

1 ULOKO (to Ogoli, his mother). . . . Did you speak for me? Did you let Ibekwe know that an injustice was being done to you by his action? did you let anyone now that, for money, the wife whom you had planned for your son was being forced from your hands and being given to someone else? Did you tell them that my life would become nothing if the one I love so much was given away to someone else? Did you?

Act II, Sc. 2, *Wedlock of the Gods 1971*

2 [There are] aspects in traditional society where customs and moral precepts set themselves at war against individual citizens.

Essay by Olu Obafemi in, *Contemporary British Dramatists,*
K.A. Berney, ed. *1993*

2728. Liv Ullman (1938–)

1 . . . we have to work to be good people, . . . goodness always involves the choice to be good.

Quoted in *Necessary Losses* by Judith Viorst* *1986*
*See 2479.

2729. Laurel Thatcher Ulrich (1938–)

1 . . . it is in the very dailiness, the exhaustive repetitious dailiness, that the real power of Martha Ballard's book lies . . . For her, living was to be measured in doing. Nothing was trivial.

A Midwife's Tale: The Life of Martha Ballard, Based on Her Diary, 1785–1812 1991

2730. Luisa Valenzuela (1938–)

1 In Victor's life, monotony and boredom had nothing to do with one another. He repeated his repertoire so often that even from miles away, Clara could follow his conversation with anyone who happened to be sitting next to him.

"The Body," Ch. 1, *Clara* (1967), Quoted in *Thirteen Short Stories and a Novel,* Hortense Carpenter and J. Jorge Castello, trs. *1976*

2 How good can freedom be if you're alone and broke, with just a few coins in the bottom of your purse, hidden in the lining, the forgotten coins nobody cares about.

Ch. 4, Ibid.

3 I am superior. I don't need any drugs, although at times I share those of others out of pure sociability, so as not to seem different. And to keep my business going: I produce drugs—no longer through my pores but in an industrial way, so others can attain, even if only in fleeting flashes, a little of the light that illuminates me.

For my personal use, I *am* the drug, the drug is I.

"The One," *The Lizard's Tale (El Brujo Hormiga Roja Señor Del Tacurú),* Gregory Rabassa, tr. *1983*

4 The initial path can be repeated forever.

Ibid.

2731. Alena Vostrá (1938–)

1 OFFSIDE. How should I put it? You have to ask yourself the question: are they governing you or are you governing them?

This is the only defense. I tell myself: this is a sort of experiment as to what one can endure and what one can make another endure . . . It is all a game. . . . Finally we all shall get it. It is a sort of a merry-go-round.

Eeny Meeny Miney Mo 1966

2732. Gloria Jean Wade-Gayles (1938–)

1 To scream, to know that you are heard, is the only right the violator has not taken from you.

"Fissures in the Moon: Sharing Pain in Order to Heal,"
Rooted Against the Wind: Personal Essays 1996

2 Perhaps I wore too heavy a scent of my fragrance in the grocery line or smiled too warmly when he cut in front of me at a traffic light. Perhaps I took the lighted darkness for granted and, as punishment, I lost the night. I whip myself.

Ibid.

2733. Natalie Wood (1938–1983)

1 The only time a woman really succeeds in changing a man is when he is a baby.

Remark *n.d.*

2734. Jane Alexander (1939–)

1 The arts have tremendous economic power; they have the ability to communicate, to heal, to offer hope—to the troubled and disadvantaged, to the young child in the inner city, to the lonely and those looking for inspiration or solace or challenge. Let that message ring out, and let us work toward getting more people into our theaters and introducing them to the arts.

Speech, Show Biz Expo-East (New York City,
6 January 1994), *American Theatre* (New York)
March 1994

2 I knew what the endowment* did, because I had performed in regional theaters—it made those not-for-profit theaters possible in those communities. It made possible 13,000 art teachers in schools across the country. It provided seed money for the performing arts, for music, writing, painting, sculpture and folk crafts all across the nation, in every district, in villages and cities.

Quoted in "Let's Support Our Artists" by Dotson Rader,
Parade Magazine 30 October 1994
*Reference to the National Endowment for the Arts.

3 There are two parts to the creative endeavor: making something, then disseminating it.

Ibid.

4 Some city people don't know why they should be taxed to subsidize wheat farmers when they don't live in a rural state. Why should childless people be taxed for public schools? Why should nonmotorists be taxed for highways, or middle-class people to pay health care for the poor? Or people be taxed to support the arts? Because it is in the good of the whole nation. The arts are vital to the life of this country.

Ibid.

5 Art can be very disturbing to people. But art is liberating. It allows people to experience their humanity in a way nothing else can. I don't think there's anything that's human which is alien to an artist, even if it sometimes offends or even frightens us.

Ibid.

2735. Paula Gunn Allen (1939–)

1 but your shaken
voice, is it a small wind
we carry in our genes?
"Suicid/ing(ed) Indian Women," I. Kyukuh, *A Cannon
between My Knees 1981*

2   Division
does not come easy to a woman,
it is against the tribe
laws which only women honor
III. Navajo, Ibid.

3 The best of the world slumps before me—minds
that eighteen years ago first turned earthward,
blinking.
oh yeah.
Wasted.
Turned off.
Tuned in to video narcosis,
stereophonic flight, transfixed.
naked angels burning their hopes, mine, on dust and
beer.
"Star Child Suit" II, St. 4,*That's What She Said,*
Rayna Green,* ed. *1984*

*See 2800.

4 We are the women of daylight; of clocks and steel
foundries, of drugstores and streetlights,
of superhighways that slice our days in two.
Our dreams are pale memories of themselves,
and nagging doubt is the false measure of our days.
"Kopis'taya," St. 3, Ibid.

5 beautiful woman. beautiful
corn woman. woman like corn:
ripe and full. sweet. self
generating. tasseled.
blowing in the wind. meeting.
"The Beautiful Woman Who Sings," Ibid.

6 There was a man who had come into her life, into her,
feeding her, feeding on her.
"The Bearer of the Sun Arises," Ibid.

7 The serene presence of the state, the faceless shadow of authority, of power, of those who controlled because they had
seen fit to entomb themselves and their sacred honor in the
vast caverns of city hall.
Untitled story, Ibid.

8 "I pay for my loving and I refuse to pay when they refuse to
love. Shit."
Ibid.

9 Human beings need to belong to a tradition and equally need
to know about the world in which they find themselves.
"Something Sacred Going On out There" (1982),
The Sacred Hoop 1986

10 [M]yth allows us to rediscover ourselves in our most human
and ennobling dimensions. Through it we are allowed to see
our own transcendent powers triumphant . . .
Ibid.

11 Myth . . . shows us our own ability to accept and allow the
eternal to be part of our selves.
Ibid.

2736. Margaret Atwood (1939–)

1 You fit into me
like a hook into an eye

a fish-hook
an open eye.
Epigraph, *Power Politics 1971*

2 I've never understood why people consider youth a time of
freedom and joy. It's probably because they have forgotten
their own.
"Hair Jewelry," *Ms.* (1976), *Dancing Girls and
Other Stories 1982*

3 She even had a kind of special position among men: she was
an exception, she fitted none of the categories they commonly
used when talking about girls; she wasn't a cock-teaser, a cold
fish, an easy lay or a snarky bitch; she was an honorary person. She had grown to share their contempt for most women.
"The Man From Mars" (*Ontario Review*, 1977), Ibid.

4 He has realized he was an intruder; the cabin, the fences, the
fires and paths were violations; now his own fence excludes
him, as logic excludes love.
Surfacing 1983

5 We are for breeding purposes: we aren't concubines, geisha
girls, courtesans. On the contrary: everything possible has
been done to remove us from that category. There is supposed
to be nothing entertaining about us.
The Handmaid's Tale 1986

6 Who knows, your very flesh may be polluted, dirty as an oily
beach, sure death to shore birds and unborn babies. Maybe a
vulture would die of eating you. . . . Women took medicines,
pills, men sprayed trees, cows ate grass, all that souped-up piss
flowed into the rivers. Not to mention the exploding atomic
power plants.
Ibid.

7 Nobody dies from lack of sex. It's lack of love we die from.
There's nobody here I can love. . . . I too am a missing person.
Ibid.

8 . . . he wants to punish her for his own addiction to her.
Ibid.

9 "What's the point of continuing, in a society like this one,
where it's always two steps forward and two back?"
"Uglypuss," *Bluebeard's Egg and Other Stories 1986*

10 [I]f art sucks and everything is only art, what has she done
with her life?
"The Sunrise," Ibid.

11 Time is not a line.
first line, *Cat's Eye 1989*

12 Nothing ever goes away
Ibid.

13 Popular art is the dream of society; it does not examine itself.
"A Question Of Metamorphosis," interview in *Malahat Review*, No. 41 (1977), *Conversations*, Earl G. Ingersoll, ed.
1990

14 If a stranger taps you on the ass and says, "How's the little
lady today!" you will probably cringe. But if he's an American,
he's only being friendly.
Ibid.

15 The beginning of Canadian cultural nationalism was not "Am I really that oppressed?" but "Am I really that boring?"
    "Dancing On the Edge Of the Precipice," interview with Joyce Carol Oates,* *Ontario Review* (Fall/Winter 1978), Ibid.

16 The basic Female body comes with the following accessories: garter belt, panti-girdle, crinoline, camisole, bustle, brassiere, stomacher, chemise, virgin zone, spike heels, nose ring, veil, kid gloves, fishnet stockings, fichu, bandeau, Merry Widow, weepers, chokers, barrettes, bangles, beads, lorgnette, feather boa, basic black, compact, Lycra stretch one-piece with modesty panel, designer peignoir, flannel nightie, lace teddy, bed, head.
    "The Female Body," *Michigan Quarterly Review* (1990), *The Best American Essays*, Joyce Carol Oates,* ed. *1991*
    *See 2722.

17 The personal is not political, thinks Tony: the personal is military. War is what happens when language fails.
    The Robber Bride 1993

18 There must be people like that around, because there are more humans alive on the earth right now than have ever lived, altogether, since humans began, and if souls are recycled then there must be some people alive today who didn't get one, sort of like musical chairs.
    Ibid.

19 Women don't want all the men eaten up by man-eaters; they want a few left over so they can eat some themselves.
    Ibid.

20 We're tired of being good all the time. When you deprive women of any notion of threat, it pretty much puts them back in the Victorian age. All innocent, and without power, except the power of being good.
    Quoted in "Zenia* Is Sort of Like Madonna"** by Laurel Graeber (p. 22), *The New York Times Book Review* *31 October 1993*
    *A character in her book *The Robber Bride*. **See 3449.

21 Men's bodies are the most dangerous things on earth.
    "Making a Man," *Good Bones and Simple Murders 1994*

22 Take some dust off the ground. Form. Breathe into the nostrils the breath of life. Simple, but effective!
    Ibid.

23 [Why is it] there are never any evil stepfathers.
    "Unpopular Gals," Ibid.

24 Women's novels leave out parts of the men as well. Sometimes it's the stretch between the belly button and the knees, sometimes it's the sense of humor.
    "Women's Novels," Ibid.

25 The use of "religion" as an excuse to repress the freedom of expression and to deny human rights is not confined to any country or time. But it is appalling that in our own time, the Prime Minister of a Commonwealth country should ban a piece of literature on the basis of "a glance at the back page," thus countenancing and indeed encouraging the outburst of threat, demonization and obscene vituperation which has pursued Lindsey Collen. Sincere practitioners of any religion should be dismayed to see their beliefs distorted in this shameful manner.*
    Letter, *Index on Censorship* (London) *1995*
    *Reference to the banning of *The Rape of Sita* by Lindsey Collen (see 3626).

26 You have soft feet.
    You don't know what it's like
    so close to bedrock.
    "Owl Burning" *1995?*

27 Men such as him do not have to clean up the messes they make, but we have to clean up our own messes, and theirs into the bargain. In that way, they are like children, they do not have to think ahead, or worry about the consequences of what they do.
    Alias Grace 1996

28 . . . the ladylike bums that have sat on this very settee, all delicate and white, like wobbly soft-boiled eggs.
    Ibid.

2737. Maria Isabel Barreno (1939–)

1 . . . all friendship between women has a uterine air about it, the air of a slow, bloody, cruel incomplete exchange, of an original situation being repeated all over again.
    New Portuguese Letters, with Maria Fatima Velho da Costa,* and Maria Teresa Horta** *1972*
    *See 2789. **See 2757.

2 The time of discipline began. Each of us the pupil of whichever one of us could best teach what each of us needed to learn.
    Ibid.

3 . . . we are still the property of men, the spoils today of warriors who pretend to be our comrades in the struggle, but who merely seek to mount us. . . .
    Ibid.

4 One lives and endures one's life with others, within matrices, but it is only alone, truly alone that one bursts apart, springs forth.
    Ibid.

5 Let no one tell me that silence gives consent, because whoever is silent dissents.
    Ibid.

2738. Mary Catherine Bateson (1939–)

1 The family is changing, not disappearing. We have to broaden our understanding of it, look for the new metaphors.
    Quoted in *A World of Ideas* by Bill Moyers *1989*

2 There are few things as toxic as a bad metaphor. You can't think without metaphors.
    Ibid.

3 Fear is not a good teacher. The lessons of fear are quickly forgotten.
    Ibid.

4 Either we have to make the leap to a vision that includes all human beings, or we are locked up in tiny, local self-interest and prejudices—and at that point, why not just get rich and enjoy yourself? It's as if the time had come to recognize that we are one.
    Ibid.

5 This is the century of the refugee.
    Ibid.

2739. Kathleen Betsko (1939–)

1 Most war tales have been about male bravery. National history seen through men's militaristic eyes. I want to record the history of England's mothers at war . . . children at war.
"Kathleen Betsko," *Interviews with Contemporary Women Playwrights*, with Rachel Koenig 1987

2 I think the theater should be a place to "get down and dirty" . . . passionate, visceral. Even unfair if necessary. Fairness is the opposite of passion.
Ibid.

3 We* were delirious with learning, discovering art, growing in self-esteem, and still doing the laundry.
Ibid.

*Disadvantaged Women for a Higher Education [DWHE] at the University of New Hampshire.

4 In my own opinion, women think and write differently than men because they have different experiences, different myths, different needs and desires and dreams and memories. As feminist scholars have pointed out, we exist as a separate culture within the dominant culture. A culture distinct from men's, no matter how intimately we may live with or love them.
Ibid.

5 When women are free to be completely honest, the theater will be rocked to its foundations; far from destroying it, I think there'll be a glorious rebirth.
Ibid.

2740. Rosellen Brown (1939–)

1 "Do you think there could be something like victims without crimes?"
"A Letter to Ismael in the Grave," *Street Games* 1974

2 "I wish you were alive. I wish, I wish, so I could hate you and get on with it."
Ibid.

3 I know how he dreams me. I know because I dream his dreams.
"How to Win," Ibid.

4 . . . I remember sort of half dreaming as if I had dozed for a few unlikely minutes down by the bay and some sea animal had crawled up, slimy, from between the pilings, had bit me painfully between the legs, and had retreated to its secret life, invisible under the water, covered with blood like something wounded. For an initiation, I assume it was about average.
"Street Games," Ibid.

2741. Gro Harlem Brundtland (1939–)

1 We need a wider definition of national security . . . The destruction of the planet's environment is making the world a less stable place, politically, economically and militarily . . . Our environmental management practices have focused largely upon after-the-fact repair of damage . . . The ability to anticipate and prevent environmental damage will require that the ecological dimensions of policy be considered at the same time as the economic, trade, energy, agricultural and other dimensions.
From television broadcast, "Only One Earth," Quoted in *Ms.* (New York) *January 1989*

2 There is resentment [against the "minimum gender" rule*]. There are only so many jobs. It is a question of power.
Quoted in "Are Women Leaders Wielding Power Differently Than Men?" by Georgia Anne Geyer,** *Seattle Times* *14 May 1989*

*The Social Democrat rule in Norway by which 40 percent of Cabinet and Parliament posts are assured for women. **See 2592.

3 There is a very close connection between being a doctor and being a politician. The doctor first tries to prevent illness, then tries to treat it if it comes. It's exactly the same as what you try to do as a politician, but with regard to society.
Quoted in "Norway's Radical Daughter" by Nancy Gibbs, *Time* (New York) *25 September 1989*

4 I do not know of any environmental group in any country that does not view its government as an adversary.
Ibid.

5 Only by educating people and giving them a fair chance to break out of poverty can we help to find a sustainable relation between population and resources.
Technology Review 1993

6 I have tried in vain to understand how the term "reproductive health care" can be read as promoting abortion as a means of family planning. Rarely, if ever, have so many misrepresentations been used to imply a meaning that was never there in the first place.
Speech, U.N. Conference on Population and Development (Cairo) *5 September 1994*

7 Morality becomes hypocrisy if it means accepting mothers' suffering or dying in connection with unwanted pregnancies and illegal abortions and unwanted children.
Ibid.

8 The myth that men are the economic providers and women, mainly, are mothers and care givers in the family has now been thoroughly refuted. This family pattern has never been the norm, except in a narrow middle-class segment.
Remark (1995), Quoted in *Women in World History Curriculum*, http://home.earthlink.net/~womenwhist/ *1996–97*

9 The environment is where we all live; and development is what we all do in attempting to improve our lot within that abode. The two are inseparable.
Quoted in *Twentieth-Century Women Political Leaders* by Claire Price-Groff 1998

2742. Siv Cedering (1939–)

1 . . . when I finish my other work
I can spend all night sweeping
the heavens.
"Letter from Caroline Herschel* (1750–1848)," St. 4, *From Songs from Unsung Worlds (Science in Poetry)*, Bonnie B. Gordon, ed. 1985

*See 653.

2 Sometimes when I am alone
in the dark, and the universe reveals
yet another secret, I say the names
of my long, lost sisters, forgotten
in the books that record
our science—

Aganice of Thessaly,
Hypatia,

Hildegard,
Catherina Hevelius,
Maria Agnesi*

St. 5, Ibid.

*See 106, 178, 568.

3   However long we live, life is short, so I
work. And however important man becomes,
he is nothing compared to the stars.
There are secrets, dear sister, and it is
for us to reveal them. Your name, like mine,
is a song.

St. 9, Ibid.

2743. Barbara Chase-Riboud (1939–)

1   Pride is never sinful when it is Justice.

Echo of Lions 1989

2744. Judy Chicago (1939–)

1   We have made a space to house our spirit, to give form to our dreams.

"Let Sisterhood Be Powerful," *Womanspace
February/March* 1973

2   . . . I suddenly knew that I was alone forever, that I could lose the people I loved any time, any moment, and that the only thing I had in this life was myself.

Ch. 1, *Through the Flower: My Struggle as a Woman Artist
1975*

3   I did not understand that wanting doesn't always lead to action.

Ch. 4, Ibid.

4   The acceptance of women as authority figures or as role models is an important step in female education. . . . It is this process of identification, respect, and then self-respect that promotes growth.

Ch. 5, Ibid.

5   We were wedded together on the basis of mutual work and goals.

Ch. 9, Ibid.

6   I believe that the conquest of nature, control of the environment, the rise of patriarchal religion, Vetruvian man as a measure, the development of the scientific and medical minds, the industrial revolution, the burning of witches, are all part of the institutionalization of patriarchal culture. The systematic burning of Jews in the Holocaust is part of the outcome of this historical situation. You can't understand the Holocaust except from a feminist perspective. Without a feminist perspective, the consequences of patriarchy will mystify you.

Quoted in "Judy Chicago," *Exposures, Women & Their Art*
by Ann Brown and Arlene Raven* 1989

*See 3020.

7   After some years in the art world trying to pretend I wasn't a woman, I decided for better or worse I had to be who I was.

Ibid.

8   When we look at the Empire State Building or the Washington Monument, nobody yells "Penis!" We are used to seeing the world through male images, not our own likenesses.

Ibid.

2745. Terry Cole-Whittaker (1939–)

1   Examine where money is an issue in your life—where the lack of it holds you back, where the abundance of it is a problem, or where the fear of having it or losing it is an obstacle. Are you a money victim or are you a money generator and curator? This doesn't have to be a have-not world.

How To Have More In A Have-Not World 1983

2746. Judy Collins (1939–)

1   In the future we will have pop song cycles like classical Lieder, but we will create our own words, music, and orchestrations, because we are a generation of whole people.

Quoted in *Rock and Other Four
Letter Words* 1968

2   I look in the mirror through the eyes of the child that was me.

"Secret Gardens of the Heart" 1972

3   Secret gardens of the heart where the old stay young forever . . .

Ibid.

2747. Yaël Dayan (1939–)

1   Within me I would be the mistress; outside, if necessary, a slave. I would knit my world together, make contact with the outside world, write the right kinds of letters, and be as I thought appropriate to different people.

New Face in the Mirror 1959

2   My father,* I remembered, had no fears at all. In that he differed greatly from me. But he could not be called a courageous man because he had no fears to overcome.

Ibid.

*Moshe Dayan, Israeli political and military leader (1915–1981).

3   High society is, of course, mainly habit . . .

Ibid.

4   He picked up some earth and poured it into the boys palm. "Grasp it, feel it, taste it. There is your God. If you want to pray, boy, pray to the sky to bring rain to our land and not virtue to your souls."

Ch. 4, *Envy the Frightened* 1960

5   It wasn't a battle really, as it wasn't a war. Nor was it a game, not when you heard the poisonous shrieking of the bullets— confused, scattered, searching above your heads—there was no feeling of deep revenge or hatred. It was almost as quiet as a day's work, only moments seemed eternal and seconds endless . . . Not a war, or a battle, but a fight.

Ch. 18, Ibid.

6   She was friendless and yet a friend to others and the same intensity with which she ignored the future marked her passionate attitude to the past.

Ch. 8, Death Had Two Sons 1967

7   How long it takes us to gather the component parts of our memory—the problems, self-appraisals, the self-analysis, our little daily dilemmas, petty quests for comfort. And how quickly they can all disappear.

Israel Journal June 1967

8   People in politics are not very kind to each other.

Quoted in the *Los Angeles Times
7 March* 1974

2748. Shelagh Delaney (1939–)

1 HELEN. The only consolation I can find in your immediate presence is your ultimate absence.

Act. I, Sc. 1, A Taste of Honey 1959

2 JO. In this country [England] there are only two seasons, winter and winter.

Sc. 2, Ibid.

3 HELEN. Why don't you learn from my mistakes? It takes half your life to learn from your own.

Ibid.

4 BOY. Women never have young minds. They are born three thousand years old.

Ibid.

5 JO. We don't ask for life, we have it thrust upon us.

Act II, Sc. 2, Ibid.

6 GEOF. You need somebody to love you while you're looking for someone to love.

Ibid.

7 JESSE. Nothing passes. Everything stays with you. Everything makes its mark.

The Lion in Love 1960

8 NELL. Some women will have any sort of a man rather than no man at all.

Ibid.

9 According to her, only a revolution will ever bring true democracy to this country and the sooner revolution comes (she said) the better and even though hundreds of innocents will be slaughtered they will die in a good cause and men must be willing to sacrifice themselves. But that depends I suppose on which men you're thinking of . . .

"Sweetly Sings the Donkey," Sweetly Sings the Donkey 1963

10 "He was very ugly but people can't help the faces they're born with."

Ibid.

11 I am here and I am safe and I am sick of it.

Ibid.

12 . . . Poles seem to be as much condemned to a diet of caviar, vodka and the Polka as the English are to rare old port and pheasant.

"Vodka and Small Pieces of Gold," Ibid.

13 He didn't play with his food anymore till it got cold; instead, down it went like fuel into a furnace keeping the ovens hot, and the energy at boiling point, as Tom hurtled through his life catching up with himself at last.

"Tom Riley," Ibid.

14 We teach you the pleasures of physical exercise—the team-spirit of games, too, for when you leave school finally you will find that life is a game, sometimes serious, sometimes fun, but a game that must be played with true team spirit—there is no room for the outsider in life.

"The Teacher," Ibid.

15 "There aren't enough secrets to go round anymore. Some spies are having to invent secrets in order to earn a living."

"My Uncle, the Spy," Ibid.

2749. Margaret Anne Doody (1939–)

1 One of the most successful literary lies is that the English claim to have invented the novel.

The True Story of the Novel 1996

2 We make a not unimportant spiritual and political as well as personal move when we open a novel and become initiates, entering upon the marshy margins of becoming.

Ibid.

2750. Margaret Drabble (1939–)

1 If I need to understand what I am doing, if I cannot act without my own approbation—and I must act, I have changed, I am no longer capable of inaction—then I will invent a morality that condones me. Though by doing so, I risk condemning all that I have been.

The Waterfall 1969

2 It appalled him, the complacency with which such friends would describe the advantages of living in a mixed area. As though they licensed seedy old ladies and black men to walk their streets, teaching their children of poverty and despair, as their pet hamsters and guinea pigs taught them of sex and death.

Pt. I, The Needle's Eye 1972

3 Rose . . . had the sense that there was something unpleasant that she had promised herself that she would do. While she gave the children their breakfast and drank a cup of tea, she tried to work out what it could be—unearthing accidentally, as she did so, a whole heaped cupboard-full of nasty obligations, such as shoe-buying and glazier-visiting, and of nagging guilts, about people she should have rung back and hadn't, birthday presents unbought and promises unfulfilled.

Ibid.

4 . . . affluence was, quite simply, a question of texture . . . The threadbare carpets of infancy, the coconut matting, the ill-laid linoleum, the utility furniture, the curious upholstery . . . had all spoken of a life too near the bones of subsistence, too little padded, too severely worn.

Ibid.

5 . . . she used to pray . . . and she still prayed, occasionally, not incessantly as she had done through childhood, but every now and then a natural or man-made calamity would push her imperiously to her knees, a massacre, an earthquake, a drowning, and she would implore justice, mercy, intercession, explanation, not praying any more for herself, as she had once so futilely done . . . wondering even as she knelt whether there were any use in such genuflections, and yet pushed down as certainly as if a hand had descended on her head to thrust her from above, crushing her hair and weighing on her skull.

Pt. II, Ibid.

6 How easy it was to underestimate what had been endured.

Ibid.

7 People like admiration more than anything. Whatever can one do about it?

"A Success Story," Spare Rib Magazine 1972

8 . . . if I'd known twenty years ago . . . A pity, really, that one couldn't have had that particular thrill then—the thrill of knowing. It wasn't worth much now.

Ibid.

9 "Much have I travelled in the realms of gold."

The Realms of Gold 1975

10 "To hear him talk of tradition and the individual talent was to enter into a world where old labels had meanings."

Ibid.

11 She taught herself, over the years, to see his death as a healing of some kind, the end of a long illness, a sacrifice. Taken from them for their better health.

Ibid.

12 We seek a utopia in the past, a possible if not ideal society. We seek golden worlds from which we are banished, they recede infinitely, for there never was a golden world, there never was anything but toil and subsistence, cruelty and dullness.

Ibid.

13 . . . the human mind can bear plenty of reality but not too much intermittent gloom.

Ibid.

14 As a geologist, he took a long view of time: even longer than Frances Wingate, archaeologist, and very much longer than Karel Schmidt, historian.

Ibid.

15 But his heart was another matter. It beat in his chest, soft and treacherous. It was invisible. Nobody had ever seen it. He had been unaware of it most of the time, until it had reminded him of its existence. And now he thought of it often, he nursed it carefully, as though it were a baby or a bird, a delicate creature that must not be shocked or offended.

Pt. I, *The Ice Age 1977*

16 People like blowing things up these days, thought Len. They prefer blowing up to building.

Ibid.

17 When nothing is sure, everything is possible.

The Middle Ground 1980

18 We gamble on the present, what else can we do?

Ibid.

19 A male world, a world of suits and ties and speeches, of meetings and money. Charles had conquered it. First he had mocked it, then he had exposed it, then he had joined it, and now he represented it.

The Radiant Way 1987

2751. Roxanne Dunbar (1939–)

1 Man, in conquering nature, conquered the female, who had worked with nature, not against it, to produce food and to reproduce the human race.

"Feminine Liberation as the Basis for Social Revolution,"
Sisterhood Is Powerful, Robin Morgan,* ed. *1970*
*See 2864.

2 We live under an international caste system, at the top of which is the Western white male ruling class, and at the bottom of which is the female of the nonwhite colonized world.

Ibid.

3 In reality, the family has fallen apart. Nearly half of all marriages end in divorce, and the family unit is a decadent, energy-absorbing, destructive, wasteful institution for everyone except the ruling class for which the institution was created.

Ibid.

2752. Marian Wright Edelman (1939–)

1 Just because a child's parents are poor or uneducated is no reason to deprive the child of basic human rights to health care, education, proper nutrition. Clearly we ignore the needs of black children, poor children, and handicapped children in the country.

Quoted in "Society's Pushed-Out Children" by
Marge Casady, *Psychology Today* (New York) *June 1975*

2 I've been struck by the upside-down priorities of the juvenile-justice system. We are willing to spend the least amount of money to keep a kid at home, more to put him in a foster home, and the most to institutionalize him.

Ibid.

3 Some school officials have forgotten the reason they are there. Expediency and efficiency in administration have somehow become more important than educating children.

Ibid.

4 Parents have become so convinced that educators know what is best for children that they forget that they themselves are really the experts.

Ibid.

5 The poor have been sent to the front lines of a federal budget deficit reduction war that few other groups were drafted to fight.

Families in Peril 1987

6 Democracy is not a spectator sport.

Ibid.

7 It is a spiritually impoverished nation that permits infants and children to be the poorest Americans.

The Measure of Our Success 1992

8 The 1990s' struggle is for America's conscience and future—a future that is being determined right now in the bodies and minds and spirits of every American child.

Ibid.

9 Children must have at least one person who believes in them. It could be a counselor, a teacher, a preacher, a friend. It could be you. You never know when a little love, a little support, will plant a small seed of hope.

Ibid.

10 . . . help America remember that the fellowship of human beings is more important than the fellowship of race and class and gender.

"25 Lessons for Life," Ibid.

11 . . . your wife is not your mother or maid, but your partner and friend.

Ibid.

12 . . . don't be afraid of hard work.

Ibid.

13 One thing the country does not understand is that we don't have a child to waste. We will not be a strong country unless we invest in every one of our children. We need the poor black kid, the poor brown kid, the poor white kid to be productive. All children are essential to America's future.

Quoted in "Make Things Better For Somebody" by
Wallace Terry, *Parade Magazine 14 February 1993*

14 If recent trends continue, by the end of the century, poverty will overtake one in every four children. We need a massive,

insistent movement telling the White House and the Congress that no American child will be left behind.

Ibid.

15 We learned [as children] that our worth was measured by what was in our heads and hearts, not by material possession.

Ibid.

16 Service to others is the rent you pay for living on this planet.

Ibid.

17 I am less concerned about whether my kids grow up Jewish or Christian than if they have inner strength and a sense of service.*

Ibid.

*Reference to her three sons' "Baptist bar mitzvahs."

18 Our worst nightmares are coming true. After years of epidemic poverty, joblessness, racial intolerance, family disintegration, domestic violence and drug and alcohol abuse, the crisis of children having children has been eclipsed by the greater crisis of children killing children.

Annual Report, Children's Defense Fund 1993

19 If we don't wake up and take care of our children, the country is going to go to hell. This is our moral and practical Achilles heel.

Quoted in Intelligence Report by Jane Ciabattari, Parade Magazine 3 May 1997

2753. Terry Garthwaite (1939–)

1 from bessie to bebe to billie to boz
there's a lot more power than the wizard of oz

"Rock and Roller" 1975

2754. Joan Goulianos (1939–)

1 . . . these . . . women [of history] . . . wrote in a world which was controlled by men, a world in which women's revelations, if they were anything but conventional, might not be welcomed, might not be recognized, and they wrote nevertheless.

Introduction, By a Woman Writt 1973

2 But, overall, it was men who were the critics, the publishers, the professors, the sources of support. It was men who had the power to praise women's work, to bring them to public attention, or to ridicule them, to doom them . . . to obscurity.

Ibid.

2755. Germaine Greer (1939–)

1 The consequences of militancy do not disappear when the need for militancy is over. Freedom is fragile and must be protected. To sacrifice it, even as a temporary measure, is to betray it.

Introduction, The Female Eunuch 1971

2 Every time a man unburdens his heart to a stranger he reaffirms the love that unites humanity.

"The Ideal," Ibid.

3 The only causes of regret are laziness, outbursts of temper, hurting others, prejudice, jealousy and envy.

Ibid.

4 Our life-style contains more Thanatos than Eros, for egotism, exploitation, deception, obsession and addiction have more place in us than eroticism, joy, generosity and spontaneity.

Ibid.

5 Every time a woman makes herself laugh at her husband's often-told jokes she betrays him. The man who looks at his woman and says "What would I do without you?" is already destroyed.

"Egotism," Ibid.

6 As soon as we find ourselves working at being indispensable, rigging up a pattern of vulnerability in our loved ones, we ought to know that our love has taken the socially sanctioned form of egotism.

Ibid.

7 Woman . . . cannot be content with health and agility: she must make exorbitant efforts to appear something that never could exist without a diligent perversion of nature. Is it too much to ask that women be spared the daily struggle for superhuman beauty in order to offer it to the caresses of a subhumanly ugly mate?

"Loathing and Disgust," Ibid.

8 Women have very little idea of how much men hate them.

Ibid.

9 Man made one grave mistake: in answer to vaguely reformist and humanitarian agitation he admitted women to politics and the professions. The conservatives who saw this as the undermining of our civilization and the end of the state and marriage were right after all; it is time for the demolition to begin.

"Revolution," Ibid.

10 Revolution is the festival of the oppressed.

Ibid.

11 Maybe I couldn't make it. Maybe I don't have a pretty smile, good teeth, nice tits, long legs, a cheeky arse, a sexy voice. Maybe I don't know how to handle men and increase my market value, so that the rewards due to the feminine will accrue to me. Then again, maybe I'm sick of the masquerade. I'm sick of pretending eternal youth. I'm sick of belying my own intelligence, my own will, my own sex. I'm sick of peering at the world through false eyelashes, so everything I see is mixed with a shadow of bought hairs; I'm sick of weighting my head with a dead mane, unable to move my neck freely, terrified of rain, of wind, of dancing too vigorously in case I sweat into my lacquered curls. I'm sick of the Powder Room. I'm sick of pretending that some fatuous male's self-important pronouncements are the objects of my undivided attention. I'm sick of going to films and plays when someone else wants to, and sick of having no opinions of my own about either. I'm sick of being a transvestite. I refuse to be a female impersonator. I am a woman, not a castrate.

"Soul: The Stereotype," Ibid.

12 Freud* is the father of psychoanalysis. It had no mother.

"The Psychological Sell," Ibid.

*Austrian physician and founder of psychoanalysis (1856–1939).

13 What is the arms race and the cold war but the continuation of male competitiveness and aggression into the inhuman sphere of computer-run institutions? If women are to cease producing cannon fodder for the final holocaust they must rescue men from the perversities of their own polarization.

Ibid.

14 If marriage and family depend upon the castration of women let them change or disappear.

Ibid.

15 Even crushed against his brother in the Tube the average Englishman pretends desperately that he is alone.
"Womanpower," Ibid.

16 Womanpower means the self-determination of women, and that means that all the baggage of paternalistic society will have to be thrown overboard.
Ibid.

17 Changing partners is such a thoroughly unspontaneous activity, so divorced from the vagaries of genuine sexual desire—no more than a variant on the square dance. In such a transaction sex is the sufferer: passion becomes lechery.
"Family," Ibid.

18 There is no such thing as security. There never has been. . . .
"Security," Ibid.

19 Loneliness is never more cruel than when it is felt in close propinquity with someone who has ceased to communicate.
Ibid.

20 Love, love, love—all the wretched cant of it, masking egotism, lust, masochism, fantasy under a mythology of sentimental postures.
"Obsession," Ibid.

21 Australia is a huge rest home, where no unwelcome news is ever wafted on to the pages of the worst newspapers in the world.
Observer (London) *1 August 1982*

22 We in the West do not refrain from childbirth because we are concerned about the population explosion or because we feel we cannot afford children, but because we do not like children.
Ch. 1, *Sex and Destiny 1984*

23 The most threatened group in human societies as in animal societies is the unmated male: the unmated male is more likely to wind up in prison or in an asylum or dead than his mated counterpart. He is less likely to be promoted at work and he is considered a poor credit risk.
Ch. 2, Ibid.

24 The management of fertility is one of the most important functions of adulthood.
Ibid.

25 All societies on the verge of death are masculine. A society can survive with only one man; no society will survive a shortage of women.
Ch. 3, Ibid.

26 It is fatally easy for Western folk, who have discarded chastity as a value for themselves, to suppose that it can have no value for anyone else. At the same time as Californians try to re-invent "celibacy," by which they seem to mean perverse restraint, the rest of us call societies which place a high value on chastity "backward."
Ch. 4, Ibid.

27 The blind conviction that we have to do something about other people's reproductive behaviour, and that we may have to do it whether they like it or not, derives from the assumption that the world belongs to us, who have so expertly depleted its resources, rather than to them, who have not.
Ch. 14, Ibid.

28 Perhaps catastrophe is the natural human environment, and even though we spend a good deal of energy trying to get away from it, we are programmed for survival amid catastrophe.
Ibid.

29 The only perfect love to be found on earth is not sexual love, which is riddled with hostility and insecurity, but the wordless commitment of families, which takes as its model mother-love. This is not to say that fathers have no place, for father-love, with its driving for self-improvement and discipline, is also essential to survival, but that uncorrected father-love, father-love as it were practised by both parents, is a way to annihilation.
Introduction, *The Madwoman's Underclothes 1986*

30 The compelled mother loves her child as the caged bird sings. The song does not justify the cage nor the love the enforcement.
"Abortion," *Sunday Times* (London, 21 May 1972), Ibid.

31 There has come into existence, chiefly in America, a breed of men who claim to be feminists. They imagine that they have understood "what women want" and that they are capable of giving it to them. They help with the dishes at home and make their own coffee in the office, basking the while in the refulgent consciousness of virtue. . . . Such men are apt to think of the true male feminists as utterly chauvinistic.
"Eternal War: Strindberg's* View of Sex," *Spectator* (London, 3 June 1978), Ibid.
*August Strindberg, Swedish playwright (1849–1912).

32 Sadism is the necessary outcome of the belief that one sex is passive and suffers sex at the hands of another. If we are to escape any of the hideous effects of this mythology, effects which include war and capital punishment, we must regain the power of the cunt.
"Lady Love Your Cunt," *Suck* (London, 1971), Ibid.

33 Only one thing is certain: if pot is legalized, it won't be for our benefit but for the authorities'. To have it legalized will also be to lose control of it.
"Flip-top Legal Pot," *Oz* (London, October 1968), Ibid.

34 The tragedy of machismo is that a man is never quite man enough.
"My Mailer* Problem," *Esquire* (New York, September 1971), Ibid.
*Norman Mailer, American writer (1923–), winner of two Pulitzer Prizes (1968, 1979).

35 The hippie is the scion of surplus value. The dropout can only claim sanctity in a society which offers something to be dropped out of—career, ambition, conspicuous consumption. The effects of hippie sanctimony can only be felt in the context of others who plunder his lifestyle for what they find good or profitable, a process known as rip-off by the hippie, who will not see how savagely he has pillaged intricate and demanding civilizations for his own parodic lifestyle.
Quoted in "Hippies in Asia," *Sunday Times* (London, 27 August 1972) Ibid.

36 Human beings have an inalienable right to invent themselves; when that right is pre-empted it is called brain-washing.
Times (London) *1 February 1986*

37 English culture is basically homosexual in the sense that the men only really care about other men.
Daily Mail (London) *18 April 1988*

38 Libraries are reservoirs of strength, grace and wit, reminders of order, calm and continuity, lakes of mental energy, neither

warm nor cold, light nor dark. The pleasure they give is steady, unorgiastic, reliable, deep and long-lasting. In any library in the world, I am at home, unself-conscious, still and absorbed.

"Still in Melbourne, January 1987," *Daddy, We Hardly Knew You* 1989

39 The older woman's love is not love of herself, nor of herself mirrored in a lover's eyes, nor is it corrupted by need. It is a feeling of tenderness so still and deep and warm that it gilds every grassblade and blesses every fly. It includes the ones who have a claim on it, and a great deal else besides. I wouldn't have missed it for the world.

Introduction, *The Change: Women, Aging and the Menopause* 1991

40 The misery of the middle-aged woman is a grey and hopeless thing, born of having nothing to live for, of disappointment and resentment at having been gypped by consumer society, and surviving merely to be the butt of its unthinking scorn.

Ibid.

41 After centuries of conditioning of the female into the condition of perpetual girlishness called femininity, we cannot remember what femaleness is.

Ch. 2, *Ibid.*

42 Developing the muscles of the soul demands no competitive spirit, no killer instinct, although it may erect pain barriers that the spiritual athlete must crash through.

Ibid.

43 All that remains to the mother in modern consumer society is the role of scapegoat; psychoanalysis uses huge amounts of money and time to persuade analysands to foist their problems on to the absent mother, who has no opportunity to utter a word in her own defence. Hostility to the mother in our societies is an index of mental health.

Ch. 3, *Ibid.*

44 The climacteric marks the end of apologizing. The chrysalis of conditioning has once for all to break and the female woman finally to emerge.

Ch. 17, *Ibid.*

45 Matters are not made easier for the whole woman if her gynecologist treats her as a pair of dead ovaries, her rheumatologist as a collection of joints, her bone specialist as a skeleton, her psychiatrist as a set of traumas, her gerontologist as an unsuitable candidate for treatment and her physician as a nuisance.

(p. 160), *Ibid.*

46 The supporters of HRT* see distress at change of life as the result of a deficiency, as diabetes is a result of a deficiency in insulin. . . . Until we know if women without symptoms have something that women with symptoms do not, we have no logical ground for describing menopausal distress as a deficiency disease.

(pp. 171–73), *Ibid.*

*Hormone replacement therapy.

2756. Matina Horner (1939–)

1 Unusual excellence in women was clearly associated for them with the loss of femininity, social rejection, personal or societal destruction or some combination of the above.

Women and Success: The Anatomy of Achievement 1964

2757. Maria Teresa Horta (1939–)

Coauthor with Maria Isabel Barreno (see 2737) and Maria Fatima Velho da Costa (see 2789).

2758. Penelope Keith (1939–)

1 Shyness is just egotism out of its depth.

Quoted in *Daily Mail* (London) *27 June 1988*

2759. Barbara Kolb (1939–)

1 . . . composing a piece of music is very feminine. It is sensitive, emotional, contemplative. By comparison, doing housework is positively masculine.

Quoted in "A Matter of Art, Not Sex," *Time* (New York) *10 November 1975*

2760. Nancy Mairs (1939–)

1 I'm no mystic, although when I was much younger, especially while I was reading Dame Julian of Norwich and St. John of the Cross, I wished that I were one. In later years I've come to think it's just as well that I'm not. If I had a mystical experience—saw Jesus, say, or felt his hand in mine—I'd behave badly, I suspect: screech, the way I do when a spider surprises me, or faint away.

"God's Will," *Ordinary Time: Cycles in Marriage, Faith and Renewal* 1993

2 Since "cure" and "heal" can be used interchangeably, I didn't reflect before making my choice. . . . The one occurrence is not necessarily more miraculous than the other, but the drama of it—the paralytic rising to his feet and trudging with his pallet past the outraged scribes, Lazarus staggering from the cave's mouth in his stinking graveclothes—distracts and delights as healing's tedium cannot do.

Ibid.

3 God is no White Knight who charges into the world to pluck us like distressed damsels from the jaws of dragons, or diseases. God chooses to become present to and through us. It is up to us to rescue one another.

Ibid.

2761. Lynn Martin (1939–)

1 In days when I grew up and before, job security meant one's union or one's company. For women it was often one's husband.

But in today's world of company closures and mergers, a union can't stop [a firm] from moving overseas or from shutting down.

Job security now has to be with each individual. This department [of Labor], no matter how well meaning, has been tied to another past.

Quoted in "Lynn Martin's new message" by Robert Lewis, *AARP Bulletin*, Vol. 33, No. 1 *January 1992*

2 It seems a little odd to be talking about the older worker; maybe that's the 90-year-old.

Ibid.

3 It isn't that family leave isn't a good idea. It's do you mandate it? Do you take away that flexibility from an employer?

Ibid.

4 It's never wise to keep the House [of Representatives] in after 11. It's like managing a nursery school without a nap.

(p. 464), Quoted in *Politics in America* 1990 ed. by Philip D. Duncan, *1991*

2762. Erika Munk (1939–)

1   . . . even in a world with five billion inhabitants, people suffer history one by one.
"The world turned upside down," *The Women's Review of Books*, Vol. XIV, No 8 *May 1997*

2   She believed in brotherhood, and it arrived as Cain and Abel.
Ibid.

3   We're back at the gates of Troy or the sack of Rome, but with better technology.
Ibid.

4   Hope is the commodity in shortest supply for all refugees.
Ibid.

5   The Bosnian conflict isn't over. Even if large-scale violence doesn't recur, nothing has been solved—the refugees aren't home, the country's not being rebuilt, its political structures are a sham and war criminals lounge untouched in sidewalk cafes. The worldwide rise of fundamentalist nationalism, with its inevitable atrocity and misogyny, remains undeterred.
Ibid.

2763. Kathrin Perutz (1939–)

1   The true man or woman must be deeply sexual; the only true intercourse between humans is sexual; levels of pleasure have almost become notches in the yardstick of goodness; and sexual variation is as necessary to marriage now as once social graces were. . . . Love must be made—or sex must be had—a prescribed number of times a week; otherwise one falls from grace and competition.
Marriage is Hell 1972

2764. Letty Cottin Pogrebin (1939–)

1   . . . lifestyles and sex roles are passed from parents to children as inexorably as blue eyes or small feet.
"Down with Sexist Upbringing," *The First Ms. Reader*, Francine Klagsbrun, ed. *1972*

2   In school books, the Dick and Jane syndrome reinforced our emerging attitudes. The arithmetic books posed appropriate conundrums: "Ann has three pies . . . Dan has three rockets . . . ." We read the nuances between the lines: Ann keeps her eye on the oven; Dan sets his sights on the moon.
Ibid.

3   . . . children's liberation is the next item on our civil right's shopping list.
Ibid.

4   Boys don't make passes at female smart-asses.
Ibid.

2765. Helen Prejean (1939–)

1   The sheer weight of his loneliness, his abandonment, draws me. I abhor the evil he has done. But I sense something, some sheer and essential humanness, and that, perhaps, is what draws me most of all.
Dead Man Walking: An Eyewitness Account of the Death Penalty in the United States 1993

2   I realize that I cannot stand by silently as my government executes its citizens. If I do not speak out and resist, I am an accomplice.
Ibid.

3   Do you really believe that Jesus, who taught us not to return hate for hate and evil for evil and whose dying words were, "Father, forgive them," would participate in these executions? Would Jesus pull the switch?*
Ibid.

* Remark to the Louisiana prison warden.

4   But each human being is a personal universe, someone of value. And the people I have accompanied to their deaths have gone there sensing their own worth and their own dignity.
Speech, Seattle, quoted in "A personal journey into death row" by John Marshall, *Seattle Post-Intelligencer*, C1–4 *16 November 1993*

5   The death penalty is an act of despair by society. It says that people can be sealed up and done away with—that there is absolutely nothing redeemable about them. And to those people and their families, it signals that they are nothing but human waste.
Ibid.

2766. Jane Bryant Quinn (1939–)

1   A poor man may still get into heaven, but after Reaganization, he may not be able to get into court.
Lawyer's Wit and Wisdom, Bruce Nash, Allan Zullo, eds.; Kathryn Zullo, compiler *1995*

2   Lawyers are . . . operators of toll bridges across which anyone in search of justice must pass.
Remark, quoted in *Newsweek* (New York) *9 October 1978*

2767. Willa Mae Reid (1939–)

1   [There is an] insidious, contradictory belief that Black women have always had it better than Black men, and still do. For example, there is the story that Black women have always enjoyed "sexual liberation," . . . The truth is that Black women, from the time of slavery to this very day, have been victimized the most by the warped sexual ideas of this racist society. As slaves, we were raped, abused, and beaten at the whim of the slave owners . . . We were bred like cattle . . . Black women were assumed to be the sexual property of the owner, his friends, visitors, and relatives.
"Changing Attitudes Among Black Women," *International Socialist Review March 1975*

2   What must be recognized is that the status of black women places us at the intersection of all the forms of subjugation in this society—racial oppression, sexual oppression, economic exploitation. We are a natural part of many different struggles—as Black people, as union members, as unemployed, as parents, as women.
Ibid.

3   The oppression of women, like the oppression of blacks, is one of the pillars of the capitalist system of exploitation. The fight to weaken any one of these pillars contributes to weakening the entire structure that victimizes all of us.
Ibid.

2768. Aline Rousselle (1939–)

1   Paradoxically, the spilling of blood, . . . symbolized the respect in which life was held by all. Everyone was insistent on the necessity of spilling blood, as it was the price that had to be paid for the survival of the community and for the salvation of each individual.
Porneia: On Desire and the Body in Antiquity, F. Pheasant, tr. *1988*

2769. Susan Sherman (1939–)

1 Analysis. Cross-reference analysis. The age of analysis.
Psychological, philosophical, poetic analysis. Not the
event, but the picture of the event.
"The Fourth Wall," St. 2, El Corno Emplumado 1966

2 *In Soweto*
the people continue to rebel
in Soweto
the people continue to fight back
In Manhattan
my student looks at the 5 o'clock news

His head is filled with facts
He knows nothing
He learns nothing

He doesn't even know "Why?"
"Facts," A Poetics of Resistance: Women Writing in El
Salvador, South Africa, and the United States,
Mary K. DeShazer, ed. 1994

2770. Grace Slick (1939–)

1 Remember what the doormouse said:
"Feed your head.
Feed your head.
Feed your head."
"White Rabbit" 1965

2771. Eleanor Smeal (1939–)

1 Just think—guns have a constitutional amendment protecting
them and women don't.
Fundraising letter, Fund for the Feminist Majority 1989

2 Any system that produces 95% men members and 5% women
members—like Congress—is sex discriminatory. We must
show how the election rules lock women out, and we must
change these rules!
Ibid.

3 Once again, this vote shows that the under-representation of
women in Congress is cheating all women. This 41% difference between men and women representatives is not a
gender gap—it's a gender *gulf*. If women made up 50% of
the House, poor women would have Medicaid funding for
abortion, and the Hyde amendment* would never have
passed.
"Congress Moves Slowly . . . " by Jyotsna Sreenivasan and
Christine Onyango, Feminist Majority Report, Vol. 5, No. 2
August–September 1993
*1976:prohibited use of Medicaid funds for abortions; upheld by
U.S. Supremem Court 30 June 1980.

2772. Loretta Swit (1939–)

1 So much of life is luck. One day you make a right turn and get
hit by a car. Turn left and you meet the love of your life. I think
I made the correct turn.
*Quoted in "M*A*S*H Supporting Players About Ready for*
Civilian Careers" by Bob Wisehart, The Times/Picayune
(New Orleans) 17 September 1981

2773. Solveig Torvik (1939–)

1 And women surely won't be able to rest easy until it becomes
just as routine for a woman to fail as Cabinet officer as it has

been for the legions of third-rate men who so ineptly have dis-
charged those duties in recent decades.
"Clinton can't please everyone," Seattle Post-Intelligencer,
Op-Ed, A7 30 December 1992

2 The world needs more mean women.
Ibid.

2774. Naomi Weisstein (1939–)

1 . . . in order to understand why people do what they do, and
certainly in order to change what people do, psychologists
must turn away from the theory of the causal nature of the
inner dynamic and look at the social context within which individuals live.
Address, "'Kinder, Kuche, Kirche' as Scientific Law:
Psychology Constructs the Female," American Studies
Association (California) 26 October 1968

2 Until psychologists realize that it is they who are limiting discovery of human potential . . . by their assumption that people move
in a context-free ether, with only their innate dispositions and
their individual traits determining what they will do, then psychology will have nothing of substance to offer in this task.
Ibid.

3 . . . there isn't the tiniest shred of evidence that . . . fantasies of
servitude and childish dependence have anything to do with
woman's true potential. . . .
Ibid.

4 Except for their genitals, I don't know what immutable differences exist between men and women. Perhaps there are some
other unchangeable differences; probably there are a number
of irrelevant differences. But it is clear that until social expectations for men and women are equal, until we provide equal
respect for both sexes, answers to this question will simply reflect our prejudices.
"Woman as Nigger," Psychology Today (New York)
October 1969

5 The problem with insight, sensitivity and intuition is that they
tend to confirm our biases. At one time people were convinced
of their ability to identify witches. All it required was sensitivity to the workings of the devil. Clinical experience is not the
same thing as empirical evidence.
Ibid.

6 . . . a typical minority-group stereotype—woman as nigger—if
she knows her place (home), she is really a quite lovable, loving creature, happy and childlike.
Ibid.

7 Psychology has nothing to say about what women are really
like, what they need and what they want, for the simple reason
that psychology does not know. Yet psychologists will hold
forth endlessly on the true nature of woman, with dismaying
enthusiasm and disquieting certitude.
Ibid.

8 Humor as a weapon in the social arsenal constructed to maintain caste, class, race, and sex inequalities is a very common
thing.
Introduction, She Needs 1973

9 Why have they been telling us women lately that we have no
sense of humor—when we are always laughing? . . . And when
we're not laughing, we're smiling.
Ibid.

10 Evidence and reason: my heroes and my guides.

"Adventures of a Woman in Science," *Women Look at
Biology Looking at Women*, Ruth Hubbard,*
Mary Sue Henifin and Barbara Fried, eds. *1979*

*See 2247.

2775. Toni Cade Bambara (1939–1995)

1 Personally, Freud's "anatomy is destiny" has always horrified me. *Kirche, Kusse, Kuche, Kinde* made me sick. Career
woman versus wife-mother has always struck me as a false
dichotomy. The-pill-'ll-make-you-gals-run-wild a lot of male
chauvinist anxiety. Dump-the-pill a truncated statement. I
think most women have pondered, those who have the heart
to ponder at all, the oppressive nature of pregnancy, the
tyranny of the child burden, the stupidity of male-female divisions, the obscene nature of employment discrimination.
And day-care and nurseries being what they are, paid maternity leaves being rare, the whole memory of wham bam
thank you ma'am and the big Getaway a horrible nightmare,
poverty so ugly, the family unit being the last word in social-
izing institutions to prepare us all for the ultimate rip-off
and perpetuate the status quo, and abortion fatalities being
what they are—of course the pill.

"The Pill," *Onyx* August 1969

2 We are involved in a struggle for liberation: liberation from
the exploitive and dehumanizing system of racism, from the
manipulative control of a corporate society; liberation from
the constrictive norms of "mainstream" culture, from the syn-
thetic myths that encourage us to fashion ourselves rashly
from without (reactive) rather than from within (creation).

Preface, *The Black Woman* 1970

3 The genocidal bloodbath of centuries and centuries of witch
hunts sheds some light on the hysterical attitude white men
have regarding their women.

Lecture, "The Scattered Sopranos," Livingston College
Black Women's Seminar, Ibid.

4 Revolution begins with the self, in the self.

Ibid.

5 Not all speed is movement . . . Ain't no such animal as an instant guerilla.

Ibid.

6 Yesterday Dada Bibi had hugged her hello and didn't even fuss
where you been little sister and why ain't you been coming
round, don't you want to know about your heritage, ain't you
got not pride? Dada Bibi never said none of them things ever.
She just hugged you and helped you do whatever it was you
thought you came to do at the Center.

"A Girl's Story," *The Sea Birds Are Still Alive* 1974

7 Being American and being proud and they weren't the same in
her head. When Dada Bibi talked about Harriet Tubman* and
them, she felt proud. She felt it in her neck and in her spine.
When the brother who ran the program for the little kids
talked about powerful white Americans robbing Africa and
bombing Vietnam and doing ugly all over the world, causing
hard times for Black folks and other colored people, she was
glad not to be American.

Ibid.

*See 908.

8 It was simpler to watch than to listen.

Ibid.

9 "What is wrong, Old Wife? What is happening to the daughters of the yam? Seem like they just don't know how to draw
up the powers from the deep like before."

The Salt Eaters 1980

10 Bless the workers and beam on me if you please.

Dedication Page, Ibid.

2776. Nobuko Albery (1940?–)

1 "Many may argue it's the lowest of the low among living creatures, to be performers. But don't forget, Buddha put us there,
and we actors live in service to the gods. . . . We, the humblest
leeches of the temples and shrines, though called untouchables,
beggars and dung-worms, by singing, dancing, giving happiness to thousands of miserable souls should be the first
amongst holy herons and peace blossoms to be allowed into
Heaven of Blissful Peace."

Ch. 1, *The House of Kanze* 1986

2 "I'd rather forgo sleep today than sleeplessly lament my lost
fortune tomorrow."

Ch. 9, Ibid.

3 "When you forget the beginner's awe, you start decaying."

Ch. 10, Ibid.

4 "Of course it is true that our art exists only when we are seen;
we are slaves to our audiences. But at the same time, we must
always be a step ahead of them. We must tantalize, not bore
them. . . . To shock, Motomasa, is a Flower of our art, like a
sting of a certain bee that is said to revive the dead."

Ch. 21, Ibid.

2777. Angeles Arrien (1940–)

1 Story opens us to discover where we really are in our journey
rather than where we think we are.

"Transformation in the Millennium," *The Fabric of the
Future: Women Visionaries of Today Illuminate the Path
to Tomorrow*, M.J. Ryan, ed. *1998*

2 We need to bless those who challenge us to be fully loving;
they mirror to us where we may withhold our love by being
closed-hearted, half-hearted, and weak-hearted. They are great
teachers for us, and remind us that the greatest remorse for
human beings is love unexpressed.

Ibid.

3 There comes a time in the spiritual journey where our patterns
of denial and our patterns of indulgence become more painful
than truly being ourselves. This is when we begin finally to
risk telling the truth about who we really are.

Ibid.

4 Whenever we experience happiness and peace in our natures,
we are at the gate where the medicines of joy, laughter, play,
fun, and humor flourish.

Ibid.

5 The experiences of solitude are those in which we feel filled by
silence, rather than empty or alone.

Ibid.

2778. Moira Bachman (fl. 1940s)

1 In my apron I carry nails, pliers, a heavy hammer, and pride.

Organization for Equal Education of the Sexes *n.d.*

2779. Elizabeth Bartholet (1940–)

1 A sane and humane society should encourage people to provide for these existing children rather than bring more children into the world.

Family Bonds: Adoption and the Politics of Parenting 1993

2 Adoption has a very bad name. All the characters in the adoption story are regularly described as victims, forced by circum- stances to live out lives that are significantly diminished in quality.

(p. 164), Ibid.

3 Despite . . . universal denigration, the available evidence shows that adoption works extremely well for all those immediately concerned. Why is the success story being suppressed? It may be too threatening. It means, among other things, that women can give away their children or lose their capacity for pregnancy and still function as full human beings. It means that children who are mistreated by their birth parents can be removed for parenting by others. It means that biology is *not* destiny. It raises questions about the goal of self-perpetuation and the value of promoting our own racial, cultural, and national groups. It forces us to think about the appropriate definition of family and community.

(p. 165), Ibid.

4 Adoption creates a family that in important ways is not "nuclear." It creates a family that is *connected* to another family, the birth family, and often to different cultures and to different racial, ethnic, and national groups as well. Adoptive families might teach us something about the value for families of connection with the larger community.

(p. 186), Ibid.

5 There may be some inborn need to procreate, but there are also inborn needs to nurture. Why does organized society seem to want to encourage its members to obsess over the former at the expense of the latter?

(p. 231), Ibid.

2780. Louise Bernikow (1940–)

1 Pep is what happened in American history before *vigah*, but it only applied to females. Pep was cheerfulness. It mysteriously resided in the Ipana smile.

"Confessions of an Ex-Cheerleader," *Ms.* (New York)
October 1973

2 Every time I say "sure" when I mean "no," every time I smile brightly when I'm exploding with rage, every time I imagine my man's achievement is my own, I know the cheerleader never really died. I feel her shaking her ass inside me and I hear her breathless, girlish voice mutter "T-E-A-M, Yea, Team."

Ibid.

3 The question arises as to whether it is possible *not* to live in the world of men and still to live in the world. The answer arises nearly as quickly that this can only happen if men are not thought of as "the world."

Introduction, *The World Split Open 1974*

4 A witch was a woman with enormous power, a woman who might change the natural world. She was "uncivilized" and in opposition to the world of the King, the court, polite society. She had to be controlled.

Ch. 1, *Among Women 1980*

5 Acknowledging the tension, distance, and conflict, where is a map of the nurturance, the connection, the ways in which the

torch is passed from mother to daughter or from daughter to mother?

Ch. 2, In Colette.* Colette is the Poet of Passion Between
Mother and Daughter. Colette Paints the Portrait of Mother
as the Tree of Life, Ibid.

*See 1341.

6 I say you hurt me. You say I scorned you. We say we care. It begins. The conversation begins.

Ch. 6, Ibid.

2781. Anita Bryant (1940–)

1 If homosexuality were the normal way, God would have made Adam and Bruce.

Remark, Quoted in *The New York Times 1977*

2782. Susan Cahill (1940–)

1 As many historians have pointed out, religious institutions, despite their petrified official hierarchies, have provided abundant opportunities for women's self-authorization and -actualization. In spite of themselves, these institutions have nurtured the love of freedom and goodness and justice within their own hidebound bodies.

Introduction, *Wise Women: Over 2000 Years of Spiritual
Writing by Women*, ed. 1996

2 The power and beauty of women's witness to a spiritual dimension of experience, of a world beyond the single separative self, resonate through centuries of writing.

Ibid.

3 What is common . . . is a desire to resolve—or a refusal to admit—the old dualisms of patriarchal religion: between self and other, body and soul, male and female, the sacred and the secular, God the Father and God the Mother. The failures of history point up the obfuscating and nullifying effects of such bifurcations and abstractions on the work of building an earth fit for human beings.

Ibid.

4 From Eros, the God/Goddess of Love, the timeless source of mystical longing, comes the sensory language of mysticism and its imagery of touching, dancing, arousal, penetration, ectasy, suckling, satisfaction.

Ibid.

2783. Maria Campbell (1940–)

1 Cheechum [grandmother] would often say scornfully of this God that he took more money from us than the Hudson's Bay store.

Halfbreed 1973

2 She taught me to see beauty in all things around me; that inside each thing a spirit lived, that it was vital too, regardless of whether it was only a leaf or a blade of grass, and by recognizing its life and beauty I was accepting God. . . . that when my body became old my spirit would leave and I'd come back and live again. She said God lives in you and looks like you, and not to worry about him floating around in a beard and a white cloak; that the Devil lives in you and in all things, and that he looks like you and not like a cow. . . . Her explanation made much more sense than anything Christianity had ever taught me.

Ibid.

3 Dreams are so important in one's life, yet when followed blindly they can lead to the disintegration of one's soul.

Ibid.

4 My Cheechum used to tell me that when the government gives you something, they take all that you have in return—your pride, your dignity, all the things that make you a living soul. When they are sure they have everything they give you a blanket to cover your shame. She said that the churches with their talk about God, the Devil, heaven and hell, and schools that taught children to be ashamed, were all part of that government. . . . She used to say that all our people wore blankets, each in his own way.

Ibid.

5 I no longer need my blanket to survive.

Ibid.

2784. Isabel do Carmo (1940–)

1 The movement must be accompanied by force. . . . There must be an armed insurrection.

Quoted in *Time* (New York) 30 October 1975

2 There can be no halfway solutions, no half measures. That won't work. We must have either pure socialism or we will go back to fascism.

Ibid.

3 In our party, being a woman is no problem. After all, it is a revolutionary party.

Ibid.

2785. Ana Carrigan (194-?–)

1 . . . back to *campesino* country, to Indian country, where there are no historical monuments or archives or television cameras to worry about, and where the casualties are politically invisible.*

The Palace of Justice, A Colombian Tragedy 1993
*Reference to the guerilla attack on 6 November 1985 on the Palace of Justice, and the army's brutal response to it.

2786. Kim Chernin (1940–)

1 The obsession [of slenderness] . . . might well be considered one of the most serious forms of suffering affecting women in America today.

The Obsession 1981

2 They could not see they were too thin because slenderness had become a statement of power. There could never be too much of it, since more implied that the will had grown even stronger in its relentless struggle to dominate matter.

Ibid.

3 And so we leave home, we leave the apron and . . . put on . . . tailored executive suits. . . . And now we take ourselves in hand, tailoring ourselves to the specifications of this world we are so eager to enter. We strip our bodies of flesh, our hearts of the overflow of feeling, our language of exuberant and dramatic imprecisions. We cut back the flight of our fancy, make our thoughts rigorous and subject (this marvelous rushing intuitive leaping capacity of ours) to measure of demonstration and proof, trying not to talk with our hands, trying hard to subdue our voices, getting our bursts of laughter under control.

The Hungry Self 1985

2787. Phyllis Chesler (1940–)

1 At this moment in history only women can (if they will) support the entry or re-entry of women into the human race.

Women and Madness 1972

2 There is a double standard of mental health—one for men, another for women—existing among most clinicians. . . . For a woman to be healthy, she must "adjust" to and accept the behavioral norms of her sex—passivity, acquiescence, self-sacrifice, and lack of ambition—even though these kinds of "loser" behaviors are generally regarded as socially undesirable (i.e. nonmasculine).

Ibid.

3 While [women] live longer than ever before, and longer than men, there is less and less use for them in the only place they have been given—within the family. Many newly useless women are emerging more publicly and visibly into insanity and institutions.

Ibid.

4 How can we deny that children bond with their birth mothers in utero, and that children suffer terribly in all kinds of ways when this bond is prematurely or abruptly terminated? . . . Today, adoption is not primarily about the welfare of children; it is about the welfare of those adults who want to "have" children.

Quoted in "Maternal triangle" by Carol Sternhell,*
The Women's Review of Books, Vol. XI, No. 1
October 1993
*See 3653.

5 The clinical distrust of mothers, simply because they are women, the eagerness to bend over backward to like fathers, simply because they are men, is mind-numbing. Mother-blaming and woman-hatred fairly sizzle on clinical pages.

Introduction, *Women and Madness*, 25th Anniversary Ed.
1997

6 . . . what we call "madness" can also be caused or exacerbated by injustice and cruelty, within the family and society; and that freedom, radical legal reform, political struggle, and kindness are crucial to psychological and moral health.

Ibid.

7 What does a feminist therapist do that's different? A feminist therapist tries to *believe* what women say. Given the history of psychiatry and psychoanalysis, this alone is a radical act.

Ibid.

8 We now understand more about what trauma is, and what it does. We understand that chronic, hidden family/domestic violence is actually more traumatic than sudden violence at the hands of a stranger, or of an enemy during war.

Ibid.

9 We understand that rape is not about love or even lust, but about humiliating another human being through forced or coerced sex and sexual shame. The intended effect of rape is always the same: to utterly break the spirit of the rape victim, to drive the victim out of her (or his) body and to make her incapable of resistance and quite often out of her mind.

Ibid.

10 Freedom and justice do wonders for one's mental health. So, in response to my brother Sigmund Freud's* infamous query, what do women want? For starters, and in no particular order: freedom, food, nature, shelter, leisure, freedom from violence, justice, music, poetry, nonpatriarchal family, community, compassionate support during chronic or life-threatening illness and at the time of death, independence, books, physical/sexual pleasure, education, solitude, the ability to defend ourselves,

love, ethical friendships, the arts, health, dignified employment, and political comrades.

Ibid.

**Austrian physician and founder of psychoanalysis (1856–1939).

11 . . . a feminist boss who occasionally yells or criticizes real errors is not breaking your spirit. Women tend to experience everything "personally."

Letter to Liza Featherstone, *Women Cross Generations to Talk About Family, Work, Sex, Love and the Future of Feminism*, Anna Bondoc and Meg Daly, eds. *1999*

2788. Anne Commire (1940?–)

1 SHAY. I finally learned when I'm alone—I'm total. I'm not rude, boring, or stupid. In fact, I become a very nice person. I like me and I don't hurt anyone. I don't like what's in here when I'm with people: jealousy, anger, boredom . . . That's why I shouldn't be allowed to run around loose. I'm sealing myself off for society's sake.

Act I, Shay 1978

2 We're being reviewed through male eyes or women with male-oriented eyes—women who want to "write like a man." It's not some great conspiracy. Most men are uncomfortable with a woman's mind . . . We like to pretend it's not an issue between (man) critic and (woman) writer. Check out the male critic's relationship with Mom and you'll see a direct connection to his receptivity toward women's themes.

"Anne Commire," *Interviews with Contemporary Women Playwrights*, Kathleen Betsko* and Rachel Koenig *1987*
*See 2739.

3 When I was younger there were always two voices bumping around inside me. One said I'd conquer Kilimanjaro; the other was right behind it, a little giggle that said, "Who, you?"

Ibid.

4 Funny, if I have any pride in my writing, it's not in what I wrote. It's because I dare to write, dare to face my demons and that enormously frightening machine daily. After fifteen years, I still face that machine with fear. Dreading there'll be nothing there. Dreading that today I'll find out I don't have an original thought left in my brain, that I squandered it on postcards to friends.

Ibid.

5 Theater risks every night. It has the possibility of soaring in the air or landing on its ass. People come for the spectacle, for the danger. Some with holly in their hearts; some like spectators at the Colosseum, rooting for the lion.

Ibid.

6 Books have been written *ad infinitum* on male-female misunderstandings. Most of Hollywood's success is based on it. And yet we've never dealt with that on a level of male critic/ female writer. We pretend that it's not even going on.

Ibid.

7 LYNNE. I've always been a bit stiff; afraid to be seen having fun. Some ride roller coasters, some wait below, holding the coats. Now, there's a T-shirt if I ever heard one.

Starting Monday 1990

2789. Maria Fatima Velho da Costa (1940?–)

Coauthor with Maria Isabel Barreno; see 2737, and Maria Teresa Horta; see 2757.

2790. Angela de Hoyos (1940–)

1 I must wait for the conquering barbarian
to learn the Spanish word for love:
HERMANO*

"Hermano," *The Woman That I Am, The Literature and Culture of Contemporary Women of Color*, D. Soyini Madison, ed. *1994*

*Brother.

2791. Jennifer Dunn (1941–)

1 I'm someone who has broken a lot of glass ceilings. I was the first woman president of our student body in the sixth grade and was the first woman Republican Party state chairman.

"Congresswoman: Leadership needs change of face" (p. 10A), *USA Today 11 November 1998*

2 I have the skills that can fill any gap. I can communicate. I can organize. I can feel what people want. I'm a woman.

Ibid.

3 I have always been a proponent of softening our [the Republican Party's] rhetoric. I believe we can pursue the same positions we have been, but we don't need to be as harsh and scary about it.

Quoted in *Biographical Dictionary of Congressional Women* by Karen Foerstel *1999*

2792. Lydia Dunn (1940–)

1 China will let Hong Kong survive not because it is just or right but because of our economic value.

Quoted in "Whither Hong Kong?" by Margaret Scott, *The New York Times Magazine October 1989*

2 We [Hong Kongers] have been told to stay out of politics and if we did we could make money. We did.

Ibid.

2793. Betty Edwards (fl. 1940s)

1 Training in perception has the same function as teaching people to read and write—that is, it reins those skills so they are honed up and useable at a conscious level, and useful for things other than just looking around, just as language skills are trained up through reading and writing, in ways that one doesn't achieve just talking.

Quoted in "Betty Edwards: Teaching the Tricks of Perception" by John Crutcher, *Common Ground of Puget Sound Fall 1989*

2 My work essentially is involved with teaching people how to better control their own brains. This is what I'm interested in. And drawing is as incidental to being an artist in that sense, as learning to read and write is to being a poet. Drawing is simply a path towards really becoming a better Captain Kirk*—of the space voyage.

Ibid.

*Fictitious character from the long-lived *Star Trek* television series.

3 Somehow or other in this century, we have psychologically blocked the training of the right hemisphere, especially for drawing, which is one of its main functions.

Ibid.

4 Computers can do all the left hemisphere processing better and faster than the human brain. So what's left for the human brain is global thinking, creative thinking, intuitive-problem solving, seeing the whole picture. All of that cannot be done

by the computer. And yet the school system goes on, churning out reading, writing, and arithmetic, spelling, grammar.

Ibid.

2794. Frances Fitzgerald (1940–)

1 By intervening in the Vietnamese struggle the United States was attempting to fit its global strategies into a world of hillocks and hamlets, to reduce its majestic concerns for the containment of Communism and the security of the Free World to a dimension where governments rose and fell as a result of arguments between two colonel's wives.

Pt. I, Ch. 1, Fire in the Lake 1972

2 Americans see history as a straight line and themselves standing at the cutting edge of it as representatives for all mankind. They believe in the future as if it were a religion; they believe that there is nothing they cannot accomplish, that solutions wait somewhere for all problems, like brides.

Ibid.

3 In a sense, the design of the Confucian world resembled that of a Japanese garden where every rock, opaque and indifferent to itself, takes on significance from its relation to the surrounding objects.

Ibid.

4 For most Americans, Southeast Asia came to look like the most complicated place in the world. And naturally enough, for the American official effort to fit the new evidence into the old official assumptions was something like the effort of the seventeenth-century astronomers to fit their observations of the planets into the Ptolemaic theory of the universe.

Ch. 2, Ibid.

5 Quite consciously, Ho Chi Minh* forswore the grand patriarchal tradition of the Confucian emperors. Consciously he created an "image" of himself as "Uncle Ho"—the gentle, bachelor relative who has only disinterested affection for the children who are *not* his own sons. As a warrior and a politician he acted ruthlessly upon occasion, but in public and as head of state he took pains to promote that family feeling which Vietnamese have often had for their leaders, and which he felt was the proper relationship between the people and their government.

Ch. 4, Ibid.

*Vietnamese nationalist leader (1890–1969); president of North Vietnam (1954–1969).

6 The Americans began by underestimating the Vietnamese guerrillas, but in the end they made them larger than life. During the invasion of Cambodia in 1970, American officials spoke of plans to capture the enemy's command head quarters for the south as if there existed a reverse Pentagon in the jungle . . . Paradoxically, the exaggeration diminished them, for in the dimension of mythology all things are fabulous and unaccountable. By turning their enemy into a mirror image of themselves, the Americans obscured the nature of the Vietnamese accomplishment.

Ibid.

7 . . . [Lyndon B.] Johnson* condemned his officials who worked on Vietnam to the excruciating mental task of holding reality and the official version of reality together as they moved farther and farther apart.

Pt. II, Ch. 13, Ibid.

*American politician (1908–1973), 36th president of the United States (1963–69).

8 . . . the Americans were once again embarked upon a heroic and (for themselves) almost painless conquest of an inferior race. . . . [They] were white men in Asia, and they could not conceive that they might fail in their enterprise, could not conceive that they could be morally wrong.

Ibid.

9 Personally, socially, politically, the disorder of the cities is a highly unstable condition—a vacuum that craves the oxygen of organized society. The Americans might force the Vietnamese to accept the disorder for years, but behind the dam of American troops and American money the pressure is building towards one of those sudden historical shifts when "individualism" and its attendant corruption gives way to the discipline of the revolutionary community.

Pt. III, Ch. 17, Ibid.

10 . . . the American government did not want to face the consequences of peace. It was, after all, one thing to wish for an end to the war and quite another to confront the issues upon which the war had begun. President Johnson had wanted to end the war; so, too, had President Kennedy.* But to end the war and not to lose it: the distinction was crucial, and particularly crucial after all the American lives that had been spent and all the political rhetoric expended.

Ibid.

*John F. Kennedy, American politican (1917–63), 35th U.S. president (1961–63); assassinated.

2795. Helen Fremont (194-?–)

1 I had been living my life with flawed vision, stumbling in the dark, bumping into things I hadn't realized were there. No one acknowledged anything. Yet each time I walked into my parents' house, I fell over something, or dropped into something, a cavernous silence, an unspoken, invisible danger.

After Long Silence 1998

2 Perhaps the war had not changed them so much as selected their strengths, reinforced them and made them rigid. Their secret was their armor, but it was a mask of silence imposed on all of us.

Ibid.

2796. Maria Mazziotto Gillan (1940–)

1 Remember me, ladies,
the silent?
I have found my voice
and my rage will blow
your house down.

"Public School 18: Paterson, New Jersey," *The Dream Book: An Anthology of Writings by Italian American Women*, Helen Barolini,* ed. *1985*

*See 2268.

2797. Sue Grafton (1940–)

1 He'd forgotten just how addictive crime can be. Repeat offenders are motivated more by withdrawal symptoms than necessity.

"H" is for Homicide 1991

2798. Laurie Graham (1940–)

1 "Blue-collar people think that if you don't want to work you get a desk job."

Singing the City 1998

2799. Judy Grahn (1940–)

1 a woman is talking to death. . . .

"A Woman is Talking to Death" 1974

2 . . . I looked into the mirror
and nobody was there to testify.

Ibid.

3 the woman who has the tattoo of a bird
the woman who puts things together
the woman who squats on her haunches
the woman whose children are all
different colors

singing i am the will of the
woman the woman
my will is unbending

when She-Who-moves-the-earth will turn over
when She who moves, the earth will turn over.

"She Who," Sts. 10–12, The Work of a Common Woman:
The Collected Poetry of Judy Grahn, 1964–1977 (repr. in
On Lies, Secrets, and Silence, 1980) 1980

4 In the sexual creative trance, metaphors, scenes, personages
speaking and moving, one's ancestors, mentors, spirit-guides of
every description from earth and sky and parts unknown arrive
with messages and meanings as the lovers pass through level
upon level of sexual and psychic feeling in a state that may go on
for hours, at or near the level of intensity immediately preceding
orgasm. . . . The orgasm is the way back from the trance.

"Modern Lesbian Sex Domains: Flaming without Burning,"
Another Mother Tongue 1984

5 The shaman/priest/artist/teacher/leader does not operate for
the sole benefit of herself and her kind but for the benefit of
the people at large and of the universe and its patterns, as becomes what she perceives as fitting into place, into her sense of
natural justice.

Ibid.

6 want of my want, I am your lust
wave of my wave, I am your crest
earth of my earth, I am your crust
may of my may, I am your must
kind of my kind, I am your best

"Funeral Poem: For Yvonne Mary Robinson" (October 10,
1939—November 22, 1974), Ibid.

2800. Rayna Green (194-?-)

1 But "identity" is never simply a matter of genetic make-up or
natural birthright. Perhaps once, long ago, it was both. But
not now. For people out on the edge, out on the road, identity
is a matter of will, a matter of choice, a face to be shaped in a
ceremonial act.

Introduction, That's What She Said, Rayna Green, ed. 1984

2 women's hands are never empty
women's mouths are never empty
women's arms are never empty

"Spider Woman," Ibid.

3 Indian silence
leaves no room to hide
except in dreams
visions of light and spirit
to wipe terror away

"Old Indian Trick," St. 6, Ibid.

4 He's run everybody's patience out, and if he'd been on fire, not
a soul would have pissed on him to save him.

"High Cotton," Ibid.

5 There's nothing like funerals for good eating.

Ibid.

2801. Joan Haggerty (1940–)

1 It was the novelty of the attraction that captivated her as much
as the woman herself.

Daughters of the Moon 1971

2 Afterwards, you know, afterwards, I often feel like being
fucked by a man too. . . . You tune me, d'you see, and then I
want a man to counter me, but we together, we just keep travelling to strung out space. We can't comfort each other.

Ibid.

2802. Molly Haskell (1940–)

1 . . . the propaganda arm of the American Dream machine, Hollywood. . . .

From Reverence to Rape 1973

2 The mammary fixation is the most infantile—and most American—of the sex fetishes. . . .

Ibid.

3 Our sexual emancipators and evangelist sometimes miss half
of the truth: that if puritanism is the source of our greatest
hypocrisies and most crippling illusions it is, as the primal anxiety whose therapy is civilization itself, the source of much,
perhaps most, of our achievement.

Ibid.

4 There have been very few heroines in literature who defined
their lives morally rather than romantically and likewise but a
handful in film. . . .

Ibid.

5 The idea that acting is quintessentially "feminine" carries with
it a barely perceptible sneer, a suggestion that it is not the noblest or most dignified of professions. Acting is role-playing,
role-playing is lying, and lying is a woman's game.

Ibid.

6 . . . her [Marilyn Monroe's]* suicide, as suicides do, casts a
retrospective light on her life. Her "ending" gives her a beginning and a middle, turns her into a work of art with a message
and a meaning.

Ibid.

*See 2323.

7 We have ample evidence of the fakery that went into creating
the stars' facades, of the misery that went on behind these, and
of the tyranny of studio despots who insisted on the image at
the expense of the human being underneath. All of which inevitably raises the question whether it is possible to be both a
star and a human being. If it isn't, how many would have
traded stardom for pale humanity?

Ibid.

8 Politics remains the most heavily—and jealously—masculine
area . . .

Ibid.

9 . . . Chaplin* and Keaton** developed wit and ingenuity the
way other men develop muscles.

Ibid.

*Charlie Chaplin, English film actor, scenarist, director
(1889–1977). **Buster Keaton, American film actor, scenarist, director (1895–1966).

10 But one of the attributes of love, like art, is to bring harmony and order out of chaos, to introduce meaning and affect where before there was none, to give rhythmic variations, highs and lows to a landscape that was previously flat.

Ibid.

11 If there has been a falling off in feminine eroticism on the screen, it is from the *loss* of humor, or that aspect of humor that gives distance and perspective, rather than from an excess of it.

Ibid.

12 One of the definitions of the loss of innocence is perhaps the fragmenting of that united self—a split that is different, and emblematic, not only for each sex, but also for each era.

Ibid.

2803. Arlie Hochschild (1940–)

1 It has become a sad commonplace to associate being old with being alone. We call isolation a punishment for the prisoner, but perhaps a majority of American old people are in some degree isolated or soon will be.

"Communal Living in Old Age," *The Future of the Family*,
Louise Kapp Howe,* ed. *1972*
*See 2566.

2 . . . the decline of the extended family creates the need for a new social shelter, another pool of friendships, another bond with society apart from family.

Ibid.

2804. Joreen (194-?–)

1 Bitches are aggressive, assertive, domineering, overbearing, strong-minded, spiteful, hostile, direct, blunt, candid, obnoxious, thick-skinned, hard-headed, vicious, dogmatic, competent, competitive, pushy, loud-mouthed, independent, stubborn, demanding, manipulative, egoistic, driven, achieving, overwhelming, threatening, scary, ambitious, tough, brassy, masculine, boisterous and turbulent. . . . A Bitch takes shit from no one. You may not like her, but you cannot ignore her.

The Bitch Manifesto 1969?

2 The mythology that women are inferior and need to be protected by men went out with the mythology about the superiority of the Aryan race.

"The 51 Percent Minority Group," *The Voice of the
Women's Liberation Movement 196–?*

2805. Aisha Kahlil (1940?–)

1 Dance is more than just a discipline for me, it's a method of healing—a prayer. If I wasn't dancing I wouldn't be alive.

Quoted in "Sweet Honey: A Cappella Activists" by
Audreen Buffalo, *Ms.* (New York) *March/April 1993*

2806. Linda Kauffman (1940/9–)

1 Writing about yourself does not liberate you, it just shows how ingrained the ideology of freedom through self-expression is in our thinking.

"The Long Goodbye: Against the Personal Testimony or, An
Infant Grifter Grows Up," Quoted in *Changing Subjects:
The Making of Feminist Literary Criticism* by
Gayle Greene* and Coppélia Kahn *1993*
*See 2946.

2 In fact, most disappointments last a lifetime, and many injuries are irremediable. The older I get, the less I'm able to construct a moral even to my own story that doesn't lie with every word.

Ibid.

2807. Linda Kaufman Kerber (1940–)

1 [Not until 1992] did the Supreme Court specifically announce that it would no longer recognize the power of husbands over the bodies of their wives. That is the moment when coverture, as a living legal principle, died.

*No Constitutional Right To Be Ladies: Women and the
Obligations of Citizenship 1998*

2 We cannot embrace the rights without acknowledging the obligations. Nor do we have the option of limiting ourselves to the voluntarily embraced duties; there waits a steel hand in a velvet glove to enforce obligation.

Ibid.

2808. Wendy Kesselman (1940–)

1 MADAME DANZARD. You have no idea how lucky we are, Isabelle. The servants I've seen in my day. (*She watches her daughter stuff potatoes in her mouth.*) They eat like birds. Always looking so neat, so perfect. You wouldn't think they were maids at all.

Sc. 4, *My Sister in This House 1981*

2809. Carmel Bird (1940–)

1 Students always think I am joking when I say give up the housework. But you have the choice of a clean house or a finished story. The choice is yours; I am assuming you will make the right choice.

"Giving up Housework," *Dear Writer 1996*

2 Life is a crude inventor; fiction will only be convincing if it is more artful than life.

"Fact or Fiction," *Automatic Teller 1997*

2810. Maxine Hong Kingston (1940–)

1 Night after night my mother would talk-story until we fell asleep. I couldn't tell where the stories left off and the dreams began, her voice the voice of the heroines in my sleep. . . . At last I saw that I too had been in the presence of great power, my mother talking-story.

(p. 23), *The Woman Warrior 1977*

2 I learned to make my mind large, as the universe is large, so that there is room for paradoxes.

(p. 35), Ibid.

3 . . . each boss two feet taller than I am and impossible to meet eye to eye . . . if I took a sword, which my hate must surely have forged out of the air, and gutted [him], I would put color and wrinkles into his shirt.

(p. 58), Ibid.

4 What we have in common are the words at our backs. . . . And I have so many words—"chink" words and "gook" words too—that they do not fit on my skin.

(pp. 62–3), Ibid.

5 "Maggots!" he shouted. "Maggots! Where are my grandsons? I want grandsons! Give me grandsons! Maggots!" He pointed at each one of us, "Maggot! Maggot! Maggot! Maggot! Mag-

got! Maggot!" Then he dived into his food, eating fast and getting seconds. "Eat, maggots," he said. "Look at the maggots chew."

"He does that at every meal," the girls told us in English.

"Yeah," we said. "Our old man hates us too. What assholes."

(p. 222), Ibid.

6 [To her mother] You lie with stories. You won't tell me a story and then say, "This is a true story," or "This is just a story." I can't tell the difference. I don't even know what your real names are. I can't tell what's real and what you made up.
(p. 235), Ibid.

7 "If that demon whips me, I'll catch the whip and yank him off his horse, crack his head like a coconut. In an emergency a human being can do miracles—fly, swim, lift mountains, throw them. Oh, a man is capable of great feats of speed and strength."

China Men 1980

8 "Where's our jazz? Where's our blues? Where's our ain't-taking-no-shit-from-nobody street-strutting language? I want so bad to be the first bad-jazz China Man bluesman of America."
Tripmaster Monkey: His Fake Book 1989

9 "You're going through the delusion of clarity . . ."
Ibid.

2811. Angela Lambert (1940–)
1 Pornography is literature designed to be read with one hand.
Independent on Sunday (London) *18 February 1990*

2812. Glenda Adams (1940–)
1 While she was away Auntie Pearl watched televion every chance she got, shows with names like "I Love Lucy" and "Father Knows Best." In America they already have colour TV and we don't even have black and white yet. I told her that Americans buy twenty-thousand television sets a day, and she said as soon as television comes to Australia, she'll be the first one knocking on Anthony Hordern's door to buy one and more than happy to contribute to Australian consumer statistics. Auntie Pearl said you can get a television, phonograph and hi-fi radio all in one piece of furniture . . . She also told us the correct pronunciation for de luxe is "delucks" not "delukes." Auntie Pearl and her cousin rode in a car called a Fairlane, 17 feet long, "surrounded by a solid cushiony comfort, as solid as the car itself," and moving with "the silent smoothness of a swan on a pond." Those were the words she used, straight from the advertisements.
The Tempest of Clemenza 1996

2813. Eunice Lipton (1940?–)
1 If you're not familiar with the New York City art world you can't possibly imagine what a dreadful place it is.
"Monkey business," *The Women's Review of Books*, Vol. XII, Nos. 10–11 *July 1995*

2 Selling is what is crucial and Now is the only moment that counts. So you can treat anyone as malevolently as you like today and tomorrow you can smile at them. And mean it. The disingenuousness and flattery one experiences if one is seen as powerful, and the rudeness if one isn't, takes the breath away.
Ibid.

2814. Beverly Lowry (194-?–)
1 Gardening and scholarship were not so different; both took long hours and single-mindedness, resiliency in the face of major setbacks, a gift for tedium and a flair for the marriage of the unusual. Both strained the eyes and lower back and depended to some degree on fate, prejudice, perspective and the intuitive flash.
Breaking Gentle 1988

2 "Soup's on," she said in so low a voice not even the broccoli could have heard her.
Ibid.

2815. Stephanie Matthews-Simonton (1940–)
1 The most powerful tool we have for changing our environment is our ability to change ourselves.
Quoted in "The Good News About Cancer" by Peggy Elman Roggenbuck, *New Age May 1978*

2 Too often we associate healing only with medical treatment . . . [but] healing is more than just physiological . . . the patient can take part in his own recovery. The family can offer a vital supportive environment in this effort.
Introduction, *The Healing Family 1984*

3 Hope is essential; human beings can't live long without it. . . . When hope is taken away, people become so depressed that no matter what the outcome, their lives are miserable.
Ch. 3, Ibid.

2816. Juliet Mitchell (1940–)
1 Socialism should properly mean not the abolition of the family, but the diversification of the socially acknowledged relationships . . . which matched the free invention and variety of men and women.
"Women-The Longest Revolution," *New Left Review November/December 1966*

2 Circumstantial accounts of the future are idealistic and, worse, static.
Ibid.

3 A fixed image of the future is in the worst sense ahistorical . . .
Ibid.

4 It seems to me that in Freud's psychoanalytical schema, here, as elsewhere, we have at least the beginnings of an analysis of the way in which a patriarchal society bequeaths its structures to each of us . . . and which, unless patriarchy is demolished, we will pass on willy-nilly to our children and our children's children. Individual experimentation with communes and so forth can do no more than register protest. . . . Present or absent, "the father" always has his place.
"On Freud* and the Distinction Between the Sexes," *Women and Analysis*, Jean Strouse,** ed. *1974*
**See 3071.

5 Anatomy may, at its point of hypothetical normality, give us two opposite but equal sexes (with the atrophied sex organs of the other present in each), but Freudian* psychoanalytic theory does not.
Ibid.
*Austrian physician and founder of psychoanalysis (1856–1939).

2817. Anne Moody (1940–)
1 I sat on the grass and listened to the speakers [28 August 1963, the March on Washington], to discover we had "dreamers" in-

stead of leaders leading us. Just about every one of them stood up there dreaming. Martin Luther King* went on and on talking about his dream. I sat there thinking that in Canton [Mississippi] we never had time to sleep, much less dream.

Coming of Age in Mississippi 1968

*American civil rights leader (1929–1968), assassinated.

2   . . . the [Civil Rights] Movement was not in control of its destiny. We were like an angry dog on a leash who had turned on its master. It could bark and howl and snap, and sometimes even bite, but the master was always in control.

Quoted in *Contemporary Authors*, Vol. 65–68 1977

2818. Bharati Mukherjee (1940–)

1   It's the tyranny of the American dream that scares me. First, you don't exist. Then you're invisible. Then you're funny. Then you're disgusting. Insult, my American friends will tell me, is a kind of acceptance. No instant dignity here.

"A Wife's Story," *The Middleman and Other Stories* 1988

2   Expensive girls' schools in Lausanne and Bombay have trained me to behave well. My manners are exquisite, my feelings are delicate, my gestures refined, my moods undetectable. They have seen me through riots, uprootings, separation, my son's death.

Ibid.

3   What novelists have the power to do is imagine the inner life of people who acted out the facts of history. And do it with sympathy for every side.

Interview by Joseph A. Cincotti (p. 7), *The New York Times Book Review* October 1993

2819. Gail Parent (1940–)

1   Do you want to live in a world where a man lies about calories?

"The Facts," *Sheila Levine Is Dead and Living in New York* 1972

2   Don't we realize we're a business, we single girls are? There are magazines for us, special departments in stores for us. Every building that goes up in Manhattan has more than fifty percent efficiency apartments . . . for the one million girls who have very little use for them.

"On Jobs and Apartments," Ibid.

3   Actually, I have only two things to worry about now: afterlife and reincarnation.

"The End," Ibid.

4   . . . volleyball is a Jewish sport. It's fun, and nobody can get hurt.

"Fire Island," Ibid.

5   *Fact*: Girls who are having a good sex thing stay in New York. The rest want to spend their summer vacations in Europe.

"Europe," Ibid.

6   Do you realize the planning that goes into a death? Probably even more than goes into a marriage. This, after all, really is for eternity.

"Enough Already," Ibid.

7   Thank you, Agatha, for the lovely bracelet, but I still haven't changed my mind. I have no desire to touch you in places that I already own. Sincerely, Sheila Levine."

Ibid.

2820. Mary Pipher (194-?–)

1   Research has shown that, since they are free to act without worrying if their behavior is feminine or masculine, androgynous adults are the most well adjusted.

Ch. 1, *Reviving Ophelia: Saving the Selves of Adolescent Girls* 1994

2   Adolescent girls are saplings in a hurricane. They are young and vulnerable trees that the winds blow with gale strength.

Ibid.

3   Women often know how everyone in their family thinks and feels except themselves. They are great at balancing the needs of their co-workers, husbands, children and friends, but they forget to put themselves into the equation.

Ibid.

4   Adolescence is the most formative time in the lives of women. Girls are making choices that will preserve their true selves or install false selves. These choices have many implications for the rest of their lives.

Ch. 4, Ibid.

5   America doesn't have clearly defined and universally accepted rules about sexuality. We live in a pluralistic culture with contradictory sexual paradigms. We hear diverse messages from our families, our churches, our schools and the media, and each of us must integrate these messages and arrive at some value system that makes sense to us.

Ch. 11, Ibid.

6   Remembering is more like taking a Rorschach test than calling up a computer file. It's highly selective and revealing of one's deep character.

Ch. 12, Ibid.

7   Of course the problems of a dysfunctional culture are reflected in the lives of each family. Many men who grow up in a misogynistic culture abuse their wives and daughters. Many mothers offer their daughters passive, diminished models of femaleness. Some parents are cultural agents who are desperate for their daughters to be popular. But when so many families have trouble, it's important to look at the cultural context. Rather than blame each family for the unhappiness of its daughters, we need to examine what it is in our culture that destroys the happiness of so many teenage girls.

Ch. 13, Ibid.

8   Let's work toward a culture in which there is a place for every human gift, in which children are safe and protected, women are respected and men and women can love each other as whole human beings. Let's work for a culture in which the incisive intellect, the willing hands and the happy heart are beloved.

Ch. 15, Ibid.

2821. Jaune Quick-to-See Smith (1940–)

1   The glaciers pushed
and the People moved.

"The Ronan Robe Series," Pt. 1, *That's What She Said*, Rayna Green,* ed. 1984

*See 2800.

2   The Jesuits enslaved the young Indians, forced them into church and put them to work on cattle ranches or in the orchards. We were forbidden to drum, sing, dance, speak our language, carry anything of our culture . . . but even with all

that people would gather in a cabin, cover the windows, and drum and sing.

> Quoted in "Jaune Quick-to-See Smith," *Exposures, Women & Their Art* by Ann Brown & Arlene Raven* 1989
> *See 3020.

3 I'm going on a journey each time I begin a canvas.

> Ibid.

2822. Pattiann Rogers (1940–)

1 Seven thousand thorns, each a water slide,
A wooden tongue licking the air dry.

> "Counting What the Cactus Contains," St. 1, *Firekeeper: New and Selected Poems 1994*

2 And under the blanket beside you in the sleigh,
If I could watch the night above the flying heads
Of the horses, if I could see our love exploded
Like stars cast in a black sky over the glassy plains
So that nothing, not even the mind of an angel,
Could ever reassemble that deed;
Well, I would go with you right now,

> "The Possible Salvation of Continuous Motion," St. 4, Ibid.

3 the studious glory of a seeded dandelion scattering
its brilliant wind of stars before the sun.

> "Investigative Logic in a Study of Love," St. 6, *Eating Bread and Honey 1997*

4 Everything I assemble, all
the constructions I have rendered
are the metal and dust of my locked
and storied bones.

> "Nearing Autobiography," St. 4, Ibid.

5 It's no wonder then that leaves
can sing all summer long, even while
knowing for certain and remembering
the waiting winter ahead

> "Silva," St. 4, *The Cortland Review*, No. 7 May 1999

2823. Patricia Schroeder (1940–)

1 However useless a defense concept, however premature its implementation, however extravagant its cost, an argument to proceed is deemed conclusive on one of two grounds. Either the Russians are doing it and therefore we must do it in order to avoid falling behind, or the Russians are not doing it and therefore we must in order to stay ahead.

> Quoted in *American Political Women* by Esther Stineman 1980

2 Everyone is always talking about our defense effort in terms of protecting women and children, but no one ever asks the women and children what they think.

> Ibid.

3 I have a brain and a uterus and I use them both.

> (1973), Ibid.

4 The government has an obligation to protect the family so that it can care for itself during a crisis. But the Reagan administration has turned its back on parents who have lost their jobs because they have missed too many days at work caring for a child dying of cancer.

The administration has shown no concern for young mothers who have returned to work after having a baby only to find that they don't have a job. It makes no allowances for parents who need time off to adopt a child.

That's certainly no way to be pro-family.

> "Parental Leave Promises Big Return for Nation's Families," *Seattle Post-Intelligencer October 1988*

5 There is an ancient Indian saying: "We do not inherit the earth from ancestors; we borrow it from our children." If we use this ethic as a moral compass, then our rendezvous with reality can also become a rendezvous with opportunity.

> Quoted in *Ms.* (New York) *February 1989*

6 What began . . . as an exciting quest for the presidency of the United States ended three months later . . . as a search for Kleenex.

> Remark referring to her brief bid for the 1987 presidential primary, Cited in *Women of Congress: A Twentieth-Century Odyssey* by Marcy Kaptur 1996

7 *24 Years of House Work . . . and the Place Is Still a Mess*

> Book title 1998

8 [Ronald Reagan* is] the Teflon president.

> Cited in *Biographical Dictionary of Congressional Women* by Karen Foerstel 1999
> *American politician, actor (1911–), governor of California (1967–75), 40th president of the United States (1980–88).

9 [Dan Quayle* thinks] *Roe versus Wade*** are two ways to cross the Potomac.***

> Ibid.

> *J. Danforth Quayle (1947–), vice president of the United States (1989–1993). **U.S. Supreme Court decision re abortion rights (1973); see Sarah Weddington, 3075. ***Potomac River, which flows into Washington, D.C.

10 If you guys were women, you'd always be pregnant. You just can't say no.

> Remark to Pentagon officials on the Armed Services Committee, Ibid.

2824. Joan Semmel (1940?–)

1 I was an abstract painter in the abstract expressionist mode until 1970 . . . My whole life changed. Feminism brought me back to the figure.

> Quoted in "Joan Semmel," *Exposures, Women & Their Art* by Ann Brown & Arlene Raven* 1989
> *See 3020.

2 My erotic nudes of the early 1970s were my part of the sexual revolution and they were erotic from a woman's point of view.

> Ibid.

2825. Karen Shepherd (1940–)

1 I wonder if we would have to cough up all this money for prisons if we had fully funded Headstart* 20 years ago. We are paying the price of benign neglect.

> Quoted by Mindy Cameron in "Win-win politics from a sisterhood of change," *Seattle Times*, Op-Ed 3 April 1994
> *A pre-school program for underprivileged children, started in the 1960s.

2826. Valerie Solanis (1940–1988)

1 Life in this society being, at best, an utter bore and no aspect of society being at all relevant to women, there remains to

civic-minded, responsible, thrill-seeking females only to over-throw the government, eliminate the money system, institute complete automation and destroy the male sex.

SCUM Manifesto* 1967–1968

*SCUM is an acronym for Society for Cutting Up Men.

2   Dropping out gives control to those few who don't drop out; dropping out is exactly what the establishment leaders want; it plays into the hands of the enemy; it strengthens the system instead of undermining it, since it is based entirely on non-participation, passivity, apathy and non-involvement. . . .

Ibid.

3   Just as humans have a prior right to existence over dogs by virtue of being more highly evolved and having a superior consciousness, so women have a prior right to existence over men. The elimination of any male is, therefore, a righteous and good act, an act highly beneficial to women as well as an act of mercy.

Ibid.

4   Our society is not a community, but merely a collection of isolated family units.

Ibid.

5   To call a man an animal is to flatter him; he's a machine, a walking dildo.

Ibid.

2827. Harriet Strong (fl. 1940s)

1   . . . it takes brains, not brawn, to make farms pay . . . We need more women farmers!

(p. 96), Quoted in *Women Pioneers* by Rebecca Stefoff 1995

2828. Yukiko Tanaka (1940–)

1   Both the [19]80s and the period from 1913–38 were periods of upheaval [in Japan], when women worked to free themselves of traditional social and psychological constraints. In both . . . we see women compelled by the pressure of history to explore unfamiliar terrain, to reinvent themselves.

Introduction, *Unmapped Territories, New Women's Fiction from Japan*, ed. & tr. 1991

2829. Jane P. Tompkins (1940–)

1   The female subject par excellence, which is her self and her experiences, has once more been elided by literary criticism.

"Me and My Shadow" (1988), *The Intimate Critique: Autobiographical Literary Criticism*, Diane P. Freedman, Olivia Frey and Frances Murphy Zauhar, eds. 1993

2830. Charlotte Vale Allen (1941–)

1   There is a damned good reason why old people died: to spare youngsters the sight of them. Who the hell wanted to know at twenty that they'd one day look like a quirky assemblage of shapeless rubbery parts tacked any which way to a set of crumbling bones?

Painted Lives 1990 Ibid.

2   Men are just like little boys with money.

Ibid.

3   "Do you dream in color or black and white?" . . .

"Color, naturally. . . . Is this some kind of imbecilic psychological test?"

"No, I'm serious. I've been dreaming lately in black and white. I think it must mean something."

"Maybe it means you're too lazy to fill in the mental colors."

Dreaming In Color 1993

4   The writer's life, at least for me, entails very little glamour and large chunks of time spent alone.

On-line interview, http://www.charlottevaleallen.com/ on_writing/index.htm 2000

2831. Michelene Wandor (1940–)

1   Every time a woman writes a play about women, then she is implicitly challenging the men still at center-stage. She may not be a conscious feminist, she may want to take no part in changing things for other women in the theatrical profession, but she will still in some way be justifying her existence as a woman playwright, and justifying the existence of her subject matter as valid.

Plays by Women, Vol. 1 1982

2   However it is true so far that on the whole women playwrights have tended to choose to write about their own sex—and actually, there is nothing at all unusual about that. Most male playwrights choose to write about their own sex—it is just that they rarely see that that is what they are doing.

Introduction, *Plays by Women*, Vol. 2 1984

3   Stupid word, that. Period. In America it means "full stop," like in punctuation. That's stupid as well. A period isn't a full stop. It's a new beginning. I don't mean all that creativity, life-giving force, earth-mother stuff, I mean it's a new beginning to the month, relief that you're not pregnant, when you don't have to have a child.

"Mother's Pride," *Guests in the Body 1986*

4   I have decided to give up heterosexuality. I have decided that, while the project of altering the balance of power within heterosexual relationships is still a valid one, it is no longer one I can espouse—so to speak—so I have therefore decided to love myself and become a lesbian.

"Meet My Mother," *Close Company: Stories of Mothers and Daughters*, Christine Park and Caroline Heaton, eds. 1987

5   ADRIENNE. How can I be serious when I hear my aunt talking of submission to her orders? Could a swallow used to sunshine agree to live with a mole in darkness?

Pt. One, Sc. 17, *The Wandering Jew* (adapt. of Eugène Sue novel), with Mike Alfreds 1987

6   If someone accuses me of ghettoizing women playwrights, I have two answers: one is unprintable, the other is that no one ever accuses the editor of an all-male anthology of plays of ghettoizing playwrights.

Quoted in "Michelene Wandor," *Interviews with Contemporary Women Playwrights* by Kathleen Betsko* and Rachel Koenig 1987

*See 2739.

2832. Ruth Weisberg (194-?–)

1   I have always felt that I've lived my life with all these extra images and experiences from other minds. I've got Goya's* mind and Rembrandt's** mind, Kathe Kollwitz's*** mind. I have access to all those other great visions of humanity, of nature,

of order. I want to be among them. I want to add my voice, my vision.

> Quoted in "Ruth Weisberg," *Exposures, Women & Their Art* by Ann Brown and Arlene Raven**** 1989
> *Francisco José de Goya Lucientes, Spanish painter and etcher (1746–1828); **Rembrandt Harmenszoon van Rijn, Dutch painter, etcher and draftsman (1606–1669); ***Kathe Kollwitz, see 1271. ****See 3020.

2 I feel nourished by teaching. I have a great sense of vocation about teaching . . .

> Ibid.

3 Time turns out to be far more precious than any other thing. I have a heightened awareness that I might not have all the time in the world. I don't want to waste it.

> Ibid.

2833. Camilla T. Crespi (1942–)

1 It wasn't going to be the usual manic Monday someone on the radio was singing about. It was going to be much worse.

> *The Trouble With A Small Raise 1991*

2 "Women have never waited for authority, have we? We just go ahead and do whatever has to be done century after century. Even when we don't get recognition or a share of the authority, we still keep doing what needs to be done."

> *The Trouble With Thin Ice 1994*

3 Depending on your mood, the fog was dreary, romantic or scary.

> *The Trouble With Hot Summer 1997*

4 "Ozone layer's thinner than a Park Avenue wife."

> Ibid.

2834. Mary Hyde (fl. 1940s–d. 1982)

1 The art of managing men has to be learned from birth. . . . It depends to some extent on one's distribution of curves, a developed instinct, and a large degree of sheer feline cunning.

> *How to Manage Men 1955*

2835. Angela Carter (1940–1992)

1 Iconic clothing has been secularized. . . . A guardsman in a dress uniform is ostensibly an icon of aggression; his coat is red as the blood he hopes to shed. Seen on a coat-hanger, with no man inside it, the uniform loses all its blustering significance and, to the innocent eye seduced by decorative colour and tactile braid, it is as abstract in symbolic information as a parasol to an Eskimo. It becomes simply magnificent.

> "Notes for a Theory of Sixties Style," *(New Society, London, 1967)*, *Arts in Society*, Paul Barker, ed. *1977*

2 Women's sexy underwear is a minor but significant growth industry of late-twentieth-century Britain in the twilight of capitalism.

> "The Bridled Sweeties," *Nothing Sacred 1977*

3 The bed is now as public as the dinner table and governed by the same rules of formal confrontation.

> "Speculative Finale," *The Sadeian Woman 1979*

4 Reciprocity of sensation is not possible because to share is to be robbed.

> Ibid.

5 The whore is despised by the hypocritical world because she has made a realistic assessment of her assets and does not have

to rely on fraud to make a living. In an area of human relations where fraud is regular practice between the sexes, her honesty is regarded with a mocking wonder.

> "Desecration of the Temple," Ibid.

6 In the mythic schema of all relations between men and women, man proposes, and woman is disposed of.

> "Polemical Preface," Ibid.

7 Fine art, that exists for itself alone, is art in a final state of impotence. If nobody, including the artist, acknowledges art as a means of knowing the world, then art is relegated to a kind of rumpus room of the mind and the irresponsibility of the artist and the irrelevance of art to actual living becomes part and parcel of the practice of art.

> Ibid.

8 Mother goddesses are just as silly a notion as father gods. If a revival of the myths of these cults gives woman emotional satisfaction, it does so at the price of obscuring the real conditions of life. This is why they were invented in the first place.

> Ibid.

9 The notion of a universality of human experience is a confidence trick and the notion of a universality of female experience is a clever confidence trick.

> Ibid.

10 We do not go to bed in single pairs; even if we choose not to refer to them, we still drag there with us the cultural impedimenta of our social class, our parents' lives, our bank balances, our sexual and emotional expectations, our whole biographies—all the bits and pieces of our unique existences.

> Ibid.

11 Pornography is a satire on human pretensions.

> Ibid.

12 If Miss means respectably unmarried, and Mrs. respectably married, then Ms. means nudge, nudge, wink, wink.

> "The Language of Sisterhood," *The State of the Language*, Christopher Ricks and Leonard Michaels, eds. *1980*

13 I think it's one of the scars in our culture that we have too high an opinion of ourselves. We align ourselves with the angels instead of the higher primates.

> *Marxism Today* (London) *January 1985*

14 Reading a book is like re-writing it for yourself. . . . You bring to a novel, anything you read, all your experience of the world. You bring your history and you read it in your own terms.

> Ibid.

15 It is far easier for a woman to lead a blameless life than it is for a man; all she has to do is to avoid sexual intercourse like the plague.

> Introduction, *Wayward Girls and Wicked Women*, editor *1986*

16 Just because we're sisters under the skin doesn't mean we've got much in common.

> *The Guardian* (London) *25 October 1990*

17 Comedy is tragedy that happens to other people.

> Ch. 4, *Wise Children 1991*

18 There's a theory, one I find persuasive, that the quest for knowledge is, at bottom, the search for the answer to the ques-

tion: "Where was I before I was born." In the beginning was . . . what? Perhaps, in the beginning, there was a curious room, a room like this one, crammed with wonders; and now the room and all it contains are forbidden you, although it was made just for you, had been prepared for you since time began, and you will spend all your life trying to remember it.

"The Curious Room," *New Writing*, Malcolm Bradbury and Judy Cooke, eds. *1992*

2836. Margot Adler (1941–)

1 Although we know that on some level we are always connected, our most common experience is one of estrangement.

Drawing Down the Moon 1986

2 Just as ecological theory explains how we are interrelated with all other forms of life, rituals allow us to re-create that unity in an explosive, non-abstract, gut-level way. Rituals have the power to reset the terms of our universe until we find ourselves suddenly and truly "at home."

Ibid.

2837. Gloria Allred (1941–)

1 Lots of men, you see, simply aren't ready for assertive women. They expect us to tiptoe in, trembling and pleading for our rights and when those rights are denied, they expect us not to cause a furor but to tiptoe away quietly. But they underestimate how much we care.

Quoted in "Home Q&A" by Marshall Berger in, *The Los Angeles Times Home Magazine 7 January 1979*

2 There are enough high hurdles to climb, as one travels through life, without having to scale artificial barriers created by laws or silly regulations . . .

Ibid.

3 . . . the media is still dominated by men, many of whom think of women in a very sexist way. They cover them in a sexist way, and they do *not* cover them because of sexism.

Quoted in *Perspectives* Fall *1996*

2838. Joan Baez (1941–)

1 Powerful Jesus gold and silver with young, hundred-year-old eyes.
You look around and you know you must have failed somewhere.

"Farewell Angelina" *1965*

2 . . . hypothetical questions get hypothetical answers.

Daybreak 1966

3 War was going on long before anybody dreamed up Communism. It's just the latest justification for self-righteousness.

Ibid.

4 If it's natural to kill why do men have to go into training to learn how?

Ibid.

5 That's all nonviolence is—organized love.

Ibid.

6 By the middle of the twentieth century men had reached a peak of insanity. They grouped together in primitive nation-states, each nation-state condoning organized murder as the way to deal with international differences. . . .

Ibid.

7 The only thing that's been a worse flop than the organization of nonviolence has been the organization of violence.

"What Would You Do?" Ibid.

8 Instead of getting hard ourselves and trying to compete, women should try and give their best qualities to men—bring them softness, teach them how to cry.

Quoted in "Sexism Seen But Not Heard" by Tracy Hotchner, *The Los Angeles Times 26 May 1974*

9 And if you're offering me diamonds and rust
I've already paid.

"Diamonds and Rust" *1975*

10 We are the warriors of the sun
Fighting postwar battles
That somehow never were won.

"Warriors of the Sun," *Live Europe 83* (album) *1983*

11 We're the children of the eighties;
Haven't we grown?
We're softer than a lotus
and tougher than stone*
And the age of innocence
Is somewhere in the garden.

"(For the) Children of the Eighties," Ibid.
*Adapted from phrase by Mohandas Gandhi, Indian nationalist and spiritual leader (1869–1948), assassinated.

12 I've never had a humble opinion in my life. If you're going to have one, why bother to be humble about it?

International Herald Tribune (Paris) *2 December 1992*

2839. Sandra Ables Benítez (1941–)

1 In her hut, Remedios listens to someone's story, and the teller is revived.
It is stories that save us, Remedios is certain.

A Place Where the Sea Remembers 1993

2 Each day, the servants gathered in the kitchen for . . . the newest installment of the [radio novella's] never-ending tale of two sisters, one wicked, one good, and of the entanglements resulting from such contrary natures.

Bitter Grounds 1997

2840. Carol Bolt (1941–)

1 EMMA. . . . freeing herself from the fear of public opinion and public condemnation will set a woman free, will make her a force hitherto unknown in the world.

Red Emma, * *Queen of the Anarchists 1974*
*Reference to Emma Goldman (see 1289).

2841. Phyllis Halperin Bramson (1941–)

1 To me, making art is a difficult, intense activity where I can do a lot of things I wouldn't do out in the world. It's an area where I can function on a dangerous and erotic level. I'm sort of watching myself do it. The safety net often becomes the formal need of making a painting work.

Quoted in "Phyllis Bramson," *Exposures, Women & Their Art* by Ann Brown & Arlene Raven* *1989*
*See 3020.

2842. Beth Brant (1941–)

1 Because in the unraveling, the threads become more apparent, each one with its distinct color and texture. And as I unravel, I also weave. I am the storyteller and the story.
Introduction, *A Gathering of Spirit*, ed. *1984*

2 We have a spirit of rage. We are angry women. Angry at white men and their perversions. Their excessive greed and abuse of the earth, sky, and water. Their techno-christian approach to anything that lives, including our children, our people. We are angry at Indian men for their refusals of us. For their limited vision of what constitutes a strong Nation. We are angry at a so-called "women's movement" that always seems to forget we exist. Except in romantic fantasies of earth mother, or equally romantic and dangerous fantasies of Indian-woman-as-victim.
Ibid.

3 I truly believe that white man hates and craves what is inside those of us who are colored. They envy our connections to the spirit, to the earth, to a community, to a people. Because they envy us; they hate us, and will do anything to get rid of us. So all the things . . . slavery, genocide of Indians on this continent, as well as in Latin America; the Holocaust,* missionaries in China, the Vietnam War . . . all of these a calculated program of extermination. And I add to that, the millions of women burned at the stake centuries ago, because we were women, because we were lesbians.
Letter to Raven** (28 December 1982), Ibid.
*The genocide of European Jews and others by the Nazis during World War II. **See 3408; a.k.a. Doris Ann Foster.

4 Helen can't imagine that she is beautiful.
That her skin is warm
like redwood and fire.
That her thick black hair moves like a current.
That her large body speaks in languages stolen from her.
That her mouth is wide and full and when she smiles people catch their breath.
"Her Name Is Helen," St. 11, *Mohawk Trail 1985*

5 Prematurely grey
they called it.

Hair Binding.

Damming the flow.
"for all my Grandmothers," St. 3 (1989), *The Woman That I Am, The Literature and Culture of Contemporary Women of Color*, D. Soyini Madison, ed. *1994*

2843. Martha Gertrude Burk (1941–)

1 . . . the problem of unwanted pregnancy is largely one of uncontrolled sperm.
"The Sperm Stops Here," *Ms.* (New York)
November/December 1997

2844. Blanche Weisen Cook (1941–)

1 Revolution is a process and not an event. The power of women to come together, to support each other in community, in creative self-criticism and love, gives us the power to intensify the economic and political struggle. Wherever groups of women come together to define their own visions, economic and personal, and make connections with other groups of women working in our own interests, politically accountable to our own needs and wants, we are affirming a network of change. We are building the future.
Women and Support Networks 1979

2845. Alma De Groen (1941–)

1 DOCTOR. You can give anybody a history that never happened and they'll believe it.
Rivers of China 1987

2 WAYNE. I live in a room—and it isn't home. I live on earth—and it isn't home.
Ibid.

2846. Donna de Matteo (1941–)

1 A new play is like a child.
"Donna de Matteo," *Interviews with Contemporary Women Playwrights*, Kathleen Betsko* and Rachel Koenig *1987*
*See 2739.

2 Watching Miss [Uta] Hagen* during rehearsals is comparable to watching a superb musician playing a fine instrument. She is a master at her craft, very detailed, and patient in her approach to a character; but at the same time, she never loses sight of her instincts and emotions, and when you see her blend all of these elements together, it all looks so natural and effortless . . . It transcends life. It's art at its best.
Ibid.

*See 2137.

3 The wonderful thing about music is that it immediately evokes certain eras of one's life, brings you back to where you've been, even if you don't want to go there.
Ibid.

4 Women, generally, are apt to put things together rather than tear them apart.
Ibid.

2847. Bridget Rose Dugdale (1941–)

1 For how long you sentence me is of no relevance; I regard it with the contempt it deserves. I am guilty and proudly so if guilty has come to describe one who takes up arms to defend the people of Ireland against the English tyrant.
Quoted in "Englishwoman Trips on Revolutionary Road" by Tom Lambert, *The Los Angeles Times 26 June 1974*

2848. Barbara Ehrenreich (1941–)

1 The witch-craze was neither a lynching party nor a mass suicide by hysterical women. Rather, it followed well-ordered, legalistic procedures. The witch-hunts were well organized campaigns, initiated, financed, and executed by Church and State.
Witches, Midwives, and Nurses: A History of Women Healers, with Deirdre English* *1973*
*Coauthor (1948–).

2 In a "world without a father," that is, without the private system of paternalism built into the . . . wage system, we will have to learn to be brothers and sisters.
The Hearts of Men: American Dreams and the Flight from Commitment 1983

3 Considering the absence of legal coercion, the surprising thing is that men have for so long, and, on the whole, so reliably, adhered to what we might call the "breadwinner ethic."
Ch. 1, *The Hearts of Men 1983*

4 It is the marketplace that calls most clearly for men to be softer, more narcissistic and receptive, and the new man is the result.
"At Last, a New Man" (*The New York Times*, 1984), *The Worst Years of Our Lives 1991*

5 Upscale people are fixated with food simply because they are now able to eat so much of it without getting fat, and the reason they don't get fat is that they maintain a profligate level of calorie expenditure. The very same people whose evenings begin with melted goat's cheese . . . get up at dawn to run, break for a mid-morning aerobics class, and watch the evening news while racing on a stationary bicycle.

"Food Worship" (1985), Ibid.

6 Exercise is the yuppie version of bulimia.

Ibid.

7 There seems to be no stopping drug frenzy once it takes hold of a nation. What starts with an innocuous HUGS, NOT DRUGS bumper sticker soon leads to wild talk of shooting dealers and making urine tests a condition for employment—anywhere.

"Drug Frenzy" (1988), Ibid.

8 Upscale young men seem to go for the kind of woman who plays with a full deck of credit cards, who won't cry when she's knocked to the ground while trying to board the six o'clock Eastern shuttle, and whose schedule doesn't allow for a sexual encounter lasting more than twelve minutes.

"The Cult of Busyness" (*The New York Times*, 1985), Ibid.

9 It seems to me that there must be an ecological limit to the number of paper pushers the earth can sustain, and that human civilization will collapse when the number of, say, tax lawyers exceeds the world's total population of farmers, weavers, fisherpersons, and pediatric nurses.

"Premature Pragmatism" (*Ms.*, New York, 1986), Ibid.

10 Marriage is socialism among two people.

"Socialism in One Household" (*Mother Jones*, 1987), Ibid.

11 So why do people keep on watching? The answer, by now, should be perfectly obvious: we love television because television brings us a world in which television does not exist. In fact, deep in their hearts, this is what the spuds crave most: a rich, new, participatory life.

"Spudding Out" (1988), Ibid.

12 A child is not a salmon mousse. A child is a temporarily disabled and stunted version of a larger person, whom you will someday know. Your job is to help them overcome the disabilities associated with their size and inexperience so that they get on with being that larger person.

"Stop Ironing the Diapers" (1989), Ibid.

13 No culture on earth outside of mid-century suburban America has ever deployed one woman per child without simultaneously assigning her such major productive activities as weaving, farming, gathering, temple maintenance, and tent-building. The reason is that full-time, one-on-one child-raising is not good for women or children.

Ibid.

14 Some of us still get all weepy when we think about the Gaia Hypothesis, the idea that earth is a big furry goddess-creature who resembles everybody's mom in that she knows what's best for us. But if you look at the historical record—Krakatoa, Mt. Vesuvius, Hurricane Charley, poison ivy, and so forth down the ages—you have to ask yourself: Whose side is she on, anyway?

"The Great Syringe Tide" (*Mother Jones*, 1988), Ibid.

15 The label of liberalism is hardly a sentence to public ignominy: otherwise Bruce Springsteen would still be rehabilitating used Cadillacs in Asbury Park and Jane Fonda, for all we know, would be just another overweight housewife.

"The Liberals' Disappearing Act" (*Mother Jones*, 1986), Ibid.

16 The Republicans hardly need a party and the cumbersome cadre of low-level officials that form one; they have a bankroll as large as the Pentagon's budget, dozens of fatted PACs, and the well-advertised support of the Christian deity.

Ibid.

17 In fact, there is clear evidence of black intellectual superiority: in 1984, 92 percent of blacks voted to retire Ronald Reagan, compared to only 36 percent of whites.

"The Unbearable Being Of Whiteness," Ibid.

18 The one regret I have about my own abortions is that they cost money that might otherwise have been spent on something more pleasurable, like taking the kids to movies and theme parks.

"Their Dilemma and Mine," Ibid.

19 If men were equally at risk from this condition—if they knew their bellies might swell as if they were suffering from end-stage cirrhosis, that they would have to go nearly a year without a stiff drink, a cigarette, or even an aspirin, that they would be subject to fainting spells and unable to fight their way onto commuter trains—then I am sure that pregnancy would be classified as a sexually transmitted disease and abortions would be no more controversial than emergency appendectomies.

Ibid.

20 The feminist anti-pornography movement, no less than the feminist movement of a century ago, encourages the assumption that male and female sexuality, and possibly morality, are as unlike as yin and yang.

"Why We Lost the E.R.A."* (*Atlantic Monthly*, 1986), Ibid.
*Equal Rights Amendment; see 1538:1.

21 No matter that patriotism is too often the refuge of scoundrels. Dissent, rebellion, and all-around hell-raising remain the true duty of patriots.

"Family Values," Ibid.

22 There can be no more ancient and traditional American value than ignorance. English-only speakers brought it with them to this country three centuries ago, and they quickly imposed it on the Africans—who were not allowed to learn to read and write—and on the Native Americans, who were simply not allowed.

"Language Barrier," Ibid.

23 Thus will the fondest dream of Phallic science be realized: a pristine new planet populated entirely by little boy clones of great scientific entrepeneurs . . . free to smash atoms, accelerate particles, or, if they are so moved, build pyramids—without any social relevance or human responsibility at all.

"Phallic Science," Ibid.

24 Given the cultural barriers to intersex conversation, the amazing thing is that we would even expect women and men to have anything to say to each other for more than ten minutes at a stretch. The barriers are ancient—perhaps rooted, as some paleontologist may soon discover, in the contrast between the occasional guttural utterances exchanged in male hunting bands and the extended discussions characteristic of female food-gathering groups.

"Tales of the Man Shortage" (*Mother Jones*, 1986), Ibid.

25 Someone has to stand up for wimps.
> "Wimps" (*The New York Times*, 1985), Ibid.

2849. Nora Ephron (1941–)

1 We have lived through the era when happiness was a warm puppy, and the era when happiness was a dry martini, and now we have come to the era when happiness is "knowing what your uterus looks like."
> "Vaginal Politics" (December 1972), *Crazy Salad* 1975

2 She [Rose Mary Woods]* has often said that she was very much impressed by him [Nixon] before she even knew him, because he kept such neat expense accounts.
> "Rose Mary Woods—The Lady or the Tiger?" (March 1974), Ibid.
> *President Richard Nixon's secretary, held responsible for 18 missing minutes of vital recorded tape related to the Watergate scandal (1972–1973).

3 . . . I cannot understand any woman's wanting to be the first woman to do anything. . . . It is a devastating burden and I could not take it, could not be a pioneer, a Symbol of Something Greater.
> "Bernice Gera, First Lady Umpire" (*January*, 1973), Ibid.

4 Consciousness-raising is at the very least supposed to bring about an intimacy, but what it seems instead to bring about are the trappings of intimacy, the illusion of intimacy, a semblance of intimacy.
> "On Consciousness-Raising" (March 1973), Ibid.

5 I am uncomfortable flirting, it requires a great deal of energy and ego, and I manage to do it only a couple of times a year, and not with interview subjects.
> "A Star Is Born" (October, 1973), Ibid.

6 It struck me that the movies had spent more than half a century saying, "They lived happily ever after" and the following quarter-century warning that they'll be lucky to make it through the weekend. Possibly now we are now entering a third era in which the movies will be sounding a note of cautious optimism: You know it just might work.
> Quoted in *The Los Angeles Times* 27 July 1989

7 No man can be friends with a woman he finds attractive. He always wants to have sex with her. Sex is always out there. Friendship is ultimately doomed and that is the end of the story.
> *When Harry Met Sally* (screenplay) 1989

8 I am continually fascinated at the difficulty intelligent people have in distinguishing what is controversial from what is merely offensive.
> "Barney Collier's Book," *Esquire* (New York) *January* 1976

2850. Sheila Mary Fitzpatrick (1941–)

1 *Homo Sovieticus* was a string-puller, an operator, a timeserver, a freeloader, a mouther of slogans and much more. But above all, he was a survivor.
> *Everyday Stalinism* 1998

2851. Fannie Flagg (1941–)

1 "It's funny, when you're a child you think time will never go by, but when you hit about twenty—time passes like you're on the fast train to Memphis."
> "December 15, 1985," *Fried Green Tomatoes at the Whistle Stop Café* 1987

2 "There's nothing in the world happier to see you than a cocker spaniel."
> "February 2, 1986," Ibid.

3 He was here—Slagtown on a Saturday night—and just one block away, white Birmingham was completely unaware that this exotic sepia spot even existed. Slagtown, where the Highland Avenue maid of that afternoon could be tonight's Queen of the Avenue, and red–caps and shoeshine boys were the leaders of Slagtown's after-dark fashion show.
> "December 30, 1934," Ibid.

4 "A lot of people might have been sad to have a birth-injured child, but I think the good Lord made him like that so he wouldn't have to suffer. He never even knew there were mean people on this earth. He just loved everybody and everybody loved him. I truly believe in my heart that he was an angel that God sent down to me, and sometimes I cain't wait to get to heaven to see him again. He was my pal, and I miss him . . . "
> "March 15, 1986," Ibid.

5 She had stayed a virgin so she wouldn't be called a tramp or a slut; had married so she wouldn't be called an old maid; faked orgasms so she wouldn't be called frigid; had children so she wouldn't be called barren; had not been a feminist because she didn't want to be called queer and a man hater; never nagged or raised her voice so she wouldn't be called a bitch . . .
> "August 8, 1986," Ibid.

6 . . . and is there anything worse than man who has a little pain? Guess that's why we have the babies . . .
> "August 10, 1954," Ibid.

7 She had joined a health club, once, but was so exhausted by the time she'd pulled herself into those awful leotards, she went home to bed.
> "October 14, 1986," Ibid.

2852. Marilyn Frye (1941–)

1 We can be taken in by this equation of servitude with love because we make two mistakes at once: we think, of both servitude and love that they are selfless or unselfish.
> (p. 73), *The Politics of Reality: Essays in Feminist Theory* 1983

2 The loving eye is a contrary of the arrogant eye.
> (p. 75), Ibid.

3 For a great many lesbians, the gap between the high hopes we had some time ago for lesbian sex and the way things have worked out has turned the phrase "lesbian sex" into something of a bitter joke.
> "Lesbian 'Sex'," *Sinister Wisdom 35 Summer/Fall 1988*

4 It has been said before by feminists that the concept of "having sex" is a phallic concept, that it pertains to heterosexual intercourse, in fact, primarily to heterosexist intercourse, i.e., male-dominant-female-subordinate-copulation-whose-completion-and-purpose-is-the-male's-ejaculation.
> Ibid.

5 The meanings one's life and experience might generate cannot come fully into operation if they are not woven into language; they are fleeting, or they hover, vague, not fully coalesced, not connected, and hence not useful for explaining or grounding interpretations, desires, complaints, theories.
> Ibid.

2853. Diane Glancy (1941–)

1 They couldn't remove us. Didn't the soldiers know we were the land? The cornstalks were our grandmothers. In our story of corn, a woman named Selu had been murdered by her sons. Where her blood fell, the corn grew. The cornstalks waved their arms trying to hold us. Their voices were the long tassels reaching the air. Our spirits clung to them. Our roots entwined.

Pushing the Bear: A Novel of the Trail of Tears 1996

2 The bear had once been a person. But he was not conscious of the consciousness he was given. His darkness was greed and self-centeredness. It was part of myself too. It was in all of us. It was part of the human being. Why else did we march? No one was free of the bear.

Ibid.

3 I unbraided my hair and covered a small girl with it to keep her from shivering. "You are a small animal," I said. "Feel your fur." I took the child's hand and rubbed it over my hair. "You are warm under your fur, little rabbit."

Ibid.

2854. Linda Gottleib (1941?–)

Co-author with Joan Silver; see 2611.

2855. Toni Grant (1941–)

1 There is a profound sense of alienation and loneliness here [in Southern California], and few traditional guidelines for behavior. I don't have any grand solutions, just my own idiosyncratic ones.

"Dial Dr. Toni for Therapy," *Time* (New York)
26 May 1980

2 . . . sometimes you have to give up an intense heat for a continuing warmth.

Quoted in "Sexy Guru for Kvetches" by Elaine Warren,
Los Angeles Herald-Examiner 20 July 1980

2856. Marie Herbert (1941–)

1 Unlike children in other countries, the Eskimos played no games of war. They played with imaginary rifles and harpoons, but these were never directed against people but against the formidable beasts that haunted the vast wastes of their land.

Ch. 5, *The Snow Children 1973*

2 The Eskimos described everyone other than themselves as Kasdlunas. They called themselves the Inuit—which simply means "the people." For centuries, since they never saw anyone else, they believed they were the only human beings in the world.

Ibid.

2857. Susan Herman (1942–)

1 Fairness is an abstract concept with no foundation in reality.

Remark to Elaine T. Partnow,* Interlocken International
Learning Center (Antrim, New Hampshire)
16 February 1984

*See 2870.

2 You can have the best service, the best service delivery plan, the sexiest product, the most efficient production system, the wisest financial plan. But without the best people, your organization simply can't function at its optimum.

Ch. 1, *Hiring Right 1994*

3 An interview is like an uncontrolled chemical reaction. Into the beaker go the characteristics (sex, age, race, physical fitness/attractiveness, previous educational and work experiences, etc.) of a particular applicant and those of a particular interviewer. Then in go the beliefs, goals, values, competencies, expectations, and prejudices of both the applicant and the interviewer, which when stirred together create both verbal and nonverbal behaviors of the applicant, to which the interviewer reacts; and of the interviewer, to which the applicant reacts. Add to the beaker the various accurate and inaccurate impressions and/or the impression that the interviewer has of other applicants and the impression the applicant has of other jobs; the degree to which the interviewer wants the applicant and the degree to which the applicant wants the job. Don't forget to include in the beaker the day, time, and place of the interview, and what might be going on in the personal and professional lives of both the applicant and the interviewers. The resulting potent chemical brew somehow transforms itself into a decision . . .

Ch. 7, *Ibid.*

2858. Elizabeth Holtzman (1941–)

1 If the mood of the country is for fiscal responsibility, then let's get at that area of government which is the biggest waster of funds—the Defense Department.

Quoted in *American Political Women* by Esther Stineman
1980

2859. Libby Houston (1941–)

1 The base emotions Plato banned
have left a radio-active and not radiant land.

"Judging Lear," *At the Mercy 1981*

2 When your dreams tire, they go underground
and out of kindness that's where they stay.

"Gold," *Necessity 1988*

2860. Shirbey Johnson (1941–)

1 . . . women are carrying a new attitude. They've cast aside the old stereotypes. They don't believe you have to be ugly or have big muscles to play sports.

Quoted in "Women in Sports: The Movement is Real,"
The Los Angeles Times 23 April 1974

2 As coaches and facilities are slowly upgraded, as girls get interested at earlier ages, they become integrated into the sports system more naturally.

Ibid.

2861. Carole King (1941–)

1 When my soul was in the lost-and-found
You came along to claim it.

"A Natural Woman" *1967*

2 You've got to get up every morning with a smile on your face
And show the world all the love in your heart
Then people gonna treat you better
You're gonna find, yes you will
That you're beautiful as you feel.

"Beautiful" *1971*

3 Doesn't anybody stay in one place anymore?

"So Far Away" *1971*

4 Winter, spring, summer or fall
All you have to do is call

And I'll be there,
You've got a friend.
                              "You've Got a Friend" *1971*

5   My life has been a tapestry of rich and royal hue.
    An everlasting vision of the everchanging view.
                              "Tapestry" *1971*

2862. Irena Klepfisz (1941–)

1   at night   the vestiges
    of other ages   influence
    us.
    "dinosaurs and larger issues," vii, *periods of stress 1975*

2   By making literature in *mame-loshn** patrilineal rather than
    matrilineal, Sholom Aleichem** instantly created a male Yid-
    dish literary dynasty. . . . Just when Yiddish was being
    championed as an authentic national *mame-loshn* [he] de-
    clared—and everyone agreed—its literature now belonged to
    the fathers.
    Introduction, *Found Treasures: Stories by Yiddish Women
    Writers*, Frieda Forman, Ethel Raicus, Sarah Silberstein
    Swartz and Margie Wolf, eds. *1994*
    *Mother tongue. **Née S— Yakov Rabinowitz, Russian writer
    who popularized Yiddish literature (1859–1916).

2863. Julia Kristeva (1941–)

1   But Judaism was founded through and beyond this tradition,
    when, around 2000 BC, Egyptian refugees, nomads, brigands
    and insurgent peasants banded together, it seems, without any
    coherent ethnic origin, without land or State, seeking at first
    merely to survive as a wandering community. Jewish monothe-
    ism is undoubtedly rooted in this will to create a community in
    the face of all the unfavorable concrete circumstances: an ab-
    stract, nominal symbolic community beyond individuals and
    their beliefs, but beyond their political organization as well.
    "On This Side," *Des Chinoises 1974*

2   FLASH—instant of time or of dream without time; inordinately
    swollen atoms of a bond, a vision, a shiver, a yet formless, un-
    namable embryo. Epiphanies. Photos of what is not yet visible
    and that language necessarily skims over from afar, allusively.
    Words that are always too distant, too abstract for this under-
    ground swarming of seconds, folding into unimaginable spaces.
    Writing them down is an ordeal of discourse, like love. What is
    loving, for a woman, the same thing as writing. Laugh. Impos-
    sible. Flash on the unnamable, weavings of abstraction to be
    torn. Let a body venture at last out of its shelter, take a chance
    with meaning under a veil of words. WORD FLESH. From one
    to the other, eternally, broken up visions, metaphors of the in-
    visible.
    "Hérethique de l'amour," *Tel Quel*, 74 *Winter 1977*

3   Our philosophies of language, embodiments of the idea, are
    nothing more than the thoughts of archivists, archaeologists,
    and necrophiliacs. Fascinated by the remains of a process
    which is partly discursive, they substitute this fetish for what
    actually produced it. Egypt, Babylon, Mycenae: we see their
    pyramids, their carved tablets, and fragmented codes in the
    discourse of our contemporaries, and think that by codifying
    them we can possess them.
    "Prolegomenon," *Revolution in Poetic Language (La revo-
    lution du langage poetique*, 1974), Margaret Waller, tr. *1984*

4   I think that in the imaginary, maternal continuity is what guar-
    antees identity. One may imagine other social systems where it

would be different. . . . The imaginary of the work of art, that is
really the most extraordinary and the most unsettling imitation
of the mother-child dependence. [It is] its substitution and its
displacement towards a limit which is fascinating because inhuman. The work of art is independence conquered through
inhumanity. The work of art cuts off natural filiation, it is patri-
cide and matricide, it is superbly solitary. But look backwards,
as does the analyst, and you will find a dependence, a secret
mother on whom this sublimation is constructed.
    "*Entretien avec* Julia Kristeva *réalisé par* Françoise Collin,"
    Les Cahiers due GRIF, 32 *1985*

2864. Robin Morgan (1941–)

1   . . . although every organized patriarchal religion works over-
    time to contribute its own brand of misogyny to the myth of
    woman-hate, woman-fear, and woman-evil, the Roman
    Catho-lic Church also carries the immense power of very di-
    rectly affecting women's lives everywhere by its stand against
    birth control and abortion, and by its use of skillful and
    wealthy lobbies to prevent legislative change. It is an obscen-
    ity—an all-male hierarchy, celibate or not, that presumes to
    rule on the lives and bodies of millions of women.
    Introduction, *Sisterhood
    Is Powerful 1970*

2   There's something contagious about demanding freedom.
                              Ibid.

3   the Conquerors.
    They're always watching,

    invisibly electroded in our brains,
    to be certain we implode our rage against each other
    and not explode it against them.
                              Ibid.

4   poetry can be quite dangerous propaganda,
    especially since all worthwhile propaganda
    ought to move its readers like a poem.
    Graffiti do that; so do some songs,
    and rarely, poems on a page.
                              Ibid.

5   . . . it isn't until you begin to fight in your own cause that you
    (a) become really committed to winning, and (b) become a
    genuine ally of other people struggling for their freedom.
                              Ibid.

6   Anthropologists continue to turn up examples which prove
    that competitive, aggressive, warlike cultures are those in
    which sexual stereotypes are most polarized, while those
    social structures allowing for an overlap of roles and func-
    tions between men and women (in tasks, childrearing,
    decision-making, etc.) tend to be collectivist, cooperative and
    peaceful.
                              Ibid.

7   Don't accept rides from strange men,
    and remember that all men are strange as hell.
                              "Letter to a Sister Underground," Ibid.

8   Some have named this space where we are
    rooted a place of death.
    We fix them with our callous eyes
    and call it, rather, a terrain of resurrection.
    "Easter Island, I: Embarcation,"
    Monster 1972

9 Meanwhile, for now, this must suffice:
that murder and resurrection are the levers of change,
that creation and complexity are one,
that miracle is contradiction.
"Easter Island, II: Arrival," Ibid.

10 All the secretaries hunch at their IBM's, snickering at keys.
What they know could bring down the government.
"On the Watergate Women," St. 7, Ibid.

11 This quality of grief
could bring down
mankind.
St. 20, Ibid.

12 And I will speak less and less to you
And more and more in crazy gibberish you cannot understand:
witches' incantations, poetry, old women's mutterings. . . .
"Monster," Ibid.

13 Only she who attempts the absurd can achieve the impossible.
Sisterhood is Global 1984

2865. Claire Goldberg Moses (1941–)

1 Women's studies, even at the graduate level, intends to change
society, not simply to fit our students into the society we inherit.
"Passing on the torch," *The Women's Review of Books,*
Vol. XV, No. 5 *February 1998*

2866. Suniti Namjoshi (1941–)

1 Circe,
all animals adore you,
you are all things to each
in the tutelary garden, at the continuous feast.
"Homage to Circe," *The Jackass and the Lady 1980*

2 I give her the rose with unfurled petals.
She smiles
and crosses her legs.
"I Give Her the Rose," Ibid.

2867. Judith Niemi (1941–)

1 On the main Amazon, sheer volume overwhelms the imagina-
tion, wipes out thought.
"Bitten by the jungle," *The Women's Review of Books,* Vol.
XII, Nos. 10–11 *July 1995*

2 Floating downstream silently in the dark, the air a perfect temperature, or no-temperature—could this be what it feels like in
the womb?
Ibid.

3 Fay raises a plastic cup of *siepte raices,* powerful sugar-cane
rum with seven roots that offer endless aphrodisiac and cura-
tive properties. It promises long life; it tastes like woody, acrid
Mogen David. She surveys the tangled jungle and in her ladylike, 75-year-old voice offers a toast: "To chaos."
Ibid.

2868. Mary O'Malley (1941–)

1 MOTHER PETER. Of course nobody ever passed any exam of
their own accord. Only prayer will get results. The best thing
each one of you can do is to pick out a particular saint and
pray to him or her to get you through. Your Confirmation
Saint perhaps, or any saint you fancy. But not St. Peter the
Apostle, if you wouldn't mind. He's my saint, so he is, and
don't any of you go annoying him now.
Act I, Sc. 1, *Once a Catholic 1977*

2869. Pamela Painter (1941–)

1 For his father it had all been said, as if words had been
stripped away like coal from the hollows and hills that had
once been farms. And he too had nothing to say as he kept his
father's silence.
"Winter Evenings: Spring Night," *Getting to Know
the Weather 1985*

2870. Elaine T. Partnow (1941–)

1 We've become such highly transient consumers of people, emotions, things that we are psychically hyperventilating. Like the
cookie monster, we eat more, buy more, love and lose more,
and have more heart attacks.
Pt. I, Ch. 3, *Breaking the Age Barrier 1981*

2 Language is a boxing match in which we must spar daily,
warding off the negative suggestions that age is our worst
enemy. Indeed, it is our best friend.
Ch. 4, Ibid.

3 You never really lose your youth. How can you? The experiences and lessons of youth belong to you. Youth is as much a
state of mind as it is a time and place in life. Just as we can be
very young in some things in our later years, so, during our so-
called "youth," we may be very old in others. Yes, youth is
something you always have at your command. . . .
What we can and often do lose is vigor . . .
Pt. II, Ch. 5, Ibid.

4 We are remarkable creatures, able to mold and shape ourselves
just as we do the world we live in. Just as having opposable
thumbs differentiates us primates from all other species, enabling us to grasp and wield tools and other objects in our
hands, having "opposable minds," if you will, enables Homo
sapiens, unlike our primate cousins, to develop logic, self-ar-
gument, inner opposition, so that we can grasp any situation
and mold it into an agreeable and useful shape with our minds.
Ch. 15, Ibid.

5 The serpent's name was Hollywood
Act I, *Hear Us Roar: A Woman's Connection 1988*

6 I have seen how heart cells from different organisms, when
placed together in the same petri dish, begin to pulsate in unison.
There is a connection between all living things, and more
so between all like things.
Ibid.

7 Everyone is your teacher.
Ibid.

8 Times change. Symbols change. And so do we. We don't bury
our hopes for the future in cedar chests and mothballs anymore. We get out there and run for our future, for our health,
for our sanity. We are the women of the eighties.
Act II, Ibid.

9 It's all an experiment, isn't it? Aren't we just one great big petri
dish in the cosmos?
Ibid.

10 Success in theater is most often measured by box office receipts.

Preface, *The Female Dramatist 1998*

11 Theater is a democratic art form—it speaks to the myriad complexities of mood, intellect, station, age, and social status that
make up an audience. If it succeeds in moving that amorphous
body, whether to laughter, tears, reflection, or anger, it is good
theater. If it happens to speak particularly to the members of
"the ruling class"—upper class, white, powerful—it may garner the reputation of great theater.

Ibid.

2871. Sally Quinn (1941–)

1 Washington is . . . a company town. Most of the interesting
people in Washington either work for the government or write
about it.

We're Going to Make You a Star 1975

2 . . . there has been such a mythology built up around the supposed glamour of television life that it's hard for the average
person to imagine turning down anything on TV.

Ibid.

2872. Judith Rascoe (1941–)

1 "There are more important rights than the so-called right to
know. That is not the right that is being violated nowadays.
People have the right to know *something*. They have the right
to know that something is being done. That is more important
than the right to know. They have the right to know how long
they will have to wait until something is done. That is more
important than the right to know. I know you would rather
know that I am doing something than know what I am doing."

"Evening's Down Under," *Yours and Mine 1973*

2 . . . the grandmother opens the envelope with the letter-opener
that Helen's first husband gave her and finds a colored photograph of Helen's second husband and his new wife, Myrna,
surrounded by Myrna's children from her first marriage: "Season's Greetings from the Hannibals!"

"Yours and Mine," Ibid.

2873. Maureen Reagan (1941–)

1 We're an ideal political family, as accessible as Disneyland.

Quoted in *The Guardian* (London) *24 December 1984*

2874. Helen Reddy (1941–)

1 I am Woman, hear me roar
In numbers too big to ignore,
And I know too much
To go back and pretend.

"I Am Woman" *1972*

2 If I have to, I can do anything
I am strong, I am invincible, I am Woman.

Ibid.

3 Women temper men. We have a good influence on them.

Interview on ABC-TV *1 March 1974*

4 The most exciting thing about women's liberation is that this
century will be able to take advantage of talent and potential
genius that have been wasted because of taboos.

Quoted in the *The Los Angeles Times 23 April 1974*

5 Gentleness is not a quality exclusive to women.

Ibid.

2875. Barbara Paul Robinson (1941–)

1 It is irresponsible for public officials, especially those who are
lawyers, to use our courts as a political football, when they
must know that an independent judiciary is essential to our
system of justice.

Editorial, *The New York Times n.d.*

2876. Lillian Sara Robinson (1941–)

1 Change of life is not the last change in life, and the problems
of the old in general and old women in particular should not
be minimized by assimilating them to those of the middle-
aged.

"Consciousness lowering," *The Women's Review of Books,*
Vol. X, No. 4, pp. 11–12 *January 1993*

2 (Greer* suggests that much of the animosity against Thatcher** originated in societal contempt for aging women. I
believe that if a stereotype was involved it was Thatcher's violation of the image of woman as nurturer. In fact, contemplating
the former Prime Minister, I think I really understand for the
first time what the term Phallic Mother means.)

Ibid.

*Germaine Greer ; see 2755. **Margaret Thatcher ; see 2285.

3 Nothing has prepared us for growing older . . .

Ibid.

2877. Buffy Sainte-Marie (1941–)

1 He's five feet two and he's six feet four.
He fights with missiles and with spears.
He's all of thirty-one and he's only seventeen.
He's been a soldier for a thousand years.

He's a Cath'lic, a Hindu, an atheist, a Jain,
A Buddhist and a Baptist and a Jew.
And he know he shouldn't kill
and he knows he always will
Kill you for me my friend and me for you.

"The Universal Soldier" *1963*

2 We'll make a space in the lives that we planned
And here I'll stay until it's time for you to go.

"Until It's Time for You to Go" *1965*

3 And yet where in your history books is the tale
of the genocide basic to this country's birth?
of the preachers who lied?
how the Bill of Rights failed.

"My Country 'Tis of Thy People You're Dying" *1966*

4 You have to sniff out joy, keep your nose to the joy-trail.

Quoted by Susan Braudy in *Ms.* (New York) *March 1975*

5 . . . red, I mean, *white* tape. . . .

Ibid.

6 Here the melting pot stands open—if you're willing to get
bleached first.

Ibid.

7 The white man wants everyone who isn't white to think white.

Ibid.

2878. Susan Fromberg Schaeffer (1941–)

1 The sky is reduced,
A narrow blue ribbon banding the lake.
Someone is wrapping things up.
"Post Mortem," St. 1, *The Witch and the Weather Report*
1972

2 What can be wrong
That some days I hug this house
Around me like a shawl, and feel
Each window like a tatter in its skin,
Or worse, bright eyes I must not look through?
"Housewife," St. 1, Ibid.

3 In her drugged state, she felt only a euphoria, as if all the pain of her life had become a vast salty water, buoying up, where she floated on the great blue waves of a vast, melodramatic sea.
Ch. 1, *Falling 1973*

4 The assistants, relying on the proverbial competition among pre-meds, had assumed there would be no help among the gladiators, no risks taken which might raise the curve. It seemed to Elizabeth that higher mathematics were useless to them in real life; the students did not care how high the curve spiraled, provided they were on top, climbing the beanstalk, collecting the golden eggs, the medical acceptances, the gallstones in jars.
Ibid.

5 "Time is only a force; it is neither good nor evil, only necessary."
Ch. 6, Ibid.

2879. Vicki Sears (1941–)

1 Now
at 57 years
she sits crying for a
barren womb stolen by Nagasaki.
tears bumping down her rippled skin
bound in pain thirty years past its time
unable to answer why.
"Nagasaki Elder," St. 4, *Backbone*, Vol. I, No. 1 *Fall 1984*

2 They went to the city only once
understanding
they had all they needed.

the city never fooled them.
"Mem & Pep," *Ikon*, second series, #4
Winter/Summer 1985

3 Almost every recent day my mind tongue tasted the bitter heat of scotch. I salivated. It seemed real again. That getting drunk would make everything better. All the world issues and ordinary life problems would fade into oblivion. Nothing would hurt. I would have control of my environment again. Fool's talk on a fool's walk. Splurges of dirges, I mused.
"Sticktalk" (1984), *Hear the Silence*, Irene Zahava, ed. *1986*

4 My father had repeatedly proven, when I was a child, that all things have their own spirits and lessons to share. I am just as the sticks and rocks. I may not always know my purpose, but it will be clear to me when I need to know. I will behave just as I am supposed to at that moment.
Ibid.

5 "You can't possess anything but yourself. Let me loose."
Ibid.

2880. Donna Shalala (1941/2–)

1 Her [Joycelyn Elders's*] style is straightforward and very American. We like plain-spoken, outspoken people in this country, particularly on health issues.
Quoted in "Blunt Style of Teen Sex And Health" by
Philip J. Hilts, *The New York Times* 14 September 1993
*See 2524.

2881. Anne Tyler (1941–)

1 Sad people are the only real ones. They can tell you the truth about things; they have always known that there is no one you can depend upon forever and no change in your life, however great, that can keep you from being in the end what you were in the beginning: lost and lonely, sitting on an oilcloth watching the rest of the world do the butterfly stroke.
(p. 85), *Celestial Navigation 1974*

2 . . . she thought of the hall lamp she used to leave on so they wouldn't be scared in the dark. Then later she'd left just the bathroom light on, further down the hall of whatever house they'd been living in; and later still just the downstairs lights if one of them was out for the evening. Their growing up amounted, therefore, to a gradual dimming of the light at her bedroom door, as if they took some radiance with them as they moved away from her.
Ch. 1, *Dinner at the Homesick Restaurant 1982*

3 "You almost died," a nurse told her. But that was nonsense. Of course she wouldn't have died; she had children. When you have children, you're obliged to live.
Ibid.

4 He was back to his boyhood, it seemed, fearing that his mother could read his mind as unhesitatingly as she read the inner temperature of a roasting hen by giving its thigh a single, contemptuous pinch.
Ch. 10, Ibid.

5 Bring a novel to read on the plane to protect yourself against chatty strangers.
The Accidental Tourist 1985

6 The effort of typing made the corners of his mouth turn down, so that no one could have guessed how much he was enjoying himself. I am happy to say that it's possible now to buy Kentucky Fried Chicken in Stockholm.
Ibid.

7 . . . . toward that sense of narrowly missed connections. They were like people who run to meet, holding out their arms, but their aim is wrong; they pass each other and keep running. It had all amounted to nothing, in the end.
Ibid.

8 . . . I am nineteen years old and I'll never be nineteen again. I'll never be alive again. I mean this is the only life I get to go through, . . . so far as I know, and I've spent this great large chunk of it sitting alone in an empty apartment too proud to make up, too scared you'd say no, but even if you did say no it can't be worse than what I got now. I'm the loneliest man in the world.
Ibid.

9 . . . While a person who'd been moved around a great deal never acquired a fixed point of reference but wandered forever in a fog—adrift upon the planet, helpless, praying that just by luck he might stumble across his destination.
Ibid.

10 I've always thought a hotel ought to offer optional small animals. . . . I mean a cat to sleep on your bed at night, or a dog of some kind to act pleased when you come in. You ever notice how a hotel room feels so lifeless?

Ibid.

11 "She thinks the people she loves are better than they really are, and so then she starts changing things around to suit her view of them."

Breathing Lessons 1988

12 "When did you decide to be ordinary?"

Ibid.

13 He had passed that early, superficial stage [in solitaire] when any number of moves seemed possible and now his choices were narrower and he had to show real skill and judgment.

Ibid.

14 "It's just time to marry, that's all . . . I'm so tired of dating! I'm so tired of keeping up a good front! I want to sit on the couch with a regular, normal husband and watch TV for a thousand years."

Ibid.

15 "It used to be 'Love Me Forever' and now it's 'Help Me Make It Through the Night.'"

Ibid.

16 I think we're each allowed one single life to live on this planet. We never get another chance in all eternity. . . And if you let that go to waste—now, that is sinning.

(p. 210), *Saint Maybe 1991*

17 He had felt he was an arrow—not an arrow shot by God but an arrow heading toward God, and if it took every bit of this only life he had, he believed that he would get there in the end.

(p. 225), Ibid.

18 See, I've always pictured life as one of those ladders you find on playground sliding boards—a sort of ladder of years where you climb higher and higher, and then, oops!, you fall over the edge and others move up behind you.

(pp. 193–94), *Ladder of Years 1995*

19 . . . how life was not a straight line—either downward or upward, either one—but something more irregular, a zigzag or a corkscrew or sometimes a scribble. "And sometimes . . . you get to what you thought was the end and you find it's a whole new beginning."

(p. 219), Ibid.

20 And I was beginning to suspect that it made no difference whether they'd married the right person. Finally, you're just with who you're with. You've signed on with her, put in half a century with her, grown to know her as well as you know yourself or even better, and she's become the right person.

A Patchwork Planet 1998

21 Just because we were related didn't mean we were any good at understanding each other.

Ibid.

22 What makes people more virtuous than others? Don't they ever feel that zingy, thrilling urge to smash the world to bits?

Ibid.

23 Over her forearm she carried a Yorkshire terrier, neatly folded like a waiter's napkin.

Ibid.

24 `A quilt of our planet . . . makeshift and haphazard, clumsily cobbled together, overlapping and crowded and likely to fall into pieces at any moment..

Ibid.

25 [He wondered] if there was any event, any at all, so tragic it could jolt him out of the odious habit of observing his own reaction to it.

Ibid.

26 " . . . how long will I have to pay for just a handful of tossed–off words?"

Ibid.

27 People changed other people's lives every day of the year. There was no call to make such a fuss about it.

(end), Ibid.

2882. Yuliya Voznesenskaya (1941?–)

1 In the West they had invented disposable nappies and plastic pants long ago. Our people were supposed to be involved in industrial espionage, so why couldn't they steal some useful secrets instead of always going for electronics?

The Women's Decameron (Damskii Dekameron),
W. B. Linton, tr. *1985*

2 "I think, Larissa," she said, "that all your strength comes precisely from your insecurity. It happens to a lot of women these days. It's not so much that we're striving to be strong ourselves, but the weakness of the men forces us to be. It's frightening how unmanly they have become. A husband in the home is just another child, only greedier."

The First Day, Story Two, Ibid.

3 "When a saint does something holy there's nothing surprising about it."

The Eighth Day, Story Five, Ibid.

2883. Judy Wenning (1941?–)

1 Women are freer to express their competitiveness now. Women's competitiveness in the past has been limited to competing for men, but those days are over. It's no longer a totally negative thing.

Quoted in "Women in Sports: The Movement is Real,"
The Los Angeles Times 23 April 1974

2884. Vivienne Westwood (1941–)

1 Every time I hear that word, I cringe. Fun! I think it's disgusting; it's just running around. It's not my idea of pleasure.

Independent on Sunday (London) *18 February 1990*

2 It is not possible for a man to be elegant without a touch of femininity.

Independent (London) *12 July 1990*

2885. Margaret Wheatley (1941–)

1 In a self-organizing world, one of the things that works on our behalf is not only that we have a natural tendency toward change, that we can constantly reorganize, or that we can structure ourselves without leaders (as long as we're well connected and informed and focused) but that, underneath it all, what we're doing is discovering our connections.

"The Unplanned" (pp. 17–23), *Noetic Sciences Review*
Spring *1996*

2 You can't change people, but people change all the time.

       Ibid.

3 Organizations are living systems, or at least the people in them are living systems. . . . We're moving away from a terribly deadening image of who we are and how we should organize. The image of the world as a machine that came into our consciousness in the seventeenth century was a wonderful metaphor that then went out of control. Ultimately, we came to believe not only that the world is a machine but that people can best be understood as machines.

       Ibid.

4 Life is intent on finding what works, not what's right.

       Ibid.

5 Life is self-organizing. It seeks to create patterns, structures, organization, without pre-planned directive leadership.

       Ibid.

6 Leadership is a series of behaviors rather than a role for heroes.

       Ibid.

7 Now, if life is an accident, that means there is nothing here to support us; so we do it all alone, and if we don't get it right, we get killed because the world is an inhospitable place. I believe this kind of thinking led to the heroic image of the great corporate leader who would craft organizations and *make* things happen—nothing would happen without this great impetus of human ingenuity and human control.

       Ibid.

8 But the new recognition of a self-organizing world tells us that we can use any period of chaos and dissipation to reorganize ourselves to a structure better suited to the environment.

       Ibid.

9 When we see a change being forced on us, we recognize it as threatening our sense of self. Resistance reflects our need to protect our sense of dignity and identity as presently defined. Resistance does not represent a fundamental tendency toward inertia, which is the old belief about human nature.

       Ibid.

10 I believe it is a travesty to think we can understand ourselves or another human being independent of being in a relationship with them. . . . when a group is together it is capable of behaviors that simply are not knowable when you study the individuals.

       Ibid.

11 We live in a world in which, when we come together, we can discover new possibilities. And we live in a world in which the discovery of new possibilities is, I believe, the reason for existing.

       Ibid.

12 It is Gaia who reaches into the void that is Chaos and pulls forth life. It is Gaia who works with the creative impulse that is Eros and creates the world. She is the created universe, the mother of all life, the great partner of chaos and creativity. In modern science, she is planet Earth, a living being who creates for herself the conditions that nourish and sustain life. And in this millennial era, Gaia is us. She is the feminine energy that compels us to care about the future of Earth. She is the feminine sensibility that inspires us to dream of harmony among all beings. She is the feminine voice that yearns to speak through us of the law of love.

    "Reclaiming Gaia, Reclaiming Life," *The Fabric of the Future: Women Visionaries of Today Illuminate the Path to Tomorrow*, M.J. Ryan, ed. 1998

13 Courageous acts are born only from the self-acknowledgment of our goodness.

       Ibid.

2886. Anne Wortham (1941–)

1 A civilized society is one whose members expect that each will address at all times, as far as possible, the rational in man; that even when I may want to bash you over the head, I will be checked by my awareness of you as a rational entity, and I will not resort to force as an expression of my disagreement with you or even my feeling that you have been unjust to me; that in my disagreements with you, I will rely on the power of persuasion.

    Quoted in *A World of Ideas* by Bill Moyers 1989

2 Rationality has the capacity for betraying itself. Rational men have the capacity to be irrational and to institutionalize irrationality. We've seen that in Nazi Germany.

       Ibid.

3 Respect means that you leave me alone, that you don't build up in your own mind scenarios for my salvation and that you respect me enough to trust me, even when I'm an idiot, even when I'm wrong.

       Ibid.

4 Government is not a savior—the American federal government has not acted as a liberator. Civil rights for minorities was no great favor, for Christ's sake! This is what they should have done two hundred years ago.

       Ibid.

2887. Susan Yankowitz (1941–)

1 BILL. Is she going to be "all there"? I don't know. But during a solar eclipse, the sun is still there, isn't it? And when a star collapses in on itself, isn't that star still there?*

    Sc. 3, *Night Sky* 1991

*Referring to woman who suffers from aphasia, the loss of the ability to use words.

2888. Ama Ata Aidoo (1942–)

1 People are worms, and even the God who created them is immensely bored with their antics.

    No Sweetness Here & Other Stories 1970

2 . . . tears . . . one of the most potent weapons in woman's bitchy and inexhaustible arsenal.

       Ibid.

3 But listen, my husband. If one day when you are not looking, a man comes and takes your farmhouse or your kraal,* and he begins doing all the things a good man should not do; sells all the yams in your barns without leaving any for planting; boils your eggs as soon as they have been laid and does not spare one for a single hen to hatch; gives great feasts to all his family and all his friends, with your lambs and calves; and generally carries on in such a way that your heart hurts as though it is falling into your bowels every time you look on; and yet you

are not able to do anything for many many years, but then one day, thanks to Allah, you get your farmhouse or your kraal back, what then do you do, my husband?

> "For Whom Things Did Not Change," Ibid.

*Corral; enclosure for animals.

4 "Our Auntie Araba is going to heaven."
If there is any heaven and God is not like man, my sister.

> "Something to Talk About on the Way to the Funeral," Ibid.

5 ANOWA. I hear in other lands a woman is nothing. And they let her know this from the day of her birth. But here, O my spirit mother, they let a girl grow up as she pleases until she is married. And then she is like any woman anywhere: in order for her man to be a man, she must not think, she must not talk.

> *Anowa* 1970

6 Eternal death has worked like a warrior rat, with a diabolical sense of duty, to gnaw at my bottom.

> "The Message," *Fragment from a Lost Diary and Other Stories*, Naomi Katz and Nancy Milton, eds. 1973

7 It's a sad moment, really, when parents first become a bit frightened of their children.

> Ibid.

2889. Isabel Allende (1942–)

1 It was a long week of penitence and fasting, during which there were no card games and no music that might lead to lust or abandon; and within the limits of possibility, the strictest sadness and chastity were observed, even though it was precisely at this time that the forked tail of the devil pricked most insistently at Catholic flesh.

> Ch. 1, *The House of the Spirits*, Magda Bogin, tr. 1982

2 A bone in Nivea's corset snapped and the point jabbed her in the ribs. She felt she was choking in her blue velvet dress, with its high lace collars, its narrow sleeves, and a waist so tight that when she removed her belt her stomach jumped and twisted for half an hour while her organs fell back into place.

> Ibid.

3 "The Congress and the armed forces are above corruption. It would be better if we used the money to buy the mass media. That would give us a way to manipulate public opinion, which is the only thing that really counts."

> Ch. 12, Ibid.

4 They were unable to bribe the members of Congress, and on the date stipulated by law the left calmly came to power. And on that date the right began to stockpile hatred.

> Ibid.

2889.1. Ghāda al-Sammān (1942–)

1 The liberated woman is not that modern doll who wears make-up and tasteless clothes.. . . . The liberated woman is a person who believes that she is as human as a man. The liberated woman does not insist on her freedom so as to abuse it.

> Remark (1961), Quoted in *Women in World History Curriculum*, www.womeninworldhistory.com 1996–97

2890. Alta (1942–)

1 [Of] course, if you think only terrible people go to prison, that solves that problem.

> Untitled poem 1972

2 if you come in me
a child is likely to
come back out.
my name is alta.
i am a woman.

> Untitled poem *1969–1973*

3 I want to say the words that take you
back there . . .
There, where
you would like to be again.

> Untitled poem, Ibid.

2891. Gloria Anzaldúa (1942–)

1 Cradled in one culture, sandwiched between two cultures, straddling all three cultures and their value systems, *la mestiza* undergoes a struggle of flesh, a struggle of borders, an inner war.

> "La conciencia de la mestiza: Towards a New Consciousness," *Borderlands/La Frontera: The New Mestiza* 1987

2 At some point, on our way to a new consciousness, we will have to leave the opposite bank, the split between the two mortal combatants somehow healed so that we are on both shores at once and, at once, see through serpent and eagle eyes.

> Ibid.

3 Because the future depends on the breaking down of paradigms, it depends on the straddling of two or more cultures.

> Ibid.

4 Indigenous like corn, like corn, the *mestiza* is a product of crossbreeding, designed for preservation under a variety of conditions. Like an ear of corn—a female seed–bearing organ—the *mestiza* is tenacious, tightly wrapped in the husks of her culture. Like kernels she clings to the cob; with thick stalks and strong brace roots, she holds tight to the earth—she will survive the crossroads.

> Ibid.

5 Men, even more than women, are fettered to gender roles. Women at least have had the guts to break out of bondage. Only gay men have had the courage to expose themselves to the woman inside them and to challenge the current mascu-linity.

> Ibid.

6 The dominant white culture is killing us slowly with its ignorance.

> Ibid.

7 "We can no longer camouflage our needs, can no longer let defenses and fences sprout around us. We can no longer withdraw. To rage and look upon you with contempt is to rage and be contemptuous of ourselves. We can no longer blame you, nor disown the white parts, the male parts, the pathological parts, the queer parts, the vulnerable parts. Here we are weaponless with open arms, with only our magic. Let's try it our way, the *mestiza* way, the Chicano way, the woman way."

> Ibid.

8 I am an act of kneading, of uniting and joining that not only has produced both a creature of darkness and a creature of light, but also a creature that questions the definitions of light and dark and gives them new meanings.

> (p. 380), Making Face, *Making Soul: Creative and Critical Perspectives by Women of Color*, ed. 1990

9 . . . I turned myself inside
out plucked my heart
and offered it to her.

"Nightvoice," St. 1, *Chicana Lesbians: The Girls Our
Mothers Warned Us About*, Carla Trujillo, ed. *1991*

10 I stood at the door
of the heaven I thought out of reach.

St. 3, Ibid.

11 my face shut like a door.

St. 5, Ibid.

2892. Sue Armstrong (1942–)

1 There is no doubt that the practice is a means of suppressing and controlling the sexual behaviour of women. Female circumcision is a physiological chastity belt.

New Scientist 2 February 1991

2893. Judy Baca (1942?–)

1 We transport the "World Wall" project to a site, then work with participants to help them image the transformation of our society to peace—both spiritual and material—which ends in balance. It's a Hopi concept that we're in the situation we're in because the world has gotten too male. So this is the male and female back in balance. Many Native Americans have been talking about the teachings of the Grandmothers and there's a lot of interest in what happens when the world gets so rational and linear that we lose the ability to make intuitive leaps and imagine other ideas, dreams. We've forgotten our dreams.

Quoted in "Judy Baca," *Exposures, Women & Their Art*
by Ann Brown and Arlene Raven* *1989*

*See 3020.

2894. Charlotte Bingham (1942–)

1 I was thinking in bed the other night I must have been out with nearly three hundred men, and I still haven't found a Superman. I don't know what a Superman is, but I know there must be one somewhere.

Ch. 1, *Coronet Among the Weeds 1963*

2 I think it must have been quite fun when women were rather mysterious and men didn't know all about them. Look at the end product of women being free. I mean, go on, look at it. It's a poor old career girl sitting in her digs, wondering whether she ought to ring up her boyfriend or not.

Ibid.

3 Beatniks were too conventional anyway. I mean they thought they were getting away from it, which is pretty corny. You never do. You just change one thing for another.

Ch. 5, Ibid.

4 An isolated outbreak of virginity like Lucinda's is a rash on the face of society. It arouses only pity from the married, and embarrassment from the single.

Ch. 1, *Lucinda 1966*

5 "And the only way to avoid playing the game is never to belong to the club, class, set, or trade union. As soon as you do, you're accepting someone else's rules, and as soon as you do that, you start looking down on the other chap with different rules."

Ch. 3, Ibid.

6 "I'm glad you understand, Mr. Flint, I'm the last person in the world who would wish to ruin my life by inheriting a fortune. There are quite enough evils in it, without complicating the issues with money."

Ch. 8, Ibid.

2895. Mary Bricker-Jenkins (1942–)

1 Having been so long in ascendancy, patriarchal ideology has also determined the interpretation and recording of history. Therefore, we women must reclaim history, exposing the myths that distort our experiences and limit our vision of our capabilities.

"A Feminist World View," *Not For Women Only*, with
Nancy R. Hooyman,* eds. *1986*

*See 3052.

2 The notion that the personal is political is a primary analytic tool in feminist practice—a precision instrument with which we examine the myths and structures of oppression that contain us. It also is another of the fundamental organizing principles of our practice: we change our world by changing our selves as we change our world. It is by this process that fundamental structural changes may occur.

Ibid.

3 We have a long and enduring history of struggle to implement such values as egalitarianism, consensus democracy, nonexploitation, cooperation, collectivism, diversity, and nonjudgmental spirituality even though these values are not ascendant in the American tradition. In the fabric of our society, these values can be reclaimed and rewoven into a transformed social order. That is the feminist agenda.

Ibid.

2896. Cynthia Joanne Carlson (1942–)

1 Today the general public places very little value on art as anything more than another commodity.

Quoted in "Cynthia Carlson," *Exposures, Women & Their
Art* by Ann Brown and Arlene Raven* *1989*

*See 3020.

2 My work is I a response to the one-dimensionality of a patriarchal ordering. Feminism or pluralism offers a variety of ideas and possibilities simultaneously, and an eclectic way of thinking.

Ibid.

2897. Martha Craig Daughtrey (1942–)

1 In the early '70s, we had a real sense that women would humanize the legal profession . . . how law was practiced and how law firms were structured. Not only has the legal profession not gotten to be more humane and a better place, it has become worse and harder to maintain a law practice and have a full and well-rounded life.

"Back to the Future," *Perspectives* Fall *1997*

2898. Barbara Garson (1942–)

1 JOHN. The Pox Americana, a sweet haze
Shelt'ring all the world in its deep shade.

Act I, Sc. 2, *MacBird 1966*

2 JOHN. Consensus is the thing.

Sc. 3, Ibid.

3 4TH VOICE. Let's get the facts. Let's go and watch TV.

Sc. 7, Ibid.

4 EGG OF HEAD. Security makes cowards of us all.

> Act II, Sc. 1, Ibid.

5 EGG OF HEAD. I know you think I'm acting like a toad
But I still choose the middle of the road.

> Ibid.

2899. Carol Glassman (1942?–)

1 For its recipients, the Welfare system carried with it most of
the hazards of "housewife and mother," and a few of the rewards. Domination by a husband was replaced with control
over every aspect of a woman's life by the welfare agency.
Strangers could knock at any hour to pass judgment on her
performance as mother, housekeeper, and cook—as well as her
fidelity to the welfare board. The welfare board, like a jealous
husband, doesn't want to see any men around who might
threaten its place as provider and authority.

> "Women and the Welfare System," *Sisterhood Is Powerful*,
> Robin Morgan,* ed. *1970*

*See 2864.

2 Throughout the welfare department one finds the combined
view that poverty is due to individual *fault*, and that *something is wrong with women who don't have men*.

> Ibid.

3 It is the woman who is ultimately held responsible for pregnancy. While not being allowed to have control over her body,
she is nevertheless held responsible for its products.

> Ibid.

2900. J. B. Goodenough (1942–)

1 Wisteria ties the roof
of the porch down; morning-
Glory anchors the mailbox;
Green peas keep the garden
Fence from taking off.

> "Among Vines," St. 1, *Dower Land 1984*

2 No, they said,
You cannot be a tree.
You are a human child.

> "Changes," Ibid.

2901. Marilyn Hacker (1942–)

1 The child of wonder, deep in his
gut, knows how long forever is,
and, like a haunted anarchist,
hears a repeated order hissed
not to exist.

> "*Chanson de L'Enfant Prodigue*," *Presentation Piece 1974*

2 I am in exile in my own land.

> "Exiles," St. 1, Ibid.

3 Between us on our wide bed we cuddle an incubus
whom we have filled with voyages. We wake
more apart than before, with open hands.

> "The Navigators, I " St. 1, Ibid.

4 "Have you done
flaunting your cunt and your pen in her face
when she's not looking? high above your bed,
like a lamppost with eyes, stern as a pay toilet,

she stands, waiting to be told off
and tolled out."

> "For Elektra," St. 2, Ibid.

5 I wish I had a lover instead of letters
from strangers. The arrival of the mail
is the only time that someone hands
me movement. Nothing real is going to happen
yet, except this desiccated ritual.

> "Waiting," St. 5, Ibid.

6 when you were gone,
swaddled in strange air, I was that alone
again, inventing life left after you.

> "Nearly a Valediction," St. 1, *Ms.* (New York)
> *March/April 1990*

7 You were the weather in my neighborhood.
You were the epic in the episode.
You were the year poised on the equinox.

> St. 4, Ibid.

8 A long week before either of us said
a compromising word acknowledging
what happened every night in the brass bed

> "For K. J., Leaving and Coming Back," St. 15, *Selected
> Poems 1965–1990 1994*

9 (There's nothing I hate—perhaps I hate
the adipose deposits on my thighs
—as much as having to stay put and wait!)

> St. 22, Ibid.

10 No one was promised a shapely life
ending in a tutelary vision.

> "Against Elegies," *Winter Numbers 1994*

11 A dozen times, she looked at the long scar
studded with staples, where I'd suckled her.

> "Cancer Winter," Ibid.

12 Dusted with flour, pine-gold, the wand of bread
protrudes from a fruit-knobbed plastic Monoprix
shopping bag, balances gallantly
on a bike basket, is tucked under a red
cardigan sleeve, blue coverall sleeve, fine gray
flannel sleeve. Everyone carries it:
acolyte's candle, torch of the athlete,
common denominator.

> "Street Sc.s III," St. 2, Ibid.

13 O blight that ate my breast like worms in fruit,
be banished by the daily pesticide
that I ingest.

> Untitled, Ibid.

14 Years now since I stroked her and sang that to her.
Since her breasts grew, I haven't seen her naked.
Infant sweat's like lavender water; hers is
womanly, pungent.

> Ibid.

2902. Judith Lewis Herman (1942–)

1 This idea of the child's right to her own body is a radical one.
In the traditional patriarchal family, there is no such concept.
The child is the legal property of the father. Only in the last
century have reforms of law and custom recognized the

mother's custodial rights to her child. The concept that the child, too, might have some individual rights or interests not represented by either parent is even more recent.

Father-Daughter Incest 1981

2　As long as fathers rule but do not nurture, as long as mothers nurture but do not rule, the conditions favoring the development of father-daughter incest will prevail.

Ibid.

3　The ordinary response to atrocities is to banish them from consciousness. Certain violations of the social compact are too terrible to utter aloud: this is the meaning of the word unspeakable.

Trauma and Recovery 1992

4　. . . while patients with simple [post traumatic stress syndrome] fear they may be losing their minds, patients with the complex disorder often feel they have lost themselves.

Ibid.

5　. . . to some degree, everyone is a prisoner of the past . . .

Ibid.

6　Commonality carries with it all the meaning of the word *common*. It means belonging to a society, having a public role, being part of that which is universal. It means having a feeling of familiarity, of being known, of communion. It means taking part in the everyday. It also carries with it a feeling of smallness, . . . of insignificance, a sense that one's own troubles are "as a drop of rain in the sea." The survivor who has received commonality with others can rest from her labors. Her recovery is accomplished; all that remains before her is her life.

Ibid.

7　The hysteria of women and the combat neurosis of men are one. Recognizing the commonality of affliction may even make it possible at times to transcend the immense gulf that separates the public sphere of war and politics—the world of men—and the private sphere of domestic life—the world of women . . .

Ibid.

8　Without the context of a political movement, it has never been possible to advance the study of psychological trauma.

Ibid.

9　In the absence of strong political movements for human rights, the active process of bearing witness inevitably gives way to the active process of forgetting.

Ibid.

2903. Janette Turner Hospital (1942–)

1　We inherit [literary] plots. . . . There are only two or three in the world, five or six at most. We ride them like treadmills.

Independent (London) *7 April 1990*

2　Like the dark wood itself, which can burgeon into anyone's sleep, Queensland is fluid in size and shape, it ebbs and flows and refuses to be anchored in space, it billows out like a net that can settle without warning over its most wayward children and pull them home.

The Last Magician 1992

3　Anything, it transpires, absolutely anything, can be the mysterious machinery of desire, can be eroticized, fetishized, tantalized, sandwiched between peanut butter and rasberry jam.

Ibid.

4　" . . . the world is crammed with messages. We'll never have time to read them all."

Ibid.

5　I didn't know what I was looking for before I saw it . . .

Ibid.

6　From time to time, I find myself inside the skin of other people. I see out of their eyes. This affliction swoops down like seasickness. It changes things irrevocably.

Ibid.

2904. Erica Jong (1942–)

1　I am thinking of the onion again,
　　. . . Not self-righteous
like the proletarian potato, nor a siren like the
　　apple. No
show-off like the banana. But a modest, self-
　　effacing
vegetable, questioning, introspective, peeling
　　itself away,
or merely radiating halos like lake ripples.

"Fruits and Vegetables," *Fruits and Vegetables 1971*

2　Everyone has talent. What is rare is the courage to follow the talent to the dark place where it leads.

"The Artist as Housewife: The Housewife as Artist,"
The First Ms. Reader, Francine Klagsbrun, ed. *1972*

3　If sex and creativity are often seen by dictators as subversive activity, it's because they lead to the knowledge that you own your own body (and with it your own voice), and that's the most revolutionary insight of all.

Ibid.

4　Perhaps all artists were, in a sense, housewives: tenders of the earth household.

Ibid.

5　. . . he never regarded himself as crazy. The world was.

Fear of Flying 1973

6　Growing up female in America. What a liability! You grew up with your ears full of cosmetic ads, love songs, advice columns, whoreoscopes, Hollywood gossip, and moral dilemmas on the level of TV soap operas. What litanies the advertisers of the good life chanted at you! What curious catechisms!

Ch. 1, Ibid.

7　There is simply no dignified way for a woman to live alone. Oh, she can get along financially perhaps (though not nearly as well as a man), but emotionally she is never left in peace. Her friends, her family, her fellow workers never let her forget that her husbandlessness, her childlessness—her selfishness, in short—is a reproach to the American way of life.

Ibid.

8　Solitude is un-American.

Ibid.

9　Q: Why does a Jew always answer a question with a question?
A: And why should a Jew *not* answer a question with a question?

Ibid.

10　Phallocentric, someone once said of Freud. He thought the sun revolved around the penis. And the daughter, too.

Ch. 2, Ibid.

11 Throughout all history, books were written with sperm, not menstrual blood.

> Ibid.

12 Europe is dusty plush,
First-class carriages
with first-class dust.

> Ch. 4, Ibid.

14 Gossip is the opiate of the oppressed.

> Ch. 6, Ibid.

15 There is nothing fiercer than a failed artist. The energy remains, but, having no outlet, it implodes in a great black fart of rage which smokes up all the inner windows of the soul.

> Ch. 9, Ibid.

16 Coupling doesn't always have to do with sex. . . . Two people holding each other up like flying buttresses. Two people depending on each other and babying each other and defending each other against the world outside. Sometimes it was worth all the disadvantages of marriage just to have that: one friend in an indifferent world.

> Ch. 10, Ibid.

17 The idea of the future is our greatest entertainment, amusement, and time-killer. Take it away and there is only the past—and a windshield spattered with dead bugs.

> Ch. 11, Ibid.

18 Men and women, women and men. It will never work.

> Ch. 16, Ibid.

19 A man assumes that a woman's refusal is just part of a game. Or, at any rate, a lot of men assume that. When a man says no, it's no. When a woman says no, it's yes, or at least maybe. There is even a joke to that effect. And little by little, women begin to believe in this view of themselves.

> Ibid.

20 It was easy enough to kill yourself in a fit of despair. It was easy enough to play the martyr. It was harder to do nothing. To endure your life. To wait.

> Ch. 17, Ibid.

21 The cure for starvation in India *and* the cure for overpopulation—both in one big swallow!

> Ch. 17, Ibid.

22 Surviving meant being born over and over.

> Ch. 19, Ibid.

23 Each month
the blood sheets down
like good red rain.

I am the gardener.
Nothing grows without me.

> "Gardener," *Half-Lives* 1973

24 I can live without it all—
love with its blood pump,
sex with its messy hungers.
men with their peacock strutting,
their silly sexual baggage,
their wet tongues in my ear

and their words like little sugar suckers
with sour centers.

> "Becoming a Nun," *About Women*, Stephen Berg and
> S. J. Marks, eds. *1973*

25 It is a sad paradox that when male authors impersonate women, they are said to be dealing with "cosmic, major concerns"—but when we impersonate *ourselves* we are said to be writing "women's fiction" or "women's poetry."

> "Colette:* The Difficulty of Loving," *Ms.* (New York)
> *April 1974*

*See 1341.

26 He had been in analysis for seven years and he regarded life as a long disease, alleviated by little fifty-minute bloodlettings of words from the couch.

> *How to Save your Own Life 1977*

27 "How do I save my own life?" the poet asked.
"By being a fool," God said.

> Ibid.

28 "The trick is not how much pain you feel—but how much joy you feel. Any idiot can feel pain. Life is full of excuses to feel pain, excuses not to live, excuses, excuses, excuses."

> Ibid.

29 Books go out into the world, travel mysteriously from hand to hand, and somehow find their way to the people who need them at the *times* when they need them. . . . Cosmic forces guide such passings-along.

> Ibid.

30 "Do you want me to tell you something really subversive? Love *is* everything it's cracked up to be. That's why people are so cynical about it."

> Ibid.

31 Friends love misery, in fact. Sometimes, especially if we are too lucky or too successful or too pretty, our misery is the only thing that endears us to our friends.

> "A day in the life . . . ," Ibid.

32 In a bad marriage, friends are the invisible glue. If we have enough friends, we may go on for years, intending to leave, talking about leaving—instead of actually getting up and leaving.

> Ibid.

33 All the cosmetics names seemed obscenely obvious to me in their promises of sexual bliss. They were all firming or uplifting or invigorating. They made you *tingle*. Or *glow*. Or feel *young*. They were all prepared with hormones or placentas or royal jelly. All the juice and joy missing in the lives of these women were to be supplied by the contents of jars and bottles.

> Ibid.

34 Advice is what we ask for when we already know the answer but wish we didn't. . . .

> Epigraph, Ibid.

35 Jealousy is all the fun you think they had. . . .

> "Bennett tells all in Woodstock . . . " Epigraph, Ibid.

36 Where is Hollywood located? Chiefly between the ears. In that part of the American brain lately vacated by God.

> "Hello to Hollywood . . . " Epigraph, Ibid.

37 No one to blame! . . . That was why most people led lives they hated, with people they hated. . . . How wonderful to have

someone to blame! How wonderful to live with one's nemesis! You may be miserable, but you feel forever in the right. You may be fragmented, but you feel absolved of all the blame for it. Take your life in your own hands, and what happens? A terrible thing: no one to blame.

"Intuition, extuition . . .," Ibid.

38 To name oneself is the first act of both the poet and the revolutionary. When we take away the right to an individual name, we symbolically take away the right to be an individual. Immigration officials did this to refugees; husbands routinely do it to wives.

"My Posthumous Life . . ." Epigraph, Ibid.

39 Every country gets the circus it deserves. Spain gets bullfights. Italy gets the Catholic Church. America gets Hollywood.

"Take the Red-Eye . . .," Epigraph, Ibid.

40 Oh Doris Lessing,* my dear—your Anna is wrong about orgasms. They are no proof of love—any more than that other Anna's fall under the wheels of that Russian train was a proof of love. It's all female shenanigans, cultural mishegoss,** conditioning, brainwashing, male mythologizing. What does a woman want? She wants what she has been told she ought to want. Anna Wulf wants orgasm, Anna Karenina, death. Orgasm is no proof of anything. Orgasm is proof of orgasm. Someday every woman will have orgasms—like every family has color TV—and we can all get on with the real business of life.

"The Street Where I Lived . . .," Ibid.
*See 2140. **Yiddish word, roughly translated as "the whole, crazy mixed up thing."

41 There is a rhythm to the ending of a marriage just like the rhythm of a courtship—only backward. You try to start again but get into blaming over and over. Finally you are both worn out, exhausted, hopeless. Then lawyers are called in to pick clean the corpses. The death has occurred much earlier.

"There Is a Rhythm to the Ending . . .," Ibid.

42 The only difference between men and women is that women are able to create new little human beings in their bodies while simultaneously writing books, driving tractors, working in offices, planting crops—in general, doing everything men do.

Quoted in "Are Men and Women Different?" by Judith Viorst*, *Redbook* (New York) *November 1978*
*See 2479.

43 Beware of the man who praises women's liberation; he is about to quit his job.

Cited in "The Dreams of Youth" by Nancy Gibbons, *Time Special Issue* (New York), *Fall 1990*

2905. Temma E. Kaplan (1942–)

1 By placing human need above other social and political requirements and human life above property, profit, and even individual rights, female consciousness creates the vision of a society that has not yet appeared.

"Female Consciousness and Collective Action: the case of Barcelona, 1910–1918," *Signs: A Journal of Women in Culture and Society*, Vol. 7 *Spring 1982*

2906. Elaine Haikyung Kim (1942–)

1 British and American scholarship traditionally placed Asians between blacks and whites on a racial continuum: if whites were born to lead, blacks were best at hard labor, and Asians were suited to carry out orders. This notion has been sedi-

mented into our interpretations of economic development in Asia today . . .

"Defining Asian American Realities through Literature," *Spring 1987*

2907. Lili Lakich (1942–)

1 . . . it was driving at night that I loved best. It was then that the darkness would come alive with brightly colored images of cowboys twirling lassos atop rearing palominos, sinuous Indians shooting bows and arrows, or huge trucks in the sky with their wheels of light spinning. These were the neon signs attempting to lure motorists to stop at a particular motel or truck-stop diner. It was always the neon signs that I remembered.

Quoted in "Lili Lakich," *Exposures, Women & Their Art* by Ann Brown and Arlene Raven* 1989
*See 3020.

2 Neon is the great American art form. America's monuments are the neon signs. Places like Times Square and Las Vegas are meccas for the American dream.

Ibid.

3 Neon is associated with the highest aspirations and fantasies of the American dream as well as the lowest expression of commercialism and banality. There is no other art form that is as symbolic of the American spirit.

Ibid.

2908. Carolyn Chappell Lougee (1942–)

1 Historical studies are the terrain on which sociologists, anthropologists, and psychologists can test the universality of their categories and the possibly limited applicability of their explanations of social continuity and change.

"Modern European History," *Signs: A Journal of Women in Culture and Society*, Vol. 2, No. 3 *Spring 1977*

2 Restoring women to the historical record not only reclaims for women their own past but also provides for modern men and women the understanding of a comprehensive past needed by the creators of a human future.

Ibid.

2909. Sarah J. McCarthy (1942–)

1 On close scrutiny, the beast within us looks suspiciously like a sheep.

"Why Johnny Can't Disobey," *The Humanist September/October 1979*

2 Despite our rich literature of freedom, a pervasive value instilled in our society is obedience to authority. Unquestioning obedience is perceived to be in the best interests of the schools, churches, families, and political institutions. Nationalism, patriotism, and religious ardor are its psychological vehicles.

Ibid.

3 Religions, which are often nothing more than cults that grew, set the stage for the credulity and gullibility required for membership in cults.

Ibid.

4 The concept of religious tolerance has been stretched to its outer limits, implying freedom from criticism and the nonpayment of taxes. Neither patriotism nor religion should be justification for the suspension of reason.

Ibid.

5 Contrary to previous theories that the instinct for self-preservation was the most basic and powerful of human drives, the Guyana* suicides demonstrate that the socialization process is even more powerful.

"Pornography, Rape, and the Cult of Macho,"
The Humanist September/October 1980
*Mass suicide (18 November 1978) at the behest of Jim Jones, American religious cult leader (1931–1978).

6 There is a long macho tradition in this culture that pronounces certain kinds of violence as perfectly appropriate, even expected. . . .

Ibid.

2910. Kate Michelman (1942–)

1 [*Roe vs. Wade*]* is solely responsible for saving women's lives, saving women's health, and saving women from shame and degradation. It is an important milestone in the quest for equality and liberation.

Quoted in interview in *USA Today 22 January 1989*
*The U.S. Supreme Court case legalizing abortions (1973); see Sarah Weddington, 3075.

2 Nobody likes abortion. It's a difficult choice. Women don't have abortions they want. They have abortions they need.

Quoted in "Whose Life Is It?" by Richard Lacayo, *Time* (New York) *1 May 1989*

2911. Janice Mirikitani (1942–)

1 if you're too dark
they will kill you
if you're too swift
they will buy you
if you're too beautiful
they will rape you

watch with eyes open
speak darkly
turn your head like the owl
behind you

"Japs," *Awake in the River 1978*

2 Loving in this world
is the sliver splinting
edge
is the dare
in the teeth of the tiger
the pain of jungle rot
the horror of flesh unsealed
the madness of surviving.

"Loving from Vietnam to Zimbabwe," St. 18 (1980), *The Woman That I Am, The Literature and Culture of Contemporary Women of Color*, D. Soyini Madison, ed. *1994*

3 Some imprisonments are permanent:
white walls encaged her
with a single syllable:
JAP.

"Generations of Women," II, St. 5 (1987), Ibid.

2912. Hedda Nussbaum (1942–)

1 I worshipped him.*

Comment, Manhattan courtroom, Quoted in "Hedda's Hellish Tale" by David Ellis, *Time* (New York) *12 December 1988*
*Response to lawyer's enquiry as to why she never left Joel Steinberg, abuser and murderer.

2913. Christiane Nüsslein-Volhard (1942–)

1 To find out whether I could be attracted to studying medicine, I did a one month course as a nurse in a hospital. This experience greatly supported my conviction not to become a doctor.

Les Priz Nobel 1995

2 I immediately loved working with flies. They fascinated me, and followed me around in my dreams.

Ibid.

3 It was difficult to be a beginner in everything, after having been an expert in almost everything in the previous lab.

Ibid.

4 We believe that the combination of several approaches and systems in one laboratory provides a powerful basis for further understanding of the development of complexity in the life of an animal.

Ibid.

2914. Rosalind Petchesky (1942–)

1 [The decades before *Roe** were] years of terror, of silently fearing pregnancy, of sneaking off to possible sterility or death, and of sex ridden with shame.

Abortion and Woman's Choice: The State, Sexuality, and Reproductive Freedom 1990
*Reference to *Roe vs. Wade*, U.S. Supreme Court decision affirming abortion rights (1973); see Sarah Weddington, 3075.

2 What if women's voices tell us things we would rather not hear, or simply cannot hear—because they express values and priorities that are different from those we espouse?

Negotiating Reproductive Rights: Women's Perspectives Across Countries and Cultures, with Karen Judd, eds. *1998*

2915. Flora Purim (1942–)

1 Clear days, feel so good and free
So light as a feather can be. . . .

"Light as a Feather" *1973*

2916. Bernice Johnson Reagon (1942–)

1 There are those of us who straddle. We are born in one place . . . sent to achieve in the larger culture, and in order to survive we work out a way to be who we are in both places or all places we move. When we are home, our elders are proud because we have done well in the white world and we are committed to the advancement of ourselves and our people; but there is ecstatic joy in the community of our birth because we can and still do raise the old common-meter hymns, we can still sing the chants, we can still dance to the sun. The people smile with pride and tell us that we remember where we came from.

The Journal of American History June 1991

2 Life's challenges are not supposed to paralyze you, they're supposed to help you discover who you are. They're the prod that moves you forward.

Quoted in "Sweet Honey: A Cappella Activists" by Audreen Buffalo, *Ms.* (New York) *March/April 1993*

3 When I work with young people, I tell them, don't hand me anything with a missing step. A missing step is a hole that will break your leg and can pull your whole project down. I have no tolerance for people who skip steps; they're dangerous to themselves, their work, and everything else. If you want to be

someplace else you have to start walking. Do the steps—I get that from my mother.

Ibid.

4 You can't even tell what you created until you give it away.

Ibid.

5 If you stay in the safety zone all the time, you'll never know about your strength, you'll never know yourself at your most brilliant.

Ibid.

2917. Marina Rivera (1942–)

1 Though hungry
we have the eyes
of successful politicians
a combination of
righteous cunning
the looks of gods denied.

"Our Side of It" (1976), *The Woman That I Am, The Literature and Culture of Contemporary Women of Color,* D. Soyini Madison, ed. *1994*

2918. Anita Roddick (1942–)

1 I am still looking for the modern-day equivalent of those Quakers who ran successful businesses, made money because they offered honest products and treated their people decently, worked hard, spent honestly, saved honestly, gave honest value for money, put back more than they took out and told no lies. This business creed, sadly, seems long forgotten.

Frontispiece, *Body and Soul 1991*

2 I hate the beauty business. It is a monster industry selling unattainable dreams. It lies. It cheats. It exploits women. Its major product lines are packaging and garbage. It is no wonder that Elizabeth Arden* once said that the cosmetics business was the "nastiest in the world."

Ch. 1, Ibid.

*See 1425.

3 . . . skin care products . . . can do nothing more than cleanse, polish and protect the skin and hair. That's it. Amen. End of story. There are no magic potions, no miracle cures, no rejuvenating creams. That is all hype and lies.

Ibid.

4 It is immoral to trade on fear. It is immoral constantly to make women feel dissatisfied with their bodies. It is immoral to deceive a customer by making miracle claims for a product. It is immoral to use a photograph of a glowing sixteen-year-old to sell a cream aimed at preventing wrinkles in a forty-year-old.

Ibid.

5 How do you ennoble the spirit when you are selling something as inconsequential as a cosmetic cream? You do it by creating a sense of holism, of spiritual development, of feeling connected to the workplace, the environment and relationships with one another. It's how to make Monday to Friday a sense of being alive rather than slow death.

Ibid.

6 Conventional retailers trained for a sale; we trained for knowledge. They trained with an eye on the balance sheet; we trained with eye on the soul.

Ch. 7, Ibid.

7 When you take the high moral road it is difficult for anyone to object without sounding like a complete fool.

Ibid.

8 Too often development aid is a process by which you collect money from poor people in rich countries and give it to rich people in poor countries.

Ch. 8, Ibid.

9 Losing the collected wisdom of the rainforest tribes would be like burning every library in the world without bothering to look what was on the shelves.

Ch. 9, Ibid.

10 You have to look at leadership through the eyes of the followers and you have to live the message. What I have learned is that people become motivated when you guide them to the source of their own power and when you make heroes out of employees who personify what you want to see in the organization.

Ch. 10, Ibid.

2919. Phyllis Rose (1942–)

1 There comes a time in your life when you dead end on the search for your identity as something unique. At that point, you start looking around for what connects you to other people, not what distinguishes you alone.

Writing of Women, Essays in a Renaissance 1985

2 . . . whether you choose to destroy or to redeem what you perceive as Other, the problem begins with perceiving it as Other.

"Helen Bannerman"*, Ibid.

*Author of *Little Black Sambo* (1899); see 1097.

3 In starkly political terms, biography is a tool by which the dominant society reinforces its values. It has ignored women; it ignores the poor and working class; it ignores the unprivileged; it ignores noncelebrities. Such a formulation is useful only up to a point, because in fact biography ignores almost everyone.

"Fact and Fiction in Biography," Ibid.

2920. Marjorie Rosen (1942–)

1 Does art reflect life? In movies, yes. Because more than any other art form, films have been a mirror held up to society's porous face.

Preface, *Popcorn Venus 1973*

2 Movies have always been a form of popular culture that altered the way women looked at the world and reflected how men intended to keep it.

Ibid.

3 Which is strongest—the reality out of which the illusion is created, the celluloid illusion itself, or the need for illusion? Do we hold the mirror up and dive in? And if we do, what are the consequences? And what are the responsibilities of the illusion makers?

Pt. I, Ch. 2, Ibid.

4 Women were the sacrificial lambs of the Depression, but amid the collective pain of the nation's empty bellies, they scarcely felt the knife.

Pt. III, Ch. 8, Ibid.

5 It's unfortunate that Hollywood could not visualize a woman of mental acumen unless she was fixing up a mess her man/

boss had made, covering a scoop to prove herself to a man, or deftly forging a life of dishonesty.

Ibid.

6 Hollywood expediently ignored reality.

Ch. 8, Ibid.

7 If proof were needed of the power of woman's film image on women in life, the number of platinum heads tells the story.

Ch. 9, Ibid.

8 Studios, purporting to ease the anguish of Depression reality, transformed movies into the politics of fantasy, the great black-and-white opiate of the masses.

Ibid.

9 On December 7, 1941, the Japanese bombed the hell out of Pearl Harbor. Johnny got his gun. America mobilized. And social roles shifted with a speed that would have sent Wonder Woman into paroxysms of power pride.

Pt. IV, Ch. 12, Ibid.

10 The forties, since dubbed the era of "women's pictures." . . . Women, neither as bored, listless, nor depressed as they had been a decade earlier, were not as malleable either; hence, where the screen had not long before created a reality for them, now the females created their own. The Hollywood product mirrored—and altered—it.

Ibid.

11 Still, we chiefly remember the fifties, not for the horror of civil defense drills or witch hunts, but for kitschy fads like hoola hoops and poodle cuts and crinolines. For Lucy and Miltie and Howdy and Kukla* . . . One of the few constants during the decade was the direction women were heading: backward.

Pt. V, Ch. 17, Ibid.

*Lucille Ball, see 1992; Milton Berle, American comedian (1908–); H— Dowdy and Kukla, Fran & Ollie, American 1950s television puppet series.

12 Women's films [in the fifties] became "how-to's" on catching and keeping a man. Veneer. Appearance. Sex Appeal. Hollywood descended into mammary madness.

Ibid.

13 Sex, drugs, rapping, a passion for total independence to "do their thing" forced renunciation of traditional values—the popular artifice of clothing, purchasing power, education, employment. Looking "natural," they created costumes out of odds and ends and nodded off in the name of peace and love. They were flower children.

Pt. VI, Ch. 21, Ibid.

14 It is ironic that sixties' and seventies' women have seized on a more productive lifestyle than ever before, but the [film] industry has turned its back on reflecting it in any constructive or analytical way.

Ch. 22, Ibid.

15 Once upon a time sex was romance . . . Today, however, to be clinical is to be in.

Ibid.

2921. Susan C. Ross (1942–)

1 No one can ever be sure how courts will interpret any new law or amendment.

The Rights of Women 1973

2 The court will even make up or accept a spurious purpose for the law in order to justify differential treatment.

Ibid.

3 The brutal fact is that convicted women . . . have not yet won the right to equal treatment in the criminal and juvenile justice system.

Ch. 5, Ibid.

4 . . . alimony is one way of compensating women for those financial disabilities aggravated, or caused, by marriage: unequal educational opportunities; unequal employment opportunities; and an unequal division of family responsibilities, with no compensation for the spouse who works in the home. . . . Thus, women should not be cowed into believing that to ask for alimony is to be unliberated, or that their husbands provide alimony out of the largess of their noble hearts.

Ch. 7, Ibid.

5 Law then is not a preordained set of doctrines, applied rigidly and unswervingly in every situation. Rather, law is molded from the arguments and decisions of thousands of persons. It is very much a human process, a game of trying to convince others . . . that your view of what the law requires is correct.

Ch. 10, Ibid.

6 The concept of *enforcing* a right gives meaning to the concept of the right itself.

Ibid.

7 For many persons, law appears to be black magic—an obscure domain that can be fathomed only by the professional initiated into its mysteries.

Ibid.

2922. Sally E. Shaywitz (1942–)

1 . . . just as breast milk cannot be duplicated, neither can a mother.

"Catch 22 for Mothers," *The New York Times Magazine*
4 March 1973

2 To be somebody, a woman does not have to be more like a man, but has to be more of a woman.

Ibid.

3 It is misleading and unfair to imply that an intelligent woman must "rise above" her maternal instincts and return to work when many intelligent, sensitive women have found that the reverse is better for them.

Ibid.

2923. Judy Sheindlin (1942–)

1 The cost of custody* should rest with the parents, not with the state.

Don't Pee on My Leg and Tell Me It's Raining,
with Josh Getlin 1996

*Reference to juvenile incarceration.

2 You're no less dead if your killer is fifteen or fifty.

Ibid.

3 Where I come from, grandparents and family members are supposed to take care of neglected children. It's an obligation, not something you do for a government paycheck.

Ibid.

2924. Barbra Streisand (1942–)

1 Success to me is having ten honeydew melons and eating only the top half of each one.

> Quoted in *Life* (New York) *20 September 1963*

2 The moral immune system of this country has been weakened and attacked, and the AIDS virus is the perfect metaphor for it. The malignant neglect of the last twelve years has led to breakdown of our country's immune system, environmentally, culturally, politically, spiritually and physically.

> "The Way We Were," *The Guardian* (London) *6 November 1992*

3 Women have come a long way. Not too long ago we were called dolls, tomatoes, chicks, babes and broads.
We've graduated to being called tough cookies, foxes, bitches and witches. I guess that's progress.

> "Women fast becoming most powerful . . . " *Seattle Post-Intelligencer*, Op-Ed, A9 *10 February 1994*

4 Until there is a critical mass of women, whether it be as senators, chief executive officers or film directors, we're not going to be able to make a difference—to effect any real change.

> Ibid.

2925. Barrie Thorne (1942–)

1 In working to create political change, feminists seek to create organizations based on power understood as energy and initiative, while challenging institutions that embody power understood as domination. Although fraught with contradictions, the feminist process uses methods of organization as a strategy for redefining political power itself.

> Review of Building Feminist Theory: Essays For Quest," *Signs: A Journal of Women in Culture and Society*, Vol. 7 *1982*

2926. Karen Uhlenbeck (1942–)

1 I didn't mind being a woman doing math [at the University of Texas], not supposed to be doing it, working on the fringes, succeeding in a small way . . . I was really sort of doing it for myself.

> Quoted in *Women in Mathematics: The Addition of Difference* by Claudia Henrion* *1997*

*See 3446.

2927. Virginia Valian (1942–)

1 . . . all prestigious professions are professions for men, not simply professions.

> *Why So Slow? The Advancement of Women 1998*

2 We all want to believe we are unbiased and unaffected by stereotypes we have consciously rejected.

> Ibid.

3 . . . girls' play shades imperceptibly into housework; boys' play remains play.

> Ibid.

4 The notion of a flat earth is a notable example of a natural concept, a concept most people's experiences seem to verify. People need very special data or specific instruction to discover that the flat-world hypothesis is false. . . . Gender schemas, I suggest, are similar to a belief that the earth is flat.

> (p. 118), Ibid.

2928. Rebecca Wells (1942?–)

1 I am her mother, though, and it is my job to teach her that you cannot escape from life. Life is not a book. You can't just set it down on the coffee table and walk away from it when it gets boring or you get tired.

> "Bookworms," *Little Altars Everywhere 1992*

2 They had a club so private it didn't even have a name.

> "E-Z Boy War," Ibid.

3 "It be good to know your children done turn out sweet. It make ever'thing less bitter. It be one of the savin things."

> "Playboys' Scrapbook," Ibid.

4 "That is just the way life happen. We done lived down the road from sadness all our lives. But you gotta know what sadness be yours and what be somebody else's, is what I say."

> Ibid.

5 "Do you remember how horrified you were as a little girl when you found the word 'vivisection' in the dictionary? Came running to me in tears, remember? Well, I'm not a Goddamn frog, Sidda. You can't figure me out. *I* can't figure me out. It's *life*, Sidda. You don't figure it out. You just climb up on the beast and *ride*."

> Ch. 6, *Divine Secrets of the Ya-Ya Sisterhood 1996*

6 You could not put your finger on it, but you knew these women shared secret lagoons of knowledge. Secret codes and lore and lingo stretching back into that fluid time before air conditioning dried up the rich, heavy humidity that used to hang over the porches of Louisiana, drenching cotton blouses, beads of sweat tickling the skin, slowing people down so the world entered them in an unhurried way. A thick stew of life that seeped into the very blood of people, so that eccentric, languid thoughts simmered inside. Thoughts that would not come again after porches were enclosed, after the climate was controlled, after all windows were shut tight, and the sounds of the neighborhood were drowned out by the noise of the television set.

> Ch. 8, Ibid.

7 "Something just cracked in Vivi. Maybe people are more like the earth than we know. Maybe they have fault lines that sooner or later are going to split open under pressure."

> Ch. 27, Ibid.

8 It was the biggest parking lot I'd ever seen. I had to blink and rub my eyes; I was disoriented to see stores and pavement where all my life there had been nothing but cotton. I'd never seen a field disappear before. I didn't know such a thing could happen. I thought a field was forever. At that age I thought that everything was forever.

> Ch. 29, Ibid.

2929. Susan Witkovsky (1942–)

1 All children are musicians; all children are artists.

> Quoted in "A New Era in Day Care" by Mildred Hamilton, *San Francisco Chronicle 19 December 1971*

2 I am opposed to the custodial idea of day care. That is a mistake. Enrichment is what we are after.

> Ibid.

3 The merits of good child care for all who need it or want it are many. The health and well-being of our society depends on it. Those unconvinced are people who have no need of high qual-

ity public programs, and who choose not to see the children and parents who suffer from lack of them.

> "The Impediments to Public Day Care Programs in San Francisco" *1974*

4 At all levels of government, the question is one of priorities and money. The contradiction between what consumers (the bulk of whom are low-income) pay out in taxes and what they receive in goods and services is simply sharper the closer it is to home.

> *Ibid.*

5 Some of us would like to ignore the institutions and the money problems. I do not see how that is possible. The provision of child care on even a moderate scale requires the use of institutional money, public money. I have no trouble with using public money. Child care and other services [are] exactly what it should be used for.

> Address, University of California Conference on Child Care (Berkeley) *April 1975*

2930. Hikari Agata (1943–)

1 "For my wife I'd rather have a good-looking woman who just sits there than an ugly one who works hard."

> "A Family Part," *Unmapped Territories, New Women's Fiction from Japan*, ed. and tr. *1991*

2 "It's strange, but now that I have my own money, I don't feel like spending it on myself."

> *Ibid.*

2931. Lourdes Arizpe (1943/6–)

1 . . . people are becoming poorer in knowledge and, what is even worse, *poorer in the confidence that they can continue to create knowledge*. . . . Rural women, those formidable sources of resilience, practical knowledge, emotional strength, and other-worldly wisdom, find their capacities and skills are undermined.

> Essay, Quoted in *The Politics of Women's Education: Perspectives from Asia, Africa, and Latin America* by Jill Ker Conway and Susan C. Bourque *1993*

2 Of far greater utility [than increasing money spent on education] would be a reassessment of the kind of society we hope to construct and the type of education likely to promote it.

> *Ibid.*

2932. Eve Babitz (1943–)

1 Culturally, Los Angeles has always been a humid jungle alive with seething L.A. projects that I guess people from other places can't see. It takes a certain kind of innocence to like L.A., anyway.

> "Daughters of the Wasteland," *Eve's Hollywood 1974*

2 When they reach the age of *fifteen* and their beauty arrives, it's very exciting—like coming into an inheritance. . . .

> "The Sheik," *Ibid.*

3 Packaging is all heaven is.

> "Rosewood Casket," *Ibid.*

4 But by the time I'd grown up, I naturally supposed that I'd grown up.

> "The Academy," *Ibid.*

5 I was always much too elated to imagine despair.

> *Black Swans 1993*

6 . . . fun was all the truth we needed.

> "Black Swans," *Ibid.*

7 Except for the National Guard and the fear, it wasn't really so bad.*

> "Expensive Regrets," *Ibid.*

*Reference to the aftermath of Los Angeles riots resulting from the Rodney King verdict (1992).

2933. Patricia Barker (1943–)

1 A woman's flesh learns slow by fire and pestle,
Like succulent meats, it must be sucked and eaten.

> "From Deep Within," St. 3, *Movement in Black 1983*

2 . . . eyes still open, limbs not yet decently arranged . . . The sun has risen. The first shaft strikes the water and creeps towards them along the bank, discovering here the back of a hand, there the side of a neck, ending the rosy glow to skin from which the blood has fled, and then, finding nothing here that can respond to it, the shaft of light passes over them and begins to probe the distant fields.

> *The Ghost Road 1996*

3 The war isn't being fought for . . . [the benefit of anyone]. Nobody benefits. Nobody's in control. Nobody knows how to stop.

> *Ibid.*

4 He might even have missed the war altogether, perhaps spent the rest of his life goaded by the irrational shame of having escaped.

> *Ibid.*

2934. Jocelyn Bell Burnell (1943–)

1 Because [physics and astronomy] are predominately male, inevitably, the standards, the norms are the male. The system doesn't always stop to think, "Has this person had a career break, perchance, or are there other constraints?" . . . Do we use a quantity of achievement as a measure of ability?

> Quoted in "The Woman Who Discovered Pulsars" by Arthur M.K. Marsh Weatherall, http://www.cramer.nmt.edu/ ~kweather/bell.html *26 October 1995*

2 A lot of my working life has been driven by family circumstances. I worked part-time for 18 years and was married to a peripatetic husband who moved around an awful lot, so I sought whatever job I could get in astronomy or physics wherever he was . . . Although we are now much more conscious about equal opportunities I think there are still a number of inbuilt structural disadvantages for women. I am very conscious that having worked part-time, having had a rather disrupted career, my research record is a good deal patchier than any man's of a comparable age . . . The life experience of a woman is rather different from that of the male . . .

> "Interview with Jocelyn Bell Burnell" by Robert Lambourne, *Education and the Profession*, Vol. 31, No. 3 *May 1996*

2935. Barbara T. Christian (1943–)

1 For she [Alice Walker]* reminded us that Art, and the thought and sense of beauty on which it is based, is the province not only of those with a room of their own, or of those in libraries, universities and literary Renaissances—that *creating* is necessary to those who work in kitchens and factories, nurture

children and adorn homes, sweep streets or harvest crops, type in offices or manage them.

> "The Highs and the Lows of Black Feminist Criticism" (1990), *The Woman That I Am, The Literature and Culture of Contemporary Women of Color*, D. Soyini Madison, ed.
> *1994*

*See 3029.

2   For those of us who came out of the sixties, the vision of women moving all over the world was not solely a claiming of our rights but also the rights of all those who had been denied their humanity.

> Ibid.

3   I sometimes wonder if we critics read stories and poems, or, if as our language indicates, our reading fare is primarily that of other critics and philosophers?

> Ibid.

4   Much, of course, can be learned by all of us from all of us who speak, read, write, including those of us who look high. But as we look high, we might also look low, lest we devalue women in the world even as we define *Woman*. In ignoring their voices, we may not only truncate our movement but we may also limit our own process until our voices no longer sound like women's voices to anyone.

> Ibid.

2936. Charlotte Bonny Cohen (1943–)

1   For the Chinese Communists, ideology is always ahead of practice.

> "Chung-kuo Fu Nu (Women of China)," *Sisterhood Is Powerful*, Robin Morgan,* ed. *1970*

*See 2327.

2   China is not our model. . . . But Mao and the Chinese Communists do show us that society is changed by changing people's daily lives. Working side by side with men partially liberates women. Freedom—however you want it—comes from new ways of living together.

> Ibid.

2937. Cecilia Danieli (1943–)

1   It's the company that's important, not me as an individual.

> Quoted in "Italy's First Lady of Steel" by Gordon M. Henry, *Time* (New York) *19 May 1986*

2938. Clarissa Pinkola Estés (1943–)

1   Don't be a fool. Go back and stand under that one red flower and walk straight ahead for the last hard mile. Go up and knock on the old weathered door. Climb up to the cave. Crawl through the window of a dream. Sift the desert and see what you find. It is the only work we *have* to do.

> You wish psychoanalytic advice?
> Go gather bones.
> Ch. 1, *Women Who Run With the Wolves 1992*

2   Intuition is the treasure of a woman's psyche.

> Ch. 2, Ibid.

3   Many women are in recovery from their "Nice-Nice" complexes, wherein, no matter how they felt, no matter who assailed them, they responded so sweetly as to be practically fattening.

> Ibid.

4   There is around and about us a constant beckoning world, one which insinuates itself into our lives, arousing and creating appetite where there was little or none before.

> Ch. 3, Ibid.

5   Without a task that challenges, there can be no transformation. Without a task there is no real sense of satisfaction.

> Ch. 5, Ibid.

6   To return to an alert innocence is not so much an effort, like moving a pile of bricks from here to there, as it is standing still long enough to let the spirit find you. It is said that all that you are seeking is also seeking you, that if you lie still, sit still, it will find you. It has been waiting for you a long time. Once it is here, don't move away. Rest. See what happens next.

> Ibid.

7   Remember, we say that a flower is blooming whether it is in half, three-quarters, or full bloom.

> Ch. 6, Ibid.

8   Women have died psychically and spiritually for trying to protect the unsanctioned child, whether it be their art, their lover, their politics, their offspring, or their soul life. At the extreme, women have been hanged, burned, and murdered for defying the village proscriptions and sheltering the unsanctioned child.

> Ibid.

9   A mother with a child who is different must have the endurance of Sisyphus, the fearsomeness of the Cyclops, and the tough hide of Caliban to go against a mean-spirited culture.*

> Ibid.

*Greek myth: Sisyphus was condemned to roll a huge rock up a hill in Hades, only to have it roll down again when he reached the top; Cyclops was a gigantic three-eyed Titan who forged the thunderbolts for the god Zeus; Caliban was the grotesque, deformed slave in Shakespeare's *The Tempest*.

10   This mother is a school we are born into, a school we are students in, a school we are teachers at, all at the same time, and for the rest of our lives. Whether we have children or not, whether we nourish the garden, the sciences, or the thunderworld of poetics, we always brush against the wild mother on our way to anywhere else.

> Ibid.

11   Some say the soul informs the body. But what if we were to imagine for a moment that the body informs the soul, helps it adapt to mundane life, parses, translates, gives the blank page, the ink, and the pen with which the soul can write upon our lives?

> Ch. 7, Ibid.

12   . . . at bottom is where the living roots of psyche are. It is there that a woman's wild underpinnings are. At bottom is the best soil to sow and grow something new again. In that sense, hitting bottom, while extremely painful, is also the sowing ground.

> Ch. 8, Ibid.

13   Don't waste your time hating a failure. Failure is a greater teacher than success. Listen, learn, go on.

> Ibid.

14   [Many] of the creation Gods through all cultures and through all time did not create perfectly the first time. . . . That has nothing to do with one's goodness and skill. It is just life, evocative and evolving.

> Ibid.

15 It was not Joplin's* music, her singing, or her creative life finally sprung loose that killed her. It was lack of instinct to recognize the traps, to know when enough was enough, to create boundaries around health and welfare, to understand that excesses break small psychic bones, then larger ones, until finally the entire underpinning of psyche collapses and a person becomes a puddle instead of a powerful force.

Ibid.

*Janis J– ; see 2980.

16 If we could realize that the work is to keep doing the work, we would be much more fierce and much more peaceful.

Ibid.

17 Creativity is not a solitary movement. That is its power. Whatever is touched by it, whoever hears it, sees it, senses it, knows it, is fed. That is why beholding someone else's creative word, image, idea, fills us up, inspires us to our own creative work. A single creative act has the potential to feed a continent. One creative act can cause a torrent to break through tone.

Ch. 10, Ibid.

18 Remember, if logic were all there really was to the world, then surely all men would ride sidesaddle.

Ibid.

19 Art is not meant to be created in stolen moments only.

Ibid.

20 When a woman has trouble letting go of anger or rage, it's often because she's using rage to empower herself. While that may have been wisdom at the beginning, now she must be careful, for ongoing rage is a fire that burns her own primary energy.

Ch. 12, Ibid.

21 So the clearing of residual rage must become a periodic hygienic ritual, one that releases us, for to carry old rage beyond the point of its usefulness is to carry a constant, if unconscious, anxiety.

Ibid.

22 Women across the world—your mother, my mother, you and I, your sister, your friend, our daughters, all the tribes of women not yet met—we all dream what is lost, what next must rise from the unconscious. We all dream the same dreams worldwide. We are never without the map. We are never without each other. We unite through our dreams.

Ch. 15, Ibid.

23 The unconscious is constantly producing teaching images.

Ibid.

24 The stories are medicine. The storyteller is the medicine maker, is the physician of the soul.

"Stories that heal the soul" by Bo Emerson (Cox), *Seattle Post-Intelligencer*, C2 *1992*

2939. Mary Flanagan (1943–)

1 Everyone turns, expectant smiles on their faces, hankies at the ready. Then they see it, seven yards of deep-purple silk chiffon falling in five tiers over Nora's slender body. The tiers are cut on the bias, so that the bottom tier hangs longer on the right side, ending in a graceful point while the left side exposes Nora's black silk-stockinged leg as far as her knee. The sleeves are trimmed at the wrist in black fur, the same fur as the hat that adorns her head, tilted at a rakish angle and covering the top of her face with a black-net veil . . .

"The Wedding Dress," *The Blue Woman and Other Stories 1994*

2940. Anna Ford (1943–)

1 Let's face it, there are no plain women on television.

Quoted in *Observer* (London) *23 September 1979*

2 The world men inhabit . . . is rather bleak. It is a world full of doubt and confusion, where vulnerability must be hidden, not shared; where competition, not co-operation, is the order of the day; where men sacrifice the possibility of knowing their own children and sharing in their upbringing, for the sake of a job they may have chosen by chance, which may not suit them and which in many cases dominates their lives to the exclusion of much else.

Men 1985

2941. Tess Gallagher (1943–)

1 I stop writing the poem
to fold the clothes. No matter who lives
or who dies, I'm still a woman.
I'll always have plenty to do.
I bring the arms of his shirt
together. Nothing can stop
our tenderness. I'll get back
to the poem. I'll get back to being
a woman. But for now
there's a shirt, a giant shirt
in my hands, and somewhere a small girl

standing next to her mother
watching to see how it's done.

"I stop writing the poem ," *in toto, Instructions to the Double 1976*

2   So the air
makes a home of us.

"Songs of the Runaway Bride," i, St. 1, Ibid.

3   Like a swarm
the heart moves with its separate
wings under the eaves.

"The Calm," St. 2, Ibid.

4 Take care when you speak to me.
I might listen . . .

"When You Speak to Me," St. 1, Ibid.

5 It is a thing I learned
without learning; a hand
is a stronger mouth, a kiss could
crack the skull . . .

St. 2, Ibid.

6 And I think it's not just people who've arrived in hard places where they are suddenly in a swamp of time, the elderly and prisoners, but people who are going along in the prisonership of their workdays who need these little islands of respite. And poetry is he best kind of island for these people because it doesn't take very long to read a poem.

Quoted "Literature Belongs to the Readers" by Allen Borders, *Elliott Bay Booknotes* (Seattle) *Spring 1988*

7 Whatever you're doing—fiction, autobiography, poetry—it's an intense kind of making, and remaking. It's an opening of the heart or of the hearts of my characters.

Ibid.

8 I feel that literature doesn't belong just to the universities and the critics. It belongs to readers, a fast-disappearing population. Really, we must protect it.

Ibid.

9   We have an amplitude of means in this country, and yet spiritual powers sometimes aren't equal to the physical means we have. So there's this kind of lag, and I think it's very painful in this country.

Ibid.

10   Raymond Carver* used to say "use it all up." I like that. Each time you're working on something, throw your whole self into the balance of what you're doing.

"A Conversation with Tess Gallagher" by Katie Bolick,
Atlantic Monthly (Boston) *10 July 1997*
*Her late husband, American writer, poet and screenwriter (1938–1988).

11   Writing fiction is more like sitting in a clearing and waiting to see if the deer will come. All that gray waiting and watching and slow magic. Poetry to me is lightning of the moment. It's second nature.

Ibid.

12   Too much teaching empties me out, because I love it and try to excel. Even the emptiness is a good emptiness.

Ibid.

2942. China Galland (1943?–)

1   Going into the wilderness involves the wilderness within us all. This may be the deepest value of such an experience, the recognition of our kinship with the natural world.

Women in the Wilderness 1980

2943. Nikki Giovanni (1943–)

1   you see, my whole life is tied up to unhappiness . . .
    it's having a job
    they won't let you work
    or no work at all
    castrating me
    (yes it happens to women too)

"Woman Poem," *Black Feeling/Black Talk/
Black Judgement 1968*

2   But on the other hand the whole point
    of points is pointless when its boiled all the
        way down
    to the least common denominator. But I was
        never one
    to deal with fractions when there are so many
        wholes
    that cannot be dissected—at least these poor
        hands
    lack both skill and tool and perhaps this poor
        heart
    lacks even the inclination to try because emo-
        tion is
    of itself a wasteful thing because it lacks the
        power
    to fulfill itself.

"Letter to a Bourgeois Friend Whom Once I Loved
(And Maybe Still Do If Love Is Valid)," Ibid.

3   there is a new game I must tell you of
    It's called Catch The Leader Lying
    (And knowing your sense of the absurd
    you will enjoy this)

"Poem for Black Boys," St. 5, Ibid.

4   His headstone said
    FREE AT LAST, FREE AT LAST

But death is a slave's freedom
We seek the freedom of free men
And the construction of a world
Where Martin Luther King could have lived
and preached non-violence

"The Funeral of Martin Luther King, Jr.,"* Ibid.
*American civil rights leader (1929–1968); assassinated.

5   A nigger can die
    We ain't got to prove we can die
    We got to prove we can kill

"The True Import of Present Dialogue, Black vs. Negro,"
Ibid.

6   Why, LBJ* has made it
    quite clear to me
    He doesn't give a
    Good goddamn what I think
    (else why would he continue to *masterbate* in public?)

"A Historical Footnote to Consider Only When
All Else Fails," St. 2, Ibid.
*Lyndon Baines Johnson, American politician (1908–1973), 36th
president of the United States (1963–1969).

7   But we can't be Black
    And not be crazy

"A Short Essay on Affirmation Explaining Why," St. 7, Ibid.

8   Mistakes are a fact of life
    It is the response to error that counts

"Of Liberation," St. 16, Ibid.

9   And you will understand all too soon
    That you, my children of battle, are your heroes
    You must invent your own games and teach us old ones
    how to play

"Poem for Black Boys," St. 8, Ibid.

10   In the name of peace
    They waged the wars
    ain't they got no shame

"The Great Pax Whitie," St. 3, Ibid.

11   and nothing is worse
    than a
    dream deferred

"From a Logical Point of View," St. 1, Ibid.

12   You could say we've lost our innocence. That's a little worse than losing the nickel to put in Sunday school, though not quite as bad as losing the dime for ice cream afterward.

Introduction, *Spin a Soft Black Song 1971*

13   You can have Jesus but give me the world. I'll take it even though it's losing twenty-five percent of its energy every one hundred years or something ridiculous.

James Baldwin *—Nikki Giovanni: A Dialogue 1973*
*American writer (1924–1987).

14   Everybody's dead.

Ibid.

15   I think one of the nicest things that we created as a generation was just the fact that we could say, Hey, I don't like white people.

Ibid.

16   You have to decide who you are going to smile at. Job or no job. Future or no future. 'Cause all those reasons you give me

for your actions don't make sense if I can't enjoy you. I think men are very different from women. But I think men build their standards on false rationales. The question is: What makes a man? The question is: Can you be a man wherever you are and whatever the circumstances?

Ibid.

17 and I sometimes wonder why I didn't become a debutante
sitting on porches, going to church all the time, wondering
is my eye make-up on straight
or a withdrawn discoursing on the stars and moon
instead of a for real Black person who must now feel
and inflict
pain

"Adulthood," St. 6 1978

2944. Louise Elisabeth Glück (1943–)

1 Birth, not death, is the hard loss.
I know. I also left a skin there.

"Cottonmouth Country" 1987

2 . . . a depth
where only the dream matters
and the bond with any one soul
is meaningless; you throw it away.

"Marathon," Pt. 9 1987

3 If there is justice in some other world, those
like myself, whom nature forces
into lives of abstinence, should get
the lion's share of all things . . .

"Vespers," St. 3, The Wild Iris 1992

4 I thought my life was over and my heart was broken. Then my heart was broken

Vita Nova 1999

5 Beauty ran in his veins; he had no need for more of it.
That and his taste for empire: that much can be verified.

"The Golden Bough," Ibid.

2945. Sylvia Alicia Gonzales (1943–)

1 todo seré . . . y hasta bastarda seré, antes de dejar de ser mujer.*

"Chicana Evolution," last stanza, Quoted by Marcela
Christine Lucero-Trujillo in "The Dilemma of the Modern
Chicana Artist and Critic," The Woman That I Am, The
Literature and Culture of Contemporary Women
of Color, D. Soyini Madison, ed. 1994

*Trans.: I will be everything . . . I will even be illegitimate before forsaking my womanhood.

2 . . . the artist must be true to her own soul and her own personal experiences, and in so doing, the message will be universal and eternal.

"Ars Poetica," De Colores (Albuquerque) n.d.

3 There are many Mexican cultural values that we can relate to, but are they reliable in our search for an identity within the Anglo American cultural tradition?

Article, Ibid.

2946. Gayle Greene (1943–)

1 . . . personal criticism, rather than a practice pitted against theory and reinforcing the usual binarisms (personal against public, female against male, concrete against abstract), may be imbricated in theory in a way which broadens the notion of theory . . .

"Looking at History," quoted in Changing Subjects:
The Making of Feminist Literary Criticism by Greene
and Coppélia Kahn 1993

2 . . . —I felt abandoned in ways I can't even begin to describe. Where was the medical profession? Where were the doctors my mother had known for decades? They were there, of course, issuing the orders that determined what medication and services she was entitled to, but from the day my mother became bedridden through the long terrible slide to the end, they were nowhere near the scene. They had vanished behind desks in posh offices, surrounded by receptionists, secretaries, nurses.

"Unhappy endings," The Women's Review of Books,
Vol. XV, No. 7 April 1998

3 . . . death, like birth, is women's work . . . And poorly paid work at that: it seemed salaries went down in proportion to nearness to the messy, awful work of tending the dying. It was a radicalizing experience, to say the least.

Ibid.

4 But there is a glut, an overexposure to melodramatic media representations of death—violent, horrific, pornographic—while there is an underexposure to the reality of death, let alone any discussion of what it might mean.

Ibid.

5 Nothing prepared me for the horror of the months I spent caring for my mother, watching her lose her functions, her faculties, her mind. I would console myself that at least this ordeal might soften the blow of death itself, but I was wrong. I emerged from it stunned, dazed, having to learn baby steps back to life.

Ibid.

2947. Susan Griffin (1943–)

1 In no state of mind can a man be accused of raping his wife. How can any man steal what already belongs to him?

Quoted in Ramparts September 1971

2 I've been inside institutions,
my family,
kindergarten,
grammar school, high
school, college and then
marriage, waiting
to be
grown up, graduated, & divorced,
but before I
turned around,
here I am
back in as the
jailor, a
mother and a
teacher.

"Letters to the Outside," Dear Sky 1973

3 sleep leads to dreaming
waking to imagination and to
imagine what we
could be, o,
what we could be.

"To Gather Ourselves," Ibid.

4   . . . rape is a form of mass terrorism, for the victims of rape are chosen indiscriminately, but the propagandists for male supremacy broadcast that it is women who cause rape by being unchaste or in the wrong place at the wrong time—in essence, by behaving as though they were free. . . . The fear of rape keeps women off the streets at night. Keeps women at home.

Keeps women passive and modest for fear that they might be thought provocative.

"Rape: The All-American Crime," *Women: A Feminist Perspective*, Jo Freeman, ed. *1975*

5   because tiredness at least
you
have always been
faithful.

"Tiredness Cycle," Ibid.

6   The legal answer
to the problem of feeding children
is ten free lunches every month,
being equal, in the child's real life,
to eating lunch every other day.
Monday but not Tuesday.
I like to think of the President
eating lunch Monday, but not
Tuesday.
And when I think of the President
and the law, and the problem of
feeding children, I like to
think of Harriet Tubman*
and her revolver.

"I Like to Think of Harriet Tubman," St. 2, *Like the Iris of an Eye 1976*

*See 812.

7   We know ourselves to be made from this earth. We know this earth is made from our bodies. For we see ourselves. And we are nature. We are nature seeing nature. We are nature with a concept of nature. Nature weeping. Nature speaking of nature to nature.

Women and Nature: The Roaring Inside Her (p. 226) *1980*

8   Every time I deny myself I commit a kind of suicide.

"The Way of All Ideology," *Pornography and Silence: Culture's Revenge against Nature 1981*

9   How old is the habit of denial? We keep secrets from ourselves that all along we know.

"Denial," *A Chorus of Stones 1992*

10   For perhaps we are like stones; our own history and the history of the world embedded in us, we hold a sorrow deep within and cannot weep until that history is sung.

Ibid.

11   What at one time one refuses to see never vanishes but returns, again and again, in many forms.

Ibid.

2948. Barbro Hedström (1943–)

1   Art should awaken the senses and compassion in people. We *shall* interfere, we *shall* protest, the rebellion must be kept alive! We must not disintegrate to silent agreement to deeds that are damaging and destructive for the earth and humanity.

Interview by Annika E. Ortmark, *Kvinna Nu*, No. 2 *1989*

2   I am one who carves away rather than builds up.

Ibid.

3   If Picasso* could then I can.

Interview by Nicole de Bouczan, *Karlstads Tidningen* 6–12 *July 1989*

*Pablo Picasso, renowned Spanish painter (1881–1973).

4   I had a "real" job for seven months. My soul fell asleep.

Ibid.

2949. Susan Isaacs (1943–)

1   He wore white shirts so starched they could carry on a life of their own.

Shining Through 1988

2950. Ada Maria Isasi-Diaz (1943–)

1   . . . women's theologies simply reclaim that, as women, we are made in the image of God.

Quoted in "A new forum for voices decrying violence against women" by Pamela K. Brubaker, *Seattle Post-Intelligencer*, Focus Section *10 January 1999*

2951. Judith Jamison (1943–)

1   That's the way the kids I knew grew up. We had that kind of discipline. There was no such thing as being taken to a store and running up and down the aisles screaming or knocking things over. We weren't squelched as children but we had a certain decorum that derived from respect for our parents, and from our knowledge that we were representing them wherever we went.

Ch. 1, *Dancing Spirit: An Autobiography 1993*

2   If you study dances from the world you realize that the older the dance, the more natural the stance—before it became totally erect or turned out. The most extraordinary thing to realize is that the basis of your movement, historically, is coming from a very "primitive" tradition.

Ch. 2, Ibid.

3   Alvin* taught me how to be generous with movement, that there is no step that is not useful to your growth, that there is no *feeling* that is not useful to your growth.

Ch. 8, Ibid.

*Alvin Quin Ailey, African-American choreographer and dance company (1931–1989).

4   When you're looking at your self in the mirror you have to remember that that image is only a part of you. *The you in inside.* If you have any kind of brain at all, any kind of sense of self, you realize how unique that is. Nobody can be you. Uniqueness needs to be celebrated. There's only one of you. You're totally and absolutely individual. . . . Self-definition is very important. You define who you are by actions, by what you do with your life.

Ch. 20, Ibid.

5   Dancers have to go "over the edge" onstage. It's no place to be safe. What's the point? What are you waiting for? The stage is the perfect arena for you to let out all the stops.

Ibid.

2952. Rosabeth Moss Kanter (1943–)

1   The [commune] movement is part of a reawakening of belief in the possibilities for utopia that existed in the nineteenth century and exist again today, a belief that by creating the right

social institution, human satisfaction and growth can be achieved.

"Getting It All Together: Communes Past, Present, and Future,"
The Future of the Family, Louise Kapp Howe,* ed. 1972
*See 2155.

2953. Sally Kempton (1943?–)

1 I became a feminist as an alternative to becoming a masochist.
"Cutting Loose," *Esquire* (New York) *July 1970*

2 All children are potential victims, dependent upon the world's good will.
Ibid.

3 Men define intelligence, men define usefulness, men tell us what is beautiful, men even tell us what is womanly.
Ibid.

4 And yet wherever there exists the display of power there is politics, and in women's relations with men there is a continual transfer of power, there is, continually, politics.
Ibid.

5 Women are natural guerrillas. Scheming, we nestle into the enemy's bed, avoiding open warfare, watching the options, playing the odds.
Ibid.

6 It is hard to fight an enemy who has outposts in your head.
Ibid.

7 When men imagine a female uprising they imagine a world in which women rule men as men have ruled women: their guilt, which is the guilt of every ruling class, will allow them to see no middle ground.
Ibid.

9 Self-love depressed becomes self-loathing.
Ibid.

10 Constance Chatterley* was a male invention; Lawrence invented her, I used to think, specifically to make me feel guilty because I didn't have the right kind of orgasms.
Ibid.
*Heroine of Lady Chatterley's Lover (1928) by D. H. L—, English author (1885–1930).

2954. Karen Kijewski (1943–)

1 "I can shoot." They looked at me. I can not only shoot, I can use correct grammar; I let that slide, though.
Alley Cat Blues 1995

2955. Billie Jean King (1943–)

1 I've always wanted to equalize things for us. . . . Women can be great athletes. And I think we'll find in the next decade that women athletes will finally get the attention they deserve.
Interview *September 1973*

2 I think self-awareness is probably the most important thing towards being a champion.
Quoted by Marlene Jensen in *The Sportswoman*
November/December 1973

3 I'm not sure if it's the environment in which you live or if it's innate, because I've always played better under pressure, even when I was a youngster.
Ibid.

4 I'd like to see women's achievements become part of the landscape, instead of an unusual occurrence. Anytime women do better, it also helps men.
People, P-I News Service (Seattle)
16 May 1998

5 No one changes the world who isn't obsessed.
Quoted in "Billie Jean King, Is There Life After Tennis"
by Jane Gross, *San Francisco Chronicle 8 August 1978*

6 I think most people think I am like the mother of modern sports.. . . . I happened to come along at a time when the world was ready for some change.
"100 Years of Great Women," *ABC News Special
with Barbara Walters* 30 April 1999*
*See 2480.

2956. Jane Lazarre (1943–)

1 . . . there is only one image in this culture of the "good mother." At her worst this mother image is a tyrannical goddess of stupefying love and murderous masochism which none of us can or should hope to emulate. But even at her best, she is . . . quietly receptive and intelligent in only a moderate, concrete way; she is of even temperament, almost always in control of her emotions. She loves her children completely and unambivalently. Most of us are not like her.
Preface, *The Mother Knot 1976*

2 But what do white students and other white people mean when they talk about being silenced? Is it wrong to feel silenced if being silenced is taken to mean feeling humbled by all one does not yet understand, including the scope of one's own prejudice?
*Beyond the Whiteness of Whiteness: Memoir of a Whte
Mother of Black Sons 1996*

2957. Susan Lydon (1943?–)

1 The Victorians had needed to repress sexuality for the success of Western industrialized society; in particular, the total repression of woman's sexuality was crucial to ensure her subjugation. So the Victorians, . . . supported by Freud, passed on to us the heritage of the double standard.
"The Politics of Orgasm," *Ramparts
December 1968*

2 Our society treats sex as a sport, with its record-breakers, its judges, its rules and its spectators.
Ibid.

2958. Sandra McPherson (1943–)

1 On the third afternoon one bud tore off its green glove
And burst out brazen as Baby New Year.
"Poppies," St. 4, *Elegies for the Hot Season 1970*

2 Math soothed you; music
Made you bold; and science, completely
Understanding.
"Helen Todd: My Birthname," St. 2,
Patron Happiness 1979

3 A thief will blind you with his flashlight
but a daughter be your bouquet
When the thief's your daughter you turn your eyes the other way
"Bad Mother Blues," St. 5, *The God
of Indeterminacy 1993*

4   Dominion—death has it, beauty has it,
    water has it, drought
    has it.
        "Path Through a Few Things that Must Be Said for Putah
        Creek, at the Foot of Monticello Dam," St. 27,
        Edge Effect 1996

2959. Joni Mitchell (1943–)

1   Moons and Junes and Ferris wheels
    The dizzy dancing way you feel
    As every fairy tale comes real
    I've looked at love that way
        "Both Sides, Now" 1969

2   I've looked up life from both sides now
    From up and down, and still somehow
    It's life's illusions I recall
    I really don't know life at all.
        Ibid.

3   Woke up, it was a Chelsea morning,
    and the first thing that I knew
    There was milk and toast and honey
    and a bowl of oranges, too
    And the sun poured in like butterscotch
    and stuck to all my senses
        "Chelsea Morning" 1969

4   Oh, won't you stay
    We'll put on the day
    And we'll talk in present tenses
        Ibid.

5   Mama thinks she spoilt me
    Papa knows somehow he set me free
    Mama thinks she spoilt me rotten
    She blames herself
    But Papa he blesses me
        "Let the Wind Carry Me" 1972

6   if you're feeling contempt
    well then you tell it
    if you're tired of the silent night
    Jesus, well then you yell it
        "Judgement of the Moon and Stars" 1972

7   Sweet bird you are
    Brighter than a falling star
    All these vain promises on beauty jars
    Somewhere in your wings of time
    You might be laughing . . .
        "Sweet Bird" 1975

8   Golden in time
    Cities under sand
    Power, ideals and beauty
    Fading in everyone's hands.
        "The Hissing of Summer Lawns" 1975

9   Critics of all express
    Judges in black and white
    Saying it's wrong
    Saying it's right
    compelled by standards
    Of some ideals we fight
        Ibid.

10 We are stardust, we are golden.
        "Woodstock" 1975

11 There are things to confess that enrich the world, and things
    that need not be said.
        Independent (London)
        13 May 1988

12 The system trains people to be purchasers manipulated by hip,
    in and out, hot and not hot. But hip is hindsight, so I stood my
    ground and plowed on. If you avoid doing what's cool, you
    won't have bell-bottom pants on your songs down the road.
        Quoted in "Joni Mitchell shelves talk of retirement . . . " by
        Carrie Bell, *Seattle Post-Intelligencer*, D1 *8 October 1998*

13 It's a racket, a business of wet dreams, and what chance in hell
    does that leave women in their 50s? Companies hang on to you
    for prestige but won't do anything to promote your work . . . It's
    like being an athlete all suited up but sitting on the bench.
        Ibid.

14 The introspective artist is like a canary in a coal mine in that
    they are the first to feel things. If they are worth a salt, they
    should turn a jaundiced eye toward society and look for a vac-
    cine. That's the difference between artists and stars. Stars are
    only concerned with twinkling.
        Ibid.

2960. Regina Morantz-Sanchez (1943–)

1   The voracious desire of evangelicals and social workers to
    know how the unmarried mothers had become pregnant sug-
    gests that they were after something more than the biological
    facts they presumably knew. Since out-of-wedlock pregnancy
    ruptured the conventional narrative of married heterosexual-
    ity, they insisted that unmarried mothers supply an alternative.
        Fallen Women, Problem Girls 1994

2961. Vicki Noble (1943?–)

1   The garden within is the sacred sanctuary where we reconnect
    with the Goddess, the deep Feminine, the underground source
    of female empowerment and expression. We were once deeply
    rooted in that place, expressing power and sexuality from
    there without any splitting. That's the unambiguous wholeness
    we see in the ancient female figurines. We were snake and bird,
    earth and sky, body and spirit. We could invite the male into
    that place for an encounter, and he came.
        Shakti Woman 1990

2962. Elaine Pagels (1943–)

1   The idea that each individual has intrinsic, God-given value
    and is of infinite worth quite apart from any social contribu-
    tion—an idea most pagans would have rejected as absurd
    —persists today as the ethical basis of western law and politics.
    Our secularized Western idea of democratic society owes much
    to that early Christian vision of a new society—a society no
    longer formed by the natural bonds of family, tribe, or nation
    but by the voluntary choice of its members.
        "The 'Paradise of Virginity' Regained," *Adam, Eve, and the
        Serpent* 1988

2   As Augustine* grew older, he argued that even the most saintly
    ascetic was not, in himself, capable of self-mastery; that all hu-
    mankind was fallen; and that the human will was incorrigibly
    corrupt. This cataclysmic transformation in Christian thought
    from an ideology of moral freedom to one of universal corrup-
    tion coincided . . . with the evolution of the Christian movement
    from a persecuted sect to the religion of the emperor himself.
        Ibid.

    *St. Augustine, philosopher (354–430); considered founder of
    theology.

3   For millennia, Jews and Christians have attempted to explain the mystery of human suffering as moral judgment—the price of Adam and Eve's sin. The creation story of Genesis, addressing the question Why do we suffer and why do we die?, makes the empirically absurd claim that death does not constitute the natural end of all lives but intruded upon our species solely because Adam and Eve made the wrong choice.

"The Nature of Nature," Ibid.

4   The human tendency to accept blame for misfortunes is as observable among today's agnostics as among the Hopi or the ancient Jews and Christians, independent of—even prior to—religious belief. For quite apart from political circumstances, many people need to find reasons for their sufferings. Had Augustine's theory not met such a need—were it not that people often *would rather feel guilty than helpless*—I suspect that the idea of original sin would not have survived the fifth century, much less become the basis of Christian doctrine for 1600 years.

Ibid.

5   I would suggest [that] . . . guilt, however painful, offers reassurance that such [disastrous] events do not occur at random but follow specific laws of causation; and that their causes, or a significant part of them, lie in the moral sphere, and so within human control.

Ibid.

6   Asserting one's own guilt for suffering may also encourage one to make specific, perhaps long overdue, changes. Guilt invites the sufferer to review past choices, to amend behavior, redress negligence, and perhaps by such means improve his or her life.

Ibid.

7   What I did *not* find in the process of this research was what I had started out to find, a "golden age" of purer and simpler early Christianity. What I discovered instead is that the "real Christianity"—so far as historical investigation can disclose it—was not monolithic, or the province of one party or another, but included a variety of voices, and an extraordinary range of viewpoints, even among the saints . . . , as well as among those denounced as heretics . . . , and even, as we have seen, within the New Testament writings themselves. From a strictly historical point of view, then, there is no single "real Christianity."

"Epilogue," Ibid.

8   When you look at the history of Christianity, you see that what the Bible says has been interpreted so many ways that one has to acknowledge that one chooses an interpretation.

Quoted in *A World of Ideas* by Bill Moyers 1989

9   There's practically no religion that I know of that sees other people in a way that affirms the others' choices. But in our century we're forced to think about a pluralistic world.

Ibid.

10 I began to reflect on how our culture has taught us that suffering and death and disease are not natural, are not part of nature, but were brought in because of human guilt and sin. That belief can lead people to blame themselves in ways that are not constructive.

Ibid.

11 Guilt involves a sense of importance in the drama. To say that one is not guilty is also to acknowledge that one is in fact quite powerless. . . . Dealing with that sense of helplessness is very much part of our condition. Religion is often a way of disguising it, a way of avoiding it, a way of pretending that we're not helpless.

Ibid.

2963. Gail Thain Parker (1943–)

1   . . . Quaker meetings [were] the first enclaves in American society in which women were encouraged to speak out in public . . . [with] the faith . . . that each individual, regardless of sex, had to act according to his own inner lights. . . .

Introduction, Pt. I, *The Oven Birds* 1972

2   Literature was a great factor in the socialization of women, and without novels (and poems) which portrayed women on an heroic scale, whole generations of nascent feminists might be stunted in their development.

Ibid.

3   Sentimentalism restructured the Calvinist model of salvation, making the capacity to feel, and above all to weep, in itself evidence of redemption.

Ibid.

4   In the process of getting ahead in the world, of becoming smart and up-to-date, they have lost the ability to really feel.

Introduction, Pt. II, Ibid.

5   What this country needs is a *good* impeachment. In itself impeachment is not evil or divisive, unless it is done cheaply. If it is done admirably and it tears the country apart, then the country is so fragile that anything could tear it apart.

Quoted in "Impeachment?" by Claire Safran, *Redbook*
(New York) *April 1974*

2964. Janice G. Raymond (1943–)

1   . . . liberal speak—the language of reproductive choice and sexual liberation—pervades not only the sex and reproductive industries but progressive feminist theory and practice as well.

"Connecting Reproductive and Sexual Liberalism,"
Radically Speaking: Feminism Reclaimed, Diane Bell
and Renate Klein, eds. 1996

2965. June Machover Reinisch (1943–)

1   When people say women can't be trusted because they cycle every month, my response is that men cycle every day, so they should only be allowed to negotiate peace treaties in the evening.

Times (London) *20 January 1992*

2966. Margaret Milner Richardson (1943–)

1   No matter how much talk we hear about the problems of the tax system or the Internal Revenue Service, we should not forget that our federal tax administration is the envy of the rest of the world.

Speech, Ohio Tax Conference (16 January 1997),
Vital Speeches of the Day
1 April 1997

2967. Gloria Gervitz (1943–)

1   Silence is a job that lasts all your life. It occurs in the most deep, in the most dark places like a mortal illness

From the Book of Yiskor 1981

2968. Sandra Scofield (1943–)

1   "If you aren't nurturing your *self*, what kind of mother can you be, anyway?"

More Than Allies 1993

2 The vastness, the emptiness, terrified me. I couldn't imagine we would ever come out on the other side.*

Ibid.

*Reference to to Texas.

3 "Everybody dreams. You have to tell yourself to remember. You have to tell yourself it's better to know."

Ibid.

2969. Susan Shnall (1943–)

1 The professed purpose of the United States military is to maintain the peace, but its methods towards this goal are destructive and have resulted in the promotion of suffering and death of foreign peoples, as well as of its own.

"Women in the Military," *Sisterhood Is Powerful*,
Robin Morgan,* ed. *1970*

*See 2327.

2 Because I wore a peace symbol, I had to have an extra interview to determine my suitability as a member of the military.

Ibid.

2970. Ann Snitow (1943–)

1 . . . the demon texts* . . . for which we have been apologizing ever since.

"Motherhood: Reclaiming the Demon Texts," *Ms.*
(New York) *May/June 1991*

*Reference to the outpouring of books produced by the Women's Movement between the mid-1960s and mid-1970s.

2 Never has the baby been so delicious. A feminist theorist tells me she is more proud of her new baby than of all her books.

Essay, *The Politics of Motherhood: Activist Voices from
Left to Right*, Alexis Jetter, Annelise Orlecks, and
Diana Taylor, eds. *1997*

2971. Dale Spender (1943–)

1 . . . for centuries there has been a long and honorable tradition of women who have resisted and protested against men and their power.

*Feminist Theorists: Three Centuries of Key Women Thinkers
1983*

2 It is partly the absence of recorded history which sends women now to the lives of women past for the detailed documentation of their daily lives.

Foreword, *All Sides of the Subject, Women and Biography*,
Teresa Iles, ed. *1992*

3 Sexual harassment is becoming the modus operandi of the new world [on-line]. . . . It is the means by which some males are conquering and claiming the new territory as their own.

Nattering on the Net: Women, Power and Cyberspace 1996

4 [John Howard* is a] tight little man who wants [Australia] to be like it was in the 1950s . . . in which the wife doesn't move past the front door.

Quoted in "Insults and Injuries: Feminism in Australia" by
Judith Colp Rubin (Australia), *WIN* (Women's International
Net, Inc., NET Issue 26B, winmagazine@geocities.com)
November 1999

*Australian prime minister (1996–).

2972. Jill Tarule (1943–)

See Mary Belenky, 2143: 1–4.

2973. Geza Teleki (1943–)

1 Of course men and women see things differently. There are things—gender, ethnicity, nationality—that we all come burdened with and these affect our science.

Introduction, Quoted in *Twentieth-Century Women
Scientists* by Lisa Yount *1996*

2974. Paula Antonia Treichler (1943–)

See Cheris Kramarae, 2715:1.

2975. Rose Tremain (1943–)

1 Life is not a dress rehearsal.

Sunday Correspondent (London) *24 December 1989*

2 Even in an age in which we wisely practise the excellent art of oblivion, certain things remain.

Restoration 1990

3 Beauty causes alteration. I'm talking about the beauty of women. Alteration may frequently result in some accident or other.

The Way I Found Her 1998

4 When you begin a book and you already know in the first line that everything is in the past, this makes you worry so for the character.

Ibid.

5 Parents think they can time everything to suit themselves: they just don't see what they might be burdening you with.

Ibid.

2976. Joanna Trollope (1943–)

1 . . . [she is] a true Oxford spinster, one of that dwindling band of elderly, dignified, clever women living out frugal lives in small flats and rooms, sustained by thinking.

The Men and the Girls 1993

2 She looked around the kitchen. Mrs. Cheng had left it as she usually did, with the floor and taps and surfaces gleaming, and all the room's intractable muddle of living piled in a reproachful heap on the table.

Ibid.

2977. Gina Valdés (1943–)

1 *Hay tantisimas fronteras*
que dividen a la gente,
pero por cada frontera
existe también un puente.

(*There are so many borders*
that divide people,
but for every border
there is also a bridge.)

Untitled, Lesley A. Hyatt, tr., *Puentes y Fronteras:
Coplas Chicanas 1982*

2978. Viva (1943–)

1 If Mother had let us go to bed whenever we wanted, not forced us to go to church, allowed us to masturbate, go to bars at night, see any movie we wanted, eat whenever we felt like it, sleep with her and Daddy, then I'm sure we'd now be exactly the way she had hoped us to be.

The Baby 1975

2   I think that he exercised a lot of restraint, limiting his kicks to the wall and a painting. I only wish that the heads of governments had the same instincts.

Ibid.

3   Like marriage, nursing was turning out to be one of those painful addictions; damned if you do, damned if you don't.

Ibid.

2979. Faye Wattleton (1943–)

1   If we can't preserve the privacy of our right to procreate, I can't imagine what rights we will be able to protect.

Quoted in "Nothing Less Than Perfect" by Richard Stengel,
Time (New York) *11 December 1989*

2   Social change rarely comes about through the efforts of the disenfranchised. The middle class creates social revolutions. When a group of people are disproportionately concerned with daily survival, it's not likely that they have the resources to go to Washington and march.

Ibid.

3   The stakes are higher for us as African-American women. It will be African-American women who will die first. We suffer disproportionately from poverty. We suffer disproportionately from despair.

Address (Chicago), *Ibid.*

4   We are not daunted by this Supreme Court decision.* It is an outrage that the Court does not see fit to protect women's rights through the Bill of Rights, but leaves it up to the vagaries of the states . . . We will fight on in every state to assure that every woman has access to a safe and legal abortion.

Life on the Line 1996
*Reference to Court's *Webster v. Reproductive Health Services* decision (3 July 1989).

5   To this day I cannot imagine challenging my mother's religious beliefs. Had she lectured me about the sin of my work, I would have listened and, as she had before me, gone on to do what I believed was right. I knew that Mama believed children to be gifts from God and that no measures should ever be taken to interfere with their creation. Yet she never attacked me.

Ibid.

6   For Mama, all of life was inalterably directed toward the realm of God, and her mission was to persuade everyone who listened to join her in seeking a place in that realm. For me, life was a more earthly endeavor consisting of day-to-day struggles, and my commitment was—and is—toward making sure that all people have the freedom and the power to make the choices they need to make it through. There was no middle ground between our two perspectives.*

Ibid.
*Wattleton's mother was a fundamentalist preacher.

7   Mama used to call the power of that moment when all anxieties disappear and one is carried forward by one's message, the "Holy spirit." I believe it is the joining together of my most essential sense of purpose with an audience brought together by similar conviction. That day,* with that cheering crowd of more than half a million people, the power between us was transcendent.

Ibid.
*Reference to the March for Women's Lives (9 April 1989).

8   I was determined that these men* and their callow ideologies not run roughshod over women's lives.

Ibid.
*Reference to members of the Senate and House Hearing Committees for Title X, 1981.

9   We don't see the issue of parenting as a matter of convenience; we see the issue of parenting as a profoundly important decision, one that has lifelong implications. The whole debate over the rights of the unborn is ethically, morally, and relligiously based. There is a wide range of views. The decision should be left to the individuals coping with the circumstances.

Testimony, Senate Committee hearing re Title X
(31 March 1981), *Ibid.*

2980. Janis Joplin (1943–1970)

1   They ain't never gonna love you any better, babe
And they're nee-eever gonna love you ri-ight
So you better dig it right now, right now.

"Kozmic Blues" *1969*

2   Don't compromise yourself. You are all you've got.

Quoted in *Reader's Digest April 1973*

3   You got to get it while you can. . . .

"Get It While You Can" *n.d.*

4   Oh Lord won't you buy me a night on the town?

"Oh Lord Won't You Buy Me a Mercedez-Benz" *n.d.*

2981. Sandra Alcosser (1944–)

1   I'd watched a woman suck coins
between her thighs and up inside her body.
How long she must have trained to let the cold world
enter so.

"By the Nape," *Except By Nature 1998*

2   If love were water
not a drop would be left

"Dancing the Tarantella at the County Farm," *Ibid.*

3   Except by nature — as a woman, I will be ungovernable

"Skiing by Moonlight," *Ibid.*

4   Babies have been conceived on sweat alone—

"Sweat," St. 8, *Ibid.*

5   I know this world, said the farmer,
I've listened to worms my whole life
stirring in slime. I know where
we come from, and despite all our slick
designs, I know where we return.

"Worms," St. 8, *Ibid.*

6   And when I went off to college I lied. I denied that I had won blue ribbons for butterscotch bars and tight little stitches in skirts, because that was female, and I denied I'd grown up in a body shop, because that was laughable, lower class, and not female. So began a dance, of learning then denying experience. Not exactly the way to build intelligence, though silence sharpens the senses, creates an oily, pungent memory.

Untitled prose poem, St. 3, *Ibid.*

7   . . . my aunt who told me I should travel slowly or I would see too much before I died . . .

"Hats," *Ibid.*

8 Surely this is not the place of women in our world, that when we are old and curled like crustaceans, young girls will laugh at us, point their fingers, run as fast as they can in the opposite direction.

Ibid.

2982. Lisa Alther (1944–)

1 I happen to feel that the degree of a person's intelligence is directly reflected by the number of conflicting attitudes she can bring to bear on the same topic.

Ch. 7, *Kinflicks* 1976

2 [French strippers are] temple prostitutes, petulant goddesses . . . Like true goddesses, they were mocking the audience for giving them the homage they demanded, an homage that would never be rewarded with anything more than amused scorn.

Five Minutes in Heaven 1995

3 "Do you know German?"
Sandy nodded.
"What else?"
"Just the opera languages—Italian, French, a little Spanish."
"And East Tennesseean."

Ibid.

4 I had to wonder . . . where modern Americans ever got the idea that physicians should somehow be more competent than the rest of us. . . . When we writers make mistakes, we erase them with our delete buttons. When doctors make mistakes, they get labeled "oafish." Yet I also remember all the trips cancelled because of my father's patients, all the family dinners presided over by his empty chair, all the sleep interrupted by desperate phone calls. I remember my father crying in his armchair over a patient who had died that day on the operating table. I remember, too , my siblings' exhaustion from long hours on duty at urban medical centers, their terror at having lives depend on their split-second decisions, their despair after sleepless nights spent mopping up after other people's brutality, addictions and misfortunes.

"American tragedies," *The Women's Review of Books*,
Vol. XII, Nos. 10–11 *July 1995*

5 . . . I have to ask if our society's current rage at the ghastly errors doctors occasionally commit might not actually be, in part, rage at our own helplessness, facing down death as we must at every moment—and ultimately failing.

Ibid.

6 . . . the therapeutic power of the writing process itself, which at its best can function as a kind of exploration and exorcism that ultimately leads to healing.

Ibid.

2983. Lynn Barber (1944–)

1 The best interviews—like the best biographies—should sing the strangeness and variety of the human race.

Independent (London) 24 February 1991

2984. Judith Barrington (1944–)

1 They want women to be like gardens
cultivated possessed
perfected by man.

"A Remarkably Vigorous Rose," *Trying to be an Honest Woman* 1985

2 Awful truths can mutter under the breastbone
hide their heads, grow fat on opulent time.

"Sonnet for a Stiff Upper Lip," Ibid.

3 They say memory resides in the head
but I say it lives in the tips of fingers
the insides of thighs and forearms

"For a Friend Whose Lover Has Left," St. 1, *History and Geography* 1989

4 That kind of longing
turns your whole torso into a cavern
where despair echoes wall to wall
and hope leaps like a fœtus.

"Body Language," St. 1, *An Intimate Wilderness, Lesbian Writers on Sexuality*, ed. 1991

2985. Ingrid Bengis (1944?–)

1 Once I had abandoned the search for everyone else's truth, I quickly discovered that the job of defining my own truth was far more complex than I had anticipated.

Introduction, *Combat in the Erogenous Zone* 1973

2 The real questions are the ones that obtrude upon your consciousness whether you like it or not, the ones that make your mind start vibrating like a jackhammer, the ones that you "come to terms with" only to discover that they are still there. The real questions refuse to be placated. They barge into your life at the times when it seems most important for them to stay away. They are the questions asked most frequently and answered most inadequately, the ones that reveal their true natures slowly, reluctantly, most often against your will.

"Man-Hating," Ibid.

3 For me words still possess their primitive, mystical, incantatory healing powers. I am inclined to use them as part of an attempt to make my own reality more real for others, as part of an effort to transcend emotional damage. For me, words are a form of action, capable of influencing change. Their articulation represents a complete, lived experience.

Ibid.

4 One of these days I'm going to put bandaids across my mouth so that smiling will become less of a reflex in uncomfortable situations.

Ibid.

5 When all of the remedies and all of the rhetorical armor have been dropped, the absence of love in our lives is what makes them seem raw and unfinished.

"Love," Ibid.

6 What about the fact that everything ever constructed by civilization seems to be a dam against disintegration.

Ibid.

7 Let me off this idiot merry-go-round. My psyche is not an ideological playground. My inner feelings, at their most genuine, are not ruled by social decree.

Ibid.

8 The real trap of fame is its irresistibility.

"Monroe* According to Mailer,"** *Ms.* (New York)
October 1973

*See 1981. **American writer (1923–).

9 Psychic starvation is a desperate business: one does not wait around for Baked Alaska.

Ibid.

10 Imagination has always had powers of resurrection that no science can match.

Ibid.

11 The form that our bodies take, particularly with women, dictates more often than we wish it would the form that a portion of our lives will take.

Ibid.

12 No amount of evidence is sufficient to compensate for the deviousness with which human beings manage to conceal themselves. . . .

Ibid.

2986. Sandra Lipsitz Bern (1944–)

1 When I entered the Stanford Universe, I entered a fast-track, high-stakes game, the likes of which I never knew existed . . .

An Unconventional Family 1998

2 . . . how much better it would be for both women and men if society would stop stereotyping virtually all aspects of the human personality as either feminine or masculine . . . if everyone were free to be their own unique blending of temperament and behavior.

Ibid.

2987. Eavan Boland (1944–)

1 . . . even in the place of death,
at the heart of legend, in the midst
of rocks full of unshed tears
ready to be diamonds by the time
the story was told, a child can be
hungry.

"The Pomegranate," St. 2, *In a Time of Violence 1994*

2 After the wolves and before the elms
the bardic order ended in Ireland.
Only a few remained to continue
a dead art in a dying land.

"My Country in Darkness" (p. 15), *The Lost Land: Poems 1998*

3 What is a colony
if not the brutal truth
that when we speak
the graves open.

And the dead walk?

"Witness" (p. 18), Ibid.

4 and memory itself
has become an emigrant. . . .

"Mother Ireland" (p. 40), Ibid.

5 Night and day
words fell on me.
Seeds.
Raindrops.

Chips of Frost.

(p. 42), Ibid.

6 How much longer
will I see girlhood in my daughter?

"The Blossom" (p. 45), Ibid.

7 . . . memory.
Which is the ghost of the body.
Or myth.
Which is the ghost of meaning.

"Daughter," Pt. One (p. 46), Ibid.

8 Beautiful morning
look at me as a daughter would
look: with that love and that curiosity:
as to what she came from.
And what she will become.

"Ceres Looks at the Morning" (p. 49), Ibid.

9 *Beautiful land* the patriot said
and rinsed it with his blood.

"Whose?" (p. 67), Ibid.

10 Spirit of irony,
my caustic author
of the past, of memory, —
and of its pain, which returns
hurts, stings — reproach me now,
remind me
that I was in those rooms,
with my child,
with my back turned to her,
searching — oh irony! —
for beautiful things.

"The Necessity for Irony," St. 5, Ibid.

2988. Rita Mae Brown (1944–)

1 One doesn't get liberated by hiding. One doesn't possess integrity by passing for "white."

Untitled Essay *March 1970*

2 To love without role, without power plays, is revolution.

Ibid.

3 I move in the shadow of the great guillotine
That rhythmically does its work
On heads remaining unbowed.

"The Self Affirms Herself" (1966), *The Hand That Rocks the Cradle 1971*

4 An army of lovers shall not fail.

"Sappho's* Reply" (1970), Ibid.

*See 50.

5 I am a comic writer, which means I get to slay the dragons, and shoot the bull.

Speech (San Jose, California) *18 November 1978*

6 This is a celebration of individual freedom, not of homosexuality. No government has the right to tell its citizens when or whom to love. The only queer people are those who don't love anybody.

Speech, Gay Games (San Francisco)
8 August 1982

7 You sell a screenplay like you sell a car. If someone drives it off a cliff, that's it.

Newsweek (New York)
9 August 1985

2989. Joan Jacobs Brumberg (1944–)

1   In the course of the twentieth century, a girl's body has come to loom very large in her sense of personal identity.

The Body Project: An Intimate History of American Girls
1997

2   There's got to be more communication among the generations about what growing up female means with respect to the body.

Ibid.

3   Can you imagine what would happen if girls took all the energy they spend worrying about their image and put it into painting, writing, theorizing, science, or sports?

Ibid.

2990. Charlotte Bunch (1944–)

1   Feminism is an entire world view or gestalt, not just a laundry list of "women's issues."

"Understanding Feminist Theory," *New Directions for
Women September/October 1981*

2   We know that priorities are amiss in the world when a man gets a military medal of honor for killing another man and a dishonorable discharge for loving one.

"Speaking Out, Reaching Out," *Passionate Politics 1987*

2991. Andrea Carlisle (1944–)

1   If the world were made of language, what kind of world would I create?

The Riverhouse Stories 1989?

2992. Nancy Chodorow (1944–)

1   To understand how men and women love requires that we understand how any particular woman or man loves; to understand femininity and masculinity and the various forms of sexuality requires that we understand how any particular woman or man creates her or his own cultural and personal gender and sexuality.

*Femininities, Masculinities, Sexualities: Freud and Beyond
1994*

2993. Mary Coombs (1944–)

1   The law has been written with men in mind. Feminist jurisprudence puts women at the center and asks, "To what extent is this doctrine or this area of law designed in a way that implicitly assumes people are men?"

Quoted in "Now for a Woman's Point of View" by
Anastasia Touflexis, *Time* (New York) *17 April 1989*

2994. Stephanie Coontz (1944–)

1   The triumph of private family values discourages us from meeting our emotional needs through mutual aid associations, political and social action groups, or other forms of public life that used to be as important in people's identity as love or family.

The Way We Never Were 1992

2   . . . families have been most successful wherever they have built meaningful, solid networks and commitments *beyond* their own boundaries.

Ibid.

3   Many of the problems commonly blamed on breakdown of the traditional family exist not because we've changed too much but because we haven't changed enough.

*The Way We Really Are: Coming to Terms with America's
Changing Families 1997*

2995. Angela Davis (1944–)

1   Expending indispensable labor for the enrichment of her [the black woman's] oppressor, she could attain a practical awareness of the oppressor's utter dependence on her—for the master needs the slave far more than the slave needs the master.

"Reflections on the Black Woman's Role in the Community
of Slaves," *The Black Scholar December 1971*

2   The master subjected her to the most elemental form of terrorism distinctly suited to the female: rape.

Ibid.

3   We, the black women of today, must accept the full weight of a legacy wrought in blood by our mothers in chains. As heirs to a tradition of perseverance and heroic resistance, we must hasten to take our place wherever our people are forging toward freedom.

Ibid.

4   Domestic labor was the only meaningful labor for the slave community.

Ibid.

5   In order to function as slave, the black woman had to be annulled as woman, that is, as woman in her historical stance of wardship under the entire male hierarchy. The sheer force of things rendered her equal to her man.

Ibid.

6   In fact, the intense levels of resistance historically maintained by black people—and thus the historical function of the Black Liberation Struggle as harbinger of change throughout society—are due in part to the greater *objective* equality between the black man and woman.

Ibid.

7   Many people are unaware of the fact that jail and prison are two entirely different institutions. People in prison have already been convicted. Jails are primarily for pretrial confinement, holding places until prisoners are either convicted or found innocent. More than half of the jail population have never been convicted of anything, yet they languish in those cells.

An Autobiography 1974

8   When the iron door was opened, sounds peculiar to jails and prisons poured into my ears—the screams, the metallic clanging, officers' keys clinking.

Ibid.

9   Many of them—both the butches and the femmes—had obviously decided to take up homosexuality during their jail terms in order to make that time a little more exciting, in order to forget the squalor and degradation around them.

Ibid.

10   I was bewildered and awed by the way in which the vast majority of the jail population had neatly organized itself into generations of families: mothers/wives, fathers/husbands, sons and daughters, even aunts, uncles, grandmothers and grandfathers.

Ibid.

11 . . . the brother . . . had painted a night sky on the ceiling of his cell, because it had been years since he had seen the moon and stars.

Ibid.

12 Jails and prisons are designed to break human beings, to convert the population into specimens in a zoo—obedient to our keepers, but dangerous to each other.

Ibid.

13 Racism, in the first place, is a weapon used by the wealthy to increase the profits they bring in by paying Black workers less for their work.

Ibid.

14 The work of the political activist inevitably involves a certain tension between the requirement that positions be taken on current issues as they arise and the desire that one's contributions will somehow survive the ravages of time.

Introduction, *Women, Culture and Politics* 1989

15 Progressive art can assist people to learn not only about the objective forces at work in the society in which they live, but also about the intensely social character of their interior lives. Ultimately, it can propel people toward social emancipation.

"Art on the Frontline" (1984), Ibid.

16 Media mystifications should not obfuscate a simple, perceivable fact; Black teenage girls do not create poverty by having babies. Quite the contrary, they have babies at such a young age precisely because they are poor—because they do not have the opportunity to acquire an education, because meaningful, well-paying jobs and creative forms of recreation are not accessible to them . . . because safe, effective forms of contraception are not available to them.

Address, "Facing Our Common Foe" (15 November 1987), Ibid.

17 Radical simply means "grasping things at the root."

Address, "Let Us All Rise Together," Spelman College" (5 June 1987), Ibid.

2996. Thadious M. Davis (1944–)

1 *Girls together* once in the city that care forgot
during hot evenings elongated summers
the two of us in the sweat of days
growing through ankle socks knee-highs
ribbons and headbands

Girls together sharing pleasures that girls will
"Reunion," Sts. 2–3 (1981), *The Woman That I Am, The Literature and Culture of Contemporary Women of Color*, D. Soyini Madison, ed. 1994

2 Growing together
we measure distance like rings on palm trees
move up out
spread frond-like in casual directions apart
at home or away in college and marriage
but with every growth we remember how
we laid by a stock of coal
to warm cold spells ahead
(those sharp seasons that come damp and certain
in exotic New Orleans and tropical girlhood)
"Reunion," St. 6 (1981), Ibid.

2997. Claudia Dreifus (1944–)

1 We spent a winter learning the feminist basics from the textbook of each other's lives. . . .

Introduction, *Woman's Fate* 1973

2 . . . girls enforce the cultural code that men invent.
"The Adolescent Experience," Ibid.

2998. Linda Ellerbee (1944–)

1 Only dead fish swim with the stream.

Move On 1991

2999. Delia Ephron (1944?–)

1 If you are a girl, worry that your breasts are too round. Worry that your breasts are too pointed. Worry that your nipples are the wrong color. Worry that your breasts point in different directions.
If you are a boy, worry that you will get breasts.
. . . If you are a boy, worry that you'll never be able to grow a mustache.
If you are a girl, worry that you have a mustache.

Teenage Romance 1981

3000. Anne Fausto-Sterling (1944–)

1 . . . in modern usage, a cuckold is the husband of an unfaithful wife—a far nastier and more humiliating state, apparently, than being the wife of a philanderer, for which in fact no word exists.

Myths of Gender 1985

2 . . . to take even very extensive animal research, define it according to uniquely human behavior, and then use it to analyze human behavior is both logically flawed and politically dangerous . . .

Ibid.

3001. Fatima Gallaire-Bourega (1944–)

1 LELLA. When the mad speak of calamity, it's best to listen.

You Have Come Back (Ah! Vous êtes venus . . . là òu il y a quelques tombes), Jill MacDougall, tr. 1988

3002. Margaret Gibson (1948?–)

1 When I say
love, I mean what we've had to lose
to be what we are.
I mean what continues without us,
and somehow,
because.

(p. 138), *Memories of the Future: the daybooks of Tina Modotti*: poems 1986

*See 1693.

2 Doing nothing, I
no longer wait for whole
other worlds to break open,
more beautiful than this one
whose wild darkness
stains my fingers,
my mouth, my tongue.
"Doing Nothing" (p. 87), *Out in the Open* 1989

4 Where
did I put it, the seed

the word that will sting me
back?
"Signs: A Progress of the Soul," *Earth Elegy: New and
Selected Poems 1997*

3003. Marcia Gillespie (1944–)

1 We have been looking at it [feminism] warily. Black women
need economic equality but it doesn't apply for me to call a
black man a male chauvinist pig. Our anger is not at our men.
I don't think they have been the enemy.
Quoted in "About Women," *The Los Angeles Times
12 May 1974*

3004. Susan Gubar (1944–)

See Sandra Gilbert, 2188.

3005. Molly Ivins (1944–)

1 Government is a tool, like a hammer. You can use a hammer
to build with or you can use a hammer to destroy.
Column, *Fort Worth Star-Telegram 1992*

2 It's all very well to run around saying regulation is bad, get the
government off our backs, etc. Of course our lives are regulated. When you come to a stop sign, you stop; if you want to
go fishing, you get a license; if you want to shoot ducks, you
can shoot only three ducks. The alternative is dead bodies at
intersections, no fish and no ducks.
Column, *Fort Worth Star-Telegram 1994*

3006. J. A. Jance (1944–)

1 Despite what the Constitution says, all men are not created
equal—not in life and not in death either. Rank hath its privilege, even in the medical examiner's wagon.
Ch. 5, *Payment in Kind 1991*

2 I know from experience that homicide is no respecter of philosophy or religion. At the moment of crisis, those who pull
the triggers of murder weapons are far beyond the pale of their
own moral imperatives, to say nothing of society's as a whole.
Ch. 7, Ibid.

3 I was struck by the fact that even after all those years, the exact
time of her child's death was still engraved in her heart and
brain. Mothers are like that, I guess.
Ch. 15, Ibid.

3007. Maireád Corrigan (1944–)

1 Love everybody and don't let flags and religions get in the way
of looking somebody in the eye and seeing the beauty of the
human person.
Interview conducted by Dawn Engle and Ivan Suvanjieff,
PeaceJam.org, website, www.peacejam.org/maguire/
interview.html, (August 14, 1995) *2000*

2 We reject the way the world is at the moment and we don't accept nuclear weapons, we don't accept the fact that we train
men and women to kill each other—we think this is immoral—
and we want to disarm human hearts and human beings, one
by one, country by country and that's a big task.
Ibid.

3 Official violence begets illegal violence as surely as night follows day.
Speech, I.P.J.E.T (International Platform of Jurists for East
Timor) Conference (Dublin), www.peacejam.org/maguire
(8 November 1996) *2000*

4 Terrorism is invariably the response of powerless people to oppression of some sort. And terrorism can become endemic to a
whole community, if solutions are not found to the sources of
oppression.
Ibid.

5 To encourage people to cross over that line, to step out and declare that they will never bear arms against another human
being, ultimately requires, for most of us, an acute spiritual
awareness of the sacredness of life.
Ibid.

6 At first, some people might imagine the silence of guns to be
nonviolence; but such a silence is merely the dim early enlightenment of anti-violence. To commit oneself to live
without arms, no matter what happens, requires a much
deeper pilgrimage—and that pilgrimage is one that many
conventional politicians who lecture terrorists have not
themselves made.
Ibid.

7 Wisdom means the tough decision to walk the path of nonviolence.
"A New Vision—An Open Letter to the IRA" Ibid.

8 I have come to know for certain that our first identity is not
nationalist or unionist, but our humanity. I have come to know
for certain that love and compassion are the greatest and
strongest forces operating in our world today.
Ibid.

3008. Leslie King-Hammond (1944–)

1 That these women* would do this: to push forward against
apparently insurmountable odds when there was absolutely no
promise of their recognition, no access for them to be received.
. . . They were women, and they were African American
women. Society did not recognize them beyond being maids,
or maybe teachers or nurses. But fine artists? American society
did not recognize that as even a remote possibility.
Quoted in "Breaking the Mold" by Sharon Fitzgerald, *Ms.*
(New York) *September/October 1996*
*Reference to traveling art exhibit, "Three Generations of African
American Women Sculptors: A Study in Paradox, curated by King-
Hammond and Tritobia Hayes Benjamin (1996–97).

2 For the better part of the nineteenth century and really until
the break of the twentieth century, women were not allowed
to be in classes with nudes. So how possibly could a woman
become a sculptor if she was denied the basic education and
experience that was necessary?
Ibid.

3009. Frances Moore Lappé (1944–)

1 . . . much agricultural land which might be growing food is
being used instead to "grow" money (in the form of coffee,
tea, etc.)
Foreword, *Diet for a Small Planet 1971*

2 The act of putting into your mouth what the earth has grown
is perhaps your most direct interaction with the earth.
Pt. I, Ibid.

3 After eleven years of research, I have come to see that *food
production and food distribution are in the midst of a revolution*, a revolution that puts people's need for food *last*. And,
the revolution is led by the largest corporations on earth and

elite-based governments. It isn't fought in the name of liberty or equality or fraternity, but in the name of profit.

Food First/Institute for Food and Development Policy
Fund-raising Letter *1980*

4   . . . the outrage of hunger amidst plenty will never be solved by "experts" somewhere. It will only be solved when people like you and me decide to act.

Ibid.

3010. Harriet Goldhor Lerner (1944–)

1   Perhaps we should first take time to contemplate why tending to relationships, like changing diapers, is predominantly women's work. . . . *in relationships between dominant and subordinate groups, the subordinate group members always possess a far greater understanding of dominant group members and their culture than vice versa.*

Ch. 1, *The Dance of Intimacy 1989*

2   In our rapidly changing society we can count on only two things that will never change. What will never change is the will to change and the fear of change.

Ch. 2, Ibid.

3   Men chart the stars, create language and culture as we know it, record history as they see it, build and destroy the world around us, and continue to run every major institution that generates power, policy, and wealth. Men define the very "reality" that—until the current feminist movement—I, for one, accepted as a given, and although women throughout history have exercised a certain power as mothers, we have not created the conditions in which we mother, nor have we constructed the predominant myths and theories about "good mothering."

Epilogue, Ibid.

4   Women often choose a spouse who will express just those traits and qualities they most need to deny within themselves, or those qualities they wish they could express themselves but can't. A woman may then rage against her spouse as he expresses the very qualities she chose him for.

Quoted in "What Qualities Do Women Most Value in Husbands?" *Viewpoint*, Vol. 16, No. 5 *n.d.*

3011. Sara Lawrence Lightfoot (1944–)

1   Part of teaching is helping students learn how to tolerate ambiguity, consider possibilities, and ask questions that are unanswerable.

Quoted in *A World of Ideas* by Bill Moyers *1989*

2   Good schools have a sense of mission that kids and adults can all articulate. They have an identity. They have a character, a quality that's their own, that feels quite sturdy. They have a set of values . . . Good schools are also disciplined places. I don't mean by that just behavioral discipline, but a place where people set goals and standards and hold each other accountable.

Ibid.

3   Somehow the American public has to get back to the great richness and mystery of learning, the playfulness and seriousness of learning, and how that can be nurtured in schools by teachers in classrooms.

Ibid.

4   Schooling is what happens inside the walls of the school, some of which is educational. Education happens everywhere, and it

happens from the moment a child is born—and some people say before—until a person dies.

Ibid.

3012. Hsui-Lein Annette Lu (1944–)

1   It took the People's Republic of China 22 years [to gain United Nations membership]. It took Korea 15 years. Taiwan has been forgotten, and the process itself will remind the world.

Quoted in "Taiwan's Don Quixote," *Parade Magazine
13 February 1994*

3013. Shena MacKay (1944–)

1   . . . carousing on a sandbank in time, music and laughter drowning the sound of tomorrow's tide.

An Advent Calendar 1997

2   Every artist leaves behind a shadowy retrospective exhibition of the pictures that were never painted.

The Artist's Widow 1999

3   " . . . we're in danger of genuine grief being whipped up into something ugly."

Ibid.

3014. Tatyana Mamonova (1944?–)

1   I, Tatyana Mamonova, the chief editor of Woman and Russia, the first free feminist publication in the Soviet Union, call the women of the whole world to solidarity with our struggle for our rights. I have been stripped of my Soviet citizenship and exiled from the Soviet Union, and now, as a citizen of the world . . . I hope that all people of good will will support . . . women's moral resistance to the forces of evil and violence.

Quoted in *New Directions for Women
November/December 1980*

3015. Emily Martin (1944–)

1   It is remarkable how femininely the egg behaves and how masculinely the sperm. The egg is seen as large and passive. It does not move or journey, but passively "is transported," "is swept," or even "drifts" along the fallopian tube. In utter contrast, sperm are small, "streamlined," and invariably active. They "deliver" their genes to the egg, "activate the developmental program of the egg," and have a "velocity" that is often remarked upon. Their tails are "strong" and efficiently powered. Together with the forces of ejaculation, they can "propel the semen into the deepest recesses of the vagina."

"The Egg and the Sperm: How Science Has Constructed a Romance Based on Stereotypical Male-Female Roles," *Signs: A Journal of Women in Culture and Society*, Vol. 16, Emily Martin Spring 1991

3016. Susan Miller (1944–)

1   PERRY. There is a moment, like the black holes in space, of complete and irrevocable loss. To allow that moment is to let go of the sides of times, to fall into another place where it is not likely any of your old friends will recognize you again.

Cross Country 1976

2   Playwriting is a real study in delayed gratification. Why do I write plays? Because I'm crazy, that's why.

Quoted in "Women do Dramatise" by Sheila Hale,
City Limits (London) *1979*

3017. Ann Oakley (1944–)

1 Being a "good" mother does not call for the same qualities as being a "good" housewife, and the pressure to be both at the same time may be an insupportable burden. Children may suffer, because the goal of housework may become the goals of child-care, and a dedication to keeping children clean and tidy may override an interest in their separate development as individuals.

Ch. 5, *Woman's Work: The Housewife, Past and Present*
1974

2 The primary function of myth is to validate an existing social order. Myth enshrines conservative social values, raising tradition on a pedestal. It expresses and confirms, rather than explains or questions, the sources of cultural attitudes and values. . . . Because myth anchors the present in the past it is a sociological charter for a future society which is an exact replica of the present one.

Ch. 7, Ibid.

3 In our defense of biology and its mystique we are blind to the dangers of power. Women as the *guardians* of children possess great power. They are the molders of their children's personalities and the arbiters of their development.

Ch. 8, Ibid.

4 Clearly, society has a tremendous stake in insisting on a woman's natural fitness for the career of mother: the alternatives are all too expensive.

Ibid.

5 Housework is work directly opposed to the possibility of human self-actualization.

Ch. 9, Ibid.

6 The family's gift to women is a direct apprenticeship in the housewife role. For this reason, the abolition of the housewife role requires the abolition of the family, and the substitution of more open and variable relationships: not man-provider, woman-housewife and dependent children, but people living together in a chosen and freely perpetuated intimacy, in a space that allows each to breathe and find her or his own separate destiny.

Ibid.

7 Men are the enemies of women. Promising sublime intimacy, unequalled passion, amazing security and grace, they nevertheless exploit and injure in a myriad subtle ways. Without men the world would be a better place: softer, kinder, more loving; calmer, quieter, more humane.

"A French Letter," *Taking It like a Woman 1984*

8 If love . . . means that one person absorbs the other, then no real relationship exists anymore. Love evaporates; there is nothing left to love. The integrity of self is gone.

"Love: Irresolution," Ibid.

9 Families are nothing other than the idolatry of duty.

"The War Between Love and The Family II," Ibid.

3018. Suzanne Osten (1944–)

1 Despair and humour are inseparable.

"Creating Theatre with Lars Norén"*, *An Introduction to
the Unga Klara Company 1993*
*Swedish playwright.

2 We at the theater always strive for clarity and always ask for clarification. . . . We keep fantasizing about the characters' lies

and illusions. . . . We become like gluttons at a banquet from all the possibilities.

Ibid.

3019. Julia Phillips (1944?–)

1 Here's how I define the role of producer: the producer is there long before the shooting starts, and way after the shooting stops.

Quoted in *American Film* (New York)
December 1975

2 It [filmmaking] has to be in your blood because three times a day you ask yourself why are you doing this. Especially when you've done it before and you know up front it's going to be pure torture. But if you love the screenplay, and the director and cast amplify it, then it's magic—and the rewards are fantastic.

Ibid.

3 As a director you become the focal point, and if you look tired your crew will feel tired. But I'm not worried about stamina. I've found that women . . . generate more energy than anyone else on a [film] set. And as a producer, I've had to build up twice as much creative energy because half of it was drained just getting a picture off the ground.

Ibid.

4 Hollywood is a place that attracts people with massive holes in their souls.

Times (London)
3 April 1991

3020. Arlene Raven (1944–)

1 In my view, the content of feminist art, and its deepest meaning, is consciousness: a woman's full awareness of herself as an entity, including her sensations, her emotions, and her thoughts—mind in its broadest sense.

"Woman's Art: The Development of
a Theoretical Perspective," *Womanspace*
February/March 1973

2 An artist who shows us his/her world without this essential sense of optimism is without hope and without power: We can empathize with that art, but it cannot inspire in us the high level of human aspiration that we need to enrich ourselves, to grow, and to change.

Ibid.

3 Animals which are traditionally referred to as female include the cow, sow, bitch and cat—all derogatory words in our language when they are applied to human beings. English does not use gender extensively, but its linguistic sexism is intact because sexism is intact.

Ibid.

4 . . . if art is about consciousness grounded in reality, good art is about high consciousness—a real world view about the real world.

Ibid.

5 Historical consciousness is in no way separate from self-consciousness. The way in which we think of ourselves has everything to do with how our world sees us and how we can see ourselves successfully acknowledged by that world.

Ibid.

3021. Mandy Rice-Davies (1944–)

1 My life has been one long descent into respectability.*
*Quoted by Lynn Barber Independent on Sunday
(London) 31 March 1991*

*In connection with 1963 reports that she was on social terms
with Sir Denis Thatcher, husband of ex-prime minister Margaret
Thatcher; see 2285.

3022. Marilynne Robinson (1944–)

1 [I] never distinguished readily between thinking and dreaming.
. . . life would be much different if I could ever say, This I have
learned from my senses, while that I have merely imagined.
Housekeeping 1996

2 All this is fact. Fact explains nothing. On the contrary, it is fact
that requires explanation.
Ibid.

3 . . . the medicalization of sorrow . . .
The Death of Adam: Essays on Modern Thought 1998

4 I miss civilization, and I want it back.
Ibid.

5 Who can imagine how the things we call ideas live in the
world, or how they change, or how they perish, or how they
can be renewed?
Ibid.

6 Put aside what we know, and it will start to speak to us again.
Ibid.

7 How do we make so little of so much? Now, I think, we are
making little of the language of social conscience and of the
traditions of activism and reform. We are losing and destroying what means we have had to do justice to one another, to
confer benefit upon one another, to assure one another a worthy condition of life.
"Darwinism," Ibid.

3023. Joyce Ellen Salisbury (1944–)

1 Things are never simple when paradigms shift and ideologies
conflict. Martyrdom represents perhaps the most vivid moment in such a clash of cultures. During the early centuries of
Christianity, individuals were willing to die, and die horribly,
to bear witness to a new idea that was displacing an old one.
Introduction, Perpetua's Passion, The Death and Memory
of a Young Roman Woman 1997*

*Vivia P—, see 98.

2 Even among modern dream analysts who allow for transcendent
or even prophetic dreams, none whose works I have read share
the ancient belief that dreams may originate from outside the
dreaming psyche. Modern dreams originate within the dreamer.
Ch. 4, Ibid.

3024. Lee Smith (1944–)

1 I hate all this active-listening shit. Ever since they learned it
last year in that class, you can't have a decent conversation
with them. If you ever could. But now I mean you come home
from school really pissed, and they say something like, "Gee,
son, you're very angry!" and then if you say "Well, yes, I am
pretty goddamn angry," they say "Yes! Yes, you are! I can tell
you're angry!" and that's it.
Family Linen 1985

3025. Robyn Smith (1944–)

1 Don't ever call me a jockette.
*Quoted in "Sportswomanlike Conduct," Newsweek
(New York) 3 June 1974*

3026. Natalie J. Sokoloff (1944–)

1 Prisons are a wasteland, places of punishment, degradation
and disempowerment; warehouses for the poor, minorities, the
disadvantaged, the disenfranchised. Above all, prisons don't
stop crime.
*"In the criminal injustice system," The Women's Review
of Books, Vol. XIV, No. 1, p. 19 October 1996*

3027. Emily Toth (1944–)

1 Advice writing looks easier than it is. You have to have curiosity, patience, intellectual and emotional intelligence. It also
helps to be Jewish: Dr. Ruth, Ann Landers,* Miss Manners
and Karen Salmansohn all are . . . Jewish mothers, I know
from experience, raise their daughters to love book-learning,
good food and great gossip—so who better to give advice?
Jesus and Freud** also had Jewish mothers.
*"Help is at hand," New Directions for Women, Vol. XIV,
No. 4 January 1997*

*See 2118. **Austrian physician and founder of psychoanalysis
(1856–1939).

3028. Alma Villanueva (1944?–)

1 Who is this woman with
words dangling from
the ends of her
hair? leaping
out from her
eyes? dripping
from her
breasts? seeping
from her
hands? Her

left foot, a
question mark.
Her right
foot, an
exclamation.
Her body, a
dictionary dying
to define life,
growth, a
yearning.
Untitled, Bloodroot c. 1977

3029. Alice Walker (1944–)

1 The sight of a Black nun strikes their sentimentality; and as I am
unalterably rooted in native ground they consider me a work of
primitive art, housed in a magical color; the incarnation of civilized, anti-heathenism, and the fruit of a triumphing idea.
*"The Diary of an African Nun," Freedomways
Summer 1968*

2 How to teach a barren world to dance? It is a contradiction
that divides the world.
Ibid.

3 I wait, beautiful and perfect in every limb, cooking supper as if
my life depended on it. Lying unresisting on his bed like a

drowned body washed to shore. But he is not happy. For he knows now that I intend to do nothing but say yes until he is completely exhausted.

"Really, *Doesn't* Crime Pay?" *In Love and Trouble: Stories of Black Women* 1973

4 A slight, pretty flower that grows on any ground, and flowers pledge no allegiance to banners of any man.

Ibid.

5 She wants to live for once. But doesn't know quite what that means. Wonders if she has ever done it. If she ever will.

"Roselily," Ibid.

6 Be nobody's darling;
Be an outcast

"Be Nobody's Darling," *Revolutionary Petunias and Other Poems* 1973

7 They stumbled blindly through their lives: creatures so abused and mutilated in body, so dimmed and confused by pain, that they considered themselves unworthy even of hope . . . exquisite butterflies trapped in an evil honey, toiling away their lives in an era, a century, that did not acknowledge them, except as "the *mule* of the world."

"In Search of Our Mother's Gardens," *Ms.* (New York) *May 1974*

8 We are together, my child and I, Mother and child, yes, but *sisters* really, against whatever denies us all that we are.

"*One* Child of One's Own," *Ms.* (New York) *August 1979*

9 We will be ourselves and free, or die in the attempt. Harriet Tubman* was not out great-grandmother for nothing.

You Can't Keep a Good Woman Down 1981
*See 812.

10 . . . the inner voice; the human compulsion when deeply distressed to seek healing counsel within ourselves, and the capacity within ourselves both to create this counsel and to receive it.

"A Letter of the Times," Ibid.

11 Somewhere in the bible it say Jesus' hair was like lamb's wool, I say. Well, say Shug, if he came to any of these churches we talking bout he'd have to have it conked before anybody paid him any attention. The last thing niggers want to think about they God is that his hair kinky.

The Color Purple 1982

12 The trouble with our people is as soon as they got out of slavery they didn't want to give the white man nothing else. But the fact is, you got to give 'em something. Either your money, your land, your woman or your ass.

Ibid.

13 But I don't know how to fight. All I know how to do is stay alive.

Letter 11, Ibid.

14 But evil all over her today. She smile, like a razor opening.

Letter 27, Ibid.

15 I think Africans are very much like white people back home, in that they think they are the center of the universe and that everything that is done is done for them.

Letter 65, Ibid.

16 Anyhow, I say, the God I been praying and writing to is a man. And act just like all the other mens I know. Trifling, forgitful, and lowdown.

Letter 73, Ibid.

17 She says, Celie, tell the truth, have you ever found God in church? I never did. I just found a bunch of folks hoping for him to show. Any God I ever felt in church I brought in with me. And I think all the other folks did too. They come to church to share God, not to find God.

Ibid.

18 Yeah, It. God ain't a he or a she, but a It.
But what do it look like? I ast.

Don't look like nothing, she say. It ain't a picture show. It ain't something you can look at apart from anything else, including yourself. I believe God is everything, say Shug. Everything that is or ever was or ever will be. And when you can feel that, and be happy to feel that, you've found it.

Ibid.

19 It [marijuana] just like whiskey, I say. You got to stay ahead of it. You know a little drink now and then never hurt nobody, but when you can't git started without asking the bottle, you in trouble.

You smoke it much, Miss Celie? Harpo ast.

Do I look like a fool? I ast. I smoke when I want to talk to God. I smoke when I want to make love. Lately I feel like me and God make love just fine anyhow. Whether I smoke reefer or not.

Letter 78, Ibid.

20 And I try to teach my heart not to want nothing it can't have.

Letter 87, Ibid.

21 I believe that the truth about any subject only comes when all sides of the story are put together, and all their different meanings make one new one. Each writer writes the missing parts to the other writer's story. And the whole story is what I'm after.

In Search of Our Mothers' Gardens: Womanist Prose 1983

22 What did it mean for a black woman to be an artist in our grandmothers' time? In our great-grandmothers' day? It is a question with an answer cruel enough to stop the blood.

"In Search of Our Mothers' Gardens," Ibid.

23 Black women are called, in the folklore that so aptly identifies one's status in society, "the *mule* of the world," because we have been handed the burdens that everyone else—*everyone else*—refused to carry.

Ibid.

24 There was never a moment for her [mother] to sit down, undisturbed, to unravel her own private thoughts; never a time free from interruption—by work or the noisy inquiries of her many children. And yet, it is to my mother—and all our mothers who were not famous—that I went in search of the secret of what has fed that muzzled and often mutilated, but vibrant, creative spirit that the black woman has inherited, and that pops out in wild and unlikely places to this day.

Ibid.

25 Guided by my heritage of a love of beauty and a respect for strength—in search of my mother's garden, I found my own.

Ibid.

26 Anybody can observe the Sabbath, but making it holy surely takes the rest of the week.

Letter to the Editor, *Ms.* (New York, August 1974), Ibid.

27 As for those who think the Arab world promises freedom, the briefest study of its routine traditional treatment of blacks (slav-

ery) and women (purdah) will provide relief from all illusion. If Malcolm X* had been a black woman his last message to the world would have been entirely different. The brotherhood of Moslem men—all colors—may exist there, but part of the glue that holds them together is the thorough suppression of women.

Ibid.

*African-American leader; né Little, (1925–65); assassinated; founder, Organization for Afro-American Unity, 1964.

28 How simple a thing it seems to me that to know ourselves as we are, we must know our mothers' names.

Ibid.

29 All partisan movements add to the fullness of our understanding of society as a whole. They never detract; or, in any case, one must not allow them to do so. Experience adds to experience.

"Brothers and Sisters" *Ms.* (New York, October 1975), Ibid.

30 It is healthier, in any case, to write for the adults one's children will become than for the children one's "mature" critics often are.

"A Writer Because of, Not in Spite of, Her Children" *Ms.* (New York, January 1976), Ibid.

31 The good news may be that Nature is phasing out the white man, but the bad news is that's who She thinks we all are.

"Nuclear Madness: What You Can Do," *Black Scholar* (Spring 1982), Ibid.

32 The diamonds on Liz's* bosom
are not as bright
as his eyes
the morning they took him
to work in the mines . . .

"The Diamonds on Liz's Bosom," *Horses Make A Landscape Look More Beautiful* 1985

*Reference to Elizabeth Taylor; see 2120.

33 To me, Central America is one large plantation; and I see the people's struggle to be free as a slave revolt.

Living by the Word (p. 177) 1988

34 . . . the reasons millions of Africans are exterminating themselves in wars is that the superpowers have enormous stores of outdated weapons to be got rid of.

The Temple of My Familiar 1989

35 In consorting with man, as he had become, woman was bound to lose her dignity, her integrity.

Ibid.

36 She was soon meditating and masturbating and finding herself dissolved into the cosmic All. Delicious.

Ibid.

37 The Secret of Joy . . . is Resistance.

Possessing the Secret of Joy 1992

38 They circumcised women, little girls, in Jesus's time. Did he know? Did the subject anger or embarrass him? Did the early church erase the record? Jesus himself was circumcised; perhaps he thought only the cutting done to him was done to women, and therefore, since he survived, it was all right.

"Tashi-Evelyn-Mrs. Johnson," Pt. 21, Ibid.

39 There are those who believe Black people possess the secret of joy and that it is this that will sustain them through any spiritual or moral or physical devastation.

Epigraph, Ibid.

40 I don't believe in marriage. It's a patriarchal construct like all of these other horrible institutions. Besides, I also like being courted.

"Alice Walker: 'Color Purple' author confronts her critics and talks about her provocative new book" by Charles Whitaker, *Ebony May 1992*

41 No one could wish for a more advantageous heritage than that bequeathed to the black writer in the South: a compassion for the earth, a trust in humanity beyond our knowledge of evil, and abiding love of justice. We inherit a great responsibility . . . for we must give voice to centuries not only of silent bitterness and hate but also of neighborly kindness and sustaining love.

(p. 104), Quoted in *Everyday Use* by Barbara T. Christian 1994

42 What can we do about the needs others have of us that we, being human and therefore limited and imperfect, cannot fulfill?

"This That I Offer You: People Get Tired; Sometimes They Have Other Things to Do," *Anything We Love Can Be Saved: A Writer's Activitism* 1997

43 I've also discovered the world is full of mothers who've done their best and still hurt their daughters: that we have daughters everywhere.

"Sunniness and Shade: Twenty-five Years with the Woman Who Made Me A Mother," Ibid.

44 As oppressed people, we ask a lot from people who stand up for us; however, a complete absence of mistakes, errors of judgment, or emotional and spiritual breakdowns should never be required. . . . to give a thought to the context of their *actions*, to study *them*, to have the humility to place gently at their feet the stone we've come to throw.

"How Long Shall They Torture Our Mothers? The Trials of Winnie Mandela,"* Ibid.

*See 2571.

45 A person's work is her only signature; we forget this at our peril. It is to the work and the life we must turn.

Ibid.

46 I was moved by [Farrakhan*], and underneath all the trappings of Islam, which I personally find frightening, I glimpsed a man of humor, a persuasive teacher, and someone unafraid to speak truth to power, a virtue that makes it easier to be patient as he struggles to subdue his flaws.

"What That Day Was Like for Me: The Million Man March,"** Ibid.

*Louis Farrakhan, African American leader (1933–); founder, Nation of Islam, 1977. **Held 16 October 1995 in Washington, D.C.

47 I did not feel left out at all. I think it is absolutely necessary that black men regroup as black men; until they can talk to each other, cry with each other, hug and kiss each other, they will never know how to do those things with me. I know whole black men can exist, and I want to see and enjoy them.

Ibid.

48 I know, from this experience, that you are good, and the world is only made better by your presence.
I love you.

Speech, Commencement Day, Spelman College (22 May 1995), Ibid.

49 " . . . I learned about orgasms. And once I learned that I could have them, and have them easily, I realized in at least that one area I was free."

By the Light of My Father's Smile 1998

50 The dead are required to finish two tasks [in Mundo* theology] before all is over with them: one is to guide back to the path someone you left behind who is lost, because of your folly; the other is to host a ceremony so that you and others you have hurt may face eternity reconciled and complete.

Ibid.

*Mundo, the Spanish word for world, is also a tribe of Indian-African mestizo people found in Mexico.

51 "You seemed to know that it is when making love that we make life. Alas, you became confused about this when your own daughter followed in your footsteps."

Ibid.

52 *Crossing* is the point, she said. Crossing is life. Being on one side or the other of the river is *beside* the point.

That is what it means to accept being alive, yes, I said. That is what the Mundo believe.

Ibid.

53 "Laughter isn't even the other side of tears. It is tears turned inside out. Truly the suffering is great, here on earth. We blunder along, shredded by our mistakes, bludgeoned by our faults. Not having a clue where the dark path leads us. But on the whole, we stumble along bravely, don't you think?

Ibid.

3030. Sherley Anne Williams (1944/54–)

1 "Oh, we have paid for our children's place in the world again, and again . . ."

Dessa Rose 1986

2 The buildings of the
Projects were arrayed
like barracks in
uniform rows we
called regulation
ugly, the World in
less than one square block.

"The Iconography of Childhood," v, St. 1 (1983), *The Woman That I Am, The Literature and Culture of Contemporary Women of Color*, D. Soyini Madison, ed. 1994

3 Showfare cost a lot
but we ran the
movies every chance
we got, mostly grade
B musicals that
became the language
of our dreams.

"The Iconography of Childhood," vi, St. 1 (1983), Ibid.

3031. Leslie Wolfe (1944–)

1 What's different between these women and my generation is that they say, "I don't want to work 70 hours a week, but I want to be vice president, and *you* have to change." We kept our mouths shut and followed the rules. They want different rules.

Cited in "The Dreams of Youth" by Nancy Gibbons, *Time Special Issue* (New York) *Fall 1990*

3032. Michelle Zimbalist Rosaldo (1944–1981)

1 . . . women's status will be lowest in conditions of sharp segregation of domestic life from the public sphere of activity, and when women are isolated from each other in homes belonging to men.

Quoted in "Blueprints for inequality" by Joni Seager, *The Women's Review of Books*, Vol. X, No. 4 *January 1993*

3033. Pat Parker (1944–1989)

1 If I close my eyes
I can feel your tongue
dart
from my ear
to my neck
to the crevice
a prospector
pauses to take samples
inspect the ore
then move on.

"aftermath," St. 2, *Jonestown & Other Madness 1985*

2 The time and need
for ruses are over.
They will come
in business suits
to buy your homes
and bring bodies to
fill your jobs.
They will come in robes
to rehabilitate
and white coats
to subjugate
and where will you be
when they come?

"Where Will You Be?" St. 5 (1978), *The Woman That I Am, The Literature and Culture of Contemporary Women of Color*, D. Soyini Madison, ed. 1994

3034. Hanan al-Shaykh (1945–)

1 How can I answer your questions about the state of the country when my chief worry is the rat occupying our kitchen?

Beirut Blues, Catherine Cogham, tr. 1995

2 Despite the regularity of the routine, I can't concentrate. I keep reliving the shock of my kidnapping and I shall never be free of it even if I'm released. . . . I no longer think about life outside.

(p. 40), Ibid.

3 A room in a nearby house had no outside wall. It was still painted blue with a dining table and chairs in the middle of it. It looked beautiful, as if it were suspended between heaven and earth.

(p. 63), Ibid.

4 The men around here spent their time laughing together, drinking arrack,* and showing off their fast cars, while the arms they displayed so prominently seemed more like a fad, like the craze for growing one fingernail long.

(p. 250), Ibid.

*Similar to rum.

3035. Ruth Ann Anderson (1945?–)

1 I have never really abandoned my childhood goal of missionary work. Only, my guidebook isn't the Bible anymore.

Quoted in "Ruth Ann Anderson," *Exposures, Women & Their Art* by Ann Brown and Arlene Raven* 1989

*See 3020.

2 Being a social worker and being a Christian are not necessarily compatible. Social work has a wider view of the world, it draws from several different disciplines and sees society as the dominant factor in personality. Prior to that, I believed God was the all determining factor.

Ibid.

3 When I first started [in the Women's Spirituality Movement], I saw the word "goddess" as being a metaphor for nature. I think now it's more an understanding of a feminine energy that I would qualify as nurturing and powerful and also terrifying in her destructive aspects—all the elements of the universe in a very powerful feminine entity who has a thousand ways of being manifested.

Ibid.

3036. Aung San Suu Kyi (1945–)

1 The country [Burma] accepts me because they trust me and they associate me with my father.*

Quoted in "The Armed Forces Seize Power," *Time* (New York) *26 September 1988*

*Aung San, Burmese nationalist hero (1915–1947).

2 Let the world know that under this administration the Burmese people are like prisoners in their own homes.

Letter to various political parties, Quoted in *Time* (New York) *31 July 1989*

3 The concept of driving somebody out of their own country is totally unacceptable to me. They have tried to pressure me to leave the country in ways that no self-respecting government should try.

Interview,* "Democracy leader vows never to leave Burma" by Phillip Shenon (14 February 1994), *Seattle Post-Intelligencer*, A2 *15 February 1994*
*This was her first opportunity to speak publicly since her house arrest in 1989.

4 It must be very exhausting for them [the government] to go on lying.

Ibid.

5 We're nowhere near democracy. I've been released, that's all.*

Speech (1995), Quoted in *Twentieth-Century Women Political Leaders* by Claire Price-Groff *1998*
*Message to crowd gathered to welcome her from six years of house arrest.

6 I only ask one thing: that should my people need me, you would help me do my duty by them.

Letter to Michael Aris, her future husband, Ibid.

7 "We must make democracy the popular creed. . . . If we should fail to do this, our people are bound to suffer. . . . " That is what my father* said. It is the reason why I am participating in this struggle.

Speech (August 1988)**, Ibid.
*General Aung San, Burmese activist and hero (1915–1947); assassinated. **The Shwedagon Pagoda protests in August 1988 during which 3,000 protesters were killed.

8 You should not let your fears prevent you from doing what you know is right. Not that you shouldn't be afraid. Fear is normal. But to be inhibited from doing what you know is right, that is what is dangerous. You should be able to lead your life in the right way—despite your fears.

Ibid.

9 It is not enough to simply "live and let live." Genuine tolerance requires an active effort to try to understand the point of view of others.

Ibid.

3037. Victoria Billings (1945–)

1 Whether he admits it or not, a man has been brought up to look at money as a sign of his virility, a symbol of his power, a bigger phallic symbol than a Porsche.

"Getting It Together," *The Womansbook 1974*

2 The best thing that could happen to motherhood already has. Fewer women are going into it.

"Meeting Your Personal Needs," Ibid.

3 Constant togetherness is fine—but only for Siamese twins.

"A Love to Believe In," Ibid.

4 Rape is a culturally fostered means of suppressing women. Legally we say we deplore it, but mythically we romanticize and perpetuate it, and privately we excuse and overlook it . . .

"Sex: We Need Another Revolution," Ibid.

5 Sexual liberation, as a slogan, turns out to be another kind of bondage. For a woman it offers orgasm as her ultimate and major fulfillment; it's better than motherhood.

"What Is Individuality?" Ibid.

6 "Physicians tend to take women's complaints less seriously so you're more apt to pay for a sympathetic smile than a diagnosis. You're also more apt to be tranquilized instead of being treated."

Ibid.

3038. Janis Lynn Birkeland (1945–)

1 Because it is identified with the "feminine," nature is regarded as existing to serve Man's physical needs (and the reverse). This association of nature and women in Patriarchal societies underwrites instrumentalism, whereby things are valued only to the extent that they are useful to Man.

Essay, *Ecofeminism: Women, Animals, Nature*, Greta Gaard, ed. *1993*

2 [Ecofeminism is] about changing from a morality based on "power over" to one based on reciprocity and responsibility ("power to").

Ibid.

3039. Kathleen Brown (1945–)

1 East Coast journalists wrote us [Californians] off after the Gold Rush, again after the 1906 earthquake, after world War II, Korea, Vietnam.

In each of those we had devastating economic times and social upheavals. But in each the spirit of California reasserted itself. I believe there is something special about California. It attracts risk-takers. It's still the West. It's not for the faint-hearted.

"Kathleen Brown knows . . . ," *Seattle Post-Intelligencer*, Op-Ed, A9 *25 January 1994*

2 I love a good fight. I prefer fair fights, but I take them as they come and I like to win.

Ibid.

3040. Susanna Coffey (1945?–)

1 Beauty is not only in the eye of the beholder, but totally within the form history has provided.

Quoted in "Susanna Coffey," *Exposures, Women & Their Art* by Ann Brown and Arlene Raven* *1989*
*See 3020.

2 I had no way of visualizing anything without a mirror and the [women's] movement gave me a mirror.

Ibid.

3 It's as if there is an ocean and when your mother is alive, she's between you and the ocean, kind of like a sea wall. After she dies, you're there, you're the sea wall.

Ibid.

3041. Wendy Mary Cope (1945–)

1 I think it's a question which particularly arises over women writers: whether it's better to have a happy life or a good supply of tragic plots.

Quoted in *Independent* (London) *March 1992*

2 I'm aiming by the time I'm fifty to stop being an adolescent.

Quoted in *Daily Telegraph* (London) *9 December 1992*

3 Bloody men are like bloody buses—
You wait for about a year
And as soon as one approaches your stop
Two or three others appear.

"Bloody Men," *Serious Concerns 1992*

3042. Lucha Corpi (1945–)

1 Steeped in tradition, mystic
and mute she was sold—
from hand to hand, night to night,
denied and desecrated, waiting for the dawn
and for the owl's song

"Marina,"* I. Marina Mother, St. 2 (1976), *The Woman
That I Am, The Literature and Culture of Contemporary
Women of Color*, D. Soyini Madison, ed. *1994*

*Doña Marina, also known as La Malinche, was an Aztec noble-woman given to Hernan Cortés upon his landing in Veracruz, Mexico. Her Indian name, Malinche, is synonymous in Mexico with treachery and betrayal.

2 a promise of milk in her breasts,
vanilla scent in her hair
cinnamon flavor in her eyes,
cocoa-flower between her legs

"Dark Romance," St. 4 (1978), Ibid.

3043. Annie Dillard (1945–)

1 We wake, if we ever wake at all, to mystery, rumors of death, beauty, violence.

Ch. 1, *Pilgrim at Tinker Creek 1974*

2 Every live thing is a survivor on a kind of extended emergency bivouac.

Ibid.

3 I am an explorer, then, and I am also a stalker, or the instrument of the hunt itself.

Ibid.

4 Cruelty is a mystery, and the waste of pain.

Ibid.

5 The world's spiritual geniuses seem to discover universally that the mind's muddy river, this ceaseless flow of trivia and trash, cannot be dammed, and that trying to dam it is a waste of effort that might lead to madness.

Ch. 2, Ibid.

6 The secret of seeing is to sail on solar wind. Hone and spread your spirit till you yourself are a sail, whetted, translucent, broadside to the merest puff.

Ibid.

7 It is ironic that the one thing that all religions recognize as separating us from our creator—our very self-consciousness—is also the one thing that divides us from our fellow creatures. It was a bitter birthday present from evolution. . . .

Ch. 6, Ibid.

8 No; we have been as usual asking the wrong question. It does not matter a hoot what the mockingbird on the chimney is singing. . . . The real and proper question is: Why is it beautiful?

Ch. 7, Ibid.

9 Somewhere, and I can't find where, I read about an Eskimo hunter who asked the local missionary priest, "If I did not know about God and sin, would I go to hell?" "No," said the priest, "not if you did not know." "Then why," asked the Eskimo earnestly, "did you tell me?"

Ibid.

10 I don't know what it is about fecundity that so appalls. I suppose it is the teeming evidence that birth and growth, which we value, are ubiquitous and blind, that life itself is so astonishingly cheap, that nature is as careless as it is bountiful, and that with extravagance goes a crushing waste that will one day include our own cheap lives. . . .

Ch. 10, Ibid.

11 The world has signed a pact with the devil; it had to . . . The terms are clear: if you want to live, you have to die; you cannot have mountains and creeks without space, and space is a beauty married to a blind man. The blind man is Freedom, or Time, and he does not go anywhere without his great dog Death. The world came into being with the signing of the contract.

Ibid.

12 I am a frayed and nibbled survivor in a fallen world and I am getting along. I am aging and eaten and have done my share of eating too.

Ch. 13, Ibid.

13 Every day is a god, each day is a god, and holiness holds forth in time.

Pt. I, *Holy the Firm 1977*

14 The day is real; the sky clicks securely in place over the mountains, locks round the islands, snaps slap on the bay.

Ibid.

15 Land is a poured thing. Nothing holds; the whole show rolls.

Ibid.

16 The universe is illusion merely, not one speck of it real, and we are not only its victims, falling always into or smashed by a planet slung by its sun—but also its captives, bound by the mineral-made ropes of our senses.

Pt. II, Ibid.

17 How boldly could you push an audience—not to, in Mother's terms, "slay them," but to please them in some grand way? How can you convince the listeners that you know what you are doing, that the payoff will come? Or conversely, how long could you lead them to think you are stupid, a dumb blonde,

to enhance their surprise at the punch line and heighten their pleasure in the story you have controlled all along? Alone, energetic and trying to fall asleep, walking the residential streets long distances every day, I pondered these things. You've got to think about something.

An American Childhood 1987

18 How very gracious is the straight man!—or, in this case, the straight woman. She spreads before her friend a gift-wrapped, beribboned gag line he can claim for his own, if only he has the sense to pick it up, instead of—as happens nauseatingly often—pausing to contemplate what a nitwit he's talking to. Those men who recognize the ability for what it is, on the other hand, usually propose marriage on the spot.

Ibid.

19 Feeding our mother lines, we were training as straight men. The straight man's was an honorable calling, a bit like that of the rodeo clown: despised by the ignorant masses, perhaps, but revered among experts who understood the skills required and the risks run. We children mastered the deliberate misunderstanding, the planted pun, the Gracie Allen remark that can make of any interlocutor an instant hero.

Ibid.

20 . . . if you ask a 21-year-old poet whose poetry he likes, he might say, unblushing, ''Nobody's.'' He has not yet understood that poets like poetry, and novelists like novels; he himself likes only the role, the thought of himself in a hat.

"Write Till You Drop," *The New York Times 28 May 1989*

21 Write as if you were dying. At the same time, assume you write for an audience consisting solely of terminal patients. That is, after all, the case. What would you begin writing if you knew you would die soon? What could you say to a dying person that would not enrage by its triviality?

Ibid.

22 The writer studies literature, not the world. She lives in the world; she cannot miss it. If she has ever bought a hamburger, or taken a commercial airplane flight, she spares her readers a report of her experience. She is careful of what she reads, for that is what she will write. She is careful of what she learns, because that is what she will know.

Ibid.

23 . . . writing sentences is difficult whatever their subject. It is no less difficult to write sentences in a recipe than sentences in ''Moby-Dick.''

Ibid.

24 One of the few things I know about writing is this: spend it all, shoot it, play it, lose it, all, right away, every time. Do not hoard what seems good for a later place in the book, or for another book; give it, give it all, give it now.

Ibid.

25 When I switched from poetry to prose, it was like switching from a single reed instrument to a full orchestra. I thought: 'My God, you can do everything with this stuff. You can do everything you do with poetry, and more besides

Quoted in "A Pilgrim's Progress" by Mary Cantwell, *The New York Times 26 April 1992*

26 [Puget Sound]* was the rough edge of the world, where the trees came smack down to the stones. The shore looked . . . as if the corner of the continent had got torn off right here, sometime near yesterday, and the dark trees kept on growing like

nothing happened. The ocean just filled in the tear and settled down.

The Living 1992

*Body of water off state of Washington.

27 It is never easy to find good fill for construction.

For the Time Being 1999

28 That mass killings and genocide's recur on earth does not mean that they are similar. Each instance of human, moral evil, and each victim's personal death, possesses its unique history and form.

Ibid.

29 For Tillich,* God's activity is by no means interference, but instead divine creativity—the ongoing creation of life with all its greatness and danger. I don't know. I don't know beans about God.

Ibid.

*Paul Johannes Tillich, German-born American theologian (1886–1965).

30 But our minds must not go slack. How can we think straight if our minds go slack?

"Numbers," Ibid.

3044. Katherine Dunn (1945–)

1 . . . from thy septic whiteness, magnate and vagabond are indistinguishable . . .

Attic 1970

2 "When your mama was the geek, my dreamlets," Papa would say, "she made the nipping off of noggins such a crystal mystery that the hens themselves yearned toward her, waltzing around her, hypnotized with longing. 'Spread your lips, sweet Lil,' they'd cluck, 'and show us your choppers!'"

This same Crystal Lil, our tar-haired mama, sitting snug on the built-in sofa that was Arty's bed at night, would chuckle at the sewing in her lap and shake her head. "Don't piffle to the children, Al. Those hens ran like whiteheads."

Ch. 1, *Geek Love 1989*

3 Miss Lick's purpose is to liberate women who are liable to be exploited by male hungers. The exploitable women are, in Miss Lick's view, the pretty ones. She feels great pity for them. . . . If all these pretty women could shed the traits that made men want them (their prettiness) then they would no longer depend on their own exploitability but would use their talents and intelligence to become powerful.

Ch. 12, Ibid.

4 I've taken her on my own hook and I have to be careful. She thinks she's adopted me, that she's doing me a kindness, that she's displaying the magisterial stature of her goodness by spending time with me. I have to watch my ass. She is hideously lonely.

Ibid.

5 " . . . Isolation is a standard cult technique but I don't use it. It's standard procedure to get the poor buggers in a low moment, hustle them off to the boonies, and surround them with a strong-arm/soft-spiel combo. . . .

"As it is, I don't need all that crap. For what I've got to say, the more exposure the folks have to the outside world, the better. Feed 'em newspapers, TV, world reports. Tell 'em about terrorist attacks, mass murders, disease, divorce, crooked politicians, pollution, war and rumors of war! Then go ahead and tell 'em that only fools and half-wits join my outfit. The first half of the news cancels out that particular message. Let the relatives and lovers loose on 'em. All they can stand. Because it's the world that drives them to me. You news guys are my allies."

Ch. 19, Ibid.

6 She is a galumphing dugong, an elvish ox, a sentimental rhino.
. . .

She mooches around for my approval. She's a sullen buffalo with the world but she's a child to me. She is bigger than Papa. She could break me with two fingers. But she can be small around me . . . It's because I like her. Arty was right. She soaks it up like booze and it turns her to water, makes her defenseless.

Ch. 27, Ibid.

3045. Buchi Emecheta (1945–)

1 That was life, she said to herself. Be as cunning as a serpent and as harmless as a dove.

Ch. 2, *Second-Class Citizen* 1974

2 But how was she to tell this beautiful creature that in her society she could only be sure of the love of her husband and the loyalty of her parents-in-law by having and keeping alive as many children as possible, and that though a girl may be counted as one child, to her people a boy was like four children put together? And if the family could give the boy a good university education, his mother would be given the status of a man in the tribe. How was she to explain all that?

Ch. 6, Ibid.

3 The whole world seemed so unequal, so unfair. Some people were created with all the good things ready-made for them, others were just created like mistakes. God's mistakes.

Ch. 9, Ibid.

4 I am a woman and a woman of Africa. I am a daughter of Nigeria and if she is in shame, I shall stay and mourn with her in shame.

Destination Biafra 1982

5 . . . shame kills faster than disease.

The Rape of Shavi 1985

3046. Abla Farhoud (1945–)

1 AMIRA. In the village, there was a woman who could take anything . . . poverty, misery, anything. She'd raised about ten kids. She took everything as it came, never complained. She didn't even mind being beaten. She just smiled. But one day, a day like any other when her husband was about to beat her, she snuck into the kitchen and grabbed a butcher knife. She looked her husband straight in the eye and said, "No, not one more time, not ever again."

The Girls from the Five and Ten, Jill MacDougall, tr. 1986

3047. Shulamith Firestone (1945–)

1 Perhaps it is true that a presentation of only the female side of things . . . is limited. But . . . is it any more limited than the prevailing male view of things, which—when not taken as absolute truth—is at least seen as "serious," relevant and impor- tant.

The Dialectic of Sex 1970

2 A man is allowed to blaspheme the world because it belongs to him to damn.

Ibid.

3 I submit that women's history has been hushed up for the same reasons that black history has been hushed up . . . and that is that a feminist movement poses a direct threat to the establishment. From the beginning it exposes the hypocrisy of the male power structure.

Ch. 2, Ibid.

4 I conclude that, contrary to what most historians would have us believe, women's rights were never won. The Women's Rights Movement did not fold because it was defeated. *Seeming* freedoms appear to have been won.

Ibid.

5 The bar is the male kingdom. For centuries it was the bastion of male privilege, the gathering place for men away from their women, a place where men could go to freely indulge in The Bull Session . . . a serious political function: the release of the guilty anxiety of the oppressor class.

"The Bar as Microcosm," *Voices for Women's Liberation*, Leslie B. Tanner, ed. 1970

3048. Lesley Hazleton (1945–)

1 Some say that a writer's life is a permanent vacation.

"Floating World," *The Women's Review of Books*, Vol. XII, Nos. 10–11 *July 1995*

2 Binoculars and a bird book sit on one corner of my desk, because what work could be more important than watching a pair of trumpeter swans swim up the channel out of the early morning mist?

Ibid.

3 There was a fine romance to this: the very American romance of taking to the road. For if the history of the United States is one of settlement, its romance is one of abandoning the settled life.

Driving to Detroit: An Automotive Odyssey 1998

4 What you are doing under the most intense physical pressure, is essentially this: you are playing a highly sophisticated game of chess at well over two hundred miles an hour. With yourself as the king.

Ibid.

5 Outside, my white horse was in fact red, and had wheels instead of legs.* But it was a magnificent steed, the kind that drew quiet nods of appreciation from exactly the kind of young men who might otherwise give me trouble, which was partly why I'd chosen it.

Ibid.

*Reference to her vehicle, a 1998 red Ford Expedition 4x4.

3049. Carter Heyward (1945–)

1 I'm a priest, not a priestess. . . . "Priestess" implies mumbo jumbo and all sorts of pagan goings-on. Those who oppose us would love to call us priestesses. They can call us all the names in the world—it's better than being invisible.

Quoted in "Who's Afraid of Women Priests?" by Malcolm Boyd, *Ms.* (New York) *December 1974*

2 It's obvious throughout secular and church history that significant legislation follows only after dramatic action.

Ibid.

3 As we come to experience the erotic as sacred, we begin to know ourselves as holy and to imagine ourselves sharing in the creation of one another and of our common well-being.

Touching Our Strength 1989

4   Openly lesbian women are dangerous to heterosexist patriarchy because, whether or not it is our intention, our visibility signals an erotic energy that has gotten out of control—out of men's control.

    "The Erotic As Sacred Power," *Coming Out and Relational Empowerment: A Lesbian Feminist Theological Perspective 1989*

5   The erotic is our most fully embodied experience of the love of God. It is the source of our capacity for transcendence, or the "crossing over" among ourselves, making connections between and among ourselves. The erotic is the divine spirit's yearning, through us, toward mutually empowering relation, which becomes our most fully embodied experience of God as love.
                                                                    Ibid.

6   Mutuality is not a static place to be. It is movement into a way of being in a relation in which both or all parties are empowered *with* one another to be more fully themselves: mutually, we come to life.
                                                                    Ibid.

3050. Dianne Highbridge (1945–)

1   . . . [to know] what it is to be irrevocably other, and to be able to call it, most of the time, peace.
                                              In the Empire of Dreams 1999

2   . . . fumbling for the right words in a language made for not explaining . . . still hopefully clapping hands before the shrines of gods who will never know them but whose indifference itself seems sweet.
                                                                    Ibid.

3051. Eva Hoffman (1945–)

1   [History] tends to dissolve as you get closer, to fragment into a billion bits of ordinariness.
                                  Exit Into History, A Journey Through the New Eastern Europe 1993

2   Every time I hear Poland described reductively as an anti-Semitic country, I bridle in revolt, for I know that the reality is far more tangled than that.
                                                                    Ibid.

3   We in the West . . . should be careful of judging whole societies that have survived an epoch when to act morally often involved not only the risk of death, but also the risk of torture.
                                                                    Ibid.

4   It must have taken a special pertinacity to maintain a distinctly Slovak identity.
                                                                    Ibid.

5   . . . [Jews] are the specter haunting Eastern Europe these days . . . an absence that is itself felt as a presence, a wrongness. . . . Perhaps, if we don't always have a conscious conscience, we have a subliminal one, from which the memory of past wrongs is not so easily erased.
                                                                    Ibid.

3052. Nancy R. Hooyman (1945–)
See Mary Bricker-Jenkins, 2343: 1–3.

3053. Ruth Iskin (1945–)

1   In the dealer-critic system, galleries exist primarily for sale purposes and it is the critic's role to promote the art product by establishing its value and providing a justification for its importance.
            "A Space of Our Own, Its Meaning and Implications," *Womanspace February/March 1973*

2   The star system: the focus on the artist and his/her entire career, which was a by-product of the sale orientation developed in the dealer-critic system, replaced the older emphasis on individual paintings and schools of painters, which prevailed in the academy.
                                                                    Ibid.

3054. Kathy Kahn (1945–)

1   There is still a natural tendency for the people of one class to look down on people who they think are lower class—as if they are less than human.
            Quoted in "Kathy Kahn: Voice of Poor White Women" by Meridee Merzer, *Viva April 1974*

2   In places like the textile mills, where superhuman production rates are set, the people have to take speed (amphetamines) in order to keep up production. . . . Virtually every factory is this country is run on speed, grass, or some other kind of upper.
                                                                    Ibid.

3   I do not believe in being paid for organizing . . . because a revolution is a revolution. And nobody—*nobody*—gets paid for making a revolution.
                                                                    Ibid.

3055. Linda Kintz (1945–)

1   The corporation is defined in spiritual terms as a natural extension of God's natural law, with the belief in the corporation and the protection of corporate activity . . . saturated with moral passion [which] . . . justifies an admonition to Americans that it is their religious and moral duty to export unregulated free enterprise to the rest of the globe.
            Between Jesus and the Market: The Emotions that Matter in Right-Wing America 1997

2   How can hate sound so *nice*?
                                                                    Ibid.

3056. Elizabeth Loftus (1944–)

1   In a chaotic world, where so much is out of control, we need to believe that our minds, at least, are under our command. We need to believe that our memories, inherently trustworthy and reliable, can reach back into the past and make sense of our lives.
            The Myth of Repressed Memory, co-writer, Kathrine Ketcham *1994*

2   Sometimes we might be better off with distorted memories. And sometimes it just plain old doesn't matter if our memory is perfectly accurate or not. It only matters when you start to use memories to accuse people, and you want to imprison them or take their money.
            "Into the Past Imperfect" by Kit Boss, *Seattle Times*, Pacific Northwest section *25 September 1994*

3   People can definitely recover true memories. You just have to go to a high-school reunion to prove that to yourself. The thing I am trying to say is: Where is the evidence that an endless stream of traumas can be buried in the unconscious, where decades later you can reliably dig them up?
    There is no scientific proof.
                                                                    Ibid.

4 I like the tall-building lawyers to know my time is worth as much as theirs.*

Ibid.

*Reference to to her $350/hour rate for forensic consulting.

3057. Karen Malpede (1945–)

1 The flowing of blood and of milk, the turning of blood into milk, renewable ecstasies—these are commonplaces of female sexuality.

Women in Theatre: Compassion and Hope (p.255) 1983

2 MICHEL. Nothing we do sullies us; why is that?

Us 1987

3 . . . in order for me to reveal the divine in "man" I had to come to feminism. There was no other way, I had to come to an understanding of the divine in women. Now I can truly be one within a long tradition of people who believe that theater is a way to reveal the spirit, the deep essence, the unrealized desires, the true holiness of humankind.

Quoted in "Karen Malpede," *Interviews with Contemporary Women Playwrights* by Kathleen Betsko* and Rachel Koenig 1987

*See 2256.

4 Pacifism is an active, assertive way of being which, when used effectively disarms. It has to do with holding to a sense of self and of community and with refusing to be part of the victor/victim scenario.

Ibid.

5 The great artist speaks a truth so personal it becomes universal. There's no way you can do that with one eye on the marketplace.

Ibid.

6 I think artists, like most other people, don't want to face the fact that we are very close to our extinction as a species and we intend to take with us all the life on earth.

Ibid.

7 Pregnancy can be a tremendously creative time in the life of a woman; the body itself is tied up in the act of creation so it's easy for the mind and heart to be similarly engaged.

Ibid.

8 The true artist is bisexual; I'm not necessarily talking about whom you choose to sleep with but about how deeply you can enter into both your own psyche and that of someone unlike you.

Ibid.

3058. Wilma Mankiller (1945–)

1 Cherokees have stated that they are ready for female leadership. . . . We all knew this was coming. . . . The issues are our programs, the breaking of the circle of poverty, not me.

*Inaugural Speech** 5 December 1985
*Elected Chief of the Cherokee Nation of Oklahoma in 1987, she was the first woman to head a major Native American tribe.

2 We can look back over the 500 years since Columbus* stumbled onto this continent and see utter devastation among our people. But as we approach the 21st century, we are very hopeful. Despite everything, we survive in 1991 as a culturally distinct group. Our tribal institutions are strong. And I think we can be confident that, 500 years from now, someone like

Wilma Mankiller will say that our languages and ceremonies from time immemorial still survive.

Quoted in "She Leads A Nation" by Hank Whittemore, *Parade Magazine* 18 August 1991
*Christopher Columbus (1451?–1506), Italian navigator and explorer who, in 1492, opened the path from the Old World to the New.

3 My ability to survive personal crises is really a mark of the character of my people. Individually and collectively, we react with a tenacity that allows us again and again to bounce back from adversity.

Ibid.

4 *Have a good mind.* No matter what situation you're in, find something good about it, rather than the negative things. And in dealing with other human beings, find the good in them as well.
    We are all interdependent. Do things for others—tribe, family, community—rather than just for yourself.
    Look forward. Turn what has been done into a better path. If you're a leader, think about the impact of your decisions on seven generations into the future.

Credo, Ibid.

5 I wept tears that came from deep within the Cherokee part of me. They were tears from my history, from my tribe's past. They were Cherokee tears.

Quoted in *Twentieth-Century Women Political Leaders* by Claire Price-Groff 1998

6 We need to really trust our own selves and our own thinking, and not allow others to convince us that our thoughts, ideas and plans and visions aren't valid.

Ibid.

3059. Bette Midler (1945–)

1 For Tillie had been (in the Days of her Youth)
Adored as a Terpsichorine.
She danced with Abandon and not too much else,
Yet never approached the Obscene.

The Saga of Baby Divine, St. 16 1983

2 "A good laugh is good for the spirits it's true,
But a good cry is good for the soul."

St. 114, Ibid.

3 "Make sure that your Life is a Rare Entertainment!
It doesn't take anything drastic.
You needn't be gorgeous or wealthy or smart
Just Very Enthusiastic!"

St. 153, Ibid.

4 There's a kind of emotional exploration you plumb with a friend that you don't really do with your family.

Quoted in "I Can't Play the Victim" by Tom Seligson, *Parade Magazine* 5 February 1989

5 Marriage involves big compromises all the time. International-level compromises. You're the U.S.A., he's the USSR, and you're talking nuclear warheads.

Ibid.

3060. Gertrude Ibengwe Mongella (1945–)

1 Women have always struggled with their men-folk for the abolition of slavery, the liberation of countries from colonialism, the dismantling of apartheid and the attainment of peace. It is now the turn of men to join women in their struggle for equality.

Speech, U.S. Fourth Conference on the World's Women 1995

3061. Honor Moore (1945–)

1 I have thought the cancer was in my control. If I decide she will recover, it will go away. . . .

Mourning Pictures (verse play) 1974

2 MARGARET. Halfway down the
stairs I stop and put the dishes down,
sit there and remember
as hard as I can where I am, hard as
I can: I am myself, a woman,
nursing a woman who may be dying.
My mother can't feed me any more.

Ibid.

3 A ring or two.
Her turquoise beads
The green-striped chair
What will she leave me
Except alone. . . .

"What Will She Leave Me?," Ibid.

4 M-A-D* is the filter through which we're pressed to see our-
selves—
If we don't, we won't get published, sold, or exhibited—
I blame none of us for not challenging it
Except not challenging it may drive us mad.

"Polemic #1" (poem) 1974

*Acronym for Male Approval Desire.

3062. Carol Muske (1945–)

1 I considered how we twisted into ourselves to live.

"An Octave Above Thunder," 1, St. 11, *An Octave Above Thunder: New and Selected Poems* 1997

2 What sense would it ever

make to them, the unread world, the getters and spenders,
if they could not hear what I heard,
not feel what I felt
nothing ruined poetry, a voice revived it,
extremity.

Sts. 12–13, Ibid.

3 Look. Messages the dead send
take time to arrive.

"Like This," St. 2, Ibid.

3063. Paula Nelson (1945–)

1 Women's battle for financial equality has barely been joined, much less won. Society still traditionally assigns to woman the role of money-handler rather than money-maker, and our as-signed specialty is far more likely to be home economics than financial economics.

Ch. 1, *The Joy of Money* 1975

2 The making of money simply is not a sex-linked skill. Women can and are turning it all around. We are discovering for our-selves the challenge—and the joy—of money.

Ibid.

3 A credit card is a money tool, *not* a supplement to money. The failure to make this distinction has "supplemented" many a poor soul right into bankruptcy.

Ch. 4, Ibid.

4 . . . launching your own business is like writing your own per-sonal declaration of independence from the corporate beehive,

where you sell bits of your life in forty-hour (or longer) chunks in return for a paycheck. . . . Going into business for yourself, becoming an entrepreneur, is the modern-day equivalent of pi-oneering on the old frontier.

Ch. 6, Ibid.

5 Americans want action for their money. They are fascinated by its self-reproducing qualities if it's put to work . . . Gold-hoard-ing goes against the American grain; it fits in better with European pessimism than with America's traditional opti-mism.

Ch. 15, Ibid.

3064. Jessye Norman (1945/6–)

1 Marian Anderson* was the personification of all that I ad-mire—wonderful, simple, pure and majestic in the human spirit. She wore the glorious crown of her voice with the grace of an empress. I have loved her all my life.

Interview (1960), Cited in "Death stills voice . . . " (AP), *Seattle Post-Intelligencer*, A9 9 April 1993

*See 1821.

3065. Carolyn M. Rodgers (1945–)

1 not too smart not too bitchy not too sapphire
not too dumb not too not to not too
a little less a little more

add here detract there

.lonely.

"Poem for Some Black Woman," St. 10 (1981), *The Woman That I Am, The Literature and Culture of Contemporary Women of Color*, D. Soyini Madison, ed. 1994

3066. Diane Sawyer (1945–)

1 When someone's life is shattered, there is only humanity.*

Quoted in "Star Power" by Richard Zoglin, *Time* (New York) 7 August 1989

*Reference to Richard Nixon (1913–1994), 37th president of the United States (1969–1974), forced to resign after the Watergate scandal.

2 We're a Madison Avenue country. I'm not sure that we make a distinction between news people and celebrities. And I think there is a distinction. The distinction lies in what you do every day—what you do to get stories and how far you will go and how much you will dig for them. All of the rest of the atten-tion that comes to you because you're on the air seems to me as irrelevance.

Ibid.

3067. Karen Anne Schmidt (1945–)

1 I've been accused of being aggressive. I wonder what they would call me if I was a man doing the same thing.

If you work and fight hard for something you believe in, why is it different depending on what sex you are?

Cited in "Olympian Woman" by Dionne Searcey, *Seattle Times*, A18 31 January 1999

3068. Karin Sheldon (1945–)

1 Environment, in all its forms and relations, sustains us. We de-pend upon it. I truly believe that the fundamental principles of

ecology govern our lives, wherever we live, and that we must wake up to this fact or be lost.

Quoted in "Found Women: Defusing the Atomic Establishment" by Anna Mayo, *Ms.* (New York) *October 1973*

3069. Carly Simon (1945–)

1   You're so vain, I'll bet you think this song is about you. . . .
"You're So Vain" *1972*

2   The thing that drugs do is they break down the barrier that's tense between people. People want to feel as *comfortable* as they possibly can and if you take drugs it makes you feel more at ease with your friends. But in fact, there is a certain thing to be gained from being *tense* with your friends.
The Dick Cavett Show, PBS-TV *1977*

3070. Jacqueline St. Joan (1945–)

1   I swallow the Sunday news
with my coffee: Yet another woman
killed by her husband-who-shot-himself-too.
But
this one,
this client might have been mine,
this one,
had I not been booked up
and had to say no,
this one,
had she had the money on Thursday
instead of on Monday,
this one.
"The Drama of the Long Distance Runners," *Ms.* (New York) *November/December 1997*

2   I stand here now, still at the kitchen sink
the belly of my dress wet and stinking
this running faucet of words
running out of my mouth,
the choking generations of daughters
spitting both privilege and bitterness
from their mothers' broken cups.
"Virginia, 1957–1977–1997," St. 5, Ibid.

3071. Jean Strouse (1945–)

1   His* authority—in his office, over railroads, in the world's capital markets—came not from what he said but from he did.
Morgan, American Financier 1999

2   . . . the country's economic welfare could no longer be left to private bankers. . . . Morgan's* extraordinary authority endangered the public welfare.
Ibid.

*John Pierpont Morgan, American financier and philanthropist (1837–1913).

3072. Deborah F. Tannen (1945–)

1   There is a sense in which every woman is seen as a receptionist—available to give information and help, perennially interruptible.
Talking from 9 to 5 1994

2   Women are less likely than men to have learned to blow their own horns . . . They may well not get credit for what they have done.
Ibid.

3   The Pavlovian view of women voters—plug the words in, and they will respond—sends a chill down my spine because it sounds like an adaptation of something I have written about communication between the sexes: When a woman tells a man about a problem, she doesn't want him to fix it; she just wants him to listen and let her know he understands. But there's a difference between a private conversation and a presidential election, between what we want from our lovers and what we want from our leaders.
"Bush's Sweet Talk," Op-Ed, *The New York Times* 20 January 2000

3073. Anne Tucker (1945–)

1   All art requires courage.
Introduction, *The Woman's Eye 1973*

2   Exploration, whether of jungles or minds, is considered unfeminine.
Ibid.

3   For centuries men have defined themselves in terms of other men, but women have been defined by and in terms of men. . . . The ubiquitous nature of masculine images of Woman has contributed significantly to the struggles of women artists because that which is publicly acceptable art does not conform with their own needs and experiences, and their own art does not conform with popular standards.
Ibid.

4   Society's double behavioral standard for women and for men is, in fact, a more effective deterrent than economic discrimination because it is more insidious, less tangible. Economic disadvantages involve ascertainable amounts, but the very nature of societal value judgments makes them harder to define, their effects harder to relate.
Ibid.

3074. Anne Waldman (1945–)

1   We benefited from the examples and trials of young women who had struggled to be creative and assertive before us, and we were certainly aware of the exciting artistic and liberal heritage of our New York City environs and yet many of us fell into the same retrograde traps. Being dominated by relationships with men—letting our own talents lag, following their lead—which could result in drug dependencies, painful abortions, alienation from family and friends . . .
Introduction, Quoted in *Women of the Beat Generation* by Brenda Knight *1996*

3075. Sarah Weddington (1945–)

1   I can't say, "I'm tired of this fight, let's do something else." To say that is to lose everything that was won.
Quoted in "For Roe v. Wade attorney, the crusade goes on" by Lily Eng, *Seattle Times*, B9 *27 September 1992*

2   Some don't realize how vulnerable and how recent Roe vs. Wade* is. We have to remember that part of the younger generation were born after the decision was passed down. They have had choice all their lives.
Ibid.

*The landmark 1973 Supreme Court ruling that alllows medical abortion; Weddington was the attorney who fought for and won the case.

3076. Leslie Kanes Weisman (1945–)

1 Malls are insular fantasy worlds where the relatively well-off pursue the study and acquisition of superfluous goods as a form of entertainment, in a society in which millions are in desperate need of something to eat and a safe, warm place to sleep.

Discrimination by Design: A Feminist Critique of the Man-Made Environment 1992

3077. Jacqueline Du Pré (1945–1987)

1 Water overflows from the gutter down one's neck and the beautiful brilliant sunshine and the blue, blue sky which go with the intense cold have given way to the grayness of the undecided season. Everyone waits, longs for the first glimpse of fresh green and from then on there will be no looking back.

Letter to her friend, Madeleine Dinkel, Quoted in *Jacqueline du Pré: Her Life, Her Music, Her Legend* by Elizabeth Wilson* 1999

*See 2659.

2 [Mstislav Rostropovich]* has spent most of his time digging away at the hysteria and extravagance which are so firmly rooted in my playing.

Ibid.

*Her teacher in Moscow.

3078. Susan Au Allen (1946–)

1 The quiet but steady revolution in affirmative action puts individual rights over group rights.

Speech, National Order of Women Legislators (11 November 1996), *Vital Speeches of the Day 1 April 1997*

3079. Hanan Ashrawi (1946–)

1 You will see that it is going to be very difficult to send these women* back to the kitchen or to relegate them to the status of second class citizens.

Palestinian Women of Gaza and the West Bank, Suha Sabbagh, ed. *1998*

*Reference to Palestinian women after the Intifada of 1987–92.

3080. Joan Barfoot (1946–)

1 I remember now that in the old life, I watched clocks. They told me everything: when to do each thing, walking, cooking, laundering, watching television, reading the newspaper, even having a cigarette. And sleeping. Time was how I counted off my life. Now I see that it was time I was accomplishing. I was not timing my tasks, but making the tasks into time; and all that is gone.

Ch. 3, *Gaining Ground* (a.k.a. *Abra*) 1978

2 "I've often thought that if we just put all our energy into raising the next generation, and they do the same and so on and so on, it makes us no better than ants, really, or bees. Save something for yourself."

Ch. 5, Ibid.

3 "I can't know anything about you if you're doing something that's a lie, and I can't be myself if I have to keep worrying about whether or not you're happy."

Ch. 14, Ibid.

3081. Ysaye Barnwell (1946–)

1 . . . it's impossible to perform and interpret* for someone else at the same time. In interpreting, you're listening to someone else and expressively transposing their statements and lyrics into another language.

Quoted in "Sweet Honey: A Cappella Activists" by Audreen Buffalo, *Ms.* (New York) *March/April 1993*
*American Sign Language, for the deaf.

2 I believe very strongly that the way African and African American music is practiced, composed, and performed embodies a set of values that ought to be applied in the broader society. Part of that is allowing yourself to be open, not controlling. Cooperation as opposed to competition.

Ibid.

3082. Georgette Bennett (1946–)

1 . . . take the profit out of drugs . . .

Crime-warps: The Future of Crime in America 1988

2 [The poor] are victimized by the most crimes, they have to live with the dealers and junkies, they suffer the most.

Ibid.

3083. Candice Bergen (1946–)

1 Hollywood is like Picasso's* bathroom.

Quoted by Sheila Graham** in *New York Post* *14 February 1967*
*Pablo Picasso, renowned Spanish painter (1881–1973). **See 1622.

2 THE MAN. Man has always been under death's dictatorship, always questioned it, always challenged it.

The Freezer 1968

3 THE MAN. You've been renovated, my sweet, like an urban renewal project!

Ibid.

4 THE MAN. Can't they realize that mankind was founded on two basic principles? *Religion and Death?* The one motivates the other. *Both* motivate the man!

Ibid.

5 I may not be a great actress but I've become the greatest at screen orgasms. Ten seconds of heavy breathing, roll your head from side to side, simulate a slight asthma attack and die a little.

Quoted in *Halliwell's Filmgoer's Companion* by Leslie Halliwell *1984*

3084. Jacqueline Bisset (1946–)

1 Character contributes to beauty. It fortifies a woman as her youth fades. A mode of conduct, a standard of courage, discipline, fortitude and integrity can do a great deal to make a woman beautiful.

Quoted by Lydia Lane in *The Los Angeles Times* *16 May 1974*

3085. Kim Campbell (1946–)

1 Charisma without substance is a dangerous thing.

Quoted in "Canada's intellectual defense chief . . ." by Joel Connelly, *Seattle Post-Intelligencer*, A8 *24 March 1993*

3086. Cher (1946–)

1 I'd like to look really great for as long as I can. If some people think that makes me terminally vain, then yes, I am that. I

don't think feminists should get upset if women want to change their looks. This is the real world and we're going to get older no matter what. It's just that I'd rather get older looking like Loretta Young than get older looking like, say, Thelma Ritter, even though she was one of my favorite actresses.

Forever Fit 1991

3087. Alison Hawthorne Deming (1946–)

1 I haven't lived anywhere long enough to be anything other than an outsider.

Temporary Homelands 1994

2 She [a brown bear] and I exist as interruptions in each other's afternoon, and that is close enough to knowing her for me.

Ibid.

3 . . . [father was] so set on making do that when he died he left us with two houses listing from wear and a collection of unusable tools—divot in the screwdriver blade, broken-handled hammer, coffee can of rusted square-cut nails, a scythe dull as a stone, and a hatchet from the Pleistocene.

Ibid.

4 Wise and frightened ancestors, tell me this: If faith blinds, makes us cold to another's suffering, must we be faithless to see?

"Exiled in America," Ibid.

3088. Sharon Doubiago (1946–)

1 Men create war to compete with women, who create life.

"The Football Player and the Poet: Mother and Child Reunion," *Clinton Street Quarterly* Fall 1986

2 "Ever since you were born, I've tried to understand why, since women birth and raise the boys, they grow up to be soldiers. Why isn't the world a more sensuous, loving place? and you know what Danny? There's almost nothing on this subject. Women and war, mothers and soldiers—the most fundamental, crucial issue."

Ibid.

3 "The football player in America is like the artist in America! The same loner, the same heroic figure so outside the mainstream, but performing for it. Both are like the shaman, the one who heals oneself, who comes back transformed from the mutilating experience to show the world how.

"Still I have these funny moments. Is this what I birthed and raised my child for? Football? What would my son be, with his perfect giant body, in a perfect society? And there remains the other great mystery. What is the function of the game for the spectators? Why do Americans love football?"

Ibid.

4 What happens to your American soul when, despite all your efforts, laying your body and soul on the line, you keep losing?

Ibid.

3089. Andrea Dworkin (1946–)

1 A commitment to sexual equality with males . . . is a commitment to becoming the rich instead of the poor, the rapist instead of the raped, the murderer instead of the murdered.

Ch. 2, Speech, "Renouncing Sexual 'Equality,'" National Organization for Women Conference on Sexuality (New York City, 12 October 1974), *Our Blood* 1976

2 In this society, the norm of masculinity is phallic aggression. Male sexuality is, by definition, intensely and rigidly phallic. A man's identity is located in his conception of himself as the possessor of a phallus; a man's worth is located in his pride in phallic identity. The main characteristic of phallic identity is that worth is entirely contingent on the possession of a phallus. Since men have no other criteria for worth, no other notion of identity, those who do not have phalluses are not recognized as fully human.

Ch. 4, Speech, "The Rape Atrocity and the Boy Next Door," State University of New York (Stony Brook, 1 March 1975), Ibid.

3 Rape is no excess, no aberration, no accident, no mistake—it embodies sexuality as the culture defines it. As long as these definitions remain intact—that is, as long as men are defined as sexual aggressors and women are defined as passive receptors lacking integrity—men who are exemplars of the norm will rape women.

Ibid.

4 Men who want to support women in our struggle for freedom and justice should understand that it is not terrifically important to us that they learn to cry; it is important to us that they stop the crimes of violence against us.

Ibid.

5 No phallic hero, no matter what he does to himself or to another to prove his courage, ever matches the solitary, existential courage of the woman who gives birth.

Ch. 5, "The Sexual Politics of Fear and Courage," Queens College, City University of New York (12 March 1975), Ibid.

6 By the time we are women, fear is as familiar to us as air. It is our element. We live in it, we inhale it, we exhale it, and most of the time we do not even notice it. Instead of "I am afraid," we say, "I don't want to," or "I don't know how," or "I can't."

Ibid.

7 For a mother the project of raising a boy is the most fulfilling project she can hope for. She can watch him, as a child, play the games she was not allowed to play; she can invest in him her ideas, aspirations, ambitions, and values—or whatever she has left of them; she can watch her son, who came from her flesh and whose life was sustained by her work and devotion, embody her in the world. So while the project of raising a boy is fraught with ambivalence and leads inevitably to bitterness, it is the only project that allows a woman to be—to be through her son, to live through her son.

Ibid.

8 A man can be a hero if he is a scientist, or a soldier, or a drug addict, or a disc jockey, or a crummy mediocre politician. A man can be a hero because he suffers and despairs; or because he thinks logically and analytically; or because he is "sensitive"; or because he is cruel. Wealth establishes a man as a hero, and so does poverty. Virtually any circumstance in a man's life will make him a hero to some group of people and has a mythic rendering in the culture—in literature, art, theater, or the daily newspapers.

Ibid.

9 I love, cherish, and respect women in my mind, in my heart, and in my soul. This love of women is the soil in which my life is rooted. It is the soil of our common life together. My life grows out of this soil. In any other soil, I would die. In whatever ways I am strong, I am strong because of the power and passion of this nurturant love.

Ch. 7, Speech, "Lesbian Pride" (28 June 1975), Ibid.

10 We as women know that there are no disembodied processes; that all history originates in human flesh; that all oppression is inflicted by the body of one against the body of another; that all social change is built on the bone and muscle, and out of the flesh and blood, of human creators.

Ch. 8, "Our Blood: The Slavery of Women in Amerika," National Organization for Women (Washington, D.C, 23 August 1975), Ibid.

11 The will to domination is a ravenous beast. There are never enough warm bodies to satiate its monstrous hunger. Once alive, this beast grows and grows, feeding on all the life around it, scouring the earth to find new sources of nourishment. This beast lives in each man who fattens on female servitude.

Ibid.

12 We think that we live in a heterosexual society because most men are fixated on women as sexual objects; but, in fact, we live in a homosexual society because all credible transactions of power, authority, and authenticity take place among men; all transactions based on equity and individuality take place among men. Men are real; therefore, all real relationship is between men; all real communication is between men; all real reciprocity is between men; all real mutuality is between men.

Ch. 9, Speech, "The Root Cause," Massachusetts Institute of Technology (Cambridge, 26 September 1975), Ibid.

13 Masculinity can only be experienced, achieved, recognized, and embodied in opposition to femininity. When men posit sex, violence, and death as elemental erotic truths, they mean this—that sex, or fucking, is the act which enables them to experience their own reality, or identity, or masculinity most concretely; that violence, or sadism, is the means by which they actualize that reality, or identity, or masculinity; and that death, or negation, or nothingness, or contamination by the female is what they risk each time they penetrate into what they imagine to be the emptiness of the female hole.

Ibid.

14 Men are rewarded for learning the practice of violence in virtually any sphere of activity by money, admiration, recognition, respect, and the genuflection of others honoring their sacred and proven masculinity. In male culture, police are heroic and so are outlaws; males who enforce standards are heroic and so are those who violate them.

Ibid.

15 Only when manhood is dead—and it will perish when ravaged femininity no longer sustains it—only then will we know what it is to be free.

Ibid.

16 While gossip among women is universally ridiculed as low and trivial, gossip among men, especially if it is about women, is called theory, or idea, or fact.

Ch. 1, *Right-Wing Women 1978*

17 Undernourished, intelligence becomes like the bloated belly of a starving child: swollen, filled with nothing the body can use.

Ch. 2, Ibid.

18 Wild intelligence abhors any narrow world; and the world of women must stay narrow, or the woman is an outlaw. No woman could be Nietzsche* or Rimbaud** without ending up in a whorehouse or lobotomized.

Ibid.

*Friedrich (Wilhelm) Nietzsche, German philosopher, poet, and classical philologist (1844–1900). **(Jean Nicolas) Arthur Rimbaud, French poet of the symbolist school (1854–91).

19 No woman needs intercourse; few women escape it.

Ch. 3, Ibid.

20 Feminism is hated because women are hated. Anti-feminism is a direct expression of misogyny; it is the political defense of women hating.

Ch. 6, Ibid.

21 Women have been taught that, for us, the earth is flat, and that if we venture out, we will fall off the edge. Some of us have ventured out nevertheless, and so far we have not fallen off. It is my faith, my feminist faith, that we will not.

Ch. 6, Sct. 2, Speech, "Redefining Nonviolence," Boston College (5 April 1975), Ibid.

22 Institutionalized in sports, the military, acculturated sexuality, the history and mythology of heroism, it [violence] is taught to boys until they become its *advocates*.

Pornography: Men Possessing Women 1981

23 She is the pinup, the centerfold, the poster, the postcard, the dirty picture, naked, half-dressed, laid out, legs spread, breast or ass protruding. She is the thing she is supposed to be: the thing that makes him erect.

Ibid.

24 The sexually liberated woman is the woman of pornography . . . Freedom is the mass-marketing of woman as whore. Free sexuality for the woman is in being massively consumed, denied an individual nature, denied any sexual sensibility other than that which serves the male.

Ibid.

25 In [the work of Marquis de] Sade,* the authentic equation is revealed: the power of the pornographer is the power of the rapist batterer is the power of the man.

Ibid.

*Donatien Alphone Françoise de Sade, French writer (1740–1814). The word "sadism" derives from the marquis.

26 Erotica is simply high-class pornography; better produced, better conceived, better executed, better packaged, designed for a better class of consumer.

Preface, Ibid.

27 Marriage as an institution developed from rape as a practice. Rape, originally defined as abduction, became marriage by capture. Marriage meant the taking was to extend in time, to be not only use of but possession of, or ownership.

Ch. 1, Ibid.

28 Male supremacy is fused into the language, so that every sentence both heralds and affirms it.

Ibid.

29 Childbearing is glorified in part because women die from it.

Ch. 2, Ibid.

30 Being a Jew, one learns to believe in the reality of cruelty and one learns to recognize indifference to human suffering as a fact.

"A Feminist Looks At Saudi-Arabia," *Letters from a War-Zone 1988*

31 Seduction is often difficult to distinguish from rape. In seduction, the rapist often bothers to buy a bottle of wine.
Speech, "Sexual Economics: The Terrible Truth" (1976), Ibid.

3090. Elizabeth Fee (1946–)

1 The voice of the scientific authority is like the male voice-over in commercials, a disembodied knowledge that cannot be questioned, whose author is inaccessible.
"Women's Nature and Scientific Objectivity," *Woman's Nature: Rationalizations of Inequality*, M. Loew and R. Hubbard, eds. 1983

3091. Judith Freeman (1946–)

1 [Las Vegas, a] . . . meta-theme park arising amidst a surreal expanse of windblown nothingness . . .
A Desert of Pure Feeling 1996

2 I've lived in the world of women all my life and yet never understood there is another world of women, heretofore unseen by me, that intersects so baldly with the raw world of men . . .
Ibid.

3092. Biruté M. F. Galdikas (1946–)

1 I remember thinking that if we understood our closest human relatives we'd understand our origins . . . maybe our own behavior.
Quoted in *Twentieth-Century Women Scientists* by Lisa Yount 1996

2 . . . fat black leeches, bloated with our blood, dropped out of our socks and off our necks and fell out of our underwear.*
Ibid.
*Describing conditions at their rough camp site, nicknamed Camp Leaky, in Borneo.

3 Sometimes I felt as though I were surrounded by wild, unruly children in orange suits* who had not yet learned their manners. . . . It was a continual battle of wits and they won!
Ibid.
*Reference to orangutans.

4 My main contribution [to science] is staying in one place, following one population longer than anyone.
Ibid.

5 [Once people] pay attention to orangutans, they also have to pay attention to the tropical rain forest, which is their only home.
Ibid.

3093. Marielle Goitschel (1946–)

1 I might have skied more recklessly if Christine* was not in first place. But I wanted to make sure that we would win two medals, so I made sure not to make any mistakes.
Quoted in "The Greater Part of Glory" by Bud Greenspan, *Parade Magazine 21 April 1991*
*Her sister, with whom she shared the silver and gold, the first and only time that two sisters have done so.

3094. Kimi Gray (1946–)

1 Poor people are allowed the same dreams as everyone else.
Quoted in "Turning Public Housing Over to Resident Owners" by Jerome Cramer, *Time* (New York) *12 December 1988*

2 People don't throw trash on the ground when they know it soon will be their turn to pick it up.
Ibid.

3095. Patricia Hampl (1946–)

1 Poetry has always laid claim to the spirit. And it probably should be no surprise that a secular society like ours conceals plenty of religious ache. Yet the assumption of a secular consciousness in American cultural life is so strong that when contemporary American poets not only address God directly but make it clear that the search for God lies at the core of their enterprise, it can become a jolt.
Review of *A Silence Opens* by Amy Clampitt*, *Virgin Time 1992*
*See 2179.

3096. Ewa Hauser (1946–)

1 These young women have not experienced any oppression themselves, have had free access to education, and have not yet gone through the drudgery of household chores and childbearing, and so they express a sincere regret that they grew up in a society where they were expected to be emancipated.
Ana's Land: Sisterhood in Eastern Europe, Tanya Renne,* ed. 1996
*See 3650.

3097. Sylvia Ann Hewlett (1946–)

1 How did the most independent and best educated women in the world come to have the least good conditions of life?
A Lesser Life, the Myth of Women's Liberation in America 1987

3098. Susan Jacoby (1946–)

1 Political détente notwithstanding, the Soviet Union is still a nation with a deeply ingrained suspicion of foreign influence.
Inside Soviet Schools 1974

2 I have always regarded the development of the individual as the only legitimate goal of education. . . .
Ibid.

3 Soviet schools are extraordinarily good at squeezing the fight out of the individuals they process.
Ibid.

4 Educational opportunity for all citizens is as much an article of social faith in the Soviet Union as it is in the United States. Everyone believes in education: party leaders, intellectuals, factory workers, farm laborers. The Soviets have much more faith than Americans in the ability of public institutions to transform their lives; schools—not Marxist-Leninist theory—are seen by parents as the key to a better future for their children.
Ibid.

5 . . . all foreigners regard other societies through the prisms of their own value systems.
Ibid.

3099. Sibyl James (1946–)

1 The Chinese government was offering me a free roundtrip, a modest salary, and housing . . . for the first time in my life I was being offered a one-year contract with medical benefits . . . And that is the heart of the tale. For these pages are the

stories and meditations of a resident foreigner, not a tourist—
and all the sickness and cures, the struggle and trust that such
a status confers.

Preface, *In China With Harpo and Karl* 1990

2 First, be short. Or stand beneath an open skylight in the bus
roof. Be thin. Be very thin. To get on or off be Kung Fu elbows
and not worry. . . . Last week at Hong Kou Park I saw a bonsai exhibition—stalls and stalls of tiny trees bent into shapes
the Chinese find pleasing, a sort of stay against the chaos of
the natural. Suddenly I understood the secret of buses. My
bones leaned together, my chest concaved. I found a space that
fit me when the doors shut.

"Busing," Ibid.

3100. Marcia Carolyn Kaptur (1946–)

1 The American people have the right to know who holds the
mortgage on America.

Congressional Speech *October 1988*

3101. Robin Lane Fox (1946–)

1 The same standards apply to heathen evidence as to biblical. Is
it based on a primary source? Is it biased, ambiguous or simply wrong? Relevant evidence is extremely scarce; what, if
anything, does silence imply? In the early parts of the Bible's
story, biblical persons have yet to be identified correctly in any
external sources. There have been many attempts, and some
confident claims, but as yet there is no good reason to identify
Moses or Joseph with any known person or period in ancient
Egyptian records.

(p. 252), *The Unauthorized Version: Truth and Fiction
in the Bible* 1992

3101.1. Barbara Lee (1946–)

1 In the past, women have been judged on the Three H's—hair,
husband and hemlines. If one woman runs, she's judged on the
Three H's; if two women run, they're considered by the press
as candidates in a cat fight. But when three run, the scrutiny of
them as women diminishes, and they are viewed as capable
people who are looked at through their accomplishments, their
agenda and their vision of the future.

Quoted in "Women Who Could Be President" by
Jane Ciabattari, *Parade Magazine 7 February 1999*

3102. Candy Lightner (1946–)

1 Death by drunken driving is a socially acceptable form of
homicide.

Quoted in "Legislature Eyes Harsher Laws . . ." by Chuck
Buxton, *San Jose Mercury 20 April 1981*

2 Victims of drunk drivers have no place to turn. Judges drink
and drive, juries drink and drive, D.A.'s drink and drive.
They're going to have sympathy for the drunk driver. They
don't have sympathy for the rapist, the murderer, the mugger.

Quoted in "Mother's Crusade to Get Drunk Drivers Off
the Streets" by Beverly Beyette, *The Los Angeles Times
11 June 1981*

3103. Genny Lim (1946–)

1 A woman is a ritual
A house that must accommodate
A house that must endure
Generation after generation

Of wind and torment, of fire and rain
A house with echoing rooms
Closets with hidden cries
Walls with stretchmarks
Windows with eyes.

"Wonder Woman," St. 6 (1981), *The Woman That I Am,
The Literature and Culture of Contemporary Women
of Color*, D. Soyini Madison, ed. 1994

3104. Kristin Carol Luker (1946–)

1 Early childbearing doesn't make young women poor; rather
poverty makes women bear children at an early age. Society
should worry not about some epidemic of "teenage pregnancy" but about the hopeless, discouraged and empty lives
that early childbearing denotes.

Dubious Conceptions: The Politics of Teenage Pregnancy
1996

2 Early childbearing would decrease if poor teenagers had better
schools and safe neighborhoods, if their mothers and fathers
had decent jobs so that teens could afford the luxury of being
children for a while longer.

Ibid.

3105. Catherine A. MacKinnon (1946–)

1 The law sees and treats women the way men see and treat
women.

"Viewpoint: Feminism, Marxism, Method, and the State:
Towards Feminist Jurisprudence," *Signs: A Journal of
Women in Culture and Society* 1983

2 Lawyers considering whether anything can be done for a
woman who is damaged in ways that make her less than the
perfect case rarely conclude that they should confront or
change the law. They look at cases the way surfers look at
waves.

Introduction, *Feminism Unmodified* 1987

3 Particularly in its upper reaches, much of what has passed for
feminism in law has been the attempt to get for men what little
has been reserved for women or to get for some women some
of the plunder that some men have previously divided (unequally) among themselves.

Ibid.

4 . . . anyone with an ounce of political analysis should know
that freedom before equality, freedom before justice, will only
further liberate the power of the powerful and will never free
what is most in need of expression.

Ibid.

5 . . . power constructs the appearance of reality by silencing the
voices of the powerless, by excluding them from access to authoritative discourse.

"Francis Biddle's* Sister: Pornography: Civil Rights
and Speech," Ibid.
*French-born American jurist and public official (1886–1968).

6 The First Amendment essentially presumes some level of social
equality among people and hence essentially equal social access to the means of expression In a context of inequality
between the sexes, we cannot presume that that is accurate.

"Linda's Life and Andrea's Work," Ibid.

7 For purposes of sex discrimination law, to be a woman means
either to be like a man, or to be like a lady. We have to meet ei-

ther the male standards for males or the male standards for females.

> "On Exceptionality: Women as Women in Law," Ibid.

8 When courts learn that sexual harassment is as vicious and pervasive and damaging to women in workplaces everywhere as rape is to women guards in male prisons, and as disruptive to production as rape is to prison security, will women be excluded from the workplace altogether?

> Ibid.

9 . . . it is only the exceptional woman who escapes gender inequality enough to be able to claim that she is injured by it. It seems that we already have to be equal before we can complain of inequality.

> Ibid.

10 Most conduct is expressive as well as active; words are as often tantamount to acts as they are vehicles for removed cerebration.

> "The Sexual Politics of the First Amendment," Ibid.

11 This has been at the heart of every women's initiative for civil equality from suffrage to the Equal Rights Amendment: the simple notion that law—only words, words that set conditions as well as express them, words that are their own kind of art, words in power, words in authority, words in life—respond to women as well as men.

> Afterword, Ibid.

3106. Jessica Tuchman Mathews (1946–)

1 The automobile reaches to the heart of the American self-image in the way the horse once did in the West. It's going to be hard to change.

> Quoted in A World of Ideas by Bill Moyers 1989

2 Countries are starting to see that they can't have economic growth without protecting their resource base. The economic growth disappears as the fisheries disappear, as the forest disappears, as soil erosion progresses. They can't have real growth without environmental management.

> Ibid.

3 We're going to need a new sense of shared destiny, that we're in this together. We, the family of nations, are going to have to develop somehow some shared sense, almost like a joint business venture, that we work together, or we're all going to suffer.

> Ibid.

4 It is hard to think abstractly about a crisis.

> Ibid.

3107. Mary McCaslin (1946?–)

1 Bury me out on the lone prairie
Near the mountains I could never see

The speakers, they all gasp to clear their lungs for their luncheon speeches
This year's new campaign is to save the canyons and the beaches

> "The Dealers" 1975

3108. Liza Minnelli (1946–)

1 In Hollywood now when people die they don't say, "Did he leave a will?" but "Did he leave a diary?"

> Quoted in Observer (London) 13 August 1989

3109. Janet Horowitz Murray (1946–)

1 . . . for now we have to listen very, very carefully to hear, amid the cacophony of cyberspace, the first fumbling chords of the awakening bard.

> Hamlet on the Holodeck: The Future of Narrative
> in Cyberspace 1997

2 Mouse-clicking through the mind of the insomniac is like a walk through a labyrinth.

> Ibid.

3 In order for electronic narrative to reach a higher level of expressiveness, the medium as a whole must make that shift that Charlotte [Brontë]* made, that is, away from adolescent rehearsal fantasies and toward the expression of more realistic desires.

> Ibid.

*See 910.

3110. Marilyn Nelson (1946–)

1 slow lips recite the credo, smother yawns,
and ask forgiveness for being so bored.

> "Churchgoing," St. 1, For the Body 1978

2 Oh, sometimes it causes me to tremble,
that they believe most, who so much have lost.

> St. 4, Ibid.

3 I have no answer to the blank inequity
of a four-year-old dying of cancer.
I saw her on TV and wept
with my mouth full of meatloaf.

> "Mama's Promise," St. 1, Mama's Promises 1985

4 I've always pictured my own death
as a closed door,
a black room,
a breathless leap from the mountaintop
with time to throw out my arms, lift my head,
and see, in the instant my heart stops,
a whole galaxy of blue.

> St. 5, Ibid.

5 I remember her promise,
and whisper it over my sweet son's sleep:

When you float to the bottom, child,
like a mote down a sunbeam,
you'll see me from a trillion miles away:
my eyes looking up to you,
my arms outstretched for you like night.

> Sts. 7–8, Ibid.

6 She wished so hard, she killed part of her heart.

> "Chosen," St. 1, The Homeplace 1990

7 On the night before a mission
you gave a buddy
your hiding places
as solemnly
as a man dictating his will.

> "Lonely Eagles ," St. 4, Ibid.

8 Oh, catfish and turnip greens,
hot-water cornbread and grits.
Oh, musty, much-underlined Bibles;
generations lost to be found,
to be found

> "The House on Moscow Street ," St. 5, Ibid.

9 Big deal,
  said Abba Jacob.
  Miracles happen all the time.
  We're here,
  aren't we?
    "Abba Jacob and Miracles," St. 2, *Magnificat 1994*

10 Reverend Father, she asks,
   what is the highest spiritual virtue?

   Abba Jacob looks to heaven
   and groans.
   Humor, he says.
   Not seriously, of course.
     "Abba Jacob and the Theologian," Sts. 1–2, Ibid.

11 Dust climbs the ladder of light.
   For this infernal, endless chore,
   for these eternal seeds of rain:
   Thank you. For dust.
     "Dusting," St. 4, Ibid.

12 The true magic is the love contained in the universe.
   This is the original enchanter.
     "The Plotinus Suite," VIII. The True Magic, St. 4, Ibid.

13 Go into yourself, look around.

   And if what you see there isn't beautiful,
   don't stop smoothing, polishing, cutting away until
   you are *wholly yourself, nothing but pure light.*
     "The Plotinus Suite," X. Ennead I.vi., St. 3, Ibid.

14 monstrous love
   that wants to make the world right.
     The Fields of Praise 1997

15 So this is freedom: the peace of hours like these.
     Ibid.

3111. Linda Niemann (1946–)

1 On-the-road books are the Ur-narratives of our invading culture; they hearken back to voyages of discovery and to the building of the roads themselves. The road was created through the westward "manifest destiny" genocidal land rush, the stories it inspired having arrival as their ending. And the impulse to go on the road is a given: it was both the initiating act of our culture and its answer to any unsolvable problem.
    "Wheels of fortune," *New Directions for Women,* Vol. XVI, No. 4 *January 1999*

3112. Laura Nyro (1946–1997)

1 And when I die
  and when I'm gone
  there'll be one child born
  and a world to carry on....
    "And When I Die" *1966*

2 I was born from love
  and my poor mother worked the mines
  I was raised on the good book Jesus
  till I read between the lines....
    "Stoney End" *1966*

3 Nothing cures like time and love....
    "Time and Love" *1970*

4 I've got a lot of patience, baby
  And that's a lot of patience to lose.
    "When I Was a Freeport" *1971*

5 money money money
  do you feel like a pawn
  in your own world?
  you found the system
  and you lost the pearl....
    "Money" *1975*

6 They say a woman's place
  is to wait and serve
  under the veil
  submissive and dear
  but I think my place is in a ship from space
  to carry me
  the hell out of here
    "The Right to Vote" *n.d.*

7 ... you will find
  your own way
  hard and true
  And I'll find mine
  cause I'm growing with you
    "To a Child. . . ." *n.d.*

3113. Virginia O'Brien (1946–)

1 Women have been in the system long enough to begin influencing it and shaping it according to their values.
    Success on Our Own Trems: Tales of Extraordinary, Ordinary Business Women 1998

2 The intrinsic value of work, the ability to have an impact and operate in relationship with others, seem to motivate women more than anything else—more than climbing to the top, more than financial reward, more than power for power's sake.
    Ibid.

3114. Susie Orbach (1946–)

1 Fat is a social disease, and fat is a feminist issue.
    Introduction, *Fat is a Feminist Issue 1978*

2 Fat is a way of saying "no" to powerlessness and self-denial.
    Ibid.

3115. Dolly Parton (1946–)

1 I've been like a captured eagle.
  You know an eagle's born to fly,

  Now that I have won my freedom, like an eagle,
  I am eager for the sky.
    "Light of a Clear Blue Morning" *1976*

2 Butterflies are colorful and bright and gentle and have no way to harm you. They go about their business and bring others pleasure while doing it, because just seeing one flying around makes people happy. I'd like to think of myself as bringing people happiness while I do my business, which is my music. I'm content with what I am, and butterflies seem to be content to be just what they are, too. They're gentle, but determined.
    Quoted in "Introduction: Hello, Dolly," *Dolly* by Alanna Nash *1978*

3 Sure we had runnin' water. When we'd run and get it!
    Ch. 1, Ibid.

4 Oh, sometimes I go walking through fields where we walked
Long ago in the sweet used to be
And the flowers still grow, but they don't smell as sweet
As they did when you picked them for me
> "Do I Ever Cross Your Mind" (1973), *Trio II* (album) *1999*

3116. Adrian Piper (1946–)

1 I would never have believed it could be so agonizingly difficult
to make verbal sense of my immediate creative impulses. I felt
dull and completely helpless. I wanted to say what I was doing,
and why, and I couldn't. Words careened into mental view, col-
lided, and joined or separated randomly, as I flailed wildly
among them, trying dimly to grasp their connections and pin
them to my thoughts. It was a nightmare.
> Essay (p. 11), *Out of Order, Out of Sight*, Vol. I *1996*

2 Performance art necessarily has human subjectivity as part of its
content. To situate human subjectivity in the role of the art object is to invite the audience to engage with it, and with its own
subjectivity, and to transcend them. But this requires a high degree of skill in interpersonal fine-tuning, and attention to the
subtle psychologistics of social interaction. Most of us, who have
been trained to pummel, slash, and besmirch objects in the isolation of our studios, have yet to achieve the requisite expertise.
> Essay (1984; p. 104), Vol. II, Ibid.

3 Doing philosophy disciplines my urge to fly, improves my
sense of direction, and enables me to soar, for a time, above
the moral cretins. But it doesn't change their behavior . . . so
they always bring me down again eventually. And there is no
escape: . . . My art practice is a reflecting mirror of light and
darkness, a high sunny window that holds out to me the
promise of release into the night.
> "Flying" (1987; p. 231–232), Ibid.

3117. Gail Pool (1946–)

1 Even with the best of maps and instruments, we can never fully
chart our journeys.
> "The war at home," *The Women's Review of Books*,
> Vol. XII, Nos. 10–11 *July 1995*

3118. Minnie Bruce Pratt (1946–)

1 She has three sisters, Lethean, Evie, and Ora Gilder.
When they aggravate her she wants to pinch
their habits off like potato bugs off the leaf.
But she meets them each weekend for cards and jokes
while months go by without her speaking to her brother.
> "My Mother Loves Women," *The Sound of One Fork 1981*

2 You had not acted like a man
and I never loved you better
> "Love Poem to an Ex-Husband," St. 4, Ibid.

3 Behind, cars rim the horizon, chrome
north south. Hundreds of tourists ramble and groan
past the silver snack truck, the man selling UFO
kites, a rescue squad, a young man grinning with suntan
oil, a heterosexual pair holding a beer, legs fanned
limp on a towel. All stare out to sea . . .
> "#70 Lower Matecumbe Beach," St. 2 (27 February 1988),
> *An Intimate Wilderness, Lesbian Writers on Sexuality*,
> Judith Barrington,* ed. *1991*
*See 2984.

4 We don't say we're too old for this.
> "#65 Parked Down by the Potomac," St. 1
> (5 October 1987), Ibid.

5 In the summer I come to her door with hair freshly cut, shorn
short as a boy's, but with soft tendrils around my ears and
neck. With hair this short, in jeans and T-shirt, I've been called
"Sir" once or twice by those who easily ignored my breasts.
Maybe now I look like a young sailor on shore leave, maybe
now I look like an adventure. When I step into her hallway,
she stares and says, "You've cut it so short. Now people will
think you're the butch." She turns away without touching me
at all, leaving me motionless in the cool passageway.
> "Green Scarf," *S/he 1995*

6 "You are not only a lesbian, but very, very queer. You love a
woman who is manly, and yet do not want her to be completely man. In fact, you desire her *because* she is both."
> "You," Ibid.

3119. Shulamit Reinharz (1946–)

1 I will never know the experience of others, but I can know my
own, and I can approximate theirs by entering their world.
This approximation marks the tragic, perpetually inadequate
aspect of social research.
> *On Becoming a Social Scientist 1984*

3120. Linda Ronstadt (1946–)

1 The thing you have to be prepared for is that other people
don't always dream your dream.
> Quoted in "Ronstadt Backed into Her Notoriety" by
> Lawrence DeVine, Knight–Ridder Newspapers
> *3 October 1986*

2 The great temper tantrum of the 60's . . .
> Ibid.

3 We were raised with the idea that we had limitless chances and
we got very shocked to learn that wasn't the case.
> Ibid.

3121. Judee Sill (1946?–)

1 The great storm raged and the power kept growin',
Dragons rose from the land below
And even now I wonder where I'm goin'
Ever since a long time ago,
I've tried to let my feelin's show.
> "The Phoenix" *1969*

3122. Barbara Smith (1946–)

1 Then there was the magazine called LIFE which promised
more about the Deaths.
> "Poem for My Sister (One) Birmingham Sunday" (1963),
> *Southern Voices August/September 1974*

2 Autonomy and separatism are fundamentally different. Whereas autonomy comes from a position of strength, separatism
comes from a position of fear. When we're truly autonomous
we can deal with other kinds of people, a multiplicity of issues,
and with difference, because we have formed a solid base of
strength.
> Introduction (p. xl), *Home Girls, A Black Feminist
> Anthology 1983*

3123. Charlene Spretnak (1946–)

1 Many feminists feel there is good reason to use female
metaphors for the divine. First, it overturns a cornerstone of

gender politics in patriarchal cultures. Second, the symbolization matches physical reality; has anyone ever seen anything spring into existence because a male finger was pointed toward it? We are not amused by the mythic narratives that steal the generative power of the female; womb envy should find less aggressive outlets.

"Essay: Wholly Writ," *Ms.* (New York) *March/April 1993*

3124. Sue Townsend (1946–)

1 Friday, January 2nd. BANK HOLIDAY IN SCOTLAND, FULL MOON. I felt rotten today. It's my mother's fault for singing "My Way" at two o-clock in the morning at the top of the stairs. Just my luck to have a mother like her. There is a chance my parents could be alcoholics. Next year I could be in a children's home.

The Secret Dairy of Adrian Mole, Aged 13 3/4 1982

2 Babies hardly take any space at all. They are only about 21 inches long.

Ibid.

3 I was racked with sexuality but it wore off when I helped my father put manure on our rose bed.

Ibid.

3125. Marilyn vos Savant (1946–)

1 Moderation may be fine for parents and politicians, but science, literature and art need the bold.

"Ask Marilyn," *Parade Magazine 18 August 1991*

2 To me, the major difference between a broken heart and a broken spirit is that people break hearts and time mends them, but *time* breaks spirits and *people* mend them. My suggestion is that you take any broken spirit you know and expose it repeatedly to the light of as many warm personalities as possible.

"Ask Marilyn," *Parade Magazine 21 February 1993*

3 I believe that a First Lady should *not* serve as a role model for women, whether they're wives or not. It demeans women to suggest that, in order to be successful, they should aspire to marry people who will become rich, powerful or famous. We don't advocate that for *men*, for heaven's sake. If a woman wants wealth, power or fame, she should aspire to earn it *herself*.

"Ask Marilyn," *Parade Magazine 28 February 1999*

4 If you're enjoying life, you can't be feeling sad. And if you're not enjoying life, you shouldn't be unhappy that it won't last forever. In other words, it makes no sense to spend precious time feeling sad that time is precious.

Notice that the previous sentence—based on logic—sounds just like a statement based on emotion. That's because *healthy emotions make good sense*. When a clear head leads the way, a warm heart can safely follow.

Ibid.

3126. Anna Lee Walters (1946–)

1 The ever swollen hills in Oklahoma have given birth many times. . . . It is a land that drinks a lot of water and never seems to swallow much.

"Autobiography" (1977), *American Indian Women, Telling Their Lives*, Gretchen M. Bataille and Kathleen Mullen Sands, eds. *1981*

2 The old folks are all gone. They were tired, prepared and they went on. Life goes on. Nothing diminishes it. We have been

taught also that life is a fragile thing. Grandma always said that it almost feels too good to be alive.

Ibid.

3127. Marina Warner (1946–)

1 For while Mary* provides a focus for the steeliest asceticism, she is also the ultimate of fertility symbols. The mountain blossoms spontaneously; so does the mother maid.

Alone of All Her Sex 1978

2 The Virgin Mary* has inspired some of the loftiest architecture, some of the most moving poetry, some of the most beautiful paintings in the world; she has filled men and women with deep joy and fervent trust; she has been an image of the ideal that has entranced and stirred men and women to the noblest emotions of love and pity and awe. But the reality her myth describes is over; the moral code she affirms has been exhausted. . . .

As an acknowledged creation of Christian mythology, the Virgin's legend will endure in its splendor any lyricism, but it will be emptied of moral significance, and thus lose its present real powers to heal and to harm.

Ibid.

*See 79.

3 The vocabulary of pleasure depends on the imagery of pain.

"Fighting Talk," *The State of the Language*, Christopher Ricks and Leonard Michaels, eds. *1990*

4 The BBC* is a fine institution which I care very deeply about, yet the striking absence of women reproduces very clearly the prejudices of the country.

"Sex, symbols and the fallen virgin," The *Times* (London) *14 January 1994*

*British Broadcasting Corporation.

5 If only life were more hospitable to children, there wouldn't be this tragic controlling tension that gives women their only power and authority. I'm all for women having authority, but it is easier to be fond of children in climates where children are welcome.

Ibid.

6 . . . I don't think behavior should disqualify people from being MPs,* not because I condone it but because MPs should be representative of us all, with all our difficulties . . .

Ibid.

*Members of Parliament (Britain).

7 . . . we know where we belong because of what we choose to believe in, a location of the mind. Myth is part of that: we tell stories that reflect the kind of people we want to be, and the society we want . . .

Ibid.

3128. Kutlu Aslihan Yener (1946–)

1 [Growing up] I almost lived at the Natural History Museum in New York.

Quoted in *Twentieth-Century Women Scientists* by Lisa Yount *1996*

2 [I] was interested in the fundamental blocks that make up the world.

Ibid.

3129. Candace B. Pert (1946–)

1 There's another form of energy that we have not yet understood. For example, here's a form of energy that appears to

leave the body when the body dies. . . . Your mind is in every cell of your body. . . . There are many phenomena that we can't explain without going into energy.

> from *Bill Moyer's Healing of the Mind*, Quoted in Ch. 1,
> *Anatomy of the Spirit: The Seven Stages of Power
> and Healing*, Caroline Myss* 1996

*See 3364.

3130. Gilda Radner (1946–1989)

1   [Audiences] all applaud, but none of them will come home with you and look at your back someplace to see if you have a pimple.

> Quoted in "The Many Faces of Gilda" by Roy Blount, Jr.,
> *Rolling Stone* (New York) 2 November 1978

2   I'd much rather be a woman than a man. Women can cry, they can wear cute clothes, and they're the first to be rescued off sinking ships.

> Quoted in "My Fair City" by Merla Zellerbach,
> *San Francisco Chronicle* 6 June 1979

3   I think of my illness [ovarian cancer] as a school, and finally I've graduated.

> Quoted in *Life* (New York) 1988

3131. Patricia Aburdene (1947?–)

1   The most important thing you can master for the next decade won't be Fiber Optics 101 but rather learning how to learn.

> "Trendspotters" (p. 60), *Working Woman Magazine*
> July 1987

2   The Industrial Age relied on brute strength, but the Information Age will rely on mental stamina—women's strong suit.

> Ibid.

3132. Paulette Bates Alden (1947–)

1   It would be funny—if it weren't so painful—how up until about the age of twenty-one the worst mistake a girl like me could make would be to have a baby before she got married, and then almost overnight the worst mistake became to get married and have a baby . . . both of which I had avoided. . . . But now I was beginning to wonder if maybe I wasn't about to make—if I hadn't already—the biggest mistake of all: I was about to miss out on having a child.

> *Crossing the Moon: A Journey Through Infertility* 1996

2   The maternal instinct waiting to be unleashed in me might turn out to be like the plant in *Little Shop of Horrors*.

> Ibid.

3133. Catherine Anderson (1947–)

1   All day she'll guide cloth along a line
of whirring needles, her arms & shoulders
rocking back & forth
with the machines—
200 porch size rugs behind her
before she can stop
to reach up, like her mother,
and pick the lint
out of her hair.

> "Womanhood," St. 2, *Working Classics:
> Poems on Industrial Life*, Peter Oresick
> and Nicholas Coles, eds. 1983

3134. Laurie Anderson (1947–)

1   You can dance. You can make me laugh. You've got x-ray eyes.
You know how to sing. You're a diplomat. You've got it all.
Everybody loves you.
You can charm the birds out of the sky. But I, I've got one thing.
You always know just what to say. And when to go.
But I've got one thing. You can see in the dark.
But I've got one thing: I loved you better.

> "Gravity's Angel," St. 1, *Spectral Display* 1984

2   All of nature talks to me. If I could just make out what it was trying to tell me. Listen!
Trees are swinging in the breeze. They're talking to me.
Insects are rubbing their legs together.
They're all talking They're talking to me. And short animals—
They're bucking up on their hind legs. Talking. Talking to me.

> "Sharkey's Way," St. 3, Ibid.

3   You know? They're growing mechanical trees.
They grow to their full height. And then they chop themselves down.
Sharkey says: All of life comes from some strange lagoon.
It rises up, it bucks up to its full height from a boggy swamp on a foggy night. It creeps into your house. It's life! It's life!

> St. 6, Ibid.

4   If I were queen for a day
I'd give the ugly people all the money.
I'd rewrite the book of love
I'd make it funny.

> "Kerjillions of Stars," *Empty Places* 1989

5   So when you see a man who's broken, pick him up and carry him
And when you see a woman who's broken, put her all into your arms
'Cause we don't know where we come from. We don't know what we are

> "Ramon," Ibid.

6   What is history? It is an angel, being blown backwards into the future. It is a pile of debris.

> "The Dream Before," Ibid.

7   The willingness to be a fool, that's what I love most about this country. We don't have the same rules as Europeans.

> Quoted in "Hitching a Ride on the Great White Whale"
> by Roselee Goldeberg, *The New York Times*,
> Arts & Leisure 3 October 1999

8   Paradise
is exactly like
Where you are right now
Only much much
Better

> "Language Is a Virus," *Laurie Anderson n.d.*

9   Well I dreamed there was an island
That rose up from the sea.
And everybody on the island
Was somebody from TV.
And there was a beautiful view
But nobody could see.
'Cause everybody on the island
Was saying: Look at me! Look at me!

> "Look at me! Look at me!," Ibid.

3135. Madeleine Blais (1947/9–)

1 "Why can't you be more obedient?"
"Dogs are obedient!"
The Heart Is an Instrument : Portraits in Journalism 1992

2 I am most often drawn to people walking the edge, curiously undefeated.

Ibid.

3136. Karen Brodine (1947–)

1 "will you hold please? I'll see if he's in."
(are you in?)
"I'm sorry, sir, he's out."

the receptionist is by definition underpaid to lie.
"The Receptionist Is By Definition," St. 3, *Workweek: Poems* by Karen Brodine 1977

3137. Octavia Butler (1947–)

1 [Religion is] a dangerous prod, because it can always be misused and get out of hand, but it's useful for keeping people on the straight and narrow.
Interview, Amazon.com *24 March 1999*

2 God
Gives shape to the universe
As the universe
Shapes God.
Ch. 1, *Parable of the Talents (Earthseed: The Books of Living) 1999*

3 Back when he vanished, dying by violence was even easier than it is today. Living, on the other hand was almost impossible.
Ibid.

4 Hyperempathy syndrome is a delusional disorder, after all. There's telepathy, no magic, no deep spiritual awareness. There's just the neurochemically-induced delusion that I feel the pain and pleasure that I see others experiencing. Pleasure is rare, pain is plentiful, and, delusional or not, it hurts like hell.
Ibid.

3138. Beatrix Campbell (1947–)

1 Sexual abuse is like a corpse on a slab, saying nothing. You've got nothing to go on. It's a police officer's nightmare. You just want it to go away.
Quoting a police source, Introduction, *Unofficial Secrets 1988*

2 Sexual abuse of children now presents society with the ultimate crisis of patriarchy, when children refuse to protect their fathers by keeping secrets.
Ch. 2, Ibid.

3 A society in which adults are estranged from the world of children, and often from their own childhood, tends to hear children's speech only as a foreign language, or as a lie. . . . Children have been treated . . . as congenital fibbers, fakers and fantasisers.
Ibid.

4 Children's bodies aren't like automobiles with assailant's fingerprints lingering on the wheel. The world of sexual abuse is quintessentially secret. It is the perfect crime.
Ibid.

3139. Hillary Rodham Clinton (1947–)

1 Women who pack lunch for their kids, or take the early bus to work, or stay out late at the PTA, or spend every spare minute tending to their aging parents do not need lectures from Washington about values.
Commencement Speech, Wellesley College *29 May 1992*

2 It is important to recognize the limited ability of the legal system to prescribe and enforce the quality of social arrangements.
Quoted in *Hillary Clinton* by Judith Warner 1993

3 We currently have a system for taking care of sickness. We do not have a system for enhancing and promoting health.
Speech 1993

4 Service means you get as well as you give, your life is changed as you change the lives of others. . . . It is the way we find meaning in our lives, both individually and collectively.
Speech, Youth Service Day (The White House, Washington, D.C.) *24 April 1993*

5 If we do nothing there will be people who will continue to profit from our existing [health care] system, while many will go without care.
Speech, Service Employees Int. Union, Cited in "A preview pitch . . . " by Robert Pear, *Seattle Post-Intelligencer*, A1, 6 *27 May 1993*

6 We lack meaning in our individual lives and meaning collectively. We lack a sense that our lives are part of some greater effort, that we are connected to one another. We need a new politics of meaning. We need a new ethos of individual responsibility and caring. We need a new definition of civil society . . . that makes us feel that we are part of something bigger than ourselves.
Speech, Texas (April 1993), Cited in "Ex-Seattle activist . . . " by Joan Connell, *Seattle Post-Intelligencer*, A14 *13 June 1993*

7 If there is one message that echoes forth from this conference, let it be that human rights are women's rights, and women's rights are human rights, for once and for all.
Speech, Fourth World Conference on Women (Beijing) *5 September 1995*

8 Freedom means the right to assemble, organize, and debate openly. It means not taking citizens away from their loved ones and jailing them, mistreating them, or denying them their freedom or dignity because of peaceful expression of their ideas and opinions.
Ibid.

9 Let us use government as we have in the past, to further the common good.
It Takes a Village and Other Lessons Children Teach Us 1996

10 It is a national shame that many Americans are more thoughtful about planning their weekend entertainment than about planning their families.
Ibid.

11 If I am going to be criticized for doing what I believe in, I might as well just keep doing what I believe in.
Remark (1994), Quoted in *The 50 Most Influential Women in American Law* by Dawn Bradley Berry 1996

12 We need to be against brain-dead politics wherever we find it!
Quoted in *The Unique Voice of Hillary Rodham Clinton* by
Claire G. Osborne *1997*

13 . . . you're a public figure, which means apparently in America
anyone can say anything about you. Even public figures have
feelings and families and reputations.
Ibid.

14 We shouldn't leave the work of politics to people who run for
public office.
Ibid.

15 The idea that I would check my brain at the White House door
is something that just doesn't make any sense to me.
Ibid.

16 You know, we've been married for 22 years. And I've learned
a long time ago that the only people who count in a marriage
are the people who are in it.
Interview with Matt Lauer, *NBC's Today Show*
27 January 1999

17 Americans are ready to consider voting for a woman President
within the next 10 years. This is good news for our country,
for qualified women willing to enter the public arena at the
highest level and for every young girl interested in public service who can be told with a straight face that she too could
grow up to be President.
Quoted in "Women Who Could Be President" by
Jane Ciabattari, *Parade Magazine 7 February 1999*

18 . . . in my big ol' dictionary at home, it says a feminist is someone who believes a woman ought to have the same social,
economic and political rights as a man . . .
Quoted in "Hillary Clinton fastens seatbelt for a bumpy
ride" by Ellis E. Conklin, *Seattle Post-Intelligencer*, A1, 6
7 February 1999

19 I think he [George Bush*] is yesterday's president. I think he
has not kept up with the demands of the world as it is now.
And that his mind-set, understandably, which was formed in a
different time, has kind of imprisoned his capacity to understand and act on the new realities.
Ibid.
*American politician (1924–); 41st president of the United States
(1989–93).

20 He [Richard Nixon]* was the first to one to start it. I think I
might have said to Bill that Richard Nixon never does anything without a purpose. Either he was getting even with me
because I was on the impeachment staff—because he has a
very long memory—or it's because he's laying the groundwork
for an attack on me, which has turned out to be the case . . . It
all goes back to Nixon's comments.
Ibid.
*American politician (1913–1994); 37th president of the United
States (1969–74). Referring to his remarks in January 1992 that her
intellect and strength would make her husband "look like a wimp."

21 We are, all of us, exploring a world that none of us understand. The only tool we have to use ultimately is our lives.
Commencement address, Wellesley College (1969), Quoted
in *Rebels in White Gloves* by Miriam Horn *1999*

3140. Sara Davidson (1947–)

1 Overexposure to women's liberation leads, I found, to
headaches, depression and a fierce case of the shakes.
Quoted in interview, *Life* (New York) *1969*

2 In that time [the Sixties], that decade which belonged to the
young, we had thought life was free and would never run out.
There were good people and bad people and we could tell them
apart by a look or words spoken in code. We were certain we belonged to a generation that was special. We did not need or care
about history because we had sprung from nowhere.
Loose Change: Three Women of the Sixties 1977

3 "I've always been so rational, so damn well-adjusted. My
problem is that I don't have any problems."
Ch. 9, Ibid.

4 He had attacked hypocrisy everywhere but at home. He could-
n't deal with pain. He was always telling stories, playing with
the energy and ranting about capitalist society. But he couldn't
face himself, Susie, their life or his problems.
Ch. 20, Ibid.

5 "I can't even deal with that picture," Susie said. "People love
it, they think it's an image of courage. But pictures lie."
Ch. 27, Ibid.

3141. Bernadette Devlin (1947–)

1 To gain that which is worth having, it may be necessary to lose
everything else.
Preface, *The Price of My Soul 1969*

2 She* attended demonstrations against abuse of power, so that
makes her guilty of disrespect for British institutions.
Quoted in "In the Name of the Mother" by Neil McCafferty,
Ms. (New York) *November/December 1997*
*Reference to her daughter, Róisín McAliskey, political activist
(1971–).

3142. Ellen Carol DuBois (1947–)

1 History never stops; it is stubborn that way. Besides, what
could be more Jewish, more Talmudic, than continuing, endless debate? As a Jew, I think I prefer it that way. it seems wiser
to remain in the diaspora, to keep the messiah just over the
horizon, where I can aspire to but never quite attain her.
Quoted on *Women in World History Curriculum* website,
www.womeninworldhistory.com/ *1996–97*

2 Extending over more than a century and including most nations of the globe, the cause of woman suffrage has been one
of the great democratic forces in human history.
Remark (1989), Ibid.

3143. Linda A. Fairstein (1947/8–)

1 Each false accusation makes too many skeptics think that
every accusation is a false one—which is a danger that cannot
be overstated.
Quoted in "Rancorous Liaisons—The Morning After"
by Cathy Young, *Reason February 1994*

3144. Mary Gallagher (1947–)

1 MARINA. Well, you can't be afraid all the time, or you won't do
anything!
Act II, Sc. 16, *Dog Eat Dog 1983*

2 Publication is the only thing that makes me stop rewriting.
Quoted in "Mary Gallagher," *Interviews with*
Contemporary Women Playwrights by Kathleen Betsko*
and Rachel Koenig *1987*
*See 2256.

3 Healthy people aren't that interesting.

Ibid.

4 Good theater incorporates the personal, the social, the political, seamlessly.

Ibid.

5 The theater brigades are a major tool for unifying the Nicaraguan people. Music, dance, poetry are taught in every community because the Sandinistas believe that Nicaraguans can't explore their national identity till they are making art.

Ibid.

6 INS* OFFICER. You think we're so tough on them**—but they still keep coming! If we coddled 'em like you folks want, every goddamn country south of Texas'd be empty!

¿De Donde? 1991

*Immigration and Naturalization Service. **Immigrants, especially from Mexico and Central America.

3145. Farooka Gauhari (1947–)

1 Concealing your identity behind a veil and watching the world through a four-by-six inch rectangle of fine mesh had certain advantages. It was a sign of respect, of growing up and womanhood.

Searching for Saleem: An Afghan Woman's Odyssey 1996

2 Whenever I sat down to write, thousands of teardrops would fall and the paper would disappear behind the shadows of my mind.

Ibid.

3146. Batya Gur (1947–)

1 "What do you think about morality and art?"

. . . "For me art isn't a matter of such. . . . I think it's more important for a great artist to love than to be loved. . . . A writer who hurts people unnecessarily all his life isn't capable of mobilizing the compassion to create characters of flesh and blood.

Literary Murder, A Critical Case, tr. by Dalya Bilu 1993

3147. Cynthia Heimel (1947–)

1 Nobody, but nobody, is as fat as she thinks she is.

Sex Tips for Girls 1983

2 Dogs act exactly the way we would act if we had no shame.

Get Your Tongue Out of My Mouth, I'm Kissing You Good-Bye! 1993

3 The only women who don't believe that sexual harassment is a real problem in this country are women who have never been in the workplace.

Ibid.

4 If you leave me, can I come too?

If You Leave Me, Can I Come Too? 1995

3148. Carolivia Herron (1947–)

1 Once the old lady was young and leaned over Myrna for a kiss, the kiss that explained what they meant, what everybody meant really when they said love will take you, passion will come, this was that kiss to make true the love lies, to clear the confusion from all they said about how love feels. . . .

She could have lived with Myrna but Myrna was breaking her own heart over being a pervert . . .

"The Old Lady," *Afrekete: An Anthology of Black Lesbian Writing,* Catherine E. McKinley and L. Joyce DeLaney, eds. 1995

3149. Linda Hogan (1947–)

1 On the bus two elderly women sat in front of her. They were both speaking and neither one listened to the other. They carried on two different conversations the way people did in the city, without silences, without listening. Trying to get it all said before it was too late, before they were interrupted by thoughts.

"New Shoes," *A Gathering of Spirit,* Beth Brant,* ed. 1984

*See 2314.

2 The land is the house
we have always lived in.
The women,
their bones are holding up the earth.

"calling myself home," St. 4, *That's What She Said,* Rayna Green,* ed. 1984

*See 2735.

3 We're full of bread and gas, getting fat on the outside
while inside we grow thin.

"Oil," St. 5, Ibid.

4 From my mother, the antique mirror
where I watch my face take on her lines.

"Heritage," St. 1, Ibid.

5 She was a keeper of the family gates as well. She closed doors on those she disliked, if they were dishonest, say, or mean, or small. There was no room for smallness in her life, but she opened the doors wide for those who moved her slightly, in any way, with stirrings of love or pity. She had lusty respect for belligerence, political rebellion, and for vandalism against automobiles or businesses or bosses, and those vandals were among those permitted inside her walls.

"Making Do" 1 (1988), *Spider Woman's Granddaughters,* Paula Gunn Allen,* ed. 1986

*See 2735.

6 Us Chickasaws have lost so much we hold on to everything. Even our muscles hold on to their aches. We love our lovers long after they are gone, better than when they were present.

2 (1988), Ibid.

7 The stories we hold secret are stories of our growth as women, our transformations, the waking moments of realization that change the direction of our lives. They are sacred stories.

Preface (p. ix), *The Stories We Hold Secret: Tales of Women's Spiritual Development,* also Carol Bruchac and Judith McDaniel, eds. 1986

8 We have survived and in that survival is our life, our strength, our spirituality. And we are telling about it . . .

(p. xiv), Ibid.

9 Now we are the "betrayers of the lie." In our speaking and writing, we betray what has harmed us and held us down. We tell on those who hurt us. We give away the truths of oppression, and we betray our own denial by allowing our art and literature, our often unconscious internal creative processes, to express what we ourselves have held in.

"Women: Doing and Being," Ibid.

10 My mother is a fire beneath stone.
My father, lava.
"The History of Fire," St. 1 (1988), *The Woman That I Am,*
The Literature and Culture of Contemporary Women
of Color, D. Soyini Madison, ed. *1994*

11 I don't remember when
the girl of myself turned her back
and walked away . . .
"The Lost Girls," St. 1 (1988), Ibid.

12 . . . dancing like stopping
would mean the end of the world
and it does.
St. 2, Ibid.

3150. Keri Hulme (1947–)

1 They were nothing more than people, by themselves. Even paired, any pairing, they would have been nothing more than people by themselves. But all together, they have become the heart and muscles and mind of something perilous and new, something strange and growing and great.
Together, all together, they are the instruments of change.
Prologue, *The Bone People 1983*

2 "I have everything I need, but I have lost the main part."
Pt. I, Ch. 2, Ibid.

3 She thought of the tools she had gathered together, and painstakingly learned to use. Future probes, Tarot and I Ching and the wide wispfingers from the stars . . . all these to scry and ferret and vex the smokethick future. A broad general knowledge, encompassing bits of history, psychology, ethology, religious theory and practices of many kinds. Her charts of self knowledge. Her library. The inner thirst for information about everything that had lived or lives on Earth that she'd kept alive long after childhood had ended.
None of them helped make sense of living.
Ibid.

4 A man can find satisfaction with enough.
Pt. IV, Ch. 10, Ibid.

3151. Karla Jay (1947–)

1 History is so precarious, it could hinge on one careless trip to the laundry without first checking the contents of the pants pockets.
Tales of the Lavender Menace 1999

3152. Shirley Childress Johnson (1947?–)

1 To interpret American Sign Language is one function. To sing is yet another function. To think about the song, the singing, and the production of the song, and to interpret that into a clear, flowing rhythmic rendition at the same time is a great, great challenge. Sweet Honey's concerts are a dialogue with the audience—an emotional, spiritual, and intellectual call and response. I'm there only to help them communicate with one another—not just the expression of words and signs, but that chemistry of thought and feeling that quickens the room.
Quoted in "Sweet Honey:* A Cappella Activists" by
Audreen Buffalo, *Ms.* (New York) *March/April 1993*
*Sweet Honey in the Rock is a vocal group; also see Bernice Johnson Reagon, 2916, and Ysaye Barnwell, 3081.

2 Interpreting music and the performing arts is very specialized. My first goal is to convey Sweet Honey's message in a way that reflects its tempo, passion, and melodious intent. My expertise in this area was earned at the School of Hard Knocks, acquired through on-the-job training and from the suggestions and input of deaf people.*
Ibid.
*Johnson is the child of deaf parents.

3153. Martha McFerren (1947–)

1 Honey, if I can park in it,
I can back out of it.
"The Best Advice I Received as an Adolescent,"
Contours for Ritual 1988

3154. Melanie (1947–)

1 don't hold the spout against the seed
don't hold this need against me. . . .
"Gather on a Hill of Wildflowers" *1975*

3155. Elizabeth Morgan (1947–)

1 For the average middle-class American, living in the D.C. jail* is a horror. It's dirty, it's noisy, it's crowded, and you have no privacy. But I chose this because the middle-class American existence is worthless to me if my daughter is being raped. The destruction of my child is not worth any possessions. Just having her safe makes me happy.
Quoted in "A Hard Case of Contempt" by Jon Elson,
Time (New York) *18 September 1989*
*Incarcerated in Washington, D.C. for refusing to disclose the whereabouts of her allegedly sexually abused five-year-old daughter.

3156. Marsha Norman (1947-)

1 I was determined [*Getting Out*] would be truthful about prison . . . they're built for us all in one form or another.
Program notes to *Getting Out* (1977), A Contemporary
Theatre, Seattle *1981*

2 JESSIE. I'm just not having a very good time and I don't have any reason to think it'll get anything but worse.
'night, Mother 1983

3 Most people get their information about the theater from the critics, not from the theater itself. . . . Too often reviews answer one question, "Should you buy it or not?" When critics approach a piece of theater with a "buy it or not" attitude, our plays are reduced to products . . .
Quoted in "Marsha Norman," *Interviews with Contemporary Women Playwrights* by Kathleen Betsko* and Rachel
Koenig *1987*
*See 2256.

4 There are things that music can do that language can never do, that painting can never do, or sculpture. Music is capable of going directly to the source of the mystery. It doesn't have to explain it. It can simply celebrate it.
Ibid.

5 As women, our historical role has been to clean up the mess. Whether it's the mess left by war or death or children or sickness. I think the violence you see in plays by women is a direct reflection of that historical role. We are not afraid to look under the bed, or to wash the sheets; we know that life is messy. We

know that somebody has to clean it up, and that only if it is cleaned up can we hope to start over, and get better.

Ibid.

6   My attitude toward the computer has changed. In the first year I owned it, I was a true believer. I wrote articles and gave interviews saying it was our only hope as writers. Now I've gone back to the yellow pad. . . . I found I was having conversations with the screen, rather than with the audience, or with myself. The screen appreciates a very particular kind of talk. You might say I was talking head-to-head rather than heart-to-heart.

Ibid.

7   Success is always something that you have to recover from.

Ibid.

8   It's all time, see, and learning how to tell.

Circus Valentine n.d.

3157. Kathleen Norris (1947–)

1   And it is precisely the skills of celibate friendship—fostering intimacy through letters, conversation, performing mundane tasks together (thus rendering them pleasurable), savoring the holy simplicity of a shared meal, or a walk together at dusk— that can help a marriage survive the rough spots.

The Cloister Walk 1996

2   And this is the purpose of celibacy, not to attain some impossibly cerebral goal mistakenly conceived as "holiness" but to make oneself available to others, body *and* soul.

Ibid.

3   I'd begun to realize that the apprenticeship as a writer that I'd embarked on in my early twenties was in essence a religious quest.

Ibid.

4   The monastic life has this in common with the artistic one: both are attempts to pay close attention to objects, events, and natural phenomena that otherwise would get chewed up in the daily grind.

Ibid.

5   Scholars speak with authority, and they must, as they are trying to convince the reader that they have a worthwhile point of view. On the other hand, poets speak with no authority but that which the reader is willing to grant them.

Ibid.

6   I have lately realized that what went wrong for me in my Christian upbringing is centered in the belief that one had to be dressed up, both outwardly and inwardly, to meet God, the insidious notion that I need to be a firm and even cheerful believer before I dare show my face in "His" church. Such a God was of little use to me in adolescence, and like many women of my generation I simply stopped going to church when I could no longer be "good," which for girls especially meant not breaking rules, not giving voice to anger or resentment, and not complaining.

Ibid.

7   No matter how much I've written or published, I always return to the blank page; and even more important, from a monastic point of view, I return to the blankness within, the fears, laziness and cowardice that, without fail, will mess up whatever I'm currently writing and, in turn, require me to revise it. The spiritual dimension of this process is humility, not

a quality often associated with writers, but lurking there, in our nagging sense of the need to revise, to weed out the lies you've told yourself and get real.

Ibid.

3158. Martha Nussbaum (1947–)

1   To be a good human being is to have a kind of openness to the world, an ability to trust uncertain things beyond your own control, that can lead you to be shattered in very extreme circumstances for which you were not to blame.

Quoted in *A World of Ideas* by Bill Moyers *1989*

2   But the life that no longer trusts another human being and no longer forms ties to the political community is not a human life any longer.

Ibid.

3   The stories that we sometimes tell ourselves, that the free will is free no matter what conditions people are living in, and that these people in misery are really okay because they have free will—those are evasive and pernicious stories, because they prevent us from looking with the best kind of compassion at the lives of other people.

Ibid.

4   The role of politics is to provide conditions of support for all the richly diverse elements in the full human life.

Ibid.

5   Often, when people are measuring the quality of life, what they're doing is measuring the opulence of the society.

Ibid.

6   Advertising simplifies us, when I think what we want to do is to become more aware of complexity, nuance, and the complicated messiness of human situations. Advertising gives us a simple, two-second message in language that has to be grasped right away whereas the great works of literature draw us into a complex, highly textured language that is much more adequate for a grasp of ethical reality.

Ibid.

3159. Camille Paglia (1947–)

1   What is pretty in nature is confined to the thin skin of the globe upon which we huddle. Scratch that skin, and nature's daemonic ugliness will erupt.

Sexual Personae 1990

2   Each generation drives its plow over the bones of the dead.

Ibid.

3   Profanation and violation are part of the perversity of sex, which never will conform to liberal theories of benevolence. Every model of morally or politically correct sexual behavior will be *subverted*, by nature's daemonic law.

Ibid.

4   Prostitution is not just a service industry, mopping up the overflow of male demand, which always exceeds female supply. Prostitution testifies to the amoral power struggle of sex, which religion has never been able to stop. Prostitutes, pornographers, and their patrons are marauders in the forest of archaic night.

Ch. 1, Ibid.

5   Capitalism is an art form, an Apollonian fabrication to rival nature. It is hypocritical for feminists and intellectuals to enjoy

the pleasures and conveniences of capitalism while sneering at it. . . . Everyone born into capitalism has incurred a debt to it. Give Caesar his due.

Ibid.

6 Is there anything more affected, aggressive, and relentlessly concrete than a Parisan intellectual behind his/her turgid text? The Parisian is a provincial when he pretends to speak for the universe.

Ibid.

7 Promiscuity in men may cheapen love but sharpen thought. Promiscuity in women is illness, a leakage of identity. The promiscuous woman is self-contaminated and incapable of clear ideas. She has ruptured the ritual integrity of her body.

Ibid.

8 Pregnancy demonstrates the deterministic character of woman's sexuality. Every pregnant woman has body and self taken over by a chthonian* force beyond her control. In the welcome pregnancy, this is a happy sacrifice. But in the unwanted one, initated by rape or misadventure, it is a horror. Such unfortunate women look directly into nature's heart of darkness. For a fetus is a benign tumor, a vampire who steals in order to live. The so-called miracle of birth is nature getting her own way.

Ibid.

*In Greek mythology, of or relating to the gods and spirits of the underworld.; Paglia explains "chthonian" as "my symbol for unregenerate nature."

9 There are no accidents, only nature throwing her weight around. Even the bomb merely releases energy that nature has put there. Nuclear war would be just a spark in the grandeur of space. Nor can radiation "alter" nature: she will absorb it all. After the bomb, nature will pick up the cards we have spilled, shuffle them, and begin her game again.

Ibid.

10 The visual is sorely undervalued in modern scholarship. Art history has attained only a fraction of the conceptual sophistication of literary criticism. . . . Drunk with self-love, criticism has hugely overestimated the centrality of language to Western culture. It has failed to see the electrifying sign language of images.

Ibid.

11 Cats are autocrats of naked self-interest. They are both amoral and immoral, consciously breaking rules. Their "evil" look at such times is no human projection: the cat may be the only animal who savors the perverse or reflects upon it.

Ch. 2, Ibid.

12 Beauty is our weapon against nature; by it we make objects, giving them limit, symmetry, proportion. Beauty halts and freezes the melting flux of nature.

Ibid.

13 How many modern transsexuals are unacknowledged shamans? Perhaps it is to poets they should go for counsel, rather than surgeons.

Ibid.

14 Popular culture is the new Babylon, into which so much art and intellect now flow. It is our imperial sex theater, supreme temple of the Western eye. We live in the age of idols. The pagan past, never dead, flames again in our mystic hierarchies of stardom.

Ch. 4, Ibid.

15 Television is actually closer to reality than anything in books. The madness of TV is the madness of human life.

Harper's (New York) *March 1991*

16 When anything goes, it's women who lose.

Observer (London) *15 December 1991*

17 Jesus was a brilliant Jewish stand-up comedian, a phenomenal improvisor. His parables are great one liners.

Sex, Art, and American Culture 1992

18 If civilization had been left in female hands we would still be living in grass huts.

Introduction, Ibid.

19 Our major universities are now stuck with an army of pedestrian, toadying careerists, Fifties types who wave around Sixties banners to conceal their record of ruthless, beaverlike tunneling to the top.

Ibid.

20 We need a new kind of feminism, one that stresses personal responsibility and is open to art and sex in all their dark, unconsoling mysteries. The feminist of the *fin de siècle* will be bawdy, streetwise, and on-the-spot confrontational, in the prankish Sixties way.

Ibid.

21 My thinking tends to be libertarian. That is, I oppose intrusions of the state into the private realm—as in abortion, sodomy, prostitution, pornography, drug use, or suicide, all of which I would strongly defend as matters of free choice in a representative democracy.

Ibid.

22 Education has become a prisoner of contemporaneity. It is the past, not the dizzy present, that is the best door to the future.

Ibid.

23 We should teach general ethics to both men and women, but sexual relationships themselves must not be policed. Sex, like the city streets, would be risk-free only in totalitarian regimes.

Ibid.

24 The greatest honor that can be paid to the work of art, on its pedestal of ritual display, is to describe it with sensory completeness. We need a science of description. . . . Criticism is ceremonial revivification.

"Sexual Personae: The Cancelled Preface," Ibid.

25 In the theory of gender I began from zero. There is no masculine power or privilege I did not covet. But slowly, step by step, decade by decade, I was forced to acknowledge that even a woman of abnormal will cannot escape her hormonal identity.

Ibid.

26 Modern bodybuilding is ritual, religion, sport, art, and science, awash in Western chemistry and mathematics. Defying nature, it surpasses it.

"Alice in Muscle Land," book review, *Boston Globe* (27 January 1991), Ibid.

27 A woman simply is, but a man must become. Masculinity is risky and elusive. It is achieved by a revolt from woman, and it is confirmed only by other men. . . . Manhood coerced into sensitivity is no manhood at all.

Ibid.

28 It is capitalist America that produced the modern independent woman. Never in history have women had more freedom of choice in regard to dress, behavior, career, and sexual orientation.

"The Big Udder," *Philadelphia Enquirer* (12 May 1991), Ibid.

29 You have to accept the fact that part of the sizzle of sex comes from the danger of sex. You can be overpowered.

Interview in *San Francisco Examiner* (7 July 1991), Ibid.

30 Women's sexual powers are enormous. All cultures have seen it. Men know it. Women know it. The only people who don't know it are feminists. Desensualized, desexualized, neurotic women.

Interview in *SPIN*, "The Rape Debate" (September 1991), Ibid.

31 Pursuit and seduction are the essence of sexuality. It's part of the sizzle.

Interview in *Playboy* (Chicago, October 1991), Ibid.

32 Gay men may seek sex without emotion; lesbians often end up in emotion without sex.

"Homosexuality at the Fin de Siècle," *Esquire* (New York, October 1991), Ibid.

33 Gay men are the guardians of the masculine impulse. To have anonymous sex in a dark alleyway is to pay homage to the dream of male freedom. The unknown stranger is a wandering pagan god. The altar, as in prehistory, is anywhere you kneel.

Ibid.

34 Teenage boys, goaded by their surging hormones . . . run in packs like the primal horde. They have only a brief season of exhilarating liberty between control by their mothers and control by their wives.

Ibid.

35 Madonna* is the true feminist. She exposes the puritanism and suffocating ideology of American feminism, which is stuck in an adolescent whining mode. Madonna has taught young women to be fully female and sexual while still exercising control over their lives.

"Madonna 1: Animality and Artifice," *The New York Times* (14 December 1991), Ibid.

*See 3449.

36 The prostitute is not, as feminists claim, the victim of men but rather their conqueror, an outlaw who controls the sexual channel between nature and culture.

"Elizabeth Taylor:* Hollywood's Pagan Queen," *Penthouse* (New York, March 1992), Ibid.

37 Elizabeth Taylor* is pre-feminist woman. This is the source of her continuing greatness and relevance. She wields the sexual power that feminism cannot explain and has tried to destroy. Through stars like Taylor, we sense the world-disordering impact of legendary women like Delilah,** Salome,*** and Helen of Troy. Feminism has tried to dismiss the femme fatale as a misogynist libel, a hoary cliché. But the femme fatale expresses women's ancient and eternal control of the sexual realm. The specter of the femme fatale stalks all men's relations with women.

Ibid.

*See 2513; **24; ***82.

3160. Sara Paretsky (1947–)

1 I believe in the dull lie—make your story boring enough and no one will question it.

Blood Shot 1988

3161. Susan Partnow (1947–)

1 It is within the families themselves where peace can begin. If families can learn to respect their members, and deal with conflict resolution, that would be the first step to keeping peace on a global level.

"Families For Peace," *Puget Sound Consumers Coop Newsletter Spring 1986*

2 War toys and [children's television] cartoons dehumanize the enemy, really glamorizing war.

The opponent has a legitimate point-of-view, too, and these cartoons don't resolve issues of conflict. There are no treaties, and no solutions in cartoons. There is no consideration given to the opponent.

Quoted in "Locals Seek Alternatives to War Toys" by Denise Fisk-Park, *The North Seattle Press 30 December 1987/12 January 1988*

3 Children learn about the world through their play. When we choose toys and games that encourage creativity, problem solving and learning, and we resolve to keep violence and racial stereotypes out of our homes, we are taking important steps towards a world without hatemongers.

Letter to the editor, The *Seattle Time 3 December 1988*

4 We need to cultivate the skill of sustaining a *calm body* with *alert mind*. Many of us have forgotten, or have never known, how to achieve this balance. We are either awake, alert, and wired for action, or we are relaxed, lethargic, and possibly sleepy.

Ch. 2, *Everyday Speaking for All Occasions*, with Elaine T. Partnow* 1998

*See 2870.

5 Every time you take the opportunity to speak from your deep convictions, you will learn more about yourself.

Ch. 10, Ibid.

3162. Angela Marie Phillips (1947–)

1 . . . children . . . need the intoxicating pleasure of the passionate devotion of someone who thinks they are the bee's knees, the cat's pajamas, or the best thing since sliced bread.

The Trouble with Boys: A Wise and Sympathetic Guide to the Risky Business of Raising Sons 1994

2 Most teenage boys are treated as a general nuisance to be swatted like flies. Men seeing a boy without a father do not think: here is a young man to talk, to listen to, to make friends with. They think: here is a young man who lacks male discipline. They wade in with orders and instructions.

Ibid.

3 The trouble with boys is that they must become men.

Ibid.

3163. Sally Priesand (1947–)

1 Clergy are father figures to many women, and sometimes they are threatened by another woman accomplishing what they see as strictly male goals. But I can see them replacing that feeling with a sense of pride that women can have that role.

Quoted in *Women at Work* by Betty Medsger *1975*

3164. Margo Sappington (1947–)

1 Choreography is more than just making up movements. It's what they express. It's how you pick up a glass, how you feel about something in that particular moment of time. It's . . . not just arbitrary jiggling around.

Quoted in "Choreographer returns to NW . . . " by R.M. Campbell, D1, *Seattle Post-Intelligencer 12 January 1999*

3165. Vera Schwarcz (1947–)

1 . . . Jews . . . had to nurture memory through prolonged exile from the land of Israel. Over time remembrance became its own homeland [and] memory has kept Jews Jewish.

Bridge Across Broken Time: Chinese and Jewish Cultural Memory 1998

2 Far from being liberating, memory seeks to arrest us in our flight toward the present moment. It would be such a relief to be done with the past, or better yet, be headed for the future with a confidence unburdened by the details of sorrows gone by. But memory won't leave us alone.

Ibid.

3166. Jill Severn (1947–)

1 Getting pregnant helps fill the void in a way that nothing else can. In spite of a lot of messages to the contrary, most teenage girls know that parents are the most important people in the world and that to become a mother is to become a VIP.

Being pregnant becomes the source of new status, new power and a new definition of self. It is a rite of passage not just from adolescence to adulthood but from alienation to connectedness. Giving birth is an opportunity to work your own personal miracle. It is a way to prove to yourself and everyone else that you are in league with the divine power of creation.

"Why teens feel pregnancy their only option," *Seattle Post-Intelligencer*, Op-Ed *27 January 1994*

3167. Martha Stewart (1947?–)

1 What follows is the story of the restoration, the renovation, the decoration, and the initial landscaping of the new old house. Each project like this is really a work in progress, an ever-changing environment that is altered by time, by weather, by whim, and by necessity. One learns, one experiments, one is frustrated, and one enjoys the extraordinary variety of problems and solutions posed by such a commitment. The thrill of near completion keeps one going.

Introduction, *Martha Stewart's New Old House 1992*

3168. Lynn Thomas (1947–)

1 There are for starters, grandeur and silence, pure water and clean air. There is also the gift of distance . . . the chance to stand away from relationships and daily ritual . . . and the gift of energy. Wilderness infuses us with its own special brand of energy. I remember lying by the Snake River in Idaho once and becoming aware I could not sleep . . . nature's forces had me in hand. I was engulfed in a dance of ions and atoms. My body was responding to the pervasive pull of the moon.

The Backpacking Woman 1980

3169. Yūko Tsushima (1947–)

1 But the more I became used to his body, the more he became a stranger to me.

"The Marsh," *Unmapped Territories, New Women's Fiction from Japan*, ed. and tr. *1991*

2 I thought that if he, who had a life with his wife and child elsewhere, was a normal human being then I, whose existence was unknown, unseen and unacceptable to his family, had to be a creature without human form, like an evil spirit that inhabits the mountains and rivers.

Ibid.

3 I have no complaints now. I sometimes wonder if I should have some, though. I feel so comfortable. I don't seem to have a desire to change anything.

Ibid.

4 I felt like teasing them and so I spoke up without thinking. It's an important issue, and we ought to give them accurate information, I said. I should've stopped there. But they were nodding their heads, you know. So I went ahead and told them how I would open my legs to let my kid see what's between them. I would let him see the hole and told him that he came out of it, I told them. It's the same hole where men stick their penises and pour in this thing that makes babies. It's the hole that blood comes out of when babies are not made. I said I told my son all these things. They looked at me with shocked faces. Don't you think it's strange? I got a bit scared afterward and felt depressed. I felt I had said something silly again . . .

Ibid.

3170. Roberta Hill Whiteman (1947–)

1 The wagon people
do not think relationship is wealth.

"In the Summer After 'Issue Year' Winter (1873)," St. 2 (1984), *The Woman That I Am, The Literature and Culture of Contemporary Women of Color*, D. Soyini Madison, ed. *1994*

3171. Petra Kelly (1947–1992)

1 We, the generation that faces the next century, can add the . . . solemn injunction "If we don't do the impossible, we shall be faced with the unthinkable."

Quoted in *Vanity Fair* (New York) *January 1993*

3172. Diane Ackerman (1948–)

1 The senses don't just *make sense* of life in bold or subtle acts of clarity, they tear reality apart into vibrant morsels and reassemble them into a meaningful pattern.

Introduction, *A Natural History of the Senses 1990*

2 How sense-luscious the world is. . . . Our senses define the edge of consciousness, and because we are born explorers and questors after the unknown, we spend a lot of our lives pacing that windswept perimeter: . . .

Ibid.

3 Smells coat us, swirl around us, enter our bodies, emanate from us. We live in a constant wash of them. Still, when we try to describe a smell, words fail us like the fabrications they are. Words are small shapes in the gorgeous chaos of the world.

"The Mute Sense," Ibid.

4 Every one of us performs or tacitly approves of small transactions with torture, death, and butchery each day. . . . In our hearts, we know that life loves life. Yet we feast on some of the other life-forms with which we share our planet; we kill to live. Taste is what carries us across that rocky moral terrain, what makes the horror palatable, and the paradox we could not defend by reason melts into a jungle of sweet temptations.

"Taste," Ibid.

5   If you lose your sense of hearing, a crucial thread dissolves and you lose track of life's logic. You become cut off from the daily commerce of the world, as if you were a root buried beneath the soil.

"The Hearing Heart," Ibid.

6   Most of all, the twentieth century will be remembered as the time when we first began to understand what our address was. . . . The fragile euphoria of the complex ecosystem that is Earth, an Earth on which, from space, there are no visible fences, or military zones, or national borders. . . . The view from space is offering us the first chance we evolutionary toddlers have had to cross the cosmic street and stand facing our own home, amazed to see it clearly for the first time.

"Vision," Ibid.

7   Perception is itself a form of grace.

"Postscript," Ibid.

8   Lovers combine their senses, blend their electrical impulses, help sense for one another. When they touch, their bodies double in size. They get under each other's skin, literally and emotionally. During intercourse, a man hides part of himself in a woman, a bit of his body disappears from view, while a woman opens up the internal workings of her body and adds another organ to it, as if it were meant to be there all along. These, in a starched, stiff, dangerous world, are ultimate risks.

Ibid.

9   The great affair, the love affair with life, is to live as variously as possible, to groom one's curiosity like a high-spirited thoroughbred, climb aboard, and gallop over the thick, sun-struck hills every day. Where there is no risk the emotional terrain is flat and unyielding, and, despite all its dimensions, valleys, pinnacles, and detours, life will seem to have none of its magnificent geography, only a length. It began in mystery, and it will end in mystery, but what a savage and beautiful country lies in between.

Ibid.

10   Why do the same images come to mind when people describe their romantic feelings? Custom, culture and tastes vary, but not love itself, not the essence of the emotion.

A Natural History of Love 1994

11   What would life be without play?

Deep Play 1999

12   We evolved through play. Our culture thrives on play. Courtship includes high theater, rituals and ceremonies of play. Ideas are playful reverberations of the mind. Language is playing with words until they can impersonate physical objects and abstract ideas.

Ibid.

13   Challenge, discovery, exploration, novelty, pushing one's limits, losing one's self in the activity—all elements of deep play . . .

Ibid.

3173. Doris Baizley (1948?–)

1   DOT. This isn't a contest I'm in up here, it's every day of my life and I'm so damned good at it I can't stop.

Mrs. California 1986

3174. Laurel Gordon Bellows (1948–)

1   Like Sisyphus . . . women have long been pushing for equal integration into the [law] profession.

Quoted in *Perspectives Winter* 1995

3175. Elizabeth Berg (1948–)

1   I do not believe the army is a good idea for people with regular human hearts.

Durable Goods 1993

2   Remember when we used to pull down our pants to look at our butts in the mirror to see his handprints, see whose was darker?

Ibid.

3   . . . he can only go so far in a good direction. Then something happens. He is all broken apart.

Ibid.

4   . . . he said, "Oh." And the bottom fell out. What I am seeing now is that it was never up to him. He could have been more generous. He could have been more sensitive. But how I felt was not up to him. I only let it be.

Pull of the Moon 1996

3176. Ellen Berman (1948?–)

1   From the time [my daughter] was 18 months old, my life changed radically. Not only because it's different to live day-to-day with someone who's handicapped, but because it's changed my sensibilities in every way. It's changed my perceptions about how people get along in the world, how they look at each other, treat each other—especially how people view other people.

Quoted in "Ellen Berman" *Exposures, Women & Their Art* by Ann Brown and Arlene Raven* 1989

*See 3020.

3177. Julia Blackburn (1948–)

1   Daisy Bates was a liar, of that I am sure, but the extent and the exact details of her lies remain a difficult territory for which no good maps have survived. . . . It would seem that for her the past had no fixed shape or pattern; it was a crystal ball into which she would gaze and she was free to interpret whatever images she saw emerging out of the glimmering refractions of light and colour.

Daisy Bates in the Desert 1994

2   It was like eternity, that place. Something about the transparency of the light and the way the land seemed to merge with the air and the water as if the elements were interchangeable and the one could become the other. But it was also the silence.

Ibid.

3178. Mary Kay Blakely (1948–)

1   . . . political depression . . . a kind of soul-grief, the personal toll exacted from caring people who live in a society where "people first" is merely a slogan.

Red, White, and Oh So Blue: A Memoir of Political Depression 1996

2   Even with all the shocking evidence of what's been going on behind closed doors, myths about the superiority of "the traditional family" continue to be stronger than our grip on reality.

Ibid.

3   With our current politicians in a protracted state of arrested development, salvation depends on the bystanders asserting their power.

Ibid.

4 Treatment for our national depression has to start by recovering our senses.

Ibid.

5 I wanted to take the whole body politic into therapy, sort of lay us all down on the couch and say, "How did we get here? What are the political systems, the media systems, that have put this in place? And how do we then start to change it?"

Ibid.

6 Mothers and wives and lovers were crucial to this war [Vietnam]: we supplied the children, arranged the funerals, made the psychiatric appointments, waited for the MIAs and POWs, cleaned up the wreckage in hamburger joints and living rooms, wept at the waste, waste, waste. Every time I visit the Vietnam Memorial I imagine a bronze figure of the Universal Bystander, a lone woman off to the side, facing the Capitol and shaking her fist.

Ibid.

7 Bertha Pappenheim* chose not to detach from the pain of her childhood—she let it move her. Then she moved the world.

Ibid.

*The real name of Freud's famously pseudonymous patient, Anna O; Freud, the Austrian physician and founder of psychoanalysis (1856–1939), believed she was only fantasizing about incestuous abuse; see 1125.

3179. Catherine Breillat (1948–)

1 It happens under the eye of the camera that the actors are transfigured, like people in love. Because the camera is a way of loving people. The way you look at them transforms them totally. That's why directors sign their films, even though they're not the ones holding the camera, or saying the words. But their vision transforms things so totally that the film belongs to them.

Quoted by Leslie Camhi in "Baring the Intricacies of Desire and Shame," *The New York Times*, Arts & Leisure
14 March 1999

2 I make moral films. But mine is a rather ambiguous, Dostoyevskian morality. I believe that human beings are forever torn between their worst and best impulses. And nothing represents that better than sex—what is most trivial, most obscene, most debased and most beautiful in human beings.

Ibid.

3 I don't make films in order to present a realistic vision of society, but rather to track down the truths we are not supposed to see. It's not realism that interests me, but reality, truth, which is very incorporeal.

Ibid.

3180. Denise Elia Chávez (1948–)

1 ISABEL. When people tell me it's an easy time to be a woman, *me río*! As far as I'm concerned, when you're a woman, no time is easy. And when you're an artist, it's worse. Those born rich suffer as much as those born poor. But I'm not complaining. I might worry, but then I either sing or pray or laugh. *Ríanse*,* as my *gramita* used to say. And love! One of the greatest powers we all possess is the ability to love.

"Novena Narrativas," *Chicana Creativity and Criticism . . . Americas Review* 15 (3–4) 1987
*Laugh.

2 JESUSITA. I'm too busy with God to be worrying about people.

Ibid.

3 MINDA. She tells me, "Don't be afraid of your body, Minda. All women are the same that way. It's beautiful! A gift from God the Mother. The female thing won't kill you, or your mother being dead. All things have to die. It's natural."

Ibid.

4 PAULINE. A freak? What's a freak? A freak is someone who wears a you-know-what in the sixth grade. A freak is someone that has already started their you-know-what in the 6th grade. That's a freak!

Ibid.

3181. Chin Ann-ping (1948–)

1 One cannot say that all China's cultural symbols and cultural assumptions were reduced to ruins. They seem to be endowed with a life of their own.

Children of China 1989

3182. Pearl Cleage (1948–)

1 MISS LEAH. I needed to be someplace big enough for all my sons and all my ghost grandbabies to roam around. Big enough for me to think about all that sweetness they had stole from me and just holler about it as loud as I want to holler.

Flyin' West 1992

2 The theater is for me—a hollering place. A place to talk about our black female lives, defined by our specific black female reality to each other first and then to others of good will who will take the time to listen and to understand.

Speech, "A Hollerin' Place" given at Literary Managers and Dramaturgs of the Americas, *LMDA Review*, Vol. 6. No. 1
June 1994

3 JENNY. No horror stories please! I can't stand it when people tell a pregnant woman horror stories, especially when I'm the pregnant woman!

Hospice (1989), *The Woman That I Am, The Literature and Culture of Contemporary Women of Color,*
D. Soyini Madison, ed. 1994

4 ALICE. Nobody chooses to be alone. You might choose your sanity, or your freedom, or some other wild thing that results in your being alone, but that's the fallout. The unavoidable consequences. Not the choice.

Ibid.

5 JENNY. When she died, the paper said it was a drug overdose, and you were furious. You told me it wasn't the drugs that killed. She died because she had to feel everything. Every time. You said nobody could live that way. Not for long.

Ibid.

6 ALICE. Ordinary people often mistake courage for insanity. It frightens them.

Ibid.

7 ALICE. You want to know what I learned in Paris? Almost twenty years abroad and you know what I learned, Sister? I learned that my name is Alice and not Simone and that the Left Bank is not as far from the West Side of Detroit as I was hoping it would be.

Ibid.

8 As a playwright I don't want to spend all my time fussing at white racism, but as a feminist, I don't want to spend all my time fussing at men . . . The responsibility is to tell the com-

plete truth, and if you do that, the whole question of role models is really moot.

> Quoted in "Making Our History" by Douglas Langworthy, *American Theatre* (New York) *July/August 1996*

3183. Marcelle Clements (1948–)

1   If I had imagined the life I now lead, I doubt I would have wanted it, but it also wouldn't have occurred to me that I could handle it, . . . so I'm surprised and pleased to find that I do.

> (p. 11), *The Improvised Woman: Single Women Reinventing Single Life 1998*

3184. Deborah S. Cohen (1948–)

1   Measured in terms of violence and prejudice, college campuses often look to be altogether nastier places than they were thirty years ago. Even the presence of Women's Studies, Jewish Studies and African American Studies doesn't stop women from being raped, Holocaust revisionists from creeping up to the door of the Hillel, Ku Klux Klan banners from making surreptitious appearances on dormitory walls.

> "Strangers in a strange land," *The Women's Review of Books*, Vol. XII, No. 4 *January 1995*

2   To listen to the critics of political correctness, one might believe the history of women and gender a formidable weed that, once introduced into a curriculum, strangles everything in its vicinity. Quite the opposite, in my limited experience. Depending upon the topic, I feel as if I'm dealing either with a shrinking violet or a hot-house flower.

> "Chronicle of higher education," *The Women's Review of Books*, Vol. XV, No. 5 *February 1998*

3   Must remember to incorporate gory or libidinous material in every lecture to ensure wakefulness.

> Ibid.

3185. Patricia Hill Collins (1948–)

1   Groups unequal in power are correspondingly unequal in their ability to make their standpoint known to themselves and others.

> "Defining Black Feminist Thought," *Black Feminist Thought 1991*

2   Being black encompasses *both* experiencing white domination *and* individual and group valuation of an independent, longstanding Afrocentric consciousness.

> Ibid.

3185.1. Deirdre English (1948–)

Co-author with Barbara Ehrenreich; see 2848:1.

3186. Connie Field (1948–)

1   Many people think that the woman who responded to the call to "do the job he left behind," were suburban housewives who trotted back to their homes after the war. The newsreels would have you believe that too. But for a majority, the women were working before, and had to work after.

> Quoted in "'Rosies' Were There When U.S. Needed Them" by Anita Alverio, *New Directions for Women July/August 1981*

2   . . . making a [documentary] film is not writing a textbook. Someone can have a terrifically wonderful story, but if they can't say it in a way that makes you want to listen, then it's not useful.

> Ibid.

3187. Shakti Gawain (1948–)

1   Creative visualization is magic in the truest and highest meaning of the word. It involves understanding and aligning yourself with the natural principles that govern the workings of our universe, and learning to use these principles in the most conscious and creative way.

> *Creative Visualization 1978*

2   Women have traditionally been in touch with their female energy but they haven't backed her up with their male energy. They have not acknowledged what they know inside. They have always acted as if they were powerless when they are really very powerful. They have gone after external validation (from men especially), rather than internally validating themselves for what they know and who they are.

> Ch. 8, *Living in the Light 1986*

3   Humanity is in an ongoing process of conscious evolution. At this time, we are taking a giant step in consciousness—a great leap in that evolutionary process.

> "Facing the Future," *The Path of Transformation 1993*

4   The overall process of physical healing takes place in our lives as we learn to feel, listen to, and trust our bodies again. Our bodies communicate to us clearly and specifically, if we are willing to listen to them.

> "Healing the Physical Level," Ibid.

5   I am convinced that life in a physical body is meant to be an ecstatic experience.

> Ibid.

3188. Tipper Gore (1948–)

1   Homelessness is a result of deinstitutionalization and urban redevelopment. We haven't provided enough mental-health services, and we allowed gentrification to make a lot of money for some people without paying enough attention to what was happening to others.

> Quoted in "I Know There Is Help" by Colin Greer, *Parade Magazine 11 September 1994*

2   Denial can have a corrosive effect. It takes a toll. It's true when you deny problems inside your family, and it takes a toll on all of us when we deny problems in our society.

> Ibid.

3   Youngsters have to know about the responsibility and rewards of parenting. They have to learn about relationships. Sex education alone is not enough. Parent education is the relationship part.

> Ibid.

4   Our society is suffering from great trauma. As we reach toward the year 2000, we have to be honest about that. We have serious addictions to deal with. Even our consumption often reaches the point of addiction. When a person has to get more and more to feel good, you're reaching the point of illness. We know overconsumption is not good for the planet. It's not good for individual people either.

> Ibid.

3189. Antonia Hernandez (1948–)

1   A court victory is important but just the beginning of the process. It must translate into empowerment. It is the people that have the power to give life to those court victories.

> Remark (1991), Quoted in *The 50 Most Influential Women in American Law* by Dawn Bradley Berry *1996*

3190. Mardy Ireland (1948–)

1 I think it is exciting to decide not to have a baby, and really to try to make room for your own creative self, but I also think it's really hard. I don't think it is easy. I think there are agonies involved. But I also think that there are agonies involved in being a mother, many of which are never spoken. . . .

Reconceiving Women 1993

3191. Sara Keays (1948–)

1 We teach our children to be honourable, to own up when they are wrong, to take responsibility for their mistakes—it is increasingly difficult when the Government won't do that, financially or sexually . . .

"The curse of Keays," The *Times* (London) *14 January 1994*

3192. Ross Shepard Kraemer (1948–)

1 Self-determination for women is only available at the cost of psychic self-destruction, at the cost of the repudiation of the feminine.

Her Share of the Blessings: Women's Religions Among Pagans, Jews, and Christians in the Greco-Roman World 1992

3192.1. Margot Kidder (1948–)

1 Abortion might be killing a life; I don't know. That to me is not an issue. If there is a sin, it is the sin that we adults perpetrate on the children of the earth who truly are innocent and defenseless by bringing those children into the world when they will not be cared for . . . There are all over the globe children starving, being raped, dying, being beaten up because they're unwanted. They suffer abuses from which they never recover . . .

The Choices We Made, Angela Bonavoglia, ed. and intro. *1991*

3193. Hermione Lee (1948–)

1 The life-writer must explore and understand the gap between the outer self . . . and the secret self.

Virginia Woolf 1997

2 Woolf's* story is reformulated by each generation.

Ibid.

*See 1481.

3194. Mizuko Masuda (1948–)

1 A bag of memories is not as sturdy as you might think. A small rip from an insignificant newspaper article quickly becomes large enough to expose the bag's contents.

"Sinking Ground," *Unmapped Territories, New Women's Fiction from Japan*, ed. and tr. *1991*

2 The words she wanted to spit out were stuck inside her, and eventually rusted away.

Ibid.

3 Rather than being shocked at his quick transformation, she was impressed by his toughness.

That energy in men—who pursue wars, create orders and construct neon-filled cities, and who boast of their accomplishments—must come from this toughness . . .

Ibid.

4 As if she believed she could keep reinventing her life, she had allowed herself to make her present life unbearable.

Ibid.

3195. Heather McHugh (1948–)

1 His crime was his belief
the universe does not revolve around
the human being: God is no
fixed point or central government
but rather is poured in waves, through
all things: all things
move.

"What He Thought ," St. 7, *Hinge & Sign: Poems 1968–1993* 1994

2 I loved pencils. I loved their long hexagons. I loved their yellow paint (leaded) and their black lead (unleaded). I loved the little lines on the metal strip that held so fast to the stubborn flesh of the eraser. . . . Given a pencil, I wanted to leave my mark; I necklaced those metal strips with toothprints. For every toothmark, there was a thought. For every thought, a music. That's why I BEGAN writing.

Interview, Amazon.com *July 1998*

3 Poetry is untoward.

Broken English: Poetry and Partiality 1999 (repr.)

4 What's done by heart to day can still
be done to night by mind.

"Ein Ander," *The Father of the Predicaments* 1999

5 Calm comes from burning.
Tall comes from fast.
Comely doesn't come from come.
Person comes from mask.

"Etymological Dirge," St. 1, Ibid.

6 Too volatile, am I? too voluble? too much a word-person?
I blame the soup: I'm a primordially
stirred person.

"Ghazal of the Better-Unbegun," St. 1, Ibid.

3196. Susanna Moore (1948–)

1 She used to say laughingly that she knew the ritual ceremony for wrapping the bones of a chief, but she could not divide fractions. She could steer an outrigger canoe through rough seas, but she had never learned to iron.

Sleeping Beauties 1993

3197. Janet Peery (1948–)

1 I was born in Kansas and lived there forty-five years. I didn't know how much I loved it, though, until I left it. I knew that in this place in order to see its beauty you had to look deep, to look closely, that in its seeming emptiness—the sky itself seems a landmark—there are riches not apparent to the eye accustomed to more flamboyant sights.

Interview, Amazon.com *July 1999*

3198. Emily Prager (1948–)

1 Beauty is the still birth of suffering, every woman knows that.

"A Visit from the Footbinder," *Close Company: Stories of Mothers and Daughters*, Christine Park and Caroline Heaton, eds. *1987*

3199. Melissa Pritchard (1948–)

1 I am having last-minute qualms about being settled, much less married, partly due to a book I am reading on self-esteem.

The Instinct For Bliss 1997

2   All he knows is my soul appears salvageable, and for all my college education, I prove remarkably easy to fool.

                Ibid.

3   Someday she'd figure out how she could let herself have great sex with such a lousy individual.

                "Hallie," *Ibid.*

3200. Nora Räthzel (1948–)

1   A faint suspicion about the degree to which we have subordinated ourselves to structures of domination might, therefore, be the rational source of "irrational" anxieties towards "Ausländer" [foreigners].

    "Harmonious 'Heimat' and Disturbing 'Ausländer'," *Feminsm and Psychology*, Vol. 4, No. 1 *February 1994*

3201. Erika Ritter (1948–)

1   NICK. I don't get it. . . . If I can do you a favour, why not? What is it, you've got your life in ledger columns? "Business." "Romance."

  CHARLIE. That's right. Just don't mix me in with business, that's all. This town is one giant office. Casting done in bars. Contracts ratified on waterbeds. People sucking up to power because it might rub off. Those macrobiotic people had it all wrong. Around here, you are *who* you eat.

        Act I, Sc. 3, *The Automatic Pilot 1978*

3202. Pamela Jean Roach (1948–)

1   If it's been a career woman, who's never been at home, never had children, never been involved in the education world, the PTA, if it's a person who's never been out there with the people, working with them, if they've never had children and stayed home with them, they're in the same position as a man.

      Quoted in "Cleaning house in government . . . " by Carol M. Ostrom, *Seattle Times*, A1–9 *2 August 1992*

3203. Wendy Rose (1948–)

1   I am hungry enough
    to eat myself and you

      "The Indian Women Are Listening: To the Nuke Devils,"
        St. 2, *A Gathering of Spirit*, Beth Brant,* ed. *1984*

  *See 2314.

2   the hope or the lie
    all the gods gave us that
    pain is a vitamin
    to make us grow.

      "Well You Caught Me Unprepared," St. 4, *Ibid.*

3   . . . chained
    to the glamor of speed

               St. 6, *Ibid.*

4   I am still convinced no matter what
    that I am stronger than any storm.
    Every song straining against the shackles
    I creep the ocean floor and don't believe
    anything about me can drown.

               St. 8, *Ibid.*

5   Nothing is old
    about us yet;
    we are still waiting,

    "Walking on the Prayerstick," St. 1, *That's What She Said*,
               Rayna Green,* ed. *1984*

  *See 2284.

6   It's our blood that gives you
    those southwestern skies.

      "Long Division: A Tribal History," *Ibid.*

3204. Friederike Roth (1948–)

1   SHE (raging). Until the day I die I will insist absolutely that shared joy is half-joy. That love sings and swings and makes you uncritical and doesn't deal in accounts paid in advance, like a greedy, shriveled-up old woman.

    Sc. 12, *Piano Plays (Klavierspiele)*, Andrea Weddington, tr. *1980*

3205. Ntozake Shange (1948–)

1   oooooooooooooh the sounds
    sneakin in under age to slug's
    to stare ata real 'artiste'
    & every word outta imamu's mouth waz gospel
    & if Jesus couldnt play a horn like shepp
    waznt no need for colored folks to bear no cross at all

      "now i love somebody more than," *for colored girls who have considered suicide/ when the rainbow is enuf 1977*

2   TOUSSAINT L'OVERTURE*
    became my secret lover at the age of 8
    i entertained him in my bedroom
    widda flashlight under my covers

    way inta the night
    we discussed strategies
    how to remove white girls from my hopscotch games
    & etc.

             "toussaint," *Ibid.*

  *Leader of Haitian independence and emancipator of black slaves (c. 1743–1803).

3   i found god in myself
    & i loved her/i loved her fiercely

          "a laying on of hands," *Ibid.*

4   I am gonna write poems til i die and when i
    have gotten outta this body i am gonna hang
    round in the wind and knock over everybody
    who got their feet on the ground.

        "advice," *Nappy Edges 1979*

5   NARRATOR. [I'm] fixing you up good & colored & you gonna
    be colored all yr life & you gonna love it
    being colored
    all yr life
    colored & love it love it
    bin colored.

             spell #7 1979

6   NARRATOR. All things are possible but ain't no colored magician in his right mind gonna make you white.

             Ibid.

7   Where there is a woman there is magic. If there is a moon falling from her mouth, she is a woman who knows her magic, who can share or not share her powers. A woman with a moon falling from her mouth, roses between her legs and tiaras of Spanish moss, this woman is a consort of the spirits.

      Sassafras, Cypress and Indigo 1982

8   I know we got to fight the white people and be better than them, Gina. It's just I'm so tired of them and I feel so much better when I'm with the colored.

          Betsey Brown 1985

9 I am a war correspondent after all . . . because I'm involved in a war of cultural and esthetic aggression. The front lines aren't always what you think they are.*

> Interview with Stella Dong, *Publishers Weekly* 3 May 1985

*One of Shange's youthful goals was to be a war correspondent.

10 livin dreams'll make ya crazy
livin dreams'll lead ya to the
end/s of yrself

> "Five" (1972), *The Woman That I Am, The Literature and Culture of Contemporary Women of Color,* D. Soyini Madison, ed. 1994

11 . . . poetry is enuf/ eisa/ it brings us to our knees

& when we look up from our puddles of sweat
the world's still right there & the children still have bruises.

> Letter to Eisa Davis, *Letters of Intent: Women Cross the Generations to Talk about Family, Work, Sex, Love, and the Future of Feminism,* Anna Bondoc and Meg Daly, eds. 1999

3206. Leslie Marmon Silko (1948–)

1 The gussucks* did not understand the story; they could not see the way it must be told, year after year as the old man had done, without lapse or silence . . .

"It began a long time ago," she intoned steadily . . . she did not pause or hesitate; she went on with the story, and she never stopped.

> "Storyteller," *Puerto del Sol* (Las Cruces, New Mexico) Fall 1975

*The whites.

2 She shook her head. "I will not change the story, not even to escape this place and go home. I intended that he die. The story must be told as it is." The attorney exhaled loudly; his eyes looked tired. "Tell her that she could not have killed him that way. He was a white man. He ran after her without a parka or mittens. She could not have planned that."

> Ibid.

3 She went because she was tired of being alone with the old woman whose body had been stiffening for as long as the girl could remember. Her knees and knuckles were swollen grotesquely and the pain had squeezed the brown skin of her face tight against the bones; it left her eyes hard like river stone. The girl asked once, what it was that did this to her body, and the old woman had raised up from sewing a sealskin boot, and stared at her.

"The joints," the old woman said in a low voice, whispering like wind across the roof, "the joints are swollen with anger."

> II, Ibid.

4 It was warm and the dogs were alert. When it got cold again, the dogs would lie curled and still, too drowsy from the cold to bark or pull at the chains. She laughed loudly because it made them howl and snarl. Once the old man had seen her tease the dogs, and he shook his head. "So that's the kind of woman you are," he said, "in the wintertime the two of us are no different from those dogs. We wait in the cold for someone to bring us a few dry fish."

> III, Ibid.

5 I grew up with storytelling. My earliest memories are of my grandmother telling me stories while she watered the morning-glories in her yard. Her stories were about incidents from long ago, incidents which occurred before she was born but which she told as certainly as if she had been there. The chanting or telling of ancient stories to effect certain cures or protect from illness and harm have always been part of the Pueblo's curing ceremonies. I feel the power that the stories still have to bring us together, especially when there is loss and grief.

> Author's note, *Ceremony* 1977

6 I will tell you something about stories,
They aren't just entertainment.
don't be fooled.
They are all we have, you see,
all we have to fight off
illness and death.

> Ibid.

7 Stolen rivers and mountains
the stolen land will eat their hearts
and jerk their mouths from the Mother.
The people will starve.

> (p. 132), Ibid.

8 What I have is a story. . . . laugh if you want to
but as I tell the story
it will begin to happen.

> (pp. 132–138), Ibid.

9 . . . storytelling for Indians is like a natural resource.

> *The Third Woman: Minority Women Writers of the United States* (p. 118), Dexter Fisher, ed. 1980

10 It will take a long time, but the story must be told. There must not be any lies.

> Quoted by Trinh T. Minha-ha* in "Grandma's Story" (1989), *The Woman That I Am, The Literature and Culture of Contemporary Women of Color,* D. Soyini Madison, ed. 1994

*See 3346.

11 Corn cobs and husks, the rinds and stalks and animal bones were not regarded by the ancient people as filth or garbage. The remains were merely resting at a midpoint in their journey back to dust. Human remains are not so different. They should rest with the bones and rinds where they all may benefit living creatures—small rodents and insects—until their return is completed.

> "Landscape, History, and the Pueblo Imagination," Ibid.

12 Implicit in the Pueblo oral tradition was the awareness that loyalties, grudges, and kinship must always influence the narrator's choices as she emphasizes to listeners this is the way *she* has always heard the story told. The ancient Pueblo people sought a communal truth, not an absolute. For them this truth lived somewhere within the web of differing versions, disputes over minor points, outright contradictions tangling with old feuds and village rivalries.

> Ibid.

13 Visibility is zero, the scream of the wind blots out all sound. Quickly the hunter realizes he is being stalked. Hunted by all the forces, by all the elements of the sky and earth around him. When at last the hunter's own muscles spasm and cause the jade knife to fall and shatter the ice, the hunter's death in the embrace of the giant ice blue bear is the foretelling of the world's end. When humans have blasted and burned the last bit of life from the earth, an immeasurable freezing will descend with a darkness that obliterates the sun.

> Ibid.

3207. Nancy Springer (1948–)

1 "I hate being a woman." He had surprised bottom-line truth out of her, and it shocked her so that she burst out to defend it, "Well, of course I do! Every book I read the whole time I was growing up, men did the important things and women brought drinks on trays."

Larque on the Wing 1994

3208. Bonnie Tiburzi (1948–)

1 Flying jets is exhilarating. . . . The airplane is . . . a world above a world—and you are in it . . . looking out and down at miracles.

Takeoff! 1984

3209. Carol Williams (1948–)

1 [My garden is] like a beach at which the tide goes in and out. Sometimes the tide of weeds is out, and the plants stand clear and lovely. Sometimes the tide is in, bringing its wrack of pig-weed, nettle, mallows, and wild roses. This is lovely in another way.

Bringing a Garden to Life 1998

2 [Gardening is] not just science but art, and not just law but lore.

Ibid.

3 . . . flowers engage the heart's affections and unlock the deepest associations.

Ibid.

4 . . . with each cut one is conversing with the rose, hearing what it has to say about where it wants to go this year. The dialogue reopens, usually a few weeks later, when the rose presents its first strong buds.

Ibid.

5 An hour before work with the dew on the ground and green leaves translucent in the long rays of dawn, half an hour while a baby naps in the afternoon, twenty minutes after dinner as colors fade to dusk. Such brief interludes can be all that is needed for there to be something to pick for supper, month after month. They can redeem the whole day.

Ibid.

3210. Christine Wiltz (1948–)

1 He was saying to her, It's been done to us too, now we understand, now we know what's like to be a victim, to be connected to death by violence . . .

Glass House 1994

2 When somebody's that afraid, I guess they be pretty scary themselves.

Ibid.

3211. Christa McAuliffe (1948–1986)

1 What are we doing here? We're reaching for the stars.
Remark upon entering astronaut program,*
Quoted in *Time* (New York)
10 February 1986
*Killed in explosion of spacecraft *Challenger*, 28 January 1986.

2 I touch the future. I teach.

Speech (August 1985), Ibid.

3212. Dorothy Allison (1949–)

1 . . . get out there and do things, girl. Make people nervous and make your old aunt glad."

Bastard Out of Carolina 1992

2 . . . the boy could turn like whiskey in a bad barrel.

Ibid.

3 I want to be able to write so powerfully I can break the heart of the world and heal it . . . remake it.
Talking About Sex, Class & Literature 1993

4 Two or three things I know for sure . . . and one of them is what it means to have no loved version of your life but the one you make.

Ibid.

5 Behind the story I tell is the one I don't . . . Behind the story you hear is the one I wish I could make you hear.

Ibid.

6 Change, when it comes, cracks everything open.
Two or Three Things I Know for Sure 1995

7 "After a while it's like a skin of oil on the water. If you look at it from the side, it would go down and down, layers and layers. All the stories you've ever told. All the pictures you've ever seen. We can put in everything. Hypertext."

Ibid.

8 Way way down three or four corridors, around a turn, I hit a wall. My story was on this wall. I stood in front of my wall. . . . words were peeling across the wall, and every word was a brick. I touched one. . . . The brick fell away and a window opened. . . .

Ibid.

9 Death changes everything.

Cavedweller 1998

10 "My daddy always said that white folks are simply crazy. He also said that black folks are crazy too, but we aren't simple."

Ibid.

3213. Aida Alvarez (1949–)

1 I realized that that was what power was about. If you stood up for your rights, you had moral authority. People actually respect you when you stand up for what you think is right.
Quoted in "She's Determined That Everyone Gets A Chance," *Parade Magazine 22 November 1998*

2 Everything you do has a price. Whatever you accomplish on one side, you have given something else up.

Ibid.

3 Affirmative action is about giving people who have demonstrated that they're successful an opportunity to continue to succeed.

Ibid.

3214. Victoria Bond (1949–)

1 The conductor traditionally has been anything but a mother figure. The conductor is much more like a general than a mother or a teacher. It's a kind of enforced leadership, the kind of leadership more likely to be expected of men than women. A woman conductor, because of those traditions, must rely

completely on being able to transmit authority purely on the grounds of her musical ability.

Quoted in *Women at Work* by Betty Medsger *1975*

3215. Paula DiPerna (1949–)

1   I do not believe meat-eating to be an environmental threat on a par with ozone depletion, nor that violence toward women is no better or worse than violence toward animals, even though there may be a common source.

"Who can save the earth?," *The Women's Review of Books*, Vol. XI, No. 1 *October 1993*

3216. Nancy E. Dowd (1949–)

1   There has been an amazing continuation of the common law tradition that an unmarried putative father owes no legal duty to [parent] his child and in effect is a "stranger" to the child.

In Defense of Single Mothers 1997

3217. Slavenka Drakulić (1949–)

1   They [refugees] have nothing to do but wait. When I ask them what they're waiting for, they are not certain. Three of the men are waiting for a foreign country to accept them as immigrants; the others do not know what they are waiting for. One woman waits for a sign that her husband is alive, another just cries.

"Women Hide Behind A Wall of Silence," *The Nation* (New York) *1 March 1993*

2   Rape is an instrument of war, a very efficient weapon for demoralization and humiliation.

Ibid.

3   . . . the last taboo; the sexual mother.
Marble Skin (1987), Greg Mosse, tr. (from French) *1994*

4   The man's touch weaves bonds between us.

Ibid.

3218. Elana Dykewomon (1949–)

1   "Sometimes it just goes that way. You start walking around in your mother's big shoes and the next time you look down, your feet are all swollen and sore, the shoes barely fit. Then it's too late to say you were just pretending, am I right?

Beyond the Pale 1997

3219. Leslie Feinberg (1949–)

1   My parents worried that I was a lightning rod that would attract a dangerous storm.

Transgender Warriors 1996

2   Why was I subject to legal harassment and arrest at all? Why was I being punished for the way I walked or dressed, or who I loved? Who wrote the laws used to harass us, and why? . . . Who decided what was normal in the first place? . . . Have we always existed? Have we always been so hated? Have we always fought back?

Ibid.

3   I don't see why I should have to legally align my sex with my gender expression, especially when this policy needs to be fought. Why am I forced to check off an *F* or an *M* on these documents in the first place? For identification? Both a driver's license and a passport include photographs! . . . Why is the categorization of sex a legal question at all?

Ibid.

3220. Mary Catherine Gordon (1949–)

1   He is my husband, I say slowly, swallowing a new exotic food. Does this mean everything or nothing? I stand with him in an ancient relationship, in a ruined age, listening beyond my understanding to the warning voices, to the promise of my own substantial heart.

"Now I Am Married," *Temporary Shelter 1987*

2   I know that I must live my life now knowing it is not my own. I can keep them from so little; it must be the shape of my life to keep them at least from the danger I could bring them.

"Safe," Ibid.

3221. Jessica Hagedorn (1949–)

1   NARRATOR. As he often told his friend, the painter Frisquito: "I can no longer tolerate contradiction. This country is full of contradiction. If I stay, I shall go crazy." (*Pause*) Frisquito told Bongbong: "There's nothing wrong with being crazy. Being crazy is good for art. The thing to do is to get comfortable with it."

Tenement Lover: no palm trees/in new york city 1981

2   In all my writing there are always these characters who have a sense of displacement, a sense of being in self-exile, belonging nowhere—or anywhere. I think these themes are the human story. When it comes down to it, it's all about finding shelter, finding your identity.

Between Worlds, Contemporary Asian-American Plays, Misha Berson, ed. *1990*

3   Wherever she looks in any of her mirrors it is always night and she is always beautiful.

Dogeaters 1990

4   hey girl, how long you been here?
did you come with yr daddy in 1959 on a second-class boat
cryin' all the while cuz you didn't want to leave the barrio
"Motown/Smokey Robinson," St. 1 (1983), *The Woman That I Am, The Literature and Culture of Contemporary Women of Color*, D. Soyini Madison, ed. *1994*

3222. Gayl Jones (1949–)

1   "My great-grandmama told my grandmama the part she lived through that my grandmama didn't live through and my mama told me what they all lived through and we were supposed to pass it down like that from generation to generation so we'd never forget."

Corregidora 1975

2   It was as if the words were helping her, as if the words repeated again and again could be a substitute for memory, were somehow more than the memory.

Ibid.

3   "I'm leaving evidence. And you got to leave evidence too. And your children got to leave evidence. And when it come time to hold up the evidence, we got to have evidence to hold up. That's why they burned all the papers, so there wouldn't be no evidence to hold up against them."

Ibid.

4   "Am got a few of them cactus plants along Dairy Mart Road, though they ain't the archetypal cactus. I think it's Dairy Mart Road and some of that poverty grass. I guess it called poverty grass 'cause it the Southwest, you know. I'm going to have to find out the names of these grasses and plants and trees so's I

can tell y'all what they is. I guess that's what I likes about the Southwest, though, the landscape. Well, I likes the people that I likes (the Perfectability Baptist Church would want me to say more about the likability of peoples and us commandments to love), but when you gets to the Southwest it got it own distinctive landscape."

Mosquito 1999

5 [Nadine imagines] . . . a true jazz story, where the peoples that listen can just enter the story and start telling it theyselves while they's reading.

Ibid.

3223. Jamaica Kincaid (1949–)

1 And what do I regret? Surely not that I stand in the knowledge of the presence of death. For knowledge is a good thing; you have said that. What I regret is that in the face of death and all that it is and all that it shall be I stand powerless, that in the face of death my will, to which everything I have ever known bends, stands as if it were nothing more than a string caught in the early-morning wind.

"At the Bottom of the River," At the Bottom of
the River 1984

2 And what are my fears? What large cows! When I see them coming, shall I run and hide face down in the gutter? Are they really cows? Can I stand in a field of tall grass and see nothing for miles and miles? On the other hand, the sky, which is big and blue as always, has its limits.

"Wingless," Ibid.

3 Wash the white clothes on Monday and put them on the stone heap; wash the color clothes on Tuesday and put them on the clothesline to dry; . . . soak your little clothes right after you take them off; . . . always eat your food in such a way that it won't turn someone else's stomach; on Sundays try to walk like a lady, and not like the slut you are so bent on becoming; . . . this is how you smile to someone you don't like too much; this is how you smile to someone you don't like at all; this is how you smile to someone you like completely; . . . this is how to make a good medicine for a cold; this is how to make a good medicine to throw away a child before it even becomes a child; . . . this is how to bully a man; this is how a man bullies you; this is how to love a man, and if this doesn't work there are other ways, and if they don't work don't feel too bad about giving up . . .

"Girl," Ibid.

4 Have you ever wondered why it is that all we [West Indians] seemed to have learned from you [the British] is how to corrupt our society and how to be tyrants? . . . You came. You took things that were not yours, and you did not even, for appearance's sake, ask first.

A Small Place 1988

5 If I had to draw a picture of my future then, it would have been surrounded by black, blacker, blackest.

Lucy 1990

6 This account of my life has been an account of my mother's life as much as it has been an account of mine . . . In me is the voice I never heard, the face I never saw, the being I came from.

The Autobiography of My Mother 1996

7 My mother died at the moment I was born, and so for my whole life there was nothing standing between myself and eternity.

Ibid.

8 She was very pleased to be who she was, and by that she meant she was pleased to be of the English people, and that made sense, because it is among the first tools you need to transgress against another human being—to be very pleased with who you are.

Ibid.

9 Everyone, everywhere, succumbs eventually to the overwhelming stillness that is death.

Ibid.

10 Even now, years later, I am still surprised by [my mother's denial of ever having made a mistake in raising us], because I spend a good part of my day on my knees in apology to my own children.

My Brother 1997

11 . . . [his life, so] like the bud that sets but, instead of opening into a flower, turns brown and falls off at your feet.

Ibid.

12 All that remained of him was lying in a plastic bag of good quality. His hair was uncombed, his face was unshaven, his eyes were wide-open and his mouth was wide-open, too, and the open eyes and the open mouth made it seem as if he was looking at something in the far distance, something horrifying coming toward him, and that he was screaming, the sound of the scream silent now (but it had never been heard, I would have been told so, it had never been heard, this scream), and this scream seemed to have no break in it, no pause for an intake of breath; this scream only came out in one exhalation, trailing off into eternity, or just trailing off to somewhere I do not know, or just trailing off into nothing.

(p. 179), Ibid.

13 And now I started a new series of betrayals of people and things I would have sworn only minutes before to die for.

Annie John 1997

14 We were politeness and kindness and love and laughter.

Ibid.

3224. Alicia Bay Laurel (1949–)

1 When we depend less on industrially produced consumer goods, we can live in quiet places. Our bodies become vigorous; we discover the serenity of living with the rhythms of the earth. We cease oppressing one another.

Living on the Earth 1971

2 Let's all go out into the sunshine, take off our clothes, dance and sing and make love and get enlightened.

Quoted in Contemporary Authors 1974

3225. Deepa Mehta (1949–)

1 Like a good wife, I had followed my husband* to his home in Canada, and we started making movies. I had unconsciously imbibed the idea that divorce made me less of a woman. I had failed to make the adjustments required of a woman—even if the relationship was unhealthy. It took me two years to get a divorce, to get out of a rotten marriage.

Quoted in "Playing with Fire" by Bapsi Sidhwa, Ms.
(New York) November/December 1997

*She was married to Canadian film producer Paul Saltzman for fourteen years.

2 Whether it's an interracial marriage, which religion to follow, or which sex to be with, when people make choices that do not harm anybody else, their choice should be respected.

Ibid.

3   When *Fire* was banned in Kenya, they said, "It will give our women ideas." Of course we have ideas. We aren't puppets.

   Ibid.

4   For me, what you don't see is far more erotic than what you see.

   Ibid.

3226. Jacqueline Moscou (1949–)

1   You come back to your roots. As I approach my 50th year, I'm increasingly interested in the African American tradition of spirituality. And believe me, that was not the way I was raised. I was raised on the picket line.

   Quoted in "'Black Nativity'* draws on tradition of spirituality" by Joe Adcock, *Seattle Post-Intelligencer*, What's Happening *11 December 1998*

   *A staged retelling of the New Testament Christmas story from an African-American perspective, originally created by poet, essayist, novelist and playwright, Langston Hughes (1902–1967).

3227. Holly Near (1949–)

1   Get off me baby, get off and leave me alone
   I'm lonely when you're gone but I'm lonelier when you're home. . . .

   "Get Off Me Baby" *1973*

2   Well if you think travelling three is a drag
   Pack up loner
   I've got my own bag full of dreams for this little child of wonder
   and you can only stay if you start to understand. . . .

   "Started Out Fine" *1973*

3   Can we be like drops of water falling on the stone
   Splashing, breaking, dispersing in air
   Weaker than the stone by far
   But be aware that as time goes by
   The rock will wear away
   And the water comes again

   "The Rock Will Wear Away," St. 3, with Meg Christian* *1976*

   *See 2496.

4   You were being Isadora,* I was being you
   Did I know I'd grow to say:
   You've got me flying, I'm flying . . .
   You inspired a sister song . . .

   "You've Got Me Flying" *1976*

   *I— Duncan; see 1264.

5   Why do we kill people who kill people to show that killing people is wrong?

   "Foolish Notion" *1980*

6   First he'll want to talk about it
   Then he'll want to fight
   Then he'll want to make love to me all night
   my man's been laid off got, trouble, got
      trouble . . .

   "Laid Off" *n.d.*

3228. Christine Dorothy Overall (1949–)

1   Prostitution is a commercial enterprise.

   "What's Wrong with Prostitution?" *Signs: A Journal of Women in Culture and Society*, Vol. 17 *Summer 1992*

2   In a culture where women's sexuality is used to sell, and women learn that sex is our primary asset, sex work is not and cannot be just a private business transaction, an exchange of benefits between equals, or an egalitarian trade.

   Ibid.

3229. Katha Pollitt (1949–)

1   Opponents often argue as if the widespread use of abortion were a modern innovation, the consequence of some aspect of contemporary life of which they disapprove (feminism, promiscuity, consumerism, Godlessness, permissiveness, individualism), and as if making it illegal would make it go away.

   "Abortion in American History," *The Atlantic Monthly* (Boston) *May 1977*

2   In one of the many curious twists that mark the history of abortion, the campaign to criminalize it was waged by the same professional group that, a century later, would play an important role in legalization: physicians.

   Ibid.

3   Legalizing abortion was a public-health triumph that for pregnant women ranked with the advent of antisepsis and antibiotics.*

   Ibid.

   *Decriminalized in 1973 by the U.S. Supreme Court in its landmark ruling in *Roe v. Wade*, which allows medical abortion; see Sarah Weddington, 3075.

4   No one asks that other oppressed groups win their freedom by claiming to be extra-good. And no other oppressed group thinks it must make such a claim in order to be accommodated fully and across the board by society. For blacks and other racial minorities, it is enough to want to earn a living, exercise one's talents, get a fair hearing in the public forum. Only for women is simple justice an insufficient argument. It is as though women don't really believe they are entitled to full citizenship unless they can make a special claim to virtue. Why isn't being human enough?

   "Are Women Morally Superior to Men?" *The Nation* (New York) *28 December 1992*

5   The central question Chodorow* poses—Why are women the primary caregivers of children?—could not even be asked before the advent of modern birth control, and can be answered without resorting to psychology. Historically, women have taken care of children because high fertility and lack of other options left most of them no choice. Those rich enough to avoid personally raising their children often did . . .

   Ibid.

   *Nancy Chodorow, feminist theorist; see 2992.

6   By arguing that the traditional qualities, tasks and ways of life of women are as important, valuable and serious as those of men (if not more so), Gilligan* and others let women feel that nothing needs to change except the social valuation accorded to what they are already doing. It's a rationale for the status quo, which is why men like it, and a burst of grateful applause, which is why women like it. Men keep the power, but since power is bad, so much the worse for them.

   Ibid.

   *Carol G—, feminist theorist; see 2628.

7   Motherhood is open to any woman who can have a baby or adopt one. *Not* to be a mother is a decision; becoming one requires merely that a woman accede, perhaps only for as long as it takes to get pregnant, to thousands of years of cumulative

social pressure. After that, she's on her own; she can soothe her child's nightmare or let him cry in the dark. Nothing intrinsic to child-raising will tell her what is the better choice for the child (each has been the favored practice at different times).

Ibid.

8 Even the loony right, which thinks the President* murdered Vincent Foster to cover up the Satanic ritual child abuse taking place in Hillary's secret love nest, will concede if pressed that the man is reasonably well informed.

"Subject to Debate," *The Nation* (New York)
18 December 1995

*Reference to William Jefferson Clinton (1946–), 42nd president of the United States (1993–2001); his wife, Hillary Rodham Clinton (1947– ; see 3139); their friend and colleague Vince Foster.

9 Ordinary Americans understand perfectly well that politicians are paid by corporations and other organized interests to do their bidding; that's why most people don't vote. But even when liberal crusaders argue the same, bemoaning the domination of politics by big money and big lobbies, they shrink from the logical conclusion, which is that their bright ideas and clever suggestions, not to mention their frequent summonses to morality and meaningfulness, are destined for the circular file.

Ibid.

10 . . . lack of information rarely explains why people, and not just Presidents, fail to do the right thing.

Ibid.

11 . . . [fetal rights] posits a world in which women will be held accountable, on sketchy or no evidence, for birth defects. . . . It imposes responsibilities without giving women the wherewithal to fulfill them, and places upon women alone duties that belong to both parents and to the community.

"Fetal Rights, Women's Wrongs," *Reasonable Creatures:*
Essays on Women and Feminism 1995

12 When did sisterhood become mother-daughterhood?

Letter to Emily Gordon, *Women Cross Generations to Talk*
About Family, Work, Sex, Love and the Future of Feminism,
Anna Bondoc and Meg Daly, eds. *1999*

13 This whole notion that writing is all about mentoring and networking and each generation smoothing the way for the next like party hacks down at the clubhouse is the wrong idea. Writing is about writing.

Ibid.

3230. Sheila Radford-Hill (1949–)

1 Black women now realize that part of the problem within the movement was our insistence that white women do for/with us what we must do for/with ourselves: namely, frame our own social action around our own agenda for change. . . . Critical to this discussion is the right to organize on one's own behalf.

"Considering Feminism as model for Social Change"
(p. 160), Quoted in *Drylongso, A Self-Portrait of*
Black America, Teresa de Lauretis, ed. *1986*

3231. Barbara Ras (1949–)

1 The landscape of one's homeland becomes so deeply ingrained in one's heart and soul and mind.

Quoted in "New Bedford native earns poetry award" by
Robert Lovinger, *The Standard-Times* (New Bedford,
Connecticut) *17 October 1998*

2 If it's true, wrong action can lead to salvation, then no need to fix anything . . .

"Margin of Error," *Bite Every Sorrow 1998*

3 Days the wind uses them to write on air, a score in 3-D, arpeggios, tremolos, paradiddles, every appendage waving, hither, there, until night when they settle down

"The Sadness of Insects," Ibid.

4 You can't bring back the dead,
but you can have the words forgive and forget hold hands
as if they meant to spend a lifetime together.

"You Can't Have It All," Ibid.

5 You can have the touch of a single eleven-year-old finger
on your cheek, waking you at one a.m. to say the hamster is back.

Ibid.

3232. Michele B. Roberts (1949–)

1 . . . she struggled for years to get the hang of how she was supposed to be holy.

Impossible Saints 1998

3233. Stephanie Salter (1949?–)

1 Once in awhile, human beings still need to feel as though they have gotten away with something they shouldn't have.

"Day game sinfully pleasant . . . ," *Seattle Post-Intelligencer,*
Op-Ed, A11 *27 May 1993*

3234. Georgia Sassen (1949–)

1 . . . [I'd gained] a heightened perception of the "other side" of competitive success, that is, the great emotional costs at which success achieved through competition is gained—an understanding which, though confused, indicates some underlying sense that something is rotten in the state in which success is defined as having better grades than everyone else.

"Success Anxiety in Women: A Constructivist Interpretation
of Its Sources and Its Significance," *Harvard Educational*
Review, No. 50 *1980*

3235. Jane Smiley (1949–)

1 The one thing . . . maybe no family could tolerate was things coming out into the open.

A Thousand Acres 1991

2 With preference came point of view; with point of view, personality; with personality, uniqueness; with uniqueness, grief.

Moo 1995

3 Pundits (of course there were none of these, since Earl's very life was largely a secret) might have doubted Earl's capacity for sincere feeling, given a hog's naturally sociable disposition combined with an unusually isolated upbringing that could have given him sociopathic tendencies, but actually, his isolation deepened Earl's pleasure in his and Bob's relationship.

Ibid.

4 Thus, I sat across from my husband. . .wondering whether he was the closed, dull, stiffly upright, and self-righteous person part of me seemed to see, or the pained, lonely, and worried person another part of me seemed to see.

The All-True Travels and Adventures of
Lidie Newton 1998

5   In K.T. [Kansas Territory], it was often the case that every version of every story was equally true and equally false.

Ibid.

6   The prolonged frigid weather made even the prospect of being hanged, shot, dismembered, killed or otherwise cleared out rather an abstract one. The possibility of being frozen to death was distinctly more likely.

Ibid.

7   [Lidie pasted her home with] . . . leaves of *The Liberator* and some other papers that Thomas had brought with him from the United States. This, he said, would serve the threefold purpose of advertising our views to our visitors, reminding ourselves of the arguments to be made in the cause, and keeping out the wind. Every leaf, according to the new laws of Kansas Territory, was treasonable.

Ibid.

3236. Marianna Torgovnick (1949–)

1   The white man's burden—but also his fate and glory—is the individuated self.

"Men," *Primitive Passions: Men, Women, and the Quest for Ecstasy 1997*

2   . . . the mystic's way seems to require mortification of the flesh. . . . Is it merely provocative, then—or only fair—to read some contemporary piercings as parables of transcendence too?

"Movements and Trends," Ibid.

3   Bad white people usurp the Indians' physical space; but good whites move into their mental and spiritual space.

Ibid.

4   . . . the most startling feature of O'Keeffe's* [art] is the absence of people.

"Women," Ibid.

*Georgia O—; see 1561.

3237. Dubravka Ugresic (1949–)

1   I am 45. I am learning an alphabet. I am dealing with the first letter N, as in Nobody.

"ABCs of Exile," *The Suitcase: Refugee Voices from Bosnia and Croatia*, Julie Mertus, Jasmina Tesanovic, Habiba Metikos, and Rada Boric, eds. *1997*

3238. Theadora Van Runkle (1949?–)

1   Death is very sophisticated. It's like a Noel Coward comedy. You light a cigarette and wait for it in the library.

Quoted in "People You Should Know" by Mary Reinholz, *Viva April 1974*

2   Just at a time when women are becoming free and buoyant, and developing sexually and in a feeling way, they're dressing to look like huge, tottering objects, like courtesans during the Renaissance period.

Ibid.

3239. Linda Susan Vance (1949–)

1   . . . the domination of women and the domination of nature go hand in hand.

"Ecofeminism and the Politics of Reality," *Ecofeminism: Women, Animals, Nature*, Greta Gaard, ed. *1993*

2   Save the rainforest in case valuable medicinal plants lie undiscovered there. Preserve wilderness as part of our "national heritage." Conserve resources for future generations. This is the rhetoric of property and progeny: the two things that matter most to a privileged few.

Ibid.

3240. Stephanie M. Wildman (1949–)

1   A fundamental tension exists whenever analogies are used to compare other oppressions to racism. The comparison perpetuates racism/ white supremacy, but is also a necessary tool to teach about the oppression being compared. Any analogy to race must be used ethically and with care. We must always consider whether we are perpetuating or deconstructing societal racism at the conclusion of any analogy of discussion.

"Obscuring the Importance of Race," with Trina Grillo, *Privilege Revealed: How Invisible Preferences Undermines America 1996*

2   Meeting needs and keeping people happy are tasks women do outside the workplace, in the home. When women arrive in the workplace, the gendered expectation is that they will still perform that caretaking role.

"Privilege in the Workplace: The Missing Element in Antidiscrimination Law," Ibid.

3241. Judith Resnik (1949–1986)

1   I think something is only dangerous if you are not prepared for it or if you don't have control over it or if you can't think through how to get yourself out of a problem.

Quoted in *Time* (New York) *10 February 1986*

3242. Nora Astorga (1949–1989)

1   I want it to be known that I participated in the operation of bringing to justice the bloody henchman.*

Quoted in "Nora and the Dog," *Time* (New York) *2 April 1984*

*Reference to assassination of General Reynaldo Perez Varga (1978).

3243. María Suárez Toro (1948–)

1   Doing feminist radio is having one ear covered, in order to listen to what's inside, and the other ear open, to listen to other.

Women's Voices on FIRE 2000

2   I realized if we don't have human rights we can't have education. Education is human rights in itself.

Quoted in "Fire in Her Belly" by Judith Colp Rubin, *WIN (Women's International Net Magazine),* Issue 32 (Part A) www.winmagazine.org *May 2000*

3   [Radio is the] venue closest to women because it's cheap and women are the poorest of the poor and there's also an intimacy about it. There's also a better chance for women to be heard for what they have to say, and not by how they look. They can also listen to the radio and do 20 things at the same time, and women are the busiest of the busy.

Ibid.

4   Feminism is about women speaking out on all issues for everybody to hear. It's also to tell the men that not only do women have a right to be half of the voices heard, but when men don't have the right to listen to women's voices a right is being taken

away from them. Because then they only get the perspective of half of the world.

Ibid.

3244. Joan Borysenko (195-?–)

1 The work of healing is in peeling away the barriers of fear and past conditioning that keep us unaware of our true nature of wholeness and love.

Introduction, *Minding the Body, Mending the Mind 1987*

2 It's only through our relations with others that we develop the outlook of hardiness and come to believe in our own capabilities and inner goodness.

Ch. 1, Ibid.

3245. Kate Braverman (1950–)

1 Except for a small group of organically damaged individuals, doing nothing at all indefinitely is quite rare. For one thing, fate and external circumstances usually don't leave us completely alone. There are always some new demands from that place out there. Sometimes the demands can be quite minimal, like getting yourself together enough to pick up your unemployment check.

"Dropping What," *Dropping In, Putting It All Back Together 1973*

2 We've been raised by books which told our parents when we were supposed to move, sit, walk, read, stop hitting the kid next door and start making out instead. We grew up with them watching to see if we were on the right page at the right age.

"Splitting," Ibid.

3 To be one woman, truly, wholly, is to be all women. Tend one garden and you will birth worlds.

Palm Latitudes 1988

4 Los Angeles is a new cosmopolitan refugee city for the world. It's a city of confluences.

Quoted in "From the Tropic of L.A." by Cristina Garcia, *Time* (New York) *20 November 1989*

5 California is looked at the way Italy used to be viewed in England. It's sexual and dangerous. Something could happen. A person could change.

Ibid.

6 I find women as writers and as characters are operating within narrow confines. They inherit a kind of ghetto of the soul.

Ibid.

7 I have to protect myself from the toxicity of this culture.

Ibid.

3246. Katie Geneva Cannon (1950–)

1 . . . throughout the history of the United States, the interrelationship of white supremacy and male superiority has characterized the Black woman's reality as a situation of struggle—a struggle to survive in two contradictory worlds simultaneously, one white, privileged, and oppressive, the other black, exploited, and oppressed.

"The Emergence of a Black Feminist Consciousness" (pp. 30–40), *Feminist Interpretations of the Bible*, Letty M. Russell, ed. *1985*

3247. Anne Regina Carson (1950–)

1 It was Sappho* who first called eros "bittersweet." No one who has been in love disputes her. What does the word mean?

Eros and the Bittersweet 1986

*See 46.

2 Whenever I visit my mother
I feel I am turning into Emily Brontë. . . .

"The Glass Essay," *Glass, Irony and God 1995*

3 I can hear little clicks inside my dream.
Night drips its silver tap
down the back.

Ibid.

4 I will do anything to avoid boredom . . .

"Short Talks," *Plainwater: Essays and Poetry 1996*

5 The librarians thought him
a talented boy with a shadow side.

Autobiography of Red: A Novel in Verse 1998

3248. Jan Clausen (1950–)

1 It is a powerful act, this absolute disowning of someone with whom one has shared a bed and so much of consciousness over many years.

Apples and Oranges: My Journey to Sexual Orientation 1999

2 Branded with a scarlet 'H' for 'het,' I'd henceforth be denounced as a lapsed woman lover, pitied as a tragic mulatto of sex.

Ibid.

3 What's got to stop is the rigging of [sexual] history to make the either/or look permanent and universal.

Ibid.

3249. Michelle Cliff (1946?–)

1 When did we (the light-skinned middle-class Jamaicans) take over for them [the whites] as oppressors? I need to see when and how this happened. When what should have been reality was overtaken by what was surely unreality. When the house nigger became master.

"If I Could Write This In Fire, I Would Write This In Fire," *The Land of Look Behind 1985*

3250. Mildred Clingerman (fl. 1950s)

1 Nobody really looks at a bartender. . . . Even the bar philosophers (the dreariest customers of all) prefer to study their own faces in the back-bar mirror. And however they accept their reflected images, whether shudderingly or with secret love, it is to this aloof image that they impart their whiskey-wisdom, not to the bartender.

Stair Trick 1952

2 She faced him as if he were Judgement and she standing up pleading for mankind.

Ibid.

3251. Tsitsi Dangarembga (1958?–)

1 They played the new rumba that, as popular music will, pointed unsystematic fingers at the conditions of the times: 'I'll beat you up if you keep asking for your money,' 'Father, I am

jobless, give me money for roora,' 'My love, why have taken a second wife?' There was swaying of hips, stamping of feet to the pulse of these social facts.

Ch. 1, *Nervous Conditions* 1988

2 Words like 'always' and 'never' were meaningless to my father, who thought in absolutes and whose mind consequently made great leaps in antagonistic directions when it leapt at all.

Ch. 2, *Ibid.*

3 "Money is a difficult thing to keep, especially when it is scarce."

Ibid.

4 The victimization, I saw, was universal. It didn't depend on poverty, on lack of education or on tradition. It didn't depend on any of the things I had thought it depended on. Men took it everywhere with them. Even heroes like Babamukuru did it. And that was the problem. . . . Femaleness as opposed and inferior to maleness.

Ch. 6, *Ibid.*

3252. Doris Davenport (195-?-)

1 it is not your business,
how i came and i can't stand
nosey people but
this is your business.

i am not going back.
so here i am.
but what
i am, really,
ain't your business.

"To the 'Majority' from A 'Minority'," Sts. 2 & 3,
Eat Thunder and Drink Rain 1982

3253. Jane Eaglen (195-?-)

1 To be honest, making the voice seamless throughout its entire range takes a lot of physical strength. Not stamina, but sheer physical strength. The strength to use your muscles, and the diaphragm and the rest of the body in the right way—never the throat. There must never be an inkling of tension in the throat. I very much use all my body to sing. I use my legs, bottom, everything.

Quoted in *Diva, The New Generation: The Sopranos and Mezzos of the Decade Discuss Their Roles* by Helena Matheopoulous 1998

3254. Laura Esquivel (1950-)

1 " . . . remember that the lazy man and the stingy man end up walking their road twice."

Ch. 1, *Like Water for Chocolate*, Carol Christensen and Thomas Christensen, trs. (1992) 1989

2 The trouble with crying over an onion is that once the chopping gets you started and the tears begin to well up, the next thing you know you just can't stop.

Ibid.

3 Naked as she was, with her loosened hair falling to her waist, luminous, glowing with energy, she might have been an angel and devil in one woman. The delicacy of her face, the perfection of her pure virginal body contrasted with the passion, the lust, that leapt from her eyes, from her every pore. These things, and the sexual desire Juan had contained for so long

while he was fighting in the mountains, made for a spectacular encounter.

Ch. 3, *Ibid.*

4 "My grandmother had a very interesting theory; she said that each of us is born with a box of matches inside us but we can't strike them all by ourselves . . . the oxygen, for example, would come from the breath of the person you love; the candle could be any kind of food, music, caress, word, or sound that engenders the explosion that lights one of the matches. . . . Each person has to discover what will set off those explosions in order to live, since the combustion that occurs when one of them is ignited is what nourishes the soul."

Ch. 6, *Ibid.*

5 When the talk turns to eating, a subject of the greatest importance, only fools and sick men don't give it the attention it deserves.

Ch. 8, *Ibid.*

6 "The truth! The truth! Look, Tita, the simple truth is that the truth does not exist; it all depends on a person's point of view."

Ch. 10, *Ibid.*

3255. Laura Farabough (195-?-)

1 A strong woman artist who is not afraid of herself, her sexuality, passion, symbols, language, who is fearless, willing to take any and all risks, often produces work that is staggeringly beautiful and at the same time frightening, dangerous, something to be reckoned with.

"Laura Farabough," *Interviews with Contemporary Women Playwrights*, Kathleen Betsko* and Rachel Koenig 1987
*See 2739.

3256. Lilian Faschinger (1950-)

1 It's a matter of you listening quietly without interrupting me. . . . If you're constantly interrupted you never get past the babble stage, a frustrating condition that results in terrible anxiety, making the one who is thinking or talking, respectively, highly unpredictable.

Magdalena the Sinner (1995), Edna McCown, tr. 1997

2 . . . the majority of Austrian Catholic men and women are of the opinion that a woman should accept the suffering, the foreordained unhappiness that nature has allotted her, with masochistic joy. . . . Should women who want to sing and dance remain in Catholic Austria, they probably will end in the madhouse, in prison, or in suicide. For women who want to sing and dance, Catholic Austria is the most unsuitable country on earth.

(p. 85), *Ibid.*

3 Her act made me think of St. George slaying the dragon. She had crossed the line, of course, drawn for a Christian, a Catholic woman, but . . . in doing so she had saved others from sure death, just as St. George had saved many others from a terrible end by slaying the dragon. . . . What a woman!

(pp. 184–185), *Ibid.*

3257. Kathy E. Ferguson (1950-)

1 Feminism does not question the efficiency or effectiveness of business practices but the moral and political legitimacy of these practices: not how best to use the power that business

accords certain groups of people (owners and managers, for example) but *why* these people are thus empowered.

"Postmodernism, Feminism, and Organizational Ethics: Letting Difference Be," *Women's Studies and Business Ethics*, Andrea Larson and R. Edward Freeman, eds. *1997*

2 The field of business has a tendency to co-opt its critics by absorbing them into its orthodoxies.

Ibid.

3 We make up our claims to truth . . . then we forget we made them up, then we forget that we forgot.

Ibid.

3258. Arden Fingerhut (195-?-)

1 It's a cellular, biological reaction. We understand images because of who we are physically.

Quoted in "The Facts of Light" by Arnold Aronson, *American Theatre* (New York) *January 1986*

3259. Diana Gabaldon (1950?-)

1 . . . what do you do if you know the future?

Outlander 1991

3260. Cheri Gaulke (195-?-)

1 Working collaboratively is not only part of who I am personally, but it's part of my politics. It's what I believe in—that people are equal, that everyone has something to contribute.

Quoted in "Cheri Gaulke," *Exposures, Women & Their Art* by Ann Brown and Arlene Raven* *1989*

*See 3020.

2 I think our sexuality is very earth-oriented and we can't really feel that connection with the earth if our feet are lifted up on high heels, if we're off balance.

Ibid.

3261. Patricia Gonzalez (195-?-)

1 [Art is] a journey of self-discovery. It's finding out what it is that you're truly interested in, what really moves you, really touches you, so you can focus more on those things.

Quoted in "Patricia Gonzalez," *Exposures, Women & Their Art* by Ann Brown and Arlene Raven* *1989*

*See 3020.

2 Everything that happens in your life somehow filters through into your work. If you're being honest, it's bound to. That's the essence of creativity: Things flow through you, are transformed, reformed and then come out of you.

Ibid.

3262. Madden Harkness (195-?-)

1 The art in Europe overwhelmed me; it disrupted my inner chords, my relationship with life.

Quoted in "Madden Harkness," *Exposures, Women & Their Art* by Ann Brown and Arlene Raven* *1989*

2 I owe a real debt to my [high school] art teacher Mrs. Peterkin. I still keep in touch with her. The courses I took in college afterward didn't compare to what she taught and how she taught it. She really encouraged me, which was one of the first times I felt personal encouragement.

Ibid.

*See 3020.

3263. Carolyn R. Jabs (1950-)

1 If you keep doing little things about it, your dream, which was amorphous at first, will begin to take shape, like a statue emerging from a chunk of marble.

Quoted in "How to Kick a Dream Into Action," *Self* (May 1986), Ch. 8, *Working from the Heart* by Jacqueline McMakin with Sonya Dyer *1993*

3264. Kathryn Jacobi (195-?-)

1 On of the most important functions of the artist at this point in history is to create symbols of continuance. Religious messages have become unsatisfactory for most of us, leaving us with a void in our experience of life continuing . . .

Quoted in "Kathryn Jacobi," *Exposures, Women & Their Art* by Ann Brown and Arlene Raven* *1989*

*See 3020.

2 The reason I like painting babies is the poignancy of the particular moment. Two weeks later, they're a different entity. You see the march of aging so much more keenly telescoped during that time than at any other phase in a person's life.

Ibid.

3 My people's history has been blown to smithereens. I could not and cannot come to terms with that idea. I am appalled that holocaust is a possibility of human behavior.

Ibid.

4 I do have an awareness of the fragility of life, an awareness of the incredible sweetness of every moment of existing in good health and good condition. I take nothing for granted. I try to capture what comes alive while making a painting, so it will live for somebody else; live and tell the truth.

Ibid.

3265. Wendy Kaminer (1950?-)

1 People find victimhood appealing because they believe it absolves them of their own misdeeds; it imbues them with a sense of righteousness.

It's All the Rage 1995

2 Murder is not only an offense against an individual; it's an offense against the social order.

Ibid.

3 Debates about crime control are rarely sensible. They're ruled by politics and fear and the mindless exchange of attitudes that dominates the worst talk shows, where people never exchange ideas.

Ibid.

4 If Lorena Bobbitt* was innocent of intentionally dismembering her husband, because she was in the grip of an irresistible impulse, then a large majority of people in prison should probably go free.

Ibid.

*American woman tried for cutting off her husband's penis.

5 If the Menendez brothers are innocent because they were abused, so are many inmates on death row. Death row is filled with people who have worse childhoods than Erik and Lyle Menendez,* in addition to worse lawyers.

Ibid.

*American teenagers tried in Los Angeles for the murder of both their parents.

3266. Marjorie Karmel (fl. 1950s)

1 It is a great pity that a man should stand back, helpless and inadequate, *de trop*, while his wife alone knows the profound experience of the birth of the child they have created together.

Ch. 3, *Thank You, Dr. Lamaze** 1959

*French physician who developed drugless, natural method of childbirth (1890–1957).

2 Who ever said that doctors are truthful or even intelligent? You're getting a lot if they know their profession. Don't ask any more from them. They're only human after all—which is to say, you can't expect much.

Ch. 7, Ibid.

3 "One-way first-name calling always means inequality—witness servants, children and dogs."

Ibid.

3267. Marie Wilson (1948–)

1 We have to change the climate in order to get Americans thinking seriously about a woman candidate. If you are a democracy, you want an opportunity for everyone to participate, and women are the untapped national resource at this level of government. It's about wanting a democracy to mirror women's voices and visions.

Quoted in "Women Who Could Be President" by Jane Ciabattari, *Parade Magazine 7 February 1999*

3268. Sara Louise Maitland (1950–)

1 Once dualistic thought gained ascendancy within Christianity, women were increasingly associated with nature and with the body, while men identified themselves happily with mind and spirit.

Sex and God: Some Varieties of Women's Religious Experience, Linda Hurcombe, ed. *1987*

2 Hagiography [the study of saints] is littered with individuals of both sexes who seem to have organized their whole lives around the greed for violence and death as the way of proving their commitment.

"Passionate Prayer: Masochistic Images in Women's Experience," Ibid.

3269. Catherine Malfitano (1948–)

1 She's not a victim [Madame Butterfly*] at all, she *chooses* her destiny. It's a very strong choice, and the way things turn out there is unfortunatey no escape for her.

Quoted in *Diva, The New Generation: The Sopranos and Mezzos of the Decade Discuss Their Roles* by Helena Matheopoulous *1998*

*Eponymous character of opera by Giacomo Puccini, Italian composer (1858–1924).

3270. Catherine Risingflame Moirai (195-?–)

1 Every morning touch the earth.
Every night praise the worms.
Listen.

"How to Make a Garden in the City," St. 2, *Fominary*, Vol. 12, No. 1 *1982*

3271. Patty Murray (1950–)

1 History would not look very kindly at a moralistic Senate that went so far as to say that having an affair and trying to keep your family and friends and the country from the embarrassment of it was an impeachable offense.

"Murray urges trial dismissal . . . ," *Seattle Times*, A20 *24 January 1999*

3272. Gloria Naylor (1950–)

1 "They love each other like you'd love a man or a man would love you—I guess."

"But I've loved some women deeper than I ever loved any man," Mattie was pondering. "And there been some women who loved me more and did more for me than any man ever did."

"Yeah." Etta thought for a moment. "I can second that but it's still different, Mattie. I can't exactly put my finger on it, but . . . "

"Maybe it's not so different," Mattie said, almost to herself. "Maybe that's why some women get so riled up about it, 'cause they know deep down it's not so different after all." She looked at Etta. "It kinda gives you a funny feeling when you think about it that way, though."

"Yeah, it does," Etta said, unable to meet Mattie's eyes.

The Women of Brewster Place 1983

2 "They wouldn't understand—not in Detroit, not on Brewster Place, not anywhere! And as long as they own the whole damn world, it's them and us, Sister—them and us. And that spells different!"

Ibid.

3 Lorraine lay pushed up against the wall on the cold ground with her eyes staring straight up into the sky. When the sun began to warm the air and the horizon brightened, she still lay there, her mouth crammed with paper bag, her dress pushed up under her breasts, her bloody pantyhose hanging from her thighs. She would have stayed there forever and have simply died from starvation or exposure if nothing around her had moved.

Ibid.

4 Like his father, he saw where the future of Wayne County—the future of America—was heading. It was going to be white: white money backing wars for white power because the very earth was white—look at it—white gold, white silver, white coal running white railroads and steamships, white oil fueling white automotives. Under the earth—across the earth—and one day, over the earth. Yes, the very sky would be white. He didn't know exactly how, but it was the only place left to go. And when they got there, they weren't taking anyone black with them—and why should they?

"Linden Hills," *Linden Hills 1985*

5 "If my brothers saw me writing poems, they'd call me a queer and then it'd be all over school and I'd have to fight my way home every day. You know, most guys think you're a sissy if you like this stuff."

"December 19th," Ibid.

6 Geometry forgotten, they sat in Lester's room for hours, reciting to each other the lines that helped to harness the chaos and confusions in their fourteen-year-old worlds. Bloody noses had made them friends, but giving sound to the bruised places in their hearts made them brothers.

Ibid.

7 Willie had left school after the ninth grade. He said there was really nothing more they could teach him. He knew how to read and write and reason. And from here on in, it was all pro-

paganda. He was not free to read the books that were important to him, not to some rusty-minded teacher. And if you wanted to write about life, you had to go where life was, among the people.

Ibid.

8   Xavier Donnell was falling in love with a black woman. It was one of the most terrifying experiences of his life.

"December 21st," Ibid.

9   Maxwell had discovered long ago that he doubled the odds of finishing first if he didn't carry the weight of that milligram of pigment in his skin. There was no feasible reason why it should have slowed him down since in mass it weighed so little, and even that was consistently distributed over his six-foot frame. But the handicap had been set centuries before it was his turn at the gate. And since he knew no tract of ground but the planet earth and no competition but the human race, he had to use the rules as written and find a way to turn a consequence into an inconsequence in his struggle to reach the finish line as a man.

Ibid.

10   "She's got this real funny idea about a diet: you don't get fat if no one sees you eating."

"December 22nd," Ibid.

11   "You there, Sister?"

Mama Day 1988

3273. Peggy Noonan (1950–)

1   TV gives everyone an image, but radio gives birth to a million images in a million brains.

Ch. 2, *What I Saw at the Revolution 1990*

2   Great speeches have always had great soundbites. The problem now is that the young technicians who put together speeches are paying attention only to the soundbite, not to the text as a whole, not realizing that all great soundbites happen by accident, which is to say, all great soundbites are yielded up inevitably, as part of the natural expression of the text. They are part of the tapestry, they aren't a little flower somebody sewed on.

Ch. 5, Ibid.

3   A speech is poetry: cadence, rhythm, imagery, sweep! A speech reminds us that words, like children, have the power to make dance the dullest beanbag of a heart.

Ibid.

4   I love eulogies. They are the most moving kind of speech because they attempt to pluck meaning from the fog, and on short order, when the emotions are still ragged and raw and susceptible to leaps.

Ch. 13, Ibid.

5   Most people aren't appreciated enough, and the bravest things we do in our lives are usually known only to ourselves. No one throws ticker tape on the man who chose to be faithful to his wife, on the lawyer who didn't take the drug money, or the daughter who held her tongue again and again. All this anonymous heroism.

Ibid.

6   The battle for the mind of Ronald Reagan was like the trench warfare of World War I: never have so many fought so hard for such barren terrain.*

Ch. 14, Ibid.

*From 1984–1988, Noonan worked as a special assistant and speechwriter to Reagan, American politician and actor (1911–), 40th president of the United States (1981–1989).

7   Beware the politically obsessed. They are often bright and interesting, but they have something missing in their natures; there is a hole, an empty place, and they use politics to fill it up. It leaves them somehow misshapen.

"Another Epilogue," Ibid.

8   Don't fall in love with politicians, they're all a disappointment. They can't help it, they just are.

Ibid.

3274. Younhee Paik (195–?–)

1   I like to think about the source or power of the universe. Both art and life are derived from the power which reigns in the universe. I believe that power is truth. All beauty comes from the truth that has always been. I don't create art or create beauty, I just discover what has always been there.

Quoted in "Younhee Paik," *Exposures, Women & Their Art*
by Ann Brown and Arlene Raven* 1989

*See 3020.

2   My art is not fun or entertaining. There is beauty but also violence in this vast space and time we occupy. We are such a tiny part of the vastness, but I try to understand what is the power and beauty that has existed from the beginning of time—and my part in it.

Ibid.

3275. Kathy Peiss (1950?–)

1   Over the decades, mothers and daughters have taught each other about cosmetics, cliques have formed around looks, women have shared their beauty secrets and, in the process, created intimacy. Not only tools of deception and illusion, then, these little jars tell a rich history of women's ambition, pleasure, and community.

Introduction, *Hope in a Jar, The Making of America's Beauty Culture 1998*

2   Nineteenth-century travelers, missionaries, anthropologists, and scientists habitually viewed beauty as a function of race. Nodding in the direction of relativism—that various cultures perceive comeliness differently—they nevertheless proclaimed the superiority of white racial beauty.

Ch. 1, Ibid.

3   Women were using makeup to mark any number of differences, asserting worldliness against insularity and sexual desire against chastity. Moving into public life, they staked a claim to public attention, demanded that others look. This was not a fashion dictated by Parisian or other authorities, but a new mode of feminine self-presentation, a tiny yet resonant sign of a larger cultural contest over women's identity.

Ch. 2, Ibid.

4   The fashionable ideal has changed many times in recent decades, but the 1920s marked the moment when mass-produced images distinctly and powerfully began to influence female self-conceptions and beauty rituals.

Ch. 5, Ibid.

5   Makeup promised personal transformation, a pledge that sounded deeply in American culture—from conversion experiences and temperance oaths to the appeals of medicine men

and faith healers. Beauty culturists had proclaimed the mutual transformation of external appearance and inner well-being.

Ibid.

6 The commercialization of men's appearance was often explained, paradoxically, by men's need for a sharp look in corporate America *and* by a new hedonism that rejected the conformity demanded by the business world.

Ch. 8, Ibid.

7 When women put on a face, they continue to express ideas of naturalness and artifice, authenticity and deception, propriety and danger, modernity and tradition. Making up remains a gesture bound to perceptions of self and body, the intimate and the social—a gesture rooted in women's everyday lives.

Ibid.

3276. Gigliola Pierobon (1950?–)

1 It is horrible to listen to men in black togas (in court) having discussions about your morals, your cystitis, your feelings, your womb, the way you straddled your legs.

"Gazette News: Abortion in Italy," *Ms.* (New York) *October 1973*

3277. Aurelia Potor (fl. 1950s)

1 Middle-aged rabbits don't have a paunch, do have their own teeth and haven't lost their romantic appeal.

Quoted in *The New York Times* 22 September 1956

3278. Marilyn Quayle (1950–)

1 I'm a great devil's advocate. I can pierce holes through anything.

Quoted in "The Best Days of their Wives" by Michael Duffy, *Time* (New York) *24 August 1992*

2 I was brought up and firmly believe that one must have compassion for all people. You have to love everyone. But you don't have to love what they do.

Quoted in "Being Tested Made us Stronger" by James Zumwalt, *Parade Magazine 5 June 1994*

3279. Sapphire (1950–)

1 "Precious what's on your mind?" I say, "What?" She say, "What you was thinking just then." I go to open my mouf. She say, "Don't say it, *write* it." I say, "I can't." She say, "Don't say that." She say, "Do what I say, write what you was thinking."

Push 1996

2 I don't know what "realism" means but I do know what REALITY is and it's a mutherfucker, lemme tell you.

Ibid.

3 Ms Rain say
walk on
go into the poem
the HEART of it
beating
like
a clock
a virus
tick
tock.

Ibid.

3280. Maurya Simon (1950–)

1 My daughters recede into my future like stars shining above my life; my parents rekindle subterranean lamps, their hearts live coals.

"Forty-fifth Birthday," St. 2, *Calyx*, Vol. 17, No. 3 *1998*

2 Brooklyn delivers itself over to winter like a novice taking the veil.

"Snow," 4. New York, Ibid.

3 *Seizure World*, your son calls it, this place of palm-treed gentility, Southern California's oasis for grey-haired denizens, for the Living.

5. Laguna Hills, Ibid.

3281. Anna Deavere Smith (1950–)

1 MRS. YOUNG-SOON HAN (former liquor store owner). At leasteh they got something back, you know. Just let's forget Korean victims or other victims who are destroyed by them. They have fought for their rights over two centuries and I have a lot of sympathy and understanding for them. Because of their effort and sacrificing, other minorities, like Hispanics or Asians, maybe we have to suffer more by mainstream. You know that's why I understand, and then I like to be part of their 'joyment. But . . . That's why I had mixed feeling as soon as I heard the verdict. I wish I could live together with eh Blacks, but after the riots there were too much differences.*

"Swallowing the Bitterness," *Twilight, Los Angeles, 1992 1994*

*Refers to the civil insurrection in Los Angeles after the announcement of the verdict in the Rodney King trial (1992).

2 The spirit of acting is the travel from the self to the other.

Article, Quoted in *Newsday October 1994*

3 My work is both political and personal. I'm trying to resolve this problem of strangeness and closeness in our world that's getting closer and closer. I'm interested in telling every side of the story.

"The Beauty of Black Art," *Time* (New York) *10 October 1994*

3282. Julia Alvarez (1950–)

1 All my childhood I had dressed like an American, eaten American foods and befriended American children. I had gone to an American school and spent most of the day speaking and reading English. At night, my prayers were full of blond hair and blue eyes and snow. All my childhood I had longed for this moment of arrival. And here I was, an American girl, coming home at last.

Comment to Brujula Compass, *American Scholar Winter 1987*

2 That is the most passionate part of the process of writing. It is only possible to discover it as it is done: upon writing the ideas a direction is found. A voice is discovered: the rhythm, the characters, but one cannot know beforehand.

Ibid.

3 The radio is all static—like the sound of the crunching metal of a car; the faint, blurry voice on the airwaves her own, trapped inside a wreck, calling for help. In English or Spanish? she wonders. That poet she met at Lucinda's party the night before argued that no matter how much of it one lost, in the

midst of some profound emotion, one would revert to one's mother tongue.

How the Garcia Girls Lost their Accents 1991

4 I believe stories have this power—they enter us, they transport us, they change things inside us, so invisibly, so minutely, that sometimes we're not even aware that we come out of a great book as a different person from the person we were when we began reading it.

Convocation speech, Appalachian State University 1994?

5 I am a Dominican, hyphen, American. As a fiction writer, I find that the most exciting things happen in the realm of that hyphen—the place where two worlds collide or blend together.

"Las Mariposas" by Ian Stevens, *Nations* (552–556)
7 November 1994

6 I write to find out what I'm thinking. I write to find out who I am. I write to understand things.

"The Politics of Fiction" by Marny Requa,
www.fronteramag.com/issue5/Alvarez/ *3 November 1997*

3283. Arianna Stassinopoulos (1950–)

1 It would be futile to attempt to fit women into a masculine pattern of attitudes, skills and abilities and disastrous to force them to suppress their specifically female characteristics and abilities by keeping up the pretense that there are no differences between the sexes.

"The Natural Woman," *The Female Woman 1973*

2 Our current obsession with creativity is the result of our current striving for immortality in an era when most people no longer believe in an after-life.

"The Working Woman," Ibid.

3 Liberation is an evershifting horizon, a total ideology that can never fulfill its promises. . . . It has the therapeutic quality of providing emotionally charged rituals of solidarity in hatred—it is the amphetamine of its believers.

"The Liberated Woman? . . . And Her Liberators," Ibid.

4 Emancipation means equal status for different roles . . . Liberation . . . is a demand for the abolition of wife and mother, the dissolution of the family . . .

"The Family Woman," Ibid.

5 Whether we regard the Women's Liberation movement as a serious threat, a passing convulsion, or a fashionable idiocy, it is a movement that mounts an attack on practically everything that women value today and introduces the language and sentiments of political confrontation into the area of personal relationships.

"The Emancipated Woman," Ibid.

6 Not only is it harder to be a man, it is also harder to become one.

"The Male Man," Ibid.

3284. Vicky Stifter (195-?–)

1 I understand the logic behind, "Let's build the gate, shut the doors, keep them [immigrants] out and we'll all be better off." . . . If we build the gate and we consume resources from within our gate, that's one thing. But the reality is that . . . we're consuming resources from all over the world. We're consuming gas, coffee, food that's grown in the countries people are com-

ing from. They're not able to survive because their land has been turned into places for exporting bananas. So they come here because they need to feed their children. . . . To say, "We can come to your countries to get your resources, but you can't come here," I think it's immoral. I think it goes to the very soul of who we are as a nation.

"Growth: enough already," *Seattle Times*, A17
22 November 1998

3285. Bibiana Suarez (195-?–)

1 I felt Chicago would be a good intermediary point, good point of departure, a place where Eastern and Western mentalities meet. But the first year was a shock. I was terrified of the winter and the first autumn was horribly depressing for me. The lack of light really affects me. In retrospect, I think that's why I'm interested in light in my drawings, in chiaroscuro, the high contrast of light and dark. I create an atmosphere of intensely lit space in my drawings to make up for the lack of light in my city.

Quoted in "Bibiana Suarez," *Exposures, Women & Their Art* by Ann Brown and Arlene Raven* 1989
*See 3020.

3286. Linda Vallejo (195-?–)

1 The sweat ceremony is like an art–making space. To make art, you have to be open, giving, honest with yourself. You get that same feeling in a good sweat ceremony. The feeling spreads out from your heart. You can open up and say whatever you want with total confidence and trust.

Quoted in "Linda Vallejo," *Exposures, Women & Their Art* by Ann Brown and Arlene Raven* 1989
*See 3020.

2 In indigenous traditions, if you receive a vision—one of those spectacular moments of understanding—you have to share it with others through music, dance, poetry or art in order for it to work its wonder.

Ibid.

3 I make art like some people make cookies. I'm always compulsively busy. I know that I can't quit.

Ibid.

3287. Sherezada Vicioso (1948–)

1 If you stay in New York too long, you begin to get worn down by it.

"An Oral History," Nina M. Scott, tr., *Breaking Boundaries: Latina Writing and Critical Readings*, Asuncion Horno-Delgado, Eliana Ortega, Nina M. Scott, and Nancy Saporta Strernbach, eds. *1989*

2 By dint of having lived in the United States, I am considered a "liberated woman," which means that the men feel they have a green light to harass me sexually while the women distrust me.

Ibid.

3288. Wendy Wasserstein (1950–)

1 RITA. The only problem with menstruation for men is that some sensitive schmuck could write about it for the Village Voice, and become the new expert on women's inner life.

Uncommon Women and Others 1978

2 LEILAH. Sometimes it's difficult having sympathy with everyone's point of view.

Ibid.

3 PAUL STUART. Now you girls have careers and *you* want a wife.
Isn't It Romantic 1984

4 LILLIAN. You tell me who has to leave the office when the kid bumps his head or slips on a milk carton.
Ibid.

5 The real reason for comedy is to hide the pain.
"Wendy Wasserstein," *Interviews with Contemporary Women Playwrights*, Kathleen Betsko* and Rachel Koenig *1987*
*See 2739.

6 The worse the boyfriend, the more stunning your American Express bill.
Bachelor Girls 1990

7 In the forties emulating an ideal woman meant bobbing your hair like Betty Grable's.* In the eighties, because of Jessica Lange,** women have to get a Pulitzer Prize-winning actor-playwright to fall in love with them, have a child by one of the world's great dancers, be nominated for two Academy Awards, and enjoy doing the laundry alone on a farm.
Ibid.
*American musical film actor (1916–1973). **American film actor (1949–).

8 I knew my friend Patti was a big-time Hollywood agent the first time I saw her dial a telephone with a pencil.
Ibid.

9 GEOFFREY. You don't know what it's like to have absolutely no idea who you are!
The Sisters Rosensweig 1992

3289. Jody Williams (1950–)

1 This work came out of the field. These were the NGOs,* the de-miners, the people putting limbs on the victims, who were trying to deal with the problem in the field and recognized pretty quickly that that wasn't enough. If we didn't go to the root of the problem, if we didn't remove the weapon itself, we would never succeed. So we came together and formed the International Campaign to Ban Landmines**, which was formally launched in 1992.
Address, "A Global Ban On Landmines," Treaty Signing Conference (Ottawa, Canada) *3 December 1997*
*Non-governmental organizations. **ICBL was awarded the Nobel Prize for peace in 1998.

2 It wasn't until the voice of civil society was raised to such a high degree that governments began to listen, that change began to move the world, with lightning and unexpected speed.
Ibid.

3 Had governments not begun to say the scary words "We need to ban the weapon," it would not have happened. And gradually, they did take steps, and gradually the base was built to make the governments of the world believe that they actually could step outside of the normal diplomatic channels and do something different.
Ibid.

4 It's sort of easy to make a challenge. It's very hard to put the full fate of your government behind the challenge and make it happen. That's real leadership.
Ibid.

5 They challenged the world to work openly with civil society, to perhaps show the world that we no longer had to see each other as adversaries, that actually governments and civil society should dialogue, that we actually are part of the same world community and should work together for change. Thank you, Canada, for that leadership.
Ibid.

6 But here we have 125 governments recognizing that the tide of history has changed, recognizing that together we are a super power. It's a new definition of super power: It is not one; it is everybody. You are all part of being a super power!
Ibid.

7 . . . But I'm still Jody Williams who didn't go to her own graduation. I'm still Jody Williams, who doesn't know what my next job's going to be. . . .
The only thing I do know is that I still, every single day of my life, get up with joy and excitement and wonder about what am I going to do today that's going to make a difference. Nobody can define what makes a difference for you. You have to figure out what makes a difference for you. . . . What matters is that it gives you joy.
Speech, University of Vermont (17 May 1998)
Christian Science Monitor 12 June 1998

3290. Barbara Wilson (1950–)

1 These are trashy novels I'm talking about, and they didn't come my way often when I was growing up in the sixties but when they did, I recognized their style immediately. As frequently as the plot allowed (and sometimes the plot allowed for a great deal of frequency), the sexual tension would build up, description and dialogue tending toward a dual but united purpose (female abandon, male release).
"The Erotic Life of Fictional Characters," *An Intimate Wilderness, Lesbian Writers on Sexuality*, Judith Barrington,* ed. *1991*
*See 2984.

2 My cat had come over to look at me, but she didn't seem alarmed. She sniffed my head and pronounced me still alive. I had seen the face of madness. I had felt her devouring breath . . . I had become her for just a millisecond. But afterwards I had returned to being me.
Blue Windows: A Christian Science Childhood 1997

3 The world is an achingly beautiful and awful place. There is meaning and even pleasure sometimes in melancholy and in wrenching, reverent grief.
Ibid.

4 A wound will never disappear, but it will fade and become part of a beloved body, a laugh line perhaps or a visible reminder of pain long gone.
Ibid.

3291. Merle Woo (195–?–)

1 Abrasive teacher, incisive comedian,
Painted Lady, dark domestic-
Sweep minds' attics; burnish our senses;
keep house, make love, wreak vengeance.
"Yellow Woman Speaks," St. 5, *Breaking Silence: An Anthology of Contemporary Asian American Poets*, Joseph Bruchac, ed. *1982*

3292. Rolanda Young (1950–)

1 She [Maya Angelou]* told me that all you have to do [to write] is take an adjective and a noun, a verb and a couple of con-

junctions, then ball them up, throw them against the wall and watch them sing.

> Quoted in "Rolanda Takes Her Show on the Road,"
> *Parade Magazine September 1994*

*See 2353.

3293. Zhang Kangkang (1950–)

1 People can trace the causes and effects of the human comedies and tragedies of their times by studying history. On the other hand history is history, a pile of classical files, a science with no material benefits. Who would be interested in studying it?

> "The Wasted Years," Shen Zhen, tr., *Seven Contemporary Chinese Women Writers*, Gladys Yang,* ed. *1982*

*See 2076.

2 "But I think history is like a mirror reflecting the truth. We understand many things better after studying it."

> Ibid.

3294. Linsey Abrams (1951–)

1 We went to the party as prostitutes, the only women who got out of the house in ancient Rome.

> *Our History in New York 1995*

2 I think it was just one of those crazy things, as if suddenly you had lived two hours out of time.

Desire is like that; it has nothing to do with anything, but is like some lighted circle of the mind into which you step with another person, leaving the rest of life behind.

> Ibid.

3295. Christine Bell (1951–)

1 If heat had a smell, it would smell like this: layers upon layers of rotting vegetation steaming on the jungle floor. . . . If heat had a sound, it would be this manic staccato of unseen birds and the on-again, off-again static of insects.

> *Saint 1985*

2 And Rosa . . . she is far from idle and far from sulking. She is sweating with responsibility. She is everywhere at once and nowhere at all. She supervises, directs, organizes, aids, like a saint in religious heat. Even when she just sits and sweats, the wheels of responsibility are turning in her head. Sometimes I hear a cluck of her tongue when the wheel hits a rut. If sweat had a sound, it would be Rosa's tongue clucking.

> Ibid.

3296. Susan Jane Blackmore (1951–)

1 Just as the design of our bodies can be understood only in terms of natural selection, so the design of our minds can be understood only in terms of memetic* selection.

> *The Meme Machine 1999*

*A contagious information pattern that replicated by parasitically infecting human minds and altering their behavior, causing them to propagate the pattern (as with icons, melodies, etc.).

3297. Phyllis Burke (1951–)

1 In our early gender training, we are taught that there is something we are able to do, but are forbidden, because of our sex. A boy is told that boys do not skip, or jump rope, but he knows that his body is capable of skipping. A girl is told not to physically fight because she is a girl, but she knows that her anger is as real as her fist.

> *Gender Shock: Exploding the Mythos of Male and Female 1996*

2 The most important thing I learned is that I am enough for my son. I can do everything for him that a man can do.

> Ibid.

3 The majority of children are suppressing a part of themselves to fit in. The children diagnosed with the disorder [GID, Gender Identity Disorder] are the ones who are not actively suppressing themselves.

> Ibid.

4 Like feminism, gender independence simply means that an individual is not precluded from feeling or doing anything because of their body.

> Ibid.

3298. Susan Taylor Chehak (1951–)

1 She was dancing on a skylight; she was turning on a floor that was made out of glass. . . . And then there was only the gentlest murmur, as a chink took root, and it splintered, and there was the cruelest crackle of shattering glass, greedy fingers, a myriad of slivers, glittery cracks, eagerly branching, multiplying, radiating away in every direction, like intricate lace, a spider's web, and an explosion of crystal, smashed.

> *Dancing on Glass 1994*

2 [Bader] rolls his fingertip over the raised flesh, and he thinks of how, over the years, he's allowed the blame for what happened to Lee and to Katherine, too, to become a part of him, like this scar. How it's attached itself to him, like an extra organ, or a tumor, not growing and taking on shape inside him, but around which he himself has grown and molded the contour of his life. . . . It's his guilt that has come to define him.

> Ibid.

3 . . . [he] stepped out into the open, where his bright white shirt reflected the afternoon sunlight like an overexposed photograph, or a space in a drawing, erased, left painfully unfinished, achingly blank.

> Ibid.

3299. Jorie Graham (1951–)

1 doesn't think it has
reached deep
enough so goes in
after it

> "Age of Reason," *Dream of the Unified Field : Selected Poems 1974–1994 1995*

2 we look in each other's hair
as in ripe shrubs bearing and withering,
we feel time glide through the room, between our legs,
round through our glance—we think we can look in the
    walled-up thoughts—
we let our nights get tangled, we try to stare.

> "Studies in Secrecy," *The Errancy 1997*

3 poor secret, did you need us?
did you need us to find you?

> Ibid.

3300. Mary Ann Gwinn (1951–)

1 I'm fascinated with the notion that what we read says a great deal about the mind-set of our time. For better or worse, what we read defines who we are . . .

> Quoted in "Inside the Times" by Michael R. Fancher,
> *Seattle Times 18 October 1998*

3301. Joy Harjo (1951–)

1 i am a dangerous woman
but the weapon is not visible
security will never find it
they can't hear the clicking
of the gun
      inside my head.
      "I Am a Dangerous Woman," St. 4, *That's What She Said*,
                    Rayna Green,* ed. *1984*

  *See 2284.

2 He's half Creek, half plains.
I'm part Creek and white.
"Which part do you want tonight?" I ask him.
      "It's the Same at Four A.M.," St. 1, Ibid.

3 Remember the earth whose skin you are.
Red earth yellow earth white earth brown earth
black earth we are earth.
Remember the plants, trees, animal life who all have their
tribes, their families, their histories, too. Talk to them,
listen to them. They are alive poems.
      "Remember," Ibid.

4 But she needs
the feel of danger,
    for life. (It Helps Her Remember)
      "Noni Daylight Remembers the Future," Sts. 3–4, Ibid.

5 The woman hanging from the 13th floor window
on the east side of Chicago is not alone.

. . . .

She is all the women of the apartment
building who stand watching her, watching themselves.
      "The Woman Hanging From the 13th Floor Window,"
                    St. 3, Ibid.

6 It's true the landscape forms the mind. If stand here long
enough I'll learn how to sing.
      "Foliage on Canyon Floor," *Secrets from the Center of the*
          World, and Stephen E. Strom, photographer *1989*

7 I am witness to
flexible eternity, the evolving past, and I know we will live
forever, as dust or breath in the face of stars, in the shifting
pattern of winds.
      "Nazlini Mudhills," Ibid.

8 In winter it is easier to see what my death might look like,
over there, disappearing into the misty, spotted rocks.
      "Nazlini Overlook—Summer," Ibid.

9 Everything arrives perfectly in time, including snow
clouds that bless the earth. And the moon, the blind eye of an
ancient mountain lion who shifts his bones on a starry branch.
      "Spider Rock Overlook," Ibid.

10 But the sacred lands have their own plans,
seep through fingers of the alcohol spirit.
Nothing can be forgotten, only left behind.
      "Autobiography," St. 1, *In Mad Love and War 1990*

11 At three my mother told me this story:

God decided to make people. He put
the first batch in the oven, kept them in too
long. They burned. These were the black
people. God put in the next batch. They

were uncooked, not done. These were the
white people. But the next batch he cooked
just right, and these were the Indian
people, just like you.
      "Autobiography," Sts. 3–4, Ibid.

12 In this language there are no words for how the real world collapses.
      "Deer Dancer," Ibid.

13 Some people see vision in a burned tortilla, some in the face of
a woman.
      Ibid.

14 To pray you open your whole self
To sky, to earth, to sun, to moon

To one whole voice that is you
And know there is more
      "Eagle Poem," Ibid.

15 I think of Wind and her wild ways the year/ we had nothing to
lose and lost it anyway . . .
      "Grace," Ibid.

16 She lies for cocaine, dangles
on the arm of cocaine. And
lies to me now for a room in the DeVargas
Hotel, where she has eaten her
lover, white powder on her lips.
      "Santa Fe," IIII, Ibid.

17 a woman can't survive
by her own breath
    alone
she must know
the voices of mountains
      "Fire," *The Woman That I Am, The Literature and Culture*
      of Contemporary Women of Color, D. Soyini Madison, ed.
                     1994

18 Oh, you have choked me, but I gave you the leash.
You have gutted me but I gave you the knife.
You have devoured me, but I laid myself across the fire.
You held my mother down and raped her,
    but I gave you the heated thing.
      "I Give You Back," St. 8 (1983), Ibid.

19 But come here, fear
I am alive and you are so afraid
    of dying.
      St. 10, Ibid.

20 The world begins at a kitchen table. No matter what, we must
eat
to live.
      "Perhaps The World Ends Here," St. 1, *The Woman Who*
                  Fell From The Sky 1994

21 Perhaps the world will end at the kitchen table, while we are
laughing
and crying, eating of the last sweet bite.
      St. 11, Ibid.

22 This god was lonely for touch, and imagined
herself as a woman, with children to suckle, to
sing with—to continue the web of the
terrifyingly beautiful cosmos of her womb.
      "Reconciliation—A Prayer," I, St. 2, Ibid.

23 All acts of kindness are lights in the war for
justice.

III, Ibid.

3302. Brenda Hillman (1951–)

1 That dithyramb of ticky-tick, boom,
brrrrr we hear when we lift
the nozzle, pull back on the black rubber
and shove it in—

"Cheap Gas," *Loose Sugar* 1997

2 My girl came to the study
and said Help me;
I told her I had a time problem
which meant:
I would die for you but I don't have ten minutes.

"Time Problem," Ibid.

3303. Barbara Holland (1951–)

1 Speech that is but percussion under melody is bones to music.
I do not understand a word you say, and yet you tell me in
your rhythms, your harmonies, and richness of their structure.

"Translation," St. 1, *The East Side Scene*,
Allen de Loach, ed. 1968

3304. Janis Ian (1951–)

1 How do you do
would you like
to be friends?
No I just want a bed for the night
someone to tell me they care.
You can fake it, that's all right
In the morning I won't be here.

"The Come On" 1974

3305. Patricia Jones (1951–)

1 I been thirsty so long that my mouth feels
like parchment/ got words written cross it/. Dead
stories bout dead feelings/ dried up/ dead

"I Done Got So Thirsty That My Mouth Waters at the
Thought of Rain," St. 2 (1981), *The Woman That I Am,
The Literature and Culture of Contemporary Women
of Color*, D. Soyini Madison, ed. 1994

3306. Fran Lebowitz (1951–)

1 All God's children are not beautiful. Most of God's children
are, in fact, barely presentable.

"Manners," *Metropolitan Life* 1978

2 There is no such thing as inner peace. There is only nervous-
ness or death. Any attempt to prove otherwise constitutes
unacceptable behavior.

Ibid.

3 Being a woman is of special interest only to aspiring male
transsexuals. To actual women it is merely a good excuse not
to play football.

"Letters," Ibid.

4 If you are of the opinion that the contemplation of suicide is
sufficient evidence of a poetic nature, do not forget that actions speak louder than words.

Ibid.

5 Nothing succeeds like address.

"The Nail Bank: Not Just Another Clip Joint," Ibid.

6 If you're going to America, bring your own food.

"Fran Lebowitz's Travel Hints," *Social Studies 1981*

7 There are two modes of transport in Los Angeles: car and am-
bulance. Visitors who wish to remain inconspicuous are
advised to choose the latter.

"Lesson 1," Ibid.

8 Your responsibility as a parent is not as great as you might imagine. You need not supply the world with the next conqueror of
disease or major motion-picture star. If your child simply grows
up to be someone who does not use the word "collectible" as a
noun, you can consider yourself an unqualified success.

"Parental Guidance," Ibid.

9 Original thought is like original sin: both happened before you
were born to people you could not have possibly met.

"People," Ibid.

10 The opposite of talking isn't listening. The opposite of talking
is waiting.

Ibid.

11 To put it rather bluntly, I am not the type who wants to go back
to the land; I am the type who wants to go back to the hotel.

"Things," Ibid.

3307. Sharman MacDonald (1951–)

1 MORAG. A woman's body is a clock that runs down very
rapidly.

When I Was a Girl, I Used to Scream and Shout 1984

3308. Deborah E. McDowell (1951–)

1 It was Daddy who suggested the compound sentence using "impeccable" and "managerial": "Mother has impeccable taste,
but she is managerial."

Leaving Pipe Shop: Memories of Kin 1997

2 When the somabitch called him a gorilla [great-grandfather]
told him he could have his gorilla job and stick it where the
sun don't shine.

Ibid.

3 . . . your Mama's so broke she can't buy a flea in a wrestling
jacket, low cut and no sleeves.

Ibid.

4 . . . once a man keeps company with an alley cat, you can be
sure that prowling is all he's got on his mind.

Ibid.

5 . . . men . . . run the streets with good-time women and then go
home to their wives.

Ibid.

6 If the outer rim [of the ear] hadn't turned dark by a certain
month, then the child was sure to be fair-skinned and marked
for success and the pain and satisfaction of others' envy.

Ibid.

7 She didn't need to drop out of high school. She could have
gone on to college, but she preferred rotgut liquor, outlaw
men, and pregnancy out of wedlock.

Ibid.

8 Don't never let no man see you low, 'cause then he'll sho'nuff try to walk all over you, and sometimes, you can't get up from it . . .

Ibid.

9 . . . a part of me still detested the very idea of her scrubbing, scouring, bleaching, and buffing, while her "boss lady" went for her Saturday manicure.

Ibid.

3309. Marlane Meyer (1951–)

1 SHERMAN. Pornography in its focus on the genital experience creates an ultimately carnal mind that is necessarily death-oriented since the body is always in a progressive state of decay. The earth begins to crawl up inside you.
SHERI. Ugh.
ETTA. We're dying anyway, who cares?

Etta Jenks 1986

3310. Sally Ride (1951–)

1 All of a sudden you know you're going. . . . There is nothing like it. . . . It literally *overwhelms* you.
"Challenger's Happy Landing," *Newsweek* (New York) *4 July 1983*

2 The rockets light! The shuttle leaps off the launch pad in a cloud of steam and a trail of fire.
To Space and Back, with Susan Okie *1986*

3 I can't remember a single time [my parents] ever told me not to do something I wanted to do.
Quoted in *Women Aviators* by Lisa Yount *1995*

4 The best part of being in space is being weightless. It feels wonderful to be able to float without effort; to slither up, down, and around the inside of the shuttle just like a seal.

Ibid.

5 [I hope to see the United States] gain routine access to space, make it an extension of the Earth's environment, not just for exploration and national pride but for things the country can actually use—medicines, improved materials.

Ibid.

3311. Starhawk (1951–)

1 Ritual is the original womb of art; its waters continue to nourish creativity.

Truth or Dare 1987

3312. Phoebe Snow (1951–)

1 I'd like to be a willow, a lover, a mountain
Or a soft refrain
But I'd hate to be a grown–up
And have to try to bear
My life in pain.
"Harpo's Blues," *Phoebe Snow 1973*

2 Sometimes this face looks so funny
That I hide it behind a book
Sometimes this face has so much class
That I have to sneak a second look.
"Either or Both," Ibid.

3 It must be Sunday
Everybody's telling the truth. . . .
"It Must Be Sunday," Ibid.

3313. Patricia Spallone (1951–)

1 Clearly, the [reproductive] technologies were not invented to serve *women's* needs, but the various needs and desires of medical scientists, research scientists, and the state, to further technological "progress" and to aid population control aims, all of which requires the use of women to those ends.
(p. 2), *Beyond Conception: The New Politics of Reproduction 1989*

3314. Paula A. Vogel (1951–)

1 CECIL. Never forget that every single organic being around us strives to increase in numbers; that each lives by a struggle at some period in its life; that heavy destruction inevitably falls either on the young or the old.
And Baby Makes Seven 1986

3315. Timberlake Wertenbaker (1951–)

1 CHORUS. They say a woman is a man turned inside out. Most evident in the genitals, his turned out, hers turned in, hers waiting for his, waiting for completion, that's what they say.
Inside Out 1982

2 CHORUS. What is the anatomy of a woman?
LI. Not what you imagine through your genitals.

Ibid.

3 PHILLIP. The Greeks believed that it was a citizen's duty to watch a play. It was a kind of work in that it required attention, judgement, patience, all social virtues.
TENCH. And the Greeks were conquered by the more practical Romans, Arthur.
COLLINS. Indeed, the Romans built their bridges but they also spent many centuries wishing they were Greeks.
Act I, Sc. 6, *Our Country's Good* (adapt. of Thomas Keneally's* *The Playmaker*) *1989*
*Austrian novelist (1935–).

3316. Patricia Williams (1951–)

1 So-called formal equal opportunity has done a lot but misses the heart of the problem . . . the rules may be color-blind, but people are not.
"The Obliging Shell: An Informal Essay on Formal Equal Opportunity," *Michigan Law Review 87 1989*

2 There's a security guard in the foyer of the building now; they hired an old black man in a blue suit with a badge, to keep out other old tired black people.
"Fire and Ice," *The Alchemy of Race and Rights: Diary of a Law Professor 1991*

3 Cultural needs and ideals change with the momentum of time; the need to redefine our laws in keeping with the spirit of cultural flux is what keeps a society alive and humane.

Ibid.

4 If our laws are thus piano-wired on the exclusive validity of literalism, if they are picked clean of their spirit, then society risks heightened irresponsibility for the consequence of abominable actions.

Ibid.

5 Yet being ruled by the cool formality of language is surely as bad as being ruled solely by one's emotions.

Ibid.

3317. Jamie Sams (1951–)

1 Our traditional Native American greeting in the Seneca language is *Na:weh Skennio*—thank you for being! Whether you know it or not, each of you represents a spark of inspiration within the Great Mystery. You are needed. You touch the lives of many and are responsible for changing the lives of others for the better. For all that you do and for who you are, I thank you for being.

"Messages for the Men of the Millennium," *The Fabric of the Future: Women Visionaries of Today Illuminate the Path to Tomorrow*, M.J. Ryan, ed. *1998*

2 When we are inspired, we funnel our creativity into fashioning something of beauty, whether it is dance, art, music, or making a meal for our families. When we finish, we exhale our creations, sending them into the world to be shared with others. Creativity is present in everything we do and is fueled by the amount of life-force we are willing to embrace.

Ibid.

3 Laughing at our personal antics is Good Medicine. It is healthy to laugh at how we tend to become myopic, getting wrapped up in our lives and how we lose the bigger picture. We thrive when we can shed the armor of too much seriousness. When we can see the cosmic joke of how we have meandered into circumstances that force us to acknowledge our humanness, we shake off our unwanted self-importance.

Ibid.

4 Wise women can dare to know for themselves and allow others to find what is right for them and we can laugh at the ridiculous one-size-fits-all type of advice that is being touted for the masses.

Ibid.

5 Reclaiming the belly-laugh can cure a world of woes.

Ibid.

3318. Jeri Allyn (1952?–)

1 I see the restaurant as a symbol for the world. How do you feed and house a soul with work that's important?

Quoted in "Jeri Allyn," *Exposures, Women & Their Art* by Ann Brown and Arlene Raven* *1989*

*See 3020.

3319. Nevada Barr (1952–)

1 There hadn't been a god for many years. Not the nightgown-clad patriarch of Sunday school coloring books; not the sensitive young man with the inevitable auburn ringlets Anna had stared through in the stained-glass windows at Mass; not the many-armed and many-faceted deities of the Bhagavad Gita that she'd worshipped alongside hashish and Dustin Hoffman in her college days. Even the short but gratifying parade of earth goddesses that had taken her to their ample bosoms in her early thirties had gone, although she remembered them with more kindness than the rest.

God was dead. Let Him rest in peace. Now, finally, the earth was hers with no taint of Heaven.

(p. 1), *Track of the Cat 1993*

2 Nature was taking back what had once been hers . . .

Liberty Falling 1999

3320. Sydney Biddle Barrows (1952–)

1 A call girl is simply someone who hates poverty more than she hates sin.

Mayflower Madam 1986

3321. Denise M. Boudrot (1952–)

1 I don't ride to beat the boys, just to win.

Quoted in *Women at Work* by Betty Medsger *1975*

3322. Meg Christian (1952?–)

1 Mama, oh, my Mama, well, do you understand
Why I've not bound myself to a man?
Is something buried in your old widow's mind
That blesses my choice of our own kind?
Oh, Mama, Mama.

"Song to My Mama," Verse 3, *I Know You Know* (album) *1974*

2 She was a big tough woman, the first to come along
That showed me being female meant you still could be strong;
And though graduation meant that we had to part,
She'll always be a player on the ballfield of my heart.

"Ode to a Gym Teacher," Chorus, *Ibid.*

*Also see 3227:3.

3323. Judith Oritz Cofer (1952–)

1 So far has she gone
into herself,
that the taunting voices
from the outside calling
her *Loca, Loca*
reach her as bright beams
of light lining the road
to the kingdom where
she is the sole ruler.

"Una Mujer Loca" (1986), *The Woman That I Am, The Literature and Culture of Contemporary Women of Color*, D. Soyini Madison, ed. *1994*

3324. Judith G. Coffin (1952–)

1 Wage policy is also family policy and gender policy.

The Politics of Women's Work: The Paris Garment Trades, 1750–1915 1996

3325. Vicki Covington (1952–)

1 Southerners love a story, even when it wounds them and ruins their reputation, wrecks their economy and sets fire to things.

The Last Hotel for Women 1996

2 "Birmingham . . . you people, I see have changed." . . . His anger is being converted; he can taste it. It's a metal, a very hard metal burning his tongue, gums, throat. He thinks of molten pig iron being tapped from the furnace, how slag floats to the top. "By-products," he says, staring at them all. "By-products of the Kennedys."

Ibid.

3326. Rita Dove (1952–)

1 You have to decide whether you're going to be *in* life or if you're going to stand by and watch it.

Quoted in "Author Dove reaches . . . " by Lynne K. Varner, *Seattle Post-Intelligencer*, C1, 4 *3 November 1992*

2   "Do you know what you're telling us? Your grandmother goes half across town to buy you the first Negro baby doll and you throw a fit, you throw her down the stairs like dirty laundry. You don't like it? You don't like being a Negro?"

Virginia stared at it—the bulging eyes, the painted head. She didn't look like that. And if she did, how could her own parents stand there and tell her so? How could they love her and show her at the same time that she was ugly?

Through the Ivory Gate 1992

3   The Chateaubriand

arrived on a bone-white plate, smug and absolute
in its fragrant crust, a black plug steaming
like the heart plucked from the chest of a worthy enemy;
one touch with her fork sent pink juices streaming.

"The Bistro Styx," St. 9, *Mother Love 1995*

4   don't think you can ever forget her
don't even try
she's not going to budge

"Lady Freedom Among Us," St. 8 (1993), *On the Bus
with Rosa Parks* 1999*

*See 2020.

5   I vowed I'd get off
somewhere grand.
Who am I kidding? Here I am.

Ibid.

6   Enough of guilt—
It's hard work staying cool.

"Used," St. 3 *n.d.*

7   I've walked there, too: he can't give
you up, so you give in until you can't live
without him. Like these blossoms, white sores
burst upon earth's ignorant flesh, at first sight
everything is innocence—
then it's itch, scratch, putrescense.

"Afield," St. 2 *n.d.*

8   In time, I lost the capacity
for resolve.

"Lost Brilliance," St. 4 *n.d.*

9   There's a way to study freedom but few have found
it; you must talk yourself to death and then beyond,
destroy time, then refashion it.

"Political," St. 1 *n.d.*

3327. Ferron (1952–)

1   But by our light be we spirit,
And by our hearts be we women,
And by our eyes be we open,
And by our hands be we wide.

"Testimony" *1980*

3328. Alice Fulton (1952–)

1   Everyday was all there was on the farm.

"Happy Dust," *The Missouri Review 198-?*

2   In my experience, it is better to keep away from saints unless you have business with them.

Ibid.

3   As he saw it, childbirth was long hours for short wages.

Ibid.

4   This long path wound grandly up through massive gates and meadows toward the sky. I suspected many pilgrims from the city never knew there could be such earth on earth.

Ibid.

5   A saint wasn't much of a livelihood, but it was better than farming.

Ibid.

6   "Perfection is a nun's purpose," she replied. "She must wash the taste of the world from her mouth with carbolic and sleep on thorns lest she sleep too well. If the chapel is cosy, let her kneel in snow. If for an instant she forgets Christ's suffering, let her take switches to her shoulders, brand herself with faggots, wear an iron chain about her waist."

Ibid.

7   Suddenly it seemed my little shut-in had been cooped up long enough. Suddenly it wanted liberty. It was coming like a locomotive headlight. It was coming quick as scat. God Almighty!

Now this baby was helping. Now this baby wanted to be born.

Ibid.

8   Nuns always want some little selfless thing in exchange for their favors, I find. God's the same way when you think about it.

Ibid.

9   He kept his ear pressed

like a safecracker's
stethoscope against
her head, kept his

recombinant endearments
tumbling toward a click.

"The Orthodox Waltz," Sts. 3–5, *Powers of Congress 1989*

10   Are we making love yet?

"The Expense of Spirit," St. 2, Ibid.

11   the birds begin their final take.
They'll never know themselves as symbols
of the sublime. Transcendent
messy shrines == whose music won't stoop
to unison or climax:
tell them I said hi.

"Call The Mainland," St. 6, *Three Poems 1994*

12   The lovers get so excited
to think—nothing comes between them.
There is nothing between them.
That's how they can consume each other,
sand each other sore.

"The Priming Is A Negligee," Sts. 4–5, *Sensual Math 1995*

13   Because life's too short to blush,
I keep my blood tucked in.

"About Face," St. 1, Ibid.

14   I do not suffer
from the excess of taste
that spells embarrassment:

St. 2, Ibid.

15   At least embarrassment is not an imitation.
It's intimacy for beginners,
the orgasm no one cares to fake.

St. 4, Ibid.

16 "My flesh hissed
and I thought I'd perished,
but the sensation of descent vanishes
once the body stops accelerating.
It's astonishing how nothingness
firms up."
　　　　"Southbound In A Northbound Lane," St. 2 (1994), Ibid.

17 Waterfalling means the story visits tributaries
at a distance from itself.
　　　　　　　　　　　　　　　　　　　　　Ibid.

18 We talked by thought which made us
　　　really close. Others
might consider her a kvetch, but we
　　　became best friends. I understood
because I was her by then, wrapped up in
　　　the electric flex of her
ideas: I learned women were debarred
　　　from sweating and vision seeking,
that the female was the prey of the
　　　species . . . adapted
to the egg's needs
　　　　　　　　　　　　　　　　"Turn: A Version," Ibid.

19 　　　The natural is what

poetry contests. Why else the line == why stanza == why
　meter and the rest.
　　　　　　　　　　　　　　　　"==," St. 7 (1994), Ibid.

20 The better part of fairness is the willingness to move toward
what is given rather than impose one's own aesthetic on a
book. This approach—a sympathetic leaning toward the work
coupled with patient rereading—is the one I've tried to realize.
　　　　　　　　　　　　　　　Feeling as a Foreign Language 1999

3329. P. J. Gibson (1952–)
1 If I live to be 150, I still won't have enough time to write about
all the black women inside of me.
　　　　　　Quoted in 9 Plays by Black Women, Margaret Wilkerson,
　　　　　　　　　　　　　　　　　　　ed. and intro. 1986

3330. Beth Henley (1952–)
1 CHICK. They say each cigarette is just a little stick of cancer. A
little death stick.
　　MEG. That's what I like about it, Chick—taking a drag off of
death. Mmm! Gives me a sense of controlling my own destiny.
What power! What exhilaration! Want a drag?
　　　　　　　　　　　　　　　Act I, Crimes of the Heart 1979

2 BABE. He started hating me, 'cause I couldn't laugh at his jokes.
I just started finding it impossible to laugh at his jokes the way
I used to. And then the sound of his voice got to where it tired
me out awful bad to hear it. I'd fall asleep just listening to him
at the dinner table.
　　　　　　　　　　　　　　　　　　　　　Ibid.

3 CARNELLE. I just don't know what you can, well, reasonably
hope for in life.
　　MacSAM. There's always eternal grace.
　　　　　　　　　　　　　　　The Miss Firecracker Contest 1980

4 Women's problems are people's problems. There are certain
subjects I mightn't get into, simply because I don't have the
necessary knowledge, but I don't think my being a woman limits my concerns.
　　　　　　　　　　　Interview, The New York Times 25 October 1981

5 . . . I find it fascinating to think about what the world is going
to be like when people won't talk anymore. There are probably brilliant people, geniuses, alive today who don't even know
how to say, "Hello, how are you?" because their minds are absorbed with electronic images.
　　　　"Beth Henley," Interviews with Contemporary Women
　　　　　Playwrights, Kathleen Betsko* and Rachel Koenig 1987
　　　*See 2256.

6 And all writing is creating or spinning dreams for other people
so they won't have to bother doing it themselves.
　　　　　　　　　　　　　　　　　　　　　Ibid.

3331. Deborah Jacobs (1952–)
1 The library is about rugged independence. You can come in as
an independent learner and learn anything. . . . That's what
makes my heart pound. The doors are open. This is where you
can grow.
　　　　　　"Deborah the Librarian" by Paula Bock, Seattle Times,
　　　　　　　　　　　　　　Northwest Living 7 February 1999

2 Libraries are the core of our community and our democracy. I
believe if you have strong libraries, you have strong communities.
　　　　　　　　　　　　　　　　　　　　　Ibid.

3 When I was in library school, I used to think if I could help
one child as a librarian, I'd forever affect the quality of life for
everybody in the universe. I still think that.
　　　　　　　　　　　　　　　　　　　　　Ibid.

4 How can I defend the library to a Christian parent who doesn't
like Madonna's "Sex" if I don't have a book for them on curing
homosexuality or teaching sexuality in a Christian home?
　　　　　　　　　　　　　　　　　　　　　Ibid.

3332. Laurie R. King (1952–)
1 There are times, after all, when a writer must twist the truth in
order to tell it.
　　　　　　　　　　　　　Acknowledgments, The Moor 1998

2 "Unsophisticated minds are apt to see corpse lights or "jacky-
twoads" where the scientist would see swamp gas, and long
and lonely nights encourage the mind to wander down paths
poorly illuminated by the light of reason."
　　　　　　　　　　　　　　　　　　Ch. 2, Ibid.

3 "Admit it, Holmes," I pressed. "The only reason you so denigrate Talmudic studies is sheer envy over the fact that others
perfected the art of deductive reasoning centuries before you
were even born."
　　　　　　　　　　　　　　　　　　　　　Ibid.

4 "Women are quite mad when it comes to hospitality."
　　　　　　　　　　　　　　　　　　Ch. 3, Ibid.

5 It was the sort of light that renders vision untrustworthy,
where the eyes cannot accept the continual lack of stimulus
and begin to invent faint wraiths and twisting shadows.
　　　　　　　　　　　　　　　　　　Ch. 4, Ibid.

6 For several weeks over the summer I had lived with the fact
that debts to the dead are heavier than those owed the living
because there is no negotiation, no forgiveness, only the stark
knowledge that failure can never be recompensed, that even
success can only restore balance.
　　　　　　　　　　　　　　　　　　Ch. 9, Ibid.

7   This particular specimen of the clergy before me did not suffer from brevity of speech, although he compensated by displaying a considerable brevity of both wit and learning.

Ch. 20, Ibid.

8   As always, the extraneous data confused issues, and as always, it was not easy to know what was extraneous and what central. The best way of trying to find a pattern that I knew of was to hold all the data in mind, and remove one piece, and if that did not cause the remaining pieces to shift and click into place replace it, and remove another.

Ch. 21, Ibid.

9   . . . a literal translation is quite often not the best.

Author's Prologue, *O Jerusalem* 1999

10   This was the land my people had clung to for more than three thousand years, I thought with irony: a squalid, stinking village whose inhabitants were kept inside their crumbling walls by the occupying British Expeditionary Forces. The streets of the Promised Land flowed not with milk and honey but with ordure, and the glories of Askalon and Asdod were faded indeed.

Ch. 1, Ibid.

11   It is an amazing thing, the difference to one's powers of concentration a pair of comfortable shoes can make.

Ch. 4, Ibid.

12   "I am not a Christian, Abbot Mattias."

"God does not mind, my child. He was, after all, your God before He was ours."

"In that case I accept your blessing, with thanks."

Ch. 17, Ibid.

13   She is a jewel, that city [Jerusalem], small and brilliant and hard, and as dangerous as any valuable thing can be. . . . It was 401 years since the Turks took the city, 820 years since the Crusaders under Godfrey of Bouillon had slaughtered every Moslem and Jew within the walls (and a good number of unrecognised native Christians as well), eighteen and a half centuries since the Romans had last razed her stones to the ground, and still she rose up within her snug, high walls, a nest of stone set to nurture the holy places of three faiths . . .

Ch. 18, Ibid.

14   "Using insult instead of argument is the sign of a small mind . . ."

Ibid.

15   "And treachery being what it is, it is always the person closest to one's heart who can wield a dagger with impunity."

Ch. 20, Ibid.

16   Prolonged stress can take the oddest outlets.

Ch. 25, Ibid.

3333. Emily Mann (1952–)

1   ANNULLA. If women would only start thinking, we could change the world.

Annulla Allen: An Autobiography of a Survivor (play) 1977

2   There is a network of caring people in theater all over the country, and outside this country, who don't care about New York reviews, but rather, care about important voices.

Quoted in *Interviews with Contemporary Women Playwrights* by Kathleen Betsko* and Rachel Koenig 1987

*See 2739.

3334. Gwendolyn Mink (1952–)

1   . . . poor single mothers [on welfare are compelled] to surrender basic constitutional rights of associational freedom and reproductive privacy as a condition of receiving economic assistance.

Welfare's End 1998

2   In place of stingy benefits doled out begrudgingly to needy mothers, welfare would become an income owed to nonmarket care–giving workers—owed to anyone who bears sole responsibility for children (or for other dependent family members).

Ibid.

3   . . . *all* caregiving is work, whatever the racial, marital or class status of the caregiver . . .

Ibid.

4   "Making fathers pay" may promote the economic and justice interests of many custodial mothers. But *making mothers* make fathers pay means trading their rights and safety for subsistence. . . . The issue is coercion of mothers who have eschewed patriarchal conventions (whether by choice or from necessity). The issue is also coercion directed towards mothers whose deviation from patriarchal norms has been associated with their racial and cultural standing.

Ibid.

3335. Patricia A. Moore (1952–)

1   In small towns . . . There isn't the infrastructure of services for elders that you find in cities. I could walk for six blocks without being able to find a restroom.* Rural elders are suffering.

Quoted in "Undercover Among the Elderly" by Michael Ryan, *Parade Magazine* 18 July 1993

*Reference to three years traveling to 116 big cities and small towns disguised as an elderly woman.

2   We have made the point, very subtly, in our society that when you age, somehow you're not as good as you were. We need to understand aging is a natural, evolutionary process. Why is younger necessarily better? We have to learn to age well in our hearts.

Ibid.

3336. Cherríe Moraga (1952–)

1   A theory of the flesh means one where the physical realities of our lives—our skin color, the land or concrete we grew up on, our sexual longings—all fuse to create a politic born out of necessity. Here we attempt to bridge the contradictions in our experience:

We are the colored in a white feminist movement.

We are the feminists among the people of our culture.

We are often the lesbians among the straight.

We do this bridging by naming our selves and by telling stories in our own words.

Introduction, *This Bridge Called My Back: Writings by Radical Women of Color*, also Gloria Anzaldúa* 1984

*See 2891.

2   When we are not physically starving, we have the luxury to realize psychic and emotional starvation. It is from this starvation that other starvations can be recognized—if one is willing to take the risk of making the connection—if one is willing to be responsible to the result of the connect.

"La Güera," Ibid.

3 In this country, lesbianism is a poverty—as is being brown, as is being a woman, as is being just plain poor. The danger lies in ranking the oppressions.

Ibid.

4 Sitting in that auditorium chair [listening to Ntozake Shange*] was the first time I had realized to the core of me that for years I had disowned the language I knew best—ignored the words and rhythms that were the closest to me. The sounds of my mother and aunts gossiping—half in English, half in Spanish—while drinking cerveza [beer] in the kitchen.

Ibid.

*See 3205.

5 The real power, as you and I well know, is collective. I can't afford to be afraid of you, nor you of me. If it takes head–on collisions, let's do it: this polite timidity is killing us.

Ibid.

6 Smell is very important. Your eyes can fool you. You can see things that aren't there. But not smell. Smell remembers and tells the future. No lying about that.

Smell can make your heart crack open no matter how many locks you have wrapped 'round it.

"La Ofrenda," OUT/LOOK No. 10
Fall 1990

7 "The only blood I like," she'd say, "is what my hand digs out of a satisfied woman."

Ibid.

8 But being a sister ain't no part-time occupation.

Ibid.

9 Tina used to say her contribution to La Causa was to keep the girlfriends of the machos happy while they were being too revolutionary to screw.

Ibid.

10 I kissed her where she had never spoken
where she had never sang

Ibid.

11 I, who have only given my breast to women.

Ibid.

12 It is the intimacy of steel melting
into steel, the fire of our individual
passion to take hold of ourselves
that makes sculpture of our lives,
builds buildings.

"The Welder," St. 5, The Woman That I Am,
The Literature and Culture of Contemporary
Women of Color, D. Soyini Madison, ed.
1994

13 I am the welder.
I understand the capacity of heat
to change the shape of things.
I am suited to work
within the realm of sparks
out of control.

St. 9, Ibid.

14 During those six minutes of darkness* . . . I understood for the first time the depth and wonder of the feminine, although I confess I have been awed by it before, as my own female face

gazes upon its glory and I press my lips to that apex in the woman I love.

Goddess of the Americas/La Diosa de las Américas: Writings on the Virgin of Guadalupe, Ana Castillo, ed. 1996

*Reference to a ceremony she attended in Mexico during the moon's eclipse of the sun.

3337. Jill Nelson (1952–)

1 There is between black women a language all our own, sometimes spoken, oftentimes not. We communicate with each other through a tilt of the head, a quick cutting of eyes, a heartfelt exhalation of breath, a quiet sucking of teeth, a fleeting smile that can transform the tenor of a bad day.

It is a feminine, coded, unwritten language. It is complex in its simplicity. Black women's language grows out of our particular experience of oppression because of our race and our gender.

How I Became a Grown-Up Black Woman 1977

2 I used to try to escape from my rage in notions of love, sex, orgasm, but my rage's appetite has become more specific. Now, it can only be satisfied by action, and not the pelvic kind.

Ibid.

3 Having given up the cornerstone of my coming-of-age and become a journalist, but still in possession of an addictive personality, I simply found another drug of choice: I mainlined information.

"Fighting the Right," The Women's Review of Books,
Vol. XII, Nos.10-11 July 1995

4 Let me say that I don't like to exercise. It's just that I've found it to be one of the few activities that decreases rage and alienation while simultaneously increasing my energy level and sense of empowerment. There's also a Zen to exercising, a meditative aspect. It clears the mind, not by any cosmic mantra but because while I'm exercising all I can think about is completing the remaining miles, laps, or set. Forget Gingrich, Clinton, the right wing, sexism, racism, poverty, my work . . . forget everything but finishing.

Ibid.

3338. Naomi Sihab Nye (1952–)

1 . . . remember the dignity of daily affirmation, whatever one does—the mother speaking to the child is also a poem.

Quoted in "Serious Play: Reading Poetry with Children" by
Eve Merriam*, The Academy of American Poetry website,
http://www.poets.org 1999

*See 2086.

3339. Suze Orman (1952–)

1 The single most important quality you need in order to change the course of your life is courage. A great deal of courage.

The Courage to Be Rich 1999

2 . . . it takes courage to be rich. Why? Because choosing wealth as a goal requires facing everything about your money bravely, honestly, with courage—which is a very, very hard thing for most of us to do. But it can be done.

Ibid.

3 I had once been poor, yet had lived with spirit, courageously. Now I was living with the trappings of wealth, but had no money. I was living a lie. I no longer had even the courage to be poor.

Ibid.

4   Money doesn't bring courage, I learned. It's the other way around. Once I took that lesson to heart, I began to rebuild my life.

Ibid.

3340. Brenda Carole Petersen (1952–)

1   The wolf is anything but lonely as he or she raises a shaggy head to howl; and yet our myths have imprisoned this creature into a symbol of isolation and separation. I suggest that it is we who are lonely, not the wolves—we who have hunted the wolf to extinction so that it is a very rare few of us who have ever even heard the call of the wolf in the wild.

"Wolves, wild women and wild men," Seattle Times, A17
20 December 1992

2   Imagine that this is a howl to call all sisters and brothers who are re-discovering their wild man and their woman who runs with the wolves, to please remember that the archetype is taken from the real, endangered animal. If that wild wolf dies out, so will our wild selves.

Ibid.

3   When we recognized that our fate was directly linked to the land, trees were holy.

"Killing Our Elders," Finding Home (quarterly) n.d.

4   Old trees like old people survive the ravages of middle-age competition for light, or limelight; they give back to their generations more oxygen, more stories; they are tall and far-sighted enough to see the future because they are so firmly rooted in the past. Old-growth trees or persons are nurturers; the young saplings planted to replace them need nurturing.

Ibid.

3341. Deborah L. Rhode (1952–)

1   The bar's ethical code miscasts professional self-interests as moral necessities.

"Ethical Perspectives on Legal Practice," 37 Stanford Law
Review 589 January 1985

2   Lawyers like to leave no stone unturned, provided they can charge by the stone.

Ibid.

3   When asked what it felt like to have gotten her job because she was a woman, Barbara Babcock* developed a stock reply: "It feels better than being rejected for the position because you're a woman."

Justice and gender : sex discrimination and the law 1989
*B— Allen B— (1938–), American lawyer, educator and author;
assistant attorney general (1977–1981).

4   Who can claim to represent the interests of women when women themselves disagree about what those interests are . . .

"Feminism and the State" (p. 107), Harvard Law Review
1181 1994

5   We should focus less on the quest for gender differences and more on the inequality they create.

The Denial of Gender Inequality 1997

6   We fail to see sexual abuse as a strategy of dominance and exclusion—a way of keeping women in their places and out of men's.

"Harassment Is Alive and Well and Living at the Water
Cooler," Ms. (New York) November/December 1997

7   Litigation is a highly imperfect response to workplace abuse. But without the threat of legal sanctions, women's voices too often go unheard. For centuries women experienced harassment but only they suffered the consequences. Now at least men who harass bear some of the costs.

Ibid.

8   When men harass, it should not be women's characters that are on trial.

Ibid.

9   We need remedies for the full range of cultural practices that make sexual coercion seem sexy.

Ibid.

10   Americans dislike the fact that legal access is for sale, but they also dislike efforts to remedy it. Justice is what we proclaim on courthouse entrances, not in redistributed policies. As a result, most Americans end up with all—and only—the justice money can buy.

Professional responsibility: ethics by the pervasive method
1998

11   Highly competitive markets are no fun for most sellers. Law is not an exception and fun is not the only casualty.

Ibid.

12   Young lawyers are wined and dined, then worked to death.

Ibid.

13   We have disputes that are too big for the courts, disputes that are too small, and disputes that should not have been disputes at all.

Ibid.

3342. Rebecca Roe (1952–)

1   If a guy gets hit over the head on the street and reports it, he's looking for justice. If a woman gets raped or assaulted and reports it, then she's looking for vengeance.

Quoted in "On A Crusade" by Linda Keene, Seattle Times,
Pacific Northwest section 26 July 1992

2   If you're a male prosecutor and you're strong and assertive, you're seeking justice. If you're a woman and you're strong and assertive, you're seeking vengeance.

Ibid.

3343. Janna Malamud Smith (1952–)

1   . . . by and large the reason not to choose adultery is that the pleasure it offers is taken in trade for harming more enduring love and more important loved ones.

"National politics: Debasing weapons fired in adultery
wars," Op-Ed Page, Seattle Post–Intelligencer
22 December 1998

2   Publicly humiliating anyone for consensual adultery is draconian, and wrong. It teaches children cynicism. What they see is how little respect there is for privacy, and how gratuitously and harshly adults will harm one another to gain a little power . . .

You might say that how and why we disapprove of adultery is as important as whether we do.

Ibid.

3344. Banu Subramaniam (1952–)

1   Traversing liminal spaces, traveling the hallways of academia, at the borderlands of disciplines . . . Almost there, but never

quite. Meandering, half mesmerized, half muddled, always mumbling. Dare I speak? Almost there, but never quite. Almost a scientist, yet a feminist; almost a feminist, yet a scientist; . . . How did I find myself in this tantalizing, much celebrated place, the home of the oxymoronic feminist scientist, this magical yet insane place . . . nowhere, yet everywhere all at once?

"A contradiction in terms," *The Women's Review of Books,* Vol. XV, No. 5 February 1998

2   I grew to understand scientific culture as a set of practices and behaviors bound by the historical roots of science in Western, anglo, male, heterosexual culture. Graduate school was a gateway to these credentials and was about policing these boundaries—the weeding out of those who cannot and will not participate in these cultural practices.

Ibid.

3   A feminist scientist, not one who merely believes in women's rights, but one who wishes her science to be informed by feminism, is a contradiction in terms.

Ibid.

4   If the sciences have developed as a world without women, then women's studies, it would seem, has developed as a world without the sciences.

Ibid.

5   And yet it would seem that through years of institutionalization, women's studies finds itself just another discipline, with its own center, culture and practices, policing its own boundaries of sacred scholarship. As our theories grow, as our jargons multiply, we find at our disposal an ever more sophisticated vocabulary to lull us back into the self-serving, self-fulfilling world of the academy.

Ibid.

3345. Amy Tan (1952–)

1   To despair was to wish back for something already lost. Or to prolong what was already unbearable.

The Joy Luck Club 1989

2   My mother believed you could be anything you wanted to be in America. You could open a restaurant. You could work for the government and get good retirement. You could buy a house with almost no money down. You could become rich. You could become instantly famous.

"Two Kinds," Ibid.

3   And then I saw what seemed to be the prodigy side of me—because I had never seen that face before. I looked at my reflection, blinking so I could see more clearly. The girl staring back at me was angry, powerful. This girl and I were the same. I had new thoughts, willful thoughts, or rather thoughts filled with lots of I won'ts.

Ibid.

4   "If she had as much talent as she has temper, she would be famous now."

Ibid.

5   "Only two kind of daughters," she shouted in Chinese. "Those who are obedient and those who follow their own mind! Only one kind of daughter can live in this house. Obedient daughter!"

"Then I wish I wasn't your daughter. I wish you weren't my mother," I shouted. As I said these things I got scared. I felt like worms and toads and slimy things were crawling out of my chest, but it also felt good, as if this awful side of me had surfaced, at last.

"Too late change this," said my mother shrilly.

Ibid.

6   We had hot and cold running servants.

The Kitchen God's Wife 1992

3346. T. Minh-Ha Trinh (1952–)

1   I write to show myself showing people who show me my own showing.

Woman, Native, Other 1989

2   The story of a people. Of us, peoples. Story, history, literature (or religion, philosophy, natural science, ethics)—all in one. They call it the tool of primitive man, the simplest vehicle of truth. When history separated itself from story, it started indulging in accumulation and facts. Or it thought it could.

"Grandma's Story," Ibid.

3   She who works at un-learning the dominant language of "civilized" missionaries also has to learn how to un-write and write anew. And she often does so by re-establishing the contact with her foremothers, so that living tradition can never congeal into fixed forms, so that life keeps on nurturing life, so that what is understood as the past continues to provide the link for the Present and the Future.

Ibid.

4   Every griotte* who dies is a whole library that burns down.

Ibid.

*French term for storyteller, often used in place of African "traditionalist."

5   Diseuse, Thought-Woman, Spider-Woman, griotte, storytalker, fortune-teller, witch. If you have the patience to listen, she will take delight in relating it to you. An entire history, an entire vision of the world, a lifetime story. . . . The world's earliest archives or libraries were the memories of women.

Ibid.

6   Speech is the materialization, externalization, and internalization of the vibrations of forces.

Ibid.

7   To be "good" a story must be built in conformity with the ready-made idea some people—Western adults—have of reality, that is to say, a set of prefabricated schemata (prefabricated by whom?) they value out of habit, conservatism, and ignorance (of other ways of telling and listening to stories).

Ibid.

8   In life, we usually don't know when an event is occurring; we think it is starting when it is already ending; and we don't see its in/significance. The present, which saturates the total field of our environment, is often invisible to us.

Ibid.

9   A story in Africa may last three months. The storyteller relates it night after night, continually, or s/he starts it one night and takes it up again from that point three months later. Meanwhile, as the occasion arises, s/he may start on yet another story.

Ibid.

3347. Theodora van den Beld (1952–)

1 The only thing you can control is your own effort.

Quoted in "Food Talk" by Lynn Steinberg, *Seattle Post–Intelligencer*, C1 *3 February 1999*

2 A house has to have soul, just like a restaurant has to have soul. How you get it is hard to explain. It has to have someone with passion behind it.

Ibid.

3 I let the ingredients inspire me.

Ibid.

3348. Iyanla Vanzant (1952/3–)

1 When you are not happy where you are and you are not quite sure if you want to leave or how to leave, you are in the meantime.

In the Meantime: Finding Yourself and the Love You Want 1998

2 If you know who walks beside you, you can never be afraid.

One Day My Soul Just Opened Up : 40 Days and 40 Nights Towards Spiritual Strength and Personal Growth 1998

3 Life is about cleaning up the crap and, while you're doing it, being okay with the fact that you have to do it. . . . A word of caution. You can't get caught up in the crap! If you do, you will surely lose sight of the real meaning of life and lose your Self.

Ibid.

3349. Michelle Wallace (1952–)

1 On April 4 King* was shot and the rioting began again, worse than ever. Praying, waiting, singing, and everything white were out. Rioting was viewed as urban guerrilla warfare, the first step toward the complete overthrow of the honky, racist government. On the cultural level everything had to be rehauled. Black poems, plays, paintings, novels, hairstyles, and apparel were springing up like weeds in Central Park. Brothers, with softly beating drums in the background, were talking about beautiful black Queens of the Nile and beautiful full lips and black skin and big asses.

Pt. I, Ch. 1, *Black Macho and The Myth of the Superwoman 1978*

*Martin Luther King, Jr., American civil rights leader and minister (1929–1968); Nobel Peace Prize (1964); assassinated.

2 I am saying, among other things, that for perhaps the last fifty years there has been a growing distrust, even hatred, between black men and black women. It has been nursed along not only by racism on the part of whites but also by an almost deliberate ignorance on the part of blacks about the sexual politics of their experience in this country.

Ibid.

3 The driving force behind the [Black Power] movement had really very little to do with bread and butter needs. The motive was revenge. It was not equality that was primarily being pursued but a kind of superiority—black manhood, black macho . . . And when the black man went as far as the adoration of his own genitals could carry him, his revolution stopped. A big Afro, a rifle, and a penis in good working order were not enough to lick the white man's world after all.

Ch. 2, Ibid.

4 From the intricate web of mythology which surrounds the black woman, a fundamental image emerges. It is of a woman of inordinate strength, with an ability for tolerating an unusual amount of misery and heavy, distasteful work. This woman does not have the same fears, weaknesses, and insecurities as other women, but believes herself to be and is, in fact, stronger emotionally than most men. Less of a woman in that she is less "feminine" and helpless, she is really more of a woman in that she is the embodiment of Mother Earth, the quintessential mother with infinite sexual, life-giving, and nurturing reserves. In other words, she is a superwoman.

Pt. II, Ch. 1, Ibid.

3350. Jeana L. Yeager (1952–)

1 Dick* [flew] the airplane and I flew him. . . . We were really one pilot. We became an extension of one another, complementing each other.

Quoted in *Women Aviators* by Lisa Yount *1995*
*Dick Rutan, highly decorated air force pilot. Reference to their 10-day journey around the world in *Voyager*, the first aircraft to make the trip without stopping and without refueling.

2 [Running gave me] a feeling of sharing the beauty and strength of horses and the ease with which they flew across the land.

Ibid.

3 Most people break up and go their separate ways. We broke up and stayed together.*

Ibid.

*Reference to her relationship with co-pilot Dick Rutan.

3351. Shoshana Zuboff (1952–)

1 I've lived in a preindustrial (rural Argentina) as well as an industrial world. You experience a different sense of time in a community that works the land. Human relationships aren't professionalized or contractualized; family and friends take primacy. Life has much more continuity than discontinuity. There's a great deal of poetry in everyday life.

Interview (pp. 66–94), *Omni April 1991*

2 One of the key things that keep people loyal is a sense that they're important and expected to make a contribution.

Ibid.

3 The dream of automation remains a powerful one—the idea of a clockwork world running without human intervention but generating enough wealth that everyone can go fishing, read books, and study art.

Ibid.

4 Computerization is part of a long-term historical process in which work has become increasingly abstract.

Ibid.

5 Managers, right up to the very top of the company, will be getting their personal rewards not from giving commands and eliciting obedience but from educating and nurturing the people under them.

Ibid.

6 Learning is the new form of labor.

Ibid.

7 Informating* creates enormous transparency in the workplace. If you use that transparency for surveillance, to police people, they react with a whole range of dysfunctional behaviors. They

sabotage the data by becoming passive. They withdraw effort and caring from their work.

Ibid.

*Word coined by Zuboff to describe what the computer is doing (taking three-dimensional objects and events and then translating and displaying them as data).

8 In a world where authority is equated with ownership of information, sharing that information becomes very threatening.

Ibid.

9 As a country, we have to get serious about education as a keystone of our economy and society. In the past the labor market had much greater diversity. You could drop out of high school and still get a decent-paying job in an auto plant or some other kind of blue-collar work. Those jobs today are few and far between.

Ibid.

10 Automation strives to substitute machines for bodily effort. . . . Computers translate the physical tasks they're automating into a symbolic medium. . . . The worker has to be able to interact with this computerized version of the physical tasks in order to understand what's going on and what to do about it.

Ibid.

3352. Benazir Bhutto (1953–)

1 Every dictator uses religion as a prop to keep himself in power.
Interview, *60 Minutes*, CBS-TV *8 August 1986*

2 A ship in port is safe, but that is not what ships are built for.
Ibid.

3 Marriage and family are too personal and too precious to barter away.
"Pakistani politician marries" (p. A–21), *Times-Picayune* (New Orleans), Associated Press *19 December 1987*

4 I haven't given myself away. I belong to myself and I always shall.*
Ibid.

*Reference to her marriage to Asif Ali Zardari in Karachi in Pakistan, on 18 December 1987.

5 When a government is run at gunpoint, the youth of the country get the impression that real power comes from holding a gun, not from laws. With the restoration of free debate, students' minds will automatically switch from guns to books.
Inaugural Speech, Quoted by Barbara Crossette in, *The New York Times 3 December 1988*

6 What is not recorded is not remembered.
Daughter of Destiny 1989

7 You can't be fueled by bitterness. It can eat you up, but it cannot drive you.
Ibid.

8 It is cold. I hear the prison clock strike one o'clock, then two o'clock. I can't sleep. The chill desert wind sweeps through the open bars of my cell . . . a huge cage, an enormous space with only a rope cot in it. I twist and turn on the cot, my teeth chattering. I have no sweater, no blanket, nothing. Only the *shalwar hameez* [a typical Pakistani style dress] I had been wearing when I was arrested. One of the jailers had felt sorry for me and (quietly) passed me a pair of socks. But she was so frightened of being caught for her charity that this morning she had asked for

them back. My bones ache. If only I could see, I could at least walk around. But the electricity is turned off in my cell at night. From seven o'clock on, there is nothing but the cold darkness.
Diary entry (1981)*, Ibid.

*Written after the first days of what became five months of solitary confinement.

9 Power is no big deal. What is more important is that the people always have respect for you.
Quoted in *Twentieth-Century Women Political Leaders* by Claire Price-Groff *1998*

10 Life is not always fair, it is not always just, but even if it is not fair, and even if it is not just, it is important to go on working for what you believe in.
Ibid.

3353. Amy Bloom (1953–)

1 In the middle of the eulogy at my mother's boring and heartbreaking funeral, I began to think about calling off the wedding.
"Love Is Not a Pie," *Come to Me 1993*

2 It was like nothing else in my life, that river of love that I could dip into and leave and return to once more and find it still flowing.
"Sleepwalking," Ibid.

3 Elizabeth knew that the bad things that had happened to her were no worse than other people's bad things; they were pretty small potatoes, in fact, compared to terminal cancer, death by famine, incest, quadriplegic paralysis . . .
(p. 132), *Love Invents Us 1997*

3354. Dionne Brand (1953–)

1 Adela, rain ants coming to cover we in water. Nothing barren here, Adela, in my eyes everything full of fullness, everything yielding . . .
In Another Place, Not Here 1997

2 They loved grief and spent every penny on it and thought it made them holy, they had each a parched well inside their chests, sacred and hungry, they went to funerals of people they did not know, they stood at grave sides looking into the despair of the mourners, their eyes became ashy with passion.
Ibid.

3 They have come here to get away from Black people, to show white people that they are harmless, just like them. This lie will kill them.
Ibid.

4 She wants to be the kind of Black girl that is dangerous. Big-mouthed and dangerous.
Ibid.

5 The volcano awash in rainlessness, yellowed light and lemurs pacing, lengthening, reaching white arms out of the volcanic garden and a woman escaping, to think and float at the same time, imagining a place to rest.
Ibid.

3355. Jill Ciment (1953–)

1 The young woman wore a tank top and no bra and her red hair, tossed and stiffened by twelve hours on the sloshing deck,

had hardened into a seascape, like one of those Japanese serigraphs where the waves, all foam and power, are forever on the verge of crashing.

Ch. 1, Teeth of the Dog 1999

2 The dogs were sisters, most likely a mix of pye-dog and Chinese shar-pei, who seemed to resemble (particularly when Finster was high) W. H. Auden. He'd found them as pups, paid them in bones, and loved them to the point where he thought he was losing his mind.

Ibid.

3 With every exhalation, he watched the smoke fly out of his mouth in the shape of his soul.

Ibid.

4 . . . the sheer newness, the unrelenting beauty, the intrigue of an unprobed culture, the mere fact of their traveling together again, would make him, if not exactly well, at least himself.

Ibid.

5 She needed to be so shamelessly desired.

Ibid.

6 In Vanduuan lore,* a boat tugs a whole new ocean behind it. Ocean eats ocean. New world devours old. The foam is the mark of its voracious appetite. Teeth of the dog, the natives call it.

Ibid.

*A fictional island people.

3356. Marcia Clark (1953–)

1 Being called a bitch by some old-time gender bigot doesn't bother me. In context, it's a compliment. It means I've stood up to him, I haven't let him have his way, and now he's throwing his little tantrum. *But from women?*

Without a Doubt, with Teresa Carpenter 1997

2 We lost because American justice is corrupted by celebrity.*

Ibid.

*Reference to O.J. Simpson, American athlete (football) (1948–), who was tried and acquitted for the murder of his estranged wife and her friend (1994); Clark was the prosecuting attorney.

3 As a matter of principle, I don't feel that the government should be in the position of market-testing its arguments.

Ibid.

4 What we needed was someone who would be temperate but decisive. Someone who would be consistent. Someone who knew enough law and had enough confidence to rule from the bench. We needed the ump of all umps. A square-jawed, rock-ribbed referee . . .

Ibid.

5 It's not unusual for a D.A. to be tweaked by a judge's day-to-day rulings, only to recall him as a fine and thoughtful jurist when the outcome is favorable.

Ibid.

3357. Rosalind Coward (1953–)

1 One of the reasons for the failure of feminism to dislodge deeply held perceptions of male and female behaviour was its insistence that women were victims, and men powerful patriarchs, which made a travesty of ordinary people's experience of the mutual interdependence of men and women.

Ch. 9, Our Treacherous Hearts 1992

3358. Anne Fadiman (1953–)

1 What the doctors viewed as clinical efficiency the Hmong viewed as frosty arrogance.

The Spirit Catches You and You Fall Down 1997

2 The more I've read about plagiarism, the more I've come to think that literature is one big recycling bin . . .

Ex Libris : Confessions of a Common Reader 1998

3 When you read silently, only the writer performs. When you read aloud, the performance is collaborative.

Ibid.

4 When I was growing up, not only did my family walk around spouting sesquipedalians, but we viewed all forms of intellectual competition as a sacrament, a kind of holy water as it were, to be slathered on at every opportunity.

"The Joy of Sesquipedalians," Ibid.

5 In my view, nineteen pounds of old books are at least nineteen times as delicious as one pound of fresh caviar.

Ibid.

6 After five years of marriage and a child, George and I finally resolved that we were ready for the more profound intimacy of library consolidation. It was unclear, however, how we were to find a meeting point between his English-garden approach and my French-garden one.

"Marrying Libraries," Ibid.

7 [The odd shelf] . . . a small, mysterious corpus of volumes whose subject matter is completely unrelated to the rest of the library, yet which, upon closer inspection reveals a good deal about its owner.

``My Odd Shelf," Ibid.

3359. Rheta Grimsley Johnson (1953–)

1 And I swear, I can't see a cypress Santa or an alligator-drawn sleigh without thinking of how my Montgomery, Ala., mother whipped up a Christmas.

"Visions of mother whipping up Christmas dance in my head," Seattle Post-Intelligencer 9 December 1998

3360. Andrea Lee (1953–)

1 I had hoped to join the *rank* of dreaming expatriates for whom Paris can become a self-sufficient universe, but my life there had been no more than a slight hysteria, filled with the experimental naughtiness of children reacting against their training. It was clear, much as I did not want to know it, that my days in France had a number, that for me the bright, frank, endlessly beckoning horizon of the runaway had been, at some point, transformed into a complicated return.

(p. 15), Sarah Phillips 1984

2 The town was green and pretty, but had the constrained, slightly unreal atmosphere of a colony or a foreign enclave, that was because the people who owned the rambling houses behind the shrubbery were black. For them—doctors, ministers, teachers who had grown up in Philadelphia row houses —the lawns and tree-lined streets represented the fulfillment of a fantasy long deferred, and acted as a barrier against the predictable cruelty of the world.

(p. 39), Ibid.

3 For as long as I could remember, the civil rights movement had been unrolling like a dim frieze behind the small pleasures and

defeats of my childhood; it seemed dull, a necessary burden on my conscience, like good grades or hungry people in India.

(pp. 39–40), Ibid.

4 "Most of the world despises gypsies, but a gypsy can always look down on a Negro! Heck, that fellow was right to spit! You can dress it up with trees and big houses and people who don't stink too bad, but a nigger neighborhood is still a nigger neighborhood."

(p. 44), Ibid.

3361. Deborah Mathis (1953–)

1 Sport hunting these days is as likely to occur on a playground as in the forest and young hunters are armed not only with semi-automatic weapons . . . but with warped designs on power; a hellish fascination with getting even; and the need to prove themselves to people utterly unworthy of the effort.
Serial failures provide the ammunition.

"'Pork' in crime bill . . . ," *Seattle Post-Intelligencer*, A10
7 September 1994

2 The homeward-bound trend is a logical product of the [women's] movement. Women have been to the men's only frontier and, in large measure, tamed it. Now, some of them are reversing course. For free-minded women, for feminists, there is no disappointment in this because it is happening as a matter of choice. Women are not being driven back to Apronland.

"Liberation gives women the freedom to choose to stay home," *Seattle Post-Intelligencer*, Op-Ed *22 October 1998*

3362. Alice McDermott (1953–)

1 "Aren't you glad that you only have to see your relatives at weddings and wakes?"

At Weddings and Wakes 1992

2 . . . science is not just unappreciated, but bent by loneliness and longing.

"The Behavior of the Hawkweeds," *Ship Fever 1996*

3 Everyone loved him . . . and if you loved him, we all knew, you pleaded with him at some point. Or you drove him to AA, waited outside the church until the meeting was over, and drove him home again. Or you advanced him whatever you could afford so he could travel to Ireland to take the pledge. If you loved him, you took his car keys away, took his incoherent phone calls after midnight. You banished him from your house until he could show up sober. You saw the bloodied scraps of flesh he coughed up in his drinks. If you loved him, then you told him at some point that he was killing himself and felt the way his indifference ripped through your affection.

Charming Billy 1998

4 With so many other forces at work in the world, brutal, sly, deceiving, unstoppable forces, what could be more foolish than staking your life on an ephemeral feeling, no more than an idea, really, a fancy, the culmination of which is a clumsy bit of nakedness, a few minutes of animal grunting and bumping, a momentary obliteration of thought, of conscience?

Ibid.

5 But the child was light as a feather in his hands and the lightness took his breath away. The baby wore a seersucker sunsuit that left his tiny arms and shoulders bare and Billy covered these with a cupped palm as he rested the child against his chest. The flesh was as sweetly warm as if the hand of God had just formed it. He blew softly across the child's downy hair and closed his eyes to say, "Now, now, little fellow. Now now."

Ibid.

6 He foresaw a grassy plot and a granite stone engraved with her name, and the dates, the last not merely marking the end of her life but the end of his youth and that glorious and astounding possibility that he had once inhabited. He foresaw his own pale fingers, which trembled anyway, tracing the carved numbers and words.

Ibid.

7 [There were] . . . long stretches when nothing happened except that one's ties to home were imperceptibly dissolved and one became a stranger to one's life.

The Voyage of Narwhal 1998

8 All five were dressed in fur jackets and breeches, with high boots made from the leg skins of white bears. The men's feet, Erasmus saw, were sheltered by the bears' feet, with claws protruding like overgrown human toenails. Walking, the men left bear prints on the snow.

Ibid.

3363. Harryette Romell Mullen (1953–)

1 By the way, my computer was stolen. Now I'm unable to process words.

"All She Wrote," *Santa Monica Review Fall 1977*

2 Please page our home and visit our sigh on the wide world's ebb. Just point and cluck at our new persuasion shoes.

"Black Nikes," Ibid.

3 I don't think there is necessarily any "feminine language" except in the sense that there is feminine clothing.

Trimmings 1991

3364. Caroline M. Myss (1953?–)

1 We do indeed weave our spirits into the events and relationships of our lives. Life is as simple as that.

Introduction, *Anatomy of the Spirit: The Seven Stages of Power and Healing 1996*

2 Power is at the root of the human experience. Our attitudes and belief patterns, whether positive or negative, are all extensions of how we define, use, or do not use power. Not one of us is free from power issues. . . . Our relationship to power is at the core of our health.

Pt. I, Ch. 1, Ibid.

3 All my earthly studies of heaven have led me to the conclusion that heaven is not a complicated realm. Therefore one's personal theology should not be complicated. Seek to believe only what heaven has issued as essential.

Ibid.

4 The truths contained in the scriptural teachings of the different religious traditions are meant to unite us, not separate us. Literal interpretation creates separation, whereas symbolic interpretation—seeing that all of them address the identical design of our spiritual natures—brings us together.

Ch. 2, Ibid.

5 The universal human journey is one of becoming conscious of our power and how to use that power. Becoming conscious of the responsibility inherent in the power of choice represents the core of this journey.

Pt. II, Ch. 1, Ibid.

6 All spiritual teachings are directed toward inspiring us to recognize that the power to make choices is the dynamic that

converts our spirits into matter, our words into flesh. Choice is the process of creation itself.

Ch. 2, Ibid.

7 Prostitution of one's energy is a more common violation than is physical prostitution, for countless women and men remain in situations that represent physical security while feeling that they are selling a part of themselves in the process.

Ibid.

8 The belief that God blesses those who strive to do good by giving them financial rewards is extremely prevalent, as is the belief that helping others out financially through charity serves to ensure that we ourselves will be protected from poverty. These and many other beliefs of the same genre reflect the grander notion that God communicates with us through our finances and, conversely, that we communicate with God by our financial actions.

Ibid.

9 Nowhere in the spiritual literature, as far as I know, is there one reported incident of a person regretting following Divine guidance.

Ibid.

3365. Maureen O'Hara (1953–)

1 If I can make culture I must act responsibly. If I can only ever be part of the creation I must act humbly.

Constructing Emancipatory Realities n.d.

3366. Anna Quindlen (1953–)

1 There are currently as many Americans in jail as in New Hampshire, but we have no coherent idea of the point of crime and punishment in our society. Rehabilitation? Interesting ideal, no reality. Deterrence? The recidivism rate and swelling prison population suggest otherwise.

Simple punishment? In an age of serial stranglings, serial cannibalism and serial pedophilia it becomes increasingly difficult to figure out the appropriate punishment for tax evasion or even for a single crime of passion . . .

"Jean Harris* gives new meaning to 'doing time'," *Seattle Post-Intelligencer*, A11 *12 March 1992*

*See 2228.

2 Shell-shocked by horrors, we want the bars and the locks, never thinking about spending wisely and well. We invest a fortune on a college for criminals, where people learn they are subhuman and act accordingly, a system called corrections that doesn't correct.

Ibid.

3 The prison staff apparently occupy themselves with the meeting of tiny minds.

Ibid.

4 The child welfare system in this country is driven by . . . the ideal that biological is always better . . . and, because of it we are victimizing thousands of children who wait in foster homes and group homes and treatment centers for parents who, like Godot, somehow never come. We demand that young children sacrifice for the sake of their parents. It's supposed to be the other way around.

"Biological might not be better," *Seattle Post-Intelligencer*, A17 *1 October 1992*

5 In the fight to keep women free it is important to remember this: freedom of speech is the bedrock of it all.

Silence is what kept us in our place for too long. If we now silence others, our liberty is false.

"More, not less, talk of abortion," *Seattle Post-Intelligencer*, A19 *13 October 1992*

6 The motto of professional athletics has been clear for some time—it isn't how you play the game, it's whether you win. Twist a biblical caution, and recent events seem almost inevitable. When money is the root of all, evil follows.

"Behind the double axels . . . ," *Seattle Post-Intelligencer*, Op-Ed *25 January 1993*

7 . . . in recent years it has sometimes seemed that [sports] officials might as well simply hang a calculator around the neck of the winner.

And it also became clear how much athletes were willing to do to win. Featherlight gymnasts, their rib cages aflutter as they stood with arms raised to the crowd, threw up their low-cal meals or didn't eat in the first place. Steroids became the breakfast of champions for the bulk-up sports. Is it really that great a leap from hurting yourself to hurting the competition?

Ibid.

8 People always blame the girl; she should have said no. A monosyllable, but conventional wisdom has always been that boys can't manage it.

"Bad guys give good bad name," *Seattle Post-Intelligencer*, A9 *13 April 1993*

9 Testosterone does not have to be toxic.

Ibid.

10 Stereotypes fall in the face of humanity.

"We human beings are best understood one at a time," *Seattle Post-Intelligencer*, Op-Ed *30 April 1993*

11 Day by day, this is how the world will change for gay men and lesbians, with the power of one—one person who doesn't fit into the straight world's fact pattern and so alters it a tiny bit. . . . Coming out is a powerful thing.

Ibid.

12 But a veneer of tolerance atop a deep pool of hatred, distrust and estrangement is no more than a shiny surface, as civil rights leaders can testify from decades of experience.

Ibid.

13 But nothing important, or meaningful, or beautiful, or interesting, or great ever came out of imitations. The thing that is really hard, and really amazing, is giving up on being perfect and beginning the work of becoming yourself. More difficult, because there is no zeitgeist to read, no template to follow, no masks to wear.

Commencement Speech, Mount Holyoke College *23 May 1999*

14 Set aside the old traditional notion of female as nurturer and male as leader; set aside, too, the new traditional notions of female as superwoman and male as oppressor. Begin with that most terrifying of all things, a clean slate. And then look, every day, at the choices you are making and when you ask yourself why you are making them, find this answer: for me, for me. Because they are who and what I am, and mean to be.

Ibid.

15 Look inside. That way lays dancing to the melodies spun out by your own heart. This is a symphony. All the rest are jingles.

Ibid.

16 . . . the straight and narrow path that often leads absolutely nowhere.

Ibid.

3367. Cathleen Schine (1953–)

1 Have you ever lost a friend? It is the saddest and most baffling experience. No one sympathizes, unless the friend dies, which she did not. I lost my best friend many years ago. She had been my best friend for a decade, for more than half my childhood, and then she evaporated, as though she had never really existed at all.

The Evolution of Jane 1998

2 I wanted to ask Martha . . . why she stopped being my friend. I wanted to ask her if she would be my friend again. Of course I could do neither. One has one's pride. Anyway, how could she explain the end of something that itself had no explanation? "What is the evolutionary reason for friendship?" I said to her. "Good morning to you too, Jane," she said, laughing. "And evolution doesn't have reasons. It's opportunistic."

Ibid.

3368. Susan Seidelman (1953–)

1 Failure is a luxury not yet afforded to women.

Quoted in "Calling Their Own Shots" by Richard Corliss, *Time* (New York) *24 March 1986*

3369. Luci Tapahonso (1953–)

1 It is said that the wind enters each newborn,
a whoosh of breath inside, and the baby gasps

Untitled poem, *Saanii Dahataal,
The Women Are Singing 1993*

2 His voice a white cloud,
plumes of chimney smoke suspended in the dark

Ibid.

3370. Lisa St. Aubin de Terán (1953–)

1 Travelling is like flirting with life. It's like saying, "I would stay and love you, but I have to go; this is my station."

Ch. 2, *Off the Rails 1989*

2 A solitary traveller can sleep from state to state, from day to night, from day to day, in the long womb of its controlled interior. It is the cradle that never stops rocking after the lullaby is over. It is the biggest sleeping tablet in the world, and no one need ever swallow the pill, for it swallows them.

Ch. 15, Ibid.

3371. Marilyn Waring (1953–)

1 What I find so offensive about it [the Moral Majority] in terms of Christian dogma is that it plays on fear, not love.

Quoted in "Gazette News:
Marilyn Wang—New Zealand's Feisty M.P."
by Robin Morgan*, *Ms.* (New York)
December 1981

*See 2864.

2 I don't use all the operative academic words, but it seems you can have power *to* , or you can have power *for*, or you can have power *over*, or you're power–*less*.

Ibid.

3 Since the patriarchy has designated to us power as consumers, then let's do actions that break down national boundaries.

Ibid.

3372. Marianne Williamson (1953–)

1 God is definitely out of the closet.

Quoted in *Vanity Fair* (New York) *June 1991*

2 Physical incarnation is highly overrated; it is one corner of universal possibility.

Ibid.

3373. Oprah Winfrey (1953–)

1 Our prisons are filled with older men who, as young men, had the living hell beat out of them. Every parent who beat them said, "I'm doing this because I love you." When my grandmother used to whip my behind, she'd say "I'm doing this because I love you." And I'd want to say, "If you loved me, you'd get that switch off my butt." I still don't think that was love.

Quoted in Ch. 1, *Oprah! by* Robert Waldron *1987*

2 I understand that there are a lot of sick people in the world. I understand that many people are victimized, and some people certainly more horribly than I have been.* But you do have to be responsible for claiming your own victories, you really do. If you live in the past and allow the past to define who you are then you never grow.

Ch. 2, Ibid.

*Winfrey was raped several times during her childhood, the first occurring when she was nine.

3 Sofia* teaches us that there is a great will and power inside us all, and that you can overcome anything. You can be down, you can even be broken, but there's always a way to mend.

Ch. 13, Ibid.

*The character portrayed by Winfrey in the film *The Color Purple* (based on Alice Walker's book; see 3029:11–20).

4 The great thing about attaining some level of success in your life is being spiritually in a place where you accept it and feel good about it and know why you are there, and not be afraid that tomorrow it's going to end.

Ch. 16, Ibid.

5 I want to be syndicated in every city known to mankind.

Ibid.

6 But somewhere I have always known that I was born for greatness in my life. Somewhere I have always felt it. I didn't mean it from an . . . an arrogant point of view, or greatness in terms of notoriety and money. Because who could have ever imagined this life that I'm living now, or that you could even make this much money? I couldn't have imagined it. But I did think that I would be able to use my life, and that my life could somehow be a force for good. I always did think that.

"100 Years of Great Women," *ABC News Special
with Barbara Walters 30 April 1999*

3374. Jill Abramson (1954–)

See Jane Mayer, 2388:1–2.

3375. Somer Brodribb (1954–)

1 As for the idea that feminists should be ragpickers in the bins of male ideas, we are not as naked as that.

"Radical Feminists 'Interrogate' Post-modernism," *Radically
Speaking: Feminism Reclaimed*, Diane Bell and
Renate Klein, eds. *1996*

2 Postmodernism is an addition to the masculinist repertoire of psychotic mind/body splitting and the peculiar arrangement of reality as Idea.

Ibid.

3376. Lorna Dee Cervantes (1954–)

1 Maybe it's here
en los campos extraños de esta ciudad
where I'll find it, that part of me
mown under
like a corpse
or a loose seed.

"Freeway 280," St. 4, *Emplumada* 1981

2 In my land there are no distinctions.
The barbed wire politics of oppression
have been torn down long ago. The only reminder
of past battles, lost or won, is a slight
rutting in the fertile fields.

"Poem For The Young White Man Who Asked Me How I,
An Intelligent, Well-Read Person, Could Believe In The War
Between Races," St. 1 (1981), *The Woman That I Am, The
Literature and Culture of Contemporary Women of Color*,
D. Soyini Madison, ed. 1994

3 I believe in revolution
because everywhere the crosses are burning,
sharp-shooting goose-steppers round every corner,
there are snipers in the schools . . .

St. 4, Ibid.

5 This world
could be a dream, this
dream, a universe.

"Lápiz Azul," *¡Floricanto Sí! A Collection of Latina Poetry*,
Bryce Milligan and Mary Guerrero-Milligan, trs. 1998

3377. Sandra Cisneros (1954–)

1 Never marry a Mexican, my ma said once and always. She said this because of my father. She said this though she was Mexican too. But she was born here in the US., and he was born there, and it's *not* the same, you know.

"Never Marry a Mexican" (1991), *Woman Hollering Creek*
1991

2 Your body doesn't lie. It's not silent like you.

Ibid.

3 The house was immaculate, as always, not a stray hair anywhere, not a flake of dandruff or a crumpled towel. Even the roses on the dining-room table held their breath. A kind of airless cleanliness that always made me want to sneeze.

Ibid.

4 Human beings pass me on the street, and I want to reach out and strum them as if they were guitars. Sometimes all humanity strikes me as lovely. I just want to reach out and stroke someone, and say There, there, it's all right, honey. There, there, there.

Ibid.

5 When I see la *Virgen de Guadalupe* I want to lift her dress as I did my dolls' and look to see if she comes with *chones* [underwear], and does her *panocha* look like mine, and does she have dark nipples too? Yes, I am certain she does.

"Guadalupe, the Sex Goddess," *Goddess of the Americas/
La Diosa de las Américas: Writings on the Virgin
of Guadalupe*, Ana Castillo, ed. 1996

6 Guadalupe the sex goddess, a goddess who makes me feel good about my sexual power, my sexual energy . . . My *Virgen de Guadalupe* is not the mother of God. She is God.

Ibid.

3378. Louise Erdrich (1954–)

1 She can't keep much trash in a Mustang,
and that's what she likes. Travel light.
Don't keep
what does not have immediate uses. The road
thinks ahead.

"The Lady in the Pink Mustang," St. 3, *That's What She
Said*, Rayna Green,* ed. 1984

*See 2284.

2 The drum breaks. There will be no parlance.
Only arrows whining, a death-cloud of nerves
swarming down on the settlers
who die beautifully, tumbling like dust weeds
into the history that brought us all here
together: this wide screen beneath the sign of the bear.

"Dear John Wayne,"* St. 3, Ibid.

*American film actor (1907–1979).

3 We get into the car
scratching our mosquito bites, speechless and small
as people are when the movie is done.
We are back in ourselves.

St. 5, Ibid.

4 For his ribs, which were cracked from a bad fall and still mending, Uncle Lawrence wore a thick white corset laced up the front with a striped sneakers lace. His glass eye and his set of dentures were still out for the night so his face puckered here and there, around its absences and scars, like a damaged but fierce little cake. Although he had a few gray streaks now, Uncle Lawrence's hair was still thick, and because he wore a special contraption of elastic straps around his head every night, two oiled waves always crested on either side of his middle part.

"American Horse," *Spider Woman's Granddaughters*,
Paula Gunn Allen,* ed. 1986

*See 2735.

5 American Horse took the butterfly, a black and yellow one, and rubbed it on Albertine's collarbone and chest and arms until the color and the powder of it were blended into her skin.

"For grace," he said.

And Albertine had felt a strange lightening in her arms, in her chest, when he did this and said, "For grace." The way he said it, grace meant everything the butterfly was. The sharp delicate wings. The way it floated over grass. The way its wings seemed to breathe fanning in the sun. The wisdom of the way it blended into flowers or changed into a leaf. In herself she felt the same kind of possibilities and closed her eyes almost in shock or pain, she felt so light and powerful at that moment.

Ibid.

6 Our tribe unraveled like a coarse rope, frayed at either end as the old and new among us were taken.

Tracks 1988

7 Land is the only thing that lasts life to life. Money burns like tinder, flows off like water. And as for government promises, the wind is steadier.

Ibid.

8 Even when you plan to have a family, you never know who the person is going to be that you decide to become a parent to. We're accidentally born to our own parents.
Quoted in A World of Ideas by Bill Moyers 1989

9 Columbus* only discovered that he was in some new place. He didn't discover America.
Ibid.

*Christopher Columbus (1451?–1506), Italian navigator and explorer who, in 1492, opened the path from the Old World to the New.

10 The ordained push West was supposed to clear the land of the native inhabitants. They were supposed to vanish before progress. That never happened. There are over three hundred tribes surviving and somehow managing to keep together language, culture, and religion. These are not visible people.
Ibid.

11 Our reservation is not real estate, luck fades when sold.
The Bingo Palace 1994

12 We saw him immediately as he entered the gym during the winter powwow. . . . We saw him edge against the wall to watch the whirling bright dancers, and immediately we had to notice that there was no place the boy could fit. He was not a tribal council honcho, not a powwow organizer, not a medic in the cop's car in the parking lot, no one we would trust with our life. He was not a member of a drum group, not a singer . . .
    He was none of these, only Lipsha, come home.
Ibid.

13 Soon we are trying to travel back to the beginning, trying to put families into order and make sense of things.
Ibid.

3379. Chris Evert (1954–)

1 Once you're been No. 1, you can never be satisfied with less.
Quoted in "Fire Over Ice" by Tom Callahan, Time (New York) 15 July 1985

2 My whole career, people have been talking about how tough I am. Now that I'm losing some, I can see how tough I was—the killer instinct, the single-mindedness, playing like a machine. Boy, that's what made me a champion.
Quoted in "I Can See How Tough I Was" by William A. Henry III, Time (New York) 11 September 1989

3 Wherever there's more money, there's going to be more downfall.
Cited by Anna Quindlen in "Behind the double axels . . . ," Seattle Post-Intelligencer, Op-Ed, A9 25 January 1994*
*See 3366.

3380. Mary Gaitskill (1954–)

1 The photograph loomed over the toiling shoppers like a totem of sexualized pathology, a vision of feeling and unfeeling chafing together. It was a picture made for people who can't bear to feel and yet still need to feel. It was a picture by people sophisticated enough to fetishize their disability publicly. It was a very good advertisement for a product called Obsession.
Because They Wanted To: Stories 1997

2 "I fixed it so I wouldn't have to wash my face off at night," she said. She said it with brisk self-deprecation, as if her face, every-

body's face, was a vaguely ridiculous thing that could come off at any moment. She also said it with pride that she'd acknowledged the problem and then gone right in there to fix it.
"Because They Wanted To," Ibid.

3 [It's] the kind of thing that I enjoy saying at the moment but that has a nasty reverb. I want it to be a joke, but I'm afraid it's not.
"The Wrong Thing," Ibid.

4 . . . he felt helplessness move through his body the way a swimmer feels a large sea creature pass beneath him.
"Tiny, Smiling Daddy," Ibid.

3381. Sylvie Germain (1954–)

1 Thousands of tiny insects of a bright phosphorescent green burst from Juliette's gaping body. They flew out of the open window in a whirl and descended on the cornfields, of which there was almost immediately nothing left but completely empty dried husks.
The Book of Nights, Christine Donougher, tr. 1993

3382. Nanci Griffith (1954–)

1   Say it isn't so
Tell me that you're someone
I'll believe in
Am I the last to know
That you don't love me anymore?
If you ever did . . .
"Say It Isn't So," Flyer (album) 1994

2 This heart was almost taken
this heart had a love of its own
This heart was reawakened
When you came along . . .
This heart hears the telephone ringin'
This heart is gonna let it go.
"This Heart," Ibid.

3 And when he dies he says he'll catch
Some blackbird's wing
then he will fly away to Heaven
come some sweet blue–bonnet spring.
"Gulf Coast Highway," Ibid.

4 . . . when the banker's swarm like locusts out there, turning away our yield.
"Trouble in the Fields," Ibid.

5 I think of my songs as little gifts that I reach out and grab. They just happen.
"Little Gifts . . . " by Michael Walsh, Time (New York) 3 October 1994

3383. Rickie Lee Jones (1954–)

1 Ask me if you want to know
The way to Coolsville
"Coolsville," RLJ 1979

2 And if she don't know your name
She knows what you got
From your matzoh balls
To the chicken-in-the-pot
"Danny's All-Star Joint" (1978), Ibid.

3 There are wounds that stir up the force of gravity:
a cold that will wipe the hope from your eyes.
"Gravity" (1983), The Magazine 1984

4 Draw the Weird Beast
   everywhere you go.
   Death speaks the foreign
   language we don't know.
   Make sure they hear him
   breathing.
                 "Rorschachs B. The Weird Beast" (1984), Ibid.

3384. Anne Lamott (1954–)

1 It's so awful, attacking your child. It is the worst thing I know, to shout loudly at this 50-pound being with his huge trusting brown eyes.
                 Traveling Mercies 1998

2 Nietzsche* said that he could only believe in a God who would dance, and I feel the same way: not Jesus as John Travolta** but Jesus as Judith Jamison,*** the great black dancer with Alvin Ailey,**** a shining, long-limbed, elegant crane.
                 Ibid.
   *Friedrich Wilhelm Nietzsche (1844-1900), German philosopher.
   **American actor, singer and dancer (1954-). ***See 2951.
   ****American choreographer, dance company director (1931– 1989).

3385. Annie Lennox (1954–)

1 There are two kinds of artists left: those who endorse Pepsi and those who simply won't.
                 The Guardian (London) *November 1990*

3386. Martha Minow (1954–)

1 Contemporary identity politics seems to offer people life rafts in the turbulent search for meaning, home, acknowledgment and redress . . . Recognition, of course, is not the only stake. Physical safety, when you are gay, or brown-skinned, or female, in the contemporary United States, is definitely at stake . . . when some people have specifically targeted others because of their race, or gender, or sexual orientation, or religion, or disability, demanding redress and acceptance *on those very grounds* is the only way not to concede those are natural or legitimate targets for injury. Hence, out of this arises identity politics.
                 Not Only For Myself: Identity, Politics, and the Law 1997

3387. Deborah Prothrow-Stith (1954–)

1 Violence is a learned behavior that's preventable. But from the first cartoon to the latest super hero movie, violence is rewarded as a great way to handle anger.
                 Quoted in "Finding alternatives . . . " by Don Williamson, *Seattle Times*, Op-Ed *8 November 1992*

3388. Darlene Marie Ricker (1954–)

1 Just like in Hollywood, image is everything in the courtroom . . .
                 Lawyer's Wit and Wisdom, Bruce Nash, Allan Zullo, eds.; Kathryn Zullo, compiler *1995*

2 Judges are, in many respects, like parents. You have to give them a good enough reason to do what you want.
                 Ibid.

3389. Milcha Sánchez-Scott (1954/55–)

1 CUBANA. I'm human. I have a green card.
                 Latina 1980

2 SARITA. See, what I actually want to be . . . I mean, what I really am is an actress. . . . I'll give you my credits. I was a barrio girl who got raped by a gang in *Police Story*, a young barrio mother who got raped by a gang in *Starsky and Hutch*, a barrio wife who got beat up by her husband who was in a gang in *The Rookies*. I was even a barrio lesbian who got knifed by an all-girl gang called the Mal-flores . . . that means Bad Flowers. It's been a regular barrio blitz on television lately. If this fad continues, I can look forward to being a barrio grandmother done in by a gang of old Hispanics called Los Viejitos Diabilitos, the old devils.
                 Act I, Ibid.

3 My early life was sheer fantasy. Eccentricity was so natural that I didn't know it was eccentricity!
                 Quoted in *On New Ground, Contemporary Hispanic-American Plays*, M. Elizabeth Osborn, ed. *1987*

4 CHATA (recalling her grandmother's words). "Ah! So you're a woman now. Got your own cycle like the moon. Soon you'll want a man. Well this is what you do. When you see the one you want, you roll the tortilla on the inside of your thigh and then you give it to him nice and warm. Be sure you give it to him and nobody else." Well, I been rolling tortillas on my thighs, on my nalgas, and God only knows where else, but I've been giving my tortillas to the wrong men . . .
                 Roosters 1987

3390. Elizabeth Tallent (1954–)

1 She did not bring seven children from Nicaragua in order for them to choose the doomed American existence of nerves rubbed raw by divorce, of quarrels, mutual contempt and lawyers' costly ministrations.
                 "Honey," *Honey 1993*

2 In a chipped sink, before a postcard of mirror, she washed in water so icy it rang in the bones of her hands.
                 Ibid.

3 James is neither brutal nor about to be, but his circumstances confuse him, and he wishes that the gun wasn't all willingness to the hand that holds it.
                 "James Was Here," Ibid.

3391. Helena María Viramontes (1954–)

1 The only way Champ knows her mother's true hair color is by her roots which, like death, inevitably rise to the truth.
                 "Miss Clairol" (1987), *The Woman That I Am, The Literature and Culture of Contemporary Women of Color*, D. Soyini Madison, ed. *1994*

2 She is too busy thinking of things people otherwise dismiss like parentheses, but sticks to her like gum, like a hole on a shirt, like a tattoo, and sometimes she wishes she weren't born with such adhesiveness.
                 Ibid.

3392. Wang Anyi (1954–)

1 How a comfortable life can improve one's tolerance of others!
                 "Life in a Small Courtyard," Ch. 1, Hu Shihui, tr., *Seven Contemporary Chinese Women Writers*, Gladys Yang,* ed. *1982*
   *See 2076.

2 How I long for some hot soup! Aping held my hands tenderly. Though I had worn two pairs of gloves, my hands were still

cold. He put them in the pockets of his overcoat. I drew them out at once. I didn't want such tenderness. What I needed badly was a stable family life, not embraces and kisses!

> Ch. 3, Ibid.

3   "Our life was so beautiful and we were so deeply in love. So we're not poor at all."

"We're only short of money," Ziao Ji added dryly. We all laughed.

> Ch. 4, Ibid.

3393. Asta Bowen (1955–)

1   Violence committed out of moral conviction is still violence. Like everything else, idealism works best in moderation, and in the newly declared war for the soul of the country, we should beware the leader who is too pure; too moral; too well-cleansed. Idealism is the father of fanaticism, and fanaticism is the mother of much injustice.

> "Ethnic cleansing: It could not happen here . . . ,"
> *Seattle Post-Intelligencer*, A7 *1 September 1992*

2   The 20th century problem with creation spirituality, like the 17th century problem with the Copernican universe, is that it spells the end of business as usual. If the Earth is holy, we lose the right to subdue it; if the human spirit is mystical, our materialism must go; if the meek are truly blessed, our concept of power has to change. If we are the product of "original blessing" and not original sin, maybe up is down and down, up; anything is possible. Maybe the Earth is round after all.

> "Can today's heretic be tomorrow's prophet?," *Seattle Post-Intelligencer*, Op-Ed *18 March 1993*

3   We are all standing our ground, ready to fight for the last pieces of Earth that have what we need to survive.

> "No one want to lose ground in NW forests," *Seattle Post-Intelligencer*, A13 *14 April 1993*

4   What I learned from Tenino (a wild wolf) is a lesson in wildness. I learned the difference between a captive wolf like Moose*—a "real" wolf genetically, but not ecologically—and a wild wolf, which is a real wolf in every way.

The difference between Tenino and Moose is the difference between ancient forest and second growth. Ancient forest is the wild forest, the real forest, Tenino's home. The tree farms we plant in their place are "real" enough genetically, but not ecologically.

For us to re-create the ancient forest is like trying to turn Moose into Tenino, to restore the wild spirit to what is no longer wild.

> Ibid.

*These wolves were visited by Bowen at Wolf Haven, a sanctuary south of Seattle, Washington. Moose was raised by humans, but Tenino was captured wild.

5   What we have forgotten in our zeal for equal rights, is that there are two ways to achieve equality; bringing the bottom up and bringing the top down.

> "The ultimate in equal opportunity," *Seattle Post-Intelligencer*, Op-Ed *18 May 1993*

6   To them [doctors], we were not authoritative sources of information about our condition; we were sets of symptoms that didn't fit a tidy diagnosis. The doctor is busy. Case dismissed.

> "Nation's health care system . . . ," *Seattle Post-Intelligencer*, Op-Ed, A11 *27 May 1993*

7   The problem with the health care industry is that it's an industry, not service. The bottom line is the profit of the owners, not the benefit of the consumers.

> Ibid.

8   The world is changing, and the women's movement will change with it.

What happens to feminism matters because at long last, what happens to women matters. A paradigm shift has taken place in our society, and it is a sign of great hope. If women matter, then men may also matter one of these days, and then who knows? Little children, or even old people, might also begin to matter. We could leave behind the -isms and -ocracies and work together, women and men, old and young, to make the next days good days for everyone.

> "Good days for women . . . ," *Seattle Post-Intelligencer* *21 January 1994*

9   The adulation we shower on movie stars and filmmakers differs little from the honor given to the shamans and storytellers of time gone by.

By whatever medium stories are transmitted, be it celluloid in a multiplex theater or a dog-eared book on a beach, the fact remains that some kind of "telling" remains fundamental to human beings.

> "The power of story . . . ," *Seattle Post-Intelligencer*, Op-Ed *6 April 1994*

10   What price silence? What price solitude? The usual assumption is, if we don't know what it's worth, it isn't worth any- thing.

> "We cannot put a price on Mother Nature . . . " *Seattle Post-Intelligencer*, Op-Ed *9 July 1997*

11   For the first time, scientists are making a serious attempt to put a price on nature's head. The total value of goods and services provided by Earth and its processes . . . is at least \$33 trillion—almost twice the world's gross national product. . . . Putting a price on nature is not unlike putting a price on parenthood; we don't call her "Mother Nature" for nothing. Both are essential; both variously have been taken for granted and esteemed beyond price; both are now under the accountant's glass.

> Ibid.

3394. Ann Deborah Braude (1955–)

1   From Biblical bans on women's voices to the attempted silencing of Hillary Clinton,* the control of women's speech has been a pillar of patriarchy.

> "Language Barrier," *The Women's Review of Books*, Vol. XV, No. 12 *September 1998*

*See 3139.

2   Puritans' obsession with the efficacy of words grew out of their faith in The Word. They departed from the Catholic church and the Church of England over their conviction that human access to God resided in the words of the Bible rather than in the church and its sacraments. . . . Yet Puritans hoped that these unique individual encounters with the divine would reflect and support religious uniformity, as well as the hierarchies of a well-ordered society. This created an inherent conflict between a desire for freedom of expression and a desire for well-governed tongues.

> Ibid.

3395. Roseanne Cash (1955–)

1   I'm not looking for your answers,
Just to know the question
Is good enough for me.

> "The Wheel," *The Wheel* (album) *1993*

2   If there's a God on my side,
    Why don't she show me her face?
                                   "If There's a God on My Side," Ibid.

3   I'll kill you if we can't be friends.
                                   "You Won't Let Me In," Ibid.

3396. Marilyn Chin (1955–)

1   for we all know
    lust drove men to greatness,
    not goodness, not decency.
            "How I Got That Name," St. 1, *The Phoenix Gone,*
                                   The Terrace Empty 1994

2   Nobody dared question his integrity given
    his nice, devout daughters
    and his bright, industrious sons
    as if filial piety were the standard
    by which all earthly men are measured.
                                                         Ibid.

3   survived by everybody and forgotten by all.
                                                St. 4, Ibid.

4   We are Americans now, we live in the tundra
    Of the logical, a sea of cities, a wood of cars.
        "We Are Americans Now, We Live in the Tundra," St. 9
        (1989), *The Woman That I Am, The Literature and Culture
        of Contemporary Women of Color,* D. Soyini Madison, ed.
                                                        1994

3397. Darrah Cloud (1955–)

1   SONG. Those who love and understand this country are the
    only ones who ever really own it.
                                   O Pioneers! * 1992
    *Adaptation of a novel by Willa Cather; also screenplay (see
    1191:2–4).

2   I have found a language writing my own gender that is secret
    and which I want to reveal, so that it becomes part of the
    norm. For in language is perspective, and in perspective is a
    whole new way of looking at things.
        Quoted by John Istel in *Contemporary Dramatists,* 5th ed.,
                                   K.A. Berney, ed. *1993*

3   All my themes are feminist because I am a woman.
                           Correspondence with the author *1995*

3398. Nancy L. Etcoff (1955–)

1   To tell people not to take pleasure in beauty is like telling them
    to stop enjoying food or sex or novelty or love.
                                   Survival of the Prettiest 1999

2   . . . men are evaluated by their income and professional status
    as harshly as women are evaluated by their looks.
                                                         Ibid.

3   What was biologically advantageous became an esthetic pref-
    erence.
                                                         Ibid.

4   Rather than denigrate one source of women's power, it would
    seem far more useful for feminists to attempt to elevate all
    sources of women's power.
                                                         Ibid.

3399. bell hooks (1955–)

1   To me feminism is not simply a struggle to end male chauvin-
    ism or a movement to ensure that women will have equal
    rights with men; it is a commitment to eradicating the ideol-
    ogy of domination that permeates Western culture on various
    levels—sex, race, and class, to name a few—and a commit-
    ment to reorganizing U.S. society so that the self-development
    of people can take precedence over imperialism, economic ex-
    pansion, and material desires.
                       (p. 194), *Ain't I A Woman: Black Women
                                   and Feminism* 1981

2   To be in the margin is to be part of the whole but outside the
    main body. As black Americans living in a small Kentucky
    town, the railroad tracks were a daily reminder of our
    marginality. Across those tracks were paved streets, stores we
    could not enter, restaurants we could not eat in, and people we
    could not look directly in the face. Across those tracks was a
    world we could work in as maids, as janitors, as prostitutes, as
    long as it was in a service capacity. We could enter that world
    but we could not live there. We had always to return to the
    margin, to cross the tracks to the shacks and abandoned
    houses on the edge of town.
            Preface, *Feminist Theory: From Margin to Center* 1984

3   Oppressed people resist by identifying themselves as subjects,
    by defining their reality, shaping their new identity, naming
    their history, telling their story.
                       (p. 43), *Tallking Back: Thinking Feminist,
                                   Thinking Black* 1989

4   For each of us, getting our hair pressed is an important rit-
    ual. It is not a sign of our longing to be white. It is not a sign
    of our quest to be beautiful. We are girls. It is a sign of our
    desire to be women. It is a gesture that says we are ap-
    proaching womanhood. It is a rite of passage. Before we
    reach the appropriate age we wear braids and plaits that are
    symbols of our innocence, our youth, our childhood. Then
    we are comforted by the parting hands that comb and braid,
    comforted by the intimacy and bliss. There is a deeper inti-
    macy in the kitchen on Saturday when hair is pressed, when
    fish is fried, when sodas are passed around, when soul music
    drifts over the talk.
            "Black Is a Woman's Color" (1988), *Callaloo,* Vol. 12,
                                   No. 2 *Spring 1989*

5   She eases her pain in poetry, using it to make the poems live,
    using the poems to keep on living.
                                                         Ibid.

6   They catch his angry words in their hands like lightning bugs.
    They store them in a jar to sort them out later.
                                                         Ibid.

7   Silenced. We fear those who speak about us, who do not speak
    to us and with us. We know what it is like to be silenced. We
    know that the forces that silence us, because they never want
    us to speak, differ from the forces that say speak, tell me your
    story. Only do not speak in a voice of resistance. Only speak
    from that space in the margin that is a sign of deprivation, a
    wound, an unfulfilled longing. Only speak your pain.
            "Choosing the Margin as a Space of Radical Openness,"
                       Yearning: Race, Gender, and Cultural Politics 1990

8   Spaces can be real and imagined. Spaces can tell stories and
    unfold histories. Spaces can be interrupted, appropriated, and
    transformed through artistic and literary practice.
                                                         Ibid.

9 We are wedded in language, have our being in words. Language is also a place of struggle. Dare I speak to oppressed and oppressor in the same voice? Dare I speak to you in a language that will move beyond the boundaries of domination—a language that will not bind you, fence you in, or hold you? Language is also a place of struggle. The oppressed struggle in language to recover ourselves, to reconcile, to reunite, to renew. Our words are not without meaning, they are an action, a resistance. Language is also a place of struggle.

Ibid.

10 In our young minds houses that belonged to women were their special domain, not as property, but as places where all that truly mattered in life took place—the warmth and comfort of shelter, the feeding of our bodies, the nurturing of our souls. There we learned dignity, integrity of being; there we learned to have faith. The folks who made this life possible, who were our primary guides and teachers, were black women.

"Homeplace (a site of resistance)," *Ibid.*

11 I want to remember these black women today. The act of remembrance is a conscious gesture honoring their struggle, their effort to keep something for their own. I want us to respect and understand that this effort has been and continues to be a radically subversive political gesture. For those who dominate and oppress us benefit most when we have nothing to give our own, when they have so taken from us our dignity, our humanness that we have nothing left, no "homeplace" where we can recover ourselves. I want us to remember these black women today, both past and present.

Ibid.

12 It is no accident that this homeplace, as fragile and as transitional as it may be, a makeshift shed, a small bit of earth where one rests, is always subject to violation and destruction. For when a people no longer have the space to construct homeplace, we cannot build a meaningful community of resistance.

Ibid.

13 We can no longer act as though sexism in black communities does not threaten our solidarity; any force which estranges and alienates us from one another serves the interests of racist domination.

Ibid.

14 . . . no level of individual self-actualization alone can sustain the marginalized and oppressed. We must be linked to collective struggle, to communities of resistance that move us outward into the world.

Sisters of the Yam: Black Women and Self-Recovery 1993

15 For some time now . . . I have seen that we cannot fully create effective movements for social change if individuals struggling for that change are not self-actualized or working towards that end. When wounded individuals come together in groups to make change our collective struggle is often undermined by all that has not been dealt with emotionally.

(pp. 4–5), *Ibid.*

16 One aspect of the myth of the "strong" black woman that continues to inform black women's self-concept is the assumption that we are somehow an earthy mother goddess who has built-in capacities to deal with all manner of hardship without breaking down, physically or mentally. Many black women accept this myth and perpetuate it. Providing a convenient mask, it can be the projected identity that hides addiction and mental illness among black women.

(p. 70), *Ibid.*

17 Working with women, especially black women, I have found that many of us are willing to acknowledge the evils of sexism, the way it wounds and hurts everyone, but are reluctant to make that conversion to feminist thinking that would require substantive changes in habits of being.

Quoted in Introduction to *Women and Madness*, 25th Anniversary Ed. by Phyllis Chesler* 1997

*See 2787.

3400. Debbie Horsfield (1955–)

1 We don't quarrel with a good review—except to ask why it's assumed that a woman can't write a play about football without wielding a sledge hammer and aiming it in the general direction of the male.

Introduction, *Plays by Women*, Vol. 1, Michelene Wandor,* ed. 1982

*See 2831.

2 PHIL. Oh, we're all dead ignorant up North, aren't we? It's dead embarrassing. How d'y'admit y've never been wind-surfing—never read Gormenghast—never heard of David Hockney? I've missed out. I'm not a Feminist, Friend-of-the-Earth, Ban-the-Bomber, Real Ale Freak. What am I? I don't know anything. Y'go to school, y'sit exams—nobody tells yer about Jean-Luc Godard or reading the *The Guardian*. Football? Oh but you don't actually go? Oh no, not me. Not much. What d'y'do if y'can't stand yoga, despise *The Hobbit*—an' thought that Donizetti was a cheap martini? How can y'be taken seriously if yer favorite film's *The Jungle Book*?

True Dare Kiss 1983

3401. Barbara Kingsolver (1955–)

1 Those times made bonds among people. The clotheslines ran from house to house and the wash ran between families like the same drab flag repeated over and over, uniting them all in the nation of washtubs and rough knuckles. There was love in that life, a kind of solid hope. Children ran heedless under the flapping laundry in a nation of their own. But it's Alice's impression that most of them grew up with hungry hearts, feeling sure that one day they would run out of everything again.

Pigs in Heaven 1993

2 This isn't a city, it's a car wash.*

Ibid.

*Reference to Seattle, Washington.

3 There's a banner over my desk and over my life that says, "Respect People."

"Fast Ride on 'Pigs'" by John Marshall, *Seattle Post-Intelligencer*, C1–2 *20 July 1993*

4 What is the conqueror's wife, if not a conquest herself? . . . That's what we yell back at history, always, always.

The Poisonwood Bible 1998

5 May Africa talk back? Might those pagan babies send *us* to hell for living too far from a jungle? Because we have not tasted the sacrament of palm nuts?

Ibid.

6 That is the story of Congo they are telling now in America: a tale of cannibals. I know about this kind of story—the lonely look down upon the hungry; the hungry look down upon the starving. The guilty blame the damaged. . . . It makes everyone feel much better.

Ibid.

7   So sorry, but Ike* should perhaps be killed now with a poi-soned arrow. . . . What sort of man would wish to murder the president of another land? None but a barbarian. A man with a bone in his hair.

Ibid.

*Dwight D. Eisenhower, (1890–1969), 34th president of the United States (1953–61).

8   [Voodoo] . . . embraces death as its company, not its enemy.

Ibid.

3402. Véronique Tadjo (1955–)

1   Be wary of your guiding star. It may fall from the heavens and disintegrate into dust and ash.

Ch. LIX, *A vol d'oiseau* (As the crow flies, or In a straight line) *1986*

2   Need one be blind not to see?
Deaf not to hear?
Mute not to cry?

Ibid. Ch. LX

3403. Judith "Judy" Perez Martinez (1955–)

1   I hope we're moving not toward focusing more on how women can conform to the [law] profession as it exists, but how we can bring women's characteristics and qualities to bet-ter the profession.

"Back to the Future," *Perspectives* Fall 1997

3404. Candia McWilliam (1955–)

1   A man that unironic would be valuable in war.

Debatable Land 1995

2   At the bow of the boat the anchor chain girned with a faint but surprisingly serious sound, as though the stone knight on a tomb were waking and beginning heavily to stir in his burden-some carapace, the stone conjunctions of his armour beginning painfully to grate into articulation.

Ibid.

3405. Louise Page (1955–)

1   [She] wrecked her life trying to keep her body whole. I did not ask her to be beautiful but to be there.

Tissue 1978

2   LEONARD. You expect everything in you to shrivel [when you get old]. All the hate and the longing. The lust. You don't ex-pect to have them any more. But there isn't much else so you have them all the more. I could kill now. If I had the strength. . . . That's not what you expect.

Salonika 1982

3   [When asked why she writes about women]: Why not? Men write about men and no one asks them why.

Quoted in "Golden Girl," *The Stage Guardian* (London) *13 April 1984*

4   Feminism is about doing what you want to do to the best of your ability and not being stopped. It's not about being told what to do by feminists.

Quoted in *The Woman's Post* (London) *n.d.*

3406. Karen Propp (1955?–)

1   In my experience, when wanting a child is a long-term, aching pain and trying to have one involves heroic medical measures,

the narcissism inherent in parenting is often exacerbated. The inability to become pregnant easily becomes a devastating fe-male failure.

"The end and the means," *The Women's Review of Books,* Vol. XV, No. 12 *September 1998*

2   When having a child entails expending so much time, effort and, yes, money, it's difficult not to make the end result—a healthy baby—into an object.

Ibid.

3407. Joyce Radtke (1955–)

1   Like Persephone, the Greek goddess of eternal spring, I jour-neyed into the dark realms and used the seeds of creativity to find my way home. By imaging myself as Persephone, I was able to escape from the pain, the grieving, the dark and barren landscape the doctors painted for me. I have returned to the light, to living moments as they come and embracing every second I have.

Artist's Statement, Art.Rage.Us exhibit, Los Angeles Public Library *March 1999*

3408. Raven (1955–)

1   I'm dying slowly. I need to feel the earth under my feet. This place resembles a tomb. I'm sealed away from the things that make living living. I need fresh air and space to move. I often ask the guards to bring me a cup of fresh air . . .

Letter to Beth Brant* (6 January 1983), *A Gathering of Spirit*, Beth Brant, ed. *1984*

*See 2842.

2   Many Christians write [to me], but I do not believe the way they do. They are really weird sometimes. I usually ignore them. They only want to save my soul. I need to save my life.

(26 January 1983), Ibid.

3409. Maureen Reddy (1955–)

1   It was only when I stopped being white, in some sense, that I began to understand what whiteness means in America. . . . [making] whiteness visible, becoming aware of whiteness as a social construction, moves out of the mainstream of whiteness. . . . In all-white groups, I feel like a secret spy.*

Crossing the Color Line: Race, Parenting, and Culture 1994

*Reference to her marriage to an African-American man.

2   . . . white people in responsible positions are usually unwilling to admit that racism exists in their environment in any form. And if the racism isn't overt—in other words, if no one is run-ning down the halls screaming "nigger" and wearing a Klan hood—you can count on a long, uphill struggle.

Ibid.

3   Someone would make a racist remark within my hearing and I would launch an assault. . . . I started to feel like a maniac, un-able to control myself and my newfound propensity for violence, a sort of Dr. Jekyll and Ms. Hyde for the twentieth century.

Ibid.

3410. Sara Roy (1955–)

1   Palestinian women leaders have consistently grappled with the subordination of women's rights to the nationalist cause. For women as for men, nationalism has always provided the only acceptable context for political activity. . . . But what happens

when nationalism dies and with it the political structure to which the women's movement so directly tied itself?

"Conflicts, challenges and changes," *New Directions for Women*, Vo. XIV, No. 4 *January 1997*

2 Perhaps the greatest and most painful loss to the [Palestinian] movement has been the destruction of its ties to the majority of women at the grassroots level, who now feel abandoned and betrayed by their leadership at a time of acute need and unprecedented hardship.

Ibid.

3 As I think of the women in this [Palestinian] family . . . it is clear that it is not just the kitchen that constrains them but, perhaps more tragically, the lack of food to prepare in it.

"One step forward, two steps back," *The Women's Review of Books*, Vol. XVI, No. 3 *December 1998*

3411. Spring Mae Selby (1955–)

1 I can polish mahogany way better than I can practice monogamy.

Stand–up act, Comedy Underground (Seattle) *12 November 1997*

2 It's not what *was* I thinking, it's that I *wasn't* thinking.

Stand-up act, Giggles Comedy Nite Club (Seattle) *5 June 1999*

3 I will not limit the amount of love that I put into the universe!

Stand-up act, Parkhurst's (Seattle) *8 August 1999*

3412. Debbie Taylor (1955?–)

1 Turn your minds—backward—Oh white-faced men—I beg you!
With your secretaries and your reports,
REMEMBER—How Africa—WAS—when you landed.
beaching your ships on our shores.
You found FIELDS—with NO FENCES.
WORK—with NO PROFIT . . . CROPS—with NO OWNERS.

"Africa, My Africa," St. 16, *Moto* (African newspaper) *April 1985*

2 Who will undo all the HARM that's been done to us?
Will you hold—one more summit?
Will you write—one more report?
Will you hold—another decade?
LISTEN TO ME! THE WOMAN—OF AFRICA.

Ibid.

3413. Terry Tempest Williams (1955–)

1 Writing becomes an act of compassion toward life, the life we so often refuse to see because if we look too closely or feel too deeply, there may be no end to our suffering. But words empower us, move us beyond our suffering and set us free. This is the sorcery of literature. We are healed by our stories.

An Unspoken Hunger: Stories from the Field 1994

2 The world's on fire, and each of us has to do our work.

Quoted in "Naturalist writes with compassion" by John Marshall, *Seattle Post-Intelligencer 12 May 1994*

3 You have to stay quiet to write.

Ibid.

3414. Deborah Winger (1955–)

1 I was never afraid of failure after that* because, I think, coming that close to death, you get kissed. With the years, the actual experience of course fades, but the flavor of it doesn't.

Quoted in "What Choice Do I Have But To Live Fully" by Lisa Birbach, *Parade Magazine 6 March 1994*
*Of her brush with death.

2 I don't believe in careers. I believe in work.

Ibid.

3415. Thalia Zepatos (1955–)

1 A procession of indigo clouds marched in, while thunder boomed like temple drums. Then the breeze drew a gauzy curtain of mist across the ravine. Within minutes the rain was falling in giant gobs.

"Galleries and gamelans," *The Women's Review of Books*, Vol. XII, Nos. 10–11 *July 1995*

2 . . . hard work has always been an equal opportunity employer.

Ibid.

3415.1. Barbara Bonney (1956–)

1 She [Ilia in Mozart's* opera *Idomeneo*] is a true blue female in the best sense of the word: the tender, nurturing sense that can make such women the salt of the earth. She is the Mother Teresa** of operatic characters because she gives without wanting anything back. It's all in one direction, it's all give. And that is something very, very special.

Quoted in *Diva, The New Generation: The Sopranos and Mezzos of the Decade Discuss Their Roles* by Helena Matheopoulous *1998*
*Wolfgang Amadeus Mozart, Austrian composer (1756–1791).
**See 1973.

3416. Rose Brady (1956–)

1 The task, then, was to dismantle the machine. He* had come up against fierce opponents of reform, and in the political-economic game that ensued he had not always played clean. But he kept his eye on the prize. The prize was a non-Communist Russia in which private property dominated the economy.

Kapitalizm: Russia's Struggle to Free Its Economy 1999
*Reference to Anatoly Chubais, aide to Boris Yeltsin, Soviet and Russian political leader *(1931–); president of Russia (1991–2000).

3417. Lucie Brock-Broido (1956–)

1 Sometimes I think I will be broken by your lukewarm Hand

"Into Those Great Countries of the Blue Sky of Which We Don't Know Anything," *The Master Letters 1995*

2 *Should you, before this reaches you, experience Immortality, Who will inform me of the exchange?*

Ibid.

3 My world is as ordered as if—as if I
had stacked the stars in the nightsky's
orchard, senseless as crates of fish
stacked glimmering, one-eyed &
blank, one atop the other of them, cold
as Rome apples or a new moon.

Ibid.

3418. Eileen Collins (1956–)

1 Because of [Amelia Earhart],* we had more women available to fly in the 1940s to help us get through World War II. And because of these women, women of my generation are able to look back and say, "Hey, they did it. They even flew military airplanes, we can do it, too."

"100 Years of Great Women," ABC News Special with Barbara Walters 30 April 1999
*See 1710.

3419. Sarah Daniels (1956–)

1 MARY (suicide note to her husband). Your dinner and my head are in the oven.

Ripen Our Darkness 1981

3420. Carrie Fisher (1956–)

1 Actors may know how to act, but a lot of them don't know how to behave.

Postcards From the Edge 1987

2 I was into pain reduction and mind expansion, but what I've ended up with is pain expansion and mind reduction.

Ibid.

3 Instant gratification takes too long.

Ibid.

4 Relationship—that silk purse turned sow's ear . . .

Ibid.

5 The message about sex and relationships that she had gotten as a child . . . was confused, contradictory. Sex was for men, and marriage, like lifeboats, was for women and children.

Surrender the Pink 1990

6 . . . [my] short list of long-term friends.

Delusions of Grandma 1994

3421. Anita Hill (1956–)

1 I had to tell the truth.

Quoted in "A Moment of Truth," *Newsweek* (New York) *21 October 1991*

2 I would have preferred not to endure what I endured . . .*

Speech, Hunter College (New York City, 25 April 1992), Cited by Deborah Sontag, *The New York Times 26 April 1992*
*Reference to the Clarence Thomas, American jurist and Supreme Court associate justice, (1948–), sexual harassment hearing held by the U.S. Senate Judiciary Committee, October 1991.

3 . . . we need to turn the question around to look at the harasser, not the target. We need to be sure that we can go out and look anyone who is a victim of harassment in the eye and say, "You do not have to remain silent anymore."

Ibid.

4 The way of modern journalism, reducing persons to icons, appeared at that moment* to have lost its skill for dealing with mere human beings.

Speaking Truth to Power 1997
*Reference to 15 October 1991, the day Clarence Thomas was confirmed as associate justice of the Supreme Court.

5 . . . I felt far removed from the hearing, the demonstrations which followed, and the Senate vote. That was all I wanted—to find the peace in my life that had vanished with the leak of my statement.

Ibid.

6 The possible violation of a woman's civil rights is not the same as the emotional pain and loss of trust that result from extramarital affairs. Equating the two promotes a form of moral fundamentalism that devalues women and the issues they face and offers only a formulaic approach to addressing them.

"Clinton-Lewinsky is not Thomas-Hill," Seattle Post-Intelligencer, Op-Ed, A7 29 September 1998

3422. Mae Jemison (1956–)

1 To me [Bessie Coleman*] is that ephemeral daydream of adventure, strength, audacity, and beauty that we all seek, hope, and somehow know must be present in the world.

Quoted in *Queen Bess: Daredevil Aviator* by Doris Rich *1993*
*See 1628.

3423. Rebecca L. Johnson (1956–)

1 The dirt in Boston is nothing like the good Ohio soil back home.

"New Moon Over Roxbury," *Ecofeminism and the Sacred*, Carol J. Adams, ed. *1993*

3424. Naomi Littlebear (1956?–)

1 You can't kill the spirit
It's like a mountain
old and strong; it lives on and on.

"Like a Mountain" 1976

3425. Emily Lyon (1956–)

1 It has been 26 years since *Roe vs. Wade.** We thought that was all that would be necessary, but now we have to continually protect that right, day after day.

Quoted in "Bombing victim builds a life . . . " by Rheta Grimsley Johnson**, *Seattle Post-Intelligencer*, A9 *6 February 1999*
*Supreme Court decision legalizing abortion (1973); also see Sarah Weddington, 3075. **See 3359.

3426. Lilian Nattel (1956–)

1 "A real writer tells the truth, and that's how he changes the world."

The River Midnight 1999

2 "I'm going to be independent like Misha was before she got herself into trouble. And who brought her down?" Ruthie asked agitatedly. "Nobody knows for sure, but it wasn't an angel, I can tell you. It was some man."

Ibid.

3 "I'm telling you plain, everything is God. Are you looking, Hayim? Are you using your eyes? The Baal Shem Tov, of blessed memory, spent days in the fields and the woods, and there he saw the Holy One arising from every living thing and also the stones."

Ibid.

3427. Mariah Burton Nelson (1956–)

1 I found that women's responses to the male-dominated sports system are as diverse and complex as their responses

to the male-dominated social, political, and economic system. . . . Dismayed by "winning is the only thing" ethic that presides over . . . "mainstream sport," many women are once again questioning the dualism and danger inherent in the male model.

Are We Winning Yet? How Women are Changing Sports and Sports are Changing Women 1991

2 By playing sports, women are challenged to see themselves not as the same as men but as equally entitled to define the nature of the games and the relationships between and among players.

Ibid.

3 The story of women in sports is a personal story, because nothing is more personal than a woman's bone, sinew, sweat and desire, and a political story, because nothing is more powerful than a woman's struggle to be free.

Introduction, *Nike Is a Goddess*, Lissa Smith, ed. *1999*

3428. Fae Myenne Ng (1956–)

1 Fault. In English or Cantonese that was the word we were all afraid of. I held it like a seed in my mouth. As kids, the three of us loved to suck on dried plums. Long after the sour and salty fruit dissolved, the seed stayed sweet, the true secret. Now I was afraid my secret guilt would start to grow sweet, and I would never want to spit it out.

Bone 1992

2 *The heart never travels.*
   I believe in holding still. I believe that the secrets we hold in our hearts are our anchors, that even the unspoken between us is a measure of our every promise to the living and to the dead. And all our promises, like all our hopes, move us through life with the power of an ocean liner pushing the sea.

Ibid.

3 Bones are what's left, they're what lasts.

Quoted in "Author digs deep into immigrant struggle" by M.L. Lyke, *Seattle Post-Intelligencer*, C1–2 *30 January 1993*

4 The old-timers were so courageous to come here. They had a phrase: "We wanted to have a better place for our children to stand."
   To *stand* . . .

Ibid.

3429. Achy Obejas (1956–)

1 To me, she was like the purest, blackest earth—that rich, sweet soil in which sugarcane grows. I always imagined her as hills in which I would roll around, happy and dirty, as if I were back in Cuba.

Memory Mambo 1996

3430. Dorothy E. Roberts (1956–)

1 American culture reveres no Black madonna. It upholds no popular image of a Black mother tenderly nurturing her child.

Killing the Black Body: Race, Reproduction, and the Meaning of Liberty 1997

2 The social order established by powerful white men was founded on two inseparable ingredients: the dehumanization of Africans on the basis of race, and the control of women's sexuality and reproduction.

Ibid.

3431. Kathy Rudy (1956–)

1 Our tendency to describe abortion one way rather than another is produced not by our own individual intention but rather by the logic of the systems which make the world intelligible to us.

Beyond Pro-Life and Pro-Choice: Moral Diversity in the Abortion Debate 1996

2 Repeal of abortion laws will not end the abortion wars, it will give them a critically different inflection. That is, we will no longer be fighting about whether the procedure should or shouldn't be legal; we will be fighting about the fundamental differences between worldviews and communities.

Ibid.

3432. Kathleen Turner (1956–)

1 Being a sex symbol has to do with an attitude, not looks. Most men think it's looks, most women know otherwise.

Quoted in *Observer* (London) *27 April 1986*

3433. Margaret Casey (1956–1985)

1 It hurts not being a contender.

Quoted in *Time* (New York) *10 June 1985*

3434. Ellen Alderman (1957–)

1 There is simply no comprehensive body of law established to deal with all of the privacy concerns arising in the digital age.

The Right to Privacy, and Caroline Kennedy* *1995*
*See 3007.

2 Even if you don't cruise the superhighway, your personal profile will. A portrait of you in I's and O's, the language of computers, will exist in cyberspace.

Ibid.

3435. Dawn Bradley Berry (1957–)

1 Female attorneys today still face the paradox that traits considered most desirable in a male attorney—self-assurance, a competitive and aggressive nature, and high ambition—are considered by many to be "unfeminine."

Quoted in *The 50 Most Influential Women in American Law* by Dawn Bradley Berry *1996*

3436. Rosemary Breslin (1957–)

1 Once in my life, off the coast of Maine, I dived off a high rock and from the moment my toes pushed off from the boulder it felt perfect . . .

Not Exactly What I Had in Mind: An Incurable Love Story 1997

2 . . . Tony* figured if I was good with all my scams, and now with the responsible repayment of my debts, he could get this to work for him. He ignited my newfound pride in doing the best job possible. And he employed it to make me a solid citizen, something I had sneered at my whole life. Tony set me up and I fell for it.

Ibid.

*Her husband, Tony Dunne.

3437. Jill Dolan (1957–)

1 How do you locate yourself on the edge of an issue? How do you not impose ethical answers but, instead, open a discussion of where the edge is and how it shifts?

Presence and Desire: Essays on Gender, Sexuality, Performance 1993

2   Feminism . . . never held my hand and comforted me. [It] has strengthened me . . . but it's also made me realize how dangerous I am and that my position, however it shifts historically, will never be safe. . . . Feminism has given me theory, and that is where I live.

(p. 82), Ibid.

3   The explicitness of pornography seems the most constructive choice for practicing cultural disruptions.

(p. 201), Ibid.

3438. Jane Hamilton (1957–)

1   I used to think if you fell from grace it was more likely than not the result of one stupendous error, or else an unfortunate accident. I hadn't learned that it can happen so gradually you don't lose your stomach or hurt yourself in the landing.

A Map of the World 1994

2   . . . the grass was so green it hurt to look at it, the air so overpoweringly sweet you had to go in and turn on the television, just to dull your senses.

Ibid.

3   I might have told him that our mission in life is . . . to fill up the endless gray void that is time.

Ibid.

4   Sometimes people get so confused by how fast everything's moving they have to throw somebody out, to make them feel better.

Ibid.

3439. Velina Hasu Houston (1957–)

1   FUMIKO. Ha. First our women put on dresses, then cut their hair, and smoke like men. . . .
KIHEIDA. You see what your Yankee freedom has done? You live in Kobe, a beautiful city ravaged by Yankee fire bombs, your own parents victims of them. How can you strut about in American clothes as Yankees walk in their ashes?
FUMIKO. (somberly). I do not look back, Obisan.

Sc. 3, Asa Ga Kimashita (Morning Has Broken) 1981

2   FUSAE SHIMADA. There is nothing but the present moment—the one we can grasp in our fists and feel.

American Dreams 1984

3   The kinds of plays that are important to me are plays that give something to the world in which we live, that recycle our emotions, spirits, and intellect to refuel and improve the world—not destroy it. Important plays are rich with cultural and political substance. They reflect a social consciousness without losing a sense of the personal. Their vision remains inextricably tied to the never-ending exploration and excavation of the human condition. For theater should not only entertain but also enlighten.

Introduction, The Politics of Life, Four Plays by Asian American Woman 1993

3440. Tama Janowitz (1957–)

1   Long after the bomb falls and you and your good deeds are gone, cockroaches will still be here, prowling the streets like armored cars.

"Modern Saint 271," Slaves of New York 1986

2   I was like a social worker for lepers. My clients had a chunk of their body they wanted to give away; for a price I was there to

receive it. Crimes, sins, nightmares, hunks of hair: it was surprising how many of them has something to dispose of. The more I charged, the easier it was for them to breathe freely once more.

Ibid.

3   With publicity comes humiliation.

International Herald Tribune (Paris) 8 September 1992

3440.1. Caroline Kennedy (1957–)
See Ellen Alderman, 3434:1–2.

3441. Myung Mi Kim (1957–)

1   One gives over to a language and then

What is given, given over?

"Into Such Assembly" 2, The Woman That I Am, The Literature and Culture of Contemporary Women of Color, D. Soyini Madison, ed. 1994

3442. Lorrie Moore (1957–)

1   Wives are like cockroaches. They will survive you after a nuclear attack.

Birds of America 1998

2   In the end, you suffer alone. But at the beginning you suffer with a whole lot of others.

Ibid.

3   There is nothing as complex in the world—no flower or stone—as a single hello from a human being.

"Which Is More Than I Can Say About Some People," Ibid.

4   Walter leaned her against his parked car. His mouth was slightly lopsided, paisley-shaped, his lips anneloid and full, and he kissed her hard. There was something numb and on hold in her. There were small dark pits of annihilation she discovered in her heart, in the loosening fist of it, and she threw herself into them, falling.

"Willing," Ibid.

5   [She was a] minor movie star once nominated for a major award.

Ibid.

6   . . . the mystery of interspecies love.

"Four Calling Birds, Three French Hens," Ibid.

7   A cynic is someone who feels like nothing is worth believing in, that it's all just trash.
I'm maybe just more of a pessimist, I think that all these ideas and these little emotional projects we hope for in the world are all worth hoping for. But that they will come about? I doubt it.

Quoted in "A generation of skeptics tunes in to Moore" by Hillel Italie, Seattle Post-Intelligencer, What's Happening 22 January 1999

8   In this culture we have this idea of mother love being different from romantic love. The great love you have for your children isn't a separate kind of love It is a romance. You are in love, physically in a similar state, and you want this person's presence all the time.

Ibid.

3443. Martina Navratilova (1957–)

1 In Czechoslovakia there is no such thing as freedom of the press. In the United States there is no such thing as freedom from the press.

Quoted in Sportswit *by Lee Green* 1984

2 I came to live in a country I love; some people label me a defector. I have loved men and women in my life; I've been labelled "the bisexual defector" in print. Want to know another secret? I'm even ambidextrous. I don't like labels. Just call me Martina.

Ch. 1, Being Myself 1985

3 Being blunt with your feelings is very American. In this big country, I can be as brash as New York, as hedonistic as Los Angeles, as sensuous as San Francisco, as brainy as Boston, as proper as Philadelphia, as brawny as Chicago, as warm as Palm Springs, as friendly as my adopted home town of Dallas, Fort Worth, and as peaceful as the inland waterway that rubs up against my former home in Virginia Beach.

Ibid.

4 People in the States used to think that if girls were good at sports their sexuality would be affected. Being feminine meant being a cheerleader, not being an athlete. The image of women is changing now. You don't have to be pretty for people to come and see you play. At the same time, if you're a good athlete, it doesn't mean you're not a woman.

Ch. 8, Ibid.

5 The moment of victory is much too short to live for that and nothing else.

The Guardian *(London)* 21 June 1989

6 Wimbledon is like a drug—once you win it, you've just got to do it again.

"3rd time is charm" *(Reuters and AP),* Seattle Times *8 July 1990*

7 As long as the body is willing, I am.

Ibid.

3444. Mia Törnqvist (1957–)

1 THE CHILD.* Nora Schahrazade is not lonely. You on the other hand could use some company. . . . You have to understand that she can't hold her mother's hand her whole life.

The Dreamed Life of Nora Schahrazade 1994

*An "angel-child," not on this plane.

3445. Bonnie Friedman (1958–)

1 An unhurried sense of time is in itself a form of wealth.

"Bit and Pieces of an Alter Ego," The New York Times, *Travel* 14 March 1999

2 Is the whole of life stripping ourselves of cliché after cliché?

Ibid.

3 Traveling, each day is several.

Ibid.

3446. Claudia Henrion (1958–)

1 . . . the identification of mathematics with formal deductive proofs fuel[s] an image of mathematics as non–human and impersonal. Because the final product, rather than the process of doing mathematics, is what is highlighted, people are seen as almost irrelevant.

Women in Mathematics: The Addition of Difference 1997

3447. Martha Kegel (1958–)

1 The proponents of this law [scientific creationism] are trying to sneak religion into the public schools. They are trying to disguise the religious nature of the doctrine of creationism. They have dressed this law with verbal fig leaves, nice-sounding phrases like "equal time" and "non-discrimination." But the fact remains that creationism is a Bible story and teaching it as science in public schools violated the rights of religious minorities.

Quoted in Daily Star *(Hammond, Louisiana* 3 December 1981

3448. Sarah Lindsay (1958–)

1 The world is large
and without a fuss has absorbed stranger things than this.

"Cheese Penguin," Primate Behavior 1997

2 She doesn't know
why this time she pushes past the surface tension
and wimples up the minute incline
on jellied stumps . . .
She feels a pocket
flex inside her neck, she gapes
at the scoured entry of demanding air.

"Lungfish Conquers Depression," Ibid.

3449. Madonna (1958–)

1 Being blond is definitely a different state of mind. I can't really put my finger on it, but the artifice of being blond has some incredible sort of sexual connotation.

Interview in Rolling Stone *(New York)* 23 March 1989

2 Catholicism is not a soothing religion. It's a painful religion. We're all gluttons for punishment.

Ibid.

3 I sometimes think I was born to live up to my name. How could I be anything else but what I am having been named Madonna? I would either have ended up a nun or this.

Vanity Fair *(New York)* April 1991

4 I love meetings with suits. I live for meetings with suits. I love them because I know they had a really boring week and I walk in there with my orange velvet leggings and drop popcorn in my cleavage and then fish it out and eat it. I like that. I know I'm entertaining them and I know that they know. Obviously, the best meetings are with suits that are intelligent, because then things are operating on a whole other level.

Ibid.

5 Everyone probably thinks that I'm a raving nymphomaniac, that I have an insatiable sexual appetite, when the truth is I'd rather read a book.

Q Magazine *(London)* June 1991

6 I always thought of losing my virginity as a career move.

Epilogue, Quoted in Madonna Unauthorized *by Christopher Andersen* 1991

7 I wouldn't have turned out the way I was if I didn't have all those old-fashioned values to rebel against.

Time *(New York, 17 December 1990), Ch. 11,* Madonna: Blonde Ambition 1992

3450. Margie Profet (1958–)

1 Sperm are vectors of disease.

Quarterly Review of Biology Fall 1993

2   I propose that menstruation functions to protect the uterus and oviducts from colonization by pathogens.

Ibid.

3   No matter what aspect of physiology you look at, the core question is: what's it there for? Maybe it is just a fluke or a by-product. But maybe it has a function. You have to know that. Otherwise you're doing blind medical intervention.

Quoted in "Darwinian Medicine"
by Terry McDermott, Seattle Times,
Pacific Northwest section 31 July 1994

4   I had this phobia of libraries. They were dusty and old, and I was afraid of going to the stacks and finding some old 18th-century scholar rotting there. Now I love them. They're like my sanctuaries.

Ibid.

5   Physicians don't look at function. Physicians seem to think if you ask what's the function of something, it's teleological. It's an intellectual theory, and there's no practical utility.

It's not important? It's the basis, it's the foundation for understanding physiology. And physiology is the basis for understanding medicine. . . .

Say we have two theories about the function of the heart. One is that it pumps blood. The second theory is that it's there to give us love and heartbreak.

In the second case it's removable. You had a bad love-ship, take out your heart.

Ibid.

6   I was constantly applying for jobs, looking at the want ads. One of my versions of hell is a world populated solely by personnel directors.

Ibid.

7   Science isn't a democracy.

Ibid.

3451. Miranda Richardson (1958–)

1   Insecurity, commonly regarded as a weakness in normal people, is the basic tool of the actor's trade.

The Guardian (London) 5 December 1990

3452. Sharon Stone (1958–)

1   If you have a vagina and an attitude in this town, then that's a lethal combination.

Empire (London) June 1992

3453. Maria Elena Moyano (1958–1992)

1   This is my life. If they're going to kill me, they're going to kill me.

I'm going to be dead one day. . . . Death is always present. . . . And if my death can serve a purpose, so be it.

Quoted in "Shining Path* slays leader . . . " by Kevin
Galvin (AP), Seattle Times, A16 23 February 1992

*A Peruvian guerilla group dedicated to overthrowing the government.

2   We're not with those who kill popular leaders, who massacre leaders of soup kitchens and the Glass of Milk program. We are not with those who . . . want to impose themselves by force and brutality.

Speech (14 February), Ibid.

3454. Kim Suzanne Bridgford (1959–)

1   He spent his time on the Internet, creating Web pages for corporations. Lately he'd been assigned to self-help. He was surprised at how much people were willing to pay for the chance of transforming their lives: to learn to be happy with their unhappiness or to be the one in a million to buy an estate from selling shampoo. He was good at what he did and was paid well, the long hours showing in his body—slightly hunched, a little graying, the urban fossil.

"Seeing Angels," Calyx, Vol. 17, No. 3 1998

2   I was forty-one years old and had just had a miscarriage; Mark was forty-five. We had waited eleven years to have a baby, but now I couldn't remember exactly what we had been waiting for.

Ibid.

3   Like a sword swallowed, I ate pain for a living; I coughed pain; I slept pain.

Anything to fill the hole there.

Ibid.

4   "Children are there to listen to what you have to say."

Ibid.

3455. Susan Faludi (1959–)

1   It has not been unusual that during periods when women have made great social strides they have been ignored or vilified.

Backlash: The Undeclared War Against American Women
1991

2   What has made women unhappy in the last decade is not their "equality"—which they don't yet have—but the rising pressure to halt, and even reverse, women's quest for that equality.

Ch. 1, Ibid.

3   Identifying feminism as women's enemy only furthers the ends of a backlash against women's equality, simultaneously deflecting attention from the backlash's central role and recruiting women to attack their own cause.

Ibid.

4   The backlash against women's rights would be just one of several powerful forces creating a harsh and painful climate for Women at Work. Reaganomics, the recession, and the expansion of a minimum-wage service economy also helped, in no small measure, to slow and even undermine women's momentum in the job market.

But the backlash did more than impede women's opportunities for employment, promotions, and better pay. Its spokesmen kept the news of many of these setbacks from women. Not only did the backlash do grievous damage to working women—it did it on the sly.

Ch. 13, Ibid.

5   Because women's hour on the stage is long, long overdue. Because, whatever new obstacles are mounted against the future march toward equality, whatever new myths invented, penalties levied, opportunities rescinded, or degradations imposed, no one can ever take from the American woman the justness of her cause.

Epilogue, Ibid.

3456. Sarah Ferguson (1959–)

1   They [British royalty] took them [Secret Service Agents] away after I got separated. My daughters still have them. It gets diffi-

cult when I'm with them, because they work for my daughters, not me. Sometimes they forget who's the mother.

Quoted in Intelligence Report by Jane Ciabattari, *Parade Magazine 3 May 1997*

3457. Christina Herrström (1959–)

1 Seduce the audience. Seduce them and make them think as well.

Correspondence with the author *1994*

2 . . . something very like love and care can be a way to keep sons and daughters and growing forces of curiosity and liveliness in control.

Ibid.

3458. Maya Lin (1959–)

1 You really can't function as a celebrity. Entertainers are celebrities. I'm an architect. I'm an artist. I make things.

Quoted in "First She Looks Inwards" by Jonathan Coleman, *Time* (New York) *6 November 1989*

2 Architecture is like a mythical fantastic. It *has* to be experienced. It can't be described. We can draw it up and we can make models of it, but it can only be experienced as a complete whole.

Ibid.

3 If you don't remember history accurately, how can you learn?

Ibid.

3459. Lydia Lunch (1959–)

1 Women are denied masturbation even more severely than men and that's another method of control—they're not taught to please themselves. . . . Most women—it takes them a while to warm up to the "situation," but once they get into it, I'm sure they're going to get just as hooked as—well, everyone I know is!

Interview in *Re/Search*, No. 13, *Angry Women* (San Francisco) *1991*

3460. Rigoberta Menchú (1959/60–)

1 In memory of 46,000 disappeared Guatemalans, let's give a cry for life. The disappeared will not die. They will be with us, and we will honor their names and their struggles.

Speech* (San Marcos, Guatemala), Cited in "Guatemalan wins Peace Prize," *Seattle Post-Intelligencer*, A1 *17 October 1992*

*Made before her townspeople, upon hearing she'd won the Nobel Peace Prize.

2 Perhaps for the first time, the world is looking at our land. They now know its name.

Ibid.

3 Today we must fight for a better world, without poverty, without racism, with peace.

Acceptance speech, Nobel Peace Prize (Oslo) *10 December 1992*

4 I consider this prize not as an award to me personally, but rather as one of the greatest conquests in the struggle for peace, for human rights and for the rights of the indigenous people who, along all the 500 years* have been . . . the victims of genocides, repression and discrimination.

Ibid.

*The award coincided with the 500th anniversary of Christopher Columbus's arrival in the West Indies.

5 When I wrote that book,* I simply did not know the commercial rules. I was just happy to be alive and tell my story.

Crossing Borders: An Autobiography, Ann Wright, ed. and tr. *1998*

*Her original auotbiography, I . . . Rigoberta Menchú, An Indian Woman in Guatamala, Elisabeth Burgos-Debray, ed. and intro., 1984.

6 The indigenous community absorbs differences, be they sexual, mental, or physical.

"The Quincentenary and the Earth Summit," Ibid.

7 Culture isn't pure, it is dynamic, it is a kind of dialectic, it is something that progresses and evolves. As for purity, who can determine what that means?

Ibid.

8 Our experience, as indigenous peoples, is that religion was used as a powerful shotgun, a powerful machine gun, a powerful arrow, to try to dismantle our cultures. . . . I want to distinguish, however, between religion as a doctrine and as the beliefs of a people.

Ibid.

9 All refugees know the immense solitude you feel. . . . Not physical . . . but spiritual and cultural solitude. . . . When I was in exile, I felt I was a nomad because I could never put down roots.

"Coming Home to Guatemala, 1988 and 1994," Ibid.

10 The liberation movements . . . had no real understanding of the struggles of women and indigenous peoples either. They understood that privation and poverty were unjust, and they knew that they had to fight for social equality. No one can deny that this profound social awareness marked a big breakthrough towards democratization. Yet it did not affect the position of women and indigenous peoples.

"The Legacy of My Parents and My Village," Ibid.

3461. Rona Munro (1959–)

1 FIIONA. I don't know what I'm going to end up looking like. I feel like I'm not born yet.

Piper's Cave 1985

2 What happens if women no longer define their sexuality in response to male sexuality? What happens if we acknowledge our own potential for physical strength, for violence, for aggression? What do we do then?

Introductory note, *Plays by Women*, Vol. 8, Mary Remnant, ed. *1990*

3 Power between men and women on a personal level is a much more complicated thing than any sweeping generalizations about the nature of society.

Correspondence with the author *1995*

4 I used to resist . . . [the] expectation that I would be concerned with "women's issues" . . . messy, sticky, biological things, babies and blood and gingerbread with no relevance, interest, or importance in the "real world." But then I came to think that sticky, biological things actually define what we are and that attempts to evade that realization lead us down the blind alleys where a large part of our culture has taken us.

Ibid.

3462. Mona Sandoval Ruiz (1959–)

1 Death seemed to be everywhere and, sadly, a lot of the homeboys didn't seem to care. I didn't know if they thought it made

them seem heroic or if the future was such a dim prospect they resigned themselves. Many talked as if they expected to die by twenty-one.

Two Badges: The Lives of Mona Ruiz 1997

2   He [her husband] wanted control over every part of my life. The idea that I could work and make money frightened him. He hated to think his grip did not extend to every part of my existence.

Ibid.

3   The abusive marriage is the ebb and flow of the hatred it breeds. In some ways, the bad times, the worse valleys, make the good times and reconciliations seem stronger, more meaningful.

Ibid.

3463. Suzanne Vega (1959–)

1   Today I am
a small blue thing
Like a marble
or an eye

"Small Blue Thing," *Suzanne Vega* (album) *1985*

2   Solitude stands by the window
She turns her head as I walk in the room
I can see by her eyes she's been waiting
Standing in the slant of the late afternoon

"Solitude Standing" *1987*

3   I believe right now if I could
I would swallow you whole
I would leave only bones and teeth
We could see what was underneath
And we could be free then.

"The Undertow" *n.d.*

3464. Margaret Wertheim (1959–)

1   All gradients of reality, all existential distinctions, have finally been annihilated.

The Pearly Gates of Cyberspace 1999

3465. Cheryl L. West (1959–)

1   MADEAR. Some folks wear dey scars on de inside . . . you jus wearin' yours on de outside. . . . You show me a woman dat ain't got a scar somewhere an I'll show you a woman dat ain't lived nuttin' but a lie.

Jar the Floor 1991

2   We [blacks] want only positive images of ourselves . . . We have the right to be suspicious of anything that makes us look anything less than pristine, because there have been so many images out there that have been negative and false . . . [but] I'm going to write about—boils, warts and all . . .

Program notes for Seattle Repertory Theatre production of *Holiday Heart 1994*

3466. Jeanette Winterson (1959–)

1   It's true that heroes are inspiring, but mustn't they also do some rescuing if they are to be worthy of their name? Would Wonder Woman matter if she only sent commiserating telegrams to the distressed?

Independent (London) *6 January 1990*

2   However it is debased or misinterpreted, love is a redemptive feature. To focus on one individual so that their desires become superior to yours is a very cleansing experience.

Times (London) *26 August 1992*

3467. Eimi Yamada (1959–)

1   Confidence and disillusionment are always warring inside me when it comes to my talent. When people applaud my finished work, I find myself a likeable person; when I paint in solitude, however, I often suffer from anxiety attacks and have to just sit on the floor, waiting for help. What help? Help from a God who would make me paint, I suppose. I don't think about God most of the time, but when I feel such helplessness, I want to put myself in the hands of something absolute. It is at such moments that I sincerely wish I were not an artist.

"When A Man Loves A Woman," *Unmapped Territories, New Women's Fiction from Japan*, ed. and tr. *1991*

2   "Having sex doesn't mean love. You can sleep with a woman just for fun, or to make money. You shouldn't worry about our having had sex once, but you should be concerned about the fact that we're in bed without making love."

Ibid.

3468. Florence Griffith Joyner (1959–1998)

1   I don't think a person has to use drugs [to excel in athletics]. There is no substitute for hard work.

Quoted in "For Speed and Style, Flo with the Go" by Ellie McGrath, *Time* (New York) *19 September 1988*

3469. Lilly Walters (1956–)

See Dottie Walters, 2171:1–2

3470. Edith Anderson (fl. c. 1960–90)

1   There were better places than East Berlin to start a new life in the grim year 1950.

Love in Exile, An American Writer's Memoir . . . 1999

2   If a woman has learned before the last day of her life to cast off alien definitions and define herself, it is not too late.

Ibid.

3   Our world was cleft by unjust, unseen powers whose doings . . . we were too ignorant and hopeful to imagine.

Ibid.

3471. Frances M. Beal (fl. c. 1960)

1   The advertising media in this country continuously informs the American male of his need for indispensable signs of his virility . . .

"Double Jeopardy: To Be Black and Female" (1969), *Sisterhood Is Powerful*, Robin Morgan,* ed. *1970*
*See 2864.

2   Let me state here and now that the black woman in America can justly be described as a "slave of a slave."

Ibid.

3   Men may be cruelly exploited and subjected to all sorts of dehumanizing tactics on the part of the ruling class, but they have someone who is below them—at least they're not women.

Ibid.

4 To die for the revolution is a one-shot deal; to live for the revolution means taking on the more difficult commitment of changing our day-to-day life patterns.

Ibid.

3472. Christine Billson (fl. c. 1960)

1 I am admired because I do things well. I cook, sew, knit, talk, work, and make love very well. So I am a valuable item. Without me he would suffer. With him I am alone. I am as solitary as eternity and sometimes as stupid as clotted cream. Ha ha ha! Don't think! Act as if all the bills are paid.

You Can Touch Me 1961

3473. Julie Burchill (1960–)

1 A woman who looks like a girl and thinks like a man is the best sort, the most enjoyable to be and the most pleasurable to have and to hold.

"Born Again Cows," *Damaged Gods: cults & heroes reappraised 1986*

2 Prostitution is the supreme triumph of capitalism. . . . Worst of all, prostitution reinforces all the old dumb clichés about women's sexuality; . . . , that women can be had, bought, as often as not sold from one man to another. When the sex war is won prostitutes should be shot as collaborators for their terrible betrayal of all women, for the moral tarring and feathering they give indigenous women who have had the bad luck to live in what they make their humping ground.

Ibid.

3 The freedom that women were supposed to have found in the Sixties largely boiled down to easy contraception and abortion; things to make life easier for men, in fact.

Ibid.

4 What Mrs. Thatcher* did for women was to demonstrate that if a woman had enough desire she could do what she wanted, do anything a man could do. . . . Mrs. Thatcher did not have one traditional feminine cell in her body.

Ibid.

*See 2285.

5 Fame is no sanctuary from the passing of youth . . . suicide is much easier and more acceptable in Hollywood than growing old gracefully.

Ch. 3, *Girls on Film 1986*

6 A good part—and definitely the most fun part—of being a feminist is about frightening men.

Quoted in *Time Out* (London) *16 November 1989*

7 Tears are sometimes an inappropriate response to death. When a life has been lived completely honestly, completely successfully, or just completely, the correct response to death's perfect punctuation mark is a smile.

Quoted in *Independent* (London) *5 December 1989*

8 Show me a frigid women and, nine times out of ten, I'll show you a little man.

"Where's the Beef?" *Arena* (London, 1988), *Sex and Sensibility 1992*

9 As with most liberal sexual ideas, what makes the world a better place for men invariably makes it a duller and more dangerous place for women.

Ibid.

10 It has been said that a pretty face is a passport. But it's not, it's a visa, and it runs out fast.

"Kiss and Sell," *Mail on Sunday* (London, 1988), Ibid.

11 Now the whole dizzying and delirious range of sexual possibilities has been boiled down to that one big, boring, bulimic word. RELATIONSHIP.

"The Dead Zone," *Arena* (London, 1988), Ibid.

3474. Beatrice Conrad (fl. 1960s)

1 Their lives had intertwined into a comfortable dependency, like the gnarled wisteria on their front porch, still twisted around the frail support which long ago it had outgrown.

"The Night of the Falling Star," *American Scene: New Voices*, Don Wolfe, ed. *1963*

2 We are poor helpless creatures on an undistinguished planet in an obscure corner of a small and fading universe.

Ibid.

3475. Chris J. Cuomo (196-?–)

1 But which women's lives matter to feminism, and ought to matter in the creation of feminist sciences and technologies? Western feminism has itself been "local," disproportionately concerned with the interests of privileged European and American women. It has all but ignored the extent to which colonialism has fed the privileged at the expense of poor women, women of color and women in Southern nations and cultures.

"Fertile hybrids," *The Women's Review of Books*, Vol. XVI, No. 3 *December 1998*

2 Like postcolonial science studies, feminist philosophies of science also find their origins in political opposition to the scientific status quo: the dearth of women in scientific professions, sexism in scientific practice, and masculinist biases that shape knowers and conceptions of knowledge.

Ibid.

3476. Virginie des Rieux (fl. 1960s)

1 "Gentlemen, in life, there is one thing that fascinates everybody, and that's rear ends. Talk about backsides and only backsides, and you will have friends everywhere always."

Ch. 1, *La Satyre 1967*

2 Marriage is a lottery in which men stake their liberty and women their happiness.

Epigram *n.d.*

3477. Greta Gaard (1960–)

1 Ecofeminism calls for an end to all oppressions, arguing that no attempt to liberate women (or any other oppressed group) will be successful without an equal attempt to liberate nature.

"Living Interconnections with Animals and Nature" (p. 1), *Ecofeminism: Women, Animals, Nature*, ed. *1993*

2 . . . ecofeminism rests on the notion that the liberation of all oppressed groups must be addressed simultaneously.

Ibid.

3478. Kaye Gibbons (1960–)

1 [She received an] easy life charm . . . the hindfoot of a white graveyard rabbit caught at midnight, under the full moon, by a cross-eyed Negro.

Charms for the Easy Life 1993

2 [She was] the first woman anybody knew with the courage not only to possess a toilet but to use it.

Ibid.

3 "I still hold that it [the Civil War] was a conflict perpetrated by rich men and fought by poor boys against hungry women and babies."

On the Occasion of My Last Afternoon 1998

3479. Nancy Gibbs (1960–)

1 Over the past 30 years, all that was orthodox has become negotiable.

"The Dreams of Youth," *Time Special Issue* (New York)
Fall 1990

2 If there is a theme among those coming of age today . . . it is that gender differences are often better celebrated than suppressed. Young women do not want to slip unnoticed into a man's world; they want that world to change and benefit from what women bring to it.

Ibid.

3 Today's young adults dismiss old gender stereotypes and limitations. They expect equal opportunities but want more than mere equality. It is their dream that they will be the ones to strike a healthy balance at last between their public and private lives: between the lure of fame and glory, and a love of home and hearth.

Ibid.

3480. Nicola Griffith (1960–)

1 There is a silence at the table and from that silence Lore understands that she is the chosen battleground of her parents, that whatever she does, however hard she tries, one of then will feel betrayed. But she is not even eleven, and she cannot help but try.

Slow River 1995

3481. Charlotte Keatley (1960–)

1 MARGARET. My parents are called, my parents are called. . . . Guilt, and . . . Duty. Wonderful, how they keep the family together . . .

Act III, Sc. 4, *My Mother Said I Never Should 1987*

3482. Enriqueta Longauex y Vasquez (fl. 1960s)

1 A woman who has no way of expressing herself and of realizing herself as a full human has nothing else to turn to but the owning of material things.

"The Mexican-American Woman," *Sisterhood Is Powerful*,
Robin Morgan,* ed. *1970*

*See 2864.

2 The Anglo woman is always there with her superiority complex.

Ibid.

3 When a family is involved in a human rights movement, as is the Mexican-American family, there is little room for a woman's liberation movement alone.

Ibid.

3483. Susanna Millar (fl. 1960s)

1 The term "play" has long been a linguistic wastepaper basket for behaviour which looks voluntary, but seems to have no obvious biological or social use.

Foreword, *The Psychology of Play 1968*

2 If animals play, this is because play is useful in the struggle for survival; because play practices and so perfects the skills needed in adult life.

Ch. 1, *Ibid.*

3 For the healthy, a monotonous environment eventually produces discomfort, irritation and attempts to vary it.

Ch. 4, *Ibid.*

4 The social life of a child starts when he is born.

Ch. 7, *Ibid.*

5 It is the business of psychologists to be puzzled by every action, but if the questions are formulated so that they require answers in terms of special motives, they soon become unsatisfactory.

Ch. 10, *Ibid.*

3484. Gina Barkhordar Nahai (1960–)

1 I never knew that Jews weren't allowed out of the ghetto [in Iran]—or that there *was* a ghetto. I thought that it was just another neighborhood.

Quoted in "Revealing 'Peacock'" is an emotional adventure" by Michelle Bisson, *Seattle Times*, L3 *9 June 1991*

2 Iranians do have incredible resilience, considering all they've been through.

Ibid.

3 Writing is my answer, my emotional reaction to all the injustices of the world.

Ibid.

3485. Vera Naufal (fl. 1960s)

1 The Palestinian woman carries all the burden. There are periods when men disappear, get jailed, killed, and the Palestinian woman is up to the challenge. I mean the traditional woman. She does everything in the house and for the children. She gets pregnant, gives birth, she builds houses and defends the camp, and goes to the first demonstration that goes out of the camp. . . . When water is cut off [to] the camp that is a woman's issue.

Remark* (1969), Quoted in *Daughters of Palestine: Leading Women of the Palestinian National Movement 1996*
*Made after witnessing the 1969 camp uprising in Lebanon.

3486. Tina Rosenberg (1961–)

1 The sicario [hired killer] did for murder in Medellin what the transistor did for the radio. Killing is easy, cheap and popular. . . .

Children of Cain: Violence and the Violent in Latin America 1991

3487. Arundhati Roy (1961?–)

1 The waiting filled Rahel until she was ready to burst. She looked at her watch. It was ten to two. She thought of Julie Andrews and Christopher Plummer* kissing each other sideways so that their noses didn't collide. She wondered whether people always kissed each other sideways. She tried to think of whom to ask.

Ch. 3, *The God of Small Things 1997*
*Starring actors in the film *The Sound of Music.*

2 Rahel froze. She was so desperately sorry for what she had said. She didin't know where those words had come from. She

didn't know that she'd had them in her. But they were out now, and wouldn't go back in. They hung about that red staircase like clerks in a government office.

Ch. 4, Ibid.

3 Her belly button protruded from her satiated satin stomach like a domed monument on a hill. Chacko laid his ear against it and listened with wonder at the rumblings from within. Messages being sent from here to there. New organs getting used to each other. A new government setting up its systems. Organizing the division of labor, deciding who would do what.

Ibid.

4 The Great Stories are the ones you have heard and want to hear again. The ones you can enter anywhere and inhabit comfortably. They don't deceive you with thrills and trick endings. They don't surprise you with the unforeseen. They are as familiar as the house you lived in. Or the smell of your lover's skin. You know how they end, yet you listen as though you don't. In the way that although you know that one day you will die, you live as though you won't. In the Great Stories you know who lives, who dies, who finds love, who doesn't. And yet you want to know again.

Ch. 11, Ibid.

5 There is something precious about living in a place where literature affects lives, creates arguments, fierce debate—it isn't just a clubhouse activity. Living and writing from here [India] calls for a great deal of maturity. You can't just play at being a cool radical. You have to be aware of the consequences of what you say.

Quoted in "Arundhati Roy: A Forceful, Daring Debut" by Jordana Hart, *Ms.* (New York) *November/December 1997*

3488. Melissa Scott (1960–)

1 Trouble's on the nets tonight, riding the high data like a cowboy, the plains of light stark around her. The data flows and writhes like grass in the virtual wind, and she glides along the shifts and shadows, a shadow herself against their virtual sun.

Trouble and Her Friends 1994

3489. Tanita Tikaram (196-?–)

1 Look my eyes are just holograms

"twist in my sobriety" *n.d.*

2 Chance, changes are all that you have

"i love you" *n.d.*

3490. Vendela (196-?–)

1 I was so lucky being born in a country where there's no war and every child has the right to be a child. I realize this is not a privilege that all children have in the world.

"The Power of Caring," *Time* (New York) *10 November 1998*

3491. A. J. Verdelle (1960–)

1 I did not want the girls' jobs. Rather than walk with the girls holding banners that said CHRIST, THE OPEN DOOR, I wanted to be where my brothers belonged. I wanted to hit a big drum with sticks.

The Good Negress 1995

2 . . . history complicates things . . .

Ibid.

3 She tell me I ain't ig'nant, that I shouldn't let nobody make me think I'm ig'nant, that my problem is my language. That I live in a country where English is spoke and I don't know how to speak it. . . . Nobody who sounds dumb will ever be important, she say, no matter how much potential they have. Nobody will ever understand you, nobody who can help you rise, unless you can speak the language of the nation.

Ibid.

3492. Irene Vilar (1969–)

1 The Nation is a mother and Lolita,* who may have had trouble in being a mother before, now would not hesitate to die for that Nation.

A Message from God in the Atomic Age, Gregory Rabassa, tr. *1996*

*L— Lebron; see 2341.

2 Soon she began to look for herself in the mirrors of motherhood. Each new pregnancy . . . must have been another way of filling hollow places.

Ibid.

3493. Octavia Waldo (fl. 1960s)

1 "Living," he had said, "like studying, needs a little practice."

"Roman Spring," *American Scene: New Voices*, Don Wolfe, ed. *1963*

2 The rain fell like a cascade of pine needles over Rome. Rain—thirty days of it. It marked the interlude between winter and spring, and spring was late in coming. There was nothing to do about it but wait. There is nothing to do about most things that are late in Rome, whether it be an appointment, or a bus, or a promise. Or even hope.

Ch. 1, Ibid.

3 ". . . Adam Maxwell, age twenty-four, husband to Ruth. A boy who wants to go to the top. As if the world had a top!"

Ibid.

4 The lazy pattern of living had reinstated itself, had returned an assuagement made of compromises and complacency. It had made things safe again between them.

Ch. 2, Ibid.

5 But sleep had been taking a vacation from her; as if she were a pariah, it visited her too infrequently, and then only out of unavoidable duty.

Ibid.

6 "The war has caved the very heart out of modesty and has left her rather bare."

Ibid.

3494. Geneviève Antoine-Dariaux (fl. 1960s–d. 1973)

1 [Habit]
is the chloroform of love.
is the cement that unites married couples.
is getting stuck in the mud of daily routine.
is the fog that masks the most beautiful scenery.
is the end of everything.

The Men in Your Life 1968

2 The stranger loses his charm the day he is no longer a stranger.

Ibid.

3   She began to think about her friends' happy tranquility, of their affection, of their two non-problem children: the boy wasn't on drugs; the girl wasn't a nymphomaniac; they weren't even quarrelsome. The kind of children nobody had any more.

Ch. 1, The Fall Collection 1973

4   Make ready-to-wear clothing like everybody else? Of course, after all, there is not much difference between the two. The creation is the same. It becomes haute couture if it's made to order with three fittings, or boutique if it's made in advance in standard sizes.

Ibid.

5   Elegance has become so rare today that a well-cut black jersey cape makes heads turn. It isn't chic to be chic anymore!

Ch. 3, Ibid.

6   The general rule should be respected without favoritism in business and there is no reason why the best workers should earn ten centimes more than the less good ones. Workers shouldn't depend on one boss' good will any more than they should be the victims of the ill will of the bad one.

Ch. 7, Ibid.

3495. Margaret Edson (1961–)

1   VIVIAN BEARING, PH.D. I have been asked "How are you feeling today?" while I was throwing up into a plastic washbasin. I have been asked as I was emerging from a four-hour operation with a tube in every orifice, "How are you feeling today?"
    I am waiting for the moment when someone asks me this question and I am dead.
    I'm a little sorry I'll miss that.

(Opening), Wit 1999

2   VIVIAN BEARING, PH.D. It is not my intention to give away the plot, but I think I die at the end. They've given me less than two hours.

Ibid.

3   VIVIAN BEARING, PH.D. Once I did the teaching, now I am taught. This is much easier. I just hold still and look cancerous. It requires less acting every time.

Ibid.

3496. Suzanne Gardinier (1961–)

1   . . . words are the bridges between our separatenesses and are sacred . . .

A World That Will Hold All the People 1996

2   Somehow Neruda's* sturdy aversion to bowing before kings weakens before patriarchs; his view of history is often through the eyes of Great Men. . . . In this telling, the American continent has no mothers nor daughters; the Canto is not a "song of all" but of fathers, brothers, and sons.

"Pablo Neruda," *Ibid.*

*Chilean poet, diplomat (1904–73); Nobel Prize for Literature (1971), Lenin Prize for Peace (1953).

3   There are voices in the *Iliad* we do not hear at length, and faces we do not see, or glimpse only briefly: Those of the people who bind the battle wounds; those of the slaves in Troy and in the Achaean camp; and those of women, who may also be the nurses and the slaves, who are ignored and derided and raped and given as prizes in athletic contests.

"Two Cities," *Ibid.*

3497. Hou Xiaotian (1961–)

1   I was not part of Tiananmen,* but Tiananmen changed me.

Cited in Close-up by Jennifer Lin, *Seattle Times*, A3
13 February 1994

*Reference to government massacre of demonstrators in Tiananmen Square in Beijing, China on 4 June 1989.

3498. Silvana Paternostro (1961?–)

1   Each light is a crowded house with no sewage system but with a color TV, an abusive husband, a frigid wife, and a desperate daughter like Mariana, who wishes she could swim across to the other side where the rich women wear thongs, live in condominiums with smoky mirrors, and where Cytotec [a chemical abortifacient] is available.

In the Land of God and Man: Confronting Our Sexual Culture 1998

3499. Susan Power (1961–)

1   Too many people don't believe in their souls, don't recognize them when they feel the spirit twist against their heart or snap across their brain. And some that do believe hand their spirits over to the care of others, just give them blithely away, though they may be tight-fisted when it comes to their coins.

The Grass Dancer 1994

3500. Elma Softic (1961–)

1   If the meaning of life is not the search for meaning, then what is it?

Sarajevo Days/Sarajevo Nights, Nada Conic, tr. 1996

2   They're exterminating the Muslims as though they were vermin or pestilence . . . setting living people on fire, roasting children alive, raping little girls, torturing men to death.

Ibid.

3   I want to remember everything. Simply so that nothing that human beings can do will ever surprise me again.

Ibid.

4   Truly it terrifies me to think that I may by choosing to stay here, find myself in a foreign land. In an enemy land. In a very new world where there will be no place for me.

Ibid.

5   I've had enough of circling like a vulture around every spot of blood on the streets of this city, describing and recording it. I'm afraid I'll develop a taste for it and start frequenting these banquets of Death.

Ibid.

6   I had one foot in the bus, but the other one was heavier . . . I can't bear not to see the end of this story. If this story doesn't outlive me.

Ibid.

3501. Debbie Tomassi (1961–)

1   If the human body is a work of art . . . I must have been designed by a cartoonist.

Quoted in "A character named Gladys . . ." by Melinda Bargreen, *Seattle Times*, M1 26 June 1994

2   Inside this body is a thin person just screaming to get out . . .
    . . . I ate her.

Ibid.

3 I don't need a man in my life . . . If I wanted something to sit around on the couch all day, I'd buy a couple of throw pillows.
Ibid.

3502. Brigit Dressel (1961–1987)

1 These are all harmless drugs.* All athletes take them. It's really nothing special.
Comment to mother, Quoted in "An Athlete Dying Young,"
Time (New York) *10 October 1988*

*Referring to use of steroids.

3503. Andrea Dunbar (1961–1991)

1 GIRL. It's not that I don't like you. I just want to be alone.
SAM. How long for? How long do you need?
GIRL. It could be a week, it could be a month, I don't know, it could be longer. I just couldn't say at this time.
SAM. But why do you need so long?
GIRL. I need that time. I gotta have it. And I'm going to get it at all costs.
Act II, Sc. 8, *The Arbor 1980*

3504. Diana, Princess of Wales (1961–1997)

1 Everywhere I go I smell fresh paint.
Quoted in *The Daily Telegraph* (London) *28 January 1988*

3505. Naima Ahmed (1962–)

1 Everybody go to the bank [in Mogadishu] with big sack on their back like Santa Claus. They come out with their money, and somebody outside is waiting with a machine gun: BOOM boom boom! I say, Hello! OK, I don't need the bank money.
Quoted in "Naima's Song" by Paula Bock, *Seattle Times,*
Pacific Northwest section *10 January 1999*

2 When I am standing on the stage and I sing, I have a lot of spirit. I forget everything and I'm gonna sing and I'm gonna dance and I'm not tired.
Ibid.

3 We're gonna sing songs about love, stories, make a show for the people because everybody, everybody has a break in their heart. When we sing, the people are gonna feel UP! Feel Good! Good! And we have power now. We have a heart now. We wake UP now!
Ibid.

3506. Karrin Allyson (1962–)

1 Don't have to call Betty Crocker
Don't have to call Sara Lee
This man has done his homework
He makes his own recipe.
"My Sweet Home Cookin' Man," *My Sweet*
Home Cookin' Man (album) *1994*

2 He's a chef of fine distinction—yes—
He comes complete with pots and pans
I've got a nick-name for him—I call him my
—Sweet home cookin' man.
Ibid.

3507. Nadia Comaneci (1962–)

1 I heard a lot of noise before I had a chance to see the scoreboard. And when I turned my head, I saw my number, 073,

and under that there was 1.00. And I thought, "No, it can't be a one! I think I did better than one." I didn't know what that meant.* And after that, they put four digits, so now they can make a 10. I like to be remembered very simply, like the first perfect 10.
"100 Years of Great Women," *ABC News Special*
with Barbara Walters 30 April 1999

*The scoreboard did not have enough digits to record a perfect score of ten, a first in Olympic history.

3508. Carolyn Ferrell (1962–)

1 I am a girl made out of brown peel, not iron and steel.
Don't Erase Me 1997

2 You could say that the fun stopped when I hit the end of my teenage years at fourteen.
Ibid.

3509. Galina Gorchakova (1962/3–)

1 They (the women in Puccini's* operas) are disposed to take their fate in their own hands, whereas Verdi** heroines tend to surrender themselves to fate. Of course, in Puccini's day the emancipation of women was beginning, and this made a huge difference to the way women came to be perceived.
(p. 100), Quoted in *Diva, The New Generation: The Sopranos and Mezzos of the Decade Discuss Their Roles* by
Helena Matheopoulous *1998*

*Giacomo Puccini, Italian operatic composer (1858-1924).
**Giuseppe Verdi, Italian composer (1813–1901).

3510. Ginu Kamani (1962–)

1 "A modern girl. And how do you propose to find a man on your own?"
Daya narrowed her eyes and sneered, "By kidnapping and raping him, how else?" She cut into her samosa with an exaggerated swing of her knife, then licked the blade clean.
"Just Between Indians," *Junglee Girl 1995*

2 I am feeding her with the only food I can give. Blood and milk.
"Shakuntala," Ibid.

3 When I grow up I will smell the meat on men and the smell will keep me hungry.
"The Smell," Ibid.

3511. Taslima Nasrin (1962–)

1 During these days in hiding I felt I was dying every moment. I was not allowed to use the telephone, and I lived in a dark room. . . . It was like living in a jail cell or in exile.*
Quoted in "Bangladesh writer surrenders" by Faris Hossaid
(AP), *Seattle Times 4 August 1994*

*Bangladesh Islamic fundamentalists called for Nasrin's execution for suggesting the Koran be revised.

2 Every religion oppresses women. I talk about the Koran because I know this book best. It allows for torture and other mistreatment, especially for women. And I despise the Sharia laws. They cannot be changed. They must be thrown out, abolished.
Quoted in "Writer with price on her head . . ."
by Barry Bearak, *Seattle Post-Intelligencer*
28 October 1998

3512. Rosie O'Donnell (1962–)

1 Lucille Ball* paved the way for every female performer, I think, today. You have to honor those who came before you and give a hand to those who are coming up after you, I think. Because we're all in it together.
"100 Years of Great Women," ABC News Special with Barbara Walters 30 April 1999
*See 1992.

3513. Michelle Shocked (1962–)

1 The secret of a long life is knowing when it's time to go.
"The Secret of a Long Life," Campfire Tapes (album) 1992

3514. Naomi Wolf (1962–)

1 We are in the midst of a violent backlash against feminism.
The Beauty Myth 1990

2 To ask women to become unnaturally thin is to ask them to relinquish their sexuality.
"Hunger," Ibid.

3 The beauty myth moves for men as a mirage; its power lies in its ever-receding nature. When the gap is closed, the lover embraces only his own disillusion.
"Sex," Ibid.

4 Pain is real when you get other people to believe in it. If no one believes in it but you, your pain is madness or hysteria.
"Violence," Ibid.

5 Women have face-lifts in a society in which women without them appear to vanish from sight.
Ibid.

6 . . . feminism . . . [may effectively exclude] women who are not sure about, or who actively oppose abortion; women who are terrified of being tarred with the brush of homophobia; women who strongly resist identifying themselves as victims; women who are uneasy with what they see as man bashing and blaming; conservative women, and men themselves.
Fire With Fire, The New Female Power and How It Will Change the 21st Century 1993

7 When women are pessimistic about their political strength and feel hopeless about changing the conditions of their lives, it is almost as if they do not believe that democracy means the country belongs to them. But it's true.
Ibid.

8 There are and always have been two different approaches within feminism. One—"victim feminism," as I define it—casts women as sexually pure and mystically nurturing, and stresses the evil done to these "good" women as a way to petition for their rights. The other, which I call "power feminism," sees women as human beings—sexual, individual, no better or worse than their male counterparts—and lays claim to equality simply because women are entitled to it.
Ibid.

9 If we stay hunkered down defensive and angry, we waste our energies. We act effectively now if we learn to relax into our power, stand upright and leave the foxholes that we have almost begun to consider a permanent home.
Ibid.

10 I have done abject deeds for sexual passion. So, I am sure, has Norman Schwarzkopf.*
Ibid.
*American army general and public figure (1934–).

11 Confucius, in his Book of Rites, held that it was a husband's duty to take care of his wife or concubine sexually as well as financially and emotionally.
Promiscuities 1997

3514.1. Naomi Levy (1963–)

1 But how many of us ever enter into *real* rest—not going on vacations or spending time on hobbies but practicing a regular discipline that can change our very selves?
To Begin Again: The Journey Toward Comfort, Strength and Faith in Difficult Times 1998

2 Even the most harried workdays become tolerable when you know a day of holy peace is shortly arriving. The days succeeding the day of rest become days of light too. They shimmer with the afterglow of a revived spirit.
Ibid.

3 Celebrating a Sabbath day is a way to take one day out of each week and live it differently. In peace. It is not only a time to stop work, it is also a time to stop thinking about work. It is not a restriction, it is a freedom.
Ibid.

3515. Jacqueline Joyner-Kersee (1962–1998)

1 Ask any athlete: we all hurt at all times. I'm asking my body to go through seven different tasks. To ask it not to ache would be too much.
Quoted in "Regal Masters of Olympic Versatility" by Tom Callahan, Time (New York) 19 September 1988

2 Jumping has always been the thing to me. It's like leaping for joy. . . .
Ibid.

3 I don't think being an athlete is unfeminine. I think of it as a kind of grace.
Ibid.

4 What Babe* did, she was able to capture the world with her talent. . . . Babe opened the door, and Wilma** continued to push the door open a little further.
"100 Years of Great Women," ABC News Special with Barbara Walters 30 April 1999
*Babe Didrickson; see 2038. **Wilma Glodean Rudolph, African-American track and field athlete (1940–1994); Olympic gold medalist (1960).

3516. Suzan-Lori Parks (1963–)

1 BLACK MAN WITH WATERMELON. There is uh Now and there is uh Then. Ssall there is. (I bein in uh Now: uh Now bein in uh Then: I bein, in Now in then, in I will be. I was be too but that's uh Then that's past. That me that was be is uh me-has-been. Thuh Then that was be is uh has-been-Then too. Thuh me-has-been sits in thuh be-me: we sit on this porch. Same porch. Same me. Thuh Then that's been somehow sits in thuh Then that will be: same Thens. I swing from uh tree. You cut me down and bring me back. Home. Here. I fly over thuh yard. I fly over thuh yard in all over. Them thens stays fixed. Fixed Thens. Thuh Thems stays fixed too. Thuh Thems that

come and take me and thuh Thems that greet me and then them Thems that send me back here. Home. Stays fixed, Them do.
The Death of the Last Black Man in the Whole World 1990

3517. Helen Sharman (1963–)

1 There is very little difference between men and women in space.
Independent on Sunday (London) *9 June 1991*

3518. Alice Thompson (1963–)

1 Inter-railers are the ambulatory equivalent of McDonalds, walking testimony to the erosion of French culture.
"Ticket to Ride the Rails of France," *Times* (London) *16 July 1992*

3519. Cathy Young (1963–)

1 The concept of feminism or of a women's movement remains too closely linked to the concept of women's advantage, of taking the woman's side.
Ceasefire! Why Women and Men Must Join Forces to Achieve True Equality 1999

3520. Tracy Chapman (1964–)

1 I love you
is all that you can't say
"Baby Can I Hold You" (1982), *Tracy Chapman* (album) *1988*

2 It won't do no good to call
The police
Always come late
If they come at all
"Behind the Wall" (1983), Ibid.

3 And those whose sole misfortune
Was having mountains o' nothing at birth.
"Mountains O' Things" (1987), Ibid.

3521. Joanne Harris (1964–)

1 "Chocolate, I am told, is not a moral issue."
Chocolat 1998

2 People who know nothing of real magic imagine it to be a flamboyant process. . . . And yet the real business is very un-dramatic; simply the focusing of the mind toward a desired objective. There are no miracles, no sudden apparitions.
Ibid.

3 "I don't think there is such a thing as a good or bad Christian. . . . Only good or bad people."
Ibid.

4 "There is a kind of sorcery in all cooking."
Ibid.

5 "It is an amazement of riches. . . . *Try me. Test me. Taste me.*"
Ibid.

3522. Christina Baker Kline (1964–)

1 "Did you ever do something—and you know that even if it didn't seem so weird at the time, someday it would change everything about you?"
Desire Lines 1999

3523. Maki Mandela (1964?–)

1 From the cradle to the grave, blacks are aliens, are prisoners. From the day you're born, your future is determined by apartheid laws. Where you are going to be born, which schools you will attend, where you can work, where you can die and be buried.
Quoted in "South African cruelty rampant . . ." by James Hodge, *Times Picayune* (New Orleans) *20 April 1988*

2 He [Tutu*] will not sing the song of the administration, but the songs of the oppressed people of South Africa.
Ibid.
*Desmond Tutu, South African prelate and antiapartheid leader (1931–); Nobel Peace Prize (1984).

3 Black women take care of white children, but no one takes care of their children.
Ibid.

3524. Patricia Pearson (1964–)

1 Women commit the majority of child homicides in the United States, a greater share of physical child abuse, an equal rate of sibling violence and assaults on the elderly, about a quarter of child sexual abuse, an overwhelming share of the killings of new-borns, and a fair preponderance of spousal assaults.
When She Was Bad: Violent Women and the Myth of Innocence 1997

2 The picture of female violence is a rich and textured tableau that we present to ourselves as monochromatic and stilted.
Ibid.

3 Narcissists easily attach to psychopaths . . . Theirs was a pas de deux between grandiose egos.
Ibid.

3525. Andrea Barrett (1965–)

1 His people had a name for Zeke, a chain of soft syllables that meant *The One Who Is Trouble.*
The Voyage of Narwhal 1998

2 . . . there are continents and seas in the moral worlds, to which every man is an isthmus or an inlet, yet unexplored by him, but that it is easier to sail many thousand miles through cold and storm and cannibals . . . than it is to explore the private sea, the Atlantic and Pacific Ocean of one's being alone.
Ibid.

3526. Marina Carr (1965–)

1 GRANDMOTHER. There's two types of people in this world, from what I can make out: them that puts their children first and them that puts their lover first. And for what it is worth, the nine-fingered fisherman and myself belongs to the latter of these. I would gladly have hurled all seven of you down the slopes of hell for one more night with the nine-fingered fisherman and may I rot eternally for such unmotherly feelings.
The Mai 1994

2 There's the word, and there's the word processor.
Quoted in "A Playwright's Post-Beckett Period" by James Larity, *The New York Times 3 November 1994*

3527. Evelyn Glennie (1965–)

1 I have perfect pitch, the ability to hear a note in my head and place it exactly in relation to other notes. And I learned to read music vertically, to look at the full score. If I'm playing a concerto, I must know what the clarinets and trumpets are doing. When I learn a piece of music, often I listen to it by placing a tape recorder between my knees and playing it.
> Quoted in "I Hear the Notes in My Head" by Gail Buchalter, *Parade Magazine* 13 February 1994

2 My deafness is something unique and I treasure it, and I don't want it to be taken away. I want to stay as I am. Sometimes, it has even helped me.
> Ibid.

3 People have the wrong idea about deafness. They think you live in a world of total silence, but that isn't the way it works.
> Quoted in "A Different Drummer" by Michael Walsh, *Time* (New York) 21 March 1994

4 I don't think in terms of loud and soft. Instead I think of sounds as thin or fat, strong or weak. The amount of sounds you can create with just one cymbal are infinite.
> Ibid.

3528. Lisa Marcus (1965–)

1 And it would be romantic of me to imagine that feminism could remain unpolluted by the lures of institutional power and star systems. But feminism has also changed institutions—productively calling into question power/knowledge forma- tions even as it was sometimes being seduced by them.
> "Feminism's Daughter," *The Women's Review of Books*, Vol. XV, No. 5 February 1998

2 Feminism isn't finished. It did not fail to reproduce; it is being reinvented every day.
> Ibid.

3 According to Sommers,* all we ever offer our students anyway is "Ms. Information": scare tactics, victim theories and bad science. Whistle, crow, squawk—we are all transgressive in the eyes of the dominant culture.
> Ibid.

*Reference to Christina Hoff Sommers.

3529. Lady Pink (1965–)

1 Teenagers have lots of energy and are looking for something to do. Some kids turn to drugs or crime. I turned to art. I saw myself as an adventurer, a pioneer woman.*
> Quoted in "Lady Pink Graffiti with Feminist Intent" by Fern Siegel, *Ms.* (New York) *March/April 1993*
*Pink was the first female grafitti artist in the world to be exhibited.

2 We were like sixties radicals, rebelling against the system. I was dodging bullets in the service of folk art, bringing art to the people.*
> Ibid.

3 If you're not harming anyone, all sexual preferences are cool.
> Ibid.

3530. Catherine Sameh (1965–)

1 Queers really are everywhere these days. Many are out, proud, and even living the good old American life—getting married, buying homes, and having babies.
> Letter to Suzanne Pharr, *Letters of Intent: Women Cross the Generations to Talk about Family, Work, Sex, Love, and the Future of Feminism*, Anna Bondoc and Meg Daly, eds. 1999

3531. Cecilia Bartoli (1966/7–)

1 I wasn't born with my voice placed in the right position . . . [We] had to work on it endlessly and painstakingly, sometimes working on a single note for days or even weeks . . . Until slowly, with time, study, hard work and the mellowing that comes with growth, I expanded my vocal range and acquired agility.
> Quoted in *Diva, The New Generation: The Sopranos and Mezzos of the Decade Discuss Their Roles* by Helena Matheopoulous 1998

3532. Edie Brickell (1966?–)

1 Philosophy is the talk on a cereal box.
> "What I Am" *n.d.*

2 There's nothing I hate more than nothing
Nothing keeps me up at night
I toss and turn over nothing
Nothing could cause a great big fight.
> "Nothing" *n.d.*

3533. Martha McCaughey (1966–)

1 . . . I was holding, in the ball of my fist, key tensions in contemporary feminist theories. . . . At the same time that enacting an aggressive posture felt empowering, it felt taboo—in my case doubly taboo as a woman and a feminist.
> *Real Knockouts: The Physical Feminism of Women's Self-Defense* 1997

2 If women abdicate violence without being capable of it anyhow, it makes less of an impact than if that abdication were a real choice.
> Ibid.

3 Because gender is not really natural it requires constant enforcement and repetition.
> Ibid.

4 Self-defense enables women to internalize a different kind of bodily knowledge. As such, self-defense is feminism in the flesh.
> Ibid.

3534. Elizabeth McCracken (1966–)

1 Her voice was a deep sticky void, the kind a woman generally gets through sin of some sort.
> *The Giant's House* 1996

2 Unrequited love turned you into a salesperson, and what you are selling was something he didn't want, couldn't use, would never miss.
> Ibid.

3 Library books are promiscuous, ready to lie in the arms of anyone who asked.
> Ibid.

4 I thought I would be better than I am.
The River Beyond the World 1996

3535. Holly Morris (1966–)

1 Feminism has been all about reacting. Now it's time to be proactive.
"Divas, not darlings" by Hugo Kugiya, *Seattle Times*, Pacific Northwest section *15 June 1997*

2 You don't have to be a martyr to do good things.
Ibid.

3 I have a perverse attraction to not knowing what's going to happen next.
Ibid.

3536. Gail Devers (1967–)

1 I have a message for people. If there are times when you feel the walls are closing in on you, when you feel there's no way out, use me as an example. If you have faith in yourself and you never give up on your dreams, or your goals, anything's possible.*
Quoted in "A testament to courage" by Steve Kelley, *Seattle Times*, C1, 7 *2 August 1992*
*From 1988 to 1990, Devers suffered from Graves' disease; she came close to having her feet amputated.

2 I wouldn't wish my disease on anyone, but I feel thankful that I've gone through it. It's changed me as a person. I'm more determined. I'm a stronger person.
Ibid.

3537. Karin Muller (1965–)

1 Dear Mom, I can't get a single, solitary soul to go down to the marketplace and try the roasted bugs with me. If only you were here.
Hitchhiking Vietnam: A Woman's Solo Journey in an Elusive Land 1998

2 There was nothing. No warbling birds, neither bullfrog nor scurrying rodent. Everything had been eaten in this overused land until the only sound left was the trill of uncooked insects.
Ibid.

3538. Laura Mary Oaks (1967–)

1 In Ireland, reproduction is a medium through which competing national origin stories that focus on Irish national identity and cultural self-determination, indeed visions of "Irishness" itself, are imagined and expressed. An emphasis on women's right to control their bodies invokes narratives of independence, struggles that resulted in Irish citizens' self-governance, whereas attention to the "rights of the unborn" perpetuates a literary-mythical image of a natural, innocent Erin or motherland threatened by hostile outsiders and in need of protection.
Essay (p. 133), *Reproducing Reproduction: Kinship, Power, and Technological Innovation*, Sarah Franklin and Helena Ragoné, eds. *1998*

3539. Liz Phair (1967–)

1 I bet
you fall in bed too easily
with the beautiful girls who are shy and brave
and you sell yourself as a man to save
but all the money in the world is not enough
"6' 1,'" Verse 1, *Exile in Guyville 1993*

2 With all of the time
in the world to spend it
wild and unwise
I wanna be
mesmerizing too
"Mesmerizing," chorus, Ibid.

3 The fire you like so much in me
Is the mark of someone adamantly free
But you can't stop yourself
from wanting worse
Cause nothing feeds a hunger
like a thirst.
"Strange Loop?" Verse 1, Ibid.

4 and I never met a man
who was so pretty inside
he's got diamonds on the bed of his thumbnails . . .
and I liked it
let me tell you I liked it more and more
"Johnny Feelgood," 1st Verse, *White Chocolate Space Egg 1998*

3540. Tabitha Soren (1967–)

1 Of all consumer goods, only cars cause more deaths than guns. And you have to license and register your car. And you have to be trained to drive.
Why shouldn't the same rules apply to guns?
"Gun violence . . . " *Seattle Post-Intelligencer*, A15 *23 February 1994*

2 Gun violence is as misunderstood as the Second Amendment.
Ibid.

3541. Elizabeth Wurtzel (1967–)

1 *Depression is all about If you loved me you would.*
"I Hate Myself and I Want to Die," Prologue, *Prozac Nation 1994*

2 I'm making plans, I'm thinking grandiose thoughts . . . I'm deciding to spend the whole night writing an epic Marxist-feminist study of Biblical villainesses which I've been meaning to get started on for years.
Ibid.

3 *In a strange way, I had fallen in love with my depression.*
Ibid.

4 It is a girl who is exquisite, or preternaturally sexy, or possessed of a talent that makes her beautiful—it is a girl who is special, radiant, a sensitive artist, a delicate flower; it is a girl whose loss to the world would be viewed as the greatest tragedy . . . she is precisely the one who is most likely to mistake her own delicacy for invincibility.
Bitch 1998

3542. Sarah McLachlan (1968–)

1 Oh my brother my sister my mother
your [sic] losing your identity
can't you see that it's you in the window
shining with intensity
"Circle," *Fumbling Towards Ecstasy 1993*

2 I love the time & in between the calm inside me
in the space where I can breathe

I believe there is a distance I have wandered
to touch upon the years of reaching out & reaching in
holding out holding in.
I believe this is heaven to no one else but me
                                              "Elsewhere," Ibid.

3   . . . your angels speak with jilted tongues
     the serpent's tale has come undone
     you have no strength to squander.
                                                     "Ice," Ibid.

4   oh you speak to me in riddles & you speak to me in rhyme
     my body aches to breathe your breath your words keep me alive
                                              "Possession," Ibid.

5   . . . every generation yields
     a new born hope unjaded by their years.
                                                    "Wait," Ibid.

3543. Edwidge Danticat (1969–)

1   There are two ways to go to the cemetery. One is on your two
     feet, the other is in a box. Either way, it is a large travail.
                                       Breath, Eyes, Memory 1994

2   According to Tante Atie, each finger had a purpose. It was the
     way she had been taught to prepare herself to become a
     woman. Mothering. Boiling. Loving. Baking. Nursing. Frying.
     Healing. Washing. Ironing. Scrubbing. It wasn't her fault, she
     said. Her ten fingers had been named for her even before she
     was born. Sometimes, she wished she had six fingers on each
     hand so she could have two left for herself.
                                                            Ibid.

3544. Ruth Forman (1969?–)

1   we don have no backyard
     frontyard neither
     we got black magic n brownstone steps
     when the sun go down
           "Young Cornrows Callin Out the Moon," *We Are the
                                           Young Magicians* 1993

2   poetry is always for the people
     and it is always a time of war.
                       "For Your Information," *in toto*, Ibid.

3   . . . poetry should ride the bus
     in a fat woman's Safeway bag
     between the greens n chicken wings
     to be served with Tuesday's dinner . . .
                                "Poetry Should Ride the Bus," Ibid.

4   . . . it is not your pen you are looking for. . . .

     it is your tongue. . . .

     it will not matter if your pockets are empty
     if you write with a green Bic or a black Bic
     or the blood of your finger
     you will write
     you will write
                                     "If You Lose Your Pen," Ibid.

3545. Lucy Lawless (1969–)

1   [Fame] is not real to me. It's absolutely not real. It has nothing
     really to do with my daily life. Real life is the cliché: You get

up and put your pants on one foot at a time like everybody
else. Then you go out and water the garden or clean up the
dishes from the night before.
           Quoted in "Zena, Web Princess" by David Sheff, Yahoo!
                                        Internet Life May 1997

2   Television itself is obviously a powerful medium, reaching the
     wide world. The Internet covers the same territory but offers
     something else. It's not just a one-way thing anymore. They're
     all connecting up. They're diverse and widespread, but it's a
     tight-knit community.
                                                            Ibid.

3   All television is at least 5 percent eye candy.
                                                            Ibid.

4   Mrs. Albright,* by naming Xena her role model,** showed
     she was amply armed with enough savvy and charm to strike
     a harmonious chord with the natives while staunchly main-
     taining a diametrically opposite view on the Anzus
     stalesmate.***
                          "Albright role model . . . " *Agence France Presse
                                                     4 August 1998*
     *Reference to Madeleine Albright ; see 2616. **Reference to tele-
     vision series, *Xena, Warrior Princess*. ***Reference to the military
     pact linking Australia and New Zealand.

5   It should be understood that New Zealand's shunning of [nu-
     clear] vessels is not isolationist . . . It is not hostile atavism but
     an act of courage, hope for the future and love for our chil-
     dren's children.
                                                            Ibid.

3546. Nina Revoyr (1969–)

1   . . . it was as if she feared that if she stopped playing well and
     receiving recognition, she would somehow cease to exist.
                                       The Necessary Hunger 1997

3547. Nancy Bank-Smith (fl. 1970s–'80s)

1   In my experience, if you have to keep the lavatory door shut
     by extending your left leg, it's modern architecture.
                          The Guardian (London) 20 February 1979

2   Anthropology is the science which tells us that people are
     the same the whole world over—except when they are dif-
     ferent.
                               The Guardian (London) 21 July 1988

3548. Michele Barrett (fl. 1970s–'90s)

1   Caring, sharing and loving would be more wide-spread if the
     family did not claim them for its own.
                    The Anti-Social Family, with Mary McIntosh* 1982
     *See 3566.

3549. Joan Busfield (fl. 1970s–'90s)

1   It is only if we can manage to create a better society that we
     are likely to enhance the mental health of the population as a
     whole. The complete eradication of mental disorder in both
     women and men is a utopian dream; some reduction in disor-
     der through making our social institutions and social arrange-
     ments less destructive and difficult is not.
                    *Men, Women and Madness: Understanding Gender and
                                         Mental Disorder 1996*

3550. Loma Chandler (fl. 1970s)

1 Sometimes asylums are just what they should be—a resting place for people who get lost in life.
"They're Expecting Us," *Reader's Digest October 1973*

2 A smile appeared upon her face as if she'd taken it directly from her handbag and pinned it there.
Ibid.

3551. E. Kitch Childs (fl. 1970s–'90s)

1 We need a whole new level of consciousness-raising groups and networks. We must learn how to speak our bitterness about each other *to* each other. It will liberate our energies to keep on working together.
Quoted in Introduction, *Women and Madness*, 25th anniversary ed. By Phyllis Chesler* *1997*
*See 2787.

3552. Amy Cohen (fl. 1970s–'90s)

1 Yet I cannot accept the politically dangerous doctrine that some sex-linked characteristic of females leads them to avoid rigorous thought.
"No safety in numbers?" *The Women's Review of Books*, Vol. XVI, No. 2 *November 1998*

2 A love for mathematics is a rare thing; it's a terrible thing to waste wherever it is found.
Ibid.

3 Doing mathematics requires a tolerance for frustration.
Ibid.

3553. Alessandra Comini (fl. 1970s–'90s)

1 One is born to it—to being an artist—by predisposition and talent; one achieves mastery of it by dint of study, hard work, thought, experimentation, doubt, observation, striving, perseverance and above all, by following an inner imperative—sometimes buoyantly joyous, sometimes fatiguingly compulsive, always mysterious.
Quoted in Foreword of *Exposures, Women & Their Art* by Ann Brown and Arlene Raven* *1989*
*See 3020.

2 To live in America in the 20th century means, for an increasing number of women, to have a chance at *multiple* creativity, artistic as well as biological.
Ibid.

3554. Margarita Cota-Cárdenas (fl. 1970s)

1 yes yes I went yelling loud too why why and they said tie her up she's too forward too flighty she thinks she's a princess thinks she's her father's daughter thinks she's hot stuff that's it doesn't know her place a real threat to the tribe take her away haul her off she's a menace to our cause that's it only learned to say crazy things accuse with HER EYES and they didn't want them troublemakers in their country.
Puppet 1985

3555. Meinrad Craighead (fl. 1970s–'90s)

1 I draw and paint from my own myth of personal origin. Each painting I make begins from some deep source where my mother and grandmother, and all my fore-mothers, still live; it is as if the line moving from pen or brush coils back to the original Matrix. Sometimes I feel like a cauldron of ripening images where memories turn into faces and emerge from my vessel. So my creative life is itself an image of God the Mother and her unbroken story of emergence in our lives.
The Mother's Songs, Images of God the Mother 1986

3556. Ani DiFranco (1970–)

1 i got the answer here
i wrote it down somewhere
i just gotta find it
"Coming Up," Verse 1, *Imperfectly* (album) *1992*

2 the urgent napkin poems
the matchbook phone numbers
all of which laundering has rendered
pulpy and strange
Ibid.

3 but i love this city, this state
this country is too large
and whoever's in charge up there
had better take the elevator down
and put more than change in our cup
or else we
are coming
up
Verse 3, Ibid.

4 every time i say something
they find hard to hear
they chalk it up to my anger
never to their own fear
"Not A Pretty Girl," Verse 2, *Not A Pretty Girl* (album) *1995*

5 don't you think every kitten
figures out how to get down
whether or not you ever show up
Verse 3, Ibid.

6 generally my generation
wouldn't be caught dead
working for the man
Ibid.

7 the river has more colors at sunset
then my sock drawer ever dreamed of
"Tiptoe," Ibid.

8 i could wake up screaming sometimes
but i don't
Ibid.

9 and you won't see me surrender
you won't hear me confess
'cuz you've left me with nothing
but i've worked with less
"Dilate," Verse 3, *Dilate* (album) *1996*

10 i found religion in the greeting card aisle
now i know hallmark was right
"Superhero," Verse 1, Ibid.

11 art may imitate life
but life imitates t.v.
Ibid.

12 and i wonder who's gonna be president
tweedle dumb or tweedle dumber?
"Fuel," Verse 2, *Little Plastic Castle* (album) *1998*

13 i don't think war is noble
and i don't like to think love is like war
but i got a big, hot cherry bomb
and i wanna slip it through the mail slot
of your front door
"Independence Day," Chorus, Ibid.

14 yeah, i would like to perfect the art
of being studiously aloof
like life is just a boring chore
and i am living proof
"Pixie," Verse 5, Ibid.

15 i've gotten out of everything
i've gotten into so far
"Virtue," *Up, Up, Up, Up, Up, Up* (album) *1999*

3557. Helen Dudar (fl. 1970s)

1 Contrary to the folklore of abortion as lifelong trauma, it is not necessarily a profoundly scarring one either.
"Abortion for the Asking," *Saturday Review of the Society April 1973*

2 In this era of radicalized and politicized clergy, it is no longer even surprising when a woman shows up at [an abortion] clinic with the blessing of her priest.
Ibid.

3558. Susan Dworkin (fl. 1970s–'90s)

1 We are genetically programmed to be too fat for American fashion. Let down your guard and you can easily look like Mrs. Khrushchev, who comes from the same basic gene pool . . .
The Book of Candy 1996

2 . . . he had entered into his compact with Candy with so much pre-existing hatred for her breed and class of woman that there was never really any chance for survival.
Ibid.

3 [The JAP*] . . . comforter, guardian, caretaker, supporting the whole Jewish nation on her soft shoulders, cushioning the descent of his soul with her plump arms and plucking him out of the nightmares, protecting his sacred work, always waiting up, always worrying.
Ibid.

*Pejorative acronym for Jewish American Princess.

3559. Alice Embree (fl. 1970s)

1 Shortly after the turn of the century, America marshaled her resources, contracted painfully, and gave birth to the New Technology. The father was a Corporation, and the New Technology grew up in the Corporate image.
"Media Images I: Madison Avenue Brainwashing—The Facts," *Sisterhood Is Powerful*, Robin Morgan,* ed. *1970*
*See 2327.

2 Humans must breathe, but corporations must make money.
Ibid.

3 The message of the media is the commercial.
Ibid.

4 America's technology has turned in upon itself; its corporate form makes it the servant of profits, not the servant of human needs.
Ibid.

5 Women are the neglected orphans of the technological age.
Ibid.

3560. Michèle Fabien (fl. 1970s)

1 JOCASTA. One does not gaze upon one's mother when she is a woman. One does not gaze upon a woman when she is one's mother.
Sc. 5, *Jocasta*, Richard Miller, tr. *1981*

3561. Marcia Falk (fl. 1970s–'90s)

1 Washing the hands, we call to mind the holiness of body.
The Book of Blessings: New Jewish Prayers for Daily Life, the Sabbath, and the New Moon Festival 1996

2 The recognition of difference is part of the very appreciation of life.
Ibid.

3 . . . let us distinguish parts within the whole and bless their differences.
Ibid.

4 Hear O Israel—
The divine abounds everywhere
and dwells in everything;
the many are One.
Sh'ma*, Ibid.

*Her interpretation of the most famous prayer in the Jewish liturgy.

3562. Carol Flinders (fl. 1970s–'90s)

1 The precious beginnings of a different kind of world are not impossibly hard to imagine, and each of us needs to be imagining them—strenuously. But we don't have to start from scratch. Important as it is to recall all those wrong turns, it may be even more crucial to identify the women and men who know, or knew, what a right turn looks like.
"Feminism Reimagined: A Civil Rights Movement Grounded in Spirituality," *The Fabric of the Future: Women Visionaries of Today Illuminate the Path to Tomorrow*, M.J. Ryan, ed. *1998*

2 At the core of patriarchy, ideologically fundamental to the nation-state, is the belief that one builds a "self"—becomes more fully human—through competition and acquisition, a creed that culminates in standing armies, colonial expansion, and ridiculously large buildings that tower over slums, a creed which is nothing more, at bottom, than materialism itself.
Ibid.

3 The selflessness, the austerity, and the communality of resistance work kindles a kind of flame.
Ibid.

4 Gandhi* saw the futility of challenging outward forms of colonial oppression without at the same time beginning to dismantle the internalized forms—the complex of beliefs, inbuilt by centuries of institutionalized racism, in one's own *inherent* unworthiness.
Ibid.

*Mohandas Gandhi, Indian nationalist leader and father of nonviolent resistance (1869–1948); assassinated.

5   Feminism has no better friend or more ardent champion than Gandhi.

Ibid.

6   . . . one of the real sticking points for would-be feminists all along—one of the reasons the movement has not attracted the large numbers of women it should have, or held all it *has* attracted—is the oppositional paradigm that we've inherited from patriarchy itself—the winner-take-all model that assumes a champion and a challenger, one who is victorious, and one who is vanquished.

Ibid.

3563. Marjorie B. Garber (fl. 1970s–'90s)

1   . . . [the] extraordinary power of the transvestite as an aesthetic and psychological agent of destabilization, desire, and fantasy.

Vested Interests: cross dressing & cultural anxiety
1992

2   Historians record dozens, probably hundreds, of . . . stories of lifelong cross-dressers whose "true" gender identities were disclosed only after death.

Ibid.

3564. Margaret Jenkins (fl. 1970s–'90s)

1   I believe that things happen when they're supposed to if one is fully engaged in the process and doing it for the right reason.

Quoted by Rita Feliciano in "Dancing Through the Fragments of Memory," Arts & Leisure, *The New York Times 28 March 1999*

2   [There is a] necessary disorder that is crucial to making work.

Ibid.

3565. Marion Jones (1976–)

1   I feel in my heart I can jump far.
"Marion Jones looks to win gold," by Jim Caple, *Seattle Post-Intelligencer 10 July 2000*

3566. Mary McIntosh (fl. 1970s–'90s)

*See Michele Barrett, 3548.

3567. Annette Motley (fl. 1970s–'80s)

1   "Ah, Second Daughter, your imagination takes you journeying as far as any traveler."
"Is that a curse, or a blessing, do you think?"
"A blessing, surely as long as imagination outstrips desire."

Pt. I, Ch. 3, *Green Dragon, White Tiger 1986*

2   How the Chinese man loved to build such walls. It was part of his temperament. He built them around his cities and his houses; around his women; and most of all around his innermost thoughts.

Ch. 4, *Ibid.*

3568. Beth Orton (1970–)

1   Why must people always want what they can't have?
"Blood Red River," *Central Reservation* (album) *1999*

2   You might as well smile
Because tomorrow you just don't know.

"Pass in Time,"
Ibid.

3   Why should I know better by now
When I'm old enough not to?

"Stolen Car,"
Ibid.

3569. Carol Polowy (fl. 1970s)

1   Educational institutions mirror the stereotypes of the larger society. The fact that education has become known as a "woman's field" stems at least in part from the identification of childcare and child-rearing as woman's work. Men frequently view teaching as a stepping stone to educational administration while women look to careers as classroom teachers.

Address, "Sex Discrimination: The Legal Obligations of Educational Institutions," *Vital Speeches of the Day 1 February 1975*

2   When textbooks are examined in terms of their presentation and reinforcement of a social order, women and minority groups are dissatisfied with the lack of reality in the presentation.

Ibid.

3570. Amy Richards (fl. 1970s)

1   For many women, our bodies have become the canvasses upon which our struggles paint themselves. Body image, in fact, may be the pivotal third wave issue—the common struggle that mobilizes the current feminist generation.

Essay, *Adiós, Barbie: Young Women Write about Body Image and Identity,* Ophira Edut, ed. *1988*

3571. Sonya Rudikoff (fl. 1970s)

1   Although there are countless alumni of the school of hard knocks, there has not yet been a move to accredit that institution.

"Women and Success," *Commentary* (New York)
October 1974

2   The embattled gates to equal rights have indeed opened up for modern women, but I sometimes think to myself: " That is not what I meant by freedom—it is only 'social progress.'"

Ibid.

3   There are surely lives which display very few of the signs of success until very late, or after life is over. There are lives of great significance which go unrecognized by peers for a very long time, there are those who achieve nothing for themselves but leave a legacy for others who come after, there are lives sacrificed for causes.

Ibid.

4   . . . the idea has gained currency that women have often been handicapped not only by a fear of failure—not unknown to men either—but by a fear of success as well.

Ibid.

5   History provides abundant examples of . . . women whose greatest gift was in redeeming, inspiring, liberating, and nurturing the gifts of others.

Ibid.

6   Should we, perhaps, see the development of the commune movement in another light, as a less expensive form of summer camp for a growing population—post-adolescent, post-industrial, post-Christian and unemployed?
> Article, Quoted in *Commentary* (New York) *1974*

3572. Sally Park Scattergood (fl. 1970s–'90s)

1   . . . childrearing, which is probably the most important task that most human beings will ever undertake, and one of vital importance for society, is ignored in our school curriculum.
> Quoted in *Boys Will Be Boys* by Myriam Miedzian *1991*

3573. Danzy Senna (1970–)

1   Before I ever saw myself, I saw my sister. When I was still too small for mirrors, I saw her as the reflection that proved my own existence. . . .

In those days, I rotated around Cole. Everything was her. I obeyed her, performed for her, followed her, studied her the way little sisters do. We were rarely far apart. We even spoke our own language. Cole insists that it began before I was born, when I was just a translucent ball in my mother's womb.
> "face" (p. 5), *Caucasia 1998*

3574. Merle Shain (fl. 1970s)

1   We tend to think of the rational as a higher order, but it is often the emotional that marks our lives. One often learns more from ten days of agony than from ten years of contentment. . . .
> Pt. I, Ch. 1, *Some Men are More Perfect Than Others 1973*

2   Most women would rather have someone whisper their name at optimum moments then rocket with contractions to the moon. . . .
> Ch. 3, Ibid.

3   So mistresses tend to get a steady diet of whipped cream, but no meat and potatoes, and wives often get the reverse, when both would like a bit of each.
> Pt. II, Ch. 4, Ibid.

3575. Wendy Shalit (1975–)

1   Today men expect to be able to treat all women like prostitutes, only without just compensation, and the virgins are the ones who are now stigmatized, told that no man will have them.
> *A Return to Modesty 1998*

2   I see so many young women around me spending half of their time sleeping with all these men, and the other half telling me how heartbroken they are. I wonder who gave them the idea that this is what they had to do in the first place?
> Ibid.

3576. Margaret Sloan (fl. 1970s)

1   We feel that there can't be liberation for less than half a race. We want *all* black people in this country to be free.
> Manifesto, National Black Feminist Organization *1975*

2   It has been hard for black women to emerge from the myriad of distorted images that have portrayed us as grinning Beulahs, castrating Sapphires, and pancake-box Jemimahs.
> Ibid.

3577. Judy Syfers (fl. 1970s)

1   My God, who *wouldn't* want a wife?
> "I Want a Wife," *The First Ms. Reader*, Francine Klagsbrun, ed. *1972*

2   The problems of an American wife stem from the fact that we live in a society which is structured in such a way as to profit only a few at the expense of the many. As long as we women tolerate such a capitalist system, all but a privileged few of us must necessarily be exploited as workers and as wives.
> Ibid.

3578. Rebecca Walker (1970–)

1   Where are the stories that challenge the notion that perfect happiness can be found in a "perfect" body? Where are the anecdotes about learning to love parts of ourselves not because of how they look or how they measure up to Cindy Crawford,* but because of how they feel to us, or how they tell a unique part of our personal history.
> Foreword, *Adiós, Barbie: Young Women Write about Body Image and Identity*, Ophira Edut, ed. *1998*

*American fashion model.

3579. Dorothy Wright Wilson (fl. 1970s)

1   If criminals wanted to grind justice to a halt, they could do it by banding together and all pleading not guilty. It's only because we have plea-bargaining that our criminal justice system is still in motion. That doesn't say much for the quality of justice.
> Quoted in *The Los Angeles Times 11 August 1974*

3580. Gwyneth Paltrow (1971–)

1   Sometimes people fall in love with people they shouldn't marry.
> Quoted in "It was a real awakening for me" by Dotson Rader, *Parade Magazine 17 January 1999*

2   You'll never be happy if you can't figure out that loving people is all there is. And that it's more important to love than to be loved. Because that is when you feel love, by loving somebody.
> Ibid.

3   My dad took me to Paris for the weekend. We had the most amazing time. On the plane back to London, he asked me, "Do you know why I took you to Paris—only you and me?" And I said, "Why?" And he said, "Because I wanted you to see Paris for the first time with a man who would always love you."
> Ibid.

3581. Bernardina Guervara Corvera (1972–)

1   Ants don't need money to eat.
    The earth belongs to them,

and their fortresses bulge with food
for these nameless days of rain.

"My Commandante Federico" (1981),
A Poetics of Resistance: Women Writing in El Salvador,
South Africa, and the United States,
Mary K. DeShazer, ed. *1994*

3582. Waris Dirie (1972?–)

1 As we traveled throughout Somalia, we met families and I played with their daughters. When we visited them again, the girls were missing. No one spoke the truth about their absence or even spoke of them at all.

Desert Flower, with Cathleen Miller *1999?*

3583. Mia Hamm (1972–)

1 Many people say I'm the best women's soccer player in the world. I don't think so. And because of that, someday I just might be.

Go for the Goal: A Champion's Guide to Winning
in Soccer and Life 1999?

2 There is no me in Mia.

Ibid.

3584. Cristina Sanchez (1972–)

1 The bullfighting world is made by and for men, but I still have the pride that I've made history. I've written golden pages in the bullfighting world.

"Woman bullfighter quits the ring in macho Spain" by
Mar Roman, Associated Press *21 May 1999*

2 It's a lovely profession, and if I was born again I would do it again.

Ibid.

3585. Heather Whitestone (1973–)

1 The most handicapped [person] in the world is a negative thinker.

People, *Seattle Post-Intelligencer September 1994*

3586. Monica Lewinsky (1974–)

1 . . . no one ever asked me to lie, and I was never promised a job for my silence.

The Starr Report: The Independent Counsel's Complete
Report to the Congress on the Investigation of
President Clinton 9 September 1998

2 He [William J. Clinton]* reminded me of my mom because like her, he was an ostrich, putting his head in the sand because he didn't like confrontation.

Quoted in *Monica's Story* by Andrew Morton *1999*
*American politician and lawyer (1946–), 42nd president of the United States (1993–2001).

3 Sex is like eating . . . Sometimes you have fast food, and sometimes you eat a gourmet meal.

Time (New York) *22 March 1999*

3587. Hwee Hwee Tan (1974–)

1 I'm at the top of the food chain, but I feel nothing.

Foreign Bodies 1998

2 I didn't want to believe. Faith is so unhip. Atheism is much more glamorous.

Ibid.

3588. Nika Turbina (1974/5–)

1 What a shame that
I'm not a fortune teller.
I would tell fortunes
only with flowers
and I would heal
the earth's wounds
with a rainbow.

"Telling Fortunes," First Draft 1987

2 What frightens me is indifference. It can devour the world, our tiny little planet, the little heart that beats in the universe.

"People" (p. 65), Time (New York) *23 November 1987*

3589. Lauryn Hill (1975–)

1 My mother always thought I'd be a star
But way before the record deal
The streets that nurtured Lauryn Hill
Made sure that I'd never go too far

"Every Ghetto Every City," 1st Verse, The Miseducation of
Lauryn Hill (album) 1998

2 Loving you is like a battle
And we both end up with scars

"Ex-Factor," 1st Verse, Ibid.

3 He was the ocean and I was the sand

"I Used to Love Him," Verse 1, Ibid.

4 Gave up my power ceased being a queen
Addicted to love like the drug of a fiend

Verse 2, Ibid.

5 Now don't you understand man universal law
What you throw out comes back to you, star
Never underestimate those who you scar
Cause karma, karma, karma comes back to you hard

"Lost Ones," last Verse, Ibid.

6 Now, some might listen and some might shun
And some may think that they've reached perfection
If you look closely you'll see what you've become
Cause you might win some but you just lost one

Ibid.

3590. Aimee Mullins (1976–)

1 Confidence is the sexiest thing a woman can have. It's much sexier than any body part.

Quoted in *"Confidence . . . "* by Elizabeth Shepard,
Parade Magazine 21 June 1998

2 Let me be the one who changes fear into understanding and makes people comfortable with amputees. Who knows? Maybe, little by little, I can change the world.

Ibid.

3 My parents didn't try to shield me from physical and emotional scars, which is why I'm not afraid of being wounded now.

Ibid.

4 The truth is, I'm sort of lucky to have this body because it forced me to find my strength and beauty within.

Ibid.

3591. Randy Albelda (fl. 1980s–'90s)

1 Without an adequate understanding of the material basis of women's inequality, there is little hope for achieving gender equality.

Economics and Feminism 1997

2 To twist one of neoclassical economics' most popular metaphors, the theory's invisible hand has kept a very tight grip—if not a stranglehold—on the credibility of feminist explanations of women's unequal status in the marketplace of economic ideas.

Ibid.

3592. Lori B. Andrews (fl. 1980s)

1 We're approaching space-age technology with Model-T statutes and cases.*

The New York Times 27 June 1984

*Describing infertility cases and the law.

3593. Mary Ellen S. Capek (fl. 1980s–'90s)

1 Fathers, especially, are . . . perhaps uncomfortable giving daughters trucks but distinctly uncomfortable giving sons dolls.

"From molehills to mountains," *The Women's Review of Books*, Vol. XVI, No. 2 *November 1998*

2 As we are finding, now that a generation of feminist leaders approaches retirement, the organizations they worked so hard to transform all too easily revert back to their old shapes.

Ibid.

3 Our culture spends an inordinate amount of time and energy making sure girls become girls and boys become boys.

Ibid.

4 By the time women and men enter the workforce, implicit assumptions about women's and men's work stack the deck against women.

Ibid.

3594. Theresa Hak Kyung Cha (fl. 1980s)

1 Truth embraces with it all other abstentions other than itself.

Dictée 1982

2 Let the one who is diseuse, Diseuse de bonne aventure.* Let her call forth. Let her break open the spell cast upon time upon time again and again.

Ibid.

*Fortune-teller.

3 The ink spills thickest before it runs dry before it stops writing at all.

Ibid.

3595. Ann Crittenden (fl. 1980s–'90s)

1 One learns, in theory and in practice, to try to resolve conflict in ways that do not involve the sheer imposition of will or brute force. One learns that violence just doesn't work.

Article, *The Nation* (New York) *1991*

3596. Maureen Dowd (fl. 1980s–'90s)

1 Here is a Congress which has boasted more concupiscent hypocrites pouncing on more nubile office girls than any institution in history except maybe Mitsubishi, and they're ready to string up Bill Clinton over sex?

"Like '50s film heroine, Monica managed to get herself a man," *Seattle Post-Intelligencer*, Op-Ed *8 October 1998*

2 It would be a waste of time trying to embarrass the Republicans on sex when they are doing such a fine job of embarrassing themselves.

Ibid.

3 People keep talking about redemption when they just want revenge.

This great capital, once a place of gravity, has been reduced to a keyhole.

"Ah, for a parallel universe, far from this nasty business," *Seattle Post-Intelligencer*, Op-Ed *15 October 1998*

3597. Dianne Dugaw (fl. 1980s–'90s)

1 We in the West may be living our way out of one of the most constrained and unimaginative epochs in the history of human sexual expression. (One can only hope.)

"Delusions of gender," *The Women's Review of Books*, Vol. XIV, No. 7 *April 1997*

2 People who have had themselves refashioned from "woman" to "man" or vice versa almost necessarily stand in a parodying relationship to the binary gender system, and may well be more aware of it as a superstructure than people whose gender has been achieved with less contrivance.

Ibid.

3598. Zlata Filipovic (1980–)

1 War has crossed out the day and replaced it with horror, and now horrors are unfolding instead of days.

Zlata's Diary 1994

3599. Melissa Green (fl. 1980s–'90s)

1 We become the people we are because of what happens to us and how our memory of it charges the rest of our lives with meaning. It is not only that we make metaphor; metaphor makes us. Language is what we own to be greater than ourselves.

Preface, *Color is the Suffering of Light: A Memoir 1994*

2 A tiny, formless child lying wrapped in white sheets in an incubator like some hothouse flower whose bloom would wither and die if touched by human hands. . . . No one held her in their arms, no one stroked her deathly pale skin. She was alone in the universe.

(p. 3), Ibid.

3 I didn't get tired of listening, really, just tired of listening so hard.

(p. 125), Ibid.

4 There didn't seem to be any difference between what was terrible in the world and what was terrible in me. I had no skin, there was no buffer, I was a spongy mass of tissue that soaked up pain, terror, suffering, despair, and defeat from everything around me. The razor made a safe, straight mark, and suddenly, because I had cut myself, there was a membrane between me and the world, and it was bleeding.

(p. 257), Ibid.

5 I hear the sound of a beating heart, and suddenly I understand— it is my heart beating. I have become myself at last, a body and

soul, fused together as nature intended, and I stretch like a cat to feel my muscle and tissue respond. I am exhausted. I am whole.

(p. 289), Ibid.

3600. Luce Irigaray (fl. 1980s)

1 Woman's desire most likely does not speak the same language as man's desire, and it probably has been covered over by the logic that has dominated the West since the Greeks.

"This sex which is not one.," *New French Feminisms: An Anthology*, Elaine Marks and Isabelle de Courtivron, eds. *1981*

2 Contradictory words seem a little crazy to the logic of reason, and inaudible for him who listens with ready-made grids, a code prepared in advance.

Ibid.

3 Must the multiple nature of female desire and language be understood as the fragmentary, scattered remains of a raped or denied sexuality? This is not an easy question to answer. The rejection, the exclusion of a female imaginary undoubtedly places woman in a position where she can experience herself only fragmentarily as waste or as excess in the little structured margins of a dominant ideology . . .

Ibid.

4 [Before woman can] arrive at the point where she can enjoy her pleasure . . . a long detour by the analysis of the various systems of oppression which affect her is certainly necessary.

Ibid.

3601. Michiko Itatani (fl. 1980s)

We are on this seemingly insignificant planet in this insignificant location in the galaxy. Being confined to this small dot, the human mind travels around the universe. Even before we could circle the earth, we started to search the inner and outer space of the universe.

Quoted in "Michiko Itatani," *Exposures, Women & Their Art* by Ann Brown and Arlene Raven* *1989*

*See 3020.

2 For me, to be an artist is an intellectual choice and a carefully chosen commitment. There is no intoxication. My painting is a painterly diagram of my cosmology. It's incomplete, fragmented and under inquiry.

Ibid.

3602. Sheila Jeffreys (fl. 1980s–'90s)

1 Prostitution does not fit here. It is not a sexual practice for the women involved, and it was not "discovered" and categorised as a perversion by sexologists in the same way [as transvestites, transsexuals, pedophiles, sadomasochists and fetishists]. Prostitution, unlike the other practices, is performed for money and has nothing to do with the "sexual tastes" of the practitioners.

The Idea of Prostitution 1997

2 The skills that all prostituted women must develop are those which allow them to *survive*, such as dissociation, being alert to danger and limiting the activities that the customers request to those [she is] prepared to accept without too much damage to her health and sense of self.

Ibid.

3 Prostituted women are being paid to receive exactly the treatment as sexual objects that other women workers are seeking to abolish.

Ibid.

3603. Shirley Geok-Lin Lim (fl. 1980s–90s)

1 If the women's movement has discovered difference to be a liberating rather than an oppressive principle, through which new visions, new understanding and new orders of society can be generated, the experiences of being an Asian American woman is an exemplar of living in difference.

Introduction (p. 10), *The Forbidden Stitch: An Asian-American Women's Anthology*, Lim, Mayumi Tsutakawa, and Margarita Donnelly, eds. *1989*

2 Life's miseries dissipated into the sharp fertility of sense through my fixed idea that all I saw and felt would become words one day. The ambition for poetry, a belief in the vital connection between language and my specific local existence, was clearly irrational, even perhaps a symptom of small madness.

Among the White Moon Faces: An Asian-American Memoir of Homelands 1996

3604. Valerie Matsumoto (fl. 1980s)

1 In the evening the air was thick with mosquitoes, gnats and moths. The cicadas buzzed in deafening chorus from every tree. They danced in frenzied legions around the porch light and did kamikaze dives into the bath water. All of them came in dusty gray hordes, as though the desert had sapped the color from them, but not their energy.

"Two Deserts" (1986), *The Forbidden Stitch: An Asian-American Women's Anthology*, Shirley Geok-lin Lim,* Mayma Tsutakawa, and M. Donnelly, eds. *1989*

*See 3603.

2 To Mattie, [a garden] was the true world of the heart, with no room for ungentle or impatient hands. It was a place of deeply sown hopes, lovingly nurtured, and its colors were the colors of unspoken dreams.

Ibid.

3605. Tahira Naqvi (fl. 1980s)

1 The immensity of the sea on film was reduced to a mere blue splash of color, its place usurped by a vastness she could scarce hold within the frame of her vision; a window opened in her head, she drew in the wonder of the sea as it touched the hem of the heavens and, despite the heat, Sakina Bano shivered involuntarily. God's touch is upon the world, she silently whispered to herself.

"Paths Upon Water," *The Forbidden Stitch: An Asian American Women's Anthology*, Shirley Geok-lin Lim,* Mayumi Tsutakawa, and M. Donnelly, eds. *1989*

*See 3603.

2 Sakina Bano couldn't understand why these men and women wished to scorch their bodies, and why, if they were here by the shore of an ocean which seemed to reach up to God, they didn't at least gaze wide-eyed at the wonder which lay at their feet. Why did they choose instead to shut their eyes and merely wallow in the heat. Their skins had rebelled, the red and darkly-pink blotches spoke for themselves. Perhaps this is a ritual they must, of necessity, follow, she mused. Perhaps they yearn to be brown as we yearn to be white.

Ibid.

3606. Charity Kaluki Ngilu (fl. 1980s–'90s)

1 He is a leader of darkness and death. . . . You can see his cowardice. Moi* is playing a game alone. He is player and referee.

Quoted in "Kenya's First Woman President?" by Andrea Useem, *Ms.* (New York) *November/December 1997*

*Reference to Daniel arap Moi, Kenyan politician (1924–), president of Kenya (1978–).

2   I had to carry water on my back, and my daughter will have to do the same.
> *The New York Times* interview, Quoted by Andrea Useem in "Kenya's First Woman President?," Ibid.

3607. B. Ruby Rich (fl. 1980s–'90s)

1   Neither group [of the argument regarding sadomasochism in film] seems to recognize fantasy as a sphere apart, shaped by social and psychological factors but lacking any inherently linear relationship to the action itself.
> "Feminism and Sexuality in the Eighties" (1986), *Chick Flicks: Theories and Memories of the Feminist Film Movement* 1998

2   The global context of contemporary life rarely enters into the theoretical debates, as though to indicate that sexuality is not really as socially constructed as claimed, as though sexual issues were not so deeply affected, after all, by history, the economy, the cold war, disease, the new conservatism, or even fashion.
> Ibid.

3   As a woman sitting in the dark, watching that film made by and for men . . . what is my experience? Don't I in fact interact with that text and that context, with a conspicuous absence of passivity?
> "In the Name of Feminist Film Criticism," Ibid.

4   [In the 1990s] . . . feminist film cold wars have dissipated and we old warriors have become congenial veterans, not unlike the CIA and KGB spies who now meet to reminisce and do each other favors.
> Essay, Ibid.

3608. Graciela "Chely" Rodriguez (1980?–)

1   I've decided to become my own role model by reminding myself who I am every day. I am an eighteen-year-old Latina, a full-figured former model. I have survived an eating disorder. And I'm learning to love my body.
> Essay, *Adiós, Barbie: Young Women Write about Body Image and Identity*, Ophira Edut, ed. 1998

3609. Georgiana Valoyce Sanchez (fl. 1980s)

1   For a moment we were equals, looking into each other's eyes, acknowledging our separateness. If not understanding, at least accepting the other's stand. It was a brief moment of union. Before the eyes looked away. Before we fell back into the hurting bones of ourselves, of our roles as husband and wife.
> "The Heart of the Flower," *The Stories We Hold Secret: Tales of Women's Spiritual Development*, Linda Hogan,* Carol Bruchac and Judith McDaniel, eds. 1986

*See 3149.

2   My mind was like a small alert bird perched atop the headboard, watching.
> Ibid.

3610. Joni Seager (fl. 1980s–'90s)

1   Machismo has given us a design ethos of buildings and cities that are shaped by metaphors of machines; large-scale public buildings that are inhumane, confusing and intimidating; dwelling and working environments that are ecologically unsustainable.
> "Blueprints for inequality," *The Women's Review of Books*, Vol. X, No. 4 *January 1993*

2   It may well be true that we cannot change society only by reforming our built environment; but it is just as true that we cannot change society if we leave its spatial conventions unexamined and intact.
> Ibid.

3611. Svetlana Slapsak (fl. 1980s–'90s)

1   All the bestialities of war were triggered by words—cliches put forward by intellectuals and eagerly appropriated by politicians.
> "Bosnia proves words can kill," *Seattle Post-Intelligencer*, Op-Ed, A11 *27 May 1993*

2   Those writings by intellectuals were recycled by journalists; soon, draftees were sent to be killed with writers' words on their lips.
> Ibid.

3   Fear, repulsion, concern for our careers—there were any number of reasons why many did not act to thwart the false prophets who have destroyed public discourse and civilization in Serbia, not to mention the destruction they caused in Bosnia and Croatia.
  We should have taken out the garbage when we first noticed the stench.
> Ibid.

3612. Meredith Small (fl. 1980s–'90s)

1   . . . the sperm is actually an unwilling participant in the reproductive process. . . . They are . . . reluctant to contact anything, and it's the egg that must pull them toward fertilization. . . . Contrary to popular belief, the egg is actually the aggressor.
> *Female Choices: Sexual Behavior of Female Primates* 1993

2   Feel the strands of DNA unravel and connect you and those brown eyes that stare back through the bars of the cage. And acknowledge that primateness, and sisterhood, extends beyond one family, one community, one race, one species.
> Ibid.

3   Sisterhood is important for female primates because it helps them remain a strong cohesive power, and lack of this power can have drastic consequences.
> Ibid.

3613. Ba Tam (fl. 1980s)

1   I was happy! It is just like heaven! Because people live here in freedom.*
> (p. 425), Quoted in *Hearts of Sorrow: Vietnamese American Lives* by James Freeman 1989

*Upon her arrival in the United States.

2   In Vietnam, in a village, from one end to another, everybody knows each other. Even in the city where I lived, we knew each other and visited one another. If I was sick, my friends visited me, and I did the same for them. I would see my friends at the market. When I think of that, I miss not having people I know nearby. It's very sad. Over here I live at home, and I cannot go anywhere.* In Vietnam, if I felt sad, I'd go to visit my friends, my fellow "sisters" . . . I am very sad and I have nowhere to go.
> (p. 426), Ibid.

*One month after her arrival.

3614. Luisah Teish (fl. 1980s–'90s)

2   The sacred symbols and practices of African, Native American, and Asian people have been usurped without respect or

compensation. These symbols have been stripped of their true meaning and reduced to the fleeting diversions of Western spiritual adolescents.

> "Sister, Can You Paradigm? Or, Whose Millennium Is It?"
> *The Fabric of the Future: Women Visionaries of Today Illuminate the Path to Tomorrow*, M.J. Ryan, ed. *1998*

3 I maintain that the biggest challenge in the new millennium could be a change of habit. We could change from a dominating commodity culture into one of true exchange in which we learn from each other in humility and respect.

> Ibid.

3615. Lynne Tillman (fl. 1980s–'90s)

1 We were a ragtag band of inhibited outsiders, each a secret and keeping secrets from the others. And ourselves, I suspect.

> *Cast in Doubt 1992*

2 I am a ride, a roller coaster, the fun house. I'm what frightens you in the palace of horror. I'm pleasure . . . fire engine red inside your brain . . . Lie down, I'll speak for you.

> The Madame Realism Complex *1992*

3616. Amaryllis Tigalo Torres (fl. 1980s–'90s)

1 The decision of the American government to educate the Filipino masses was not an act of magnanimity. Education was correctly perceived to be the most effective way to pacify the nation.

> Essay, Quoted in *The Politics of Women's Education: Perspectives from Asia, Africa, and Latin America* by Jill Ker Conway and Susan C. Bourque *1993*

2 [Education should transmit] concepts, perspectives, and skills that respond to the needs of people for good-paying and self-fulfilling jobs, for democratic processes, and for peace and security in their daily lives.

> Ibid.

3617. Brita Westergaard (fl. 1980s)

1 We are not just changing Norway.* When people realize that this is possible in the Cabinet of one country, they must realize it is possible everywhere.

> Quoted in "An Experiment in Woman Power" by Michael S. Serrill, *Time* (New York) *6 October 1986*

*Reference to stunning increase in the number of women selected to serve on the Norwegian Cabinet by Gro Brundtland; see 2258.

3618. Lucinda Williams (fl. 1980s–'90s)

1 Mr. Johnson sings over in a corner by the bar
Sold his soul to the devil so he can play guitar.

> "2 Kool 2 Be 4-Gotten," 1st Verse, *Car Wheels On A Gravel Road* (album) *1998*

2 He asked me: Would you jump into the water with me?
I told him: No way, baby, that's your own death, you see

> 3rd Verse, Ibid.

3 Somewhere in Louisiana my sugar's doing time
But he can't spent time with me

> "Concrete and Barbed Wire," 5th Verse, Ibid.

4 Some kind of savior singin' the blues
A derelict in your duct tape shoes

> "Drunken Angel," Ibid.

5 I think I lost it
Let me know if you come across it
Let me know if I let it fall
Along a back road somewhere

> "I Lost it," chorus and 2nd Verse, Ibid.

6 Not a day goes by I don't think about you
You left your mark on me. It's permanent, a tattoo

> "Right In Time," 1st Verse, Ibid.

3619. Lucia Annunziata (fl. 1990s)

1 A haze of sentiment has traditionally clouded America's perception of Italy: Americans love the country, but it is a love based on cliché.

> "The Fall of the Cold War Order," *The Nation* (New York) *5 April 1993*

2 But this is exactly the nature of the Italian political system: It has worked by being both in turmoil and unchangeable, corrupt yet efficient. For almost five decades, paralysis and farce have been not the "underdeveloped" face of a modern nation but two faces of the same coin. This paradox has been our Berlin wall.

> Ibid.

3620. Margalynne Armstrong (fl. 1990s)

1 . . . white people have the privilege of escaping people of color, and . . . anyone who can afford to is entitled to abandon the urban poor.

> "Privilege in Residential Housing," Quoted in *Privilege Revealed: How Invisible Preference Undermines America* by Stephanie M. Wildman* *1996*

*See 3240.

2 The lesson our society must learn from the rising that followed the Simi Valley*acquittals is that those to whom the pledge of equality was made have not forgotten America's promises and refuse to allow themselves to be forgotten.

> Ibid.

3 Our system allows easy circumvention of fair housing law when discrimination takes the form of financial requirements or if exclusion is attributed to protection of property interests.

> Ibid.

4 The American represented by Rodney King and South Central Los Angeles* lives in segregated cities, while the America of the police defendants and Ventura County jurors resides in segregated suburbs. "Two nations" is a recurring metaphor for the racial configuration of the United States.

> Ibid.

*Reference to the Simi Valley, California jury acquittal of the police officers accused of beating King that led to the uprising in south central Los Angeles Watts in 1992.

3621. Virginia Ayllón Soria (fl. 1990s)

1 And I put in my prayers, day and night, clasping my hands together to keep them from stealing, sealing off my mouth and my rage to keep from drinking and drinking not knowing where I'll end up. I go to church every Sunday, and I take the children, too, doing everything that the Bible says to do, that the priest and the sisters say to do, but nothing happens.

> "Prayer to the Goddesses," Kathy S. Leonard, tr., *Fire from the Andes: Short Fiction by Women from Bolivia, Ecuador and Peru*, Kathy S. Leonard and Susan Benner, eds. *1998*

3622. Aparna Basu (fl. 1990s)

1 History is no longer just a chronicle of kings and statesmen, of people who wielded power, but of ordinary women and men engaged in manifold tasks. Women's history is an assertion that women have a history.

Web site, *Women in World History Curriculum*, www.womeninworldhistory.com *1996–97*

3623. Chris Bright (fl. 1990s)

1 Even the worst chemical spills are dumb. They cannot reproduce and they dissipate over time. But smart pollution* proliferates and spreads.

Cited in "Plants, bugs, animals turn up in places they don't belong" by Davis Briscoe, *Seattle Times*, A21 *11 October 1998*

*I.e., biological (e.g., exotic species of plants, bugs and animals).

2 Invasion itself is an ancient process. What's new is that the integration of the global economy is spreading more and more creatures around.

Ibid.

3624. C. Carr (fl. 1990s)

1 Finley* represents a frightening and rare presence—an unsocialized woman.

On Edge: Performance at the End of the Twentieth Century 1994

*Karen Finley, American performance artist.

2 Bohemia was always part of the exile tradition, the place where the lost ones went to find each other. But it was exile from one tangible place to another. Now that there is no place, the exiles have become nomads, and there's a whole culture of the disappeared.

Ibid.

3 As a media creature since childhood, [Michael Jackson]* thinks he's all image. He has, in fact, abandoned his body, in order to inhabit its simulacrum. I think of him as a sort of radical "body artist." He doesn't want to be black, yet I don't think he wants to be white.

And I don't think he wants to have a gender . . .

(p. 244), Ibid.

*American singer and composer (1958–).

3625. Sue-Ellen Case (fl. 1990s)

1 The economic situation has created two choices for women: the relative economic poverty of child-rearing, or the emotional alienation of success within the structures of capitalism.

Feminism and Theatre 1988

2 . . . the Church [by the late Middle Ages] had secured the notion that such immoral conduct was the proven of women: that is, that prostitutes caused prostitution. Therefore the control of prostitutes would control prostitution, or, more specifically, banning women from the stage would prevent the stage from becoming the site for immoral sexual conduct.

Ibid.

3626. Lindsey Collen (fl. 1990s)

1 Another day of being colonized.

The Rape of Sita 1993

*Banned by the Mauritian prime minister, Sir Aneerood Jugnauth.

2 "God, or god," "God, or Gods," "Sir or Madam" . . . are we allowed out?

Ibid.

3 Wait for the silence, girls. For the gods if they ever spaketh in the past, hath stopped in the present.

Ibid.

3627. Anne-Christine d'Adesky (fl. 1990s)

1 "Why do these people from the outside only care what's happening to us after someone dies or is murdered?"

Under the Bone 1994

2 I who am left here as witness, passive eye in the center of a terrible storm.

Ibid.

3628. Robbie Davis-Floyd (fl. 1990s)

1 [The experience of childbirth was] irrevocably altered by the Pitocin that made the contractions too painful to bear, by the Demerol that made me woozy and unable to cope, by the institutional policy that would not let me eat even though I was starving, by the long steel hook that broke my waters and made it essential that the birth happen within a certain amount of time, by the deadly cold metal table on which I now lay, by the epidural anesthesia that cut me off from all sensation below my upper chest, and by the green curtain that cut me off from even visual contact with my huge belly and my emerging child.

"technobirth," *Cyborg Babies: From Techno-Sex to Techno-Tots*, Davis-Floyd and Joseph Dumit, eds. *1998*

2 The IV, for example, is the umbilical cord to the hospital, mirroring in microcosm the fact that we are all umbilically linked to the technocracy, dependent on society and its institutions for our nurturance and our life.

Ibid.

3 The fact that the baby's image on the ultrasound screen is often more real to the mother than its movement inside her reflects our cultural fixation on experience one step removed on TV and computer screens.

Ibid.

3629. Catherine De Vinck (fl. 1990s)

1 [My writing is] soaked in a theology of hope, that is, in the knowledge that death has no dominion, that light overcomes darkness, and that love is a divine power of transformation and renewal.

Quoted in *Wise Women: Over 2000 Years of Spiritual Writing by Women*, Susan Cahill,* ed. *1996*

*See 2782.

2 I am a God of a thousand names:
    why cannot one of them be
Woman Singing?

"The Womanly Song of God," ll., *Wise Women: Over 2000 Years of Spiritual Writing by Women*, Susan Cahill,* ed. *1996*

*See 2782.

3 Did you know the concordance
that links not only heaven and earth
but the most antique fragment of baked clay
to the very blood that pumps your heart
full of desire and dream?

"Venus—Aghia Sophia," St. 1, Ibid.

4 Is happiness controlled, pulled
    by strings held
    in some enormous hidden will?
    Or is it born of water and flame,
    of unbetrayed trust, of pain
    that grinds flesh and bone
    into a fine powder that the wind lifts?

St. 2, Ibid.

3630. Diane DiPerna (fl. 1990s)

1 When the heads of state assembled for their group photo, they no longer seemed agents of progress but rather mere wooden soldiers, impotent from a lack of courage or penetrating ideas.

*"Thinking globally, acting locally,"
The Women's Review of Books, Vol. X, No. 4,
pp. 6–7 January 1993*

2 Route 20, the arrow-straight road that once took American pioneers west across New York, traverses what would have been my Congressional district. At night, only blackness fills the rearview mirror; one can feel like an astronaut alone in the void except for an occasional flash of red, a deer or raccoon's eye, or the face-on too-bright headlights of some other late night space traveler.

Ibid.

3 But people will choose change only if they believe things can change for them . . .

Ibid.

4 In the end, politics is only as remote and as tarnished as we ordinary citizens let it become.

Ibid.

3631. Lisa Dodson (fl. 1990s)

1 In the face of stigma, irrational regulations, peril to children, and a woman's despair, [a researcher's] neutrality is known only as collusive silence.

*Don't Call Us Out of Name: The Untold Lives of Women
and Girls in Poor America 1998*

2 More than anything, they spoke of little erosions which finally wear you down into someone you don't want to be. They spoke of chronic exhaustion. They spoke of having no car, no warm coats, no baby clothes, no functioning laundry in the building no elevator and many stairs, no heat sometimes, no Pampers, no tampons, of long lines at clinics, and of being able to go only to stores which accept food stamps, and, above all, of having no one to "offer a kind word."

Ibid.

3632. Jessie Duarte (fl. 1990s)

1 Now we use it to wipe
    arses, then to blow noses
    or to write a poem on..
    or better still . . .
    we use it to write
    an impassioned plea for
    release to minister of law and order
    who then stuffs it in
    his ear!

*"Toilet Paper," A Poetics of Resistance: Women Writing in
El Salvador, South Africa, and the United States
Mary K. DeShazer, ed. 1994*

3633. Leslie Forbes (fl. 1990s)

1 My sister was simply one language I no longer spoke, another country I'd lost.

Bombay Ice 1998

2 "Facts are like butterflies, madam. Most difficult to catch, and often lacking in beauty when finally pinned down."

Ibid.

3 . . . the precision of all men whose souls do not exceed the limits of their uniforms.

Ibid.

3634. Annette Gordon-Reed (fl. 1990s)

1 There is, apparently, nothing like a story involving race, sex and interracial family lines to capture the American imagination.

*Conference paper, cited in "Taking New Measurements for
Jefferson's Pedestal" by Nicholas Wade, The New York
Times, National 7 March 1999*

2 Women harvested his [Thomas Jefferson's*] crops while he sat writing letters and thinking great thoughts. When he died penniless, the majority of them were scattered to the four winds, losing family, home and friends. All these activities—all of these things done to black women—have been taken in and washed clean of their import for those who style themselves as the keepers of Jefferson's flame.

Ibid.

*American philosopher, educator and architect (1743–1826), 3rd president of the United States (1801–09). Reference to recent discovery that he fathered children with his African-American house slave-mistress.

3635. Elizabeth Haiken (fl. 1990s)

1 . . . the surgical solution has allowed us to hold on to an idealized self-image:. . . . We are realists, pragmatists . . . bent on creating and recreating ourselves in the most modern of all possible ways.

Venus Envy: A History of Cosmetic Surgery 1997

2 In the 1970s, women insisted that the personal is political; they defined appearance and beauty as social issues rather than individual problems. A decade later . . . popular conceptions of feminism began to reflect the same emphasis on individual achievement and fulfillment that swept through the larger culture.

Ibid.

3636. Rayda Jacobs (fl. 1990s)

1 The middle people* have had it better than the black people, yes, but the middle people have suffered too. . . . At least, if you have a black skin, you know you're black. The devil isn't at your elbow telling you to just get into the white section of the train 'cause there you'll have a seat, or leave out your race on the job ap because you're damn qualified and want the job. Whiteskins are tempted everyday into falseness and deceit . . . We've all been fucked by apartheid.

*"For the Smell of the Sea" (p. 143), The Middle Children
1994*

*Term used for multi-racial or "coloured" people in South Africa.

2 They couldn't possibly be serious about a monkey for a president, and the vote for everyone.

"Give Them Too Much" (p. 149), Ibid.

3 Living in exile is hard. A South African going home for a holiday doesn't tell the truth. He can't afford to let on. He keeps up the show, promotes his new home. The freedom and opportunities. But he's not free in his soul. The first thing that hits you in a new country is the loneliness.

"Miss Pretorious" (p. 158), Ibid.

4 I saw for the first time my black brothers and sisters. I didn't know them in 1968. They were not on my street, not in my school, not in my thoughts. But I watched now, through the smoke and tear gas, and was ashamed that the middle children have had it better than them.

"Make the Chicken Run," Ibid.

5 The emotional damage of apartheid is large. It clogs the pores, deadens the heart.

Ibid.

6 I left my soul at the foot of Table Mountain. I want it back.

"The Middle Children," Ibid.

3637. Beth Kephart (fl. 1990s)

1 What, in the end, are you fighting for: Normal? Is normal possible? Can it be defined?. . . . And is normal superior to what the child inherently is, to what he aspires to, fights to become, every second of his day?

A Slant of Sun: One Child's Courage 1998

2 Nothing erodes it [a mother's love]. It is not sand on a beach. It is the nuclear heart of things—hard as the rock of this earth.

Ibid.

3 [Our son is] different in a million wonderful ways, and also different in ways that need our help.

Ibid.

4 The future is a blank book with a million uncut pages.

Ibid.

5 . . . my concern has been to look beyond labels and medical methodology so as to discover the extraordinary spirit of a little boy.

Flap copy, Ibid.

3638. Sarah Kerr (fl. 1990s)

1 Certain economic crises, precisely because they occur at an abstract remove, have some of the sickening allure of a horror story, or of a myth in which a merciless god threatens to wipe out a city at some unspecified date in the future.

"The Confidence Men," *The New York Review of Books*
10 August 1995

2 Some new word or even epistemological category might be needed to describe how, regarding Mexico, an optimistic scenario has been floated for years like an option, to become indistinguishable from the truth as long as enough people invested in it.

Ibid.

3 That the market-based approach works best of all is a given. Therefore the market-based approach deserves our confidence. And only if we trust in the market-based approach, as it deserves, will it show you doubters that it works best of all. A roundabout piece of reasoning, requiring an almost religious faith.

Ibid.

4 So while credibility is reassuring it can also be callous.

Ibid.

3639. Baleka Kgositsile (fl. 1990s)

1 Rhythm
feet so precise
to the left
to the right
to the songs
we sing now
our voices beckoned
from the past of the future
will be pronounced
medicine or poison
rhythm
this dance is our future.

"Umkhonto," *A Poetics of Resistance: Women Writing in El Salvador, South Africa, and the United States*
Mary K. DeShazer, ed. *1994*

3640. Ynestra King (fl. 1990s)

1 The very condition of disability provides a vantage point of a certain lived experience in the body, a lifetime of opportunity for the observation of reaction to bodily deviance, a testing ground for reactions to persons who are readily perceived as having something wrong or being different. It is fascinating, maddening, and disorienting. It defies categories of "sickness" and "health," "broken" and "whole." It is in between.

"The Other Body," *Ms.* (New York) *March/April 1993*

2 The wish that the body should be irrelevant has been one of my most fervent lifelong wishes. The knowledge that it isn't is my most intense lifelong experience.

Ibid.

3 The mythology of autonomy perpetuates in terrible ways the oppression of the disabled. It also perpetuates misogyny—and the destruction of the planet.

Ibid.

4 . . . the potential for human growth and creativity is infinite—but it is not groundless. The common ground for the person—the human body—is a place of shifting sand that can fail us at any time. It can change shape and properties without warning; this is an essential truth of embodied existence.

Ibid.

3641. Nan Levinson (fl. 1990s)

1 To move, to go, to travel; the need can be so great as to be almost a sickness, away-sickness, maybe, an untamably sweet longing to go somewhere that will never be your home among people you'll never know well enough to belong to.

"Out of Place," *The Women's Review of Books*, Vol. XV,
No. 10–11 *July 1998*

2 Travel is sweet because it doesn't wear out its welcome, bittersweet because it puts time and place in perspective and reminds us how small we are.

Ibid.

3 Being a tourist must be the single most disconcerting occupation in the world.

Ibid.

4 We travel to look at people who have stayed put.

Ibid.

5 To know how a society functions, transact business at the post office. To know how a society falls apart, fall in love.

Ibid.

3642. Vera Litrichin (fl. 1990s)

1 We know that if we are to say aloud who we are and what we want, there will be no historically accepted political patterns for our experience or our language. And yet here we are.

"Serbian nation," with Lepa Mladjenovic* (p. 185),
Ana's Land: Sisterhood in Eastern Europe,
Tanya Renne,** ed. *1996*

*See 3644. **See 3650.

3643. Nora Bermúdez Méndez (fl. 1990s)

1 We believed
before they tortured us
that we carried
all the sensitivity of the world
in the soft plains of our skin.
And now we understand,
compañeros,
that conviction and faith
can't be carried on the skin
because if this were so
they would have killed us
a long time ago.

"Testimonies," *A Poetics of Resistance: Women Writing in
El Salvador, South Africa, and the United States* Mary K.
DeShazer, ed. *1994*

3644. Lepa Mladjenovic (fl. 1990s)

See Vera Litrichin, 3642.

3645. Khawar Mumtaz (fl. 1990s)

See Farida Shaheed, 3652: 1–2.

3646. Martha Nichols (fl. 1990s)

1 . . . we no longer see the zeroes and ones of machine code, but the logic of programming still rules what hackers create. Computer interaction forces users into an analytical, problem-solving mode, which is why the adventure-game format . . . was such a good match for early computer stories. There's just one hitch: problem-solving, especially in a binary universe, is not the only thing we do in life or art.

"Cyber, cyber, burning bright," *The Women's Review
of Books,* Vol. XV, No. 4 *January 1998*

2 The conservative politics that now hold sway are a good first for cyberspace's love of anarchy and individualism, and its sense of boyish rebellion.

Ibid.

3647. Urszula Nowakowska (fl. 1990s)

1 Catholic fundamentalism and the ideology of a free-market economy constitute the biggest threat to women's rights and their status in society. Women are the most visible victims of the period of transition, and they are going to pay the biggest price.

Ana's Land: Sisterhood in Eastern Europe,
Tanya Renne,* ed.
1996

*See 3650.

3648. Mary Orr (fl. 1990s)

1 Journal writing and travel go together like chai and samosas. Each can stand alone, but both are enhanced by the other.

"Passages in India," *The Women's Review of Books,*
Vol. XII, Nos. 10–11 *July 1995*

2 I asked the waiter what kind of fish they had: "Sorry madame, no fish today."

No problem. I had my alternative. I asked what they put in their noodles, knowing perfectly well I'd order them even with the tedious carrots and cabbage. "Sorry madame, no noodles today."

This surprised me. Too hungry to look further, long past the ability to make a decision, I grasped for the old standby: *biryani:* "Sorry madame, no *biryani.*"

I gave up. "What *do* you have, then?"

"Sorry, madame, no food today."

Ibid.

3 Standing behind me, the room boy placed his hands at the base of my neck, applying pressure. "Massage, madame?"

I showed him the door. I barricaded it with the other bed in the room. Then I angrily bolted the doors to the balcony, which connected with the rooms on either side of mine. Because of this Lothario I had to sleep in a stuffy cell. Land of the Buddha indeed.

Ibid.

3649. Charlotte Pierce-Baker (fl. 1990s)

1 For black women, where rape is concerned, race has preceded issues of gender. We are taught that we are first black, then women. . . . Black women have survived by keeping quiet, not solely out of shame, but out of a need to preserve the race and its image. In our attempts to preserve racial pride, we black women have often sacrificed our souls.

*Surviving the Silence: Black Women's
Stories of Rape 1998*

2 The way out is to tell: speak the acts perpetrated upon us, speak the atrocities, speak the injustices, speak the personal violations of the soul. Someone will listen, someone will believe our stories, someone will join us.

Ibid.

3650. Tanya Renne (fl. 1990s)

1 . . . decades of mono-ideology had left the people without a structure to create or deal with choice. "Options" as a concept had disappeared from social memory . . .

Introduction, *Ana's Land: Sisterhood in Eastern Europe,*
intro. and ed. *1996*

2 For feminism, the fall of communism has meant categorical rejection. It is seen either as an imported Western ideology to be rejected out of hand or as an old communist principle to be proudly refused . . .

Ibid.

3651. Alexandra Richie (fl. 1990s)

1 . . . for a few brief sparkling years the city attracted a sheer concentration of talent which had not yet been equaled in Europe. Berlin heralded a new vision of modernity, and introduced it to Germany.

Faust's * *Metropolis: A History of Berlin 1998*
*Reference to *Faust,* the play by German poet, novelist and dramatist, Johann Wolfgang von Goethe (1749–1832).

2 . . . that bizarre mixture of cynicism, self-interest, political naiveté and sheer petulance which has, throughout [Berlin's] entire history, stood in the way of clear-headed political decisions.

Ibid.

3 Rather than . . . claiming that Berlin was traditionally a city of immigrants they might protect its minorities from increasingly

frequent attacks; rather than trying to remove the Soviet war memorial at Treptow they might ask why so little is known about the war-time treatment of Russian prisoners, over 3 million of whom were killed by the Nazis. Rather than . . . complain about how much is written about the concentration camps they might ask how it was that in 1991 Ravensbrück, only 35 miles from Berlin, barely escaped being transformed into a shopping mall and car park.

Ibid.

3652. Farida Shaheed (fl. 1990s)

1 . . . transforming the educational system requires a two-pronged approach: one led by mainstream educators and the other led by mobilized communities. And, given the powerfully patriarchal nature of the society, special efforts on every level must be made for women.

"Women's Education in Pakistan," with Khawar Mumtaz,*
Quoted in *The Politics of Women's Education: Perspectives from Asia, Africa, and Latin America* by Jill Ker Conway and Susan C. Bourque *1993*

2 Pakistan's educational system is a poor imitation of the one the colonial powers left behind.

Ibid.

3653. Carol Sternhell (fl. 1990s)

I believe reproductive technologies . . . are good because they help women who want children desperately to have them, they enable single women and lesbian and gay couples to become parents, they give us more control over our bodies, not less, and most of all because they turn all our ideas about "proper" families and acceptable social arrangements inside out. They're good because they help us use our biology to challenge biology And adoption, I believe, is good because it moves us beyond the constraints of biology, expands our notions of love, and places us in a much broader human community.

"Maternal triangle," *The Women's Review of Books,*
Vol. XI, No. 1 *October 1993*

2 "These days," I wrote in my college's Twentieth Reunion Book, "I look at raindrops swimming down my windowpane and think they look like sperm. So do July Fourth fireworks, the ones that shoot across the sky trailing long tails."

Ibid.

3 Why is it that some feminists who are militantly prochoice when it comes to abortion suddenly become antichoice when the subject turns to adoption, surrogacy, or technology? Why is ending an unwanted pregnancy liberating, but proceeding with it and yet choosing not to mother so disturbing? Many anti-abortion activists strongly believe that no woman who has had an abortion ever ceases to mourn her lost child. That's exactly what anti-adoption activists believe about birthmothers. But—in both cases—it simply isn't true.

Ibid.

4 Difference causes problems in a society that fears it.

Ibid.

5 *This* child, through some accident of fate, this particular child and no other has become mine. He could be living anywhere, not just in Iowa; if his birthmother had chosen someone else, or I had looked somewhere else, he could be the child of Republican bankers in Southern California or Christian evangelists in Mississippi or old hippies in Vermont. Benjamin, my son, would be a different person—and the miracle is, so would I.

Ibid.

6 Motherhood, like sisterhood, may be powerful. It's certainly complicated. Just as we learned, slowly and painfully, not to make generalizations about "women"; just as we learned that there are many feminisms; so we have to recognize the multiple, contradictory forms of mothering.

"Motherhood is powerful," *The Women's Review of Books,*
Vol. XIV, No. 7 *April 1997*

7 Just like motherhood, feminism was all-consuming; like motherhood, it changed—transformed, exploded—my life.

Ibid.

8 So far, I've loved everything about motherhood except chicken pox. . . . I love re-experiencing all the little corners of the world I'd forgotten to notice for decades.

Ibid.

3654. Yelena Tarasova (fl. 1990s)

1 Plastic surgery can correct a horrible nose, but the soul carries the scars from the operation. Everything that heals in the body continues to bleed and fester in the soul. That's what she thought when she was young, and if she were to remember everything now the way it happened, she would see her soul: a fat, melancholy blob, always sighing heavily.

"She Who Bears No Ill," *Half a Revolution: Contemporary Fiction by Russian Women,* Masha Gessen, ed. and tr. *1995*

3655. Jelica Todosijevic (fl. 1990s)

1 Now we are no longer imprisoned by state limitations and censorship. . . . since we are receiving so much information, we have a wonderful opportunity to collect other people's experiences and apply it in our work. Sometimes it introduces revolutionary ideas, which makes our work much easier . . . Most of the time, though, learning about the successes of women-in-struggle itself gives us a lot of positive energy to go on.

NEWW On-line, Cited by Sonia Jaffe Robbins in "Lost in cyberspace," *The Women's Review of Books,* Vol. XIV, No. 2 *November 1996*

3656. Terry Wolverton (fl. 1990s)

1 I know the way your mind works.

You think because I say "I," I am revealing myself to you. You assume that the first person is personal. You believe you know something about me. This is how you get your power. You feel free to pass judgments; you decide that I'm tough or smart, wounded or seriously disturbed.

This is how Freud* ruined literature.

Bailey's Beads 1996
*Austrian physician and founder of psychoanalysis (1856–1939).

2 Once I'm drunk I can float in that sensation; it doesn't matter if his skin smells like raw beef from his job at the butcher shop, blood under his nails; it doesn't matter that he barely touches me before he rams into me; it doesn't matter that he leaves me feeling sticky and unmoved.

"Landmarks," *Calyx,* Vol. 17, No. 3 *1998*

3 Recovery is so difficult to navigate because one is required to travel simultaneously in two directions: to walk again through the familiar landscapes of the past and to journey at the same time into unknown territory, to live as one has never before lived.

Ibid.

4 Since my mother and stepfather were going out, I dropped a tab of mescaline and spent the evening on that glorious chemical

edge, limbs turned to Jell-O, brain racing after a scattering of elusive thoughts, eyes staring at the patterns of energy in the air.

Ibid.

5 I am ashamed to confess this; my reputation as an inveterate partier is essential to me.

Ibid.

6 I made rules: never call her after noon Eastern time. Never pick up the phone when it rings; always listen to the message on the answering machine to see if it's her, how drunk she sounds. Visit infrequently, never stay more than a few days. During those visits, spend time in shopping malls, play cards. Never ask her for anything I really need. Never tell her anything true about my life.

Ibid.

7 Whispered subterfuge, the miasma of the double life, a blur of truth and lies, a constant fear of discovery: these things too affect the body's chemistry, jolt the nervous system. Even the daily ritual of rolling joints—smoking before breakfast on the way to work, in the parking lot on break, on the drive home, after dinner, before bed—pales before the adrenaline rush of infidelity.

Ibid.

8 Patterns of behavior are woven early, whether in our homes or in our DNA.*

Ibid.

*Acronym for deoxyribonucleic acid, the fundamental building block of all living things.

9 She switched from gin to wine, her solution to the problem she believes she doesn't have.

Ibid.

3657. Stasa Zajovic (fl. 1990s)

1 Has the body of a woman ever belonged to herself?

Ana's Land: Sisterhood in Eastern Europe, Tanya Renne,* ed. *1996*

*See 3650.

Biographical Index

Every contributor is listed alphabetically and her contributor number given (these numbers will be found in page headings throughout the Quotations section). Women well known by a name other than the one used as the heading of their entries in the Quotation section are cross-indexed here. All coauthors are listed except "as told to" authors.

Brief biographical information is given for each woman: her full name (those parts of her name not commonly used are in brackets), and any hereditary or honorary title she is known to hold or to have held; her nationality and—if different—her country (or countries, when each has been substantial) of residence (e.g., Austrian/Cuban/Amer., as is the case of Riane Eisler, indicates she was born in Austria, lived a substantial portion of her life in Cuba, but now resides in the United States). Nationality is followed by other appellations by which she has been known—everything from nicknames to pseudonyms to birth names. Next come notable family relations, if any, including brief biographical data on those relations, when available. If another woman included in that citing is also listed in the book, her name is marked with an asterisk (*). Notable achievements, including "firsts," discoveries, inventions, record settings, and so on, follow, after which come major awards and honors. The latter is by no means comprehensive or, when it comes to European and Asian countries, consistent; it is simply meant as an indicator of the woman's status in her profession.

A word about alphabetization of names: many women nobles, women of the Middle Ages, and many Asian women are alphabetized by what may not be a surname. Letter-by-letter alphabetization is used.

Abbreviations for relatives of the woman being quoted are in relation to her—the *contributor's* relationship to the other rather than the other's relationship to her (e.g. "*daughter* of . . . " rather than "father . . .")—and are as follows:

w.	wife	m.	mother
gm.	grandmother	s.	sister
d.	daughter	gd.	granddaughter
p.	partner	a.	aunt
ga.	grandaunt	mn.	married name
gn.	grandniece	m.-in-law	mother-in-law
c.	cousin	d.-in-law	daughter-in-law
n.	niece		

All other kinship terms are spelled out in full. Other names may be indicated by a.k.a. (*also known as,* for aliases), a.s.a. (*also seen as,* for different spellings), and pseud. (*pseudonyms,* or pen names).

The term *educator* encompasses teachers, professors (whether full, associate or assistant) and other instructors. The term *composer* designates one who writes classical music; *songwriter* is used for popular music. The term *theatrician* (first coined in the first edition of *The Quotable Woman* in 1978 and since in wider use) connotes one who has worked in almost every capacity in theater (producer, director, actor, designer, etc.).

Various organizations and affiliations that are often repeated are abbreviated, as follows:

AAP: Academy of American Poets

AAAL: American Academy of Arts and
  Letters

ABA: American Book Award, Before Columbus
  Foundation

ACTRA: Alliance of Canadian Cinema, Television
  and Radio Artists

ASL: American Sign Language

Blackburn: Susan Smith Blackburn Prize

Bollingen: Bollingen Prize in Poetry

C.B.E.: Commander of the Order of the British
  Empire

DCA: Dramalogue Critics Award GFN

DCCA: Drama Critics Circle Award

DDA: Drama Desk Award

Ford: Ford Foundation (grants and awards)
Fulbright: Fulbright scholarship
Golden Globe: Golden Globe award for excellence in film and television (Hollywood Foreign Press Association)
Grammy: Statuette awarded by National Academy of Recording Arts and Sciences
Guggenheim: Guggenheim Foundation (grants and awards)
Hugo: Hugo Award from the World Science Fiction Convention
Emmy: Statuette awarded by Academy of Television Arts and Sciences
MacArthur: John D. and Catherine T. MacArthur Foundation Fellowship
McKnight: McKnight Composer Fellowship
MP: Member of Parliament
NAACP: National Association for the Advancement of Colored People
NASA: National Aeronautics and Space Administration
NBA: National Book Award
NBCCA: National Book Critics Circle Award

NEA: National Endowment for the Arts fellowship or grant
Nebula: Nebula Award from the Science Fictions Writers of America
NEH: National Endowment for the Humanities fellowship or grant
Newbery: Newbery Medal for American literature for children
NOW: National Organization for Women
NIAL: National Institute of Arts and Letters
NSF: National Science Foundation fellowship or grants
NYDCCA: New York Drama Critics Circle Award
ODCCA: Outer Drama Critics Circle Award
Obie: Village Voice Award for exceptional achievement in off-Broadway theater
PEN: Award from PEN international literary organization
Pushcart: Pushcart Press Prize
Rockefeller: Rockefeller Foundations fellowships and grants
Tony: Antoinette Perry Award sponsored by the American Theatre Wing for outstanding Broadway theater

A

Abbagnano, Nicola (1901–1990) 1807
Ital. philosopher

Abbot, Sidney (1937–) 2661
Amer. writer

Abbott, Berenice (1898–1991) 1737
Amer. photographer, writer; technical pioneer of photographic equipment

Abbott, Wenonah Stevens (1865–1950) 1255
Amer. journalist, poet

Abel of Beth-maacah, Woman of (fl. 1040s–970s B.C.E.) 29
Isr. peacemaker

Abigail (fl. 990s B.C.E.) 34
Judean biblical figure; w. Navah (1) and David (2), m. Chileab

Abrams, Linsey (1951–) 3294
Amer. novelist

Abramson, Jill (1954–) 3374
Amer. author, journalist

Aburdene, Patricia (1947?–) 3131
Amer. social forecaster, author; w. John Naisbitt (writer); Medal of Italy from Senate of Italy, 1990

Abutsu (?–1283?) 224
Jap. nun, poet

Abzug, Bella (1920–1998) 2180
Amer. lawyer, politician, activist; née Savitsky; U.S.

congresswoman (D-N.Y.), 1971–77; cofounder, National Women's Political Caucus; first Jewish woman in Congress (1970)

Ace, Jane (1905–1974) 1875
Amer. comedian, radio personality; neé Epstein; w. Goodman A— (TV & radio comedy writer, 1899–1982)

Ackerman, Diane (1948–) 3172
Amer. nonfiction writer, journalist, naturalist, poet; AAP Poetry Prize, 1972; Rockefeller 1974–1976; NEA, 1976, 1986

Adams, Abigail (1744–1818) 634
Amer. first lady, letter writer, feminist; née Smith; w. John A— (1735–1826; 2nd U.S. president), m. John Quincy A— (1767–1848; 6th U.S. president), m.-in-law Louisa Catherine A—,* s. Elizabeth Peabody*

Adams, Glenda (1940–) 2812
Austral./Amer. novelist, educator; Miles Franklin Award, 1987, New South Wales Premier's Award, 1987; National Book Council Banjo Award, 1990, Age Fiction Book of the Year Award, 1990.

Adams, Grace (1900–?) 1753
Amer. psychologist; née Kinckle

Adams, Louisa Catherine (1775–1852) 755
Eng./Amer. first lady; née Johnson; w. John Quincy A— (1767–1848; 6th U.S. pres.), d.-in-law Abigail A—,* gm. Henry B. A— (1838–1919; historian)

Adams, Maude (1872–1953) 1328
Amer. actor; famed for portrayal of Peter Pan

Adams, Sarah Flower (1805–1848) 870
Eng. hymnist

Adamson, Joy (1919–1980) 2145
Aust./Kenyan naturalist, photographer, painter, author; née Joy-Friederike Victoria Gessner; w. George A— (naturalist)

al-Adawiya, Rabi'a (712/17–801) 135
Persian poet, slave, Sufi mystic, Islamic saint, scholar; a.k.a. R— the mystic; pivotal figure in the early development of Sufism

Addams, Jane (1860–1935) 1204
Amer. social worker; founder of Hull House, Chicago; Nobel Peace Prize, 1931; Hall of Fame, 1965

Addison, Mrs. (fl. 1810s) 887
poet

Adelwip see HADEWIJCH OF BRABANT

Adler, Freda (1934–) 2549
Amer. nonfiction writer, educator

Adler, Margot [Carole] (1941–) 2836
Amer. writer

Adler, Polly (1900–1962) 1774
Pol./Amer. author, madam

Adler, Renata (1938–) 2703
Ital./Amer. writer, philosopher, film critic

Adnan, Etel (1925–) 2264
Lebanese/Fr./Amer. poet, novelist, filmmaker, documentary

Agata, Hikari (1943–) 2930
Jap. writer; New Writers' Prize, 1982

Agnes the Martyr (1500–1535) 292
Eng. Protestant martyr

Agnesi, Maria Gaëtana (1718–1799) 568
Ital. scholar, mathematician; established a hospice for elderly infirm women; cubic curve known as the "witch of Agnesi" named for her careful description of it

Agreda, María de (1602–1664/65) 411
Span. abbess, essayist, philosopher, mystic; née Maria Fernandez Coronel, a.k.a. Sister Maria de Jesús

Dyer, Mary (fl. 1630s–d. 1660) 448
Eng./Amer. Quaker martyr;
née Barrett, a.s.a. Dyre

Dykewomon, Elana [Nachman]
(1949–) 3218
Amer. writer

E

Eaglen, Jane (195-?–) 3253
Eng. opera singer

Eane, Elizabeth *see* ABERGAVENNY,
FRANCES

Earhart, Amelia (1897–1937) 1710
Amer. writer, women's rights
activist, pacifist, aviator, social worker; w. George P.
Putnam (American publisher);
first woman to fly across Atlantic (1928) and to fly solo
across Atlantic (1932); first
person to fly solo from
Hawaii to San Francisco
(1935); set cross-country
speed record; co-found
Ninety-Nines, first women's
aviator organization (1930);
first woman to receive French
Legion of Honor, Distin-
guished Flying Cross 1932;
Women's Sports Hall of Fame,
1980

Earle, Sylvia A. (1935–) 2589
Amer. nonfiction writer, ma-
rine biologist, explorer,
environmental activist; a.k.a.
Her Deepness; Conservation
Service Award, U.S. Dept. of
Interior, 1970

Eastman, Crystal (1881–1928) 1465
Amer. attorney; industrial
safety pioneer

Eastwood, Alice (1859–1953) 1196
Can./Amer. nonfiction writer,
botanist, botany curator; honorary pres. of 7th Int.
Botanical Congress, 1950

Eberhardt, Isabelle
(1877–1904) 1402
Russ. adventurer

Eckenstein, Lina
(fl. 1890s–1931) 1597
Amer. writer, educator

Eddy, Mary Baker (1821–1910) 953
Amer. pastor, writer, theologian; founder, Christian
Science, 1866, and *The Christian Science Monitor*, 1908

Edelman, Marian Wright
(1939–) 2752
Amer. lawyer, children's rights
advocate, nonprofit adminis-
trator; founder, Children's
Defense Fund, 1973; Gandhi
Peace Award 1989;
MacArthur, 1985; NAACP
Roy Wilkins Civil Rights
Award 1984; Rockefeller,
1981

Edelstein, Jean (192-?–) 2153
Amer. painter

Eden, Emily (1797–1869) 835
Eng./Ind. novelist; a.k.a. Lady
Auckland; d. William E—, 1st
baron of Auckland, s. George
E—, earl of Auckland

Ederle, Gertrude (1906–) 1886
Amer. athlete (swimmer); first
woman to swim the English
Channel, 1926; Olympic
medalist

Edgeworth, Maria
(1767–1849) 723
Ir. essayist, novelist

Edna (fl. 720s B.C.E) 45
Mede biblical figure; w.
Raguel, m. Sarah

Edson, Margaret (1961–) 3495
Amer. playwright, educator,
public school; Pulitzer,1999

Edwards, Amelia
(1831–1889) 1002
Eng. writer, Egyptologist

Edwards, Anne (1927–) 2334
Amer. writer, scenarist

Edwards, Betty (fl. 1940s) 2793
Amer. author, researcher,
artist

Edwards, Marie (1926?–) 2296
Amer. psychologist; née Babare

Edwards, Sarah Pierpont
(1710–1758) 555
Amer. Puritan mystic, householder; great-gd. Rev.
Thomas Hooker (English-born
American colonizer and cleric,
1586?–1647; founder, city of
Hartford, Conn., 1636), d.
James Pierpont, a.s.a. Pierrepont (pastor and cofounder of
Yale college), w. Jonathan Edwards (American theologian
and philosopher, 1703–1758;
president, College of New Jersey [now Princeton],
1703–1758)

Egburg (fl. 8th century) 143
Eng. nun

Egeria (fl. 380s–d. 384) 107
Span. abbess

Egeria *see* HEMANS, FELICIA

Egerton, Sarah F[yge Field]
(1670–1723) 508
Eng. poet; possibly youngest
feminist polemicist on record

Eglui, Ellen
(fl. late 19th century) 1754
Amer. inventor; invented the
clothes wringer for washing
machines; sold the patent
rights in 1888 for $18.00

Ehrenreich, Barbara
(1941–) 2848
Amer. columnist, author;
Guggenheim, 1987

Eifuku, Empress (1271–1342) 223
Jap. poet, noble

Eisenhower, Mamie [Geneva] Doud
(1896–1979) 1703
Amer. society leader, first
lady; w. Dwight "Ike" D. E—
(American general and politician, 1890–1969; 34th U.S.
president, 1953–61)

Eisler, Riane [Tennenhaus]
(1931–) 2459
Aus./Cuban/Amer. author, social historian; w. David Loye
(philosopher); founder, Center
for Partnership Studies, International Partnership Network

Elders, Joycelyn "Minnie"
(1933–) 2524
Amer. civil servant, pediatri-
cian, endocrinologist; U.S.
Surgeon General, 1993–1994

Eleanor of Aquitaine
(1122?–1204) 182
Fr./Eng. queen; w. Louis VII of
France (1) and Henry II of England (2), m. Richard I (the
Lion Heart) and John of England

Elia, Bridget *see* LAMB, MARY

Elion, Gertrude B.
(1918–1999) 2131
Amer. chemist & biologist;
Nobel Prize in Physiology and
Chemistry, 1988, with George
Hitchens (1905–1998), for
their discoveries of important
principles for drug treatment

Eliot, George (1819–1880) 930
Eng. writer; née Marian
Evans; mn. Cross

Eliott, Ethelinda *see* BEERS, ETHEL

Elisabeth, Saint
(fl. 20s B.C.E–? C.E.) 78
Judean saint; w. Zechariah, m.
John the Baptist, c. Virgin
Mary*

Elisabeth of Brandenburg
(1485–1545) 280
Ger. noble; s. Christian II of
Denmark, w. Joachim I (elec-
tor of Brandenburg), m.
Elizabeth of Braunschweig*

Elizabeth *see* ARNIM, MARY

Elizabeth, Caroline Amelia
(1768–1821) 726
Ger./Eng. queen; second w.
George IV of England
(1762–1830), m. Charlotte
Augusta (1762–1830)

Elizabeth, Helene Marie Phillipine
(1764–1794) 708
Fr. noble, French; s. Louis
XVI, king of France
(1754–93)

Elizabeth, Queen Mother
(1900–) 1755
Eng. queen; née Lady E— Angela Marguerite Bowes-Lyon;
w. King George VI
(1895–1952), m. Elizabeth II*

Elizabeth I of England, Queen
(1533–1603) 331
Eng. queen; a.k.a. Elizabeth
Tudor; d. Henry VIII of En-
gland (1491–1597) and Ann
Boleyn,* half-s. Mary I of
England* and Edward VI
(1537–53; king of England,
1447–53), gd. Elizabeth of
York,* first c. Mary, Queen of
Scots*

Elizabeth II of England, Queen
(1926–) 2297
Eng. queen, spokesperson; d.
Queen Mother Elizabeth* and
King George VI (1895–1952);
w. Phillip Mountbatten, duke
of Edinburgh (1921—)

Elizabeth of Braunschweig
(1510–1558) 300
Ger. noble; d. Elisabeth of
Brandenburg*, w. Erich, duke
of Braunschweig-Calenberg,
m. Anna Maria of B—*

Elizabeth of Romania *see* SYLVA,
CARMEN

Elizabeth of Thuringia, Saint
(1206/07–1231) 213
Ger. queen, Franciscan ter-
tiary; d. Andrew II of
Hungary (1205–35), w. Ludwig (landgrave of Thuringia)

Elizabeth of York
(1465/66–1503) 267
Eng. queen, poet; d. Edward
IV, king of England (1442–83)
and Elizabeth Woodville-
Grey,* m. Henry VII, king of
England (1485–1509), gm.
Elizabeth I*

Ellerbee, Linda [Jane]
(1944–) 2998
Amer. journalist; Peabody
Award, 1992

Elliot, Jean (1727–1805) 586
Scot. poet, songwriter; a.s.a.
Jane E—

Elliott, Anna (fl. 1770s) 732
Amer. householder

Elliott, Charlotte (1789–1871) 795
Eng. hymnist

Elliott, Maxine (1871–1940) 1320
Amer. actor, theater owner-
manager

Ellis, Alice Thomas (1932–) 2489
Brit. author; a.k.a. Anna Hay-
craft

Ellis, Sarah (1812–1872) 898
Eng. writer, missionary; w.
William E—; cofounder, Raw-
don House School for Girls

Elmendorf, Mary J[ohnson]
(fl. 1920s) 2154
Amer. poet

Elstob, Elizabeth (1683–1756) 520
Eng. governess, Anglo-Saxon
scholar; a.k.a. The Saxon
Lady; n. Rev. Charles E—

MacLeod, Jean Sutherland (1908–) 1921
Eng. novelist, poet; pseud. Catherine Airlie, Phila Henrietta Case

MacLeod, Mairi (1569–1674?) 366
Scot. nurse, poet; d. Red Alastair (poet)

MacPherson, Myra (1935?–) 2600
Amer. journalist, author

Macuilxochitl (1435–1499?) 255
Aztec poet; d. Tlacaelel (counselor to Itzcoatl)

Macy, Joanna [Rogers] (1929–) 2386
Amer. Buddhist scholar, nonfiction writer, workshop leader; Fulbright; Ford 1979, 1980

Madan, Judith (fl. 1750s) 647
Eng. poet; née Cowper; s. William Cowper (1664?–1723; jurist; Lord High Chancellor of England, 1707–10 and 1714–18)

Madison, Dolley (1768–1849) 728
Amer. society leader, first lady; née Dorothea Payne; w. John Todd (1) and James M— (2; 1751–1836; politician; 4th U.S. president, 1809–1849)

Madonna (1958–) 3449
Amer. actor, singer; née M— Louise Veronica Ciccone

Magdeburgh, Mechtild von see MECHTILD VON MAGDEBURG

Magdelene, Mary see MARY MAGDALENE

Magnani, Anna (1918–1973) 2125
Egyp./Ital. actor; Academy Award, 1955

Mahādēviyakka (fl. 12th century) 205
Ind. poet, Hindu saint; a.s.a. Mahadevi; w. King Kausika

Mahlah, Noah, Hoglah, Milcah and Tirzah, Five Daughters of Zelophehad (fl. 1240s–1200 B.C.E) 18
Hebrew biblical figures; demanded right of father's inheritance if no son living; first women to win legal property rights

Mahler, Alma see WERFEL, ALMA

Mahler, Margaret (1897–1985) 1720
Hung./Amer. psychiatrist, psychoanalyst, lecturer, nonfiction writer; née Schoenberger

Mahler-Werfel, Alma (1879–1964) 1440
Aus./Amer. diarist, society figure, composer; née Schindler; m. Anna M— (sculptor); widow of Gustav Mahler (1860–1911; 1, Aus. composer & conductor); Franz Werfel (1890–1945; 2, Aus. writer)

Mahodahi (fl. 7th–11th century) 128
Ind. poet

Mahsati (fl. 12th century) 206
Iran. poet

Maintenon, Françoise de (1635–1719) 460
Fr. letter writer; née d'Aubigné, a.s.a. marquise or Mme de M—; w. Paul Scarron (1; 1610–60; writer), mistress and w. Louis XIV (2; 1638–1715, king of France, 1643–1715); founded school for daughters of impoverished noblemen at St.-Cyr, 1686

Mairs, Nancy (1939–) 2760
Amer. essayist

Maitland, Sara Louise (1950–)3268
Eng. writer, religious

Makeba, Miriam (1932–) 2503
S. Afr./Amer. political activist, singer; a.k.a. Mama Africa; ex-w. Stokely Carmichael (Amer. civil rights activist; a.k.a. Kwame Toure)

Makhfi (1639–1703) 463
Ind. princess, poet, patron of poets, patron of scholars; a.k.a. Zibu'n-Nisa (a.s.a. Zeb-un-Nissa)

Makhubu, Lydia Phindile (1937–) 2683
Swazi chemist, research scientist, university administrator; first Swazi woman to earn a Ph.D.; founder, Royal Swaziland Society of Science and Technology, 1977; cofounder, Third World Organization of Women in Science (TWOWS), 1989; first woman to head Association of Commonwealth Universities

Makin, Bathsua (1608/12?–1674/5?) 419
Eng. author, tutor, scholar; d. John Pell, s. John Pell II (mathematician); royal tutor to Princess Elizabeth and other children of Charles II (1630–85; king of England, 1660–85)

Malcolm, Janet (1934–) 2570
Cuban-born Amer. writer, critic

Malfitano, Catherine (1948–) 3269
Ital. opera singer

Malone-Mayes, Vivienne (1932–1995) 2504
? mathematician

Malpede, Karen (1945–) 3057
Amer. theater historian, peace activist, playwright, educator; w. George Bartenieff (actor-producer); cofounder, New Cycle Theatre, Brooklyn (1976–84); with Bartenieff,

cofounder, Theater Three Collaborative

Mamonova, Tatyana (1944?–) 3014
Sov./Aus. critic, translator, painter, feminist, poet

Mancini, Maria Anna (1649–1714) 477
Ital./Fr. salonist; d. Michele Lorenzo Mand Girolama Mazzarino, s. Laure, Olympe, Marie, and Hortense M—, w. Godefroy Maurice de la Tour, duc de Bouillon, n. Jules Mazarin Ital.-born French cardinal1602–61); patron of Jean de La Fontaine (1621–95; Fr. writer), Pierre Corneille (Fr. playwright, 1606–84), and Jean-Baptiste Molière (1622–73; Fr. playwright)

Mandela, [Nomzamo] Winnie [Madikizela] (1934–) 2571
S. Afr. political activist, social worker (medical), political leader; a.k.a. Umama Wethu, the Mother of the Nation; ex-w. Nelson M— (1918–; anti-apartheid activist and leader; president, So. Africa, 1994– ; Nobel Peace Prize, 1993), m. Maki M—*

Mandela, Maki (1964?–) 3523
S. Afr. political activist, sociologist; d. Nelson M— (1918– ; anti-apartheid activist and leader; president, So. Africa, 1994– ; Nobel Peace Prize, 1993) and Winnie M—*

Mankiller, Wilma Pearl (1945–) 3058
Amer. social worker, Native American rights activist, politician; chief of the Cherokee Nation of Oklahoma, 1987–95; first woman to head a major Native American tribe

Manley, Delariviere (1663/72–1724) 494
Eng. author, editor, playwright; a.k.a. (Mary) D—M—; pseud. Mrs. Crackenthorpe; née Daniels; first Englishwoman to be a political journalist, to author a best-seller, and to be arrested for her writings

Manley, Joan [Adele] (1932–) 2505
Amer. publisher; née Daniels

Mann, Emily (1952–) 3333
Amer. playwright; w. Gerry Banman (actor, writer); Guggenheim, 1983; NEA 1984, 1986; Tony, 1994; Obie, 1981

Mann, Erika (1905–1969) 1872
Ger. writer, lecturer, journalist; d. Thomas M— (writer,

1875–1955), w. W. H. Auden (Eng./Am. author, 1907–73)

Manner, Eeva-Liisa (1921–) 2186
Finn. playwright, writer, poet

Mannering, Julia see BINGHAM, MADELINE

Manners, Diane see COOPER, DIANA

Manners, Frances, Lady see ABERGAVENNY, FRANCES

Mannes, Marya (1904–) 1847
Amer. writer, journalist

Manoah, Wife of (fl. 1080 B.C.E) 25
Hebrew biblical figure; w. M— of Zorah, m. Samson (Old Testament Isr. judge)

Mansfield, Katherine (1888–1923) 1564
N.Z./Eng. writer, literary critic; née K— Beauchamp Murry

Mantua, marquise of see ESTE, ISABELLA D'

Mara, Gertrude Elizabeth (1749–1833) 645
Ger. singer; née Schmaling

Maraini, Dacia (1936–) 2601
Ital. feminist, political activist, writer, playwright, poet; w. Alberto Moravia (né Pincherle; 1907–90; fiction writer); founder, La Maddalena (feminist theater), Rome, 1972

Marbury, Elisabeth (1856–1933) 1163
Amer. theater manager, literary agent, playwright, translator

Marcelle, countess de (fl. 1540s) 335
Fr. nun

Marchant, Catherine see COOKSON, CATHERINE

Marchocka, Anna Maria (1603–1652) 413
Pol. Carmelite nun; a.k.a. Sister Teresa

Marcos, Imelda (1929–) 2387
Filipina public figure; née Romualdez; w. Ferdinand M— (1917–89; politician; president of Phillipines, 1966–86); governor of metropolitan Manila, 1975–86; cabinet member, 1978–86; Miss Manila, 1953

Marcus, Lisa (1965–) 3528
Amer. educator (ethnic literature & feminist theory)

Margaret of Alençon see MARGUERITE OF NAVARRE

Margaret of Angoulême see MARGUERITE OF NAVARRE

Margaret of Anjou (1430–1482) 254
Eng. military hero, queen; w. Henry VI (1421–71; king of

Merman, Ethel (1908–1984)   1934
Amer. actor, singer; née E—
Agnes Zimmerman; Tony,
1951; Grammy, 1959

Merriam, Eve (1916–1992)   2086
Amer. playwright, feminist,
writer, poet, director; Obie,
1977

Merry, Anne Brunton
(1769–1808)   729
Eng./Amer. theater manager,
actor; a.k.a. Mrs. Wignell,
Mrs. Warren; w. Robert M—
(1; poet, playwright, politician), Thomas Wignell (2;
theater producer, manager),
and William Warren (3; theater producer, manager)

Mettika (fl. 6th century B.C.E)   48
Chin. Buddhist nun

Metzger, Deena [Posy]
(1936–)   2637
Amer. poet, writer

Mew, Charlotte (1869–1928)   1286
Eng. writer, poet

Meyer, Agnes [Elizabeth Ernst]
(1887–1970?)   1551
Amer. translator, social
worker, writer, journalist

Meyer, Marlane (1951–)   3309
Amer. playwright, TV writer;
née M— Emily Huapala Go-
mard; DCA, 1986; Blackburn,
1990; NEA

Meynell, Alice Christiana
(1845/47–1922)   1109
Eng. poet, literary critic; née
Thompson

Michaelis, Aline Triplett
(1885–?)   1520
Amer. poet, journalist

Michal
(fl. 1010s–970 B.C.E)   32
Hebrew queen; d. Saul, king
of Israel, s. Merab (first be-
trothed of David), first w.
David, king of Israel

Michel, Louise (1830–1905)   995
Fr. revolutionary; pseud.
Clemence

Michelman, Kate (1942–)   2910
Amer. civic organization administrator, women's rights
activist; executive director,
National Abortion Rights Action League (NARAL), 1985–

Michiel, Renier Giustina
(1755–1832)   671
Ital. botanist, noble

Michiner, Harry, Mrs.   see IRVING,
MINNA

Michitsuna, Mother of
(fl. 950s–d. 974)   159
Jap. diarist; a.k.a. Lady Gossamer; mistress of Fujiwara no
Kane-iye (statesman), w. Re-
gent Kaneie, m. Udaish«
Michitsuna no haba

Midler, Bette (1945–)   3059
Amer. actor, singer, writer;
a.k.a. The Divine Miss M;
Grammy, 1973, 1980 (2);
Tony, 1973; Emmy 1978

Mihru'n-Nisa of Heart   see MEHRI

Mikulski, Barbara [Ann]
(1936–)   2638
Amer. politician; U.S. House
of Representatives (D-Maryland), 1977–1987; U.S.
senator (D-Maryland),
1987– ; first woman to hold a
Senate leadership post

Milan, duchess of   see ESTE, BEAT-
RICE D'

Milbanke, Anne Isabella
(1792–1860)   811
Eng. poet; a.k.a. Lady Byron,
Annabella; w. George Gordon
(a.k.a. Lord Byron, poet,
1788–1824); m. Augusta Ada
Byron

Milcah   see MAHLAH, NOAH,
HOGLAH, MILCAH AND TIRZAH, FIVE
DAUGHTERS OF ZELOPHEHAD

Mildmay, Lady   see SHERRINGTON,
GRACE

Miles, Josephine
(1911–1985)   1979
Amer. literary critic, educator,
poet

Mill, Harriet Taylor
(1807/08–1858)   881
Eng. suffragist; w. John Stuart
M— (1806–73; philosopher,
economist)

Millar, Margaret Ellis
(1915–1994)   2053
Can./Amer. fiction writer; née
Sturm; w. Kenneth M—
(pseud. Ross Macdonald;
writer)

Millar, Susanna (fl. 1960s)   3483
Eng. writer, psychologist

Millay, Edna St. Vincent
(1892–1950)   1632
Amer. poet, playwright,
writer; pseud. Nancy Boyd; w.
Eugene Boissevain; Pulitzer,
1923

Miller, Alice (193-?–)   2435
Ger. arts-in-education specialist, painter

Miller, Alice Duer
(1874–1942)   1356
Amer. poet, novelist; mn.
Wise

Miller, Casey Geddes
(1919–1997)   2148
Amer. etymologist; pioneer in
study of non-sexist language

Miller, Emily (1833–1913)   1020
Amer. poet, social reformer,
writer, journalist, editor;
a.k.a. E— Clarke Huntingdon

Miller, Helen [Day] Hill
(1899–?)   1742
Amer. writer, journalist

Miller, Isabel   see ROUTSONG,
ALMA

Miller, Jean Baker (1927–)   2342
Amer. psychiatrist, psychoanalyst, editor, teacher, author

Miller, Lee (1907–1977)   1908
Amer. model, photographer;
w. Sir Roland Algernon Penrose (1900–84; Eng. art critic,
collector, painter)

Miller, Susan (1944–)   3016
Amer. playwright; Obie,
1979; NEA, 1976, 1983;
Rockefeller, 1975

Millet, Kate (1934–)   2574
Amer. sculptor, writer,
feminist

Miner, Dorothy Eugenia
(1904–1973)   1853
Amer. librarian, scholar

Minh-ha, Trinh   see TRINH, T.
MINH-HA

Mink, Gwendolyn (1952–)   3334
Amer. community activist

Mink, Patsy [Takemoto]
(1927–)   2343
Amer. lawyer, politician; first
Asian-American elected to
Congress (D-Hawaii),
1965–1977 and 1990– ; co-
founder, National Women's
Political Caucus; cofounder,
Women USA

Minnelli, Liza (1946–)   3108
Amer. singer, actor; d. Judy
Garland* and Vincent M—
(film director, 1910–), s.
Lorna Luft (singer, 1952–)

Minow, Martha (1954–)   3386
Amer. educator (law)

Mirabai (1498–1547)   288
Ind. Hindu saint, poet,
princess

Miriam (fl. 1250s–30s B.C.E)   16
Hebrew poet, prophet; d.
Jochebed, s. Moses (Hebrew
prophet, lawgiver) and Aaron,
w. Hur

Mirikitani, Janice (1942–)   2911
Amer. poet, book editor, nonprofit administrator

Mirrielees, Edith Ronald
(1878–1962)   1424
Amer. editor, writer, educator

Mistral, Gabriela
(1889–1957)   1583
Chilean educator, diplomat,
educational activist, poet; née
Lucila Godoy y Alcayaga;
Chilean consul in Naples,
Madrid, and Lisbon; first
Latina to win Nobel Prize,
1945

Mitchell, Helen Porter   see MELBA,
NELLIE

Mitchell, Joni (1943–)   2959
Can./Amer. singer, songwriter;
Grammy, 1969

Mitchell, Juliet (1940–)   2816
N.Z./Eng. editor, lecturer,
writer

Mitchell, Margaret
(1900–1949)   1772
Amer. writer; mn. Marsh;
Pulitzer, 1937

Mitchell, Maria (1818–1889)   922
Amer. astronomer, educator;
first woman astronomer in
U.S.; first woman member of
American Academy of Arts and
Sciences; discovered new comet,
1847; Hall of Fame, 1905

Mitchell, Martha
(1918–1976)   2127
Amer. public figure; née Jennings; w. John M— (1913–88;
lawyer; attorney general of
U.S., 1968–72)

Mitford, Jessica [Lucy]
(1917–1996)   2108
Eng./Amer. social critic,
writer; mn. Treuhaft

Mitford, Mary Russell
(1787–1855)   784
Eng. author, playwright, poet;
a.k.a. Sancho Panza in Petticoats

Mitford, Nancy (1904–1973)   1854
Eng./Fr. novelist, biographer;
a.k.a. N— Freeman M—
Rodd; d. David Bertram
Ogilvy (2nd baron Redesdale)

Mladjenovic, Lepa (fl. 1990s)   3644
Serb. political activist

Mock, Geraldine Fredritz
(1925–)   2280
Amer. aviator, radio & TV
host; a.k.a. the flying housewife; first woman to fly alone
around the world

Modjeska, Helena
(1840–1920)   1061
Pol. actor; née Opid

Modotti, Tina (1896–1942)   1693
Ital./Amer./Mex. actor, revolutionary, photographer;
companion to Edward Weston
(1; 1850–1936; Eng/Am. photographer), Julio Antonio
Mella (2; Cuban revolutionary; assassinated, 1928)

Moffat, Mary Jane (1938?–)   2719
Amer. actor, writer,
educator

Moirai, Catherine Risingflame
(195-?–)   3270
Amer. poet

Moïse, Penina (1797–1880)   836
Amer. Jewish hymnist, poet

Mojtabai, A.G. [Ann Grace]
(1937–)   2720
Amer. novelist, nonfiction
writer

Molesworth, Mary Louisa
(1839–1921)   1055
Dutch/Eng. essayist, author;
a.k.a. Ennis Graham

Mongella, Gertrude Ibengwe (1945–) 3060
Tanz. diplomat; Secretary General of United Nations Fourth Conference on the World's Women, 1995

Monica (340–395) 104
Numidian letter writer; a.s.a. Monnica; w. Patricius, m. St. Augustine (354–430; theologian, bishop of Hippo), Navigius and Perpetuals

Monk, Mary (?–1715) 563
Ir. noble, poet; née Molesworth, a.s.a. Monck, pseud. Marinda

Monroe, Anne Shannon (1877–1942) 1403
Amer. writer, lecturer

Monroe, Harriet (1860–1936) 1206
Amer. editor, poet

Monroe, Marilyn (1926–1962) 2323
Amer. screen actor; née Norma Jean Baker; ex-w. Joe DiMaggio (2, 1914–99; baseball hero), Arthur Miller (3, playwright, 1915–)

Montagu, Elizabeth (1720–1800) 572
Eng. essayist, letter writer; née Robinson; first Bluestocking

Montagu, Lily (1873–1963) 1347
Ger. religious figure; a.k.a. Lillian Helen M—

Montagu, Mary Wortley, Lady (1689–1762) 527
Eng. poet, essayist, letter writer; d. Evelyn Pierrepont (marquess of Dorchester and 1st duke of Kingston) w. Edward W— M— I, m. Edward W— M— II (writer, traveler)

Montansier, La see BRUNET, MARGUERITE

Montessori, Maria (1870–1952) 1311
Ital. physician, educator, writer; originator of Montessori Method of education; first Italian woman to receive M.D. from University of Rome

Montgomery, countess of see WROTH, MARY SIDNEY

Montgomery, Lucy Maud (1874–1942) 1357
Can. writer

Montgomery, Roselle Mercier (1874–1933) 1354
Amer. poet

Montolieu, Jeanne Isabelle (1751–1832) 656
Swiss novelist

Montpensier, duchess of see ORLÉANS, ANN-MARIE-LOUISE

Moodie, Susanna (1803–1885) 866
Can. writer, poet

Moody, Anne (1940–) 2817
Amer. writer, activist

Moore, Grace (1901–1947) 1794
Amer. actor, opera singer

Moore, Honor (1945–) 3061
Amer. playwright, poet

Moore, Julia A (1847–1920) 1108
Amer. poet

Moore, Liz (1922–) 2209
Amer. environmental & health activist; cofounder, Colorado Coalition for the Prevention of Nuclear War; founder, Solar Action Network of the American Solar Energy Society; creator of "The Ten Commandments for HMOs"

Moore, Lorrie (1957–) 3442
Amer. educator (English), fiction writer; a.k.a. Marie Lorena M—

Moore, Marianne [Craig] (1887–1972) 1560
Amer. literary editor, poet; NBA, 1952; Pulitzer, 1952

Moore, Martha Milca (1740–1829) 621
Amer. poet, educator

Moore, Patricia A. (1952–) 3335
Amer. industrial designer, lecturer

Moore, Susanna (1948–) 3196
Amer. novelist; AAAL, 1983

Moore, Virginia [E.] (1903–) 1828
Amer. biographer, poet

Moorhead, Sarah Parsons (fl. 1740s) 617
Amer. poet

Mora, Elizabeth Catlett (1916?–) 2077
Amer. political activist, sculptor

Moraga, Cherríe (1952–) 3336
Amer. educator, essayist, anthologist, playwright, poet; cofounded (with Audre Lorde* and Barbara Smith*) the first publishing collective by women of color, Kitchen Table: Women of Color Press; ABA, 1986; NEA

Morantz-Sanchez, Regina (1943–) 2960
Amer. nonfiction writer, educator (history); née R— Ann Markell; NEH 1975, 1981, 1987

Morata, Olimpia (1526–1555) 322
Ital. poet, scholar

More, Hannah (1745–1833) 636
Eng. philanthropist, reformer, writer; a.k.a. The Laureate of the Bluestockings, Stella; pseud. Will Chip

Moreau, Jeanne (1928–) 2367
Fr. actor

Morgan, Angela (1874?–1957) 1368
Amer. poet, writer, lecturer

Morgan, Barbara [Brooks] (1900–) 1762
Amer. photographer

Morgan, Elaine [Neville] (1920–) 2162
Welsh writer, educator, anthropologist

Morgan, Elizabeth (1947–) 3155
Amer. physician, prisoner, author

Morgan, Julia (1872–1957) 1330
Amer. architect; first woman awarded degree in architecture from L'Ecole des Beaux-Arts, Paris

Morgan, Marabel (1937–) 2684
Amer. writer; née Hawk

Morgan, Marlo (1934–) 2575
Amer. health care professional, author

Morgan, Robin (1941–) 2864
Amer. poet, writer, anthologist, feminist

Morgan, Ruth (1920–1978) 2176
Amer. novelist

Morgan, Sydney Owenson, Lady (c.1776/83–1859) 759
Ir./Eng. novelist, actor, historian, poet; a.k.a. Gloriana; first woman in Great Britain to receive a pension for service to the world of letters

Mori, Nobuko (1932–) 2506
Jap. politician

Morpeth, Mary (fl. 1650s) 479
Scot. poet

Morphonios, Ellen James (1929–) 2389
Amer. attorney

Morpurgo, Rahel (1790–1871) 802
Ital./Hebrew turner, seamstress, poet; née Luzzatto, a.s.a. Rachel; gd. Isaac Luzzatto (1729–?), c. Samuel David Luzzatto

Morra, Isabella da (1520–1546) 313
Ital. poet; d. Giovanni Michele di M—

Morris, Esther Hobart McQuigg Slack (1813/14–1902) 902
Amer. attorney

Morris, Holly (1966–) 3535
Amer. publisher, TV host & producer, editor, feminist; d. Jeannie M— (sports writer, broadcaster) and Johnny M— (football player and sports broadcaster)

Morris, Jan (1926–) 2312
Welsh journalist, writer; née James Humphrey M—

Morris, Margaret (1737?–1816) 613
Amer. healer, diarist; née Hill

Morris, Mary [Elizabeth] (1913–1986) 2018
Amer. editor, nonfiction writer, author, columnist; née Davis

Morris, Nobuko see ALBERY, NOBUKO

Morrison, Toni (1931–) 2469
Amer. novelist, book editor; née Chloe Anthony Wofford; first black woman to win Nobel Prize, 1993; Pulitzer, 1988

Morrow, Elizabeth Cutter (1873–1955) 1342
Amer. poet, writer; m. Anne Morrow Lindberg*, mn. Whitney

Mortimer, Penelope (1918–1999) 2121
Eng. writer; née Fletcher

Morton, Sarah Wentworth (1759–1846) 690
Amer. poet; née Apthorp; a.k.a. Constantia, Philenia, A Lady of Boston, The American Sappho, The American Montague

Moscou, Jacqueline (1949–) 3226
Amer. stage director

Moses, Claire Goldberg (1941–) 2865
Amer. educator (women's studies), journal editor, nonfiction writer

Moses, Grandma (1860–1961) 1208
Amer. painter; née Anna Mary Robertson

Mossell, N[athan] F[rancis], Mrs. (1856–1946) 1165
Amer. writer

Motley, Annette (fl. 1970s–80s) 3567
Eng. novelist

Motoni, Nomura (1806–1867) 877
Jap. poet, political activist

Mott, Lucretia (1793–1880) 820
Amer. abolitionist, suffragist, Quaker minister; née Coffin; founder, The Female Anti-Slavery Society, 1833; with Elizabeth Cady Stanton,* organized the first women's rights convention, Seneca Falls, New York, 1848

Moulton, Louise (1835–1908) 1032
Amer. poet, writer; née Chandler

Mountain Wolf Woman (1881–1960) 1472
Amer. autobiographer; née Kehachiwinga

Mowatt, Anna Cora (1819–1870) 929
Amer./Fr. public speaker, actor, playwright, poet; cofounder, Mount Vernon Association (first time a group of women was allowed to band together and purchase property)

Ronell, Ann (1908–1993)   1924
Amer. orchestra conductor, songwriter; first woman to conduct and compose for film

Ronstadt, Linda (1946–)   3120
Amer. singer; Grammy (4)

Roosevelt, [Anna] Eleanor (1884–1962)   1513
Amer. lecturer, humanitarian, first lady, government official, writer; w. Franklin D. R— (1882–1945; politician; 32nd U.S. president, 1933–45), m. Alice R— Halsted,* n. Theodore R— (1858–1919; war hero, politician; 26th U.S. president, 1901–09), Corinne R— Robinson,* c. Edith Carow R—* and Alice R— Longworth*; U.S. delegate to United Nations, 1945–53, 1961; United Nations Prize, 1968

Roosevelt, Edith Carow (1861–1948)   1222
Amer. society leader; d. Theodore R— (1858–1919; war hero, politician 26th U.S. president, 1901–09), n. Corinne R. Robinson,* a. Anna R— Halsted,* c. Eleanor R—*, s. Alice R— Longworth*

Rosaldo, Michelle Zimbalist (1944–1981)   3032
Amer. anthropologist

Rose, Ernestine [Potowski] (1810–1892)   893
Pol./Amer. socialist, feminist, abolitionist

Rose, Phyllis (1942–)   2919
Amer. biographer, educator, literary critic; née Davidoff

Rose, Wendy [Elizabeth] (1948–)   3203
Amer. poet, artist, editor

Rosen, Marjorie (1942–)   2920
Amer. writer, film historian

Rosenberg, Ethel (1915–1953) 2059
Amer. public figure; née Greenglass; w. Julius R—; only U.S. citizen, with her husband, to be executed for treason

Rosenberg, Tina (1961–)   3486
Amer. nonfiction writer, political journalist, speech writer; MacArthur, 1987; NBA, 1995; Pulitzer, 1996

Rosenstein, Harriet (1932?–) 2510
Amer. writer

Rosenthal, Ida (1886–1973)   1547
Russ./Amer. dressmaker, political activist, inventor, philanthropist; née Kaganovich; invented the first modern brassiere, Maiden Form, 1922

Rosenthal, Rachel (1930?–)   2443
Fr./Amer. performance artist; founder, director, Instant Theatre, Los Angeles, 1956–66

Ross, Lillian (1927–)   2345
Amer. writer, journalist

Ross, Susan C. (1942–)   2921
Amer. civil rights activist, educator, writer, lawyer

Rossetti, Christina [Georgina] (1830–1894)   994
Eng. poet, writer; pseud. Ellen Alleyne; s. Dante Gabriel R— (1828–82; poet, painter)

Rossi, Alice (1922–)   2213
Amer. author, educator, scholar, editor

Rossner, Judith (1935–)   2606
Amer. writer

Roth, Friederike (1948–)   3204
Ger. philosopher, translator, linguist, radio writer, playwright, poet

Roulet, Elaine, Sister (1931–) 2472
Amer. nun, teacher, prison reformer

Rourke, Constance [Mayfield] (1885–1941)   1525
Amer. writer

Rousselle, Aline (1939–)   2768
Fr. historian

Routsong, Alma (1924–)   2254
Amer. feminist, writer; pseud. Isabel Miller

Row, Amanda (1931–)   2473
Amer. writer, educator

Rowe, Elizabeth (1674–1736/37)   511
Eng. poet, author; a.k.a. E— Singer; pseud. Philomela

Rowland, Helen (1876–1950) 1392
Amer. journalist, humorist, writer

Rowlandson, Mary [White] (1635?–post-1678)   459
Amer. pioneer, author

Rowson, Susanna Haswell (1762–1824)   702
Eng./Amer. novelist, playwright, actor, poet, editor, textbook writer

Roy, Arundhati (1961–)   3487
Ind. screenwriter, novelist; w. Pradip Krishen (filmmaker); Booker Prize, 1997

Roy, Gabrielle (1909–1983)   1945
Can. novelist; Governor General's Award (3)

Roy, Sara (1955–)   3410
Amer. researcher

Royall, Anne Newport (1769–1854)   731
Amer. author, newspaper publisher, traveler; née Newport; a.k.a. "Grandma of the Mudrakers"; sometimes called the first American newspaperwoman

Royden, [Agnes] Maude (1877–1956)   1407
Eng. religious leader

Ruarowna, Margareta (fl. 1620s)   430
Pol. author (religion), poet; d. Marcin Ruar

Rubin, Vera C. (1927?–)   2346
Amer. astrophysicist; w. Robert R— (mathematician); Gold Medal of the Royal Astronomical Society (London), the first woman to be awarded this medal since Caroline Herschel* in 1828

Rubinstein, Helena (1870–1965)   1312
Pol./Amer. writer, cosmetic manufacturer, business executive; a.k.a. Princess Gourielli-Tchkonia

Ruckelshaus, Jill (1937–)   2691
Amer. civil servant, lecturer; née Strickland; w. William R— (1932–); officer, U.S. Commission of Civil Rights, 198?–?

Ruddick, Sara (1935–)   2607
Amer. teacher, pacifist, author, philosopher

Rudikoff, Sonya (fl. 1970s)   3571
Amer. writer

Rudy, Kathy (1956–)   3431
Amer. educator (ethics & women's studies)

Ruether, Rosemary Radford (1937–)   2692
Amer. theologian, nonfiction writer, feminist, educator (theology)

Ruiz, Mona Sandoval (1959–)   3462
Amer. police officer

Rukeyser, Muriel (1913–1980)   2029
Amer. biographer, writer, civil rights activist, poet, translator, film editor; NIAL, 1942; AAAL, 1942

Rule, Jane (1931–)   2474
Amer./Can. writer

Runkle, Bertha (1878–1958)   1423
Amer. writer; mn. Bash

Russell, Anna (1911–)   1981
Eng./Amer. singer, comedian

Russell, Countess see ARNIM, MARY

Russell, Dora [Winifred], countess (1894–1986)   1679
Brit. pacifist, author, feminist, campaigner; née Black; ex-w. Lord Bertrand R— (1872–1970; philosopher and mathematician); cofounder, Beacon Hill School, West Sussex, 1927 (progressive school); pioneer of women's rights

Russell, Elizabeth Hoby, Lady (1528–post-1603)   323
Eng. diarist, courtier; d. Anthony Cooke (1442–83; tutor to Edward IV; king of England, 1461–83), s. Anne Cooke Bacon,* Lady Mildred Burleigh and Catherine Killigrew,* w. Sir Thomas H— (1; author, translator) and Lord John R— (2), m. Elizabeth, Ann and Thomas Posthumous H—, m.-in-law Lady Margaret H—*; earliest known English woman diarist

Russell, Lady   see HARINGTON, LUCY

Russell, Rachel, Lady (1636–1723)   461
Eng. letter writer; née R— Wriothesley; w. Vaughn (1), Lord William R— (2)

Russell, Rosalind (1911–1976)   1990
Amer. philanthropist, screen actor; mn. Brisson; cofounder, Independent Artists, Inc., 1947; Tony, 1953

Ruth (fl. 1100s B.C.E)   23
Moabite biblical figure; d.-in-law Naomi,* w. Mahlon (1) and Boaz (2), m. Obed, great-gm. David; founder, with Boaz, of the House of David

Rutherford, Alison   see COCKBURN, ALICIA

Ru Zhijuan (1925–)   2283
Chin. editor, writer

Ryan, Sarah (1724?–1768)   581
Eng. Methodist leader, school housekeeper; friend of John Wesley (1703–1791; preacher; founder of Methodism, 1784) and Mary Fletcher*

S

Sabin, Florence [Rena] (1871–1953)   1322
Amer. writer, anatomist, public health scientist, educator

Sabina, Poppæa (fl. 50s–60 C.E.)   91
Roman courtier; mistress of Nero

Sablé, Madeleine de Souvré de, Marquise (1599–1678)   401
Fr. salonist

Sachs, Nelly (1891–1970)   1617
Ger./Swed. translator, poet, playwright; Prize of the Swedish Poets Association, 1958; Nobel Prize, 1966

Sackville, Margaret, Lady (1881–1963)   1474
Eng. poet

Sackville-West, Vita (1892–1962)   1634
Eng. writer

Siddons, Sarah (1755–1831)   670
Eng. sculptor, actor; d. Roger
Kemble (actor, theater manager), s. John Phillip Kemble
(1757–1823; actor–manager),
w. William S— (actor, business manager), a. Fanny
Kemble*

Sidney, Margaret (1844–1924) 1093
Amer. writer; née Harriet
Stone; mn. Mulford and
Lothrop

Sidqi (?–1703)   545
Turk. Sufi poet; d. Qamr
Muhammad (scholar)

Siebert, Muriel (1932–)   2512
Amer. feminist, securities analyst; first woman to hold seat
on New York Stock Exchange

Sigea, Luisa (1522–1560)   318
Portuguese scholar; tutor to
Maria, princess of Portugal

Signoret, Simone (1921–1985) 2192
Fr. screen actor; née
Kaminker; w. Yves Allégret
(1), Yves Montand (2; 1921– ;
actor); m. Catherine Allégret
(actress); Academy Award,
1959

Sigourney, Lydia Howard
(1791–1865)   807
Amer. magazine editor, author,
poet, teacher; née Huntley,
a.k.a. the Sweet Singer of Hartford, the American Hemans,
the Female Milton; second w.
Charles S— ; first professional
female poet in the U.S.

Sila (fl. 7th–11th century)   129
Ind. poet

Šilabhlaṭṭarikā
(fl. 7th–11th century)   130
Ind. poet

Silko, Leslie Marmon (1948–) 3206
Amer. novelist, poet; NEA,
1974; Pushcart, 1977;
MacArthur, 1983

Sill, Judee (1946?–)   3121
Amer. songwriter, singer

Sills, Beverly (1929–)   2397
Amer. opera singer, arts ad-
ministrator; née Belle
Silverman; Grammy, 1976;
Presidential Medal of Free-
dom, 1980

Silver, Joan Micklin (1935–)   2611
Amer. writer, film producer

Silverberg, Frances (1916–)   2080
Amer. writer

Simmons, Laura (1877–1949) 1405
Amer. poet

Simon, Carly (1945–)   3069
Amer. songwriter, singer; w.
James Taylor (1948– ; singer);
Grammy, 1971

Simon, Kate [Grobsmith]
(1912–1990)   2003
Amer. writer, historian

Simon, Maurya (1950–)   3280
Amer. poet, educator (writing)

Simon, Patricia (1934–)   2580
Amer. writer

Simonton, Stephanie   see
MATTHEWS-SIMONTON, STEPHANIE

Simos, Miriam   see STARHAWK

Simpson, Becky (1936–)   2651
Amer. social activist

Simpson, Nancy (1938–)   2726
Amer. poet

Singer, June (1918–)   2122
Amer. nonfiction writer, psychoanalyst

Singer, Maxine [Frank]
(1931–)   2475
Amer. biochemist

Sinha, Kabita (1931–)   2476
Bengalese poet, novelist

Sitwell, Edith [Louisa], Dame
(1887–1964)   1554
Eng. editor, poet, literary critic

Siunetsi, Sahakdoukht
(fl. 8th century)   147
Armen. teacher, poet, musician

Skau, Annie (1916?–)   2081
Nor. nurse, Evangelical nun

Skinner, Cornelia Otis
(1901–1979)   1803
Amer. entertainer, actor,
writer; d. Otis S—
(1858–1942; actor)

Skrine, Agnes Higgenson   see
O'NEILL, MOIRA

Slapsak, Svetlana
(fl. 1980s–90s)   3611
Yug. novelist, linguist, historian, cultural

Slave girl who was a soothsayer (fl.
50s C.E.)   90
Greek slave

Slick, Grace (1939–)   2770
Amer. songwriter, singer; née
Wing

Sloan, Margaret [Bentson]
(fl. 1970s)   3576
Amer. civil rights activist; cofounder, National Black
Feminist Organization

Slocumb, Mary (1760–1836)   700
Amer. patriot, plantation
manager; née Hooks

S. M. [The Scottish Minstrel]   see
NAIRNE, CAROLINA

Small, Meredith
(fl. 1980s–90s)   3612
? sociologist

Smart, Elizabeth (1913–1986) 2030
Can. poet, author

Smeal, Eleanor [Marie Cutri]
(1939–)   2771
Amer. feminist, nonprofit administrator, civil rights
activist; president, NOW,
1977–87

Smedley, Agnes (1894?–1950) 1674
Amer. author, lecturer

Smiley, Jane [Graves] (1949–) 3235
Amer. writer, author; Fulbright, 1976–77; NEA, 1978,
1987; Pulitzer, 1991; NBCCA,
1991

Smith, Anna Deavere (1950–) 3281
Amer. educator, actor, play-
wright; MacArthur, 1996;
Obie, 1992; DCCA; DDA

Smith, Anna Young
(1756–1780?)   675
Amer. poet; pseud. Sylvia; n.
Elizabeth Graeme Ferguson*

Smith, Arabella [Eugenia]
(1844–1916)   1088
Amer. poet

Smith, Barbara (1946–)   3122
Amer. anthologist, poet; cofounded (w/ Audre Lorde*
and Cherrie Moraga*) the
first publishing collective by
women of color, Kitchen
Table: Women of Color Press

Smith, Bessie (1898–1937)   1724
Amer. songwriter, singer

Smith, Betty (1896–1972)   1699
Amer. writer

Smith, Charlotte (1749–1806)   644
Eng. novelist, translator, poet;
née Turner; d. Catherine
Dorset (poet)

Smith, Dodie (1896–1990)   1707
Eng./Amer. novelist, screen-
writer, playwright; pseud. C.
L. Anthony; née Dorothy
Gladys Beesley

Smith, Dorothy E. (1926–)   2318
Amer. sociologist, feminist

Smith, Elizabeth Oakes
(1806–1893)   880
Amer. lecturer, writer, suffragist, social reformer; née Prince,
pseud. Ernest Helfenstein

Smith, Evelyn Elizabeth
(1937?–)   2694
Amer. writer

Smith, Hazel Brannon
(1914–1994)   2045
Amer. newspaper publisher, editor, journalist; Pulitzer, 1964

Smith, Janna Malamud
(1952–)   3343
Amer. psychotherapist, writer;
d. Bernard M— (writer,
1914–86)

Smith, Laura Frost (1893–)   1647
Amer. pacifist, nurse; oldest
known living (as of 1999)
American veteran of World
War I

Smith, Lee (1944–)   3024
Amer. writer

Smith, Lillian [Eugenia]
(1897–1966)   1715
Amer. writer, social critic

Smith, Liz (1923–)   2232
Amer. columnist; née Mary
Elizabeth S—

Smith, Margaret Bayard
(1778–1844)   762
Amer. journalist, author

Smith, Margaret Chase
(1897–1995)   1709
Amer. politician; U.S. congresswoman, 1940–49,
Senator (R-Maine), 1949–73;
first woman elected to both
U.S. House and Senate;
longest serving woman in Senate history

Smith, May Riley
(1842–1927)   1075
Amer. writer, poet

Smith, Nora Archibald
(1859–1934)   1193
Amer. writer, poet, educator;
s. Kate Douglas Wiggin*

Smith, Robyn [Carolyn]
(1944–)   3025
Amer. jockey; w. Fred Astaire
(1899–1987; dancer, film
star); first woman jockey to
win a major stakes horse race

Smith, Sophia (1796–1870)   828
Amer. philanthropist; founder,
Smith College (Northampton,
Massachusetts)

Smith, Stevie (1902–1971)   1815
Eng. writer, poet; née Florence
Margaret S—

Smyth, Ethel Mary, Dame
(1858–1944)   1185
Eng. feminist, conductor,
composer

Snitow, Ann (1943–)   2970
Amer. writer

Snow, Helen Foster
(1907–1997)   1903
Amer. writer, educator, researcher; pseud. Nym Whales;
w. Edgar S—

Snow, Phoebe (1951–)   3312
Amer. songwriter, singer

Sofola, Zulu (1938–)   2727
Nigerian educator, play-
wright; first published and
established female Nigerian
dramatist; Ford, 1969–72;
Fulbright, 1988

Softic, Elma (1961–)   3500
Serb. educator, philosophy, diarist

Sokoloff, Natalie J(ean)
(1944–)   3026
Amer. nonfiction writer, educator (sociology), prison
reform activist

Solanas, Valerie (1940–1988) 2826
Amer. feminist, actor, painter

Somerset, duchess of   see THYNNE,
FRANCES

Somerville, Mary (1780–1872) 769
Scot. translator, mathematician, astronomer, physical
geographer; née Fairfax; w.
William S— (2)

Tait, Katherine (1923–) 2235
Eng. public figure; d. Bertrand Russell (1872–1970; mathematician, philosopher)

Tallent, Elizabeth (Ann) (1954–) 3390
Amer. writer; NEA, 1983

Talmadge, Betty Shingler (1924–) 2258
Amer. businesswoman, cookbook writer, meat broker

Talvi *see* ROBINSON, THERESE

Tam, Ba (fl. 1980s) 3613
Viet. diarist

Tamar (fl. 990s B.C.E) 35
Hebrew princess; d. David (king of Israel) and Maacah, s. Absalom, half-s. Amnon

Tan, Amy [Ruth] (1952–) 3345
Amer. novelist, writer

Tan, Hwee Hwee (1974–) 3587
Singaporean novelist

Tanaka, Yukiko (1940–) 2828
Jap./Amer. translator, nonfiction writer, anthologist

T'ang Wan, Lady (fl. 12th century) 207
Chin. poet; w. Lu Yu (poet)

Tannen, Deborah F[rances] (1945–) 3072
Amer. nonfiction writer, linguist; NEH (3); Rockefeller, 1982–1983

Tanner, Beatrice Stella *see* CAMPBELL, PATRICK

Tanner, Nancy Makepeace (1933–1989) 2548
Amer. scientist

Tapahonso, Luci (1953–) 3369
Amer. poet, writer; Southwestern Association Indian Affairs Literature fellowship, 1981; New Mexico Eminent Scholar Award, New Mexico Commission of Higher Education 1989

Tapp, June L. (1930–) 2446
Amer. educator, psychologist

Tappan, Eva March (1854–1930) 1155
Amer. writer, poet, historian, editor

Tarabotti, Arcangela (1604–1652) 414
Ital. scholar, writer, nun; née Elana Cassandra T—; a.k.a. Galerana Baratotti

Tarasova, Yelena (fl. 1990s) 3654
Russ. writer

Tarbell, Ida [Minerva] (1857–1944) 1174
Amer. historian, biographer, editor

Tarule, Jill (1943–) 2972
Amer. educator, author; née Mattuck

Tattlewell, Mary (fl. 1640s) 467
Eng. author

Taylor, Ann (1782–1866) 774
Eng. poet; a.k.a. Mrs. Gilbert; s. Jane T—*; developed, with her sister, the "awful warning" school of poetry

Taylor, Arie P. (1927/28–) 2348
Amer. military officer; first black noncommissioned officer in charge of women's Air Force training

Taylor, Debbie (1955?–) 3412
Afr. poet

Taylor, Elizabeth (1932–) 2513
Eng./Amer. actor, entrepreneur, AIDS activist; w. Conrad "Nicky" Hilton (1; 1926–78; hotel chain heir), Michael Wilding (2; 1912–79; actor), Mike Todd (3; 1907–58; film producer), Eddie Fisher (4; 1928– ; singer), Richard Burton (5; 1925–84; actor), John W. Warner (6; 1927– ; U.S. senator– Virginia), and Larry Fortenski (7; construction worker); Academy Award, 1960, 1966; Jean Hersholt Humanitarian Award, 1992, C.B.E., 2000

Taylor, Jane (1783–1824) 777
Eng. poet; s. Ann T—*; developed, with her sister, the "awful warning" school of poetry

Taylor, Mrs. (fl. 1680s) 516
Eng. poet

Teasdale, Sara (1884–1933) 1509
Amer. poet; mn. Filsinger; Pulitzer, 1918

Teish, Luisah (fl. 1980s–90s) 3614
Amer. performer, writer, priestess

Tekoa, Woman of (fl. 940s B.C.E) 39
Hebrew biblical figure

Teleki, Geza (1943–) 2973
Hung./Amer. scientist, primatologist

Telesilla (fl. 5th century B.C.E) 58
Greek military leader, poet, hero

Temple, Countess *see* CHAMBER, ANNA

Temple, Shirley *see* BLACK, SHIRLEY

Tencin, Claudine Alexandrine [Guerin] de (1685–1749) 522
Fr. salonist, author

Teng Ying-ch'ao (1903–) 1830
Chin. public figure, government official; w. Zhou Enlai (Chou En-lai; 1898–1976; statesman)

Terán, Lisa St. Aubin de (1953–) 3370
Brit. author

Teresa [of Calcutta], Mother (1910–1997) 1973
Albanian/Ind. Roman Catholic nun, missionary; née Agnes Gonxha Bojaxhiu; founder, Missionaries of Charity, 1948; first Pope John XXIII Peace Prize; Nobel Peace Prize, 1979

Teresa of Avila, Saint (1515–1582) 306
Span. nun, poet; née Teresa de Cepeda y Ahumada, a.s.a. Theresa, a.k.a. St. Teresa of Jesús; founded nine convents, reformed the Carmelite Order, with Saint James of Santiago, copatron saint of Spain

Teresa, Sister *see* MARCHOCKA, ANNA

Terracina, Laura (1519?–1577?) 308
Ital. poet

Terrell, Mary Church (1863–1954) 1239
Amer. public speaker, women's rights & black rights activist, educator; cofounder, Colored Women's League of Washington, 1892; cofounder & first president, National Association of Colored Women, 1896; founding member, NAACP, 1909

Terry, Ellen [Alice], Dame (1848–1928) 1117
Eng. actor

Terry, Lucy (1731?–1822?) 599
Amer. poet, slave

Terry, Megan (1932–) 2514
Amer. playwright; née Marguerite Duffy; cofounder, Women's Theater Council (NY); Obie, 1970; NEA; Guggenheim

Thatcher, Margaret (1925–) 2285
Eng. scientist, chemist, attorney, tax, political leader; née M— Hilda Roberts; a.k.a. the Iron Lady; M.P., 1959; prime minister of Britain, 1979–1990; first woman to head a major government in modern Europe; took up lifetime seat in House of Lords, 1992; Baroness Kesteven (1992)

Thaxter, Celia (1835–1894) 1029
Amer. poet; née Laighton

Theano (fl. 420s B.C.E) 63
Greek priestess

Theodora, Empress (508?–d. 547/48) 112
Byzantine empress, dancer, actor; w. Justinian I (483–565, emperor 527–65)

Theodosia *see* STEELE, ANNE

Therbusch, Anna Dorothea Lisiewka *see* LISIEWSKA-THERBUSCH, ANNA

Thermuthis *see* PHARAOH'S DAUGHTER

Thomas, Audrey [Callahan] (1935–) 2612
Amer./Can. writer

Thomas, Edith [Matilda] (1854–1925) 1154
Amer. poet

Thomas, Elizabeth (1675/77?–1730/31) 512
Eng. letter writer, poet; pseud. Corinna

Thomas, Louisa [Carroll Jackson] (1865–?) 1244
? poet

Thomas, Lynn (1947–) 3168
Amer. magazine editor; née Massimino

Thomas, Martha [Carey] (1857–1935) 1170
Amer. college administrator, educator, suffragist, writer; cofounder, Bryn Mawr College, 1885

Thomas, Minnie (1933?–) 2543
Amer. social reformer

Thompson, Alice (1963–) 3518
Brit. journalist, travel writer

Thompson, Clara (1893–1958) 1651
Amer. lecturer, physician, psychiatrist, writer, educator

Thompson, Dorothy (1894–1961) 1676
Amer. writer, journalist; ex-w. Sinclair Lewis (novelist, 1885–1951)

Thompson, Kay (1911–1998) 1984
Amer. writer (children)

Thorne, Barrie (1942–) 2925
Amer. professor (women's studies & sociology)

Thornton, Alice (1627–1707) 446
Eng. author, householder

Thorpe, Rose Hartwick (1850–1939) 1133
Amer. songwriter, writer

Thrale, Hester Lynch or Mrs. Henry *see* PIOZZI, HESTER

Thundercloud, Katherine *see* WITT, SHIRLEY

Thynne, Frances (?–1754) 665
Eng. poet; a.k.a. duchess of Somerset; pseud. Cleora, Eusebia

Tibergeau, Marchioness de (fl. 17th century) 539
Fr. poet, patron of literature; née Silery; n. La Rochefoucauld (1613–80; moralist)

Tibors (1130?–1182) 186
Provençal trobairitz; s. Raimbaut d'Orange (troubadour), w. Bertrand des Baux

Tiburzi, Bonnie Linda (1948–) 3208
Amer. aviator; first woman to be hired as a pilot by a major U.S. airline

and Maria de Salinas (lady-in-waiting to Catherine of Aragon*), second w. Charles Brandon, duke of Suffolk (1), w. Richard Bertie (2)

Willson, Dixie (1896–?) 1692
Amer. poet, writer

Wilner, Eleanor (1937–) 2700
Amer. poet; NEA, 1976–77; MacArthur, 1991

Wilson, Augusta Jane *see* EVANS, AUGUSTA)

Wilson, Barbara (1950–) 3290
Amer. publisher, book, short story writer, novelist

Wilson, Dorothy Wright (fl. 1970s) 3579
Amer. educator, university administrator

Wilson, Elizabeth (1936–) 2659
Brit. journalist, author

Wilson, Harriette (1789–1846) 790
Eng. diarist

Wilson, Marie (1948–) 3267
Amer. women's rights activist, nonprofit administrator

Wilson, Martha (1758–post-1848) 679
Amer. householder; née Stewart; friend of George Washington (1732–99; military leader; 1st U.S. president, 1789–97)

Wiltz, Christine (1948–) 3210
Amer. novelist

Winchilsea, Lady *see* FINCH, ANNE

Windsor, Wallis Simpson, duchess of (1896–1986) 1706
Amer./Eng. public figure; née Warfield; w. duke of W— (1894–1972; king of Great Britain, 1936–37; abdicated)

Winegarten, Renee [Cecile] (1922–) 2215
Eng. literary critic, writer

Winfrey, Oprah (1953–) 3373
Amer. TV personality & producer, screen actor

Winger, Deborah (1955–) 3414
Amer. actor

Winn, Mary Day (1888–1965) 1571
Amer. writer

Winnemucca, Sarah (1844–1891) 1085
Amer. Indian rights activist, army scout, interpreter, lecturer, teacher; d. Old Chief W— (18??–1882); gd. Captain Truckee

Winslow, Anna Green (1759–1780) 686
Can./Amer. diarist, poet

Winslow, Anne Goodwin (1875–?) 1371
Amer. writer, poet

Winslow, Thyra Samter (1903–1961) 1833
Amer. literary & drama critic, scenarist

Winters, Shelley (1922–) 2216
Amer. stage, screen actor; née Shirley Shrift; Academy Award, 1959, 1965; Emmy, 1964

Winterson, Jeanette (1959–) 3466
Eng. author

Winthrop, Margaret (1591?–1647) 393
Eng./Amer. letter writer; née Tyndal; w. John W— (1588–1649; colonial administrator; first governor of Massachusetts Bay Colony)

Winwar, Frances (1900–) 1768
Ital./Amer. writer, translator, literary critic; née Francesca Vinciguerra

Wiseman, Jane (fl. 1700s) 541
Eng. tavern keeper, playwright, servant

Witkovsky, Susan (1942–) 2929
Amer. pre-school consultant, adult education specialist; wrote model city program (San Francisco) for Headstart, 1971

Witt, Shirley Hill (1934–) 2582
Amer. Indian rights activist, anthropologist, educator, writer, poet; a.k.a. Katherine Thundercloud

Wittig, Monique (1935/36–) 2615
Fr. writer

Woffington, Peg (1720–1760) 570
Eng. actor, author

Wolf, Beverly Hungry *see* HUNGRY WOLF, BEVERLY

Wolf, Christa (1929–) 2400
Ger. pacifist, feminist, novelist, writer

Wolf, Naomi (1962–) 3514
Amer. feminist, nonfiction writer; Rhodes Scholar, 1986

Wolfe, Leslie (1944–) 3031
Amer. nonprofit administrator

Wolff, Charlotte (1904–) 1849
Ger./Eng. psychiatrist, writer

Wolitzer, Hilma (1930–) 2451
Amer. writer, educator

Wollstonecraft, Mary (1759–1797) 687
Eng. author, feminist; w. William Godwin (1756–1836; political philosopher), m. Mary W— Shelley*; s.-in-law, Hannah Godwin*

Wolverton, Terry (fl. 1990s) 3656
Amer. literary editor, writer, poet

Wong, Nellie (1934–) 2583
Amer. writer, feminist, poet, activist

Woo, Merle (195-?–) 3291
Amer. poet

Wood, Ellen (1813–1887) 901
Eng. playwright, journalist, writer; née Price

Wood, J. R., Mrs. *see* CHAMBERS, JESSIE

Wood, Natalie (1938–1981) 2733
Amer. actor; née Gurdin; d. Nicholas (architect and set designer) and Maria G— (ballet dancer), s. Lana W— (actress, 1946–); w. Robert Wagner (1 & 3; 1930– ; actor), Richard Gregson (2; British producer); m. Natasha Wagner (actress)

Wood, Sally Sayward (1759–1855) 691
Amer. novelist; née Barrell, a.k.a. Sarah Sayward Keating

Woodhull, Victoria Claflin (1838–1927) 1051
Amer. spiritualist, actor, writer, political activist, editor, stock broker, feminist; s. Tennessee C—*; published *The Woodhull & Claflin Weekly*, 1870–76; ran for U.S. president, 1870; formed Equal Rights Party, 1872; published *The Humanitarian*, 1892–1901

Woodman, Marion (1928–) 2373
Can. Jungian analyst, author

Woodruff, Julia [Louise M.] (1833–1909) 1017
Amer. writer; pseud. W. M. L. Jay

Woodville-Grey, Elizabeth *see* GREY, ELIZABETH

Woolf, Virginia (1882–1941) 1481
Eng./Eng. writer, literary critic; b. Adeline V— Stephen; a.k.a. V— Stephen, V— Adeline W—; d. Sir Leslie Stephen (biographer, ciritic, scholar); w. Leonard W— (economist, publisher, writer); with Leonard, founder and operator of Hogarth Press, 1917; with brother Thoby Stephen, founder of *Hyde Park Gate News*, 1891–1895

Woolley, Hannah (1621/23?–1675/76?) 435
Eng. governess, pioneer educator

Woolsey, Mary (1832–1864) 1011
Amer. poet, social worker; mn. Howland

Woolsey, Sarah Chauncey *see* COOLIDGE, SUSAN

Wordsworth, Dorothy (1771–1855) 745
Eng. diarist, naturalist; s. William W— (1770–1850; poet); s.-in-law of Mary W—*; a. Elizabeth W—*

Wordsworth, Elizabeth (1840–1932) 1064
Amer. poet; great-n. William W-(1770–1850; poet) and Mary W—*; n. Dorothy W—*

Wordsworth, Mary (1770–1859) 740
Eng. letter writer; née Hutchinson; w. William W— (poet, 1770–1850); s.-in-law Dorothy W—*, great-a. Elizabeth W—*

Wortham, Anne (1941–) 2886
Amer. scholar, sociologist

Worthington, Robin (1932–) 2516
Amer. writer

Wray, Fay (1907–1995) 1913
Amer. screen actor

Wright, Frances (1795–1852) 825
Scot./Amer. poet, lecturer, philanthropist, author, feminist, social reformer; a.s.a. Fanny W; w. William D'Arusmont

Wright, Susanna (1697–1784) 537
Eng./Amer. painter, frontierswoman, poet, letter writer, scholar

Wroth, Mary Sidney (1586/7–1640/51) 386
Eng. poet, patron of poets; a.s.a. Wroath, a.k.a. countess of Montgomery; d. Robert, earl of Leicester, n. M— S— Herbert* and Sir Phillip S— (poets), c. Elizabeth Manners (poet, d. Sir Phillip S—)

Wu, Chien-Shiung *see* CHIEN SHIUNG WU

Wu Tse-t'ien (624–705) 120
Chin. empress, poet; only empress in Chinese history to rule alone, 689–705

Wurtzel, Elizabeth [Leigh] (1967–) 3541
Amer. rock and roll critic, writer

Wyatt, Edith Franklin (1873–1958) 1345
Amer. writer

Wylie, Elinor [Morton] (1885–1928) 1523
Amer. writer, poet; née Hoyt; w. William Rose Benét (1886–1950; writer and editor), s.-in-law, Stephen Vincent B— (1898–43; writer)

X

Xanthippe (fl. 5th century B.C.E) 59
Greek householder; w. Socrates (philosopher, 469–399 B.C.E)

Xue Tao (768–831) 139
Chin. concubine, poet, calligrapher, hostess

Career and Occupation Index

Contributors have been indexed according to the major career paths their lives have taken and are listed alphabetically, within each category, with reference to contributor numbers.

Careers and Occupations are divided into the following divisions and categories:

A. ACADEMIA AND CRITICISM

Art Patrons and Collectors
Arts, Media and Literary Critics
Biographers, Historians, Scholars and Social Critics
Education, Civic and Foundation/Association Administrators and Consultants
Educators and Instructors
Librarians, Curators and Preservationists
Philosophers

B. ARTS AND ENTERTAINMENT

Actors, Entertainers and Performers
Comedians, Humorists, Cartoonists and Wits
Courtesans, Mistresses and Prostitutes
Dancers, Choreographers and Dance Critics
Designers—Architectural, City, Industrial and Interiors
Designers—Costume and Fashion
Designers—Graphic, Print and Illustration
Directors—Stage, Film and Television
Film, Video and Media Producers, Designers, Specialists and Technicians
Lecturers, Public Speakers and Workshop Leaders
Musicians, Singers and Conductors
Painters, Sculptors, Artisans and Other Visual Artists
Photographers
Radio and Television Personalities
Songwriters, Arrangers, Composers and Lyricists
Theater Producers, Artistic Directors, Designers, et al.

C. POLITICAL, SOCIAL AND JUDICIAL ARENA

Activists, Reformers and Revolutionaries
Criminologists, Police Workers and Investigators
Diplomats, Civil Servants, Government Officials and Spies
Feminists and Suffragists
Heads of State, Presidents, Premiers, Governors, et al.
Judges, Lawyers and Legal Scholars
Labor Leaders
Politicians
Public Figures and Society Leaders

D. PRINTED WORD

Diarists and Letter Writers
Dramatists—Librettists, Playwrights, Scriptwriters and Dramaturgs
Journalists, Columnists, Reporters and Editors
Poets
Printed Media Publishers, Proprietors, Agents, et al.
Translators, Linguists and Interpreters
Writers—Fiction and Nonfiction

E. SCIENCE AND MEDICINE

Computer Specialists and Trainers
Engineers
Healing Arts—Physicians, Psychiatrists, Midwives, Healers, et al.
Naturalists
Nutritionists, Chefs, Cookbook Writers and Food Specialists
Psychotherapists, Analysts and Counselors
Scientists—Biological
Scientists—Cultural
Scientists—Earth
Scientists—Physical
Social Science and Psychology

F. OTHER

Adventurers, Frontier Settlers, Heroes and Pilots
Athletes, Sports and Fitness Figures

Business Executives, Entrepreneurs, Industrialists and
    Consultants
Economists, Financial Specialists and Bankers
Farmers, Ranchers, Horticulturists and Agriculturists
Householders, Laborers, Office Workers, Slaves and
    Miscellaneous

Inventors
Military Personnel, Soldiers and Patriots
Occultists, Witches and Prophets
Philanthropists and Humanitarians
Religious Figures, Leaders and Theologians
Royalty and Courtiers

A. ACADEMIA AND CRITICISM

ART PATRONS AND COLLECTORS

Cavendish, Georgiana   677
Dodge, Mabel   1438
Este, Isabella d'   272
Gonzaga, Elisabetta   271
Gonzaga, Giulia   304
Harington, Lucy   381
Herbert, Mary Sidney   358
Jeanne of Navarre   222
Makhfi   463
Marguerite of Navarre   285
Medici, Lucrezia de'   251
Pompadour, Jeanne-Antoinette
    Poisson de   574
Renée de France   302
Stein, Gertrude   1363
Tibergeau, Marchioness de   539
Wroth, Mary Sidney   386

ARTS, MEDIA AND LITERARY CRITICS

Adler, Renata   2703
Allen, Paula Gunn   2735
Ayllón Soria, Virginia   3621
Bogan, Louise   1716
Christian, Barbara T.   2935
Clark, Eleanor   2013
Condé, Maryse   2670
Crist, Judith   2200
Deutsch, Babette   1683
Dilke, Emilia   1057
Dolan, Jill   3437
Drew, Elizabeth   1556
Faure, Elie   1375
Finch, Anne   491
Gilliatt, Penelope   2493
Goulianos, Joan   2754
Greene, Gayle   2946
Gwinn, Mary Ann   3300
Hardwick, Elizabeth   2071
Haskell, Molly   2802
Jacobson, Ethel   1864
Jameson, Anna Brownwell   822
Janeway, Elizabeth   2016
Johnson, Pamela Hansford   2006
Jones, Patricia   3305
Kael, Pauline   2138
Kauffman, Linda   2806
Keatley, Charlotte   3481
King, Georgiana Goddard   1317
Krásnohorská, Eliška   1110
Lejeune, Caroline   1718
Leslie, Amy   1207
Lowell, Amy   1353
Malcolm, Janet   2570
Mamonova, Tatyana   3014

Mansfield, Katherine   1564
Mason-Manheim, Madeline   1922
McCarthy, Mary   2009
McDowell, Deborah E.   3308
Meynell, Alice Christiana   1109
Miles, Josephine   1979
Orlova, Raisa Davydovna   2100
Ostriker, Alicia Suskin   2688
Peery, Janet   3197
Peterson, Virgilia   1852
Pool, Gail   3117
Raine, Kathleen Jessie   1923
Rich, B. Ruby   3607
Riding, Laura (Jackson)   1808
Rittenhouse, Jessie   1292
Rose, Phyllis   2919
Sitwell, Edith   1554
Spacks, Patricia Meyer   2398
Spretnak, Charlene   3123
Staël, Germaine de   717
Sternhell, Carol   3653
Stimpson, Catharine R.   2653
Tompkins, Jane P.   2829
Trevisan, Anna F.   1868
Tucker, Anne   3073
Van Rensselaer, Mariana Griswold
    1139
Vendler, Helen Hennessy   2545
Vicioso, Sherezada   3287
Vreeland, Diana   1750
West, Rebecca   1639
Winegarten, Renee   2215
Winslow, Thyra Samter   1833
Winwar, Frances   1768
Woolf, Virginia   1481
Wurtzel, Elizabeth   3541

BIOGRAPHERS, HISTORIANS, SCHOLARS AND SOCIAL CRITICS

Aburdene, Patricia   3131
Agnesi, Maria Gaëtana   568
Aidoo, Ama Ata   2888
Aiken, Lucy   772
Albery, Nobuko   2776
Arendt, Hannah   1896
Armstrong, Mary F.   1442
Bateson, Mary Catherine   2738
Baudonivia   116
Baynard, Anne   509
Beard, Mary Ritter   1394
Bedford, Sybille von Schoenbeck
    1976
Belenky, Mary Field   2522
Benedict, Ruth   1553
Benét, Laura   1517
Berenson, Mary   1242
Bern, Sandra Lipsitz   2986
Beruriah   215

Betsko, Kathleen   2739
Bird, Caroline   2049
Blackburn, Julia   3177
Blind, Mathilde   1066
Bowen, Catherine Drinker   1717
Bowen, Marjorie   1567
Brady, Rose   3416
Brett, Dorothy   1501
Brodie, Fawn M.   2063
Brooke, Frances   582
Brookner, Anita   2356
Brumberg, Joan Jacobs   2989
Cam, Helen M.   1530
Capek, Mary Ellen S.   3593
Carson, Anne Regina   3247
Carter, Elizabeth   567
Cartland, Barbara   1792
Cary, Elizabeth Tanfield   384
Case, Sue-Ellen   3625
Caulkins, Frances Manwaring   826
Cereta, Laura   269
Chambers, Jessie   1555
Chapone, Hester   585
Christina of Sweden   442
Christine de Pisan   242
Coffin, Judith G.   3324
Coleridge, Mary   1212
Comnena, Anna   175
Cooper, Anna Julia   1187
Corday, Charlotte   725
Cornelia   71
Cruz, Juana Inés de la   481
Dacier, Anne   482
Dauenhauer, Nora   2332
Davis, Rebecca Harding   1009
Decter, Midge   2333
Dodson, Lisa   3631
Durant, Ariel   1733
Dworkin, Andrea   3089
Edwards, Amelia   1002
Edwards, Betty   2793
Eisler, Riane   2459
Elstob, Elizabeth   520
Emerson, Mary Moody   752
Epstein, Cynthia Fuchs   2525
Faure, Elie   1375
Fedele, Cassandra   268
Fee, Elizabeth   3090
Ferguson, Kathy E.   3257
Fields, Annie Adams   1024
Fitzpatrick, Sheila Mary   2850
Fraiberg, Selma   2128
Franz, Marie-Louise von   2050
Fraser, Antonia   2491
Fuller, Margaret   891
Gelfant, Blanche H.   2202
Gilchrist, Marie   1643
Gilman, Charlotte Perkins   1205

Ginzburg, Eugenia   1905
Green, Mary A. E.   926
Green, Rayna   2800
Grote, Harriet   814
Guyon, Jeanne-Marie de la Motte
    475
Hamilton, Edith   1273
Hammond, Eleanor Prescott   1261
Han Suyin   2095
Harrison, Jane   1132
Hazan, Marcella   2229
Hebard, Gracy   1218
Heilbrun, Carolyn G.   2300
Higginson, Ella   1230
Hill, Ruth Beebe   2015
Himmelfarb, Gertrude   2205
Hochschild, Arlie Russell   2803
Home, Anne   628
hooks, bell   3399
Huang Zongying   2276
Hubbard, Barbara Marx   2382
Iskin, Ruth   3053
Jacobs, Jane   2072
Jeffreys, Sheila   3602
Jordan, June   2634
Jung, Emma   1484
Kaminer, Wendy   3265
Kanner, Barbara   2277
Kaplan, Temma E.   2905
Kelly-Gadol, Joan   2363
Keuls, Eva Clara   2364
King, Georgiana Goddard   1317
Kraemer, Ross Shepard   3192
Krásnohorská, Eliška   1110
Landowska, Wanda   1437
Lape, Esther   1470
Leech, Margaret   1658
Lerner, Gerda   2160
Le Sueur, Meridel   1788
Lewis, Edith   1451
Liljestrom, Rita   2365
Lim, Shirley Geok-Lin   3603
Lipton, Eunice   2813
Li Qingzhao   176
Lively, Penelope   2534
Lougee, Carolyn Chappell   2908
Luce, Gay Gaer   2432
MacKinnon, Catherine A.   3105
Macy, Joanna   2386
Makin, Bathsua   419
Malpede, Karen   3057
Marguerite of Navarre   285
Martineau, Harriet   855
Matthews, Glenna C.   2718
McCarthy, Mary   2009
McIntosh, Peggy   2572
Miner, Dorothy Eugenia   1853
Mitford, Jessica   2108

Mitford, Nancy 1854
Moore, Virginia 1828
Morata, Olimpia 322
Morgan, Sydney Owenson 759
Murray, Janet Horowitz 3109
Nogarola, Isotta 250
Nussbaum, Martha 3158
Oliphant, Margaret 987
Pagels, Elaine 2962
Paglia, Camille 3159
Pankhurst, Sylvia 1485
Pardoe, Julia 876
Peiss, Kathy 3275
Petchesky, Rosalind 2914
Pulcheria, Aelia 108
Rabi'a al-Adawiya 137
Räthzel, Nora 3200
Raven, Arlene 3020
Repplier, Agnes 1186
Rich, B. Ruby 3607
Richie, Alexandra 3651
Richter, Gisela 1489
Ripley, Sarah Alden 818
Robinson, Therese Albertine Louise 834
Rose, Phyllis 2919
Rosen, Marjorie 2920
Rossi, Alice 2213
Rousselle, Aline 2768
Roy, Sara 3410
Rukeyser, Muriel 2029
St. John, Christopher 1384
Salisbury, Joyce Ellen 3023
Schneir, Miriam 2538
Schreiner, Olive 1159
Schurman, Anna Maria van 417
Schwarcz, Vera 3165
Seton, Julia 1580
Sewell, Sarah Ann 1302
Sforza, Costanza Varano 252
Sheehy, Gail 2650
Sigea, Luisa 318
Simon, Kate 2003
Slapsak, Svetlana 3611
Smith, Lillian 1715
Snow, Helen Foster 1903
Sontag, Susan 2540
Stanton, Elizabeth Cady 907
Stern, Edith Mendel 1801
Stowe, Harriet Beecher 896
Strouse, Jean 3071
Tappan, Eva March 1155
Tarabotti, Arcangela 414
Tarbell, Ida 1174
Toth, Emily 3027
Treichler, Paula Antonia 2974
Ts'ai Yen 97
Tuchman, Barbara 2010
Tucker, Anne 3073
Walker, Barbara G. 2449
Wandor, Michelene 2831
Warren, Mercy Otis 589
Webb, Beatrice Potter 1184
Weil, Simone 1948
Weimer, Joan Myers 2657
Willard, Nancy 2658
Wortham, Anne 2886
Wright, Susanna 537

Zaturenska, Marya 1814

EDUCATION, CIVIC AND FOUNDATION/ASSOCIATION ADMINISTRATORS AND CONSULTANTS

Alexander, Jane 2734
Astor, Brooke 1823
Braude, Ann Deborah 3394
Brown, Trisha 2585
Burk, Martha Gertrude 2843
Capek, Mary Ellen S. 3593
Catt, Carrie Chapman 1195
Dole, Elizabeth Hanford 2625
Edelman, Marian Wright 2752
Gildersleeve, Virginia 1412
Girsh, Faye Joan 2531
Harris, Jean 2228
Hooyman, Nancy R. 3052
Horner, Matina 2756
Kahlil, Aisha 2805
Lord, Betty Bao 2717
Makhubu, Lydia Phindile 2683
Michelman, Kate 2910
Mirikitani, Janice 2911
Norman, Marsha 3156
Palmer, Alice Freeman 1157
Parker, Gail Thain 2963
Putnam, Emily James 1253
Sills, Beverly 2397
Smeal, Eleanor 2771
Stifter, Vicky 3284
Sutherland, Efua Theodora 2257
Thomas, Martha 1170
Wattleton, Faye 2979
Wilson, Dorothy Wright 3579
Wilson, Marie 3267
Wolfe, Leslie 3031

EDUCATORS AND INSTRUCTORS

Adler, Freda 2549
Aguirre, Isidora 2132
Aidoo, Ama Ata 2888
Akalaitis, JoAnne 2662
Albelda, Randy 3591
Alcosser, Sandra 2981
Allen, Paula Gunn 2735
Aloni, Shulamit 1861
Anastasi, Anna 1914
Anthony, Katharine 1410
Anzaldúa, Gloria 2891
Arrien, Angeles 2777
Ashton-Warner, Sylvia 1933
Aspasia 62
Baker, Dorothy Gillam 1884
Bambara, Toni Cade 2775
Bartholet, Elizabeth 2779
Basu, Aparna 3622
Bates, Katherine Lee 1190
Bateson, Mary Catherine 2738
Bazan, Emilia Pardo 1143
Beecher, Catharine Esther 849
Belenky, Mary Field 2522
Benedict, Agnes E. 1581
Benston, Margaret Lowe 2665
Berry, Mary Frances 2707
Bethune, Mary McLeod 1380
Bieber, Margarete 1441

Blackmore, Susan Jane 3296
Blais, Madeleine 3135
Bonaparte, Marie L. 1473
Borysenko, Joan 3244
Botta, Anne 906
Botume, Elizabeth 1297
Bovasso, Julie Anne 2457
Bowen, Asta 3393
Bradley, Marion Zimmer 2408
Bridgford, Kim Suzanne 3454
Brookner, Anita 2356
Brown, Charlotte 1486
Brown, Rita Mae 2988
Brown, Tabitha Moffatt 766
Bunch, Charlotte 2990
Bunting, Mary Ingraham 1953
Burnell, Jocelyn Bell 2934
Burroughs, Nannie Helen 1494
Burrows, Eva 2410
Cahill, Susan 2782
Calderone, Mary Steichen 1860
Calisher, Hortense 1977
Cam, Helen M. 1530
Campan, Jeanne Louise 659
Carew, Elizabeth 383
Carney, Julia A. 963
Case, Sue-Ellen 3625
Castellani, Maria 2411
Cather, Katherine Dunlap 1954
Catt, Carrie Chapman 1195
Caulkins, Frances Manwaring 826
Cervantes, Lorna Dee 3376
Chesler, Phyllis 2787
Chiang Kai-shek, Madam 1722
Chin, Marilyn 3396
Chin Ann-ping 3181
Chisholm, Shirley 2244
Christian, Barbara T. 2935
Cisneros, Sandra 3377
Clappe, Louise Amelia 935
Clarenbach, Kathryn 2272
Cleyre, Voltairine de 1258
Clifton, Lucille 2624
Clinchy, Blythe M. 2412
Cohen, Amy 3552
Cohen, Deborah S. 3184
Cohen, Sherry Suib 2556
Coleridge, Mary 1212
Collins, Patricia Hill 3185
Comini, Alessandra 3553
Cone, Helen Gray 1192
Conrad, Beatrice 3474
Cook, Blanche Weisen 2844
Coombs, Mary 2993
Cooper, Anna Julia 1187
Corey, Shirley Trusty 2413
Crapsey, Adelaide 1415
Cumming, Patricia 2488
Cuomo, Chris J. 3475
Daly, Mary 2358
Dauenhauer, Nora 2332
Davidson, Laura Lee 1302
Davis, Angela 2995
Davis, Thadious M. 2996
Delany, Sarah "Sadie" 1578
Dinnerstein, Dorothy 2224
Doody, Margaret Anne 2749
Dove, Rita Frances 3326

Dowd, Nancy E. 3216
Dresselhaus, Mildred Spiewak 2415
DuBois, Ellen Carol 3142
Dugaw, Dianne 3597
Dunbar-Nelson, Alice 1373
Duncan, Isadora 1416
Eckenstein, Lina 1597
Edson, Margaret 3495
Elstob, Elizabeth 520
Epstein, Cynthia Fuchs 2525
Evans, Mari 2225
Fausto-Sterling, Anne 3000
Fee, Elizabeth 3090
Fitzpatrick, Sheila Mary 2850
Flanagan, Hallie 1605
Flinders, Carol 3562
Fremantle, Anne 1940
Fuller, Margaret 891
Fulton, Alice 3328
Gallagher, Tess 2941
Gardiner, Lisa 1773
Gawain, Shakti 3187
Gearhart, Sally 2460
Gelfant, Blanche H. 2202
Gelpi, Barbara C. 2529
Germain, Sylvie 3381
Geyer, Georgia Anne 2592
Gilbert, Sandra 2627
Gillan, Maria Mazziotto 2796
Gilman, Caroline 823
Ginsberg, Ruth Bader 2530
Giovanni, Nikki 2943
Glendon, Mary Ann 2712
Glück, Louise Elisabeth 2944
Godwin, Gail 2674
Goldberger, Nancy Rule 2561
Gorbachev, Raisa Maxima 2519
Gordon-Reed, Annette 3634
Graham, Isabella 627
Graham, Martha 1681
Greer, Germaine 2755
Griffin, Susan 2947
Grimké, Sarah Moore 812
Gubar, Susan 3004
Guest, Judith 2630
Hagen, Uta 2137
Hamilton, Elizabeth 683
Hardwick, Elizabeth 2071
Harjo, Joy 3301
Harris, Janet 2051
Harris, Jean 2228
Harris, Patricia Roberts 2246
Haskins, Minnie 1382
Hazan, Marcella 2229
Hazleton, Lesley 3048
Hebard, Gracy 1218
Heilbrun, Carolyn G. 2300
Henley, Nancy M. 2563
Herbert, Marie 2856
Herman, Susan 2857
Heyward, Carter 3049
Hill, Anita 3421
Himmelfarb, Gertrude 2205
Hochschild, Arlie Russell 2803
Hogan, Linda 3149
hooks, bell 3399
Hooyman, Nancy R. 3052

LIBRARIANS, CURATORS AND PRESERVATIONISTS

PHILOSOPHERS

Nussbaum, Martha 3158
O'Brien, Mary Mamie 2327
Pilgrim, Peace 1932
Piper, Adrian 3116
Rand, Ayn 1880
Roth, Friederike 3204
Ruddick, Sara 2607
Weil, Simone 1948

B. ARTS AND ENTERTAINMENT

ACTORS, ENTERTAINERS AND PERFORMERS

Adams, Maude 1328
Ahmed, Naima 3505
Aimée, Anouk 2482
Akhmadulina, Bella 2663
Alexander, Jane 2734
Anderson, Judith 1738
Anderson, Laurie 3134
Angelou, Maya 2353
Arnould, Sophie 620
Atkins, Eileen 2550
Bacall, Lauren 2241
Bai Fengxi 2484
Ball, Lucille 1992
Bankhead, Tallulah 1834
Bardot, Brigitte 2551
Barr, Nevada 3319
Barrymore, Ethel 1436
Berg, Gertrude 1744
Bergen, Candice 3083
Bergman, Ingrid 2066
Bernhardt, Sarah 1092
Bisset, Jacqueline 3084
Black, Shirley Temple 2354
Boesing, Martha Gross 2619
Bonal, Denise 2406
Bovasso, Julie Anne 2457
Braverman, Kate 3245
Bronaugh, Anne 1398
Burke, Billie 1532
Burnett, Carol 2622
Campbell, Mrs. Patrick 1251
Carroll, Vinnette [Justine] 2198
Centlivre, Susanna 505
Charke, Charlotte 693
Chase, Ilka 1878
Cher 3086
Childress, Alice 2178
Cleage, Pearl 3182
Clive, Catherine 558
Cooper, Diana 1641
Crothers, Rachel 1422
Cryer, Gretchen 2587
Cushman, Charlotte Saunders 912
Daisy, Princess of Pless 1335
Dane, Clemence 1570
Davis, Bette 1937
De Wolfe, Elsie 1257
Desbordes-Valmore, Marceline 783
Desjardins, Marie-Catherine 453
Dietrich, Marlene 1809
Dirie, Waris 3582
Douglas, Helen Gahagan 1781
Dressler, Marie 1336
Duse, Eleanora 1189
Elliott, Maxine 1320

Estés, Clarissa Pinkola 2938
Evans, Edith 1574
Field, Kate 1046
Fields, Gracie 1730
Fisher, Carrie 3420
Fiske, Minnie 1250
Fonda, Jane 2671
Furness, Betty 2087
Gabor, Zsa Zsa 2136
Gallagher, Mary 3144
Garbo, Greta 1882
Gardner, Ava 2218
Garland, Judy 2217
Garrick, Eva Maria 583
Gaulke, Cheri 3260
Gingold, Hermione 1721
Gordon, Ruth 1705
Grant, Lee 2379
Grenfell, Joyce Phipps 1968
Guilbert, Yvette 1252
Guinan, Texas 1508
Gwyn, Nell 480
Hagedorn, Jessica Tarahata 3221
Hagen, Uta 2137
Handle, Irene 1806
Harris, Julie 2274
Hayes, Helen 1787
Haywood, Eliza 526
Hedström, Barbro 2948
Henley, Beth 3330
Hepburn, Audrey 2402
Hepburn, Katherine 1942
Holbrook, Ann 844
Hoper, Mrs. 616
Huang Zongying 2276
Janis, Elsie 1582
Jellicoe, Ann 2336
Kalisch, Shoshana 2362
Kanin, Fay 2115
Keatley, Charlotte 3481
Kemble, Fanny 886
Kidder, Margot 2809
Lanchester, Elsa 1817
Langtry, Lily 1150
Launey, de 937
Lawless, Lucy 3545
Lawrence, Gertrude 1795
Leachman, Cloris 2249
Lee, Gypsy Rose 2039
Le Gallienne, Eva 1752
Leigh, Vivien 2027
Lenya, Lotta 1734
Leslie, Amy 1207
Lillie, Beatrice 1736
Lincoln, Abbey 2431
Littlewood, Joan 2033
Livingstone, Belle 1383
Lloyd, Marie 1305
Loren, Sophia 2568
Lovell, Marie 861
Lupino, Ida 2119
MacDonald, Sharman 3307
MacLaine, Shirley 2569
Madonna 3449
Magnani, Anna 2125
Mercouri, Melina 2291
Merman, Ethel 1934
Merry, Anne Brunton 729

Midler, Bette 3059
Miller, Lee 1908
Minnelli, Liza 3108
Modjeska, Helena 1061
Modotti, Tina 1693
Moffat, Mary Jane 2719
Monroe, Marilyn 2323
Moore, Grace 1794
Moreau, Jeanne 2367
Morgan, Sydney Owenson 759
Mowatt, Anna Cora 929
Mullins, Aimee 3590
Munro, Rona 3461
Neal, Patricia 2313
Neuber, Friederika Karoline 535
Oakley, Annie 1201
O'Casey, Eileen 1866
O'Donnell, Rosie 3512
O'Malley, Mary 2868
O'Neill, Carlotta Monterey 1572
Otero, Caroline 1282
Paltrow, Gwyneth 3580
Parker, Suzy 2536
Partnow, Elaine T. 2870
Perón, Eva Duarte 2144
Phyrne 64
Pickford, Mary 1662
Piper, Adrian 3116
Pollock, Sharon 2642
Radner, Gilda 3130
Reagan, Nancy 2188
Reed, Donna 2193
Richards, Beah 2282
Richardson, Miranda 3451
Riefenstahl, Leni 1812
Robinson, Mary 682
Rollin, Betty 2648
Rosenthal, Rachel 2443
Rowson, Susanna Haswell 702
Russell, Rosalind 1990
Scott, Hazel 2177
Scott-Maxwell, Florida 1502
Shore, Dinah 2167
Siddons, Sarah 670
Signoret, Simone 2192
Skinner, Cornelia Otis 1803
Smith, Anna Deavere 3281
Solanis, Valerie 2826
Stanwyck, Barbara 1912
Stone, Sharon 3452
Streisand, Barbra 2924
Swanson, Gloria 1748
Swit, Loretta 2772
Taylor, Elizabeth 2513
Teish, Luisah 3614
Terry, Ellen 1117
Theodora 112
Tomlin, Lily 2654
Treadwell, Sophie 1535
Trevor, Claire 2004
Turner, Kathleen 3432
Tyler, Priscilla Cooper 913
Ullman, Liv 2728
Vendela 3490
Vestris, Eliza 806
Viva 2978
Wagner, Jane 2350
Wanatee, Adeline 1963

Webster, Margaret 1873
Wells, Rebecca 2928
Wertheim, Margaret 3464
West, Mae 1663
Winfrey, Oprah 3373
Winger, Deborah 3414
Winters, Shelley 2216
Woffington, Peg 570
Wood, Natalie 2733
Woodhull, Victoria Claflin 1051
Wray, Fay 1913
Zetterling, Mai 2286

COMEDIANS, HUMORISTS, CARTOONISTS AND WITS

Ace, Jane 1875
Bacon, Josephine Dodge 1397
Ball, Lucille 1992
Beard, Miriam 1791
Bombeck, Erma 2328
Bracken, Peg 2109
Brice, Fanny 1612
Burnett, Carol 2622
Cornuel, A. M. Bigot de 416
Diller, Phyllis 2093
Ephron, Delia 2999
Gingold, Hermione 1721
Hamilton, Gail 1016
Hay, Lucy 399
Heimel, Cynthia 3147
Holley, Marietta 1039
Houdetot, Sophie de la Briche 597
Lebowitz, Fran 3306
Leslie, Eliza 785
Lillie, Beatrice 1736
Longworth, Alice Roosevelt 1518
Loos, Anita 1576
McGinley, Phyllis 1879
Mumford, Ethel Watts 1418
Ostenso, Martha 1775
Parker, Dorothy 1653
Radner, Gilda 3130
Rice, Alice Caldwell 1309
Ritter, Erika 3201
Rivers, Joan 2604
Rowland, Helen 1392
Russell, Anna 1981
Selby, Spring Mae 3411
Tomassi, Debbie 3501
Tomlin, Lily 2654
Tracy, Honor 2024
Weisstein, Naomi 2774
Wells, Carolyn 1290
Yamada, Eimi 3467

COURTESANS, MISTRESSES AND PROSTITUTES

Albrecht of Johannsdorf, Mistress of 227
Ambapali 54
Barrows, Sydney Biddle 3320
Chao Luan-luan 142
d'Aragona, Tullia 299
Franco, Veronica 341
Hollander, Xaviera 2632
Jerusalem (mother of the dead child), Prostitute of 36

873

Cunningham, Agnes "Sis" 2032
Curie, Ève 1844
David-Néel, Alexandra 1283
Dietrich, Marlene 1809
DiFranco, Ani 3556
Diller, Phyllis 2093
Du Pré, Jacqueline 3077
Eaglen, Jane 3253
Ferron 3327
Fields, Gracie 1730
Gabrielli, Caterina 596
Garden, Mary 1413
Garland, Judy 2217
Garthwaite, Terry 2753
Genlis, Stephanie Félicité 639
Glennie, Evelyn 3527
Gorchakova, Galina 3509
Griffith, Nanci 3382
Guillet, Pernette du 311
Guppy, Shusha 2713
Harjo, Joy 3301
Hill, Lauryn 3589
Holiday, Billie 2060
Horne, Lena 2096
Horne, Marilyn 2564
Houdetot, Sophie de la Briche 597
Hsüeh T'ao 138
Hunter, Alberta 1686
Ian, Janis 3304
Jackson, Mahalia 1988
Jacquet de la Guerre, Elisabeth-
    Claude 496
Jones, Rickie Lee 3383
Joplin, Janis 2980
Kahlil, Aisha 2805
Kahn, Kathy 3054
Kalisch, Shoshana 2362
Kaptur, Marcy 3100
Kesselman, Wendy 2808
King, Carole 2861
King, Coretta Scott 2339
Lais 65
Landowska, Wanda 1437
Lehman, Lotte 1575
Lennox, Annie 3385
Lenya, Lotta 1734
Lincoln, Abbey 2431
Lind, Jenny 942
Li Yeh 146
Lunch, Lydia 3459
Lynn, Loretta 2502
Madonna 3449
Makeba, Miriam 2503
Malfitano, Catherine 3269
Mara, Gertrude Elizabeth 645
McCaslin, Mary 3107
McLachlan, Sarah 3542
McRae, Carmen 2208
Melanie 3154
Melba, Nellie 1249
Merman, Ethel 1934
Midler, Bette 3059
Minnelli, Liza 3108
Mitchell, Joni 2959
Moore, Grace 1794
Near, Holly 3227
Norman, Jessye 3064
Nye, Naomi Sihab 3338

Nyro, Laura 3112
Orton, Beth 3568
Parra, Violeta 2102
Parton, Dolly 3115
Phair, Liz 3539
Previn, Dory 2439
Price, Leontyne 2344
Purim, Flora 2915
Reagon, Bernice Johnson 2916
Reddy, Helen 2874
Reynolds, Malvina 1778
Ronell, Ann 1924
Ronstadt, Linda 3120
Russell, Anna 1981
Sainte-Marie, Buffy 2877
Schumann-Heink, Ernestine 1219
Scott, Hazel 2177
Selby, Spring Mae 3411
Shocked, Michelle 3513
Shore, Dinah 2167
Sill, Judee 3121
Sills, Beverly 2397
Simon, Carly 3069
Siunetsi, Sahakdoukht 147
Slick, Grace 2770
Smith, Bessie 1724
Smyth, Ethel Mary 1185
Snow, Phoebe 3312
Sorrels, Rosalie 2541
Speyer, Leonora 1329
Stampa, Gaspara 319
Storace, Nancy 715
Streisand, Barbra 2924
Sutherland, Joan 2320
Tikaram, Tanita 3489
Tipton, Billy 2042
Truman, Margaret 2259
Tucker, Sophie 1516
Vega, Suzanne 3463
Waring, Marilyn 3371
Weisstein, Naomi 2774

PAINTERS, SCULPTORS, ARTISANS
AND OTHER VISUAL ARTISTS
Adamson, Joy 2145
Aguirre, Isidora 2132
Aldis, Mary Reynolds 1325
Allyn, Jeri 3318
Anderson, Ruth Ann 3035
Anguissola, Sofonisba 332
Angus, Rita 1928
Applebroog, Ida 2404
Arnim, Bettina von 780
Baca, Judy 2893
Barnes, Djuna 1638
Bashkirtseff, Marie [Konstantinovna]
    1178
Berman, Ellen 3176
Bramson, Phyllis Halperin 2841
Brett, Dorothy 1501
Carlson, Cynthia Joanne 2896
Carr, Emily 1321
Carriera, Rosalba 513
Carrington, Leonora 2090
Cassatt, Mary 1094
Cedering, Siv 2742
Chang, Diana 2554
Chase-Riboud, Barbara 2743

Chicago, Judy 2744
Coffey, Susanna 3040
Craighead, Meinrad 3555
de Hoyos, Angela 2790
Delany, Mary 543
DeWit, Antoinette 2223
Dilke, Emilia 1057
Drexler, Rosalyn 2295
Edelstein, Jean 2153
Edwards, Betty 2793
Fanshawe, Catherine Marie 716
Fukuzoyo Chiyo 544
Gentileschi, Artemisia 395
Gonzales, Sylvia Alicia 2945
Gonzalez, Patricia 3261
Guest, Barbara 2155
Harkness, Madden 3262
Hartigan, Grace 2203
Hedström, Barbro 2948
Hemans, Felicia 815
Hepworth, Barbara 1836
Hildegarde von Bingen 178
Hoffman, Malvina 1529
Hosmer, Harriet 996
Howells, Mildred 1333
Hulme, Keri 3150
Hunter, Clementine 1490
Itatani, Michiko 3601
Jacobi, Kathryn 3264
Johnston, Henrietta 499
Kahlo, Frida 1966
Killigrew, Anne 489
Kollwitz, Käthe 1271
Kuan Tao-shêng 221
Lakich, Lili 2907
Laurel, Alicia Bay 3224
Laurencin, Marie 1527
Layton, Elizabeth 1961
Li Yeh 146
Lin, Maya 3458
Lisiewska-Therbusch, Anna
    Dorothea 575
Loy, Mina 1488
Mamonova, Tatyana 3014
Merian, Maria Sibylla 474
Miller, Alice 2435
Millet, Kate 2574
Mora, Elizabeth Catlett 2077
Moses, Grandma 1208
Neel, Alice 1935
Nevelson, Louise 1749
O'Keeffe, Georgia 1561
O'Neill, Rose 1361
Ono, Yoko 2535
Ormes, Cicely 321
Owens, Rochelle 2640
Paik, Younhee 3274
Pink, Lady 3529
Potter, Beatrix 1265
Poulsson, Emilie 1152
Quick-to-See Smith, Jaune 2821
Radtke, Joyce 3407
Remington, Deborah 2603
Rose, Wendy 3203
Sanchez, Carol Lee 2577
Schapiro, Miriam 2255
Schurman, Anna Maria van 417
Scudder, Janet 1337

Semmel, Joan 2824
Sheridan, Clare 1521
Shikishi 212
Siddons, Sarah 670
Solanis, Valerie 2826
Spencer, Lilly Martin 955
Spero, Nancy 2319
Suarez, Bibiana 3285
Swerda, Patricia 2083
Toklas, Alice B 1414
Treiman, Joyce 2214
Vallejo, Linda 3286
Vigée-Lebrun, Elisabeth 673
Viva 2978
Waldo, Octavia 3493
Wayne, June 2142
Weisberg, Ruth 2832
Wright, Susanna 537

PHOTOGRAPHERS
Abbott, Berenice 1737
Adamson, Joy 2145
Arbus, Diane 2238
Beals, Jessie Tarbox 1308
Bergen, Candice 3083
Bourke-White, Margaret 1894
Cameron, Julia Margaret 905
Cones, Nancy Ford 1294
Cunningham, Imogen 1500
Gilpin, Laura 1620
Gore, Tipper 3188
Kasebier, Gertrude 1146
Lange, Dorothea 1682
Lord, Betty Bao 2717
Miller, Lee 1908
Modotti, Tina 1693
Morgan, Barbara 1762
Onassis, Jacqueline Kennedy 2403
Stark, Freya Madeline 1668
Wells, Alisa 2399
Welty, Eudora 1946

RADIO AND TELEVISION PERSONALI-
TIES
Ace, Jane 1875
Barrett, Rona 2705
Bennett, Georgette 3082
Cartland, Barbara 1792
Child, Julia 1993
Ford, Anna 2940
Fraser, Antonia 2491
Furness, Betty 2087
Graham, Virginia 2012
Grant, Toni 2855
Hagedorn, Jessica Tarahata 3221
Houston, Libby 2859
Kilgallen, Dorothy 2026
Loud, Pat 2309
McBride, Mary Margaret 1746
Mock, Geraldine Fredritz 2280
Morris, Holly 3535
Murray, Kathryn 1901
Myerson, Bess 2252
O'Donnell, Rosie 3512
Perón, Eva Duarte 2144
Peterson, Virgilia 1852
Pipher, Mary 2820
Ritter, Erika 3201

PRINTED MEDIA PUBLISHERS, PROPRIETORS, AGENTS, ET AL.

TRANSLATORS, LINGUISTS AND INTERPRETERS

E. SCIENCE AND MEDICINE

COMPUTER SPECIALISTS AND TRAINERS

ENGINEERS

HEALING ARTS—PHYSICIANS, PSYCHIATRISTS, MIDWIVES, HEALERS, ET AL.

Ethnicity and Nationality Index

Contributors have been arranged according to the nation of their *birth*, rather than the nation of their residence and/or death: those citations may be found in the Biographical Index. Additionally, to serve multicultural studies programs, women of color have been arranged, whenever possible, according to their race and/or ethnic background within the context of their nation of birth.

Ancient lands and nations no longer extant have been annotated with the present-day nations of their geographic origins. Within appropriate categories, contributors are listed alphabetically.

AFGHAN

Gauhari, Farooka 3145

AFRICAN

Taylor, Debbie 3412

ALBANIAN

Teresa, Mother 1973

ALGERIAN

Bonal, Denise 2406
Gallaire-Bourega, Fatima 3001

AMERICAN

Abbot, Sidney 2661
Abbott, Berenice 1737
Abbott, Wenonah Stevens 1255
Abrams, Linsey 3294
Abramson, Jill 3374
Aburdene, Patricia 3131
Abzug, Bella 2180
Ace, Jane 1875
Ackerman, Diane 3172
Adams, Abigail 634
Adams, Grace 1753
Adams, Maude 1328
Addams, Jane 1204
Adler, Freda 2549
Adler, Margot 2836
Akalaitis, JoAnne 2662
Akers, Elizabeth Chase 1013
Akins, Zoë 1543
Albelda, Randy 3591
Albright, Madeleine 2616
Alcosser, Sandra 2981
Alcott, Louisa May 1012

Alden, Ada 1171
Alden, Paulette Bates 3132
Alderman, Ellen 3434
Aldis, Mary Reynolds 1325
Alexander, Mrs. 970
Alexander, Jane 2734
Alexander, Shana 2265
Allen, Dede 2266
Allen, Florence Ellinwood 1515
Allen, Mary Wood 1067
Allerton, Ellen Palmer 1027
Allison, Dorothy E. 3212
Allred, Gloria 2837
Allyn, Jeri 3318
Allyson, Karrin 3506
Alston, Theodosia Burr 776
Alta 2890
Alther, Lisa Reed 2982
Anastasi, Anna 1914
Anderson, Catherine 3133
Anderson, Edith 3470
Anderson, Laurie 3134
Anderson, Margaret 1656
Anderson, Ruth Ann 3035
Andrews, Lori B. 3592
Annan, Annie Rankin 1116
Anthony, Katharine 1410
Anthony, Susan B. 949
Antrim, Minna 1209
Applebroog, Ida 2404
Arbus, Diane 2238
Arensberg, Ann 2664
Arnold, Margaret Shippen 696
Arnow, Harriette 1915
Arrien, Angeles 2777
Arzner, Dorothy 1780

Ashmun, Margaret Eliza 1376
Astor, Brooke 1823
Astor, Madeline Talmage 1601
Astor, Nancy 1439
Atherton, Gertrude 1176
Atkinson, Ti-Grace 2704
Auel, Jean M. 2617
Austin, Mary Hunter 1278
Avary, Myrta Lockett 1175
Axline, Virginia Mae 1975
Babitz, Eve 2932
Bacall, Lauren 2241
Bache, Sarah 633
Bachman, Moira 2778
Bacon, Josephine Dodge 1397
Bailey, Urania Locke 941
Baizley, Doris 3173
Baker, Dorothy 1906
Baker, Dorothy Gillam 1884
Baldwin, Faith 1660
Ball, Lucille 1992
Ballard, Bettina 1832
Bankhead, Tallulah 1834
Bannerman, Helen 1232
Banning, Margaret Culkin 1622
Barker, Elsa 1293
Barker, Myrtie Lillian 1951
Barnes, Djuna 1638
Barnes, Margaret Ayer 1545
Barney, Natalie Clifford 1400
Barolini, Helen 2268
Barr, Nevada 3319
Barrett, Andrea 3525
Barrett, Michele 3548
Barrett, Rona 2705
Barrows, Sydney Biddle 3320

Barrymore, Ethel 1436
Barton, Clara [Harlowe] 954
Bates, Katherine Lee 1190
Bateson, Mary Catherine 2738
Beale, Frances M. 3471
Beals, Jessie Tarbox 1308
Beard, Mary Ritter 1394
Beard, Miriam 1791
Beecher, Catharine Esther 849
Beers, Ethel Lynn 981
Belenky, Mary Field 2522
Bell, Christine 3295
Bell, Helen Olcott 1000
Bellows, Laurel Gordon 3174
Bender, Marilyn 2270
Benedict, Agnes E. 1581
Benedict, Ruth 1553
Benét, Laura 1517
Bengis, Ingrid 2985
Benston, Margaret Lowe 2665
Berenson, Mary 1242
Berg, Elizabeth 3175
Berg, Gertrude 1744
Bergen, Candice 3083
Berman, Ellen 3176
Bern, Sandra Lipsitz 2986
Bernard, Jessie Shirley 1825
Bernikow, Louise 2780
Berriault, Gina 2293
Berry, Dawn Bradley 3435
Bianchi, Martha Dickinson 1264
Billings, Victoria 3037
Bingham, Anne Willing 709
Bingham, Sallie 2666
Birch, Alison Wyrley 2195
Bird, Caroline 2049

Subject Index

Numbers: numbers preceding colons are contributor numbers (guides to these numbers are found at the top of each page in the Quotations section); numbers following colons reflect specific numbered quotations. If several quotations for that contributor are cited under the same subject, they are separated by commas. Semicolons separate one contributor from another.

Word forms: singular is used except in those instances when the plural helps to distinguish the connotation of the word (as in "speech" and "speeches" or "appearance" and "appearances"); reader should presume plurals when applicable (for example, under

"change" is the subheading "nothing"; one *assumes* the phrase "nothing changes")

"The" is used sparingly and must often be assumed (e.g., "dead"); however, when it distinguishes the *meaning* of a subject, it is applied (e.g., "English, the").

The tilde (~) is used in subclassifications to replace the main subject word; its placement varies and is meant to aid definition, thus — "marriage, ~ laws", "population, over- ~", "African American, achievement of ~ women".

Like subjects are often sandwiched together with a slash, as in "mother/hood," "nurse/nursing" and "Europe/an." Entries are filed letter-by-letter.

2540:47; point of ~, 1618:21;
practical ~, 950:6

behavior   see also specific
emotions; COMPORTMENT; CON-
DUCT; HUMAN NATURE;
SOCIALIZATION, analyzing human
~, 3000:2; childish ~, 901:3;
civilian ~, 1929:5; guidelines for
~, 2855:1; patterns of ~, 3656:8;
refinement of ~, 907:11; ~ towards loved ones, 1048:7;
unconscious ~, 2438:5

Behn, Aphra, 454:1; 491:7; 528:1, 2

beingness   see also IDENTITY,
396:1; 2117:4; reason for ~,
2248:1; state of ~, 1363:9;
2455:10

Beirut, Lebanon, 2264:3

Belafonte, Harry, 2462:1

belief   see also CONVICTIONS;
FAITH; RELIGION, 1560:9;
1652:2; 1721:4; 2100:1; 2191:1;
2610:4; discussing ~, 1881:10;
history of ~, 1530:7; ~ in another, 1728:; ~ in oneself,
2190:6; 3244:2; incapable of ~,
1715:10; inclusiveness of ~,
2469:35; personal ~, 2240:25;
power of ~, 2408:1

bell, 1716:1

bellicosity, 2540:65

Bellow, Saul, 2370:26

belonging (member)   see also CON-
NECTEDNESS/CONNECTION,
1804:5; 2634:26; sense of ~,
3127:7; ~ to another, 1688:1

belongings   see also POSSESSION,
2675:4; relinquish ~, 397:1

beneficiary/benefit, 2353:30; personal ~, 2245:5

benevolence, 2068:32

bereavement, 1735:1; 2149:15

Berlin, Germany, 3651:1; ~ in 1950,
3470:1; personality of ~, 3651:2;
political denial in ~, 3651:3

Berra, Yogi, 1560:27

berry, 1325:1

best, 46:13; 2325:2; doing one's ~,
964:10; giving your ~, 1090:2

Bethlehem, Israel, 2287:27

betrayal   see also TRAITOR, 807:19;
1429:1; 1503:1; 1719:1; 1777:1;
1915:6; 2282:5; 2606:6;
3223:13; ~ of nation, 2095:18;
pain of ~, 3421:6; victim of ~,
1341:37

betterment, working for ~, 2292:3

Beverly Hills, California, 2501:1

bewilderment   see also CONFUSION,
151:3; 157:8; 705:21; 1481:49;
1564:25

bias, 2774:6; ~ vs. women, 1181:9

Bible   see also BIBLICAL FIGURES
AND BOOKS; GOSPEL; KORAN;
MAGNIFICAT; SACRAMENT; SCRIP-
TURE; TEN COMMANDMENTS,
283:1; 509:2; 871:2; 907:48, 55;
951:2; 959:1; 1241:1; 1457:6;

1760:1; 1841:5; 1858:2;
1881:15; 2459:6; feminism and
~, 2692:1; history in ~, 3101:1;
influence of ~, 907:32; interpretation of ~, 979:15; 2962:8;
studying ~, 931:2; translation of
~, 812:1; women and ~, 363:1;
women in ~, 907:31, 33, 37;
2347:2

bickering   see also ARGUMENT;
QUARREL, 186:1; 1557:10

bigotry, 2634:17

bill, paying ~, 1748:1

biofeedback, 2357:1

biographer/biography   see also AU-
TOBIOGRAPHY, 1341:38;
1410:12; 1451:1; 1481:57;
1541:1; 1553:19; 1557:1;
1639:18; 1948:75; 2002:23;
3193:1; elitism of ~, 2919:3;
facts and fiction in ~, 1717:8;
writing ~, 1639:27

biology, 1632:18; 2183:9; enthusiasm for ~, 1213:1; possibilities of
~, 2648:1

bird   see also specific varieties,
158:1; 263:1; 484:1; 824:6;
842:15; 942:1; 976:12; 1029:1;
1172:1; 1363:10; 1740:1;
1775:1; 3328:11; ~ -song, 711:1;
976:24; 1285:6; 1517:3; 1609:3;
2000:4; 3043:8; caged ~, 582:12;
1159:17; 1370:1; 1528:4; ~ in
summer, 2700:2; migration of ~,
1775:1; scarcity of ~, 1904:11; ~
watching, 3048:2

Birmingham, Alabama, 2851:3;
3325:2

birth   see also BABY; CHILDBIRTH;
PREGNANCY/PREGNANT; REBIRTH,
121:4; 452:9; ~ -injured child,
2851:4; ~ and death, 2944:1;
miracle of ~, 70:1; 2416:12; ~ of
boy, 835:8; ~ of parents, 2714:1;
philosophy of ~, 2327:1; time of
~, 1410:10; trauma of ~, 2479:11

birth control   see also CONTRACEP-
TION; FAMILY, ~ PLANNING,
1289:22; 1497:10, 13, 18, 20, 26;
1636:44; 1680:3; 1885:1; 2049:1;
2213:7; 2490:4; ~ and law,
1497:17; attitudes toward ~,
2140:7; 2210:3; carrying condom
for ~, 2524:5; ~ pill, 2775:1; ~
programs, 2648:2; right to ~   see
also ABORTION, ~ RIGHTS, 2530:2

birthday, 76:1; 537:2; 994:5;
1783:1; ~ wishes, 612:3

bisexual/ity   see also ANDROGYNY;
HOMOSEXUALITY; SEX, 1271:10;
1448:3; 1634:31; 2029:22;
2314:7; 2384:2

bitch (pejorative), 1840:3; 2012:2;
3356:1; woman as ~, 2804:1

bitterness   see also RESENTMENT,
783:4; 1543:10; 1653:16;
1771:2, 9; 2373:9; 3352:7; eliminating ~, 1247:1

black (color), 2383:1

Black Mass, 2219:1

blackmail, diplomatic ~, 1709:8

blacks   see also AFRICA/N; AFRICAN
AMERICAN, 662:2; 1239:8;
1494:3; 1551:7; 2057:1; 2775:7;
2943:7; ~ Americans, 1187:2; autonomy of ~, 1227:1; 2160:1;
average ~, 1610:2; ~ child of
slave owner, 971:1; color of ~,
2227:3; communication between
~ women, 3337:1; control of ~,
2455:18; ~ culture of gangstas,
2448:1; dangerous ~, 3354:4;
destiny of ~, 788:26; educated ~,
788:23; 2466:4; education for ~,
1486:1; enslavement of ~   see
also RIGHTS, BLACK ~, 3029:9;
3576:1; equality between ~ men
and women, 2995:6; exploitation
of ~ musicians, 2168:1; family
life and ~, 2686:4; ~ girls in
South, 1187:3; growing up ~,
2943:17; ~ hair, 3029:11; ~ heritage, 1380:4; ~ identity, 2246:1;
2462:1; 2466:1; 3205:5; image of
~, 3465:2; ~ in relation to Africa,
2465:8; ~ in relation to America,
2465:8; ~ in relation to whites,
823:4; 2308:9; 2324:3; 2353:16;
2380:16; 2469:2; 2943:15;
3029:12; 3205:2, 6, 8; 3272:4;
3354:3; intellect of ~, 2848:17;
joy of ~, 3029:39; ~ lesbian,
2584:7; marginalization of ~,
3399:2; ~ men, 3029:47; 3272:9;
murder and ~, 2943:5; murder of
~, 1227:5; 1239:9; 2060:1; music
of ~, 959:4; normalcy of ~,
2584:9; obstacles of ~, 1239:3;
oppression of ~, 788:24; 1227:2;
1239:1, 7; 1949:1; 2469:22;
2686:1; 2767:3; 3029:7; political
consciousness of ~, 2571:4; ~
power movement, 2584:19;
3349:3; prejudice against ~,
2378:7; ~ pride, 1239:; 1380:4;
1494:4; 2431:1; 2584:1; 3349:1;
racism among ~, 1494:2; relations between ~ men and women,
2388:2; 3349:2; reparation to ~,
837:17; revolution of ~, 1978:2;
self-hatred among ~, 1613:1; sexism among ~, 837:10; 2496:1;
3399:13; ~ succeeding in white
world, 2916:1; survival skills of
~, 2584:17; ~ sycophant, 1494:6;
~ teenage girls, 2995:16; the ~
experience, 3185:2; theater and
~, 3182:2; ~ tokenism, 2344:2;
victim mentality among ~,
1613:5; ~ women, 837:9; 864:2;
1187:1; 1239:10; 1486:2;
2160:2; 2353:6; 2469:2, 7;
2767:1, 2; 2995:1, 3; 3003:1;
3029:23; 3246:1; 3272:8;
3349:4; 3399:11, 16; 3429:1;
3520:2; 3576:2; 3649:1; ~

women and appearance, 1494:1;
~ women artists, 3029:22; ~
women as caretakers, 3523:3; ~
women as teachers, 3399:10; ~
women in America, 3430:1

Blake, William, 1295:1

blame, 2904:37; accepting ~,
2962:4; attached to ~, 3298:2;
hierarchy of ~, 3401:6; ~ oneself,
2732:2; placing ~, 2634:19

blasphemy   see also PROFANENESS;
SACRILEGE, 41:1

bleeding   see also BLOOD, 2031:6;
2466:6

blessed, to be ~, 3378:5

blindness, 513:3; ~ in newborn,
976:4; ~ of humankind, 800:13

bliss   see also HAPPINESS; JOY,
233:4; 705:15; 939:3; 1180:2; attaining ~, 917:6

blonde, 3449:1; ~ bombshell,
2497:1

blood   see also BLEEDING, bond of
~, 2279:14; menstrual ~, 3336:7;
spilling of ~, 2768:1

bloom, 2958:1

blooming, 1632:43; 2938:7

blossom, 2240:29

blue, 1259:1

bluebell, 1301:1

bluntness, 2480:3

blush, 854:1; 1958:1; 3328:13

boasting, 285:; 1082:4; 2285:17;
2393:16; women and ~, 3072:2

boat/ing   see also SHIP, 3355:6; ~
adrift, 151:3; ~ anchor, 3404:2

Bobbitt, Lorena, 3265:4

body (human), 1800:1; 3377:2;
3501:1; aging ~, 2295:7; appreciation of ~, 3578:1; awareness of
~, 3187:4; calm ~, 3161:4; commercialization of women's ~,
2981:1; concealed ~, 1802:17;
condition of ~, 1813:5; 3443:7;
control over ~, 2380:15;
2459:38; enjoyment of ~, 3187:5;
female ~, 2736:16; 3180:3;
3307:1; 3657:1; girl's ~ image,
2989:1; ~ image, 3570:1; in tune
with ~, 2432:3; limitations of ~,
2461:3; maintaining ~, 1739:4;
male ~, 2736:21; metaphysics of
~, 2613:5; ~ of lover, 2393:32;
passions of ~, 2508:4; ~ piercing,
3236:2; politics of ~, 2459:33;
reclaiming women's ~, 2669:4;
relevancy of ~, 3640:2; religion
and ~, 904:1; rhythms of ~,
2432:4; ~ size, 753:46; vulnerability of ~, 1608:11; 1841:11;
3640:4

bodybuilding, 3159:26

Bohemian, 3624:2

Boleyn, Anne, 298:7

Bolshevist, 1485:11

bomb/ing   see also LAND MINES,
dropping ~, 2700:4; 3440:1; remnants of ~, 3034:3

bone, 3428:3

bonsai, 3099:2

book   *see also* FICTION; LITERATURE; NOVEL/IST; READING; TEXTBOOK, 510:1; 636:8; 753:52; 754:6; 791:22; 993:35; 1034:1; 1152:1; 1164:1; 1290:1, 11; 1343:1; 1353:2, 7; 1377:5; 1446:1; 2240:15; 2904:11, 29; abridgment of ~, 2213:8; ~ as educational tool, 922:8; ~ at home, 1636:40; bad ~, 2374:1; beginning~, 2975:4; ~ by person of importance, 2016:8; ~ by women, 363:2; children's ~, 2473:1; cook- ~ *see also* COOKING, ~ RECIPE, 796:1; ~ design, 1853:1; exploitative ~, 2210:16; good ~, 1718:3; identification with ~, 2425:4; library ~, 3534:3; marketing ~, 2505:2; old ~, 3358:5; paperback ~, 1879:26; publication of ~, 1632:77; 1905:3; self-help ~, 2636:4; travel ~, 3111:1; unfinished ~, 2425:3; writing ~ *see also* WRITER; WRITING, 425:8; 1771:16; 2071:13

bookkeeping, 2849:2

border, abolishing ~, 1634:2

bore/dom   *see also* MONOTONY, 661:19; 671:1; 717:21; 723:37; 753:12; 987:15; 1306:1; 1341:64; 1867:1; 1984:3; 2463:6; 2540:14, 34; 2579:4; 2730:1; 3483:3; avoiding ~, 3247:4; intolerance of ~, 1341:55

Bosnia/n, 2547:15; 3611:3; conflict in ~, 2762:5

Boston, Massachusetts, 392:3; 1416:1; 3423:1; ~ Symphony Orchestra, 2242:3; ~ Tea Party, 587:1

botany, 2276:2; studying ~, 1820:8

bottom, hitting ~, 2938:12; room at ~, 1705:7

bourgeoisie   *see also* CLASS [SOCIAL], 1169:6; 1327:3; demise of ~, 2640:12; ~ in Soviet Union, 1327:4; materialism of ~, 1948:12

boxing, 1805:4

boy   *see also* CHILD/REN; SON, 800:7; 1341:39; 1363:38; 1478:3; 1879:23; birth of ~, 835:8; conditioning of ~, 2611:3; 3089:22; 3272:5; ~ growing up, 2999:1; ~ kept indoors, 1544:4; role of ~, 1360:2; 1802:13; teenage ~ *see also* ADOLESCENCE/ADOLESCENT; TEENAGE/R, 3162:2; trouble with ~, 3162:3; upbringing of ~, 2277:1

boycott, 2426:2, 3

boyfriend, 3288:6; dissatisfied with ~, 2579:4

braggart, 1418:6

Brahms, Johannes, 2526:1

brain   *see also* MIND, 361:1; 975:5; 993:22; 1205:27; 1481:64; 1994:2; 2370:24; 2385:11; ~ of woman, 1840:17; training of ~, 2793:2, 3, 4

brainwashing, 2338:2

Branch Davidians, 2725:2

brassiere   *see also* UNDERWEAR, 2708:1

bravery   *see also* COURAGE; VALOR, 306:14; 692:1; 705:10; 1403:1; 1460:1; 1772:5; 2375:19; ~ in woman, 931:8; lack of ~, 2507:20; ~ of men and women, 2299:4

Brazil/ian, 1809:2; 1991:6, 8

bread, 668:1; 2116:1; commercial ~, 1507:3; loaf of ~, 2901:12

breadwinner   *see also* WAGE, man as ~, 2848:3

breakfast, 1263:1; 2959:3

breast, 2999:1; exposing ~, 837:13; ~ fixation, 2802:2; 2920:12; ~ milk, 2922:1; ~ size, 2708:1; women's ~, 54:3; 1547:1; 2755:

breast-feeding, 370:1; 2978:3; trends in ~, 2009:11

breath/ing, 1516:3; 2169:1

breeding, bad ~, 2125:2; good ~, 1346:7

brevity, 401:8; 559:1; 1653:21; 2479:6

Briand, Aristide, 1395:9

bribery, 2455:1; 2889:4

bridge, 2634:2

Brisbane, Arthur, 1604:4

British Museum, 1481:32

British Navy, 1137:12

British   *see also* ENGLISH; SCOT/LAND; WELSH, 638:1; 2140:68

Broadway (New York City), 1934:1; theater on ~, 2514:5

broken/ness, mending what's ~, 1772:16; repair ~, 1715:1; ~ spirit, 3417:1

Brontë, Emily, 910:, 23; 3247:2

brook, 1421:5

Brooklyn, New York, 1699:1; 3280:2

brothel   *see also* PROSTITUTE/PROSTITUTION, 1774:1; 1809:5

brother   *see also* SIBLING; SISTER, 713:7; 753:20; 1179:1; 2578:7; death of ~, 358:5; 815:11; ~ in relation to sister, 855:22

brotherhood   *see also* ESPRIT DE CORPS; FELLOWSHIP; SISTERHOOD, 2723:2; 2762:2

Brown, Antoinette Blackwell, 949:19

Brown, John, 990:1; 1215:9

Brown, Rap, 2462:1

Browning, Elizabeth Barrett, 1353:26

brute/brutishness, 1010:12; ~ force, 1967:4; women and ~, 2517:36

Brutus, 77:1; 891:9

Bryn Mawr College, 2469:10

Buckingham Palace, bombing of ~, 1755:2

bud, brown ~, 3223:11

Buddha/Buddhism, 166:17; 1553:7; 2560:1

budget, family ~, 2021:1; 2256:1; ignoring ~, 2588:19; national ~, 2256:1

buffalo, 1218:2

bug, cooking ~, 3537:1

bulb (plant), 746:6

bullfighting, 3584:2; women in ~, 3584:1

bullfinch, 674:1

bum, 2312:9

Bunche, Ralph, 2462:1

buoyancy, 2019:17

burden, bearing one's ~, 2540:48

bureaucracy/bureaucrat   *see also* RED TAPE, 1304:13; 1327:6, 7; 1637:2; 2009:17; red tape of ~, 2877:5

burial   *see also* CEMETERY; DEATH; DYING; FUNERAL; GRAVE, 2436:1; tears at ~, 896:33

burlesque, 785:5; ~ dancer, 3059:1

Burma, 3036:3, 5; 3037:1; government of ~, 3036:2; 3037:2; leadership in ~, 3036:1

Burns, Robert, 773:8; 1714:1

Burr, Aaron, 807:19

Burton, Sir Richard, 1007:5; 2513:2

bus, crowded ~, 3099:2

Bush, George W., 2537:1; 3139:19

business   *see also* COMMERCE; CORPORATION; ENTERPRISE; MANAGEMENT; MERCHANT, 776:1; 791:20; 868:1; 1663:28; 1684:1; 1701:4; ~ acumen, 1761:1; big ~, 1550:4; ~ creed, 2918:1; ~ critic, 3257:2; dislike of ~, 723:9; favoritism in ~, 3494:6; feminism and ~, 3257:1; home ~, 2262:2; ~ in relation to employees, 2918:10; interdependence of ~, 1880:15; 1927:1; launching ~, 3063:4; minding one's ~ *see also* NOSINESS, 1772:13; 2287:1; mix ~ with pleasure, 3201:1; ~ of others, 444:7; 1951:1; reading habits of ~ men, 2270:5; unconventional ~, 2918:6; woman in ~, 2070:1; women in cosmetic ~, 1312:1

businessperson, 896:2; 1784:19; 1813:1; woman ~ *see also* CAREER, ~ WOMAN; WOMAN/WOMEN, ~ IN BUSINESS, 2786:3

bustle, 776:1

busyness, 2210:6

butterfly, 724:1; 758:1; 807:1; 1157:1; 1783:5; 3115:2

buttocks, fascination with ~, 3476:1; woman's ~, 2736:28

Byron, Lord George Gordon, 773:8; 779:11; 853:5; 1653:10

bystander, 2292:6; passivity of ~, 2292:4

C

cabinet, U.S., 2127:1

Cabrini, Mother, 1680:2

cactus, 2822:1

Caesar, Gaius Julius, 395:3

Cain and Abel, 2762:2

Cairo, 2594:2

cajolery, 24:1

cake, 1048:3

Calais, France, 297:1; 582:2

calamity, 644:20; 3001:1

Calamity Jane, 1142:2

calculation, 1828:3

calendar, 3614:3

California, 1308:5; 2588:15, 36; 2722:17; 3039:1; 3245:5; Simi Valley ~, 3620:2; Southern ~, 2855:1

calm, 1946:9; appearance of ~, 1039:3; continuous ~, 2036:2; intolerance for ~, 1653:12

Calvin, John, 768:12

Calvinism/Calvinist, 335:1; 2963:3

Cambridge, ~ men, 2517:1

camel, 1471:11; 1560:23

Camelot, 2285:25

camera   *see also* PHOTOGRAPHER/PHOTOGRAPHY, 1682:2; 2238:5; 2540:36; motion picture ~, 3179:1; ~ on vacation, 2540:37

camp (style), 2540:11, 13, 14, 15

campaign   *see also* POLITICS, political ~ *see also* ELECTION, 867:1; political smear ~, 1513:31; ~ promise, 2146:3; ~ reform, 3229:9

campfire, 1580:3

Canada/Canadian, 1321:8; leadership of ~, 3289:5; ~ nationalism, 2736:15; prosperity in ~, 1316:4

cancer, 3063:1; 3130:3; breast ~, 2901:13; cigarettes and ~, 3330:1; overcoming ~, 2403:8; ~ patient, 2540:43

candle, 398:6

candor   *see also* FRANKNESS; OPENNESS, 526:15; 896:34; 2654:2; ~ of children, 157:6

capability, 896:36; 2469:6; individual ~, 1831:4; ~ of women, 515:8

capital, ~ and labor, 1457:23

capital punishment   *see also* DEATH SENTENCE; EXECUTION, 298:3; 765:1; 869:47; 2765:5; 3227:5; ~ as deterrent, 1675:4; opposition to ~, 2765:2

capitalism   *see also* FREE ENTERPRISE; PROFIT, 1169:10, 15; 1184:1; 1289:20; 1304:4, 5; 1457:11, 25; 1550:5; 2226:2; 2459:17; 2640:10; 2641:1; 3159:5; advocate of ~, 2511:6; crisis in ~, 2226:3; evils of ~, 2767:3; faults of ~, 1603:5; im-

2879:2; ~ street, 842:10; thriving ~, 911:1; ugly ~, 2140:18; whirl of ~, 785:1

city hall, 2735:5

civil disobedience   *see also* NONVI-OLENCE; PROTEST/ER; RESISTANCE, 871:7; 1101:6; 1181:5, 7, 12; 1570:4; 1719:5; 1896:42, 44; 2057:9; reason for ~, 1181:1

civility, 1128:2; voice of ~, 3289:2

civilization   *see also* CULTURE; SO-CIETY, 949:6; 1204:18; 1281:1; 1530:5; 1564:2; 1632:76; 1802:10; 1880:1; 2149:4; 2385:4; 3022:4; advances of ~, 717:5; 948:1; 979:22; 1967:1; 2339:1; 2552:3; ancient ~, 2040:1; development of ~, 2215:3; disintegration of ~, 2985:6; effects of ~ on individ-ual, 2210:4; ~ left to women, 3159:18; precariousness of ~, 826:2; rebuilding ~, 2535:1; rele-vancy of ~, 2183:11; remains of ~, 2140:2; roots of ~, 2238:6; standardization of ~, 1375:1; test of ~, 855:3; unnaturalness in ~, 1634:30; ~ vs. barbarism, 1394:11; women and ~, 2300:6

civil rights   *see also* LIBERATION; RIGHTS, CIVIL ~, 2530:2; 2886:4; ~ of children   *see also* CHILD/REN, RIGHTS OF ~, 2764:3

civil rights movement, childhood memory of ~, 3360:3

civil war, 1664:5

Civil War, American, 1009:11, 12; 1072:1; 3478:3; black soldiers in ~, 908:3

clarity   *see also* SIMPLICITY, 568:1; 1560:21; 1796:1; 2046:5; 2810:9

class (social), 632:23; 670:11; 768:1; 1169:13; blurring of ~, 3044:1; commercial ~, 980:2; conditions of lower ~, 3498:1; differences between ~, 866:11; 1452:1; 2426:5; doing away with ~, 1840:14; lower ~, 1121:11; 1497:1; middle ~   *see also* BOURGEOISIE, 1363:5; 1586:12; 1716:13; middle ~ women, 1110:2; polarization of ~, 820:5; 2638:2; resentment of ruling ~, 1254:13; rising middle ~, 1184:1; ruling ~, 2640:10; 2641:1, 2; sta-tus and middle ~, 2009:27; stodginess of middle ~, 1564:3; struggle of working ~, 1788:5; taxes on middle ~, 1879:30; training lower ~, 636:19; upper ~   *see also* AFFLUENCE/AFFLUENT; WEALTH, 1651:5; 1730:1; 1958:9; working ~   *see also* PROLETARIAT, 1174:4; 1307:4

class (style), test of ~, 2118:10

class consciousness, 975:4; 1840:14; 3223:2; absence of ~, 1420:2

classification, 2276:2

classroom   *see also* SCHOOL, ~ at-mosphere, 3011:3; challenges of ~, 2391:3; ~ scholar

cleaning   *see also* HOUSEKEEPING, 2328:5; 2474:7; 3156:5; ~ dishes, 3070:2

cleanliness   *see also* TIDINESS, 1502:11; 1837:7; 1927:2; 2074:2; 3377:3; household ~, 2470:3

clergy   *see also* CHURCH; MINISTER; MISSIONARY; PREACHER/PREACH-ING; PRIEST/HOOD; RELIGIOUS LIFE, 182:1; 354:1; 753:25; 773:17; 910:18; 1917:1; 3332:7; ~ attitude toward women, 907:34; impotence of ~, 306:2; ~ in relation to politics, 1670:1; ~ man, 723:32; pomp of Catholic ~, 282:1; protection of ~, 546:1; radicalization of ~, 3557:2; women in the ~, 1031:3; 1138:3; 2422:1; 3049:1; 3163:1

cleverness, 359:1; 685:4, 7; 1064:1; 2535:10; ~ in women, 878:3

cliché   *see also* BANALITY, 3445:2; ~ of critics, 2493:7

climate, ~ control, 2928:6

clinic, women's ~, 2490:8

Clinton, Hillary Rodham, 2239:1

Clinton, William Jefferson, 2239:2; 2537:2; 3586:2; 3596:1; right wing and ~, 3229:8

clique   *see also* ELITISM, govern-ment ~, 1722:12

clock   *see also* TIME, ~ PIECE; WATCH, 2469:21; 2588:4; na-ture's ~, 1278:6; ~ watching, 2666:2; 3080:1

close mindedness   *see also* NAR-ROW-MINDEDNESS, 954:3; 1178:7; 1450:8; 1558:1; 1715:10

clothing   *see also specific articles*; FASHION; WARDROBE, 924:5; 984:1; 998:4; 1000:1; 1015:1; 1344:9; 1653:8; 1968:1; actor's ~, 1910:1; emblematic ~, 2835:1; influence of ~, 2140:43; non-military ~, 2234:20; practical ~, 1269:8; ready-made ~, 2474:6; 3494:4; sex and ~, 1857:2; women's ~, 924:5; 1402:3; 1842:1; 2270:1; 2671:10

cloud, 1203:1

clover, four-leaf ~, 1230:2

clown, 993:38

cloying, 2938:3

club, private ~, 2928:2

clumsiness, 3044:6

coalition, meaningful ~, 2584:14

coarseness, 383:2

cocaine, 3301:16; ~ addiction, 1834:3

cock/fight, 2285:17; 2640:8

cocker spaniel, 2851:2

cockroach, 2584:2; 3440:1

cocktail   *see also* DRINKING; DRUNKARD/DRUNKENNESS, 1705:4

cocoa, 2175:4

coercion, 1344:7

coffee, 1878:4

coffin, 2158:1; 2563:2

cold (weather), 1524:1; 3383:3; pro-tection from ~, 2853:3

coldness (temperament), ~ in woman, 1817:8

Coleman, Bessie, 3422:1

Colette, 1977:6; 2780:5

collaboration, ~ in research, 1820:9; ~ with women, 2295:3

collectivism, 1880:8; 2032:2

college   *see also* EDUCATION; SCHOOL; UNIVERSITY, 1883:1; 2724:1; ~ administration, 2049:7; ~ campus malevolence, 3184:1; compulsory ~, 2049:8; goal in ~, 2692:5; ~ in relation to earnings, 2049:12; investment of ~ fund, 2049:9; ~ life, 688:1; rea-son to attend ~, 2049:13; women and ~, 2309:1

colloquialism, 1705:8

Colombia, life in ~, 3498:1; murder in ~, 3486:1

colonialism, 1050:2; 1112:2; 1658:3; 2106:10; 2987:3; 3626:1; aftermath of ~, 3223:4; failure of ~, 2040:3

color, 166:13; 208:1; 784:7; 1257:2; ~ perception, 2101:11

Columbia University, New York, 2511:6

columbine, 1238:3

Columbus, Christopher, 2280:3; 3378:9

columnist, advice ~, 3027:1; gossip ~, 2232:2

combat   *see also* FIGHT/ING; SOL-DIER; WAR, ~ on Western Frontier, 459:2; women in ~, 2348:1

comedian   *see also* COMEDY; HUMOR; HUMORIST, 1612:2; 1817:2; woman ~, 1981:1; 2604:2

comedy   *see also* COMEDIAN; HUMOR, 505:1; 1336:3; 1525:5; 1912:4; 2604:5; 2835:17; perfor-mance of ~, 2622:1; reason for ~, 3288:5; ~ routine, 2604:7; sense of ~, 1525:3; straight man in ~, 3043:19

comfort, 272:5; 853:10; 1013:5; 1088:1; 1229:5; 1341:3; 1359:1; 1632:69; 1942:11; 3392:1; seeking ~, 1481:44; throw off ~, 705:19

command, 14:1; possessing ~, 1585:5

commandment, moral ~, 1880:12

commerce   *see also* BUSINESS; MAR-KETING, loathsomeness of ~, 1082:10

commercialism, 980:4; 1258:2; 2141:2; 2203:1; 2270:2; ~ in cre-ative works, 3156:3; ~ in United States, 1674:5

commitment, 1453:1; half-hearted ~, 1395:3

common ground, seeking ~, 2234:5

common sense, 1114:8; 1363:55; 1395:10; 1439:6; 1495:1; 1840:27; 2517:8; 2658:5

commonality, 2902:6

commoner, 1957:2; disparagement of ~, 1471:9; life of ~, 2567:1

commonplace   *see also* ORDINARI-NESS, 1095:1; disinterested in ~, 1812:4; ~ life, 1335:4

communal society/commune   *see also* COMMUNITY, 2634:10; 2704:1; 2952:1; 3571:6

communication, 306:3; 630:4; 1106:5; 1145:7; 1341:59; 1513:14, 38; 2604:8; 3303:1; ~ between men and women, 1344:11; 3072:3; desire for ~, 2439:4; difficulties of ~, 1319:2; 1819:5; 2068:21; 2231:8; evolu-tion of ~, 1363:41; extraterrestrial ~, 2149:33; face-to-face ~, 2416:1; family ~, 1933:18; future ~, 3330:5; im-pulse for ~, 2393:54; inner ~, 1639:15; lack of ~, 1639:14; 1881:22; 1911:10; 1975:2; 2522:1; tools of ~, 363:7; 1352:2; ~ with women, 1867:2; withholding ~, 2864:12; ~ with-out words, 2399:2

communism/communist, 1327:5; 1394:7; 1533:3; 1550:5; 1778:5; 1781:2; 2540:52; 2838:3; argu-ment against ~, 1513:29; combating ~, 1676:1; economy of ~, 1513:15; ~ in relation to peasants, 1664:5; intellectuals and ~, 1840:13; member of ~, 1363:49

Communist Party, ~ China, 2010:16; ~ in America, 1603:5

community   *see also* AFFILIATION; COMMUNAL SOCIETY/COMMUNE, background of ~, 2455:3; ~ in America, 2660:14; ~ in relation to children, 1636:45; 2469:23; lack of ~, 1788:1; 2342:6; 3158:2; 3613:2; necessity of ~, 2602:10; post-national ~, 2040:5; ~ quality of life, 2703:3; sense of ~, 2602:7

companion   *see also* FRIEND, 1756:3; 2959:4; faithful ~, 1028:4; identification with ~, 2227:14; lasting ~, 1354:5; life ~   *see also* MATE, SOUL ~; SPOUSE, 1433:5

companionship   *see also* FRIEND-SHIP, 753:50; 993:14; 1083:4; 1132:2; 1167:1; 1341:61;

1576:8; 2251:5; need for ~, 1937:17; 2164:1; seeking ~, 152:1

company, choosing one's ~, 1357:4; good ~, 1663:8; ~ of self, 1576:5

compassion *see also* HUMANENESS; PITY, 682:2; 875:11; 1321:6; 1439:6; 1586:5; 2005:1; 2041:3; 2152:2; 3278:2; ~ for all, 1082:9; ~ for elderly, 242:18; ~ for past, 869:42; lack of ~, 36:1; 2018:2; 3158:3; need for ~, 2969:1; power of ~, 3007:8

compatibility, 443:8

competence, 2279:18; 2647:7; attaining ~, 401:3

competition, 1184:1; 1201:1; 2038:2; 2058:4; 2069:2; 2591:2; 3321:1; 3433:1; ~ between men and women, 1169:17; ~ between nations, 2823:1; children and ~, 2206:9; cutthroat ~, 2556:1; 2654:6; emotional cost of ~, 3234:1; healthy ~, 1397:1; individual ~, 2569:15; intellectual ~, 3358:4; refrain from ~, 658:1; women and ~, 1822:6; 2183:23; 2199:2; 2883:1; worthy ~, 822:7

competitiveness, 1822:1; ~ between people, 2602:9

complaint/complainer, 298:5; 372:7; 583:1; 2609:4; ~ of child, 1942:3

completeness, lack of ~, 2493:3; sense of ~, 2494:5

complex (psychological), 1621:6; Cinderella ~, 2711:2

complexity, 2332:1

complication, ~ everywhere, 1918:1

complicity, 378:1; despise ~, 2455:12

compliment, 1366:1; ~ to poet, 468:5

comportment *see also* BEHAVIOR; CONDUCT, 260:1

composure, 1498:4; 2175:5

compromise, 661:16; 761:3; 853:11; 1277:12; 1513:7; 1582:2; 1632:53; 1660:2; 1771:2; 1879:15; 2898:5; 2980:2; 3213:2; 3493:4; life's ~, 3213:2; need for ~, 2044:2; ~ oneself, 3364:7; shun ~, 1815:4

compulsion *see also* OBSESSION, 1484:1; 2517:16

computer *see also* CYBERSPACE; INTERNET, 2793:4; ~ gone berserk, 2675:8; ~ in relation to humans, 3351:10; ~ programming, 3646:1; writer and ~, 3156:5

computerization, 3351:4

comrade, 3336:8

concealment, 661:3

conceit/edness *see also* EGOCENTRICITY/EGOTISM; SELF-CENTEREDNESS, 644:14; 779:2; 930:17, 28; 1012:11

concentration, 2469:14

concentration camp, ~ brands, 1782:1; death in ~, 1896:5

concept *see also* IDEA, carrying out of ~, 725:3; global ~, 2793:4

conception *see* BIRTH; FERTILITY, 178:3; 2981:4

concern, 1526:7; practical ~, 400:5

conciliation, 706:2

conclusion, drawing ~, 1634:22

concreteness, 2385:27

condemnation, 661:26; ~ of others, 1764:1

conduct *see also* BEHAVIOR; COMPORTMENT; MANNERS, 271:1; 348:1; 1042:2; 1471:5; 1629:1; 1979:4; 2699:1; cheap ~, 1622:3; control of ~, 601:1; disapproving ~, 1471:7; mis- ~, 791:13; ~ of women, 1622:1; poor ~, 661:15; upright ~, 460:1; 718:1

conference, 2140:41

confession, 1142:2; 1223:5; 2959:1; ~ between lovers, 1392:12; Catholic ~, 800:6; 2123:19; forced ~, 371:3

confidence *see also* SELF-CONFIDENCE, 757:6; 1513:36; 3590:1; ~ in oneself, 1377:8; sharing ~, 2455:13; 2562:6

confinement *see also* IMPRISONMENT, 216:1; 505; 2280:1; self-imposed ~, 2201:8

conflict *see also* STRIFE; STRUGGLE, 1277:2; 1431:5; 2050:3; cause of international ~, 1948:31; inner ~, 703:2; 1004:1; 1184:8; 1526:, 9; 1656:2; 1752:3; 1837:26; 2121:6; 2303:2; 2523:6; 2722:35; 2788:3; national ~, 637:1; resolution and ~, 1487:4; 2660:3; 3161:1; 3595:1

conformist/conformity *see also* CONVENTION; PROPRIETY, 582:10; 840:3; 1481:11; 1717:2; 1722:12; 1857:4; 1880:23; 2306:10; 2998:1; demand for ~, 2137:6; 2590:1; ease of ~, 2183:12; ~ in America, 2416:9

Confucianism, 87:1; 2794:3; ~ on marriage, 3514:11

confusion *see also* BEWILDERMENT, 848:2; 1560:19; 1796:1; 3438:4; emotional ~, 185:1; ~ of life, 1653:27; 2029:7

Congo, story of ~, 3401:6

Congress, U.S. *see also* LAWMAKER; LEGISLATION; LEGISLATOR; POLITICIAN, 2009:2; 2180:4, 5; 2823:7; hypocrisy of ~, 3596:1; ~ in relation to legislation for women, 1051:12; members of ~ *see also* LAWMAKERS; LEGISLATOR, 1970:1; 2244:4; 2537:3; 2979:8; seniority system of ~, 2244:9; sexism in ~, 2771:2; under-representation of women in ~, 2771:3; women in ~

see GOVERNMENT, WOMEN IN ~; 1461:2; 2180:7

connectedness/connection *see also* ONENESS, 963:1; 2207:5; 2624:2; 2836:1, 2; 2885:1; 2919:1; 2977:1; ~ among people, 1877:2; ~ among women, 2844:1; hidden ~, 1621:7; missed ~, 2881:7; need for ~, 2465:5; ~ of all life, 875:6; 2117:9; 3612:2; 3629:3; personal ~, 1229:9; sacredness of ~, 2459:31; ~ with right person, 1545:2

Connecticut, 2146:4

conqueror, 2864:3; myths of ~, 1788:8; ~ of self, 1012:2

conquest, 998:11; 2351:1; ~ by invading forces, 3500:4; desire for ~, 930:61; fear of ~, 1082:7

conscience, 339:13; 469:13; 499:1; 713:2; 862:3; 896:2; 976:6; 993:24; 1128:6; 1148:1; 1289:14; 1517:1; 1837:7; 2308:4; 2400:13; 2722:18; awakened ~, 234:4; clear ~, 339:8; 348:1; 831:2; 1881:16; guilty ~ *see also* GUILT/Y, 346:1; 1866:1; 2013:1; 2128:1; listening to ~, 869:10; overdeveloped ~, 1661:4; political ~, 1236:2; search one's ~, 658:3; 717:12

conscientious objector, 1632:61, 62; 2685:1

conscientiousness, 1585:2; 2544:2

consciousness *see also* SELF-CONSCIOUSNESS; UNCONSCIOUS/NESS, 869:34; 1321:4; 1687:5; 1743:2; 2050:1; 2459:26; 2529:4; 3045:1; awakening of ~, 780:3; changes in ~, 2459:42; collective ~ of women, 1788:17; expanding one's ~, 2590:2; forgetting ~ of self, 2095:13; historical ~, 3020:5; intimacy of ~ -raising, 2849:4; raising, 2076:1; 2160:7; 2581:3; 2997:1; 3551:1; ~ -raising group, 2333:7; 2849:4; ~ of world, 3187:3; stream of ~, 1782:2; 1789:4; 2863:2; the new ~, 2891:2

conscription, 959:6; 1395:1; 1633:1; ~ in Great Britain, 2010:4; mother and ~, 1448:7; ~ of women, 1275:2

consensus, 2898:2; ~ in politics, 2285:16

consequence, equal ~, 2326:9

conservation (environment) *see also* ECOLOGY, 1904:12; 3092:5; ~ of game, 262:3; politics of ~, 3239:2; river ~, 1620:3

conservatism/conservative (political) *see also* MORAL MAJORITY; REACTIONARY, 1416:3; women ~, 2573:1

consistency, 910:4; 1816:5

consolation, 220:1; 1082:5; 1583:15

constancy *see also* LOYALTY, 331:25; 339:19; 469:15

Constitution, U.S. *see also* AMENDMENT, 1942:14; 2298:2; exclusivity of ~, 2660:10; First Amendment of ~, 3105:6; preamble of ~, 949:14; preserving ~, 2660:7; representation of women in ~, 2151:1; 2622:2; 2771:1; sexism in ~, 923:9

constructiveness, 879:8

consumer/ism *see also* SHOPPING, 1205:7; 2213:11; 2870:1; 3224:1; ~ frenzy, 3188:4; ~ in relation to art, 2385:31; power of ~, 3371:3; ~ services, 2929:4

container, 1290:10

contemplation *see also* MEDITATION, 322:3; 1948:18; life of ~, 1283:2; 2016:10

contempt *see also* SCORN, ~ for men, 666:3; ~ for women, 2736:3; object of ~, 418:15; 2800:4

contentiousness, 166:21; 763:4

contentment, 343:1; 567:1; 571:2; 572:8; 791:13; 794:2; 998:19; 1457:9; 1666:2; 3115:2; 3169:3; ~ of partner, 1933:9; ~ of spirit, 791:12

contest, skiing ~, 3093:1

continuation, 2140:36

continuity, ~ of life, 3112:1

contraception *see* BIRTH CONTROL, ~ for teenagers, 2524:6; lack of ~, 2372.1:4

contradiction *see also* PARADOX, 1089:3; 2419:2; 3600:2; ~ in terms, 2463:7

contrariness, 2132:1; rule of ~, 901:9

contrast, 1650:21; life of ~, 1678:7

contribution, full ~, 1728:22; ~ of men, 1513:61

control *see also* SELF-CONTROL, 1012:9; 1209:6; 1341:54; 1464:4; 3347:1; lack of ~, 1819:4; 2817:2; letting go of ~, 1639:12; loss of ~, 515:4; 1450:9; 2722:37; majority ~, 1277:20; ~ of circumstance, 840:1; ~ of mind, 3056:1; ~ of others, 1543:4; those in ~, 2864:3; 3401:9

controversy, understanding ~, 2849:8

convenience, 670:11

convent, 382:1; 1092:1; ~ education, 1608:25; life in ~, 481:27; motivation to enter ~, 481:10

convention/ality, 1121:, 19; 1279:2; 2300:7; breaking through ~, 901:5; sticking with ~, 1285:2

conversation *see also* DIALOGUE, 589:20; 769:4; 833:8; 1039:4; 1186:15; 1363:19; 1491:2; 1634:15; 1639:14; 1808:4; 2046:2; art of ~, 636:15; 1803:9; 2480:1; ~ between the sexes, 2848:24; cautious ~, 2606:12;

diligence   *see also* EFFORT; INDUS-TRIOUSNESS; PERSEVERANCE, 567:3; 632:1; 679:3; 1362:2; 2776:2; 3468:1; rewards of ~, 699:1; 852:1

dining   *see also specific meals*; EAT-ING; FEAST; FOOD, ~ alone, 823:7; 1341:34; importance of ~ well, 1481:27; ~ on steak, 3326:3

dinner, 1512:2; ~ announcement, 2814:2

Diogenes, 536:3

diploma, value of ~, 2049:9

diplomacy/diplomat, 930:35; 1207:3; 1497:12; 2010:18; 2420:1; restraints of ~, 2467:1

direction, best ~, 2505:1; finding ~, 1771:7; 1787:7; heading in wrong ~, 515:4; right ~, 3562:1

directness, 2654:2

dirt   *see also* SOIL, 754:12; 2641:15

disabled/disability   *see also* HANDI-CAP, 1502:6; 1682:3; children with ~, 2313:2; 2602:6; 2851:4; oppression of ~, 3640:3; physical ~, 1819:6; 2223:2; 3640:1; psy-chological ~, 2140:22

disagreement, 791:2; philosophical ~, 2979:6; working out ~, 2326:8

disappearance, 166:15; 1341:39; 2361:4; impossibility of ~, 2438:3; wish for ~, 1790:3

disappointment, 923:4; 984:2; 1080:1; 2019:6; 2806:2; ~ in life, 1528:15; ~ in self, 3534:4; little ~, 685:1

disapproval, 661:26; 1635:6; 1983:3; 2703:5; expressing ~, 580:1

disarmament, 3007:2

disaster, 1485:4; 1618:25; 2173:2; 2441:1; absence of ~, 2588:16

disciple, 1012:33

discipline   *see also* SELF-DISCIPLINE, 896:24; 917:13; 1728:29; 1942:8; 2737:2; ~ for children, 1311:2; 1937:7; ~ in relation to liberty, 1311:7

disclosure, 1145:11; 1338:32; 2584:28; need for ~, 3649:2; per-sonal ~, 1639:36; public ~, 2722:54

discontent, 383:4; 1586:33; 2534:4; 3156:2; ~ of citizenry, 272:2

discourse, 2398:5; theoretical ~, 2689:1

discovery, 2076:1; 2475:3; 2694:2; fear of ~, 1084:1; 2401:13; mo-ment of ~, 1944:4; 2494:12

discretion, 1136:15; lack of ~, 166:12

discrimination   *see also* PREJUDICE, 2244:7; eliminating ~, 1513:57; 2485:1; racial ~, 1757:42; sex ~, 2530:5; ~ vs. women, 2464:3; 2574:7; ~ vs. women writers, 469:14

disease   *see also specific disorders; specific illnesses*; ILLNESS; SICK-NESS, 953:8, 11, 14; 2048:1; 2540:46; attitudes toward ~, 2962:10; dread of ~, 1132:7; psy-chic ~, 2337:4; study of ~, 1855:3; symptoms of ~, 950:3

disembodiment, 218:2

disembowelment, 2517:22

disfavor, 452:2

disguise, 401:11

disillusionment, 1789:6; 3112:2; fear of ~, 1503:2; ~ of youth, 1341:77

disinfectant, odor of ~, 2722:5

disloyalty, 515:3

disorder, 1841:10; 2189:6; 3564:2

displacement, 157:1

disposition   *see also* HUMAN NA-TURE; PERSONALITY; TEMPER/AMENT, 671:2; good-na-tured ~, 664:12; importance of ~, 600:1

dispute   *see also* ARGUMENT, legal ~, 3341:13; settling ~, 1461:16

dissatisfaction, 289:4; 304:2; 713:15, 16; 907:22; 1632:14; im-petus of ~, 1158:15

dissembling, 1341:69; difficulty of ~, 628:1; power of ~, 1881:25

dissension, ~ between mother and daughter, 2230:2

dissent, 2056:1

dissident, political ~, 2220:1

dissipation, 1639:20; life of ~, 1608:15

distance, disappearance of ~, 1370:2

distinction   *see also* INDIVIDUALITY, 773:14; achieving ~, 1209:11; de-sire for ~, 443:10; 589:4; 661:18; woman of ~   *see also* WOMAN/WOMEN, ~ LEADERS; WOMAN/WOMEN, ~ OF GENIUS, 515:1

distraction, 1363:25

distribution, 1880:2

distrust   *see also* MISTRUST, 930:56

dive, perfect ~, 3436:1

diversion   *see also* AMUSEMENT; PLEASURE, 567:5; 767:1; inces-sant ~, 441:3; 723:10; indifference to ~, 429:2

diversity   *see also* MULTI-RACIAL/ISM; VARIETY, appreciation of ~, 1802:11; cut off from ~, 1550:2; elimination of ~, 1802:10; importance of ~, 1802:3

divestment, 281:5

divine/divinity   *see also* GOD, GOD-DESS, GODS, 299:1; 856:10; 2446:5; feminine in ~, 979:5; 3123:1; gender of ~, 2194:1; om-nipresence of ~, 1112:7, 8; 3561:4; search for ~, 2160:10

division, ~ among people, 1636:29

divisiveness, 2977:1

divorce   *see also* ALIMONY; COUPLE, ~ SPLITTING UP; MARRIAGE, END OF ~, 1153:10; 1223:4; 1341:8; 1392:3, 11, 24, 31; 1510:4; 1665:3; 1840:7; 2427:1; 3248:1; ~ among rich, 2231:6; children and ~, 1805:6; 2118:11; impact of ~, 2231:4; impermissible ~, 1665:14; ~ in America, 1392:29; ~ laws, 949:8; 2490:3; ~ lawyer, 2004:1; New York ~, 1229:1; privilege of ~, 855:9; ~ rate, 2183:24; reasons for ~, 1655:19; 2605:3; women and ~, 1840:6

DNA (deoxyribonucleic acid), 3612:2

doctor   *see* MEDICAL PROFESSION; HEALER; PHYSICIAN; THERAPIST, holiday for ~, 2517:24; ~ in for-eign culture, 3358:1; women ~, 950:12

Dodge, Mabel, 1501:1

doe, 2234:2

dog   *see also* SPECIFIC BREEDS, 398:1; 845:1; 1190:3; 1229:24; 1352:1; 1374:5; 1544:1; 1563:18; 1583:9; 1614:1; 1692:1; 2227:2; 2295:5; 3147:2; admiration of ~, 666:3; 1721:2; companionship of ~, 1414:6; eyes of ~, 632:7; ~ in relation to mas-ter, 1495:5; ~ in relation to people, 956:1; 1586:32; love for ~, 604:2; 644:8; 956:2; 1178:3; 3355:2; loyalty of ~, 1357:11; naughty ~, 139:2; teasing ~, 3206:4

doll, 1097:1; black ~, 3326:2

Doll's House, A, Nora of ~, 2071:5

domain, personal ~, 1841:18

domesticity   *see also* TAMENESS, 636:16; 2070:1; early ~, 1802:28; limitations of ~, 907:7; perils of ~, 853:4; pleasures of ~, 2722:46; rewards of ~, 1801:2; women and ~, 768:9; 1344:8; 2532:3

domination, 1841:5; admiration of ~, 2459:47; dissolution of male ~, 2490:4; effective ~, 2459:34; maintenance of ~, 2459:21; male ~, 2459:16; ~ of nature, 3239:1; ~ of women, 3239:1; ~ over oth-ers, 2635:2; power of ~, 1880:5; structures of ~, 3200:1; will to ~, 3089:11

dominion, 2958:4

Don Quixote, 818:1

donkey, 1216:2

Donner Party, 1026:2

doodle, 2610:13

doom, 824:13

door, ~ bell, 1672:2

doorman, 2026:3

Dostoevsky, Feodor, 1103:2

double standard   *see also* SEXISM, 1098:1; 1665:13; 2459:43; 2957:1; ~ for men and women,

3073:4; ~ in child-rearing, 1198:4; ~ in manners, 2012:5; ~ in politics, 2478:2; ~ of Christian Church, 979:8

double talk, 664:8; 2009:34

double-crosser   *see also* TRAITOR, 3212:2

doubt   *see also* UNCERTAINTY, 260:3; 1037:1; 1715:9; un-founded ~, 886:8

Douglas, Helen Gahagan, 1513:31

dove, 799:2

Dover, White Cliffs of, England, 1356:5

down to earth, 2356:14

downfall, ~ of kings, 1260:2

dowry, 298:2

Dracula, 2430:6

dragon, 1560:25

dragonfly, 1173:1

drama (life), 2380:18

drama (play)   *see also* STAGE PLAY, 2316:3; 2567:5

drawing, 2793:2, 3; skill at ~, 2435:2

dread   *see also* FEAR, 883:3; 2400:9; avoiding ~, 2588:34

dream   *see also* DAYDREAM; DREAMING; NIGHTMARE, 102:1; 807:25; 815:, 12; 831:6; 833:1; 991:1; 1114:7; 1159:20; 1341:49; 1431:3; 1435:5; 1666:1; 1814:1; 1909:1; 2588:45; 2722:57; 2740:3; 2742:1; 2901:2; 3247:3; 3376:5; American ~, 3345:2; ~ analysis, 3023:2; birth of ~, 2353:29; color of ~, 2830:3; ~ come true, 1427:1; 3263:1; conscious of ~, 1911:1; controlling one's ~, 1464:4; depth of ~, 2944:2; deso-late ~, 1632:54; destroying ~, 1636:17; distant ~, 1946:8; ex-pired~, 2859:2; facts of ~, 1638:6; faded ~, 154:1; following ~, 2783:3; forgotten ~, 2893:1; function of ~, 1638:9; 2590:2; good ~, 162:1; holding a ~, 1462:6; impact of ~, 917:10; in search of ~, 1730:2; interpreta-tion of ~, 2540:3; living ~, 3205:10; meaning of ~, 2674:10; ~ of castles in the air, 1353:6; ~ of evil, 2375:20; ~ of flying, 2494:5; ~ of humanity, 1715:8; ~ of love, 916:3; 1109:10; ~ of the future, 1190:2; political ~, 1896:39; realizing one's ~, 2330:3; 2416:17; remembering ~, 2968:3; sad ~, 1716:16; shared ~, 3120:1; staving off ~, 2624:12; surrender of ~, 1212:6; unattain-able ~, 2438:2; understanding ~, 2590:3

dreamer   *see also* VISIONARY, 968:9; 1012:29; 1815:1

dreaming   *see also* DREAM, 3022:1

dress *see also* CLOTHING; FASHION, shopping for ~, 1678:1; stunning ~, 2939:1; unadmired ~, 1100:2

drinking *see also* COCKTAIL; LIQUOR, 1428:1; attitude towards ~ alcohol, 1287:4; ~ habits, 1576:6; habitual ~, 1567:6; social ~, 2112:2; succumbing to ~, 866:12

driver/driving, ~ at night, 2907:1; 3630:2; drunk ~, 3102:1; victims of drunk ~, 3102:2

dross, ~ vs. gold, 1655:4

drought, 2747:4; casualties of ~, 1278:4

drowning, 420:1

drudgery, 2517:37; freedom from ~, 49:1; ~ of kitchen, 50:1; women in ~, 2029:2

drug addict/ion *see also* ADDICTION; DRUGS; DRUNKARD/DRUNKENNESS, 2060:8; 2112:3; 2334:1; 2549:5; ~ among Native Americans, 1974:1; impact of ~ on loved ones, 2060:9; ~ overdose, 3182:5; women and ~, 2543:1

drugs *see also specific drugs*; ADDICTION; DRUG ADDICT/ION, addictive to ~, 896:9; balm of ~, 681:1; 1140:1; battle vs. ~ use, 2848:7; ~ culture, 1757:5; decriminalization of ~, 3082:1; effect of ~, 2878:3; 3069:2; hallucinogenic ~, 1837:39; ~ in Hollywood, 1937:13; mescaline ~, 3656:4; overuse of prescription ~, 2068:22; prescription ~, 2112:3; social ~, 2730:3; speed ~, 2650:8; steroid ~, 3502:1; workers on ~, 3054:2

drunkard/drunkenness *see also* HANGOVER, 146:1; 285:11; 364:2; 503:2; 2095:5; men and ~, 1363:27; sex when ~, 3656:2

duality, 1563:5; 2361:2; inner ~, 1536:1; ~ of events, 1163:4; ~ of the sexes, 891:6; wish for ~, 1936:16

Dulles, John Foster, 1513:59

dullness, 683:5; advantages of ~, 1661:1; ~ of life, 2278:2

Duncan, Isadora, 3227:4

duplicity *see also* DECEIT/DECEPTION, 331:18; 783:34; 869:45; 1929:4; 2120:2; 2149:16; 2203:1; 2358:2; 2747:1; 2780:2; ~ of life, 2400:6

Duse, Eleonora, 1768:1

dust, 1653:36; 2014:2; 2517:18; 3110:11

duty *see also* OBLIGATION; RESPONSIBILITY, 401:20; 768:14; 832:1; 909:1; 976:25; 1033:2; 1205:; Christian ~, 910:4; demands of ~, 1176:2; doing one's ~, 1399:1; forgetting one's ~, 2106:24; keeping to one's ~,

773:22; ~ of friendship, 896:34; path of ~, 1104:1; rewards of ~, 893:1

dying *see also* BURIAL; DEAD; DEATH; DEATH SENTENCE; GRAVE, 361:5; 589:18; 1114:11; 2306:9; 2370:27; 2508:2; 2517:30; ~ at home, 2306:7; ~ by violence, 3137:3; choice of ~, 2531:1; experience of ~, 2609:6; fear of ~, 1271:9; process of ~, 2584:26; romantic notion of ~, 285:2; ~ slowly, 2946:5; solitude of ~, 1114:12; tending the ~, 2946:3; women ~, 1771:1; words of the ~, 61:2; ~ young, 791:10

E

eagle, 1523:6; 3115:1

Earhart, Amelia, 1797:1; 3418:1

earliness, 253:1

earning *see* LIVELIHOOD; WAGE

Earth *see also* WORLD, 1047:11; 1589:7; 2375:16; 2385:48; 2641:13, 14; 2726:1; 3393:3; abundance of ~, 1589:6; ~ as mother, 1997:4; caring for ~, 1370:4; 2709:1; 2823:5; connectedness to ~, 2015:4; 3270:1; 3301:3; 3408:1; damage to ~, 2948:1; desecration of ~ *see also* ENVIRONMENT, DESTRUCTION OF ~, 632:22; 697:1; enduring ~, 419:4; evolution of ~, 2143:1; future of ~, 2315:3; interaction with ~, 3009:2; living organism of ~, 2885:12; love of ~, 1285:1; lying on ~, 2152:7; magic of ~, 2312:5; preservation of ~, 2358:12; protecting ~, 178:6; rescuing ~, 2587:6; story of ~, 1904:6; 3149:2; survival of ~, 2443:2; troubled ~, 2219:13; unfriendly ~, 313:1; use of ~ resources *see also* NATURAL RESOURCES, 2140:74; worship ~, 2641:15

easiness, 443:8; 572:8

East Bengal, India, 2106:6

Easter, 990:3

eating *see also specific meals*; DIGESTION; DINING; FOOD, 1700:3; 3009:2; 3254:5; communion of ~ together, 1939:6; ~ habits, 523:1; 3537:2; ~ habits of youth, 2748:13; over- ~ *see also* DIET/ER, 788:18

eccentric/ity, 1554:20; 2175:7; 2498:1; 3389:3; ~ looking, 3378:4; ~ of English, 2493:8

echo, 723:11

ecofeminism *see also* ECOLOGY; ECOSYSTEM; ENVIRONMENT, 3038:2; 3477:1, 2

ecology *see also* CONSERVATION [ENVIRONMENT]; ECOSYSTEM; ENVIRONMENT; POLLUTION, 1073:2; 1775:6; 2098:1; balance

of ~, 2040:7; battles of ~, 3393:3; management of ~, 2741:1; principles of ~, 3068:1; unbalanced ~, 1802:37; world ~, 2386:5

economics/economy (system) *see also* INFLATION, 892:4; 1805:3; ~ as cause of exploitation, 2640:14; backbone of American ~, 2135:3; city ~, 2072:10; cooperative ~, 1550:5; depressed ~, 783:15; 1487:2; development of ~ *see also* DEVELOPMENT, ~ ECONOMIC, 2072:6; false ~, 572:10; growth of ~ *see also* DEVELOPMENT, ~ ECONOMIC, 1896:31; 2044:3; ~ in relation to art, 1338:35; market-based approach to ~, 3638:3; national ~, 3106:2; ~ of plenty, 2021:3; ~ of scarcity, 2638:2; ~ of supply and demand, 1184:4; ~ of world trade, 1394:12; theory of ~, 3591:2; unstable ~, 659:4; 1513:19; vital interests of ~, 1948:31; women and ~, 2665:1

ecosystem *see also* ECOFEMINISM; ECOLOGY; ENVIRONMENT, ~ of forest, 2589:4; understanding ~, 3172:6

ecstasy, physical ~, 3187:5; spiritual ~, 1776:4

Eden, Garden of *see also* HEAVEN; PARADISE, finding ~ *see* RAPTURE, 783:2

editor, crusading ~, 2045:3; woman ~, 1467:1

education *see also* COLLEGE; INSTRUCTION; SCHOOL; STUDY; TRAINING, 632:4; 694:2; 788:19; 952:4; 1226:2; 1311:22; 1439:5; 1457:18; 1581:1; 1715:14; 1757:1; 2123:8; 2140:62; 3011:4; American ~ *see also* UNITED STATES, EDUCATION IN ~, 2793:4; ~ and speech, 1311:9; arts in ~, 2413:1, 2; 3144:5; ~ at birth, 1311:21; bureaucracy in ~, 1862:1; children and ~, 419:9; 1464:3; 1514:1; 1608:25; 2085:14; 2200:3; 2581:15; Christian ~, 754:9; co- ~, 2358:18; concept of ~, 1311:24; cost of ~, 820:3; danger of traditional ~, 1889:9; effect of ~ on morals, 591:11; equality in ~, 825:5; financial assistance for ~, 922:6; focus of ~, 2206:8; 3161:6; ~ for black children, 788:23; ~ for disadvantaged women, 2739:3; global public ~, 2459:61; goals of ~, 2390:4; 3616:2; good ~, 1056:1; government influence of ~, 1412:2; holistic ~, 1722:10; impact of early ~, 2825:1; ~ in relation to society, 2931:2; ~ in Soviet Union, 3098:4; lack of ~, 809:2;

1355:4; 2085:1; liberal ~, 1344:1; 2469:10; 3150:3; liberal arts ~, 2049:10; money and ~, 2490:7; Montessori ~, 2206:7; multiplicity in ~, 2390:5; nature and ~, 1311:8; ~ of nation, 3616:1; ~ of girls, 460:3; 1440:5; 2433:3; parent ~, 3188:3; partnership ~, 2459:62; physical ~, 2486:1; pleasure of ~, 1273:18; power of ~, 723:28; practical ~, 653:1; problems of ~, 2390:9; public ~, 1121:8; 1513:2; 1551:6; purpose of ~, 687:18; 754:1; 822:5; 896:36; 3098:2; reforming system of ~, 3652:1; religious ~, 506:2; 509:2; reverence for ~, 2062:4; rural ~, 980:1; self- ~, 1001:2; sex ~ *see also* SEX, ~ EDUCATION, 1860:1, 3; 2459:52; 2524:4, 6; 3169:4; 3188:3; sexism in ~, 166:1; 242:2; 655:2; 2390:1; 2764:2; 3569:1, 2; shortcomings in ~, 1289:30; systems of ~, 1262:3; timing of ~, 2085:8; universal higher ~, 2049:11; women and ~, 320:10; 363:3; 419:5; 438:20; 504:1; 788:6; 807:6; 828:1; 855:5; 869:52; 1042:1; 1889:4; 2183:16; 2294:1; 2390:2; 2533:1; work and ~, 3351:9

educator *see* PROFESSOR; TEACHER

Edward VI of England, 326:1

efficiency, 1661:8; ~ of people, 2432:1

effort *see also* DILIGENCE; ENDEAVOR, 2140:13; 2520:2; futility of ~, 363:8

egalitarianism *see also* EQUALITY; GYLANY, 856:17; 1550:3; 3393:8; men and ~, 2581:2

egg, 1341:53; boiled ~, 753:27

ego *see also* IDENTITY; SELF; SELF-IMAGE, 481:15; 1114:3; 1880:10; building one's ~, 1879:10; competitive ~, 1232:2; differentiated ~, 2373:1; feeding ~, 1930:2; lack of ~, 3583:2; male ~, 1937:4; rapacious ~, 1771:3; submission of ~, 2514:6; throwing off ~, 1893:5

egocentricity/egotism *see also* CONCEIT/EDNESS; SELF-CENTEREDNESS; SELF-INTEREST; SELFISHNESS, 401:2, 17; 443:9; 494:3; 834:1; 840:2; 869:45; 892:14; 930:17, 28; 1012:19; 1418:6; 1543:15; 1560:34; 1576:10; 1582:5; 1638:2; 1640:4; 2231:8; 2416:6; 2755:6; 3134:9

Egypt, 950:7; polygamy in ~, 855:23; poverty in ~, 2594:4; women in ~, 855:21

Eichmann, Adolf, 1896:27; 2555:6

Eiffel Tower (Paris), 1004:7

duration of ~, 1178:2; hopeless ~, 875:12; lasting ~, 1841:14; love of ~, 3354:2; measure of ~, 1431:9; overcoming ~, 45:1; uncontrolled ~, 959:8; universal ~, 892:10; unspoken ~, 1037:3; women's ~, 959:7

grievance, remedy for ~, 1450:2

Griffith, D. W., 1576:15; 1604:1

grooming, ~ of man, 1557:9; ~ of women, 630:7; 1803:3; 1832:4

group, effectiveness of ~, 1538:2; ~ encounter, 2596:1; ~ spirit, 1277:11; success of ~, 1277:8

growing up   see also CHILDHOOD; YOUTH, 896:8; 1565:1; 1778:1; 1932:1; 2060:3; 2101:8; 2118:4; 2179:3; 2479:12; 2507:24; 2547:18; 2881:2; 2900:2; disappointments of ~, 1012:6; ~ female; 2989:2

growth, 1204:2; 1575:3; 1634:7; 2342:5; 238:17; 2674:14; 2737:4; 3154:1; aiding ~ of others, 2342:4; artistic ~, 1338:7; economic ~   see also DEVELOPMENT, ECONOMIC ~ , 3106:2; inner ~, 1112:10; lack of ~, 2410:1; 2674:13; need for ~, 891:2; ~ of artist, 2951:3; personal ~   see also MATURITY, 869:43, 53; 907:66; 930:79; 1311:24; 1321:4; 1635:18; 2285:15; 3112:7; spiritual ~ see also SPIRIT/UALITY, DEVELOPMENT OF ~, 166:22

guardian, ~ of child, 1660:13

Guatemala, 3460:2; disappearances in ~, 3460:1

guest   see also VISIT/OR, 1341:14; perfect ~, 1504:1; 1560:6; treatment of ~, 2012:1; welcome ~, 788:32; woman ~, 1496:2

guidance/guide, 1711:3; 3402:1; 3436:2; divine ~, 3364:9; lack of ~, 1319:4; need for ~, 2465:6; 2560:1; spiritual ~, 2617:1

guilt/y, 450:4; 833:2; 924:4; 965:3; 976:6; 1093:7; 1132:5; 1503:1; 1560:10; 2013:1; 2353:10; 2375:1; 2479:7; 2722:3; 2732:2; 2962:4, 5, 6, 11; 3298:2; 3326:6; admitting ~, 1896:25; assumption of ~, 2300:1; secret ~, 3428:1; tinge of ~, 339:4

guitar, playing ~, 3618:1

gullibility, 243:3; 304:1; 443:21; 604:6; 1205:29; 2632:1; ~ of citizenry, 254:1

gun   see also ARMS; SHOOTING; WEAPON, 2771:1; ~ control, 2527:1; 3540:1; fascination with ~, 2611:3; power of ~, 3352:5; shooting ~, 1145:6; ~ use, 3390:3; ~ violence, 3540:1, 2

Guyana, 2184:2

gylany   see also EGALITARIANISM; EQUALITY, 2194:2

gym, work out at ~, 2163:3

gymnast, scoring ~, 3507:1

gynecologist   see also MEDICAL PROFESSION; PHYSICIAN, 1837:11

gypsy, 934:4; 3360:4; character of ~, 1007:5

H

habit   see also CUSTOM, 1481:8; 1618:3; 2314:10; 3494:1; breaking ~, 1359:2; evil ~, 807:2; simple ~, 754:4

hacienda, life on ~, 2643:1

Hagen, Uta, 2846:2

hair, 3355:1; ~ color, 2239:1; ~ dresser, 2588:25; dyed ~, 3391:1; grey ~, 1826:1; 2842:5; straight ~, 1087:2; ~ style, 1278:1; 2178:3; 3399:4; ~ type, 2227:15; white ~, 2624:13

half-breed   see also MESTIZO; MULATTO, 3301:2

Hamlet, 1751:1

hand (human), 142:2; 713:1; 788:14; 1457:19; 1636:55; 2722:23; 2941:5; beautiful ~, 824:9; flaccid ~, 1674:6; holding ~, 2317:5; ~ washing, 3561:1; work of ~, 1457:

handbag, 2201:13

handicap   see also CHILD/REN, HANDICAPPED ~; DISABLED/DISABILITY, 3585:1; physical ~, 988:3; 3590:4

handshake, 1457:12

hangover   see also DRUNKARD/DRUNKENNESS, 176:7

Hannah, 370:1; 374:1

haphazardness, 1424:2

happiness   see also BLISS; JOY; UNHAPPINESS, 338:1; 398:10; 490:2; 536:6; 572:4; 582:7, 9; 600:1; 601:3; 661:23; 684:2; 717:23; 759:1; 803:1; 869:37, 39; 994:7; 1089:3; 1229:10; 1338:10; 1353:5; 1359:2; 1362:18, 21; 1389:3; 1392:23; 1544:3; 1583:8; 1852:1; 1869:1; 1880:9; 1946:18; 1998:1, 4; 2149:13; 2397:6; 2401:9; 2547:4; 2777:4; 2849:1; 3629:4; demand for ~, 1896:50; domestic ~, 823:8; ephemerality of ~, 630:11; 644:3; 1466:2; fear of ~, 1840:29; feigned ~, 664:11; finding ~, 582:1; 1276:1; 1335:2; hungry for ~, 1309:5; intermittent ~, 1553:17; loss of ~, 386:2; 680:1; meager ~, 1043:2; money and ~, 1377:4; pursuit of ~, 705:28; 791:12; road to ~, 683:2; shunning ~, 824:20

harassment   see also SEXUAL HARASSMENT, legal ~, 3219:2

harbor, 1119:1

hardship   see ADVERSITY; LIFE, STRUGGLE OF ~; OBSTACLE; TROUBLE

Hari Krishna, 288:2

Harlem, New York City, ~ uprising of 1935, 1494:7

harm, inflict ~, 443:3

harmlessness, 3047:1

harmony   see also COOPERATION, 449:3; 891:4; inner ~, 1184:8; living in ~, 896:27; ~ with nature, 1946:22

Harvard University, women of ~ Business School, 2512:1

harvest, 1290:6

hate/hatred   see also HOSTILITY, 269:1; 349:2; 784:5; 930:1; 1192:1; 1433:4; 1837:13; 2006:1; 2103:1; 2117:10; 2385:39; 2675:17; 3055:2; 3283:3; creative ~, 1338:6; eliminating ~, 1247:1; look of ~, 930:30; object of ~, 1209:11; ~ of self   see also SELF-HATRED, 1936:17; 1961:1; 2601:3; ~ of wife, 1783:2; unconscious ~, 1089:7

Hawaii/ans, 1050:1, 2

hawk, 641:1; 1740:1, 2; 2722:58

head of state   see also *specific positions*; LEADER/SHIP; RULE/R; STATESMAN, 331:8; 339:19; accountability of ~, 339:15; 2106:7; concerns of ~, 526:7; credibility of ~, 254:1; 283:3; demands on ~, 591:5, 10; friend of ~, 340:1; impotence of ~, 3630:1; pressures of ~, 659:2; woman ~, 302:2

Headstart, funding for ~, 2825:1

healer   see also PHYSICIAN, 979:11; 1593:1

healing   see also CURE; RECOVERY; REMEDY, 953:13; 1673:1; 2373:10; 2459:58; 2507:4; 2815:2; 3112:3; 3244:1; 3373:3; 3588:1; ~ arts   see also MEDICAL PROFESSION, 1704:3; miracle of ~, 2760:2; ~ oneself, 3029:10; 3187:4; ~ others, 1263:7

health   see also WELL-BEING, 272:5; 852:1; 1496:5; 1564:20; 1813:5; 2432:2; good ~, 1019:3; 2564:5; holistic ~, 922:7; importance of ~, 1366:3; improved ~, 1564:21; mind and ~, 953:18; poor ~, 527:19; principles of ~, 1073:4; ~ problems, 1229:8; promoting ~, 3139:3; psychological ~, 2787:6; reproductive ~, 2478:3; science of ~, 952:3;   seeking ~, 785:1; study of ~, 1855:3; teaching ~, 1475:1

health care, ~ coverage, 2478:3; ~ industry, 3393:7; national ~, 3139:5; reproductive ~, 2741:6

health club, 2851:7

hearing (senses), 3172:5

hearsay, 1639:36

Hearst, William Randolph, 2233:1

heart   see also EMOTION; FEELING; LOVE, 132:3; 165:4; 267:1; 291:1; 310:1; 515:5; 717:32; 1549:1; 1632:45; 2189:6; 2941:3; ~ attack, 2870:1; big ~, 1163:2; bountiful ~, 1109:11; care of ~, 2750:15; cold ~, 799:1; denying one's ~, 3029:20; fluttering ~, 2014:1; following one's ~, 2620:2; free ~, 876:2; 994:7; good ~, 917:14; graceless ~, 1251:4; hard ~, 1841:7; 2018:2; human ~, 939:8; judgment of ~, 2517:4; light ~, 884:5; logic of ~, 601:6; lonely ~, 773:16; loving ~, 2861:2; master of ~, 1254:10; mind and ~, 3195:4; narrow ~, 2717:2; noble ~, 408:3; open ~, 2227:14; secrets of ~, 910:1; 2746:3; song of ~, 1053:7; stolen one's ~, 238:1; submissive ~, 452:1; weak ~, 1114:13; willing ~, 705:13; 773:6; win one's ~, 471:2; 521:2; 649:2; woman's ~, 320:2; 505:14; 878:7; 930:68

heartbeat, 2517:25

heartbreak   see also LOVE, LOST, 46:9; 149:2; 551:3; 875:38; 993:30, 36; 1329:5; 1636:17; 2370:23; 2717:1; 2944:4; consolation for ~, 1353:10

heartlessness, ~ in society, 2278:4

heat, 1544:13; 3295:1

heathen   see also PAGAN/ISM, 548:1

heather, 672:1

heaven   see also PARADISE, 46:3; 241:1; 281:6; 888:1; 950:5; 1166:1; 1289:35; 1988:4; 2239:3; 2307:3; 2932:3; 3364:3; arrival in ~, 658:3; 1255:1; blocked from ~, 450:4; door of ~, 2891:10; fly to ~, 3382:3; focus on ~, 2213:13; going to ~, 1048:4; ~ on earth, 875:34; personal ~, 3542:2; reward in ~, 2581:31; road to ~, 791:4; 856:3; 1615:2;   seeking ~, 757:8; unbelief in ~, 1567:4; women in ~, 2888:4

Hebrew, 1728:8

Hedda Gabler, 2071:5, 12

hedonism, 361:6

hegemony, science and ~, 2635:3

heir/ess, American ~, 2009:20

heirloom, family ~, 2540:41

hell   see also DAMNATION/DAMNED; PURGATORY, 140:3; 148:3; 283:4; 411:1; 2430:6; 2717:3; condemned to ~, 1636:28; 3043:9; real ~, 1948:16; world going to ~, 2310:7

Héloïse, 177:9

help/fulness, 1082:8; asking for ~, 2705:2; creed of ~, 1578:5; devotion to ~, 2609:2; giving ~, 910:; 976:9; 1081:1; 3134:5; ~ oneself, 460:12; 3029:10

helplessness, 2962:11; 3380:4

idleness   *see also* LAZINESS, 262:4; 361:9; 460:12; 622:2; 636:1; 1004:4; 1089:2; 1261:1; 1311:10; 1543:2; 1881:19; 2074:6; 2308:1; maintaining ~, 3245:1

idol/atry   *see also* HERO/INE, 157:3; 604:5; 636:6; 875:3; 1570:5; 2912:1; adoration of ~, 219:3; age of ~, 3159:14; desire for ~, 1353:1; function of ~, 2270:2; ~ of women, 2299:6; ~ worship, 452:1

ignorance   *see also* STUPIDITY, 311:2; 325:1; 331:17; 407:1; 931:1; 1163:1, 3; 1481:9; 1881:5; 2101:1; 2353:12; 2562:1; 2606:12; 2610:1; advantages of ~, 1450:5; embarrassment of ~, 3400:2; harm of ~, 1557:12; ~ in America, 2848:22; ~ of masses, 922:4; ~ of times, 452:7; perception of ~, 3491:3

Iliad, The, women in ~, 3496:3

illiteracy   *see also* READING, 636:13; 837:2; 2353:2; ~ of women, 630:3

illness   *see also specific disorders*; DISEASE; SICKNESS, 1841:13; 1898:1; 1946:3; 2540:42; affect of ~ on attitude, 1338:22; association of ~, 2540:57; cure for ~ *see also* CURE, 1028:2; 1638:4; 2303:4; ~ in relation to community, 1184:12; privacy of ~, 2241:2; 2354:6; psychosomatic ~ *see also* HYPOCHONDRIA; MENTAL ILLNESS; MIND, DISEASE OF ~, 331:13; 418:2; 757:11; 784:1

illumination   *see also* INSPIRATION, 2455:11

illusions, 994:17; 1229:5; 2046:11; 2088:2; 2217:4; 2959:2; creating ~, 2920:3; dupe to ~, 1136:12; giving up ~, 2186:7; lost ~, 791:28; ~ of self, 869:30; search for ~, 1678:1; women's ~, 2356:12

image   *see also* IDENTITY, addiction to ~, 2540:35; bad self-~, 1089:5; creating ~, 1840:28; 2071:8; iconic use of male ~, 2744:8; language of ~, 3159:10; maximizing ~, 2320:2; need new ~, 930:12; understanding ~, 3258:1

imagination, 285:13; 661:4; 747:2; 791:5; 835:6; 993:29; 1117:1; 1357:1; 1392:35; 1525:2; 1832:3; 2385:32, 55; 3567:1; conflict of ~, 2393:39; curbing ~, 687:19; freeing human ~, 2459:20; lack of ~, 987:24; ~ of child, 1819:7; power of ~, 2985:10; repressing ~, 2900:2; soaring ~, 644:12; spell of ~ *see also* REVERIE, 824:7; tortuous ~,

1837:6; ~ vs. reality, 1357:7; 1457:21; women and ~, 753:10; 2068:20; 2398:4

imitation, 1363:52; 1575:6; 1700:4; 3366:13

immigrant/immigration   *see also* EMIGRANT/EMIGRATION; REFUGEE, 819:3; 3144:6; 3221:4; 3389:1; barring ~, 3284:1; children of ~, 1204:12; 2583:1; 3390:1; courage of ~, 3428:4; ~ in America, 1477:5; 2416:8; 2818:1; 3345:2; 3396:4; 3613:1; ~ parents, 1775:7; treatment of ~, 1856:1

immorality   *see also* MORALITY, LACK OF ~, 687:3; 1513:5

immortality, 165:1; 938:7; 976:15; 1053:6; 1196:2; 1323:1; 1788:11; 1896:21; 2306:12; 3417:2; belief in ~, 1674:3; 2231:15; desire for ~, 1632:30; ~ of youth, 1655:8; striving for ~, 3283:2

impartiality   *see also* OBJECTIVITY, 428:1

impassivity, 2493:1; 2494:1; learning ~, 934:7

impatience   *see also* PATIENCE, 746:1; 1251:1; 2089:2; 2537:4

impeachment, 2963:5; ~ of American president, 2660:11

imperfection, 2234:11

imperialism, 1497:8; 2095:16; American ~, 1636:27

impertinence, 1093:6

imperturbability, 2818:2

imperviousness, 3567:2

importance   *see also* SIGNIFICANCE, 931:6; 1632:1; feeling of ~, 1513:44; lack of ~, 1618:4

impossibility   *see also* POSSIBILITY, 285:17; 841:2; 1494:9; 2311:1; 2419:3; desire for ~, 3539:3; overcoming ~, 2864:13; 3171:1

impotence, feeling of ~, 2334:2

impression, leaving an ~, 2356:25

Impressionism, 1919:8

imprisonment   *see also* ENSLAVEMENT; PRISONER, ; 390:1; 475:1; 2995:11; advantages of ~, 436:3; effects of ~, 2201:19; 2565:1; escaping ~, 2261:3; fear of ~, 2507:5; misery of ~, 3352:8

improvement   *see also* SELF-IMPROVEMENT, 632:16; 1269:3; ~ for future, 3058:4; lack of ~, 300:2; 632:3; ~ of succeeding generations, 987:17; resisting ~, 759:5

improvisation, 2071:10

imprudence, 2356:2

impudence, 661:5

inaction, 2687:14

incentive, lack of ~, 1239:7; work ~, 1899:2

incest, 10:1; 35:1; 2016:24; 2902:2; ~ in Bible, 10:1

inclusiveness, 2584:16; necessity of ~, 2935:4

income   *see also* SALARY; WAGE, ~ in relation to God, 2353:4; inequality of women's ~, 2437:2; living within one's ~, 242:16; men and ~, 2210:7; ~ of college graduate, 2049:12; regular ~, 1481:31

incompatibility, 2736:1

incompetence, mark of ~, 1679:1

inconsiderateness, 1158:16; 1341:14

inconstancy, 469:2

indebtedness, 1292:2

indecency, 1481:5; 1566:1

indecision   *see also* DECISION, 553:1; 556:1; 661:17; 2634:28; image of ~, 2068:9

independence, 687:2; 896:10; 945:2; 949:17; 1094:1; 1154:3; 1713:1; 1802:41; 2060:2; 2070:2; 2240:9; 2356:14; 2541:1; 2783:5; 3029:6; 3352:4; attaining ~, 2465:5; desire for ~, 1311:17; ~ for women, 907:59; 1840:2; illusion of ~, 2178:2; necessity for ~, 2163:2; personal ~, 1410:13; test of ~, 1988:1; ~ vs. individuality, 1169:12; women of ~, 100:1; 866:4; 1051:1; 1631:2; 3426:2

indestructibility, 2584:2

index/ing, 2028:10

India/n, 2106:6; 2337:3, 6, 7; 2581:26; children in ~, 2106:13; corruption in ~, 2106:14; democracy in ~, 2106:8, 12, 26; disease in ~, 2337:4; equality of the sexes in ~, 1786:5; fashion in ~, 1245:1; hunger in ~, 2106:15; ~ in relation to whites, 1513:20; independence of ~, 2106:10; national life in ~, 1431:7; poverty of ~, 2569:7; racism in ~, 1112:1; starvation in ~, 2904:21; women in ~, 1245:2; 1431:7; ~ writer, 1786:7; youth in ~, 2106:2

indifference   *see also* DETACHMENT, 1564:23; 1567:14; 1653:11; 2191:2; 2252:1; 2621:2; 3588:2; ~ of yesterday, 1708:2

indigenous people   *see also specific groups*; NATIVE, 3460:6; differences between sexes of ~, 1802:31; oppression of ~, 3460:4; religion and ~, 3460:8; rights of ~, 2130:2

indiscretion, 76:6

indispensability, 1159:25; 2755:6

individual   *see also* PEOPLE; PERSON, assessment of ~, 1808:15; dangerous ~, 443:5; 779:11; dignity of ~, 1728:13; importance of ~, 3317:1; ~ in relation to society, 1277:4; intrinsic worth of ~, 2962:1; personal world of ~, 2765:4; ~ vs. group, 2569:15

individuality   *see also* NONCONFORMIST/NONCONFORMITY; SINGULARITY, 856:19; 917:8; 1338:36; 1564:22; 1772:11; 1875:3; 1920:1; 2373:2; 2490:5; 3236:1; effacement of ~, 840:3; finding one's ~, 3366:13; historicity of ~, 3642:1; ignoring one's ~, 1652:6; importance of ~, 3080:2; loss of ~, 1857:4; suppression of ~, 2569:3; women of ~, 1586:20

indolence, 429:2; 442:4; attitude toward ~, 661:21; ~ in children, 166:14

indomitability, 2084:1

indoors, women and ~, 1808:18

indulgence, 1043:10; 1567:7; ~ of society, 2056:2; self- ~, 779:4; 1105:1; slight ~, 1305:1

Industrial Revolution, 1184:1

industrialization/industry   *see also* AGE [ERA], INDUSTRIAL ~, 2665:3; development of ~, 1304:5; dominance of ~, 1904:13; effects of ~, 1009:1; 1651:6; effects of ~ on family function, 1818:3; ~ in relation to Wall Street, 1784:6; inhumanity of ~, 1174:4; local ~, 980:1; ~ of West, 2106:18; women and ~, 1169:1

industriousness   *see also* DILIGENCE, 622:2; 987:19

inebriation   *see also* ALCOHOL/ALCOHOLISM; DRINKING, 1991:22

inequality, 1972:5; charges of ~, 3105:9

inequity   *see also* FAIRNESS, LACK OF ~; INJUSTICE, ~ of life, 3110:3; ~ of world, 3047:5

inertia, 1543:20, 20

inexpressible, 1771:5

infant   *see also* BABY; NEWBORN, 705:5; 713:3; 3487:3; birth of ~ *see also* CHILDBIRTH, 291:2; death of ~ *see also* LOVED ONE, DEATH OF ~, 164:1; 308:1; 551:4; 655:1; 744:3; 781:1; 783:12; ~ in relation to mother, 2230:4; 2787:4

infatuation   *see also* LOVE, 595:1; 1632:70

inferiority, ~ of women's place, 1651:3; sense of ~ *see also* SELF-ESTEEM, LOW ~) 1513:1

infertility, 3406:1; surmounting ~, 3406:2

infidelity   *see also* ADULTERY; PHILANDERER, 166:20; 878:6; 2046:8; excitement of ~, 3656:7; hiding ~, 384:3; rationalization for ~, 2442:3; woman's ~, 285:1; 435:2

infinite, 896:21

infinity, 1632:67

inflation   *see also* ECONOMICS/ECONOMY [SYSTEM], 1778:4; 2044:3

2675:2; 3411:1; men and ~, 1401:1

monotony *see also* BORE/DOM, 1474:1; 2730:1

Monroe, Marilyn, 2802:6

monster, 833:5; man-made ~, 2265:4

Montessori, Maria, 2206:7

monument, 489:6; ~ to women, 996:1

mood, 2430:2; dark ~, 2613:3

Moon, 305:1; 527:24; 644:7; 891:3; 976:20; 1353:29; 1488:4, 6; 2031:9; 2219:8; 3301:9; crescent ~, 644:1; eclipse of ~, 1290:4; hidden ~, 943:3; light of ~, 703:4; pull of ~, 2207:3; symbology of ~, 2664:2

moor, 993:29

Moral Majority *see also* CONSERVATISM; RIGHT WING, 3371:1

morality *see also* ETHICS, 687:16; 717:10; 769:4; 871:12; 1036:1; 1153:14; 1289:13; 1505:1; 1621:2; 1813:9; 1880:14; 2069:6; 2149:22; 2474:7; 2549:3; 2660:5; changing ~, 582:2; 2183:26; clash of ~, 1204:4; conflicts of ~, 3179:2; decaying ~, 807:19; defining ~, 2385:12; demise of ~, 1709:5; feminine ~, 2385:43; fight over ~ issues, 2655:1; government and ~, 2685:2; impact of art on ~, 2540:32; ~ in nature, 573:6; inventing ~, 2750:1; lack of ~ *see also* IMMORALITY, 1649:1; lax standards, 3159:16; middle class ~, 2016:22; objecting to ~, 2918:7; ~ of nation, 2010:27; ~ of women, 2581:1; 2628:3; ~ sensibility, 1189:10; standards of ~, 1948:45; 2068:6; teaching ~, 866:10; test of ~, 1363:3; upholding ~, 601:1; ~ vs. profit, 2244:5

More, Henry, 773:8

More, Thomas, 2231:15

mores *see also* CUSTOM, changing ~, 669:2; 1513:33

Morgan, J. P., 1493:1; 3071:1, 2

Mormon/ism, 2063:3

morning *see also* DAWN; DAY; SUNRISE, 380:1; 1095:4; 1096:1; 2100:3; 2987:8; mood of ~, 1263:1; spring ~, 1707:4; sunny ~, 2959:3

morning glory, 2900:1

mortality *see also* DEATH, awareness of ~, 1785:1; 2650:10; decreasing ~ rates, 1818:5

Moscow, U.S.S.R., 1786:4; 2267:1

Moses, 17:1; 1383:2; 1494:5; 2134:2

Moslem *see also* ISLAM, 2123:11; brotherhood of ~, 3029:27

Mother Hubbard, 845:1

mother-in-law, 1933:13

mother/hood *see also* PARENT/HOOD; STEPMOTHER, 80:2; 101:1; 370:3; 490:1; 774:2; 823:3; 883:2; 923:17; 1012:21; 1093:4; 1121:3, 26, 27; 1159:9; 1160:1; 1205:14, 17; 1341:33; 1491:1; 1492:2; 1497:22; 1576:9; 1639:35; 1868:2; 1893:3; 2019:22; 2046:15; 2055:2; 2162:4; 2182:1; 2309:2; 2338:1, 2; 2393:19; 2471:3; 2547:2, 14; 2607:2, 3; 2648:3; 2922:1; 2968:1; 3006:3; 3043:2; 3149:10; 3220:2; 3229:7; 3247:2; 3308:1; advice from ~, 2190:1; aging ~, 1936:22; alcoholic ~, 3656:6; anger at ~, 2380:8; anguish of ~, 746:5; ~ as poet, 2624:8; ~ as servant, 1410:9; ~ as storyteller, 2810:1; aspects of ~, 1410:1; bad ~, 2505:3; benefits of ~, 942:3; broken ~, 2688:6; character of ~, 821:1; complexity of ~, 3653:6; conflicts of working ~, 1786:1; constant activity of ~, 3029:24; death of ~ *see also* DEATH, ~ OF MOTHER, 566:1; 783:3; 1341:22; 1919:1; 2303:7; 2375:21; 2471:2; demands of ~, 2279:15; 3017:1; desire for ~, 438:12; 1788:2; 3132:1; destiny of ~, 1497:23; difficulties of ~, 1341:7; dying ~, 3061:2; education and ~, 2390:2; expectant ~ *see also* PREGNANCY/PREGNANT, 687:23; function of ~, 1435:4; glorification of ~, 2648:2; hostility to ~, 2755:43; illness of ~, 2230:5; 2881:3; image of ~, 2224:2; 2956:1; ~ in kitchen, 1915:3; ~ in patriarchy, 2393:27, 64; ~ in relation to adult child, 1502:2; 2058:3; 2673:3; ~ in relation to adult daughter, 1583:6; 2901:14; ~ in relation to baby, 981:3; 1541:1; ~ in relation to child, 37:1; 323:3; 357:1; 364:1; 370:1; 631:2; 1223:6; 1720:1; 2239:2; 2393:25; 2541:5; 2863:4; 2881:2; 3112:7; 3155:1; 3223:10; 3227:2; ~ in relation to daughter, 443:1; 714:1; 716:1; 1361:2; 1719:9; 2112:1; 2425:1; 2780:5; 2958:3; 3029:8, 43; 3229:12; 3302:2; ~ in relation to feminism, 2605:8; ~ in relation to husband *see also* WIFE, ~ IN RELATION TO HUSBAND, 1881:25; ~ in relation to son *see also* SON, ~ IN RELATION TO MOTHER, 168:3; 1392:6; 1555:1; 3088:2, 3; 3089:7; 3297:2; ~ in relation to teenaged child, 2310:3; ineffectual ~, 1813:7; influence of ~, 788:1, 7; 807:29;

1698:2; internalized ~, 2461:2; invincible ~, 1582:4; Jewish ~, 3027:1; joy of ~, 3653:8; lack of maternal instinct in ~, 1698:1; limitations of ~, 949:19; ~ love *see also* LOVE, MOTHER ~, 2698:6; love for ~, 2484:2; love of ~, 791:19; 3442:8; 3637:2; lower income ~, 1410:1; mirrors of ~, 3492:2; motivations for ~, 1497:14; nursing ~ *see also* BREAST, ~ FEEDING, 975:12; ~ of different child, 2938:9; ~ of only child, 2848:13; ~ of soldier, 1868:4; overbearing ~, 723:29; overprotective ~, 1136:1; patience of ~, 981:4; power of ~, 3017:3; preparation for ~, 832:3; 907:42; price of ~, 1416:7; promise of ~, 3110:5; protective ~, 2517:32; reasons for ~, 2426:6; religious beliefs of ~, 2979:5; resentment toward ~, 2901:4; responsibilities of ~, 1205:8; rights of ~, 642:4; 1416:10; 1805:5; role of ~, 2479:11; 2928:1; sexuality of ~, 3217:3; single ~, 2262:1; slave ~, 1497:4; snooping ~, 1879:18; society's need for ~, 3017:4; stage ~, 2039:1; starving ~, 3510:2; supportive ~, 1619:1; taboo of ~, 3560:1; theories of ~, 3010:3; transformed by ~, 3653:7; unwed ~, 1636:43; 2052:1; 2074:5; 2960:1; welfare ~ *see also* SOCIAL WELFARE, SINGLE MOTHERS ON ~, 2074:5; 2690:4; white ~ of black child, 2956:2; wild ~ within, 2938:10; wisdom of ~, 907:40; working ~, 1121:28; 1410:2; 1728:24; 2190:5; young ~, 2678:2

motivation, 2020:1; 2243:2; 3083:4; inducing ~, 1112:9; understanding ~, 2774:4

mountain *see also* HILL, 1295:2; 1421:2; ~ climbing, 1460:3; ~ pass, 220:2

mourning *see also* GRIEF, 136:1; 164:1; 235:1; 242:15; 353:1; 657:3; 785:3; 831:1; 1391:7; 1554:12; 1743:6; dress for ~, 892:3; national ~, 1658:4

mouth (human), 471:2

movement (physical) *see also* ACTIVITY, 1681:1, 2

movement (socio-political) *see also* specific movements; PROTEST/ER, 2073:1; extremist ~, 2215:6; ~ for change, 2581:16; ~ for social change, 3399:15; grass roots ~, 2459:56; ~ in America, 2160:5; men and women in ~, 3060:1; partisan ~, 3029:29; progress of ~, 2775:5; reform ~, 1538:5; social potential ~, 2382:1; socialist ~, 1169:2

Mozart, Wolfgang Amadeus, works of ~, 1639:21

MP (Member of Parliament), 3127:6

Ms. (magazine), 2581:33; 2835:12

mudslinging *see also* ACCUSATION, 2271:5

Mugabe, Robert, 2140:56

mule, 1772:12

multi-racial/ism *see also* HALF-BREED; MESTIZO; MULATTO, 1636:46; 2577:3; 2891:8; benefits of ~, 1553:4; tribulations of being ~, 2380:1; 2891:1

multifariousness, ~ of women, 1631:1

mundane, ~ activity, 2487:2

murder/er *see also* KILLER; KILLING; MASSACRE, 599:1; 763:6; 1590:1; 1618:1, 15; 1841:6; 2469:36; 3006:2; 3265:2; 3627:1; avenging ~, 757:4; ~ by poisoning, 800:16; child ~, 2722:8; commonness of ~, 1930:3; condoned ~, 283:1; defending victim of ~, 950:8; effect of ~ on others, 1862:3; identity of ~, 1946:24; incarcerated ~, 2765:1; intentional ~, 3206:2; sanctioned ~, 1948:32; target of ~, 2567:3; victim of ~, 2923:2

Muses *see also* VARIOUS ART FORMS, 489:1; 705:2; 891:14; 904:4; ill use of ~, 308:2

museum, impact of ~, 3128:1

Museum of Modern Art (New York City), 2295:6

music *see also* MELODY; OPERA; SINGER/SINGING; SONG; SYMPHONY, 438:2; 780:3; 1329:2; 1632:49; 1883:7; 2085:2; 2958:2; 3156:4; African ~, 3081:2; American ~, 1416:12; big ~, 2959:13; blues ~, 1988:3; 2208:1; classical ~, 2470:11; composing ~, 1575:4; 2759:1; disinterested in ~, 2470:11; ~ education, 2526:1; experiencing ~, 1568:1; 2461:4; god of ~, 1154:5; gospel ~, 1988:2; great ~, 1568:2; ~ in one's soul, 1717:9; ~ in relation to dance, 1416:6; ~ in relation to gender, 2368:1; jazz ~, 2208:1; 2608:2; ~ lover, 639:4; 3205:1; ~ lyrics, 1575:1; martial ~ *see also* BAND, 661:28; ~ of past, 1437:1; popular ~, 3251:1; power of ~, 869:25; 2846:3; reading ~, 3527:1; recording ~, 2344:1; rock ~, 2326:6; 2587:1; ~ score, 1440:7; teaching ~ *see also* TEACHER, MUSIC ~, 1290:5; understanding ~, 1636:53; woman ~ conductor, 3214:1; women in ~, 2502:1; writing ~, 1249:3

New York City, 1205:26; 1308:5; 1507:2; 1771:3; 2026:2; 2123:20; 2333:3; 2416:8; 2540:49; 2588:1; 2594:2; 2606:10; 2647:6; 3287:1; people of ~, 1638:12; 2514:7; poverty in ~, 2071:2; robbery in ~, 837:14; young women in ~, 1746:3

New Zealand, ~ and nuclear power, 3545:5; ~ women, 946:1

Nguyen Cao Ky, 2416:5

Niagara Falls, 807:4

Nicaragua, art education in ~, 3144:5

nickname, 298:7

Nietzsche, Friedrich Wilhelm, 3384:2

night *see also* EVE/NING; MIDNIGHT, 129:1; 297:1; 711:4; 824:10; 863:1; 1032:1; 1638:8; 2385:21; 2667:1; 3247:3; beautiful ~, 1637:3; cloak of ~, 1975:1; fear of ~, 503:1; ~ in country, 1357:12; ~ on town, 2980:4; secrets of ~, 172:1; shelter of ~, 786:1; shortest ~, 1632:52; sleepless~, 165:6

nightingale, 46:12; 582:12; 644:2; 1421:4

nightmare *see also* DREAM, 1872:4; 2212:5; 2430:; 2606:3

Nimrod, 1374:1

Nixon, Richard M., 1513:31, 58, 62; 1680:6; 1781:2; 2120:1, 2; 2244:14; 2849:2; 3139:20

Nobel Prize, 2469:27; ~ Committee, 1470:1; ~ for Peace, 3460:4; women recipients of ~, 1636:13

noble/nobility (rank)*see also* ARISTOCRACY; COURTIERS; RANK; ROYAL/TY, 994:15; 2387:1; desire to be ~, 501:4; ~ in relation to subjects, 339:

nobleness, 1474:4

noise *see also* SOUND, 717:24; ~ of the world, 284:7; surrounding ~, 2385:10

nomad *see also* VAGABOND; WANDERER, 770:2; 1634:2, 8

nonconformist/nonconformity *see also* INDIVIDUALITY, 1136:10; 2068:7; 2540:30; 2988:3; 3554:1; hostility toward ~, 1471:4; women and ~, 2938:8

nonsense, 234:3

nonviolence *see also* PACIFISM/PACIFIST, 2552:3; 2838:5, 7; 3007:5, 6, 7

noon, 992:14

normality, 1363:14; 3140:3; 3637:1; ~ in children, 2397:2

Norris, Kathleen, 1653:26

North/erners (U.S.), ~ in relation to South, 862:4

North, Oliver, 2120:7

North America, ~ in relation to South America, 2592:3

Norway, women in government of ~, 2741:2; 3617:1

nose (human) *see also* SMELL, 669:1; 866:2

nosiness *see also* BUSINESS, MINDING ONE'S ~), 303:2; 1142:2; 1145:2; 1557:23; 1772:13; 1951:1; 2640:1; 3252:1

nostalgia *see also* SENTIMENTALITY, 339:; 401:18; 640:2; 2178:8; 2470:4; 2750:12; 3115:4

note/book, 2461:1; scattered ~, 3556:2

nothing/ness, 475:3; 536:5; 723:6; 1608:9; 1635:14; 1790:3; 1881:3, 19; 2234:9; 2290:3; 2493:5; 2507:, 13; 2736:12; 3328:16; 3532:2; achieving ~, 3245:1; doing ~, 2904:20; fear of ~, 1745:9

notoriety, 1817:6

noun, 1277:18

nourishment *see also* NUTRITION/IST, self ~, 1771:19

novel/ist *see also* BOOK; FICTION; LITERATURE; READING; WRITER, 753:41; 1400:6; 2287:20; 2370:20; 2510:2; 2749:2; 2818:3; anonymity of ~, 2028:11; art of ~, 166:16; bad ~, 1653:31; beginning of ~, 1634:11; disposable ~, 2300:8; ending of ~, 791:26; fledgling ~, 1636:56; insights of ~, 1184:10; invention of ~, 2749:1; modern satirical ~, 2703:1; mystery ~, 1650:40; political ~, 1229:23; protagonists of ~, 2511:8; romantic ~, 585:4; stream of consciousness ~, 2028:1; tedious ~, 1481:40; trashy ~, 3290:1; women's ~, 2736:23; writing ~, 2245:7; 2356:8

novelty *see also* ORIGINALITY, 661:25

November, 297:1

NOW (National Organization for Women), 2299:7, 8; administration of ~, 2326:2

nuclear power *see also* ATOMIC BOMB, uses of ~, 2193:1; ~ weapons, 2552:2

nuclear weaponry *see also* WAR; WEAPONRY, 3007:2; ~ in relation to pacifism, 1655:17

nudity, 527:8; 984:1; 1448:5; 1707:7; 2367:7

nuisance, 1767:1

numbers, knowledge of ~, 527:14

nun, 148:5; 442:7; 781:2; 1129:4; 1625:1; 2468:1; 2576:2; activity of ~, 952:8; black ~, 3029:1; education of ~, 1597:1; favor of ~, 3328:8; hypocrisy of ~, 1370:8; inner conflicts of ~, 1782:4; purpose of ~, 3328:6

Nuremberg, Germany, ~ Trials, 1896:27

nurse/nursing *see also* MEDICAL PROFESSION, 768:24; 950:1;

1395:7; 1655:2; dedication to ~, 1686:1; ~ in relation to patient, 1686:1; ~ in war, 1647:4; obstinacy of ~, 907:41; training of ~, 1450:1

nursemaid, 370:3

nursery, children's ~

nurturing *see also* CARING, men and ~, 2587:5; need for ~, 2779:5; women and ~, 2628:4

nutrition/ist *see also* DIET/ER; FOOD; NOURISHMENT, 1168:2; 2310:1; 2421:4; effect of ~ on state of mind, 1855:2; good ~, 1855:1; longevity of ~, 1855:6; ~ research, 1855:7; science of ~, 1073:3

O

Oates, Joyce Carol, 2370:26

oath *see also* PROMISE; SWEARING, 331:11; 392:1; 494:1; 800:8; false ~, 515:3; keeping one's ~, 791:1; legal ~, 1816:7

obedience, 11:2; 300:1; 1129:2; 3135:1; blind ~, 871:7; 2909:2; habit of ~, 2010:13; ~ in child, 1262:1; ~ of women, 924:9; ~ to god, 1129:4; total ~, 1949:3

obesity *see also* DIET/ER; FAT/NESS; PLUMPNESS; WEIGHT, 727:1; 1540:1

obituary, 1661:, 3

objectification *see also* DEHUMANIZATION, ~ OF others, 2523:2; 2919:2; ~ of women *see also* WOMAN/WOMEN, OBJECTIFICATION OF ~, 3089:23

objectivity *see also* DETACHMENT; IMPARTIALITY, 1159:28; 1219:1; 1513:27; 1837:33; 1936:1; pursuit of ~, 2318:1

obligation *see also* DUTY; RESPONSIBILITY, 909:2; 2016:26; feeling of ~, 2101:12; fulfilling ~, 1632:34; 2750:3

oblivion, 284:11; art of ~, 2975:2

obscenity, anti-~ laws, 2581:11

obscurity, 2393:9

observation, 601:2; 668:4; 1481:60; 1561:2; 2775:8; 3402:2; ~ of sick, 950:2; powers of ~, 467:3; 869:31; 1283:3; 1586:7; shared ~, 2207:2

observatory, 2133:2

obsession *see also* COMPULSION, 1186:7; ~ with cleanliness, 1837:7

obstacle *see also* ADVERSITY; TROUBLE, 833:4; 2385:37; creating ~, 1361:6; 1528:13; 2837:2; overcoming ~, 166:11; 359:1; 1183:11; 1403:3; 1578:3; 1705:6; 2415:1; 3536:2

obstetrician/obstetrics *see* medical profession), 1369:2

obstinacy *see also* STUBBORNNESS, 1634:14; ~ of life, 833:7

obviousness, 1339:3; 2370:13

occupation, 567:5; 600:4; 1986:2; change of ~, 1458:1; enduring ~, 417:1; ~ for sexes, 1802:14; necessity of ~, 1650:16; sex and ~, 1802:7

ocean *see also* SEA; TIDE; WAVE [OCEAN], ~ territories, 331:3; threats to ~, 2589:2

October, 992:18; 2140:6

odds, going vs. ~, 2198:1; ~ vs. one, 2251:1

odds and ends, 1059:1

oeuvre, 1977:4

offense, 2849:8; causing ~, 2480:7

office (position), running for ~, 1513:11

Ohio, 3423:1

oil, 802:4; ~ on Indian reservation, 1557:16; ~ spill, 3623:1

Oklahoma, 3126:1

O'Keeffe, Georgia, 3236:4

old age *see also* AGE/AGING; ELDERLY/ELDERS; MIDDLE AGE; YEARS OF AGE, 46:10; 54:1; 436:5; 481:11; 558:5; 604:7; 623:2; 678:2; 869:40, 46; 936:5; 973:4; 1010:18; 1102:2; 1114:2; 1132:6; 1229:12; 1299:1; 1341:19; 1353:9; 1363:20; 1462:5; 1502:1, 5, 9; 1636:52; 1661:9; 1683:4; 1728:27; 1865:3, 10; 1936:25; 1970:2, 5; 2021:4; 2114:4; 2123:1; 2215:5; 2547:3; 2722:33; accepting ~, 1641:5; attaining ~, 960:2; beauty of ~, 2172:2; dependency in ~, 1223:9; dreams of ~, 2498:1; fear of ~, 1802:43; happy ~, 856:18; 1271:8; 1865:11; hating ~, 2114:3; horror of ~, 661:10; 2830:1; ~ in relation to youth, 2981:8; infirmities of ~, 1502:6; isolation of ~, 2803:1; limitations of ~, 947:1; routine of ~, 2089:8; sex and ~ *see also* SEX, 2096:1; social class and ~, 1936:24; virtue in ~, 1341:17; women and ~, 433:1; 2385:23; work and ~, 1271:3

omnipotence *see also* POWER, 1443:1; illusions of ~ *see also* MEGALOMANIA, 3063:1; ~ of divine, 956:3

O'Neill, Eugene, 1572:1, 2, 4

oneness *see also* CONNECTEDNESS/CONNECTION; INSEPARABILITY; UNITY, 1880:8; ~ of all life, 1112:7; ~ of humankind, 856:10; questioning ~, 1991:16

onion, 2904:1

onlooker, 2356:31

openness *see also* CANDOR, 712:1; 788:32; 1080:2; 1158:7; 1476:1; 2202:2; 2210:27; 2575:1; 2624:11

scared of ~, 2881:8; ~ taking, 100:1; 752:2; 1564:22; 1632:59; 3172:9; 3422:5

rite/ritual, 1132:9; 2836:2; 3311:1; black woman's ~ of passage, 3399:4; decline of ~, 2421:2; ~ of eating, 2421:4; woman's ~ of passage, 2385:22; 2477:2

Ritter, Thelma, 3086:1

rivalry, ~ in love, 1012:5; 1638:7

river, 313:2; 439:3; 632:21; 1620:1; 1804:6; 1922:2; ~ at night, 847:1; flowing ~, 2624:16; names of ~, 815:1

road, country ~, 3048:3

roaming   *see also* WANDERLUST, 1423:1

roast beef, 1557:1

Robinson, Jack, 661:7

rock   *see also* STONE, ~ wearing away, 3227:3

Rodeo Drive (Beverly Hills, California), 2501:1

Roe vs. Wade   see also ABORTION, 2823:9; 2910:1; 2914:1; 3075:1, 2; protecting ~, 3425:1

Rogers, Samuel, 744:1

role model   *see also* EXEMPLAR, 807:26; 3182:8; following ~, 1664:4; women ~, 2744:4

Rolf, Ida, 1704:1

romance   *see also* LOVE, 753:49; 1858:4; 2338:3; 2479:6; 2634:27; 3574:2; images of ~, 3172:10

Roman/Rome, ancient, 3315:3; entertainment in ~, 1273:10; women in ~, 3294:1

Roman Empire, Holy, 92:1

romanticism, 2356:23; ~ in poverty, 1770:3

Rome, Italy, 272:3; 2904:39; 3493:2; Christianity in early ~, 94:1; sack of ~, 2762:3

Rooney, Mickey, 2217:2

Roosevelt family, Eleanor, 1781:3, 5; Franklin Delano R—, 1487:3, 5; 1680:4; Theodore R—, 990:2; 1658:6

rooster, 1418:6

rootlessness, 2881:9

roots   *see also* HERITAGE, deep ~, 1551:5; ~ of humankind, 1808:10; return to ~, 2916:1

rose, 612:1; 810:1; 973:8; 1338:43; 1363:8; 1564:4; 2013:5; 2375:11; 2634:27; 3209:4; beauty of ~, 1850:1; ~ bud, 810:2; fragrance of ~, 783:37; ~ garden, 2494:4; unopened ~, 2866:2

Rose Bowl (Pasadena, California), 2328:5

Roth, Phillip, 2370:26

rouge, 1726:1

Rousseau, Jean Jacques, 604:4; 2459:39

routine   *see also* RUT, 800:4; 3493:4; daily ~, 752:1; imprison-

ment of ~, 2435:3; ~ of life, 2089:8

Rowe, Elizabeth Singer, 551:2

royal/ty   *see also* COURTIERS; KING; NOBLE/NOBILITY [RANK]; PRINCE/SS; QUEEN, 442:6; 636:5; control of ~, 1570:8; English ~, 926:1; ~ family, 2297:3; line of ~, 15:1; marriage among ~, 279:4; mother of ~, 3456:1; notions of ~, 808:1

rudeness   *see also* SURLINESS, 166:15

Rudolph, Wilma, 3515:4

ruin   *see also* DESTRUCTION/DESTRUCTIVENESS, 632:15; 779:4; 1305:2; mocking one's ~, 56:3; road to ~, 661:18

rule/r   *see also* HEAD OF STATE; LEADER/SHIP, 14:1; 477:1; 1424:3; ~ by emotion, 3316:5; command of ~, 591:2; difference in ~, 1428:8; follow ~, 998:3; ~ of elite, 1567:8; oppressive ~, 1636:4; play by ~, 2591:4; victorious ~, 251:1

rules (regulations)   *see also* LAW, 2593:7; 2894:5; mistaken ~, 491:8; questioning ~, 2016:21

rumba, 3251:1

rumor   *see also* GOSSIP; SCANDAL, 157:10; 661:12

Rumpelstiltskin, 2385:29

running away, 2121:7; 3360:1; women who ~, 2675:14

Rushdie, Salmon, 2227:24

Ruskin, John, 1128:3

Russia/n   *see also* SLAV; UNION OF SOVIET SOCIALIST REPUBLICS, 717:20; 934:5; 1289:28; 1483:1; 1513:; ~ Army, 2010:3; life in ~, 1416:4; reform in ~, 3416:1; ~ Revolution, 1602:4

rut   *see also* ROUTINE, 1705:11; daily ~, 2083:2

ruthlessness   *see also* CRUELTY, 2039:1

S

Sabbath, 1112:5; 3514.1:2, 3; holiness of ~, 3029:26; keeping the ~, 993:16

Sacco and Vanzetti, 1603:9; 1788:5

sacrament, ~ before death, 187:2

sacredness   *see also* HOLINESS, ~ of every day, 1112:5; ~ of life, 1465:3; place of ~, 67:1

sacrifice   *see also* SELF-SACRIFICE, 51:5; 127:2; 1031:10; 1336:5; 1678:7; 2095:4; 2191:3; 3141:1; necessity of ~, 1486:4; personal ~, 1999:1; reality of ~, 1728:; reasons for ~, 2628:2; religious ~, 481:20

sacrilege   *see also* BLASPHEMY, 1948:53

Sade, marquis de, 2421:5; 3089:25

sadism, 2755:32

sadness   *see also* MELANCHOLY, 310:3; 1262:8; 2928:4; lessons of ~, 2881:1

sadomasochism, 2459:40

safari, ecology ~, 2540:36

safe/ty   *see also* SECURITY, 987:2; 1006:1; 2532:2; 2624:4; ~ living, 2788:7; playing it ~, 717:27; 2916:5

sage (wisdom), 630:12; 986:1; forgotten ~, 2095:5

sailing, 2122:3

sailor, 500:1; 793:2; 1987:1

saint/liness, 896:1; 1363:11, 45; 1600:4; 1752:3; 1879:37; 2006:1; 2882:3; dealing with ~, 3328:2; ~ in relation to God, 450:3; lives of ~, 3268:2; mock ~, 1254:9; study of ~, 3268:2

St. Ansalam, 180:1

St. Augustine, 2219:10; 2962:2, 4

St. Francis of Assisi, 1159:29; 1948:39

St. Paul, 59:2; 94:1

St. Teresa of Avila, 1363:11

salad days, 620:3

salamander, 319:1; 2324:5

salary   *see also* INCOME; WAGE, commensurate ~, 596:1

salmon, 1804:6; preserving the wild ~, 2207:4

saloon   *see* BARS AND PUBS; BARROOM

salvation   *see also* REDEMPTION, 354:2; 1311:15; 2523:1; 2963:3; 3231:2; ~ from heathenism, 2455:2

Salvation Army, 2410:1

Samaritan, Good, 83:1

sameness   *see also* SIMILARITY, 823:1; 994:3; 2361:3; 2682:2

Samson, 579:2

San Francisco, California, 1546:7; 2528:1; 19th century ~, 935:1

sand, 2430:3; 2687:15

Sand, George, 875:10; 891:11

Sandinistas, art and ~, 3144:5

sandpiper, 1029:1

Sanger, Margaret, 1680:3

sanity, 2310:2

San Juan Capistrano, California, 1546:2

Santa Claus, belief in ~, 2354:4

Sao Paulo, Brazil, 2222:2

Sappho, 454:1; 1353:26; 3247:1

Sarah, 370:1

Sarajevo, Bosnia-Herzegovina, sacking of ~, 3500:2

Satan   *see also* DEVIL, 302:1; deliverance from ~, 377:1

satiety, 788:18; 1209:17

satire, 527:21; 675:3

satisfaction, 567:5; 791:17; 1560:11; 2539:3; 3150:4; lack of ~, 2609:4

Saturday, 2053:1; ~ night, 718:1

sausage, 2258:1

savage/ry   *see also* BARBARIAN/BARBARISM, 400:3; 505:21; ~ of man, 489:10; ~ of men, 97:2; ~ within, 1481:45

savior   *see also* HERO/INE; RESCUE, 1494:5

scandal   *see also* RUMOR, 166:19; 510:7

Scandinavia   *see also individual nations*, 1482:1

scapegoat, 1933:6

scar, 3290:4; 3465:1

scarecrow, 455:1

Scarlet Pimpernel, The, 1254:4

scavenger, 1278:4

scent, sweet ~, 1353:

scheming, 2634:3

scholar/ship   *see also* RESEARCH, 469:16; 1896:22; 2001:1; 2814:1; authority of ~, 3157:5; ~ award, 922:6; limitations of ~, 2213:2; mediocrity of ~, 1269:7

scholasticism, isolation of ~, 1883:3

school   *see also specific levels*; CLASSROOM; COLLEGE; EDUCATION; UNIVERSITY, 823:6; ~ administration, 2752:3; ~ board bureaucracy, 1862:1; boarding ~, 1482:2; ~ book, 1047:9; ~ building, 921:1; care of children in ~, 2390:7; Catholic ~, 2279:11; corporal punishment in ~, 1045:1; ~ curriculum, 1269:5; 2390:1; discrimination in ~, 1513:57; divinity ~, 1059:2; ~ drop-out, 2089:9; 3272:7; favoritism in ~, 644:15; finishing ~, 1159:7; 2818:2; gender difference in ~, 949:11; good ~, 3011:2; ~ house, 1583:2; independence of child at ~, 2085:11; learning from ~ life, 1205:11; ~ lunch program, 2947:6; military ~, 1608:25; problems of ~, 687:17; punishment at ~, 1121:7; ~ recital, 1633:5; reforming ~ system, 1121:8; unjustly treated ~ -child, 2085:11; ~ vacation, 2175:1

schooling   *see also* EDUCATION; SCHOOL, 3011:4; free ~, 2490:7

Schwarzkopf, Norman, 3514:10

science   *see also specific branches of science*, 349:4; 1031:5; 1186:22; 1269:6, 9; 1406:1; 1551:9, 14; 1848:1; 2123:7; 2475:1, 2; 2958:2; 3422:3; 3450:7; admirers of ~, 1004:9; advances of ~, 717:8; age of ~, 1071:1; appreciation of ~, 2683:2; art and ~, 1696:2; authority of ~, 3090:1; black women of ~, 1754:1; cautions of ~, 1802:1; contribution towards ~, 3092:4; criticism of ~, 975:3; culture of ~, 3344:2; dearth of women in ~, 3475:2; discoveries of ~, 1426:2; dream of ~, 2848:23; empirical ~, 1184:5; ex-

2227:7; misspent ~, 272:5; passage of ~, 297:2; 436:5; 537:2; 570:1; 623:4; 661:6; 705:21; 930:75; 968:3; 973:4; 1013:1; 1159:28; 1523:1; 1589:7; 1653:14; 2101:19; 2236:3; ~ piece *see also* CLOCK; WATCH, 753:24; preciousness of ~, 2832:3; 3125:4; ravages of ~, 682:10; relativity of ~, 468:3; 661:8; 815:6; 1557:2; 1586:25; 1615:1; 1705:4; 2288:1; 2750:14; right ~, 1410:10; speed of passing ~, 2851:1; spending ~, 2046:24; 3539:2; spending ~ with loved one, 3302:2; telling ~, 2469:21; ~ to oneself, 331:6; unhurried ~, 3445:1; use of ~, 452:21; 565:1; 685:3; 787:3; 1832:4; 1936:2; 3080:1; wasted ~, 1083:1; 2392:1, 1; 2588:18; 2666:2; ~ well-spent, 777:2

timeliness, 1586:6; 2300:2

Times Square, New York, 2907:2

timidity, 515:5; 2227:8

tiredness *see also* EXHAUSTION; FATIGUE, 2947:5

Titanic, ~ survivor, 1559:1

titles, 2835:12

today *see also* HERE AND NOW; PRESENT [TIME], 968:10; 973:3; 1431:11; living for ~, 491:5

togetherness, 875:14; 994:16; 2140:24; 3037:3; 3043:3; ~ in dreams, 1164:5

toil, 2009:19; ~ of life, 1771:13

toilet, 3478:2; ~ paper, 2028:3; 3632:1

tokenism, 2344:2; 2358:7; 2584:15; ~ at workplace, 2495:3

tolerance, 418:3; 1457:14; 3392:1; lukewarm ~, 1137:4; ~ of differing opinions, 1094:3; requirements of ~, 3036:9; specious ~, 3366:12

Tolstoy, Leonid, 1089:8

Toluca, Mexico, 1966:2

tombstone, 1287:3

tomorrow *see also* FUTURE, 491:5; 1052:5; 1378:1; 2513:1; unknown ~, 3568:2

tongue, holding one's ~, 467:3; sharp ~, 2375:18

tool, 1632:76

Torah, 473:1, 2

torch, passing ~, 3512:1

torture, 1891:2; 2292:5; 2459:40; 2571:5; 3643:1; ~ of prisoner, 2007:5; ~ of women, 327:1; physical ~, 2405:1

Tory Party (Great Britain), 606:1

totalitarianism, 1896:3, 24; supporters of ~, 1896:2

touch, 2251:5; bond of ~, 3217:4; human ~, 3231:5; sense of ~, 3172:8

toughness *see also* RESILIENCE, 1362:12; 1636:35; 2528:2; ~ in

men, 3194:3; ~ in woman, 2057:3; underside of ~, 2584:8

tourism/tourist, 2551:2; 3641:3; effect of ~ on historical preservation, 1958:8; ~ in relation to nature, 1654:1

Toussaint L'Ouverture, François Dominique, 3205:2

town, new ~, 1391:11; small ~, 869:8; 2308:1

toy *see also* GAME; PLAY/ING, adult ~, 1112:9; children's ~; :3; foolish ~, 1311:10; war ~, 2611:3; 2856:1; 3161:2, 3

trade *see also* OCCUPATION, 1986:2; woman at helm of ~, 1879:8

tradition *see also* CUSTOM; HABIT; RITE, 1575:3; 1665:1; 2421:1; 2522:6; 2750:10; at odds with ~, 1719:2; belonging to ~, 2735:9; breaking with ~, 1328:1; challenges to ~, 3479:1; different spiritual ~, 3614:3; ~, 3286:2; influence of ~, 1109:3; inheritance of ~, 1665:11; loss of ~, 869:24; 1896:18; 2775:9; oral ~, 3206:12; questioning ~, 2016:14; worn out ~, 1195:8

tragedy, 1236:3; 1273:7; 1474:5; 1528:9; 1639:12; surviving ~, 2403:12

trail, carving out ~, 1218:2

train, 1183:8; 2095:22; 2630:2; express ~, 1481:63; freight ~, 1667:2; ~ in France, 3518:1

training *see also* EDUCATION, 2297:4; physical ~, 1283:1; spiritual ~, 1283:1

traitor *see also* BETRAYAL; DISSIDENT; DOUBLE-CROSSER; TREASON, 807:19; 1523:5; 2095:18

trance, group ~, 2095:13; sexual ~, 2799:4

tranquility, 177:6; 469:33; foe of ~, 661:3; satisfied with ~, 910:5

tranquilizer *see also* DRUGS, effects of ~, 1739:2

transcendence, ~ of gender, 1841:15

transformation, 1617:1; time for ~, 2650:16

transgression, requirements of ~, 3223:8

transience, 945:2; 1338:43; 1567:1; 1710:1; 2101:19; 2345:2; 2861:3; 2980:3; 3087:1; ~ of time, 1634:7

transition, age of ~, 1979:8

translation/translator, 817:1; 1273:11; 1979:9; 2385:47; literal ~, 3332:9

transportation, modes of ~, 1362:6

transsexual/ism *see also* CROSS-DRESSING; GENDER, ~ IDENTITY, 2042:1; 2654:1; 3159:13; 3563:2; 3597:2; cultural response to ~, 2312:6

transvestite, 3563:1

trap *see also* PITFALL, 1106:4; 1329:1; 2698:1; caught in ~, 1630:5; 2064:1; 2101:10; nature's ~, 2152:9

trauma, post ~ stress syndrome, 2902:4; psychological ~, 2902:8

travel *see also* JOURNEY; TRAVELER; TRIP; VACATION, 418:10; 1094:4; 1362:6; 1636:12; 1976:1; 1991:14; 2245:6; 3370:1; 3445:3; 3641:2; ~ abroad, 930:38; 987:7; 1033:3; 2009:30; ~ alone, 2534:5; Americans and ~, 3111:1; benefits of ~, 632:16; 785:1; ~ by air, 1641:4; 1890:1; ~ by automobile, 2174:1; ~ by land, 839:1; desire to ~, 1534:1; 3641:1; food and ~, 2881:6; foreign ~, 1229:15; 1991:13; ~ in India, 3648:2; incessant ~, 754:11; 791:14; ~ journal, 1485:10; 3648:1; lessons of ~, 922:2; ~ light, 3378:1; mind ~, 947:1; need to ~, 1352:3; pace of ~, 2981:7; reason for ~, 3641:4; spoiled by ~, 661:14; vicissitudes of ~, 443:15

traveler *see also* TRAVEL; VISIT/OR, 855:24; 1608:13; 1890:1; 1922:5; 2750:9; American ~, 2567:6; armchair ~, 1946:19; food and ~, 2400:4; ignorant ~, 540:1; passing ~, 1212:4; poor ~, 1794:2; solitary ~, 3370:2; tales of ~, 1634:4; woman ~ alone, 3648:3 women ~, 634:8; 1045:6

Travolta, John, 3384:2

treachery, 3332:15

treason *see also* TRAITOR, 452:5; 733:1; 1639:33; 2264:3

treasure, hidden ~, 2063:1; personal ~, 713:8

treaty, 115:2

tree *see also specific varieties*, 182:1; 623:2; 1338:4; 1695:5; 2152:3; 2380:14; 3340:3; ~ blossom, 173:1; 220:2; city ~, 1179:2; 1699:1; cultivating ~, 1039:5; dead ~, 1460:1; felled ~, 807:21; ~ in winter, 745:2; logging ~, 3134:3; old-growth ~, 3340:4; planting ~, 977:1; redwood ~, 1654:1; reverence for ~, 907:56; sapling ~, 977:2; sick ~, 2569:2

trial, 421:1; ~ by fire, 405:2; ~ of character *see also* METTLE, TEST ONE'S ~, 589:15

tribalism *see also* ABORIGINAL, 115:2; demise of ~, 3378:6

trick/ery *see also* DECEIT/DECEPTION; MISCHIEVOUSNESS, 289:3

trick/ster *see also* MISCHIEF, 1344:2

trip *see also* JOURNEY; TRAVEL, 76:4; preparation for ~, 1890:8

trivia/lity *see also* SUPERFICIALITY, 375:2; 768:17, 20; 1560:4

trouble *see also* ADVERSITY; OBSTACLE, 278:1; 312:2; 452:17; 824:1; 2118:8; always in ~, 3525:1; handling ~, 505:29; 791:14; petty ~, 773:1; 901:1; put away your ~, 1950:1; response to ~, 901:10; self-imposed ~, 418:6; 644:; women and ~, 1362:15

troublemaker, 398:1; 406:1

trousers, 1109:7

trout, river ~, 1421:6

Troy, gates of ~, 2762:3

Truman, Harry S., 1996:3

trust, 780:2; 886:8; 921:9; 1038:1; 1560:14; gaining child's ~, 1397:3; ~ in one's people, 3058:6; ~ in others, 871:10; ~ in self *see also* SELF-TRUST, 331:7; lack of ~ *see also* MISTRUST, 604:8; 705:18; 3158:2

truth *see also* HONESTY, 4:1; 166:17; 249:4; 302:1; 361:10; 418:7; 448:2; 450:5; 457:3; 489:2; 687:10; 800:10; 820:6; 822:4; 837:12; 891:18; 904:3; 907:36; 930:43; 936:1, 2; 953:19; 965:2; 1082:2; 1131:5; 1137:9; 1158:8; 1164:3; 1273:4; 1463:1; 1481:58; 1495:2; 1519:2; 1523:4; 1586:11; 1808:4, 6, 7; 1813:13; 1896:46; 1936:27; 1946:7; 1948:68; 2009:18; 2010:26; 2041:2; 2067:5; 2068:14; 2078:1; 2079:3; 2149:4, 22; 2219:9; 2287:5; 2314:2; 2408:4; 2463:4; 2540:1; 2671:3; 2722:18, 21; 3254:6; 3257:3; 3312:3; 3421:1; 3594:1; all sides of ~, 3029:21; aspects of ~, 2240:1; awareness of ~, 1563:13; awful ~, 2984:2; blind to ~, 375:3; 773:24; claim of ~, 1481:42; communal ~, 3206:12; defense of ~, 106:2; 1989:2; dismiss ~, 508:3; gaining ~, 1509:14; grain of ~, 2201:18; impact of ~, 494:2; ~ in relation to facts, 2353:25; locating ~, 1481:32; lover of ~, 1410:11; maintaining ~, 1783:7; making up ~, 2654:4; opposite of ~, 2540:16; personal ~, 2985:1; ~ prevails, 1134:8; propagation of ~, 871:3; refining one's sense of ~, 1338:7; requirements of ~, 1722:18; sacrifice for ~, 2628:2; seeking ~, 979:1; 1481:55; 1576:6; 1936:1; selling ~, 1932:4; slanted ~, 993:32; spark of ~, 2037:1; spurning ~, 2141:8; study of ~, 401:1; 1004:3; submerged ~, 1481:29; telling ~, 54:2, 3; 1335:1; 1851:1; 2029:24; 2068:10; 2356:18; 3206:2, 10; 3433:1; test of ~,

motive for ~, 1819:8; 3484:3; ~ of everyday, 2279:12; ~ of nature, 2234:2; ~ on oneself, 2806:1; ~ out of emotions, 2540:51; permanence of ~, 2140:70; power of ~, 964:6; 2459:6; 3212:3; 3413:1; preparation for ~, 479:1; 848:3; 3282:2; prolific ~, 930:76; purpose of ~, 675:1; 2523:7; reality in ~, 1718:5; reasons for ~, 2046:7; 3282:6; rhythm of ~, 2608:6; satisfaction of ~, 1564:26; ~ sentence, 3043:23; slipshod ~, 1329:11; spiritual ~, 3629:1; styles of ~, 2483:2; subject of ~, 2332:1; teaching ~, 3279:1; technique of ~, 2483:3; 3156:6; 3413:3; therapeutic power of ~, 2982:6; time for ~, 2809:1; weeping and ~, 3145:2; ~ with whole self, 2941:10; woman ~ about women, 3405:3; women and ~, 2400:7; 2669:4; word selection in ~, 2013:4; working at ~, 1481:59; 2380:18

wrong   see also RIGHT AND WRONG; SIN/NER; VICE, being ~, 2419:1; convinced of ~, 713:17; ~ of women, 800:1; past ~, 3051:5; ~ redressed, 1171:2; stopping ~, 940:1

wrongdoing, fighting ~, 856:9

X

Xena, the Warrior Princess, 3545:4
Xenocrates, 64:1
xenophobia   see also PREJUDICE, ~ AGAINST FOREIGNERS, 1603:9; 1854:3

Y

year, close of ~, 831:8
yearning   see also LONGING, 2300:20; 2674:14
years of age, 10 ~, 723:16; 2031:1; 100 ~, 1627:1, 3; 12 ~, 2101:8; 14 ~, 1815:2; 15 ~, 790:1; 1462:3; 2932:2; 16 ~, 842:6; 19 ~, 2881:8; 20 ~, 869:40; 21 ~, 1596:1; 25 ~, 518:1; 3 ~, 723:16; 30 ~, 442:8; 770:1; 1771:18; 2442:2; 2479:3; 2701:2; 38 ~, 644:4; 40 ~, 527:7; 1396:2; 46 ~, 1481:69; 49 ~, 2227:4; 50 ~, 573:8; 1336:6; 1481:72; 6 ~, 723:16; 60 ~, 2183:30; 70 ~, 788:30; 1502:1; 1513:28; 1728:17; 74 ~, 1705:15; 80 ~, 1502:1; 90 ~, 1114:2
Yeats, William Butler, 1716:5
yesterday   see also PAST, 1933:17
yielding   see also FLEXIBILITY, 2717:4
yoga, science of ~, 1739:5
Yorkshire terrier, 2881:23

young   see also YOUTH, 2307:2; ~ in relationship to elders, 242:18
Young, Loretta, 3086:1
youth   see also ADOLESCENCE/ADOLESCENT; CHILDHOOD; GROWING UP; TEENAGE/R; YEARS OF AGE, 597:1; 644:20; 759:11; 775:1; 788:29; 831:3; 998:17; 1131:1; 1353:14; 1400:12; 1498:12; 1632:53; 1661:9; 1724:1; 1763:1; 1831:1; 2959:10; 3140:2; agonies of ~, 1851:4; 2736:2; attitudes of ~, 536:6; 869:40; clinging to ~, 1863:3; concerns of ~, 723.1:1; conditioning of ~   see also BOY, CONDITIONING OF ~; GIRL, CONDITIONING OF ~, 3352:5; dissatisfaction of ~, 1938:4; 2175:2; end of ~, 770:1; 791:25; equality among ~, 644:15; eternal ~, 783:32; expectations of ~, 3479:3; fountain of ~, 2183:31; freedom in ~, 1634:27; happiness of ~, 830:1; immortal ~, 1655:8; impatience of ~, 1938:1; improvidence of ~, 1462:4; ~ in relation to elderly, 1972:1; ~ in wartime, 1792:1; 1867:3; inexperienced ~, 1194:1; joy of ~, 783:4; lost ~, 527:28; 620:3; 1186:5; 1509:14; 1635:11; 1655:7; 2140:16; 2507:24; 2735:3; 2870:3; main-

taining ~, 1158:12; misspent ~, 2356:11; options of ~, 2650:9; passing ~, 1481:1; ~ past, 1543:17; prodigal ~, 1634:1; provisions for ~, 1204:7; rebellion of ~, 2333:4; recollections of ~, 644:5; 1543:17; regained ~, 1662:1; 2438:6; return to one's ~, 921:6; 1013:1; scars of ~, 1159:1; self-involvement of ~, 1785:6; sex and ~   see also SEX, ADOLESCENT ~; SEX, YOUTH AND ~, 2051:4; sheltered ~, 723:29; spent ~, 1381:3; ~ spreading wings, 1019:2; vigor of ~, 2378:11; wasted ~, 685:3
youthfulness, 998:16
yuppie, food and ~, 2848:5; ~ men in relation to women, 2848:8

Z

zealotry, 1784:16
zebra, 1560:1
Zen, 2776:3
Zeus, 322:1
Zimbabwe, beauty of ~, 2140:54; independence in ~, 2140:56; leadership in ~, 2140:55
Zion, sinners of ~, 525:1
Zionism/Zionist   see also ISRAEL/I, 1728:
zoo, 713:5; 2016:11
Zoroaster, 856:7

0048   03